A London
Bibliography of the
Social Sciences

BRITISH LIBRARY OF POLITICAL AND ECONOMIC SCIENCE

A London Bibliography of the Social Sciences

Seventh Supplement
1969-72

VOLUME XXV

Intervention
—
Negroes – History

MANSELL LONDON 1973

*This Bibliography has been reproduced from
cards forming the subject catalogue of the
British Library of Political and Economic Science by
Mansell Information/Publishing Limited
3 Bloomsbury Place, London WC 1A 2QA*

SBN 7201 0297 9
Library of Congress Card Number 31–9970

*The paper on which this Bibliography has
been printed is based on requirements established
by the late William J. Barrow for a permanent/
durable book paper. It is laboratory certified
to meet or exceed the following values:
Substance 89 gsm
pH cold extract 9.4
Fold endurance (MIT ½ kg tension) 1200
Tear resistance (Elmendorf) 73 (or 67 × 3)
Opacity 90.3%.*

Printed and bound in England
© 1973 *The British Library of Political and Economic Science*

Preface

This supplement to *A London Bibliography of the Social Sciences* is the second to use the method of photographic reproduction direct from the cards filed in the subject catalogue of the British Library of Political and Economic Science. Thus works are included which appeared in print less than a year ago. Entries listed are identical with those in the Library's author catalogue. More recent ones no longer give the names of publishers or the titles of publishers' series.

As with the previous supplement, speed of publication has meant the omission of cross-references. Readers are, as a guide, referred to the 'List of subject headings used in the Bibliography arranged under topics', which has always been a feature of the Bibliography, and which is to be found at the end of the final volume of this supplement. This list also includes under the section *Geography, history and topography* a list of individual countries and places used as main headings, a feature which was re-introduced in the previous supplement. The 'Complete list of headings and subdivisions used, in the order they occur' is no longer included.

D. A. Clarke *June 1972*

Contents

VOLUMES I-XXVIII

VOLUMES I–IV *Original Compilation*

Holdings up to 1929 of the
British Library of Political and Economic Science
Edward Fry Library of International Law
Goldsmith's Library of Economic Literature,
 University of London
National Institute of Industrial Psychology
Royal Anthropological Institute
Royal Institute of International Affairs
Royal Statistical Society

Special collections in the libraries of
The Reform Club (political and historical pamphlets)
*University College, London (the Hume, Ricardo and
 other economic and political collections)*
*The University of London (works on economics and
 related subjects)*

VOLUME V *First Supplement*

Additions from 1929 to 1931 to the collections
included in Volumes I–IV

VOLUME VI *Second Supplement*

Additions from 1931 to 1936 to the
British Library of Political and Economic Science
Edward Fry Library of International Law
Goldsmith's Library of Economic Literature

VOLUMES VII–IX *Third Supplement*

Additions from 1936 to 1950, other than works in
 the Russian language, to the
British Library of Political and Economic Science
Edward Fry Library of International Law

VOLUMES X–XI *Fourth Supplement*

Additions from 1950 to 1955 in all languages, and also
 from 1936 to 1950 in Russian, to the
British Library of Political and Economic Science
Edward Fry Library of International Law

VOLUMES XII–XIV *Fifth Supplement*

Additions from 1955 to 1962 to the
British Library of Political and Economic Science
Edward Fry Library of International Law

VOLUMES XV–XXI *Sixth Supplement*

Additions from 1962 to 1968 to the
British Library of Political and Economic Science
Edward Fry Library of International Law
Volume XXI contains indexes to Volumes XV–XXI

VOLUMES XXII–XXVIII *Seventh Supplement*

Additions from 1969 to 1972 to the
British Library of Political and Economic Science
Edward Fry Library of International Law
Volume XXVIII contains an index to
Volumes XXII–XXVIII

PERIODICALS LISTS

An alphabetical list of the periodicals in the British
Library of Political and Economic Science in 1929
is given in Volume IV; supplementary lists up to 1936
are given in Volumes V and VI, after which they
have been discontinued.

AUTHOR INDEX

Author indexes are given in Volumes IV (for Volumes
I–III), V, and VI, but not in later volumes.
*Volumes I–XIV were published by the
British Library of Political and Economic Science,
Houghton Street, London WC2*

A LONDON BIBLIOGRAPHY OF THE SOCIAL SCIENCES

INTERVENTION (INTERNATIONAL LAW)

LOTH (HEINRICH) Kolonialismus und Humanitätsintervention: Kritische Untersuchung der Politik Deutschlands gegenüber dem Kongostaat 1884-1908. Berlin, 1966. pp. 117. bibliog.

ORGANIZATION OF AMERICAN STATES. 1966. Differences between intervention and collective action. (Official Records. OEA/Series I/VI.2. CIJ. 81) Washington, 1966. pp. iii, 31.

LAWYERS COMMITTEE ON AMERICAN POLICY TOWARDS VIETNAM. Consultative Council. Vietnam and international law: an analysis of the legality of the U.S. military involvement. Flanders, O'Hare, 1967. pp. 162. 21cm.

BASTID (S.) Remarques sur l'interdiction d'intervention. in Mélanges offerts à Juraj Andrassy. La Haye, 1968.

FALK (RICHARD A.) Legal order in a violent world. Princeton, U.P., 1968. pp. xvi, 610 $23\frac{1}{2}$cm.

HULL (ROGER H.) and NOVOGROD (JOHN C.) Law and Vietnam. Dobbs Ferry, Oceana, 1968. pp. xi, 211. bibliog. $22\frac{1}{2}$cm.

CHAKRABARTI (RADHARAMAN) Intervention and the problem of its control in the 20th century: case studies of the crises in Spain, the Congo, Hungary, Czechoslovakia and Vietnam; [Ph. D. (London) thesis]. 1969. fo. 257. bibliog. Typescript: unpublished. This thesis is the property of London University and may not be removed from the Library

BOEHME (ECKART) Tankerunfälle auf dem Hohe Meer: die Zulässigkeit staatlicher Massnahmen zur Gefahrenabwehr. Hamburg, 1970. pp. 92. bibliog. (Hamburg. Hansische Universität. Forschungsstelle für Völkerrecht und Ausländisches Öffentliches Recht. Werkhefte. 13)

SCHWARZ (URS) Auslandredaktor of Neue Zürcher Zeitung. Confrontation and intervention in the modern world. New York, 1970. pp. 218.

INTERVENTION in international politics: texts of the lectures delivered at the conference organised by the Netherlands Institute of International Affairs on...its 25th anniversary on 19 and 20 November 1970; edited by Louis G.M. Jacquet. The Hague, 1971. pp. 124

INTERVIEWING

U.K. 1951. Social Survey. The effect of interviewers own opinions about minorities and foreigners on the opinions about negroes which they obtain or record from informants; by H. D. Willcock. (Papers. Methodological Series. No.M.45) [London], 1951. pp. 5. 33cm.

U.K. 1951. Social Survey. Hindsight on interviewer X; by H. D. Willcock and K. E. Hoy. (Papers. Methodological Series. No.M. 43) [London, 1951] pp. 4. 33cm.

U.K. 1951. Social Survey. Research on interviewing; by H. D. Willcock. (Papers. Methodological Series. No.M.36) [London], 1951. pp. 8. 33cm.

[U.K. 1952. Social Survey]. Interviewer research. Paper 2. Description of work in progress; ([by] H. D. Willcock). ([Papers. Methodological Series]. No.M.48) [London, 1952] pp. 9. 33cm.

[U.K. 1952. Social Survey]. Interviewer research. Paper 3. Some data relating to refusals and refusal-prone interviewers, based on performance on routine inquiries; [by H. D. Willcock]. ([Papers. Methodological Survey]. No.M.49) [London, 1952] pp. 10. 33cm.

U.K. 1952. Social Survey. Interviewer research. Paper 5. Interviewer efficiency as assessed by test and by regional organisers; by H. D. Willcock. (Papers. Methodological Series. No.M.51) [London], 1952. pp. 2. 33cm.

U.K. 1952. Social Survey. Interviewer research. Paper 6. The grading of interviewers: an examination of visible and concealed interviewer errors as revealed by the grading tests, and some suggestions for future grading procedure; by Muriel Harris. (Papers. Methodological Series. No.M.52) [London], 1952. pp. 5. 33cm.

U.K. 1952. Social Survey. Some effects of bonus payments in interviewer performance; by D. L. Lamberth. (Papers. Methodological Series. No.M.56) [London], 1952. pp. 13. 33cm.

U.K. 1952. Social Survey. Some facts about interviewer turnover; by Muriel Harris. (Papers. Methodological Series. No.M.47) [London], 1952. pp. 3. 33cm.

[U.K. 1956. Social Survey]. Examples of interviewer variability taken from two sample surveys; [by] Percy G. Gray. ([Papers. Methodological Series]. No.M.82) [London, 1956] pp. 10. bibliog. 33cm.

ITALY. Commissione Nazionale per lo Studio e la Determinazione dei Profili Professionali. Raccolta di Profili Professionali. 17. Profilo professionale presuntivo della intervistatrice: addetta alle ricerche sulle opinioni pubbliche; compilatori; Gino Santini [and] Giuseppe Conti. Roma, Ente Nazionale Prevenzione Infortuni, 1958. pp. 19. bibliog. $24\frac{1}{2}$cm.

U.K. 1960. Social Survey. The use of the telephone for making interview appointments; by Christopher Scott and Stuart Jackson. (Papers. Methodological Series. No.M.92) [London], 1960. pp. 4. 33cm.

U.K. 1961. Social Survey. Should the respondent be interviewed alone?; by D. Sheppard. (Papers. Methodological Series. No.M.101) [London], 1961. pp. 5. 33cm.

INTERVIEWING (Cont'd.)

SPIELBERGER (KARLHEINZ) Über die Möglichkeiten und Grenzen des standardisierten Interviews in der Marktforschung. [Erlangen-Nürnberg, 1967?]. pp. 175. bibliog.

U.K. Social Survey. Papers. Methodological Series. No. M. 136. A handbook for interviewers; by Jean Atkinson: a manual for Government Social Survey interviewing staff, describing practice and procedures on structured interviewing. [London] 1967. pp. 165.

DEUTSCHER (I.) Asking questions cross-culturally: some problems of linguistic comparability. in Becker (Howard Saul) and others, eds. Institutions and the person. Chicago, 1968.

RICH (JOHN) Interviewing children and adolescents. London, Macmillan, 1968. pp. viii, 120. bibliog. 21½cm.

ROEDE (HANS) Befrager und Befragte: Probleme der Durchführung des soziologischen Interviews. Berlin, 1968. pp. 250.

DIDCOTT (PETER J.) Field strategies and response bias in a survey of adolescent boys. [London, 1969]. pp. 94. (London. University. London School of Economics and Political Science. Survey Research Centre)

DEXTER (LEWIS ANTHONY) Elite and specialized interviewing. Evanston, 1970. pp. 205. bibliog.

U.K. Social Survey. Papers. Methodological Series. No. M. 136. Handbook for interviewers; by Jean Atkinson: a manual for Social Survey interviewing staff, describing practice and procedures on structured interviewing. 2nd ed. London, 1971. pp. 170.

INTRACOASTAL WATERWAYS

- India

INDIA. Sethusamudram Project Committee. 1956. Report. [A. Ramaswami Mudaliar, chairman]. [New Delhi?, 1956?]. pp. 52,26.

INTUITION

CHUEVA (I. P.) Intuitivizm kak raznovidnost' antiintellektualizma. in Uchenye Zapiski Kafedr Obshchestvennykh Nauk Vuzov G. Leningrada. Filosofiia. vyp.3. Leningrad, 1961.

CONFERENCE ON INTUITIONISM AND PROOF THEORY, BUFFALO, 1968. Intuitionism and proof theory: proceedings of the Summer Conference...; edited by A. Kino [and others]. Amsterdam, 1970. pp. 516. bibliogs.

INTUITION (PSYCHOLOGY)

WESTCOTT (MALCOLM R.) Toward a contemporary psychology of intuition: a historical, theoretical, and empirical inquiry. New York, Holt, [1968]. pp. xi, 228. bibliog. 22½cm.

INVENTIONS

UNITED STATES. Congress. Joint Economic Committee. Invention and the patent system. Washington, 1964. pp. ix, 247.

KINGSTON (WILLIAM HENRY GILES) Invention and monopoly. London, Woolwich Polytechnic, Department of Economics and Business Studies, [1967]. pp. 39. 21cm. (Woolwich Economic Papers. No.15).

MORISHIMA (M.) and SAITO (M.) An economic test of Sir John Hicks's theory of biased induced inventions. in Wolfe (James Nathaniel) ed. Value, capital, and growth. Edinburgh, 1968.

JEWKES (JOHN) and others. The sources of invention. 2nd ed. London, 1969. pp. 372.

- Germany

BRUGGER (KARL) Der Schutz geistigen Eigentums: Patent, Gebrauchsmuster, Warenzeichen. 4th ed. Stuttgart, 1968. pp. 64.

- Russia

EREMEEV (BORIS IVANOVICH) Sotsial'no-ekonomicheskie problemy tekhnicheskogo tvorchestva v SSSR. Moskva, 1967. pp. 124.

- United Kingdom

PROSSER (RICHARD BISSELL) Birmingham inventors and inventions: being a contribution to the industrial history of Birmingham;...[reprint of work] originally published for private circulation, Birmingham, 1881. Wakefield, 1970. pp. 251.

INVENTIONS, EMPLOYEES'

PEDRAZZINI (M.M.) Bemerkungen zur Struktur der Diensterfindung. in Zuerich. Universität. Rechts- und Staatswissenschaftliche Fakultät. Die Rechtsordnung im technischen Zeitalter. Zürich, 1961.

- Poland

PILAWSKI (BRONISŁAW) Wynalazczość pracownicza: rozstrzyganie sporów. Warszawa, CRZZ, 1967. pp. 215. bibliog. 17cm.

- Sweden

SWEDEN. Statens Offentliga Utredningar. 1946. 21. Betänkande med utredning och förslag angående ratten till arbetstagares uppfinningar; avgivet av särskilt tillkallade sakkunniga. Stockholm, 1946. pp. 71. 24cm.

- United States

NEUMEYER (FRIEDRICH) The employed inventor in the United States: R[esearch] and D[evelopment] policies, law and practice;...with legal analysis by John C. Stedman. Cambridge, Mass., [1971]. pp. 540. bibliog.

- Yugoslavia

JANJIĆ (MIODRAG) Pravni režim pronalazaka stvorenih u radnom odnosu, etc. Beograd, 1965. pp. 175. bibliog. (Institut za Uporedno Pravo. Monografije. 18) With French summary.

INVENTORIES

HAEHLING VON LANZENAUER (CHRISTOPH) Optimale Lagerhaltung im Produktionsprozess. Bonn, 1966. pp. 138. bibliog.

BUFFA (ELWOOD S.) Production-inventory systems: planning and control. Homewood, Irwin, 1968. pp.xiii,457. Bibliogs. 23cm.

WENZEL (KONRAD) Geldentwertung und Erhaltung des Unternehmens, dargestellt am Beispiel des Vorratsvermögens. [Erlangen, imprint, 1969?]. pp. 275. bibliog.

- Mathematical models

IGLEHART (DONALD L.) and LALCHANDANI (A.P.) An allocation model and its application to a multi-echelon inventory problem. Ithaca, Cornell University, Department of Industrial Engineering and Operations Research, [1965]. pp. 30. bibliog. 28cm.

EL-SHAFEI (AL WALID A. M.) and MAHDY (M.A.M.) On determining reorder point and reorder quantity in a probabilistic inventory model: (a simulation model). Cairo, [1968]. pp. 18. 28cm. (U.A.R. Institute of National Planning. Memos. No. 842)

HILTON (KENNETH) The level of stocks in British manufacturing industry. Southampton, 1968. fo. 37. bibliog. (Southampton. University. Discussion Papers in Economics and Econometrics. No.6801)

MARWAH (KANTA) Inventory investment and distributed lag responses. [Ottawa, 1968?]. fo. 24. (Carleton University. Carleton Economic Papers)

POPP (WERNER) Einführung in die Theorie der Lagerhaltung. Berlin, 1968. pp. 173. bibliog.

WINDER (JOHN W.L.) Tests of alternative models of inventory behaviour: a case study of the U.S. copper industry. Toronto, 1968. fo. 28. (Toronto. University. Institute for the Quantitative Analysis of Social and Economic Policy. Working Paper Series. No. 6813)

BELSLEY (DAVID A.) Industry production behavior: the order-stock distinction. Amsterdam, 1969. pp. 233. bibliog.

HOCHSTAEDTER (DIETER) Stochastische Lagerhaltungsmodelle. Berlin, 1969. pp. 269. bibliog.

HEES (R.N.VAN) and MONHEMIUS (W.) Produktiebesturing en voorraadbeheer: theoretische achtergronden. Deventer, [1970]. pp. 395. bibliog.

- Germany

MUELLER (JUERGEN) Konjunktur und Lagerhaltung: eine lagerwirtschaftliche Analyse verschiedener Branchen im Zeitreihenvergleich. [Bamberg, imprint], 1964. pp. 167. bibliog.

- United Kingdom

HILTON (KENNETH) The level of stocks in British manufacturing industry. Southampton, 1968. fo. 37. bibliog. (Southampton. University. Discussion Papers in Economics and Econometrics. No.6801)

TRIVEDI (PRAVINCHANDRA KANTILAL) An econometric study of inventory behaviour in the U.K. manufacturing sector, 1956-67; [Ph. D. (London) thesis]. 1969 [or rather 1970]. fo. 293. bibliog. Typescript: unpublished. This thesis is the property of London University and may not be removed from the Library.

- United States

UNITED STATES. 1961. Availability and reliability of inventory data needed to study economic change; (a report prepared by Elmer C. Bratt). (Bureau of the Budget Statistical Evaluation Reports. No.4) Washington, 1961. pp. iii, 211. 26½cm.

HILTON (KENNETH) The level of stocks in British manufacturing industry. Southampton, 1968. fo. 37. bibliog. (Southampton. University. Discussion Papers in Economics and Econometrics. No.6801)

INVENTORS, AMERICAN

NEUMEYER (FRIEDRICH) The employed inventor in the United States: R[esearch] and D[evelopment] policies, law and practice;...with legal analysis by John C. Stedman. Cambridge, Mass., [1971]. pp. 540. bibliog.

INVENTORS, BRITISH

PROSSER (RICHARD BISSELL) Birmingham inventors and inventions: being a contribution to the industrial history of Birmingham;...[reprint of work] originally published for private circulation, Birmingham, 1881. Wakefield, 1970. pp. 251.

CHALONER (WILLIAM HENRY) People and industries. London, 1963. pp. (iv), 151. bibliogs.

INVESTMENT BANKING

FRIEND (IRWIN) and others. Investment banking and the new issues market. Cleveland, World Publishing Company, [1967]. pp. ix, 598. 21cm. (World Series in Economics)

- Argentine Republic

ARGENTINE REPUBLIC. Consejo Federal de Inversiones: 1960. El Consejo Federal de Inversiones: finalidades practicas y argentinas; ([by] Juan Quilici [and] Julian F. Freaza). Buenos Aires, 1960. pp. 24.

ARGENTINE REPUBLIC. Consejo Federal de Inversiones. 1960. Los fondos comunes de inversión y el desarrollo regional. Buenos Aires, 1960. pp. 47.

- Egypt

ELHAMY (MOHAMED ADEL) and KNAUTHE (ERHART) Concepts of investment financing with reference to the GDR Investment Bank and the UAR Investment Fund. Cairo, 1966. pp. 32. 28cm. (U.A.R. Institute of National Planning. Memos. No. 747.)

INVESTMENT BANKING (Cont'd.)

- Germany, Eastern

ELHAMY (MOHAMED ADEL) and KNAUTHE (ERHART) Concepts of investment financing with reference to the GDR Investment Bank and the UAR Investment Fund. Cairo, 1966. pp. 32. 28cm. (U.A.R. Institute of National Planning. Memos. No. 747.)

- United States

SHERIDAN (JAMES R.) Employment of temporary funds for commercial banks. Boston, [1967]. pp. 132. bibliog.

CAROSSO (VINCENT P.) Investment banking in America: a history. Cambridge, Mass., 1970. pp. 569. bibliog. (Harvard University. Harvard Studies in Business History. 25)

INVESTMENT OF PUBLIC FUNDS

SOMMER (ERDMUTE) Ansatzpunkte zur Beurteilung der Wachstumswirkungen öffentlicher Investitionen. München, [imprint, 1966?]. pp. 231. bibliog.

ARROW (KENNETH JOSEPH) and KURZ (MORDECAI) Public investment, the rate of return, and optimal fiscal policy. Baltimore, [1970]. pp. 218. bibliog.

FREY (RENE L.) Infrastruktur: Grundlagen der Planung öffentlicher Investitionen. Tübingen, 1970. pp. 132.

- America, Latin

WHITEHEAD (LAURENCE) Public sector activities in Latin America. Oxford, 1970. pp. 45. (Oxford. University. St. Antony's College. Latin American Centre. Occasional Papers. 1)

- Brazil

BRAZIL. Ministerio do Planejamento e Coordenação Econômica. Programa de investimentos publicos. a., 1965, 1967; ceased pbln. [Rio de Janeiro].

BRAZIL. Ministerio do Planejamento e Coordenação Econômica. Grupo de Acompanhamento do Programa de Investimentos. Programa de investimentos publicos: distribuição regional. a., 1965. [Rio de Janeiro].

- Germany

STOERMER (KARL HEINZ) Öffentliche Investitionen in das Sozialkapital und Wirtschaftswachstum in der Bundesrepublik Deutschland von 1950-1964. Düsseldorf, 1967. pp. 177. bibliog.

- New Zealand

EVANS (L.) Some thoughts on public investment in New Zealand's inland transport. Wellington, Victoria University of Wellington, Department of Economics, 1966. fo. 34. 25½cm.

INVESTMENT TAX CREDIT

- United States

AMERICAN ENTERPRISE INSTITUTE FOR PUBLIC POLICY RESEARCH. Legislative Analyses. No. 11. The investment tax credit : should it be repealed?; an analysis of the tax credit repeal provision in the surcharge tax proposal. Washington, 1969. pp. 19.

TAX incentives and capital spending; Gary Fromm, editor: papers presented at a conference of experts held on November 3, 1967, [at the Brookings Institution]. Washington, D.C., [1971]. pp. 301. bibliog. (Brookings Institution. National Committee on Government Finance. Studies of Government Finance.)

INVESTMENT TRUSTS

RASSI (FAOUZI) "Investment trusts": gestion et fiscalité; etude comparée. Paris Pichon et Durand-Auzias, 1964. pp. 226. bibliog. 25cm. (Bibliothèque de Science Financière. tome 3)

FOSSATI (GIORGIO) Borsa, azionariato popolare, fondi comuni di investimento. Milano, 1969. pp. 201. bibliog.

RAW (CHARLES) and others. Do you sincerely want to be rich?: Bernard Cornfeld and IOS: an international swindle. London, 1971. pp. 464.

- Belgium

REQUETTE (FRANCIS) Les fonds communs de placement en Belgique. Bruxelles, Bruylant, 1968. pp. 206. 22½cm.

- Canada

CANADA. Committee on Mutual Funds and Investment Contracts. 1969. Report... provincial and federal study: [Gordon E. Grundy, chairman]. Ottawa, 1969. pp. 825.

- Caribbean Area

CARIBBEAN ECONOMIC DEVELOPMENT CORPORATION. Investing in the Caribbean. San Juan, 1970. 3 vols.

- France

DEGAND (JEAN) Les sociétés d'investissement mobilières et immobilières: les S.I.C.A.V. Paris, 1969. pp. 318.

- Germany

BAUSCH (THOMAS) Deferred profit sharing trust plan: Darstellung der amerikanischen Gewinnbeteiligung mit aufgeschobener Auszahlung ... in den USA und in der BRD. [Erlangen, imprint], 1968. pp. 229. bibliog.

- South Africa

SOUTH AFRICA. Bureau of Statistics. National Accounts and Finance Reports. No.40. Census of investment companies and other financial enterprises, 1962-63. Pretoria, [1965]. pp. 1 . 32. 33cm. In Afrikaans and English.

SOUTH AFRICA. Bureau of Statistics. Reports.
No. 04-05-01. Census of investment
companies and other financial enterprises,
1964-65. [Pretoria, 1968]. pp. viii, 15.
30cm. In English and Afrikaans.

- **United Kingdom**

BURTON (H.) and CORNER (D.C.) Investment and unit
trusts in Britain and America. London, [1968].
pp. (xii), 409. bibliog.

UNIT TRUST YEAR BOOK, THE. 1969.
London, 1969. pp. 176. 23½cm.
Specimen issue.

U.K. Board of Trade. 1969. Particulars of
dealers in securities and of unit trusts,
1969; published under the Prevention of
Fraud (Investments) Act, 1958. London,
1969. pp. 72. 24½cm.

MORLEY (M. F.) A guide to the taxation of
investment institutions. London, [1971].
pp. 50. bibliog.

U.K. Department of Trade and Industry. 1971.
Particulars of dealers in securities and of
unit trusts, 1971; published under the
Prevention of Fraud (Investments) Act, 1958.
London, 1971. pp. 79.

- **United Kingdom - Directories**

ASSOCIATION OF UNIT TRUST MANAGERS. Directory
of unit trusts, 1969. London, 1969. pp. 134.
23cm.

- **United States**

BAUSCH (THOMAS) Deferred profit
sharing trust plan: Darstellung
der amerikanischen Gewinnbeteiligung mit aufgeschobener Auszahlung
... in den USA und in der BRD.
[Erlangen, imprint], 1968. pp.
229. bibliog.

BURTON (H.) and CORNER (D. C.) Investment and
unit trusts in Britain and America. London,
Elek, [1968]. pp. (xii), 409. bibliog. 24½cm.

INVESTMENTS

LORENZ (DETLEF) Probleme und Ansätze einer
kapazitätsorientierten Investitionspolitik.
Berlin, [1958]. pp. 158. bibliog. (Berlin.
Freie Universität. Wirtschafts- und Sozialwissenschaftliche Fakultät. Wirtschaftswissenschaftliche Abhandlungen. Heft 8)

FRANCE. Direction Générale du Génie Rural et de
l'Hydraulique Agricole. 1960. La rentabilité
des investissements de génie rural: séminaire
de Sancerre, 25-28 mai 1959; rapport de synthèse.
[Paris], 1960. pp. 205. 21cm.

NARDI (G. DI) Osservazioni sui criteri di scelta
degli investimenti. in vol. 2 of Saggi di
economia aziendale e sociale in memoria di Gino
Zappa. Milano, 1961.

ISMAR (HEINZ H.) and others. Die Konsum- und
Investitionsfunktion: Untersuchung für die
Bundesrepublik Deutschland. Köln,
Westdeutscher Verlag, 1962. pp. 419.
bibliog. 29½cm. (North Rhine-Westphalia.
Forschungsberichte des Landes Nordrhein-
Westfalen. Nr. 1024)

KLEIN (ALFRED W.) Objetivos del desarrollo y
politica de inversion;...capítulo 11 del libro
La productividad como criterio de inversión...
editado por el Departamento de Investigaciones
Industriales del Banco de México. [Santo
Domingo?, 1962?] fo. 10.

FARRAR (DONALD E.) The investment decision under
uncertainty. Englewood Cliffs, 1964. pp. 90.
bibliog. (Ford Foundation. Doctoral Dissertation
Series. 1961)

UNITED ARAB REPUBLIC. 1964. Outline of course
[on] operations research techniques and investment criterion; by A.S.A. El Tigi. (Institute
of National Planning Memos. No. 437) Cairo,
1964. pp. 11. bibliog. 27½cm.

WEDIG (WILHELM) Zur Behandlung der
Investierungen in Modellen gleich-
gewichtigen Wachstums. [Berlin,
imprint], 1964. pp. 142. bibliog.

WILLIAMS (BRUCE RODDA) Investment and technology in growth. Manchester, Statistical
Society, 1964. pp. 20. 21½cm.

GUHR (HANS MARTIN) Kapitalanlagen in
schottischem Whisky. Frankfurt am Main,
Nowack, 1965. pp. 119. bibliog. 21cm.

PORTERFIELD (JAMES T.S.) Investment decisions
and capital costs. Englewood Cliffs, Prentice-
hall, [1965]. pp. viii, 152. 21½cm. (Prentice-
hall Foundations of Finance Series)

KRICKE (MANFRED) Zum Prognosewert un-
ternehmerischer ex ante-Tendenzan-
gaben in der Investitionserhebung
des Ifo-Instituts für Wirtschaftsforschung. [Mannheim?], 1966. pp.
204. bibliog.

TAGI (GIORGIO) Gli investitori istituzionali
e il contributo del risparmio al mercato dei
titoli mobiliari. Milano, Giuffrè, 1966.
pp. viii, 131. 25cm. (Milan. Università Commerciale Luigi Bocconi. Istituto di Studi
sulle Borse Valori A. Lorenzetti. Pubblicazioni. N.19)

URSELMANN (THEO) Probleme der Abgrenzung
und Fixierung des Verhältnisses zwischen
Eigen- und Fremdkapital. [Cologne,
imprint], 1966. pp. 91. bibliog.

CARRINGTON (A.S.) Profitability estimates for
investment projects. Wellington, N.Z., 1967.
pp. 22. 21cm. (New Zealand Institute of Economic
Research. Discussion Papers. No.13)

CECCANTI (GASTONE) Gli investimenti delle aziende
industriali: tendenze, politiche, piani. Firenze,
[imprint], 1967. pp. xii, 340. bibliog. 24cm.

EZEKIEL (HANNAN) The pattern of investment
and economic development. Bombay, University, 1967. pp. (vii), 119. 21½cm.
(Economics Series. No. 13)

FRERK (PETER) Wirtschaftlichkeit öffentlicher Investitionen. Köln, Grote,
1967. pp. 78, 11. 23½cm. (Kommunale
Gemeinschaftsstelle für Verwaltungs-
vereinfachung. Veröffentlichungen)

INVESTMENTS (Cont'd.)

KATZENSTEIN (ROBERT) Die Investitionen und ihre Bewegung im staatsmonopolistischen Kapitalismus, etc. Berlin, Akademie-Verlag, 1967. pp.226. 24cm. (Deutsche Akademie der Wissenschaften zu Berlin. Institut für Wirtschaftswissenschaften. Schriften. Nr.23)

KAUFMANN (ERNST) Die Zinsempfindlichkeit der Investitionen. Zürich, 1967. pp. 163. bibliog.

LEHNERT (GUENTER) Kommunale Investitionen und Wirtschaftswachstum. Reinheim, 1967. pp. (ii), 143. bibliog. 24cm.

LEVI (EUGENIO) La scelta degli investimenti. Torino, Boringhieri, 1967. pp. 133. bibliog. 21cm. (Serie di Ricerca Operativa. 9)

ORGANISATION FOR ECONOMIC CO-OPERATION AND DEVELOPMENT. Committee for Invisible Transactions. Capital Markets Study. [vol.1] Capital markets study: general report; (with Statistical annex). [Paris, 1967]. 2 vols. (in 1). 24cm.

ORGANISATION FOR ECONOMIC CO-OPERATION AND DEVELOPMENT. Committee for Invisible Transactions. Capital Markets Study. [vol.] 4. Utilization of savings; rapporteur Prof. J.S.G. Wilson, etc, [Paris, 1967]. pp. 552.

WOLFF (JUERGEN H.) Zur Frage der idealen Produktionsfaktorintensitäten von Investitionen in Entwicklungsländern. Freiburg i Br., 1967. pp. 45. bibliog. (Arnold-Bergstraesser-Institut für Kulturwissenschaftliche Forschung. Materialien) With summaries in English and French.

ARROW (K.J.) Optimal capital policy with irreversible investment. in Wolfe (James Nathaniel) ed. Value, capital, and growth. Edinburgh, 1968.

COLLOQUE JURIDIQUE INTERNATIONAL, PARIS, 1967. Les investissements et le développement économique des pays du tiers-monde. Paris, Pedone, 1968. pp. xv, 443. 25cm.

DOBRSKA-WOYDT (Z.) Criteria for evaluation of investment projects in manufacturing industry. Dar Es Salaam, [1968]. pp. 29. (Dar Es Salaam. University. Economic Research Bureau. ERB Papers. 68. 18)

GINSBURG (LOUIS) The meaning of investment in an age of plenty. London, Harrap 1968. pp.238. 21½cm.

HANSSMANN (FRED) Operations research techniques for capital investment. New York, Wiley, [1968]. pp. ix, 269. bibliog. 22½cm.

HELLIWELL (JOHN F.) Public policies and private investment. Oxford, Clarendon P., 1968. pp. xiii, 238. 21½cm.

HINTERHUBER (GIOVANNI) La politica degli investimenti nelle imprese industriali. 2nd ed. Milano, [1968]. pp. 386. bibliog. (Milan. Università Cattolica del Sacro Cuore. Saggi e Ricerche. Serie 3. Scienze Economiche. 1)

JENSEN (OLAV HARALD) Foretakets finanseringsproblemer. Oslo, Bedriftsøkonomens Forlag, 1968. pp. 295. bibliog. 24cm. (Norges Handelshøjskole. Skrifter. Økonomiske Avhandlinger. Nr. 11)

JEYNES (PAUL H.) Profitability and economic choice. Ames, Iowa State P., 1968. pp. xvii, 622. bibliog. 23cm.

KNAGGE (BERNHARD) Unternehmerische Investitionsentscheidungen im Verkehrssektor: Determinanten und staatliche Einflussmöglichkeiten. Göttingen, Vandenhoeck und Ruprecht, 1968. pp. 189. bibliog. 24cm. (Muenster in Westfalen. Westfälische Wilhelms-Universität. Institut für Verkehrswissenschaft. Beiträge. Heft 49)

MAINIE (PHILIPPE) and others. Effects of credit policy on the choice of investment in a "heavy" industry...; translated from the French. London, 1968. pp. 21. (U.K. Forestry Commission. Research and Development Papers. No. 69)

RAÏSSIS (MARIE LOUISE) Les investissements et la planification. Nice, 1968. pp. 449. bibliog. 24cm.

RASHLEIGH (J.) Portfolio investments: aids to decision taking. [London, 1968]. pp. 39. bibliog. (Institute of Chartered Accountants in England and Wales. Summer Courses. 1968)

SEMINAR ON THE FINANCING OF INDUSTRIAL DEVELOPMENT, BARCELONA, 1967. The financing of industrial development; [seminar held in] Barcelona, 16th-20th May 1967. [Paris], Organisation for Economic Co-operation and Development, [1968]. pp. 140.

SHACKLE (GEORGE LENNOX SHARMAN) Expectations, investment and income. 2nd ed. Oxford, Clarendon P., 1968. pp. xxxvi, 130. 21½cm.

SPRECKELSEN (ALBERT VON) Der Investitionskoeffizient: Wachstum und Investitionen im industriellen Unternehmen. Bonn, 1968. pp. 169. bibliog.

BUHL (AXEL) Die Sicherung des finanziellen Gleichgewichtes als Aufgabe in der Investitionsplanung. Hamburg, 1969. pp. 230. bibliog.

CARR (J. LAURIE) Investment economics. London, Routledge & Kegan Paul, 1969. pp. viii, 104. bibliog. 18½cm. (Students Library of Economics)

HILLIER (FREDERICK S.) The evaluation of risky interrelated investments. Amsterdam, 1969. pp. 113. bibliog.

HOELLER (HEINZ A.) Staatliche Investitionsplanung und Wirtschaftswachstum. Köln, 1969. pp. 182. bibliog. (Institut für Mittelstandsforschung. Abhandlungen zur Mittelstandsforschung. Nr. 37)

HUTCHINSON (B.G.) The economic evaluation of urban transportation investments. London, 1969. pp. 40. bibliog. (Centre for Environmental Studies. Working Papers. 39)

KOSKENKYLA (HEIKKI) An evaluation of the predictive value of the investment survey of the Bank of Finland Institute for Economic Research. [Helsinki], 1969. fo. 12. (Suomen Pankki. Taloustieteellinen Tutkimuslaitos. Julkaisuja. Sarja D. 23)

INVESTMENTS (Cont'd.)

- Taxation - Sweden

NITARE (G.) and REHN (GOSTA) Investment reserves allowances in Swedish fiscal policy: information memorandum. Stockholm, 1961. fo. 11. 30cm.

- America, Latin - Bibliography

PAETZ (JUERGEN) Das Arbeits-, Sozial- und Investitionsrecht iberoamerikanischer Länder: eine Auswahl deutscher und ausländischer Veröffentlichungen. Hamburg, Institut für Iberoamerika-Kunde, 1963. pp. 62. 20½cm. (Reihe Bibliographie und Dokumentation. Heft 1)

- Angola

ANGOLA. Junta de Desenvolvimento Industrial. 1963. How to invest in Angola; [by Walter Marques]. [Luanda, 1963]. pp. 43. bibliog.

- Argentine Republic

ALEMANN (JUAN E.) La inversion bursatil. Buenos Aires, 1962. pp. 188.

- Asia

GROPENGIESSER (PETER) Determinanten der Investitionsentscheidung in südasiatischen Entwicklungsländern. Berlin, 1965. pp. (iv), 316. bibliog. 20½cm.

- Belgium

DEBOIS (J. M.) Analyse économique des investissements dans l'agriculture belge: étude de la substitution capital-travail 1950-1965; par J.M. Debois sous la direction de G. Bublot. Bruxelles, 1968. fo. 92,(5). bibliog. 29cm. (Belgium. Cahiers de l'Institut Économique Agricole. No.83)

MAKART (J.) and BRIMIOULLE (J.) Investissements industriels et fonction de production. Bruxelles, Bruylant, 1968. pp. 63. bibliog. 24cm. (Liège. Université. Séminaire Interdisciplinaire des Professeurs Harsin et Davin. Travaux. No. 6)

- Bolivia

BOLIVIA. Comite Nacional de Inversiones. 1962. Perspectivas que ofrece Bolivia al inversionista. [La Paz], 1962. pp. 112. Parts in English, Spanish, German, French and Japanese.

- Brazil - Pernambuco

PERNAMBUCO. Comissão de Desenvolvimento Econômico. 1962. Incentivos aos investimentos em Pernambuco:...I. Vantagens em localizar-se no nord este;...II. Vantagens em localizar-se em Pernambuco. 2nd ed. Recife, 1962. pp. 21. 23½cm.

- Canada

CANADA'S INTERNATIONAL INVESTMENT POSITION; ([pd. by] Statistics Canada). a., 1926/1967 (1st issue)- Ottawa.

EVANS (R.G.) Canadian inventory investment. [Ottawa], 1969. pp. 48. bibliog. (Bank of Canada. Staff Research Studies. No. 2)

LORANGER (JEAN GUY) Investissement et financement manufacturiers au Canada: séries chronologiques sur les variables financières des compagnies, 1946-1964. Montréal, 1969. pp. 618. Appendix in English.

- Colombia

SHEAHAN (J.) Imports, investment, and growth: Colombia. in Papanek (Gustav F.) ed. Development policy. Cambridge, [Mass.], 1968.

- Europe

PORTA (G.D.) Problemi generali e specifici del movimento dei capitali nella C[omunità] E[conomica] E[uropea] con particolare referimento all'allargamento del M[ercato] E[uropeo] C[omune]. in Ferrara. Università. Centro di Documentazione e Studi sulle Comunità Europee. Quaderni. 7. Milano, 1963.

PALMA (MAURIZIO DI) ed. Il rapporto capitale-prodotto: evoluzione per settori in Italia ed in alcuni paesi occidentali. Torino, Boringhieri, 1967. pp. 132. 21 cm. (Centro di Studi e Piani Economici. Quaderni. Studi sulle Strutture Economiche. N. 5)

INVESTMENT RESEARCH GROUP. Key figures of European securities. [Amsterdam], 1970. pp. 95.

- European Economic Community countries

CANE (ALFREDO) Considerazioni sul problema del movimento dei capitali nei paesi della Comunità Economica Europea; [and]... Immigrazione in Europa di capitali statunitensi [by] Alberto de Vincolis. Firenze, the Camera, 1962. pp. 43. 17cm. (Florence. Camera di Commercio, Industria e Agricoltura. Quaderni. 19)

[JASAY (ANTHONY DE)] Les moyens d'améliorer l'apport des fonds de pension aux marchés des capitaux dans les pays de la C[ommunauté] E[conomique] E[uropéenne]. Bruxelles, [European Economic Community], 1969. 2 pts. (Etudes: Série Economie et Finances. 7) In English and French.

- France

FRANCE. 1954. Plan d'échantillonnage de l'enquête agricole sur l'auto investissement en 1951. (Institut National de la Statistique et des Études Économiques) Paris, [1954]. pp. (xi), 44.

COLLOQUE UNIVERSITÉ-INDUSTRIE, 1962, LYON. Le financement des entreprises et le Marché Commun; par J. Austruy [and others]. Paris, Dunod, 1963. pp. xiv, 150. 24cm. (Bibliothèque d'Administration des Entreprises)

- Germany

SIGRIST (WERNER) Unternehmensfinanzierung und Marktwirtschaft: ein Beitrag zum Problem der Unternehmenskonzentration und Eigentumsstreuung im Hinblick auf die Konzeption der sozialen Marktwirtschaft. [Mannheim?], 1963. pp. 170. bibliog.

MERTENS (DIETER) and KIRNER (WOLFGANG) Input-Output-Rechnung; Investitionsverflechtung in der Bundesrepublik Deutschland 1950 bis 1970. Berlin, Duncker & Humblot, 1967. pp. 79. (Deutsches Institut für Wirtschaftsforschung. DIW-Beiträge zur Strukturforschung. Heft 1)

SEMINAR ON THE NEEDS OF SPECIALIST PERSONNEL FOR THE PREPARATION AND EVALUATION OF INVESTMENT PROJECTS, ATHENS, 1968. Needs in specialist personnel for the preparation and evaluation of investment projects; [Seminar held in] Athens, 21st-25th October, 1968. Paris, Organisation for Economic Co-operation and Development, 1969. pp. 126. bibliog.

CLAASSEN (EMIL M.) Analyse des liquidités et théorie du portefeuille. Paris, 1970. pp. 178. bibliogs.

JEAN (WILLIAM H.) The analytical theory of finance: a study of the investment decision process of the individual and the firm. New York, [1970]. pp. 206. bibliogs.

MERRETT (ANTHONY JOHN WATKIN) Valuation of ordinary shares. London, 1970. pp. various.

SCHEINMAN (WILLIAM X) Why most investors are mostly wrong most of the time. New York, [1970]. pp. 268.

KREGEL (J.A.) Rate of profit, distribution and growth: two views. London, 1971. pp. 222.

LUND (PHILIP J.) Investment: the study of an economic aggregate. Edinburgh, 1971. pp. 167. bibliog.

PROBLEMS of investment: [a seminar series held at the Graduate Business Centre of the City University]; edited with an introduction by Sir Robert Shone. Oxford, [1971]. pp. 110.

SCHWERNA (WOLFGANG) Untersuchungen zur Theorie der Investition. Tübingen, 1971. pp. 108. bibliog. (Kiel. Universität. Institut für Weltwirtschaft. Kieler Studien. 115)

- Bibliography

BURGESS (NORMAN) How to find out about banking and investment. Oxford, Pergamon P., 1969. pp. xii, 300. bibliogs. 19½cm.

- Mathematical models

BLOECH (JUERGEN) Untersuchung der Aussagefähigkeit mathematisch formulierter Investitionsmodelle mit Hilfe einer Fehlerrechnung. Göttingen, 1966. pp. 226. bibliog.

BAUMAN (W. SCOTT) and KLEIN (THOMAS A.) Investment profit correlation: a regression model of profits from common stock investments. Ann Arbor, University of Michigan, Bureau of Business Research, [1968]. pp. (vi), 51. bibliog. 22½cm. (Michigan Business Reports. No. 55)

AHNER (HEINRICH) Kriterien der Anwendung von Operations Research-Modellen bei Entscheidungen über regionale Verkehrsinvestitionen. [Clausthal-Zellerfeld, imprint], 1969. pp. 258. bibliog.

REUTLINGER (SHLOMO) Techniques for project appraisal under uncertainty. [Washington], International Bank for Reconstruction and Development, 1970. pp. 95. bibliog. (World Bank Staff Occasional Papers. No. 10).

SHARPE (WILLIAM F.) Portfolio theory and capital markets. New York, [1970]. pp. 316. bibliog.

BARRON (MICHAEL J.) Investment decisions under uncertainty: the time-state preference model and some theoretical shortcomings of two widely accepted decision criteria. [Reading], 1971. pp. 12. bibliog. (Reading. University. Department of Economics. Discussion Papers in Economics. No. 29)

SAARBRUECKEN. Universität. Annales Universitatis Saraviensis. Rechts- und Wirtschaftswissenschaftliche Abteilung. Heft 47. Portefeuilleanalyse: Entscheidungskriterien und Gleichgewichtsprobleme; von Jörg Ebel. Köln, 1971. pp. 173. bibliog.

SCHAFFRANEK (MANFRED) Zur prognostischen Bedeutung von quantitativen Investitionsplänen aus Erhebungen des Ifo-Instituts für Wirtschaftsforschung: ein Versuch, die Aussagekraft durch klassifizierende Informationsauswertung zu erhöhen. [Bamberg], 1971. pp. 174. bibliog.

WESTPHAL (LARRY E.) Planning investments with economies of scale. Amsterdam, 1971. pp. 380. bibliog.

- Mathematics

LEVI (E.) Le valutazioni di bilancio degli investimenti a lunga scadenza dal punto di vista della matematica finanziaria. in vol. 2 of Saggi di economia aziendale e sociale in memoria di Gino Zappa. Milano, 1961.

GORMAN (W.M.) Measuring the quantities of fixed factors. in Wolfe (James Nathaniel) ed. Value, capital, and growth. Edinburgh, 1968.

BARRON (MICHAEL J.) The notional rate method of solving portfolio analysis problems when short sales are permitted. Reading, [1969]. pp. irreg. bibliog. (Reading. University. Department of Economics. Discussion Papers in Economics. No.16)

OOSTERHAVEN (J.A.) Portfolio selection based on security analysts' predictions. (Rotterdam], 1969. fo. 12. (Nederlandsche Economische Hoogeschool. Econometric Institute. Reports. 6905)

SILBER (WILLIAM L.) Portfolio behavior of financial institutions: an empirical study with implications for monetary policy, interest-rate determination, and financial model-building. New York, [1970]. pp. 142. bibliog.

TAYLOR (BASIL) ed. Investment analysis and portfolio management: readings from British publications. London, [1970]. pp. 536.

STONE (BERNELL KENNETH) Risk, return and equilibrium: a general single-period theory of asset selection and capital-market equilibrium. Cambridge, Mass., [1970]. pp. 150. bibliog.

WILLIAMSON (JOHN PETERKIN) Investment: new analytic techniques. London, 1971. pp. 325. bibliogs.

- Taxation

ORGANISATION FOR EUROPEAN ECONOMIC CO-OPERATION. 1960-61. Taxation systems applicable to investments: fiscal encouragement (in the overseas countries associated with member countries of OEEC as at 31st December 1959). [Paris], 1960-61. 2 vols.

WATTER (WOLFGANG) Anlageinvestitionen
und Anlagevermögen in Berlin (West),
1950 bis 1965. Berlin, Duncker und
Humblot, 1967. pp. 104. 29½cm.
(Deutsches Institut für Wirtschaftsforschung. DIW-Beiträge zur Strukturforschung. Heft 2)

JANSEN (PAUL GUENTER) Infrastrukturinvestitionen als Mittel der Regionalpolitik. Gütersloh, [1968]. pp. 158.
bibliog. (Zentralinstitut für Raumplanung. Beiträge zur
Raumplanung. Band 3)

KNOBLAUCH (PETER) Der zuwachsende Gasanschluss
als Investitionsentscheidung. Hamburg,
1968. pp. 219. bibliog.

KRENGEL (ROLF) La productivité du capital de
21 branches industrielles dans la république
fédérale d'Allemagne de 1950 à 1975.
Bruxelles, [European Economic Community],
1968. pp. 132. bibliog. 27cm. (Études:
Série Économie et Finances.6)

RINGLE (GUENTHER) Investitionen und Investitionspolitik genossenschaftlicher Wirtschafts-
gebilde. Hamburg, 1968. pp. 200. bibliog.

DICHTL (ERWIN) Die absatz- und kostenwirtschaftliche
Prüfung eines Investitionsobjekts im Einzelhandel,
erläutert an Hand einer authentischen Fallstudie.
Berlin, [1969]. pp. 65. bibliog.

THOLEN (ALFRED) Die Anlagepolitik
der Kreditbanken und Sparkassen:
betriebs- und volkswirtschaftliche
Probleme. Hamburg, 1969. pp. 297.
bibliog.

- Hungary

NAGY (SÁNDOR) Beruházások generál-
organizációja. Budapest. Közgazdasági és Jogi Könyvkiadó, 1964.
pp. 242. bibliog. 20cm.

- India

INDIA. 1965. Capital issues control: a
booklet containing principles and policy
followed in the administration of the
Capital Issues (Control) Act, 1947.
(Department of Economic Affairs, Ministry
of Finance) New Delhi, 1965. pp. 25.
24½cm.

CHAKRAVARTI (ILA) Investment criteria in relation
to agricultural development in India.
[Bhagalpur], 1967. pp. 196. bibliog.

VAISH (M.C.) An analysis of investments and advances
of scheduled banks in India during 1951-1966.
Agra, [1969]. pp. 288. bibliog.

- Italy

PALMA (MAURIZIO DI) ed. Il rapporto capitale-
prodotto: evoluzione per settore in Italia
ed in alcuni paesi occidentali. Torino,
Boringhieri, 1967. pp. 132. 21½cm. (Centro
di Studi e Piani Economici. Quaderni. Studi
sulle Strutture Economiche. N.5)

RICOSSA (SERGIO) and others. Il problema degli investimenti e i suoi
riflessi sulla occupazione operaia.
[Turin], Centro di Ricerca e Documentazione Luigi Einaudi, [1967]. pp.
83. 20cm.

IETTO (GRAZIA) La funzione degli investimenti
nei modelli econometrici: aspetti teorici e applicazione
all'economia italiana. Milano, 1969. pp. 123.
bibliog.

SABA (ANDREA) La politica di incentivazione degli
investimenti industriali in Italia e Europa.
Roma, [1969]. pp. 210. (Rome. Università. Istituto
di Economia Politica. Collana di Studi. 1)

- Ivory Coast

IVORY COAST. Statutes, etc. 1959. Les investissements privés dans la République de Côte
d'Ivoire: loi No.59/134 du 3 septembre 1959
et modalités d'application. Abidjan, Ministère des Finances, des Affaires Economiques
et du Plan, [1959]. pp. 31.

IVORY COAST. Statutes, etc. 1959. Private
investments in the Republic of Ivory Coast:
law No.59/134 of September 3, 1959 and terms
of application. Abidjan, Ministry of Finance
and Economic Affairs, [1959?]. pp. 27.

- Japan

ORGANISATION FOR ECONOMIC CO-OPERATION AND DEVELOP-
MENT. Committee for Invisible Transactions. 1968.
Liberalisation of international capital movements:
Japan. Paris, 1968. pp. 179.

- Netherlands

LINDEIJER (A.G.F.) De investeringsaftrek:
handleiding voor de ondernemer. Leiden,
Nederlandsche Uitgevers, [1963]. pp. 80.
15cm.

- Nicaragua

NICARAGUA. Instituto de Fomento Nacional. 1962.
Nicaraguan: our industrial progress in your
hands. Managua, [1962]. pp. 30.

- Nigeria

NIGERIA (EASTERN REGION). 1963. In search of
investment; by M.I. Okpara:(Addresses...during
his economic tour in the United States of
Americ). (Office of the Premier) Enugu, 1963.
pp. 32. 18½cm.

- Norway

NAERINGSØKONOMISK FORSKNINGSINSTITUT.
Økonomi. Nr.49. Renten som omkostnings-
faktor i en periode med lavrentepolitikk
og kredittregulering;([by] Morten Tu-
veng; [and] Finansieringen av de offent
lige investeringer i etterkrigstiden;
([by] Bernhard Nestaas). Oslo, 1966.
pp. 108. bibliogs. .22½cm.

ANDREASSEN (TORMOD) En analyse av industriens
investeringsplaner; an analysis of the
industries investment plans. Oslo, 1969.
pp. 23. (Norway. Statistiske Centralbyrå.
Artikler. Nr. 29) With English summary.

- Pakistan

PAKISTAN. Department of Investment Promotion and
Supplies. 1963. Investment proposals sanctioned
by the Investment Promotion Wing, Department of
Investment Promotion and Supplies, April, 1959,
to December, 1962. Karachi, 1963. pp. 46.

INVESTMENTS - Pakistan (Cont'd.)

BAQAI (MOINUDDIN) Problems of domestic resource mobilization; ...background paper for the P.I.D.E. seminar on the current economic problems of Pakistan. Karachi, [1967?]. pp. 14.

SAFIULLAH (M.) Corporate saving in Pakistan, 1959-63. Dacca, 1967. pp. 82. bibliog.

- Poland

KNYZIAK (ZYGMUNT) and LISSOWSKI (WITOLD) Ekonomika i programowanie inwestycji przemysłowych. 2nd ed. Warszawa, 1967. pp. 337. bibliog. With English and Russian summaries.

- Portugal

PORTUGAL. 1964. Plano de fomento para 1959-1964: programa de financiamento para 1964 aprovado em Conselho Económico. (Direcção de Serviços de Planeamento) Lisboa, 1964. fo. 25. 28½cm.

BANCO DE FOMENTO NACIONAL. Investments in Portugal. 2nd ed. Lisbon, 1968. pp. 205.

- Siam

BEITZEL (GEORGE B.) and others. Expanding private investment for Thailand's economic growth: a special report prepared by a team under the direction of George B. Beitzel. Bangkok, Board of Investment, 1959. pp. vi, 22. 25cm.

SIAM. Board of Investment. 1959. Brief information concerning investment in Thailand. Bangkok, [1959]. pp. 40, xli. 24cm.

- Sweden

JOHANSSON (SVEN ERIK) and EDENHAMMAR (HANS) Investeringfonders lönsamhet. Stockholm, Ekonomiska Forskningsinstitutet, 1968. pp. 150. bibliog. 24cm.

ELIASSON (GUNNAR) The credit market, investment planning and monetary policy: an econometric study of manufacturing industries. Stockholm, Almqvist & Wiksell, [1969]. pp. 111. bibliog. 21½cm.

- United Kingdom

SCIENCE and the city: papers presented for [a] conference (on 14 and 15 November, 1963, in the City of London); sponsored by Hambros Bank and the New Scientist. [London], 1963. pp. 77.

RABB (THEODORE K.) Enterprise and empire: merchant and gentry investment in the expansion of England, 1575-1630. Cambridge, Harvard U.P., 1967. pp. xiii, 420. bibliog. 23½cm.

SHAPIRO (SEYMOUR) Capital and the cotton industry in the industrial revolution. Ithaca, Cornell U.P., 1967. pp. xv, 203. bibliog. 23cm.

ECONOMIC DEVELOPMENT COMMITTEE FOR HOTELS AND CATERING. Investment in hotels and catering. London, H.M.S.O., 1968. pp. v, 68. 24½cm.

HALL (ALAN ROSS) ed. The export of capital from Britain, 1870-1914. London, Methuen, 1968. pp. ix, 190. bibliog. 20½cm. (Debates in Economic History)

POLANYI (GEORGE) Comparative returns from investment in nationalised industries. London, Institute of Economic Affairs, 1968. fo. 28. 30cm. (Background Memoranda. 1)

ROCKLEY (LAWRENCE EDWIN) Capital investment decisions a manuel for profit planning. London, Business Books, 1968. pp. x, 260. bibliog. 23½cm. (Business Management Books)

U.K. Department of Trade and Industry. Business monitor: Miscellaneous series. M5. Insurance companies and private pension funds' investment. q., 1970- London.

BRISTON (R.J.) The Stock Exchange and investment analysis. London, 1970. pp. 493. bibliog.

CUMMINGS (GORDON) The complete guide to investment. 5th ed. Harmondsworth, 1970. pp. 239.

TAYLOR (BASIL) ed. Investment analysis and portfolio management: readings from British publications. London, [1970]. pp. 536.

INVESTORS' CHRONICLE and Stock Exchange Gazette. Beginners, please. 4th ed. London, 1971. pp. 332. bibliog.

- United Kingdom - Ireland, Northern

IRELAND, NORTHERN. Cmd. 564. Review of economic and social development in Northern Ireland: report of the Joint Review Body. Belfast, 1971. pp. 15.

- United Kingdom - Wales

WELSH COUNCIL. Investment incentives. [Cardiff?], 1971. pp. various.

- United States

KENTUCKY. Commission on Economy and Efficiency. Opportunities for administration of inactive state funds to secure increased yields; staff report. Frankfort, 1964. pp. 18. 28cm.

NEW YORK (CITY). Stock Exchange. The corporate director and the investing public. [New York, Stock Exchange, 1965]. pp. 48. 23½cm.

HAMBURGER (MICHAEL J.) The impact of monetary variables: a selected survey of the recent empirical literature. [Washington, 1967]. fo. 20, iv. bibliog. 26½cm. (United States. Board of Governors of the Federal Reserve System. Staff Economic Studies. No. 34.)

ALMON (SHIRLEY) The lags between investment decisions and their causes. [Washington, 1968]. fo.(iii), pp. 31. bibliog. 26½cm. (United States. Board of Governors of the Federal Reserve System. Staff Economic Studies. No. 42.)

HAVEMAN (ROBERT H.) and KRUTILLA (JOHN V.) Unemployment, idle capacity, and the evaluation of public expenditures: national and regional analyses;...with the assistance of Robert M. Steinberg. Baltimore, Johns Hopkins P., [1968]. pp. xi, 159. 24cm.

JONES (LAWRENCE D.) Investment policies of life insurance companies. Boston, Harvard University, Graduate School of Business Administration, Division of Research, 1968. pp. xxi, 568. bibliog. 20½cm.

RICKENBACKER (WILLIAM F,) Death of the dollar: personal investment survival in monetary disaster. New Rochelle, Arlington House, [1968]. pp. 189. 20½cm.

ROLO (CHARLES J.) and NELSON (GEORGE J.) eds. The anatomy of Wall Street: a guide for the serious investor. Philadelphia, Lippincott, [1968]. pp. xii, 307. bibliog. 23cm.

SMITH (ADAM) pseud. The money game. London, Joseph, 1968. pp. ix, 302. 21½cm.

WEST (DAVID A.) The investor in a changing economy. Englewood Cliffs, Prentice-Hall, [1968]. pp. x, 133. bibliog. 20cm.

- United States - Alaska

UNITED STATES. Area Redevelopment Administration. A technical study of investment opportunities in Southeastern Alaska, with an evaluation of the economic impact of the "marine highway" system. Washington, 1965. pp. v, 244. bibliog.

- Yugoslavia

PEJOVSKI (VLADIMIR) Yugoslav investment policy. Beograd, Medunarodna Politika, 1965. pp. 42. 20cm. (Studies. No. 3)

PEJOVSKI (VLADIMIR) Yugoslav investment policy, 1966-1970. Beograd, Medunarodna Stampa, 1967. pp. 38. 20cm. (Studies. No. 21)

YUGOSLAVIA. Statutes, etc. 1967. Propisi o investicionoj izgradnji...; priredio Milivoj Bosanac. Zagreb, 1967. pp. 105.

INVESTMENTS, AMERICAN

UNITED STATES. International Development Agency. United States government memorandum to businessmen ...subject: aids to business, overseas investment. Washington, 1963. pp. ii, 46.

COHEN (BENJAMIN J.) Voluntary foreign investment curbs: a plan that really works. Princeton, 1967. pp. irreg. (Princeton University. Department of Economics and Sociology. International Finance Section. Reprints in International Finance. No. 6.

LAFAVE (WAYNE R.) and HAY (PETER) eds. International trade, investment, and organization. Urbana, U. of Illinois P., 1967. pp. x, 506. bibliog. 25½cm.

SYMPOSIUM ON INTERNATIONAL BUSINESS IN 1967: PROBLEMS AND SOLUTIONS OF PRIVATE INVESTORS ABROAD, DALLAS, 1967. Private investors abroad: problems and solutions in international business in 1967;...editor Virginia Shook Cameron. Albany, N.Y., 1967. pp. 400.

HOFFMEYER (ERIK) Die amerikanische Herausforderung und die Theorie der Forschungsintensität. Tübingen, 1969. pp. 13. (Kiel. Universität. Institut für Weltwirtschaft. Kieler Vorträge. Neue Folge. 58)

KINDLEBERGER (CHARLES POOR) American business abroad: six lectures on direct investment. New Haven, Yale U.P., 1969. pp. ix, 225. 20cm.

WILKINS (MIRA) The emergence of multinational enterprise: American business abroad from the colonial era to 1914. Cambridge, Mass., 1970. pp. 310. bibliog.

- America, Latin.

SELSER (GREGORIO) Diplomacia garrote y dolares en América Latina. Buenos Aires, Palestra, 1962. pp. 372. 19½cm. (Colección Vertientes de la Libertad)

UNITED STATES. Congress. Joint Economic Committee. Private investment in Latin America: hearings, etc. Washington, 1964. pp. iv, 492.

FOURNIAL (GEORGES) Pauvres ou riches Amériques?. Paris, [1968]. pp. 86.

HIRSCHMAN (ALBERT O.) How to divest in Latin America, and why. Princeton, 1969. pp. 24. (Princeton University. Department of Economics and Sociology. International Finance Section. Essays in International Finance. No. 76)

MIKESELL (RAYMOND FRECH) and others. Foreign investment in the petroleum and mineral industries: case studies of investor-host country relations;... [sponsored by] Resources for the future, Inc. Baltimore, [1971]. pp. 459. bibliog.

- Australia

BRASH (D.T.) American investment in Australian industry. London, 1966. pp. 366. bibliog.

- Brazil

RAMOS (ARNALDO) Como o Brasil ajuda os E.U.A. [Rio de Janeiro], Editôra Problemas Contemporâneos, [1963]. pp. 76. 18cm. (União Nacional dos Estudantes. Centro Popular de Cultura. Coleçao Reportagem. 1)

ROJAS (ROBINSON) Estados Unidos en del [sic] Brasil. Santiago de Chile, Prensa Latinoamericana, [1965]. pp. 205. 19½cm.

- Europe

VINCOLIS (A. DE) Immigrazione in Europa di capitali statunitensi. in Cané (Alfredo) Considerazioni sul problema del movimento dei capitali nei paesi della Comunità Economica Europea; [and]...Immigrazione in Europa di capitali statunitensi [by] Alberto de Vincolis. Firenze, 1962.

LAYTON (CHRISTOPHER) Trans-Atlantic investments. Boulogne-sur-Seine, [1966?]. pp. 141. (Atlantic Institute. Atlantic Papers)

LAYTON (CHRISTOPHER) Trans-Atlantic investments. 2nd ed. Boulogne-sur-Seine, [1968]. pp. 144. (Atlantic Institute. Atlantic Papers.)

DUNNING (JOHN HARRY) European and U.S. trade patterns, U.S. foreign investment and the technological gap. Reading, 1969. fo.various. (Reading. University. Department of Economics. Discussion Papers in Economics. No.17)

CONFERENCE: "DIRECT INVESTMENT IN THE ATLANTIC AREA", WASHINGTON, 1969. The multinational corporation in the world economy: direct investment in perspective; edited by Sidney E. Rolfe, Walter Damm. New York, 1970. pp. 169.

INVESTMENTS, AMERICAN - Europe (Cont'd.)

HELLMANN (RAINER) The challenge to U.S. dominance of the international corporation;... translated by Peter Ruof. New York, [1970]. pp. 348. bibliog.

HELLMANN (RAINER) Weltunternehmen nur amerikanisch?: das Ungleichgewicht der Investitionen zwischen Amerika und Europa. Baden-Baden, [1970]. pp. 301. bibliog.

- European Economic Community countries

EUROPEAN ECONOMIC COMMUNITY. Études: Série Industrie. 1. L'industrie électronique des pays de la communauté et les investissements américains. Bruxelles, 1969. pp. 168.

- Formosa

SCHREIBER (JORDAN C.) U.S. corporate investment in Taiwan. New York, [1970]. pp. 133. bibliog.

- France

VIEILLARD (GEORGES) L'affaire Bull. [Paris, 1969]. pp. 248.

DICKIE (ROBERT B.) Foreign investment: France: a case study. Leyden, 1970. pp. 135. bibliog.

- Germany

STRATTHAUS (GERHARD) Überfremdung unserer Wirtschaft?: US-Investitionen in der Bundesrepublik. Mannheim, [1968]. pp. 36. bibliog.

- Mexico

AMERICAN MANAGEMENT ASSOCIATION. Management Bulletins. 57. Doing business in Mexico: prospects in a growing market. New York, [1964]. pp. 24. 28cm.

- Netherlands

STUBENITSKY (FRANK) American direct investment in the Netherlands industry: a survey of the year 1966. Rotterdam, 1970. pp. 191. bibliog.

- Spain

AMERICAN MANAGEMENT ASSOCIATION. Management Bulletins. 38. New business opportunities in Spain, etc. New York, [1964]. pp. 32. 28cm.

- United Kingdom

ASH (BILL) and others. Vietnam, United States and Britain: the facts of entanglement. London, [imprint, 1968]. pp. 24. 21½cm.

STEUER (M.D.) American capital and free trade: effects of integration. London, 1969. pp. 53. (Atlantic Trade Study. Papers)

- Venezuela

MÁRQUEZ (POMPEYO) Hacia una patria libre. [Caracas], La Muralla, [1967]. pp. 179. bibliog. 19cm.

INVESTMENTS, BRITISH

U.K. Central Office of Information. Reference Division. 1966. Britain's overseas investments. London, 1966. pp. 52. bibliog. 23½cm.

ATKIN (JOHN MICHAEL) British overseas investment, 1918-1931; [Ph.D. (London) thesis]. [1968]. fo. vii, 351. bibliog. 25½cm. Typescript: unpublished. This thesis is the property of London University and may not be removed from the Library.

DUNNING (JOHN HARRY) The costs and benefits of foreign investment to the investing country: the U.K. experience. [Reading], 1968. fo. 26. bibliog. (Reading. University. Department of Economics. Discussion Papers in Economics. No.9)

REDDAWAY (WILLIAM BRIAN) Effects of U.K. direct investment overseas: final report; ...in collaboration with S.J. Potter and C.T. Taylor. Cambridge, C.U.P., 1968. pp. 197-408. 23½cm. (Cambridge. University. Department of Applied Economics. Occasional Papers. 15)

NATIONAL AND GRINDLAYS BANK. Private overseas investment: a survey of its importance in selected areas of the developing world, and of the part played by National and Grindlays Bank in promoting the flow of investment. [London], 1969. unpaged.

INDUSTRIAL POLICY GROUP. Studies. No. 4. The case for overseas direct investment. London, 1970. pp. 48.

U.K. Central Office of Information. Reference Division. Reference Pamphlets. 98. Britain's international investment position. London, 1971. pp. 67. bibliog.

- Argentine Republic

ORTEGA PEÑA (RODOLFO) and DUHALDE (EDUARDO LUIS) Baring Brothers y la historia política argentina: la banca británica y el proceso histórico nacional de 1824 a 1890. Buenos Aires, Sudestada, 1968. pp. 213. 18cm.

- India

SEN (A. K.) The pattern of British enterprise in India 1854-1914: a causal analysis. in Singh (Baljit) and Singh (Vidya Bhusan) eds. Social and economic change. Bombay, 1967.

- South Africa

NATIONAL ASSOCIATION OF BRITISH MANUFACTURERS. The British stake in South Africa. London, 1962. pp. 16.

LABOUR RESEARCH DEPARTMENT and AFRICAN NATIONAL CONGRESS (SOUTH AFRICA). South Africa, apartheid and Britain. London, 1970. pp. 19.

- United States

ADLER (DOROTHY R.) British investment in American railways, 1834-1898;...edited by Muriel E. Hidy. Charlottesville, 1970. pp. 253. bibliogs.

INVESTMENTS, EUROPEAN

- European Economic Community Associated countries

EUROPEAN ECONOMIC COMMUNITY. Commission. Directorate General of Overseas Countries and Territories. Directorate of Research. 1959. Investments in overseas countries associated with the European Economic Community: methods, sources of finance, stage of progress reached. Brussels, 1959. pp. various. 30cm.

- United States

HELLMANN (RAINER) The challenge to U.S. dominance of the international corporation;... translated by Peter Ruof. New York, [1970]. pp. 348. bibliog.

HELLMANN (RAINER) Weltunternehmen nur amerikanisch?: das Ungleichgewicht der Investitionen zwischen Amerika und Europa. Baden-Baden, [1970]. pp. 301. bibliog.

FAITH (NICHOLAS) The infiltrators: the European business invasion of America. London, 1971. pp. 242.

INVESTMENTS, FOREIGN

FRISCH (RAGNAR) Optimal investments under limited foreign resources: part I and part II. Oslo, Institute of Economics, University of Oslo, 1959. fo. iv, 190. 29½cm. (Memoranda)

CARNEIRO (OTAVIO AUGUSTO DIAS) Movimentos internacionais de capital e desenvolvimento econômico. Recife, Comissão de Desenvolvimento Econômico, 1961. pp. 148.

INTERNATIONAL INVESTMENT SYMPOSIUM, 1962. Aspects of international investment: record of the proceedings of an International Investment Symosium held at Pembroke College, Cambridge, 22nd to 28 July 1962. London, Hepburn, [1962]. pp. 465. 26½cm.

BRUNNER (JOHANN) Die mittelfristige Exportfinanzierung als Problem der Investitionsgüterlieferungen nach den Entwicklungsländern. Winterthur, 1965. pp. 77. bibliog.

KECSKÉS (GYULA) Private Investitionen in Entwicklungsländern in der Nachkriegszeit. [Kiel, imprint], 1965. pp. 1 bibliog.

AMMANN (ULRICH) Der Schutz ausländischer Privatinvestitionen in Entwicklungsländern aus völkerrechtlicher, volkswirtschaftlicher und betriebswirtschaftlicher Sicht. Zürich, Polygraphischer Verlag, [1967]. pp. xi,180. bibliog. 24cm. (St. Gall. Handelshochschule. Schweizerisches Institut für Aussenwirtschafts- und Marktforschung. Schriftenreihe für Wirtschaftsprobleme der Entwicklungsländer. Band 3)

CREMONESE (MASSIMO) Terzo mondo: problematica di sviluppo economico e di aiuti internazionali. Roma, Abete, [1967]. pp. 135. 21cm.

DESAI (MEGHNAD J.) Costs and returns of overseas investment from the point of view of the host country. [Brighton], 1967. fo. 13. ([Brighton. University of Sussex. Institute of Development Studies. Mimeo Series. No. 25])

BLOOMFIELD (ARTHUR I.) Patterns of fluctuation in international investment before 1914. Princeton, Princeton University, International Finance Section, Department of Economics, 1968. pp. 55. 23cm. (Princeton Studies in International Finance. No. 21)

STIKKER (DIRK UIPKO) The role of private enterprise in investment and promotion of exports in developing countries. (TD/35/Rev. 1) New York, United Nations, 1968. pp. 112.

UNITED NATIONS. Department of Economic and Social Affairs. 1968. Foreign investment in developing countries. (E/4446) New York, 1968. pp. 61. bibliog.

WANGENHEIM (EBERHARD VON) Die Wirkungen zwischenstaatlichen Kapitalverkehrs auf Wechselkurse und Zahlungsbilanzen: eine theoretische Untersuchung. Berlin, Duncker & Humblot, [1968]. pp. 137. bibliog. 23cm. (Volkswirtschaftliche Schriften. Heft 124)

BALOGH (THOMAS) Government measures to support private overseas investment in less developed countries. Brighton, 1969. pp. 26. (Brighton. University of Sussex. Institute of Development Studies. Mimeo Series. No. 21)

FRANKEL (SALLY HERBERT) Gold and international equity investment, a study of investment in gold mining and the lessons for the international market in equity capital. London, Institute of Economic Affairs, 1969. pp. 54. 21½cm. (Hobart Papers. 45)

GRAY (CLIVE S.) Resource flows to less-developed countries: financial terms and their constraints. New York, 1969. pp. 305. bibliog.

HEIDHUES (FRANZ) Zur Theorie der internationalen Kapitalbewegungen: eine kritische Untersuchung unter besonderer Berücksichtigung der Direktinvestitionen. Tübingen, 1969. pp. 210. bibliog.

INVESTISSEMENTS étrangers et arbitrage entre états et personnes privées: la Convention B.I.R.D. du 18 mars 1965; [proceedings of the journée d'étude of the Société Française pour le Droit International, Dijon, 27 avril 1968]. Paris, Pedone, 1969. pp. iv. 196. 24cm.

LIPTON (MICHAEL) The flow of private investment from rich to poor countries: some research proposals. Brighton, 1969. pp. 15. (Brighton. University of Sussex. Institute of Development Studies. Mimeo Series. No.20)

STREETEN (PAUL PATRICK) New approaches to private overseas investment. Brighton, 1969. pp. 12. (Brighton. University of Sussex. Institute of Development Studies. Mimeo Series. No. 19)

UNITED NATIONS INDUSTRIAL DEVELOPMENT ORGANIZATION. Monographs on Industrial Development. Industrialization of Developing Countries: Problems and Prospects. No. 16. Domestic and external financing; based on the proceedings of the International Symposium on Industrial Development, Athens, November-December 1967. (ID/40/16). New York, United Nations, 1969. pp. 48. bibliog.

DUNNING (JOHN HARRY) Studies in international investment. London, 1970. pp. 400. bibliog.

INVESTMENTS, FOREIGN (Cont'd.)

> LITVAK (ISAIAH A.) and MAULE (CHRISTOPHER JOHN) eds. Foreign investment: the experiences of host countries. New York, 1970. pp. 406. bibliog.
>
> ORGANISATION FOR ECONOMIC CO-OPERATION AND DEVELOPMENT. 1970. Investing in developing countries: facilities for the promotion of foreign private investment in developing countries. Paris, 1970. pp. 120.
>
> BERTIN (GILLES Y.) L'investissement public international. Paris, 1971. pp. 204. bibliog.
>
> ROBINSON (HARRY JOSEPH) Prospectus preparation for international private investment: a guide for the developing countries. New York, 1971. pp. 103.

INVESTMENTS, FOREIGN
See also INTERNATIONAL CENTRE FOR SETTLEMENT OF INVESTMENT DISPUTES

- Law and legislation

> ORGANISATION FOR ECONOMIC CO-OPERATION AND DEVELOPMENT. 1962. Code of liberalisation of capital movements; (with Amendments). [in French and English] [Paris], 1962. pp. 69.
>
> ORGANISATION FOR ECONOMIC CO-OPERATION AND DEVELOPMENT. 1965. Code of liberalisation of capital movements, June, 1965. [Paris], 1965. pp. 165. 27cm. In English and French. For 1962 edition see ORGANISATION FOR ECONOMIC CO-OPERATION AND DEVELOPMENT. 1962.
>
> HENDERSON (JULIAN) Foreign investment laws and agriculture: a study of the legislative and other measures taken by developing countries to attract and regulate foreign private investment, with special reference to agriculture, including forestry, fisheries and related industries. Rome, Food and Agriculture Organization, 1970. pp. 224. bibliog. (Food and Agriculture Organization. Legislative Series. No. 9.)
>
> SZÁSZY (ISTVÁN) Conflicts of laws arising from investments in developing countries. Budapest, 1970. pp. 25. (Magyar Tudományos Akademia. Afro Azsiai Kutato Központ. Studies on Developing Countries. No. 32)

- Law and legislation - Colombia

> POSADA URIBE (CARLOS A.) Estatuto legal para las inversiones privadas de los extranjeros en Colombia. Bogotá, Kelly, 1966. pp. 110. bibliog. 23½cm.

- Law and legislation - Korea

> KOREA (REPUBLIC). Statutes, etc. 1966. Foreign capital inducement law, with its enforcement decree and working rules for implementation. [Seoul?, 1967?] pp. 85.
>
> KOREA (REPUBLIC). Statutes, etc. 1953-1970. The laws and regulations pertaining to foreign capital inducement. [Seoul], 1970. pp. 311.

- Law and legislation - Mexico

> WRIGHT (HARRY K.) Foreign enterprise in Mexico: laws and policies. Chapel Hill, [1971] pp. 425. (American Society of International Law. Studies in Foreign Investment and Economic Development)

- Law and legislation - Yugoslavia

> SUKIJASOVIĆ (MIODRAG) Yugoslav foreign investment legislation at work: experiences so far. 2nd ed. Belgrade, 1970. pp. 178. bibliog.

- Africa

> HELLEINER (GERALD KARL) New forms of private foreign investment in Africa. Brighton, 1969. pp. 17. (Brighton. University of Sussex. Institute of Development Studies. Mimeo Series. No. 23)
>
> LARDNER (G.E.A.) Some aspects of the role of foreign private enterprise in developing countries in Africa. Brighton, 1969. pp.27. (Brighton. University of Sussex. Institute of Development Studies. Mimeo Series. No. 24.

- Africa, North

> NEHRT (LEE CHARLES) The political climate for private foreign investment, with special reference to North Africa. New York, 1970. pp. 391. bibliog.

- Africa, West

> WEST AFRICA COMMITTEE. Foreign investment: its role in the development of Commonwealth West Africa. London, 1968. pp.25. 24cm.

- America, Latin

> MONTENEGRO (CARLOS) Las inversiones extranjeras en América Latina. Buenos Aires, Coyoacán, 1962. pp. 87. 18cm. (Ediciones Coyoacán. 35)
>
> INTER-AMERICAN DEVELOPMENT BANK. 1966. La participación de Europa en el financiamiento del desarrollo de América Latina. Mexico, Centro de Estudios Monetarios Latinoamericanos, 1966. pp. vii, 412. 21cm.
>
> RICHMOND (LEONARD T.) La crises de inversiones en America Latina: un nuevo enfoque de los problemas económicos Latino Americanos; The Latin American investment crisis: a new approach to economic problems in Latin America. Montevideo, Barreiro y Ramos, [1967]. pp. 229. 19½cm. In English and Spanish.
>
> GANNON (THOMAS A.) ed. Doing business in Latin America. [New York], American Management Association, [1968]. pp. 127. 22½cm.
>
> MULTINATIONAL investment in the economic development and integration of Latin America; Round Table [organized by the Inter-American Development Bank] Bogota, Inter-American Development Bank, 1968. pp. 381.
>
> WIONCZEK (MIGUEL S.) Lateinamerika und das ausländische Kapital. Hamburg, [1969]. pp. 77. bibliog. (Institut für Iberoamerika-Kunde, Schriftenreihe Band 15)
>
> ECONOMIST INTELLIGENCE UNIT. Q[uarterly] E[conomic] R[eview] Specials. No. 6. Investment in Latin America; by Penelope Roper. London, 1970. pp. 38. bibliog.

MIKESELL (RAYMOND FRECH) and others. Foreign investment in the petroleum and mineral industries: case studies of investor-host country relations;... [sponsored by] Resources for the future, Inc. Baltimore, [1971]. pp. 459. bibliog.

ORGANIZATION OF AMERICAN STATES. 1971. External financing for Latin American development. Baltimore, [1971]. pp. 248.

- Argentine Republic

LAURANT (HENRY W.) Factors affecting foreign investment in Argentina. Menlo Park, Stanford Research Institute, International Development Center, 1963. pp. xii, 64. bibliog. 28cm. (Investment Series. 5)

KATZ (JORGE M.) Production functions, foreign investment and growth: a study based on the Argentine manufacturing sector, 1946-1961. Amsterdam, 1969. pp. 203. bibliog. 22½cm.

MINKNER (MECHTHILD) and BOHRISCH (ALEXANDER) Investitionsklima und Auslandskapital in Argentinien. Hamburg, 1970. pp. 181. bibliog. (Institut für Iberoamerika-Kunde. Private Auslandsinvestitionen in Lateinamerika. Nr.2)

- Asia

MURRAY (ANN) ed. Foreign investment and development in Asia: a seminar report. [Singapore], 1969. fo. 27. (Singapore. University. Economic Research Centre. Seminar Series. No.1)

- Australia

AUSTRALIA. Australian News and Information Bureau, [Canberra]. 1966. Australia: an economic and investment reference. [Canberra?, 1966]. pp. 106. bibliog. 30cm.

AUSTRALIA. Australian News and Information Bureau, [Canberra]. 1968. Australia: an economic and investment reference. [new ed.] [Canberra, 1968]. pp. 112. bibliog. 30½cm.

HOGAN (WARREN P.) Foreign investment and capital inflows. [Brisbane], U. of Queensland P., 1968. pp. 32. bibliog. 21cm. (English, Scottish and Australian Bank. Research Lectures, 1968)

AUSTRALIA. Commonwealth Bureau of Census and Statistics. 1969-70. Overseas participation in Australian manufacturing industry, 1962-63 and 1966-67. Canberra, [1969-1970]. 2 pts.

- Australia - Western Australia

WESTERN AUSTRALIA. 1964. Key to investment: Western Australia. [Perth, 1964?]. pp. 24. 27½cm.

- Belgium

INSTITUT BELGE D'INFORMATION ET DE DOCUMENTATION. Foreign investments in Belgium. Brussels, Ministry of Foreign Affairs and External Trade, 1968. pp. 7. (Belgian News. No.3c)

- Bolivia

ROCABADO ALCOCER (RENÉ) Bolivia a precio de costo: subasta de las universidades, zinc y petróleo. [Cochabamba], Universidad de San Simón, Centro de Estudiantes de Derecho, 1967. pp. 73. 17½cm. (Cuadernos).

- Brazil

BASTOS (HUMBERTO) Desenvolvimento ou escravidão: aspectos de influências externas na formação econômica do Brasil. São Paulo, Martins, 1964. pp. 391. bibliog. 21cm.

FERREIRA (PINTO) Capitais estrangeiros e dívida externa do Brasil. [São Paulo], Editôra Brasiliense, [1965]. pp. viii, 230. 21cm.

RABELO (GENIVAL) O capital estrangeiro na imprensa brasileira. Rio de Janeiro, Civilização Brasileira, 1966. pp. (viii), 287. 21cm. (Retratos do Brasil. vol.49)

SCHILLING (PAULO R.) Una historia sucia: el capital extranjero en el Brasil. [Montevideo, L.Y.S., 1968]. pp. 80. 16½cm. (Colección Cerro Corá. 2)

JOLOWICZ (HANS) Erfahrungen ausländischer Investoren in Brasilien. Hamburg, 1970. pp. 107. bibliog. (Institut für Iberoamerika-Kunde. Private Auslandsinvestitionen in Lateinamerika. Nr.1)

JOLOWICZ (HANS) Wirtschaftliche und rechtliche Aspekte des Investitionsklimas in Brasilien. Hamburg, 1970. pp. 154. bibliog. (Institut für Iberoamerika-Kunde. Private Auslandsinvestitionen in Lateinamerika. Nr. 3)

- Canada

CANADA. Task Force on the Structure of Canadian Industry. 1968. Foreign ownership and the structure of Canadian industry; report; (prepared for the Privy Council Office). Ottawa, 1968. pp. 427.

REUBER (GRANT LOUIS) and ROSEMAN (FRANK) The take-over of Canadian firms, 1945-61: an empirical analysis. Ottawa, 1969. pp. viii, 242. 25cm. (Canada. Economic Council of Canada. Special Studies. No. 10.)

CAVES (RICHARD E.) and REUBER (GRANT LOUIS) Capital transfers and economic policy: Canada, 1951-1962. Cambridge, Mass., 1971. pp. 432. bibliog. (Harvard University. Harvard Economic Studies. vol. 135)

- Caribbean Area

CARIBBEAN ECONOMIC DEVELOPMENT CORPORATION. Investing in the Caribbean. San Juan, 1970. 3 vols.

- Colombia

COLOMBIA. Ministerio de Relaciones Exteriores. Subsecretaria de Asuntos Economicos. 1957. Garantias al capital extranjero. Bogota, 1957. pp. 108.

- Europe

ORGANISATION FOR EUROPEAN ECONOMIC CO-OPERATION. Committee for Invisible Transactions. 1961. Liberalisation of current invisibles and capital movements by the OEEC. Paris, 1961. pp. 47.

PARIS. Université. Institut d'Administration des Entreprises and ASSOCIATION POUR LE DEVELOPPEMENT DES ETUDES DE GESTION DES ENTREPRISES. Les investissements étrangers en Europe: seminaire...; avec la collaboration de P.Uri [and others]. Paris, Dunod, 1968. pp. xi, 267. 24cm.

INVESTMENTS, FOREIGN (Cont'd.)

- Europe, Eastern

POSSONY (STEFAN THOMAS) Wirtschaftshilfe oder Aussenhandel mit dem Osten?: Perspektiven wirtschaftlicher Zusammenarbeit. Bonn, [1967]. pp. 43.

BANDERA (VLADIMIR NICHOLAS) Foreign capital as an instrument of national economic policy: a study based on the experience of East European countries between the World Wars. 2nd. ed. The Hague, Nijhoff, 1968. pp. xiv, 156. bibliog. 24cm.

- European Economic Community countries

PARIS. Université. Faculté de Droit et des Sciences Économiques. Travaux et Recherches. Série "Europe". No.7. La politique industrielle de l'Europe intégrée et l'apport des capitaux extérieurs; Paris, 23-27 mai 1966. Paris, P.U.F., 1968. pp. xvi, 410. 24cm.

- France

MANUALI (LOUIS) La France face à l'implantation étrangère. Paris, Société d'Éditions Économiques et Financières, 1967. pp. 130. 27cm.

- Germany

KRAUSHAAR (ROLF) Die steuerlichen Vorteile ausländischer Kapitalgesellschaften gegenüber inländischen bei Direktinvestitionen in der Bundesrepublik Deutschland unter besonderer Berücksichtigung des gespaltenen Körperschaftsteuersatzes, etc. [Bamberg, imprint], 1966. pp. 186. bibliog.

NORTH RHINE-WESTPHALIA. 1967. Die Kapitalverflechtung der Montanindustrie in Nordrhein-Westfalen mit dem Ausland. (Forschungsberichte des Landes Nordrhein-Westfalen. Nr. 1681) Köln, Westdeutscher Verlag, 1967. pp. 225. 24cm.

ADOLF-WEBER-STIFTUNG. Schriften. Aspekte der Stabilitäts- und Wachstumspolitik: Professoren-Kolloquien der...Stiftung. Berlin, [1969]. pp. 131.

AUSLANDSKAPITAL in der deutschen Wirtschaft; herausgegeben von...Winfried Schmitz-Esser. Bonn, [1969]. pp. 520.

- Ghana

GHANA. President, 1960-1966 (Nkrumah). 1962. Overseas capital and investment in Ghana: text of a speech by Kwame Nkrumah... March 24th, 1962. London, [1962]. pp. (3).

BREUER (HELMUT) and others. Estimation of foreign capital requirements as a guide to economic policy: the case of Ghana for 1968-1972. Berlin, 1969. pp. 92. bibliog.

- Greece

COMMERCIAL BANK OF GREECE, and others. Investment guide to Greece. rev. ed. Athens, 1969. pp. 118.

- Guatemala

CENTRO DE DESARROLLO Y PRODUCTIVIDAD INDUSTRIAL [GUATEMALA]. Guia del inversionista; [by] Ruben Ayala Muñoz. [Guatemala], 1964. pp. 104. (Estudios y Publicaciones)

- India

ALL INDIA SEMINAR ON FOREIGN COLLABORATION, UNIVERSITY OF BOMBAY, 1965. Foreign collaboration: report and proceedings of the seminar held by the Centre of Advanced Studies, Department of Economics, University of Bombay, February 1-3, 1965; edited by Professor R.K. Hazari. Bombay, 1967. pp. 271. (Bombay (City). University. Economic Series. No. 15)

BREUER (HELMUT) Die Industrialisierung Indiens unter dem Druck der steigenden Auslandsverschuldung: eine Konfliktanalyse der bisherigen Planstrategien. Berlin, Duncker und Humblot, 1967. pp. 162. bibliog. 23cm. (Volkswirtschaftliche Schriften. Heft 112)

SHIVARAMU (SHIVANNA) Foreign ventures in India: the Swedish case. Stockholm, Svenska Bokförlaget, [1967]. pp. ix, 134. bibliog. 21cm. (Scandinavian University Books)

RESERVE BANK OF INDIA. Foreign collaboration in Indian industry: survey report. Bombay, 1968. pp. viii, 140. 27cm.

SEMINAR ON INTERNATIONAL INVESTMENT: INDIA, NEW DELHI, 1968. [Proceedings, background papers, and speeches,...held at Vigyan Bhavan, New Delhi, 27-29 November, 1968]. New Delhi, 1969. pp. xi, 205.

TOMLINSON (JAMES W.C.) The joint venture process in international business: India and Pakistan. Cambridge, Mass., [1970]. pp. 227. bibliog.

- India - Directories

DIRECTORY of foreign collaborations in India; (compiled and edited by J.N. Gupta [and others]). Delhi, [1968]. 2 vols.

- Indonesia

INDONESIA. Department of Information. 1968. Investment: new policies and procedures on Indonesia's foreign capital investment. Djakarta, [1968]. pp. 152. 18cm.

- Israel

[BEN-SHAHAR (HAIM)] Public international development financing in Israel. New York, Columbia University, School of Law, 1963. pp. vi, 136. 27½cm. (Public International Development Financing [Research Project]. Reports. No. 5.)

ISRAEL. Investment Authority. 1968. Israel investors' manual. 2nd ed. [Tel Aviv], 1968. pp. 99. 22cm.

- Italy

ORTELLI (FAUSTO) Il contributo degli investimenti esteri allo sviluppo dell'economia italiana, sino al 1961. [Zürich, Polygraphischer Verlag], 1966. pp. (x), 167. bibliog. (Staatswissenschaftliche Studien. Neue Folge. Band 57)

SOCIETÀ RICERCHE E STUDI. Effetti degli investimenti esteri in Italia. Milano, Etas Kompass, 1968. pp. 359. 24cm.

- Jamaica

JAMAICA. Industrial Development Corporation. Information Pamphlets. No.1. Opportunities for industrial investment. Kingston, 1961. fo. 13. 28cm.

- Japan

ORGANISATION FOR ECONOMIC CO-OPERATION AND DEVELOPMENT. Committee for Invisible Transactions. 1968. Liberalisation of international capital movements: Japan. Paris, 1968. pp. 179.

- Korea

KIM (SEUNG HEE) Foreign capital for economic development: a Korean case study. New York, 1970. pp. 206. bibliog. (New York (City). University. Center for International Studies. Studies in Peaceful Change)

- Malaya

JACKSON (JAMES C.) Planters and speculators: Chinese and European agricultural enterprise in Malaya. 1786-1921. Kuala Lumpur, U. of Malaya P., 1968. pp. xxi, 312. bibliog. 21½cm.

- Mexico

WIONCZEK (MIGUEL S.) El nacionalismo mexicano y la inversión extranjera. México, Siglo Veintuno, 1967. pp. viii, 314. bibliog. 17½cm. (El Mundo del Hombre. Economía y Demografia)

BOHRISCH (ALEXANDER) Probleme privater Auslandsinvestitionen in Mexico. Hamburg, 1969. pp. 130. bibliog. (Institut für Iberoamerika-Kunde. Schriftenreihe. 11)

- Netherlands

NETHERLANDS. Ministerie van Economische Zaken. 1968- Guide to the establishing of industrial operations in the Netherlands. The Hague, 1968 in progress. Loose-leaf binder.

NETHERLANDS. Ministerie van Economische Zaken. 1969. Industrial operations in the Netherlands: facts and figures. The Hague, 1969. pp. 41. Map in front pocket.

- New Zealand

NEW ZEALAND. Department of Industries and Commerce. 1957. Investment in New Zealand. [Wellington, 1957]. fo. 57.

NEW ZEALAND. Department of Industries and Commerce. 1966. New Zealand - a sound investment. Wellington, 1966. 6 pts (in 1.)

DEANE (RODERICK S.) Foreign investment in New Zealand manufacturing. Wellington, N.Z., 1970. pp. 540. bibliog.

- Nigeria

NIGERIA (WESTERN REGION). 1959. Western Nigeria: gateway to Africa. London, [1959]. pp. 31.

ECONOMIST INTELLIGENCE UNIT. Investment opportunities in Eastern Nigeria. [Enugu, 1960] pp. 56. bibliog.

NIGERIA (EASTERN REGION). Ministry of Commerce. 1962. Investment opportunities in Eastern Nigeria. 2nd ed. Enugu, 1962. pp. 53. bibliog.

NIGERIA (EASTERN REGION). Ministry of Commerce. 1966 Investment opportunities in Eastern Nigeria. 3rd ed. Enugu, 1966. pp. 96.

NIGERIA (NORTH CENTRAL STATE). Ministry of Trade and Industry. 1967. Trade and industry: a comprehensive review of trade and industrial potential in the six northern states of the Federation of Nigeria. Kaduna, [1967?]. pp. 71. 25cm.

MUMMERY (DAVID R.) The protection of international private investment: Nigeria and the world community. New York, Praeger, 1968. pp. xxvii, 198. bibliog. 23½cm. (Praeger Special Studies in International Economics and Development)

- Pakistan

TOMLINSON (JAMES W.C.) The joint venture process in international business: India and Pakistan. Cambridge, Mass., [1970]. pp. 227. bibliog.

- Peru

MALPICA (CARLOS) El mito de la ayuda exterior. Lima, Moncloa, 1967. pp. 239. 22cm. (Toda la Realidad. 4)

- Rhodesia and Nyasaland, Federation of

FEDERATION OF RHODESIA AND NYASALAND. 1957. Final report of the American investment adviser to the Federation of Rhodesia and Nyasaland [Geo. F. Spaulding] covering the portion of his assignment spent in the Federation, April 23rd, 1956 to May 26th, 1957; (with Supplement on agriculture). [Salisbury, 1957]. pp. 21,7. 30cm.

- Russia

SVERDLOV (N.V.) Zakhvatnicheskaia politika inostrannykh kapitalistov na rysskom Dal'nem Vostoke i ee krakh, 1900-1917 gg. in Iz istorii sovetskogo Dal'nego Vostoka, Khabarovsk, 1963.

McKAY (JOHN P.) Pioneers for profit: foreign entrepreneurship and Russian industrialization, 1885-1913. Chicago, 1970. pp. 442. bibliog.

- Sierra Leone

SIERRA LEONE. Ministry of Information and Broadcasting. 1965. Investment opportunities in Sierra Leone. [London], [1965?] pp. 47.

- Singapore

HUGHES (HELEN) and SENG (YOU POH) eds. Foreign investment and industrialisation in Singapore. Canberra, 1969. pp. 226.

- Spain

SPAIN. 1963. Oportunidades del capital extranjero en España. (Organización Sindical Española) 2nd ed. [Madrid], 1963. pp. 78.

INVESTMENTS, FOREIGN (Cont'd.)

- Switzerland

SCHILTKNECHT (KURT) Beurteilung der Gentlemen's Agreements und Konjunkturbeschlüsse der Jahre 1954-1966, unter besonderer Berücksichtigung der Auslandgelder. [Zurich, 1969?]. pp. 200. bibliog.

- United Kingdom

U.K. Department of Trade and Industry. Business monitor: Miscellaneous series. M4. Overseas transactions. a., 1969- London.

MILLARD (PATRICIA) British made?...just how much British-made is really made in Britain. Havant, Mason. 1969. pp. 187. 21½cm.

U.K. Central Office of Information. Reference Division. Reference Pamphlets. 98. Britain's international investment position. London, 1971. pp. 67. bibliog.

- United States

UNITED STATES. Business Economics Office. Foreign business investments in the United States. Washington, 1962. pp. v, 58.

CONFERENCE: "DIRECT INVESTMENT IN THE ATLANTIC AREA", WASHINGTON, 1969. The multinational corporation in the world economy: direct investment in perspective; edited by Sidney E. Rolfe, Walter Damm. New York, 1970. pp. 169.

- Venezuela

CRAZUT (RAFAEL J.) Consideraciones acerca de las inversiones privadas extranjeras en Venezuela. Caracas, Comisión Nacional del Cuatricentenário de la Fundación de Caracas, [1967]. pp. 147. 23cm. (Ediciones del Cuatricentário de Caracas. Série de Obras Económicas)

- Vietnam

VIET-NAM (REPUBLIC). Department of National Economy. 1957. Investing in Viet-Nam. Saigon, [1957?]. pp. 65.

- Yugoslavia

ORGANISATION FOR ECONOMIC CO-OPERATION AND DEVELOPMENT. Committee for Invisible Transactions. 1970. Foreign investment in Yugoslavia. Paris, 1970. pp. 30.

INVESTMENTS, FOREIGN (INTERNATIONAL LAW)

LAUTERPACHT (E.) The World Bank convention on the settlement of international investment disputes. in Recueil d'études de droit international en hommage à Paul Guggenheim. Genève, 1968.

SCHWARZENBERGER (GEORG) Foreign investments and international law. London, Stevens, 1969. pp. xxiii, 237. bibliog. 24cm. (London Institute of World Affairs. Library of World Affairs. No. 68)

INVESTMENTS, FRENCH

- Cameroun

CAMEROUN. Service d'Information. 1959. Cameroons: 10 years of investments and progress under the leadership of France. [Yaoundé?, 1959?]. pp. 39.

- Italy

GILLE (BERTRAND) Les investissements français en Italie, 1815-1914. Torino, 1968. pp. 433. bibliog. (Italy. Istituto per la Ricostruzione Industriale. Archivio Economico dell'Unificazione Italiana. Serie 2. Vol. 16)

INVESTMENTS, GERMAN

SEIFERT (HUBERTUS) Die deutschen Direktinvestitionen im Ausland: ihre statistische Erfassung als Instrument der internationalen technisch-wirtschaftlichen Zusammenarbeit. Köln, Westdeutscher Verlag, 1967. pp. 125. bibliog. 24cm. (Aachen. Technische Hochschule. Forschungsinstitut für Internationale Technisch-Wirtschaftliche Zusammenarbeit. Internationale Kooperation. 1) With English summary.

GROSCHE (GUENTER) and LEHMANN-RICHTER (ROLF) Die Gewinne aus deutschen Direktinvestitionen in Entwicklungsländern:...unter besonderer Berücksichtigung der reinvestierten Gewinne. Düsseldorf, [1970]. pp. 98. bibliog. (Bochum. Ruhr-Universität. Institut für Entwicklungsforschung und Entwicklungspolitik. Bochumer Schriften zur Entwicklungsforschung und Entwicklungspolitik. Band 11)

- Taxation - Chile

NORTHMANN (R.J.) Die Besteuerung deutscher Privatinvestitionen in Chile. Herme, Neue Wirtschafts-Briefe, 1967. pp. 150, bibliog. 21cm. (Munich. Forschungsstelle für Internationales Steuerrecht. Schriftenreihe "Steuern in Entwicklungsländern". Heft 3)

- Africa

HEIDELBERG (WOLFGANG) Grundzüge des Niederlassungsrechts in den afrikanischen Staaten. Hamburg, the Institut, 1965 in progress. bibliog. 24cm. (Deutsches Institut für Afrika-Forschung. Hamburger Beiträge zur Afrika-Kunde)

- Russia

LEVIN (I.I.) Germanskie kapitaly v Rossii. S.-Peterburg, 1914. pp. 87.

- Tunis

WIEDENSOHLER (GUENTER) Der Schutz deutschen Privatinvestitionen in Tunesien. Hamburg, Hamburgisches Weltwirtschafts-Archiv, 1966. pp. 73. bibliog. 20½cm.

INVESTMENTS, ITALIAN

- Nigeria

ITALY. Italian Embassy, Lagos. Commercial Office. 1967. Italians in Nigeria: a story of successful international co-operation. Lagos, [1967]. pp. 132. 24½cm.

INVESTMENTS, NORWEGIAN

- Taxation

BORGENVIK (HALLVARD) Inntekts- og formuesskattlegging av norske Kapitalplasseringer i utlandet; income and net wealth taxes of Norwegian investment in foreign countries. Oslo, 1969. pp. 38. 23½cm. (Norway, Statistiske Centralbyrå. Artikler. Nr.27) With English summary.

INVESTMENTS, SWEDISH

- India

SHIVARAMU (SHIVANNA) Foreign ventures in India: the Swedish case. Stockholm, Svenska Bokförlaget, [1967]. pp. ix, 134. bibliog. 21cm. (Scandinavian University Books)

INVESTMENTS, SWISS

BROGLE (URS) Zur Frage des schweizerischen Kapitalexports. Zurich, Polygraphischer Verlag, 1963. pp. vii, 82. bibliog. 22½cm. (Staatswissenschaftliche Studien. Neue Folge. Band 50)

KECSKÉS (GYULA) Private Investitionen in Entwicklungsländern in der Nachkriegszeit. [Kiel, imprint], 1965. pp. 182 bibliog.

IORGA (NICOLAE)

GEORGESCU (T.) Nicolae Iorga, historien roumain, dans la lutte contre l'hitlérisme. in Comité National des Historiens de la République Socialiste de Roumanie. Nouvelles études d'histoire. Bucarest, 1965.

NETEA (V.) Nicolae Iorga, historien et défenseur des peuples d'Autriche-Hongrie. in Comité National des Historiens de la République Socialiste de Roumanie. Nouvelles études d'histoire. Bucarest, 1965.

GEORGESCU (TITU) Nicolae Iorga împotriva hitlerismului. București, 1966. pp. 146.

IPL (COMPUTER PROGRAMME LANGUAGE)
See I. P. L. (COMPUTER PROGRAMME LANGUAGE)

IPSWICH

- Biography

PUBLIC men of Ipswich and East Suffolk: a series of personal sketches re-printed from the Suffolk Mercury. Ipswich, Scopes, 1875. pp. xvi, 295. 18cm. Title page bears the ascription "By Richard Gowing"

- Civic improvement

SHANKLAND, COX AND ASSOCIATES. Expansion of Ipswich: designation proposals; consultants' study of the town in its sub-region; a report to the Minister of Housing and Local Government (with Expansion of Ipswich: comparative costs; a supplementary report) London, H.M.S.O., 1966-68. 2 pts. 29½cm.

SHANKLAND, COX AND ASSOCIATES. Ipswich draft basic plan: consultants' proposals for the expanded town: a report to the Minister of Housing and Local Government and Ipswich County Borough Council. London, H.M.S.O., 1968. pp. 151.

SUFFOLK. East Suffolk. County Council and IPSWICH. Corporation. Ipswich fringe area: interim planning statement [by] C.W. Smith [and] G.I. Ramsdale. [Ipswich], 1970. pp. 17. bibliog.

- Harbour

GWILLIAM (KENNETH MASON) A pilot study of the haven ports of Harwich, Felixstowe and Ipswich. London, [1967]. pp. 93. (Leeds. University. Centre for Transport Studies. Reprint Series. No. 3)

IQUITOS

- Social conditions

CENTRO DE INVESTIGACIONES SOCIALES POR MUESTREO. Estudio de la ciudad de Iquitos: movilidad ocupacional, educacion, migracion, encuesta de hogares de Iquitos. Lima, 1968. 1 vol.(various pagings).

IRAK
See IRAQ

IRAN

FRYE (RICHARD NELSON) Persia. rev. ed. London, Allen and Unwin, 1968. pp. 128. bibliog. 18cm.

- Boundaries

IRAQ. Ministry of Foreign Affairs. 1960. Facts concerning the Iraqi-Iranian frontier. [Baghdad], 1960. pp. 36.

- Census

IRAN. Census, 1966. National census of population and housing, November 1966: total country - settled population. [Tehran], 1968. pp. (xxvi, xxxii, 190). 29cm. In English and Persian.

- Commerce

INDIA. British Indian Commercial Mission to South-Eastern Persia, 1904-1905. Reports by A. H. Gleadowe-Newcomen. Calcutta, 1906. pp. (ii), 156. 34cm. Map in front pocket.

FRANCE. Direction de la Documentation. La Documentation Française. Notes et Études Documentaires. No. 2,982. Le commerce extérieur de l'Iran. Paris, 1963. pp. 16. 30½cm.

BAIBURTIAN (VAGAN ARAKELOVICH) Armianskaia koloniia Novoi Dzhul'fy v XVII veke: rol' Novoi Dzhul'fy v irano-evropeiskikh politicheskikh i ekonomicheskikh sviaziakh. Erevan, 1969. pp. 167. With English summary.

- Commerce - Statistics

INTERNAL TRADE STATISTICS IN IRAN; ([pd. by] Bureau of Statistics [Iran]). a., 1968- Tehran.

IRAN - Commerce - Statistics (Cont'd.)

    IRAN. Bureau of Statistics. Trends in industrial and commercial statistics. [in English and Persian] Tehran, irreg., [1968] [2nd series, no. 1] to date. 27cm.

- Constitution

    IRAN. Constitution. 1906. The Iranian constitution with amendments; translated by A. P. Saleh. (Ministry of Foreign Affairs) Teheran, 1961. pp. 39. 27cm.

- Economic conditions

    IRAN. 1957. An economic survey of Iran. (Iranian Embassy, London) London, 1957. pp. 54. bibliog. 24½cm.

    INTERNATIONAL STUDENT CONFERENCE. Research and Information Commission. Iran: a report ...1961/62. Leiden, 1962. pp. 36.

    RAZAWI (HOSSEIN) Die Strukturveränderungen der iranischen Wirtschaft unter besonderer Berücksichtigung von Landwirtschaft, Industrie und Verkehr. [Cologne, imprint, 1962?]. pp. 267. bibliog.

    UNITED STATES. International Commerce Bureau. A market for U.S. products in Iran. Washington pp. x, 50. bibliog. 1966.

    BUDGET OF THE IMPERIAL GOVERNMENT OF IRAN, THE; [pd. by] Central Bureau of the Budget, Plan Organization [Iran]. a., 1347 (1968/9)- Tehran. File includes suppl., Prime Minister's report to Parliament on economic conditions, etc. 1971/2-

- Economic conditions - Bibliography

    BARTSCH (WILLIAM HENRY) and BHARIER (JULIAN) compilers. The economy of Iran, 1940-1970: a bibliography. Durham, 1971. pp. 114. (Durham. University. Centre for Middle Eastern and Islamic Studies. Publications. No.2)

- Economic history

    BHARIER (JULIAN) Economic development in Iran, 1900-1970. London, 1971. pp. 314. bibliog.

- Economic policy

    IRAN. 1958. The Plan Organization of Iran: historical review, September 25, 1955-March 20, 1958; (based on a report by A.H. Ebtehaj to the Iranian legislature) [Tehran, 1958?] pp. 59. 25cm.

    IRAN. 1960. Iran plans for the future: a summary of activities, the Plan Organization of Iran. Tehran, 1960. pp. (ii), 47. 22cm.

    IRAN. Plan Organization. Division of Economic Affairs. 1960. Review of the second seven year plan program of Iran, March 10, 1960. Tehran, 1960. pp. 159.

    SADRI (AMIR) L'état et le financement du développement économique sur l'exemple iranien. Téhéran, 1965. pp. 205. bibliog. 24cm.

    IRAN. Plan Organization. 1968. Fourth national development plan, 1968-1972. Tehran, 1968. pp. 335.

    BUDGET OF THE IMPERIAL GOVERNMENT OF IRAN, THE; [pd. by] Central Bureau of the Budget, Plan Organization [Iran]. a., 1347 (1968/9)- Tehran. File includes suppl., Prime Minister's report to Parliament on economic conditions, etc. 1971/2-

- Foreign relations

    TAQIZADEH (S.H.) Memorandum on Persia's wishes and her aspirations addressed to the Peace Conference of Paris. The Hague, 1919. pp. 6.

    KAZEMZADEH (FIRUZ) Russia and Britain in Persia, 1864-1914: a study in imperialism. New Haven, Yale U.P., 1968. pp. xii, 711. bibliog. 23½cm. (Yale Russian and East European Studies. 6)

- Foreign relations - Azerbaijan

    ABDURAKHMANOV (ASIM AKHMED OGLY) Азербайджан во взаимоотношениях России, Турции и Ирана в первой половине XVIII в. Баку, АН Азерб. ССР, 1964. pp. 99. 20½cm.

- Foreign relations - Russia

    IUSUPOV (I. A.) Ustanovlenie i razvitie sovetsko-iranskikh otnoshenii, 1917-1927 gg. Tashkent, 1969. pp. 225. bibliog.

- Foreign relations - United Kingdom

    ELLIS (EDWARD ROGER INGRAM) British policy towards Persia and the defence of British India, 1798-1807; [Ph.D. (London) thesis]. [1968]. fo. xxi, 378. bibliog. 27½cm. Typescript: unpublished. This thesis is the property of London University and may not be removed from the Library.

- Foreign relations - United States

    HERAVI (MEHDI) Iranian-American diplomacy. Brooklyn, 1969. pp. 161. bibliog.

- History

    ARUTIUNIAN (GEORGII SAMVELOVICH) Иранская революция 1905-1911 гг. и большевики Закавказья. Ереван, 1956. pp. 163.

    The CAMBRIDGE history of Iran. Cambridge, C.U.P., 1968 in progress. bibliogs. 23cm.

    KAZEMZADEH (FIRUZ) Russia and Britain in Persia, 1864-1914: a study in imperialism. New Haven, Yale U.P., 1968. pp. xii, 711. bibliog. 23½cm. (Yale Russian and East European Studies. 6)

    SHABAN (M.A.) The 'Abbásid revolution. Cambridge, 1970. pp. 181. bibliog.

- Industries - Statistics

    IRAN. Bureau of Statistics. Trends in industrial and commercial statistics. [in English and Persian] Tehran, irreg., [1968] [2nd series, no. 1] to date. 27cm.

    IRANIAN INDUSTRIAL STATISTICS; ([pd. by] Bureau of Statistics [Iran]). a., 1968- Tehran.

    STATISTICS ON LARGE INDUSTRIAL ESTABLISHMENTS OF IRAN; ([pd. by] Bureau of Statistics [Iran]). a., 1968- Tehran.

- Kings and rulers

> BAYNE (E.A.) Persian kingship in transition: conversations with a monarch whose office is traditional and whose goal is modernization. New York, [1968]. pp. 288. bibliog.

- Neutrality

> IRAN. 1919. Requête adressée par le Gouvernement Persan à la Conférence des Préliminaires de Paix à Paris afin d'être admis à y participer. Paris, 1919. pp. 4.

- Politics and government

> INTERNATIONAL STUDENT CONFERENCE. Research and Information Commission. Iran: a report ...1961/62. Leiden, 1962. pp. 36.
>
> ROUZBEH (KHOSROV) Mein Herz schlägt für Irans Zukunft. Berlin, Dietz, 1964. pp. 169. 18cm.
>
> The REVOLUTION of the Shah and the people. London, Transorient, 1967. 11pts. (in 1). 21cm.
>
> SANGHVI (RAMESH) Aryamehr: the Shah of Iran; a political biography. London, Macmillan, 1968. pp. xxvi, 390. bibliog. 21½cm.
>
> NIRUMAND (BAHMAN) Iran: the new imperialism in action...; translated by Leonard Mins. New York, Monthly Review P., [1969]. pp. 192. 20cm.

- Population

> CHASTELAND (JEAN CLAUDE) and others. Etude sur la fécondité et quelques caracteristiques démographiques des femmes mariées dans quatre zones rurales d'Iran. Teheran, 1968. pp. 316.

- Rural conditions

> GHARATCHEHDAGHI (CYRUS) Distribution of land in Varamin: an opening phase of the agrarian reform in Iran. Opladen, Leske, 1967. pp. 179. bibliog. 24cm. (Deutsches Orient-Institut. Schriften. Materialien und Dokumente)

- Social life and customs

> ARASTEH (A. REZA) Faces of Persian youth: a sociological study. Leiden, 1970. pp. 268.

- Social policy

> IRAN. 1958. The Plan Organization of Iran: historical review, September 25, 1955-March 20, 1958; (based on a report by A.H. Ebtehaj to the Iranian legislature) [Tehran, 1958?] pp. 59. 25cm.
>
> IRAN. 1960. Iran plans for the future: a summary of activities, the Plan Organization of Iran. Tehran, 1960. pp. (ii), 47. 22cm.
>
> IRAN. Plan Organization. Division of Economic Affairs. 1960. Review of the second seven year plan program of Iran, March 10, 1960. Tehran, 1960. pp. 159.
>
> IRAN. Plan Organization. 1968. Fourth national development plan, 1968-1972. Tehran, 1968. pp. 335.

IRAQ

- Boundaries

> IRAQ. Ministry of Foreign Affairs. 1960. Facts concerning the Iraqi-Iranian frontier. [Baghdad], 1960. pp. 36.

- Commerce - Statistics

> UNITED NATIONS. Economic and Social Office in Beirut. 1967. Foreign trade statistics of Iraq, 1960-1963; reclassified according to the United Nations Standard International Trade Classification, 1960 revision (SITC, Revised) (ST/ESA/BEIRUT/2). New York, 1967. pp. 274.
>
> IRAQ. Central Statistical Organization. Department of Foreign Trade Statistics. Quarterly bulletin of foreign trade statistics. S[tandard] I[nternational] T[rade] C[lassification]. q., Ja/Mr 1969 [1st]- Baghdad.

- Constitution

> FRANCE. Direction de la Documentation. La Documentation Française. Notes et Etudes Documentaires. No. 3,205. La constitution intérimaire de la République d'Irak (10 mai 1964). Paris, 1965. pp. 9.
>
> FRANCE. Direction de la Documentation. La Documentation Française. Notes et Études Documentaires. No. 3,569. Constitution, provisoire de la République d'Irak (21 septembre 1968). Paris, 1969. pp. 11. 27cm.

- Description and travel

> AL-FEEL (MUHAMMAD RASHID) Iraq: geographic study, social and economic development. Baghdad, Ministry of Culture and Guidance, 1964. pp. 61,(25). bibliog. (Foreign Languages Books. 2)

- Economic conditions

> AL-FEEL (MUHAMMAD RASHID) Iraq: geographic study, social and economic development. Baghdad, Ministry of Culture and Guidance, 1964. pp. 61,(25). bibliog. (Foreign Languages Books. 2)
>
> MELICZEK (HANS) Die wirtschaftlichen und sozialpolitischen Verhältnisse im Irak unter besonderer Berücksichtigung von Agrarverfassung und Agrarreform. Frankfurt am Main, DLG-Verlag, 1966. pp. xvi, 309. bibliog. 21cm. (Zeitschrift für Ausländische Landwirtschaft. Materialsammlungen. Heft 6)
>
> KHODAYER ABBAS AL-MOOHOOR. Der Beitrag der Ölindustrie zur Entwicklung der irakischen Volkswirtschaft. [Bamberg, imprint, 1967]. pp. iv, a-c, 173, ix. bibliog.
>
> DIDDEN (HORST) Irak: eine sozio-ökonomische Betrachtung. Opladen, 1969. pp. 278. (Deutsches Orient-Institut. Schriften. Materialien und Dokumente)

- Economic policy

> IRAQ. Higher Committee for the Celebrations of the 14th July Revolution. 1959. The Iraqi revolution: one year of progress and achievement...1958-1959. [Baghdad, 1959]. pp. 128.

IRAQ - Economic policy (Cont'd.)

IRAQ. Ministry of Guidance. 1959. Provisional economic plan. [Baghdad, 1959?]. pp. 210.

IRAQ. Higher Committee for the Celebrations of the 14th July Revolution. 1960. The Iraqi revolution in its second year. Baghdad, 1960. pp. 437.

- Foreign relations

IRAQ. Prime Minister. 1956. Address by... Sayid Nuri as-Said, broadcast from Baghdad Radio on Dec. 16, 1956. Baghdad, [1956?]. pp. 26.

IRAQ. Embassy (U.K.) Office of the Press Attaché. 1965. Iraq: official statements of policy on internal, Arab and foreign affairs; (replacing the issue of the Bulletin of the Republic of Iraq for the months of November-December, 1965). London, 1965. pp. 63.

- Foreign relations - United Kingdom

MENTESHASHVILI (AL'BERT MIKHAILOVICH) Ирак в годы английского мандата. Москва, 1969. pp. 288. bibliog. With English summary.

FULEIHAN (DAVID ELLIS) The development of British policy in Iraq from 1914 to 1926; [Ph.D. (London) thesis]. 1970. fo. 233. bibliog. Typescript: unpublished. This thesis is the property of London University and may not be removed from the Library.

- History

MENTESHASHVILI (AL'BERT MIKHAILOVICH) Ирак в годы английского мандата. Москва, 1969. pp. 288. bibliog. With English summary.

FULEIHAN (DAVID ELLIS) The development of British policy in Iraq from 1914 to 1926; [Ph.D. (London) thesis]. 1970. fo. 233. bibliog. Typescript: unpublished. This thesis is the property of London University and may not be removed from the Library.

- Industries - Statistics

IRAQ. Central Statistical Organization. Industrial Statistics Department. Industrial statistics of small establishments. [in English and Arabic] a., 1969- [Baghdad]

- Nationalism

MENTESHASHVILI (AL'BERT MIKHAILOVICH) Ирак в годы английского мандата. Москва, 1969. pp. 288. bibliog. With English summary.

- Politics and government

IRAQ. Higher Committee for the Celebrations of the 14th July Revolution. 1959. The Iraqi revolution: one year of progress and achievement...1958-1959. [Baghdad, 1959]. pp. 128.

IRAQ. Higher Committee for the Celebrations of the 14th July Revolution. 1960. The Iraqi revolution in its second year. Baghdad, 1960. pp. 437.

IRAQI STUDENTS SOCIETY. Stop murder in Iraq. London, [1963]. s.sh.

IRAQ. Embassy (U.K.) Office of the Press Attaché. 1965. Iraq: official statements of policy on internal, Arab and foreign affairs; (replacing the issue of the Bulletin of the Republic of Iraq for the months of November-December, 1965). London, 1965. pp. 63.

RUINDEZH (D.) Борьба Иракского народа против Багдадского пакта, 1954-1959 гг. Баку, АН Азербайджанской ССР, 1966. pp. 121. bibliog. 20cm.

DANN (URIEL) Iraq under Qassem: a political history, 1958-1963. New York, Praeger, 1969. pp. xviii, 405. bibliog. $22\frac{1}{2}$cm.

KHADDURI (MAJID) Republican 'Iraq: a study in 'Iraqi politics since the revolution of 1958. London, 1969. pp. 318.

OIL, oppression and resistance in Iraq: [interview given by a leading member of the Iraqi Communist Party Central Command]. Nottingham, [1970]. pp. 8. (Spokesman, The. Pamphlets. No. 9)

- Sanitary affairs

IRAQ. Ministry of Guidance. 1960. Health in the republican regime. Baghdad, 1960. pp. 27.

- Social conditions

MELICZEK (HANS) Die wirtschaftlichen und sozialpolitischen Verhältnisse im Irak unter besonderer Berücksichtigung von Agrarverfassung und Agrarreform. Frankfurt am Main, DLG-Verlag, 1966. pp. xvi, 309. bibliog. 21cm. (Zeitschrift für Ausländische Landwirtschaft. Materialsammlungen. Heft 6)

DIDDEN (HORST) Irak: eine sozio-ökonomische Betrachtung. Opladen, 1969. pp. 278. (Deutsches Orient-Institut. Schriften. Materialien und Dokumente)

FERNEA (ROBERT A.) Shaykh and effendi: changing patterns of authority among the El Shabana of Southern Iraq. Cambridge, Mass., 1970. pp. 225. bibliog. (Harvard University. Center for Middle Eastern Studies. Harvard Middle Eastern Studies. 14)

- Social policy

IRAQ. Higher Committee for the Celebrations of the 14th July Revolution. 1959. The Iraqi revolution: one year of progress and achievement...1958-1959. [Baghdad, 1959]. pp. 128.

IRAQ. Higher Committee for the Celebrations of the 14th July Revolution. 1960. The Iraqi revolution in its second year. Baghdad, 1960. pp. 437.

- Statistics

IRAQ. Central Statistical Organization. Quarterly bulletin of statistics (formerly M. bulletin of statistics). Baghdad, quarterly, 1940-1968, with gap.

IRAQ. Central Bureau of Statistics. 1968. Statistical handbook of the Republic of Iraq for the years 1957-1967. Baghdad, 1968. pp. 261.

IRELAND

- Antiquities

NORMAN (EDWARD ROBERT) and ST. JOSEPH (JOHN KENNETH SINCLAIR) The early development of Irish society: the evidence of aerial photography. Cambridge, 1969. pp. 125. bibliog.

- Army - History

O'CASEY (SEAN) The story of the Irish citizen army; by P. O Cathasaigh [pseud.]. Dublin, Maunsel, 1919. pp.vii, 72. 18cm.

- Boundaries

IRISH BOUNDARY COMMISSION. Report...1925; introduction by Geoffrey J. Hand. Shannon, Irish University Press, [1969]. pp. various. 2 maps in end pocket.

- Church history

WATT (J.A.) The church and the two nations in medieval Ireland. Cambridge, 1970. pp. 251. bibliog.

- Civilization

NORMAN (EDWARD ROBERT) and ST. JOSEPH (JOHN KENNETH SINCLAIR) The early development of Irish society: the evidence of aerial photography. Cambridge, 1969. pp. 125. bibliog.

O'FAOLAIN (SEAN) The Irish. 2nd ed. Harmondsworth, 1969. pp. 173.

- Commerce - Congresses

ALL-IRELAND INDUSTRIAL CONFERENCE, 4TH, GALWAY, 1908. Proceedings. Galway, [1908]. pp. 56.

- Commerce - United Kingdom

CLARKE (THOMAS BROOKE) The case of Ireland, setting forth various difficulties experienced in its commercial intercourse with Great Britain, since the Union, in a letter to the Rt. Hon. Henry Addington, Chancellor of the Exchequer, etc. London, Cadell and Davies, 1802. pp. 39. 23cm.

CULLEN (LOUIS MICHAEL) Anglo-Irish trade, 1660-1800. Manchester, Manchester U. P., [1968]. pp. viii, 252. bibliog. 21½cm.

-Description and travel

FREEMAN (THOMAS WALTER) Ireland: a general and regional geography. 4th ed. London, Methuen, 1969. pp. xix, 557. bibliog. 21½cm. (Advanced Geographies)

IRISH geographical studies in honour of E. Estyn Evans; edited by Nicholas Stephens and Robin E. Glasscock. [Belfast], 1970. pp. 403. bibliogs.

- Dictionaries and encyclopaedias

ENCYCLOPAEDIA of Ireland; [principal editor Victor Meally]. Dublin, Figgis, 1968. pp. 463. bibliogs. 28cm.

- Economic conditions

ATHERTON (HENRY) Remarks on the condition of Ireland. [Lewes, 1873?] pp. 10.

FOX (JOSEPH HOYLAND) A visit to Ireland: a reprint of a lecture delivered in the Town Hall, Wellington, Somerset, June 19th, 1888. Taunton, [1888]. pp. 14.

La PRIMA fra le piccole nazioni: paragone tra l'Irlanda e le piccole nazioni libere d'Europa. [192-?]. pp. 19.

CLAMPETT (G. J. T.) Some economic needs of Ireland. Dublin, 1922. pp. 24.

O'HIGGINS (KEVIN) Three years hard labour: an address delivered to the Irish Society of Oxford University on the 31st October, 1924. [Dublin, 1924]. pp. 16.

FREEMAN (THOMAS WALTER) Ireland: a general and regional geography. 4th ed. London, Methuen, 1969. pp. xix, 557. bibliog. 21½cm. (Advanced Geographies)

IRISH geographical studies in honour of E. Estyn Evans; edited by Nicholas Stephens and Robin E. Glasscock. [Belfast], 1970. pp. 403. bibliogs.

- Economic history

FACTS for the repealers: originally published in the Dublin Evening Post during the months of January and February 1834. Dublin, Page, 1834. pp. 24.

McCRACKEN (EILEEN) The Irish woods since Tudor times: distribution and exploitation. Newton Abbot, [1971]. pp. 184. bibliog.

- Economic history - Sources

PETTY (Sir WILLIAM) M.D., Surveyor-General of Ireland to Charles II. The history of the survey of Ireland, commonly called the Down Survey;...A.D. 1655-1656; [facsimile reprint of the edition originally published in 1851]. New York, Kelley, 1967. pp. xxiii, 426. 22½cm. (Reprints of Economic Classics)

- Economic policy

LYSAGHT (EDWARD E.) Self-government and business interests: a memorandum on the economic and fiscal aspects of the question. Dublin, Maunsel and Company, 1918. pp. 33. 21½cm.

- Emigration and immigration

MR. TUKE'S FUND. Executive Committee. Emigration from Ireland; being the third report of the Committee...together with reports by Mr. Tuke, etc. London, [1884]. pp. 38.

GREENHILL (BASIL) The great migration: crossing the Atlantic under sail. London, H.M.S.O., 1968. pp. 32.

- Foreign relations

WARD (ALAN J.) Ireland and Anglo-American relations, 1899-1921. London, London School of Economics and Political Science, [1969]. pp. xii, 291. bibliog. 21½cm.

IRELAND (Cont'd.)

- Gentry

O'HART (JOHN) The Irish and Anglo-Irish landed gentry; [reprint of the first edition of 1884 with a new] introduction by Edward MacLysaght. Shannon, 1969. pp. 773.

- Historical geography

IRISH geographical studies in honour of E. Estyn Evans; edited by Nicholas Stephens and Robin E. Glasscock. [Belfast], 1970. pp. 403. bibliogs.

- History

CHAUVIRE (ROGER) History of Ireland;...translated by the Earl of Wicklow. Dublin, 1952. pp. 127. bibliog.

CONNOLLY (JAMES) Irish Republican Leader. The re-conquest of Ireland: [reprint of the work originally published in 1917]. Dublin, 1968. pp. 78.

COSTIGAN (GIOVANNI) A history of modern Ireland, with a sketch of earlier times. New York, [1969]. pp. 380. bibliogs.

LYONS (FRANCIS STEWART LELAND) Ireland since the famine. London, [1971]. pp. 852. bibliog.

NORMAN (EDWARD ROBERT) A history of modern Ireland. London, 1971. pp. 330. bibliog.

O'FARRELL (PATRICK JAMES) Ireland's English question: Anglo-Irish relations 1534-1970. London, 1971. pp. 336. bibliog.

- History - Bibliography

JOHNSTON (EDITH MARY) compiler. Irish history: a select bibliography. London, Historical Association 1969. pp. 63. (Helps for Students of History. No. 73)

- History - Historiography

OSIPOVA (T.S.) Trudy F. Engel'sa po istorii Irlandii v sovetskoi medievistike. in Engel's i problemy istorii. Moskva, 1970.

IRISH historiography, 1936-70; edited by T.W. Moody [for the] Irish Committee of Historical Sciences. Dublin, 1971. pp. 155.

- History - Sources

A JACOBITE narrative of the war in Ireland, 1688-1691; [ascribed to Nicholas Plunket]; ([edited by] John T. Gilbert); [reprint of the work first published in Dublin in 1892, with an] introduction by J.G. Simms. Shannon, [1971]. pp. 328.

MOODY (THEODORE WILLIAM) and SIMMS (JOHN GERALD) eds. The Bishopric of Derry and the Irish Society of London, 1602-1705. Dublin, 1968 in progress. 25cm.

- History - 17th century

SIMMS (JOHN GERALD) Jacobite Ireland, 1685-91. London, 1969. pp. 297. bibliog.

BOTTIGHEIMER (KARL S.) English money and Irish land: the 'adventurers' in the Cromwellian settlement of Ireland. Oxford, 1971. pp. 226. bibliog.

- History - 1625-1649

UNITED KINGDOM. Parliament. 1643. A declaration of the Lords and Commons...concerning the present lamentable estate and miserable condition of Ireland...; [dated 16 June, 1643]. London, Wright, 1643. pp. 8. 18½cm. Wing E 1395.

UNITED KINGDOM. Parliament. 1643. An ordinance or declaration of the Lords and Commons...for the encouragement of adventurers to make new subscriptions for townes, cities, and lands in Ireland...;[dated 14 July, 1643]. London, Wright, 1643. pp. 10. 19cm. Wing E 2114.

A DECLARATION of the gallant service performed by...Hugh Peters in the West of England concerning the bringing in of the Irish army to the obedience of the Parliament of England, etc. London, Woodnoth, 1646. pp. 6. 18½cm. Wing D 672.

PETERS (HUGH) Severall propositions presented to the Members of the Honourable House of Commons. concerning the Presbyterian ministers of this kingdome: (Mr. Peters reports...concerning the speedy reducing of the Irish rebels), etc. London, J.G., 1646. pp. 6. 19cm. Wing P 1718.

BOURKE (ULICK) Marquis of Clanricarde. A declaration of the resolutions of His Majesties forces, published by the Marquisse of Clanricka against the Parliament of England; also a declaration signed by the officers in Ulster; and a copy of a letter from Collonell Jones to the Lord Inchequeen. London, A.H., 1648. pp. 19cm. Wing C 4406.

A GREAT victory at sea against the Irish rebels, by Captaine Robert Dare, commander of the English, etc. London, Ibbitson, 1648. pp. 6. 19cm. Wing G 1764.

- History - Rebellion of 1641

The APPREHENDING of Captayne Butler at Portchmouth in the county of Southampton and his followers who were bound with bullets and ammuniton [sic] for Ireland...; as also the true relation of a terrible sea fight by the states of Holland, against a fleet of the Spannish, etc. London, F. C[oles] and T. B[anks], 1641 [O.S.] pp. 6. 18½cm. Wing A 3583.

EXCEEDING good newes from the Isle of Wight: being a true relation of a great quantity of ammunition...lately taken there from a ship which was going to the rebels in Ireland, etc. London, Thomas, 1641[O.S.]. pp. 5. 17½cm. Wing E 3739.

LONDON. Court of Common Council. A petition of the Major, aldermen, and Common-Councell of the citie of London, to His Majestie; together with His Majesties gracious answer thereunto. London, Barker and Bill, 1641. pp. 14. 18½cm. Wing P 1819.

NEWROBE (RICHARD) The mutuall joyes of the King, Parliament, and subjects;...as also the resolution of the House of Commons...concerning Bishops...; with a true relation of a sudden mutiny arising amongst the rebels in Ireland, at Bravers in the county of Munster, etc. London, Howell, 1641. pp. (6). 17½cm. Wing N 944.

CHARLES I., King of Great Britain and Ireland. His Majesties message to the House of Commons concerning an order made by them for the borrowing of one hundered thousand pounds of the adventurers money for Ireland; together with the answer of the House of Commons in Parliament thereunto. London, Husband and Franck, 1642. pp. 15. 18½cm. Wing C 2478.

TWO petitions of the knights, gentlemen, freeholders, and others of the inhabitants of the county of Hertford: the one to the right honourable House of Peers; the other to the...House of Commons assembled in Parliament; delivered... January 25, 1641 [O.S.] London, Sweeting, 1642. pp. 6. 19cm. Wing T 3511.

CHARLES I., King of Great Britain and Ireland. The grounds and motives inducing His Majesty to agree to a cessation of armes for one whole yeare, with the Roman Catholiques of Ireland; together with the articles of cessation...; whereunto is added an instrument touching the manner of payment of 30800. pound sterling, etc. Oxford, Lichfield, 1643. pp. 22. 17½cm. Wing G 2134.

UNITED KINGDOM. Parliament. 1643. An ordinance of the Lords and Commons...whereby the commissioners named in a late Act of Parliament for raising the subsidy of 400,000£...are authorized to take...all such moneys, victuals, armes...and commodities as have been lately collected for the reliefe of Ireland...;[dated 17 May, 1643]. London, Wright, 1643. pp. (5). 19½cm. Wing E 2106.

SAPRYKIN (IURII MIKHAILOVICH) Ирландское восстание XVII века. Москва, Университет, 1967. pp. 267. 20см.

- History - 1642-1649

UNITED KINGDOM. Parliament. 1643. A declaration of the Lords and Commons...concerning the present lamentable and miserable condition of Ireland...; whereunto are added the severall propositions made by the committee of the House of Commons...; [dated 16-24 June, 1643]. London, Miller, 1643. pp. 14. 18½cm. Wing E 1394.

- History - War of 1689-1691

A JACOBITE narrative of the war in Ireland, 1688-1691; [ascribed to Nicholas Plunket]; [[edited by] John T. Gilbert); [reprint of the work first published in Dublin in 1892, with an] introduction by J.G. Simms. Shannon, [1971]. pp. 328.

- History - 18th century

TONE (THEOBALD WOLFE) Life of Theobald Wolfe Tone...; edited by his son William Theobald Wolfe Tone with a brief account of his own education and campaigns, etc. Washington, [imprint], 1826. 2 vols. 23cm.

- History - Rebellion of 1798

PAKENHAM (THOMAS) The year of liberty: the story of the great Irish rebellion of 1798. London, 1969. pp. 416. bibliog.

- History - The Union, 1800

JOHNSON (WILLIAM) One of the Justices of the Court of Common Pleas, Ireland. A letter to Joshua Spencer, esq., on an union. London, Hatchard, [1798]. pp. 23. 23cm.

CLARKE (THOMAS BROOKE) The case of Ireland, setting forth various difficulties experienced in its commercial intercourse with Great Britain, since the Union, in a letter to the Rt. Hon. Henry Addington, Chancellor of the Exchequer, etc. London, Cadell and Davies, 1802. pp. 39. 23cm.

- History - 19th century

O'HERLIHY (T.) The famine, 1845-1847: a survey of its ravages and causes. [Drogheda?, 19--]. pp. 87.

DENIEFFE (JOSEPH) A personal narrative of the Irish revolutionary brotherhood: [reprint of work originally published in 1906]; introduction by Seán Ó Lúing. Shannon, 1969. pp. 293.

McGILL (JAMES) and REDMOND (TOM) The story of the Manchester martyrs. [London, Connolly Association, 1963]. pp. 11. 19cm.

HURST (MICHAEL) Maria Edgeworth and the public scene: intellect, fine feeling and landlordism in the age of reform. Coral Gables, [1969]. pp. 206. bibliog.

Ó BROIN (LEON) Fenian fever: an Anglo-American dilemma. London, 1971. pp. 264. bibliog.

- History - 20th century

BRITISH AND IRISH COMMUNIST ORGANISATION. Pamphlets. No. 4. The working class in the Irish national revolution, 1916-23. [London, Murphy, 1966]. pp. 37.

CONNOLLY. [London], Murphy, 1966. pp. 13. 25½cm. (Irish Communist Organisation. Pamphlets. No. 5)

CONNOLLY (RODDY) The Republican struggle in Ireland. [London, Murphy, 1966?]. pp. v, 48-61. 25½cm. (Irish Communist Organisation. Pamphlets. No. 6)

O'FAOLÁIN (SEÁN) Constance Markievicz. [new ed.] London, Sphere, [1967]. pp. 220. 18cm.

YOUNGER (CALTON) Ireland's civil war. London, 1968. pp. viii, 534. bibliog.

NOWLAN (KEVIN B.) and WILLIAMS (T. DESMOND) eds. Ireland in the war years and after, 1939-51. Dublin, 1969. pp. 216.

WARD (ALAN J.) Ireland and Anglo-American relations, 1899-1921. London, London School of Economics and Political Science, [1969]. pp. xii, 291. bibliog. 21½cm.

HAMILTON (IAIN) The Irish tangle. [London], 1970. pp. 18. (Current Affairs Research Services Centre. Conflict Studies. No. 6)

FORESTER (MARGERY) Michael Collins: the lost leader. London, 1971. pp. 371. bibliog.

GREAVES (CHARLES DESMOND) Liam Mellows and the Irish revolution. London, 1971. pp. 416.

- History - Sinn Fein Rebellion, 1916

PANKHURST (ESTELLE SYLVIA) and others. Rebel Ireland. London, [1917?]. pp. 16.

IRELAND - History - Sinn Fein Rebellion 1916 (Cont'd.)

DEVOY (JOHN) Recollections of an Irish rebel: [facsimile reprint of the work originally published in New York in 1929]; with an introduction by Sean O Luing. Shannon, 1969. pp. 491.

GREAVES (CHARLES DESMOND) 1916-1966: the Easter Rising as history. London, Communist Party of Great Britain, Historians' Group, 1966. pp. 19. 25½cm. (Our History, No. 43)

HEUSTON (JOHN M.) Headquarters battalion: army of the Irish Republic, Easter week, 1916. [Dublin, 1966]. pp. 73.

COFFEY (THOMAS M.) Agony at Easter: the 1916 Irish uprising. Toronto, 1969. pp. 271.

FITZGIBBON (CONSTANTINE) Out of the lion's paw: Ireland wins her freedom. London, 1969. pp. 126.

NOWLAN (KEVIN B.) ed. The making of 1916: studies in the history of the Rising. (Commissioned by Coiste Chuimhneacháin 1916). Dublin, Stationery Office, 1969. pp. xiii, 338. 22cm.

MAC LOCHLAINN (PIARAS F.) ed. Last words: letters and statements of the leaders executed after the Rising at Easter, 1916. Dublin, 1971. pp. 217. In English or Irish.

- Nationalism

NEWMAN (A.) What Emmet means in 1915: a tract for the times. Dublin, [1915?]. pp. 15.

NOWLAN (KEVIN B.) Charles Gavan Duffy and the repeal movement. [Dublin], 1963. pp. 24. (National University of Ireland. O'Donnell Lectures. No.7.)

EDWARDS (OWEN DUDLEY) and others. Celtic nationalism. London, Routledge & Kegan Paul, 1968. pp. 358. 21½cm.

Ó CUÍV (B.) The Gaelic cultural movements and the new nationalism. in Nowlan (Kevin B.) ed. The making of 1916. Dublin, 1969.

HAMILTON (IAIN) The Irish tangle. [London], 1970. pp. 18. (Current Affairs Research Services Centre. Conflict Studies. No. 6)

- Officials and employees

Ó BROIN (LEON) The chief secretary: Augustine Birrell in Ireland. London, 1969. pp. 232. bibliog.

- Parliament

A CRITICAL review of the liberties of British subjects; with a comparative view of the proceedings of the H-e of C-s of I-d, against an unfortunate exile [Charles Lucas] of that country...; by a gentleman of the Middle-Temple. 2nd ed. London, printed for R. Watkins, 1750. pp. 119.

- Politics and government

BOYLE (R.) 1st Earl of Cork. A worthie, learned, and religious speech. in United Kingdom. Parliament. House of Commons. 1642. A copie of a letter sent by Mr. Speaker...; also a worthie, learned, and religious speech, delivered by the Earl of Cork,etc. London, 1642.

An ADDRESS to the people of Ireland, with a brief report of parliamentary proceedings on Irish affairs: containing a summary view of the principal measures discussed and an abstract and index of all the statutes passed for that part of the United Kingdom, in the second session of the first united Parliament, 42 Geo. III. 1802. London, Cadell and Davies, 1802. pp. 98. 22½cm.

IRELAND: her evils and remedies. London, Spiers, 1841. pp. iv, 5-16. 22½cm.

ROLLESTON (THOMAS WILLIAM HAZEN) Ireland and Poland: a comparison. London, 1917. pp. 21.

O'HIGGINS (KEVIN) Three years hard labour: an address delivered to the Irish Society of Oxford University on the 31st October, 1924. [Dublin, 1924]. pp. 16.

THEY mutilated Ireland, and other things to remember when you vote. [London, 1964] pp. 12. (Reprinted from the Irish Democrat, June 1964)

CONNOLLY (JAMES) Irish Republican Leader. The reconquest of Ireland: [reprint of the work originally published in 1917]. Dublin, 1968. pp. 78.

HURST (MICHAEL) Maria Edgeworth and the public scene: intellect, fine feeling and landlordism in the age of reform. Coral Gables, [1969]. pp. 206. bibliog.

Ó BROIN (LEON) The chief secretary: Augustine Birrell in Ireland. London, 1969. pp. 232. bibliog.

HAMILTON (IAIN) The Irish tangle. [London], 1970. pp. 18. (Current Affairs Research Services Centre. Conflict Studies. No. 6)

LENIN (VLADIMIR IL'ICH) Lenin on Ireland. [Dublin, 1970] pp. 35.

MARX (KARL) and ENGELS (FRIEDRICH) Ireland and the Irish question: [collected writings on Ireland]. Moscow, 1971. pp. 518.

Ó BROIN (LEON) The prime informer: a suppressed scandal. London, 1971. pp. 174. bibliog.

- Relations (general) with the United States

HERNON (JOSEPH M.) Celts, catholics, and copperheads: Ireland views the American Civil War. [Columbus], Ohio State U.P., [1968]. pp. ix, 150. bibliog. 23½cm.

- Rural conditions

CONNELL (KENNETH HUGH) Irish peasant society: four historical essays. Oxford, Clarendon P., 1968. pp. xiii, 167. 21½cm.

BROEKER (GALEN) Rural disorder and police reform in Ireland, 1812-36. London, 1970. pp. 254. bibliog.

- Sanitary affairs

GRIMSHAW (THOMAS WRIGLEY) Remarks on impending sanitary legislation for Ireland. Dublin, 1874. pp. 20.

GRIMSHAW (THOMAS WRIGLEY) Remarks on the Public Health (Ireland) Bill 1874. Dublin, 1874. pp. 8.

- Social conditions

ATHERTON (HENRY) Remarks on the condition of Ireland. [Lewes, 1873?] pp. 10.

MARX (KARL) and ENGELS (FRIEDRICH) Ireland and the Irish question: [collected writings on Ireland]. Moscow, 1971. pp. 518.

- Social history

MARX (KARL) The Fenians. London, 1967. pp. 49. (Irish Communist Organisation. Pamphlets. No. 7)

CONNELL (KENNETH HUGH) Irish peasant society: four historical essays. Oxford, Clarendon P., 1968. pp. xiii. 167. 21½cm.

- Social history - Sources

CRAWFORD (W.H.) and TRAINOR (B.) Aspects of Irish social history, 1750-1800: documents. Belfast, H.M.S.O., 1969. pp. 199. bibliog.

- Surveys

PETTY (Sir WILLIAM) M. D., Surveyor-General of Ireland to Charles II. The history of the survey of Ireland, commonly called the Down Survey;...A.D. 1655-1656; [facsimile reprint of the edition originally published in 1851]. New York, Kelley, 1967. pp. xxiii, 426. 22½cm. (Reprints of Economic Classics)

IRELAND (REPUBLIC)

- Civilization

SHEEHY (MICHAEL) Is Ireland dying?: culture and the Church in modern Ireland. London, Hollis & Carter, 1968. pp. 256. bibliog. 21½cm.

- Commerce

EIRE. Department of Finance. 1961. Official import and export lists, 1961. rev. ed. Dublin, 1961. pp. 96. 24½cm.

EIRE. Committee on Industrial Organisation, 1962. Second interim report: joint export marketing. Dublin, [1962]. pp. 9. 24½cm.

EIRE. Department of Finance. 1962. Official import and export lists, 1963; issued under the authority of the Minister for Finance and the Revenue Commissioners, etc. Dublin, [1962]. pp. 133. 24½cm.

EIRE. Department of Finance. 1968. Official import and export lists...January, 1968. rev. ed. Dublin, 1968. pp. 133.

McALEESE (DERMOT) A study of demand elasticities for Irish imports. Dublin, 1970. pp. 40. bibliog. (Economic and Social Research Institute. Papers. No. 53)

- Commerce - Directories

STUBBS' DIRECTORY: manufacturers, merchant shippers, and professional. London, annual, 1968/9. 26½cm.

- Constitution

EIRE. Dáil Éireann. Committee on the Constitution. 1967. Report of the committee on the constitution, December, 1967: [George Colley chairman]. (Pr. 9817) Dublin, [1967] pp. iv, 144. bibliog. 24½cm.

LANGROD (GEORGES) and CLIFFORD-VAUGHAN (MICHALINA E. F.) L'Irlande. Paris, Pichon and Durand-Auzias, [1968]. pp. 303. bibliog. 19cm. (Comment ils sont Gouvernés. tome 16)

AYEARST (MORLEY) The Republic of Ireland: its government and politics. London, 1970. pp. 241. bibliog.

- Description and travel

ZHELEZNOVA (IRINA L'VOVNA) and LEBEDEV (IGOR' ALEKSEEVICH) Erin izumrudnyi. Moskva, 1970. pp. 159.

- Economic conditions

THE NEW querist, containing several queries, proposed to the consideration of the public. Dublin, 1933. pp. 34.

EIRE. National Industrial Economic Council. Economy in [ ] and the prospects for [ ]. Dublin, annual, 1967 [1st rep.] to date. 20½cm.

ECONOMIC RESEARCH INSTITUTE. Papers. No. 39. The Irish economy in 1967. Dublin, the Institute, 1967. pp. (60). bibliog. 33cm.

McGILVRAY (JAMES) Irish economic statistics. Dublin, Institute of Public Administration, 1968. pp. viii, 180. 23cm.

O'SULLIVAN (PATRICK MICHAEL) Transport networks and the Irish economy. London, [1969]. pp. 62. (London. University. London School of Economics and Political Science. Department of Geography. Geographical Papers. No. 4)

EIRE. Central Statistics Office. 1970. Input-output tables for 1964. Dublin, [1970]. pp. 41.

McALEESE (DERMOT) A study of demand elasticities for Irish imports. Dublin, 1970. pp. 40. bibliog. (Economic and Social Research Institute. Papers. No. 53)

- Economic conditions - Bibliography

KAIM-CAUDLE (P.R.) and JOHNSON (NUALA) eds. Abstract of published papers, 1961-1969. [Dublin], 1969. pp. 48.

- Economic history

MEENAN (JAMES) The Irish economy since 1922. Liverpool, 1970. pp. 442. bibliog.

IRELAND (REPUBLIC) (Cont'd.)

- Economic policy

ROBERTS (HENRY NEVILLE) The fruits of freedom: a new Ireland through economic nationalism. Dublin, Talbot P., [1934]. pp.32. 18cm.

EIRE. 1963. Second programme for economic expansion; laid by the government before each House of the Oireachtas, August, 1963. Dublin, [1963]. pp. 67. 21cm.

EIRE. 1964. Second programme for economic expansion: a digest. Dublin, [1964]. pp. 25.

EIRE. 1964. Second programme for economic expansion. pt. 2, laid by the Government before each House of the Oireachtas, July, 1964. Dublin, [1964]. pp. 340. 21cm.

EIRE. National Industrial Economic Council. 1964. Interim report on second programme for economic expansion. Dublin, [1964]. pp. 7. 24½cm.

EIRE. National Industrial Economic Council. [Reports. No.2]. Report on procedure for continuous review of progress under the second programme for economic expansion. Dublin, [1964]. pp. 19. 21cm.

EIRE. 1966. Report on arrangements for planning at industrial level. (National Industrial Economic Council Reports. No. 15) (Pr. 8879) Dublin, [1966]. pp. 24. 21cm.

EIRE. 1966. The work of N[ational] I[ndustrial] E[conomic] C[ouncil], 1963-1966. (National Industrial Economic Council Occasional Publications. No.2) (Pr.9090) Dublin, [1966]. pp. 72. 21cm.

ECONOMIC RESEARCH INSTITUTE. Papers. No. 39. The Irish economy in 1967. Dublin, the Institute, 1967. pp. (60). bibliog. 33cm.

NEWMAN (JEREMIAH) New dimensions in regional planning: a case study of Ireland. Dublin, National Institute for Physical Planning and Construction Research, 1967. pp. 128. Development Series. 1.)

O'MAHONY (DAVID) The Irish economy: an introductory description. 2nd ed. Cork, Cork U.P., 1967. pp. x, 190. bibliog. 22cm.

SEMINAR ON INDUSTRIAL DEVELOPMENT AND THE DEVELOPMENT PLAN, DUBLIN, 1966. Proceedings. Dublin, National Institute for Physical Planning and Construction Research, 1967. pp. 52.

BRISTOW (JOHN A.) and TAIT (ALAN A.) Economic policy in Ireland. Dublin, Institute of Public Administration, 1968. pp. 314. 25cm.

EIRE. National Industrial Economic Council. 1968. Comments on second programme review of progress 1964/67. Dublin, [1968]. pp. 16. (Reports. No.24)

EIRE. Stationery Office. 1968. Second programme for economic expansion: review of progress, 1964-67. Dublin, [1968]. pp. 120.

FITZGERALD (GARRET) Planning in Ireland: a PEP study. Dublin, Institute of Public Administration, 1968. pp. viii, 246. 23cm.

SIMPSON (DAVID) Economist. A medium term planning model for Ireland. Dublin, Economic and Social Research Institute, 1968. pp. vii, 32. 27½cm. (Papers. No. 41)

CHUBB (BASIL) and LYNCH (PATRICK) eds. Economic development and planning. Dublin, 1969. pp. 369. (Institute of Public Administration, Dublin. Readings in Irish Public Administration. vol.1)

EIRE. 1969. Third programme: economic and social development, 1969-72. Dublin, 1969. pp. 275. 21½cm.

CONFEDERATION OF IRISH INDUSTRY. Signpost: industry in the seventies; [assignment carried out by Michael Sweetman]. Dublin, 1971. pp. 39.

- Emigration and immigration

HANNAN (DAMIAN) Rural exodus: a study of the forces influencing the large-scale migration of Irish youth. London, 1970. pp. 348.

WALSH (BRENDAN M.) Religion and demographic behaviour in Ireland...; with appendix, Migration between Northern Ireland and the Republic of Ireland, by R.C. Geary and J.G. Hughes. [Dublin], 1970. pp. 50. (Economic and Social Research Institute. Papers. No. 55)

- Executive departments

The CONSTRUCTIVE work of Dail Eireann. No. 2.... 1. The Department of Agriculture and the Land Settlement Commission; 2. The Commission of Inquiry into the Resources and Industries of Ireland; 3. The Department of Trade and Commerce. Dublin, Talbot Press, 1921. pp. 36. 21½cm.

MUIMHNEACHÁIN (M.) The functions of the Department of the Taoiseach. Dublin, 1960. pp. 19. (Institute of Public Administration, Dublin. Department of State Series. 1)

EIRE. Public Services Organisation Review Group. 1969. Report...1966-1969. Dublin, 1969. pp. 497.

HOCTOR (DANIEL) The department's story: a history of the Department of Agriculture [of the Republic of Ireland]. Dublin, 1971. pp. 304. bibliog.

- Foreign relations - United Kingdom - British Empire

HARKNESS (D.W.) The restless dominion: the Irish Free State and the British Commonwealth of Nations, 1921-31. London, Macmillan, 1969. pp. xviii, 312. bibliog. 21½cm.

- Full employment policies

EIRE. 1967. Report on full employment. (National Industrial Economic Council Reports. No. 18) (Pr. 9188) Dublin [1967]. pp. 129. 21½cm.

- History

PAKENHAM (FRANCIS AUNGIER) 7th Earl of Longford, and O'NEILL (THOMAS P.) Eamon de Valera. London, 1970. pp. 499.

- Industries

EIRE. Committee on Industrial Organisation. 1962. Third interim report: creation of adaptation councils to promote measures of rationalisation, co-operation, etc. in individual industries. Dublin, [1962]. pp. 7. 24½vm.

NEVIN (EDWARD THOMAS) The capital stock of Irish industry. Dublin, the Institute, 1963. pp. 22. 28½cm. (Economic Research Institute. Papers. No.17)

EIRE. National Industrial Economic Council. Economy in [ ] and the prospects for [ ]. Dublin, annual, 1967 [1st rep.] to date. 20½cm.

SEMINAR ON INDUSTRIAL DEVELOPMENT AND THE DEVELOPMENT PLAN, DUBLIN, 1966. Proceedings. Dublin, National Institute for Physical Planning and Construction Research, 1967. pp. 52.

EIRE. National Industrial Economic Council. 1969. Report on physical planning. Dublin, [1969]. pp. 20. (Reports. No.26)

[INDUSTRIAL CREDIT COMPANY]. Focus on industrial credit. Dublin, 1969. pp. 60.

PRASAD (S. BENJAMIN) Enterprise in Ireland. Milwaukee, [1969]. pp. 106. bibliog.

JEFFERSON (C.W.) Capital statistics for Irish manufacturing industry. Dublin, 1971. pp. 42. (Economic and Social Research Institute Papers. No. 60)

KENNEDY (KIERAN A.) Productivity and industrial growth: the Irish experience. Oxford, 1971. pp. 281. bibliog.

O'MALLEY (PATRICK) Irish industry: structure and performance. Dublin, 1971. pp. 141. bibliog.

- Languages

EIRE. Commission on the Restoration of the Irish Language, 1963. Summary, in English, of final report, 13th July, 1963: [An tAthair Tomás Fiaich, chairman]. Dublin, [1963]. pp. 143. 24½cm.

EIRE. 1966. White paper on the restoration of the Irish language: progress report for the period ended 31 March, 1966. (Pr.9088) Baile Átha Cliath, 1966. pp. 39. 24½cm. In English and Irish; See also EIRE. 1965. The restoration of the Irish language.

Ó CUÍV (B.) The Gaelic cultural movements and the new nationalism. in Nowlan (Kevin B.) ed. The making of 1916. Dublin, 1969.

- Oireachtas

EIRE. Oireachtas. Joint Committee on a Scheme for Contributory Pensions for members. 1960. Report. Dublin,[1960]. pp. xiv. 24½cm.

- Oireachtas - Elections

EIRE. Dáil Éireann. 1957. Election results and transfer of votes in general election, March, 1957, for sixteenth Dáil and bye-elections to fifteenth Dáil, 1954-1957. Dublin, 1957. pp. 60. 33cm.

EIRE. 1962. Election results and transfer of votes in general election, October, 1961, for seventeenth Dáil, and bye-elections to sixteenth Dail, 1957-1961. (Dáil Eireann) Dublin, [1962]. pp. 60. 33cm.

EIRE. 1966. Election results and transfer of votes in general election, April, 1965, for eighteenth Dáil, and bye-elections to seventeenth Dáil, 1961-1965. (Dáil Eireann) Dublin, [1966]. pp. 60. 33cm.

- Oireachtas - Privileges and immunities

EIRE. Dáil Éireann. Committee on Procedure and Privileges. 1964. Report... on a statement reported in the press to have been made by a member; (with Proceedings). Dublin, [1964]. pp. vii. 24½cm. In English and Irish.

- Oireachtas - Rules and practice

EIRE. Seanad Éireann. 1961. Standing orders relative to public business; with appendices containing, 1. Oireachtas library rules; 2. regulations as to travelling facilities. [In English and Erse]

EIRE. Seanad Éireann. Committee on Procedure and Privileges on Amendment of Standing Orders. 1961. Report. Dublin, [1961]. pp. xix. 24cm.

EIRE. Dáil Éireann. Committee on Procedure and Privileges. 1962. Report ... on Amendments to Standing Orders relating to sittings of the Dáil, private members business and quorum. [in English and Irish] Dublin, [1962]. pp. xi. 24½cm.

EIRE. Dáil Éireann. 1964. Standing orders relative to public business together with Oireachtas library rules, regulations and notes as to travelling facilities to members and Oireachtas allowances to members regulations, 1963. Dublin, [1964]. pp. xix, 164. 18cm. In English and Irish.

- Oireachtas - Dáil

EIRE. Dáil Éireann. Returns relating to sittings and business. sess., Ap 21 1965/My 22 1969 (18th Dáil)- Dublin.

- Oireachtas - Seanad

GARVIN (THOMAS) The Irish Senate. Dublin, 1969. pp. 100. (Institute of Public Administration, Dublin. Research Series. 1)

- Politics and government

DE VALERA (EAMON) The foundation of the Republic of Ireland in the vote of the people: results of the general election of December, 1918; a national plebiscite held under British law and British supervision. [Melbourne?, 1918?] 1 pamphlet (unpaged)

GRIFFITH (ARTHUR) Arguments for the Treaty. Dublin, [1922?]. pp. 32.

FERRIS (WILLIAM) The Gaelic commonwealth: being the political and economic programme for the Irish Progressive Party. Dublin, Talbot P., 1923. pp. xi, 161. 17½cm.

IRELAND (REPUBLIC) - Politics and government (Cont'd.)

GALLACHER (WILLIAM) Ireland: can it remain neutral? London, 1941. pp. 23. (Communist Party of Great Britain. Communist Policy Series. No.8)

CONNOLLY ASSOCIATION. Ireland! not the Commonwealth: a reply to Lord Pakenham and those who wish to promote the bankers' reconquest of Ireland;...an appeal to Irishmen to remain Irish. London, 1961. pp. 8. 22cm.

BRITISH AND IRISH COMMUNIST ORGANISATION. Pamphlets. No. 8. Liam Mellowes. [London], 1966 repr. 1969. pp. 17.

The CONNOLLY Association. London, Murphy, [1967?]. pp. 32. 25½cm. (Irish Communist Organisation. Pamphlets. No. 10)

The IRISH Republican Congress. 2nd ed. London, Murphy, 1967. pp. 38. 25½cm. (Irish Communist Organisation. Pamphlets. No. 3)

BOYD (ANDREW) The two Irelands. London, Fabian Society, 1968. pp. 27. 21½cm. (Research Series. [No.] 269)

LANGROD (GEORGES) and CLIFFORD-VAUGHAN (MICHALINA E. F.) L'Irlande. Paris, Pichon and Durand-Auzias, [1968]. pp. 303. bibliog. 19cm. (Comment ils sont Gouvernés. tome 16)

BRITISH AND IRISH COMMUNIST ORGANISATION. The crisis in the Unionist Party. [Belfast, 1969]. pp. 13.

GARVIN (THOMAS) The Irish Senate. Dublin, 1969. pp. 100. (Institute of Public Administration, Dublin. Research Series. 1)

HARKNESS (D.W.) The restless dominion: the Irish Free State and the British Commonwealth of Nations, 1921-31. London, Macmillan, 1969. pp. xviii, 312. bibliog. 21½cm.

AYEARST (MORLEY) The Republic of Ireland: its government and politics. London, 1970. pp. 241. bibliog.

CARTY (XAVIER) ed. Violence and protest, including statement of the hierarchy. [Dublin, 1970]. pp. 17.

CHUBB (BASIL) The government and politics of Ireland;...with a historical introduction by David Thornley. Stanford, Calif., 1970. pp. 364. bibliog.

COMMUNICATIONS CONFERENCE, DUBLIN, 1969. Government and people: creative dialogue; a report of the 1969/70 Communications Conference; by Xavier Carty. Dublin, 1970. pp. 52. (Tuairim. Tuairim Pamphlets. 16)

MANNING (MAURICE) The Blueshirts. Dublin, [1970]. pp. 276. bibliog.

- Population

SYMES (DAVID GILYARD) The population resources of the...Gaeltacht: an analysis of the employment potential; a memorandum to the Board of Gaeltarra Eireann. Hull, University, Department of Geography, 1965. 2 vols. (in 1). (Miscellaneous Series. Nos. 1-2)

WALSH (BRENDAN M.) Some Irish population problems reconsidered. Dublin, Economic and Social Research Institute, 1968. pp. viii, 41. 28cm. (Papers. No. 42)

GEARY (ROBERT CHARLES) and HUGHES (J.G.) Internal migration in Ireland; with appendix, County migration; an alternative approach, by C.J. Gillman. [Dublin], 1970. pp. 82. (Economic and Social Research Institute. Papers No. 54.)

WALSH (BRENDAN M.) Religion and demographic behaviour in Ireland...; with appendix, Migration between Northern Ireland and the Republic of Ireland, by R.C. Geary and J.G. Hughes. [Dublin], 1970. pp. 50. (Economic and Social Research Institute. Papers. No. 55)

- Religion

WALSH (BRENDAN M.) Religion and demographic behaviour in Ireland...; with appendix, Migration between Northern Ireland and the Republic of Ireland, by R.C. Geary and J.G. Hughes. [Dublin], 1970. pp. 50. (Economic and Social Research Institute. Papers. No. 55)

- Rural conditions

LUCEY (DENIS I.F.) and KALDOR (DONALD R.) Rural industrialization: the impact of industrialization on two rural communities in Western Ireland. London, 1969. pp. 208. bibliog.

MESSENGER (JOHN C.) Inis Beag: isle of Ireland. New York, [1969]. pp. 136. bibliog.

HANNAN (DAMIAN) Rural exodus: a study of the forces influencing the large-scale migration of Irish youth. London, 1970. pp. 348.

- Social conditions

ARENSBERG (CONRAD MAYNADIER) and KIMBALL (SOLON TOOTHAKER) Family and community in Ireland. 2nd ed. Cambridge, Mass., 1968. pp. 471.

- Social history

FOX (J.R.) Kinship and land tenure on Tory island. [Belfast], 1967. pp. 17. (Reprinted from Ulster Folklife, vol. 12, 1966)

- Social life and customs

MESSENGER (JOHN C.) Inis Beag: isle of Ireland. New York, [1969]. pp. 136. bibliog.

- Social policy

McCARTHY (CHARLES) The distasteful challenge. Dublin, Institute of Public Administration, 1968. pp. 116. 22½cm.

EIRE. 1969. Third programme: economic and social development, 1969-72. Dublin, 1969. pp. 275. 21½cm.

IRELAND, NORTHERN

IRELAND, NORTHERN. 1962. Northern Ireland: its people, resources, history and government, by Hugh Shearman. [rev. ed.] Belfast, 1962. pp. 40. 21½cm.

LYSAGHT (D.R. O'CONNOR) The making of Northern Ireland. Dublin, [1970?]. pp. 48.

- Army - Regulations

U.K. Ministry of Defence. 1969- . Regulations for the Ulster Defence Regiment. [London], 1969 in progress. Loose-leaf binder.

- Census

IRELAND, NORTHERN. Census, 1966. Census of population, 1966: general report. Belfast, 1968. pp. 1, 177, (2). 33½cm.

IRELAND, NORTHERN. Census, 1971. Census of population, 1971: preliminary report. Belfast, 1971. pp. 16.

- Constitution

IRELAND, NORTHERN. Constitution. The constitution of Northern Ireland; being the Government of Ireland Act, 1920 as amended; prepared for the Clerk of the Parliaments of Northern Ireland in the Statutory Publications Office. [rev. ed.] Belfast, 1960. pp. 56. 24½cm.

SHEARMAN (HUGH) How Northern Ireland is governed: central and local government in Northern Ireland. 2nd ed. Belfast, H.M.S.O., 1963. pp. 31. 20½cm.

IRELAND, NORTHERN. Constitution. The constitution of Northern Ireland: being the Government of Ireland Act 1920, as amended to 31st December 1968, etc. Belfast, 1969. pp. 61.

- Constitutional history

WALLACE (MARTIN) Northern Ireland: fifty years of self-government. Newton Abbot, [1971]. pp. 192. bibliog.

- Constitutional law

CALVERT (HARRY) Constitutional law in Northern Ireland: a study in regional government. London, Stevens, 1968. pp. xxi, 400. 24cm.

- Description and travel

SHEARMAN (HUGH) Northern Ireland. Belfast, H.M.S.O., 1968. pp. 92.

- Economic conditions

COMMUNIST PARTY OF IRELAND. Craigavon in the dock. Belfast, 1938. pp. 28. 18cm.

BOYD (ANDREW) and IRELAND (JOHN) of Dublin. The new partition of Ireland: a symposium on the state of Ireland's economic and political life. Belfast, [1965?]. pp. unpaged.

- Economic history - Sources

IRELAND, NORTHERN. 1967. Exhibition of Irish economic documents, the Law Courts Building, May Street, Belfast, March-September 1967. (Public Record Office) Belfast, 1967. fo (ii), pp. 18. 21½cm.

- Economic policy

IRELAND, NORTHERN. Cmd. 547. Northern Ireland development programme 1970-75: government statement. Belfast, 1970. pp. 29.

PARKINSON (JOHN RICHARD) Economic development in Northern Ireland. [Nottingham, 1970] pp. 24.

- Emigration and immigration

WALSH (BRENDAN M.) Religion and demographic behaviour in Ireland...; with appendix, Migration between Northern Ireland and the Republic of Ireland, by R.C. Geary and J.G. Hughes. [Dublin], 1970. pp. 50. (Economic and Social Research Institute. Papers. No. 55)

- History

EDWARDS (OWEN DUDLEY) The sins of our fathers: roots of conflict in Northern Ireland. Dublin, [1970]. pp. 353.

RIDDELL (PATRICK) Fire over Ulster. London, 1970 pp. 208. bibliog.

FITZGIBBON (CONSTANTINE) Red hand: the Ulster colony. London, [1971]. pp. 367.

- Industries

IRELAND, NORTHERN. Ministry of Commerce. Industries development assistance: report. 22nd Nov.1966/31st March 1968 [1st] to date included in IRELAND, NORTHERN. Parliament. House of Commons. [Papers].

IRELAND, NORTHERN. Distributive Industry Training Board. Report and statement of accounts. May 16th 1969/March 31st 1971 [1st] to date included in IRELAND, NORTHERN. Parliament. House of Commons. [Papers].

COE (W.E.) The engineering industry of the North of Ireland. Newton Abbot, David & Charles, [1969]. pp. 224. bibliog. 21cm. (Industrial History)

JEFFERSON (C.W.) Capital statistics for Irish manufacturing industry. Dublin, 1971. pp.42. (Economic and Social Research Institute. Papers. No. 60)

- Industries - Directories

IRELAND, NORTHERN. Ministry of Commerce. 1968. Who makes what in Northern Ireland: a directory of goods made...with the names of the firms making them, etc. 6th ed. Belfast, 1968. pp. xl, 428, xli-lxvii, 21cm. In English, French, German, and Spanish.

IRELAND, NORTHERN. Ministry of Commerce. 1970. Who makes what in Northern Ireland, 1970: a trade directory of Northern Ireland. 7th ed. Belfast, 1970. pp. 498. In English, French, German, and Spanish.

- Parliament

IRELAND, NORTHERN. H.C. 1813. Special report from the Joint Select Committee on the Kitchen and Refreshment Rooms. Belfast, 1967. pp. 11.

IRELAND, NORTHERN. H.C. 1886. Special report from the Joint Select Committee on the Kitchen and refreshment rooms. Belfast, 1968. pp. 11.

IRELAND, NORTHERN - Parliament (Cont'd.)

IRELAND, NORTHERN. Cmd. 560. The future development of the parliament and government of Northern Ireland: a consultative document. Belfast, 1971. pp. 12.

- Parliament - Elections

BRITISH AND IRISH COMMUNIST ORGANISATION. The Stormont elections: a working class analysis; produced jointly by the...organisation and a group of communist workers in the 6 counties. [Belfast, 1969]. pp. 10.

- Parliament - Salaries, pensions, etc.

IRELAND, NORTHERN. H.C. 1557. Report from the Select Committee on Ministerial Salaries and Allowances of Members of the Senate and the House of Commons, etc. Belfast, [1963]. pp. 160.

- Politics and government

COMMUNIST PARTY OF IRELAND. Craigavon in the dock. Belfast, 1938. pp. 28. 18cm.

BLYTHE (ERNEST) A new departure in Northern policy: appeal to the leaders of nationalist opinion. Dublin, Clancy, [1956?]. pp. 31. 24½cm.

SHEARMAN (HUGH) How Northern Ireland is governed: central and local government in Northern Ireland. 2nd ed. Belfast, H.M.S.O., 1963. pp. 31. 20½cm.

BOYD (ANDREW) and IRELAND (JOHN) of Dublin. The new partition of Ireland: a symposium on the state of Ireland's economic and political life. Belfast, [1965?]. pp. unpaged.

MAGEE UNIVERSITY COLLEGE. Extra Mural Studies. Public administration in Northern Ireland. Londonderry, [1967]. pp. (iii). 124. 24½cm.

BOYD (ANDREW) The two Irelands. London, Fabian Society, 1968. pp. 27. 21½cm. (Research Series. [No.] 269)

[BRITISH AND IRISH COMMUNIST ORGANISATION]. The situation in the North. Cork, 1969. pp. 5.

EGAN (BOWES) and McCORMACK (VINCENT) Burntollet. [London, 1969]. pp. 64.

GREAVES (CHARLES DESMOND) Northern Ireland: civil rights and political wrongs. London, [1969]. pp. 11. (Communist Party of Great Britain. Communist Party Pamphlets)

IRELAND, NORTHERN. Cmd. 532. Disturbances in Northern Ireland: report of the Commission appointed by the Governor of Northern Ireland. Belfast, 1969. pp. 124.

IRELAND, NORTHERN. Cmd. 534. A commentary by the government of Northern Ireland to accompany the Cameron report.

KENNEDY (D.) Ulster unionism and the new nationalism. in Nowlan (Kevin B.) ed. The making of 1916. Dublin, 1969.

KROMBACH (UWE) ed. Revolution in Nordirland?: vom Religionskrieg zur Organisierung des Klassenkampfes. München, [1969]. pp. 72.

NORTHERN FRIENDS' PEACE BOARD and SOCIETY OF FRIENDS. Ulster Quarterly Meeting. Peace Committee. Orange and green: a Quaker study of community relations in Northern Ireland. [Sedbergh, Yorks.], 1969. pp. 51.

O'NEILL (TERENCE) Ulster at the crossroads. London 1969. pp. 201.

ULSTER UNIONIST PARTY. Ulster: the facts. Belfast, 1969. unpaged.

BLADES (M.) and SCOTT (D.) What price Northern Ireland? London, 1970. pp. 24. (Young Fabian Group. Young Fabian Pamphlets. 22)

BOYD (ANDREW) Holy war in Belfast. 2nd ed. Tralee, 1970. pp. 220. bibliog.

CARTY (XAVIER) ed. Violence and protest, including statement of the hierarchy. [Dublin, 1970]. pp. 17.

CASTERAN (CHRISTIAN) Guerre civile en Irlande. [Paris], 1970. pp. 217.

EDWARDS (OWEN DUDLEY) The sins of our fathers: roots of conflict in Northern Ireland. Dublin, [1970]. pp. 353.

FARRELL (MIKE) The struggle in the north. London, [1970]. pp. 34.

R[EVOLUTIONARY] S[OCIALIST] S[TUDENTS'] F[EDERATION]. Special Papers. The struggle in Ireland. n.p., [1970?]. 1 pamphlet (unpaged) bibliog.

STETLER (RUSSELL) The battle of Bogside: the politics of violence in Northern Ireland. London, 1970. pp. 212. bibliog.

CAMPAIGN FOR SOCIAL JUSTICE IN NORTHERN IRELAND and ASSOCIATION FOR LEGAL JUSTICE. Northern Ireland: the mailed fist; a record of army and police brutality from Aug. 9 - Nov. 9, 1971; with a foreword by Tony Smythe, etc. n.p., [1971]. pp. 71.

HARWOOD (JEREMY) and others. Ireland: our Cuba? London, [1971?]. 1 pamphlet (unpaged)

IRELAND, NORTHERN. Cmd. 560. The future development of the parliament and government of Northern Ireland: a consultative document. Belfast, 1971. pp. 12.

McCANN (EAMONN) The British press and Northern Ireland. London, [imprint], [1971]. pp. 28.

Ó TUATHAIL (SEAMAS) compiler. They came in the morning. n.p., [1971]. pp. 41.

ROSE (RICHARD) Governing without consensus: an Irish perspective. London, 1971. pp. 567.

WALLACE (MARTIN) Northern Ireland: fifty years of self-government. Newton Abbot, [1971]. pp. 192. bibliog.

YOUNG SOCIALISTS. National Committee. Northern Ireland. n.p., [1971]. pp. 11.

CALVERT (HARRY) The Northern Ireland problem. London, [1972]. pp. 15.

IRELAND, NORTHERN. Cmd. 566. Violence and civil disturbances in Northern Ireland in 1969: report of tribunal of inquiry, Mr. Justice Scarman, chairman. Belfast, 1972. 2 vols.

IRELAND, NORTHERN. Cmd. 568. Political settlement: statements issued on Friday 24 March 1972 by the Prime Minister and the government. Belfast, 1972. pp. 8.

McCANN (EAMONN) What happened in Derry. London, [1972]. pp. 14. (Socialist Worker. Pamphlets)

- Race question

NORTHERN IRELAND SOCIETY OF LABOUR LAWYERS. Discrimination: pride for prejudice. Belfast, [1969]. pp. 16.

- Religion

NORTHERN FRIENDS' PEACE BOARD and SOCIETY OF FRIENDS. Ulster Quarterly Meeting. Peace Committee. Orange and green: a Quaker study of community relations in Northern Ireland. [Sedbergh, Yorks.], 1969. pp. 51.

BOYD (ANDREW) Holy war in Belfast. 2nd ed. Tralee, 1970. pp. 220. bibliog.

EDWARDS (OWEN DUDLEY) The sins of our fathers: roots of conflict in Northern Ireland. Dublin, [1970]. pp. 353.

- Social conditions

NORTHERN FRIENDS' PEACE BOARD and SOCIETY OF FRIENDS. Ulster Quarterly Meeting. Peace Committee. Orange and green: a Quaker study of community relations in Northern Ireland. [Sedbergh, Yorks.], 1969. pp. 51.

EDWARDS (OWEN DUDLEY) The sins of our fathers: roots of conflict in Northern Ireland. Dublin, [1970]. pp. 353.

- Social policy

IRELAND, NORTHERN. Cmd. 534. A commentary by the government of Northern Ireland to accompany the Cameron report.

IRELAND, NORTHERN. Cmd. 547. Northern Ireland development programme 1970-75: government statement. Belfast, 1970. pp. 29.

IRETON (HENRY) Lord Deputy of Ireland

The CRUELL tragedy or inhumane butchery, of Hamor and Shechem, with other their adherents, lately revived and reacted heere in England, by Fairfax and Ireton, upon the persons of Sir Charles Lucas and Sir George Lisle, in Colchester, the 28. Aug. 1648, etc. [London], 1648. pp. (ii), 16. 19½cm. Wing C 7422.

IRIGOYEN (HIPÓLITO)

LUNA (FÉLIX) Yrigoyen. Buenos Aires, Editorial Desarrollo, [1964]. pp. 447. 22½cm.

PUIGGRÓS (RODOLFO) El yrigoyenismo. Buenos Aires, Alvárez, [1965] pp. 245. 19½cm. (Historia Crítica de los Partidos Políticos Argentinos. 2)

GIUFFRA (EDUARDO F.) Hipolito Yrigoyen en la historia de las instituciones argentinas. Buenos Aires, 1969. pp. 482.

IRISH

CONNERY (DONALD S.) The Irish. London, Eyre & Spottiswoode, 1968. pp. 256. 21½cm.

- Caricatures and cartoons

CURTIS (LEWIS PERRY) Apes and angels: the Irishman in Victorian caricature. Newton Abbot, [1971]. pp. 126. bibliog.

IRISH IN THE UNITED STATES

LESLIE (Sir JOHN RANDOLPH SHANE) The Irish issue in its American aspect: a contribution to the settlement of Anglo-American relations during and after the Great War. New York, Scribner, 1917. pp. 207. 19cm.

COLEMAN (JAMES WALTER) The Molly Maguire riots: industrial conflict in the Pennsylvania coal region;... [reprint of original edition of 1936]. New York, 1969. pp. 189. bibliog.

HERNON (JOSEPH M.) Celts, catholics, and copperheads: Ireland views the American Civil War. [Columbus], Ohio State U.P., [1968]. pp. ix, 150. bibliog. 23½cm.

WARD (ALAN J.) Ireland and Anglo-American relations, 1899-1921. London, London School of Economics and Political Science, [1969]. pp. xii, 291. bibliog. 21½cm.

Ó BROIN (LEON) Fenian fever: an Anglo-American dilemma. London. 1971. pp. 264. bibliog.

IRISH LANGUAGE

Ó CUÍV (BRIAN) ed. A view of the Irish language. Dublin, Stationery Office, 1969. pp. x, 156. 21½cm.

IRISH PROGRESSIVE PARTY

FERRIS (WILLIAM) The Gaelic commonwealth: being the political and economic programme for the Irish Progressive Party. Dublin, Talbot P., 1923. pp. xi, 161. 17½cm.

IRISH QUESTION

TONE (THEOBALD WOLFE) An address to the people of Ireland. n.p. 1796; [Belfast, Connolly Books, 1969]. pp. 35.

BRIDGES (JOHN HENRY) Irish disaffection: four letters addressed to the editor of the Bradford Review. Bradford, Hanson, 1868. pp. 24. 17cm.

NEALE (JOHNSTOUN O'NEALE) The real remedy for Ireland: an engineering solution. London, Routledge, 1868. pp. 17. 21cm.

ATHERTON (HENRY) Remarks on the condition of Ireland. [Lewes, 1873?]. pp. 10.

NULTY (THOMAS) Bishop of Meath. Letter...to Joseph Cowen, Esq., M.P., on the state of public affairs in Ireland. Dublin, [imprint], 1881. pp. 36.

IRISH QUESTION (Cont'd.)

BIALE (LAWRENCE) A glance at the history of Ireland till the Act of Union. London, [1887]. pp. 14. (Liberal and Radical Printing and Publishing Association. National Liberal Pamphlets. No. 12)

FOX (JOSEPH HOYLAND) A visit to Ireland: a reprint of a lecture delivered in the Town Hall, Wellington, Somerset, June 19th, 1888. Taunton, [1888]. pp. 14.

LAING (SAMUEL) the Younger. The government and the Irish people: a speech delivered at Brighton, February 9th, 1889. [London, National Liberal Federation, Home Counties Division], 1889. pp. 7.

BLAKE (EDWARD) M.P. The Irish situation: speech... at Glasgow, December, 1898. Dublin, [imprint], 1899. pp. 24. 17½cm.

FRY (Sir EDWARD) Lord Justice of the Court of Appeal. James Hack Tuke; a memoir. London, Macmillan, 1899. pp. xii, 354. 20½cm.

SPENCER (JOHN POYNTZ) 5th Earl Spencer. Earl Spencer, K.G., at Eastbourne, 5th March, 1902. London, Collard, 1902. pp. 7. 21½cm.

MACDONAGH (MICHAEL) The viceroy's post-bag: correspondence hitherto unpublished of the Earl of Hardwicke, first lord lieutenant of Ireland after the union. London, Murray, 1904. pp. ix, 466. 22cm.

LEATHAM (JAMES) The deep fact of nationalism: the cases of Scotland and Ireland contrasted; a sexcentenary study, some ancient history with an immediate moral. Cottingham, Cottingham P., [1914?]. pp. 12. 22cm.

LESLIE (Sir JOHN RANDOLPH SHANE) The Irish issue in its American aspect: a contribution to the settlement of Anglo-American relations during and after the Great War. New York, Scribner, 1917. pp. 207. 19cm.

La PRIMA fra le piccole nazioni: paragone tra l'Irlanda e le piccole nazioni libere d'Europa. [192-?]. pp. 19.

McHUGH (CHARLES) Letters to the press...on the Lloyd-George partition proposals. [Derry?, 1920?]. pp. 24.

ULSTER. Unionist Council. [Publications]. 127. The Labour Party and Ireland: the deputation's report: analysis and criticism. Belfast, the Council, [1920?]. pp. 11. 24½cm.

GWYNN (DENIS ROLLESTON) Daniel O'Connell: the Irish liberator. London, [1930]. pp. 288.

BARRA (LIAM DE) The Irish revival - do we mean it? [Cork, imprint, 1943]. pp. 64. 18cm.

GREAVES (CHARLES DESMOND) The Irish case against partition: ...full facts and programme of action. 2nd ed. London, 1961. pp. 36. (Connolly Association. Pamphlets)

O'DONNELL (PEADAR) There will be another day. Dublin, Dolmen Press, 1963. pp. 132. 18cm.

FITT (GERARD) and others. Gerry Fitt's speech and contributions by delegates; (the Irish question; challenge to democratic Britain; report of conference 25 Feb., 1967). n.p., [1967?]. pp. 47.

BOYD (ANDREW) The two Irelands. London, Fabian Society, 1968. pp. 27. 21½cm. (Research Series. [No.] 269)

CURTIS (LEWIS PERRY) Anglo-Saxons and Celts: a study of anti-Irish prejudice in Victorian England. Bridgeport, Conn., [1968]. pp. 162. bibliog. (Bridgeport, Connecticut. University. Conference on British Studies. Studies in British History and Culture. vol. 2)

McCAFFREY (LAWRENCE J.) The Irish question, 1800-1922. Lexington, U. of Kentucky P., [1968]. pp. (v), 202. bibliog. 21½cm. (Kentucky Paperbacks. KP 117)

The ECONOMICS of partition. [London, 1969]. pp. 52. (Irish Communist Organisation. Pamphlets. No. 16)

EDWARDS (R.W.D.) The decline and fall of the Irish nationalists at Westminster. in Nowlan (Kevin B.) ed. The making of 1916. Dublin, 1969.

HURST (MICHAEL) Maria Edgeworth and the public scene: intellect, fine feeling and landlordism in the age of reform. Coral Gables, [1969]. pp. 206. bibliog.

BROEKER (GALEN) Rural disorder and police reform in Ireland, 1812-36. London, 1970. pp. 254. bibliog.

DE PAOR (LIAM) Divided Ulster. Harmondsworth, 1970. pp. 207.

McDOWELL (ROBERT BRENDAN) The Irish convention, 1917-18. London, 1970. pp. 240. bibliog.

MARX (KARL) and ENGELS (FRIEDRICH) Ireland and the Irish question: [collected writings on Ireland]. Moscow, 1971. pp. 518.

O'FARRELL (PATRICK JAMES) Ireland's English question: Anglo-Irish relations 1534-1970. London, 1971. pp. 336. bibliog.

ROSE (RICHARD) Governing without consensus: an Irish perspective. London, 1971. pp. 567.

IRISH REPUBLICAN ARMY

BELL (J. BOWYER) The secret army: a history of the IRA, 1916-1970. London, 1970. pp. 405. bibliog.

COOGAN (TIMOTHY PATRICK) The I.R.A. London, 1970. pp. 373. bibliog.

IRKUTSK

VOROB'EV (VLADIMIR VASIL'EVICH) and SDASIUK (GALINA VASIL'EVNA) Иркутск: экономико-географическая характеристика. Иркутск, 1966. pp. 77. bibliog.

- History

KUDRIAVTSEV (FEDOR ALEKSANDROVICH) and VENDRIKH (GERMAN ALEKSANDROVICH) Иркутск: очерки по истории города. Иркутск, 1958. pp. 515. bibliog.

IRKUTSK (OBLAST')

- Economic history

VYBOROV (M. M.) Иркутские большевики в борьбе за повышение трудовой активности трудящихся крестьян, 1921-1925 гг, Иркутск, 1961. pp. 70. 19½cm. (Irkutsk. Irkutskii Gosudarstvennyi Pedagogicheskii Institut. Uchenye Zapiski. вып.18(5)). On title page вып. given as 17.

- History

ZEMLIA Irkutskaia, 1917-1967. Irkutsk, 1967. pp. 447.

- History - Revolution, (1917-1921)

DVORIANOV (NIKOLAI VASIL'EVICH) and DVORIANOV (VLADIMIR NIKOLAEVICH) В тылу Колчака. 2nd ed. Москва, Мысль, 1966. pp. 252. 20cm.

- Industries

PROBLEMY... Проблемы развития и размещения промышленности и транспорта Иркутской области. Иркутск, 1965. pp. 151. bibliog.

- Sanitary affairs

К... К истории развития здравоохранения Иркутской области. ч.1. Иркутск, 1968. pp. 157. (Иркутский Государственный Медицинский Институт. Научные Труды. вып. 93)

- Statistics

IRKUTSK (OBLAST') Statisticheskoe Upravlenie. Народное хозяйство Иркутской области: статистический сборник. Иркутск, Статистика, 1967. pp. 196. 21½см.

IRON AND STEEL WORKERS

- Belgium

BELGIUM. Office National de l'Emploi. 1966. Les aides accordées aux travailleurs licenciés des industries du charbon et de l'acier: activités particulières de l'Office National de l'Emploi. [Bruxelles, 1966]. pp. 33. 20½cm.

- European Economic Community countries

ORGANISATION FOR EUROPEAN ECONOMIC CO-OPERATION. European Productivity Agency. Industrial Versions. No. 2. Steel workers and technical progress: a comparative report on six national studies; (by Olive Banks and J.D. Reynaud). Paris, 1959. pp. 65.

BURKART (LUTZ) and WILLENER (ALFRED) Niveau de mécanisation et mode de rémunération:...rapport de synthèse d'une recherche effectuée dans la sidérurgie par des instituts des six pays de la Communauté. Luxembourg, European Coal and Steel Community, 1960. pp. 149.

EUROPEAN COAL AND STEEL COMMUNITY. 1961. Décision complémentaire à la décision relative à l'application de l'article 69 du traité du 18 avril 1951 instituant la Communauté européenne du charbon et de l'acier. [Luxembourg], 1961. pp. 89. 28cm. In Dutch, French, German and Italian.

EUROPEAN COAL AND STEEL COMMUNITY. 1963. La représentation des travailleurs sur le plan de l'entreprise et du secteur d'industrie: tableaux comparatifs; document authentifié par la Commission mixte Employeurs-Travailleurs pour l'harmonisation des conditions de travail dans l'industrie sidérurgique. (Haute Autorité) [Luxembourg, 1963]. pp. 131. 20½ x 29cm.

- France

HARDACH (GERD H.) Der soziale Status des Arbeiters in der Frühindustrialisierung: eine Untersuchung über die Arbeitnehmer in der französischen eisenschaffenden Industrie zwischen 1800 und 1870. Berlin, [1969]. pp. 221. bibliog.

- Germany

KRAHN (KARL) Mobilitätsorientierung und Fluktuationsbereitschaft: eine empirisch-soziologische Untersuchung in einem Hüttenwerk. Berlin, [1971]. pp. 160. bibliog.

- Hong Kong

HONG KONG. Machine Shop and Metal Working Industrial Committee. 1969. Report...on the manpower survey of the machine shop and metal working trades (2nd April - 11th April, 1968). Hong Kong, 1968 [or rather 1969]. pp. 151.

- India

INDIA. Study Group on Iron and Steel Industry. 1968. Report. Delhi, 1968. pp. 112.

- Russia

LIUDI... Люди огня и металла. Москва, 1969. pp. 316.

- United Kingdom

SHEFFIELD STEEL WORKERS' GROUP. Steel workers next step. [Nottingham, 1968]. pp. irreg. (Institute for Workers' Control. Pamphlet Series. No.7)

SCUNTHORPE GROUP. The threat to steel workers: a discussion pamphlet. Nottingham, [1971]. pp. 16. (Institute for Workers' Control. Pamphlet Series. No. 23)

- United States

FOSTER (WILLIAM ZEBULON) Unionizing steel. New York, 1936. pp. 46.

ADDUCCI (G.) and MARILLIER (J.) The 116-day strike of the American steel workers. London, [1959]. pp. 40.

ROWAN (RICHARD L.) The negro in the steel industry. Philadelphia, [1968]. pp. 148. (Pennsylvania University. Wharton School of Finance and Commerce. Industrial Research Unit. Racial Policies of American Industry. Report No. 3)

IRON INDUSTRY AND TRADE

INTERNATIONAL IRON AND STEEL INSTITUTE. Conference. Report of proceeding. Los Angeles, annual 1967. (1st) to date. 27½cm.

DELFORGE (JACQUES) Développements récents dans l'industrie des minerais de fer. Mons, Centre Universitaire de l'Etat à Mons, 1968. pp. 120. bibliog. 27cm.

UNITED NATIONS. Economic Commission for Europe. 1968. The world market for iron ore. (ST/ECE/STEEL/24). New York, 1968. pp. 333.

PASCHEN (HERBERT) Die Messung der Betriebs- und Unternehmenskonzentration; mit einer quantitativen Untersuchung über die Konzentration in der Eisen- und Stahlindustrie der EGKS-Länder. Freiburg i. Br., [1969]. pp. 222. bibliog. (Heidelberg. Universität. Institut für International Vergleichende Wirtschafts- und Sozialstatistik. Schriftenreihe. Band 8)

UNITED NATIONS INDUSTRIAL DEVELOPMENT ORGANIZATION. Monographs on Industrial Development Industrialization of Developing Countries: Problems and Prospects. No.5. Iron and steel industry; based on the proceedings of the International Symposium on Industrial Development, Athens, November-December 1967. (ID/40/5). New York, United Nations, 1969. pp. 78. bibliog.

MANNERS (GERALD) The changing world market for iron ore, 1950-1980: an economic geography. Baltimore, [1971]. pp. 384. bibliog.

POUNDS (NORMAN JOHN GREVILLE) The geography of iron and steel. 5th ed. London, 1971. pp. 175. bibliogs.

- America, Latin

BOAS (ERNEST ARTHUR) Die eisenschaffende Industrie Latein-Amerikas: Aufbau und Entwicklung. Berlin, Duncker und Humblot, [1966]. pp. 174. bibliog. 23cm. (Volkswirtschaftliche Schriften. Heft 100).

BOAS (ERNEST ARTHUR) Latin-America's steel industry: present and future. Berlin, Duncker & Humblot, 1968. pp. 160. 23½cm.

- Austria

KLEINER (OTMAR) Österreichs Eisen- und Stahlindustrie und ihre Aussenhandelsverflechtung. Wien, 1969. pp. 184. bibliog. (Vienna. Hochschule für Welthandel. Geographisches Institut. Wiener Geographische Schriften. 31/32) With English summary.

- Benelux

FRANCE. Direction de la Documentation. La Documentation Française. Notes et Etudes Documentaires. No. 3,191. Les sidérurgies du Benelux. Paris, 1965. pp. 25.

- Canada

CANADA. Mineral Resources Division. Mineral Information Bulletins. 74. Economic aspects of iron ore in a changing market; [by] R.B. Elver. Ottawa, 1964. pp. 32. bibliog. With French summary.

CANADA. 1967. Report by the Tariff Board relative to the inquiry ordered by the Minister of Finance respecting iron or steel products used in the shipbuilding industry. (Reference No.139) Ottawa, 1967. pp. 98. 25cm.

WITTUR (G. E.) Primary iron and steel in Canada. Ottawa, 1968. pp. ix, 116. 24½cm. (Canada. Mineral Resources Division. Mineral Information Bulletins. 92.)

CANADA. Dominion Bureau of Statistics. Productivity Research and Analysis Section. 1970. Productivity trends in industry. Report no. 2. Indexes of output per person employed and per man-hour, 1959-68: iron and steel mills. Ottawa, 1970. pp. 20.

SCHNEIDER (V.B.) Canadian primary iron and steel statistics to 1969. Ottawa, 1970 [or rather 1971]. pp. 27. (Canada. Mineral Resources Division. Mineral Information Bulletins. 113)

- Czechoslovakia

FRANCE. Direction de la Documentation. La Documentation Française. Notes et Études Documentaires. No. 3,388. La sidérurgie tchécoslovaque. Paris, 1967. pp. 19. 30½cm.

- Europe

PASCHEN (HERBERT) Die Messung der Betriebs- und Unternehmenskonzentration; mit einer quantitativen Untersuchung über die Konzentration in der Eisen- und Stahlindustrie der EGKS-Länder. Freiburg i. Br., [1969]. pp. 222. bibliog. (Heidelberg. Universität. Institut für International Vergleichende Wirtschafts- und Sozialstatistik. Schriftenreihe. Band 8)

- European Economic Community countries

EUROPEAN COAL AND STEEL COMMUNITY. Direction Générale Problèmes du Travail, Assainissement et Reconversion. 1962. Le perfectionnement des cadres dans l'industrie, sidérurgique de la Communauté: rapport d'un groupe d'experts des organisations professionnelles. [Luxembourg], 1962. pp. 40. 29cm.

COMMISSION MIXTE POUR L'HARMONISATION DES CONDITIONS DE TRAVAIL DANS L'INDUSTRIE SIDÉRURGIQUE. 1963. Les répercussions de l'évolution technique sur la productivité, les salaires, la durée du travail et l'emploi: étude globale. [Luxembourg, European Coal and Steel Community, 1963]. pp. 15, (39). 29cm.

EUROPEAN COAL AND STEEL COMMUNITY. Direction Générale Problèmes du Travail, Assainissement et Reconversion. 1963. Progrès technique et formation professionnelle dans l'industrie sidérurgique. [Luxembourg]. 1963. pp. 49. 29cm.

MASSOTH (KARL) Le progrès technique et l'organisation de l'entreprise dans les industries de la C[ommunauté] E[uropéenne du] C[harbon et de l'] A[cier]: (exposé... présenté lors du séminaire sur l'automation dans le secteur administratif, tenu à Bruxelles du 19 au 21 février 1963). [Luxembourg], European Coal and Steel Community, 1963. pp. 34, (7). 29cm.

EUROPEAN COAL AND STEEL COMMUNITY. High Authority. 1965. Les entreprises sidérurgiques de la Communauté. [Luxembourg], 1965. 1 vol. (loose-leaf) In various languages.

EUROPEAN COAL AND STEEL COMMUNITY. 1966. Les entreprises de la Communauté... état 1.12.1966. (Direction Générale Administration et Finances) [Luxembourg, 1966]. 2 pts. 21cm. x 30cm.

EUROPEAN COAL AND STEEL COMMUNITY. Direction Générale Administration et Finances. Division Études et Analyses. 1967. Bilanzen der eisenschaffenden Unternehmen der Gemeinschaft; Balance sheets of the steel companies of the Community, 1950-1966. [7th ed.] [Luxembourg, 1967]. fo. 314. In various languages.

EUROPEAN COMMUNITIES. Commission. 1969. Étude sur la question des charbons à coke et cokes destinés à la sidérurgie de la Communauté. Bruxelles, 1969. 2 vols. (Série Énergie. No. 2) In English and French.

- France

BIARD (ROGER) Les mines de fer de Lorraine: (une richesse nationale en péril). Paris, Editions Sociales, [1966]. pp. 359. 19cm.

VIAL (JEAN) L'industrialisation de la sidérurgie française, 1814-1864. Paris, Mouton, 1967. 2 vols. bibliog. 24cm. (Paris. École Pratique des Hautes Études. Section des Sciences Économiques et Sociales. Centre de Recherches Historiques. Industrie et Artisanant. 3)

GILLE (BERTRAND) La sidérurgie française au XIXe siècle: recherches historiques. Genève, Droz, 1968. pp. 317. 23cm. (Travaux de Droit, d'Économie, de Sociologie et de Sciences politiques. No. 66)

JURGONS (RAINER) Die Hüttenstandorte Dünkirchen, Ijmuiden, Bremen und Lübeck: eine vergleichende Betrachtung. Wiesbaden, 1969. pp. 157. bibliog.

- France - Taxation

ESSER (JOSEF) Professor at Mainz University. Die steuerliche Belastung der Eisen- und Stahlindustrie in der Bundesrepublik und in Frankreich. Düsseldorf, Stahleisen, 1963. pp. 79. 21cm. (Wirtschaftsvereinigung Eisen- und Stahlindustrie. Schriftenreihe zur Wirtschafts- und Industriepolitik. Heft 5)

- Germany

KRAFT (MAX) Der Eisenhüttenindustrie der Rheinprovinz. Berlin, [1888?]. pp. 30. (Sonder-Abdruck aus Glaser's Annalen für Gewerbe und Bauwesen, 1888, Bd. 23)

SCHROEDTER (E.) Fuenf und zwanzig Jahre deutscher Eisenindustrie: Vortrag...24. April 1904. [Düsseldorf, 1904?]. pp. 11. (Sonder-Abdruck aus Stahl und Eisen, 1904)

DECKUNG des Eisen- und Stahlbedarfs im Rahmen des Marshall-Planes unter besonderer Berücksichtigung der durch die Demontage entstehenden Engpässe: Coverage of the iron and steel demand, etc. Düsseldorf, [1948]. pp. 31. In German and English.

HERMAN (OTTO) Wirtschaftliche Studie über die...Um- und Neubauten von Werksanlagen in einem gemischten Hüttenwerk: erörtert am Beispiel eines Werkes der Phoenix-Rheinrohr AG, Vereinigte Hütten- und Röhrenwerke. Marburg, 1962. pp. 163. bibliog

LECKEBUSCH (GUENTHER) Die Beziehungen der deutschen Seeschiffswerften zur Eisenindustrie an der Ruhr in der Zeit von 1850 bis 1930. Köln, Rheinisch-Westfälisches Wirtschaftsarchiv, 1963. pp. 147. bibliog. 24cm. (Cologne. Archiv für Rheinisch-Westfälische Wirtschaftsgeschichte. Schrifte zur Rheinisch-Westfälischen Wirtschaftsgeschichte. Band 8)

BANKMANN (JÖRG) Eine Untersuchung über den Einfluss der Steuerpolitik auf die Selbstfinanzierung der Eisen- und Stahlindustrie in der Bundesrepublik Deutschland seit 1948. Düsseldorf, [imprint], 1965. pp. 111. bibliog. 21cm.

MEYER (FRANZ) Die Investitionstätigkeit eisenschaffender Industrieunternehmungen seit 1953 im Spiegel ihrer Bilanzen: Methoden und Ergebnisse. Bonn, 1965. pp. 195. bibliog.

KOESTER (HERMANN) Der Einfluss der europäischen Integration auf die Entwicklung der Eisen- und Stahlindustrie in der Bundesrepublik Deutschland. München, 1966. pp. 129. bibliog.

HARDACH (KARL W.) Die Bedeutung wirtschaftlicher Faktoren bei der Wiedereinführung der Eisen- und Getreidezölle in Deutschland 1879. Berlin, Duncker und Humblot, [1967]. pp. 219. bibliog. 23cm. (Schriften zur Wirtschafts- und Sozialgeschichte. Band 7)

SCHMIDT (JOCHEN) Strukturwandlungen des Eisenhandels in der Bundesrepublik als Folge veränderter Marktverhältnisse. [Munich, imprint, 1968?]. pp. 238. bibliog.

WEINERT (LOTHAR) Ökonometrische Analyse der deutschen Eisen- und Stahlindustrie. [Bonn, 1968?]. pp. 139. bibliog.

JURGONS (RAINER) Die Hüttenstandorte Dünkirchen, Ijmuiden, Bremen und Lübeck: eine vergleichende Betrachtung. Wiesbaden, 1969. pp. 157. bibliog.

- Germany - Taxation

ESSER (JOSEF) Professor at Mainz University. Die steuerliche Belastung der Eisen- und Stahlindustrie in der Bundesrepublik und in Frankreich. Düsseldorf, Stahleisen, 1963. pp. 79. 21cm. (Wirtschaftsvereinigung Eisen- und Stahlindustrie. Schriftenreihe zur Wirtschafts- und Industriepolitik. Heft 5)

- Germany - North Rhine - Westphalia

NORTH RHINE-WESTPHALIA. Statistisches Landesamt. Beiträge zur Statistik des Landes Nordrhein-Westfalen. Heft. 233. Die Eisen- und Stahlindustrie in Nordrhein-Westfalen, 1958-1966. Düsseldorf, 1967. pp. 85. 29½cm.

- Germany - Prussia

LINDOW (CONRAD) Die Bedeutung der gewerblichen Sozialpolitik in der brandenburg-preussischen Merkantilzeit, insbesondere auf dem Gebiete des Bergbaues und der Eisen-Industrie. Giessen, 1928. pp. 115. bibliog.

IRON INDUSTRY AND TRADE (Cont'd.)

- Germany - Saarland

SAARGEBIET. Statistisches Amt. Saarland in Zahlen. Sonderhefte. 6. Die eisenschaffende Industrie des Saarlandes, Ende 1958: ein Entwicklungs-und Strukturbild. [Saarbrücken], 1959. pp. 31. 30cm.

- India

BEGBIE (L.F.) A monograph on the iron and steel industry in the Central Provinces. Nagpur, Secretariat Press, 1908. pp. 61.

BALIGA (B.S.) Prospects of an iron and steel industry in Madras... with a last chapter on present position of iron and steel industry in Madras, prepared by the Department of Industries, Labour and Co-operation. Madras, 1960. pp. 205. bibliog.

SENGUPTA (PHULRANI) The ferreous metallurgical industry of India: its problems and prospects. [paper read to the] 20th International Geographical Congress, London, 21-28 July, 1964. New Delhi, Office of the Registrar General, India, [1964]. pp. 7. bibliog.

NATIONAL COUNCIL OF APPLIED ECONOMIC RESEARCH. Long term projections for iron and steel. New Delhi, 1968. pp. xiv, 470.

STANG (FRIEDRICH) Die indischen Stahlwerke und ihre Städte: eine wirtschafts- und siedlungsgeographische Untersuchung zur Industrialisierung und Verstädterung eines Entwicklungslandes. Wiesbaden, 1970. pp. 169. bibliog.

- Ireland (Republic)

EIRE. Committee on Industrial Organisation. 1963. Report on survey of the iron and steel manufactures industry. Dublin, [1963]. pp. 168. 24½cm.

- Italy

ITALY. Direzione Generale delle Imposte Dirette. 1959. Studio orientativo sul commercio ferro e acciaio: approvato nella riunione di Ispettori Compartimentali tenuta a Firenze nei giorni 12-15 novembre 1958. Roma, 1959. pp. 43. 20cm.

FRUMENTO (A.) Notizie siderurgiche intorno alla Stato di Milano nel censimento di Carlo VI, 1719-1725. in vol. 2 of Saggi di economia aziendale e sociale in memoria di Gino Zappa. Milano, 1961.

VERZI (G.) Struttura attuale a caratteristiche di di gestione dell'industria siderurgica italiana. in vol.3 of Saggi di economia aziendale e sociale in memoria di Gino Zappa. Milano, 1961.

MANUELLI (ERNESTO) La sidérurgie maritime italienne. Lausanne, Centre de Recherches Européennes, 1962. pp. 28. 24cm.

MORI (GIORGIO) L'industria del ferro in Toscana dalla restaurazione alla fine del granducato, 1815-1859. Torino, 1966. pp. 602. (Italy. Istituto per la Ricostruzione Industriale. Archivio Economico dell'Unificazione Italiana. Serie 2. Vol. 13) Map in end pocket.

BERTAMINI (TULLIO) Il centro siderurgico di Villadossola nelle antiche e recenti attività ossolane. [Domodossola, imprint, 1967]. pp. 79. 24cm.

ROSA (LUIGI DE) Iniziativa e capitale straniero nell'industria metalmeccanica del Mezzogiorno, 1840-1904. Napoli, Giannini, [1968]. pp. xiii, 324. 21½cm. (Economia e Società. 1)

- Japan

BIENFAIT (JEAN) La sidérurgie japonaise. Lausanne, Centre de Recherches Européennes, 1965. pp. 103. 24cm. (Revised and expanded version of an article in Revue de Géographie de Lyon, vol. 38, no. 4.)

FRANCE. Direction de la Documentation. La Documentation Française. Notes et Études Documentaires. No. 3,557. La sidérurgie japonaise. Paris, 1969. pp. 41. 27cm.

- Netherlands

JURGONS (RAINER) Die Hüttenstandorte Dünkirchen, Ijmuiden, Bremen und Lübeck: eine vergleichende Betrachtung. Wiesbaden, 1969. pp. 157. bibliog.

- Poland

SYREK (MIECZYSŁAW) Wydajność pracy w polskim hutnictwie żelaza i stali. Katowice, Śląsk, 1964. pp. 300. bibliog. 23½cm.

FRANCE. Direction de la Documentation. La Documentation Française. Notes et Études Documentaires. No. 3,594. La sidérurgie polonaise. Paris, 1969. pp. 24. 27cm.

- Poland - Silesia

OSTEUROPA-INSTITUT IN BRESLAU. Bergbau- und Hüttenkunde Abteilung. Beiträge zur oberschlesischen Frage: 1. Oberschlesien und die Umgestaltung der europäischen Schwerindustrie durch den Versailler Vertrag; 2. Die wirtschaftliche Zugehörigkeit der Kreise Pless und Rybnik zur oberschlesischen Montanindustrie: Denkschrift. Breslau, 1921. pp. 26.

- Russia

BELAN (ROMAN VASIL'EVICH) and DENISENKO (IVAN MARKOVICH) Perspektivy razvitiia chernoi metallurgii SSSR. Moskva, 1962. pp. 191. bibliog.

STOSKOVA (NINA NIKOLAEVNA) Первые металлургические заводы России. Москва, Академия Наук, 1962. pp. 106. 21½cm.

KAGANOV (G. A.) and SURIN (P. P.) Rezervy dosrochnogo vypolneniia plana bez dopolnitel'nykh kapitalovlozhenii. Moskva, 1963. pp. 44.

BALDANOV (BATO-MUNKO BALDANOVICH) Ekonomicheskoe stimulirovanie effektivnogo ispol'zovaniia oborotnykh sredstv v promyshlennosti: po materialam predpriiatii chernoi metallurgii SSSR i riada promyshlennykh predpriiatii Buriatskoi ASSR. Ulan-Ude, 1965. pp. 27.

LELIUKHINA (NINA DMITRIEVNA) Perspektivy razvitiia chernoi metallurgii tsentral'nykh raionov SSSR. Moskva, 1966. pp. 196.

SHPALTAKOV (V. P.) Finansirovanie nauchno-issledovatel'skikh i proektno-konstruktorskikh rabot, izobretatel'stva i ratsionalizatsii v chernoi metallurgii SSSR v 50-e gody. in Cheliabinskii Politekhnicheskii Institut. Sbornik Nauchnykh Trudov. Nr.55. Problemy politicheskoi ekonomii sotsializma. Cheliabinsk, 1968.

OSINTSEV (ARKADII STEPANOVICH) Экономика черной металлургии СССР. 2nd ed. Москва, 1969. pp. 342.

- South Africa

SOUTH AFRICA. Board of Trade and Industries. Industrial Development Series. [Reports]. No.6. Investigation into the iron and steel, metallurgical and engineering industries. Pretoria, [1968-69]. 5 pts.

- Spain

CHILCOTE (RONALD H.) Spain's iron and steel industry. Austin, University of Texas, Bureau of Business Research, 1968. pp. xvi, 174. bibliog. 23cm. (Research Monographs. No. 32)

SPAIN. Comisaria del Plan de Desarrollo Economico y Social. 1968. (II Plan de desarrollo economico y social): industrias basicas del hierro y del acero. [Madrid, 1968]. pp. 337.

- Sweden

ADAMSON (ROLF) De svenska järnbrukens storleksutveckling och avsättningsinriktning, 1796-1860. Göteborg, 1963. pp. 160. (Meddelanden. 4)

ADAMSON (ROLF) Den svenska järnhanteringens finansieringsförhållanden: förlagsinteckningar 1800-1884. Göteborg, 1963. pp. 67. (Meddelanden. 3) Instructions on use of tables in end pocket.

ADAMSON (ROLF) Järnavsättning och bruksfinansiering, 1800-1860. Göteborg, Universitet, Ekonomisk-Historiska Institutionen, 1966. pp. xv,195,28. bibliog. 29½cm. (Meddelanden. 7) With English summary.

- Ukraine

[TRIDTSAT']... 30 пламенных лет; (литературная запись) Донецк, 1964. pp. 189.

- United Kingdom

JOHNSON (JOSEPH) Iron merchant, Liverpool. On the state and prospects of the iron trade in Scotland and South Wales in May, 1839; ([with] Appendix: statistics of the iron-works in Staffordshire and Shropshire). London, Middleton, [1840]. pp. 22, 4. 22cm. (Extracted from the Mining Review, no. 18 (new series) June, 1839)

TARIFF COMMISSION. Memorandum on the iron and steel trades; (with Statistical memorandum on the iron and steel industry in the United Kingdom; and Covering letter). London, [1904]. 3 pts. 28cm.

BRITISH IRON AND STEEL FEDERATION. Iron and Steel Bill: some arguments for and against. London, the Federation, [1949]. pp. (ii), 62. 23cm.

ROEPKE (H.G.) Ore supply and location of the British iron and steel industry. in Malcolm Jarvis Proudfoot memorial volume. Evanston, 1957.

250TH anniversary of the first successful use of coke in ironmaking: anniversary meeting, 23rd-25th September, 1959, Birmingham and Coalbrookdale; programme [with historical introduction by W.K.V. Gale]. [London?, 1959]. pp. 28. bibliog.

EUROPEAN COAL AND STEEL COMMUNITY. Direction Générale Problèmes du Travail, Assainissement et Reconversion. 1961. La formation des cadres dans la sidérurgie britannique: rapport d'un voyage d'information effectué en Grande-Bretagne du 7 au 11 novembre 1960. [Luxembourg, 1961. pp. 33. 29cm.

SCOPES (FREDERICK) The development of Corby works. [London], Stewarts & Lloyds, 1968. pp. xiv, 283. bibliog. 24cm.

FRANCE. Direction de la Documentation. La Documentation Française. Notes et Études Documentaires. No. 3,601. La sidérurgie du Royaume-Uni. Paris, 1969. pp. 42. 27cm.

GALE (WALTER KEITH VERNON) Iron and steel. London, Longmans, 1969. pp. xviii, 152. bibliog. 21½cm. (Industrial Archaeology Series)

ROLT (LIONEL THOMAS CASWELL) Waterloo ironworks: a history of Taskers of Andover, 1809-1968. Newton Abbot, [1969]. pp. 240.

WARREN (KENNETH) The British iron and steel sheet industry since 1840: an economic geography. London, 1970. pp. 313.

- United Kingdom - Scotland

VAMPLEW (W.) The railways and the iron industry: a study of their relationship in Scotland. in Reed (M.C.) ed. Railways in the Victorian economy. Newton Abbot, [1969].

- United States - Pennsylvania

BINING (ARTHUR CECIL) Pennsylvania iron manufacture in the eighteenth century. Harrisburg, 1938. pp. 227. bibliog. 23cm. (Pennsylvania. Pennsylvania Historical and Museum Commission. Publications. Vol. 4)

- Venezuela

BALESTRINI (CESAR) La industria del mineral de hierro en Venezuela. [Caracas, 1967]. pp. 347. bibliog.

IRON MINES AND MINING

- Russia

BARSUKOV (FEDOR ALEKSANDROVICH) and RACHKOVSKII (SOLOMON IAKOVLEVICH) Ekonomicheskaia effektivnost' kapital'nykh vlozhenii v zhelezorudnuiu promyshlennost'. Moskva, 1964. pp. 112. bibliog.

- Sweden

JONSSON (BO) Staten och malmfälten: en studie i svensk malmfältspolitik omkring sekelskiftet. Stockholm, Almqvist & Wiksell, 1969. pp. 388. bibliog. 23cm. (Uppsala. Statsvetenskapliga Föreningen. Skrifter. 49) With English summary.

IRON MINES AND MINING (Cont'd.)

- Ukraine

SHOSTAK (AFANASII GRIGOR'EVICH) Горно-добывающая промышленность Украинской ССР: горнорудная промышленность Украинской ССР: железная и марганцевая руда. Москва, 1967. pp. 285. bibliog.

- United Kingdom

SELLICK (ROGER J.) The West Somerset Mineral Railway and the story of Brendon Hills iron mines;...with contributions by J.R. Hamilton and M.H. Jones. 2nd ed. Newton Abbot, 1970. pp. 128. bibliog.

IRON ORES

UNITED NATIONS. Economic Commission for Europe. 1968. The world market for iron ore. (ST/ECE/STEEL/24). New York, 1968. pp. 333.

MANNERS (GERALD) The changing world market for iron ore, 1950-1980: an economic geography. Baltimore, [1971]. pp. 384. bibliog.

- Transportation

BOCTOR (ADEL LOUIS) The classical transportation problem and its application in iron-ore industry (U.A.R.); prepared by A.L.Boctor supervised by Roshdi Amer. Cairo, 1966. pp. 57. bibliog. (U.A.R. Institute of National Planning. Memos. No. 682)

HEECKT (HUGO) Grundlagen und Tendenzen der Bildung von Kostenfrachtraten in der Eisenerzfahrt. Tübingen, Mohr, 1968. pp. vi, 84. bibliog. 23½cm. (Kiel. Universität. Institut für Weltwirtschaft. Kieler Studien. 86)

- Canada

CANADA. Geological Survey. Economic Geology Reports. No. 22. Geology of iron deposits in Canada; by G.A. Gross. Ottawa, 1965 in progress. bibliogs. 24½cm. Maps in end pockets.

JANES (T.H.) and LAFLEUR (P.) The Canadian iron ore industry: its position and outlook. Ottawa, 1970. pp. 23. (Canada. Mineral Resources Division. Mineral Information Bulletins. 112)

- Norway - Transportation

OUREN (T.) Norges fraktbalanse og transitten av svensk jernmalm over Narvik. in Gothenburg. Handelshögskolan. Skriftserie. 1959. Nr. 1. Göteborg, 1959.

- Russia

BRAUN (GRIGORII ANISIMOVICH) Zhelezorudnaia baza chernoi metallurgii SSSR. 2nd ed. Moskva, 1970. pp. 310. bibliog.

- United Kingdom

ROEPKE (H.G.) Ore supply and location of the British iron and steel industry. in Malcolm Jarvis Proudfoot memorial volume. Evanston, 1957.

ANDREWS (CHARLES REGINALD) The story of Wortley Ironworks : a record of its history and traditions, and eight centuries of Yorkshire iron-making; .. edited and revised ... by Mary Andrews. 2nd ed. Nottingham, Milward, 1956. pp. (ix), 97. bibliog. 21cm.

IRONBRIDGE

MORTON (G.R.) and MOSELEY (A.F.) An examination of fractures in the first iron bridge at Coalbrookdale. [Wolverhampton], 1970. pp. 8. (West Midlands Studies. Special Publications. No.2)

IROQUOIS INDIANS

PARKER (ARTHUR C.) Parker on the Iroquois;... edited with an introduction by William N. Fenton. Syracuse, Syracuse U.P., [1968]. pp. vii, 158. 22½cm.

GOLDSTEIN (ROBERT A.) French-Iroquois diplomatic and military relations, 1609-1701. The Hague, 1969. pp. 208. bibliog.

NAMMACK (GEORGIANA C.) Fraud, politics, and the dispossession of the Indians: the Iroquois land frontier in the colonial period. Norman, Okla., [1969]. pp. 128. bibliog.

IRRELIGION

CAMPBELL (COLIN BARNSLEY) Toward a sociology of irreligion. London, 1971. pp. 171. bibliog.

IRRIGATION

The ECONOMICS of irrigation development: a symposium. Reading, 1969. pp. 67. (Reading. University. Faculty of Agriculture and Horticulture. Agricultural Economics Department. Development Studies. No. 6)

CLARK (COLIN GRANT) The economics of irrigation. 2nd ed. Oxford, 1970. pp. 155.

- Australia

RUTHERFORD (J.) Government irrigation and its physical environment. in Dury (George Harry) and Logan (M.I.) eds. Studies in Australian geography. London, 1968.

DAVIDSON (BRUCE ROBINSON) Australia wet or dry?: the physical and economic limits to the expansion of irrigation. [Melbourne], 1969. pp. 264. bibliog.

- Australia - Queensland

DRISCOLL (E.M.) The irrigation settlements of the lower Burdekin, Queensland, Australia. [Liverpool, 1970]. pp. 75. bibliog.

- Australia - Victoria

VICTORIA. 1965. Pedology of the Goulburn Valley area, Victoria. part 1. Stratigraphy of layers. part 2. Application in irrigated horticulture; by B. Cockroft. (Department of Agriculture Technical Bulletins. No. 19) Melbourne, 1965. pp. 27. bibliog. 27½cm.

- Bolivia

> CASTRILLO JUSTINIANO (RENAN) Aprovechamiento de las aguas del Pilcomayo: el regadio de Villa Montes. La Paz, 1961. pp. 39. (Bolivia. Direccion Nacional de Informaciones. Tercer Gobierno de la Revolucion Nacional. 8)

- Botswana

> UPTON (MARTIN) A report on the economic potential for irrigation in Botswana. Reading, 1969. pp. 74. (Reading. University. Faculty of Agriculture and Horticulture. Agricultural Economics Department. Development Studies. No. 5)

- Brazil

> BRAZIL. 1962. Relatório da Comissão de Planejamento da Irrigação. (Superintendência do Plano de Valorização Econômica da Região da Fronteira Sudoeste do Pais) Pôrto Alegre, 1962. fo.20. 28cm.

- Ceylon

> CEYLON. Ministry of Land, Irrigation and Power, Plan [of development, 1966-70] implementation report. a., 1966/7- Colombo.
>
> CEYLON. Ministry of Land, Irrigation and Power. 1966. Plan of development of Ministry of Land, Irrigation and Power, 1966-1970. [Colombo, 1966.] pp. 302.
>
> CEYLON. Ministry of Land, Irrigation and Power. Plan of development, 1966-70: implementation programme and targets. a., 1967/8- Colombo.
>
> FOOD AND AGRICULTURE ORGANIZATION. 1968. Report of the irrigation program review - Ceylon: FAO/IBRD Co-operative Program. [Colombo], Ministry of Planning and Economic Affairs, 1968. pp. 118.
>
> FOOD AND AGRICULTURE ORGANIZATION. Development Programme. 1969. Mahaweli Ganga irrigation and hydropower survey, Ceylon: final report. vol.1. General, etc. (FAO/SF:55/CEY-7) Rome, 1969. pp. 140.
>
> CEYLON. Gal Oya Project Evaluation Committee. 1970. Report. Colombo, 1970. pp. 203. (Parliament. Sessional Papers. 1970. No.1)
>
> SIRINANDA (KOKUHENNEDIGE UPAJEEVA) Water supply and irrigation in the dry zone of Ceylon, [Ph.D. (London) thesis]. 1970. fo. 462. bibliog. Typescript: unpublished. This thesis is the property of London University and may not be removed from the Library.

- Egypt

> FOOD AND AGRICULTURE ORGANIZATION. Development Programme. 1967. Pilot project for drainage of irrigated land: United Arab Republic: final report. (FAO/SF:30/UAR) Rome, 1967. pp. 49. bibliog.

- Ghana

> FOOD AND AGRICULTURE ORGANIZATION. Development Programme. 1968. Land and water survey in the upper and northern regions: Ghana: final report. vol.1. General, etc. (FAO/SF:31/GHA-6) Rome, 1968. pp. 118. [maps in end pocket]

- Greece

> LANDIS (WALTER) Dynamische und lineare Programmierung zur optimalen Dimensionierung eines Bewässerungsprojektes. [Freiburg i. Br., imprint, 1968?]. pp. 86. bibliog.

- India

> INDIA. Planning Commission. Programme Evaluation Organisation. Publications. No. 40. Study of the problems of minor irrigation. Delhi, 1961. pp. 264.
>
> INDIA Planning Commission. Programme Evaluation Organisation. Publications. No. 50. Evaluation of major irrigation projects: some case studies. [New Delhi], 1965 [or rather 1966]. pp. 253. $20\frac{1}{2}$cm.
>
> THORNTON (D.S.) Contrasting policies in irrigation development: Sudan and India. Reading, University, Faculty of Agriculture and Horticulture, Agricultural Economics Department, 1966. pp. (vi), 54, x. $25\frac{1}{2}$cm. (Development Studies. No. 1)
>
> UNITED STATES. International Agricultural Development Service. Agricultural water management in India. [Washington], 1966. pp. 57.
>
> BIEHL (MAX) Die Intensivierung der Flächennutzung durch Landbewässerung in Indien. Tübingen, Mohr, 1968. pp. vii, 179. bibliog. $23\frac{1}{2}$cm. (Kiel. Universität. Institut für Weltwirtschaft. Kieler Studien. 92)
>
> SYMPOSIUM ON ECONOMICS AND FINANCING OF IRRIGATION, DRAINAGE AND FLOOD CONTROL WORKS, NEW DELHI, 1961. [Report.] Delhi, 1967 [or rather 1968]. pp. 114. (India. Central Board of Irrigation and Power. Publications. No. 85.)

- India - Rates

> ANSARI (NASIM) Economics of irrigation rates: a study in Punjab and Uttar Pradesh. Bombay, [1968]. pp. 360.

- India - Madras

> MADRAS. 1959. Power and irrigation projects of Madras State. (Director of Information and Publicity) Madras, 1959. pp. ii, 5-29, 16cm.
>
> ADICEAM (EMMANUEL) La géographie de l'irrigation dans le Tamilnad. Paris, the École, 1966. pp. xviii, 525. bibliog. 25cm. (Saigon. École Français d'Extrême-Orient. Publications Hors-Série)

- Italy

> ITALY. Cassa per Opere Straordinarie di Pubblico Interesse nell'Italia Meridionale. Convegno Tecnico, 3°, 1954. Atti...:i problemi dell' irrigazione a pioggia nelle zone sub-aride del bacino del Mediterraneo. [Rome], 1955. pp. 381. $24\frac{1}{2}$cm.
>
> ITALY. Cassa per Opere Straordinarie di Pubblico Interesse nell'Italia Meridionale. Convegno Tecnico, 4°, 1956. Atti...: giornate di studio sui problemi dell' esercizio irriguo collettivo nell Mezzogiorno. Roma, 1957. pp. 283. 24cm.

IRRIGATION - Italy (Cont'd.)

ITALY. Direzione Generale della Bonifica e della Colonizzazione. Quaderni di Studio e di Informazione. 7. Il problema della irrigazione in Italia; a cura di Gaetano Nevano. Bologna, [1961?]. pp. 32. 31cm. (Estratto dalla Rivista Agricoltura, agosto 1961).

BUFFA (EUSEBIO) Il Canale Cavour e il progresso economico e sociale del Novarese e della Lomellina. [Pavia, 1968]. pp. 594. bibliog. Summaries in various languages.

- Kenya

FOOD AND AGRICULTURE ORGANIZATION. Development Programme. 1968. Survey of the irrigation potential of the Lower Tapa River Basin, Kenya: final report. vol.1. General, etc.(FAO/SF:53/KEN-3) Rome, 1968. pp. 182. bibliog.

GOLKOWSKY (RUDOLF) Bewasserungsland-wirtschaft in Kenya: Darstellung grundsätzlicher Zusammenhänge am Beispiel des Mwea Irrigation Settlement. München, [1969]. pp. 141. bibliog. (Ifo-Institut für Wirtschaftsforschung. Afrika-Studien. 39)

- Kirghizia

ILEBAEV (UICHUMAN ILEBAEVICH) Правовой режим орошаемых земель в Киргизской ССР в современный период. Фрунзе, 1966. pp. 187. bibliog.

BUDIANSKII (DAVID MIRONOVICH) Zemel'no-vodnaia reforma v Iuzhnoi Kirgizii, 1927-1928 gg. Frunze, 1968. pp. 170.

- Mediterranean

ITALY. Cassa per Opere Straordinarie di Pubblico Interesse nell'Italia Meridionale. Convegno Tecnico, 3°, 1954. Atti...: problemi dell' irrigazione a pioggia nelle zone sub-aride del bacino del Mediterraneo. [Rome], 1955. pp. 381. 24½cm.

- Pakistan

ETIENNE (GILBERT) Progrès agricole et maîtrise de l'eau: le cas du Pakistan. Paris, P.U.F., 1967. pp. 187. bibliog. 24cm. (Paris. Université, Institut d'Etude du Développement Economique et Social. Collection Tiers-Monde)

CARRUTHERS (I.D.) Irrigation development planning: aspects of Pakistan experience. Ashford, London, University, Wye College, Department of Economics, 1968. pp. vi, 67. 21cm. (Agrarian Development Studies. Reports. No. 2)

- Pakistan, East

FAROUK (A.) Irrigation in a monsoon land: economics of farming in the Ganges-Kobadak. Dacca, University of Dacca, Bureau of Economic Research, [1968]. pp. viii, 169. 24cm.

- Pakistan, West

MOHAMMAD (GHULAM) Programme for the development of irrigation and agriculture in West Pakistan: a preliminary analysis of some of the major recommendations in the bank consultants report. Karachi, 1967. pp. 63.

- Peru

BUCH (ALFRED) Das Bewässerungsprojekt "Tinajones" Peru: ein Modellfall zur Lösung wirtschaftlicher und sozial-politischer Probleme in Entwicklungs-ländern. 2nd ed. Hamburg, Übersee-Verlag, 1965. pp. 40. 21cm. (Übersee-Schriftenreihe. Heft 7)

- Poland

ŁOJEWSKI (STANISŁAW) Wpływ melioracji na wydajność gleb lekkich. Warszawa, 1970. pp. 139. bibliog.

- Russia

ASKOCHENSKII (ALEKSANDR NIKOLAEVICH) Oroshenie i obvodnenie v SSSR. Moskva, 1967. pp. 216.

KOPANEV (GERMAN VIKTOROVICH) Ekonomika i organizatsiia obvodneniia pastbishch. Moskva, 1967. pp. 255. bibliog.

EKONOMIKA... Экономика мелиорации земель. Москва, 1968. pp. 256. Colophon has subtitle: орошение и обводнение.

ILEBAEV (UICHUMAN ILEBAEVICH) Теоретические основы правового режима орошаемых земель в СССР. Фрунзе, 1968. pp. 208.

KUZNETSOV (IVAN ALEKSEEVICH) Komplek-snoe osvoenie vodnykh resursov rav-ninnykh basseinov i irrigatsiia. Moskva, 1968. pp. 134. bibliog.

- Russia - Siberia

MICHKOV (VALENTIN ANDREEVICH) Каменская ГЭС на Оби и орошение Кулунды. Новосибирск, Академия Наук СССР, 1964. pp. 60. 20½cm.

- South Africa

WALKER (G.N.) A preliminary report on the water resources of the Orange Free State. Bloemfontein, 1964. 3 vols. bibliog.

SOUTH AFRICA. Planning and Resources Advisory Council. 1967. Noord-Kaapland-streekstudie...; 'n verslag deur 'n Hulpkomitee. Pretoria, 1967. 5 vols. (in 1). bibliogs. With English summaries.

- Soviet Central Asia

MAMEDOV (ALI MURTUZAEVICH) Ирригация Средней Азии: экономический очерк. Москва, 1969. pp. 189.

- Spain

SPAIN. Comisaría del Plan de Desarrollo Económico y Social. 1964. Transformación en regadios: [anexo al Plan de...1964 a 1967]. [Madrid, 1964]. pp. 410. 30cm.

SPAIN. Comisaria del Plan de Desarrollo Economico y Social. 1967. (II Plan de desarrollo economico y social): transformacion en regadios. [Madrid, 1967]. pp. 614.

- Sudan

> THORNTON (D.S.) Contrasting policies in irrigation development: Sudan and India. Reading, University, Faculty of Agriculture and Horticulture, Agricultural Economics Department, 1966. pp. (vi), 54, x. 25½cm. (Development Studies. No. 1)

- United Kingdom - Maps

> HOGG (W.H.) Atlas of long-term irrigation needs for England and Wales. [London, H.M.S.O.], 1967. pp. (240). Loose-leaf binder

- United States

> ALMEIDA (POLIBIO FERNANDO AMARO VALENTE DE) Irrigação e cooperativismo nos Estados Unidos da America. Lisboa, 1968. pp. 236. bibliog. (Portugal. Junta de Investigações do Ultramar. Centro de Estudos Politicos e Sociais. Estudos de Ciências Politicas e Sociais. No. 82)

- Uzbekistan

> MAMEDOV (ALI MURTUZAEVICH) Razvitie irrigatsii v Uzbekistane. Tashkent, 1967. pp. 297. bibliog.

IRVINE (ROBERT FRANCIS)

> McFARLANE (BRUCE) Professor Irvine's economics in Australian labour history, 1913-1933. Canberra, Australian Society for the Study of Labour History, 1966. pp. 71. 25½cm.

IRVINE

- Civic improvement

> SCOTLAND. 1966. New Towns Act, 1946: Draft New Town (Irvine) Designation Order 1966; memorandum by the Secretary of State for Scotland. (Scottish Development Department) Edinburgh, 1966. pp. 15. 24½cm.

> WILSON (HUGH) and WOMERSLEY (LEWIS) Firm. Irvine New Town: final report on planning proposals... to the Secretary of State for Scotland, etc. Edinburgh, H.M.S.O., 1967. pp. (vii), 240. 30cm. Map in end pocket.

ISAACS (ISAAC ALFRED)

> COWEN (ZELMAN) Isaac Isaacs. Melbourne, O.U.P., 1967. pp. viii, 272. 21½cm.

ISAACS (SUSAN SUTHERLAND)

> GARDNER (DOROTHY ELLEN MARION) Susan Isaacs. London, Methuen Educational, 1969. pp. 191. bibliog. 21½cm.

ISÈRE (DEPARTMENT)

- Church history

> BERNARDIS (LAZZARO MARIA DE) L'instaurazione della costituzione civile del clero nel dipartimento dell'Isère. Milano, Giuffrè, 1968. pp. vii, 209. bibliog. 25cm. (Genoa. Università. Facoltà di Giurisprudenza. Annali. Collana. 16)

ISLE OF MAN

- Census

> ISLE OF MAN. Census, 1966. Isle of Man census 1966: report. [Douglas, 1966]. pp. 21.

- Constitution

> ISLE OF MAN. Commission on the Isle of Man Constitution. 1959. Report... (and Appendices). [Rt. Honourable Lord MacDermott, chairman] Douglas, [1959]. 2 vols. 24½cm.

> U.K. Joint Working Party on the Constitutional Relationship between the Isle of Man and the United Kingdom. 1969. Report: [Lord Stonham, chairman]. London, 1969. pp. 126. bibliog.

- Economic conditions

> FREEMAN (THOMAS WALTER) and others. Lancashire, Cheshire and the Isle of Man. London, [1966] repr 1968. pp. 308. bibliog.

- Statistics

> ISLE OF MAN. Government Office. 1891. Statistical abstract in each year from 1880-1 to 1889-90. [Douglas], 1891. pp. 45. 24cm.

ISLINGTON

- Civic improvement

> REGENTS CANAL GROUP. Design Schemes. No. 5. Duncan terrace gardens: conservation and change. London, the Group, 1967. pp. (41). 30cm.

ISMAY (HASTINGS LIONEL) 1st Baron Ismay

> WINGATE (Sir RONALD) Lord Ismay: a biography. London, 1970. pp. 232.

ISRAEL

> McINTYRE (IAN) The proud doers: Israel after twenty years. London, British Broadcasting Corporation, 1968. pp. (iv), 192. 21cm.

> NIKITINA (GALINA STEPANOVNA) Государство Израиль: особенности экономического и политического развития. Москва, Наука, 1968. pp. 413. 20см.

> HADOW (MICHAEL) and others. Israel today. London, 1970. pp. 32. (Anglo-Israel Association. Pamphlets. No. 26)

> SOME recent studies of Israel; [reports from] Wyndham Deedes Scholars. London, 1970. pp. 32. (Anglo-Israel Association. Pamphlets. No. 25)

- Army

> PERLMUTTER (AMOS) Military and politics in Israel: nation-building and role expansion. London, Cass, 1969. pp. xiv, 161. bibliog. 21½cm.

> ALLON (YIGAL) The making of Israel's army. London, 1970. pp. 273.

ISRAEL (Cont'd.)

- Constitution

LIKHOVSKI (ELIAHU S.) Israel's parliament: the law of the Knesset. Oxford, 1971. pp. 236. bibliog.

- Constitutional history

PERLMUTTER (AMOS) Anatomy of political institutionalization: the case of Israel and some comparative analyses. [Cambridge, Mass., 1970]. pp. 60. (Harvard University. Center for International Affairs. Occasional Papers in International Affairs. No.25)

- Constitutional law

LIKHOVSKI (ELIAHU S.) Israel's parliament: the law of the Knesset. Oxford, 1971. pp. 236. bibliog.

- Defences

INTERNATIONAL INSTITUTE FOR STRATEGIC STUDIES. Adelphi Papers. No. 52. Arms and security: the Egypt-Israel case; by Geoffrey Kemp. London, 1968. pp. 26.

PERES (SHIMON) David's sling. London, [1970]. pp. 322.

JABBER (FUAD) Israel and nuclear weapons: present option and future strategies. London, 1971. pp. 164. bibliog.

- Description and travel

BEN-ARIEH (YEHOSHUA) The changing landscape of the central Jordan valley. Jerusalem, 1968. pp. 131. bibliog. (Hebrew University. Scripta Hierosolymitana. vol. 15. Studies in Geography. No. 3)

KARMON (YEHUDA) Israel: a regional geography. London, [1971]. pp. 345. bibliogs. Map in end pocket.

- Economic conditions

MEISSNER (HANS GUENTHER) Die Wirtschaft Israels: Aufbau, Struktur, Entwicklung. Köln, Schmidt, 1962. pp. 78. 23cm. (Germany (Bundesrepublik). Bundesstelle für Aussenhandelsinformation. Aussenhandel und Weltwirtschaft. Heft 7).

HOROWITZ (DAVID) A policy on trial. Jerusalem, 1963. pp. 9. (Article published in the Jerusalem Post, September 6, 1963)

HOROWITZ (DAVID) The enigma of economic growth: the case of Israel: (lecture)... at the London School of Economics. London, Anglo-Israel Association, 1965. pp. 16. 24cm. (Pamphlets. No. 9)

ISRAEL. Economic Planning Authority. 1968. Israel economic development: past progress and plan for the future: final draft. Jerusalem, 1968. pp. 551. 24cm.

SZERESZEWSKI (ROBERT) Essays on the structure of the Jewish economy in Palestine and Israel. Jerusalem, Maurice Falk Institute for Economic Research in Israel, 1968. pp. xii, 99. bibliog. 23½cm.

SHIBL (YUSUF) ed. Essays on the Israeli economy. Beirut, 1969. pp. 276. bibliog. (Palestine Research Center. Palestine Books. No. 15)

DOUEK (ISAAC) and DOUEK (JOSEPHINE) Scientists in Israel; and The Israel economy, with special reference to wages policy; by David Metcalf. London, 1970. pp. 35. bibliogs.

EISENSTADT (SHMUEL N.) and others, eds. Integration and development in Israel. London, 1970. pp. 703. bibliog.

SHEFER (MICHAEL) Monopoly and competition in small economies with special reference to Israel; [Ph. D. (London) thesis]. 1970. fo. 422. bibliog. Typescript: unpublished. This thesis is the property of London University and may not be removed from the Library.

GAATHON (A.L.) Economic productivity in Israel. New York, 1971. pp. 280. bibliog.

KARMON (YEHUDA) Israel: a regional geography. London, [1971]. pp. 345. bibliogs. Map in end pocket.

PACK (HOWARD) Structural change and economic policy in Israel. New Haven, 1971. pp. 273. bibliog.

- Economic policy

HOROWITZ (DAVID) A policy on trial. Jerusalem, 1963. pp. 9. (Article published in the Jerusalem Post, September 6, 1963)

HESSE (KURT) Planungen in Entwicklungsländern: eine Einführung in Wesen und Praxis des Entwicklungsplanens an Hand von sechs Beispielen. Berlin, Duncker und Humblot, [1965]. pp. xx, 618. bibliog. 23cm.

HOROWITZ (DAVID) The enigma of economic growth: the case of Israel: (lecture)... at the London School of Economics. London, Anglo-Israel Association, 1965. pp. 16. 24cm. (Pamphlets. No. 9)

ISRAEL. 1965. Israel industry, 1970. (Investment Authority) Tel-Aviv, 1965. pp. 47. 27cm.

WILDHABER-CREUX (SIMONE ANNE MARIE) Wachstum und Strukturwandel in der israelischen Wirtschaft. [Stuttgart, imprint], 1967. pp. 186. bibliog.

BEHAM (MIRIAM) Monetary aspects of the 1962 devaluation. Jerusalem, Maurice Falk Institute for Economic Research in Israel, 1968. pp. 106. 24cm.

HALEVI (NADAV) and KLINOV-MALUL (RUTH) The economic development of Israel. New York, Praeger, 1968. pp. xviii, 321. bibliog. 23½cm. (Praeger Special Studies in International Economics and Development)

ISRAEL. Economic Planning Authority. 1968. Israel economic development: past progress and plan for the future: final draft. Jerusalem, 1968. pp. 551. 24cm.

HELOU (ANGELINA) Interaction of political, military and economic factors in Israel. Beirut, 1969. pp. 175. bibliog. (Palestine Research Centre. Palestine Monographs. 16)

SHIBL (YUSUF) ed. Essays on the Israeli economy. Beirut, 1969. pp. 276. bibliog. (Palestine Research Center. Palestine Books. No. 15)

WILLNER (DOROTHY) Nation-building and community in Israel. Princeton, Princeton U.P., 1969. pp. xi, 478. bibliog. 21½cm.

PACK (HOWARD) Structural change and economic policy in Israel. New Haven, 1971. pp. 273. bibliog.

- Emigration and immigration

ISAACS (HAROLD ROBERT) American Jews in Israel. New York, Day, [1967]. pp. 253. 20cm.

RESEARCH GROUP FOR EUROPEAN MIGRATION PROBLEMS. Publications. 16. The return movement of Jews to Austria after the Second World War, with special consideration of the return from Israel; by F. Wilder-Okladek. The Hague, 1969. pp. 130. bibliog.

DESHEN (SHLOMO A.) Immigrant voters in Israel: parties and congregations in a local election campaign. Manchester, [1970]. pp. 239. bibliog.

HERODOTUS pseud. British settlers in Israel. London, 1971. pp. 36. (Anglo-Israel Association. Pamphlets. No. 30)

SHOKEID (MOSHE) The dual heritage: immigrants from the Atlas mountains in an Israeli village. Manchester, [1971]. pp. 245. bibliog.

- Executive departments

ISRAEL. State Comptroller's Office. 1965. State control in Israel. Jerusalem, 1965. pp. 26. 24cm.

- Foreign relations

SOME aspects of Israel; [reports of three lectures and two essays, 1960-61]; (by Solomon Gaon) [and others]. London, [1963]. pp. 54.

DRAPER (THEODORE) Israel and world politics: roots of the third Arab-Israeli war. New York, Viking P., 1968. pp. x. 278. 19½cm.

JANSEN (G.H.) Whose Suez?: aspects of collusion, 1967. Beirut, 1968. pp. 36. (Institute for Palestine Studies. Monographs Series. No. 13)

FRIEDLAENDER (SAUL) Réflexions sur l'avenir d'Israël. Paris, Éditions du Seuil, [1969]. pp. 189. 20½cm.

ZWEIG (FERDYNAND) Israel: the sword and the harp; the mystique of violence and the mystique of redemption; controversial themes in Israeli society London, Heinemann, 1969. pp. x, 326. 21½cm.

CORM (GEORGES G.) Israel in the international strategy of the western powers. Beirut, [1970]. pp. 24.

ECKARDT (ALICE) and ECKARDT (ARTHUR ROY) Encounter with Israel: a challenge to conscience. New York, [1970]. pp. 304.

SIONIZM - otravlennoe oruzhie imperializma: dokumenty i materialy; (sbornik sostavlen po publikatsiiam sovetskoi pechati) Moskva, 1970. pp. 319.

- Foreign relations - Africa

FRANCE. Direction de la Documentation. La Documentation Française. Notes et Études Documentaires. No. 2,949. Les relations d'Israël avec les nouveaux états d'Afrique. Paris, 1962. pp. 31. bibliog. 30½cm.

- Foreign relations - Asia

KOCHAN (RAN) Israel's relations with Asian states east of Iran, 1948-1967; [Ph.D. (London) thesis]. 1970. fo. 370. bibliog. Typescript: unpublished. This thesis is the property of London University and may not be removed from the Library.

- Foreign relations - France

ARON (RAYMOND) De Gaulle, Israël et les Juifs. [Paris], Plon, [1968]. pp. 186. 20cm. (Tribune Libre)

ARON (RAYMOND) De Gaulle, Israel and the Jews... (essays). London, 1969. pp. 160.

- Foreign relations - Germany

BURG (J.G.) pseud. [i.e. Josef GINSBURG] Sündenböcke: Grossangriffe des Zionismus auf Papst Pius XII. und auf die deutschen Regierungen. [Munich], 1968. pp. 334.

VOGEL (ROLF) ed. The German path to Israel: a documentation. London, 1969. pp. 325.

DEUTSCHKRON (INGE) Bonn and Jerusalem: the strange coalition. Philadelphia, [1970]. pp. 357. bibliog.

DEUTSCHKRON (INGE) Israel und die Deutschen: zwischen Ressentiment und Ratio. Köln, [1970]. pp. 367.

- Foreign relations - Jordan

HUSSEIN, King of Jordan. My "war" with Israel; as told to and with additional material by Vick Vance and Pierre Lauer; (translated from the French). London, 1969. pp. 176.

- Foreign relations - Russia

ISRAEL. Ministry for Foreign Affairs. Information Division. 1967. The USSR and Arab belligerency. Jerusalem, 1967. pp. 87. 23½cm.

DAGAN (AVIGDOR) Moscow and Jerusalem: twenty years of relations between Israel and the Soviet Union. London, 1970. pp. 255. bibliog.

- Foreign relations - United States

MOHAMAD (FADHIL ZAKY) Congress and foreign policy: a case study of the role of the U.S. Congress in shaping the American stand toward Palestine. Baghdad, Ministry of Culture and Guidance, 1965. pp. 54. bibliog. (Foreign Languages Books. 9)

KADI (LEILA S.) A survey of American-Israeli relations. Beirut, Palestine Research Center, 1969. pp. 278. bibliog. 17cm. (Palestine Monographs. 56)

- Historical geography - Maps

VILNAY (ZEV) The new Israel atlas: Bible to present day;...maps prepared by Carta, Jerusalem. London, Humphrey, 1968. pp. 112. 29cm.

ISRAEL (Cont'd.)

- History

THE PARTITION of Palestine, 29 November, 1947: an analysis. Beirut, 1967. pp. 55. (Institute for Palestine Studies. Monographs Series. No.9)

WEIZMANN (CHAIM) The letters and papers...; edited by Leonard Stein in collaboration with Gedalia Yogev. London, O.U.P., 1968 in progress. 23½cm.

LOUVISH (MISHA) The challenge of Israel. Jerusalem, Israel U.P., 1968. pp. xix, 281. bibliog. 21½cm.

WEINSTOCK (NATHAN) Le sionisme contre Israël. Paris, 1969. pp. 622. bibliog.

ECKARDT (ALICE) and ECKARDT (ARTHUR ROY) Encounter with Israel: a challenge to conscience. New York, [1970]. pp. 304.

SAMUEL (EDWIN) 2nd Viscount Samuel. A lifetime in Jerusalem: the memoirs of the second Viscount Samuel. London, 1970. pp. 335.

SEGRE (V.D.) Israel: a society in transition. London, 1971. pp. 227.

- History - Sources

LAQUEUR (WALTER ZE'EV) ed. The Israel-Arab reader: a documentary of history of the Middle East conflict. London, Weidenfeld & Nicolson, 1969. pp. xii, 371. bibliog. 21½cm.

- History, Military

ALLON (YIGAL) The making of Israel's army. London, 1970. pp. 273.

- Industries

ISRAEL. 1965. Israel industry, 1970. (Investment Authority) Tel-Aviv, 1965. pp. 47. 27cm.

ISRAEL. Central Bureau of Statistics. Census of Industry, 1965. Census of industry and crafts, 1965. Jerusalem, 1966-70. 13 pts. (in 4 vols.) In English and Hebrew.

TEL-AVIV. Department of Research and Statistics. Special Surveys. No.25. Development of industry and crafts in Tel-Aviv-Yafo. [Tel-Aviv], 1967. pp. irreg. In English and Hebrew.

- Knesset

ZIDON (ASHER) Knesset: the parliament of Israel...; translated from the Hebrew by Aryeh Rubinstein and Gertrude Hirschler. New York, Herzl P., [1967]. pp. x, 342. 21cm.

- Knesset - Rules and practice

LIKHOVSKI (ELIAHU S.) Israel's parliament: the law of the Knesset. Oxford, 1971. pp. 236. bibliog.

- Maps

ISRAEL. Survey of Israel. 1970. Atlas of Israel: cartography, physical geography, human and economic geography, history. 2nd ed. Amsterdam, Elsevier, 1970. pp. various. bibliogs.

- Nationalism

HERMAN (SIMON N.) Israelis and Jews: the continuity of an identity. New York, [1970]. pp. 331. bibliog.

- Officials and employees

ISRAEL. 1963. Civil Service Commission: report no.12: summary, covering the period 1.4.61 to 31.3.62. Jerusalem, 1963. pp. 26. 24cm. The other of the Commission's reports have been issued in Hebrew only.

ISRAEL. Statutes, etc. 1955-61. State service laws. (Civil Service Commission) (Reprinted from Laws of the State of Israel) Jerusalem, 1964. pp. 37. 24cm.

ISRAEL. Civil Service Commission. 1968. Twenty years of service. Jerusalem, 1968 pp. 89. 24cm.

- Politics and government

ISRAEL. Knesset. Divrei haKnesset: Records of the Knesset. Sess., F 14/S 12 1949 ([1st Knesset] 1st session)- Jerusalem. English summary of Divrei haKnesset. For 1st Knesset (F 14 1949 - Ag 20 1951) file includes Indices only; some issues for 1949-1965 are xerographic reprints.

SOME aspects of Israel; [reports of three lectures and two essays, 1960-61]; (by Solomon Gaon) [and others]. London, [1963]. pp. 54.

BURG (J.G.) pseud. [i.e. JOSEF GINSBURG] Schuld und Schicksal: Europas Juden zwischen Henkern und Heuchlern. 4th ed. München, 1965. pp. 370.

SCHUERHOLZ (FRANZ) Innenpolitische Kräfte in Israel. Bonn, 1966. pp. 40. 26cm. (Germany (Bundesrepublik). Bundeszentrale für Politische Bildung. Schriften)

FREUDENHEIM (YEHOSHUA) Government in Israel; ... translated from the Hebrew by Meir Silverstone and Chaim Ivor Goldwater. Dobbs Ferry, Oceana Publications, 1967. pp. x, 309. 23cm.

ARIAN (ALAN) Ideological change in Israel. Cleveland, Case Western Reserve U.P., [1968]. pp. xvii, 220. bibliog. 21cm.

COLLOQUE DE JURISTES ARABES SUR LA PALESTINE, ALGER. 1967. La question palestinienne. [Algiers, Société Nationale d'Édition et de Diffusion, 1968]. pp. 237. 23cm.

FEIN (LEONARD J.) Israel: politics and people; (revised edition of Politics in Israel). Boston, Little, [1968]. pp. xiv, 338. 20cm.

LOUVISH (MISHA) The challenge of Israel. Jerusalem, Israel U.P., 1968. pp. xix, 281. bibliog. 21½cm.

DROR (YEHEZKEL) From management science to the improvement of public policymaking: the experience of Israel; outline and background material. n.p., 1969. pp. 39.

HELOU (ANGELINA) Interaction of political, military and economic factors in Israel. Beirut, 1969. pp. 175. bibliog. (Palestine Research Centre. Palestine Monographs. 16)

HILLEL (MARC) Israël en danger de paix. [Paris], Fayard, [1969]. pp. 350. 21½cm.

ISRAEL. State Comptroller's Office. 1969. Norms for public administration: based on the State Comptroller's reports during the term of office of Dr. S. Moses 5709-5721 · 1949-1961; edited and with introductions by Dr. M. Gilon. Jerusalem, 1969. pp. 308.

PERLMUTTER (AMOS) Military and politics in Israel: nation-building and role expansion. London, Cass, 1969. pp. xiv, 161. bibliog. 21½cm.

PRITTIE (TERENCE CORNELIUS FARMER) Eshkol of Israel: the man and the nation. London, Museum P., 1969. pp. xiv, 368. bibliog. 23½cm.

WILLNER (DOROTHY) Nation-building and community in Israel. Princeton, Princeton U.P., 1969. pp. xi, 478. bibliog. 21½cm.

ZIONISM and the Arab revolution: the myth of progressive Israel. New York, 1969. pp. 31.

BENTWICH (NORMAN DE MATTOS) Israel: two fateful years, 1967-69. London, [1970]. pp. 115. bibliog.

CAIDEN (GERALD ELLIOT) Israel's administrative culture. Berkeley, 1970. pp. 118. bibliog.

ECKARDT (ALICE) and ECKARDT (ARTHUR ROY) Encounter with Israel: a challenge to conscience. New York, [1970]. pp. 304.

EISENSTADT (SHMUEL N.) and others, eds. Integration and development in Israel. London, 1970. pp. 703. bibliog.

WEINSTOCK (NATHAN) and ROTHSCHILD (JON) The truth about Israel and Zionism. New York, 1970. pp. 15.

SEGRE (V.D.) Israel: a society in transition. London, 1971. pp. 227.

- Population

SHIBL (YUSUF) ed. Essays on the Israeli economy. Beirut, 1969. pp. 276. bibliog. (Palestine Research Center. Palestine Books. No. 15)

EISENSTADT (SHMUEL N.) and others, eds. Integration and development in Israel. London, 1970. pp. 703. bibliog.

- Public buildings

ISRAEL. Ministry of Housing. 1968. Israel builds: 1948-1968. [Jerusalem], [1968?]. pp. (48). 26½cm.

- Relations (general) with Russia

NISSES (EFIM IAKOVLEVICH) Komu sluzhat sionisty. Simferopol', 1969. pp. 64.

SIONIZM - otravlennoe oruzhie imperializma: dokumenty i materialy; (sbornik sostavlen po publikatsiiam sovetskoi pechati) Moskva, 1970. pp. 319.

- Relations (general) with the United Kingdom

SAMUEL (EDWIN) 2nd Viscount Samuel. Anglo-Israel contacts, 1948-1968: a catalogue. London, 1969. pp. 45. (Anglo-Israel Association. Pamphlets. No. 24)

- Relations (military) with France

[COMITE DE SOLIDARITE FRANÇAISE AVEC ISRAEL]. La solidarité française avec Israël: les Français contre l'embargo. Paris, [1969]. pp. 24.

- Religion

LESLIE (SAMUEL CLEMENT) The rift in Israel: religious authority and secular democracy. London, 1971. pp. 185.

- Rural conditions

GLIKSON (ARTUR) Two case studies of rural planning and development in Israel: prepared for the United Nations Seminar on Regional Planning, Tokyo, 1958. [Jerusalem], Ministry of Labour, 1961. fo. 40. bibliog. 27cm.

- Sanitary affairs

ISRAEL. Ministry of Health, 1968. Health services in Israel; edited by Th. Grushka. [3rd ed.] Jerusalem, 1968. pp. xix, 455. bibliogs. 23½cm.

- Social conditions

IDELSON (BEBA) The power of good will: Moetzet Hapoalot in 1964. [Tel-Aviv, 1964] pp. 33.

SOME social and educational aspects of Israel; [reports from] William Deedes Scholars. London, 1964. pp. 29. (Anglo-Israel Association. Pamphlets. No. 6)

LOUVISH (MISHA) The challenge of Israel. Jerusalem, Israel U.P., 1968. pp. xix, 281. bibliog. 21½cm.

MNACKO (LADISLAV) Die Aggressoren: von der Schuld und Unschuld der Schwachen. Wien, Molden, [1968]. pp. 272. 21cm.

FRIEDLAENDER (SAUL) Réflexions sur l'avenir d'Israël. Paris, Éditions du Seuil, [1969]. pp. 189. 20½cm.

HILLEL (MARC) Israël en danger de paix. [Paris], Fayard, [1969]. pp. 350. 21½cm.

KLEINBERGER (AHARON F.) Society, schools and progress in Israel. Oxford, 1969. pp. 337.

SAMUEL (EDWIN) 2nd Viscount Samuel. The structure of society in Israel. New York, [1969]. pp. 184. bibliog.

ZWEIG (FERDYNAND) Israel: the sword and the harp; the mystique of violence and the mystique of redemption; controversial themes in Israeli society. London, Heinemann, 1969. pp. x, 326. 21½cm.

BENTWICH (NORMAN DE MATTOS) Israel: two fateful years, 1967-69. London, [1970]. pp. 115. bibliog.

ECKARDT (ALICE) and ECKARDT (ARTHUR ROY) Encounter with Israel: a challenge to conscience. New York, [1970]. pp. 304.

EISENSTADT (SHMUEL N.) and others, eds. Integration and development in Israel. London, 1970. pp. 703. bibliog.

PERES (SHIMON) David's sling. London, [1970]. pp. 322.

ISRAEL (Cont'd.)

- Social policy

ISRAEL. Ministry of Housing. 1966. Housing in relation to the national level of economic and social development in Israel: series of articles prepared for the 28th World Congress for Housing and Planning... 1966, Tokyo. Jerusalem, 1966. pp. (30). 26½cm.

- Year-books

FACTS ABOUT ISRAEL; [published by] Ministry for Foreign Affairs, Information Division, [Israel]. Jerusalem, annual, 1968 to date. 18½cm.

ISRAEL. Press Office. Israel's [ ] year. [Jerusalem?], annual, 1968 to date. 27½cm.

ISRAEL AND THE DIASPORA

HERMAN (SIMON N.) Israelis and Jews: the continuity of an identity. New York, [1970]. pp. 331. bibliog.

ISRAEL- ARAB BORDER CONFLICTS, 1949-

BELL (J. BOWYER) The long war: Israel and the Arabs since 1946. Englewood Cliffs, [1969]. pp. 467. bibliog.

ISRAEL- ARAB WAR, 1967

CENTRO STUDI AZIONE COMUNE. Quaderni. 2. La crisi del medio oriente: Israele '67. Milano, Azione Comune, [1967]. pp. 106. 21cm.

DAYAN (YAEL) Israel journal: June, 1967. New York, McGraw-Hill, [1967]. pp. (v), 113. 20½cm.

ISRAEL. Ministry for Foreign Affairs. Information Division. 1967. The Arab war against Israel: [statements and documents]. Jerusalem, 1967. pp. 55. 24cm.

ISRAEL. Ministry for Foreign Affairs. Information Division. 1967. From words to guns: Nasser's blueprint for war. Jerusalem, 1967. pp. 38. 24cm.

ISRAEL. Ministry for Foreign Affairs. Information Division. 1967. The USSR and Arab belligerency. Jerusalem, 1967. pp. 87. 23½cm.

JAPHETH (M. D.) and RAJIV (P. K.) The Arab Israel conflict. Bombay, 1967. pp. 107.

ROULEAU (ERIC) and others. Israel et les Arabes: le 3ᵉ combat. Paris, Éditions du Seuil, [1967]. pp. 187. 20½cm. (L'Histoire Immédiate)

SEGUEV (SAMUEL) La guerre de six jours: opération "drap rouge"; (traduit de l'hébreu par Maurice Saporta et Claude Feigelman). Paris, Calmann-Lévy, [1967]. pp. 307. 23cm.

STONE (ISIDOR F.) For a new approach to the Israeli-Arab conflict. [New York], 1967. pp. 22. (Reprinted from the New York Review of Books, August 3, 1967)

AGWANI (MOHAMMED SHAFI) The West Asian crisis, 1967. Meerut, Meenakshi Prakashan, 1968. pp. viii, 196. 21½cm.

ARAB WOMEN'S INFORMATION COMMITTEE. The Arabs under Israeli occupation: memorandum submitted by the Arab Women's Information Committee to the Regional Conference on Human Rights, Beirut, 1968. [Beirut, 1968]. unpaged.

ARON (RAYMOND) De Gaulle, Israël et les Juifs. [Paris], Plon, [1968]. pp. 186. 20cm. (Tribune Libre)

BONDY (RUTH) and others, eds. Mission survival: the people of Israel's story in their own words, from the threat of annihilation to miraculous victory. London, Allen, 1968. pp. 504. bibliog 21½cm.

DOUGLAS-HOME (CHARLES) The Arabs and Israel: a background book. London, Bodley Head, 1968. pp. 121. 18½cm. (Background Books)

DRAPER (THEODORE) Israel and world politics: roots of the third Arab-Israeli war. New York, Viking P., 1968. pp. x, 278. 19½cm.

JANSEN (G.H.) Whose Suez?: aspects of collusion, 1967. Beirut, 1968. pp. 36. (Institute for Palestine Studies. Monograph Series. No. 13)

KEESING'S CONTEMPORARY ARCHIVES. Research Reports. The Arab-Israeli conflict: the 1967 campaign. [London], Keesing's Publications, [1968]. pp. 55. bibliog. 18½cm.

KHADDURI (MAJDIA D.) ed. The Arab-Israeli impasse: expressions of moderate viewpoints on the Arab-Israeli conflict by well known western writers. Washington, Luce, [1968]. pp. 223. 20cm.

KHOURI (FRED JOHN) The Arab-Israeli dilemma. Syracuse, Syracuse U.P., [1968]. pp. xi, 436. bibliog. 22½cm.

KIMCHE (DAVID) and BAWLY (DAN) The sandstorm: the Arab-Israeli war of June 1967: prelude and aftermath. London, Secker & Warburg, 1968. pp. 319. 21½cm.

LALL (ARTHUR S.) The UN and the Middle East crisis, 1967. New York, Columbia U.P., 1968. pp. ix, 322. 22½cm.

WAGENLEHNER (GUENTHER) Eskalation im Nahen Osten: die politische und psychologische Problematik eines Konflikts. Stuttgart-Degerloch, [1968]. pp. 284. bibliog.

AL JOUNDI (SAMI) Le drame palestinien: pour sortir de l'impasse; [translated from the German]. Paris, Fayard, [1969]. pp. 155. 21½cm. (Le Monde sans Frontières)

ARON (RAYMOND) De Gaulle, Israel and the Jews...(essays). London, 1969. pp. 160.

BERINDRANATH (DEWAN) War and peace in west Asia. New Delhi, 1969. pp. 214.

BERKMAN (EDWARD O.) Sabra: de rol van de sabra's in de oorlog en hun betekenis voor Israël. Paris, 1969. pp. 267.

BINDRA (ATAM PARKASH SINGH) Suez thrombosis: causes and prospects. Delhi, [1969]. pp. 159. bibliog.

CATTAN (HENRY) Palestine, the Arabs and Israel: the search for justice. London, Longmans, 1969. pp. viii, 281. 22cm.

CRANE (PEGGY) Peace in Palestine? London, 1969. pp. 32. bibliog.

HUSSEIN, King of Jordan. My "war" with Israel; as told to and with additional material by Vick Vance and Pierre Lauer; (translated from the French). London, 1969. pp. 176.

INTERNATIONAL SYMPOSIUM ON INEVITABLE WAR OR INITIATIVES FOR PEACE, TEL AVIV, 1969. To make war or make peace: proceedings [of the symposium]; March 27,29,30, 1969, Tel Aviv, Kibbutz Gan Shmuel, Jerusalem. Tel Aviv, 1969. pp. 285. Reprinted from special issue of New Outlook

PALESTINE RESEARCH CENTER. Palestine Monographs. 55. The Arabs under Israeli occupation. Beirut, 1969. pp. 114. 17cm.

PRITTIE (TERENCE CORNELIUS FARMER) Eshkol of Israel: the man and the nation. London, Museum P., 1969. pp. xiv. 368. bibliog. 23½cm.

ROSENSAFT (MENACHEM Z.) Not backward to belligerency a study of events surrounding the "Six-Day War" of June, 1967. New York, [1969]. pp. 181.

ABU-LUGHOD (IBRAHIM) ed. The Arab-Israeli confrontation of June 1967: an Arab perspective. Evanston, 1970. pp. 201. bibliog.

KANOVSKY (ELIYAHU) The economic impact of the Six-day War: Israel, the occupied territories; Egypt, Jordan. New York, 1970. pp. 451. bibliog.

PERES (SHIMON) David's sling. London, [1970]. pp. 322.

The SEVENTH day: soldiers' talk about the Six-day War; recorded and edited by a group of young kibbutz members. London, 1970. pp. 247.

- Blockades

ISRAEL. Ministry for Foreign Affairs, Information Division. 1967. Egypt's unlawful blockade of the Gulf of Aqaba. Jerusalem, [1967]. pp. 28. 24½cm.

- Occupied territories

TEVETH (SHABTAI) The cursed blessing: the story of Israel's occupation of the West Bank. London, 1970. pp. 372.

- Refugees

DODD (PETER) and BARAKAT (HALIM) River without bridges: a study of the exodus of the 1967 Palestinian Arab refugees. Beirut, 1969. pp. 64. (Institute for Palestine Studies. Monographs Series. No.10)

ISTANBUL

- History

MILLER (DEAN A.) Imperial Constantinople. New York, [1969]. pp. 226. bibliog.

ISTANBUL UNIVERSITY

ISTANBUL. Üniversitesi. Hukuk Fakültesi. Mukayeseli Hukuk Enstitüsü. Yönetmelik. Istanbul, 1949. pp. 32. 24cm. [in Turkish, French, English, German and Italian]

ISTRIA

- Annexation to Italy

BRATULIĆ (VJEKOSLAV) Dokumenti o obrani i istrebljenju hrvatskih škola u Istri pod Italijom. Zagreb, 1955. pp. 95. bibliog. Documents in Italian.

ISUV (IOSIF ANDREEVICH)

GARVI (PETR ABRAMOVICH) Revoliutsionnye siluety. New York, 1962. pp. 43. (Inter-University Project on the History of the Menshevik Movement)

ITALIAN LANGUAGE

MIGLIORINI (BRUNO) Saggi sulla lingua del Novecento. 2nd ed. Firenze, Sansoni, 1942. pp. 259. 18cm. (Biblioteca di Lingua Nostra. 1)

HALL (ROBERT A.) Italian for modern living. Philadelphia, [1961] repr. 1966. pp. 427.

MAURO (TULLIO DE) Storia linguistica dell'Italia unita. [2nd ed.] Bari, 1970. pp. 573. bibliog.

- Dictionaries

DIZIONARIO Garzanti della lingua italiana; realizzato della Redazione Lessicografica Garzanti, diretto da Giorgio Cusatelli. Milano, 1965. repr. 1969. pp. 1990.

DEVOTO (GIACOMO) Avviamento alla etimologia italiana: dizionario etimologico. 2nd ed. Firenze, 1968. pp. 501.

- Dictionaries - English

CASSELL AND COMPANY. Italian-English, English-Italian dictionary; prepared by Piero Rebora with the assistance of Francis M. Guercio and Arthur L. Hayward. 7th ed. London, Cassell, 1967. pp. xxi, 1096. 21cm.

CENTRO LESSICOGRAFICO SANSONI. Dizionario delle lingue italiana e inglese;...realizzato...sotto la direzione di Vladimiro Macchi. Firenze, 1970 in progress.

- Grammar, Historical

ROHLFS (GERHARD) Grammatica storica della lingua italiana e dei suoi dialetti. rev. ed. Torino, 1966-69. 3 vols. bibliog.

- Idioms, corrections, errors.

VITALE (GRAZIA) Principali espressioni idiomatiche italiane. Genova, 1964. pp. 265.

SATTA (LUCIANO) Come si dice: uso e abuso della lingua italiana. Firenze, [1968]. pp. 420.

ITALIAN LITERATURE

- Bio-bibliography

NICOLINI (FAUSTO) Saggio d'un repertorio biobibliografico di scrittori nati o vissuti nell'antico regno di Napoli. Napoli, the Banco, 1966. pp. 857. bibliog. 24½cm. (Banco di Napoli. Bollettino dell'Archivio Historico. Biblioteca. 11)

ITALIAN NEWSPAPERS

MATTEINI (NEVIO) Il "Rimino", una del prime "Gazzette" d'Italia: saggio storico sui primordi della stampa. [Bologna], Cappelli, [1967]. pp. 107. 24½cm.

ITALIAN PERIODICALS

LICATA (GLAUCO) La Rassegna Nazionale: conservatori e cattolici liberali italiani attraverso la loro rivista, 1879-1915. Roma, 1968. pp. 614. With extensive indexes to the periodical.

- Directories

GUARDA (GUIDO) Guida della stampa periodica (italiana). Roma, 1969. pp. 317.

ITALIAN QUESTION, 1848-1870

FERRARI (GIUSEPPE) Political Writer. La federazione repubblicana; a cura di Salvatore Onufrio; [originally published 1851]. Firenze, 1969. pp. 209.

I PARTITI del'opposizione e la maggioranza: cenni politici. Napoli, [imprint], 1862. pp. 24. 19½cm.

SAITTA (ARMANDO) Sinistra hegeliana e problema italiano negli scritti di A.L. Mazzini: [with appendix of Mazzini's works reprinted]. Roma, 1967-1968. 3 vols. (Istituto Storico Italiano per l'Età Moderna e Contemporanea. Italia e Europa. Collezione per il Primo Centenario dell'Unità.)

BUSH (JOHN W.) S.J. Venetia redeemed: Franco-Italian relations, 1864-1866. New York, Syracuse U.P., [1967]. pp. xv, 160. bibliog. 22½cm.

TOMEUCCI (LUIGI) Massimo D'Azeglio: autore e padre della questione italiana. Bologna, 1969. pp. 312. bibliog.

ITALIANS IN AUSTRIA-HUNGARY

VEITER (THEODOR) Die Italiener in der Österreichisch-ungarischen Monarchie: eine volkspolitische und nationalitätenrechtliche Studie. München, Oldenbourg, [1965]. pp. 112. bibliog. 20½cm. (Österreich Archiv)

ITALIANS IN CANADA

BOISSEVAIN (JEREMY FERGUS) The Italians of Montreal: social adjustment in a plural society. Ottawa, 1970. pp. 87. bibliog. (Canada. Royal Commission on Bilingualism and Biculturalism, 1963. Studies. 7)

ITALIANS IN FOREIGN COUNTRIES

FIORE (ILARIO) L'italiano di Ponte Cayumba. Firenze, Vallecchi, [1967]. pp. 352. 22cm.

ITALIANS IN FRANCE

MONGÉ (RENÉ) Le travailleur italien en France et la famille italienne en France; Il Lavoratore italiano, la famiglia italiana in Francia. Paris, Éditions Sociales Françaises. [1966]. pp. 71. 21cm. In French and Italian

ITALIANS IN GERMANY

BRITSCHGI-SCHIMMER (INA) Die wirtschaftliche und soziale Lage der italienischen Arbeiter in Deutschland: ein Beitrag zur ausländischen Arbeiterfrage. Karlsruhe i.B., Braun, 1916. pp. xii, 178. bibliog. 24¼cm.

NANN (EBERHARD) Die Kriminalität der italienischen Gastarbeiter im Spiegel der Ausländerkriminalität. Hamburg, Kriminalistik Verlag, 1967. pp. 207. bibliog. 22½cm. (Deutsche Kriminologische Gesellschaft. Kriminologische Schriftenreihe. Band 28)

ITALIANS IN RUSSIA

FILATOV (GEORGII SEMENOVICH) Восточный поход Муссолини. Москва, 1969. pp. 183. bibliog.

ITALIANS IN SPAIN

PIKE (RUTH) Enterprise and adventure: the Genoese in Seville and the opening of the new world. Ithaca, Cornell University Press, 1966. pp. xiii, 243. bibliog. 21½cm.

ITALIANS IN SWITZERLAND

ROBBIANI (DARIO) Socialisti e Italiani in Svizzera. Milano, Edizioni Azione Comune, [1968]. pp. xvii, 159. 21cm.

BRAUN (RUDOLF) of Zuerich. Sozio-kulturelle Probleme der Eingliederung italienischer Arbeitskräfte in der Schweiz. Erlenbach-Zürich, [1970]. pp. 589. bibliog.

ITALIANS IN THE UNITED STATES

ROLLE (ANDREW F.) The immigrant upraised: Italian adventurers and colonists in an expanding America. Norman, U. of Oklahoma P., [1968]. pp. xvi, 391. bibliog. 22½cm.

ETS (MARIE HALL) Rosa: the life of an Italian immigrant. Minneapolis, [1970]. pp. 254.

NELLI (HUMBERT STEVEN) Italians in Chicago, 1880-1930: a study in ethnic mobility. New York, 1970. pp. 300.

ITALIANS IN YUGOSLAVIA

VIGILANS pseud. Italija pruža ruku... znači li to poboljšanje položaja Hrvata i Slovenaca pod Italijom? Zagreb, Demos, [1936]. pp. 32. 22½cm.

RADETIĆ (ERNEST) Istra pod Italijom, 1918-1943. Zagreb, 1944. pp. 276. 22cm.

RAPOTEC (VINKO) Praksa Italije s slovenci in hrvati, 1918-1940. Koper, 1952. pp. 76. bibliog. 21cm.

BRATULIĆ (VJEKOSLAV) Dokumenti o obrani i istrebljenju hrvatskih škola u Istri pod Italijom. Zagreb, 1955. pp. 95. bibliog. Documents in Italian.

ITALO-ABYSSINIAN WAR, 1935-1936

GALLO (MAX) L'affaire d'Éthiopie, aux origines de la guerre mondiale. [Paris], Centurion, [1967]. pp. 292. bibliog. 21cm. (Un Brûlant Passé)

LAURENS (FRANKLIN D.) France and the Italo-Ethiopian crisis, 1935-1936. The Hague, Mouton, 1967. pp. 432. bibliog. 24cm. (Studies in European History. 7)

BARKER (A.J.) The civilizing mission: the Italo-Ethiopian War, 1935-6. London, Cassell, 1968. pp. xiv, 354. bibliog. 21cm.

PRETI (LUIGI) Impero fascista: africani ed ebrei. Milano, Mursia, [1968]. pp. 375. 21cm. (Testimonianze fra Cronaca e Storia. 28)

BOCA (ANGELO DEL) The Ethiopian war, 1935-1941; ...translated from the Italian by P.D. Cummins. Chicago, 1969. pp. 289.

ROCHAT (GIORGIO) Militari e politici nella preparazione della campagna d'Etiopia: studio e documenti 1932-1936. Milano, [1971]. pp. 514. (Istituto Nazionale per la Storia del Liberazione in Italia. [Publications]. 2)

ITALY

ITALY. Presidenza del Consiglio dei Ministri. 1962. Italy today. Rome, 1962. pp.(ii), 353. 24cm.

GRINDROD (MURIEL) Italy. London, Benn, 1968. pp. 260. bibliog. 21½cm. (Nations of the Modern World)

- Appropriations and expenditures

CARABBA (MANIN) Spesa pubblica e iniziativa imprenditoriale: le erogazioni pecuniarie dello stato a favore dell'attività economica. Torino, Einaudi, [1968]. pp. 233. 22cm. [Serie di Politica Economica)

ONIDA (VALERIO) Le leggi di spesa nella costituzione. Milano, 1969. pp. 890. bibliog. (Milan. Università. Facoltà di Giurisprudenza. Pubblicazioni. Serie 2b. Studi di Diritto Pubblico. N.4)

TARQUINIO (OSVALDO) Significati delle entrate e delle spese dello Stato per regioni, 1951-1965. Roma, 1969. pp. 150. (Associazione per lo Sviluppo dell'Industria nel Mezzogiorno. Centro per gli Studi sullo Sviluppo Economico. Collana Francesco Giordani)

PARTITO REPUBBLICANO ITALIANO. Osservazioni al Libro Bianco sulla spesa pubblica. Roma, 1971. pp. 115. (Documenti. 3)

- Army - History

BIASE (CARLO DE) L'aquila d'oro: storia dello Stato Maggiore Italiano, 1861-1945. Milano, [1969]. pp. 473.

PANSA (GIAMPAOLO) L'esercito di Salo nei rapporti riservati della guardia nazionale repubblicana, 1943-44. [Milan], Istituto Nazionale per la Storia del Movimento di Liberazione, [1969]. pp. 216. (Movimento di Liberazione in Italia, Il. Quaderni. 3)

- Biography

LUI, chi è? Torino, [1969]. 2 vols.

- Boundaries

RUSINOW (DENNISON I.) Italy's Austrian heritage, 1919-1946. Oxford, 1969. pp. 423. bibliog.

NOVAK (BOGDAN C.) Trieste, 1941-1954: the ethnic, political and ideological struggle. Chicago, 1970. pp. 526. bibliog.

- Census

ITALY. Istituto Centrale di Statistica. Censimento, 1961. 10° censimento generale della popolazione, 15 ottobre 1961. [volume series]. Roma, 1963-70. 10 vols. (in 13).

- Civilization

ROMAGNOSI (GIOVANNI DOMENICO) Dell' indole e dei fattori dell'incivilimento con esempio del suo risorgimento in Italia. Milano, Editori degli Annali Universali delle Scienze e dell' Industria, 1832. pp. 272. 22½cm.

RICCIO (STEFANO) I fattori culturali e morali del Risorgimento italiano. Napoli, Istituto Editoriale del Mezzogiorno, 1962. pp. 111. 20½cm.

- Colonies

CAIOLI (ALDO) Fatti e figure della politica coloniale italiana, Eritrea 1897-1900. [Pistoia, 1968?] pp. 40.

MIEGE (JEAN LOUIS) L'impérialisme colonial italien de 1870 à nos jours. Paris, SEDES, 1968. pp. 419. bibliog. (Regards sur l'Histoire, 2. Histoire Générale.2)

- Colonies - History

ITALY. 1965. L'Italia in Africa. Serie storica. La politica coloniale dell'Italia negli atti, documenti e discussioni parlamentari; testo di Giacomo Perticone e note redazionali di richiamo agli atti parlamentari a cura di Guglielmo Guglielmi. (L'Italia in Africa) Roma, 1965. pp. xvii, 359. 24cm.

FINAZZO (GIUSEPPINA) L'Italia nel Benadir: l'azione di Vincenzo Filonardi, 1884-1896. Roma, Ateneo, [1966]. pp. xvi, 480. 22cm. (Nuovi Saggi. 53)

MALTESE (PAOLO) La terra promessa: la guerra italo-turca e la conquista della Libia, 1911-1912. [Milan], Sugar, [1968]. pp. 377. bibliog. 20½cm. (Nuova Biblioteca Storica. 2)

ITALY (Cont'd.)

- Commerce

DEMARIA (GIOVANNI) Problemi attuali e di lungo momento del commercio estero italiano; (III Convegno Nazionale per il Commercio Estero, relazione generale). Milano, Camera di Commercio, Industria e Agricoltura, 1949. pp. 24. 24½cm.

MELIS (F.) Il giornale a partita doppia presso un'azienda fiorentina nel 1391. in vol.3 of Saggi di economia aziendale e sociale in memoria di Gino Zappa. Milano, 1961.

CAO-PINNA (VERA) ed. Le esportazioni italiane: prospettive al 1970. Torino, Boringhieri, 1965. pp. 209. 21½cm. (Centro di Studi e Piani Economici. Quaderni. Studi sulle Strutture Economiche. N.1)

RENOUARD (YVES) Italia e Francia nel commercio medievale; con prefazione e a cura di Pier Fausto Palumbo. Rome, Edizioni del Lavoro, 1966. pp. xviii, 370. bibliog. 24cm. (Biblioteca Storica. 6)

REY (GUIDO M.) Relazioni tra il commercio estero dell'Italia e la domanda interna ed internazionale. [Rome], Ente per gli Studi Monetari, Bancari e Finanziari Luigi Einaudi, [1967]. pp. 50. bibliog. 24cm. (Quaderni di Ricerche. Num. 1)

CENTRO STUDI PER LO SVILUPPO DELL'INDUSTRIA CHIMICA. Quaderni. 1. Le importazioni italiane di prodotti chimici. Firenze, Vallecchi, [1968]. pp. vii, 115. 23½cm.

Le IMPORTAZIONI italiane di prodotti chimici. Firenze, [1968]. pp. vii, 115. (Centro Studi per lo Sviluppo dell'Industria Chimica. Quaderni. 1)

KEBSCHULL (DIETRICH) Italien. Hamburg, Verlag Weltarchiv, 1968. pp.137. bibliog. 24cm. (Hamburg. Hamburgisches Welt-Wirtschafts-Archiv. Studien zur Exportförderung)

TAGLIACARNE (GUGLIELMO) ed. La carta commerciale d'Italia con le sue 442 aree e subaree di attrazione del commercio al dettaglio e le relative quote di mercato. 2nd ed. [Milan], Giuffrè, 1968. pp. vii, 415. bibliog. 34cm. Map in end pocket.

UNIONE ITALIANA DELLE CAMERE DI COMMERCIO, INDUSTRIA E AGRICOLTURA. Corso di Aggiornamento sul Commercio Estero, 30, 1967. Le nuove prospettive del commercio estero italiano. Milano, Giuffrè, 1968. pp. 576. bibliog. 24cm.

FRANCE. Direction de la Documentation. La Documentation Française. Notes et Études Documentaires. No. 3,580. L'organisation de l'expansion du commerce extérieur de l'Italie, 1960-1968. Paris, 1969. pp. 74. bibliog. 27cm.

COLOMBO (VITTORINO) Commercio estero e politica di piano. Milano, 1970. pp. 222.

- Commerce - China

REGHIZZI (GABRIELE CRESPI) Legal aspects of trade with China: the Italian experience. [Cambridge, Harvard University], Harvard Law School, [1968]. pp. 85-139. 23cm. (Studies in Chinese Law. No. 8.) (Reprinted from Harvard International Law Journal, vol. 9, no. 1, 1968)

- Commerce - France

IZZO (LUIGI) Storia delle relazioni commerciali tra l'Italia e la Francia dal 1860 al 1875. Napoli, Edizioni Scientifiche Italiane, 1965. pp. xxvii, 452. bibliog. 25cm. (Naples. Istituto Universitario Navale. Istituto di Storia del Commercio. Collana di Storia del Commercio. 1)

RENOUARD (YVES) Italia e Francia nel commercio medievale; con prefazione e a cura di Pier Fausto Palumbo. Rome, Edizioni del Lavoro, 1966. pp. xviii, 370. bibliog. 24cm. (Biblioteca Storica. 6)

- Commerce - Switzerland

SWITZERLAND. Office Suisse d'Expansion Commerciale. Rapports Spéciaux. Série B. No. 56. L'économie italienne à l'heure du Marché commun et le commerce italosuisse; par Auguste Hurni. Lausanne, 1960. pp. 24. Tirage à part des Informations Économiques.

- Commerce - United States

UNITED STATES. International Commerce Bureau. Industry and opportunity in Italy. Washington, 1963. pp. 32.

ITALY - Commercial policy
See also EUROPEAN ECONOMIC COMMUNITY - Italy

- Constitution

NENNI (PIETRO) Legge truffa e costituzione: ragioni dell'ostruzionismo socialista. Milano, Avanti!, 1953. pp. 40. 21½cm. (Attualità. 2)

ITALY. Comitato Nazionale per la Celebrazione del Primo Decennale della Promulgazione della Costituzione. 1958. Guida alla costituzione; ([edited by] Coraldo Piermani [and others]). Roma, 1958. pp. 270. 21cm.

GITTI (CISO) Aspetti giuridici della pianificazione in Italia. 1. Programmazione e pianificazione nella costituzione italiana. Milano, the Istituto, 1962. fo. (iii), 106. 28cm. (Istituto Lombardo per gli Studi Economici e Sociali. Progetti di Ricerca. Fasc. IX. 8. La Finanza Pubblica.)

CHELI (ENZO) Potere regolamentare e struttura costituzionale. Milano, Giuffrè, 1967. pp. xi, 490. bibliog. 25cm.

ESPOSITO (ENRICO) Lo stato e i cittadini in Italia. 2nd ed. Roma, Società Editrice Universo, 1967. pp. vii, 313. 23½cm.

JACINI (STEFANO) La riforma dello stato e il problema regionale; a cura di Francesco Traniello. Brescia, [1968]. pp. 253.

BRUNETTI (LEANDRO) Discorso sulla costituzione. Orvieto, [1969]. pp. 29.

DOLCE (GIOVANNI) and PREDIERI (ALBERTO) Scuola e stato. Firenze, 1969. pp. 248.

LACONI (RENZO) Parlamento e costituzione: (scritti e discorsi); a cura di Enrico Berlinguer e Gerardo Chiaromonte. Roma, 1969. pp. 166.

STUDI per il ventesimo anniversario dell'Assemblea Costituente. Firenze, [1969]. 6 vols.

- Constitutional history

ASTUTI (GUIDO) **La formazione dello stato moderno in Italia: lezioni di storia del diritto italiano.** Torino, Giappichelli, [1967 in progress]. 25cm.

MARANINI (GIUSEPPE) Storia del potere in Italia 1848-1967. 2nd ed. Firenze, Vallecchi, 1967 repr. 1968. pp. 540. 22cm. (Collana Storica. 80)

STUDI per il ventesimo anniversario dell'Assemblea Costituente. Firenze, [1969]. 6 vols.

- Constitutional law

ITALY. Presidenza del Consiglio dei Ministri. Ufficio Regioni. 1958. Ordinamento delle regioni: quadri sinottici comparativi delle competenze legislative e amministrative delle regioni a statuto normale e speciale, comprese le province autonome di Bolzano e di Trento. Roma, 1958. pp. 62. 29cm.

BORGHESE (SOFO) Nozioni di diritto costituzional Milano, Pirola, 1963. pp. 118. 17cm.

SARACENO (DIVO) Funzione dialettica del controllo tra i poteri dello stato: saggi di diritto amministrativo. Roma, Ciranna, [1965]. pp. 234. 20½cm. (Experientia. 12)

STUDI in memoria di Guido Zanobini. Milano, 1965. 5 vols. bibliog. A few articles in Spanish.

TUCCARI (EMANUELE) Saggio per una teoria sulla legge regionale. Milano, Giuffrè, 1966. pp. 110. 25cm. (Messina. Università. Istituto di Scienze Giuridiche, Economiche, Politiche e Sociali. Pubblicazioni. No. 78)

BARILE (PAOLO) Scritti di diritto costituzionale. Padova, CEDAM, 1967. pp. vii, 749. 25cm.

CARUSO (CORRADO) Lineamenti di diritto costituzionale nei rapporti tra parlamento e governo. Roma, De Luca, 1967. pp. 174. bibliog. 24cm.

BARBERA (AUGUSTO) Leggi di piano e sistema delle fonti. Milano, Giuffrè, 1968. pp. 138. bibliog. 25cm. (Giurisprudenza Costituzionale. Quaderni. 6)

CARBONARO (SALVATORE) Ordinamento dello Stato italiano e legislazione scolastica sull'istruzione elementare. Firenze, 1968 repr. 1969. pp. 267.

CARBONE (CARMELO) I doveri pubblici individuali nella costituzione. Milano, Giuffrè, 1968. pp. 282. 25cm.

FENUCCI (FULVIO) I limiti dell'inchiesta parlamentare. Napoli, Jovene, 1968. pp. xxiv, 342. 24cm. (Naples. Università. Facoltà Giuridica. Pubblicazioni. 112)

SIMONE (SAVERIO DE) Il diritto scolastico nella costituzione italiana. Milano, 1968. pp. 384. bibliog.

CARBONARO (SALVATORE) Diritto costituzionale. 2nd ed. Firenze, 1969. pp. 278.

CONSO (GIOVANNI) Costituzione e processo penale: dodici anni di pagine sparse; 1956-1968. Milano, 1969. pp. 557.

LUPONE (GIUSEPPE) La Regione a statuto ordinario in Italia. Roma, [1969]. pp. 218.

ONIDA (VALERIO) Le leggi di spesa nella costituzione. Milano, 1969. pp. 890. bibliog. (Milan. Università. Facoltà di Giurisprudenza. Pubblicazioni. Serie 2b. Studi di Diritto Pubblico. N.4)

STUDI per il ventesimo anniversario dell'Assemblea Costituente. Firenze. [1969]. 6 vols.

STUDI sull'art. 41 della costituzione. Bologna, [1969]. pp. 355. (Messina. Università. Istituto di Diritto Commerciale e del Lavoro. [Publications]. 1)

PROBLEMI dello statuto regionale: l'organizzazione politico-costituzionale della Regione; progetto di statuto, documentazione e atti del convegno, 20 e 21 marzo 1970 ([of the] Unione Regionale delle Province Toscane). Firenze, 1970. pp. 669.

STUDI in onore di Ferdinando Carbone nel cirquantunesimo anno di servizio allo Stato, etc. Milano, 1970. pp. 1277.

- Description and travel

LAVELEYE (EMILE DE) Baron. L'Italie actuelle, (1878-1879): lettres à un ami. Londres, 1880. pp. 394.

FERRARA (GUIDO) L'architettura del paesaggio italiano: (The Italian landscape). [Bologna, 1968]. pp. 183. bibliog. With English summary.

- Economic conditions

SWITZERLAND. Office Suisse d'Expansion Commerciale. Rapports Spéciaux. Série B. No. 56. L'économie italienne à l'heure du Marché commun et le commerce italosuisse; par Auguste Hurni. Lausanne, 1960. pp. 24. Tirage à part des Informations Économiques.

ITALY. Ministero del Bilancio. 1962. Problemi e prospettive dello sviluppo economico italiano: nota presentata al Parlamento dal Ministro del Bilancio, On. Ugo La Malfa il 22 maggio 1962. Roma, 1962. pp. 48. 29cm.

BONASERA (FRANCESCO) Il problema delle fonti nella geografia economica. Milano, Giuffrè, 1963. pp. 33. bibliog. 24½cm.

ITALY. Direzione Generale della Produzione Industriale. Economia nazionale, produzione e scambi con l'estero nell'industria. Roma, annual, 1964/1966 to date. 14 x 20cm.

PARETO (V.) Libre-échangisme, protectionnisme et socialisme. in vol. 4 of Pareto (Vilfredo) Oeuvres complètes. Genève, 1965.

SCROFANI (SERAFINO) Sicilia e mezzogiorno. Bologna, Pàtron, [1967 in progress]. 24cm.

ITALY - Economic conditions (Cont'd.)

EUROPEAN ECONOMIC COMMUNITY. Études: Série Économie et Finances. 5. Étude pour la création d'un pôle industriel de développement en Italie méridionale. Bruxelles, 1967. 2 vols. 27cm.

ITALY. [Cassa per Opere Straordinarie di Pubblico Interesse nell'Italia Meridionale. 1967]. The Cassa per il Mezzogiorno. [Rome, 1967?]. pp. 129. [In English].

PARRILLO (FRANCESCO) Aspetti e problemi dell'economia italiana:(relazione tenuta all'Assemblea annuale dell'Associazione Nazionale "L.Luzzatti" fra le Banche Popolari, Roma, 24 febbraio 1967). Roma, [Credito Popolare], 1967. pp. 26. 26cm. (Estratto dalla Rivista "Credito Popolare", 1967, Nos. 1-2)

RETZLAFF (CHRISTINE) Kulturgeographische Wandlungen in der Maremma unter besonderer Berücksichtigung der italienischen Bodenreform nach dem Zweiten Weltkrieg. Kiel, Universität, Geographisches Institut, 1967. pp. 204. bibliog. 24cm. (Schriften. Band 27. Heft 2)

CONTI DEGLI ITALIANI, I: compendio della vita economica nazionale; ([pd. by] Istituto Centrale di Statistica, Italy). a., 1968 [2nd issue]- Roma.

BOLLINO (ALDO) Geografia economica dell'Italia d'oggi. [Bologna], Cappelli, [1968]. pp. 145. 19½cm. (Io So, Tu Sai)

GAY (FRANÇOIS) and WAGRET (PAUL) L'économie de l'Italie. 3rd ed. Paris, P.U.F., 1968. pp. 127. bibliog. 17½cm. (Que Sais-Je? No. 1007)

TAGLIACARNE (GUGLIELMO) ed. La carta commerciale d'Italia con le sue 442 aree e subaree di attrazione del commercio al dettaglio e le relative quote di mercato. 2nd ed. [Milan], Giuffrè, 1968. pp. vii, 415. bibliog. 34cm. Map in end pocket.

GRAZIANI (AUGUSTO) and others. Lo sviluppo di un'economia aperta. [Naples, 1969]. pp. 253.

ITALY. Comitato dei Ministri per il Mezzogiorno. 1969 Studi monografici sul Mezzogiorno: a corredo della "Relazione sull'attuazione del piano di coordinamento degli interventi pubblici nel Mezzogiorno e sui provvedimenti per le aree depresse del Centro Nord", etc. Roma, 1969. pp. 167.

LENTI (LIBERO) Inventario dell'economia italiana. 2nd ed. [Milan], 1969. pp. 299.

NEGRO (NANNI) L'Italia economica: agricoltura, industria e servizi nell'Italia d'oggi. Milano, 1969. pp. 158.

PALMERIO (GIOVANNI) Il ruolo del progresso tecnico nello sviluppo economico italiano, 1951-1965. Milano, 1969. pp. 111. (Istituto Nazionale per lo Studio della Congiuntura. Collana. N. 1)

SARACENO (PASQUALE) Ricostruzione e pianificazione, 1943-1948; a cura...di Piero Barucci. Bari, 1969. pp. 494.

SPINOSA (ANTONIO) Come si vive in Italia oggi. [Bologna, 1969]. pp. 139.

PARETO (V.) La liberté économique et les événements d'Italie. in tome 14 of Pareto (Vilfredo) Oeuvres complètes. Genève, 1970.

PEGGIO (EUGENIO) Capitalismo italiano anni '70. Roma, [1970]. pp. 186.

LO BELLO (NINO) The Vatican's wealth. London, 1971. pp. 186.

- Economic conditions - Statistics

BARBERI (BENEDETTO) and MARZANO (CARLO) The 1959 input-output table for Italy;...([paper presented to the] International Conference on Input-Output Techniques...1961) n. p. [1961?] fo. 37. bibliog. 30½cm.

CONFEDERAZIONE GENERALE DELL'INDUSTRIA ITALIANA. Servizio Studi e Rilevazioni. Statistiche comparative dell'economia italiana e britannica: comparative statistics between Italian and British economy. [Rome], the Confederazione, 1963. pp. 69. 17cm.

- Economic history

FERRARI AGGRADI (MARIO) Cento anni di economia italiana. Roma, Presidenza del Consiglio dei Ministri, Servizio delle Informazioni, 1962. pp. 47. 21cm. (Lo Stato per il Cittadino. 2)

MASSACHUSETTS INSTITUTE OF TECHNOLOGY. Center for International Studies. Italy Project. Development of regional economic differentials in Italy: North and South at the time of unification. [Cambridge, 1962?] pp. 37. 28cm.

STUDI in onore di Amintore Fanfani. Milano, Giuffrè, 1962. 6 vols. 24cm.

BENZONI (A.) Il Mezzogiorno nello stato italiano. Parisi (Achille) and Zappa (Goffredo) eds. Mezzogiorno e politica di piano. Bari, 1964.

CAFAGNA (L.) Intorno alle origini del dualismo economico italiano. in Caracciolo (Alberto) ed. Problemi storici della industrializzazione e dello sviluppo. Urbino, [1965].

CINGARI (GAETANO) Problemi del Risorgimento meridionale. Messina, D'Anna, 1965. pp. 249. 25cm. (Messina. Universita. Facolta di Magistero. Pubblicazioni. 5)

ROSA (LUIGI DE) Iniziativa e capitale straniero nell'industria metalmeccanica del Mezzogiorno 1840-1904. Napoli, Giannini, [1968]. pp. xiii, 324. 21½cm. (Economia e Società. 1)

BASINI (GIAN LUIGI) Finanza pubblica ed aspetti economici negli stati italiani del Cinque e del Seicento. Parma, 1966 repr. 1969. pp. 136. bibliog.

MORANDI (RODOLFO) Storia della grande industria in Italia. Torino, Einaudi, [1966] pp. 294. 18cm. (Piccola Biblioteca Einaudi. 82) Reprint of the first edition of 1931 with a new preface.

ALESSANDRO (ALESSANDRO D') Disegno storico dell'economia italiana. Roma, Bulzoni, [1967]. pp. 178. bibliog. 21cm.

LUZZATTO (GINO) Per una storia economica d'Italia; con un saggio introduttivo di Bruno Caizzi. Bari, Laterza, 1967. pp. 205. bibliog. 18cm. (Universale Laterza. 56)

ROMANI (MARIO) Storia economica d'Italia nel secolo XIX (1815-1914); con una scelta di testi e documenti. Milano, Giuffrè, 1968 in progress. 25cm.

MATASSI (LUIGI) La civiltà dell'industria in Italia, 1789-1967. Roma, [1968]. pp. 133. bibliog.

PANE (LUIGI DAL) La storia come storia del lavoro: discorsi di concezione e di metodo. Bologna, [1968]. pp. 275. bibliog.

PARRILLO (FRANCESCO) Impegno unitario per lo sviluppo del Mezzogiorno. Roma, 1968. pp. 20. 25cm. (Estratto dalla rivista Credito Popolare, nn.3-4, marzo-aprile 1968)

CARACCIOLO (ALBERTO) ed. La formazione dell'Italia industriale: discussioni e ricerche; [by] L. Spaventa [and others]. Bari, Laterza, 1969. pp. 303. (Libri del Tempo. 112)

CATALANO (FRANCO) L'economia italiana di guerra: la politica economico-finanziaria del fascismo dalla guerra d'Etiopia alla caduta del regime, 1935-1943. [Milan], 1969. pp. 143. bibliog. (Movimento di Liberazione in Italia, Il. Quaderni. 5)

MOLHO (ANTHONY) ed. Social and economic foundations of the Italian renaissance. New York, [1969]. pp. 239. bibliog.

WILLIS (F. ROY) Italy chooses Europe. New York, 1971. pp. 373. bibliog.

- **Economic history - Historiography**

    ROMEO (ROSARIO) **Risorgimento e capitalismo: [two essays]. [3rd ed.] Bari. 1970. pp. 191.**

- **Economic history - Sources**

    ORLANDELLI (GIANFRANCO) ed. Due relazioni sulla erezione dei monti di pubbliche prestanze in Bologna, 1655-1744. Milano, Giuffrè, 1968. pp. xxiv, 138. 27cm. (Fondazione Italiana per la Storia Amministrativa. Acta Italica. 14)

- **Economic policy**

    VANONI (EZIO) Discorsi sul programma di sviluppo economico. Roma, Istituto Poligrafico dello Stato, 1956. pp. xx, 297. 24cm.

    FERRARI AGGRADI (MARIO) Le partecipazioni statali nella politica di sviluppo; (discorsi sul bilancio del Ministero delle Partecipazioni Statali, istruzioni e direttive agli enti e società dipendenti). Roma, Ministero delle Partecipazioni Statali, 1959-60. 2 vols.

    ITALY. Consiglio Nazionale dell'Economia e del Lavoro. Segretariato Generale. 1959. Raccolte di studi e relazioni dei consiglieri per i lavori del C.N.E.L. Roma, 1959. pp. 267. (Consiglio Nazionale dell'Economia e del Lavoro. Bollettino di informazioni. Appendici.)

    GASPARINI (I.) L'economia italiana di fronte al Mercato comune europeo. in Ferrara. Università. Centro di Documentazione e Studi sulle Comunità Europee. Quaderni. 1. Milano, 1960, repr. 1963.

    ITALY. Ministero del Bilancio. 1960. Per una economia di sviluppo senza inflazione: discorso pronunciato al Senato il 4 ottobre 1960 a chiusura della discussione sull'esercizio finanziario 1960-61; ([by)] Giuseppe Pella, Ministero del Bilancio). Roma, 1960. pp. 40. 19cm.

    ITALY. 1961. Il Consiglio Nazionale dell'Economia e del Lavoro nel triennio 1958-1960. Roma, 1961. pp. xliii, 567. 27cm.

    ITALY. Commissione Nazionale Italiana UNESCO. Convegno Italo-Jugoslavo, 1961. Gli aspetti sociali dello sviluppo economico: atti del Convegno, etc. Milano, Società Editrice Vita e Pensiero, 1961. pp. 155. bibliog. 24½cm.

    PROSPETTIVE DELL'INDUSTRIA ITALIANA, LE (formerly Previsioni di sviluppo dell'industria italiana); ([pd. by] Confederazione Generale dell'Industria Italiana, Servizio Studi e Rilevazioni). 1962/1965, 1963/1966, 1964/1966; annual, 1967/1970- Roma.

    AMENDOLA (GIORGIO) Lotta di classe e sviluppo economico dopo la liberazione. Roma, Editori Riuniti, 1962. pp. 105. bibliog. 21cm. (Nostro Tempo)

    BULTRINI (GIAN FILIPPO) and others. Industrializzazione del Mezzogiorno e sviluppo economico nazionale, etc. Roma, Opere Nuove, 1962. pp. 103. 17½cm. (Partito Socialista Democratico Italiano. Commissione Studi e Programmi. Orientamenti. 2)

    FORTUNATI (PAOLO) Programmazione economica democratica e trasformazione della struttura: (discorso pronunciato al Senato nella seduta del 24 luglio 1962). Roma, [imprint, 1962]. pp. 26. 21cm.

    GITTI (CISO) Aspetti giuridici della pianificazione in Italia. 1. Programmazione e pianificazione nella costituzione italiana. Milano, the Istituto, 1962. fo. (iii), 106. 28cm. (Istituto Lombardo per gli Studi Economici e Sociali. Progetti di Ricerca. Fasc. IX. 8. La Finanza Pubblica.)

    ITALY. Ministero del Bilancio. 1962. Problemi e prospettive dello sviluppo economico italiano: nota presentata al Parlamento dal Ministro del Bilancio, On. Ugo La Malfa il 22 maggio 1962. Roma, 1962. pp. 48. 29cm.

    ITALY. Statutes, etc. 1950-1961. Raccolta leggi: decreti e circolari riguardanti la Cassa per il Mezzogiorno. Napoli, 1961 [or rather 1962]. pp. xxvii, 363. 23½cm.

    ITALY. Cassa per Opere Straordinarie di Pubblico Interesse nell'Italia Meridionale. 1963. The "Cassa per il Mezzogiorno" and the economic development of Southern Italy. Rome, 1963. fo. 108.

ITALY - Economic policy (Cont'd.)

MARZANO (CARLO) Il bilancio dello stato e la programmazione economica. Milano, Giuffre, 1963. pp. 55. 24½cm. (Messina. Università. Facoltà di Economia e Commercio. Istituto di Scienze Economiche. Collana di Studi e Saggi Economici. 7)

CONFEDERAZIONE GENERALE ITALIANA DEL LAVORO. CGIL e programmazione economica: (documenti). vol. [1]-2. [Rome, 1964-6]. 2 vols.

PARISI (ACHILLE) and ZAPPA (GOFFREDO) eds. Mezzogiorno e politica di piano. Bari, Laterza, 1964. pp. xviii, 465. 20½cm. (Libri del Tempo. n.85)

[PARTITO COMUNISTA ITALIANO Comitato Regionale del Lazio] Linee per un programma di sviluppo economico del Lazio: (progetto di documento). Roma, [imprint, 1964]. pp. 58. 23½cm.

ITALY. 1965. Politica nuova per il Mezzogiorno: discorso pronunciato alla Camera dei Deputati il 18 maggio 1965; ([by] Giulio Pastore). Roma, 1965. pp. 46. 24cm.

PARETO (V.) Libre-échangisme, protectionnisme et socialisme. in vol. 4 of Pareto (Vilfredo) Oeuvres complètes. Genève, 1965.

RICOSSA (SERGIO) Documenti di politica economica italiana. Torino, Giappichelli, [1965]. pp. 113. 25cm. (Corsi Universitari)

STUDI in onore di Gaetano Zingali. Milano, 1965. 3 vols. bibliog. (Catania. Università. Facoltà di Giurisprudenza. Pubblicazioni. 53)

ANTONIO (MARIO D') Commento al programma economico nazionale: il programma di sviluppo economico per il quinquennio 1966-1970; illustrato con note esplicative e con i resoconti e le risultanze dei dibattiti parlamentari, etc. [Bologna], Cappelli, [1966?]. pp. xix, 1262. 23½cm.

BRACCO (ROBERTO) Le Camere di Commercio della Toscana e la programmazione economica regionale; ...[and] Impostazione, metodo e programmi di ricerche per la elaborazione di un piano di sviluppo economico per la Toscana, a cura del dott. Franco Archibugi. Padova, 1966. pp. 135. (Unione Regionale delle Camere di Commercio della Toscana. Studi e Ricerche per il Piano Regionale Toscano di Sviluppo Economico. 1)

CICOGNA (FURIO) Cinque anni di lotta per la libertà economica. Roma, 1966. pp. 284. 24cm.

CONFEDERAZIONE GENERALE ITALIANA DEL LAVORO. CGIL e programmazione economica: (documenti). [Rome, Editrice Sindacale Italiana, 1964 in progress]. 21½cm.

ITALY. 1966. Linee di una nuova politica industriale per il mezzogiorno: discorsi alle assemblee dell'IRFIS e dell'ISVEIMER, Palermo-Napoli, aprile 1966; ([by] Giulio Pastore). Roma, [1966]. pp. 38. 24½cm.

ITALY. 1966. Nord e sud in una nuova politica di sviluppo; [speech delivered at the] conferenza tenuta alla Camera di Commercio di Milano...29 gennaio, 1966; [by] Giulio Pastore, Ministro per gli Interventi Straordinari nel Mezzogiorno). Roma, [imprint], 1966. pp. 19. 24½cm.

ITALY. Comitato dei Ministri per il Mezzogiorno. 1966. Piano di coordinamento degli interventi pubblici nel Mezzogiorno... 1 ottobre 1966-31 dicembre 1969. Roma, 1966. pp. 340.

MISSERI (SALVATORE CORRADO) Logica della programmazione in Italia. Bologna, Calderini, [1966]. pp. viii, 131. bibliog. 21cm.

PROBLEMI economici e giuridici del programma quinquennale: convegno di studi, Roma, 28-30 aprile 1965; [organised by Fondazione Luigi Einaudi]. [Florence], Sansoni, [1966]. pp.xv,300. 21½cm.

SCROFANI (SERAFINO) Sicilia e mezzogiorno. Bologna, Pàtron, [1967 in progress]. 24cm.

MEZZOGIORNO e triangolo industriale: (relazioni del convegno di Taranto, "Il Mezzogiorno degli anni '70"); [by] M. Barnabei [and others]. Manduria, Lacaita, 1967. pp. 226. 22cm. (Uomini e cose della Nuova Italia. N. 25)

MUSCARÀ (CALOGERO) La geografia dello sviluppo; sviluppo industriale e politica geografica nell'Italia del secondo dopoguerra. Milano, Edizione di Communita, 1967. pp.277. bibliog. 22½cm. (Studi e Ricerche di Scienze Sociali. 34)

PARTITO COMUNISTA ITALIANO. Comitato Regionale del Lazio. Le scelte per un programma democratico di sviluppo economico di Roma e del Lazio. [Rome, 1967?]. pp. 15. 21cm.

POLA (GIANCARLO) Il programma economico italiano 1966-70 : in appendice il testo integrale del piano. Milano, Etas Kompass, 1967. pp. 266. 24cm.

RICOSSA (SERGIO) and others. Il problema degli investimenti e i suoi riflessi sulla occupazione operaia. [Turin], Centro di Ricerca e Documentazione Luigi Einaudi, [1967]. pp. 83. 20cm.

SEPE (GIOVANNI) Le tre occasioni: politica di piano, Ministero dell'Urbanistica e Unità Nazionale. Napoli, Fiorentino, [1967]. pp. xxiii, 433. 22½cm.

UNIONE REGIONALE DELLE CAMERE DI COMMERCIO DEL PIEMONTE. Centro Studi e Ricerche Economico-Sociali. I problemi dell'agricoltura piemontese di fronte allo sviluppo economico: contributo alla programmazione economica regionale. Torino, 1967. pp. xii, 638.

VERGOTTINI (GIUSEPPE DE) Pianificazione statale e interventi comunitari. Milano, 1967. pp. vii, 388. (Rome. Università. Istituto di Diritto Pubblico. Monografie. Nuova Serie. 38)

AMÉRICA Latina, Italia y la Comunidad Económica Europea; [Seminar], Roma, 24-26 de Junio de 1968. Milano, Giuffrè, 1968. pp. xx, 713. 24cm.

ASSOCIAZIONE PER LO SVILUPPO DELL'INDUSTRIA NEL MEZZOGIORNO. Il Mezzogiorno nelle ricerche della SVIMEZ, 1947-1967. Roma, Giuffrè, 1968. pp. xi, 799. 24cm.

BARBATO (LUIGI) Politica meridionalista e localizzazione industriale, dalla Legge Pastore all'Alfa Sud, etc. Padova, 1968. pp. 262.

BRIGIDA (FRANCO) La programmazione in Italia. Padova, Marsilio, 1968. pp.120. 21cm. (Attualità politica. 5)

CAPERDONI (ENRICO) Lo sviluppo italiano del dopoguerra. Padova, 1968. pp. 191.

COLLIDA (ADA) and others. Sviluppo economico e crescita urbana in Italia: un modello d'interdipendenza. Milano, 1968. pp. 219. bibliogs. (Istituto per gli Studi sullo Sviluppo Economico e il Progresso Tecnico. Collana Isvet. n. 8)

COMPAGNA (FRANCESCO) Il Mezzogiorno tra due legislature: [articles reprinted from various journals]. Milano, 1968. pp. 149.

CONVEGNO SUI PROBLEMI DELLA MONTAGNA, 5°, 1968. Atti. Torino, [1968]. pp. 337.

DEMOCRAZIA CRISTIANA. Comitato Regionale. Piano di sviluppo dell'Emilia-Romagna: proposta. Roma, Cinque Lune, [1968]. pp. 226. 24cm. (Democrazia Cristiana dell'Emilia-Romagna. Contributi alla Programmazione Regionale. 1)

FRANCE. Direction de la Documentation. La Documentation Française. Notes et Études Documentaires Nos. 3,537-3,538. Le plan économique italien, 1966-1970. Paris, 1968. pp. 84. 27cm.

GAY (FRANÇOIS) and WAGRET (PAUL) L'économie de l'Italie. 3rd ed. Paris, P.U.F., 1968. pp. 127. bibliog. 17½cm. (Que Sais-Je? No. 1007)

ITALY. Cassa per Opere Straordinarie di Pubblico Interesse nell'Italia Meridionale. 1968. Programma quinquennale, 1965-69. Roma, 1968. pp. 640. Map in end pocket.

LIBERTINI (LUCIO) Integrazione capitalistica e sottosviluppo: i nuovi termini della questione meridionale. Bari, Laterza, [1968]. pp. 239. 18cm. (Tempi Nuovi. 3)

MERUSI (FABIO) Disciplina e organizzazione dei finanziamenti pubblici nelle leggi per il Mezzogiorno. Roma, Giuffrè, 1968. pp. vi, 69. 24cm. (Associazione per lo Sviluppo dell'Industria nel Mezzogiorno. Centro per gli Studi sullo Sviluppo Economico. Collana Francesco Giordani)

NORD e Sud nella società e nell'economia italiana di oggi: atti del convegno promosso dalla Fondazione Luigi Einaudi, Torino, 30 marzo - 8 aprile 1967. Torino, 1968. pp. 542. (Fondazione Luigi Einaudi. Studi. 1)

PARRILLO (FRANCESCO) Impegno unitario per lo sviluppo del Mezzogiorno. Roma, 1968. pp. 20. 25cm. (Estratto dalla rivista Credito Popolare, nn.3-4, marzo-aprile 1968)

SANTARELLI (ANTONINO) Saggi sulla politica economica meridionalistica. Venezia, 1968. pp. 214. (Venice. Istituto Universitario di Economia e Commercio, etc. Collana Ca'Foscari)

SEMINARIO SULLA PROGRAMMAZIONE ECONOMICA E L'ASSETTO TERRITORIALE, BOLOGNA, 1967. Atti del seminario... tenuto nel corso di tecnica urbanistica presso l'Istituto di Architettura...([by M. Allione [and others]). Bologna, 1968. pp. 269. (Bologna. Università. Istituto di Architettura e Urbanistica. Quaderni. Serie Ricerca Tecnico-Scientifica. 1)

VECCHIO (GUSTAVO DEL) Politica economica: cronache 1910-1960. [Torino, 1968]. pp. 322.

VITO (FRANCESCO) La nuova fase della politica di sviluppo economico del Mezzogiorno. Milano, Giuffrè, 1968. pp. 72. 25cm. (Messina. Università. Istituto di Scienze Economiche. [Publications]. 11)

CIAMPI (VITTORIO) Mezzogiorno perchè. [Naples, 1969]. pp. 285.

ITALY. Comitato dei Ministri per il Mezzogiorno. 1969. Relazione sull'attuazione del piano di coordinamento degli interventi pubblici nel Mezzogiorno e sui provvedimenti per le aree depresse del Centro-Nord, etc. Roma, 1969. pp. 219.

LENTI (LIBERO) Inventario dell'economia italiana. 2nd ed. [Milan], 1969. pp. 299.

MARZANO (FERRUCCIO) Un'interpretazione del processo di sviluppo economico dualistico in Italia. Milano, 1969. pp. 497. bibliog. (Rome. Università. Facoltà di Economia e Commercio. Pubblicazioni. 35)

MISASI (RICCARDO) Quale politica economica?: discorsi, scritti, interviste. [Rome, 1969?]. pp. 173.

NEGRO (NANNI) L'Italia economica: agricoltura, industria e servizi nell'Italia d'oggi. Milano, 1969. pp. 158.

PACINI (MARCELLO) Programmazione e società: le istituzioni e la programmazione economica in Italia negli anni '70. Milano, 1969. pp. 195.

RADI (LUCIANO) Potere democratico e forze economiche. Roma, 1969. pp. 97.

SARACENO (PASQUALE) Ricostruzione e pianificazione, 1943-1948; a cura...di Piero Barucci. Bari, 1969. pp. 494.

COLOMBO (VITTORINO) Commercio estero e politica di piano. Milano, 1970. pp. 222.

CONFEDERAZIONE GENERALE DELL'INDUSTRIA ITALIANA. Servizio Studi e Rilevazioni. Collana di Studi e Documentazione. 24. La politica di sviluppo economico del Mezzogiorno; (a cura di Nicola La Marca). Roma, 1970. pp. 308.

Il CONTROLLO dell'economia nel breve periodo: rapporto del gruppo di studio sui problemi di analisi economica e di politica economica a breve termine; [by] Lucio Izzo [and others]. Milano, [1970]. pp. 192. (Istituto Nazionale per lo Studio della Congiuntura. Collana. N. 3)

ITALY - Economic policy (Cont'd.)

FRANCE. Direction de la Documentation. La Documentation Française. Notes et Etudes Documentaires. Nos.3,655-3,656. La planification italienne dans la perspective des années 1970: [translation of Progetto 80: rapporto preliminare al programma economico nazionale, 1971-75]. Paris, 1970. pp. 73.

GOLINELLI (GAETANO M.) Le finanziarie di sviluppo nell'esperienza italiana: problemi e prospettive. Milano, 1970. pp. 198. bibliog.

PARETO (V.) La liberté économique et les événements d'Italie. See tome 14 of Pareto (Vilfredo) Oeuvres complètes. Genève, 1970.

PARRILLO (FRANCESCO) Lo sviluppo economico italiano. 3rd ed. Milano, 1970. pp. 641. bibliog.

PARTITO REPUBBLICANO ITALIANO. La politica economica nei documenti del PRI, 1964-1971; prefazione di Ugo La Malfa. Roma, 1971. pp. 147.

WILLIS (F. ROY) Italy chooses Europe. New York, 1971. pp. 373. bibliog.

-Emigration and immigration

CAFIERO (S.) Le migrazioni dal Mezzogiorno. in Parisi (Achille) and Zappa (Goffredo) eds. Mezzogiorno e politica di piano. Bari, 1964.

CAVAZZA (FABIO LUCA) Italy and Latin America. Santa Monica, [1967]. pp. 91. (Rand Corporation. Memoranda. 5400)

CINANNI (PAOLO) Emigrazione e imperialismo. Roma, 1968. pp. 258.

MANZOTTI (FERNANDO) La polemica sull'emigrazione nell'Italia unita. 2nd ed. Milano, 1969. pp. 203. (Nuova Rivista Storica. Biblioteca. N.28)

PASSIGLI (STEFANO) Emigrazione e comportamento politico. Bologna, [1969]. pp. 251.

VENTURINI (FIORENZA) Nudi col passaporto: la verità sull'emigrazione italiana in Svizzera. Milano, 1969. pp. 333.

- Executive departments

ITALY. Direzione Generale dell'Urbanistica. Servizio Urbanistico del Consiglio Superiore. 1956. Attività urbanistica dell'amministrazione dei lavori pubblici: esperienze e prospettive; introduzione dell'on. ing. Giuseppe Romita. Roma, 1956. pp. 57. 30cm.

ITALY. Statutes, etc. 1950-57. Current legislation on the Cassa per il Mezzogiorno; translation. Rome, Cassa per il Mezzogiorno, 1958. fo. vi, 97. 31½cm.

MEDICI (GIUSEPPE) Conoscere per amministrare. 3rd ed. Roma, 1958. pp. 102. 24cm.

SULLO (FIORENTINO) Il Comitato Centrale per la Previdenza e l'Assistenza Sociale. Roma, Ministero del Lavoro e della Previdenza Sociale, Rassegna del Lavoro, 1960. pp. 11. 27cm.

AMMINISTRAZIONE PER LE ATTIVITÀ ASSISTENZIALI ITALIANE E INTERNAZIONALI. P[ublic] R[elations] and Press Office. Administration for Italian and International Welfare Activities. Roma, [1961] pp. (8). 23½cm.

ITALY. 1961. Il Consiglio Nazionale dell'Economia e del Lavoro nel triennio 1958-1960. Roma, 1961. pp. xliii, 567. 27cm.

ITALY. Consiglio Nazionale dell' Economia e del Lavoro. 1962. Parere sull'ordinamento delle partecipazioni statali: assemblea, 13 febbraio, n. 4/27. Roma, 1962. pp. 138. 26½cm

ITALY. Statutes, etc. 1950-1961. Raccolta leggi: decreti e circolari riguardanti la Cassa per il Mezzogiorno. Napoli, 1961 [or rather 1962]. pp. xxvii, 363.

MARONGIU (G.) Aspetti giuridico-organizzativi. in Parisi (Achille) and Zappa (Goffredo) eds. Mezzogiorno e politica di piano. Bari, 1964.

JONA CELESIA (LIONELLO) Il Tesoro e le riserve valutarie. 2nd ed. Milano, 1969. pp. 204. (Turin. Università. Laboratorio di Economia Politica S. Cognetti de Martiis. Studi. 3a Serie. vol. 5)

SALVEMINI (MARIA TERESA) La politica di tesoreria. Milano, 1969. pp. 107. bibliog. (Rome. Università. Istituto di Politica Economica e Finanziaria. Pubblicazioni. 8)

- Foreign economic relations

ZAGARI (MARIO) Le relazioni economiche dell'Italia con i paesi europei ad economia di stato nella prospettiva della politica commerciale della CEE: conferenza etc. [Milano, 1966]. pp. 22. 20cm.

FRANCE. Direction de la Documentation. La Documentation Française. Notes et Études Documentaires. No. 3,580. L'organisation de l'expansion du commerce extérieur de l'Italie, 1960-1968. Paris, 1969. pp. 74. bibliog. 27cm.

ITALY - Foreign economic relations
See also EUROPEAN ECONOMIC COMMUNITY

- Foreign economic relations - France

VECCHIO (EDOARDO DEL) Di Robilant e la crisi nei rapporti marittimi italo-francesi. Milano, 1970. pp. 194. (Rome. Università. Istituto di Studi Storici e Politici. [Publications]. 19)

- Foreign economic relations - Spain

PISTOLESE (GENNARO E.) Spagna e Italia: le due economie. Roma, [1969]. pp. 214.

- Foreign economic relations - United Kingdom

BOLCHINI (PIERO) La Gran Bretagna e la formazione del mercato italiano, 1861-1883. Genova, [1969?]. pp. 264. bibliog. (Genoa. Università. Istituto di Storia Moderna e Contemporanea. Miscellanea Storica Ligure. Nuova Serie Periodica. Anno 1. N. 2)

- Foreign opinion, French

MILZA (PIERRE) L'Italie fasciste devant l'opinion française, 1920-1940. Paris, Colin, [1967] pp. 263. bibliog. 18cm. (Kiosque. 32)

- Foreign relations

QUINET (EDGAR) La croisade autrichienne, française, napolitaine, espagnole contre la République romaine. 3rd ed. Paris, Chamerot, 1849. pp. 36. 17½cm.

LOMBARDI (RICCARDO) and others. Resoconto del dibattito sulla politica estera in Parlamento. [Rome, imprint, 1961]. pp. 53. 21cm.

SIEBERT (FERDINAND) Italiens Weg in den Zweiten Weltkrieg. Frankfurt am Main, 1962. pp. 460. bibliog.

OSTELLINO (PIERO) L'Italia tra atlantismo e neutralismo. Torino, Centro di Ricerca e Documentazione Luigi Einaudi, [1964] pp. 155. 24cm.

AMOJA (FULVIO D') Declino e prima crisi dell'Europa di Versailles: studio sulla diplomazia italiana ed Europea, 1931-1933. Milano, Giuffrè, 1967. pp. iv, 510. bibliog. 25cm. (Messina. Università. Istituto di Scienze Giuridiche, Economiche, Politiche e Sociali. Pubblicazioni. N.80)

ANDRÈ (GIANLUCA) L'Italia e il Mediterraneo. alla vigilia della prima guerra mondiale: i tentativi di intesa mediterranea, 1911-1914. Milano, Guiffrè, 1967. pp. (111) 318. 25cm. (Rome. Università. Istituto di Studi Storici e Politici. [Publications]. 16)

BONANNI (MASSIMO) ed. La politica estera della Repubblica Italiana. Milano, Edizioni di Comunità, 1967. 3 vols. (in 1). 22½cm. (Studi e Ricerche di Scienze Sociali. 33)

BETTINI (EMILIO) ed. Il trattato contro la proliferazione nucleare. Bologna, Il Mulino, [1968]. pp. 216. 21cm.

GRAZIANO (LUIGO) La politica estera italiana nel dopoguerra. Padova, Marsilio, 1968. pp. 189. 21½cm.

MORANDI (CARLO) La politica estera dell'Italia da Porta Pia all'età giolittiana; ... a cura di Fernando Manzotti. new ed Firenze, Le Monnier, 1968. pp. xxiii, 354. bibliog. 20cm. (Quaderni di Storia)

RUMI (GIORGIO) Alle origini della politica estera fascista, 1918-1923. Bari, 1968. pp. 327. (Istituto Nazionale per la Storia del Movimento di Liberazione in Italia. Serie di Studi. 5)

CAROCCI (GIAMPIERO) La politica estera dell'Italia fascista, 1925-1928. Bari, Laterza, 1969. pp. vii, 391. 20cm. (Storia Società)

SCOTT (IVAN) The Roman question and the powers, 1848-1865. The Hague, 1969. pp. 390. bibliog.

CASSELS (ALAN) Mussolini's early diplomacy. Princeton, 1970. pp. 425. bibliog.

GANAPINI (LUIGI) Il nazionalismo cattolico: i cattolici e la politica estera in Italia dal 1871 al 1914. Bari, 1970. pp. 224.

SALVEMINI (GAETANO) La politica estera italiana dal 1871 al 1915; a cura di Augusto Torre. Milano, [1970]. pp. 603. (Opere di Gaetano Salvemini. 3. Scritti di Politica Estera. vol. 4)

ITALY - Foreign relations
See also EUROPEAN ECONOMIC COMMUNITY

- Foreign relations - Treaties

VEDOVATO (GIUSEPPE) ed. Il trattato di pace con l'Italia, Parigi, 10 febbraio 1947. Firenze, 1971. pp. 624.

- Foreign relations - Albania

PASTORELLI (PIETRO) L'Albania nella politica estera italiana, 1914-1920. Napoli, 1970. pp. 418. (Bari. Università. Facoltà Giuridica. Pubblicazioni. 27)

- Foreign relations - Austria

ITALY. Ministero degli Affari Esteri. 1960. Alto Adige: documents presented to the Italian Parliament by the Minister of Foreign Affairs, Signor A. Segni, the 16th September, 1960. [Rome, 1960]. pp. 105. 30cm.

ITALY. Presidenza del Consiglio dei Ministri. 1960. The De Gasperi-Gruber Agreement on the Alto Adige, from the historical and political background to the implementation of the Agreement within the Italian constitutional system. Rome, 1960. 24½cm. pp. 211.

AUSTRIA. 1961. Memorandum der österreichischen Bundesregierung zur Südtirolfrage vom 10. Oktober 1961; [with, Beilagen]. [Vienna], 1961. 8 pts.

ITALY. Ministero degli Affari Esteri. 1961. Alto Adige: documents presented to the Italian Parliament by the Minister for Foreign Affairs, Signor A. Segni, on 19th September, 1961. [Rome, 1961]. pp. 140. 30cm.

CAJOLI (RENATO) Alto Adige addio! Milano, Borghese, [1967]. pp 341. 19½cm. (I Libri del Borghese. vol. 60)

- Foreign relations - Balkan States

COLLOTTI (ENZO) and others. L'Italia nell' Europa danubiana durante la seconda guerra mondiale; saggi. [Milan], Istituto Nazionale per la Storia del Movimento di Liberazione in Italia, [1966]. pp. 123. 22cm. (Movimento di Liberazione in Italia, Il. Quaderni)

SMIRNOVA (NINA DMITRIEVNA) Балканская политика фашистской Италии: очерк дипломатической истории, 1936-1941. Москва, 1969. pp. 279.

- Foreign relations - East (Near East)

CENTRO STUDI AZIONE COMUNE. Quaderni. 2. La crisi del medio oriente: Israele '67. Milano, Azione Comune, [1967]. pp.106. 21cm.

- Foreign relations - Europe

WILLIS (F. ROY) Italy chooses Europe. New York, 1971. pp. 373. bibliog.

ITALY (Cont'd.)

- Foreign relations - France

BUSH (JOHN W.) S.J. Venetia redeemed: Franco-Italian relations, 1864-1866. New York, Syracuse U.P., [1967]. pp. xv, 160. bibliog. 22½cm.

LAURENS (FRANKLIN D.) France and the Italo-Ethiopian crisis, 1935-1936. The Hague, Mouton, 1967. pp. 432. bibliog. 24cm. (Studies in European History. 7)

- Foreign relations - Germany

TOSCANO (MARIO) The origins of the Pact of Steel. Baltimore, Johns Hopkins P., [1967]. pp. xiv, 417. 23cm.

PLEHWE (FRIEDRICH KARL VON) The end of an alliance: Rome's defection from the Axis in 1943. London, 1971. pp. 161.

- Foreign relations - Somaliland

ITALY. Ministero degli Affari Esteri. 1961. L'amministrazione fiduciaria della Somalia e i rapporti dell'Italia con la Repubblica somala: relazione presentata al Parlamento italiano. Roma, 1961. pp. 208. 29cm.

- Foreign relations - Turkey

MALTESE (PAOLO) La terra promessa: la guerra italo-turca e la conquista della Libia, 1911-1912. [Milan], Sugar, [1968]. pp. 377. bibliog. 20½cm. (Nuova Biblioteca Storica. 2)

- Foreign relations - United Kingdom

MALINVERNI (BRUNO) Il primo accordo per il Mediterraneo: febbraio-marzo 1887. Milano, Marzorati, [1967]. pp. 192. 21¼cm. (Collani di Studi Storici.)

- Government property

CASSESE (SABINO) I beni pubblici: circolazione e tutela. Milano, 1969. pp. 540. (Rome. Università. Istituto di Diritto Pubblico. Monografie. Nuova Serie. 40)

MARTINI (GASTONE) Dei beni pubblici destinati alle comunicazioni. Milano, 1969. pp. 259.

- History

MISCELLANEA Walter Maturi. Torino, Giappichelli, 1966. pp. 526. bibliog. 25cm. (Turin. Università. Facoltà di Lettere e Filosofia. Storia. vol. 1)

PIERI (PIERO) Scritti vari. Torino, Giappichelli, [1966]. pp. vii, 496. bibliog. 25cm. (Turin. Università. Facolta di Magistero. Pubblicazioni. 29)

HUGHES (SERGE) The fall and rise of modern Italy. New York, Macmillan, [1967]. pp. xiv, 322. bibliog. 21cm.

CLOUGH (SHEPARD BANCROFT) and SALADINO (SALVATORE) A history of modern Italy: documents, readings, and commentary. New York, Columbia U.P., 1968. pp. xi, 657. bibliog. 23½cm.

FLORITA (GIORGIO) Le due Italie. Milano, [1968]. pp. 193.

WISKEMANN (E.) Germany, Italy and Eastern Europe. in vol. 12 of The New Cambridge modern history. 2nd ed. Cambridge, 1968.

GALASSO (GIUSEPPE) Dal comune medievale all'unità: linee di storia meridionale. Bari, Laterza, 1969. pp. 198. bibliog. 21½cm. (Biblioteca di Cultura Moderna. 661)

RAGIONIERI (ERNESTO) and others, eds. Italia giudicata, 1861-1945: ovvero la storia degli italiani scritta dagli altri. Bari, 1969. pp. 873.

Il RISORGIMENTO e l'Europa: (studi in onore di Alberto Maria Ghisalberti); a cura di Vittorio Frosini. Catania, 1969. pp. 349. (Istituto per la Storia del Risorgimento Italiano. Comitato di Catania. Studi Risorgimentali. 7)

SPADOLINI (GIOVANNI) Il mondo di Giolitti. Firenze, 1969 repr. 1970. pp. 460.

CAPONE (ALFREDO) L'opposizione meridionale nell'età della Destra. Roma, 1970. pp. 407.

CHABOD (FEDERICO) De Machiavel à Benedetto Croce; études présentées par Henri Lapeyre. Genève, 1970. pp. 239.

PROCACCI (GIULIANO) History of the Italian people; ...translated by Anthony Paul. London, [1970]. pp. 394.

BERNARD (JACK F.) Italy: an historical survey. Newton Abbot, 1971. pp. 534. bibliog.

GRAMSCI (ANTONIO) Selections from the prison notebooks...; edited and translated by Quintin Hoare and Geoffrey Nowell Smith. London, 1971. pp. 483.

- History - Bibliography

CAMPANELLA (ANTHONY P.) compiler. Giuseppe Garibaldi e la tradizione garibaldina: una bibliografia dal 1807 al 1970. Ginevra, 1971. 2 vols.

- History - Historiography

BULLOUGH (DONALD A.) Italy and her invaders. Nottingham, University, [1968?]. pp. 30. 21cm. (Inaugural Lectures)

VALIANI (LEO) L'historiographie de l'Italie contemporaine; version française par Maurice Chevallier. Genève, Droz, 1968. pp. 171. 24cm. (Travaux d'Histoire Éthico-Politique. 17)

GALASSO (GIUSEPPE) Croce, Gramsci e altri storici. Milano, 1969. pp. 335.

VALSECCHI (FRANCO) L'età contemporanea nella recente storiografia. Milano. [1969]. pp. 47.

- History - Sources

CURATULO (GIACOMO EMILIO) Garibaldi, Vittorio Emanuele, Cavour nei fasti della patria: documenti inediti; dieci lettere di Vittorio Emanuele a Garibaldi nel 1860, scritti di Cavour, etc. Bologna, Zanichelli, 1911. pp. xxvii, 445. 29½cm.

IMBRIANI (VITTORIO) Vittorio Imbriani intimo: lettere familiari e diari inediti; a cura di Nunzio Coppola. Roma, the Istituto, 1963. pp. 403. 25cm. (Istituto per la Storia del Risorgimento Italiano. Pubblicazioni. 2a Serie: Fonti. vol. 48)

IMBRIANI (VITTORIO) Voci di esuli politici meridionali: lettere e documenti dal 1849 al 1861 con appendici varie; a cura di Nunzio Coppola. Roma, the Istituto, 1965. pp. 528. 25cm. (Istituto per la Storia del Risorgimento Italiano. Pubblicazioni. 2a Serie: Fonti. vol. 53)

MURAT FAMILY. Les archives Murat (1767-1966); inventaire; préface par André Chamson; avant-propos par le Prince Charles Murat. Paris, 1967. pp. liv, (13),303. (France. Archives Nationales. Inventaires et Documents).

ALBERTINI (LUIGI) Epistolario, 1911-1926; a cura di Ottavio Barié. [Milan]. 1968. 4 vols.

Gli ARCHIVI dei regi commissari nelle province del Veneto e di Mantova, 1866. Roma, 1968. 2 vols. (in 1). bibliog. (Italy. Ufficio Centrale degli Archivi di Stato. Pubblicazioni degli Archivi di Stato. 62)

MACK SMITH (DENIS) ed. The making of Italy, 1769-1870. London, Macmillan, 1968. pp. xii, 428. bibliog. 23cm. (Documentary History of Western Civilization)

WALKER (MACK) ed. Plombières: secret diplomacy and the rebirth of Italy. New York, O.U.P., 1968. pp. xii, 3-262. bibliog. 20cm. (Problems in European History: a Documentary Collection)

- History - Study and teaching

AQUARONE (ALBERTO) and others. Gli studi di storia e di diritto contemporaneo. Milano, 1968. pp. 158. bibliog. (Comitato per le Scienze Politiche e Sociali. Rapporti sulle Scienze Sociali. Quaderno n. 1)

- History - 476-1492

VOLPE (GIOACCHINO) L'Italia che nasce. Firenze, 1969. pp. 307.

WALEY (DANIEL) The Italian city-republics. London, Weidenfeld & Nicolson, 1969. pp. 254. bibliog. 19cm. (World University Library)

- History - 476-1268

FASOLI (GINA) Dalla "civitas" al comune nell'Italia settentrionale. Bologna, 1969. pp. 181. bibliog.

- History - 1559-1789

LEPRE (AURELIO) Storia del mezzogiorno nel risorgimento. Roma, 1969. pp. 290.

- History - 18th century

VENTURI (F.) Gli anni '30 del Settecento. in Miscellanea Walter Maturi. Torino, 1966.

MARTIN (GEORGE) b. 1926. The red shirt and the cross of Savoy: the story of Italy's Risorgimento, 1748-1871. London, 1970. pp. 782. bibliog.

- History - 1789-1900

PISACANE (CARLO) Opere complete...a cura di Aldo Romano. Milano, 1957-64. 8 vols.

- History - 1789-1870

LEPRE (AURELIO) Storia del mezzogiorno nel risorgimento. Roma, 1969. pp. 290.

MARTIN (GEORGE) b. 1926. The red shirt and the cross of Savoy: the story of Italy's Risorgimento, 1748-1871. London, 1970. pp. 782. bibliog.

- History - 1789-1815

RODOLICO (NICCOLO) Il popolo agli inizi del risorgimento nell'Italia meridionale 1798-1801: ristampa xerografica (della edizione del 1926) presentata da Francesco Cataluccio. Firenze, [1969?] pp. 312.

- History - 19th century

LUCATI (VENOSTO) Il garibaldino Luigi Mazzucchelli nelle battaglie per l'unità d'Italia e per l'ideale democratico: Cantù 1835 - Como 1896. Como, Noseda, 1961. pp. 32. bibliog 24cm.

VENTURA (TOMMASO) La verità storica sulla prima e seconda guerra d'indipendenza, sull'opera risorgimentale di Mazzini, di Garibaldi, di Cavour, sul significato del 20 settembre 1870: appunti critici. Milano, [1968]. pp. 155.

- History - 1815-1870

QUINET (EDGAR) La croisade autrichienne, française, napolitaine, espagnole contre la République romaine. 3rd ed. Paris, Chamerot, 1849. pp. 36. 17½cm.

BARIGAZZI (MICHELE) L'Italia dal 1820 al 1870: storia del nostro risorgimento narrata al popolo. Pisa, Valenti, 1882. pp. xiii, 301. 23cm.

MAURICI (ANDREA) L'opera della Sicilia per la cessazione del potere temporale e la liberazione di Roma e di Venezia all' inizio del Regno d'Italia, 1861-1862. Palermo, Priulla, 1914. pp. 397. 22cm.

MONTI (ANTONIO) L'idea federalistica nel risorgimento italiano: saggio storico. Bari, Laterza, 1922. pp. viii, 196. 20cm. (Biblioteca di Cultura Moderna)

CURATULO (GIACOMO EMILIO) Scritti e figure del risorgimento italiano; con documenti inediti. Torino, Bocca, 1926. pp. xi, 316. 20½cm. (Piccola Biblioteca di Scienze Moderni. No. 336)

LUCARELLI (ANTONIO) Il brigantaggio politico del Mezzogiorno d'Italia dopo la seconda restaurazione borbonica, 1815-1818 [first published at Bari, 1942]; e Il brigantaggio politico delle Puglie dopo il 1860 [2nd ed. published at Bari, 1946]. Milano, Longanesi, [1968]. pp. 533. 18cm. (I Cento Libri. vol. 18)

GREW (R.) How success spoiled the Risorgimento. in Black (Eugene Charlton) ed. European political history, 1815-1870. New York, 1967.

RAMM (AGATHA) The risorgimento. London, 1962 repr. 1967. pp. 28. bibliog. (Historical Association. General Series. G. 50)

ITALY - History - 1815-1870 (Cont'd.)

RICCIO (STEFANO) I fattori culturali e morali del Risorgimento italiano. Napoli, Istituto Editoriale del Mezzogiorno, 1962. pp. 111. 20½cm.

CINGARI (GAETANO) Problemi del Risorgimento meridionale. Messina, D'Anna, 1965. pp. 249. 25cm. (Messina. Universita. Facolta di Magistero. Pubblicazioni. 5)

GRAMSCI (ANTONIO) Sul risorgimento; a cura di Elsa Fubini. 4th ed. Roma, 1967. pp. 134. bibliog.

SALVESTRINI (ARNALDO) Il movimento antiunitario in Toscana 1859-1866. Firenze, Olschki, 1967. pp. vii, 297. 21cm. (Unione Regionale delle Provincie Toscane. Biblioteca di Storia Toscana Moderna e Contemporanea. Studi e Documenti. 3)

ROMEO (ROSARIO) Cavour e il suo tempo. Bari, 1969 in progress.

Il RISORGIMENTO e l'Europa: (studi in onore di Alberto Maria Ghisalberti); a cura di Vittorio Frosini, 1969. pp. 349. (Istituto per la Storia del Risorgimento Italiano. Comitato di Catania. Studi Risorgimentali. 7)

HOLT (EDGAR) 1900- Risorgimento: the making of Italy, 1815-1870. London, 1970. pp. 320. bibliog.

MACK SMITH (DENIS) Victor Emanuel, Cavour, and the risorgimento. London, 1971. pp. 381.

- History - Revolution of 1848

ARLINCOURT (CHARLES VICTOR PRÉVÔT D') Vicomte. L'Italia rossa; o, Storia delle rivoluzioni di Roma, Napoli, Palermo, Messino, Firenze, Modena, Torino, Milano e Venezia dall'elezione di Pio IX al di lui ritorno in sua capitale, giugno 1846-april 1850;... e ridotta in italiano con note da Francesco Giuntini. Firenze, a spese dell'editore, 1851. pp. 360. 17cm.

BERTOTTI (E.) Goffredo Mameli e Repubblica romana nel 1849 Genova, Studio Editoriale Genovese, 1927. pp. 151. bibliog. 20½cm.

VAINI (MARIO) I contadini mantovani nella rivoluzione nazionale, 1848-1860: contributo al dibattito storiografico sulle vicende del Mantovano negli ultimi cento anni. Milano, Gallo, 1966. pp. 196. 29cm. (Strumenti di Lavoro: Archivi del Movimento Operaio. N. 10)

MINNOCCI (CARLO) Pietro Sterbini e la rivoluzione romana, 1846-1849. Marcianise, Edizioni La Diana, 1967. pp. 169. 24½cm.

CATTANEO (CARLO) L'insurrezione di Milano nel 1848 e la successiva guerra; a cura di Lilia Borri Motta. Torino, Loescher, 1968. pp. 315. 21½cm.

AMBROSOLI (LUIGI) ed. La insurrezione milanese del marzo 1848: memorie di Cesare Correnti [and others]. Milano, 1969. pp. 167.

CLINI (PIERO) Le speranze d'Italia nelle cinque giornate di Milano. Milano, 1970. pp. 279. bibliog.

- History - 1849-1870

GUERRAZZI (FRANCESCO DOMENICO) La patria e le elezioni; etc. Firenze, Grazzini, 1861. pp. (ii), 80. 18½cm.

PROVENZANO (PIETRO) Sensi politici di giovine studente. [1870?]. pp. 14. 15½cm.

MANFREDI (CRISTOFORO) La spedizione Sarda in Crimea nel 1855-56, narrazione...compilata con la scorta dei documenti esistenti nell'archivio del corpo di Stato Maggiore, edita nell'anno 1896. Roma, Stato Maggiore Esercito, Ufficio Storico, 1956. pp. 312. bibliog. 24cm.

COMPOSTO (RENATO) I democratici dall'unità ad Aspromonte. Firenze, Le Monnier, 1967. pp. x, 255. 20cm.

FONZI (FAUSTO) I partiti politici italiani e la polemica sul sessantasei: [with facsimile reprints of I partiti politici nel parlamento italiano; by Ruggero Bonghi; and, Di chi è la colpa?; o sia, La pace e la guerra; by P. Villari]. Parma, Studium Parmense, 1968. pp. 81, c.

TORRE (PAOLO DALLA) L'anno di Mentana: contributo ad una storia dello Stato Pontificio nel 1867. Milano, Martello, [1968]. pp. xxvii, 548. bibliog. 22½cm.

WALKER (MACK) ed. Plombières: secret diplomacy and the rebirth of Italy. New York, O.U.P., 1968. pp. xii, 3-262. bibliog. 20cm. (Problems in European History: a Documentary Collection)

JACO (ALDO DE) ed. Il brigantaggio meridionale: cronaca inedita dell'unità d'Italia; a cura di Aldo De Jaco. Roma, 1969. pp. 351.

SCIROCCO (ALFONSO) I democratici italiani da Sapri a Porta Pia. [Naples, 1969]. pp. 549.

TALAMO (GIUSEPPE) De Sanctis politico, e altri saggi. Roma, 1969. pp. 301.

TIBERIIS (GIUSEPPE F. DE) Le ragioni del sud. Napoli, [1969]. pp. 301. bibliog.

CADORNA (RAFFAELE) La liberazione di Roma nell'anno 1870 ed il plebiscito; a cura di Giuseppe Talamo. [Milan], 1970. pp. 527. With 3 folded maps.

FEO (ITALO DE) Roma 1870: l'Italia dalla morte di Cavour a Porta Pia. Milano, 1970. pp. 332. bibliog.

- History - War of 1859

VALSECCHI (FRANCO) Italia ed Europa nel 1859. Firenze, Monnier, 1965. pp. vii, 215. 20cm. (Quaderni di Storia)

- History - 1870-1915

BIASE (CORRADO DE) L'Italia dalla neutralità all'intervento nella prima guerra mondiale. Modena, [1965-66]. 2 vols.

VIGEZZI (BRUNELLO) Da Giolitti a Salandra. Firenze, [1969]. pp. 410.

- History - 1914-1945

    SILVESTRI (CLAUDIO) Dalla redenzione al
    fascismo: Trieste, 1918-1922. 2nd ed.
    Udine, Del Bianco, 1966. pp. 162. bibliog.
    17½cm. (Deputazione Regionale per la
    Storia del Movimento di Liberazione nel
    Friuli e Venezia Giulia. Lotta Politica
    e Resistenza nel Friuli e Venezia Giulia.
    Saggi e Documenti. No. 2)

    VIVARELLI (ROBERTO) Il dopoguerra in Italia
    e l'avvento del fascismo, 1918-1922.
    Napoli, Istituto Italiano per gli Studi
    Storici, 1967 in progress. 24cm.

    BOCCA (GIORGIO) Storia d'Italia nella guerra
    fascista, 1940-1943. Bari, 1969. pp. 650. bibliog.

    CORDOVA (FERDINANDO) Arditi e legio-
    nari dannunziani. Padova, 1969.
    pp. 245.

    MELOGRANI (PIERO) Storia politica della grande
    guerra, 1915-1918. Bari, 1969. pp. 579.

    RUSINOW (DENNISON I.) Italy's Austrian heritage,
    1919-1946. Oxford, 1969. pp. 423. bibliog.

    VAILATI (VANNA) L'armistizio e il regno del sud.
    Milano, [1969]. pp. 599.

- History - 1922-1945

    SCORZA (CARLO) La notte del Gran Consiglio. Milano,
    1968 repr. 1969. pp. 222.

- History - Allied occupation, 1943-1947

    PERMOLI (PIERGIOVANNI) La costituente e i
    partiti politici italiani. [Bologna],
    Cappelli, [1966]. pp. 173. 18½cm.
    (Universale Cappelli. Serie Storia e
    Politica. 114)

- History - 1945-

    WISKEMANN (ELIZABETH) Italy since 1945. London,
    1971. pp. 142. bibliog.

- History, Military

    PISACANE (CARLO) Opere complete...a cura di Aldo
    Romano. Milano, 1957-64. 8 vols.

    ROCHAT (GIORGIO) Militari e politici nella preparazione
    della campagna d'Etiopia: studio e documenti
    1932-1936. Milano, [1971]. pp. 514. (Istituto
    Nazionale per la Storia del Liberazione in Italia.
    [Publications]. 2)

- History, Naval

    BRAGADIN (MARC'ANTONIO) Il dramma della Marina
    italiana 1940-1945. [Verona], Mondadori, 1968.
    pp. vii, 453. 21cm.

- Industries

    ITALY. Istituto Centrale di Statistica. Metodi
    e Norme. Serie A. N. 4. Calcolo delle
    variazioni stagionali negli indici della
    produzione industriale. Roma, 1960. 2 pts.
    22cm.

    PROSPETTIVE DELL'INDUSTRIA ITALIANA, LE (formerly
    Previsioni di sviluppo dell'industria italiana);
    ([pd. by] Confederazione Generale dell'Industria
    Italiana, Servizio Studi e Rilevazioni).
    1962/1965, 1963/1966, 1964/1966; annual, 1967/1970-
    Roma.

    BULTRINI (GIAN FILIPPO) and others. Industrial-
    izzazione del Mezzogiorno e sviluppo economico
    nazionale, etc. Roma, Opere Nuove, 1962.
    pp. 103. 17½cm. (Partito Socialista Democrat-
    ico Italiano. Commissione Studi e Programmi.
    Orientamenti. 2)

    ITALY. Istituto Centrale di Statistica.
    Note e Relazioni. N. 18. Il valore
    aggiunto delle imprese nel periodo
    1951-1959. Roma, 1962. pp. 215. 26cm.

    ITALY. Direzione Generale della Produzione
    Industriale. Economia nazionale, produzione e
    scambi con l'estero nell'industria. Roma, annual,
    1964/1966 to date. 14 x 20cm.

    MANNA (D.) Aspetti territoriali della politica di
    sviluppo industriale. in Parisi (Achille) and
    Zappa (Goffredo) eds. Mezzogiorno e politica
    di piano. Bari, 1964.

    PETRILLI (GIUSEPPE) L'I[stituto]di R[icostruzione]
    I[ndustriale] nell'economia italiana, etc. Milano,
    Giuffrè, 1964. pp. 63. 24cm. (Messina. Università.
    Istituto di Scienze Economiche. [Publications]. 8)

    SCOTTI (E.) Lo sviluppo industriale. in Parisi
    (Achille) and Zappa (Goffredo) eds. Mezzogiorno
    e politica di piano. Bari, 1964.

    MARIANI (G. NINO) Una politica economica e
    sindacale per l'industria minore. [Rome],
    Edizioni "Confapi", [1965] pp. vii, 176.
    24½cm.

    ZANETTI (GIOVANNI) and FILIPPI (ENRICO)
    Finanza e sviluppo della grande
    industria in Italia. 2nd ed. [Milan],
    Angeli, 1966-67. 2 vols. 23cm. (Turin.
    Università. Scuola di Amministrazione
    Industriale. Centro di Ricerche sull'
    Impresa e lo Sviluppo. [Stato e Pros-
    pettive dello Sviluppo Industriale
    in Italia]. 1)

    CICOGNA (FURIO) Cinque anni di lotta per
    la libertà economica. Roma, 1966. pp.
    284. 24cm.

    CONFEDERAZIONE GENERALE DELL'INDUSTRIA ITALIANA.
    Servizio Studi e Rilevazioni. Collana di Studi
    e Documentazione. 14. Il processo di
    sviluppo a medio termine dell'industria
    italiana nelle previsioni degli operatori
    economici. Roma, 1966. pp. xi, 173. 23cm.

    GIOVANNELLI (V.) and CALANDRA (P.) Problemi
    giuridici dei consorzi di sviluppo
    industriale nel Mezzogiorno. Roma, Giuffrè,
    1966. pp. viii, 228. 24cm. (Associazione per
    lo Sviluppo dell'Industria nel Mezzogiorno.
    Centro per gli Studi sullo Sviluppo Economico.
    Collana Francesco Giordani)

    MORANDI (RODOLFO) Storia della grande indus-
    tria in Italia. Torino, Einaudi, [1966]
    pp. 294. 18cm. (Piccola Biblioteca Einaudi.
    82) Reprint of the first edition of 1931
    with a new preface.

    EUROPEAN ECONOMIC COMMUNITY. Études: Série Écono-
    mie et Finances. 5. Étude pour la création
    d'un pôle industriel de développement en Italie
    méridionale. Bruxelles, 1967. 2 vols. 27cm.

    MEZZOGIORNO e triangolo industriale: (relazioni
    del convegno di Taranto, "Il Mezzogiorno degli
    anni '70"); [by] M. Barnabei [and others].
    Manduria, Lacaita, 1967. pp. 226. 22cm.
    (Uomini e cose della Nuova Italia. N. 25)

ITALY - Industries (Cont'd.)

MUSCARÀ (CALOGERO) La geografia dello sviluppo; sviluppo industriale e politica geografica nell'Italia del secondo dopoguerra. Milano, Edizione di Communita, 1967. pp.277. bibliog. 22½cm. (Studi e Ricerche di Scienze Sociali. 34)

CONFEDERAZIONE GENERALE DELL'INDUSTRIA ITALIANA. I quadri dell'organizzazione industriale. Roma, 1968. pp. 410. 24cm.

FORTE (FRANCESCO) and others. L'economia industriale italiana al 1980. Roma, 1968. pp. 18, 11 folded leaves. (Centro di Studi e Piani Economici. Contributi Occasionali. n. 53)

MATASSI (LUIGI) La civiltà dell'industria in Italia, 1789-1967. Roma, [1968]. pp. 133. bibliog.

ARINGA (CARLO DELL') Occupazione, salari e prezzi: un'analisi empirica per l'industria italiana, 1953-1967. Milano, 1969. pp. 174.

CALORO (BONAVENTURA) Pionieri dell'industria italiana Milano, Martello, [1969?]. pp. xxvii, 266. 22½cm.

SABA (ANDREA) La politica di incentivazione degli investimenti industriali in Italia e Europa. Roma, [1969]. pp. 210. (Rome. Universita. Istituto di Economia Politica. Collana di Studi. 1)

- Industries - Directories

CONFEDERAZIONE GENERALE DELL'INDUSTRIA ITALIANA. I quadri dell'organizzazione industriale. Roma, [the Confederazione], 1966. pp. 401. 24cm.

- Intellectual life

LAVELEYE (EMILE DE) Baron. L'Italie actuelle, (1878-1879): lettres à un ami. Londres, 1880. pp. 394.

IMBRIANI (VITTORIO) Gli hegeliani di Napoli ed altri corrispondenti letterati ed artisti; a cura di Nunzio Coppola. Roma, the Instituto, 1964. pp. 584. 25cm. (Istituto per la Storia del Risorgimento Italiano. Pubblicazioni. 2ª Serie:Fonti. vol.50)

SPAVENTA (BERTRANDO) Unificazione nazionale ed egemonia culturale; a cura...di G. Vacca. Bari, 1969. pp. 333.

COCHRANE (ERIC) ed. The late Italian renaissance, 1525-1630: [readings]. London, 1970. pp. 462.

- Nationalism

GAETA (FRANCO) Nazionalismo italiano. Napoli, Edizioni Scientifiche Italiane, [1965]. pp. 247. 21cm. (L'Acropoli. 16)

MOLINELLI (RAFFAELE) Per una storia del nazionalismo italiano: studi storici. Urbino, Argalia, [1966]. pp. 209. 21cm.

MOLINELLI (RAFFAELE) Pasquale Turiello, precursore del nazionalismo italiano: studi storici. Urbino, [1968]. pp. 110. bibliog.

PERFETTI (FRANCESCO) ed. Il nazionalismo italiano. Milano, [1969]. pp. 332. bibliog.

SCOTT (IVAN) The Roman question and the powers, 1848-1865. The Hague, 1969. pp. 390. bibliog.

LEONI (FRANCESCO) Origini del nazionalismo italiano. Napoli, [1970]. pp. 123. bibliog.

- Neutrality

BIASE (CORRADO DE) L'Italia dalla neutralità all'intervento nella prima guerra mondiale. Modena, [1965-66]. 2 vols.

- Officials and employees

ITALY. Statutes, etc. 1928-1957. Raccolta coordinata della legislazione concernente l'E[nte] N[azionale di] P[revidenza ed] A[ssistenza per i Dipendenti] S[tatali]; aggiornata al 1° gennaio 1958. Roma, [1958]. pp. 363. 24cm.

ITALY. Statutes, etc. 1942-57. Raccolta coordinata della legislazione concernente l'E[nte] N[azionale di] P[revidenza ed] A[ssistenza per i Dipendenti] S[tatali] aggiornata al 1° gennaio 1958. Roma, [1958]. pp. 363. 24cm.

ITALY. Ente Nazionale di Previdenza e Assistenza per i Dipendenti Statali. Servizio Studi e Statistica. 1959. La protection des employés de l'état selon le système de prévoyance italien. Rome, 1959. pp. 85. 24cm.

ITALY. Statutes, etc. 1942-1961. Raccolta di giurisprudenza sull'E[nte] N[azionale di] P[revidenza ed] A[ssistenza per i D[ipendenti] S[tatali]. Roma, 1962. pp. 137. 24½cm.

SCARPAT (ORLANDO) La misura della produttività nella pubblica amministrazione; con particolare riferimento alla situazione italiana. Milano, 1970. pp. 154. bibliog. (Istituto per gli Studi sullo Sviluppo Economico e il Progresso Tecnico. Collana Isvet. 12)

- Officials and employees - Salaries, allowances, etc.

ITALY. Statutes, etc. 1956-1957. Trattamento economico e di quiescenza del personale delle amministrazioni dello stato. Roma, 1959. pp. 108. 20cm.

- Parliament

ITALY. Assemblea Costituente, 1946-1947. (Stato sovrano e ipoteca clericale): gli atti dell'Assemblea Costituente sull'Art. 7, con il testo dei Patti lateranensi e il discorso del Croce al Senato; a cura di Aldo Capitini e Piero Lacaita. Perugia, 1959 [or rather 1960]. pp. 614.

MOHRHOFF (FEDERICO) I Vicepresidenti delle Assemblee legislative. [Rome], Editore Colombo, [1962]. pp. 50. 21½cm.

STURZO (LUIGI) Scritti di carattere giuridico: discorsi e attività parlamentare, 1951-1959. Bologna, Zanichelli, [1962] pp. viii, 396. 23½cm. (Istituto Luigi Sturzo. Opera Omnia di Luigi Sturzo. 3a Serie vol. 3)

PICCARDI (LEOPOLDO) and others. La sinistra davanti alla crisi del parlamento: [proceedings of a conference held 14-15 May 1966]. Milano, Giuffrè, [1967]. pp. 222. 20½cm.

AMATO (GIULIANO) L'ispezione politica del Parlamento. Milano, Giuffrè, 1968. pp. 169. 25cm. (Rome. Università. Istituto di Studi Giuridici. Pubblicazioni. Serie 5.N.7)

MARONGIU (ANTONIO) Medieval parliaments: a comparative study; ... translated and adapted by S.J. Woolf. London, Eyre & Spottiswoode, 1968. pp. 306. bibliog. 22cm. (International Commission for the History of Representative and Parliamentary Institutions. Studies. 32)

LACONI (RENZO) Parlamento e costituzione: (scritti e discorsi); a cura di Enrico Berlinguer e Gerardo Chiaromonte. Roma, 1969. pp. 166.

RIZZO (FRANCO) Il controllo del parlamento sugli enti pubblici. [Milan], 1969. pp. 173.

STUDI per il ventesimo anniversario dell'Assemblea Costituente. Firenze, [1969]. 6 vols.

- Parliament - Biography

SARTI (TELESFORO) Il parlamento subalpino e nazionale: profili e cenni biografici di tutti i deputati e senatori eletti e creati dal 1848 al 1890, legislature XVI; con appendice contenente i profili e cenni biografici dei deputati i senatori eletti e creati durante le legislature XVII, XVIII e XIX, etc. Roma, [imprint] 1896. pp. 1068. 26cm.

- Parliament - Elections

ZAVATTERO (DOMENICO) Il giuoco della borghesia. 2nd ed. Rimini, L'Iniziativa Editrice, 1907. pp. 16. 16cm.

ITALY. Direzione Generale dell'Amministrazione Civile. Divisione Servizi Elettorali. Servizi Tecnici. 1958. Elezioni politiche del 1946, 1948, 1953: compendio dei risultati. Roma, 1958. pp. xxxi, 99. 29cm.

ITALY. Istituto Centrale di Statistica. 1958. Elezioni della Camera dei Deputati e del Senato della Repubblica, 25 maggio 1958: dati riassuntivi. Roma, 1958. pp. 55. 26½cm.

ITALY. Presidenza del Consiglio dei Ministri. Servizio Informazioni. 1958. Le elezioni politiche, 1946, 1948, 1953. [Roma, 1958] pp. 83. 21cm. Supplemento al N.76 di Documenti di Vita Italiana.

- Parliament - History

MOHRHOFF (FEDERICO) Introduzione ad uno studio sugli aspetti storico-politici, giuridico-costituzionali e regolamentari-consuetudinari dell'Istituto presidenziale del Parlamento italiano, 1848-1963, etc. [Rome], Colombo, [1962]. pp. 78. 21cm.

- Parliament - Rules and practice

ITALY. Camera dei Deputati. 1965. Circolari e disposizioni interpretative del regolamento emanate dal Presidente della Camera, 1948-1964. [Rome], 1965. pp. 121. 24cm. (Bolletino di informazioni costituzionali e parlamentari. Supplementi. Nuova serie. [N.1])

FENUCCI (FULVIO) I limiti dell'inchiesta parlamentare. Napoli, Jovene, 1968. pp. xxiv, 342. 24cm. (Naples. Università. Facoltà Giuridica. Pubblicazioni. 112)

LONGI (VINCENZO) and STRAMACCI (MAURO) Il regolamento della Camera dei Deputati illustrato con i lavori preparatori...1848-1968. 2nd ed. Milano, Giuffrè, 1968. pp. (ii), 249.

BUCCISANO (IOLE) Le interrogazioni e le interpellanze parlamentari. Milano, 1969. pp. 116. (Messina. Università. Istituto di Scienze Giuridiche, Economiche, Politiche e Sociali. Pubblicazioni. N. 85)

- Politics and government

RACCOLTA di opuscoli contenenti uno studio di nuove idee sulla società federativa. Genova, Stamperia Nazionale, 1800. pp. 43.

GHISLERI (ARCANGELO) Democrazia in azione: scritti politici e sociali. Roma, Casa Editrice Italiana, [1953?]. pp. xvi, 224. bibliog. 17cm. (Scrittori Politici Italiani)

ITALY. Presidenza del Consiglio dei Ministri. Ufficio per la Riforma dell'Amministrazione. 1956. Costi dell'attività e del lavoro amministrativo: atti del secondo Convegno di tecnica della organizzazione nelle Pubbliche Amministrazioni, Milano, 24-25 aprile, 1955. Roma, 1956. pp. 188. bibliog. 24½cm.

ITALY. 1965. Discorsi parlamentari di Vittorio Emanuele Orlando, publicati per deliberazione della Camera dei Deputati. Roma, 1965. 4 vols.(in 2) 26½cm.

ENTE PER LA STORIA DEL SOCIALISMO E DEL MOVIMENTO OPERAIO ITALIANO. Attività parlamentare dei socialisti italiani. Roma. E.S.M.O.I., 1967. in progress. 24cm.

CONGRESSO CELEBRATIVO DEL CENTENARIO DELLE LEGGI AMMINISTRATIVE DI UNIFICAZIONE. La tutela del cittadino;...a cura di Giovanni Miele ([and] Paolo Barile; atti del congresso, etc.). [Vicenza], 1967-8. 2 vols. (in 1).

ESPOSITO (ENRICO) Lo stato e i cittadini in Italia. 2nd ed. Roma, Società Editrice Universo, 1967. pp. vii, 313. 23½cm.

GANCI (SALVATORE MASSIMO) L'Italia antimoderata: radicali, repubblicani, socialisti, autonomisti dall'Unità a oggi. Parma, Guanda, 1968. pp. 467. 21 cm. (Problemi d'Oggi)

SPEZZANO (FRANCESCO) La lotta politica in Calabria, 1861-1925. Manduria, Lacaita, 1968. pp. 235. 22cm. (Uomini e Cose della Nuova Italia. N.26)

CONGRESSO CELEBRATIVO DEL CENTENARIO DELLE LEGGI AMMINISTRATIVE DI UNIFICAZIONE. Sommario dell'opera; indici degli undici volumi; (atti del congresso, etc.). [Vicenza, 1969]. pp. 70.

PERTICONE (GIACOMO) Scritti di storia e politica del post-Risorgimento. Milano, 1969. pp. 467. (Rome. Università. Istituto di Studi Storici e Politici. [Publications] 18)

TAGLIACOZZO (ENZO) Risorgimento e postrisorgimento. Cagliari, [1969]. pp. 376.

WALEY (DANIEL) The Italian city-republics. London, Weidenfeld & Nicolson, 1969. pp. 254. bibliog. 19cm. (World University Library)

ITALY - Politics and government (Cont'd.)

RUFFILLI (ROBERTO) La questione regionale dall'unificazione alla dittatura, 1862-1942. Milano, 1971. pp. 485. bibliog. (Istituto per la Scienza dell'Amministrazione Pubblica. Pubblicazioni. Studi e Testi. 2)

- Politics and government - Periodicals

LICATA (GLAUCO) La Rassegna Nazionale: conservatori e cattolici liberali italiani attraverso la loro rivista, 1879-1915. Roma, 1968. pp. 614. With extensive indexes to the periodical.

- Politics and government - 1789-1900

CRISPI (FRANCESCO) L'anima di Francesco Crispi: carteggio intimo sulla politica del risorgimento italiano; con proemio e note biografiche di' G. Pipitone-Federico. Palermo, Trimarchi, 1910. pp. lx, 192. 19cm.

MAURICI (ANDREA) L'opera della Sicilia per la cessazione del potere temporale e la liberazione di Roma e di Venezia all' inizio del Regno d'Italia, 1861-1862. Palermo, Priulla, 1914. pp. 397. 22cm.

FERRARI (GIUSEPPE) Political Writer. I partiti politici italiani dal 1789 al 1848: la rivoluzione e i rivoluzionarii in Italia; la rivoluzione e le riforme in Italia. Città di Castello, Il Solco, 1921. pp. xxvii, 287. 19cm. (Biblioteca di Cultura Storica)

GIOBERTI (VINCENZO) Il pensiero politico di Vincenzo Gioberti; ([selected and with an introduction and commentary by] Tullio Vecchietti). Milano, Istituto per gli Studi di Politica Internazionale, [1941]. pp. 421. 19cm. (Documenti di Storia e di Pensiero Politico. 13)

DORSO (GUIDO) La rivoluzione meridionale: (il Mezzogiorno d'Italia de Cavour a Mussolini); [edited by Carlo Muscetta]. 2nd ed. [Milan], 1945 repr. 1969. pp. 370.

ALBERTONI (ETTORE A.) La teoria della classe politica nella crisi del parlamentarismo. Milano, Istituto Editoriale Cisalpino, [1968]. pp. 123. (Collana Documenti e Saggi. N. 6)

JACINI (STEFANO) La riforma dello stato e il problema regionale; a cura di Francesco Traniello. Brescia, [1968]. pp. 253.

LAGERSVÄRD (JOHAN CLAES) Lettere a Giovanni Ferri de Saint-Constant;...a cura di Vittorio E. Giuntella. Roma, 1968. pp. 181. (Istituto per la Storia del Risorgimento Italiano. [Pubblicazioni]. Serie 2a: Fonti. vol. 55.)

PISACANE (CARLO) La rivoluzione in Italia; a cura di Aurelio Lepre. [Rome], Editori Riuniti, 1968. pp. 225. 18½cm. (Le Idee. 17)

TALAMO (GIUSEPPE) La formazione politica di Agostino Depretis. Milano, 1970. pp. 246.

- Politics and government - 1849-1870

PREZZOLINI (PIETRO) Le speranze del partito reazionario e l'Italia al cospetto delle potenze dell' Europa. [Firenze, imprint, 1859]. pp. 14. 18½cm.

I PARTITI del'opposizione e la maggioranza: cenni politici. Napoli, [imprint], 1862. pp. 24. 19½cm.

MANTEGAZZA (PAOLO) Ordine e libertà: conversazioni di politica popolare. Milano, Bernardoni, 1864. pp. 192. 18½cm.

MANIN (DANIELE) and PALLAVICINO TRIVULZIO (GIORGIO GUIDO) Marquis. Daniele Manin e Giorgio Pallavicino: epistolario politico, 1855-1857; con note e documenti per B.E.Maineri. Milano, Bortolotti, 1878. pp. xc, 648. 23cm.

IMBRIANI (VITTORIO) Vittorio Imbriani intimo: lettere familiari e diari inediti; a cura di Nunzio Coppola. Roma, the Istituto, 1963. pp. 403. 25cm. (Istituto per la Storia del Risorgimento Italiano. Pubblicazioni. 2a Serie: Fonti. vol. 48)

IMBRIANI (VITTORIO) Voci di esuli politici meridionali: lettere e documenti dal 1849 al 1861 con appendici varie; a cura di Nunzio Coppola. Roma, the Istituto, 1965. pp. 528. 25cm. (Istituto per la Storia del Risorgimento Italiano. Pubblicazioni. 2a Serie: Fonti. vol. 53)

FONZI (FAUSTO) I partiti politici italiani e la polemica sul sessantasei: [with facsimile reprints of I partiti politici nel parlamento italiano; by Ruggero Bonghi; and, Di chi è la colpa?; o sia, La pace e la guerra; by P. Villari]. Parma, Studium Parmense, 1968. pp. 81, c.

SPAVENTA (BERTRANDO) Unificazione nazionale ed egemonia culturale; a cura...di G. Vacca. Bari, 1969. pp. 333.

- Politics and government - 1870-1915

LAVELEYE (EMILE DE) Baron. L'Italie actuelle, (1878-1879): lettres à un ami. Londres, 1880. pp. 394.

MINGHETTI (MARCO) I partiti politici e la pubblica amministrazione; a cura di Bruno Widmar. [Bologna, 1881 repr. 1969]. pp. 139.

ZAVATTERO (DOMENICO) Il giuoco della borghesia. 2nd ed. Rimini, L'Iniziativa Editrice, 1907. pp. 16. 16cm.

CICOTTI (FRANCESCO) Il "caso Ferri" e la partecipazione dei Socialisti al governo. Firenze, Nerbini, 1910. pp. 34. 19½cm.

BISSOLATI (LEONIDA) Sulla politica del ministero: discorso...,Camera dei Deputati, seduta 8 aprile 1911. [Roma], 1911. pp. 269-284. 25cm. (Reprinted from: "L'Eloquenza," 1911)

VILLARI (PASQUALE) Storia, politica e istruzione: saggi critici. Milano, 1914. pp. 440.

ROSSELLI (CARLO) Filippo Turati e il movimento socialista italiano; a cura di Salvo Tomaselli. Roma, I.E.P.I., [194-]. pp. 96. bibliog. 17cm.

VALLAURI (CARLO) La politica liberale di Giuseppe Zanardelli, dal 1876 al 1878. Milano, Giuffrè, 1967. pp. xi, 498. 25cm. (Rome. Università. Istituto di Studi Storici e Politici. [Publications]. 15)

SALVEMINI (GAETANO) Carteggi. vol. 1. 1895-1911; a cura di Elvira Gencarelli. Milano, Feltrinelli, 1968. pp. xxxi, 568. 21½cm. (Opere di Gaetano Salvemini. 9).

NEPPI MODONA (GUIDO) Sciopero, potere politico e magistratura 1870-1922. Bari, 1969. pp. 486. (Centro Nazionale di Prevenzione e Difesa Sociale. Indagine su "L'Amministrazione della Giustizia e la Società Italiana in Trasformazione". 6)

SANCTIS (FRANCESCO DE) I partiti e l'educazione della nuova Italia; a cura di Nino Cortese. Torino, 1970. pp. 555. (Opere di Francesco De Sanctis. 16)

- Politics and government - 20th century

DORSO (GUIDO) La rivoluzione meridionale: (il Mezzogiorno d'Italia de Cavour a Mussolini); [edited by Carlo Muscetta]. 2nd ed. [Milan], 1945 repr. 1969. pp. 370.

BERGAMO (MARIO) Nazionalcomunismo. Milano, Edizioni Mondiali, [1965]. pp. 427. 20½cm.

AZIONE, L'. L'Azione, 1905-1922; a cura di Carlo Bello. Roma, Cinque Lune, 1967. pp. lvi, 606. 21cm. (Le Antologie. 2)

FEDERZONI (LUIGI) Italia di ieri: per la storia di domani. [Verona], Mondadori, 1967. pp. 319. 21cm.

PONT (ADRIANO DAL) and ZOCCHI (LINO) eds. Pionieri dell'Italia democratica: vita e scritti di combattenti antifascisti. Roma, A.N.P.P.I.A., [1967]. pp. xv, 343. bibliog. 24cm.

SEPE (GIOVANNI) Le tre occasioni: politica di piano, Ministero dell'Urbanistica e Unità Nazionale. Napoli, Fiorentino, [1967]. pp. xxiii, 433. 22½cm.

CALAMANDREI (PIERO) Lettere 1915-1956; a cura di G. Agosti e A. Galante Garrone. Firenze, La Nuova Italia, 1968. 2 vols. 20 cm. (Documenti di Storia Italiana. 3a Serie. 3. Opere Politiche e Letterarie di Piero Calamandrei. 3)

JEMOLO (ARTURO CARLO) Costume e diritto. Venezia, Neri Pozza, 1968. pp. xviii, 490. 21½cm. (Nuova Biblioteca di Cultura. 30)

JEMOLO (ARTURO CARLO) Anni di prova. Vicenza, 1969. pp. 266.

EARLE (JOHN) Journalist. Italy's troubles. [London], 1970. pp. 13. (Institute for the Study of Conflict. Conflict Studies. No. 9)

- Politics and government - 1914-1945

PANTALEONI (MAFFEO) La fine provvisoria di un'epopea. Bari, Laterza, 1919. pp. viii, 319. 20½cm.

PARTITO SOCIALISTA ITALIANO. Congresso Nazionale, 18°, Milano, 1921. Il Partito socialista italiano sulla via del riformismo: discorsi dei delegati della Internazionale comunista al...congresso...; ([by] C. Zetkin ed E. Walecki); [reprint of the original edition of 1921]. [Milan, Feltrinelli, 1966?] pp. 79. 19cm. (Biblioteca dell' Internazionale Comunista. 10)

GIULIANO (BALBINO) L'esperienza politica dell'Italia. Firenze, Vallecchi, [1924]. pp. 332. 19½cm. (Uomini e Idee)

PIAZZA (GIUSEPPE) La fiamma bilingue: momenti del dissidio ideale, 1913-1923. Milano, Corbaccio, 1924. pp. 277. 19cm. (Res Publica. vol. 4)

PARTITO COMUNISTA ITALIANO. Il Partito Comunista d'Italia davanti al Tribunale Speciale fascista: testo della sentenza di rinvio della Camera di Consiglio del Tribunale Speciale. Milan, Feltrinelli, [1966?]. pp. 64. 21cm. Reprinted from the original edition published by Edizioni del P.C.I. in Paris in 1928.

OMODEO (ADOLFO) Per la riconquista della libertà: raccolta di pagine politiche. Napoli, Macchiaroli, 1944. pp. 117. 20cm.

BARTELLINI (ERMANNO) La rivoluzione in atto, e altri scritti. Firenze, "La Nuova Italia" Editrice, 1967. pp. lxii, 249. 21cm. (Maestri e Compagni. Biblioteca di Studi Critici e Morali. 32)

KOBYLIANSKII (K. V.) Velikii Oktiabr' i revoliutsionnoe dvizhenie v Italii, 1917-1921. Moskva, 1968. pp. 263. bibliog.

LOPUKHOV (BORIS REMOVICH) Фашизм и рабочее движение в Италии, 1919-1929 гг. Москва, 1968. pp. 413. bibliog.

PELLICANI (ANTONIO) Il filo nero. [Milan], Sugar, [1968]. pp. 402. 21cm. (Nuova Biblioteca Storica. 4)

RIZZO (FRANCO) Profeti del nuovo Mezzogiorno. Roma, [1968]. pp. 181.

SALVEMINI (GAETANO) L'Italia vista dall' America; a cura di Enzo Tagliacozzo. Milano, Feltrinelli, [1969]. 2 vols. (in 1). 21½cm. (Opere di Gaetano Salvemini. 7)

- Politics and government - 1922-1945

ROSSELLI (CARLO) Oggi in Spagna, domani in Italia; con la prefazione di Gaetano Salvemini alla prima edizione. [Turin], Einaudi, 1938, repr. 1967. pp. xxxiii, 182. 17½cm. (Nuova Universale Einaudi. 86)

SCHIAVI (ALESSANDRO) Esilio e morte di Filippo Turati, 1926-1932. Roma, Opere Nuove, 1956. pp. 606. bibliog. 19½cm.

LEGNANI (MASSIMO) Politica e amministrazione nelle repubbliche partigiane: studio e documenti. [Milan]. Istituto Nazionale per la Storia del Movimento di Liberazione, [1967?]. pp. 175. bibliog. 22cm. (Movimento di Liberazione in Italia, Il. Quaderni. 2)

PALUMBO (PIER FAUSTO) Il governo dei quarantacinque giorni, e Diario della resistenza a Roma. Roma, 1967. pp. 265.

VALIANI (LEO) and others. L'altra Europa 1922-1945: momenti e problemi. Torino, Giappichelli, 1967. pp. ix, 294. 23cm. (Turin. Università. Istituto di Storia. Collana. 3)

ITALY - Politics and government - 1922-1945 (Cont'd.)

ACERBO (GIACOMO) Fra due plotoni di esecuzione: avvenimenti e problemi dell'epoca fascista. [Bologna], Cappelli, [1968]. pp. 775. 20½cm. (Testimoni per la Storia del Nostro Tempo: Collana di Memorie, Diari e Documenti. 42)

VENERUSO (DANILO) La vigilia del fascismo: il primo ministero Facta nella crisi dello stato liberale in Italia. Bologna, Il Mulino, [1968]. pp. 552. 21½cm. (Saggi. 80)

COLAPIETRA (RAFFAELE) La lotta politica in Italia dalla liberazione di Roma alla Costituente. Bologna, [1969]. pp. 578.

CASSELS (ALAN) Mussolini's early diplomacy. Princeton, 1970. pp. 425. bibliog.

- Politics and government - 1945-

RIZZONE (STEFANO) Dal fascismo alla democrazia. Modica, [imprint], 1946. pp. 149. 25cm.

CROCE (BENEDETTO) Due anni di vita politica italiana 1946-47. Bari, Laterza, 1948. pp. viii, 204. 20cm. (Biblioteca di Cultura Moderna. N. 442)

NENNI (PIETRO) Legge truffa e costituzione: ragioni dell'ostruzionismo socialista. Milano, Avanti!, 1953. pp. 40. 21½cm. (Attualità. 2)

STURZO (LUIGI) Politica di questi anni: consensi e critiche, dal gennaio 1950 al giugno 1951. rev. ed. Bologna, Zanichelli, [1957] pp. 477. 23½cm. (Istituto Luigi Sturzo. Opera Omnia di Luigi Sturzo. 2a Serie. vol. 11)

DAL Congresso di Napoli al Governo Fanfani; [reprinted in part from Il Popolo, 1962]. [Rome], Spes, [1962]. fo. 25. 28cm. (Documentazione Spes)

MORO (ALDO) La continuità della politica di sviluppo democratico promossa, in Italia, dalla Democrazia Cristiana. [Rome], Spes, [1962]. pp. 72. 16cm. (Collana Documenti e Studi Spes. 13)

PARTITO LIBERALE ITALIANO. La sfiducia al governo di centro-sinistra: discorsi alla Camera dei Deputati nelle sedute del 5-6-7-8 e 10 marzo 1962; ([by] Aldo Bozzi [and others]). Roma, [the Partito, 1962]. pp. 151. 20½cm.

NENNI (PIETRO) Elezioni dominate dalla ragione e dalla volontà di rinnovamento:(il discorso... alla Camera del 25 gennaio 1963). [Rome, imprint, 1963]. pp. 30. 20cm.

SARAGAT (GIUSEPPE) Il rafforzamento elettorale del P.S.D.I. è condizione di sviluppo del Centro-Sinistra: discorso pronunciato alla Camera dei Deputati...24 gennaio 1963, etc. Roma, P.S.D.I., 1963. pp. 39. 19cm.

TANASSI (MARIO) Per lo sviluppo della democrazia italiana: discorso pronunciato alla Camera dei Deputati... 13 dicembre 1963. [Rome, imprint, 1963]. pp. 24. 21cm.

ITALY. 1964. Il governo Moro. (Vita Italiana: documenti e informazioni. Supplementi). [Rome, 1964]. pp. 104. 20cm. Includes speeches by Aldo Moro.

OSTELLINO (PIERO) L'Italia tra atlantismo e neutralismo. Torino, Centro di Ricerca e Documentazione Luigi Einaudi, [1964] pp. 155. 24cm.

SARAGAT (GIUSEPPE) La grande prospettiva del socialismo democratico: discorso pronunciato...il 1 marzo 1964. Roma, P.S.D.I., 1964. pp. 32. 19cm.

MONDO OPERAIO. Mondo operaio, 1956-1965; antologia a cura di Gaetano Arfé; introduzione di Pietro Nenni. [Florence], Landi, [1966-67]. 2 vols. 23½cm. (Biblioteca di Politica e Sociologia. 4)

BON VALSASSINA (MARINO) La società dei nostri giorni osservata da un uomo di destra. Roma, Volpe, [1966]. pp. 259. 21cm.

LEPRE (AURELIO) La svolta di Salerno. Roma, Editori Riuniti, 1966. pp. 159. 18½cm. (Enciclopedia Tascabile. 102)

PARTITO LIBERALE ITALIANO. L'azione politica e legislativa del PLI, 1963-1965. [Rome, the Partito, 1966?] pp. 341. 21cm.

FERMOLI (PIERGIOVANNI) La costituente e i partiti politici italiani. [Bologna], Cappelli, [1966]. pp. 173. 18½cm. (Universale Cappelli. Serie Storia e Politica. 114)

RINASCITA. Rinascita, 1944-1962: antologia; a cura di Paolo Alatri. [Florence], Landi, [1966]. 3 vols. 23cm. (Biblioteca di Politica e Sociologia. 3)

WOLLEMBORG (LEO J.) Italia al rallentatore: cronache politiche 1949-1966. Bologna, Il Mulino, [1966]. pp. 501. 21½cm. (La Specola Contemporanea)

SALVEMINI (GAETANO) Lettere dall'America, 1944-(1949): a cura di Alberto Merola. Bari, Laterza, 1967-68. 2 vols. 20cm. (Libri del Tempo. 102-105)

CAVALLARI (ALBERTO) Il potere in Italia. [Verona], Mondadori, 1967. pp. 128. 21cm. (Le Scie)

FEO (ITALO DE) L'ultima Italia. Torino, Edizioni Rai Radiotelevisione Italiana, [1967]. pp. 203. bibliog. 30cm.

LA GUIDARA (FRANCO) ed. 25 anni caldi: [articles by Italian journalists]. Roma, Edizioni Internazionali, 1967. pp. 478. 21cm.

MARINO (GAETANO DI) La confederazione di Bonomi nella vita politica italiana. Roma, Editrice Cooperativa, [1967]. pp. 103. 21½cm.

PISTELLI (NICOLA) Scritti politici; a cura di Enrico De Mita. Firenze, 1967. pp. 945.

ROSELLI (ENRICO) A cuore aperto: appunti di un deputato: (scelta e revisione dei testi a cura di Luciano Guaraldo). Roma, Città Nuova, [1967]. pp. 280. bibliog. 20cm.

BONARDI (ETTORE) La rivoluzione è la rivoluzione. Milano, Edizioni Socialiste, 1968. pp. 140. 21cm.

CONTE (LUIGI) La via italiana alla democrazia. [Bologna, 1968]. pp. 141.

ERAMO (PACIFICO D') La liberazione dall'antifascismo. Roma, L'Orologio, 1968. pp. 187. 20½cm.

FERRI (MAURO) I socialisti in parlamento: discorsi parlamentari nella quarta legislatura. Roma, Lerici, [1968]. pp. 259. 21cm. (Saggi. 41)

GERMINO (DANTE LEE) and PASSIGLI (STEFANO) The government and politics of contemporary Italy. New York, Harper & Row, [1968]. pp. ix, 212. bibliog. 20½cm. (Harper's Comparative Government Series)

LA MALFA (UGO) Ideologia e politica di una forza di sinistra. Milano, Il Saggiatore di Alberto Mondadori, 1968. pp. 147. 21cm.

LIBERTINI (LUCIO) Dieci tesi sul partito di classe. Roma, Samonà e Savelli, [1968]. pp. 75. 18cm. (Cultura Politica. 16)

ORLANDI (FLAVIO) Socialismo giorno per giorno; a cura di T. Meli. [Bologna], Cappelli, [1968]. pp. 357. 21cm.

PICCOLI (FLAMINIO) Democrazia possibile in un paese che cambia. Roma, 1968. pp. 151.

POGGI (GIANFRANCO) Le preferenze politiche degli italiani: analisi di alcuni sondaggi pre-elettorali. Bologna, [1968]. pp. 69. (Istituto di Studi e Ricerche "Carlo Cattaneo". Quaderni. 2)

RAFFAELE (LUCIANO) Democrazia di sinistra: sinistra democrazia. Roma, Volpe, [1968]. pp. 90. 21½cm.

La RIFORMA dello stato: atti del convegno promosso dall'Istituto Gramsci, Roma, 16-18 gennaio 1968. Roma, Riuniti, 1968. pp. 559. 21½cm. (Nuova Biblioteca di Cultura. 79)

SERNINI (MICHELE) La disputa sui partiti. Padova, Marsilio, 1968. pp. 158. bibliog. 21½cm. (Collana di Attualità Politica. No. 3)

SOLARI (FERMO) Una nuova prospettiva. n.p., Movimento Socialisti Autonomi del Friuli-Venezia Giulia. [1968?]. fo.60.

STURZO (LUIGI) Politica di questi anni: consensi e critiche, dal gennaio 1954 al dicembre 1956. rev. ed. Bologna, Zanichelli, [1968]. pp. 403. 23½cm. (Istituto Luigi Sturzo. Opera Omnia di Luigi Sturzo. 2a Serie. vol.13)

VALITUTTI (SALVATORE) La riforma dello stato. Firenze, Le Monnier, 1968. pp. xxvii, 342. 22½cm.

CAPUA (GIOVANNI DI) Come l'Italia aderì al patto atlantico. [Rome?, 1969]. pp. 253.

FERRARI (PIERRE) and MAISL (HERBERT) Les groupes communistes aux Assemblées parlementaires italiennes, 1958-1963, et françaises, 1962-1967;...préface de Maurice Duverger. Paris, 1969. pp. 214. bibliog. (Paris. Université. Faculté de Droit et des Sciences Economiques. Travaux et Recherches. Série "Science Politique." No. 16)

GASPERI (ALCIDE DE) Discorsi politici; a cura di Tommaso Bozza. Roma, 1956 repr. 1969. pp. 661.

ITALY. Consiglio di Stato. 1969. Il Consiglio di Stato nel quinquennio 1961-65: relazione al Presidente del Consiglio dei Ministri, (with Appendice. Il Consiglio di Giustizia Amministrativa per la Regione Siciliana). Roma, 1969. 5 vols.

KHOLODKOVSKII (KIRILL GEORGIEVICH) Рабочее движение в Италии, 1959-1963. Москва, 1969. pp. 897.

PALUMBO (PIER FAUSTO) L'Italia dalla resistenza alla "legge-truffa": cronache degli anni "difficili", 1944-1953. Roma, 1969. pp. 302. bibliog. (Saggi. 5)

RADI (LUCIANO) Potere democratico e forze economiche. Roma, 1969. pp. 97.

STUDI per il ventesimo anniversario dell'Assemblea Costituente. Firenze, [1969]. 6 vols.

CAPUA (GIOVANNI DI) Un anno caldo. Firenze, 1970. pp. 347.

RIZZO (FRANCO) Dal riformismo alla contestazione. Roma, [1970]. pp. 229.

ZANGRANDI (RUGGERO) Inchiesta sul SIFAR: (schedature, fascicoli, indagini, interessi e legami in un documentato resoconto sulle degenerazioni dei servizi di sicurezza militare). Roma, 1970. pp. 126.

SOMMA (LUIGI) Operazione Quirinale. Roma, [1971]. pp. 249.

WILLIS (F. ROY) Italy chooses Europe. New York, 1971. pp. 373. bibliog.

ITALY, (1969-1970): new tactics and organisation. London, [1972]. pp. 61.

- **Population**

COLETTI (FRANCESCO) Due massime forze d'Italia: l'uomo e l'acqua; conferenza tenuta a Firenze il 28 maggio 1916, etc. (Le Pagine dell'Ora.17) Milano, Treves, 1917. pp. (iii),79. 19cm.

PINNA (MARIO) La carta della densità della popolazione in Italia, Cens. 1951; presentazione di Roberto Almagià. (Consiglio Nazionale delle Ricerche). [Rome], Consiglio Nazionale delle Ricerche, 1960. pp. 73, 1 map. bibliog. 24½cm. (Contributi alla Carta della Distribuzione della Popolazione in Italia)

ZANGHERI (RENATO) La popolazione italiana in età napoleonica: studi sulla struttura demografica del Regno italico e dei Dipartimenti francesi. Bologna, 1963. pp. 220, ciii. 24cm. (Extracted from Bollettino del Museo del Risorgimento, anno VIII, 1963)

ITALY. Direzione Generale della Produzione Industriale. Economia nazionale, produzione e scambi con l'estero nell'industria. Roma, annual, 1964/1966 to date. 14 x 20cm.

ITALY. Commissione Nazionale Italiana UNESCO. Convegno Italo-Svizzero, 1965. L'esodo rurale e lo spopolamento della montagna nella società contemporanea: atti del Convegno..., 24-26 maggio 1965. Milano, Società Editrice Vita e Pensiero, 1966. pp.xxiv, 337. bibliogs. 24cm.

ITALY - Population (Cont'd.)

GRASSI (CORRADO) Le migrazioni interne italiane nel secolo unitario: cause e conseguenze. Torino, Giappichelli, [1967]. pp. xxxi, 236. bibliog. 24½cm. (Corsi Universitari)

ITALY. Istituto Centrale di Statistica. 1967. Popolazione residente e presente dei comuni ai censimenti dal 1861 al 1961: circoscrizioni territoriali al 15 ottobre 1961. Roma, 1967. pp. ix, 419. 26cm.

NAPOLI (CATALDO DI) I meridionali nel Nord Italia. Roma, Editoriale Idea, [1967]. pp. 172. 22cm. (Collana Sociologia e Vita. N. 3)

BARBERI (BENEDETTO) Teoria e politica della popolazione. Roma, 1969. pp. 293. (Centro di Ricerche e Studi Economici. Studi sulla Dinamica Economica. 4)

PELLICCIARI (GIOVANNI) ed. L'immigrazione nel triangolo industriale: scritti di G. Albertelli [and others]. Milano, 1970. pp. 681. bibliog.

- Presidents

ANTONELLI (SERGIO) Le immunità del Presidente della Repubblica italiana. Milano, [1971]. pp. 379.

CAPUA (GIOVANNI DI) Le chiavi del Quirinale da De Nicola a Saragat, la strategia del potere in Italia. Milano, 1971. pp. 292.

- Public works

ITALY. Direzione Generale dell'Urbanistica. Servizio Urbanistico del Consiglio Superiore. 1956. Attività urbanistica dell'amministrazione dei lavori pubblici: esperienze e prospettive; introduzione dell'on. ing. Giuseppe Romita. Roma, 1956. pp. 57. 30cm.

ITALY. Ministero dei Lavori Pubblici. 1958. Les travaux publics dans l'après-guerre: ouvrages et réalisations. [Rome, 1958] pp. 156. 30½cm.

ITALY. Ragioneria Generale dello Stato. 1960. La revisione dei prezzi delle pubbliche forniture e degli appalti e concessioni di opere pubbliche. 2nd ed. Roma, 1960. pp. xxxvii, 521. bibliog. 26cm.

PARTITO COMUNISTA ITALIANO. Libro bianco sulla tragedia del Vajont: prima documentazione presentata dalla delegazione parlamentare del PCI al Presidente della Repubblica, etc. [Rome, imprint, 1963] pp. 87. 20½cm.

ALESSI (NICOLO) Opere pubbliche comunali, ed esecuzione dei lavori pubblici nei grandi e piccoli comuni. Milano, 1969. pp. 425.

- Relations (general) with Africa

VEDOVATO (GIUSEPPE) Studi africani e asiatici. Firenze, [1964]. 3 vols. (Rivista di Studi Politici Internazionali. Biblioteca. Serie 3. N. 1-3)

- Relations (general) with the Balkan States

PACOR (MARIO) Italia e Balcani dal Risorgimento alla Resistenza. Milano, Feltrinelli, 1968. pp. 359. bibliog. 22cm.

- Relations (general) with Europe

Il RISORGIMENTO e l'Europa: (studi in onore di Alberto Maria Ghisalberti); a cura di Vittorio Frosini. Catania, 1969. pp. 349. (Isitituto per la Storia del Risorgimento Italiano. Comitato di Catania. Studi Risorgimentali. 7)

- Relations (general) with Latin America

CAVAZZA (FABIO LUCA) Italy and Latin America. Santa Monica, [1967]. pp. 91. (Rand Corporation. Memoranda. 5400)

- Relations (general) with Russia

KIROVA (KIRA EMANUILOVNA) Русская революция и Италия, март - октябрь 1917 г. Москва, 1968. pp. 328. bibliog.

ROSSIIA... Россия и Италия: из истории русско-итальянских культурных и общественных отношений. Москва, 1968. pp. 464.

KONFERENTSIIA SOVETSKIKH I ITAL'IANSKIKH ISTORIKOV, 3-aia, MOSKVA, 1968. Dokumenty sovetsko-ital'-ianskoi konferentsii istorikov, 8-10 aprelia 1968 goda: absoliutizm v Zapadnoi Evrope i Rossii; russko-ital'ianskie sviazi vo vtoroi polovine XIX veka. Moskva, 1970. pp. 374.

- Relations (general) with the United States

SYMPOSIUM DI STUDI AMERICANI, 2, FIRENZE, 1966. Italia e Stati Uniti nell'età del Risorgimento e della Guerra Civile: atti. Firenze, 1969. pp. 401. (Florence. Università degli Studi di Firenze. Istituto di Studi Americani. Pubblicazioni. 2)

- Relations (general) with Yugoslavia

RAPOTEC (VINKO) Praksa Italije s slovenci in hrvati, 1918-1940. Koper, 1952. pp. 76. bibliog. 21cm.

- Rural conditions

ITALY. Commissione Nazionale Italiana UNESCO. Convegno Italo-Svizzero, 1965. L'esodo rurale e lo spopolamento della montagna nella società contemporanea: atti del Convegno..., 24-26 maggio 1965. Milano, Società Editrice Vita e Pensiero, 1966. pp.xxiv, 337. bibliogs. 24cm.

COLCLOUGH (NEVILLE THOMAS) Land, politics and power in a southern Italian village; [Ph.D. (London) thesis]. 1969. fo. 222. bibliog. Typescript: unpublished. This thesis is the property of London University and may not be removed from the Library.

GIORIO (GIULIANO) Organizzazione di comunità, con particolare riferimento all'ambiente rurale italiano. Padova, 1969. pp. 319.

BENVENUTI (BRUNO) Cooperazione agricola e modernizzazione dell'agricoltura: indagine sociologica. Padova, 1970. pp. 258. (Istituto Federale delle Casse di Risparmio delle Venezie. Studi e Ricerche. 5)

- Sanitary affairs

ITALY. Istituto Centrale di Statistica. Note e Relazioni. N. 10. Indagine speciale su alcuni aspetti delle condizioni igieniche e sanitarie della popolazione. Roma, 1960 pp. 78. 26cm.

PICCININO (RENATO) I delitti contro la salute pubblica. Milano, 1968. pp. 394.

- Social conditions

ALBERTI (SALVATORE) Condizioni di abitazione e stati morbosi. Roma, 1958. pp. 56. 24cm. [with Italian, English, French and German summaries].

ITALY. Istituto Centrale di Statistica. Note e Relazioni. N.2. Indagine speciale su alcuni aspetti delle condizioni di vita della popolazione; (relazione del dott. Luigi Pinto). Roma, 1958. pp. 63. 26cm.

ZAPPA (G.) La questione meridionale: aspetti sociali e culturali. in Parisi (Achille) and Zappa (Goffredo) eds. Mezzogiorno e politica di piano. Bari, 1964.

GRAMSCI (ANTONIO) La questione meridionale; a cura di Franco De Felice e Valentino Parlato [Rome], Editori Riuniti, 1966. pp. 160. 18½cm. (Le Idee. 5)

DEMARCHI (FRANCO) Sociologia della provincia: relazione tenuta al Convegno di studi promosso dalla Democrazia Cristiana su "Realtà e prospettive dello sviluppo economico e sociale nella provincia isontina", Grado 16-17 settembre 1967. [Gorizia, 1967?] pp. 26. (Quadrante Est. Quaderni)

MARTINELLI (FRANCO) Introduzione ai problemi sociali della società italiana. Roma, 1967. pp. 136.

RETZLAFF (CHRISTINE) Kulturgeographische Wandlungen in der Maremma unter besonderer Berücksichtigung der italienischen Bodenreform nach dem Zweiten Weltkrieg. Kiel, Universität, Geographisches Institut, 1967. pp. 204. bibliog. 24cm. (Schriften. Band 27. Heft 2)

DAVIS (JOHN HORSLEY RUSSELL) Land tenure and social change in a South Italian town; [Ph. D. (London) thesis]. 1968. fo. vi, 284. bibliog. 25½cm. Map in end pocket. Typescript: unpublished. This thesis is the property of London University and may not be removed from the Library.

LIBERTINI (LUCIO) Integrazione capitalistica e sottosviluppo: i nuovi termini della questione meridionale. Bari, Laterza, [1968]. pp. 239. 18cm. (Tempi Nuovi. 3)

HYTTEN (EYVIND) Esperienze di sviluppo sociale nel mezzogiorno. Roma, 1969. pp. 189. (Associazione per lo Sviluppo dell'Industria nel Mezzogiorno. Centro per gli Studi sullo Sviluppo Economico. Collana Francesco Giordani)

JEMOLO (ARTURO CARLO) Anni di prova. Vicenza, 1969. pp. 266.

SPINOSA (ANTONIO) Come si vive in Italia oggi. [Bologna, 1969]. pp. 139.

ITALY. Consiglio Nazionale dell'Economia e del Lavoro. 1970. Rapporto sulla situazione sociale del paese; a cura del CENSIS, Centro Studi Investimenti Sociali. Milano, 1970. pp. 236.

PELLICCIARI (GIOVANNI) ed. L'immigrazione nel triangolo industriale: scritti di G. Albertelli [and others]. Milano, 1970. pp. 681. bibliog.

- Social conditions - Statistics

MIANI-CALABRESE (DONATO) Metodologia statistica e statistica di fenomeni sociali: appendice di aggiornamento. 2nd ed. Milano, 1969. pp. 173. bibliogs.

- Social history

CARACCIOLO (ALBERTO) Stato e società civile: problemi dell'unificazione italiana. 2nd ed. Torino, 1960. pp. 170. bibliog.

SOCIETÀ e costume: panorama di storia sociale e tecnologica. vol. 6. L'Italia nel Seicento e nel Settecento; ([by] Franco Valsecchi) Torino, UTET, 1967. pp. xi, 889. bibliog. 25½cm.

VILLANI (PASQUALE) Feudalità, riforme, capitalismo agrario: panorama di storia sociale italiana tra Sette e Ottocento. Bari, Laterza, 1968. pp. 173. 21½cm. (Biblioteca di Cultura Moderna. 642)

MOLHO (ANTHONY) ed. Social and economic foundations of the Italian renaissance. New York, [1969]. pp. 239. bibliog.

- Social life and customs

ETS (MARIE HALL) Rosa: the life of an Italian immigrant. Minneapolis, [1970]. pp. 254.

- Social policy

AMICIS (EDMONDO DE) Osservazioni sulla questione sociale: conferenza...detta...11 febbraio 1892 all'Associazione Universitaria Torinese. Torino, 1892. pp. 33. 22½cm.

ITALY. Statutes, etc. 1950-57. Current legislation on the Cassa per il Mezzogiorno; translation. Rome Cassa per il Mezzogiorno, 1958. fo. vi, 97.

SULLO (FIORENTINO) Il Comitato Centrale per la Previdenza e l'Assistenza Sociale. Roma, Ministero del Lavoro e della Previdenza Sociale, Rassegna del Lavoro, 1960. pp. 11. 27cm.

ITALY. Comitato dei Ministri per il Mezzogiorno Documenti. No. 5. Formazione professionale e attività sociali nel Mezzogiorno. Roma, 1961. pp. 47. 24½cm.

ITALY. Statutes, etc. 1950-61. Raccolta leggi: decreti e circolari riguardanti la Cassa per il Mezzogiorno. Napoli, 1961 [or rather 1962]. pp. xxvii, 363.

ITALY. Comitato dei Ministri per il Mezzogiorno. 1966. Piano di coordinamento degli interventi pubblici nel Mezzogiorno... 1 ottobre 1966-31 dicembre 1969. Roma, 1966. pp. 340.

FRANCE. Direction de la Documentation, La Documentation Française. Notes et Études Documentaires Nos. 3,537-3,538. Le plan économique italien, 1966-1970. Paris, 1968. pp. 84. 27cm.

CIAMPI (VITTORIO) Mezzogiorno perchè. [Naples, 1969]. pp. 285.

ITALY - Social policy (Cont'd.)

HYTTEN (EYVIND) Ed sperienze di sviluppo sociale nel mezzogiorno. Roma, 1969. pp. 189. (Associazione per lo Sviluppo dell'Industria nel Mezzogiorno. Centro per gli Studi sullo Sviluppo Economico. Coana Francesco Giordani)

ITALY. Comitato dei Ministri per il Mezzogiorno. 1969. Relazione sull'attuazione del piano di coordinamento degli interventi pubblici nel Mezzogiorno e sui provvedimenti per le aree depresse del Centro-Nord, etc. Roma, 1969. pp. 219.

STUDI per il ventesimo anniversario dell'Assemblea Costituente. Firenze, [1969]. 6 vols.

- Statistics

ASSOCIAZIONE PER LO SVILUPPO DELL'INDUSTRIA NEL MEZZOGIORNO. Statistics on southern Italy, 1861-1953. Rome, [1954?]. pp. 341.

ITALY. Istituto Centrale di Statistica. 1961. Cromografie statistiche dell'Italia: sintesi grafica dei dati contenuti nell'Annuario Statistico Italiano. [Rome, 1961]. fo.(75) 26½cm.

ITALY. Istituto Centrale di Statistica. 1961. Dal censimento dell'unità al censimenti del centenario: un secolo di vita della statistica italiana, 1861-1961; (testo di Roberto Fracassi). [Rome, 1961]. pp. 205. 22cm.

- Statistics, Vital

ITALY. Istituto Centrale di. Statistica. 1958. Cause di morte, 1887-1955. Roma, 1958. pp. 271. 26½cm.

ITALY. Istituto Centrale di Statistica. Note e Relazioni. N.7. Indagine campionaria sulla morbosità della popolazione italiana; (relazione del prof. Mario de Vergottini). Roma, 1959. pp. 57. 26cm.

BRUNO (VINCENZO) Evoluzione della mortalità per cause di morte nella prima metà del secolo XX in base alle tavole di mortalità del 1899-1902 e 1950-1953. Pisa, 1960. pp. 27. 24½cm.

- Yearbooks

ITALIA: annuario dell'economia, della politica, della cultura (formerly Annuario Politico Italiano); a cura del Centro Italiano di Ricerche e Documentazione. Milano, annual, 1963 [1st issue] to date. 24½cm.

ITSEKIRIS

IKIME (OBARO) Merchant prince of the Niger delta: the rise and fall of Nana Olomu, last Governor of the Benin River. London, Heinemann, 1968. pp. xiv, 218. 21½cm.

IKIME (OBARO) Niger delta rivalry: Itsekiri-Urhobo relations and the European presence, 1884-1936. London, 1969. pp. 301. bibliog.

ITTIHAD VE TERAKKI CEMIYETI
See YOUNG-TURKISH PARTY

ITURBIDE (AGUSTIN DE)

BARQUIN Y RUIZ (ANDRES) Agustin de Iturbide, campeon del hispanoamericanismo. Mexico, 1968. pp. 203.

IURUKOV (DANIIL)

IURUKOV (DANIIL) Спомени из политическия живот на България. София, 1932. pp. 276. Bound with the author's Брацигово, which see.

IUZHNOROSSIISKII SOIUZ RABOCHIKH

ITENBERG (B.) "Южнороссийский союз рабочих" - первая пролетарская организация в России. Москва, Госполитиздат, 1954. pp. 88. 20cm.

IVAN IV, Tsar of Russia

NOSOV (NIKOLAI EVGEN'EVICH) Становление сословно-представительных учреждений в России: изыскания о земской реформе Ивана Грозного. Ленинград, 1969. pp. 601. With English table of contents.

IVANENKO (VASILII IVANOVICH)

IVANENKO (VASILII IVANOVICH) Тропою памяти. Москва, 1968. pp. 120.

IVANO-FRANKOVSK (OBLAST')

- Statistics

IVANO-FRANKOVSK (OBLAST'). Statystychne Upravlinnia. Народне господарство Івано-Франківської області в 1967 році: статистичний збірник. Львів, 1968. pp. 149.

IVANOV (AMANGEL'DY)

NURKANOV (AIAP) Народный батыр. Москва, Госполитиздат, 1962. pp. 64. 20cm.

IVANOVO

- History

CHERNOVA (E. I.) Иванововознесенский пролетариат - создатель одного из первых Советов рабочих депутатов. Москва, Профиздат, 1955. pp. 76. 20cm.

- Politics and government

ISTORIIA... История Ивановской городской партийной организации: научно-теоретическая конференция. Иваново, 1967. pp. 173. 16½см.

IVANOVO (OBLAST')

- Economic history - Sources

VOSSTANOVLENIE tekstil'noi promyshlennosti Ivanovo-Voznesenskoi gubernii, 1920-1925 gg.: sbornik dokumentov i materialov. Ivanovo, 1966. pp. 264.

- History

VSEOBSHCHAIA... Всеобщая стачка Иваново-Вознесенских рабочих в 1905 году: сборник документов и материалов. Иваново, Книжное Издательство, 1955. pp. 261. 20см.

- History - Sources

> KOMMUNISTICHESKAIA PARTIIA SOVETSKOGO SOIUZA. Ivanovskii Oblastnoi Komitet. Partiinyi Arkhiv. Листовки Иваново-Вознесенской большевистской организации, 1900-1917 гг. Иваново, Книжное Издательство, 1957. pp. 217. 20см.

-Politics and government

> OCHERKI... Очерки истории Ивановской организации КПСС. ч.2. 1917-1967. Ярославль, Верхне-Волжское Книжное Издательство, 1967. pp. 516.

- Rural conditions

> SHAKHANOV (N. P.) Krest'ianskoe dvizhenie na territorii I[vanovskoi] P[romyshlennoi] O[blasti]. Ivanovo, 1931. pp. 89. bibliog.

IVENS (JORIS)

> MEYER (HAN) Joris Ivens, de weg naar Vietnam. Utrecht, 1970. pp. 260.

IVORY COAST

- Colonization

> BINDER-KRAUTHOFF (KRISTINE) Phasen der Entkolonialisierung: eine Analyse kolonialpolitischer Relikte in Afrika...in Ghana und in der Elfenbeinküste. Berlin, [1970]. pp. 185. bibliog.

- Economic conditions

> FRANCE. Direction de la Documentation. La Documentation Française. Notes et Études Documentaires. No. 3,308. La République de Côte d'Ivoire. Paris, 1966. pp. 51. bibliog. 30½cm.

> UNITED STATES. International Commerce Bureau. A market for U.S. products in the Ivory Coast. Washington, 1966. pp. viii, 86. bibliog.

> IVORY COAST. Ministère du Plan. Direction des Études de Développement. 1969. Les comptes de la nation, 1966-1967. [Abidjan, 1969]. 3 vols.(in one). 31cm.

> IVORY COAST. Ministère du Plan. Direction des Études de Développement. 1969. Les comptes de la nation: comptes provisoires, 1968. [Abidjan], 1969. fo. 52. 31cm.

- Politics and government

> COMITÉ NATIONAL POUR LA LIBÉRATION DE LA CÔTE D'IVOIRE. La situation politique en Côte d'Ivoire et l'indépendance nationale. Conakry, [1959]. pp. 40. 20½cm.

> FRANCE. Direction de la Documentation. La Documentation Française. Notes et Études Documentaires. No. 3,308. La République de Côte d'Ivoire. Paris, 1966. pp. 51. bibliog. 30½cm.

> ZOLBERG (ARISTIDE R.) One-party government in the Ivory Coast. rev. ed. Princeton, 1969. pp. 400. bibliog.

- Population

> IVORY COAST. Ministère du Plan. 1967. Population: études régionales 1962-1965, synthèse; rédigée par Louis Roussel. Abidjan, 1967. pp. 208. bibliog. 27cm.

- Social conditions

> FRANCE. Direction de la Documentation. La Documentation Française. Notes et Études Documentaires. No. 3,308. La République de Côte d'Ivoire. Paris, 1966. pp. 51. bibliog. 30½cm.

- Statistics

> GERMANY (BUNDESREPUBLIK). Statistisches Bundesamt. Länderkurzberichte: Elfenbeinküste. Wiesbaden, irreg., 1969 [1st issue] to date. 29½cm.

IXIL INDIANS

> COLBY (BENJAMIN N.) and VAN DEN BERGHE (PIERRE LOUIS) Ixil country: a plural society in highland Guatemala. Berkeley, 1969. pp. 218. bibliog.

IYENGAR (KASTURI RANGA)

> NARASIMHAN (V.K.) Kasturi Ranga Iyengar;... with a foreword by C.P. Ramaswami Aiyar. Delhi, 1963. pp. 239. (Builders of Modern India)

IZQUIERDA NACIONAL
See PARTIDO SOCIALISTA DE LA IZQUIERDA NACIONAL

JABŁOŃSKI (HENRYK)

- Bibliography

> NARÓD i państwo; prace ofiarowane Henrykowi Jabłońskiemu w 60 rocznicę urodzin. Warszawa, 1969. pp. 434.

JACKSON (ANDREW) President of the United States

> GATELL (FRANK OTTO) ed. The Jacksonians and the money power, 1829-1840. Chicago, [1967]. pp. 59.

> REMINI (ROBERT VINCENT) Andrew Jackson and the Bank War: a study in the growth of presidential power. New York, Norton, [1967]. pp. 192. bibliog. 20½cm. (Norton Essays in American History)

> COLE (DONALD BARNARD) Jacksonian democracy in New Hampshire, 1800-1851. Cambridge, Mass., 1970. pp. 283. bibliog.

> VAN DEUSEN (GLYNDON GARLOCK) The rise and decline of Jacksonian democracy;... [with readings]. New York, [1970]. pp. 262. bibliog.

JACKSON (GEORGE LESTER)

> JACKSON (GEORGE LESTER) Soledad brother: the prison letters of George Jackson; introduction by Jean Genet. London, 1971. pp. 290.

JACOBINS

REVUNENKOV (VLADIMIR GEORGIEVICH) Marksizm i problema iakobinskoi diktatury: istoriograficheskii ocherk. Leningrad, 1966. pp. 176.

SOBOUL (ALBERT) Paysans, sans-culottes et Jacobins. Paris, Clavreuil, [1966]. pp. 387. 22½cm.

GRAB (WALTER) Norddeutsche Jakobiner: demokratische Bestrebungen zur Zeit der französischen Revolution. Hamburg, Europäische Verlagsanstalt, [1967]. pp. 139. bibliog. 20½cm. (Hamburger Studien zur Neueren Geschichte. Band 8)

WANGERMANN (ERNST) From Joseph II to the Jacobin trials: government policy and public opinion in the Habsburg dominions in the period of the French revolution. 2nd ed. London, 1969. pp. 218. bibliog.

WOLOCH (ISSER) Jacobin legacy: the democratic movement under the Directory. Princeton, 1970. pp. 455. bibliog.

JACOBINS, ENGLISH
See RADICALISM IN THE UNITED KINGDOM

JACOBITES

A JACOBITE narrative of the war in Ireland, 1688-1691; [ascribed to Nicholas Plunket]; ([edited by] John T. Gilbert); [reprint of the work first published in Dublin in 1892, with an] introduction by J.G. Simms. Shannon, [1971]. pp. 328.

GREENWOOD (DAVID) William King: Tory and Jacobite. Oxford, 1969. pp. 386. bibliog.

JAHN (FRIEDRICH LUDWIG)

STOECKER (GERHARD) Friedrich Ludwig Jahn und das Problem der Volkserziehung. Köln, 1966. pp. 350. bibliog. 20½cm.

JAIPUR

- Economic conditions

MATHUR (M.V.) and others. Economic survey of Jaipur city. Jaipur, [1965?]. pp. 97,vi.

JAKSCH (WENZEL)

JAUERNIG (EDMUND) Sozialdemokratie und Revanchismus: zur Geschichte und Politik Wenzel Jakschs und der Seliger-Gemeinde. Berlin, 1968. pp. 291. bibliog.

JAM

UNITED KINGDOM. Social Survey. 1944. Jam buying; by Gertrude Wagner. [mimeographed]. n.p. 1944. pp. 5. 33cm.

JAMAICA

[LESLIE (CHARLES) of Jamaica] A new and exact account of Jamaica. wherein the antient and present state of that colony, its importance to Great Britain, laws, trade, manners and religion...; are described with a particular account of the sacrifices, libations, etc. at this day in use among the negroes. Edinburgh, Kincaid, 1739. pp. (iii), ii, 358. 17cm.

- Biography

WHO'S who in Jamaica 1963;...edited by Clifton Neita. Kingston, 1963. pp. 430.

- Census

FRANCIS (O.C.) The people of modern Jamaica: [a study summarizing and commenting on the main results of the 1960 census]. [Kingston], Department of Statistics, [1963?]. pp. various.

JAMAICA. Census, 1970. Population census, 1970: preliminary report. Kingston, [1970]. pp. 33.

- Commerce

JAMAICA. Industrial Development Corporation. Information Pamphlets. No.12. Jamaica in world trade. Kingston, 1961. fo.8. 28cm.

JAMAICA. Department of Statistics. 1966. Indices of external trade, 1965. Kingston, [1966?]. pp. 11.

- Description and travel

JAMAICA. Industrial Development Corporation. Information Pamphlets. No.13. Moving to Jamaica. Kingston, 1961. fo.17. 28cm.

- Economic conditions

EVES (C. WASHINGTON) Jamaica and the Royal Jubilee Exhibition Liverpool 1887. London, 1887. pp. 91.

FRANCIS (O.C.) The people of modern Jamaica: [a study summarizing and commenting on the main results of the 1960 census]. [Kingston], Department of Statistics, [1963?]. pp. various.

PALMER (RANSFORD W.) The Jamaican economy. New York, Praeger, 1968. pp. xvii, 185. bibliog. 23½cm. (Praeger Special Studies in International Economics and Development)

WALSH (B. THOMAS) Economic development and population control: a fifty-year projection for Jamaica. New York, 1971. pp. 134. bibliogs.

- Economic history

JAMAICA. Industrial Development Corporation. Office of Economic Research. 1962. A review of industrial development in Jamaica. rev. ed Kingston, 1962. fo. (51). 28cm. Xerox copy.

- Economic policy

JAMAICA. 1946. A ten-year plan of development for Jamaica: (third draft). Kingston, 1946. pp. 63.

JAMAICA. 1951. Report on the revision of the ten-year plan of development for Jamaica; as approved by the House of Representatives on 28th November, 1951. Kingston, 1951. pp. 28.

JAMAICA. 1963. Five year independence plan, 1963-1968: a long term development programme for Jamaica. [Kingston, 1963]. pp. (ix), 241.

- Foreign relations

> GREEN (IRENE) The effects of the population explosion on Jamaica's international relations. Johannesburg, South African Institute of International Affairs, 1966. pp. 85. bibliog. 22cm.

- History

> BRIDGES (GEORGE WILSON) The annals of Jamaica; [facsimile reprint of the first edition of 1828] London, Cass, 1968. 2 vols. 21½cm. (Cass Library of West Indian Studies. 1)

- History - Maroon War, 1795-1796

> ROBINSON (CAREY) The fighting Maroons of Jamaica. [Kingston], 1969. pp. 160. bibliog.

- Industries

> JAMAICA. Industrial Development Corporation. Information Pamphlets. No.1. Opportunities for industrial investment. Kingston, 1961. fo. 13. 28cm.

> JAMAICA. Industrial Development Corporation. Information Pamphlets. No.2. Starting and operating an industrial enterprise in Jamaica. Kingston, 1961. fo. 14. 28cm.

> JAMAICA. Industrial Development Corporation. Information Pamphlets. No.3. Industrial incentive laws. Kingston, 1961. fo. 10. 28cm.

> JAMAICA. Industrial Development Corporation. Office of Economic Research. 1962. A review of industrial development in Jamaica. rev. ed Kingston, 1962. fo. (51). 28cm. Xerox copy.

> JAMAICA. Industrial Development Corporation. Office of Economic Research. 1962. Statistical report of manufacturing enterprises operating under industrial incentive laws. Kingston, 1962. fo. iii, 26. 28cm. Xerox copy.

> JAMAICA. Department of Statistics. 1963. Industrial activity: mining, manufacture, construction, 1960: report on a survey of establishments. Kingston, [1963]. pp. xiv, 275. 27½cm.

> JAMAICA. Department of Statistics. Employment Statistics Unit. 1966. Employment and earnings in large establishments, 1963-64. Kingston, [1966]. pp. 198.

> JAMAICA. Department of Statistics. Economic Accounts Section. 1970. Cost, output and investment survey programme: vol. 2.1: production costs and output in large establishments: manufacturing (provisional report), 1964. Kingston, [1970]. pp. 238.

> JAMAICA. Department of Statistics. Economic Accounts Section. 1971. Cost, output and investment survey programme: vol. 1.2: summary of liabilities and assets in private non-corporate establishments, 1964-66. Kingston, [1971]. pp. 107.

- Parliament

> JAMAICA. 1964. 300 years of parliamentary tradition in Jamaica, 1664-1964. [Kingston, 1964]. pp. 36. 15cm x 23cm.

- Parliament - Elections

> JAMAICA. 1967. General election results. London, 1967. pp. 6. From Jamaica Monthly Newsletter, March 1967.

- Politics and government

> NETTLEFORD (REX) Manley and the politics of Jamaica: towards an analysis of political change in Jamaica, 1938-1968. Mona, Jamaica, 1971. pp. 72. (Social and Economic Studies. Supplements)

- Population

> FRANCIS (O.C.) The people of modern Jamaica: [a study summarizing and commenting on the main results of the 1960 census]. [Kingston], Department of Statistics, [1963?]. pp. various.

> GREEN (IRENE) The effects of the population explosion on Jamaica's international relations. Johannesburg, South African Institute of International Affairs, 1966. pp. 85. bibliog. 22cm.

> TEKSE (KALMAN) Internal migration in Jamaica. [Kingston], 1967. pp. v, 42. bibliog. 28cm.

> WALSH (B. THOMAS) Economic development and population control: a fifty-year projection for Jamaica. New York, 1971. pp. 134. bibliogs.

- Race question

> HENRIQUES (LOUIS FERNANDO) Family and colour in Jamaica. 2nd ed. London, MacGibbon and Kee, 1968. pp. 208. bibliog. 22cm.

- Social conditions

> FRANCIS (O.C.) The people of modern Jamaica: [a study summarizing and commenting on the main results of the 1960 census]. [Kingston], Department of Statistics, [1963?]. pp. various.

> HENRIQUES (LOUIS FERNANDO) Family and colour in Jamaica. 2nd ed. London, MacGibbon and Kee, 1968. pp. 208. bibliog. 22cm.

- Social history

> BRATHWAITE (EDWARD) The development of Creole society in Jamaica, 1770-1820. Oxford, 1971. pp. 374. bibliog.

- Social policy

> JAMAICA. 1963. Five year independence plan, 1963-1968: a long term development programme for Jamaica. [Kingston, 1963]. pp. (ix), 241.

> MAU (JAMES A.) Social change and images of the future: (a study of the pursuit of progress in Jamaica). Cambridge, Mass., [1968]. pp. 145.

- Statistics

> GERMANY (BUNDESREPUBLIK). Statistisches Bundesamt. Länderkurzberichte: Jamaika. Wiesbaden, irreg., 1969 [1st issue] to date. 29½cm.

JAMAL (HAKIM ABDULLAH)

> JAMAL (HAKIM ABDULLAH) From the dead level: Malcolm X and me. London, 1971. pp. 240.

JAMES I., King of Great Britain and Ireland

EGLISHAM (GEORGE) The fore-runner of revenge; being two petitions: the one to the Kings most excellent Majesty; the other to the most honourables [sic] Houses of Parliament; wherein is expressed divers actions of the late Earle of Buckingham, etc. London, 1642. pp. (16). 19cm.

JAMES (RICHARD)

LARIN (BORIS ALEKSANDROVICH) Русско-английский словарь-дневник Ричарда Джемса, 1618-1619 гг. Ленинград, 1959. pp. 423.

JAMES (WILLIAM)

AYER (ALFRED JULES) The origins of pragmatism: studies in the philosophy of Charles Sanders, Peirce and William James. London, Macmillan, 1968. pp. 347. 21½cm.

WILSHIRE (BRUCE) William James and phenomenology: a study of "The principles of psychology". Bloomington, Indiana U.P., 1968. pp. xi, 251. bibliog. 23½cm.

WILD (JOHN DANIEL) The radical empiricism of William James. Garden City, N.Y., 1969. pp. 430. bibliog.

EISENDRATH (CRAIG R.) The unifying moment: the psychological philosophy of William James and Alfred North Whitehead. Cambridge, Mass., 1971. pp. 290.

JAMESON (WILLIAM WILSON)

GOODMAN (NEVILLE MARRIOTT) Wilson Jameson: architect of national health. London, 1970. pp. 216. bibliogs.

JAMESON'S RAID, 1895-1896

BUTLER (JEFFREY ERNEST) The Liberal Party and the Jameson raid. Oxford, Clarendon P., 1968. pp. xii, 336. bibliog. 21½cm.

JAMESTOWN

- History - Sources

BARBOUR (PHILIP L.) ed. The Jamestown voyages under the first charter, 1606-1609. Cambridge, 1969. 2 vols. (Hakluyt Society. Works. Second Series. No. 136)

JAMMU AND KASHMIR

- Constitution

JAMMU AND KASHMIR. Ministry of Information. 1953. India and Kashmir: constitutional aspect. [New Delhi, 1953?]. pp. 23.

JAMMU AND KASHMIR. Constitution. 1956-61. The constitution of Jammu and Kashmir; (with the constitution of Jammu and Kashmir, first (and second, and third) amendment Act, 1959(-61). [Srinagar, 1956-[61]]. pp. 71,(6).

JAMMU AND KASHMIR. Constitution. 1956. The constitution of Jammu and Kashmir. rev. ed. [Srinagar], 1957. pp. 112.

- Economic conditions

JAMMU AND KASHMIR. Ministry of Information. 1953. Five years: [1951-52 to 1955-56]. [New Delhi, 1953] pp. 31.

JAMMU AND KASHMIR. Ministry of Information. 1953. Jammu and Kashmir today. [Srinagar, 1953]. pp. 56.

NATIONAL COUNCIL OF APPLIED ECONOMIC RESEARCH. Techno-economic survey of Jammu and Kashmir. New Delhi, [1969]. pp. 268.

- Economic policy

JAMMU AND KASHMIR. Prime Minister. 1953. Kashmir averts national disaster: Bakhshi Ghulam Mohammad's call to people...on August 9, 1953, from Radio Kashmir, Srinagar. [Srinagar, 1953]. pp. 16.

JAMMU AND KASHMIR. Prime Minister. 1955. Aid from India: text of the speech of...Bakhshi Ghulam Mohammed [sic]...in the State Assembly on March 17, 1955. Srinagar, 1955. pp. 7. (Kashmir Today Series. 2)

- History

DAS GUPTA (JYOTI BHUSAN) Jammu and Kashmir. The Hague, Nijhoff, 1968. pp. xiv, 428. bibliog.

- Politics and government

JAMMU AND KASHMIR. Ministry of Information. 1953. Five years: [1951-52 to 1955-56]. [New Delhi, 1953] pp. 31.

JAMMU AND KASHMIR. Ministry of Information. 1953. Unanimous vote of confidence in Bakshi government: an account of the proceedings of the state legislature on the motion of confidence in Bakshi government adopted on 5th October, 1953. [Srinagar, 1953]. pp. 44.

JAMMU AND KASHMIR. Prime Minister. 1953. Kashmir averts national disaster: Bakhshi Ghulam Mohammad's call to people...on August 9, 1953, from Radio Kashmir, Srinagar. [Srinagar, 1953]. pp. 16.

JAMMU AND KASHMIR. Prime Minister. 1955. A reply to critics: text of the speech of...Bakhshi Ghulam Mohammed...in the State Assembly on March 5, 1955. Srinagar, [1955]. pp. 9. (Kashmir today Series. 1)

JAMMU AND KASHMIR. Prime Minister. 1955. Report on general administration: text of the speech of Bakhshi Ghulam Mohammad...in the State Assembly on March 19, 1955. Srinagar, 1955. pp. 9. (Kashmir Today Series. 3)

- Social conditions

JAMMU AND KASHMIR. Ministry of Information. 1953. Five years: [1951-52 to 1955-56]. [New Delhi, 1953] pp. 31.

JAMMU AND KASHMIR. Ministry of Information. 1953. Jammu and Kashmir today. [Srinagar, 1953]. pp. 56.

JAN SANGH
See JANA SANGH

JANA SANGH

BAXTER (CRAIG) The Jana Sangh: a biography of an Indian political party. Philadelphia, [1969]. pp. 352. bibliog.

KISHORE (MOHAMMED ALI) Jana Sangh and India's foreign policy. New Delhi, [1969]. pp. 248. bibliog.

JANSENISTS

BENEDIKT (H.) Der Josephinismus vor Joseph II. in Institut für Österreichische Geschichtsforschung and Vienna. Katholische Akademie. Österreich und Europa. Graz, 1965.

JANSEN (P.) Attachée de recherches au C.N.R.S. Le Cardinal Mazarin et le mouvement janséniste français, 1653-1659; d'après les documents inédits conservés dans les archives du Ministère des Affaires Étrangères. Paris, Vrin, 1967. pp. 274. bibliog. 22½cm. (Société d'Histoire Ecclésiastique de la France. Bibliothèque)

ADAM (ANTOINE) Du mysticisme à la révolte: les jansénistes du XVIIe siècle. [Paris], Fayard, [1968]. pp. 349. bibliog. 21½cm. (L'Histoire sans Frontières)

BOLTON (CHARLES A.) Church reform in 18th century Italy: the Synod of Pistoia, 1786. The Hague, 1969. pp. 162. bibliog.

JAPAN

UNITED STATES. Army Department. Pamphlets. No. 550/30. U[nited] S[tates] army area handbook for Japan. 2nd ed. Washington, 1964. pp. xi, 820. bibliogs.

VAHLEFELD (HANS WILHELM) 100 Millionen Aussenseiter: die neue Weltmacht Japan. Düsseldorf, 1969. pp. 334. bibliog.

- Bibliography

WENCKSTERN (ADOLPH VON) compiler. A bibliography of the Japanese Empire: being a classified list of all books, essays and maps in European languages... published...from 1859-93; [a reprint of the work first published in 1895]; to which is added a...reprint of Leon Pages, Bibliographie japonaise depuis le XVe siècle jusqu'à 1859; [first published in 1859]. Stuttgart, 1970. pp. 338, 68.

HARVARD UNIVERSITY. Library. Widener Library Shelflists. [No]. 14. China, Japan and Korea. Cambridge, Harvard U.P., 1968. pp. 494. 28cm.

- Census

JAPAN. Census, 1965. 1965 population census of Japan. vol.5. [Tokyo, 1969]. 2 vols. Vols.1-4 out of print. Vol.6 not acquired. In English and Japanese.

JAPAN. Census, 1970. 1970 population census of Japan: [volume series]. [Tokyo, 1971 in progress]. In English and Japanese.

- Civilization

BRAMELD (THEODORE BURGHARD HURT) Japan: culture, education, and change in two communities. New York, Holt, [1968]. pp. xx, 316. bibliog. 22½cm.

PYLE (KENNETH B.) The new generation in Meiji Japan: problems of cultural identity, 1885-1895. Stanford, 1969. pp. 240. bibliog.

KAHN (HERMAN) The emerging Japanese superstate: challenge and response. London, 1971. pp. 274. bibliog.

- Civilization - Occidental influences

GOODMAN (GRANT KOHN) The Dutch impact on Japan, 1640-1853. Leiden, Brill, 1967. pp. ix, 242. bibliog. 25½cm. (Monographies du T'oung Pao. vol. 5)

KEENE (DONALD) The Japanese discovery of Europe, 1720-1830. rev. ed. Stanford, Calif., 1969. pp. 255. bibliog.

HAVENS (THOMAS R.H.) Nishi Amane and modern Japanese thought. Princeton, 1970. pp. 253. bibliog.

- Commerce

JAPAN. 1960. Exports and wages: the case of Japan. (Ministry of Foreign Affairs) [Tokyo], 1960. pp. 20. 23½cm.

WATANABE (AKIHIKO) L'économie japonaise et la C.E.E. Nancy, Université, Centre Européen Universitaire, 1964. pp. viii, 76. bibliog. 24cm. (Collection des Mémoires. No. 9)

HOLLERMAN (LEON) Japan's dependence on the world economy: the approach toward economic liberalization. Princeton, Princeton U.P., 1967. pp. xv, 291. 21½cm.

ALLEN (GEORGE CYRIL) Japan's place in trade strategy: larger role in Pacific region. London, Atlantic Trade Study, 1968. pp. vi, 62. 21½cm.

CORBET (HUGH) ed. Trade strategy and the Asian-Pacific region. London, 1970. pp. 221.

FRANCE. Direction de la Documentation. La Documentation Française. Notes et Études Documentaires. Nos.3,651-3,652. Les méthodes et l'expansion du commerce extérieur au Japon. Paris, 1970. pp. 70. bibliog.

GUILLAIN (ROBERT) The Japanese challenge;...translated from the French by Patrick O'Brian. London, 1970. pp. 345. bibliog.

YOSHINO (M.Y.) The Japanese marketing system: adaptations and innovations. Cambridge, Mass., [1971]. pp. 319. bibliog.

- Commerce - Australia

COMMITTEE FOR ECONOMIC DEVELOPMENT OF AUSTRALIA. Discussions with an industrial mission from the International Management Association of Japan; memorandum for the information of trustees. Melbourne, 1968. fo. (23). 26cm. x 20½cm.

- Commerce - Netherlands

DEKKER (F.). De betrekkingen tusschen de Oost-Indische Compagnie en Japan. 'S-Gravenhage, Boucher, 1941. pp. 128. 23cm.

JAPAN (Cont'd.)

- Commerce - New Zealand

CASTLE (L.V.) and McDOUGALL (I.) Japan as a market for New Zealand exports of meat and dairy products. [Wellington], 1969. pp. 43. (New Zealand Institute of Economic Research. Research Papers. No. 14)

- Commerce - Siam

KULTHONGKHAM (SAWAENG) Report on the Japan market for Thai agricultural products. Bangkok, Division of Agricultural Economics, Ministry of Agriculture, [1958] pp. (33), 21. $26\frac{1}{2}$cm. In English and Thai.

- Commerce - Switzerland

NAKAI (PAUL AKIO) Das Verhältnis zwischen der Schweiz und Japan: vom Beginn der diplomatischen Beziehungen 1859 bis 1868. Bern, Haupt, [1967]. pp. x, 150 bibliog. $22\frac{1}{2}$cm.

- Commerce - United States

UNITED STATES. International Commerce Bureau. Doing business in Japan. Washington, [1963]. pp. 16.

LYNCH (JOHN) Ph.D. Toward an orderly market: an intensive study of Japan's voluntary quota in cotton textile exports. Tokyo, 1968. pp. 215. bibliog.

- Commercial policy

KOJIMA (KIYOSHI) Japan and a Pacific Free Trade Area. London, 1971. pp. 195.

- Commercial treaties - Australia

AUSTRALIA. 1963. Agreement on commerce between Australia and Japan: 1963 revision. in Australia Parliamentary papers, 1962-63, vol. 7.

- Constitution

HENDERSON (DAN FENNO) ed. The constitution of Japan: its first twenty years, 1947-67. Seattle, [1968]. pp. 323. (Seattle. University of Washington. School of Law. Asian Law Series. No. 1)

KEVENHOERSTER (PAUL) Das politische System Japans. Köln, 1969. pp. 330. bibliog.

- Constitutional law

MINEAR (RICHARD H.) Japanese tradition and Western law: emperor, state and law in the thought of Hozumi Yatsuka. Cambridge, Mass., 1970. pp. 244. bibliog. (Harvard University. East Asian Research Center. Harvard East Asian Series. 48)

- Defences

JAPAN. Defense Agency. Public Information Office. 1958. Defense strength of Japan. [Tokyo], 1958. pp. 22.

WEINSTEIN (MARTIN E.) Japan's postwar defense policy, 1947-1968. New York, 1971. pp. 158. bibliog. (Columbia University. East Asian Institute. Studies)

- Economic conditions

JAPAN SCIENCE REVIEW, THE: Economic Sciences; [pd. by] Japan Union of Associations of Economic Sciences. irreg., 1953-1964 (nos. 1-10). Tokyo.

JAPAN. 1961. The income-doubling plan and the growing Japanese economy. (Ministry of Foreign Affairs) [Tokyo], 1961. pp. 19. 23cm.

ECONOMIST INTELLIGENCE UNIT. The Japanese economy: a survey prepared for the F.B.I. London, Federation of British Industries, 1962. pp. vi, 126. $21\frac{1}{2}$cm.

JAPAN. 1963. Development of the Japanese economy after World War II. (Ministry of Foreign Affairs) Tokyo, 1963. pp. 32. 24cm.

JAPAN. 1963. The growth of the national economies of Japan and the Soviet Union: a comparison of economic growth rate. (Ministry of Foreign Affairs) [Tokyo], 1963. pp. viii, 45. 24cm.

DEMPSTER (PRUE) Japan advances: a geographical study. London, 1967. pp. 329. bibliog.

HOLLERMAN (LEON) Japan's dependence on the world economy: the approach toward economic liberalization. Princeton, Princeton U.P., 1967. pp. xv, 291. $21\frac{1}{2}$cm.

KIGA (KENZO) Characteristics of Japan's economic growth. Budapest, Hungarian Academy of Sciences, Center for Afro-Asian Research, 1968. pp. 32. $23\frac{1}{2}$cm. (Studies on Developing Countries. No.18)

LOCKWOOD (WILLIAM WIRT) The economic development of Japan: growth and structural change. 2nd ed. Princeton, Princeton U.P., 1968. pp. xv, 686. 20cm.

PEZEU-MASSABUAU (JACQUES) Géographie du Japon. Paris, Presses Universitaires de France, 1968. pp. 128. bibliog. $17\frac{1}{2}$cm. ("Que Sais-Je?". № 1292)

DEMPSTER (PRUE) Japan advances: a geographical study. 2nd ed. London, 1969. pp. 332. bibliog.

GIEBEL (J.) Japan 1968: een economische oriëntatie. 's-Gravenhage, Staatsuitgeverij, 1969. pp. 93.

SCHARNAGL (WILFRIED) Japan: die konzentrierte Aggression. München, [1969]. pp. 275. bibliog.

STONE (PETER B.) Japan surges ahead: Japan's economic rebirth. London, Weidenfeld & Nicolson, [1969]. pp. xiv, 206. bibliog. $21\frac{1}{2}$cm.

BIEDA (KEN) The structure and operation of the Japanese economy. Sydney. [1970]. pp. 292.

GUILLAIN (ROBERT) The Japanese challenge;...translated from the French by Patrick O'Brian. London, 1970. pp. 345. bibliog.

INTERNATIONAL CONFERENCE ON AGRICULTURE AND ECONOMIC DEVELOPMENT, TOKYO, 1967. Agriculture and economic growth: Japan's experience; edited by Kazushi Ohkawa, Bruce F. Johnston, [and] Hiromitsu Kaneda. [Tokyo], 1970. pp. 433.

SHINOHARA (MIYOHEI) Structural changes in Japan's economic development. Tokyo, 1970. pp. 445. (Tokyo. Hitotsubashi University. Institute of Economic Research. Economic Research Series. No. 11)

YAO (JIRO) ed. Monetary factors in Japanese economic growth. Kobe, [1970]. pp. 241. (Kobe. University. Research Institute for Economics and Business Administration. Kobe Economic and Business Research Series. No. 3)

KAHN (HERMAN) The emerging Japanese superstate: challenge and response. London, 1971. pp. 274. bibliog.

KURIHARA (KENNETH K.) The growth potential of the Japanese economy. Baltimore, [1971]. pp. 148. bibliog.

- Economic conditions - Mathematical models

JAPAN. Economic Research Institute. Economic Bulletins. No. 15. Econometric analysis of postwar business cycles in Japan. Tokyo, 1967. pp. 55. bibliog.

- Economic history

IKITA (S.) Saving and economic growth in post war Japan. in Sinha (Manas Ranjan) ed. The problem of world liquidity and other essays. Bombay, 1964. pp. vi, 114.

INTERNATIONAL CONFERENCE ON ECONOMIC GROWTH, TOKYO, 1966. Economic growth: the Japanese experience since the Meiji era; proceedings of the conference of the Japan Economic Research Center; edited by Lawrence Klein and Kazushi Ohkawa. Homewood, Irwin, 1968. pp. xv, 424. 21½cm. (Yale University. Economic Growth Center. Publications)

LOCKWOOD (WILLIAM WIRT) The economic development of Japan: growth and structural change. 2nd ed. Princeton, Princeton U.P., 1968. pp. xv, 686. 20cm.

TSURU (SHIGETO) Essays on economic development. Tokyo, Kinokuniya, 1968. pp. vi, 257. 21cm. (Tokyo. Hitotsubashi University. Institute of Economic Research. Economic Research Series. No. 9)

TAKAHASHI (KAMEKICHI) The rise and development of Japan's modern economy: the basis for "miraculous" growth. Tokyo, [1969]. pp. 389.

- Economic policy

NAKAYAMA (SOHEI) Japan's economy is turning toward a new direction. New York, 1965. pp. 4. (Reprinted from The Commercial and Financial Chronicle. September 23, 1965)

HOLLERMAN (LEON) Japan's dependence on the world economy: the approach toward economic liberalization. Princeton, Princeton U.P., 1967. pp. xv, 291. 21½cm.

JAPAN. Economic Planning Agency. 1967. Economic and social development plan, 1967-1971. [Tokyo], 1967. pp. (vii), 199. 25½cm.

DIMOCK (MARSHALL EDWARD) The Japanese technocracy: management and government in Japan. New York, 1968. pp. 197. bibliog.

IDEMITSU (SAZO) If Karl Marx had been born in Japan. n.p., [1968?]. pp. (v), 140. 25½cm.

KIGA (KENZO) Characteristics of Japan's economic growth. Budapest, Hungarian Academy of Sciences, Center for Afro-Asian Research, 1968. pp. 32. 23½cm. (Studies on Developing Countries. No.18)

LOCKWOOD (WILLIAM WIRT) The economic development of Japan: growth and structural change. 2nd ed. Princeton, Princeton U.P., 1968. pp. xv, 686. 20cm.

TSURU (SHIGETO) Essays on economic development. Tokyo, Kinokuniya, 1968. pp. vi, 257. 21cm. (Tokyo. Hitotsubashi University. Institute of Economic Research. Economic Research Series. No. 9)

MADDISON (ANGUS) Economic growth in Japan and the U.S.S.R. London, Allen & Unwin, 1969. pp. xxviii, 174. bibliog. 21½cm.

BIEDA (KEN) The structure and operation of the Japanese economy. Sydney. [1970]. pp. 292.

GRIMM (HERMANN O.) Die Grundlagen der japanischen Einfuhr ausländischer Technologie. Köln, 1970. pp. 229. bibliog. (Aachen. Technische Hochschule. Forschungsinstitut für Internationale Technisch-Wirtschaftliche Zusammenarbeit. Internationale Kooperation. 4)

IKEDA (KOTARO) and others. Die industrielle Entwicklung in Japan unter besonderer Berücksichtigung seiner Wirtschafts- und Finanzpolitik. Berlin, [1970]. pp. 234.

YAO (JIRO) ed. Monetary factors in Japanese economic growth. Kobe, [1970]. pp. 241. (Kobe. University. Research Institute for Economics and Business Administration. Kobe Economic and Business Research Series. No. 3)

LOERCHER (SIEGFRIED) Wirtschaftsplanung in Japan 1955-1969: ein Beitrag zur Theorie staatlicher Makroplanung. Göppingen, 1971. pp. 183. bibliog.

- Foreign economic relations

ORGANISATION FOR ECONOMIC CO-OPERATION AND DEVELOPMENT. 1963. Mémorandum d'accord entre l'Organisation de Coopération et de Développement Economiques et le gouvernement du Japon relatif à l'acceptation par le gouvernement du Japon des obligations du membre de l'Organisation. Memorandum of understanding between the Organisation... and the government of Japan concerning the assumption by the government of Japan of the obligations of membership of the Organisation. [in English and French] [Paris, 1963]. pp. (21).

- Foreign economic relations - America, Latin

LATIN America and Japan: a symposium on investment and trade at Sophia University, Tokyo, Japan 20-30 March 1968: proceedings; edited by Vendelino Lorscheiter and Gustavo Andrade. Tokyo, 1968. pp. 181. In Japanese and English.

JAPAN (Cont'd.)

- Foreign economic relations - Asia, South-East

FRANCE. Direction de la Documentation. La Documentation Française. Notes et Etudes Documentaires. No. 2,625. Les relations économiques entre le Japon et le Sud-Est asiatique; texte établi par la Maison franco-japonaise de Tokyo, sur la base de documents de presse japonais, avec la collaboration de Hiroshi Kurimoto. Paris, 1960. pp. 24.

- Foreign economic relations - Australia

COMMITTEE FOR ECONOMIC DEVELOPMENT OF AUSTRALIA. Discussions with an industrial mission from the International Management Association of Japan; memorandum for the information of trustees. Melbourne, 1968. fo. (23). 26cm. x 20½cm.

- Foreign economic relations - United States

HADLEY (ELEANOR M.) Antitrust in Japan. Princeton, 1970. pp. 528.

IGNATUSHCHENKO (STEPAN KIRILLOVICH) Iaponiia i SSHA: partnery i konkurenty. Moskva, 1970. pp. 306.

- Foreign opinion

ANETHAN (ALBERT D') Baron. The d'Anethan dispatches from Japan 1894-1910: the observations of Baron Albert d'Anethan...; selected, translated and edited, with a historical introduction by George Alexander Lensen. Tokyo, [1967]. pp. 272.

- Foreign relations

WENDT (INGEBORG Y.) Geht Japan nach links? Reinbek bei Hamburg, Rowohlt, 1964. pp. 158. 19cm. (Rowohlts Deutsche Enzyklopädie)

ANETHAN (ALBERT D') Baron. The d'Anethan dispatches from Japan 1894-1910: the observations of Baron Albert d'Anethan...; selected, translated and edited, with a historical introduction by George Alexander Lensen. Tokyo, [1967]. pp. 272.

YU (TE-JEN) The Japanese struggle for world empire. New York, Vantage P., [1967]. pp. 330. 20cm.

AUSTRALIAN NATIONAL UNIVERSITY. Research School of Pacific Studies. Department of International Relations. Papers on modern Japan, 1968: [seminar papers], edited by D.C.S. Sissons. Canberra, 1968. pp. (iii), 137. 25cm.

STOCKWIN (JAMES ARTHUR AINSCOW) The Japanese Socialist Party and neutralism: a study of a political party and its foreign policy. Melbourne, Melbourne U.P., 1968. pp. xv, 197. bibliog. 21½cm.

KAJIMA (MORINOSUKE) Modern Japan's foreign policy. Rutland, Vermont, 1969 repr. 1970. pp. 327. bibliog.

GUILLAIN (ROBERT) The Japanese challenge;...translated from the French by Patrick O'Brian. London, 1970. pp. 345. bibliog.

OKAMOTO (SHUMPEI) The Japanese oligarchy and the Russo-Japanese war. New York, 1970. pp. 355. bibliog. (Columbia University. East Asian Institute. Studies)

OLSON (LAWRENCE) Japan in postwar Asia. London, 1970. pp. 288. bibliog.

KAHN (HERMAN) The emerging Japanese superstate: challenge and response. London, 1971. pp. 274. bibliog.

- Foreign relations - Treaties

HARADA (KUMAO) Baron. Saionji-Harada memoirs: fragile victory; Prince Saionji and the 1930 London Treaty issue from the memoirs of Baron Harada Kumao; translated with an introduction and annotations by Thomas Francis Mayer-Oakes. Detroit, Wayne State U.P., 1968. pp. 330. 25½cm.

- Foreign relations - China

JANSEN (MARIUS B.) The Japanese and Sun Yat-sen. Stanford, 1954 repr. 1970. pp. 274. bibliog.

MAO (TSE-TUNG) Oppose capitulationist activity, June 30, 1939. Peking, 1969. pp. 12.

RICHARDS (PETER) British policy towards China, with special reference to the Shantung question, 1918-1922; [Ph.D. (London) thesis]. 970. fo. 452. bibliog. Typescript: unpublished. This thesis is the property of London University and may not be removed from the Library.

- Foreign relations - Germany

MARTIN (BERND) Deutschland und Japan im Zweiten Weltkrieg: vom Angriff auf Pearl Harbor bis zur deutschen Kapitulation. Göttingen, [1969]. pp. 326. bibliog. (Arbeitskreis für Wehrforschung, etc. Studien und Dokumente zur Geschichte des Zweiten Weltkrieges. Band 11)

- Foreign relations - India

HAYASHIDA (TATSUO) Netaji Subhas Chandra Bose: his great struggle and martyrdom;...English translation edited by Biswanath Chatterjee. Bombay, 1970. pp. 183.

- Foreign relations - Korea

KIM (KWAN BONG) The Korea-Japan treaty crisis and the instability of the Korean political system. New York, 1971. pp. 350. bibliog.

- Foreign relations - Philippine Islands

GOODMAN (GRANT KOHN) Davao: a case study in Japanese-Philippine relations. [Lawrence], University of Kansas, Center for East Asian Studies, [1967]. pp. (viii), 117. 23cm. (International Studies, East Asian Series. Research Publications. No. 1.)

- Foreign relations - Russia

HATA (IKUHIKO) Reality and illusion: the hidden crisis between Japan and the U.S.S.R., 1932-1934. New York, Columbia University, East Asian Institute, [1967]. pp. (v), 60. 23cm. (Occasional Papers)

HELLMANN (DONALD C.) Japanese foreign policy and domestic politics: the peace agreement with the Soviet Union. Berkeley, 1969. pp. 202. bibliog.

KRIEGER (KONRAD SIEGFRIED) Das sowjetisch-japanische Verhältnis 1931-1941: Auswirkungen auf die Entwicklungspolitik in Ost- und Südostasien. Mainz, [1970]. pp. 78. bibliog. (Institut für Internationale Solidarität. Schriftenreihe. Band 11)

LENSEN (GEORGE ALEXANDER) Japanese recognition of the U.S.S.R.: Soviet-Japanese relations, 1921-1930. Tokyo, [1970]. pp. 419. bibliog.

- Foreign relations - Switzerland

NAKAI (PAUL AKIO) Das Verhältnis zwischen der Schweiz und Japan: vom Beginn der diplomatischen Beziehungen 1859 bis 1868. Bern, Haupt, [1967]. pp. x, 150 bibliog. 22½cm.

- Foreign relations - United Kingdom

HARADA (KUMAO) Baron. Saionji-Harada memoirs: fragile victory; Prince Saionji and the 1930 London Treaty issue from the memoirs of Baron Harada Kumao; translated with an introduction and annotations by Thomas Francis Mayer-Oakes. Detroit, Wayne State U.P., 1968. pp. 330. 25½cm.

FOX (GRACE) Britain and Japan, 1858-1883. Oxford, 1969. pp. 627. bibliog.

KENNEDY (MALCOLM D.) The estrangement of Great Britain and Japan 1917-35. Manchester, [1969]. pp. 363. bibliog.

LOWE (PETER) Lecturer in History at Manchester University. Great Britain and Japan, 1911-15: a study of British Far Eastern policy. London, Macmillan, 1969. pp. 343. bibliog. 21½cm.

- Foreign relations - United States

ASSOCIATION FOR PROMOTION OF OKINAWA'S LIBERATION AND ITS RETURN TO THE FATHERLAND. Okinawa, island of tragedy. Tokyo, 1963. pp. (iii), 87. 25½cm.

KOGINOS (MANNY T.) The Panay incident: prelude to war. Lafayette, Purdue University Studies, 1967. pp. ix, 154. bibliog. 22½cm.

NEU (CHARLES E.) An uncertain friendship: Theodore Roosevelt and Japan, 1906-1909. Cambridge, Harvard U.P., 1967. pp. xi, 347. bibliog. 21cm.

BUHITE (RUSSELL D.) Nelson T. Johnson and American policy toward China, 1925-1941. East Lansing, Michigan State U.P., 1968. pp. ix, 163. bibliog. 23½cm.

FRIEDMAN (DONALD J.) The road from isolation: the campaign of the American Committee for Non-Participation in Japanese Aggression, 1938-1941. Cambridge Harvard U.P., 1968. pp. ix, 122. bibliog. 25½cm. (Harvard University. East Asian Research Center. Harvard East Asian Monographs. 25)

GEORGETOWN UNIVERSITY. Center for Strategic and International Studies. Special Report Series. No.7. United States-Japanese political relations: the critical issues affecting Asia's future. Washington, D.C., 1968. pp. 102.

MORRIS (MORTON DAN) Okinawa: a tiger by the tail. New York, Hawthorn Books, 1968. pp. (v), 238. bibliog. 22½cm.

OSGOOD (ROBERT ENDICOTT) and others. Japan and the United States in Asia. Baltimore, [1968]. pp. 65. (Johns Hopkins University. Washington Center of Foreign Policy Research. Studies in International Affairs. No. 8)

ASIAN dilemma: United States, Japan and China; a special report [on a conference between Japanese and American members of government] from the Center for the Study of Democratic Institutions; edited by Elaine H. Burnell. Santa Barbara, 1969. pp. 238. (Center for the Study of Democratic Institutions. Occasional Papers)

WATANABE (AKIO) The Okinawa problem: a chapter in Japan-U.S. relations. Carlton, Victoria, 1970. pp. 220. bibliog.

- History

YU (TE-JEN) The Japanese struggle for world empire. New York, Vantage P., [1967]. pp. 330. 20cm.

VIE (MICHEL) Histoire du Japon: des origines à Meiji. Paris, 1969. pp. 125. bibliog.

CROWLEY (JAMES BUCKLEY) ed. Modern East Asia: essays in interpretation. New York, [1970]. pp. 385. bibliogs.

HALL (JOHN WHITNEY) Japan from prehistory to modern times. London, [1970]. pp. 395. bibliog.

- History - Sources

ANETHAN (ALBERT D') Baron. The d'Anethan dispatches from Japan 1894-1910: the observations of Baron Albert d'Anethan...; selected, translated and edited, with a historical introduction by George Alexander Lensen. Tokyo, [1967]. pp. 272.

- History - Tokugawa period, 1600-1867

TSUKAHIRA (TOSHIO GEORGE) Feudal control in Tokugawa Japan: the sankin kōtai system. Cambridge, Harvard U.P., 1966. pp. xii, 228. bibliog. 25½cm. (Harvard University. East Asian Research Center. Harvard East Asian Monographs. 20)

TOTMAN (CONRAD D.) Politics in the Tokugawa bafuku, 1600-1843. Cambridge, Harvard U.P., 1967. pp. (vii), 346. bibliog. 23½cm. (Harvard University. East Asian Research Center. Harvard East Asian Studies. 30)

HALL (JOHN WHITNEY) and JANSEN (MARIUS B.) eds. Studies in the institutional history of early modern Japan;... contributors Harumi Befu [and others]. Princeton, Princeton U.P., 1968. pp. xi, 396. 23½cm.

HAROOTUNIAN (HARRY D.) Toward restoration: the growth of political consciousness in Tokugawa Japan. Berkeley, 1970. pp. 421.

- History-Restoration, 1853-1870

AKAMATSU (PAUL) Meiji, 1868: révolution et contre-révolution au Japon. Paris, Calmann-Lévy, [1968]. pp. 382. bibliog. 21cm. (Les Grandes Vagues Révolutionnaires)

- History - Meiji period, 1867-1912

AKAMATSU (PAUL) Meiji, 1868: révolution et contre-révolution au Japon. Paris, Calmann-Lévy, [1968]. pp. 382. bibliog. 21cm. (Les Grandes Vagues Révolutionnaires)

MASON (R.H.P.) Japan's first general election, 1890. Cambridge, C.U.P., 1969. pp. ix, 254. bibliog. 21½cm. (Cambridge. University. Faculty of Oriental Studies. University of Cambridge Oriental Publications. No. 14)

JAPAN - History - Meiji period, 1867-1912 (Cont'd.)

PYLE (KENNETH B.) The new generation in Meiji Japan: problems of cultural identity, 1885-1895. Stanford, 1969. pp. 240. bibliog.

SCHEINER (IRWIN) Christian converts and social protest in Meiji Japan. Berkeley, 1970. pp. 268. bibliog.

- History - 20th century

BROWNE (COURTNEY) Tojo: the last Banzai. New York, Holt, [1967]. pp. ix, 260. bibliog. 21cm.

- History - 1912-1945

TOLAND (JOHN) Writer on World War II. The rising sun: the decline and fall of the Japanese Empire, 1936-1945. London, 1971. pp. 954. bibliog.

- History - Allied occupation, 1945-1952

FEIS (HERBERT) Contest over Japan. New York, Norton, [1967]. pp. vi, 187. 20½cm.

- Industries

BALLON (ROBERT J.) ed. Joint ventures and Japan. Tokyo, Sophia University, 1967. pp. xiii, 138. 23cm.

FAMINU (N. A.) Report of Japan's seminar on smaller enterprise development course for 1967. Ibadan, Ministry of Economic Planning and Social Development, 1967. fo. 16.

VEPA (RAM K.) Small industries in Japan. Bombay, Vora, 1967. pp. xii, 237. 21cm.

JAPAN. Bureau of Statistics. 1968. General report on the unincorporated enterprise survey, 1952-1966. [Tokyo, 1968]. pp. 124. In English and Japanese.

SHINOHARA (MIYOHEI) and FISHER (DOUGLAS) The role of small industry in the process of economic growth. The Hague, 1968. pp. 218. bibliog. (International Committee for Social Sciences Documentation. Conference. vol. 7)

YOSHINO (M. Y.) Japan's managerial system: tradition and innovation. Cambridge, M.I.T. Press, [1968]. pp. xvi, 292. bibliog. 22½cm.

GRIMM (HERMANN O.) Die Grundlagen der japanischen Einfuhr ausländischer Technologie. Köln, 1970. pp. 229. bibliog. (Aachen. Technische Hochschule. Forschungsinstitut für Internationale Technisch-Wirtschaftliche Zusammenarbeit. Internationale Kooperation. 4)

IKEDA (KOTARO) and others. Die industrielle Entwicklung in Japan unter besonderer Berücksichtigung seiner Wirtschafts- und Finanzpolitik. Berlin, [1970]. pp. 234.

- Industries - Statistics

JAPAN. Establishment Census, 1966. 1966 establishment census of Japan. Vols. 1,4-7. [Tokyo, 1968]. 5 vols. Vols. 2 and 3 out of print.

JAPAN. Establishment Census, 1969. 1969 establishment census of Japan. [Tokyo, 1970] in progress. In English and Japanese.

- Intellectual life

GOODMAN (GRANT KOHN) The Dutch impact on Japan, 1640-1853. Leiden, Brill, 1967. pp. ix, 242. bibliog. 25½cm. (Monographies du T'oung Pao. vol. 5)

ARIMA (TATSUO) The failure of freedom: a portrait of modern Japanese intellectuals. Cambridge, Mass., 1969. pp. 296. bibliog. (Harvard University. East Asian Research Center. Harvard East Asian Studies. 39)

HAROOTUNIAN (HARRY D.) Toward restoration: the growth of political consciousness in Tokugawa Japan. Berkeley, 1970. pp. 421.

HAVENS (THOMAS R.H.) Nishi Amane and modern Japanese thought. Princeton, 1970. pp. 253. bibliog.

- Kings and rulers

WEBB (HERSCHEL) The Japanese imperial institution in the Tokugawa period. New York, Columbia U.P., 1968. pp. xvi, 296. bibliog. 21½cm. (Columbia University. East Asian Institute. Studies)

- Nationalism

MARSHALL (BYRON KIPLING) Capitalism and nationalism in prewar Japan: the ideology of the business elite, 1868-1941. Stanford, U.P., [1967]. pp. xi, 163. bibliog. 21½cm.

WILSON (GEORGE M.) Radical nationalist in Japan: Kita Ikki, 1883-1937. Cambridge, Mass., 1969. pp. 230. bibliog. (Harvard University. East Asian Research Center. Harvard East Asian Studies. 37)

- Officials and employees

KUBOTA (AKIRA) Higher civil servants in post-war Japan: their social origins, educational backgrounds, and career patterns. Princeton, Princeton U.P., 1969. pp. xv, 197. bibliog. 21½cm.

- Politics and government

WENDT (INGEBORG Y.) Geht Japan nach links? Reinbek bei Hamburg, Rowohlt, 1964. pp. 158. 19cm. (Rowohlts Deutsche Enzyklopädie)

NAJITA (TETSUO) Hara Kei in the politics of compromise, 1905-1915. Cambridge, Harvard U.P., 1967. pp. xix, 314. bibliog. 21cm. (Harvard University. East Asian Research Center. Harvard East Asian Series. 31)

TOTMAN (CONRAD D.) Politics in the Tokugawa bafuku, 1600-1843. Cambridge, Harvard U.P., 1967. pp. (vii), 346. bibliog. 23½cm. (Harvard University. East Asian Research Center. Harvard East Asian Studies. 30)

AUSTRALIAN NATIONAL UNIVERSITY. Research School of Pacific Studies. Department of International Relations. Papers on modern Japan, 1968: [seminar papers], edited by D.C.S. Sissons. Canberra, 1968. pp. (iii), 137. 25cm.

BAKKE (EDWARD WIGHT) Revolutionary democracy: challenge and testing in Japan. Hamden, Archon Books, [1968]. pp. xi, 343. bibliog. 21½cm.

DIMOCK (MARSHALL EDWARD) The Japanese technocracy: management and government in Japan. New York, 1968. pp. 197. bibliog.

DUUS (PETER) Party rivalry and political change in Taisho Japan. Cambridge, Harvard U.P., 1968. pp. x, 317. bibliog. 23½cm. (Harvard University. East Asian Research Center. Harvard East Asian Studies. 35)

SINHA (SASADHUR) Aspects of Japan. London, Asia Publishing House, [1968]. pp. xii, 138. 21½cm.

WARD (ROBERT EDWARD) ed. Political development in modern Japan;...[by] Ardath W. Burks [and others]. Princeton, U.P., 1968. pp. xii, 637. 20cm. (Association for Asian Studies. Conference on Modern Japan)

WEBB (HERSCHEL) The Japanese imperial institution in the Tokugawa period. New York, Columbia U.P., 1968. pp. xvi, 296. bibliog. 21½cm. (Columbia University. East Asian Institute. Studies)

YANAGA (CHITOSHI) Big business in Japanese politics. New Haven, Yale P., 1968. pp. xi, 371. bibliog. 23½cm. (Yale University. Yale Studies in Political Science. 22)

BELLIENI (STEFANO) Zengakuren Zenkyoto: (Giappone; rapporto su una generazione in rivolta). Milano, 1969. pp. 361.

HELLMANN (DONALD C.) Japanese foreign policy and domestic politics: the peace agreement with the Soviet Union. Berkeley, 1969. pp. 202. bibliog.

KEVENHOERSTER (PAUL) Das politische System Japans. Köln, 1969. pp. 330. bibliog.

THAYER (NATHANIEL B.) How the conservatives rule Japan. Princeton, N.J., 1969. pp. 349. bibliog. (Columbia University. East Asian Institute. Studies)

CROWLEY (JAMES BUCKLEY) ed. Modern East Asia: essays in interpretation. New York, [1970]. pp. 385. bibliogs.

FUKUI (HARUHIRO) Party in power: the Japanese Liberal-Democrats and policy-making. Canberra, 1970. pp. 301. bibliog.

OKAMOTO (SHUMPEI) The Japanese oligarchy and the Russo-Japanese war. New York, 1970. pp. 355. bibliog. (Columbia University. East Asian Institute. Studies)

- Population

JAPAN. Public Information and Cultural Affairs Bureau. 1957. Japan's population problems; by Ayanori Okasaki. [Tokyo], 1957. pp. 28.

JAPAN. Bureau of Statistics. 1970. Population estimates of Japan. [Tokyo, 1970.] pp. 235. (Population Estimates Series. No.36) In English and Japanese.

- Public works

U.K. 1964. Department of Scientific and Industrial Research. Public works and roads in Japan; by C. R. S. Manders. (Reports from U.K. Scientific Attachés and Advisers. Japan. 42) London, 1964. pp. 10. 30cm.

- Relations (general) with Latin America

OHARA (YOSHINORI) Japan and Latin America. Santa Monica, 1967. pp. 68. (Rand Corporation. Research Memoranda. 5388)

- Relations (general) with the Netherlands

GOODMAN (GRANT KOHN) The Dutch impact on Japan, 1640-1853. Leiden, Brill, 1967. pp. ix, 242. bibliog. 25½cm. (Monographies du T'oung Pao. vol. 5)

- Relations (general) with Russia

OKTIABR'... Октябрь и Япония: по материалам симпозиума. Москва, Наука, 1968. pp. 88. 20см.

- Relations (general) with the United Kingdom

FOX (GRACE) Britain and Japan, 1858-1883. Oxford, 1969. pp. 627. bibliog.

- Religion

JAPAN. Ministry of Education. Research Bureau. Religious Affairs Section. 1959. Religions in Japan. [Tokyo], 1959. pp. 136.

BASABE (FERNANDO M.) Japanese youth confronts religion: a sociological survey;...in collaboration with Anzai Shin and Alphonso M. Nebreda. Tokyo, Sophia University, 1967. pp. vi, 183. bibliog. 25½cm.

BASABE (FERNANDO M.) Religious attitudes of Japanese men: a sociological survey;...in collaboration with Anzai Shin and Federico Lanzaco. Tokyo, [1968]. pp. 135.

HORI (ICHIRO) Folk religion in Japan: continuity and change; ... edited by Joseph M. Kitagawa and Alan L. Miller. Chicago, Chicago U.P., 1968. pp. x, 278. bibliog. 21½cm. (Chicago University. Haskell Foundation Institute. Haskell Lectures on History of Religions. New Series. No. 1)

SIEFFERT (RENÉ) Les religions du Japon. Paris, P.U.F., 1968. pp. 133. 17½cm. (Mythes et Religions. 59)

- Rural conditions

FUKUTAKE (TADASHI) Asian rural society: China, India, Japan. Seattle, U. of Washington P., [1967]. pp. xiv, 207. 22½cm.

- Social conditions

SOCIOLOGICAL REVIEW, THE; [published by] University of Keele. Monographs No.10. Japanese sociological studies; edited by Paul Halmos. Keele, the University, 1966. pp. 212. 21½cm.

TAKEDA (R.) The problem of civil society in Japan. in Sociological Review, The; [published by] University of Keele. Monographs No. 10. Keele, 1966.

DEMPSTER (PRUE) Japan advances: a geographical study. London, 1967. pp. 329. bibliog.

BRAMELD (THEODORE BURGHARD HURT) Japan: culture, education, and change in two communities. New York, Holt, [1968]. pp. xx, 316. bibliog. 22½cm.

JAPAN - Social conditions (Cont'd.)

DEMPSTER (PRUE) Japan advances: a geographical study. 2nd ed. London, 1969. pp. 332. bibliog.

PYLE (KENNETH B.) The new generation in Meiji Japan: problems of cultural identity, 1885-1895 Stanford, 1969. pp. 240. bibliog.

NAKANE (CHIE) Japanese society. London, [1970]. pp. 157.

TSURUMI (KAZUKO) Social change and the individual: Japan before and after defeat in World War II. Princeton, 1970. pp. 441. bibliog.

- Social history

YAZAKI (TAKEO) Social change and the city in Japan from earliest times through the industrial revolution. San Francisco, [1968]. pp. 549. bibliog.

SCHEINER (IRWIN) Christian converts and social protest in Meiji Japan. Berkeley, 1970. pp. 268. bibliog.

SHIPMAN (M.D.) Education and modernisation. London, 1971. pp. 276.

- Social life and customs

OKADA (Y.) Social organisation of the Li tribe of Hainan Island. in Sociological Review, The; [published by] University of Keele. Monographs No. 10. Keele, 1966.

- Social policy

JAPAN. Economic Planning Agency. 1967. Economic and social development plan, 1967-1971. [Tokyo], 1967. pp. (vii), 199. 25½cm.

- Statistics, Vital

STATISTICS RELATING TO MATERNAL AND CHILD HEALTH IN JAPAN; [pd. by] Maternal and Child Health Section, Children and Families Bureau, Ministry of Health and Welfare [Japan]. a., 1968- [Tokyo]

JAPANESE IN BRAZIL

SAITO (HIROSHI) O cooperativismo e a comunidade. [2nd ed] São Paulo, Editôra Sociologia e Política, [1964?] pp. 205. bibliog. 23cm.

JAPANESE IN CANADA

HENRY (FRANKLIN J.) Perception of discrimination among Negroes and Japanese-Canadians in Hamilton: a report submitted to the Ontario Human Rights Commission. [Hamilton], McMaster University, Department of Sociology and Anthropology, 1965. pp. xii, 97. 28cm.

JAPANESE IN INDONESIA

NETHERLANDS. 1942. Ten years of Japanese burrowing in the Netherlands East Indies: official report of the Netherlands East Indies Government on Japanese subversive activities in the Archipelago during the last decade; published...by the Netherlands Information Bureau. New York, 1942 repr. 1944. pp. 132.

JAPANESE IN PARAGUAY

STEWART (NORMAN R.) Japanese colonization in eastern Paraguay. Washington, National Research Council, 1967. pp. xiii, 202. bibliog. 23½cm. (Publications. [No.] 1490)

JAPANESE IN THE UNITED STATES

KITANO (HARRY HARUS LEE) Japanese Americans: the evolution of a subculture. Englewood Cliffs, Prentice-Hall, [1969]. pp. xvii, 186. bibliog. 22½cm. (Ethnic Groups in American Life Series)

JAPANESE LANGUAGE

MILLER (ROY ANDREW) The Japanese language. Chicago, 1967. pp. 428. bibliog.

JAPANESE PERIODICALS

- Bibliography

KURODA (YASUMASA) compiler. A guide to social and behavioral science journals in Japan. [Honolulu], 1969. fo. 157.bibliog. (Hawaii University. East-West Center. Institute of Advanced Projects. Occasional Papers of Research Publications and Translations. Annotated Bibliography Series. No. 6)

JARRY (GEDEON)

LOISEAU (IVAN) 89; ou, La Révolution manquée; [and other essays]. Paris, La Palatine, [1964]. pp. 135. 18cm.

JASPERS (KARL)

DIETRICH (R.) Karl Jaspers als Geschichtsdenker. in Dietrich (Richard) ed. Historische Theorie und Geschichtsforschung der Gegenwart. Berlin, 1964.

GALIASKAROV (V. G.) O filosofsko-psikhologicheskikh vozzreniiakh K. Iaspersa na nekotorye problemy soznaniia. in Soznanie i obshchenie. Frunze, 1968.

LONG (EUGENE THOMAS) Jaspers and Bultmann: a dialogue between philosophy and theology in the existentialist tradition. Durham, Duke U.P., 1968. pp. ix, 155. 21½cm.

RIGALI (NORBERT) Die Selbstkonstitution der Geschichte im Denken von Karl Jaspers. Meisenheim am Glan, 1968. pp. 128. bibliog.

JATAVS

LYNCH (OWEN M.) The politics of untouchability: social mobility and social change in a city of India. New York, 1969. pp. 251. bibliog.

JATS

WESTPHAL-HELLBUSCH (SIGRID) and WESTPHAL (HEINZ) Zur Geschichte und Kultur der Jat. Berlin, Duncker & Humblot, [1968]. pp. 367. bibliog. 23cm. (Forschungen zur Ethnologie und Sozialpsychologie. Band 7)

JAURÈS (JEAN)

DOMMANGET (M.) Sur Jaurès, historien de la Révolution française. in Société des Études Robespierristes. La pensée socialiste devant la Révolution française. Paris, 1966.

DOMMANGET (M.) Trois lettres inédites de Jaurès sur l'histoire de la Révolution française. in Société des Études Robespierristes. La pensée socialiste devant la Révolution française. Paris, 1966.

REBERIOUX-AMOUDRUZ (M.) Jaurès, historien de la Révolution française. in Société des Études Robespierristes. La pensée socialiste devant la Révolution française. Paris, 1966.

CROIX (ALEXANDRE) Jaurès et ses détracteurs: l'histoire à travers la polémique. [Paris], Éditions du Vieux Saint-Ouen, [1967]. pp. 337. 20½cm.

FONVIEILLE-ALQUIER (FRANÇOIS) Ils ont tué Jaurès!: 31 juillet 1914. Paris, Laffont, [1968]. pp. 364. 24cm. (Ce Jour-Là)

LEFRANC (GEORGES) Jaurès et le socialisme des intellectuels. Paris, Aubier-Montaigne, [1968]. pp. 231. bibliog. 19cm. (Histoire du Travail et de la Vie Économique)

ROBINET (ANDRÉ) Péguy entre Jaurès, Bergson et l'église: métaphysique et politique. [Paris], Seghers, [1968]. pp. 347. 20cm. (Recherches)

MOLCHANOV (NIKOLAI NIKOLAEVICH) Жорес. Москва, 1969. pp. 396. bibliog.

JAVA

- Economic conditions

CASTLES (LANCE) Religion, politics and economic behavior in Java: the Kudus cigarette industry. [New Haven], Yale University, [1967]. pp. x, 158. bibliog. 23cm. (Yale University. [Council on] Southeast Asia Studies. Cultural Report Series. No. 15)

- Politics and government

WIDJOJO (NITISASTRO) and ISMAEL (J.E.) The government, economy and taxes of a central Javanese village. Ithaca, 1959. pp. 37. (Cornell University. Department of Asian Studies. Southeast Asia Program. Modern Indonesia Project. Monograph Series)

- Rural conditions

WIDJOJO (NITISASTRO) and ISMAEL (J.E.) The government, economy and taxes of a central Javanese village. Ithaca, 1959. pp. 37. (Cornell University. Department of Asian Studies. Southeast Asia Program. Modern Indonesia Project. Monograph Series)

- Social life and customs

PEACOCK (JAMES L.) Rites of modernization: symbolic and social aspects of Indonesian proletarian drama. Chicago, U. of Chicago P., 1968. pp. xxv, 306. bibliog. 22½cm.

BENSA (ALBAN) Le sacré à Java et à Bali: chamanisme, sorcellerie, et transe;... ([report of the] Mission Merry Ottin). Paris, [1969]. pp. 241.

JAVANESE IN SINGAPORE

BIN JOHARI (ABDUL AZIZ) The Javanese people of Singapore... with special reference to those who regard themselves as Javanese but who are in fact Singapore/Malaya born. [1961]. fo. 106. bibliog. Microfilm of typescript.

JAY (WILLIAM) of New York

TUCKERMAN (BAYARD) William Jay and the constitutional movement for the abolition of slavery. London, Osgood, 1893. pp. xxiii, 185. bibliog. 22½cm.

JAY'S TREATY, 1794

COMBS (JERALD A.) The Jay treaty: political background of the founding fathers. Berkeley, 1970. pp. 254. bibliog.

JAZIRAH

See JEZIRE

JAZZ MUSIC

KRAEHENBUEHL (PETER) Der Jazz und seine Menschen: eine soziologische Studie. Bern, [1968]. pp. 139. bibliog.

JEFFERSON (THOMAS)

GOODMAN (PAUL) ed. The Federalists vs. the Jeffersonian Republicans. New York, Holt, [1967]. pp. 122. bibliog. 23½cm. (American Problem Studies)

FRIED (ALBERT) ed. The Jeffersonian and Hamiltonian traditions in American politics: a documentary history. New York, Doubleday, 1968. pp. xv, 581. bibliog. 18cm. (Anchor Books)

DAVIS (DAVID BRION) Was Thomas Jefferson an authentic enemy of slavery?;... an inaugural lecture, etc. Oxford, 1970. pp. 29.

PETERSON (MERRILL DANIEL) Thomas Jefferson and the new nation: a biography. New York, 1970. pp. 1072. bibliog.

BENSON (C. RANDOLPH) Thomas Jefferson as social scientist. Rutherford, [1971]. pp. 333. bibliog.

ELLIS (RICHARD E.) The Jeffersonian crisis: courts and politics in the young republic. New York, 1971. pp. 377. bibliog.

JEHOVAH'S WITNESSES

BARTOSHEVICH (EDUARD MIKHAILOVICH) and BORISOGLEBSKII (EVGENII IVANOVICH) Свидетели Иеговы. Москва, 1969. pp. 214.

JELLICOE (JOHN RUSHWORTH) 1st Earl Jellicoe

NAVY RECORDS SOCIETY. Publications. vols. 108, 111. The Jellicoe papers: selections from the private and official correspondence of Admiral of the Fleet Earl Jellicoe of Scapa; with an appendix on the papers of Vice-Admiral J. E. T. Harper; edited by A. Temple Patterson. London, the Society, 1966-68. 2 vols. 22½cm.

PATTERSON (A. TEMPLE) Jellicoe: a biography. London, Macmillan, 1969. pp. 277. bibliog. 21½cm.

JEMOLO (ARTURO CARLO)

JEMOLO (ARTURO CARLO) Anni di prova. Vicenza, 1969. pp. 266.

JENGHIS KHAN, Great Khan of the Moguls

GROUSSET (RENÉ) Conqueror of the world; translated [from the French] by Denis Sinor and Marian MacKellar, with preface notes and bibliography by Denis Sinor. Edinburgh, Oliver & Boyd, 1967. pp. xvii, 300. 22½cm.

JENKINS (DAVID) One of the judges for South Wales

SALUS populi solus rex: the peoples safety is the sole soveraignty; or, The royalist out-reasoned: calculated for the hopefull recovery of the considerate royalist, from the dangerous infection of the slie sophistry of Iudge Ienkings, etc. [London, White], 1648. pp. 22. 18½cm. Wing S 515.

BALL (WILLIAM) of Barkham. The power of kings discussed; or, An examen of the fundamentall constitution of the free-borne people of England: in answer to severall tenents of M. David Jenkins. London, Harris, 1649. pp. 13. 18¼cm. Wing B 594.

JEROME, Saint

ADAMS (JEREMY DUQUESNAY) The populus of Augustine and Jerome: a study in the patristic sense of community. New Haven, 1971. pp. 278. bibliog.

JERRAM (Sir THOMAS MARTYN) Admiral

NISH (IAN HILL) Admiral Jerram and the German Pacific fleet, 1913-15. [New York, 1970]. pp. 411-422. (Reprinted from The Mariner's Mirror, vol. 56, no. 4, 1970)

JERSEY

- Constitutional history

BOIS (F. DE L.) A constitutional history of Jersey. [St. Helier], States' Greffe, 1970. pp. 276.

JERUSALEM

- Census

ISRAEL. Central Bureau of Statistics. 1968-70. Census of population and housing 1966/67: east Jerusalem. Jerusalem, 1968-70. 2 pts. (in 1 vol.)

- History

ISRAEL. Ministry for Foreign Affairs. Information Division. 1967. Desecration: twenty years of Jordanian 'guardianship'. Jerusalem, 1967. pp.(58). 28cm. [in English, French and Spanish].

LAUTERPACHT (ELIHU) Jerusalem and the Holy Places. London, Anglo-Israel Association, 1968. pp. 85. 23cm. (Pamphlets. No.19)

- History - Latin Kingdom, 1099-1244

BEN-AMI (AHARON) Social change in a hostile environment: the crusaders' kingdom of Jerusalem. Princeton, 1969. pp. 193. bibliog. (Princeton University. Program in Near Eastern Studies. Princeton Studies on the Near East)

- Politics and government

PFAFF (RICHARD H.) Jerusalem: keystone of an Arab-Israeli settlement. Washington, D.C., 1969. pp. 54. (American Enterprise Institute for Public Policy Research. Middle East Research Project. Analyses. No. 13)

JESNESS INVENTORY

U.K. 1967. Home Office The use of the Jesness inventory on a sample of British probationers; by Martin Davies. (Studies in the Causes of Delinquency and the Treatment of Offenders. 12) London, 1967. pp. iv, 20. bibliog. 24cm.

MOTT (JOY) The Jesness Inventory: application to approved school boys. London, 1969. pp. iv, 26. bibliog. 24½cm. (U.K. Home Office. Studies in the Causes of Delinquency and the Treatment of Offenders. 13)

JESSEN (JOHANN VON)

DZIALLAS (P.) Johann von Krafftheim und Johann von Jessen. in Schulz (Eberhard G.) ed. Leistung und Schicksal. Köln, 1967.

JESUITS

[KENNET (WHITE) Bishop of Peterborough]. Dr. Snape instructed in some matters especially relating to convocations and converts from popery; by a member of the Convocation. London, Knapton, 1718. pp. 96. 19½cm.

- Education

MARTÍN (LUIS) The intellectual conquest of Peru: the Jesuit College of San Pablo, 1568-1767. New York, Fordham U.P., 1968. pp. xiii, 194. bibliog. 21½cm.

PADBERG (JOHN W.) College in controversy: the Jesuit schools in France from revival to suppression, 1815-1880. Cambridge, Mass., 1969. pp. 321. bibliog. (Harvard University. Harvard Historical Studies. vol. 83)

- History

McCABE (JOSEPH) A candid history of the Jesuits. London, 1913. pp. 451.

- Missions

MURATORI (LODOVICO ANTONIO) A relation of the missions of Paraguay; wrote originally in Italian...and now done into English from the French translation. London, printed for J. Marmaduke, 1759. pp. xvi, 296.

LIGUE POUR LA PROTECTION ET L'EVANGELISATION DES NOIRS. M. Vandervelde se refait une virginité: réponse...aux articles récents du Peuple contre les missionnaires. [Brussels], 1913. pp. 29. (Mouvement des Missions. Suppléments)

SUAREZ (SOFIA) El fenomeno sociologico del trabajo industrial en las misiones jesuiticas. Buenos Aires, 1920. pp. 400. bibliog.

POPESCU (ORESTE) El sistema económico en las misiones jesuiticas: un vasto experimento de desarrollo indoamericano. 2nd ed. Barcelona, Ariel, 1967. pp. 198. bibliog. 22cm. (Colección Zetein. Estudios y Ensayos. 21)

SILVA (ANTONIO DA) Mentalidade missiológica dos Jesuitas em Moçambique antes de 1759; esboço ideológico a partir do nucleo documental. Lisboa, 1967. 2 vols. bibliog. (Portugal. Junta de Investigações do Ultramar. Estudos Missionarios. No. 2) With summaries in French and English.

GELFAND (MICHAEL) ed. Gubulawayo and beyond: letters and journals of the early Jesuit missionaries to Zambesia, 1879-1887. London, Chapman, 1968. pp. 496. 21½cm.

JESUITS IN BRAZIL

VELLINHO (MOYSÉS) Brazil South: its conquest and settlement; translated from the Portuguese by Linton Lomas Barrett and Marie McDavid Barrett. New York, Knopf, 1968. pp. xv, 282, x. bibliog. 21cm. (Borzoi Books)

JESUITS IN CANADA

DALTON (ROY C.) The Jesuits' estates question, 1760-1888: a study of the background for the agitation of 1889. Toronto, [1968]. pp. 201. bibliog. (Social Science Research Council of Canada. Canadian Studies in History and Government. No. 11)

JESUITS IN FRANCE

PADBERG (JOHN W.) College in controversy: the Jesuit schools in France from revival to suppression, 1815-1880. Cambridge, Mass., 1969. pp. 321. bibliog. (Harvard University. Harvard Historical Studies. vol. 83)

JESUITS IN LATIN AMERICA

ALEGRE (FRANCISCO JAVIER) Memorias para la historia de la provincia que tuvo la Compañia de Jesus en Nueva España;... publicalas J. Jijon y Caamaño. Mexico, 1940-41. 2 vols. (in 1).

POPESCU (ORESTE) El sistema económico en las misiones jesuiticas: un vasto experimento de desarrollo indoamericano. 2nd ed. Barcelona, Ariel, 1967. pp. 198. bibliog. 22cm. (Colección Zetein. Estudios y Ensayos. 21)

JESUITS IN MOZAMBIQUE

SILVA (ANTONIO DA) Mentalidade missiológica dos Jesuitas em Moçambique antes de 1759: esboço ideológico a partir do núcleo documental. Lisboa 1967. 2 vols. bibliog. 24cm. (Portugal. Junta de Investigações do Ultramar. Estudos Missionários. No. 2) With summaries in French and English.

JESUITS IN PARAGUAY

MURATORI (LODOVICO ANTONIO) A relation of the missions of Paraguay; wrote originally in Italian...and now done into English from the French translation. London, printed for J. Marmaduke, 1759. pp. xvi, 296.

SUAREZ (SOFIA) El fenomeno sociologico del trabajo industrial en las misiones jesuiticas. Buenos Aires, 1920. pp. 400. bibliog.

ROJAS (ALBERTO) Los jesuitas en el Paraguay. Asuncion 1936. pp. 140. 22½cm.

LUGON (CLOVIS) A república comunista cristã dos Guaranis, 1610-1768. Rio de Janeiro, Paz e Terra, 1968. pp. (iii), 353. bibliog. 21cm. (Serie Ecumenismo e Humanismo. vol. 12)

JESUITS IN PERU

MARTÍN (LUIS) The intellectual conquest of Peru: the Jesuit College of San Pablo, 1568-1767. New York, Fordham U.P., 1968. pp. xiii, 194. bibliog. 21½cm.

JESUITS IN SOUTHERN RHODESIA

GELFAND (MICHAEL) ed. Gubulawayo and beyond: letters and journals of the early Jesuit missionaries to Zambesia, 1879-1887. London, Chapman, 1968. pp. 496. 21½cm.

JESUITS IN ZAMBIA

GELFAND (MICHAEL) ed. Gubulawayo and beyond: letters and journals of the early Jesuit missionaries to Zambesia, 1879-1887. London, Chapman, 1968. pp. 496. 21½cm.

JESUS CHRIST

VANE (Sir HENRY) Two treatises: viz. I. An epistle general to the mystical body of Christ on earth, the Church Universal in Babylon; II. The face of the times, etc. [London], 1662. pp. (v), 99. 19½cm. Wing V 80.

BARTON (BRUCE) The man nobody knows. Indianapolis, 1925 repr. 1962. pp. 133.

BELYEA (D.) Christ the model for history. in Dunphy (William) ed. The new morality. London, 1968.

- Art

KATZENELLENBOGEN (A.) The image of Christ in the early middle ages. in Hoyt (Robert Stuart) ed. Life and thought in the early middle ages. Minneapolis, [1967].

- Biography

SMITH (ARTHUR DENNER HOWELL) Jesus not a myth. London, 1942. pp. 210. bibliog.

JESUS CHRIST (Cont'd.)

- Biography - Apocryphal and legendary literature

ROBERTSON (JOHN MACKINNON) The Jesus problem. London, 1917. pp. 264.

- Historicity

RYLANDS (LOUIS GORDON) Did Jesus ever live? London, 1935. pp. 120.

- Kingdom

HOADLY (BENJAMIN) successively Bishop of Bangor, of Hereford, of Salisbury and of Winchester. The nature of the kingdom, or church, of Christ: a sermon preach'd before the King...March 31, 1717. 14th ed. London, Knapton, 1717. pp. 31. 19½cm.

[SYKES (ARTHUR ASHLEY)] A letter to the Reverend Dr. Sherlock, one of the committee of Convocation appointed to draw up a representation concerning the Bishop of Bangor's Preservative and Sermon, comparing the dangerous...doctrines contained in the doctor's sermon...with those charged upon the bishop, etc. London, Burleigh, 1717. pp. 27. 19½cm. Signed A.V.

SYKES (ARTHUR ASHLEY) A second letter to the Reverend Dr. Sherlock, being a reply to his Answer, etc. ...; to which is added a Postscript ...by...Benjamin Lord Bishop of Bangor. London, Knapton, [1717]. pp. 93. 19½cm.

- Miracles

BAYLY (BENJAMIN) The truth of the Christian revelation prov'd from...its miracles; and of the usefulness and necessity of creeds in general, in opposition to deists and free-thinkers: in two sermons, etc. London, Wyat, 1713. pp. viii,48. 19cm.

- Rationalistic interpretations

BENNETT (DE ROBIQUE MORTIMER) An open letter to Jesus Christ, etc. New York, [1878?]. pp. 27.

SOURY (JULES) Morbid psychology: studies on Jesus and the Gospels; [with] The religion of Israel: a study in comparative mythology;...translated...by Annie Besant. London, 1881. pp. 79,80.

RENESSE (CAMILLE DE) Comte. Jesus Christ: his apostles and disciples in the twentieth century;.. translated... by William Heaford. London, 1903. pp. 76.

GORHAM (CHARLES TURNER) The first Easter dawn: an inquiry into the evidence for the resurrection of Jesus. London, 1908. pp. 320. bibliog.

ROBERTSON (JOHN MACKINNON) The Jesus problem. London, 1917. pp. 264.

WHITEHEAD (GEORGE) F.R. Econ. S. Jesus Christ: man, god or myth; with a special chapter on Was Jesus a socialist? London, [1921]. pp. 125.

RHYS (JOCELYN) Shaken creeds: the resurrection doctrines. London, 1924. pp. 268.

RYLANDS (LOUIS GORDON) The evolution of Christianity. London, 1927. pp. 230. bibliog.

DUJARDIN (EDOUARD) Ancient history of the god Jesus;...abridged English version by A. Brodie Sanders. London, 1938. pp. 172.

DU CANN (CHARLES GARFIELD LOTT) The faults and failings of Jesus Christ. London, [1941]. pp. 18.

- Resurrection

GORHAM (CHARLES TURNER) The first Easter dawn: an inquiry into the evidence for the resurrection of Jesus. London, 1908. pp. 320. bibliog.

RHYS (JOCELYN) Shaken creeds: the resurrection doctrines. London, 1924. pp. 268.

JESÚS DE MACHACA

BONILLA MAYTA (HERACLIO) and FONSECA MARTEL (CÉSAR) Tradición y conservadorismo en el area cultural del Lago Titicaca: Jesús de Machaca, una comunidad Aymara del Altiplano andino. Lima, 1967. pp. 140.

JET PLANES - Noise
See AEROPLANES - Noise

JEWELLERY TRADE

- Canada

CANADA. Dominion Bureau of Statistics. Jewellery stores (independent): operating results (formerl Operating results and financial structure: independent jewellery stores). Ottawa, triennia_ (formerly biennial), 1959 to date. 28cm.

- Germany

UNITED STATES. Business and Defense Services Administration. The market for costume jewellery in West Germany. Washington, 1963. pp. iv, 28.

- United States

UNITED STATES. Wage and Hour and Public Contracts Divisions. Foreign competition in the jewellery and silverware industry in the United States. Washington, 1965. pp. xv, 67, 58.

JEWISH-ARAB RELATIONS

INTERNATIONAL COMMITTEE OF THE RED CROSS. The International Committee of the Red Cross in Palestine. Geneva, 1948. pp. 23.

TANNOUS (IZZAT) Tension and peace in the Middle East;...an account of the tragedy of the holyland. New York, [1957]. pp. 40.

ANDRAWOS (ELIAS) The Jews: do they have the right to establish a state of their own in Palestine? Cairo, [196-]. pp. 24.

BENN (ANTHONY NEIL WEDGWOOD) Lecture...on Arab-Israel relations, 1963, in the grand committee room, House of Commons. London, Anglo-Israel Association, 1963. pp. 20. 22½cm. (Pamphlets. No. 1.)

MANDEL (N.) Turks, Arabs and Jewish immigration into Palestine, 1882-1914. in St. Antony's Papers. No. 17. Middle Eastern affairs. No. 4. London, 1965.

SA'B (HASAN) Zionism and racism. Beirut, 1965. pp. 34. (Palestine Research Center. Palestine Essays. No. 2.)

ISKANDER (MARWAN) The Arab boycott of Israel.
Beirut, Palestine Liberation Organization,
Research Center, 1966. pp. 55. 18cm.
(Palestine Monographs. 6)

SHUKAIRY (AHMAD) Liberation, not negotiation.
Beirut, 1966. pp. 141. (Palestine Research
Centre. Palestine Books. No.3)

1967

BHARGAVA (G. S.) India and West Asia: a
survey of public opinion. New Delhi,
Popular Book Services, 1967. pp. 109.
21½cm.

CARR (MAURICE) Forward to peace. Jerusalem,
1967. pp. 36. 24cm.

CATTAN (HENRY) The dimensions of the Palestine
problem, 1967. Beirut, 1967. pp. 17.
(Institute for Palestine Studies. Monographs
Series, No. 6)

The CHINESE people firmly support the Arab people's
struggle against aggression. Peking, 1967.
pp. 53.

COMMUNIST PARTY OF GREAT BRITAIN.
Communist Party Pamphlets. The back-
ground to the Middle East crisis.
[London, 1967]. pp. 7.

COUNCIL FOR THE ADVANCEMENT OF ARAB — BRITISH
UNDERSTANDING. The Arab-Israeli conflict:
a British view of the Arab case. [London],
1967. pp. 16. 20½cm.

HERZ (ISRAEL) It is time to negotiate:
discussions with the left on the Middle East
crisis. London, [1967]. pp. 16.

INDIAN SOCIETY OF INTERNATIONAL LAW.
The Arab-Israeli conflict: documents
& comments. New Delhi, 1967. pp. viii,
306. 24cm.

INTERNATIONAL INSTITUTE FOR STRATEGIC STUDIES.
Adelphi Papers. No. 41. Israel and the Arab
world: the crisis of 1967; by Michael Howard
and Robert Hunter. London, 1967. pp. 51.

ISRAEL. Ministry for Foreign Affairs. Information Division. 1967. Desecration: twenty
years of Jordanian 'guardianship'. Jerusalem
1967. pp.(58). 28cm. [in English, French
and Spanish].

ISRAELI SOCIALIST ORGANIZATION and PALESTINIAN
DEMOCRATIC FRONT. Joint Israeli-Arab
statement on the Middle East crisis. London,
[1967]. pp. 12.

LINDSAY (KENNETH) Israel, the Middle East and
world powers, [and] Commentary on current
situation in Israel; by George Weidenfeld.
London, 1967. pp. 23. (Anglo-Israel
Association. Pamphlets. No. 15)

PARKES (JAMES WILLIAM) Arabs and Jews in the
Middle East: a tragedy of errors. London,
1967. pp. 32.

RABBATH (EDMOND) Les thèmes juridiques du colloque
d'Alger sur le problème palestinien, 1967.
Beyrouth, 1967. pp. 23. (Reprinted from L'Orient,
Beyrouth, 14-15 août 1967)

RAMELSON (BERT) The Middle East: crisis,
causes, solution. [London], Communist
Party of Great Britain, [1967]. pp. 42.
21½cm. (Communist Party Pamphlets)

SALEM (ELIE ADIB) War and peace in the Middle
East: the role of the university and the
intellectual. Beirut, 1967. pp. 8.

1968

ADAMS (MICHAEL) 1920- . **Chaos or rebirth:
the Arab outlook.** London, British Broadcasting Corporation, 1968. pp. x, 170.
21cm.

AGWANI (MOHAMMED SHAFI) The West Asian
crisis, 1967. Meerut, Meenakshi Prakashan,
1968. pp. viii, 196. 21½cm.

ARNONI (M. S.) Rights and wrongs in the Arab-
Israeli conflict: to the anatomy of the forces
of progress and reaction in the Middle East.
Passaic, Minority of One P., [1968]. pp. 191.
bibliog. 20½cm.

AVNERY (URI) Israel without Zionists:
a plea for peace in the Middle East.
New York, Macmillan, [1968]. pp. 215.
21cm.

BALDACCI (GAETANO) Arabi o ebrei. Milano, [1968].
pp. 270.

BERL (EMMANUEL) Nasser tel qu'on le loue.
[Paris], Gallimard, [1968]. pp.155. 16½cm.
(Idées Actuelles. 151)

COLLOQUE DE JURISTES ARABES SUR LA PALESTINE,
ALGER, 1967. La question palestinienne.
[Algiers, Société Nationale d'Edition et
de Diffusion, 1968]. pp. 237. 23cm.

DAVIS (JOHN HERBERT) The evasive peace:
a study of the Zionist-Arab problem.
London, Murray, [1968]. pp. x, 124.
bibliog. 21½cm.

DÉMERON (PIERRE) Contre Israel. [Paris],
Pauvert, [1968]. pp. 191. 18cm. (Libertés
Nouvelles. 7)

DOUGLAS-HOME (CHARLES) The Arabs and
Israel: a background book. London,
Bodley Head, 1968. pp. 121. 18½cm.
(Background Books)

FRANCOS (ANIA) Les Palestiniens. [Paris], Julliard,
[1968]. pp. 318. bibliog. 20cm.

GOODHART (ARTHUR LEHMAN) Israel, the United
Nations and aggression; (Lecture...) at the
Royal Society of Arts. London, Anglo-Israel
Association, 1968. pp. 47. 23cm. (Pamphlets.
No. 17)

HADAWI (SAMI) Palestine in focus;...
edited by Yusif A. Sayigh. Beirut,
Palestine Research Center, 1968. pp.
122. bibliog. 20cm. (Palestine Essays.
No. 7)

HAMZEH (FUAD S.) United Nations conciliation
commission for Palestine, 1949-1967. Beirut,
1968. pp. 68. (Institute for Palestine Studies.
Monographs Series. No. 17)

HILLIER (BILL) Israel and Palestine. London,
1968. pp. 32.

JEWISH-ARAB RELATIONS (Cont'd.)

HODES (AUBREY) Dialogue with Ishmael: Israel's future in the Middle East. New York, [1968]. pp. 258.

INTERNATIONAL ASSOCIATION OF DEMOCRATIC LAWYERS. Le conflit du Moyen-Orient: notes et documents, 1915-1967. Bruxelles, [1968]. pp. 142. 24cm.

INTERNATIONAL INSTITUTE FOR STRATEGIC STUDIES. Adelphi Papers. No. 52. Arms and security: the Egypt-Israel case; by Geoffrey Kemp. London, 1968. pp. 26.

INTERNATIONAL INSTITUTE FOR STRATEGIC STUDIES. Adelphi Papers. No. 53. Fedayeen action and Arab strategy; by Y. Harkabi. London, 1968. pp. 43. bibliog.

JARGY (SIMON) Guerre et paix en Palestine; ou, L'histoire du conflit israélo-arabe, 1917-1967. Neuchâtel, La Baconnière, [1968]. pp. 218. bibliog. 21½cm. (Histoire et Société d'Aujourd'hui)

KEESING'S CONTEMPORARY ARCHIVES. Research Reports. The Arab-Israeli conflict: the 1967 campaign. [London], Keesing's Publications, [1968]. pp. 55. bibliog. 18½cm.

KHADDURI (MAJDIA D.) ed. The Arab-Israeli impasse: expressions of moderate viewpoints on the Arab-Israeli conflict by well known western writers. Washington, Luce, [1968]. pp. 223. 20cm.

KHOURI (FRED JOHN) The Arab-Israeli dilemma. Syracuse, Syracuse U.P., [1968]. pp. xi, 436. bibliog. 22½cm.

KIMCHE (DAVID) and BAWLY (DAN) The sandstorm: the Arab-Israeli war of June 1967: prelude and aftermath. London, Secker & Warburg, 1968. pp. 319. 21½cm.

LAKHANPAL (P.L.) Documents and notes on the Arab-Israeli question. Delhi, 1968. pp. 400.

MacLEISH (RODERICK) The sun stood still: perspectives on the Arab-Israeli conflict. London, Macdonald, 1968. pp xv, 174. 20cm.

MERLIN (SAMUEL) The search for peace in the Middle East: the story of President Bourguiba's campaign for a negotiated peace between Israel and the Arab states. South Brunswick, Yoseloff, [1968]. pp. 490. 23cm.

PALESTINE; [compiled for Free Palestine by Dr. Yusef Sayegh]. [London, 1968?]. pp. 22.

RODINSON (MAXIME) Israel and the Arabs: translated by Michael Perl. Harmondsworth, Penguin, 1968. pp. 240. 18cm. (Penguin Special. S263)

SEMINAR OF ARAB JURISTS ON PALESTINE, ALGIERS, 1967. The Palestine question; translated from French by Edward Rizk. Beirut, 1968. pp. 203. (Institute for Palestine Studies. Monographs Series. No. 18)

STEPPAT (FRITZ) Zionism-Judaism: some historical aspects of the clash between Zionism and Arab nationalism. Beirut, 1968. pp. 13.

1969

ABDUL-RAHMAN (AS'AD) Memoirs of a prisoner. Beirut, 1969. pp. 151. (Palestine Research Center. Palestine Monographs. 51)

AL-FATEH. Address by the Al-Fateh delegation to the second International Conference in Support of the Arab Peoples. Cairo, 1969. pp. 7.

AL-FATEH. Revolution until victory. [Beirut?, 1969?]. unpaged.

AL JOUNDI (SAMI) Le drame palestinien: pour sortir de l'impasse; [translated from the German]. Paris, Fayard, [1969]. pp. 155. 21½cm. (Le Monde sans Frontières)

ASSOCIATION FOR PEACE. Four solutions to the Palestinian problem. Tel Aviv, [1969?]. pp. 35.

BELL (J. BOWYER) The long war: Israel and the Arabs since 1946. Englewood Cliffs, [1969]. pp. 467. bibliog.

BINDRA (ATAM PARKASH SINGH) Suez thrombosis: causes and prospects. Delhi, [1969]. pp. 159. bibliog.

CATTAN (HENRY) Palestine, the Arabs and Israel: the search for justice. London, Longmans, 1969. pp. viii, 281. 22cm.

COMMUNISTE, LE. Numéro Spécial. Juin-Juillet, 1969. Un jour ou l'autre, l'état d'Israel disparaîtra. 3rd ed. Paris, 1969. pp. 62.

FRIEDLAENDER (SAUL) Réflexions sur l'avenir d'Israël. Paris, Éditions du Seuil, [1969]. pp. 189. 20½cm.

HILLEL (MARC) Israël en danger de paix. [Paris], Fayard, [1969]. pp. 350. 21½cm.

[HUMAN RIGHTS REGIONAL CONFERENCE, BEIRUT, 1968]. Zionism and Arab resistance. Beirut, Palestine Research Center, 1969. pp. 223. 17cm. (Palestine Monographs. 54)

INTERNATIONAL ASSOCIATION OF DEMOCRATIC LAWYERS. The Middle East conflict; notes and documents, 1915-1967. Brussels, [1969]. pp. 136.

INTERNATIONAL SYMPOSIUM ON INEVITABLE WAR OR INITIATIVES FOR PEACE, TEL AVIV, 1969. To make war or make peace: proceedings [of the symposium]; March 27,29,30, 1969, Tel Aviv, Kibbutz Gan Shmuel, Jerusalem. Tel Aviv, 1969. pp. 285. Reprinted from special issue of New Outlook

LAQUEUR (WALTER ZE'EV) ed. The Israel-Arab reader: a documentary of history of the Middle East conflict. London, Weidenfeld & Nicolson, 1969. pp. xii, 371. bibliog. 21½cm.

NUTTING (HAROLD ANTHONY) The tragedy of Palestine from the Balfour declaration to today. London, [1969]. pp. 15.

PALESTINE RESEARCH CENTER. Palestine Monographs. 55. The Arabs under Israeli occupation. Beirut, 1969. pp. 114. 17cm.

PARKES (JAMES WILLIAM) The long haul to peace in the Middle East; (lecture)...at the Royal Society of Arts. London, 1969. pp. 18. (Anglo-Israel Association. Pamphlets. No. 22)

PFAFF (RICHARD H.) Jerusalem: keystone of an Arab-Israeli settlement. Washington, D.C., 1969. pp. 54. (American Enterprise Institute for Public Policy Research. Middle East Research Project. Analyses. No. 13)

[ROBERTS (JOHN CHARLES DE VILLAMAR)] Middle East. London, [1969]. pp. 24. (British Association for World Government. Crisis Pamphlets. No. 2)

ROSENSAFT (MENACHEM Z.) Not backward to belligerency: a study of events surrounding the "Six-Day War" of June, 1967. New York, [1969]. pp. 181.

SHARABI (HISHAM B.) Palestine and Israel: the lethal dilemma. New York, [1969]. pp. 224.

SMITH (BARBARA) Author of Israel's unfinished war. Israel's unfinished war. London, The Economist, [1969]. pp. 24. bibliog. 21½cm. (Briefs. 15)

WAJSMAN (P.) and TEISSEDRE (R.F.) Nos politiciens face au conflit israélo-arabe. [Paris, 1969]. pp. 202. bibliog.

WARBURG (JAMES PAUL) Crosscurrents in the Middle East: a primer for the general reader, including a history of the region, a survey of recent developments, an appraisal of Western responsibility and the prospects for peace. London, Gollancz, 1969. pp. x, 244. bibliog. 21½cm.

YA'ATEH (ALI) The Middle East crisis and the Palestine cause;...the text of the report presented...to the Temporary National Committee of the Party of Liberation and Socialism... February 23, 1969. [Casablanca?, 1969?]. unpaged.

1970

AIMS of the Palestinian resistance movement with regard to the Jews: quotations from resistance leaders and documents. [Beirut, 1970]. pp. 14.

BENTWICH (NORMAN DE MATTOS) Israel: two fateful years, 1967-69. London, [1970]. pp. 115. bibliog.

BURDETT (WINSTON) Encounter with the Middle East: an intimate report on what lies behind the Arab-Israeli conflict. London, 1970. pp. 384.

COHEN (AHARON) Israel and the Arab world;... [translated from the Hebrew edition of 1964 with updating of the last chapter]. London, 1970. pp. 576.

CRISIS in the Middle East : the Arab-Israeli dispute and its effect on the western alliance; report of a seminar held at the Royal United Service Institution on Wednesday, 3 December 1969; chairman Alastair Buchan. [London, 1970?]. pp. 18.

DEMERON (PIERRE) Against Israel; translated from the French by H. Dee Bachour. Damascus, 1970. pp. 96.

DODD (C. H.) and SALES (MARY E.) eds. Israel and the Arab world. London, 1970. pp. 247. bibliog.

ECKARDT (ALICE) and ECKARDT (ARTHUR ROY) Encounter with Israel: a challenge to conscience. New York, [1970]. pp. 304.

FEINBERG (NATHAN) The Arab-Israel conflict in international law: a critical analysis of the colloquium of Arab jurists in Algiers. Jerusalem, 1970. pp. 120.

GASPAR (LORAND) Palestine année 0: un dialogue israélo-arabe. Paris, 1970. pp. 103.

GINIEWSKI (PAUL) Le point de vue juif. Bruxelles, 1970. pp. 287.

JOHN (ROBERT) 1921- , and HADAWI (SAMI) The Palestine diary. Beirut, [1970]. 2 vols. bibliog.

KIMCHE (JON) The second Arab awakening. London, [1970]. pp. 288. bibliog.

MASON (HERBERT) ed. Reflections on the Middle East crisis. Paris, [1970]. pp. 236.

PARTISANS. No. 52. Le peuple palestinien en marche. Paris, 1970. pp. 199.

PERES (SHIMON) David's sling. London, [1970]. pp. 322.

REISMAN (MICHAEL) The art of the possible: diplomatic alternatives in the Middle East. Princeton, 1970. pp. 161.

SAYEGH (FAYEZ A.) Palestine, Israel and peace. Beirut, 1970. pp. 38. (Palestine Research Center. Palestine Essays. No. 17)

SAYIGH (YUSIF ABDALLAH) Towards peace in Palestine;...address delivered on April 15, 1970, at Central Hall, Westminster, London, under the sponsorship of the Council for the Advancement of Arab-British understanding. Beirut, [1970]. pp. 29.

TAYLOR (ALAN R.) of the American University in Washington, and TETLIE (RICHARD N.) eds. Palestine: a search for truth: approaches to the Arab-Israeli conflict. Washington, [1970]. pp. 284.

1971

AL-FATEH and others. Documents of the Palestinian resistance movement. New York, 1971. pp. 23.

AMERICAN ACADEMIC ASSOCIATION FOR PEACE IN THE MIDDLE EAST. Annual Conference, 3rd, Philadelphia, 1970. People and politics in the Middle East: proceedings of the annual conference...; edited by Michael Curtis. New Brunswick, [1971]. pp. 325.

The ARAB-Israeli dispute: [seminar held at Sidney Sussex College, Cambridge University, 11-13 December, 1970, by the Institute for the Study of Conflict]. [London], 1971. pp. 42. (Institute for the Study of Conflict. Conflict Studies. Special Reports)

KHALIDI (WALID) ed. From haven to conquest: readings in Zionism and the Palestine problem until 1948. Beirut, 1971. pp. 914. (Institute for Palestine Studies. Anthology Series. No. 2)

KIMCHE (JON) Can Israel contain the Palestine revolution? London, 1971. pp. 11. (Institute for the Study of Conflict. Conflict Studies. No. 13)

VATIKIOTIS (PANAYIOTIS J.) Conflict in the Middle East. London, 1971. pp. 224. bibliog.

JEWISH-ARAB RELATIONS (Cont'd.)

- Bibliography

FIFTH OF JUNE SOCIETY. A selected reading list on the Palestine problem and Arab-Israeli conflict; prepared under the guidance of Professor Walid Khalidi. Beirut, [1969?]. pp. 7.

JEWISH AUTONOMOUS OBLAST'

EVREISKAIA... Еврейская автономная область. Хабаровск, Книжное Издательство, 1965. pp. 32. 19½cm.

JEWISH LAW
See LAW, JEWISH

JEWISH LEARNING AND SCHOLARSHIP

LANCZOS (CORNELIUS) Judaism and science. [Leeds], 1970. pp. 22. (Leeds. University. Selig Brodetsky Memorial Lectures. No. 11)

JEWISH PERIODICALS

- Bibliography

FRAENKEL (JOSEF) compiler. The Jewish press of the world. 6th ed. London, World Jewish Congress, Cultural Department, 1967. pp. 116. 21½cm.

JEWISH QUESTION

[INGE (WILLIAM RALPH)] The Jews. London, Joint Press Committee, [1922]. pp. 8. (Reprinted from the Jewish Guardian)

GAJIĆ (E. B.) Jugoslavija i "jevrejski problem". Beograd, Gregorić, 1938. pp. 96. 21cm.

INTERNATIONAL CONFERENCE OF CHRISTIANS AND JEWS, OXFORD, 1946. Freedom, justice and responsibility: reports and recommendations of the...Conference. London, [1946]. pp. 44.

WORLD JEWISH CONGRESS. British Section. Jewish Topics of Today. No. 7. Three areas of Jewish life; addresses to a meeting of the...world executive, July 1964. London, [1965]. pp. 32. 21cm.

IKOR (ROGER) Peut-on être juif aujourd'hui? Paris, Grasset, [1968]. pp. 283. 20½cm.

LÉON (ABRAHAM) La conception matérialiste de la question juive; edition revue et préfacée par Maxime Rodinson;...textes complémentaires de Isaac Deutscher et Léon Trotsky. [new ed.]. Paris, Études et Documentation Internationales, [1968]. pp. xlvii, 206. 20½cm.

LÉVAI (JENŐ) Hungarian Jewry and the papacy: Pope Pius XII did not remain silent; reports, documents and records from church and state archives;... translated by J.R. Foster. London, Sands, [1968]. pp. xii, 132. 22cm.

BAR-NIR (DOV) A letter to a left-wing friend. London, [1969?]. pp. 8.

GREIVE (HERMANN) Theologie und Ideologie: Katholizismus und Judentum in Deutschland und Österreich, 1918-1935. Heidelberg, 1969. pp. 320. bibliog. (Cologne. Universität. Martin-Buber-Institut. Arbeiten. Band 1)

LAMM (HANS) Karl Marx und das Judentum. München, 1969. pp. 78.

BELOFF (MAX) The intellectual in politics and other essays. London, [1970]. pp. 346.

GRUENAGEL (FRIEDRICH) Die Judenfrage: die geschichtliche Verantwortung der Kirchen und Israels. Stuttgart, [1970]. pp. 46.

IKOR (ROGER) Lettre ouverte aux juifs. Paris, [1970]. pp. 158.

TROTSKII (LEV DAVYDOVICH) On the Jewish question. New York, 1970. pp. 31.

JEWS

WOLF (LUCIEN) Are the Jews a separate people?: the problems of race and intermarriage. n.p., [1904?]. pp. 4. 21cm. (Extracted from an article in the Jewish Quarterly Review, October 1904)

MAGNUS (Sir PHILIP) Jewish action and Jewish ideals. London, [imprint], 1917. pp. 11. 21½cm. (Reprinted from the Jewish Chronicle, November 13, 1891)

BIKERMAN (IOSIF MANASIEVICH) K samopoznaniiu evreia: chem my byli, chem my stali, chem my dolzhny byt'; [translated from German]. Parizh, 1939. pp. 105.

WORLD JEWISH CONGRESS. British Section. Jewish Topics of Today. No. 8. World Jewry and the international scene: a survey, 1964-1965. London, 1965. pp. 26. 21½cm.

BAR-ZOHAR (MICHEL) The avengers;...translated from the French by Len Ortzen. London, Barker, [1968]. pp. 287. bibliog. 21½cm.

DEUTSCHER (ISAAC) The non-Jewish Jew, and other essays;... edited with an introduction by Tamara Deutscher. London, O.U.P., 1968. pp. xi, 164. 21½cm.

LITVINOFF (BARNET) A peculiar people: inside world Jewry today. London, Weidenfeld & Nicolson, [1969]. pp. (v), 308. bibliog. 21½cm.

HEBREW UNIVERSITY. Institute of Contemporary Jewry, and INSTITUTE OF JEWISH AFFAIRS. Jewish population studies, 1961-1968; edited by U.O. Schmelz and P. Glikson. Jerusalem, 1970. pp. 174. bibliog.

The JEWISH communities of the world: demography, political and organizational status, religious institutions, education, press;...published for the Institute of Jewish Affairs in association with the World Jewish Congress. London, 1971. pp. 128.

- Bibliography

SCHMELZ (URIEL OSCAR) compiler. Jewish demography and statistics bibliography for 1920-1960;...with the assistance of R. Shebath. Jerusalem, 1961. pp. (829).

- Biography

LEVITAN (TINA NELLIE) Jews in American life. New York, [1969]. pp. 253.

- Civilization

GUEDEMANN (MORITZ) Geschichte des Erziehungswesens und der Cultur der abendländischen Juden während des Mittelalters und der neueren Zeit; [reprint of edition originally published 1880-88]. Amsterdam, 1966. 3 vols.

EPSTEIN (ISIDORE) Judaism: a historical presentation. Harmondsworth, Penguin Books, 1959, repr. 1968. pp. 349. bibliog. 18cm. (Pelican Books. A440)

GORDIS (ROBERT) The root and the branch: Judaism and the free society. Chicago, U. of Chicago P., 1962. pp. xv, 254. 21½cm.

DAWIDOWICZ (LUCY S.) ed. The golden tradition: Jewish life and thought in Eastern Europe. London, Vallentine, 1967. pp. (vi), 502. bibliog. 21cm.

KAUPP (PETER) Toynbee und die Juden: eine kritische Untersuchung der Darstellung des Judentums im Gesamtwerk Arnold J. Toynbees, etc. Meisenheim am Glan, Hain, 1967. pp (xi), 300. bibliog. 23cm. (Mainz. Universität. Institut für Vergleichende Kulturwissenschaft. Archiv für Vergleichende Kulturwissenschaft. Band 1)

JUBILEE volume dedicated to Curt C. Silberman; edited by Herbert A. Strauss [and] Hans G. Reissner. New York, 1969. pp. 132.

NEUSNER (JACOB) Politics and theology in Talmudic Babylonia. [Syracuse], 1969. pp. 25. (Syracuse University. B.G. Rudolph Lectures in Judaic Studies. 1969)

- Converts to Christianity

DOMÍNGUEZ ORTIZ (A.) Los conversos de origen judío despries de la expulsión. in tome 3 of Consejo Superior de Investigaciones Cientificas. Instituto "Balmes" de Sociologia. Departamento de Historia social. Estudios de historia social de España. Madrid, 1955.

- Diaspora

SAMUEL (EDWIN) 2nd Viscount Samuel. The Jewish civil services of the Diaspora. London, World Jewish Congress, British Section, 1958. pp. 8. 21½cm. (Noah Barou Memorial Lectures. 1958)

SHAPIRO (JUDAH J.) Contemporary Jewish community life and the Zionist movement: dangers and challenges;...comments by Zvi Lurie. Jerusalem, 1965. pp. 38.

- Dictionaries and encyclopaedias

The NEW standard Jewish encyclopedia; Cecil Roth and Geoffrey Wigoder, editors-in-chief. rev. ed. London, 1970. 2028 columns.

ENCYCLOPAEDIA judaica; [editor in chief, Cecil Roth]. Jerusalem, [1971-72]. 16 vols. bibliogs.

- Education

GUEDEMANN (MORITZ) Geschichte des Erziehungswesens und der Cultur der abendländischen Juden während des Mittelalters und der neueren Zeit; [reprint of edition originally published 1880-88]. Amsterdam, 1966. 3 vols.

EDUCATION AID SOCIETY. Objects, methods and progress. [London, 1926?]. pp. 10. 21½cm.

ORT UNION. Report on the ORT activities, August 1946-July 1947, submitted to the meeting of the Central Board of the World ORT Union, Paris July 6th-7th 1947. Paris, 1947. fo. 125. 29cm.

- History

HEER (FRIEDRICH) God's first love: Christians and Jews over two thousand years;...translated from the German by Geoffrey Skelton. London, [1970]. pp. 530. bibliog.

- History - Maps

GILBERT (MARTIN) Jewish history atlas;... cartography by Arthur Banks. London, Weidenfeld & Nicolson, [1969]. pp. (v), 112, (14). bibliog. 25½cm.

- History - To 70 A.D.

ROBINSON (HENRY WHEELER) The history of Israel: its facts and factors. London, Duckworth, 1941. pp. 262. bibliog. 18½cm.

BRUCE (FREDERICK FYVIE) Israel and the nations from the exodus to the fall of the second temple Exeter, [1963] repr. 1969. pp. 254. bibliog.

FOSTER (RAYMOND S.) The restoration of Israel: a study in exile and return. London, 1970. pp. 239.

MAHLER (RAPHAEL) A history of modern Jewry:... [an abridged translation of the Hebrew revised text of 1960]. London, 1971 in progress. bibliog.

- Intellectual life

JOSPE (ALFRED) ed. Tradition and contemporary experience: essays on Jewish thought and life. New York, [1970] repr. 1971. pp. 372.

- Law

STEINBERG (DAYAN MEYER) Responsum on problems of adoption in Jewish law...;edited...by Rabbi Maurice Rose. London, 1969. pp. 45.

- Legal status, laws, etc.

[HOFFMANN (BRUNO)] Die Ausnahmegesetzgebung gegen die Juden von 1933-1945, unter besonderer Berücksichtigung der Synagogengemeinde Köln. [Cologne, 1963?]. pp. 121. bibliog.

HAHN (ROLF) Das "schändliche Dekret" vom 17.3.1808 und seine Auswirkung auf die rechtliche Stellung der Kölner Juden. [Cologne, imprint, 1967?]. pp. 117. bibliog.

- Mental illness

MALZBERG (BENJAMIN) Mental disease among Jews in Canada: a study of first admissions to mental hospitals, 1950-1952. Albany, Research Foundation for Mental Hygiene, 1963. fo. 88. 28cm.

- Migration

LEE (SAMUEL J.) Moses of the new world: the work of Baron de Hirsch. New York, [1970]. pp. 313.

JEWS (Cont'd.)

- Persecutions

RUSSO-JEWISH COMMITTEE. Russian atrocities, 1881: supplementary statement issued in confirmation of the Times narrative. London, [imprint], 1882. pp. 35. 21cm.

LONDON. London Committee of Deputies of the British Jews and ANGLO-JEWISH ASSOCIATION. Conjoint Committee. Massacre of Jews in Russia: report of the protest meeting at Queen's Hall, January 8th, 1906; with extract from the report made to the Russo-Jewish Committee by Mr C. Stettauer, a member of the Commission which recently journeyed through Russia to organize the distribution of the relief fund. London, 1906. pp. 47. (Reprinted from the Jewish World, January 12th, 1906)

JEWISH LABOUR LEAGUE. Jewish Labour League; ...to the workers of Great Britain. [Manchester, imprint, 1915]. pp. (4). 22cm.

KEMPNER (ROBERT M. W.) Edith Stein und Anne Frank: zwei von Hunderttausend: die Enthüllungen über die NS-Verbrechen in Holland vor dem Schwurgericht in München: die Ermordung der "nichtarischen" Mönche und Nonnen. Freiburg im Br., 1968. pp. 189.

MORSE (ARTHUR D.) While six million died. London, Secker & Warburg, 1968. pp. vi, 420. bibliog. 21½cm.

PRESSER (JACOB) Ashes in the wind: the destruction of Dutch Jewry. London, Souvenir P., [1968]. pp. xiv, 556. 21½cm.

GINIEWSKI (PAUL) Le point de vue juif. Bruxelles, 1970. pp. 287.

- Political and social conditions

BEER (MAX) Socialist. Social struggles in antiquity;... translated by H.J. Stenning and revised by the author. London, 1922 repr. 1925. pp. 222.

SCHAEFFER (HENRY) Hebrew tribal economy and the jubilee as illustrated in Semitic and Indo-European village communities. Leipzig, Hinrichs, 1922. pp. viii, 198. 22cm.

SAMUEL (EDWIN) 2nd Viscount Samuel. The Jewish civil services of the Diaspora. London, World Jewish Congress, British Section, 1958. pp. 8. 21½cm. (Noah Barou Memorial Lectures. 1958)

WORLD JEWISH CONGRESS. British Section Jewish Topics of Today. No. 7. Three areas of Jewish life; addresses to a meeting of the...world executive, July 1964. London, [1965]. pp. 32. 21cm.

CHARIM (ALEXANDER) Die toten Gemeinden. Wien, Europa Verlag, [1966]. pp. 51. 19cm. (Dokumentationsarchiv des Österreichischen Widerstandes. Monographien zur Zeitgeschichte)

GOITEIN (SOLOMON DOB FRITZ) A Mediterranean society: the Jewish communities of the Arab world as portrayed in the documents of the Cairo Geniza. Berkeley, U. of California P., 1967 in progress. 23½cm.

BISGYER (MAURICE) Challenge and encounter: behind the scenes in the struggle for Jewish survival. New York, Crown, [1967] pp. xxiii, 279. 21cm.

HASSELMEIER (HANS HEINRICH) Die Stellung der Juden in Schaumburg-Lippe von 1648 bis zur Emanzipation. Bückeburg, 1967. pp. 138. bibliog. (Historische Arbeitsgemeinschaft für Schaumburg. Schaumburger Studien. Heft 19)

FISCHER (HORST) Judentum, Staat und Heer in Preussen im frühen 19. Jahrhundert: zur Geschichte der staatlichen Judenpolitik. Tübingen, Mohr, 1968. pp. viii, 232. bibliog. 23cm. (Leo Baeck Institute of Jews from Germany. Schriftenreihe Wissenschaftlicher Abhandlungen. 20)

FREID (JACOB) ed. Judaism and the community: new directions in Jewish social work. New York, Yoseloff, [1968]. pp. 248. 21cm.

GINIEWSKI (PAUL) Le point de vue juif. Bruxelles, 1970. pp. 287.

JEWS - Religion
See JUDAISM

- Restoration

HERZL (THEODOR) Der Judenstaat: (Versuch einer modernen Lösung der Judenfrage); Neudruck der Erstausgabe 1896. Osnabrück, Zeller, 1968. pp. 88. bibliog. 22½cm. (Milliaria. 12)

CHLENOV (EFIM VLADIMIROVICH) Der Krieg, die russische Revolution und der Zionismus: Rede...auf der Delegierten-Konferenz der russischen Zionisten in Petrograd,...1917. Copenhagen, 1917. pp. 24.

ZIONIST ORGANIZATION OF AMERICA. Summary of the position of the...Organization...in conference with Dr. Weizmann and associates; submitted by the President...and adopted by the National Executive Committee at its meeting March 19-20th, 1921. n.p., [1921]. pp. 29. 20½cm.

SIDEBOTHAM (HERBERT) The future of Palestine. London, 1922. pp. 8.

ANDRAWOS (ELIAS) The Jews: do they have the right to establish a state of their own in Palestine? Cairo, [1960]. pp. 24.

EUROPEAN ZIONIST CONFERENCE, BASLE, 1964. In search of new paths. Jerusalem, [1964]. pp. 53.

BURG (J.G.) pseud. [i.e. JOSEF GINSBURG] Schuld und Schicksal: Europas Juden zwischen Henkern und Heuchlern. 4th ed. München, 1965. pp. 370.

MANDEL (N.) Turks, Arabs and Jewish immigration into Palestine, 1882-1914. in St. Antony's Papers. No.17. Middle Eastern affairs. No.4. London, 1965.

SA'B (HASAN) Zionism and racism. Beirut, 1965. pp. 34. (Palestine Research Center. Palestine Essays. No. 2.)

SAYEGH (FAYEZ A.) Zionist colonialism in Palestine. Beirut, Palestine Liberation Organization, Research Center, 1965. pp. vi, 78. 18cm. (Palestine Monographs. 1)

SHAPIRO (JUDAH J.) Contemporary Jewish community life and the Zionist movement: dangers and challenges;...comments by Zvi Lurie. Jerusalem, 1965. pp. 38.

JEFFRIES (JOSEPH MARY NAGLE) The Balfour Declaration. Beirut, 1967. pp. 20. (Institute for Palestinian Studies. Monographs Series. No. 7)

SAYEGH (FAYEZ A.) Do Jews have a "divine right" to Palestine. Beirut, 1967. pp. 13. (Palestine Liberation Organization. Research Center. Palestine Essays. No. 4)

WEIZMANN (CHAIM) The letters and papers...; edited by Leonard Stein in collaboration with Gedalia Yogev. London, O.U.P., 1968 in progress. 23½cm.

ARIAN (ALAN) Ideological change in Israel. Cleveland, Case Western Reserve U.P., [1968]. pp. xvii, 220. bibliog. 21cm.

AVNERY (URI) Israel without Zionists: a plea for peace in the Middle East. New York, Macmillan, [1968]. pp. 215. 21cm.

BURG (J.G.) pseud. [i.e. Josef GINSBURG] Sündenböcke: Grossangriffe des Zionismus auf Papst Pius XII. und auf die deutschen Regierungen. [Munich], 1968. pp. 334.

DAVIS (JOHN HERBERT) The evasive peace: a study of the Zionist-Arab problem. London, Murray, [1968]. pp. x, 124. bibliog. 21½cm.

KIMCHE (JON) The unromantics: the great powers and the Balfour declaration. London, 1968. pp. 87.

ROSE (NORMAN ANTHONY) Gentile zionism and Anglo-Zionist diplomacy, 1929-39: some aspects of the role played by Gentile zionists in relations between the British government and the Jewish agency. [Ph.D.(London) Thesis]. 1968. fo. 445. bibliog. 25½cm. Typescript: unpublished. This thesis is the property of London University and may not be removed from the Library.

SEMINAR OF ARAB JURISTS ON PALESTINE, ALGIERS, 1967. The Palestine question; translated from French by Edward Rizk. Beirut, 1968. pp. 203. (Institute for Palestine Studies. Monographs Series. No. 18)

SOUSTELLE (JACQUES) La longue marche d'Israel. [Paris], Fayard, [1968]. pp. 338. bibliog. 21½cm.

STEPPAT (FRITZ) Zionism-Judaism: some historical aspects of the clash between Zionism and Arab nationalism. Beirut, 1968. pp. 13.

WEISBORD (ROBERT G.) African Zion: the attempt to establish a Jewish colony in the East Africa Protectorate, 1903-1905. Philadelphia, Jewish Publication Society of America, 1968. pp. ix, 347. bibliog. 21cm.

AUERBACH (ELIAS) Pionier der Verwirklichung: ein Arzt aus Deutschland erzählt vom Beginn der zionistischen Bewegung und seiner Niederlassung in Palästina kurz nach der Jahrhundertwende. Stuttgart, [1969]. pp. 411.

BOROCHOV (BER) Die Grundlagen des Poalezionismus. Frankfurt/M, 1969. pp. 116.

GINIEWSKI (PAUL) Le sionisme d'Abraham a Dayan. Brussels, 1969. pp. 568. 20½cm.

HALPERN (BEN) The idea of the Jewish state. 2nd ed. Cambridge, Mass., 1969. pp. 493. bibliog. (Harvard University. Center for Middle Eastern Studies. Harvard Middle Eastern Studies. 3.)

HILLEL (MARC) Israël en danger de paix. [Paris], Fayard, [1969]. pp. 350.

[HUMAN RIGHTS REGIONAL CONFERENCE, BEIRUT, 1968]. Zionism and Arab resistance. Beirut, Palestine Research Center, 1969. pp. 223. 17cm. (Palestine Monographs. 54)

NISSES (EFIM IAKOVLEVICH) Komu sluzhat sionisty. Simferopol', 1969. pp. 64.

NUTTING (HAROLD ANTHONY) The tragedy of Palestine from the Balfour declaration to today. London, [1969]. pp. 15.

PRAGG (H. VAN) and WERBLOWSKY (RAPHAEL JEHUDA ZWI) Antisemitisme: antizionisme. Bussum, [1969]. pp. 102.

RUBIN (JACOB A.) Partners in state-building: American Jewry and Israel. New York, [1969]. pp. 283. bibliog.

SAYEGH (FAYEZ A.) The Zionist diplomacy. Beirut, 1969. pp. 160. (Palestine Research Center. Palestine Monographs. 13)

WEINSTOCK (NATHAN) Le sionisme contre Israël. Paris, 1969. pp. 622. bibliog.

JOHN (ROBERT) 1921- , and HADAWI (SAMI) The Palestine diary. Beirut, [1970]. 2 vols. bibliog.

LICHTHEIM (RICHARD) Rückkehr: Lebenserinnerungen aus der Frühzeit des deutschen Zionismus. Stuttgart, [1970]. pp. 387.

(The REBIRTH of Yasha Kazakov: the road from Moscow to Jerusalem); revival of national Jewish consciousness; impact of six-day war on the young generation; return to the homeland. [London], 1970. pp.12.

SILVERBERG (ROBERT) If I forget thee O Jerusalem: American Jews and the State of Israel. New York, 1970. pp. 620. bibliog.

SIONIZM - otravlennoe oruzhie imperializma: dokumenty i materialy; (sbornik sostavlen po publikatsiiam sovetskoi pechati) Moskva, 1970. pp. 319.

TALMON (JACOB LAIB) Israel among the nations. London, [1970]. pp. 199.

WEINSTOCK (NATHAN) and ROTHSCHILD (JON) The truth about Israel and Zionism. New York, 1970. pp. 15.

WORLD ZIONIST ORGANIZATION. The Central Zionist Archives. Jerusalem, 1970. pp. 31.

ELON (AMOS) The Israelis: founders and sons. New York, [1971]. pp. 359. bibliog.

KAYE (SOLLY) Zionism: a socialist view. London, [1971]. pp. 10. (Communist Party of Great Britain. Communist Party Pamphlets)

JEWS - Restoration (Cont'd.)

KHALIDI (WALID) ed. From haven to conquest: readings in Zionism and the Palestine problem until 1948. Beirut, 1971. pp. 914. (Institute for Palestine Studies. Anthology Series. No. 2)

SEGRE (V.D.) Israel: a society in transition. London, 1971. pp. 227.

- Societies

ORT UNION. Report on the ORT activities, August 1946-July 1947, submitted to the meeting of the Central Board of the World ORT Union, Paris July 6th-7th 1947. Paris, 1947. fo. 125. 29cm.

JEWS, MOROCCAN

SHOKEID (MOSHE) The dual heritage: immigrants from the Atlas mountains in an Israeli village. Manchester, [1971]. pp. 245. bibliog.

JEWS AS SOLDIERS

FISCHER (HORST) Judentum, Staat und Heer in Preussen im frühen 19. Jahrhundert: zur Geschichte der staatlichen Judenpolitik. Tübingen, Mohr, 1968. pp. viii, 232. bibliog. 23cm. (Leo Baeck Institute of Jews from Germany. Schriftenreihe Wissenschaftlicher Abhandlungen. 20)

JEWS IN AUSTRALIA

MEDDING (P.Y.) From assimilation to group survival: a political and sociological study of an Australian Jewish community; introduction by Marshall Sklare. Melbourne, 1968. pp. 309. bibliog.

GETZLER (ISRAEL) Neither toleration nor favour: the Australian chapter of Jewish emancipation. Melbourne, 1970. pp. 153. bibliog.

JEWS IN AUSTRIA

BAUM (PHIL) and WEISBROD (CAROL) Shadow over Austria. London, [1966]. pp. 32. (World Jewish Congress. British Section. Jewish Topics of Today. No. 9)

MOSER (JONNY) Die Judenverfolgung in Österreich 1938-1945. Wien, Europa Verlag, [1966]. pp. 55. bibliog. 19cm. (Dokumentationsarchiv des Österreichischen Widerstandes. Monographien zur Zeitgeschichte)

ROSENKRANZ (HERBERT) Reichskristallnacht: 9. November 1938 in Österreich. Wien, Europa Verlag, [1968]. pp. 68. 19cm. (Dokumentationsarchiv des Österreichischen Widerstandes. Monographien zur Zeitgeschichte)

RESEARCH GROUP FOR EUROPEAN MIGRATION PROBLEMS. Publications. 16. The return movement of Jews to Austria after the Second World War, with special consideration of the return from Israel; by F. Wilder-Okladek. The Hague, 1969. pp. 130. bibliog.

WEINZIERL (ERIKA) Zu wenig Gerechte: Österreicher und Judenverfolgung 1938-1945. Graz, [1969]. pp. 208. bibliog.

JEWS IN BELGIUM

AJZENBERG-KARNY (MINNA) and WOLF (ALBERT) of Liège. À propos de..."Les Belges face à la persécution raciale 1940-1944" par Betty Garfinkels...un soufflet! Liège, [1966]. pp. 8.

JEWS IN CANADA

ROSENBERG (LOUIS) Use of the terms "racial origin" and "religion" in the Canadian Census and other official statistical reports, and its effect upon the Jewish community in Canada. n.p., 1946. fo. 12.

GORDON (M. EDMUND) Political and legal aspects of Jewish history in Canada. [Montreal, 1959] fo. 13.

ROSENBERG (LOUIS) A study of the growth and changes in the distribution of the Jewish population of Winnipeg, 1961. Montreal, [1961?]. fo. 30. (Canadian Jewish Congress. Bureau of Social and Economic Research. Canadian Jewish Population Studies. Canadian Jewish Community Series. Vol. 2, no. 1)

ROSENBERG (LOUIS) Two centuries of Jewish life in Canada, 1760-1960. Montreal, [1961]. pp. 28-49. (Canadian Jewish Congress. Bureau of Social and Economic Research. Canadian Jewish Population Studies. Population Characteristics Series. No. 3) (Reprinted from The American Jewish Year Book, 1961, vol. 62)

ROSENBERG (LOUIS) A statistical study of the number and percentage of Jewish children in the Protestant schools of greater Montreal and the suburb of Chomedey as at April 30, 1964. Montreal, 1964. fo. 7. (Canadian Jewish Congress. Bureau of Social and Economic Research. Research Papers. Series E. No. 3)

ROSENBERG (LOUIS) Changes in the geographical distribution of the Jewish population of metropolitan Montreal in the decennial periods from 1901 to 1961 and the estimated possible changes during the period from 1961 to 1971: a preliminary study. Montreal, 1966. fo. 5. (Canadian Jewish Congress. Bureau of Social and Economic Research. Research Papers. Series A. No. 7)

ROSENBERG (LOUIS) The number, age and sex distribution and marital status of Jews 60 years of age and over in the metropolitan census area of Montreal and in the larger municipal areas within metropolitan Montreal in 1961. Montreal, 1966. fo. 7. (Canadian Jewish Congress. Bureau of Social and Economic Research. Research Papers. Series. A. No. 6)

ROSENBERG (LOUIS) A preliminary study of the number of Jewish children of elementary school age and Jewish teenagers in Canada and its larger Jewish communities. Montreal, 1966. fo. 8. (Canadian Jewish Congress. Bureau of Social and Economic Research. Research Papers. Series A. No. 5)

VINEBERG (ETHEL) The history of the National Council of Jewish Women of Canada. Montreal, National Council of Jewish Women of Canada, 1967. pp. 84. 18cm.

VAUGEOIS (DENIS) Les juifs et la Nouvelle France. Trois-Rivières, [1968]. pp. 154. bibliog.

JEWS IN CHINA

WHITE (WILLIAM CHARLES) Chinese Jews: a compilation of matters relating to the Jews of K'ai-fêng Fu. 2nd ed. New York, Paragon Book Reprint Corporation, [1966]. pp. xii, 228. 24½cm.

JEWS IN CZECHOSLOVAKIA

RYCHNOVSKY (ERNST) and others, eds. Masaryk a židovství, etc. Praha, 1931. pp. 333.

KISCH (GUIDO) Die Prager Universität und die Juden 1348-1848; (Nachdruck der Ausgabe 1935). Amsterdam, 1969. pp. 239. bibliog.

INSTITUTE OF JEWISH AFFAIRS. Background Papers. No. 11. Jewish aspects of the changes in Czechoslovakia. [London]. 1968. pp. 26.

KESTENBERG-GLADSTEIN (RUTH) Neuere Geschichte der Juden in den böhmischen Ländern. Tübingen, 1969 in progress. bibliog. (Leo Baeck Institute of Jews from Germany. Schriftenreihe Wissenschaftlicher Abhandlungen. 18)

JEWS IN DENMARK

YAHIL (LENI) The rescue of Danish Jewry: test of a democracy; ...translated from the Hebrew by Morris Gradel. Philadelphia, 1969. pp. 536. bibliog.

JEWS IN DUTCH GUIANA

ESSAI historique sur la colonie de Surinam...avec la description et l'etat actuel de la colonie...avec l'histoire de la nation juive portugaise et allemande y etablie;...[by Moses Pereira de Leon and others]. Paramaribo, 1788; [Amsterdam, 1968]. 2 vols. (in 1). Facsimile.

JEWS IN EAST AFRICA

WEISBORD (ROBERT G.) African Zion: the attempt to establish a Jewish colony in the East Africa Protectorate, 1903-1905. Philadelphia, Jewish Publication Society of America, 1968. pp. ix, 347. bibliog. 21cm.

JEWS IN EASTERN EUROPE

DAWIDOWICZ (LUCY S.) ed. The golden tradition: Jewish life and thought in eastern Europe. London, Vallentine, 1967. pp. (vi), 502. bibliog.

ZECHLIN (EGMONT) Die deutsche Politik und die Juden im Ersten Weltkrieg. Göttingen, [1969]. pp. 592. bibliog.

JEWS IN EGYPT

LANDAU (JACOB M.) Jews in nineteenth-century Egypt. New York, 1969. pp. 354. bibliog. (New York (City). University. Studies in Near Eastern Civilization. No. 2)

JEWS IN EUROPE

RUSSELL (EDWARD FREDERICK LANGLEY) 2nd Baron Russell of Liverpool. The trial of Adolf Eichmann. London, Heinemann, 1962. pp. xxviii, 324. 21½cm.

BURG (J.G.) pseud. [i.e. JOSEF GINSBURG] Schuld und Schicksal: Europas Juden zwischen Henkern und Heuchlern. 4th ed. München, 1965. pp. 370.

LEVENBERG (SHNEUR) European Jewry today. Leeds, University Press, 1967. pp. 26. 21½cm. (Leeds. University. Selig Brodetsky Memorial Lectures. No. 8)

MORSE (ARTHUR D.) While six million died. London, Secker & Warburg, 1968. pp. vi, 420. bibliog. 21½cm.

JEWS IN FRANCE

La RÉVOLUTION française et l'émancipation des Juifs; [reprints of works originally published 1787-1806]. Paris, Éditions d'Histoire Sociale, [1968]. 8 vols. 21cm.

GUEDEMANN (MORITZ) Geschichte des Erziehungswesens und der Cultur der abendländischen Juden während des Mittelalters und der neueren Zeit; [reprint of edition originally published 1880-88]. Amsterdam, 1966. 3 vols.

BLUM (LÉON) Souvenirs sur l'affaire. Paris, Gallimard, [1935]. pp. 181. 18½cm.

HERTZBERG (ARTHUR) The French enlightenment and the Jews. New York, Columbia U.P., 1968. pp. xii, 420. bibliog. 22½ cm.

SZAJKOWSKI (ZOSA) Jews and the French revolutions of 1789, 1830 and 1848; [a collection of studies]. New York, 1970. pp. 1161.

MARRUS (MICHAEL R.) The politics of assimilation: a study of the French Jewish community at the time of the Dreyfus affair. Oxford, 1971. pp. 300. bibliog.

JEWS IN GERMANY

GUEDEMANN (MORITZ) Geschichte des Erziehungswesens und der Cultur der abendländischen Juden während des Mittelalters und der neueren Zeit; [reprint of edition originally published 1880-88]. Amsterdam, 1966. 3 vols.

NEUMANN (KURT H.) Die jüdische Verfälschung des Sozialismus in der Revolution von 1848. Berlin, Junker und Dünnhaupt, 1939. pp. 80. bibliog. 23 cm. (Deutsche Hochschule für Politik. Forschungsabteilung. Veröffentlichungen. Geschichte. Band 3)

[HOFFMANN (BRUNO)] Die Ausnahmegesetzgebung gegen die Juden von 1933-1945, unter besonderer Berücksichtigung der Synagogengemeinde Köln. [Cologne, 1963?]. pp. 121. bibliog.

SCHNEE (HEINRICH) Das Hoffaktorentum in der deutschen Geschichte. Göttingen, [1964?]. pp. 30. bibliog. (Ranke-Gesellschaft. Historisch-Politische Hefte. Heft 14)

BRESLAUER (WALTER) and GOLDSCHMIDT (F.) The work of the Council of Jews from Germany in the sphere of indemnification. London, 1966. pp. 29.

OPPLER (FRIEDRICH) Das falsche Tabu: Betrachtungen über das deutsch-jüdische Problem. Stuttgart, Seewald, [1966]. pp 331. 20½cm.

JEWS IN GERMANY (Cont'd.)

ARNOLD (HERMANN) Von den Juden in der Pfalz. Speyer, Pfälzische Gesellschaft zur Förderung der Wissenschaften, 1967. pp. vii, 127. bibliog. 24cm. (Veröffentlichungen. Band 56)

DEUTSCHE und Juden: Beiträge von Nahum Goldmann [and others]. Frankfurt a. M., [1967]. pp. 123.

GRUENFELD (FRITZ V.) Das Leinenhaus Grünfeld: Erinnerungen und Dokumente... eingeleitet und herausgegeben von Stefi Jersch-Wenzel. Berlin, Duncker und Humblot, [1967]. pp. 237. bibliog 23½cm. (Schriften zur Wirtschafts- und Sozialgeschichte. Band 12)

HAHN (ROLF) Das "schändliche Dekret" vom 17.3.1808 und seine Auswirkung auf die rechtliche Stellung der Kölner Juden. [Cologne, imprint, 1967?]. pp. 117. bibliog.

HANKE (PETER) Zur Geschichte der Juden in München zwischen 1933 und 1945. München, Stadtarchiv, 1967. pp. 353. bibliog. (Munich. Stadtarchiv. Neue Schriftenreihe. Band 19)

HASSELMEIER (HANS HEINRICH) Die Stellung der Juden in Schaumburg-Lippe von 1648 bis zur Emanzipation. Bückeburg, 1967. pp. 138. bibliog. (Historische Arbeitsgemeinschaft für Schaumburg. Schaumburger Studien. Heft 19)

JERSCH-WENZEL (STEFI) Jüdische Bürger und kommunale Selbstverwaltung in preussischen Städten 1808-1848. Berlin, De Gruyter, 1967. pp. xi, 265. bibliog. 23½cm. (Berlin. Freie Universität. Friedrich-Meinecke-Institut. Historische Kommission zu Berlin. Veröffentlichungen. Band 21)

OPPENHEIMER (WALTER W. JACOB) Jüdische Jugend in Deutschland. München, Juventa Verlag, [1967]. pp. 207. bibliog. 23cm.

ROTHSCHILD (L.) Judentum in Ostdeutschland. in Schulz (Eberhard G.) ed. Leistung und Schicksal. Köln, 1967.

SCHEIDL (FRANZ J.) Deutschland und die Juden in Vergangenheit und Gegenwart; [with] Nachtrag. Wien, Scheidl, [1967?]. pp. 321. 20cm.

SCHEIDL (FRANZ J.) Die Wahrheit über die Millionenvergasung von Juden. Wien, Scheidl, [1967?]. pp. 255. 20cm. (Geschichte der Verfemung Deutschlands. Band 4)

BURG (J.G.) pseud. [i.e. Josef GINSBURG] Sündenböcke: Grossangriffe des Zionismus auf Papst Pius XII. und auf die deutschen Regierungen. [Munich], 1968. pp. 334.

DUEWELL (KURT) Die Rheingebiete in der Judenpolitik des Nationalsozialismus vor 1942: Beitrag zu einer vergleichenden zeitgeschichtlichen Landeskunde. Bonn, Röhrscheid, 1968. pp. 328. bibliog. 23cm. (Bonn. Universität. Institut für Geschichtliche Landeskunde der Rheinlande. Rheinisches Archiv. 65)

GLANZ (RUDOLF) Geschichte des niederen jüdischen Volkes in Deutschland: eine Studie über historisches Gaunertum, Bettelwesen und Vagantentum. New York, [imprint], 1968. pp. (vi), 366. 22½cm.

HAMBURGER (ERNEST) Juden im öffentlichen Leben Deutschlands: Regierungsmitglieder, Beamte und Parlamentarier in der monarchischen Zeit 1848-1918. Tübingen, Mohr, 1968. pp. xxiv, 595. bibliog. 23cm. (Leo Baeck Institute Jews from Germany. Schriftenreihe Wissenschaftlicher Abhandlungen. 19)

KATCHER (LEO) Post mortem: the Jews and Germany, now. London, Hamish Hamilton, 1968. pp. x, 258.

KEIM (ANTON M.) ed. Tagebuch einer jüdischen Gemeinde 1941/43; (herausgegeben und kommentiert von Anton Keim). Mainz, [1968]. pp. 112. bibliog.

KOPP (AUGUST) Die Dorfjuden in der Nordpfalz: dargestellt an der Geschichte der jüdischen Gemeinde Alsenz ab 1655. Meisenheim am Glan, Hain, 1968. pp. (xi), 458. bibliog. 23cm.

LINN (DOROTHEE) Das Schicksal der jüdischen Bevölkerung in Memmingen von 1933 bis 1945: Jahresbericht einer Primanerin. Stuttgart, [1968]. pp. 90. bibliog.

MEIER (KURT) Kirche und Judentum: die Haltung der evangelischen Kirche zur Judenpolitik des Dritten Reiches. Göttingen, 1968. pp. 153. (Evangelische Kirche in Deutschland. Kommission für die Geschichte des Kirchenkampfes. Arbeiten zur Geschichte des Kirchenkampfes. Ergänzungsreihe. Band 7)

PAUCKER (ARNOLD) Der jüdische Abwehrkampf gegen Antisemitismus und Nationalsozialismus in den letzten Jahren der Weimarer Republik. Hamburg, Leibniz-Verlag, [1968]. pp. 311. bibliog. 22cm. (Hamburg. Forschungsstelle für die Geschichte des Nationalsozialismus in Hamburg. Hamburger Beiträge zur Zeitgeschichte. Band 4)

STAERKER als die Angst: den sechs Millionen, die keinen Retter fanden; (herausgegeben...von Heinrich Fink). Berlin, Union, 1968. pp. 260. 19cm.

WINTER (DAVID ALEXANDER) Geschichte der jüdischen Gemeinde in Moisling/Lübeck; mit einer Biographie des Verfassers von Hans Chanoch Meyer. Lübeck, 1968. pp. 224. (Lübeck. Archiv. Veröffentlichungen zur Geschichte der Hansestadt Lübeck. Band 20)

ADLER (HANS GUENTHER) The Jews in Germany: from the enlightenment to national socialism. Notre Dame, [1969]. pp. 152. bibliog.

FRIEDLANDER (SAUL) Counterfeit Nazi: the ambiguity of good;...translated from the French and German by Charles Fullman. London, Weidenfeld & Nicolson, 1969. pp. xvii, 228. 21½cm.

GERSHON (KAREN) ed. Postscript: a collective account of the lives of Jews in West Germany since the second world war. London, 1969. pp. 191.

GRAUPE (HEINZ MOSCHE) Die Entstehung des modernen Judentums: Geistegeschichte der deutschen Juden 1650-1942. Hamburg, [1969]. pp. 386. bibliog.

JUBILEE volume dedicated to Curt C. Silberman; edited by Herbert A. Strauss [and] Hans G. Reissner. New York, 1969. pp. 132.

SAUER (PAUL) Die Schicksale der jüdischen Bürger Baden-Württembergs während der nationalsozialistischen Verfolgungszeit, 1933-1945: statistische Ergebnisse, etc. Stuttgart, Kohlhammer, 1969. pp. xvi, 468. bibliog. (Baden-Württemberg. Staatlicher Archivverwaltung. Veröffentlichungen. Band 20)

SPIEGEL (MARGA) Retter in der Nacht. Frankfurt/Main, [1969]. pp. 104.

ZECHLIN (EGMONT) Die deutsche Politik und die Juden im Ersten Weltkrieg. Göttingen, [1969]. pp. 592. bibliog.

DEUTSCHKRON (INGE) Bonn and Jerusalem: the strange coalition. Philadelphia, [1970]. pp. 357. bibliog.

DEUTSCHKRON (INGE) Israel und die Deutschen: zwischen Ressentiment und Ratio. Köln, [1970]. pp. 367.

DIAMANT (ADOLF) Chronik der Juden in Chemnitz, heute Karl-Marx-Stadt: Aufstieg und Untergang einer jüdischen Gemeinde in Sachsen. Frankfurt/Main, [1970]. pp. 183.

ENGELMANN (BERNT) Deutschland ohne Juden: eine Bilanz. München, [1970]. pp. 524. bibliog.

GEGENWART im Rückblick: Festgabe für die Jüdische Gemeinde zu Berlin 25 Jahre nach dem Neubeginn; herausgegeben von Herbert A. Strauss und Kurt R. Grossmann. Heidelberg, 1970. pp. 374. bibliogs. In German or English.

MOSSE (GEORGE L.) Germans and Jews: the Right, the Left and the search for a "third force" in pre-Nazi Germany. New York, 1970. pp. 260.

SCHLEUNES (KARL A.) The twisted road to Auschwitz: Nazi policy toward German Jews, 1933-1939. Urbana, [1970]. pp. 280. bibliog.

SCHOEPS (HANS JOACHIM) Bereit für Deutschland!: der Patriotismus deutscher Juden und der Nationalsozialismus; frühe Schriften 1930 bis 1939: eine historische Dokumentation. Berlin, [1970]. pp. 316.

BLOCH (ERICH) Geschichte der Juden von Konstanz im 19. und 20. Jahrhundert: eine Dokumentation. Konstanz, [1971]. pp. 300. bibliog.

MOSSE (WERNER EUGEN) and PAUCKER (ARNOLD) eds. Deutsches Judentum in Krieg und Revolution 1916-1923: ein Sammelband. Tubingen, 1971. pp. 704. bibliog. (Leo Baeck Institute of Jews from Germany. Schriftenreihe Wissenschaftlicher Abhandlungen. 25)

NIEWYK (DONALD L.) Socialist, anti-semite and Jew: German Social Democracy confronts the problem of anti-semitism, 1918-1933. Baton Rouge, [1971]. pp. 254. bibliog.

JEWS IN HUNGARY

BISS (ANDREAS) Der Stopp der Endlösung: Kampf gegen Himmler und Eichmann in Budapest. Stuttgart, Seewald, [1966]. pp. 358. 20cm.

LÉVAI (JENŐ) Hungarian Jewry and the papacy: Pope Pius XII did not remain silent; reports, documents and records from church and state archives;... translated by J.R. Foster, London, Sands, [1968]. pp. xii, 132. 22cm.

JEWS IN INDIA

STRIZOWER (SCHIFRA) The children of Israel: the Bene Israel of Bombay. Oxford, [1971]. pp. 176. bibliog.

JEWS IN ITALY

GUEDEMANN (MORITZ) Geschichte des Erziehungswesens und der Cultur der abendländischen Juden während des Mittelalters und der neueren Zeit; [reprint of edition originally published 1880-88]. Amsterdam, 1966. 3 vols.

FERORELLI (NICOLA) Gli ebrei nell'Italia meridionale dall'eta romana al secolo xviii. Bologna, Forni, [1966]. pp. xxiv, 261. bibliog. 25cm. Reprint of the edition of 1915.

KATZ (ROBERT) Black sabbath: a journey through a crime against humanity. Toronto, [1969]. pp. 398. bibliog.

FORMIGGINI (GINA) Stella d'Italia, stella di David: gli ebrei dal Risorgimento alla Resistenza. Milano, [1970]. pp. 470.

JEWS IN LATIN AMERICA

SCHVARTZMAN (PABLO) Judíos en América. Buenos Aires, Instituto Amigos del Libro Argentino, 1963. pp. 143. 19½cm. (Colección Ensayos. vol. 2)

GARCIA DE PROODIAN (LUCIA) Los judios en América: sus actividades en los virreinatos de Nueva Castilla y Nueva Granada, s. xvii. Madrid, Consejo Superior de Investigaciones Cientificas, Instituto Arias Montano, 1966. pp. xxii, 567. bibliog. 24cm. (Publicaciones. Serie E. No. 2)

- Directories

MONK (ABRAHAM) and ISAACSON (JOSÉ) eds. Comunidades judías de Latinoamérica. 2nd ed. Buenos Aires, Instituto de Relaciones Humanas, Comité Judío Americano, Oficina Latinoamericana, 1968. pp. 287. bibliog.

JEWS IN NORTH AFRICA

BENSIMON-DONATH (DORIS) Évolution du judaisme marocain sous le protectorat français, 1912-1956. Paris, 1968. pp. 149. bibliog. (Paris. École Pratique des Hautes Études. Section des Sciences Économiques et Sociales. Études Juives. 12)

CHOURAQUI (ANDRÉ N.) Between East and West: a history of the Jews of North Africa; translated from the French by Michael M. Bernet, Philadelphia, Jewish Publication Society of America, 1968. pp. xxii, 376. bibliog. 21½cm.

JEWS IN PALESTINE

SZERESZEWSKI (ROBERT) Essays on the structure of the Jewish economy in Palestine and Israel. Jerusalem, Maurice Falk Institute for Economic Research in Israel, 1968. pp. xii, 99. bibliog. 23½cm.

GERIES (SABRI) Les Arabes en Israël; précédé de Les Juifs et la Palestine, par Eli Lobel. Paris, 1969. pp. 216. Text varies from the Lebanese edition.

JEWS IN POLAND

KRONIKA getta Łódzkiego; z oryginału do druku przygotowali, wstępem i przypisami zaopatrzyli Danuta Dąbrowska i Lucjan Dobroszycki. Łódź, Wydawnictwo Łódzkie, 1965 in progress. 24cm.

INSTITUTE OF JEWISH AFFAIRS. Background Papers. No. 9. The student unrest in Poland and the anti-Jewish and anti-Zionist campaign. [New York], 1968. pp. 35. 30cm.

IRANEK-OSMIECKI (KAZIMIERZ) "Kto ratuje jedno życie...": Polacy i Zydzi, 1939-1945. London, 1968. pp. 323. (Studium Polski Podziemnej)

ROSENFELD (ELSE) and LUCKNER (GERTRUD) eds. Lebenszeichen aus Piaski: Briefe Deportierter aus dem Distrikt Lublin 1940-1943. München, Biederstein, [1968]. pp. 184. 20cm.

BARTOSZEWSKI (WŁADYSŁAW) and LEWIN (ZOFIA) eds. Righteous among nations: how Poles helped the Jews, 1939-1945. London, Earlscourt Publications, 1969. pp. lxxxvii, 834. 21cm.

HYAMS (JOSEPH) A field of buttercups. London, Muller, 1969. pp. 220. 21½cm.

KOWALSKI (ISAAC) A secret press in Nazi Europe: the story of a Jewish united partisan organization. New York, [1969]. pp. 416. bibliog.

KARSOV (NINA) and SZECHTER (SZYMON) Monuments are not loved;... translated by Paul Stevenson. London, [1970]. pp. 285.

IRANEK-OSMIECKI (KAZIMIERZ) He who saves one life. New York, [1971]. pp. 336.

JEWS IN PRUSSIA

ASCHKEWITZ (MAX) Zur Geschichte der Juden in Westpreussen. Marburg (Lahn), [Johann Gottfried Herder-Institut], 1967. pp. (vii), 276. bibliog. 20½cm. (Wissenschaftliche Beiträge zur Geschichte und Landeskunde Ost-Mitteleuropas. Nr.81)

NEUBACH (HELMUT) Die Ausweisungen von Polen und Juden aus Preussen, 1885/86: ein Beitrag zu Bismarcks Polenpolitik und zur Geschichte des deutsch-polnischen Verhältnisses. Wiesbaden, Harrassowitz, 1967. pp. xi, 293. bibliog. 24cm. (Johann Gottfried Herder Forschungsrat Marburger Ostforschungen. Band 27)

FISCHER (HORST) Judentum, Staat und Heer in Preussen im frühen 19. Jahrhundert: zur Geschichte der staatlichen Judenpolitik. Tübingen, Mohr, 1968. pp. viii, 232. bibliog. 23cm. (Leo Baeck Institute of Jews from Germany. Schriftenreihe Wissenschaftlicher Abhandlungen. 20)

JEWS IN ROUMANIA

SIMA (HORIA) Osservazioni sull'articolo del R.P. Angelo Martini S.I.: La Santa Sede e gli ebrei della Romania durante la seconda guerra mondiale; [with reprint of Martini's article]. [Munich], 1963. pp. various.

JEWS IN RUSSIA

RUSSO-JEWISH COMMITTEE. Russian atrocities, 1881: supplementary statement issued in confirmation of the Times narrative. London, [imprint], 1882. pp. 35. 21cm.

PRELOOKER (JAAKOFF) From holy orthodox Russia: a Studist appeal to Christian Britain. Edinburgh, [189-?]. pp. 7.

POMOSHCH'... Помощь евреям, пострадавшим от неурожая: литературно-художественный сборник. С.-Петербург, Гольдберг, 1901. pp. ix, 505. 29см.

LONDON. London Committee of Deputies of the British Jews and ANGLO-JEWISH ASSOCIATION. Conjoint Committee. Massacre of Jews in Russia: report of the protest meeting at Queen's Hall, January 8th, 1906; with extract from the report made to the Russo-Jewish Committee by Mr C. Stettauer, a member of the Commission which recently journeyed through Russia to organize the distribution of the relief fund. London, 1906. pp. 47. (Reprinted from the Jewish World, January 12th, 1906)

JEWISH LABOUR LEAGUE. Jewish Labour League; ...to the workers of Great Britain. [Manchester, imprint, 1915]. pp. (4). 22cm.

CHLENOV (EFIM VLADIMIROVICH) Der Krieg, die russische Revolution und der Zionismus: Rede...auf der Delegierten-Konferenz der russischen Zionisten in Petrograd,...1917. Copenhagen, 1917. pp. 24.

LESKOV (NIKOLAI SEMENOVICH) Евреи в России: несколько замечаний по еврейскому вопросу; с портретом Н. С. Лескова и вступительной статьей Ю. Гессена. Петроград, 1919. pp. 96. Xerographic reprint by Lounz, 1969.

EVREISKII krest'ianin. Sb. no.1. Moskva, 1925. pp. 160.

KAMENSHTEIN (M.) Советская власть, еврейское землеустроение и "Озет". Москва, 1928. pp. 56.

EVREISKII... Еврейский народ в борьбе против фашизма: материалы III антифашистского митинга представителей еврейского народа и III пленума еврейского антифашистского комитета в СССР. Москва, Дер Эмес. 1945. pp. 151. 20cm.

RABINOVICH (SOLOMON) Jews in USSR. [Moscow, 1965] pp. 42.

RUSSIAN Jewry 1860-(1967); edited by Jacob Frumkin [and others]. New York, [1966-69]. 2 vols.

AL'TSHULER (MOISEI SOLOMONOVICH) Что есть иудаизм? Москва, Московский Рабочий, 1968. pp. 112. 16см. (Беседы о Религии)

AMERICAN JEWISH CONFERENCE ON SOVIET JEWRY. White paper on Soviet Jewry. New York, [1968]. pp. 23.

AMI (BEN) Les Juifs en Union Soviétique; traduction de Jacques Sert. [Paris], Fayard, [1968]. pp. 163. 21½cm. (Le Monde sans Frontières)

DEUTSCHER (I.) La révolution russe et le problème juif: conférence prononcée...le 29 octobre 1964, à la Jewish Society de la London School of Economics. in Léon (Abraham) La conception matérialiste de la question juive. [new ed.] Paris, [1968].

NOVE (ALEXANDER) Soviet Jewry and the fiftieth anniversary of the Russian revolution; [lecture] delivered at... University College, London, on Thursday 4th January, 1968. London, [1968]. pp. 22. (World Jewish Congress. British Section. Noah Barou Memorial Lectures. 1967)

PELSENEER (JEAN) Les persécutions contre les savants et les intellectuels en U.R.S.S., 1917-1967: syllabus. Bruxelles, 1968. pp. 13.

RUBIN (RONALD I.) ed. The unredeemed: anti-semitism in the Soviet Union. Chicago, Quadrangle Books,]1968]. pp. 316. bibliog. 23½cm.

ANTIN (MARY) The promised land. 2nd ed. Boston, 1969. pp. 373.

CONFERENCE ON SOVIET JEWRY, LONDON, 1969. Light on Soviet Jewry: report of a conference on Jews in the USSR..., etc. London, [1969]. pp. 56.

NISSES (EFIM IAKOVLEVICH) Komu sluzhat sionisty. Simferopol', 1969. pp. 64.

CANG (JOEL) The silent millions: a history of the Jews in the Soviet Union. New York, 1970. pp. 246. bibliog.

DECTER (MOSHE) ed. Redemption...:Jewish freedom letters from Russia. New York, 1970. pp. 91.

KOCHAN (LIONEL EDMUND) ed. The Jews in Soviet Russia since 1917. London, 1970. pp. 357. bibliogs.

LAWRENCE (GUNTHER) Three million more? Garden City, 1970. pp. 214. bibliog.

MENDELSOHN (EZRA) Class struggle in the Pale: the formative years of the Jewish Workers' Movement in Tsarist Russia. Cambridge, 1970. pp. 180. bibliog.

SOVIET Jews reject Zionist "protection": Novosti Press Agency round table discussion February 5, 1971. Moscow, 1971. pp. 30.

JEWS IN SPAIN

DOMÍNGUEZ ORTIZ (A.) Los conversos de origen judío despríes de la expulsión. in tome 3 of Consejo Superior de Investigaciones Cientificas. Instituto "Balmes" de Sociologia. Departamento de Historia social. Estudios de historia social de España. Madrid, 1955.

NETANYAHU (BENZION MILEIKOWSKY) The Marranos of Spain, from the late XIVth to the early XVIth century: according to contemporary Hebrew sources. New York, American Academy for Jewish Research, 1966. pp. ix, 254. 23cm.

TORROBA BERNALDO DE QUIRÓS (FELIPE) Los judios españoles. Madrid, 1967. pp. 366. 17cm.

JEWS IN THE ARGENTINE REPUBLIC

GERCHUNOFF (ALBERTO) The Jewish gauchos of the pampas;... translated by Prudencio de Pereda. rev. ed. London, Abelard-Schuman, 1959. pp. xvii, 169. 20½cm.

LIEBERMANN (JOSÉ) Los judios en la Argentina. Buenos Aires, Libra, 1966. pp. 277. bibliog. 20cm.

SEBRELI (JUAN JOSE) La cuestion judia en la Argentina. Buenos Aires, [1968]. pp. 259.

JEWS IN THE MEDITERRANEAN

GOITEIN (SOLOMON DOB FRITZ) A Mediterranean society: the Jewish communities of the Arab world as portrayed in the documents of the Cairo Geniza. Berkeley, U. of California P., 1967 in progress. 23½cm.

JEWS IN THE NEAR EAST

JABES (ANDRE) Jews in Arab countries: Egypt, Iraq, Syria, Libya; a survey of events since August, 1967. [London], 1971. fo. 19. (Institute of Jewish Affairs. Background Papers. No. 22)

JEWS IN THE NETHERLANDS

KEMPNER (ROBERT M. W.) Edith Stein und Anne Frank: zwei von Hunderttausend: die Enthüllungen über die NS-Verbrechen in Holland vor dem Schwurgericht in München: die Ermordung der "nichtarischen" Mönche und Nonnen. Freiburg im Br., 1968. pp. 189.

PRESSER (JACOB) Ashes in the wind: the destruction of Dutch Jewry. London, Souvenir P., [1968]. pp. xiv, 556. 21½cm.

KLEIN (W.F.) and KOPUIT (M.) De joden in Nederland: een beeld van hun leven na 1945. Assen, 1969. pp. 143.

MEIJER (JAAP) Hoge hoeden, lage standaarden: de Nederlandse joden tussen 1933 en 1940. Baarn, 1969. pp. 192.

JEWS IN THE UNITED KINGDOM

ROSENBAUM (S.) Writer on Jewish affairs. Suggested methods for computing the Jewish population of the United Kingdom. [London?, 1904?] fo.14,3.

HYAMSON (ALBERT MONTEFIORE) The Jews of England: an historical survey. n.p., [193-?]. pp. 24.

RUTTKE (FALK) Geld ersetzt nicht Blut: britische Bevölkerungssorgen. Berlin, 1940. pp. 84. (Nationalsozialistische Deutsche Arbeiterpartei. Schriftenreihe. Gruppe 5. Band 11)

GARTNER (LLOYD P.) The Jewish immigrant in England, 1870-1914. London, Allen & Unwin, 1960. pp. 320. bibliog. 21 cm. (Studies in Society. No. 4)

JEWS IN THE UNITED KINGDOM (Cont'd.)

KIMMEL (HANS) The structure and regime of the Board of Deputies of British Jews: a communal and social study. London, the Author, 1968. pp. 19. 21½cm. (Jewish Public Affairs. No.4)

BERMANT (CHAIM ICYK) Troubled Eden: an anatomy of British Jewry. London, 1969. pp. 274.

CARRIER (JOHN WOOLFE) Working class Jews in present-day London: a sociological study; [M.Phil. (London) thesis]. 1969. fo. 386. bibliog. Typescript: unpublished. This thesis is the property of London University and may not be removed from the Library.

HOMA (BERNARD) Orthodoxy in Anglo-Jewry, 1880-1940. London, [1969]. pp. 52. bibliog.

ARIS (STEPHEN) The Jews in business. London, 1970. pp. 255. bibliog.

GARRARD (JOHN A.) The English and immigration, 1880-1910. London, 1971. pp. 244. bibliog.

JEWS IN THE UNITED STATES

PESSIN (DEBORAH) History of the Jews in America; ...illustrations by Ruth Gikow. New York, Abelard-Schuman, [1957]. pp. 287.

SCHOENER (ALLON) ed. Portal to America: the Lower East Side, 1870-1925. New York, Holt, [1967]. pp. 256. 25½cm.

SOLOMON (GUS J.) Jewish role in the American civil rights movements. London, 1967. pp. 27.

BERMAN (LOUIS A.) Jews and intermarriage: a study in personality and culture. New York, Yoseloff, [1968]. pp. 707. bibliog. 20cm.

BIRMINGHAM (STEPHEN) "Our crowd": the great Jewish families of New York. London, Longmans, 1968. pp. xi, 404. 22cm.

FREID (JACOB) ed. Judaism and the community: new directions in Jewish social work. New York, Yoseloff, [1968]. pp. 248. 21cm.

GOLDSTEIN (SIDNEY) and GOLDSCHEIDER (CALVIN) Jewish Americans: three generations in a Jewish community. Englewood Cliffs, Prentice-Hall, [1968]. pp. xvii, 274. bibliog. 22½cm. (Ethnic Groups in American Life Series)

KAHN (ROGER) of the Saturday Evening Post. The passionate people: what it means to be a Jew in America. New York, Morrow, 1968. pp. x, 350. 23½cm.

MINTZ (JEROME R.) Legends of the Hasidim: an introduction to Hasidic culture and oral tradition in the New World. Chicago, U. of Chicago P., 1968. pp. x, 462. bibliog. 22½cm.

TELLER (JUDD L.) Strangers and natives: the evolution of the American Jew from 1921 to the present. New York, [1968]. repr. 1969. pp. 308.

WEYL (NATHANIEL) The Jew in American politics. New Rochelle, Arlington House, [1968]. pp. viii, 375. 20½cm.

YAFFE (JAMES) **The American Jews.** New York, [1968]. pp. 338. bibliog.

JUBILEE volume dedicated to Curt C. Silberman; edited by Herbert A. Strauss [and] Hans G. Reissner. New York, 1969. pp. 132.

KORN (BERTRAM WALLACE) The early Jews of New Orleans. Waltham, Mass., 1969. pp. 382.

LEVITAN (TINA NELLIE) Jews in American life. New York, [1969]. pp. 253.

MILLER (ALAN W.) God of Daniel S.: in search of the American Jew. London, [1969]. pp. 245. bibliog.

POLL (SOLOMON) The Hasidic community of Williamsburg: a study in the sociology of religion. [2nd ed.] New York, 1969. pp. 308. bibliog.

ROSE (PETER ISAAC) ed. The ghetto and beyond: essays on Jewish life in America. New York, [1969]. pp. 499.

RUBIN (JACOB A.) Partners in state-building: American Jewry and Israel. New York, [1969]. pp. 283. bibliog.

FEINGOLD (HENRY L.) The politics of rescue: the Roosevelt administration and the Holocaust, 1938-1945. New Brunswick, [1970]. pp. 394. bibliog.

GOREN (ARTHUR A.) New York Jews and the quest for community: the Kehillah experiment, 1908-1922. New York, 1970. pp. 361. bibliog.

HARRIS (LOUIS) and SWANSON (BERT E.) Black-Jewish relations in New York City. New York, 1970. pp. 234.

KAPLAN (MORDECAI MENAHEM) The religion of ethical nationhood: Judaism's contribution to world peace. London, [1970]. pp. 205.

SILVERBERG (ROBERT) If I forget thee O Jerusalem: American Jews and the State of Israel. New York, 1970. pp. 620. bibliog.

- Bibliography

GLANZ (RUDOLF) compiler. The German Jew in America: an annotated bibliography including books, pamphlets and articles of special interest. Cincinnati, 1969. pp. 192. (Hebrew Union College-Jewish Institute of Religion. Bibliographica Judaica. No. 1)

JEWS IN YUGOSLAVIA

GAJIĆ (E. B.) Jugoslavija i "jevrejski problem". Beograd, Gregorić, 1938. pp. 96. 21cm.

JIMÉNEZ (MARCOS PÉREZ)
See PÉREZ JIMÉNEZ (MARCOS)

JINNAH (MOHAMMED ALI)

ALLANA (GULAM ALI) Quaid-e-Azam Jinnah: the story of a nation. Karachi, [1967]. pp. 537. bibliog.

JOB ANALYSIS

DANSK ARBEJDSGIVERFORENING and LANDSORGANISATIONEN DE SAMVIRKENDE FAGFORBUND. Outline agreement on work study; agreed February 20, 1963, by the Danish Employers' Confederation and the Danish Federation of Trade Unions. [Copenhagen, imprint], n.d. pp. 7. 21cm.

ORGANISATION FOR EUROPEAN ECONOMIC CO-OPERATION. European Productivity Agency. Stockholm Seminar on Job Evaluation, 1958. Job evaluation: report on the Scandinavian Conference held at Rüno, Sweden, from 10th-13th June, 1958. Paris, [1958?] pp. 81.

U.K. 1960. Social Survey. A comparison of workers' and their employers' statements about the status of the workers within an industry; by D. Sheppard. (Papers. Methodological Series. No. M. 89) [London], 1960. pp. 3. 33cm.

SOUTHERN RHODESIA. Commission of Inquiry into the Organization and Development of the Southern Rhodesia Public Services. 1961-63. First (-third) report. [T.T.Paterson, commissioner]. [Salisbury], 1961-63. 3 vols. (in 1). 33cm. (Legislative Assembly. [Sessional Papers]. 1962. C.S.R.9, 1962. C.S.R. 35, 1963. C.S.R.2) Fourth report unpublished.

ORGANISATION FOR ECONOMIC CO-OPERATION AND DEVELOPMENT. 1965. Job re-design and occupational training for older workers: International Management Seminar, London, 30th September-2nd October 1964: final report; ([and] Supplement). (International Seminars. 1964. 2) Paris, 1965. 2 pts. 24cm - 29cm.

ORGANISATION FOR ECONOMIC CO-OPERATION AND DEVELOPMENT. 1965. Work requirement data for farm management purposes. (Documentation in Food and Agriculture. 1965 Series.72) [Paris, 1965]. pp. 110. 24cm.

UNITED STATES. Employment Security Bureau. BES-No. E-3. Training and reference manual for job analysis. Washington, 1965. pp. vi, 91. bibliog.

OTTOLENGHI (GIORGIO) Analisi e valutazione del lavoro. [Milan], Etas Kompass, 1966. pp. 482. bibliog. 20½cm. (Biblioteca di Economia Sociologia Organizzazione. 30)

ROBERTS (GEOFFREY) Demarcation rules in shipbuilding and ship repairing. Cambridge, C.U.P., 1967. pp. 45. 24cm. (Cambridge. University. Department of Applied Economics. Occasional Papers. 14)

U.K. National Coal Board. Production Department. 1967. Method study in the coal industry. [London, 1967]. pp. (28). 21cm x 30cm.

ARBEITSKLASSIFIZIERUNG: Grundlagen und Methode; [by] R. Emmrich [and others]. Berlin, 1968. pp. 186. bibliog. (Sozialistische Arbeitswissenschaft. [Publications]. 14.)

PAY, PRODUCTIVITY AND PROFITABILITY CONFERENCE, STRATFORD-UPON-AVON, 1968. Conference papers: [J. Sawkill, chairman]. [With supplement.] [London, 1968] pp. 77; 11.

THOMASON (GEORGE F.) Personnel manager's guide to job evaluation. London, Institute of Personnel Management, 1968. pp. 49. 21cm.

COLLINS (RAY) Job evaluation and workers' control. [Nottingham], 1969. pp. 19. (Institute for Workers' Control. Pamphlet Series. No. 16).

MAASDORP (GAVIN G.) The attitudes of Indians to heavy manual work: a job study; [and] The educational and employment position of Indian women in a Natal North coast area. [Durban, 1969]. pp. 55. (Natal University. Department of Economics. Occasional Paper Series. Nos. 1/2)

SCOVILLE (JAMES G.) The job content of the U.S. economy, 1940-1970. New York, McGraw-Hill, [1969]. pp. xiv, 144. bibliog. 23 cm. (Wertheim Committee. Publications)

TASK analysis; by J. Annett [and others]. London, H.M.S.O., 1971. pp. 24. bibliog. (Training Information Papers. 6.)

JOB SATISFACTION

HERZBERG (FREDERICK) and others. Job attitudes: review of research and opinion. Pittsburgh, Psychological Service, 1957, repr. 1967. pp. xii, 279. bibliog. 23cm.

BJØRVIK (KJELL INGE) Ansvars- og myndighetsforhold: forholdet mellom oppfatning av ansvars- og myndighetsforhold, grad av autoritaer personlighet, trivsel og innstilling til arbeidsledelse; en studie på et utvalg produksjonsformenn i norsk industri. Bergen, Norges Handelshøyskole, Instituttet for Arbeidspsykologi og Personalforvaltning, 1967. fo. (164). bibliog. 29½cm. (Stensiltrykk. Nr. 18)

GREEN (R. L.) and others. Why they leave: a study of morale and the reasons for resignation of public servants in the Wellington area, during April and May, 1966. [Wellington, N.Z.], 1967. pp. 128.

CANT (R.G.) and WOODS (MARY J.) An analysis of factors which cause job-satisfaction or dissatisfaction among farm workers in New Zealand. [Christchurch, N.Z., 1968] pp. 38. (Christchurch, New Zealand. University of Canterbury. Lincoln College. Agricultural Economics Research Unit. Technical Papers. No. 2)

PORTER (LYMAN W.) and LAWLER (EDWARD E.) Managerial attitudes and performance. Homewood, Irwin, 1968. pp. viii, 209. bibliog. 22½cm. (Irwin-Dorsey Series in Behavioral Science)

STOLLBERG (RUDHARD) Arbeitszufriedenheit: theoretische und praktische Probleme. Berlin, 1968. pp. 143.

CHADWICK-JONES (JOHN K.) Automation and behaviour: a social psychological study. London, [1969]. pp. 168. bibliogs.

FORD (ROBERT N.) Motivation through the work itself. [New York], American Management Association, [1969]. pp. 265. 23cm.

GRAEN (GEORGE) Instrumentality theory of work motivation: some experimental results and suggested modifications. [Lancaster, Pa.], 1969. pp. 25. bibliog. (Journal of Applied Psychology. Monographs. 1969)

BARAN (JÓZEF) Wychowawcze funkcje zakładu pracy. Warszawa, 1970. pp. 211. bibliog.

BERG (IVAR E.) Education and jobs: the great training robbery. New York, 1970. pp. 200.

JOB SATISFACTION (Cont'd.)

HUIZINGA (GERARD) Maslow's need hierarchy in the work situation. Groningen, 1970. pp. 207 and appendices. bibliog.

PATCHEN (MARTIN) Participation, achievement, and involvement on the job. Englewood Cliffs., N.J., [1970]. pp. 285. bibliog.

RONAN (W.W.) Individual and situational variables relating to job satisfaction. Atlanta, 1970. pp. 31. (Journal of Applied Psychology. Monographs. vol. 54, no. 1, Part 2, February, 1970)

VEROFF (JOSEPH) and FELD (SHEILA) Marriage and work in America: a study of motives and roles. New York, [1970]. pp. 404. bibliog.

BUTTERISS (MARGARET) Job enrichment and employee participation: a study. London, 1971. pp. 71.

COTGROVE (STEPHEN FREDERICK) and others. The nylon spinners: a case study in productivity bargaining and job enlargement. London, 1971. pp. 151.

SHEPARD (JON M.) Automation and alienation: a study of office and factory workers. Cambridge, Mass., [1971]. pp. 163. bibliog.

JOB VACANCIES

NATIONAL INDUSTRIAL CONFERENCE BOARD. Studies in Business Economics. No. 109. Job vacancies in the firm and the labor market; by John G. Myers. New York, [1969]. pp. 106. bibliog.

RAY (M.E.) Practical job advertising. London, 1971. pp. 67.

JOHANNESBURG

- Civic improvement

JOHANNESBURG. City Engineer's Department. Central area: Johannesburg; report. [Johannesburg], 1967. pp. 57.

- Guide books

SUTTNER (SHEILA) Egoli: a guide to Johannesburg for Africans. 2nd ed. Johannesburg, 1967. pp. 63.

- Native races

JOHANNESBURG. Non-European Affairs Department. Activities of the Non-European Affairs Department. Johannesburg, 1964. pp. 29.

SUTTNER (SHEILA) Cost of living in Soweto, 1966. Johannesburg, 1966. pp. 23. bibliog.

HELLMANN (ELLEN P.) Soweto, Johannesburg's African city; an address given to the Natal Region of the S.A. Institute of Race Relations in 1967. Johannesburg, [1967]. pp. 28.

JOHANNESBURG. Non-European Affairs Department. Your Bantu servant and you: a few suggestions to facilitate happier relations between employer and employee. Johannesburg, 1967. pp. 10.

- Race question

LEVER (HENRY) Ethnic attitudes of Johannesburg youth. Johannesburg, Witwatersrand U.P., 1968. pp. xv, 192. bibliog. 21cm.

- Social conditions

GUTSCHE (THELMA) The changing social pattern of Johannesburg. Johannesburg, 1967. pp. 17. (Institute for the Study of Man in Africa. Papers. No. 24)

JOHANNESBURG. Non-European Affairs Department. Your Bantu servant and you: a few suggestions to facilitate happier relations between employer and employee. Johannesburg, 1967. pp. 10.

LEVER (HENRY) Ethnic attitudes of Johannesburg youth. Johannesburg, Witwatersrand U.P., 1968. pp. xv, 192. bibliog. 21cm.

JOHN, of Damascus, Saint

ADELMANN (F.J.) The theory of will in St. John Damascene. in Adelmann (Frederick J.) ed. The quest for the absolute. Chestnut Hill, [1966].

JOHN XXIII., Pope. (Angelo Giuseppe RONCALLI)

GORRESIO (VITTORIO) La nuova missione. Milano, Rizzoli, 1968. pp. 223. 22cm.

LAI (BENNY) Vaticano aperto. Milano, Longanesi, 1968. pp. 485. 18cm. (Il Mondo Nuovo. vol. 88)

JOHNSON (HIRAM W.)

OLIN (SPENCER C.) California's prodigal sons: Hiram Johnson and the Progressives, 1911-1917. Berkeley, U. of California P., 1968. pp. x, 253. bibliog. $21\frac{1}{2}$cm.

JOHNSON (JAMES)

AYANDELE (EMMANUEL AYANKANMI) Holy Johnson: pioneer of African nationalism, 1836-1917. London, 1970. pp. 417. bibliog.

JOHNSON (LYNDON BAINES) President of the United States

JOESTEN (JOACHIM) The dark side of Lyndon Baines Johnson. London, Dawnay, 1968. pp. 272. 21cm.

JOHNSON (LYNDON BAINES) President of the United States. Quotations from chairman LBJ. New York, Simon and Schuster, [1968]. pp. 189. $13\frac{1}{2}$cm.

JOHNSON (LYNDON BAINES) President of the United States. To heal and to build: the programs of President Lyndon B. Johnson; edited by James MacGregor Burns. New York, McGraw-Hill, [1968]. pp. xiv, 506. $22\frac{1}{2}$cm.

LINCOLN (EVELYN) Kennedy and Johnson. New York, Holt, [1968]. pp. xiii, 209. 21cm.

SIDEY (HUGH SWANSON) A very personal presidency: Lyndon Johnson in the White House. New York, Atheneum, 1968. pp. xi, 305.

STEINBERG (ALFRED) Sam Johnson's boy: a close-up of the president from Texas. New York, Macmillan, [1968]. pp. 871. bibliog. $23\frac{1}{2}$cm.

GOLDMAN (ERIC FREDERICK) The tragedy of Lyndon
Johnson. London, Macdonald, 1969. pp. xii,
531, xxi. 22cm.

WICKER (TOM) JFK and LBJ: the influence of personality
upon politics. Baltimore, 1969 repr. 1970.
pp. 297.

HEREN (LOUIS) No hail, no farewell. London, 1970.
pp. 277.

JOHNSON (NELSON TRUSLER)

BUHITE (RUSSELL D.) Nelson T. Johnson and American
policy toward China, 1925-1941. East Lansing,
Michigan State U.P., 1968. pp. ix, 163. bibliog.
23½cm.

JOHORE

- Sanitary affairs

JOHORE. [Medical Department]. Report of the medical
and health services of the State of Johore
(formerly Medical report, previously Territorial
medical report). Johore Bahru, annual, 1922-1934;
1936; 1938 (pt.2 only); 1940. 20-32cm.

JOHST (HANNS)

PFANNER (HELMUT F.) Hanns Johst: vom Expressionismus zum Nationalsozialismus. The Hague,
1970. pp. 326. bibliog.

JOINT ADVENTURES

BALLON (ROBERT J.) ed. Joint ventures and Japan.
Tokyo, Sophia University, 1967. pp. xiii, 138.

FRIEDMANN (WOLFGANG GASTON) and MATES (LEO) eds.
Joint business ventures of Yugoslav enterprises
and foreign firms; international colloquium,
Belgrade, June 12-14, 1967. Belgrade, Institute
of International Politics and Economy, 1968.
pp. 192.

HILTEN (HENDRIK WILLEM VAN) Joint ventures: enkele
facetten van de joint business venture. Deventer,
1968. pp. 183. bibliog. English summary.

TOMLINSON (JAMES W.C.) The joint venture process
in international business: India and Pakistan.
Cambridge, Mass., [1970]. pp. 227. bibliog.

JOINT FAMILY

- Bulgaria

FROLEC (V.) The joint family and its dwelling in
western Bulgaria. in Lockwood (William G.) ed.
Essays in Balkan ethnology. Berkeley, 1967.

JONAH

NEALE (FRANCIS) A tale of a whale; or, The
strange adventures of the prophet Jonah.
Birmingham, 1874. pp. 32.

JONES (Sir WILLIAM) the Orientalist

MUKHERJEE (S.N.) Sir William Jones: a study in
eighteenth-century British attitudes to India.
Cambridge, C.U.P., 1968. pp. viii, 199. bibliog.
21½cm. (Cambridge South Asian Studies. No. 6)

JORDAN

- Census

ISRAEL. Central Bureau of Statistics. Census of
Population, 1967. Publications. No. 1. Census
of population 1967: West Bank of the Jordan,
Gaza Strip and Northern Sinai, Golan Heights:
data from full enumeration. 3rd ed. Jerusalem,
1967. pp. xxxvii, 204. 27cm. In English and
Hebrew.

- Commerce

JORDAN. Department of Statistics. External trade
statistics and shipping activity in Aqaba port.
Amman, quarterly, July/Sept. 1967 to date. 27cm.

UNITED NATIONS. Economic and Social Office
in Beirut. 1967. Foreign trade statistics
of Jordan, 1960-1963: reclassified according
to the United Nations Standard International
Trade Classification, 1960 revised (SITC,
Revised). (ST/ESA/BEIRUT/1). New York, 1967.
pp. 283.

- Constitution

FRANCE. Direction de la Documentation. La
Documentation Française. Notes et Etudes
Documentaires. No. 3,329. Constitution
du royaume de Jordanie Hachémite (texte
mis à jour en 1965). Paris, 1966. pp. 13.

- Economic conditions

ISRAEL. Economic Planning Authority. 1967.
Economic survey of the West Bank: (summary).
Jerusalem, 1967. pp. 34.

JORDAN. Department of Statistics. 1968.
The Jordan economy. [Amman], 1968.
fo. various. (Some Economic Indicators. 2)

WANDER (HILDE) Bevölkerungsprobleme im Wirtschaftsauf-
bau kleiner Länder: das Beispiel Jordanien.
Tübingen, 1969. pp. 228. bibliog. (Kiel. Universität. Institut für Weltwirtschaft. Kieler Studien.
99)

CENTRAL BANK OF JORDAN. Department of Research and
Studies. Annual report. a., 1970 (7th)- [Amman].

- Economic policy

JORDAN. Development Board. 1966. Seven year
program for economic development, 1964-1970.
[Amman, 1966?]. pp. 360. 23½cm.

- Foreign relations - Israel

HUSSEIN, King of Jordan. My "war" with Israel;
as told to and with additional material by
Vick Vance and Pierre Lauer; (translated from
the French). London, 1969. pp. 176.

- Industries

JORDAN. Department of Statistics. Census of
Industries. 1967. Manufacturing industrial
census, 1967. Amman, 1968. fo. 93. 27cm.
In English and Arabic.

- Population

WANDER (HILDE) Bevölkerungsprobleme im Wirtschaftsauf-
bau kleiner Länder: das Beispiel Jordanien.
Tübingen, 1969. pp. 228. bibliog. (Kiel. Universität. Institut für Weltwirtschaft. Kieler Studien.
99)

JORDAN (Cont'd.)

- Social policy

JORDAN. Development Board. 1966. Seven year program for economic development, 1964-1970. [Amman, 1966?]. pp. 360. 23½cm.

- Statistics

JORDAN. Department of Statistics. Quarterly bulletin of current statistics. q., Jl/S 1961 - Ja/Mr 1967; ceased pbln. Amman.

JORDAN, RIVER

BEN-ARIEH (YEHOSHUA) The changing landscape of the central Jordan valley. Jerusalem, 1968. pp. 131. bibliog. (Hebrew University. Scripta Hierosolymitana. vol. 15. Studies in Geography. No. 3)

SALIBA (SAMIR N.) The Jordan river dispute. Hague, Nijhoff, 1968. pp. ix, 164. bibliog. 24cm.

JORDANS VILLAGE

HAYWARD (ARTHUR L.) Jordans: the making of a community; a history of the early years. London, 1969. pp. 186.

JOS

- Social conditions

PLOTNICOV (LEONARD) Strangers to the city: urban man in Jos, Nigeria. Pittsburgh, U. of Pittsburgh P., [1967]. pp. xiii, 320. bibliog. 20½cm.

JOSEPH II, Emperor of Germany

WAGNER (H.) Staatsarchivar. Die Reise Josephs II. nach Frankreich 1777 und die Reformen in Österreich. in Institut für Österreichische Geschichtsforschung and Vienna. Katholische Akademie. Österreich und Europa. Graz, 1965.

BERNARD (PAUL PETER) Joseph II. New York, [1968]. pp. 155. bibliog.

WANGERMANN (ERNST) From Joseph II to the Jacobin trials: government policy and public opinion in the Habsburg dominions in the period of the French revolution. 2nd ed. London, 1969. pp. 218. bibliog.

JOSEPHINISM

BENEDIKT (H.) Der Josephinismus vor Joseph II. in Institut für Österreichische Geschichtsforschung and Vienna. Katholische Akademie. Österreich und Europa. Graz, 1965.

ZOELLNER (E.) Bemerkungen zum Problem der Beziehungen zwischen Aufklärung und Josephinismus. in Institut für Österreichische Geschichtsforschung and Vienna. Katholische Akademie. Österreich und Europa. Graz, 1965.

JOSSELIN (RALPH)

MACFARLANE (ALAN DONALD JAMES) The family life of Ralph Josselin: a seventeenth-century clergyman; an essay in historical anthropology. Cambridge, 1970. pp. 241. bibliog.

JOURNALISM

VERANTWORTUNG: eine Festschrift; Willy Bretscher zum 60. Geburtstag. Zürich, [1957]. pp. 233. In various languages.

HOHENBERG (JOHN) The professional journalist: a guide to the practices and principles of the news media. 2nd ed. New York, [1969]. pp. 532.

RUEHL (MANFRED) Die Zeitungsredaktion als organisiertes soziales System. Bielefeld, [1969]. pp. 205. bibliog.

- Social aspects

LYLE (JACK) ed. The black American and the press; [by] Armistead S. Pride [and others]. Los Angeles, [1968]. pp. 86.

- Study and teaching

BARTON (FRANK) African assignment: the story of IPI's six-year training programme in tropical Africa. Zurich, 1969. pp. 75.

- Africa, Subsaharan

BARTON (FRANK) African assignment: the story of IPI's six-year training programme in tropical Africa. Zurich, 1969. pp. 75.

- Germany

KOLLER (HELLMUT) Die nationalsozialistische Wirtschaftsidee im Völkischen Beobachter. München, [1939?]. pp. 175. bibliog.

SILEX (KARL) Mit Kommentar: Lebensbericht eines Journalisten. Frankfurt am Main, Fischer, 1968. pp. 301. 21cm.

- Italy

ISTITUTO NAZIONALE PER LA STORIA DEL GIORNALISMO. Congresso, 5°, 1966. Il giornalismo italiano dal 1861 al 1870; dagli atti del...Congresso, etc. Torino, Edizioni 45 Parallelo, 1966. pp. xxviii, 264. 28cm.

RADIUS (EMILIO) Cinquant'anni di giornalismo. Milano, [1969]. pp. 281.

- Italy - Bibliography

MAMBELLI (ANTONIO) Il giornalismo in Romagna: rassegna di tutta la stampa quotidiana e periodica dalle origini ad oggi. Forlì, Camera di Commercio, Industria, e Agricoltura, 1966. pp.xii,437. 23½cm.

- Russia

OCHERKI istorii russkoi sovetskoi zhurnalistiki, 1917-1932. Moskva, 1966. pp. 509.

MAKSIMOV (ALEKSEI ALEKSANDROVICH) У истоков советской журналистики. Ленинград, 1967. pp. 112.

OCHERKI... Очерки истории русской советской журналистики, 1933-1945. Москва, Наука, 1968. pp. 502. 25½см.

PEL'T (VLADIMIR DANILOVICH) M.Gor'kii - zhurnalist, 1928-1936. Moskva, 1968. pp. 426.

PROKHOROV (EVGENII PAVLOVICH) Publitsistika v zhizni obshchestva. Moskva, 1968. pp. 100.

BEREZHNOI (ALEKSANDR FEODOSEEVICH) Русские предшественники ленинской печати. Ленинград, 1969. pp. 128.

BEREZINA (VALENTINA GRIGOR'EVNA) Русская журналистика второй четверти XIX века (1840-е годы). Ленинград, 1969. pp. 112. bibliog.

ALFEROV (V.N.) Vozniknovenie i razvitie rabsel'korovskogo dvizheniia v SSSR. Moskva, 1970. pp. 302.

V. I. Lenin i problemy pechati. Leningrad, 1970. pp. 180.

CHEREPAKHOV (M.S.) Problemy teorii publitsistiki. Moskva, 1971. pp. 191.

- Switzerland

NEUE ZUERCHER ZEITUNG. Unsere Zeitung: Willy Bretscher zum 70. Geburtstag. [Zürich, 1967]. pp. 254. 24cm.

- United Kingdom

PRESS TRAMP, pseud. Fleet Street a.m and p.m.; humorously illustrated by H.E.F. London, 1909. pp. 94.

- United States

GRAMLING (OLIVER) AP: the story of news. New York, Farrar & Rinehart, [1940]. pp. x, 506. 22½cm.

AXELRAD (JACOB) Philip Frensau: champion of democracy. Austin, University of Texas P., [1967]. pp. xii, 480. bibliog. 23cm.

MISSOURI UNIVERSITY. Freedom of Information Center. Annual Conference, 8th 1965. Race and the news media; edited by Paul L. Fisher and Ralph L. Lowenstein; [papers of the conference jointly sponsored by the Center and the Anti-Defamation League of B'nai B'rith]. [New York, 1967]. pp. 158.

HOHENBERG (JOHN) The news media: a journalist looks at his profession. New York, [1968]. pp. xiii, 320. 22½cm.

DINSMORE (HERMAN H.) All the news that fits: a critical analysis of the news and editorial contents of The New York Times. New Rochelle, N.Y., [1969]. pp. 376. bibliog.

JOURNALISM, COMMERCIAL

- Germany

WINSCHUH (JOSEF) Über Wirtschaft schreiben: Wirtschaftspublizistik im Wandel der Zeit. Baden-Baden, Lutzeyer, 1963. pp. 42. 21cm.

JOURNALISM, COMMUNIST

- Germany

WINKLER (KURT) Presse im Freiheitskampf: eine Dokumentation über die illegale Presse der Kommunistischen Partei Deutschlands. Berlin, 1961. pp. 45. (Verband der Deutschen Journalisten. Schriftenreihe. Heft 19)

JOURNALISM, LABOUR

- Roumania

DEAC (A.) Les premiers journaux ouvriers de Roumanie et leur rôle pour le renforcement des associations professionelles. in Comité National des Historiens de la République Socialiste de Roumanie. Nouvelles études d'histoire. Bucarest, 1965.

- United Kingdom

HOLLIS (PATRICIA) The pauper press: a study in working-class radicalism of the 1830s. London, 1970. pp. 348. bibliog.

JOURNALISM, MILITARY

- Germany

SCHNITTER (HELMUT) Militärwesen und Militärpublizistik: die Militärische Zeitschriftenpublizistik in der Geschichte des bürgerlichen Militärwesens in Deutschland. Berlin, Deutscher Militärverlag, 1967. pp. 274. bibliog. 21½cm. (Deutsche Akademie der Wissenschaften zu Berlin. Institut für Geschichte. Abteilung Militärgeschichte. Militärhistorische Studien. Neue Folge. 9)

- Russia

ZHUKOV (SEMEN IOSIFOVICH) Frontovaia pechat' v gody Velikoi Otechestvennoi voiny. Moskva, 1968. pp. 147.

JOURNALISM, SOCIALIST

SCHEU (FRIEDRICH) Die Emigrationspresse der Sozialisten 1938 bis 1945. Wien, [1968]. pp. 43. bibliog. (Dokumentationsarchiv des Osterreichischen Widerstandes. Monographien zur Zeitgeschichte)

- Austria

MIERSCH (KLAUSJUERGEN) Die Arbeiterpresse der Jahre 1869 bis 1889 als Kampfmittel der österreichischen Sozialdemokratie. Wien, [1969]. pp. 203. bibliog. (Arbeitsgemeinschaft für Geschichte der Arbeiterbewegung in Osterreich. Veröffentlichungen. 6)

- Germany

SCHLESINGER (MAXIMILIAN) Eine Reise nach Utopien. Breslau, 1877. pp. 43. (Separat-Abdruck aus "Die Wahrheit")

JENSEN (JUERGEN) Presse und politische Polizei: Hamburgs Zeitungen unter dem Sozialistengesetz, 1878-1890. Hannover, Dietz, [1966]. pp. 193. bibliog. 23½cm.

JOURNALISM, SOCIALIST - Germany (Cont'd.)

LENZ (REIMAR) Manipulation von links?: die Konkret Story: Konkret vor Gericht. Köln, 1969. unpaged.

- Germany, Eastern

POMMERT (JOCHEN) Zu einigen Fragen der Argumentation und Polemik in der sozialistischen Presse. Berlin, 1963. pp. 39. (Verband der Deutschen Journalisten. Schriftenreihe. Heft 21)

- Russia

BEISOV (PETR SERGEEVICH) Свободное слово бессмертно: из истории революционной литературы в старом Симбирске, 1905-1912 гг. Саратов, 1966. pp. 194. bibliog.

- Switzerland

RENSCHLER (REGULA) Die Linkspresse Zürichs im 19. Jahrhundert. Zürich, Europa Verlag, [1967]. pp. (iv). 295. bibliog. 21cm.

JOURNALISTS

- Legal status, law, etc. - Poland

MICHALSKI (BOGDAN) Działałność zawodowa dziennikarza a ochrona czci obywatela w prawie karnym PRL. Toruń, PWN, 1966. pp. 146. 24cm. (Toruńo Towarzystwo Naukowe. Studia Iuridica. t.7, zeszyt 1) With German summary.

- France

LACROIX (JEAN PAUL) 1914- . La presse indiscrète. [Paris, 1967]. pp. 281. bibliog.

FAUCHER (JEAN ANDRE) and JACQUEMART (NOEL) Le quatrième pouvoir: la presse française de 1830 à 1960. Paris, 1968. pp. 335. (Écho de la Presse et de la Publicité, L'. Hors Série)

- Germany

KESSLER (HEINRICH) Wilhelm Stapel als politischer Publizist: ein Beitrag zur Geschichte des konservativen Nationalismus zwischen den beiden Weltkriegen. Nürnberg, Spindler, 1967. pp. (iv), 326. bibliog. 20½cm.

EDEN (HARO) Die Mitwirkungsrechte des Betriebsrats bei Kündigungen im Zeitungswesen. Darmstadt, Stoytscheff, 1968. pp. 192. bibliog. 21cm.

- India

INDIA. Study Group for Newspaper Industry. 1968. Report. Delhi, 1968. pp. 36.

- Poland

KUPIS (TADEUSZ) Zawód dziennikarza w Polsce Ludowej. Warszawa, Książka i Wiedza, 1966. pp. 348. bibliog. 20cm. With Russian and English summaries.

- Russia

EIDEL'MAN (NATAN IAKOVLEVICH) Тайные корреспонденты "Полярной звезды". Москва, 1966. pp. 309.

BEREZHNOI (ALEKSANDR FEDOROVICH) and SMIRNOV (SERGEI VASIL'EVICH) compilers. Бойцы революции: сотрудники большевистской печати: биобиблиографический справочник. Ленинград, 1969. pp. 274. bibliog.

LENIN v "Pravde": vospominaniia. Moskva, 1970. pp. 350. bibliog.

- United Kingdom

MYTTON-DAVIES (CYNRIC) Journalist alone: the story of the freelance and the Freelance Section of the Institute of Journalists. [London, 1968]. pp. 88.

ANDREWS (Sir WILLIAM LINTON) and TAYLOR (HENRY ARCHIBALD) Lords and laborers of the press: men who fashioned the modern British newspaper. Carbondale, [1970]. pp. 330. bibliog.

TUNSTALL (JEREMY) The Westminster lobby correspondents: a sociological study of national political journalism. London, 1970. pp. 142. bibliogs.

- United Kingdom - Directories

DIRECTORY OF BRITISH JOURNALISM, THE: the a. register of Britain's journalists and the news organisations they represent. a., 1971. London.

- United States

FORD FOUNDATION. The newsman's scope. [New York, 1968]. pp. 32.

LEAB (DANIEL J.) A union of individuals: the formation of the American Newspaper Guild, 1933-1936. New York, 1970. pp. 362. bibliog.

JOURNALISTS, AMERICAN, (ENGLISH, ETC.). See JOURNALISTS - United States, (United Kingdom, etc.).

JOVELLANOS Y RAMIREZ (GASPAR MELCHOR DE)

DOERIG (J. A.) Ein spanischer Vorläufer moderner Gedanken zur Förderung der Landwirtschaft: Gaspar Melchor Jovellanos. in Zukunftsaufgaben in Wirtschaft und Gesellschaft. Zürich, 1963.

JOYCE (WILLIAM HENRY)

Ó BROIN (LEON) The prime informer: a suppressed scandal. London, 1971. pp. 174. bibliog.

JUÁREZ (BENITO)

SIERRA BRABATA (CARLOS J.) Presencia de Juárez en los gobiernos de la revolución, 1911-1963. Mexico, Secretaria de Hacienda y Credito Publico, 1964. pp. 135.

SIERRA BRABATA (CARLOS J.) Juárez en la inmortalidad del 21 de Marzo. Mexico, Secretaria de Hacienda y Credito Publico, 1965. pp. 162.

SCHOLES (WALTER V.) Mexican politics during the Juárez regime, 1855-1872. Columbia, Missouri, 1969. pp. 190. (Missouri University. Studies. vol.30)

JUDAEA

- Census

ISRAEL. Central Bureau of Statistics. Census of Population, 1967. Publications. No. 2. Census of population 1967: housing conditions, household equipment, welfare assistance and farming in the administered areas. Jerusalem, 1967 [or rather 1968]. pp. xxxv, 50. 27cm.

ISRAEL. Central Bureau of Statistics. Census of Population, 1967. Publications. No. 3. Demographic characteristics of the population in the administered territories: data from sample enumeration. Jerusalem, 1968. pp. xxxiii, 76. 27cm.

ISRAEL. Central Bureau of Statistics. Census of Population, 1967. Publications. No.5. The administered territories: additional data from the sample enumeration. Jerusalem, 1970. pp. 79. In English and Hebrew.

JUDAISM

In earlier volumes of A London Bibliography, etc. similar material will be found entered under the heading JEWS — Religion.

SOURY (JULES) Morbid psychology: studies on Jesus and the Gospels; [with] The religion of Israel: a study in comparative mythology;...translated...by Annie Besant. London, 1881. pp. 79,80.

ALTMANN (ALEXANDER) Tolerance and the Jewish tradition. London, Council of Christians and Jews, 1957. pp. 19. 21½cm. (Robert Waley Cohen Memorial Lectures. 1957)

EPSTEIN (ISIDORE) Judaism: a historical presentation. Harmondsworth, Penguin Books, 1959, repr. 1968. pp. 349. bibliog. 18cm. (Pelican Books. A440)

GORDIS (ROBERT) The root and the branch: Judaism and the free society. Chicago, U. of Chicago P., 1962. pp. xv, 254. 21½cm.

BELEN'KII (MOISEI SOLOMONOVICH) Иудаизм. Москва, Политиздат, 1966. pp. 239. 16½cm. (Библиотека "Современные Религии")

AL'TSHULER (MOISEI SOLOMONOVICH) Что есть иудаизм? Москва, Московский Рабочий, 1968. pp. 112. 16см. (Беседы о Религии)

HOLLADAY (WILLIAM) Is the Old Testament Zionist? Beirut, 1968. pp. 23.

INSTITUTE OF JEWISH AFFAIRS and WORLD JEWISH CONGRESS. [Publications]. No.1. Christian attitudes on Jews and Judaism : a periodical survey. London, 1968. pp. 15.

COUNCIL OF CHRISTIANS AND JEWS. Facing realities: aspects of Christian-Jewish understanding. London, [1969?]. pp. 31. bibliog.

MARMORSTEIN (EMILE) Heaven at bay: the Jewish Kulturkampf in the holy land. London, 1969. pp. 215. bibliog.

MILLER (ALAN W.) God of Daniel S.: in search of the American Jew. London, [1969]. pp. 245. bibliog.

PARKES (JAMES WILLIAM) Prelude to a dialogue: Jewish-Christian relationships. London, [1969]. pp. xi, 227. 21½cm.

JOSPE (ALFRED) ed. Tradition and contemporary experience: essays on Jewish thought and life. New York, [1970] repr. 1971. pp. 372.

KAPLAN (MORDECAI MENAHEM) The religion of ethical nationhood: Judaism's contribution to world peace. London, [1970]. pp. 205.

NEUSNER (JACOB) Judaism in the secular age: essays on fellowship, community and freedom. London, 1970. pp. 181.

JUDAISM AND SOCIAL PROBLEMS

LEEUWEN (C. VAN) Le développement du sens social en Israël avant l'ère chrétienne. Assen, Van Gorcum, 1955. pp. 247. bibliog. 24cm. (Studia Semitica Neerlandica)

JUDAISM AND STATE

LESLIE (SAMUEL CLEMENT) The rift in Israel: religious authority and secular democracy. London, 1971. pp. 185.

JUDGE-MADE LAW

DAWSON (JOHN PHILIP) The oracles of the law. Ann Arbor, 1968. pp. 520. (Michigan. University. Law School. Thomas M. Cooley Lectures. 1959)

JAFFE (LOUIS LEVENTHAL) English and American judges as lawmakers. Oxford, 1969. pp. 116.

- United Kingdom

SCARMAN (Sir LESLIE) Codification and judge-made law: a problem of co-existence;...a lecture delivered...20th October, 1966. Birmingham, University, Faculty of Law, 1966. pp. 21. 24½cm.

JUDGES

- Canada

CANADA. 1967. The special joint committee of the Senate and of the House of Commons respecting Justice Landreville: joint chairmen: Daniel A. Lang and Ovide Laflamme: minutes of proceedings and evidence. nos. 1-2, 4-7; (with Second and third, final, reports). (27th Parliament. 1st Session) Ottawa, 1967. 6 pts. (in 1) 25cm. Minute No. 3 out of print. Landreville inquiry filed at

CANADA. Statutes, etc. 1952-67. Office consolidation of the Judges Act, R.S.C. 1952, c.159, as amended by 1952-53, c.4, etc. Ottawa, 1967. pp. 15.

- Colombia

COLOMBIA. Oficina de Estudios Criminologicos. 1962. Magistrados y jueces superiores para la reforma: determinacion estadistica. [Bogota], 1962. pp. 97. (Reforma judicial, 1961-1962. Tomo 3.)

JUDGES (Cont'd.)

- France

PICCA (GEORGES) Le juge de l'application des peines. Melun, Direction de L'Administration Pénitentiaire, 1961. pp. 23. 24cm. (France. Administration Pénitentiaire. Études et Documentation)

CHAZELLE (RENE) Pour une réforme des institutions judiciaires. Paris, 1969. pp. 133.

SYNDICAT DE LA MAGISTRATURE. La formation du magistrat: (Livre blanc sur le Centre national d'études judiciaires). Paris, [1969]. pp. 122.

- Germany

GERMANY. [Allied Occupying Powers, 1944-1955. British Zone]. 1948. Justiz und Verfassung: Beiträge und Vorschläge zur Stellung der Rechtspflege im Staat aus Anlass der westdeutschen Verfassungsberatungen. (Zentral-Justizblatt für die Britische Zone. Sonderveröffentlichungen. 4) Hamburg, Rechts- und Staatswissenschaftlicher Verlag, [1948]. pp. 157. 20½cm.

ZWINGMANN (KLAUS) Zur Soziologie des Richters in der Bundesrepublik Deutschland. Berlin, De Gruyter, 1966. pp. xx, 164. bibliog. 22cm. (Cologne. Universität. Rechtswissenschaftliche Fakultät. Neue Kölner Rechtswissenschaftliche Abhandlungen. Heft 44)

BUCHHEIT (GERT) Richter in roter Robe: Freisler, Präsident des Volksgerichtshofes. München, List, [1968]. pp. 295. bibliog. 21cm.

IM Namen des Volkes?: vier Richter über Justiz und Recht; (by Theo Rasehorn and others) [Neuwied, 1968]. pp. 239.

RICHTER (WALTHER) Zur soziologischen Struktur der deutschen Richterschaft. Stuttgart, 1968. pp. 45.

- Italy

MORIONDO (EZIO) L'ideologia della magistratura italiana. Bari, 1967. pp. xx, 351. (Centro Nazionale di Prevenzione e Difesa Sociale. Indagine su "L'Amministrazione della Giustizia e la Società Italiana in Trasformazione". 1)

FEDERICO (GIUSEPPE DI) La giustizia come organizzazione: il reclutamento dei magistrati. Bari, Laterza, 1968. pp. xv, 157. 21½cm. (Centro Nazionale di Prevenzione e Difesa Sociale. Indagine su "L' Amministrazione della Giustizia e la Società Italiana in Trasformazione." 2)

- Mauritius - Salaries, pensions, etc.

U.K. Commonwealth Office. 1967. General scheme of retirement benefits for pensionable officers who are members of Her Majesty's Overseas Civil Service or Her Majesty's Overseas Judiciary or who are designated officers under the Overseas Service (Mauritius) Agreement, 1961. [Port Louis], 1967. pp. iv, 20. 25cm. (Mauritius. Legislative Assembly. Sessional Papers. 1967. No. 3)

- Russia

PRUSAKOV (NIKOLAI STEPANOVICH) Народный судья. Москва, Юридическая Литература, 1965. pp. 48. 20cm.

GOLUBEVA (LIUDMILA MIKHAILOVNA) Uchastie obshchestvennosti v osushchestvlenii pravosudiia. Frunze, 1968. pp. 129.

- United Kingdom

PUGH (RALPH BERNARD) Itinerant justices in English history. [Exeter], 1967. pp. 30. (Exeter. University. Harte Memorial Lectures in Local History. 1965)

LEON (HENRY CECIL) The English judge. London, 1970. pp. 177. (Hamlyn Lectures. 22nd Series)

- United States

PELTASON (JACK WALTER) Federal courts in the political process. New York, [1955]. pp. viii, 81.

DUNHAM (ALLISON) and KURLAND (PHILIP B.) eds. Mr. Justice: (biographical studies of twelve Supreme Court justices). rev. ed. Chicago, University of Chicago Press, 1964. pp. xi, 344. 20½cm. (Phoenix Books)

BOWEN (DON RAMSEY) The explanation of judicial voting behavior from sociological characteristics of judges. 1965. fo. (iv), 206. Microfilm of typescript. 1 reel.

SCHUBERT (GLENDON AUSTIN) The judicial mind: the attitudes and ideologies of supreme court justices, 1946-1963. Evanston, [1965]. pp. 295.

JUDGMENT

SHELLY (MAYNARD W.) and BRYAN (GLENN L.) eds. Human judgments and optimality. New York, [1964]. pp. 436. bibliogs.

KLEINMUNTZ (BENJAMIN) Formal representation of human judgment;...[by] Raymond B. Cattell [and others]; the third of an annual series of symposia in the area of cognition under the sponsorship of Carnegie-Mellon University. New York, Wiley, [1968]. pp. xiii, 273. bibliog. 22½cm.

LA CHARITÉ (RAYMOND C.) The concept of judgment in Montaigne. The Hague, Nijhoff, 1968. pp. ix, 149. bibliog. 24cm.

STROEBE (WOLFGANG) An experimental and theoretical study of social judgment. [Ph.D.(London) Thesis]. 1968. fo. 255. bibliog. 25½cm. Typescript: unpublished. This thesis is the property of London University and may not be removed from the Library.

EISER (JOHN RICHARD) Context effects in absolute judgement: adaptation or concept attainment?; [Ph. D. (London) thesis]. 1969. fo. 302. bibliog. Typescript: unpublished. This thesis is the property of London University and may not be removed from the Library.

JUDGMENT (LOGIC)

LALANDE (ANDRÉ) La raison et les normes: essai sur le principe et sur la logique des jugements de valeur. 2nd ed. Paris, Hachette, [1963]. pp. 263. 18½cm. (À la Recherche de la Vérité)

JUDGMENT DAY

BRANDON (SAMUEL GEORGE FREDERICK) The judgment of the dead: the idea of life after death in the major religions. New York, [1967]. pp. 300. bibliog. 21cm.

JUDGMENTS

- Poland

HANAUSEK (STANISŁAWA) Orzeczenie sądu rewizyjnego w procesie cywilnym. Warszawa, PWN, 1966. pp. 355. bibliog 19cm.

KAFTAL (ALFRED) Prawomocność wyroków sądowych w polskim prawie karnym procesowym. Warszawa, Wydawnictwo Prawnicze, 1966. pp. 309. bibliog. 20½cm. With Russian and English summaries.

JUDGMENTS, CRIMINAL

ASPECTS of the international validity of criminal judgments; [by H. Grützner and others]. Strasbourg, Council of Europe, 1968. pp. 164.

JUDGMENTS, FOREIGN

- Netherlands

KOKKINI-IATRIDOU (D.) and VERHEUL (J.P.) Les effets des jugements et sentences étrangers aux Pays-Bas. Deventer, 1970. pp. 56.

- Norway

HAMBRO (E) Norwegian attitude to international and foreign judgments: recent developments. in Mélanges offerts à Juraj Andrassy. La Haye, 1968.

- Switzerland

GUTZWILLER (PETER MAX) Jurisdiktion und Anerkennung ausländischer Entscheidungen im schweizerischen internationalen Ehescheidungsrecht, auf der Grundlage der Rechtsprechung, etc. Bern, 1969. pp. 103.

JUDICIAL ASSISTANCE

ORGANIZATION OF AMERICAN STATES. 1955. Observaciones al informe sobre la uniformidad de legislación relativa a la cooperación internacional en procedimientos judiciales, asistencia judicial; sometido por el Comité Jurídico, etc. (CIJ 26) Washington, 1955. pp. 80. 27cm.

ORGANIZATION OF AMERICAN STATES. 1962. Report on uniformity of legislation on international cooperation in judicial procedures, judicial assistance: prepared ([by the] Inter-American Juridical Committee), etc. (Official Records. OEA/Ser.I/VI.2.13. CIJ 15) Washington, 1962. pp. (ii), 40. 27cm.

MANGIN (GILBERT) La cooperation judiciaire avec les états d'Afrique Noire, de Madagascar et du Laos. Paris, Institut des Hautes Études d'Outre-Mer, 1965. pp. 60. 27cm.

ASPECTS of the international validity of criminal judgments; [by H. Grützner and others]. Strasbourg, Council of Europe, 1968. pp. 164.

- America

ORGANIZATION OF AMERICAN STATES. 1963. International cooperation in judicial procedures: resolution approved on August 27, 1963. (Official Records. OEA/Ser.I/VI.2 CIJ 69) Washington, 1963. 2 pts. 27½cm. In English and Spanish.

JUDICIAL DISCRETION

STERN (KLAUS) Ermessen und unzulässige Ermessensausübung: eine Analyse der subjektiven und objektiven Elemente. Berlin, [1964]. pp. 37. (Berlin. Freie Universität. Institut für Staatslehre, Staats- und Verwaltungsrecht. Studien und Gutachten. Heft 4)

- Germany

ARNAU (FRANK) Die Straf-Unrechtspflege in der Bundesrepublik. München, Desch, 1967. pp. 223. bibliog. 20cm. (Dokumente zur Zeit)

JUDICIAL POWER

LONDOÑO HOYOS (FERNANDO) El poder del juez. Bogotá, Kelly, 1967. pp. 102. bibliog.

- United States

KUTLER (STANLEY IRA) Judicial power and reconstruction politics. Chicago, U. of Chicago P., 1968. pp. xi, 178. bibliog. 21½cm.

JUDICIAL PROCESS

SCHUBERT (GLENDON AUSTIN) and DANELSKI (DAVID J.) eds. Comparative judicial behavior: cross-cultural studies of political decision-making in the East and West. New York, 1969. pp. 412.

SHAMBAUGH CONFERENCE ON JUDICIAL RESEARCH, IOWA CITY, 1967. Frontiers of judicial research: [papers presented at the Conference]; edited by Joel B. Grossman and Joseph Tanenhaus. New York, Wiley, [1969]. pp. xix, 492. 23cm. (Iowa University. Benjamin F. Shambaugh Lectures in Political Science. 1967)

JUDICIAL REVIEW

- Canada

STRAYER (BARRY L.) Judicial review of legislation in Canada. Toronto, U. of Toronto P., [1968]. pp. xiv, 275. 22½cm.

- Mexico

BAKER (RICHARD D.) Judicial review in Mexico: a study of the amparo suit. Austin, Texas, [1971]. pp. 304. bibliog.

- Poland

ŚLIWOWSKI (JERZY) Sądowy nadzór penitencjarny. Warszawa, Wydawnictwo Prawnicze, 1965. pp. 408. 20½cm. With French summary.

JUDICIAL REVIEW (Cont'd.)

- Russia

PROKURORSKI... Прокурорский надзор в СССР. Москва, Юридическая Литература, 1966. pp. 331. bibliog. 20cm.

AKTY prokurorskogo nadzora: obraztsy osnovnykh aktov. Moskva, 1968. pp. 124.

NIKOLAEVA (LIDIIA ALEKSANDROVNA) and TIGI (IURII RUDOL'FOVICH) Общественность и прокуратура: по материалам общенадзорной практики органов прокуратуры. Ленинград, 1968. pp. 46.

TADEVOSIAN (VRAMSHAPU SAMSONOVICH) Прокурорский надзор в СССР: учебное пособие. Москва, Знание, 1968. pp. 80. bibliog. 21см. (Народный Университет. Факультет Правовых Знаний. 4)

ZHOGIN (NIKOLAI VENEDIKTOVICH) Прокурорский надзор за предварительным расследованием уголовных дел. Москва, Юридическая Литература, 1968. pp. 262. 20см.

GRUN (ALEKSANDR IAKOVLEVICH) Пересмотр приговоров в порядке судебного надзора. Москва, Юридическая Литература, 1969. pp. 159.

PROKURORSKII... Прокурорский надзор в СССР. 2nd ed. Москва, 1969. pp. 406. bibliog.

SAFONOV (ALEKSANDR PETROVICH) Predstavlenie prokurora ob ustranenii obstoiatel'stv, sposobstvovavshikh sovershenii prestupleniia. Moskva, 1970. pp. 53.

- United Kingdom - British Empire

SWINFEN (D.B.) Imperial control of colonial legislation, 1813-1865: a study of British policy towards colonial legislative powers. Oxford, 1970. pp. 202. bibliog.

- United States

BERGER (RAOUL) Congress v. the Supreme Court. Cambridge, Mass., 1969. pp. 424. bibliog.

JUDICIAL REVIEW OF ADMINISTRATIVE ACTS

TSOUTSOS (ATHOS G.) Les notions d'administration et de juridiction: leur nature et leurs relations. Paris, Pichon et Durand-Auzias, 1968. pp. 63. 19cm.

JUDICIAL control of the administrative process: report of a conference at Ditchley Park, 4-7 July, 1969; by Professor J.F. Garner and A.R. Galbraith. Enstone, 1969. pp. 38. (Ditchley Foundation. Ditchley Papers. No. 22)

- European Economic Community countries

AUBY (JEAN MARIE) and FROMONT (MICHEL) Les recours contre les actes administratifs dans les pays de la Communauté Economique Européenne, etc. Paris, 1971. pp. 473.

- France

DRAN (MICHEL) Le contrôle juridictionnel et la garantie des libertés publiques. Paris, Pichon et Durand-Auzias, 1968. pp. xv, 655. bibliog. 25cm. (Bibliothèque Constitutionnelle et de Science Politique. Tome 32)

LANDON (PIERRE) Le recours pour excès de pouvoir depuis 1954: douze ans de jurisprudence. Paris, Pichon et Durand-Auzias, 1968. pp. v, 182.

- Germany

OSSENBUEHL (FRITZ) Die Rücknahme fehlerhafter begünstigender Verwaltungsakte. Berlin, De Gruyter, 1964. pp. xxviii, 132. bibliog. 21½cm. (Cologne. Universität. Rechtswissenschaftliche Fakultät. Neue Kölner Rechtswissenschaftliche Abhandlungen. Heft 29)

SAARBRUECKEN. Universität. Annales Universitatis Saraviensis. Rechts- und Wirtschaftswissenschaftliche Abteilung. Heft 25. Die massgebliche Rechts- und Sachlage für die gerichtliche Beurteilung von Verwaltungsakten; von Peter Bähr. Köln, Heymann, 1967. pp. 156. bibliog. 20½cm.

- Hungary

TOLDI (FERENC) Az államigazgatási rendelkezések megsemmisítése és megváltoztatása. Budapest, Közgazdasági és Jogi Könyvkiadó, 1965. pp. 292. bibliog. 20cm. With Russian and French tables of contents.

- India

FAZAL (MD. ABUL) Judicial control of administrative action in India and Pakistan: a comparative study of principles and remedies. Oxford, Clarendon P., 1969. pp. xxxv, 345. bibliog. 21½cm.

- Israel

ETZION (DAVID) Le contrôle juridictionnel de l'administration en Israël: étude de droit comparé. Paris, 1970. pp. 194. bibliog.

- Netherlands

ANGEREN (J.A.M.VAN) De gewone rechter en de administratieve rechtsgangen. Deventer, 1968. pp. 240. With French summary.

- Pakistan

FAZAL (MD. ABUL) Judicial control of administrative action in India and Pakistan: a comparative study of principles and remedies. Oxford, Clarendon P., 1969. pp. xxxv, 345. bibliog. 21½cm.

- Poland

DĄBROWSKI (WITOLD FRANCISZEK) Prokuratorska kontrola decyzji administracyjnych. Poznań, 1963. pp. 208. bibliog. 23cm. (Poznań. Poznańskie Towarzystwo Przyjaciół Nauk. Wydział Historii i Nauk Społecznych. Komisja Nauk Społecznych. Prace. tom 11, zeszyt 2) With Russian summary.

- Roumania

> TARHON (V. GH.) Răspunderea patrimonială a organelor administrației de stat și controlul jurisdicțional indirect al legalității actelor administrative. București, 1967. pp. 224.

- United Kingdom

> DE SMITH (STANLEY ALEXANDER) Judicial review of administrative action. 2nd ed. London, Stevens, 1968. pp. lii, 629. 24½cm.

> STREET (HARRY) Justice in the welfare state. London, Stevens, 1968. pp. x, 130. 18½cm. (Hamlyn Lectures. 20th series)

> U.K. Law Commission. Published Working Papers. No. 40. Remedies in administrative law. London, 1971. pp. 120.

JUDICIAL STATISTICS

- Belgium

> BELGIUM. Office Central de Statistique. Statistique judiciaire de la Belgique. Bruxelles, 1931/1940. 29cm.

- Benelux

> UNION ÉCONOMIQUE BENELUX. Commission de Coordination des Statistiques. 1956. Rapport concernant les statistiques judiciaires dans les pays de Benelux: essai de comparaison de quelques résultats; Rapport over de gerechtelijke statistieken in de Beneluxlanden: proeve van vergelijking van enige uitkomsten. Bruxelles, 1956. pp. 178. in French and Dutch.

- Germany - North Rhine - Westphalia

> NORTH RHINE-WESTPHALIA. Statistisches Landesamt. Beiträge zur Statistik des Landes Nordrhein-Westfalen. Heft. 240. Das Rechtswesen in Nordrhein-Westfalen, 1956-1966. Düsseldorf, 1968. pp. 227. 29½cm.

- Norway

> NORWAY. Statistiske Centralbyrå. Sivilrettsstatistikk: Civil judicial statistics (formerly Civil law statistics). Oslo, annual, 1959 [1st issue] to date. 29½cm.

JUDKIN FAMILY

> COLLIDGE (WILLIAM HENRY) A short history of Judkins of Hayford, Northamptonshire and Judkins quarries at Nuneaton. [Nuneaton, inprint, 1966]. pp. 36. bibliog. 25½cm.

JULIÃO (FRANCISCO)

> BARRETO (LEDA) Julião, Nordeste, revolução. Rio de Janeiro, Editôra Civilização Brasileira, 1963. pp. xi, 145. 20½cm. (Retratos do Brasil. vol. 23)

JULIUS II., Pope

> ERASMUS (DESIDERIUS) The Julius exclusus...; translated by Paul Pascal,...critical notes by J. Kelley Sowards. Bloomington, Indiana U.P., [1968]. pp. 141. 21cm.

JUNAID KHAN (MUHAMMAD QURBAN)

> ALEKSEENKOV (P.) Хивинское восстание 1916 года. Ташкент, 1980. pp. 56. Xerographic copy. Lacks pp.50,51.

JUNG (CHARLES GUSTAVE)

> FORDHAM (FRIEDA) An introduction to Jung's psychology. 3rd ed. Harmondsworth, Penguin Books, 1966 repr. 1968. pp. 159. bibliog. 18cm. (Pelican Books. A 273)

> BERTINE (ELEANOR) Jung's contribution to our time: the collected papers of Eleanor Bertine; edited by Elizabeth C. Rohrbach. New York, Putnam, [1967]. pp. xvi, 271. bibliog. 21cm.

> JACOBI (JOLAN) The psychology of C.J. Jung: an introduction with illustrations. 7th ed. London, Routledge & Kegan Paul, 1968. pp. xvi, 199. bibliog. 21½cm.

> HOCHHEIMER (WOLFGANG) The psychotherapy of C.G. Jung...; translated by Hildegard Nagel. London, [1969]. pp. 160. bibliog.

> MORENO (ANTONIO) Jung, gods and modern man. Notre Dame, Ind., [1970]. pp. 274. bibliog.

JUNG (EDGAR JULIUS)

> JENSCHKE (BERNHARD) Zur Kritik der konservativ-revolutionären Ideologie in der Weimarer Republik: Weltanschauung und Politik bei Edgar Julius Jung. München, [1971]. pp. 200. bibliog. (Munich. Universität. Institut für Politische Wissenschaft. Münchener Studien zur Politik. 16. Band)

JURA

- History

> REYNOLD (GONZAGUE DE) Destin du Jura: origine et prise de conscience; l'histoire; vers une conclusion. Lausanne, Rencontre, [1968]. pp. 371. 17½cm.

- Nationalism

> BAERTSCHI (KONRAD) Los von Bern!; Wohin?; der Jura-Separatismus als schweizerisches Problem. Bern, Die Fähre, [1966]. pp. (1), 45. 20½cm.

> SOCIÉTÉ DE SECOURS EN FAVEUR DES VICTIMES DE LA LUTTE POUR LA PATRIE JURASSIENNE. Histoire et procès du Front de liberation jurassien. [Delemont], Jura Libre, 1967. pp. 257. 22½cm.

JURISDICTION

- Germany

> BASSE (HERMANN) Das Verhältnis zwischen der Gerichtsbarkeit des Gerichtshofes der Europäischen Gemeinschaften und der deutschen Zivilgerichtsbarkeit. Berlin, Duncker & Humblot, [1967]. pp. 464. bibliog. 23cm. (Schriften zum Prozessrecht. Band 10)

- Italy

> BUSCEMA (SALVATORE) La giurisdizione contabile: fondamento e tipologia della giurisdizione in materia di contabilità dello stato, delle regioni, degli enti locali, degli enti pubblici istituzionali. Milano, 1969. pp. 672.

JURISDICTION (Cont'd.)

- Russia

TILLE (ANATOLII ALEKSANDROVICH) Время, пространство, закон: действие Советского закона во времени и пространстве. Москва, Юридическая Литература, 1965. pp. 203. 20см.

- Switzerland

GUTZWILLER (PETER MAX) Jurisdiktion und Anerkennung ausländischer Entscheidungen im schweizerischen internationalen Ehescheidungsrecht, auf der Grundlage der Rechtsprechung, etc. Bern, 1969. pp. 103.

- United States

ARONOW (EDWARD I.) Memorandum in behalf of Earl Russell Browder, submitted in support of letter dated March 5th, 1942, addressed to Hon. Mathias F. Correa, United States Attorney for the southern district of New York. New York, [1942]. pp. 16.

JURISDICTION (INTERNATIONAL LAW)

HAMBRO (EDVARD) Jurisdiksjonsvalg og lovalg. Oslo, Universitetsforlaget, 1957. pp. xvi, 406. bibliog. (Norges Handelshøyskole. Skrifter. Almene Emner. Nr.4)

FUMEL (HENRYK DE) Les réserves dans les déclarations d'acceptation de la juridiction obligatoire de la Cour Internationale de Justice. Nancy, Université, Centre Européen Universitaire, 1962. pp. xi, 32. bibliog. 24cm. (Collection des Mémoires. 4)

REICHLIN (KURT) Schweizerischer Staatsschutz gegen ausländisches Wirtschaftsrecht: zum Konflikt zwischen Art. 271 und 273 StGB und der Überspannung ausländischer Zuständigkeit im internationalen Wirtschaftsrecht. Zürich, 1964. pp. 23. bibliog. (Reprinted from Schweizerisches Zentralblatt für Staats- und Gemeindeverwaltung, 1964)

TOMKO (JÁN) The domestic jurisdiction of states and the UNO. Bratislava, Slovak Academy of Sciences, 1967. pp. 374. bibliog. 20cm.

BERNHARDT (R.) Das Gegenseitigkeitsprinzip in der obligatorischen internationalen Gerichtsbarkeit. in Recueil d'études de droit international en hommage à Paul Guggenheim. Genève, 1968.

BRIGGS (H.W.) The optional protocols of Geneva, 1958 and Vienna, 1961, 1963 concerning the compulsory settlement of disputes. in Recueil d'études de droit international en hommage à Paul Guggenheim. Genève, 1968.

KATZ (MILTON) The relevance of international adjudication. Cambridge, Mass., Harvard U.P., 1968. pp. (v), 165. 21cm.

SCHNITZER (A. F.) Internationale Gerichtsbarkeit und Rechtsanwendung. in Recueil d'études de droit international en hommage à Paul Guggenheim. Genève, 1968.

RIDEAU (JOEL) Juridictions internationales et contrôle du respect des traités constitutifs des organisations internationales. Paris, Pichon & Durand-Auzias, 1969. pp. xv, 382. bibliog. 24½cm. (Bibliothèque de Droit International. Tome 47)

CSABAFI (IMRE ANTHONY) The concept of state jurisdiction in international space law: a study in the progressive development of space law in the United Nations. The Hague, 1971. pp. 197 bibliog.

KEITH (KENNETH JAMES) The extent of the advisory jurisdiction of the International Court of Justice. Leyden, 1971. pp. 271.

JURISDICTION OVER SHIPS AT SEA

POULANTZAS (NICHOLAS M.) The right of hot pursuit in international law. Leyden, 1969. pp. 451. bibliog. (Utrecht. Rijiksuniversiteit. Volkenrechtelijk Instituut. Nova et Vetera Iuris Gentium. Series A. Modern International Law. No.5)

JURISPRUDENCE

HOHFELD (WESLEY NEWCOMB) Fundamental legal conceptions as applied in judicial reasoning; edited by Walter Wheeler Cook, with a new foreword by Arthur L. Corbin. New Haven, [1919] rep.1966. pp. 114.

TEORIIA... Теория государства и права. Москва, Госюриздат, 1955. pp. 460. 21½см.

DRATH (MARTIN) Grund und Grenzen der Verbindlichkeit des Rechts: Prolegomena zur Untersuchung des Verhältnisses von Recht und Gerechtigkeit. Tübingen, Mohr, 1963. pp. 60. 22½cm. (Recht und Staat in Geschichte und Gegenwart. Heft 272/273)

GRAY (JOHN CHIPMAN) The nature and sources of the law; second edition from the author's notes, by Roland Gray. Boston, [Mass.] Beacon Press, 1963 pp. xviii, 348. 20½cm. (Columbia University. Carpentier Lectures. 1908-09.)

HALL (JEROME) From legal theory to integrative jurisprudence. [Cincinnati, University, 1964]. pp. (ii), 53. 25cm. (Cincinnati. University. School of Law. Robert S. Marx Lectures) (Reprinted from University of Cincinnati Law Review 1964, vol. 33, No. 2)

VRAČAR (STEVAN K.) Socijalna sadržina funkcije državnopravnog poretka: razmatranje o ulozi države i prava u procesu političkog konstituisanja društva. Beograd, 1965. pp. 253.

MacGUIGAN (MARK R.) Jurisprudence: readings and cases. 2nd ed. Toronto, 1966 repr. 1968. pp. 666.

VIDWANS (M.D.) Principles of jurisprudence in a co-operative commonwealth. Poona, University, 1966. pp. (iii), 198. 24½cm.

VOPROSY... Вопросы теории советского права: сборник докладов к конференции по итогам научно-исследовательской работы. Новосибирск, 1966. pp. 169.

ZIEMBIŃSKI (ZYGMUNT) Logiczne podstawy prawoznawstwa: wybrane zagadnienia. Warszawa, Wydawnictwo Prawnicze, 1966. pp. 264. 20½cm. With English summary.

CHKHIKVADZE (VIKTOR MIKHAILOVICH) Gosudarstvo, demokratiia, zakonnost': leninskie idei i sovremennost'. Moskva, 1967. pp. 503.

KEIZEROV (NIKOLAI MIRONOVICH) Vlast' bez budushchego: kritika burzhuaznykh teorii o budushchem gosudarstva i prava. Moskva, 1967. pp. 167.

MOROZOV (VLADIMIR PETROVICH) Pravovye vzgliady i uchrezhdeniia pri sotsializme. Moskva, 1967. pp. 134.

STOYANOVITCH (K.) Le domaine du droit. Paris, Pichon & Durand-Auzias, 1967. pp. vi, 519. 22½cm.

BABKIN (VOLODYMYR DMYTROVYCH) and others. Радянське право і комуністична мораль, etc. Київ, 1968. pp. 195.

FULLER (LON L.) Anatomy of the law. New York, Praeger, 1968. pp. v, 122. 23½cm. (Britannica Perspectives)

HAHLO (HERMAN ROBERT) and KAHN (ELLISON) The South African legal system and its background. Cape Town, Juta, 1968. pp. xxxix, 603. bibliog. 24cm.

KLECATSKY (HANS R.) and others, eds. Die Wiener rechtstheoretische Schule: Schriften von Hans Kelsen, Adolf Merkl, Alfred Verdross. Wien, Europa, [1968]. 2 vols. 21 cm.

LLOYD (DENNIS) Baron Lloyd of Hampstead. Law. London, Heinemann, 1968. pp. 122. 19½cm. (Concept Books. 3)

LUEDERSSEN (KLAUS) ed. Theorie der Erfahrung in der Rechtswissenschaft des 19. Jahrhunderts: zwei methodische Schriften ([by] Paul Johann Anselm Feuerbach und Karl Joseph Anton Mittermaier; [published in 1804 and 1819 respectively]). Frankfurt am Main, 1968. pp. 155. (Theorie. 1)

TEORIIA... Теория государства и права. Москва, Юридическая Литература, 1968. pp. 640. 20см.

MARTENS (WOLFGANG) Öffentlich als Rechtsbegriff. Bad Homburg, Gehlen, [1969]. pp. 235. bibliog. 23cm.

OSNOVY... Основы теории государства и права. Москва, 1969. pp. 384.

OSTROUMOV (G. S.) Pravovoe osoznanie deistvitel'nosti. Moskva, 1969. pp. 172.

PAWLOWSKI (HANS MARTIN) Das Studium der Rechtswissenschaft: eine Einführung in das Wesen des Rechts. Tübingen, 1969. pp. 347.

TROLLER (ALOIS) The law and order: an introduction to thinking about the nature of law. Leyden, 1969. pp. 90.

BENTHAM (JEREMY) An introduction to the principles of morals and legislation; edited by J.H. Burns and H.L.A.Hart. London, 1970. pp. 343. (The Collected Works of Jeremy Bentham. Principles of Legislation)

BENTHAM (JEREMY) Of laws in general; edited by H.L.A. Hart. London, 1970. pp. 342. (The Collected Works of Jeremy Bentham. Principles of Legislation)

DIAS (REGINALD WALTER MICHAEL) Jurisprudence. 3rd ed. London, 1970. pp. 606. bibliogs.

HARRIS (JAMES WILLIAM) When and why does the grundnorm change? Cambridge, 1971. pp. [31]. Reprinted from the Cambridge Law Journal, 1971.

HOBBES (THOMAS) A dialogue between a philosopher and a student of the common laws of England; edited...by Joseph Cropsey. Chicago, 1971. pp. 168.

OLIVECRONA (KARL) Law as fact. 2nd ed. London, 1971. pp. 320. bibliog.

- Bibliography

DIAS (REGINALD WALTER MICHAEL) A bibliography of jurisprudence. 2nd ed. London, 1970. pp. 445.

- History

CHKHIKVADZE (VIKTOR MIKHAILOVICH) Karl Marks o gosudarstve i prave. Moskva, 1968. pp. 207. bibliog.

- History - Germany

BLUEHDORN (J.) and RITTER (JOACHIM) eds. Philosophie und Rechtswissenschaft: zum Problem ihrer Beziehung im 19. Jahrhundert. Frankfurt am Main, [1969]. pp. 184. (Fritz Thyssen Stiftung. Neunzehntes Jahrhundert. Studien zur Philosophie und Literatur des Neunzehnten Jahrhunderts. Band 3)

CANARIS (CLAUS WILHELM) Systemdenken und Systembegriff in der Jurisprudenz entwickelt am Beispiel des deutschen Privatrechts. Berlin, 1969. pp. 169. bibliog.

- History - Italy

ARENA (GIUSEPPE ANTONIO) Stato e diritto in Giuseppe Palmieri. Napoli, 1968. pp. 127.

- History - Russia

KOKIS (PAVEL PAVLOVICH) Filosofskie problemy v trudakh P. I. Stuchki. Riga, 1967. pp. 239. bibliog.

CERRONI (UMBERTO) Il pensiero giuridico sovietico. Roma, 1969. pp. 260.

Z zagadnień teorii prawa i teorii nauki Leona Petrażyckiego: studia opracowane dla upamiętnienia stulecia urodzin. Warszawa, 1969. pp. 204.

PLOTNIEK (ANDRIS ADAMOVICH) Petr Stuchka i istoki sovetskoi pravovoi mysli. Riga, 1970. pp. 265. bibliog.

- History - United Kingdom

STEIN (PETER GONVILLE) Roman law and English jurisprudence yesterday and today: an inaugural lecture. Cambridge, 1969. pp. 30.

- History - United States

CASPER (GERHARD) Juristischer Realismus und politische Theorie im amerikanischen Rechtsdenken. Berlin, Duncker & Humblot, [1967]. pp. 206. bibliog. 3cm. (Schriften zur Rechtstheorie. Heft 10)

JURISTIC PERSONS

- Europe, Eastern

SLAPNICKA (HELMUT) Die sozialistische Kollektivperson: Funktion und Struktur der juristischen Person in den europäischen Volksdemokratien. Wien, 1969. pp. 323. (Österreichisches Ost- und Südosteuropa-Institut. Veröffentlichungen. Band 7)

- Russia

CHECHOT (DMITRII MIKHAILOVICH) Субъективное право и формы его защиты. Ленинград, Университет, 1968. pp. 72. 21см.

JURY

- United Kingdom

ERSKINE (THOMAS) Baron Erskine, and WELCH (W.) Barrister at law. The rights of juries vindicated: the speeches of the Dean of St. Asaph's counsel in the Court of King's Bench... November, 1784, in shewing cause why a new trial should be granted...; taken in short hand by William Blanchard. London, Johnson, 1785. pp. 81. 20cm.

NAPIER (RODGER) Murder by jury: a layman's inquiry. London, 1931. pp. 48.

PROGRESSIVE LEAGUE. Jury service: a memorandum submitted to the Home Office Departmental Committee on Jury Service. London, 1963. 1 pamphlet (unpaged).

CORNISH (WILLIAM R.) The jury. London, Lane, 1968. pp. 298. 22cm.

- United States

SIMON (RITA JAMES) The jury and the defense of insanity. Boston, Little, [1967]. pp. xiv, 269. bibliog. 23cm.

JUSTICE

ZYRO (EMILIA) Pojęcie sprawiedliwości u Karola Marksa. Warszawa, Książka i Wiedza, 1966. pp. 186. bibliog. 19½cm. (Biblioteka Studiów nad Marksizmem) With Russian and English summaries and tables of contents.

BIRD (OTTO A.) The idea of justice. New York, Praeger, 1967. pp. xvi, 192. bibliog. 24cm. (Institute for Philosophical Research. Concepts in Western Thought Series)

SCARPELLI (UBERTO) Esistenzialismo e marxismo: saggio sulla giustizia. 3rd ed. Torino, 1968. pp. 124.

CASAMAYOR ( ) La justice pour tous. Paris, [1969]. pp. 216.

DUERRENMATT (FRIEDRICH) Monstervortrag über Gerechtigkeit und Recht; nebst einem helvetischen Zwischenspiel: Eine kleine Dramaturgie der Politik. Zürich, [1969]. pp. 119.

PUMILIA (NINO) La giustizia umana e il "neo diritto socialcristiano". Roma, 1970. pp. 273. bibliog.

JUSTICE, ADMINISTRATION OF

ABRAHAM (HENRY JULIAN) The judicial process: an introductory analysis of the courts of the United States, England and France. New York, 1962. pp. 381. bibliog.

CHITIVA CÁRDENAS (GUILLERMO) Tres funciones del ministerio público en el proceso penal [Bogotá], 1965. pp. 64. bibliog. 23½cm.

ABRAHAM (HENRY JULIAN) The judicial process: (an introductory analysis of the courts of the United States, England and France]. 2nd ed. New York, O.U.P., 1968. pp. xiv, 496. bibliog. 20½cm.

- Africa, Subsaharan

L'ORGANISATION judiciaire en Afrique noire: études; colloque organisé par le Centre d'Histoire et d'Ethnologie juridiques sous la direction de John Gilissen. Bruxelles, 1969. pp. 290. bibliog. (Brussels. Université Libre. Institut de Sociologie. Centre d'Histoire et d'Ethnologie Juridiques. Etudes d'Histoire et d'Ethnologie Juridiques. 10)

ALLOTT (ANTONY NICOLAS) ed. Judicial and legal systems in Africa. 2nd ed. London, 1970. pp. 314.

- Algeria

LAPASSAT (ÉTIENNE JEAN) La justice en Algérie, 1962-1968. Paris, 1969. pp. 183. bibliog. (Fondation Nationale des Sciences Politiques. Centre d'Étude des Relations Internationales. Série θ: Etudes Maghrébines. 9)

- Argentine Republic

BERTOTTO (JOSÉ GUILLERMO) Politica y justicia argentinas. Montevideo, Ceibo, 1945. pp. 319. 23½cm.

- Botswana

LESOTHO. Judicial Department. Annual report of the Judicial Department, (Basutoland, the Bechuanaland Protectorate and Swaziland). n.p., annual, 1953-1956. 33cm.

- Canada

NELLIGAN (JOHN P.) Justice: luxury or necessity?;...an address delivered to the John Howard Society, Ottawa, Ontario, March 18, 1964. Toronto, [1964]. pp. 7.

CANADA. Parliament. House of Commons. Standing Committee on Justice and Legal Affairs. Minutes of proceedings and evidence. [in English and French] Ottawa, irreg., March 4 1969(28th Parl., 1st session, no.7) to date. 25cm.

- Canada - New Brunswick

NEW BRUNSWICK. 1959. Report of the Committee on Administration of Justice in New Brunswick: [Gordon F. Nicholson, chairman]. Fredericton, 1959. pp. 32. 23cm.

- China

> LENG (SHAO-CHUAN) Justice in communist China: a survey of the judicial system of the Chinese People's Republic. Dobbs Ferry, Oceana, 1967. pp. xviii, 196. bibliog. 23½cm.
>
> SHIGA (S.) Some remarks on the judicial system in China: historical development and characteristics. in Buxbaum (David C.) ed. Traditional and modern legal institutions in Asia and Africa. Leiden, 1967.
>
> UNITED STATES. Library of Congress. Guide to selected legal sources of mainland China: a listing of laws and regulations, etc. Washington, 1967. pp. ix, 357. bibliogs.

- Colombia

> COLOMBIA. Ministerio de Justicia. Memoria del Ministro de Justicia al Congreso. a., 1949, 1961, 1962, 1964. Bogota.
>
> COLOMBIA. Oficina de Estudios Criminológicos. 1962. Necesidades de la justicia colombiana: respuesta de los tribunales superiores de distrito, los juzgados superiores y los juzgados del circuito a una encuesta de la Oficina de Estudios Criminologicos. [Bogota], 1962. pp. 530. (Reforma judicial, 1961-1962. Tomo 4.)
>
> MOLANO SÁNCHEZ (ERNESTO) Los juzgados permanentes de Bogotá, D.E. Bogotá, 1963. pp. 81. bibliog. 22cm.
>
> CHITIVA CÁRDENAS (GUILLERMO) Tres funciones del ministerio público en el proceso penal. [Bogotá], 1965. pp. 64. bibliog. 23½cm.

- Czechoslovakia

> BOGUSZAK (JIŘÍ) Základy socialistické zákonnosti v ČSSR. Praha, Československá Akademie Věd, 1963. pp. 218. 20½cm. With Russian and German summaries.

- France

> FRANCE. Ministère de la Justice. Compte général de l'administration de la justice criminelle et de la justice civile et commerciale: métropole et départments d'outre-mer. a., 1966- Paris.
>
> DEBAUVE (HENRY JEAN LOUIS) La justice révolutionnaire dans le Morbihan: essai sur l'organisation judiciaire du Morbihan de 1790 à 1795. Paris, 1965. pp. 568. bibliog. 25cm.
>
> LAROCHE-FLAVIN (CHARLES) La machine judiciaire. [Paris], Éditions du Seuil, [1968]. pp. 144. bibliog. 18cm. (Société. 30)
>
> AGOR (ANDRE) pseud. Histoire d'un procès; ou, Pour une justice électronique. Paris, [1969]. pp. 393.
>
> CALDUS, pseud. Pour une réforme de la justice. Paris, [1969]. pp. 189.
>
> HAMELIN (JACQUES) Entretiens sur la justice contemporaine. Paris, 1970. pp. 127.

- Gambia

> GAMBIA. Judicial Department. Annual report. a., 1956. Bathurst.

- Germany

> SCHMIDT (E.) Politische Rechtsbeugung und Richteranklage. in Germany. [Allied Occupying Powers, 1944-1955. British Zone]. 1948. Justiz und Verfassung. Hamburg, [1948].
>
> BIEDERBICK (KARL HEINZ) and RECKTENWALD (WOLF) Das Bundesministerium der Justiz. Frankfurt a.M., [1967]. pp. 103. bibliog.
>
> HANACK (ERNST WALTER) Zur Problematik der gerechten Bestrafung nationalsozialistischer Gewaltverbrecher. Tübingen, Mohr, 1967. pp. (iii), 61. 18½cm.
>
> SCHMID (RICHARD) Justiz in der Bundesrepublik. Pfullingen, [1967]. pp. 80.
>
> FRAENKEL (ERNST) Zur Soziologie der Klassenjustiz; und, Aufsätze zur Verfassungskrise 1931-32; mit einem Vorwort zum Neudruck; [collection of one monograph and four articles originally published 1927 and 1931-32]. Darmstadt, 1968. pp. xiv, 103. 22cm.
>
> IM Namen des Volkes?: vier Richter über Justiz und Recht; (by Theo Rasehorn and others) [Neuwied, 1968]. pp. 239.
>
> SINZHEIMER (HUGO) and FRAENKEL (ERNST) Die Justiz in der Weimarer Republik: eine Chronik. Neuwied, Luchterhand, [1968]. pp. 488. bibliog. 20½cm. (Politica. Band 29)
>
> WEINKAUFF (HERMANN KARL AUGUST) Die deutsche Justiz und der Nationalsozialismus: ein Überblick; [and] Die Umgestaltung der Gerichtsverfassung und des Verfahrens- und Richterrechts im nationalsozialistischen Staat; ([by] Albrecht Wagner). Stuttgart, Deutsche Verlags-Anstalt, 1968. pp. 383. (Institut für Zeitgeschichte. Quellen und Darstellungen zur Zeitgeschichte. Band 16/1)
>
> SCHWARZ (WALTER) In den Wind gesprochen?: Glossen zur Wiedergutmachung des nationalsozialistischen Unrechts. München, 1969. pp. 95.
>
> TILFORD (R.B.) and PREECE (R.J.C.) Federal Germany: political and social order. London, Wolff, 1969. pp. 176. bibliogs. 21½cm.
>
> ECHTERHOELTER (RUDOLF) Das öffentliche Recht im nationalsozialistischen Staat. Stuttgart, 1970. pp. 343. (Institut für Zeitgeschichte. Quellen und Darstellungen zur Zeitgeschichte. Band 16/2)

- India

> THEOBALD (W.) Indian tracts. Nos. 1-3. London, Benning, 1857. 3 pts. 21½cm.
>
> JAIN (B.S.) Administration of justice in seventeenth century India: a study of salient concepts of Mughal justice. Delhi, 1970. pp. 153. bibliog.

- Ireland (Republic)

> KELLY (JOHN MAURICE) Fundamental rights in the Irish law and constitution. 2nd ed. Dublin, Figgis, 1967. pp xxxiii, 355. 21cm.

JUSTICE, ADMINISTRATION OF (Cont'd.)

- Israel

BAKER (HENRY EDMEADES) The legal system of Israel. Jerusalem, Israel U.P., 1968. pp. (vi), 277. bibliog. 21½cm.

- Italy

NULLI (ATTILIO) Governo e magistrativa di fronte ai socialisti. Bologna, Zanichelli, 1895. pp. (ii), 51. 23cm.

PERA (GIUSEPPE) Un mertiere difficile: il magistrato. Bologna, Il Mulino, [1967]. pp. 209. 21½cm. (La Specola Contemporanea)

CASTELLANO (CESARE) and others. l'efficienza della giustizia italiana e i suoi effetti economico-sociali. Bari, Laterza, 1968. pp. 312. 21cm. (Centro Nazionale di Prevenzione e Difesa Sociale. Indagine su "L'Amministrazione della Giustizia e la Società Italiana in Trasformazione". 3)

FEDERICO (GIUSEPPE DI) La giustizia come organizzazione: il reclutamento dei magistrati. Bari, Laterza, 1968. pp. xv, 157. 21½cm. (Centro Nazionale di Prevenzione e Difesa Sociale. Indagine su "L' Amministrazione della Giustizia e la Società Italiana in Trasformazione." 2)

PALLADINO (ALFONSO) Giustizia e democrazia. Milano, 1969. pp. 139.

- Lesotho

LESOTHO. Judicial Department. Annual report of the Judicial Department, (Basutoland, the Bechuanaland Protectorate and Swaziland). n.p., annual, 1953-1956. 33cm.

- Madagascar

MASSIOT (MICHEL) L'organisation politique, administrative financière et judiciaire de la République Malgache. [Tananarive, 1970]. pp. 487. bibliog.

- Mauritius

ÉTUDES de droit privé français et mauricien: congrès tenu à Saint-Denis de la Réunion, 1er-4 juillet 1965; [Gérard Conac, chairman]. Paris, 1969. pp. 230. (Université d'Aix Marseille. Faculté de Droit et des Sciences Économiques d'Aix. Annales. 57)

- New Guinea

NASH (PATRICK GERARD) Some problems of administering law in the Territory of Papua and New Guinea: inaugural lecture. [Port Moresby], University of Papua and New Guinea, [1967?] pp. 44. 21cm.

- Nigeria

NIGERIA (NORTHERN REGION). 1959. Statement by the government...on the reorganisation of the legal and judicial systems of the Northern Region. Kaduna, 1959. pp. 8.

- Pakistan

PAKISTAN. Law Reform Commission. 1970. The report of the...Commission, 1967-70. Karachi, 1970. pp. 491. bibliog.

- Poland

ŁĘTOWSKI (JANUSZ) Sądy powszechne i praworządność w administracji. Wrocław, Ossolineum, 1967. pp. 184. 21cm. With Russian and French summaries.

XXV lat wymiaru sprawiedliwości PRL. Warszawa, 1969. pp. 483.

- Portugal - Colonies

WILENSKY (ALFREDO HECTOR) La administracion de justicia en Africa continental portuguesa: contribucion para su estudio. Lisboa, 1971. pp. 301. bibliog. (Portugal. Junta de Investigações do Ultramar. Centro de Estudos Politicos e Sociais. Estudos de Ciências Politicas e Sociais. No.85)

- Rhodesia

TREDGOLD (Sir ROBERT CLARKSON) The Rhodesia that was my life. London, Allen & Unwin, 1968. pp. 271. 21½cm.

- Russia

KALININ (M. I.) О социалистической законности. Москва, Известия, 1959. pp. 187. 20cm.

POPOVA (VERA IVANOVNA) Работа местных Советов депутатов трудящихся по обеспечению социалистической законности. Москва, Госюриздат, 1959. pp. 141. 20cm.

BERCHENKO (A. IA.) XXII съезд КПСС и дальнейшее укрепление социалистической законности в СССР. Москва, ВПШ и АОН, 1963. pp. 88. 20cm.

ALEKSEEV (SERGEI SERGEEVICH) Механизм правового регулирования в социалистическом государстве. Москва, Юридическая Литература, 1966. pp. 187. 20cm.

CONQUEST (ROBERT) Justice and the legal system in the U.S.S.R. London, Bodley Head, 1968. pp. 152. bibliog. 21½cm. (Soviet Studies Series)

VLASOV (IL'IA SEMENOVICH) and TIAZHKOVA (IRINA MIKHAILOVNA) Ответственность за преступления против правосудия. Москва, 1968. pp. 134.

HAZARD (JOHN NEWBOLD) and others. The Soviet legal system: contemporary documentation and historical commentary. rev. ed. Dobbs Ferry, 1969. pp. 667. bibliog.

KUCHEROV (SAMUEL) The organs of Soviet administration of justice: their history and operation. Leiden, [1970]. pp. 754. bibliog.

- St. Vincent

ST. VINCENT. Report of the Registrar of the Supreme Court. Kingstown, 1962/1966 to date. 34cm.

- Salvador

SALVADOR. Constitution. 1950. Constitución politica de la República de El Salvador: Ley de procedimientos constitucionales; Ley organica del poder judicial; Ley reglamentaria de la carrera judicial, etc. San Salvador, 1960. pp. 261.

- Seychelles

   SEYCHELLES. Judicial Department. Annual report. Mahé, annual, 1968 <u>to date</u>. 33cm.

- Swaziland

   LESOTHO. Judicial Department. Annual report of the Judicial Department, (Basutoland, the Bechuanaland Protectorate and Swaziland). n.p., annual, 1953-1956. 33cm.

- Trinidad and Tobago

   REPORT on the system of administration of justice in the Colony [of Trinidad and Tobago: Sir Albert Napier, chairman]. [Port-of-Spain], 1956. pp. 88.

- United Kingdom

   CHARLES I., King of Great Britain and Ireland. The Kings Maiesties charge sent to all the judges of England, to be published in their respective circuits, by His Maiesties speciall command. London, Blaiklock, 1642. pp. 5. 17½cm. Wing C 2156.

   UNITED KINGDOM. Parliament. 1643. A declaration of the Lords and Commons...concerning His Majesties proclamation for adjourning the terme to Oxford,...: [dated 21 Jan. 1643]. London, Wright, 1642 [O.S.] pp. (6). 18½cm. Wing E 1374. Another copy is at Tt(54).

   UNITED KINGDOM. Parliament. 1643. The desire and advice of the Lords and Commons...to His Majesty that the next assize and generall goale-delivery may not be holden, etc.; with His Majesties gratious answer thereunto, February 21, 1642 [O.S.]. Oxford, Lichfield, [or rather, London], 1642. [O.S.] pp. 5. 19cm.

   UNITED KINGDOM. Parliament. House of Commons. 1642. Articles of impeachment...against Sir Thomas Gardiner, Recorder of the city of London, for severall great crimes and misdemeanours committed by him: [dated 23 May, 1642]. London, Walkley, 1642. pp.(6). 19cm. Wing E2523.

   UNITED KINGDOM. Parliament. 1643. A declaration of the Lords and Commons...concerning a late proclamation of His Majesties for the keeping of Trinity Terme at Oxford...; [dated 30 May, 1643]. London, Wright, 1643. pp. 6. 18½cm. Wing E 1358.

   UNITED KINGDOM. Parliament. 1643. A declaration of the Lords and Commons...shewing the reasons why they cannot consent to the keeping of Easter Tearme at Oxford, but in the usuall places...: [dated 18 April, 1643]. London, Wright, 1643. pp. (6). 18½cm. Wing E 1459.

   UNITED KINGDOM. Parliament. House of Commons. 1648. A Committee appointed by the Commons...to consider of such grievances as have been promised to the people to be redressed;... [dated 8 January, 1648]. London, Husband, 1647[O.S.]. pp. 7. 18½cm. Wing E 2539.

   [TWYSDEN (Sir ROGER)] The commoners liberty; or, The English-mans birth-right. [London], 1648. pp. 33. 17½cm. Wing T 3550.

   LONDON. London County Council. Standing Joint Committee. Memorandum of the chairman... relative to the unnecessary cost, delay, and inconvenience connected with the present administration of justice in London; with suggestions for an enquiry by Royal Commission or otherwise. London, 1890. pp. 20.

   WALKER (RONALD JACK) and WALKER (MICHAEL GEORGE) The English legal system. London, Butterworths, 1967. pp xxix, 520. 24½cm.

   ABEL-SMITH (BRIAN) and STEVENS (ROBERT BOCKING) In search of justice: society and the legal system. London, Lane, 1968. pp. 384. 22cm.

   COUNTER (KENNETH NORMAN SAMUEL) The framework and functions of English law: an introduction to the English legal system. Oxford, Pergamon, 1968. pp. ix, 136. 19½cm. (Commonwealth and International Library. Pergamon Modern Legal Outlines)

   VICK (RICHARD WILLIAM) and SHOOLBRED (CLAUDE FREDERICK) The administration of civil justice in England and Wales. Oxford, 1968. pp. xxi, 279. (Commonwealth and International Library. Pergamon Modern Legal Outlines)

   WALKER (RONALD JACK) and WALKER (MICHAEL GEORGE) The English legal system. 2nd ed. London, 1970. pp. 536.

   RADCLIFFE (GEOFFREY REYNOLDS YONGE) and CROSS (ARTHUR GEOFFREY NEALE) Baron Cross of Chelsea. The English legal system; fifth edition by Lord Cross of Chelsea and G.J. Hand. London, 1971. pp. 472.

   U.K. Royal Commission on Assizes and Quarter Sessions, 1966. Special statistical survey; report by G.N.G. Rose. London, 1971. pp. 81. Royal Commission's report, 1969, published as Cmnd. 4153 in British Parliamentary Papers, session 1968-69.

   U.K. Royal Commission on Assizes and Quarter Sessions, 1966. Written evidence submitted to the Commission under the chairmanship of Lord Beeching. London, 1971. pp. 506. Royal Commission's report, 1969, published as Cmnd. 4153 in British Parliamentary Papers, 1968-69.

   BUTLER (DAVID J.) Quarter sessions and the justices of the peace in West Sussex. Chichester, 1972. pp.13.

- United Kingdom - Scotland

   UNITED KINGDOM. 1822. Proceedings...on Mr Abercromby's motion for enquiring into the conduct of the Lord Advocate and other law officers, in connection with the public press of Scotland; with an appendix of documents. 2nd ed. Edinburgh, Dick, 1822. pp. 54.

   WALKER (DAVID MAXWELL) The Scottish legal system: an introduction to the study of Scots law. 3rd ed. Edinburgh, 1969. pp. 488. bibliogs.

- United States

   UNITED STATES. 12417/1479. Study of the Federal Judicial System: report. Washington, 1962. pp. ii, 13.

JUSTICE, ADMINISTRATION OF - United States (Cont'd.)

UNITED STATES. President's Commission on Law Enforcement and Administration of Justice. National Symposium on Science and Criminal Justice. Washington, 1966. pp. vii, 189.

CARLIN (JEROME E.) and others. Civil justice and the poor: issues for sociological research. New York, 1967. pp. 81. (Reprinted from the Law and Society Review, 1966)

FORD FOUNDATION. ...and justice for all. New York, 1967. pp. 47. 17cm.

FRIENDLY (ALFRED) and GOLDFARB (RONALD L.) Crime and publicity: impact of news on the administration of justice. New York, Twentieth Century Fund, 1967. pp. (v), 335. 23cm.

UNITED STATES. President's Commission on Law Enforcement and Administration of Justice. Task Force Reports. Science and technology: prepared by the Institute for Defense Analyses. Washington, 1967. pp. xiv, 288.

FRANK (JOHN PAUL) American law: the case for radical reform; (lectures...upon the dedication of the Earl Warren Legal Center, University of California). [Toronto, 1969]. pp. 216.

UNITED STATES. National Commission on the Causes and Prevention of Violence. Law and order reconsidered report of the Task Force on Law and Law Enforcement Washington, [1969?]. pp. 597. bibliogs.

KLONOSKI (JAMES R.) and MENDELSOHN (ROBERT I.) eds. The politics of local justice: [readings] Boston, [Mass], [1970]. pp. 255.

- United States - California

JONES (EDGAR A.) Some observations on the computerization of the legal system of the state of California. Los Angeles, 1964. fo. 14. (California University. Institute of Government and Public Affairs. [Publications]. MR-24)

- United States - District of Columbia

UNITED STATES. District of Columbia Committee on the Administration of Justice under Emergency Conditions. Justice in time of crisis. Washington, 1969. pp. 180. bibliog.

- Viêtnam

O'NEILL (FRANK) The legal system of Viet Nam; [excerpts from a speech given before the Saigon (Central) Lions Club on September 22, 1969]. [Saigon, 1969]. pp. 7.

JUSTICE AND POLITICS

CHARVIN (ROBERT) Justice et politique: évolution de leurs rapports. Paris, Pichon and Durand-Auzias, 1968. pp. xi, 542. bibliog. 25cm.

FRAENKEL (ERNST) Zur Soziologie der Klassenjustiz; und, Aufsätze zur Verfassungskrise 1931-32; mit einem Vorwort zum Neudruck; [collection of one monograph and four articles originally published 1927 and 1931-32]. Darmstadt, 1968. pp. xiv, 103. 22cm.

ENZENSBERGER (HANS MAGNUS) ed. Freisprüche: Revolutionäre vor Gericht. Frankfurt am Main, 1970. pp. 458. bibliogs.

- Italy

GOVERNATORI (FEDERICO) Stato e cittadino in tribunale: valutazioni politiche nelle sentenze...: ricerca affidata all'Istituto lombardo di studi economici e sociali, etc. Bari, 1970. pp. 280. (Centro Nazionale di Prevenzione e Difesa Sociale. Indagine su "L'Amministrazione della Giustizia e la Società Italiana in Trasformazione." 9)

- United States

TODD (ALDEN L.) Justice on trial: the case of Louis D. Brandeis. Chicago, U. of Chicago P., [1964] repr. 1968. pp. ix, 275. bibliog. 20cm. (Phoenix Books)

HARRIS (RICHARD) Staff Writer for the New Yorker. Justice: the crisis of law, order and freedom in America. London, 1970. pp. 268.

GLICK (HENRY ROBERT) Supreme courts in state politics: an investigation of the judicial role. New York, [1971]. pp. 166. (Temple University. Center for the Study of Federalism. Studies in Federalism. 2)

JUSTICES OF THE PEACE

- United Kingdom

GLEASON (JOHN HOWES) The justices of the peace in England, 1558 to 1640: a later Eirenarcha. Oxford, 1969. pp. 285.

HARRIS (BRIAN) The criminal jurisdiction of magistrates. London, 1969. pp. 365.

MOIR (ESTHER ALINE LOWNDES) The Justice of the Peace. Harmondsworth, 1969. pp. 205. bibliog.

MOIR (ESTHER ALINE LOWNDES) Local government in Gloucestershire, 1775-1800: a study of the justices of the peace. [Bristol], 1969. pp. 191. bibliog. (Bristol and Gloucestershire Archaeological Society Records Section. vol. 8)

McGREGOR (OLIVER ROSS) and others. Separated spouses: a study of the matrimonial jurisdiction of magistrates' courts. London, 1970. pp. 281.

- United Kingdom - Scotland

TAIT (GEORGE) of Edinburgh. A summary of the powers and duties of a Justice of the Peace in Scotland...; with forms of proceedings etc.; comprising a short view of the criminal duty, and of the greater part of the civil duty, of sheriffs of magistrates of burghs. Edinburgh, Anderson, 1815. pp. viii, 375,54. 21 cm.

JUSTIFICATION

[LEGH (GEORGE)] A letter from Edinburgh to Dr. Sherlock, rectifying the committee's notions of sincerity: defending the whole of the B. of Bangor's doctrine...; by Gilbert Dalrymple, D.D. 2nd ed. London, Roberts. 1718. pp. 48. 19½cm.

JUSTO (JUAN BAUTISTA)

CÚNEO (DARDO) Juan B. Justo y las luchas sociales en Argentina. Buenos Aires, Alpe, 1956. pp. 472. 19cm.

PAN (LUIS) Justo y Marx: el socialismo en la Argentina. Buenos Aires, 1964. pp. 173.

JUTE

MALIK (SALEEM H.) Der Jutemarkt und seine Organisation. [Erlangen-Nürnberg, 1966?]. pp. 233. bibliog.

FOOD AND AGRICULTURE ORGANIZATION. Commodity Bulletin Series. 46. Impact of synthetics on jute and allied fibers. Rome, 1969. pp. 114.

- India

INDIA. Jute Enquiry Committee. 1958. Report...1957. [Delhi, 1958]. pp. v, 128.

INDIA. Central Wage Board for Jute Industry. 1964. Report...1963. Delhi, 1964. pp. 227.

INDIAN JUTE MILLS ASSOCIATION. Loom and spindle statistics, corrected up to 1st January 1964. Calcutta, [1964]. pp. 35.

INDIA. 1965. Report on survey of labour conditions in jute factories in India. (Labour Bureau) [Delhi, 1965] pp. vii, 109. 24cm.

- India - Bengal, West

WEST BENGAL. State Statistical Bureau. 1950. A draft report on the statistical study on the output of jute in West Bengal in relation to capital and labour employed and fuels and raw materials consumed. [Calcutta, 1950]. pp. 75, (40). Available for consultation only by special permission of the Librarian.

NATIONAL COOPERATIVE DEVELOPMENT AND WAREHOUSING BOARD, [INDIA]. Study Team on Cooperative Marketing. Report on cooperative marketing of jute in West Bengal; by the Study Team on Cooperative Marketing. New Delhi, 1961. pp. 80.

- Pakistan

HABIBULLAH (M.) Some aspects of productivity in the jute industry of Pakistan. Dacca, [1968?]. pp. 180. bibliog.

PAKISTAN. Bureau of National Research and Reference. 1968. The growth of jute industry in Pakistan. Rawalpindi, [1968]. pp. 56.

- United Kingdom

WOODHOUSE (THOMAS) and KILGOUR (P.) The jute industry from seed to finished cloth. London, 1921. pp. 133.

U.K. Department of Trade and Industry. Business monitor: Production series. P 108. Jute. q., 1971- London.

JUVENILE AUTOMOBILE DRIVERS

- United Kingdom

U.K. Ministry of Transport. 1969. Driver training for young people: suggestions to heads of schools and others. London, 1969. pp. 36.

JUVENILE COURTS

VEILLARD-CYBULSKA (HENRYKA) La protection judiciaire de la jeunesse dans le monde: ses débuts: (étude historique publiée à l'occasion du 7me Congrès de l'Association Internationale des Magistrats de la Jeunesse, Paris 1966). Bruxelles, Association Internationale des Magistrats de la Jeunesse, 1966. pp. 160. 23½cm.

- Bibliography

CAMBRIDGE. University. Institute of Criminology. Bibliographical Series. No.2. Family courts and councils: a select bibliography, with special reference to the White Paper, 'The child, the family and the young offender', 1965 (Cmnd. 2742), compiled by John A. Seymour. Cambridge, [1967]. fo. 18.

- Russia

PRONINA (VERA SERGEEVNA) Комментарий к положениям о комиссиях по делам несовершеннолетних. Москва, 1968. pp. 144.

- United Kingdom

MORRISON (ARTHUR CECIL LOCKWOOD) Notes on juvenile court law:...a summary of the principal statutes and statutory instruments dealing with children and young persons, etc. 3rd ed. Chichester, Justice of the Peace and Local Government Review, 1959. pp. (ii), 28. 15¼cm.

CAVENAGH (WINIFRED ELIZABETH) Juvenile courts, the child and the law. rev. ed. Harmondsworth, Penguin Books, 1967. pp. 300. bibliog. 18cm. (Pelican Books. A 796) First published as The child and the court.

MUMFORD (GILBERT HENRY FRANCIS) A guide to juvenile court law. 6th ed. London, Jordan, 1968. pp. xxx, 334.

- United Kingdom - Ireland, Northern

IRELAND, NORTHERN. Child Welfare Council. 1960. Operation of juvenile courts in Northern Ireland: report. [F.Crilly, chairman]. Belfast, 1960. pp. 24. 21cm.

- United Kingdom - Scotland

SCOTLAND. Scottish Office. Social Work Services Group. 1970. Children's hearings: notes on Part 3 of the Social Work (Scotland) Act, 1968. Edinburgh, 1970. pp. 42.

- United States

KETCHAM (ORMAN W.) and PAULSEN (MONRAD GOTKE) Cases and materials relating to juvenile courts. Brooklyn, 1967. pp. 558.

JUVENILE COURTS - United States (Cont'd.)

BROWN (HOWARD G.) and DOWNS (WILLIAM T.)
Juvenile courts and the Gault decision.
[Washington, Children's Bureau], 1968. pp.
86-96. 26cm. Xerox copy of article in
Children, May-June, 1968, vol. 15, no. 3.

LEMERT (EDWIN M.) Social action and legal change:
revolution within the juvenile court. Chicago,
1970. pp. 248.

- United States - California

CALIFORNIA. 1959. First interim report of
the special study commission on juvenile
justice: [Mildred M. Prince, chairman].
Sacramento, 1959. pp. 41. 22½cm.

JUVENILE DELINQUENCY

COMFORT (ALEXANDER) Delinquency; a lecture delivered
at the Anarchist Summer School, London, August
1950. London, 1951. pp. 14.

DITTSCHLAG (WERNER) Wohlstandsdelinquenz der
Jugendlichen: Versuch einer Deutung und
Analyse. Hamburg, 1967. pp. 84.

U.K. 1967. Home Office. Types of
delinquency and home background: a
validation study of Hewitt and Jenkins'
hypothesis; by Elizabeth Field. (Studies
in the Causes of Delinquency and the
Treatment of Offenders. 10) London,
1967. pp. vi, 21. bibliog. 24cm.

VAZ (EDMUND W.) ed. Middle-class juvenile delinquency: [readings]. New York, [1967]. pp. 289.

BOSSHARD (PETER) Bildung als kriminologischer
Faktor: Untersuchungen über kriminalsoziologische
Zusammenhänge zwischen Bildungsgrad und kriminel-
lem Verhalten Jugendlicher. Zürich, 1968.
pp. 153. bibliog. (Zürich. Universität. Rechts- und
Staatswissenschaftliche Fakultät. Zürcher Beiträge
zur Rechtswissenschaft. Neue Folge. Heft 298)

COHEN (STANLEY) Hooligans, vandals and the community
a study of social reaction to juvenile delinquency;
[Ph. D. (London) thesis]. 1969. fo. 644. bibliog.
Typescript: unpublished. This thesis is the property of London University and may not be removed
from the Library.

HEUYER (GEORGES) La délinquance juvénile: étude
psychiatrique. Paris, 1969. pp. 308.

McDONALD (LYNN) Social class and delinquency.
London, Faber, 1969. pp. 240. bibliog. 21½cm.
(Society Today and Tomorrow)

SPERGEL (IRVING) Community problem solving: the
delinquency example. Chicago, 1969. pp. 342.
bibliog.

WATSON (JOHN ARTHUR FERGUS) Which is the justice?
London, Allen & Unwin, 1969. pp. 242. 21½cm.

FRANKENSTEIN (CARL) Varieties of juvenile delinquency.
London, [1970]. pp. 252. bibliog.

GIBBONS (DON C.) Delinquent behavior. Englewood
Cliffs, [1970]. pp. 276.

MOSER (TILMANN) Jugendkriminalität und
Gesellschaftsstruktur: zum Verhältnis von
soziologischen, psychologischen und
psychoanalytischen Theorien des Verbrechens.
Frankfurt am Main, [1970]. pp. 377. bibliog.

SIMON (FRANCES H.) Prediction methods in
criminology, including a prediction study of
young men on probation; (a Home Office Research
Unit report). London, 1971. pp. 233. bibliog.
(U.K. Home Office. Home Office Research Studies.
7)

- Bibliography

UNITED STATES. National Institutes of Health.
Crime and delinquency abstracts. Bethesda, Md.
[1964] to date.

- Research - United Kingdom

BELSON (WILLIAM A.) and DIDCOTT (PETER J.) Causal
factors in the development of stealing by London
boys. [London, 1969] in progress. (London. University. London School of Economics and Political
Science. Survey Research Centre)

- Australia - New South Wales

NEW SOUTH WALES. Child Welfare Department.
Research Branch. 1952. Statistical survey of
one thousand children committed to institutions
in New South Wales; conducted by E.M. Corkery.
[Sydney, 1952]. pp. 23.

- Belgium

RACINE (AIMÉE) La délinquance juvénile
en Belgique en 1960, 1961 et 1962.
Bruxelles, CEDJ, 1966. pp. 53. 24cm.
(Centre d'Étude de la Délinquance Juvénile.
Publications. No. 16)

RACINE (AIMÉE) and others. Les blousons
noirs: un phénomène socio-culturel de
notre temps. Paris, Éditions Cujas,
1966. pp. 236. 24cm. (Centre d'Étude
de la Délinquance Juvénile. Publications.
No. 14)

RACINE (AIMÉE) La délinquance juvénile en
Belgique en 1963, 1964 et 1965. Bruxelles,
Centre d'Étude de la Délinquance Juvénile,
1968. pp. 45. 24cm. (Publications. No. 22)

JUNGER (J.) De jeugdmisdadigheid aan de kust.
Brussel, 1969. pp. 137. (Studiecentrum voor
Jeugdmisdadigheid. Publicaties. Nr. 25)

- Colombia

MOGOLLÓN TORRES (MARTHA) and GÓMEZ SARMIENTO
(MARIA TERESA) De la delincuencia juvenil.
Bogotá, 1968. pp. 103. bibliog.

- Czechoslavakia

SCHUBERT (LADISLAV) Problémy s kri-
minalitou mládeže. Bratislava,
1967. pp. 157. With Russian and
English summaries.

- Europe

MIDDENDORFF (WOLF) Kriminelle Jugend in Europa: eine vergleichende Übersicht über Jugendgerichtsbarkeit und Jugendkriminalität. Freiburg im Breisgau, Lambertus, 1953. pp. 102. bibliog. 21cm. (Jugendwohl. Beiträge zur Jugendhilfe. Heft 5)

COLLOQUE DE VARSOVIE, 1964. La délinquance juvénile en Europe: actes du colloque, etc. Bruxelles, Université Libre, Institut de Sociologie, [1968]. pp. 192. 24cm.

- France

ANDRÉ (LÉONCE) La lutte contre la criminalité juvénile: étude critique et de législation comparée sur la minorité pénale. Paris, Rousseau, 1912. pp. 440. 22cm.

- Germany

SAARBRUECKEN. Universität. Annales Universitatis Saraviensis. Rechts- und Wirtschaftswissenschaftliche Abteilung. Heft 19. Anwendungsbereich und Wirksamkeit der bestimmten Jugendstrafe: Untersuchungen an 180 Häftlingen der Jugendstrafanstalt Saarbrücken; von Richard Bellon. Köln, Heymann, 1966. pp. 225. bibliog. 21cm.

SAARBRUECKEN. Universität. Annales Universitatis Saraviensis. Rechts- und Wirtschaftswissenschaftliche Abteilung. Heft 38. Zum Erziehungserfolg der Jugendstrafe von unbestimmter Dauer: ein Beitrag zur kriminologischen Wirkungslehre; von Egon Müller. Köln, 1969. pp. 185. bibliog.

ABELS (DIETRICH MENO) Wege ins Verbrechen: Versuch einer Motivationsanalyse kriminellen Verhaltens. Stuttgart, 1970. pp. 176. bibliog.

- India

VARMA (S.C.) The young delinquents: a sociological inquiry. Lucknow, 1970. pp. 105.

- Italy

BERTOLINI (PIERO) and others. Deliquenza e disadattamento minorile: esperienze rieducative. Bari, Laterza, 1964. pp. 158. bibliog. 21½cm. (Convegno su "La scuola e la Società Italiana in Trasformazione". Ricerche. 16)

- Latvia

GREK (A.) and others. Kakim ty budesh', paren'? Riga, 1967. pp. 110.

KLIUCHINSKAIA (LEONIDA AL'BERTOVNA) and BERGERE (LIUTSIIA ALEKSANDROVNA) Несовершеннолетние и уголовный закон: исследование эффективности уголовного наказания по материалам Латвийской ССР; под редакцией Г. Я. Клявы. Рига, 1967. pp. 182.

KLIUCHINSKAIA (LEONIDA AL'BERTOVNA) Комиссии по делам несовершеннолетних: научно-практический комментарий к Положению о комиссиях по делам несовершеннолетних и опыт их работы. Рига, 1969. pp. 169.

- Mexico

ROSENQUIST (CARL M.) and MEGARGEE (EDWIN I.) Delinquency in three cultures. Austin, [1969]. pp. 554. bibliog.

- Moldavian Republic

SANTALOV (A. I.) ed. Соблюдать законы об ответственности несовершеннолетних. Кишинев, Картя Молдовеняскэ, 1965. pp. 159. 20cm.

- Netherlands

NETHERLANDS. Ministerie van Justitie. 1955. Strafbejegening: een studie over de toepassing van de jeugdgevangenis; door een Werkgroep van het Studie-en Documentatiecentrum van het Nederlandse Gevangeniswezen, thans opgegaan in het Studie- en Voorlichtingscentrum van het Ministerie van Justitie. 's-Gravenhage, 1955. pp. 121.

VASSART (CHR.) and RACINE (AIMÉE) Provos et provotariat: un an de recherche participante en milieu provo. Bruxelles, Centre d'Étude de la Délinquance Juvénile, 1968. pp. 160. bibliog. 24cm. (Publications. No. 21)

- Poland

ZAKRZEWSKI (PAWEŁ) Współdziałanie w przestępstwie młodocianych i dorosłych z nieletnimi. Kraków, Uniwersytet Jagielloński, 1960. pp. 168. bibliog. 25cm. (Rozprawy i Studia) With English summary.

KHARSHAK (E.) Nekotorye voprosy bor'by s prestupnost'iu nesovershennoletnikh v Pol'skoi Narodnoi Respublike. in Santalov (A.I.) ed. Sobliudat' zakony ob otvetstvennosti nesovershennoletnikh. Kishunev, 1965.

SZYMANOWSKI (TEODOR) Młodociani w polskim prawie karnym i penitencjarnym. Warszawa, WP, 1967. pp. 212. 20½cm. (Ośrodek BadańPrzestępczości. Prace) With Russian and English summaries.

- Russia

GRABOVSKAIA (NONNA PETROVNA) Ugolovno-pravovaia bor'ba s prestupleniiami nesovershennoletnikh v SSSR. Leningrad, 1961. pp. 79.

FILIMONOV (BORIS ALEKSANDROVICH) Protsessual'nye voprosy dosrochnogo osvobozhdeniia ot nakazaniia nesovershennoletnikh. Moskva, 1965. pp. 96.

PREDUPREZHDENIE... Предупреждение преступности несовершеннолетних. Москва, 1965. pp. 287.

GUKOVSKAIA (NATAL'IA ISIDOROVNA) Деятельность следователя и суда по предупреждению преступлений несовершеннолетних: методическое пособие. Москва, 1967. pp. 112.

BABAEV (MIKHAIL MATVEEVICH) Индивидуализация наказания несовершеннолетних. Москва, 1968. pp. 118.

JUVENILE DELINQUENCY - Russia (Cont'd.)

VOPROSY... Вопросы борьбы с преступностью несовершеннолетних. Алма-Ата, Наука, 1968. pp. 167. 20см.

ORLOV (VIKTOR SEMENOVICH) Подросток и преступление: основные пути предупреждения преступлений несовершеннолетних. Москва, Университет, 1969. pp. 202. 21см.

KAREV (DMITRII STEPANOVICH) ed. Izuchenie i preduprezhdenie pravonarushenii sredi nesovershennoletnikh: sbornik statei. Moskva, 1970. pp. 146.

- South Africa

VENTER (J.D.) The incidence of juvenile crime in South Africa: an analysis of the problem based on available information. [Pretoria, 1959] repr. 1964. pp. 71, fo.xxxiii. (South Africa. National Bureau of Educational and Social Research. Research Series. No. 2.)

SMITH (PIETER RETIEF) De gesinslewe van die jeugdige oortreder met besondere verwysing na gesinsonvolledigheid: 'n vergelykende kriminologiese ondersoek na 100 oortredende en 100 nie-oortredende jeugdiges. Pretoria, 1967. fo. 143,12. bibliog.

- Sweden

BÖRJESON (BENGT) Om påföljders verkningar: en undersökning av prognosen för unga lagöverträdare efter olika slag av behandling. Stockholm, Almqvist & Wiksell, 1966. pp. 259. bibliog. 22cm. (Stokholms Högskola. Acta Universitatis Stockholmiensis. Stockholm Studies in Educational Psychology. 12) With English summary.

- United Kingdom

LONDON. London County Council. Education Officer's Department. Report of the Education Officer on juvenile delinquency. London, 1937. pp. 23.

U.K. 1967. Home Office The use of the Jesness inventory on a sample of British probationers; by Martin Davies. (Studies in the Causes of Delinquency and the Treatment of Offenders. 12) London, 1967. pp. iv, 20. bibliog. 24cm.

U.K. Social Survey. [Reports. New Series.] 352 Deterrents and incentives to crime among youth aged 15-21 years, 1963; by H.D.Willcock, assisted by Judy Stokes; an inquiry undertaken for the Home Office. [London], 1968 in progress.

DAVIES (MARTIN) Probationers in their social environment: a study of male probationers aged 17-20, together with an analysis of those reconvicted within twelve months; (a Home Office Research Unit report). London, 1969. pp. 204. bibliog. (U.K. Home Office. Home Office Research Studies. 2.)

MOTT (JOY) The Jesness Inventory: application to approved school boys. London, 1969. pp. iv, 26. bibliog. 24½cm. (U.K. Home Office. Studies in the Causes of Delinquency and the Treatment of Offenders. 13)

WEST (DONALD JAMES) Present conduct and future delinquency: first report of the Cambridge study in delinquent development. London, 1969. pp. 207. bibliog. (Cambridge. University. Institute of Criminology. Cambridge Studies in Criminology. vol. 25)

DAVIES (MARTIN) Financial penalties and probation; (a Home Office Research Unit report). London, 1970. pp. 38. (U.K. Home Office. Home Office Research Studies. 5)

HALLORAN (JAMES D.) and others. Television and delinquency. Leicester, 1970. pp. 221. (Television Research Committee. Working Papers. No. 3.)

STRATTA (ERICA) The education of borstal boys: a study of their educational experiences prior to, and during, borstal training. London, 1970. pp. 228. bibliog.

BLANDY (MARY) Harvest from rotten apples: an account of experimental work with detached youth. London, 1971. pp. 190.

COCKETT (R.) Drug abuse and personality in young offenders. London, [1971]. pp. 166.

TAYLOR (MARILYN) Study of the juvenile Liaison scheme in West Ham, 1961-1965; (a Home Office Research Unit Report). London, 1971. pp. 45. (U.K. Home Office. Home Office Research Studies. 8)

WILDE (EDWARD) The forgotten years: dealing with the younger offender. London, 1971. pp. 28. (Bow Group. Memoranda)

- United Kingdom - Bibliography

CAMBRIDGE. University. Institute of Criminology. Bibliographical Series. No.1. Deprivation of liberty for young offenders: a select bibliography on approved schools, attendance centres, borstals, detention centres and remand homes, 1940-1965; compiled by Keith Hawkins. Cambridge, [1967]. fo. 48.

- United Kingdom - Congresses

CHILDREN in trouble: proceedings of a conference held at the University of Leeds on 26th October 1968 to discuss the white paper, Cmnd. 3601. Leeds, [1968]. pp. 28.

- United Kingdom - Scotland

MACK (JOHN ALEXANDER) Police juvenile liaison: practice and evaluation;...reporting a training course for the police juvenile liaison officers. Glasgow, University, School of Social Study, [1968]. pp. 30. 21½cm.

- United Kingdom - Wales

JUVENILE delinquency and incidence of maladjustment: Cardiff survey; published by the Cardiff Teachers' Association [and] National Union of Teachers. Cardiff, 1969. pp. 84. bibliog.

- United States

LONGSTRETH (LANGDON E.) Delinquency prediction. Los Angeles, 1961. fo. 9. (Los Angeles. University of Southern California. Youth Studies Center. Working Papers. 5)

UNITED STATES. Education Office. Role of the school in prevention of juvenile delinquency. Washington, 1963. pp. v, 101.

UNITED STATES. 12618/1519 and 1608. Juvenile delinquency: report[s], etc. Washington, 1964. 2 pts.

STEEL (RONALD) ed. New light on juvenile delinquency. New York, Wilson, 1967. pp. 221. bibliog. 18½cm. (The Reference Shelf. vol 39, no.4)

U.K. 1967. Home Office. The use of the Jesness inventory on a sample of British probationers; by Martin Davies. (Studies in the Causes of Delinquency and the Treatment of Offenders. 12) London, 1967. pp. iv, 20. bibliog. 24cm.

UNITED STATES. President's Commission on Law Enforcement and Administration of Justice. Task Force Reports. Juvenile delinquency and youth crime: report on juvenile justice and consultants' papers. Washington, 1967. pp. xii, 428. bibliog.

UNITED STATES. Welfare Administration. The handling of juveniles from offense to disposition. [Introduction, cases one to five, and instructor's guide]. Washington, 1967. 3 pts.

SHORT (JAMES F.) ed. Gang delinquency and delinquent subcultures. New York, Harper & Row, [1968]. pp. viii, 328. 20½cm. (Readers in Social Problems)

STRATTON (JOHN R.) and TERRY (ROBERT M.) eds. Prevention of delinquency: problems and programs. New York, Macmillan, [1968]. pp. xiii, 334. 23½cm.

WINSLOW (ROBERT WALLACE) ed. Juvenile delinquency in a free society: selections from the President's Commission on Law Enforcement and Administration of Justice. Belmont, Dickenson, [1968]. pp. ix, 237. 23cm.

AMERICAN ACADEMY OF POLITICAL AND SOCIAL SCIENCE. Annals. vol. 381. The future of corrections; special editor...John P. Conrad. Philadelphia, 1969. pp. xiii, 230. 23½cm.

HIRSCHI (TRAVIS) Causes of delinquency. Berkeley, 1969. pp. 309. bibliog.

KEISER (R. LINCOLN) The vice lords: warriors of the streets. New York, [1969]. pp. 83. bibliog.

MOTT (JOY) The Jesness Inventory: application to approved school boys. London, 1969. pp. iv, 26. bibliog. 24½cm. (U.K. Home Office. Studies in the Causes of Delinquency and the Treatment of Offenders. 13)

PLATT (ANTHONY M.) The child savers: the invention of delinquency. Chicago, 1969. pp. 230. bibliog.

ROSENQUIST (CARL M.) and MEGARGEE (EDWIN I.) Delinquency in three cultures. Austin, [1969]. pp. 554. bibliog.

SELLIN (JOHAN THORSTEN) and WOLFGANG (MARVIN EUGENE) eds. Delinquency: selected studies. New York, [1969]. pp. 161.

SHAW (CLIFFORD ROBE) and McKAY (HENRY DONALD) Juvenile delinquency and urban areas: a study of rates of delinquency in relation to differential characteristics of local communities in American cities. rev. ed. Chicago, 1969. pp. 394.

GARABEDIAN (PETER G.) and GIBBONS (DON C.) eds. Becoming delinquent: young offenders and the correctional process. Chicago, 1970. pp. 304. bibliog.

LERMAN (PAUL) ed. Delinquency and social policy. New York, 1970. pp. 488.

RUBIN (SOL) Crime and juvenile delinquency: a rational approach to penal problems. 3rd ed. Dobbs Ferry, New York, 1970. pp. 234.

- United States - Bibliography

UNITED STATES. Children's Bureau. A selected bibliography on juvenile delinquency. rev. ed. [Washington], 1964. pp. 72.

- Upper Volta

HOCHET (JEAN) Inadaptation sociale et délinquance juvénile en Haute-Volta. Paris, C.N.R.S. — C.V.R.S., 1967. pp. 199. bibliog. 22cm. (Recherches Voltaïques. 9)

KABABISH

ASAD (TALAL) The Kababish Arabs: power, authority and consent in a nomadic tribe. London, [1970]. pp. 263. bibliog.

KABARDINO-BALKARIAN REPUBLIC

KABARDINO-BALKARIIA... Кабардино-Балкария под солнцем Великого Октября: сборник статей. Нальчик, Кабардино-Балкарское Книжное Издательство, 1967. pp. 282. 21½см.

- Economic history

TSAVKILOV (B. KH.) ed. Pod znamenem Lenina: k 40-letiiu sovetskoi avtonomii Kabardino-Balkarii. Nal'chik, 1961. pp. 105.

KUMYKOV (TUGAN KHABASOVICH) Экономическое и культурное развитие Кабарды и Балкарии в XIX веке. Нальчик, Кабардино-Балкарское Книжное Издательство, 1965. pp. 419. 21см.

KARDANOV (ABUBA TITUEVICH) Narodnoe khoziaistvo Kabardino-Balkarskoi ASSR v gody semiletki, 1959-1965 gg.: istoricheskii ocherk. Nal'chik, 1968. pp. 105.

- History

ISTORIIA Kabardino-Balkarskoi ASSR s drevneishikh vremen do nashikh dnei. Moskva, 1967. 2 vols.

- Industries

KHAPACHEV (PSHIKAN GERIKHANOVICH) Promyshlennost' i stroitel'stvo Kabardino-Balkarii na novom pod"eme. Nal'chik, 1963. pp. 46.

- Nationalism

MASAEV (SHEKHIM-GERI) Leninskaia natsional'naia politika i sozdanie avtonomii Kabardino-Balkarii. Nal'chik, 1961. pp. 59.

KABARDINO-BALKARIAN REPUBLIC (Cont'd.)

- Politics and government

TAZIEV (KHAZHMURAT FITSOVICH) Ideino-vospitatel'naia rabota Kabardino-Balkarskoi partiinoi organizatsii mezhdu XX i XXII sezdami KPSS: pod redaktsiei U. A. Uligova. Nal'chik, 1962. pp. 109.

- Social life and customs

GARDANOV (B. A.) ed. Materialy po obychnomu pravu kabardintsev: pervaia polovina XIX v. Nal'chik, 1956. pp. 427,

KABIR (HUMAYUN)

DATTA (DIPANKAR) Humayun Kabir: a political biography. London, [1969]. pp. 80.

KADALIE (CLEMENTS)

KADALIE (CLEMENTS) My life and the ICU: the autobiography of a black trade unionist in South Africa;...edited... by Stanley Trapido. London, 1970. pp. 230.

KÁDÁR (JÁNOS)

KÁDÁR (JÁNOS) Vorwärts auf dem Wege des Sozialismus: Reden und Artikel; Auswahl aus den Jahren 1960-1966. Budapest, Corvina Verlag, 1967. pp. 478. 19½cm.

KÁDÁR (JÁNOS) Izbrannye stat'i i rechi, oktiabr' 1964 g. - aprel' 1970 g.; [perevod s vengerskogo] Moskva, 1970. pp. 648.

KADUNA RIVER

NIGERIA. [Ministry of Transport]. 1959. Proposals for dams on the Niger and Kaduna Rivers. Lagos, 1959. pp. 30.

KAFIRS (AFRICAN PEOPLE)

HOLDEN (WILLIAM CLIFFORD) British rule in South Africa: illustrated in the story of Kama and his tribe and of the war in Zululand. London, the author, [1879; Pretoria, State Library, 1969]. pp. viii, 218. 18cm. (Reprints. No.37) Facsimile reprint.

ALBERTI (JOHANN CHRISTOPH LUDWIG) Account of the tribal life and customs of the Xhosa in 1807; translated by Dr. William Fehr from the original manuscript in German of The Kaffirs of the south coast of Africa. Cape Town, Balkema, 1968. pp. xiv, 117. 22cm.

MAYER (PHILIP) Townsmen or tribesmen: conservatism and the process of urbanization in a South African city...; with contributions by Iona Mayer. 2nd ed. Cape Town, 1971. pp. 329. bibliog.

KAIRA

- Industries

AMIN (RAMDAS KISHORDAS) A survey of the industrial potential of Kaira district. Vallabh Vidyanagar, Sardar Patel University, Department of Economics, 1966. pp. viii, 135. 21½cm. (Studies in Economics. 5)

KAISER WILHELM (KIEL) CANAL

HEECKT (HUGO) Alte und neue Aspekte der wirtschaftlichen Bedeutung des Nord-Ostsee-Kanals. Tübingen, 1969. pp. 91. bibliog. (Kiel. Universität. Institut für Weltwirtschaft. Kieler Studien. 98)

KALABARI

- Tribal government

NIGERIA (EASTERN REGION). Commission of Inquiry into the Kalabari Chieftaincy Dispute. 1959. Report: [Nwabuto Uwechia, commissioner]. Enugu, [1959]. pp. 12.

KALABARI (AFRICAN PEOPLE)

- Religion

NIGERIA. Nigeria Magazine. Special Publications. 3. The Gods as guests: an aspect of Kalabari religious life; by Robin Horton. Lagos, 1960. pp. 71. 24½cm.

KALAMATA

- Civic improvement

ETHNIKON METSOVION POLYTECHNEION. Spoudastērion Poleodomikōn Ereunōn. Master plan of the town and region of Kalamata. Athens, 1971. pp. 194, 59 maps and charts. In Greek with English summary. 7 maps in end pocket.

KALASHNIK (MIKHAIL KHARITONOVICH)

KALASHNIK (MIKHAIL KHARITONOVICH) Ispytanie ognem. Moskva, 1971. pp. 462.

KALEDIN (ALEKSEI MAKSIMOVICH)

MEL'NIKOV (NIKOLAI MIKHAILOVICH) А. М. Каледин: герой Луцкого прорыва и Донской Атаман. [Париж], 1968. pp. 374. bibliog.

KALEP (TEODOR FERDINAND GEORGIEVICH)

ZIL'MANOVICH (DMITRII IAKOVLEVICH) Teodor Kalep, 1866-1913. Moskva, 1970. pp. 171. bibliog.

KALININGRAD

- Industries

CHUPRAKOVA (IRINA MIKHAILOVNA) Сила общественности. Калининград, Книжное Издательство, 1963. pp. 16. 19½cm.

KALININGRAD (OBLAST')

- Statistics

KALININGRADSKAIA... Калининградская область в цифрах. Калининград, 1968. pp. 138.

KALISZ

KALISZ; (wstęp J. Parandowskiego) Poznań, Wydawnictwo Poznańskie, 1967. pp. 98. 21cm.

KÁLLAI (GYULA)

KÁLLAI (GYULA) Szocializmus, népfront, demokrácia. Budapest, 1971. pp. 413.

KALMYK REPUBLIC

- History

OCHERKI istorii Kalmytskoi ASSR: do-oktiabr'skii period. Moskva, 1967. pp. 479.

KICHIKOV (MERGEN LIDZHINOVICH) Vo imia pobedy nad fashizmom: ocherki istorii Kalmytskoi ASSR v gody Velikoi Otechestvennoi voiny. Elista, 1970. pp. 207.

OCHERKI istorii Kalmytskoi ASSR: epokha sotsializma. Moskva, 1970. pp. 432.

- Intellectual life

IZ... Из истории культуры дореволюционной Калмыкии. Волгоград, Нижне-Волжское Книжное Издательство, 1967. pp. 72. bibliog. 20cm.

TASHNINOV (NIKOLAI SHAVEL'EVICH) Ocherki istorii prosveshcheniia Kalmytskoi ASSR. Elista, 1969. pp. 213.

- Nationalism

SVERDLIN (MATVEI ABRAMOVICH) and ROGACHEV (PETR MIKHAILOVICH) Kommunizm i natsii. Elista, 1964. pp. 96. bibliog.

- Politics and government

KALMYK REPUBLIC. Verkhovnyi Sovet. Zasedaniia: stenograficheskii otchet. Elista, sessional, Dec.1966 (3rd series, 7th session). 22cm.

- Social history - Sources

IZ... Из истории движения за национальную школу в Калмыкии: к 60-летию союза учителей "Хальмаг тангачин туг"; сборник документов и материалов. Элиста, 1967. pp. 99.

KALMYKS IN THE UNITED STATES

RUBEL (PAULA G.) The Kalmyk Mongols: a study in continuity and change. Bloomington, [1967]. pp. 282. (Indiana University. Graduate School. Publications. Uralic and Altaic Series. vol. 64)

KALUGA (OBLAST')

- Politics and government

SPIVAK (VENIAMIN MIKHAILOVICH) and SHURKIN (PAVEL ANDREEVICH) Ocherki istorii Kalughskoi organizatsii KPSS. ch.1. 90-e gg. XIX v. - 1918 g. Kaluga, 1959. pp. 247.

OCHERKI... Очерки истории Калужской организации КПСС. [Тула], Приокское Книжное Издательство, 1967. pp. 410. 21см.

- Statistics

KALUGA (OBLAST'). Statisticheskoe Upravlenie. Калужская область за 50 лет: статистический сборник. Калуга, 1967. pp. 168. 20см.

KAMA RIVER

DUBROVIN (L. I.) and others. Камское водохранилище. Пермь, Книжное Издательство, 1959. pp. 159,[15]. bibliog. 20cm.

KAMBAS

INTERNATIONAL AFRICAN INSTITUTE. Ethnographic Survey of Africa. East Central Africa. Part 5. The central tribes of the north-eastern Bantu: the Kikuyu...and the Kamba of Kenya; by John Middleton and Greet Kershaw. rev. ed. London, the Institute, 1965. pp. 103. bibliog. 24½cm.

KAMCHATKA

- Commerce

KURIN (K.) Torgovlia i obshchestvennoe pitanie na Kamchatke. Petropavlovsk-Kamchatskii, 1963. pp. 75.

- Economic conditions

PARMUZIN (IURII PAVLOVICH) Северо-Восток и Камчатка: очерк природы. Москва, Мысль, 1967. pp. 368. bibliog. 19½см.

- History

GARUSOV (IVAN SERGEEVICH) Разгром белогвардейщины в Охотско-Камчатском крае. Магадан, Книжное Издательство, 1963. pp. 71. 16½cm.

- History - Revolution, 1917-1921

PERVYI Sovdep: dokumenty i materialy o Petropavlovsom Sovete rabochikh i soldatskikh deputatov. Petropavlovsk-Kamchatskii. 1967. pp. 140.

KAMCHATKA

- History - Revolution - 1917-1921 - Sources

ZA... За власть Советов: из истории борьбы за установление Советской власти в Камчатской области, 1920-1922 гг.; документы и материалы. Владивосток. 1967. pp. 182.

- Statistics

KAMCHATKA. Statisticheskoe Upravlenie. Narodnoe khoziaistvo Kamchatskoi oblasti: statisticheskii sbornik. Khabarovsk, 1966. pp. 150.

KAMENEV (LEV BORISOVICH)

KAMENEV i Zinov'ev v 1917 g.: fakty i dokumenty. Moskva, [1926?]. pp. 61.

KAMENSKII (S.)

KAMENSKII (S.) Vek minuvshii: vospominaniia. Parizh, 1967. pp. 190.

KAMLOOPS, BRITISH COLUMBIA

- Economic conditions

BRITISH COLUMBIA. Bureau of Economics and Statistics. 1961. The Kamloops region: an economic survey. Victoria, B.C., 1961. pp. (v), iv, 68.

KAMMERER (PAUL)

KOESTLER (ARTHUR) The case of the midwife toad. London, 1971. pp. 187. bibliog.

KAMO.
See TER-PETROSIAN (SIMON ARSHAKOVICH) called KAMO

KAMP (JOSEPH P.)

FRIENDS OF DEMOCRACY INC. Joe Kamp: peddler of propaganda and hero of the pro-fascists. New York, [194-?]. pp. 23. 28cm.

KAMPALA

- Description

VORLAUFER (KARL) Physiognomie, Struktur und Funktion Gross-Kampalas: ein Beitrag zur Stadt-geographische Tropisch-Afrikas. Frankfurt/Main, Universität, Seminar für Wirtschaftsgeographie, 1967. 2vols. bibliog. 21cm. (Frankfurter Wirtschafts- und Sozialgeographische Schriften. Band 1-2) Vol. 2 consists of maps.

- Economic conditions

VORLAUFER (KARL) Physiognomie, Struktur und Funktion Gross-Kampalas: ein Beitrag zur Stadt-geographische Tropisch-Afrikas. Frankfurt/Main, Universität, Seminar für Wirtschaftsgeographie, 1967. 2vols. bibliog. 21cm. (Frankfurter Wirtschafts- und Sozialgeographische Schriften. Band 1-2) Vol. 2 consists of maps.

- Politics and government

PARKIN (DAVID) Neighbours and nationals in an African city ward. London, Routledge & Kegan Paul, 1969. pp. xvii, 228. bibliog. 21½cm.

- Social conditions

VORLAUFER (KARL) Physiognomie, Struktur und Funktion Gross-Kampalas: ein Beitrag zur Stadt-geographische Tropisch-Afrikas. Frankfurt/Main, Universität, Seminar für Wirtschaftsgeographie, 1967. 2vols. bibliog. 21cm. (Frankfurter Wirtschafts- und Sozialgeographische Schriften. Band 1-2) Vol. 2 consists of maps.

PARKIN (DAVID) Neighbours and nationals in an African city ward. London, Routledge & Kegan Paul, 1969. pp. xvii, 228. bibliog. 21½cm.

KAMPONG HENDERSON

HORSLEY (J. A. T.) Resettlement of a community: discussion of the problems arising from the disorganisation of a community in Singapore. 1955. fo. v, 186. bibliog. Microfilm of typescript.

KANNENBÄCKERLAND

- Economic conditions

SCHMIDT-NICOLAI (INGE) Das Kannenbäckerland: Struktur und Wandel einer agrarischen Tonwirtschaftslandschaft. Bonn, 1968. pp. 205. bibliog.

KANO

- Civic improvement

TREVALLION (BERNARD A.W.) Metropolitan Kano: report on the twenty year development plan, 1963-1983. [London], Neame, [1966]. 2 vols. 29½cm. The second volume contains two maps only.

KANPUR

- Industries

INTERNATIONAL SEMINAR ON URBAN AND INDUSTRIAL GROWTH OF KANPUR REGION, 1967. Regional perspective of industrial and urban growth: the case of Kanpur: papers and proceedings...;[edited by] P.B. Desai [and others]. Bombay, 1969. pp. 406.

KANSAS

- Constitution

DRURY (JAMES WESTBROOK) The government of Kansas. rev. ed., Lawrence, Kansas, [1970]. pp. 492.

-Executive departments

DRURY (JAMES WESTBROOK) The government of Kansas. rev. ed., Lawrence, Kansas, [1970]. pp. 492.

- History

SCHRUBEN (FRANCIS W.) Kansas in turmoil, 1930-1936. Columbia, Missouri, [1969]. pp. 240. bibliog.

- Politics and government

CLANTON (O. GENE) Kansas populism: ideas and men. Lawrence, Kansas, [1969]. pp. 330. bibliog.

- Social history

DYKSTRA (ROBERT R.) The cattle towns. New York, 1968. pp. 386, x.

KANSAS CITY

- Economic conditions

KANSAS CITY. City Planning Department. Economic base study. Part 2. Kansas City Metropolitan Area: trade, transportation and services. Kansas City, 1967. pp. (vii, 4, 16), x, 225. 28cm. (Kansas City. Community Renewal Program. Reports. 2)

- Politics and government

DORSETT (LYLE W.) The Pendergast machine. New York, O.U.P., 1968. pp. xv. 163. 21cm.

KANSK- ACHINSK BROWN COAL BASIN

GRIGOR'EV (KLAVDII NIKOLAEVICH) Канско-Ачинский угольный бассейн: геологическое строение, угленосность и перспективы развития. Москва, Недра, 1968. pp. 184. bibliog. 26см.

KANT (IMMANUEL)

BAEUMLER (ALFRED) Das Irrationalitätsproblem in der Ästhetik und Logik des 18. Jahrhunderts bis zur Kritik der Urteilskraft; (reprographischer Nachdruck der 1. Auflage, Halle an der Saale 1923); mit einem Nachwort zum Neudruck. Darmstadt, 1967. pp. 354.

DE MONTMORENCY (HERVEY GUY FRANCIS EDWARD) From Kant to Einstein. Cambridge, Heffer, 1926. pp. 39 21½cm.

GOLDMANN (LUCIEN) Introduction à la philosophie de Kant; [first published by Presses Universitaires de France in 1948]. [Paris], Gallimard, [1967]. pp. 311. 16½cm. (Idées. 146)

KANT (IMMANUEL) Introduction to logic and his essay on the mistaken subtilty of the four figures; translated by Thomas Kingsmill Abbott...; with a few notes by Coleridge. New York, [1963]. pp. 100.

KANT (IMMANUEL) On history;...[selected] and edited, with an introduction, by Lewis White Beck. Indianapolis, [1963]. pp. 154. bibliog.

FEIGL (H.) What Hume might have said to Kant. in Bunge (Mario Augusto) ed. The critical approach to science and philosophy. New York, [1964].

BATIN (V.N.) Kategoriia schast'ia v etike Kanta. in Uchenye Zapiski Kafedr Obshchestvennykh Nauk Vuzov G. Leningrada. Filosofiia. vyp. 6. Leningrad, 1965.

VODZINSKII (EVGENII IVANOVICH) Russkoe neokantianstvo kontsa XIX - nachala XX vekov: marksistsko-leninskaia kritika ontologii i gnoseologii. Leningrad, 1966. pp. 79.

SUPPES (P.) Some extensions of Randall's interpretation of Kant's philosophy of science. in Anton (John Peter) ed. Naturalism and historical understanding. Albany, [1967].

GRAM (MOLTKE S.) Kant, ontology, and the a priori. Evanston, 1968. pp. 194.

HARTNACK (JUSTUS) Kant's theory of knowledge; ...translated by M. Holmes Hartshorne. London, Macmillan, 1968. pp. (iv), 146. 21½cm.

KLEIN (ZIVIA) La notion de dignité humaine dans la pensée de Kant et de Pascal. Paris, Vrin, 1968. pp. 134. bibliog. 22½cm. (Bibliothèque d'Histoire de la Philosophie)

LAMANNA (EUSTACHIO PAOLO) Studi sul pensiero morale e politico di Kant; a cura di Domenico Pesce. Firenze, Le Monnier, [1968]. pp. ix, 318. 21½cm. First published in Cultura Filosofica, 1914-16.

PHILONENKO (A.) Théorie et praxis dans la pensée morale et politique de Kant et de Fichte en 1793. Paris, Vrin, 1968. pp. 227. 25cm. (Bibliothèque d'Histoire de la Philosophie)

SAARBRUECKEN. Universität. Annales Universitatis Saraviensis. Rechts- und Wirtschaftswissenschaftliche Abteilung. Heft 34. Das Problem von Sein und Sollen in der Philosophie Immanuel Kants; von Günter Ellscheid. Köln, Heymann, 1968. pp. 193. bibliog. 21cm.

SCHWARTLAENDER (JOHANNES) Der Mensch ist Person: Kants Lehre vom Menschen. Stuttgart, [1968]. pp. 266.

SELLARS (WILFRID STALKER) Science and metaphysics: variations on Kantian themes. London, Routledge & Kegan Paul, 1968. pp x, 246. 21½cm. (International Library of Philosophy and Scientific Method)

WILLIAMS (T.C.) The concept of the categorical imperative: a study of the place of the categorical imperative in Kant's ethical theory. Oxford, Clarendon P., 1968. pp. xi, 142. bibliog. 22cm.

WOLF (ROBERT PAUL) ed. Kant: a collection of critical essays. London, Macmillan, 1968. pp. (iii), 416. bibliog. 17cm. (Modern Studies in Philosophy)

BLUEHDORN (J.) and RITTER (JOACHIM) eds. Philosophie und Rechtswissenschaft: zum Problem ihrer Beziehung im 19. Jahrhundert. Frankfurt am Main, [1969]. pp. 184. (Fritz Thyssen Stiftung. Neunzehntes Jahrhundert. Studien zur Philosophie und Literatur des Neunzehnten Jahrhunderts. Band 3)

HOPPE (HANSGEORG) Kants Theorie der Physik: eine Untersuchung über das Opus postumum von Kant. Frankfurt am Main, Klostermann, [1969]. pp. viii, 144. bibliog. (Philosophische Abhandlungen. Band 31)

LEHMANN (GERHARD) Beiträge zur Geschichte und Interpretation der Philosophie Kants. Berlin, De Gruyter, 1969. pp. viii, 427. bibliog. 23cm. 4 plates in end pocket.

PENELHUM (TERENCE) and MACINTOSH (JOHN JAMES) eds. The first critique: reflections on Kant's Critique of pure reason. Belmont, Calif., [1969]. pp. 146.

SWING (THOMAS KAEHAO) Kant's transcendental logic. New Haven, 1969. pp. 388. bibliog.

GRAYEFF (FELIX) Kant's theoretical philosophy: a commentary to the central part of the Critique of pure reason; translated from the German by David Walford. Manchester, [1970]. pp. 232.

MURPHY (JEFFRIE G.) Kant: the philosophy of right. London, 1970. pp. 186. bibliog.

REISS (HANS SIEGBERT) ed. Kant's political writings;... translated by H.B. Nisbet. Cambridge, 1970. pp. 210. bibliog.

WOOD (ALLEN W.) Kant's moral religion. Ithaca, 1970. pp. 283. bibliog.

GOLDMANN (LUCIEN) Immanuel Kant. London, 1971. pp. 236.

KANTOROWICZ (ALFRED)

KANTOROWICZ (ALFRED) Im 2. Drittel unseres Jahrhunderts: Illusionen, Irrtümer, Widersprüche, Einsichten, Voraussichten. Köln, [1967]. pp. 216. 20½cm.

WACHE im Niemandsland: zum 70. Geburtstag von Alfred Kantorowicz; herausgegeben von Heinz-Joachim Heydorn; Beiträge und Briefe von Ernst Bloch [and others]. Köln, [1969]. pp. 133. In various languages.

KAOLIN

HUDSON (KENNETH) The history of English china clays: fifty years of pioneering and growth. Newton Abbot, [1969]. pp. 189.

KAPP (FRIEDRICH)

KAPP (FRIEDRICH) Vom radikalen Frühsozialisten des Vormärz zum liberalen Parteipolitiker des Bismarckreichs: Briefe 1843-1884; herausgegeben...von Hans-Ulrich Wehler. Frankfurt a.M., [1969]. pp. 156.

KARACHAI - CHERKESS AUTONOMOUS OBLAST'

- Economic conditions

VOPROSY... Вопросы экономики Карачаево-Черкесии. Черкесск, 1968. pp. 220.

- History

OCHERKI istorii Karachaevo-Cherkesii. t.1. S drevneishikh vremen do Velikoi Oktiabr'skoi sotsialisticheskoi revoliutsii. Stavropol', 1967. pp. 600.

- Politics and government

K istorii partiinykh organizatsii Stavropol'skogo kraia i Karachaevo-Cherkesskoi avtonomnoi oblasti. Stavropol', 1967. pp. 116.

KARACHI

KHAN (MOHAMMAD ZAFAR AHMAD) Karachi: a pre-industrial city in transition. [Ph.D.(London) Thesis]. 1968. fo. 514. bibliog. 25½cm. Typescript: unpublished. This thesis is the property of London University and may not be removed from the Library.

- Growth

PAKISTAN. Planning Commission. Physical Planning and Housing Section. Studies. No. P.P. & H. 19. Urban biographies (Karachi, Lahore, Dacca); by Grenfell Rudduck. [Karachi], 1965. pp. 127. 24cm.

- Population

HASHMI (SULTAN S.) and others. The people of Karachi: data from a survey. Karachi, Pakistan Institute of Development Economics, 1964. pp. xii, 368. 24½cm. (Statistical Papers. No.2)

- Statistics

HASHMI (SULTAN S.) and others. The people of Karachi: data from a survey. Karachi, Pakistan Institute of Development Economics, 1964. pp. xii, 368. 24½cm. (Statistical Papers. No.2)

KARADZIC (VUK STEFANOVIC)

HAHN (F.) Deutsch-serbische Begegnung in der Person und im Schaffen von Vuk Stefanović Karadžić. in Steinitz (Wolfgang) and others, eds. Ost und West in der Geschichte des Denkens und der kulturellen Beziehungen. Berlin, 1966.

NIKITIN (S.A.) Vuk Karadzhich i Rossiia. in Nikitin (Sergei Aleksandrovich) Ocherki po istorii iuzhnykh slavian i russko-balkanskikh sviazei v 50-70-e gody XIX v. Moskva, 1970.

KARAGANOV (AMFILOGII ALEKSANDROVICH)

MIASNIKOV (ALEKSANDR KONSTANTINOVICH) and others, defendants. Дело Мясниковых: стенографический отчет И.К. Маркузе. Санкт-Петербург, 1872. pp. viii, 406.

KARA-KALPAK REPUBLIC

- Economic conditions

MATERIALY... Материалы по производительным силам Узбекистана. вып.10. Природные условия и ресурсы низовьев Аму-Дарьи Кара-Калпакская АССР и Хорезмская област УзССР. Ташкент, АН УзССР, 1959. pp. 353. 25½см.

EKONOMICHESKIE... Экономические основы специализации и размещения ведущих отраслей народного хозяйства Каракалпакской АССР. Ташкент, 1969. pp. 241. bibliog.

- Economic history

KARAKALPAKIIA... Каракалпакия в период победы социализма и коммунистического строительства. Ташкент, 1969. pp. 266. bibliog.

- History - Revolution, 1917-1921

DOSUMOV (IANGIBAI MUKHAMEDOVICH) Победа Великой Октябрьской социалистической революции в Кара-Калпакии. Ташкент, 1958. pp. 142. bibliog.

- Intellectual life

KOSYMBETOV (I.) Kul'turnoe stroitel'stvo v natsional'nykh respublikhakh Srednei Azii. in Iz istorii vypolneniia vtoroi programmy, partii v oblasti kul'turnogo stroitel'stva. Moskva, 1968.

PANABERGENOV (ABISH) Partiinaia organizatsiia Karakalpakii v bor'be za osushchestvlenie kul'turnoi revoliutsii, 1917-1941 gg. Nukus, 1969. pp. 339. bibliog.

- Native races

> BHALEKENOV (U. KH.) Казаки низовьев
> Амударьи: к истории взаимоотношений
> народов Каракалпакии в XVIII-XX вв.
> Ташкент, 1966. pp. 336. bibliog.

KARA-KALPAKS

> KAMALOV (SABIR KAMALOVICH) Каракалпаки
> в XVIII-XIX веках: к истории взаимоот-
> ношений с Россией и среднеазиатскими
> ханствами. Ташкент, 1968. pp. 327.
> bibliog.

KARA-KUM CANAL

> GOKOV (REDZHEPMURAD) Знаменосцы
> большой стройки. Ашхабад, 1965.
> pp. 55.

KARDELJ (EDVARD)

> KARDELJ (EDVARD) Белешке о нашој
> друштвеној критици. Београд, Кул-
> тура, 1966. pp. 198. 18cm.

KARELIA

- History - Sources

> BALAGUROV (IAKOV ALEKSEEVICH) ed. Ре-
> волюционные события в Карелии в годы
> первой русской революции, 1905-1907 гг.:
> сборник документов и материалов. Пет-
> розаводск, Госиздат КФССР, 1955. pp.
> 182. bibliog. 20cm.

- Intellectual life

> KOLOSENOK (STANISLAV VITAL'EVICH) and MONOSOV
> (IOSIF MIKHAILOVICH) Kul'tura Sovetskoi Karelii.
> Petrozavodsk, 1967. pp. 155.

- Politics and government

> KARELIA. Verkhovnyi Sovet. Zasedaniia: stenograficheskii
> otchet. Petrozavodsk, sessional, Dec.1964 - Nov.1966
> (6th series, 4th-8th sessions), with gap (7th session).
> 22cm.

> PETROZAVODSK. Universitet. Uchenye Za-
> piski. t.14, vyp.5. Istoricheskie Na-
> uki. Вопросы истории КПСС: сборник
> статей кафедры истории КПСС. Петроза-
> водск, 1967. pp. 135.

KARIRI INDIANS

> RABELLO (SYLVIO) Os artesãos do Padre Cícero;
> condições sociais e econômicas do artesanato
> de Juàzeiro do Norte. Recife, Instituto
> Joaquin Nabuco de Pesquisas Sociais,
> 1967. pp. 156, (22). bibliog. 22½cm.

KARL-MARX-STADT

- History

> DIAMANT (ADOLF) Chronik der Juden in Chemnitz,
> heute Karl-Marx-Stadt: Aufstieg und Untergang
> einer jüdischen Gemeinde in Sachsen. Frankfurt/Main,
> [1970]. pp. 183.

- Politics and government

> KARL-MARX-STADT. Polizeiamt. Politische
> Abteilung. Der Polizeidirektor be-
> richtet; ein Polizeibericht über die
> Arbeiterbewegung in Chemnitz am Vor-
> abend des ersten Weltkrieges; einge-
> leitet und erläutert von Rudolph
> Strauss. Karl-Marx-Stadt, Stadtarchiv,
> 1962. pp. 85. 20cm. (Beiträge zur
> Heimatgeschichte von Karl-Marx-Stadt.
> Heft 11)   R/WA 3100/285780

KARLOVY VARY

- Politics and government

> ROTAVSKÁ tragédie: sborník z dějin
> dělnického hnutí a Komunistické
> strany Československa na Karlovarsku.
> Plzeň, Krajské Nakladatelství, 1961.
> pp. 131. 21cm.

KARLSRUHE

- Economic conditions

> ISENBERG (GERHARD) Zur wirtschaft-
> lichen Entwicklung des Stadt- und
> Landkreises Karlsruhe: Wirtschafts-
> gutachten. Karlsruhe, 1962. pp.
> 79.

KAROSAS (JONAS)

> KAROSAS (JONAS) Mówią kamienie Wilna;
> przekład z litewskiego Anny Lau-
> Gniadowskiej. Warszawa, Książka i
> Wiedza, 1968. pp. 366. 19½cm.

KARSOV (NINA)

> KARSOV (NINA) and SZECHTER (SZYMON) Monuments
> are not loved;... translated by Paul Stevenson.
> London, [1970]. pp. 285.

KASHIPUR

- Economic conditions

> MANDAL (G. C.) and SENGUPTA (SUNIL C.) Kashipur,
> West Bengal 1956-60: a report on re-survey of
> a village. Santiniketan, Visva-Bharati [Uni-
> versity], Agro-Economic Research Centre, 1962.
> pp. vii, 105. 24½cm. (Studies in Rural Change)

KASHMIR
See JAMMU AND KASHMIR

KASHMIR QUESTION

> MAHAJAN (MEHR CHAND) Accession of Kashmir to
> India: the inside story. Sholapur, [1962?].
> pp. 28.

> PAKISTAN. Embassy (U.S.A.). Information
> Division. 1962. Double-think on Kashmir:
> background report. Washington, [1962].
> pp. 17.

> PAKISTAN. Embassy (U.S.A.). Information
> Division. 1962. Kashmir and the United
> Nations, 1962: background report. Washington,
> [1962]. pp. 39.

> WORLD opinion on Kashmir. Rawalpindi,
> Press Information Department, 1962.
> pp. 24. 24½cm.

KASHMIR QUESTION (Cont'd.)

PAKISTAN. President, 1958-1969 (Ayub Khan). 1964. Broadcast to the nation by Mohammad Ayub Khan, 1st March, 1964. Karachi, [1964]. pp. 11.

REVOLT in Kashmir: British views on Kashmir dispute; editorial comments in the U.K. press. London, Information Department, High Commission for Pakistan, [1964]. pp. (12). 23cm.

KHAN (MOHAMMAD AYUB) President's monthly broadcast to the nation [delivered on November 1st, 1965]. London, Pakistan High Commission, Information Division, 1965. fo. 7.

KHAN (RAHMATULLAH) Kashmir and the United Nations. Delhi, [1965]. pp. 199. bibliog.

PAKISTAN. High Commission (U.K.). Information Department. 1965. India's aggression against Pakistan: defiance of U.N. sparks revolt in Kashmir; the only solution. London, [1965]. pp. 8.

PAKISTAN. [Ministry of External Affairs]. 1965. Kashmir in arms: the hour of reckoning; broadcast talk by Zulfikar Ali Bhutto, Foreign Minister of Pakistan, September 3, 1965. [Karachi, 1965]. pp. 12.

KHAN (MOHAMMAD AYUB) President explains implications of Tashkent meeting: [excerpts from broadcast on January 14th, 1966]. London, Information Division, Pakistan High Commission, 1966. fo. 3.

MAUDUDI (SAYYID ABUL ALA) Kashmir: a call to the conscience of humanity. Lahore, 1966. pp. 60.

BAZAZ (PREM NATH) Kashmir in crucible. New Delhi, Pamposh Publications, 1967. pp. vii, 318. 21½cm.

DAS GUPTA (JYOTI BHUSAN) Jammu and Kashmir. The Hague, Nijhoff, 1968. pp. xiv, 428. bibliog. 24cm.

ROY (A.C.) The second Kashmir war: as seen from different angles. Calcutta, 1969. pp. 258.

KATANGA

- Bibliography

WALRAET (MARCEL) Bibliographie du Katanga 1824-[1949]. Bruxelles, 1954-60. 3 vols. (in 1) 24½cm. (Académie Royale des Sciences d'Outre-Mer. Classe des Sciences Morales et Politiques. Mémoires in -8°. Tome 32. Fasc. 3 and Nouvelle Série. Tome 14. Fasc. 1, Tome 22. Fasc. 4)

- Politics and government

DAVISTER (PIERRE) and TOUSSAINT (PHILIPPE) Croisettes et casques bleus: récits et documents. Bruxelles, Éditions Actuelles, [1962]. pp. 269.

KATOWICE (PROVINCE)

- Economic conditions

GRABANIA (MAREK) and MRZYK (JÓZEF) Województwo katowickie: krótka charakterystyka gospodarcza. Katowice, Slask, 1967. pp. 182. bibliog. 16 cm.

- History

GOŁĘBIOWSKI (JANUSZ WOJCIECH) and RECHOWICZ (HENRYK) eds. Studia i materiały z dziejów województwa katowickiego w Polsce Ludowej. Katowice, Śląsk, 1966. pp. 320. 24cm. With Russian and English summaries.

- Industries

SYREK (MIECZYSŁAW) Rozwój i przemiany strukturalne przemysłu województwa katowickiego w 25-leciu Polski Ludowej. Katowice, 1971. pp. 268. bibliog.

KATYN FOREST MASSACRE, 1940

ZBRODNIA katyńska w świetle dokumentów; z przedmową Władysława Andersa. Londyn, Gryf, 1948. pp. 384. 21½cm.

KAUNDA (KENNETH DAVID)

HALL (RICHARD) The high price of principles: Kaunda and the white South. London, Hodder & Stoughton, 1969. pp. 256. 21½cm.

KAUTSKY (KARL)

LENIN (VLADIMIR IL'ICH) The proletarian revolution and renegade Kautsky; [with explanatory notes]. London, 1935. pp. 110.

REDZIC (E.) Kautsky o naciji i nacionalnom pitanju. in Redžić (Enver) Prilozi o nacionalnom pitanju. Sarajevo, 1963.

TROTSKII (LEV DAVYDOVICH) On Engels and Kautsky. New York, 1969. pp. 30.

KAY (RICHARD)

KAY (RICHARD) 1716-1751. The diary of Richard Kay, 1716-51, of Baldingstone, near Bury, a Lancashire doctor; extracts edited...by W. Brockbank and F. Kenworthy. Manchester, Chetham Society, 1968. pp. (iii), 179. (Remains, Historical and Literary, connected with the Palatine Counties of Lancaster and Chester. 3rd Series. vol. 16)

KAZAKOV (YASHA)

(The REBIRTH of Yasha Kazakov: the road from Moscow to Jerusalem); revival of national Jewish consciousness; impact of six-day war on the young generation; return to the homeland. [London], 1970. pp.12.

KAZAKS

BHALEKENOV (U. KH.) Казаки низовьев Амударьи: к истории взаимоотношений народов Каракалпакии в XVIII-XX вв. Ташкент, 1966. pp. 336. bibliog.

VOSTROV (VENIAMIN VASIL'EVICH) and MUKANOV (MARAT SABITOVICH) Родоплеменной состав и расселение казахов, конец XIX - начало XX в. Алма-Ата, 1968. pp. 255. 21см.

KAZAKS IN CHINA

MOSELEY (GEORGE) A Sino-Soviet cultural frontier: the Ili Kazakh autonomous Chou. Cambridge, Harvard U.P., 1966. pp. viii, 163. 25½cm. (Harvard University. East Asian Research Center. Harvard East Monographs. 22)

KAZAKSTAN

ZVEREV (NIKOLAI VASIL'EVICH) and others. Полвека созидания. Алма-Ата, Казахстан, 1967. pp. 399. 21см.

SOVETSKII Kazakhstan. Alma-Ata, 1970. pp. 588.

- Annexation to Russia

BEKMAKHANOV (ERMUKHAN BEKMAKHANOVICH) Prisoedinenie Kazakhstana k Rossii. Moskva, 1957. pp. 342. bibliog.

- Bibliography

ANTROPOVA (Z. L.) and others, compilers. Освоение целины: указатель литературы по экономике и культуре областей Северного Казахстана. Алма-Ата, Казахстан, 1966. pp. 96. 20см.

- Commerce

ROZMANOV (M. M.) Nekotorye problemy sovetskoi torgovli Kazakhstana. Alma-Ata, 1966. pp. 231.

- Constitutional history

TUGANBAEV (AKAN SHARIPOVICH) Октябрьская революция и развитие Казахской Советской национальной государственности. Алма-Ата, Казахстан, 1967. pp. 132. 20см.

KENZHEBAEV (SAKEN MAMAZHANOVICH) Советы в борьбе за построение социализма: история советского строительства в Казахстане, 1917-1987 гг. Алма-Ата, 1969. pp. 358.

ZIMANOV (SALYK ZIMANOVICH) V.I. Lenin i sovetskaia natsional'naia gosudarstvennost' v Kazakhstane. Alma-Ata, 1970. pp. 303.

- Constitutional history - Sources

POKROVSKII (S. N.) ed. Obrazovanie Kazakhskoi ASSR: sbornik dokumentov i materialov. Alma-Ata, 1957. pp. 368.

- Description and travel

KAZAKH Soviet Socialist Republic. Moscow, [1967]. pp. various.

- Economic conditions

PROBLEMY SOVREMENNOI EKONOMIKI KAZAKHSTANA: sbornik statei; [published by] Akademiia Nauk Kazakhskoi SSR, Institut Ekonomiki. Alma-Ata, annual, 1965 (vyp.1) to date. 22cm.

PROBLEMY fizicheskoi, ekonomicheskoi i meditsinskoi geografii Kazakhstana: materialy nauchnykh konferentsii, posviashchennykh 50-letiiu Velikoi Oktiabr'skoi sotsialisticheskoi revoliutsii. Alma-Ata, 1967. pp. 159. bibliog.

RAZVITIE... Развитие и размещение производительных сил Казахской ССР. Москва, Наука, 1967. pp. 259. bibliog. 21см. (Академия Наук СССР. Совет по Изучению Производительных Сил. Развитие и Размещение Производительных Сил СССР)

GEOGRAFIIA... География районов освоения Казахстана. Алма-Ата, Казахстан, 1968. pp. 132. bibliog. 21см. (Академия Наук Казахской ССР. Сектор Физической Географии. Вопросы Географии Казахстана вып.14)

KAZAKHSTAN... Казахстан. Москва, 1969. pp. 481. bibliog. (Академия Наук СССР. Институт Географии. Природные Условия и Естественные Ресурсы СССР)

BAISHEV (SAKTAGAN BAISHEVICH) and CHECHELEVA (T.V.) eds. Tempy, struktura i effektivnost' obshchestvennogo proizvodstva Kazakhskoi SSR. Alma-Ata, 1970. pp. 289.

- Economic history

SARMURZIN (ALTAI GAISIEVICH) Partiinoe rukovadstvo dvizheniem za kommunisticheskii trud v Kazakhstane, noiabr' 1958-1963gg. Alma-Ata, 1964. pp. 169.

BAISHEV (SAKTAGAN BAISHEVICH) and CHULANOV (G. CH.) eds. Razvitie narodnogo khoziaistva Kazakhstana za 50 let Sovestskoi vlasti. Alma-Ata, 1967. pp. 463.

INTER-REGIONAL STUDY TOUR AND SEMINAR ON THE SEDENTARISATION OF NOMADIC POPULATIONS IN THE SOVIET SOCIALIST REPUBLICS OF KAZAKHSTAN AND KIRGHIZIA, 1966. Report on the Inter-Regional Study Tour...5 to 30 September 1966. (ILO/TAP/INT/R.13) Geneva, International Labour Office, 1967. pp. 96. (Development Programme: Technical Assistance Sector. [International]. R.13)

SUZHIKOV (MARAT MUKHAMBETKALIEVICH) Социально-экономические проблемы национальной консолидации: из опыта перехода казахского народа к социализму, минуя капитализм; под редакцией и с предисловием...М. С. Джунусова. Алма-Ата, Наука, 1968. pp. 379. 19½см.

- Economic policy

BAISHEV (SAKTAGAN BAISHEVICH) ed. Материально-техническая база коммунизма и ее экономические проблемы в Казахстане, etc. Алма-Ата, 1966. pp. 440.

- Emigration and immigration

TURSUNBAEV (A. B.) Из истории крестьянского переселения в Казахстан. Алма-Ата, 1950. pp. 101.

- Foreign relations - Russia

BASIN (VALENTIN IAKOVLEVICH) Rossiia i kazakhskie khanstva v XVI-XVIII vv.: Kazakhstan v sisteme vneshnei politiki rossiiskoi imperii. Alma-Ata, 1971. pp. 275.

KAZAKSTAN (Cont'd.)

- History

ISTORIIA Kazakhskoi SSR: epokha sotsializma. [3rd] ed. Alma-Ata, 1967. pp. 751.

BEISEMBAEV (SERKBAI BEISEMBAEVICH) Ленин и Казахстан, 1897-1924 гг. Алма-Ата, Казахстан, 1968. pp. 534. 19½см.

KAZAKHSTAN... Казахстан в XV - XVIII веках: вопросы социально-политической истории; [сборник статей] Алма-Ата, 1969. pp. 201.

- History - Bibliography

AGEEVA (E. I.) and others, compilers. Bibliografiia po istorii Kazakhstana: annotirovannyi ukazatel'. vyp.1. Dorevoliutsionnyi period. Alma-Ata, 1964. pp. 410.

- History - Chronology

U... У истоков Коммунистической партии Казахстана: летопись важнейших событий. ч.1. Конец XIX века - февраль 1917 года. Алма-Ата, Казахстан, 1966. pp. 379. 20см.

- History - Historiography

NUSUPBEKOV (AKAI) and BISENOV (KHAMID) Фальсификация истории и историческая правда. Алма-Ата, Казахстан, 1964. pp. 219. 20см.

DAKHSHLEIGER (GRIGORII FEDOROVICH) Историография Советского Казахстана: очерк. Алма-Ата, 1969. pp. 189. bibliog.

- History - Sources

KAZAKHSTAN... Казахстан в период Великой Отечественной войны Советского Союза, 1941-1945: сборник документов и материалов. Алма-Ата, Наука, 1964-67. 2 vols. 26см.

- History - Revolution, 1917-1921

ROMANOV (IURII IVANOVICH) Дружба, рожденная в борьбе: из истории содружества трудящихся Российской Федерации и Казахстана в годы гражданской войны. Алма-Ата, 1964. pp. 120. bibliog.

POBEDA... Победа Советской власти в Средней Азии и Казахстане. Ташкент, Фан, 1967. pp. 771. 22см.

NURPEISOV (KENES) Sovety Kazakhstana v bor'be za uprochenie vlasti rabochikh i krest'ian, noiabr' 1917 g. - iiun' 1918 g. Alma-Ata, 1968. pp. 172.

POKROVSKII (SERGEI NIKOLAEVICH) Lenin i pobeda Sovetskoi vlasti v Kazakhstane. Alma-Ata, 1970. pp. 149.

- History - Revolution, 1917-1921 - Sources

INOSTRANNAIA... Иностранная военная интервенция и гражданская война в Средней Азии и Казахстане: май 1918 г. - (декабрь 1920 г.) Алма-Ата, АН КазССР, 1968-64. 2 vols. bibliog. 21см. (Из Истории Гражданской Войны в СССР: Документы и Материалы)

VELIKAIA... Великая Октябрьская социалистическая революция в Казахстане. Алма-Ата, 1967. pp. 458.

- Industries

ASHIMBAEV (TUIMEBAI ASHIMBAEVICH) Проблемы повышения эффективности основных фондов: на материалах промышленности Казахстана. Алма-Ата, 1967. pp. 388.

BAISHEV (SAKTAGAN BAISHEVICH) История индустриализации Казахской ССР, 1926-1941. Алма-Ата, 1967. 2 vols. bibliog. (История Индустриализации СССР: Документы и Материалы)

ADAMCHUK (V. A.) and DVOSKIN (BENIAMIN IAKOVLEVICH) Проблемы развития промышленных узлов: на примере Казахстана. Москва, 1968. pp. 269.

EFFEKTIVNOST'... Эффективность капитальных вложений в промышленности Казахстана. Алма-Ата, Наука, 1969. pp. 242. 20см.

KOL'TSOV (VASILII IVANOVICH) Tempy i proportsii razvitiia promyshlennosti Kazakhstana. Alma-Ata, 1970. pp. 135.

SIMAKOV (KAIUM MUKHAMEDZHANOVICH) Ocherk razvitiia promyshlennosti Kazakhstana. Alma-Ata, 1970. pp. 211.

- Intellectual life

KUL'TURNOE stroitel'stvo v Kazakhstane, 1918-1932 gg.: sbornik dokumentov i materialov. t.1. Alma-Ata, 1965. pp. 566.

SULEIMENOV (RAMAZAN BIMASHEVICH) and BISENOV (KHAMID IZNEEVICH) Социалистический путь культурного прогресса отсталых народов: история строительства Советской культуры Казахстана, 1917-1965гг Алма Ата, 1967. pp. 320.

- Nationalism

KIIKBAEV (NIGMATULLA KUSENOVICH) Торжество ленинской национальной политики в Казахстане. Алма-Ата, Казахстан, 1968. pp. 342. 19½см.

SUZHIKOV (MARAT MUKHAMBETKALIEVICH) Социально-экономические проблемы национальной консолидации: из опыта перехода казахского народа к социализму, минуя капитализм; под редакцией и с предисловием...М. С. Джунусова. Алма-Ата, Наука, 1968. pp. 379. 19½см.

ERZHANOV (AKHMET ERZHANOVICH) Успехи национальной политики КПСС в Казахстане, 1946-1958 гг. Алма-Ата, 1969. pp. 248.

ZIMANOV (SALYK ZIMANOVICH) V.I. Lenin i sovetskaia natsional'naia gosudarstvennost' v Kazakhstane. Alma-Ata, 1970. pp. 303.

- Politics and government

IZ istorii partiinykh organizatsii Urala, Kazakhstana i Uzbekistana: sbornik statei. Sverdlovsk, 1963. pp. 190.

ASYLBEKOV (MALIK KHANTEMIRULY) Железнодорожники Казахстана в первой русской революции, 1905-1907 гг. Алма-Ата, Наука, 1965. pp. 182. 20см.

TOMSK. Universitet. Uchenye Zapiski. No.53. Iz istorii partiinykh organizatsii Zapadnoi Sibiri i Kazakhstana posle XX s"ezda KPSS: sbornik rabot aspirantov kafedry istorii KPSS. vyp.2. Tomsk, 1965. pp. 177.

ZIMANOV (SALYK ZIMANOVICH) and ATISHEV (ARYSTANBEK ATISHEVICH) Политические взгляды Чокана Валиханова. Алма-Ата, Наука, 1965. pp. 249. pp. 20.

BAISHEV (SAKTAGAN BAISHEVICH) В. И. Ленин и Советский Казахстан. Алма-Ата, 1969. pp. 325.

- Population

NASELENIE i trudovye resursy gorodov Severnogo Kazakhstana. Alma-Ata, 1970. pp. 275. bibliog.

- Rural conditions

KUL'TURA i byt kazakhskogo kolkhoznogo aula. Alma-Ata, 1967. pp. 303.

SOSKIN (SEMEN NAUMOVICH) O preodolenii sotsial'no-ekonomicheskikh i kul'turno-bytovykh razlichii mezhdu gorodom i derevnei v period stroitel'stva kommunizma. Alma-Ata, 1967. pp. 221.

TURSUNBAEV (ABDE BACHINOVICH) Kazakhskii aul v trekh revoliutsiiakh. Alma-Ata, 1967. pp. 483.

TURSUNBAEV (ABDE BOCHINOVICH) Dorogoi bor'by i svershenii: iz istorii kazakhskogo aula. Alma-Ata, 1971. pp. 166.

- Social conditions

SARSENBAEV (TABIGAT SARSENBAEVICH) Социализм и свобода личности: на примере Казахстана и Средней Азии. Алма-Ата, 1969. pp. 95.

- Social history - Sources

ASTAPOVICH (ZOIA ANTONOVNA) and others, eds. Velikii Oktiabr' i raskreposhchenie zhenshchin Srednei Azii i Kazakhstana, 1917-1936 gg.: sbornik dokumentov i materialov. Moskva, 1971. pp. 464.

- Social life and customs

SARSENBAEV (NURULLA SARSENBAEVICH) Обычаи и традиции в развитии. Алма-Ата, Казахстан, 1965. pp. 326. bibliog. 19½см.

- Statistics

KAZAKSTAN. Tsentral'noe Statisticheskoe Upravlenie. 1968. Народное хозяйство Казахстана: статистический сборник. Алма-Ата, Казахстан, 1968. pp. 416. 21см.

KAZAN'

- History

IONENKO (I.M.) Bor'ba bol'shevikov Kazani za upravlenie voiskami i provedenie demobilizatsii staroi armii v Kazanskom voennom okruge, noiabr' 1917 - fevral' 1918. in Kazan'. Universitet. Uchenye Zapiski. tom 122, kn. 2. Iz istorii klassovoi bor'by i obshchestvennoi mysli v Povolzh'e i Priural'e: sbornik statei. Kazan', 1962.

- Politics and government

IZ istorii kazanskogo revoliutsionnogo podpol'ia 80-kh godov XIX veka. Kazan', 1970. pp. 74.

KAZAN' (GUBERNIIA)

- Politics and government

ZAKHAROV (NIKOLAI STEPANOVICH) and EMEL'IANOVA (IRINA ARDAL'ONOVNA) Советы Среднего Поволжья в период подготовки Октябрьской революции: по материалам Казанской губернии. Казань, Университет, 1967. pp. 129. 21см.

KAZASOV (DIMO)

KAZASOV (DIMO) Vidiano i prezhiviano, 1891-1944. Sofiia, 1969. pp. 702.

KEATS (JOHN)

PEDERSON-KRAG (G.) "O poesy! For thee I hold my pen". in Wilbur (George B.) and Muensterberger (Warner) eds. Psychoanalysis and culture:... [reprint of the volume originally published in 1951]. New York, 1967.

KEELE UNIVERSITY

SOCIOLOGICAL REVIEW, THE; [published by] University of Keele. Monographs. [No.] 12. The foundation year in the University of Keele: a report by A.H. Iliffe. Keele, 1968. pp. xix, 115. 22cm.

KEI (HARA)
See HARA (SATOSHI)

KEKCHI INDIANS

CARTER (WILLIAM E.) New lands and old traditions: Kekchi cultivators in Guatemalan lowlands. Gainesville, 1969. pp. 153. bibliog. (Florida University. School of Inter-American Studies. Latin American Monographs. 2nd Series. No. 6)

KELANTAN

- Politics and government

KELANTAN. Administration report. [Kota Bharu], annual, 1925-1931. 25cm.

KELANTAN (Cont'd.)

- Sanitary affairs

KELANTAN. Medical Department. Annual report. [Kota Bharu?], annual, 1927-1934, 1936. 25-33cm

KELSEN (HANS)

VONLANTHEN (ALBERT) Zu Hans Kelsens Anschauung über die Rechtsnorm. Berlin, Duncker und Humblot, [1965]. pp. 92. 23cm. (Schriften zur Rechtstheorie. Heft 6)

MILIBAND (R.) Marx y el estado. in Marx, el derecho y el estado. Barcelona, 1969.

KEMANTS

GAMST (FREDERICK C.) The Qemant: a pagan-Hebraic peasantry of Ethiopia. New York, [1969]. pp. 128. bibliog.

KEMEROVO (OBLAST')

- Statistics

KEMEROVSKAIA ordenonosnaia: statisticheskii sbornik. Kemerovo, 1968. pp. 122.

KENNA (MICHAEL)

WENDT (LLOYD) and KOGAN (HERMAN) Bosses in lusty Chicago: the story of Bathhouse John and Hinky Dink; [reprint, with a new introduction, of the work originally published in 1943 as Lords of the Levee]. Bloomington, Indiana U.P., 1967. pp. xviii, 9-384. bibliog. 20cm. (Midland Books. M. B. 109)

KENNEDY (JOHN FITZGERALD) President of the United States

AKAHATA. Kennedy and U.S. imperialism: a commentator's article in Akahata, organ of the Central Committee of the Communist Party of Japan, March 10, 1964. Peking, Foreign Languages P., 1964. pp. 80. 18½cm.

UNITED STATES. President's Commission on the Assassination of President Kennedy. Investigation of the assassination of President John F. Kennedy: hearings. Washington, 1964. 26 vols.

MEAGHER (SYLVIA) Accessories after the fact; the Warren Commission, the authorities, and the report. Indianapolis, Bobbs-Merrill, [1967]. pp. xxxiii, 477. 22¼cm.

SPARROW (JOHN) Warden of All Souls College, Oxford. After the assassination: a positive appraisal of the Warren report. New York, Chilmark P., [1967]. pp. (iii), 77. bibliog. 18cm.

GROMYKO (ANATOLII ANDREEVICH) 1036 дней президента Кеннеди. Москва, 1968. pp. 279.

LANE (MARK) A citizen's dissent: Mark Lane replies. New York, Holt, 1968. pp. xiii, 290. 20½cm.

LINCOLN (EVELYN) Kennedy and Johnson. New York, Holt, [1968]. pp. xiii, 209. 21cm.

WHITE (STEPHEN) Should we now believe the Warren report? New York, Macmillan, [1968]. pp. x, 309. 23cm.

HEATH (JIM F.) John F. Kennedy and the business community. Chicago, 1969. pp. 198. bibliog.

KENNEDY (ROBERT FRANCIS) 13 days: the Cuban missile crisis, October 1962. [London], Macmillan, [1969]. pp. 190. 20cm.

SORENSEN (THEODORE CHAIKIN) The Kennedy legacy. London, 1970. pp. 414. First published 1969.

WICKER (TOM) JFK and LBJ: the influence of personality upon politics. Baltimore, 1969 repr. 1970. pp. 297.

MEL'NIKOV (IURII MIKHAILOVICH) Vneshnepoliticheskie doktriny SHA: proiskhozhdenie i sushchnost' programmy "Novykh rubezhei" prezidenta D. Kennedi. Moskva, 1970. pp. 494.

- Bibliography

UNITED STATES. Library of Congress. John F. Kennedy, 1917-1963: a chronological list of references. Washington, 1964. pp. viii, 68.

CROWN (JAMES TRACY) The Kennedy literature: a bibliographical essay on John F. Kennedy. New York, New York P., 1968. pp. viii, 181. 22½cm.

KENNEDY (ROBERT FRANCIS)

HALBERSTAM (DAVID) The unfinished odyssey of Robert Kennedy. London, [1968]. pp. 211.

KIMBALL (PENN) Bobby Kennedy and the new politics. Englewood Cliffs, Prentice-Hall, [1968]. pp. (v), 214. 22½cm.

LAING (MARGARET) Robert Kennedy. London, Macdonald, 1968. pp. xi, 236. 21½cm.

SORENSEN (THEODORE CHAIKIN) The Kennedy legacy. London, 1970. pp. 414. First published 1969.

WITCOVER (JULES) 85 days: the last campaign of Robert Kennedy. New York, [1969]. pp. 347.

NEWFIELD (JACK) Robert Kennedy: a memoir. London, 1970. pp. 318.

KENT

- Economic conditions

KENT. Planning Department. Kent development plan quinquennial review, 1963: report on the survey and analysis. Part 4. Sample surveys of households. [Maidstone], the Council, 1964 in progress. 30cm.

SOUTH EAST ECONOMIC PLANNING COUNCIL. South east Kent study. [London, H.M.S.O.], 1969. pp. 79.

- Economic policy

KENT. County Council. Kent development plan: written statement; ([with] Kent development plan, 1967 revision: amendment to written statement). [Maidstone], 1958-67. 3 pts. (in 1 vol.).

- Population

    KENT. Planning Department. Kent development plan quinquennial review, 1963: report on the survey and analysis. Part 4. Sample surveys of households. [Maidstone], the Council, 1964 in progress. 30cm.

- Social history

    JORDAN (WILBUR KITCHENER) Social institutions in Kent, 1480-1660: a study of the changing pattern of social aspirations. Maidstone, 1961. pp. x, 172. (Kent Archaeological Society. Archaeologia Cantiana. vol. 75)

KENT STATE UNIVERSITY

MICHENER (JAMES ALBERT) Kent State: what happened and why. London, 1971. pp. 563.

TOMPKINS (PHILLIP K.) and ANDERSON (ELAINE VANDEN BOUT) Communication crisis at Kent State: a case study. New York, [1971]. pp. 153.

KENTUCKY

- Economic conditions

    FULMER (JOHN L.) and PITTS (JAMES E.) Kentucky employment trends from 1951 to 1963 with projections to 1965-75. Lexington, Bureau of Business Research, University of Kentucky, 1965. pp. v, 79. 28cm.

- Economic policy

    KENTUCKY. 1944. Kentucky government, 1939-1943: a report on the executive and administrative work, etc. [Frankfort?, 1944?]. pp. 74. 23cm.

- Politics and government

    KENTUCKY. 1944. Kentucky government, 1939-1943: a report on the executive and administrative work, etc. [Frankfort?, 1944?]. pp. 74. 23cm.

    KENTUCKY. 1965. Commission on economy and efficiency: general report: [Shelby C. Kinkead, chairman]. Frankfort, 1965. pp. (iii), 29. 27½cm.

    JEWELL (MALCOLM EDWIN) and CUNNINGHAM (EVERETT W.) Kentucky politics. Lexington, U. of Kentucky P., 1968. pp. vii, 278. 23½cm.

- Population

    BOWMAN (MARY JEAN) and HAYNES (WILLIAM WARREN) Resources and people in East Kentucky: problems and potentials of a lagging economy. Baltimore, John Hopkins Press, [1963]. pp. xxv, 449. 24cm.

- Public works

    KENTUCKY. 1955. The State Property and Buildings Commission and its Division of Engineering: report of activities, July 1, 1944 to December 31, 1953. [Frankfort, 1955?]. fo. (iii), 42. 27½cm.

KENTUCKY UNIVERSITY

KENTUCKY UNIVERSITY. College of Commerce. Bureau of Business Research. Research Briefs. Forty-five years of property tax classification: Kentucky's experience; [and] The Bureau of Business Research 1965-66. Lexington, the Bureau, 1966. pp. 42. 28cm.

KENYA

- Bibliography

    WEBSTER (JOHN B.) and others, compilers. A bibliography on Kenya. Syracuse, University, Maxwell Graduate School of Citizenship and Public Affairs, Program of Eastern African Studies, [1967]. pp. xvii, 461. 23cm. (Eastern African Bibliographical Series. No. 2.)

- Boundaries - Somaliland

    MITCHELL (CHRISTOPHER ROGER) The dispute over the Northern Frontier District of Kenya, 1963-1967: a study in strategies of conflict resolution; [Ph. D. (London) Thesis]. 1971 [or rather 1972]. 1 vol. (various foliations). Typescript: unpublished. This thesis is the property of London University and may not be removed from the Library.

- Census

    KENYA. Census, 1969. Kenya population census, 1969: [volume series]. [Nairobi], 1970 in progress.

- Description and travel

    HOBLEY (CHARLES WILLIAM) Kenya: from chartered company to crown colony; thirty years of exploration and administration in British East Africa. 2nd ed. London, 1970. pp. 256.

- Economic conditions

    KENYA. Ministry of Economic Planning and Development. 1966. Three years of independence: building for a better future. [Nairobi], 1966. pp. 38. 24½cm.

    OMINDE (SIMEON HONGO) Land and population movements in Kenya. London, Heinemann, 1968. pp. xii, 204. bibliog.

    SOJA (EDWARD W.) The geography of modernization in Kenya: a spatial analysis of social, economic, and political change. Syracuse, Syracuse U.P., 1968. pp. xi, 143. bibliog. 26cm. (Syracuse Geographical Series. No. 2)

- Economic policy

    INTERNATIONAL BANK FOR RECONSTRUCTION AND DEVELOPMENT. 1962. The economic development of Kenya: report of an economic survey mission: [Edmund H. Leavey, Chief of Mission]. [Nairobi], 1962. pp. 270.

    KENYA. Sessional Papers. 1963. No. 1. Observations on the report of an economic survey mission from the International Bank for Reconstruction and Development. [Nairobi], 1963. pp. 20. 25cm.

    KENYA. Ministry of Economic Planning and Development. 1966. Towards a better future for our people. [Nairobi], 1966. pp. (iii), 39. 24½cm.

    VAN ARKADIE (BRIAN) Development and the mode of production: the case of Kenya. Brighton, 1970. pp. 8. (Brighton. University of Sussex. Institute of Development Studies. Communications. No.57)

KENYA (Cont'd.)

- Emigration and immigration

CABLE (VINCENT) Whither Kenyan emigrants? London, Young Fabian Group, 1969. pp. 31. bibliog. 22cm. (Young Fabian Pamphlets. [No.] 18)

- Foreign relations - Zanzibar

KENYA. Sessional Papers. 1961. No. 9. The Kenya coastal strip: report of the Commissioner [James W. Robertson]. [Nairobi, 1961]. pp. 48.

- History

WERE (GIDEON S.) A history of the Abaluyia of western Kenya. Nairobi, East African Publishing House, 1967. pp. 206. bibliog. 21½cm. (Peoples of East Africa)

KENYATTA (JOMO) Suffering without bitterness: the founding of the Kenya nation. Nairobi, East African Publishing House, 1968. pp. 348. 21½cm.

MACPHEE (A. MARSHALL) Kenya. London, Benn, 1968. pp. 238. bibliog. 21 cm. (Nations of the Modern World.)

SORRENSON (MAURICE PETER KEITH) Origins of European settlement in Kenya. Nairobi, O.U.P., 1968. pp. xii, 320. bibliog. 22cm. (British Institute of History and Archaeology in East Africa. Memoirs. No. 2)

HOBLEY (CHARLES WILLIAM) Kenya: from chartered company to crown colony; thirty years of exploration and administration in British East Africa. 2nd ed. London, 1970. pp. 256.

- History - Sources

FEDHA (NATHAN W.) and WEBSTER (JOHN B.) compilers. A catalogue of the Kenya National Archive collection on microfilm at Syracuse University. Syracuse, N.Y., 1967. unpaged.

WERE (GIDEON S.) Western Kenya historical texts: Abaluyia, Teso and Elgon Kalenjin. Nairobi, East African Literature Bureau, 1967. pp. (iii), 196. bibliog. 20½cm.

- Legislative Council

KENYA. Council of State. 1959. Report...to the Legislative Council under section 56 (2) (a) (i) of the Kenya (Constitution) Order in Council, 1958: subject: the Legislative Council (Constituency Elected Members) Bill, 1959. [Nairobi, 1959?] pp. 6, 2.

KENYA. Sessional Papers. 1961. No. 1. Amendments to the standing orders of Legislative Council. [Nairobi], 1961. fo. 2.

- National Assembly

SLADE (HUMPHREY) The parliament of Kenya. Nairobi, 1967. pp. 64.

- Nationalism

KENYATTA (JOMO) Suffering without bitterness: the founding of the Kenya nation. Nairobi, East African Publishing House, 1968. pp. 348. 21½cm.

- Native races

KENYA. 1948. A Bill to provide for local government in native areas and for the establishment of African district councils and other matters incidental thereto. [Nairobi] 1948. pp. 20.

KENYA. 1961. Report of a survey of problems of child welfare in Kenya. [Nairobi], 1961. pp. 65. bibliog.

- Officials and employees

KENYA. Sessional Papers. 1961. No. 6. Limited compensation scheme. [Nairobi], 1961. fo. 4, 4, (5).

KENYA. Sessional Papers. 1963/64. No. 2. [The general services]: proposals by the government of Kenya for the implementation of the recommendations contained in the report of the commission on the Kenya civil service, the Kenya teaching service, etc. [Nairobi], 1964. pp. 23. 25cm.

- Officials and employees - Salaries, allowances, etc.

KENYA. Public Service Salaries Review Commission. 1967. Report. [Nairobi], 1967. pp. 138. 25cm.

KENYA. Sessional Papers. 1967. No. 10. Proposals by the government of Kenya for the implementation of the recommendations contained in the report of the public service salaries review commission, 1967. [Nairobi?], 1967. pp. 24. 25cm.

- Politics and government

RUKARI (ZEEKY) Who rules Kenya? [n.p. 196-] pp. 29.

KENYA. Sessional Papers. 1961. No. 9. The Kenya coastal strip: report of the Commissioner [James W. Robertson]. [Nairobi, 1961] pp. 48.

KENYA. President, 1964- (Jomo Kenyatta). Main address...at the state opening of Parliament on 15th February, 1967. [Nairobi, 1967]. pp. 7. 25cm.

KENYATTA (JOMO) Suffering without bitterness: the founding of the Kenya nation. Nairobi, East African Publishing House, 1968. pp. 348. 21½cm.

MACPHEE (A. MARSHALL) Kenya. London, Benn, 1968. pp. 238. bibliog. 21½cm. (Nations of the Modern World.)

NYAGAH (S.) The politicalization of administration in East Africa: a comparative analysis of Kenya and Tanzania. Nairobi, K.I.A., 1968. pp. (1), 32. bibliog. 24½cm. (Kenya Institute of Administration. K.I.A. Occasional Papers. No. 1.)

GERTZEL (CHERRY) The politics of independent Kenya., 1963-8. London, 1970. pp. 180.

GHAI (YASH P.) and McAUSLAN (J. PATRICK W.B.) Public law and political change in Kenya: a study of the legal framework of government from colonial times to the present. Nairobi, 1970. pp. 536.

MBOYA (THOMAS JOSEPH) The challenge of nationhood: a collection of speeches and writings. London, 1970. pp. 278.

- Population

> MORGAN (WILLIAM THOMAS WILSON) and SHAFFER (N. MANFRED) Population of Kenya: density and distribution: a geographical introduction to the Kenya Population Census, 1962. Nairobi, 1966. pp. 36. 4 maps in end pocket.
>
> OMINDE (SIMEON HONGO) Land and population movements in Kenya. London, Heinemann, 1968. pp. xii, 204. bibliog. 27½cm.

- Rural conditions

> EDUCATION, employment and rural development; the proceedings of a conference held at Kericho, Kenya in September, 1966; James R. Sheffield, editor. Nairobi, East African Publishing House, 1967. pp. xxvi, 499. 21½cm.
>
> SYRACUSE UNIVERSITY. Maxwell Graduate School of Citizenship and Public Affairs. Program of Eastern African Studies. Occasional Papers. No.30. Two variables affecting rural transformation in Kenya : the settlement case ; by Brack E. S. Brown. [Syracuse, N.Y., 1967?]. fo. 29.

- Sanitary affairs

> KENYA. Sessional Papers. 1960/61. No. 8. Report of the Committee Appointed to Consider the Role of the Medical Services Rendered by the Missions in Relation to those Provided by Central and Local Government: [T.F. Anderson, chairman]. [Nairobi], 1960. pp. 37.

- Social conditions

> SOJA (EDWARD W.) The geography of modernization in Kenya: a spatial analysis of social, economic, and political change. Syracuse, Syracuse U.P., 1968. pp. xi, 143. bibliog. 26cm. (Syracuse Geographical Series. No. 2)

- Social policy

> KENYA. 1958. Social development report, 1956/57. Nairobi, 1958. pp. 24.
>
> KENYA. Ministry of Economic Planning and Development. 1966. Towards a better future for our people. [Nairobi], 1966. pp. (iii), 39. 24½cm.

KENYANS IN THE UNITED KINGDOM

> STEEL (DAVID) 1938- . No entry: the background and implications of the Commonwealth Immigrants Act, 1968. London, Hurst, [1969]. pp. (vii), 263. 21½cm.

KENYATTA (JOMO)

> KENYA. President, 1964- (Jomo Kenyatta). Main address...at the state opening of Parliament on 15th February, 1967. [Nairobi, 1967]. pp. 7. 25cm.
>
> KENYATTA (JOMO) Suffering without bitterness: the founding of the Kenya nation. Nairobi, East African Publishing House, 1968. pp. 348. 21½cm.

KEPLER (JOHANN)

> KOYRÉ (ALEXANDRE) La révolution astronomique: Copernic, Kepler, Borelli. Paris, Hermann, [1961]. pp. 525. 21cm. (Paris. École Pratique des Hautes Études. Histoire de la Pensée. 3)

KERALA

- Boundaries

> INDIA. Commission on Maharashtra — Mysore — Kerala Boundary Disputes. 1967. Report: [Mehr Chand Mahajan, sole commissioner]. Delhi, 1967. 2 vols.
>
> ANTULAY (A. RAHMAN) Mahajan report uncovered. Bombay, Allied Publishers, 1968. pp. (iv), 192. 21½cm.

- History

> KRISHNA AYYAR (K.V.) A short history of Kerala. Ernakulam, Pai, 1966. pp. ix, 218. 21cm.
>
> MENON (ALAPPAT SREEDHARA) A survey of Kerala history. Kottayam, National Book Stall, [1967]. pp. (ix), 446, xx. bibliog. 20½cm.

- Industries

> NATIONAL COUNCIL OF APPLIED ECONOMIC RESEARCH. Industrial programmes for the fourth plan: Kerala. New Delhi, [1969]. pp. 156.

- Legislative Assembly - Elections

> KRISHNA MURTHY (K. G.) and LAKSHMANA RAO (G.) Political preferences in Kerala: an electoral analysis of the Kerala general elections, 1957, 1960, 1965 and 1967. Delhi, Radha Krishna, [1968]. pp. xii, 99. 22cm.

- Politics and government

> NAMBOODIRIPAD (E.M.S.) What really happened in Kerala: the story of the disruptive game played by right-wing communists. Calcutta, 1966. pp. 71.

- Population

> NAMBOODIRI (N. KRISHNAN) The changing population of Kerala. [Delhi, 1968.] pp. 123. (India. Census, 1961. Monograph Series. No.7.)

- Rural conditions

> KLAUSEN (ARNE MARTIN) Kerala fishermen and the Indo-Norwegian pilot project. Oslo, Universitetsforlaget, [1968]. pp. 201. bibliog. 22½cm. (International Peace Research Institute. Prio Monographs. No. 1)

KERICHO

- Economic conditions

> KENYA. Committee to Carry Out an Economic Survey of South Nyanza and Kericho District with a View to Advising whether the Economic Potential would justify Rail Development. 1957. Report: [C.J. Martin, chairman]. Nairobi, 1957. pp. (150).

KERMANSHAH

- Economic conditions

CLARKE (JOHN INNES) and CLARK (BRIAN D.) Kermanshah: an Iranian provincial city. Durham, University of Durham, Centre for Middle Eastern and Islamic Studies, 1969. pp. (6), 137. 24cm. (Publications. No. 1)

- Growth

CLARKE (JOHN INNES) and CLARK (BRIAN D.) Kermanshah: an Iranian provincial city. Durham, University of Durham, Centre for Middle Eastern and Islamic Studies, 1969. pp. (6), 137. 24cm. (Publications. No. 1)

KERN (JONANN KONRAD)

SCHOOP (ALBERT) Johann Konrad Kern: Jurist, Politiker, Staatsmann. Frauenfeld, Huber, [1968 in progress]. bibliog. 23cm.

KERŠOVANI (OTOKAR)

KERŠOVANI OTOKAR ed. Izbor članaka; izbor, napomene, predgovor i pogovor Nusret Seferović. Beograd, 1960. pp. 459.

KERSTEN (FELIX)

KERSTEN (FELIX) The Kersten memoirs, 1940-1945;...translated from the German by Constantine Fitzgibbon and James Oliver. London, 1956. pp. 314.

KESSLER (HARRY) Graf.

KESSLER (HARRY) Graf. Tagebücher 1918-1937. Frankfurt am Main, [1961]. pp. 799.

KESSLER (HARRY) Graf. The diaries of a cosmopolitan: Count Harry Kessler, 1918-1937; translated and edited by Charles Kessler. London, 1971. pp. 535.

KETELS (ROBERT H.)

KETELS (ROBERT H.) Révision...des idées!: et souvenirs 1914-1951. [Brussels, the author, 1953]. pp. 221. bibliog. (Le Racisme Paneuropéen)

KETSKHOVELI (VLADIMIR ZAKHAR'EVICH)

LADO Ketskhoveli: sbornik dokumentov i materialov. Tbilisi, 1969. pp. 253.

KETU

- History

PARRINDER (EDWARD GEOFFREY SIMONS) The story of Ketu: an ancient Yoruba kingdom;... second edition, edited by I.A. Akinjogbin. Ibadan, University Press, 1967. pp. viii,106. bibliog. 21½cm.

KEYNES (JOHN MAYNARD) 1st Baron Keynes

The CRISIS: Marx versus Keynes; a criticism of the theories of Lord Keynes and of the policies arising therefrom. n.p., [194-?]. fo. 21.

WINKLER (ERNST) John Maynard Keynes und Silvio Gesell; ein Vortrag gehalten am 10.Februar 1951 im Internationalen Presseklub Heidelberg, nach dem Stenogramm übertragen. Heidelberg-Ziegelhausen, Vita-Verlag, [1951]. pp. 30. 29½cm. (Gesellschaft für Wirtschaftswissenschaftliche und Soziologische Forschung. Berichte. 2)

GEIGER (RUDOLF) Economist. Die Entwicklungstendenzen des Kapitalismus bei Keynes, Schumpeter und Burnham. Zürich, Polygraphischer Verlag, 1959. pp. ix, 102. bibliog. 22½cm.

DEMARIA (GIOVANNI) I fondamenti logici dei modelli keynesiani per la sistematica dell'interesse. Milano, Giuffrè 1961. pp. 851-858. 24cm. (Estratto da Studi in memoria del Prof. Gino Zappa. vol.2).

GHAUSSY (ABDUL GHANIE) Verbrauchen und Sparen: Versuch einer kritischen Überprüfung der Keynes'schen Konsumfunktion an Hand der langfristigen Sparentwicklung in den USA. Berlin, Duncker und Humblot, [1964]. pp. 236. bibliog. 23cm. (Hamburg. Hansische Universität. Institut für das Spar-, Giro- und Kreditwesen. Untersuchungen über das Spar-, Giro- und Kreditwesen. Band 16)

KEMPSKI (JUERGEN VON) Recht und Politik: Studien zur Einheit der Sozialwissenschaft. Stuttgart, Kohlhammer, [1965]. pp. 231. 23cm.

DASGUPTA (A. K.) Marx and Keynes. in Singh (Baljit) and Singh (Vidya Bhusan) eds. Social and economic change. Bombay, 1967.

STEWART (MICHAEL JAMES) Keynes and after. Harmondsworth, Penguin Books, 1967. pp. 271. bibliog. 18cm. (Pelican Books. A 908)

LEIJONHUFVUD (AXEL) On Keynesian economics and the economics of Keynes: a study in monetary theory. New York, O.U.P., 1968. pp. xiv, 431. 22½cm.

PHILBROOK (C. E.) The conservative face of Keynes. in Beadles (Nicholas Aston) and Drewry (L. Aubrey) eds. Money, the market, and the state. Athens, Ga, [1968].

STÁDNÍK (MILOŠ) Theses for Harvard. Praha, 1968. pp. 171.

WRIGHT (D. M.) Is there a Keynesian system? in Beadles (Nicholas Aston) and Drewry (L. Aubrey) eds. Money, the market, and the state. Athens, [1968].

LAMBERT (PAUL) The evolution of Keynes's thought from the Treatise on money to the General theory. Liège, International Centre of Research and Information on Public and Co-operative Economy, 1969. pp. 21. 23½cm. (Annals of Public and Co-operative Economy)

LEIJONHUFVUD (AXEL) Keynes and the classics: two lectures on Keynes' contribution to economic theory. London, 1969. pp. 46. bibliog. (Institute of Economic Affairs. Occasional Papers. 30)

MATTICK (PAUL) Marx and Keynes: the limits of the mixed economy. Boston, Mass., [1969]. pp. 364. bibliog.

TURNER (CARL B.) An analysis of Soviet views on John Maynard Keynes. Durham, N.C., 1969. pp. 183. bibliog.

JOHNSON (HARRY GORDON) The Keynesian revolution and the monetarist counter-revolution. n.p., [1970]. fo. 17. bibliog. (American Economic Association. Richard T. Ely Lectures. 1970)

MARSHALL (NATALIE) ed. Keynes: updated or outdated?: [readings]. Lexington, Mass., [1970]. pp. 142. bibliog.

KEYNES (JOHN MAYNARD) 1st Baron Keynes. The collected writings of John Maynard Keynes; (edited by Elizabeth Johnson). London, 1971 in progress.

KEYNESIAN ECONOMICS
See ECONOMICS - 1876-

KGATLAS

ROBERTS (SIMON) A restatement of the Kgatla law of domestic relations. Gaborone, Government Printer, [1970]. pp. 30.

ROBERTS (SIMON) A restatement of the Kgatla law of succession to property. Gaborone, Government Printer, [1970]. pp. 23.

ROBERTS (SIMON) A restatement of the Kgatla law relating to land and natural resources. Gaborone, Government Printer, [1970]. pp. 33.

KHABAROVSK (KRAI)

- Economic policy

GOGOLEV (N. A.) Avangardnaia rol' Khabarovskoi kraevoi partiinoi organizatsii v okazanii trudiashchimisia kraia pomoshchi frontu v period Velikoi Otechestvennoi voiny. in Iz istorii sovetskogo Dal'nego Vostoka: materialy mezhvuzovskoi nauchnoi konferentsii, posviashchennoi 40-letiiu osvobozhdeniia Dal'nego Vostoka ot interventov i belogvardeitsev, sentiabr' 1962. Khabarovsk, 1963.

- Intellectual life

BENSMAN (ESFIR' GRIGOR'EVNA) Kul'turnoe stroitel'stvo v Khabarovskom krae. Khabarovsk, 1965. pp. 111.

- Politics and government

SHTEIN (M. G.) Iz istorii partiinoi organizatsii Khabarovskogo zavoda "Dal'dizel'". in Iz istorii sovetskogo Dal'nego Vostoka: materialy mezhvuzovskoi nauchnoi konferentsii, posviashchennoi 40-letiiu osvobozhdeniia Dal'nego Vostoka ot interventov i belogvardeitsev, sentiabr' 1962. Khabarovsk, 1963.

KHAITUN (DAVID EFIMOVICH)

TADZHIKSKII GOSUDARSTVENNYI UNIVERSITET. Trudy. Seriia Istoricheskaia. vyp.2. Voprosy istorii SSSR. Dushanbe, 1966. pp. 331.

KHAKASIA

- Economic history

VOPROSY sotsial'no-ekonomicheskogo razvitiia Khakasii: istoriia, ekonomika, kul'tura, nauka. Abakan, 1968. pp. 179.

KHAN (MOHAMMAD AYUB)

SAHNI (NARESH CHANDER) Political struggle in Pakistan. Jullundur City, 1969. pp. 239.

ZIRING (LAWRENCE) The Ayub Khan era: politics in Pakistan, 1958-1969. Syracuse, N.Y., [1971]. pp. 234. bibliog.

KHAN (MUHAMMAD REZA)

KHAN (ABDUL MAJED) The transition in Bengal, 1756-1775: a study of Saiyid Muhammad Reza Khan. Cambridge, 1969. pp. 376. bibliog. (Cambridge. University. Centre of South Asian Studies. Cambridge South Asian Studies. No. 7)

KHAN (Sir SYED AHMAD)

MUHAMMAD (SHAN) Sir Syed Ahmad Khan: a political biography; ...with a foreword by Dr. Tara Chand. Begum Bridge, [1969]. pp. 272. bibliog.

KHARKOV (OBLAST')

- History - Revolution - 1917-1921

KULICHENKO (MIKHAIL IVANOVICH) Большевики Харьковщины в борьбе за власть Советов, 1918-1920 гг. Харьков, Университет, 1966. pp. 248. 20см.

KHARTOUM

SUDAN. 1963. Khartoum: capital of the Republic of the Sudan; (booklet issued on the occasion of African Finance Ministers Conference on the Establishment of the African Development Bank, July/August 1963). [Khartoum, 1963]. pp. (60).

KHAS TRIBE

NAKANE (CHIE) Garo and Khasi: a comparative study in matrilineal systems. Paris, Mouton, [1967]. pp. 187. bibliog. 24cm. (Paris. École Pratique des Hautes Études. Section des Sciences Économiques et Sociales. Cahiers de l'Homme. Nouvelle Série. 2)

KHERSON (OBLAST')

- Statistics

KHERSON (OBLAST'). Statisticheskoe Upravlenie. Народное хозяйство Херсонской области: статистический сборник. Одесса, 1969. pp. 201.

KHETAGUROV (KONSTANTIN LEVANOVICH)

ABAEV (VLADIMIR DAVIDOVICH) Коста Хетагуров и его время. Тбилиси, 1961. pp. 200.

KHIVA KHANATE

KAMALOV (SABIR KAMALOVICH) Каракалпаки в XVIII-XIX веках: к истории взаимоотношений с Россией и среднеазиатскими ханствами. Ташкент, Фан, 1968. pp. 327. bibliog. 21½см.

- Commerce - Russia

SADYKOV (ATABAI SADYKOVICH) Экономические связи Хивы с Россией во второй половине XIX - начале XX вв. Ташкент, Наука, 1965. pp. 183. 21½см. (Tashkent. Universitet. Nauchnye Trudy. вып.296 [being also] Istoricheskie Nauki. кн.57)

- Foreign relations - Russia

TUKHTAMETOV (TUKHTAMET GAFUROVICH) Rossiia i Khiva v kontse XIX - nachale XX v.; pobeda Khorezmskoi narodnoi revoliutsii. Moskva, 1969. pp. 141.

- History

ALEKSEENKOV (P.) Хивинское восстание 1916 года. Ташкент, 1980. pp. 56. Xerographic copy. Lacks pp.50,51.

BECKER (SEYMOUR) Russia's protectorates in Central Asia: Bukhara and Khiva, 1865-1924. Cambridge, Harvard U.P., 1968. pp. xiv, 416. bibliog. 23½cm. (Harvard University. Russian Research Center. Studies. 54)

POGOREL'SKII (IVAN VASIL'EVICH) Очерки экономической и политической истории Хивинского ханства конца XIX и начала XX вв., 1873-1917 гг. Ленинград, Университет, 1968. pp. 148. 21см.

KHMER LANGUAGE

UNITED STATES. State Department. Cambodian: basic course. Washington, 1966 in progress.

KHOKHLOV (NIKOLAI EVGEN'EVICH)

KHOKHLOV (NIKOLAI EVGEN'EVICH) Pravo na sovest'. Frankfurt, Posev, 1957. pp. 614. Cover has false author and title: Iu. Dol'd-Mikhailik.

KHOREZM' (OBLAST')

- Economic conditions

MATERIALY... Материалы по производительным силам Узбекистана. вып.10. Природные условия и ресурсы низовьев Аму-Дарьи Кара-Калпакская АССР и Хорезмская область УзССР. Ташкент, АН УзССР, 1959. pp. 353. 25½см.

KHOREZM PEOPLE'S SOVIET REPUBLIC

TUKHTAMETOV (TUKHTAMET GAFUROVICH) Rossiia i Khiva v kontse XIX - nachale XX v.; pobeda Khorezmskoi narodnoi revoliutsii. Moskva, 1969. pp. 141.

KHRUSHCHEV (NIKITA SERGEEVICH)

PREBYVANIE... Пребывание Н. С. Хрущева в Германской Демократической Республике, 4-12 марта 1959 г. Москва, Госполитиздат, 1959. pp. 158. 20см.

DEUERLEIN (ERNST) Deutschland wie Chruschtschow es will: Zielbestimmung der sowjetischen Deutschlandpolitik 1955-1961: eine kommentierte Dokumentation. Bonn, 1961. pp. 216. bibliog.

EVANS (ARTHUR H.) On Khruschov and others. London, David-Goliath Publication, [1963?] pp. (iii), 34. 21½cm.

The KHRUSHCHEV-Tito revisionist group concoct new plans against the cause of socialism. Tirana, 1963. pp. 37. (Reprinted from Zëri i Popullit, January 8, 1963)

KERUSCHEV again in the role of a demagogue, a slanderer and sower of dissension. Tirana, "Naim Frashëri" State Publishing Enterprise, 1964. pp. 53. 18cm. (Reprinted from Zëri i Popullit, April 18, 1963)

KHRUSCHEV and Tito hatch new plots. Tirana, "Naim Frashëri" State Publishing Enterprise, 1964. pp. 13. 14½cm. (Reprinted from Zëri i Popullit, August 22, 1963)

KHRUSCHEV rehabilitates the agents of imperialism and supports the murderers of communists. Tirana, "Naim Frashëri" State Publishing Enterprise, 1964. pp. 23. 14½cm. (Reprinted from Zëri i Popullit, August 27, 1963)

VERNYI leninets, bezzavetnyi borets za mir i kommunizm: serdechnye pozdravleniia i dobrye pozhelaniia v sviazi s 70-letiem so dnia rozhdeniia N. S. Khrushcheva. Moskva, 1964. pp. 148.

WHY Khrushchov fell. Peking, 1964. pp. 12. (Reprinted from Hongqi, nos. 21-22, 1964)

EXPOSE to the end the double-faced stand of the Khruschevite revisionists towards the struggle of the Vietnamese people. Tirana, 1965. pp. 22.

WHAT lies behind the divisive meeting of March 1 which the Khrushchevite revisionists are getting up. Tirana, 1965. pp. 20.

ZERI I POPULLIT. Alliance and complete harmony between Titoite clique and Soviet Khrushchevite revisionist leaders. Tirana, 1965. pp. 35.

HYLAND (WILLIAM) and SHRYOCK (RICHARD WALLACE) The fall of Khrushchev. New York, Funk & Wagnalls, [1968]. pp. xi, 209. 20cm.

TATU (MICHEL) Power in the Kremlin: from Krushchev's decline to collective leadership;...translated by Helen Katel. London, Collins, 1969 [or rather 1968]. pp. 570. 22½cm.

BARKER (Sir WILLIAM) N.S. Khrushchev: an assessment. Liverpool, 1970. pp. 32. bibliog. (Liverpool. University. Inaugural Lecture Series)

KHRUSHCHEV remembers; with an introduction, commentary and notes by Edward Crankshaw; translated and edited by Strobe Talbott; [attributed to N.S. Khrushchev]. London, 1971. pp. 639.

KHRYPFFS (NICOLAUS) de Cusa, Cardinal

BATTAGLIA (FELICE) Metafisica, religione e politica nel pensiero di Nicolo' da Cusa. Bologna, Pàtron, [1965]. pp 93. 25cm. (Scienze Filosofiche)

KHUDIAKOV (IVAN ALEKSANDROVICH)

BAZANOV (V.G.) I.A. Khudiakov i ego "Kratkoe opisanie Verkhoianskogo okruga." in Khudiakov (Ivan Aleksandrovich) Kratkoe opisanie Verkhoianskogo okruga. Leningrad, 1969.

KIDNAPPING

- United Kingdom

DEELEY (PETER) and WALKER (CHRISTOPHER) Murder in the Fourth Estate: an investigation into the roles of press and police in the McKay case. London, 1971. pp. 192.

KIEL CANAL
See KAISER WILHELM (KIEL) CANAL

KIEL UNIVERSITY

- Institut für Weltwirtschaft

KIEL. Universität. Institut für Weltwirtschaft. Das Institut für Weltwirtschaft und Seeverkehr: wirtschaftswissenschaftliche Forschungs- und Lehranstalt an der Universität Kiel: ein Wegweiser für Studierende. Kiel, 1922. pp. 24.

KIELCE (PROVINCE)

KIELECKIE: rozwój województwa w Polsce Ludowej. Warszawa, 1970. pp. 282. bibliog.

- Politics and government

Z dziejów ruchu ludowego na Kielecczyźnie: materiały z sesji popularnonaukowej zorganizowanej w Kielcach dnia 21-22 stycznia 1967 roku na 70-lecie powstania ruchu ludowego w Polsce; pod redakcja Stanisława Lato. Kraków, 1970. pp. 365.

- Social history

JARECKA-KIMLOWSKA (STANISŁAWA) Kielecki Związek Młodzieży Wiejskiej Wici, 1928-1939: z problemów ruchu młodzieżowego w okresie międzywojennym. Warszawa, Ludowa Spółdzielnia Wydawnicza, 1968. pp. 197. bibliog.

KIELMANSEGG (JOHANN ADOLF) Graf.

CONSILIO non imperio; on the occasion of the sixtieth birthday of General Johann Adolf, Graf von Kielmansegg. Cologne, Markus, 1966. pp. 62. 22½cm.

KIERKEGAARD (SØREN AABYE)

GARELICK (HERBERT M.) The anti-Christianity of Kierkegaard: a study of Concluding unscientific postscript. The Hague, 1965 repr. 1969. pp. 73.

HAGEN (EDUARD VON) Abstraktion und Konkretion bei Hegel und Kierkegaard. Bonn, 1969. pp. 108. bibliog.

KIESINGER (KURT GEORG)

NORDEN (ALBERT) Hitler's chief agitator, chancellor candidate in Bonn: report...at the international press conference on 22 November 1966 in Berlin. [Dresden, 1966]. 1 pamphlet (unpaged).

HOFF (KLAUS) Kurt Georg Kiesinger: die Geschichte seines Lebens. Frankfurt/M., [1969]. pp. 157.

KLARSFELD (BEATE) Die Geschichte des PG 2 633 930 Kiesinger: Dokumentation; mit einem Vorwort von Heinrich Böll. Darmstadt, [1969]. pp. 160.

KIEV

- Statistics

KIEV. Statystychne Upravlinnia. Київ в цифрах: статистичний збірник. Київ, Статистика, 1966. pp. 162. 14см.

KIEV (OBLAST')

STAROVOITENKO (IVAN PAVLOVYCH) Київська область: географічний нарис. 2nd ed., Київ, Радянська Школа, 1967. pp. 139. bibliog. 19½см. (Області Української РСР)

-Description and travel

STAROVOITENKO (IVAN PAVLOVYCH) Київська область: географічний нарис. 2nd ed. Київ, Радянська Школа, 1967. pp. 141. bibliog. 19½см. (Області Української РСР)

- Statistics

KIEV (OBLAST'). Statystychne Upravlinnia. Narodne hospodarstvo Kyïvs'koï oblasti: statystychnyi zbirnyk. Kyïv, 1967. pp. 238.

KIKI (ALBERT MAORI)

KIKI (ALBERT MAORI) Kiki: ten thousand years in a lifetime; a New Guinea autobiography. London, Pall Mall P., [1968]. pp. (v), 190. 21½cm.

KIKUYUS

INTERNATIONAL AFRICAN INSTITUTE. Ethnographic Survey of Africa. East Central Africa. Part 5. The central tribes of the north-eastern Bantu: the Kikuyu...and the Kamba of Kenya; by John Middleton and Greet Kershaw. rev. ed. London, the Institute, 1965. pp. 103. bibliog. 24½cm.

KENYATTA (JOMO) My people of Kikuyu and the life of chief Wangombe. Nairobi, 1966. pp. 59.

KILOMBERO VALLEY

JAETZOLD (RALPH) The Kilombero Valley, Tanzania: characteristic features of the economic geography of a semihumid East African flood plain and its margins;...with a review of development plans and possibilities in the Kilombero Valley, by E. Baum. München, Weltforum Verlag, [1968]. pp. 147. bibliog. (Ifo-Institut für Wirtschaftsforschung. Afrika-Studien. 28)

KIM (IL- SUNG)

CHOSON NODONGDANG. Central Committee. Party History Institute. Brief history of the revolutionary activities of comrade Kim Il Sung. Pyongyang, 1969. pp. 294.

KIMMOCHI (SAIONJI) Prince.
See SAIONJI (KIMMOCHI) Prince

KINDERGARTEN

The PLACE and value of the free kindergarten or nursery school in our national scheme of education. [London, 1910?] pp. 8.

BELGIUM. Ministère des Affaires Etrangères et du Commerce Extérieur. 1967. Infant school education. Brussels, 1967. pp. 44. bibliog. (Memo from Belgium. No. 90-91)

KINDERGARTENS

- United Kingdom

MICHAELIS FREE KINDERGARTEN. Michaelis Free Kindergarten, 11 St. Ann's Villas, Darnley Road, Notting Hill. [London, 190-?] pp. 7.

KING (CECIL HARMSWORTH)

KING (CECIL HARMSWORTH) Strictly personal: some memoirs. London, Weidenfeld & Nicolson, 1969. pp. viii, 232. 21½cm.

KING (CORETTA SCOTT)

KING (CORETTA SCOTT) My life with Martin Luther King, Jr. London, 1970. pp. 384.

KING (MARTIN LUTHER)

BENNETT (LERONE) What manner of man: a biography of Martin Luther King, Jr. 3rd ed. Chicago, Johnson, 1968. pp. (x), 251. 23½cm.

DUVALIER (FRANÇOIS) A tribute to the martyred leader of non-violence, Reverend Dr. Martin Luther King, Jr. Port-au-Prince, Presses Nationales, [1968]. pp. 167. 21½cm.

MURDER in Memphis: Martin Luther King and the future of the black liberation struggle; by Paul Boutelle [and others]. New York, 1968 repr. 1969. pp. 15.

HUIE (WILLIAM BRADFORD) He slew the dreamer: my search, with James Earl Ray for the truth about the murder of Martin Luther King. London, 1970. pp. 222.

KING (CORETTA SCOTT) My life with Martin Luther King, Jr. London, 1970. pp. 384.

LEWIS (DAVID L.) Martin Luther King: a critical biography. London, 1970. pp. 459. bibliog.

WALTON (HANES) The political philosophy of Martin Luther King, Jr. Westport, Conn., [1971]. pp. 137. bibliog.

WILLIAMS (JOHN ALFRED) The King God didn't save: reflections on the life and death of Martin Luther King, Jr. London, 1971. pp. 222.

KING (RUFUS)

ERNST (ROBERT) Rufus King: American federalist Chapel Hill, U. of North Carolina P., [1968]. pp. xiii, 446. 22½cm.

KING (WILLIAM)

GREENWOOD (DAVID) William King: Tory and Jacobite. Oxford, 1969. pp. 386. bibliog.

KING ISLAND

- Economic policy

TASMANIA. 1965. King Island development: report of select committee of the Legislative Council, with minutes of proceedings: [Tom D'Alton, chairman] in Tasmania. Parliament. Journals and printed papers. 1965. Part 1. No.10.

KINGS AND RULERS

MACCHIAVELLI (NICCOLÒ) Princeps; ex Silvestri Telii...traductione...emendatus; adjecta sunt ejusdem argumenti aliorum...contra Machiavellum scripta, de potestate et officio principum contra tyrannos; quibus...accessit Antonii Possevini Iudicium de Nicolai Machiavelli et Ioannis Bodini scriptis. Lugduni Batavorum, ex officina H. de Vogel, 1643. pp. 456.

SWADLIN (THOMAS) The soveraignes desire peace, the subjects dutie obedience. London, 1643. pp. 39. 18½cm. Wing S 6227.

A VINDICATION of kings and nobles against that ungodly paper called, The alarum to the head quarters; by T.H. London, R.L., 1647. pp. (6). 18½cm. Wing H 146.

A DECLARATION to all His Majesties loving subjects within the kingdome of England and dominion of Wales concerning a King and his representative councell, touching the government of his people, according to the known laws of the realme;...[signed G.N.]. London, 1648. pp. 6. 18½cm. Wing N 17.

GREAT Britans vote; or, God save King Charles; etc. London, G.M. and W.H., 1648. pp. 49. 18½cm. Wing G 1670.

STURMY (DANIEL) A sermon preach'd, etc., October the 31st, 1708, on the death of His Royal Highness the prince. London, Midwinter, 1708. pp. 14. 19cm.

QUEVEDO VILLEGAS (FRANCISCO DE) Política de Dios, govierno de Christo; edicion de James O. Crosby. Urbana, University of Illinois P., 1966. pp. 604. bibliog. 23½cm.

ULLMANN (WALTER) The Carolingian renaissance and the idea of kingship. London, Methuen, 1969. pp. xiv, 201. 21½cm. (Cambridge. University. Trinity College. Birkbeck Lectures in Ecclesiastical History. 1968-9)

KINGS AND RULERS (IN RELIGION, FOLK-LORE, ETC.)

DENNETT (RICHARD EDWARD) At the back of the black man's mind: or, Notes on the kingly office in West Africa; [facsimile reprint of the edition first published in 1906]. London, Cass, 1968. pp. xvi, 288. 21½cm. (Cass Library of African Studies. General Studies. No. 70)

WOOD (DOROTHY) Leo VI's concept of divine monarchy: illustrated in a cave chapel. London, [1964]. pp. 64. bibliog. (Monarchist Press Association. Historical Series. No. 1)

CHANEY (WILLIAM A.) The cult of kingship in Anglo-Saxon England: the transition from paganism to Christianity. Manchester, [1970]. pp. 276.

KINGS COLLEGE, BUDO

McGREGOR (G.P.) King's College, Budo: the first sixty years. Nairobi, O.U.P., 1967. pp. x, 168. bibliog. 21cm.

KING'S LYNN

- Commerce

ARMES (WILLIAM) The port of King's Lynn: its position and prospects. King's Lynn, [1853]. pp. 56.

- Harbour

ARMES (WILLIAM) The port of King's Lynn: its position and prospects. King's Lynn, [1853]. pp. 56.

- Politics and government

REPORT of an enquiry into the affairs of the Corporation of King's Lynn ... held before the Commissioners appointed for that purpose, in the Guildhall ... 1833; taken by John Thew. Stamford, Thew, 1833. pp. 55. 23½cm.

THEW (JOHN) ed. A correct copy of the poll as taken at the election for burgesses to serve in parliament for .... King's Lynn ..... Jan. 1835; to which is prefixed a detail of the proceedings, speeches, and events connected with the election. Lynn, Garland, 1835. pp. 87, (19). 21cm.

KINGSTON, CANADA

- Social history

PRESTON (RICHARD ARTHUR) R.M.C. and Kingston: the effect of imperial and military influences on a Canadian community. [Durham, N.C., 1968]. pp. irreg. (Duke University. Commonwealth Studies Center. Reprint Series. No. 27) (Reprinted from Ontario History, vol. 60, No. 3)

KINGSTOWN, EIRE
See DUN LAOGHAIRE

KINLOCH (GEORGE)

TENNANT (CHARLES GAIRDNER DALRYMPLE) The radical laird: a biography of George Kinloch, 1775-1833. Kineton, Warwicks., 1970. pp. 255. bibliog.

KINSHASA

- Politics and government

LA FONTAINE (JEAN SYBIL) City politics: a study of Léopoldville, 1962-63. Cambridge, 1970. pp. 246. bibliog. (Cambridge. University. African Studies Centre. African Studies Series. 1)

KINSHIP

MORGAN (LEWIS HENRY) Systems of consanguinity and affinity of the human family. [Washington, 1871]. pp. xii, (604). 33cm. (United States. Smithsonian Institution. Smithsonian Contributions to Knowledge. vol. 17)

ENCYCLOPAEDIA BRITANNICA. Kinship; [by B. Malinowski]. [1929]. pp. 403-409. bibliog. 27½cm. Xerox copy of the article.

CUNNISON (IAN GEORGE) Kinship and local organisation on the Luapula: a preliminary account of some aspects of Luapula social organization. Livingstone, Rhodes-Livingstone Institute, 1950, repr. 1965. fo. (iii), 32. 32½cm. (Communications. No. 5)

CANADA. National Museum of Canada. Bulletins. No. 196. Igluligmiut kinship and local groupings: a structural approach; by David Damas. Ottawa, 1963. pp. 216. bibliog. With French summary.

SCHMITZ (CARL A.) Grundformen der Verwandtschaft. Basel, Schwabe, 1964. pp. 134. bibliog. 24cm. (Geographisch-Ethnologische Gesellschaft and Basel. Museum für Völkerkunde und Schweizerisches Museum für Volkskunde. Basler Beiträge zur Geographie und Ethnologie. Ethnologische Reihe. Band 1)

BANERJEE (BHAVANI) Marriage and kinship of the Gangadikara Vokkaligas of Mysore. Poona, Deccan College, 1966. pp. xxiv, 212. bibliog. 24½cm. (Deccan College Dissertation Series. 27)

FOX (J.R.) Kinship and land tenure on Tory island. [Belfast], 1967. pp. 17. (Reprinted from Ulster Folklife, vol. 12, 1966)

BAKER (HUGH D.R.) A Chinese lineage village: Sheung Shui. London, Cass, 1968. pp. xiv, 237. 21½cm.

BOHANNAN (PAUL) and MIDDLETON (JOHN) eds. Kinship and social organization. Garden City, Natural History P., 1968. pp. xiii, 391. bibliog. (American Museum of Natural History. American Museum Sourcebooks in Anthropology)

FARBER (BERNARD) Comparative kinship systems: a method of analysis. New York, Wiley, [1968]. pp. ix, 147. 21cm.

HUBERT (JANE) and others. Methods of study of middle-class kinship in London: a working-paper on the history of an anthropological project, 1960-65. London, University, London School of Economics and Political Science, Department of Anthropology, 1968. pp. iv, 149. 30cm. (Occasional Papers)

KINSHIP (Cont'd.)

RIVERS (WILLIAM HALSE RIVERS) Kinship and social organization;...together with, The genealogical method of anthropological enquiry; [works first published in 1914 and 1910 respectively] with commentaries by Raymond Firth and David M. Schneider. London, Athlone P., 1968. pp. vi, 116. 21½cm. (Monographs on Social Anthropology. No. 34)

SCHNEIDER (DAVID MURRAY) American kinship: a cultural account. Englewood Cliffs, Prentice-Hall, [1968]. pp. x, 117. (Anthropology of Modern Societies Series)

CONFERENCE ON BAND ORGANIZATION, OTTAWA, 1965. Contributions to anthropology: band societies: proceedings of the Conference...; edited by David Damas. Ottawa, 1969. pp. 295. bibliogs. (Canada. National Museum of Canada. Bulletins. No.228. Anthropological Series. No.84) Chart in end pocket.

FIRTH (RAYMOND WILLIAM) and others. Families and their relatives: kinship in a middle-class sector of London; an anthropological study by Raymond Firth [and others] with the team of the 'London Kinship Project'. London, [1970]. pp. 476.

GOODY (JOHN RANKINE) Comparative studies in kinship. London, 1969. pp. 261. bibliogs.

LÉVI-STRAUSS (CLAUDE) The elementary structures of kinship: Les structures élémentaires de la parenté; revised edition translated from the French by James Harle Bell [and others]. London, Eyre & Spottiswoode, 1969. pp. xix, 541. bibliog. 23cm.

NUKUNYA (GODWIN KWAKU) Kinship and marriage among the Anlo Ewe. London, 1969. pp. 217. bibliog. (London. University. London School of Economics and Political Science. Monographs on Social Anthropology. No. 37)

RIGBY (PETER) Cattle and kinship among the Gogo: a semi-pastoral society of central Tanzania. Ithaca, N.Y., 1969. pp. 355. bibliog.

TYLER (STEPHEN A.) ed. Cognitive anthropology: readings, etc. New York, 1969. pp. 521.

FORTES (MEYER) Kinship and the social order: the legacy of Lewis Henry Morgan. London, 1970. pp. 347. bibliog. (Rochester, N.Y. University. Lewis Henry Morgan Lectures. 1963)

HARRIS (CHRISTOPHER) ed. Readings in kinship in urban society. Oxford, 1970. pp. 397. bibliogs.

FARBER (BERNARD) Kinship and class: a midwestern study. New York, [1971]. pp. 210. bibliog.

FOX (RICHARD G.) Kin, clan, Raja, and rule: state-hinterland relations in preindustrial India. Berkeley, 1971. pp. 187. bibliog.

GULLIVER (PHILIP HUGH) Neighbours and networks: the idiom of kinship in social action among the Ndendeuli of Tanzania. Berkeley, 1971. pp. 366. bibliog.

KINSHIP and culture: [mainly papers presented at a symposium at Burg Wartenstein, 1966, under the sponsorship of the Wenner-Gren Foundation for Anthropological Research]; edited by Francis L.K. Hsu. Chicago, 1971. pp. 510. bibliog.

RETHINKING kinship and marriage: [derived mainly] from material presented at a conference on kinship and marriage, sponsored by the Association of Social Anthropologists of the Commonwealth, held at the University of Bristol...1970); edited by Rodney Needham. London, 1971. pp. cxvii, 276. bibliogs.

SELGIN (FRANCES CLARE) Respect relationships in the little tradition of Java; [M.Phil. (London) thesis]. 1971. fo. 230. bibliog. Typescript: unpublished. This thesis is the property of London University and may not be removed from the Library.

KIRCHHEIM

- History

NEUER (DIETER) 1200 Jahre Kirchheim, 767-1967. Heidelberg, [1966?]. pp. 32. bibliog.

KIRGHIZIA

- Constitutional history

NURBEKOV (KUBANYCHBEK) Vozniknovenie Kirgizskoi Sovetskoi natsional'noi gosudarstvennosti. Frunze, 1964. pp. 151.

NURBEKOV (KURBANYCHBEK) Istoriia gosudarstva i prava Kirgizskoi SSR. vyp.1. Frunze, 1965. pp. 153.

- Economic conditions

RAZVITIE proizvoditel'nykh sil Kirgizskoi SSR v perspektive. Frunze, 1966. pp. 75.

ISLAMOV (SAGID UMEROVICH) Effektivnost' obshchestvennogo proizvodstva i ekonomicheskoe razvitie. Frunze, 1969. pp. 253.

- Economic history

AITTBAEV (MUKASH TOKTOKHODZHEVICH) Sotsial'no-ekonomicheskie otnosheniia v kirgizskom aile v XIX i nachale XX vekov. Frunze, 1962. pp. 195.

TOPTYGINA (NADEZHDA ILLARIONOVNA) Leninskii printsip vzaimopomoshchi osnova razvitiia sovetskikh narodov. Frunze, 1962. pp. 36.

MATERIALY po istorii i ekonomike Kirgizii. Frunze 1963. pp. 149.

SHERSTOBITOV (VIKTOR PAVLOVICH) Новая экономическая политика в Киргизии, 1921-1925; под редакцией... К. К. Орозалиева. Фрунзе, 1964. pp. 610. bibliog.

BAIBULATOV (BEGALY BAIBULATOVICH) Bor'ba partorganizatsii Kirgizii za provedenie osedaniia kochevogo naseleniia. Frunze, 1965. pp. 224. bibliog.

DZHUNUSHEV (KERIM) Развитие товарно-денежных отношений в дореволюционной Киргизии. Фрунзе, 1965. pp. 143.

TABYSHALIEV (SALMORBEK TABYSHALIEVICH) Kirgiziia v period zaversheniia stroitel'stva sotsializma. Frunze, 1965. pp. 227.

INTER-REGIONAL STUDY TOUR AND SEMINAR ON THE SEDENTARISATION OF NOMADIC POPULATIONS IN THE SOVIET SOCIALIST REPUBLICS OF KAZAKHSTAN AND KIRGHIZIA, 1966. Report on the Inter-Regional Study Tour...5 to 30 September 1966. (ILO/TAP/INT/R.13) Geneva, International Labour Office, 1967. pp. 96. (Development Programme: Technical Assistance Sector. [International]. R.13)

SAPELKIN (ALEKSEI ALEKSANDROVICH) К истории феодализма в Киргизии в конце XIX - начале XX вв.: административное устройство и налоговая система. Фрунзе, 1968. pp. 125. bibliog.

DZHAMANKULOVA (GULBUBU D.) Sotsial'no-ekonomicheskie preobrazovaniia i puti dal'neishego razvitiia Kirgizii. Frunze, 1969. pp. 431.

KARAKEEV (KURMAN-GALI KARAKEEVICH) and ALYSHBAEV (DZHUMAGUL ALYSHBAEVICH) V. I. Lenin i sotsialisticheskoe stroitel'stvo v Kirgizstane. Frunze, 1970. pp. 133.

V.I.Lenin i razvitie sotsialisticheskoi ekonomiki Kirgizii. Frunze, 1970. pp. 197.

- Economic policy

DZHAMANKULOVA (GULBUBU D.) Sotsial'no-ekonomicheskie preobrazovaniia i puti dal'neishego razvitiia Kirgizii. Frunze, 1969. pp. 431.

- History

USENBAEV (KUSHPEK USENBAEVICH) Восстание 1916 года в Киргизии; под редакцией...А. Х. Хасанова. Фрунзе, 1967. pp. 326. bibliog.

ISTORIIA... История Кирги́зской ССР. Фрунзе, Кыргызстан, 1968. 2vols. (in 3). 21cm.

- History - Revolution, (1917-1921)

KABEL'KOVA (MARIIA TERENT'EVNA) Sovety Kirgizii v 1918 godu. Frunze, 1967. pp. 136.

UEZDNO-gorodskie partiinye organizatsii Kirgizii, 1918-1924 gg: sbornik dokumentov i materialov. Frunze, 1968. pp. 660.

- Industries

CHYIMYLOVA (BUBUKAN) and UMETOV (DZHUMALI) Развитие промышленности Киргизии в годы довоенных пятилеток, 1928 г. - июнь 1941 г.; под редакцией...Ш. Х. Шириязданова. Фрунзе, Илим, 1967. pp. 168. 21½см.

- Intellectual life

KAZAKBAEV (ABDYKAIR KAZAKBAEVICH) Kompartiia Kirgizii v bor'be za dal'neishee razvitie sotsialisticheskoi kul'tury kirgizskogo naroda, 1956-1961 gg. Frunze, 1963. pp. 247.

KARAKEEV (KURMAN-GALI K.) Iz istorii kul'turnogo stroitel'stva v Kirgizstane; pod redaktsiei...V.P. Sherstobitova. Frunze, 1968. pp. 174. bibliog.

LENIN i nauka Sovetskogo Kirgizstana. Frunze, 1970. pp. 391.

- Nationalism

DZHAMGERCHINOV (BEGAMAALY DZHAMGERCHINOVICH) Marksistsko-leninskoe reshenie natsional'nogo voprosa. Frunze, 1969. pp. 160.

- Politics and government

USENBAEV (KUSHBEK USENBAEVICH) Revoliutsionnoe dvizhenie v Kirgizii nakanune Oktiabr'skoi revoliutsii. Frunze, 1965. pp. 75. Bibliog.

DZHAMGERCHINOV (BEGAMAALY DZHAMGERCHINOVICH) Ocherk politicheskoi istorii Kirgizii XIX veka, pervaia polovina. Frunze, 1966. pp. 191.

KIRGHIZIA. Verkhovnyi Sovet. Zasedaniia: stenograficheskii otchet. Frunze, sessional, Dec.1966 (6th series, 11th session). 22cm.

ALTMYSHBAEV (ASYLBEK ALTMYSHBAEVICH) Lenin i propaganda marksizma v Kirgizii, 1905-1923 gg. Frunze, 1967. pp. 271. bibliog.

- Religion

SHIBAEVA (Iu. A.) Nekotorye religiozno-bytovye perezhitki u kirgizov Vostochnogo Pamira. in Tadzhikskii Gosudarstvennyi Universitet. Trudy. Seriia Istoricheskaia. vyp.2. Voprosy istorii SSSR. Dushanbe, 1966.

- Rural conditions

SHERSTOBITOV (VIKTOR PAVLOVICH) Ленин и крестьянство Советского Востока: на материале Киргизской ССР. Фрунзе, 1969. pp. 720.

- Social history

AITBAEV (MUKASH TOKTOKHODZHEVICH) Sotsial'no-ekonomicheskie otnosheniia v kirgizskom aile v XIX i nachale XX vekov. Frunze, 1962. pp. 195.

PLOSKIKH (VLADIMIR MIKHAILOVICH) Ocherki patriarkhal'no- feodal'nykh otnoshenii v Iuzhnoi Kirgizii, 50-70-e gody XIX v. Frunze, 1968. pp. 150. bibliog.

- Statistics

KIRGHIZIA. Tsentral'noe Statisticheskoe Upravlenie. 1966. Советский Киргистан за 40 лет, 1926-1966: статистический сборник. Фрунзе, 1966. pp. 160.

KIRGHIZIA. Tsentral'noe Statisticheskoe Upravlenie. 1967. Киргистан за 50 лет Советской власти: статистический сборник. Фрунзе, 1967. pp. 223. 21см.

KIRKBY STEPHEN

- Economic history

WILLAN (THOMAS STUART) An eighteenth-century shopkeeper: Abraham Dent of Kirkby Stephen. Manchester, [1970]. pp. 208.

KIROV (SERGEI MIRONOVICH)

TROTSKII (LEV DAVYDOVICH) La bureaucratie stalinienne et l'assassinat de Kirov; [reprint of the work originally published about 1935 by Editions Librairie du Travail]. Milan, 1967. pp. 44.

SINIAEV (V.S.) O revoliutsionnoi deiatel'nosti S.M.Kirova v Tomske. in Revoliutsionnoe dvizhenie v Sibiri i na Dal'nem Vostoke. vyp.1. Tomsk, 1960.

MOSTIEV (BORIS MUKHARBEKOVICH) Voprosy kul'tury v publitsistike S. M. Kirova; po materialam gazety "Terek", 1909-1917 gg. Ordzhonikidze, 1965. pp. 60.

KIROV (SERGEI MIRONOVICH) О народном просвещении и воспитании. Москва, 1969. pp. 198.

NASH Mironych: vospominaniia o zhizni i deiatel'nosti S.M. Kirova v Leningrade. Leningrad, 1969. pp. 464.

KIROV (OBLAST')

- Bibliography

CHERNIAKHOVSKII (GEORGII SERGEEVICH) and ZABOLOTSKII (VLADISLAV VLADIMIROVICH) Iz istorii knigoizdatel'skogo dela v Kirovskoi oblasti. Kirov, 1964. pp. 27. bibliog.

- Economic conditions

VOLGO-VIATSKII... Волго-Вятский район: экономико-географический обзор. Горький, Волго-Вятское Книжное Издательство, 1964. pp. 287. bibliog. 20cm.

- Economic history

PIAT'DESIAT... Пятьдесят советских лет: Кировская область. Киров, 1967. pp. 240.

-History - Revolution, 1917-1921

POPOVA (EMILIIA DMITRIEVNA) Krest'ianskie komitety Viatskoi gubernii v 1917 godu. Kirov, 1966. pp. 40.

- Industries

IOSIFOV (PAVEL ANDREEVICH) Lesnaia promyshlennost' Kirovskoi oblasti za 50 let. Kirov, 1968. pp. 60. bibliog.

- Maps

ATLAS Kirovskoi oblasti. Moskva, 1968. pp. 38.

- Politics and government

OCHERKI istorii Kirovskoi organizatsii KPSS. ch.2. 1918-1968. Gor'kii, 1969. pp. 532.

- Statistics

KIROV (OBLAST'). Statisticheskoe Upravlenie. Кировская область к 50-летию Октября: статистический сборник. Горький, 1967. pp. 175.

KIRUNDI LANGUAGE

UNITED STATES. State Department. Kirundi: basic course. Washington, [1965]. pp. lxi, 526.

KISANGANI

- Social conditions

PONS (VALDO GUSTAVE) Stanleyville: an African urban community under Belgian administration. London, O.U.P., 1969. pp. xxiv, 356. bibliog. 24½cm.

KISHINEV

- Politics and government

50 let kishinevskoi partiinoi organizatsii: materialy nauchno-teoreticheskoi konferentsii, etc. Kishinev, 1968. pp. 163.

KITA (IKKI)

WILSON (GEORGE M.) Radical nationalist in Japan: Kita Ikki, 1883-1937. Cambridge, Mass., 1969. pp. 230. bibliog. (Harvard University. East Asian Research Center. Harvard East Asian Studies 37)

KITCHEN UTENSILS

UNITED STATES. Tariff Commission. Earthenware table and kitchen articles. Washington, 1963. fo. ii, 55.

UNITED STATES. Tariff Commission. Household china tableware and kitchenware. Washington, 1963. fo. ii, 50.

KITEEZI

- Social conditions

KLEIN (EBERHARD C.) Sozialer Wandel in Kiteezi/Buganda, ein Dorf im Einflussbereich der Stadt Kampala. München, [1969]. pp. 160. bibliog. (Ifo-Institut für Wirtschaftsforschung. Afrika-Studien. 46)

KLÁCEL (FRANTISEK MATAUS)

SVOBODA (L.) F.M. Klácels "Briefe eines Freundes an eine Freundin über den Ursprung des Sozialismus und Kommunismus". in Steinitz (Wolfgang) and others, eds. Ost und West in der Geschichte des Denkens und der kulturellen Beziehungen: Festschrift für Eduard Winter zum 70. Geburtstag. Berlin, Akademie-Verlag, 1966. pp. 816.

KLAGES (LUDWIG)

KASDORFF (HANS) Ludwig Klages: Werk und Wirkung; Einführung und kommentierte Bibliographie. Bonn, 1969. pp. 795. bibliogs.

KLAUSNER (JOSEPH)

KLING (SIMCHA) Joseph Klausner. New York, [1970]. pp. 161. bibliog.

KLEIN (FÉLIX)

MANEGOLD (KARL HEINZ) Universität, technische Hochschule und Industrie: ein Beitrag zur Emanzipation der Technik im 19. Jahrhundert unter besonderer Berücksichtigung der Bestrebungen Felix Kleins. Berlin, [1970]. pp. 330. bibliog.

KLEIN (MANFRED)

KLEIN (MANFRED) Jugend zwischen Diktaturen, 1945-1956. Mainz, [1968]. pp. 151.

KLEIST-SCHMENZIN (EWALD VON)

SCHEURIG (BODO) Ewald von Kleist-Schmenzin: ein Konservativer gegen Hitler. Oldenburg, Stalling, [1968]. pp. 296. bibliog. 21cm.

KLIUCHEVSKII (VASILII OSIPOVICH)

KLIUCHEVSKII (VASILII OSIPOVICH) Письма, дневники, афоризмы и мысли об истории. Москва, Наука, 1968. pp. 526. bibliog. 21½см.

KLOSTER VALLEY

LERCHENMUELLER (FRANK) Das Klostertal: Bevölkerung und Wirtschaft. Innsbruck, 1970. pp. 183. bibliog.

KNIT GOODS

CANADA. Tariff Board. 1960. Report...relative to the investigation ordered by the Minister of Finance respecting hosiery and knitted goods. [Ottawa, 1960]. pp. 210.

KNIT GOODS INDUSTRY

- India

INDIA. Working Group for the Hosiery, Knitting and Embroidery Industries. 1962. Report of the Working Group [etc.]. Delhi, Ministry of Commerce and Industry, 1962. pp. 71. 24½cm.

- Ireland, (Republic)

EIRE. Committee on Industrial Organisation. 1963. Report on the hosiery and knitwear industry. Dublin, [1963]. pp. 172. 24½cm.

EIRE. Committee on Industrial Progress. 1970. Report on hosiery and knitwear industry. Dublin, [1970]. pp. 106.

- Russia

SUKNOVALOV (ALEKSANDR EVGEN'EVICH) and FOMENKOV (IVAN NIKIFOROVICH) Фабрика "Красное Знамя": очерки истории Ленинградской государственной ордена Ленина трикотажно-чулочной фабрики "Красное Знамя", 1855-1967. Ленинград, Лениниздат, 1968. pp. 448. bibliog. 21½см.

- United Kingdom

ECONOMIC DEVELOPMENT COMMITTEE FOR THE HOSIERY AND KNITWEAR INDUSTRY. The compleat exporter: a guide to exporting. London, [1968]. pp. (v), 31. bibliog. 24½cm.

ASSOCIATED INDUSTRIAL CONSULTANTS LTD. Hosiery and knitwear in the 1970s: a study of the industry's future market prospects; a report prepared ...for the Marketing Action Group of the Economic Development Committee for the Hosiery and Knitwear Industry. London, H.M.S.O., 1970. pp. 182.

ECONOMIC DEVELOPMENT COMMITTEE FOR THE HOSIERY AND KNITWEAR INDUSTRY. Industrial report...on the economic assessment to 1972. London, National Economic Development Office, 1970. pp. 19.

ECONOMIC DEVELOPMENT COMMITTEE FOR THE HOSIERY AND KNITWEAR INDUSTRY. Statement to the industry. [London, National Economic Development Office, 1971.] fo. 13.

KNOWLEDGE, SOCIOLOGY OF

IZZO (ALBERTO) Sociologia della conoscenza. Roma, Armando, 1966. pp. 189. 21½cm. (Problemi di Sociologia. 12)

REMMLING (GUNTER WERNER) Road to suspicion: a study of modern mentality and the sociology of knowledge. New York, Appleton, [1967]. pp. xiii, 220. 23½cm. (Sociology Series)

BALANDIER (GEORGES) and others, eds. Perspectives de la sociologie contemporaine: hommage a Georges Gurvitch. Paris, 1968. pp. 468.

REMMLING (GUNTER WERNER) Wissenssoziologie und Gesellschaftsplanung: das Werk Karl Mannheims. Dortmund, 1968. pp. 315. bibliog.

POLANYI (MICHAEL) Knowing and being; essays...edited by Marjorie Grene. London, Routledge & Kegan Paul, 1969. pp. xvii, 246. 21½cm.

CURTIS (JAMES E.) and PETRAS (JOHN W.) eds. The sociology of knowledge: a reader. London, 1970. pp. 724.

KURUCZ (JENO) Falsches Bewusstsein und geronnener Geist: ein Beitrag zur Theorie und Anwendung der Wissenssoziologie. Koln, [1970]. pp. 84. bibliog.

HAVELOCK (RONALD G.) and others. Planning for innovation through dissemination and utilization of knowledge. Ann Arbor, [1971]. 1 vol. (various pagings). bibliog.

WILLER (JUDITH) The social determination of knowledge. Englewood Cliffs, [1971]. pp. 150.

KNOWLEDGE, THEORY OF

KRAFT (VIKTOR) Professor der Philosophie an der Universität Wien. Die Grundformen der wissenschaftlichen Methoden:...vorgelegt in der Sitzung [of the Akademie der Wissenschaften in Wien] am 29. April 1925. Wien, 1925. pp. 304. (Osterreichische Akademie der Wissenschaften. Philosophisch-Historische Klasse. Sitzungsberichte. 203. Band. 3. Abhandlung) Xerographic copy.

WELLS (HERBERT GEORGE) World encyclopaedia. [London, 1936]. pp. 26.

JUHOS (BÉLA) Die Erkenntnis und ihre Leistung: die naturwissenschaftliche Methode. Wien, 1950. pp. 263.

SCHELER (MAX FERDINAND) Gesammelte Werke; (herausgegeben von Maria Scheler). Bern, [1954 in progress]. bibliogs.

KNOWLEDGE, THEORY OF (Cont'd.)

VODZINSKII (E. I.) Reaktsionnaia sushchnost' gnoseologii russkogo neokantianstva. in Uchenye Zapiski Kafedr Obshchestvennykh Nauk Vuzov G. Leningrada. Filosofiia. vyp. 3. Leningrad, 1961.

BARTLEY (W. W.) Rationality versus the theory of rationality. in Bunge (Mario Augusto) ed. The critical approach to science and philosophy. New York, [1964].

BERNAYS (P.) Reflections on Karl Popper's Epistemology. in Bunge (Mario Augusto) ed. The critical approach to science and philosophy. New York, [1964].

FEIGL (H.) What Hume might have said to Kant. in Bunge (Mario Augusto) ed. The critical approach to science and philosophy. New York, [1964].

KOLMAN (ARNOST) Considerations about the certainty of knowledge; edited...by Robert S. Cohen and Dirk J. Struik. New York, [1965]. pp. 12. (American Institute for Marxist Studies. Occasional Papers. No.2)

MANNHEIM (KARL) Ideologie und Utopie;...[introduction and chapter 1 translated from the English by Heinz Maus]. 4th ed. Frankfurt/Main, 1965 repr. 1969. pp. 302. bibliog.

BLAKELEY (T. J.) The salient features of the Marxist-Leninist theory of knowledge. in Adelmann (Frederick J.) ed. The quest for the absolute. Chestnut Hill, [1966].

DEUGD (C. DE) The significance of Spinoza's first kind of knowledge. Assen, Van Gorcum, 1966. pp. (iii), 283. bibliog. 23½cm. (Wijsgerige Teksten en Studies. 15)

ERKENNTNISTHEORETISCHE und methodologische Probleme der Wissenschaft; (deutsche Answahlausgabe besorgt von Günter Kröber). Berlin, Akademie-Verlag, 1966. pp. 209. 21½cm.

GRECO (P.) Piaget; ou, L'épistémologie nécessaire. in Psychologie et épistémologie génétiques. Paris, 1966.

KLAUS (GEORG) Kybernetik und Erkenntnistheorie. Berlin, Deutscher Verlag der Wissenschaften, 1966. pp. xi, 411. bibliog. 23cm.

KLAUS (GEORG) Spezielle Erkenntnistheorie: Prinzipien der wissenschaftlichen Theorienbildung. Berlin, Deutscher Verlag der Wissenschaften, 1966. pp. 383. bibliog. 21½cm.

KRAUSS (W.) Fontenelle und Helvétius. in Steinitz (Wolfgang) and others, eds. Ost und West in der Geschichte des Denkens und der kulturellen Beziehungen. Berlin, 1966.

SINGER (GERWULF) Das Objekt der Nationalökonomie als ontologisches und erkenntnistheoretisches Problem: eine wissenschaftstheoretische Untersuchung. [Erlangen, imprint, 1966?]. pp. 192. bibliog.

VODZINSKII (EVGENII IVANOVICH) Russkoe neokantianstvo kontsa XIX - nachala XX vekov: marksistsko-leninskaia kritika ontologii i gnoseologii. Leningrad, 1966. pp. 79.

CHOMSKY (N.) Recent contributions to the theory of innate ideas. in Boston Colloquium for the Philosophy of Science. Proceedings, 1964-1966. Boston studies in the philosophy of science, vol.3. Dordrecht, 1967.

ENCYCLOPÉDIE DE LA PLÉIADE. Logique et connaissance scientifique;...sous la direction de Jean Piaget. [Paris, 1967] pp. 1345. bibliogs.

FISCHER (ANTON) Die philosophischen Grundlagen der wissenschaftlichen Erkenntnis. 2nd ed. Wien, 1967. pp. 226. bibliogs.

GOODMAN (N.) The epistemological argument. in Boston Colloquium for the Philosophy of Science. Proceedings, 1964-1966. Boston studies in the philosophy of science, vol.3. Dordrecht, 1967.

KOSING (ALFRED) Wissenschaftstheorie als Aufgabe der marxistischen Philosophie. Berlin, 1967. pp. 31. (Deutsche Akademie der Wissenschaften zu Berlin. Sitzungsberichte. 1967. Nr. 1)

AYER (Sir ALFRED JULES) and WINCH (RAYMOND) eds. British empirical philosophers Locke, Berkeley, Hume, Reid and J.S. Mill. New York, Simon & Schuster, 1968. pp. 560. 20½cm. (Clarion Books)

BACHELARD (GASTON) Essai sur la connaissance approchée. 2nd ed. Paris, Vrin, 1968. pp. 310. bibliog. 21½cm. (Bibliothèque des Textes Philosophiques)

BAUSOLA (ADRIANO) Conoscenza e moralità in Franz Brentano. Milano, Vita e Pensiero, 1968. pp. vii, 218. bibliog. 24cm. (Milan. Università Cattolica del Sacro Cuore. Contributi. Serie 3. Scienze Filosofiche. 13)

CELLÉRIER (GUY) and others. Cybernétique et épistémologie. Paris, P.U.F., 1968. pp. 143. bibliog. 21½cm. (Études d'Épistémologie Génétique. 22)

COLISH (MARCIA L.) The mirror of language: a study in the medieval theory of knowledge. New Haven, Yale U.P., 1968. pp. xxiii, 404. bibliog. 23½cm. (Yale University. Yale Historical Publications. Miscellany. 88)

DANTO (ARTHUR C.) Analytical philosophy of knowledge. Cambridge, C.U.P., 1968. pp. xiv, 270. 23cm.

HABERMAS (JUERGEN) Erkenntnis und Interesse. Frankfurt am Main, 1968. pp. 363.

HARTNACK (JUSTUS) Kant's theory of knowledge;...translated by M. Holmes Hartshorne. London, Macmillan, 1968. pp. (iv), 146. 21½cm.

HEERDEN (PIETER J. VAN) The foundation of empirical knowledge: with a theory of artificial intelligence. Wassenaar, Wistik, [1968]. pp. xii, 143. bibliogs. 23½cm.

KRAFT (VIKTOR) Professor der Philosophie an der Universität Wien. Die Grundlagen der Erkenntnis und der Moral. Berlin, Duncker und Humblot, [1968]. pp. 146. 23cm. (Erfahrung und Denken. Band 28)

KURSANOV (G. A.) ed. Современная идеалистическая гносеология: критические очерки. Москва, 1968. pp. 585.

MORRA (GIANFRANCO) Sociologia e antropologia. Forlì, Edizioni di Ethica, 1968. pp. 263. bibliog 21cm.

MUSGRAVE (ALAN EDWARD) Impersonal knowledge: a criticism of subjectivism in epistemology; [Ph. D. (London) thesis]. 1968. fo. 358. bibliog. 30cm. Typescript: unpublished. This thesis is the property of London University and may not be removed from the Library.

ONG (WALTER JACKSON) ed. Knowledge and the future of man: an international symposium. New York, Holt, [1968]. pp. x, 276. 20½cm.

REZNIKOV (LAZAR' OSIPOVICH) Erkenntnistheoretische Fragen der Semiotik; (aus dem Russischen übertragen). Berlin, 1968. pp. 299.

SELLARS (WILFRID STALKER) Science and metaphysics: variations on Kantian themes. London, Routledge & Kegan Paul, 1968. pp. x, 246. 21½cm. (International Library of Philosophy and Scientific Method)

SIGEL (IRVING E.) and HOOPER (FRANK H.) eds. Logical thinking in children: research based on Piaget's theory. New York, Holt, Rinehart & Winston, [1968]. pp. xvii, 541. 23cm.

YOLTON (JOHN W.) John Locke and the way of ideas. Oxford, 1968. pp. 235. bibliog.

SEIFFERT (HELMUT) Einführung in die Wissenschaftstheorie. München, [1969 in progress]. bibliogs.

BOSTON COLLOQUIUM FOR THE PHILOSOPHY OF SCIENCE. Proceedings, 1966-1968. Boston studies in the philosophy of science, vol. 4;...edited by Robert S. Cohen and Marx W. Wartofsky. Dordrecht, [1969 pp. 537.

DUCASSE (CURT JOHN) Truth, knowledge and causation. London, Routledge & Kegan Paul, 1968 [or rather 1969]. pp. viii, 255. 21½cm. (International Library of Philosophy and Scientific Method)

EAMES (ELIZABETH RAMSDEN) Bertrand Russell's theory of knowledge. London, Allen & Unwin, 1969. pp. 240. bibliog. 21½cm.

FOUCAULT (MICHEL) L'archéologie du savoir. [Paris, 1969]. pp. 279.

GOTSHALK (DILMAN WALTER) The structure of awareness: introduction to a situational theory of truth and knowledge. Urbana, Ill., [1969]. pp. 139.

GRENE (MARJORIE GUCKSMAN) ed. The anatomy of knowledge; papers presented to the Study Group on Foundations of Cultural Unity, Bowdoin College, 1965 and 1966. London, Routledge & Kegan Paul, 1969. pp. xii, 367. 21 cm.

KLAUS (GEORG) Semiotik und Erkenntnistheorie. 2nd ed. Berlin, 1969. pp. 182. bibliog.

KLEMKE (ELMER D.) The epistemology of G. E. Moore. Evanston, [Ill.], 1969. pp. 205. bibliog.

MANSON (RICHARD) The theory of knowledge of Giambattista Vico. [Hamden, Connecticut], 1969. pp. 83. bibliog.

MOULOUD (NOEL) Langage et structures: essais de logique et de séméiologie. Paris, [1969]. pp. 252. bibliog.

POLANYI (MICHAEL) Knowing and being; essays...edited by Marjorie Grene. London, Routledge & Kegan Paul, 1969. pp. xvii, 246. 21½cm.

POPPER (Sir KARL RAIMUND) Conjectures and refutations: the growth of scientific knowledge. 3rd ed. London, 1969. pp. xiii, 431.

QUINE (WILLARD VAN ORMAN) Ontological relativity and other essays. New York, 1969. pp. 165. (Columbia University. John Dewey Essays in Philosophy. No. 1)

SCHMIDT (ALFRED) of Frankfurt University, ed. Beiträge zur marxistischen Erkenntnistheorie:...Aufsätze von György Márkus [and others]. Frankfurt a.M., [1969]. pp. 264.

WITTGENSTEIN (LUDWIG) On certainty;...edited by G.E.M. Anscombe and G.H. von Wright [and] translated by Denis Paul and G.E.M. Anscombe. Oxford, 1969. pp. various. In German and English.

HARVEY (MARK OLIVER) Structure and dialectics: a critical analysis of the origins and development of Jean Piaget's epistemology; [Ph.D. (London) thesis]. 1969[or rather 1970]. fo.376 bibliog. Typescript: unpublished. This thesis is the property of London University and may not be removed from the Library.

HEIDEGGER (MARTIN) Hegel's concept of experience; with a section from Hegel's Phenomenology of spirit, in the Kenley Royce Dove translation. New York, [1970]. pp. 155.

HOFFMAN (ROBERT) Language, minds and knowledge. London, 1970. pp. 164. bibliog.

LANDESMAN (CHARLES) ed. The foundations of knowledge: [readings]. Englewood Cliffs, [1970]. pp. 184. bibliog.

PIAGET (JEAN) Genetic epistemology;...translated by Eleanor Duckworth. New York, 1970. pp. 84. (Columbia University. Woodbridge Lectures. No. 8)

ROYAL INSTITUTE OF PHILOSOPHY. Lectures. vol. 3. Knowledge and necessity. London, 1970. pp. 284.

RYAN (ALAN) The philosophy of John Stuart Mill. London, 1970. pp. 268. bibliog.

SLOTE (MICHAEL A.) Reason and scepticism. London, 1970. pp. 224.

STUDIES in the theory of knowledge; essays by Norman Malcolm [and others]. Oxford, 1970. pp. 132. (American Philosophical Quarterly. Monograph Series. No. 4)

AARON (RICHARD ITHAMAR) Knowing and the function of reason. Oxford, 1971. pp. 276.

GURVICH (GEORGII DAVYDOVICH) The social frameworks of knowledge;...translated from the French by Margaret A. Thompson and Kenneth A. Thompson. Oxford, 1971. pp. 292. bibliog.

PIEPE (ANTHONY) Knowledge and social order. London, 1971. pp. 81.

KNOWLEDGE, THEORY OF (RELIGION)

SMITH (J. E.) Randall's interpretation of the role of knowledge in religion. in Anton (John Peter) ed. Naturalism and historical understanding. Albany, [1967].

KNOX (JOHN)

MACKIE (JOHN DUNCAN) John Knox. rev. ed. London, Historical Association, 1968. pp. 24. bibliog. 21½cm. (General Series. G. 20)

KNUTZEN (MATTHIAS)

KNUTZEN (MATTHIAS) Matthias Knutzen: ein deutscher Atheist und revolutionärer Demokrat des 17.Jahrhunderts: Flugschriften und andere zeitgenössische sozialkritische Schriften; herausgegeben und eingeleitet von Werner Pfoh. Berlin, Akademie-Verlag, 1965. pp. 95. bibliog. 20cm. (Philosophische Studientexte)

KOBLENZ
- History

BELLINGHAUSEN (HANS) ed. 2000 Jahre Koblenz: Geschichte der Stadt an Rhein und Mosel;...mit Beiträgen von Erich Franke [and others]. Boppard am Rhein, 1971. pp. 502. bibliogs.

KOCIOŁ (JAN DĄB-)
See DĄB-KOCIOŁ (JAN)

KOEPPEN (PETER VON)

GRASSHOFF (H.) Aus dem Briefwechsel Therese Jakob-Talvjs an P. I. Köppen. in Steinitz (Wolfgang) and others, eds. Ost und West in der Geschichte des Denkens und der kulturellen Beziehungen. Berlin, 1966.

KOESTRING (ERNST)

KOESTRING (ERNST) General Ernst Köstring: der militärische Mittler zwischen dem Deutschen Reich und der Sowjetunion, 1921-1941; bearbeitet von Hermann Teske. Frankfurt am Main, Mittler, [1965]. pp. 334. (Profile bedeutender Soldaten. Band 1)

KOFYARS

NETTING (ROBERT McCORKLE) Hill farmers of Nigeria: cultural ecology of the Kofyar of the Jos plateau. Seattle, U. of Washington P., [1968]. pp. xx, 259. bibliog. 21½cm. (American Ethnological Society. Monographs. 46)

KOGĂLNICEANU (MIHAIL)

KOGĂLNICEANU (MIHAIL) Texte social-politice alese; (volum alcătuit de Dan Berindei [and others]). București, 1967. pp. 423.

KOLAROV (VASIL PETROV)

KOLAROV (VASIL PETROV) Детство, юношество, възмъжаване: спомени; [with an introduction by Todor Pavlov]. София, Народна Младеж, 1966. pp. 149. 20cm.

KOLB (FRANZ SALES)

KRAMER (H.) Franz Kolb, ein Tiroler Politiker und Historiker. in Institut für Österreichische Geschichtsforschung and Vienna. Katholische Akademie. Österreich und Europa. Graz, 1965.

KOLCHAK (ALEKSANDR VASIL'EVICH)

RAZGROM... Разгром Колчака: воспоминания. Москва, 1969. pp. 293.

KOLLONTAI (ALEKSANDRA MIKHAILOVNA)

ITKINA (ANNA MARKOVNA) Revoliutsioner, tribun, diplomat: stranitsy zhizni Aleksandry Mikhailovny Kollontai. 2nd ed. Moskva, 1970. pp. 287.

KOŁOBRZEG
- History

LESIŃSKI (HENRYK) ed. Dzieje Kołobrzegu, X - XX wiek. Poznań, Wydawnictwo Poznańskie, 1965. pp. 243. 24cm. (Polskie Towarzystwo Historyczne. Oddział i Stacja Naukowa Województwa Koszalińskiego w Słupsku. Biblioteka Słupska. t.14)

KOŁODZIEJ (STANISŁAW)

KOŁODZIEJ (STANISŁAW) Wspomnienia, 1915-1945. Warszawa, Książka i Wiedza, 1967. pp. 251. 19½cm.

KOLOKOL'NIKOV (PRAVEL NIKOLAEVICH)

GARVI (PETR ABRAMOVICH) Revoliutsionnye siluety. New York, 1962. pp. 43. (Inter-University Project on the History of the Menshevik Movement)

KOL'SKII UEZD
See MURMANSK (OBLAST')

KOMEITO
See SOKAGAKKAI

KOMI-PERMIAK NATIONAL OKRUG
- Politics and government

VSESOIUZNYI LENINSKII KOMMUNISTICHESKII SOIUZ MOLODEZHI. Komi-Permiatskii Okruzhnoi Komitet. Komi-permiatskii komsomol v tsifrakh i faktakh, 1918-1968 gg. Kudymkar, 1968. pp. 52.

KOMI REPUBLIC

SOTSIALISTICHESKIE... Социалистические преобразования в Коми АССР: историко-филологический сборник. вып.9. Сыктывкар, Коми Книжное Издательство, 1965. pp. 168. 22см.

- Economic history

IVANOV (NIKOLAI DMITRIEVICH) Первые шаги к социализму: революционные преобразования в экономике Коми края в 1918-1920 гг. Сыктывкар, 1967. pp. 94.

- **Industries**

> KUDRIAVTSEV (N.P.) and others, eds. Istoriia industrializatsii Severnogo raiona: Arkhangel'-skaia, Vologodskaia oblasti i Komi ASSR, 1926-1941 gg. Arkhangel'sk, 1970. pp. 670. bibliog.

- **Intellectual life**

> BEZNOSIKOV (IAKOV NIKOLAEVICH) Культурная революция в Коми АССР. Москва, Наука, 1968. pp. 295. 21см.

- **Maps**

> ATLAS... Атлас Коми Автономной Советской Социалистической Республике. Москва, ГУГК, 1964. pp. 112. 32см.

- **Statistics**

> KOMI REPUBLIC. Statisticheskoe Upravlenie. 1967. Коми АССР к 50-летию Советской власти: статистический сборник. Сыктывкар, 1967. pp. 192. 20см.

KON (FELIKS IAKOVLEVICH)

> KON (FELIKS IAKOVLEVICH) Escape from the gallows. London, [1932]. pp. 47.

KON FAMILY

> LESMAN (BOLESŁAW) Recepta na miliony: z dziejów rodu Konów. Warszawa, Książka i Wiedza, 1967. pp. 466. 19½cm.

KONDRAT'EV (PETR VLADIMIROVICH)

> KONDRAT'EV (PETR VLADIMIROVICH) Polet skvoz' gody. Moskva, 1970. pp. 327.

KONDRAT'EV (ZAKHAR IVANOVICH)

> KONDRAT'EV (ZAKHAR IVANOVICH) Дороги войны; (литературная запись). Москва, Воениздат, 1968. pp. 357. 20см. (Военные Мемуары)

KONEV (IVAN STEPANOVICH)

> KONEV (IVAN STEPANOVICH) L'invasion du IIIe Reich: mémoires de guerre, 1945; [translated from the Russian by René Huntzbucler]. [Paris], Plon, [1968]. pp. 315. 20cm.

KONGOS

> BALANDIER (GEORGES) The sociology of black Africa: social dynamics in central Africa...; translated by Douglas Garman. London, 1970. pp. 540.

> MacGAFFEY (WYATT) Custom and government in the lower Congo. Berkeley, Calif., [1970]. pp. 322. bibliog.

KONI (ANATOLII FEDOROVICH)

> KONI (ANATOLII FEDOROVICH) Priemy i zadachi prokuratury: iz vospominanii sudebnogo deiatelia, etc. Petrograd, 1923. pp. 116.

> KONI (ANATOLII FEDOROVICH) Собрание сочинений. Москва, 1966-1969. 8 vols.

KONIAGUI (AFRICAN PEOPLE)

> GESSAIN (MONIQUE) Les migrations de Coniagui et Bassari; publié avec le concours du Centre National de la Recherche Scientifique Paris, Société des Africanistes, Musée de l'Homme, 1967. pp. 106. bibliog. 28cm.

KORCZAK (JANUSZ)

> HYAMS (JOSEPH) A field of buttercups. London, Muller, 1969. pp. 220. 21½cm.

KOREA

> UNITED STATES. Army Department. Pamphlets. No. 550-41. U.S. Army area handbook for Korea, [rev. ed.] Washington, 1964. pp. xii, 595. bibliogs.

> KOREA SEEN FROM ABROAD; (pd. by the Korea Information Service). Seoul, annual, 1968 (v.4) to date. 21cm.

- **Army**

> KIM (IL-SUNG) On the 20th anniversary of the founding of the Korean People's Army; speech at the banquet...February 8, 1968. Pyongyang, 1968. pp. 13.

- **Bibliography**

> KANG (SANGWOON) compiler. A list of articles on Korea in the western languages, 1800 [or rather 1890]-1964. Seoul, [1967]. pp. 192. Title and foreword in English and Korean.

> HARVARD UNIVERSITY. Library. Widener Library Shelflists. [No]. 14. China, Japan and Korea. Cambridge, Harvard U.P., 1968. pp. 494. 28cm.

- **Commerce**

> KOREA (REPUBLIC). Korea Trade Promotion Corporation. 1966. Korea trade guide, 1967. Seoul, 1966. pp. 640. 26½cm.

> KOREA (REPUBLIC). Ministry of Public Information. Korea Series. No. 7. Foreign trade. [Seoul, 1967?] pp. 30. 21cm.

> KOREA (REPUBLIC). Ministry of Commerce and Industry. Office of Planning and Management. Commerce and industry statistics review. [in Korean and English] irreg., S/Oc, N/D 1968 (v.6, nos.7,8); Mr/My 1969 (v.7, no.3)- [Seoul?]

- **Constitution**

> FRANCE. Direction de la Documentation. La Documentation Française. Notes et Études Documentaires. No. 3,333. Constitution de le Republique de Corée (1962). Paris, 1966. pp. 14. 30½cm.

> KOREA (REPUBLIC). Ministry of Public Information. Korea Series. No. 3. Constitution. [Seoul, 1966] pp. 41. 21cm.

- **Description and travel**

> IVANENKO (VASILII IVANOVICH) Тропою памяти. Москва, 1968. pp. 120.

> KOREA (REPUBLIC). Ministry of Public Information. 1968. Facts about Korea. Seoul, 1968. pp. 138.

KOREA (Cont'd.)

- Economic conditions

FRANCE. Direction de la Documentation. La Documentation Française. Notes et Études Documentaires. No. 2,897. La Corée du Nord depuis l'armistice de Panmunjom. Paris, 1962. pp. 43. 30½cm.

KOREA (REPUBLIC). Ministry of Commerce and Industry. 1964. Development of the Korean industry. Seoul, 1964. pp. iii, 137.

KOREA (REPUBLIC). Korea Trade Promotion Corporation. 1966. Korea trade guide, 1967. Seoul, 1966. pp. 640. 26½cm.

KOREA (REPUBLIC). Ministry of Public Information. 1966. Korean economy: about to take off. Seoul, [1966]. pp. 233. 26cm.

BANK OF KOREA. Economic progress in Korea. [Seoul?], 1967. pp. 35.

FRANCE. Direction de la Documentation. La Documentation Française. Notes et Études Documentaires. No. 3,404. La république de Corée depuis 1945. Paris, 1967. pp. 33. bibliog. 30½cm.

KOREA (REPUBLIC). Ministry of Public Information. Korea Series. No. 9. Basic industries. [Seoul, 1967]. pp. 21. 21cm.

KIM (SEUNG HEE) Foreign capital for economic development: a Korean case study. New York, 1970. pp. 206. bibliog. (New York (City). University. Center for International Studies. Studies in Peaceful Change.)

- Economic policy

RODONG SHINMOON. Self-reliance and independent national economic construction. Peking, 1963. pp. 17.

YOUNG (SEEK CHOUE) The way to Korea's prosperity;... translated by Jae Min Noh. Seoul, 1967. pp. 88.

PRACTICAL approaches to development planning: Korea's second five-year plan; [from a conference held in St. Charles, Illinois, June 1968]; edited by Irma Adelman. Baltimore, [1969]. pp. 306. bibliog.

COLE (DAVID C.) and LYMAN (PRINCETON N.) Korean development: the interplay of politics and economics. Cambridge, Mass., 1971. pp. 320. bibliog.

- Foreign relations

FRANCE. Direction de la Documentation. La Documentation Française. Notes et Études Documentaires. No. 2,897. La Corée du Nord depuis l'armistice de Panmunjom. Paris, 1962. pp. 43. 30½cm.

FRANCE. Direction de la Documentation. La Documentation Française. Notes et Études Documentaires. No. 3,404. La république de Corée depuis 1945. Paris, 1967. pp. 33. bibliog. 30½cm.

KOH (BYUNG CHUL) The foreign policy of North Korea. New York, Praeger, 1969. pp. xxiii, 237. bibliog. 23½cm. (Praeger Special Studies in International Politics and Public Affairs)

INTERNATIONAL INSTITUTE FOR STRATEGIC STUDIES. Adelphi Papers. No. 80. Moving the glacier: the two Koreas and the powers; by Morton Abramowitz. London, 1971. pp. 26.

KIM (IL-SUNG) On immediate political and economic policies of the Democratic People's Republic of Korea and some international problems: answers to questions raised by newsmen of Japanese newspaper "Yomiuri Shimbun", January 10, 1972. Pyongyang, 1972. pp. 46.

- Foreign relations - China

LIU (SHAO-CHI) and CHOI (YONG KUN) Joint statement of Chairman Liu Shao-Chi and President Choi Yong Kun. Peking, Foreign Languages P., 1963. pp. 17. 18½cm.

CHIEN (FREDERICK FOO) The opening of Korea: a study of Chinese diplomacy, 1876-1885. [Hamden], 1967. pp. xiii, 364. bibliog. 21½cm.

CHO (M.Y.) Die Entwicklung der Beziehungen zwischen Peking und P'yongyang, 1949-1967: Analyse und dokumente; eine Studie über die Auswirkungen des sowjetisch-chinesischen Konfliktes. Wiesbaden, Harrassowitz, [1967]. pp. 175. bibliog. 24cm. (Hamburg. Institut für Asienkunde. Schriften. Band 20)

PREMIER Chou En-lai visits the Democratic People's Republic of Korea. Peking, 1970. pp. 97.

- Foreign relations - Japan

KIM (KWAN BONG) The Korea-Japan treaty crisis and the instability of the Korean political system. New York, 1971. pp. 350. bibliog.

- Foreign relations - United States

UNITED STATES. State Dept. Far Eastern Series. 115. A historical summary of United States-Korean relations, with a chronology of important developments 1834-1962. Washington, 1962. pp. vi, 138.

KOREA (REPUBLIC). Ministry of Foreign Affairs Publications. 65/M-1. Documents on Korea-United States relations, 1943-1965. Seoul, 1965. pp. xi, 302. 23cm.

HONOLULU CONFERENCE, 1968. Honolulu Conference: a milestone of the Asian-Pacific era. Seoul, 1968. pp. 95. 26cm.

U.S. imperialism: the sworn enemy of the Korean people. Pyongyang, 1969. pp. 158.

- Government publications

KOREA (REPUBLIC). National Assembly Library. 1966. Government publications in Korea, 1948-1965. [Seoul, 1966?] pp. (iv), 58. 26cm. Mostly of Korean titles with a few English.

- History

SHABSHINA (FANIA ISAAKOVNA) Очерки новейшей истории Кореи, 1945-1953 гг. Москва, Госполитиздат, 1958. pp. 307. bibliog. 19½cm.

KOREA (REPUBLIC). Ministry of Public Information. Information Series. No. 1. The history of Korea. [Seoul, 1966] pp. 30. 21cm.

LI (OGG) Histoire de la Corée. Paris, P.U.F., 1969. pp. 128. bibliog. 17½cm. (Que Sais-Je? No. 1310)

U.S. imperialism: the sworn enemy of the Korean people. Pyongyang, 1969. pp. 158.

- History - Bibliography

HENTHORN (WILLIAM E.) compiler. A guide to reference and research materials on Korean history: an annotated bibliography. Honolulu, East-West Center, Institute of Advanced Projects, 1968. fo. iii, 152. 28cm. (Occasional Papers of Research Publications and Translations. Annotated Bibliography Series. No. 4)

- Industries

KOREA (REPUBLIC). Ministry of Commerce and Industry. 1964. Development of the Korean industry. Seoul, 1964. pp. iii, 137.

KOREA DEVELOPMENT BANK. Research Department. Report on sample survey for mining and manufacturing establishments;...64. Seoul, [1965]. pp. 147. 26cm. In English and Korean.

KOREA (REPUBLIC). Economic Planning Board. 1967. Report on mining and manufacturing census, [19]66. [Seoul, 1967]. 3 vols. 26cm. In English and Korean.

KOREA (REPUBLIC). Ministry of Public Information. Korea Series. No. 9. Basic industries. [Seoul, 1967]. pp. 21. 21cm.

KOREA DEVELOPMENT BANK. Industry in Korea, 1967. Seoul, [1967]. pp. 335. 28cm.

KOREA (REPUBLIC). Ministry of Commerce and Industry. Office of Planning and Management. Commerce and industry statistics review. [in Korean and English irreg., S/Oc, N/D 1968 (v.6, nos.7,8); Mr/My 1969 (v.7, no.3)- [Seoul?]

KOREA DEVELOPMENT BANK. Industry in Korea, 1970. Seoul, [1970]. pp. 337.

- National Assembly

KOREA (REPUBLIC). National Assembly. House of Representatives. Secretariat. 1967. The National Assembly of the Republic of Korea. Seoul, 1967. pp. 169. 26cm. In Korean, English, French and German.

- Nationalism

REES (DAVID) The new pressures from North Korea. [London], 1970. pp. 14. (Current Affairs Research Services Centre. Conflict Studies. No. 3)

- Politics and government

FRANCE. Direction de la Documentation. La Documentation Française. Notes et Études Documentaires. No. 2,897. La Corée du Nord depuis l'armistice de Panmunjom. Paris, 1962. pp. 43. 30½cm.

RODONG SHINMOON. Self-reliance and independent national economic construction. Peking, 1963. pp. 17.

FRANCE. Direction de la Documentation. La Documentation Française. Notes et Études Documentaires. No. 3,404. La république de Corée depuis 1945. Paris, 1967. pp. 33. bibliog. 30½cm.

HAHM (PYONG-CHOON) The Korean political tradition and law: essays in Korean law and legal history. Seoul, Hollym, [1967]. pp. ix, 249. bibliog. 20½cm. (Royal Asiatic Society. Korean Branch. Monograph Series. No. 1)

KIM (CHONG-SHIN) Seven years with Korea's Park Chung-hee;... translated by Park Yune-hee. Seoul, Hollym Corporation, [1967]. pp. x, 306. 18½cm.

KIM (IL-SUNG) Let us embody more thoroughly the revolutionary spirit of independence, self-sustenance and self-defence in all fields of state activity; political programme of the Government of the Democratic People's Republic of Korea, announced at the first session of the fourth Supreme People's Assembly of the D.P.R.K., December 16, 1967. Pyongyang, Foreign Languages Publishing House, 1967. pp. 89

KOH (BYUNG CHUL) ed. Aspects of administrative development in South Korea. Kalamazoo, Korea Research and Publication, Inc., [1967]. pp. vii, 144. bibliog. 27½cm.

KOREA (REPUBLIC). Ministry of Public Information Korea Series. No. 4. Structure of government [Seoul, 1967?]. pp. 105. 21cm.

CHOSON NODONGDANG. Central Committee. Party History Institute. Among the people. Pyongyang, 1968. pp. 146.

HENDERSON (GREGORY) Korea: the politics of the vortex. Cambridge, Harvard U.P., 1968. pp. xvii, 482. bibliog. 23½cm.

KIM (IL-SUNG) On socialist construction and the South Korean revolution in the Democratic People's Republic of Korea. Pyongyang, 1968. pp. 68.

LEE (HAHN BEEN) Korea: time, change and administration. Honolulu, East-West Center P., 1968. pp. xiii, 240. bibliog. 23cm

MOLDEN (OTTO) Zweikampf um das Gelbe Reich: wer überlebt in Ostasien? Wien, Molden, [1968]. pp. 269. bibliog. 21cm.

OH (JOHN KIE-CHIANG) Korea: democracy on trial. Ithaca, Cornell U.P., 1968. pp. xiv, 240. bibliog. 21½cm.

CHOSON NODONGDANG. Central Committee. Party History Institute. Brief history of the revolutionary activities of comrade Kim Il Sung. Pyongyang, 1969. pp. 294.

FOR the peaceful unification of the country: important documents. Pyongyang, 1969. pp. 155.

KIM (IL-SUNG) Answers to the questions raised by general manager of "Dar-el-Tahrir", for printing and publishing of the United Arab Republic, July 1, 1969. Pyongyang, 1969. pp. 18.

KIM (IL-SUNG) Answers to the questions raised by the delegation of the Democratic Youth League of Finland, for the "Kansan Uutiset", central organ of the Communist Party of Finland, September 2, 1969. Pyongyang, 1969. pp. 32.

KIM (IL SUNG) Answers to the questions raised by the Iraqi news agency, July 1, 1969. Pyongyang, 1969. pp. 9.

KIM (BYONG SIK) Modern Korea: the socialist North revolutionary perspectives in the South, and unification. New York, [1970]. pp. 319.

KOREA - Politics and government (Cont'd.)

KIM (IL-SUNG) The great idea of Lenin on the national liberation struggle in colonies in the East is triumphing. Pyongyang, 1970. pp. 14. (Reprinted from Pravda, April 16, 1970)

KIM (IL-SUNG) Report on the work of the Central Committee to the Fifth Congress of the Workers' Party of Korea, November 2, 1970. Pyongyang, 1970. pp. 169.

PARK (CHUNG-HEE) The country, the revolution and I;... [English version by Leon Sinder]. 2nd ed. Seoul, 1970. pp. 191.

PARK (CHUNG-HEE) Major speeches by Korea's Park Chung Hee; compiled by Shin Bum Shik. Seoul, 1970. pp. 386.

PARK (CHUNG-HEE) Our nation's path: ideology of social reconstruction. 2nd ed. Seoul, 1970. pp. 240.

REES (DAVID) The new pressures from North Korea. [London], 1970. pp. 14. (Current Affairs Research Services Centre. Conflict Studies. No. 3)

INTERNATIONAL INSTITUTE FOR STRATEGIC STUDIES. Adelphi Papers. No. 80. Moving the glacier: the two Koreas and the powers; by Morton Abramowitz. London, 1971. pp. 26.

KIM (IL SUNG) The youth must take over and carry forward the revolution. Pyongyang, 1971. pp. 20.

KIM (KWAN BONG) The Korea-Japan treaty crisis and the instability of the Korean political system. New York, 1971. pp. 350. bibliog.

KIM (IL-SUNG) On immediate political and economic policies of the Democratic People's Republic of Korea and some international problems: answers to questions raised by newsmen of Japanese newspaper "Yomiuri Shimbun", January 10, 1972. Pyongyang, 1972. pp. 46.

- Rural conditions

KIM (IL-SUNG) Theses on the socialist rural question in our country; adopted at the Eighth Plenary Meeting of the Fourth Central Committee of the Workers' Party of Korea, February 25, 1964. Pyongyang, 1968. pp. 69.

- Social conditions

KIM (CHONG IK EUGENE) and CHEE (CH'ANGBOH) eds. Aspects of social change in Korea. Kalamazoo, [1969]. pp. 272. (Korea Research and Publications, Inc. Series on Contemporary Korean Problems. vol. 5)

- Social life and customs

CRANE (PAUL SHIELDS) Korean patterns. 2nd ed. Seoul, 1968. pp. 244. (Royal Asiatic Society. Korea Branch. Handbook Series. No. 1)

- Statistics

KOREA DEVELOPMENT BANK. Research Department. Report on sample survey for mining and manufacturing establishments;...'64. Seoul, [1965]. pp. 147. 26cm. In English and Korean.

- Year-books

KOREA; [published by] Ministry of Culture and Information, Republic of Korea. Seoul, annual, 1968 [vol.2] to date. 30cm.

KOREAN REUNIFICATION QUESTION (1945-)

FOR the peaceful unification of the country: important documents. Pyongyang, 1969. pp. 155.

KOREAN WAR, 1950-1953

YOO (TAE-HO) The Korean War and the United Nations: a legal and diplomatic historical study. Louvain, Desbarax, 1965. pp.216. Bibliog. 24cm.

PAIGE (GLENN D.) The Korean decision, June 24-30, 1950. New York, Free P., [1968]. pp. xxvii, 394. bibliog. 21cm.

STONE (ISIDOR F.) The hidden history of the Korean War. 2nd ed. New York. 1969. pp. 368.

- Atrocities

ON the criminal acts committed by the U.S. imperialist aggression troops in Korea. Pyongyang, 1970. pp. 112.

- Naval operations

UNITED STATES. [Navy Department]. History of United States naval operations, Korea. Washington, 1962. pp.xv,499. bibliog.

- Prisoners and prisons

MEYERS (SAMUEL M.) and BIDERMAN (ALBERT DAVID) eds. Mass behavior in battle and captivity: the communist soldier in the Korean war; research studies directed by William C. Bradbury. Chicago, U. of Chicago P., 1968. pp. xxx, 377. bibliog. 22½cm.

- China

KIM (TAEKHOAN) Die Vereinten Nationen und ihr kollektives Sicherheitssystem: Studie über die UN-Aktion gegen die Intervention der Volksrepublik China im Korea Krieg. München, UNI-Druck, [1968]. pp. vi, 246. bibliog. 21cm.

- United States

UNITED STATES. [Navy Department.] History of United States naval operations, Korea. Washington, 1962. pp. xv, 499. bibliog.

GUTTMANN (ALLEN) ed. Korea and the theory of limited war. Boston, Heath, [1967]. pp. x, 118. bibliog. 23½cm. (Problems in American Civilization)

CARIDI (RONALD J.) The Korean war and the American politics: the Republican party as a case study. Philadelphia, [1968]. pp. 319. bibliog.

NAKED act of aggression by U.S. imperialism against the Korean people: information on activities of the armed spy ship "Pueblo" of U.S. imperialist aggressor army which intruded deep into the territorial waters of the Democratic People's Republic of Korea. [No.] 3. Pyongyang, 1968. pp. 81.

KOREANS IN JAPAN

MITCHELL (RICHARD HANKS) The Korean minority in Japan. Berkeley, University of California Press, 1967. pp (viii), 186. bibliog. 21½cm.

KOREANS IN RUSSIA

KIM (SYN KHVA) Очерки по истории советских корейцев. Алма-Ата, Наука, 1965. pp. 251. bibliog. 20cm.

KORNILOV (LAVR GEORGIEVICH)

IVANOV (NIKOLAI IAKOVLEVICH) Корниловщина и ее разгром: из истории борьбы с контрреволюцией в 1917 г. Ленинград, Университет, 1965. pp. 239. 21½см.

KAPUSTIN (MIKHAIL IVANOVICH) Заговор генералов: из истории корниловщины и ее разгрома. Москва, Мысль, 1968. pp. 261. 20см.

KOROS

NA'IBI (MALLAM SHUAIBU) and HASSAN (ALHAJI) The Gwari, Gade and Koro tribes. [Ibadan], 1969. pp. 54.

KORSCH (KARL)

KORSCH (KARL) Marxism and philosophy: and other articles; translated from the German and edited by Fred Halliday. London, 1970. pp. 159.

KOŚCIUSZKO (TADEUSZ ANDRZEJ BONAWENTURA)

TATARINOFF-EGGENSCHWILER (ADELE) Tadeusz Kościuszko, 1746-1817; Kampf und Opfer für die Freiheit. Solothurn, [imprint], [1967?]. pp. 107. bibliog. 23cm. (Separatdruck aus dem Jahrbuch für Solothurnische Geschichte, Band 40, 1967)

DIHM (JAN) Kościuszko nieznany. Wrocław, Ossolineum, 1969. pp. 447. 24cm.

KOSIOR (STANISLAV VIKENT'EVICH)

POHREBINS'KYI (M. B.) Stanislav Vikentiiovych Kosior. Kyïv, 1967. pp. 301.

KOSOVO AND METOHIJA

AKSIĆ (STANOJE) Položaj autonomnih pokrajina u ustavnom sistemu Socijalističke Federativne Republike Jugoslavije, sa posebnim osvrtom na položaj i razvoj autonomne pokrajine Kosova i Metohije: doktorska teza, etc. Beograd, 1967. pp. 148. bibliog. With Russian and French summaries. In Cyrillic.

TITO (JOSIP BROZ) Razgovori i govori na Kosovu i Metohiji. Beograd, 1967. pp. 70.

- Constitution

AUTONOMNE pokrajine u Jugoslaviji: društveno-politički i pravni aspekti; referati i diskusija sa Simpozijuma održanog u Novom Sadu 8, 9. i 10. juna 1967. Beograd, 1967. pp. 400.

- Economic policy

WOLFSON (MARGARET S.) and others. Regional project of Kosovo-Metohija, Yugoslavia. Paris, 1968. pp. 94. (Technical Assistance Evaluation Studies)

- Politics and government

LIDHJA SOCIALISTE TË POPULLIT PUNUES TË SERBIS PËR KOSOVË E METOHI. Konferenca, e 6, 1960. Konferenca, etc. Prishtinë, 1961. pp. 163.

NIKOLIĆ (MIODRAG) Autonomous province of Kosovo and Metohija. Beograd, 1965. pp. 43. (Međunarodna Politika. Studies. No.5)

KOSSUTH (LAJOS)

VAS (ZOLTÁN) Ha még egyszer azt üzeni... [sic]: Kossuth Lajos élete az emigrációban, 1849-1861. Budapest, 1967. pp. 679.

KÖSTRING
See KOESTRING

KOSTROMA (OBLAST')

VOROB'EV (LEONID IVANOVICH) Разбуженная рамень: очерки истории, экономики и культуры Кологривского района Костромской области. Кострома, Книжное Издательство, 1960. pp. 172. bibliog. 14 см. (Города и Районы Родного Края)

- History - Revolution, 1917-1921 - Chronology.

ZA vlast' Sovetov: khronika revoliutsionnykh sobytii v Kostromskoi gubernii, fevral' 1917 - mart 1918. Iaroslavl', 1967. pp. 188.

- Politics and government

OCHERKI istorii Kostromskoi organizatsii KPSS. Iaroslavl', 1967. pp. 404.

KOSZALIN (PROVINCE)

KOSZALIŃSKIE: rozwój województwa w Polsce Ludowej. Warszawa, 1970. pp. 225. bibliog.

- Social conditions

CHMIELEWSKA (BOZENNA) Społeczno-kulturowe mechanizmy i kierunki awansu młodego pokolenia: na przykładzie województwa koszalińskiego. Poznań, 1970. pp. 141. (Polskie Towarzystwo Historyczne. Oddział w Słupsku. Biblioteka Słupska. t.23)

KOTA

- Industries

VAID (KANWAL N.) The new worker: a study in Kota. London, Asia Publishing House, [1968]. pp. xvi, 196. bibliog. 21cm.

KŌTOKU (DENJIRO)

NOTEHELFER (F.G.) Kōtoku Shūsui: portrait of a Japanese radical. Cambridge, 1971. pp. 227. bibliog.

KŌTOKU (SHŪSUI)
See KŌTOKU (DENJIRO)

KOTSIUBINSKII (MIKHAIL MIKHAILOVICH)

M... М. М. Коцюбинський як громадський діяч: документи, матеріали, публікації. Київ, Наукова Думка, 1968. pp. 191. 21½см.

KOVALEVSKAIA (SOF'IA VASIL'EVNA)

KOVALEVSKAIA (SOF'IA VASIL'EVNA) Нигилистка. Женева, Вольная Русская Типография, 1892. pp. 112. 19½см.

KOVALEVSKII (MAKSIM MAKSIMOVICH)

KAZAKOV (ANATOLII PAVLOVICH) Teoriia progressa v russkoi sotsiologii kontsa XIX veka: P.L. Lavrov, N.K. Mikhailovskii, M.M. Kovalevskii. Leningrad, 1969. pp. 129.

KOWLOON

- Riots

HONG KONG. Kowloon Disturbances Claims Assessment Board. 1966. Report. [T.L. Yang, chairman]. Hong Kong, [1966]. pp. 24.

KOWLOON disturbances, 1966: report of commission of inquiry. [Sir Michael Hogan, chairman]. Hong Kong, 1967. pp. 167.

KOZICKA (MARJA DUNIN-)
See DUNIN-KOZICKA (MARJA)

KOZLOV (IVAN ANDREEVICH)

KOZLOV (IVAN ANDREEVICH) Ни время, ни расстояние. Москва, Молодая Гвардия, 1966. pp. 318. 20cm.

KOZLOV (IVAN ANDREEVICH) Наш последний и решительный. Москва, 1969. pp. 333.

KOZLOV (VASILII IVANOVICH)

KOZLOV (VASILII IVANOVICH) Veren do kontsa. Moskva, 1970. pp. 415.

KRAFFTHEIM (JOHANN CRATO VON)
See CRATO VON KRAFFTHEIM (JOHANN)

KRAFT (JOHANN)
See CRATO VON KRAFFTHEIM (JOHANN)

KRAIGHER (BORIS)

KRAIGHER (BORIS) O reformi. Ljubljana, "Komunist", 1967. pp. 288. 18½cm. Selected speeches and articles.

KRASIKOV (PETR ANAN'EVICH)

GINDIN (ARON MENDELEVICH) and GINDIN (GRIGORII MIKHAILOVICH) С Лениным в сердце: жизнь Петра Красикова. Москва, ИПЛ, 1968. pp. 263. 16½см.

KRASIN (LEONID BORISOVICH)

ZARNITSKII (STANISLAV VASIL'EVICH) and TROFIMOVA (LIDIIA IVANOVNA) Советской страны дипломат. Москва, ИПЛ, 1968. pp. 262. 15½см.

KRASNIANSKAIA (ANNA PETROVNA)

GARVI (PETR ABRAMOVICH) Revoliutsionnye siluety. New York, 1962. pp. 43. (Inter-University Project on the History of the Menshevik Movement)

KRASNODAR (KRAI)

- History - Revolution, 1917-1921 - Personal narratives

SHEVTSOV (IVAN BORISOVICH) Особое задание. 2nd ed. Москва, Политиздат, 1965. pp. 144. 20cm.

- Social life and customs

KUBANSKIE... Кубанские станицы: этические и культурно-бытовые процессы на Кубани. Москва, 1967. pp. 356.

- Statistics

KRASNODAR (KRAI). Statisticheskoe Upravlenie. Krasnodarskii krai za 50 let Sovetskoi vlasti: statisticheskii sbornik. Krasnodar, 1967. pp. 178.

KRASNOYARSK (KRAI)

- History

KRASNOIARSKII GOSUDARSTVENNYI PEDAGOGICHESKII INSTITUT. Uchenye Zapiski. t.26, vyp.1. Iz istorii Krasnoiarskogo kraia. Krasnoiarsk, 1964. pp. 101.

- Industries

ZUBKOV (ANATOLII IVANOVICH) and GORIZONTOV (BORIS BORISOVICH) Край великого будущего: развитие промышленных районов Красноярского края. Красноярск, Книжное Издательство, 1959. pp. 144. 19½см.

- Politics and government

IAKOVLEV (BORIS VLADIMIROVICH) Ленин в Красноярске: документальный очерк. Москва, Политиздат, 1965. pp. 207. bibliog. 20cm.

IZ istorii Krasnoiarskoi partiinoi organizatsii. Krasnoiarsk, 1968. pp. 157.

- Social conditions

USTINOV (VALENTIN ALEKSEEVICH) and DEEV (ALEKSANDR FEDOROVICH) Opyt primeneniia EVM v sotsiologicheskikh issledovaniiakh: na materialakh biudzhetov vremeni trudiashchikhsia Krasnoiarskogo kraia. Novosibirsk, 1967. pp. 243.

- Statistics

KRASNOYARSK (KRAI). Statisticheskoe Upravlenie. Народное хозяйство Красноярского края: статистический сборник. Красноярск, Книжное Издательство, 1967. pp. 259. 21½см.

KRAUS (KARL)

FIELD (FRANK) The last days of mankind: Karl Kraus and his Vienna. London, Macmillan, 1967. pp. xi, 280. bibliog. 21½cm.

IGGERS (WILMA ABELES) Karl Kraus: a Viennese critic of the twentieth century. The Hague, Nijhoff, 1967. pp. xvii, 248. bibliog. 23½cm.

KRAVCHINSKII (SERGEI MIKHAILOVICH)
See STEPNIAK (SERGEI) ps.

KREFELD

- Economic history

KISCH (HERBERT) Prussian mercantilism and the rise of the Krefeld silk industry: variations upon an eighteenth-century theme. Philadelphia, 1968. pp. 50. (American Philosophical Society. Transactions. New Series. vol. 58, part 7)

KREUTZER (RUDOLF)

KREUTZER (RUDOLF) Meine Ziele: ein Unternehmerschicksal in bewegter Zeit. München, Moderne Industrie, [1967]. pp. 161.

KROCK (ARTHUR)

KROCK (ARTHUR) Memoirs: intimate recollections of twelve American presidents from Theodore Roosevelt to Richard Nixon. London, 1970. pp. 508.

KROEBER (ALFRED LOUIS)

SCHNEIDER (D. M.) Rivers and Kroeber in the study of kinship. in Rivers (William Halse Rivers) Kinship and special organization. London, 1968.

KROKHMAL' (VIKTOR NIKOLAEVICH)

GARVI (PETR ABRAMOVICH) Revoliutsionnye siluety. New York, 1962. pp. 43. (Inter-University Project on the History of the Menshevik Movement)

KRONSTADT

- History - Revolt, 1921

TROTSKII (LEV DAVYDOVICH) Hue and cry over Kronstadt. London, [1938?]. pp. 10. (Socialist Labour League. Pamphlets)

KATKOV (G.) The Kronstadt rising. in St. Antony's Papers. No. 6. Soviet affairs; No. 2. London, 1959.

POLLACK (EMANUEL) The Kronstadt rebellion: the first armed revolt against the Soviets. New York, Philosophical Library, 1959. pp. (xi), 98. bibliog. 20½cm.

METT (IDA) La rivolta di Kronstadt: il ruolo della marina nella rivoluzione russa: pagine inedite di storia sovietica; (a cura dei Gruppi d'Azione Carlo Pisacane). Milano, Edit. Azione Comune, [1962]. pp. 107. 20½cm.

KOOL (FRITS) and OBERLAENDER (ERWIN) eds. Arbeiter-Demokratie oder Parteidiktatur. Olten, Walter, 1967. pp. 536. bibliog. 22cm. (Dokumente der Weltrevolution. Band 2)

METT (IDA) The Kronstadt commune. [London], Solidarity: for workers' power, [1967]. pp. xv, 56. bibliog. 25½cm. (Pamphlets. No. 27)

AVRICH (PAUL HENRY) Kronstadt 1921. Princeton, 1970. pp. 271. bibliog.

KRONSTEIN (HEINRICH)

KRONSTEIN (HEINRICH) Briefe an einen jungen Deutschen. 2nd ed. München, Beck, 1968. pp. 323. 20cm.

KROPOTKIN (PETR ALEKSEEVICH) Prince

KROPOTKIN (PETR ALEKSEEVICH) Prince. Записки революционера;...примечания Н. К. Лебедева, предисловие П.П. Парадизова. Москва, 1933. pp. 362. First published version of the Russian MS original; almost complete.

KROPOTKIN (PETR ALEKSEEVICH) Prince. Записки революционера; (предисловие и примечания В. А. Твардовской) Москва, Мысль, 1966. pp. 504. 21cm. Slightly abridged reprint of the 1933 Russian ed. of the "almost complete text" of the original MS in Russian.

HULSE (JAMES W.) Revolutionists in London: a study of five unorthodox socialists. Oxford, 1970. pp. 246. bibliog.

KRUGER (STEPHANUS JOHANNES PAULUS)

SCHREUDER (D.M.) Gladstone and Kruger: Liberal government and colonial 'home rule', 1880-85. London, 1969. pp. 558. bibliog.

KRUPP (ALFRED)

ALFRED Krupp: der Treuhänder eines deutschen Familienunternehmens; ein Beitrag zur westdeutschen Wirtschaftsgeschichte im 19. Jahrhundert; [and] Rheinische Bibliographie 1937; [by Hermann Corsten]. Düsseldorf, 1938. pp. 304. bibliog.

KRUPP FAMILY

ENGELMANN (BERNT) Krupp: Legenden und Wirklichkeit. München, [1969]. pp. 590. bibliog.

KRUPP FAMILY (Cont'd.)

MANCHESTER (WILLIAM) The arms of Krupp, 1587-1968. London, Joseph, 1969. pp. 1053. bibliog. 21½cm.

KRUPP VON BOHLEN UND HALBACH (ALFRIED FELIX ALWYN)

MANCHESTER (WILLIAM) The arms of Krupp, 1587-1968. London, Joseph, 1969. pp. 1053. bibliog. 21½cm.

KRUPSKAIA (NADEZHDA KONSTANTINOVNA)

OSOVSKII (EFIM GRIGOR'EVICH) Роль Н. К. Крупской в строительстве социалистической профессиональной школы. Москва, 1967. pp. 63.

GONCHAROV (N. K.) and others, eds. Педагогические взгляды и деятельность Н. К. Крупской. Москва, Просвещение, 1969. pp. 400. bibliog. 21½см.

RIADOM... Рядом с Лениным, воспоминания о Н. К. Крупской: к столетию со дня рождения. Москва, 1969. pp. 431.

KRZECZKOWSKI (KONSTANTY)

BALICKA-KOZŁOWSKA (HELENA) Konstanty Krzeczkowski: badacz życia społecznego. Warszawa, Książka i Wiedza, 1966. pp. 344. bibliog. 20cm. (Z Prac Instytutu Gospodarstwa Społecznego)

KSIĘŻARCZYK (FRANCISZEK)

KSIĘŻARCZYK (FRANCISZEK) Droga w ogniu. Warszawa, Ministerstwo Obrony Narodowej, 1966. pp. 332. 19½cm.

KUBAN'

- Economic history

KUBAN' za piat'desiat sovetskikh let. Krasnodar, 1967. pp. 350.

- History - Revolution, 1917-1921 - Campaigns

SKOBTSOV (D. E.) Три года революции и гражданской войны на Кубани. Париж, 1962. 2 vols (in 1).

- History - Revolution, 1917-1921 - Personal narratives

SKOBTSOV (D. E.) Три года революции и гражданской войны на Кубани. Париж, 1962. 2 vols (in 1).

KUBITSCHEK DE OLIVEIRA (JUSCELINO)

BOURNE (RICHARD) Political leaders of Latin America: Che Guevara, Alfredo Stroessner, Eduardo Frei Montalva, Juscelino Kubitschek, Carlos Lacerda, Eva Peron. New York, 1970. pp. 310, x. bibliog. First published by Penguin Books in 1969.

KUENZLER (JACOB)

ALAMUDDIN (IDA) Papa Kuenzler and the Armenians. London, 1970. pp. 167.

KUIBYSHEV (VALERIAN VLADIMIROVICH)

KUIBYSHEV (VALERIAN VLADIMIROVICH) Izbrannye stat'i i rechi, 1931-1934. Moskva, 1944. pp. 206.

SINIAEV (V. S.) V.V. Kuibyshev v Naryme. in Revoliutsionnoe dvizhenie v Sibiri i na Dal'nem Vostoke. vyp.2. Tomsk, 1963.

VALERIAN... Валериан Владимирович Куйбышев: биография. Москва, Политиздат, 1966. pp. 859. 20см.

EVSEEV (MIKHAIL PAVLOVICH) Вопросы социалистической экономики в работах В. В. Куйбышева. Томск, 1967. pp. 122.

KUIBYSHEV

- History

ISTORIIA... История Кишинева. Кишинев, Картя Молдовеняскэ, 1966. pp. 563. 24см.

GOROD... Город Куйбышев за 50 лет Советской власти: цифры и факты. Куйбышев, 1967. pp. 121.

KUIBYSHEV (OBLAST')

- Politics and government

PREBYVANIE... Пребывание руководителей партии и правительства в Куйбышевской области. [Куйбышев], Книжное Издательство, 1958. pp. 84. 20cm.

RUTBERG (GRIGORII NAUMOVICH) Самарские большевики в годы реакции и нового революционного подъема, 1907-1914 гг. Куйбышев, 1961. pp. 144.

KU-KLUX-KLAN

JACKSON (KENNETH THERRY) The Ku Klux Klan in the city, 1915-1930. New York, O.U.P., 1967. pp. xix, 326. 21cm. (Urban Life in America Series)

LOWE (DAVID) Ku Klux Klan: the invisible empire. New York, Norton. [1967]. pp. 128. 23½cm.

KU-KLUX-KLAN IN MISSISSIPPI

WHITEHEAD (DON) Attack on terror: the FBI against the Ku Klux Klan in Mississippi. New York, [1970]. pp. 321.

KULIAB BEYLIC

- History

IUSUPOV (SHARKI) Ocherki istorii Kuliabskogo bekstva v kontse XIX i nachale XX veka. Dushanbe, 1964. pp. 126. (Akademiia Nauk Tadzhikskoi SSR. Institut Istorii Arkheologii i Etnografii. Trudy. 41)

KULUNDA STEPPE

MICHKOV (VALENTIN ANDREEVICH) Каменская ГЭС на Оби и орошение Кулунды. Новосибирск, Академия Наук СССР, 1964. pp. 60. 20½см.

KULYAB
See KULIAB

KUMAO (HARADA) Baron
See HARADA (KUMAO) Baron

KUN (BÉLA)

KUN (BÉLÁné) Kun Béla: emlékezések. Budapest, Magvető, 1966. pp. 420, (30). 18cm.

KUNBAJA

- History

FLACH (PAUL) Geschichte von Kunbaja: Werden und Vergehen einer deutschen Gemeinde in der Nordbatschka. München, 1967. pp. 190. bibliog. 20½cm. (Landsmannschaft der Deutschen aus Ungarn in Bayern. Die Deutschen aus Ungarn. 2)

KUOMINTANG

DOMES (JUERGEN) Die Kuomintang-Herrschaft in China. [Hannover, 1970] pp. 116. bibliog. (Niedersächsische Landeszentrale für Politische Bildung. Schriftenreihe. Neue Weltmacht China. 2)

KURDS

KARADAGHY (MOHAMAD SALIH) Kurdistan and Kurds. [London], Kurdish Students Society in Europe, U.K. Branch, [1962]. pp. 20. 14cm.

BLAU (JOYCE) Le problème kurde: essai sociologique et historique. Bruxelles, the Centre, 1963. pp. 80. bibliog. 19cm. (Centre pour L'Étude des Problèmes du Monde Contemporain. Le Monde Musulman Contemporain: Initiations. 4)

KHALFIN (NAFTULA ARONOVICH) Борьба за Курдистан: курдский вопрос в международных отношениях XIX века. Москва, ИВЛ, 1963. pp. 171. bibliog. 20cm.

MAURIÈS (RENÉ) Le Kurdistan ou la mort. Paris, Laffont, [1967]. pp. 240. 20cm. (Enquêtes, Actualités)

CHATOEV (KHALIT MURADOVICH) Uchastie kurdov Sovetskogo Soiuza v Velikoi Otechestvennoi voine, 1941-1945 gg. Erevan, 1970. pp. 172.

KURDS IN IRAQ

KAMAL' (M. A.) Национально-освободительное движение в Иракском Курдистане, 1918-1932 гг. Баку, Азернешр, 1967. pp. 183. bibliog. 19½см.

KURDS IN RUSSIA

ARISTOVA (TAT'IANA FEDOROVNA) Kurdy Zakavkaz'ia: istoriko-etnograficheskii ocherk. Moskva, 1966. pp. 210.

KURELLA (ALFRED)

KURELLA (ALFRED) Unterwegs zu Lenin: Erinnerungen. Berlin, 1967. pp. 159.

KURGAN (OBLAST')

- History

GORELOV (VENEDIKT ALEKSEEVICH) Курганские большевики в революции 1905-1907 годов: исторический очерк. Челябинск, 1965. pp. 175.

OCHERKI... Очерки истории Курганской области. Челябинск, Южно-Уральское Книжное Издательство, 1968. pp. 480. 20см.

KURSK (OBLAST')

- History - Sources

REVOLIUTSIONNYE... Революционные события 1905-1907 гг. в Курской губернии: сборник документов и материалов. Курск, Книжное Издательство, 1955. pp. 268. 22см.

- History - Revolution, 1917-1921 - Sources

KURSKAIA... Курская губерния в годы иностранной военной интервенции и гражданской войны, 1918-1920. Воронеж, Центрально-Черноземное Книжное Издательство, 1967. pp. 359. 21½см.

KURSK, BATTLE OF, 1943

KOLTUNOV (G. A.) and SOLOV'EV (B. G.) Курская битва. Москва, 1970. pp. 396.

PAROT'KIN (I. V.) ed. Kurskaia bitva. Moskva, 1970. pp. 543.

KURSKAIA (ANNA SERGEEVNA)

KURSKAIA (ANNA SERGEEVNA) Пережитое. Москва, Московский Рабочий, 1965. pp. 259. 20см.

KURSKII (DMITRII IVANOVICH)

KURSKAIA (ANNA SERGEEVNA) Пережитое. Москва, Московский Рабочий, 1965. pp. 259. 20см.

KURZYNA (MIECZYSŁAW)

KURZYNA (MIECZYSŁAW) 20 lat próby; wybór z artykułów drukowanych w latach 1946-1964. Warszawa, PAX, 1965. pp. 278. 19cm.

KUTEPOV (ALEKSANDR PAVLOVICH)

GENERAL... Генерал Кутепов: сборник статей. Париж, 1934. pp. 378.

KUTUZOV (MIKHAIL ILARIONOVICH) Prince of Smolensk

MUN'KOV (NIKOLAI PETROVICH) M. I. Kutuzov - diplomat. Moskva, 1962. pp. 141.

KUWAIT

- Census

KUWAIT. Census, 1965. [Results of the population census of Kuwait for the year 1965. Kuwait, 1965? pp. 368]. Entirely in Arabic.

- Commerce

UNITED NATIONS. Economic and Social Office in Beirut. 1967. Foreign trade statistics of Kuwait, 1960-1963: reclassified according to the United Nations Standard International Trade Classification, 1960 revision (SITC, Revised) (ST/ESA/BEIRUT/5). New York, 1967. pp. 116.

- Constitution

FRANCE. Direction de la Documentation. La Documentation Française. Notes et Etudes Documentaires. No. 3,201. Constitution de l'Etat de Koweït. (11 novembre 1962). Paris, 1965. pp. 14.

- Economic conditions

UNITED STATES. International Commerce Bureau. Kuwait: a market for U.S. products. Washington, [1963]. pp. viii, 21.

BROER (HANS JOACHIM) Wirtschaftliche Entwicklung in Kuweit: ein Beispiel für die Rolle der Mentalität in einem Entwicklungsland. [Cologne, imprint], 1965. pp. 257. bibliog.

EL MALLAKH (RAGAEI) Economic development and regional cooperation: Kuwait. Chicago, U. of Chicago P., 1968. pp. xxi, 265. bibliog. 21½cm. (Chicago. University. Center for Middle Eastern Studies. Publications. No.3.)

- Nationalism

IRAQ. Ministry of Foreign Affairs. 1961. The truth about Kuwait. 1. [Baghdad], 1961. pp. 27.

- Social conditions

BROER (HANS JOACHIM) Wirtschaftliche Entwicklung in Kuweit: ein Beispiel für die Rolle der Mentalität in einem Entwicklungsland. [Cologne, imprint], 1965. pp. 257. bibliog.

- Statistics

GERMANY (BUNDESREPUBLIK). Statistiches Bundesamt. Länderkurzberichte: Kuwait. irreg., 1970 [1st issue] - Wiesbaden.

KUZNETSK BASIN

- Economic history

IZ istorii rabochego klassa v Kuzbasse, 1917-1965. вур.2: Материалы к научной конференции. Кемерово, 1966. pp. 189.

SAVOSTENKO (VIKTOR MIKHAILOVICH) Коммунисты Кузбасса - организаторы творческого подъема масс, 1929-1937 годы. Алма-Ата, 1967. pp. 163.

ZELKIN (IOSIF ISAAKOVICH) Кузнецкий угольный бассейн в годы Великой Отечественной войны. Москва, 1969. pp. 183. bibliog.

- Economic history - Sources

KUZBASS... Кузбасс в период восстановления народного хозяйства, 1920-1926 гг. Кемерово, Книжное Издательство, 1966. pp. 183. 20см.

- History - Sources

PARTIINYE... Партийные организации Кузбасса в годы Великой Отечественной войны, 1941-1945 гг. Кемерово, Книжное Издательство, 1962-65. 2 vols. 20см.

KVIRING (EMMANUIL IONOVICH)

BACHINSKII (PETR PAVLOVICH) and KVIRING (VIKTOR EMMANUILOVICH) Emmanuïl Ionovych Kvirinh. Kyïv, 1964. pp. 122.

BACHINSKII (PETR PAVLOVICH) and others Эммануил Ионович Квиринг. Москва, 1968. pp. 135.

KWAKIUTL INDIANS

ROHNER (RONALD P.) The people of Gilford: a contemporary Kwakiutl village. Ottawa, 1967. pp. xiv, 179. bibliog. 24½cm.

ROHNER (RONALD P.) and ROHNER (EVELYN C.) The Kwakiutl: Indians of British Columbia. New York, [1970]. pp. 111. bibliog.

KYOTO UNIVERSITY

- Center for Southeast Asian Studies

KYOTO. University. Center for Southeast Asian Studies. SEAS: the first five years, 1963-1968. Kyoto, 1969. pp. 50.

LA BARRE (GASPARD ALEXIS DE) Comte

[LA BARRE (GASPARD ALEXIS DE) Comte] Un colon sur sa plantation: [letters edited by] (G. Debien), Dakar, [the Université], 1959. pp. 185. 25cm. (Dakar. Université. Faculté des Lettres et Sciences Humaines. Section d'Histoire. Publications. No. 1)

LABELS

RESEARCH INSTITUTE FOR CONSUMER AFFAIRS. Informative labelling: the Swedish system. [London, the Institute, 1963]. pp. 16. 24cm.

DAVIS (ALEC) Package and print: the development of container and label design. London, Faber, 1967. pp. 112. bibliog 28cm.

LABOR-PROGRESSIVE PARTY
See COMMUNIST PARTY - Canada

LABORATORIES

- Bibliography

ORGANISATION FOR ECONOMIC CO-OPERATION AND DEVELOPMENT. 1962. Laboratories and lecture rooms: bibliography; [by the Netherlands Instituut voor Documentatie en Registratuur]. (Directorate for Scientific Affairs) [Paris], 1962. pp. 110. 24cm.

LABORATORY TECHNICANS

CANADA. Dominion Bureau of Statistics. Health and Welfare Division. Institutions Section. 1970. Health manpower in hospitals: laboratory technologists, 1961-68. Ottawa, 1970. pp. 21.

LABOUR AND LABOURING CLASSES

ROBERT, du Var. Histoire de la classe ouvrière, depuis l'esclave jusqu'au prolétaire de nos jours, etc. Paris, Michel, 1845-50. 4 vols. (in 2). 26½cm. Vol.1 is of the 3rd ed. 1850, vol.2 is of 1847 (2nd ed.?), vol.3 is of 1850 (3rd ed.?), vol.4 is of 1845.

GIRARDIN (ÉMILE DE) Questions de mon temps 1836 à 1856: questions économiques, tome 12. Paris, Serrière, 1858. pp. 528. 21½cm. Author's holograph dedication to Charles Bradlaugh on half-title page.

LARNED (J.N.) Talks about labor, and, Concerning the evolution of justice between the laborers and the capitalists. New York, 1876. pp. 162.

LEAVITT (JOHN McDOWELL) Kings of capital and knights of labor. New York, [1886]. pp. 681.

MARTEL (HENRI) Livre dédié aux classes ouvrières. new ed. Bruxelles, [imprint], 1892. pp. 132.

INDEPENDENT LABOUR PARTY. National Administrative Council. Labour catechism. [Manchester, imprint, 1895?] pp. 4. (Independent Labour Party. Caroline Martyn Memorial Library. No. 3)

GARRIGUET (LÉON) Régime du travail. Paris, 1908-1909. 2 vols. bibliog.

QUELCH (HARRY) Economics of labour: a lecture delivered...to the Economic Club of the Borough Polytechnic Institute, London. London, 1908. pp. 16.

ARGENTE (BALDOMERO) La esclavitud proletaria. Madrid, Renacimiento, 1913. pp. 260. 19cm.

[RED INTERNATIONAL OF LABOUR UNIONS]
The economic struggle of the working class in capitalist countries. n.p., [192-?]. fo. 45. Mimeographed copy, unpublished.

AS to politics: a discussion upon the relative importance of political action and of class-conscious economic action and the urgent nesesity of both; [edited by Daniel De Leon]. Glasgow, 1920. pp. 91.

NETTLAU (MAX) Verantwortlichkeit und Solidarität im Klassenkampf: ihre gegenwärtigen Grenzen und möglichen Ausdehnungen. Berlin, [1922?]. pp. 15.

YOUNG COMMUNIST INTERNATIONAL. Exekutiv-Komitee. The child of the worker: collection of facts and the remedy. Berlin, 1923. pp. 61.

KANITZ (OTTO FELIX) Das proletarische Kind in der bürgerlichen Gesellschaft. Jena, 1925. pp. 95.

NATIONAL MINORITY MOVEMENT. British imperialism: an outline of workers' conditions in the colonies. London, n.d. pp. 48.

RED INTERNATIONAL OF LABOUR UNIONS. Central Council. The tasks of the revolutionary trade union organisations in the work at the factories resolution of the VIIIth session of the... Council, etc. [London, 193-]. pp. 8.

RED INTERNATIONAL OF LABOUR UNIONS. Central Council. Position of the R.I.L.U. sections and their role in the leadership of the economic struggles and unemployed movement; theses adopted by the eighth session of the... Council, etc. London, [1932?]. pp. 25.

LENIN (VLADIMIR IL'ICH) The proletarian revolution and renegade Kautsky; [with explanatory notes]. London, 1935. pp. 110.

PIECK (WILHELM) Der Vormarsch zum Sozialismus: Bericht, Schlusswort und Resolution zum 1. Punkt der Tagesordnung des Kongresses: Rechenschaftsbericht über die Tätigkeit des Exekutivkomitees der Kommunistischen Internationale. Moskau, 1935; Milano 1967. pp. 131.

DORTMUND. Sozialakademie Dortmund. Internationale Tagung, [1958]. Stellung der Arbeitnehmer in der modernen Wirtschaftspolitik; herausgegeben von Hans Bayer. Berlin, Duncker und Humblot, [1959]. pp. 349. 23cm.

ORGANIZACION REGIONAL INTERAMERICANA DE TRABAJADORES. Report on the 5th continental congress of the Inter-American Regional Organization of Workers [ORIT] Rio de Janeiro, Brazil, 20-25 de agosto de 1961. Mexico City, 1961. pp. 103.

DAVYDOV (IURII NIKOLAEVICH) Труд и свобода. Москва, Высшая Школа, 1962. pp. 132. 19½см.

DEUTSCHE STIFTUNG FÜR ENTWICKLUNGSLÄNDER. Studienstelle. Der Übergang vom traditionellen zum industriellen Arbeitsverhalten in Entwicklungsländern: Bericht über eine Literaturstudie. Berlin, 1962. fo. iv, pp. 94. bibliog. 29½cm.

BAR-NIR (DOV) A short history of the international labour movement. Tel-Aviv, [1963]. pp. 25.

LABOUR AND LABOURING CLASSES (Cont'd.)

KOGON (EUGEN) Die Rolle der Arbeiterbewegung in der Kultur einer humanitären Welt. Wien, Verlag des Österreichischen Gewerkschaftsbundes, 1963. pp. 30. 20cm. (Aktuelle Probleme unserer Zeit)

GRIGOR'EV (GERASIM SERGEEVICH) Труд - первая человеческая потребность: диалектика процесса труда. Пермь, 1965. pp. 159.

TIMOFEEV (TIMUR TIMOFEEVICH) The working class is the leading force. [Moscow, 1965]. pp. 32.

ZAOSTROVTSEV (PAVEL GRIGOR'EVICH) О непосредственно общественном труде при социализме и коммунизме. Ленинград, Университет, 1965. pp. 115. 20cm.

ENGELS (FRIEDRICH) Anteil der Arbeit an der Menschwerdung des Affen. Berlin, 1966. pp. 21.

GOLOSOV (VIKTOR FEDOTOVICH) Труд и человек: очерки по истории возникновения и развития гуманистической идеологии трудящихся масс. Красноярск, 1966. pp. 510. bibliog.

CACÈRES (BÉNIGNO) compiler. Le mouvement ouvrier: [extract from contemporary documents and other writings]. Paris, Éditions du Seuil, [1967]. pp. 285. bibliog.

ELVERS (GERD) Gewerkschaftliche Einflussmöglichkeiten auf den Wirtschaftsablauf einer Marktwirtschaft ohne Berücksichtigung der aussenwirtschaftlichen Beziehungen. [Munich, imprint], 1967. pp. 234. bibliog.

FESTSCHRIFT für Otto Brenner zum 60. Geburtstag; dargebracht von Wolfgang Abendroth [and others]; herausgegeben von Peter von Oertzen. Frankfurt am Main, Europäische Verlagsanstalt, [1967]. pp. 492.

FISCHER (WOLFRAM) and BAJOR (GEORG) eds. Die soziale Frage: neuere Studien zur Lage der Fabrikarbeiter in den Frühphasen der Industrialisierung. Stuttgart, Koehler, [1967] pp. 324. bibliog. 20cm.

FOHLEN (CLAUDE) Le travail au XIXe siècle. Paris, Presses Universitaires de France, 1967. pp. 128. bibliog. 17½cm. (Que Sais-Je? No. 1289)

KRIVOGUZ (IGOR' MIKHAILOVICH) and MOLCHANOV (IURII LEONIDOVICH) Ленин и борьба за единство рабочего движения. Ленинград, Лениздат, 1967. pp. 295. 20cm.

MARIÁTEGUI (JOSÉ CARLOS) La organizacion del proletariado. Lima, Bandera Roja, 1967. pp. 264. 18cm.

HISTORY OF SOCIALISM YEAR BOOK; [published by] the Institute of the History of Socialism. [with articles in English, French or German] Prague, annual, 1968 (1st) to date.

ANDREEV (MIKHAIL VASIL'EVICH) Католицизм и проблемы современного рабочего и национально-освободительного движения. Москва, Мысль, 1968. pp. 343. bibliog. 19½см.

BUITER (JAN HENDRIK) Modern salariaat in wording een sociologische studie over posities en orientaties van werknemers. Rotterdam, 1968. pp. 316. bibliog. With English summary.

La CLASE obrera contemporanea: composicion, situacion, cambios; materiales del intercambio de opiniones organizado por Revista Internacional. [Buenos Aires], 1968. pp. 351.

EVOLUTION économique et salut de l'homme; session nationale des aumôniers de l'A.C.O. à Versailles, septembre 1967: ([by] M. Parodi and others). Paris, [1968]. pp. 348.

KUCZYNSKI (JUERGEN) Die Theorie der Lage der Arbeiter. Berlin, Akademie-Verlag, 1968. pp. viii, 167. 24cm. (Die Geschichte der Lage der Arbeiter unter dem Kapitalismus. Band 36)

LONGO (LUIGI) and BERLINGUER (ENRICO) L'unità del movimento operaio. [Rome], Editori Riuniti, [1968]. pp. 99. 18½cm. (Il Punto. 3)

PANE (LUIGI DAL) La storia come storia del lavoro: discorsi di concezione e di metodo. Bologna, [1968]. pp. 275. bibliog.

PROBLEMY... Ленинизм и некоторые проблемы рабочего движения: (материалы международной научной сессии "Ленинизм и некоторые проблемы рабочего движения", состоявшейся в Москве 12-15 апреля 1967 г.) Москва, Мысль, 1968. pp. 501. 20см

QUADERNI ROSSI. Luttes ouvrières et capitalisme d'aujourd'hui; traduit de l'Italien par Nicole Rouzet. Paris, Maspero, 1968. pp. 247. 21½cm. (Cahiers Libres. 118, 119)

RABOCHII... Рабочий класс в борьбе против империализма, за революционное обновление мира: материалы международной научной конференции "50-летие Октября и международный рабочий класс". Москва, Наука, 1968. pp. 312. 19½см.

RUPPRECHT (FRANK) Ideal und Wirklichkeit: das revolutionäre Gesellschaftsideal der Arbeiterklasse in historisch-materialistischer Sicht. Berlin, 1968. pp. 159. bibliog.

USENIN (VLADISLAV IVANOVICH) Социальное партнерство или классовая борьба? Москва, 1968. pp. 269.

AYMONE (FIORELLA) and others, eds. Sviluppo economico e rivoluzione: [a collection of most of the essays previously issued in a privately printed volume celebrating the 65th birthday of Lelio Basso]. Bari, 1969. pp. 255.

BOAS (GEORGE) Vox populi: essays in the history of an idea. Baltimore, 1969. pp. 292. bibliog.

BROWN (MICHAEL BARRATT) Opening the books. [Nottingham, 1969?]. unpaged. (Institute for Workers' Control. Pamphlet Series. No. 4)

CONGRES NATIONAL DU TRAVAIL, 2ND, PORT-AU-PRINCE, 1969. Actes. [Port-au-Prince, 1969]. 2 vols.

HUNTER (LAURENCE C.) and ROBERTSON (DONALD JAMES) Economics of wages and labour. London, Macmillan, 1969. pp. 544. bibliogs. 21½cm.

INTERNATIONAL LABOUR OFFICE. 1969. The I.L.O. in the service of social progress. Geneva, 1969. pp. 209.

LAFARGUE (PAUL) Le droit à la paresse; présentation nouvelle de Maurice Dommanget. Paris, 1969. pp. 157.

LENIN... Ленин и международное рабочее движение. Москва, 1969. pp. 606.

POSTER WORKSHOP. Calendar, 1970. [London, 1969?] 1 pamphlet (unpaged)

RABOCHII... Рабочий класс и антимонополистическая борьба: материалы Международной научной конференции "50-летие Октября и международный рабочий класс". Москва, 1969. pp. 478.

TENZLER (WOLFGANG) and BOGISCH (MANFRED) eds. Die richtige Seite: bürgerliche Stimmen zur Arbeiterbewegung. Berlin, [1969]. pp. 291. bibliog.

THOMAS (KONRAD) Arbeiter im Betrieb. Hannover, 1969. pp. 109. bibliog. (Niedersaechsische Landeszentrale für Politische Bildung. Schriftenreihe. Gesellschaft und Politik. 3)

CHERKASOV (GELII NIKOLAEVICH) Sotsiologiia truda i profsoiuzy. Moskva, 1970. pp. 190.

FLEISHER (BELTON MENDEL) Labor economics: theory and evidence. Englewood Cliffs, N.J., 1970. pp. 304. bibliog.

FOMIN (V. T.) ed. Osnovnye problemy rabochego dvizheniia v razvitykh kapitalisticheskikh stranakh. Moskva, 1970. pp. 287.

JACKSON (JOSEPH M.) Wages and labour economics. London, [1970]. pp. 244.

SELLIER (FRANÇOIS) and TIANO (ANDRÉ) Economie du travail. 2nd ed. Paris, [1970]. pp. 672. bibliogs.

SILVESTRE (PAUL) Le mouvement ouvrier jusqu'à la deuxieme guerre mondiale. Paris, [1970]. pp. 96. bibliog.

SINGH (VIDYA BHUSAN) ed. Role of labour in economic development;... [articles taken mainly from the Indian Journal of Labour]. Bombay, 1970. pp. 276.

SOTSIAL'NAIA deiatel'nost' OON: organizatsiia Ob"edinennykh Natsii i sotsial'nye problemy trudiashchikhsia. Moskva, 1970. pp. 232.

WILLIAMS (C. GLYN) Labor economics. New York, [1970]. pp. 489. bibliogs.

CHIARAVIGLIO (CURIO) Il lavoro e la proprietà universale: introduzione allo studio dei piani di sviluppo rivolti a valorizzare le forze di lavoro, etc. Firenze, 1971. pp. 255.

DEPPE (FRANK) Das Bewusstsein der Arbeiter: Studien zur politischen Soziologie des Arbeiterbewusstseins; mit einem Anhang von Helga Deppe-Wolfinger: Gewerkschaftliche Jugendbildung und politisches Bewusstsein. Köln, [1971]. pp. 359. bibliog.

FISHER (MALCOLM R.) The economic analysis of labour. London, [1971]. pp. 303.

ISSUES in labor policy; papers [presented at a symposium] in honor of Douglass Vincent Brown; edited by Stanley M. Jacks. Cambridge, Mass., [1971]. pp. 182.

KOZAK (VLADIMIR EVGEN'EVICH) Proizvoditel'nyi i neproizvoditel'nyi trud: ocherk teorii. Kiev, 1971. pp. 211.

- Bibliography

UNITED STATES. United States Information Service, London. Library. Books on labor and business management. London, 1960. pp. 54.

INTERNATIONAL LABOUR OFFICE. Library. 1968. Subject index to International Labour Documentation, 1957-1964. Boston, Mass., Hall, 1968. 2 vols.

CLARKE (R.O.) and others. Workers' participation and industrial democracy: a bibliography. n.p., 1969. pp.various.

- Congresses

LECTURE and conference on management, labour and the community; [held for the Stafford Cripps Memorial, Bristol, 22 November 1958]. n.p., [1958]. pp. 42.

CICLO DE ESTUDIOS SOBRE NORMAS NACIONALES E INTERNATIONALES DEL TRABAJO, LIMA, 1966. Informe del Ciclo...para funcionarios de la administracion del trabajo de países de America Latina...3-15 de octubre de 1966. (OIT/TAP/LAT/R.8) Ginebra, 1967. pp. 15. (International Labour Office. Development Programme: Technical Assistance Sector. [Latin America].

- Dictionaries and encyclopaedias

SACHSE (EKKEHARD) and FREYER (H.) eds. Taschenwörterbuch. Berlin, 1966. pp. 475. (Sozialistische Arbeitswissenschaft. [Publications].)

- Dwellings

MULLER (ÉMILE) and CACHEUX (ÉMILE) Les habitations ouvrières en tous pays; 2e édition, entièrement refondue; (with Supplément par Émile Cacheux). Paris, Baudry, 1889-[1903]. pp. 668, with vol. of plates and suppl. vol. bibliogs. 25½ - 28½cm.

- Education

GAY (NARCISO) Veladas del obrero ó la moral, la hijiene, la economía privada y las cuestiones economico-sociales de actualidad, puestas al alcance de las clases populares. Barcelona, Administración del Plus Ultra, 1857. pp. (iv). 245. 19cm.

CONGRÈS INTERNATIONAL DES MOUVEMENTS OUVRIERS CHRÉTIENS, 5E, ROME, 1961. Ve Congrès International des Mouvements Ouvriers Chrétiens, Rome, mai 1961: [proceedings]. Bruxelles, Fédération Internationale des Mouvements Ouvriers Chrétiens, 1961. pp. 96. 21½cm. (Tour d'Horizon. Numéros Spéciaux)

LABOUR AND LABOURING CLASSES - Education (Cont'd.)

COLLOQUE UNIVERSITÉ-INDUSTRIE, 1963, LYON. La promotion sociale;...par B. Lebigre [and others]. Paris, Dunod, 1965. pp. xv, 75. 24cm. (Bibliothèque d'Administration des Entreprises)

TETERUK (IVAN MYKYTOVYCH) Presa i trudove vykhovannia. Kyïv, 1965. pp. 99.

FREITAS (IVAN GONCALVES DE) Mão-de-obra industrial na Guanabara. Rio de Janeiro, Instituto de Ciências Sociais, 1967. pp. 106. bibliog. 21½cm. (Monografias. vol. 4)

MAHIEU (JAIME MARIA DE) Proletariado y cultura: los nuevos barbaros; Cultura para el proletariado; La cultura sindical. Buenos Aires, Maru, 1967. pp. 80. 19½cm.

NEGT (OSKAR) Soziologische Phantasie und exemplarisches Lernen: zur Theorie der Arbeiterbildung. Frankfurt am Main, Europäische Verlagsanstalt, [1968]. pp. 103. bibliog. 20½cm. (Theorie und Praxis der Gewerkschaften)

- Education - Audio-visual aids

CONGRESS OF INDUSTRIAL ORGANIZATIONS. Department of Education and Research. Film Division. Pamphlets. No. 176. Films for labor and how to use them. 4th ed. Washington, D.C., [1952]. pp. 45.

- Medical care

GIRON (MANUEL ANTONIO) Medicina social y trabajo; (primera Semana de Informacion Profesional). 2nd ed. Guatemala, [1958?]. pp. 56. bibliog. 16cm.

RASKIN (B. V.) Marks i Engel's o gegemonii proletariata v burzhuazno-demokraticheskoi revoliutsii, o polozhenii i zdorov'e trudizshchikhcia pri kapitalizme. in Kofman (F. Ia.) Sotsial'nye problemy zdravookhraneniia. Moskva, 1967.

FELSTEIN (IVOR) Snakes and ladders: medical and social aspects of modern management. London, 1971. pp. 197.

- Research

DERBER (MILTON) Research in labor problems in the United States. New York, Random House, [1967]. pp. vii 184. 18½cm. (Studies in Labor)

- Statistics

VANDERVELDE (ÉMILE) Les bureaux de statistique du travail. Bruxelles, Weissenbruch, 1893. pp. 20. 25½cm. (Extrait de la Revue de Belgique)

[U.K. Ministry of Labour]. Oversea Division. Statistics Branch. Oversea information. Southport, 1939 (nos. 1-9); 1940 (nos. 1-8); 1941 (nos. 1-7).

UNITED STATES. Labor Statistics Bureau. BLS Reports. No. 302. How to establish current reporting of employment, hours, and earnings in developing countries. Washington, 1966. pp. vi, 150.

KASHKAREVA (LIUDMILA NIKOLAEVNA) Организация К. Марксом и Ф. Энгельсом рабочей статистики труда; под редакцией проф. Петрова А. И. Москва, 1968. pp. 75.

RUSSIA (U.S.S.R.) Tsentral'noe Statisticheskoe Upravlenie. 1968. Труд в СССР: статистический сборник. Москва, 1968. pp. 341.

· Abyssinia

INTERNATIONAL LABOUR OFFICE. Development Programme: Technical Assistance Sector. [Ethiopia]. R.9. Report to the government of Ethiopia on labour administration. (ILO/TAP/Ethiopia/R.9) Geneva, 1968. pp. 47.

Africa - Bibliography

UNITED STATES. Labor Statistics Bureau. Bulletins. No. 1473. Bibliography on labor in Africa, 1960-64. Washington, 1965. pp. v, 121.

· Africa, East

NEULOH (OTTO) ed. Der ostafrikanische Industriearbeiter zwischen Shamba und Maschine: Untersuchungen über den sozialen und personalen Wandel in Ostafrika. München, [1969]. pp. 422. (Ifo-Institut für Wirtschaftsforschung. Afrika-Studien. 43)

· Africa, North

RABOCHEE... Рабочее движение в странах Азии и Северной Африки на современном этапе. Москва, 1969. pp. 366.

· Algeria

INTERNATIONAL LABOUR OFFICE. Development Programme: Technical Assistance Sector. [Algeria]. R.12. Rapport au gouvernement de l'Algérie sur l'administration du travail. (OIT/TAP/Algérie/R.12) Genève, 1969. pp. 132.

- Algeria - Education

INTERNATIONAL LABOUR OFFICE. Regular Programme of Technical Assistance. [Algeria]. R.10. Rapport sur l'éducation ouvrière en République Algérienne Démocratique et Populaire. (OIT/OTA/Algérie/R.10) Genève, 1967. pp. 29. 30cm.

- America, Latin

ORGANIZACIÓN REGIONAL INTERAMERICANA DE TRABAJADORES and INTERNATIONAL CONFEDERATION OF FREE TRADE UNIONS. Publicaciones Especiales. La Alianza para el Progreso y los trabajadores. México, ORIT, [1961?]. pp. (14). 22½cm.

RUIZ-MARCOS (JOSÉ M.) Unternehmensreform in Lateinamerika: Einstellung der lateinamerikanischen Unternehmer zur Unternehmensreform. Hannover, Verlag für Literatur und Zeitgeschehen, [1966]. pp. 109. bibliog. 23½cm. (Friedrich-Ebert Stiftung. Forschungsinstitut. Schriftenreihe. A. Sozialwissenschaftliche Schriften)

CICLO DE ESTUDIOS SOBRE NORMAS NACIONALES E INTERNATIONALES DEL TRABAJO, LIMA, 1966. Informe del Ciclo...para funcionarios de la administracion del trabajo de países de America Latina...3-15 de octubre de 1966. (OIT/TAP/LAT/R.8) Ginebra, 1967. pp. 15. (International Labour Office. Development Programme: Technical Assistance Sector. [Latin America]. R.8)

RAMA (CARLOS M.) Historia del movimiento obrero y social latinoamericano contemporaneo. Buenos Aires, Editorial Palestra, 1967. pp. 143. 19½cm. (Colección Historia Viva)

ROMUALDI (SERAFINO) Presidents and peons: recollections of a labor ambassador in Latin America. New York, Funk & Wagnalls, [1967]. pp. xvi, 524. 22½cm.

ALBA (VÍCTOR) Politics and the labor movement in Latin America. Stanford, U.P., 1968. pp. (iii), 404. bibliog. 23cm.

PROLETARIAT... Пролетариат Латинской Америки. Москва, 1968. pp. 430. bibliog.

- America, Latin - Bibliography

AMERICAN INSTITUTE FOR MARXIST STUDIES. Bibliographical Series. No. 1. A bibliography of the history of the Latin-American labor and trade union movements. rev. ed. New York, [1967]. fo. 18.

RAMA (CARLOS M.) Die Arbeiterbewegung in Lateinamerika: Chronologie und Bibliographie 1492-1966. Bad Homburg, [1967]. pp. 294. bibliog. (Kontaktprogramm zur Sozialwissenschaftlichen Forschung in Lateinamerika. Beiträge zur Soziologie und Sozialkunde Lateinamerikas. Band 1)

- Arabia

THE ROLE of the workers: in the struggle of British-occupied Arabia. London, [1966?] pp. 13.

- Argentine Republic

BIALET MASSE (JUAN) El estado de las clases obreras argentinas a comienzos del siglo; prologo y notas de Luis A. Despontin; [reprint of work originally published 1904]. Cordoba, Argentina, 1968. pp. 665.

PAN (LUIS) Política y gremialismo en la era de Frondizi. Buenos Aires, Monserrat, 1963. pp. 95. 18cm.

PANETTIERI (JOSE) Los trabajadores en tiempos de la inmigracion masiva en Argentina, 1870-1910. La Plata, [1966]. pp. 195. bibliog. (La Plata. Universidad Nacional. Facultad de Humanidades y Ciencias de la Educacion. Departamento de Historia. Monografias y Tesis. 8)

ABAD DE SANTILLÁN (DIEGO) Estudios sobre la Argentina: la inmigracion europea; trayectoria del movimiento obrero argentino; la Argentina de mañana. Buenos Aires, Cajica, [1967]. pp. 444. bibliog. 14cm. (Biblioteca Cajica de Cultura Universal. 32)

IPARRAGUIRRE (HILDA) and PIANETTO (OFELIA) La organización de la clase obrera en Córdoba, 1870-1895. Córdoba, Universidad Nacional de Córdoba, Dirección General de Publicaciones, 1968. pp. 67. bibliog. 23cm. (Separata de la Revista de la Universidad Nacional de Córdoba)

SPALDING (HOBART A.) La clase trabajadora argentina: documentos para su historia, 1890/1912. Buenos Aires, 1970. pp. 639.

- Armenia

ALLAKHVERDIAN (SERGEI ALEKSANDROVICH) Роль рабочего класса в победе колхозного строя в Армении, 1927-1935. Ереван, АН Армянской ССР, 1969. pp. 208. bibliog. 20см.

- Asia

RABOCHEE... Рабочее движение в странах Азии и Северной Африки на современном этапе. Москва, 1969. pp. 366.

- Australia

HUGHES (WILLIAM MORRIS) The case for Labor: [reprint of the first edition published in 1910]. Sydney, 1970. pp. 144, xiii-xxxiv.

MINORITY MOVEMENT [AUSTRALIA]. Tramway Section. Five years of reformism: the case for militant organisation among tram workers: a critical analysis of the fruits of the policy of reformism and arbitration in the tramway industry, and a statement of the M.M. policy to overcome it. [Sydney?, 1934?]. pp. 6.

McFARLANE (BRUCE) Professor Irvine's economics in Australian labour history, 1913-1933. Canberra, Australian Society for the Study of Labour History, 1966. pp. 71. 25½cm.

AUSTRALIAN SOCIETY FOR THE STUDY OF LABOUR HISTORY. Labour and the gold fields. Canberra, 1968. pp. 35.

HILL (E. F.) Democracy for whom? n.p., [1968?] unpaged.

HARRIS (JOE) The bitter fight: (a pictorial history of the Australian labor movement). Brisbane, [1970]. pp. 310. bibliog.

- Australia - Queensland

HARRIS (W.J.H.) First steps: Queensland workers' moves towards political expression, 1857-1893. Canberra, Australian Society for the Study of Labour History, 1966. pp. 34. 25½cm.

- Austria

HEINISCH (THEODOR) Österreichs Arbeiter für die Unabhängigkeit, 1934 bis 1945. Wien, [1968]. pp. 39. (Dokumentationsarchiv des Österreichischen Widerstandes. Monographien zur Zeitgeschichte)

- Austria - Bibliography

STEINER (HERBERT) 1923-, compiler. Bibliographie zur Geschichte der österreichischen Arbeiterbewegung, 1867-(1945). Wien, 1962-[70]. 3 vols.

LABOUR AND LABOURING CLASSES (Cont'd.)

- Austria - Periodicals - Bibliography

EBERLEIN (ALFRED) compiler. Die Presse der Arbeiterklasse und der sozialen Bewegungen von den dreissiger Jahren des 19. Jahrhunderts bis zum Jahre 1967: Bibliographie, etc. Frankfurt/Main 1968-70. 5 vols. (Deutsche Akademie der Wissenschaften zu Berlin. Institut für Geschichte. Abteilung Dokumente und Materialien zur Geschichte der Deutschen Arbeiterbewegung. Archivalische Forschungen, etc. Band 6)

- Azerbaijan

RABOCHEE... Рабочее движение в Азербайджане в годы нового революционного подъема, 1910-1914 гг.: документы и материалы. Баку, 1962. 2 vols.

IZ... Из истории советского рабочего класса Азербайджана. Баку, АН АзССР, 1964. pp. 256. 25cm.

AZERBAIDZHAN... Азербайджан в годы первой русской революции: сборник статей. Баку, АН АзССР, 1965. pp. 258. 21см.

GADZHINSKII (DZHAMO) В огне революционной борьбы: промысловые и заводские комиссии в бакинском нефтепромышленном районе в годы первой русской революции. Баку, Академия Наук Азербайджанской ССР, 1965. pp. 180. 19½см.

DZEBRAILOV (N. F.) Rabochii klass Azerbaidzhana v gody semiletki, 1959-1965. in Iz istorii rabochego klassa SSSR. Moskva, 1968.

STEL'NIK (BETIA IAKOVLEVNA) Бакинский пролетариат в годы реакции, 1907-1910 гг. Баку, 1969. pp. 202.

- Bashkir Republic

IVANKOV (V. P.) ed. Из истории рабочего класса Башкирской АССР. Уфа, 1967. pp. 91. 21½см.

- Belgium

BRUSSELS. Comité de Patronage des Habitations Ouvrières et des Institutions de Prévoyance. L'habitation ouvrière; notice sur les facilités et avantages concédés aux travailleurs. Bruxelles, 1893. pp. 15. In French and Flemish.

SCHAERBEEK. Conseil Communal. Commission Spéciale. Habitations ouvrières: conclusions;...rapport de la Commission Spéciale. Bruxelles, 1898. pp. 19.

FOYER SCHAERBEEKOIS S.A. Historique de la Société. Schaerbeek, 1905. pp. 64.

LOUVAIN. Bureau de Bienfaisance. Notice sur les maisons ouvrieres. Louvain, 1905. pp. 7.

ROYER (ÉMILE) Prose pour Jean Prolo. Bruxelles, Milot, 1908. pp. viii, 370. 19cm.

BERTRAND (LOUIS PHILIPPE) L'ouvrier belge depuis un siècle. Bruxelles, 1924. pp. 448.

GESCHIEDENIS van de socialistische arbeidersbeweging in België; (hoofdredakteur: Jan Dhondt). Antwerpen, 1960-[68]. 20 pts. (in 1 vol.). bibliog.

BAYER-LOTHE (JEANNINE) Documents relatifs au mouvement ouvrier dans la province de Namur au XIXe siècle. Leuven, Nauwelaerts, 1967 in progress. 24cm. (Centre Interuniversitaire d'Histoire Contemporaine. Cahiers. 45)

JOYE (PIERRE) and LEWIN (ROSINE) L'Église et le mouvement ouvrier en Belgique. Bruxelles, Société Populaire d'Éditions, 1967. pp. 385. 21cm.

OUKHOW (CATHERINE) compiler. Documents relatifs à l'histoire de la première Internationale en Wallonie. Leuven, Nauwelaerts, 1967. pp. lv, 376. 24cm. (Centre Interuniversitaire d'Histoire Contemporaine. Cahiers. 47)

TOUSSAINT (FRANCINE) and others. Essai d'étude du comportement electoral des travailleurs lors des élections aux conseils d'entreprise de 1963. Bruxelles, the Centre, 1967. 3 vols. 25cm. (Centre National d'Études et de Recherches Socio-Économiques. Collection Économie Concertée)

- Belgium - Education

BUSET (MAX) and DELSINNE (LÉON) L'éducation ouvrière en Belgique. Bruxelles, Centrale d'Éducation Ouvrière, [1931?]. pp. 40. 24cm.

- Belgium - Statistics

BELGIUM. Institut National de Statistique. Statistiques sociales. q., 1970, no.1- Bruxelles.

- Bessarabia

ESAULENKO (A. S.) and others, eds. Bor'ba trudiashchikhsia Bessarabii za svoe osvobozhdenie i vossoedinenie s sovetskoi rodinoi, 1918-1940 gg. Kishinev, 1970. pp. 735.

- Bolivia

ANTEZANA (FERNANDO) Los braceros bolivianos: drama humano y sangria nacional. La Paz, Icthus, [1966]. pp. 44. 21cm.

LORA (GUILLERMO) Historia del movimiento obrero boliviano. La Paz, 1967 in progress. bibliog.

- Brazil

SIMÃO (AZIS) Sindicato e estado: suas relações na formação do proletariado de São Paulo. São Paulo, Dominus, Editôra da Universidade, 1966. pp. 245. bibliog. 20½cm. (Ciências Sociais. 7)

FREITAS (IVAN GONCALVES DE) Mão-de-obra industrial na Guanabara. Rio de Janeiro, Instituto de Ciências Sociais, 1967. pp. 106. bibliog. 21½cm. (Monografias. vol. 4)

MARTINS RODRIGUES (LEONCIO) La clase obrera en el Brasil. Buenos Aires, [1969]. pp. 148.

FISCHLOWITZ (ESTANISLAU) Valorização dos recursos humanos do Brasil. Rio de Janeiro, 1970. pp. 421.

VINHAS (MOISES) Estudos sôbre o proletariado brasileiro. Rio de Janeiro, 1970. pp. 279. bibliog.

- Bulgaria

TISHEV (DIMITŬR) Za sŭiuz mezhdu rabotnitsite i selianite, 1917-1923 g. Sofiia, 1964. pp. 192.

CHERNIAVSKII (GEORGII IOSIFOVICH) Рабочее движение в Болгарии в период частичной стабилизации капитализма, 1925-1929 годы. Харьков, 1968. pp. 200. 21½см.

- Cameroons

STOECKER (HELMUTH) ed. Kamerun unter deutscher Kolonialherrschaft: Studien. Berlin, 1960-68. 2 vols. 24cm. (Berlin. Humboldt-Universität. Institut für Allgemeine Geschichte. Schriftenreihe. Bände 5 and 12)

- Canada

CONGRÈS DES RELATIONS INDUSTRIELLES DE L'UNIVERSITÉ LAVAL. (Études préparées pour le congrès). Québec, annual, 1946 (1er cong.) to date, with gap (1948, 3e)

CANADA. Parliament. Senate. Standing Committee on Immigration and Labour. Proceedings. Ottawa, irreg., June 16th 1966 (27th Parl., 1st session, no.1) to date. 25cm.

CANADA. Parliament. House of Commons. Standing Committee on Labour and Employment. Minutes of proceedings and evidence. Ottawa. irreg., Feb.22/May 17-Dec.13 1966 (27th Parl., 1st session nos. 1-10); Jan.26/Feb.1 - March 14/19 1968 (2nd session, nos.1-13). 25cm.

CANADA. 1966. Vital partner of workers and employers. (Department of Labour) Ottawa, 1966. pp. (16). 21½cm. x 28cm.

CANADA. Parliament. House of Commons. Standing Committee on Labour, Manpower and Immigration. Minutes of proceedings and evidence. Ottawa, irreg., Oct. 17 1968 (28th Parl., 1st session, no. 1) to date.

- Canada - Bibliography

CANADA. Department of Public Printing and Stationery. Publications Branch. Sectional Catalogues. No. 10. Canadian government publications relating to labour; Publications du gouvernement canadien sur les sujets relatifs au travail. 2nd ed. Ottawa, 1963. pp. 336. In English and French.

- Canada - Statistics

CANADA. Dominion Bureau of Statistics. Labour Division. 1969. Inventory of federal government company and establishment surveys collecting labour data, 1968. Ottawa, 1969. pp. (128). 28cm.

CANADA. Statistics Canada. Notes on labour statistics. a., 1971 (1st issue)- Ottawa.

- Canada - Alberta

ALBERTA. Bureau of Statistics. Working conditions survey: Alberta. a., Ag 1968 - Edmonton.

- Canada - British Columbia

BRITISH COLUMBIA. 1964. Excerpts from an address during debate on the speech from the throne by the Honourable L.R. Peterson, Minister of Labour, Minister of Education, first session of the 27th Legislative Assembly...January 29th, 1964. Victoria, B.C., 1964. pp. (iii), 14.

BRITISH COLUMBIA. Department of Labour. 1967. History of British Columbia Department of Labour (1917-1967). Victoria, 1967. pp.(13).

- Canada - New Brunswick

[NEW BRUNSWICK. Department of Labour. 1960.] [Address by] Hon. K.J. Webber, Minister of Labour, Legislative Assembly, November 24, 1960. [Fredericton, 1960]. fo. 13.

- Canada - Nova Scotia

NOVA SCOTIA. Department of Labour. Annual report. a., 1968/9- Halifax, N.S.

ECONOMIC AND LABOUR STATISTICS FOR NOVA SCOTIA; [pd. by] Economics and Research Division, Nova Scotia Department of Labour. q., 1969, 3rd quarter; susp. pbln. Halifax, N.S.

- Caucasus

SHIGABUDINOV (MAGOMED SHIGABUDINOVICH) Борьба рабочих Северного Кавказа накануне и в период революции 1905-1907 гг. Махачкала, 1964. pp. 183. bibliog. 22cm.

GALOIAN (GALUST ANUSHAVANOVICH) Rabochee dvizhenie i natsional'nyi vopros v Zakavkaz'e, 1900-1922. Erevan. 1969. pp. 507.

- Chile

RECABARREN (LUÍS EMILIO) Obras escogidas, Tomo 1. Los albores de la revolución social en Chile; Ricos y pobres; La Rusia obrera y campesina. Santiago de Chile, 1965. pp. 191. bibliog.

TRONCOSO ROJAS (HERNÁN) Participación popular y gobierno popular. Santiago de Chile, [Editorial Orbe], 1965. pp. 268. 19cm..

LANDSBERGER (HENRY A.) and CANITROT M. (FERNANDO) Iglesia, intelectuales y campesinos: la huelga campesina de Molina. Santiago de Chile, Pacífico, [1967]. pp. 358. 26cm.

TELLA (TORCUATO S. DI) and others. Sindicato y comunidad: dos tipos de estructura sindical latinoamericana. [Santiago de Chile], Universidad de Chile, Instituto de Sociología, 1967. pp. 389. 19½cm. (Serie Naranja. Sociología)

- China

MALONE (CECIL L'ESTRANGE) The slavery of China:...the facts about the coolie wages which the capitalists maintain to undercut western conditions and which the British forces are being used to defend. London, [193-?]. pp. 8.

CHESNEAUX (JEAN) The Chinese labor movement, 1919-1927; translated from the French by H.M. Wright. Stanford, Stanford U.P., 1968. pp. xvi, 574. bibliog. 23cm.

RABOCHEE dvizhenie v Kitae 1945-1949 gg.; dokumenty i materialy. Moskva, 1969. pp. 243. bibliog.

- Chuvash Republic

LENIN i trudiashchiesia Chuvashii: dokumenty, materialy, vospominaniia. Cheboksary, 1970. pp. 359. bibliog.

LABOUR AND LABOURING CLASSES (Cont'd.)

- Colombia

URRUTIA (MIGUEL) The development of the Colombian labor movement. New Haven, 1969. pp. 297. bibliog.

COLOMBIA. Ministerio de Trabajo y Seguridad Social. Memoria. a., 1970- Bogota.

- Communist countries

RUKOVODIASHCHAIA rol' rabochego klassa v sotsialisticheskikh stranakh. Moskva, 1970. pp. 341.

- Congo (Kinshasa)

UNITED STATES. Labor Statistics Bureau. Foreign labor information: labor in the Belgian Congo. [Washington], 1959. pp. 35.

- Cuba

RIVERO MUNIZ (JOSE) El movimiento obrero durante la primera intervencion: apuntes para le historia del proletariado en Cuba. [Santa Clara], 1961. pp. 223.

VENTOCILLA (ELEODORO) Cuba 1967: la situación de los trabajadores. México, 1967. pp. 142. 18½cm.

MESA LAGO (CARMELO) The labor sector and socialist distribution in Cuba. New York, Praeger, 1968. pp. xix, 250. bibliog. 23½cm. (Praeger Special Studies in International Economics and Development)

- Czechoslovakia

BOJOVALO se o léta budoucí: sborník dokumentů k dějinám dělnického hnutí a KSČ ve Východočeském kraji v letech 1917 až 1921. Havlíčkův Brod, Krajské Nakladatelství, 1961. pp. 151. 21cm.

KARLOVA UNIVERSITA. Acta Universitatis Carolinae. 1961. Philosophica et Historica. O revoluční jednotu československého dělnického hnutí: sborník statí pracovníku katedry dějin KSČ filosofické fakulty, etc. Praha, Universita Karlova, 1961. pp. 223. With Russian and German summaries.

JORDÁN (FRANTIŠEK) Problémy rozkolu dělnického hnutív českých zemích na umírněné a radikály, 1879-1889. Praha, Státní Pedagogické Nakladatelství, 1965. pp. 173. bibliog. 23½cm. (Brno. Universita Spisy. 105) With German summary.

VEBER (VÁCLAV) Postavení dělnické třídy v českých zemích, 1924-1929. Praha, Práce, 1965. pp. 198. bibliog. 20cm.

MALÝ (KAREL) Policejní a soudní perzekuce dělnické třídy v druhé polovině 19.století v Čechách. Praha, Academia Věd, 1967. pp. 282. 20½cm. (Československá Akademie Věd. Pravněhistoricka Knižnice. sv.8) With German summary.

HISTORY OF SOCIALISM YEAR BOOK; [published by] the Institute of the History of Socialism. [with articles in English, French or German] Prague, annual, 1968 (1st) to date.

- Dahomey

INTERNATIONAL LABOUR OFFICE. Development Programme: Technical Assistance Sector. [Dahomey]. R.10. Rapport au gouvernement de la République du Dahomey sur l'administration du travail. (OIT/TAP/Dahomey/R.10) Genève, 1967. pp. 66.

- Denmark

NIELSEN (VILLY) and SVANE (VIGGO) eds. Arbejdsforhold: historisk og aktuelt. 3rd ed. [Copenhagen?], Arbejdernes Oplysningsforbund i Danmark, 1966. pp. 323. bibliog. 21cm.

- East (Far East) - Congresses

CONGRESS OF THE TOILERS OF THE FAR EAST, 1ST, MOSCOW AND LENINGRAD, 1922. The First Congress of the Toilers of the Far East; held in Moscow, January 21st-February 1st, 1922; closing session in Petrograd, February 2nd 1922; [reprint of the work originally published in Petrograd, 1922]. London, 1970. pp. 242.

- Egypt

BADR (GHASSAN ZAKI) Probleme der Industrialisierung Agyptens: Rekrutierung und Weiterbildung neuer Arbeitskräfte. Winterthur, Keller, 1965. pp. 88. bibliog. 22½cm.

- Europe

ABENDROTH (WOLFGANG) Sozialgeschichte der europäischen Arbeiterbewegung. Frankfurt, Suhrkamp, [1965]. pp. 192. bibliog. 17½cm.

GORZ (ANDRÉ) Réforme et révolution. Paris, [1969]. pp. 248.

MITCHELL (HARVEY) and STEARNS (PETER N.) Workers and protest: the European labor movement, the working classes and the origins of social democracy, 1890-1914. Itasca, Ill., [1971]. pp. 250. bibliog.

- European Economic Community countries

CIAMAGA (LUCJAN) Podział pracy w przemyśle krajów Europejskiej Wspólnoty Gospodarczej: wybrane problemy specjalizacji i lokalizacji produkcji. Warszawa, 1969. pp. 235. bibliog. (Polska Akademia Nauk. Komitet Przestrzennego Zagospodarowania Kraju. Studia. t.30) With Russian and English summaries.

- Far Eastern Republic

AVDEEVA (N. A.) Ukreplenie soiuza rabochikh i krest'ian v Dal'nevostochnoi respublike. in Iz istorii sovetskogo Dal'nego Vostoka. Khabarovsk, 1963.

- France

LA FARELLE (F. FÉLIX DE) Plan d'une réorganisation disciplinaire des classes industrielles en France, précédé et suivi d'études historiques sur les formes anciennes et modernes du travail humain. Paris, Guilhaumin, 1842. pp. 246.

WIBRATTE (F.) Le travail et la misère: lettres d'un campagnard. Paris, Garnier, 1848. pp. 160. 22½cm.

RONDELET (ANTONIN) Les réunions publiques et les congrès d'ouvriers. Paris, Lecoffre, 1869. pp. 304. 18½cm.

INTERNATIONAL WORKING MEN'S ASSOCIATION. Conseil Fédéral Parisien. Procès de l'Association Internationale des Travailleurs: première et deuxième commissions du bureau de Paris. 2nd ed. Paris, 1870; [Paris, Editions d'Histoire Sociale, 1968]. pp. 212. Facsimile reprint.

TROTSKII (LEV DAVYDOVICH) Die Fragen der Arbeiterbewegung in Frankreich und die Kommunistische Internationale: zwei Reden, gehalten auf der Konferenz der Erweiterten Exekutive...1922 in Moskau. Hamburg, 1922. pp. 31. (Communist International. Bibliothek. 30)

VINCENT (Sir CHARLES EDWARD HOWARD) The popular front in France: a short history of the French working class from 1934 to 1938. London, [1938]. pp. 55.

NAVILLE (PIERRE) La classe ouvrière et le régime gaulliste. Paris, Etudes et Documentation Internationales, [1964]. pp. 489. 21cm. (Questions du Socialisme 1.)

BÉRÉGI (THÉODORE) A travers l'histoire du mouvement ouvrier. [Paris, P.T.T. Syndicaliste, 1967]. pp. 198. bibliog. 21cm. (P.T.T. Syndicaliste. No.200. Supplément)

BRANCIARD (MICHEL) Société française et luttes de classes, 1789-(1967). Lyon, Chronique Sociale de France, [1967]. 2 vols. (in 1). bibliogs. 22cm. (Chronique Sociale de France. L Essentiel. 2,3.)

GRYSON (EMILE) Les premières manifestations du socialisme et la fondation de la section locale du P.O.B. à Comines, 1894-1914; édition... par Jean-Marie Duvosquel. Comines, 1967. pp. 72.

BRON (JEAN) Histoire du mouvement ouvrier français. Paris, Les Editions Ouvrières, [1968 in progress].

GOSSEZ (R.) Les ouvriers de Paris. [Paris, 1968 in progress]. bibliog. (Société d'Histoire de la Révolution de 1848. Bibliothèque. Tome 24)

KESSEL (PATRICK) Le prolétariat français. [Paris], Plon, [1968 in progress] 20cm.

BENOIT (JOSEPH) Confessions d'un prolétaire, Lyon 1871; présentées par Maurice Moissonnier. Paris, Éditions Sociales, [1968]. pp. 310. 21cm.

COHN-BENDIT (DANIEL) and COHN-BENDIT (GABRIEL) Le gauchisme: remède à la maladie sénile du communisme. Paris, Éditions du Seuil, [1968]. pp. 271.

COHN-BENDIT (DANIEL) and COHN-BENDIT (GABRIEL) Obsolete Communism: the left-wing alternative. London, Deutsch, 1968. pp. 256. 19½cm.

IBARROLA (JÉSUS) Structures d'une population active de type traditionnel, Grenoble 1848. Paris, Mouton, [1968]. pp. 127. bibliog. 22½cm. (Grenoble. Université. Centre de Recherche d'Histoire Économique, Sociale et Institutionnelle. Série Histoire Sociale. vol. 3)

KAËS (RENÉ) Images de la culture chez les ouvriers français. Paris. Cujas, [1968]. pp. x,347. bibliog. 24cm. (Temps de l'Histoire)

MAUPEOU-ABBOUD (NICOLE DE) Les blousons bleus: étude sociologique des jeunes ouvriers de la région parisienne. Paris, Colin, [1968]. pp. 261. (Paris. Université. Institut des Sciences Sociales du Travail. Centre de Recherches. Collection Sciences Sociales du Travail. 3)

PERGEAUX (YVES) ed. Réalités du troisième âge: enquêtes sur les ouvriers retraités du bâtiment et des travaux publics. Paris, Dunod, 1968. pp. xiii, 223. bibliog. 24cm.

RAUCH (MALTE J.) and SCHIRMBECK (SAMUEL H.) Die Barrikaden von Paris: der Aufstand der französischen Arbeiter und Studenten. Frankfurt a. M., [1968]. pp. 227.

WILLIAMS (GWYN ALFRED) Artisans and Sans-Culottes: popular movements in France and Britain during the French revolution. London, Arnold, 1968. pp. viii, 128. bibliog. 20cm. (Foundations of Modern History)

BOUVIER-AJAM (MAURICE) Histoire du travail en France depuis la révolution. Paris, Pichon & Durand-Auzias, 1969. pp. 604. 23cm.

GEISMAR (ALAIN) and others. Vers la guerre civile. Paris, Éditions et Publications Premières, [1969]. pp. 440. 22½cm. (Collection Stratégies)

GRETTON (JOHN) Students and workers: an analytical account of dissent in France, May-June, 1968. London, Macdonald, 1969. pp. 320. bibliog. 21½cm.

GUIN (YANNICK) La commune de Nantes. Paris, 1969. pp. 176.

KULSTEIN (DAVID I.) Napoleon III and the working class: a study of government propaganda under the Second Empire. [Los Angeles], California State Colleges, [1969]. pp. xii, 250. bibliog. 19½cm.

LEUWERS (JEAN MARIE) Un peuple se dresse: luttes ouvrières, mai 1968. Paris, [1969]. pp. 370.

MALLET (SERGE) La nouvelle classe ouvrière. [4th ed.] Paris, [1969]. pp. 253. bibliog.

MANCEAU (HENRI) Des luttes ardennaises. Paris, [1969]. pp. 231. bibliog.

Un OUVRIER parle: enquête; ([edited by] Juliette Minces). Paris, Éditions du Seuil, [1969]. pp. 85. 18cm.

AGULHON (MAURICE) Une ville ouvrière au temps du socialisme utopique: Toulon de 1815 à 1851. Paris, [1970]. pp. 368. bibliog. (Paris. Ecole Pratique des Hautes Etudes. Section des Sciences Economiques et Sociales. Centre de Recherches Historiques. Civilisations et Sociétés. 18)

L'OUVRIER français: enquête nationale auprès de 1116 ouvriers d'industrie; ([by] Gérard Adam [and others]). Paris, 1970. pp. 276. (Fondation Nationale des Sciences Politiques. Travaux et Recherches de Science Politique. 13)

LABOUR AND LABOURING CLASSES (Cont'd.)

- France - Education

GUIEYSSE (CHARLES) Les universités populaires et le mouvement ouvrier. Paris, Cahiers de la Quinzaine, [1901]. pp. 75. 19cm. (3me Série. 2me cahier).

CAHIERS DE LA QUINZAINE. 3me Série. 10me [and] 20me Cahiers. Les universités populaires, 1900-1901. Paris, [1902]. 2 vols. (in 1). 19cm.

- Galicia (Eastern Europe)

MAKAIEV (VOLODYMYR KYRYLOVYCH) Робітничий клас Галичини в останній третині XIX ст. Львів, 1968. pp. 205.

- Germany

RIEHL (WILHELM HEINRICH) Die deutsche Arbeit. Stuttgart, Cotta, 1861. pp. x, 330. 20cm.

STUTTGART. Arbeiter-Sekretariat. Jahresbericht. Stuttgart, 1897, 1898.

ERKELENZ (ANTON) Die freiheitlich-nationale Arbeiterbewegung. München, Buchhandlung Nationalverein, 1910. pp. 139. 22cm. (Politische Handbücherei. Heft 1)

CHRISTLICH-NATIONALE ARBEITER-BEWEGUNG. Ausschuss. Die christlich-nationale Arbeiterbewegung im neuen Deutschland. Köln, 1917. pp. 48

LENSCH (PAUL) Was wird aus der deutschen Arbeiterbewegung?: Partei oder Gewerkschaften?; herausgegeben von "Aufbau und Werden", Gesellschaft für praktische Volksaufklärung und Steigerung der nationalen Arbeitskraft. Berlin, [1920]. pp. 27.

LABOUR RESEARCH DEPARTMENT. Labour White Papers. No. 21. British capital and German workers. London, [1926?].

[KRUEGER (OSKAR) ed.] 2. Mai 1933: die Befreiung des deutschen Arbeiters. München, 1934. pp. 216.

EDEL (FRITZ) German labour service. Berlin, 1937. pp. 31. (Terramare Office. Publications. No. 6)

DORTMUND. Sozialakademie Dortmund. Internationale Tagung, [1958]. Stellung der Arbeitnehmer in der modernen Wirtschaftspolitik; herausgegeben von Hans Bayer. Berlin, Duncker und Humblot, [1959]. pp. 349. 23cm.

ENGELS (FRIEDRICH) Die preussische Militärfrage und die deutsche Arbeiterpartei. Berlin, Dietz, 1963. pp. 72. 20cm. (Kleine Bücherei des Marxismus-Leninismus)

ULBRICHT (WALTER) Vergangenheit und Zukunft der deutschen Arbeiterbewegung: Referat auf der 2.Tagung des ZK der SED 10. bis 12.April 1963. Berlin, Dietz, 1963. pp. 64. 20cm.

BOROZNIAK (A. I.) Rabochii klass Rurskoi oblasti v bor'be protiv kapitalisticheskikh monopolii v 1946-1947 gg. in Moscow. Moskovskii Gosudarstvennyi Pedagogicheskii Institut. Uchenye Zapiski. no.205. Moskva, 1964.

CONZE (WERNER) Möglichkeiten und Grenzen der liberalen Arbeiterbewegung in Deutschland: das Beispiel Schulze-Delitzschs. Heidelberg, Winter, 1965. pp. 28. 25cm. (Heidelberg. Akademie der Wissenschaften. Philosophisch-historische Klasse. Sitzungsberichte. 1965. 2.Abhandlung)

FISHER (WALTER) Die Fürther Arbeiterbewegung von ihren Anfängen bis 1870. [Erlangen?, 1965?]. pp. 218 bibliog. 20½cm.

GOTTSCHOL (RUDOLF) and GOTTSCHOL (ANNELIES) Die Görlitzer Arbeiterbewegung in der Zeit von 1871 bis 1903. Görlitz, Rat, 1965. pp. 164. bibliog. 23cm. (Görlitz. Ratsarchiv. Beiträge zur Geschichte der Görlitzer Arbeiterbewegung. 2)

LEMMNITZ (ALFRED) Staatsmonopolistische Regulierung und Klassenkampf in Westdeutschland. Berlin, Dietz, 1965. pp. 158. 20cm. (Sozialistische Einheitspartei Deutschlands. Zentralkomitee. Abteilung Propaganda. Sozialistische Bildungshefte zum Studium des Programms der SED)

GRUENER (ERNST) Die hallesche Arbeiterbewegung von ihren Anfängen bis zum Jahre 1914. [Halle, 1966 in progress]. (Sozialistische Einheitspartei Deutschlands. Stadtleitung Halle. Kommission zur Erforschung der Geschichte der örtlichen Arbeiterbewegung. Aus der Geschichte der Halleschen Arbeiterbewegung. 3)

CONZE (WERNER) and GROH (DIETER) Die Arbeiterbewegung in der nationalen Bewegung: die deutsche Sozialdemokratie vor, während und nach der Reichsgründung. Stuttgart, Klett, [1966]. pp. 133. 21cm. (Arbeitskreis für Moderne Sozialgeschichte. Industrielle Welt. Band 6)

FESTSCHRIFT für Otto Brenner zum 60. Geburtstag; dargebracht von Wolfgang Abendroth [and others]; herausgegeben von Peter von Oertzen. Frankfurt am Main, Europäische Verlagsanstalt, [1967]. pp. 492.

HABEDANK (HEINZ) Um Mitbestimmung und Nationalisierung während der Novemberrevolution und im Frühjahr 1919. Berlin, [1967]. pp. 360.

HAUSER (ROLF) and MEYER (GERHARD) Aktion Mitbestimmung: der Kampf der Arbeiterklasse Westdeutschlands um Mitbestimmung in der Wirtschaft. Berlin, Staatsverlag der Deutschen Demokratischen Republik, 1967. pp. 275. 21cm.

KALEX (GUENTER) Wirtschaftsunternehmen der Arbeiterbewegung in Westdeutschland. Berlin, Dietz, 1967. pp. 236. 20cm.

NEUBAUER (WALTER F.) Selbsteinschätzung und Idealeinschätzung junger Arbeiter als Gegenstand sozialpsychologischer Verhaltensforschung. [Erlangen-Nürnberg, 1967?]. pp. 261. bibliog.

SCHARMANN (THEODOR) ed. Lebensplanung und Lebensgestaltung junger Arbeiter aus der Metallindustrie der Bundesrepublik und der Schweiz, etc. Bern, Huber, [1967]. pp. 368. bibliogs. 23cm. (Munich. Deutscher Jugendinstitut, and Erlangen. Universität. Institut für Wirtschafts- und Sozialpsychologie. Der Junge Arbeiter: Studien zu einer Genealogie des Industriebürgers. Band 1).

SCHNEIDER (LOTHAR) Der Arbeiterhaushalt im 18. und 19. Jahrhundert: dargestellt am Beispiel des Heim- und Fabrikarbeiters. Berlin Duncker & Humblot, [1967]. pp. 166. 23cm. (Beiträge zur Okonomie von Haushalt und Verbrauch. Heft 4)

SCHULT (JOHANNES) Geschichte der Hamburger Arbeiter, 1890-1919. Hannover, Dietz, [1967]. pp. 371. bibliog.

ECKERT (HUGO) Liberal- oder Sozialdemokratie: Frühgeschichte der Nürnberger Arbeiterbewegung. Stuttgart, [1968]. pp. 336. bibliog. (Arbeitskreis für Moderne Sozialgeschichte. Industrielle Welt. Band 9)

KLOCKHAUS (RUTH) Junge Arbeiter als Staatsbürger: Ergebnisse einer empirischen Untersuchung über Industriearbeiter in der Bundesrepublik. [Nuremberg, 1968?]. pp. 212. bibliog.

KUCZYNSKI (JUERGEN) Studien zur Geschichte der Lage des arbeitenden Kindes in Deutschland von 1700 bis zur Gegenwart. Berlin, Akademie-Verlag, 1968. pp. (vii), 372. 24cm. (Die Geschichte der Lage der Arbeiter unter dem Kapitalismus. Band 19)

OBERMANN (KARL) Joseph Weydemeyer: ein Lebensbild, 1818-1866. Berlin, Dietz, 1968. pp. 470. 20cm.

PIECHOCKI (WERNER) Der Volkspark als Kultur- und Bildungsstätte der halleschen Arbeiter 1907-1914 Halle, 1968. pp. 46. bibliog. (Sozialistische Einheitspartei Deutschlands. Stadtleitung Halle. Kommission zur Erforschung der Geschichte der Örtlichen Arbeiterbewegung. Aus der Geschichte der Halleschen Arbeiterbewegung. 6)

SCHMITZ (HEINRICH KARL) Anfänge und Entwicklung der Arbeiterbewegung im Raum Düsseldorf: die Arbeiterbewegung in Düsseldorf 1859-1878 und ihre Auswirkungen im linken Niederrheingebiet. Hannover, [1968]. pp. 167. bibliog. (Friedrich-Ebert-Stiftung. Forschungsinstitut. Schriftenreihe. B. Historisch-politische Schriften)

SCHNEIDER (DIETER) and KUDA (RUDOLF) Arbeiterräte in der Novemberrevolution: Ideen, Wirkungen, Dokumente. Frankfurt a.M., [1968]. pp. 173. bibliog.

EZHOV (VSEVOLOD DMITRIEVICH) Рабочее движение в Западной Германии, 1945-1968. Москва, 1969. pp. 383. bibliog.

GREBING (HELGA) The history of the German labour movement: a survey;...with a chapter on foreign policy by Mary Saran; (translated [from the German] by Edith Körner). London, Wolff, 1969. pp. 227. bibliog. 21½cm.

HOPPE (RUTH) ed. Dokumente zur Geschichte der Lage des arbeitenden Kindes in Deutschland von 1700 bis zur Gegenwart. Berlin, Akademie-Verlag, 1969. pp. xii, 347. 24cm. (Die Geschichte der Lage der Arbeiter unter dem Kapitalismus. Band 20)

SAL'KOVSKII (OLEG VLADIMIROVICH) Социальная политика буржуазии и пролетариат: по материалам ФРГ. Москва, 1969. pp. 319.

SCHNORBUS (AXEL) Arbeit und Sozialordnung in Bayern vor dem Ersten Weltkrieg 1890-1914. München, 1969. pp. 269. bibliog. (Munich. Stadtarchiv. Neue Schriftenreihe. Band 36)

DOWE (DIETER) Aktion und Organisation: Arbeiterbewegung, sozialistische und kommunistische Bewegung in der preussischen Rheinprovinz 1820-1852. Hannover, [1970]. pp. 341. bibliog. (Friedrich-Ebert-Stiftung. Forschungsinstitut. Schriftenreihe. Band 78)

SCHMIERER (WOLFGANG) Von der Arbeiterbildung zur Arbeiterpolitik: die Anfänge der Arbeiterbewegung in Württemberg 1862/63-1878. Hannover, [1970]. pp. 309. bibliog. (Friedrich-Ebert-Stiftung. Forschungsinstitut. Schriftenreihe. B. Historisch-politische Schriften)

DEPPE (FRANK) Das Bewusstsein der Arbeiter: Studien zur politischen Soziologie des Arbeiterbewusstseins; mit einem Anhang von Helga Deppe-Wolfinger: Gewerkschaftliche Jugendbildung und politisches Bewusstsein. Köln, [1971]. pp. 359. bibliog.

- Germany - Education

HITPASS (JOSEF) and others. Einstellungen der Industriearbeiterschaft zu höherer Bildung: eine Motivuntersuchung. Ratingen, [1965]. pp. 78. bibliog.

- Germany - Periodicals

ALLGEMEINE ARBEITER-ZEITUNG. Die Allgemeine Frankfurter Arbeiter-Zeitung von 1848: (unveränderter Neudruck); mit einer Einführung von Max Quark; (aus Grünbergs Archiv für die Geschichte des Sozialismus, Bd. XI, 1925). Frankfurt a.M., 1968. pp. various.

- Germany - Periodicals - Bibliography

EBERLEIN (ALFRED) compiler. Die Presse der Arbeiterklasse und der sozialen Bewegungen von den dreissiger Jahren des 19. Jahrhunderts bis zum Jahre 1967: Bibliographie, etc. Frankfurt/Main 1968-70. 5 vols. (Deutsche Akademie der Wissenschaften zu Berlin. Institut für Geschichte. Abteilung Dokumente und Materialien zur Geschichte der Deutschen Arbeiterbewegung. Archivalische Forschungen, etc. Band 6)

- Germany - Prussia

VOLKMANN (HEINRICH) Die Arbeiterfrage im preussischen Abgeordnetenhaus 1848-1869. Berlin, Duncker und Humblot, [1968]. pp. 218. bibliog. 23cm. (Schriften zur Wirtschafts- und Sozialgeschichte. Band 13)

LABOUR AND LABOURING CLASSES (Cont'd.)

- Germany, Eastern

BEZIRKSKOMMISSION ZUR ERFORSCHUNG DER GESCHICHTE DER ARBEITERBEWEGUNG IM BEZIRK HALLE and SOZIALISTISCHE EINHEITSPARTEI DEUTSCHLANDS. Bezirksleitung Halle. Dokumente und Materialien zur Geschichte der Arbeiterbewegung im Bezirk Halle. Halle, 1965 in progress.

SIEGEL (HORST) Der Kampf um die Schaffung antifaschistisch-demokratischer Selbstverwaltungsorgane in Halle, 1945/1946. [Halle, 1965]. pp. 56. bibliog. (Sozialistische Einheitspartei Deutschlands.Stadtleitung Halle. Kommission zur Erforschung der Geschichte der örtlichen Arbeiterbewegung. Aus der Geschichte der Halleschen Arbeiterbewegung. 2)

SOZIALISTISCHE ARBEITSWISSENSCHAFT (formerly Arbeitsökonomik); theoretische Zeitschrift für arbeitswissenschaftliche Disziplinen; ([published by] Zentrales Forschungsinstitut für Arbeit des Staatlichen Amtes für Arbeit und Löhne beim Ministerrat der DDR). Berlin, 8 a yr., 1969 (13.Jhrg.) to date. 23½cm.

ARBEITERKLASSE und Kultur; [edited by] Marianne Lange. Berlin, 1969. pp. 334.

EGGERATH (WERNER) Unruh im engen Tal: Reportage über Ruhla und seine Schrittmacher. Berlin, 1969. pp. 208.

- Germany, Eastern - Education

KINDZORRA (OTTO) and SANDER (HORST) Arbeiterklasse und Wissenschaft: die Gewerkschaften und der Verflechtungsprozess von Wissenschaft und Produktion. Berlin, 1969. pp. 52.

- Ghana

GHANA. Labour Department. 1961. Information on labour matters, Ghana. [Accra], 1961. pp. (99).

- Ghana - Education

INTERNATIONAL LABOUR OFFICE. Regular Programme of Technical Assistance. [Ghana]. R.12. Report on workers' education in Ghana. (ILO/OTA/Ghana/R.12) Geneva, 1968. pp. 28.

- Guatemala

MEJIA (MEDARDO) El movimiento obrero en la revolución de octubre. Guatemala, 1949. pp. 219. 23cm.

GUATEMALA. Statutes, etc. 1958. Reglamento del Departamento Administrativo de Trabajo. Guatemala, 1958. pp. 29. 16cm.

GUATEMALA. Statutes, etc. 1959. Reglamento interior del Consejo Tecnico del Ministerio de Trabajo y Bienestar Social. Guatemala, 1960. pp. 12. 16cm.

- Hungary

VILÁGHY (ERNŐ) Die Sozialstruktur der ungarischen Industrie. Göttingen, 1969. pp. 203. bibliog.

BORSÁNYI (GYÖRGY) "Munkát! Kenyeret!": a proletariátus tömegmozgalmai Magyarországon, a gazdasági válság éveiben, 1929-1933. Budapest, 1971. pp. 305.

- Hungary - Education

SZILÁGYI (JÁNOS) Munkásosztályunk általános műveltségi helyzete 1919-1945 között. Budapest Akadémiai Kiadó, 1964. pp. 132. 20cm. (Magyar Tudományos Akadémia. Történettudományi Intézet. Értekezések a Történeti Tudományok Köréből. Új Sorozat. 35)

- Hungary - Statistics

HUNGARY, 1961. A munkások helyzete az iparvállalatoknál. (Statisztikai Időszaki Közlemények. 41. kötet) Budapest, 1961. pp. 207,(2). 28cm. With English summary.

HUNGARY. Központi Statisztikai Hivatal Statisztikai Időszaki Közlemények. 52. kötet. A munkások szakképzettsége és kereseti arányai. Budapest, 1963. pp. 122. 28½cm. With English summary.

HUNGARY. 1966. A munkások és alkalmazottak száma, keresete a munka jellege szerint: 15,000 háztartás adatai. (Statisztikai Időszaki Közlemények. 85. kötet) Budapest, 1966. pp. 91, (2). 28cm. With English summary.

HUNGARY. Központi Statisztikai Hivatal. Statisztikai Időszaki Közlemények. 82. kötet. Az ipari munkások létszámarányai, munkakörülményei és bérhelyzete. Budapest, 1966. pp. 341,(2). With English summary.

- India

EMPLOYEES' ASSOCIATION. Reforms enquiry and labour representation. Calcutta, 1925. s. sh.

INDIA. Labour Investigation Committee. 1946. Main report. Delhi, 1946. pp. 468.

CURRENT problems of labour in India. [Delhi, Manager of Publications, 1957.] pp. 64.

INDIA. Parliament. Lok Sabha. Secretariat. 1959. India and the International Labour Organisation. New Delhi, 1959. pp. 18.

BRICKE (DIETER) Die Arbeitspolitik im System der indischen Wirtschafts- und Sozialpolitik und ihre weltanschauliche Beeinflussung: ein Beitrag zum Problem der sozialpolitischen Ergänzungsnotwendigkeit bei der wirtschaftlichen Entfaltung von Entwicklungsländern. [Mannheim, imprint], 1965. pp. 234. bibliog.

INDIAN NATIONAL TRADE UNION CONGRESS. Labour policies and programmes in fourth five year plan: (INTUC suggestions on). New Delhi, 1965. pp. 66. 24cm.

RAMANUJAM (G.) From the babul tree: story of Indian labour. New Delhi, Indian National Trade Union Congress, 1967. pp. xvi, 252. 21½cm.

SINGH (VIDYA BHUSAN) An introduction to the study of Indian labour problems. Agra, Agarwala, 1967. pp. iv, 194, v. 21cm.

DATAR (B.N.) Labour economics. Bombay, 1968. pp. 303.

GHOSH (SRI KANTA) Impact of industrialisation on law and order. Bombay, 1968. pp. 200. bibliog.

VAID (KANWAL N.) The new worker: a study in Kota. London, Asia Publishing House, [1968]. pp. xvi, 196. bibliog. 21cm.

INDIA. National Commission on Labour. 1969. Indian worker: a changing profile, 1947-1967. Delhi, 1969. pp. 232.

INDIA. National Commission on Labour. 1969. Indian worker: an industry-wise review, 1947-1968. Delhi, 1969. pp. 210. bibliogs.

INDIA. National Commission on Labour. 1969. Report. Delhi, 1969. pp. 503, 178.

INDIA. Study Group for Tribal Labour (Agricultural and Industrial). 1969. Report. Delhi, 1969. pp. 120. bibliog.

SINGH (VIDYA BHUSAN) ed. Role of labour in economic development;... [articles taken mainly from the Indian Journal of Labour]. Bombay, 1970. pp. 276.

- India - Congresses

INDIA. Department of Labour and Employment. 1968 Tripartite conclusions 1942-1967. [2nd ed.] [Delhi, 1968.] pp. 351.

- India - Education

MAHARASHTRA. 1964. Bombay Labour Institute: prospectus. Bombay, 1964. pp. 29.

INDIA. Committee on Workers' Education. 1968. Report. Delhi, 1968. pp. 66.

- India - Research

LABOUR research in India; [papers from two seminars organized by the Indian Society of Labour Economics in 1961 and 1962]; edited by V.B.Singh. Bombay, 1970. pp. 225.

- India - Statistics

INDIA. Labour Bureau. Labour statistics under the Annual survey of industries: Summary report. a., 1963- Simla.

- India - Gujarat

GUJARAT. Working Group on Labour, Welfare, Social Welfare and Welfare of Backward Classes. 1968 - . Fourth five year plan, 1969-70 to 1973-74: report. [Ahmedabad, 1968?] in progress.

- India - Mysore

KATTI (A. P.) Seasonal in-migrants in rural Shimoga, Mysore State. Dharwar, [1966]. pp. 101.

- Iran

SHAMIDE (ALI ISMAILOVICH) Rabochee i profsoiuznoe dvizhenie v Irane posle vtoroi mirovoi voiny, 1946-1953 gg. Baku, 1965. pp. 212.

- Ireland (Republic)

IRISH WORKERS' LEAGUE. Executive Committee. Irish workers' road to freedom: manifesto. Dublin, 1949. 1 pamphlet (unpaged).

HILLERY (BRIAN) and LYNCH (PATRICK) Ireland in the International Labour Organisation. Dublin, Department of Labour, 1969. pp. 49.

- Italy

CHIESA (PIETRO) and MURIALDI (GINO) Il Partito Socialista e l'organizzazione economica del proletariato industriale: ([papers read to the] Congresso Nazionale del Partito Socialista Italiano, Imola 6-7-8 settembre 1902). Imola, [imprint], 1902. pp. 49.

AMBRIS (ALCESTE DE) L'unità operaia e i tradimenti confederali. Parma, S.E.L.I., 1913; [Milan, Feltrinelli, 196-] pp. 72. 17cm. (Biblioteca de l'Internazionale. Serie Pubblicazioni d'Attualità. N.4) Facsimile reprint.

PARTITO COMUNISTA ITALIANO. Bollettino... settembre-ottobre 1925. [Rome, imprint], 1925;[Milan], Feltrinelli, [196-]. Facsimile reprint.

RUSSELL (G.) and BRANNAN (HUGH) The Italian revolution. [Glasgow, 1943?] pp. 32.

GHISLERI (ARCANGELO) Giuseppe Mazzini e gli operai. Roma, 1946. pp. 111.

GORI (PIETRO) Pagine di vagabondaggio. 3rd ed. Milano, Editrice Moderna, 1948. pp. 96. 17½cm. (Opere. vol. 10)

NAPOLITANO (GIORGIO) Movimento operaio e industria di stato. Roma, Editori Riuniti, [1962]. pp. 68. 21cm. (Nostro Tempo).

CAPITINI MACCABRUNI (NICLA) La Camera del Lavoro nella vita politica e amministrativa fiorentina dalle origini al 1900. Firenze, Olschki, [1965]. pp. 397. bibliog. 21cm. (Unione Regionale delle Provincie Toscane. Biblioteca di Storia Toscana Moderna e Contemporanea. Studi e Documenti. 2)

CASSINIS (UMBERTO) Aspetti e problemi del mercato del lavoro nel Mezzogiorno. Milano, Giuffrè, 1965. pp. vii, 115. 24cm. (Associazione per lo Sviluppo dell'Industria nel Mezzogiorno. Centro per gli Studi sullo Sviluppo Economico. Collana Francesco Giordani)

CARRIA (RENZO DEL) Proletari senza rivoluzione: storia delle classi subalterne italiane dal 1860 al 1950. Milano, Edizioni Oriente, 1966. 2 vols. (in 1). bibliog. 21½cm.

MAITAN (LIVIO) Il movimento operaio in una fase critica, etc. Roma, Samonà e Savelli, [1966]. pp. 275. 18½cm.

BONICELLI (GAETANO) Lavoro e concilio: i problemi del lavoro alla luce del Vaticano II. Milano, Opera della Regalità di N.S. Gesù Cristo, 1967. pp. 117. 17cm. (Temi Conciliari. 3)

GIUDICE (RICCARDO DEL) Scritti di storia e diritto del lavoro. Roma, Edizioni Ricerche, 1967. pp. 297. 24cm.

LABOUR AND LABOURING CLASSES - Italy (Cont'd.)

IL MOVIMENTO operaio bergamasco: Carlo Zilocchi, Memorie di un socialista, 1905-1965; Circolo Socialista (Bergamo), Verbale Assemblee Riunioni 1904-1913; La scissione di Livorno nelle carte di A. Piccinini. Milano, Edizioni del Gallo, 1967. pp. (x), 333. 29cm. (Strumenti di Lavoro: Archivi del Movimento Operaio. N. 16)

RICOSSA (SERGIO) and others. Il problema degli investimenti e i suoi riflessi sulla occupazione operaia. [Turin], Centro di Ricerca e Documentazione Luigi Einaudi, [1967]. pp. 83. 20cm.

AMENDOLA (GIORGIO) La classe operaia italiana. Roma, [1968]. pp. 213.

BRAVO (GIAN MARIO) Torino operaia: mondo del lavoro e idee sociali nell'età di Carlo Alberto. Torino, 1968. pp. 300. (Fondazione Luigi Einaudi. Studi. 2)

GIBELLI (ANTONIO) Genova operaia nella Resistenza. Firenze, Istituto Storico della Resistenza in Liguria, 1968. pp. 371. 22cm. (Contributi.c.2)

LOPUKHOV (BORIS REMOVICH) Фашизм и рабочее движение в Италии, 1919-1929 гг. Москва, 1968. pp. 413. bibliog.

FLAMINI (GIANNI) Operai nell'Italia industriale. Bologna, [1969]. pp. 199. bibliog.

KHOLODKOVSKII (KIRILL GEORGIEVICH) Рабочее движение в Италии, 1959-1963. Москва, 1969. pp. 397.

PARTITO COMUNISTA ITALIANO. Conferenza Nazionale Operaia, 5a, 1970. La conferenza operaia, Milano, 28 febbraio-1 marzo 1970. [Rome], 1970. pp. 405.

- Italy - Bibliography

ENTE PER LA STORIA DEL SOCIALISMO E DEL MOVIMENTO OPERAIO ITALIANO. Centro Bibliografico. Bibliografia del socialismo e del movimento operaio italiano. Roma, Edizioni E.S.M.O.L., 1956-68. 2 vols. (in 6). 24½cm.

- Italy - Education

I LAVORATORI studenti: testimonianze raccolte a Torino; a cura di Giorgina Levi Arian [and others]. Torino, [1969]. pp. 350.

- Japan

RINDL (PETER) Die gehorsamen Rebellen: Arbeiter in Japan. Wien, [1968]. pp. 231. bibliog.

BALLON (ROBERT J.) ed. The Japanese employee. Tokyo, [1969]. pp. 317.

IDEMITSU (SAZO) Capitalism of working people. n. p., [1969]. pp. 113.

EVANS (ROBERT) The labor economies of Japan and the United States. New York, 1971. pp. 276. bibliog.

- Japan - Statistics

JAPAN INSTITUTE OF LABOUR. 1967. Japan's labor statistics. Tokyo, 1967. pp. 178.

- Karelia

BALAGUROV (IAKOV ALEKSEEVICH) Фабрично-заводские рабочие дореволюционной Карелии. Петрозаводск, 1968. pp. 214. bibliog.

- Kazakstan

SARMURZIN (ALTAI GAISIEVICH) Partiinoe rukovadstvo dvizheniem za kommunisticheskii trud v Kazakhstane, noiabr' 1958-1963gg. Alma-Ata, 1964. pp. 169.

- Kirghizia

ISTORIIA sovetskogo rabochego klassa Kirgizstana. Frunze, 1966. pp. 488.

- Komi Republic

STARTSEV (VLADIMIR VASIL'EVICH) Rabochii klass Komi ASSR v bor'be za kommunizm; pod...redaktsiei i s predisloviem...V.N. Davydova. Syktyvkar, 1965. pp. 53.

- Kuwait - Education

INTERNATIONAL LABOUR OFFICE. Regular Programme of Technical Assistance. [Kuwait]. R.2. Report on workers' education in Kuwait. (ILO/OTA/Kuwait/R.2) Geneva, 1967. pp. 26. 30cm.

INTERNATIONAL LABOUR OFFICE. Development Programme: Technical Assistance Sector. [Kuwait]. R.3. Report to the government of Kuwait on workers' education. (ILO/TAP/Kuwait/R.3) Geneva, 1969. pp. 24.

- Liberia

UNITED STATES. Labor Statistics Bureau. Foreign Labor Information. Labor in Liberia. [Washington] 1960. pp. iii, 22.

- Lithuania

SURBLIS (K. Z.) Razvitie rabochego klassa Litovskoi SSR i izmeneniia v ego sostave. in Sovetskii rabochii klass na sovremennom etape. Moskva, 1964.

- Malaya

GENERAL LABOUR COMMITTEE, BRITISH MALAYA. Report of the executive...on Indian labour and labourers; [by W. Duncan and A.B. Milne; C. Ward-Jackson, secretary]. Kuala Lumpur, 1920. pp. 25.

BLYTHE (WILFRED LAWSON) Methods and conditions of employment of Chinese labour in the Federated Malay States: report. Kuala Lumpur, 1938. pp. ii, 74. 33cm.

- Malaysia - Education

INTERNATIONAL LABOUR OFFICE. Regular Programme of Technical Assistance. [Malaysia]. R. 22 Report on audio-visual teaching aids and lecture techniques in workers' education in Malaysia. (ILO/OTA/Malaysia/R. 22) Geneva, 1967. pp. 31. 30cm.

- Mari Republic - Education

VASENEV (SERGEI ANDREEVICH) Ideologicheskoe vospitanie trudiashchikhsia. Ioshkar-Ola, 1964. pp. 51. bibliog.

- Mexico

QUIRÓS MARTINEZ (ROBERTO) El problema del proletariado en México. México, 1934. pp. xlvii, 736. 23½cm.

CERDA SILVA (ROBERTO DE LA) El movimiento obrero en Mexico. Mexico, Instituto de Investigaciones Sociales, U.N.A.M., 1961. pp. 187. bibliog. 23½cm.

ARAIZA (LUIS) Historia del movimiento obrero mexicano. Mexico, 1964-65. 4 vols. (in 1).

ASHBY (JOE C.) Organized labor and the Mexican Revolution under Lázaro Cárdenas. Chapel Hill, U. of North Carolina P., [1967]. pp. xi, 350. bibliog. 23cm.

- Mexico - Statistics

MEXICO. Dirección General de Muestreo Estadístico. 1965. La población económicamente activa de Mexico en abril de 1965. vols. 4-7. México, 1965. 4 vols. (in 1). 23cm. Vols. 1-3 not obtainable.

MEXICO. Dirección General de Muestreo Estadístico. 1968. La población económicamente activa del Distrito Federal, junio de 1968. Mexico, 1968. pp. 80. 23cm.

- Moldavian Republic

BARBULAT (V. K.) Развитие рабочего класса Молдавской ССР, 1945-1955 гг. Кишинев, 1969. pp. 177.

- Mongolia

TUDEV (BATYN) Формирование и развитие рабочего класса Монгольской Народной Республики. Москва, 1968. pp. 146.

- Netherlands

BEKIUS (H.J.) and BERGMAN (R.A.M.) Rijswerkers bij de Zuiderzeewerken in 1956. Amsterdam, Stichting voor het Bevolkningsonderzoek in de Drooggelegde Zuiderzeepolders, 1963. pp. 58. 25cm. (Publicaties. No. 29) With English summary.

- New Zealand

DUNEDIN. Dunedin Metropolitan Regional Planning Authority. Regional Planning Series. Reports. No. 1. Labour force, employment and industry in the Dunedin urban area. Dunedin, 1967. fo. 60. 26cm.

- Nigeria

TOYO (ESKOR) The working class and the Nigerian crisis. Ibadan, imprint, [1967?]. pp. 112, vii. 17½cm.

KRIZSÁN (LÁSZLÓ) Aspects of an analysis of the labour structure of the Nigerian working class. Budapest, 1970. pp. 21. (Magyar Tudományos Akademia. Afro Azsiai Kutato Központ. Studies on Developing Countries. No. 37)

- Nigeria - Education

INTERNATIONAL LABOUR OFFICE. 1963. Report on workers' education in Nigeria. Geneva, 1963. pp. ii, 24.

- Norway

ANKER-ORDING (AAKE) Betriebsdemokratie: Wege zur sozialistischen Gesellschaft in Norwegen. Frankfurt a.M., 1966, repr. 1969. pp. 135.

NORWAY. Statistiske Centralbyra. 1969. Sysselsatte lønnstakere etter bosted og arbeidssted, 31. mars 1968; salaried employees and wage earners by residence and place of work, 31 March 1968; (prepared under the supervision of Sverre Hovind). Oslo, 1969. pp. 61. (Norges Offisielle Statistikk. Rekke A. 284.) In Norwegian and English.

- Pakistan, West

KHAN (MOHAMMAD AKRAM) Non-agricultural labour conditions in West Pakistan: analysis, evaluation, suggestions. Basel, 1966. pp. xi, 138. bibliog. 20½cm.

- Panama

PANAMA. Direccion de Estadistica y Censos. Estadistica panameña. Serie O. Estadisticas del trabajo. a., 1968 (año 29)- Panama.

INTERNATIONAL LABOUR OFFICE. Development Programme: Technical Assistance Sector. [Panama]. R. 6. Informe al gobierno de la Republica de Panama sobre la administracion y legislacion del trabajo. (OIT/TAP/Panama/R. 6) Ginebra, 1968. pp. 53.

- Paraguay

GAONA (FRANCISCO) Introducción a la historia gremial y social del Paraguay. Asunción, Arandú, 1967 in progress. 19½cm.

- Peru

FAJARDO (J. V.) Sindicalismo libre en el Peru: la realidad histórica del sindicalismo y algunas conquistas en la legislación laboral del Perú. Lima, Editorial Mercurio, [1965]. pp. 169. 19½cm.

- Poland

POLAND. Główny Urząd Statystyczny. Rocznik statystyczny pracy. a., 1945/1968 [1st]- Warszawa.

ŹRÓDŁA do dziejów klasy robotniczej na ziemiach polskich. Warszawa, PWN, 1962 in progress. 24cm.

KOWALSKI (JÓZEF) Zarys historii polskiego ruchu robotniczego w latach 1918-1939. cz.1. Lata 1918-1928. 2nd ed. Warszawa, 1962. For cz.2 see his Trudne lata.

LABOUR AND LABOURING CLASSES - Poland (Cont'd.)

CZUBIŃSKI (ANTONI) and MAKOWSKI (EDMUND) Klasowy ruch robotniczy w Wielkopolsce w okresie II Rzeczypospolitej. t.1. Lata 1918-1928. Poznań, Wydawnictwo Poznańskie, 1963. pp. 423. 20½cm.

CIECHOCIŃSKA (MARIA) Położenie klasy robotniczej w Polsce, 1929-1939: studia i materiały. Warszawa, Książka i Wiedza, 1965. pp. 347. bibliog. 24cm. (Gospodarka Polski 1918-1939)

KOWALSKI (JÓZEF) Trudne lata: problemy rozwoju polskiego ruchu robotniczego 1929-1935. Warszawa, Książka i Wiedza, za, 1966. pp. 795. bibliog. 24cm.

STETSKEVICH (STANISLAV MIKHAILOVICH) Rabochee dvizhenie v Pol'she v 1918-1919 godakh, noiabr' 1918 - iiul' 1919 goda. Leningrad, 1966. pp. 264.

TURSKI (RYSZARD) Między miastem a wsią: struktura społeczno-zawodowa chłopów-robotników w Polsce. Warszawa, PWN, 1965. pp. 305. bibliog. 20cm.

HISTORIA polskiego ruchu robotniczego 1864-1964. Warszawa, 1967. 2 vols. bibliog.

Z dziejów ruchu robotniczego w Łodzi: materiały do szkolenia partyjnego. Łódź, Wydawnictwo Łódzkie, 1967. pp. 407. bibliog. 19½cm.

ZIL'BERMAN (MARKO IOSYPOVYCH) Революційна боротьба трудящих Західної України, 1924-1928 рр. Львів, 1968. pp. 198.

OSIPOV (GENNADII VASIL'EVICH) and SZCZEPAŃSKI (JAN) eds. Социальные проблемы труда и производства: советско-польское сравнительное исследование. Москва, 1969. pp. 510.

POLAND. Główny Urząd Statystyczny. Seria "Statystyka Polski: Materiały Statystyczne". zeszyt 44(166). Zatrudnienie w gospodarce narodowej, 1950-1968. Warszawa, 1969. pp. 194.

TULSKI (JÓZEF) Postawy młodych robotników wobec pracy zawodowej. Warszawa, 1969. pp. 246. bibliog.

BARAN (JÓZEF) Wychowawcze funkcje zakładu pracy. Warszawa, 1970. pp. 211. bibliog.

ERMOLAEVA (ROZALIIA ALEKSANDROVNA) and MANUSEVICH (ALEKSANDR IAKOVLEVICH) Lenin i pol'skoe rabochee dvizhenie. Moskva, 1971. pp. 503.

LANDAU (ZBIGNIEW) and TOMASZEWSKI (JERZY) Robotnicy przemysłowi w Polsce: materialne warunki bytu, 1918-1939. Warszawa, 1971. pp. 755. bibliog.

- Poland - Bibliography

KORMANOWA (ŻANNA) compiler) Materiały do bibliografii polskiego ruchu robotniczego, 1918-1939. t.1. Druki zwarte. Warszawa, PWN, 1960. pp. 581. 24cm. Continuation of Materały do bibliografii druków socjalistycznych na Ziemiach polskich w latach 1866-1918, published in 1935.

- Poland - Education

CZAPÓW (CZESŁAW) Kształtowanie postaw młodzieży pracującej: z zagadnień startu zawodowego młodych robotników. Warszawa, 1969. pp. 234. bibliog. With Russian and English summaries.

- Poland - Silesia

HREBENDA (ADAM) Klasa robotnicza Zagłębia Dąbrowskiego w latach 1929-1933: położenie i walka robotników Zagłębia Dąbrowskiego w latach kryzysu gospodarczego, 1929-1933. Katowice, 1969. pp. 202. bibliog.

RABA (JOEL) Robotnicy śląscy. 1850-1870: praca i byt. Londyn, Odnowa, 1970. pp. 208. bibliog. With English and German summaries.

- Portugal - Statistics

FUNDO DE DESENVOLVIMENTO DA MÃO-DE-OBRA. Divisão de Estatistica. Algumas estatisticas do trabalho em Portugal. q., Mr 1970 (no. 1)- Lisboa.

- Rhodesia - Statistics

RHODESIA. Census of Employees, 1961. Final report on the September 1961 census of employees. (Central Statistical Office) Salisbury, 1965. pp. 53. 33cm. For preliminary report see FEDERATION OF RHODESIA AND NYASALAND. Census, 1961.

- Roumania

MATEI (G.) L'importance historique des luttes des cheminots et des ouvriers du pétrole de janvier-février 1933 en Roumanie. in Comité National des Historiens de la Republique Socialiste de Roumanie. Nouvelles études d'histoire. Bucarest, 1965.

MIȘCAREA muncitorească din România, 1893-1900. București, 1965. pp. 455.

DOCUMENTE din istoria mișcării muncitorești din România, 1916-1921. București, Editura Politică, 1966. pp. 790. 21½cm.

- Russia

RUBINER (FRIDA) Die Grundlagen des Sowjetstaates: ein Elementarkursus in vier Abenden. Berlin, 1927. pp. 128. bibliog.

ZIELONKA (EDUARD) and SCHMIDT (MARTIN) of Düsseldorf. Als sozialdemokratische Arbeiter in der Sowjetunion. Berlin, [1931]. pp. 32.

YVON (M.) What has become of the Russian revolution. New York, [1937]. pp. 63.

GOR'KII (MAKSIM) pseud. [i.e. Aleksei Maksimovich PESHKOV]. Wenn der Feind sich nicht ergibt wird er vernichtet: gesammelte Aufsätze 1927 bis 1935. Paris, [1938]. pp. 510.

AMOSOV (N.) Что дала советская власть трудящимся. 2nd ed. Москва, Профиздат, 1946. pp. 48. 17см.

PROZHOGIN (V.) Эстетика труда в творчестве М. Горького. Киев, 1955. pp. 321.

INOZEMTSEV (GEORGII ALEKSANDROVICH) U istokov rabochego dvizheniia na Donu. Rostov-na-Donu, 1956. pp. 56.

DANIELIAN (M. S.) Марксизм-ленинизм о противоположности между умственным и физическим трудом. Ереван, АН АрмССР, 1957. pp. 211. 16½см.

LEVIN (I. M.) Планирование труда и заработной платы на промышленных предприятиях. Москва, Госполитиздат, 1958. pp. 191. 20см.

CHUBAROV (G. S.) Планирование труда и заработной платы на промышленных предприятиях. Москва, Госпланиздат, 1960. pp. 159. 20см.

ZAOZERSKAIA (ELIZAVETA IVANOVNA) Рабочая сила и классовая борьба на текстильных мануфактурах России в 20-60 гг. XIII в. Москва, АН, 1960. pp. 450. 21½см. Continues her Развитие легкой промышленности в Москве в первой четверти XVIII века, which see.

HRABOVS'KYI (VOLODYMYR KLYMENTIIOVYCH) Spivrobitnytstvo ta vzaiemodopomoha vsikh pratsivnykiv suspil'stva - forma vyrobnychykh vidnosyn sotsializmu. Kyïv, 1961. pp. 63.

LOSEV (A. A.) Rol' brigad kommunisticheskogo truda v stroitel'stve kommunizma. in Uchenye Zapiski Kafedr Obshchestvennykh Nauk Vuzov G. Leningrada. Filosofiia. vyp.3. Leningrad, 1961.

PRUDENSKII (GERMAN ALEKSANDROVICH) ed. Внерабочее время трудящихся. Новосибирск, 1961. pp. 256.

ISTORIIA rabochego klassa Leningrada. vvp.1, 2. Leningrad, 1962-63. 2 vols [in 1].

FITISOV (VASILII ANISIMOVICH) Организация отдыха трудящихся. Москва, 1963. pp. 47.

IZ... Из истории рабочего класса СССР. Львов, Университет, 1963. pp. 198. 21½см. (Odessa. Одесский Гидрометеорологический Институт. Труды. вып. 30)

POTOLOV (SERGEI IVANOVICH) Рабочие Донбасса в XIX веке. Москва, Академия Наук, 1963. pp. 256. 21см.

WORKERS in the Soviet economy: industrial labour and living standards. 1963. pp. 31.

BUIKO (ALEKSANDR MIKHAILOVICH) Put' rabochego: vospominaniia putilovtsa. Leningrad, 1964. pp. 148.

IVANOV (VALENTIN IVANOVICH) Общественное бюро нормирования труда. Москва, 1964. pp. 61.

KRUK (DAVID MOISEEVICH) and CHERTKOV (DAVID GRIGOR'EVICH) Ot chego zavisit uroven' zhizni trudiashchikhsia v SSSR. Moskva, 1964. pp. 78.

MASLOV (K. P.) Из истории борьбы рабочего класса за власть Советов и ее упрочение: "Красное Сормово" на великом рубеже. Горький, 1964. pp. 230. 21½см.

SOVETSKII... Советский рабочий класс на современном этапе. Москва, Мысль, 1964. pp. 188. 20см.

SOVETY i soiuz rabochego klassa i krest'ianstva v oktiabr'skoi revoliutsii: sbornik statei. Moskva, 1964. pp. 228.

EL'MEEV (VASILII IAKOVLEVICH) and others. Коммунизм и преодоление разделения между умственным и физическим трудом. Ленинград, Университет, 1965. pp. 142. 21½см.

GOLIKOVA (NINA BORISOVNA) Наемный труд в городах Поволжья в первой четверти XVIII века. Москва, Университет, 1965. pp. 176. 21см.

IVASENKO (PAVEL IVANOVICH) and MERKIN (NIKOLAI KONSTANTINOVICH) Kollektivnaia organizatsiia i oplata truda v promyshlennosti i stroitel'stve. Moskva, 1965. pp. 151.

IZ... Из истории рабочего класса и крестьянства Пермского края: сборник статей. Пермь, 1965. pp. 174.

SHELOMOVA (L. I.) Vliianie sovmeshcheniia professii na rabotnika proizvodstva. in Uchenye Zapiski Kafedr Obshchestvennykh Nauk Vuzov g. Leningrada. Filosofiia. vyp 6. Leningrad, 1965.

VAL'TUKH (KONSTANTIN KURTOVICH) Общественная полезность продукции и затраты труда на ее производство. Москва, Мысль, 1965. pp. 287. 20см

DAVTIAN (MAVR MKHITAROVICH) Protiv antiobshchestvennogo otnosheniia k trudu. Erevan, 1966. pp. 95.

GAGOSHIDZE (G. D.) Tsel' sotsialisticheskogo proizvodstva i stoimost': k teorii neposredstvenno obshchestvennogo truda. Dushanbe, 1966. pp. 69.

IZ istorii rabochego klassa v Kuzbasse, 1917-1965. vyp.2: Materialy k nauchnoi konferentsii. Kemerovo, 1966. pp. 189.

KAZAKEVICH (ROZA ABRAMOVNA) and SUSLOVA (FAINA MIKHAILOVNA) Mister Paips fal'sifitsiruet istoriiu: o knige R. Paipsa "Sotsial-demokratiia i rabochee dvizhenie v S.-Peterburge, 1885-1897". Leningrad, 1966. pp. 182.

KOTELKIN (VLADIMIR IVANOVICH) Sovershenstvovanie normirovaniia truda v promyshlennosti: ekonomicheskie problemy. Leningrad, 1966. pp. 142.

LABOUR AND LABOURING CLASSES - Russia
(Cont'd.)

MAMEDOV (MIUSIUM) Нэп и политическое воспитание рабочего класса. Баку, 1966. pp. 125.

MANEVICH (EFIM L'VOVICH) Проблемы общественного труда в СССР. Москва, Экономика, 1966. pp. 190. 21см.

SEMANOV (SERGEI NIKOLAEVICH) Петербургские рабочие накануне первой русской революции. Москва, Наука, 1966. pp. 171. 21½см.

SPRAVOCHNIK... Справочник работника общественного бюро технического нормирования. Москва, Экономика, 1966. pp. 206. 20см.

ALEKSEEVA (VALENTINA MIKHAILOVNA) Развитие союза рабочих и крестьян в период перехода к коммунизму. Ленинград, 1967. pp. 109.

BOR (MIKHAIL ZAKHAROVICH) and LINDE (E. V.) eds. Upravlenie proizvodstvom i organizatsiia truda. Moskva, 1967. pp. 213.

BUGROV (ALEKSANDR PORFIR'EVICH) and CHUBAREV (GEORGII STEPANOVICH) Отраслевые и межотраслевые нормативы по труду. Москва, Экономика, 1967. pp. 282. 19½см.

CHELOVEK... Человек и его работа: социологическое исследование. Москва, Мысль, 1967. pp. 392. 19½см.

DIAGILEV (D. V.) and others, eds. Iz istorii bor'by za razvitie kommunisticheskikh form truda: sbornik dokumentov i materialov. Moskva, 1967. pp. 502.

FREIDLIN (BORIS MIRONOVICH) Ocherki istorii rabochego dvizheniia v Rossii v 1917g. Moskva, 1967. pp. 339.

KAPUSTIN (EVGENII IVANOVICH) Arbeit und Arbeitslohn. Berlin, 1967. pp. 183. (Sozialistische Arbeitswissenschaft. [Publications]. 11.)

LITVINOV (LEONID NIKIFOROVICH) Vospitanie lichnosti v trude i v bytu: na opyte dvizheniia za kommunisticheskii trud i byt. Tula, 1967. pp. 182. bibliog.

OSTRIAKOV (VIKTOR VASIL'EVICH) and STEPANOVICHIUS (AL'BINAS IONOVICH) Социально-политические факторы формирования коммунистической сознательности трудящихся. Москва, 1967. pp. 160.

POLETAEV (VLADIMIR EVGEN'EVICH) Рабочие Москвы на завершающем этапе строительства социализма, 1945-1958 гг. Москва, 1967. pp. 276.

ROL' rabochego klassa v rasvitii sotsialisticheskoi kul'tury. Moskva, 1967. pp. 149.

SLEZINGER (GRIGORII EMMANUILOVICH) Trud v upravlenii promyshlennym proizvodstvom. Moskva, 1967. pp. 256.

1968

BORISOV (IURII STEPANOVICH) and others, eds. Краткая история советского рабочего класса, 1917-1967. Москва, ИПЛ, 1968. pp. 430. 20см.

CHUKHNO (ANATOLII ANDREEVICH) and others. Вознаграждение за труд при социализме. Киев, Университет, 1968. pp. 280. 20см.

ETNOGRAFICHESKOE... Этнографическое изучение быта рабочих: по материалам отдельных промышленных районов СССР Москва, 1968. pp. 208. bibliog.

EZHOV (VIKTOR ANATOL'EVICH) Rabochie Leningrada v poslevoennye gody, 1946-1950. Leningrad, 1968. pp. 119. bibliog.

GLAZACHEV (AFANASII ALEKSEEVICH) and MOLDAVAN (VASILII SAVEL'EVICH) Труд и всестороннее развитие личности. Москва, Мысль, 1968. pp. 118. 19½см.

IAKOVENKO (VIACHESLAV ANDRIIOVYCH) Поділ праці при переході до комунізму: питання теорії і методології. Харків, Університет, 1968. pp. 143. 21см. With Russian summary.

IZ... Из истории рабочего класса СССР. Москва, 1968. pp. 199.

KAIDALOV (DMITRII PETROVICH) Закон перемены труда и всестороннее развитие человека. Москва, Мысль, 1968. pp. 319. 19½см.

KAPLAN (FREDERICK I.) Bolshevik ideology and the ethics of Soviet labor, 1917-1920: the formative years. New York, Philosophical Library, [1968]. pp. ix, 521. bibliog. 21cm.

KOSOLAPOV (RICHARD IVANOVICH) Коммунистический труд: природа и стимулы. Москва, 1968. pp. 88.

NAUCHNO-ISSLEDOVATEL'SKII INSTITUT KOMPLEKSNYKH SOTSIAL'NYKH ISSLEDOVANII. Uchenye Zapiski. vyp.3. Chelovek i obshchestvo; pod obshchei redaktsiei... B.G. Anan'eva,... D.A.Kerimova. Leningrad, 1968. pp. 248.

OVSIANKIN (V. A.) ed. Рабочий класс СССР на современном этапе. Ленинград, Университет, 1968. pp. 168. 21½см.

RABOCHII... Рабочий класс в управлении государством, 1926-1937 гг. Москва, Мысль, 1968. pp. 239. 20см.

RAUD (VIACHESLAV MIKHAILOVICH) Социалистическая организация общественного труда. Москва, Мысль, 1968. pp. 253. 20см.

ROL'... Роль рабочего класса в социалистическом преобразовании деревни в СССР. Москва, Мысль, 1968. pp. 255. 19½см.

SELUNSKAIA (VALERIIA MIKHAILOVNA) Рабочий класс и Октябрь в деревне: рабочий класс во главе Октябрьской социалистической революции в деревне. Октябрь 1917-1918 г. Москва, Мысль, 1968. pp. 296. 19½см.

SKARZHINSKII (M. I.) Труд в непроизводственной сфере. Москва, 1968. pp. 127.

VOLKOV (A. P.) and others, eds. Труд и заработная плата в СССР. Москва, Экономика, 1968. pp. 471. 20см.

1969

ALEKSANDROV (NIKOLAI GRIGOR'EVICH) ed. Khoziaistvennaia reforma, trud i pravo. Moskva, 1969. pp. 178.

BATUKHTIN (IVAN LUKIIANOVICH) Анализ труда и заработной платы на предприятии. Москва, 1969. pp. 229.

BELOUSOV (REM ALEKSANDROVICH) Общественно необходимые затраты труда и уровень оптовых цен. Москва, Мысль, 1969. pp. 276. 20см.

BURMISTROVA (TAT'IANA IUL'EVNA) Национальный вопрос и рабочее движение в России: ленинская политика пролетарского интернационализма, 1907-1917 гг. Москва, 1969. pp. 274. bibliog.

KALININ (ANANII ILLARIONOVICH) Rol' truda v razvitii lichnosti v usloviiakh stroitel'stva kommunizma. Cheboksary, 1969. pp. 544.

LENINSKOE... Ленинское учение о союзе рабочего класса с крестьянством. Москва, 1969. pp. 348.

NESTEROV (VLADIMIR GAVRILOVICH) Trud i moral' v sovetskom obshchestve: problemy vzaimosviazi. Moskva, 1969. pp. 187.

OSIPOV (GENNADII VASIL'EVICH) and SZCZEPAŃSKI (JAN) eds. Социальные проблемы труда и производства: советско-польское сравнительное исследование. Москва, 1969. pp. 510.

PODMARKOV (VALENTIN GEORGIEVICH) Социальные проблемы организации труда. Москва, 1969. pp. 212.

RABOCHII... Рабочий класс и развитие сельского хозяйства СССР. Москва, 1969. pp. 246.

RABOCHII... Рабочий класс СССР, 1951-1965 гг. Москва, 1969. pp. 558.

SLASTENENKO (V. A.) and MOSIN (V. P.) eds. Kollektivnost' - osnova sotsialisticheskogo proizvodstva. Moskva, 1969.

SMYSHLIAEV (VALENTIN ALEKSEEVICH) По ленинским заветам. Ленинград, 1969. pp. 166.

VEDUSHCHAIA sila sovetskogo obshchestva. Moskva, 1969. pp. 86.

1970

BEILINA (EVGENIIA ELIBEROVNA) Rabochii klass i novye formy sorevnovaniia, 1959-1965gg. Moskva, 1970. pp. 303.

BRINTON (MAURICE) The Bolsheviks and workers' control 1917 to 1921: the state and counter-revolution. London, 1970. pp. 89.

GAPONENKO (LUKA STEPANOVICH) Rabochii klass Rossii v 1917 godu. Moskva, 1970. pp. 579. bibliog.

POLOZOV (VLADIMIR ROMANOVICH) Sotsial'no-ekonomicheskaia struktura obshchestvennogo truda pri perekhode k kommunizmu. Leningrad, 1970. pp. 168.

ROSSIISKII proletariat: oblik, bor'ba, gegemoniia. Moskva, 1970. pp. 361.

SHKARATAN (OVSEI IRMOVICH) Problemy sotsial'noi struktury rabochego klassa SSSR: istoriko-sotsiologicheskoe issledovanie. Moskva, 1970. pp. 472.

TIAPKIN (NIKOLAI KAPITONOVICH) Kommunisticheskaia organizatsiia obshchestvennogo truda: voprosy teorii. Moskva, 1970. pp. 283.

TRUD, tekhnika, ekonomika. Moskva, 1970. pp. 318.

VOPROSY istoriografii rabochego klassa SSSR. Moskva, 1970. pp. 327.

1971

GERSHBERG (SEMEN RAKHMIL'EVICH) Rabota u nas takaia: zapiski zhurnalista-pravdista tridtsatykh godov. Moskva, 1971. pp. 445.

KREVNEVICH (VALENTINA VIACHESLAVOVNA) Vliianie nauchno-tekhnicheskogo progressa na izmenenie struktury rabochego klassa SSSR: itogi i perspektivy. Moskva, 1971. pp. 391.

SELITSKII (VLADISLAV IOSIFOVICH) Massy v borb'e za rabochii kontrol', mart - iiul' 1917 g. Moskva, 1971. pp. 235.

SENIAVSKII (SPARTAK LEONIDOVICH) and TEL'PUKHOVSKII (VLADIMIR BORISOVICH) Rabochii klass SSSR, 1938-1965 gg. Moskva, 1971. pp. 533. bibliog.

- Russia - Dictionaries and encyclopaedias

POPOV-CHERKASOV (IGOR' NIKOLAEVICH) ed. Kratkii slovar'-spravochnik po voprosam truda i zarabotnoi platy. Moskva, 1967. pp. 311.

- Russia - Education

VOSPITATEL'NAIA... Воспитательная работа профсоюзных организаций. Москва, Профиздат, 1959. pp. 130. 20см.

VOPROSY... Вопросы воспитательной работы в коллективах коммунистического труда: материалы научной конференции. вып.1. Красноярск, 1961. pp. 274. 20см.

PARFENOV (DMITRII ANDREEVICH) Umstvennyi i fizicheskii trud v SSSR: ekonomicheskie predposylki preodoleniia sushchestvennykh razlichii. Moskva, 1964. pp. 144.

LABOUR AND LABOURING CLASSES - Russia - Education (Cont'd.)

TSVETKOV (VASILII IAVNOVICH) Как у нас ведется воспитательная работа: записки председателя завкома. Москва, Профиздат 1964. pp. 94. 16½cm. (Библиотечка Профсоюзного Активиста.

VOSPITANIE... Воспитание коммунистической сознательности. Москва, Мысль, 1964. pp. 316. 20cm.

MAMONTOV (IVAN SEMENOVICH) ФЗМК и коммунистическое воспитание трудящихся. Москва, Профиздат, 1965. pp. 96. 16cm. (Библиотечка Профсоюзного Активиста. 8/99)

FORMIROVANIE lichnosti v proizvodstvennom kollektive. Moskva, 1968. pp. 168.

PROKOPOVA (ZINAIDA GAVRILOVNA) Kommunisticheskoe vospitanie molodykh rabochikh, 1959-1965 gg. Moskva, 1971. pp. 77.

- Russia - Medical care

KAZIEV (MAMED IAKUBOVICH) Забота профсоюзов о здоровье трудящихся. Москва, 1969. pp. 157.

ZAKHAROV (FEDOR GALAKTIONOVICH) Organizatsiia meditsinskoi pomoshchi promyshlennym rabochim Rossii i SSSR: ocherki istorii. Moskva, 1969. pp. 279.

- Russia - Songs and music

AKIMOVA (TAT'IANA MIKHAILOVNA) and ARKHANGEL'SKAIA (VERA KONSTANTINOVNA) Революционная песня в Саратовском Поволжье: очерки исторического развития. Саратов, Университет, 1967. pp. 168. 20см.

GIPPIUS (EVGENII VLADIMIROVICH) and SHIRIAEVA (PELAGEA GRIGOR'EVNA) "Krasnoe znamia": iz istorii pesni trekh russkikh revoliutsii. Moskva, 1969. pp. 168.

- Russia - Statistics

STATISTIKA... Статистика труда. Москва, 1967. pp. 215.

- Russia - Siberia

MOSKOVSKII (ALEKSEI STEPANOVICH) Рабочий класс Западной Сибири в годы первой пятилетки. Новосибирск, Академия Наук, 1964. pp. 113. 20½cm.

SIBIR'... Сибирь периода капитализма. вып. 1. Предпосылки Октябрьской революции в Сибири. Новосибирск, Академия Наук. 1964. pp. 260. 25½cm.

BORZUNOV (VALENTIN FEDOROVICH) Пролетариат Сибири и Дальнего Востока накануне первой русской революции: по материалам строительства Транссибирской магистрали, 1891-1904 гг. Москва, Наука, 1965. pp. 198. 20cm.

MOSKOVSKII (ALEKSEI STEPANOVICH) Формирование и развитие рабочего класса Сибири в период строительства социализма. Новосибирск, 1968. pp. 300.

MOSKOVSKII (ALEKSEI STEPANOVICH) Рост трудовой активности рабочего класса Сибири в борьбе за победу социализма. Новосибирск, 1968. pp. 170.

ZOL'NIKOV (DMITRII MARKOVICH) Рабочее движение в Сибири в 1917 г. Новосибирск, 1969. pp. 382.

- Ruthenia

SPIVAK (BORYS IVANOVYCH) Нариси історії революційної боротьби трудящих Закарпаття в 1930-1945 роках. Львів, Університет, 1963. pp. 256. 20см.

- Senegal

PFEFFERMANN (GUY) Industrial labor in the Republic of Senegal. New York, Praeger, 1968. pp. xxi, 325. bibliog. 23½cm. (Praeger Special Studies in International Economics and Development)

Seychelles

SEYCHELLES. Labour Department. Biennial report. Mahé, biennial, 1967/1968 [1st] to date.

Siam

INTERNATIONAL LABOUR OFFICE. Development Programme: Technical Assistance Sector. [Thailand]. R.27. Report to the government of Thailand on labour administration. (ILO/TAP/Thailand/R.27). Geneva, 1967. pp. 36.

- Siam - Statistics

SIAM. Department of Labour. Yearbook of labour statistics. [in Siamese and English] [Bangkok], annual, 1965 (1st) to date. 30cm.

INTERNATIONAL LABOUR OFFICE. Development Programme: Technical Assistance Sector. [Thailand]. R.28. Report to the government of Thailand on labour statistics. (ILO/TAP/Thailand/R.28) Geneva, 1968. pp. 43.

· South Africa

NEW REFORM CLUB. Political Committee. [Leaflets] No. 2. Rand magnates and British labour. [London, 1904?] pp. 8.

INTERNATIONAL LABOUR CONFERENCE. Special report on the Director-General on the application of the declaration concerning the policy of "apartheid" of the Republic of South Africa. a., 1965 [1st]- Geneva.

WORLD FEDERATION OF TRADE UNIONS. Workers and trade unions against apartheid. n.p., [1966?]. pp. 43.

GORODNOV (VALENTIN PETROVICH) Южно-Африканский рабочий класс в борьбе против реакции и расизма, 50-60-е годы XX века. Москва, Наука, 1969. pp. 156. bibliog. 20см.

SIMONS (HAROLD JACK) and SIMONS (RAY ESTHER) eds. Class and colour in South Africa 1850-1950. Harmondsworth, 1969. pp. 702. bibliog.

BIRLEY (Sir ROBERT) The African worker in South Africa. [Leeds], 1971. pp. 29. (Leeds. University. Montague Burton Lectures on International Relations. No.29)

- Soviet Far East

BORZUNOV (VALENTIN FEDOROVICH) Пролетариат Сибири и Дальнего Востока накануне первой русской революции: по материалам строительства Транссибирской магистрали, 1891-1904 гг. Москва, Наука, 1965. pp. 198. 20cm.

- Soviet North

AKADEMIIA NAUK SSSR. Sovet po Izucheniiu Proizvoditel'nykh Sil. Komissiia po Problemam Severa. Problemy Severa. vyp. 14. Trud i zdorov'e cheloveka na Krainem Severe. Moskva, 1970. pp. 219.

- Spain

ROVIROSA (GUILLERMO) Militantes obreros. Madrid, 1965. pp. 377.

TUÑÓN DE LARA (MANUEL) Introducció a la història del moviment obrer. Barcelona, Editorial Nova Terra, 1966. pp. 375. bibliog. 17cm. (Colleció Síntesi. 21)

ABAD DE SANTILLÁN (DIEGO) Historia del movimiento obrero español. Madrid, ZYX, 1967 in progress. 20cm. (Biblioteca Promoción del Pueblo)

RUIZ GONZÁLEZ (DAVID) El movimiento obrero en Asturias: de la industrialización a la segunda republica. Oviedo, 1968. pp. 283. bibliog.

DIAZ DEL MORAL (JUAN) Historia de las agitaciones campesinas andaluzas: Cordoba; antecedentes para una reforma agraria. [new ed.], Madrid, 1967 repr. 1969. pp. 508. bibliog.

MARAVALL (JOSE MARIA) El desarrollo economico y la clase obrera: un estudio sociologico de los conflictos obreros en España. Caracas, 1970. pp. 259.

NUÑEZ DE ARENAS (MANUEL) and TUÑON DE LARA (MANUEL) Historia del movimiento obrero español. Barcelona, 1970. pp. 264.

- Sweden

AHLANDER (FREDRIK E.) The archive of the Swedish labour movement. Stockholm, [1925?]. pp. 4.

SWEDEN. Arbetsmarknadsstyrelsen. 1960. Samhällsservice och lokaliseringsverksamhet: ett inom arbetsmarknadsstyrelsen sammanställt material belysande närings- och bebyggelsestrukturen, företagens krav på lokaliseringssorten och samhällets möjligheter att förbättra lokaliseringsförutsättningarna. Karlshamn, [imprint], 1960. pp. 272. 24cm.

- Switzerland

ERB (HANS) Zur Vorgeschichte des Landesgeneralstreiks 1918 in der Schweiz. Zürich, Allgemeine Geschichtsforschende Gesellschaft der Schweiz, 1961. pp. 321-377, 433-522. 22½cm. (Extracted from Schweizerische Zeitschrift für Geschichte, 11/3-4, 1961)

NEUBAUER (WALTER F.) Selbsteinschätzung und Idealeinschätzung junger Arbeiter als Gegenstand sozialpsychologischer Verhaltensforschung. [Erlangen-Nürnberg, 1967?]. pp. 261. bibliog.

SCHARMANN (THEODOR) ed. Lebensplanung und Lebensgestaltung junger Arbeiter aus der Metallindustrie der Bundesrepublik und der Schweiz, etc. Bern, Huber, [1967]. pp. 368. bibliogs. 23cm. (Munich. Deutscher Jugendinstitut and Erlangen. Universität. Institut für Wirtschafts- und Sozialpsychologie. Der Junge Arbeiter: Studien zu einer Genealogie des Industriebürgers. Band 1).

GRUNER (ERICH) Die Arbeiter in der Schweiz im 19. Jahrhundert: soziale Lage, Organisation, Verhältnis zu Arbeitgeber und Staat. Bern, Francke, [1968]. pp. 1136. bibliog. 23cm. (Bern. Universität. Forschungszentrum für Geschichte und Soziologie der schweizerischen Politik. Helvetia Politica. Series A. vol.3)

- Switzerland - Education

GIROD (R.) Le degré d'instruction de la main-d'oeuvre. in Atteslander (Peter M.) and Girod (Roger) eds. Soziologische Arbeiten. 1. Bern, 1966.

- Switzerland - Periodicals - Bibliography

EBERLEIN (ALFRED) compiler. Die Presse der Arbeiterklasse und der sozialen Bewegungen von den dreissiger Jahren des 19. Jahrhunderts bis zum Jahre 1967: Bibliographie, etc. Frankfurt/Main 1968-70. 5 vols. (Deutsche Akademie der Wissenschaften zu Berlin. Institut für Geschichte. Abteilung Dokumente und Materialien zur Geschichte der Deutschen Arbeiterbewegung. Archivalische Forschungen, etc. Band 6)

- Switzerland - Statistics

SWITZERLAND. Bureau Fédéral de Statistique. Recensement des Entreprises, 1965. Recensement fédéral des entreprises, septembre 1965: personnes occupées dans les communes; d'après les secteurs économiques. Berne, 1968. pp. 134. 29cm. (Switzerland. Bureau Fédéral de Statistique. Statistiques de la Suisse. 438e fasc.) In French and German.

- Syria - Education

INTERNATIONAL LABOUR OFFICE. Regular Programme of Technical Assistance. [Syria]. R.4. Rapport sur l'éducation ouvrière dans la République arabe syrienne. [OIT/OTA Syrie/R.12) Genève, 1967. pp. 39.

- Tajikistan

KOMMUNISTICHESKAIA... Коммунистическая партия в борьбе за формирование и развитие рабочего класса в Таджикистане. Душанбе, 1967. pp. 326.

- Trinidad and Tobago - Education

INTERNATIONAL LABOUR OFFICE. Development Programme: Technical Assistance Sector. [Trinidad]. R. 7. Report on the organisation and development of a Labour studies institute in Trinidad and Tobago. (ILO/TAP/Trinidad and Tobago/R. 7) Geneva, 1968. pp. 41.

- Tunis

INTERNATIONAL LABOUR OFFICE. Regular Programme of Technical Assistance. [Tunisia]. R.22. Rapport au gouvernement de la Tunisie sur l'éducation ouvrière en Tunisie. (OIT/OTA/Tunisie/R.22) Genève, 1969. pp. 87.

LABOUR AND LABOURING CLASSES (Cont'd.)

- Uganda - Statistics

EAST AFRICA HIGH COMMISSION. East African Statistical Department. 1949. Uganda Protectorate: report on the enumeration of African labour, March, 1949. [Nairobi], 1949. fo. 14,(37). 33½cm.

- Ukraine

MAKSIMOV (ALEKSANDR MIKHAILOVICH) Revoliutsionnaia bor'ba proletariata Donbassa v 1905 godu. Stalino, 1956. pp. 83.

LOS' (FEDOR EVDOKIMOVICH) Робітничий клас України в 1907-1913 роках. Київ, АН УРСР, 1962. pp. 196. 22cm.

POTOLOV (SERGEI IVANOVICH) Рабочие Донбасса в XIX веке. Москва, Академия Наук, 1963. pp. 256. 21cm.

SHARLAI (G. N.) Shefskaia pomoshch' rabochikh Ukrainy v nalazhivanii organizatsionnoi i kul'turno-vospitatel'noi raboty na sele po razvertyvaniiu massovogo kolkhoznogo dvizheniia. in Iz istorii rabochego klassa SSSR. L'vov, 1963.

ZINYCH (VOLODYMYR TYKHONOVYCH) Sotsialistychni peretvorennia parostky novoho komunistichnoho v kul'turi ta pobuti robitnykiv Radians'koï Ukraïny. Kyïv, 1963. pp. 176.

KUDLAI (OLEKSANDR STEPANOVYCH) Робітничий клас Української РСР у боротьбі за відбудову і розвиток промисловості в післявоєнний період. Київ, Наукова Думка, 1965. pp. 296. 19½cm. With Russian summary.

MYTIUKOV (OLEKSANDR HEORHIEOVYCH) Рабочий класс Украины в борьбе за развитие промышленности, 1956-1961 гг. Киев, Наукова Думка, 1965. pp. 200. 20cm.

ROBITNYCHYI rukh na Ukraïni v roky reaktsiï: cherven' 1907 r. - zhovten' 1910 r.; zbirnyk dokumentiv. Kyïv, 1965. pp. 334.

LAVROV (PAVEL ARSENT'EVICH) Рабочее движение на Украине в период нового революционного подъема, 1910-1914 гг. Киев, Політвидав, 1966. pp. 224. 20см.

PROMYSHLENNOST'... Промышленность и рабочий класс Украинской ССР в период построения фундамента социалистической экономики, 1926-1932 годы: сборник документов и материалов. Киев, Политиздат Украины, 1966. pp. 594. 21см.

RABOCHEE... Рабочее движение на Украине в период первой мировой империалистической войны, июль 1914 г. - февраль 1917; сборник документов и материалов. Киев, 1966. pp. 432.

HOSHKO (IURII HRYHOROVYCH) Громадський побут робітників Західної України, 1920-1939 pp. Київ, Наукова Думка, 1967. pp. 263. 16½см.

EPSHTEIN (ARKADII ISAKOVYCH) Робітники України в боротьбі за створення матеріально-технічної бази соціалізму, 1928-1932 pp. Харків, 1968. pp. 195.

ZIL'BERMAN (MARKO IOSYPOVYCH) Революційна боротьба трудящих Західної України, 1924-1928 pp. Львів, 1968. pp. 198.

OSTRIANIN (DANIIL FOMICH) ed. Svidomist' robitnyka v period budivnytstva komunizmu. Kharkiv, 1969. pp. 172.

KOMPANIIETS' (IVAN IVANOVYCH) Ленін та інтернаціональна єдність українських і російських трудящих у трьох революціях. Київ, 1970. pp. 229.

STELIIA (BORYS IVANOVYCH) Vykhovannia novoï liudyny - sprava partiina: z dosvidu roboty partorhanizatsii po komunistychnomu vykhovanniu pratsivnykiv promyslovosti Ukrainy, 1956-1965rr. Kyïv, 1970. pp. 200.

- Ukraine - Education

KURNOSOV (IURII OLEKSIIOVYCH) Роль інтелігенції України в комуністичному вихованні трудящих, 1959-1965. Київ, 1968. pp. 181. With Russian summary.

- United Kingdom

MAYHEW (HENRY) The unknown Mayhew: selections from the Morning Chronicle, 1849-1850; edited and introduced by E.P. Thompson and Eileen Yeo. London, 1971. pp. 489.

METROPOLITAN ASSOCIATION FOR IMPROVING THE DWELLINGS OF THE INDUSTRIOUS CLASSES. Healthy homes: report of a public meeting to consider the best method of extending the operations of the... Association;...also, charge to the grand jury of Birmingham on the connexion between disease and crime, delivered by M.D. Hill. London, Bowie, [1854]. pp. 64. 20½cm.

WARREN (SAMUEL) Barrister-at-Law. Labour: its rights, difficulties, and consolations; a lecture read...January 3, 1856. rev. ed. London, [1856]. pp. 32.

POTTER (GEORGE) Political tracts for the people...: the conservative working man, the liberal working man. [London?, 1883] pp. 7. Proof copy.

[DE RICCI (JAMES HERMAN)] The welfare of the people. 5th ed. Bedford, 1885. pp. 23.

ENGELS (FRIEDRICH) The condition of the working-class in England in 1844; with a preface written in 1892; translated by Florence Kelley Wischnewetzky; reprinted 1952 with the dedication written by Engels in English in 1845. London, Allen & Unwin, 1968. pp. xxii, 300. 18½cm.

TALBOT (EDWARD STUART) Bishop of Winchester. The religious aspirations of labour. London, SPCK, 1895. pp. 16. 17cm.

GUYOT (YVES) Labour socialism and strikes. London, Wilson, 1896. pp. 122. 18cm.

GARNETT (Mrs. CHARLES) The story of the Navvy Mission. London, 1898. pp. 24.

BRADLAUGH (CHARLES) Labour's prayer. n.p., [19--]. pp. 7.

FARNINGHAM (MARIANNE) A working woman's life: an autobiography. London, Clarke, 1907. pp. 281. 19cm.

HUMPHREY (ARTHUR WILFRID) The class war: facts, history, and a policy for wage-earners. London, [1910]. pp. 16.

GLASS (JAMES) Better times for working people. London, Ormiston and Glass, [1913?]. pp. 128. 18½cm.

COMMUNIST PARTY OF GREAT BRITAIN. Peterloo: the story of the terrible massacre of the Lancashire workers at St. Peter's Fields, Manchester, on August 16th, 1819, and the lessons of Peterloo. London, 1928. pp. 15.

NATIONAL MINORITY MOVEMENT. Now for action': the policy of the National Minority Movement; a report of the Sixth Annual Conference. London, 1929. pp. 40.

DUTT (RAJANI PALME) Fight for the workers' charter. London, Minority Movement, [193-?]. pp. 11. 21½cm.

FIRST NATIONAL WORKERS' CHARTER CONVENTION, LONDON, 1931. Road to victory; resolutions ...[of April 12th, 1931, at Bermondsey Town Hall, London]; chairman, Tom Mann. London, [1931]. pp. 16.

NATIONAL MINORITY MOVEMENT. Trade Union Congress and the workers. London, [1932?]. pp. 15.

ARNOT (ROBERT PAGE) Slavery or socialism. London, [1933?]. pp. 16.

BRAMLEY (TED) We are many! London, [1940?]. pp. 16.

[WORKERS' INTERNATIONAL LEAGUE. 2nd National Conference, London, 1943]. The world revolution, and the tasks of the British working class. London, [1943]. pp. 32. 21cm.

POSTGATE (RAYMOND WILLIAM) A pocket history of the British working class. 2nd ed. Tillicoultry, 1947. pp. 99.

[COMMUNIST PARTY OF GREAT BRITAIN. East Midlands District]. 500 years of struggle: a peoples history of Nottingham. [Nottingham, 1949]. pp. 16.

GUROVICH (POLINA VENIAMINOVNA) Pod"-em rabochego dvizheniia v Anglii v 1918-1921 gg. Moskva, 1956. pp. 222. bibliog.

MARSHALL (J.D.) Nottinghamshire labourers in the early nineteenth century. n.p., 1960. pp. 18. (Reprinted from the Transactions of the Thoroton Society, 1960)

DAVIES (BOB) Pages from a worker's life, 1916-26. London, Communist Party of Great Britain, Historians' Group, 1961. pp. 18. 25½cm. (Our History. No. 23)

BARNSBY (GEORGE) The Dudley working class movement, 1832-1860. Dudley, Dudley Public Libraries, Local History and Archives Department, 1967. pp. 48. 26cm. (Transcript Series. No. 8)

GUROVICH (POLINA VENIAMINOVNA) Английское рабочее движение накануне второй мировой войны. Москва, 1967. pp. 357. bibliog.

The AFFLUENT worker: industrial attitudes and behaviour; [by] John H. Goldthorpe [and others]. Cambridge, 1968. pp. 206. bibliog.

The AFFLUENT worker: political attitudes and behaviour; by John H. Goldthorpe [and others]. Cambridge, 1968. pp. vii, 95.

GORBIK (VIACHESLAV ALEKSANDROVICH) Правящий класс и рабочее движение в Англии, 1959-1964. Киев, 1968. pp. 156.

JACKSON (BRIAN) Working class community: some general notions raised by a series of studies in northern England. London, Routledge and Kegan Paul, 1968. pp vii, 184. 21 cm. (International Library of Sociology and Social Reconstruction)

KUNINA (VALERIA EMMANUILOVNA) Карл Маркс и английское рабочее движение, 1845-1883. Москва, Мысль, 1968. pp. 422. 10½см.

LAWRENCE (JOHN) of Workers Mutual Aid. Workers mutual aid. London, [1968?]. pp. 10.

MOCHUL'SKII (NIKOLAI FEDOS'EVICH) Rabochee dvizhenie v Anglii nakanune vtoroi mirovoi voiny, 1934-1939 gg. Moskva, 1968. pp. 352.

PELLING (HENRY MATHISON) Popular politics and society in late Victorian Britain: essays. London, Macmillan, 1968. pp. vii, 188. 21½cm.

ROSE (GORDON) The working class. London, Longmans 1968. pp. vii, 151. bibliog. 19½cm. (Aspects of Modern Sociology: the Social Structure of Modern Britain)

WILLIAMS (GWYN ALFRED) Artisans and Sans-Culottes: popular movements in France and Britain during the French revolution. London, Arnold, 1968. pp. viii, 128. bibliog. 20cm. (Foundations of Modern History)

ZAITSEV (VALENTIN PAVLOVICH) Рабочий класс Англии в борьбе против наступления монополий, 1956-1966 гг. Москва, 1968. pp. 214.

The AFFLUENT worker in the class structure; [by] John H. Goldthorpe [and others]. Cambridge, 1969. pp. 239. bibliog.

CHALONER (WILLIAM HENRY) The skilled artisans during the industrial revolution, 1750-1850. London, 1969. pp. 16. (Historical Association. Aids for Teachers Series. No. 15)

MITCHELL (JACK) Robert Tressell and The ragged trousered philanthropists. London, [1969]. pp. 200.

KUNINA (V.E.) Fridrikh Engel's - istorik rabochego i sotsialisticheskogo dvizheniia Anglii. in Engel's i problemy istorii: sbornik statei. Moskva, 1970.

POPULAR movements, c. 1830-1850; edited by J.T. Ward. London, 1970. pp. 206. bibliogs.

YOUNG SOCIALISTS. National Committee. A charter for young workers. [London, 1970] pp. 16.

LABOUR AND LABOURING CLASSES - United Kingdom (Cont'd.)

DUBINSKII (LEONID SEMENOVICH) Sovremennye problemy vosproizvodstva i ispol'zovaniia rabochego naseleniia v Anglii. Moskva, 1971. pp. 103.

ENGELS (FRIEDRICH) The condition of the working class in England; translated and edited by W.O. Henderson and W.H. Chaloner. 2nd ed. Oxford, 1971. pp. 386.

ESSAYS in labour history, [vol. 2], 1886-1923; edited by Asa Briggs and John Saville. London, 1971. pp. 360.

HINDESS (BARRY) The decline of working-class politics. London, 1971. pp. 191.

MUNBY (LIONEL M.) ed. The Luddites and other essays: [reprints of studies which first appeared in Our History] ...; with an introduction by Eric J. Hobsbawm. London, 1971. pp. 281.

ODDY (DEREK JOHN) The working-class diet 1886-1914; [Ph.D. (London) thesis]. 1970 [or rather 1971]. fo. 370. bibliog. Typescript: unpublished. This thesis is the property of London University and may not be removed from the Library.

ROBERTS (ERNIE) The Industrial Relations Act!, the U.C.S. struggle!, unemployment.': the solution is workers' control. Nottingham, [1971]. pp. 15. (Spokesman, The. Pamphlets. No. 19)

ROBERTS (ROBERT) of the Prison Department. The classic slum: Salford life in the first quarter of the century. Manchester, [1971]. pp. 219. bibliog.

- United Kingdom - Bibliography

BROOK (MICHAEL) compiler. A bibliography of British labour history, 1945-54; [with] Soviet writings on British labour history published in 1945-1961; part 1...by E. Loone. n.p., [1961?]. pp. 16-58.

[COMMUNIST PARTY OF GREAT BRITAIN. Historians' Group]. Select bibliography of the history of the British labour movement, 1760-1939. [London, the Party, 1961]. pp. iii, 19. bibliog. 25½cm.

- United Kingdom - Congresses

[INSTITUTE FOR WORKERS' CONTROL]. Archives in Trade Union History and Theory. Series 1. No. 4. What happened at Leeds: a report of the Leeds Convention of June 3rd, 1917; [reprint of work originally published in 1917]. [Nottingham, 1965?] pp. 16.

- United Kingdom - Education

PATON (JOHN BROWN) Secondary education for the industrial classes of England: a memorandum prepared by request of the Council of the Recreative Evening Schools Association for the Royal Commission on Secondary Education. London, [1895]. pp. 8.

LITCHFIELD (RICHARD B.) The beginnings of the Working Men's College. London, [1902]. pp. 371-380. (Supplement to the Working Men's College Journal, October, 1902)

WORKERS' EDUCATIONAL ASSOCIATION. The Workers' Educational Association: its aims and ideals. [London, 1907?] pp. 16.

CENTRAL LABOUR COLLEGE. The prospectus of the Central Labour College, Oxford. Oxford, [1911?]. 2 parts.

GORE (CHARLES) successively Bishop of Worcester, of Birmingham, and of Oxford. Address delivered...at the eighth annual meeting of the Association in Manchester, October, 1911. London, [1911]. pp. 7. (Workers' Educational Association. Leaflets. 9)

[CENTRAL LABOUR COLLEGE]. The Central Labour College policy and work: issued...to the representatives of the Parliamentary Committee at an inquiry,... held at the College on July 27th, 1914. [London, 1914?] pp. 4. (Reprinted from September number of the "Plebs" Magazine, 1914)

GEORGE (REUBEN) Unconventional approaches to adult education: our school among the hills and hedgerows;...a paper read at the annual convention ([of] the Workers' Educational Association) held in the University College, Nottingham, on October 18th, 1919. London, [1919?]. pp. 8.

WORKERS' EDUCATIONAL TRADE UNION COMMITTEE. The right to an opinion: a straightforward appeal to all trade unionists. [London, 1931] pp. 7

CATHOLIC WORKERS' COLLEGE. Annual report, 1961-62. Oxford, [1962]. pp. 19.

WORKERS' EDUCATIONAL ASSOCIATION. Central Council. Action and advance: the W.E.A. on the march; report...for 1964-1967. London, [1967]. pp. 54.

ALLAWAY (ALBERT JOHN) Challenge and response: W.E.A. East Midland District, 1919-1969. [Nottingham], 1969. pp. 131.

CORFIELD (A.J.) Epoch in workers' education: a history of the Workers' Educational Trade Union Committee. London, 1969. pp. 272.

- United Kingdom - Societies

NATIONAL FREE LABOUR ASSOCIATION. The National Free-Labour Association: its foundation, history and work. London, 1898. pp. 96.

- United Kingdom - Statistics

BRITISH LABOUR STATISTICS; year book; [pd. by] Department of Employment [U.K.]. a., 1969 [1st issue]- London.

U.K. Department of Employment. 1971. British labour statistics: historical abstract, 1886-1968. London, 1971. pp. 436.

- United Kingdom - Ireland

INTERNATIONAL SOCIALIST CONGRESS, 1919. Ireland at Berne: being the reports and memoranda presented to the International Labour and Socialist Conference held at Berne, February, 1919. Dublin, Talbot P., [1919]. pp. 52. 21½cm.

BRITISH AND IRISH COMMUNIST ORGANISATION. Pamphlets. No. 4. The working class in the Irish national revolution, 1916-23. [London, Murphy, 1966]. pp. 37.

- United Kingdom - Ireland, Northern

MURPHY (J.D) Strike at Hitler! [Belfast, 1942]. 1 pamphlet (unpaged).

- United Kingdom - Scotland

GALLACHER (WILLIAM) The Clyde in wartime: sketches of a stormy period. Glasgow, Collet's, [1920?] pp. 32. 18½cm.

- United States

STEIN (LEON) and TAFT (PHILIP) eds. Religion, reform, and revolution: labor panaceas in the nineteenth century; [reprints of pamphlets originally published 1830-1885, selected and] edited by Leon Stein and Philip Taft. New York, 1969. pp. various.

STEIN (LEON) and TAFT (PHILIP) eds. Wages, hours, and strikes: labor panaceas in the twentieth century; [reprints of pamphlets originally published 1887-1937, selected and] edited by Leon Stein and Philip Taft. New York, 1969. pp. various.

LOVESTONE (JAY) 1928: the presidential election and the workers. New York, 1928. pp. 46.

DEALTRY (WILLIAM) The laborer: a remedy for his wrongs; [reprint of the work originally published 1869]. New York, 1969. pp. 420.

LARCOM (LUCY) An idyl of work; [facsimile reprint of the work published in 1875]. Westport, Conn., 1970. pp. 183.

GLADDEN (WASHINGTON) Working people and their employers; [reprint of work originally published 1876]. New York, 1969. pp. 241.

NEW YORK (CITY). Citizens' Union. Committee on Labor and Social Reform. Workingmen as citizens New York, [1897?]. pp. 16.

GOMPERS (SAMUEL) Labor and the common welfare; [reprint of work originally published 1919]. New York, 1969. pp. 306.

INDUSTRIAL WORKERS OF THE WORLD. The silent defense: a story of the remarkable trial of members of the Industrial Workers of the World held at Sacramento, California. Chicago, [1919?]. pp. 47.

LEISERSON (WILLIAM MORRIS) Adjusting immigrant and industry; [reprint of work originally published 1924]. New York, 1969. pp. 356.

HILL (HELEN) Foreign trade and the worker's job. Boston, 1935. pp. 40. (World Peace Foundation. Popular Pamphlets on World Problems. No. 1)

BROWDER (EARL RUSSELL) Production for victory. New York, 1942. pp. 48.

BROWDER (EARL RUSSELL) America's decisive battle. New York, 1945. pp. 31.

AMERICUS pseud. Labor and socialism in America. n.p., 1948. pp. 46.

BAUER (KASPER) Watchman, what of the night? Chicago, [1951-?]. 1 pamphlet (unpaged).

BOYER (RICHARD O.) and MORAIS (HERBERT MONTFORT) A history of the American labour movement. London, Calder, 1956. pp. 402. bibliog. 21cm.

IMAN (RAYMOND S.) and KOCH (THOMAS W.) compilers. Labor in American society: [selected passages with introductions]. Chicago, Scott, [1965]. pp. 176. 23cm. (Scott Foresman Problems in American History)

LABOUR NEWS FROM THE UNITED STATES; published by the United States Information Service. London, every months, July/Aug.1967 to date. 22½-25½cm.

DERBER (MILTON) Research in labor problems in the United States. New York, Random House, [1967]. pp. vii 184. 18½cm. (Studies in Labor)

The LABOUR movement: a re-examination; a conference in honour of David J. Saposs, January 14-15, 1966; edited under the direction of Jack Barbash. [Madison, 1967]. pp. 162. bibliog.

MELTZER (MILTON) Bread - and roses: the struggle of American labor, 1865-1915. New York, Knopf, [1967]. pp. 231. bibliog. 21cm. (The Living History Library)

MONTGOMERY (DAVID) Beyond equality: labor and the radical Republicans, 1862-1872. New York, Knopf, 1967. pp. xiv, 508, xix, bibliog. 21cm.

PESSEN (EDWARD) Most uncommon Jacksonians: the radical leaders of the early labor movement. Albany, N.Y., [1967]. pp. 208.

GARRATY (JOHN ARTHUR) ed. Labor and capital in the gilded age: testimony taken by the Senate Committee upon the Relations between Labor and Capital, 1883. Boston, [Mass], 1968. pp. 178.

GUÉRIN (DANIEL) Le mouvement ouvrier aux États-Unis, 1867-1967. Paris, Maspero, 1968. pp. 174. bibliog. 18cm. (Petite Collection Maspero. 23)

JACOBSON (JULIUS) ed. The Negro and the American labor movement. Garden City, Doubleday, 1968. pp. vii, 430. 18cm. (Anchor Books. A 495)

OBERMANN (KARL) Joseph Weydemeyer: ein Lebensbild, 1818-1866. Berlin, Dietz, 1968. pp. 470. 20cm.

ROWAN (RICHARD L.) and NORTHRUP (HERBERT ROOF) eds. Readings in labor economics and labour relations. Homewood, Irwin, 1968. pp. ix, 573. 25cm.

SWADOS (HARVEY) A radical at large: American essays. London, Hart-Davis, 1968. pp. 311. 21½cm.

AUERBACH (JEROLD S.) ed. American labor: the twentieth century. Indianapolis, [1969]. pp. 474.

The AUTOBIOGRAPHIES of the Haymarket martyrs; [by Albert R. Parsons and others]; edited and with an introduction by Philip S. Foner. New York, 1969. pp. 198. bibliog.

NEWCOMB (SIMON) A plain man's talk on the labor question; [reprint of the work originally published in New York, 1886, with a new introduction]. New York, 1969. pp. 195.

WILLIAMSON (JOHN) Communist. Dangerous Scot: the life and work of an American "undesirable". New York, [1969]. pp. 221.

LABOUR AND LABOURING CLASSES - United States (Cont'd.)

WORTMAN (MAX S.) ed. Critical issues in labor: text and readings. New York, Macmillan, [1969]. pp. xiii, 466. 23½cm.

YELLOWITZ (IRWIN) The position of the worker in American society, 1865-1896. Englewood Cliffs, [1969]. pp. 118. bibliog.

ZIEGER (ROBERT H.) Republicans and labor, 1919-1929. Lexington, Kentucky, 1969. pp. 303. bibliog.

ASKOL'DOVA (S.M.) Amerikanskoe rabochee dvizhenie v rabotakh Engel'sa. in Engel's i problemy istorii. Moskva, 1970.

BERNSTEIN (IRVING) The turbulent years: (a history of the American worker, 1933-1941). Boston, [Mass.], 1970. pp. 873.

COHEN (SANFORD) Labor in the United States. 3rd ed. Columbus, Ohio, [1970]. pp. 660.

HOWE (LOUISE KAPP) ed. The white majority: between poverty and affluence. New York, [1970]. pp. 303. bibliog.

JACOBS (JIM) and LASKOWSKI (LARRY) The new rebels in industrial America. San Francisco, [1970]. pp. 18. (Reprinted from Leviathan, March 1969, with postscript, 1970)

LENIN (VLADIMIR IL'ICH) Lenin on the United States; [compiled by C. Leiteizen]. New York, [1970]. pp. 674.

MKRTCHIAN (ANATOLII ASHOTOVICH) Rabochee dvizhenie v SShA: sovremennye problemy i tendentsii. Moskva, 1970. pp. 214. bibliog.

TAFT (PHILIP) Corruption and racketeering in the labor movement. 2nd ed. Ithaca, N.Y., 1970. pp. 77. (Cornell University. New York State School of Industrial and Labor Relations. Bulletins. No. 38)

EVANS (ROBERT) The labor economies of Japan and the United States. New York, 1971. pp. 276. bibliog.

HAUSER (STUART T.) Black and white identity formation: studies in the psychosocial development of lower socioeconomic class adolescent boys. New York, [1971]. pp. 160. bibliog.

- United States - Statistics

CLAGUE (EWAN) The Bureau of Labor Statistics. New York, Praeger, 1968. pp. xv, 271. bibliog. 21cm. (Library of U.S. Government Departments and Agencies)

- United States - California

TAFT (PHILIP) Labor politics American style: the California State Federation of Labor. Cambridge, Harvard U.P., [1968]. pp. viii, 288. 23cm.

- United States - Illinois

ILLINOIS UNIVERSITY. Institute of Labor and Industrial Relations. Atlas of Illinois resources, section 5: manpower resources. Urbana, 1963. pp. (ii), 64. bibliog. 30cm.

- United States - Massachusetts

THERNSTROM (STEPHAN) Poverty and progress: social mobility in a nineteenth century city. Cambridge, Mass, Harvard University Press, 1964. pp. xiii, 286. 21cm. (Massachusetts Institute of Technology and Harvard University. Joint Center for Urban Studies. Publications)

- United States - Michigan

LEGGETT (JOHN C.) Class, race and labor: working-class consciousness in Detroit. New York, O.U.P., 1968. pp. xvii, 252. bibliog. 21cm.

- United States - Rhode Island

GOODMAN (JAY S.) The Democrats and labor in Rhode Island, 1952-1962: changes in the old alliance. Providence, Brown U.P., 1967. pp. xi, 154. 21½cm.

- United States - Washington (State)

O'CONNOR (HARVEY) Revolution in Seattle: a memoir. New York, Monthly Review Press, 1964. pp. xvii, 300. bibliog. 20½cm.

- Uruguay

UNITED STATES. Labor Statistics Bureau. Foreign Labor Information. Labor in Uruguay. [Washington], 1959. pp. iii, 26.

- Uzbekistan

ISTORIIA... История рабочего класса Узбекистана. Ташкент, Наука, 1964-66. 3 vols. bibliog. 22cm.

PULATOV (KHAKIM) Kommunisticheskii trud - faktor razvitiia proizvodstva. Tashkent, 1969. pp. 208.

- Viêt-Nam

VIET-NAM (REPUBLIC). Secrétariat d'Etat au Travail. 1959. Aperçu sur les activités du Secrétariat d'Etat au Travail. [Saigon], 1959. pp. 77.

- Vietnam - Education

INTERNATIONAL LABOUR OFFICE. Regular Programme of Technical Assistance. [Viet-Nam]. R.18. Rapport sur l'éducation ouvrière au Viet-Nam. (OIT/OTA/Viet-Nam/R.18) Genève, 1966. pp.

- White Russia

BOR'BA... Борьба трудящихся Западной Белоруссии за социальное и национальное освобождение и воссоединение с БССР: документы и материалы. том 1. 1921-1929 гг. Минск, Госиздат БССР, 1962. pp. 620. 21½cm.

SALADKAŬ (TSIMAFEI ERAFEEVICH) Bor'ba trudiashchikhsia Belorussii protiv tsarizma, 1907-1917 gg. Minsk, 1967. pp. 373.

ZAVALEEV (NIKOLAI EVTIKHIEVICH) Рабочий класс Белоруссии в борьбе за социализм, 1917-1932 гг. Минск, 1967. pp. 312. bibliog.

ABEZGAUZ (ZALMAN EVNOVICH) Razvitie promyshlennosti i formirovanie proletariata Belorussii vo vtoroi polovine XIX veka. Minsk, 1971. pp. 179. bibliog.

- Yugoslavia

> SOCIJALISTIČKI SAVEZ RADNOG NARODA JUGOSLAVIJE, Kongres, 5-i, 1960. Peti kongres, etc. Beograd, [1960], pp. 324.
>
> SOCIJALNA struktura i pokretljivost radničke klase Jugoslavije. tom 1. Beograd, Institut Društvenih Nauka, 1963. pp. 542. 24cm.
>
> TODOROVIĆ (ALEKSANDAR) Razvoj radničke svesti u socijalističkom društvu. Beograd, 1967. pp. 282. With French and Russian tables of contents.
>
> BALTIĆ (ALEKSANDR) and DESPOTOVIĆ (MILAN) Osnovi radnog prava Jugoslavije: sistem radnih odnosa Jugoslavije, i osnovni problemi sociologije rada. 2nd ed. Beograd, 1968. pp. 507.
>
> BREKIĆ (JOVO) ed. Organizacija rada u samoupravnim odnosima. Zagreb, 1970. pp. 671. bibliog. With English and Russian summaries.

LABOUR AND LABOURING CLASSES - Yugoslavia - Slovenia.
See also SOCIALISTIČNA ZVEZA DELOVNEGA LJUDSTVA SLOVENJE

- Zambia - Education

> INTERNATIONAL LABOUR OFFICE. Regular Programme of Technical Assistance. [Zambia]. R.3. Report on workers' education in Zambia. (ILO/OTA/Zambia/R.3) Geneva, 1968. pp. 47.

- Zanzibar

> EAST AFRICAN COMMON SERVICES ORGANIZATION. East African Statistical Department. 1963. The pattern of income, expenditure and consumption of unskilled workers in Zanzibar: report on a survey carried out in April, 1962. [Nairobi], 1963. pp. 25. 27½cm.

LABOUR AND LABOURING CLASSES IN LITERATURE

> ROEHNER (EBERHARD) Arbeiter in der Gegenwartsliteratur. Berlin, Dietz, 1967. pp. 256. 20cm.

LABOUR BUREAUS

- Germany

> GERMANY. Reichsanstalt für Arbeitsvermittlung und Arbeitslosenversicherung. Hauptstelle 1938. Zehn Jahre Reichsanstalt für Arbeitsvermittlung und Arbeitslosenversicherung, 1927-1937. Berlin, Elsner, [1938?]. pp. 79. 30cm.

- Italy

> BALBONI (ENZO) Le origini della organizzazione amministrativa del lavoro. Milano, Giuffrè, 1968. pp. xi, 153. 24cm. (Istituto per la Scienza dell'Amministrazione Pubblica. Quaderni ISAP. 4)

- Sweden

> SWEDEN. Arbetsmarknadsstyrelsen. 1961. Organization of the labour market administration; translation of office memorandum. rev.ed. Stockholm, 1961. fo. 6. 30cm.

- Viêtnam

> VIET-NAM. (REPUBLIC). Secrétariat d'Etat au Travail. 1959. Aperçu sur les activités du Secrétariat d'Etat au Travail. [Saigon], 1959. pp. 77.

LABOUR CAMPS

- United Kingdom

> HAZELL (WALTER) A social experiment: being an account of the working of Bird Green Test Farm for the Unemployed, from May, 1891 to December, 1894. [London, 1895]. pp. 13.

- United States

> UNITED STATES. Labor Standards Bureau. Bulletins. 235. Housing for migrant agricultural workers: labor camp.standards. rev. ed. Washington, 1962. pp. iv, 112.

LABOUR CONTRACT

> MEYERS (FREDERIC) Ownership of jobs: a comparative study. Los Angeles, [1964]. pp. 114. (California University. Institute of Industrial Relations. Industrial Relations Monographs. 11)

- America, Latin

> RENDON (GEORGES) Le droit du travail en Amérique Latine: le contrat de travail. Paris, 1970. pp. 72. bibliog. (Paris. Université. Faculté de Droit et des Sciences Economiques. Travaux et Recherches. Série "Droit Privé". No. 7)

- Belgium

> THONE (HENRI) Commentaire des lois sur le contrat d'emploi et de la loi du 30 juillet 1963 fixant le statut des représentants de commerce. Angleur-Liège, Damier, 1963. pp. 117. 24cm.

- Cape Verde Islands

> CID (FRANCISCO DE PAULA) La main d'oeuvre aux îles de Cabo Verde. Lisbonne, [imprint], 1914. pp. 15. 25½cm. Paper read at Congrès International d'Agriculture Tropicale, 3ème, Londres, 1914.

- Colombia

> CASTAÑEDA ALARCÓN (JOSÉ A.) Apuntes sobre derecho del trabajo: contrato de trabajo. Bogotá, 1962. pp. 93. bibliog. 24cm.
>
> DUQUE GÓMEZ (MARTHA) El contrato de trabajo en la legislación colombiana. Bogota, 1962. pp. 134. bibliog. 23½cm.
>
> VALENCIA CAICEDO (RODRIGO) La estabilidad en el empleo. Bogotá, 1968. pp. 129. bibliog.

LABOUR CONTRACT (Cont'd.)

- France

ORLIAC (CLAUDE) Le contrat de travail. Paris, P.U.F., 1969. pp. 128. bibliog. 17½cm. (Que Sais-Je? No. 1332)

- Germany

ZEISS (CARL) FIRMA. Arbeitsvertrag der Optischen Werkstaette von Carl Zeiss in Jena vom 15. Juli 1897, mit den Abänderungen vom 12. Februar 1900, 14. März 1900 und 8. März 1901. [Jena], 1901. pp. 34.

WIESZNER (GOETZ) Das mittelbare Arbeitsverhältnis. [Augsburg, imprint], 1940. pp. 109. bibliog.

BECKER (KLAUS) 1934- Das Aushilfsarbeitsverhältnis. [Göttingen?], 1962. pp. 161. bibliog.

DIETRICH (THOMAS) Die betrieblichen Normen nach dem Tarifvertragsgesetz vom 9.4.1949. Heidelberg, Verlagsgesellschaft Recht & Wirtschaft, [1964]. pp. xi, 123. bibliog. 20½cm. (Abhandlungen zum Arbeits- und Wirtschaftsrecht. Band 12)

UNTERSEHER (LUTZ) Arbeitsvertrag und innerbetriebliche Herrschaft: eine historische Untersuchung. Frankfurt am Main, [1969]. pp. 87. bibliog.

- Israel

GENERAL FEDERATION OF LABOUR IN ISRAEL. National Union of Metal Workers, and ISRAEL MANUFACTURERS' ASSOCIATION. Contract. [Tel Aviv, 1958]. fo. 29, 8.

- Italy

CACCIARI (MASSIMO) ed. Che fare: il '69-'70, classe operaia e capitale di fronte ai contratti. Padova, 1969. pp. 160.

- Portugal

LIMA (ADOLPHO) O contrato do trabalho: esboço historico, critica do actual contrato do trabalho, contrato collectivo de trabalho. Lisboa, Bastos, 1909. pp. 415. bibliog. 22½cm. (Estudos de Economia Social)

- United Kingdom

DIX (DOROTHY KNIGHT) Contracts of employment, with special reference to the Redundancy Payments and Contracts of Employment Acts. 3rd ed. London, Butterworths, 1968. pp. xxxii, 351.

NATIONAL JOINT COUNCIL FOR THE BUILDING INDUSTRY. National working rules for the building industry, as at 2nd March, 1970. London, [1970]. pp. 100. With appendices.

SAMUELS (HARRY) and PEARSON (NEVILLE STEWART) Redundancy payments: an annotation and guide to the Redundancy Payments Act, 1965. 2nd ed. London, 1970. pp. 197.

LABOUR COSTS

- Canada

CANADA. Dominion Bureau of Statistics. Labour costs in manufacturing. [in English and French]. Ottawa, annual, 1967 to date.

CANADA. Dominion Bureau of Statistics. Labour Division. Employment Section. 1969. Labour costs in manufacturing, 1967. Ottawa, 1969. pp. 120. In English and French.

CANADA. Dominion Bureau of Statistics. Labour Division. Employment Section. 1971. Labour costs in Canada: mines, quarries and oil wells; Coûts de la main-d'oeuvre au Canada: mines, carrières et puits de pétrole, 1969. Ottawa, 1971. pp. 104. In English and French.

- Europe

SALARI e costo del lavoro nell'Europa Occidentale; a cura di Gianni Scaiola, con la collaborazione di Paolo Gardin [and others]. Milano, Angeli, 1968. pp. 623. 22cm.

- Russia

KOMINA (LENA FEDOROVNA) Полные трудовые затраты: методология измерения и применения. Москва, 1969. pp. 182.

- United Kingdom

ECONOMIC DEVELOPMENT COMMITTEE FOR HOTELS AND CATERING. Service in hotels: a study of the labour costs of providing personal services in hotels with suggestions for cost savings. London, H.M.S.O., 1968. pp. v, 38. 24½cm.

U.K. Department of Employment and Productivity. 1968. Labour costs in Great Britain in 1964. London, 1968. pp. 22. 27½cm.

KOTAS (RICHARD) Labour costs in restaurants: a study of labour costs in catering establishments in the Greater London area. London, 1970. pp. 210. bibliog.

- United States

UNITED STATES. Agriculture Department. Economic Research Service. Agricultural Economic Reports No. 70. Utilization and cost of labor for ginning cotton. Washington, 1965. pp. iv, 31.

LABOUR COURTS

CONGRÈS DES RELATIONS INDUSTRIELLES DE L'UNIVERSITÉ LAVAL, 16e, 1961. Les tribunaux du travail. See CONGRÈS DES RELATIONS INDUSTRIELLES DE L'UNIVERSITÉ LAVAL. (Études, etc.), 1961.

- Belgium

HUBERT (ÉMILE) Les conseils de prud'hommes: leur origine, leur fonctionnement, les lois qui s'y rattachent, réformes nécessaires. Bruxelles, [imprint], 1906. pp. 39. 18½cm.

VEROUGSTRAETE (WILLEM) La procédure devant les nouvelles juridictions du travail. Bruxelles, 1969. pp. 134. Loose-leaf.

- Canada

> WANCZYCKI (JAN K.) Judicial review of decisions of labour relations boards in Canada. Ottawa, Department of Labour, 1969. pp. 37. 23cm.

- Denmark

> DENMARK. Statutes, etc. 1964. The labour court. [Copenhagen, imprint], n.d. pp. 12. 21cm.

- Europe

> COUNCIL OF EUROPE. 1961. Settlement of disputes in social law: report adopted by the Social Committee of Western European Union in May 1960. Strasbourg, 1961. pp. 60. 23cm.

> AARON (BENJAMIN) ed. Labor courts and grievance settlement in Western Europe...; essays by Xavier Blanc-Jouvan [and others]. Berkeley, 1971. pp. 342.

- Germany

> TRINKHAUS (HANS) and MENKENS (HEINZ) Geschichte und Rechtsprechung der bremischen Arbeitsgerichtsbarkeit. Berlin, Duncker & Humblot, [1967]. pp. 441. bibliog. 23cm.

- India

> MALHOTRA (L.C.) Law and practice relating to industrial adjudications. Allahabad, University Book Agency, 1967. pp. (viii), 239. 24cm.

- Ireland (Republic)

> EIRE. Redundancy Appeals Tribunal. Annual report. Dublin, annual, 1968 (1st) to date.

- Poland

> JACKOWIAK (CZESŁAW) Zakładowe organy wymiaru sprawiedliwości w sporach ze stosunku pracy. Poznań, 1965. pp. 197. bibliog. 25. (Poznań. Poznańskie Towarzystwo Przyjaciół Nauk.Wydział Historii i Nauk Społecznych. Komisja Nauk Społecznych. Prace. tom 12, zeszyt 3) With German summary.

LABOUR DISCIPLINE

- Czechoslovakia

> KALENSKÁ (MARIE) Socialistická pracovní kázeň. Praha, ČSAV, 1965. pp. 170. bibliog. 20cm.

- France

> SOINNE (BERNARD) L'analyse juridique du règlement intérieur d'entreprise. Paris, 1970. pp. 207.

- Germany, Eastern

> POGUNDKE (DIETER) and others. Arbeitsökonomische Aufgaben im sozialistischen Handelsbetrieb. Berlin, Die Wirtschaft, 1963. pp. 102.

- Hungary

> WELTNER (ANDOR) A munkafegyelem. Budapest, Közgazdasági és Jogi Könyvkiadó, 1966. pp. 277. 20cm. (Munkajogi Kézikönyvek)

- Russia

> PASHKOV (ALEKSEI STEPANOVICH) and OREKHOV (V.V.) eds. Trudovaia distsiplina kak ob"ekt sotsial'nogo planirovaniia v proizvodstvennykh kollektivakh. Leningrad, 1971. pp. 88.

- United Kingdom - British Empire

> AVINS (ALFRED) Employees' misconduct as cause for discipline and dismissal in India and the Commonwealth. Allahabad, Law Book Co., 1968. pp. cxxiv, 731. 24cm.

LABOUR DISPUTES

- Canada

> ARTHURS (HARRY W.) Labour disputes in essential industries. Ottawa, 1968 [or rather] 1970. pp. 305. bibliog. (Canada. Task Force on Labour Relations. Studies. No.8.) With French summary.

> VERGE (PIERRE) Les critères des conflits créant une situation d'urgence. Ottawa, 1967 [or rather] 1971. pp. 252. bibliog. (Canada. Task Force on Labour Relations. Studies. No. 23.) With English summary.

- Ceylon

> CEYLON. Commission on Industrial Disputes. 1968. Interim report. Colombo, 1968. pp. 14. 24½cm. (Parliament. Sessional Papers. 1968. 14)

> CEYLON. Commission on Industrial Disputes. 1970. Report...1966-69. Colombo, 1970. pp. 482. (Parliament. Sessional Papers. 1970. No.4)

- Europe

> AARON (BENJAMIN) ed. Dispute settlement procedures in five western European countries; papers by Xavier Blanc-Jouvan [and others]. Los Angeles, [1969]. pp. 90.

> AARON (BENJAMIN) ed. Labor courts and grievance settlement in Western Europe...; essays by Xavier Blanc-Jouvan [and others]. Berkeley, 1971. pp. 342.

- Fiji Islands

> GOULD (Sir TREVOR) Report...on the trade dispute between the Airport, Hotel and Catering Workers' Union and Qantas Empire Airways Ltd. in FIJI. Legislative Council. Journal. Sessions of 1967, which see.

- Germany

> RAJEWSKY (XENIA) Arbeitskampfrecht in der Bundesrepublik. Frankfurt am Main, 1970. pp. 87. bibliog.

- India

> ROW (V.G.) Law relating to industrial disputes. 3rd ed. Madras, 1967. pp. 869.

> MALHOTRA (O.P.) The law of industrial disputes. Bombay, 1968. pp. 1085.

> PANDEY (SHIV MOHAN) Government employees' strike: a study in white collar unionism in India. Meerut, [1969]. pp. 106.

LABOUR DISPUTES (Cont'd.)

- Italy

REGINI (MARINO) and REYNERI (EMILIO) Lotte operaie e organizzazione del lavoro. Padova, 1971. pp. 191.

- New Zealand

COMMUNIST PARTY OF NEW ZEALAND. Watersiders! harbour board workers! tally clerks! foremen stevedores! wharf foremen! drivers! railwaymen! seamen! timekeepers! unite to free N.Z. from foreign shipping monopoly. Auckland, 1965. pp. 32. 21½cm.

- Russia

McAULEY (MARY) Labour disputes in Soviet Russia, 1957-1965. Oxford, Clarendon, 1969. pp. ix, 269. bibliog. 21½cm.

KLIUEV (ANATOLII ALEKSEEVICH) and MAVRIN (ALEKSANDR VENEDIKTOVICH) Spravochnik chlena komissii po trudovym sporam. 3rd ed. Moskva, 1971. pp. 272.

- Switzerland

VETSCH (G.) Arbeitsgerichte, ordentliche Gerichte und Schiedsgerichte in Arbeitsstreitigkeiten. in Zukunftsaufgaben in Wirtschaft und Gesellschaft. Zurich, 1963.

- United Kingdom

ROBERTS (GEOFFREY) Demarcation rules in shipbuilding and ship repairing. Cambridge, C.U.P., 1967. pp. 45. 24cm. (Cambridge. University. Department of Applied Economics. Occasional Papers. 14)

ELDRIDGE (JOHN E. T.) Industrial disputes: essays in the sociology of industrial relations. London, Routledge & Kegan Paul, 1968. pp. x, 277. bibliog.

WEDDERBURN (KENNETH WILLIAM) and DAVIES (P. L.) Employment grievances and disputes procedures in Britain. Berkeley, 1969. pp. 301.

REPORT of a Committee of Inquiry into the difference between the Newlyn Pier and Harbour Commissioners and the Transport and General Workers Union over the reinstatement of former employees: [W. Hagenbuch, chairman]. London, H.M.S.O., 1970. pp. 11.

REPORT of a Court of Inquiry under Professor John C. Wood, LL.M., into a dispute between Pilkington Brothers Ltd. (and subsidiaries of that company) and certain of their employees. London, H.M.S.O., 1970. pp. 25.

- United States

STEIN (LEON) and TAFT (PHILIP) eds. Wages, hours, and strikes: labor panaceas in the twentieth century; [reprints of pamphlets originally published 1887-1937, selected and] edited by Leon Stein and Philip Taft. New York, 1969. pp. various.

STEIN (LEON) ed. The Pullman strike; [reprint of pamphlets originally published 1894-1913] selected and edited by Leon Stein. New York, 1969. pp. various.

LA BOURDONNAIS (BERTRAND FRANÇOIS MAHÉ DE)
See MAHÉ DE LA BOURDONNAIS (BERTRAND FRANÇOIS)

LABOUR ECONOMICS
See LABOUR AND LABOURING CLASSES

LABOUR EXCHANGES

DENIS (HECTOR) Robert Owen: les principes et l'experimentation du labour exchange. Bruxelles, 1895. pp. 21. (Extrait des Annales de l'Institut des Sciences Sociales)

LEVINE (LOUIS) b. 1907. The public employment service in social and economic policy: deliberations of a working party. Paris, Organisation for Economic Co-operation and Development, 1969. pp. 59. (Employment and Training)

- America, Latin

INTERNATIONAL LABOUR OFFICE. Regular Programme of Technical Assistance. [Latin America]. R.7. Informe del curso sobre los servicios del empleo, Lima, Peru, 1.° de agosto - 16 de diciembre de 1966. (OIT/OTA/LAT/R.7) Ginebra, 1967. pp. 27.

- Austria

VIENNA. Landesarbeitsamt. 20 Jahre Landesarbeitsamt Wien, 1945-1965. Wien, Landesarbeitsamt, 1965. pp. 108. 29cm.

DANIMANN (FRANZ) Die Arbeitsämter unter dem Faschismus. Wien, [1966]. pp. 55. bibliog.

- Ireland (Republic)

INSTITUTE OF PUBLIC ADMINISTRATION, DUBLIN. Report...on the Placement and Guidance Service: [J.A. Agnew, chairman of the Steering Committee]. Dublin, [1968]. pp. 131.

- Italy

PETRUZZELLI (FRANCESCO) I collocamenti obbligatori; corso di aggiornamento per i Collocatori comunali della provincia di Bari, etc. Bari, [1960?] pp. 23. 24½cm.

ROBERTIS (GIUSEPPE DE) La funzione del collocamento; corso di aggiornamento per i Collocatori comunali della provincia di Bari, etc. Bari, [1960?] pp. 73 24½cm.

VELLA (MICHELE) Il servizio del collocamento; corso di aggiornamento per i Collocatori comunali della provincia di Bari, etc. Bari, [1960?]. pp. 69. 24½cm.

- Jordan

INTERNATIONAL LABOUR OFFICE. Development Programme: Technical Assistance Sector. [Jordan]. R.10. Report to the government of the Hashemite Kingdom of Jordan on the programme for the establishment of an employment service. (ILO/TAP/Jordan/R.10) Geneva, 1967. pp. 11.

- Tanzania

> INTERNATIONAL LABOUR OFFICE. Development Programme: Technical Assistance Sector. [Tanzania]. R.5. Report to the government of the United Republic of Tanzania on the national employment service (ILO/TAP/Tanzania/R.5) Geneva, 1969. pp. 52.

- Tunis

> INTERNATIONAL LABOUR OFFICE. Development Programme. Technical Assistance Sector. [Tunisia], R.20. Rapport au gouvernement de la République de Tunisie sur l'organisation et le fonctionnement de l'Office de la formation professionnelle. (OIT/TAP/Tunisie/R.20) Genève, 1969. pp. 103.

- United Kingdom

> LEC MEMORANDUM; issued by the Department of Employment and Productivity for the information of local employment committees. London, irreg., 1946 to date.

> U.K. Central Office of Information. Reference Division. 1967. Government employment and training services in Britain. rev. ed. London, 1967. pp. 8. bibliog. 23½cm.

- United States

> NEW YORK (STATE). Governor's Commission on Unemployment Relief. 1935. The public employment services in the state of New York: their organization, operation and relationship to relief administration. Albany, 1935. pp. 141.

> NEMORE (ARNOLD L.) and MANGUM (GARTH LEROY) Reorienting the federal-state employment service. Ann Arbor, 1968 repr. 1969. pp. 67. (Michigan University and Wayne State University. Institute of Labor and Industrial Relations. Policy Papers in Human Resources and Industrial Relations. No. 8)

> ADAMS (LEONARD P.) The public Employment Service in transition, 1933-1968: evolution of a placement service into a manpower agency. Ithaca, 1969. pp. 246. (Cornell University. New York State School of Industrial and Labor Relations. Studies in Industrial and Labor Relations. vol. 16)

LABOUR INJUNCTIONS

- Canada - Ontario

> REPORT of a study on the labour injunction in Ontario; A.W.R. Carrothers, Director; E.E. Palmer, Deputy Director. [Toronto, Ontario Department of Labour], 1966. 2 vols. (in 1).

LABOUR INSPECTION

> INTERNATIONAL LABOUR CONFERENCE. 52nd Session. Reports. 5. Fifth item on the agenda: labour inspection in agriculture. Geneva, 1967-68. 2 pts.

> INTERNATIONAL LABOUR CONFERENCE. 53rd Session. Reports. 4. Fourth item on the agenda: labour inspection in agriculture. Geneva, 1968-69. 2 pts.

- Dominican Republic

> INTERNATIONAL LABOUR OFFICE. Development Programme: Technical Assistance Sector. [Dominican Republic]. R.4. Informe al gobierno de la Republica Dominicana sobre la inspeccion del trabajo (OIT/TAP/Rep. Dominicana/R. 4) Ginebra, 1968. pp. 142.

- Europe

> COUNCIL OF EUROPE. Social Committee. 1967. Labour inspection: scope, organisation and administration. Strasbourg, 1967. pp. 35. (Social Co-operation in Europe.)

- Italy

> CRESTA (ATTILIO) L'Ispettorato del lavoro: compiti e natura giuridica. Milano, Giuffrè, 1966. pp. 155. 22cm.

- Venezuela

> INTERNATIONAL LABOUR OFFICE. Development Programme: Technical Assistance Sector. [Venezuela]. R.8. Informe al gobierno de la Republica de Venezuela sobre la inspeccion del trabajo. (OIT/TAP/Venezuela/R.8) Ginebra, 1967. pp. 40.

LABOUR LAWS AND LEGISLATION

> CORNIL (M.) Particularités du droit social comparé. in Brussels. Université Libre. Faculté de Droit. Travaux et Conférences. 10. [Brussels], [1962].

> UNITED STATES. Women's Bureau. Women in the World Today. International Reports. 5. Protective labor legislation for women in 91 countries. Washington, 1963. pp. v, 33, iii.

> SZAKSZERVEZETI tevékenység a Munka Törvénykönyve alapján. Budapest, 1966. pp. 365.

> LAW and industrial relations:...proceedings [of conference sponsored by the Centre for Industrial Relations, Toronto University, and the Osgoode Hall Law School], May 26-27, 1966; H.W. Arthurs and John H.G. Crispo, editors. Toronto, 1967. pp. 106.

> MAYER-MALY (THEO) and others, eds. Festschrift für Hans Schmitz zum 70. Geburtstag. Wien, Herold, [1967]. 2 vols. 24cm.

> SZÁSZY (ISTVÁN) International labour law: a comparative survey of the conflict rules affecting labour legislation and regulations ... edited by Louis A. De Pinna. Leyden, Sijthoff, 1968. pp. (vi), 465. bibliog. 23½cm.

> VIRTON (PAUL) Histoire et politique du droit du travail. Paris, Spes, [1968]. pp. 254. 21cm. (Bibliothèque de la Recherche Sociale)

- Study and teaching

> ZACHER (HANS F.) Die Lehre des Sozialrechts an den Universitäten in der Bundesrepublik Deutschland. Wiesbaden, Chmielorz, 1968. pp. 109. bibliog. 22cm. (Schriftenreihe des Deutschen Sozialgerichtsverbandes. Band 3)

- Aden

> ADEN. 1960. Industrial legislation, 1960: statement of policy presented to the Legislative Council on the 1st August, 1960 by the Member-in-Charge [T. Fallows] Labour, Welfare and Local Government. Aden, [1960]. pp. 19. 25cm.

LABOUR LAWS AND LEGISLATION (Cont'd.)

- America, Latin - Bibliography

PAETZ (JUERGEN) Das Arbeits-, Sozial- und Investitionsrecht iberoamerikanischer Länder: eine Auswahl deutscher und ausländischer Veröffentlichungen. Hamburg, Institut für Iberoamerika-Kunde, 1963. pp. 62. 20½cm. (Reihe Bibliographie und Dokumentation. Heft 1)

- Australia

CONFERENCE OF STATE MINISTERS FOR LABOUR AND INDUSTRY RE UNIFORMITY OF LEGISLATION AND ADMINISTRATION, SYDNEY, 1947. Conference of State Ministers for Labour and Industry re Uniformity of Legislation and Administration, 11th,12th and 13th February, 1947. Sydney, 1947. pp. 48.

FOENANDER (ORWELL DE RUYTER) Recent developments in Australian industrial regulation. Melbourne, 1970. pp. 207.

- Austria

MAYER-MALY (THEO) Österreichisches Arbeitsrecht. Wien, 1970. pp. 262.

- Azerbaijan

KHALAFOV (M. S.) Мероприятия Советской власти в Азербайджане в области трудового права, 1917-1918 гг. Баку, Академия Наук Азербайджанской ССР, 1964. pp. 84. 19cm.

- Belgium

SYNDICAT DES EMPLOYÉS TECHNICIENS ET CADRES DE BELGIQUE. Droits et protection de l'employé. [Brussels, Leclercq, 1967]. pp. xii, 210. 17½cm.

BLANPAIN (ROGER) Handboek van het belgisch arbeidsrecht. 2nd ed. Gent, Story-Scientia, 1968 in progress. 24cm.

SEYFARTH, SHAW, FAIRWEATHER AND GERALDSON. Labor relations and the law in Belgium and the United States: a comparative study. Ann Arbor, Michigan, [1969]. pp. 455. bibliog. (Michigan University. Bureau of Business Research. Program in International Business. Michigan International Labor Studies. vol. 2)

PIRON (JACQUES) and DENIS (PIERRE) Chargé de cours à la Faculté de Droit de l'Université Catholique de Louvain. Le droit des relations collectives du travail en Belgique. Bruxelles, 1970. pp. 301. bibliogs.

- Botswana

CATCHPOLE (F.C.) Report on labour legislation in the Bechuanaland Protectorate. [Mafeking], 1960. fo. various.

- Brazil

BRAZIL. Ministerio do Trabalho e Previdência Social. Boletim. s-a. (formerly 4 nos. in 1 a yr.), Ja/D 1961 (nos. 1/4)- ; susp. pbln. Jl 1967 - Je 1968. Rio de Janeiro.

SILVA (C.A. BARATA) and SANVICENTE (BRENO) Introdução ao direito brasileiro do trabalho: comentários à consolidação das leis do trabajo, artigos 1 a 12. Pôrto Alegre, Sulina, 1963. pp. 472, vii. bibliogs. 22½cm.

CAMPANHOLE (ADRIANO) Consolidação das leis do trabalho. 19th ed. São Paulo, Atlas, 1968. pp. 333. 21 cm.

CAMPANHOLE (ADRIANO) Consolidação das leis do trabalho. 20th ed. São Paulo, Atlas, 1968. pp. 335. 20½cm. (Biblioteca Legislação Trabalhista)

- Bulgaria

ZLATINCHEV (IORDAN) Борбата за трудово законодателство в България, 1878-1944 г. София, Профиздат, 1961. pp. 389. 20cm.

MIRKOV (DIMITŬR) Trudovo pravorazdavane v Narodna Republika Bŭlgariia; prerabotil i dopŭlnil...Zh. Stalev. Sofiia, 1964. pp. 226.

- Burundi

INTERNATIONAL LABOUR OFFICE. Development Programme: Technical Assistance Sector. [Burundi]. R.2. Rapport au gouvernement du Burundi sur la legislation et l'administration du travail. (OIT/TAP/Burundi/R.2). Genève, 1967. pp. ix, 203. 30cm.

- Canada

CANADA. Statutes, etc. 1954-66. Rules of procedure of the Canada Labour Relations Board (with amendments, June, 1966). Ottawa, 1957-66. 2 pts. 25cm.

CANADA. Department of Labour. 1965. The Canada Labour (Standards) Code. [Ottawa, 1965]. pp. 27. Code and regulations in end pocket.

CANADA. Department of Labour. Legislation Branch. 1970. Labour relations in Canada; [by Eileen Sufrin]. Ottawa, 1970. pp. 180.

- Canada - New Brunswick

NEW BRUNSWICK. Department of Labour. 1964. Canadian labour standards legislation versus discrimination, prejudice and exploitation. [Fredericton, 1964?]. pp. iii, 39. 28cm.

- Canada - Nova Scotia

McKINNON (ALEXANDER H.) Report of fact-finding body re labour legislation. Antigonish, 1962. pp. 153.

LABOUR LEGISLATION IN NOVA SCOTIA; [pd.by] Nova Scotia Department of Labour. a., 1969- Halifax, N.S.

- Canada - Quebec (Province)

CONGRÈS DES RELATIONS INDUSTRIELLES DE L'UNIVERSITÉ LAVAL, 20e, 1965. Le code du travail du Québec, 1965. See CONGRÈS DES RELATIONS INDUSTRIELLES DE L'UNIVERSITÉ LAVAL. (Études, etc.), 1965.

CUTLER (PHILIP) Labour relations and court review: a study in the supervision and control of administrative tribunals. Montreal, Tundra Books, 1968. pp. x, 332. bibliog. 23½cm.

- Canada - Saskatchewan

SASKATCHEWAN. Statutes, etc. 1944-58. Saskatchewan labour legislation, April, 1958. [Regina], Department of Labour, 1958. pp. 82.

SASKATCHEWAN. Statutes, etc. 1944-63. Saskatchewan labour legislation, August, 1963. [Regina], Department of Labour, 1963. pp. 110.

SASKATCHEWAN. Statutes, etc. 1944-65. Saskatchewan labour legislation, August, 1965. [Regina, Department of Labour], 1965. pp. 114.

SASKATCHEWAN. Statutes, etc. 1944-67. Saskatchewan labour legislation, April, 1967. [Regina], Department of Labour, 1967. pp. 118.

- Chile

JARA (ALVARO) Fuentes para la historia del trabajo en el Reino de Chile: legislación. Santiago de Chile, Universidad de Chile, Centro de Investigaciones de Historia Americana, 1965 in progress. (Serie Documental y Bibliográfica. 1)

- Colombia

CASTAÑEDA ALARCÓN (JOSÉ A.) Apuntes sobre derecho del trabajo: contrato de trabajo. Bogotá, 1962. pp. 93. bibliog. 24cm.

COLOMBIA. Statutes, etc. 1959-61. Disposiciones legales en materia laboral. Bogota, 1962. pp. 29.

ESCOBAR TÉLLEZ (JORGE ENRIQUE) Colombia frente a las principales normas marítimas de derecho laboral internacional. Bogotá, 1967. pp. 127. bibliog. 24cm.

NAVARRETE DOMINGUEZ (GERMAN) El sindicalismo como asociación profesional. Bogotá, 1968. pp. 142. bibliog.

VALENCIA CAICEDO (RODRIGO) La estabilidad en el empleo. Bogotá, 1968. pp. 129. bibliog.

- Congo (Kinshasa)

INTERNATIONAL LABOUR OFFICE. Development Programme. Technical Assistance Sector [Congo/Kin] R.13. Rapport au gouvernement de la République Démocratique du Congo sur l'administration et la législation du travail. (OIT/TAP/Congo (Kin)/R.13) Geneva, 1969. pp. 54.

- Cuba

CUBA. Statutes, etc. 1959-1960. La revolución en el campo laboral: 5 leyes básicas en materia de trabajo, dictadas por el gobierno revolucionario de Cuba. (Ministerio del Trabajo) [Havana, 1960?] pp. 245. 18cm.

- Czechoslovakia

CZECHOSLOVAKIA. Statutes, etc. 1965. Zákoník práce a předpisy souvisící. Praha, Práce, 1966. pp. 557. 14cm.

BERNARD (FRANTIŠEK) and PAVLÁTOVÁ (JARMILA) Pracovní poměr. Praha, Práce, 1967. pp. 307. 20½cm. (Pracovněprávní Knižnice. svazek 14)

MAŘÍK (VLADIMIR) and URBANEC (ALFONS) Die tschechoslowakischen Gewerkschaften und das Arbeitsrecht. Prag, 1967. pp. 114.

WITZ (KAREL) ed. Československé pracovní právo: učebnice, etc. Praha, Orbis, 1967. pp. 446. bibliog. 20cm.

CZECHOSLOVAKIA. Statutes, etc. 1968. Zákoník práce a předpisy souvisící. 3rd ed. Praha, Práce, 1968. pp. 515. 14½cm.

TEJKAL (JIŘÍ) and others. Zákonník práce v otázkach a odpovediach. Bratislava, 1968. pp. 317.

- Dominican Republic

DOMINICAN REPUBLIC. Statutes, etc. 1951. Código de trabajo: votado por la Ley No. 2920 del Congreso Nacional, promulgada por el Poder Ejecutivo el 11 de junio de 1951 y publicada en la Gaceta Oficial No. 7309 bis, del 23 de julio, 1951. 3rd ed. Ciudad Trujillo, 1957. pp. 226. 23cm.

- Egypt

UNITED STATES. Labor Statistics Bureau. BLS Reports. No. 275. Labor law and practice in the United Arab Republic, Egypt. Washington, 1965. pp. 100. bibliog.

- Europe

ROSE (ARNOLD MARSHALL) Migrants in Europe: problems of acceptance and adjustment. Minneapolis, [1969]. pp. 194.

- Europe, Eastern

PASHERSTNIK (A. E.) Трудовое право стран народной демократии. Москва, Госюриздат, 1955. pp. 140. 20cm.

- European Economic Community countries

EUROPEAN COAL AND STEEL COMMUNITY. 1956. Arrangement en exécution de la décision relative à l'application de l'article 69 du Traité instituant la Communauté Européenne du Charbon et de l'Acier. [Luxembourg], 1956. pp. (54). 28½cm.

MONJAU (MAX WERNER) Das Arbeitskampfrecht in den Ländern der Europäischen Wirtschaftsgemeinschaft. München, imprint, 1967. pp. xxxvi, 188. bibliog. 24cm.

BONTEMPS (JEAN) Liberté d'établissement et libre prestation des services dans le Marché commun: directives de suppression des restrictions et directives de mesures transitoires. Bruxelles, Bruylant, 1968. pp. 316. 22cm.

- France

GIVERT (JACQUES) Mémento de législation sociale et hygiène: imprimerie de labeur. 3rd ed. Paris, Institut National des Industries et Arts Graphiques, 1966. pp. 146. 20½cm.

DESPAX (MICHEL) Le droit du travail. Paris, P.U.F., 1967. pp. 128. bibliog. 17½cm. (Que Sais-Je? No. 1268)

BRUN (ANDRÉ) and GALLAND (H.) Droit du travail: bilan de dix années, avec les ordonnances de 1967. rev. ed. [Paris], Sirey, 1968. pp. vi, 317. 24cm. (Traités Sirey)

DESPAX (MICHEL) Le droit du travail. 2nd ed. Paris, 1970. pp. 126. bibliog.

LABOUR LAWS AND LEGISLATION - France (Cont'd.)

SUET (PHILIPPE) L'application pratique de la législation du travail dans les entreprises. 2nd ed. Paris, 1970. pp. 382.

- France - Colonies

FRANCE. Statutes, etc. 1952. Code du travail: loi no. 52, 1322, du 15 décembre 1952 instituant un code du travail dans les territoires et territoires associés relevant du Ministère de la France d'Outre-Mer. Tananarive, 1953. pp. 37.

- Germany

LANGE (PAUL) Die soziale Bewegung der kaufmännischen Angestellten. Berlin, Zentralverband der Angestellten, 1920. pp. viii, 229. 24½cm.

LANDESVEREINIGUNG DER INDUSTRIELLEN ARBEITGEBER-VERBÄNDE NORDRHEIN-WESTFALENS. Geschäftsführerkonferenz, Berlin, 1962. Die Entwicklung des Arbeitsrechts in Ost und West: Vorträge, etc. [Düsseldorf, imprint, 1962?]. pp. 69. (Landesvereinigung der Industriellen Arbeitgeberverbände Nordrhein-Westfalens. Schriftenreihe. Heft 19)

APITZ (HANS JOACHIM) Entstehung und Bedeutung der deutschen Sozialgesetzgebung für Heimarbeiter und Angestellte in den Jahren 1896 bis 1914. Berlin, 1967. pp. 154. bibliog.

TRINKHAUS (HANS) and MENKENS (HEINZ) Geschichte und Rechtsprechung der bremischen Arbeitsgerichtsbarkeit. Berlin, Duncker & Humblot, [1967]. pp. 441. bibliog. 23cm.

BALLERSTEDT (KURT) and others, eds. Recht und Rechtsleben in der sozialen Demokratie: Festgabe für Otto Kunze zum 65.Geburtstag. Berlin, 1969. pp. 306. bibliog.

SEYFARTH, SHAW, FAIRWEATHER AND GERALDSON. Labor relations and the law in West Germany and the United States: a comparative study. Ann Arbor, Michigan, [1969]. pp. 606. bibliog. (Michigan University. Bureau of Business Research. Program in International Business. Michigan International Labor Studies. vol. 3)

WELLER (BERNHARD) Arbeitslosigkeit und Arbeitsrecht: Untersuchung der Möglichkeiten zur Bekämpfung der Arbeitslosigkeit unter Einbeziehung der Geschichte des Arbeits- und Sozialrechts. Stuttgart, 1969. pp. 268. bibliog.

- Germany, Eastern

LANDESVEREINIGUNG DER INDUSTRIELLEN ARBEITGEBER-VERBÄNDE NORDRHEIN-WESTFALENS. Geschäftsführerkonferenz, Berlin, 1962. Die Entwicklung des Arbeitsrechts in Ost und West: Vorträge, etc. [Düsseldorf, imprint, 1962?]. pp. 69. (Landesvereinigung der Industriellen Arbeitgeberverbände Nordrhein-Westfalens. Schriftenreihe. Heft 19)

POGUNDKE (DIETER) and others. Arbeitsökonomische Aufgaben im sozialistischen Handelsbetrieb. Berlin, Die Wirtschaft, 1963. pp. 102.

MAMPEL (SIEGFRIED) Arbeitsverfassung und Arbeitsrecht in Mitteldeutschland. Stuttgart, Kohlhammer, [1966]. pp. 567. 23cm.

Das SOZIALISTISCHE Arbeitsrecht im neuen ökonomischen System: Materialien der 23. Sitzung der Volkskammer am 23. November, 1966 mit dem Wortlaut des Zweiten Gesetzes zur Änderung und Ergänzung des Gesetzbuches der Arbeit der DDR. [Berlin], 1966. pp. 96. (Aus der Tätigkeit der Volkskammer und ihrer Ausschüsse. 4. Wahlperiode. Heft 10)

GERMANY (DEUTSCHE DEMOKRATISCHE REPUBLIK). Ministerrat. Staatliches Amt für Arbeit und Löhne. 1968. Gesetzbuch der Arbeit, und eine Auswahl anderer Bestimmungen arbeitsrechtlichen Inhalts. Berlin, 1968. 2 vols. (in 1). 21cm.

MICHAS (JOACHIM) ed. Arbeitsrecht der DDR...: eine systematische Darstellung und Erläuterung des Gesetzbuches der Arbeit der Deutschen Demokratischen Republik in der Neufassung vom 23.November 1966, etc. Berlin, Staatsverlag, 1968. pp. 526. 21cm.

- Guatemala

GUATEMALA. Statutes, etc. 1947-56. Codigo de trabajo, decreto numero 330 del Congreso, y sus reformas contenidas en decreto numero 570 del presidente de la republica. Guatemala, 1956. pp. 245. 16½cm.

GUATEMALA. Ministerio de Trabajo y Bienestar Social. 1958. Exposición de motivos y proyecto de ley del estatuto de los trabajadores del estado. (Separata de la Revista del Ministerio de Trabajo y Bienestar Social) Guatemala, Ministerio de Educación Pública, 1958. pp. 71. 24cm.

- Hungary

MOLNÁR (DÁNIEL) Munkajogi gyakorlatok. Budapest, Táncsics, 1965. pp. 231. 20cm.

RUDOLF (LORÁNT) Határidők a polgári jogban és a munkajogban. Budapest, Közgazdasági és Jogi Könyvkiadó, 1965. pp. 217. 18cm. With Russian and German tables of contents.

BOGYAY (GÉZA) Vállalati munkajogi kézikönyv. 2nd ed. Budapest, Közgazdasági és Jogi Könyvkiadó, 1966. pp. 640. 20cm.

MIHOLICS (TIVADAR) and others. Hatályos munkajogi állásfoglalások 1966. Budapest, Táncsics Könyvkiadó, 1966. pp. 143. 20cm.

WELTNER (ANDOR) Fundamental traits of socialist labour law, with special regard to Hungarian legislation. Budapest, 1970. pp. 218.

- India

INDIA. Ministry of Labour and Employment. 1961. Employers' obligations under labour laws. [Delhi], 1961. pp. 46.

ARYA (V.P.) A guide to settlement of industrial disputes. 2nd ed. Calcutta, Oxford and IBH Publishing Co., 1967. pp. 122. 21½cm.

DAWSON (WILLIAM ALBERT) An introductory guide to central labour legislation. London, Asia Publishing House, [1967]. pp. xi, 240. 21cm.

MALHOTRA (L.C.) Dismissal, discharge, termination of service and punishment. Allahabad, University Book Agency, 1967. pp. 3, 192. 24cm.

MALHOTRA (L.C.) Law and practice relating to industrial adjudications. Allahabad, University Book Agency, 1967. pp. (viii), 239. 24cm.

VOHRA (D.N.) Dismissal, discharge and punishment, lay-off and retrenchment in the private sector; [edited by Inder Jit]. 4th ed. New Delhi, Labour Law Publishers, 1967. pp. x, 348. 23½cm.

INDIA. Study Group on Labour Legislation. 1968. Final report; with draft labour code. Delhi, 1968. pp. 200.

INDIA. Study Group on Labour Legislation. 1968. Interim report. Delhi, 1968. pp. 53.

KOTHARI (GANPATLAL M.) A study of industrial law, labour laws. Bombay, 1968. pp. 705. bibliog.

MALHOTRA (L.C.) Dismissal, discharge, termination of service and punishment. 2nd ed. Allahabad, 1968. pp. 279.

VARKEY (N.K.) A handbook of labour legislation in India. Bombay, Lalvani, 1968. pp. ix, 175. 22cm.

INDIA. Central Working Group on Labour Administration. 1969. Report. Delhi, 1969. pp. 131.

INDIA. Working Group on Labour Administration (Eastern Region). 1969. Report. Delhi, 1969. pp. 126.

INDIA. Working Group on Labour Administration (Northern Region). 1969. Report. Delhi, 1969. pp. 157.

INDIA. Working Group on Labour Administration (Southern Region). 1969. Report. Delhi, 1969. pp. 162.

INDIA. Working Group on Labour Administration (Western Region). 1969. Report. Delhi, 1969. pp. 190.

NATIONAL SEMINAR ON INDUSTRIAL RELATIONS IN A DEVELOPING ECONOMY, 4TH, 1968. Issues in Indian labour policy: papers and conclusions...; edited by C.K. Johri. New Delhi, [1969]. pp. 344.

- India - Rajasthan

JINDEL (S.K.) and JINDEL (B.M.) Rajasthan labour code. Jodhpur, 1968. 2 vols.

- Iran

UNITED STATES. Labor Statistics Bureau. BLS Reports. No. 276. Labor law and practice in Iran. Washington, 1964. pp. iv, 63. bibliog.

- Iraq

IRAQ. Statutes, etc. 1958-61. Labour law, No. 1 for 1958: (and Amendments). Baghdad, 1958-62. 2 pts.

- Italy

ITALY. Statutes, etc. 1923-1959. Provvedimenti per l'artigianato: raccolta di disposizioni legislative ed amministrative. 2nd ed. Roma, 1961. 192. 20½cm.

ITALY. Statutes, etc. 1956-1961. Codice del lavoro: raccolta completa della legislazione vigente corredata di ampie note illustrative e commentata articolo con la guirisprudenza, la prassi amministrativa...; appendice di aggiornamento al 31 dicembre 1961. Roma, Sapi, 1962. 2 vols. (in 1).

CORRADO (RENATO) Trattato di diritto del lavoro. [Turin], Unione Tipografico-Editrice Torinese, 1965-66. 2 vols. bibliog. 24cm.

ALFONSO (VICENZO ROBERTO) La sicurezza sociale del lavoratore italiano all'estero e dello straniero in Italia: tutela giuridica e previdenziale, convenzioni internazionali; manuale teorico-pratico etc. Milano, Pirola, 1967. pp. 447. bibliog. 24cm.

GIUDICE (RICCARDO DEL) Scritti di storia e diritto del lavoro. Roma, Edizioni Ricerche, 1967. pp. 297. 24cm.

ITALY. Statutes, etc. 1942-66. Italian law of companies, labour, enterprise and economic organisation: the Italian civil code, book five; translated, annotated and with an introduction by V.G. Venturini. Deventer, Kluwer, 1967. pp. 245.

ARCECI (GIULIO) Legislazione sociale. 2nd ed. Parma, 1968. pp. 492. bibliog.

BALBONI (ENZO) Le origini della organizzazione amministrativa del lavoro. Milano, Giuffrè, 1968. pp. xi, 153. 24cm. (Istituto per la Scienza dell'Amministrazione Pubblica. Quaderni ISAP. 4)

ITALY. Ministero del Lavoro e della Previdenza Sociale. Rassegna del Lavoro. Quaderni. 47. Giurisprudenza del lavoro, 1967. Roma, 1968. pp. 191.

BARBARANELLI (FABRIZIO) Manuale dell'agitatore operaio: salari istituti normativi, contratti, accordi interconfederali. Roma, [1969]. pp. 121.

ITALY. Ministero del Lavoro e della Previdenza Sociale. Rassegna del Lavoro. Quaderni. 51. Giurisprudenza del lavoro, 1968. Roma, 1969. pp. 195.

MAZZONI (GIULIANO) Manuale di diritto del lavoro. 3rd ed. Milano, 1969. pp 1186. bibliog.

SEYFARTH, SHAW, FAIRWEATHER AND GERALDSON. Labor relations and the law in Italy and the United States: a comparative study. Ann Arbor, 1970. pp. 464. bibliog. (Michigan University. Bureau of Business Research. Program in International Business. Michigan International Labor Studies. vol. 4)

- Jamaica

JAMAICA. Industrial Development Corporation. Information Pamphlets. No.10. Legislation affecting labour. Kingston, 1961. fo.9. 28cm.

LABOUR LAWS AND LEGISLATION (Cont'd.)

- Kenya

KENYA. Sessional Papers. 1963/65. No. 7. International Labour Conference: proposed action by the Republic of Kenya on certain conventions and recommendations adopted by the...Conference [Nairobi], 1965. pp. 31. 25cm.

KENYA. Sessional Papers. 1969. No. 3. International Labour Organization: proposed action by the Republic of Kenya on certain conventions and recommendations adopted by the International Labour Conference. [Nairobi, 1969]. pp. 68.

- Laos

UNITED STATES. Labor Statistics Bureau. BLS Reports. No. 290. Labor law and practice in the Kingdom of Laos. Washington, 1965. bibliog. pp. iv, 59.

- Latvia

ZONNE (OSVALD IANOVICH) Возникновение важнейших институтов советского трудового права в Латвийской ССР, 1940-1941 г.г. Рига, 1968. pp. 56.

ZONNE (OSVALD IANOVICH) Pravovoe regulirovanie truda v burzhuaznoi Latvii i ego ekspluatatorskaia sushchnost', 1920-1940 gg. Riga, 1969. pp. 59.

- Lebanon

UNITED STATES. Labor Statistics Bureau. BLS Reports. No. 304. Labor law and practice in Lebanon. [Washington, 1966] pp. vi, 98. bibliog.

- Malaysia

UNITED STATES. Labor Statistics Bureau [BLS Reports. No. 274]. Labor law and practice in Malaysia and Singapore. Washington, [1965]. pp. iv, 105. bibliog.

- Morocco

UNITED STATES. Labor Statistics Bureau. BLS Reports. No. 282. Labor law and practice in Morocco. Washington, [1965] pp. iv, 73. bibliog.

- Mozambique

SALDANHA (EDUARDO D'ALMEIDA) Moçambique — União de Africa do Sul: as bases para a convenção. Lisboa, [imprint], 1928. pp. (256). 24cm.

- New Zealand

MATHIESON (D.L.) Industrial law in New Zealand. Wellington, 1970 in progress.

- New Zealand - Bibliography

ROTH (H.O.) Labour legislation in New Zealand: a bibliography. Auckland, University of Auckland, 1964. pp. 43. 21½cm. (Bulletins. Library Series. 1)

- Nicaragua

UNITED STATES. Labor Statistics Bureau. BLS Reports. No. 265. Labor law and practice in Nicaragua. Washington, 1964. pp. iv, 99. bibliog.

TIJERINO MEDRANO (JOSÉ ANTONIO) Proyecto de reformas inmediatas a la legislación laboral de Nicaragua. Managua, 1966. pp. 174. bibliog. 19cm.

- Nigeria

ADEOGUN (A. A.) The legal framework of industrial relations in Nigeria: [supplementary paper at the Seminar for Trade Union Leaders, Ahmadu Bello University, 1969]. [Zaria, 1969]. pp. 38.

- Pakistan

UNITED STATES. Labor Statistics Bureau. BLS Reports. No. 271. Labor law and practice in Pakistan. Washington, 1964. pp. iv, 68. bibliog.

- Pakistan, East

AZAD (K.M.) Procedure of disciplinary action in factories and commercial establishment. Dacca, 1968. pp. 63.

- Peru

FAJARDO (J. V.) Sindicalismo libre en el Peru: la realidad histórica del sindicalismo y algunas conquistas en la legislación laboral del Perú. Lima, Editorial Mercurio, [1965]. pp. 169. 19½cm.

- Philippine Islands

UNITED STATES. Bureau of Labor Statistics. BLS Reports. No. 253. Labor law and practice in the Philippines. Washington, 1963. pp. 85. bibliog.

- Poland

CONGRESS OF POLISH TRADE UNIONS. Workmen's protective legislation in Poland: 20 years co-operation with the International Labor Organization. London, [1941]. pp. 48. 19½cm.

ZIELIŃSKI (JÓZEF) Prawo pracy: przepisy, orzecznictwo i wyjaśnienia; zebrał i opracował Józef Zieliński; uzupełnienie pierwsze. Warszawa, Wydawnictwo Prawnicze, 1965. pp. 152. 24cm.

MATEY (MARIA) Pracownicy umysłowi: zagadnienia prawne i społeczne. Warszawa, PWN, 1967. pp. 211. bibliog. 20cm. With French and Russian summaries.

MIROŃCZUK (ALBIN) Odpowiedzialność karno-administracyjna za wykroczenia przeciwko przepisom prawa pracy; według stanu prawnego na dzień 15 listopada 1966 r. Warszawa, 1967. pp. 67.

PIŁAT (ZBIGNIEW) O odpowiedzialności materialnej pracowników. Warszawa, CRZZ, 1967. pp. 140. 16cm. (Drogowskazy).

ŚWIĘCICKI (MACIEJ) Prawo pracy. Warszawa, PWN, 1968. pp. 648. bibliog. 24cm.

JAŚKIEWICZ (WIKTOR) and others. Prawo pracy: zarys wykładu. Warszawa, 1970. pp. 414.

KLIMEK (JÓZEF) Pracownik a Kodeks karny: odpowiedzialność i ochrona. Warszawa, 1970. pp. 205.

SALWA (ZBIGNIEW) Prawo pracy. 4th ed. Warszawa, 1970. pp. 316.

ZIELIŃSKI (JÓZEF) compiler. Prawo pracy: przepisy, orzecznictwo i wyjaśnienia; zebrał i opracował Józef Zieliński; stan prawny na dzień 1.2.1970 r. Warszawa, 1970. 2 vols.

BIŃCZYCKA-MAJEWSKA (TERESA) Opinie o pracownikach w świetle prawa. Warszawa, 1971. pp. 160. bibliog. With Russian summary.

- Portugal - Colonies

COUTINHO (MARTINHO DE FRANÇA DA GAMA PEREIRA) O trabalho indígena nas colónias portuguesas. Lisboa, Instituto Superior de Ciências Económicas e Financeiras, 1936. pp. 47. bibliog. 25cm. (Reprinted from Anais, vol.4)

- Roumania

ROUMANIA. Statutes, etc. 1950. The labour code of the Rumanian People's Republic. n.p., [1950?] pp. 69.

CÂMPIANU (VIRGIL I.) Dreptul muncii. București, 1967. pp. 446.

- Russia

SOVETSKOE trudovoe pravo na novom etape: sbornik statei. Moskva, 1931. pp. 127.

LEISTRITZ (HANS KARL) Der bolschewistische Weltbetrug: Theorie und Wirklichkeit der sowjetischen Arbeitsverfassung. Berlin, 1943. pp. 155.

VOPROSY sovetskogo grazhdanskogo i trudovogo prava. Moskva, 1952. pp. 208.

OSTROVSKII (LEONID IAKOVLEVICH) Рабочее время по советскому трудовому законодательству. Минск, Академия Наук БССР, 1968. pp. 157. 20см.

UNITED STATES. Labor Statistics Bureau. BLS Reports. No. 270. Labor law and practice in the U.S.S.R. Washington, 1964. pp. iv, 85. bibliog.

ARTEM'EV (FEDOR ANDREEVICH) Трудовые права медицинских работников. Москва, Юридическая Литература, 1965. pp. 144. 20cm.

KOMMENTARII k zakonodatel'stvu o trude. Moskva, 1966. pp. 832.

SPRAVOCHNIK... Справочник по условиям труда работников сельского хозяйства РСФСР. Москва, 1966. pp. 480.

ASTRAKHAN (EVGENII IVANOVICH) and others. Трудовое право: пособие для судей. 2nd ed. Москва, 1967. pp. 280.

DVORNIKOV (IVAN SEMENOVICH) and others. Трудовое законодательство: справочная книга для профактива. Москва, Профиздат, 1967. pp. 528. 19½см.

GENKIN (LAZAR' BORISOVICH) Stanovlenie novoi distsipliny truda. Moskva, 1967. pp. 200.

GORSHENIN (KONSTANTIN PETROVICH) Кодификация законодательства о труде: теоретические вопросы. Москва, Юридическая Литература, 1967. pp. 224. 20см.

PASHKOV (ALEKSEI STEPANOVICH) ed. Pravovye osnovy nauchnoi organizatsii truda. Moskva, 1967. pp. 247.

KLENOV (EVGENII ALEKSANDROVICH) and MALOV (VIACHESLAV GRIGOR'EVICH) Материальная ответственность рабочих и служащих на предприятии. Москва, 1968. pp. 152.

KRATKII iuridicheskii spravochnik v pomoshch' profaktivu. Moskva, 1968. pp. 476.

NIKOLAEVA (LIUDMILA ALEKSANDROVNA) Судебная защита трудовых прав граждан. Алма-Ата, 1968. pp. 192.

PROBLEMY... Проблемы трудового права. Москва, Юридическая Литература, 1968. pp. 224. 19½см.

SMIRNOV (OLEG VLADIMIROVICH) Эффективность правового регулирования организации труда на предприятии. Москва, Юридичейкая Литература, 1968. pp. 183. 19½см.

ALEKSANDROV (NIKOLAI GRIGOR'EVICH) ed. Khoziaistvennaia reforma, trud i pravo. Moskva, 1969. pp. 178.

BRONINA (ALINA BORISOVNA) and CHUBAIS (BORIS MAREEVICH) Trudovye prava rabotnikov lesnoi promyshlennosti: spravochnoe posobie. Moskva, 1969. pp. 142.

IAMPOL'D (GUSTAV MAKSOVICH) Основы советского гражданского и трудового права. 2nd ed. Москва, 1969. pp. 391.

SKOBELKIN (VLADIMIR NIKOLAEVICH) Юридические гарантии трудовых прав рабочих и служащих. Москва, 1969. pp. 183.

SPRAVOCHNIK... Справочник профсоюзного работника, 1969: труд, etc. Москва, 1969. pp. 639.

BATYGIN (KONSTANTIN STEPANOVICH) ed. Sovetskoe trudovoe pravo; Osnovy grazhdanskogo prava: uchebnoe posobie. Moskva, 1970. pp. 448.

GORSHENIN (KONSTANTIN PETROVICH) Novoe v zakonodatel'stve o trude. Moskva, 1970. pp. 103.

KHOZIAISTVENNAIA reforma i trudovoe pravo: materialy nauchnoi konferentsii. Moskva, 1970. pp. 383.

LABOUR LAWS AND LEGISLATION - Russia (Cont'd.)

KHVOSTOV (ADAM MOISEEVICH) Vina v sovetskom trudovom prave. Minsk, 1970. pp. 119.

KLIUEV (ANATOLII ALEKSEEVICH) and MAVRIN (ALEKSANDR VENEDIKTOVICH) Rukovediteliu predpriiatiia o trudovom zakonodatel'stve. Moskva, 1970. pp. 233.

LENIN o trude i prave. Leningrad, 1970. pp. 178.

DVORNIKOV (IVAN SEMENOVICH) and others. Trudovoe zakonodatel'stvo: spravochnaia kniga dlia profaktiva. 2nd ed. Moskva, 1971. pp. 543.

- Salvador

SALVADOR. Statutes, etc. 1956. Ley de riesgos profesionales y ley sobre seguridad e higiene del trabajo. San Salvador, 1956. pp. 77. 18cm.

SALVADOR. Statutes, etc. 1961. Ley procesal de trabajo. San Salvador, [1961?]. pp. 46. (Salvador. Secretaria de Informacion. [Publications]. 3)

- Senegal

SENEGAL. Statutes, etc. 1961. Code du travail: loi no. 61-34 du 15 juin 1961 instituant un code du travail. [Dakar, 1961?]. fo. (viii), 73. 31cm.

- Singapore

UNITED STATES. Labor Statistics Bureau. [BLS Reports. No. 274.] Labor law and practice in Malaysia and Singapore. Washington, [1965]. pp. iv, 105. bibliog.

- South Africa

SCHAEFFER (M.) and HEYNE (J.F.) Industrial law in South Africa. Pretoria, Van Schaik, 1968. pp. (xvi), 302. 22cm.

HEPPLE (ALEXANDER) South Africa: workers under apartheid. London, Christian Action Publications, 1969. pp. vi, 86. 21cm.

HEPPLE (ALEXANDER) South Africa: workers under apartheid. 2nd ed. London, 1971. pp. 88.

- Spain

GARRIGUES (JOAQUIN) Tres conferencias en Italia sobre el fuero del trabajo. Madrid, 1939. pp. 87.

LEGAZ Y LACAMBRA (LUIS) and ARAGON GOMEZ (BARTOLOME) Cuatro estudios sobre sindicalismo vertical. Zaragoza, 1939. pp. 124.

UNITED STATES. Labor Statistics Bureau. BLS Reports. No.289. Labor law and practice in Spain. Washington, 1965. bibliog. pp. iv, 58.

PEREZ LENERO (JOSE) Jurados de empresa y participacion en la gestion: comentarios a sus reglamentos. Valladolid, 1966. pp. 567.

MADRID. Universidad. Facultad de Derecho. Seminarios de Derecho del Trabajo. 4. Quince lecciones sobre conflictos colectivos de trabajo. Madrid, 1968. pp. 352. bibliog. 21cm.

- Spain - Colonies

CANALDA PALAU (GUILLERMO) España y Mejico: el derecho laboral en "Nueva España"; siglos xvi y xvii. Madrid, [Ediciones del Movimiento], 1968. pp. 87. bibliog. 21cm. (Coleccion Nuevo Horizonte. Serie Temas de Colaboración)

- Sweden

UNITED STATES. Labor Statistics Bureau. BLS Reports. No. 285. Labor law and practice in Sweden. Washington, [1965]. pp. iv, 68. bibliog.

SCHMIDT (FOLKE FREDRIK) Das kollektive Arbeitsrecht Schwedens; (aus dem Schwedischen übertragen, etc.). [5th ed.] Stuttgart, Fischer, 1968. pp. viii, 240. 21cm. (Arbeits- und Sozialrechtliche Studien. Heft 10)

- Switzerland

HUG (WALTHER) Die Kodifikation des Arbeitsrechts. in Zukunftsaufgaben in Wirtschaft und Gesellschaft. Zürich, 1963.

- Tunis

TUNIS. 1959. Aperçu sur les institutions sociales et le droit social en Tunisie. (Secrétariat d'Etat à la Santé Publique et aux Affaires Sociales) [Tunis, 1959?] fo. 39. 30½cm.

UNITED STATES. Labor Statistics Bureau. BLS Reports. No. 294. Labor law and practice in Tunisia. Washington, 1965. pp. iv, 68. bibliog.

- Turkestan

SAGDULLAEV (TALAT SAGDULLAEVICH) Sozdanie i razvitie sovetskogo trudovogo prava v Turkestanskoi ASSR, 1917-1924. Tashkent, 1966. pp. 181.

- Ukraine

UKRAINE. Statutes, etc. 1965. Кодекс законов про працю Української РСР: офіціальний текст із змінами на 15 червня 1965 року та з додатками систематизованих матеріалів. Київ, 1966. pp. 438. bibliog.

- United Kingdom

ANDERSON (ADELAIDE MARY) Legislation affecting the conditions of employment in home work and domestic industries in England. London, 1900. pp. 31.

BAUER (STEPHEN) Address delivered...at the meeting of the Executive Committee of the British Association for Labour Legislation, on July 20th, 1905. [London, imprint, 1905]. pp. 4.

KAHN-FREUND (OTTO) Labour law: old traditions and new developments. Toronto, 1968. pp. xii, 92. (Saskatchewan. University. College of Law. W.M. Martin Lectures. 1967)

SEYFARTH, SHAW, FAIRWEATHER AND GERALDSON. Labor relations and the law in the United Kingdom and the United States: a comparative study. Ann Arbor, University of Michigan, Graduate School of Business Administration, Program in International Business, [1968]. pp. xxvii, 634. bibliog. 23cm. (Michigan International Labor Studies. vol. 1)

DRAKE (CHARLES DOMINIC) Labour law. London, 1969. pp. 311.

SIM (R.S.) and POWELL-SMITH (VINCENT) Casebook on industrial law. London, Butterworths, 1969. pp. 387.

CRONIN (J.B.) and GRIME (R.P.) Labour law. London, 1970. pp. 500.

RAMELSON (BERT) Carr's Bill, and how to kill it: a class analysis. London, [1970]. pp. 23. (Communist Party of Great Britain. Communist Party Pamphlets)

SPOKESMAN, THE. Pamphlets. No. 11. Trade unionists: we can defeat the Tory bill. [Nottingham, 1970]. pp. 15.

U.K. Department of Employment and Productivity. 1970. Industrial Relations Bill: consultative document. [London, 1970]. pp. 27.

AIKIN (OLGA) and REID (JUDITH) Employment, welfare and safety at work: (labour law, 1) Harmondsworth, 1971. pp. 416.

BROWN (KENNETH D.) Labour and unemployment, 1900-1914. Newton Abbot, [1971]. pp. 219. bibliog.

CONSERVATIVE CENTRAL OFFICE. It's a fair deal: the Industrial Relations Act. London, 1971. pp. 23.

FABIAN SOCIETY. Fabian Tracts. [No.] 406. Divide and rule: the Industrial Relations Bill; [by] Giles Radice [and] J.O.N. Vickers. London, 1971. pp. 20.

HAMPTON (PETER) The Industrial Relations Bill: a declaration of war. [London, 1971]. 1 pamphlet (unpaged).

HARVEY (RICHARD JON STANLEY) Industrial relations...: including the Industrial Relations Act 1971 with annotations by G.R.N. Cusworth. London, 1971. pp. 448.

HENDERSON (JOAN) A guide to the Industrial Relations Bill. London, 1971. pp. 19.

HENDERSON (JOAN) The Industrial Relations Act at work. London, 1971. pp. 28.

HEPPLE (BOB ALEXANDER) and O'HIGGINS (PAUL) Individual employment law: an introduction. London, 1971. pp. 203.

LABOUR RESEARCH DEPARTMENT. Industrial Relations Act, 1971: trade unionist's guide. London, [1971]. pp. 40.

SELWYN (NORMAN M.) Guide to the Industrial Relations Act, 1971. London, 1971. pp. 153.

SHERMAN (BARRIE) The Immigration Bill and the Industrial Relations Bill: a combined threat to trade unions. n.p., [1971]. fo. 9.

SPOKESMAN, THE. Pamphlets. No. 16. Can we kill that Bill?: an appeal to trade unionists to defend democracy; [drafted by Ken Coates]. Nottingham, [1971]. 1 pamphlet (unpaged)

WEDDERBURN (KENNETH WILLIAM) The worker and the law. 2nd ed. Harmondsworth, 1971. pp. 587. bibliog.

- United Kingdom - Ireland, Northern

IRELAND, NORTHERN. 1967. A general guide to the Office and Shop Premises Act (Northern Ireland) 1966. (Ministry of Health and Social Services. O.S.P. Leaflets. 1) Belfast, [1967]. pp. 46. 20½cm.

- United Kingdom - Scotland

MILLER (ISAAC P.) Industrial law in Scotland. Edinburgh, 1970. pp. 461.

- United States

MARKHAM (EDWIN) and others. Children in bondage: (a complete and careful presentation of the anxious problem of child labor, its causes, its crimes, and its cure); [reprint of the work originally published in New York, 1914]. New York, 1969. pp. 411. bibliog.

MASON (ALPHEUS THOMAS) Organized labor and the law; (with especial reference to the Sherman and Clayton Acts); [reprint of the work originally published in Durham, N.C., 1925]. New York, 1969. pp. 265. bibliog.

OPINION RESEARCH CORPORATION. Public Opinion Index for Industry. Did the people get the Labor Law they want?: special analysis detailing how closely the public's wishes in labor reform have been enacted into corrective legislation. Princeton, N.J., [1959]. fo. 6.

UNITED STATES. Labor Standards Bureau. Bulletins. 262. Federal labor laws and programs. Washington, 1964. pp. vi, 180.

COX (ARCHIBALD) and BOK (DEREK CURTIS) Cases and materials on labor law; (with 1966 Statutory supplement) 6th ed. Brooklyn, Foundation P., 1965-66. 2 pts. 25cm. (University Casebook Series)

STATE labor and social legislation: a symposium in honor of Elizabeth Brandeis Raushenbush, May 20, 1966. [Madison], University of Wisconsin, Industrial Relations Research Institute and the Department of Economics, [1966]. pp. vi, 112. 22½cm.

TURNER (MARJORIE BROOKSHIRE SHEPHERD) The early American labor conspiracy cases: their place in labor law; a reinterpretation. San Diego, 1967. pp. 86. (San Diego. San Diego State College. Social Science Monograph Series. vol. 1, no. 3)

MANGUM (GARTH LEROY) M[anpower] D[evelopment and] T[raining] A[ct]: foundation of federal manpower policy. Baltimore, Johns Hopkins P., [1968]. pp. viii, 184. 22½cm.

RUBIN (RICHARD S.) A summary of state collective bargaining law in public employment. Ithaca, Cornell University, New York State School of Industrial and Labor Relations, [1968]. pp. iii, 52. 28cm. (Public Employee Relations Reports. 3)

SEYFARTH, SHAW, FAIRWEATHER AND GERALDSON. Labor relations and the law in the United Kingdom and the United States: a comparative study. Ann Arbor, University of Michigan, Graduate School of Business Administration, Program in International Business, [1968]. pp. xxvii, 634. bibliog. 23cm. (Michigan International Labor Studies. vol. 1)

SUMMERS (CLYDE WILSON) and WELLINGTON (HARRY H.) Cases and materials on labor law. New York, 1968. pp. 1229.

WELLINGTON (HARRY H.) Labor and the legal process. New Haven, Yale U.P., 1968. pp. xi, 409. 20½cm.

LABOUR LAWS AND LEGISLATION - United States (Cont'd.)

AMERICAN ENTERPRISE INSTITUTE FOR PUBLIC POLICY RESEARCH. Legislative Analysis. No.3. Proposals to deal with national emergency strikes. rev.ed. Washington, D.C., 1969. pp. 94. bibliog.

AUERBACH (JEROLD S.) ed. American labor: the twentieth century. Indianapolis, [1969]. pp. 474.

SELZNICK (PHILIP) Law, society and industrial justice. [New York, 1969]. pp. 282.

SEYFARTH, SHAW, FAIRWEATHER AND GERALDSON. Labor relations and the law in Belgium and the United States: a comparative study. Ann Arbor, Michigan, [1969]. pp. 455. bibliog. (Michigan University. Bureau of Business Research. Program in International Business. Michigan International Labor Studies. vol. 2)

SEYFARTH, SHAW, FAIRWEATHER AND GERALDSON. Labor relations and the law in West Germany and the United States: a comparative study. Ann Arbor, Michigan, [1969]. pp. 606. bibliog. (Michigan University. Bureau of Business Research. Program in International Business. Michigan International Labor Studies. vol. 3)

SEYFARTH, SHAW, FAIRWEATHER AND GERALDSON. Labor relations and the law in Italy and the United States: a comparative study. Ann Arbor, 1970. pp. 464. bibliog. (Michigan University. Bureau of Business Research. Program in International Business. Michigan International Labor Studies. vol. 4)

BLUMROSEN (ALFRED W.) Black employment and the law. New Brunswick, N.J., [1971]. pp. 416.

TAYLOR (BENJAMIN J.) and WITNEY (FRED) Labor relations law. Englewood Cliffs, [1971]. pp. 684. bibliog.

- United States - Arizona

ARIZONA. Statutes, etc. Labor laws of the State of Arizona. (State Labor Department). rev. ed. Phoenix, 1957. pp. 59. 23½cm.

- United States - Minnesota

STIEBER (JACK W.) Ten years of the Minnesota labor relations act. Minneapolis, the Center, [1949]. pp. iv, 32. 23cm. (Minnesota University. Industrial Relations Center. Bulletins. 9)

- United States - New York

HANSLOWE (KURT L.) New York State Labor relations Law, 1964. [Ithaca], Cornell University, New York State School of Industrial and Labor Relations, [1964]. pp. 244-259. 23cm. (Reprint Series. No. 169) (Reprinted from Syracuse Law Review. vol. 16, no. 2, 1964)

- Uruguay

FOTI (ROQUE) Estudio preparatorio para una legislación laboral, etc. Montevideo, Instituto Nacional del Trabajo, 1958. pp. 48. 24½cm.

- Venezuela

RIVAS BELANDRIA (JOSÉ JUAN) Antecedentes coloniales de nuestra legislación laboral. Mérida, Universidad de los Andes, Facultad de Derecho, 1965. pp. 71. bibliog. 23cm. (Colección Justitia et Jus. No.14)

- Vietnam

VIET-NAM (REPUBLIC). Statutes, etc. 1952-1955. Code du travail: ordonnance no. 15 du 8 juillet 1952, complétée et modifiée par les ordonnances nos. 9 et 10 du 8 février 1955. Saigon, 1958. pp. 341. In French and Vietnamese.

VIET-NAM (REPUBLIC). Statutes, etc. 1950-1953. [Code du travail des entreprises agricoles, ordonnance no. 26 du 26 juin 1953; Régime des allocations familiales, etc., ordonnance no. 2 du janvier 1953; Régime des associations et syndicats professionnels, ordonnances, nos. 10 et, 23 des 6 aout 1950 et 16 Novembre 1952] [Saigon], 1961. pp. 215, 75, 93. Title-page in Vietnamese, text in Vietnamese and French.

- Yugoslavia

PERIC (BOŠKO K.) Радно право ФНРЈ. Сараево, Одбор за Издавање Уџбеника и Скрипата за Студенте Универзитета и Високих Школа НР БиХ, 1950. pp. 684. bibliog. 23cm.

STANKOVIĆ (RADOMIR) and RADIVOJEVIĆ (ĐORĐE) Osnovni zakon o radnim odnosima, sa objašnjenjima. Beograd, Naučna Knjiga, 1965. pp. (iv), 152. 20cm.

PETROVIĆ (VOJISLAV I.) Osnovi prava, sa privrednim i radnim pravom. Beograd, 1967. pp. 260.

BALTIĆ (ALEKSANDR) and DESPOTOVIĆ (MILAN) Osnovi radnog prava Jugoslavije: sistem radnih odnosa Jugoslavije, i osnovni problemi sociologije rada. 2nd ed. Beograd, 1968. pp. 507.

LABOUR LAWS AND LEGISLATION, INTERNATIONAL

INTERNATIONAL ASSOCIATION FOR LABOUR LEGISLATION. Spanish Section. Memoria de los Trabajos de la Sección, etc. Madrid, 1910-1912 (4th-6th year). 23cm.

SALDANHA (EDUARDO D'ALMEIDA) Moçambique — União de Africa do Sul: as bases para a convenção. Lisboa, [imprint], 1928. pp. (256). 24cm.

NEW ZEALAND. [General Assembly]. House of Representatives. 1962. International Labour Conference: proposed action by the government of New Zealand on certain international instruments adopted at the 44th session 1960, and the 45th session 1961. Wellington, 1962. pp. 7.

INTERNATIONAL LABOUR OFFICE. Revision of conventions Nos.35,36,37,38,39 and 40 concerning invalidity, old-age and survivors' pensions. in International Labour Office. 1964. Date, place and agenda of the 50th, 1966, session of the International Labour Conference: (with Appendices 1-4) (G.B.160/2/1) Geneva, 1964.

INTERNATIONAL LABOUR OFFICE. Revision of the holidays with pay convention, 1936. in International Labour Office. 1964. Date, place and agenda of the 50th, 1966, session of the International Labour Conference: (with Appendices 1-4) (G.B.160/2/1) Geneva, 1964.

GAITÁN GÓMEZ (JULIO) Derecho internacional del trabajo. Bogotá, 1965. pp. 99. bibliog. 24cm.

INTERNATIONAL LABOUR ORGANISATION. 1965. International standards and guiding principles, 1944-1964. Geneva, 1965. pp. 196. bibliogs. (Labour-Management Relations Series. No. 24)

INTERNATIONAL LABOUR CONFERENCE. 51st Session. Reports.4. Fourth item on the agenda: revision of Conventions Nos. 35,36,37,39,39 and 40 concerning old-age, invalidity and survivors pensions. Geneva, 1966-67. 2 pts.

INTERNATIONAL LABOUR CONFERENCE. 52nd Session. Reports. 6. Sixth item on the agenda: revision of Conventions Nos. 24 and 25 concerning sickness insurance. Geneva, 1967-68. 2 pts.

ALFONSO (VICENZO ROBERTO) La sicurezza sociale del lavoratore italiano all'estero e dello straniero in Italia: tutela giuridica e previdenziale, convenzioni internazionali; manuale teorico-pratico etc. Milano, Pirola, 1967. pp. 447. bibliog. 24cm.

ESCOBAR TÉLLEZ (JORGE ENRIQUE) Colombia frente a las principales normas marítimas de derecho laboral internacional. Bogotá, 1967. pp. 127. bibliog. 24cm.

INTERNATIONAL LABOUR CONFERENCE. 51st Session. Reports.3. Third item on the agenda: information and reports on the application of conventions and recommendations. Geneva, 1967. 4 pts.

INTERNATIONAL LABOUR CONFERENCE. 53rd Session. Reports. 5. Fifth item on the agenda: revision of Conventions Nos. 24 and 25 concerning sickness insurance. Geneva, 1968-69. 2 pts.

INTERNATIONAL LABOUR CONFERENCE. 52nd Session. Reports. 3. Third item on the agenda: information and reports on the application of conventions and recommendations. Geneva, 1968. 4 pts.

PLATA-CASTILLA (ALFONSO) La D.I.T. y el derecho international del trabajo. Bogotá, 1968. pp. (6),iv,222. bibliog.

SZÁSZY (ISTVÁN) International labour law: a comparative survey of the conflict rules affecting labour legislation and regulations ... edited by Louis A. De Pinna. Leyden, Sijthoff, 1968. pp. (vi), 465. bibliog. 23½cm.

INTERNATIONAL LABOUR CONFERENCE. 53rd Session. Reports. 3. Third item on the agenda: information and reports on the application of conventions and recommendations, etc. Geneva, 1969. 4 pts.

INTERNATIONAL LABOUR ORGANISATION. 1969. International standards and guiding principles, 1944-1968. Geneva, 1969. pp. 255. bibliog. (Labour-Management Relations Series. No. 34.)

INTERNATIONAL LABOUR ORGANISATION. 1969. Rights of trade union representatives at the level of the undertaking; documents of a technical meeting [held at] Geneva, 20-29 November 1967. Geneva, 1969. pp. 105. (Labour-Management Relations Series. No.32).

JENKS (CLARENCE WILFRED) Social justice in the law of nations: the ILO impact after fifty years. London, 1970. pp. 94. (Cambridge. University. Faculty of Law. Hersch Lauterpacht Lectures. 1969)

AMETISTOV (ERNEST MIKHAILOVICH) Mezhdunarodnoe trudovoe pravo i rabochii klass. Moskva, 1970. pp. 184.

LABOUR LITERATURE SOCIETY

LABOUR LITERATURE SOCIETY. Rules. Glasgow, 1895. pp. 15.

LABOUR MOBILITY

ORGANISATION FOR ECONOMIC CO-OPERATION AND DEVELOPMENT. 1964. International joint seminar on geographical and occupational mobility of manpower, Castelfusano, 19th to 22nd November, 1963: final report (by Guy Routh; and Supplement). (International Seminars, 1963. 3) Paris, 1964. 2 pts. 24cm - 29½cm.

ANTUNES (MARIA DA GRAÇA MARQUES) Problemas de mão-de-obra rural nos países em desenvolvimento. Lisboa, 1965. pp. 157. bibliog. (Fundo de Desenvolvimento da Mão-de-Obra. Cadernos. 9) With abstracts in English, French and German.

ORGANISATION FOR ECONOMIC CO-OPERATION AND DEVELOPMENT. 1965. Geographic and occupational mobility of rural manpower; [by C. E. Bishop]. (Documentation in Food and Agriculture. 1965 Series. 75). [Paris, 1965]. pp. 87. 24cm.

GEOGRAPHICAL and occupational mobility of workers in the aircraft and electronics industries: regional trade union seminar, Paris, 21st-22nd September, 1966; final report (with Supplement). Paris, Organisation for Economic Co-operation and Development, [1966-67]. 2 pts. 24cm and 27cm. (Social Affairs Division. International Seminars. 1966.3)

UNITED STATES. Congress. Joint Economic Committee. Economic policies and practices. Paper no. 8. Programs for relocating workers used by governments of selected countries. Washington, 1966. pp.ix, 76.

LANSING (JOHN BELCHER) and MUELLER (EVA) The geographic mobility of labor. Ann Arbor, University of Michigan, Institute for Social Research, 1967. pp. xiv, 421. 23cm.

HUNTER (LAURENCE C.) and REID (GRAHAM L.) Urban worker mobility. [Paris], Organisation for Economic Co-operation and Development, [1968]. pp. 215. bibliog. 24cm. (Social Affairs Division. Labour Mobility. 5.)

BODENHOEFER (HANS JOACHIM) Arbeitsmobilität und regionales Wachstum: ein Beitrag zur Strukturanalyse von Wachstumsprozessen. Berlin, [1969]. pp. 196. bibliog.

LABOUR MOBILITY (Cont'd.)

CULLINGWORTH (JOHN BARRY) Housing and labour mobility: a preliminary report. [Paris], Organisation for Economic Co-operation and Development, [1969]. pp. 73. (Social Affairs Division. Labour Mobility. 6)

HARLOFF (HANS JOACHIM) Der Einfluss psychischer Faktoren auf die Mobilität der Arbeit. Berlin, [1970]. pp. 234. bibliog. (Berlin. Freie Universität. Wirtschafts- und Sozialwissenschaftliche Fakultät. Wirtschaftswissenschaftliche Abhandlungen. Heft 27)

- Mathematical models

DEAN (MICHAEL) and PYATT (FRANK GRAHAM) A model of manpower movements in an industry. Coventry, 1970. fo. various. (University of Warwick. Centre for Industrial and Business Studies. Warwick Research in Industrial and Business Studies. No. 7)

- Belgium

BELGIUM. Office National de l'Emploi. Études Économiques et Sociales. Le mouvement des "navetteurs" dans l'arrondissement d'Alost. Bruxelles, 1970. pp. 29.

- Canada

CANADA. 1967. The geographic mobility of the 1955 class of graduates from Canadian universities in science and engineering; by D.Dyck. (Department of Manpower and Immigration) Ottawa, 1967. pp. x, 49.

NICKSON (MAY) Geographic mobility in Canada, October 1964- October 1965. Ottawa, 1967. pp. 23. 28cm. (Canada. Dominion Bureau of Statistics. Special Labour Force Studies. No. 4.)

- Canada - Quebec

LEGENDRE (CAMILLE) La mobilité de la main-d'oeuvre dans l'industrie forestière: annexe technique au plan de développement pour la région pilote du Bas St-Laurent, de la Gaspésie et des Îles de la Madeleine. Ottawa, 1968. pp. iii, 21. 28cm. (Canada. Department of Forestry and Rural Development. ARDA Rapports Abrégés. RA-No.18.)

- Europe

INTERNATIONAL LABOUR OFFICE. 1965. International differences in factors affecting labour mobility: study of inter-industry, occupational and geographical mobility in selected countries of Western Europe;(with Appendix: twelve case studies);(by F. Sellier and C. Zarka)(AUT/DOC/7). Geneva, 1965. 2 pts. 29½cm.

FRANCE. Direction de la Documentation. La Documentation Française. Notes et Etudes Documentaires. No.3,603. Les migrations intra-européennes de main-d'oeuvre; [by] Hélène Rivière d'Arc...sous la direction de Bernard Kayser. Paris, 1969. pp. 76. bibliog.

ROSE (ARNOLD MARSHALL) Migrants in Europe: problems of acceptance and adjustment. Minneapolis, [1969]. pp. 194.

HUNTER (LAURENCE C.) and REID (GRAHAM L.) European economic integration and the movement of labour. Kingston, Ontario, 1970. pp. 38. (Kingston, Ontario. Queen's University. Industrial Relations Centre. Research Series. No. 9)

- European Economic Community countries

[CLUZEL (HUBERT) and FRAIGNEAUD (ROGER)] Aides apportées aux agriculteurs migrants dans les pays de la C[ommunauté] É[conomique] E[uropéenne]. Bruxelles, [European Economic Community]. 1966. pp. 91. 27cm. (Études: Série Agriculture.22)

ITALY. Ministero del Lavoro e della Previdenza Sociale. Rassegna del Lavoro. Quaderni. 43. Libertà di stabilimento e prestazione dei servizi nella Comunità. Roma, 1967. pp. 183. bibliog. 26½cm.

BENYOUSSEF (AMOR) Dimensions humaines de la Communauté Économique Européenne: éléments d'une doctrine de l'intégration. Paris, 1968. pp. xv, 120. bibliog. (Observation Économique. 26) With English summary.

BONTEMPS (JEAN) Liberté d'établissement et libre prestation des services dans le Marché commun: directives de suppression des restrictions et directives de mesures transitoires. Bruxelles, Bruylant, 1968. pp. 316. 22cm.

BOUSCAREN (ANTHONY TRAWICK) European Economic Community migrations. The Hague, 1969. pp. 155. bibliog.

ITALY. Ministero del Lavoro e della Previdenza Sociale. Rassegna del Lavoro. Quaderni. 52. La libera circolazione dei lavoratori. Roma, 1969. pp. 74. bibliog.

ROYAL INSTITUTE OF INTERNATIONAL AFFAIRS and POLITICAL AND ECONOMIC PLANNING. European Series. No. 10. Trade unions and free labour movement in the EEC; [by] R. Colin Beever. London, 1969. pp. 50. 21cm.

BÖHNING (W. R.) and STEPHEN (DAVID) The EEC and the migration of workers: the EEC's system of free movement of labour and the implications of United Kingdom entry. London, [1971]. pp. 43.

- Germany

SCHWANSE (PETER) Der Einfluss der Beschäftigungsmobilität auf Produktivität und Sozialprodukt in der Bundesrepublik Deutschland 1950 bis 1960. Berlin, 1964. pp. 150. bibliog.

KRAHN (KARL) Mobilitätsorientierung und Fluktuationsbereitschaft: eine empirisch-soziologische Untersuchung in einem Hüttenwerk. Berlin, [1971]. pp. 160. bibliog.

- Poland

GOLACHOWSKI (STEFAN) and GOLDZAMT (EDMUND) eds. Problemy osadnictwa robotniczego na wsi. Warszawa, 1971. pp. 345. With Russian and English summaries.

- Portugal

> ANTUNES (MARIA DA GRAÇA MARQUES) Problemas de mão-de-obra rural nos países em desenvolvimento. Lisboa, 1965. pp. 157. bibliog. (Fundo de Desenvolvimento da Mão-de-Obra. Cadernos. 9) With abstracts in English, French and German.

- Russia - Siberia

> ANTOSENKOV (E. G.) ed. Опыт исследования перемены труда в промышленности: по результатам экономического и социологического обследования текучести рабочих кадров. Новосибирск, 1969. pp. 181.

- Spain

> HIGUERAS ARNAL (ANTONIO M.) La emigración interior en España. Madrid, Mundo del Trabajo, 1967. pp. 131. bibliog. 17½cm. (Colección Mundo del Trabajo. Series Estudios. 15)

- Sweden

> SWEDEN. Arbetsmarknadsstyrelsen. 1961. Measures to stimulate the mobility of manpower in Sweden; full verbatim translation of official printed documents. Stockholm, 1961. fo. 6,3, 5. 30cm.

- United Kingdom

> HOUSE (JOHN WILLIAM) and KNIGHT (E.M.) Pit closure and the community. [Newcastle-upon-Tyne], University, Department of Geography, 1967. pp. (iv), 144. 30cm. (Papers on Migration and Mobility in Northern England. No. 5)

> HOUSE (JOHN WILLIAM) and others. Mobility of the northern business manager;...report to the Ministry of Labour. Newcastle upon Tyne University, Department of Geography, 1968. pp. (v), 133. 30cm. (Papers on Migration and Mobility in Northern England. No. 8)

> THOMAS (RON) ed. An exercise in redeployment: the report of a trade union study group. Oxford, Pergamon, 1969. pp. xiii, 266. 19½cm. (Commonwealth and International Library)

> CHILD (PETER STUART) Location aspects of office development in Croydon: with special reference to earnings; [Ph.D. (London) thesis]. 1970 [or rather 1971]. fo. 194. bibliog. 2 maps in end pocket. Typescript: unpublished. This thesis is the property of London University and may not be removed from the Library.

- United States

> STOLNITZ (GEORGE J.) Manpower movements: a proposed approach to measurement. Bloomington, Indiana University, International Development Research Center, [1964]. pp. 165-174. 23cm. (Reprint Series. Papers. No. 5)

> UNITED STATES. Social Security Administration. Research Reports No. 18. Interindustry labor mobility in the United States 1957 to 1960. Washington, 1967. pp. v, 330. bibliog.

> PENCAVEL (JOHN H.) An analysis of the quit rate in American manufacturing industry. Princeton, 1970. pp. 65. (Princeton University. Department of Economics and Sociology. Industrial Relations Section. Research Report Series. No. 114)

- Yugoslavia

> SOCIJALNA struktura i pokretljivost radničke klase Jugoslavije. tom 1. Beograd, Institut Drušstvenih Nauka, 1963. pp. 542. 24cm.

> HAMMEL (EUGENE ALFRED) The pink yo-yo: (occupational mobility in Belgrade, ca. 1915-1965). Berkeley, [1969]. pp. 96. bibliog. (California University. Institute of International Studies. Research Series. No. 13)

LABOUR PARTY

- Australia

> HUGHES (WILLIAM MORRIS) The case for Labor: [reprint of the first edition published in 1910]. Sydney, 1970. pp. 144, xiii-xxxiv.

> AUSTRALIAN LABOUR PARTY. Platform, constitution and rules. Canberra, 1965. pp. 47.

> TRUMAN (TOM) Ideological groups in the Australian Labor Party and their attitudes. St. Lucia, University of Queensland Press, 1965. pp. 45-165. 24cm. (Queensland University. Department of History and Political Science. Papers. vol. 1, no. 2)

> AUSTRALIAN LABOUR PARTY. Platform, constitution and rules as approved by the 27th Commonwealth Conference, Adelaide, 1967. Canberra, Wyndham, 1967. pp. 66. 24cm.

> BLACKBURN (SUSAN) Maurice Blackburn and the Australian Labor Party, 1934-1943: a study of principle in politics. [Canberra], 1969. pp. 58. bibliog.

> MURRAY (ROBERT) of the Australian Financial Review. The split: Australian Labor in the fifties. Melbourne, 1970. pp. 388. bibliog.

> KENNAN (JAMES) Australian labour: a time of challenge London, 1971. pp. 28. (Young Fabian Group. Young Fabian Pamphlets. 25)

- Belgium

> CLAEYS-VAN HAEGENDOREN (MIEKE) 25 jaar Belgisch socialisme: evolutie van de verhouding van de Belgische Werkliedenpartij tot de parlementaire democratie in België van 1914 tot 1940. Antwerpen, 1967. pp. 509. bibliog. With English summary.

- Canada

> SCOTTON (CLIFFORD A.) Canadian labour and politics:.. a short history of the development of the Canadian labour movement and its relationship to and influence on the Canadian political scene. n.p., [196-?]. pp. 40.

> ROBIN (MARTIN) Radical politics and Canadian labour. Kingston, Ontario, 1968. pp. 321. bibliog.

- New Zealand

> HOBBS (LESLIE) The thirty-year wonders. Christchurch, Whitcombe & Tombs, 1967. pp. 192. 20½cm.

- South Africa

> MILES-CADMAN (CECIL FRANK) Socialism for South Africa. 3rd ed. Johannesburg, South African Labour Party, 1943. pp. 186. 18½cm.

LABOUR PARTY (Cont'd.)

- Trinidad and Tobago

MALIK (YOGENDRA K.) East Indians in Trinidad: a study in minority politics. London, 1971. pp. 199. bibliog.

- United Kingdom

HENDERSON (FRED) Socialism of the I.L.P. London, Independent Labour Party, n.d. pp. 10. 21½cm. (Programme Pamphlets. No.1)

INDEPENDENT LABOUR PARTY. Circulars. 3. An appeal to trade unionists, co-operators and workers generally. London, 1894. pp. 4.

INDEPENDENT LABOUR PARTY. National Administrative Council. Labour catechism. [Manchester, imprint, 1895?] pp. 4. (Independent Labour Party. Caroline Martyn Memorial Library. No. 3)

INDEPENDENT LABOUR PARTY. Metropolitan District Council. Reception to the Labour Representation Committee and other socialist Members of Parliament and parliamentary candidates...at the Royal Horticultural Hall..., February 15th, 1906: (programme). [London, 1906]. 1 pamphlet (unpaged)

INDEPENDENT LABOUR PARTY. Eisteddfod, 1st annual, 1909. [Programme;...chairman, Keir Hardie; and] J. Keir Hardie, M.P.: the prize epic...; a translation from the Welsh of Daniel Owen, etc. [Mountain Ash?, 1909]. 1 pamphlet (in 2 pts.)

LABOUR PARTY. Report to the International Congress, Copenhagen, 1910. n.p., [1910]. pp. 8.

The GOSPEL of Labour;...[by] Will Crooks [and others]. [London, 1912]. pp. 94.

HARDIE (JAMES KEIR) The red dragon and the red flag: being an exposition of the case for socialism and the Labour Party. London, Labour Pioneer Printing and Publishing Co., 1912. pp. 18. 21cm. (Pioneer Pamphlets. No. 1) Summary in Welsh.

TO the workers of the world: an appeal for personal religion by eight labour members of parliament, etc. London, [1913?]. pp. 93. 18cm.

The SOUL of Labour as voiced by eight Labour Members of Parliament; [by] William Adamson [and others]. London, [1914?]. pp. 78.

BRITISH SOCIALIST PARTY. Executive Committee. Labour and the government: manifesto...to the delegates at adjourned Labour Party conference, August 21st, 1917. London, [1917]. pp. (2).

LABOUR PARTY. Memorandum on the issues of the war. London, 1917. pp. 8. 24½cm.

COMMUNIST PARTY OF GREAT BRITAIN. Executive Committee. The Communist Party and Labour Party affiliation: some questions and answers addressed to all workers affiliated to the Labour Party. London, [c.1920]. pp. 4.

INDEPENDENT LABOUR PARTY. The I.L.P. and the 3rd International: being the questions submitted by the I.L.P. delegation to the executive of the 3rd International and its reply, with an introductory statement by the National Council of the I.L.P. Manchester, National Labour P., 1920. pp. 64. 17½cm.

PERRY (S.F.) The Co-operative Party and the proposed Labour and Co-operative Political Alliance. Manchester, 1920. pp. 10.

WEBB (SIDNEY) 1st Baron Passfield. To the men and women electors of the Seaham Division of Durham: letter of acceptance...of the position of prospective labour candidate for the Seaham division; together with some particulars of Mr. Webb's career. Seaham Harbour, [1920]. pp. 11.

MACMANUS (ARTHUR) and WALLHEAD (RICHARD COLLINGHAM) Communism or I.L.P. ism?: verbatim report of debate held in St. Andrew's Hall, Glasgow, on August 30th, 1921. London, [1921]. pp. 12.

BRACHER (SAMUEL VEALE) The "Herald" book of labour members; with foreword by Hamilton Fyfe; [with] 1924 Supplement. London, 1923-24. 2 vols.

MYERS (TOM) Liberalism and socialism: an open letter to Sir John Simon. London, Trades Union Congress and the Labour Party, [1923]. pp. 16. 24½cm.

YATES (EDWIN GEORGE) ed. Labour personalities in the House of Commons. Watford, Watford Printers Limited, 1923. pp. (32). 25cm.

The CAUSE of Labour is the hope of the world: to welcome the Labour victors in the general election of 1923. [London?, 1924?]. unpaged.

COLYER (WILLIAM THOMAS) Anti-Labour legislations: why the workers should demand their repeal. London, [1924?]. pp. 22.

COMMUNIST PARTY OF GREAT BRITAIN. The record of the Labour Government. London, [1924]. pp. 32.

GALLACHER (WILLIAM) Can Labour govern?: the first Labour government and the struggle of the workers. London, [1924?] pp. 15.

LONDON. London Labour Party. Fifty points for municipal electors: facts and arguments for the labour programme briefly and brightly recorded; things that everyone ought to know. London, 1925. pp. 64.

WOOLWICH. Borough Council. Six years of Labour administration, 1919-25. [Woolwich, Barefoot, 1925]. pp. 31. 18½cm.

JOWETT (FREDERICK WILLIAM) Socialism in our time; (address of the chairman... I.L.P. annual conference, Whitley Bay, April 4th, 1926. London, [1926]. pp. 13.

SOCIALISM in our time: Labour's road to power: the policy of the living income. London, [1926]. pp. 15.

INDEPENDENT LABOUR PARTY. Conference, 1927. Souvenir of the 35th annual conference to be held at Leicester, Easter, 1927. [London, 1927]. pp. 48.

VAUGHAN (J.J.) Towards a labour government: the policy and programme of the National Left-Wing Movement. London, [1927]. pp. 24.

CAMPBELL (JOHN ROSS) Is Labour lost? The new labour party's programme examined. London, [1928]. pp. 19.

WILLIAMS (BERT) The record of the Labour Government. London, [1929]. pp. 16.

ELTON (GODFREY) 1st Baron Elton. Why National Labour? London, [193-]. pp. 8.

LINDSAY (KENNETH) National labour and leadership. London, National Labour Committee, [193-]. pp. 8. 24cm.

MURPHY (JOHN THOMAS) The Labour government: an examination of its record. [London], Modern Books, [1930]. pp. 96. 21½cm.

NATIONAL LABOUR COMMITTEE. Labour Party - the crisis and the nation; by a Labour candidate, 1924-1931. London, [1931]. pp. 20. 21½cm.

LABOUR PARTY. The Labour Party and the I.L.P.: the clear issue. [London, 1932]. pp. (4) 24½cm.

INDEPENDENT LABOUR PARTY. Conference, 1934. Decisions of the forty-second I.L.P. annual conference together with the statement of I.L.P. policy endorsed at the conference. London, [1934]. pp. 15.

INDEPENDENT LABOUR PARTY. I.L.P. and the Communist International: full text of the correspondence. London, [1934]. pp. 19.

MACDONALD (JAMES RAMSAY) National Labour and National government; speech...at the National Labour Conference...28th October, 1935. London, [1935?]. pp. 15.

INDEPENDENT LABOUR PARTY. Conference, 1936. Resolutions for forty-fourth annual conference Temperance Hall, Keighley April 11th to 14th, 1936; chairman, James Maxton, M.P. London, [1936]. pp. 23.

MACDONALD (JAMES RAMSAY) National Labour and the Labour movement; a speech...at the Second Annual Conference of the National Labour Committee. [London, c.1936]. pp. 8.

SACKVILLE (HERBRAND EDWARD DUNDONALD BRASSEY) 9th Earl De La Warr. Today and tomorrow. London, 1938. pp. 11. (National Labour Organisation. Pamphlets. No. 8)

FORWARD from victory!: Labour's plan; six essays based on lectures prepared for the Fabian Society; by Rt. Hon. Herbert Morrison [and others]. London, 1946. pp. 88.

HENDERSON (FRED) Socialism of the I.L.P.; (with the constitution of the Party). London, the Party, [1948?]. pp. 10. 21½cm.

LABOUR PARTY. Labour Party election manifesto. London, [1951]. fo. 2. Photocopy.

POZZANI (SILVIO) La revisione critica del laborismo. Milano, Istituto per gli Studi di Economia, 1953. pp. 94. 21cm.

BARKER (SARA ELIZABETH) How the Labour Party works. rev. ed. London, Labour Party, [1955?] pp. 16. 21½cm.

LABOUR PARTY. Programme for prices: a Labour Party policy for the cost of living. [London], 1955. pp. 31.

LABOUR PARTY. Labour's colonial policy: II. Economic aid. London, [1957?]. pp. 45.

BROWN (TOM) Nationalisation and the new boss class. London, the Federation, [1958?]. pp. 16. 20½cm. (Syndicalist Workers' Federation. Direct Action Pamphlets. No. 3)

LABOUR PARTY. Labour's housing policy. [London, 1958] pp. 35.

ALPATOVA (G.M.) Bor'ba techenii v leiboristskoi partii Anglii nakanune parlamentskikh vyborov 1951 g. in Problemy istorii rabochego i demokraticheskogo dvizheniia v stranakh Zapadnoi Evropy. Ufa, 1963.

LABOUR PARTY. Labour's election who's who: main list...parliamentary candidates general election, 1964. London, [1964]. pp. 147.

LABOUR PARTY. What the new Britain will be like when Labour wins: 21 questions, 21 answers. London, [1964]. pp. 15. 22cm.

ZILLIACUS (KONNI) the Younger. Labour's crisis: its nature, cause and cure. [London], the Author, [1966]. pp. 37. 20½cm.

DARNBOROUGH (ANNE) Labour's record on southern Africa: an examination of attitudes before October 1964 and actions since. London, Anti-Apartheid Movement, 1967. pp. 27. 21½cm.

GUROVICH (POLINA VENIAMINOVNA) Английское рабочее движение накануне второй мировой войны. Москва, 1967. pp. 357. bibliog.

HEALY (GERRY) The alternative to Wilson. London, 1967. pp. 16. (Socialist Labour League. Pamphlets)

MILLER (KENNETH E.) Socialism and foreign policy: theory and practice in Britain to 1931. The Hague, Nijhoff, 1967. pp. viii, 301. bibliog. 24cm.

SOCIALISM and affluence: (four Fabian essays); [by] Brian Abel-Smith [and others]. London, Fabian Society, 1967. pp. 93. 22½cm.

BARKER (RODNEY STEVEN) The educational policies of the Labour Party, 1900-1961; [Ph.D. (London) thesis]. 1968. fo. 508. bibliog. 25½cm. Typescript: unpublished. This thesis is the property of London University and may not be removed from the Library.

BURGESS (TYRRELL) and others. Matters of principle: Labour's last chance. Harmondsworth, Penguin Books, 1968. pp. 128. 18cm. (Penguin Specials. S 267)

CHRIST (GEORGE ELGIE) The myth of Munich. London, [1968?]. pp. 26.

LABOUR PARTY - United Kingdom (Cont'd.)

COATES (KEN) and TOPHAM (ANTHONY) The Labour Party's plans for industrial democracy. [Nottingham, 1968]. pp. irreg. (Institute for Workers' Control. Pamphlet Series. No.5)

GOLLAN (JOHN) Crisis: the communist answer. London, Communist Party, [1968]. pp. 22. 21½cm.

HOWARD (MICHAEL) and LAMONT (NORMAN) "Through a glass darkly": an examination of the Labour Party's mid term manifesto. London, [1968]. pp. 8. (Bow Group. Memoranda)

JANOSIK (EDWARD GABRIEL) Constituency Labour parties in Britain. London, Pall Mall, 1968. pp. (iii), 222. bibliog. 21½cm.

KRASIL'NIKOV (ALEKSEI NIKOLAEVICH) Внешняя политика Англии и лейбористская партия, 1951-1964. Москва, 1968. pp. 435. bibliog.

PELLING (HENRY MATHISON) A short history of the Labour Party. 3rd ed. London, Macmillan, 1968 pp. vii, 150. 21½cm.

READING (BRIAN) Government by deceit. London, Conservative Political Centre, 1968. pp. 51. 21½cm. ([Publications]. No. 412)

Das RINGEN um eine Wende: 50 Jahre Kampf von Kommunisten und linken Sozialisten um eine Alternative. [Berlin, 1968?]. pp. 139. (Berlin. Humboldt-Universität. Fichte-Schriften. 5)

ESSAYS on modern politics and history, written in honor of Harold M. Vinacke; edited by Han-Kyo Kim. Athens, Ohio, [1969]. pp. 255.

FABIAN SOCIETY. Fabian Tracts. [No.] 396. Labour's pension plan; [by] Tony Lynes. London, 1969. pp. 32. 21½cm.

GORDON (MICHAEL R.) Conflict and consensus in Labour's foreign policy 1914-1965. Stanford, California, 1969. pp. 333. bibliog.

HASELER (STEPHEN MICHAEL ALAN) The Gaitskellites revisionism in the British Labour Party, 1951-64. London, 1969. pp. 286. bibliog.

LABOUR PARTY. The fight against world poverty: Labour's commitment. [London], 1969. pp. 38.

LABOUR PARTY. Labour's economic strategy. London, [1969]. pp. 80.

LABOUR PARTY. Labour's social strategy. London, 1969. pp. 113.

LABOUR PARTY. National Executive Committee. Agenda for a generation; a statement...presented to the Labour Party annual conference, Brighton, 1969. [London, 1969]. pp. 13.

LABOUR PARTY. National Executive Committee. Chemical and bacteriological weapons; a statement of policy presented...to the Party annual conference, Brighton, 1969. [London, 1969]. s. sh.

LABOUR PARTY. National Executive Committee. Labour and the Common Market, 1969: a statement of policy presented...to the Party annual conference, Brighton, 1969. [London, 1969]. s. sh.

MARTEN (NEIL) Their's not to reason why: a study of the Anguillan operation as presented to Parliament. London, 1969. pp. 22. (Conservative Political Centre. [Publications]. No. 437)

NAYLOR (JOHN F.) Labour's international policy: the Labour Party in the 1930's. London, Weidenfeld & Nicolson, [1969]. pp. viii, 380. 21½cm.

PEREGUDOV (SERGEI PETROVICH) Antivoennoe dvizhenie v Anglii i leiboristskaia partiia, 1957-1968 gg. Moskva, 1969. pp. 245.

READING (BRIAN) In place of growth: a critique of Labour's economic strategy. London, 1969. pp. 48. (Conservative Political Centre. [Publications]. No. 452)

STANSKY (PETER) ed. The Left and war: the British Labour Party and World War I: [documentary material]. New York, O.U.P., 1969. pp. x, 335. bibliog. 20½cm. (Problems in European History)

TOBIN (JOSEPH) The extremists move in. [London, 1969]. pp. 11.

WAKEFORD (GEOFFREY) The great Labour mirage: an indictment of socialism in Britain. London, Hale, [1969]. pp. 240. 21½cm.

BEALEY (FRANK) ed. The social and political thought of the British Labour Party. London, [1970]. pp. 233.

BEAMISH (Sir TUFTON VICTOR HAMILTON) Half Marx;...with a postscript by Tibor Szamuely. London, [1970]. pp. 208.

CROUCH (COLIN) Politics in a technological society. London, 1970. pp. 36. (Young Fabian Group. Young Fabian Pamphlets. 23)

DERRICK (PAUL) Socialism in the seventies?: a co-operative contribution to Labour policies. London, 1970. pp. 38.

FABIAN SOCIETY. Fabian Tracts.[No.] 401. A socialist foreign policy?; [by] Rodney Fielding. London, 1970. pp. 24.

FABIAN SOCIETY. Fabian Tracts. [No.]403. Labour and inflation; [by] Thomas Balogh. London, 1970. pp. 64.

JENKINS (PETER) The battle of Downing Street. London, 1970. pp. 171.

LABOUR in action. Leicester, [1970]. pp. 202.

LAPPING (BRIAN) The Labour government, 1964-1970. Harmondsworth, 1970. pp. 219.

PARKINSON (MICHAEL) The Labour Party and the organization of secondary education,1918-65. London, 1970. pp. 139. bibliog.

READING (BRIAN) The great mess myth. [London], 1970. pp. 38. (Conservative Research Department. Old Queen Street Papers. No. 15)

TATARINTSEV (V.M.) "Politika dokhodov" leiboristskogo pravitel'stva v Anglii i bor'ba rabochego klassa za svoi prava. in Fomin (V.T.) ed. Osnovnye problemy rabochego dvizheniia v razvitykh kapitalisticheskikh stranakh. Moskva, 1970.

BROWN (KENNETH D.) Labour and unemployment, 1900-1914. Newton Abbot, [1971]. pp. 219. bibliog.

COATES (KEN) The crisis of British socialism: essays on the rise of Harold Wilson and the fall of the Labour Party. Nottingham, 1971. pp. 243.

COWLING (MAURICE JOHN) The impact of Labour, 1920-1924: the beginnings of modern British politics. Cambridge, 1971. pp. 570. bibliog.

DUFF (PEGGY) Left, left, left: a personal account of six protest campaigns, 1945-65. London, 1971. pp. 278.

FABIAN SOCIETY. Fabian Tracts. [No.] 407. The Labour Party: an organisational study; [by] Anthony Wedgwood Benn [and others]; [edited by] Inigo Bing. London, 1971. pp. 56.

FABIAN SOCIETY. Fabian Tracts. [No.] 411. Politicians, equality and comprehensives; [by] Dennis Marsden. London, 1971. pp. 36.

JAINE (T.W.M.) and STOREY (R.A.) compilers. [List of general correspondence and related papers of the Labour Representation Committee]; (with Index to the...list). [London], Historical Manuscripts Commission, 1971. 2 vols.

LABOUR and the common market: report of a special conference of the Labour Party, Central Hall, Westminster, 17 July 1971. London, [1971]. pp. 50.

PEREGUDOV (S.) Leiboristskaia partiia v sisteme vlasti. in Sotsial'no-politicheskie sdvigi v stranakh razvitogo kapitalizma. Moskva, 1971.

WILSON (HAROLD) The Labour government, 1964-1970: a personal record. London, 1971. pp. 836.

WORSTHORNE (PEREGRINE) The socialist myth. London, 1971. pp. 256.

YOUNG SOCIALISTS. National Committee. A fighting programme for Labour. n.p., [1971]. pp. 8.

- United Kingdom - Bibliography

LABOUR PARTY. Library. The Labour Party: a select reading list, excluding Labour Party publications. [London, 1971]. pp. 24.

LABOUR SERVICE

- Germany

SEIPP (PAUL) and SCHEIBE (WOLFGANG) Spaten und Ähre: das Handbuch der deutschen Jugend im Reichsarbeitsdienst; Herausgeber: v. Gönner. Heidelberg, 1937. pp. 239.

- Ghana

GHANA. 1958. National Workers Brigade. Accra, [1958?]. pp. 7.

- Russia

GUREEV (PETR ANTONOVICH) Льготы при оргнаборе и общественном призыве. Москва, Юридическая Литература, 1968. pp. 135. 20см.

- Ukraine

TROFIMOV (G.N.) К вопросу о возникновении движения бригад и ударников коммунистического труда на промышленных предприятиях г. Одессы. in Из истории рабочего класса СССР. Львов, 1968.

LABOUR SUPPLY

ORGANISATION FOR EUROPEAN ECONOMIC CO-OPERATION. Directorate for Scientific Affairs. 1961. Manpower assessments: a preliminary outline of objectives and methodology; by F.H. Harbison. Paris, 1961. pp. 10.

INTERNATIONAL LABOUR OFFICE. 1962. Report of the meeting of experts on the assessment of manpower requirements for economic development, Geneva, 1-12 October 1962. (G.B.153/7/12) Geneva, 1962. pp. 3, 34. 30cm.

BEDRIJFSSOCIOLOGISCHE STUDIEDAGEN 1963. Verschuivingen in de arbeidsvoorziening: inleidingen gehouden op de...Studiedagen...georganiseerd door het Sociologisch Instituut van de Rijksuniversiteit te Leiden [and] Nederlandsche Economische Hoogeschool te Rotterdam; door P. van Berkel [and others]. Leiden, Stenfert Kroese, 1963. pp. ix, 169. 23cm.

ORGANISATION FOR ECONOMIC CO-OPERATION AND DEVELOPMENT. 1964. International trade union seminar on active manpower policy, Vienna, 17th-20th September, 1963: final report; ([and] supplement). (International Seminars. 1963. 1) Paris, 1964. 2 pts. 24cm-30cm.

ORGANISATION FOR ECONOMIC CO-OPERATION AND DEVELOPMENT. 1965. Active manpower policy: International Management Seminar Brussels, 14th-17th April 1964; final report; ([and] supplement). (International Seminars. 1964. 1) Paris, 1965. 2 pts. 24cm - 29cm.

ROMERO (FERNANDO) Trabajo, educación y bienestar: política del empleo para el desarrollo económico. Lima, Universidad Nacional Mayor de San Marcos, Departamento de Publicaciones, 1965. pp. 385. 24½cm. (Biblioteca de Estudios Superiores.)

TECHNICAL MEETING CONCERNING CERTAIN ASPECTS OF LABOUR-MANAGEMENT RELATIONS WITHIN THE UNDERTAKING, GENEVA, 1964. Certain aspects of labour-management relations within the undertaking: documents of a Technical Meeting [held in] Geneva, 5-14 October 1964. Geneva, International Labour Organisation, 1965. pp. 389. (Labour Management Relations Series. No. 25.)

MANPOWER problems in the service sector: (background report for a trade union seminar); (with Supplement). Paris, Organisation for Economic Co-operation and Development, 1966-67. 2 pts. 24cm. and 27cm. (Social Affairs Division. International Seminars. 1966.2)

BLOCH (GILBERT) and PRADERIE (MICHEL) La population active dans les pays développés. [Paris], Cujas, 1966. pp. 366. 18½cm.

CONGRÈS DES RELATIONS INDUSTRIELLES DE L'UNIVERSITÉ LAVAL, 21e, 1966. Une politique globale de la main-d'oeuvre? See CONGRÈS DES RELATIONS INDUSTRIELLES DE L'UNIVERSITÉ LAVAL. (Études, etc.), 1966.

LABOUR SUPPLY (Cont'd.)

MANPOWER aspects of automation and technical change: European conference, Zurich, 1st-4th February 1966. Paris, Organisation for Economic Co-operation and Development, [1966]. 2 pts. 24cm. and 27cm. (Social Affairs Division. International Seminars. 1966. 1)

BRAUNREUTHER (KURT) and others, eds. Soziologische Aspekte der Arbeitskräftebewegung: internationales Kolloquium, Berlin, Juni 1966: gesammelte Beiträge. Berlin, Akademie-Verlag, 1967. pp. 437. bibliog. 24cm. (Deutsche Akademie der Wissenschaften zu Berlin. Institut für Wirtschaftswissenschaften. Schriften. Nr. 24)

INTERNATIONAL LABOUR OFFICE. Studies and Reports. New Series. No. 71. Human resources for industrial development: some aspects of policy and planning. Geneva, 1967. pp. 237.

ORGANISATION FOR ECONOMIC CO-OPERATION AND DEVELOPMENT. Social Affairs Division. Industrial Relations Aspects of Manpower Policy. 4. Technical change and manpower planning: co-ordination at enterprise level: (a series of national case studies edited by Solomon Barkin). [Paris, 1967]. pp. 287. 24cm.

INSTITUTE OF APPLIED MANPOWER RESEARCH. Reports. No. 3. Manpower research 1967. New Delhi, 1968. pp. xi, 298. 24½cm.

The LABOUR market and inflation: the proceedings of a symposium held at the International Institute for Labour Studies in Geneva, 24-26 October 1966, under the chairmanship of Pierre Massé; edited by Anthony D. Smith; with a preface by R.W. Cox. London, Macmillan, 1968. pp. xx, 247. 21½cm.

LEROY (ROBERT) Essai sur la population active: théories économiques récentes et analyse régionale de l'emploi féminin. Louvain, 1968. pp. 224. bibliog.

McCORMICK (BRIAN JOSEPH) and SMITH (E. OWEN) eds. The labour market: selected readings. Harmondsworth, Penguin Books, 1968. pp. 393. 18cm. (Penguin Modern Economics. X55)

MANPOWER aspects of educational planning: problems for the future. Paris, Unesco, 1968. pp. 265.

ROBINSON (DEREK) Wage drift, fringe benefits and manpower distribution: a study of employer practices in a full employment labour market. [Paris], Organisation for Economic Co-operation and Development, [1968], pp. 180. bibliog. (Social Affairs Division. Labour Mobility. 7)

UNITED NATIONS INDUSTRIAL DEVELOPMENT ORGANIZATION. Training for Industry Series. No. 2. Estimation of managerial and technical personnel requirements in selected industries. (ID/SER.D/2). New York, United Nations, 1968. pp. 250. bibliogs.

WEDDERBURN (DOROTHY) Enterprise planning for change: co-ordination of manpower and technical planning. [Paris], Organisation for Economic Co-operation and Development, [1968]. pp. 140. bibliog. 24cm. Social Affairs Division. Industrial Relations Aspects of Manpower Policy. 5.

COST-benefit analysis of manpower policies: proceeding of a North American conference; editors: C.G. Somers and W.D. Wood...; sponsored by Canadian Department of Manpower and Immigration [and] United States Department of Labour. Kingston, [1969]. pp. 272.

DAVIS (N.H.W.) Some methods of analysing cross-classified census data: the case of labour force participation rates. Ottawa, 1969. pp. 37. bibliog. (Canada. Dominion Bureau of Statistics. Special Labour Force Studies. Series B. No. 3)

FAIR (RAY C.) The short-run demand for workers and hours. Amsterdam, North-Holland Publishing Co., 1969. pp. xiii, 225. bibliog. 22½cm. (Contributions to Economic Analysis. 59)

JOLLY (RICHARD) The purpose of manpower planning and its implications for planning techniques. Brighton, 1969. pp. 8. (Brighton. University of Sussex. Institute of Development Studies. Communications. No.45)

LEVINE (LOUIS) b. 1907. The public employment service in social and economic policy: deliberations of a working party. Paris, Organisation for Economic Co-operation and Development, 1969. pp. 59. (Employment and Training)

MATHUR (ASHOK KUMAR) Manpower planning, education and economic development: a process analysis approach; [Ph.D. (London) thesis]. 1969. fo. 323. Typescript: unpublished. This thesis is the property of London University and may not be removed from the Library.

PERLMAN (RICHARD) Labor theory. New York, Wiley, [1969]. pp. xi, 237. 22½cm.

UNITED NATIONS INDUSTRIAL DEVELOPMENT ORGANIZATION. Monographs on Industrial Development. Industrialization of Developing Countries: Problems and Prospects. No. 14. Manpower for industry: based on the proceedings of the International Symposium on Industrial Development, Athens, November-December 1967. (ID/40/14). New York, United Nations, 1969. pp. 54. bibliog.

WEINTRAUB (LEON) International manpower development: a role for private enterprise in foreign assistance. New York, 1969. pp. 135. bibliog.

WIT (YNTO BRAM DE) Arbeidsmarkt en economische ontwikkeling in arme landen: elementen van algemene economische arbeidsmarkttheorie speciaal met betrekking tot e ontwikkeling van arme landen. Groningen, 1969. pp. 258. bibliog. With English summary.

BLAZEK (ALFRED) Die Wirkung der Besteuerung auf das Arbeitsangebot. Berlin, [1970]. pp. 137. bibliog.

FLEISHER (BELTON MENDEL) Labor economics: theory and evidence. Englewood Cliffs, N.J., 1970. pp. 304. bibliog.

HYMAN (RICHARD) Economic motivation and labour stability. Coventry, [1970]. fo. 29. (University of Warwick. Centre for Industrial and Business Studies. Warwick Research in Industrial and Business Studies. No. 2)

JACKSON (JOSEPH M.) Wages and labour economics. London, [1970]. pp. 244.

LOCAL labour markets and wage structures; editor Derek Robinson; [papers of a conference sponsored by the Engineering Employers' Federation]. London, 1970. pp. 296.

REYNOLDS (LLOYD GEORGE) Labor economics and labor relations. 5th ed. Englewood Cliffs, [1970]. pp. 692. bibliogs.

ROBERTSON (DONALD JAMES) and HUNTER (LOUIS CLARE) eds. Labour market issues of the 1970s. Edinburgh, [1970]. pp. 223. bibliogs. (Reprinted from Scottish Journal of Political Economy, vol. 17, no. 2)

SOME statistical techniques in manpower planning; [by D.J. Bartholomew and others]; edited by A.R. Smith. London, H.M.S.O., 1970. pp. 43. bibliog. (Civil Service College [U.K.]. Occasional Papers. No. 15.)

WICKENS (MICHAEL R.) A theory of the labour market. [Bristol], 1970. pp. various. (Bristol. University. Department of Economics. Discussion Papers in Economics. No. 36)

ADEBAHR (HUBERTUS) Die Fluktuation der Arbeitskräfte: Voraussetzungen und wirtschaftliche Wirkungen eines sozialen Prozesses. Berlin, [1971]. pp. 262. bibliog.

ASPECTS of manpower planning: a volume of papers published for the Manpower Society and edited by D.J. Bartholomew and B.R. Morris. London, 1971. pp. 130.

DOERINGER (PETER B.) and PIORE (MICHAEL J.) Internal labor markets and manpower analysis. Lexington, Mass., [1971]. pp. 214.

ISSUES in labor policy; papers [presented at a symposium] in honor of Douglass Vincent Brown; edited by Stanley M. Jacks. Cambridge, Mass., [1971]. pp. 182.

READINGS in labor market analysis; edited by John F. Burton [and others]. New York, [1971]. pp. 523. bibliogs.

- Bibliography

ORGANISATION FOR ECONOMIC CO-OPERATION AND DEVELOPMENT. Directorate for Scientific Affairs. 1962. Mediterranean Regional Project:...provisional selected bibliography. Paris, 1962. pp. 8.

KEAVENY (TIMOTHY J.) and HERMAN (GEORGIANNA) Compilers. Manpower planning: a research bibliography. Minneapolis, Minnesota University, Industrial Relations Center, 1966. pp. iii, 37. 23cm. (Bulletins. 45)

SOUTH AFRICA. Department of Education. Library. 1967. Manpower: selected bibliography. Pretoria, 1967. fo. 56.

LEWIS (C.G.) ed. Manpower: a bibliography. London, [1969]. pp. 96.

- Mathematical models

REDFERN (PERCY) Statistician. Input-output analysis and its application to education and manpower planning. London, H.M.S.O., 1967. pp. 18. bibliog. (Centre for Administrative Studies [U.K.]. Occasional Papers. No. 5)

REYNOLDS (LLOYD GEORGE) A critique of labor surplus models. Cairo, 1967. pp. 14. 28cm. (U.A.R. Institute of National Planning. Memos. No. 720.)

- Statistics

INTERNATIONAL LABOUR OFFICE. Development Programme: Technical Assistance Sector. [Nigeria]. R.10. Report to the government of Nigeria on programming for the development of manpower and labour statistics. (ILO/TAP/Nigeria/R.10) Geneva, 1967, pp. 87. 30cm.

DELDYCKE (T.) and others. La population active et sa structure: the working population and its structure;...under the supervision of P. Bairoch. Bruxelles, Université Libre, Institut de Sociologie, Centre d'Économie Politique, [1968]. pp. viii, 236. bibliog. 27cm. (Statistiques Internationales Rétrospectives. vol. 1) In English and French.

- Africa

LOKEN (ROBERT D.) Manpower development in Africa. New York, Praeger, 1969. pp. xi, 152. bibliog. 23½cm. (Praeger Special Studies in International Economics and Development)

- Algeria

TREBOUS (MADELEINE) Migration and development: the case of Algeria; manpower requirements in Algeria and vocational training in Europe. Paris, Organisation for Economic Co-operation and Development, 1970. pp. 242. bibliog. (Development Centre. Studies)

- America, Latin

BANNON (JOHN FRANCIS) ed. Indian labor in the Spanish Indies: was there another solution? Boston, [Mass.], Heath, [1966]. pp. xii, 105. bibliog. 23½cm. (Problems in Latin American Civilization)

ORGANISATION FOR ECONOMIC CO-OPERATION AND DEVELOPMENT. Directorate for Scientific Affairs. 1967. Problems of human resources planning in Latin America and in the Mediterranean regional project countries: long-term forecasts of manpower requirements and educational policies; report on the seminar held at Lima in March 1965 and complementary documents. [Paris, 1967]. pp. 279.

ORGANISATION FOR ECONOMIC CO-OPERATION AND DEVELOPMENT. Directorate for Scientific Affairs. 1967. Problems of human resources planning in Latin America and in the Mediterranean regional project countries: long-term forecasts of manpower requirements and educational policies; report on the seminar held at Lima in March 1965 and complementary documents. [Paris, 1967]. pp. 279.

RAMOS (JOSEPH R.) Labor and development in Latin America. New York, 1970. pp. 281. bibliog.

- Argentine Republic

ARGENTINE REPUBLIC. Departamento Nacional del Trabajo. División de Estadística. 1943. Ocupación y desocupación. Buenos Aires, 1943. pp. 20. (Serie B: Estadistica y Censos. No. 13)

LABOUR SUPPLY - Argentine Republic (Cont'd.)

ARGENTINE REPUBLIC. Instituto Nacional de Estadística y Censos. 1971. Encuesta de empleo y desempleo. [Buenos Aires, 1971?]. 6 pts. (in 1 vol.)

- Argentine Republic - Cordoba (Province)

ENCUESTA SOBRE EMPLEO Y DESEMPLEO EN LA CIUDAD DE CÓRDOBA; [published by] Dirección General de Estadística, Censos e Investigaciones [Córdoba], Facultad de Ciencias Económicas [Universidad Nacional de Córdoba] [and] Consejo Nacional de Desarrollo [Argentine Republic]. Córdoba, annual, 1966/7 to date. 33½cm.

- Australia

AUSTRALIA. 1965. Wage and salary earners in employment, June, 1961 to June, 1965. (Commonwealth Bureau of Census and Statistics) (S.B.295) Canberra, [1965]. pp. 66. 33cm. For 1947/1960 see AUSTRALIA. 1962; For 1954/1961 see AUSTRALIA. 1966.

AUSTRALIA. Commonwealth Bureau of Census and Statistics. Labour force: preliminary estimates. Canberra, quarterly, Aug. 1966/Feb 1969 (1st issue) to date. 29½cm.

AUSTRALIA. 1966. Wage and salary earners in employment, June, 1954 to June, 1961. (Commonwealth Bureau of Census and Statistics) (S.B.412) Canberra, [1966]. pp. 127. 33cm. For 1947/1960 see AUSTRALIA. 1962; for 1961/1965 see AUSTRALIA. 1965.

HORN (ROBERT VICTOR) Labour economics: Australia. Melbourne, 1969. pp. 96. bibliog.

- Australia - New South Wales

LINGE (GODFREY JAMES RUTHERFORD) Report on the future work-force of Canberra with special reference to industrial development;...(for the National Capital Development Commission). Canberra, 1960. fo. 43,(42).

STEINKE (JOHN C.) and others. Employment and unemployment in Illawarra: a report to the Illawarra Regional Development Committee. n.p., [1964]. fo. 34.

- Australia - Western Australia

WESTERN AUSTRALIA. Commonwealth Bureau of Census and Statistics, Western Australian Office. Statistics of Western Australia: Labour and prices. a., 1969 [1st issue]- Perth.

- Austria

VIENNA. Kammer für Arbeiter und Angestellte. Wirtschaftswissenschaftliche Abteilung. Probleme des österreichischen Arbeitsmarktes: eine Untersuchung. Wien, [1962]. pp. 78. (Vienna. Kammer für Arbeiter und Angestellte. Schriftenreihe)

BEIRAT FÜR WIRTSCHAFTS- UND SOZIALFRAGEN. [Publikationen. 5.] Vorausschätze des österreichischen Arbeitskräftepotentials bis 1980. Wien, 1965. pp. 40.

ORGANISATION FOR ECONOMIC CO-OPERATION AND DEVELOPMENT. Reviews of Manpower and Social Policies. 5. Manpower policies and problems in Austria. [Paris, 1967]. pp. 145. 24cm.

- Baltic States

TRUDOVYE... Трудовые ресурсы Прибалтийских Советских республик. Рига, Зинатне, 1967. pp. 148. 21½см.

- Belgium

BOGAERTS (GEORGES) Les besoins de l'industrie en personnel qualifié: estimation des besoins de l'industrie belge, etc. Bruxelles, Office Belge pour l'Accroissement de la Productivité, 1962. pp. 37. 24½cm. (Études sur le Chômage et l'Expansion)

EUROPEAN COMMUNITIES. Office Statistique. Statistiques Sociales. Série Speciale: Structure et Répartition des Salaires, 1966. 2. Enquête sur structure et la répartition des salaires, 1966: Belgique. [Luxembourg, 1969]. pp. 510. In various languages.

ROMPUY (PAUL VAN) De vraag naar arbeid: een econometrische studie van conjuncturele tewerkstellingsfuncties. Antwerpen, 1969. pp. 200. bibliog. (Louvain. Université. Institut de Recherches Economiques, Sociales et Politiques. Centre de Recherches Economiques. [Publications]. 28.) With English summary.

ORGANISATION FOR ECONOMIC CO-OPERATION AND DEVELOPMENT. Manpower and Social Affairs Committee. 1971. Manpower policy in Belgium. Paris, 1971. pp. 187. (Reviews of Manpower and Social Policies. 9)

- Botswana

PRATT (T.P.) Report of the 1967/68 labour census of Botswana. [Gaberones], 1969. fo. 14. (Botswana. Central Statistics Office. Statistical Publications. No. 1.)

- Brazil

VILLAÇA (MARIA JOSÉ) A fôrça do trabalho no Brasil. São Paulo, Pioneira, 1967. pp. 309. bibliog. 23cm. (Biblioteca Pioneira de Administração e Negócios)

FISCHLOWITZ (ESTANISLAU) Valorização dos recursos humanos do Brasil. Rio de Janeiro, 1970. pp. 421.

- British East Africa

UNITED COMMITTEE FOR TAXATION OF LAND VALUES. More jobs than men: remarkable conclusions of a famous army surgeon, who made the Panama canal possible; together with labour problems in British East Africa; evidence and report from East African Protectorate, Native Labour Commission, 1912-13. London, [1915?]. pp. 7.

- Bulgaria

APER'IAN (VLADIMIR EREMEEVICH) Социализм и трудовые ресурсы: из опыта социалистического строительства в Народной Республике Болгарии. Москва, ИМО, 1968. pp. 214. 19½см.

- Burma

KOOP (JOHN CLEMENT) Sample survey of labour force in Rangoon: a study in methods. Rangoon, 1956. pp. 101. bibliog.

INTERNATIONAL LABOUR OFFICE. Development Programme: Technical Assistance Sector. [Burma]. R. 32. Report to the government of the Union of Burma on manpower assessment and planning. (ILO/TAP/Burma/R.32) Geneva, 1968. pp. iii, 37. 30cm.

- Canada

CANADA. Dominion Bureau of Statistics. Seasonally adjusted employment indexes [in English and French]. Ottawa, annual, Jan.1961/March 1967 (1st ed.) to date. 28cm.

CANADA. Department of Labour. Economics and Research Branch. Professional Manpower Reports. No. 12. Employment and earnings in the scientific and technical professions, 1958-1961. Ottawa, 1962. pp. 31.

CANADA. Department of Labour. Economics and Research Branch. 1965. Chartbook: manpower trends in Canada. Ottawa, 1965. pp. 40.

CANADA. Department of Labour. Economics and Research Branch. Occasional Papers. No. 2. Changes in the occupational composition of the Canadian labour force, 1931-1961; by Noah M. Meltz. Ottawa, 1965. pp. 136. bibliog.

CANADA. Dominion Bureau of Statistics. Labour Division. Research and Analysis Section. 1965. Estimates of employees by province and industry, 1961-64. Ottawa, 1965. pp. 24. For current estimates see CANADA. Dominion Bureau of Statistics. Estimates of employees by province and industry.

LABOUR-MANAGEMENT CONFERENCE ON ECONOMIC AND TECHNOLOGICAL CHANGE IN THE SIXTIES, VANCOUVER, 1965. [Proceedings]; edited by Noel A. Hall. Vancouver, University of British Columbia, Institute of Industrial Relations, [1965]. pp. 164. 28cm.

CANADA. Parliament. Senate. Standing Committee on Immigration and Labour. Proceedings. Ottawa, irreg., June 16th 1966 (27th Parl., 1st session, no.1) to date. 25cm.

ORGANISATION FOR ECONOMIC CO-OPERATION AND DEVELOPMENT. Directorate for Scientific Affairs. 1966. Training of and demand for high-level scientific and technical personnel in Canada. Paris, 1966. pp. 136. (Reviews of National Policies for Education)

WALTON (F.T.) and McDONALD (D.J.) Atlantic provinces population and labour force projections to 1971. Fredericton, the Centre, 1966. fo. iv, 42. 28cm. (Atlantic Provinces Economic Council. Research Centre. Research Papers. No. 2)

WHITTINGHAM (FRANK J.) Educational attainment of the Canadian population and labour force, 1960-1965. Ottawa, 1966. pp. 40. 28cm. (Canada. Dominion Bureau of Statistics. Special Labour Force Studies. No.1.)

CANADA. Department of Manpower and Immigration. Annual report. Ottawa, annual, 1967/8 to date.

ALLINGHAM (JOHN D.) Women who work: part 1. The relative importance of age, education and marital status for participation in the labour force. Ottawa, 1967. pp. 26. 28cm (Canada. Dominion Bureau of Statistics. Special Labour Force Studies No. 5)

BRITTAIN (E. LOUISE) and others. Manpower requirements of the hospitality industry: a survey of opinion, etc. Ottawa, Canadian Department of Manpower and Immigration, 1967. pp. v, 57. 28cm.

CANADA. Department of Manpower and Immigration. Manpower Information and Analysis Branch. 1967. Career outlook, university graduates, 1967-1968. Ottawa, 1967. pp. 95. 25cm.

CANADA. Department of Manpower and Immigration. Professional Labour Market Section. 1967. Career outlook, technological institute graduates, 1966-67. Ottawa, 1967. pp. 37.

CANADA. Economic Council. 1967. A declaration on manpower adjustments to technological and other change. Ottawa, 1966[or rather] 1967. pp. 14, 15. In English and French.

OSTRY (SYLVIA) The occupational composition of the Canadian labour force. Ottawa, D.B.S., 1967. pp. x, 88. 23cm. (Canada. Dominion Bureau of Statistics. Census Division. 1961 Census Monographs.)

WHITTINGHAM (FRANK J.) and WILKINSON (BRUCE W.) Work patterns of the Canadian population, 1964. Ottawa, 1967. pp. 35. 28cm. (Canada. Dominion Bureau of Statistics. Special Labour Force Studies. No. 2.)

CANADA. Parliament. House of Commons. Standing Committee on Labour, Manpower and Immigration. Minutes of proceedings and evidence. Ottawa, irreg., Oct.17 1968 (28th Parl., 1st session, no.1) to date. 25cm.

ALLINGHAM (JOHN D.) and SPENCER (BYRON G.) Women who work: part 2. Married women in the labour force: the influence of age, education, child-bearing status and residence. Ottawa, 1968. pp. 21. (Canada. Dominion Bureau of Statistics. Special Labour Force Studies. Series B. No. 2)

DAVIS (N.H.W.) and GUPTA (MOTI LAL) Labour force characteristics of post-war immigrants and native-born Canadians, 1956-67. Ottawa, 1968. pp. 45. 28cm. Canada. Dominion Bureau of Statistics. Special Labour Force Studies. No. 6.

KRUGER (ARTHUR M.) and MELTZ (NOAH M.) eds. The Canadian labour market: readings in manpower economics. Toronto, University of Toronto, Centre for Industrial relations, 1968. pp. xix, 312. 21½cm.

MELTZ (NOAH M.) and PENZ (G. PETER) Canada's manpower requirements in 1970. Ottawa, Department of Manpower and Immigration, 1968. pp. x, 68. 28cm.

OSTRY (SYLVIA) Provincial differences in labour force participation. Ottawa, D.B.S., 1968. pp. viii, 37. 23cm. (Canada. Dominion Bureau of Statistics. Census Division. 1961 Census Monographs.)

AHAMAD (B.) A projection of manpower requirements by occupation in 1975: Canada and its regions. Ottawa, Queen's Printer, 1969. pp. 315.

CANADA. Dominion Bureau of Statistics. Labour Division. Employment Section. 1969. Estimates of employees by province and industry, 1961-1968. Ottawa, 1969. pp. 31. In English and French.

LABOUR SUPPLY - Canada (Cont'd.)

CANADA. Dominion Bureau of Statistics. Regional Statistics, Research and Integration. 1969. Growth patterns in manufacturing employment by counties and census divisions, 1949-1959-1961-1965. Ottawa, 1969. pp. 146. bibliog. In English and French.

DAVIS (N.H.W.) Some methods of analysing cross-classified census data: the case of labour force participation rates. Ottawa, 1969. pp. 37. bibliog. (Canada. Dominion Bureau of Statistics. Special Labour Force Studies. Series B. No. 3)

MELTZ (NOAH M.) Manpower in Canada, 1931 to 1961: historical statistics of the Canadian labour force. Ottawa, Queen's Printer, 1969. pp. 288.

TANDAN (NAND K.) Underutilization of manpower in Canada. Ottawa, 1969. pp. 36. (Canada. Dominion Bureau of Statistics. Special Labour Force Studies. No. 8)

ATKINSON (A.G.) and others. Canada's highly qualified manpower resources. Ottawa, Information Canada, 1970. pp. 304.

DENTON (FRANK T.) The growth of manpower in Canada. Ottawa, 1970. pp. 83. (Canada. Dominion Bureau of Statistics. Census Division. 1961 Census Monographs.)

LACASSE (FRANÇOIS D.) Women at home: the cost to the Canadian economy of the withdrawal from the labour force of a major proportion of the female population. Ottawa, 1970. pp. 28. (Canada. Royal Commission on the Status of Women in Canada, 1967. Studies. 2.)

SPENCER (BYRON G.) and FEATHERSTONE (DENNIS C.) Married female labour force participation: a micro study. [Ottawa], 1970. pp. 99. bibliog. (Canada. Dominion Bureau of Statistics. Special Labour Force Studies. Series B. No. 4.)

CANADA. Statistics Canada. Notes on labour statistics. a., 1971 (1st issue)- Ottawa.

CANADA. Dominion Bureau of Statistics. Consumer Finance Research Staff. 1971. Earnings and work experience of the 1967 labour force. Ottawa, 1971. pp. 45.

CANADA. Dominion Bureau of Statistics. Regional Statistics, Research and Integration. 1971. Growth patterns in manufacturing employment by counties and census divisions; La croissance de l'emploi dans les industries manufacturières, par comtés et par divisions de recensement, 1961-1967. Ottawa, 1971. pp. 138. Bibliog. In English and French.

DAVIS (N.H.W.) Cycles and trends in labour force participation. 1953-1968. Ottawa, 1971. pp. 91. (Canada. Dominion Bureau of Statistics. Special Labour Force Studies. Series B.No. 5.)

KEYS (B. A.) and others. Meeting managerial manpower needs: a survey of managerial manpower planning and development in Canadian business. Ottawa, Information Canada, 1971. pp. 74. bibliog.

MILLER (RICHARD ULRIC) and ISBESTER (A. FRASER) eds. Canadian labour in transition. Scarborough, Ont., [1971]. pp. 266.

CANADA. Statistics Canada. Quarterly report on job vacancies. [in English and French] q., 1972 (v.1, no.1)- Ottawa.

CANADA. Statistics Canada. Labour force: employment-unemployment. w. Ottawa. Current issues only kept.

- Canada - British Columbia

MONTAGUE (J.T.) and VANDERKAMP (JOHN) The British Columbia Labour force: a study in labour market adjustment. [Vancouver], University of British Columbia, 1966. pp.(iii), 134. 28cm.

- Canada - New Brunswick

RAPHAEL (LLOYD F.) Labour force of New Brunswick, 1951-1971. [Fredericton], New Brunswick Department of Labour, 1963. pp. (iv), 143. 28cm.

NEW BRUNSWICK. Department of Labour. Studies. No.3. Some aspects of the manpower problem in New Brunswick woodlands. Fredericton, 1967. pp. ii, 53. bibliog. 28½cm.

- Canada - Nova Scotia

JUDEK (STANISLAW) Manpower training requirements for Nova Scotia, 1970 and 1975. Halifax, Department of Labour, [1965] repr. 1968. fo. 100. bibliog.

COMEAU (ROBERT L.) Manpower requirements in the construction industry in Nova Scotia. Halifax, N.S., Nova Scotia Department of Labour, 1966. pp. 88.

SCHAFER (D. P.) A study of employment trends in the services sector of the American, Canadian and Nova Scotia economies (1921-1961). Halifax, 1966. pp. 119. bibliog. (Nova Scotia. Voluntary Planning Board. Special Studies. No.2)

- Canada - Ontario

MEHMET (OZAY) Methods of forecasting manpower requirements: with special reference to the province of Ontario. Toronto, University of Toronto, 1965. pp. (v), 57, xvi. bibliog. 25cm.

- Cape Verde Islands

CID (FRANCISCO DE PAULA) La main d'oeuvre aux îles de Cabo Verde. Lisbonne, [imprint], 1914. pp. 15. 25½cm. Paper read at Congrès International d'Agriculture Tropicale, 3ème, Londres, 1914.

- Ceylon

SRIVASTAVA (R.K.) Manpower approach to educational planning. [Colombo, Ministry of Planning and Economic Affairs, 1966?]. fo. 8.

SRIVASTAVA (R.K.) Manpower situation in Ceylon: a preliminary note. Colombo, Department of National Planning, 1966. pp. 15.

CEYLON. Planning Committee on Manpower and Education. 1967. Report...on education, health, housing and manpower: [M.J. Perera, chairman]. [Colombo], Ministry of Planning and Economic Affairs, 1967. pp. 107.

SRIVASTAVA (R.K.) A note on the technical aspects of the proposed labour force survey. [Colombo, Ministry of Planning and Economic Affairs, 1967?]. fo. 12, 4.

CEYLON. Official Committee on Mobilisation of Surplus Manpower for Development. 1968. Report. [Colombo, 1968?]. fo. 26.

INTERNATIONAL LABOUR OFFICE. 1968. Interim report to government of Ceylon on manpower assessment and planning; [by R.K.Srivastava]. Geneva, 1968. fo. 25.

SELVARATNAM (S.) Education and manpower needs: prepared at the request of the Ministry of Education and Cultural Affairs. Colombo, [Ministry of Planning and Economic Affairs], 1968. fo. 14. bibliog.

SELVARATNAM (S.) and SRIVASTAVA (R.K.) Employment trends in Ceylon: a preliminary analysis. Colombo, Ministry of Planning and Economic Affairs, 1968. fo. 11.

SRIVASTAVA (R.K.) Ceylon: demand and supply of skilled engineering craftsmen and vocational training needs: a preliminary exercise. [Colombo], Department of National Planning, [1968?]. fo.various.

SRIVASTAVA (R.K.) and others. UNDP - SF: national economic planning and programming project: employment in the industrial sector, 1967-1969. [Colombo], Ministry of Planning and Economic Affairs, 1969. fo. various.

- Chile

GUADAGNI (ALIETO A.) La estructura ocupacional y el desarrollo económico de Chile. [Buenos Aires], Instituto Torcuato di Tella, Centro de Investigaciones Económicas, 1965. fo. 25. 27cm. (Documentos de Trabajo. 24) (Reprinted from Journal of Inter-American Studies, vol.6, 1964)

CHILE. Servicio Nacional del Empleo. Informe trimestral sobre la situacion del empleo. q., D 1970- Santiago.

- China

UNITED STATES. Census Bureau. International Population Statistics Reports. Series P-90. No. 21. Nonagricultural employment in Mainland China, 1949-1958. Washington, 1965. pp. x, 24. bibliog.

HOWE (CHRISTOPHER) Employment and economic growth in urban China, 1949-1957. Cambridge, 1971. pp. 170. bibliog. (London. University. School of Oriental and African Studies. Contemporary China Institute. Publications)

- Colombia

ZSCHOCK (DIETER K.) Manpower perspective of Colombia. Princeton, Princeton University, Department of Economics, Industrial Relations Section, 1967. pp. x, 151. bibliog. 21½cm. (Research Report Series. No. 110)

INTERNATIONAL LABOUR OFFICE. 1970. Towards full employment: a programme for Colombia; prepared by an inter-agency team organised by the International Labour Office. Geneva, 1970. pp. 471.

- Communist countries

DEGTIAR' (L. S.) Трудовые ресурсы и их использование в зарубежных социалистических странах-членах СЭВ. Москва, 1969. pp. 157.

MIKUL'SKII (KONSTANTIN IVANOVICH) Trudovye resursy evropeiskikh stran sotsializma. Moskva, 1969. pp. 197. bibliog.

- Cyprus

CYPRUS. Ministry of Labour and Social Insurance. Labour Research and Statistics Section. Report on the Island-wide manpower survey of establishments employing 10 or more persons. a., 1967 (2nd)- [Nicosia] 1968 (3rd) catalogued separately and filed at R(0) 564(95).

CYPRUS. Ministry of Labour and Social Insurance. Labour Research and Statistics Section. Review of labour market developments. a., 1967 (3rd)- Nicosia.

- Denmark

JØRGENSEN (ERLING) Arbejdsmarkedets marginalgrupper: de unges, de ældres og de gifte kvinders placering på arbejdsmarkedet; The marginal groups of the labour market: the labour market situation of the young, the aged and the married women. København, Teknisk Forlag, 1969. pp. 102. (Socialforskningsinstituttet. Publikationer. 39) With English abstract, summary, and translation of tables.

- Egypt

SEMINAR ON MANPOWER PLANNING, CAIRO, 1968. Seminar... organized jointly by the Organization for Economic Co-operation and Development and the Institute of National Planning. [Cairo, 1968]. pp. (273).

- Europe

UNITED STATES. Labor Department. Manpower and Research Bulletins. No. 11. Manpower policy and programs in five Western European countries. Washington, 1966. pp. viii, 59. bibliog.

CHORAFAS (DIMITRIS N.) The knowledge revolution: an analysis of the international brain market and the challange to Europe. London, Allen & Unwin, 1968. pp. 142. 21½cm.

INTERNATIONAL LABOUR OFFICE. 1969. Manpower aspects of recent economic developments in Europe. Geneva, 1969. pp. iv, 175. 24cm.

- Europe, Eastern

PERSPEKTIVPLANUNG der Arbeitskräfte: Erfahrungen sozialistischer Länder; herausgegeben von E. Sachse. Berlin, [1966]. pp. 175. (Sozialistische Arbeitswissenschaft. [Publications]. 7.)

- European Economic Community countries

EUROPEAN ECONOMIC COMMUNITY. Commission. 1961. L'évolution de l'emploi dans les états membres, 1954-1958. [Brussels], 1961. pp. 280. 25cm.

LABOUR SUPPLY - European Economic Community countries (Cont'd.)

VITAL (MARIA ODETE) Aspectos relacionados com as políticas de emprego e formação profissional e de rendimentos no âmbito do programa de política económica a médio prazo (1966-1970) da Comunidade Económica Europeia. Lisboa, 1967. pp. 23. 30cm. (Fundo de Desenvolvimento da Mão-de-Obra. Boletim bimestral. Suplementos. N.º 14) With abstracts in English and French.

- Fiji Islands

ELKAN (WALTER) Fiji Manpower Resources Council and manpower planning; report on a visit...20th August - 10th September, 1968. in Fiji. Legislative Council. Journal. Sessions of 1969, which see.

- France

FRANCE. Institut National de la Statistique et des Études Économiques. Direction Régionale de Limoges. 1957. Allure du renouvellement de la population active masculine en Haute-Vienne de 1954 à 1970: réflexions sur le sort de générations de jeunes filles; texte d'une conférence faite à Limoges le dimanche 31 mars 1957...par Louis Pichard. [Limoges, 1957]. pp. 8. 27cm.

FRANCE. Institut National de la Statistique et des Études Économiques. Direction Régionale de Nantes. 1959. L'ensemble industriel de la Basse-Loire: ses zones d'influence. Nantes, [1959?]. pp. (7). 27cm. Issued with another part, under the cover title Ensemble industriel de la XIème région statistique.

FRANCE. Institut National de la Statistique et des Études Économiques. Direction Régionale de Nantes. 1959. Ensembles industriels: Tours, Angers, Le Mans. Nantes, [1959]. pp. 11 26¾cm.

FRANCE. Institut National de la Statistique et des Études Économiques. Direction Régionale de Nantes, and CHOLET. Chambre de Commerce. 1959. La zone industrielle choletaise par l'état de sa population: centre de haute pression démographique; carrefour de l'emploi régional. Nantes, [1959]. pp. 36. 26½cm.

FRANCE. Commission de la Main-d'Oeuvre. 1966. Ve Plan, 1966-1970: rapport général. [Paris, La Documentation Française], 1966. pp. 423. 24cm.

BALLAN (J.J.) La structure de l'emploi en Aquitaine: analyse qualitative et perspectives d'évolution. Paris, Gauthier-Villars, 1967. 2 vols. (in 1). bibliog. 27½cm. (Bordeaux. Université. Faculté de Droit. Institut d'Économie Régionale du Sud-Ouest. Techniques Économiques Modernes. No. 8/9)

FRANCE. Institut National de la Statistique et des Études Économiques. Structure des emplois au 1er janvier. (Les Collections de l'I.N.S.E.E. Série D) a., 1968- Paris.

GEREMEK (BRONISLAW) Le salariat dans l'artisanat parisien aux XIIIe-XVe siècles: étude sur le marche de la main-d'oeuvre au moyen âge; traduit du polonais, etc. Paris, 1968. pp. 147. (Paris. Ecole Pratique des Hautes Etudes. Section des Sciences Economiques et Sociales. Industrie et Artisanat. 5)

MAILLARD (JEAN PHILIPPE) Le nouveau marché du travail. [Paris], Seuil, [1968]. pp. 142. bibliog. 18cm. (Société. 24)

HUGUES (PHILIPPE D') and PESLIER (MICHEL) Les professions en France - évolution et perspectives. Paris, P.U.F., 1969. pp. 473. (France. Institut National d'Etudes Démographiques. Travaux et Documents. Cahiers. No. 51.)

EUROPEAN COMMUNITIES. Office Statistique. Statistiques Sociales. Série Spéciale: Structure et Répartition des Salaires, 1966. 4. Enquête sur la structure et la répartition des salaires, 1966: France. [Luxembourg, 1970]. pp. 600. In various languages.

VINCENS (JEAN) La prévision de l'emploi. Paris, 1970. pp. 204. bibliog.

FRANCE. Commission de l'Emploi. 1971. Préparation du VIe Plan: rapport. Paris, 1971. 2 pts.

- Germany

TAFEL (W.) Arbeitszwang und Arbeitslust. Gotha, 1919. pp. 40.

GERMANY (BUNDESREPUBLIK). Statistisches Bundesamt. 1964-66. Arbeitsstättenzählung vom 6. Juni 1961. Stuttgart, 1964-66. 7 pts. (in 1 vol.)

EUROPEAN COMMUNITIES. Office Statistique. Statistiques Sociales. Série Spéciale: Structure et Répartition des Salaires, 1966. 3. Enquête sur la structure et la répartition des salaires, 1966: Deutschland (B.R.). [Luxembourg, 1969]. pp. 610. In various languages.

STEDEN (WERNER) Der Arbeitsmarkt der bayrischen Industrie: ein interregionaler Vergleich. Berlin, [1969]. pp. 212. bibliog.

NORTH RHINE-WESTPHALIA. Statistisches Landesamt. Beiträge zur Statistik des Landes Nordrhein-Westfalen. Heft 270. Erwerbstätige in Nordrhein-Westfalen, 1959-1969: Ergebnisse des Mikrozensus. Düsseldorf, 1971. pp. 113.

- Greece

ORGANISATION FOR EUROPEAN ECONOMIC CO-OPERATION. Directorate for Scientific Affairs. 1961. Mediterranean Regional Project: statistics, Greek National Study Team. Paris, 1961. pp. 17.

- Hawaiian Islands

HAWAII. Bureau of Employment Security. Staff Service Division. 1958. OAHU looks forward to 1961: a report on future manpower requirements and training needs. Honolulu, 1958. pp. 51. 28cm.

- Hong Kong

INTERNATIONAL LABOUR OFFICE. Development Programme: Technical Assistance Sector. [Hong Kong]. R.3. Report to the government of Hong Kong on manpower assessment. (ILO/TAP/Hong Kong/R.3) Geneva, 1967. pp. 30.

HONG KONG. Special Committee on Higher Education. 1968. Second interim report, 1968. Hong Kong, 1968. pp. iii, 126.

- Hungary

HUNGARY. 1965. Munkaerőhelyzet, 1949-1964. január 1. (Statisztikai Időszaki Közlemények. 76. kötet) Budapest, 1965. pp. 214,(3). 28cm. With English summary.

HUNGARY. Központi Statisztikai Hivatal. Statisztikai Időszaki Közlemények. 110. kötet. Munkaerőhelyzet megyék szerint, 1949-1966. Budapest, 1967. pp. 126. 29cm.

- India

INDIA. Scientific Manpower Committee. 1949. Basic report on survey and assessment. New Delhi, 1949. pp. 312.

INDIA. Ministry of Community Development, Panchayati Raj and Cooperation. 1963. Defence labour bank; [by] S.K. Dey. Delhi, 1963. pp. (10).

RAY (K.) Scientific and technical personnel. New Delhi, [1966]. pp. ix, 88. bibliog. (India. Census, 1961. Monograph Series. No. 1)

MITRA (LALIT KUMAR) Employment and output in small enterprises of India: a techno-economic study. Calcutta, Bookland, 1967. pp. vii, 199. bibliog. 21½cm.

INSTITUTE OF APPLIED MANPOWER RESEARCH. Fact book on manpower. 2nd ed. New Delhi, 1968-1970. 3 vols. bibliogs. (Reports. 1968. No. 1, 1969. Nos. 4-5)

BURGESS (TYRRELL) and others. Manpower and educational development in India, 1961-1986. Edinburgh, Oliver & Boyd, 1968. pp. xii, 89. 24 cm. (London. University. London School of Economics and Political Science. Unit for Economic and Statistical Studies on Higher Education. Reports. 3)

DAS (NABAGOPAL) Unemployment and employment planning. Bombay, 1968. pp. 100. bibliog.

INDIA. Census. Papers. 1967. No.1. Census of India, 1961...: subsidiary tables B-I.6 and B-II.3: workers from 1901/11 to 1961 by states and union territories and by cities. [Delhi, 1968]. pp. 145.

TOBIAS (GEORGE) and QUEENER (ROBERT S.) India's manpower strategy revisited, 1947-1967. [Bombay], 1968. pp. 265.

AGARWAL (SATYA PRAKASH) Manpower supply: concepts and methodology. Meerut, [1969]. pp. 187. bibliog.

BASU (SAROJ KUMAR) and others. Labour market behaviour in a developing economy. Calcutta, 1969. pp. 126.

SANGHVI (PRAFULLA) Surplus manpower in agriculture and economic development; with special reference to India. London, [1969]. pp. 343. bibliogs.

- Iran

IRAN. Ministry of Labour. 1959. National manpower resources and requirements survey, Iran, 1958. Washington, Governmental Affairs Institute, 1959. fo. 90.

BARTSCH (WILLIAM HENRY) Labour supply and employment-creation in the urban areas of Iran, 1956-1966; [Ph.D. (London) thesis]. 1970. fo.347. bibliog. Typescript: unpublished. This thesis is the property of London University and may not be removed from the Library.

- Ireland (Republic)

EIRE. National Industrial Economic Council. [Reports. No.3]. Report on manpower policy. Dublin,[1964]. pp. 23. 21cm.

SYMES (DAVID GILYARD) The population resources of the...Gaeltacht: an analysis of the employment potential; a memorandum to the Board of Gaeltarra Eireann. Hull, University, Department of Geography, 1965. 2 vols. (in 1). (Miscellaneous Series. Nos. 1-2)

ROSEINGRAVE (TOMAS) Manpower in an industrial growth centre: a survey in Waterford: report. Dublin, Stationery Office, [1969]. pp. 63.

DEENY (JAMES) The Irish worker: a demographic study of the labour force in Ireland. Dublin, 1971. pp. 97. (Institute of Public Administration, Dublin. Research Series. 4)

- Israel

ISRAEL. 1964. Development towns in Israel: first report on 21 development towns; translated from the Hebrew by Asher Weill. (Manpower Planning Authority) [Jerusalem], 1964. fo. 39. 27cm.

HOCHWALD (I.) Employment and mobility of employees in Tel Aviv—Yafo. Tel Aviv, Department of Research and Statistics, 1966. pp. x, 22. 24cm. (Special Surveys. No.19) In English and Hebrew.

ISRAEL. Ministry of Labour. Manpower Planning Authority. 1966. Projection of manpower: post-elementary education. [Jerusalem], 1966. pp. 65.

SHIBL (YUSUF) ed. Essays on the Israeli economy. Beirut, 1969. pp. 276. bibliog. (Palestine Research Center. Palestine Books. No. 15)

TEL-AVIV. Department of Research and Statistics. Special Surveys. No. 32. Labour force and employment in Tel Aviv-Yafo, 1961-1968. Tel-Aviv, 1969. pp.irregular. bibliog. (In English and Hebrew)

- Italy

ALAURO (ORLANDO D') ed. Studi regionali sull'occupazione: Liguria, etc. Lussemburgo, European Coal and Steel Community, 1957. pp. 74. (Studies and Documents)

ITALY. Istituto Centrale di Statistica. Metodi e Norme. Serie A. N. 3. Rilevazioni campionarie delle forze di lavoro. Roma, 1958. pp. 58. 22cm.

ITALY. Istituto Centrale di Statistica. Note e Relazioni. N.1. Alcuni principali risultati delle rilevazioni delle forze di lavoro negli anni 1954-1957; (relazione del prof. Benedetto Barberi). Roma, 1958. pp. 81. 26cm.

LABOUR SUPPLY - Italy (Cont'd.)

ITALY. Istituto Centrale di Statistica. Note e Relazioni. N.4. Rilevazione nazionale delle forze di lavoro, 8 novembre 1957; (relazione del dott. Carlo Viterbo). Roma, 1958. pp. 54. 26cm.

ARINGA (CARLO DELL') Occupazione, salari e prezzi: un'analisi empirica per l'industria italiana, 1953-1967. Milano. 1969. pp. 174.

EUROPEAN COMMUNITIES. Office Statistique. Statistiques Sociales. Série Speciale: Structure et Répartition des Salaires, 1966. 5. Enquête sur la structure et la répartition des salaires, 1966: Italia. [Luxembourg, 1970]. pp. 606. In various languages.

- Jamaica

SMITH (MICHAEL GARFIELD) A report on labour supply in rural Jamaica. Kingston, [imprint], 1956. pp.(iii),167. 25cm.

JAMAICA. Department of Statistics. Employment Statistics Unit. 1966. Employment and earnings in large establishments, 1963-64. Kingston, [1966]. pp. 198.

- Japan

JAPAN. Bureau of Statistics. 1952. Report on the labor force survey, 1947-1952. [Tokyo], 1952. pp. 172.

JAPAN. Bureau of Statistics. 1955. Report on the labor force survey, no. 2. [Tokyo], 1955. pp. 195.

JAPAN. Bureau of Statistics. 1957. Revised figures of the labor force survey prior to April 1957. [Tokyo], 1957. pp. 124.

JAPAN. Bureau of Statistics. 1959. Figures of labor force survey concerning the population 15 years old and over, January, 1953-December, 1958. [Tokyo], 1959. pp. 95.

UNITED STATES. Department of Labor. Employment policies of the United States and Japan: report of the joint United States-Japan Employment Study. Washington, 1968. pp. 126.

TAIRA (KOJI) Economic development and the labor market in Japan. New York, 1970. pp. 280. bibliog. (Columbia University. East Asian Institute. Studies)

- Jordan

JORDAN. Department of Statistics. Monthly employment survey for large establishments. Amman, irreg., Jan./March 1967 (no. 1) to date. 27cm.

Not published July-Dec. 1967.

- Kazakstan

NASELENIE i trudovye resursy gorodov Severnogo Kazakhstana. Alma-Ata, 1970. pp. 275. bibliog.

- Kenya

KENYA. Labour Department. 1949. Report on African labour census, 1948. [Nairobi], 1949. pp. 7, (31).

EDUCATION, employment and rural development, the proceedings of a conference held at Kericho, Kenya in September, 1966; James R. Sheffield, editor. Nairobi, East African Publishing House, 1967. pp. xxvi, 499. 21½cm.

- Kirghizia

CHERNOVA (ELENA PETROVNA) Trudovye resursy promyshlennosti Kirgizii. Frunze, 1970. pp. 271.

- Korea

MANPOWER DEVELOPMENT RESEARCH INSTITUTE. Handbook of manpower statistics, 1968. n.p., 1968. pp. xii, 226. 26cm. In English and Korean.

- Latvia

TRUDOVYE... Трудовые ресурсы Латвийской ССР. Рига, АН Латвийской ССР, 1964. pp. 184. 21½cm.

- Liberia

WECKSTEIN (R.S.) Wages and labor scarcity: Liberia. in Papanek (Gustav F.) ed. Development policy. Cambridge, Mass., 1968.

- Libya

INTERNATIONAL LABOUR OFFICE. Development Programme: Technical Assistance Sector. [Libya]. R.16. Report to the government of the Kingdom of Libya on the development of a manpower information programme. (ILO/TAP/Libya/R.16). Geneva, 1969. pp. 95.

LIBYA. Census and Statistical Department. Monthly Statistics of production and employment in selected large manufacturing establishments. [in English and Arabic] q., Ja/Mr 1970 [1st issue]- Guimada El-Tani.

- Luxembourg

EUROPEAN COMMUNITIES. Office Statistique. Statistiques Sociales. Série Speciale: Structure et Répartition des Salaires. 1966. 7. Enquête sur la structure et la répartition des salaires, 1966: Luxembourg. [Luxembourg, 1970]. pp. 285. In various languages.

ORGANISATION FOR ECONOMIC CO-OPERATION AND DEVELOPMENT. Manpower and Social Affairs Committee. 1970. Manpower policy in Luxembourg. Paris, 1970. pp. 149. (Reviews of Manpower and Social Policies. 8)

- Malawi

MALAWI. Department of Census and Statistics. Quarterly report on earnings and employment. Zomba, quarterly, March [1st issue] - Nov. 1969; ceased publication.

MALAWI. National Statistical Office. Reported employment and earnings: annual report. a., 1970 [1st issue]- Zomba.

- Mali (Republic)

INTERNATIONAL LABOUR OFFICE. Development Programme: Technical Assistance Sector. [Mali].R.10. Rapport au gouvernement de la République du Mali sur l'organisation et la planification de la formation professionnelle. (OIT/TAP/Mali/R.10) Geneva, 1969. pp. 63.

- Malta

MALTA. 1957. Report by Mr. German on the labour problems of Malta, 1956. [Valletta, 1957]. pp. 30.

INTERNATIONAL LABOUR OFFICE. Development Programme: Technical Assistance Sector. [Malta]. R.3. Report to the government of Malta on the assessment of the present and future manpower situation. (ILO/TAP/Malta/R.3) Geneva, 1967. pp. 53.

MALTA. Census, 1967. Malta census, 1967: report on economic activities. Valletta, [1971?] 2 vols. (in 1).

- Mauritania

INTERNATIONAL LABOUR OFFICE. Development Programme: Technical Assistance Sector. [Mauritania]. R.7. Rapport au gouvernement de la République islamique de Mauritanie sur l'évaluation et la planification de la main-d'oeuvre. (OIT/TAP/Mauritanie/R.7) Genève, 1967. pp. ii, 79. 30cm.

- Mediterranean

ORGANISATION FOR ECONOMIC CO-OPERATION AND DEVELOPMENT. Directorate for Scientific Affairs. 1961-62. Mediterranean Regional Project:...National Directors' Group: (summary record[s] of the first [-third] meeting[s]). Paris, 1961-62. 3 pts.

ORGANISATION FOR ECONOMIC CO-OPERATION AND DEVELOPMENT. Directorate for Scientific Affairs. 1961. Mediterranean Regional Project: analysis of educational needs and priorities for specialised manpower in relation to economic development: ...note on methodology. Paris, 1961. pp. 12.

ORGANISATION FOR ECONOMIC CO-OPERATION AND DEVELOPMENT. Directorate for Scientific Affairs. 1961. The methodological content of the work; proposed research activities relating to the...Mediterranean Regional Project; (prepared by H.S. Parnes). Paris, 1961. pp. 4.

ORGANISATION FOR EUROPEAN ECONOMIC CO-OPERATION. Directorate for Scientific Affairs. 1961. Mediterranean Regional Project: first meeting of national directors...Paris, 3-5 July 1961: further activities of O.E.E.C. Secretariat. Paris, 1961. pp. 5.

ORGANISATION FOR ECONOMIC CO-OPERATION AND DEVELOPMENT. Directorate for Scientific Affairs. 1962. Mediterranean Regional Project on targets and programmes for education and priorities for specialised manpower in relation to economic development. Paris, 1962. pp. 8.

ORGANISATION FOR ECONOMIC CO-OPERATION AND DEVELOPMENT. Directorate for Scientific Affairs. 1967. Problems of human resources planning in Latin America and in the Mediterranean regional project countries: long-term forecasts of manpower requirements and educational policies; report on the seminar held at Lima in March 1965 and complementary documents. [Paris, 1967]. pp. 279. 24cm.

- Nepal

INTERNATIONAL LABOUR OFFICE. Development Programme: Technical Assistance Sector. [Nepal]. R.2. Report to His Majesty's Government of Nepal on the establishment of a manpower assessment and planning programme. (ILO/TAP/Nepal/R.2) Geneva, 1968. pp. 95.

NEPAL. Ministry of Economic Planning. 1968. Technical and vocational training in Nepal (1966-67). Kathmandu, [1968?]. pp. 80.

NEPAL. National Planning Commission. 1969. Employment of graduates in Nepal (1964-1966). Kathmandu, [1969]. 2 pts.

- Netherlands

BEDRIJFSSOCIOLOGISCHE STUDIEDAGEN 1963. Verschuivingen in de arbeidsvoorziening: inleidingen gehouden op de...Studiedagen...georganiseerd door het Sociologisch Instituut van de Rijksuniversiteit te Leiden [and] Nederlandsche Economische Hoogeschool te Rotterdam; door P. van Berkel [and others]. Leiden, Stenfert Kroese, 1963. pp. ix, 169. 23cm.

ORGANISATION FOR ECONOMIC CO-OPERATION AND DEVELOPMENT. Reviews of Manpower and Social Policies. 6. Manpower and social policy in the Netherlands. [Paris, 1967]. pp. 301. 24cm.

EUROPEAN COMMUNITIES. Office Statistique. Statistiques Sociales. Série Speciale: Structure et Répartition des Salaires, 1966. 6. Enquête sur la structure et la répartition des salaires, 1966: Nederland. [Luxembourg, 1969]. pp. 520. In various languages.

- New Hebrides

INTERNATIONAL LABOUR OFFICE. Development Programme: Technical Assistance Sector. [New Hebrides]. R.1. Report to the governments of Great Britain and France on manpower assessment in the New Hebrides. (ILO/TAP/New Hebrides/R.1). Geneva, 1969. pp. 39.

- New Zealand

NEW ZEALAND. Department of Statistics. 1965. New Zealand population and labour force projections, 1965-1990. Wellington, 1965. pp. 58. 27cm.

NATIONAL DEVELOPMENT CONFERENCE, WELLINGTON, 1969. Labour Committee. Report. [Wellington, Government Printer], 1969. pp. 55. ([Reports]. N.D.C. 21.)

NEW ZEALAND. Department of Statistics. 1969. New Zealand population and labour force projections, 1968-2000. Wellington, 1968 [or rather 1969]. pp. 40. (Monthly abstract of statistics. Special supplement, December 1968)

- Nigeria

NIGERIA. National Manpower Board. Annual report. Lagos, annual, 1962/64 [1st] to date. 24cm.

CALLAWAY (A.) School leavers and the developing economy of Nigeria. in Tilman (Robert O.) and Cole (Taylor) eds. The Nigerian political scene. Durham, N.C., 1962.

INTERNATIONAL LABOUR OFFICE. Development Programme: Technical Assistance Sector. [Nigeria]. R.10. Report to the government of Nigeria on programming for the development of manpower and labour statistics. (ILO/TAP/Nigeria/R.10) Geneva, 1967. pp. 87. 30cm.

LABOUR SUPPLY - Nigeria (Cont'd.)

INTERNATIONAL SEMINAR ON MANPOWER PROBLEMS IN ECONOMIC DEVELOPMENT, LAGOS, 1964. Manpower problems and economic development in Nigeria; report...edited by T.M. Yesufu. Ibadan, 1969. pp. 328.

NIGERIA. National Manpower Board. Manpower Studies. No. 9. Health manpower survey, 1965: hospitals and clinics, dispensaries and maternity centres, health centres, health offices and specialist units. Lagos, 1969. pp. 84. Map in end pocket.

NIGERIA. National Manpower Board. Manpower Studies. No. 10. A survey of labour requirements, 1965: sectoral study. Lagos, [1969?]. pp. 112.

YESUFU (TIJANI M.) Management in Nigerian industries; (a pilot survey). Lagos, 1968 [or rather 1969]. pp. 45. (Nigeria. National Manpower Board. Manpower Studies. No. 8)

- Norway

NORWAY. Statistiske Centralbyrå. Arbeidsmarkedstatistikk: Labour market statistics. Oslo, annual, 1967 [1st issue] to date.

NORWAY. Statistiske Centralbyrå. Norges Offisielle Statistikk. Rekke A. 236. Arbeidsmarkedstatistikk, 1967: Labour market statistics, 1967. Oslo, 1968. pp. 52. 29cm. In Norwegian and English.

- Pakistan

SEMINAR ON POPULATION PROBLEMS IN THE ECONOMIC DEVELOPMENT OF PAKISTAN, KARACHI, 1967. Background papers; [read at the Seminar held on 2-3 June, 1967]; [by] Farhat Yusuf [and others]. Karachi, 1967. pp. various.

PAKISTAN. Labour and Social Welfare Division. Research and Statistics Branch. Quarterly review of employment market trends in employment exchange areas. q., Ap/Je 1970-   [Karachi]

- Pakistan, East

EAST PAKISTAN. Planning Department. 1969. Manpower planning in East Pakistan: medium term projections, problems and policies: (first report of the Skilled Manpower Project). Dacca, 1969. pp. 174.

- Panama

PANAMA. Direccion de Estadistica y Censos. Estadistica panameña. Serie O. Estadisticas del trabajo. a., 1968 (año 29)-   Panama.

- Peru

ROMERO (FERNANDO) Trabajo, educación y bienestar: política del empleo para el desarrollo económico. Lima, Universidad Nacional Mayor de San Marcos, Departamento de Publicaciones, 1965. pp. 585. 24½cm. (Biblioteca de Estudios Superiores.)

PLAN piloto de recursos humanos, Peru 1967. [Lima?], 1967. 1 vol. various pagings.

PERU. Junta Nacional de Mano de Obra. 1969. Informe sobre la situación ocupacional del Perú. Lima, [1969]. fo. 47,(14).

- Poland

UNITED STATES. Census Bureau. International Population Statistics Reports. Series P-90. No. 20. The labor force of Poland. Washington, 1964. pp. ii, 46.

MAHL (JERZY) Problemy zatrudnienia i rynku pracy w Województwie Wrocławskim w latach 1956-1960. Wrocław, Zakład Narodowy im. Ossolińskich, 1965. pp. 199. bibliog. 24cm. (Monografie Śląskie. 10) With English summary.

SAJKIEWICZ (ALICJA) Planowanie pracochłonności, zatrudnienia i funduszu płac. Warszawa, PWE, 1967. pp. 174. bibliog. 20cm. (Biblioteka Służby Ekonomicznej Przemysłu. 4)

SARAPATA (ADAM) Płynność i stabilność kadr. Warszawa, CRZZ, 1967. pp. 231. 19½cm.

- Portugal

CORREIA (HERMÍNIA GALVÃO) Estimativas da evolução da população e do emprego nos distritos do continente português, 1950-1965. Lisboa, 1966. pp. 78. 30½cm. (Fundo de Desenvolvimento da Mão-de-Obra. Boletim bimestral. Suplementos. N.° 8.) With abstracts in English and French.

FUNDO DE DESENVOLVIMENTO DA MÃO-DE-OBRA. Boletim bimestral. Suplementos. N.° 5. Recolha de elementos sobre mão-de-obra, 1965: níveis de emprego, estrutura profissional, [etc.]. Lisboa, 1966. pp. 174. 30½cm.

FUNDO DE DESENVOLVIMENTO DA MÃO-DE-OBRA. Boletim bimestral. Suplementos. N.° 11. Estrutura da população por divisões regionais do S[erviço] N[acional de] E[mprego], em 1960: 1 vol: Beja [and] Faro. Lisboa, 1967. pp. 143. With abstracts in English and French.

FUNDO DE DESENVOLVIMENTO DA MÃO-DE-OBRA. Boletim bimestral. Suplementos. N.°12. Recolha de elementos sobre mão-de-obra, 1965: emprego, remunerações, [etc.] Lisboa, 1967. pp. 79. 30cm.

FUNDO DE DESENVOLVIMENTO DA MÃO-DE-OBRA. Boletim bimestral. Suplementos. N.° 13. Actividades e profissões salientes por divisões regionais do S[erviço] N acional de] E[mprego], em 1960. Lisboa, 1967. pp. 29. 30cm. With abstracts in English and French.

FUNDO DE DESENVOLVIMENTO DA MÃO-DE-OBRA. Estatísticas internas. Lisboa, every 2 months, nov./dez. 1968 (núm.1) to date. 30cm.

FUNDO DE DESENVOLVIMENTO DA MÃO-DE-OBRA. Relatória e contas da gerência. a., 1968-   Lisboa.

FUNDO DE DESENVOLVIMENTO DA MÃO-DE-OBRA. Boletim bimestral. Suplementos. N.° 16. Estrutura da população por divisões regionais do S[erviço] N[acional de] E[mprego], em 1960: 2 vol: Évora [and] Lisboa. Lisboa, 1968. pp. 137. 30cm. With abstracts in English and French.

FUNDO DE DESENVOLVIMENTO DA MÃO-DE-OBRA. Boletim bimestral. Suplementos. N.° 20. Inquerito: necessidades de mão-de-obra, 1967: variação semestral do emprego; dificuldades de recrutamento de pessoal; necessidades de formação profissional; [edited by] Salome de Sousa [and] Vitor Viegas. Lisboa, 1968. pp. 69. With abstracts in English and French.

FUNDO DE DESENVOLVIMENTO DA MÃO-DE-OBRA. Boletim bimestral. Suplementos. N.° 21. Inquerito: emprego, 1968; variação semestral do emprego (1.° semestre 1968); [edited by] Jesuvina de Sousa Vaz [and] Vitor Viegas. Lisboa, 1968. pp. 19. With abstracts in English and French.

FUNDO DE DESENVOLVIMENTO DA MÃO-DE-OBRA. Boletim bimestral. Suplementos. N.°25. Inquérito: emprego/2.° semestre 1968: variação do emprego; [edited by] Jesuvina de Sousa Vaz [and] Vitor Viegas. Lisboa, 1969. pp. 21. 30cm. With abstracts in English and French.

MURTEIRA (MARIO) and others. Recursos humanos em Portugal (síntese de informação estatística). Lisboa, 1969. pp. 107. (Fundo de Desenvolvimento da Mão-de-Obra. Cadernos. 31.) With summaries in English, French and German.

VAZ (JESUVINA DE SOUSA) and VIEGAS (VITOR) Variação anual do emprego em Portugal metropolitano (1968). Lisboa, 1969. pp. 33. (Fundo de Desenvolvimento da Mão-de-Obra. Cadernos. 30) With abstracts in English, French and German.

FUNDO DE DESENVOLVIMENTO DA MÃO-DE-OBRA. Orçamento da receita e despesa. a., 1970 [1st issue]- Lisboa.

FUNDO DE DESENVOLVIMENTO DA MÃO-DE-OBRA. Divisão de Estatistica. Algumas estatisticas do trabalho em Portugal. q., Mr 1970 (no. 1)- Lisboa.

FUNDO DE DESENVOLVIMENTO DA MÃO-DE-OBRA. Serviço Nacional de Emprego. Analise do mercado de emprego. m., Ja 1970 (no.1)- Lisboa.

- Portugal - Colonies

COUTINHO (MARTINHO DE FRANÇA DA GAMA PEREIRA) O trabalho indígena nas colónias portuguesas. Lisboa, Instituto Superior de Ciências Económicas e Financeiras, 1936. pp. 47. bibliog. 25cm. (Reprinted from Anais, vol.4)

- Puerto Rico

FULL EMPLOYMENT AND UNDEREMPLOYMENT IN PUERTO RICO; [published by] Bureau of Labor Statistics, Labor Force Statistics Division, [Puerto Rico]. [in Spanish and English] [Hato Rey], Oct. 1952/Oct. 1967 annual, 1966/7 to date. 22 x 36cm.

EMPLOYMENT, HOURS AND EARNINGS IN THE MANUFACTURING INDUSTRIES IN PUERTO RICO: special report with averages for calendar years and fiscal years. [pd. by] Bureau of Labor Statistics [Puerto Rico]. [in English and Spanish] a., 1968/1969- n.p. 1957/1964 and 1960/1967 catalogued separately and filed at R(O.S.) Y 1518e and Y 1693 respectively.

PUERTO RICO. 1965. Employment, hours and earnings in the manufacturing industries in Puerto Rico: special report with averages for calendar years 1957 to 1964 and fiscal years 1957-58 to 1963-64. (Bureau of Labor Statistics) [Hato Rey], 1965. fo. 37, vii. 22cm. x 28cm. In English and Spanish.

EMPLOYMENT AND UNEMPLOYMENT IN PUERTO RICO. [annual/fiscal year] [pd. by] Bureau of Labor Statistics, Labor Force Statistics Division [Puerto Rico]. [In English and Spanish] a., 1967-8/1968-9 to date. n.p. Each issue covers 2 fiscal yrs. 1966-7/1967-8 catalogued separately and filed at R(O.S.) Y 1692.

PUERTO RICO. 1966. Full employment and underemployment in Puerto Rico, January 1965 to April 1966. (Special Reports on the Labor Force. No. 43) [Hato Rey, 1966]. fo. 16. 22cm. x 36cm. In English and Spanish.

EMPLOYMENT AND UNEMPLOYMENT IN PUERTO RICO [annual/calendar year]; [pd. by] Bureau of Labor Statistics, Labor Force Statistics Division [Puerto Rico]. [in English and Spanish] a., 1968/1969- n.p. Each issue covers 2 calendar yrs. 1967/1968 catalogued separately and filed at R(O.S.) Y 1694.

PUERTO RICO. Bureau of Economic and Social Analysis. 1967. Manpower report to the Governor: a report on a society in transition: an assessment of manpower requirements, utilization, and training needs to 1975. [San Juan?, 1967?]. pp. 130.

PUERTO RICO. Bureau of Labor Statistics. Labor Force Statistics Division. Special Reports on the Labor Force. No. 49. Estadísticas sobre empleo y desempleo en Puerto Rico 1960-67: cifras revisadas de 1960 a 1966; employment and unemployment statistics for Puerto Rico 1960-67: revised figures from 1960 to 1966. [San Juan], 1967. fo.(i), 42. 21½cm. x 35½cm. In English and Spanish.

EMPLOYMENT, HOURS AND EARNINGS IN THE MANUFACTURING ESTABLISHMENTS PROMOTED BY THE ECONOMIC DEVELOPMENT ADMINISTRATION OR THE PUERTO RICO INDUSTRIAL DEVELOPMENT COMPANY: special report with averages for calendar years and fiscal years; [pd. by] Bureau of Labor Statistics, [Puerto Rico]. [in English and Spanish] a., 1968/1969- n.p.

EMPLOYMENT, HOURS AND EARNINGS IN THE MANUFACTURING ESTABLISHMENTS PROMOTED BY THE ECONOMIC DEVELOPMENT ADMINISTRATION OR THE PUERTO RICO INDUSTRIAL DEVELOPMENT COMPANY; [published by] Bureau of Labor statistics, Puerto Rico. [in Spanish and English] Hato Rey, annual, 1969 to date.

DURAND (JOHN DANA) and HOLDEN (KAREN C.) Methods for analysing components of change in size and structure of the labor force with application to Puerto Rico, 1950-60. Philadelphia, 1969. pp. 100. (Pennsylvania. University. Population Studies Center. Analytical and Technical Reports. No. 8)

PUERTO RICO. Bureau of Labor Statistics. Labor Force Statistics Division. Special Reports on the Labour Force. No. 54. Regularidad de trabajo en Puerto Rico: años naturales 1960 a 1967: cifras revisadas de 1960 a 1966; work experience in Puerto Rico: calendar years 1960 to 1967: revised figures from 1960 to 1966. [San Juan], 1969. fo. (i), 18. 21½cm x 35½cm. In English and Spanish.

LABOUR SUPPLY - Puerto Rico (Cont'd.)

PUERTO RICO. Bureau of Labor Statistics. Labor Force Statistics Division. Special Reports [on the Labor Force]. No. 56. Empleo y desempleo ajustados estacionalmente enero de 1963 a diciembre de 1968; seasonall adjusted employment and unemployment: January 1963 to December 1968. [San Juan, 1969]. fo.(iii), 15. 21½cm. x 35½cm. In English and Spanish.

- Roumania

ROUMANIA. Direcţia Centrală de Statistica. 1966. Forţa de Muncă în Republica Socialistă România: culegere de date statistice. Bucureşti, 1966. pp. 448. 25½см. With separate booklet of English captions.

GRIGORESCU (CONSTANTIN) and others. Utilizarea forţei de muncă: factori, caracteristici, tendinţe în România. Bucureşti 1968. pp. 248. (Academia Republicii Socialiste România. Institutul de Cercetări Economice. Bibliotheca Oeconomica. 6) With English, French and Russian tables of contents.

- Russia

BLIAKHMAN (L. S.) and others. Движение рабочей силы на промышленных предприятиях. Москва, Экономика, 1965. pp. 151. bibliog. 20cm.

KOSTAKOV (VLADIMIR GEORGIEVICH) and LITVIAKOV (PAVEL PETROVICH) Баланс труда: содержание и методика разработки. Москва, Экономика, 1965. pp. 312. 20см.

RUSANOV (EFIM STEPANOVICH) Занятость населения и использование трудовых ресурсов. Москва, Экономика, 1965. pp. 148. 20cm.

VOPROSY vosproizvodstva rabochei sily v promyshlennosti SSR na sovremennom etape: sbornik statei. Saratov, 1965. pp. 291.

PISAREV (I.IU.) Naselenie i trud v SSSR. Moskva, 1966. pp. 151.

NARODONASELENIE... Народонаселение и экономика. Москва, 1967. pp. 187.

RUZAVINA (EKATERINA IVANOVNA) Территориальные балансы трудовых ресурсов. Москва, 1967. pp. 169.

URZHINSKII (KONSTANTIN PAVLOVICH) Трудоустройство граждан в СССР. Москва, Юридическая Литература, 1967. pp. 144. 20см.

NASELENIE i trudovye resursy Severo-Vostoka SSSR. Moskva, 1968. pp. 142.

STANLEY (EMILO J.) Regional distribution of Soviet industrial manpower, 1940-60. New York, Praeger. 1968. pp. xxv, 208. bibliog. 23½cm. (Praeger Special Studies in International Economics and Development)

DOROSHIN (IGOR' IVANOVICH) Opredelenie narodnokhoziaistvennoi trudoemkosti produktsii na osnove mezhotraslevogo balansa. Moskva, 1969. pp. 55.

LITVIAKOV (PAVEL PETROVICH) ed. Демографические проблемы занятости. Москва, Экономика, 1969. pp. 215. 19½см.

PROFESSIONAL'NAIA... Профессиональная адаптация молодежи. Москва, 1969. pp. 126.

SCIENTIFIC COORDINATING CONFERENCE ON QUESTIONS OF THE ECONOMICS OF EDUCATION, MOSCOW, 1964. The economics of education in the U.S.S.R.; edited and translated by Harold J. Noah. New York, Praeger, 1969. pp. xxii, 227. 23½cm. (Praeger Special Studies in International Economics and Development)

PROBLEMY migratsii naseleniia i trudovykh resursov. Moskva, 1970. pp. 224.

NASELENIE, trudovye resursy SSSR: problemy razmeshcheniia i puti ikh resheniia. Moskva, 1971. pp. 300.

RUSANOV (EFIM STEPANOVICH) Raspredelenie i ispol'zovanie trudovykh resursov SSSR. Moskva, 1971. pp. 215.

- Russia - Mathematical models

BEZRUKOV (VLADIMIR BORISOVICH) Primenenie ekonomiko-matematicheskikh metodov v raschetakh balansa trudovykh resursov. Moskva, 1971. pp. 149.

- Russia - Siberia

PRUDENSKII (GERMAN ALEKSANDROVICH) ed. Вопросы трудовых ресурсов в районах Сибири. Новосибирск, 1961. pp. 171.

PEREVEDENTSEV (VIKTOR IVANOVICH) Миграция населения и трудовые проблемы Сибири. Новосибирск, 1966. pp. 191.

VOPROSY trudovykh resursov i urovnia zhizni naseleniia vostochnykh raionov: materialy k nauchnoi konferentsii po probleme "Regional'nye osobennosti organizatsii promyshlennogo proizvodstva i razvitiia ekonomicheskikh raionov". vyp.7. Novosibirsk, 1966. pp. 112.

- Samoa

INTERNATIONAL LABOUR OFFICE. Development Programme: Technical Assistance Sector. [Western Samoa]. R. 1. Report to the government of Western Samoa on the assessment of manpower situation. (ILO/TAP/Western Samoa/R. 1) Geneva, 1969. pp. 52.

- Siam

BOWEN (IAN) Seven lectures on manpower planning, with special reference to Thailand. Nedlands, University of Western Australia, Centre for Asian Studies, 1967. pp. (95). 26½cm. (Working Paper in Asian Studies. No.2)

SIAM. Department of Labour. 1967. Labour statistics and employment market information, January, 1967: Bangkok-Thonburi. [Bangkok], 1967. pp. 110. 30½cm. In English and Thai.

SIAM. Department of Labour. 1967. Labour
statistics and employment market information,
April 1967: Changwat Mahasarakham. [Bangkok],
1967. pp. 34. 29½cm. In English and Thai.

SIAM. National Statistical Office. 1967.
Report of the labor force survey: Bangkok-
Thon Buri municipal areas, 1965-1966.
[Bangkok, 1967]. pp. 152. 29½cm. In
English and Thai.

INTERNATIONAL LABOUR OFFICE. Development Programme: Technical Assistance Sector. [Thailand].
R.29. Report to the government of Thailand on
manpower assessment and planning. (ILO/TAP/
Thailand/R.29) Geneva, 1968. pp. 43.

SIAM. Department of Labour. 1968. Labour statistics
and employment market information, January, 1968:
Bangkok-Thonburi, Samutprakan, Nonthaburi, Pathum
Thani. [Bangkok], 1968. pp. 66. 29½cm. In English
and Thai.

SIAM. National Statistical Office. 1968.
Final report of the labor force survey:
Bangkok-Thon Buri municipal areas, 1966-
1967. [Bangkok, 1968]. pp. 123. 29½cm.
In English and Thai.

SIAM. National Statistical Office. 1968.
Final report of the labor force survey:
rural areas, 1966-1967. [Bangkok, 1968].
pp. 133. 29½cm. In English and Thai.

SIAM. National Statistical Office. 1968.
Preliminary report of the labor force
survey: Bangkok-Thon Buri municipal areas,
1966-1967. [Bangkok, 1968]. pp. 38. 29½cm.
In English and Thai.

SIAM. National Statistical Office. 1969.
Final report of the labor force survey: all
municipal areas, August-October 1967.
[Bangkok, 1969]. pp. 89. In English and
Thai.

SIAM. National Statistical Office. 1969.
Final report of the labor force survey:
all municipal areas, February - April
1968. [Bangkok, 1969]. pp. 89. In
English and Thai.

SIAM. National Statistical Office. 1969.
Preliminary report of the labor force
survey: all municipal areas, February -
April, 1968. [Bangkok, 1969]. pp. 35.
29cm. In English and Thai.

- Singapore

BLAKE (D.J.) Employment and unemployment in
Singapore. Singapore, University of Singapore,
Economic Research Centre, [1967?]. pp. 166-
191. 21cm. (Reprint Monograph Series. No. 8)
(Reprinted from Crucial issues in industrial
relations in Singapore by W.E. Chalmers)

- Somaliland

NIGAM (SHYAM BEHARI LAL) The manpower situation
in Somalia: report submitted to the government
of Somalia. Mogadiscio, Department of Labour,
1965. pp. v, 322.

INTERNATIONAL LABOUR OFFICE. Development Programme:
Technical Assistance Sector. [Somalia]. R.5.
Report to the government of the Republic of
Somalia on manpower assessment and planning.
(ILO/TAP/Somalia/R.5) Geneva, 1970. pp. 192.

- South Africa

DARLINGTON. Labour Representation
Committee. Leaflets. No.1. White
labour or yellow slaves?: the facts
concerning a gigantic conspiracy.
[Darlington, 1904?]. pp. 7.

SOUTH AFRICA. Embassy (Paris). 1955.
La main-d'oeuvre bantoue dans l'industrie:
un nouvel aspect. [Paris, 1955]. pp. 15.
21cm. (Connaissance de l'Afrique du Sud)

OWEN (KEN) Foreign Africans: summary of the
report of the Froneman committee.
Johannesburg, South African Institute of
Race Relations, 1964. pp. 65. 25½cm.

SOUTH AFRICA. National Bureau of Educational and
Social Research. Research Series. No.67. An
estimate of the demand for and supply of White
manpower in 1971 according to occupational
groups for the Republic of South Africa; by
S.S. Terblanche. [Pretoria], 1968. pp. 18.

HORRELL (MURIEL) South Africa's workers, their
organizations and the patterns of employment.
Johannesburg, 1969. pp. 153.

KOOY (G.A.) and others. Apartheid en arbeids-
bestel in Zuid-Afrika. Bussum, 1969. pp. 270.

- South Africa - Bibliography

SOUTH AFRICA. Department of Education. Library.
1967. Manpower: selected bibliography.
Pretoria, 1967. fo. 56.

- Soviet Far East

VOPROSY trudovykh resursov i urovnia
zhizni naseleniia vostochnykh raionov: materialy k nauchnoi konferentsii po probleme "Regional'nye osobennosti organizatsii promyshlennogo proizvodstva i razvitiia ekonomicheskikh raionov". vyp.7. Novosibirsk,
1966. pp. 112.

NASELENIE i trudovye resursy Severo-Vostoka SSSR. Moskva, 1968.
pp. 142.

VOSPROIZVODSTVO... Воспроизводство
трудовых ресурсов Дальнего Востока.
Москва, 1969. pp. 125.

- Soviet North

NASELENIE i trudovye resursy Severo-Vostoka SSSR. Moskva, 1968.
pp. 142.

- Spain

SPAIN. Ministerio de Educación y Ciencia.
Dirección General de Promoción y Cooperación
Científica. 1966. Las necesidades de graduados
en España en el período 1964-1971: enseñanzas
media y superior. Madrid, 1966. pp. 279. 25cm.

- Sweden

SWEDEN. Arbetsmarknadsstyrelsen. 1961. Labour
market policy and the community. Stockholm,
1961. pp. 36. 30cm. Translation of published text in Arbetsmarknadsinformation L:
1, 1960.

LABOUR SUPPLY - Sweden (Cont'd.)

LANDSORGANISATIONEN I SVERIGE. Labour market policy: a Swedish trade union programme, 1967. [Stockholm, 1967]. pp. 53. 21cm.

SWEDEN. [Arbetsmarknadsstyrelsen]. Labour market policy: AMS' budget proposal for the fiscal year. a., 1969/70- [Stockholm]

FRANCE. Direction de la Documentation. La Documentation Française. Notes et Etudes Documentaires. No. 3,596. Stratégie économique et politique de l'emploi dans une économie de croissance: le système suédois; [by] Raoul Danaho. Paris, 1969. pp. 71. 27cm.

- Tajikistan

TSAI (M. A.) Trudovye resursy Tadzhikistana v period razvernutogo stroitel'stva kommunizma. Dushanbe, 1964. pp. 76.

- Tanzania

SKOROV (GEORGE) Integration of educational and economic planning in Tanzania. Paris, Unesco, 1966. pp. 78. bibliog. (International Institute for Educational Planning African Research Monographs. 6)

- Tonga

INTERNATIONAL LABOUR OFFICE. Development Programme: Technical Assistance Sector. [Tonga] R.1. Report to the government of the Kingdom of Tonga on manpower assessment and planning. (ILO/TAP/Tonga/R.1.) Geneva, 1969. pp. 48.

- Turkey

ROBINSON (RICHARD DUNLOP) High-level manpower in economic development in the Turkish case. Cambridge, Harvard U.P., 1967. pp. xiii, 134. bibliog. 21cm. (Harvard University. Center for Middle Eastern Studies. Harvard Middle Eastern Monographs. 17)

- Uganda

BARYARUHA (AZARIAS) Factors affecting industrial employment: a study of Ugandan experience, 1954 to 1964. Nairobi, O.U.P., 1967. pp. vi, 83. 21cm. (Makerere Institute of Social Research. Occasional Papers. No. 1)

- United Kingdom

BRITISH ASSOCIATION FOR COMMERCIAL AND INDUSTRIAL EDUCATION. Economic growth and manpower. in its Spring Conference. Papers presented, etc., 1963.

U.K. 1967. Ministry of Labour. Efficient use of manpower: report of a study group composed of directors and senior managers of well-known firms in the Midlands: [A.J. Nicol, chairman]. London, 1967. pp. iv, 20. 24½cm.

STANIC (VLADIMIR) and PYM (DENIS) Brains down the drain: the misuse of highly-qualified manpower. London, Anbar Publications, [1968]. pp. 39. bibliog. 21cm. (Anbar Monographs. No. 12)

HUNTER (LAURENCE C.) and ROBERTSON (DONALD JAMES) Economics of wages and labour. London, Macmillan, 1969. pp. 544. bibliogs. 21½cm.

An INVESTIGATION into the demand for manpower and its supply in the engineering industries: a pilot study; by Keith Cowling [and others]. Coventry, 1969. pp. various. (University of Warwick. Centre for Industrial and Business Studies. Warwick Research in Industrial and Business Studies. No. 1)

McPHERSON (KLIM) and GAITSKELL (JULIA) Immigrants and employment: two case studies in East London and in Croydon. London, [1969]. pp. 96. (Institute of Race Relations. Special Series)

CHAPMAN (J.S.) London employment survey: methodology. [London], 1970. pp. 158. (London. Greater London Council. Department of Planning and Transportation. Research Memoranda. 246.)

CREYKE (TIMOTHY) and others. Labour availability estimates for London boroughs in 1981: a second estimate. [London], 1970. fo. 6,(5); pp. 5. (London. Greater London Council. Department of Planning and Transportation. Research Memoranda. 221.)

HUNTER (LAURENCE C.) and others. Labour problems of technological change. London, 1970. pp. 363. (Glasgow. University. Department of Economic and Social Research. Social and Economic Studies. New Series. No. 18)

LOMAS (GRAHAM M.) and WOOD (PETER A.) Employment location in regional economic planning: a case study of the west Midlands. London, 1970. pp. 158.

ORGANISATION FOR ECONOMIC CO-OPERATION AND DEVELOPMENT. Manpower and Social Affairs Committee. 1970. Manpower policy in the United Kingdom. Paris, 1970. pp. 230. (Reviews of Manpower and Social Policies. 7)

GREEN (REUBEN) The evolution of manpower policy in Great Britain from the fifteenth century to the mid-nineteen sixties; [Ph.D. (London) thesis]. 1971. fo. 341. bibliog. Typescript: unpublished. This thesis is the property of London University and may not be removed from the Library.

LABOUR markets under different employment conditions; [by] D.I. Mackay [and others]. London, 1971. pp. 433. (Glasgow University. Department of Economic and Social Research. Social and Economic Studies. New Series. No. 22)

QUALIFIED manpower and economic performance: an inter-plant study in the electrical engineering industry; ([by] P.R.G. Layard [and others]). London, 1971. pp. 267. bibliog. (London. University. London School of Economics and Political Science. Higher Education Research Unit. L.S.E. Studies on Education)

SOUTH EAST JOINT PLANNING TEAM. Strategic plan for the South East. Studies. Vol.1. Population and employment. London, H.M.S.O., 1971. pp. 265.

U.K. Census, 1966. Sample census, 1966: Great Britain: qualified manpower tables. London, 1971. pp. 175.

U.K. Census, 1966. Sample census, 1966: Great Britain: scientific and technological qualifications. London, 1971. pp. 55.

U.K. Central Statistical Office. 1971. Qualified manpower in Great Britain: the 1966 census of population. London, 1971. pp. 52. (Studies in Official Statistics. No. 18)

U.K. Department of Trade and Industry. 1971. Persons with qualifications in engineering, technology and science, 1959 to 1968. London, 1971. pp. 134. (Studies in Technological Manpower. No. 3.)

WORKING GROUP ON SCIENTIFIC AND TECHNOLOGICAL MANPOWER [U.K.] Qualified manpower in the electronics industry: a preliminary report: [G.D. Sims, chairman]. London, National Economic Development Office, 1971. pp. 44. bibliog.

- United Kingdom - Ireland, Northern

IRELAND, NORTHERN. 1967. Manpower: an appraisal of the position, 1964-1970. (Northern Ireland Economic Council) Belfast, 1967. pp. 44. 24cm.

- United States

WOYTINSKY (WLADIMIR SAVELEVICH) The labor supply of the United States: occupational statistics of the 1930 census tabulated by class of work and industry, as well as by sex, race, and age groups. Washington, Committee on Social Security, 1936. fo. 129. 32½cm.

UNITED STATES. 1962. Employment in New England, 1947-1961: manufacturing, non-manufacturing, total employment. (Bureau of Labor Statistics, New England Regional Office) Boston, 1962. fo. (16). 27cm.

UNITED STATES. Labor Statistics Bureau. Employment in relation to U.S. imports, 1960. [Washington, 1962]. pp.14.

NATIONAL INDUSTRIAL CONFERENCE BOARD. Jobs profits economic growth: prepared for the 47th annual meeting...1963. New York, [1963]. pp. 36.

ORGANISATION FOR ECONOMIC CO-OPERATION AND DEVELOPMENT. Directorate for Scientific Affairs. 1963. Higher education and the demand for scientific manpower in the United States. Paris, 1963. pp. 101. (Reviews of National Policies for Science and Education).

HILDEBRAND (GEORGE H.) The 1966 manpower report of the president and the secretary of labor. [Ithaca, 1966]. pp. 10. (Cornell University. New York State School of Industrial and Labor Relations. Reprint Series. No. 220)

NATIONAL EDUCATION ASSOCIATION OF THE UNITED STATES. Research Division. Research Reports. R. 16. Teacher supply and demand in public schools, 1966. Washington, [1966]. pp. 80. 28cm.

UNITED STATES. Senate. Labor and Public Welfare Committee. History of employment and manpower policy in the United States. Washington, 1966. 2 vols.

LEVITAN (SAR A.) and MANGUM (GARTH LEROY) Making sense of federal manpower policy. Ann Arbor, 1967. pp. 42. (Michigan University and Wayne State University. Institute of Labor and Industrial Relations. Policy Papers in Human Resources and Industrial Relations. No. 2)

MANGUM (GARTH LEROY) Contributions and costs of manpower development and training. Ann Arbor, Michigan University, Institute of Labor and Industrial Relations, 1967. pp. (vi), 85. 21 cm. (Policy Papers in Human Resources and Industrial Relations. No. 5)

SIEGEL (IRVING H.) ed. Manpower tomorrow: prospects and priorities; report on a conference commemorating two decades of service of the W.E.Upjohn Institute for Employment Research. New York, Kelley, 1967. pp. viii, 219. 22½cm.

BARKER (ROBERT L.) and BRIGGS (THOMAS L.) Differential use of social work manpower: an analysis and demonstration-study. New York, National Association of Social Workers, 1968. pp. 270. 22½cm.

DELEHANTY (GEORGE E.) Nonproduction workers in U.S. manufacturing. Amsterdam, North-Holland Publishing Company, 1968. pp. xii, 256. bibliog. 22½cm. (Contributions to Economic Analysis. 54)

EASTERLIN (RICHARD AINLEY) Population, labor force, and long swings in economic growth: the American experience. New York, National Bureau of Economic Research, 1968. pp. xx, 298. bibliog. 22½cm. [Publications]. No. 86)

GINZBERG (ELI) Manpower agenda for America. New York, McGraw-Hill, [1968]. pp. xi, 250. bibliog. 22½cm.

GINZBERG (ELI) and others. Manpower strategy for the metropolis. New York, Columbia U.P., 1968. pp. xiii, 321. bibliog. 21½cm.

JAFFE (ABRAM J.) and FROOMKIN (JOSEPH N.) Technology and jobs: automation in perspective. New York, Praeger, 1968. pp. xvii, 284. 23½cm.

TRENT (JAMES W.) and MEDSKER (LELAND L.) Beyond high school: a psychosociological study of 10,000 high school graduates. San Francisco, Jossey-Bass, 1968. pp. xxiv, 333. bibliog. 22½cm. (Series in Higher Education)

UNITED STATES. Department of Labor. Employment policies of the United States and Japan: report of the joint United States-Japan Employment Study. Washington, 1968. pp. 126.

ZELLER (FREDERICK ANTHONY) and MILLER (ROBERT WILEY) eds. Manpower development in Appalachia: an approach to unemployment. New York, Praeger, 1968. pp. xxxv, 270. 23½cm. (Praeger Special Studies in U.S. Economic and Social Development)

BOLINO (AUGUST C.) Manpower and the city. Cambridge, Mass., [1969]. pp. 282. bibliog.

BOWEN (WILLIAM GORDON) and FINEGAN (T. ALDRICH) The economics of labor force participation. Princeton, 1969. pp. 897.

FREEDMAN (MARCIA) The process of work establishment;...assisted by Gretchen Maclachlan. New York, Columbia U.P., 1969. pp. xvii, 135. 22cm.

LECHT (LEONARD ABE) Manpower needs for national goals in the 1970's. New York, Praeger, 1969. pp. xxxi, 183. 21cm.

PUBLIC-PRIVATE manpower policies; edited by Arnold R. Weber [and others]. [Madison, Wisconsin, 1969]. pp. 210.

LABOUR SUPPLY - United States (Cont'd.)

SCOVILLE (JAMES G.) The job content of the U.S. economy, 1940-1970. New York, McGraw-Hill, [1969]. pp. xiv, 144. bibliog. 23½cm. (Wertheim Committee Publications)

BORUS (MICHAEL E.) and TASH (WILLIAM R.) Measuring the impact of manpower programs: a primer. Ann Arbor, 1970. pp. 81. bibliog. (Michigan University and Wayne State University. Institute of Labor and Industrial Relations. Policy Papers in Human Resources and Industrial Relations. No. 17)

DEVINE (EUGENE J.) Analysis of manpower shortages in local government: case studies of nurses, policemen, and teachers. New York, 1970. pp. 171. bibliog.

FOLK (HUGH) The shortage of scientists and engineers. Lexington, Mass., [1970]. pp. 364.

LEVITAN (SAR A.) and others. Economic opportunity in the ghetto: the partnership of government and business. Baltimore, [1970]. pp. 84.

REES (ALBERT) and SHULTZ (GEORGE PRATT) Workers and wages in an urban labor market. Chicago, 1970. pp. 236. (Chicago. University. School of Business. Studies in Business and Society)

RUTTENBERG (STANLEY H.) and GUTCHESS (JOCELYN) The federal-state employment service: a critique. Baltimore, 1970. pp. 105.

RUTTENBERG (STANLEY H.) and GUTCHESS (JOCELYN) Manpower challenge of the 1970s: institutions and social change. Baltimore, [1970]. pp. 126.

SOCIAL economics for the 1970's: (programs for social security, health and manpower); [based on a series of symposia held in 1969 under the auspices of the Institute for Social Economics and Policy Research at Temple University, Philadelphia]; edited by George F. Rohrlich. New York, [1970]. pp. 189.

STANBACK (THOMAS M.) and KNIGHT (RICHARD V.) The metropolitan economy: the process of employment expansion. New York, 1970. pp. 279.

PATTEN (THOMAS H.) Manpower planning and the development of human resources. New York, [1971]. pp. 737. bibliog.

READINGS in labor market analysis; edited by John F. Burton [and others]. New York, [1971]. pp. 523. bibliogs.

- United States - Bibliography

KEAVENY (TIMOTHY J.) and HERMAN (GEORGIANNA) Compilers. Manpower planning: a research bibliography. Minneapolis, Minnesota University, Industrial Relations Center, 1966. pp. iii, 37. 23cm. (Bulletin 45)

- United States - Alabama

MORLEY (BURTON R.) Characteristics of the labor market in Alabama related to the administration of unemployment compensation. University, Alabama, University, Bureau of Business Research, 1937. pp. (iv),82,(33). 23½cm. (Printed Series. No.1)

- United States - Kentucky

FULMER (JOHN L.) and PITTS (JAMES E.) Kentucky employment trends from 1951 to 1963 with projections to 1965-75. Lexington, Bureau of Business Research, University of Kentucky, 1965. pp. v, 79. 28cm.

- United States - New York

NEW YORK (STATE). Division of Employment. Research and Statistics Office. 1969- . A handbook of statistical data. [Albany], 1969 in progress.

- United States - Washington (State)

WASHINGTON (STATE). 1964. Distribution of 1985 population and employment to analysis zones for land use Plan B; by Rajanikant N. Joshi. (Puget Sound Regional Transportation Study Staff Reports. No. 17) Seattle, 1964. fo. vii, 55, (16).

WASHINGTON (STATE). 1964. Forecasting the distribution of 1985 population and employment to analysis zones for Plan A; by Charles H. Graves. (Puget Sound Regional Transportation Study Staff Reports. No. 15) preliminary ed. Seattle, 1964. fo. ix, 80, (24). 28cm.

- Uzbekistan

TRUDOVYE resursy Uzbekistana: problemy raspredeleniia i ispol'zovaniia. Tashkent, 1970. pp. 220.

- Yugoslavia

UNITED STATES. Census Bureau. International Population Statistics Reports. Series P-90. No. 22. The labor force of Yugoslavia. Washington, 1965. pp. 41.

- Zambia

ZAMBIA. 1966. Manpower report: a report and statistical handbook on manpower, education, training and Zambianisation, 1965-6; (issued by the Cabinet Office). Lusaka, 1966. pp. vi, 194. bibliog. 25½cm.

ZAMBIA. Development Division. 1969. Zambian manpower. Lusaka, 1969. pp. 122.

JOLLY (RICHARD) Skilled manpower as a constraint to development in Zambia. [Brighton], 1970. pp. 47. (Brighton. University of Sussex. Institute of Development Studies. Communications. No. 48)

LABOUR TURNOVER

NANZ (CLAUS E.) Personalfluktuation: das Problem und betriebliche Massnahmen seiner Minderung. [Mannheim], 1965. pp.vi, 262. bibliog. 21cm.

- Germany

WILHELM (WOLFRAM) Fluktuation und Absentismus: eine Untersuchung der Bedingungen und Motivationen zu ihrem Auftreten in einem Industriebetrieb. [Mannheim], 1964. pp. 292. bibliog.

LUX (EUGEN) Ausmass und Ursachen der Fluktuation der Arbeitnehmer in der Industrie der Bundesrepublik Deutschland. [Cologne, 1965]. pp. iv, 196. bibliog. 19½cm.

- Germany, Eastern

>BERNARD (GUENTER) and others. Fluktuation eine praxisverbundene, wissenschaftlich begründete Betrachtung über Begriff, Ursachen, Folgen und Eindämmung der Fluktuation im sozialistischen Industriebetrieb. Berlin, Tribüne, 1965. pp. 104. 20½cm.

- New Zealand

>GREEN (R. L.) and others. Why they leave: a study of morale and the reasons for resignation of public servants in the Wellington area, during April and May, 1966. [Wellington, N.Z.], 1967. pp. 128.

- Siam

>SIAM. Department of Labour. 1967. Labour statistics and employment market information, January, 1967: Bangkok-Thonburi. [Bangkok], 1967. pp. 110. 30½cm. In English and Thai.

>SIAM. Department of Labour. 1967. Labour statistics and employment market information, April 1967: Changwat Mahasarakham. [Bangkok], 1967. pp. 34. 29½cm. In English and Thai.

>SIAM. Department of Labour. 1968. Labour statistics and employment market information, January, 1968: Bangkok-Thonburi, Samutprakan, Nonthaburi, Pathum Thani. [Bangkok], 1968. pp. 66. 29½cm. In English and Thai.

- United Kingdom

>U.K. 1952. Social Survey. Some facts about interviewer turnover; by Muriel Harris. (Papers, Methodological Series. No.M.47) [London], 1952. pp. 3. 33cm.

>ECONOMIC DEVELOPMENT COMMITTEE FOR THE CLOTHING INDUSTRY. Labour turnover. London, 1967. pp. (iii), 18. 24¼cm. (Occasional Papers. No. 1)

>ECONOMIC DEVELOPMENT COMMITTEE FOR FOOD MANUFACTURING. A study of labour turnover: (undertaken by the Centre for Applied Social Research of the Tavistock Institute of Human Relations). London, [1968]. pp. 37. bibliog. 24½cm.

>ECONOMIC DEVELOPMENT COMMITTEE FOR THE RUBBER INDUSTRY. Costing your labour turnover. London, [1968]. pp. 20. 24¼cm.

>NATIONAL ECONOMIC DEVELOPMENT OFFICE. Labour turnover; a manager's guide to action. London, [1968?]. pp. (i, 14). 21½cm.

>U.K. Department of Employment and Productivity. Manpower Papers. No. 1. Company manpower planning. London, 1968. pp. v, 54. bibliog. 24cm.

>ECONOMIC DEVELOPMENT COMMITTEE FOR HOTELS AND CATERING. Staff turnover; [based on a study carried out by the Centre for Applied Social Research of the Tavistock Institute of Human Relations.] London, H.M.S.O., 1969. pp. vii, 60. 24½cm.

>NEWSHAM (D.B.) The challenge of change to the adult trainee: a study of labour turnover during and following training of middle-aged men and women for new skills. London, H.M.S.O., 1969. pp. v, 39. bibliog. 24½cm. (Training Information Papers. 3)

>ROAD TRANSPORT INDUSTRY TRAINING BOARD [U.K.] Manpower in the road transport industry: (survey of manpower and labour turnover...1968) [Wembley, 1969]. pp. 76.

>SAMUEL (P.J.) Labour turnover?: towards a solution. London, 1969. pp. 55. bibliog.

>ECONOMIC DEVELOPMENT COMMITTEE FOR ELECTRONICS. Labour losses in the electronics industry. [London, National Economic Development Office, 1970.] pp. 10.

>SOCIAL SURVEYS (GALLUP POLL) LIMITED. The attitude of seafarers to their employment; report submitted to the Committee of Inquiry into Shipping. London, Board of Trade, 1970. 3 vols (in 1).

LABRADOR

- Social history

>KLEIVAN (HELGE) The Eskimos of northeast Labrador: a history of Eskimo-white relations, 1771-1955. Oslo, Norsk Polarinstitutt, 1966. pp. 195. bibliog. 26cm. (Norske Polarinstitut. Skrifter. Nr. 139)

LABRIOLA (ANTONIO)

>PROTO (MARIO) Labriola politico. Manduria, Lacaita, 1967. pp. 136. bibliog. 22cm. (Uomini e Cose della Nuova Italia. 21)

>NERI (SERGIO) Antonio Labriola, educatore e pedagogista. Modena, [1968]. pp. 175.

LABRIOLA (ARTURO)

>MARUCCO (D.) L'ambiente politico napoletano nell'esperienza giovanile di Arturo Labriola. in Miscellanea Walter Maturi. Torino, 1966.

LAC

>SIAM. 1964. Lac products of Thailand. (Ministry of Economic Affairs). 2nd ed. [Bangkok, 1964]. pp. 12. 19cm.

LACCADIVE ISLANDS

- Social conditions

>DUBE (LEELA) Matriliny and Islam: religion and society in the Laccadives. Delhi, 1969. pp. 125. bibliog. (University of Saugar. Monographs in Anthropology and Sociology)

LACE AND LACE MAKING

- United Kingdom

>FREEMAN (CHARLES) Pillow lace in the East Midlands. Luton, 1958 repr. 1966. pp. 51. bibliog.

- United Kingdom - Ireland

>BOYLE (ELIZABETH) The Irish flowerers. Holywood, Co. Down, 1971. pp. 160. bibliog.

LACERDA (CARLOS)

BOURNE (RICHARD) Political leaders of Latin America: Che Guevara, Alfredo Stroessner, Eduardo Frei Montalva, Juscelino Kubitschek, Carlos Lacerda, Eva Peron. New York, 1970. pp. 310, x. bibliog. First published by Penguin Books in 1969.

LACLOS (PIERRE AMBROISE FRANÇOIS CHODERLOS DE)
See CHODERLOS DE LACLOS (PIERRE AMBROISE FRANÇOIS)

LA CORUÑA
See CORUNNA

LACTOSE

EUROPEAN ECONOMIC COMMUNITY. 1965. Proposition de règlement du Conseil relatif au glucose et au lactose, présentée par la Commission au Conseil. (VI/COM. 65, 54 final) Bruxelles, 1965. pp. 3, 4. 29½cm.

LACUNAE IN LAW

PERELMAN (CHAÏM) ed. Le probleme des lacunes en droit: etudes. Bruxelles, Bruylant, 1968. pp. 554. 23¾cm. (Centre National de Recherches de Logique. Travaux)

LA CURNE DE SAINTE PALAYE (JEAN BAPTISTE DE)

GOSSMAN (LIONEL) Medievalism and the ideologies of the enlightenment: the world and work of La Curne de Sainte-Palaye. Baltimore, Johns Hopkins P., [1968]. pp. xvii. 377. 22½cm.

LA FAYETTE (MARIE JEAN PAUL ROCH YVES GILBERT MOTIER) Marquis de
See MOTIER (MARIE JEAN PAUL ROCH YVES GILBERT) Marquis de la Fayette

LAFORGE (MARCEL)

LAFORGE (MARCEL) Au fil des jours en Orient: Grèce, Égypte, Pakistan, Jérusalem, 1922-1958. Bruxelles, Librairie Encyclopédique, 1967. pp. 319. 23cm.

LAFTA
See LATIN AMERICAN FREE TRADE ASSOCIATION

LAGERSVÄRD (JOHAN CLAES)

LAGERSVÄRD (JOHAN CLAES) Lettere a Giovanni Ferri de Saint-Constant;...a cura di Vittorio E. Giuntella. Roma, 1968. pp. 181. (Istituto per la Storia del Risorgimento Italiano. [Pubblicazioni]. Serie 2a: Fonti. vol. 55.)

LAGOS

- History

LOSI (JOHN B.) History of Lagos; [originally published by Tika-Tore Press in 1914]. Lagos, African Education P., 1967. pp. ii, 95. 20¼cm.

- Markets

NIGERIA. 1959. Report of an inquiry by R.N. Rapson into alleged irregularities by the Lagos Town Council in connection with the collection of money and the issue of permits and the allocation of market stalls in respect of proposed temporary markets at Ereko and Oko-Awo. Lagos, 1959. pp. 29.

- Politics and government

NIGERIA. [Commission on Lagos Local Government]. 1959. Report by Sir John Imrie into the relationship between the Federal Government and the Lagos Town Council. Lagos, 1959. pp. 40.

NIGERIA. Lagos Executive Development Board Tribunal of Inquiry. 1968. Report...for the period 1st October, 1960 to 31st December, 1965. Lagos, 1968. pp. x, 292. 24½cm.

LAGOS UNIVERSITY

LAGOS. University. The installation of the chancellor and conferment of honorary degrees and first degrees of the University: addresses and citations at the congregation, 18th January and 23rd March, 1968. [Lagos, 1968]. pp.22. 23½cm.

LAHARPE (FREDERIC CESAR)

BOEHTLINGK (ARTHUR) Frédéric-César Laharpe, 1754-1838, précepteur du Tsar Alexandre Ier, antagoniste de Napoléon...; adaptation française du Oscar Forel. [Neuchâtel, 1969]. pp. 426.

LAHORE

- Growth

PAKISTAN. Planning Commission. Physical Planning and Housing Section. Studies. No. P.P. & H. 19. Urban biographies (Karachi, Lahore, Dacca); by Grenfell Rudduck. [Karachi], 1965. pp. 127. 24cm.

LAI (BENNY)

LAI (BENNY) Vaticano aperto. Milano, Longanesi, 1968. pp. 485. 18cm. (Il Mondo Nuovo. vol. 88)

LAISSEZ-FAIRE

RICHTER (EMIL) Ein Licht der Manchestristen. Leipzig, 1873. pp. 59.

HENSEL (K. PAUL) Marktwirtschaft: Wirtschaftsordnungen bürgerlicher Planung. Hannover, 1965. pp. 79. bibliog.

ACTON (HARRY BURROWS) The morals of markets: an ethical exploration. London, 1971. pp. 104.

LĀJPAT RĀYA

ARGOV (DANIEL) Moderates and extremists in the Indian nationalist movement, 1883-1920, with special reference to Surendranath Banerjea and Lajpat Rai. London, Asia Publishing House, [1967]. pp. xix, 246. bibliog. 21½cm.

LAKE DISTRICT, UNITED KINGDOM

- Economic history

MARSHALL (J.D.) and DAVIES-SHIEL (M.) The industrial archaeology of the Lake counties. Newton Abbot, [1969]. pp. 287. bibliog.

MARSHALL (J.D.) and DAVIES-SHIEL (M.) The Lake District at work: past and present. Newton Abbot, 1971. pp. 112. bibliog.

LAKES

ORGANIZATION OF AMERICAN STATES. 1963. Industrial and agricultural use of international rivers and lakes: study and draft convention prepared by the Inter-American Juridical Committee during its 1963 Meeting. (Official Records. OEA/Ser.I/VI.2 CIJ-67) Washington, 1963. 2 pts. 27½cm. In English and Spanish. For a later edition see ORGANIZATION OF AMERICAN STATES. 1965.

ORGANIZATION OF AMERICAN STATES. 1965. Industrial and agricultural use of international rivers and lakes: revised report and draft convention, etc. (Official Records. OEA/SeriesI/VI.2 CIJ. 79) Washington, 1965. pp. iii, 22. 27cm. For an earlier edition see ORGANIZATION OF AMERICAN STATES. 1963.

- Germany

BRENDEL (RUEDIGER) Das Münchener Naherholungsgebiet im Bereich des Ammersees und des Starnberger Sees: eine sozialgeographische Studie. [Munich?], 1967. pp. 237. bibliog.

HIRT (HARTMUT) Die Bedeutung der Seen des niedersächsischen Tieflandes für den Fremdenverkehr. Hildesheim, 1968. pp. 100. bibliog. (Göttingen. Universität. Niedersächsisches Institut für Landeskunde und Landesentwicklung. Veröffentlichungen. Reihe A1. Band 86)

LA MATANZA

NEWTON (JORGE) El Partido Bonaerense de La Matanza. Buenos Aires, [imprint], [1963]. pp. 255. 28cm. (Geografía Humana de las Poblaciones Argentinas)

LAMB (EDWARD)

LAMB (EDWARD) "Trial by battle": the case history of a Washington witch-hunt. [Santa Barbara], Center for the Study of Democratic Institutions, [1964]. pp. 24. 28cm. (Occasional Papers)

LAMB (MEAT)

MUTTON AND LAMB SITUATION, THE; published by Bureau of Agricultural Economics,...Australia. Canberra, annual, June 1966 (no. 1) to date. 23 cm-24 cm.

LAMBETH

- Sanitary affairs

ST. THOMAS'S HOSPITAL. Medical School. Department of Clinical Epidemiology and Social Medicine. St. Thomas's health survey in Lambeth, report 3, 1.1.67 - 31.4.67. London, [1967]. fo. (48); pp. (25).

LAMBRUSCHINI (RAFELLO)

GENTILI (RINO) Lambruschini: un liberale cattolico dell''800. Firenze, La Nuova Italia, 1967. pp. xxx, 245. bibliog. 20½cm. (Educatori Antichi e Moderni. 220)

LAMBTON (JOHN GEORGE) 1st Earl of Durham

REPORT of the public reception, and the speeches delivered at the dinner to Lord Durham, on Wednesday, 29th October, 1834; taken in short hand by Simon McGregor. Glasgow, McPhun, 1834. pp. 33.

LAMONTAGNE (PIERRE)

CANADA. 1965. Special public inquiry 1964: report of the Commissioner, Frederic Dorion, Chief Justice of the Superior Court for the Province of Quebec; ([with] Modification). [Ottawa], 1965. pp. 151.

LAMPSON (GRAHAM CURTIS) 2nd Baron Killearn

EVANS (TREFOR E.) Mission to Egypt, 1934-1946: Lord Killearn, High Commissioner and Ambassador; an inaugural lecture delivered at...Aberystwyth on 2 December 1970. Cardiff, 1971. pp. 25.

LAMUT LANGUAGE

AGBLEMAGNON (F. N'SOUGAN) Sociologie des sociétés orales d'Afrique noire: les Eve du Sud-Togo. Paris, 1969. pp. 216. bibliog. (Paris. Ecole Pratique des Hautes Etudes. Section des Sciences Economiques et Sociales. Le Monde d'Outre-Mer Passé et Présent. 1ère Série. Etudes. 35)

LAMZDORF (VLADIMIR NIKOLAEVICH) Graf.

LAMZDORF (VLADIMIR NIKOLAEVICH) Graf. Дневник, 1891-1892; под редакцией и с предисловием Ф. А. Ротштейна; подготовил к печати В. М. Хвостов; перевод с французского, etc. Москва, 1934. pp. 402, 22см. (Центральный Государственный Архив РСФСР. Русские Мемуары: Дневники, Письма и Материалы) Lacks final pages.

LANCASHIRE

- Bibliography

HORROCKS (SIDNEY) compiler. Lancashire Acts of Parliament, 1266-1957. Manchester, 1969. pp. 350. (Joint Committee on the Lancashire Bibliography. Contributions towards a Lancashire Bibliography. 2)

- Directories

TUPLING (GEORGE HENRY) compiler. Lancashire directories, 1684-1957; revised, enlarged and edited by Sidney Horrocks. rev. ed. Manchester, 1968. pp. 78. bibliog. (Joint Committee on the Lancashire Bibliography. Contributions Towards a Lancashire Bibliography. 1)

- Economic conditions

RUST (WILLIAM) What's wrong with Lancashire? Manchester, [imprint], [1934?]. pp. 12.

LANCASHIRE - Economic conditions (Cont'd.)

   FREEMAN (THOMAS WALTER) and others. Lancashire, Cheshire and the Isle of Man. London, [1966] repr 1968. pp. 308. bibliog.

   MATTHEW (ROBERT), JOHNSON-MARSHALL AND PARTNERS and ECONOMIC CONSULTANTS LTD. Central Lancashire new town proposal: impact on north east Lancashire; (consultants' appraisal). London, H.M.S.O., 1968. pp. (vi), 304. 30cm.

- Industries

   LANCASHIRE COMMUNIST PARTY. Better times for Lancashire. Manchester, [1939?]. pp. 13.

   ALLEN (ERIC GEORGE WALTER) Post-war industrial development in Lancashire and Merseyside. [Manchester], Manchester Statistical Society, [1963]. pp. 29. 21½cm.

   HOPWOOD (EDWIN) A history of the Lancashire cotton industry and the Amalgamated Weavers' Association:...the Lancashire weavers story. Manchester, Amalgamated Weavers Association, [1969]. pp. (ix), 199. 24½cm.

- Politics and government

   CLARKE (P.F.) Lancashire and the new Liberalism. Cambridge, 1971. pp. 472. bibliog.

- Sanitary affairs

   MIDWINTER (ERIC CLARE) Social administration in Lancashire, 1830-1860: poor law, public health and police. Manchester, [1969]. pp. 193. bibliog.

- Social history

   MIDWINTER (ERIC CLARE) Law and order in early Victorian Lancashire. York, St. Anthony's 1968. pp. 42. 21½cm. (York. University. Borthwick Institute of Historical Research. Borthwick Papers. No. 34)

   MIDWINTER (ERIC CLARE) Social administration in Lancashire, 1830-1860: poor law, public health and police. Manchester, [1969]. pp. 193. bibliog.

- Social life and customs

   KAY (RICHARD) 1716-1751. The diary of Richard Kay, 1716-51, of Baldingstone, near Bury, a Lancashire doctor; extracts edited...by W. Brockbank and F. Kenworthy. Manchester, Chetham Society, 1968. pp. (iii), 179. 21cm. (Remains, Historical and Literary, connected with the Palatine Counties of Lancaster and Chester. 3rd Series. vol. 16)

   PEEL (EDGAR) and SOUTHERN (PAT) The trials of the Lancashire witches: a study of seventeenth-century witchcraft. Newton Abbot, [1969]. pp. 192. bibliog.

LANCASHIRE AND YORKSHIRE RAILWAY

   MARSHALL (JOHN) Writer on Railways. The Lancashire and Yorkshire Railway. Newton Abbot, [1969-72]. 3 vols.

   NOCK (OSWALD STEVENS) The Lancashire and Yorkshire Railway: a concise history. London, 1969. pp. 159.

   BROADBRIDGE (SEYMOUR ALBERT) Studies in railway expansion and the capital market in England, 1825-1873. [London], 1970. pp. 215. bibliog.

LAND

   HILLS (G. A.) The ecological basis for land-use planning. [Toronto], 1961. pp. vi,204. bibliog. 28cm. (Ontario. Department of Lands and Forests. Research Reports. No.46)

   ORGANISATION FOR ECONOMIC CO-OPERATION AND DEVELOPMENT.1965. Obstacles to shifts in the use of land: ([by] J. Klatzmann [and others]). (Documentation in Food and Agriculture. 1965 Series. 74) [Paris, 1965]. pp. 155. 24cm.

   ROGERS (ANDREI) An investigation of retail land use forecasting models. [Berkeley], Bay Area Transportation Study Commission, [1966?]. pp. 82. bibliogs. 28cm.

   HEERDEGEN (RICHARD G.) ed. Land use and planning: readings in regional development;... six lectures presented to the Manawatu Branch, New Zealand Geographical Society, Inc., in 1966. Palmerston North, Manawatu Branch, 1967. pp. v, 141. 21cm.

   STEINER (DIETER) compiler. Index to the use of aerial photographs for rural land use studies. Bad Godesberg, Bundesanstalt für Landeskunde und Raumforschung, 1967. pp. 232. bibliog. (Landeskundliche Luftbildauswertung im mitteleuropäischen Raum. Sonderfolge. Geographische Luftbildinterpretation. 1)

   CHISHOLM (MICHAEL) Rural settlement and land use: an essay in location. 2nd ed. London, Hutchinson, 1968. pp. 183. bibliog. 20½cm. (Hutchinson University Library. Geography)

   DREIER (WILHELM) Raumordnung als Bodeneigentums- und Bodennutzungsreform. Köln, Bachem, 1968. pp. 304. bibliog. 22cm.

   DUCKWORTH (ROBERT P.) and others. The land reserves system: an approach to the possible application of land bank techniques to the bi-county region. Silver Spring, 1968. pp. iv, 39. bibliog. 28cm. (Maryland-National Capital Park and Planning Commission. Working Papers. No. 13)

   INSTITUTE OF BRITISH GEOGRAPHERS. Special Publications. No. 1. Land use and resources: studies in applied geography; a memorial volume to Sir Dudley Stamp. London, 1968. pp. 269. bibliog.

   SYMPOSIUM ON LAND EVALUATION, CANBERRA, 1968. Land evaluation: papers of a CSIRO symposium organized in cooperation with UNESCO...; edited by G.A. Stewart. Melbourne, Macmillan of Australia, 1968. pp. (ii), 392. bibliogs. 24½cm.

   DENMAN (DONALD ROBERT) Land use and the constitution of property; an inaugural lecture. Cambridge, 1969. pp. 26.

   POLSKA AKADEMIA NAUK. Instytut Geografii. Geographia Polonica. 19. Essays on agricultural typology and land utilization; edited by Jerzy Kostrowicki and Wieslawa Tyszkiewicz. Warszawa, 1970. pp. 290.

   ANDREWS (RICHARD BRUCE) Urban land economics and public policy. New York, [1971]. pp. 159. bibliog.

BLUNDEN (W.R.) The land-use/transport system: analysis and synthesis. Oxford, 1971. pp. 318. bibliog.

- Bibliography

COUNCIL OF PLANNING LIBRARIANS. Exchange Bibliographies. 63 to date. Monticello, Ill., 1968. to date.

FOOD AND AGRICULTURE ORGANIZATION. Documentation Center. 1968. Index: land and water, (1945-1966). (PU:DC/Sp.8) [Rome], 1968. pp. iv, 31,220,9,165. 28cm.

- Maps

COMMITTEE FOR THE WORLD ATLAS OF AGRICULTURE. World atlas of agriculture, under the aegis of the International Association of Agricultural Economists: land utilisation maps and relief maps. Novara, Istituto Geografico De Agostini, 1969 in progress. 48cm. Looseleaf.

- Taxation

BECKER (ARTHUR P.) ed. Land and building taxes: their effect on economic development; (proceedings of a symposium sponsored by the Committee on Taxation, Resources and Economic Development...at the University of Wisconsin, Milwaukee, 1966). Madison, 1969. pp. 308. (Committee on Taxation, Resources and Economic Development. Publications. 4)

- Taxation - Germany

MUSSLER (HANS PETER) Die steuerliche Behandlung und betriebswirtschaftliche Bedeutung von Grundstückspacht und Erbbaurecht. München. 1967. pp. 227. bibliog.

- Taxation - India

HUSAIN (IMTIAZ) Land revenue policy in north India: the ceded and conquered provinces, 1801-33. Calcutta, New Age Publishers, 1967. pp. (viii), 298. bibliog. 21cm.

- Taxation - India - Andhra Pradesh

ANDHRA PRADESH. Land Revenue Reforms Committee. 1959. Report: 1958-1959. Hyderabad, 1959. 2 vols (in 1). bibliog.

- Taxation - India - Bombay

BOMBAY rural land systems. Melbourne, [imprint], [c.1927]. pp. 8.

- Taxation - India - Gujarat

PATHAK (MAHESH T.) and PATEL (ARUN S.) Agricultural taxation in Gujarat. London, [1970]. pp. 93.

- Taxation - India - Madras

[MADRAS]. 1834. Replies to the Governor-General Lord William Bentinck's queries respecting the ryotwar system of revenue administration in the presidency of Fort St. George, by the principal collectors of Coimbatore and Salem; [including replies by John Orr]. [Madras], 1834. pp. 31.

MADRAS. 1951. The Land Revenue Reforms Committee, Madras [M.V.Subramanian, chairman]: first (and second) report. Madras, 1951. 2 pts.

- Taxation - India - Orissa

JENA (KRISHNACHANDRA) Land revenue administration in Orissa during the nineteenth century. Delhi, 1968. pp. 249. bibliog.

- Taxation - Jamaica

MURRAY (JOHN FRANCIS NOWELL) Report to the government of Jamaica on valuation, land taxation and rating. Kingston, [imprint], 1957. pp. ii,55. 25cm.

- Taxation - Nepal

REGMI (MAHESH CHANDRA) Land tenure and taxation in Nepal. Berkeley, 1963-8. 4 vols. bibliogs. 23½cm. (California University. Institute of International Studies. Research Series. Nos. 3,4,8,12)

- Taxation - New Zealand

NEW ZEALAND. Valuation Department. Research Papers. 68-1. A critical study of the unimproved value of land: its basis, determination and uses. Wellington, 1968. pp. iv, 104. 23½cm.

NEW ZEALAND. Valuation Department. Research Papers. 71-1. Betterment levy on land: submissions made to Commission of Inquiry into Housing, January and March 1971. Wellington, 1971. pp. 24.

- Taxation - Poland

FRANZ (JÓZEF) Niektóre podatki i opłaty terenowe: teksty i objaśnienia według stanu prawnego na dzień 30.VI.1969 r. 3rd ed. Warszawa, 1969. pp. 143.

- Taxation - Sweden

SWEDEN. Finansdepartementet. Fastighetstaxeringskommittéer. 1968. 1965 års allmänna fastighetstaxering: huvudresultat beträffande skattepliktiga fastigheter inom kommuner, kommunblock och län. Stockholm, 1968. pp. 166. 24cm. (Sweden. Statens Offentliga Utredningar. 1968. 31.)

SWEDEN. Finansdepartementet. Fastighetstaxeringskommittéer. 1968. Fastighetstaxeringens regler och organisation: förslag till vissa ändringar. Stockholm, 1968. pp. 145. 24cm. (Sweden. Statens Offentliga Utredningar. 1968. 32.)

- Taxation - Switzerland

BAER (GUY) Die Verkehrswertbesteuerung der Liegenschaften als Mittel der Bodenpolitik. Bern, [1970]. pp. 179. bibliog.

- Taxation - United Kingdom

NATIONAL ANTI-CORN-LAW LEAGUE. The constitutional right to a revision of the land-tax; being the argument on a case submitted to counsel on behalf of the... League. London, Ridgway, 1842. pp. (ii) 57. 21½cm.

MANCHESTER. Manchester Land Values League. Tale of two cities. Manchester, [191-?]. 1 pamphlet (unpaged).

WHITE (JAMES DUNDAS) Economic justice. London, 1918. pp. 96.

LAND - Taxation - United Kingdom (Cont'd.)

LAND UNION. Work of the Land Union. London, 1920. pp. 15. 12½cm.

ENGLISH LEAGUE FOR THE TAXATION OF LAND VALUES. [Leaflets]. New Series. No. 2. After the war. London, [1945?]. s.sh.

CLAYTON (DAVID) of Reading University, and others. Capital taxation and land ownership in England and Wales: a preliminary assessment. Reading, University of Reading, Agricultural Economics Department, 1967. pp. (iii), 43. 25½cm. (Miscellaneous Studies. No. 44)

WELLS (Sir HENRY WESTON) The Land Commission and the legal profession. [London], The Law Society, [1967?]. pp. 30. 21cm.

HUGHES (PERCY F.) and others. The betterment levy. London, 1968. pp. 862.

JOHNSON (T. A.) ed. Current aspects of law and valuation; ...[by] B. C. Berkinshaw-Smith [and others]. [Reading, 1969]. pp. 119.

SUDDARDS (ROGER W.) and JOSEPH (CLIFFORD) Land Commission definitions. London, [1969]. pp. 68.

U.K. Land Commission. 1969. Land Commission betterment levy: case notes: a guide to detailed provisions of part 3 of the Land Commission Act, 1967. London, 1969. pp. 67.

- Taxation - United Kingdom - Scotland

SCOTLAND. Scottish Development Department. 1967. Betterment levy: Scotland: an explanatory memorandum on part 3 of the Land Commission Act, 1967. Edinburgh, 1967. pp. vi, 48.

- Taxation - United States - Maryland

MEYERS (CAROL S.) Taxation and development: the use of tax policies for preserving open space and improving development patterns in the bi-county region. Silver Spring, 1968. pp. ii, 82. bibliog. 21½cm. x 28cm. (Maryland-National Capital Park and Planning Commission. Working Papers. No. 4)

- Afghanistan

FOOD AND AGRICULTURE ORGANIZATION. 1965. Report on survey of land and water resources: Afghanistan. vol.1. General report; [by] N. D. Tkachev [and others]). (FAO/SF: 9/AFG) Roma, 1965. 2 pts. 28cm.

- Africa, Subsaharan

SOUTHERN AFRICAN REGIONAL COMMITTEE FOR THE CONSERVATION AND UTILIZATION OF THE SOIL. Sub-Committee on Systems of Land Use for the Semi-Arid Regions of Southern Africa. 1960. Report. [Pretoria, 1960]. pp. 42-90. 23cm. (Reprinted from African Soils, vol.4, no.4) In English and French.

- Algeria

RUEDY (JOHN) Land policy in colonial Algeria: the origins of the rural public domain. Berkeley, U. of California P., 1967. pp. xiii, 115. bibliog. 25½cm. (California University. Near Eastern Center. Near Eastern Studies. 10)

- America, Latin

HARDOY (JORGE) and others. Politica de la tierra urbana y mecanismo para su regulacion en America del Sur. Buenos Aires, 1968. pp. 113. bibliog.

- Arabia

FOOD AND AGRICULTURE ORGANIZATION. Development Programme. 1966. Land and water surveys in the Wadi Tizan Kingdom of Saudi Arabia: final report, etc. (FAO/UNDP/SF:23/SAA) Rome, 1966. pp. 100 [maps in end pocket]

- Australia

AUSTRALIA. Parliament. Joint Committee on the Australian Capital Territory. 1965. Report on the supply of residential blocks in Canberra. in Australia. Parliament. [Parliamentary papers], 1964-65-66, vol. 9.

AUSTRALIA. Commonwealth Scientific and Industrial Research Organization. Land Research Series. No. 24. Lands of the Queanbeyan-Shoalhaven area, A.C.T. and N.S.W.; comprising papers by R.H. Gunn [and others]. Melbourne, 1969. pp. 164. bibliogs. 3 maps in end pocket.

- Australia - Queensland

AUSTRALIA. Commonwealth Scientific and Industrial Research Organization. Land Research Series. No. 21. Lands of the Dawson-Fitzroy area, Queensland; comprising papers by N.H. Speck [and others]. Melbourne, 1968. pp. 200. bibliogs. 24cm. 2 maps in end pocket.

- Australia - South Australia

ADELAIDE. City Engineer and Surveyor's Department. The city of Adelaide: report on 1967 land use survey. [Adelaide], 1968. pp. 76.

- Australia - Victoria

SKENE (J.K.M.) Soils and land use in the Deakin irrigation area, Victoria. Melbourne, 1963. pp. 43. 27½cm. (Victoria. Department of Agriculture. Technical Bulletins. No.16). Map in end pocket.

VICTORIA. 1964. Soils and land use in the Rochester and Echuca districts, Victoria, including the Rochester irrigation area, Campaspe irrigation district, and Echuca East irrigation settlement; by J.K.M. Skene and L.B. Harford. (Department of Agriculture Technical Bulletins. No.17) Melbourne, 1964. pp. 50, (21). bibliog.

VICTORIA. 1966. Soils and land use near Swan Hill, Victoria. (Department of Agriculture. Technical Bulletins. No. 20) Melbourne, 1966. pp. 58, 12 maps. 27cm.

HOUSING INDUSTRY ASSOCIATION. Land Usage Committee. A study in land usage; prepared ...to examine the future development of Melbourne to the year 2000. [Melbourne, 1968]. pp. 36.

- Australia - Western Australia

AUSTRALIA. Bureau of Agricultural Economics. 1970. The economics of land development on the Esperance Sand Plain, Western Australia; [with] Supplement; [by G.M. Scobie]. Canberra, 1970. pp. 125;8. (Wool Economic Research Reports. No. 17)

- Azores

CALLENDER (J.M.) and HENSHALL (J.D.) The land use of Faial in the Azores. in World Land Use Survey. [Regional] Monographs. No. 5. Four island studies. Bude, 1968.

PRINCE (H.C.) The land use of Santa Maria in the Azores. in World Land Use Survey. [Regional] Monographs. No. 5. Four island studies. Bude, 1968.

- Botswana

BAWDEN (M.G.) and STOBBS (A.R.) The land resources of Eastern Bechuanaland. Tolworth, Forestry and Land Use Section, Directorate of Overseas Surveys, 1963, repr. 1968. pp. 75. bibliog. 6 maps in end pocket.

BLAIR RAINS (A.) and McKAY (A.D.) The Northern State Lands, Botswana. Tolworth, 1968[or rather 1969]. pp. 124. bibliog. (U.K. Directorate of Overseas Surveys, Land Resources Division. Land Resource Studies. No. 5) Map in end-pocket.

BLAIR RAINS (A.) and YALALA (A.M.) The central and southern state lands, Botswana. Tolworth, 1972. pp. 115. bibliog. (U.K. Overseas Development Administration. Land Resources Division. Land Resource Studies. No. 11) 4 maps in end pocket.

- British East Africa

UNITED COMMITTEE FOR THE TAXATION OF LAND VALUES. More jobs than men: remarkable conclusions of a famous army surgeon, who made the Panama canal possible; together with labour problems in British East Africa; evidence and report from East African Protectorate, Native Labour Commission, 1912-13. London, [1915?]. pp. 7.

- Canada

CANADA LAND INVENTORY. The Canada Land Inventory...: objectives, scope and organization. Ottawa, Queen's Printer, 1965. pp. 12. (Reports. No. 1)(Canada. Department of Forestry. Publications. No.1088)

- Canada - Classification

McCORMACK (R. J.) Land capability classification for forestry. Ottawa, Queen's Printer, 1967. pp. 26. (Canada Land Inventory. Reports. No.4)

- Canada - British Columbia

FORWARD (CHARLES N.) Land use of the Victoria area, B.C. Ottawa, 1969. pp. 25. (Canada. Geographical Branch. Geographical Papers. No.43.) 4 maps in end pocket.

- Canada - Manitoba

WINNIPEG. Metropolitan corporation of Greater Winnipeg. Planning Division. Technical Reports. An economic land use study of South Point Douglas. [Winnipeg], 1966. fo. various. bibliog.

- Canada - New Brunswick

ST. JOHN, NEW BRUNSWICK. Town Planning Commission. Comprehensive community plan, St. John, New Brunswick: planning; [by] Proctor, Redfern, Bousfield, and Bacon [and] Read Voorhees and Associates Ltd. [Toronto], 1967-69. 5 vols.

- Canada - Ontario

FACTORS affecting land use in a selected area in Southern Ontario: a land use and geographic survey of Louth Township in Lincoln County; by the Ontario Department of Agriculture [and others]...; compiled by R.M. Irving. [Toronto] 1957. pp. x, 145. 27½cm.

- Canada - Prince Edward Island

BEAULIEU (ANDREE) Land adjustment problems in Prince Edward Island: a cartographic presentation. Ottawa, 1970. pp. 22. 1 map. bibliog. (Canada. Department of Energy, Mines and Resources. Policy Research and Coordination Branch. Geographical Papers. No. 45.) In English and French.

- Ceylon

CEYLON. Land Utilization Committee. 1968. Report...August 1967. Colombo, 1968. pp. iii, 121. 24cm. (Ceylon. Parliament. Sessional Papers. 1968. 11)

- Fiji Islands

FRAZER (R.M.) A Fiji-Indian rural community. Wellington, Victoria, Department of Geography, 1968. pp. (iii), 48. bibliog. 24½cm. (Pacific Viewpoint Monographs. No. 3)

- Formosa

FORMOSA. 1958. Land use conditions in Taiwan; by Emile C.H.Hsia. (Joint Commission on Rural Reconstruction Forestry Series. No.5) 2nd ed. Taipei, 1958. pp.(vii). 57. bibliog. 26cm.

- Germany

DOHRS (F.E.) Land use regions of the middle Neckar basin. in Malcolm Jarvis Proudfoot memorial volume. Evanston, 1957.

- Germany - Saarland

WERKMEISTER (HANS FRIEDRICH) and WESTPHAL (WALTER) Landschaftsplan „Mittleres Saartal": Erläuterungsbericht. Bad Godesberg, 1969. pp. 77. bibliog. (Germany (Bundesrepublik). Institut für Raumordnung. Mitteilungen. Heft 54) 2 maps in end-pocket.

- Grenada

GRENADA. Department of Forestry and Lands. Report. in Grenada. Council papers. St. George's, 1959 to date.

- Hong Kong

LIANG (CHI-SEN) Urban land-use in Hong Kong and Kowloon. Hong Kong, [1966-68]. 2 pts. (in 1 vol.). (Hong Kong. Chinese University. Chung Chi College. Research Institute of Far Eastern Studies. Geography Research Papers. Nos. 1-2) (Reprinted from the Chung Chi Journal, vol. 6, no. 1; vol. 8, no. 1)

LAND (Cont'd.)

- India

INDIA. Study Group on Distribution of Land between Foodgrains and Cotton under the Fourth Plan. 1967. Report. Delhi, 1967. p. 27.

WHYTE (ROBERT ORR) Land, livestock and human nutrition in India. New York, Praeger, 1968. pp. xvii, 309. bibliog. 23½cm. (Praeger Special Studies in International Economics and Development)

MERILLAT (HERBERT CHRISTIAN LAING) Land and the constitution in India. New York, 1970. pp. 321. bibliog.

- India - Assam

VERMA (BRIND BIHARI) Agriculture and land ownership system among primitive people of Assam. Delhi, [1956]. pp. 29. bibliog.

- India - Uttar Pradesh

MOHIUDDIN (IQBAL) Land use and nutrition in Lucknow district; [M. Phil. (London) thesis]. 1968. fo. 268, and vol. of maps. bibliog. 29 cm. Typescript: unpublished. This thesis is the property of London University and may not be removed from the Library.

SINGH (VIJAYA RAM) Land use patterns in Mirzapur and environs. Varanasi, 1970. pp. 152. bibliog.

- Kenya

KENYA. 1960. Report on unalienated crown land and undeveloped or under-developed land in other areas. [Nairobi], 1960. pp. 9.

OMINDE (SIMEON HONGO) Land and population movements in Kenya. London, Heinemann, 1968. pp. xii, 204. bibliog. 27½cm.

- Lebanon

KLAER (WENDELIN) Eine Landnutzungskarte von Libanon. Heidelberg, Keyser, 1962. pp. 55. bibliog. 23cm. (Heidelberger Geographische Arbeiten. Heft 10)

- Lesotho

BAWDEN (M.G.) and CARROLL (D.M.) The land resources of Lesotho. Tolworth, Land Resources Division, Directorate of Overseas Surveys, 1968. pp. viii, 87. bibliog. 29½cm (U.K. Directorate of Overseas Surveys. Land Resources Division. Land Resource Studies. No. 3.) 6 maps in end pocket.

- Madeira

SMITH (C.D.) The land use of Eastern Madeira. in World Land Use Survey. [Regional] Monographs. No. 5. Four island studies. Bude, 1968.

- New Guinea

AUSTRALIA. Commonwealth Scientific and Industrial Research Organization. Land Research Series. No.20. Lands of Bougainville and Buka Islands, Territory of Papua and New Guinea; comprising papers by R.M. Scott [and others]. Melbourne, 1967. pp. 184. bibliogs. 24cm. 3 maps in end pocket.

AUSTRALIA. Commonwealth Scientific and Industrial Research Organization. Land Research Series. No.22. Lands of the Wewak-Lower Sepik area, Territory of Papua and New Guinea; comprising papers by H.A. Haantjens [and others]. Melbourne, 1968. pp. 150. bibliogs. 24cm. 2 maps in end pocket.

AUSTRALIA. Commonwealth Scientific and Industrial Research Organization. Land Research Series. No. 23. Lands of the Kerer Vailala area, Territory of Papua and New Guinea; comprising papers by B.P. Ruxton [and others]. Melbourne, 1969. pp. 158. bibliogs. 24cm. 3 maps in end pocket.

- New Zealand

WARD (J.T.) and PARKES (E.D.) An economic analysis of large-scale land development for agriculture and forestry. [Christchurch, N.Z.], University of Canterbury, Lincoln College, Agricultural Economics Research Unit, [1966]. pp. 158. 24cm. (Publications. No. 27)

FORESTRY DEVELOPMENT CONFERENCE, WELLINGTON, 1969. Production Forestry Working Party. Land Resources Sub-Committee. Report on land resources for...[the] Working Party, etc. [Wellington, Government Printer, 1969.] pp. 12.

NATIONAL DEVELOPMENT CONFERENCE, WELLINGTON, 1969. Physical Environment Committee. Report. [Wellington, Government Printer], 1969. pp. 24. ([Reports]. N.D.C. 15)

PARKES (E. D.) Land development by the state: an economic analysis of the Hindon block, Otago. [Christchurch, N.Z.], 1969. pp. 53. bibliog. (Christchurch, New Zealand. University of Canterbury. Lincoln College. Agricultural Economics Research Unit. Research Reports. No.61)

- Nigeria

BAWDEN (M. G.) and TULEY (P.) The land resources of Southern Sardauna and Southern Adamawa Provinces, Northern Nigeria: with a short study of the high altitude grasslands. Tolworth, Land Resources Division, Directorate of Overseas Surveys, 1966. pp. xi, 119. bibliog. 32½cm. (U.K. Directorate of Overseas Surveys. Land Resources Division. Land Resource Studies. No.2) 2 maps in end pocket.

NIGERIA (NORTHERN REGION). Ministry of Town and Country Planning. 1967. A handbook of the Ministry of Town and Country Planning on: A. Land. B. Mining titles. C. Administrative boundaries. Kaduna, [1967?]. pp. 205. Loose-leaf binder.

HILDEBRAND (F. H.) A reconnaissance survey of the Serti area, Sardauna Province, Northern Nigeria. Zaria, 1968. pp. 34. (Ahmadu Bello University. Institute for Agricultural Research. Soil Survey Bulletins. No.37)

- Pakistan

PAKISTAN. Department of Agricultural Economics and Statistics. 1963. Land and crop statistics of Pakistan. 2nd ed. Karachi, 1962[or rather 1963]. pp. 329.

- Pakistan, West

UNITED STATES. Report on land and water development in the Indus plain. Washington, 1964. pp. ii, 454.

RAHMAN (MUSHTAQUR) Deh Dali Nandi, West Pakistan: a study of cultural factors in land use. Karachi, Karachi University, Department of Geography, Pakistan Institute of Geography, 1965. pp. x, 54. bibliog. 24cm. (Monographs. No. 1)

- Poland

GRABOŃ (WŁADYSŁAW) and PAKIER (MAURYCY) Gospodarka terenami w miastach i osiedlach: przepisy i objaśnienia; stan prawny na dzień 1.I.1967 r. Warszawa, Wydawnictwo Prawnicze, 1967. pp. 180. 21cm.

WINIARZ (JAN) Użytkowanie wieczyste. Warszawa, PWN, 1967. pp. 344. bibliog. 19½cm. With German and Russian summaries.

- Rhodesia

COMMISSION FOR TECHNICAL CO-OPERATION IN AFRICA SOUTH OF THE SAHARA. 1954. Review of soil conservation and land use planning in native areas in Southern Rhodesia. provisional ed. [Salisbury, 1954?]. pp. 15. 23cm. (Inter-African Soils Conference, 1954. [Papers]. III)

RHODESIA. Report of the Secretary for Lands. Salisbury, annual, 1968[1st] to date. 25½cm.

- Russia

PRAVIL'NOE... Правильное и полное использование земли, важное условие подъема экономики колхозов и совхозов: сборник материалов областной экономической конференции. Калуга, 1960. pp. 198. bibliog.

VNUTRIKHOZIAISTVENNOE... Внутрихозяйственное землеустройство совхозов. Москва, 1964. pp. 168.

BURIKHIN (N. N.) and others. Экономическое обоснование землеустройства колхозов нечерноземной зоны РСФСР. Москва, Колос, 1967. pp. 287. 20см.

PEPSHIN (PAVEL NIKOLAEVICH) ed. Экономические основы советского земельного кадастра. Киев, Наукова Думка, 1969. pp. 228. 20см.

- Russia - Classification

POSOSHNIKOVA (KLAVDIIA PORFIR'EVNA) and ADAMIAN (LEVON IVANOVICH) Ekonomicheskaia otsenka zemli. Erevan, 1970. pp. 215.

- Siam

SIAM. Ministry of Agriculture. Division of Agricultural Economics. 1963. Land utilization of Thailand, 1961. Bangkok, [1963]. pp.(35). 26cm. In English and Thai.

SIAM. Ministry of Agriculture. Division of Agricultural Economics. 1968. Land utilization of Thailand, 1965. [4th ed.] Bangkok, [1968]. pp. 27. 26½cm. In English and Thai.

- Sicily

MILONE (FERDINANDO) Memoria illustrativa della carta della utilizzazione del suolo della Sicilia...;con una introduzione di Carmelo Colamonico. Roma, Consiglio Nazionale delle Ricerche, [1959]. pp. 210. 25cm.

- Singapore

SINGAPORE. Land clearance and Resettlement Working Party. 1956. Report. [S G. Burlock, chairman]. Singapore, 1956. pp. 17. 25cm.

- Somaliland

FOOD AND AGRICULTURE ORGANIZATION. Development Programme. 1967. Agricultural and water surveys, Somalia: final report. vol.1. General, etc. (FAO/SF:36/SOM) Rome, 1967. pp. 275.

- South Africa

DULY (LESLIE CLEMENT) British land policy at the Cape, 1795-1844: a study of administrative procedures in the Empire. Durham, Duke U.P., 1968. pp. xix, 226. bibliog. 23½cm. (Duke Historical Publications)

BEAVON (KEITH S.O.) Land use patterns in Port Elizabeth: a geographical analysis in the environs of Main Street. Cape Town, 1970. pp. 138. bibliog.

- Soviet Central Asia

MAL'TSEV (ANATOLII EFIMOVICH) Земельно-водные ресурсы Средней Азии и их сельскохозяйственное использование. Фрунзе, 1969. pp. 252. bibliog.

- Switzerland

SCHMID (WERNER) Wenn der Boden knapp wird. Bern, 1962. pp. 14.

- Tanzania

SPOONER (R. J.) and JENKIN (R. N.) The development of the lower Mgeta river area of the United Republic of Tanzania. Tolworth, Land Resources Division, Directorate of Overseas Surveys, 1966. pp. xiii, 102. bibliog. 32½cm. (U.K. Directorate of Overseas Surveys. Land Resources Division. Land Resource Studies. No. 1) 11 maps in end pocket.

LUDWIG (HEINZ DIETER) Ukara: ein Sonderfall tropischer Bodennutzung in Raum des Victoria-Sees: eine wirtschaftsgeographische Entwicklungsstudie. München, Weltforum, [1967]. pp. 251. bibliog. 23cm. (IFO-Institut für Wirtschaftsforschung. Afrika-Studien. 22) 4 maps in end pocket.

BERRY (LEN) and BERRY (EILEEN) Land use in Tanzania by districts. Dar es Salaam, 1969. pp. 14. bibliog. (Dar es Salaam. University College. Bureau of Resource Assessment and Land Use Planning. Research Notes. No.6) In English and Swahili.

LAND - Tanzania (Cont'd.)

RALD (J.) Land use in a Buhaya village: a case study from Bukoba District, West Lake Region. Dar es Salaam, 1969. pp. 63. bibliog. (Dar es Salaam. University College. Bureau of Resource Assessment and Land Use Planning. Research Papers. No. 5) In English and Swahili.

PITBLADO (J. ROGER) A review of agricultural land use and land tenure in Tanzania. [Dar Es Salaam], 1970. pp. 41. bibliog. (Dar Es Salaam. University. ~~College.~~ Bureau of Resource Assessment and Land Use Planning. Research Notes. No. 7)

THOMAS (IAN D.) Some notes on population and land use in the more densely populated parts of the Uluguru mountains of Morogoro district. [Dar Es Salaam], 1970. pp. 51. (Dar Es Salaam. University. Bureau of Resource Assessment and Land Use Planning. Research Notes. No. 8)

THOMAS (IAN D.) Some notes on population and land use in the North Pare mountains. [Dar Es Salaam], 1970. pp. 61. (Dar Es Salaam. University. Bureau of Resource Assessment and Land Use Planning. Research Notes. No. 9)

- Tasmania

TASMANIA. Parliament. Joint Committee on Town and Country Planning. 1970. Preservation of foreshore areas; interim report: [R.W. Baker, chairman]. in Tasmania. Parliament. Journals and Printed Papers, 1970, no. 27.

TASMANIA. Parliament. Joint Committee on Town and Country Planning. 1970. Report...with minutes of proceedings: [R.W. Baker, chairman]. in Tasmania. Parliament. Journals and Printed Papers, 1970, no. 103.

- Trinidad and Tobago

TRINIDAD AND TOBAGO. Central Statistical Office. 1958. Land utilization, agricultural production, 1956. [Port-of-Spain], 1958. pp. 55.

- Ukraine

DAVYDOV (A. M.) Agrarnye preobrazovaniia i formirovanie sotsialisticheskogo zemlepol'zovaniia d Uzbekskoi SSR. Tashkent, 1965. pp. 271. bibliog.

- United Kingdom

NATIONAL UNION OF CONSERVATIVE AND UNIONIST ASSOCIATIONS Land questions. London, [1913?]. pp. 211-262,iii.

WIBBERLEY (GERALD PERCY) Land planning and agriculture. Ashford, 1958. pp. 11. (London. University. Wye College. Reprints. New Series. No.114)

U.K. Ministry of Housing and Local Government. Handbook of statistics. London, annual, 1965 [1st issue] to date. 24½cm.

WIBBERLEY (GERALD PERCY) Pressures on Britain's land resources. Sutton Bonington, 1965. pp. 12. (Nottingham. University. School of Agriculture. Department of Agricultural Economics. Heath Memorial Lectures. No. 10)

BOURNEMOUTH. County Borough Council, and others. First report on a land use and transportation study of south east Dorset and south west Hampshire. Bournemouth, 1967. pp. 137. 21 x 30½cm.

FREEMAN (THOMAS WALTER) Geography and planning. 3rd ed. London, Hutchinson, 1967. pp. 192. 21cm.

COLEMAN (ALICE M.) Land use Survey handbook: an explanation of the second land use survey of Britain on the scale of 1:25,000. 5th ed. London, 1968. pp. 32.

HALL (P.G.) Land use - the spread of towns into the country. in Young (Michael Dunlop) ed. Forecasting and the social sciences. London, 1968.

MARTINDALE (LAWRENCE) Demography and land use in the late seventeenth and eighteenth centuries in Middlesex; [Ph.D.(London) thesis]. [1968]. fo. xi, 483. bibliog. 25½cm. Typescript: unpublished. This thesis is the property of London University and may not be removed from the Library.

NATIONAL BUILDING AGENCY. Land costs and housing development: a study based on a sample of 16,300 housing society dwellings in England and Wales. London, 1968. pp. 31. bibliog.

RURAL planning methods: (a brief report of a research exercise in rural planning developed by a team from the Ministry of Agriculture, Fisheries and Food, the Forestry Commission, the Countryside Commission (then National Parks Commission), the Nature Conservancy, Hampshire County Council, with assistance from the Ministry of Housing and Local Government). [London], Countryside Commission, 1968. unfoliated.

BEST (ROBIN H.) and CHAMPION (A.G.) Regional conversions of agricultural land to urban use in England and Wales, 1945-1967. London, 1969. pp. 35. bibliog. (Centre for Environmental Studies. University Working Papers. 3)

NICHOLLS (D.C.) Use of land for forestry within the proprietary land unit: a study of land use on wooded private estates in England and Wales. London, 1969. pp. 78. bibliog. (U.K. Forestry Commission. Bulletins. No. 39)

TRAFFIC RESEARCH CORPORATION. Merseyside area land use/transportation study: technical reports, nos. 1-24. Liverpool, 1969. 3 pts. (in 5 vols.).

APPLETON (JAMES HENRY) Disused railways in the countryside of England and Wales; a report to the Countryside Commission; with a section on disused railways and agriculture by Richard J. Appleton. London, H.M.S.O., 1970. pp. 82.

FAIRBROTHER (NAN) New lives, new landscapes. London, 1970. pp. 397. bibliog.

PATMORE (JOHN ALLAN) Land and leisure in England and Wales. Newton Abbot, [1970]. pp. 332.

THOMAS (DAVID) Reader in Geography, University College London. London's green belt. London, 1970. pp. 248.

U.K. Central Office of Information. Reference Division. 1970. Land conservation in Britain. London, 1970. pp. 19. bibliog.

U.K. Ministry of Housing and Local Government. 1970. Development plans: a manual on form and content. London, 1970. pp. 105; various.

WIBBERLEY (GERALD PERCY) The future of Britain's rural land. Newton Abbot, 1970. pp. 15. (Devon County Agricultural Association. Lectures. 1970)

LAND and industry: the landed estate and the industrial revolution; a symposium edited by J.T. Ward and R.G. Wilson. Newton Abbot, [1971]. pp. 280.

- United Kingdom - Classification

KAYE (G.M.) National land use classification: an approach. [London], 1970. pp. various. (London. Greater London Council. Department of Planning and Transportation. Research Memoranda. 251.)

- United Kingdom - Ireland

BOTTIGHEIMER (KARL S.) English money and Irish land: the 'adventurers' in the Cromwellian settlement of Ireland. Oxford, 1971. pp. 226. bibliog.

- United Kingdom - Scotland

McVEAN (D.N.) and LOCKIE (J.D.) Ecology and land use in upland Scotland. Edinburgh, 1969. pp. 134. bibliog.

- United States

HAAR (CHARLES MONROE) Land-use planning: a casebook on the use, misuse and re-use of urban land. Boston, Little, Brown, 1959. pp. xxxv, 790. 24½cm. (Law School Casebook Series)

UNITED STATES. Public Roads Bureau. Land use conference...Washington...1963. Washington, 1964 pp. 29.

ELIAS (C.E.) Land development and local public finance. in California University. Real Estate Research Program. Essays in urban land economics. Los Angeles, 1966.

NATIONAL RESEARCH COUNCIL. Highway Research Board. Highway Research Records. No. 126. Land use forecasting concepts: 7 reports. Washington, D.C., 1966. pp. 87.

CLAWSON (MARION) The federal lands since 1956: recent trends in use and management. Washington, Resources for the Future, Inc. [1967]. pp. xiii. 113. 25½cm.

CLAWSON (MARION) The land system of the United States: an introduction to the history and practice of land use and land tenure. Lincoln, U. of Nebraska P., [1968]. pp. ix, 145. 20cm.

DUCKWORTH (ROBERT P.) and others. The land use intensity system: a study of its meaning for and application to the bi-county region. Silver Spring, 1968. pp. iv, 29. bibliog. 28cm. (Maryland-National Capital Park and Planning Commission. Working Papers. No. 11)

UNITED STATES. National Commission on Urban Problems. Research Reports. No. 2. Problems of zoning and land-use regulation. Washington, 1968. pp. 80. bibliog.

UNITED STATES. National Commission on Urban Problems. Research Reports. No. 12. Three land research studies: Trends in the value of real estate and land 1956 to 1966; Land use in 106 large cities; Estimating California land values from independent statistical indicators. Washington, 1968. pp. 62

UNITED STATES. National Commission on Urban Problems. Research Reports. No. 15. Alternatives to urban sprawl: legal guidelines for governmental action. Washington, 1968. pp. 69.

URBAN LAND INSTITUTE. Technical Bulletins. [No.] 60. From horse and buggy to the nuclear age: the changing principles of land economics, fifteen 20th century revolutions that have changed land economics; by Homer Hoyt. Washington, D.C., [1968]. pp. 23. 28cm.

DELAFONS (JOHN) Land-use controls in the United States. 2nd ed. Cambridge, Mass., 1969. pp. 203.

UNITED STATES. National Commission on Urban Problems. Research Reports. No. 18. Fragmentation in land-use planning and control. Washington, 1969. pp. 91.

LAND USE SYMPOSIUM, 1st, 1969. Land: recreation and leisure; abstracted from the first annual Land Use Symposium. Washington, D.C., [1970]. pp. 97. bibliog.

- Viêt-Nam

VIET-NAM (REPUBLIC). Commissariat General for Land Development. 1960. The work of land development in Viet-Nam up to June 30, 1959, achievements up to June, 1960, attached. [Saigon, 1960]. pp. 31, iv.

- White Russia

MEDVEDEV (ANDREI GRIGOR'EVICH) and others. Kachestvennaia otsenka zemel' v kolkhozakh i sovkhozakh BSSR; pod redaktsiei... S.G. Skoropanova. Minsk, 1971. pp. 327.

- Zanzibar

CAISTOR (M.E.) The land use of Zanzibar Island. in World Land Use Survey. [Regional] Monographs. No. 5. Four island studies. Bude, 1968.

LAND, NATIONALIZATION OF

STIRLING (JAMES HUTCHISON) The community of property: nationalisation of land. Edinburgh, Oliver and Boyd, 1885. pp. 40. 18½cm.

DEUTSCHER BAUERNTAG, 1.-2., 1886, 1894. 1. Deutscher Bauerntag im Sofiensaale zu Wien am 20. März 1886; (and 2. Deutscher Bauerntag in Wien am 27. März 1894); Kundgebungen, etc. [Horn, Berger, 1894]. pp. 18. 21cm.

FORDHAM (MONTAGUE EDWARD) Homes and the land: practical politics for country people. London, [1908?]. pp. 14.

LEATHAM (JAMES) Can the British get Britain for nothing?: a reply to an impossibilist difficulty. Cottingham, Gateway, [1913?]. pp. 12. 22cm.

BURMA. Statutes, etc. 1948. The Land Nationalization Act, 1948. Rangoon, 1948. pp. 41.

LAND, NATIONALIZATION OF (Cont'd.)

BURMA. Statutes, etc. 1953-54. The Land Nationalization Act, 1953...; as amended... 1954. [Rangoon, 1955]. pp. 26.

WEST BENGAL. Statutes, etc. 1954-59. West Bengal Act I of 1954: the West Bengal Estates Acquisition Act, 1953 as modified up to the 1st April, 1959. Alipore, 1960. pp. ii, 39. 24½cm.

FRITZ (WALTER) Ideen zur Sozialisierung des Bodens: eine dogmengeschichtliche Untersuchung. [Zurich, 1969?]. pp. 178. bibliog.

LENINSKII dekret "O zemle" i sovremennost? Moskva, 1970. pp. 384.

LAND BANKS

- Georgia

SANAKOEV (MURAD PETROVICH) Deiatel'nost' Krest'-ianskogo pozemel'nogo banka v Gruzii, 1906-1917 gg. Tbilisi, 1971. pp. 110. bibliog.

LAND COMPANIES

- United States

SUSQUEHANNAH COMPANY. The Susquehannah Company papers;...edited by Julian P. Boyd ([and] Robert J. Taylor); published for Wyoming Historical and Geological Society. Ithaca, 1930-71. 11 vols. Vols. 1-4 reprinted 1962. Maps in end pocket of vols. 1 and 2.

LAND RESEARCH

SALTER (LEONARD AUSTIN) A critical review of research in land economics; ... with and introductory essay by M.M.Kelso. Madison, U. of Wisconsin P., 1967. pp. xxi, 258. 23½cm.

LAND SETTLEMENT

AKADEMIE FÜR RAUMFORSCHUNG UND LANDES-PLANUNG. Ausschuss Historische Raumforschung. Historische Raumforschung. 4. Raumordnung in Renaissance und Merkantilismus. Hannover, Jänecke, 1963. pp. vii, 125. 25cm.

FOOD AND AGRICULTURE ORGANIZATION. Rural Institutions Division. Land reform, land settlement and co-operatives. Rome, semi-annual, 1965 (no.1) to date. 28cm.

LAGLER (KARL F.) ed. Man-made lakes: planning and development. Rome, Food and Agriculture Organization, 1969. pp. 71. bibliog.

- Mathematical models

ALDSKOGIUS (HANS) Modelling the evolution of settlement patterns: two studies of vacation house settlement. Uppsala, 1969. pp. 108. bibliog. (Uppsala. Universitet. Kulturgeografiska Institutionen. Geografiska Regionstudier. Nr. 6)

- Africa, Subsaharan

CHAMBERS (ROBERT J.H.) Settlement schemes in tropical Africa: a study of organizations and development. London, 1969. pp. 294. bibliog.

- Australia - New South Wales

BUXTON (G.L.) The Riverina, 1861-1891: an Australian regional study. Melbourne, U.P., 1967. pp. xi, 338. bibliog. 21½cm.

LANGFORD-SMITH (T.) Murrumbidgee land settlement 1817 to 1912. in Dury (George Harry) and Logan (M. I.) eds. Studies in Australian geography. London, 1968.

- Bolivia

MONHEIM (FELIX) and KESSLER (ALBRECHT) Beiträge zur Landeskunde von Peru und Bolivien. Wiesbaden, 1968. pp. 89. bibliogs. (Geographische Zeitschrift. Beihefte. Erdkundliches Wissen. Heft 20)

- Canada - Manitoba

MANITOBA. 1914. First province of Western Canada: own a farm of your own in Manitoba. (Department of Agriculture and Immigration) [Winnipeg, 1914]. pp. 79. 24cm.

- Ceylon

CEYLON. Ministry of Land, Irrigation and Power. Plan [of development, 1966-70] implementation report. a., 1966/7- Colombo.

CEYLON. Ministry of Land, Irrigation and Power. 1966. Plan of development of Ministry of Land, Irrigation and Power, 1966-1970. [Colombo, 1966.] pp. 302.

CEYLON. Ministry of Land, Irrigation and Power. Plan of development, 1966-70: implementation programme and targets. a., 1967/8- Colombo.

- Dominica

BARBADOS. Delegation Appointed to Visit Dominica to Examine the Possibilities of a. Land Settlement Scheme there for Barbadians. 1960. Report. [Bridgetown, 1960]. pp. 7.

- East (Near East)

DEVELOPMENT CENTRE ON LAND POLICY AND SETTLEMENT FOR THE NEAR EAST, TRIPOLI, 1965. Land policy in The Near East: proceedings of the Development Centre...held in Tripoli, Libya, from 16 to 28 October 1965...; compiled by Mohamad Riad El-Ghonemy. Rome, Food and Agriculture Organization, 1967. pp. 417.

- Finland

HAUTAMÄKI (LAURI) Development of settlement in some rural communes in western Finland since 1920. Helsinki, 1967. pp. 98. bibliog. 25cm. (Fennia: bulletins de la Société de Géographie Finlandaise. vol. 96, no. 2)

- Germany

HERRMANN (JOACHIM) Siedlung, Wirtschaft und gesellschaftliche Verhältnisse der slawischen Stämme zwischen Oder/Neisse und Elbe: Studien auf der Grundlage archäologischen Materials. Berlin, 1968. pp. 374. bibliog. (Deutsche Akademie der Wissenschaften zu Berlin. Sektion für Vor- und Frühgeschichte. Schriften. Band 23) 8 maps in end pocket.

- Ghana

    CHAMBERS (ROBERT J.H.) ed. The Volta resettlement experience. London, 1970. pp. 286. bibliog.

- Israel

    WILLNER (DOROTHY) Nation-building and community in Israel. Princeton, Princeton U.P., 1969. pp. xi, 478. bibliog. 21½cm.

- Kenya

    SYRACUSE UNIVERSITY. Maxwell Graduate School of Citizenship and Public Affairs. Program of Eastern African Studies. Occasional Papers. No.30. Two variables affecting rural transformation in Kenya : the settlement case by Brack E. S. Brown. [Syracuse, N.Y., 1967?]. fo. 29.

    KENYA. Ministry of Finance and Economic Planning. Statistics Division. Farm Economic Survey Reports. No. 27. An economic appraisal of the settlement schemes, 1964/65-1967/68. [Nairobi, 1971]. pp. 165. bibliog. Map in end pocket.

- Nigeria

    RICHARDS (DAVID ALBERT) Problems of resettlement administration in the areas of the Niger dam; [M. Sc. (Econ.) (London) thesis]. 1971. fo. 172. bibliog. Typescript: unpublished. This thesis is the property of London University and may not be removed from the Library

    ROIDER (WERNER) Farm settlements for socio-economic development: the Western Nigerian case. München, [1971]. pp. 214. bibliog. (Ifo-Institut für Wirtschaftsforschung. Afrika-Studien. 66)

- Peru

    MONHEIM (FELIX) and KESSLER (ALBRECHT) Beiträge zur Landeskunde von Peru und Bolivien. Wiesbaden, 1968. pp. 89. bibliogs. (Geographische Zeitschrift. Beihefte. Erdkundliches Wissen. Heft 20)

- Poland

    WIELGOSZ (ZBIGNIEW) Wielka własność cysterska w osadnictwie pogranicza Śląska i Wielkopolski. Poznań, PWN, 1964. pp. 181. bibliog. 25cm. (Poznań. Poznańskie Towarzystwo Przyjaciół Nauk. Wydział Historii i Nauk Społecznych. Komisja Historyczna. Prace. tom 21, zeszyt 1) With French summary.

- Rhodesia

    RHODESIA. Agricultural Land Settlement Board. Report. a., 1970 [1st]- Salisbury.

- Russia

    GOEHRKE (CARSTEN) Die Wüstungen in der Moskauer Rus': Studien zur Siedlungs-, Bevölkerungs- und Sozialgeschichte. Wiesbaden Steiner, 1968. pp. xii, 357. bibliog. 24cm. (Quellen und Studien zur Geschichte des Östlichen Europa. Band 1)

- Siam

    SIAM. Department of Public Welfare. 1959. Self-help land settlement in Thailand. [Bangkok, 1959], pp.(iii),42. 26½cm.

    SITTON (GORDON R.) and others. Farm success and project administration cooperative land settlement project, part 1;...in cooperation with the Department of Land Cooperatives, Ministry of National Development. Bangkok, 1962. pp. 194. (Bangkok. Kasetsart University. Department of Agricultural Economics. Kasetsart Economic Reports. No. 17)

- Sicily

    TRASSELLI (CARMELO) Il popolamento dell'isola di Ustica nel secolo XVIII. Caltanissetta, Sciascia, 1966. pp.193. 18½cm. (Unione delle Camere di Commercio, Industria, Artigianato e Agricoltura della Regione Siciliana. Storia Economica di Sicilia. Testi e Ricerche. 7)

- South Africa

    INTERNATIONAL DEFENCE AND AID FUND [FOR SOUTHERN AFRICA]. South Africa: resettlement -- the new violence to Africans. London, 1969. pp. 46.

- Sweden

    ALDSKOGIUS (HANS) Modelling the evolution of settlement patterns: two studies of vacation house settlement. Uppsala, 1969. pp. 108. bibliog. (Uppsala. Universitet. Kulturgeografiska Institutionen. Geografiska Regionstudier. Nr. 6)

- Tanzania

    SYRACUSE UNIVERSITY. Maxwell Graduate School of Citizenship and Public Affairs. Program of Eastern African Studies. Occasional Papers. No.29. Settlement patterns and rural development in Tanganyika...: (preliminary draft, etc.); by Nikos Georgulas. [Syracuse, N.Y.], 1967. fo. 40.

- Uganda

    LANGLANDS (B. W.) and OBOL-OWIT (L. E. C.) Essays on the settlement geography of east Acholi. Kampala, 1968. pp. 54. (Makerere University College. Department of Geography. Occasional Papers. No. 7)

- Ukraine

    AUERBACH (HANS) Die Besiedelung der Südukraine in den Jahren 1774-1787. Wiesbaden, Harrassowitz, 1965. pp. 136. bibliog. 24cm. (Osteuropa-Institut, München. Veröffentlichungen. Band 25)

- United Kingdom

    U.K. 1967. Ministry of Housing and Local Government. Settlement in the countryside: a planning method. (Planning Bulletins. 8) London, 1967. pp. 12. bibliog. 30cm. Maps in end pocket.

- United Kingdom - Wales

    JONES (PHILIP NICHOLAS) Colliery settlement in the South Wales coalfield, 1850-1926. [Hull], 1969. pp. 109. (Hull. University. Department of Geography. Occasional Papers in Geography. No. 14)

LAND SETTLEMENT (Cont'd.)

- United States

SUSQUEHANNAH COMPANY. The Susquehannah Company papers;...edited by Julian P. Boyd ([and] Robert J. Taylor); published for Wyoming Historical and Geological Society. Ithaca, 1930-71. 11 vols. Vols. 1-4 reprinted 1962. Maps in end pocket of vols. 1 and 2.

ROHRBOUGH (MALCOLM JUSTIN) The Land Office business: the settlement and administration of American public lands, 1789-1837. New York, O.U.P., 1968. pp.xiii, 331. bibliog. 22½cm.

SWIERENGA (ROBERT P.) Pioneers and profits: land speculation on the Iowa frontier. Ames, Iowa, 1968. pp. 260.

BURTON (IAN) and others. The human ecology of coastal flood hazard in megalopolis. Chicago, University of Chicago, Department of Geography, 1969. pp. xiv, 196. bibliog. 23cm. (Research Papers. No. 115)

- Zambia

NORTHERN RHODESIA. Department of Lands. 1925. Land for settlers. Livingstone, 1925. pp. 3.

LAND SUBDIVISION

- United States

THROWER (NORMAN JOSEPH WILLIAM) Original survey and land subdivision: a comparative study of the form and effect of contrasting cadastral surveys. Chicago, Rand McNally, [1966]. pp. xxii, 160. bibliog. 21½cm. (Association of American Geographers. Monograph Series. No. 4)

LAND TENURE

BRISTOL LEAGUE FOR SOCIAL REFORM BY LAND RESTORATION. War: a moral and economic analysis. [Bristol, 192-?]. pp. (4). 19cm.

HOWARD (W.H.) The land question and Christian justice: essays. Melbourne, [imprint], [1939?]. pp. 96.

BECKWITH (L.D.) Caution!: unless you can refute its argument, this book will change you greatly, you'll never again be the person you were. n.p., [1946]. unpaged.

VAZ FERREIRA (CARLOS) Sobre la propiedad de la tierra. Montevideo, 1953. pp. 375. (Biblioteca Artigas. Coleccion de Clasicos Uruguayos. vol.6.)

UNITED NATIONS. Department of Economic and Social Affairs. 1962- . Progress in land reform:... report, etc. New York, 1962 in progress.

FOOD AND AGRICULTURE ORGANIZATION. Rural Institutions Division. Land reform, land settlement and co-operatives. Rome, semi-annual, 1965 (no.1) to date. 28cm.

INTERNATIONAL SEMINAR ON LAND TAXATION, LAND TENURE, AND LAND REFORM IN DEVELOPING COUNTRIES, UNIVERSITY OF HARTFORD, 1966. [Proceedings]; editors Archibald M. Woodruff [and others]; sponsored by the John C. Lincoln Foundation, Phoenix, Arizona. West Hartford, University of Hartford, John C. Lincoln Institute, [1966]. pp. xiii, 598. 23cm.

MYRDAL (GUNNAR) Land reform in its broader economic and social setting: opening address at the second World Land Reform Conference, held at FAO Headquarters in Rome, June 20, 1966. Stockholm, 1966. fo. 26.

COLLOQUE INTERNATIONAL D'URBANISME, 2EME, TOULOUSE, 1967. Propriété et urbanisme; organisé du 14 au 18 avril 1967 par La Municipalité de Toulouse, l'Union Internationale des Architectes et l'Institut des Etudes juridiques de l'Urbanisme et de la Construction. Paris, 1968. pp. 278.

JACOBY (ERICH H.) Agrarian reconstruction. Rome, Food and Agriculture Organization, 1968. pp. 82. (Freedom from Hunger Campaign. Basic Studies. No. 18.)

WHETHAM (EDITH H.) Co-operation, land reform and land settlement: report on a survey in Kenya, Uganda, Sudan, Ghana, Nigeria and Iran. London, Plunkett Foundation for Co-operative Studies, 1968. pp. xiv, 79. 21½cm.

WARRINER (DOREEN) Land reform in principle and practice. Oxford, Clarendon P., 1969. pp. xx, 457. bibliog. 21½cm.

JACOBY (ERICH H.) Man and land: the fundamental issue in development;...in collaboration with Charlotte F. Jacoby. London, 1971. pp. 400. bibliog.

- Bibliography

FOOD AND AGRICULTURE ORGANIZATION. Documentation Center. 1971. Land reform: annotated bibliography; author and subject index; FAO publications and documents (1945-April 1970). (DC/Sp. 20) [Rome, 1971]. 1 vol. (various pagings). In various languages.

- Abyssinia

HUNTINGFORD (G.W.B.) ed. The land charters of northern Ethiopia. Addis Ababa, Haile Sellassie I University, Institute of Ethiopian Studies and the Faculty of Law, 1965. pp. xii, 132. bibliog. 24cm. (Monographs in Ethiopian Land Tenure. No.1)

MANN (HARBANS SINGH) Land tenure in Chore, Shoa: a pilot study. Addis Ababa, Haile Sellassie I University, Institute of Ethiopian Studies and the Faculty of Law, 1965. pp. 78. 24cm. (Monographs in Ethiopian Land Tenure. No.2)

PANKHURST (RICHARD KEIR PETHICK) State and land in Ethiopian history. Addis Ababa, Haile Sellassie I University, Institute of Ethiopian Studies and Faculty of Law, 1966. pp. vii, 211. 23½cm. (Monographs in Ethiopian Land Tenure. No. 3)

- Africa

MACHYO (B. CHANGO) Land ownership and economic progress. [London, 1963]. pp. 36. (Africana Study Group. Lumumba Memorial Publications)

- Africa - Law

MIFSUD (FRANK M.) Customary land law in Africa: with reference to legislation aimed at adjusting customary tenures to the needs of development. Rome, Food and Agriculture Organization, 1967. pp. 96. bibliog. (Legislative Series. No. 7)

- Africa, East - Law

MAINI (KRISHAN M.) Land law in East Africa. Nairobi Oxford U.P., 1967. pp. xvii, 270 21½cm.

- Africa, North

VERDIER (JEAN MAURICE) and others. Structures foncières et développement rural au Maghreb. Paris, 1969. pp. 165. (Paris. Université. Faculté de Droit et des Sciences Économiques. Travaux et Recherches. Série "Afrique". No. 4)

- Africa, Subsaharan

LEYS (NORMAN MACLEAN) Land law and policy in tropical Africa. London, 1922. pp. 16. (League of Nations Union. [Publications]. No. 94)

BACHELET (MICHEL) Systèmes fonciers et réformes agraires en Afrique noire. Paris, Pichon et Durand-Auzias, 1968. pp. xvi, 677. bibliog. 27cm.

SAUTTER (GILLES) Les structures agraires en Afrique tropicale. Paris, [1968]. pp. 267. bibliog.

- Africa, West - Law

KOUASSIGAN (GUY-ADJETE) L'homme et la terre: droits fonciers coutumiers et droit de propriété en Afrique occidentale. Paris, Office de la Recherche Scientifique et Technique Outre-Mer, 1966. pp. 283. bibliog. (L'Homme d'Outre-Mer. Nouvelle Série. No. 8.)

- America, Latin

SOCIEDAD, economia y reforma agraria; [by] Horacio C.E. Giberti [and others]. Buenos Aires, [1965]. pp. 127.

GARCIA (ANTONIO) Reforma agraria y economia empresarial en America Latina. [Santiago de Chile], Universitaria, 1967. pp. 305. bibliog. 18cm. (Colección Imagen de América Latina)

LÓPEZ DE SEBASTIÁN (JOSÉ) Reforma agraria y poder social. Madrid, 1968. pp. 190.

STAVENHAGEN (RODOLFO) ed. Agrarian problems and peasant movements in Latin America: [a selection of essays]. New York, 1970. pp. 583.

- Argentine Republic

FRIGERIO (REINALDO A.) Introduccion al estudio del problema agrario argentino. Buenos Aires, [1953]. pp. 168. bibliog.

[FRONDIZI (ARTURO) and others]. El problema agrario argentino. Buenos Aires, Editorial Desarrollo, 1965. pp. 159. 18cm.

GARCÍA (JOSÉ MARIA) El campo argentino y la reforma agraria. Buenos Aires, Calicanto, 1968. pp. 281. bibliog.

KOHEN (ALBERTO) Clases sociales y programas agrarios. [Buenos Aires], Quipo, [1968]. pp. 298. 19½cm.

- Argentine Republic - Law

HORNE (BERNARDINO C.) Politica agraria y regulacion eocnomica. Buenos Aires, 1942 repr. 1945. pp. 280.

- Assam

DUTTA (NARENDRA CHANDRA) Land problems and land reforms in Assam. Delhi, 1968. pp. 159. bibliog

- Australia

AUSTRALIA. 1963. Petition from certain people of Yirrkala relating to the excision of land from the Aboriginal Reserve in Arnhem Land. in Australia. Parliamentary papers, 1962-63, vol.7.

- Bessarabia

MALINSKII (V.) Agrarnaia "reforma" 1918-1924 gg. v Bessarabii; pdd redaktsiei...Grosul Ia.S. Kishinev, 1949. pp. 144.

- Bolivia

BOLIVIA. Subsecretaria de Prensa, Informaciones y Cultura. 1954. El libro blanco de la reforma agraria. La Paz, [1954]. pp. 180. Lacks pp. 19-22.

BELTRÁN ARANÍBAR (FAUSTO) and FERNÁNDEZ BUSTOS (JOSÉ) Dónde va la reforma agraria boliviana?: estudio critico. La Paz, 1960. pp. 225. 19cm.

PÉREZ PATON (ROBERTO) La reforma agraria en Bolivia : sus resultados. La Paz, Universidad Mayor de San Andrés, 1961.fo. 29 bibliog. 32 cm.

MONHEIM (FELIX) and KESSLER (ALBRECHT) Beiträge zur Landeskunde von Peru und Bolivien. Wiesbaden, 1968. pp. 89. bibliogs. (Geographische Zeitschrift. Beihefte. Erdkundliches Wissen. Heft 20)

- Bolivia - Law

HEATH (DWIGHT B.) and others. Land reform and social revolution in Bolivia. New York, 1969. pp. 464. bibliog.

- Botswana - Law

ROBERTS (SIMON) A restatement of the Kgatla law relating to land and natural resources. Gaborone, Government Printer, [1970]. pp. 33.

- Brazil

SIGAUD (GERALDO DE PROENÇA) Arcebispo de Diamantina, and others. Reforma agrária: questão de consciência. 4th ed. São Paulo, Vera Cruz, 1962. pp. xvii, 497. 23cm. (Coleção Tradição, Familia, Propriedade)

LAND TENURE - Brazil (Cont'd.)

SUND (MICHAEL) Land tenure and economic performance of agricultural establishments in Northeast Brazil. Madison, 1965. fo. 42. (Wisconsin University. Land Tenure Center. Research Papers. No. 17)

SCHILLING (PAULO R.) Brasil de los latifundistas. [Montevideo], 1967. pp. 175.

LUDWIG (ARMIN K.) and TAYLOR (HARRY W.) Brazil's new agrarian reform: an evaluation of its property classification and tax systems. New York, 1969. pp. 186. bibliog.

CLINE (WILLIAM R.) Economic consequences of a land reform in Brazil. Amsterdam, 1970. pp. 213. bibliog.

- Bulgaria

DOLINSKII (N. V.) Vŭprosi iz oblastta na bŭlgarskoto zemlevladenie. Varna, 1928. pp. 123.

TSANKOVA-PETKOVA (GENOVEVA) За аграрните отношения в средновековна България, XI-XIII в.; Sur les rapports agraires en Bulgarie au moyen âge, XI-XIIIe s. София, БАН, 1964. pp. 210. 20cm. With Russian and French summaries.

- Burma

BURMA. Revenue Department. 1936. Report on rural indebtedness in the Nyaunglebin East, Pegu and Thanatpin townships of the Pegu District. Rangoon, 1936. pp. 15.

- Buryat Republic

EGUNOV (NIKIFOR PETROVICH) Колониальная политика царизма и первый этап национального движения в Бурятии в эпоху империализма. Улан-Удэ, Бурятское Книжное Издательство, 1963. pp. 316. bibliog. 20cm.

- Cameroons

STOECKER (HELMUTH) ed. Kamerun unter deutscher Kolonialherrschaft: Studien. Berlin, 1960-68. 2 vols. 24cm. (Berlin. Humboldt-Universität. Institut für Allgemeine Geschichte. Schriftenreihe. Bände 5 and 12)

- Cameroons - Law

KRAUSS (HEINRICH) Die moderne Bodengesetzgebung in Kamerun 1884-1964. Berlin, Springer, 1966. pp. xii, 156. bibliog. 23cm. (IFO-Institut für Wirtschaftsforschung. Afrika-Studien. 12)

- Canada

GATES (LILLIAN F.) Land policies of Upper Canada. Canada, U. of Toronto P., [1968]. pp. ix, 378. bibliog. 24½cm. (Social Science Research Council of Canada. Canadian Studies in History and Government. No. 9)

- Caucasus

GIOEV (MIKHAIL IL'ICH) Bor'ba bol'shevikov Tereka za razreshenie agrarnogo voprosa v period pobedy sotsialisticheskoi revoliutsii i ustanovleniia Sovetskoi vlasti, mart 1917 - fevral' 1919 gg. Ordzhonikidze, 1966. pp. 175.

- Chile

AHUMADA CORVALÁN (JORGE) En vez de la miseria. 5th ed. Santiago de Chile, Editorial del Pacífico, 1965. pp. 190. 18cm.

INTER-AMERICAN COMMITTEE FOR AGRICULTURAL DEVELOPMENT. 1966. Chile: tenencia de la tierra y desarrollo socio-económico del sector agrícola. 2nd ed. [Washington?], 1966. pp. 405. bibliog.

ROGERS SOTOMAYOR (JORGE) Dos caminos para la reforma agraria en Chile, 1945-1965. Santiago de Chile, Orbe, 1966. pp. 342. 18cm.

OLIVARES (JOSÉ) Programación del uso de la tierra en una zona de reforma agraria. [Santiago de Chile], 1968. pp. 131. bibliog. (Santiago de Chile. Universidad de Chile. Instituto de Economia. Publicaciones. No. 107)

TENENCIA de la tierra y campesinado en Chile. Buenos Aires, 1968. pp. 186.

KIRBY (JOHN MALCOLM) The uplands of central Chile: the geographical implications of the ley de reforma agraria, No. 16640; [Ph.D. (London) thesis]. 1969. fo.286. bibliog. Typescript: unpublished. This thesis is the property of London University, and may not be removed from the Library.

KAY (CRISTOBAL) Comparative development of the European manorial system and the Latin American hacienda system: an approach to a theory of agrarian change for Chile. 1971. fo. 253. bibliog.

- China

TSENG (HSIAO) The theory and practice of land reform in the Republic of China. 2nd ed. Taipei, China Research Institute of Land Economics, 1968. pp. 143. 20½cm.

HSIAO (TSO-LIANG) The land revolution in China, 1930-1934: study of documents. Seattle, [1969?]. pp. 361. bibliog.

- Colombia

COLOMBIA. Ministerio de Agricultura. 1961. Reforma social agraria. [vol. 2]. Bogota, [1961]. pp. 154. Vol. 1 out of print.

INSTITUTO COLOMBIANO DE LA REFORMA AGRARIA. Oficina de Divulgacion. Segundo año de reforma agraria, 1963. [Bogota, 1964]. pp. 109.

AMAYO PULIDO (STELLA) El cooperativismo y la reforma agraria. Bogotá, 1965. pp. 79. bibliog. 24cm.

SALAZAR MORAN (JORGE A.) Régimen de la expropiación en Colombia. [Bogotá], 1965. pp. 110. bibliog. 23½cm.

QUIMBAYA (ANTEO) El problema de la tierra en Colombia. Bogota, 1967. pp. 239.

DUFF (ERNEST A.) Agrarian reform in Colombia. New York, Praeger, 1968. pp. xiii, 240. bibliog. 23½cm. (Praeger Special Studies in International Economics and Development)

- Colombia - Law

COLOMBIA. Statutes, etc. 1936. Ley 200 de 1.936, diciembre 30, sobre regimen de tierras. [Bogota, 1936?]. fo. 14.

INSTITUTO COLOMBIANO DE LA REFORMA AGRARIA. Oficina de Divulgacion. La reforma agraria. Bogotá, 1965. pp. 17. Tomado de la Carta Economica del Banco Cafatero, vol.II, No.2 de Marzo de 1.965. (Serie Divulgacion. No.29)

INSTITUTO COLOMBIANO DE LA REFORMA AGRARIA. Subgerencia Juridica. La expropiacion en el derecho Colombiano: la constitucionalidad de la Ley de Reforma Agraria: demanda, conceptos y sentencia de la Corte Suprema de Justicia del 11 de Diciembre de 1964. [Bogotá, 1965]. pp. 200. (Serie Juridica. No. 3)

- Cuba

DOCUMENTOS escogidos de la revolución cubana. Bogotá, Ediciones Paz y Socialismo, 1963. pp. 101. 20cm. (Colección Cuba Nueva. 1)

- Czechoslovakia

OTÁHAL (MILAN) Zápas o pozemkovou reformu v ČSR. Praha, ČSAV, 1963. pp. 265. bibliog. 21cm. With Russian summary.

- Czechoslovakia - Law

FÁBRY (VALER) Základní otázky československého pozemkového práva. Praha, 1967. pp. 525. bibliog. With German summary.

- Ecuador

ECUADOR. Junta Nacional de Planificacion y Coordinacion Economica. 1961. Memorandum que el gobierno del Ecuador presenta al Banco Interamericano de Desarrollo, etc. Quito, 1961. fo. ii, 70.

EISENLOHR (EDDA) Agrarreform in Ecuador im entwicklungspolitischen Kräftespiel. Dortmund, 1969. pp. 267. bibliog. (Kontaktprogramm zur Sozialwissenschaftlichen Forschung in Lateinamerika. Arbeitsunterlage zur Lateinamerikaforschung. 30/31)

- Egypt

MATHUR (SURESH CHANDRA) Report on agrarian reform in the United Arab Republic. Delhi, Manager of Publications, 1966. pp. 22.

EL-SHAGI (EL-SHAGI) Neuordnung der Bodennutzung in Ägypten: drei Fallstudien. München, [1969]. pp. 167. bibliog. (Ifo-Institut für Wirtschaftsforschung. Afrika-Studien. 36)

- Europe

TOWARD modern land policies: studies in the development of national policy toward land in selected countries; [sponsored by the Institute of Agricultura Economics and Policy, University of Padua]; Davis McEntire and Danilo Agostini, editors. Padua, [1970]. pp. 490. bibliogs.

- Fiji Islands

FRANCE (PETER) The charter of the land: custom and colonization in Fiji. Melbourne, 1969. pp. 229. bibliog.

- Formosa

FORMOSA (PROVINCIAL GOVERNMENT). 1961. Land reform in Taiwan. (Land Bureau) [Taipei], 1961. pp. 22. 26½cm.

KOO (ANTHONY Y.C.) The role of land reform in economic development: a case study of Taiwan. New York, Praeger, 1968. pp. xix, 197. bibliog. 23½cm. (Praeger Special Studies in International Economics and Development)

CHEUNG (STEVEN N.S.) The theory of share tenancy: with special application to Asian agriculture and the first phase of Taiwan land reform. Chicago, 1969. pp. 188. bibliog.

YANG (MARTIN M.C.) Socio-economic results of land reform in Taiwan. Honolulu, 1970. pp. 563. bibliog.

- France

PLAISSE (ANDRÉ) L'évolution de la structure agraire dans la Campagne du Neubourg. Paris, Mouton, 1964. pp. 126. bibliog. 24cm. (Paris. École Pratique des Hautes Études. Section des Sciences Économiques et Sociales. Cahiers des Études Rurales. 2) 24 colour slides in end-pocket.

CHADEFAUD (MICHEL) Evolution des structures agraires dans le canton de Verteillac. Bordeaux, 1965. pp. 99. (Bordeaux. Université. Faculté de Droit. Institut d'Economie Régionale du Sud-Ouest. Collection. 16. Tome 1)

- France - Law

BOBIN (GEORGES) Exploitation agricole et politique des structures. Paris, 1969. pp. 313. bibliog.

CHIANEA (GERARD) La condition juridique des terres en Dauphiné au 18e siècle, 1700-1789. Paris, 1969. pp. 368. bibliog. (Grenoble. Université. Centre de Recherche d'Histoire Economique, Sociale et Institutionnelle. Série Histoire Institutionnelle. vol. 2)

- Germany

KELLERMANN (BERNHARD) and others. Was sollen wir tun?; mit Diskussionsbeiträgen von Theodor Plievier [and others]. Berlin, 1946. pp. 48.

- Germany - Law

MUSSLER (HANS PETER) Die steuerliche Behandlung und betriebswirtschaftliche Bedeutung von Grundstückspacht und Erbbaurecht. München, 1967. pp. 227. bibliog.

OHLMER (HENNING) and WALPER (KARL HEINZ) Eine bessere Bodenverfassung - aber wie? Köln-Mülheim, [1969]. pp. 32. (Deutscher Verband für Wohnungswesen, Städtebau und Raumplanung. Kleine Schriften. 13)

LAND TENURE - Germany - Law (Cont'd.)

ERNST (WERNER) Bodenrecht: Fragen zur Neuordnung. Köln-Mülheim, [1970]. pp. 22. bibliog. (Deutscher Verband für Wohnungswesen, Städtebau und Raumplanung. Kleine Schriften. 22)

- Germany - Silesia

MEYER (WALDTRAUT) Gemeinde, Erbherrschaft und Staat im Rechtsleben des schlesischen Dorfes vom 16. bis 19. Jahrhundert; dargestellt auf Grund von Schöppenbüchern an Beispielen aus Nieder- und Oberschlesien. Würzburg, Holzner, 1967. pp. xvi, 196. bibliog. 23cm. (Historische Kommission für Schlesien. Quellen und Darstellungen zur Schlesischen Geschichte. 12. Band)

- Germany, Eastern

GROSS (REINER) Die bürgerliche Agrarreform in Sachsen in der ersten Hälfte des 19. Jahrhunderts. Weimar, 1968. pp. 245. bibliog. (Dresden. Staatsarchiv. Schriftenreihe. Band 8)

- Greece

LONGNON (JEAN) and TOPPING (PETER W.) eds. Documents sur le régime des terres dans la principauté de Morée au 14e siècle. Paris, 1969. pp. 326. (Paris. Ecole Pratique des Hautes Etudes. Section des Sciences Economiques et Sociales. Documents et Recherches sur l'Economie des Pays Byzantins, Islamiques et Slaves et leurs Relations Commerciales au Moyen Age. 9)

- Hawaiian Islands - Law

HAWAII. Statutes, etc. 1895. Land Act, 1895. Honolulu, 1895. pp. 47. 21½cm.

- India

NARAYAN (JAYAPRAKASH) A picture of Sarvodaya social order. 4th ed. Tanjore. [1957]. pp. 139.

INDIA. Planning Commission. 1963. Progress of land reform. Delhi, 1963. pp. 276.

UNITED STATES. Agriculture Department. Economic Research Service. ERS-Foreign. 82. Land reform in western India. [Washington], 1964. pp. ii, 46.

LADEJINSKY (WOLF) A study on tenurial conditions in package districts. [Delhi, 1965]. pp. 59.

INDIA. National Development Council. Land Reforms Implementation Committee. 1966. Implementation of land reforms: a review. New Delhi, 1966. pp. 283.

SEMINAR ON LAND REFORMS, NEW DELHI, 1966. Proceedings and papers. Delhi, 1966. pp. 231. (India. Planning Commission. Socio-Economic Research Division. SER Publications. Seminar Series. No. 1.)

SIRCAR (DINES CHANDRA) ed. Land system and feudalism in ancient India. Calcutta, University, Centre of Advanced Study in Ancient Indian History and Culture, 1966. pp. (iii), 140. 21½cm. (Lectures and Seminars. No. 1-B)

MORELAND (WILLIAM HARRISON) The agrarian system of moslem India: a historical essay with appendices. 2nd ed. Delhi, 1968. pp. 296. bibliog.

FRYKENBERG (ROBERT ERIC) ed. Land control and social structure in Indian history. Madison, 1969. pp. 256.

PATEL (GOVINDLAL DALSUKHBAI) The land systems of union territories of India. Anand, 1970. pp. 578.

- India - Bengal, West - Law

WEST BENGAL. Statutes, etc. 1955-59. The West Bengal Land Reforms Act, 1955, as modified up to the 1st July, 1959. Alipore, 1959. pp. ii, 23. 24½cm.

- India - Kerala

VARGHESE (T.C.) Agrarian change and economic consequences: land tenures in Kerala, 1850-1960. Bombay, 1970. pp. 275. bibliog.

- India - Orissa

JENA (KRISHNACHANDRA) Land revenue administration in Orissa during the nineteenth century. Delhi, 1968. pp. 249. bibliog.

- India - Uttar Pradesh - Law

UTTAR PRADESH. Statutes, etc. 1956. The Uttar Pradesh Urban Areas Zamindari Abolition and Land Reforms Act, 1956. [Allahabad], 1957. pp. 29. 24½cm.

- Iran

GHARATCHEHDAGHI (CYRUS) Distribution of land in Varamin: an opening phase of the agrarian reform in Iran. Opladen, Leske, 1967. pp. 179. bibliog. 24cm. (Deutsches Orient-Institut. Schriften. Materialien und Dokumente)

LAMBTON (ANN KATHERINE SWYNFORD) The Persian land reform, 1962-1966. Oxford, 1969. pp. 386.

- Iraq

BAALI (FUAD) Relation of the people to the land in southern Iraq. Gainesville, University of Florida Press, 1966. pp. (vii), 64. 23cm. (Florida University. Monographs. Social Sciences No. 31)

- Iraq - Law

IRAQ. Statutes, etc. 1958. Agrarian reform law, no. 30 of 1958. Baghdad, 1959. pp. 13.

- Italy

BOTTERI (TULLIO) Le cooperative nella riforma fondiaria italiana. Roma, La Rivista della Cooperazione, 1961. pp. xv, 333. 24½cm. (Italy. Direzione Generale della Cooperazione. Biblioteca de "La Rivista della Cooperazione")

[ITALY. Direzione Generale della Bonifica e della Colonizzazione.] 1962. Land reform in Italy. Rome, 1962. pp. 27. 22½cm.

ITALY. Ministero dell' Agricoltura e delle Foreste. Ente Maremma. 1962. Objectives and achievements (of the land reform in the Maremma in Tuscany and Latium), 1951-1961. Rome, 1962. pp. 28. 24½cm.

ASSANTE (FRANCA) Calopezzati: proprietà fondiaria e classi rurali in un comune della Calabria, 1740-1886. Napoli, [1964] repr. 1969. pp. 142. bibliog. (Naples. Università. Istituto di Storia Economica e Sociale. Biblioteca degli Annali. 8)

ITALY. 1964. Land reform. (Ministry of Agriculture and Forestry). [Rome, 1964?]. pp. 44.

ITALY. Direzione Generale della Bonifica e della Colonizzazione. Quaderni di Studio e d'Informazione. 9. Strutture e servizi per lo sviluppo produttivistico delle campagne: realizzati o promossi dagli enti di riforma fondiaria. [Rome, 1964?].

RETZLAFF (CHRISTINE) Kulturgeographische Wandlungen in der Maremma unter besonderer Berücksichtigung der italienischen Bodenreform nach dem Zweiten Weltkrieg. Kiel, Universität, Geographisches Institut, 1967. pp. 204. bibliog. 24cm. (Schriften. Band 27. Heft 2)

BANDINI (MARIO) and GUERRIERI (GIUSEPPE) Istituzioni di economia e politica agraria. Bologna, Edizioni Agricole, [1968]. pp. x, 516. bibliog. 23cm.

DAVIS (JOHN HORSLEY RUSSELL) Land tenure and social change in a South Italian town; [Ph. D. (London) thesis]. 1968. fo. vi, 284. bibliog. 25½cm. Map in end pocket. Typescript: unpublished. This thesis is the property of London University and may not be removed from the Library.

COLCLOUGH (NEVILLE THOMAS) Land, politics and power in a southern Italian village; [Ph.D. (London) thesis]. 1969. fo. 222. bibliog. Typescript: unpublished. This thesis is the property of London University and may not be removed from the Library.

KING (RUSSELL) Land reform in theory and practice: a geographical case study of Italy; [Ph.D.(London) thesis]. 1970. fo.506. bibliog. Typescript: unpublished. This thesis is the property of London University and may not be removed from the Library.

- Jamaica

NORRIS (KATRIN) Law and custom in Jamaica: a conflict between two systems of family responsibility and land-inheritance. 1964. fo. (ii), 120. bibliog. Typescript. Thesis for Diploma in Anthropology (London): unpublished.

- Kenya

KENYA. Sessional Papers. 1959/60. No. 6. Land tenure and control outside the native lands. Nairobi, 1960. pp. 8.

- Kenya - Law

MUNRO (A. P.) Land law in Kenya. in Hutchison (Thomas W.) and others, eds. Africa and law: developing legal systems in African Commonwealth nations. Madison, 1968.

- Kirghizia

PLOSKIKH (VLADIMIR MIKHAILOVICH) Очерк земельных отношений в Южной Киргизии накануне вхождения в состав России. Фрунзе, 1965. pp. 61. bibliog.

BUDIANSKII (DAVID MIRONOVICH) Zemel'no-vodnaia reforma v Iuzhnoi Kirgizii, 1927-1928 gg. Frunze, 1968. pp. 170.

- Kokand Khanate

TROITSKAIA (ANNA LEONIDOVNA) Materialy po istorii kokandskogo khanstva XIX v.: po dokumentam arkhiva kokandskikh khanov. Moskva, 1969. pp. 154.

- Latvia

HANCHETT (W. S.) The communists and the Latvian countryside, 1919-1949. in Sprudzs (Adolf) and Rusis (Armins) eds. Res baltica. Leyden, 1968.

- Libya

FOOD AND AGRICULTURE ORGANIZATION. Funds in Trust. 1969. Report to the government of Libya on development of tribal lands and settlements project. (FAO/LIB/TF/20). Rome, 1969. 4 vols.

- Luxembourg - Law

FISCHBACH (MARCEL) Reformnotwendigkeit des Bauern-Erbrechtes in Luxemburg. Luxemburg, 1941. pp. 150. bibliog.

- Malawi

CHIPETA (W.) Land tenure and problems in Malawi. Blantyre, [1971]. pp. 10. (Reprinted from the Society of Malawi Journal, January 1971, vol.24, no. 1)

- Mexico

BARBA GONZALEZ (SILVANO) La lucha por la tierra. Mexico, 1956-64. 4 vols.

VILLALPANDO R. (ABELARDO) El problema del indio y la reforma agraria. Potosi, Universidad Tomás Frias, Departamento de Cultura, 1960. pp. (vii), 162. 19cm.

ROMERO ESPINOSA (EMILIO) La reforma agraria en México a médio siglo de iniciada. México, Cuadernos Americanos, 1963. pp. 161. bibliog. 21cm.

FRIEDRICH (JUERGEN) Die Agrarreform in Mexiko: Bedeutung und Verbreitung des Ejido-Systems in den wichtigsten Anbaugebieten des Landes. [Erlangen], Universität, Wirtschafts- und Sozialgeographisches Institut, 1968. pp. viii, 236, ix-xix. bibliog. 20½cm. (Nürnberger Wirtschafts- und Sozialgeographische Arbeiten. Band 7)

GONZÁLEZ NAVARRO (MOISÉS) La confederación nacional campesina: un grupo de presión en la reforma agraria mexicana. México, 1968. pp. 335. bibliog.

TELLO (CARLOS) La tenencia de la tierra en México. México, Instituto de Investigaciones Sociales, 1968. pp. 143.

ADLER (JUDITH) The politics of land reform in Mexico, with special reference to the Comarca Lagunera, 1935-1967; [M.Phil. (London) thesis]. 1970. fo. 246. bibliog. Typescript: unpublished. This thesis is the property of London University and may not be removed from the Library.

LAND TENURE - Mexico (Cont'd.)

FRIEDRICH (PAUL WILLIAM) Agrarian revolt in a Mexican village. Englewood Cliffs, [1970]. pp. 158. bibliog.

TOWARD modern land policies: studies in the development of national policy toward land in selected countries; [sponsored by the Institute of Agricultural Economics and Policy, University of Padua]; Davis McEntire and Danilo Agostini, editors. Padua, [1970]. pp. 490. bibliogs.

- Mexico - Law

FABILA (MANUEL) Cinco siglos de legislación agraria, 1493-1940. vol. 1. México, 1941. pp. 800. bibliog. No more published?

CHAVEZ PADRON DE VELAZQUEZ (MARTHA) El derecho agrario en Mexico. 2nd ed. Mexico, 1970. pp. 409.

- Moldavian Republic

ITKIS (M. B.) Крестьянское движение в Молдавии в 1917 году и претворение в жизнь ленинского декрета о земле; под редакцией., И. И. Минца. Кишнев, 1970. pp. 299.

- Nepal

REGMI (MAHESH CHANDRA) Land tenure and taxation in Nepal. Berkeley, 1963-8. 4 vols. bibliogs. 23½cm. (California University. Institute of International Studies. Research Series. Nos. 3,4,8,12)

CAPLAN (LIONEL) Land and social change in East Nepal: a study of Hindu-tribal relations. London, 1970. pp. 224. bibliog.

- Netherlands

FOCKEMA ANDREAE (S. J.) Grondeigenaars en grondgebruikers in een hoekje van Holland. in Studiekring voor de Geschiedenis van de Landbouw. Agronomisch-Historische Bijdragen. 6. Ceres en Clio. Wageningen, 1964.

- New Zealand

PEOPLE'S VOICE. Government plans the last big grab of Maori land, and in the process exposes 'capital democracy'; [reprint of articles]. n.p., 1968. pp. 7.

- Nicaragua

NICARAGUA. Statutes, etc. 1963. Ley de reforma agraria. Managua, 1963. pp. 881-904. Gaceta: diario oficial. año 67, no. 85.

- Nigeria

NIGERIA (WESTERN REGION). 1956. Land tenure in Ijebu province; by C.W. Rowling. Ibadan, 1956. pp. 67.

AHMADU BELLO UNIVERSITY. Institute of Administration. Traditional land tenure surveys [in northern Nigeria]. [Zaria, the Institute, 1965 in progress]. 32cm.

- Niue Island

NEW ZEALAND. Department of Maori and Islands Affairs, 1968. Report on land tenure in Niue. Wellington, 1968. pp. 14.

- Pakistan, West

WEST PAKISTAN. Land Reforms Commission. 1959. Report. Lahore, 1959. pp. iii,74,ix,12.

BERINGER (CHRISTOPH) and HADI (ABDUL) Land fragmentation and size of agricultural holdings in the former North-West Frontier Province of West Pakistan. Peshawar, University, Board of Economic Enquiry, 1962. pp. x, 47. 24cm. (Publications. No.8)

· Peru

SANCHEZ (LUIS ALBERTO) El Peru: retrato de un pais adolescente. 2nd ed. Lima, Universidad Nacional Mayor de San Marco, 1963. pp. 254. 21cm.

HEYSEN (LUIS E.) Fundamentos sociologicos del desarrollo regional: la reforma agraria en función del desarrollo integral de los pueblos. 3rd ed. Lima, Nuevo Dia, 1964. pp. 36. 24cm.

MAC-LEAN Y ESTENOS (ROBERTO) La reforma agraria en el Peru. Mexico, Universidad Nacional Autonoma de Mexico, Instituto de Investigaciones Sociales, Biblioteca de Ensayos Sociologicos, 1965. pp. 266.

INTER-AMERICAN COMMITTEE FOR AGRICULTURAL DEVELOPMENT. 1966. Tenencia de la tierra y desarrollo socio-económico del sector agrícola: Peru. Washington, Organization of American States, 1966. pp. 496. bibliog.

THORBECKE (ERIK) Some notes on the macroeconomic implications of and the cost of financing agrarian reform in Peru. Ames, 1966. pp. 7. (Iowa State University of Science and Technology. Department of Economics and Sociology. International Studies in Economics. Monographs. No. 3)

FAVRE (HENRY) and others. La hacienda en el Perú. Lima, Instituto de Estudios Peruanos, 1967. pp. 235-395. 24½cm. (Separata de la Revista del Museo Nacional, tomo 33, 1964)

VILLANUEVA (VICTOR) Hugo Blanco y la rebelion campesina. Lima, 1967. pp. 197.

MONHEIM (FELIX) and KESSLER (ALBRECHT) Beiträge zur Landeskunde von Peru und Bolivien. Wiesbaden, 1968. pp. 89. bibliogs. (Geographische Zeitschrift. Beihefte. Erdkundliches Wissen. Heft 20)

HARGOUS (SABINE) Les oubliés des Andes. Paris, 1969. pp. 120. bibliog.

- Peru - Law

PERU. Statutes, etc. Reglamentación de la reforma agraria en el Perú...; (edición preparada por Gregorio Rueda Sánchez). Lima, Editorial "Thesis", 1965 in progress. 16½cm.

- Poland

> ĆWIEK (ZBIGNIEW) Z dziejów wsi koronnej XVII wieku. Warszawa, Państwowe Wydawnictwo Naukowe, 1966. pp. 271. bibliog. 24cm.
>
> GRONIOWSKI (KRZYSZTOF) Kwestia agrarna w Królestwie Polskim 1871-1914. Warszawa, Państwowe Wydawnictwo Naukowe, 1966. pp. 267. bibliog. 23½cm.

- Poland - Law

> GRABOŃ (WŁADYSŁAW) and PAKIER (MAURYCY) Gospodarka terenami w miastach i osiedlach: przepisy i objaśnienia; stan prawny na dzień 1.I.1967 r. Warszawa, Wydawnictwo Prawnicze, 1967. pp. 180. 21cm.

- Poland - Silesia

> MEYER (WALDTRAUT) Gemeinde, Erbherrschaft und Staat im Rechtsleben des schlesischen Dorfes vom 16. bis 19. Jahrhundert; dargestellt auf Grund von Schöppenbüchern an Beispielen aus Nieder- und Oberschlesien. Würzburg, Holzner, 1967. pp. xvi, 196. bibliog. 23cm. (Historische Kommission für Schlesien. Quellen und Darstellungen zur Schlesischen Geschichte. 12. Band)

- Polynesia

> PANOFF (MICHEL) Les structures agraires en Polynésie française: rapport d'une mission effectuée dans le cadre de la Recherche Scientifique et Technique d'Outre-Mer 1961-1963. [Paris], École Pratique des Hautes Études, Centre Documentaire pour l'Océanie, (Rapports et Documents.1) 1964. pp. 147. bibliog. 26½cm.

- Portugal

> CUNHAL (ALVARO) A questão agrária em Portugal. Rio de Janeiro, 1968. pp. 393.

- Puerto Rico

> VILLAR ROCES (MARIO) Puerto Rico y su reforma agraria. Rio Piedras, Edil, 1968. pp. 196. bibliog. 21½cm.

- Rhodesia

> SOUTHERN RHODESIA. Native Land Board. Report. Salisbury, annual, 1932/3-1935/6. 33cm.
>
> SOUTHERN RHODESIA. 1959. First report of the select committee on resettlement of natives etc: [H.J. Quinton, chairman]. (L.A.S.C.4-1959) Salisbury, 1959. pp. 25.
>
> SOUTHERN RHODESIA. 1960. Second report of the select committee on resettlement of natives, etc: [H.J. Quinton, chairman]. (L.A.S.C. 3-1960) Salisbury, 1960. pp. (iii), 116. Maps in end pocket. For first report see SOUTHERN RHODESIA. 1959. First report, etc.
>
> PALMER (R.H.) Aspects of Rhodesian land policy, 1890-1936. Salisbury, 1968. pp. 54. (Central Africa Historical Association. Local Series. No. 22)

- Roumania

> ADANILOAIE (N.) La réforme agraire de 1864 reflétée dans l'historiographie roumaine. in Comité National des Historiens de la République Socialiste de Roumanie. Nouvelles études d'histoire. Bucarest, 1965.

- Russia

> SHKREDOV (VLADIMIR PETROVICH) Sotsialisticheskaia zemel'naia sobstvennost'. Moskva, 1967. pp. 152.
>
> VESELOVSKII (STEPAN BORISOVICH) Исследования по истории класса служилых землевладельцев; (под редакцией... В. И. Шункова и... С. М. Каштанова) Москва, 1969. pp. 582. bibliog.
>
> FRENCH (R. ANTONY) and SMITH (ROBERT ERNEST FREDERICK) The terminology of settlements and their lands in late medieval Russia. Birmingham, 1970. pp. 69. (Birmingham. University. Centre for Russian and East European Studies. Discussion Papers. Series RC/D. No. 7)
>
> LENINSKII dekret "O zemle" i sovremennost? Moskva, 1970. pp. 384.
>
> PODOLINSKY (SERGEJ SERGEJEWITSCH VON) Russland vor der Revolution: die agrarsoziale Lage und Reformen;... herausgegeben von Arnold Harttung. Berlin, [1971]. pp. 239. bibliog.

- Russia - Law

> SEREDA (IVAN EMEL'IANOVICH) Pravo priusadebnogo zemlepol'zovaniia kolkhoznogo dvora. Moskva, 1964. pp. 59.
>
> BOGOLEPOV (RUSLAN DMITRIEVICH) and others. Sovetskoe zemel'noe pravo: uchebnik dlia srednikh iuridicheskikh shkol. Moskva, 1965. pp. 240.
>
> SAKHAROV (PETR DMITRIEVICH) Землеустроительный процесс в СССР. Москва, Юридическая Литература, 1968. pp. 158. 20см.
>
> PRAVOVOE... Правовое обеспечение рационального использования земли в СССР. Москва, 1969. pp. 215.
>
> ZHARIKOV (IURII GEORGIEVICH) Pravo sel'skokhoziaistvennogo zemlepol'zovaniia. Moskva, 1969. pp. 196.

- Russia - Siberia - Law

> PRUDNIKOVA (Т. Р.) Подготовка землеустроительного законодательства для Западной Сибири, 60-90 годы XIX века: доклад на итоговой научной конференции профессорско-преподавательского состава. Новосибирск, 1967. pp. 29.

- Sicily

> FORTUNATI (PAOLO) Aspetti sociali dell'assalto al latifondo. Roma, I.N.C.F., [1941]. pp. 64. 22cm. (Istituto Nazionale Fascista di Cultura. Quaderni. Serie 11. No. 3)

LAND TENURE (Cont'd.)

- Sicily - Law

SICILY. Statutes, etc. 1950. Riforma agraria in Sicilia: legge approvata dalla Assemblea Regionale nella seduta del 21.11.1950. Palermo, 1950. pp. 61. 20cm.

SANTORO (RAIMONDO) La riforma agraria in Sicilia: aspetti giuridici. Palermo, [1958]. pp. 64. 24½cm.

LAZZARA (CARMELO) I rapporti agrari consuetudinari in Sicilia nell'attuale momento legislativo. Milano, 1969. pp. 199. (Catania. Università. Facoltà di Giurisprudenza. Pubblicazioni. 64)

- South Africa

CAPE OF GOOD HOPE. Parliament. House of Assembly. Select Committee on Granting Lands in Freehold to Hottentots. 1854-56. Report; (with Minutes of evidence). Cape Town, 1854-56. 2 pts. (in 1).

SOUTH AFRICA. Commission of Inquiry into European Occupancy of the Rural Areas. 1960. Report. [François Jacobus Du Toit, chairman] Pretoria, [1960]. pp. vi, 64. bibliog. 33cm.

SOUTH AFRICA. Department of Agricultural Credit and Land Tenure. Annual report. 1966/1968 [1st] to date included in SOUTH AFRICA. Parliament. House of Assembly. Votes and proceedings; (with Printed annexures).

SOUTH AFRICA. Parliament. House of Assembly. Select Committee on the Subject of the Removal of Restrictions Bill. 1967. Report...(with Proceedings) (S.C. 7-'67) in SOUTH AFRICA. Parliament. House of Assembly. Select Committee Reports.

- South West Africa

HORRELL (MURIEL) South-west Africa. Johannesburg, South African Institute of Race Relations. 1967. pp. iii, 94. 21½cm.

- Spain

CAMPOS NORDMANN (RAMIRO) Estructura agraria de España: estudio sobre los elementos y relaciones que la caracterizan. Madrid, Zyx, 1967. pp. 319. 20cm. (Biblioteca Promoción del Pueblo. 18)

LÓPEZ DE SEBASTIAN (JOSÉ) Reforma agraria en España: Sierra Morena en el S[iglo] 18. Madrid, Zyx, [1968]. pp. 231. 20cm. (Biblioteca Promoción del Pueblo. 23)

LÓPEZ DE SEBASTIAN (JOSÉ) Reforma agraria y poder social. Madrid, 1968. pp. 190.

MALEFAKIS (EDWARD E.) Agrarian reform and peasant revolution in Spain: origins of the Civil War. New Haven, 1970. pp. 469. bibliog.

MARTINEZ ALIER (JUAN) Labourers and landowners in southern Spain. London, 1971. pp. 352. bibliog. (Oxford. University. St. Antony's College. Publications. No. 4)

- Switzerland - Law

WINTERBERGER (GERHARD) Bodenrecht und Landesplanung. Zürich, [1966?]. pp. 11. (Wirtschaftsförderung: Gesellschaft zur Förderung der schweizerischen Wirtschaft. Stimmen zur Staats- und Wirtschaftspolitik. 36)(Sonderdruck aus Schweizer Monatshefte, Heft 5, 1966)

SIEBER (HUGO) Bodenpolitik und Bodenrecht. Bern, [1970]. pp. 214. bibliog.

- Tanzania

McKAY (JOHN) Planning for development: a review of studies of traditional rural settlement in Tanzania. Dar Es Salaam, [1967]. pp. 34. bibliog. (Dar Es Salaam. University College. Bureau of Resource Assessment and Land Use Planning. Research Notes. No. 2)

NELSON (ANTON) The freemen of Meru. Nairobi, O.U.P., 1967. pp. xii, 227. bibliog. 21 cm.

- Uganda - Bibliography

UGANDA. Ministry of Land Tenure. 1957. Bibliography of land tenure. [Entebbe], 1957. pp. (iv), 57. 33cm.

- Ukraine

SVEZHYNS'KYI (PETRO VOLODYMYROVYCH) Ahrarni vidnosyny na Zakhidnii Ukraïni v kintsi XIX - na pochatku XX st. L'viv, 1966. pp. 191.

- United Kingdom

BRADLAUGH (CHARLES) The land, the people and the coming struggle. 4th ed. London, [imprint], n.d. pp. 16. 17½cm.

VERINDER (FREDERICK) Land for the landless: Spence and Spence's plan, 1775; inter neo-Spencean appendix, 1896;...compiled by J. Morrison Davidson. London, 1896. pp. 19.

SLATER (J.) The land question: a lecture, etc. Belper, 1898. pp. 14.

PETAVEL (JAMES WILLIAM) Decentralisation or protection?: to end Great Britain's perils. London, [1902]. pp. 15. (Reprint, with notes and appendices, of an article in The Reformer, May, 1902)

COUNTRY LANDOWNERS' ASSOCIATION. Rules of the Association. London, 1924. pp. 14.

OXFORD. Oxford Historical Society. [Publications]. New Series. vols. 14 and 20. Survey of Oxford; by the late Rev. H.E. Salter; edited by W.A. Pantin and W.T. Mitchell. Oxford, Clarendon Press, 1960-69. 2 vols. 22cm.

CLAYTON (DAVID) of Reading University, and others. Capital taxation and land ownership in England and Wales: a preliminary assessment. Reading, University of Reading, Agricultural Economics Department, 1967. pp. (iii), 43. 25½cm. (Miscellaneous Studies. No. 44)

NEWMAN (W. L.) The land-laws. in Guttsman (Wilhelm Leo) ed. A plea for democracy. London, 1967.

WAITES (BRYAN) Moorland and vale-land farming in north-east Yorkshire: the monastic contribution in the thirteenth and fourteenth centuries. York, St. Anthony's P., 1967. pp. (ii), 35. 21½cm. (York. University. Borthwick Institute of Historical Research. Borthwick Papers. No. 32)

POSTAN (M.M.) Chronology of labour services. rev. ed. in vol. 1 of Minchinton (Walter Edward) ed. Essays in agrarian history...; reprints, etc. Newton Abbot, [1968].

SUTHERLAND (DOUGLAS) The landowners. London, Blond, 1968. pp. x, 180. bibliog. 23cm.

YOUINGS (J.A.) The terms of the disposal of the Devon monastic lands, 1536-58; ([with Postscript). in vol. 1 of Minchinton (Walter Edward) ed. Essays in agrarian history...; reprints, etc. Newton Abbot, [1968].

SMITH (R.B.) Land and politics in the England of Henry VIII: the West Riding of Yorkshire: 1530-46. Oxford, 1970. pp. 318.

- United Kingdom - Law

WELLS (Sir HENRY WESTON) The Land Commission and the legal profession. [London], The Law Society, [1967?]. pp. 30. 21cm.

HAWKINS (A.J.) Law relating to owners and occupiers of land. London, 1971. pp. 260.

- United Kingdom - Ireland

CANNON (WILLIAM J.) Outline of a plan for the relief and improvement of Ireland. London, Mann, 1849. pp. 12. 20½cm.

NULTY (THOMAS) Back to the land. Melbourne, 1939. pp. 64.

EIRE. Irish Manuscripts Commission. 1967. Books of Survey and Distribution: being abstracts of various surveys and instruments of title, 1636-1703: vol. IV, County of Clare reproduced from the manuscript in the Public Record Office of Ireland;...introductions by R.C. Simington; index...by Breandan Mac Giolla Choille. Dublin, 1967. pp. xlviii, 609. 27cm. x 38cm. 2 maps in end-pocket.

HILL (F. H.) Ireland. in Guttsman (Wilhelm Leo) ed. A plea for democracy. London, 1967.

- United States

TREAT (PAYSON JACKSON) The national land system, 1785-1820; [reprint of the work originally published in 1910]. New York, Russell, 1967. pp. xv, 426. bibliog. 21½cm.

BLESER (CAROL K. ROTHROCK) The promised land: a history of the South Carolina Land Commission, 1869-1890. Columbia, S.C. 1969. pp. 189. bibliog. (South Carolina Tricentennial Commission, Tricentennial Studies. No. 1.)

- Uruguay

PORTA (ELISEO SALVADOR) Uruguay: realidad y reforma agraria. 2nd ed. Montevideo, Ediciones de la Banda Oriental, 1964. pp. 79. 16½cm. (Ediciones de la Banda Oriental.

TORRE (NELSON DE LA) and others. La revolucion agraria artiguista, 1815-1816; etc. Montevideo, 1969. pp. 444.

- Uzbekistan - Law

DZHALILOV (I.) Vozniknovenie i razvitie sovetskogo zemel'nogo prava v Uzbekistane. Tashkent, 1970. pp. 272. bibliog.

- Venezuela

PLAZA (SALVADOR DE LA) Reforma agraria en Venezuela: objetivos y evaluacion. Caracas, Universidad Central de Venezuela, 1964. pp. 73. 16cm.

MARQUEZ (POMPEYO) Imperialismo, dependencia, latifundismo. [Caracas], 1968. pp. 258.

La OBRA Pía de Chuao, 1568-1825; estudios introductorios Eduardo Arcila Farias [and others]; compiladores, Carlos Salazar [and others]. Caracas, Universidad Central de Venezuela, 1968 in progress. 23cm.

REFORMA agraria venezolana: concepcion, evaluacion y perspectivas; [a forum held as part of a project of the Universidad Central de Venezuela]; ponentes Salvador de la Plaza [and others]. [Caracas], 1968. pp. 302. (Caracas. Universidad Central de Venezuela. Coleccion Foros y Seminarios. Serie Foros. 3)

- Venezuela - Law

LOSADA ALDANA (RAMON) Venezuela: latifundio y subdesarrollo; estudio sociojuridico sobre la cuestion agraria venezolana. Caracas, 1969. pp. 283. bibliog. (Caracas. Universidad Central de Venezuela. Direccion de Cultura. Coleccion Humanismo y Ciencia. 7)

- Vietnam

VIET-NAM (REPUBLIC). Secretariat of State for Land Property and Agrarian Reform. 1960. Land reform program before 1954 and land reform program and achievements since July 1954. [Saigon, 1960?] fo. 48.

- Zanzibar

ZANZIBAR. 1956. Report on the inquiry into claims to certain land at or near Ngezi, Vitongoji, in the Mudiria of Chake Chake, in the district of Pemba; by Sir John Gray. Zanzibar, 1956. pp. 54.

LAND TITLES

- Registration and transfer - Germany

MEYER (WALDTRAUT) Gemeinde, Erbherrschaft und Staat im Rechtsleben des schlesischen Dorfes vom 16. bis 19. Jahrhundert; dargestellt auf Grund von Schöppenbüchern an Beispielen aus Nieder- und Oberschlesien. Würzburg, Holzner, 1967. pp. xvi, 196. bibliog. 23cm. (Historische Kommission für Schlesien. Quellen und Darstellungen zur Schlesischen Geschichte. 12. Band)

- Registration and transfer - Ireland (Republic)

EIRE. Statutes, etc. 1964. Registration of Title bill, 1963, as passed by both Houses of the Oireachtas and enacted as the Registration of Title Act, 1964: explanatory memorandum. [Dublin, 1967]. pp. 40. 25cm.

LAND TENURE (Cont'd.)

- Registration and transfer - Mauritius

MAURITIUS. Legislative Council. Sessional Papers. 1961. No. 4. Report on matters concerning the registration of title to land and the cadastral map of Mauritius; by L. S. Himely. Port Louis, 1961. pp. (iii), 65. 33cm.

- Registration and transfer - Nigeria

NIGERIA. 1957. A report on the registration of title to land in Lagos; by S. Rowton Simpson. Lagos, 1957. pp. 45.

- Registration and transfer - Poland

MEYER (WALDTRAUT) Gemeinde, Erbherrschaft und Staat im Rechtsleben des schlesischen Dorfes vom 16. bis 19. Jahrhundert; dargestellt auf Grund von Schöppenbüchern an Beispielen aus Nieder- und Oberschlesien. Würzburg, Holzner, 1967. pp. xvi, 196. bibliog. 23cm. (Historische Kommission für Schlesien. Quellen und Darstellungen zur Schlesischen Geschichte. 12. Band)

- Registration and transfer - South Africa

SOUTH AFRICA. Parliament. House of Assembly. Select Committee on the Registration of Sectional Titles Bill. 1969. Report...(with Proceedings and Minutes of Evidence)(S.C. 7-69) in South Africa. Parliament. House of Assembly. Select Committee Reports.

SOUTH AFRICA. Commission of Inquiry into the Registration of Sectional Titles Bill. Report: [Chairman, J.H. Visse] (R.P.27/1971). in South Africa. Parliament. House of Assembly. Votes and proceedings; (with Printed annexures).

- Registration and transfer - Tanzania

UNITED REPUBLIC OF TANZANIA. Land Registry Division. Annual report. a., 1968- [Dar es Salaam].

- Registration and transfer - United Kingdom

LAND UNION. The Land Union's latest test case: the King v. the Ministry of Health. London, 1920]. pp. 4. 12½cm.

THOMPSON (F.M.L.) **The land market in the nineteenth century; [first published 1957]. in vol. 2 of Minchinton (Walter Edward) ed. Essays in agrarian history...; reprints, etc. Newton Abbot, [1968].**

U.K. Land Registry. 1968. Registration of title to land. London, 1968. pp. 20. 33cm.

U.K. Law Commission. Published Working Papers. No. 32. First programme, item IX. Transfer of land: land registration (first paper). London, 1970. pp. 61.

U.K. Law Commission. Published Working Papers. No. 37. First programme, item IX. Transfer of land: land registration (second paper). London, 1971. pp. 65.

LANDAU (JACQUES)

LANDAU (JACQUES) Defendant. Le procès du "Bonnet Rouge": plaidoirie pour Jacques Landau; par Henry Torrès. Paris, [1929]. pp. 103. 18½cm. (Documents pour l'Histoire)

LANDAUER (GUSTAV)

KALZ (WOLF) Gustav Landauer: Kultursozialist und Anarchist. Meisenheim am Glan, Hain, 1967. pp. (v), 161. bibliog. 23cm. (Schriften zur Politischen Wissenschaft. Band 6)

LANDBEACH

- History

RAVENSDALE (J. R.) Landbeach in 1549: Ket's rebellion in miniature. in Munby (Lionel M.) ed. East Anglian studies. Cambridge, 1968.

LANDES (DEPARTMENT)

- Economic conditions

BELLIARD (J.L.) Les comptes économiques du département des Landes. Paris, Gauthier-Villars, 1966. pp. 272, vii. 27½cm. (Bordeaux Université. Faculté de Droit. Institut d'Économie Regionale du Sud-Ouest. Techniques Économiques Modernes. No. 1)

LANDESRING DER UNABHÄNGIGEN

SCHWENDIMANN (ARMIN) Wirtschafts- und sozialpolitische Ideen im Landesring der Unabhängigen bis 1947. Zürich, 1971. pp. 198. bibliog.

LANDLORD AND TENANT

- Australia - New South Wales

NEW SOUTH WALES. 1961. Farm tenancy in New South Wales;...Division 1. The Agricultural Holdings Act, 1941, and its application. Division 2. Procedure for settling disputes under the Agricultural Holdings Act, 1941. (Department of Agriculture) 3rd ed. Sydney, 1961. pp. 71. 21cm.

- Canada

SOCIOLOGICAL REVIEW, THE [published by] University of Keele. Monographs. [No.] 14. Sociological studies in economics and administration; edited by Paul Halmos. Keele, 1969. pp. 163.

- Ceylon

CEYLON. Special Committee on Housing (1970). 1971. Interim report. 1. Rental housing. Colombo, 1971. pp. 52. (Ceylon. Parliament. Sessional Papers. 1971. No. 5)

- Czechoslovakia

ADLER (JAROSLAV) Práva a povinnosti nájemníků a pronajímatelů bytů a jiných místností. Praha, Orbis, 1960. pp. 167. 21cm.

- France

RAMAIN (FRANÇOISE) Le droit de reprise du bailleur rural à travers la loi et la jurisprudence de la cour de cassation de 1945 à 1963. Paris, Mouton, [1967]. pp. viii, 102. bibliog. 23cm. (Grenoble. Université. Faculté de Droit et des Sciences Économiques. Centre de Recherche Économique et Sociale. Série Agriculture et Devenir Social)

- Ireland (Republic)

EIRE. 1967. Landlord and Tenant (Ground Rents) Bill, 1965: explanatory memorandum. Dublin, [1967]. pp. 5.

EIRE. 1967. Report on occupational tenancies under the Landlord and Tenant Act, 1931. (Landlord and Tenant Commission) (Pr. 9685) Dublin, [1967]. pp. vi, 82. 24½cm.

EIRE. Landlord and Tenant Commission. 1968. Report on certain questions arising under the Landlord and Tenant Acts, 1958 and 1967: [John C. Conroy, chairman]. Dublin, [1968]. pp. 50.

- Pakistan, East

EAST PAKISTAN. Statutes, etc. 1885-1955. Act VIII of 1885: The Bengal Tenancy Act, 1885; as modified up to the 31st December, 1955. Dacca, 1954 [or rather 1956]. pp. 181.

- Russia

FEL'DMAN (ARKADII MOISEEVICH) Права и обязанности нанимателя жилого помещения. Киев, Будівельник, 1966. pp. 139. 16½cm.

- Salvador

SALVADOR. Statutes, etc. 1961. Reforma a la ley de inquilinato: rebaja de los alquileres de las piezas de mesones. San Salvador, [1961?]. pp. 11. (Salvador. Secretaria de Informacion. [Publications]. 4)

- United Kingdom

NATIONAL UNION OF CONSERVATIVE AND UNIONIST ASSOCIATIONS. Land questions. London, [1913?]. pp. 211-262, iii.

U.K. Ministry of Housing and Local Government. 1957. Rent Act, 1957: the Rent Act and you: questions and answers for landlord and tenant. [London, 1957]. pp. 24.

TIMS (MARGARET) Ealing Tenants Ltd.: pioneers of co-partnership. [Ealing, Local History Society], 1966. pp. 48. bibliog. 20½cm. (Ealing. Local History Society. Members' Papers. No. 8)

LEWIS (JOHN ROYSTON) and HOLLAND (JOHN ANTHONY) Landlord and tenant. London, Sweet & Maxwell, 1968. pp. xxviii, 317. 18½cm. (Concise College Texts)

ROSENBERG (STEPHEN) Room for improvement. London, Fair Rent Association, 1968. fo. 17. 25½cm.

U.K. Law Commission. Published Working Papers. No. 16. Working party's provisional proposals relating to termination of tenancies. London, 1968. pp. iii, 39. 33cm.

U.K. Ministry of Housing and Local Government 1968. Rent Act 1968: tables of comparison: showing I. how the enactments repealed are dealt with by the Act; II. the derivation of the provisions of the Act. London, 1968. pp. 27. 24½cm.

WOODFALL (WILLIAM) Barrister-at-Law. Law of landlord and tenant; twenty-seventh edition by Lionel A. Blundell and V.G. Wellings. London, Sweet & Maxwell, 1968. 2 vols. 24½cm. (Property and Conveyancing Library. No.8)

BARNETT (MALCOLM JOEL) The politics of legislation: the Rent Act of 1957. London, Weidenfeld & Nicolson, [1969]. pp. (xx), 293. bibliog. 21½cm.

U.K. Ministry of Agriculture, Fisheries and Food. 1969. Agricultural land: rights and obligations of landlords and tenants in England and Wales. 5th ed. London, 1969. pp. iv, 26. 24½cm.

HILL (HAROLD ARTHUR) and REDMAN (JOSEPH HAWORTH) Law of landlord and tenant; fifteenth edition by Michael Barnes [and] George Dobry. London, 1970. pp. 1899.

U.K. Law Commission. Published Working Papers. No. 25. First programme, item VIII: the law of landlord and tenant: Working Party's provisional proposals relating to covenants restricting dispositions, parting with possession, change of user and alterations. London, 1970. pp. 105.

U.K. Lord Chancellor's Office. 1970. Security of tenure of business premises: how landlord and tenant are affected. 4th ed. [London], 1970. pp. 21.

LANDREVILLE (LEO ALBERT)

CANADA. 1967. The special joint committee of the Senate and of the House of Commons respecting Justice Landreville: joint chairmen: Daniel A. Lang and Ovide Laflamme: minutes of proceedings and evidence. nos. 1-2, 4-7; (with Second and third, final, reports). (27th Parliament. 1st Session) Ottawa, 1967. 6 pts. (in 1) 25cm. Minute No. 3 out of print. Landreville inquiry filed at R(0)/71(1442)

LANDSCAPE

HUTCHINSON (G. E.) On being a meter and a half long. in Oehser (Paul Henry) ed. Knowledge among men. Washington, [1966].

FERRARA (GUIDO) L'architettura del paesaggio italiano: (The Italian landscape). [Bologna, 1968]. pp. 183. bibliog. With English summary.

COLVIN (BRENDA) Land and landscape: evolution, design and control. 2nd ed. London, 1970. pp. 412. bibliog.

TUAN (YI-FU) China. London, 1970. pp. 225.

LANDSCAPE ARCHITECTURE

IRELAND, NORTHERN. Ministry of Development. 1969. Landscape aspects of road design. Belfast, 1969. pp. 19. bibliog.

CANADA. Department of Public Works. Design Branch. 1971. Landscape and site development. Ottawa, 1971. pp. 88. bibliog.

LANDSCAPE PROTECTION

- Czechoslovakia

MĚKOTA (RUDOLF) Ochrana přírody v československom práve. Bratislava, SAV, 1968. pp. 199. bibliog. 20½cm. With Russian and German summaries.

- Europe

JACKSON (R. T.) Mining settlements in Western Europe: the landscape and the community. in Beckinsale (Robert P.) M.A. and Houston (James M.) eds. Urbanization and its problems. Oxford, 1968.

- Germany

OLSCHOWY (GERHARD) Landschaft und Technik: Landespflege in der Industriegesellschaft. Hannover, [1970]. pp. 328. bibliog. Map in end pocket.

- Ireland (Republic)

O NEILL (ANTHONY M.) The hill of Howth: a conservative study made for An Taisce, the National Trust for Ireland. Dublin, 1971. pp. 53,13.

- United Kingdom

[CONFERENCE ON] THE COUNTRYSIDE IN 1970. 2nd Conference, London, 1965. The countryside in 1970; second conference, London, 10-12 November 1965: a review of the preparatory studies. London, Royal Society of Arts, [1965]. pp. 48. 24½cm. R(P)

CADBURY (PAUL STRANGMAN) and WISE (MICHAEL JOHN) The expansion of Birmingham into the green belt area. Birmingham, Cadbury Brothers Ltd., 1968. pp. 32. 24cm.

EAST Hampshire: area of outstanding natural beauty: a study in countryside conservation. [Winchester], 1968. pp. 62.

U.K. Central Office of Information. Reference Division. Reference Pamphlets. 9. Town and country planning in Britain. London, 1968. pp. 32. bibliog. 23½cm.

U.K. National Parks Commission. Regional Coastal Conference, Preston, 1966. Coastal preservation and development: a study of the coastline of England and Wales: the coasts of North-west England: [J.A. Steers, chairman]. London, 1968. pp. v, 88. bibliog. 24½cm. Map in end-pocket.

U.K. National Parks Commission. Regional Coastal Conference, Ipswich, 1967. Coastal preservation and development: a study of the coastline of England and Wales: the coasts of East Anglia: [J.A. Steers, chairman]. London, 1968. pp. v, 81. 24½cm. Map in end-pocket.

U.K. National Parks Commission. Regional Coastal Conference, Newcastle-upon-Tyne, 1967. Coastal preservation and development: a study of the coastline of England and Wales: the coasts of North-east England: [J.A. Steers, chairman]. London, 1968. pp. vii, 74. 24½cm. Map in end-pocket.

U.K. National Parks Commission. Regional Coastal Conference, York. 1967. Coastal preservation and development: a study of the coastline of England and Wales: the coasts of Yorkshire and Lincolnshire: [J.A. Steers, chairman]. London, 1968. pp. v, 69. 24½cm. Map (2 sheets) in end-pocket.

RUBINSTEIN (DAVID) and SPEAKMAN (COLIN) Leisure, transport and the countryside. London, Fabian Society, 1969. pp. 27. 23cm. (Research Series. [No.] 277)

BRACEY (HOWARD EDWIN) People and the countryside. London, 1970. pp. 310. bibliog.

COLVIN (BRENDA) Land and landscape: evolution, design and control. 2nd ed. London, 1970. pp. 412. bibliog.

CONFERENCE ON THE COUNTRYSIDE IN 1970. 3rd Conference, London, 1970. Reports of advisory committees and groups. [London, 1970.] 1 vol. (paged variously)

[JOINT PLANNING ADVISORY COMMITTEE FOR BERKSHIRE, HAMPSHIRE AND SURREY.] Blackwater river valley landscape restoration and recreation study. [Reading], 1970. pp. 21.

U.K. Countryside Commission. 1970. [Coastal preservation and development]: the coastal heritage: a conservation policy for coasts of high quality scenery. London, 1970. pp. 99, 8 maps. 2 maps in end pocket.

- United Kingdom - Scotland

COUNTRYSIDE COMMISSION FOR SCOTLAND. Report. a., Ap/D 1968 (1st)- Perth.

NATIONAL TRUST FOR SCOTLAND. Year book. Edinburgh, annual, 1969 to date.

- United Kingdom - Wales

U.K. National Parks Commission. Regional Coastal Conference, Dolgellau, 1966. Coastal preservation and development: a study of the coastline of England and Wales: the coasts of North Wales: [J.A. Steers, chairman]. London, 1968. pp. v, 78. bibliog. 24½cm. Map in end-pocket.

LANDSLIDES

U.K. Advisory Committee on Tip Safety. 1969. Guidance notes for the initial inspection of disused tips. London, 1969. pp. iii, 20. 21cm.

LANE (MARK)

LANE (MARK) A citizen's dissent: Mark Lane replies. New York, Holt, 1968. pp. xiii, 290. 20½cm.

LANG (ANDREW)

COCQ (ANTONIUS PETRUS LEONARDUS DE) Andrew Lang, a nineteenth century anthropologist. Tilburg, Zwijsen, 1968. pp. 151. 23cm.

LANG (JOHN THOMAS)

FOOTT (BETHIA) Dismissal of a Premier: the Philip Game papers. Sydney, Morgan, 1968. pp. (iii), 223. 21½cm.

COOKSEY (ROBERT) Lang and socialism: a study in the Great Depression. Canberra, 1971. pp. 96. bibliog.

L'ANGE (FRANÇOIS JOSEPH)

IOANNISSIAN (A.) La première ébauche du "plan" de Lange. in Société des Études Robespierristes. La pensée socialiste devant la Révolution française. Paris, 1966.

L'ANGE (FRANÇOIS JOSEPH) Oeuvres; introduction et notes par Paul Leutrat. Paris, [1968]. pp. 239. bibliog.

LANGETON (WALTER) Bishop of Coventry and Lichfield
See LANGTON (WALTER) Bishop of Coventry and Lichfield

LANGIEWICZ (MARIAN)

RZADKOWSKA (HELENA) Marian Langiewicz. Warszawa, PWN, 1967. pp. 436. 19½cm

LANGLOIS (DENIS)

LANGLOIS (DENIS) Le cachot. Paris, Maspero, 1967. pp. 141. 19½cm. (Cahiers Libres. 97)

LANGTON (WALTER) Bishop of Coventry and Lichfield

CAMDEN SOCIETY. [Publications]. 4th Series. vol. 6. Records of the trial of Walter Langeton, Bishop of Coventry and Lichfield, 1307-1312; edited...by Alice Beardwood. London, Royal Historical Society, 1969. pp. v, 370. 21½cm.

LANGUAGE, UNIVERSAL

KINDLEBERGER (CHARLES POOR) The politics of international money and world language. Princeton, the Department, 1967. pp. 11. 23cm. (Princeton University. Department of Economics and Sociology. International Finance Section. Essays in International Finance. No.61)

LANGUAGE AND LANGUAGES

SPITZER (LEO) Anti-Chamberlain: Betrachtungen eines Linguisten über Houston Stewart Chamberlains Kriegsaufsätze und die Sprachbewertung im allgemeinen. Leipzig, 1918. pp. 82.

FIRTH (JOHN RUPERT) The tongues of men; and, Speech; [a reprint of the editions of 1937 and 1930 respectively]. London, O.U.P., 1964, repr. 1966. pp. x, 211. 19½cm. (Language and Language Learning. 2)

BOAS (FRANZ) Race, language and culture. New York, Free P., [1940], repr. 1966. pp. xx, 647. 21cm. (Free Press Paperbacks)

KOFLER (LEO) Marxismus und Sprache: zu Stalins Untersuchung über den Marxismus in der Sprachwissenschaft. Köln, 1952. pp. 53.

MANY-sided language; Robert F. Spencer, editor. Minneapolis, University of Minnesota, Graduate School Research Center, 1964. pp. iii, 108. bibliog. 22½cm. (Annual Public Discussions on Problems of Current Interest in the Social Sciences. 15)

BRITISH AND FOREIGN BIBLE SOCIETY. The Gospel in many tongues: specimens of 872 languages in which the British and Foreign Bible Society has published or circulated some portion of the Bible. London, the Society, 1965. pp. 189, 20, iv. 22cm.

BRICEÑO GUERRERO (J.M.) America Latina en el mundo. Caracas, [1966]. pp. 228.

DEUTSCHER KONGRESS FÜR PHILOSOPHIE, 8th, HEIDELBERG, 1966. Das Problem der Sprache; Herausgeber Hans-Georg Gadamer. München, 1967 pp. 566.

GRIMSLEY (R.) Jean-Jacques Rousseau and the problem of "original" language. in Barber (William H.) and others, eds. The age of the enlightenment.

ONG (WALTER JACKSON) The presence of the work: some prolegomena for cultural and religious history. New Haven, Yale University Press, 1967. pp. xv, 360. bibliog. 20cm. (Yale University. Terry Lectures. 1967)

BOLINGER (DWIGHT) Aspects of language. New York, [1968]. pp. 326.

CHAO (YUEN REN) Language and symbolic systems. Cambridge, C.U.P., 1968. pp. xv, 240. bibliog. 20cm.

ENCYCLOPÉDIE DE LA PLÉIADE. Le langage;... publié sous la direction d'André Martinet. [Paris, Gallimard, 1968]. pp. xv, 1525. bibliogs. 17cm.

GLEESON (PATRICK) and WAKEFIELD (NANCY) eds. Language and culture. Columbus, [1968]. pp. 200.

LINGUAGGI nella società e nella tecnica: convegno promosso dalla Ing. C. Olivetti & C., S.p.A. per il centenario della nascita di Camillo Olivetti...Milano, 1968. Milano, [1970]. pp. 608. bibliogs. In various languages with English translations.

OLDFIELD (RICHARD CHARLES) and MARSHALL (J. C.) eds. Language: selected readings. Harmondsworth, 1968. pp. 392. bibliogs.

WHYTE (W. F.) and BRAUN (R. R.) On language and culture. in Becker (Howard Saul) and others, eds. Institutions and the person. Chicago, 1968.

MOULOUD (NOËL) Langage et structures: essais de logique et de sémeiologie. Paris, [1969]. pp. 252. bibliog.

NEW YORK (CITY). University. Institute of Philosophy, 9th, 1968. Language and philosophy: a symposium; edited by Sidney Hook. [New York], 1969. pp. 301.

PAULUS (JEAN) La fonction symbolique et le langage. Bruxelles, [1969]. pp. 173. bibliog.

SCHAFF (ADAM) Langage et connaissance: suivi de six essais sur la philosophie du langage. Paris, [1969]. pp. 372. bibliog.

STEINER (GEORGE) Language and silence: essays, 1958-1966. New ed. Harmondsworth, 1969. pp. 368.

KOFLER (LEO) Stalinismus und Bürokratie: zwei Aufsätze. Neuwied, 1970. pp. 182.

LANGUAGE AND LANGUAGES (Cont'd.)

- Abbreviations

BRITISH STANDARDS INSTITUTION. Recommendations for symbols for languages geographical areas and authorities: B.S. 3862; 1965. London, 1965. pp. 18.

- Dictionaries

AKHMANOVA (OL'GA SERGEEVNA) Словарь лингвистических терминов. Москва, Советская Энциклопедия, 1966. pp. 607. 20см.

- Origin

HAAS (MARY ROSAMUND) The prehistory of languages. The Hague, 1969. pp. 120. bibliog.

- Style

FOWLER (ROGER) ed. Essays on style and language: linguistic and critical approaches to literary style. London, Routledge & Kegan Paul, 1966 repr. 1967. pp. ix, 188. 21½cm.

WILLIAMS (C.B.) Style and vocabulary: numerical studies;...with a foreword by Randolph Quirk, etc. London, 1970. pp. 161. bibliog.

LANGUAGE LABORATORIES

U.K. Department of Education and Science. Building Bulletins. 43. Secondary school design: modern languages. London, 1968. pp. 76. bibliog. 30cm.

U.K. Department of Education and Science. Education Surveys. 3. Language laboratories. London, 1968 pp. vi, 32. 24½cm.

STILL (P.R.) and others. Report on the assessment of language laboratories. Farnborough, 1969. pp. 107. (Royal Aircraft Establishment. Technical Reports. 69100.)

LANGUAGE QUESTION IN THE CHURCH

- Roumania

ŞESAN (M. P.) Über die Bemühungen um die Einführung der Volkssprache in die rumänische Kirche. in Steinitz (Wolfgang) and others, eds. Ost und West in der Geschichte des Denkens und der kulturellen Beziehungen. Berlin, 1966.

LANGUAGES

- Philosophy

HAYAKAWA (SAMUEL ICHIYÉ) and others. Language in thought and action. 2nd ed. New York, Harcourt, [1964]. pp. xvii, 350. bibliog. 21½cm.

LAZAREV (V.V.) Nekotorye aspekty gnoseologicheskogo analiza kontseptual'nogo apparata lingvistiki i semiotiki. in Voprosy teoreticheskogo nasledstva V.I. Lenina. Krasnoiarsk, 1966.

DANTO (A. C.) Reflections upon Randall's theory of language. in Anton (John Peter) ed. Naturalism and historical understanding. Albany, [1967].

DEUTSCHER KONGRESS FÜR PHILOSOPHIE, 8th, HEIDELBERG, 1966. Das Problem der Sprache; Herausgeber Hans-Georg Gadamer. München, 1967 pp. 566.

PUTNAM (H.) The 'innateness hypothesis' and explanatory models in linguistics. in Boston Colloquium for the Philosophy of Science. Proceedings, 1964-1966. Boston studies in the philosophy of science, vol.3. Dordrecht, 1967.

WILSON (JOHN) 1928- . Language and the pursuit of truth. Cambridge, C.U.P., 1956, repr. 1967. pp. 105. bibliog. 18½cm.

BLACK (MAX) The labyrinth of language. London, Pall Mall P., [1968]. pp. vii, 178. bibliog. 23½cm. (Britannica Perspectives)

EHRLICH (STEPHANE) Les mécanismes du comportement verbal. Paris, 1968. pp. 383. bibliog.

SCHMIDT (SIEGFRIED J.) Sprache und Denken als sprachphilosophisches Problem von Locke bis Wittgenstein. Den Haag, 1968. pp. 202. bibliog.

BUYSSENS (ERIC) Vérité et langue [and,] Langue et pensée. [Bruxelles], 1969. pp. 46. (Brussels Université Libre. Institut de Sociologie. Collection de Sociologie Générale et Philosophie Sociale)

CAVELL (STANLEY) Must we mean what we say?: a book of essays. New York, [1969]. pp. 365.

CLACK (ROBERT J.) Bertrand Russell's philosophy of language. The Hague, 1969. pp. 100. bibliog.

GILSON (ETIENNE HENRY) Linguistique et philosophie: essai sur les constantes philosophiques du langage. Paris, 1969. pp. 309.

LEWIS (DAVID K.) Convention: a philosophical study. Cambridge, Mass., 1969. pp. 213.

OLSHEWSKY (THOMAS M.) Problems in the philosophy of language. New York, [1969]. pp. 774. bibliogs.

SCHAFF (ADAM) Langage et connaissance: suivi de six essais sur la philosophie du langage. Paris, [1969]. pp. 372. bibliog.

WATKINS (JOHN WILLIAM NEVILLE) The human condition: two criticisms of Hobbes; an inaugural lecture delivered at the London School of Economics on October 14, 1969. [London, 1969]. fo. 33.

BLACK (MAX) Margins of precision: essays in logic and language. Ithaca, N.Y., 1970. pp. 277.

LORENZ (KUNO) Elemente der Sprachkritik: eine Alternative zum Dogmatismus und Skeptizismus in der Analytischen Philosophie. Frankfurt am Main, 1970. pp. 267. bibliog.

MEILAND (JACK W.) Talking about particulars. London, 1970. pp. 168.

RASMUSSEN (DAVID M.) Mythic-symbolic language and philosophical anthropology: a constructive interpretation of the thought of Paul Ricoeur. The Hague, 1971. pp. 158. bibliog.

ROSENBERG (JAY F.) and TRAVIS (CHARLES) Ph.D., eds. Readings in the philosophy of language. Englewood Cliffs, [1971]. pp. 645. bibliogs.

- Political aspects

RICE (FRANK A.) ed. Study of the role of second languages: in Asia, Africa, and Latin America. Washington, Center for Applied Linguistics, 1962. pp. vii, 123. 23cm.

CONSEIL DE LA VIE FRANÇAISE EN AMERIQUE. Nothing more: nothing less; a French-Canadian view of bilingualism and biculturalism. Toronto, Holt, Rinehart and Winston, [1967]. pp. vii, 79. bibliog. 23½cm.

DAKIN (JULIAN) and others. Language in education: the problem in Commonwealth Africa and the Indo-Pakistan sub-continent. London, O.U.P., 1968. pp. xii, 177. 21½cm. (Language and Language Learning Series. 20)

MEYNAUD (JEAN) Le problème des langues dans l'administration fédérale helvétique. [Montréal], 1968. pp. 182.

NAYAR (BALDEV RAJ) National communication and language policy in India. New York, [1969]. pp. 310. bibliog. (McGill University. Centre for Developing-Area Studies. McGill Studies in Development. No. 3)

EPSTEIN (ERWIN H.) ed. Politics and education in Puerto Rico: a documentary survey of the language issue. Metuchen, N.J., 1970. pp. 257.

KLAUS (GEORG) Sprache der Politik. Berlin, 1971. pp. 294.

THOMAS (NED) The Welsh extremists: a culture in crisis. London, 1971. pp. 127. bibliog.

LANGUAGES - Psychology
See PSYCHOLINGUISTICS

LANGUAGES - Sociological aspects
See SOCIOLINGUISTICS

LANGUAGES, MIXED

RICE (FRANK A.) ed. Study of the role of second languages: in Asia, Africa, and Latin America. Washington, Center for Applied Linguistics, 1962. pp. vii, 123. 23cm.

HEINE (BERND) Status and use of African lingua francas. München, [1970]. pp. 198. bibliog. (IFO-Institut Für Wirtschaftsforschung. Afrika-Studien. 49)

PIDGINIZATION and creolization of languages: proceedings of a conference held at the University of the West Indies, Mona, Jamaica, April 1968; edited by Dell Hymes. Cambridge, 1971. pp. 530. bibliogs.

LANGUAGES, MODERN

COPENHAGEN. Handelshøjskolen. Afhandlinger fra Handelshøjskolen i København, udsendt i anledning af højskolens 50 års jubilaeum den 1. oktober 1967. København, 1967. pp. 456. bibliogs.

- Study and teaching

SWEET (HENRY) M.A. The practical study of languages: a guide for teachers and learners; [reprinted from the Dent edition of 1899]. London, O.U.P., 1964. pp. xv, 276. 19½cm. (Language and Language Learning)

COUNCIL OF EUROPE. Education in Europe. Section 4. No. 1. Recent developments in modern language teaching: resolutions of the Second and Third Conferences of European Ministers of Education; and Summary report of three...Courses presented by D.C. Riddy. Strasbourg, 1964. pp. 43. 23cm.

COUNCIL OF EUROPE. Education in Europe. Section 4. No. 3. Research and techniques for the benefit of modern language teaching; report of the refresher course held at Strasbourg on 22nd and 23rd March 1963 by the Regional Branch of the Association of Modern Language Teachers in collaboration with the Council, etc. Strasbourg, 1964. pp. 187. 23cm.

MODERN languages in colleges of education; report of a conference organized jointly by the Department of Education and Science and the Modern Languages Section of the ATCDE, Harrogate, 8-11 October, 1965; edited by B.G. Palmer. [London], the Department, 1966. pp. 58. 21cm.

HEALEY (F.G.) Foreign language teaching in the universities. Manchester, U.P., [1967]. pp. xix, 271. bibliog. 20½cm.

BENNETT (W. A.) Aspects of language and language teaching. Cambridge, 1968. pp. 175. bibliog.

RIVERS (WILGA MARIE) Teaching foreign-language skills. Chicago, 1968. pp. 403. bibliog.

SANTOS (R.A.) Philippines: language education and science education. in Thomas (Robert Murray) and others. Strategies for curriculum change. Scranton, [1968].

THOMAS (R.M.) Indonesia: the English language curriculum. in Thomas (Robert Murray) and others. Strategies for curriculum change. Scranton, [1968].

U.K. Committee on Research and Development in Modern Languages. 1968. First report; [L. Farrer-Brown, chairman]. London, 1968. pp. vii, 39.

MACKEY (WILLIAM FRANCIS) Language teaching analysis. London, 1969. pp. 554. bibliog.

U.K. Department of Education and Science. Schools Council. Working Papers. No. 19. Development of modern language teaching in secondary schools. London, 1969. pp. 25.

LESTER (MARK) ed. Readings in applied transformational grammar. New York, [1970]. pp. 314.

U.K. Committee on Research and Development in Modern Languages. 1971. Second report: [L. Farrer-Brown, chairman]. London, 1971. pp. 29.

- Study and teaching - Audio-visual aids

RENARD (RAYMOND) L'enseignement des langues vivantes par la méthode audio-visuelle et structuro-globale de Saint-Cloud-Zagreb. Bruxelles, [1965]. pp. 127. bibliog.

- Study and teaching - Bibliography

CENTRE FOR INFORMATION ON LANGUAGE TEACHING and BRITISH COUNCIL. English-Teaching Information Centre. A language-teaching bibliography. Cambridge, C.U.P., 1968. pp. x, 244. 21cm.

LANGUAGES, MODERN (Cont'd.)

- Study and teaching - Mathematical models

CROTHERS (EDWARD) and SUPPES (PATRICK). Experiments in second-language learning. New York, Academic P., 1967. pp. ix, 374. bibliog. 22½cm.

- Testing

DAVIES (ALAN) ed. Language testing symposium: a psycholinguistic approach. London, 1968. pp. 214. bibliog.

LANGUEDOC

- Economic conditions

BADOUIN (ROBERT) and others. Région et développement: l'économie du Languedoc-Roussillon. Paris, Gauthier-Villars, 1968. pp. ix, 7-294. 24cm. (Centre Régional de la Productivité et des Études Économiques (Xe Région Économique) Travaux)

SOUCHON (MARIE FRANÇOISE) La Compagnie Nationale d'Amenagement de la Région du Bas-Rhône Languedoc. [Paris, 1969]. pp. 196. bibliog. (Grenoble. Université. Institut d'Etudes Politiques. Cahiers. 3)

- Statistics, Vital

GODECHOT (JACQUES) and MONCASSIN (SUZANNE) Démographie et subsistances en Languedoc du XVIIIe au début du XIXe siècle. Paris, Imprimerie Nationale, 1965. pp. 48. (France. Commission d'Histoire Economique et Sociale de la Révolution Française. [Instructions, Bibliographies et Recueils de Textes. Nouvelle Série.] 6)

LANKA SAMA SAMAJA PARTY

[GOONEWARDENE (LESLIE)] A short history of the Lanka Sama Samaja Party. [Colombo, 1960.] pp. 66. 18cm.

LERSKI (GEORGE JAN) Origins of trotskyism in Ceylon: a documentary history of the Lanka Sama Samaja Party, 1935-1942. Stanford, University, Hoover Institution on War, Revolution and Peace, 1968. pp. xix, 288. bibliog. 20cm. (Hoover Institution Publications)

LANTIERI (GIACOMO)

BARBIERI (G.) Il trattatello "Della economica" di Giacomo Lantieri, letterato e architetto bresciano del secolo XVI. in vol.1 of Saggi di economia aziendale e sociale in memoria di Gino Zappa. Milano, 1961.

LANZONI (FRANCESCO)

BEDESCHI (LORENZO) Lineamenti dell'antimodernismo: il caso Lanzoni. Parma, 1970. pp. 280.

LAOS

- Constitution

FRANCE. Direction de la Documentation. La Documentation Française. Notes et Etudes Documentaires. No.3,627. Constitution du Royaume du Laos (30 juillet 1961). Paris, 1969. pp. 7.

- Description and travel

GUBER (ALEKSANDR ANDREEVICH) Bomby, peshchery, liudi: reportazh iz raionov Laosa, kontroliruemykh patrioticheskim frontom. Moskva, 1969. pp. 86.

SEMENOV (IULIAN SEMENOVICH) Вьетнам, Лаос, 1968. Москва, 1969. pp. 190.

- Economic conditions

FRANCE. Direction de la Documentation. La Documentation Française. Notes et Etudes Documentaires. No.3,630. Le Laos; [by] Guy Brossollet [and] François Joyaux; (with Annexe: Les accords de Genève, 28 juillet 1962). Paris, 1969. pp. 36, 7. bibliog.

- Foreign relations

INTERNATIONAL CONFERENCE ON THE SETTLEMENT OF THE LAOTIAN QUESTION, 2ND, GENEVA, 1961-2. [Summary record of proceedings and basic documents; edited with a preliminary commentary] by George Modelski. Canberra, the University, 1962. pp. vi, 156. 25½cm. (Australian National University. Research School of Pacific Studies. Department of International Relations. Working Papers. No. 2)

CHITTENDEN (GEOFFREY MARTIN) Laos and the powers, 1954-1962; [Ph. D. (London) thesis]. 1969. fo. 186. bibliog. 29½cm. Typescript: unpublished. This thesis is the property of London University and may not be removed from the Library.

FRANCE. Direction de la Documentation. La Documentation Française. Notes et Etudes Documentaires. No.3,630. Le Laos; [by] Guy Brossollet [and] François Joyaux; (with Annexe: Les accords de Genève, 28 juillet 1962). Paris, 1969. pp. 36, 7. bibliog.

DOMMEN (ARTHUR J.) Conflict in Laos: the politics of neutralization. rev ed. New York, 1971. pp. 454. bibliog.

- Foreign relations - United States

DOUZE années d'intervention et d'agression des impérialistes américains au Laos. [Laos], 1966. pp. 135.

TWELVE years of American intervention and aggression in Laos. n.p., Neo Lao Haksat Publications, 1966. pp. 129. 18cm.

GUBER (ALEKSANDR ANDREEVICH) Bomby, peshchery, liudi: reportazh iz raionov Laosa, kontroliruemykh patrioticheskim frontom. Moskva, 1969. pp. 86.

ADAMS (NINA S.) and McCOY (ALFRED W.) eds. Laos: war and revolution. New York, 1970. pp. 482. bibliog.

BURCHETT (WILFRED G.) Second Indochina war: Cambodia and Laos today. London, [1970]. pp. 160.

- Foreign relations - Vietnam

LANGER (PAUL FRITZ) and ZASLOFF (JOSEPH JEREMIAH) North Vietnam and the Pathet Lao: partners in the struggle for Laos. Cambridge, Mass., 1970. pp. 262. bibliog. (Rand Corporation. Research Studies)

- History

U.K. Central Office of Information. Reference Division. 1967. Laos. rev. ed. London, 1967. pp. 58. bibliog. 23½cm.

U.K. Central Office of Information. Reference Division. 1968. Vietnam, Laos, and Cambodia: chronology of events, 1945-68. rev. ed. London, 1968. pp. (151). 23½cm.

FRANCE. Direction de la Documentation. La Documentation Française. Notes et Etudes Documentaires. No.3,630. Le Laos; [by] Guy Brossollet [and] François Joyaux; (with Annexe: Les accords de Genève, 28 juillet 1962). Paris, 1969. pp. 36, 7. bibliog.

ADAMS (NINA S.) and McCOY (ALFRED W.) eds. Laos: war and revolution. New York, 1970. pp. 482. bibliog.

U.K. Central Office of Information. Reference Division. 1971. Vietnam, Laos and Cambodia: chronology of events 1968-70. London, 1970 [or rather 1971]. 1 pamphlet (unpaged).

- Neutrality

DOMMEN (ARTHUR J.) Conflict in Laos: the politics of neutralization. rev ed. New York, 1971. pp. 454. bibliog.

- Politics and government

PHOUKOUT stronghold. n.p., 1967. pp. 22.

U.K. Central Office of Information. Reference Division. 1967. Laos. rev. ed. London, 1967. pp. 58. bibliog. 23½cm.

IN the liberated zone of Laos; [by Van Son and others]. Hanoi, 1968. pp. 53.

NEO LAO HAKSAT. Political program of the Neo Lao Haksat, (Lao Patriotic Front). n.p., 1968. pp. 21.

TOYE (HUGH) Laos: buffer state or battleground. London, O.U.P., 1968. pp. xvii, 245. bibliog. 21½cm.

CHITTENDEN (GEOFFREY MARTIN) Laos and the powers, 1954-1962; [Ph. D. (London) thesis]. 1969. fo. 186. bibliog. 29½cm. Typescript: unpublished. This thesis is the property of London University and may not be removed from the Library.

FALL (BERNARD B.) Anatomy of a crisis: the Laotian crisis of 1960-1961. New York, 1969. pp. 283. bibliog.

LANGER (PAUL FRITZ) and ZASLOFF (JOSEPH JEREMIAH) North Vietnam and the Pathet Lao: partners in the struggle for Laos. Cambridge, Mass., 1970. pp. 262. bibliog. (Rand Corporation. Research Studies)

DOMMEN (ARTHUR J.) Conflict in Laos: the politics of neutralization. rev ed. New York, 1971. pp. 454. bibliog.

- Statistics

LAOS. Service National de la Statistique. Statistiques essentielles. a., 1969- [Vientiane]

GERMANY (BUNDESREPUBLIK). Statistisches Bundesamt. Länderkurzbericht: Laos. irreg., 1971 [1st issue]- Wiesbaden.

LAO-TZU

OPITZ (PETER JOACHIM) Lao-Tzu: die Ordnungsspekulation im Tao-tê-ching. München, List, [1967]. pp. 202. bibliog. 23cm. (Schriftenreihe zur Politik und Geschichte)

LA PLATIÈRE (ROLAND DE)
See ROLAND DE LA PLATIÈRE (JEAN MARIE)

LAPPS

DIKKANEN (SIRI LAVIK) Sirma: residence and work organization in a Lappish-speaking community. Oslo, Universitetsforlaget, 1965. pp. 47. bibliog. 24cm. (Norsk Folkemuseum. Samiske Samlinger. Bind. 8)

LARCENY

- France

GASSIN (R.) La notion de vol dans la jurisprudence française contemporaine. in L'Évolution du droit criminel contemporain. Paris, 1968.

- Russia

BOR'BA s khishcheniiami gosudarstvennogo i obshchestvennogo imushchestva. Moskva, 1971. pp. 254.

- United Kingdom

GRIEW (EDWARD JAMES) The Theft Act 1968. London, Sweet & Maxwell, 1968. pp. xx, 174. 24½cm.

SMITH (JOHN CYRIL) The law of theft. London, Butterworths, 1968. pp. xxii, 226. 23½cm.

LARKIN (JAMES)

DEASY (JOSEPH) Fiery cross: the story of Jim Larkin. [Dublin, 1963] pp. 39.

LARNER (WILLIAM)

LARNER (WILLIAM) A vindication of every freemans libertie against all arbitrary power and government; or, A letter...to Sir Henry Vane junior,...; wherein is set forth his unjust imprisonment and cruell hard dealings towards the said William Larner. [London, 1646]. pp. 4. 18½cm. Wing L 445A.

A TRUE relation of all the remarkable passages and illegall proceedings of some Sathannicall or Doeg-like accusers of their brethren againt [sic] William Larner...for selling eight printed sheets of paper intituled, Londons last warning, etc. [London, Larner's last press, 1646]. pp. 16. 19cm. Wing T 2899.

LA ROCHE (BENEDIKT)

VOEGELIN (H. A.) Benedikt La Roche, 1802-1876. in Verein fuer Wirtschaftshistorische Studien. Schweizer Pioniere der Wirtschaft und Technik. 18. Zürich, 1967.

LASAULX (ERNST VON)

DOCEKAL (HERTA URSULA) Ernst von Lasaulx: ein Beitrag zur Kritik des organischen Geschichtsbegriffs. Münster, [1970]. pp. 141. bibliog.

LASKI (HAROLD JOSEPH)

LASKI (HAROLD JOSEPH) and HUEBSCH (BENJAMIN W.) Copies of letters from Harold J. Laski to Benjamin W. Huebsch, 22nd December, 1914-13th April, 1949, with letters from Benjamin W. Huebsch to Harold J. Laski, 3rd April, 1940-12th September, 1944. [1914-1944]. fo. (204). 27½cm. Xerographic copies of the originals in the Library of Congress.

[WINTRINGHAM (THOMAS HENRY) Review of Harold J. Laski's book entitled Communism. 1927?] fo. 9. Typescript.

SARMA (G.N.) The political thought of Harold J. Laski. Bombay, Orient Longmans, 1965. pp. (v), 138. bibliog. 20½cm.

ZYLSTRA (BERNARD) From pluralism to collectivism: the development of Harold Laski's political thought. Assen, Van Gorcum, 1968. pp. (vi), 236. bibliog. 23½cm.

SHARMA (SURYA KANT) The origins and nature of Laski's opinions on international politics; [Ph.D. (London) thesis]. 1971 [or rather 1972]. fo. 395. bibliog. Typescript: unpublished. This thesis is the property of London University and may not be removed from the Library.

LA SPEZIA (PROVINCE)

- Statistics

LA SPEZIA. Camera di Commercio, Industria, Artigianato e Agricoltura. Ufficio Provinciale di Statistica. Compendio statistico della provincia della Spezia, 1968. [La Spezia, 1969]. pp. 359.

LASSALLE (FERDINAND JOHANN GOTTLIEB)

OBERWINDER (HEINRICH) Sozialismus und Sozialpolitik: ein Beitrag zur Geschichte der sozialpolitischen Kämpfe unserer Zeit. Berlin, Staude, 1887. pp. iv, 164. 20½cm.

FERDINAND Lassalle der Volkstribun: sozialpolitische Studie. Leipzig-Gautzsch, 1919. pp. 15.

NA'AMAN (SHLOMO) Lassalle. Hannover, [1970]. pp. 890. (Institut für Sozialgeschichte Braunschweig. Veröffentlichungen)

LASSO DE LA VEGA (GARCÍA)

COX (CARLOS MANUEL) Utopia y realidad en el Inca Garcilaso: pensamiento económico, interpretación histórica. Lima, the Universidad, [1965]. pp. 235. 24cm. (Lima. Universidad Nacional Mayor de San Marcos. Departamento de Publicaciones. Biblioteca de Estudios Superiores)

VARNER (JOHN GRIER) El Inca: the life and times of Garcilaso de la Vega. Austin, Texas, [1968]. pp. 413. bibliog.

LASSWELL (HAROLD DWIGHT)

ROGOW (ARNOLD A.) ed. Politics, personality, and social science in the twentieth century: essays in honor of Harold D. Lasswell. Chicago, 1969. pp. 455. bibliog.

LASTENAUSGLEICH (1949-)

SCHAEFER (KARL HEINZ) Fundstellen zum Recht des Lastenausgleichs: Bundesrecht, Landesrecht, internationales Recht... Stand 1.Oktober 1963. Frankfurt am Main, Verlag für Wirtschaft und Verwaltung, 1963. pp. 100. 21cm.

LATERITE

MAIGNIEN (R.) Review of research on laterites. Paris, United Nations Educational, Scientific and Cultural Organization, 1966. pp. 148. bibliog. 24cm. (Natural Resources Research. 4)

PERSONS (BENJAMIN S.) Laterite: genesis, location, use. New York, 1970. pp. 103.

LATERZA (GIOVANNI)

RUSSO (L.) Ricordo di Giovanni Laterza. in Milan. Biblioteca Comunale. Mostra storica della Casa editrice Laterza, Milano 16 novembre - 16 dicembre, 1961. [Milan, 1961].

LATHAM (HAROLD S.)

LATHAM (HAROLD S.) My life in publishing. London, Sidgwick & Jackson, 1966. pp. 256. 19½cm.

LATIN AMERICAN FEDERATION

HAYA DE LA TORRE (VICTOR RAÚL) Problema e imperative de la unidad continental. Lima, 1963. pp. 25. 18cm. (Serie Doctrina) (Reproducido de Revista Política, no. 9, mayo 1960).

MARTZ (JOHN D.) Justo Rufino Barrios and Central American union. Gainesville, University of Florida Press, 1963. pp. 51. bibliog. 22½cm. (Florida University. School of Inter-American Studies. Latin American Monographs. 21)

PUIGGRÓS (RODOLFO) Integración de América Latina: factores ideológicos y políticos. Buenos Aires, Alvárez, 1965. pp. 80. 17½cm.

DEUTSCH (KARL WOLFGANG) and others. Integracion y formacion de comunidades politicas: analisis sociologico de experiencias historicas. Buenos Aires, Instituto Para la Integracion de America Latina, 1966. pp. 256.

RODRÍGUEZ R. (JULIO E.) Por una comunidad política latinoamericana: hacia la federación. Bogotá, 1966. pp. 99. bibliog. 24cm.

ALDUNATE UNDURRAGA (JOSÉ M.) Verdadero origen de la política de integración total latinoamericana; en lo cultural, económico y político. Santiago de Chile, [1967?]. pp. 60. 19cm.

BETANCOURT (RÓMULO) Hacia América Latina democrática e integrada. Caracas, Senderos, 1967. pp. 215. 23cm.

GABAY (MARCOS) and GUTIERREZ (CARLOS MARIA) eds. Integracion latinoamericana?: de la Alianza para el Progreso a la OLAS. Montevideo, 1967. pp. 285.

COCHRANE (JAMES DUNDAS) The politics of regional integration: the central American case. New Orleans, 1969. pp. 225. (Tulane University of Louisiana. Tulane Studies in Political Science. vol. 12)

LATIN AMERICAN FREE TRADE ASSOCIATION

GARCIA REYNOSO (PLACIDO) Integracion economica latinoamericana: primera etapa 1960-1964. Mexico, 1965. pp. 282.

HAAS (ERNST BERNARD) and SCHMITTER (PHILIPPE C.) The politics of economics in Latin American regionalism: the Latin American Free Trade Association after four years of operation. Denver, [1965]. pp. 78. (Denver. University. Social Science Foundation and Graduate School of International Studies. Monograph Series in World Affairs. vol. 3. No. 2)

MAGARIÑOS DE MELLO (M.) Die Lateinamerikanische Freihandelsassoziation (LAFTA, ALALC). in St.Gall. Handelshochschule. Lateinamerikanisches Institut. Integration in Lateinamerika. Zürich, 1965.

ABAL (J. D.) El régimen jurídico de la Asociacion Latinoamericana de Libre Comercio...y los problemas que a su respecto puedan suscitarse: soluciones posibles. in Mexico. 1966. Ensayos de derecho administrativo y tributario para conmemorar el XXX aniversario de la ley de justicia fiscal. Mexico, [1966].

ASPECTOS legales de la Asociacion Latinoamericana de Libre Comercio: Seminario organizado por Federacion Interamericana de Abogados, [and others]; realizado en Montevideo, del 20 al 29 de Noviembre de 1963. Montevideo, 1966. pp. 482.

ECONOMIST INTELLIGENCE UNIT. Q[uarterly] E[conomic] R[eview] Specials. No. 1. The crisis in Latin American integration. London, [1968]. pp. 12.

INTER-AMERICAN INSTITUTE OF INTERNATIONAL LEGAL STUDIES. Instrumentos relativos a la integracion economica de America Latina. 2nd ed. [Washington], 1968. pp. 508.

INTER-AMERICAN INSTITUTE OF INTERNATIONAL LEGAL STUDIES. Instruments relating to the economic integration of Latin America. Dobbs Ferry, Oceana Publications, 1968. pp. x; 452. bibliog. 24½cm.

UNITED STATES. Department of State. Publications. No. 8448. Latin American Free Trade Association: progress, problems, prospects. Washington, 1969. pp. 61. bibliog.

CENTRO DE ESTADISTICAS NACIONALES Y COMERCIO INTERNACIONAL DEL URUGUAY. Manual practico de la ALALC, etc. 2nd ed. Montevideo, 1970. pp. 237. bibliog.

- Bolivia

JORDÁN SANDOVAL (SANTIAGO) Alternativa de Bolivia para ingresar a la Zona Libre de Comercio; ampliación de la conferencia disertada en el paraninfo de la Universidad Mayor de San Andrés, bajo los auspicios del Centro de Estudiantes de la Facultad de Economía, el 25 de Mayo de 1962. La Paz, 1962. pp. 100. 18½cm. (Biblioteca Boliviana de Autores Contemporáneos)

BARRIENTOS ORTUÑO (RENE) Bolivia y la integracion economica de America Latina. Buenos Aires, Instituto para la Integracion de America Latina, 1969. pp. 168.

- Mexico

SCHMITTER (PHILIPPE C.) and HAAS (ERNST BERNARD) Mexico and Latin American economic integration. Berkeley, California University, Institute of International Studies, 1964. pp. 43. bibliog. 23½cm. (Research Series. No.5)

LATIN AMERICAN FREE TRADE ASSOCIATION COUNTRIES

- Commerce - Argentine Republic

DAGNINO PASTORE (JOSÉ MARÍA) Argentina en la ALALC: estadísticas comerciales, 1959-1963. 2nd ed. Buenos Aires, Instituto Torcuato di Tella, Centro de Investigaciones Económicas, 1965. pp. xxvi, 143. 27½cm. (Documentos de Trabajo. 10)

- Commerce - Mexico

MEXICO. Direccion General de Estadistica. Anuario estadistico del comercio de los Estados Unidos Mexicanos con los paises de la Asociacion Latinoamericana de Libre Comercio. a., 1964, 1969- Mexico.

- Statistics

BANCO CENTRAL DE VENEZUELA. Departamento de Investigaciones Economicas y Estadisticas. Seccion ALALC. Algunas estadisticas de los paises de ALALC. [Caracas], 1968. pp. 121.

LATIN AMERICAN LITERATURE

GUATEMALA. Seminario de Integración Social Guatemalteca. Cuadernos. Primera Serie. No. 3. America Latina en el espejo de su literatura; ([by] Roger Bastide; versión de Jorge Luis Arriola). Guatemala, 1959. pp. 36. 21cm. (De la revista Annales, no. 1, janvier-mars 1958)

LATIN AMERICAN NEWSPAPERS

- Bibliography - Union lists

CHARNO (STEVEN M.) compiler. Latin American newspapers in United States libraries: a union list; compiled in the Serial Division, Library of Congress. Austin, University of Texas Press, 1968. pp. 619. bibliog. (Conference on Latin American History. Publications. No. 2.)

LATIN AMERICAN PERIODICALS

- Bibliography

ORGANIZATION OF AMERICAN STATES. 1958. Repertorio de publicaciones periódicas actuales latinoamericanas; Directory of current Latin American periodicals. [Paris], Unesco, 1958. pp. 266. (Unesco Bibliographical Handbooks. [8])

HARVARD UNIVERSITY. Library. Widener Library Shelflists. Nos. 5-6. Latin America and Latin American periodicals. Cambridge, Mass., Harvard University Press, 1966. 2 vols.

LATIN AMERICAN PERIODICALS - Bibliography (Cont'd.)

LEVI (NADIA) and others, compilers.
Guía de publicaciones periódicas de universidades latinoamericanas. México, Universidad Nacional Autónoma de México, 1967. pp. 406. 23½cm.

LATIN American serial documents: a holdings list. Ann Arbor, 1968 in progress. (Florida University. Libraries. Documents Department)

COMMITTEE ON LATIN AMERICA. Latin American economic and social serials. London, Bingley, 1969. pp. 189. bibliog. 21½cm.

- Indexes

ORGANIZATION OF AMERICAN STATES. Pan American Union. Columbus Memorial Library. 1962-68. Index to Latin American periodical literature, 1929-1960; ([with] First supplement 1961-1965). Boston, Mass., Hall, 1962-1968. 10 vols.

LATIN AMERICAN STUDIES

ORGANIZATION OF AMERICAN STATES. 1959. Survey of investigations in progress in the field of Latin American studies; compiled by Basil C. Hedrick. (Department of Cultural Affairs) Washington, 1959. pp. 76. 21cm. For a later survey see ORGANIZATION OF AMERICAN STATES. 1962.

ORGANIZATION OF AMERICAN STATES. 1962. Survey of investigations in progress in the field of Latin American studies; compiled by Philip F. Flemion and Murdo J. MacLeod. (Department of Cultural Affairs) Washington, 1962. pp. 80. 21cm. For a previous survey see ORGANIZATION OF AMERICAN STATES. 1959.

UNITED STATES. State Department. Resources survey for Latin American countries. Washington, 1965. pp (iii), 640.

LATIN America in transition: problems in training and research; (proceedings of a conference held at the State University of New York at Stony Brook, 22-23 March 1968); edited by Stanley R. Ross. Albany, [N.Y.], [1970]. pp. 150.

- Europe - Directories

DIRECTORIO de latinoamericanistas europeos: Directory of European Latin Americanists; ([edited by] H. Hoetink [and others]). Amsterdam, 1969. pp. 96. (In Spanish and English).

- Russia

OSWALD (J. GREGORY) Soviet image of contemporary Latin America: a documentary history, 1960-1968; compiled and translated from Russian by J. Gregory Oswald;...edited by Robert G. Carlton. Austin, Texas, [1970]. pp. 365. (Conference on Latin American History. Publications. No. 3.)

- United States

SPELL (LOTA M.) Research materials for the study of Latin America at the University of Texas. Austin, U. of Texas P., 1954. pp. ix, 107. (Texas University. Institute of Latin American Studies. Latin American Studies. 14)

SHIRES (PAMELA) compiler. Latin American activities and resources at the University of California, Los Angeles, December, 1966. [Los Angeles, California University, Latin American Center], 1966. fo. (v), 136. 27½cm.

GOMEZ (R.A.) The study of Latin American politics in university programs in the United States. Tucson, [1967]. pp. 75. bibliog. (Arizona University. Institute of Government Research. Comparative Government Studies. No. 2)

LATIN LANGUAGE

- Study and teaching

GOODYEAR (FRANCIS RICHARD DAVID) The future of Latin studies in English education; an inaugural lecture. London, 1967. pp. 14.

- Words - History

PELLICER (ANDRÉ) Natura: étude sémantique et historique du mot latin. Paris, P.U.F., 1966. pp. 524. bibliog. 25cm. (Montpellier. Université. Faculté des Lettres et Sciences Humaines. Publications. 27)

LATIN LANGUAGE, MEDIEVAL AND MODERN

- Glossaries, vocabularies, etc.

FISHER (JOHN LIONEL) A medieval farming glossary of Latin and English words taken mainly from Essex records. London, National Council of Social Service, [1968]. pp. (viii), 41. 21½cm.

LATIN LANGUAGE, VULGAR

HERMAN (JOSEPH) Le latin vulgaire. Paris, 1967. pp. 125. bibliog.

VÄÄNÄNEN (VEIKKO) Introduction au latin vulgaire; nouvelle édition revue et complétée d'une anthologie avec commentaires. Paris, 1967. pp. 274. bibliog. 23cm. (Strasbourg. Université. Faculté des Lettres. Centre de Philologie et de Littératures Romanes. Bibliothèque Française et Romane. Series A: Manuels et Études Linguistiques. 6)

LATIN LITERATURE

- Study and teaching

GOODYEAR (FRANCIS RICHARD DAVID) The future of Latin studies in English education; an inaugural lecture. London, 1967. pp. 14.

LATIN LITERATURE, MEDIEVAL AND MODERN

FRAZER (Sir J. G.) Mediaeval Latin fabulists. in Frazer (Sir James George) Creation and evolution in primitive cosmogonies, and other pieces; [reprint of the work originally published in 1935]. London, 1968.

LA TORRE (LISANDRO DE)

GONZALES ARRILI (BERNARDO) Vida de Lisandro de la Torre. Buenos Aires, [1962]. pp. 194. bibliog.

LATROBE VALLEY, VICTORIA

- Economic conditions

VICTORIA. 1964. Development of the Latrobe Valley: progress achieved to 1st January, 1964 and plans for further development; compiled by the Latrobe Valley Development Advisory Committee. Melbourn [1964] pp. iii, 38. 25½cm.

LATTER DAY SAINTS
See MORMONS AND MORMONISM

LATVIA

- Bibliography

PŪCE (O.) and VEINBERGS (J.) compilers. Latvijas PSR, 1940-1960: literatūras rādītajs; Латвийская ССР, 1940-1960: указатель литературы. Riga, 1961. pp. 578.

- Commerce

ZITRON (HIRSCH) Aussenhandel und Handelspolitik Lettlands und die Frage der baltischen Zollunion. Riga, 1935. pp. 109. bibliog.

- Commercial policy

ZITRON (HIRSCH) Aussenhandel und Handelspolitik Lettlands und die Frage der baltischen Zollunion. Riga, 1935. pp. 109. bibliog.

- Constitution

GOSUDARSTVENNO-PRAVOVOE... Государственно-правовое строительство Латвийской ССР. Рига, Зинатне, 1968. pp. 312. 19½см.

ŠKAPARE (BALVA) Rol' postoiannykh komissii mestnykh Sovetov v obespechenii sotsialisticheskoi zakonnosti: po materialam Latviiskoi SSR. Riga, 1969. pp. 83.

- Constitutional history

MILLER (VISVARIS OTTOVICH) Создание Советской государственности в Латвии. Рига, 1967. pp. 528. bibliog.

- Economic conditions

BILMANIS (ALFRED) compiler. Latvia in the present world crisis: facts and figures. Washington, Latvian Legation, [1949?]. pp. 8.

GULIAN (PETR VATSLAVOVICH) Latviia v sisteme narodnogo khoziaistva SSSR. Riga, 1967. pp. 386. bibliog.

LATVIISKII GOSUDARSTVENNYI UNIVERSITET. Uchenye Zapiski. tom 108. Latvijas PSR tautas saimniecības attīstības jautājumi. Riga, 1968. pp. 156. Articles in Latvian and Russian.

PROBLEMY razvitiia narodnogo khoziaistva Latviiskoi SSR. Riga, 1970. pp. 333.

- Economic history

OCHERKI... Очерки экономической истории Латвии, 1900-1917: из истории экономических предпосылок Великой Октябрьской социалистической революции в Латвии. Рига, 1968. pp. 345. bibliog.

V bratskoi sem'e narodov SSSR: trudy kafedr obshchestvennykh nauk vysshikh uchebnykh zavedenii. Riga, 1969. pp. 181.

- Economic policy

DELO... Дело всех, дело каждого: из опыта работы органов народного контроля Латвийской ССР по выявлению и использованию резервов производства. Рига, Лиесма, 1968. pp. 142. 20см.

PIATILETKU... Пятилетку - досрочно!: из опыта работы партийных организаций Латвийской ССР по использованию резервов и повышению эффективности производства. Рига, Лиесма, 1968. pp. 232. 20см.

- Foreign relations

SIPOLS (VILNIS IANOVICH) Тайная дипломатия: буржуазная Латвия в антисоветских планах империалистических держав, 1919-1940 гг. Рига, Лиесма, 1968. pp. 347. 21см.

- Foreign relations - United Kingdom

VARSLAVAN (A.) Politika angliiskogo imperializma v otnoshenii burzhuaznoi Latvii, 1920-1923. Riga, 1966. pp. 183.

- History

GRUENER (VIKTOR) Von der Willkür zum System: zum Verständnis des lettischen Bolschewismus. Berlin, [1919]. pp. 45.

BILMANIS (ALFRED) compiler. Latvia in the present world crisis: facts and figures. Washington, Latvian Legation, [1949?]. pp. 8.

- History - Historiography

LATVIISKII GOSUDARSTVENNYI UNIVERSITET. Uchenye Zapiski. t. 82. Istoricheskie Nauki. vyp. 5. Voprosy istoriografii Latviiskoi SSR. Riga, 1967. pp. 63.

BIRON (ANATOLII KARLOVICH) and DOROSHENKO (VASILII VASIL'EVICH) Советская историография Латвии. Рига, 1970. pp. 497.

- History - Sources

HENRICUS de Ymera. Хроника Ливонии; введение, перевод [с латинского] и комментарии С.А. Аннинского, предисловие В.А. Быстрянского. 2nd ed. Ленинград, 1938. pp. 251.

MY obviniaem. Riga, 1967. pp. 316. With appendix of facsimiles and photographs.

LATVIA (Cont'd.)

- Industries

STURE (E.) Вопросы перспективного планирования комплексной механизации промышленности. in Эффективность комплексного развития техники в промышленности. Москва, 1966.

IANOV (IAN ALEKSANDROVICH) Effektivnost' kontsentratsii proizvodstva i optimal'nye razmery predpriiatii. Riga, 1969. pp. 151.

EKONOMICHESKOE stimulirovanie povysheniia effektivnosti proizvodstva. Riga, 1970. pp. 91.

SVILPE (KARL IANOVICH) Совершенствование организации повышения качества продукции. Рига, 1970. pp. 228. bibliog.

- Intellectual life

LATVIA. Tsentral'noe Statisticheskoe Upravlenie. 1967. Печать и культурно-просветительные учреждения Латвийской ССР: статистический сборник. Рига. 1967. pp. 179. 14см.

- Moral conditions

MORGUNOV (I. G.) Всестороннее развитие личности. Рига, 1967. pp. 238.

- Nationalism

GORIS (A.) Latyshskie burzhuazno-natsionalisticheskie emigranty - orudie antikommunisticheskoi politiki imperialisticheskoi reaktsii. in Antikommunizm - orudie imperialisticheskoi reaktsii. Moskva, 1967.

GERMANIS (U.) The idea of independent Latvia and its development in 1917. in Sprudzs (Adolf) and Rusis (Armins) eds. Res baltica. Leyden, 1968.

MIŠKE (V.) Этого нельзя забывать: как латышская националистическая буржуазия предавала родину и народ в 1917-1919 годах; (перевод с латышского) Рига, Лиесма, 1968. pp. 135. 16½см.

- Politics and government

MILLER (VISVARIS OTTOVICH) Создание Советской государственности в Латвии. Рига, 1967. pp. 528. bibliog.

RAPOPORT (G.B.) Budni podpol'ia. 3rd ed. Riga, 1970. pp. 348.

- Politics and government - Bibliography

PŪCE (O.) compiler. Cīņa par Padomju varu Latvijā: izraksti no revolucionāras periodikas, 1920-1940; literaturas rāditajs; Bor'ba za Sovetskuiu vlast' v Latvii: analiticheskaia rospis' revoliutsionnoi periodiki, 1920-1940; ukazatel' literatury. Riga, 1969. pp. 495. bibliog.

- Religion

BALEVITS (ZIGMUND VLADISLAVOVICH) Православная церковь Латвии под сенью свастики, 1941-1944. Рига, 1967. pp. 90.

ATEIZM... Атеизм и религия; некоторые проблемы атеистического воспитания в Латвийской ССР. Рига, 1969. pp. 207.

- Sanitary affairs

GRIGORASH (FEDOR FEDOROVICH) and ARONS (KARL IANOVICH) Здравоохранению Советской Латвии 20 лет. Рига, 1960. pp. 106.

LATVIA. Ministerstvo Zdravookhraneniia. 1965. 25 лет здравоохранения Советской Латвии; Padomju Latvijas veselības aizsardzībai 25 gadi. Рига, Звайгзне, 1965. pp. 157, xxxviii. 24см. In Latvian and Russian.

- Social policy

MORGUNOV (I. G.) Всестороннее развитие личности. Рига, 1967. pp. 238.

- Statistics

LATVIA. Latviiskaia SSR v tsifrakh v...godu: kratkii statisticheskii sbornik. (Tsentral'noe Statisticheskow Upravlenie) Riga, annual, 1961 to date. 14cm.

LATVIA. Tsentral'noe Statisticheskoe Upravlenie. 1966. Padomju Latvijas ekonomika un kultūra; Экономика и культура Советской Латвии: statistisko datu krājums; статистический сборник. Rīga, 1966. pp. 508. In Latvian and Russian.

LATVIA. Tsentral'noe Statisticheskoe Upravlenie. 1967. Latviia za gody Sovetskoi vlasti: statisticheskii sbornik. Riga, 1967. pp. 403.

LATVIA. Tsentral'noe Statisticheskoe Upravlenie. 1968. Narodnoe khoziaistvo Sovetskoi Latvii: statisticheskii sbornik. Riga, 1968. pp. 541. In Latvian and Russian.

LATVIANS IN SPAIN

BORTSY Latvii v Ispanii, 1936-1939: vospominaniia i dokumenty. Riga, 1970. pp. 560.

LAUCA, RIVER

BOLIVIA. Ministerio de Relaciones Exteriores y Culto. 1962. La desviacion del rio Lauca: antecedentes y documentos. La Paz, 1962. pp. 310.

LAUD (WILLIAM) Archbishop of Canterbury

ALL to Westminster: newes from Elizium; or, A packet of wonders, brought over in Charons ferry-boat last spring tyde; discovering many notable things worth observation, 1641. [London] 1641. pp. 6. 18½cm. Wing A 949.

The BISHOPS potion; or, A dialogue betweene the Bishop of Canterbury, and his phisitian, wherein he desireth the doctor to have a care of his bodie, and to preserve him from being let blood in the neck, when the signe is in Taurus. [London], 1641. pp. 4. 18½cm.

A BRIEFE recitall of the unreasonable proceedings of Dr. Laud against T.W. Minister of the Word of God which he conveyed into his hands in a letter very lately sent to him in the Tower; together with his absurd answer to the same. London, Overton, 1641. pp. 5. 17½cm. Wing W 112.

BROWNE (JOHN) Jesuit. A discovery of the notorious proceedings of William Laud, Archbishop of Canterbury, in bringing innovations into the Church, and raising up troubles in the state, etc. London, Walker, 1641. pp. (5). 18½cm. Wing B 5119.

CANTERBURIES dreame: in which the apparition of Cardinall Wolsey did present himselfe unto him on the fourtenth [sic] of May last past: it being the third night after my Lord of Strafford had taken his fare-well to the world. [London], 1641. pp. (6). 18½cm. Wing C 458.

CANTERBURIE[S] pilgrimage: in the testimony of an accused conscienc[e] for the bloud of Mr. Burton, Mr. Prynne, and Doctor Bastwicke; and the deserved sufferings he lyes under, etc. London, Walker, 1641. pp. (6). 17½cm. Wing C 459. Title-page cropped.

CANTERBURIES potion: wherein is shewed the great art of his doctor in finding out the nature of his disease; together with the medicines hee applied, and the strange effects they wrought in him, to the great ease of his surcharged body, collected from the doctors owne hand. n.p., 1641. pp. (5). 18½cm. Wing C 460.

CANTERBURY'S will; with a serious conference betweene his scrivener and him; also a loving admonition to his brethren the bishops. [London], 1641. pp. 8. 17½cm. Wing C 461.

An EXACT copy of a letter, sent to William Laud late Arch-bishop of Canterbury, now prisoner in the Tower, November the 5, 1641...and... some private discourse with him; [the letter signed: A]. London, H.W[alker?] and T.B[ates?] 1641. pp. 6. 18½cm. Wing A 2.

GULTER (GILES) The archbishops crueltie, made knowne in a true story of one Mr. Edward Rood, who was Minister at Saint Helens in Abingdon, and dismissed of his meanes and ministery by him, etc. [London], 1641. pp. (6). 17½cm. Wing G 2229.

LAUD (WILLIAM) Archbishop of Canterbury. The copie of a letter sent...the 28 of June MDCXLI unto the Vniversitie of Oxford specifying, his willingnesse to resigne his Chancellor-ship, and withall deploring his sad estate now in the time of his imprisonment: [suppositious]. [London], 1641. pp. 2. 18½cm. Wing L 581.

LAUD (WILLIAM) Archbishop of Canterbury. The copy of a letter sent...to the Universitie of Oxford wherein he relates his present condition, and resignes the office of his Chancellourship, with an advertisement, for the election of another: [suppositious]. [London], 1641. pp. 3. 17½cm. Wing L 580.

LAUD (WILLIAM) Archbishop of Canterbury. A letter sent...with divers manuscripts to the Vniversity of Oxford...with the answer which the Vniversiti sent him, wherein is specified their integrity, as he is their Chancellor,...; [translated from the Latin]. [London], 1641. pp. 5. 17½cm. Wing L 590.

LAUD (WILLIAM) Archbishop of Canterbury. The true copie of a letter sent...to the Vniversity of Oxford, when he resign'd his office of Chancellour; published by occasion of a base libell and forgery that runs under this title; and also the answer of the Vniversity to the said letter. Oxford, Lichfield, 1641. pp. 8. 18½cm. Wing L 601.

A NEW play called Canterburie his change of diot, etc. [London], 1641. pp. (6). 17½cm. Wing N 702.

[PRYNNE (WILLIAM)] Canterburies tooles: or, Instruments wherewith he hath effected many rare feats, and egregious exploits, as is very well known, and notoriously manifest to all men, etc. [London], 1641. pp. 6. 18½cm. Wing P 3918.

PYM (JOHN) M.P. The speech or declaration...to the Lords of the upper House, upon the delivery of the articles of the Commons assembled in Parliament, against William Laud, Archbishop of Canterbury, in maintenance of their accusation, whereby he stands charged of high treason; together with a true copie of the said articles. London, Mabb, 1641. pp. 34. 18½cm. Wing P 4295.

ROMES ABC, being a short perambulation, or rather articular accusation of a late tyrannicall oppressour; with a petition to the Archbishop of Canterbury, now prisoner in the Tower. [London], 1641. pp. 6. 18½cm. Wing L 95.

[TAYLOR (JOHN) the Water Poet] The Pope's benediction; or, His generall pardon to be purchased onely wirh [sic] mony and without penance: sent into England by Ignatius Holy-water a Jesuit, to the Archbishop of Canterbury, and to the rest of his subjects there. London, 1641. pp. 5. 18½cm. Wing T 497.

WRAY (Sir JOHN) Three speeches made...to the House of Commons assembled in Parliament: 1. Against Thomas, Earle of Strafford, and the Bishop of Canterbury; 2. Being a motion for the taking of an oath to maintaine the religion and vowes established; 3. Against the oath and canons made by the Assembly at the last Convocation. London, 1641. pp. 8. 17½cm. Wing W 3670.

A COPIE of a letter written from his Holinesse Court at Rome, to his Grace of Canterburies palace now in the Tower deploring his sequestration from his liberty, but commending him for his late care in performing his Holinesse desires. London, [Norton?], 1642. pp. 4. 17½cm. Wing C 6171.

[LAUD (WILLIAM) Archbishop of Canterbury]. A letter sent from the Arch-bishop of Canterbury, now prisoner in the Tower, to the Vice-Chancellor, doctors, and the rest of the Convocation at Oxford, intimating his humble desires to His Majesty, for a speedy reconcilement between him and His High Court of Parliament: [probably suppositious]. London, Vere, [1642]. pp. 8. 18½cm. Wing L 591.

LAUD (WILLIAM) Archbishop of Canterbury (Cont'd.)

LAUD (WILLIAM) Archbishop of Canterbury. The copy of the petition presented to the Honourable Houses of Parliament, by the Lord Arch-Bishop of Canterbury, etc.: wherein the said Arch-Bishop desires that he may not be transported beyond the seas into New England with Master Peters, in regard of his extraordinary age and weakenesse. London, Smith, 1643. pp. (5). 18½cm. Wing L 582.

UNITED KINGDOM. Parliament. 1643. An ordinance of the Lords and Commons...concerning the Arch-Bishop of Canterbury, who by reason of many great and weighty businesses, cannot as yet be brought to his tryall: [dated 16 May, 1643]. London, Wright, 1643. pp. (3). 18½cm. Wing E 1815.

UNITED KINGDOM. Parliament. 1643. An ordinance of the Lords and Commons...that all the temporall livings...belonging unto William [Laud] Lord Arch-bishoppe of Canterbury, be forthwith sequestered...and that he shall be suspended...; [dated 16 May and 10 June, 1643]. [London], Wright, 1643. pp. (6). 19cm. Wing E 2084.

UNITED KINGDOM. Parliament. House of Commons. 1644. Articles of the Commons...in maintenance of their accusation against William Laud, Arch-bishop of Canterbury, whereby he stands charged with high treason; also, further articles of impeachment...; [dated 17 January, **1644**]. [London], Wright, 1643[O.S.]. pp. 14. 18½cm. Wing E 2527.

[HEYLYN (PETER)] A briefe relation of the death and sufferings of the...Archbishop of Canterbury, etc. Oxford[or rather London], 1644 [O.S.]. pp. 30. 18½cm. Wing H 1685.

LAUD (WILLIAM) Archbishop of Canterbury. The Archbishop of Canterbury's speech; or, His funeral sermon, preacht by himself on the scaffold on Tower-Hill, on Friday the 10. of Ianuary, 1644[O.S.], etc. London, Cole, 1644[O.S.]. pp. 5-19. 18½cm. Wing L 599.

[BURTON (HENRY) Rector of St.Matthews, Friday Street] A full and satisfactorie answere to the Arch-bishop of Canterburies speeh [sic], or, funerall sermon, etc. London, Coe, 1645. **pp. 23.** 18½cm. Wing B 6162A.

[PARKER (HENRY) of Lincoln's Inn] [Jus regum; or, A vindication of the regall power against all spirituall authority...; in a brief discourse occasioned by the observation of some passages in the Archbishop of Canterburies last speech]. [London, Bostock, 1645]. pp. 38. 17½cm. Wing P 404. Lacks title page.

The TRUE informer. [London], 4/11 Jan., 1645 (no. 61). 18½cm.

LAUNCESTON

- Sewerage

TASMANIA. 1965. Launceston Corporation: reimbursement for installation of water, sewerage and drainage: report of joint committee of both Houses of Parliament, with minutes of proceedings: [W.H. Fraser, chairman] in Tasmania. Parliament. Journals and printed papers. 1965. Part 2. No.77.

- Water-supply

TASMANIA. 1965. Launceston Corporation: reimbursement for installation of water, sewerage and drainage: report of joint committee of both Houses of Parliament, with minutes of proceedings: [W.H. Fraser, chairman]. in Tasmania. Parliament. Journals and printed papers. 1965. Part 2. No.77.

LAUNDRIES, PUBLIC

COMMITTEE FOR PROMOTING THE ESTABLISHMENT OF BATHS AND WASH-HOUSES FOR THE LABOURING CLASSES. Baths and wash-houses for the labouring classes: report by the engineer to the committee [P.Prichard Baly]. London, 1852. pp. 40.

LAUNDRY INDUSTRY

- Canada

CANADA. Dominion Bureau of Statistics. Power laundries, dry cleaning and dyeing plants (formerly Laundries, cleaners and dyers). Ottawa, annual, 1958 to date. 28cm.

LAVAL (PIERRE)

WARNER (GEOFFREY) Pierre Laval and the eclipse of France. London, Eyre & Spottiswoode, 1968. pp. xix, 461. bibliog. 22cm.

GOUNELLE (CLAUDE) Le dossier Laval. [Paris, 1969]. pp. 764.

LAVAL UNIVERSITY

QUEBEC. Université Laval. Comité de Développement et de Planification de l'Enseignement et de la Recherche. Un projet de réforme pour l'Université Laval; rapport préparé pour le Conseil de l'Université; [chairman, Lorenzo Roy]. Québec, 1968. pp. 170.

LAVELLE (LOUIS)

HARDY (GILBERT G.) La vocation de la liberté chez Louis Lavelle. Louvain, 1968. pp. 128. bibliog.

LA VERBENA

- Economic conditions

GUATEMALA. Direccion General de Obras Publicas. Seccion de Estudios Geograficos. 1968. Barrios marginales; informe sobre la Colonia La Verbena, Finca "La Verbena" Zona 7, Ciudad de Guatemala. [Guatemala, 1968]. pp. 59.

- Social conditions

GUATEMALA. Direccion General de Obras Publicas. Seccion de Estudios Geograficos. 1968. Barrios marginales; informe sobre la Colonia La Verbena, Finca "La Verbena" Zona 7, Ciudad de Guatemala. [Guatemala, 1968]. pp. 59.

LAVRADIO (LUIS DE ALMEIDA PORTUGAL SOARES) 2nd Marquis of

ALDEN (DAURIL) Royal government in colonial Brazil: with special reference to the administration of the Marquis of Lavradio, Viceroy, 1769-1779. Berkeley, U. of California P., 1968. pp. xxvii, 545. bibliog. 23½cm.

LAVROV (PETR LAVROVICH)

TROITSKII (N.A.) Osnovanie zhurnala P.L. Lavrova "Vpered!" in Iz istorii obshchestvennoi mysli i obshchestvennogo dvizheniia v Rossii. Saratov, 1964.

KAZAKOV (ANATOLII PAVLOVICH) Teoriia progressa v russkoi sotsiologii kontsa XIX veka: P.L. Lavrov, N.K. Mikhailovskii, M.M. Kovalevskii. Leningrad, 1969. pp. 129.

VOLODIN (A.I.) and ITENBERG (B.S.) Fridrikh Engel's i Petr Lavrov. in Engel's i problemy istorii. Moskva, 1970.

LAW (JOHN)

HYDE (HARFORD MONTGOMERY) John Law: the history of an honest adventurer. new ed. London, 1969. pp. 228. bibliog.

LAW

BRUSSELS. Université Libre. Faculté de Droit. Travaux et Conférences. 7. Bruxelles, Larcier, 1959. pp. 145. 24½cm.

KEMPSKI (JUERGEN VON) Recht und Politik: Studien zur Einheit der Sozialwissenschaft. Stuttgart, Kohlhammer, [1965]. pp. 231. 23cm.

MOKICHEV (К. А.) ed. Теория государства и права. Москва, Юридическая Литература, 1965. pp. 519. 21½см.

SCRITTI giuridici in memoria di Marcello Barberio Corsetti; [presented by the Consiglio dell'Ordine degli Avvocati di Roma]. Milano, 1965. pp. 807.

STUDI in memoria di Guido Zanobini. Milano, 1965. 5 vols. bibliog. A few articles in Spanish.

KADELBACH (GERD) ed. Wissenschaft und Gesellschaft: Einführung in das Studium von Politikwissenschaft, neuere Geschichte, Volkswirtschaft, Recht, Soziologie. Frankfurt a. M, 1967. pp. 343. (Frankfurt am Main. Universität and Hessischer Rundfunk. Funk-Kolleg zum Verständnis der modernen Gesellschaft. Band 1)

SCRITTI in memoria di Antonino Giuffrè. Milano, Giuffrè, 1967. 4 vols.

STUDI in onore di Antonio Segni. Milano, 1967. 4 vols. (Rome. Università. Facoltà di Giurisprudenza. Pubblicazioni. 28-31) In various languages.

FESTSCHRIFT für Walther Hug, Professor Dr. iur., S.J.D. Harvard: zum 70. Geburtstag 14. April 1968; (herausgegeben von Riccardo L. Jagmetti und Walter R. Schluep). Bern, [1968]. pp. 707. bibliog. In various languages.

La FUNZIONE del diritto nell'attuale momento storico: (scritti di giuristi italiani e stranieri in celebrazione del decennale della costituzione legale dell'Istituto Internazionale di Studi Giuridici) Roma, 1969. pp. 223.

KIRCHHEIMER (OTTO) Politics, law, and social change: selected essays...; edited by Frederic S. Burin and Kurt L. Shell. New York, Columbia U.P., 1969. pp. xlii, 483. bibliog. 23½cm.

DROR (YEHEZKEL) Law as a tool of directed social change: a framework for policymaking. n.p., 1970. pp. 12.

- Bibliography

BRAZIL. Ministério da Justiça e Negócios Interiores. Serviço de Documentação. Biblioteca. 1961. Catálogo da Biblioteca: direito (1941-1955). [Rio de Janeiro?, 1961]. pp. 572. 23cm.

PRICE (MILES OSCAR) and BITNER (HARRY) Effective legal research: student edition revised. Boston, Little, Brown, 1962 repr. 1966. pp. xx, 496. 23½cm.

- Codification

VANDERLINDEN (JACQUES) Le concept de code en Europe occidentale du XIIIe au XIXe siècle: essai de définition. Bruxelles, Université Libre, Institut de Sociologie, [1967]. pp. 500. bibliog. 24cm. (Études d'Histoire et d'Ethnologie Juridiques)

- Dictionaries and encyclopaedias

SAUNDERS (JOHN BEECROFT) ed. Words and phrases legally defined. 2nd ed. London, Butterworths, 1969 in progress. 24½cm.

DIETL (CLARA ERIKA) Wörterbuch der Wirtschafts-, Rechts- und Handelssprache...Band I. Anglo/amerikanisch-deutsch. Schloss Bleckede, [1971]. pp. 302.

- History and criticism

MACDONELL (Sir JOHN) and MANSON (EDWARD) eds. Great jurists of the world; (first published by Little, Brown, in 1914). South Hackensack, Rothman Reprints, 1968. pp. xxxii, 607. 22½cm. (Association of American Law Schools. Continental Legal History Series. vol. 2)

LE BRAS (GABRIEL) and others. L'age classique, 1140-1378: sources et théorie du droit. Paris, Sirey, [1965] pp. xii, 608. 25cm. (Histoire du Droit et des Institutions de l'Église en Occident. Tome 7)

DAWSON (JOHN PHILIP) The oracles of the law. Ann Arbor, 1968. pp. 520. (Michigan. University. Law School. Thomas M. Cooley Lectures. 1959)

MARXISTISCHE Beiträge zur Rechtsgeschichte. Berlin, 1968. pp. 236. (Berlin. Humboldt-Universität. Wissenschaftliche Schriftenreihe)

OURLIAC (PAUL) and MALAFOSSE (J. DE) Histoire du droit privé. tome 3. Le droit familial. Paris, P.U.F., 1968. pp. vii, 554. 18cm. (Thémis)

THIEME (H. W.) Rechtsgeschichte und Zeitgeschichte. in vol. 1 of Sieber (Marc) ed. Discordia concors. Basel, [1968].

LAW - History and criticism (Cont'd.)

KANTOROWICZ (HERMANN U.) Rechtshistorische Schriften...; herausgegeben von Helmut Coing und Gerhard Immel. Karlsruhe, 1970. pp. 468. bibliog. (Freiburg im Breisgau. Universität. Rechts- und Staatswissenschaftliche Fakultät. Freiburger Rechts- und Staatswissenschaftliche Abhandlungen. Band 30)

- History and criticism - Bibliography

GILISSEN (JOHN) ed. Bibliographical introduction to legal history and ethnology. Bruxelles, Université Libre, Institut de Sociologie, [1963 in progress]. 26cm. (Études d'Histoire et d'Ethnologie Juridiques) Loose leaf. In English or French.

- International unification

SCHMITTHOFF (CLIVE MACMILLAN) The unification of the law of international trade. Göteborg, 1964. pp. 28. (Gothenburg. Handelshögskolan. Skriftserie. 1964.5)

WIEBRINGHAUS (HANS) Die Bemühungen des Europarats um eine Rechtsangleichung auf wirtschaftlichem Gebiet. Göttingen, Schwartz, 1967. pp. 101-139. bibliog. 20½cm. (Göttingen. Universität. Institut für Völkerrecht. Beiträge zum Internationalen Wirtschaftsrecht und Atomenergierecht. Band 2. Heft 4)

- Interpretation and construction

KRIELE (MARTIN) Theorie der Rechtsgewinnung entwickelt am Problem der Verfassungsinterpretation. Berlin, Duncker und Humblot, [1967]. pp. 334. bibliog. 23½cm. (Schriften zum "Öffentlichen Recht." Band 41)

- Periodicals

BLAUSTEIN (ALBERT P.) Manual on foreign legal periodicals and their index. Dobbs Ferry, Oceana, 1962. pp. (vii), 137. 22½cm. (Columbia University. Parker School of Foreign and Comparative Law. Studies in Foreign and Comparative Law.)

MAX-PLANCK-GESELLSCHAFT ZUR FÖRDERUNG DER WISSENSCHAFTEN. Zeitschriftenverzeichnis der juristischen Max-Planck-Institute, ZVJM: Zeitschriften, Jahrbücher, periodische Gesetz- und Entscheidungssammlungen, Parlamentaria; Stand 15.1.1969. München, [1969]. pp. 365.

- Periodicals - Bibliography

LONDON. University. Institute of Advanced Legal Studies. Union Catalogues. No. 1. Union list of legal periodicals: a location guide to holdings of legal periodicals in libraries in the United Kingdom. 3rd ed. London, 1968. pp. xv, 179. 24cm.

- Philosophy

[BERTOLINI ( ) Abbé] Analyse raisonnée de l'Esprit des loix. Pise, Grazioli, 1784. pp. 126. 18½cm

FEUERBACH (P.J.A.) Über Philosophie und Empirie in ihren Verhältnis zur positiven Rechtswissenschaft: eine Antrittsrede. in Luederssen (Klaus) ed. Theorie der Erfahrung in der Rechtswissenschaft des 19. Jahrhunderts:...[published in 1804]. Frankfurt am Main, 1968.

CHEVALLEY (E.) La théorie des différents ordres de lois, d'après Montesquieu, et son application à l'histoire: le divorce de Napoléon. Le Caire, [190-?]. pp. 163. 25cm.

KRUPA (HANS) Otto von Gierke und die Probleme der Rechtsphilosophie; Neudruck der Ausgabe Breslau 1940. Aalen, 1969. pp. 64.

LOEFFELHOLZ (THOMAS) Die Rechtsphilosophie des Pragmatismus: eine kritische Studie. Meisenheim am Glan, Hain, 1961. pp. xi, 156. bibliog. 23cm. (Monographien zur Philosophischen Forschung. Band 31)

CONGRESSO NAZIONALE DI FILOSOFIA DEL DIRITTO, 6°, PISA, 1963. Dommatica, teoria generale e filosofia del diritto: stato di diritto e stato di giustizia: atti...a cura di Rinaldo Orecchia. 2. Comunicazioni. Milano, 1964. pp. xiv, 339.

HALL (JEROME) From legal theory to integrative jurisprudence. [Cincinnati, University, 1964]. pp. (ii), 53. 25cm. (Cincinnati. University. School of Law. Robert S. Marx Lectures) (Reprinted from University of Cincinnati Law Review. 1964, vol. 33, No. 2)

KASSIMATES (GRÉGORIOS P.) L'état, la société et le droit: études sur l'évolution de la pensée politique, sociale et juridique de notre temps. Paris, Sirey, [1964]. pp. 206. 24cm.

VONLANTHEN (ALBERT) Zu Hans Kelsens Anschauung über die Rechtsnorm. Berlin, Duncker und Humblot, [1965]. pp. 92. 23cm. (Schriften zur Rechtstheorie. Heft 6)

BERCHENKO (ALEKSANDR IAKOVLEVICH) Воспитательная роль советского права. Москва, Мысль, 1966. pp. 79. 20cm.

CONGRESSO NAZIONALE DI FILOSOFIA DEL DIRITTO, 7, ROMA, 1965. Diritto e potere: il problema dell'interpretazione e dell'applicazione del diritto; atti...a cura di Rinaldo Orecchia. Milano, Giuffrè, 1966. 2 vols. (in 1). 25cm.

Die MODERNE Demokratie und ihr Recht; Modern constitutionalism and democracy; Festschrift für Gerhard Leibholz zum 65. Geburtstag. Tübingen, 1966. 2 vols. bibliog. 23cm.

BRIMO (ALBERT) Les grands courants de la philosophie du droit et de l'état. Paris, Pedone, 1967. pp. 436. bibliogs. 22½cm. (Collection: Philosophie Comparée du Droit et de l'État)

BUCHDAHL (G.) Semantic sources of the concept of law. in Boston Colloquium for the Philosophy of Science. Proceedings, 1964-1966. Boston studies in the philosophy of science, vol.3. Dordrecht, 1967.

COLLOQUE DE PHILOSOPHIE DU DROIT COMPARÉE. 2e Colloque, Toulouse, 1966. La logique juridique: travaux, etc. Paris, Pedone, 1967. pp. 262. 24cm. (Collection Philosophie Comparée du Droit et de l'État. 2) (Extrait des Annales de la Faculté de Droit et des Sciences Économiques de Toulouse)

LONDOÑO HOYOS (FERNANDO) El poder del juez. Bogotá, Kelly, 1967. pp. 102. bibliog. 24cm.

MARCIC (R.) Die Würde des Rechts und die Freiheit des Menschen. in Roegele (Otto Bernhard) ed. Die Freiheit des Westens. Graz, [1967].

MORIONDO (EZIO) L'ideologia della magistratura italiana. Bari, Laterza, 1967. pp. xx, 351. 21½cm. (Centro Nazionale di Prevenzione e Difesa Sociale. Indagine su "L'Amministrazione della Giustizia e la Società Italiana in Trasformazione"1)

VECCHIO (GIORGIO DEL) Nuova silloge di temi giuridici e filosofici. Torino, Giappichelli, [1967]. pp. 202. 23cm.

WEBER (MAX) Rechtssoziologie; aus dem Manuskript herausgegeben und eingeleitet von Johannes Winckelmann. 2nd ed. Neuwied am Rhein, Luchterhand, 1967. pp. 452. Bibliog. 19cm. (Soziologische Texte. Band 2)

CONDE SALGADO (REMIGIO) Sociedad, estado y derecho en la filosofía marxista. Madrid, Cuadernos para el Diàlogo, 1968. pp. 232. bibliog. 18½cm. (Divulgación Universitaria. No. 2)

DIESSELHORST (MALTE) Ursprünge des modernen Systemdenkens bei Hobbes. Stuttgart, [1968]. pp. 54. (Mannheim. Universität. Veröffentlichungen. Band 22)

DUBISCHAR (ROLAND) Grundbegriffe des Rechts: eine Einführung in die Rechtstheorie. Stuttgart, Kohlhammer, 1968. pp. 105. 23cm.

KLECATSKY (HANS R.) and others, eds. Die Wiener rechtstheoretische Schule: Schriften von Hans Kelsen, Adolf Merkl. Alfred Verdross. Wien, Europa, [1968]. 2 vols. 21½cm.

LLOMPART (JOSE) Die Geschichtlichkeit in der Begründung des Rechts im Deutschland der Gegenwart. Frankfurt am Main, 1968. pp. 182. bibliog.

PERELMAN (CHAÏM) Droit, morale et philosophie. Paris, Pichon et Durand-Auzias, 1968. pp. vii, 149. 25cm. (Bibliothèque de Philosophie du Droit. vol. 8)

QUAESTIONES et responsa: ein rechtphilosophisches Gespräch für Erik Wolf zum 65. Geburtstag veranstaltet am 15. Juli 1967 von Schülern und Freunden unter Leitung von Thomas Würtenberger. Frankfurt, [1968]. pp. 43.

SCHAPP (JAN) Sein und Ort der Rechtsgebilde: eine Untersuchung über Eigentum und Vertrag. Den Haag, Nijhoff, 1968. pp. xiii, 192. bibliog.

SCHMIDT (JOACHIM) Das "Prinzipielle" in der Freirechts-Bewegung: eine Studie zum Frei-Recht, seiner Methode und seiner Quelle. Bonn, Bouvier, 1968. pp. xii, 192. bibliog. (Schriften zur Rechtslehre und Politik. Band 62)

SUMMERS (ROBERT S.) ed. Essays in legal philosophy. Oxford, Blackwell, 1968. pp. viii, 307. bibliog. 21½cm.

ARCHIVES DE PHILOSOPHIE DU DROIT. [Nouvelle série]. No. 14. Le droit et la crise universitaire; [and] Récents apports sociologiques à la philosophie du droit. Paris, 1969. pp. 404.

BENDER (GERHARD) Probleme des Rechtsdenkens: einführende Texte zum Gewohnheitsrecht, Gesetzesrecht, Naturrecht. Frankfurt am Main, 1969. pp. 101. bibliog.

BOCKELMANN (PAUL) and others, eds. Festschrift für Karl Engisch zum 70. Geburtstag, etc. Frankfurt, Klostermann, 1969. pp. xii, 736. bibliog. 23½cm.

GYSIN (ARNOLD) Rechtsphilosophie und Grundlagen des Privatrechts: Begegnung mit grossen Juristen. Frankfurt am Main, [1969]. pp. 358.

HOBBES (THOMAS) The elements of law, natural and politic; ...edited...by Ferdinand Tönnies; second edition, with a new introduction, by M. M. Goldsmith. London, 1969. pp. 226.

MAIHOFER (WERNER) ed. Ideologie und Recht: (Referate des Kongresses der Deutschen Sektion der Internationalen Vereinigung für Recht- und Sozialphilosophie, im Frühjahr 1966). Frankfurt, [1969]. pp. 176.

MARCIC (RENE) Rechtsphilosophie: eine Einführung. Freiburg, 1969. pp. 312.

PERTICONE (GIACOMO) Scritti di filosofia giuridica e politica. Milano, 1969. pp. 449. (Pisa. Università. Facoltà di Giurisprudenza. Pubblicazioni. 26)

ROELLECKE (GERD) Der Begriff des positiven Gesetzes und das Grundgesetz. Mainz, Hase & Koehler, [1969]. pp. 316. bibliog. (Sozialwissenschaftliche Bibliothek. Sonderbände)

RYFFEL (HANS) Grundprobleme der Rechts- und Staatsphilosophie: philosophische Anthropologie des Politischen. Neuwied, [1969]. pp. 544.

SAMELI (KATHARINA) Freiheit und Sicherheit im Recht: zum Problem der Wertantinomie im Recht auf der Grundlage der Wertlehre Nicolai Hartmanns. Zürich, 1969. pp. 181. bibliog. (Zuerich. Universität. Rechts- und Staatswissenschaftliche Fakultät. Zürcher Beiträge zur Rechtswissenschaft. Neue Folge. Heft 307)

VECCHIO (GIORGIO DEL) Man and nature: selected essays...; Ralph A. Newman, editor; translated by A.H. Campbell. Notre Dame, [1969]. pp. 197.

VILLEY (MICHEL) Seize essais de philosophie du droit, dont un sur la crise universitaire. Paris, Dalloz, 1969. pp. 370. 22½cm. (Collection "Philosophie du Droit". 12)

WUERTENBERGER (THOMAS) ed. Phänomenologie, Rechtsphilosophie, Jurisprudenz: Festschrift für Gerhart Husserl zum 75. Geburtstag. Frankfurt a. M., [1969]. pp. 276. bibliog.

BRODERICK (ALBERT) ed. The French institutionalists: Maurice Hauriou, Georges Renard, Joseph T. Delos. Cambridge, Mass., 1970. pp. 370. bibliog. (Association of American Law Schools. Twentieth Century Legal Philosophy Series. vol. 8)

FINCH (JOHN D.) Introduction to legal theory. London, 1970. pp. 145.

INTERNATIONALE VEREINIGUNG FÜR RECHTS- UND SOZIAL-. PHILOSOPHIE. Kongress, 1967. Sein und Sollen im Erfahrungsbereich des Rechtes: Vorträge...herausgegeben...von Peter Schneider. Wiesbaden, 1970. pp. 256. (Archiv für Rechts- und Sozialphilosophie. Beihefte. Neue Folge. Nr.6) With summaries in various languages.

LAW - Philosophy (Cont'd.)

McBRIDE (WILLIAM LEON) Fundamental change in law and society: Hart and Sartre on revolution. The Hague, 1970. pp. 235. bibliog.

PASHUKANIS (EVGENII BRONISLAVOVICH) La théorie générale du droit et le marxisme. Paris, [1970]. pp. 173.

PASSERIN D'ENTRÈVES (ALEXANDER) Natural law: an introduction to legal philosophy. 2nd ed. London, 1970. pp. 208.

PENNOCK (JAMES ROLAND) and CHAPMAN (JOHN WILLIAM) eds. Political and legal obligation. New York, 1970. pp. 455. (American Society for Political and Legal Philosophy. Nomos. 12)

PLATO. The laws; translated with an introduction by Trevor J. Saunders. Harmondsworth, 1970. pp. 550. bibliog.

RAZ (JOSEPH) The concept of a legal system: an introduction to the theory of legal system. Oxford, 1970. pp. 212. bibliog.

SCHEFOLD (CHRISTOPH) Die Rechtsphilosophie des Jungen Marx von 1842, mit einer Interpretation der 'Pariser Schriften' von 1844. München, [1970]. pp. 301. bibliog. (Munich. Universität. Institut für Politische Wissenschaft. Münchener Studien zur Politik. 15. Band)

STEPHANITZ (DIETER VON) Exakte Wissenschaft und Recht: der Einfluss von Naturwissenschaft und Mathematik auf Rechtsdenken und Rechtswissenschaft in zweieinhalb Jahrtausenden; ein historischer Grundriss. Berlin, 1970. pp. 273. bibliog. (Muenster in Westfalen. Westfälische. Wilhelms-Universität. Rechts- und Staatswissenschaftliche Fakultät. Muensterische Beiträge zur Rechts- und Staatswissenschaft. Heft 15)

ARCHIVES DE PHILOSOPHIE DU DROIT. [Nouvelle Série]. No.16. Le droit investi par la politique. Paris, 1971. pp. 506.

- Sources

LE BRAS (GABRIEL) and others. L'age classique, 1140-1378: sources et théorie du droit. Paris, Sirey, [1965]. pp. xii, 608. 25cm. (Histoire du Droit et des Institutions de l'Église en Occident. Tome 7)

- Study and teaching

EHRLICH (EUGEN) Recht und Leben: gesammelte Schriften zur Rechtstatsachenforschung und zur Freirechtslehre;...ausgewählt und eingeleitet von Manfred Rehbinder. Berlin, Duncker & Humblot, [1967]. pp. 252. 23cm. (Berlin. Freie Universität. Institut für Rechtssoziologie und Rechtstatsachenforschung. Schriftenreihe. Band 7)

- Study and teaching - Asia

ASIAN JUDICIAL CONFERENCE, 2nd, TOKYO, 1965. Proceedings. [Tokyo, 1966?] pp. 320.

- Study and teaching - Italy

LENTZE (H.) George Phillips und die italienische Rechtsgeschichte. in Institut für Österreichische Geschichtsforschung and Vienna. Katholische Akademie. Österreich und Europa. Graz, 1965.

AQUARONE (ALBERTO) and others. Gli studi di storia e di diritto contemporaneo. Milano, 1968. pp. 158. bibliog. (Comitato per le Scienze Politiche e Sociali. Rapporti sulle Scienze Sociali. Quaderno n. 1)

- Study and teaching - United Kingdom

MEGARRY (Sir ROBERT EDGAR) The law lecture: (an examination of a mysterious longevity). Birmingham, 1970. pp. 12. (Birmingham. University. Holdsworth Club. Presidential Addresses. 1970)

- Study and teaching - Zambia

NORTHERN RHODESIA. Legal Profession (Entry and Training) Committee. 1962. Report: [D.W. Conroy, chairman]. Lusaka, 1962. pp. 16.

- Terms and phrases

PHILIP (J.R.) The use of English in the law courts: address delivered to the English Association in Edinburgh. Edinburgh, 1948. pp. 18. (Reprinted from The Scottish Law Review and Sheriff Court Reports November and December, 1947)

- Abyssinia

REDDEN (KENNETH) and others. The law making process in Ethiopia. Addis Ababa, 1966. pp. 37.

- Africa

GONIDEC (PIERRE FRANÇOIS) Les droits africains: évolution et sources. Paris, Pichon et Durand-Auzias, 1968. pp. ii, 278. 25cm. (Bibliothèque Africaine et Malgache. Droit et Sociologie Politique. tome 1)

BIPOUN-WOUM (JOSEPH MARIE) Le droit international africain: problemes generaux, reglement des conflits. Paris, 1970. pp. 327. bibliog.

- Africa, East

SEMINAR ON LAW AND SOCIAL CHANGE IN EAST AFRICA, DAR ES SALAAM, 1966. East African law and social change: [papers given at a seminar held at University College, Dar es Salaam, 1966]; edited by G.F.A. Sawyerr. Nairobi, East African Publishing House, 1967. pp. 307. bibliog. 21½cm. (East African Institute of Social and Cultural Affairs. Contemporary African Monographs. No. 6)

- Africa, Subsaharan

HAZARD (JOHN NEWBOLD) Classifying Africa's law. Beograd, Institut za Uporedno Pravo, 1966. pp. 217-232. bibliog. 23½cm. (Extrait du Recueil des Travaux Relatifs au Droit Etranger et Droit Comparé, vol. 4)

ALLOTT (A.N.) African law. in Derrett (John Duncan Martin) ed. An introduction to legal systems. London, 1968.

HUTCHISON (THOMAS W.) and others, eds. Africa and law: developing legal systems in African Commonwealth nations. Madison, University of Wisconsin Press, 1968. pp. xviii, 181. 23½cm. Reprinted from Wisconsin Law Review, 1966.

AFRICA in the seventies and eighties: issues in development; [based on the Symposium, Africa in the 1980s, Chicago, 1969 under the auspices of the Adlai Stevenson Institute of International Affairs]; edited by Frederick S. Arkhurst. New York, 1970. pp. 405.

ALLOTT (ANTONY NICOLAS) New essays in African law. London, 1970. pp. 348.

- America

ORGANIZATION OF AMERICAN STATES. 1964. Manual: Quinta Reunión del Consejo Interamericano de Jurisconsultos, San Salvador, 25 de enero de 1965. (Documentos oficiales. OEA/Ser.I/VI.2, español. CIJ-76) Washington, 1964. pp. vi, 51. 27cm.

ORGANIZATION OF AMERICAN STATES. 1965. Acta final de la quinta reunión del Consejo Interamericano de Jurisconsultos, San Salvador, El Salvador, 25 de enero al 5 de febrero de 1965. (Documentos oficiales. OEA/Ser.C/IV.5, español. CIJ-77) Washington, 1965. pp. vii, 64. 27½cm.

LAW - America
See also INTER-AMERICAN COUNCIL OF JURISTS; INTER-AMERICAN JURIDICAL COMMITTEE

- America, Latin

SARRIA RUIZ (JORGE) Funciones del derecho en la vida social. Bogotá, 1963. pp. 84. bibliog. 24cm.

- America, Latin - Bibliography

UNITED STATES. Library of Congress. Hispanic Law Division. 1961- . Index to Latin American legislation, 1950-1960; (with Supplement[s]). Boston, G.K. Hall, 1961 in progress.

- America, Latin - History and criticism

OTS CAPDEQUI (JOSE M.) Historia del derecho español en America y del derecho indiano. Madrid, 1969. pp. 367.

- Asia

BUXBAUM (DAVID C.) ed. Traditional and modern legal institutions in Asia and Africa. Leiden, Brill, 1967. pp. (vii), 151. 24cm. (International Studies in Sociology and Social Anthropology. vol.5) Reprinted from Journal of Asian and African Studies, vol.2, nos.1-2, 1967.

- Assyria

LUTZ (HENRY FREDERICK) Legal and economic documents from Ashjâly. Berkeley, U. of California P., 1931. pp. 184. 26½cm. (California University. Publications in Semitic Philology. Vol. 10, no. 1)

- Australia

[HILL (E.F.)] Towards the police state: some analyses of repressive laws in Australia. [1963]. pp.40. 21½cm.

SAWER (GEOFFREY) The Australian and the law. Harmondsworth, Penguin, 1968. pp. 288. 18cm. (Pelican Books. A 977)

BAALMAN (JOHN) Outline of law in Australia; third edition by Jean Malor. Sydney, 1969. pp. 257. bibliog.

- Australia - Bibliography

CAMPBELL (ENID M.) and MACDOUGALL (DONALD) Associate Professor in Law. Legal research: materials and methods. Sydney, 1967. pp. 240.

- Australia - History and criticism

CURREY (CHARLES HERBERT) The brothers Bent: Judge-Advocate Ellis Bent and Judge Jeffery Hart Bent. [Sydney], Sydney U. P., 1968. pp. 176. 21½cm.

- Australia - Societies

AUSTRALIAN UNIVERSITIES LAW SCHOOLS ASSOCIATION. Directory of members, 1971; editor, Peter G. Heffey. Sydney, [1971?]. pp. 34.

- Austria

CONGRÈS INTERNATIONAL DE DROIT COMPARÉ, 1966. 7e Congrès. Österreichische Landesreferate zum VII. Internationalen Kongress für Rechtsvergleichung in Uppsala 1966. Wien, Manz, 1966. pp. 164. 23cm. (Wiener Rechtswissenschaftliche Studien. Band 3)

- Austria - History and criticism

FESTSCHRIFT Hans Lentze zum 60. Geburtstage dargebracht von Fachgenossen und Freunden; herausgegeben von Nikolaus Grass und Werner Ogris. Innsbruck, 1969. pp. 626. bibliog.

- Azerbaijan

ISTORIIA... История государства и права Азербайджанской ССР. [v.1]. Великая Октябрьская социалистическая революция и создание Советской государственности в Азербайджане. Баку, АН АзССР, 1964. pp. 318. bibliog. 22cm.

AZERBAIJAN. Statutes, etc. 1938-1966. Сборник законов Азербайджанской ССР и указов Президиума Верховного Совета Азербайджанской ССР, 1938-1966 гг. Баку, 1966-67. 2 vols. 21½см.

- Babylonia

LUTZ (HENRY FREDERICK) Legal and economic documents from Ashjâly. Berkeley, U. of California P., 1931. pp. 184. 26½cm. (California University. Publications in Semitic Philology. Vol. 10, no. 1)

- Bahamas

BAHAMAS. Statutes, etc. 1799-1965. The statute law of the Bahama Islands, 1799-1965, in force on the 1st April 1965; revised edition ...by Sir Ralph Hone. Nassau, 1965. 7 vols.

- Baltic States - Bibliography

KLESMENT (JOHANNES) and others. Legal sources and bibliography of the Baltic states: Estonia, Latvia, Lithuania. New York, [1963]. pp. 197. bibliog.

LAW (Cont'd.)

- Belgium

Les CODES Larcier...contenant toutes les dispositions législatives d'intérêt général et les lois spéciales les plus usuelles en vigueur en Belgique avec notes de concordance et de jurisprudence...publiés sous la direction juridique de Joseph Guissart [and others]. Bruxelles, 1970. 5 vols.

- Belgium - Bibliography

GUIDE to foreign legal materials: Belgium, Luxembourg, Netherlands; by Paul Graulich [and others]. Dobbs Ferry, Oceana, 1968. pp. x, 258. bibliog. 23cm. (Columbia University. Parker School of Foreign and Comparative Law. Guides to Foreign Law. vol. 3)

- British Virgin Islands

BRITISH VIRGIN ISLANDS. Statutes, etc. 1839-1961. The revised laws of the Virgin Islands: prepared under the authority of the Revised Edition of the Laws Ordinance, 1959; by P. Cecil Lewis. Tortola, 1965. 8 vols. 25cm.

- Bulgaria

BULGARIA. Statutes, etc. 1953-1963. Сборник постановления и тълкувателни решения на Върховния съд на НР-България, 1953-1963. София, 1965. pp. 529.

- Bulgaria - Interpretation and construction

TULKUVATELNI... Тълкувателни решения на Президиума на Народното събрание, 1948-1967: справочник. София, Наука и Изкуство, 1968. pp. 382. 19½см.

- Canada

CANADA. Statutes, etc. 1867-1960. A consolidation of the British North America Acts, 1867 to 1960; prepared by Elmer A. Driedger; consolidated as of January 1, 1964. Ottawa, 1964. pp. 50.

CANADA. Statutes, etc. 1867-1970. Revised statutes of Canada, 1970 proclaimed and published under the authority of chapter 48 of the Statutes of Canada, 1964-65. Ottawa, 1970 in progress.

- Canada - Bibliography

CANADA. Department of Public Printing and Stationery. Publications Branch. Canadian Government Publications Price Lists. No. 1. Canadian government publications: statutes of Canada, price list revised September 30, 1960. 3rd ed. Ottawa, 1960. pp. 57.

- Canada - History and criticism

LASKIN (BORA) The British tradition in Canadian law. London, 1969. pp. 138. (Hamlyn Lectures. 21st series)

- China

CHINA. Statutes, etc. 1949-1958. Fundamental legal documents of communist China; edited by Albert P. Blaustein. South Hackensack, 1962. pp. 603.

COHEN (JEROME ALAN) ed. Contemporary Chinese law: research problems and perspectives; with contributions by Harold J. Berman [and others]. Cambridge, Mass., 1970. pp. 380. bibliog. (Harvard University. Harvard Studies in East Asian Law. 4)

- China - Bibliography

UNITED STATES. Library of Congress. Guide to selected legal sources of mainland China: a listing of laws and regulations, etc. Washington, 1967. pp. ix, 357. bibliogs.

- China - History and criticism

BODDE (DERK) and MORRIS (CLARENCE) Law in imperial China, exemplified by 190 Ch'ing Dynasty cases, translated from the Hsing-an hui-lan, with historical, social and juridical commentaries. Cambridge, Harvard U.P., 1967. pp. xiii, 615. bibliog. 23½cm. (Harvard University. Harvard Studies in East Asian Law. 1)

McALEAVY (H.) Chinese law. in Derrett (John Duncan Martin) ed. An introduction to legal systems. London, 1968.

- Colombia

COLOMBIA. Statutes, etc. 1949-1961. Prontuario de Legislacion nacional colombiana, comprende el periodo de 9 de noviembre de 1949 a 31 de diciembre de 1961; arreglado por Carlos Julio Angel con la colaboracion de Julio J. Benetti Salgar. Bogota, 1963. pp. 418.

SÁNCHEZ CAMARGO (BERNARDO) Normatividad de algunas leyes canónicas en derecho colombiano. Bogotá, Kelly, 1965. pp. 112 bibliog. 23½cm.

- Communist countries

MOROZOV (VLADIMIR PETROVICH) Pravovye vzgliady i uchrezhdeniia pri sotsializme. Moskva, 1967. pp. 134.

HAZARD (JOHN NEWBOLD) Communists and their law: a search for the common core of the legal systems of the Marxian socialist states. Chicago, 1969. pp. 560. bibliog. (Columbia University. Research Institute of Communist Affairs. Studies)

- Czechoslovakia

BIANCHI (LEONARD) Die Tschechoslowakische Republik als bürgerlich-demokratischer Staat: ein Rückblick auf die Jahre 1918-1938. Frankfurt, 1969. pp. 61. (Gesellschaft für Rechtsvergleichung. Arbeiten zur Rechtsvergleichung. 44)

- Dominican Republic

ORGANIZATION OF AMERICAN STATES. 1964. A statement of the laws of the Dominican Republic in matters affecting business;... revised and enlarged by Antonio Tellado. (Department of Legal Affairs) 3rd ed. Washington, 1964. pp. xiii, 300. bibliog. 27cm. For the second edition see ORGANIZATION OF AMERICAN STATES. 1953-58. R(0)

- Europe

CAEMMERER (ERNST VON) and others, eds. Vom deutschen zum europäischen Recht: Festschrift für Hans Dölle. Tübingen, Mohr, 1963. 2 vols. bibliog. 23cm.

VISINE (FRANÇOIS) ABC de l'Europe. Paris, 1967 in progress.

VISINE (FRANÇOIS) ABC de l'Europe. Paris, 1967-69. 3 vols.

WIEBRINGHAUS (HANS) Gerichtshof für Europa?: Voraussetzungen und Möglichkeiten der Gründung eines obersten europäischen Gerichtshofs mit allgemeiner Kompetenz. 2nd ed. Leiden, Sijthoff, 1967. pp. 129 23cm. (Council of Europe. European Aspects. Series E: Law. No.6)

- Europe - Bibliography

EUROPEAN law libraries guide; prepared by the International Association of Law Libraries...; [edited by Elizabeth M. Moys]. [London, 1971]. pp. 678. In English or French.

- Europe - History and criticism

The PROGRESS of continental law in the nineteenth century; by various authors (first published in 1918 by Little, Brown). South Hackensack, Rothman Reprints, 1969. pp. xlix, 558. 23cm. (Association of American Law Schools. Continental Legal History Series. vol. 11)

- European Economic Community countries

EVERLING (ULRICH) Rechtsprobleme der gemeinsamen Handelspolitik in der Europäischen Wirtschaftsgemeinschaft. Göttingen, Schwarz, 1965. pp. 189-230. 20½cm. (Goettingen. Universität. Institut für Völkerrecht. Beiträge zum Internationalen Wirtschaftsrecht und Atomenergierecht. Band 1. Heft 5)

SEMAINE DE BRUGES, 1965. Droit communautaire et droit national: community law and national law; [by] N. Catalano [and others]. Bruges, De Tempel, 1965. pp. 412. 23cm. (College of Europe. Cahiers de Bruges. Nouvelle Série. [no.] 14) In English or French.

SACERDOTI (GIORGIO) L'efficacia del diritto delle Comunità europee nell'ordinamento giuridico italiano. Milano, Giuffrè, 1966. pp. xi, 176. bibliog. 25cm.

EUROPEAN COMMUNITIES. Commission. Service Juridique. Decisions nationales relative au droit communautaire: liste sélective de références publiées. irreg., [1967] (no.1/2)- Bruxelles.

BUELCK (HARTWIG) ed. Zur Stellung der Mitgliedstaaten im Europarecht; von Erich Bülow [and others]. Berlin, Duncker und Humblot, [1967]. pp. 245. 23cm. (Spires. Hochschule für Verwaltungswissenschaften. Schriftenreihe. Band 32)

CONSTANTINIDÈS-MÉGRET (COLETTE) Le droit de la Communauté Économique Européenne et l' ordre juridique des états membres. Paris, Pichon et Durand-Auzias, 1967. pp. v, 224. bibliog. 23cm. (Bibliothèque de Droit International. tome 41)

GAUDET (MICHEL) Conflits du droit communautaire avec les droits nationaux. Nancy, Université, Centre Européen Universitaire, [1967]. pp. 59. 21cm. (Collection des Conférences Européennes. No. 4)

MONACO (RICCARDO) Diritto delle Comunità europee e diritto interno. Milano, Giuffrè, 1967. pp. (ii), 237. 25cm.

SAINT-ESTEBEN (ROBERT) Droit communautaire et droits nationaux. Paris, Presses Universitaires de France, 1967. pp. viii, 94. bibliog. 24cm. (Paris. Université. Faculté de Droit et des Sciences Economiques. Travaux et Recherches. Série "Europe". No.4)

TRABUCCHI (A.) Per una visione sistematica del diritto comunitario. in Ferrara. Università. Centro di Documentazione e Studi sulle Comunità Europee. Quaderni. 9. Milano, 1967.

BERNINI (GIORGIO) Profili di diritto delle Comunità Europee. Napoli, [1968]. pp. 449.

CONSERVATIVE POLITICAL CENTRE. [Publications]. No. 393. Europe and the law: studies on the implementation of the EEC'S common policy and its impact on United Kingdom laws. London, 1968. pp. 96. 21½cm.

DONNER (ANDRÉ M.) The role of the lawyer in the European Communities. Evanston, Northwestern U.P., [1968]. pp. xvii, 86. 20cm. (Northwestern University. School of Law. Rosenthal Lectures. 1966)

SCHOENTJES-MERCHIERS (YVETTE) De waardebeveiligingsbedingen in het recht van de landen der Europese Economische Gemeenschap. Brussel, 1968. pp. 483. bibliog.

BRINKHORST (L.J.) and SCHERMERS (H.G.) Judicial remedies in the European Communities. Deventer, 1969. pp. 275.

LOUIS (JEAN VICTOR) Les reglements de la Communauté Économique Européenne. Bruxelles, P.U. de Bruxelles, 1969. pp. xxxi, 514. bibliog. 33½cm. (Brussels. Université Libre. Institut d'Études Européennes. Thèses et Travaux Juridiques. 3)

WALL (EDWARD HAROLD) Europe: unification and law. Harmondsworth, 1969. pp. 220.

ZULEEG (MANFRED) Das Recht der Europäischen Gemeinschaften im innerstaatlichen Bereich. Köln, Heymann, 1969. pp. xx, 448. bibliog. 22½cm. (Cologne. Universität. Institut für das Recht der Europäischen Gemeinschaften. Kölner Schriften zum Europarecht. Band 9)

MEGRET (JACQUES) and others. Le droit de la Communauté Economique Européenne: commentaire du traité et des textes pris pour son application. Bruxelles, 1970 in progress. bibliogs. (Brussels. Université Libre. Institut d'Etudes Européennes. Thèses et Travaux Juridiques)

FINE (RICHARD I.) The nature of a restrictive practice under Article 85 and 86 of the Treaty of Rome. [Washington], 1970-71. 2 pts. (Reprinted from The Journal of International Law and Economics, vol. 4, no.2; vol. 5, no.2)

LECOURT (ROBERT) Le juge devant le Marché commun. Genève, 1970. pp. 69. (Geneva. Graduate Institute of International Studies. Etudes et Travaux. No. 10)

TORRELLI (MAURICE) L'individu et le droit de la Communauté économique européenne. Montréal, 1970. pp. 396. bibliog.

LAW (Cont'd.)

- **European Economic Community countries - Bibliography**

   EUROPEAN COMMUNITIES. 1966. Rapports entre le droit communautaire et le droit national: (Bibliographie sélective) (Service de Presse et d'Information) Bruxelles, 1966. pp. 32. 29½cm.

- **Flanders - History and criticism**

   WARNKOENIG (LEOPOLD AUGUST) Flandrische Staats- und Rechtsgeschichte bis zum Jahr 1305; (unveränderter Neudruck der Ausgabe von 1835-42). Wiesbaden, Sändig, 1967. 3 vols. 20½cm. Map and facsimile of document in end pocket of vol.1. Facsimile reprint.

- **France**

   MANCINI (JEAN GABRIEL) Répertoire des droites et obligations des Français résidant hors de France. Paris, Les Éditions Sociales Françaises, [1967] pp. 309. 24cm.

   FRANCE. Assemblée Nationale. Recueil des lois: motions et résolutions: tables des réponses aux questions orales. 2 a yr., 1968/9- Paris.

   UNIVERSITÉ D'AIX-MARSEILLE. Faculté de Droit et des Sciences Economiques d'Aix. Études offertes à André Audinet, doyen honoraire à la Faculte de Droit et des Sciences Economiques d'Aix-en-Provence. Paris, 1968. pp. 348. bibliog.

   SOCIETE DE LEGISLATION COMPAREE. Livre du centenaire de la Société...; un siècle de droit comparé en France, 1869-1969; les apports du droit comparé au droit positif français. Paris, [1969]. pp. 382.

- **France - Abbreviations**

   SPRUDZS (ADOLF) Foreign law abbreviations: French. Dobbs Ferry, Oceana, 1967. pp. 103. 28cm.

- **France - History and criticism**

   OURLIAC (PAUL) and MALAFOSSE (J. DE) Histoire du droit privé. Paris, P.U.F., 1961-68. 3 vols. bibliogs. vol.1 is of the new ed.

   BRISSET (JACQUELINE) L'adoption de la communauté comme régime légal dans le code civil. Paris, Presses Universitaires de France, 1967. pp. viii, 91. bibliog. 24cm. (Paris. Université. Faculté de Droit et des Sciences Économiques. Travaux et Recherches. Série "Droit Privé" No.3)

   RASENACK (CHRISTIAN A. L.) Gesetz und Verordnung in Frankreich seit 1789. Berlin, Duncker & Humblot, [1967]. pp. 282. bibliog. 23cm. (Schriften zum Öffentlichen Recht. Band 55)

   ARNAUD (ANDRÉ JEAN) Les origines doctrinales du code civil français. Paris, 1969. pp. 326. bibliog.

   ETUDES d'histoire du droit parisien; par Marie-Hélène Bourquin [and others]. Paris, 1970. pp. 456. bibliogs. (Paris. Université. Faculté de Droit et des Sciences Economiques. Travaux et Recherches. Série "Sciences Historiques". No. 16)

- **Georgia**

   SURGULADZE (I. I.) Istoriia gosudarstva i prava Gruzii. Tbilisi, 1968. pp. 335.

- **Germany**

   LUEBECK. Statutes, etc. Der Kayserlichen freyen Reichs Stadt Lübeck Statuta; oder, Das so wohl in denen Städten Holsteins als in der Reichs Stadt Lübeck gebräuchliche Stadt-Recht sammt angehengter Hansee-Städtischer Schiffs-Ordnung und See-Recht, etc. Glückstadt, Lehmann, 1724. pp. (297). 33cm.

   SCHINNERER (ERICH) German law and legislation. Berlin, 1938. pp. 32. (Terramare Office. Publications. No. 4)

   CAEMMERER (ERNST VON) and others, eds. Vom deutschen zum europäischen Recht: Festschrift für Hans Dölle. Tübingen, Mohr, 1963. 2 vols. bibliog. 23cm.

   DEMOKRATIE und Grundrechte: ausgewähltes und überarbeitetes Protokoll der wissenschaftlichen Konferenz: Der Kampf der Arbeiterklasse und ihrer Partei um die Entwicklung der sozialistischen Persönlichkeit, etc. Berlin, Staatsverlag der DDR, 1967. pp. 192. bibliog 21cm.

   COHN (ERNST JOSEPH) and others. Manual of German law. 2nd ed. London, 1968-71. 2 vols. bibliog. (British Institute of International and Comparative Law. Comparative Law Series. Nos. 14, 15)

   BADER (HANS HEINZ) Staat, Wirtschaft, Gesellschaft: Grundlagen der Staats- und Rechtslehre, Gesellschafts- und Wirtschaftslehre. 3rd ed. Hamburg, Decker, 1968. pp. xxv, 419. bibliog. 20½cm. (Schriftenreihe für Industrie und Wirtschaft. Band 1)

   TUEBINGEN. Universität. Rechts- und Wirtschaftswissenschaftliche Fakultät. Rechtswissenschaftliche Abteilung. Tübinger Festschrift für Eduard Kern; ...[edited by Jürgen Baumann]. Tübingen, Mohr, 1968. pp. viii, 498. bibliog. 23cm. (Tübinger Rechtswissenschaftliche Abhandlungen. Band 24)

   FESTSCHRIFT für Eduard Bötticher zum 70. Geburtstag am 29. Dezember 1969; herausgegeben von Karl August Bettermann und Albrecht Zeuner. Berlin, 1969. pp. 461. bibliog.

   CHREZVYCHAINOE zakonodatel'stvo FRG. Moskva, 1970. pp. 278.

- **Germany - Bibliography**

   BIBLIOTHECA iuridica: Handbuch der gesamten juristischen und staatswissenschaftlichen Literatur: eine Zusammenstellung aller... Jahren 1750-1876 in Deutschland und den benachbarten Staaten erschienenen Schriften; herausgegeben von T.C.F. Enslin [and others; reprint of the edition published in Leipzig by Engelmann, 1840-49, and Rossberg, 1867-77]. 2nd ed. Aalen, Scientia-Verlag, 1968. 4 vols. 20cm.

GESELLSCHAFT FÜR RECHTSVERGLEICHUNG. Bibliographie des deutschen Rechts in englischer und deutscher Sprache eine Auswahl;...mit einer Einführung in das deutsche Recht von Fritz Baur;...Stand 31. Dezember 1963; (with Supplement 1964-1968) Karlsruhe, 1964-1969. 2 vols.

SCHNEIDER (FRANZ) of Karlsruhe. Bibliographie der Veröffentlichungen von Willi Geiger. Tübingen, 1969. pp. 24.

- Germany - History and criticism

QUELLEN zur neueren Privatrechtsgeschichte Deutschlands im Auftrag der Strassburger Wissenschaftlichen Gesellschaft an der Universität Frankfurt herausgegeben und gemeinsam mit Wolfgang Kunkel und Hans Thieme bearbeitet von Franz Beyerle. Weimar, Böhlau, 1936 in progress. 27½-28½cm.

EBEL (WILHELM) Jacob Grimm und die deutsche Rechtswissenschaft. Göttingen, 1963. pp. 32. bibliog.

HERRMANN (MANFRED) Der Schutz der Persönlichkeit in der Rechtslehre des 16.-18. Jahrhunderts, dargestellt an Hand der Quellen des Humanismus, des aufgeklärten Naturrechts und des Usus modernus. Stuttgart, Kohlhammer, 1968. pp. 89. bibliog. (Cologne. Universität. Institut für Neuere Privatrechtsgeschichte. Beiträge zur Neueren Privatrechtsgeschichte. Band 2)

LLOMPART (JOSE) Die Geschichtlichkeit in der Begründung des Rechts im Deutschland der Gegenwart. Frankfurt am Main, 1968. pp. 182. bibliog.

RUETHERS (BERND) Die unbegrenzte Auslegung: zum Wandel der Privatrechtsordnung im Nationalsozialismus. Tübingen, Mohr, 1968. pp. xx, 496. bibliog. 23cm.

- Germany, Eastern

DEMOKRATIE und Grundrechte: ausgewähltes und überarbeitetes Protokoll der wissenschaftlichen Konferenz: Der Kampf der Arbeiterklasse und ihrer Partei um die Entwicklung der sozialistischen Persönlichkeit, etc. Berlin, Staatsverlag der DDR, 1967. pp. 192. bibliog 21cm.

WEITERE Ausgestaltung der Sozialistischen Rechtsordnung: Materialien der 9. Tagung der Volkskammer der DDR am 11. Juni, 1968. [Berlin], 1968. pp. 94. (Aus der Tätigkeit der Volkskammer und ihrer Ausschüsse. 5. Wahlperiode. Heft 11.)

GERMANY (DEUTSCHE DEMOKRATISCHE REPUBLIK). Ministerium der Justiz. 1969- . Kommentar zum Ordnungswidrigkeitsrecht der DDR; (Verfasser Rudolf Hartwig [and others]). Berlin, 1969 in progress.

GERMANY (DEUTSCHE DEMOKRATISCHE REPUBLIK). Statutes. 1954-68. Gesetz zur Bekämpfung von Ordnungswidrigkeiten, OWG, und ergänzende gesetzliche Bestimmungen, etc. Berlin, 1969. pp. 159.

- Ghana

ASANTE (S.K.B.) Law and society in Ghana. in Hutchison (Thomas W.) and others, eds. Africa and law. Madison, 1968.

- Gibraltar

GIBRALTAR. Statutes. 1868-1940. The revised edition of the laws of Gibraltar in force on the 31st day of December 1935; prepared... by H. Ralph Hone; (with 1941 Supplement). Gibraltar, Miles, 1936-41. 5 vols. 24½cm. For annual supplements 1941-1946 see GIBRALTAR. Statutes. The laws of Gibraltar.

- Greece

KOKKINI-IATRIDOU (D.) Introduction au droit hellénique. Deventer, 1969. pp. 63. bibliog.

- Grenada

GRENADA. Statutes, 1934. The revised laws of Grenada, in force on the 31st day of December, 1934; compiled by C. Mansel Reece. London, 1935. 3 vols. 25cm.

- Honduras

ORGANIZATION OF AMERICAN STATES. 1965. A statement of the laws of Honduras in matters affecting business;...revised and enlarged by Francisco Zacapa [and others]. (Department of Legal Affairs). Washington, 1965. pp. xi, 276.

- Hong Kong

HONG KONG. Statutes, etc. 1844- . The laws of Hong Kong; revised edition 1964; prepared... by H.A. de Barros Botelho; (with Amendments). Hong Kong, 1964 in progress. 17 vols. 25cm. Loose-leaf.

- Hungary

HUNGARY. Statutes, etc. 1945-1958. Hatályos jogszabályok gyűjteménye, 1945-1958. 4. kötet. Nemzetközi szerződések összesített szám- és tárgymutató, etc. Budapest, 1960. pp. 368. 27½cm.

HUNGARY. Statutes, etc. 1945-1963. Hatályos miniszteri rendeletek, 1945-1963; készült a Magyar Forradalmi Munkás-Paraszi Kormány 2016/1963. (VII.14.) számú határozata alapján. Budapest, 1964. 2 vols. 27cm.

HUNGARY. Statutes, etc. 1945-1963. Hatályos törvények és törvényerejű rendeletek, 1945-1963, etc. Budapest, 1965. pp. 835. 27cm.

HUNGARY. Statutes, etc. 1945-1968. Hatályos jogszabályok gyűjteménye, 1945-1968. 2. kötet. Kormányrendeletek és kormányhatározatok. Budapest, 1969. pp.901.

HUNGARY. Statutes, etc. 1945-1968. Hatályos jogszabályok gyűjteménye, 1945-1968. 3. kötet. Miniszteri rendeletek. Budapest, 1970. pp. 816.

HUNGARY. Statutes, etc. 1945-1968. Hatályos jogszabályok gyűjteménye, 1945-1968. 4.kötet. Miniszteri rendeletek. Budapest, 1970. pp. 2031.

HUNGARY. Statutes, etc. 1945-1968. Hatályos jogszabályok gyűjteménye, 1945-1968. 5.kötet. Nemzetközi szerződések összesített szám- és tárgymutató. Budapest, 1970. pp. 1135.

LAW (Cont'd.)

- India

INDIA. Statutes, etc. Acts of Parliament: with a table showing the effect of legislation and an index. a., 1950- New Delhi.

DERRETT (JOHN DUNCAN MARTIN) Religion, law and the state in India. London, Faber, [1968]. pp. 615. bibliog. 21½cm.

JAIN (MAHABIR PRASHAD) Outlines of Indian legal history. 2nd ed. Bombay, Tripathi, 1966. pp. xxv, 746. 22cm.

- India - History and criticism

KULSHRESHTHA (V.D.) Landmarks in Indian legal history and constitutional history. 2nd ed. Lucknow, 1968. pp. 438. bibliog.

JAIN (B.S.) Administration of justice in seventeenth century India: a study of salient concepts of Mughal justice. Delhi, 1970. pp. 153. bibliog.

- India - Sources

LINGAT (ROBERT) Les sources du droit dans le système traditionnel de l'Inde. Paris, Mouton, 1967. pp. 322. bibliog. 24cm. (Paris. Ecole Pratique des Hautes Etudes. Section des Sciences Économiques et Sociales. Le Monde d'Outre-Mer Passé et Présent. 1 ière Série. Etudes. 32)

- Israel

LIVNEH (ERNST) Development of Israel law in 1958-1959. Jerusalem, Hebrew University, Institute for Legislative Research and Comparative Law, 1960. pp. 36. 24cm. ([Publications] 1) With a preface in Hebrew.

HETH (MEIR) The legal framework of economic activity in Israel. New York, Praeger, 1967. pp. xv, 275. bibliog. 23½cm. (Praeger Special Studies in International Economics and Development)

BAKER (HENRY EDMEADES) The legal system of Israel. Jerusalem, Israel U.P., 1968. pp. (vi), 277. bibliog. 21½cm.

- Israel - Bibliography

LIVNEH (ERNST) compiler. Israel legal bibliography in European languages. Jerusalem, Hebrew University Students Press, 1963. pp. viii, 85. 21cm. (Hebrew University. Institute for Legislative Research and Comparative Law. [Publications]. 7)

- Italy

STURZO (LUIGI) Scritti di carattere giuridico: discorsi e attività parlamentare, 1951-1959. Bologna, Zanichelli, [1962] pp. viii, 396. 23½cm. (Istituto Luigi Sturzo. Opera Omnia di Luigi Sturzo. 3a Serie vol. 3)

SCRITTI giuridici in memoria di Marcello Barberio Corsetti; [presented by the Consiglio dell'Ordine degli Avvocati di Roma]. Milano, 1965. pp. 807.

STUDI in memoria di Guido Zanobini. Milano, 1965. 5 vols. bibliog. A few articles in Spanish.

STUDI in onore di Gaetano Zingali. Milano, 1965. 3 vols. bibliog. (Catania. Università. Facoltà di Giurisprudenza. Pubblicazioni. 53)

SACERDOTI (GIORGIO) L'efficacia del diritto delle Comunità europee nell'ordinamento giuridico italiano. Milano, Giuffrè, 1966. pp. xi, 176. bibliog. 25cm.

BATTAGLINI (ERNESTO) Scritti giuridici. Milano, Giuffrè, 1967. 2 vols. 25cm.

SCRITTI in memoria di Antonino Giuffrè. Milano, Giuffrè, 1967. 4 vols.

STUDI in onore di Antonio Segni. Milano, 1967. 4 vols. (Rome. Università. Facoltà di Giurisprudenza. Pubblicazioni. 28-31) In various languages.

ITALY. Statutes, etc. 1930-1967. I cinque codici; a cura di Rosario Nicolò [and] Giovanni Leone. Rev. ed. Milano, 1968. pp. irreg.

- Italy - History and criticism

BERLINGUER (LUIGI) Sui progetti di codice di commercio del regno d'Italia, 1807-1808: considerazioni su un inedito di D. A. Azuni. Milano, 1970. pp. 168.

- Italy - Study and teaching

AQUARONE (ALBERTO) and others. Gli studi di storia e di diritto contemporaneo. Milano, 1968. pp. 158. bibliog. (Comitato per le Scienze Politiche e Sociali. Rapporti sulle Scienze Sociali. Quaderno n. 1)

- Japan - History and criticism

HENDERSON (D. F.) Promulgation of Tokugawa statutes. in Buxbaum (David C.) ed. Traditional and modern legal institutions in Asia and Africa. Leiden, 1967.

- Kabardino-Balkarian Republic

GARDANOV (B. A.) ed. Materialy po obychnomu pravu kabardintsev: pervaia polovina XIX v. Nal'chik, 1956. pp. 427.

- Korea

KOREAN LEGAL CENTER. Laws of the Republic of Korea: six major laws with main fundamental procedural administrative and economic laws, etc. Seoul, the Center, [1964?] pp. xxvii, 1327. 20½cm.

- Korea - History and criticism

HAHM (PYONG-CHOON) The Korean political tradition and law: essays in Korean law and legal history. Seoul, Hollym, [1967]. pp. ix, 249. bibliog. 20½cm. (Royal Asiatic Society. Korean Branch. Monograph Series. No. 1)

- Latvia

GOSUDARSTVENNO-PRAVOVOE... Государственно-правовое строительство Латвийской ССР. Рига, Зинатне, 1968. pp. 312. 19½см.

MEL'KISIS (E.A.) Создание первых организационно-правовых форм социалистического контроля в Латвии, 1917-1919 гг. in Latviiskii Gosudarstvennyi Universitet. Uchenye Zapiski. № 105. Riga, 1968.

- Lebanon - Bibliography

NASSIF (ALBERT) Bibliographie juridique libanaise. Beyrouth, [Université St. Joseph, Faculté de Droit et des Sciences Économiques], 1958. pp. 57. 22½cm. (Annales)

- Luxembourg - Bibliography

GUIDE to foreign legal materials: Belgium, Luxembourg, Netherlands; by Paul Graulich [and others]. Dobbs Ferry, Oceana, 1968. pp. x, 258. bibliog. 23cm. (Columbia University. Parker School of Foreign and Comparative Law. Guides to Foreign Law. vol. 3)

- Madagascar

MADAGASCAR. Statutes, etc. 1939-1949. Textes concernant l'état civil autochtone à Madagascar et dépendances. (Haut Commissariat de la République Française à Madagascar et Dépendances) Tananarive, 1954. pp. 19. 31cm.

- Malawi

BENDA-BECKMANN (FRANZ VON) Rechtspluralismus in Malawi: geschichtliche Entwicklung und heutige Problematik. München, [1970]. pp. 207. bibliog. (Ifo-Institut für Wirtschaftsforschung. Afrika-Studien. 56) With English summary.

- Malaysia

[FEDERATION OF MALAYSIA] Statutes, etc. Acts. Kuala Lumpur, annual, 1964 to date.

- Mauritius

ÉTUDES de droit privé français et mauricien: congrès tenu à Saint-Denis de la Réunion, 1er-4 juillet 1965; [Gérard Conac, chairman]. Paris, 1969. pp. 230. (Université d'Aix Marseille. Faculté de Droit et des Sciences Économiques d'Aix. Annales. 57)

- Mexico

MEXICO. Statutes, etc. 1808-1967. Leyes fundamentales de México, 1808-1967; dirección y efemerides de Felipe Tena Ramírez. 3rd ed. México, Porrua, 1967. pp. xv, 968. 23cm.

- Moldavian Republic

MOLDAVIAN REPUBLIC. Statutes, etc. 1967. Сборник нормативных актов: в помощь работникам местных Советов. Кишинев, Картя Молдовеняскэ, 1968. pp. 732. 21см.

- Netherlands

ALGRA (N.E.) and JANSSEN (H.C.J.G.) Rechtsingang: een oriëntatie in het recht. Groningen, 1969. pp. 192.

OP de grenzen van komend recht: opstellen aangeboden aan...J.H. Beekhuis. Deventer, [1969]. pp. 353. bibliog.

- Netherlands - Bibliography

GUIDE to foreign legal materials: Belgium, Luxembourg, Netherlands; by Paul Graulich [and others]. Dobbs Ferry, Oceana, 1968. pp. x, 258. bibliog. 23cm. (Columbia University. Parker School of Foreign and Comparative Law. Guides to Foreign Law. vol. 3)

- Netherlands - Codification

AA (HANS) and others, eds. Bronnen van de nederlandse codificatie sinds 1798. Utrecht, 1968 in progress. (Vereeniging tot Uitgave der Bronnen van het Oude Vaderlandsche Recht. Oude Vaderlandsche Rechtsbronnen. Derde Reeks. No. 22)

- Netherlands - History and criticism

AA (HANS) and others, eds. Bronnen van de nederlandse codificatie sinds 1798. Utrecht, 1968 in progress. (Vereeniging tot Uitgave der Bronnen van het Oude Vaderlandsche Recht. Oude Vaderlandsche Rechtsbronnen. Derde Reeks. No. 22)

KUNST (A.J.M.) Historische ontwikkeling van het recht. 2nd ed. Zwolle, 1969 in progress.

- New Zealand

NEW ZEALAND. Statutes, etc. 1908-1957. Reprint of the statutes of New Zealand, 1908-1957, (with amendments incorporated). Wellington, 1958-1961. 16 vols.

O'KEEFE (J.A.B.) and FARRANDS (W.L.) Introduction to New Zealand law. Wellington, 1969. pp. 451.

- Nicaragua

ORGANIZATION OF AMERICAN STATES. 1965. A statement of the laws of Nicaragua in matters affecting business: third edition revised and enlarged by J. J. Lugo Marenco. (General Legal Division) Washington, 1965. pp. x, 312. 27cm. For the second edition see ORGANIZATION OF AMERICAN STATES. 1957-60.

- Nigeria

BUXBAUM (DAVID C.) ed. Traditional and modern legal institutions in Asia and Africa. Leiden, Brill, 1967. pp. (vii), 151. 24cm. (International Studies in Sociology and Social Anthropology. vol.5) Reprinted from Journal of Asian and African Studies, vol.2, nos.1-2, 1967.

ELIAS (TASLIM OLAWALE) Law in a developing society: inaugural lecture delivered... 17 January 1969. [Lagos], 1969. pp. 26. (Lagos. University. Inaugural Lecture Series. 3)

- Panama

UNITED STATES. [Defense Department]. Country law study for Panama. [Washington, 1965]. pp.51.

- Poland

POLAND. Statutes, etc. 1550-1726. Inwentarz konstytucyy koronnych y W. X. Litewskiego, przez M... M... Ładowskiego... od roku pańskiego 1550. do r. 1683 krotko zebrany... y suplementem obszernym od roku 1683 az do ostatniey konstytucyi Seymu 1726 inclusive opatrzony. Lipsk, Weidmann, 1733. pp. 680. 35cm.

LAW - Poland (Cont'd.)

POLISH YEARBOOK OF INTERNATIONAL LAW; [pd. by] Polish Institute of International Affairs, Institute of Legal Sciences of Polish Academy of Sciences [and] Polish Branch of International Law Association. a., 1966/7 (1)- Wrocław.

ROLA prawa w integracji Ziem Zachodnich: materiały sesji naukowj prawników odbytej we Wrocławiu w dniach 4 i 5 czerwca 1965 roku z okazji XX-lecia PRL. Warszawa, Wydawnictwo Prawnicze, 1966. pp. 200. 20½cm.

ZIEMBIŃSKI (ZYGMUNT) Logiczne podstawy prawoznawstwa: wybrane zagadnienia. Warszawa, Wydawnictwo Prawnicze, 1966. pp. 264. 20½cm. With English summary.

POLISH ROUND TABLE: yearbook; ([published by] Polish Association of Political Sciences). Warsaw, annual, 1967 (1) to date.

BORUCKA-ARCTOWA (MARIA) O społecznym działaniu prawa. Warszawa, PWN, 1967. pp. 282. bibliog. 20cm. With English summary.

POLSKA AKADEMIA NAUK. Instytut Nauk Prawnych. Introduction à l'étude du droit polonais; [sous la direction de Stefan Rozmaryn]. Varsovie, PWN, [1967]. pp. 588. bibliog. 23cm.

ÉTUDES sur le droit polonais actuel: oeuvre collective de Professeurs de la Faculté de Droit de Poznan; préparée sous la direction d'Adam Lopatka. Paris, Mouton, [1968]. pp. 185. 23cm. (Grenoble. Université. Faculté de Droit et des Sciences Économiques. Centre de Recherche Juridique. Série Droits Étrangers et Droit Comparé. vol. no. 1)

JANKOWSKI (HENRYK) Prawo i moralność. Warszawa, Książka i Wiedza, 1968. pp. 263. 20cm.

PODGÓRECKI (ADAM) Zarys socjologii prawa. Warszawa, 1971. pp. 485. With Russian and English summaries.

- Poland - Bibliography

POLSKA bibliografia prawnicza, 1944-(   ); (Bibliographie juridique polonaise). Warszawa, Państwowe Wydawnictwo Naukowe, 1962 in progress. 24cm. In Polish and French.

SIEKANOWICZ (PETER) Legal sources and bibliography of Poland. New York, Praeger, [1964]. pp. (xii), 311. 21½cm. (Praeger Publications in Russian History and World Communism. No. 22)

- Poland - Dictionaries and encyclopaedias

WISZNIEWSKI (JERZY) Zarys encyklopedii prawa. 6th ed. Warszawa, 1968. pp. 433.

- Poland - History and criticism

WAGNER (WENCESLAS JOSEPH) ed. Polish law throughout the ages. Stanford, California, [1970]. pp. 476. (Stanford University. Hoover Institution on War, Revolution and Peace. Hoover Institution Publications)

- Poland - Interpretation and construction

NOWACKI (JÓZEF) Analogia legis. Warszawa, PWN, 1966. pp. 234. 20cm. With German summary.

- Poland - Mathematical models

KISZA (ANDRZEJ) Model cybernetyczny powstawania i działania prawa. Wrocław, 1970. pp. 204. bibliog. (Breslau. Wrocławskie Towarzystwo Naukowe. Prace. Seria A. Nr.133) With English summary.

- Roumania - Bibliography

STOICOIU (VIRGILIU) Legal sources and bibliography of Roumania. New York, Praeger, [1964]. pp. (xii), 237. 21½cm. (Praeger Publications in Russian History and World Communism. No. 24)

IONAŞCU (TRAIAN) and others, compilers. Bibliographie juridique roumaine; Bibliografie juridică română, 1944-1968. Bucureşti, 1969. pp. 410. In French and Roumanian.

- Russia

RUSSIA (R.S.F.S.R.). Statutes, etc. 1917. Decrees, orders and proclamations of the Provisional Workmen's and Peasants' Government of the Russian Republic, vol.1, October 25 - December 1, 1917. Petrograd, 1918. pp. 28. (Russia (R.S.F.S.R.). Narodnyi Komissariat Inostrannykh Del. Department of Foreign Political Literature. Russian Revolutionary Pamphlets)

RUSSIA (R.S.F.S.R.). Statutes, etc. 1917-1918. Dekrety Sovetskoi vlasti. t.1. 25 oktiabria 1917 g. - 16 marta 1918 g. Moskva, 1957. pp. 626.

RUSSIA (R.S.F.S.R.). Statutes, etc. 1918. Dekrety Sovetskoi vlasti. t.2. 17 marta - 10 iiulia 1918 g. Moskva, 1959. pp. 686.

ISTORIIA gosudarstva i prava SSSR. ch.2. Istoriia Sovetskogo gosudarstva i prava. Moskva, 1962. pp. 444.

GABRICHIDZE (BORIS NIKOLAEVICH) and RIABKO (IVAN FEDOROVICH) Mestnye Sovety i vospitanie sotsialisticheskogo pravosoznaniia trudiashchikhsia. Rostov-na-Donu, 1964. pp. 74.

TOMSK. Universitet. Doklady itogovoi nauchnoi konferentsii iuridicheskikh fakul'tetov, dekabr' 1964 g. Tomsk, 1964. pp. 154.

VOPROSY gosudarstva i prava. Leningrad, 1964. pp. 203.

MOKICHEV (K. A.) ed. Теория государства и права. Москва, Юридическая Литература, 1965. pp. 519. 21½см.

SARATOVSKII IURIDICHESKII INSTITUT. Uchenye Trudy. vyp.2. (Issledovaniia... po aktual'nym voprosam gosudarstva i prava). Saratov, 1965. pp. 301.

SARATOVSKII IURIDICHESKII INSTITUT.
Uchenye zapiski. vyp.12. Voprosy
gosudarstva i prava. Saratov, 1965.
pp. 182.

KONI (ANATOLII FEDOROVICH) Собрание сочинений. Москва, 1966-1969. 8 vols.

BERCHENKO (ALEKSANDR IAKOVLEVICH)
Воспитательная роль советского права.
Москва, Мысль, 1966. pp. 79. 20cm.

KALINYCHEV (FEDOR IVANOVICH) Советское законодательство в период строительства коммунизма. Москва, Мысль, 1966. pp. 102. 20см.

VOPROSY... Вопросы теории советского права: сборник докладов к конференции по итогам научно-исследовательской работы. Новосибирск, 1966. pp. 169.

RUSSIA (R.S.F.S.R.). Statutes, etc. 1967. Систематическое собрание законов РСФСР, указов Президиума Верховного Совета РСФСР и решений Правительства РСФСР. Москва, 1967 in progress.

AKTUAL'NYE... Актуальные проблемы Советского государства и права в период строительства коммунизма. Ленинград, 1967. pp. 519.

BERMAN (HAROLD JOSEPH) and MAGGS (PETER B.) Disarmament inspection under Soviet law. Dobbs Ferry, Oceana, 1967. pp. vii, 154. bibliog. 22½cm.

DENISOV (ANDREI IVANOVICH) ed. Teoriia gosudarstva i prava. Moskva, 1967. pp. 416

ISTORIIA gosudarstva i prava SSSR. ch.1. Moskva, 1967. pp. 651.

KONKRETNO-sotsiologicheskie issledovaniia v pravovoi nauke: materialy nauchnoi konferentsii, Kiev, 26-27 oktiabria 1965 g. Kiev, 1967. pp. 192.

PETROV (L. A.) and others, eds. Некоторые вопросы социологии и права: материалы научно-теоретической конференции "Конкретно-социологические исследования правовых отношений". Иркутск, 1967. pp. 292. 21½см.

[PIAT'DESIAT]... 50 лет Советской власти и актуальные проблемы правовой науки: материалы к конференции по итогам научно-исследовательской работы за 1966 г. Саратов, (Юридический Институт), 1967. pp. 204. 21½см.

RUSSIA (R.S.F.S.R.). Statutes, etc. 1961-1966. Постановления Пленума Верховного Суда РСФСР. Москва, 1967. pp. 168.

BABKIN (VOLODYMYR DMYTROVYCH) and others. Радянське право і комуністична мораль, etc. Київ, 1968. pp. 195.

CHECHOT (DMITRII MIKHAILOVICH) Субъективное право и формы его защиты. Ленинград, Университет, 1968. pp. 72. 21см.

LATVIISKII GOSUDARSTVENNYI UNIVERSITET. Uchenye Zapiski. № 105. Октябрьская революция и развитие права: о становлении науки советского права и социалистической законности. Рига, 1968. pp. 174.

MAL'TSEV (GENNADII VASIL'EVICH) Социалистическое право и свобода личности: теоретические вопросы. Москва, Юридическая Литература, 1968. pp. 143. 19½см.

MIRONOV (NIKOLAI VLADIMIROVICH) Советское законодательство и международное право. Москва, 1968. pp. 195. bibliog.

RUSSIA (R.S.F.S.R.). Statutes, etc. 1918-1919. Dekrety Sovetskoi vlasti. t.4. 10 noiabria 1918 g. - 31 marta 1919 g. Moskva, 1968. pp. 731.

RUSSIA (U.S.S.R.). Statutes, etc. 1938-1967. Сборник законов СССР и указов Президиума Верховного Совета СССР, 1938-1967. Москва, 1968. 2 vols. 21cm.

SHEBANOV (ALEKSANDR FILIPPOVICH) Форма советского права. Москва, 1968. pp. 212.

SOVETSKOE narodnoe zakonodatel'stvo. Moskva, 1968. pp. 447.

ALEKSANDROV (NIKOLAI GRIGOR'EVICH) Sushchnost' sotsialisticheskogo gosudarstva i prava: uchebnoe posobie. Moskva, 1969. pp. 125. bibliog.

CHKHIKVADZE (V. M.) ed. Проблемы советского социалистического государства и права в современный период: некоторые теоретические вопросы. Москва, 1969. pp. 311.

CHKHIKVADZE (V.M.) ed. The Soviet state and law: essays by V.M.Chkhikvadze [and others]. Moscow, 1969. pp. 333.

DOZORTSEV (ABRAM VLADIMIROVICH) ed. Советское право, etc. Москва, 1969. pp. 607.

HAZARD (JOHN NEWBOLD) and others. The Soviet legal system: contemporary documentation and historical commentary. rev. ed. Dobbs Ferry, 1969. pp. 667. bibliog.

MATUZOV (NIKOLAI IGNAT'EVICH) Sotsialisticheskoe pravo i kommunisticheskaia moral' v ikh vzaimodeistvii. Saratov, 1969. pp. 90.

OSNOVY... Основы теории государства и права. Москва, 1969. pp. 384.

OSNOVY... Основы советского государственного строительства и права: учебное пособие. 3rd ed. Москва, 1969. pp. 574.

OSTROUMOV (G. S.) Pravovoe osoznanie deistvitel'nosti. Moskva, 1969. pp. 172.

LAW - Russia (Cont'd.)

STERNIK (ISAAC BORISOVICH) В. И. Ленин - юрист: юридическая деятельность В. И. Ульянова (Ленина). Ташкент, 1969. pp. 269.

VOLKOV (B. A.) and others. Юридический справочник для населения: в вопросах и ответах. Минск, Беларусь, 1969. pp. 494. 19½см.

BERCHENKO (ALEKSANDR IAKOVLEVICH) Leninskie printsipy sovetskogo prava. Moskva, 1970. pp. 255.

HAZARD (JOHN NEWBOLD) Union of Soviet Socialist Republics law digest. n.p., 1970. fo. [14]. (Reprinted from Martindale-Hubbell law directory, 1970)

IAKUBA (ELENA ALEKSANDROVNA) Pravo i nravstvennost' kak reguliatory obshchestvennykh otnoshenii pri sotsializme. Khar'kov, 1970. pp. 208. bibliog.

IOFFE (OLIMPIAD SOLOMONOVICH) ed. Osnovy sovetskogo prava. 2nd ed. Minsk, 1970. pp. 599.

OSNOVY Sovetskogo gosudarstva i prava. Moskva, 1970. pp. 374.

ALEKSEEV (SERGEI SERGEEVICH) Sotsial'naia tsennost' prava v sovetskom obshchestve. Moskva, 1971. pp. 223.

- Russia - Bibliography

KULAZHNIKOV (MIKHAIL NIKITICH) compiler. Teoriia gosudarstva i prava: bibliografiia, 1954-1964. Rostov, 1964. pp. 220.

BUTLER (WILLIAM E.) Writings on Soviet law and Soviet international law: a bibliography of books and articles published since 1917 in languages other than East European. Cambridge, 1966. pp. xi, 165. 20cm. (Harvard University. Harvard Law School Library)

KULAZHNIKOV (M. N.) compiler. Теория государства и права: библиография, 1917-1968. Москва, 1969. pp. 371.

- Russia - Codification

GORSHENIN (KONSTANTIN PETROVICH) Кодификация законодательства о труде: теоретические вопросы. Москва, Юридическая Литература, 1967. pp. 224. 20см.

POLENINA (SVETLANA VASIL'EVNA) Основы гражданского законодательства и гражданские кодексы. Москва, 1968. pp. 190.

RAZVITIE... Развитие кодификации советского законодательства. Москва, Юридическая Литература, 1968. pp. 248. 19½см.

MISHUTIN (A. N.) ed. Подготовка и издание систематических собраний действующего законодательства. Москва, 1969. pp. 342.

SHVEKOV (GEORGII VASIL'EVICH) Pervyi sovetskii Ugolovnyi kodeks. Moskva, 1970. pp. 207.

- Russia - Dictionaries and encyclopaedias

IURIDICHESKII... Юридический справочник для населения. Москва, Юридическая Литература, 1968. pp. 504. 21½см.

PRISCHEPENKO (NICHOLAS PIGOT) Russian-English law dictionary...; completed and edited by the New York University School of Law. New York, 1969. pp. 146.

- Russia - History and criticism

PFAFF (DIETER) Die Entwicklung der sowjetischen Rechtslehre. Köln, Verlag Wissenschaft und Politik, [1968]. pp. 286. bibliog. 22 cm. (Bundesinstitut für Ostwissenschaftliche und Internationale Studien. Abhandlungen. Band 19)

ROL'... Роль В. И. Ленина в становлении и развитии советского законодательства. Москва, 1969. pp. 477.

- Russia - Mathematical models

VOPROSY kibernetiki i pravo. Moskva, 1967. pp. 312.

PRAVOVAIA kibernetika. Moskva, 1970. pp. 334. bibliog.

- St. Kitts

ST. CHRISTOPHER-NEVIS. Statutes, etc. 1681-1961. The revised laws of St. Christopher Nevis and Anguilla: prepared under the authority of the revised edition of the Laws Ordinance, 1959, by P. Cecil Lewis. [Basseterre], 1964. 9 vols. 24½cm.

- St. Vincent

ST. VINCENT. Statutes, etc. 1784-1926. The laws of Saint Vincent...in force on the 4th day of May, 1926...; prepared...by James Stanley Rae. rev. ed. London, 1927. 2 vols.

ST. VINCENT. Statutes, etc. 1784-   . The laws of St. Vincent in force on the 31st day of December 1966...; prepared...by Keith Hennessey Conrad Alleyne; (with Supplement) rev. ed. Kingstown, 1970 in progress. Vol. 6, Chronological tables and index and vol. 9, Supplement and looseleaf.

- Sardinia

SARDINIA. Consiglio Regionale. Attività legislativa. sess., My 28 1949/My 7 1953 - Jl 3 1961/Je 12 1965 (1a - 4a legislatura). Cagliari.

- Scandinavia - Bibliography

GINSBURG (RUTH BADER) A selective survey of English language studies on Scandinavian law. South Hackensack, 1970. pp. 53.

- Siam

WENK (KLAUS) Gerichtsverfassung und Zivilprozess in Thailand; ein Überblick; mit einem Anhang; Verzeichnis der wichtigsten Gesetze Thailands. Frankfurt am Main, Metzner, [1960]. pp. viii, 75. bibliog. $23\frac{1}{2}$cm. (Hamburg. Institut für Asienkunde. Schriften. Band 6)

- Somaliland

CONTINI (PAOLO) The Somali Republic: an experiment in legal integration. London, 1969. pp. 92. bibliog.

- South Africa

SOUTH AFRICA. Statutes, etc. 1910- . Statutes of the republic of South Africa classified and annotated from 1910. Durban, [1967]in progress. 21 vols. Loose leaf binders.

MAASDORP (Sir ANDRIES FERDINAND STOCKENSTROM) Institutes of South African law...[edited] by C.G.Hall. vols. 1-2 are of the 9th ed., vol. 3 of the 8th. Cape Town, 1968-71. 3 vols.

HAHLO (HERMAN ROBERT) and KAHN (ELLISON) The South African legal system and its background. Cape Town, Juta, 1968. pp. xxxix, 603. bibliog. 24cm.

SOUTH AFRICA. Department of Foreign Affairs. 1968. South Africa and the rule of law. Pretoria, 1968. pp. 68. 24cm.

- Spain

JOVELLANOS Y RAMÍREZ (GASPAR MELCHOR DE) Obras. Tomos 1, 2, 4. Madrid, Mellado, 1845-46. 3 vols. $15\frac{1}{2}$cm.

VILLARROYA (JOAQUÍN TOMÁS) El sistema político del estatuto real: 1834-1836. Madrid, Instituto de Estudios Políticos, 1968. pp. 649. 21cm. (Colección História Política)

- Spain-Colonies

ARRIAGA COPETE (LIBARDO) El por que de un mundo: evaluación jurídica de la obra de España en América. [Bogota], 1965. pp. 141. $22\frac{1}{2}$cm.

- Spain - History and criticism

PROCTER (EVELYN EMMA STEFANOS) The judicial use of pesquisa (inquisition) in León and Castille 1157-1369. London, 1966. pp. 41. bibliog. (English Historical Review. Supplements. 2)

- Sudan

THOMPSON (C. F.) The sources of law in the new nations of Africa: a case study from the Republic of the Sudan. in Hutchison (Thomas W.) and others, eds. Africa and law. Madison, 1968.

- Sudan - History and criticism

MUSTAFA (ZAKI) The common law in the Sudan: an account of the "justice, equity and good conscience" provision. Oxford, 1971. pp. 272. bibliog.

- Swaziland

SWAZILAND. Statutes. etc. Statutes of Swaziland; prepared by the Attorney General. [rev. ed.] Mbabane, [1971 in progress]. Loose-leaf binders.

- Switzerland

SCHWEIZERISCHER JURISTENVEREIN. Regards sur le droit suisse aujourd'hui et demain: Das schweizerische Recht; Besinnung und Ausblick; recueil publié...à l'occasion de l'Exposition nationale suisse Lausanne 1964, etc. Bâle, 1964. pp. 339. bibliog. 24cm.

- Tajikistan

TAJIKISTAN. Statutes, etc. 1965. Sbornik zakonodatel'stva Tadzhikskoi SSR dlia mestnykh Sovetov deputatov trudiashchikhsia. Dushanbe, 1966. pp. 558.

- Turkey

ANSAY (TUĞRUL) and WALLACE (DON) eds. Introduction to Turkish law. Ankara, Society of Comparative Law, 1966. pp. xvi, 254. bibliog. $23\frac{1}{2}$cm.

- Turkmenistan

TURKMENISTAN. Statutes, etc. 1925-1944. Хронологическое собрание законов Туркменской ССР, указов Президиума Верховного Совета, постановлений и распоряжений правительства Туркменской ССР. т.1. 1925-1944. Ашхабад, 1960. pp. 393. 22cm.

TURKMENISTAN. Statutes, etc. 1945-1951. Хронологическое собрание законов Туркменской ССР, указов Президиума Верховного Совета, постановлений и распоряжений правительства Туркменской ССР. т.2. 1945-1951. Ашхабад, 1962. pp. 400. $21\frac{1}{2}$см.

TURKMENISTAN. Statutes, etc. 1952-1956. Хронологическое собрание законов Туркменской ССР, указов Президиума Верховного Совета, постановлений и распоряжений правительства Туркменской ССР. т.3. 1952-1956. Ашхабад, 1962. pp. 589. 21cm.

TURKMENISTAN Statutes, etc. 1957-1960. Хронологическое собрание законов Туркменской ССР, указов Президиума Верховного Совета, постановлений и распоряжений правительства Туркменской ССР. т.4. 1957-1960. Ашхабад, 1963. pp. 928. 21см.

- Uganda

BROWN (DOUGLAS) M.A., LL.B. and ALLEN (PETER AUSTIN PHILIP JERMYN) An introduction to the law of Uganda. London, Sweet & Maxwell, 1968. pp. vii, 136. $21\frac{1}{2}$cm. (Law in Africa. No. 25)

- Ukraine

ISTORIIA derzhavy i prava Ukraïns'koï RSR. Kyïv, 1967. 2 vols.

- Ukraine - Codification

TKACH (ARKADII PETROVYCH) Istoriia kodyfikatsiï dorevoliutsiinoho prava Ukraïny. Kyïv, 1968. pp. 170.

LAW (Cont'd.)

- United Kingdom

JENKINS (DAVID) One of the Judges for South Wales. To the honorable societies of Grayes-Inne and of the rest of the innes of court and to all the professors of the law; (Lex terrae); [dated 28. Aprilis, 1647]. [London, 1647]. pp. (32). 19cm. Wing J 612.

BALL (WILLIAM) of Barkham. The power of kings discussed; or, An examen of the fundamentall constitution of the free-borne people of England: in answer to severall tenents of M. David Jenkins. London, Harris, 1649. pp. 13. 18½cm. Wing B 594.

METCALFE (OSWALD KILLINGBRECK) General principles of English law; eighth edition by John Westwood. London, Cassell, 1967. pp. xiv, 300. 21¾cm.

WALKER (RONALD JACK) and WALKER (MICHAEL GEORGE) The English legal system. London, Butterworths, 1967. pp. xxix, 520. 24½cm.

UNITED KINGDOM. Statutes, etc. Halsbury's statutes of England; third edition [by A.D. Yonge and others] London, Butterworths, 1968 in progress. 24½cm.

CONSERVATIVE POLITICAL CENTRE. [Publications]. No. 393. Europe and the law: studies on the implementation of the EEC'S common policy and its impact on United Kingdom laws. London, 1968. pp. 96. 21¼cm.

COUNTER (KENNETH NORMAN SAMUEL) The framework and functions of English law: an introduction to the English legal system. Oxford, Pergamon, 1968. pp. ix, 136. 19½cm. (Commonwealth and International Library. Pergamon Modern Legal Outlines)

MONTROSE (JAMES LOUIS) Precedent in English law, and other essays; edited by Harold Greville Hanbury. Shannon, Irish U.P., 1968. pp. v, 368. bibliog. 24cm.

RADCLIFFE (CYRIL JOHN) Viscount Radcliffe. Not in feather beds: some collected papers. London, Hamilton, 1968. pp. xviii, 277. 21½cm.

FRANK (WILLIAM FRANCIS) The general principles of English law. 4th ed. London, 1969. pp. 216. bibliog.

JAMES (PHILIP SEAFORTH) Introduction to English law. 7th ed. London, Butterworths, 1969. pp. 501, 32. 20½cm.

TENCH (DAVID) The law for consumers. London, [1969]. pp. 130.

PRITT (DENIS NOWELL) Law, class and society. London, 1970 in progress.

PHILLIPS (OWEN HOOD) A first book of English law. 6th ed. London, 1970. pp. 346.

SALMON (Sir CYRIL BARNET) The law and individual liberty. London, 1970. pp. 15. (London. University. Birkbeck College. Haldane Memorial Lectures. 34)

WALKER (RONALD JACK) and WALKER (MICHAEL GEORGE) The English legal system. 2nd ed. London, 1970. pp. 536.

FOX (CHARLES) Solicitor. The countryside and the law. Newton Abbot, [1971]. pp. 206.

LAW STUDENTS' ANNUAL. London, annual. 21½cm. Current issue only kept.

- United Kingdom - Codification

SCARMAN (Sir LESLIE) Codification and judge-made law: a problem of co-existence;...a lecture delivered...20th October, 1966. Birmingham, University, Faculty of Law, 1966. pp. 21. 24½cm.

- United Kingdom - Dictionaries and encyclopaedias

RADIN (MAX) Law dictionary; edited by Lawrence G. Greene. Dobbs Ferry, 1955 repr. 1966. pp. 408.

MOZLEY (HERBERT NEWMAN) and WHITELEY (GEORGE CECIL) Law dictionary; eighth edition by John B. Saunders. London, 1970. pp. 389.

STROUD (FREDERICK) Judicial dictionary of words and phrases; fourth edition by John S. James. London, 1971 in progress.

- United Kingdom - Digests

WILLIAMS (THOMAS WALTER) A compendious digest of the statute law, comprising the substance and effect of the most material clauses in all the public acts of parliament in force within Great Britain, from Magna Charta in the ninth year of King Henry III to the forty-eighth year of his present majesty King George III inclusive. 3rd ed., London, Kearsley, 1809. 21cm. 2 vols.

- United Kingdom - History and criticism

USHER (ROLAND GREENE) The rise and fall of the High Commission;... [reprinted from the 1913 original] with a new introduction by Philip Tyler [and an additional bibliography]. Oxford, 1968. pp. 380. bibliog.

KIRALFY (A.K.R.) English law. in Derrett (John Duncan Martin) ed. An introduction to legal systems. London, 1968.

POLLOCK (Sir FREDERICK) and MAITLAND (FREDERIC WILLIAM) The history of English law before the time of Edward I...; second edition reissued with a new introduction and select bibliography by S.F.C. Milsom. Cambridge, C.U.P., 1968. 2 vols. 23cm.

LEVIN (JENNIFER) The charter controversy in the city of London, 1660-1688, and its consequences. London, 1969. pp. 119. bibliog.

MILSOM (STROUD FRANCIS CHARLES) Historical foundations of the common law. London, Butterworths, 1969. pp. xiv, 466. 21½cm.

LITTLE (DAVID) Religion, order, and law: a study in pre-revolutionary England. Oxford, 1970. pp. 269. bibliog.

VEALL (DONALD) The popular movement for law reform, 1640-1660. Oxford, 1970. pp. 259. bibliog.

WHAT'S wrong with the law?: [the revised version of nine broadcast talks]; by Lord Devlin [and others]; [edited by] Michael Zander. London, 1970. pp. 126.

BAKER (J.H.) An introduction to English legal history. London, 1971. pp. 330. bibliogs.

RADCLIFFE (GEOFFREY REYNOLDS YONGE) and CROSS (ARTHUR GEOFFREY NEALE) Baron Cross of Chelsea. The English legal system; fifth edition by Lord Cross of Chelsea and G.J. Hand. London, 1971. pp. 472.

- United Kingdom - Interpretation and construction

MAXWELL (Sir PETER BENSON) On the interpretation of statutes; twelfth edition by P.St. J. Langan. London, 1969. pp. 391.

STROUD (FREDERICK) Judicial dictionary of words and phrases; fourth edition by John S. James. London, 1971 in progress.

CRAIES (WILLIAM FEILDEN) On statute law; seventh edition by S.G.G. Edgar. London, 1971. pp. 640.

- United Kingdom - Societies

SOCIETY FOR PROMOTING THE AMENDMENT OF THE LAW. (Rules and regulations) [and list of officers and members]. London, 1845. pp. 23. 18cm.

- United Kingdom - Study and teaching

LAW SOCIETY. Associate Members' Group. The prospective lawyer: blue-print for the future; a memorandum on legal education and training, etc. London, [1968]. pp. 71. 21cm.

TRAINING for the law : report of a conference at Ditchley Park, 7-10 July 1967. Enstone, [1968?] pp. 51. (Ditchley Foundation. Ditchley Papers. No.11.)

SOCIETY OF LABOUR LAWYERS. Legal education: report. London, Fabian Society, 1969. pp. 40. 21½cm. (Research Series [No.] 276)

- United Kingdom - Vocational guidance

U.K. Central Youth Employment Executive. 1970. Law. 4th ed. [London], 1970. pp. 51. (Choice of Careers. 26.)

- United Kingdom - Scotland

GLOAG (WILLIAM MURRAY) and HENDERSON (ROBERT CANDLISH) Introduction to the law of Scotland; seventh edition [by] Alastair M. Johnston and J.A.D. Hope, etc. Edinburgh, Green, 1968. pp. cxix, 875. 24cm.

WALKER (DAVID MAXWELL) The Scottish legal system: an introduction to the study of Scots law. 3rd ed. Edinburgh, 1969. pp. 488. bibliogs.

STAIR SOCIETY. [Publications]. 26. Miscellany One; by various authors;..... Edinburgh, 1971. pp. 282.

- United Kingdom - Scotland - History and criticism

SMITH (ADAM) LL.D., F.R.S. Four autograph letters of Adam Smith to Lord Hailes, 1769 Kirkcaldy; facsimile printed by Yushodo Booksellers Ltd. Tokyo, imprint, [1968]. pp. (16).

- United Kingdom - British Empire

CONFERENCE ON INTERNATIONAL AND COMPARATIVE LAW OF THE COMMONWEALTH, 1966. International and comparative law of the Commonwealth; [papers presented by] Ralph Braibanti [and others]; edited by Robert R. Wilson. Durham, N.C., Duke U.P., 1968. pp. (x), 247. 23cm. (Duke University. Commonwealth Studies Center. Publications. 33)

- United States

INGERSOLL (EDWARD) A digest of the laws of the United States of America, from March 4th, 1789, to May 15th, 1820; including also the constitution, and the old Act of Confederation, etc. Philadelphia, Maxwell 1821. pp. (iii), 850. 23½cm.

ORGANIZATION OF AMERICAN STATES. 1964. A statement of the laws of the United States in matters affecting business; [edited by] Robert B. Glynn. (General Legal Division). Washington, 1964. pp. vi, 200. 27cm.

AMERICAN ASSEMBLY [32nd[?] Assembly, 14 March 1968] Law in a changing America: [papers for background reading; edited by Geoffrey C. Hazard]. Englewood Cliffs, Prentice-Hall, [1968]. pp. xiii, 207. 21 cm.

FREUND (PAUL ABRAHAM) On law and justice. Cambridge, Mass., Belknap, 1968. pp. vii, 259. 21cm.

LIEBHAFSKY (HERBERT HUGO) American government and business. New York, [1971]. pp. 587.

- United States - Bibliography

The LAW in the United States of America: a selective bibliographical guide; [compiled by] Joseph L. Andrews [and others]. New York, University P., [1966]. pp. ix, 100. 21cm.

LONDON. University. Institute of Advanced Legal Studies. Union Catalogues. No. 3. Union list of United States legal literature: holdings of legislation, law reports and digests in libraries in Oxford, Cambridge and London...as at Oct. 1966. 2nd ed. London, the Institute, 1967. pp. x, 82. 24½cm.

- United States - Dictionaries and encyclopaedias

RADIN (MAX) Law dictionary; edited by Lawrence G. Greene. Dobbs Ferry, 1955 repr. 1966. pp. 408.

HEIMANSON (RANDOLPH) Dictionary of political science and law. Dobbs Ferry, Oceana Publications, 1967. pp. 188. 21½cm.

- United States - History and criticism

HONNOLD (JOHN) ed. The life of the law: readings on the growth of legal institutions. Glencoe, Free P., [1964]. pp. xv, 581. 23½cm.

HUSTON (LUTHER A.) and others. Roles of the Attorney General of the United States. Washington, American Enterprise Institute for Public Policy Research, 1968. pp. vi, 158. bibliog. 21½cm.

HURST (JAMES WILLARD) The legitimacy of the business corporation in the law of the United States 1780-1970. Charlottesville, 1970. pp. 191. bibliog. (Virginia University. Page-Barbour Lectures. 1969)

- Uruguay

REAL (ALBERTO RAMÓN) Los principios generales de derecho en la constitución uruguaya. 2nd ed. Montevideo, 1965. pp. 66. bibliog. 23cm.

LAW (Cont'd.)

- Uzbekistan

SOVETSKOE... Советское право Узбекистана в период развернутого строительства коммунизма. Ташкент, 1964. pp. 211.

UZBEKISTAN. Statutes, etc. 1938-1964. Сборник законов Узбекской ССР и указов Президиума Верховного Совета Узбекской ССР, 1938-1964 гг. Ташкент, 1964. pp. 527. 21½cm.

VOPROSY sovershenstvovaniia zakonodatel'stva Uzbekskoi SSR. Tashkent, 1970. pp. 380.

- Uzbekistan - History and criticism

ISTORIIA... История Советского государства и права Узбекистана. Ташкент, 1960-1968. 3 vols.

- White Russia

VOLKOV (B. A.) and others. Юридический справочник для населения: в вопросах и ответах. Минск, Беларусь, 1969. pp. 494. 19½см.

- Yugoslavia

LEGRADIĆ (RUDOLF) Sociologija prava. Beograd, "Savremena Administracija", 1965. pp. 313. 24cm. (Biblioteka Društvenih Nauka)

PETROVIĆ (VOJISLAV I.) Osnovi prava, sa privrednim i radnim pravom. Beograd, 1967. pp. 260.

- Yugoslavia - Bibliography

GJUPANOVICH (FRAN) and ADAMOVITCH (ALEXANDER) Legal sources and bibliography of Yugoslavia. New York, [1964]. pp. 353.

- Zambia

ZAMBIA. Legal Affairs Division. Annual report. Lusaka, annual, 1967/1968 [1st] to date. 32½cm.

LAW, ANCIENT

MYTH and law among the Indo-Europeans: studies in Indo-European comparative mythology; edited by Jaan Puhvel; [a symposium of the Center for the Study of Comparative Folklore and Mythology]. Berkeley, 1970. pp. 276. bibliog. (California University. Center for the Study of Comparative Folklore and Mythology. Publications. 1)

LAW, BANTU

SEYMOUR (S. M.) Bantu law in South Africa. 3rd ed. Cape Town, 1970. pp. 429.

LAW, BYZANTINE

SVORONOS (NICOLAS G.) ed. Recherches sur la tradition juridique à Byzance: la Synopsis major des basiliques et ses appendices. Paris, P.U.F. 1964. pp. viii, 210. 23½cm. (Bibliothèque Byzantine. Etudes. 4)

LAW, COMPARATIVE

ROTONDI (MARIO) Diritto comparato. Torino, Unione Tipografico-Editrice Torinese, [196-]. pp. 24. 19½cm. (Estralto dal Novissimo Digesto Italiano).

INTERNATIONAL SYMPOSIUM ON COMPARATIVE LAW. Proceedings;...under the patronage of the Canadian and Foreign Law Research Centre. [in French or English]. Ottawa (formerly Montréal), annual, 1963 (1st) to date. 22cm.

CAEMMERER (ERNST VON) and others, eds. Vom deutschen zum europäischen Recht: Festschrift für Hans Dölle. Tübingen, Mohr, 1963. 2 vols. bibliog. 23cm.

AMERICAN JOURNAL OF COMPARATIVE LAW, THE. The American Journal of Comparative Law reader; edited, with foreword by Hessel E. Yntema. Dobbs Ferry, Oceana, 1966. pp. xvii, 493. 21cm.

CONGRÈS INTERNATIONAL DE DROIT COMPARÉ, 1966. 7ᵉ Congrès. Österreichische Landesreferate zum VII. Internationalen Kongress für Rechtsvergleichung in Uppsala 1966. Wien, Manz, 1966. pp. 164. 23cm. (Wiener Rechtswissenschaftliche Studien. Band 3)

MATEESCO (MIRCEA) Le droit maritime et le droit aérien de l'U.R.S.S. à l'heure de la coexistence pacifique. Paris, Pedone, 1967. pp. 383. bibliog. 25cm.

WILHELM (GEORGES) La responsabilité civile des administrateurs de sociétés anonymes: études de droit comparé; droits français, allemand et suisse. Genève, Droz, 1967. pp. 198. bibliog. 23cm. (Travaux de Droit, d'Économie, de Sociologie et de Sciences Politiques. No. 59)

CONFERENCE ON INTERNATIONAL AND COMPARATIVE LAW OF THE COMMON-WEALTH, 1966. International and comparative law of the Commonwealth; [papers presented by] Ralph Braibanti [and others]; edited by Robert R. Wilson. Durham, N.C., Duke U.P., 1968. pp. (x), 247. (Duke University. Commonwealth Studies Center. Publications. 33)

DAVID (RENÉ) and BRIERLEY (JOHN E.C.) Major legal systems in the world today: an introduction to the comparative study of law. London, Stevens, 1968. pp. xvii, 528. bibliog. 21½cm. This is a translation and adaptation of Les grands systèmes de droit contemporains, 2nd ed., 1966, by René David.

DERRETT (JOHN DUNCAN MARTIN) ed. An introduction to legal systems. London, Sweet and Maxwell, 1968. pp. xix, 203. bibliogs. 21½cm.

CAEMMERER (ERNST VON) and others, eds. Ius privatum gentium: Festschrift für Max Rheinstein zum 70. Geburtstag am 5. Juli 1969. Tubingen, 1969. 2 vols. bibliog. In various languages.

ÉTUDES de droit privé français et mauricien: congrès tenu à Saint-Denis de la Réunion, 1er-4 juillet 1965; [Gérard Conac, chairman]. Paris, 1969. pp. 230. (Université d'Aix Marseille. Faculté de Droit et des Sciences Économiques d'Aix. Annales. 57)

HAZARD (JOHN NEWBOLD) Communists and their law: a search for the common core of the legal systems of the Marxian socialist states. Chicago, 1969. pp. 560. bibliog. (Columbia University. Research Institute of Communist Affairs. Studies)

SOCIETE DE LEGISLATION COMPAREE. Livre du centenaire de la Société...; un siècle de droit comparé en France, 1869-1969; les apports du droit comparé au droit positif français. Paris, [1969]. pp. 382.

BOZEMAN (ADDA BRUEMMER) The future of law in a multicultural world. Princeton, 1971. pp. 229. bibliog.

SAARBRUECKEN. Universität. Annales Universitatis Saraviensis. Rechts- und Wirtschaftswissenschaftliche Abteilung. Band 62. Rechtsvergleichung; ([by] Léontin-Jean Constantinesco). Band 1. Einführung in die Rechtsvergleichung. Köln, 1971. pp. 298. bibliog.

LAW, GERMANIC

FEINE (HANS ERICH) Reich und Kirche: ausgewählte Abhandlungen zur deutschen und kirchlichen Rechtsgeschichte; eingeleitet und herausgegeben von Friedrich Merzbacher. Aalen, Scientia Verlag, 1966. pp. xi, 322. bibliogs. 24½cm.

LAW, GREEK

BERNEKER (ERICH) ed. Zur griechischen Rechtsgeschichte; [reprint of articles published in various periodicals between 1906 and 1964]. Darmstadt, Wissenschaftliche Buchgesellschaft, 1968. pp. vi, 788. bibliog. 19½cm. (Wege der Forschung. Band 45)

LAW, HINDU

DERRETT (J.D.M.) Hindu law. in Derrett (John Duncan Martin) ed. An introduction to legal systems. London, 1968.

LAW, ISLAMIC
See LAW, MOHAMMEDAN

LAW, JEWISH

FALK (Z.W.) Jewish law. in Derrett (John Duncan Martin) ed. An introduction to legal systems. London, 1968.

LAW, MOHAMMEDAN

ALLMENDINGER (KARL HEINZ) Die Beziehungen zwischen der Kommune Pisa und Ägypten im hohen Mittelalter: eine rechts- und wirtschaftshistorische Untersuchung. Wiesbaden, Steiner, 1967. pp. viii, 109. bibliog. 24cm. (Vierteljahrschrift für Sozial- und Wirtschaftsgeschichte. Beihefte. Nr. 54)

COULSON (N. J.) Islamic law. in Derrett (John Duncan Martin) ed. An introduction to legal systems. London, 1968.

LAW, PRIMITIVE

BARKUN (MICHAEL) Law without sanctions: order in primitive societies and the world community. New Haven, Yale U.P., 1968. pp. (vi) 179. bibliog. 23½cm.

OTS CAPDEQUI (JOSE M.) Historia del derecho español en America y del derecho indiano. Madrid, 1969. pp. 367.

DIAMOND (ARTHUR SIGISMUND) Primitive law, past and present. London, 1971. pp. 410.

- Bibliography

GILISSEN (JOHN) ed. Bibliographical introduction to legal history and ethnology. Bruxelles, Université Libre, Institut de Sociologie, [1963 in progress]. 26cm. (Études d'Histoire et d'Ethnologie Juridiques) Loose leaf. In English or French.

LAW, SAXON

GRYPHIANDER (JOANNES) De weichbildis saxonicis, sive colossis rulandinis urbium quarundam saxonicarum, commentarius historico-juridicus, etc. Argentorati, sumptibus T.H. Hauensteini, 1666. pp. (xxii), 204, (28). 19cm.

LAW, SLAVIC

KADLEC (KAREL) Introduction à l'étude comparative de l'histoire du droit public des peuples slaves. Paris, 1933. pp. 328. bibliog.

LAW AND ART

HARTLIEB (HORST VON) Die Freiheit der Kunst und das Sittengesetz. München-Pullach, [1969]. pp. 67. (Archiv für Urheber-, Film-, Funk- und Theaterrecht. Schriftenreihe der UFITA. Heft 33)

MUELLER (FRIEDRICH) Dr. jur. Freiheit der Kunst als Problem der Grundrechtsdogmatik. Berlin, 1969. pp. 161. bibliog.

LAW AND ETHICS

GINSBERG (MORRIS) Morality, law and the climate of opinion. [London], 1964. pp. irreg. bibliog.

DEVLIN (PATRICK ARTHUR) Baron Devlin. The enforcement of morals. London, 1965 repr. 1969. pp. 139.

KNEALE (WILLIAM CALVERT) The responsibility of criminals. Oxford, Clarendon P., [1967]. pp. 32. 21 cm. (Oxford University. Exeter College. Marett Memorial Lectures, 1967)

JANKOWSKI (HENRYK) Prawo i moralność. Warszawa, Książka i Wiedza, 1968. pp. 263. 20cm.

LE BARON (BENTLEY) Responsible obedience and disobedience: an inquiry into the limits and conditions of obligation to law; [Ph. D. (London) thesis]. 1968. fo. 291. bibliog. 25½cm. Typescript: unpublished. This thesis is the property of London University and may not be removed from the Library.

MADDEN (EDWARD HENRY) Civil disobedience and moral law in nineteenth-century American philosophy. Seattle, U. of Washington P., [1968]. pp. vii, 214. bibliog. 21½cm.

PERELMAN (CHAIM) Droit, morale et philosophie. Paris, Pichon et Durand-Auzias, 1968. pp. vii, 149. 25cm. (Bibliothèque de Philosophie du Droit. vol. 8)

LAW AND ETHICS (Cont'd.)

UNIONE GIURISTI CATTOLICI ITALIANI. Convegno Nazionale di Studio, 19°, 1968. Diritto e moralità pubblica in Italia. Roma, 1969. pp. 185. (Iustitia. Quaderni. 20)

UTLEY (THOMAS EDWIN) What laws may cure: a new examination of morals and the law. London, 1968. pp. 15. (Conservative Political Centre. [Publications]. No. 409)

FULLER (LON L.) The morality of law. 2nd ed. New Haven, [1969]. pp. 262. (Yale University. Storrs Lectures. 1963)

LEONHARDT (RUDOLF WALTER) Wer wirft den ersten Stein?: Minoritäten in einer züchtigen Gesellschaft. München, [1969]. pp. 435. bibliog.

DUSTER (TROY) The legislation of morality: law, drugs and moral judgment. New York, [1970]. pp. 274.

LAW AND FACT

- Poland

BAFIA (JERZY) Zmiana kwalifikacji prawnej czynu w procesie karnym. Warszawa, WP, 1964. pp. 252. bibliog. 20cm.

- Russia

IVANOV (O. V.) Printsip ob"ektivnoi istiny v sovetskom grazhdanskom protsesse: lektsiia dlia studentov vechernego otdeleniia. Moskva, 1964. pp. 77.

- Switzerland

L'HUILLIER (L.) L'appréciation juridique des faits. in Geneva. Université. Faculté des Sciences Économiques et Sociales. Publications. vol. 11. Genève, 1950.

LAW AND GOSPEL

CORBET (JOHN) Nonconformist Divine. A vindication of the magistrates and ministers of the city of Gloucester from the calumnies of Mr. Robert Bacon in his printed relation of his usage there which he intitles, The spirit of prelacy yet working, etc. London, Bostock, 1646. pp. (ii), 30. 17½cm. Wing C 6250.

CARTWRIGHT (THOMAS) Puritan. Helpes for discovery of the truth in point of toleration: being the judgment of that eminent scholler Tho. Cartwright...wherein the power and duty of the magistrate in relation to matters of religion is discussed;...occasionally handled in a controversie betweene the said publike Professor T.C. and Doctor Whitgift, etc. London, Banks, 1648. pp. 14. 18½cm. Wing C 700.   R(S.R.R.) : S.R. 11/Ff 3

LAW AND POLITICS

BUERGI (W. F.) Probleme des Rechtes im Zeitalter der Integrationen. in Zukunftsaufgaben in Wirtschaft und Gesellschaft. Zurich, 1963.

JONES (H. W.) Law and politics. in Parsons (Malcolm B.) ed. Perspectives in the study of politics. Chicago, [1968].

ARCHIVES DE PHILOSOPHIE DU DROIT. [Nouvelle Série]. No. 16. Le droit investi par la politique. Paris, 1971. pp. 506.

LAW AND SOCIALISM

GINDEV (PANAIOT) За някои категории на диалектическия материализъм и тяхното приложение в наказателното право и наказателния процес. София, БАН, 1956. pp. 264. bibliog. 20cm.

PETZOLD (SIEGFRIED) ed. Fragen der Staats- und Rechtstheorie: sowjetische Beiträge;...zusammengestellt vom Institut für Theorie des Staates und des Rechts/Staatsrecht an der Deutschen Akademie, etc. Potsdam-Babelsberg, the Akademie, 1963. 2 vols. (in 1). 20½ cm. (Deutsche Akademie für Staats- und Rechtswissenschaft "Walter Ulbricht". Aktuelle Beiträge zur Staats- und Rechtswissenschaft aus den sozialistischen Ländern. Hefte 2-3)

MACHT und Recht im kommunistischen Herrschaftssystem: (Boris Meissner zum 50. Geburtstag...; Redaktion Dietrich Frenzke und Alexander Uschakow). Köln, Verlag Wissenschaft und Politik, [1965]. pp. 335. 22½cm.

HOERZ (HERBERT) Ergebnisse und Aufgaben einer marxistischen Theorie des objektiven Gesetzes. Berlin, 1968. pp. 28. (Deutsche Akademie der Wissenschaften zu Berlin. Sitzungsberichte. 1968. Nr.7)

MAL'TSEV (GENNADII VASIL'EVICH) Sotsialisticheskoe pravo i svoboda lichnosti: teoreticheskie voprosy. Москва, Юридическая Литература, 1968. pp. 143. 19½см.

MATUZOV (NIKOLAI IGNAT'EVICH) Sotsialisticheskoe pravo i kommunisticheskaia moral' v ikh vzaimodeistvii. Saratov, 1969. pp. 90.

eÖRSI (GYULA) Fundamental problems of socialist civil law. Budapest, 1970. pp. 134. (Magyar Tudomanyos Akademia. Allam-és Jogtudomanyi Intézet. Series in Foreign Languages. No. 6)

LAW ENFORCEMENT

- Russia

SOVETSKAIA... Советская общественность и укрепление правопорядка. Минск, АН БССР, 1961. pp. 284. 20cm.

- United States

UNITED STATES. President's Commission on Law Enforcement and Administration of Justice. National Symposium on Science and Criminal Justice. Washington, 1966. pp. vii, 189.

UNITED STATES. House of Representatives. Committee on the Judiciary. Anti-crime program: hearings before Subcommittee No. 5 ... ninetieth Congress, first session on H. R. 5037, ... Serial No. 3. Washington, 1967. pp. x, 1551

UNITED STATES. President's Commission on Law
Enforcement and Administration of Justice.
Field Surveys. 1.
Report on a pilot study in the District of
Columbia, on victimization and attitudes
toward law enforcement: by Albert D Biderman
[and others]. Washington, 1967. pp. v, 176,
(88).

UNITED STATES. President's Commission on Law
Enforcement and administration of Justice.
Field Surveys. 2.
Criminal victimization in the United States:
a report of a national survey; by Philip H.
Ennis. Washington, 1967. pp. ix. 111.

UNITED STATES. President's Commission on Law
Enforcement and Administration of Justice.
Field Surveys. 3.
Studies in crime and law enforcement in major
metropolitan areas: by Albert J. Reiss [and
Donald J. Black]. Washington, 1967. 2 vols.

UNITED STATES. President's Commission on Law
Enforcement and Administration of Justice.
Task Force Reports.
Crime and its impact: an assessment.
Washington, 1967. pp. xi, 220.

UNITED STATES. President's Commission on Law
Enforcement and Administration of Justice.
Task Force Reports.
Organised crime: annotations and consultants'
papers. Washington, 1967. pp. vii, 126.

ELDEFONSO (EDWARD) and others. Principles of law
enforcement. New York, Wiley, [1968]. pp. (v),
284. bibliog. 22cm.

JONES (HARRY W.) The efficacy of law. Evanston,
Ill., [1969]. pp. 113. (Northwestern University.
Julius Rosenthal Foundation for General Law.
Lectures. 1968)

NORRGARD (DAVID L.) Regional law enforcement: a
study of intergovernmental cooperation and
coordination. Chicago, [1969]. pp. 58.

PACKER (HERBERT L.) The limits of the criminal
sanction. Stanford, Stanford U.P., 1969. pp.
xi, 385. bibliog. 23cm.

UNITED STATES. National Commission on the Causes and
Prevention of Violence. Law and order reconsidered:
report of the Task Force on Law and Law Enforcement.
Washington, [1969]. pp. 597. bibliogs.

LAW LIBRARIES

U.K. Treasury Solicitor. Legal Library. 1967.
Catalogue of the Legal Library of the
Treasury Solicitor; compiled by the Librarian.
2nd ed. London, 1967. pp. 236. 20cm.

EUROPEAN law libraries guide; prepared by the
International Association of Law Libraries...;[edited
by Elizabeth M. Moys]. [London, 1971]. pp.
678. In English or French.

LAW REFORM

- Australia

SUTTON (K.C.T.) The pattern of law reform in
Australia. St. Lucia, [1970]. pp. 22.
(Queensland University. Inaugural Lectures)

- Austria

NOVAK (FRANZ) Österreichs "grosse Rechtsreform"
und die Zivilgerichtsbarkeit...; mit einem
Nachwort und mit einem Verzeichnis der
Publikationen Novaks versehen von Franz
Matscher. Salzburg, [1968.] pp. 27. bibliog.
(Salzburg. Universtät. Salzburger Univer-
sitätsreden. Heft 29)

- Canada - British Columbia

BRITISH COLUBIA. Law Reform Commission. Annual
report. a., 1970 [1st]- Vancouver.

- France

AGOR (ANDRE) pseud. Histoire d'un procès; ou,
Pour une justice électronique. Paris, [1969].
pp. 393.

CHAZELLE (RENE) Pour une réforme des institutions judiciaires. Paris, 1969. pp. 133.

- Germany

ZITSCHER (WOLFRAM) Rechtssoziologische und
organisationssoziologische Fragen der Justizreform. Köln, 1969. pp. 72.

JUSTIZREFORM: Beiträge von Jan-Wolfgang Berlit
[and others]; herausgegeben von Rudolf Wassermann
(Aktionskomitee Justizreform). [Neuwied, 1970].
pp. 188.

- Hong Kong

HONG KONG. Law Reform Committee. 1957-65.
First (to fifth) report[s]. [Sir Michael
Hogan, chairman]. Hong Kong, 1957-65. 5 pts.

- Ireland (Republic)

EIRE. Department of Justice 1962.
Programme of law reform, laid before
each House of the Oireachtas, January,
1962. Dublin, [1962]. pp. 16. 24½cm.

- New Zealand

NEW ZEALAND. Department of Justice. 1969. The
machinery of law reform in New Zealand. Wellington, [1969]. pp. 18.

NEW ZEALAND. Law Review Commission. Report.
a., 1970/71 [1st]- Wellington.

- Pakistan

PAKISTAN. Law Reform Commission. 1970. The
report of the...Commission, 1967-70. Karachi,
1970. pp. 491. bibliog.

- United Kingdom

U.K. Law Commission. [Publications]. No. 23.
Civil liability for animals. London, 1967.
pp. 50. 24½cm.

GARDNER (EDWARD) and others. Rough justice.
London, Conservative Political Centre,
1968. pp. 22. 21½cm. ([Publications].
No. 424)

SCARMAN (Sir LESLIE) Law reform: the new
pattern. London, Routledge, 1968. pp. 64.
18½cm. (Keele. University. Lindsay Memorial
Lectures. 1967)

LAW REFORM - United Kingdom (Cont'd.)

U.K. Law Commission [Publications]. No.14. Second programme of law reform. London, 1968. pp. 8. 24cm.

U.K. Law Commission. Published Working Papers. No. 15. Second programme, item XIX. Family law: arrangements for the care and upbringing of children: (section 33 of the Matrimonial Causes Act, 1965); report by Mr. John Hall. London, 1968. pp. ii, 53. 33cm.

U.K. Law Commission. Published Working Papers. No. 16. Working party's provisional proposals relating to termination of tenancies. London, 1968. pp. iii, 39. 33cm.

U.K. Law Commission. Published Working Papers. No. 17. Second programme, item XVIII. Codification of the criminal law: general principles. London, 1968. pp. 47. 33cm.

U.K. Law Commission. Published Working Papers. No. 18. Provisional proposals relating to amendments to sections 12-15 of the Sale of Goods Act, 1893, and contracting out of the conditions and warranties implied by those sections. London, 1968. pp. 45. 33cm.

U.K. Law Commission. Published Working Papers. No. 19. First programme, item XV: the actions for loss of services, loss of consortium, seduction and enticement. [London], 1968. pp. 57. 33cm.

U.K. Law Commission. Published Working Papers. No. 20. First programme -- Item x. Family law: nullity of marriage. London, 1968. pp. 52. 33cm.

U.K. Law Commission. Published Working Papers. No. 21. Polygamous marriages. London, 1968. pp. 57. 33cm.

LONDON. University. Institute of Advanced Legal Studies. List of official committees, commissions and other bodies concerned with the reform of the law. 5th ed. London, 1969 pp. 55.

U.K. Law Commission.[Publications]. No.25. Family law: report on financial provision in matrimonial proceedings. London, 1969. pp. 154. Another copy filed with British Parliamentary Papers, 1968/69, H.C. 448.

U.K. Law Commission. Published Working Papers. No. 22. Second programme, item XIX. Family law: restitution of conjugal rights. London, 1969. fo. 8. 30cm.

U.K. Law Commission. Published Working Papers. No. 23. Second programme, item XVIII(2)(a). Criminal law: malicious damage. London, 1969. pp. ii, (51). 33cm.

U.K. Law Commission. Published Working papers. No.24. First programme, item IX. Transfer of land: rentcharges. London, 1969. pp.33. 33cm.

BENNION (FRANCIS ALAN ROSCOE) Tangling with the law: reforms in legal process. London, 1970. pp. 158. bibliog.

BORRIE (GORDON JOHNSON) Law reform: a damp squib?; an inaugural lecture delivered in the University of Birmingham on 5th November 1970. Birmingham, 1970. pp. 15.

U.K. Law Commission. Published Working Papers. No. 25. First programme, item VIII: the law of landlord and tenant: Working Party's provisional proposals relating to covenants restricting dispositions, parting with possession, change of user and alterations. London, 1970. pp. 105.

U.K. Law Commission. Published Working Papers. No. 26. Second programme, item XVIII (2) (a). Criminal law: forgery. London, 1970. pp. 61.

U.K. Law Commission. Published Working Papers. No. 27. First programme, item VI B. Personal injury litigation: assessment of damages: itemisation of pecuniary loss and the use of actuarial tables as an aid to assessment. London, 1970. pp. various.

U.K. Law Commission. Published Working Papers. No. 28. Family law: jurisdiction in matrimonial causes (other than nullity). London, 1970. pp. 60.

U. K. Law Commission. Published Working Papers. No.29. Second programme, item XVIII. Codification of the criminal law: subject 3: territorial and extraterritorial extent of the criminal law. London, 1970. pp. 69.

U.K. Law Commission. Published Working Papers. No.30. Second programme, item XVIII. Codification of the criminal law: strict liability and the enforcement of the Factories Act 1961 report by members of the Sub-Faculty of Law of the University of Kent. London, 1970. pp. 66.

U.K. Law Commission. Published Working Papers. No. 31. Second programme, item XVIII. Codification of the criminal law: general principles: the mental element in crime. London, 1970. pp. 65.

U.K. Law Commission. Published Working Papers. No. 32. First programme, item IX. Transfer of land: land registration (first paper). London, 1970. pp. 61.

U.K. Law Commission. Published Working Papers. No. 33. Second programme, item XVIII, subject (2)(a). Criminal law: perjury and kindred offences. London, 1970. pp. 58.

VEALL (DONALD) The popular movement for law reform, 1640-1660. Oxford, 1970. pp. 259. bibliog.

WHAT'S wrong with the law?: [the revised version of nine broadcast talks]; by Lord Devlin [and others]; [edited by] Michael Zander. London, 1970. pp. 126.

U.K. Law Commission. Published Working Papers. No. 34. Second programme, item XIX. Family law: jactitation of marriage. London, 1971. pp. 8.

U.K. Law Commission. Published Working Papers. No. 35. Solemnisation of marriage in England and Wales...: provisional proposals of the Joint Working Party of the Law Commission and the Registrar General. (Second programme, item XIX. Family law). London, 1971. pp. 120.

U.K. Law Commission. Published Working Papers. No. 36. First programme, item IX. Transfer of land: appurtenant rights. London, 1971. pp. 141.

U.K. Law Commission. Published Working Papers. No. 37. First programme, item IX. Transfer of land: land registration (second paper). London, 1971. pp. 65.

U.K. Law Commission. Published Working Papers. No. 38. (Second programme, item XIX.) Family law: jurisdiction in suits for nullity of marriage. London, 1971. pp. 16.

U.K. Law Commission. Published Working Papers. No. 39. The exclusion of liability for negligence in the sale of goods, and exemption clauses in contracts for the supply of services and other contracts; joint document containing the provisional proposals of the Law Commission and the Scottish Law Commission. London, 1971. pp. 103.

U.K. Law Commission. Published Working Papers. No. 40. Remedies in administrative law. London, 1971. pp. 120.

U.K. Law Commission. Published Working Papers. No. 41. First programme, item VI(b). Personal injury litigation: assessment of damages. London, 1971. pp. 171.

U.K. Law Commission. Published Working Papers. No. 42. Second programme, item XIX. Family law: family property law. London, 1971. pp. 328.

- United Kingdom - Scotland

SCOTLAND. Scottish Law Commission. 1965. Law Commissions Act, 1965: first programme of the Scottish Law Commission. Edinburgh, 1965. pp. 8.

SCOTLAND. 1966. Law Commissions Act 1965: first programme of consolidation and statute law revision of the Scottish Law Commission, etc. Edinburgh, 1966. pp. 7.

SCOTLAND. 1967. Proposal for reform of the law of evidence relating to corroboration. (Scottish Law Commission) Edinburgh, [1967]. pp. 12. 24½cm.

SCOTLAND. Scottish Law Commission. 1968. Second programme of law reform. Edinburgh, 1968. pp. 8. (Scot. Law Com. No. 8.)

- United States

FRANK (JOHN PAUL) American law: the case for radical reform; (lectures...upon the dedication of the Earl Warren Legal Center, University of California). [Toronto, 1969.] pp. 216.

LAW REPORTS, DIGESTS, ETC.

- Bulgaria

IANEV (NIKOLA) and ZLATINOV (DIMITŬR) Финансови начети: систематизирани решени: на Върховния съд на НРБ за 1953-1956 г. София, Наука и Изкуство, 1957. pp. viii, 244. bibliog. 22cm.

NAKAZATELNOPRAVNA... Наказателноправна и гражданскоправна защита на социалистическата собственост: литература, текст, съдебна практика, etc. София, Наука и Изкуство, 1959. pp. 212. bibliog. 22cm.

BULGARIA. Statutes, etc. 1953-1963. Сборник постановления и тълкувателни решения на Върховния съд на НР-България, 1953-1963. София, 1965. pp. 529.

TŬLKUVATELNI... Тълкувателни решения на Президиума на Народното събрание, 1948-1967: справочник. София, Наука и Изкуство, 1968. pp. 832. 19½см.

- Congo (Kinshasa)

PAUWELS (JOHAN M.) Répertoire de droit coutumier congolais: jurisprudence et doctrine: 1954-1967. Kinshasa, Office National de la Recherche et du Développement, 1970. pp. 443.

- Europe

EUROPEAN COMMISSION OF HUMAN RIGHTS. 1969. Collection of decisions of national courts referring to the Convention: (European Convention on Human Rights). [Strasbourg], Council of Europe, 1969. various.

- Germany

STORZ (KARL ALFRED) Die Rechtsprechung des Obersten Gerichtshofes für die Britische Zone in Strafsachen. Tübingen, Mohr, 1969. pp. xii, 155. bibliog. 23cm. (Tuebingen. Universität. Rechts- und Wirtschaftswissenschaftliche Fakultät. Rechtswissenschaftliche Abteilung. Juristische Studien. Band 13)

FONTES JURIS GENTIUM. Series A. Sectio 2. Tomus 4. Rechtsprechung der höchsten Gerichte der Bundesrepublik Deutschland in völkerrechtlichen Fragen...1949-1960; bearbeitet... von Karl Doehring [and others]. Köln, 1970. pp. 1435. With English, French and German summaries.

- Hungary

HUNGARY. Legfelsőbb Bíróság. 1964. Polgári jogi döntvénytár Bírósági határozatok, 1953-1963. Budapest, 1964. pp. 736.

HUNGARY. Legfelsőbb Bíróság. 1966. Buntetőjogi Döntvénytár Bírósági Határozatok, 1963.november - 1965.december. Budapest, 1966. pp. 713.

- Ireland (Republic)

IRISH REPORTS, THE; containing reports of cases determined in the High Court and in the Court of Criminal Appeal...; published by the Incorporated Council of Law Reporting for Ireland. Dublin, 4 a yr., 1960 to date. 24½cm.

LAW REPORTS, DIGESTS, ETC. (Cont'd.)

- Poland

ŚWIĘCICKI (WITOLD) and PIASECKI (KAZIMIERZ) eds. Orzecznictwo Sądu Najwyższego w składach powiększonych: zbiór wytycznych i uchwał zgromadzenia ogólnego Całej Izby i składu siedmiu sędziów Sadu Najwyższego w sprawach cywilnych za lata 1945-1959. Warszawa, Wydawnictwo Prawnicze, 1961. pp. 463. 24½cm.

- Roumania

ROUMANIA. Statutes, etc. 1955-1964. Repertoriu de practică arbitrală, 1955-1964. Bucureşti, 1965. pp. 384.

- Russia

RUSSIA (R.S.F.S.R.). Statutes, etc. 1957-1959. Сборник постановлений Президиума и определений Судебной коллегии по уголовным делам Верховного суда РСФСР, 1957-1959 гг. Москва, 1960. pp. 250. 20cm.

RUSSIA (U.S.S.R.). Statutes, etc. 1946-1962. Сборник постановлений Пленума и определений коллегий Верховного Суда СССР по вопросам уголовного процесса, 1946-1962 гг. Москва, 1964. pp. 334.

RUSSIA (R.S.F.S.R.). Statutes, etc. 1961-1966. Постановления Пленума Верховного Суда РСФСР. Москва, 1967. pp. 168.

BORODIN (STANISLAV VLADIMIROVICH) ed. Voprosy ugolovnogo prava i protsessa v praktike Verkhovnykh Sudov SSSR i RSFSR, 1938-1969 gg. 2nd ed. Moskva, 1971. pp. 445.

- United Kingdom

LAW TIMES REPORTS, THE. London, weekly, Nov.1859 - Dec.1947 (vols.1-177). 25cm.

DANIEL (WILLIAM THOMAS SHAVE) The history and origin of the Law Reports, together with a compilation of various documents shewing the progress and result of proceedings taken for their establishment, etc. London, Wildy, [1884 repr.1968]. pp. (vi),363. 22½cm.

The ENGLISH and Empire digest, with complete and exhaustive annotations: replacement volumes; (with continuation volumes and cumulative supplement). [2nd ed] London, 1950-70. 56 vols.

SELDEN SOCIETY. Publications. vols. 85,86. Year books of Edward II. vol. 26. The Eyre of London, 14 Edward II, A.D. 1321; edited by...Helen M. Cam. London, 1968-69. 2 vols. (Year Books Series. vol. 26) In various languages.

LONDON. London Record Society. Publications. vol. 6. The London eyre of 1244; edited by Helena M. Chew and Martin Weinbaum. London, 1970. pp. 174.

LAWRENCE (ERNEST ORLANDO)

DAVIS (NUEL PHARR) Lawrence and Oppenheimer. London, Cape, 1969. pp. 384. bibliog. 23cm.

LAWRENCE (Sir HENRY)

MORISON (JOHN LYLE) Lawrence of Lucknow, 1806-1857: being the life of Sir Henry Lawrence retold from his private and public papers. London, Bell, 1934. pp. viii, 348. 22cm.

LAWRENCE (THOMAS EDWARD)

KNIGHTLEY (PHILLIP) and SIMPSON (COLIN) The secret lives of Lawrence of Arabia. London, 1969. pp. 293. bibliog.

LAWYERS

MACDONELL (Sir JOHN) and MANSON (EDWARD) eds. Great jurists of the world; (first published by Little, Brown, in 1914). South Hackensack, Rothamn Reprints, 1968. pp. xxxii, 607. 22½cm. (Association of American Law Schools. Continental Legal History Series. vol. 2)

LAWTON (Sir FREDERICK HORACE) The role and responsibility of the advocate: being a public lecture...in the University of Bristol. 4th November 1966. [Bristol, University of Bristol, 1966?] pp. 11. 24½cm.

- Egypt

ZIADEH (FARHAT J.) Lawyers, the rule of law and liberalism in modern Egypt. Stanford, University, Hoover Institution on War, Revolution and Peace, 1968. pp. xi, 177. bibliog. 21½cm.

- Germany

BOERGEN (RUDIGER) Die vertragliche Haftung des Rechtsanwalts. Berlin, Duncker & Humblot, [1968]. pp. 178. bibliog. 23cm. (Schriftenreihe zur Rechtssoziologie und Rechtstatsachenforschung. Band 13)

KAUPEN (WOLFGANG) Die Hüter von Recht und Ordnung: die soziale Herkunft, Erziehung und Ausbildung der deutschen Juristen: eine soziologische Analyse. Neuwied, [1969]. pp. 268. bibliog.

- Italy

MARTINES (LAURO) Lawyers and statecraft in renaissance Florence. Princeton, U.P., 1968. pp. xiii, 531. bibliog. 23½cm.

- Nigeria

NIGERIA. Committee on the Future of the Nigerian Legal Profession. 1959. Report: [E.I.G. Unsworth, chairman]. Lagos, 1959. pp. 29.

- Russia

SUDEBNYE... Судебные речи известных русских юристов: сборник. 2nd ed. Москва, Госюриздат, 1957. pp. 871. 21½cm.

[SOROK]... 40 лет советской адвокатуры: доклады научной конференции Ленинградских адвокатов, 1-2 июня, 1962. Ленинград, 1962. pp. 107. 19½cm.

GINZBURG (GRIGORII ALEKSANDROVICH) and others. Советский адвокат. Москва, 1968. pp. 199.

RUSSIA (R.S.F.S.R.) Iuridicheskaia Komissiia. 1968. Sovetskaia advokatura: zadachi i deiatel'nost'. Moskva, 1968. pp. 143.

SUKHAREV (I. IU.) compiler. Rechi sovetskikh advokatov. Moskva, 1968. pp. 171.

LATVIISKII GOSUDARSTVENNYI UNIVERSITET. Kafedra Ugolovnogo Prava, Ugolovnogo Protsessa i Kriminalistiki. Сборник нормативных актов и инструктивных материалов к изучению курса "Организация суда и прокуратуры в СССР"; составитель А. Рейгас. Рига, 1969. pp. 204.

VATMAN (DAVID PETROVICH) and ELIZAROV (VLADIMIR ALEKSANDROVICH) Адвокат в гражданском процессе; под редакцией И. И. Склярского. Москва, 1969. pp. 198.

- Serbia

IGNJATOVIĆ (BORISAV M.) Advokatura u Srbiji. Doboj, [the author], 1966. pp. 254. bibliog. 20cm.

- South Africa

SOUTH AFRICA. Bureau of Statistics. Special Reports. No.266. Census of legal services, 1961-62. Pretoria, [1964]. pp.iv, 13. 32½cm. in Afrikaans and English.

- United Kingdom

COOK (JOHN) Solicitor-General for the High Court of Justice. The vindication of the professors and profession of the law:...wherein is declared what manner of persons Christian magistrates, judges, and lawyers ought to be,...; occasioned by way of answer to a printed sheet intituled, Advertisements for the new election of members for the House of Commons. London, Walbancke, 1646. pp. (xxii), 96. 17½cm. Wing C 6029.

LUND (Sir THOMAS GEORGE) A guide to the professional conduct and etiquette of solicitors. London, Law Society, 1960 repr. 1967. pp. vii, 176. 20½cm.

ZANDER (MICHAEL) Court of Appeal: Norbert F. Rondel, plaintiff-appellant, against Michael D.L. Worsley, defendant-respondent; brief for Norbert F. Rondel, appellant. [London, 1966]. fo. (iii, 116). 32½cm. Typescript.

ZANDER (MICHAEL) Memorandum of evidence to the Monopolies Commission in regard to restrictive practices in the legal profession. London, 1967. pp. (iv), vi, 240. 30cm.

ABEL-SMITH (BRIAN) and STEVENS (ROBERT BOCKING) In search of justice: society and the legal system. London, Lane, 1968. pp. 384. 22cm.

CORDERY (ARTHUR) Law relating to solicitors; sixth edition by Graham J. Graham-Green, assisted by Duncan S. Gordon. London, Butterworths, 1968. pp. cxxxvii, 769. 24½cm.

LAW SOCIETY. Associate Members' Group. The prospective lawyer: blue-print for the future; a memorandum on legal education and training, etc. London, [1968]. pp. 71. 21cm.

SOCIETY OF LABOUR LAWYERS. Justice for all; Society of Labour Lawyers report. London, Fabian Society, 1968. pp. 76. 22cm. (Research Series. [No.] 273)

ZANDER (MICHAEL) Lawyers and the public interest: a study in restrictive practices. London, Weidenfeld & Nicolson, [1968]. pp. xi, 342. bibliog. 21½cm.

JUSTICE (BRITISH SECTION OF THE INTERNATIONAL COMMISSION OF JURISTS) Complaints against lawyers: (a report); chairman of committee; Geoffrey Garrett. London, 1970. pp. 34.

SWEET AND MAXWELL, LIMITED. Guide to a career in the law. 7th ed. London, 1971. pp. 85.

- United Kingdom - Fees

The STAR Chamber epitomized; or, A dialogue betweene Inquisition a newes smeller, and Christopher Cob-web a keeper of the records for the Star-chamber, as they met at the office in Grayes-Inne: wherein they discourse how the clarkes used to exact fees, and of the likely alteration. [London], 1641. pp. 6. 18½cm. Wing S 5264.

- Zambia

NORTHERN RHODESIA. Legal Profession (Entry and Training) Committee. 1962. Report: [D.W. Conroy, chairman]. Lusaka, 1962. pp. 16.

LAWYERS IN POLITICS

GAUDEMET (YVES HENRI) Les juristes et la vie politique de la IIIe République. Paris, 1970. pp. 120. bibliog. (Paris. Université. Faculté de Droit et des Sciences Économiques. Travaux et Recherches. Série "Science Politique". No. 21)

LAY DAYS

SUMMERSKILL (MICHAEL BRYNMOR) Laytime. London, Sweet & Maxwell, 1966. pp. xxvii, 282. 24½cm.

LAYOFF SYSTEMS

MOONMAN (ERIC) Security of employment. London, [1963] pp. 14.

IRELAND, NORTHERN. Redundancy Fund account, together with the report of the Comptroller and Auditor-General thereon. 6th Dec 1965/31st March 1966 [1st] to date included in IRELAND, NORTHERN. Parliament. House of Commons. [Papers].

SLUITING van ondernemingen: (colloquium), Leuven 25 mei 1968. Antwerpen, 1968. pp. 264. bibliog. French title: Les fermetures d'entreprises. Text in French or Flemish.

GRUNFELD (CYRIL) The law of redundancy. London, 1971. pp. 279.

LAZIO

- Economic conditions

[PARTITO COMUNISTA ITALIANO Comitato Regionale del Lazio] Linee per un programma di sviluppo economico del Lazio: (progetto di documento). Roma, [imprint, 1964]. pp. 58. 23½cm.

UNIONE ITALIANA DELLE CAMERE DI COMMERCIO, INDUSTRIA E AGRICOLTURA. Monografie Regionali per la Programmazione Economica. Lazio; a cura dell'Associazione Regionale delle Camere di Commercio del Lazio. [Milan], Giuffrè, [1965]. pp. xi, 227. bibliog. 24cm.

LAZIO - Economic conditions (Cont'd.)

ISTITUTO DI RICERCHE ECONOMICO SOCIALI "PLACIDO MARTINI". Comitato Scientifico. Ricerca preliminare sulle opere pubbliche; direttore della ricerca; E. Peggio. [Rome], 1967. pp. 167. bibliog. 28cm.

ISTITUTO DI RICERCHE ECONOMICO SOCIALI "PLACIDO MARTINI". Comitato Scientifico. Ricerca sul mercato creditizio e finanziario nel Lazio...; direttore della ricerca: V. Selan. [Roma], 1967. 2 vols.(in 1).

ISTITUTO DI RICERCHE ECONOMICO SOCIALE "PLACIDO MARTINI". Comitato Scientifico. Ricerca sulla finanza pubblica nel Lazio...; direttore della ricerca: V. Selan. [Roma], 1967. 2 vols.

PARTITO COMUNISTA ITALIANO. Comitato Regionale del Lazio. Le scelte per un programma democratico di sviluppo economico di Roma e del Lazio. [Rome, 1967?]. pp. 15. 21cm.

ISTITUTO DI RICERCHE ECONOMICO SOCIALI "PLACIDO MARTINI". Studio delle zone depresse del Lazio...; direttore della ricerca: Fausto Pitigliani. 2nd ed. Roma, 1968. pp. 370. 31cm.

- Sanitary affairs

ISTITUTO DI RICERCHE ECONOMICO SOCIALI "PLACIDO MARTINI". Comitato Scientifico. Ricerca preliminare sui servizi sanitari; direttore della ricerca; E. Peggio. [Rome], 1967. pp. 27, (84). bibliog. 28cm.

- Social conditions

ISTITUTO DI RICERCHE ECONOMICO SOCIALI "PLACIDO MARTINI". Comitato Scientifico. Ricerca preliminare sul patrimonio edilizio e sulle abitazioni; direttore della ricerca: E. Peggio. [Rome], 1967. pp. 172. bibliog. 28cm.

ISTITUTO DI RICERCHE ECONOMICO SOCIALI "PLACIDO MARTINI". Comitato Scientifico. Ricerca preliminare sulla assistenza sociale. [Rome], 1967. pp. 153. bibliog. 28cm.

LAZZARINI (RENATO)

MODENATO (FRANCESCA) Intenzionalità e storia in Renato Lazzarini. Bologna, Pàtron, [1967]. pp. 116. bibliog. 22cm. (Scienze Filosofiche. 9)

LEAD INDUSTRY AND TRADE

SCHMITZ (EBERHARD) Der Bleimarkt unter dem Einfluss neuerer Strukturwandlungen Bonn, 1963. pp. 300. bibliog. pp. 20.

- United Kingdom

BURT (ROGER) The lead industry of England and Wales, 1700-1880; [Ph.D. (London) thesis]. 1970 [or rather 1971]. fo. 434. bibliog. Typescript: unpublished. This thesis is the property of London University and may not be removed from the Library.

LEAD MINES AND MINING

- United Kingdom

BUSHELL (THOMAS) The case of Thomas Bushell... truly stated; together with his progresse in minerals, and the desires of severall merchants and others that are willing and ready to advance so good a work for the benefit of the nation: humbly tendred to the serious consideration of the Honourable House of Commons, etc. London, 1649. pp. 16. 17½cm. Wing B 6242.

KIRKHAM (NELLIE) Derbyshire lead mining through the centuries. Truro, Bradford Barton, 1968. pp. 132. bibliog. 21cm.

PEAK DISTRICT MINES HISTORICAL SOCIETY. Lead mining in the Peak District;...edited by Trevor D. Ford and J. H. Rieuwerts. Bakewell, Peak Park Planning Board, 1968. pp. iv, 124. bibliog. 21½cm.

BURT (ROGER) The lead industry of England and Wales, 1700-1880; [Ph.D. (London) thesis]. 1970 [or rather 1971]. fo. 434. bibliog. Typescript: unpublished. This thesis is the property of London University and may not be removed from the Library.

HUNT (CHRISTOPHER JOHN) The lead miners of the northern Pennines in the eighteenth and nineteenth centuries. Manchester, [1970]. pp. 282. bibliog.

- United States

WRIGHT (JAMES E.) The Galena Lead district: federal policy and practice, 1824-1847. Madison, State Historical Society of Wisconsin, 1966. pp. xv, 148. bibliog. 23cm.

LEAD POISONING

NEW SOUTH WALES. Board of Trade. 1921. Report... on white lead as used in the painting industry: its dangers and their prevention. Sydney, 1921. pp. lxxix. Issued without the evidence of witnesses, etc., listed in the contents.

HAYHURST (EMERY ROE) Lead poisoning: its chief causes, with observations on its diagnosis and prevention. [Ohio, 1923]. pp. 11. bibliog. (Monthly Bulletin, Ohio Department of Health, May, 1914, revised, July, 1923).

NATIONAL UNION OF SOCIETIES FOR EQUAL CITIZENSHIP. Women and the Lead Paint (Protection Against Poisoning) Bill: statement on clause II of the Bill, submitted to the House of Commons. [London], 1926. pp. 6.

LEADERSHIP

CASSAU (THEODOR O.) Das Führerproblem innerhalb der Gewerkschaften. Berlin-Hessenwinkel, 1925. pp. 20.

McDOWELL (FLOYD M.) That problem of leadership. Independence, 1943. pp. 100.

NAYACAKALOV (RUSIATE RAIBOSA) Fijian leadership in a situation of change. 1963. fo. 388. bibliog. 25½cm. [typescript] Ph.D.(London) thesis: unpublished. This thesis is the property of London University and may not be removed from the Library.

BENJAMIN (JOE) In search of adventure: a study in play leadership. 2nd ed. London, National Council of Social Service, 1966. pp. 106. bibliog. 23cm.

HERRERA Y OBES (MANUEL) and PRUDENCIO BERRO (BERNARDO) El caudillismo y la revolución americana: polémica; prólogo de Juan E. Pivel Devoto. Montevideo, 1966. pp. 57. (Biblioteca Artigas. Colección de Clásicos Uruguayos. Vol.110)

MAUD (JOHN PRIMATT REDCLIFFE) Baron Redcliffe-Maud. Leader-ship and democracy. [London, 1966]. pp. 12. (London. University. Birkbeck College. Foundation Orations. 1966)

PUNEKAR (S.D.) and MADHURI (S.) Trade union leadership in India: a survey;... conducted by Tata Institute of Social Sciences, Bombay and sponsored by International Institute for Labour Studies, Geneva. Bombay, Lalvani, 1967. pp. xiii, 192. 21½cm. (Tata Institute of Social Sciences. Tata Institute of Sciences Series. No. 16)

LEADERSHIP and authority: a symposium [held at the University of Singapore, 8-13 December 1963]; edited by Gehan Wijeyewardene. Singapore, U. of Malaya P., 1968. pp. 337. 21½cm.

LEMAY (MICHEL) Les groupes de jeunes inadaptés: rôle du jeune meneur. 2nd ed. Paris, P.U.F., 1968. pp. 247. bibliog. 17½cm. (Paideia)

PRABHAKAR (PURUSHOTTAM) Leadership pattern in China: a study in the emerging leadership. Delhi, 1968. pp. 142.

SARTIN (PIERRETTE) Les cadres et l'intelligence. [Paris], Hachette, [1968]. pp. 235. bibliog. 20cm. (On en parle)

WILLNER (ANN RUTH) Charismatic political leader-ship: a theory. Princeton, Princeton University, Center of International Studies, 1968. pp. v, 113, 27½cm. (Research Monographs. No. 32)

GIBB (CECIL A.) ed. Leadership: selected readings. Harmondsworth, 1969. pp. 439. bibliogs.

LACOUTURE (JEAN) Quatre hommes et leurs peuples: sur-pouvoir et sous-développement. Paris, [1969]. pp. 282. bibliog.

L'ETANG (HUGH) The pathology of leadership. [London], 1969. pp. 218. bibliogs.

McFARLAND (ANDREW S.) Power and leadership in pluralist systems. Stanford, 1969. pp. 273. bibliog.

PIERSON (GEORGE WILSON) The education of American leaders: comparative contributions of U.S. colleges and universities. New York, Praeger, 1969. pp. xxxii, 261. 25½cm. (Praeger Special Studies in U.S. Economic and Social Development)

ROSEN (NED ARNOLD) Leadership change and work-group dynamics: an experiment. Ithaca, 1969. pp. 261. bibliog.

VESSIGAULT (GABRIEL) The status and training of youth leaders: problems and achievements. Strasbourg, Council for Cultural Co-operation, 1969. pp. 352. bibliog.

WALTER-RAYMOND-STIFTUNG. Veröffentlichungen. Band 11. Führung in einer freiheitlichen Gesellschaft. Köln, 1969. pp. 269. bibliog.

BREEN (TIMOTHY HALL) The character of the good ruler: a study of Puritan political ideas in New England, 1630-1730. New Haven, 1970. pp. 301. bibliog. (Yale University. Yale Historical Publications. Miscellany. 92)

MILLER (DELBERT CHARLES) International community power structures: comparative studies of four world cities. Bloomington, [1970]. pp. 320.

POLITICAL leadership in Eastern Europe and the Soviet Union; [papers of a conference held in November 1968 under the auspices of the Comparative Politics Program at Northwestern University]; edited by R. Barry Farrell. Chicago, 1970. pp. 359.

VEEN (P.) Meebeslissen: een veldexperiment in een hockeyclub. Assen, 1970. pp. 347. bibliog. With English summary.

KNOWLES (HENRY P.) and SAXBERG (BORJE O.) Personality and leadership behavior. Reading, Mass., [1971]. pp. 164. bibliog.

LACOUTURE (JEAN) The demigods: charismatic leadership in the Third World;...translated from the French by Patricia Wolf. London, 1971. pp. 300,vi. bibliog.

OSTERGAARD (GEOFFREY NIELSEN) and CURRELL (MELVILLE) The gentle anarchists: a study of the Sarvodaya movement for non-violent revolution in India. Oxford, 1971. pp. 421. bibliog.

PERSONALITY and power: studies in political achievement: [texts of a series of radio broadcasts]; edited by Graham Tayar. London, 1971. pp. 107. bibliog.

LEAFLETS DROPPED FROM AIRCRAFT

ERDMANN (JAMES MORRIS) Leaflet operations in the Second World War: the story of the how and why of the 6,500,000,000 propaganda leaflets dropped on Axis forces and homelands in the Mediterranean and European theaters of operations. [Denver, 1969]. pp. 422. bibliog.

LEAGUE OF ARAB STATES

LEAGUE OF ARAB STATES. General Secretariat. Information Department. Press releases. [Cairo], irreg., Jan. 2, 1969 (no. 1) to date. 25½cm.

LEAGUE OF BRITISH JEWS

MAGNUS (LAURIE) Old lamps for new: an apologia for the League of British Jews. London, [imprint], 1918. pp. 16. 21½cm.

LEAGUE OF NATIONS

LEAGUE OF NATIONS SOCIETY OF IRELAND. A memorandum stating the case for an immediate declaration of national rights for the subject peoples of Europe to form the charter and a basis of a league of nations and a method for its achievement. Dublin, 1918. pp. 6.

LEAGUE TO ENFORCE PEACE. Executive Committee. Tentative draft of a treaty for a league of nations approved by the...Committee...April 11, 1918. [New York?, 1918]. fo. (2).

DEUTSCHE LIGA FÜR VÖLKERBUND. [Constitution, prospectuses, list of publications, report for 1919, etc.] [Berlin?, 1919-20]. 5 pts.

LEAGUE OF NATIONS (Cont'd.)

GARNETT (JAMES CLERK MAXWELL) The brotherhood of nations. [London, 192-?] pp. 8. (Central Committee for Church Crusades. Crusade Leaflets. No. 18)

AUSTRALIAN LEAGUE OF NATIONS UNION. New South Wales Branch. The League and its critics: a report... by a Committee appointed to investigate recent criticism of the League of Nations. Sydney, [1922?]. pp. 20.

DRUMMOND (JAMES ERIC) 16th Earl of Perth. The League of Nations. London, 1933. pp. 27. (British Broadcasting Corporation. Broadcast National Lectures. 12)

REYNOLDS (ERNEST EDWIN) The League experiment. London, 1939. pp. 163. bibliog.

MEIENBERGER (NORBERT) Entwicklungshilfe unter dem Völkerbund: ein Beitrag zur Geschichte der internationalen Zusammenarbeit in der Zwischenkriegszeit unter besonderer Berücksichtigung der technischen Hilfe an China. Winterthur, Keller, 1965. pp. xvi, 150. bibliog. 22½cm.

CASELLA (ALESSANDRO) Le conflit sino-japonais de 1937 et La Société des Nations. Paris, Librairie Générale de Droit et de Jurisprudence, 1967. pp. 150. bibliog.

DEXTER (BYRON VINSON) The years of opportunity: the League of Nations, 1920-1926. New York, Viking P., [1967]. pp. xxiii, 264. 21cm.

STONE (RALPH A.) ed. Wilson and the League of Nations: why America's rejection? New York, Holt, [1967]. pp. 122. bibliog. 23½cm. (American Problem Studies)

PROTOPOPOV (ANATOLII SERGEEVICH) СССР, Лига Наций и ООН. Москва, 1968. pp. 167. (История и Современность)

VERMA (D.N.) India and the League of Nations. Patna, Bharati Bhawan, 1968. pl. xii, 350. bibliog. 21½cm.

BARROS (JAMES) Betrayal from within: Joseph Avenol, Secretary-General of the League of Nations, 1933-1940. New Haven, 1969. pp. 285. bibliog.

BARROS (JAMES) The League of Nations and the great powers: the Greek-Bulgarian incident, 1925. Oxford, 1970. pp. 143.

BHUINYA (NIRANJAN) International organisations: a critical study of League of Nations, United Nations and International Court of Justice. New Delhi, [1970]. pp. 159. bibliog.

RINGGENBERG (CECILE M.) Die Beziehungen zwischen dem Roten Kreuz und dem Völkerbund. Bern, 1970. pp. 108. bibliog.

BECK (PETER JAMES) Britain and the peace-keeping rôle of the League of Nations, 1924-29; [Ph.D. (London) thesis]. 1971. fo. 458. bibliog. Typescript: unpublished. This thesis is the property of London University and may not be removed from the Library.

- Officials and employees

ROVINE (ARTHUR W.) The first fifty years: the Secretary-General in world politics, 1920-1970. Leyden, 1970. pp. 498. bibliog.

LEAGUE OF NATIONS UNION

LEAGUE OF NATIONS UNION. [Publications]. Series 2. [Pamphlets]. No. 10. The League of Nations Union. London, 1919. pp. 17.

LEAGUE OF NATIONS UNION. Education in world affairs: a report...for 1932. London, [1933]. pp. 27.

LEAMINGTON SPA

- Race question

JENKINS (SIMON) Here to live: a study of race relations in an English town;...research [by] Victoria Randall. London, [1971]. pp. 43.

LEARNED INSTITUTIONS AND SOCIETIES

THIRWALL (CONNOP) Bishop of St. David's. The advantages of literary and scientific institutions for all classes; a lecture delivered at the Town Hall, Carmarthen,... 1849. London, Longman, 1850. pp. 37. 20½cm.

VAVRA (J.) Die Olmützer Societas incognitorum und die Petersburger Akademie der Wissenschaften. in Steinitz (Wolfgang) and others, eds. Ost und West in der Geschichte des Denkens und der kulturellen Beziehungen. Berlin, 1966.

LEARNING, PSYCHOLOGY OF

COFER (CHARLES N.) ed. Verbal learning and verbal behavior;...proceedings of a conference sponsored by the Office of Naval Research and New York University. New York, McGraw-Hill, 1961. pp. vii, 241. bibliogs. 22½cm. (McGraw-Hill Series in Psychology)

COFER (CHARLES N.) and MUSGRAVE (BARBARA S.) eds. Verbal behavior and learning: problems and processes;...proceedings of the second conference sponsored by the Office of Naval Research and New York University. New York, McGraw-Hill, [1963] pp. x, 397. bibliogs. 22½cm. (McGraw-Hill Series in Psychology)

BORGER (R.) and SEABORNE (A.E.M.) The psychology of learning. Harmondsworth, 1966 repr. 1969. pp. 249. bibliog.

HATWELL (Y.) À propos de notions d'assimilation et d'accommodation dans les processus cognitifs. in Psychologie et épistémologie génétiques. Paris, 1966.

PSYCHOLOGY OF LEARNING AND MOTIVATION, THE: advances in research and theory. London, annual, 1967 (vol.1) to date. 23½cm.

FITTS (PAUL M.) and POSNER (MICHAEL I.) Human performance. Belmont, [1967]. pp. xi, 162. bibliog.

KOHNSTAMM (GELDOLPH A.) Piaget's analysis of class inclusion: right or wrong? The Hague, Mouton, [1967]. pp.(iv), 153. bibliog. 23cm. (Psychological Studies. Minor Series 1)

LINDGREN (H. C.) Theories of human learning revisited. in Bower (Eli Michael) and Hollister (William G.) eds. Behavioral science frontiers in education. [New York, 1967].

SLAMECKA (NORMAN J.) ed. Human learning and memory: selected readings. London, 1967. pp. 543. bibliogs.

SUCHMAN (J. R.) The pursuit of meaning: models for the study of enquiry. in Bower (Eli Michael) and Hollister (William G.) eds. Behavioral science frontiers in education. [New York, 1967].

CIBA FOUNDATION. Symposia. The role of learning in psychotherapy;...edited by Ruth Porter. London, Churchill, 1968. pp. xii, 340. bibliogs. 22½cm.

DIXON (THEODORE R.) and HORTON (DAVID L.) eds. Verbal behavior and general behavior theory. Englewood-Cliffs, Prentice-Hall, [1968]. pp. ix, 596. bibliogs. 23cm. (Prentice-Hall Psychology Series)

EHRLICH (STEPHANE) Les mécanismes du comportement verbal. Paris, 1968. pp. 383. bibliog.

FELLOWS (BRIAN J.) The discrimination process and development. Oxford, 1968 repr. 1969. pp. 218. bibliog.

JUDD (WILSON A.) The effects of task characteristics on response latency and latency trends during learning and overlearning. Pittsburgh, University of Pittsburgh, Learning Research and Development Center, 1968. pp. iii, 88. bibliog. 27½cm. (Technical Reports. 7)

LOVEJOY (ELIJAH) Attention in discrimination learning: a point of view and a theory. San Francisco, [1968]. pp. 133. bibliog.

LUNZER (ERIC A.) and MORRIS (JOHN FREDERICK) eds. Development in human learning. London, Staples P., 1968. pp. xix, 487. bibliogs. 22cm. (Development in Learning. 2)

LUNZER (ERIC A.) and others. The regulation of behaviour. London, Staples P., 1968. pp. xix, 392. bibliogs. 22cm. (Development in Learning. 1)

NUTTIN (JOSEPH) and GREENWALD (ANTHONY G.) Reward and punishment in human learning: elements of a behavior theory. New York, Academic P., 1968. pp. x, 205. bibliog. 23cm.

STAATS (ARTHUR WILBUR) Learning, language, and cognition: theory, research and method for the study of human behavior and its development. New York, Holt, [1968]. pp. xix, 614. bibliog. 22½cm.

TRABASSO (TOM) and BOWER (GORDON H.) Attention in learning: theory and research. New York, Wiley, [1968]. pp. xiii, 253. bibliog. 23cm. (Series in Psychology)

UNITED STATES. National Institute of Child Health and Human Development. Perspectives on human deprivation: biological, psychological, and social. Washington, 1968. pp. 323. bibliogs.

ANNETT (JOHN) Feedback and human behaviour: the effects of knowledge of results, incentives and reinforcement on learning and performance. Harmondsworth, 1969. pp. 196. bibliog.

BANDURA (ALBERT) Principles of behavior modification. New York, [1969]. pp. 677. bibliog.

GELFAND (DONNA M.) ed. Social learning in childhood: readings in theory and application. Belmont, Calif., [1969]. pp. 415. bibliog.

GIBSON (ELEANOR J.) Principles of perceptual learning and development. New York, [1969]. pp. 537. bibliog.

GILBERT (R.M.) and SUTHERLAND (NORMAN STUART) eds. Animal discrimination learning. London, Academic P., 1969. pp. xvi, 501. 23cm.

McFARLAND (H.S.N.) Human learning: a developmental analysis. London, 1969. pp. 128. bibliog.

MARX (MELVIN HERMAN) ed. Learning: processes. London, [1969.] repr. 1970. pp. 515. bibliogs.

GAGNE (ROBERT MILLS) The conditions of learning. 2nd ed. London, [1970]. pp. 407. bibliog.

GARRY (RALPH) and KINGSLEY (HOWARD L.) The nature and conditions of learning. 3rd ed. Englewood Cliffs, [1970]. pp. 593. bibliogs.

KINTSCH (WALTER) Learning, memory and conceptual processes. New York, [1970]. pp. 498. bibliog.

LEARNING and memory; by Jean-François le Ny [and others]; translated by Louise Elkington. London, 1970. pp. 376. bibliog.

LEGGE (DAVID) ed. Skills: selected readings. Harmondsworth, 1970. pp. 378. bibliog.

SLUCKIN (WLADYSLAW) Early learning in man and animal. London, 1970. pp. 123.

LEARNING ABILITY

MALNUTRITION, learning and behavior; edited by Nevin S. Scrimshaw and John E. Gordon; proceedings of an International Conference, co-sponsored by the Nutrition Foundation, Inc., and the Massachusetts Institute of Technology, held at Cambridge, Massachusetts, March 1 to 3, 1967. Cambridge, M.I.T. Press, [1968]. pp. xiii, 566. 22½cm.

GELFAND (DONNA M.) ed. Social learning in childhood: readings in theory and application. Belmont, Calif., [1969]. pp. 415. bibliog.

LEARNING AND SCHOLARSHIP

HOLBERG (LUDVIG AF) Baron. Des Herrn Baron von Holbergs übrige kleine Schriften übersetzt. Kopenhagen, 1755.

MEURERS (J.) Freiheit und Wissenschaft. in Roegele (Otto Bernhard) ed. Die Freiheit des Westens. Graz, [1967].

- Czechoslovakia

CZECHOSLOVAKIA past and present; edited by Miloslav Rechcigl. The Hague, 1968. 2 vols. bibliog. Mainly consisting of papers presented at the 2nd congress of the Czechoslovak Society of Arts and Sciences in America.

- United Kingdom

HALSEY (ALBERT HENRY) and TROW (MARTIN A.) The British academics. London, 1971. pp. 560. bibliog.

LEARNING BY DISCOVERY

BELBIN (R.M.) The discovery method: an international experiment in retraining. [Paris], Organisation for Economic Co-operation and Development, [1969]. pp. 85. bibliog. 24cm. Social Affairs Division. Employment of Older Workers.

LEARNING BY DISCOVERY (Cont'd.)

BELBIN (R.M.) The discovery method in training: a report based on a more detailed study by the Organisation for Economic Co-operation and Development in Austria, Sweden, the United States and the United Kingdom. London, H.M.S.O., 1969. pp. 43. (Training Information Papers. 5)

LEASES

PORTALE (ANTONINO) Il leasing: una moderna tecnica finanziaria e le sue possibilità di utilizzazione in Italia. Milano, Etas, 1967. pp. 205. bibliog. 24cm.

- Ireland (Republic)

EIRE. Ground Rents Commission. 1964. Report on ground rents [John C. Conroy, chairman]. Dublin, [1964]. pp. vi, 53. 25cm.

- United Kingdom

LONDON LEASEHOLDERS' ASSOCIATIONS. The case for leasehold reform (enfranchisement), with an amending parliamentary bill. [London], 1953. pp. 20.

MACMILLAN (S.K.) Law of leases. London, [1970]. pp. 410.

LEAST SQUARES

PARK (SOO BIN) Two-stage least-squares estimation with inequality constraints on the coefficients. [Ottawa], 1968. fo. 41. bibliog. (Carleton University. Carleton Economic Papers)

ABRAHAMSE (ADRIAAN PIETER JOHANNES) and KOERTS (JOHANNES) New estimators of disturbances in regression analysis. [Rotterdam], 1969. fo. 12. bibliog. (Nederlandsche Economische Hoogeschool. Econometric Institute. Reports. 6906)

GUPTA (Y. P.) A note on the Durbin's method of fitting a linear regression model with auto-correlated disturbances. Rotterdam, 1969. fo. 14. (Nederlandsche Economische Hoogeschool. Econometric Institute. Reports. 6907)

SPRENT (PETER) Models in regression and related topics. London, 1969. pp. 173. bibliog.

CASSON (M.C.) Linear regression with error in the deflating variable. [Reading], 1970. fo. 26. (Reading. University. Department of Economics. Discussion Papers in Economics. No. 26)

GABRIELSEN (ARNE) An interpretation of the probability limit of the least squares estimator in linear models with errors in variables. Oslo, 1970. fo. 29. (Oslo. Universitet. Sosialøkonomiske Institutt. Memoranda)

HUANG (DAVID SHIH-LI) Regression and econometric methods. New York, [1970]. pp. 274. bibliog.

LEATHER INDUSTRY AND TRADE

BREITENACHER (MICHAEL) Leder- und Schuhindustrie: strukturelle Probleme und Wachstumschancen. Berlin, Duncker und Humblot, [1967]. pp. 99. 23½cm. (IFO-Institut für Wirtschaftsforschung. Struktur und Wachstum. Reihe Industrie. Heft 18)

- Afghanistan

INTERNATIONAL LABOUR OFFICE. Development Programme: Technical Assistance Sector. [Afghanistan]. R. 9. Report to the government of Afghanistan on small-scale leather industries: model tannery, leather tanning project, charicar. (ILO/TAP/Afghanistan/R.9). Geneva, 1967. pp. ii, 73. 30cm.

- Australia

AUSTRALIA. Department of Trade. Industries Division. Industry Study Series. The Australian leather industry. Melbourne, 1960. pp. 30.

- Europe

INTERNATIONAL TRADE CENTRE UNCTAD/GATT. 1968. Major markets for hides, skins and leather in Western Europe. Geneva, 1968. pp. 331. bibliog.

- France

FRANCE. Direction de la Documentation. La Documentation Française. Notes et Etudes Documentaires. No. 3,167. L'industrie française du cuir. Paris, 1965. pp. 31.

FRANCE. Comité sectoriel des Industries de l'Habillement. 1971. Préparation du VIe Plan...: rapports des Comités: industrie de l'habillement; industrie du cuir et de la chaussure. Paris, 1971. pp. 123.

- India

MADRAS. 1954. Report of the committee for leather industry and trade: [B.M.Das, chairman] (Industries, Labour and Co-operation Department Madras, 1954. pp. 63. 24½cm.

INDIA. Ministry of Commerce. 1966. Report on the leather and allied industries of India. New Delhi, [1966]. pp. 254. bibliog.

- United Kingdom

U.K. Department of Trade and Industry. Business monitor: Production series. P 105. Leather and fellmongery. q., 1971- London.

U.K. Department of Trade and Industry. Business monitor: Production series. P 106. Leather goods. q., 1971- London.

LEATHER WORKERS

- India

INDIA. Labour Investigation Committee. 1946. Report on labour conditions in tanneries and leather goods factories; by Ahmad Mukhtar. [Delhi], 1946. pp. 94.

INDIA. Labour Bureau. 1969. Report on survey of labour conditions in tanning and leather finishing factories in India, 1965-66. [Delhi, 1969] pp. 68.

LEBANON

- Biography

WHO'S who in Lebanon:... dictionnaire biographique des principales personnalités libanaises ainsi que des étrangers notables résidant au Liban... 1970-1971. 4th ed. Beyrouth, [1971]. 1 vol. (various pagings).

- Commerce - Statistics

UNITED NATIONS. Economic and Social Office in Beirut. 1967. Foreign trade statistics of Lebanon, 1960-1963: reclassified according to the United Nations Standard International Trade Classification, 1960 revision (SITC, Revised) (ST/ESA/BEIRUT/3). New York, 1967. pp. 302.

- Economic conditions

FRANCE. Direction de la Documentation. La Documentation Française. Notes et Etudes Documentaires. No.3,608. L'économie et les finances du Liban. Paris, 1969. pp. 28.

HACHEM (NABIL) Libanon: sozio-ökonomische Grundlagen. Opladen, 1969. pp. 374. bibliog. (Deutsches Orient-Institut. Schriften. Materialien und Dokumente)

KHALAF (NADIM G.) Economic implications of the size of nations, with special reference to Lebanon. Leiden, 1971. pp. 259. bibliog.

- Economic conditions - Statistics

LEBANESE REPUBLIC. Direction Centrale de la Statistique. Comptes économiques. Beyrouth, annual, 1964 (vol. 1) to date, with gap (1964, vol. 2).

- Economic policy

AZHARI (NAAMAN) L'évolution du système économique libanais; ou, La fin du laisser faire. Paris, 1970. pp. 134.

- Government publications - Bibliography

BEIRUT. American University. Department of Political Studies and Public Administration. A selected and annotated bibliography of Lebanese government documents, 1920-1958. Beirut, 1960. fo. 16.

- History

TIBAWI (ABDUL LATIF) A modern history of Syria, including Lebanon and Palestine. London, 1969. pp. 441. bibliog.

- Industries

LEBANESE REPUBLIC. Census of Industries, 1964. Recensement de l'industrie au Liban: résultats pour 1964; preparés et edités par la Direction Centrale de la Statistique au Ministère du Plan. [Beyrouth, 1967]. pp. 174. 28cm.

- Politics and government

HARIK (ILIYA F.) Politics and change in a traditional society: Lebanon, 1711-1845. Princeton, Princeton U.P., 1968. pp. xi, 324. bibliog. 21½cm.

HUDSON (MICHAEL C.) The precarious republic: political modernization in Lebanon. New York, Random House, [1968]. pp. xvi, 364. bibliog. 23½cm.

- Social conditions

VALIN (EMILE) Le pluralisme socio-scolaire au Liban. Beirut, [1969]. pp. 196. bibliog. (Centre Culturel Universitaire. Publications. Hommes et Sociétés du Proche-Orient. No. 1)

- Social history

HARIK (ILIYA F.) Politics and change in a traditional society: Lebanon, 1711-1845. Princeton, Princeton U.P., 1968. pp. xi, 324. bibliog. 21½cm.

LEBOWA TERRITORY

- Politics and government

SOUTH AFRICA. Report of the Controller and Auditor-General on the accounts of the Lebowa Territorial Authority and of the accounts of lower authorities in its area. 1969/70 [1st] to date included in SOUTH AFRICA. Parliament. House of Assembly. Votes and proceedings; (with Printed annexures).

LE BRET (CARDIN)

COMPARATO (VITTOR IVO) Cardin Le Bret: "royauté" e "orde" nel pensiero di un consigliere del '600. Firenze, Olschki, 1969. pp. 211. 24½cm. (Il Pensiero Politico. Biblioteca. 2)

LECCE (PROVINCE)

- Economic conditions

LAUDISA (FIORAVANTE) Prospettive di sviluppo economico e programma quinquennale 1966-70 per la Provincia di Lecce. Lecce, Amministrazione Provinciale di Lecce, [1966?]. pp. 132. 24cm.

LECHIN OQUENDO (JUAN)

LECHIN y la revolución nacional. [La Paz, 1969?]. pp. 168.

LECTURE METHOD IN TEACHING

McLEISH (JOHN) The lecture method. [Cambridge], 1968. pp. 60. bibliog. (Cambridge. University. Institute of Education. Cambridge Monographs on Teaching Methods. 1)

BLIGH (DONALD A.) What's the use of lectures? London, 1971. pp. 216. bibliog.

LECTURES AND LECTURING

- Germany

LINNERT (PETER) Die Finanzierung der Unternehmungen des Vortrags- und Aufführungswesens. Hamburg, 1964. pp. 259. bibliog.

LEDEBOUR (GEORG THEODOR)

RATZ (URSULA) Georg Ledebour 1850-1947: Weg und Wirken eines sozialistischen Politikers. Berlin, 1969. pp. 281. bibliog. (Berlin. Freie Universität. Friedrich-Meinecke-Institut. Historische Kommission zu Berlin. Veröffentlichungen. Band 31)

LEE (KUAN YEW)

JOSEY (ALEX) Lee Kuan Yew. Singapore, Moore, 1968. pp. xi, 657. 22½cm.

LEE VALLEY REGIONAL PARK

LEE VALLEY REGIONAL PARK AUTHORITY. Report on the development of the Regional Park with plan of proposals. [Enfield, 1969]. pp. 81.

LEEDS

- Benevolent and moral institutions

HOLLOWAY (JOY) They can't fit in: a study of destitute men under thirty in St. George's crypt, Leeds. London, [1970]. pp. 78. bibliog. (National Council of Social Service. Publications. 793)

- Civic improvement

LEEDS. Council. Planning and transport: the Leeds approach. London, H.M.S.O., 1969. pp. 38.

- Office buildings

FACEY (M.V.) and SMITH (G.B.) Offices in a regional centre: a study of office location in Leeds. London, Location of Offices Bureau, 1968. pp. 109, 33cm. (Research Papers. No. 2)

LOCATION OF OFFICES BUREAU. Research Papers. No. 3. Offices in a regional centre: follow-up studies on infrastructure and linkages; based on report by M.J. Croft. London, 1969. pp. 119.

- Race question

BUTTERWORTH (ERIC) Leeds, West Riding of Yorkshire. [London, 1964] pp. 8. (Institute of Race Relations. Area Reports on Cities and Boroughs with Substantial Immigrant Settlements. 2)

- Transit systems

LEEDS. Council. Planning and transport: the Leeds approach. London, H.M.S.O., 1969. pp. 38.

LEEWARD ISLANDS

- Economic conditions

O'LOUGHLIN (CARLEEN) Economic and political change in the Leeward and Windward Islands. New Haven, Yale U.P., 1968. pp. ix, 260. bibliog. 23½cm. (Caribbean Series. 10)

- Politics and government

O'LOUGHLIN (CARLEEN) Economic and political change in the Leeward and Windward Islands. New Haven, Yale U.P., 1968. pp. ix, 260. bibliog. 23½cm. (Caribbean Series. 10)

LEFT (POLITICAL SCIENCE)
See RIGHT AND LEFT (POLITICAL SCIENCE)

LEFT- AND RIGHT-HANDEDNESS

DOUGLAS (JAMES WILLIAM BRUCE) and others. The relationship between handedness attainment and adjustment in a national sample of school children. [London, 1966?]. pp. irreg. bibliog.

FRITSCH (VILMA) La gauche et la droite: vérités et illusions du miroir. Paris, Flammarion, [1967]. pp.250. bibliog. 21cm. (Nouvelle Bibliothèque Scientifique)

LEFT BOOK CLUB

LEWIS (JOHN) B.Sc., Ph.D. The Left Book Club: an historical record;... with a foreword by Dame Margaret Cole. London, 1970. pp. 163. bibliog.

LEGAL AID

- Canada

ONTARIO. 1965. Report of the joint committee on legal aid:...William B. Common, chairman, etc. [Toronto], 1965. pp. 126. 24½cm.

- United Kingdom

U.K. Department of Health and Social Security. [Circulars]: FIN [Finance]. London, irreg., Aug. 1962 to date.

SOCIETY OF LABOUR LAWYERS. Justice for all; Society of Labour Lawyers report. London, Fabian Society, 1968. pp. 76. 22cm. (Research Series. [No.] 273)

CHILD POVERTY ACTION GROUP. Legal Committee. A policy to establish the legal rights of low income families: legal aid and advice; memorandum drawn up by Rosalind Brooke [and others]. London, 1969. pp. 12. bibliog.

LAW SOCIETY. Legal advice and assistance: second memorandum of the Council of the Law Society. [London, 1969] pp. 15.

PATERSON (ALAN) A report on legal aid as a social service. London, [1970]. pp. 82. bibliog.

MATTHEWS (EDWIN JAMES THOMAS) and OULTON (ANTHONY DEREK MAXWELL) Legal aid and advice under the Legal Aid Acts 1949 to 1964. London, 1971. pp. 555.

- United Kingdom - Ireland, Northern

INCORPORATED LAW SOCIETY OF NORTHERN IRELAND. Report... on the Legal Aid Scheme..., and the comments and recommendations made by the Advisory Committee. 1965/6 (1st) to date included in IRELAND, NORTHERN. Parliament. House of Commons. [Papers].

- United States

UNITED STATES. Welfare Administration. Conference proceedings: the extention of legal services to the poor... 1964, Washington. Washington, 1965. pp. xi, 202.

- Zambia

ZAMBIA. Department of Legal Aid. Annual report. a., 1970 [1st issue]- Lusaka.

LEGAL COMPOSITION

PHILIP (J.R.) The use of English in the law courts: address delivered to the English Association in Edinburgh. Edinburgh, 1948. pp. 18. (Reprinted from The Scottish Law Review and Sheriff Court Reports November and December, 1947)

PIESSE (EDMUND LEONLIN) The elements of drafting...; fourth edition by J.K. Aitken. Sydney, Law Book Company, 1968. pp. xiv, 166. bibliog. 17½cm.

LEGAL DOCUMENTS

- Russia

MITIAEV (K. G.) and MITIAEVA (E. K.) Административная документация: дело-производство в советских учреждениях; под редакцией... А. В. Чернова. Ташкент, Узбекистан, 1964. pp. 285. bibliog. 20cm.

SVERDLOVSK. Sverdlovskii Iuridicheskii Institut. Sbornik sudebnykh ugolov-no-protsessual'nykh dokumentov. Sverdlovsk, 1968. pp. 225.

LEGAL ETHICS

- United Kingdom

FORBES (ARTHUR HAROLD) Legal ethics...: a lecture. Birmingham, the University, 1966. pp. 19. 24½cm.

- United States

AMERICAN BAR ASSOCIATION. Code of professional responsibility and canons of judicial ethics. n.p., [1969]. pp. 51.

LEGAL RESEARCH

- Australia

CAMPBELL (ENID M.) and MACDOUGALL (DONALD) Associate Professor in Law. Legal research: materials and methods. Sydney, 1967. pp. 240.

- Europe

EXCHANGE OF INFORMATION ON RESEARCH IN EUROPEAN LAW; issued by the Directorate of Legal Affairs, Council of Europe. [in English and French]. irreg., 1971 (1)- Strasbourg.

- United States

SURRENCY (ERWIN C.) and others. A guide to legal research; (with Supplement) New York, Oceana, 1959. pp. 124. 22½cm.

PRICE (MILES OSCAR) and BITNER (HARRY) Effective legal research: student edition revised. Boston, Little, Brown, 1962 repr. 1966. pp. xx, 496. 23½cm.

LEGENDS

- Buryat Republic

MAKHATOV (BATOR PROKOP'EVICH) Былы и предания байкало-кударинских бурят. Улан-Удэ, Бурятское Книжное Издательство, 1963. pp. 43. 16½cm.

LEGENDS, BASQUE

REICHER (GIL G.) Les légendes basques dans la tradition humaine. Paris, Maisonneuve, 1946. pp 148. bibliog. 22½cm.

LEGENDS, JEWISH

NEALE (FRANCIS) A tale of a whale; or, The strange adventures of the prophet Jonah. Birmingham, 1874. pp. 32.

SNOWDEN (KEIGHLEY) Myth and legend in the Bible. London, 1915. pp. 200.

LEGISLATION

BENTHAM (JEREMY) Principes de législation et d'économie politique; ([edited by] S. Raffalovich). Paris, Guillaumin, [1888]. pp. lxxi, 160. bibliog. (Petite Bibliothèque Économique Française et Étrangère)

- Canada

CANADA. Parliament. House of Commons. Special Committee on Statutory Instruments. 1969- Minutes of proceedings and evidence; [Mark MacGuigan, chairman]. Ottawa, 1969 in progress. 25cm.

CANADA. Parliament. House of Commons. Standing Committee on Justice and Legal Affairs. Minutes of proceedings and evidence. [in English and French] Ottawa, irreg., March 4 1969 (28th Parl., 1st session, no.7) to date . 25cm.

CANADA. Parliament. Senate. Standing Senate Committee on Legal and Constitutional Affairs. Proceedings. Ottawa, irreg., Feb.13th 1969 (28th Parl., 1st session, no.1) to date. 25cm.

- Communist countries

KOVACHEV (DIMITR ATANASOVICH) Законодательный процесс в европейских социалистических государствах. Москва, Юридическая Литература, 1966. pp. 185. 20cm.

- Europe

COUNCIL OF EUROPE. Directorate of Legal Affairs. Exchange of information between the member states on their legislative activity and regulations. a., 1967 (n.s., no.1)- Strasbourg.

- France

WIENER (CELINE) Recherches sur le pouvoir réglementaire des ministres. Paris, 1970. pp. 298. bibliog.

- Germany

SCHINNERER (ERICH) German law and legislation. Berlin, 1938. pp. 32. (Terramare Office. Publications. No. 4)

ELLWEIN (THOMAS) and others. Parlament und Verwaltung. Stuttgart, [1967-68]. 2 vols. bibliogs.

ODEWALD (JENS) Der parlamentarische Hilfsdienst in den Vereinigten Staaten von Amerika und in der Bundesrepublik Deutschland. Berlin, Duncker und Humblot, [1967]. pp. 165. bibliog. 23cm. (Schriften zum Öffentlichen Recht. Band 64)

RITTER (ERNST HASSO) Verfassungsrechtliche Gesetzgebungspflichten. Bonn, 1967. pp. 171. bibliog.

RODE (KARLHEINZ) Die Ausfertigung der Bundesgesetze. Berlin, Duncker & Humblot, [1968]. pp. 106. bibliog. 23cm. (Schriften zum Öffentlichen Recht. Band 78)

- India

RASHIDUZZAMAN (M.) The central legislature in British India, 1921-1947. Dacca, 1965. pp. 282. bibliog.

LEGISLATION (Cont'd.)

- Ireland (Republic)

EIRE. Seanad Éireann. Select Committee on Statutory Instruments. 1959-61. Second (and Third) report[s]. Dublin, [1959-61]. 2pts. 24½cm.

EIRE. Seanad Éirann. Select Committee on Statutory Instruments, 1966- Report[s] of the Select Committee on Statutory Instruments appointed 7th July, 1965. Dublin, 1966 in progress.

- Italy

BARBERA (AUGUSTO) Leggi di piano e sistema delle fonti. Milano, Giuffrè, 1968. pp. 138. bibliog. 25cm. (Giurisprudenza Costituzionale. Quaderni. 6)

ISTITUTO PER LA DOCUMENTAZIONE LEGISLATIVA. Indagine sull'attività normativa del governo. Milano, Giuffrè, [1968]. pp. xi, 657. 23cm. (Pubblicazioni dell'ISLE. 17)

SANDULLI (ALDO M.) L'attività normativa della pubblica amministrazione: origini, funzione, caratteri. Napoli, 1970. pp. 117.

- Kirghizia

VOPROSY razvitiia zakonodatel'stva Kirgizskoi SSR: sbornik statei. Frunze, 1968. pp. 226.

- Russia

KERIMOV (DZHANGIR ALI-ABASOVICH) ed. Законодательная техника. Ленинград, Университет, 1965. pp. 148. 21½cm.

TOKAREV (IURII SERGEEVICH) Народное правотворчество накануне Великой Октябрьской социалистической революции, март - октябрь 1917 г. Москва, Наука, 1965. pp. 186. 21½см.

PIGOLKIN (AL'BERT SEMENOVICH) Подготовка проектов нормативных актов: организация и методика. Москва, Юридическая Литература, 1968. pp. 167. 20см.

- Sicily

SICILY. Assemblea Regionale. Segretariato Generale. Ufficio Studi Legislativi. 1955. Attività legislativa dell'Assemblea nella IIa legislatura, 2 luglio 1951-5 aprile 1955. Palmerno, 1955. pp. 530. 24½cm.

- Switzerland

FLUECKIGER (MAX) Die Anhörung der Kantone und der Verbände im Gesetzgebungsverfahren. Bern, Stämpfli, 1968. pp. xv, 192. bibliog. 23cm. (Abhandlungen zum Schweizerischen Recht. Neue Folge. Heft 383)

- United Kingdom

ZAKRZEWSKI (WITOLD) Ustawa i delegacja ustawodawcza w Anglii; De anglorum legibus earundemque ferendarum potestate. Kraków, 1960. pp. 190. bibliog. 25cm. (Cracow. Uniwersytet Jagielloński. Rozprawy i Studia. tom 28) With English summary.

WALKLAND (S.A.) The legislative process in Great Britain. London, Allen & Unwin, 1968. pp. 109. bibliog. 21½cm. (Studies in Political Science. 3)

BARNETT (MALCOLM JOEL) The politics of legislation: the Rent Act of 1957. London, Weidenfeld & Nicolson, [1969]. pp. (xx), 293. bibliog. 21½cm.

- United Kingdom - British Empire

SWINFEN (D.B.) Imperial control of colonial legislation, 1813-1865: a study of British policy towards colonial legislative powers. Oxford, 1970. pp. 202. bibliog.

- United States

ODEWALD (JENS) Der parlamentarische Hilfsdienst in den Vereinigten Staaten von Amerika und in der Bundesrepublik Deutschland. Berlin, Duncker und Humblot, [1967]. pp. 165. bibliog. 23cm. (Schriften zum Öffentlichen Recht. Band 64)

KEEFE (WILLIAM J.) and OGUL (MORRIS S.) The American legislative process: Congress and the States. 2nd ed. Englewood Cliffs, Prentice-Hall, [1968]. pp. xxi, 521. 23½cm.

PATTERSON (SAMUEL C.) ed. American legislative behavior: a reader. Princeton, Van Nostrand, [1968]. pp. xii, 451. bibliog. 23cm. (Van Nostrand. Political Science Series)

MASNATA-RUBATTEL (CLAIRE) L'Amérique blanche et les droits des noirs: la loi de 1964; contribution à l'étude du processus de décision aux États-Unis d'Amérique. Genève, Droz, 1969. pp. 295. bibliog. (Travaux de Droit, d'Économie, de Sociologie et de Sciences Politiques. No. 74)

MACRAE (DUNCAN) Issues and parties in legislative voting: methods of statistical analysis. New York, [1970]. pp. 329. bibliog.

LEGISLATIVE BODIES

MYCIELSKI (ANDRZEJ) Z zagadnień techniki parlamentarnej. Wrocław, 1965. pp. 102. bibliog. 21cm. (Breslau. Wrocławskie Towarzystwo Naukowe. Prace. Seria A. Nr.104) With English summary.

INTER-PARLIAMENTARY UNION. 2nd International Symposium, Geneva, 1968. Le parlement et ses moyens de contact avec l'opinion publique par la presse, la radio et la télévision:...rapports et débats. Genève, International Centre for Parliamentary Documentation, 1968. pp. xxi, 311. 29cm. In English or French.

KORNBERG (ALLAN) and MUSOLF (LLOYD DARYL) eds. Legislatures in developmental perspective. Durham, N.C., 1970. pp. 590.

WILSON (CHARLES HENRY) Parliaments, people and mass media; a report on the Geneva Symposium organized by the Inter-Parliamentary Union in December 1968. London, 1970. pp. 144. bibliog.

LEGISLATIVE BODIES
See also the names of individual legislative bodies under the names of countries or of states of a federal union

- Freedom of debate

BAR (CARL LUDWIG VON) Die Redefreiheit der Mitglieder gesetzgebender Versammlungen mit besonderer Beziehung auf Preussen. Leipzig, 1868; Frankfurt/Main, 1969. pp. 55.

- Privileges and immunities

BELAVADI (S. H.) The press and the parliamentary privileges. Ahmedabad, 1965. pp. 16. (Harold Laski Institute of Political Science. Laski Memorial Lectures. 1965)

- Upper Chambers

MAIN (JACKSON TURNER) The upper house in revolutionary America, 1763-1788. Madison, U. of Wisconsin P., 1967. pp. xii, 311. 23½cm.

LEGISLATIVE BODIES - Upper Chambers
See also the names of upper chambers under the names of countries

- Bulgaria

RADEV (IAROSLAV) Държавни представителни органи в България, 1944-1947; State representative organs in Bulgaria, 1944-1947. София, 1965. pp. 180. With Russian and English summaries and table of contents.

KHRISTOFOROV (VESELIN GEORGIEV) Държавните учреждения - правна същност и административно-правен режим. София, 1966. pp. 185. bibliog.

- Europe

INTERNATIONAL COMMISSION FOR THE HISTORY OF REPRESENTATIVE AND PARLIAMENTARY INSTITUTIONS. Studies. 1. (Histoire des assemblées d'états); [reprint of articles originally published in 1937]. Bruxelles, Librairie Encyclopédique, 1967. pp. 68. bibliog. 26cm. (Reprinted from Bulletin of the International Committee of Historical Sciences, t. 9, fasc. 4, no. 37, 1937) In English and French.

KOENIGSBERGER (HELMUT GEORG) The powers of deputies in sixteenth century assemblies. Louvain, 1961. pp. 214-243. (Reprinted from Album Helen Maud Cam)

MARONGIU (ANTONIO) Medieval parliaments: a comparative study; ... translated and adapted by S.J. Woolf. London, Eyre & Spottiswoode, 1968. pp. 306. bibliog. 22cm. (International Commission for the History of Representative and Parliamentary Institutions. Studies. 32)

- European Economic Community countries

ROYAL INSTITUTE OF INTERNATIONAL AFFAIRS and POLITICAL AND ECONOMIC PLANNING. European Series. No. 17. The EEC: national parliaments in community decision-making; [by] Michael Niblock. London, 1971. pp. 112. bibliog.

- Germany

JAEGER (HANS) Unternehmer in der deutschen Politik, 1890-1918. Bonn, Röhrscheid, 1967. pp. 383. bibliog. 23cm. (Bonner Historische Forschungen. Band 30)

KRAMER (HELMUT) Fraktionsbindungen in den deutschen Volksvertretungen 1819-1849. Berlin, [1968]. pp. 296. bibliog.

LEGISLATIVE BODIES - Germany - Berlin
See BERLIN - Abgeordnetenhaus

- Micronesia

MELLER (NORMAN) The Congress of Micronesia: development of the legislative process in the Trust Territory of the Pacific Islands; with the assistance of Terza Meller. Honolulu, U. of Hawaii P., 1969. pp. xi, 480. 22½cm.

- Poland

GEBETHNER (STANISŁAW) and others. System organów państwowych w Polskiej Rzeczypospolitej Ludowej. Warszawa, Książka i Wiedza, 1966. pp. 167. bibliog. 20cm. (Biblioteka Wychowania Obywatelskiego)

- Rhodesia

WILLSON (FRANCIS MICHAEL GLENN) and PASSMORE (GLORIA C.) Southern Rhodesia: holders of administrative and ministerial office, 1894-1964 and members of the Legislative Council, 1899-1923 and Legislative Assembly, 1924-1964. Salisbury, University College of Rhodesia and Nyasaland, Department of Government, 1966. pp. v, 77. 23cm. (Source Book Series. No. 3)

- Rome, Ancient

DEININGER (JUERGEN) Die Provinziallandtage der römischen Kaiserzeit von Augustus bis zum Ende des dritten Jahrhunderts n. Chr. München, Beck, 1965. pp. xvi, 220. bibliog. 24cm. (Vestigia. Band 6)

- Russia

MANOKHIN (VASILII MIKHAILOVICH) Organy sovetskogo gosudarstvennogo upravleniia: voprosy formirovaniia. Saratov, 1962. pp. 163.

EROSHKIN (NIKOLAI PETROVICH) История государственных учреждений России до Великой Октябрьской Социалистической революции: учебное пособие. Москва, 1965. pp. 417. bibliog. Xerographic copy.

GRIGORIAN (LEVON ARMENAKOVICH) Sovety - organy vlasti i narodnogo samoupravleniia. Moskva, 1965. pp. 235.

VASILENKOV (PETR TARASOVICH) Organy Sovetskogo gosudarstva i ikh sistema na sovremennom etape. Moskva, 1967. pp. 302.

KIRICHENKO (MIKHAIL GAVRILOVICH) Vysshie organy gosudarstvennoi vlasti RSFSR. Moskva, 1968. pp. 244.

KLEANDROVA (VALENTINA MIKHAILOVNA) Organizatsiia i formy deiatel'nosti VTsIK, 1917-1924 gg. Moskva, 1968. pp. 126.

LEGISLATIVE BODIES - Russia (Cont'd.)

KUZNETSOV (IGOR' NIKOLAEVICH) Компетенция высших органов власти и управления СССР. Москва, 1969. pp. 140.

MUKSINOV (IREK SHARIFOVICH) Совет Министров союзной республики. Москва, 1969. pp. 208.

- Switzerland - Privileges and immunities

LANZ-BAUR (REGULA) Die parlamentarische Immunität in Bund und Kantonen der schweizerischen Eidgenossenschaft. Zürich, Schulthess, 1963. pp. xx, 97. bibliog. 22½cm. (Zürcher Beiträge zur Rechtswissenschaft. Neue Folge. Heft 239)

- Ukraine

MARCHUK (VALENTIN MEFODIEVICH) Organy gosudarstvennogo upravleniia USSR na sovremennom etape. Kiev, 1964. pp. 192.

- United States

FRANCIS (WAYNE L.) Legislative issues in the fifty states: a comparative analysis. Chicago, Rand McNally, [1967]. pp. xiii, 129. 22½cm. (American Politics Research Series)

LACY (ALEX B.) ed. Power in American state legislatures: case studies of the Arkansas, Louisiana, Mississippi, and Oklahoma legislatures. New Orleans, Tulane University, 1967. pp. viii, 179. 23cm. (Tulane Studies in Political Science. vol. 11)

CRANE (WILDER W.) and WATTS (MEREDITH W.) State legislative systems. Englewood Cliffs, Prentice-Hall, [1968]. pp. ix, 118. 23cm. (Foundations of State and Local Government Series)

NATIONAL MUNICIPAL LEAGUE. Staff and services for state legislatures. New York, 1968. pp. 40.

HERZBERG (DONALD GABRIEL) and UNRUH (JESS) Essays on the state legislative process. New York, [1970]. pp. 116.

- White Russia

ORGANY... Органы государственного управления Белорусской ССР, 1919-1967 гг. Минск, Наука и Техника, 1968. pp. 828. 21½см.

LEGISLATIVE POWER

YEMIN (EDWARD) Legislative powers in the United Nations and specialised agencies. Leyden, 1969. pp. 227. bibliog.

- France

DOUENCE (JEAN CLAUDE) Recherches sur le pouvoir réglementaire de l'administration. Paris, Pichon et Durand-Auzias, 1968. pp. xiii, 7-534. bibliog. 25cm. (Bibliothèque de Droit Public. tome 81)

- Italy

LUCIFREDI (PIER GIORGIO) L'iniziativa legislativa parlamentare. Milano, Giuffrè, 1968. pp. xii, 350. 25cm. (Rome. Università. Istituto di Studi Giuridici. Pubblicazioni. Serie 5. N.6)

LEGITIMACY OF GOVERNMENTS

BOTANA (NATALIO) La légitimité: problème politique. Buenos Aires, 1968. pp. 261. bibliog.

HARRIS (JAMES WILLIAM) When and why does the grundnorm change? Cambridge, 1971. pp. [31]. Reprinted from the Cambridge Law Journal, 1971.

LEGITIME

- United Kingdom

TYLER (EDWARD LAWSON GRIFFIN) Family provision. London, 1971. pp. 207.

LEGIUNEA ARHANGHELUL MIHAIL

CANTACUZINO (ALEXANDRU) Opere complete. München, 1969. pp. various.

LEGNICA

BRESLAU. Wrocławskie Towarzystwo Naukowe. Naukowa Sesja Wyjazdowa, 1965. Problemy Legnicko-Głogowskiego Okręgu Miedzi. Wrocław, 1966. pp. 109. 21½cm.

LEI (FENG)

CHEN (KUANG-SHENG) Lei Feng, Chairman Mao's good fighter. Peking, Foreign Languages P., 1968. pp. 102.

LEIBNIZ (GOTTFRIED WILHELM VON) Baron

LEIBNIZ (GOTTFRIED WILHELM VON) Baron. Die philosophischen Schriften...; herausgegeben von C. I. Gerhardt. Hildesheim, Olms, 1965. 7 vols. 23½cm. (Olms Paperbacks. Bände 11-17) Facsimile reprint of the Berlin edition of 1875-1890.

GUGGENBERGER (ALOIS) Leibniz; oder, Die Hierarchie des Geistes. Stuttgart, [1947]. pp. 48.

BARBER (W. H.) Mme. du Châtelet and Leibnizianism: the genesis of the Institutions de physique. in Barber (William H.) and others, eds. The age of the enlightenment. Edinburgh, 1967.

KLINE (G. L.) Randall's reinterpretation of the philosophies of Descartes, Spinoza, and Leibniz. in Anton (John Peter) ed. Naturalism and historical understanding. Albany, [1967].

JOURNÉES LEIBNIZ, 1966. Leibniz, 1646-1716: aspects de l'homme et de l'oeuvre. Paris, Aubier-Montaigne, [1968]. pp. 294. bibliog. 22cm.

SIMONOVITS (ANNA) Dialektisches Denken in der Philosophie von Gottfried Wilhelm Leibniz. Budapest, Akadémiai Kiadó, 1968. pp. 239. bibliog. 21cm.

VOISÉ (W.) Gottfried Wilhelm Leibniz, ou l'historiographie d'un conciliateur. in vol.1 of Sieber (Marc) ed. Discordia concors. Basel, [1968].

LEIBNIZ (GOTTFRIED WILHELM VON) Baron. Philosophical papers and letters: a selection translated and edited, with an introduction by Leroy E. Loemker. 2nd ed. Dordrecht, [1969]. pp. 736. bibliog.

PEURSEN (CORNELIS ANTHONIE VAN) Leibniz...; English edition translated by Hubert Hoskins, with additional matter by the author. London, 1969. pp. 128. bibliog.

GUITTON (JEAN) Profils parallèles: Pascal-Leibniz Renan-Newman, Teilhard-Bergson, Claudel-Heidegger. [Paris, 1970]. pp. 496.

LEICESTER

- History

ELLIS (COLIN D. B.) History in Leicester, 55 B.C.- A.D. 1969. 2nd ed. Leicester, 1969. pp. 146. bibliogs.

- Transit systems

SHARP (CLIFFORD) Problems of urban passenger transport: with special reference to Leicester. Leicester, University Press, 1967. pp. 118. 20½cm.

LEISURE

INTERNATIONAL LABOUR CONFERENCE. 6th Session. Questionnaires. 1. Development of facilities for the utilisation of workers' leisure: first item of the agenda. Geneva, 1923. pp. 30. 22cm.

BECQUET (YVONNE) L'organisation des loisirs des travailleurs. Paris, Pedone, 1939. pp. 272. bibliog. 24½cm.

DOGLIO (C.) I "tempi d'ozio" come incentivo di attività industriali. in vol.2 of Trentino-Alto Adige. 1956. L'economia industriale della regione Trentino-Alto Adige. pt.1. Trento, 1956.

PRUDENSKII (GERMAN ALEKSANDROVICH) ed. Внерабочее время трудящихся. Новосибирск, 1961. pp. 256.

FITISOV (VASILII ANISIMOVICH) Организация отдыха трудящихся. Москва, 1963. pp. 47.

MECHELEN (FRANS VAN) and others. Vrijetijdsbesteding in Vlaanderen. Antwerpen, Uitgeverij s.m. Ontwikkeling, 1964-66. 2 vols. bibliog. 22cm. (Volksopvoeding. Verhandelingen. 5,6)

BOLGOV (V. I.) Внерабочее время и уровень жизни трудящихся. Новосибирск, 1964. pp. 185. bibliog. Cover and colophon have В. А. Болгов.

LAPORTA (RAFFAELE) and others. Il tempo libero giovanile e la sua organizzazione educativa. Bari, Laterza, 1964. pp. 206. bibliog. 21½cm. (Convegno su "La Scuola e la Società Italiana in Trasformazione". Ricerche. 14)

KRIAZHEV (VIKTOR GRIGOR'EVICH) Внерабочее время и сфера обслуживания. Москва, 1966. pp. 144.

SMITH (CYRIL S.) Young people at leisure: a report on Bury. Manchester, imprint, 1966. pp. 62. 21½cm.

ĆWIAKOWSKI (MAREK) Problemy społeczne wolnego czasu. Warszawa, CRZZ, 1967. pp. 226. bibliog. 21cm.

MARTIN (PETER A.) ed. Leisure and mental health: a psychiatric viewpoint. Washington, American Psychiatric Association, Committee on Leisure Time and its Uses, 1967. pp. (vii), 126. 23cm.

GOVAERTS (FRANCE) Loisirs des femmes et temps libre. Bruxelles, [1969]. pp. 312. bibliog. (Centre National de Sociologie du Travail. Section "Loisir et culture modernes". Etudes)

RUBINSTEIN (DAVID) and SPEAKMAN (COLIN) Leisure, transport and the countryside. London, Fabian Society, 1969. pp. 27. 23cm. (Research Series. [No.] 277)

ANDREAE (CLEMENS AUGUST) Ökonomik der Freizeit: zur Wirtschaftstheorie der modernen Arbeitswelt. Reinbek bei Hamburg, 1970. pp. 247. bibliog.

ENTWISTLE (HAROLD) Education, work and leisure. London, 1970. pp. 119. bibliog.

Die FREIE Zeit als Problem: soziologische Untersuchungen in Bulgarien, Polen, Ungarn und der Sowjetunion; [by] Boris Grušin [and others; three of the four contributions reprinted from Probleme des Friedens und des Sozialismus, Prague]; herausgegeben von Arnold Harttung. Berlin, [1970]. pp. 187.

GLASSER (RALPH) Leisure, penalty or prize. London, 1970. pp. 221.

ROBERTS (KENNETH) Leisure. London, 1970. pp. 133. bibliog.

FRANCE. Intergroupe Loisirs. 1971. Préparation du VIe Plan: rapport. Paris, 1971. pp. 191.

PARKER (STANLEY ROBERT) The future of work and leisure. London, 1971. pp. 160.

- Bibliography

DUMAZEDIER (JOFFRE) and others, compilers. Les sciences sociales du loisir et l'organisation du loisir: bibliographie française et guide d'orientation documentaire. Paris, Éducation et Vie Sociale, afterwards Cujas, [1961 in progress]. 21cm.

PINKERTON (JAMES R.) and PINKERTON (MARJORIE J.) compilers. Outdoor recreation and leisure: a reference guide and selected bibliography. Colombia, University of Missouri, School of Business and Public Administration, Research Center, 1969. pp. (vi), 322. bibliog. 23cm.

LEITH-ROSS (Sir FREDERICK WILLIAM)

LEITH-ROSS (Sir FREDERICK WILLIAM) Money talks: fifty years of international finance; the autobiography of Sir Frederick Leith-Ross. London, Hutchinson, 1968. pp. viii, 364. 21cm.

LELEWEL FAMILY

LELEWEL (PROT ADAM JACEK) Pamiętniki i diariusz domu naszego; przygotowała do druku i opatrzyła przypisami Irena Lelewel-Friemannowa. Wrocław, Ossolineum, 1966. pp. 536. 23cm.

LE MANS

- Population

FRANCE. Institut National de la Statistique et des Études Économiques. Direction Régionale de Nantes. 1959. Ensembles industriels: Tours, Angers, Le Mans. Nantes, [1959]. pp. 11. 26¾cm.

LEMIRE (JULES AUGUSTE) Abbé

MAYEUR (JEAN MARIE) Un prêtre démocrate l'Abbé Lemire 1853-1928. [Tournai, 1968]. pp. 698. bibliog.

LEMKE (WILLIAM)

BENNETT (DAVID H.) Demagogues in the depression: American radicals and the Union Party, 1932-1936. New Brunswick, [1959]. pp. 341. bibliog.

LEMMER (ERNST)

NATIONALE FRONT DES DEMOKRATISCHEN DEUTSCHLAND. Nationalrat. Ernst Lemmer: Goebbels journalist, Nazi informer, revenge minister; excerpts from the documentation published by the National Council, etc. [Dresden, 1964] pp. 60.

LENA RIVER

ANTONOV (VASILII SEMENOVICH) Ust'-evaia oblast' reki Leny: gidrologicheskii ocherk. Leningrad, 1967. pp. 107.

LEND-LEASE OPERATIONS (1941-1945)

JONES (ROBERT HUHN) The roads to Russia: United States lend-lease to the Soviet Union. Norman, U. of Oklahoma P., [1969]. pp. xix, 326. bibliog. 22½cm.

KIMBALL (WARREN F.) The most unsordid act: lend-lease, 1939-1941. Baltimore, Maryland, [1969]. pp. 281. bibliog.

LENGLET DU FRESNOY (NICOLAS)

RICUPERATI (G.) Giannone e i suoi contemporanei: Lenglet du Fresnoy, Matteo Egizio, e Gregorio Grimaldi. in Miscellanea Walter Maturi. Torino, 1966.

LENIN (VLADIMIR IL'ICH)

ZINOV'EV (GRIGORII EVSEEVICH) N. Lénine (W.J. Oulianov): sa vie et son activité. Petrograd, 1919. pp. 52.

HOSCHILLER (MAX) Le mirage du soviétisme. Paris, Payot, 1921. pp. 253. 17½cm. (Bibliothèque Politique et Économique)

SERGE (VICTOR) pseud. [i.e. Viktor L'vovich KIBAL'CHICH] Lenine, 1917. Paris, Librairie du Travail, [1924?] pp. 72. (Faits et Documents. No. 2)

STALIN (IOSIF VISSARIONOVICH) The theory and practice of leninism. London, 1925. pp. 130.

ADLER (MAX) Helden der sozialen Revolution. Berlin, 1926. pp. 53.

YOUNG COMMUNIST LEAGUE [OF GREAT BRITAIN]. Lenin and the youth movement. London, [193-?]. pp. 7.

GORBUNOV (N. P.) Lenin: Erinnerungen eines Sekretärs des Rats der Volkskommissare. Moskau, Verlagsgenossenschaft Ausländischer Arbeiter in der UdSSR, 1934. pp. 40. 18½cm.

ZETKIN (CLARA) Reminiscences of Lenin. New York, [1934]. pp. 64.

[PANNEKOEK (ANTON)] Lenin als Philosoph: kritische Betrachtung der philosophischen Grundlagen des Leninismus; von J. Harper [pseud.]. [Amsterdam], [1938]. pp. 112. (Gruppe Internationaler Kommunisten in Holland. Bibliothek der "Räte-korrespondenz". No.1)

GLASSER (M.) Über die Arbeitsmethoden der Klassiker des Marxismus-Leninismus. Berlin, [1948]. pp. 102.

The 20TH congress (C.P.S.U.) and world Trotskyism: a documented analysis. New York, 1957. pp. 124.

BESSONOV (A.P.) О работе В.И. Ленина над заглавиями своих статей. in Leningrad. Universitet. Uchenye Zapiski. No.245. Leningrad, 1957.

MIKHLIN (E.) В. И. Ленин о возможности мирного развития революции в 1917 году. Ленинград, 1958. pp. 40. 20cm.

KARAVAEV (A.) Lenin: chelovek, politik, filosof, revoliutsioner. Frankfurt, Posev, 1959. pp 198.

LENIN (VLADIMIR IL'ICH) Lenin on state and democracy; [with commentary by] A. Spirkin. Moscow, [196-?]. pp. 63.

AZIZBEKOVA (P. A.) Руководство В. И. Ленина социалистическим строительством в Азербайджане в 1920-1923 гг. Баку, АН АзССР, 1960. pp. 267. bibliog. 21cm.

IZ istorii revoliutsionnoi i gosudarstvennoi deiatel'nosti V. I. Lenina: k 90-letiiu so dnia rozhdeniia V. I. Lenina, 1870-1960; sbornik statei. Moskva, 1960. pp. 457.

SAMARKAND. Universitet. Trudy. Novaia Seriia. vyp.108. Voprosy leninskoi natsional'noi politiki i kommunisticheskogo stroitel'stva: sbornik statei kafedr obshchestvennykh nauk. Samarkand, 1960. pp. 173. Some articles in Uzbek.

MAKSA (N.) Ленин в Праге. in Kommunisticheskaia Partiia Sovetskogo Soiuza. Tsentral'nyi Komitet. Uchenye Zapiski Kafedr Istorii Kommunisticheskoi Partii Sovetskogo Soiuza Vysshei Partiinoi Shkoly i Mestnykh Partiinykh Shkol. vyp.3. Moskva, 1961.

SHAKHNOVICH (MIKHAIL IOSIFOVICH) Lenin i problemy ateizma: kritika religii v trudakh V.I.Lenina. Leningrad, 1961. pp. 671.

VASINA (EMILIIA LEONIDOVNA) Leninskii plan postroeniia marksistskoi partii v Rossii; Bor'ba leninskoi "Iskry" za sozdanie partii; lektsiia dlia studentov-zaochnikov gosudarstvennykh universitetov. Moskva, 1962. pp. 40.

KRASAVIN (VITALII PETROVICH) Bor'ba G.V. Plekhanova protiv "ekonomizma" v zagranichnoi organizatsii RSDRP. Perm', 1964. pp. 78.

PERSOV (M.S.) Nekotorye problemy istoricheskogo opyta v rabotakh V.I. Lenina 1907-1914 godov. in Iz istorii obshchestvennoi mysli i obshchestvennogo dvizheniia v Rossii. Saratov, 1964.

POTULOV (BORIS MIKHAILOVICH) В. И. Ленин и советское здравоохранение. Москва, Медицина, 1964. pp. 183. bibliog. 20cm.

REISBERG (ARNOLD) Lenin und die Aktionseinheit in Deutschland. Berlin, Dietz, 1964. pp. 190. 20cm.

SAIDASHEVA (MUNIRA ABDULLOVNA) and BURNASHEVA (IU. V.) compilers. V. I. Lenin i Tatariia: sbornik dokumentov, materialov i vospominanii. Kazan', 1964. pp. 359. bibliog.

SANZHIEV (BUIANTO SAINTSAKOVICH) В. И. Ленин и проблемы Сибири: краткое обозрение. [Иркутск], Восточно-Сибирское Книжное Издательство, 1964. pp. 28. 20cm.

VOSPOMINANIIA medikov o V.I. Lenine. Moskva, 1964. pp. 235.

ALLILUEVA (N.S.) and others. Tagebuch der Sekretäre W.I. Lenins, 21. November 1922 bis 6. März 1923. Berlin, Dietz, 1965. pp. 99. 18cm.

ANDREEV (ANDREI ANDREEVICH) О Владимире Ильиче Ленине. 2nd ed. Москва, Политиздат, 1965. pp. 62. 20cm.

CHELOVEKU... Человеку, другу, вождю: саратовцы В. И. Ленину и о В. И. Ленине; сборник документов, 1918-1924 гг. Саратов, Приволжское Книжное Издательство, 1965. pp. 103. 20cm.

HONGQI. A great victory for Leninism: in commemoration of the 95th anniversary of the birth of Lenin; Hongqi editorial, No.4. 1965. Peking, Foreign Languages P., 1965. pp. 14. 18½cm.

IAKOVLEV (BORIS VLADIMIROVICH) Ленин в Красноярске: документальный очерк. Москва, Политиздат, 1965. pp. 207. bibliog. 20cm.

KEDROV (BONIFATII MIKHAILOVICH) Как изучать книгу В. И. Ленина "Материализм и эмпириокритицизм". 2nd ed. Москва, Политиздат, 1965. pp. 200. 20cm.

LAPTIN (MIKHAIL NIKOLAEVICH) Lenin on material incentive and enthusiasm of the masses. [Moscow, 1965]. pp. 16.

LUKÁCS (GEORG) Marxist. Lénine. Paris, Etudes et Documentation Internationales, [1965]. pp. 128. 20cm.

MRACHKOVSKAIA (IRINA MIKHAILOVNA) О содержании второго выпуска работы В.И. Ленина "Что такое "друзья народа" и как они воюют против социал-демократов?". Москва, 1965. pp. 64.

NAZIMOVA (EKATERINA MIKHAILOVNA) Pervyi den': V.I. Lenin v Petrograde 4 aprelia 1917 goda. Leningrad, 1965. pp. 79.

POCHKAI (IL'IA BORISOVICH) and CHASHNIKOV (IVAN PETROVICH) В. И. Ленин и научная информация. Москва, 1965. pp. 41.

SEVRIUGINA (N.) Lessons of history: from the history of Lenin's struggle with the "Leftists" in the international Communist movement, 1918-1922. [Moscow, 1965]. pp. 23.

IVANOV (VLADIMIR VASIL'EVICH) Принцип историзма в произведениях В. И. Ленина 90-х годов. Томск, Университет, 1966. pp. 207. 21½см.

KHVARTSKIIA (MDZHYT SH.) Zashchita i razvitie V. I. Leninym programmy RSDRP v period reaktsii, 1907-1910 gg. Sukhumi, 1966. pp. 175.

L'VOV (IVAN ANDREEVICH) and NIKITIN (PETR EROFEEVICH) Lenin v Razlive. Leningrad, 1966. pp. 94.

MALYI (IL'IA GRIGOR'EVICH) Статистика в труде В. И. Ленина "Империализм, как высшая стадия капитализма". Москва, Статистика, 1965. pp. 127. 20cm.

MAMIKONIAN (KARAPET AVETOVICH) Bor'ba V. I. Lenina za sozdanie i ukreplenie bol'shevistskikh organizatsii Zakavkaz'ia, 1903-1905 gg. Erevan, 1966. pp. 127.

NA putiakh k kommunizmu: sbornik statei. Leningrad, 1966. pp. 203.

PANCHENKO (MYKOLA PYLYPOVYCH) Ленін про розширене соціалістичне відтворення. Київ, Політвидав, 1966. pp. 161. 19½см.

SAVENKOV (ALEKSEI ALEKSEEVICH) Iskusstvo ubezhdat': iz tvorcheskoi laboratorii V. I. Lenina - propagandista i agitatora. Leningrad, 1966. pp. 166.

TADZHIKSKII GOSUDARSTVENNYI UNIVERSITET. Trudy. Seriia Istoricheskaia. vyp.2. Voprosy istorii SSSR. Dushanbe, 1966. pp. 331.

LENIN (VLADIMIR IL'ICH) (Cont'd.)

TARASENKO (ANATOLII ALEKSANDROVICH) Zhivoe slovo. Moskva, 1966. pp. 248.

VOPROSY teoreticheskogo nasledstva V. I. Lenina. Krasnoiarsk, 1966. pp. 162.

1967

ALTMYSHBAEV (ASYLBEK ALTMYSHBAEVICH) Lenin i propaganda marksizma v Kirgizii, 1905-1923 gg. Frunze, 1967. pp. 271. bibliog.

ANOSHKIN (IVAN FEDOROVICH) Analiz V. I. Leninym internatsional'nykh uslovii perekhoda k sotsializmu v SSSR. Saratov, 1967. pp. 106.

CHAGIN (BORIS ALEKSANDROVICH) Lenin o roli subektivnogo faktora v istorii. Leningrad, 1967. pp. 147.

CHAGIN (BORIS ALEKSANDROVICH) and others. Razvitie V. I. Leninym istoricheskogo materializma posle Velikoi Oktiabr'skoi sotsialisticheskoi revoliutsii. Leningrad, 1967. pp. 152.

EKONOMICHESKAIA... Экономическая теория Маркса-Ленина и современный капитализм. Москва, 1967. pp. 407.

[FELD (CHARLES) ed.] Quand Lénine vivait à Paris. Paris, Club Messidor, [1967]. pp. 237. bibliog. 28cm.

FOTIEVA (LIDIIA ALEKSANDROVNA) Из жизни В. И. Ленина. Москва, ИПЛ, 1967. pp. 320. 16½cm. With illustrations.

GARIBDZHANIAN (GEVORG BAGRATOVICH) В. И. Ленин и большевистские организации Закавказья, 1893-1924. Ереван, АН Армянской ССР, 1967. pp. 571. 19½см. With English summary.

GONCHAROV (ALEKSANDR DMITRIEVICH) and LUNIAKOV (PAVEL IVANOVICH) V I. Lenin i krest'ianstvo. Moskva, 1967. pp. 199.

GOR'KII (MAKSIM) pseud. [i.e. Aleksei Maksimovich PESHKOV]. Lenin: a biographical essay; introduced by Z. A. B. Zeman. Edinburgh, University Texts, [1967]. pp. 62. 21½cm. (University Texts. 1)

KOENIG (HELMUT) Lenin und der italienische Sozialismus, 1915-1921: ein Beitrag zur Gründungsgeschichte der Kommunistischen Internationale. Tübingen, Böhlau, 1967. pp. x, 240. bibliog. 23cm. (Arbeitsgemeinschaft für Osteuropaforschung. Forschungsberichte und Untersuchungen zur Zeitgeschichte. Nr. 13)

KOGAN (S.N.) V.I. Lenin o vzaimosviazi obshchedemokraticheskoi i sotsialisticheskoi bor'by proletariata v period revoliutsii 1905-1907 gg. in Voprosy istorii KPSS. Cheliabinsk, 1967.

KOMIAKOV (L.V.) V.I. Lenin o vneshnikh ekonomicheskikh sviaziakh Sovetskoi respubliki. in Voprosy istorii KPSS. Cheliabinsk, 1967.

KRASIN (IURII ANDREEVICH) Ленин, революция, современность: проблемы ленинской теории социалистической революции. Москва, Наука, 1967. pp. 563. 20см.

KRIVOGUZ (IGOR' MIKHAILOVICH) and MOLCHANOV (IURII LEONIDOVICH) Ленин и борьба за единство рабочего движения. Ленинград, Лениздат, 1967. pp. 295. 20см.

KURELLA (ALFRED) Unterwegs zu Lenin: Erinnerungen. Berlin, 1967. pp. 159.

LALOY (JEAN) Le socialisme de Lénine. [Paris], Desclée de Brouwer, [1967]. pp. 317. bibliog. 19½cm.

LENIN, partiia, Oktiab': [sbornik statei]. Leningrad, 1967. pp. 256.

LENIN... Ленин в 1917 году: воспоминания. Москва, ИПЛ, 1967. pp. 388. 20см.

LENINSKIE... Ленинские принципы партийного руководства массами в первые годы строительства Советского общества, 1917 1923 гг. Москва, Мысль, 1967. pp. 238. 19½см.

LIBKIND (ARON SOLOMONOVICH) Analiz amerikanskikh sel'skokhoziaistvennykh tsenzov v rabotakh V. I. Lenina. Moskva, 1967. pp. 132.

LIUBIMOV (VASILII NIKOLAEVICH) and IULDASHBAEV (BILAL KHAMITOVICH) Ленин и самоопределение наций: на примере народов Среднего Поволжья и Приуралья. Чебоксары, Чувашское Книжное Издательство, 1967. pp. 239. bibliog. 19½см.

MY... Мы наш, мы новый мир построим. Москва, Политиздат, 1967. pp. 591. 20cm. Earlier vols. entitled: У истоков партии; Партия шагает в революцию; Светок ленинских идей; Ленинская гвардия планеты.

NAGY (LASZLO) Lénine et sa révolution. [Lausanne], Rencontre, [1967]. pp. 204. 24cm.

NEEF (HELMUT) ed. W.I. Lenins Ruf: "An alle!": 50 Jahre Dekret über den Frieden. Berlin, Dietz, 1967. pp. 298. 20cm.

NELIDOV (NIKOLAI VASIL'EVICH) and BARCHUGOV (PAVEL VASIL'EVICH) Leninskaia shkola v Lonzhiumo. Moskva, 1967. pp. 78.

OVSIENKO (VALENTIN ERMOLAEVICH) and VITALINA (ELIZAVETA GRIGOR'EVNA) Вопросы статистической науки в трудах В. И. Ленина. Москва, Статистика, 1967. pp. 207. bibliog. 20см.

POTULOV (BORIS MIKHAILOVICH) В. И. Ленин и охрана здоровья советского народа. Ленинград, 1967. pp. 390.

REZNIKOV (ANDREI ILLARIONOVICH) Роль теоретического наследия В. И. Ленина в борьбе за марксистскую философию против идеализма. Харьков, 1967. pp. 240.

ROBERTS (H. L.) Lenin and power. in Krieger (Leonard) and Stern (Fritz Richard) eds. The responsibility of power. Garden City, 1967.

RODIONOV (PETR ALEKSANDROVICH) Коллективность - высший принцип партийного руководства: разработка, развитие и воплощение ленинского принципа коллективности в деятельности КПСС. Москва, Политиздат, 1967. pp. 287. 20см.

SHNITMAN (ABRAM MOISEEVICH) Из истории интернациональных связей В. И. Ленина с революционным рабочим движением в Болгарии, 1896-1923 гг. Мурманск, 1967. pp. 477. bibliog.

TRAPEZNIKOV (SERGEI PAVLOVICH) Leninizm i agrarno-krest'ianskii vopros. Moskva, 1967. 2 vols.

TRUSH (MIKHAIL IVANOVICH) Vneshne-politicheskaia deiatel'nost' V. I. Lenina 1921-1923, den' za dnem. Moskva, 1967. pp. 408.

TRUSH (MIKHAIL IVANOVICH) and DZHU-SUPBEKOV (S. D.) Великое наследие: новые документы полного собрания сочинений В. И. Ленина. Алма-Ата, 1967. pp. 110.

UCHENIE V. I. Lenina ob imperializme i sovremennost'. Moskva, 1967. pp. 464.

URAZAEV (SHAVKAT ZAKARIEVICH) V. I. Lenin i stroitel'stvo Sovetskoi gosudarstvennosti v Turkestane. Tashkent, 1967. pp. 518. bibliog.

V.I. Lenin i Sovetskie Vooruzhennye Sily. Moskva, 1967. pp. 446.

WOLFE (BERTRAM DAVID) The bridge and the abyss: the troubled friendship of Maxim Gorky and V.I.Lenin. London, Pall Mall P., 1967. pp. xiii, 180. bibliog. 20cm. (Stanford University. Hoover Institution on War, Revolution and Peace. Hoover Institution Publications)

1968

BEISEMBAEV (SERKBAI BEISEMBAEVICH) Ленин и Казахстан, 1897-1924 гг. Алма-Ата, Казахстан, 1968. pp. 534. 19½см.

FRÉVILLE (JEAN) Lénine à Paris. Paris, Éditions Sociales, [1968]. pp. 247. 19cm.

GALKIN (I.S.) Борьба В.И. Ленина против центризма в годы первой мировой войны. in Первая мировая война, 1914-1918. Москва, 1968.

GARAUDY (ROGER) Lénine. Paris, P.U.F., 1968. pp. 109. bibliog.

KHESSIN (NIKOLAI VLADIMIROVICH) В. И. Ленин о сущности и основных признаках товарного производства. Москва, 1968. pp. 190.

KOROLEV (NIKOLAI EGOROVICH) Ленин и международное рабочее движение, 1914-1918. Москва, 1968. pp. 296. bibliog.

LAPTIN (MIKHAIL NIKOLAEVICH) and PONOMAREV (E. I.) В. И. Ленин и социалистическое хозяйствование. Москва, Мысль, 1968. pp. 332. 20см.

LENIN (VLADIMIR IL'ICH) Lenin on politics and revolution: selected writings; edited and introduced by James E. Connor. New York, [1968]. pp. 375. bibliog.

LEWIN (MOSHE) Lenin's last struggle; translated from the French by A.M. Sheridan Smith. New York, Pantheon Books, [1968]. pp. xxiv, 193. 21cm.

LIKHTENSHTEIN (E.S.) Lenin i kniga. in Piat'sot let posle Gutenberga, 1468-1968. Moskva, 1968.

NIKISHOV (SERAFIM IVANOVICH) Leninskaia kritika filosofskikh osnov religii. Moskva, 1968. pp. 372.

NIKOL'NIKOV (GEORGII L'VOVICH) Выдающаяся победа ленинской стратегии и тактики: Брестский мир, от заключения до разрыва. Москва, Мысль, 1968. pp. 374. 19½см.

NOVIKOV (VIKTOR IVANOVICH) В. И. Ленин и Псковские искровцы. Ленинград, Лениздат, 1968. pp. 112. 19см.

POSPELOV (PETR NIKOLAEVICH) Problemy istorii: stat'i i rechi. Moskva, 1968. pp. 208.

SHAPKO (VALERII MAKAROVICH) Обоснование В.И. Лениным принципов государственного руководства. Москва, 1968. pp. 343.

STEPANOV (V. N.) Ленин и русская организация "Искры", 1900-1903. Москва, Мысль, 1968. pp. 398. 16½см.

SUSLOV (IVAN PETROVICH) Политическая статистика в работах В. И. Ленина. Москва, Статистика, 1968. pp. 160. 20см.

TAUBIN (RAFAIL ABRAMOVICH) V. I. Lenin ob ideologii i ideologakh predshestvennikov revoliutsionnoi sotsial-demokratii v Rossii. Ul'ianovsk, 1968. pp. 134.

TEMKIN (IAKOV GRIGOR'EVICH) Ленин и международная социал-демократия, 1914-1917. Москва, 1968. pp. 623.

UL'IANOV (DMITRII IL'ICH) Vospominaniia o Vladimire Il'iche. 3rd ed. Moskva, 1968. pp. 127.

V... В. И. Ленин и историческая наука. Москва, Наука, 1968. pp. 551. 21см.

VALENTINOV (NIKOLAI VLADISLAVOVICH) pseud. [i.e. Nikolai Vladislavovich VOL'SKII] Encounters with Lenin; translated from the Russian by Paul Rosta and Brian Pearce. London, OUP, 1968. pp. xix, 273. 21½cm.

LENIN (VLADIMIR IL'ICH) (Cont'd.)

VOL'PER (IZRAIL' NAUMOVICH) Psevdonimy V. I. Lenina. 2nd ed. Leningrad, 1968. pp. 158.

1969

VOSPOMINANIIA o Vladimire Il'iche Lenine. Moskva, 1969-70. 5 vols.

AKBARDIIA (K.) Leninskoe uchenie o gnoseologicheskikh posylkakh svobody i neobkhodimosti. Tbilisi, 1969. pp. 311.

ALTHUSSER (LOUIS) Lénine et la philosophie. Paris, 1969. pp. 59.

ASHIMBAEV (TUIMEBAI ASHIMBAEVICH) Leninskie idei tekhnicheskogo progressa i ikh osushchestvlenie v Kazakhstane. Alma-Ata, 1969 pp. 181.

ASTAKHOV (VIKTOR IVANOVICH) and SHERMAN (ISAI L'VOVICH) В. И. Ленин - историк советского общества. Харьков, 1969. pp. 855.

BAGIROV (Z. N.) V. I. Lenin i dialekticheskoe ponimanie otritsaniia. Baku, 1969. pp. 221.

BAISHEV (SAKTAGAN BAISHEVICH) В. И. Ленин и Советский Казахстан. Алма-Ата, 1969. pp. 325.

BONCH-BRUEVICH (VLADIMIR DMITRIEVICH) Воспоминания о Ленине. 2nd ed. Москва, 1969. pp. 517.

BURMISTROVA (TAT'IANA IUL'EVNA) Национальный вопрос и рабочее движение в России: ленинская политика пролетарского интернационализма, 1907-1917 гг. Москва, 1969. pp. 274. bibliog.

CHERNENKO (ANATOLII MYKHAILOVYCH) V. I. Lenin i zakordonni bil'shovits'ki orhanizatsii. Kyïv, 1969. pp. 159.

CHERNUKHA (HRYHORII OLEKSANDROVYCH) В. І. Ленін у боротьбі за зміцнення партії нового типу, 1908-1905 pp. Харків, 1969. pp. 175.

CHERNYKH (ANNA GRIGOR'EVNA) В. И. Ленин - историк пролетарской революции в России. Москва, 1969. pp. 382.

CHUEVA (IZIDA PANTELEIMONOVA) Ленин об идейных истоках антикоммунизма. Ленинград, 1969. pp. 289.

DOROGOI... Дорогой товарищ Ленин: телеграммы и письма трудящихся Петрограда и Петроградской губернии Владимиру Ильичу Ленину, 1917-1924. Ленинград, 1969 pp. 399.

DRIZULIS (ALEKSANDR ARVIDOVICH) V.I. Lenin and the revolutionary movement in Latvia. Riga, 1969. pp. 30.

EL'SBERG (IAKOV EFIMOVICH) Ленинское наследие, жизнь и литература. Москва, 1969. pp. 253.

FEDOTOV (VASILII PAVLOVICH) В. И. Ленин об организационных отношениях экономики переходного к социализму общества. Ленинград, Университет, 1969. pp. 80. 21½см.

FEIGIN (IA. G.) Ленин и социалистическое размещение производительных сил. Москва, 1969. pp. 222. bibliog.

FIGUERES (LEO) Le trotskisme, cet antiléninisme. Paris, [1969]. pp. 257. bibliog.

FURMANOV (GRIGORII L'VOVICH) Leninskaia teoriia sotsialisticheskoi revoliutsii i sovremennost'. Moskva, 1969. pp. 50. bibliog.

GENKINA (ESFIR' BORISOVNA) Государственная деятельность В. И. Ленина, 1921-1923. Москва, 1969. pp. 519.

ILLICHEVSKII (ANATOLII FOMICH) Ленин в художественной литературе Запада. Киев, 1969. pp. 285. bibliog.

IUFEREVA (EKATERINA VASIL'EVNA) Ленинское учение о госкапитализме в переходный период к социализму. Москва, 1969. pp. 221.

KAK V.I.Lenin gotovil svoi trudy. Moskva, 1969. pp. 190.

KALININ (ANATOLII FROLOVICH) and MANDEL' (SEMEN ZAKHAROVICH) Ленин и Петербургский университет. Ленинград, 1969. pp. 269. bibliog.

KALTAKHCHIAN (SUREN TIGRANOVICH) Ленинизм о сущности нации и пути образования интернациональной общности людей. Москва, 1969. pp. 461.

KARAMYSHEV (ALEKSANDR LEONT'EVICH) and TOMUL' (ANTONINA IVANOVNA) Vospitanie v sem'e Ul'ianovykh. 2nd ed. Saratov, 1969. pp. 124.

KAZAKEVICH (EMMANUIL GENRIKHOVICH) The blue notebook; (translated from the Russian by Ralph Parker and Valentina Scott). Moscow, 1962 repr.1969. pp. 105.

KHARMANDARIAN (SEGVARD VAGARSHAKHOVICH) Ленин и становление Закавказской Федерации, 1921-1923. Ереван, 1969. pp. 455. bibliog.

KHASANOV (KUCHKAR) В. И. Ленин и Туркбюро ЦК РКП/б/. Ташкент, 1969. pp. 151.

KHROMOV (PAVEL ALEKSEEVICH) V. I. Lenin o proizvoditel'nosti truda. Moskva, 1969. pp. 141.

KISELEV (ASKOL'D ALEKSANDROVICH) В. И. Ленин и вопросы этики. Львов, 1969. pp. 207.

KLIUCHNYKOV (VALENTYN PAVLOVYCH) Metodolohichni osnovy krytyky V. I. Leninym idealizmu. Kyïv, 1969. pp. 202.

KOL'TSOV (ANATOLII VASIL'EVICH) Ленин и становление Академии наук как центра Советской науки. Ленинград, 1969. pp. 279.

KOPNIN (PAVEL VASIL'EVICH) Философские идеи В. И. Ленина и логика. Москва, Наука, 1969. pp. 483. 21½см.

KOPNIN (PAVEL VASIL'EVICH) В. И. Ленин и материалистическая диалектика. Киев, 1969. pp. 194.

KORABLEV (IURII IVANOVICH) V. I. Lenin - sozdatel' Krasnoi Armii. Moskva, 1969. pp. 159.

KOTOV (VIKTOR NIKIFOROVICH) V. I. Lenin - osnovopolozhnyk radians'koï istorychnoï nauky. Kyïv, 1969. pp. 267.

KRETOV (FEDOR DMITRIEVICH) Bor'ba V. I. Lenina za sokhranenie i ukreplenie RSDRP v gody stolypinskoi reaktsii. Moskva, 1969. pp. 193.

LENIN and revolution in the East; [by B. Gafurov and others]. Moscow, 1969. pp. 120.

LENIN... Ленин и международное рабочее движение. Москва, 1969. pp. 606.

LENIN... Ленин и московские большевики. Москва, 1969. pp. 543.

LENIN v vospominaniiakh revoliutsionerov Latvii. Riga, 1969. pp. 298.

LENIN... Ленин - вождь Октября. Москва, 1969. pp. 316.

LENINIZM... Ленинизм и экономические проблемы коммунистического строительства в СССР. Москва, 1969. pp. 285.

LENINS'KA... Ленінська теоретична спадщина в українській радянській історіографії. Київ, 1969. pp. 333.

LENINS'KE vchennia pro material'ni i moral'ni stymuly ta ioho zdiisnennia v period budivnytstva komunizmu. Kyïv, 1969. pp. 287.

LENINSKIE printsipy sotsialisticheskogo khoziaistvovaniia. Leningrad, 1969. pp. 204.

LENINSKOE... Ленинское учение о союзе рабочего класса с крестьянством. Москва, 1969. pp. 343.

LEONT'EV (LEV ABRAMOVICH) Ленинская теория империализма. Москва, 1969. pp. 549.

MAKAROVA (GALINA PETROVNA) Осуществление ленинской национальной политики в первые годы Советской власти, 1917-1920 гг. Москва, 1969. pp. 268.

MASLOV (NIKOLAI NIKOLAEVICH) Ленин как историк партии. 2nd ed. Ленинград, Лениздат, 1969. pp. 255. 16½см.

MATUSHKIN (PETR GEORGIEVICH) Lenin ob Urale. 2nd ed. Cheliabinsk, 1969. pp. 540.

MELESHCHENKO (IURII SERGEEVICH) and SHUKHARDIN (SEMEN VIKTOROVICH) Ленин и научно-технический прогресс. Ленинград, 1969. pp. 326. bibliog.

PANNEKOEK (ANTON) Lenin als Philosoph; herausgegeben von Alfred Schmidt. Frankfurt am Main, [1969]. pp. 140.

PIS'MA... Письма В. И. Ленину из-за рубежа. 2nd ed. Москва, 1969. pp. 468.

POSPELOV (PETR NIKOLAEVICH) ed. Ленин и Академия наук: сборник документов. Москва, 1969. pp. 341.

POTULOV (BORIS MIKHAILOVICH) В. И. Ленин и охрана здоровья советского народа. 3rd ed. Ленинград, 1969. pp. 537. bibliog.

PROTASENKO (ZOIA MIKHAILOVNA) Lenin kak istorik filosofii. Leningrad, 1969. pp. 108.

RAZVITIE... Развитие статистической науки в трудах В. И. Ленина. Москва, 1969. pp. 328.

RAZVITIE... Развитие В. И. Лениным экономической теории социализма и коммунизма. Москва, 1969. pp. 413.

ROL'... Роль В. И. Ленина в становлении и развитии советского законодательства. Москва, 1969. pp. 477.

ROMANOV (VALENTIN VIKTOROVICH) Борьба В. И. Ленина против антипартийной группы "демократического централизма". Москва, 1969. pp. 216.

ROZENTAL' (M. M.) ed. Ленин как философ. Москва, 1969. pp. 447.

RYBALKA (IVAN KLYMENT'EVYCH) В. І. Ленін і Україна. Харків, 1969. pp. 122. bibliog.

SAIDASHEVA (MUNIRA ABDULLOVNA) Ленин и социалистическое строительство в Татарии, 1918-1923. Москва, 1969. pp. 325.

SAVITSKAIA (RAISA MALAKHOVNA) Очерк государственной деятельности В. И. Ленина, март-июль 1918 г. Москва, 1969. pp. 434.

SHERSTOBITOV (VIKTOR PAVLOVICH) Ленин и крестьянство Советского Востока: на материале Киргизской ССР. Фрунзе, 1969. pp. 720.

SHIMODA (MIKIO) Lenin, his religion on socialism. [Tokyo, 1969]. pp. 11. (Reprinted from The Waseda Journal of Social Science, No. 6,7, 1969)

SIDEL'NIKOV (IVAN IVANOVICH) V. I. Lenin o zashchite sotsialisticheskogo otechestva. Moskva, 1969. pp. 106.

STERNIK (ISAAK BORISOVICH) В. И. Ленин - юрист: юридическая деятельность В. И. Ульянова (Ленина). Ташкент, 1969. pp. 269.

LENIN (VLADIMIR IL'ICH) (Cont'd.)

TORZHESTVO... Торжество ленінських філософських ідей на Україні. Київ, 1969. pp. 349.

TSEITLIN (ALEKSANDR GRIGOR'EVICH) Стиль Ленина - публициста. Москва, 1969. pp. 277.

V... В. И. Ленин и А. М. Горький. 3rd ed. Москва, 1969. pp. 630.

V. I. Lenin i filosofs'ki problemy suchasnosti. Kyïv, 1969. pp. 270.

V... В. І. Ленін і критика буржуазної ідеології. Київ, 1969. pp. 244.

V.I.Lenin i problemy naukovo-tekhnichnoï revoliutsiï. Kyïv, 1969. pp. 283. bibliog.

V... В. И. Ленин и русская общественно-политическая мысль XIX - начала XX в. Ленинград, 1969. pp. 399.

V... В. И. Ленин и советская внешняя политика. Москва, 1969. pp. 302.

V... В. И. Ленин и Советские Вооруженные Силы. 2nd ed. Москва, 1969. pp. 414.

V... В. И. Ленин о социалистическом государстве и праве. Москва, 1969. pp. 411.

V... В. И. Ленин об историческом опыте Великого Октября: сборник статей. Москва, 1969. pp. 473.

VALENTINOV (NIKOLAI VLADISLAVOVICH) pseud. [i.e. Nikolai Vladislavovich VOL'SKII] The early years of Lenin...; translated and edited by Rolf H.W. Theen, etc. Ann Arbor, [1969]. pp. 302.

VASILEVSKII (EFIM GRIGOR'EVICH) Развитие взглядов В. И. Ленина на империализм, 1898-1917 гг. Москва, 1969. pp. 211.

ZHVANIIA (GRIGORII KONDRAT'EVICH) V.I. Lenin, TsK partii i bol'sheviki Zakavkaz'ia. Tbilisi, 1969. pp. 273.

1970

ADAMO (HANS) Antileninismus in der BRD:... Tendenzen, Inhalt und Methoden der Leninfälschung in der Bundesrepublik, etc. Frankfurt/Main, [1970]. pp. 85.

ALEKSANDROV (V. S.) and LASHIN (A. G.) eds. Razvitie V. I. Leninym teorii nauchnogo kommunizma. Moskva, 1970. pp. 427.

ALEKSEEV (EGOR EGOROVICH) Po puti polnogo ukrepleniia vlasti samikh trudiashchikhsia: rol' V.I. Lenina v istoricheskikh sud'bakh narodov Iakutii. Iakutsk, 1970. pp. 273. bibliog.

ALEKSEEV (NIKOLAI SERGEEVICH) and LUKASHEVICH (VLADIMIR ZAKHAROVICH) Ленинские идеи в советском уголовном судопроизводстве: возбуждение уголовного дела и предварительное расследование. Ленинград, 1970. pp. 190.

ARAKELIAN (ARTASHES ARKAD'EVICH) V. I. Lenin i tekhnicheskii progress. Erevan, 1970. pp. 84.

ARISMENDI (RODNEY) Lenin, la revolucion y America Latina. Montevideo, [1970]. pp. 483.

BERCHENKO (ALEKSANDR IAKOVLEVICH) Leninskie printsipy sovetskogo prava. Moskva, 1970. pp. 255.

BIALIK (BORIS ARONOVICH) Vlastiteli dum i chuvstv V.I. Lenin i M. Gor'kii. Moskva, 1970. pp. 246.

BURLATSKII (FEDOR MIKHAILOVICH) Lenin, gosudarstvo, politika. Moskva, 1970. pp. 522. bibliog.

BUSLOV (KAZIMIR PAVLOVICH) ed. Problemy gumanizma v trudakh V.I.Lenina. Minsk, 1970. pp. 269. bibliog.

CHERNETSOVSKII (IURII MIKHAILOVICH) Lenin i bor'be protiv mezhdunarodnogo revizionizma. Leningrad, 1970. pp. 471.

COGNIOT (GEORGES) Présence de Lénine. Paris, [1970]. 2 vols. (in 1).

The CREATIVE force of the Leninist ideas. Bucharest, 1970. pp. 304. (Academia Republicii Socialiste România. Secţia di Ştiinţe Istorice, Filozofice şi Economico-Juridice. Bibliotheca Historica Romaniae. Studies. 31)

DEUTSCHER (ISAAC) Lenin's childhood. London, 1970. pp. 67.

DUBOVSKAIA (E.) and ELEKS (V.) V. I. Lenin i Latviia: v pomoshch' izuchaiushchim biografiiu V. I. Lenina v sisteme partiinogo i komsomol'skogo prosveshcheniia. Riga, 1970. pp. 180. bibliog.

ESAIASHVILI (V. G.) V. I. Lenin i Gruziia. Tbilisi, 1970. pp. 285.

FAIN (LEONID EFREMOVICH) Istoriia razrabotkii V.I.Leninym kooperativnogo plana. Moskva, 1970. pp. 332.

FOND dokumentov V. I. Lenina. Moskva, 1970. pp. 307.

GORODETSKII (EFIM NAUMOVICH) Ленин основоположник советской исторической науки: история советского общества в трудах В. И. Ленина. Москва, 1970. pp. 550. bibliog.

GRINISHIN (DANIL MAKSIMOVICH) O voennoi deiatel'nosti V.I. Lenina. Moskva, 1970. pp. 257. bibliog.

IAKUSHEVSKII (IGOR' TITOVICH) Leninizm i "sovetologiia": leninskii printsip edinstva teorii i praktiki i "sovetologiia". Leningrad, 1970. pp. 453. bibliog.

IDEI Lenina zhivut i pobezhdaiut. Leningrad, 1970. pp. 269.

INTERNATSIONAL'NA syla lenins'kykh idei: V.I. Lenin i revoliutsiinyi rukh u kraïnakh Tsentral'noï i Pivdenno-Skhidnoï Ievropy. Kyïv, 1970. pp. 519.

IOVCHUK (MIKHAIL TRIFONOVICH) Leninizm, filosofskie traditsii i sovremennost'. Moskva, 1970. pp. 334. bibliog.

IOVCHUK (MIKHAIL TRIFONOVICH) and MSHVENIERADZE (V. V.) eds. Leninizm i filosofskie problemy sovremennosti. Moskva, 1970. pp. 652.

IURCHENENKO (OLEKSANDR TIMOFIIOVYCH) В. І. Ленін і більшовицькі організації України. Київ, 1970. pp. 619.

IUROV (IURII MIKHAILOVICH) Podpisano Leninym. Moskva, 1970. pp. 254.

IVANOV (VSEVOLOD MIKHAILOVICH) and SHMELEV (ANATOLII NIKOLAEVICH) Leninizm i ideino-politicheskii razgrom trotskizma. Leningrad, 1970. pp. 503.

KARAKEEV (KURMAN-GALI KARAKEEVICH) and ALYSHBAEV (DZHUMAGUL ALYSHBAEVICH) V. I. Lenin i sotsialisticheskoe stroitel'stvo v Kirgizstane. Frunze, 1970. pp. 133.

KARPOV (GEORGII GEORGIEVICH) Ленин о культурной революции. Ленинград, 1970. pp. 405.

KIM (IL-SUNG) The great idea of Lenin on the national liberation struggle in colonies in the East is triumphing. Pyongyang, 1970. pp. 14. (Reprinted from Pravda, April 16, 1970)

KOMPANIIETS' (IVAN IVANOVYCH) Ленін та інтернаціональна єдність українських і російських трудящих у трьох революціях. Київ, 1970. pp. 229.

KOPNIN (PAVEL VASIL'EVICH) Dialektik, Logik, Erkenntnistheorie: Lenins philosophisches Denken; Erbe und Aktualität; [translated from the Russian]. Berlin, 1970. pp. 543. bibliog.

KORABLEV (IURII IVANOVICH) V.I. Lenin i sozdanie Krasnoi Armii. Moskva, 1970. pp. 461.

KOSTIN (ALEKSANDR FEDOROVICH) Ленин - создатель партии нового типа, 1894-1904 гг. Москва, 1970. pp. 366.

LENIN: istoriko-biograficheskii atlas. Moskva, 1970. pp. 66.

LENIN: Mensch, Denker, Revolutionär; [by F.D. Ryzhenko and others; translated from the Russian]. Schwerte/Ruhr, [1970]. pp. 335.

LENIN... Ленин и исторические судьбы Болгарского народа. Москва, 1970. pp. 246.

LENIN i latyshskaia revoliutsionnaia sotsial-demokratiia. Riga, 1970. pp. 161.

LENIN... Ленин и национально-освободительное движение в странах Востока. Москва, 1970. pp. 504.

LENIN i nauka Sovetskogo Kirgizstana. Frunze, 1970. pp. 391.

LENIN... Ленин и Польша: проблемы, контакты, отклики. Москва, 1970. pp. 418.

LENIN i trudiashchiesia Chuvashii: dokumenty, materialy, vospominaniia. Cheboksary, 1970. pp. 359. bibliog.

LENIN o trude i prave. Leningrad, 1970. pp. 178.

LENIN und die Wissenschaft:...Beiträge zum 100. Geburtstag von W.I. Lenin. Berlin, 1970. 2 vols.

LENIN v bor'be za revoliutsionnyi Internatsional. Moskva, 1970. pp. 672.

LENIN v "Pravde": vospominaniia. Moskva, 1970. pp. 350. bibliog.

LENINISM or social-imperialism?: in commemoration of the centenary of the birth of the great Lenin; by the editorial departments of Renmin Ribao, Hongqi and Jiefangjun Bao, April 22, 1970. Peking, 1970. pp. 65. bibliog.

LENINISMO e rivoluzione socialista; (risultato di ricerche e dibattiti svolti da una équipe del Centro Studi Marxisti di Roma). Bari, [1970]. pp. 284.

LENINIZM i aktual'ni problemy suchasnosti. L'viv, 1970. pp. 343.

LENINIZM... Ленинизм и диалектика общественного развития. Москва, 1970. pp. 444.

LENINIZM i sovremennye problemy istoriko-filosofskoi nauki. Moskva, 1970. pp. 619.

LENINIZM - velikoe znamia stroitelei kommunizma. Baku, 1970. pp. 334.

LENINS'KI pryntsypy sotsialistychnoho hospodariuvannia i ekonomichna reforma. Kyïv, 1970. pp. 210.

LENINSKIE... Ленинские идеи в изучении истории первобытного общества, рабовладения и феодализма: сборник статей. Москва, 1970. pp. 233.

LENINSKIE... Ленинские идеи живут и побеждают. Москва, 1970. pp. 894.

LENINSKII kooperativnyi plan i ego osushchestvlenie v Tatarii. Kazan' 1970. pp. 332.

LENINSKOE nasledie i izuchenie fol'klora. Leningrad, 1970. pp. 197. bibliog.

LENINSKOE... Ленинское учение о диктатуре пролетариата. Москва, 1970. pp. 255. bibliog.

LUKÁCS (GEORG) Marxist. Lenin: a study on the unity of his thought; (translated by Nicholas Jacobs); [with a postscript 1967 by the author]. London, 1970. pp. 104.

LUNIAKOV (PAVEL IVANOVICH) and GONCHAROV (ALEKSANDR DMITRIEVICH) Lenin and the peasantry. Moscow, [1970]. pp. 117.

LENIN (VLADIMIR IL'ICH) (Cont'd.)

MAKARENKO (IAKOV IVANOVICH) С Россией в сердце; В. И. Ленин в Польше в 1912-1914 годах. 2nd ed. Москва, 1970. pp. 253.

MAMALUI (ALEKSANDR PROKOF'EVICH) ed. Lenins'kyi etap u rozvytku politychnoï ekonomiï, Kharkiv, 1970. pp. 343.

MANUCHAR'IANTS (SHUSHANIKA NIKITICHNA) V biblioteke Vladimira Il'icha. 2nd ed. Moskva, 1970. pp. 114.

MEILAKH (BORIS SOLOMONOVICH) Lenin i problemy russkoi literatury XIX - nachala XX vv. 4th ed. Leningrad, 1970. pp. 493.

MIKHAILOV (NIKOLAI ALEKSANDROVICH) Ленин и мир книги. Москва, 1970. pp. 125.

MIKOIAN (ANASTAS IVANOVICH) Mysli i vospominaniia o Lenine. Moskva, 1970. pp. 238.

MNATSAKANIAN (ARAMAIS NAVASARDOVICH) Lenin i reshenie natsional'nogo voprosa v SSSR. Erevan, 1970. pp. 363.

MODRZHINSKAIA (ELENA DMITRIEVNA) Leninizm i sovremennaia ideologicheskaia bor'ba. Moskva, 1970. pp. 350.

MULTYKH (HEORHII MYNOVYCH) Lenins'ka teoriia sotsialistychnoï revoliutsiï i suchasnist'. Kyïv, 1970. pp. 112.

NAUMOV (KONSTANTIN VASIL'EVICH) Literaturnoe masterstvo Lenina - publitsista: ocherki i issledovaniia. L'vov, 1970. pp. 174.

NIKISHOV (SERAFIM IVANOVICH) ed. V.I.Lenin i aktual'nye problemy istoricheskogo materializma. Moskva, 1970. pp. 317.

POKROVSKII (SERGEI NIKOLAEVICH) Lenin i pobeda Sovetskoi vlasti v Kazakhstane. Alma-Ata, 1970. pp. 149.

POLIAKOV (VASILII FILATOVICH) Po puti progressa. Moskva, 1970. pp. 158.

RAZVITIE V.I. Leninym teorii nauchnogo kommunizma v period podgotovki i provedeniia Velikoi Oktiabr'skoi sotsialisticheskoi revoliutsii. Minsk, 1970. pp. 223.

ROTHSTEIN (ANDREW) Lenin in Britain. London, [1970]. pp. 31.

SAVENKOV (ALEKSEI ALEKSEEVICH) Prizyv - deistvie: V.I.Lenin ob organizatorskom znachenii propagandistskikh i agitatsionnykh vystuplenii. Leningrad, 1970. pp. 253.

SEN (SATYA BRATA) The relevance of Lenin's party theory: special emphasis being on the criticisms of tnis theory in American political science, history and sociology. Hamburg, 1970. pp. 210. bibliog. With German summary.

SHAPKO (VALERII MAKAROVICH) Begründung der Prinzipien der staatlichen Leitung durch W.I. Lenin. Berlin, 1970. pp. 331.

SHATAGIN (NIKOLAI IVANOVICH) ed. Развитие ленинского учения о партии: в послеоктябрьский период. Москва, 1970. pp. 214.

STEKLOV (VLADIMIR IUR'EVICH) V.I. Lenin i elektrifikatsiia. Moskva, 1970. pp. 343. bibliog.

STOLIARENKO (MIKHAIL ANDREEVICH) В. И. Ленин и революционные моряки: В. И. Ленин и работа партии большевиков в военно-морском флоте, 1903-1917 гг. Москва, 1970. pp. 143.

SVANIDZE (S.) V. I. Lenin o formirovanii kommunisticheskikh obshchestvennykh otnoshenii. Tbilisi, 1970. pp. 306.

SWEEZY (PAUL MARTOR) and MAGDOFF (HARRY) eds. Lenin today: eight essays on the hundredth anniversary of Lenin's birth. New York, [1970]. pp. 125.

TEORIIA, preobrazuiushchaia mir: v pomoshch' izuchaiushchim marksizm-leninizm. Minsk, 1970. pp. 331. bibliog.

V... В. И. Ленин и историческая наука. Ленинград, 1970. pp. 226.

V... В. И. Ленин и история классов и политических партий в России. Москва, 1970. pp. 518.

V. I. Lenin i Kommunisticheskii Internatsional. Moskva, 1970. pp. 561.

V.I. Lenin i mezhdunarodnoe kommunisticheskoe dvizhenie. Moskva, 1970. pp. 277.

V. I. Lenin i Novgorodskaia guberniia: dokumenty, materialy, vospominaniia. Leningrad, 1970. pp. 192.

V. I. Lenin i problemy filosofskikh nauk i nauchnogo kommunizma. Leningrad, 1970. pp. 163.

V... В. И. Ленин и проблемы истории: статьи и исследования. Ленинград, 1970. pp. 433.

V. I. Lenin i problemy pechati. Leningrad, 1970. pp. 180.

V. I. Lenin i problemy politicheskoi ekonomii sotsializma. Moskva, 1970. pp. 484.

V. I. Lenin i problemy stroitel'stva sotsializma. Leningrad, 1970. pp. 164.

V.I.Lenin i razvitie sotsialisticheskoi ekonomiki Kirgizii. Frunze, 1970. pp. 197.

V.I. Lenin i teoreticheskie osnovy stroitel'stva ko. Kazan', 1970. pp. 215.

V.I.Lenin i tyl Sovetskikh Vooruzhennykh Sil. Moskva, 1970. pp. 110.

V... В. І. Ленін і Український народ: збірник документів. Київ, 1970. pp. 980.

V.I.Lenin o nauchnykh osnovakh rukovodstva sotsialisticheskim obshchestvom. Moskva, 1970. pp. 398.

V... В. И. Ленин о социальной структуре и политическом строе капиталистической России. Москва, 1970. pp. 317.

V. I. Lenin - osnovopolozhnik politicheskoi ekonomii sotsializma. Kazan', 1970. pp. 253.

V. I. Lenin pro osvitu, navchannia i komunistychne vykhovannia. Kyïv, 1970. pp. 211. With brief Russian summaries.

V. I. Lenin pro rozvytok sotsialistychnoï ekonomiky. Kyïv, 1970. pp. 305.

V... В. И. Ленин в Октябре и в первые годы Советской власти. Ленинград, 1970. pp. 346.

V... В. И. Ленин - великий теоретик. 2nd ed. Москва, 1970. pp. 463.

VOLLRATH (ERNST) Lenin und der Staat: zum Begriff des Politischen bei Lenin. Wuppertal, [1970]. pp. 92.

VOPROSY filosofskogo naslediia V.I.Lenina. Moskva, 1970. pp. 212.

VOPROSY filosofskogo nasllediia V.I. Lenina. Riga, 1970. pp. 219. bibliog. (Latviiskii Gosudarstvennyi Universitet. Uchenye Zapiski. t.131)

VOPROSY istorii sovetskogo obshchestva v trudakh V.I.Lenina. Moskva, 1970. pp. 285.

VOSKRESENSKAIA (NINA ALEKSANDROVNA) V.I.Lenin - organizator sotsial'isticheskogo kontrolia. Moskva, 1970. pp. 322.

WORLD FEDERATION OF TRADE UNIONS. International trade union meeting on the occassion [sic] of the centenary memorial of the birth of V.I. Lenin, Ulyanovsk, April 16-17, 1970. [Prague], 1970. pp. 82.

ZAPADOV (ALEKSANDR VASIL'EVICH) Mysl' i slovo: iz nabliudenii nad literaturnoi rabotoi V.I.Lenina Moskva, 1970. pp. 357.

ZARODOV (KONSTANTIN IVANOVICH) Leninizm i sovremennye problemy bor'by za sotsializm. Moskva, 1970. pp. 400.

ZERNITSKII (MARK SOLOMONOVICH) Velikii master publitsistiki: iz opyta isskedovaniia vystuplenii V.I.Lenina v pechati v 1918-1920 gg. Minsk, 1970. pp. 249. bibliog.

ZHIZNENNAIA... Жизненная сила ленинских принципов партийного строительства. Москва, 1970. pp. 437.

ZIMANOV (SALYK ZIMANOVICH) V.I. Lenin i sovetskaia natsional'naia gosudarstvennost' v Kazakhstane. Alma-Ata, 1970. pp. 303.

1971

ALTHUSSER (LOUIS) Lenin and philosophy, and other essays; translated from the French by Ben Brewster. London, 1971. pp. 229.

AZOVTSEV (NIKOLAI NIKOLAEVICH) V. I. Lenin i sovetskaia voennaia nauka. Moskva, 1971. pp. 359. bibliog.

BALYCHEVA (GALINA DMITRIEVNA) Kritika V.I.Leninym "eticheskogo sotsializma" i ee znachenie dlia sovremennosti. Moskva, 1971. pp. 181.

BEREZHNOI (ALEKSANDR FEODOSEEVICH) Lenin - sozdatel' pechati novogo tipa, 1893-1914 gg. Leningrad, 1971. pp. 343.

ERMOLAEVA (ROZALIIA ALEKSANDROVNA) and MANUSEVICH (ALEKSANDR IAKOVLEVICH) Lenin i pol'skoe rabochee dvizhenie. Moskva, 1971. pp. 503.

ISTORIIA marksistskoi dialektiki: ot vozniknoveniia marksizma do leninskogo etapa. Moskva, 1971. pp. 536.

KHALIPOV (ALEKSEI SEMENOVICH) Bor'ba V.I.Lenina za vykhod iz partiinogo krizisa posle II s"ezda RSDRP. Minsk, 1971. pp. 170.

KOLESNIKOV (ANDREI KONSTANTINOVICH) Leninskie printsipy organizatsionnogo rukovodstva KPSS, oktiabr' 1917-1923 g. Moskva, 1971. pp. 332.

KORNEEVA (ANNA IVANOVNA) Leninskaia kritika makhizma i bor'ba protiv sovremennogo idealizma. Moskva, 1971. pp. 239.

KUZ'MINOV (IVAN IVANOVICH) and others, eds Ekonomicheskoe uchenie V.I. Lenina i sovremennost'. Moskva, 1971. pp. 319.

ROSMER (ALFRED) Lenin's Moscow; translated by Ian H. Birchall. London, 1971. pp. 253.

SLADKOVSKII (M.I.) and others, eds. Lenin i problemy sovremennogo Kitaia: sbornik statei. Moskva, 1971. pp. 286.

TROTSKII (LEV DAVYDOVICH) On Lenin: notes towards a biography;... translated and annotated by Tamara Deutscher, with an introduction by Lionel Kochan. London, 1971. pp. 204.

ZAZERSKII (EVGENII IAKOVLEVICH) and LIUBARSKII (ANATOLII VLADIMIROVICH) Lenin, emigratsiia, Peterburg. Leningrad, 1971. pp. 405. bibliog.

- Bibliography

BAHMUT (OSIP ANDRIANOVYCH) and SHMORHUN (PETRO) Твори В. І. Леніна на Україні: видання, розповсюдження і переклад. Київ, 1960. pp. 143.

V... В. И. Ленин и Сибирь: библиографический указатель. Томск, 1964. pp. 246. bibliog.

LEVIN (L.A.) Библиография произведений марксизма-ленинизма в СССР. in Вопросы библиографии общественно-политической литературы. Москва, 1967.

LENIN (VLADIMIR IL'ICH) - Bibliography (Cont'd.)

ALAGARDIAN (S. G.) and STEPANISHVILI (N. N.) compilers. V. I. Lenin o Zakavkaz'e: annotirovannaia bibliografiia. Tbilisi, 1969. pp. 197.

PAEGLIS (J.) and DRUVA (M.) compilers. K. Markss, F. Engelss, V. I. Ļeņins latviešu valoda: bibliografija; K. Marks, F. Ehgel's, V. I. Lenin na latyshskom iazyke: bibliografiia. Riga, 1969. pp. 361.

V. I. Lenin i sovetskoe zdravookhranenie: bibliograficheskii ukazatel'. Moskva, 1970. pp. 66.

MATVEEVA (T.Z.) and others, compilers. V.I. Lenin i Dal'nii Vostok: bibliograficheskii ukazatel'. Vladivostok, 1971. pp. 215.

- Bibliography - Statistics

RUSSIA (U.S.S.R.). Vsesoiuznaia Knizhnaia Palata. 1969. Ленин в печати: издание произведений В. И. Ленина, книг и брошюр о нем; статистический сборник. Москва, 1969. pp. 207.

LENINGRAD

LUNEV (VASILII STEPANOVICH) and SHILOV (VLADIMIR VASIL'EVICH) Невский район. Ленинград, Лениздат, 1966. pp. 166. bibliog. 20cm.

- Civic improvement

CATTELL (DAVID T.) Leningrad: a case study of Soviet urban government. New York, Praeger, [1968]. pp. xxiv, 171. bibliog. 23½cm. (Special Studies in International Politics and Public Affairs)

KAMENSKII (VALENTIN ALEKSANDROVICH) Город смотрит в завтра: генеральный план развития Ленинграда. Ленинград, 1968. pp. 344.

- Economic history

ISTORIIA rabochego klassa Leningrada. vyp.1, 2. Leningrad, 1962-63. 2 vols [in 1].

EZHOV (VIKTOR ANATOL'EVICH) Rabochie Leningrada v poslevoennye gody, 1946-1950. Leningrad, 1968. pp. 119. bibliog.

- Economic history - Sources

VOSSTANOVLENIE i nachalo rekonstruktsii promyshlennosti Leningrada, 1921-1928gg. dokumenty i materialy. t.1. Vosstanovlenie promyshlennosti Leningrada, 1921-1924 gg. Leningrad, 1963. pp. 452.

- History

BIBIKOV (IU. K.) and MALYSHKIN (V. F.) Возникновение и деятельность профсоюзов Петербурга, 1905-1907 годы. Москва, Профиздат, 1956. pp. 54. 20cm.

KHAIDAROV (G. KH.) Краткий очерк истории Ленинабада. Ленинабад, 1965. pp. 142.

BURDZHALOV (EDUARD NIKOLAEVICH) Вторая русская революция: восстание в Петрограде. Москва, Наука, 1967. pp. 407. 22cm.

- History - Sources

KOMMUNISTICHESKAIA PARTIIA SOVETSKOGO SOIUZA. Leningradskii Oblastnoi Komitet. Institut Istorii Partii. Листовки петроградских большевиков, 1917-1920. т.3. [Ленинград], Лениздат, 1957. pp. 472. 21½cm.

- History - Revolution, 1917-1921

OKTIABR'SKOE... Октябрьское вооруженное восстание в Петрограде: сборник статей. Ленинград, АН, 1957. pp. 444. 22cm.

POTEKHIN (MIKHAIL NIKOLAEVICH) Первый Совет пролетарской диктатуры: очерки по истории Петроградского Совета рабочих и солдатских депутатов, 1917-1918 гг. Ленинград, Лениздат, 1966. pp. 339. 20cm.

OKTIABR'SKOE... Октябрьское вооруженное восстание. Ленинград, Наука, 1967. 2 vols. 21cm.

KHAIDAROV (G. KH.) and MOROZOV (N. M.) Первые шаги Ходжентского Совета, март 1917 г. - февраль 1919 г. Душанбе, Ирфон, 1968. pp. 58. 20см.

FRAIMAN (ANTON L'VOVICH) Форпост социалистической революции: Петроград в первые месяцы Советской власти. Ленинград, 1969. pp. 395.

- History - Revolution, 1917-1921 - Personal narratives

KNIAZEV (S. P.) and KONSTANTINOV (A. P.) eds. Октябрьское вооруженное восстание в Петрограде. Ленинград, Лениздат, 1956. pp. 424. 19½cm.

GEROI... Герои Октября: биографии активных участников подготовки и проведения Октябрьского вооруженного восстания в Петрограде. Ленинград, 1967. 2 vols.

V... В огне революционных боев: районы Петрограда в двух революциях 1917 г.; сборник воспоминаний старых большевиков-питерцев. Москва, Мысль, 1967. pp. 583. 21см.

- History - Revolution, 1917-1921 - Sources

BASTIONY... Бастионы революции: сборник материалов из истории ленинградских заводов в 1917 году. Ленинград, Лениздат, 1957. pp. 824. 19½см.

- Industries

BURMISTROVA (V.A.) Промышленность Ленинграда в первый период Великой Отечественной войны, 1941-1942 гг. in Вопросы политической экономии. Москва, 1968.

VOSSTANOVLENIE i nachalo rekonstruktsii promyshlennosti Leningrada, 1921-1928gg. dokumenty i materialy. t.1. Vosstanovlenie promyshlennosti Leningrada, 1921-1924 gg. Leningrad, 1963. pp. 452.

KHIZHNIAK (PAVEL DENISOVICH) and BAKHANOVICH (ALEKSANDR IVANOVICH) Mekhanizatsiia i avtomatizatsiia na leningradskikh predpriiatiiakh: iz opyta raboty. Leningrad, 1964. pp. 172.

EKONOMICHESKAIA... Экономическая эффективность производства. Ленинград, Лениздат, 1966. pp. 180. 20cm.

LAVRIKOV (IURII ALEKSANDROVICH) and others. Очерк экономического развития ленинградской индустрии за 1917-1967 гг. Ленинград, Лениздат, 1968. pp. 392. 21½см.

- Politics and government

[TYSIACHA]... 1905 год в Петербурге. вып.1. Социал-демократические листовки. Ленинград, Госиздат, 1925. pp. xvi, 446. 23cm.

SPUSTEK (IRENA) Polacy w Piotrogrodzie, 1914-1917. Warszawa, Państwowe Wydawnictwo Naukowe, 1966. pp. 466. 19½cm.

STREL'TSINA (L. P.) and SHVEDOV (V. V.) Большевистская легальная печать Петербурга в годы первой революции в России, 1905-1907 гг. Ленинград, 1967. pp. 169. bibliog.

CATTELL (DAVID T.) Leningrad: a case study of Soviet urban government. New York, Praeger, [1968]. pp. xxiv, 171. bibliog. 23½cm. (Special Studies in International Politics and Public Affairs)

OCHERKI... Очерки истории Ленинградской организации ВЛКСМ. Ленинград, 1969. pp. 510.

- Siege, 1941-1944

MUSHNIKOV (A. N.) Балтийцы в боях за Ленинград, 1941-1944. Москва, Воениздат, 1955. pp. 207. 20cm.

KARASEV (A. V.) Ленинградцы в годы блокады 1941-1943. Москва, Академия Наук, 1959. pp. 315. 22см.

SOBOLEV (GENNADII LEONT'EVICH) Uchenye Leningrada v gody Velikoi Otechestvennoi voiny, 1941-1945. Moskva, 1966. pp. 172.

OBORONA... Оборона Ленинграда, 1941-1944: воспоминания и дневники участников; предисловие...М. В. Захарова. Ленинград, Наука, 1969. pp. 792. 21½см. (Вторая Мировая Война в Исследованиях, Воспоминаниях, Документах)

PAVLOV (DMITRII VASIL'EVICH) Ленинград в блокаде. Москва, 1969. pp. 268.

SALISBURY (HARRISON EVANS) The siege of Leningrad. London, Secker & Warburg, 1969. pp. xiii, 635. bibliog. 24cm.

NEPOKORENNYI Leningrad: kratkii ocherk istorii goroda v period Velikoi Otechestvennoi voiny. Leningrad, 1970. pp. 412.

INBER (VERA MIKHAILOVNA) Leningrad diary;...translated by Serge M. Wolff and Rachel Grieve. London, 1971. pp. 207.

- Social history

SEMANOV (SERGEI NIKOLAEVICH) Петербургские рабочие накануне первой русской революции. Москва, Наука, 1966. pp. 171. 21½см.

DELA... Дела и люди Ленинградской милиции: очерки истории. Ленинград, Лениздат, 1967. pp. 376. 20cm.

- Statistics

LENINGRAD. Statisticheskoe Upravlenie and LENINGRAD (OBLAST'). Statisticheskoe Upravlenie. Ленинград и Ленинградская область в цифрах: статистический сборник. Лениздат, 1964. pp. 251. 14см.

LENINGRAD. Statisticheskoe Upravlenie. Ленинград за 50 лет: статистический сборник. Ленинград, Лениздат, 1967. pp. 175. 21½см.

LENINGRAD (OBLAST')

- Economic conditions

SEVERO-ZAPADNYI... Северо-Западный экономический район. Москва, Наука, 1967. pp. 302. 21см. (Академия Наук СССР. Совет по Изучению Производительных Сил. Развитие и Размещение Производительных Сил СССР)

- Industries

TIUL'PANOV (S. I.) ed. Завершение восстановления промышленности и начало индустриализации Северо-Западного района, 1925-1928 гг. Ленинград, 1964. pp. xxiv, 394. 26cm. (История Индустриализации СССР: Документы и Материалы)

- Maps

ATLAS Leningradskoi oblasti. Moskva, 1967. pp. 82.

- Politics and government

OCHERKI... Очерки истории Ленинградской организации КПСС. ч.1. 1883-октябрь 1917 гг. Ленинград, Лениздат, 1962. pp. 608. 21см.

- Statistics

LENINGRAD (OBLAST'). Statisticheskoe Upravlenie. Ленинградская область за 50 лет: статистический сборник. Ленинград, Лениздат, 1967. pp. 184. 21½см.

LENINGRAD UNIVERSITY

KALININ (ANATOLII FROLOVICH) and MANDEL' (SEMEN ZAKHAROVICH) Ленин и Петербургский университет. Ленинград, 1969. pp. 269. bibliog.

LENINGRAD UNIVERSITY (Cont'd.)

KLUSHIN (VLADIMIR IVANOVICH) Bor'ba za istoricheskii materializm v Leningradskom gosudarstvennom universitete, 1918-1925 gody. Leningrad, 1970. pp. 114.

LENSHINA (ALICE)

ZAMBIA. 1965. Report of the commission of inquiry into the former Lumpa Church. Lusaka, 1965. pp. 36. 25½cm.

LENTHALL (WILLIAM)

LENTHALL (WILLIAM) A declaration...shewing the grounds and reasons which moved him to absent himselfe from attending the service of the House on Fryday the 30th of July, 1647. London, Whittington, 1647. pp. 7. 18½cm. Wing L 1071.

LEO VI, called the Philosopher, Emperor of the East

WOOD (DOROTHY) Leo VI's concept of divine monarchy: illustrated in a cave chapel. London, [1964]. pp. 64. bibliog. (Monarchist Press Association. Historical Series. No. 1)

LEONI (BRUNO)

OMAGGIO a Bruno Leoni. Milano, 1969. pp. 166. bibliog. (Politico, Il. Quaderni.n.7)

LEONTIEF (WASSILY W.)

BORCHERT (MANFRED) Das Heckscher-Ohlin Theorem und das Leontief Paradoxon. [Erlangen, imprint, 1967?]. pp. 141. bibliog.

LEOPOLD II, Emperor of Germany

WANGERMANN (ERNST) From Joseph II to the Jacobin trials: government policy and public opinion in the Habsburg dominions in the period of the French revolution. 2nd ed. London, 1969. pp. 218. bibliog.

LEOPOLD I, King of the Belgians

PAGE (JAMES) Queen Victoria and King Leopold I of the Belgians. London, [1966?]. fo. 4. (Monarchist Press Association. Occasional Papers)

ARONSON (THEO) The Coburgs of Belgium. London, Cassell, 1969. pp. xxviii, 323. bibliog.

LEOPOLD II, King of the Belgians

COLLINS (ROBERT O.) King Leopold, England, and the Upper Nile, 1899-1909. New Haven, Yale U.P., 1968. pp. xvii, 346. bibliog. 21½cm.

ARONSON (THEO) The Coburgs of Belgium. London, Cassell, 1969. pp. xxviii, 323. bibliog.

LEOPOLD III, King of the Belgians

BELGIUM. Secrétariat du Roi. 1946. Livre blanc, 1936-1946. I. Mémoire. [Brussels], 1946. pp. 508.

ARONSON (THEO) The Coburgs of Belgium. London, Cassell, 1969. pp. xxviii, 323. bibliog.

LEPCHAS

WEST BENGAL. 1962. The Lepchas of Darjeeling district; [by] Amal Kumar Das and Swapan Kumar Banerjee. (Bulletins of the Cultural Research Institute. Special Series. [vol. 1]. No.2) [Calcutta], 1962. pp. (vi), 168. bibliog. 22cm.

GORER (GEOFFREY) Himalayan village: an account of the Lepchas of Sikkim. 2nd ed. London, 1967. pp. 488.

LEPINI MOUNTAINS

- Economic conditions

CONVEGNO DEI SINDACI E DEI CONSIGLIERI COMUNALI DELLE COLLINE DEI LEPINI, 1°, 1962. [Proceedings]. Priverno, 1962. pp. 14. 21½cm.

- Social conditions

CONVEGNO DEI SINDACI E DEI CONSIGLIERI COMUNALI DELLE COLLINE DEI LEPINI, 1°, 1962. [Proceedings]. Priverno, 1962. pp. 14. 21½cm.

LE PLAY (PIERRE GUILLAUME FREDERIC)

BROOKE (MICHAEL Z.) Le Play: engineer and social scientist: the life and work of Frédéric Le Play. London, 1970. pp. 193. bibliog.

LEPROSY

BROWNE (STANLEY GEORGE) The changing pattern: (a general review of leprosy in the world today and the future role of the Leprosy Mission). London, [1966]. pp. 13.

FOLLEREAU (RAOUL) Love one another;...translated by Barbara Wall. London, Burns & Oates, 1968. pp. x, 270. 21½cm.

- Hospitals - India

ASKEW (ALBERT DENNIS) A sound of marching: (the story of the Purulia Leprosy Home and Hospital). London, Leprosy Mission, [1968]. pp. 66. 18½cm.

- Hospitals - New Guinea

BOCK (VALERIE) Ge hama. London, [1970]. pp. 67.

- Hospitals - South Africa

DE VILLIERS (SIMON A.) Robben Island: out of reach, out of mind; a history of Robben Island. Cape Town, 1971. pp. 169. bibliog.

- South Africa

SOUTH AFRICA. Department of the Interior. 1913. Report by the Government Research Bacteriologist (Leprosy) on the necessity or advisability of segregation in relation to the conditions and spread of leprosy in South Africa at the present time, etc. (U.G. 24/1913) in South Africa. Parliament. House of Assembly. Votes and proceedings; (with Printed annexures).

LES VERRIÈRES

- Social history

LOEW (FERNAND) Les Verrières: la vie rurale d'une communauté du Haut-Jura au moyen âge. Neuchâtel, Société d'Histoire et d'Archéologie [du Canton de Neuchâtel], 1954. pp. 398. bibliog 24cm. (Publications. Nouvelle Série. Tome 4)

LESBIANISM

BRITTAIN (VERA MARY) Radclyffe Hall: a case of obscenity? [London], Femina Books, 1968. pp. 186. 21½cm.

LESOTHO

- Appropriations and expenditures

SYMON (A.C.B.) Economic and financial report on the High Commission Territories. [London, H.M.S.O.], 1954. pp. 131. 24½cm.

- Bibliography

SYRACUSE UNIVERSITY. Maxwell Graduate School of Citizenship and Public Affairs. Program of Eastern African Studies. Occasional Bibliographies. No.9. A bibliography on Lesotho; compiled by John B. Webster [and] Paulus Mohome. Syracuse, N.Y., 1968. fo. 59.

- Census

LESOTHO. Census, 1966. 1966 population census report: [volume series]. Maseru, 1969 in progress.

- Constitution

LESOTHO. Constitutional Reform Committee. 1958. Report on constitutional reform and chieftainship affairs: [report of the Constitutional Reform Committee, George Berenge, chairman and the Chieftainship Committee, Mopeli Jonathan Molapo, chairman]. Maseru, 1958. pp. 130.

LESOTHO. Basutoland Constitutional Commission. 1963. Report: [W.P. Stanford, chairman]; (with U.K. Government statement and The High Commission Territories: a British Government statement). Maseru, 1963. 3 pts.

- Description and travel

SMIT (P.) Lesotho: a geographical study. Pretoria, Africa Institute, 1967. pp. (iv), 44. 26½cm. (Communications. No. 6)

- Economic conditions

SYMON (A.C.B.) Economic and financial report on the High Commission Territories. [London, H.M.S.O.], 1954. pp. 131. 24½cm.

LEISTNER (G.M.E.) Lesotho: economic structure and growth. Pretoria, Africa Institute, 1966. pp. (iv), 56. bibliog. 26cm. (Communications. No. 5)

SMIT (P.) Lesotho: a geographical study. Pretoria, Africa Institute, 1967. pp. (iv), 44. 26½cm. (Communications. No. 6)

- Economic policy

LESOTHO. Central Planning and Development Office. 1970. Lesotho first five-year development plan, 1970/71-1974/75. Maseru, 1970. pp. 262, 5 maps.

- Foreign relations - South Africa

GLASS (HAROLD M.) South African policy towards Basutoland. Johannesburg, 1966. pp. 36. bibliog.

- History

BECKER (PETER) of Johannesburg. Hill of destiny: the life and times of Moshesh, founder of the Basotho. London, 1969. pp. 294. bibliog.

- Industries

LESOTHO. Bureau of Statistics. Census of production. a., 1966 [2nd]- Maseru.

- Politics and government

SPARKS (ALLISTER) Lesotho, Botswana, Swaziland: the implications of independence. Port Elizabeth, 1967. pp. 12.

VAN WYK (A. J.) Lesotho: a political study. Pretoria, 1967. pp. (iv), 61, vii. bibliog. (Africa Institute. Communications. No.7)

SPENCE (JOHN EDWARD) Lesotho: the politics of dependence. London, O.U.P., 1968. pp. (iv), 88. 20½cm.

- Rural conditions

WALLMAN (SANDRA SUZANNE) Take out hunger: two case studies of rural development in Basutoland. London, 1969. pp. 178. bibliog. (London. University. London School of Economics and Political Science. Monographs on Social Anthropology. No. 39)

- Social conditions

SYMON (A.C.B.) Economic and financial report on the High Commission Territories. [London, H.M.S.O.], 1954. pp. 131. 24½cm.

- Social policy

LESOTHO. Central Planning and Development Office. 1970. Lesotho first five-year development plan, 1970/71-1974/75. Maseru, 1970. pp. 262, 5 maps.

- Statistics

LESOTHO. Bureau of Statistics. Annual statistical bulletin. Maseru, annual, 1963/1964 [1st] to date. 32cm.

GERMANY (BUNDESREPUBLIK). Statistisches Bundesamt. Länderkurzberichte: Lesotho. irreg., 1971 [1st issue]- Wiesbaden.

LESSEPS (FERDINAND MARIE DE)

PUDNEY (JOHN) Suez: De Lesseps' canal. London, Dent, 1968. pp. xiv, 242. 21½cm.

LETTERS OF CREDIT

- India

MITRA (B.C.) The law relating to bankers' letters of credit. Allahabad, Indian P., 1964. pp. xvi, 274. 23½cm.

- United Kingdom

GUTTERIDGE (HAROLD COOKE) and MEGRAH (MAURICE HENRY) The law of bankers' commercial credits. 4th ed. London, Europa, 1968. pp. xxiii, 262. bibliog. 24½cm.

LEVASSEUR (ÉMILE)

CLAVAL (PAUL) and NARDY (JEAN PIERRE) Pour le cinquantenaire de la mort de Paul Vidal de la Blache: études d'histoire de la géographie. Paris, Les Belles Lettres, 1968. pp. 130. 24cm. (Besançon. Université. Cahiers de Géographie de Besançon. No. 16)

LEVELLER MUTINY, 1649

SEA-green and blue, see which speaks true; or, Reason contending with treason in discussing the late unhappy difference in the army, which now men dream is well composed; wherein also is weighed, the testimony of one lately risen from the dead, concerning the levellers, etc. [London], 1649. pp. (18). 19cm. Wing S 2169.

WOOD (JOHN) Leveller, and others. The levellers (falsly so called) vindicated; or, The case of the twelve troops (which by treachery in a treaty) was lately surprised, and defeated at Burford, truly stated...; by a faithful remnant, late of Col. Scroops, Commissary General Iretons, and Col. Harrisons regiments, etc. [London, 1649] pp. 12. 19cm. Wing L 1900 A.

LEVELLERS

The FREE mans plea for freedom, against the arbitrarie unwarrantable actions and proceedings of the apostate associates, commonly called by others, Levellers...; by R.L., a member of the army. London, White, 1648. pp. 13 19cm. Wing L 54.

A REPLY to the House of Commons, or rather to an impostor, giving answer in their names to the Londoners petition, presented to the said Honourable House, Sept. 11, 1648. London, Larnar, 1648. pp. 13. 17½cm.

UNITED KINGDOM. Parliament. House of Commons. 1648. A declaration of some proceedings of Lt. Col. John Lilburn, and his associates; with some examination, and animadversion upon papers lately printed, and scattered abroad, one called The earnest petition of many free-born people of this kingdome; another, The mournfull cries of many thousand poor tradesmen, etc. London, Harward, 1648. pp. 62. 18½cm.

COLLINS (CHARLES) Apprentice, and others. An outcry of the youngmen and apprentices of London; or, An inquisition after the lost fundamentall lawes and liberties of England...: [ascribed to John Lilburne]. [London, 1649] pp. 12. 19cm. Wing L 2152.

FRESE (JAMES) The levellers vindication; or, A tragicall story, presented unto this commonwealth, city, and army; together with a letter directed to His Excellency, and the Councell of Warre...concerning the great cruelty and oppression still continued in this land, etc. London, Lindsey, [1649]. pp. 8. 19cm. Wing F 2197 B.

LILBURNE (JOHN) and others. Englands new chains discovered; or, The serious apprehensions of a part of the people, in behalf of the commonwealth; (being presenters, promoters, and approvers of the large petition of September 11. 1648), etc. [London, 1649] pp. (15). 19cm. Wing L 2106.

LILBURNE (JOHN) and others. The picture of the Councel of State, held forth to the free people of England by Lieut. Col. John Lilburne [and others]...or, A full narrative of the late extrajudicial and military proceedings against them, etc. [London], 1649. pp. 54. 18½cm. Wing L 2154.

LILBURNE (JOHN) and others. The second part of Englands new-chaines discovered; or, A sad representation of the uncertain and dangerous condition of the common-wealth; directed to the supreme authority of England, the representors of the people in Parliament assembled, etc. London, 1649. pp. 18. 19cm. Wing L 2181.

LONDON. Apprentices. The thankfull acknowledgment and congratulation of divers well-affected apprentices within the ward of Cripplegate without, unto...Lieutenant Colonel John Lilburn, Mr. William Walwyn, [and others]...now prisoners in the Tower of London, etc. [London, 1649] single sheet. 29cm. Wing T 835.

OVERTON (RICHARD) Defyance of the act of pardon; or, The copy of a letter to the citizens usually meeting at the Whale-Bone in Lothbury behinde the Royal Exchange; and others commonly (though unjustly) styled levellers. London, 1649. pp. 8. 19cm. Wing O 627.

PRINCE (THOMAS) The silken independents snare broken;...turning the mischief intended upon him, in Walwyns Wyles, upon the seven independent authors thereof, viz. William Kiffin [and others] London, W.L[arner], 1649. pp. 10. 19cm. Wing P 3479.

The REMONSTRANCE of many thousands of the free-people of England; together with the resolves of the yong-men [sic] and apprentices of the city of London, in behalf of themselves, and those called levellers, for the attainment of their just requests in their petition of May 20. 1647, etc. London, 1649. pp. 8. 18½cm. Wing R 995.

THOMPSON (WILLIAM) Member of an Association formed to resist the tyranny of the Army, etc. Englands standard advanced; or, A declaration from M.Will. Thompson and the oppressed people of this nation, now under his conduct in Oxfordshire, dated at their randezvous, May 6. 1649. [London, 1649] pp. 3. 19cm. Wing T 1017

WARD (ROBERT) Soldier, and others. The hunting of the foxes from New-market and Triploe-heaths to White-hall, by five small beagles (late of the armie); or, The grandie-deceivers unmasked (that you may know them)...; [variously ascribed to John Lilburne, Richard Overton and William Walwyn]. [London], 1649. pp. 1-14, 17-28. 18½cm. Wing L 2115.

WINSTANLEY (GERARD) A letter to the Lord Fairfax and his councell of war; proving it an undeniable equity, that the common people ought to dig, plow, plant and dwell upon the commons, without hiring them, or paying rent to any; delivered to the Generall...on Saturday, June 9 [1649]. London, Calvert, 1649. pp. 13. 17½cm. Wing W 3046.

DAVIDSON (JOHN MORRISON) The wisdom of Winstanley the Digger: being outlines of the Kingdom of God on earth. London, 1904. pp. 43.

MORTON (ARTHUR LESLIE) Leveller democracy: fact or myth? London, 1968. pp. 22. (Communist Party of Great Britain. Historians' Group. Our History. No. 51)

MORTON (ARTHUR LESLIE) The world of the Ranters: religious radicalism in the English revolution. London, 1970. pp. 224. bibliog.

LEVERKUSEN

- Civic improvement

PRIVATINITIATIVE im Städtebau: Modellfall Leverkusen; (ein Pressegespräch am 15. Oktober. 1969) mit Dr. Carl Schaetzle [and others]. Bonn, [1970]. pp. 26. (Deutscher Verband für Wohnungswesen, Städtebau und Raumplanung. Kleine Schriften. 21)

LEVI (PAUL)

BERADT (CHARLOTTE) Paul Levi: ein demokratischer Sozialist in der Weimarer Republik. Frankfurt a. M., [1969]. pp. 155. bibliog.

LEVI (PAUL) Zwischen Spartakus und Sozialdemokratie: Schriften, Aufsätze, Reden und Briefe; herausgegeben und eingeleitet von Charlotte Beradt. Frankfurt am Main, [1969]. pp. 335.

LÉVI-STRAUSS (CLAUDE)

POUILLON (J.) L'oeuvre de Claude Lévi-Strauss; [originally published in 1961]. in Lévi-Strauss (Claude) Race et histoire. [Paris, 1968].

MOORE (TIM) Claude Lévi-Strauss and the cultural sciences. Birmingham, [1968]. pp. 50. bibliog. (Birmingham. University. Centre for Contemporary Cultural Studies. Occasional Papers. No.4)

SIMONIS (YVAN) Claude Lévi-Strauss;ou,La "passion de l'inceste"; introduction au structuralisme. Paris, Aubier Montaigne, [1968]. pp. 380. bibliog. 20cm. (Collection Recherches Économiques et Sociales. 8)

HAYES (E. NELSON) and HAYES (TANYA) eds. Claude Lévi-Strauss: the anthropologist as hero. Cambridge, Mass., [1970]. pp. 264. bibliog.

LEACH (EDMUND RONALD) Lévi-Strauss. London, 1970. pp. 126. bibliog.

PAZ (OCTAVIO) Claude Lévi-Strauss: an introduction; translated from the Spanish by J.S. Bernstein and Maxine Bernstein. Ithaca, 1970. pp. 159. bibliog.

LEVSKI (VASIL)

KIRCHEV (M. I.) Левски: човекът на делото; етюд от М. И. Кирчев. София, 1928. pp. 18.

BAKALOV (GEORGI) Нашите революционери: Раковски. Левски, Ботев. София, Нов Път, 1924. pp. 72. 20cm.

LEWANIKA (LUBOSI)

CLAY (GERVAS) Your friend, Lewanika: the life and times of Lubosi Lewanika, Litunga of Barotseland, 1842 to 1916. London, Chatto & Windus, 1968. pp. xvi, 192. bibliog. 23½cm. (Robins Series. No. 7)

LEWIN (KURT)

KAUFMANN (PIERRE) Kurt Lewin: une théorie du champ dans les sciences de l'homme. Paris, Vrin, 1968. pp. 382. bibliog. 22½cm. (Sciences de l'Homme)

MAILHIOT (GÉRALD BERNARD) Dynamique et genèse des groupes: actualité des découvertes de Kurt Lewin. Paris, Épi, [1968]. pp. 275. bibliog. 20cm.

LEWIS (CLARENCE IRVING)

LEWIS (CLARENCE IRVING) Collected papers of Clarence Irving Lewis; edited by John D. Goheen and John L. Mothershead. Stanford, California, 1970. pp. 444.

LEWIS (EARL RUPERT)

LEWIS (EARL RUPERT) The whites and the coloureds: London, [1963]. pp. 13. 21½cm.

LEWIS (SINCLAIR)

SILHOL (ROBERT) Les tyrans tragiques: un témoin pathétique de notre temps, Sinclair Lewis. Paris, 1969. pp. 443. (Paris. Université. Faculté des Lettres et Sciences Humaines. Publications. Série Recherches. Tome 51)

LEWISHAM

- Civic improvement

LEWISHAM. Borough Council. Planning and Development Committee. Lewisham central area: an interim report illustrating the long term concept for the centre, prepared by Stephen P. Byrne. [London], 1970. pp. 50.

LEWSEY (ERNEST W. WALTON)
See WALTON-LEWSEY (ERNEST W.)

LEXICOGRAPHY

HALLIG (RUDOLF) and WARTBURG (WALTHER VON) Begriffssystem als Grundlage für die Lexikographie: Versuch eines Ordnungsschemas, etc. 2nd ed. Berlin, Akademie-Verlag, 1963. pp. 316. bibliog. 24cm. (Deutsche Akademie der Wissenschaft zu Berlin. Institut für Romanische Sprachwissenschaft. Veröffentlichungen. Nr.19) With French and German preface and introduction.

HOUSEHOLDER (FRED W.) and SAPORTA (SOL) eds. Problems in lexicography; (report of the conference on lexicography held at Indiana University, November 11-12, 1960). 2nd ed. Bloomington, Indiana U., 1967. pp. viii, 286. 25cm. (Indiana University. Research Center in Anthropology, Folklore, and Linguistics. Publications. 21)

LEXICOGRAPHY (Cont'd.)

HOGBEN (LANCELOT THOMAS) The vocabulary of science;... with the assistance of Maureen Cartwright. London, 1969. pp. 184.

LEXINGTON, KENTUCKY

- Growth

BAHL (ROY W.) A bluegrass leapfrog. Lexington, University of Kentucky, College of Commerce, Bureau of Business Research, 1963. pp. iv, 27. 28cm.

LEZGHIANS

IKHILOV (MIKHAIL MATATOVICH) Народности лезгинской группы: этнографическое исследование прошлого и настоящего лезгин, табасаранцев, рутулов, цахуров, агулов. Махачкала, 1967. pp. 367.

LIABILITY FOR ANIMALS

- United Kingdom

U.K. Law Commission. [Publications]. No. 23. Civil liability for animals. London, 1967. pp. 50. 24½cm.

LIABILITY FOR MARINE ACCIDENTS

KROEGER (BERND.) Haftungsprobleme im Übersee-Container-Verkehr: Vortrag. Hamburg, 1967. pp. 15. (Deutscher Verein für Internationales Seerecht. Schriften. Reihe A: Berichte und Vorträge. Heft 11)

RAMBERG (JAN) Unsafe ports and berths: a comparative study of the charterer's liability in Anglo-American and Scandinavian law. Oslo, 1967. pp. 126. bibliog.

LIABILITY FOR NUCLEAR DAMAGES

EUROPEAN NUCLEAR ENERGY AGENCY. 1964. Convention on third party liability in the field of nuclear energy, 29th July 1960. (Text incorporating the provisions of the Additional Protocol...signed in Paris on 28th January 1964). In English and French. Paris, 1964. pp. 73.

LIABILITY FOR ROAD ACCIDENTS

- New Zealand

SZAKATS (ALEXANDER) Compensation for road accidents: a study on the question of a, absolute liability and social insurance. Wellington, Sweet & Maxwell, 1968. pp. ix, 173. bibliog. 21½cm.

LIBEL AND SLANDER

STARKIE (THOMAS) Traité sur la répression de la licence dans les écrits, les emblêmes et les paroles: extrait de l'anglais par L. Hubert. Paris, Rondonneau, 1817. pp. xxxii, 323. 21cm.

LLOYD (HERBERT) The legal limits of journalism. Oxford, Pergamon P., 1968. pp. xviii, 121. bibliog. 21cm. (Library of Industrial and Commercial Education and Training)

- Europe, Eastern

FRANCE. Direction de la Documentation. La Documentation Française. Notes et Études Documentaires. No. 3,332. Le droit de la presse et le statut juridique de publication dans les pays socialiates européens; [by] Georges Henri Mond. Paris, 1966. pp. 42. 30½cm.

- United Kingdom

FOOTE (GEORGE WILLIAM) ed. The Hall of Science libel case: with a full and true account of 'The Leeds Orgies'. London, Forder, [1895]. pp. 58. 17½cm.

COURTNEY (ANTHONY TOSSWILL) Sailor in a Russian frame. London, 1968. pp. 256.

- United Kingdom - Cases

HYDE (HARFORD MONTGOMERY) Their good names: twelve cases of libel and slander, with some introductory reflections on the law. London, 1970. pp. 406. bibliog.

- United States

COOPER (THOMAS) M.D., one of the judges of the Supreme Court, Pennsylvania. A treatise on the law of libel and the liberty of the press;...[originally published in 1830]. New York, 1970. pp. 184.

LIBERAL DEMOCRATIC PARTY (JAPAN)

FUKUI (HARUHIRO) Party in power: the Japanese Liberal-Democrats and policy-making. Canberra, 1970. pp. 301. bibliog.

LIBERAL-DEMOKRATISCHE PARTEI DEUTSCHLANDS

LIBERAL-DEMOKRATISCHE PARTEI DEUTSCHLANDS. Zentralvorstand. Thesen zur Geschichte der Liberal-Demokratischen Partei Deutschlands. Berlin, [1965]. pp. 123. (Liberal-Demokratische Partei Deutschlands. Schriften. Heft 1)

DIECKMANN (JOHANNES) Johannes Dieckmann: aus seinen Leben und Wirken. Berlin, Der Morgen, [1968] pp. 394. bibliog. 19cm.

LIBERAL FEDERATION OF CANADA

LIBERAL FEDERATION OF CANADA. Constitution. [Ottawa], 1966. pp. irreg. In English and French.

LIBERAL PARTY

- Australia

SMITH (Hon. BRUCE) K.C. Some thoughts in regard to an anti-socialist - "liberal" - programme for the Australian Federal Parliament, etc. [Sydney, 1908]. pp. 11. 21½cm.

WEST (KATHARINE) The Australian Liberal Party. Croydon, Victoria, 1968. pp. 48. bibliog.

- Canada

The GUELPH papers: [based on the Liberal caucus policy conference at Guelph University, in 1969]; edited by Robert F. Nixon. Toronto, [1970]. pp. 149.

- Colombia

FUENTES (MILTON) Historia del Partido Liberal Colombiano. 2nd ed. Bogota, 1961. pp. 665.

- Denmark

HVIDT (KRISTIAN) Venstre og forsvarssagen, 1870-1901. 2nd ed. Aarhus, 1971. pp. 220. bibliog. (Jysk Selskab for Historie. Skrifter. 7)

- Germany

NATIONALLIBERALE PARTEI DEUTSCHLANDS. Centralbureau. Taschenbuch für Nationalliberale Wähler; abgeschlossen Oktober 1911. Berlin, 1911. pp. 312.

DEUTSCHER Liberalismus im Zeitalter Bismarcks: ein politische Briefsammlung; Neudruck der Ausgabe 1925-(1926). Osnabrück, Biblio, 1967. 2 vols. 23cm. (Bayerische Akademie der Wissenschaften. Historische Kommission. Deutsche Geschichtsquellen des 19. Jahrhunderts. Bände 18, 24)

- Italy

PARTITO LIBERALE ITALIANO. L'azione politica e legislativa del PLI, 1963-1965. [Rome, the Partito, 1966?] pp. 341. 21cm.

PARTITO LIBERALE ITALIANO. Congresso Nazionale, 10°, 1966. [Proceedings]. [Rome, the Partito, 1967?] 2 vols. (in 1). 21cm.

- South Africa

LIBERAL PARTY OF SOUTH AFRICA. Blueprint for the future: the Liberal Party plans a new South Africa. [Pietermaritzburg, c.1960]. pp. 8. 22cm.

LIBERAL PARTY OF SOUTH AFRICA. How much time have we left, etc.? Pietermaritzburg, [1957?]. 1 pamphlet (unpaged).

- United Kingdom

REPORT of the public reception, and the speeches delivered at the dinner to Lord Durham, on Wednesday, 29th October, 1834; taken in short hand by Simon McGregor. Glasgow, McPhun, 1834. pp. 33.

REPORT of the speeches at the dinner to Earl Grey, on Monday, 15th September, 1834; taken in short hand by Simon McGregor. Edinburgh, Hamilton, 1834. pp. 39.

[MACCOLL (MALCOLM)] Is Liberal policy a failure?; by Expertus [pseud.] London, 1870. pp. 53.

CONFERENCE ON PARLIAMENTARY REFORM, LEEDS, 1883. List of representatives. n.p. [1883]. pp. 30.

FREMANTLE (WILLIAM HENRY) Christianity and liberal politics;...being an address delivered as President of the Liberal Association, Canterbury...1885, etc. [London], 1885. pp. 32.

MARTIN-LEAKE (MARY) The organisation and work of women's liberal associations. London, [19--]. pp. 12. 21½cm.

REES (J. AUBREY) "Our aims and objects". London, [19--?]. pp. 8. (National League of Young Liberals. Young Liberal Pamphlets. No. 1)

LEAGUE OF LIBERALS AGAINST AGGRESSION AND MILITARISM. Pamphlets. No. 11. Liberals and organisation: the part of the individual Liberal. London, [1902]. pp. 8.

ASQUITH (HERBERT HENRY) Earl of Oxford and Asquith. The three capital issues: a speech delivered...December 10th, 1909. London, Liberal Publication Department, 1910. pp. 12. 21½cm.

MANCHESTER. Liberal Federation. Draft of the liberal programme of the...Federation. Manchester, [1918?]. pp. 4.

GREY (EDWARD) 1st Viscount Grey of Fallodon. Liberal policy; a speech... December 13th, 1926. [London, 1927?]. pp. 12.

LIBERAL PUBLICATION DEPARTMENT. Liberalism: what it is, what it has done, what it will do. London, 1927. pp. 16.

GREY (EDWARD) 1st Viscount Grey of Fallodon, and SAMUEL (HERBERT LOUIS) 1st Viscount Samuel. The duty of a liberal party in support of a national government: speeches delivered...on the occasion of a dinner...1931. London, [1931?]. pp. 16.

NATIONAL LEAGUE OF YOUNG LIBERALS and UNION OF LIBERAL STUDENTS. Joint Political Committee. New orbits: a draft to be presented at the Operation Manifesto Congress, Manchester, 18th and 19th April, 1959. London, 1959. pp. 70.

LIBERAL PARTY ORGANISATION. Liberal Special Assembly: agenda, Central Hall, Westminster, 4th and 5th September 1964. London, [1964]. pp. 12.

ITIAEVA (L.I.) "Agrarnaia kampaniia" liberalov 1913 goda v Anglii. in Mordovskii Gosudarstvennyi Universitet. Uchenye Zapiski. No.51. Seriia Istoricheskikh Nauk. vyp.1. Saransk, 1965.

CRATON (MICHAEL) and McCREADY (H. W.) The great Liberal revival, 1903-6. London, [1966]. pp. 47. bibliog.

MAHER (TERRY) and others. Effective politics. [London, 1966]. pp. 21.

YOUNG LIBERAL MOVEMENT. Red Guard. [Manchester, 1966?]. pp. 4.

THORPE (JEREMY) The Liberal crusade, people count: the Liberal plan for power. London, [1967]. pp. 36.

BANKS (DESMOND) Why Britain suffers! London, Liberal Publication Department, [1968]. pp. 19. 21½cm.

BUTLER (JEFFREY ERNEST) The Liberal Party and the Jameson raid. Oxford, Clarendon P., 1968. pp. xii, 336. bibliog. 21½cm.

ROWLAND (PETER) The last Liberal governments: the promised land, 1905-1910. London, Barrie & Rockliff, 1968. pp. xviii, 404. 22½cm.

LIBERAL PARTY - United Kingdom (Cont'd.)

EMY (HUGH VINCENT) The Liberal party and the social problem, 1892-1914; [Ph.D. (London) thesis]. 1969. fo. vii, 617. bibliog. 25½cm. Typescript: unpublished. This thesis is the property of London University and may not be removed from the Library.

LIBERAL COMMISSION. Liberals look ahead: report. London, [1969]. pp. 81.

LIBERAL PARTY. The constitution of the Liberal Party. Rev. ed. London, 1969. pp. 23.

SCOTT (CHRISTOPHER) The Liberals, the Common Market, and the S.N.P. n.p., [1970]. pp. 15.

VINOGRADOV (K.B.) Эволюция английской либеральной партии в свете трудов В.И. Ленина. in В.И. Ленин и историческая наука. Ленинград, 1970.

CLARKE (P.F.) Lancashire and the new Liberalism. Cambridge, 1971. pp. 472. bibliog.

DOUGLAS (ROY) The history of the Liberal Party, 1895-1970. London, 1971. pp. 331. bibliog.

- United Kingdom - Year-books

POLITICAL WORLD YEAR BOOK AND STATESMAN'S ENCYCLOPEDIA, THE. a., 1887-1889 [1st-3rd issues]; ceased pbln. London. 1887-1888 as The Liberal and radical year book and statesman's encyclopedia.

- United Kingdom - Scotland

[SCOTTISH LIBERAL PARTY]. Scottish Liberals today. Edinburgh, [imprint], [1971]. pp. 25.

LIBERALISM

[VIEUSSEUX (ANDRE)] Essay on liberalism; being an examination of the nature and tendency of the liberal opinions; with a view of the state of parties on the continent of Europe; by the author of "Italy and the Italians in the nineteenth century." London, Pewtress, 1823. pp.xii,238. 21cm. Manuscript leaf criticizing "this pretended Essay on liberalism" is bound with the end-papers and appears to be signed "J.S.M.", but is not in J.S. Mill's handwriting.

DONOSO CORTÉS (JUAN FRANCISCO MANUEL MARIA DE LA SALUD) Marquis de Valdegamas. Essai sur le catholicisme, le libéralisme et le socialisme. Liége, Lardinois, 1851. pp. vii, 5-256. 19½cm. (Bibliothèque Historique, Philosophique et Littéraire. 8e année. 1er ouvrage)

DONOSO CORTÉS (JUAN FRANCISCO MANUEL MARIA DE LA SALUD) Marquis de Valdegamas. Saggio sul cattolicismo liberalismo, e socialismo;...prima traduzione italiana. Fuligno, [imprint], 1852. pp. 416. 20cm.

FIORENTINO (FRANCESCO) Lo stato moderno e le polemiche liberali, etc. Roma, Alberti, 1924. pp. 72. 19½cm. (Studi Politici. 1)

BERGER-PERRIN (R.) ed. Vitalité libérale: physionomie et avenir du libéralisme renaissant. Paris, SEDIF, 1953. pp. 93. 20cm.

PAUCK (WILHELM) The heritage of the reformation; [reprint of the work originally published 1961]. rev. ed. London, O.U.P., 1968. pp. xi, 399. 20½cm.

COATES (WILLSON HAVELOCK) and others. The emergence of liberal humanism: an intellectual history of Western Europe, vol. 1: from the Italian renaissance to the French revolution. New York, [1966]. pp. x, 357.

BLACK (EUGENE CHARLTON) ed. European political history, 1815-1870: aspects of liberalism. New York, Harper & Row, 1967. pp. 253. 20cm. (Contemporary Essays Series)

BENAERTS (PIERRE) and others. Nationalité et nationalisme, 1860-1878. new ed. Paris, P.U.F., 1968. pp. 761. 21cm. (Peuples et Civilisations. Histoire Générale)

FRUMENTO (ARMANDO) Il liberalismo per una società guista e di sviluppo, etc. [Roma], Fondazione Luigi Einaudi per Studi di Politica Economica e per la Pubblicistica Relativa, 1968. pp. 31. 26cm.

PONTEIL (FÉLIX) L'éveil des nationalités et le mouvement libéral, 1815-1848. new ed. Paris, P.U.F., 1968. pp. viii, 786. 21cm. (Peuples et Civilisations. 15)

RODÓ (JOSÉ ENRIQUE) Ariel; Liberalismo y jacobinismo; Ensayos. Mexico, Porrua, 1968. pp. xlvi, 257. bibliog. 22cm. (Colección Sepan Cuantos. No. 87) Reprint of essays published between 1899 and 1913.

SELIGER (M.) The liberal politics of John Locke. London, Allen & Unwin, 1968. pp. 387. bibliog. 21½cm.

STRALEK (ARNOLD) Die politische Ordnungskonzeption des Neoliberalismus. [Cologne, 1968?]. pp. 204. bibliog.

STRAUSS (LEO) Liberalism: ancient and modern. New York, Basic Books, [1968]. pp. xi, 276. 23½cm.

BERTELÈ (ALDO) and CANTORE (ANTONIO) Liberalismo e socialismo. Firenze, 1969. pp. 380.

CUMMING (ROBERT DENOON) Human nature and history: a study of the development of liberal political thought. Chicago, 1969. 2 vols.

THORNTON (NEIL SYLVESTER) The problem of liberalism in the thought of John Stuart Mill; [Ph. D. (London) thesis]. [1969]. fo. 335. bibliog. 25½cm. Typescript: unpublished. This thesis is the property of London University and may not be removed from the Library.

COATES (WILLSON HAVELOCK) and WHITE (HAYDEN V.) The ordeal of liberal humanism: an intellectual history of western Europe, vol. 2: since the French Revolution. New York, [1970]. pp. 499. bibliog.

HOUGHTON (D. HOBART) Enlightened self-interest and the liberal spirit. Johannesburg, [1970]. pp. 17. (South African Institute of Race Relations. Hoernlé Memorial Lectures. 1970)

VACHET (ANDRE) L'idéologie libérale: l'individu et sa propriété. Paris, [1970]. pp. 567.

Das WAGNIS der Mündigkeit: Beiträge zum Selbstverständnis des Liberalismus; Festschrift für Paul Luchtenberg. Neustadt/Aisch, 1970. pp. 282.

LIBERALISM (RELIGION)

- Catholic Church

PRELOT (MARCEL) compiler. Le libéralisme catholique; textes choisis et présentés...avec la collaboration de Françoise Gallouédec Genuys. Paris, [1969]. pp. 479. bibliog.

LIBERALISM IN AUSTRIA

ELBOGERN (FRIEDRICH) Die neue Aera; ein Aufruf. Wien, the author, 1895. pp. 15. 21cm.

LIBERALISM IN AUSTRIA-HUNGARY

WINTER (EDUARD J.) Frühliberalismus in der Donaumonarchie: religiöse, nationale und wissenschaftliche Strömungen von 1790-1868. Berlin, 1968. pp. 365. bibliog.

WINTER (EDUARD J.) Revolution, Neoabsolutismus und Liberalismus in der Donaumonarchie. Wien, [1969]. pp. 246. bibliog.

LIBERALISM IN BELGIUM

WILS (LODE) De liberale Antwerpse dagbladen, 1857-1864. Leuven, Nauwelaerts 1962. pp. 59. 24cm. (Centre Interuniversitaire d'Histoire Contemporaine. Cahiers. 26)

DAENENS (RAYMOND) Origine et esprit du libéralisme belge. [Heule], 1969. pp. 98.

LIBERALISM IN CANADA

KELLEY (ROBERT LLOYD) The transatlantic persuasion: the liberal democratic mind in the age of Gladstone. New York, 1969. pp. 433. bibliog.

LIBERALISM IN COLOMBIA

ROMERO AGUIRRE (ALFONSO) Ayer, hoy y mañana del liberalismo colombiano. 3rd ed. Bogota, 1949. 4 vols.(in 1).

LIBERALISM IN DENMARK

CHRISTENSEN (J.V.) Liberalism i Danmark. København, 1930. pp. 31.

LIBERALISM IN EUROPE

COLLINS (I.) Liberalism in nineteenth-century Europe. in Black (Eugene Charlton) ed. European political history, 1815-1870. New York, 1967.

LIBERALISM IN GERMANY

DEUTSCHER Liberalismus im Zeitalter Bismarcks: ein politische Briefsammlung; Neudruck der Ausgabe 1925-(1926). Osnabrück, Biblio, 1967. 2 vols. 23cm. (Bayerische Akademie der Wissenschaften. Historische Kommission. Deutsche Geschichtsquellen des 19. Jahrhunderts. Bände 18, 24)

LAATHS (ERWIN) Der Nationalliberalismus im Werke Gustav Freytags. [Wuppertal-Beyenburg, imprint, 1934]. pp. 122. bibliog.

PEIFFER (EVA) Wilhelm Joseph Behr: Studie zum bayerischen Liberalismus der Metternich-Zeit. Emsdetten, Lechte, 1936. pp. 106. bibliog. 22½cm.

WINKLER (HEINRICH AUGUST) Preussischer Liberalismus und deutscher Nationalstaat: Studien zur Geschichte der Deutschen Fortschrittspartei, 1861-1866. Tübingen, 1964. pp. 134. bibliog.

FRIEDRICH NAUMANN-STIFTUNG. Schriftenreihe zur Politik und Zeitgeschichte. Bd.10. Geschichte des deutschen Liberalismus. Köln, Westdeutscher Verlag, 1966. pp. 190. bibliog. 20½cm.

POLITISCHER Liberalismus und Evangelische Kirche; (Bischof D. Hermann Kunst... zum 60.Geburtstag) Köln, Westdeutscher Verlag, 1967. pp. 128. 20½cm. (Friedrich Naumann-Stiftung. Schriftenreihe zur Politik und Zeitgeschichte. Band 11)

ELM (LUDWIG) Zwischen Fortschritt und Reaktion : Geschichte der Parteien der liberalen Bourgeoisie in Deutschland 1893-1918. Berlin, 1968. pp. 330. bibliog. (Deutsche Akademie der Wissenschaften zu Berlin. Institut für Geschichte. Schriften. Reihe 1. Band 32)

GALL (LOTHAR) Der Liberalismus als regierende Partei: das Grossherzogtum Baden zwischen Restauration und Reichsgründung. Wiesbaden, Steiner, 1968. pp. xiii, 524. bibliog. 23½cm. (Institut für Europäische Geschichte Veröffentlichungen. Band 47)

WEGNER (KONSTANZE) Theodor Barth und die Freisinnige Vereinigung: Studien zur Geschichte des Linksliberalismus im wilhelminischen Deutschland 1893-1910. Tübingen, Mohr, 1968. pp. xii, 159. bibliog. 23cm. (Tübinger Studien zur Geschichte und Politik. Nr.24)

DEHLER (THOMAS) Reden und Aufsätze. Köln, Westdeutscher Verlag, 1969. pp. 234. (Friedrich-Naumann-Stiftung. Schriftenreihe zur Politik und Zeitgeschichte. Band 13)

EKSTEINS (MODRIS) Theodor Heuss und die Weimarer Republik: ein Beitrag zur Geschichte des deutschen Liberalismus. Stuttgart, [1969]. pp. 204. bibliog.

Das WAGNIS der Mündigkeit: Beiträge zum Selbstverständnis des Liberalismus; Festschrift für Paul Luchtenberg. Neustadt/Aisch, 1970. pp. 282.

LIBERALISM IN INDIA

AIYAR (SADASHIV PPABHAKAR) Liberalism and the modernization of India: an interpretation. Ahmedabad, 1967. pp. 38. (Harold Laski Institute of Political Science. Annual Lectures. 12th, 1966)

LIBERALISM IN ITALY

RABUAZZO (ANTONINO) L'atteggiamento dei Liberali dal 1919 al 1922. Bologna, [imprint], 1966. pp. 30. bibliog. 24½cm.

LIBERALISM IN ITALY (Cont'd.)

BIGNARDI (AGOSTINO) Ritratti liberali e libri letti. Bologna, 1969. pp. 153.

ORSELLO (GIAN PIERO) ed. Critica liberale: per una storia della sinistra liberale attraverso le riviste, 1952-1966. [S. Giovanni Valdarno], 1969. 2 vols.

LIBERALISM IN MEXICO

HALE (CHARLES A.) Mexican liberalism in the age of Mora, 1821-1853. New Haven, Yale U.P., 1968. pp. xi, 347. bibliog. 23½cm. (Caribbean Series. 11)

PARCERO (MARIA DE LA LUZ) Lorenzo de Zavala: fuente y origen de la reforma liberal en Mexico. Mexico, 1969. pp. 292. bibliog. (Instituto Nacional de Antropologia e Historia. Serie Historia. 20.)

LIBERALISM IN PARAGUAY

PASTORE (CARLOS) Temas del Congreso del Liberalismo Paraguayo. Montevideo, Editorial Antequera, [1951]. pp. 14. 20cm.

LIBERALISM IN RUSSIA

PIPES (RICHARD EDGAR) Struve: liberal on the left, 1870-1905. Cambridge, Mass., 1970. pp. 415. bibliog. (Harvard University. Russian Research Center. Studies. No. 64)

LIBERALISM IN SOUTH AFRICA

ROBERTSON (JANET) Liberalism in South Africa, 1948-1963. Oxford, 1971. pp. 252. bibliog.

LIBERALISM IN SPAIN

PARKER (A.A.) Liberalism and Carlism in nineteenth century Spain. [Dublin, 1936] pp. 26. (Lingard Society. Lingard Papers. N.S. No. 20)

DEROZIER (ALBERT) Martin de Garay; ou, Le liberalisme des compromissions: contribution aux recherches sur le liberalisme en Espagne au XIX siècle. Paris, 1968. pp. 136. (Besançon. Université. Annales Littéraires. [2e Série]. vol. 100)

LIBERALISM IN SWEDEN

BJÖRKLUND (STEFAN) Oppositionen vid 1823 års riksdag: jordbrukskris och borgerlig liberalism. Stockholm, Norstedt, [1964]. pp. 62. bibliog. 23cm. (Uppsala. Universitet. Historiska Institutionen. Studia Historica Upsaliensia. 16)

LIBERALISM IN THE ARGENTINE REPUBLIC

SOMMI (LUIS V.) La crisis del liberalismo argentino. Buenos Aires, 1957. pp. 45.

RONDANINA (ESTEBÁN F.) Liberalismo, masonería y socialismo en la evolución nacional. Buenos Aires, Ediciones Libera, 1965. pp. 302. 17cm.

LIBERALISM IN THE UNITED KINGDOM

KELLEY (ROBERT LLOYD) The transatlantic persuasion: the liberal democratic mind in the age of Gladstone. New York, 1969. pp. 433. bibliog.

LIBERALISM IN THE UNITED STATES

DOUGLAS (LEWIS WILLIAMS) The liberal tradition: a free people and a free economy. New York, Van Nostrand, 1935. pp. xxiii, 136. 21cm. (Harvard University Godkin Lectures. 1935)

GOLDWIN (ROBERT ALLEN) ed. Left, right and center: essays on liberalism and conservatism in the United States; by Frank S. Meyer [and others]. Chicago, Rand McNally, [1965]. pp.(v),169. 21½cm. (Rand McNally Public Affairs Series)

WHEELER (JOHN HARVEY) The rise and fall of liberal democracy. [Santa Barbara], Center for the Study of Democratic Institutions, [1966]. pp. 26. 28cm. (Occasional Papers)

EKIRCH (ARTHUR ALPHONSE) The decline of American liberalism. [New ed.] New York, Atheneum, 1967. pp. xix, 401. 18½cm. (Atheneum Paperbacks. 111)

GETTLEMAN (MARVIN E.) and MERMELSTEIN (DAVID) eds. The great society reader: the failure of American liberalism. New York, Random House, [1967]. pp. xiv, 551. bibliog. 21cm.

KAUFMAN (ARNOLD SAUL) The radical liberal: new man in American politics. New York, Atherton P., 1968. pp. xxi, 175. bibliog. 21½cm.

SPROAT (JOHN G.) "The best men": liberal reformers in the gilded age. New York, O.U.P., 1968. pp. xi, 356. bibliog. 20½cm.

WEINSTEIN (JAMES) The corporate ideal in the liberal state: 1900-1918. Boston, [Mass.], [1968]. pp. 263.

WOLFF (ROBERT PAUL) The poverty of liberalism. Boston, Beacon P., [1968]. pp. 200. 20cm.

BAILEY (HUGH C.) Liberalism in the new South: Southern social reformers and the progressive movement. Coral Gables, [1969]. pp. 290. bibliog.

CARSON (CLARENCE B.) The flight from reality. New York, 1969. pp. 548.

LIBERIA

UNITED STATES. Army Department. Pamphlets. No. 550-38. U.S. Army area handbook for Liberia. Washington, 1964. pp. xiii, 419. bibliogs.

- Census

LIBERIA. Census, 1962. The 1962 population census: handbook of census education for schools. Monrovia, 1961. pp. 47, (16).

LIBERIA. Census, 1962. The 1962 population census. Document No. M/DS/A. District supervisor's manual. Monrovia, [1962?]. pp. 23. (32).

LIBERIA. Census, 1962. The 1962 population census. Document No. M/ENUM(A). Enumerator's reference manual. Monrovia, [1962?]. pp. 68, (39).

LIBERIA. Census, 1962. The 1962 population census. Document No. M/FS/A. Field supervisor's manual. Monrovia, [1962?]. pp. 32, (28).

LIBERIA. Census, 1962. The 1962 population census. Document No. M/PES. Interviewer's reference manual for the post-enumeration survey. Monrovia, [1962?]. pp. 40.

- Commerce

U.K. Embassy (Liberia). 1968. Liberia: commercial and economic report. [London], 1968. pp. ii, 20. 30cm.

- Commerce - Statistics

LIBERIA. Bureau of Statistics. 1954. Statistical classification of merchandise, schedule A, with rates of duty and tariff and paragraphs and regulations for the collection of Foreign trade statistics, etc. rev. ed. Monrovia, 1954. pp. xxx, 71. 28cm.

- Constitution

LIBERIA. Constitution. 1955. The constitution of the Republic of Liberia and Declaration of independence; with notes by Alfonso K. Dormu. New York, [1970]. pp. 119. bibliog.

- Description and travel

LIBERIA. Information Service, 1958. The Republic of Liberia: the nation, its government, people and potential. [London, 1958], pp. 3.

LIBERIA. Information Service. 1960. Liberia: story of progress. London, 1960. pp. 76.

- Economic conditions

LIBERIA. Information Service. 1958. Some useful information: businessman's guide to Liberia. [London, 1958]. pp. (3).

FRANCE. Direction de la Documentation. La Documentation Francaise. Notes et Études Documentaires. No. 3,174. Le Libéria. Paris, 1965. pp. 35. bibliog. 30½cm.

UNITED STATES. International Commerce Bureau. A market for U.S. products in Liberia. Washington, 1965. pp. iv, 39.

LIBERIA. Department of Information and Cultural Affairs. 1967. Liberia: open door to travel and investment. Monrovia, 1967. pp. 95,(6). 23cm.

LIBERIAN TRADING AND DEVELOPMENT BANK. Liberia: basic data and information, 1968. Monrovia, 1968. pp. 107.

U.K. Embassy (Liberia). 1968. Liberia: commercial and economic report. [London], 1968. pp. ii, 20. 30cm.

- Economic policy

LIBERIA. Statutes, etc. 1953. An act approving the nine-year program for the economic development of the Republic of Liberia, L. 1953-54, ch. XX. [Monrovia, 1953?] fo. 27. 33cm.

CONRAD (A.H.) Econometric models in development planning: Pakistan, Argentina, Liberia. in Papanek (Gustav F.) ed. Development policy. Cambridge, [Mass.], 1968.

- Foreign relations

TUBMAN (WILLIAM VACANARAT SHADRACH) Speeches... during...state visit to the United States, Haiti and Jamaica 1954, etc. [Washington, 1954?]. pp. 59. 27cm.

TUBMAN (WILLIAM VACANARAT SHADRACH) The official papers of William V.S. Tubman, President of the Republic of Liberia: covering addresses, messages, speeches and statements 1960-67: edited by E. Reginald Townsend... assisted by Abeodu Bowen Jones, etc. Monrovia, 1968. pp. xxi, 687. 25cm.

- History

LIEBENOW (J. GUS) Liberia: the evolution of privilege. Ithaca, 1969. pp. 247. bibliog.

WEST (RICHARD LEAF) Back to Africa: a history of Sierra Leone and Liberia. London, 1970. pp. 357. bibliog.

BLYDEN (EDWARD WILMOT) Black spokesman: selected published writings of Edward Wilmot Blyden; edited by Hollis R. Lynch. London, 1971. pp. 354. bibliog.

WILSON (CHARLES MORROW) Liberia: black Africa in microcosm. New York, [1971]. pp. 242. bibliog.

- Politics and government

TUBMAN (WILLIAM VACANARAT SHADRACH) President Tubman of Liberia speaks; edited by E. Reginald Townsend. London, Consolidated Publications, 1959. pp. 301. 24cm.

FRANCE. Direction de la Documentation. La Documentation Francaise. Notes et Études Documentaires, No. 3,174. Le Libéria. Paris, 1965. pp. 35. bibliog. 30½cm.

TUBMAN (WILLIAM VACANARAT SHADRACH) The official papers of William V.S. Tubman, President of the Republic of Liberia: covering addresses, messages, speeches and statements 1960-67: edited by E. Reginald Townsend... assisted by Abeodu Bowen Jones, etc. Monrovia, 1968. pp. xxi, 687. 25cm.

LIEBENOW (J. GUS) Liberia: the evolution of privilege. Ithaca, 1969. pp. 247. bibliog.

BERG (ELLIOT J.) Politics, privilege and progress in Liberia: a review article. Ann Arbor, [1970]. pp. 175-183. (Michigan University. Center for Research on Economic Development. Cred Reprints. New Series. No. 17) (Reprinted from Liberian Studies Journal, vol. 2, no. 2, 1970)

- Population

JUERGENS (HANS WILHELM) Beiträge zur Binnenwanderung und Bevölkerungsentwicklung in Liberia. Berlin, 1965. pp. 92. (Ifo-Institut für Wirtschaftsforschung. Afrika-Studien. 4)

LIBERIA (Cont'd.)

- Public works

LIBERIA. Information Service. 1958.
Building the nation: Liberia's public
works programme. [London, 1958].
pp. (3)

- Sanitary affairs

LIBERIA. Information Service. 1958. Nation's
health. [London, 1958]. pp. (3).

- Social conditions

FRANCE. Direction de la Documentation. La Documentation Francaise. Notes et Études Documentaires.
No. 3,174. Le Libéria. Paris, 1965. pp. 35.
bibliog. 30½cm.

LIBERIA. Department of Information and
Cultural Affairs. 1967. Liberia: open
door to travel and investment. Monrovia,
1967. pp. 95,(6). 23cm.

- Statistics

GERMANY (BUNDESREPUBLIK). Statistisches Bundesamt.
Länderkurzberichte: Liberia. Wiesbaden, irreg.,
1968 to date. 29½cm.

LIBERTY

ENGLANDS birth-right justified against all
arbitrary usurpation, whether regall or
parliamentary, or under what vizor soever...;
by a well-wisher to the just cause for which...
John Lilburne is unjustly imprisoned...;
[attributed to John Lilburne]. 2nd ed. [London],
1645. pp. 49. 19cm.

[LILBURNE (JOHN)] England's miserie and
remedie: in a judicious letter from an
utter-barrister...concerning Leiutenant [sic]
Col. Lilburn's imprisonment in Newgate,
Sept. 1645. [London, 1645]. pp. 8. 19cm.
Wing L 2105.

BALL (WILLIAM) of Barkham. Constitutio liberi
populi; or, The rule of a free-born people.
[London], 1646. pp. (ii), 22. 19½cm. Wing
B 588.

LARNER (WILLIAM) A vindication of every freemans libertie against all arbitrary power
and government; or, A letter...to Sir Henry Vane
junior,...; wherein is set forth his unjust
imprisonment and cruell hard dealings towards
the said William Larner. [London, 1646]. pp.
4. 18½cm. Wing L 445A.

OVERTON (RICHARD) An arrow against all tyrants
and tyrany shot from the prison of New-gate
into the prerogative bowels of the arbitrary
House of Lords and all other usurpers and tyrants
whatsoever, etc. Printed at the backside of the
Cyclopian Mountains by Martin Claw-Clergy, [i.e.
London], 1646. pp. 20. 19cm. Wing O 622.

VOX plebis; or, The peoples outcry against
oppression, injustice, and tyranny; wherein the
liberty of the subject is asserted, Magna Charta
briefly but pithily expounded, Lieutenant
Colonell Lilburnes sentence published and
refuted, etc. London, 1646. pp. 69. 18½cm.
Wing V 726.

SACHEVERELL (HENRY) False notions of liberty in
religion and government destructive of both:
a sermon preach'd before the...House of Commons,
etc. London, Clements, 1713. pp. 23. 20cm.

FREIMUETHIGE Betrachtungen eines philosophischen
Weltbürgers über wichtige Gegenstände entsprechend den Bedürfnissen unsers Zeitalters und
des Menschengeschlechts. [Copenhagen], 1793.
pp. 206.

LORINI (GIUSEPPE) Religione e libertà: sermone
detto nella chiesa metropolitana di Firenze...
il di 19 marza 1848. Firenze, Mariani, 1848.
pp. 28. 22½cm.

[VASEY (GEORGE)] Individual liberty, legal, moral,
and licentious; in which the political fallacies
of J.S. Mill's essay "On liberty" are pointed out;
by Index [pseud.]. London, Vasey, 1867. pp.
xii, 172.

HERBERT (AUBERON EDWARD WILLIAM MOLYNEUX)
The free mind in the free body: a statement
of principles and measures. [London 1885]
pp. 7. (Anti-Force Papers. No. 1)

CHALLAMEL (AUGUSTIN) Histoire de la liberté
en France. Paris, Jouvet, 1886. 2 vols.
22cm.

[KOL (HENRI HUBERT VAN)] Socialisme en vrijheid;
door Rienzi, [pseud]. Amsterdam, 1893. pp.
213.

HAMON (AUGUSTIN FRÉDÉRIC) Discours de cloture
prononcé le 21 septembre 1912 ([to the] Grand
Orient de France, Assemblée Générale de 1912).
Paris, 1912. pp. 20.

IEZOWER (IGNAZ) ed. Die Befreiung der
Menschheit: Freiheitsideen in Vergangenheit
und Gegenwart; unter Mitwirkung von Paul
Adler [and others]. Berlin, Bong, [1921].
pp. xii, xxiv, 222, 186, 44. 31cm.

NITTI (FRANCESCO SAVERIO) La libertà; [first
published in 1926]. in vol. 11 of his Edizione
nazionale delle opere di Francesco Saverio
Nitti. Bari, 1961.

MARITAIN (JACQUES) Du régime temporel et
de la liberté. Paris, Desclée de Brouwer,
[1933] pp. x, 271. 19cm.

ARON (ROBERT) Dictature de la liberté. Paris,
Grasset, [1935] pp. 289.

TEMPLE (WILLIAM) successively Archbishop of
York and of Canterbury. Faith and freedom.
London, 1935. pp. 26. (British Broadcasting
Corporation. Broadcast National Lectures. 16)

GALLACHER (WILLIAM) Communism and liberty:
a letter to Bill. London, Communist
Party of Great Britain, 1949. pp. 16.
16cm. (Communist Party Pamphlets)

MILLIS (WALTER) Individual freedom and the common defense. New York, [1957]. pp. 80.

MENDE (GEORG) Freiheit und Verantwortung: kleine Essays. Berlin,
Deutscher Verlag der Wissenschaften,
1958. pp. 212. 21½cm.

KAPANI (MUNCI) Freedom to destroy freedom: its meaning
and implications. Ankara, Universitesi [196-?]. pp.
18. 24cm. Reprinted from the collection of essays
in honour of Professor E. Hirsch.

CONGRESS FOR CULTURAL FREEDOM. Conference, Berlin, 1960. Progress in freedom: a discussion of human ideals in modern society; [reports of] study groups I-IV. Berlin, 1960. 4 pts. (in 1 vol.)

DAVYDOV (IURII NIKOLAEVICH) Труд и свобода. Москва, Высшая Школа, 1962. pp. 132. 19½cm.

ESVELD (N. E. H. VAN) Vrijheid van arbeid. Alphen aan den Rijn, Samsom, 1963. pp. 28. 22cm. (Geschriften Recht, Bestuur, Economie. Nr.20)

LE MAY (GODFREY HUGH LANCELOT) Freedom and authority. Johannesburg, Witwatersrand U.P., 1963. pp. 18. 21cm. (Johannesburg. University of Witwatersrand. Republic in a Changing World. Lectures. No.2)

SHAH (A.B.) Liberty in the modern state. Ahmedabad, 1964. pp. 24. (Harold Laski Institute of Political Science. Annual Lectures. 1963)

STEININGER (HERBERT) Was ist Freiheit? Berlin, 1964. pp. 69. (Institut für Gesellschaftswissenschaften. ABC des Marxismus Leninismus)

THIELICKE (HELMUT) Der Einzelne und der Apparat: von der Freiheit des Menschen im technischen Zeitalter. Hamburg, Furche-Verlag, [1964]. pp. 126. 18cm. (Stundenbücher. 34)

BIRLEY (Sir ROBERT) Concepts of freedom; ...three public lectures given at the university of Cape Town, 18-22 August, 1966. Cape Town, 1966. pp. various.

DODDS (ELLIOTT) and REISS (ERNA) The logic of liberty. [London, Liberal Publication Department, 1966]. pp. 35. 21½cm. (Unservile State Group. Unservile State Papers. No. 11)

PRANDSTRALLER (GIAN PAOLO) Valori e libertà: contributo ad una sociologia del pluralismo politico occidentale. [Milan], Comunità, 1966. pp. 247. bibliog. 22½cm. (Studi e Ricerche di Scienze Sociali. 31)

ROGGERONE (GIUSEPPE AGOSTINO) Benedetto Croce et la fondazione del concetto di libertà. Milano, Marzorati, [1966]. pp. 306. 21½cm. (Genoa. Università. Istituto di Filosofia. Pubblicazioni 40)

ABBATE (MICHELE) Libertà e società di massa. Bari, Laterza, [1967] pp. 194. 20cm. (Libri del Tempo Laterza. 95).

AFTALION (FRED) Libres, égaux, fraternels? [Paris], Plon, [1967]. pp. 249. 20cm.

APTHEKER (HERBERT) The nature of democracy, freedom, and revolution. New York, [1967], repr. 1969. pp. 128.

CIARDO (MANLIO) La decadenza della libertà nel mondo moderno: genesi e forme. Bologna, Pàtron, [1967]. pp. xv, 274. 21cm.

DAVIDOVICH (VSEVOLOD EVGEN'EVICH) Problemy chelovecheskoi svobody. L'vov, 1967. pp. 248.

HYMAN (HAROLD MELVIN) and LEVY (LEONARD W.) eds. Freedom and reform: essays in honor of Henry Steele Commager. New York, [1967]. pp. 400. bibliog.

KAEGI (W.) Freedom and power in history. in Krieger (Leonard) and Stern (Fritz Richard) eds. The responsibility of power. Garden City, 1967.

MARSHALL (T.H.) Freedom as a factor in social development. in Singh (Baljit) and Singh (Vidya Bhusan) eds. Social and economic change. Bombay, 1967.

PIKE (FREDRICK BRAUN) ed. Freedom and reform in Latin America. [new ed.] Notre Dame, University of Notre Dame Press, [1967]. pp. xlv, 308. bibliog. 20cm.

PRÉPOSIET (JEAN) Spinoza et la liberté des hommes. [Paris], Gallimard, [1967]. pp. 315. bibliog. 18½cm. (Essais. 130)

ROEGELE (OTTO BERNHARD) ed. Die Freiheit des Westens: Wesen, Wirklichkeit, Widerstände. Graz, Styria, [1967]. pp. 631. 20½cm.

SHELL (KURT LEO) Erich Fromm's Escape from freedom: a critical commentary. New York, [1967]. pp. 63. bibliog.

SHUSTER (GEORGE NAUMAN) ed. Freedom and authority in the West: [papers prepared for a conference held at the University of Notre Dame in October 1966]. Notre Dame, U. of Notre Dame P., [1967]. pp. xv, 199. 23cm. (Notre Dame. University. Committee on International Relations. International Studies)

LAKEBRINK (BERNHARD) Die europäische Idee der Freiheit. Leiden, 1968 in progress.

CERRONI (UMBERTO) La libertà dei moderni. Bari, [1968]. pp. 295.

COFRANCESCO (DINO) Appunti sull'ideologia: marxismo e libertà. Milano, [1968]. pp. 255.

ERIKSON (ERIK HOMBURGER) Insight and freedom. Cape Town, 1968. pp. 18. (Cape Town. University. T.B. Davie Memorial Lectures. 9)

GRASS (GUENTER) and KOHOUT (PAVEL) Briefe über die Grenze: Versuch eines Ost-West-Dialogs. Hamburg, [1968]. pp. 118.

HARDY (GILBERT G.) La vocation de la liberté chez Louis Lavelle. Louvain, 1968. pp. 128. bibliog.

HERMAND (JOST) ed. Von deutscher Republik, 1775-1795. Frankfurt am Main, [1968]. 2 vols. bibliogs.

MAL'TSEV (GENNADII VASIL'EVICH) Социалистическое право и свобода личности: теоретические вопросы. Москва, Юридическая Литература, 1968. pp. 143. 19½см.

MASSUH (VICTOR) La libertad y la violencia. Buenos Aires, [1968]. pp. 350.

MILNE (ALAN JOHN MITCHELL) Freedom and rights. London, Allen and Unwin, 1968. pp. 376. 21½cm.

LIBERTY (Cont'd.)

RANDALL (PETER) Human rights and the human spirit. Johannesburg, [1968]. pp. 15. (South African Institute of Race Relations. Topical Talks. No.13)

SIMON (YVES RENÉ MARIE) Freedom and community;... edited by Charles P. O'Donnell. New York, Fordham U.P., 1968. pp. xxi, 201. bibliog. 21cm.

STOCKS (MARY DANVERS) Baroness Stocks. Where is liberty? London, Epworth P., [1968]. pp. 61. 18½cm.

WOLFF (ROBERT PAUL) The poverty of liberalism. Boston, Beacon P., [1968]. pp. 200. 20cm.

BERLIN (Sir ISAIAH) Four essays on liberty. London, O.U.P., 1969. pp. lxiii, 213. 20½cm. (Oxford Paperbacks. No. 116)

CHADWICK (WILLIAM OWEN) Freedom and the historian: an inaugural lecture [delivered in the University of Cambridge on 27 November, 1968]. Cambridge, C.U.P., 1969. pp. 42. 18cm.

DESHUSSES (JEROME) La gauche réactionnaire. [Paris, 1969]. pp. 145.

FREIHEIT und Verantwortung in Gesellschaft und Erziehung: (Festschrift für Erwin Stein ...; herausgegeben von Johann Peter Ruppert; unter Mitwirkung von Wolfgang Böhme [and others]). Bad Homburg, [1969]. pp. 289.

FROMM (EBERHARD) and others. Verfassung und Freiheit. Berlin, 1969. pp. 94.

HOFMANN (HANS) Discovering freedom. Boston, [1969]. pp. 100.

MARCUSE (HERBERT) An essay on liberation. London, Penguin P., 1969. pp. xi, 91. 23cm.

MAYER (MILTON) On liberty: Man v. the state;...with a Center discussion. Santa Barbara, Calif., [1969]. pp. 191. (Center for the Study of Democratic Institutions. Occasional Papers.)

ROCHE (GEORGE CHARLES) Legacy of freedom. New Rochelle, N.Y., [1969]. pp. 356. bibliog.

SAMELI (KATHARINA) Freiheit und Sicherheit im Recht: zum Problem der Wertantinomie im Recht auf der Grundlage der Wertlehre Nicolai Hartmanns. Zürich, 1969. pp. 181. bibliog. (Zuerich. Universität. Rechts- und Staatswissenschaftliche Fakultät. Zürcher Beiträge zur Rechtswissenschaft. Neue Folge. Heft 307)

SPENCER (HERBERT) The man versus the state, with four essays on politics and society; (first published 1884, 1892); edited and with an introduction by Donald MacRae. Harmondsworth, [1969]. pp. 350. bibliog.

SZAMUELY (TIBOR) Communism and freedom. London, 1969. pp. 19. (Conservative Political Centre. [Publications]. No. 442)

WEINSTEIN (FRED) and PLATT (GERLD M.) The wish to be free: society, psyche, and value change. Berkeley, 1969. pp. 319.

ARON (RAYMOND) An essay on freedom;... translated from the French by Helen Weaver. New York, 1970. pp. 161.

BOWKER (GORDON) ed. Freedom: reason or revolution? London, 1970. pp. 176.

CRITCHLEY (THOMAS ALAN) The conquest of violence: order and liberty in Britain. London, 1970. pp. 225. bibliog.

PAPANDREOU (ANDREAS GEORGE) Man's freedom. New York, [1970]. pp. 71. (Carnegie-Mellon University. Benjamin F. Fairless Memorial Lectures. 1969)

SCHLESINGER (ARTHUR MEIER) the Younger. The vital center: the politics of freedom;... with a new foreword by the author. new ed. London, 1970. pp. 274.

SCHMIDTCHEN (GERHARD) Manipulation: Freiheit negativ. Neuwied, [1970]. pp. 80.

WHATLEY (DOUGLAS BRYAN) The concept of civil liberties; [Ph. D. (London) thesis]. 1970. fo. 212. bibliog. Typescript: unpublished. This thesis is the property of London University and may not be removed from the Library.

PARSONS (JACK) Population versus liberty. London, 1971. pp. 417. bibliog.

LIBERTY IN LITERATURE

WEDGWOOD (JOSIAH CLEMENT) 1st Baron Wedgwood and NEVINS (ALLAN) Forever freedom; being an anthology in prose and verse from England and America. Harmondsworth, 1940. pp. 222.

FOCKE (A.) Freiheit in der Literatur. in Roegele (Otto Bernhard) ed. Die Freiheit des Westens. Graz, [1967].

LIBERTY OF CONSCIENCE

REALI (EUSEBIO) Della libertà di coscienza nelle sue attinenze col potere temporale de'Papi. Torino, Franco, 1861. pp. 194. 18cm.

GIRMAN (IURII IVANOVICH) В чем сущность свободы совести? Москва, Мысль, 1966. pp. 88. bibliog. 20cm

LIBERTY OF CONTRACT

- Italy

BARCELLONA (PIETRO) Intervento statale e autonomia privata nella disciplina dei rapporti economici. Milano, 1969. pp. 300. (Catania. Università. Facoltà di Giurisprudenza. Pubblicazioni. 55)

LIBERTY OF INFORMATION

- United Kingdom

IVENS (MICHAEL WILLIAM) The right to speak. London, [1964]. pp. 13.

LIBERTY OF SPEECH

TOM MANN RELEASE MOVEMENT. Who dares - free speech? London, [1932?]. pp. 2.

DOUGLAS (W.O.) The society of the dialogue. in Cohen (Arthur Allen) ed. Humanistic education and western civilization. New York, [1964].

- France

PROUDHON (PIERRE JOSEPH) La justice poursuivie par l'église: appel du jugement rendu par le tribunal de police correctionnelle de la Seine le 2 juin 1858 contre P.J. Proudhon. Bruxelles, 1858. pp. 184.

- South Africa

AUERBACH (F. E.) Freedom and authority in education. Johannesburg, [1967]. pp. 14. (South African Institute of Race Relations. Topical Talks. No.18)

- United Kingdom

NATIONAL COUNCIL FOR CIVIL LIBERTIES. Indecency in church: hypocrisy, dishonesty, injustice at Brighton. [London, 1966?]. pp. 8. 21cm.

- United States

SUMMERS (MARVIN) ed. Free speech and political protest. Boston, Heath, 1967. pp. viii, 136. bibliog. 21cm. (Problems in Political Science)

LIBERTY OF THE PRESS

BELLOC (JOSEPH HILAIRE PIERRE) The free press. London, 1918. pp. 102.

SCHOLLER (HEINRICH J.) Person und Öffentlichkeit: zum Spannungsverhältnis von Pressefreiheit und Persönlichkeitsschutz. München, Beck, 1967. pp. xviii, 455. 23½cm. (Münchener Öffentlich-rechtliche Abhandlungen. 3.Heft)

ES geht nicht nur um Springer: Material und Meinungen zur inneren Pressefreiheit; mit Beiträgen von Walter Mallmann [and others]; (Herausgeber Otto Wilfert). Mainz, [1968]. pp. 78. bibliog.

DUERRENMATT (PETER) Wie frei ist die Presse?: Grundlagen moderner Publizistik am Beispiel Schweiz. Bern, [1971]. pp. 308. bibliog.

HOHENBERG (JOHN) Free press - free people: the best cause. New York, 1971. pp. 514.

- Bibliography

McCOY (RALPH EDWARD) compiler. Freedom of the press; an annotated bibliography. Carbondale, Ill., 1968. pp. unpaged.

GERMANY (BUNDESREPUBLIK). Deutscher Bundestag. Wissenschaftliche Dienste. 1970. Pressefreiheit, Pressekonzentration, Presserechtsrahmengesetz: Auswahlbibliographie; [compiled by Dr. Chronz in collaboration with Frau Dr. Geissler]. Bonn, 1970. pp. 71. (Bibliographien. 24)

- Belgium

INSTITUT BELGE D'INFORMATION ET DE DOCUMENTATION. The topical press under the sign of freedom. Brussels, Ministry of Foreign Affairs and External Trade, 1967. pp. 19. bibliog. (Belgian News. No.1a)

- Czechoslovakia

HAMŠÍK (DUŠAN) Writers against rulers;...translated by D. Orpington. London, 1971. pp. 208.

- France

SCHWOEBEL (JEAN) La presse, le pouvoir et l'argent. Paris, Seuil, [1968]. pp. 287. 20½cm.

- Germany

JENSEN (JUERGEN) Presse und politische Polizei: Hamburgs Zeitungen unter dem Sozialistengesetz 1878-1890. Hannover, Dietz, [1966]. pp. 193. bibliog. 23½cm.

BUNN (R.F.) West Germany: the Spiegel affair. in Bunn (Ronald F.) and Andrews (William George) eds. Politics and civil liberties in Europe. Princeton, [1967].

BUNN (RONALD F.) German politics and the Spiegel affair: a case study of the Bonn system. Baton Rouge, Louisiana State U.P., [1968]. pp xxv, 230. 21½cm.

FORSTHOFF (ERNST) Der Verfassungsschutz der Zeitungspresse. Frankfurt a.M., 1969. pp pp. 77.

MARX (KARL) and ENGELS (FRIEDRICH) Pressefreiheit und Zensur; herausgegeben und eingeleitet von Iring Fetscher. Frankfurt, [1969]. pp. 235. 21cm.

EISENHARDT (ULRICH) Die kaiserliche Aufsicht über Buchdruck, Buchhandel und Presse im Heiligen Römischen Reich Deutscher Nation, 1496-1806: ein Beitrag zur Geschichte der Bücher- und Pressezensur. Karlsruhe, 1970. pp. 168. bibliog.

- India

ISLAMIC REVIEW. The Indian Press Act: an open letter to the Secretary of State for India from the editor, etc. London, [1914?]. pp. 16.

BELAVADI (S. H.) The press and the parliamentary privileges. Ahmedabad, 1965. pp. 16. (Harold Laski Institute of Political Science. Laski Memorial Lectures. 1965)

NATARAJAN (SWAMINATH) Democracy and the press. Bombay, 1965. pp. 38. 24½cm. (Samaj Prabodhan Sanstha. Acharya Javadekar Memorial Lectures. 1964)

- Italy

LAZZARO (GIORGIO) La libertà di stampa in Italia dall'Editto albertino alle norme vigenti. Milano, 1969. pp. 255. (Centro di Studi sul Giornalismo "Gino Pestelli". Comitato Scientifico. Studi e Ricerche sul Giornalismo. 1)

LIBERTY OF THE PRESS (Cont'd.)

- Mexico

ENRÍQUEZ SIMONÍ (GUILLERMO) La libertad de prensa en México: una mentira rosa. México, Costa-Amic, 1967. pp. 130. 19½cm.

- Russia

FRANCE. Direction de la Documentation. La Documentation Française. Notes et Etudes Documentaires. Nos. 3,679-3,680. La presse, les intellectuels et le pouvoir en Union Soviétique et dans les autres pays socialistes européens. 1. L'Union Soviétique; [by] Georges H. Mond. Paris, 1970. pp. 58. bibliog.

- Salvador

SALVADOR. Presidencia. Departamento de Relaciones Publicas. 1958. La libertad de prensa en el Salvador. San Salvador, 1958. pp. 171. (Salvador. Presidencia. Publicaciones)

- South Africa

DE VILLIERS (RENE M.) The press and the people; an address to the southern Transvaal Region of the Institute, Johannesburg, November, 1967. Johannesburg, [1967]. pp. 9. (South African Institute of Race Relations. Topical Talks. No. 8)

- Spain

MEMORIA sobre la libertad política de la imprenta, leida en la Junta de Instrucción Pública por uno de sus vocales D.J.I.M. y aprobada por la misma junta. Sevilla, Muñoz Alvarez, 1809. pp. 32.

DUEÑAS (GONZALO) La ley de prensa de Manuel Fraga. [Colombes?, 1969]. pp. 161.

- United Kingdom

BIRLEY (ROBERT) Printing and democracy. London, Monotype Corporation, 1964. pp. 29. 25cm. Privately printed.

- United States

COOPER (THOMAS) M.D., one of the judges of the Supreme Court, Pennsylvania. A treatise on the law of libel and the liberty of the press;...[originally published in 1830]. New York, 1970. pp. 184.

LINTON (WILLIAM JAMES) Editorial right: a question of honesty and plain speech. [New Haven, Conn.?, 1879]. pp. 8.

COWEN (ZELMAN) and others. Fair trial vs. a free press. [Santa Barbara], Center for the Study of Democratic Institutions, [1965]. pp. 36. 27½cm. (Occasional Papers)

NELSON (HAROLD LEWIS) ed. Freedom of the press from Hamilton to the Warren Court. Indianapolis, Bobbs-Merrill, [1967]. pp. lxviii, 420. bibliog. 20½cm. (American Heritage Series)

HACHTEN (WILLIAM A.) The Supreme Court on freedom of the press: decisions and dissents. Ames, Iowa State U.P., 1968. pp. xxi, 316. bibliog. 23cm.

LIBRARIANS

[SKAWRAN (PAUL ROBERT)] The intelligence of the adult (its problems and methods). 2. The intelligence of the scientist (practical part). [Pt.]A. The intelligence of the librarian. Pretoria, National Institute for Personnel Research, 1969. fo. 69; various. bibliog. (South Africa. Council for Scientific and Industrial Research. CSIR Special Reports. PERS 119)

- Recruiting - United Kingdom

JORDAN (PETER) ed. Working conditions in libraries: a survey;...contributors Graham Crowther [and others]. [London], Association of Assistant Librarians, 1968. pp. 71. 31cm.

- Salaries, pensions, etc. - United Kingdom

JORDAN (PETER) ed. Working conditions in libraries: a survey;...contributors Graham Crowther [and others]. [London], Association of Assistant Librarians, 1968. pp. 71. 31cm.

- Africa, Subsaharan

VARLEY (DOUGLAS HAROLD) The role of the librarian in the new Africa: an inaugural lecture given in the University College of Rhodesia and Nyasaland on 5 October, 1962. London, O.U.P., 1963. pp. 24. 21½cm.

- United Kingdom

HUNT (KENNETH GEOFFREY) The Association of Metropolitan Chief Librarians: an account of its work for library services in their relation to London local government. London, the Association, 1967. pp. (iii), 37. 21cm. (Library Association. Pamphlets. No. 29)

U.K. Central Youth Employment Executive. 1968. Library, information and archive work. 6th ed. [London], 1968. pp. 27. 21½cm. (Choice of Careers. 4)

U.K. Civil Service Commission. 1969. Librarians in government service. London, 1969. pp. 30.

LIBRARIES

BUCH, Bibliothek, Leser: Festschrift für Horst Kunze zum 60. Geburtstag; (herausgegeben von Werner Dube [and others]). Berlin, 1969. pp. 651. bibliogs. In various languages, with German summaries.

BENGE (RONALD C.) Libraries and cultural change. London, 1970. pp. 278. bibliog.

- Automation

UNITED STATES. Library of Congress. Automation and the Library of Congress. Washington, 1963. pp.vii, 88.

UNITED STATES. Library of Congress. Libraries and automation: proceedings of the Conference on Libraries and Automation.... 1963. Washington, 1964. pp. xii, 268. bibliogs.

BATTY (CHARLES DAVID) ed. The library and the machine: selected papers and discussions from a study conference held at Nottingham 19-22 April, 1966, on library applications of computers and data processing equipment. Scunthorpe, North Midland Branch of the Library Association, 1966. pp. 56. 20½cm.

CONFERENCE ON COMPUTERS IN CANADIAN LIBRARIES, QUEBEC, 1966. A report prepared for the Canadian Association of College and University Libraries. [Vancouver], University of B.C. Library, 1966. fo.13. 28cm.

BATTY (CHARLES DAVID) ed. Libraries and machines today;...proceedings of a 24-hour computer workshop held at Nottingham, 19-20 April, 1967. London, North Midland Branch of the Library Association, 1967. pp. 50. bibliog. 24½cm.

CANADIAN ASSOCIATION OF COLLEGE AND UNIVERSITY LIBRARIES. Workshop on Library Automation, Vancouver, 1967. Automation in libraries. [Ottawa], 1967. pp. vi, 154. 28cm.

WARD (GWENDOLINE ALICE TYNE) and others. The automatic production of library catalogue cards: (progress reports 1 and 2). Wellington, Applied Mathematics Division, 1968-69. 2 pts.

CARROLL (RAYMOND ALBERT) ed. Papers on computers presented at the week-end school, Cheltenham, April, 1967. London, 1968. pp. 19.

PFLUG (GUENTHER) and ADAMS (BERNHARD) eds. Elektronische Datenverarbeitung in der Universitätsbibliothek Bochum: Ergebnisse, Erfahrungen, Pläne. Bochum, [1968]. pp. 147. bibliog. With summaries in English.

EVANS (A.J.) and others. Periodicals data automation project. Loughborough, 1969. pp. 39.

INTERFACE: library automation with special reference to computing activity; [including papers presented at the Newcastle seminar on the management of computing activity in academic libraries, 10-13 January, 1969]; edited by C.K. Balmforth and N.S.M. Cox. Newcastle, 1971. pp. 251. bibliog.

UNESCO-SEMINAR ELECTRONIC DATA PROCESSING IN LIBRARIES, REGENSBURG, 1970. [Proceedings] in LIBRI, vol. 21, 1971.

- Automation - Bibliography

BERGMANN (WERNER) and POHLMANN (CHRISTA) compilers. Bibliotheken und elektronische Datenverarbeitung: ein bibliographischer Wegweiser. Leipzig, 1968. pp. 72. bibliog. (Deutsche Bücherei. Bibliographischer Informationsdienst. Nr.14)

CAYLESS (C.F.) and POTTS (HILARY) compilers. Bibliography of library automation, 1964-1967. [London], Council of the British National Bibliography, 1968. pp. 107. 25½cm.

- Directories

WALES (ALEXANDER PETER) ed. International library directory: a world directory of libraries;...1969/70. 3rd ed. London, Wales, [1968]. pp. 1222. 24cm.

INTERNATIONALES Bibliotheks-Handbuch: World guide to libraries; ([compiled by] Klaus G. Saur). 3rd ed. München-Pullach, 1970. 4 vols. Pagination continuous.

- Special collections

SOURCE materials for business and economic history; proceedings of a colloquium convened at the Graduate School of Business Administration, Harvard University, October 20-22, 1966; Laurence J. Kipp, editor. Boston, Mass., Baker Library, 1967. pp. (ii), 154. 28cm.

- America

ORGANIZATION OF AMERICAN STATES. 1962. The Inter-American Program of Library and Bibliographic Development of the Organization of American States: a statement of principles and practices. (Cuadernos Bibliotecológicos. No. 11) Washington, 1962. pp. 5. 28cm.

ORGANIZATION OF AMERICAN STATES. 1963. Books and libraries in the Americas: recommendations of Inter-American conferences, 1947-1962; compiled by the Library Development Program of the Pan American Union. (Estudios Bibliotecarios. No. 7) Washington, 1963. pp. viii, 286. 27½cm.

- America, Latin

ORGANIZATION OF AMERICAN STATES. 1963. Bibliotecas públicas y escolares en America Latina;...por Marietta Daniels. (Estudios Bibliotecarios. No. 5) Washington, 1963. pp. (vii), 136. 27½cm.

- America, North - Special collections

ASH (LEE) and LORENZ (DENIS) compilers. Subject collections: a guide to special book collections and subject emphases as reported by university, college, public and special libraries in the United States and Canada. 3rd ed. New York, Bowker, 1967. pp. ix, 1221. 25cm.

- Brazil

BRAZIL. 1967. Informe sôbre o Servico de Bibliotecas Escolares Ambulantes da Superintendência da Fronteira Sudoeste do Pais por Miriam Mara Dantur de la Rocha: (V Congresso Brasileiro de Biblioteconomia e Documentação, São Paulo, 8 a 15 de janeiro de 1967...Tema 3: bibliotecas gerais). (Superintendência do Plano de Valorização Econômica da Região Fronteira Sudoeste do Pais) [Pôrto Alegre, 1967]. fo. 13. bibliog. 33cm.

- Canada

CONFERENCE ON COMPUTERS IN CANADIAN LIBRARIES, QUEBEC, 1966. A report prepared for the Canadian Association of College and University Libraries. [Vancouver], University of B.C. Library, 1966. fo.13. 28cm.

- Europe - Directories

LEWANSKI (RICHARD CASIMIR) compiler. European library directory: a geographical and bibliographical guide, etc. Firenze, Olschki, 1968. pp. xxvii, 774. 23½cm.

LIBRARIES (Cont'd.)

- Finland

[KAUPPI (HILKKA M.)] ed. Libraries in Finland. 2nd ed. [Helsinki, Finnish Library Association, 1967]. pp. 47. 14½cm.x21cm.

- France

HASSENFORDER (JEAN) Développement comparé des bibliothèques publiques en France, en Grand-Bretagne et aux États-Unis dans la seconde moitié du XIXe siècle 1850-1914. Paris, Cercle de la Librairie, 1967. pp. 210. bibliog. 25cm. (Bibliographie de la France. Partie Chronique)

- Germany

ANDRAE (FRIEDRICH) ed. Volksbücherei und Nationalsozialismus: Materialien zur Theorie und Politik des öffentlichen Büchereiwesens in Deutschland, 1933-1945. Wiesbaden, 1970. pp. 200. (Deutscher Büchereiverband and Verein der Bibliothekare an Öffentlichen Büchereien. Beiträge zum Büchereiwesen. Reihe B. Quellen und Texte. Heft 3)

- Germany, Eastern

THILO (MARTIN) Das Bibliothekswesen in der Sowjetischen Besatzungszone Deutschlands. Bonn, 1964. pp. 191. bibliog. 20½cm. (Germany (Bundersrepublik). Bundesministerium für Gesamtdeutsche Fragen. Bonner Berichte aus Mittel- und Ostdeutschland)

THILO (MARTIN) Das Bibliothekwesen in der sowjetischen Besatzungszone Deutschlands. 2nd ed. Bonn, 1965. pp. 243. bibliog. 20½cm. (Germany (Bundesrepublik). Bundesministerium für Gesamtdeutsche Fragen. Bonner Berichte aus Mittel- und Ostdeutschland)

- Ireland (Republic) - Directories

LIBRARY ASSOCIATION. Address list of public library authorities in the United Kingdom and the Republic of Ireland, with a select list of academic, government and national libraries. [4th ed.] London, [1969]. pp. 59.

- Italy

CARINI DAINOTTI (VIRGINIA) La biblioteca pubblica in Italia tra cronaca e storia, 1947-1967: scritti, discorsi, documenti. Firenze, 1969. 2 vols.

- Pakistan

PAKISTAN. Central Bureau of Education. 1967. Second five-year plan development projects and their evaluation. [Karachi], 1967. pp. 56.

- Russia - Directories

BIBLIOTEKI SSSR obshchestvenno-politicheskogo, filologicheskogo i iskusstvovedcheskogo profilia: spravochnik. Moskva, 1969. pp. 343.

- Russia - Siberia

IZ istorii knigi, bibliotechnogo dela i bibliografii v Sibiri. Novosibirsk, 1969. pp. 284.

- Scandinavia - Special collections

ÅBO. Akademi. Acta Academiae Aboensis. Humaniora. 27.3. British and American literary letters in Scandinavian public collections: a survey; by Nils Erik Enkvist. Åbo, 1964. pp. 110.

- Scandinavia - Union lists

ÅBO. Akademi. Acta Academiae Aboensis. Humaniora. 27.3. British and American literary letters in Scandinavian public collections: a survey; by Nils Erik Enkvist. Åbo, 1964. pp. 110.

- South Africa

SOUTH AFRICA. Interdepartmental Committee on the Libraries of the Union of South Africa. 1937. Report; [Robert B. Young, chairman] Cape Town, 1937. pp. 64,66. bibliog. 24½cm. In English and Afrikaans.

Die SUID-Afrikaanse Biblioteek: sy geskiedenis, versamelinge en bibliotekarisse, 1818-1968; bydraes aangebied by geleentheid van die honderd-en-vyftigjarige bestaan onder redaksie van C. Pama. [Cape Town], 1968. pp. 216.

- United Kingdom

BRITISH LIBRARIANSHIP AND INFORMATION SCIENCE; ed. by H.A. Whatley; [pd. by] the Library Association. quinquennial, 1966/1970 [1st issue]- London.

WOOD (BRUCE) The public library service. London, London University, London School of Economics and Political Science, Greater London Group, 1966. pp. 34. 30cm. (Town Government in South East England. Research Studies. No. 3)

HASSENFORDER (JEAN) Développement comparé des bibliothèques publiques en France, en Grand-Bretagne et aux États-Unis dans la seconde moitié du XIXe siècle 1850-1914. Paris, Cercle de la Librairie, 1967. pp. 210. bibliog. 25cm. (Bibliographie de la France. Partie Chronique)

ASTBURY (RAYMOND GEORGE) ed. Libraries and the book trade: papers delivered at a symposium held at Liverpool School of Librarianship, May 1967. London, Bingley, 1968. pp. 194. 21½cm.

JORDAN (PETER) ed. Working conditions in libraries: a survey;...contributors Graham Crowther [and others]. [London], Association of Assistant Librarians, 1968. pp. 71. 31cm.

U.K. Department of Education and Science. Education and science. a., 1969- London.

EAGLE (SELWYN) ed. Library resources in London and South East England. London, Library Association, Reference, Special and Information Section, South Eastern Group, 1969. pp. viii, 380.

KAUFMAN (PAUL) Libraries and their users: collected papers in library history. London, 1969 repr. 1971. pp. 233.

The WRITER in the market place: papers delivered at a symposium held at Liverpool School of Librarianship, April 1968, and edited by Raymond Astbury. London, 1969. pp. 176.

ADAMSON (DONALD) Dusty heritage: a national policy for museums and libraries. London, [1971]. pp. 41.

- United Kingdom - Directories

ASSOCIATION OF SPECIAL LIBRARIES AND INFORMATION BUREAUX. Aslib directory...; edited by Brian J. Wilson. 3rd ed. London, Aslib, 1968-70. 2 vols.

LIBRARY ASSOCIATION. Address list of public library authorities in the United Kingdom and the Republic of Ireland, with a select list of academic, government and national libraries. London, [1969]. pp. 59. [4th ed.]

WALKER (GREGORY) ed. Directory of libraries and special collections on Eastern Europe and the U.S.S.R. London, 1971. pp. 159.

- United Kingdom - Special collections

WALKER (GREGORY) ed. Directory of libraries and special collections on Eastern Europe and the U.S.S.R. London, 1971. pp. 159.

- United Kingdom - Union lists

JOHNSON (R.S.) compiler. Foreign theses in British libraries. Cardiff, 1971. pp. 27.

- United Kingdom - Scotland

SMITH (COLIN) b. 1919, and others, eds. Library resources in Scotland;...industrial adviser Douglas Roxburgh. Glasgow, Scottish Library Association, 1968. pp. viii, 107.

STANDARDS for the public library service in Scotland: report of a working party appointed by the Secretary of State for Scotland: [I.M. Robertson, chairman]. Edinburgh, H.M.S.O., 1969. pp. 48.

- United States

BOSTWICK (ARTHUR ELMORE) ed. The Library and society: reprints of papers and addresses; [reprint of the work originally published by the H. W. Wilson Company in 1921]. Freeport, Books for Libraries P., 1968. pp. 474. 21cm. (Essay Index Reprint Series)

MOORE (EVERETT THOMSON) Issues of freedom in American libraries. Chicago, 1964. pp. 80. (Reprinted from the A.L.A. Bulletin, volumes 54-57, June, 1960-June, 1963)

HASSENFORDER (JEAN) Développement comparé des bibliothèques publiques en France, en Grand-Bretagne et aux États-Unis dans la seconde moitié du XIXe siècle 1850-1914. Paris, Cercle de la Librairie, 1967. pp. 210. bibliog. 25cm. (Bibliographie de la France. Partie Chronique)

ILLINOIS UNIVERSITY. Graduate School of Library Science. Institute, 1966. Federal legislation for libraries; papers presented at an institute...: edited by Winifred Ladley. Champaign, Ill., Illini Union Bookstore, [1967] pp. vii, 104. 23cm. (Allerton Park Institute. [Publications]. No. 13)

MEISE (NORMAN R.) Conceptual design of an annotated national library system. Metuchen, N.J., 1969. pp. 234. bibliog.

NELSON ASSOCIATES INCORPORATED. Public library systems in the United States: a survey of multi-jurisdictional systems. Chicago, American Library Association, 1969. pp. xvi, 368. 24cm.

- United States - Special collections

ENGLISH (THOMAS H.) Roads to research: distinguished library collections of the Southeast. Athens, Georgia, [1968]. pp. 116. bibliog.

- United States - Year-books

BOWKER ANNUAL OF LIBRARY AND BOOK TRADE INFORMATION, THE;...sponsored by the Council of National Library Associations. New York, annual, 1968 (13th ed.). 24cm.

- Uruguay

ESPINOSA BORGES (I.A.) Problemas bibliotecarios del Uruguay: el libro en nuestra sociologia cultural. Montevideo, 1968. pp. 286.

LIBRARIES, COUNTY

STOCKHAM (K.A.) ed. British county libraries, 1919-1969. London, 1969. pp. 126. bibliog.

LIBRARIES, DEPOSITORY

- United States

MECHANIC (SYLVIA) Annotated list of selected United States government publications available to depository libraries; compiled for...the New York State Library. New York, 1971. pp. 407.

LIBRARIES, GOVERNMENTAL, ADMINISTRATIVE, ETC.

GRIEKEN (E. VAN) La bibliothèque du Ministère des Affaires Africaines: son rôle, ses collections et ses ouvrages précieux. Bruxelles, Académie Royale des Sciences d'Outre-Mer, Commission d'Histoire, 1962. pp. 186-201. 24½cm. ([Publications]. No.82) (Extrait du Bulletin de l'Academie...nouvelle serie, tome 8, fasc. 2)

KOREA (REPUBLIC). National Assembly Library. 1964. Guide to the National Assembly Library [Seoul, 1964]. pp. (iv), 43. 21cm. In English and Korean.

U.K. Parliament. House of Commons. Library. 1966. The library of the House of Commons: handbook, etc. [London], 1966. pp. 56. 21½cm.

U.K. Civil Service Commission. 1969. Librarians in government service. London, 1969. pp. 30.

U.K. Parliament. House of Commons. Library. 1970. The library of the House of Commons: handbook, etc. [rev. ed.] [London], 1970. pp. 20.

LIBRARIES, NATIONAL

- Australia

NATIONAL LIBRARY OF AUSTRALIA. Annual report of the Council. 1960/61 (1st) to date.
in Australia. Parliament. [Parliamentary papers].

- Denmark

DENMARK. 1927. Betaenkning vedrørende Statens Biblioteksvaesen; afgiven af det af Undervisningsministeriet under 11. oktober 1924 nedsatte Udvalg. København, 1927. pp. 247. 25½cm.

- Russia

MORACHEVSKII (NIKOLAI IAKOVLEVICH) Guide to the M.E. Saltykov-Shchedrin State Public Library Leningrad...an English translation by Raymond H. Fisher. Los Angeles, 1963. fo. 48. (California University. Library. Occasional Papers. No. 14)

- South Africa

Die SUID-Afrikaanse Biblioteek: sy geskiedenis, versamelinge en bibliotekarisse, 1818-1968; bydraes aangebied by geleentheid van die honderd-en-vyftigjarige bestaan onder redaksie van C. Pama. [Cape Town], 1968. pp. 216.

- United Kingdom

U.K. Department of Education and Science. 1969. National Lending Library for Science and Technology. [2nd ed.] [London], 1969. pp. 17. 23cm.

U.K. National Libraries Committee. 1969. Principal documentary evidence submitted to the...Committee. London, H.M.S.O., 1969. 2 vols. (in 1). Report of the Committee published as British Parliamentary Papers Session 1968/69, Cmnd. 4028.

WATSON (PETER G.) Great Britain's National Lending Library. Los Angeles, 1970. pp. 93. bibliog.

LIBRARIES, PRIVATE

- United Kingdom

UNITED KINGDOM. Parliament. 1643. An ordinance by the Lords and Commons...for the preservation and keeping together for publique use, such books, evideuees [sic], records and writings sequestred or taken by distresse or otherwise, as are fit to be so preserved: [dated 18 November, 1643]. London, Husbands, 1643. pp. 6. 18½cm. Wing E 1780.

LIBRARIES, SPECIAL

- United Kingdom

BURKETT (JACK) ed. Trends in special librarianship: based on a series of lectures delivered at Ealing Technical College, April 1968. London, Bingley, 1968. pp. 205. 21½cm.

- United States

ASSOCIATION OF RESEARCH LIBRARIES. Minutes of the meeting. Washington, D.C., semi-annual, Jan.1968 (71st) to date. 28cm.

LIBRARIES, STORAGE

ELLSWORTH (RALPH EUGENE) The economics of book storage in college and university libraries. Metuchen, N.J., 1969. pp. 135. bibliog.

LIBRARIES, SUBSCRIPTION

GRIEST (GUINEVERE L.) Mudie's circulating library and the Victorian novel. Bloomington, Ind., [1970]. pp. 272. bibliog.

LIBRARIES, UNIVERSITY AND COLLEGE

CHICAGO. University. Graduate Library School. 19th Annual Conference. The function of the library in the modern college: the nineteenth annual conference, ...June 14-18, 1954; edited by Herman H. Fussler. Chicago, U. of Chicago P., 1954, repr. 1967. pp. vii, 117. 24cm. (Studies in Library Science)

BUCKLAND (M.K.) and WOODBURN (I.) An analytical approach to duplication and availability. Lancaster, 1968. pp. 24. (Lancaster. University. Library. Occasional Papers. No. 2)

GELFAND (MORRIS A.) University libraries for developing countries. [Paris], United Nations Educational, Scientific and Cultural Organization, 1968. pp. 157. bibliog. (Public Library Manuals. 14)

SAUNDERS (WILFRED LEONARD) ed. University and research library studies: some contributions from the University of Sheffield, Postgraduate School of Librarianship and Information Science. Oxford, Pergamon P., 1968. pp. ix, 221. 22½cm. (International Series of Monographs in Library and Information Science. vol. 8)

DURHAM. University. Project for Evaluating the Benefits from University Libraries. Final report. [Durham], 1969 repr. 1970. pp. various. bibliogs.

ELLSWORTH (RALPH EUGENE) The economics of book storage in college and university libraries. Metuchen, N.J., 1969. pp. 135. bibliog.

SYSTEMS analysis of a university library: final report on a research project; by M.K. Buckland [and others]. [Lancaster], 1970. pp. 57. bibliog. (Lancaster. University. Library. Occasional Papers. No. 4)

METCALF (KEYES DEWITT) and ELLSWORTH (RALPH EUGENE) Planning the academic library: Metcalf and Ellsworth at York; edited by Harry Faulkner Brown. Newcastle upon Tyne, 1971. pp. 97.

ROGERS (RUTHERFORD DAVID) and WEBER (DAVID CARTER) University library administration. New York, 1971. pp. 454. bibliogs.

- Canada

> CANADIAN ASSOCIATION OF COLLEGE AND UNIVERSITY LIBRARIES. University Library Standards Committee. Guide to Canadian university library standards: report... 1961-1964. [Waterloo], 1965. fo. v, 53. 28cm.

- Finland

> GRONROOS (HENRIK) and MYLLYNIEMI (KAIJA) Helsinki university library: a short survey. 2nd rev.ed. Helsinki, 1965. pp. 35. bibliog.

- Germany

> HAMBURG. Staats- und Universitäts-Bibliothek. Der Wiederaufbau der Staats- und Universitäts-Bibliothek Hamburg: 10. bis 12. Jahresbericht umfassend die Jahre 1954/55, 1955/56, 1956/57. Hamburg, 1957. pp. 132.

> BURR (VIKTOR) and WENIG (OTTO) Universitäts-Bibliothek Bonn: erfüllte Bauaufgaben; ein Bericht. Bonn, 1962. pp. 55.

- Japan

> OSAKA (CITY). University. Library. Katalog der Werner Sombart-Bibliothek in der städtischen Universität Osaka. [Osaka], 1967. pp. 350.

- United Kingdom

> HEADICAR (BERTIE MASON) Aids to research...; with select bibliographies...by C. Fuller. London, 1931. pp. 16. (Reprinted from Bulletins of the British Library of Political and Economic Science)

> ASSOCIATION OF UNIVERSITY TEACHERS. The university library. London. 1964. pp. 7.

> BRYAN (HARRISON) A critical survey of university libraries and librarianship in Great Britain. Adelaide, 1966. pp. iii, 255. bibliog. 23cm. (Libraries Board of South Australia. Occasional Papers in Librarianship. No. 4)

> OXFORD. University. Committee on University Libraries. Report; [chairman, R. Shackleton]. [Oxford, University Press, 1966]. pp. 210. 21½cm. Supplement No.1 to the University Gazette, vol.97, November 1966.

> **RESEARCH into library services in higher education; papers presented at a conference held at the University of London on Friday November 3rd 1967** London, 1968. pp. 31.

> **STANDING CONFERENCE OF LIBRARIANS OF LIBRARIES OF THE UNIVERSITY OF LONDON. Guide to the admission of academic staff, students and other visitors to libraries within the University of London.** [London], 1968. pp. 19. 21½cm.

> NEAL (K. W.) British university libraries. Wilmslow, 1970. pp. 149. bibliogs.

> YORK. University. Library Guides. No. 8. Notes on using the catalogues. [York, 1970] pp. 12.

- United States

> SPELL (LOTA M.) Research materials for the study of Latin America at the University of Texas. Austin, U. of Texas P., 1954. pp. ix, 107. (Texas University. Institute of Latin American Studies. Latin American Studies. 14)

> KNAPP (PATRICIA B.) and others. The Monteith College library experiment. New York, Scarecrow P., 1966. pp. 293. 21½cm.

> AMERICAN LIBRARY ASSOCIATION. Library Administration Division. Library statistics of colleges and universities, 1965-66: institutional data. Chicago, 1967. pp. 234. 27cm.

> HARVARD UNIVERSITY. Library. Guides to the Harvard Libraries. No. 10. Afro-American Studies: a guide to resources of the Harvard University Library. Cambridge, [Mass.], 1969. pp. 36. bibliog.

> **RAFFEL (JEFFREY A.) and SHISHKO (ROBERT) Systematic analysis of university libraries: an application of cost-benefit analysis to the M.I.T. libraries.** Cambridge, Mass., [1969]. pp. 107. bibliog.

LIBRARIES AND READERS

> HEADICAR (BERTIE MASON) Aids to research...; with select bibliographies...by C. Fuller. London, 1931. pp. 16. (Reprinted from Bulletins of the British Library of Political and Economic Science)

> MOORE (EVERETT THOMSON) Issues of freedom in American libraries. Chicago, 1964. pp. 80. (Reprinted from the A.L.A. Bulletin, volumes 54-57, June, 1960-June, 1963)

> BUCKLAND (M.K.) and WOODBURN (I.) An analytical approach to duplication and availability. Lancaster, 1968. pp. 24. (Lancaster. University. Library. Occasional Papers. No. 2)

> KISTER (KENNETH F.) Social issues and library problems: case studies in the social sciences. New York, Bowker, 1968. pp. xxvii, 190. bibliog. 23cm.

> KAUFMAN (PAUL) Libraries and their users: collected papers in library history. London, 1969 repr. 1971. pp. 233.

> SLATER (MARGARET) and FISHER (PAMELA) Use made of technical libraries. London, Aslib, [1969]. pp. vi, 86. bibliog. 29½cm. (Occasional Publications. No. 2)

> **WHOLE earth library and switchboard:...report to [Keele University] Union general meeting; prepared by Dave Wickens [and others]. [Keele, 1972]** 1 pamphlet (unpaged).

LIBRARIES AND STATE

- Germany

ANDRAE (FRIEDRICH) ed. Volksbücherei und National-sozialismus: Materialien zur Theorie und Politik des öffentlichen Büchereiwesens in Deutschland, 1933-1945. Wiesbaden, 1970. pp. 200. (Deutscher Büchereiverband und Verein der Bibliothekare an Öffentlichen Büchereien. Beiträge zum Büchereiwesen. Reihe B. Quellen und Texte. Heft 3)

- United Kingdom

RADCLIFFE (CYRIL JOHN) Viscount Radcliffe. Government by contempt: a speech in the House of Lords;...with some relevant documents. London, Chatto and Windus, 1968. pp. 32. 19½cm.

LIBRARY ADMINISTRATION

BUCKLAND (M.K.) and WOODBURN (I.) An analytical approach to duplication and availability. Lancaster, 1968. pp. 24. (Lancaster. University. Library. Occasional Papers. No. 2)

BUCKLAND (M.K.) and WOODBURN (I.) Some implications for library management of scattering and obsolescence. Lancaster, 1968. pp. 25. (Lancaster. University. Library. Occasional Papers. No. 1)

MORSE (PHILIP McCORD) Library effectiveness: a systems approach. Cambridge, M.I.T Press, [1968]. pp. xi, 207. 23cm.

RAFFEL (JEFFREY A.) and SHISHKO (ROBERT) Systematic analysis of university libraries: an application of cost-benefit analysis to the M.I.T. libraries. Cambridge, Mass., [1969]. pp. 107. bibliog.

ROBINSON (F.) and others. Systems analysis in libraries. Newcastle-upon-Tyne, 1969. pp. 55.

THOMAS (P.A.) and EAST (H.) The use of bibliographic records in libraries. London, Aslib, [1969]. pp. v, 51. bibliog. 29cm. (Occasional Publications. No. 3)

SYSTEMS analysis of a university library: final report on a research project; by M.K. Buckland [and others]. [Lancaster], 1970. pp. 57. bibliog. (Lancaster. University. Library. Occasional Papers. No. 4)

ROGERS (RUTHERFORD DAVID) and WEBER (DAVID CARTER) University library administration. New York, 1971. pp. 454. bibliogs.

LIBRARY ARCHITECTURE

LIBRARY technology and architecture: report of a conference held at the Harvard Graduate School of Education, February 9, 1967. Cambridge, Harvard University, Graduate School of Education, Library, 1968. pp. ix, 51. 25½cm.

LIBRARY ASSOCIATIONS

HUNT (KENNETH GEOFFREY) The Association of Metropolitan Chief Librarians: an account of its work for library services in their relation to London local government. London, the Association, 1967. pp. (iii), 37. 21cm. (Library Association. Pamphlets. No. 29)

LIGUE DES BIBLIOTHEQUES EUROPEENNES DE RECHERCHE. Statuts. [Strasbourg?, 1971] fo. 5.

LIBRARY FITTINGS AND SUPPLIES

DEWE (MICHAEL) Library supply agencies in Europe. London, 1968. pp. 205. bibliog.

LIBRARY LEGISLATION

- Germany

NITZE (ANDREAS) Die Rechtsstellung der wissenschaftlichen Bibliotheken: zugleich ein Beitrag zum Anstaltsrecht. Berlin, Duncker & Humblot, [1967]. pp. 172. bibliog. 23cm. (Schriften zum Öffentlichen Recht. Band 67)

LIBRARY OF CONGRESS

UNITED STATES. Library of Congress. Automation and the Library of Congress. Washington, 1963. pp. vii, 88.

MacCLOSKEY (MONRO) Our national attic: the Library of Congress, the Smithsonian Institution, the National Archives. New York, Richards Rosen P., 1968. pp. 191. 21cm.

LIBRARY PLANNING

METCALF (KEYES DEWITT) and ELLSWORTH (RALPH EUGENE) Planning the academic library: Metcalf and Ellsworth at York; edited by Harry Faulkner Brown. Newcastle upon Tyne, 1971. pp. 97.

LIBRARY RESOURCES ON SOUTHEASTERN ASIA

[HULL. University.] South-East Asia Library Group. Survey of library resources. [Hull, 1969 in progress]. Looseleaf.

LIBRARY SCHOOLS AND TRAINING

ORGANIZATION OF AMERICAN STATES. 1964. Guia de escuelas y cursos de bibliotecologia en América Latina;...compilado por Carmen Rovira. (Bibliographic Series. No. 36, Rev. 2) 3rd ed. Washington, 1964. pp. viii, 66. 27cm. For second edition see ORGANIZATION OF AMERICAN STATES. 1959.

INTERNATIONAL CONFERENCE ON LIBRARIANSHIP, URBANA, 1967. Library education: an international survey edited by Larry Earl Bone; papers...; conducted by the University of Illinois, Graduate School of Library Science, June 12-16, 1967. [Urbana], University of Illinois, Graduate School of Library Science, [1968]. pp. xiii, 388. 22½cm.

LIBRARY ADVISORY COUNCIL (ENGLAND) A report on the supply and training of librarians. London, H.M.S.O., 1968. pp. viii, 64. 24½cm.

SCHUR (H.) and others. Education and training for scientific and technological library and information work. London, H.M.S.O., 1968. pp. vii, 79. bibliog. 24½cm.

BRAMLEY (GERALD A.J.) A history of library education. London, Bingley, 1969. pp. 131. 21½cm.

SEMINAR ON HUMAN ASPECTS OF LIBRARY INSTRUCTION, READING, 1969. Proceedings (held at the University of Reading, 9th December); [organised by the] Standing Conference on National and University Libraries. Cardiff, [1970]. pp. 63.

LIBRARY SCIENCE

BRITISH LIBRARIANSHIP AND INFORMATION SCIENCE; ed. by H. A. Whatley; [pd. by] the Library Association. quinquennial, 1966/1970 [1st issue]- London.

FUENFZEHN Jahre Bibliotheksarbeit der Deutschen Forschungsgemeinschaft, 1949-1964: Ergebnisse und Probleme; herausgegeben von Wieland Schmidt und Dieter Oertel. Frankfurt am Main, [1966]. pp. 196. (Zeitschrift für Bibliothekswesen und Bibliographie. Sonderhefte. 4)

CUNHA (GEORGE DANIEL MARTIN) Conservation of library materials: a manual and bibliography on the care, repair and restoration of library materials. Metuchen, Scarecrow P., 1967. pp. x, 405. 21½cm.

KISTER (KENNETH F.) Social issues and library problems: case studies in the social sciences. New York, Bowker, 1968. pp. xxvii, 190. bibliog. 23cm.

COUNCIL ON LIBRARY RESOURCES. Annual report. a., 1969/70 (14th)- Washington, D.C.

BUCH, Bibliothek, Leser: Festschrift für Horst Kunze zum 60. Geburtstag; (herausgegeben von Werner Dube [and others]). Berlin, 1969. pp. 651. bibliogs. In various languages, with German summaries.

DAVINSON (DONALD E.) The periodicals collection: its purpose and uses in libraries. London, 1969. pp. 212.

MACKENZIE (A. GRAHAM) and STUART (IAN M.) eds. Planning library services: proceedings of a research seminar held at the University of Lancaster, 9-11 July, 1969. [Lancaster], 1969. pp. various. bibliogs. (Lancaster. University. Library. Occasional Papers. No. 3)

PENNA (CARLOS V.) The planning of library and documentation services; second edition, revised and enlarged by P.H. Sewell and Herman Liebaers. Paris, United Nations Educational, Scientific and Cultural Organization, 1970. pp. 158. bibliog. (Public Library Manuals. 17)

- Abstracts

UNITED STATES. Education Office. Library science dissertations, 1925-60: an annotated bibliography of doctoral studies. Washington, 1963. pp. viii, 120

- Bibliography

Die FACHLITERATUR zum Buch- und Bibliothekswesen. 8th ed. München-Pullach, Dokumentation, 1967. pp. viii, 636. 21cm. (Handbuch der technischen Dokumentation und Bibliographie. Band 2)

MAXWELL (ROBERT) AND COMPANY. Documentation Centre. New reference tools for librarians; 1966/67 edition, with a bibliography of new books on the library sciences; compiled and edited by the editorial staff of the Documentation Centre. [3rd ed.]. Oxford, Maxwell, [1969]. pp.vi,230.

REYNOLDS (ROSE) compiler. A selective bibliography on measurement in library and information services. London, [1970]. pp. 19.

- Dictionaries and encyclopaedias

VOCABULARIUM bibliothecarii Nordicum: Engelsk, Dansk, Norsk, Svensk, Finsk; udgivet af Nordisk Videnskabeligt Bibliotekarforbund ved Torben Nielsen. København, 1968. pp. 278.
Cataloguing Room

PIPICS (ZOLTÁN) ed. Dictionarium bibliothecarii practicum; ad usum internationalem in XX linguis; Wörterbuch des Bibliothekars in zwanzig Sprachen; The librarian's practical dictionary in twenty languages. 4th ed. München-Pullach, [1970]. pp. 375.
Cataloguing Room

- Periodicals - Bibliography

WINCKLER (PAUL A.) Library periodicals directory: a selected list of periodicals currently published throughout the world relating to library work. Brookville, N.Y., 1967. pp. 76.

- Research

RESEARCH into library services in higher education; papers presented at a conference held at the University of London on Friday November 3rd 1967. London, 1968. pp. 31.

LIBRARY SCIENCE AS A PROFESSION

UNITED STATES. Employment Security Bureau. Occupations in the field of library science. [Washington, 1966]. pp. vi, 58.

LIBRARY STATISTICS

AMERICAN LIBRARY ASSOCIATION. Library Administration Division. Library statistics of colleges and universities, 1965-66: institutional data. Chicago, 1967. pp. 234. 27cm.

INTERNATIONAL FEDERATION OF LIBRARY ASSOCIATIONS. The international standardisation of library statistics: a progress report; [the proceedings of conferences held at The Hague, 1966, and Paris, 1967]. London, 1968. pp. 216.

FUSSLER (HERMAN HOWE) and SIMON (JULIAN L.) Patterns in the use of books in large research libraries. Chicago, 1969. pp. 210. bibliog. (Chicago. University. Studies in Library Science)

LIBRARY SUPPLY AGENCIES

DEWE (MICHAEL) Library supply agencies in Europe. London, 1968. pp. 205. bibliog.

LIBYA

- Census

LIBYA. Census, 1964. General population census, 1964. Tripoli, [1965?] pp. 86. In English and Arabic.

- Commerce

LIBYA. Census and Statistical Department. Imports by oil companies. bien., 1969/1970- [Tripoli]

LIBYA. Census and Statistical Department. 1969. Trends in Libyan imports and exports, 1962-1968. [Tripoli, 1969]. 2 pts (in 1.) In English and Arabic.

- Commerce - India

INDIAN INSTITUTE OF FOREIGN TRADE. [Country survey report]: export market report on Libya; prepared for the Ministry of Commerce, Government of India. New Delhi, 1966. pp. 297. bibliog.

- Commerce - United States

UNITED STATES. International Commerce Bureau. Libya: a market for U.S. products. Washington, 1962. pp. x, 65. bibliog.

- Constitutional history

PELT (ADRIAN) Libyan independence and the United Nations: a case of planned decolonization...; foreword by U Thant. New Haven, 1970. pp. 1016. Map in end pocket.

- Description and travel

WRIGHT (JOHN) Civil servant. Libya. London, Benn, 1969. pp. 304. bibliog. 21½cm. (Nations of the Modern World)

- Economic conditions

UNITED STATES. International Commerce Bureau. Libya: a market for U.S. products. Washington, 1962. pp. x, 65. bibliog.

INDIAN INSTITUTE OF FOREIGN TRADE. [Country survey report]: export market report on Libya; prepared for the Ministry of Commerce, Government of India. New Delhi, 1966. pp. 297. bibliog.

INTERNATIONAL LABOUR OFFICE. 1967. Report to the government of Libya on the role of handicrafts in a rapidly developing economy. (ILO/TF/Libya/R.14) Geneva, 1967. pp. 67.

ELDBLOM (LARS) Structure foncière: organisation et structure sociale; une étude comparative sur la vie socio-économique dans les trois oasis libyennes de Ghat, Mourzouk et particulièrement Ghadamès. Lund, Uniskol, 1968. pp. 424. bibliog. 23½cm. (Lund. Universitet, Geografiska Institution. Meddelanden. Avhandlingar. 55) Map in end pocket. With English summary.

FRANCE. Direction de la Documentation. La Documentation Française. Notes et Études Documentaires. No. 3,525. L'économie de la Libye. Paris, 1968. pp. 16. 27cm.

- Economic history

ANDERSEN (PETER) Die wirtschaftliche Entwicklung Libyens auf der Grundlage seiner Erdölindustrie. Bonn, 1969. pp. 184. bibliog.

- Economic policy

LIBYA. 1958-59. Financing of development programmes: a report on development expenditures planned and made in the years 1952/3 to 1957/8; (and Report on development expenditures, 1957/1958 to 1959/60). (Development Council) [Tripoli], 1958-[59?] 2pts. 32cm.

FARLEY (RAWLE) Planning for development in Libya: the exceptional economy in the developing world. New York, 1971. pp. 349. bibliog.

- History

WRIGHT (JOHN) Civil servant. Libya. London, Benn, 1969. pp. 304. bibliog. 21½cm. (Nations of the Modern World)

- Industries

LIBYA. Census and Statistical Department. Monthly statistics of production and employment in selected large manufacturing establishments. [in English and Arabic] q., Ja/Mr 1970 [1st issue]- Guimada El-Tani.

- Population

LIBYA. Census and Statistical Department. 1969. Report on the first phase of the household sample survey. [Paper 1.] Tripoli Town. [Tripoli, 1969.] pp. 10,39. In English and Arabic.

LIBYA. Census and Statistical Department. 1969. Report on the first phase of the household sample survey. [Paper 2.] Benghazi Town. [Tripoli, 1969.] pp. 10,39. In English and Arabic.

LIBYA. Census and Statistical Department. 1970. Report on the first phase of the household sample survey. (Papers 3 and 4.) Tripoli and Benghazi: economically active population. [Tripoli, 1970.] fo. xvi, pp. 28. In English and Arabic.

LIBYA. Census and Statistical Department. 1970. Report on the first phase of the household sample survey. (Paper 5.) Tripoli and Benghazi: economically inactive population. [Tripoli, 1970.] fo. xii, pp. 14. In English and Arabic.

- Social conditions

ELDBLOM (LARS) Structure foncière: organisation et structure sociale; une étude comparative sur la vie socio-économique dans les trois oasis libyennes de Ghat, Mourzouk et particulièrement Ghadamès. Lund, Uniskol, 1968. pp. 424. bibliog. 23½cm. (Lund. Universitet, Geografiska Institution. Meddelanden. Avhandlingar. 55) Map in end pocket. With English summary.

LICENCE SYSTEM

- Canada - British Columbia

BRITISH COLUMBIA. Liquor Control Board. Annual report. Victoria, B.C., annual, 1939/40-1941/2, 1943/4, 1944/5, 1946/7, 1947/8 (19th-21st, 23rd, 24th, 26th, 27th reps.). 26½cm.

- Canada - Saskatchewan

SASKATCHEWAN. Liquor Sales Outlets Inquiry Committee. 1958. Report. [Peter A. Howe, Chairman]. Regina, 1958. pp. 48.

- New Zealand

NEW ZEALAND. [General Assembly]. House of Representatives. Licensing Committee. 1960. Mr. R.A. Keeling. chairman. Wellington, 1960. pp. 96.

- United Kingdom

THEN and now!: a contrast;...Messrs. Cardwell and Harcourt and their constituents; great meeting in the Town Hall. London, [1873?]. pp. 12. (From the Oxford Chronicle, January 4th, 1873)

PATERSON (JAMES) Barrister-at-Law. Licensing acts; seventy-seventh edition...by J.N. Martin. London, Butterworths, 1969. pp. lxxi,1735,240. 19½cm.

- United Kingdom - Ireland, Northern

IRELAND, NORTHERN. H.C. 2047. Report from the Committee of Privileges together with the proceedings..., minutes of evidence and appendices: complaint concerning articles in the Belfast Telegraph of 8th July, 1970. Belfast, 1970. pp. 39.

- United Kingdom - Scotland

SCOTLAND. Scottish Home and Health Department. 1968. Temperance polls, 1962-67: return of voting areas in Scotland in which polls under part 8 of the Licensing (Scotland) Act, 1959, were taken during the period 1962-67 [etc.] Edinburgh, 1968. pp. (3).

LICENCES

- India

HAZARI (RABINDRA KISHEN) Industrial planning and licensing policy: final report. [Delhi], Planning Commission, [1967-68]. 2 vols. (in 6).

HAZARI (RABINDRA KISHEN) Industrial planning and licensing policy: interim report to Planning Commission. [Delhi, Ministry of Industry, 1967]. pp. 96. 24cm.

MOHNOT (SOHAN RAJ) Monopoly, concentration and industrial licensing. Calcutta, 1968. pp. 171.

INDIA. Industrial Licensing Policy Inquiry Committee. 1969. Report; [with] Appendices 1-4. [Delhi]. 1969. 5 pts. (in 1).

- South Africa

SOUTH AFRICA. 1913. Financial Relations Bill: memorandum showing the revenue licences in force in the respective provinces, etc. (U.G. 29/1913). in South Africa. Parliament. House of Assembly. Votes and proceedings; (with Printed annexures).

SOUTH AFRICA. Committee of Enquiry into the Financial Relations between the Central Government, the Provinces and Local Authorities. 1964. Sixth interim report...: trading and other licences: [C.L.F. Borckenhagen, chairman]. Pretoria, [1964]. fo. 33.

- United Kingdom

U.K. Ministry of Transport. 1967. Proposals for a new system of carrier licensing: note by the Minister of Transport. [London, 1967]. pp. 6. 33cm.

STREET (HARRY) Justice in the welfare state. London, Stevens, 1968. pp. x,130. 18½cm. (Hamlyn Lectures. 20th series)

LICHTENBERG (GEORG CHRISTOPH) the Elder

LICHTENBERG (GEORG CHRISTOPH) the Elder. Lichtenberg: aphorisms and letters; translated and edited by Franz Mautner and Henry Hatfield. London, 1969. pp. 124. bibliog.

LIDHJA SOCIALISTE TË POPULLIT PUNUES TË SERBIS PËR KOSOVË E METOHI

- Congresses

LIDHJA SOCIALISTE TË POPULLIT PUNUES TË SERBIS PËR KOSOVË E METOHI. Konferenca, e 6, 1960. Konferenca, etc. Prishtinë, 1961. pp. 163.

LIDICE

WHEELER (ELEANOR) Lidice. Prague, Orbis, 1957. pp. 34. 20cm.

LIE ALGEBRAS

BOURBAKI (NICOLAS) pseud. Eléments de mathématique...: groupes et algèbres de Lie. Paris, 1968 in progress. bibliog.

LIE GROUPS

FREUDENTHAL (HANS) and VRIES (HILLE DE) Linear Lie groups. New York, 1969. pp. 547.

LIEBKNECHT (KARL)

ADLER (MAX) Helden der sozialen Revolution. Berlin, 1926. pp. 53.

BADIA (GILBERT) Le spartakisme: les dernières années de Rosa Luxemburg et de Karl Liebknecht, 1914-1919. Paris, L'Arche, [1967]. pp. 438. bibliog. 18cm.

LIEBKNECHT (KARL) (Cont'd.)

HANNOVER-DRUECK (ELISABETH) and HANNOVER (HEINRICH) eds. Der Mord an Rosa Luxemburg und Karl Liebknecht: Dokumentation eines politischen Verbrechens. Frankfurt am Main, Suhrkamp, 1967. pp. 185. 18cm.

SCHIEL (ILSE) and MILZ (ERNA) eds. Karl und Rosa: Erinnerungen; zum 100. Geburtstag von Karl Liebknecht und Rosa Luxemburg. Berlin, 1971. pp. 300. bibliog.

TROTSKII (LEV DAVYDOVICH) Martyrs of the Third International; Karl Liebknecht, Rosa Luxemburg. London, [1971]. pp. 15.

LIEBKNECHT (WILHELM PHILIPP MARTIN CHRISTIAN LUDWIG)

CHUBINSKII (VADIM VASIL'EVICH) Вильгельм Либкнехт - солдат революции. Москва, 1968. pp. 214.

LIECHTENSTEIN

- Constitutional history

PAPPERMANN (ERNST) Die Regierung des Fürstentums Liechtenstein. Bigge, 1967. pp. 159. bibliog.

- Economic conditions

SCHNETZLER (HANSWERNER) Beiträge zur Abklärung der Wirtschaftsstruktur des Fürstentums Liechtenstein. Winterthur, Schellenberg, 1966. pp. xviii, 329. bibliog. 22½cm.

- History

RATON (PIERRE) Liechtenstein: history and institutions of the principality. Vaduz, [1970]. pp. 150. bibliog.

- Politics and government

PAPPERMANN (ERNST) Die Regierung des Fürstentums Liechtenstein. Bigge, 1967. pp. 159. bibliog.

RATON (PIERRE) Liechtenstein: history and institutions of the principality. Vaduz, [1970]. pp. 150. bibliog.

LIEGE

- Economic history - Sources

LINOTTE (LEON) Les manifestations et les grèves à Liège de l'an IV à 1914: (inventaire sommaire des archives de la police de la ville de Liège). Leuven, 1969. pp. 140. (Centre Interuniversitaire d'Histoire Contemporaine. Cahiers. 53)

- Industries

MAKART (J.) and BRIMIOULLE (J.) Investissements industriels et fonction de production. Bruxelles, Bruylant, 1968. pp. 63. bibliog. 24cm. (Liège. Université. Séminaire Interdisciplinaire des Professeurs Harsin et Davin. Travaux. No. 6)

LIEGE (PROVINCE)

- Economic conditions

LIÈGE. Administration Communale. Échevinat des Services Sociaux et de la Famille. La région liégeoise: démographie, logement, industrie, commerce, services; l'évolution depuis 1947 et les données du recensement général de 1961. Liège, 1966. pp. 174. 31cm.

- Industries

BELGIUM. Ministère des Affaires Etrangères et du Commerce Extérieur. 1967. Liège and industry. Brussels, 1967. pp. 16. (Memo from Belgium. No. 85.)

- Population

LIÈGE. Administration Communale. Échevinat des Services Sociaux et de la Famille. La région liégeoise: démographie, logement, industrie, commerce, services; l'évolution depuis 1947 et les données du recensement général de 1961. Liège, 1966. pp. 174. 31cm.

LIENS

WUERDINGER (HANS) Das Brüsseler Haftungsabkommen von 1957 und seine Bedeutung für die Schiffsgläubigerrechte: Vortrag...am 17. Januar 1962. Hamburg, 1962. pp. 16. (Deutscher Verein für Internationales Seerecht. Schriften. Reihe A: Berichte und Vorträge. Heft 8)
R(P)

ASSER (JAN) Maritime liens and mortgages in the conflict of laws. Göteborg, Gumpert, 1963. pp. 31. 22½cm. (Gothenburg. Handelshögskolan. Skriftserie. 1963.5)

SANDSTRÖM (JAN) Befälhavareavtal och sjöpanträtt Göteborg, Akademiförlaget, 1969. pp. 394. bibliog. 22½cm. (Gothenburg. Handelshögskolan. Skriftserie. 1969. 1) With English summary.

- Netherlands

HEYNING-PLATE (L.S.C.) Eigenrichting tot zekerheid: de exceptio non adimpleti contractus en het retentierecht. Zwolle, [1969?]. pp. 291. bibliog.

LIFE

PANTSKHAVA (IL'IA DIOMIDOVICH) Chelovek, ego zhizn' i bessmertie. Moskva, 1967. pp. 191.

TROTIGNON (PIERRE) L'idée de vie chez Bergson, et la critique de la métaphysique. Paris, 1968. pp. 635. bibliog.

HOFMANN (HANS) Discovering freedom. Boston, [1969]. pp. 100.

LIFE-SAVING

CONVENTION ON ACCIDENT PREVENTION AND LIFE SAVING, 1963. [Proceedings of a public convention held by the] Royal College of Surgeons of England Working Party on Accident Prevention and Life Saving, etc. [London, 1963]. pp. 74. bibliog.

LIGA NARODOWA

KOZICKI (STANISŁAW) Historia Ligi Narodowej: okres 1887-1907. Londyn, Myśl Polska, 1964. pp. 622. 21cm.

LIGHT

BROGLIE (LOUIS DE) Matter and light: the new physics;....translated by W.H. Johnston; [reprint of the edition originally published in 1939]. New York, Dover Publications, [196-?]. pp. 300. 20cm. (Dover Books Explaining Science. Paperbounds. T35)

LIGHTING

U.K. Department of Employment and Productivity. Safety, Health and Welfare. New Series. No.39. Lighting in offices, shops, and railway premises. London, 1969. pp. 34. bibliog. 21½cm.

- Patents

COUNCIL OF EUROPE. 1966. International classification of patents for invention under the European Convention of 19th December 1954: elaboration of section F, mechanics, lighting and heating; prepared by the classification working party of the committee of experts on patents, etc. Strasbourg, 1966. pp. xv, 691. 26½cm.

LIGNITE

- Germany, Eastern

HERTIG (WOLFRAM) Entwicklung der Selbstkosten für die Gewinnung von Rohbraunkohle in den Tagebauen des Industriezweiges Braunkohlenbergbau der DDR von 1957 bis 1961, etc. Leipzig, VEB Deutscher Verlag für Grundstoffindustrie, 1966. pp. 104. bibliog. 24cm. (Freiberg. Bergakademie. Freiberger Forschungshefte. A 359)

- Russia

GRIGOR'EV (KLAVDII NIKOLAEVICH) Канско-Ачинский угольный бассейн: геологическое строение, угленосность и перспективы развития. Москва, Недра, 1968. pp. 184. bibliog. 26см.

LIGURIA

- Economic conditions

ALAURO (ORLANDO D') ed. Studi regionali sull'occupazione: Liguria, etc. Lussemburgo, European Coal and Steel Community, 1957. pp. 74. (Studies and Documents)

UNIONE ITALIANA DELLE CAMERE DI COMMERCIO, INDUSTRIA E AGRICOLTURA. Monografie Regionali per la Programmazione Economica. Liguria; a cura dell'Unione Regionale delle Camere di Commercio della Liguria. [Milan], Giuffrè, [1966]. pp. xv, 241. bibliog. 24cm.

SAVONA. Camera di Commercio, Industria, Agricoltura. Centro Studi Economici. Quaderni di Ricerche. 4. Lo sviluppo economico dei bacini delle Bormide. [Savona], 1968. pp. 151.

- Economic policy

La PROGRAMMAZIONE economica regionale nell'Italia del Nord: Veneto, Liguria; conferenza del Innocenzo Gasparini...[and] conferenza del Augusto Pedulla. Milano, [1968]. pp. 52. (Centro Regionale di Studi Urbanistici della Lombardia. Notiziario. 2)

SAVONA. Camera di Commercio, Industria, Agricoltura. Centro Studi Economici. Quaderni di Ricerche. 4. Lo sviluppo economico dei bacini delle Bormide. [Savona], 1968. pp. 151.

LILBURNE (JOHN)

[LILBURNE (JOHN)] England's miserie and remedie: in a judicious letter from an utter-barrister...concerning Leiutenant [sic] Col. Lilburn's imprisonment in Newgate, Sept. 1645. [London, 1645]. pp. 8. 19cm. Wing L 2105.

[LILBURNE (JOHN)] Innocency and truth justified: first against the unjust aspertions of W. Prinn, called A fresh discovery of prodigious new wandring blazing stars...; next, by a...reply, to his other pamphlet called The lyar confounded...; unto which reply is annext...a letter written by L.C.L. to one of his...friends, etc. [London], 1645[O.S.]. 2 pts. (in 1). 18½cm. Wing L 2118.

A PEARLE in a dounghill; or, Lieu. Col. John Lilburne in New-gate, etc. [London, 1646]. pp. 4. 19cm. Wing P 968.

A REMONSTRANCE of many thousand citizens, and other free-born people of England, to their owne House of Commons occasioned through the illegall and barbarous imprisonment of...John Lilburne, etc; [ascribed to Richard Overton]. [London, Larner's last press], 1646. pp. 20. 19cm. Wing R 993.

SHEPPARD (SAMUEL) The false alarum; or, An answer to a libell lately published, entituled, An alarum to the House of Lords against their insolent usurpation of the Commons liberties, and the rights of this nation, etc. London, Hardesty, 1646. pp. (ii), 12. 18½cm. Wing S 3162.

VOX plebis; or, The peoples outcry against oppression, injustice, and tyranny; wherein the liberty of the subject is asserted, Magna Charta briefly but pithily expounded, Lieutenant Colonell Lilburnes sentence published and refuted, etc. London, 1646. pp. 69. 18½cm. Wing V 726.

LILBURNE (JOHN) The additional plea of Lieut. Col. John Lilburne, prerogative prisoner in the Tower of London, the 28 of October, 1647, which he sent unto the Committee of the House of Commons,...with a letter...: [a continuation of 'The grand plea of Lieut. Col. John Lilburne']. [London, 1647]. pp. 17-24. 18½cm. Not entered separately in Wing.

LILBURNE (JOHN) The oppressed mans oppressions declared; or, An epistle...in which the...cruelty of all the gaolers of England is declared, and particularly the Lieutenants of the Tower, etc. [London, 1647]. pp. 28. 18½cm. Wing L 2149.

LILBURNE (JOHN) (Cont'd.)

LILBURNE (JOHN) Rash oaths unwarrantable: and the breaking of them is inexcusable; or, A discourse, shewing that the two Houses of Parliament had little ground to make those oaths they have made, etc. [London], 1647. pp. 56. 18½cm. Wing L 2167.

LILBURNE (JOHN) The resolved mans resolution, to maintain with the last drop of his heart blood, his civill liberties and freedomes, granted unto him by the good, just, and honest declared lawes of England, etc. [London, 1647]. pp. 40. 18½cm. Wing L 2174.

MASTERSON (GEORGE) The triumph stain'd: being an answer to Truths triumph, i.e., a pamphlet so called, and lately set forth by Mr. John Wildman...; with a full...account of an information...given in to the House of Lords...January the 18. 1647[O.S.] against Lieut.Col. John Lilburn and John Wildman. London, Field, 1647 [O.S.] pp. 26. 18½cm. Pp. 25-6 have been supplied from another copy. Wing M 1063.

ENGLANDS weeping spectacle; or, The sad condition of Lievtenant Colonell John Lilburne: crying to all who have any conscience or compassion, for assistance and deliverance from his unjust, long and cruell sufferings, etc. [London], 1648. pp. 13. 19cm. Wing L 2107.

UNITED KINGDOM. Parliament. House of Commons. 1648. A declaration of some proceedings of Lt. Col. John Lilburn, and his associates; with some examination, and animadversion upon papers lately printed, and scattered abroad, one called The earnest petition of many free-born people of this kingdome; another, The mournfull cries of many thousand poor tradesmen, etc. London, Harward, 1648. pp. 62. 18½cm. Wing D 625.

LILBURNE (JOHN) A discourse betwixt Lieutenant Colonel Iohn Lilburn, close prisoner in the Tower of London, and Mr Hugh Peter, upon May 25, 1649. London, 1649. pp. 8. 19cm. Wing L 2100.

LILBURNE (JOHN) and others. The picture of the Councel of State, held forth to the free people of England by Lieut. Col. John Lilburne [and others]...or, A full narrative of the late extrajudicial and military proceedings against them, etc. [London], 1649. pp. 54. 18½cm. Wing L 2154.

LONDON. Apprentices. The thankfull acknowledgment and congratulation of divers well-effected apprentices within the ward of Cripplegate without, unto...Lieutenant Colonel John Lilburn, Mr. William Walwyn, [and others]...now prisoners in the Tower of London, etc. [London, 1649] single sheet. 29cm. Wing T 835.

LILLE

FRANCE. Direction de la Documentation. La Documentation Française. Notes et Études Documentaires. No. 3, 206. Les grandes villes françaises: Lille-Roubaix-Tourcoing; [by] Pierre Bruyelle. Paris, 1965. pp. 111. bibliog. 30½cm.

- History

LILLE. Université. Faculté des Lettres. Histoire de Lille; (sous la direction de Louis Trenard). Lille, [1970] in progress. bibliog.

LILLY (WILLIAM) the Astrologer

The LATE storie of Mr. William Lilly, which (as it passed several hands of the better sort of cavaliers) was apprehended for a truth, and so committeed to the presse; [by Colonel Th.] London, 1648. pp. 12. 18½cm. Wing L 2226 & L 559.

LIMA

- Economic conditions

PERU. Servicio del Empleo y Recursos Humanos. 1969. Empleo, salarios y horas de trabajo en 1968: informe de Lima-Callao. [Lima], 1969. pp. 56. (Serie de Investigaciones en Centros de Trabajo).

LIMA (CITY)

CAPELO (J.) Sociologia de Lima. Lima, 1895-1902. 4 vols (in 1). 15cm.

- Politics and government

AUSTIN (ALLAN G.) and LEWIS (SHERMAN) Urban government for metropolitan Lima. New York, 1970. pp. 186. bibliog. (Institute of Public Administration, New York. International Urban Studies. No. 6)

- Poor

MATOS MAR (JOSÉ) Estudio de las barriadas limeñas: informe presentado a Naciones Unidas en diciembre de 1966. Lima, [Universidad Nacional Mayor de San Marcos, Facultad de Letras y Ciencias Humanas, Departamento de Antropologia], 1966. pp. 97. 25cm. (Série Urbanización, Migraciones y Cambios en la Sociedad Peruana. No. 1)

- Social conditions

GAMBOA VILLARROEL (MIRYAM) and ALONSO HERNANDEZ (E. JAVIER) La familia en Lima: avance de diagnóstico sociopastoral. Lima, 1968. pp. 143. (Centro Arquidiocesano de Pastoral. Colección Santo Toribio de Mogrovejo. 2)

SALAZAR BONDY (SEBASTIÁN) Lima la horrible. 3rd ed. México, Era, 1968. pp. 133. 19½cm.

LIMBURG (PROVINCE)

- History

WOUTERS (H.H.E.) Grensland en bruggehoofd: historische studies met betrekking tot het Limburgse Maasdal en, meer in het bijzonder, de stad Maastricht. Assen, 1970. pp. 472. bibliog. (Limburg. Sociaal Historisch Centrum. Maaslandse Monografieën. 11) With French and German summaries.

- Population

BELGIUM. 1966. L'évolution de la population, de l'emploi, de la mobilité géographique de la main-d'oeuvre et du chômage dans la province du Limbourg au cours de la période 1958-1964. (Études Économiques et Sociales de l'Office National de l'Emploi) Bruxelles, [1966?]. pp. 8, (6). 29½cm.

LIME INDUSTRY

- France

VARINOT (JEAN PIERRE) L'industrie de la chaux d'aciérie en Lorraine. Nancy, Centre d'Études pour la Région Économique de Lorraine, 1967. pp. 198, bibliog. 24cm.

- Germany

SAARBRUECKEN. Universität. Annales Universitatis Saraviensis. Rechts- und Wirtschaftswissenschaftliche Abteilung. Heft 39. Zur Planung des optimalen Fertigungsprogramms, dargestellt am Beispiel der Kalkindustrie; von Hans-Josef Brink. Köln, 1969. pp. 170. bibliog.

LIMEHOUSE

- Poor

ST. ANNE'S [LIMEHOUSE] PARISH, MIDDLESEX. Vestry. Report from a committee of Vestry on the maintenance and employment of the poor, January-November 1818. London, [imprint, 1818?]. pp. 25. 20cm.

LIMESTONE

- Canada

HEWITT (D.F.) The limestone industries of Ontario. Toronto, 1960. ppx,177. 28cm. (Ontario. Department of Mines. Industrial Mineral Circulars. No.5)

LIMITATION OF ACTIONS

SYMPOSIUM OF WAR CRIMES, CRIMES AGAINST HUMANITY AND STATUTORY LIMITATIONS, JERUSALEM, 1968. [Papers of a symposium sponsored by the Institute of Criminology of the Hebrew University and the World Jewish Congress]. [Jerusalem, 1968]. pp. 38. (Hebrew University. Institute of Criminology. Publications. No. 15)

- Germany

VOGEL (ROLF) ed. Ein Weg aus der Vergangenheit: eine Dokumentation zur Verjährungsfrage und zu den NS-Prozessen. Frankfurt/M., [1969]. pp. 222.

- United Kingdom - Scotland

SCOTLAND. Scottish Law Commission. 1970. Reform of the law relating to prescription and limitation of actions. Edinburgh, 1970. pp. 75. (Scot. Law Com. No. 15.)

- United States

CERVERA (ALEJO DE) The statute of limitations in American conflicts of law. Rio Piedras, University of Puerto Rico P.,1966. pp. ix, 189. 21½cm.

LIMITED LIABILITY

WUERDINGER (HANS) Das Brüsseler Haftungsabkommen von 1957 und seine Bedeutung für die Schiffsgläubigerrechte: Vortrag...am 17. Januar 1962. Hamburg, 1962. pp. 16. (Deutscher Verein für Internationales Seerecht. Schriften. Reihe A: Berichte und Vorträge. Heft 8)

UNITED STATES. Senate. Foreign Relations Committee. Hague protocol to Warsaw convention: hearings. Washington, 1965. pp. iii, 126.

LIMOGES

FRANCE. Direction de la Documentation. La Documentation Française. Notes et Etudes Documentaires. Nos. 3,677-3,678. Les villes françaises: Limoges; [by] Raymond Lazzarotti. Paris, 1970. pp. 64. bibliog.

LIMOUSIN

- Economic conditions

FRANCE. Direction de la Documentation. La Documentation Française. Notes et Études Documentaires. No. 3,118. Économies régionales et planification: Le Limousin; [by] Francis Morch. Paris, 1964. pp. 62. bibliog. 30½cm.

- Population

FRANCE. [Institut National de la Statistique et des Études Économiques. Direction Régionale de Limoges].1957. Population de la région de Limoges en 1936-1946-1954. Limoges, [1957]. pp. 8. 27cm. (Extraits du Bulletin Régional de Statistique de la D[irection] R[égionale] de Limoges, no. 4, 1954 et no. 3, 1957).

LINCOLN (ABRAHAM) President of the United States

POLLARD (FRANCIS EDWARD) Abraham Lincoln: [review of the biography by Lord Charnwood]. Sheffield, [imprint, 1916?] fo. 510-20. (Reprinted from the Friends' Quarterly Examiner)

ABRAHAM LINCOLN ASSOCIATION. Papers. [vol. 13]. Lincoln, the constitution and democracy, by Andrew C. McLaughlin; A philosopher looks at Lincoln, by T.V. Smith. Springfield, Illinois, 1937. pp. 82. 23cm.

HESSELTINE (WILLIAM BEST) Lincoln and the war governors. New York, Knopf, 1948 repr. 1955. pp. x, 405, xxii. bibliog. 23cm.

HESSELTINE (WILLIAM BEST) Lincoln's plan of reconstruction; [reprint of the work originally published in 1960]. Chicago, Quadrangle Books, 1967. pp. 154. bibliog. 21cm. (Quadrangle Paperbacks. 41)

FEHRENBACHER (DON EDWARD) The changing image of Lincoln in American historiography:... an inaugural lecture delivered before the University of Oxford on 21 May 1968. Oxford, Clarendon, 1968. pp. 24. 21½cm.

LINCOLN (ROBERT TODD) A portrait of Abraham Lincoln in letters by his oldest son; edited by Paul M. Angle with the assistance of Richard G. Case. Chicago, [1968]. pp. 92.

LINCOLN (ABRAHAM) President of the United States (Cont'd.)

FEHRENBACHER (DON EDWARD) ed. The leadership of Abraham Lincoln: [readings]. New York, [1970]. pp. 194. bibliog.

WRIGHT (JOHN S.) Lincoln and the politics of slavery. Reno, Nevada, 1970. pp. 215. bibliog.

LINCOLN (GEORGE ARTHUR)

NYE (R. H.) George A. Lincoln: architect in national security. in Jordan (Amos Azariah) ed. Issues of national security in the 1970s. New York, 1967.

LINCOLN (DIOCESE)

- History

BOWKER (MARGARET) The secular clergy in the diocese of Lincoln, 1495-1520. Cambridge, 1968. pp. 253. bibliog.

LINCOLN

- Hospitals

LINCOLN HEATH HOSPITAL MANAGEMENT COMMITTEE. A booklet to mark the one hundred and fiftieth anniversary of the Lawn Hospital, Lincoln: instituted November 4th, 1819; opened for the reception of patients March 25th, 1820. [Sheffield, 1969]. pp. 20.

MELTON (BEATRICE LOUISE) One hundred and fifty years at the Lawn. [Sheffield, 1969]. pp. 24.

LINCOLNSHIRE

- Maps

SYMES (DAVID GILYARD) and others. The Yorkshire and Humberside planning region: an atlas of population change, 1951-66. [Hull], 1968. pp. various. Map in end pocket. (Hull. University. Department of Geography. Miscellaneous Series. No. 8)

LINDET (JEAN BAPTISTE ROBERT)

DUPRE (HUNTLEY) Two brothers in the French Revolution: Robert and Thomas Lindet. [Hamden], Archon Books, 1967. pp. xi, 174. 21½cm.

LINDET (ROBERT THOMAS)

DUPRE (HUNTLEY) Two brothers in the French Revolution: Robert and Thomas Lindet. [Hamden], Archon Books, 1967. pp. xi, 174. 21½cm.

LINDLEY (DANIEL)

SMITH (EDWIN WILLIAM) The life and times of Daniel Lindley, 1801-80: missionary to the Zulus, pastor of the Voortrekkers, Ubebe Omhlope. London, 1949. pp. 456.

LINDSAY (JOHN VLIET)

LINDSAY (JOHN VLIET) Journey into politics: some informal observations. New York, Dodd, [1967]. pp. viii, 152. 19½cm. (Apollo Editions. A176)

HENTOFF (NAT) A political life: the education of John V. Lindsay. New York, 1969. pp. 354.

KLEIN (WOODY) Lindsay's promise: the dream that failed. New York, [1970]. pp. 349.

LINEAR PROGRAMMING

FRISCH (RAGNAR) The multiplex method for linear and quadratic programming. Oslo, 1957. fo. ii, 62. (Oslo. Universitet. Socialøkonomiske Institutt. Memoranda)

FRISCH (RAGNAR) A numerical example of a linear programming problem. Oslo, Universitetet i Oslo, Socialøkonomisk Institutt, 1958. fo. 3. 29½cm. (Memoranda)

MADHYA PRADESH. 1958. Application of linear programming techniques in economic planning; by G.P. Khare. (Technical Papers. No. 1) Bhopal, 1958. pp. 14. bibliog. 25cm.

CHARNES (ABRAHAM) and COOPER (WILLIAM WAGER) Optimizing engineering designs under inequality constraints. Evanston, 1962. fo. 9. bibliog. (Northwestern University. Technological Institute. O.N.R. Research Memoranda. No. 64)

FRISCH (RAGNAR) Mixed linear and quadratic programming by the multiplex method: [technical presentation]. Oslo, 1960 [or rather 1964]. fo. 34. (Oslo. Universitet. Socialøkonomiske Institutt. Memoranda)

STUHR (ROLF) Anwendungen und Lösungsverfahren der ganzzahligen Linearen Programmierung. Göttingen, 1964. pp. 298. bibliog. 20½cm.

URFF (WINFRIED VON) Produktionsplanung in der Landwirtschaft unter besonderer Berücksichtigung der Methode des Linear Programming. Berlin, Duncker & Humblot, [1964]. pp. 318. bibliog. 23cm. (Frankfurt am Main. Universität. Wirtschafts- und Sozialwissenschaftliche Fakultät. Frankfurter Wirtschafts- und Sozialwissenschaftliche Studien. Heft 11)

PANNE (C. VAN DE) and WHINSTON (ANDREW) An alternative interpretation of the primal-dual method and some related parametric methods. [Charlottesville], 1965. fo. 24. bibliog. (Virginia University. Department of Economics. O.N.R. Research Memoranda. No. 1)

KNEIPP (STANLEY) and others. GAC: a computer program for analysis of linear covariance. Iowa City, the Department, [1967]. fo.(ii), 34. 28cm. (Iowa State University. Department of Geography. Discussion Paper Series. No. 6)

MAURIN (HENRI) Programmation linéaire appliquée. Paris, Technip, 1967. pp. xiv, 375. bibliog. 24cm. (Institut Français du Pétrole. Collection Science et Technique du Pétrole. No. 8.)

NOWAK (DIETER) Modellanalyse der verkehrsbetrieblichen Investitionsentscheidung. Hamburg, 1967. pp. xix, 282. bibliog. 20½cm.

CARRILLO-ARRONTE (RICARDO) An empirical test on interregional planning: a linear programming model for Mexico. Den Haag, 1968. pp. (230). bibliogs. 23cm.

ECKAUS (RICHARD S.) and PARIKH (KIRIT S.) Planning for growth: multisectoral, intertemporal models applied to India. Cambridge, M.I.T. Press, [1968]. pp. xvi, 208. 25½cm. (Studies in the Economic Development of India. 6)

FRAZER (J. RONALD) Applied linear programming. Englewood Cliffs, Prentice-Hall, [1968]. pp. xi, 174. 23cm.

GREATOREX (M.) An example of the use of linear programming in statistics. Southampton, University of Southampton, 1968. fo. (29). 30cm. (Discussion Papers in Economics and Econometrics. No.6802)

NAEGELE (HELMUT) Langfristige Finanzplanung in industriellen Grossunternehmen und die Anwendungsmöglichkeiten der linearen Planungsrechnung. Göttingen, 1968. pp. 181. bibliog.

TULKENS (HENRY) Programming analysis of the postal service: a study in public enterprise economics. Louvain, Librairie Universitaire, 1968. pp. xi, 316. bibliog. 24cm. (Louvain. Université. Faculté des Sciences Économiques, Sociales et Politiques. [Publications]. Nouvelle Série, No. 34)

WILSON (ALAN GEOFFREY) Inter-regional commodity flows: entropy maximising approaches. London, 1968. pp. 39. bibliog. (Centre for Environmental Studies. Working Papers. 19)

ANTONIO (MARIANO D') Lo sviluppo delle regioni italiane: un modello di programmazione lineare. Napoli, 1969. pp. 151. bibliog.

GASS (SAUL I.) Linear programming: methods and applications. 3rd ed. New York, [1969]. pp. 358. bibliog.

IUDIN (DAVID BERKOVICH) and GOL'SHTEIN (EVGENII GRIGOR'EVICH) Линейное программирование: теория, методы и приложения. Москва, Наука, 1969. pp. 424. bibliog. 19½см. (Экономико-Математическая Библиотека)

THROSBY (CHARLES DAVID) Elementary linear programming. New York, [1970]. pp. 242.

PANNE (C. VAN DE) Linear programming and related techniques. Amsterdam, 1971. pp. 364. bibliog.

VANDERMEULEN (DANIEL CARLSON) Linear economic theory. Englewood Cliffs, [1971]. pp. 543. bibliogs.

LINEN

BAILEY (WILLIAM) Register to the Society for the Encouragement of Arts, etc. A treatise on the better employment, and more comfortable support, of the poor in workhouses; together with some observations on the growth and culture of flax, with divers new inventions... for the improvement of the linen manufacture, etc. London, the Author, 1758. pp. 79.

- Belgium

BASTIN (J.) De Gentse lijnwaadmarkt en linnenhandel in de 17e eeuw. Gent, Rijksuniversiteit, Seminaries voor Geschiedenis, 1968. pp. 32. 24½cm. ('Studia Historica Gandensia. 87) (Overdruk uit Handelingen der Maatschappij voor Geschiedenis en Oudheidkunde te Gent, Nieuwe Reeks, dl.21, 1967)

- Germany

SCHMITZ (EDITH) Leinengewerbe und Leinenhandel in Nordwestdeutschland, 1650-1850. Köln, Rheinisch-Westfälisches Wirtschaftsarchiv, 1967. pp. 134. bibliog. 24cm. (Schriften zur Rheinisch-Westfälischen Wirtschaftsgeschichte. Band 15)

- Ireland (Republic)

EIRE. Committee on Industrial Organisation. 1962. Report on the cotton, linen and rayon industry. Dublin, [1962]. pp. 122. 25cm.

- United Kingdom - Ireland

LINEN BOARD. Letters and papers relating to the Linen Board of Ireland. [Dublin], 1827. pp.(85)

- United Kingdom - Scotland

COWPER (A.S.) Linen in the Highlands: (a nine years plan) 1753-1762. Edinburgh, 1969. pp. 54. (Edinburgh College of Commerce. Library. Occasional Papers. No. 1)

LINGUISTIC ANALYSIS (LINGUISTICS)

BUNKER (H.A.) and LEWIN (B.D.) A psychoanalytic notation on the root GN, KN, CN. in Wilbur (George B.) and Muensterberger (Warner) eds. Psychoanalysis and culture;...[reprint of the volume originally published in 1951]. New York, 1967.

CHOMSKY (NOAM) and MILLER (GEORGE ARMITAGE) L'analyse formelle des langues naturelles. Paris, 1968. pp. 174. bibliog. (Paris. École Pratique des Hautes Études. Section des Sciences Économiques et Sociales. Mathématiques et Sciences de l'Homme. 8)

LINGUISTIC GEOGRAPHY

SPRACHATLANTEN: Berichte über sprachgeographische Forschungen... von Martin Durrell [and others]. Wiesbaden, 1969 in progress. bibliogs. (Zeitschrift für Dialektologie und Linguistik. Beihefte. Neue Folge. Nr. 8)

LINGUISTIC RESEARCH

METELLI DI LALLO (CARMELA) and others. Problemi psicopedagogici: scuola e linguaggio. Bari, Laterza, 1964. pp. 206. bibliog. 21½cm. (Convegno su "La Scuola e la Società Italiana in Trasformazione". Ricerche. 4)

SLETSJØE (LEIF) Maskinene og språkstudiet;... tiltredelsesforelesning... 15.februar 1967. [Bergen], Norges Handelshøyskole, 1967. pp. 25. 21cm. (Skrifter. Almene Emner. Nr.8)

LINGUISTICS

MOHRMANN (CHRISTINE) and others, eds. Trends in modern linguistics; edited...on the occasion of the ninth International Congress of Linguists... 1962, etc. Utrecht, Spectrum, 1963. pp. 118. bibliogs. 22cm.

HALL (ROBERT A.) Introductory linguistics. Philadelphia, [1964] repr. 1967. pp. 508. bibliog.

BUYSSENS (ERIC) Linguistique historique: homonymie, stylistique, semantique, changements phonetiques. Bruxelles, 1965. pp. 158. (Brussels. Université Libre. Faculté de Philosophie et Lettres. Travaux. Tome 28)

ALLEN (WILLIAM SIDNEY) and others. Five inaugural lectures; edited...by Peter Strevens. London, O.U.P., 1966. pp. ix, 129. 19½cm. (Language and Language Learning)

FRIES (CHARLES CARPENTER) Linguistics: the study of language; chapter two of Linguistics and reading. New York, Holt, 1966. pp. xii, 92, 223-232. 21cm.

GREENBERG (JOSEPH H.) Language universals: with special reference to feature hierarchies. The Hague, 1966. pp. 89.

TRENDS in European and American linguistics, 1930-1960; edited on the occasion of the ninth International Congress of Linguistics...by Christine Mohrmann, Alf Sommerfelt and Joshua Whatmough. Utrecht, 1966. pp. 299. bibliogs. In English, German, French or Italian.

BROWN (ROGER LANGHAM) Wilhelm von Humboldt's conception of linguistic relativity. The Hague, Mouton, 1967. pp. 132. bibliog. 22½cm.

BUYSSENS (ERIC) La communication et l'articulation linguistique. Bruxelles, Presses Universitaires, [1967]. pp. 175. 24cm. (Brussels. Université Libre. Faculté de Philosophie et Lettres. Travaux. Tome 31)

LEHMANN (WINIFRED PHILIPP) ed. A reader in nineteenth-century historical Indo-European linguistics. Bloomington, [1967]. pp. 266.

PIKE (KENNETH LEE) Language in relation to a unified theory of the structure of human behavior. 2nd ed. The Hague, Mouton, 1967. pp. 762. bibliog. 26cm. (Janua Linguarum. Series Maior. 24)

ROBINS (ROBERT HENRY) A short history of linguistics. London, Longmans, 1967. pp. viii, 248. bibliogs. 21¼cm. (Longmans' Linguistics Library)

STEIBLE (DANIEL) Concise handbook of linguistics. London, Owen, 1967. pp. 146. 21½cm.

TO honor Roman Jakobson: essays on the occasion of his seventieth birthday, 11 October, 1966. The Hague, Mouton, 1967. 3 vols. bibliogs. 26cm. (Janua Linguarum. Studia Memoriae Nicolai Van Wijk Dedicata. Series Maior. 31-33)

BACH (EMMON) and HARMS (ROBERT T.) eds. Universals in linguistic theory [a symposium held at the University of Texas on April 13-15, 1967]; [by] Charles J. Fillmore, Paul Kiparsky and James D. McCawley. New York, [1968]. pp. 210. bibliog.

CRYSTAL (DAVID) What is linguistics? London, Arnold, 1968. pp. viii, 84. bibliog. 18½cm.

DAVIES (EIRIAN) Aspects of general linguistics. London, 1968. pp. 107. (London. University. University College. Communication Research Centre Programme in Linguistics and English Teaching. Papers. No. 8)

DOUGHTY (P.S.) Linguistics and the teaching of literature. London, 1968. pp. 86. (London. University. University College. Communication Research Centre. Programme in Linguistics and English Teaching. Papers. No. 5)

FIRTH (JOHN RUPERT) Selected papers..., 1952-59; edited by F.R. Palmer. London, Longmans, 1968. pp. x, 209. bibliog. 21½cm. (Longmans' Linguistics Library)

HALL (ROBERT A.) An essay on language. Philadelphia, [1968]. pp. 160. bibliog.

INFORMATION in the language sciences; proceedings of the conference held at Airlie House, Warrenton, Virginia, March 4-6, 1966, under the sponsorship of the Center for Applied Linguistics; edited by Robert R. Freeman, [and others]. New York, 1968. pp. 247. bibliogs.

LANGACKER (RONALD WAYNE) Language and its structure: some fundamental linguistic concepts. New York, [1968]. pp. 260. bibliog.

LANGENDOEN (D. TERENCE) The London school of linguistics: a study of the linguistic theories of B. Malinowski and J.R. Firth. Cambridge, M.I.T. Press, [1968]. pp. xiii, 123. bibliog.

LYONS (JOHN) Introduction to theoretical linguistics. Cambridge, C.U.P., 1968. pp. x, 519. bibliog. 21cm.

POTTIER (BERNARD) Lingüística moderna y filologia hispánica. Madrid, Gredos, 1968. pp. 246. 20cm. (Biblioteca Románica Hispánica. [Serie 2.] Estudios y Ensayos. 110)

STALIN (IOSIF VISSARIONOVICH) Concerning marxism in linguistics: [facsimile of a work originally published in 1950 with a new preface]. [Belfast, 1968]. pp. 40.

KING (ROBERT D.) Historical linguistics and generative grammar. Englewood Cliffs, [1969]. pp. 230. bibliog.

LINGUISTICS today; edited by Archibald A. Hill; (from a series of lectures broadcast by the Voice of America). New York, [1969]. pp. 291.

WALLWORK (JEAN F.) Language and linguistics: an introduction to the study of language. London, Heinemann, 1969. pp. viii, 184. bibliog. 21½cm.

BIERWISCH (MANFRED) and HEIDOLPH (KARL ERICH) eds. Progress in linguistics: a collection of papers, selected [from the Tenth International Congress of Linguists, Bucharest, 1967]. The Hague, 1970. pp. 344. In English, German and Russian.

CHAFE (WALLACE L.) Meaning and the structure of language. Chicago, 1970 repr. 1971. pp. 360. bibliog.

INTERNATIONAL CONFERENCE OF NORDIC AND GENERAL LINGUISTICS, REYKJAVIK, 1969. The Nordic languages and modern linguistics: proceedings of the International Conference..., University of Iceland, Reykjavík, July 6-11, 1969; edited by Hreinn Benediktsson. Reykjavík, 1970. pp. 616. bibliogs. (Vísindafélag Islendinga. Occasional Publications. vol. 39)

LINGUISTIC INSTITUTE CONFERENCE ON LINGUISTIC METHOD, LOS ANGELES, 1966. Method and theory in linguistics: (conference...organized by the Bunker-Ramo Corporation); edited by Paul L. Garvin. The Hague, 1970. pp. 336. bibliogs.

LYONS (JOHN) Chomsky. London, 1970. pp. 120. bibliog.

CHOMSKY (NOAM) Chomsky: selected readings; edited by J.P.B. Allen and Paul van Buren. London, 1971. pp. 166. bibliog.

COWAN (WILLIAM GEORGE) Workbook in comparative reconstruction. New York, [1971]. pp. 112. bibliog.

INTERNATIONAL CONGRESS OF APPLIED LINGUISTICS, 2ND, CAMBRIDGE, 1969. Applications of linguistics: selected papers of the...Congress...; edited by G.E. Perren and J.L.M. Trim. Cambridge, 1971. pp. 498. bibliogs.

LINGUISTICS at large: the fourteen linguistic lectures presented by the Institute of Contemporary Arts, London, 1969-70; edited by Noel Minnis. London, 1971. pp. 328. bibliogs.

- Bibliography

CENTRE FOR INFORMATION ON LANGUAGE TEACHING and BRITISH COUNCIL. English-Teaching Information Centre. A language-teaching bibliography. Cambridge, 1968. pp. x, 244.

LINGUISTICS, STATISTICAL

WILLIAMS (C.B.) Style and vocabulary: numerical studies;... with a foreword by Randolph Quirk, etc. London, 1970. pp. 161. bibliog.

LINGUISTICS, STRUCTURAL
See STRUCTURAL LINGUISTICS

LINZ

- Social life and customs

GRUENN (HELENE) Volkskunde der heimatvertriebenen Deutschen im Raum von Linz. Wien, 1968. pp. 152. (Österreichisches Museum für Volkskunde Veröffentlichungen. Band 13)

LIPETSK (OBLAST')

- Statistics

LIPETSK (OBLAST'). Statisticheskoe Upravlenie. Narodnoe khoziaistvo Lipetskoi oblasti za gody Sovetskoi vlasti: statisticheskii sbornik. Voronezh, 1967. pp. 166.

LIPPMANN (WALTER)

WELLBORN (CHARLES) Twentieth century pilgrimage: Walter Lippmann and the public philosophy. Baton Rouge, [1969]. pp. 200. bibliog.

LIPSKI (JÓZEF)

LIPSKI (JÓZEF) (Diplomat in Berlin 1933-1939): papers and memoirs of Józef Lipski; Ambassador of Poland; edited by Wacław Jedrzejewicz. New York, Columbia U.P., 1968. pp. xxxviii, 679. bibliog. 23½cm.

LIQUEFIED PETROLEUM GAS

ITALY. Direzione Generale delle Imposte Dirette. 1959. Distribuzione gas liquido: studio approvato dagli Ispettori Compartimentali nella riunione di Firenze dal 12 al 15 novembre 1958. Roma, 1959. pp. 19. 20cm.

LIQUIDATION

- Italy

NICOLETTI (DOMENICO) Liquidazione coatta amministrativa: schema generale e leggi speciali. Roma, [1957]. pp. 292. bibliog. 18½cm. (Italy. Direzione Generale della Cooperazione. Collana di Studi Cooperativi. 33)

LIQUIDITY (ECONOMICS)

DUECHTING (HANS) Liquidität und unternehmerische Entscheidungsmodelle. [Munich?], 1965. pp. 204. bibliog.

EGGSPUEHLER (WALTER) Liquidität und Steuern. Zürich, Juris Druck & Verlag, 1967. pp. 114. bibliog.

MARZANO (ANTONIO) Teoria e politica del grado di liquidità. Padova, Cedam, 1967. pp. 234. 24½cm. (Rome. Università. Istituto di Studi Economici, Finanziari e Statistici. Raccolta di Scritti. Serie 2. vol. 7)

WOODWORTH (GEORGE WALTER) The management of cyclical liquidity of commercial banks. Boston, Mass., [1967]. pp. 140.

HARTMAN (ROLAND) Optimale Liquiditätsvorsorge durch Planung liquider Reservemittel in industriellen Unternehmungen. Zürich, 1968. pp. 197. bibliog.

UZAWA (H.) Time preference, the consumption function, and optimum asset holdings. in Wolfe (James Nathaniel) ed. Value, capital, and growth. Edinburgh, 1968.

BECKER (JUERGEN) Die kontinuierliche Liquiditätsversorgung des Bankensystems. Berlin, [1969]. pp. 145. bibliog. (Institut für Empirische Wirtschaftsforschung. Veröffentlichungen. Band 3)

HUEBL (LOTHAR) Bankenliquidität und Kapitalmarktzins. Berlin, Duncker & Humblot, [1969]. pp. 155. bibliog. 23cm. (Institut für Empirische Wirtschaftsforschung. Veröffentlichungen. Band 2)

MONTANARO (ELISABETTA) La banca centrale e il governo della liquidità. Milano, 1969. pp. 329. bibliog. (Milan. Università Commerciale Luigi Bocconi. Istituto di Economia Aziendale. Serie 6. N.15)

LIQUIDITY (ECONOMICS) (Cont'd.)

CLAASSEN (EMIL M.) Analyse des liquidités et théorie du portefeuille. Paris, 1970. pp. 178. bibliogs.

SAARBRUECKEN. Universität. Annales Universitatis Saraviensis. Rechts- und Wirtschaftswissenschaftliche Abteilung. Band 53. Liquidität und Besteuerung: der Einfluss der Besteuerung auf die Liquidität unter besonderer Berücksichtigung der vermögen- und schuldabhängigen Steuern; von Hans Kaiser. Köln, 1971. pp. 232. bibliog.

LIQUIDITY (ECONOMICS)
See also INTERNATIONAL LIQUIDITY

LIQUOR LAWS

- Guatemala

GUATEMALA. Statutes, etc. 1899. Ley de licores y sus reformas. Guatemala, 1899. pp. 63. 26cm.

LIQUOR PROBLEM

- Canada - New Brunswick

NEW BRUNSWICK. 1961. Report of the New Brunswick liquor inquiry commission:[G.F.G. Bridges, chairman] [Fredericton, 1961]. pp. 56. 23cm.

- France

FRANCE. Haut Comité d'Étude et d'Information sur l'Alcoolisme. 1962. Rapport au Premier Ministre sur l'activité du Haut Comité d'Étude et d'Information sur l'Alcoolisme. [Paris, 1962]. pp. 147. 27cm.

- Germany

MAUSS (DIETER) Sozialhygienische Erhebungen über Familien Hamburger Trinker und Trinkerinnen aus den Wohnlagern der Sozialbehörde. Bielefeld, Bertelsmann, 1965. pp. iii, 155. bibliog. 20½cm. (Hamburg. Hansische Universität. Lehranstalt für Allgemein- und Sozialhygiene. Sozialhygienische Forschungen. Band 14)

- South Africa

SOUTH AFRICA. 1965. The drinking pattern of the Bantu in South Africa; by J. D. Miles. (National Bureau of Educational and Social Research Research Series. No. 18) [Pretoria], 1965. pp. xi, 177. bibliog. 24½cm.

SOUTH AFRICA. 1965. The drinking pattern of the whites in South Africa; by J. D. Venter. (National Bureau of Educational and Social Research Research Series. No. 17) [Pretoria], 1965. pp. xi, 223. bibliog. 24½cm.

- United Kingdom

SORENSEN (REGINALD WILLIAM) Baron Sorensen. The liberty of the subject. London, 1964. pp. 8. (Ernest Winterton Memorial Lectures. 15)

HAMMERSMITH. Health Education Service. The social drinking scene: a survey of attitudes, habits and impressions contributed by young people; presented by V.T. Searle-Jordan. [Hammersmith], 1970. pp. 29.

ALCOHOL and the family: a second pilot study in the methodology of social inquiry...; [by] H.D. Chalke [and others]. London, 1971. pp. 19.

- United States

ALLSOP (KENNETH) The bootleggers: the story of Chicago's prohibition era; (with new introduction). [new ed.] London, Hutchinson, 1968. pp. xxvii, 13-379. bibliog. 22½cm.

JESSOR (RICHARD) and others. Society, personality and deviant behavior: a study of a tri-ethnic community. New York, Holt, [1968]. pp. xi, 500. bibliogs. 22½cm.

LIQUOR TRAFFIC

- Africa, Subsaharan

ABORIGINES PROTECTION SOCIETY. The liquor traffic in Africa. London, [1895?]. pp. 13. (Reprinted from the Aborigines' Friend, July 1895)

- Finland

NYBERG (AARNI) Alkoholijuomien kulutus ja hinnat: tutkimus alkoholijuomien kulutuksen vaihteluista suomessa vuosina, 1949-1965, etc. [Helsinki], the Tutkimussäätiö, [1967]. pp. 188. bibliog. 25cm. (Väkijuomakysymyksen Tutkimussäätiö. [Publications]. No. 15) With English summary.

- South Africa

PRETORIA. University of Pretoria. Bureau of Financial Analysis. Reports. No. B2. Inter firm comparative survey, retail bottle stores in South Africa, 1967. Pretoria, 1969. pp. 62. With a summary in Afrikaans.

LIQUORS

- Tables, standards, etc.

SIERRA LEONE. Sessional Papers. 1923. No.3. Despatch dated 30 January, 1923, from the Secretary of State for the Colonies on the definitions of admissible spirits. Freetown, 1923. pp. 10.

LIST (GEORG FRIEDRICH)

LENZ (FRIEDRICH BERNHARD HERMANN) Friedrich List's Staats- und Gesellschaftslehre: eine Studie zur politischen Soziologie. Neuwied, Luchterhand, [1967]. pp. 111. bibliog. (Soziologische Essays)

SCIENCE COUNCIL OF JAPAN. Division of Economics, Commerce and Business Administration. Economic Series. No.40. James Stewart, Adam Smith and Friedrich List; by Noboru Kobayashi. Tokyo, 1967. pp. (iii), 37. 21cm.

ROUSSAKIS (EMMANUEL N.) Friedrich List, the Zollverein, and the uniting of Europe. Bruges, 1968. pp. 159. bibliog. (College of Europe. Studies in Contemporary European Issues. 1)

STROESSLIN (WERNER) Friedrich Lists Lehre von der wirtschaftlichen Entwicklung: zur Geschichte von Entwicklungstheorie und -politik. Basel, Kyklos-Verlag, 1968. pp. viii, 102. bibliog. 23cm. (List Gesellschaft. Veröffentlichungen. Band 56)

LITERARY AGENTS

HEPBURN (JAMES) The author's empty purse and the rise of the literary agent. London, O.U.P., 1968. pp. (iv), 135. bibliog. 21½cm.

LITERARY FORGERIES AND MYSTIFICATIONS

[GUILLON (AIMÉ)] Machiavel commenté par Non. Buonaparte, manuscrit trouvé dans le carrosse de Buonaparte, après la bataille de Mont-saint-Jean, le 18 juin 1815; [actually by Aimé Guillon]. Paris, Nicolle, 1816. pp. lxxxii, 336. 20cm.

LITERARY SOCIETIES

- United Kingdom

ALBANY, THE. Albany 69. 2nd ed. [London], 1969. pp. 22.

LITERATURE

VARGAS VALDÉS (JOSÉ JOAQUÍN) José Joaquín Vargas Valdés: artículos y ensayos; introducción y selección de Aníbal Vargas Barón. Eugene, University of Oregon Books, 1963. pp. 197. 23cm.

- Dictionaries and encyclopaedias

KRATKAIA literaturnaia entsiklopediia. Moskva, 1962 in progress.

- History and criticism

LUKÁCS (GEORG) Marxist. Werke. Neuwied, [1962 in progress]. bibliogs. Band 8 is of the third edition.

DYSON (A.E.) Literature, 1895-1939. in The New Cambridge modern history. vol. 12. 2nd ed. Cambridge, 1968.

POULET (GEORGES) Mesure de l'instant. [Paris] Plon, [1968]. pp. 379. 20½cm. (Études sur le Temps Humain. 4)

SANTAYANA (GEORGE) Selected critical writings...; edited by Norman Henfrey. Cambridge, C.U.P., 1968. 2 vols. 21½cm.

HOGGART (RICHARD) Speaking to each other; essays. London, 1970. 2 vols.

- Philosophy

LEFEBVRE (HENRI) Introduction à la modernité: préludes. Paris, [1962]. pp. 375.

BODMER (M.) Chorus Mysticus: ein Symbol des Weltschrifttums. in [Lehmann-Haupt (Hellmut)] ed. Homage to a bookman. Berlin, 1967.

LEVI (ALBERT WILLIAM) Humanism and politics: studies in the relationship of power and value in the western tradition. Bloomington, [1969]. pp. 498.

- Study and teaching

DOUGHTY (P.S.) Linguistics and the teaching of literature. London, 1968. pp. 86. (London. University. University College. Communication Research Centre. Programme in Linguistics and English Teaching. Papers. No. 5)

LITERATURE, IMMORAL

PARETO (V.) Le mythe vertuiste et la littérature immorale. See tome 15 of Pareto (Vilfredo) Oeuvres complètes; publiées sous la direction de Giovanni Busino. Genève, 1971.

LITERATURE, MODERN

- 20th century

MEYLAN (JEAN PIERRE) La Revue de Genève: miroir des lettres européennes, 1920-1930. Genève, 1969. pp. 524.

LITERATURE AND HISTORY

MORTON (ARTHUR LESLIE) Shakespeare's idea of history. London, 1964. pp. 18. (Communist Party of Great Britain. Historians' Group. Our History. No. 33)

KOZ'MIN (BORIS PAVLOVICH) Литература и история: сборник статей. Москва, 1969. pp. 527.

LITERATURE AND SCIENCE

KREUZER (HELMUT) ed. Literarische und naturwissenschaftliche Intelligenz: Dialog über die "zwei Kulturen". Stuttgart, [1969]. pp. 273. bibliog.

LITERATURE AND SOCIETY

WARNER (CHARLES DUDLEY) A little journey in the world: [a novel; reprint of original edition of 1889] with a new introduction by Rita K. Gollin. New York, 1969. pp. 396.

BLATCHFORD (ROBERT) Spangles of existence: [a novel]. London, 1921. pp. 229.

AYMÉ (MARCEL) Le confort intellectuel. Paris, Flammarion, [1949, repr. 1967]. pp. 206. 18½cm.

LEFEBVRE (HENRI) Introduction à la modernité: préludes. Paris, [1962]. pp. 375.

ESCARPIT (ROBERT) Sociology of literature;...translted by Ernest Pick. Painesville, Ohio, 1965. pp. 103.

FINKELSTEIN (SIDNEY) Existentialism and alienation in American literature. New York, [1965] repr. 1968. pp. 314.

GOLDMANN (LUCIEN) Pour une sociologie du roman. [Paris, 1965 repr. 1969]. pp. 372.

LITERATURE AND SOCIETY (Cont'd.)

BERLIN. Humboldt-Universität. Englisch -- Amerikanisches Institut. Life and Literature of the Working Class. Essays in honour of William Gallacher; [with] supplement: Thomas Spence, The history of Crusonia, and other writings. Berlin, 1966. pp. 354.

BRUSSELS. Université Libre. Institut de Sociologie Solvay and PARIS. École Pratique des Hautes Études. Section des Sciences Économiques et Sociales. Colloque, 1964. Littérature et société: problèmes de méthodologie en sociologie de la littérature. Bruxelles, the Institut, 1967. pp. 223. 24cm.

HOGGART (RICHARD) The literary imagination and the study of society. Birmingham, [1967]. pp. 12. (Birmingham. University. Center for Contemporary Cultural Studies. Occasional Papers. No. 3)

LOFFLER (PAUL A.) Chronique de la littérature prolétarienne française de 1930 à 1939. Rodez, Subervie, 1967. pp. 84. bibliog. 19cm.

PILLECYN (PHILIP H. DE) Sociaal probleem en verhalend proza 1830-1886: een sociografische literatuurstudie. Antwerpen, Standard Wetenschappelijke Uitgeverij, 1967. pp. 195. bibliog. 24cm. (Bibliotheek voor Literatuurwetenschap. 2)

WOLFF (KURT HEINRICH) and MOORE (BARRINGTON) eds. The critical spirit: essays in honor of Herbert Marcuse. Boston, Beacon P., [1967]. pp. xi, 436. bibliog. 22½cm.

BERGONZI (BERNARD) Innovations: essays on art and ideas. London, Macmillan, 1968. pp. 252. 21½cm.

BRONSON (B.H.) The writer. in Clifford (James Lowry) ed. Man versus society in eighteenth-century Britain. Cambridge, 1968.

CHAPMAN (RAYMOND) The Victorian debate: English literature and society, 1832-1901. London, Weidenfeld & Nicolson, [1968] pp. (v), 377. bibliog. 21½cm. (Literature and Society)

ESCARPIT (ROBERT) Sociologie de la littérature. 4th ed. Paris, 1968. pp. 128. bibliog.

GILBERT (JAMES BURKHART) Writers and partisans: a history of literary radicalism in America. New York, Wiley, [1968]. pp. xv, 303. bibliog. 21cm. (American Cultural History Series)

OTTO (ULLA) Die literarische Zensur als Problem der Soziologie der Politik. Stuttgart, Enke, 1968. pp. xi, 168. bibliog. 24cm. (Bonn. Universität. Institut für Soziologie. Bonner Beiträge zur Soziologie. Nr. 3)

PEACOCK (JAMES L.) Rites of modernization: symbolic and social aspects of Indonesian proletarian drama. Chicago, U. of Chicago P., 1968. pp. xxv, 306. bibliog. 22½cm.

ROSENGREN (KARL ERIK) Sociological aspects of the literary system. Stockholm, Natur och Kultur, [1968]. pp. 216. bibliog. 23cm.

STROMBERG (ROLAND N.) ed. Realism, naturalism, and symbolism: modes of thought and expression in Europe, 1848-1914. London, Macmillan, 1968. pp. xxxvi, 296. bibliog. 23cm. (Documentary History of Western Civilization)

VERMA (RAJENDRA) Royalist in politics: T.S. Eliot and political philosophy. London, Asia Publishing House, [1968]. pp. xi, 193. 21½cm.

GROSS (JOHN) The rise and fall of the man of letters: aspects of English literary life since 1800. London, Weidenfeld and Nicolson, [1969]. pp. xiv, 322. bibliog. 21½cm.

HARRIS (RONALD WALTER) Romanticism and the social order, 1780-1830. London, Blandford P., 1969. pp. 426.

HOGGART (RICHARD) Contemporary cultural studies: an approach to the study of literature and society. Birmingham, University, Centre for Contemporary Cultural Studies, 1969. pp. 24. 21½cm. (Occasional Papers. No. 6)

KIRK (RUSSELL) Enemies of the permanent things: observations of abnormity in literature and politics. New Rochelle, N.Y., [1969]. pp. 311.

KREUZER (HELMUT) ed. Literarische und naturwissenschaftliche Intelligenz: Dialog über die "zwei Kulturen". Stuttgart, [1969]. pp. 273. bibliog.

NEW MASSES. New Masses: an anthology of the rebel thirties; edited with a prologue by Joseph North. New York, [1969]. pp. 318.

SILHOL (ROBERT) Les tyrans tragiques: un témoin pathétique de notre temps, Sinclair Lewis. Paris, 1969. pp. 443. (Paris. Université. Faculté des Lettres et Sciences Humaines. Publications. Série Recherches. Tome 51)

La SOCIETE française, 1815-1914, vue par les romanciers; [by] Pierre Guiral [and others]. Paris, [1969]. pp. 250. bibliog.

SOLZHENITSYN (ALEKSANDR ISAEVICH) Les droits de l'écrivain. Paris, Éditions du Seuil, [1969]. pp. 93. 18cm. (Combats)

WEST (Dame REBECCA) pseud. [i.e. Cicily Isabel ANDREWS]. McLuhan and the future of literature. [London], 1969. pp. 19.

Das BUCH in der dynamischen Gesellschaft: Festschrift für Wolfgang Strauss zum 60. Geburtstag; herausgegeben von Werner Adrian [and others]. Trier, [1970]. pp. 308. bibliog.

GOODLAD (JOHN SINCLAIR ROBERTSON) An analysis of the social content of popular drama, 1955-1965; [Ph.D. (London) thesis]. 1969 [or rather 1970]. fo. 329. bibliog. Typescript: unpublished. This thesis is the property of London University and may not be removed from the Library.

OTHMER (SIEGLINDE C.) Berlin und die Verbreiung des Naturrechts in Europa: kultur- und sozialgeschichtliche Studien zu Jean Barbeyracs Pufendorf-Ubersetzungen und eine Analyse seiner Leserschaft. Berlin, 1970. pp. 244. bibliog. (Berlin. Freie Universität. Friedrich-Meinecke-Institut. Historische Kommission zu Berlin. Veröffentlichungen. Band 30)

BRADBURY (MALCOLM) The social context of modern English literature. Oxford, [1971]. pp. 277. bibliog.

GOODLAD (JOHN SINCLAIR ROBERTSON) A sociology of popular drama. London, 1971. pp. 230. bibliogs.

WILLIAMS (DUNCAN) Trousered apes: a study in the influence of literature on contemporary society. Enfield, Middx., 1971. pp. 132.

LITERATURE AND STATE

WALDO (DWIGHT) The novelist on organization and administration: an inquiry into the relationship between two worlds. Berkeley, University of California, Institute of Governmental Studies, 1968. pp. 158. bibliog. 28cm.

LITERATURE AND TECHNOLOGY

SUSSMAN (HERBERT L.) Victorians and the machine: the literary response to technology. Cambridge, Harvard U.P., 1968. pp. xii, 261. bibliog. 21cm.

LITHUANIA

- Constitutional history

DOMAŠEVIČIUS (KESTUTIS) Tarybinio valstybingumo vystymasis Lietuvoje. Vilnius, Mintis, 1966. pp. 195. 20cm.

- Economic conditions

LITHUANIA. Finansų Ministerija. 1924. Economy and cooperation of Lithuania: statistical study. Kaunas, 1924. pp. 36.

VAITIEKUNAS (VYTAUTAS) ed. A survey of developments in captive Lithuania in 1965-1968. New York, [1968?]. pp. 160. bibliog.

- Economic history

LITVA... Литва за полвека новой эпохи. Вильнюс, 1967. pp. 447.

- Foreign relations - Russia

SUDUVIS (N. E.) Allein, ganz allein: Widerstand am Baltischen Meer. [Munich], 1964. pp. 134. bibliog.

TSENTRAL'NYI GOSUDARSTVENNYI ARKHIV LITOVSKOI SSR. Tarybų valdžios atkūrimas Lietuvoje, 1940-1941 metais: dokumentų rinkinys. Vilnius, 1965. pp. 347. 21cm.

- History

SUDUVIS (N. E.) Allein, ganz allein: Widerstand am Baltischen Meer. [Munich], 1964. pp. 134. bibliog.

VAITIENKUNAS (VYTAUTAS) Lithuania. New York, Assembly of Captive European Nations, 1965. pp. 48. bibliog. 22½cm. (Publications. No. 58)

GITLEROVSKAIA... Гитлеровская оккупация в Литве: сборник статей. Вильнюс, Минтис, 1966. pp. 360. 21см.

SKWARCZYNSKI (P.) Poland and Lithuania. in vol. 3 of The New Cambridge modern history. Cambridge, 1968.

VETRY... Ветры революции: сборник воспоминаний о пролетарской революции 1918-1919 гг. в Литве. Вильнюс, 1968. pp. 308.

SNIEČKUS (ANASTAS) Sovetskaia Litva na puti rastsveta; (perevod s litovskogo) Vil'nius, 1970. pp. 157. bibliog.

- History - Sources

TSENTRAL'NYI GOSUDARSTVENNYI ARKHIV LITOVSKOI SSR. Tarybų valdžios atkūrimas Lietuvoje, 1940-1941 metais: dokumentų rinkinys. Vilnius, 1965. pp. 347. 21cm.

BOR'BA... Борьба за Советскую власть в Литве в 1918-1920 гг.; сборник документов. Вильнюс, 1967. pp. 475. (Iz Istorii Grazhdanskoi Voiny v SSSR) With English summary and list of documents.

- Industries

ORGANIZATSIIA... Организация производственных объединений в легкой промышленности Литовской ССР. Вильнюс, 1968. pp. 226.

- Intellectual life

OCHMAŃSKI (JERZY) Litewski ruch narodowo - kulturalny w XIX wieku, do 1890 r. Białystok, 1965. pp. 201. (Białystok. Białostockie Towarzystwo Naukowe. Prace. Nr.5) With Lithuanian summary.

LITHUANIA. Tsentral'noe Statisticheskoe Upravlenie. 1967. Экономика и культура Литовской ССР: статистический сборник, посвященный 50-летию Великого Октября. Вильнюс, 1967. pp. 416. 21½см.

- Learned institutions and societies

MATULIS (IU. IU.) Akademiia nauk Litovskoi SSR: XXV. Vil'nius, 1965. pp. 140.

- Nationalism

COLLIANDER (BORJE ERLAND) En konspiratörs minnen 1911-1916. Åbo, 1965. pp. 40. (Åbo. Akademi. Acta Academiae Aboensis. Humaniora. 31. 1)

- Politics and government

FAJNHAUZ (DAWID) Ruch konspiracyjny na Litwie i Białorusi, 1846-1848. Warszawa, PWN, 1965. pp. 403. 19cm.

VAITIEKUNAS (VYTAUTAS) ed. A survey of developments in captive Lithuania in 1965-1968. New York, [1968?]. pp. 160. bibliog.

LITHUANIA (Cont'd.)

- Religion

RIMAITIS (J.) Religion in Lithuania. Vilnius, 1971. pp. 33.

- Social conditions

VAITIEKUNAS (VYTAUTAS) ed. A survey of developments in captive Lithuania in 1965-1968. New York, [1968?]. pp. 160. bibliog.
R : X 35,268

- Statistics

LITHUANIA. Tsentral'noe Statisticheskoe Upravlenie. 1965. Народное хозяйство Литовской ССР в 1965 году: статистический сборник. Вильнюс, 1965. pp. 482. 21cm.

LITHUANIANS IN GERMANY

HUBATSCH (WALTHER) Masuren und Preussisch-Litthauen in der Nationalitätenpolitik Preussens 1870-1920. Marburg, Elwert, 1966. pp. 91.

LITTLE ENTENTE, 1920-1939

KISZLING (RUDOLF) Die militärischen Vereinbarungen der Kleinen Entente 1929-1937. München, 1959. pp. 91. (Munich. Südost-Institut München. Südosteuropäische Arbeiten. 54)

CAMPUS (E.) La position de la Petite Entente devant le plan austro-allemand d'union douanière de 1931. in Comité National des Historiens de la République Socialiste de Roumanie. Nouvelles études d'histoire. Bucarest, 1965.

LITTLETON (EDWARD) 1st Baron Littleton

LITTLETON (EDWARD) 1st Baron Littleton. A submissive and petitionary letter subscribed to the right honourable the Lords of Parliament, etc. [London, 1642] pp. 7. 18½cm.
Wing L 2585.

LITVINOV (PAVEL MIKHAILOVICH)

REVE (K. VAN HET) ed. Letters and telegrams to Pavel M. Litvinov, December 1967 [to] May 1968; (translated...by Brian Pearce). Dordrecht, [1969]. pp. 199. In English and Russian.

LIU (SHAO-CHI)

LIU (SHAO-CHI) Collected works. Kowloon, [1968-69]. 3 vols. bibliog.

LIVERMORE (ROBERT)

LIVERMORE (ROBERT) Bostonians and bullion: the journal of Robert Livermore, 1892-1915; edited by Gene M. Gressley. Lincoln, U. of Nebraska P., [1968]. pp. xxix, 193. 23cm.

LIVERPOOL

- Civic improvement

MUCHNICK (DAVID M.) Urban renewal in Liverpool: a study of the politics of redevelopment. London, 1970. pp. 120. (Social Administration Research Trust. Occasional Papers on Social Administration. No. 33)

- Commerce

LATHAM (FRANK A.) Timber town:... a history of the Liverpool timber trade. [Liverpool, 1967?]. pp. 41. (Articles reprinted from Timber Trades Journal, 1962-67)

- Economic history

HARRIS (JOHN RAYMOND) ed. Liverpool and Merseyside: essays in the economic and social history of the port and its hinterland. London, Cass, 1969. pp. xiv, 287. 21½cm.

VIGIER (FRANÇOIS) Change and apathy: Liverpool and Manchester during the industrial revolution. Cambridge, Mass, [1970]. pp. 236. bibliog.

HYDE (FRANCIS EDWIN) Liverpool and the Mersey: an economic history of a port, 1700-1970. Newton Abbot, [1971]. pp. 269. bibliog.

- Growth

VIGIER (FRANÇOIS) Change and apathy: Liverpool and Manchester during the industrial revolution. Cambridge, Mass, [1970]. pp. 236. bibliog.

- Politics and government

VIGIER (FRANÇOIS) Change and apathy: Liverpool and Manchester during the industrial revolution. Cambridge, Mass, [1970]. pp. 236. bibliog.

- Race question

LIVERPOOL. Liverpool Youth Organisations Committee. Special but not separate; a report, etc. Liverpool. [1969]. pp. 20.

- Religion

HUME (ABRAHAM) LL.D., F.S.A. Condition of Liverpool, religious and social; including notices of the state of education, morals, pauperism, and crime. 2nd ed. Liverpool, 1858. pp. 40.

- Social conditions

HUME (ABRAHAM) LL.D., F.S.A. Condition of Liverpool, religious and social; including notices of the state of education, morals, pauperism, and crime. 2nd ed. Liverpool, 1858. pp. 40.

- Social history

LIVERPOOL and slavery: an historical account of the Liverpool-African slave trade;... by a genuine "Dicky Sam". Liverpool, 1884; [Newcastle-Upon-Tyne, F. Graham, 1969]. pp. 137.

HARRIS (JOHN RAYMOND) ed. Liverpool and Merseyside: essays in the economic and social history of the port and its hinterland. London, Cass, 1969. pp. xiv, 287. 21½cm.

LIVERPOOL AND MANCHESTER RAILWAY

CARLSON (ROBERT E.) The Liverpool and Manchester Railway project, 1821-1831. Newton Abbot, [1969]. pp. 292. bibliog.

LIVONIA

- Description and travel

HENRICUS de Ymera. Хроника Ливонии; введение, перевод [с латинского] и комментарии С.А. Аннинского, предисловье В.А. Быстрянского. 2nd ed. Ленинград, 1938. pp. 251.

- History - Sources

HENRICUS de Ymera. Хроника Ливонии; введение, перевод [с латинского] и комментарии С.А. Аннинского, предисловье В.А. Быстрянского. 2nd ed. Ленинград, 1938. pp. 251.

LIVORNO (PROVINCE)

- Economic conditions

RONCIONI (MANFREDO) and HECK (B. VAN) eds. Studio sulla situazione economica e sociale delle province di Pisa e Livorno. Pisa, Lischi, 1966. pp. 250. 24½cm.

LJUBLJANA

- Civic improvement

[ŠTEFE (TOMO)] Prebivalci Ljubljane in urbanizem: sociološka anketa o nekaterih urbanističnih alternativah v mestu: Public attitudes toward urban problems in Ljubljana, etc. Ljubljana, Urbanistični Inštitut SRS, 1967. fo. 54, 44. 29cm. (American-Yugoslav Project in Regional and Urban Planning Studies. Research Reports) In English and Slovene.

- Social conditions

[JAMBREK (PETER)] and others. Sociološke karakteristike manjših naselitvenih okolišev in pregled ustrezne literature: Social area analysis. Ljubljana, Urbanistični Inštitut SR Slovenije, 1967. fo. 64, 6. bibliog. 28½cm. (American-Yugoslav Project in Regional and Urban Planning Studies. Research Reports) In Slovene with English summary.

[ŠTEFE (TOMO)] Prebivalci Ljubljane in urbanizem: sociološka anketa o nekaterih urbanističnih alternativah v mestu: Public attitudes toward urban problems in Ljubljana, etc. Ljubljana, Urbanistični Inštitut SRS, 1967. fo. 54, 44. 29cm. (American-Yugoslav Project in Regional and Urban Planning Studies. Research Reports) In English and Slovene.

LLANTRISANT

- Civic improvement

WELSH COUNCIL. Llantrisant: its place in the strategy for South Wales. [Cardiff?], 1970. pp. 14.

LLOYD GEORGE (DAVID)
See GEORGE (DAVID LLOYD) 1st Earl Lloyd George

LOADING AND UNLOADING

HARLOFF (ALBERT) Om lønnsomheten av overtidsarbeid ved lasting og lossing. Bergen, 1966. fo. 35.

LOANDO DE SAO PAULO
See LUANDA DE SAO PAULO

LOANS

LONDON. Court of Common Council. A true copie of the master-piece of all those petitions which have formerly beene presented by the Major, Aldermen, and the rest of the Common Counsell of the citie of London, etc. London, J.B., 1641 [O.S.]. pp. (10). 17½cm. Wing T 2650.

- Italy

BERTONI (ALBERTO) Aspetti dei prestiti bancari alle imprese pubbliche. Milano, Giuffrè, 1968. pp. 19. 24cm. (Milan. Università Commerciale Luigi Bocconi. Istituto di Economia Aziendale. Serie Relazioni. N. 53)

- United Kingdom

UNITED KINGDOM. Parliament. 1643. An ordinance of the Lords and Commons...whereby the commissioners named in a late Act of Parliament for raising the subsidy of 400,000£...are authorized to take...all such moneys, victuals, armes...and commodities as have been lately collected for the reliefe of Ireland...;[dated 17 May, 1643]. London, Wright, 1643. pp. (5). 18½cm. Wing E 2106.

[CHAMBERLEN (PETER)] The poore mans advocate; or, Englands Samaritan: powring oyle and wyne into the wounds of the nation by making present provision for the souldier and the poor, by reconciling all parties, by paying all arreares to the Parliament army, all publique debts, etc. London, Calvert, [1649]. pp. (vi), 51. 19cm. Wing C 1901.

INTERNATIONAL CONFERENCE ON INSTALMENT CREDIT LAW, CAMBRIDGE, 1968. Instalment credit, edited...by Aubrey L. Diamond. London, 1970. pp. 239. bibliog. (British Institute of International and Comparative Law. Studies in International and Comparative Law. No. 4)

- United States

UNITED STATES. 1965. Banking market structure and performance in metropolitan areas: a statistical study of factors affecting rates on bank loans; by Theodore G. Flechsig. (Board of Governors of the Federal Reserve System). [Washington], 1965. pp. ix, 73. bibliog. 26cm.

MURPHY (NEIL B.) A test of the deposit relationship hypothesis. [Washington, 1967.] fo.(ii, 6). 26½cm. (United States. Board of Governors of the Federal Reserve System. Staff Economic Studies. No. 38).

LOANS, FOREIGN

UNITED STATES. House of Representatives. Committee on Banking and Currency. Bretton Woods Agreements Act amendment: hearings. Washington, pp. iv, 165.

LOANS, FOREIGN (Cont'd.)

BIBLIOTHECA VISSERIANA DISSERTATIONUM IUS INTERNATIONALE ILLUSTRANTIUM. vol. 18. 35. Problèmes juridiques des emprunts internationaux; ([by] G. van Hecke). 2nd ed. Lugduni Batauorum, Brill, 1964. pp. xix, 332. bibliog. 24cm.

EL-IMAM (M.M.) Foreign loans and economic development. Cairo, 1967-68. 3pts. 27½cm. (U.A.R. Institute of National Planning. Memos. No. 779)

KNAUTHE (ERHART) The impact of licences, loans and foreign trade on industrialization. Cairo, 1967. pp. 32. 28cm. (U.A.R. Institute of National Planning. Memos. No. 782)

WIELENS (HANS) Die Emission von Auslandsanleihen: eine Analyse ihrer Marktelemente, ihrer Entwicklung seit 1945 und ihrer Bedeutung für die Integration der Kapitalmärkte. Wiesbaden, [1968]. pp. various. bibliog. (Münster in Westfalen. Westfälische Wilhelms-Universität. Institut für Kreditwesen. Schriftenreihe. Band 6)

HUMBERT (CHRISTIAN) Aufgaben, Bedeutung und Grundprobleme internationaler Anleihen. [Augsburg, imprint, 1969?]. pp. 264. bibliog.

- Austria

KLINGENSTEIN (GRETE) Die Anleihe von Lausanne; ein Beitrag zur Geschichte der ersten Republik in den Jahren 1931-1934. Wien, Stiasny, [1965]. pp. 172. bibliog. 24cm. (Oesterreichisches Institut für Zeitgeschichte. Publikationen. Band 5)

- Israel

[BEN-SHAHAR (HAIM)] Public international development financing in Israel. New York, Columbia University, School of Law, 1963. pp. vi, 136. 27½cm. (Public International Development Financing [Research Project]. Reports. No. 5.)

- New Zealand

FRANKEL (Z.) New Zealand overseas borrowing. [Wellington], New Zealand Institute of Economic Research, 1968. pp. 138. 20½cm. (Research Papers. No. 11)

- Switzerland

BERTHOUD (LUC) Les emprunts étrangers en Suisse, depuis 1945. Zurich, Keller, 1967. pp. xiii, 261. bibliog.

LOANS, GERMAN

- Switzerland

FELDMANN (HUBERT) Le problème de l'harmonisation des impôts dans le cadre de la Communauté Économique Européenne. Duisburg, [imprint], 1967. pp. 174. bibliog. 21½cm.

LOANS, PERSONAL

- Canada

CANADA. Parliament. Special Joint Committee of the Senate and House of Commons on Consumer Credit. 1964-65. Proceedings...; joint chairman: David A Croll and J. J. Greene. Ottawa, 1964-65. 18 pts. (in 1 vol.) 25cm.

- Canada - Nova Scotia

NOVA SCOTIA. Royal Commission on the Cost of Borrowing Money, Cost of Credit and related matters in the Province of Nova Scotia, 1963. Final report: [Arthur R. Moreira, Commissioner] [Halifax, 1965]. pp. 411,xvii,6,(60). bibliog. 35½cm.

- Germany

THOMSEN (HORST) Die Kleinkredite der Grossbanken an Lohn- und Gehaltsempfänger. [Erlangen-Nürnberg, 1966?]. pp. 120. bibliog.

- Ireland, (Republic)

EIRE. Tribunal of Inquiry into the Television Programme on Illegal Moneylending. 1970. Inquiry into the programme on illegal moneylending broadcast on television by Radio Telefís Éireann on 11th November, 1969: report of Tribunal appointed by An Taoiseach on 22nd December, 1969. Dublin, 1970. pp. 136.

- Netherlands

JONGMAN (C.D.) De markt voor onderhandse leningen in Nederland. Deventer, 1970. pp. 44. bibliog. (Nederlands Instituut voor het Bank- en Effectenbedrijf. Publikaties. No.4)

- United States - New York (State)

CHAPMAN (JOHN MARTIN) and SHAY (ROBERT PAUL) Licensed lending in New York. [New York, 1970]. pp. 114.

LOBBYISTS

- United States

SCOTT (ANDREW MacKAY) and HUNT (MARGARET A.) Congress and lobbies: image and reality. Chapel Hill, U. of North Carolina P., [1966]. pp. xv, 106. 21½cm.

HALL (DONALD R.) Cooperative lobbying: the power of pressure. Tucson, [1969]. pp. 347. bibliog.

ZEIGLER (LUTHER HARMON) and BAER (MICHAEL A.) Lobbying: interaction and influence in American state legislatures. Belmont, [1969]. pp. 210.

GRAY (GIBSON HENDRIX) The lobbying game: a study of the 1953 campaign of the State Council for a Pennsylvania Fair Employment Practice Commission. Tyler, Texas, 1970. pp. 226. bibliog.

FARKAS (SUZANNE) Urban lobbying: mayors in the federal arena. New York, 1971. pp. 335. bibliog.

LOBSTER FISHERIES

- Canada

CANADA. 1967. An economic appraisal of the Canadian lobster fishery; by J.B. Rutherford [and others]. (Fisheries Research Board. Bulletins. 157) Ottawa, 1967. pp. x, 126. bibliog. 25cm.

LOCAL BUDGETS

- Canada

PAPROSKI (DENNIS M.) An introduction to comprehensive forward budgeting for smaller communities. Ottawa, 1968. pp. 35. bibliog.

- Canada - Quebec

QUEBEC (PROVINCE). Bureau of Statistics. Public Finance Section. Analyse budgétaire: municipalités du Québec. Québec, annual, 1968/9 to date.

- Nigeria

ADEWUMI (JAMES) District councils and district council budgeting in Ilorin Emirate. Zaria, 1965. fo. 8. (Ahmadu Bello University. Institute of Administration. Information Memoranda. No. 21)

- Russia

MENCHINSKII (VSEVOLOD VLADIMIROVICH) Organizatsiia biudzhetnoi raboty v mestnykh finansovykh organakh. Moskva, 1965. pp. 152.

MOROZOV (I.G.) Ispolnenie biudzheta raiona. Moskva, 1968. pp. 111.

POLIAK (GEORGII BORISOVICH) Бюджет Москвы. Москва, Экономика, 1968. pp. 208. 20см.

- United Kingdom

PROGRAMME budgeting: the concept and the application; report of an IMTA seminar held at the London Hilton, 30 October 1969. London, [1969]. pp. 29.

- United States - California

HIRSCH (WERNER ZVI) State and local government program budgeting. Los Angeles, 1966. fo. 28. (California University. Institute of Government and Public Affairs. [Publications]. MR-66)

LOCAL FINANCE

La FINANZA degli enti locali nella dottrina contemporanea, 1947-1967. Milano, Giuffrè, 1968. pp. 110. bibliog. (Istituto per la Scienza dell'Amministrazione Pubblica. Quaderni ISAP. 5)

MARSHALL (ARTHUR HEDLEY) ed. Local government finance: 33 national reports and a general report prepared for the 1969 IULA congress in Vienna. The Hague, [1969]. pp. 537.

- Accounting

MUNDHENKE (EHRHARD) Kommunales Finanzwesen bei integrierter Datenverarbeitung: Modell einer Neuordnung mit Hilfe der Elektronischen Datenverarbeitung als Beitrag zur Organisations- und Verwaltungslehre. Göttingen, 1967. pp. v, 309. bibliog. 20½cm.

- Australia - Accounting

AUSTRALIA. Commonwealth Bureau of Census and Statistics. Public authority finance. a., 1963-4/1967-8 [1st isssue]- Canberra.

- Austria

AUSTRIA. 1960. Gebarungsübersichten 1958 für die Bundesländer, Bezirksfürsorgeverbände und Gemeinden, bearbeitet im Osterreichischen Statistischen Zentralamt in Zusammenarbeit mit dem Bundesministerium für Finanzen. (Beiträge zur Österreichischen Statistik. Heft 49) Wien, 1960. pp. 243. 23cm.

SCHACHNER-BLAZIZEK (PETER) Kommunale Finanzwirtschaft in Österreich. Graz, 1970. pp. 205. bibliog.

- Botswana

BOTSWANA. Town and district councils: estimates of revenue and expenditure. a., 1971- Gaberone.

- Canada

HODGINS (BRUCE W.) Maritime claims relative to the prairie provinces land subsidy and to the northern lands question;...prepared by the government of Prince Edward Island for the Conference of the Premiers of the Atlantic Provinces, September 23 and 24, 1957. [Charlottetown], 1957. fo. 53.

VICQ (JACK) Local government finance. Regina, 1965. pp. 69. bibliog. (Saskatchewan. Royal Commission on Taxation, 1963. Research Studies. No.1)

CANADA. 1967. A review of conferences on municipal finance statistics: Dominion-Provincial Conferences, 1937-58; Queen's University Conference, 1966. (Dominion Bureau of Statistics) Ottawa, 1967. pp. 173. 28cm.

CANADIAN FEDERATION OF MAYORS AND MUNICIPALITIES. Annual Conference, 31st, 1968. The politics of government finance: proceedings of the ... Conference...; edited by Henry Alan Lawless. Ottawa, [1968?]. pp. 117.

- Canada - Manitoba

MANITOBA. Royal Commission on Local Government Organization and Finance, 1963. Report... April, 1964: [Roland Michener, chairman]. Winnipeg, 1964. pp. 306. bibliog. 5 maps in end pocket.

- Canada - New Brunswick

NEW BRUNSWICK. Royal Commission on Finance and Municipal Taxation, 1962. [Final] report of the ... Commission [etc.]. Fredericton, 1963. pp. xviii, 330,(114). 27cm.

LOCAL FINANCE (Cont'd.)

- Canada - Ontario

ONTARIO. Department of Municipal Affairs. Summary of financial reports of municipalities. a., 1968 [1st]- [Toronto]

- Canada - Quebec

QUEBEC (PROVINCE). Bureau of Statistics. Public Finance Section. Renseignements statistiques: municipalités du Québec. Québec, annual, 1967 [1st issue] to date.

- Canada - Saskatchewan

SASKATCHEWAN. 1956. Brief submitted...to the government of Canada on the subject of financing provincial and local government capital expenditures. [Regina], 1956. fo. 5.

SASKATCHEWAN. Local Government Continuing Committee. 1961. Local government finances in Saskatchewan: a technical reference document to the report Local Government in Saskatchewan; submitted to the Government of Saskatchewan, March 1, 1961. [Regina, 1961]. fo. 332.

VICQ (JACK) Local government finance. Regina, 1965. pp. 69. bibliog. (Saskatchewan. Royal Commission on Taxation, 1963. Research Studies. No.1)

- Germany

FUCHS (HELMUT) Die Entwicklung des Finanzausgleichs unter den Ländern von 1949 bis 1958. [Bonn, 1963]. pp. xvi, 186. bibliog. 20½cm.

EHLERS (HANS JUERGEN) Die Gemeindebesteuerung in Deutschland. [Zürich?, 1964?]. pp. iii, 138. bibliog. 22½cm.

MONZ (HEINZ) Der Haushaltsplan der Stadt Trier. Teil 1. Die Haushaltspläne von 30 Städten im Vergleich. Trier, 1964. pp. 25. (Trier. Statistisches Amt. Schriftenreihe zur Statistik der Stadt Trier. Heft 4)

MUELHAUPT (LUDWIG) and OETTLE (KARL) eds. Gemeindewirtschaft und Unternehmerwirtschaft: Festgabe für Rudolf Johns zum 65. Geburtstag am 15. Juli 1965. Göttingen, Schwartz, 1965. pp. xi, 384. bibliog. 22½cm. (Frankfurt am Main. Forschungsgesellschaft für Staats- und Kommunalwirtschaft. Studien. Band 4)

GLOTH (HANS) Die Entwicklung des Kommunalkredits: eine Untersuchung der Beziehungen zum Steueraufkommen. Berlin, Duncker und Humblot, [1967]. pp. 229. bibliog. 23½cm. (Bonn. Universität. Institut für das Spar-, Giro- und Kreditwesen. Untersuchungen über das Spar-, Giro- und Kreditwesen. Band 36) With English and French summaries.

KOCH (K.) Die Forschungsarbeit auf dem Gebiet der Kommunalfinanzen. in Finanzwissenschaftliche Forschung und Lehre an der Universität zu Köln, 1927-1967. Berlin, [1967].

BLUME (JUERGEN) Die Finanzwirtschaft der Gemeindeverbände in der Bundesrepublik Deutschland. Bonn, 1969. pp. 239. bibliog.

Der KOMMUNALE Finanzausgleich in der Bundesrepublik Deutschland: eine kritische Gesamtdarstellung. Bonn, 1971. pp. 90. (Institut Finanzen und Steuern. Schriftenreihe. Heft 97)

ZWILLING (ERNST) Untersuchungen zu einem rationalen Steuersystem der Gemeinden. Meisenheim am Glan, 1971. pp. 176. bibliog.

- Germany - North Rhine - Westphalia

REICHSTEIN (SUSANNE) Die Kassenbestände im ausserordentlichen Haushalt der Gemeinden: die Problematik des § 92(2) Gemeindeordnung Nordrhein-Westfalen. Berlin, Duncker & Humblot, 1964. pp. 93. bibliog. 23cm. (Finanzwissenschaftliche Forschungsarbeiten. Band Nr. 31)

- Germany - Saarland

SAARGEBIET. Statistisches Amt. Einzelschriften zur Statistik des Saarlandes. No. 21. Die Finanzen der Gemeinden und Gemeindeverbände im Rechnungsjahr 1954. Saarbrücken, 1957. pp. 139.

- Ghana

GHANA. [Legislative Council. Sessional Papers]. 1949. No. 3. Revenue and expenditure of native authorities in the Colony, Ashanti and the Northern Territories for the year ending 31st March, 1948. Accra, 1949. pp. 13.

GHANA. [Legislative Council. Sessional Papers] 1952. No. 2. Report on local government finance, 1951. Accra, 1952. pp. 68.

- Iceland

ICELAND. 1967. Sveitarsjódareikningar, 1953-62. (Hagskýrslur Íslands. 2. [Series]. 37). Reykjavík, 1967. pp. 57. 24½cm. With table headings in English.

ICELAND. Hagstofa. 1968. Sveitarsjódareikningar 1963-65; Communal finance 1963-65. Reykjavík, 1968. pp. 93. (Hagskýrslur Íslands. 2. [Series] 44) With English translations of table headings.

- India

RASTOGI (K.M.) Local finance: its theory and working in India. Gwalior, Kailash Pustak Sadan, 1967. pp. xi, 230, iv. bibliog. 21 cm.

- India - Bombay

RAO (N. RAJAGOPALA) Finances of municipalities in North Kanara district: a monograph study of local finance. Kumta, 1968. pp. 104. bibliog.

- India - Madhya Pradesh

MINOCHA (A.C.) Finances of urban local bodies in Madhya Pradesh: a case study of Bhopal, Mahakoshal and Vindhya Pradesh regions. Bombay, All-India Institute of Local Self-Government, 1965. pp. v, 266. bibliog. 24cm.

- India - Rajasthan

>BHAMBHRI (CHANDRA PRAKASH) Municipalities and their finances: an empirical study of the municipalities of Rajasthan. Jaipur, 1969. pp. 144.

- Ireland (Republic)

>EIRE. Interdepartmental Committee on Local Finance and Taxation. 1967. Report on exemptions from and remissions of rates. Dublin, [1967]. pp. 38

- Italy

>BOSISIO (OLIVIERO) L'imposta di famiglia ed altre imposte comunali. 9th ed. Milano, Pirola, 1966. pp. 175. bibliog. 23½cm.

>GIOVINE (GAETANO E. DI) L'ordinamento finanziario dei comuni. Empoli, Caparrini, [1967]. pp. 566. 24cm.

>ROME. Università. Istituto di Economia e Finanza. Studi di Finanza Pubblica. 8. Studi sulla finanza locale. Milano, Giuffrè, 1967. pp. xii, 221. 24cm.

>SARTORATI (GIANNI) Teoria, amministrazione e riforma dell'imposizione comunale sui consumi. Milano, Giuffrè, 1967. pp. iv, 197. 24cm. (Rome. Università. Istituto di Economia e Finanza. Studi di Finanza Pubblica. 10)

>CONVEGNO DI STUDI DI SCIENZA DELL' AMMINISTRAZIONE, 13°, 1967. I problemi della entrata e della spesa nella finanza degli enti locali: (atti). Milano, 1969. pp. 446.

>VILLANI (ANDREA) L'indebitamento degli enti locali. Milano, 1969. pp. 252. (Istituto per la Scienza dell'Amministrazione Pubblica. Quaderni ISAP. 8)

>ZACCARIA (FRANCESCO) Il bilancio dello Stato, delle Regioni, delle Province e dei Comuni: lezioni tenute nell'anno accademico 1968-69. Cagliari, [1970?]. pp. 266. bibliog.

>GABOARDI (ATTILIO) La finanza locale in Italia: la crisi, i problemi, le prospettive del risanamento. Milano, [1971]. pp. 183.

- Mexico

>MARGÁIN M. (E.) La hacienda municipal. in Mexico. 1966. Ensayos de derecho administrativo y tributario para conmemorar el XXX aniversario de la ley de justicia fiscal. Mexico, [1966].

- Netherlands

>NETHERLANDS. Centraal Bureau voor de Statistiek. 1966. De gemeentefinanciën in economische categorieën: methodologie en uitkomsten 1957-1960. Hilversum, de Haan, 1966. pp. 109. 29cm. With English summary.

- New Zealand

>NEW ZEALAND. Royal Commission on Local Authority Finance, 1958. Report. [Chairman: Sir Joseph Stanton]. Wellington, 1958. pp. 171.

>NEW ZEALAND. 1965. A comparison of rating systems: Onehunga borough. (Valuation Department) [Wellington, 1965]. fo. 16. 24cm.

>NEW ZEALAND. 1966. A comparison of rating systems: the city of Wellington. (Valuation Department Research Papers. No. 661) [Wellington, 1966]. fo. 20. 24cm.

>NEW ZEALAND. 1966. Local rating in New Zealand: a study of its development; by J.S.H. Robertson. (Valuation Department Research Papers. No.663) Wellington, [1966]. fo. 50. 24cm.

>NEW ZEALAND. 1966. A study in rating change: Milton borough. (Valuation Department Research Papers. No. 665) Wellington, 1966. fo. 11. bibliog. 24cm.

- Russia

>DZHUN' (BORIS MIKHAILOVICH) Effektivnost' ispol'zovaniia osnovnykh fondov kommunal'nogo khoziaistva. Kiev, 1969. pp. 166.

- South Africa

>SOUTH AFRICA. Bureau of Statistics. Divisional council statistics. [in Afrikaans and English] Pretoria, annual, 1965 [1st] to date. 30cm.

>HOLMES (IVOR QUINTON) Local government finance in South Africa; second edition by J. W. Cowden. Durban, 1969. pp. 536. bibliog.

- United Kingdom

>LONDON. London County Council. Local Government and Statistical Department. Debt of great towns, 1905-6: return showing for each town in the United Kingdom having an estimated population exceeding 250,000, the net debt outstanding at the end of the financial year 1905-6 and the annual charge in respect thereof. London, 1907. pp. 9.

>NATIONAL UNION OF CONSERVATIVE AND UNIONIST ASSOCIATIONS. The Conservative scheme of rating relief and local government reform: (supplement). [London], 1929. pp. 20. The Scheme is shelved at HJ/D 84.

>RATE REBATES IN ENGLAND AND WALES; [pd. by] Department of the Environment [U.K.]. a., 1967/68- London.

>DEW (RODNEY) and others. Motor tax as a source of local government finance. London, Institute of Municipal Treasurers and Accountants, 1968. pp. 30. 21cm.

>HILDERSLEY (STANLEY HECTOR HAMILTON) and NOTTAGE (RAYMOND) Sources of local revenue;...memorandum prepared for the Royal Commission on Local Government in England. London, Royal Institute of Public Administration, 1968. pp. 52. 21½cm.

>INSTITUTE OF MUNICIPAL TREASURERS AND ACCOUNTANTS. Sources of Local Government Finance. Local charges as a source of local government finance;[by] F.R. Flexman [and others]. London, 1968. pp. 35.

>Another copy at HJ/B 38

LOCAL FINANCE - United Kingdom (Cont'd.)

SALES tax as a source of local government finance. London, 1968. pp. 26.

ILERSIC (ALFRED ROMAN) Rates as a source of local government finance. London, Institute of Municipal Treasurers and Accountants, 1969. pp. 47. 21cm.

INSTITUTE OF MUNICIPAL TREASURERS AND ACCOUNTANTS. Sources of Local Government Finance. Local income tax as a source of local government finance; [by] Rodney Dew [and others]. London, 1969. pp. 43.

BOADEN (NOEL) Urban policy-making: influences on county boroughs in England and Wales. Cambridge, 1971. pp. 150. bibliog.

FREEMAN (ROLAND) Financing the elected member. London, 1971. pp. 9.

HEPWORTH (NOEL PEERS) The finance of local government. 2nd ed. London, 1971. pp. 349. bibliog.

LYNCH (E.J.F.) Local authority capital programmes: circular 2/70 and all that. London, 1971. pp. 22.

MARSHALL (ARTHUR HEDLEY) New revenues for local government. London, 1971. pp. 27. (Fabian Society. Research Series. No. 295)

- United Kingdom - Accounting

DISTRICT AUDITORS' SOCIETY. Works Department Panel. Financial control in local authority building department: a study. London, Institute of Municipal Treasurers and Accountants, [1967]. pp. 52. bibliog. 20½cm.

MANUAL of principles of financial and management control for local authorities carrying out new construction by direct labour: report by a working party set up by the Minister of Housing and Local Government in agreement with the local authority associations. London, H.M.S.O., 1969. pp. vii, 34. bibliog. 24½cm.

U.K. Working Party on the Housing Revenue Account. 1969. Housing revenue accounts: report: [J. Delafons, chairman]. London, 1969. pp. viii, 104. 24½cm.

- United Kingdom - Law

RYDE (WALTER CRANLEY) On rating: the law and practice; twelfth edition by David Widdicombe [and others]. London, Butterworths, 1968. pp. cxxv, 1451, 86. 24cm. (Butterworths Modern Textbooks. No.3)

- United Kingdom - Scotland

RATE REBATES IN SCOTLAND; ([pd. by] Scottish Development Department). a., 1968/69- Edinburgh.

PAGE (C.S.) and CANAWAY (E.E.) Administrative costs of local authorities; local taxation. Edinburgh, 1969. pp. 59. (Scotland. Royal Commission on Local Government in Scotland, 1966. Research Studies. 1.)

- United States

LINDMAN (ERIK L.) State school support and municipal government costs: a local tax allocation correction factor for use in apportioning state school funds. Los Angeles, 1965. fo. 24. (California University. Institute of Government and Public Affairs. [Publications]. MR-27)

ELIAS (C.E.) Land development and local public finance. in California University. Real Estate Research Program. Essays in urban land economics Los Angeles, 1966.

BRAZER (HARVEY ELLIOT) ed. Essays in state and local finance. Ann Arbor, Michigan University, 1967. pp. ix, 148. 23cm. (Michigan Governmental Studies. No. 49)

NATIONAL INDUSTRIAL CONFERENCE BOARD. Studies in Business Economics. No. 96. Financing local government; by Juan de Torres. New York, [1967]. pp. vi, 146. bibliog. 22½cm.

CONNECTICUT. Tri-State Transportation Commission. 1968. Government capital expenditure trends. New York, 1968. pp. 4. (Regional Profiles. Vol. 1. No. 1C.)

URBAN LAND INSTITUTE. Research Monographs. 15. "Do single-family homes pay their way?" : a comparative analysis of costs and revenues for public services; by Ruth L. Mace and Warren J. Wicker. Washington, D.C., 1968. pp. 46.

JOHNSON (HARRY L.) ed. State and local tax problems; [Festschrift in honor of Dr. Charles P. White]. Knoxville, [1969]. pp. 190.

MAXWELL (JAMES ACKLEY) Financing state and local governments. rev. ed. Washington, D.C., 1969. pp. 275. bibliog. (Brookings Institution. National Committee on Government Finance. Studies of Government Finance)

MUSHKIN (SELMA J.) and COTTON (JOHN F.) Sharing federal funds for state and local needs: grants-in-aid and PPB systems. New York, 1969. pp. 207. bibliog.

HIRSCH (WERNER ZVI) The economics of state and local government. New York, [1970]. pp. 333.

REUSS (HENRY S.) Revenue-sharing: crutch or catalyst for state amd local governments? New York, 1970. pp. 170. bibliog.

- United States - Illinois

FISHER (GLENN WILLIAM) and FAIRBANKS (ROBERT P.) Illinois municipal finance: a political and economic analysis. Urbana, U. of Illinois P., 1968. pp. xiii, 242. 22½cm.

FISHER (GLENN WILLIAM) Taxes and politics: a study of Illinois public finance. Urbana, 1969. pp. 332.

- United States - Kentucky

KENTUCKY. Commission on Economy and Efficiency. Opportunities for administration of inactive state funds to secure increased yields; staff report. Frankfort, 1964. pp. 18. 28cm.

- United States - North Carolina

>WICKER (WARREN J.) and HOWARD (S. KENNETH) Perspectives on local finance in North Carolina: instructional material. Chapel Hill, 1967. fo. 98.
>R . X 36 480

- United States - West Virginia

>BAHL (ROY W.) and SAUNDERS (ROBERT J.) Intercounty differences in West Virginia government expenditures. Morgantown, 1967. pp. 68. (West Virginia University. Business and Economic Studies. vol. 10, no. 3)

- Yugoslavia

>BOGOEV (KSENTE) Lokalne finansije Jugoslavije. Beograd, 1964. pp. 376. 19cm. (Savez Ekonomista Jugoslavije. Ekonomska Biblioteka. 20) With Russian and English tables of contents.

- Zambia

>NORTHERN RHODESIA. Committee Appointed to Review the Financing of Services and Amenities Provided for Africans in Urban Areas. 1961. Report: [S.W. Coleman, chairman]. Lusaka, 1961. pp. 93.

LOCAL GOVERNMENT

>ATTERBURY (FRANCIS) Bishop of Rochester. A sermon preach'd at the Guild-Hall chapel...Septemb. 28. 1706, being the day of the election of...the Lord Mayor. London, Bowyer, 1706. pp. 13. 19cm.

>HUMES (SAMUEL) and MARTIN (EILEEN M.) The structure of local government: (a comparative survey of 81 countries). 2nd ed. The Hague, 1969. pp. 674. bibliogs. (International Union of Local Authorities. Publications. 96)

>LONDON. University. Institute of Commonwealth Studies. Collected seminar papers on autonomy and dependence in 'parochial' politics. London, [1969]. pp. 113. (London. University. Institute of Commonwealth Studies. Collected Seminar Papers. No. 7)

>NATIONAL COMPUTING CENTRE. Computer application packages in local government. Manchester, 1969. pp. 55.

>LEEMANS (A. F.) Changing patterns of local government. The Hague, 1970. pp. 224. bibliog. (International Union of Local Authorities. [Publications] 97)

>UNITED NATIONS. Public Administration Division. 1970. Administrative aspects of urbanization: based on a comparative study...and on the United Nations Workshop on Administrative Aspects of Urbanization, held...at The Hague...1968. (ST/TAO/M/51). New York, 1970. pp. 228. bibliog.

>The USE of computers in local government: report of a survey group appointed by the Minister for Local Government, etc. Dublin, Stationery Office, [1970]. pp. 63.

>WICKWAR (WILLIAM HARDY) The political theory of local government. Columbia, S.C., 1970. pp. 118. bibliog.

>STEWART (JOHN DAVID) Management in local government: a viewpoint. London, 1971. pp. 197.

- Congresses

>INTERNATIONAL CONGRESS OF LOCAL AUTHORITIES. 5th Congress, 1932. Programme, May 23rd to 28th. [London], 1932. pp. 24. (International Union of Local Authorities. Publications. No. 41)

- Periodicals - Bibliography

>JOINT COMMITTEE ON EUROPEAN REGIONAL PLANNING. 1963. List of European and North American periodicals dealing with questions concerning regional economy and planning and local administration; drawn up by the Documentation Section and Library, etc. (AS-CPL/Am(63)20). [Strasbourg, Council of Europe, 1963]. pp. ii. fo. 50. 26½cm.

- State supervision - Italy

>SCUDIERO (MICHELE) I controlli sulle regioni sulle province e sui comuni nell'ordinamento costituzionale italiano. [Naples], Morano, [1963 in progress] 24cm.

- Africa

>CONFERENCE ON LOCAL DEVELOPMENT IN AFRICA, WASHINGTON, 1967. Local development in Africa: a summary report of a conference jointly sponsored by: the Foreign Service Institute of the Department of State; the Africa Subcommittee of the Foreign Area Research Coordination Group; the Agency for International Development. [Washington], Department of State, 1967. pp. 37.

>CONFERENCE ON AFRICAN LOCAL INSTITUTIONS AND RURAL TRANSFORMATION, 1967. [Proceedings of the conference held by the Institute of African Government of Lincoln University. Narberth?, 1967?] fo. ii, 95. Wanting title-page.

- Africa, West

>WEST African chiefs: their changing status under colonial rule and independence, [an international seminar, held by the Institute of African Studies of the University of Ife]; edited by Michael Crowder and Obaro Ikime. New York, 1970. pp. 453. bibliogs.

- Algeria

>ALGERIA. Ministère de l'Information. 1968. La Commune en Algérie. [Algiers, 1968]. pp. 97. bibliog.

- Australia

>ADELAIDE. University. Department of Adult Education. Publications. No. 5. Local government: selected papers from two schools held at Port Augusta and Mount Gambier, October, 1966. Adelaide, 1967. pp. 133.

- Australia - Dictionaries and encyclopedias

>GIFFORD (KENNETH H.) The Australian local government dictionary. Melbourne, 1967. pp. 309.

- Austria

>KLABOUCH (JIŘÍ) Die Gemeindeselbstverwaltung in Österreich, 1848-1918. München, Oldenbourg, 1968. pp. 180. bibliog. 20½cm. (Institut für Österreichkunde. Österreich Archiv)

LOCAL GOVERNMENT (Cont'd.)

- Botswana

BOTSWANA. Local Government Committee. 1964. Report. [Gaberones?], 1964. pp. various. In English and Tswana.

BOTSWANA. Ministry of Local Government and Lands. Annual report. a., 1967- Gaberones.

- Canada

CANADIAN FEDERATION OF MAYORS AND MUNICIPALITIES. Submission to the government of Canada, April 21st, 1969. Ottawa, 1969. fo. (87). 28cm. In English and French.

ROWAT (DONALD CAMERON) The Canadian municipal system: essays on the improvement of local government. Toronto, [1960]. pp. 242. bibliog.

- Canada - Manitoba

MANITOBA. Royal Commission on Local Government Organization and Finance, 1963. Report... April, 1964: [Roland Michener, chairman]. Winnipeg, 1964. pp. 306. bibliog. 5 maps in end pocket.

- Canada - New Brunswick

WHALEN (H.J.) The development of local government in New Brunswick. [Fredericton, Department of Municipal Affairs, 1964]. pp. 125.

- Canada - Saskatchewan

SASKATCHEWAN. Local Government Continuing Committee. 1960. Progress report. Regina, 1960. pp. 16.

SASKATCHEWAN. Local Government Continuing Committee. 1961. Consultations on local government: a technical reference document to the report Local government in Saskatchewan submitted to the Government of Saskatchewan, March 1, 1961. [Regina, 1961] fo. 290.

SASKATCHEWAN. Local Government Continuing Committee. 1961. Local government in Saskatchewan: a report submitted to the government of Saskatchewan, March, 1961. [Regina, 1961] pp. 119.

- China

GILLIN (DONALD G.) Warlord: Yen Hsi-shan in Shansi province, 1911-1949. Princeton, U.P., 1967. pp. xiv, 334. bibliog. 20cm.

- Colombia

RIZO OTERO (HAROLD) Hacia una reforma integral de la administración local en Colombia y proyecto de reforma a la estructura administrativa del municipio de Cali. [Bogotá, 1968]. pp. 135. bibliog.

- Communist countries

BORISOV (B. L.) Местные органы государственной власти европейских стран народной демократии. Москва, Госюриздат, 1955. pp. 132. 22cm.

IAKIMOVICH (IADVIGA VLADIMIROVNA) Mestnye organy gosudarstvennoi vlasti evropeiskikh stran narodnoi demokratii. Moskva, 1964. pp. 206.

- Congo (Kinshasa)

DEMUNTER (P.) L'administration locale au Congo. II. Bruxelles, 1969. fo. 29. (Centre de Recherche et d'Information Socio-Politiques. Etudes Africaines du C.R.I.S.P. [Series] 2) Part I published in Courrier Africain, no. 85 du 6 décembre 1968, which see.

Cyprus

HAYWARD (T.C.) Report on local government in Cyprus. Nicosia, 1957. pp. 31, xi. 33½cm.

- Czechoslovakia

BYDŽOVSKÝ (LADISLAV) and LUKEŠ (ZDENĚK) eds. Priestupky a previnenia: vysvetlivky k zákonu o úlonách národných výborov pri zabezpečovaní socialistického poriadku a k zákonu o miestnych ľudových súdoch. Bratislava, Osveta, 1962. pp. 239. 21cm.

- Denmark

HOLSTEIN (FREDERIK ADOLPH) Lensgreve. Om de danske raadgivende Provindsial-Staenders Vaesen og Vaerd. 2nd ed. Kjøbenhavn, 1832. pp. 94.

- East (Far East)

EASTERN REGIONAL ORGANIZATION FOR PUBLIC ADMINISTRATION. General Assembly, 2nd, 1962. Report on local governments: an integration of the discussions on local governments at the 1960 Manila first general assembly and the 1961 Tokyo seminar...prepared by Ernesto M. Vergara. Manila, 1963. pp. 60.

- Europe

INTERNATIONAL UNION OF LOCAL AUTHORITIES. Europe Day, 1957. Local authorities and European economic integration. The Hague, 1957-8. 2pts. (in 1 vol.). 22½cm.

EUROPEAN CONFERENCE OF LOCAL AUTHORITIES. Yearbook. [in French and English] a. Strasbourg. Current issues only kept.

- European Economic Community countries

GUERNIERI (ANGELO MARIA) I circondari e le province degli stati della Comunità Economica Europea: cenni sulle amministrazioni pubbliche locali, collegati all'esame di alcuni bilanci di previsione. [Rome?, 1969]. 2 vols. (in 1). bibliog.

- France

[NECKER (JACQUES)] Mémoire donné au roi par M. Neker en 1778. Londres [Paris?], 1781. pp. 32. 21½cm.

BELORGEY (GÉRARD) Le gouvernement et l'administration de la France. Paris, Colin, 1967. pp. 447. bibliog. 23½cm. (Collection U. Série Société Politique)

BILLAUDOT (FRANÇOISE) L'installation des services extérieurs de l'état dans un nouveau département de la région parisienne: l'exemple des Hauts-de-Seine. Paris, P.U.F., 1967. pp. vii, 86. bibliog. 24cm. (Paris. Université. Faculté de Droit et des Sciences Économiques. Travaux et Recherches. Série "Science Administrative". No. 1)

KESSELMAN (MARK) The ambiguous consensus: a study of local government in France. New York, Knopf, [1967]. pp. xii, 201, v. bibliog. 21cm.

ARCY (FRANÇOIS D') Structures administratives et urbanisation: la Société Centrale pour l'Équipement du Territoire (SCET). Paris, 1968. pp. 301.

DETTON (HERVÉ) and HOURTICQ (JEAN) L'administration régionale et locale de la France. 5th ed. Paris, P.U.F., 1968. pp. 128. bibliog. 17½cm. (Que Sais-Je? No. 598)

SOUCHON (MARIE FRANCOISE) Le maire, élu local dans une société en changement. Paris, [1968]. pp. 270. bibliog. (Grenoble. Université. Institut d'Etudes Politiques. Cahiers. 2)

BERNARD (PAUL) Docteur en droit. Le grand tournant des communes de France: des communautés nouvelles à l'épreuve de l'équipement. Paris, Colin, [1969]. pp. 351. 18cm. (Collection U. Série "Science Administrative")

BOURJOL (MAURICE) Les institutions régionales de 1789 à nos jours. Paris, Berger-Levrault, 1969. pp. 368. bibliog. 20½cm. (L'Administration Nouvelle: Série Histoire)

DAWSON (GEORGE) L'évolution des structures de l'administration locale déconcentrée en France: l'exemple du Département du Pas-de-Calais et de la Région du Nord. Paris, Pichon & Durand-Auzias, 1969. pp. 567. bibliog. 25cm. (Bibliothèque de Science Administrative. tome 1)

LYONNET (ALAIN) and MENARD (LUC ALEXANDRE) Recherches sur l'administration de mission dans la vie locale. Paris, 1969. pp. 157. bibliogs. (Paris. Université. Faculté de Droit et des Sciences Économiques. Travaux et Recherches. Série "Science Administrative". No. 2)

PISANI (EDGARD) La région—pour quoi faire?; ou, Le triomphe des Jacondins. [Paris, 1969]. pp. 228.

- Germany

BAUMANN (FRITZ ACHIM) Die allgemeine untere staatliche Verwaltungsbehörde im Landkreis. Berlin, Duncker und Humblot, [1967]. pp. 117. bibliog. 23cm. (Spires. Hochschule für Verwaltungswissenschaften. Schriftenreihe. Band 35)

FONK (FRIEDRICH) Die Behörde des Regierungspräsidenten: Funktionen, Zuständigkeiten, Organisation. Berlin, Duncker und Humblot, [1967]. pp. 286. bibliog. 23cm. (Spires. Hochschule für Verwaltungswissenschaften. Schriftenreihe. Band 36)

WEBER (WERNER) Dr. Jur. Staats- und Selbstverwaltung in der Gegenwart. 2nd ed. Göttingen, Schwartz, 1967. pp. 165. 23cm. (Goettingen. Universität. Juristische Fakultät. Goettinger Rechtswissenschaftliche Studien? Band 9)

GERMANY (BUNDESREPUBLIK). Institut für Raumordnung. Seminar, 2, Bad Godesberg, 1968. Raumordnung und Verwaltungsreform: Tagungsbericht über das Seminar [etc]. Bad Godesberg, 1968. pp. (297). bibliog. (Germany (Bundesrepublik). Institut für Raumordnung. Mitteilungen. Heft 64)

KOETTGEN (ARNOLD) Kommunale Selbstverwaltung zwischen Krise und Reform: ausgewählte Schriften. Stuttgart, [1968]. pp. ix, 292. (Verein für Kommunalwissenschaften. Schriftenreihe. Band 25)

FREIBERG (WERNER) Grundfragen der Kommunalpolitik. Mainz, [1970]. pp. 148.

MATZERATH (HORST) Nationalsozialismus und kommunale Selbstverwaltung. Stuttgart, [1970]. pp. 503. bibliog. (Verein für Kommunalwissenschaften. Schriftenreihe. Band 29)

- Germany - Rhineland-Palatinate

CRAMER (HUBERTUS) Sozial-ökonomische Struktur und Funktion der Gemeinden im Lande Rheinland-Pfalz 1960/61. Bonn, Forschungsgesellschaft für Agrarpolitik und Agrarsoziologie, 1967. fo. 70. 29cm. ([Publications]. 182)

- Germany - Saarland

SAARBRUECKEN. Universität. Annales Universitatis Saraviensis. Rechts- und Wirtschaftswissenschaftliche Abteilung. Heft 37. Das Saarländische Kreisrecht, ausgenommen die haushalt- und kassenrechtlichen Vorschriften; von Gert Jenewein. Köln, Heymann, 1968. pp. 279. bibliog. 20½cm.

- Germany, Eastern

ZIENERT (HANS) Die Stadt im sozialistischen Staat: zur Funktion der Stadtverordnetenversammlung und ihrer Organe im System der staatlichen Leitung. Berlin, Staatsverlag der D.D.R., 1968. pp. 196. 21cm.

- Hong Kong

HONG KONG. Urban Council. 1969. Report on the reform of local government. Hong Kong, 1969. pp. iii, 10; iii, 13. 21cm. In English and Chinese.

- Hungary

HUNGARY. 1966. Községeink főbb adatai, 1960-1964. (Statisztikai Időszaki Közlemények. 80. kötet) Budapest, 1966. pp. 349. 28cm. With English summary.

- India

INDIA. Department of Community Development. 1961. Panchayati Raj: the ten point test. [Delhi, 1961]. pp. 28.

LOCAL GOVERNMENT - India (Cont'd.)

INDIA. Department of Community Development. 1961. Training of non-officials. rev. ed. Simla, 1961. pp. 16.

INDIA. Ministry of Information and Broadcasting. Publications Division. 1961. Panchayati Raj; issued on behalf of Ministry of Community Development and Co-operation. Delhi, 1961. pp. 19.

INDIA. Department of Community Development. 1962. Panchayats at a glance, as on 31st March, 1961. [New Delhi, 1962]. pp. 19.

INDIA. Planning Commission. 1962. Report on Indian and state administrative services and problems of district administration; by V.T. Krishnamachari. [Delhi], 1962. pp. 108.

KURUKSHETRA. [Special Numbers]. vol. 10, no. 12. New Delhi conferences special. Delhi, 1962. pp. 36.

KURUKSHETRA. [Special Numbers]. vol. 11, no. 1. Tenth anniversary number. Delhi, 1962. pp. 112.

INDIA. Ministry of Health and Family Planning. Rural- Urban Relationship Committee. 1966. Report. New Delhi, 1966. 3 vols. (in 1). 24½cm.

JAIN (SUGAN CHAND) Community development and Panchayati Raj in India. Bombay, Allied Publishers, 1967. pp. xii, 656. bibliog. 24½cm.

SHARMA (MAHADEO PRASAD) Local self-government in India. 6th ed. Allahabad, Kitab Mahal, 1967. pp. vii, 168. 18cm.

DAS (R.B.) and SINGH (D.P.) eds. Deliberative and executive wings in local government. Lucknow, 1968. pp. 168.

GUPTA (BHARAT BHUSHAN) Local government in India. Allahabad, 1968. pp. 190. bibliog.

INDIA. Administrative Reforms Commission. Study Team on District Administration. 1968. Report ...February, 1967. Delhi, 1967 [or rather] 1968. pp. 170.

CHATTERJEE (BISHWA BANDHU) ed. Micro-studies in community development, panchayati raj and co-operation. Delhi, 1969. pp. 213. bibliog.

GAIKWAD (VIJAY SINGH RAMESHWAR RAO) Panchayati raj and bureaucracy: a study of the relationship patterns. Hyderabad, 1969. pp. 77.

KHAN (ILTIJA H.) Government in rural India. Bombay, [1969]. pp. 185. bibliog.

VENKATARANGAIYA (MAHIDIPUDI) and PATTABHIRAM (M.) eds. Local government in India: select readings. Bombay, 1969. pp. 515.

INAMDAR (N.R.) Functioning of village panchayats. Bombay, 1970. pp. 368.

INDIA. Administrative Reforms Commission. 1970. Report on state administration. [Delhi, 1970] pp. 155.

MADDICK (HENRY) Panchayati raj: a study of rural local government in India. London, 1970. pp. 402. bibliog.

NARAYAN (JAYAPRAKASH) Communitarian society and panchayati raj;...edited with an introduction by Brahmanand. Varanasi, 1970. pp. 155.

SEMINAR ON PANCHAYATI RAJ, HYDERABAD, 1969. Local government institutions in rural India: some aspects: proceedings...; edited by R.N. Haldipur [and] V.R.K. Paramahamsa. Hyderabad, 1970. pp. 347. bibliog.

VALSAN (E.H.) Community development programs and rural local government: comparative case studies of India and the Philippines;... foreword by Fred W. Riggs. New York, [1970]. pp. 485. bibliog.

FOX (RICHARD G.) Kin, clan, Raja, and rule: state-hinterland relations in preindustrial India. Berkeley, 1971. pp. 187. bibliog.

- India - Andhra Pradesh

ANDHRA PRADESH. Administrative Reforms Committee. 1960. Report. Hyderabad, 1960. pp. 112.

- India - Madras

MADRAS. [Rural Development and Local Administration Department]. 1967- . Manual on Panchayat administration. Madras, 1967 in progress.

- India - Rajasthan - Bibliography

SEMINAR ON PANCHAYATI RAJ, PLANNING AND DEMOCRACY, 1964. A select bibliography on Panchayati Raj, planning and democracy. Jaipur, Rajasthan University Library, 1964. fo. v, 70. 25cm.

- Ireland (Republic)

EIRE. Department of Local Government. 1962. Notes on the powers vested in the elected members of local authorities. 2nd ed. Dublin, 1962. pp. 45. 16cm.

The USE of computers in local government: report of a survey group appointed by the Minister for Local Government, etc. Dublin, Stationery Office, [1970]. pp. 63.

- Italy

ITALY. Presidenza del Consiglio dei Ministri. Ufficio Regioni. 1958. Ordinamento delle regioni: quadri sinottici comparativi delle competenze legislative e amministrative delle regioni a statuto normale e speciale, comprese le province autonome di Bolzano e di Trento. Roma, 1958. pp. 62. 29cm.

STURZO (LUIGI) Il programma municipale dei cattolici italiani:(il testo del discorso... pronunciato al Convegno di Caltanissetta... 1902). Roma, Cinque Lune, 1961. pp. 64. 20cm. (Reprinted from his "Croce di Constantino pp. 261-291, published in 1958)

PARTITO SOCIALISTA DEMOCRATICO ITALIANO. Convegno Regionale Marchigiano, Ancona, [1962?]. Per una politica socialdemocratica negli enti locali: [proceedings]. [Rome, imprint, 1962?] pp. 89. 16½cm. (Partito Socialista Democratico Italiano. Commissione Centrale Enti Locali. Collana di Documentazione. Opuscoli. N.3)

PARTITO SOCIALISTA ITALIANO. Il programma del P.S.I. per le elezioni amministrative 22 novembre 1964. Roma, 1964. pp. 14. 19½cm.

TUCCARI (EMANUELE) Saggio per una teoria sulla legge regionale. Milano, Giuffrè, 1966. pp. 110. 25cm. (Messina. Università. Istituto di Scienze Giuridiche, Economiche, Politiche e Sociali. Pubblicazioni. No. 78)

CONGRESSO CELEBRATIVO DEL CENTENARIO DELLE LEGGI AMMINISTRATIVE DI UNIFICAZIONE. L'ordinamento comunale e provinciale;... a cura di Massimo Severo Giannini ([and] Antonio Amorth; atti del congresso, etc.). [Vicenza], 1967-8. 2 vols. (in 1).

DEMARCHI (FRANCO) Sociologia della provincia: relazione tenuta al Convegno di studi promosso dalla Democrazia Cristiana su "Realtà e prospettive dello sviluppo economico e sociale nella provincia isontina", Grado 16-17 settembre 1967. [Gorizia, 1967?] pp. 26. (Quadrante Est. Quaderni)

ROTELLI (ETTORE) L'avvento della regione in Italia dalla caduta del regime fascista alla Costituzione repubblicana, 1943-1947. Milano, Giuffrè, 1967. pp. xxi, 427. bibliog. 24cm. (Istituto per la Scienza dell'Amministrazione Pubblica. Pubblicazioni. Studi e Testi. 3)

BERTI (GIORGIO) Caratteri dell'amministrazione comunale e provinciale. Padova, 1969. pp. 227.

COLCLOUGH (NEVILLE THOMAS) Land, politics and power in a southern Italian village; [Ph.D. (London) thesis]. 1969. fo. 222. bibliog. Typescript: unpublished. This thesis is the property of London University and may not be removed from the Library.

La PROVINCIA nell'ordinamento regionale: atti del convegno di studi indetto nel quadro delle manifestazioni celebrative del centenario della costituzione dell'Amministrazione Provinciale di Roma, Roma...1968. Roma, [1968?]. pp. 356.

VILLANI (ANDREA) Il potere locale: regioni, province e comuni in Italia. Milano, 1969. pp. 243.

ARBIZZANI (LUIGI) and ALFONSO (ALDO D') eds. Comuni e province nella storia dell'Emilia-Romagna: cento anni di politica di sinistra. Roma, 1970. pp. 313.

- Kenya

KENYA. 1948. A Bill to provide for local government in native areas and for the establishment of African district councils and other matters incidental thereto. [Nairobi], 1948. pp. 20.

PARKER (MARY) Political and social aspects of the development of municipal government in Kenya with special reference to Nairobi. [London], Colonial Office, [1949]. pp. 278, (22). bibliog. 32½cm.

KENYA. Sessional Papers. 1961. No. 2. The reconstitution of local authorities. Nairobi, 1961. pp. 6.

KENYA. Local Government Commission of Inquiry. 1966. Report. [Nairobi], 1966. pp. 71. 24½cm.

KENYA. Sessional Papers. 1967. No. 12. Proposed action by the government of Kenya on the report of the local government commission of inquiry. [Nairobi?], 1967. pp. 33. 25cm.

- Latvia

ŠKAPARE (BAIVA) Rol' postoiannykh komissii mestnykh Sovetov v obespechenii sotsialisticheskoi zakonnosti: po materialam Latviiskoi SSR. Riga, 1969. pp. 83.

- Malta

BOISSEVAIN (JEREMY FERGUS) Saints and fireworks: religion and politics in rural Malta; [with a postscript, 1968]. 2nd ed. London, Athlone P., 1969. pp. xii, 162. bibliog. 21½cm. (London. University. London School of Economics and Political Science Monographs on Social Anthropology. No. 30)

- Netherlands

NETHERLANDS. Ministerie van Binnenlandse Zaken. Commissie van Advies inzake Herziening van de Provinciale Wet. 1954. Verslag van de Commissie... ingesteld bij beschikking van de Minister... 17 December 1948. 's-Gravenhage, 1954. pp. 61.

NETHERLANDS. Staatscommissie Bestuursvorm Grote Gemeenten. 1955. Verslag van de Staatscommissie...ingesteld bij Koninklijk besluit van 1 November 1952, No. 32. 's-Gravenhage, 1955. pp. 47.

- New Guinea

MORAUTA (LOUISE HELEN MARGARET) Beyond the village: a study of contemporary politics in the hinterland of Madang, New Guinea; [Ph.D. (London) thesis]. [1972]. fo.562. bibliog. Typescript: unpublished. Survey schedules in end pocket. This thesis is the property of London University and may not be removed from the Library.

- New Zealand

NEW ZEALAND. [General Assembly]. House of Representatives. Local Bills Committee. 1960. Inquiry into the structure of local government; H.L.J. May, chairman. Wellington, 1960. pp. 203.

NEW ZEALAND. Board of Health. 1968. Health responsibilities of local government. rev. ed. [Wellington], 1968. pp. 28. (Report Series. No. 11.)

ROBERTS (JOHN L.) and SIDEBOTHAM (ROY) Local government in the Wellington region: the challenge of chaos. [Wellington, 1968]. pp. 53.

NEW ZEALAND. Local Government Commission. 1969. Local Government Commission statements: main provisions of the Local Government Commission Act 1967 and related observations of the Commission. [Wellington], 1969. pp. 31.

LOCAL GOVERNMENT - New Zealand (Cont'd.)

NEW ZEALAND. Local Government Commission. 1969. Wellington local government area scheme: provisional scheme and explanatory statement. [Wellington], 1969. pp. 122.

REGAN (DAVID EDWARD) Political parties in New Zealand local government; [Ph.D. (London) thesis]. [1969]. fo. 436. bibliog. Typescript: unpublished. This thesis is the property of London University and may not be removed from the Library.

NEW ZEALAND. Local Government Commission. 1970. Basic statistics of local authorities, descriptive diagrams and related data. [Wellington], 1970. 1 pamphlet (unpaged).

NEW ZEALAND. Local Government Commission. 1970. Wellington local government area: decisions of the...Commission on objections to provisional area scheme. [Wellington], 1970. pp. 94.

- Nigeria

ADEWUMI (JAMES) District councils and district council budgeting in Ilorin Emirate. Zaria, 1965. fo. 8. (Ahmadu Bello University. Institute of Administration. Information Memoranda. No. 21)

NIGERIA (NORTHERN REGION). 1965. A white paper on the government's policy for the rehabilitation of the Tiv Native Authority. Kaduna, 1965. pp. 24. 24½cm.

NIGERIA (WESTERN REGION). Ministry of Local Government and Chieftaincy Affairs. Local government circulars. Ibadan, annual, 1966 [1st?] to date.

NIGERIA (WESTERN REGION). Ministry of Home Affairs and Information. 1967. Guide to new administrative units, Western Nigeria. Ibadan, 1967. pp. (15).

OTTENBERG (S.) Local government and the law in Southern Nigeria. in Buxbaum (David C.) ed. Traditional and modern legal institutions in Asia and Africa. Leiden, 1967.

MURRAY (D. J.) The work of administration in Nigeria; case studies. London, 1969. pp. 153.

NATIONAL CONFERENCE ON LOCAL GOVERNMENT, UNIVERSITY OF IFE, 1969. The future of local government in Nigeria; the report of the national conference... held at the Institute of Administration...; from April 29 to May 3, 1969. Ife, 1969. pp. 154.

GAILEY (HARRY A.) The road to Aba: a study of British administrative policy in Eastern Nigeria. New York, 1970. pp. 184. bibliog.

SMOCK (AUDREY C.) Ibo politics: the role of ethnic unions in Eastern Nigeria. Cambridge, Mass., 1971. pp. 274. bibliog.

- Nigeria - Dictionaries and encyclopaedias

CAMPBELL (MICHAEL J.) Word list of government and local government terms: English-Hausa, for use in northern Nigeria. [Kaduna, imprint, 1963?]. pp. 23. 20½cm.

- Pakistan

HASAN (MASUDUL) Text book of basic democracy and local government in Pakistan. Lahore, 1968. pp. 551.

MAHMOOD (MIR NASEEM) and MAHMUD (SATNAM) The case method and cases in Pakistan administration. Lahore, 1968. pp. 126. bibliog.

- Pakistan, East

WHEELER (RICHARD S.) Divisional councils in East Pakistan, 1960-1965: an evaluation. [Durham, N.C., 1967]. pp. 78. bibliog. (Duke University. Commonwealth-Studies Center. Program in Comparative Studies on Southern Asia. Monograph and Occasional Papers Series. No. 4)

RASHIDUZZAMAN (M.) Politics and administration in the local councils: a study of union and district councils in East Pakistan. Karachi, 1968. pp. 124. bibliog.

- Pakistan, West

CHAUDHARI (HAIDER ALI) Union councils: a study of Sahiwal and Lyallpur Districts. [Islamabad], Ministry of Information and Broadcasting, 1967 [or rather 1968]. pp. 117.

- Philippine Islands

VALSAN (E.H.) Community development programs and rural local government: comparative case studies of India and the Philippines;... foreword by Fred W. Riggs. New York, [1970]. pp. 485. bibliog.

- Poland

GEBERT (STANISLAW) Komentarz do ustawy o radach narodowych: stan prawny na dzień 15 marca 1964 r. Warszawa, Wydawnictwo Prawnicze, 1964. pp. xv, 431. 20cm.

RYBICKI (ZYGMUNT) and KAWALEC (WINCENTY) Administracja gospodarki terenowej. Warszawa, Wydawnictwo Prawnicze, 1964. pp. 159. 21cm. With Russian summary.

BIGO (TADEUSZ) and others. Pozycja Ustrojowa komisji rady narodowej: opracowanie syntetyczne na podstawie materiałów wybranych komisji rad narodowych województw zachodnich. Wrocław, Ossolineum, 1966. pp. 165. 21cm.

PALIWODA (JÓZEF) Kierowanie rolnictwem przez rady narodowe: zagadnienia administracyjnoprawne. Wrocław, Ossolineum, 1967. pp. 331. 23½cm. With Russian and German summaries.

SOKOLEWICZ (WOJCIECH) Przedstawicielstwo i administracja w systemie rad narodowych PRL. Wrocław, 1968. pp. 420. (Polska Akademia Nauk. Instytut Nauk Prawnych)

RYBICKI (ZYGMUNT) System rad narodowych w PRL. Warszawa, 1971. pp. 442. With Russian and French tables of contents.

- Rhodesia

> SOUTHERN RHODESIA. Commission of Inquiry into the Organization and Development of the Southern Rhodesia Public Services. 1961-63. First (-third) report. [T.T.Paterson, commissioner]. [Salisbury], 1961-63. 3 vols. (in 1). 33cm. (Legislative Assembly. [Sessional Papers]. 1962. C.S.R.9, 1962. C.S.R. 35, 1963. C.S.R.2) Fourth report unpublished.

> PASSMORE (GLORIA C.) Local government legislation in Southern Rhodesia up to September 30th, 1963. Salisbury, University College of Rhodesia and Nyasaland, Department of Government, 1966. pp. vii, 65. bibliog. (Source Book Series. No. 4)

> HOLLEMAN (JOHAN FREDERIK) Chief, council and commissioner: some problems of government in Rhodesia. Assen, 1969. pp. 391. bibliog.

> WEINRICH (A.K.H.) Chiefs and councils in Rhodesia: transition from patriarchal to bureaucratic power. London, 1971. pp. 252. bibliog.

- Roumania

> VALENTIN (H.) Organizarea controlului obştesc din experienta consiliilor locale ale sindicatelor Brăila şi Constanta. Bucureşti, Editura Politică, 1963. pp. 47. 20cm.

- Russia

> AZOVKIN (IVAN AKIMOVICH) Организация работы в исполкоме районного Совета. Москва, Госюриздат, 1959. pp. 104. 19½см.

> NEMTSEV (VIKTOR ALEKSANDROVICH) and PERTTSIK (VADIM ARKAD'EVICH) Сессии областных (краевых) Советов депутатов трудящихся. Москва, Госюриздат, 1959. pp. 88. 19½см.

> POPOVA (VERA IVANOVNA) Работа местных Советов депутатов трудящихся по обеспечению социалистической законности. Москва, Госюриздат, 1959. pp. 141. 20см.

> RUSSIA (U.S.S.R.). 1961. Итоги выборов и состав депутатов местных Советов депутатов трудящихся, 1961.: статистический сборник. Москва, 1961. pp. 121.

> OSLONOVSKII (ALEKSANDR DMITRIEVICH) Внештатный отдел исполкома Совета. Свердловск, Книжное Издательство, 1963. pp. 52. 20см. (На Общественных Началах)

> PERTTSIK (VADIM ARKAD'EVICH) Problemy mestnogo samoupravleniia v SSSR. Irkutsk, 1963. pp. 306. (Irkutsk. Universitet. Trudy. tom 32. Seriia Iuridicheskaia. vyp.6, ch.2)

> VYPOLNIAIA nakazy izbiratelei... Belgorod, 1963. pp. 44.

> VISHNIAKOV (VIKTOR GRIGOR'EVICH) Участие депутатов местных Советов в распределении жилой площади. Москва, 1964. pp. 70.

> FRANCE. Direction de la Documentation. La Documentation Française. Notes et Etudes Documentaires. No. 3,234. Les soviets locaux: l'organisation locale du pouvoir en Union Soviétique; [by] Patrice Gelard. Paris, 1965. pp. 20. bibliog.

> MESTNYE... Местные Советы на современном этапе. Москва, Наука, 1965. pp. 349. 19½см.

> RIABCHUK (GRIGORII FEDOROVICH) Poselkovyi Sovet deputatov trudiashchikhsia. Moskva, 1965. pp. 66.

> STAROVOITOV (NIKOLAI GEORGIEVICH) Порядок организации и проведения выборов в местные Советы. Москва, Юридическая Литература, 1965. pp. 56. 20см.

> CHEKHARIN (IVAN MIKHAILOVICH) Postoiannye komissii mestnykh Sovetov. Moskva, 1966. pp. 89.

> ELEONSKII (VLADIMIR ALEKSANDROVICH) Nabliudatel'nye komissii. Moskva, 1966. pp. 127.

> SHEREMET (KONSTANTIN FILIPPOVICH) Сельский Совет: проблемы правового положения. Москва, Юридическая Литература, 1966. pp. 144. 19½см.

> AIMBETOV (ALDAN AIMBETOVICH) and others. Problemy sovershenstvovaniia organizatsii i deiatel'nosti mestnykh Sovetov. Alma-Ata, 1967. pp. 242.

> GRISHAEV (VASILII VASIL'EVICH) Stroitel'stvo sovetov v derevne v pervyi god sotsialisticheskoi revoliutsii. Moskva, 1967. pp. 86.

> VASENIN (VASILII KUZ'MICH) Deputat mestnogo Soveta. Moskva, 1967. pp. 79.

> VASIL'EV (RUSLAN FEDOROVICH) Resheniia mestnykh Sovetov s administrativnoi sanktsiei. Moskva, 1967. pp. 108.

> BYKOVSKII (DZHON IAKOVLEVICH) Организация работы исполкомов местных Советов. Москва, Юридическая Литература, 1968. pp. 80. 20см. (Организационно-Массовая Работа Местных Советов)

> SHEREMET (KONSTANTIN FILIPPOVICH) Компетенция местных Советов. Москва, 1968. pp. 168.

> TARASENKO (MIKHAIL NIKIFOROVICH) Ispolnenie reshenii mestnykh Sovetov. Moskva, 1968. pp. 102.

> VASIL'EV (VSEVOLOD IVANOVICH) ed. В помощь депутату местного Совета: практическое пособие. Москва, Юридическая Литература, 1968. pp. 157. 19½см.

> NOSOV (NIKOLAI EVGEN'EVICH) Становление сословно-представительных учреждений в России: изыскания о земской реформе Ивана Грозного. Ленинград. 1969. pp. 601. With English table of contents.

LOCAL GOVERNMENT - Russia (Cont'd.)

RUSSIA (U.S.S.R.). Statutes, etc. 1969. Spravochnik dlia rabotnikov sel'skikh i poselkovykh Sovetov. Moskva, 1969] 2 vols.

RUSSIA (U.S.S.R.). Verkhovnyi Sovet. Prezidium. Otdel po Voprosam Raboty Sovetov. 1969. Itogi vyborov i sostav deputatov mestnykh Sovetov deputatov trudiashchikhsia, 1969 g.: statisticheskii sbornik. Moskva, 1969. pp. 226.

KIM (VLADIMIR ALEKSANDROVICH) and NECHITAILO (GRIGORII VASIL'EVICH) Otrazhenie interesov naseleniia v deiatel'nosti mestnykh Sovetov deputatov trudiashchikhsia. Alma-Ata, 1970. pp. 218.

MIKHALKEVICH (VITALII NIKOLAEVICH) Postoiannye komissii sotsial'nogo obespecheniia mestnykh Sovetov. Moskva, 1970. pp. 32.

OSNOVIN (VIKTOR STEPANOVICH) ed. Mestnye Sovety i zakonnost'. Moskva, 1970. pp. 197.

"TEKHNOLOGIIA" raboty postoiannykh komissii. Moskva, 1970. pp. 128.

LOCAL GOVERNMENT - Russia
See also SOVIETS

- Samoa

WESTERN SAMOA. Commission to Inquire into and Report upon the Organization of District and Village Government in Western Samoa. 1951. Report. Wellington, Government Printer, 1951. pp. 75. 24½cm.

- Siam

SIAM. 1958. Local government in Thailand; (by Nai Winyoo Angkanaraksa). (Department of Interior) Bangkok, 1958. pp. 23. 19cm.

- Sicily

SILVESTRI (ENZO) and SAITTA (NAZARENO) Rassegna di giurisprudenza sull'ordinamento degli enti locali in Sicilia. Milano, Giuffrè, 1967. pp. (ii), 474. 25cm.

SPATARO (SALVATORE) Commento teorico practico alla legge sull' ordinamento amministrativo degli enti locali in Sicilia. 3rd ed. Milano, Giuffrè, 1968 in progress. bibliog. 25cm. Library has vol. 1.

- South Africa - Transvaal

TRANSVAAL. Provincial Council. Select Committee on Local Authorities. 1915. Report [Colin Wade, Chairman]. (T.P.S.C.8-1914-15) Pretoria 1915. pp. 3. 33½cm.

- Spain

SPAIN. Comisaría del Plan de Desarrollo Económico y Social. 1964. Obras y servicios de las corporaciones locales: sanidad y asistencia social: [anexo al Plan de... 1964 a 1967]. [Madrid, 1964]. pp. 159. 30cm.

- Sudan

SUDAN. Commission on Coordination between the Central and Local Government. 1960. Report. [M.A. Abu Rabbat, chairman] 2nd ed. [Khartoum, 1960?] pp. 102.

- Sweden

WALLIN (GUNNAR) and others, eds. Kommunerna i förvandling. Stockholm, Almqvist och Wiksell, [1966] pp. 247. bibliog. 21½cm.

SWEDEN. Statens Offentliga Utredningar. 1967. 50. Kommunala befogenheter inom turistväsendet: kommunalrättskommitténs betänkande 9. Stockholm, 1967. pp. 70. 24cm.

SWEDEN. Statens Offentliga Utredningar. 1967. 58. Enhetlig kommuntyp städernas auktionsmonopol m.m. kommunalrättskommitténs betänkande 10. Stockholm, 1967. pp. 165. 24cm.

- Switzerland

CODDING (GEORGE ARTHUR) Governing the commune of Veyrier: politics in Swiss local government. Boulder, Colorado University, Bureau of Governmental Research, [1967]. pp. xi, 98. bibliog. 23cm.

- Syria

OFFICE ARABE DE PRESSE ET DE DOCUMENTATION. Les principes de base du project de loi sur l'administration locale: texte intégral. Damas, 1968. fo. ix, 31.

- Tanzania

DRYDEN (STANLEY) Local administration in Tanzania. Nairobi, East African Publishing House, 1968. pp. viii, 178. bibliog. 21½cm. (EAPH Political Studies. 5)

- Turkey

MUTAFCHIEVA (V.P.) L'institution de l'ayanlik pendant les dernières décennies du XVIIIe siècle. in Études Balkaniques. 2-3. Sofia, 1965.

- Uganda

VINCENT (JOAN) African elite: the big men of a small town. New York, 1971. pp. 309.

- Ukraine

UKRAINE. Gosudarstvennaia Planovaia Komissia. 1932. Культурно-бытовое строительство, коммунальное хозяйство и жилищное строительство в Донбассе. Харьков, 1932. pp. 38.

FEDONIUK (KOSTIATYN IEVHENOVYCH) Orhanizatsiina diial'nist' vykonavchykh komitetiv mistsevykh Rad deputativ trudiashchykh URSR. L'viv, 1962. pp. 235.

MISTSEVI rady Ukraïns'koï RSR i komunistychne budivnytstvo: udoskonalennia form i metodiv diial'nosti mistsevykh Rad deputativ trudiashchykh URSR u gospodars'komu i sotsial'no-kul'turnomu budivnytstvi. Kyïv, 1970. pp. 238. With Russian summary and table of contents.

- United Kingdom

LONDON. London County Council. Procedure of local authorities and the London County Council. London, 1932. pp. 53.

HAMMOND (J.L.) The historical background. in London. University. London School of Economics and Political Science. Public lectures in celebration of the local government centenary, 1835-1935. [London, 1935].

LABOUR PARTY. Research Department. Local government handbook, 1951-52: England and Wales. [London, 1951]. pp. 231.

CONVENTION ON PRODUCTIVITY IN LOCAL GOVERNMENT, LONDON, 1963. Proceedings. London, Institution of Municipal and County Engineers, 1963. fo. iv, 40. 28½cm. Xeroxed copy.

LOCAL GOVERNMENT WORK STUDY GROUP. Publications. No. 1. The introduction of work study in a local authority. London, 1964. pp. 16. 24cm.

NATIONAL COUNCIL ON INLAND TRANSPORT. Rail closure procedure: preparing a case of objection. London, [1964]. pp. 8.

COUNTY COUNCILS ASSOCIATION. Local government reorganisation in England: memorandum approved by the Executive Council on the 28th July, 1965, for submission to the Minister of Housing and Local Government. [London], 1965. pp. 4. 27½cm.

COUNTY COUNCILS ASSOCIATION. Royal Commission on Local Government in England: supplement to the Association's evidence: Analysis of existing county services. London, the Association, 1966. pp. (iii), 36. 27½cm.

GOLDRICK (MICHAEL KEVIN D'ARCY) and WOOD (BRUCE) Public interest in local government: a survey of published data, supplemented by personal interviews. London, London University, London School of Economics and Political Science, Greater London Group, 1966. pp. 48. bibliog. 30cm. (Town Government in South East England. Research Studies. No. 4)

LONDON. University. London School of Economics and Political Science. Greater London Group. Memoranda of evidence to the Committee on Management in Local Government: Maud Committee, 1966. fo. 26. 33½cm.

U.K. Royal Commission on Local Government in England, 1966. Minutes of evidence. [parts] 1-13 (and Appendix, supplementary memoranda and index). London, 1967-69. 14pts. (in 1vol.) 24½cm.

BOWLBY (C. JAMES) Co-partnership in local government. n.p., [1967?]. pp. 53.

NORFOLK. County Council. Finance and General Purposes Committee, and others. Growth in Norfolk. n.p., [1967]. pp. 6.

BARON (GEORGE) and HOWELL (DAVID ANTONY) School management and government. London, H.M.S.O. 1968. pp. v, 144. 24½cm. (U.K. Royal Commission on Local Government in England, 1966. Research Studies. 6)

BIRMINGHAM. University. Institute of Local Government Studies. Aspects of administration in a large local authority. London, H.M.S.O., 1968. pp. vii, 208. 24½cm. (U.K. Royal Commission on Local Government in England, 1966. Research Studies. 7.)

CONSERVATIVE RESEARCH DEPARTMENT. Old Queen Street Papers. [No]. 7. The reform of local government. London, 1968. pp. 15.

DAVIES (BLEDDYN) Social needs and resources in local services: a study of variations in standards of provision of personal social services between local authority areas. London, Joseph, 1968. pp. 341. bibliog. 22½cm.

FREEMAN (THOMAS WALTER) Geography and regional administration: England and Wales, 1830-1968. London, Hutchinson University Library, 1968. pp. 200. 21cm. (Geography. 117)

HARROGATE CONFERENCE. 3rd Conference, 1968. Productivity in Local government. London, Local Authorities Conditions of Service Advisory Board, 1968. pp. iii, 318. 24cm.

HART (Sir WILLIAM EDWARD) and HART (Sir WILLIAM OGDEN) Introduction to the law of local government and administration; eighth edition by Sir William O. Hart. London, Butterworths, 1968. pp. lxxi, 784, 92. 21½cm.

HOLT (L.) Planning, introducing and controlling work study;...paper given at the third Harrogate Conference on Productivity in Local Government, March 5th, 1968. [London, 1968?]. fo.6.

LABOUR PARTY. Local government advance. [London, 1968]. pp. 30. 18cm.

LONDON. University. London School of Economics and Political Science. Greater London Group. The lessons of the London government reforms. London, H.M.S.O., 1968. pp. ix, 79. 24½cm. (U.K. Royal Commission on Local Government in England, 1966. Research Studies. 2)

MACKINTOSH (JOHN PITCAIRN) The devolution of power: local democracy, regionalism and nationalism. London, Chatto & Windus, 1968. pp. 207. 21½cm. (Reform Series. 1)

MACLEOD (ROY M.) Treasury control and social administration: a study of establishment growth at the Local Government Board, 1871-1905. London, Bell, 1968. pp. 62. 21½cm. (Social Administration Research Trust. Occasional Papers on Social Administration. No. 23)

ROBSON (WILLIAM ALEXANDER) Local government in crisis. 2nd ed. London, 1968. pp. 175.

ROYAL INSTITUTE OF PUBLIC ADMINISTRATION. Conference, 1967. Management of local government: the Maud Committee report; report of a conference ... Westminster, 12-13 December 1967, etc. London, 1968. pp. 69. 21½cm.

RURAL DISTRICT COUNCILS ASSOCIATION. Maud for R.D.Cs: suggestions for applying the Maud report on management in local government to the internal organisation of rural district councils. [London], 1968. pp. 40. 18½cm.

LOCAL GOVERNMENT - United Kingdom (Cont'd.)

U.K. Joint Review Body on Local Authority Purchasing. 1968. Report of the Joint Review Body. London, H.M.S.O., 1968. pp. iv, 20. 24½cm.

WOOLF (MYRA) Local authority services and the characteristics of administrative areas. London, H.M.S.O. 1968. pp. v, 41. 24½cm. (U.K. Royal Commission on Local Government in England, 1966. Research Studies. 5.)

YOUNG CONSERVATIVE AND UNIONIST ORGANISATION. Regional Government Research Group. Local freedom: a Young Conservative study of regional government. London, Conservative Political Centre, 1968. pp. 30. 21½cm.

BANSTEAD. Urban District Council. Royal Commission on Local Government in England: statement by Banstead Urban District Council on the report of the Royal Commission. Banstead, 1969. pp. 8.

[BEECHEY (R.M.) and STEPHENSON (C.)] Review of committees and sub-committees and devolution to officers. n.p. [1969?]. pp. 17.

BIRMINGHAM. University. Institute of Local Government Studies. Administration in a large local authority: a comparison with other county boroughs. London, H.M.S.O., 1969. pp. v, 62. 24½cm. (U.K. Royal Commission on Local Government in England, 1966. Research Studies. 10.)

CAIRNS (MARY BELL) The law of tort in local government. 2nd ed. London, 1969. pp. 272.

CLARKE (JOHN JOSEPH) Outlines of local government of the United Kingdom. 20th ed. London, Pitman, 1969. pp. x, 245. 21½cm.

COUNTY COUNCILS ASSOCIATION. Royal Commission on Local Government in England: memorandum of views on the report of the Commission, etc. London, 1969. pp. 13.

DIAMOND (D.R.) and LEVIN (P.H.) The reorganization of local government in North Wiltshire: a study of the recommendations made by the Royal Commission on Local Government in England, with special reference to the Swindon area. [Swindon, 1969]. pp. 39. 13 maps in end pocket.

EDDEY (KEITH J.) An outline of local government law. London, Butterworths, 1969. pp. xvi, 233. 21½cm.

FRIEND (JOHN K.) and JESSOP (W. NEIL) Local government and strategic choice: an operational research approach to the processes of public planning. London, Tavistock Publications, 1969. pp. xxvi, 296. 23½cm.

INSTITUTE OF MUNICIPAL TREASURERS AND ACCOUNTANTS. Cost benefit analysis in local government. London, [1969]. pp. 124. bibliog. 30cm.

LABOUR PARTY. Discussion Document. Local government reform in England. [London], 1969. pp. 24.

RESEARCH SERVICES LIMITED. Community attitudes survey: England; prepared for the Government Social Survey. London, H.M.S.O., 1969. pp. vi, 185. 24½cm. (U.K. Royal Commission on Local Government in England, 1966. Research Studies. 9.)

RURAL DISTRICT COUNCILS ASSOCIATION. The democratic alternative to Maud: a policy statement on the Royal Commission Report...presented to the Secretary of State...in October, 1969. London, [1969]. pp. 14.

SHARP (EVELYN) Baroness Sharp. The Ministry of Housing and Local Government. London, 1969. pp. 253. bibliogs. (Royal Institute of Public Administration. New Whitehall Series. No. 14)

SHERMAN (T. P.) O and M in local government. Oxford, Pergamon P., 1969. pp. x, 264. bibliog. 19½cm. (Commonwealth and International Library. Social Administration, Training, Economics and Production Division)

STANDING CONFERENCE ON LONDON AND SOUTH EAST REGIONAL PLANNING. Report of the Royal Commission on Local Government in England: joint report by the administrative and technical panels, summarising their appended report. [London], 1969. pp. 4.

INTERNATIONAL UNION OF LOCAL AUTHORITIES. British Section. Papers presented at National Conference. a., 1970- London.

U.K. Department of the Environment. Circulars. irreg., N 12 1970 (no.1)- London.

ANDREWS (J.A.) ed. Welsh studies in public law: (to mark the services to Welsh legal education of D.J. Llewelfryn Davies). Cardiff, 1970. pp. 178.

CONFERENCE papers on management and administration in the local government service, 1969-70; editor, R. Greenwood. [Birmingham], 1970. pp. 133. (Birmingham. University. Institute of Local Government Studies. Occasional Papers. Series A. No.4)

GARNER (JOHN FRANCIS) Administrative law. 3rd ed. London, 1970. pp. 473. bibliog.

HILLS (JILL) Councils of social service and local government change, London, 1957-67. London, [1970]. pp. 56. bibliog.

LABOUR PARTY. Guide for the new councillor and candidate. [London, 1970] pp. 29.

LABOUR PARTY. Principles for local government reform in England. London, [1970]. pp. 23.

MORTON (JANE) The best laid schemes?: a cool look at local government reform. London, 1970. pp. 104.

REDLICH (JOSEF) The history of local government in England: being a reissue of Book I of Local government in England by Josef Redlich and [edited by] Francis W. Hirst; second edition with an introduction and epilogue by Bryan Keith-Lucas. London, 1970. pp. 284. bibliog.

RICHARDS (PETER GODFREY) The new local government system. 2nd ed. London, 1970. pp. 200. bibliog.

RIPLEY (B.J.) Administration in local authorities. London, 1970. pp. 157.

ROSE (BARRY) ed. England looks at Maud: (an anthology on the Royal Commission on Local Government (1969) and the subsequent White Paper (1970), etc.). n.p. [1970]. pp. 213.

ROYAL INSTITUTE OF PUBLIC ADMINISTRATION. Local Government Operational Research Unit. Cheshire county council: report on the cost of local government reform. [Chester, 1970]. 2 pts. (in 1 vol.).

SHERMAN (ALFRED V.) Local government reorganisation and industry: a critical footnote to the Maud Report. London, [1970]. pp. 21. (Aims of Industry. Studies. No. 27)

SPIRES (N.S.) Local government reform: statement by the chairman of Banstead Urban District Council. [Banstead, 1970]. unpaged.

STEED (MICHAEL) and others. The Maud report: Michael Steed on the politics; Bryan Keith-Lucas on the grassroots; Peter Hall on the social geography; with a summary of the report. [London, 1970]. unpaged.

WISEMAN (HERBERT VICTOR) ed. Local government in England 1958-69. London, 1970. pp. 206. bibliog.

BANSTEAD. Urban District Council. Local government reorganisation: statement to support continuance of a separate District Council for the area of the present Urban District. Banstead, 1971. pp. 24.

BOADEN (NOEL) Urban policy-making: influences on county boroughs in England and Wales. Cambridge, 1971. pp. 150. bibliog.

CROSS (CHARLES ALBERT) Principles of local government law. 4th ed. London, 1971. pp. 518,32.

LUBENOW (WILLIAM C.) The politics of government growth: early Victorian attitudes toward state intervention, 1833-1848. Newton Abbot, 1971. pp. 237. bibliog.

MILLER (J.V.) The measurement of output of public services. London, 1971. pp. 10.

REES (IOAN BOWEN) Government by community. London, 1971. pp. 247.

ROSE (GORDON) Local councils in metropolitan areas. London, 1971. pp. 32. (Fabian Society. Research Series. [No.] 296)

THORNHILL (WILLIAM) ed. The growth and reform of English local government. London, [1971]. pp. 256.

U.K. Department of the Environment. 1971. [Consultation papers issued in connection with the reorganisation of local government in England]. [London, 1971]. 1 vol. (various pagings).

- United Kingdom - Ireland, Northern

IRELAND, NORTHERN. Cmd. 517. The reshaping of local government: statement of aims. pp. 33. Z. Belfast, 1967.

BOW GROUP. Ulster Section. Local government in Ulster: a new organisation structure. London, [1969]. pp. 20. (Bow Group. Occasional Papers)

IRELAND, NORTHERN. Cmd. 546. Review Body on Local Government in Northern Ireland, 1970; Chairman: Patrick A. Macrory. Report. Belfast, 1970. pp. 68.

- United Kingdom - Scotland

SCOTLAND. Scottish Home and Health Department. 1967. Local authority records: report by a committee appointed by the Secretary of State for Scotland; [J. McBoyle, chairman]. Edinburgh, 1967. pp. 31. $24\frac{1}{2}$cm.

RESEARCH SERVICES LIMITED. Community survey: Scotland; prepared for the Government Social Survey. Edinburgh, 1969. pp. 119. (Scotland. Royal Commission on Local Government in Scotland, 1966. Research Studies. 2)

CORNFORD (J.P.) The Wheatley Report. [Edinburgh, 1971] fo. 16. (Edinburgh. University. Department of Politics. Waverley Papers. Series 1. European Political Studies: Occasional Papers. 2)

- United Kingdom - Wales

U.K. Welsh Office. 1971. The reform of local government in Wales: consultative document. Cardiff, 1971. pp. 31.

- United States

FORDHAM (JEFFERSON BARNES) A larger concept of community. Baton Rouge, [1956]. pp. 117.

SCOTT (ILEY STANLEY) ed. Local government in a changing world: a seminar for city and county managers, 1965-1966. Berkeley, University of California, 1967. pp. xiii, 200. $22\frac{1}{2}$cm.

BUELL (ERWIN C.) and BRIGMAN (WILLIAM E.) eds. The grass roots: readings in state and local government. Glenview, Scott, Foresman and Co., [1968]. pp. (v), 534. 23cm.

DYE (THOMAS R.) Politics in states and communities. Englewood Cliffs, [1969]. pp. 479.

KOTLER (MILTON) Neighborhood government: the local foundations of political life. Indianapolis, [1969]. pp. 111.

MEDARD (JEAN FRANÇOIS) Communauté locale et organisation communautaire aux Etats-Unis. Paris, 1969. pp. 313. bibliog. (Fondation Nationale des Sciences Politiques. Cahiers. 172)

FLINN (THOMAS A.) Analyzing decision-making systems: local government and politics. Glenview, 1970. pp. 180. bibliog.

SATO (SHO) and VAN ALSTYNE (ARVO) State and local government law. Boston, 1970. pp. 1165.

- United States - Kansas

DRURY (JAMES WESTBROOK) The government of Kansas. rev. ed. Lawrence, Kansas, [1970]. pp. 492.

LOCAL GOVERNMENT (Cont'd.)

- Yugoslavia

VLADISAVLJEVIĆ (ŽIVKO) and MILOSAVLEVSKI (SLAVKO) Saveti narodnih odbora - organizacija i funkcionisanje. Beograd, Institut Društvenih Nauka, 1963. pp. 142. 24cm.

YUGOSLAVIA. Savezni Zavod za Statistiku. Studije, Analize i Prikazi. 17. Privredno statistički presek komuna Jugoslavije u 1961. godini. Economic and statistical pattern of the communes in Yugoslavia 1961. Beograd, 1963. With English summary.

KOVAČEVIĆ (MILIVOJE) Комунални систем и комунална политика, etc. Београд, 1965. pp. xii, 275. bibliog.

MILIVOJEVIĆ (DRAGOLJUB) The Yugoslav commune. Beograd, 1965. pp. 40. (Međunarodna Politika. Studies. No.8)

ŠTEFE (TOMO) and SHOULBERG (TED) Participation in planning: a case study of the Yugoslav commune. Ljubljana, Urbanistični Institut SRS, 1968. fo. 32. 29½cm.

- Yugoslavia - Statistics

JUGOSLOVENSKO STATISTIČKO DRUŠTVO. Sastanak, 7-i, 1963. VII sastanak Jugoslovenskog statističkog društva, Ohrid, 19. do 21. septembra, 1963.godine. Beograd, [1964?]. pp. 629. 24cm. With French summaries.

- Zambia

NORTHERN RHODESIA. Committee Appointed to Inquire into the Participation of Africans in Local Government in Municipal and Township Areas. 1960. Report: [S.W. Coleman, chairman]. Lusaka, 1960. pp. 54.

MITCHELL (MARGARET T.) Basic information on the structure of local government in Northern Rhodesia at 31 December, 1962. Salisbury, Department of Government, University College of Rhodesia and Nyasaland, 1963, pp. ii, 40. 33cm.

LOCAL GOVERNMENT OFFICIALS AND EMPLOYEES

UNITED NATIONS. Department of Economic and Social Affairs. 1966. Local government personnel systems. (ST/TAO/M/33) New York, 1966. pp. 103.

- Canada

Statistics Canada.
CANADA. ~~Dominion Bureau of Statistics.~~ Municipal government employment. [in English and French] Ottawa, quarterly, 1967 (vol.1) to date. 28cm.

CANADA. Dominion Bureau of Statistics. Governments Division. 1968. Municipal government employment, 1961-1966. Ottawa, 1968. pp. 47. In English and French.

- Ceylon - Salaries, pensions, etc.

CEYLON. Committee on Salary Anomalies in the Local Government Service. 1968. Final report. Colombo, 1968. pp. 155. (Parliament. Sessional Papers. 1968. 6).

CEYLON. Committee on Salary Anomalies in the Local Government Service. 1968. Interim report. Colombo, 1968. pp. 53. (Parliament. Sessional Papers. 1968. 2).

- France

GIRARD (LOUIS) and others. Les conseillers généraux en 1870: étude statistique d'un personnel politique. Paris, P.U.F., 1967. pp. 211. 25cm. (Paris. Université. Faculté des Lettres et Sciences Humaines. Série "Recherches". tome 34)

- Ireland (Republic) - Salaries, pensions, etc.

EIRE. Review Body on Higher Remuneration in the Public Sector. 1969. Report on findings of Local Authority Officers' Arbitration Board on claims by local authority engineers and county accountants. Dublin, 1969. pp. 40.

- Italy

DEMARCHI (FRANCO) and others. La burocrazia periferica e locale in Italia: analisi sociologica. Milano, 1969. 2 vols. (Istituto per la Scienza dell'Amministrazione Pubblica. Archivio ISAP. 3,4)

[ITALY. Consiglio Nazionale delle Ricerche. Gruppo Regioni. 1969]. La burocrazia nelle regioni a statuto speciale. Milano, Giuffrè, 1969. pp. viii, 327. 24cm. (Istituto per la Scienza dell'Amministrazione Pubblica. Pubblicazioni. Contributi. 2)

- Nigeria - Appointment, qualifications, tenure, etc.

FAIRHOLM (G.W.) Native authority personnel. Zaria, Ahmadu Bello University, Institute of Administration, 1965. fo. 13. 25½cm. (Information Memoranda. No. 23)

- Norway - Salaries, pensions, etc.

NORWAY. Statistiske Centralbyrå. Lønnsstatistikk for kommunale arbeidstakere: Wage statistics for local government employees. bien., 1969- Oslo.

- United Kingdom

ASSOCIATION OF GENERAL AND FAMILY CASEWORKERS and others. Standing Joint Committee. The professional social workers in local authority health and welfare services. London, 1961. pp. 8. 24½cm.

GREY (ELEANOR) Workloads in children's departments; (a Home Office Research Unit report). London, 1969. pp. 74. (U.K. Home Office. Home Office Research Studies. 1.)

LOWRY (PATRICIA) Ancillary staff in children's departments: a report by the Home Office Research Unit. [London, H.M.S.O.], 1969. pp. 31.

HOPPE (MALCOLM) Death of a doctrine: the campaign against direct labour building. London, [1970]. pp. 19.

SHARP (EVELYN) Baroness Sharp. Transport planning: the men for the job: a report to the Minister of Transport. London, H.M.S.O., 1970. pp. 138.

U.K. Central Youth Employment Executive. 1970. Local government. 4th ed. [London], 1970. pp. 53. (Choice of Careers. 28.)

- United Kingdom - Salaries, pensions, etc.

U.K. Ministry of Housing and Local Government. 1967. Local Government Superannuation Act, 1953: Local Government Superannuation (Benefits) Regulations, 1954: tables prepared by the Government Actuary, etc. London, 1967. pp. 6. 24½cm.

- United Kingdom - Scotland

SCOTLAND. Royal Commission on Local Government in Scotland, 1966. Research Studies. 3. Manpower surveys; the ratio of councillors to electors in the different types of local authorities in Scotland; percentage polls and contested seats. Edinburgh, 1969. pp. 42.

- United Kingdom - Scotland - Salaries, pensions, etc.

UNITED KINGDOM. Government Actuary's Department. 1967. Local Government Superannuation Act, 1953: Local Government Superannuation Benefits (Scotland) Regulations, 1954: tables. Edinburgh, 1967. pp. 4.

- United States

WALSH (ROBERT E.) Sorry no government today; unions vs. city hall. Boston, [1969]. pp. 325.

DEVINE (EUGENE J.) Analysis of manpower shortages in local government: case studies of nurses, policemen, and teachers. New York, 1970. pp. 171. bibliog.

LOCAL TRANSIT

ALTFELD (JUERGEN) Anpassungsmöglichkeiten bei kurzfristigen Nachfrageänderungen im öffentlichen Personen-Nahverkehr. Hamburg, 1969. fo. 190. bibliog.

FICHELET (MONIQUE) and others. Pour une approche écologique de l'utilisation des moyens de transport: analyse critique des méthodes d'étude des déplacements de personnes dans les grandes agglomérations urbaines. Paris, [1969]. fo. various.

GRADOSTROITEL'STVO... Градостроительство: проблемы скоростного транспорта в крупных городах. Киев, 1969. pp. 104.

HUTCHINSON (B.G.) Structuring urban transportation planning decisions: the use of statistical decision theory. London, 1969. pp. 25. (Centre for Environmental Studies. Working Papers. 44)

WILSON (ALAN GEOFFREY) and KIRWAN (R.M.) Measures of benefit in the evaluation of urban transport improvements. London, 1969. pp. 36. bibliog. (Centre for Environmental Studies. Working Papers. 43)

CREIGHTON (ROGER L.) Urban transportation planning. Urbana, [1970]. pp. 375.

MOHRING (HERBERT DICK) Optimization and scale economies in urban bus transportation. Minneapolis, 1971. fo. 38. bibliog. (Minnesota University. Center for Economic Research. Discussion Papers. No. 5)

- Bibliography

INTERNATIONAL UNION OF PUBLIC TRANSPORT. Metro, 1967-1968-1969: (bibliography), etc. Bruxelles, [1970]. pp. 199.

- Congresses

URBAN transportation; report of a conference at Ditchley Park, 28 February to 3 March, 1969. Enstone, [1969]. pp. 31. (Ditchley Foundation. Ditchley Papers. No. 19)

- Europe

WYSE (WILLIAM JOHN) European urban transport;... being the text of a paper presented as a background lecture to the electric traction course at Imperial College, London University, on 23rd January 1964. London, 1964. pp. 24.

- France

FRANCE. Commission des Transports. 1967. Ve Plan, 1966-1970: rapports particuliers: les transports urbains de province; la régie autonome des transports parisiens; les voies férrées d'intérêt local non urbaines. [Paris, La Documentation française, 1967]. pp. 102. 27cm.

GERONDEAU (CHRISTIAN) Les transports urbains. Paris, 1969. pp. 126. bibliog.

FRANCE. Intergroupe Transports Collectifs Urbains. 1971. Préparation du VIe Plan...: rapport. Paris, 1971. pp. 51.

- New Zealand

NEW ZEALAND. Committee of Inquiry into Urban Passenger Transport. 1970. Urban passenger transport in New Zealand: report: [D.J. Carter, chairman]. Wellington, 1970. pp. 62.

- Russia

STRAMENTOV (ANDREI EVGEN'EVICH) and others. Gorodskoi transport. 2nd ed. Moskva, 1969. pp. 422. bibliog.

CHEREPANOV (VLADIMIR ALEKSANDROVICH) Transport v planirovke gorodov. Moskva, 1970. pp. 303. bibliog.

- United Kingdom

SHARP (CLIFFORD) Problems of urban passenger transport: with special reference to Leicester. Leicester, University Press, 1967. pp. 118. 20½cm.

LOCAL TRANSIT (Cont'd.)

- United States

BREUER (ROBERT) Principal Transportation Analyst, New York State, and SHAFER (JOHN) Transit evaluation: demand and non-demand aspects. New York, State Department of Transportation, [1968?] pp. 26.

McINTOSH (P.T.) Notes on a visit to U.S.A., January 1968. [London], 1968. pp. 9. (London. Greater London Council. Department of Highways and Transportation. Research Memoranda. 59.)

SMERK (GEORGE M.) ed. Readings in urban transportation. Bloomington, Indiana U.P., [1968]. pp. xi, 336. 23½cm.

LATENT demand for urban transportation; [by] Lester A. Hoel [and others]. Pittsburgh, Carnegie-Mellon University, Transportation Research Institute, [1969]. variously paged. bibliogs. (Carnegie-Mellon University. Transportation Research Institute. Research Report Series. 2)

PRYTULA (GEORGE) Community mobility systems. Washington, D.C., [1970]. pp. 30. (Urban Land Institute. Special Reports)

- United States - Washington (State)

WASHINGTON (STATE). 1965. Plan A transit study system tests; by David S. Gendell. (Puget Sound Regional Transportation Study Staff Reports. No. 19) rev. ed. Seattle, 1965. fo. (iv), 35. 28cm.

LOCARNO CONFERENCE, 1925

FREYMOND (J.) Locarno: un nouveau départ? in vol. 1 of Sieber (Marc) ed. Discordia concors. Basel, [1968].

URBANITSCH (PETER) Grossbritannien und die Verträge von Locarno. Wien, 1968. pp. 329. bibliog. (Vienna. Universität. Dissertationen. 16)

ROESSLER (HELLMUTH) and HOELZLE (ERWIN) eds. Locarno und die Weltpolitik 1924-1932; für die Ranke-Gesellschaft herausgegeben, etc. Göttingen, Musterschmidt, [1969]. pp. 213. 21cm.

ALEXANDER (MANFRED) Der deutsch-tschechoslowakische Schiedsvertrag von 1925 im Rahmen der Locarno-Verträge. München, 1970. pp. 212. bibliog. (Ludwigshafen. Collegium Carolinum. Veröffentlichungen. Band 24)

LOCKE (JOHN)

HARTNACK (JUSTUS) Analysis of the problem of perception in British empiricism. Copenhagen, Munksgaard, 1950. pp. 203. bibliog. 23cm.

MARTIN (CHARLES BURTON) and ARMSTRONG (DAVID MALET) eds. Locke and Berkeley: a collection of critical essays. Garden City, Doubleday, 1968. pp. x, 463. bibliog. 18cm. (Modern Studies in Philosophy. AP. 6)

SELIGER (M.) The liberal politics of John Locke. London, Allen & Unwin, 1968. pp. 387. bibliog. 21½cm.

YOLTON (JOHN W.) John Locke and the way of ideas. Oxford, 1968. pp. 235. bibliog.

DUNN (JOHN) The political thought of John Locke: an historical account of the argument of the "Two treatises of government". Cambridge, C.U.P., 1969. pp. xv, 290. bibliog. 21½cm.

EUCHNER (WALTER) Naturrecht und Politik bei John Locke. Frankfurt am Main, [1969]. pp. 316. bibliog.

YOLTON (JOHN W.) ed. John Locke: problems and perspectives; a collection of new essays. Cambridge, 1969. pp. 278. 23cm.

YOLTON (JOHN W.) Locke and the compass of human understanding: a selective commentary on the "Essay". Cambridge, 1970. pp. 234. bibliog.

SCHOCHET (GORDON J.) ed. Life, liberty and property: essays on Locke's political ideas. Belmont, Calif., [1971]. pp. 182. bibliog.

WOOLHOUSE (R.S.) Locke's philosophy of science and knowledge: a consideration of some aspects of An essay concerning human understanding. Oxford, 1971. pp. 204. bibliog.

LOCKS AND KEYS

WEST BENGAL. State Statistical Bureau. 1961. Locks and keys industry in Howrah: a type-study. [Alipore], 1961. pp. 42.

LOCOMOTIVE WORKS

SHISHOV (K.) Борьба Калужского завода за советскую машину. Москва, Гострансиздат, 1932. pp. 31. 17½см.

LOCOMOTIVES

NOCK (OSWALD STEVENS) Steam locomotive: the unfinished story of steam locomotives and steam locomotive men on the railways of Great Britain. 2nd ed. London, Allen & Unwin, 1968. pp. 273. 21½cm.

- Construction

ISTORIIA... История Харьковского паровозостроительного завода, 1917-1932: сборник документов и материалов. Харьков, Прапор, 1965. pp. 455. 20cm.

ZHDANOV (GENNADII VASIL'EVICH) and KOMPANIETS (ZINOVII L'VOVICH) V kommune ostanovka: istoricheskii ocherk o Luganskom lokomotivostroitel'nom zavode. Donetsk, 1967. pp. 151.

- Construction - Russia

TRADITSII... Традиции зовут вперед: из истории ордена Трудового Красного Знамени Красноярского паровозо-вагоноремонтного завода - старейшего предприятия Красноярского края. Красноярск, Книжное Издательство, 1965. pp. 308. 20см.

- Repairing - Latvia

> GINDIN (R.) ed. Из истории Даугавпилсского локомотиворемонтного завода. Рига, Звайгзне, 1968. pp. 118. bibliog. 20cm.

LODGING-HOUSES

- United Kingdom

> DALE (MARIANNE) The necessity for provision of municipal lodging houses for women. London, [1911?]. pp. 12.

LODZ

> ŁÓDŹ: rozwój miasta w Polsce Ludowej. Warszawa, 1970. pp. 258. bibliog.

- Economic conditions

> CHARDONNET (JEAN) Métropoles économiques: deuxième série, Manchester, Rotterdam, Hambourg, Cologne, Salzgitter, Dunkerque, Grenoble, Bilbao, Bâle, Zürich, Lodz, Zagreb. Paris, Colin, 1968. pp. 243. bibliog. 24cm. (Fondation Nationale des Sciences Politiques. Cahiers. 158)

- Economic history

> BRODOWSKA (HELENA) ed. Studia i materiały do dziejów Łodzi i okręgu łódzkiego: uwłaszczenie chłopów i mieszczan-rolników. Łódź, Wydawnictwo Łódzkie, 1966. pp. 388. 24cm.

- Economic history - Sources

> RYNKOWSKA (ANNA) ed. Początki rozwoju kapitalistycznego miasta Łodzi, 1820-1864: źródła. Warszawa, Książka i Wiedza, 1960. pp. 555. 23½cm.

- History - Sources

> KARWACKI (WŁADYSŁAW LECH) Łódzka organizacja Polskiej Partii Socjalistycznej - Lewicy, 1906-1918. Łódź, Wydawnictwo Łódzkie, 1964. pp. 457. bibliog. 24cm.

> KRONIKA getta łódzkiego; z oryginału do druku przygotowali, wstępem i przypisami zaopatrzyli Danuta Dąbrowska i Lucjan Dobroszycki. Łódź, 1965 in progress.

- Industries

> WŁÓKNIARZE Łódzcy: monografia. Łódź, Wydawnictwo Łódzkie, 1966. pp. 625. 23½cm. Table of contents in Russian, English and German.

- Politics and government

> KARWACKI (WŁADYSŁAW LECH) Łódzka organizacja Polskiej Partii Socjalistycznej - Lewicy, 1906-1918. Łódź, Wydawnictwo Łódzkie, 1964. pp. 457. bibliog. 24cm.

- Social conditions

> PIOTROWSKI (WACŁAW) Społeczno-przestrzenna struktura M. Łodzi: studium ekologiczne. Wrocław, Ossolineum, 1966. pp. 217. 21cm. With Russian and English summaries.

ŁÓDŹ (PROVINCE)

- Economic conditions

> STRASZEWICZ (LUDWIK) Województwo Łódzkie: zarys geograficzno-ekonomiczny. Warszawa, PWN, 1967. pp. 184. bibliog. 24cm.

- Economic history

> WACHOWSKA (BARBARA) Strajki okupacyjne w łódzkim okręgu przemysłowym w latach kryzysu gospodarczego, 1929-1933. Łódź, Wydawnictwo Łódzkie, 1967. pp. 288. bibliog. 23cm.

> Z dziejów ruchu robotniczego w Łodzi: materiały do szkolenia partyjnego. Łódź, Wydawnictwo Łódzkie, 1967. pp. 407. bibliog. 19½cm.

- Industries

> BANDURKA (MIECZYSŁAW) and others. Źródła do historii przemysłu włókienniczego okręgu łódzkiego w XIX w. Warszawa, Książka i Wiedza, 1966. pp. 674. 23½cm. (Polska Akademia Nauk. Instytut Historii. Materiały do Historii Miast, Przemysłu i Klasy Robotniczej w Okręgu Łódzkim. t.3)

- Social history

> FIJAŁEK (JAN) Instytucje pomocy materialno-zdrowotnej w Łodzi i okręgu łódzkim: wiek XIX do roku 1870. Łódź, 1962. pp. 238. bibliog. 24cm. (Łódzkie Towarzystwo Naukowe. Wydział 2. [Prace]. Nr.43)

- Social life and customs

> BARANOWSKI (BOHDAN) Zanik tradycyjnego chowu krów oraz wierzeń i zabobonów z nim związanych na terenie obecnego województwa łódzkiego. Łódź, 1967. pp. 115. 24½cm. (Łódź. Łódzkie Towarzystwo Naukowe. Wydział 2 Nauk Historycznych i Społecznych. Prace. Nr.66)

LOEBE (PAUL)

> SCHOLZ (ARNO) and OSCHILEWSKI (WALTHER GEORG) eds. Ein grosses Vorbild: Paul Löbe zum Gedächtnis. Berlin, 1968. pp. 59.

LOEWENSTEIN (HUBERTUS FRIEDRICH ZU) Prince

> LOEWENSTEIN (HUBERTUS FRIEDRICH ZU) Prince. Towards the further shore: an autobiography. London, Gollancz, 1968. pp. 448. 21½cm.

LOEWITH (KARL)

> RIESTERER (BERTHOLD P.) Karl Löwith's view of history: a critical appraisal of historicism. The Hague, 1969. pp. 108. bibliog.

LOGAN (JAMES)

WOLF (E.) James Logan's correspondence with William Reading, librarian of Sion College. in [Lehmann-Haupt (Hellmut)] ed. Homage to a bookman. Berlin, 1967.

LOGIC

CRAIK (WILLIAM WHITE) Student's outlines... philosophic logic; the theory of historical development; economics, marxian. Halifax, Halifax Branch of the Central Labour College, [191-?]. pp. (iv), 72.

FRYE (ALBERT MYRTON) and LEVI (ALBERT WILLIAM) Rational belief: an introduction to logic. New York, [1941] repr. 1969. pp. 482.

NIKOLAEV (I.V.) Учение о понятии в диалектической логике. in Uchenye Zapiski Kafedr Obshchestvennykh Nauk Vuzov g. Leningrada. Filosofiia. vyp.3. Leningrad, 1961.

KAESBAUER (MAX) and KUTSCHERA (FRANZ VON) eds. Logik und Logikkalkül; (Wilhelm Britzelmayr zum siebzigsten Geburtstag...gewidmet). Freiburg im Breisgau, Alber, [1962]. pp. 249. bibliogs. 22½cm.

ZINKERNAGEL (PETER) Conditions for description;...translated from the Danish by Olaf Lindum. New York, Humanities Press, 1962. pp. vii, 264. 21½cm. (International Library of Philosophy and Scientific Method)

KANT (IMMANUEL) Introduction to logic and his essay on the mistaken subtilty of the four figures; translated by Thomas Kingsmill Abbott...; with a few notes by Coleridge. New York, [1963]. pp. 100.

GIEDYMIN (J.) Strength, confirmation, compatibility. in Bunge (Mario Augusto) ed. The critical approach to science and philosophy. New York, [1964].

GOODMAN (NELSON) Fact, fiction and forecast. 2nd ed. Indianapolis, [1965]. pp. 128.

NOVACK (GEORGE) An introduction to the logic of Marxism. 4th ed. New York, 1966. pp. 124.

RESCHER (NICHOLAS) ed. The logic of decision and action. Pittsburgh, U. of Pittsburgh P., [1966]. pp. ix, 226. 24cm.

BRADLEY (RAYMOND D.) Logic, physics & metaphysics. Auckland, N.Z., 1967. pp. 27.

COPI (IRVING MARMER) and GOULD (JAMES ADAMS) eds. Contemporary readings in logical theory. New York, Macmillan, [1967]. pp. (vi), 344. bibliog. 23½cm.

ENCYCLOPÉDIE DE LA PLÉIADE. Logique et connaissance scientifique;...sous la direction de Jean Piaget. [Paris, 1967] pp. 1345. bibliogs.

HAUSMAN (ALAN) and WILSON (FRED) Carnap and Goodman: two formalists. The Hague, Nijhoff, 1967. pp. viii, 225. bibliog. (Iowa State University. Iowa Publications in Philosophy. vol. 3)

STRAWSON (PETER FREDERICK) Philosophical logic. London, O.U.P., 1967. pp. 177. bibliog. 20½cm. (Oxford Readings in Philosophy)

TULANE UNIVERSITY OF LOUISIANA. Tulane Studies in Philosophy. vol. 16. Philosophical logic. The Hague, Nijhoff, 1967. pp. (v), 161. 23cm.

AYERS (MICHAEL RICHARD) The refutation of determinism: an essay in philosophical logic. London, Methuen, 1968. pp. viii, 188. bibliog. 21½cm.

BROAD (CHARLIE DUNBAR) Induction, probability and causation: selected papers. Dordrecht, Reidel, 1968. pp. xi, 296. 22cm. (Synthese Library)

COPI (IRVING MARMER) Introduction to logic. 3rd ed. New York, Macmillan, [1968]. pp. xiii, 482. 23½cm.

DURBIN (PAUL R.) Logic and scientific enquiry. Milwaukee, Bruce, [1968]. pp. ix, 132. bibliog. 23cm. (Christian Culture and Philosophy Series)

GEACH (PETER THOMAS) A history of the corruptions of logic: an inaugural lecture. Leeds, Leeds U.P., 1968. pp. 22. 21½cm.

HERBRAND (JACQUES) Écrits logiques; avec...une notice biographique par Claude Chevalley et Albert Lautmann et une note sur la pensée de Herbrand par Claude Chevalley. Paris, P.U.F., 1968. pp. 244. 21½cm. (Bibliothèque de Philosophie Contemporaine)

INTERNATIONAL COLLOQUIUM IN THE PHILOSOPHY OF SCIENCE, LONDON, 1965. The problem of inductive logic; proceedings...vol. 2; edited by Imre Lakatos. Amsterdam, North-Holland Publishing Co., 1968. pp. viii, 417. 22½cm. (Studies in Logic and the Foundations of Mathematics)

LENK (HANS) Kritik der logischen Konstanten: philosophische Begründungen der Urteilsformen vom Idealismus bis zur Gegenwart. Berlin, 1968. pp. 687. bibliog. 23cm.

MURAKAMI (YASUSUKE) Logic and social choice. London, Routledge & Kegan Paul, 1968. pp. vi, 135 bibliog. 17½cm. (Monographs in Modern Logic)

RESCHER (NICHOLAS) Topics in philosophical logic. Dordrecht, Reidel, [1968]. pp. xiv, 347. bibliogs. 22½cm. (Synthese Library)

SCHOLZ (HEINRICH) Esquisse d'une histoire de la logique; traduit de l'allemand, etc. Paris, Aubier-Montaigne, [1968]. pp. 160. bibliog. 22½cm. (Analyse et Raisons. 10)

STUDIES in logical theory; essays by James W. Cornman [and others]. Oxford, 1968. pp. 152. (American Philosophical Quarterly. Monograph Series. No.2)

THIEL (CHRISTIAN) Sense and reference in Frege's logic. Dordrecht, Reidel, [1968]. pp. ix, 172. bibliog. 22½cm.

VAZIULIN (VIKTOR ALEKSEEVICH) Логика "Капитала" К. Маркса. Москва, Университет, 1968. pp. 295. 19½см.

WRIGHT (GEORG HENRIK VON) An essay in deontic logic and the general theory of action, with a bibliography of deontic and imperative logic. Amsterdam, North-Holland Publishing Co., 1968. pp. 110. bibliog. 25cm. (Societas Philosophica Fennica. Acta Philosophica Fennica. Fasc. 21)

ALEXANDER (PETER) An introduction to logic: the criticism of arguments. London, Allen & Unwin, 1969. pp. xi, 278. bibliog. 21cm.

BECKER (WERNER) Hegels Begriff der Dialektik und das Prinzip des Idealismus: zur systematischen Kritik der logischen und der phänomenologischen Dialektik. Stuttgart, 1969. pp. 168.

DAVIS (J.W.) and others, eds. Philosophical logic. Dordrecht, [1969]. pp. 277.

ELEY (LOTHAR) Metakritik der formalen Logik: sinnliche Gewissheit als Horizont der Aussagenlogik und elementaren Prädikatenlogik. Den Haag, 1969. pp. 380. bibliog.

ESSAYS in honor of Carl G. Hempel: a tribute on the occasion of his sixty-fifth birthday; essays by Donald Davidson [and others]; edited by Nicholas Rescher, etc. Dordrecht, [1969]. pp. 272. bibliog.

GRITSENKO (IVAN IVANOVICH) Istoricheskoe i logicheskoe v marksistskoi filosofii. Rostov-na-Donu, 1969. pp. 153.

HEGEL (GEORG WILHELM FRIEDRICH) Science of logic; translated by A. V. Miller. London, Allen & Unwin, 1969. pp. 844. 21½cm. (Muirhead Library of Philosophy)

KOPNIN (PAVEL VASIL'EVICH) Философские идеи В. И. Ленина и логика. Москва, Наука, 1969. pp. 483. 21½см.

The LOGICAL way of doing things; (dedicated to the memory of Henry S. Leonard); edited by Karel Lambert. New Haven, 1969. pp. 325. bibliog.

MICHALOS (ALEX C.) Principles of logic. Englewood Cliffs, [1969]. pp. 433. bibliogs.

NOVACK (GEORGE) An introduction to the logic of Marxism. 5th ed. New York, [1969]. pp. 144.

PRZELECKI (MARIAN) The logic of empirical theories. London, Routledge, 1969. pp. v, 108. bibliog. 17½cm. (Monographs in Modern Logic Series)

VEATCH (HENRY BABCOCK) Two logics: the conflict between classical and neo-analytic philosophy. Evanston, Ill., 1969. pp. 280.

WRIGHT (GEORG HENRIK VON) Time, change and contradiction. Cambridge, [1969]. pp. 31. (Cambridge. University. Arthur Stanley Eddington Memorial Lectures. 1968)

ACKERMANN (ROBERT JOHN) Modern deductive logic: an introduction to its techniques and significance. London, 1970. pp. 261. bibliog.

BLACK (MAX) Margins of precision: essays in logic and language. Ithaca, N.Y., 1970. pp. 277.

COLLOQUIUM ON FREE LOGIC, MODAL LOGIC AND RELATED AREAS, UNIVERSITY OF CALIFORNIA, IRVINE, 1968. Philosophical problems in logic: some recent developments, edited by Karel Lambert. Dordrecht, [1970]. pp. 176. bibliog.

HAMBLIN (C.L.) Fallacies. London, 1970. pp. 326. bibliog.

HOFFMAN (ROBERT) Language, minds and knowledge. London, 1970. pp. 164. bibliog.

INDUCTION, acceptance and rational belief: (papers...presented at a symposium held at the University of Pennsylvania...1968); edited by Marshall Swain. Dordrecht, [1970]. pp. 232. bibliog.

INTERNATIONAL COLLOQUIUM ON LOGIC, PHYSICAL REALITY, AND HISTORY, 1ST, DENVER, 1966. Physics, logic, and history: based on the...Colloquium held at the University of Denver,...1966; edited by Wolfgang Yourgrau and Allen D. Breck. New York, 1970. pp. 336.

KOPNIN (PAVEL VASIL'EVICH) Dialektik, Logik, Erkenntnistheorie: Lenins philosophisches Denken; Erbe und Aktualität; [translated from the Russian]. Berlin, 1970. pp. 543. bibliog.

KÖRNER (STEPHAN) Categorial frameworks. Oxford, 1970. pp. 85.

LARGEAULT (JEAN) Logique et philosophie chez Frege. Paris, 1970. pp. 486. bibliogs. (Paris. Université. Faculté des Lettres et Sciences Humaines. Publications. Série Recherches. tome 50)

PROBLEMS of the logic of scientific knowledge; edited by P.V. Tavanec; (translated from the Russian by T.J. Blakeley). Dordrecht, [1970]. pp. 429. bibliogs.

QUINE (WILLARD VAN ORMAN) Philosophy of logic. Englewood Cliffs, [1970]. pp. 109. bibliog.

VAX (LOUIS) L'empirisme logique de Bertrand Russell à Nelson Goodman. Paris, 1970. pp. 123. bibliog.

- Terminology

STAHL (G.) Logical terminology and theory of meaning. in Bunge (Mario Augusto) ed. The critical approach to science and philosophy. New York, [1964].

LOGIC, SYMBOLIC AND MATHEMATICAL

FITCH (FREDERIC BRENTON) Symbolic logic: an introduction. New York, [1952]. pp. 238.

BOOLE (GEORGE) Studies in logic and probability. London, Watts, 1952, repr. 1953. pp. 500. 21½cm.

BETH (EVERT WILLEM) Semantic construction of intuitionistic logic. Amsterdam, 1956. pp. 357-388. bibliog. (Nederlandse Akademie Van Wetenschappen. Afdeling Letterkunde. Medelingen. Nieuwe Reeks. Deel 19. No.11)

BETH (EVERT WILLEM) Semantic entailment and formal derivability. Amsterdam, 1961. pp. 309-342. (Nederlandse Akademie Van Wetenschappen. Afdeling Letterkunde. Medelingen. Nieuwe Reeks. Deel 18. No. 13)

LOGIC, SYMBOLIC AND MATHEMATICAL (Cont'd.)

KAESBAUER (MAX) and KUTSCHERA (FRANZ VON) eds. Logik und Logikkalkül; (Wilhelm Britzelmayr zum siebzigsten Geburtstag...gewidmet). Freiburg im Breisgau, Alber, [1962]. pp. 249. bibliogs. 22½cm.

CURRY (H.B.) The elimination of variables by regular combinators. in Bunge (Mario Augusto) ed. The critical approach to science and philosophy. New York, [1964].

KUTSCHERA (FRANZ VON) Die Antinomien der Logik: semantische Untersuchungen. Freiburg, Alber, [1964]. pp. 107. bibliog. 21½cm.

SLININ (IA.A.) Основные модальные категории и современные логические исчисления. in Uchenye Zapiski Kafedr Obshchestvennykh Nauk Vuzov g. Leningrada. Filosofiia. vyp.7. Leningrad, 1965.

HAMILL (LOUIS) A note on tree diagrams, set theory and symbolic logic. [Washington], 1966. pp. 224-226. bibliog. 23cm. (From The Professional Geographer, vol. 18, no. 4) Xerox copy.

ACKERMANN (ROBERT JOHN) An introduction to many valued logics. London, 1967. pp. 90. bibliog. (Monographs in Modern Logic)

COPI (IRVING MARMER) Symbolic logic. 3rd ed. New York, Macmillan, [1967]. pp. xvi, 400. 20½cm.

E. W. BETH MEMORIAL COLLOQUIUM, PARIS, 1964. Logic and foundations of science; Paris, Institut Henri Poincaré, 19-21 May 1964; edited by Jean-Louis Destouches. Dordrecht, Reidel, [1967]. pp. viii, 137. bibliog. 22cm. In French or English.

KREISEL (GEORG) and KRIVINE (J.L.) Elements of mathematical logic: model theory. Amsterdam, North-Holland, 1967. pp. xi, 222. 22½cm. (Studies in Logic and the Foundations of Mathematics)

SHOENFIELD (JOSEPH ROBERT) Mathematical logic. Reading, Mass., Addison-Wesley, [1967]. pp. viii, 344. 23½cm. (Addison-Wesley Series in Logic)

SŁUPECKI (JERZY) and BORKOWSKI (LUDWIK) Elements of mathematical logic and set theory. Oxford, 1967. pp. 346.

VAN HEIJENOORT (J.) Logic as calculus and logic as language. in Boston Colloquium for the Philosophy of Science. Proceedings, 1964-1966. Boston studies in the philosophy of science, vol. 3. Dordrecht, 1967.

ÁDÁM (A.) Truth functions and the problem of their realization by two-terminal graphs. Budapest, 1968. pp. 206. bibliog.

EHLERS (HENRY) Logic by way of set theory. New York, Holt, [1968]. pp. xi, 386. 23cm.

KAC (MARK) and ULAM (STANISLAW MARCIN) Mathematics and logic: retrospect and prospects. New York, Praeger, 1968. pp. ix, 170. 23½cm.

KYBURG (HENRY ELY) Philosophy of science: a formal approach. New York, Macmillan, [1968]. pp. xiii, 332. bibliogs. 23½cm.

LOGIC and foundations of mathematics; dedicated to Prof. A. Heyting on his 70th birthday. Groningen, 1968. pp. 248.

ROOTSELAAR (B. VAN) and STAAL (J.F.) eds. Logic, methodology and philosophy of science 3: proceedings of the third International Congress for Logic, Methodology and Philosophy of Science, Amsterdam, 1967. Amsterdam, North-Holland Publishing Company, 1968. pp. xiii, 554. bibliogs. 22cm. (Studies in Logic and the Foundations of Mathematics)

SCHOCK (ROLF) Logics without existence assumptions. Stockholm, [1968]. pp. 134. bibliog.

SMULLYAN (RAYMOND M.) First-order logic. New York, 1968. pp. 158. bibliog.

SUMMER SCHOOL IN LOGIC, LEEDS, 1967. Proceedings...: N.A.T.O. Advanced Study Institute meeting of the Association for Symbolic Logic; edited by M. H. Löb. Berlin, 1968. pp. 331. bibliogs.

FEYS (ROBERT) and FITCH (FREDERIC BRENTON) eds. Dictionary of symbols of mathematical logic. Amsterdam, North-Holland Publishing Company, 1969. pp. xiv, 171. 22½cm. (Studies in Logic and the Foundations of Mathematics)

FITTING (MELVIN CHRIS) Intuitionistic logic, model theory and forcing. Amsterdam, 1969. pp. 191. bibliog.

FREGE (GOTTLOB) Funktion, Begriff, Bedeutung: fünf logische Studien; herausgegeben...von Günther Patzig. 3rd ed. Göttingen, 1969. pp. 103. bibliog.

GENTZEN (GERHARD) The collected papers...; edited by M. E. Szabo. Amsterdam, 1969. pp. 338.

HARRISON (FRANK R.) Deductive logic and descriptive language. Englewood Cliffs, [1969]. pp. 534.

HINTIKKA (KAARLO JAAKKO JUHANI) ed. The philosophy of mathematics. London, 1969. pp. 186. bibliog.

INTERNATIONAL SYMPOSIUM ON THE APPLICATIONS OF MODEL THEORY TO ALGEBRA, ANALYSIS AND PROBABILITY, PASADENA, CALIFORNIA, 1967. Applications of model theory to algebra, analysis and probability; edited by W.A.J. Luxemburg. New York, [1969]. pp. 307. bibliogs.

KEENE (GEOFFREY BOURTON) The relational syllogism: a systematic approach to relational logic, Exeter, [1969]. pp. 35.

LEISENRING (A. C.) Mathematical logic and Hilbert's E-symbol. London, [1969]. pp. 142. bibliog.

POLLOCK (JOHN L.) Introduction to symbolic logic. New York, [1969]. pp. 241.

ROBBIN (JOEL W.) Mathematical logic; a first course. New York, 1969. pp. 212.

ROBISON (GERSON B.) An introduction to mathematical logic. Englewood Cliffs, Prentice-Hall, [1969]. pp. xii, 212. 22½cm.

STIAZHKIN (N.I.) History of mathematical logic
from Leibniz to Peano. Cambridge, Mass., [1969].
pp. 333.

BETH (EVERT WILLEM) Aspects of modern logic;
(translated from the Dutch). Dordrecht, [1970].
pp. 176. bibliog.

CARNEY (JAMES D.) Introduction to symbolic logic.
Englewood Cliffs, [1970]. pp. 252. bibliog.

COHEN (LAURENCE JONATHAN) The implications of
induction. London, 1970. pp. 248.

CONFERENCE ON INTUITIONISM AND PROOF THEORY, BUFFALO,
1968. Intuitionism and proof theory: proceedings
of the Summer Conference...; edited by A. Kino
[and others]. Amsterdam, 1970. pp. 516. bibliogs.

DELONG (HOWARD) A profile of mathematical logic.
Reading, Mass., [1970]. pp. 304. bibliog.

ŁUKASIEWICZ (JAN) Selected works; edited by L.
Borkowski. Amsterdam, 1970. pp. 405. bibliog.

MASSEY (GERALD J.) Understanding symbolic logic.
New York, [1970]. pp. 428.

PÖRN (INGMAR) The logic of power. Oxford, 1970.
pp. 86. bibliog.

SALZBURG COLLOQUIUM IN THE PHILOSOPHY OF SCIENCE,
1968. Induction, physics and ethics: proceedings
and discussions of the...Colloquium...; edited
by Paul Weingartner and Gerhard Zecha. Dordrecht,
[1970]. pp. 382.

SCOTT (DANA) Outline of a mathematical theory
of computation. Oxford, 1970. pp. 24.
(Oxford. University. Computing Laboratory.
Programming Research Group. Technical Monographs. PRG 2)

STOLIAR (ABRAM ARONOVICH) Introduction to elementary
mathematical logic; (translation edited by Elliott
Mendelson). Cambridge, Mass., [1970]. pp.
209. bibliog.

THOMASON (RICHMOND H.) Symbolic logic: an introduction. London, [1970]. pp. 367.

FREGE (GOTTLOB) Schriften zur Logik und Sprachphilosophie; aus dem Nachlass;... herausgegeben
von Gottfried Gabriel. Hamburg, [1971]. pp.
224. bibliog.

ROGERS (ROBERT) Mathematical logic and formalized
theories: a survey of basic concepts and results.
Amsterdam, 1971. pp. 235. bibliog.

ROSSI (LAURI) Notes on the syntax and semantics
of probability logic. [Helsinki, 1971]. pp.
40. bibliog. (Helsinki. Kauppakorkeakoulu. Julkaisuja.
Sarja C.II: 9)

- Congresses

LOGIC COLLOQUIUM, 11TH, HANNOVER, 1966. Contributions
to mathematical logic: proceedings...; edited
by H. Arnold Schmidt [and others]. Amsterdam,
North-Holland Publishing Company, [1968]. pp.
xi, 298. bibliogs. 22cm. (Studies in Logic and
the Foundations of Mathematics) In English or
German.

LOGICAL POSITIVISM

ALLAKHVERDIAN (SIAMARA DERENIKOVNA)
Неопозитивизм в современной социологии. Ереван, 1964. pp. 99.

STATERA (GIANNI) Logica, linguaggio e sociologia:
studio su Otto Neurath e il neopositivismo.
Torino, Taylor, 1967. pp. 197. bibliog. 23cm.
(Documenti e Ricerche)

FEIGL (HERBERT) The Wiener Kreis in America.
[Cambridge, Mass.], 1968. pp. 630-673.
(Reprinted from Perspectives in American History,
vol. 2, 1968)

ACHINSTEIN (PETER) and BARKER (STEPHEN FRANCIS)
eds. The legacy of logical positivism: studies
in the philosophy of science. Baltimore, [1969].
pp. 300.

WELLMER (ALBRECHT) Kritische Gesellschaftstheorie
und Positivismus. Frankfurt a.M., 1969. pp.
147.

LOGICAL TREES
See **FLOW CHARTS**

LOGISTICS

LARGE scale provisioning systems: the proceedings
of a conference under the aegis of the NATO Scientific Affairs Committee [held at] Athens 4th-8th
September 1967; edited by J. Ferrier. London,
English Universities Press, 1968. pp. (vi),
530. bibliogs. 23cm.

LOIR-ET-CHER

- Politics and government

CHAFFARD (GEORGES) Les orages de mai: histoire
exemplaire d'une élection. Paris, [1968].
pp. 228.

LOIRE-ATLANTIQUE (DEPARTMENT)

- Population

FRANCE. Institut National de la Statistique
et des Études Économiques. Direction Régionale de Nantes. 1959. L'ensemble industriel
de la Basse-Loire: ses zones d'influence.
Nantes, [1959?]. pp. (7). 27cm. Issued with
another part, under the cover title Ensemble
industriel de la XIème région statistique.

LOKERMAN (ALEKSANDR SAMOILOVICH)

GARVI (PETR ABRAMOVICH) Revoliutsionnye siluety. New York, 1962.
pp. 43. (Inter-University Project on the History of the Menshevik Movement)

LOLA RIBAR (IVO)

LOLA RIBAR (IVO) Članci i govori;
(predgovor Milovan Djilas) Beograd, 1953. pp. 330. In Cyrillic.

LOLME (JEAN LOUIS DE)

MACHELON (JEAN PIERRE) Les idées politiques de J.L. de Lolme, 1741-1806. Paris, 1969. pp. 132. bibliog. (Paris. Université. Faculté de Droit et des Sciences Economiques. Travaux et Recherches. Série "Science Politique". No. 15)

LOMBARD LOANS

BRAND (ROLF) Wesen und Fignung des Effektenlombards als eine Form passiven und aktiven Bankkredits. Berlin, [1968]. pp. 164. bibliog.

LOMBARDO TOLEDANO (VICENTE)

UNZUETA (GERARDO) Lombardo Toledano y el marxismo leninismo. México, Fondo de Cultura Popular, 1966. pp. 229. 19½cm.

LOMBARDS

TAGLIAFERRI (AMELIO) ed. Problemi della civiltà e dell'economia longobarda: scritti in memoria di Gian Piero Bognetti. Milano, Giuffrè, 1964. pp. 301. bibliog. 24cm. (Economia e Storia. Biblioteca. 12)

LOMBARDY

- Constitutional history

DILCHER (GERHARD) Die Entstehung der lombardischen Stadtkommune: eine rechtsgeschichtliche Untersuchung. Aalen, Scientia Verlag, 1967. pp. xix, 208. bibliog. 24½cm. (Untersuchungen zur Deutschen Staats- und Rechtsgeschichte. Neue Folge. Band 7)

- Economic conditions

UNIONE ITALIANA DELLE CAMERE DI COMMERCIO, INDUSTRIA E AGRICOLTURA. Monografie Regionali per la Programmazione Economica. Lombardia; a cura dell'Unione Regionale delle Camere di Commercio della Lombardia. [Milan], Giuffrè, [1967]. pp. xix, 291. bibliog. 24cm.

- Economic history

CAIZZI (BRUNO) Industria, commercio e banca in Lombardia nel XVIII secolo. Milano, Banca Commerciale Italiana, 1968. pp. (x), 289. 24½cm. (Studi e Ricerche di Storia Economica Italiana nell'età del Risorgimento)

- History

RATH (REUBEN JOHN) The provisional Austrian regime in Lombardy-Venetia 1814-1815. Austin, [1969]. pp. 412. bibliog.

- History - Bibliography

DEPUTAZIONE DI STORIA PATRIA PER LE ANTICHE PROVINCIE E LA LOMBARDIA. Pubblicazioni, 1833-1935. Torino, 1935. pp. 133. (Da Dervieux E.) L'opera cinquantenaria, vol.2°, 1935-XIII)

- Sanitary affairs

BRUNI (GIAN CARLO) Un piano sanitario per la Lombardia. Milano, 1969. pp. 554. bibliog.

LONDON (ARTUR)

LONDON (ARTUR) On trial;...translated by Alastair Hamilton. London, 1970. pp. 453.

LONDON (JACK) the Novelist

LONDON (JACK) the Novelist. Letters from Jack London: containing an unpublished correspondence between London and Sinclair Lewis; edited by King Hendricks and Irving Shepard. New York, Odyssey P., [1965]. pp. ix, 502. 23½cm.

LONDON

- Amusements

LONDON. London County Council. Places of public entertainment: regulations and rules with regard to requirements as to structure and lighting, heating, electrical, ventilating and mechanical installations. London, 1934. pp. 51.

LONDON. London County Council. Places of public entertainment: rules with regard to the management of places of public entertainment and for ensuring order and decency at theatres. London, 1938. pp. 69.

- Antiquities

LONDON. London County Council. Tyburn gallows. London, 1909. pp. 24.

HORNIMAN MUSEUM AND LIBRARY. A handbook to the cases illustrating stages in the evolution of the domestic arts. London, 1910. 2 pts. bibliogs.

HORNIMAN MUSEUM AND LIBRARY. The ascent of man: a handbook to the cases illustrating the structure of man and the great apes. London, 1920. pp. 74. bibliog.

HORNIMAN MUSEUM AND LIBRARY. From stone to steel: a handbook to the cases illustrating the ages of stone, bronze and iron. 2nd ed. London, 1923. pp. 81. bibliog.

HORNIMAN MUSEUM AND LIBRARY. A handbook to the cases illustrating stages in the evolution of the domestic arts. 2nd ed. London, 1924-25. 2 pts. bibliogs.

HORNIMAN MUSEUM AND LIBRARY. A handbook to the cases illustrating simple means of travel and transport by land and water. London, 1925. pp. 71. bibliog.

HORNIMAN MUSEUM AND LIBRARY. From stone to steel: a handbook to the cases illustrating the ages of stone, bronze, and iron. 3rd ed. London, 1936. pp. 98. bibliog.

- Antiquities, Roman

LONDON. London County Council. Ship of the Roman period discovered on the site of the new County Hall. London, 1910. pp. 20.

- Benevolent and moral institutions and societies.

LONDON. London County Council. Central Public Health Committee. Handbook of information as to rescue and preventive institutions including homes and hostels for those suffering from venereal disease.

LONDON. London County Council. Central Public Health Committee. Handbook of information as to rescue and preventive institutions including homes and hostels for those suffering from venereal disease, an appendix of institutions dealing with cases of mental deficiency, and alphabetical and classified indexes of the homes. London, 1924. pp. 50.

LONDON. London County Council. Central Public Health Committee. Shelters, refuges and institutions to which homeless or destitute persons may be referred. London, 1927. pp. 9.

LONDON. London County Council. Central Public Health Committee. Handbook of information as to rescue and preventive institutions including homes and hostels for those suffering from venereal disease, an appendix of institutions dealing with cases of mental deficiency and alphabetical and classified indexes of the homes. London, 1927. pp. 51.

LONDON. London County Council. Central Public Health Committee. Shelters, refuges and institutions to which homeless or destitute persons may be referred. London, 1930. pp. 11.

LONDON. London County Council. Central Public Health Committee. Handbook of information as to rescue and preventive institutions including homes and hostels for those suffering from venereal disease and alphabetical and classified indexes of the homes. London, 1933. pp. 37.

- Biography

WOODHEAD (J.R.) The rulers of London, 1660-1689: a biographical record of the Aldermen and Common Councilmen of the City of London. London, London & Middlesex Archaeological Society, [1965]. pp. 204. 24cm.

- Bridges

LONDON. London County Council Bridges Committee. Bridges: notes on the acquisition, construction, works and maintenance of the county bridges, tunnels, ferry, embankments, and river prevention of floods works in the county of London...; by Maurice Fitzmaurice. London, 1906. pp. 99.

- Buildings

UNITED KINGDOM. Statutes, etc. 1894. ch. 213. The London Building Act, 1894, with the by-laws and regulations at present in force in relation to buildings in London. London, 1895. pp. 245.

UNITED KINGDOM. Statutes. etc. 1894. ch. 213. The London Building Act, 1894, and The London Building Act, 1894 (Amendment) Act, 1898; with the byelaws and regulations at present in force in relation to buildings in London. London, 1901. pp. 359.

LONDON. London County Council. Construction of buildings in London. London, 1938. pp. 237.

LONDON. Greater London Council. Department of Architecture and Civic Design. GLC architecture 1965/70: the work of the...Department of Architecture and Civic Design. [London, 1970.] pp. 119.

- Census

RENDEL (E.) Index of factors used in GLC 1966 census tables. [London], 1970. pp. 35. (London. Greater London Council. Department of Planning and Transportation. Research Memoranda. 241.)

THOMPSON (ERIC J.) ed. Demographic, social and economic indices for wards in Greater London. [London, 1970.] pp. 232. (London. Greater London Council. Research and Intelligence Unit. Greater London Research. Occasional Papers. No.3)

KELLY (FRANCES) Classifications of the London boroughs. London, [1971]. pp. 49. (London. Greater London Council. Intelligence Unit. Greater London Research. Research Reports. No. 9.)

- Charities

ST. BOTOLPH WITHOUT ALDERSGATE, LONDON. A statement of all charities connected with the parish, and their annual value when bequeathed, and on the 25th March 1865, also a return of parish estates, etc. London, 1869. pp. 174.

LONDON. London County Council. Memorandum on the work of children's care committees. rev. ed. London, 1908. pp. 8.

BLIGH (H.W.) Twickenham and the Anthony Death charities: how rents from Strawberry Hill and Twickenham provided scholarships for boys of London. Twickenham, 1966. pp. 22. (Twickenham. Borough of Twickenham Local History Society. Papers. No.7)

IMRAY (JEAN) The charity of Richard Whittington; a history of the trust administered by the Mercers' Company, 1424-1966. London, Athlone P., 1968. pp. viii, 138. 21½cm.

LOW'S handbook to the charities of London... 1967-68. London, Maxclif, [1968]. pp. xl, 144. 18cm.

- Charities, Medical

[WESTERN DISPENSARY] Western Dispensary, Broadway, corner of York Street, Westminister, instituted 1789, for gratuitously administering advice, medicines and attendance to the poor inhabitants of the City of Westminster, and places adjacent, etc. [London], 1859. pp. 32.

LONDON (Cont'd.)

- Charters, grants, privileges, etc.

LEVIN (JENNIFER) The charter controversy in the city of London, 1660-1688, and its consequences. London, 1969. pp. 119. bibliog.

- Churches

UNITED KINGDOM. Parliament. 1646. An ordinance of the Lords and Commons...for making the Covent-Garden Church parochiall, and for dividing the same from the parish of Martins in the Fields, upon severall articles and conditions ...; [dated 7 and 31 January, 1645]. London, Beesley, 1646. pp. 13. 18½cm. Wing E 1896.

- Civic improvement

LONDON. London County Council. Town Planning Committee. County of London plan: reports submitted to the Council at its meeting on 17th July, 1945, [by] the Town Planning Committee [and] the Finance Committee. London, 1945. pp. 9.

LONDON. London County Council. Town Planning Committee. Town and Country Planning Act, 1944: declaration of area of extensive war damage: Southwark and Lambeth (Elephant and Castle) reconstruction area: statement of planning proposals (as included in the report...submitted to the Council on 25th March, 1947). London, 1947. pp. 3.

LONDON. London County Council. Town and Country Planning Act, 1944: application for declaratory order under Section 1: Bermondsey reconstruction area: statement of planning proposals. London, 1948. pp. 6.

LONDON. London County Council. Town Planning Committee. County of London plan: reports submitted to the Council at its meeting on 17th July, 1945, [by] the Town Planning Committee [and] the Finance Committee. London, 1949. pp. 9.

LONDON. London County Council. Town Planning Committee. Draft development plan and new planning standards: report submitted to the Council at its meeting on 28th June, 1949. London, 1949. pp. 7.

LONDON. London County Council. Town Planning Committee. Administrative County of London development plan, 1951: report submitted to the Council at its meeting on 3rd July, 1951. London, 1951. pp. 3.

LONDON. London County Council. Town Planning Committee. Administrative County of London development plan, 1951: reports submitted to the Council at its meeting on 18th December, 1951, [by] the Town Planning Committee [and] the Finance Committee. London, 1951. pp. 6.

LONDON. London County Council. Town Planning Committee. New planning standards: report submitted to the Council at its meeting on 8th May, 1951. London, 1954. pp. 4.

HOLFORD (WILLIAM GRAHAM) Baron Holford. Piccadilly Circus: future development: proposals for comprehensive development...March, 1962. London, London County Council, 1962. pp. 21. bibliog.

LONDON. Greater London Council. Woolwich-Erith: a riverside project. London, 1966. pp. 40.

LONDON. Greater London Council. Thamesmead: a riverside development. London, 1967. pp. 32.

BARNSBURY environmental study: report. [London], 1968. pp. vi, 128. 30cm.

COVENT GARDEN PLANNING TEAM. Covent Garden area draft plan; [by the] consortium of Greater London Council, City of Westminster, London Borough of Camden. [London, 1968]. pp. 118, 20 maps.

The CENSUS of population as a source of information for local authority planning departments: proceedings of a seminar held by the London boroughs in March 1969: [S.P. Byrne, chairman]. London, 1969. pp. 28. (London. Greater London Council. Research and Intelligence Unit. Greater London Research. Occasional Papers. No. 2)

HALL (PETER GEOFFREY) London 2000. 2nd ed. London, 1969. pp. 287.

LONDON. Greater London Council. Greater London development plan: report of studies. London, [1969]. pp. 327. (Publications. No. 254.)

LONDON. Greater London Council. Greater London development plan: statement: draft text, March, 1969. [London, 1969]. pp. 115. 30cm. Map in end-pocket.

LONDON. Greater London Council. Greater London development plan: statement. London, [1969]. pp. 78. (Publications. No. 255.)

LONDON. Greater London Council. Strategic Planning Committee. Report: (extract from the agenda paper for the Council meeting on Tuesday 25 March 1969). London, 1969. pp. 13. 29½cm.

LONDON. Greater London Council. Tomorrow's London: a background to the Greater London development plan. London, [1969]. pp. 128.

ROYAL INSTITUTE OF BRITISH ARCHITECTS. London 1981: a report by the London Region of the Royal Institute of British Architects on the Greater London Development Plan. [London], 1969. pp. 59.

LONDON. Greater London Council. Greater London development plan: (inquiry proof[s] and inquiry support [papers]). London, 1970 in progress. For description of library holdings see succeeding cards.

LONDON. Greater London Council. Greater London development plan inquiry: notes of the preliminary session[s and hearings] held...at the County Hall, etc. [Court 1]. Days 1-237. London, 1970-72. 34 vols. Hearings held in Courts 1,2 and 3 on the same day are respectively denoted: 122x, 122y, 122z.

BEER (J.) and HECTOR (SUSAN) Planning surveys. [London], 1970. pp. 123. (London. Greater London Council. Department of Planning and Transportation. Research Memoranda. 242)

BUCHANAN (COLIN) AND PARTNERS. North East London: some implications of the Greater London development plan; a report to the Greater London Council. [London], 1970. pp. 140.

LONDON. Greater London Council. Department of Architecture and Civic Design. GLC architecture 1965/70: the work of the...Department of Architecture and Civic Design. [London, 1970.] pp. 119.

SOUTH EAST ECONOMIC PLANNING COUNCIL. South East Economic Planning Council: views on Greater London development plan. London, the Council, 1970. fo. 9.

COVENT GARDEN JOINT DEVELOPMENT COMMITTEE. Covent Garden: the next step: the revised plan for the proposed comprehensive development area. London, 1971. pp. 33.

LONDON. Greater London Council. Greater London development plan inquiry: notes of proceedings of the hearing[s] held...at the County Hall, etc. [Court 2]. Days 122y-124y, 126y-133y, 170y-171y. London, 1971. 13 pts. (in 1 vol.) Hearings held in Courts 1,2 and 3 on the same day are respectively denoted: 122x, 122y, 122z.

LONDON. Greater London Council. Greater London development plan inquiry: notes of proceedings of the hearing[s] held...at the County Hall, etc. [Court 3]. Days 122z-124z, 126z-129z, 134z. London, 1971. 8 pts. (in 1 vol.) Hearings held in Courts 1,2 and 3 on the same day are respectively denoted: 122x, 122y, 122z.

PLANNING for London: edited by Judy Hillman. Harmondsworth, 1971. pp. 152. bibliog.

SELF (PETER J.O.) Metropolitan planning: the planning system of Greater London. London, [1971]. pp. 54. (London. University. London School of Economics and Political Science. Greater London Group. Greater London Papers. No. 14)

- Climate

BRAZELL (J. H.) London weather. London, H.M.S.O., 1968. pp. 270. bibliog. 24½cm.

- Commerce

HARVEY (JOHN) Gent. Londons lawles [sic] liberty; or, A Gozmonian partie licensed: being a true discovery of a pack of...knaves, who have under pretence of an Act of Common Councell...seized...from divers free-men... their...goods, etc. London, 1647. pp. 10. 18½cm. Wing H 1082.

- Defences

LONDON. London County Council. Notes on training for rescue parties in the administrative county of London part of the London civil defence region. London, 1941. pp. 108.

- Description

LONDON. London County Council. London in pictures: a collection of illustrations of the services administered by London local governing authorities, with descriptive letterpress. London, 1937. pp. 122.

MARSHALL (DOROTHY) Dr. Johnson's London. New York, Wiley, [1968] pp. xv, 293. 21cm. (New Dimensions in History. Historical Cities)

VORONIKHINA (LIUDMILA NIKOLAEVNA) London. Leningrad, 1969. pp. 245. bibliog.

LONDON, Greater London Council. Survey of London. vol. 36. The parish of St. Paul, Covent Garden. London, 1970. pp. 388, 84.

- Description - Guide books

BARTHOLOMEW (JOHN GEORGE) The pocket atlas and guide to London. London, Walker, 1899. pp. 16, 16, 14 plates.

BARTHOLOMEW (JOHN GEORGE) The pocket atlas and guide to London. Enlarged ed. London, Walker, 1911. pp. 32, 18 plates.

SAUNDERS (NICHOLAS) Alternative London. 2nd ed. London, 1971. pp. 282.

- Directories

LONDON. London Council of Social Service. Information Department. Administration of the social services in the London boroughs; [with amendments, August, 1971]. London, [1971]. fo. 33,7.

SAUNDERS (NICHOLAS) Alternative London. 2nd ed. London, 1971. pp. 282.

KELLY'S POST OFFICE LONDON DIRECTORY. London, annual. 28cm.

- Economic conditions

A CANDLE for the blinde citizens of London, to see by; by a Freeman of the same city, etc. [London], 1648. pp. 8. 17½cm. Wing C 424.

ECONOMISTS ADVISORY GROUP. A summary of an economic study of the city of London. [London, 1968]. fo. (iii), 30.

WABE (J. S.) Labour force participation rates in the London metropolitan region. Coventry, 1968 fo. 28. (Warwick. University. Department of Economics. Warwick Economic Research Papers. No.2)

- Economic history

WILSON (AUBREY) London's industrial heritage; ... photographs by Joseph McKeown. Newton Abbot, David & Charles, [1967] pp. 160. 28cm.

WHETHAM (EDITH H.) The London milk trade, 1900-1930. [Reading], 1970. pp. 16. (Reading. University. Institute of Agricultural History. Research Papers. No. 3)

- Evening and continuation schools

HEADLAM (STEWART DUCKWORTH) The first session of free evening schools: a reply to criticisms...April 5th, 1900. n.p., [1900]. pp. 10.

LONDON. London County Council. Education Officer's Department. Privilege of Citizenship Series. No. 1. A guide to continued education in London. new ed. London, 1925. pp. 60.

LONDON - Evening and continuation schools (Cont'd.)

    LONDON. London County Council. The London scheme of further education adopted... under the Education Act, 1944. ([Publications]. No. 3672) London, 1949. pp. 153. 25cm.

    LONDON. London County Council. On from school: educational provision for young people under the age of 18 who have left school. ([Publications]. No. 4154) London, 1962. pp. 71. 25cm.

- Exhibitions

    RIDLEY (T.M.) and SMITH (PAUL PRESTWOOD) The traffic demands of a national exhibition centre at Crystal Palace. [London], 1966. pp. 32. (London. Greater London Council. Department of Highways and Transportation. Research and Development Group. Reports. No. HT/RD-3.)

    SMITH (PAUL PRESTWOOD) Travel survey of the Building Exhibition at Olympia, 1965. London, 1966. pp. 21. (London. Greater London Council. Department of Highways and Transportation. Research and Development Group. Reports. No. HT/RD-2.)

    SMITH (PAUL PRESTWOOD) and LATCHFORD (J.C.R.) Travel survey of the International Motor Show, Earl's Court. 1965. [London], 1966. pp. 22. (London. Greater London Council. Department of Highways and Transportation. Research and Development Group. Reports. No. HT/RD-1.)

- Fires and fire prevention

    LONDON. London County Council. Fire Brigade Committee. Note book on the fire brigade. London, 1903. pp. 111.

    LONDON. London County Council. Fire Brigade Committee. Note book on the fire brigade. rev. ed. London, 1908. pp. 130.

    LONDON. London County Council. Fire Brigade Committee. London Fire Brigade: notes on the history and development of the...Brigade with an account of the present staff and equipment, etc. 3rd ed. London, 1913. pp. 111.

    LONDON. London County Council. Fire Brigade. The London Fire Brigade; (with Statistical information). London, 1962. pp. 5,46. bibliog.

- Foreign population

    RICHTER (ROBERT) 1938- . Studien zur Londoner Emigration. Berlin, 1966. pp. 149. bibliog.

- Fortifications

    UNITED KINGDOM. Parliament. 1643. An ordinance and declaration of the Lords and Commons... that the Lord Major and citizens of...London shall have full power...to trench...all high-waies leading into the said city...;also, an ordinance...for an assessment...for the reliefe of maymed souldiers...[dated 6-7 March 1643]. London, Wright, 1642 [O.S.]. pp. 6. 19cm. Wing E 1775.

- Gilds

    WARLOW (WILLIAM MEYLER) A history of the charities of William Jones...at Monmouth and Newland. Bristol, 1899. pp. xiv, 444.

- Gilds - Carpenters' Company

    ALFORD (BERNARD WILLIAM ERNEST) and BARKER (THEODORE CARDWELL) A history of the Carpenters Company. London, Allen & Unwin, 1968. pp. 271. 21½cm.

- Gilds - Company of Fletchers

    OXLEY (JAMES E.) The Fletchers and Longbowstringmakers of London. London, Worshipful Company of Fletchers, [1968]. pp. 160. 24½cm.

- Gilds - Company of Longbowstringmakers

    OXLEY (JAMES E.) The Fletchers and Longbowstringmakers of London. London, Worshipful Company of Fletchers, [1968]. pp. 160. 24½cm.

- Gilds - Glass Sellers' Company

    MOORE (JOHN) compiler. The Glass Sellers Company; compiled from the ancient charter, the original Bye-laws and the minute books of the Company. [London, The Glass Sellers Company], 1899. pp. 61, 7. 23cm.

- Gilds - Mercers' Company

    IMRAY (JEAN) The charity of Richard Whittington; a history of the trust administered by the Mercers' Company, 1424-1966. London, Athlone P., 1968. pp. viii, 138. 21½cm.

- Gilds - Scriveners' Company

    LONDON. London Record Society. Publications. vol. 4. Scriveners' Company common paper, 1357-1628 with a continuation to 1678; edited by Francis W. Steer. [London], 1968. pp. xxviii, 158. 25½cm.

- Gilds - Skinners' Company

    FOX (ADAM) A brief description of the Worshipful Company of Skinners. 3rd ed. London, [imprint], 1968. pp. 72. 21½cm.

- Gilds - Society of Apothecaries

    COPEMAN (WILLIAM SYDNEY CHARLES) The Worshipful Society of Apothecaries of London: a history, 1617-1967. Oxford, Pergamon Press, [1967]. pp. 112. 23½cm.

- Growth

    BAKER (RICHARD FAULKNER) Transport in the urban development of Kentish Thames-side since the late eighteenth century; [M.A. (London) thesis]. 1968. pp. 199. bibliog. 25½cm. Typescript: unpublished. This thesis is the property of London University and may not be removed from the Library.

    BROWNE (KENNETH) and others. Clapham townscape study. [London, 1959] pp. 21.

    HALL (PETER GEOFFREY) London 2000. 2nd ed. London, 1969. pp. 287.

SOUTHWARK. Department of Architecture and Planning. Living in a development area: a simple guide to a number of problems confronting owners and occupiers of properties in development areas. [London, c.1970]. 1 pamphlet (unpaged).

THOMAS (DAVID) Reader in Geography, University College London. London's green belt. London, 1970. pp. 248.

SELF (PETER J.O.) Metropolitan planning: the planning system of Greater London. London, [1971]. pp. 54. (London. University. London School of Economics and Political Science. Greater London Group. Greater London Papers. No. 14)

- Historic houses, etc.

LONDON. London County Council. No. 17, Fleet Street. London, 1906. pp. 20.

LONDON. London County Council. Indication of houses of historical interest in London. London, the Council, 1915-38. 6 vols. Vol. 1 is of the second edition.

LONDON. London County Council. Marble Hill House: a historical and descriptive account. London, 1930. pp. 15.

LONDON. London County Council. Prince Henry's room, No. 17, Fleet Street. 3rd ed. London, 1933. pp. 29.

LONDON. London County Council. Commemorative tablets on houses of historical interest. London, 1960. pp. 31.

- History

A TERRIBLE plot against London and Westminster discovered: shewing how Colonell Lunsford the Papist that should have bin Lieutenant in the Tower, should in a conspiracy among the Jesuites and other Papists have blowne up the city of London, etc. London, Greensmith, 1642. pp. (5). Wing T 774.

LONDON. London County Council. The Council and the war; prepared by the Clerk of the Council. ([Publications]. No. 2015). London, [1920]. pp. v, 65. 25cm. Another copy at R(O)/421(61)

STUDIES in London history presented to Philip Edmund Jones; edited by A.E.J. Hollaender and William Kellaway. London, [1969]. pp. 509.

RUDÉ (GEORGE E.) Hanoverian London, 1714-1808. London, 1971. pp. 271. bibliog.

SHEPPARD (FRANCIS HENRY WOLLASTON) London 1808-1870: the infernal wen. London, 1971. pp. 427. bibliog.

- History - Sources

LONDON. London County Council. Court minutes of the Surrey and Kent Sewer Commission. vol. 1. comprising the minutes of the first two Commissions whose records exist, and covering the period from 1569 to 1579, and index. [London], 1909. pp. 352.

LONDON. London County Council. Court rolls of Tooting Beck Manor. vol. 1. comprising the rolls in the Council's possession, dating from 1394 to 1422, with introduction, notes, appendix containing earlier rolls of the manor in the possession of King's College, Cambridge and index. London, 1909. pp. 259.

LONDON. Corporation. Records Office. Plea and Memoranda Rolls. Calendar of plea and memoranda rolls preserved among the archives of the Corporation of the City of London at the Guildhall, a.d. 1437-1457; edited by Philip E. Jones. Cambridge, 1954. pp. 229.

LONDON. London County Council. Guide to the records in the London County Record Office, part 1. Records of the predecessors of the the London County Council except the Board of Guardians; by Ida Darlington. ([Publications]. No. 4183). London, 1962. pp. 63. 20½cm.

SELDEN SOCIETY. Publications. vols. 85,86. Year books of Edward II. vol. 26. The Eyre of London, 14 Edward II, A.D. 1321; edited by...Helen M. Cam. London, 1968-69. 2 vols. (Year Books Series. vol. 26) In various languages.
L : Annexe

LONDON. London Record Society. Publications. vol. 4. Scriveners' Company common paper, 1357-1628 with a continuation to 1678; edited by Francis W. Steer. [London], 1968. pp. xxviii, 158. 25½cm.

LONDON. London Record Society. Publications. vol. 5. London radicalism 1830-1843: a selection from the papers of Francis Place; edited by D.J. Rowe. London, 1970. pp. 266.

LONDON. London Record Society. Publications. vol. 6. The London eyre of 1244; edited by Helena M. Chew and Martin Weinbaum. London, 1970. pp. 174.

LONDON. London Record Society. Publications. vol. 7. The cartulary of Holy Trinity Aldgate; edited by Gerald A.J. Hodgett. [London], 1971. pp. 291.

- Hospitals

HADEN (FRANCIS SEYMOUR) Mr. Haden's statement of the origin, progress, and present position, of the Hospital for Incurables. London, [1852]. pp. 19.

LOWDER (CHARLES FUGE) S. Katharine's Hospital; its history and revenues...considered in a letter to...the Lord Bishop of London. London, 1867. pp. 16.

LOCH (Sir CHARLES STEWART) The abuse of the out-patient departments of hospitals. [London, 1896?]. pp. 8. (Family Welfare Association. Occasional Paper. Second Series. No. 15) (Reprinted from the British Medical Journal, August 15, 1896)

ST. BARTHOLOMEW'S HOSPITAL. St. Bartholemew's hospital: a brief account...from its foundation in 1123. [London], 1912. pp. 11.

LONDON. London County Council. Hospitals and Medical Services Committee. Handbook of general and special hospitals and ancillary services, 1936. London, 1937. pp. 168.

LONDON - Hospitals (Cont'd.)

    LONDON. London County Council. Hospitals and Medical Services Committee. General and special hospitals services 1938. London, 1938. pp. 28.

    BUTRYM (ZOFIA T.) Medical social work in action: a report of a study of medical social work at Hammersmith Hospital. London, Bell, 1968. pp. 128. 21½cm. (Social Administration Research Trust. Occasional Papers on Social Administration. No. 26)

    MEDICAL and nursing care of children at Paddington General Hospital (now renamed St.Mary's, Harrow Road): David Tomlinson, deceased: report of Committee of Inquiry (inquiry under the provisions of section 70 of the National Health Service Act 1946): [David Stinson, chairman]. [London, H.M.S.O.], 1969. fo. 55.

    PRIESTLEY (H.E.) The Evelina: the story of a London children's hospital, 1869-1969. [London] 1969. pp. 34.

    AYERS (GWENDOLINE M.) England's first state hospitals and the Metropolitan Asylums Board, 1867-1930. London, 1971. pp. 370. bibliog. (Wellcome Institute of the History of Medicine. Publications. New Series. vol.19)

- Industries

    LONDON. University. London School of Economics and Political Science. Graduate Geography Department. Discussion Papers. No. 8. Multivariate analysis of activity patterns in the city centre: a London example; [by] John Goddard. London, 1967. fo. 18. 30cm.

    SEAMAN (JAMES MICHAEL) The location of manufacturing in south east London: a study in industrial geography; [M.Sc. (London) thesis]. 1970. fo. 331. bibliog. Typescript: unpublished. This thesis is the property of London University and may not be removed from the Library.

- Intellectual life

    BELL (QUENTIN) Bloomsbury. London, Weidenfeld & Nicolson, [1968]. pp. 126. bibliog. 21½cm. (Pageant of History)

- Libraries

    IRWIN (RAYMOND) and STAVELEY (RONALD) eds. The libraries of London. 2nd ed. with corrections and addenda. London, 1964. pp. 332.

- Lodging-houses

    LONDON. London County Council. "The house": London's public assistance institutions. London, 1939. pp. 52.

- Maps

    LONDON. London County Council. School-Board map of London. London, n.d. 12 maps.

    BARTHOLOMEW (JOHN GEORGE) The pocket atlas and guide to London. London, Walker, 1899. pp. 16, 16, 14 plates.

    LONDON. London County Council. Building Act Committee. Map showing districts of surveyors under the London Building Act, 1894, and also shewing the metropolitan boroughs; prepared by the Superintending Architect of Metropolitan Buildings. London, [1903].

    LONDON. London County Council. River steamboat service: map of the River Thames within the city of London, shewing the steamboat piers, approaches thereto, and public buildings near the river. London, 1905.

    LONDON. London County Council. Local Government and Statistical Department. Map of the county of London showing the property under the control of the...Council. London, 1906. pp. 59.

    LONDON. London County Council. Tramway map of London and suburbs including the county of London showing the L.C.C. tramways and their connections with other tramways and tube railways. London, 1910.

    BARTHOLOMEW (JOHN GEORGE) The pocket atlas and guide to London. Enlarged ed. London, Walker, 1911. pp. 32, 18 plates.

    LONDON. London County Council. Valuation Department. Municipal map of London: index containing a reference to streets, public buildings, etc. London, 1914. 5 pts (in 1 vol).

    ATLAS of London and the London region; prepared under the direction of Emrys Jones... and D. J. Sinclair. Oxford, [1968]. pp. 70.

    LONDON. University. London School of Economics and Political Science. Graduate Geography Department. Discussion Papers. No. 13. Statistical data and other reference material held by the atlas of London; [by] June Fielding; with introduction [by] Emrys Jones. London, 1968. pp. (37). 30cm.

- Markets

    LONDON. Metropolitan Board of Works. General Purposes Committee. Fish market sites: supplemental report by the engineer and superintending architect, with estimates and further details. London, 1881. pp. 89.

    LONDON. London County Council. Notes having reference to fishing grounds, fishermen, fishing vessels, fishing gear, fish transit, markets, fish salesmen, fishmongers, and fish consumers; with a proposal for a new central market; by G.H. Andrews. London, 1890. pp. 23.

    COVENT GARDEN PLANNING TEAM. Covent Garden area draft plan; [by the] consortium of Greater London Council, City of Westminster, London Borough of Camden. [London, 1968]. pp. 118, 20 maps.

    LONDON, Greater London Council. Survey of London. vol. 36. The parish of St. Paul, Covent Garden. London, 1970. pp. 388, 84.

    COVENT GARDEN JOINT DEVELOPMENT COMMITTEE. Covent Garden: the next step: the revised plan for the proposed comprehensive development area. London, 1971. pp. 33.

- Moral conditions

[GIBBS (GEORGE) Baptist preacher?] An appeal to the clergy, addressed more particularly to the bishops and dignataries of the Church of England on the state of religion, morals and manners, in the British metropolis, etc. London, Holdsworth & Ball, 1831. pp. 223.

VARLEY (HENRY) The new London Pavilion Music Hall: an appeal to the men and women of England, etc. London, [1885?]. pp. 20.

- Office buildings

ROBINSON (ALAN) Working in the city: the interim report of a survey carried out by... assistant medical officer for the City. [London, Corporation], 1962. pp. 20. 32½cm.

The OFFICE: a facet of urban growth; by Peter Cowan [and others]. London, 1969. pp. 280. bibliog.

ROFFEY (GEORGE EDWARD) The distribution of offices in central London with special reference to the City of Westminster: a study of some aspects of urban land use; [M.Sc. (Econ.)(London) thesis]. 1970 [or rather 1971]. fo.323. bibliog. Typescript: unpublished. This thesis is the property of London University and may not be removed from the Library.

- Officials and employees

LONDON. London County Council. The Council's service and the opportunities afforded to boys for obtaining adult employment therein. London, 1910. pp. 51.

LONDON. London County Council. Record of service in the Great War 1914-18 by members of the Council's staff. London, 1922. pp. 212,203.

LONDON. London County Council. General Purposes Committee. Matters affecting members of the Council and co-opted members and their position in relation to interest in contracts and places of profit. London, 1934. pp. 15.

WOODHEAD (J.R.) The rulers of London, 1660-1689: a biographical record of the Aldermen and Common Councilmen of the City of London. London, London & Middlesex Archaeological Society, [1965]. pp. 204. 24cm.

- Officials and employees - Salaries, pensions, etc.

TAYLOR (R.) [Return of the wages paid by the Vestries and District Boards of London] [London, 1893] s. sh.

LONDON. London County Council. Superannuation and provident fund, amended scheme. [London], 1913. pp. 16.

- Parks

LONDON. London County Council. Parks and Open Spaces Committee. Parks and open spaces: particulars of districts, places therein, and district sub-committees of management. London, 1889. pp. 16.

LONDON. London County Council. Provisional Parks, Commons and Open Spaces Committee. Statement as to the existing arrangements with respect to the parks, gardens, commons and open spaces which will on the 1st April, 1889 come under the control of the Parks, etc., Committee of the...Council. London, 1889. pp. 45.

LONDON. London County Council. Dedication to the public of Deptford Park; by W.J. Collins, chairman of the Council, on Whit-Monday, 7th June 1897, at 11.30. a.m. London, 1897. pp. 8.

LONDON. London County Council. Note book of the parks, gardens, recreation grounds, and open spaces of London; with maps showing each place and its surroundings. London, 1897. pp. 45.

LONDON. London County Council. Parks Committee. Note book on the parks, gardens, recreation grounds, and open spaces of London. 3rd ed. London, 1902. pp. 66.

LONDON. London County Council Parks and Open Spaces Committee. Regulations relating to the playing of games at parks and open spaces under the control of the Council. London, 1904. pp. 18.

LONDON. London County Council. London parks and open spaces: notes on the acquisition, history and maintenance of the parks, gardens, recreation grounds and open spaces under the control of the council, etc. London, 1906. pp. 91.

LONDON. London County Council. Parks and Open Spaces Committee. Regulations relating to the playing of games; together with particulars of the facilities afforded for such games and general recreation at parks and open spaces under the control of the Council. 2nd ed. London, 1906. pp. 27.

LONDON. London County Council. Parks and open spaces: regulations relating to games; together with particulars of the facilities afforded for general recreation. 3rd ed. London, 1909. pp. 32.

LONDON. London County Council. Parks and open spaces: regulations relating to games; together with particulars of the facilities afforded for general recreation. 4th ed. London, 1915. pp. 41.

LONDON. London County Council. Parks and open spaces: regulations relating to games; together with particulars of the facilities afforded for general recreation. 5th ed. London, 1915. pp. 41.

UNITED COUNCIL FOR SUNDAY PROTECTION. Sunday games in parks and open spaces: verbatim report of the great united meeting of protest against the decision of the London County Council on July 11th, 1922, to sanction Sunday games in the London parks, etc. London, [1923?]. pp. 19.

LONDON. London County Council. Parks Department. Green islands: the parks service of the London County Council. [London, 1962]. pp. 47.

LONDON - Parks (Cont'd.)

LONDON. Greater London Council. Planning Department. Surveys of the use of open spaces. London, 1968 in progress. bibliog. (London. Greater London Council. Research and Intelligence Unit. Greater London research. Research Papers. No. 2.)

SAUNDERS (ANN) Regent's Park: a study of the development of the area from 1086 to the present day. Newton Abbot, [1969]. pp. 244. bibliog.

MYSON (W.) and others, eds. Wimbledon and Putney Commons, 1871-1971: a centenary record. London, [1971]. pp. 45.

- Police

TIMEWELL (JAMES) The Royal Commission on the Metropolitan Police: the truth about the enquiry. London, [1907?]. pp. 16.

LAURIE (PETER) Scotland Yard; a personal inquiry. London, [1970]. pp. 295.

- Politics and government

THREE looks over London; or, Plain dealing is a jewell. London, I.H. and Ro.Smith, 1643. pp. (6). 18½cm. Wing T 1104.

UNITED KINGDOM. Parliament. 1647. An ordinance of the Lords and Commons...for the putting out of the cities of London and Westminster, and late lines of communication, and twenty miles distant, for six moneths, all delinquents ...; with an order...concerning chusing of Common-Councell men...; [dated 17 December, 1647]. London, Wright, 1647. pp. 6. 18½cm. Wing E 2009.

A CANDLE for the blinde citizens of London, to see by; by a Freeman of the same city, etc. [London], 1648. pp. 8. 17½cm. Wing C 424.

HEADS of the charge against the King, drawn up by the Generall Councell of the Armie; also, His Majesties speech...concerning the present condition of himself, and his three kingdomes...; an ordinance of Parliament concerning the city of London...: [a newsletter]. London, T.R., 1648. pp. 6. 18½cm. Wing H 1293.

LONDON. Court of Common Council. The humble petition of the Lord Major, aldermen, and commons of the city of London, in Common-Councell assembled, presented to the Right honourable the Lords and Commons in Parliament assembled; with the answer of both Houses to the said petition. London, Cotes, 1648. pp. 6. 19cm. Wing H 3543.

LONDON. Court of Common Council. The humble petition of the Lord Major, aldermen, and commons of the city of London in Common-Councell assembled: to the...Lords and Commons ...; together with the answers of both Houses to the said petition. London, Cotes, 1648. pp. 6. 18½cm. Wing H 3538.

LONDON. Court of Common Council. Three petitions; the first, the humble petition of divers well-affected citizens and inhabitants in and about the city of London,...; the second...of the Lord Major, aldermen, and commons in Common-councell assembled,...; the third of the aforesaid citizens, etc. London, Cotes, 1648. pp. 10. 18½cm. Wing T 1110.

LONDONS new colours displaid; or, The snake in the cities grasse-green petition discovered for preventing the horrid mischiefs thereby intended, against the Army, and all the well-affected people in city and countrey. [London, 1648]. pp. 16. 17½cm. Wing L 2942.

LONDON. Remembrancer of the City of London. An analysis...of the Municipal Boroughs (Metropolis) Bill, County of London Bill, and Corporation of London Bill; with observations on those Bills. [London?, 1870?]. pp. 19.

LONDON. London Trades Council. L.C.C. election, 1898, South Hackney Division: an appeal to trade unionists. [London, 1898]. pp. 8.

DICKINSON (WILLOUGHBY HYETT) 1st Baron Dickinson. London's past and future: a retrospect of the various attempts to give municipal government to the metropolis and...the dangers of separate metropolitan municipalities. [London, 1899] pp. 30.

LONDON. London County Council. By-laws and regulations. rev. ed. London, 1903. pp. 334.

LONDON. London County Council. Rules of committees; revised to 31st December, 1905. London, 1906. pp. 248.

LONDON. London County Council. Parliamentary Committee. London statutes: a collection of acts relating specially to the adminstrative county of London and of local and personal acts affecting the powers and duties of the... Council from 1750 to 1907; prepared...by G.L. Gomme and Seager Berry. London, 1907. 2 vols.

LONDON. London County Council. By-laws and regulations. London, 1908. pp. 506.

LONDON. London County Council. Classification and description of the powers and duties of the London County Council. London, 1910. pp. 24.

MUNICIPAL reform v. progressive socialism: which is the better policy for you? London, [imprint], [1911]. pp. 19.

WHAT municipal reform really means: a reply to Municipal Reform Leaflet No. 177. [London, 1913?] pp. 39.

LONDON. London County Council. Guide to the County Hall. London, 1923. pp. 52.

LONDON. London County Council. Guide to the County Hall; with a brief summary of the work of the...Council. 3rd ed. London, 1924. pp. 22.

LONDON. London County Council. Guide to the County Hall; with a brief summary of the work of the...Council. 4th ed. London, 1927. pp. 22.

LONDON. London County Council. Guide to the County Hall; with a brief summary of the work of the...Council. 5th ed. London, 1930. pp. 24.

LONDON. London County Council. By-laws and statutory regulations in force, May, 1931. London, 1931. pp. 341.

LONDON. London County Council. Procedure of local authorities and the London County Council. London, 1932. pp. 53.

LONDON. London County Council. Guide to the County Hall; with a brief summary of the work of the...Council. 6th ed. London, 1934. pp. 32.

LONDON. London County Council. Twenty-five years of London government: an account of the development, 1910-1935, of the government and services of London, prepared on the occasion of an exhibition at The County Hall, 1st-7th June, 1935, to celebrate the jubilee of His Majesty King George V. London, 1935. pp. 80.

LONDON. London County Council. London in pictures: a collection of illustrations of the services administered by London local governing authorities, with descriptive letterpress. London, 1937. pp. 122.

LONDON. London County Council. The London County Council 1938: an annual publication of the Council London, 1938. pp. xxvii, 243, xxviii-lxviii.

LONDON. London County Council. Guide to the County Hall; with a brief summary of the work of the...council. 7th ed. London, 1939. pp. 24.

LONDON. London County Council. Local Government Act, 1929: Administrative County of London Administrative Scheme, 1940. [London, 1941] pp. 12.

LONDON. London County Council. The London County Council: a brief summary of the constitution and work of the London County Council. London, 1947. pp. 8.

LONDON. London County Council. Some interesting facts and figures about the Council's service, 1951. ([Publications]. No. 3726). London, 1951. pp. 48. 18½cm.

LONDON. London County Council. Royal Commission on Local Government in Greater London: statement of evidence by the... Council. London, [1958]. pp. 17.

LONDON. London County Council. Index to statutes relating to London County Council and metropolitan borough councils. London, 1960-63. pp. 235. Includes Amendments nos. 1-4.

SURREY. County Council. Surrey's opposition to the greater London plan. Kingston-upon-Thames, [1962]. 1 pamphlet (unpaged).

LONDON. Greater London Council. Minutes of proceedings. irreg., Ap 1965- London.

U.K. Central Office of Information, Reference Division. 1965. The Corporation of the City of London. London, 1965. pp. 9. 23½cm.

LONDON. Greater London Council. Index to the London Government Act 1963 and orders made thereunder and to certain local act provisions in force in Greater London. London, 1967 in progress. Includes Amendment Lists.

SHERMAN (ALFRED V.) Londoners foot the bill:... failures in direct labour building. London, [1968]. pp. 16.

TINKER (ANTHEA) The Inner London Education Authority: a study of divisional administration, London, H.M.S.O., 1968. pp. vii, 63. 24cm. (U.K. Royal Commission on Local Government in England, 1966. Research Studies. 8.)

GREENWOOD (R.) M.Soc.Sc., and others. Recent reforms in the management structure of local authorities: the London boroughs. Birmingham, 1969. pp. 53. (Birmingham. University. Institute of Local Government Studies. Occasional Papers. Series A. No. 2)

LONDON. Greater London Council. Inner London Education Authority. Inner London Education Authority standing orders, revised to 7 May 1969. London, 1969. fo. 36.

CULLINGWORTH (JOHN BARRY) Report to the Minister of Housing and Local Government on proposals for the transfer of GLC housing to the London boroughs. [London], Ministry of Housing and Local Government, 1970. pp. 2 vols. (in 1.)

LONDON. Greater London Council. Department of Architecture and Civic Design. GLC architecture 1965/70: the work of the...Department of Architecture and Civic Design. [London, 1970.] pp. 119.

RHODES (GERALD) The government of London: the struggle for reform. London, [1970]. pp. 320.

RUCK (S. KENNETH) and RHODES (GERALD) The government of greater London. London, 1970. pp. 197.

YOUNG (MICHAEL DUNLOP) The Hornsey plan: a role for neighbourhood councils in the new local government. London, [1970]. fo. 23.

KELLY (FRANCES) Classifications of the London boroughs. London, [1971]. pp. 49. (London. Greater London Council. Intelligence Unit. Greater London Research. Research Reports. No. 9.)

LONDON. London Council of Social Service. Information Department. Administration of the social services in the London boroughs; [with amendments, August, 1971]. London, [1971]. fo. 33,7.

TOWN AND COUNTRY PLANNING ASSOCIATION. Region in crisis: an independent view of the greater London development plan. London, 1971. pp. 53.

GREATER LONDON SERVICES; ([pd.by] Inner London Education Authority, Greater London Council). a. London. Current issue only kept.

- Politics and government - Bibliography

A SELECT bibliography in the reorganisation of local government in Greater London;...compiled... by Wimbledon Public Libraries [and others]; [with supplement]. [London, 1962-63] pp. 6, 2.

LONDON - Politics and government - Bibliography (Cont'd.)

    LONDON. London County Council. Library. Book Lists. No. 5. The London County Council: a select bibliography. London, 1963. pp. 13.

- Poor

    MAYHEW (HENRY) The unknown Mayhew: selections from the Morning Chronicle, 1849-1850; edited and introduced by E.P. Thompson and Eileen Yeo. London, 1971. pp. 489.

    GRANT (L.) Reminiscences of my tract district: a faithful account of four years' labour amongst brick-makers. London, 1863. pp. 144.

    [PRESTON (WILLIAM CARNALL)] The bitter cry of outcast London; [ascribed to] Andrew Mearns; with leading articles from the Pall Mall Gazette of October 1883 and articles by Lord Salisbury, Joseph Chamberlain and Forster Crozier; edited with an introduction by Anthony S. Wohl. Leicester, 1970. pp. 155.

    BOOTH (Right Hon. CHARLES) Charles Booth's London: a portrait of the poor at the turn of the century, drawn from his "Life and labour of the people in London;" selected and edited by Albert Fried and Richard M. Elman; [reprinted from the works originally published 1889-1903]. London, Hutchinson, 1969. pp. xxxix, 342. bibliog. 23cm.

    U.K. Poor Law Board. 1891. Orders of the Poor Law Board and of the Local Government Board relating to the Board of Management of the Metropolitan Asylum District and the several institutions under their control;...revised to 31st January, 1891. London, McCorquodale, 1891. pp. vii, 318, liv.

    LONDON. London County Council. Public Assistance Committee. Administration of relief. London, 1931. pp. 24.

    LONDON. London County Council. Public Assistance Committee. General information relating to the... Committee and its sub-committees; the local public assistance committees, etc. London, 1932. pp. 34.

    LONDON. London County Council. Public Assistance Committee. Administration of relief; with an appendix on the determination of transitional payments. London, 1933. pp. 29.

    LONDON. London County Council. Public Assistance Committee. Administration of relief. London, 1935. pp. 42.

    LONDON. London County Council. Public Assistance Department. London's homeless: arrangements made by the...Council, in co-operation with voluntary societies, for dealing with homeless destitute persons. London, 1937. pp. 44.

    LONDON. London County Council. Public Assistance Committee. Administration of relief. London, 1938. pp. 47.

    BOOTH (Right Hon. CHARLES) On the city: physical pattern and social structure: selected writings, edited and with an introduction by Harold W. Pfautz. Chicago, U. of Chicago P., 1967. pp. vi, 314. bibliog. 20½cm. (Heritage of Sociology)

    PARKER (TONY) People of the streets. London, Cape, 1968. pp. 256. 19½cm.

    CHESNEY (KELLOW) The Victorian underworld. London, [1970]. pp. 398. bibliog.

    BRANDON (DAVID) Homeless in London. [London, 1971]. pp. 17. bibliog.

    STEDMAN-JONES (GARETH) Outcast London: a study in the relationship between classes in Victorian society. Oxford, 1971. pp. 424. bibliog.

- Population

    LONDON. London County Council. Local Government Committee. Census, 1911: report by the Clerk of the Council upon the statistics relating to London contained in the various volumes of the Census of England and Wales, 1911. London, 1915. pp. xxi-xxxvi, 31-95. (Reprinted from London Statistics, vol. 24, pp. xxi-xxxvi and 31-95)

    AJO (REINO) London's field response in terms of population change. Helsinki, 1964. 2 pts. bibliogs. (Reprinted from Acta Geographica, 18, Nos. 2 and 3)

    AJO (REINO) On the structure of population density in London's field. Helsinki, 1965. pp. 17. bibliog. (Reprinted from Acta Geographica, 18, No. 4)

    TEPER (SUSAN) Patterns of fertility in Greater London: a comparative study: population trends project supported in the Department of Statistics, London School of Economics, by the Greater London Council (Research and Intelligence Unit). London, 1968. pp. 31. 30cm. (London. Greater London Council. Research and Intelligence Unit. Greater London research. Occasional Papers. No. 1)

    LUND. Universitet. Geografiska Institution. Lund Studies in Geography. Series B. Human Geography. No. 33. County of London: population changes, 1801-1901; by Karl Gustav Grytzell. Lund, 1969. pp. 129. bibliog.

    FORBES (THOMAS ROGERS) Chronicle from Aldgate: life and death in Shakespeare's London. New Haven, 1971. pp. 251. bibliog.

    KELLY (FRANCES) Classifications of the London boroughs. London, [1971]. pp. 49. (London. Greater London Council. Intelligence Unit. Greater London Research. Research Reports. No. 9.)

- Port

    LONGLANDS (HENRY) A review of the warehousing system as connected with the Port of London; taken from parliamentary reports and official documents. London, Richardson, 1824. pp. xii, 59.

    LOVELL (JOHN) Stevedores and dockers: a study of trade unionism in the Port of London, 1870-1914. London, 1969. pp. 270. bibliog.

    LONDON. Port of London Authority. Shipping services to overseas markets. London, 1970. pp. 56.

- Port - Port charges

LONDON DOCK COMPANY. Table of the rates and charges of the London Dock Company on goods sent to the docks for shipment. London, Truscott, 1841. pp. 36. 21½cm.

- Prisons and reformatories

HOLFORD (GEORGE PETER) An account of the general penitentiary at Millbank;...to which is added an appendix on the form and construction of prisons, etc. London, Rivington, 1828. pp. lxiv, 394.

LONDON. London County Council. Education Committee. Special Schools Sub-Committee. Handbook containing general information with reference to special and industrial schools, places of detention, reformation, etc.; revised to 31st December, 1912. London, 1913. pp. 195.

LONDON. London County Council. Education Committee. Special Schools Sub-Committee. Handbook containing general information with reference to special and industrial schools and places of detention; revised to 31st December, 1924. London, 1925. pp. 214.

- Public buildings

LONDON. London County Council. Guide to the County Hall. London, 1923. pp. 52.

LONDON. London County Council. Guide to the County Hall; with a brief summary of the work of the...Council. 3rd ed. London, 1924. pp. 22.

LONDON. London County Council. Guide to the County Hall; with a brief summary of the work of the...Council. 4th ed. London, 1927. pp. 22.

LONDON. London County Council. Guide to the County Hall; with a brief summary of the work of the...Council. 5th ed. London, 1930. pp. 24.

LONDON. London County Council. Guide to the County Hall; with a brief summary of the work of the...Council. 6th ed. London, 1934. pp. 32.

LONDON. London County Council. Guide to the County Hall; with a brief summary of the work of the...council. 7th ed. London, 1939. pp. 24.

- Public works

LONDON. Metropolitan Board of Works. Inquiry Committee into Charges made against the Board. First report adopted at St. James's Hall, on December 21, 1888. London, 1889. pp. 11.

LONDON. London County Council. Works Department. General orders to foremen. [London, 1893] pp. 26.

CADOUX (GASTON) La vie des grandes capitales: études comparatives sur Londres, Paris, Berlin, Vienne, Rome. 2nd ed. Paris, 1913. pp. 372.

- Restaurants, lunch rooms, etc.

KOTAS (RICHARD) Labour costs in restaurants: a study of labour costs in catering establishments in the Greater London area. London, 1970. pp. 210. bibliog.

- Riots

The RISING and routing of the mutiniers in the city of London on Sunday and Munday the 9th and 10th of Aprill, 1648, etc. London, Becke, 1648. pp. 6. 17½cm. Wing R 1538.

- Sanitary affairs

[MURRAY (THOMAS ARCHIBALD)] Remarks on the situation of the poor in the metropolis, as contributing to the progress of contagious diseases, with a plan for the institution of houses of recovery, for persons infected by fever. London, Hatchard, 1801. pp. vii, 47.

DUDFIELD (T. ORME) Notification of infectious disease, metropolitan hospital accommodation, and ambulance service; introductory address ([to the] Conference of Medical Officers of Health). London, 1899. pp. 409-427. (Excerpt from Vol. XX Part III, of The Journal of the Sanitary Institute)

ROBINSON (ALAN) Working in the city: the interim report of a survey carried out by... assistant medical officer for the City. [London, Corporation], 1962. pp. 20. 32½cm.

LONDON. City of London Occupational Health Service. Port and City of London Health Committee. Report; [with] appendix, Health and efficiency in the City;...by...Alan Robinson. [London, 1963] pp. 2, 7.

PSYCHIATRIC REHABILITATION ASSOCIATION. The mental health of East London; [by] Peter McCowan [and others]. [London], 1966. fo. 48.

FORBES (THOMAS ROGERS) Chronicle from Aldgate: life and death in Shakespeare's London. New Haven, 1971. pp. 251. bibliog.

- Schools

LONDON. London County Council. School-Board map of London. London, n.d. 12 maps.

LONDON. School Board for London. Reports [of committees]. s-a., etc., 1878-1886, with gap.

CONFERENCE OF MANAGERS REPRESENTATIVE OF ALL THE METROPOLITAN BOARDS OF GUARDIANS, 1896. Poor law schools: a criticism of the report of the Departmental Committee. London, 1897. pp. 36.

SCHOOL BOARD FOR LONDON ASSOCIATION OF HEAD TEACHERS OF HIGHER GRADE SCHOOLS. Memorandum on higher grade schools. [London?], 1904. pp. 14.

LONDON. London County Council. Education Committee. Elementary schools handbook. London, 1912. pp. 188.

LONDON - Schools (Cont'd.)

LONDON. London County Council. Education Committee. Special Schools Sub-Committee. Handbook containing general information with reference to special and industrial schools, places of detention, reformation, etc.; revised to 31st December, 1912. London, 1913. pp. 195.

LONDON. London County Council. Education Committee. Elementary schools handbook; revised to 31st July, 1923. London, 1923. pp. 153.

LONDON. London County Council. Education Committee. Special Schools Sub-Committee. Handbook containing general information with reference to special and industrial schools and places of detention; revised to 31st December, 1924. London, 1925. pp. 214.

LONDON. London County Council. Education Committee. Elementary schools handbook; revised to 31st July, 1928. London, 1928. pp. 155.

LONDON. London County Council. London's open-air schools. London, 1929. pp. 29.

AVERY (JOHN) Bishopsgate schools, 1702-1899. [London, 1932]. pp. 31. Privately printed.

LONDON. London County Council. Education Committee. Elementary schools handbook; revised to 31st March, 1939. London, 1939. pp. 188.

LONDON. London County Council. Education Officer's Department. Senior elementary schools in London, report by the Council's Chief Inspector, J. Brown. London, 1939. pp. 42.

LONDON. London County Council. Replanning London schools: a short account of the development plan for primary and secondary education prepared...under the Education Act, 1944. ([Publications]. No. 3608) London, 1947. pp. 64. 23½cm. For the plan see the Councils London school plan.

LONDON. London County Council. Education Officer's Department. New boarding schools for London's handicapped children. London, 1951. pp. 23.

LONDON. London County Council. The organisation of comprehensive secondary schools: some preliminary suggestions for the consideration of teachers. ([Publications]. No. 3857). rev.ed. London, 1954. pp. 31. bibliog. 18½cm.

RUBINSTEIN (DAVID) School attendance in London, 1870-1904: a social history. Hull, 1969. pp. 137. bibliog. (Hull. University. Occasional Papers in Economic and Social History. No 1.)

- Sewerage

LONDON SEWAGE COMPANY. Report upon the various plans proposed for rendering available the manure contained in the sewage water of the metropolis; with a detailed explanation of the plan...and an estimate of the cost of the works...; by Thomas Wicksteed. London, 1845. pp. 57.

METROPOLITAN COMMISSION OF SEWERS. Reports...; by J.W. Bazalgette [and others] on the high level line for the interception of the drainage north of the Thames, and on the intercepting lines south of the river. London, 1853. pp. 25.

METROPOLITAN COMMISSION OF SEWERS. North side of the Thames: report by Robert Stephenson... on the report of Joseph William Bazalgette and William Haywood on the sewage interception and main drainage of the districts north of the Thames. London, 1854. pp. 62.

METROPOLITAN COMMISSION OF SEWERS. North side of the Thames: report upon the sewage interception and main drainage of the districts north of the Thames; by Joseph William Bazalgette [and others]. London, 1854. pp. 36.

METROPOLITAN COMMISSION OF SEWERS. Report to Viscount Palmerston, upon the system of drainage pursued in the metropolis; by Richard Jebb. London, 1854. pp. 21.

METROPOLITAN COMMISSION OF SEWERS. Report upon the most advantageous mode of dealing with the sewage matter of the metropolis with a view to the preparation of sewage manure; by Thomas Wicksteed. London, 1854. pp. 47.

METROPOLITAN COMMISSION OF SEWERS. Data employed in determining the sizes and estimating the cost of the works designed for the main drainage of the metropolis...; by J.W. Bazalgette. London, 1855. pp. 19.

METROPOLITAN COMMISSION OF SEWERS. Estimates of the cost of the works referred to in reports by the engineers, on the extension of the late Mr. Forster's plan, for the main drainage of districts south of the Thames, and modification of its branches. London, 1855. pp. 11.

METROPOLITAN COMMISSION OF SEWERS. Memorandum by F.O. Ward in the data employed by Mr. Bazalgette in determining the sizes and estimating the cost of the works designed for the main drainage of the metropolis. London, 1855. pp. 19.

METROPOLITAN COMMISSION OF SEWERS. Reports by the engineers, on the extension of the late F. Forster's plan for the main drainage of the districts south of the Thames and modification of its branches. London, 1855. pp. 32.

LONDON. London County Council. Main Drainage Committee. Main drainage of London: joint report of Sir Benjamin Baker and the Chief Engineer of the Council (Alex. R. Binnie). London, 1894. pp. 35.

LONDON. London County Council. Main Drainage Committee. Report upon the main drainage of London; by Sir Alexr. R. Binnie, Chief Engineer. London, 1899. pp. 34.

LONDON. London County Council. Court minutes of the Surrey and Kent Sewer Commission. vol. 1. comprising the minutes of the first two Commissions whose records exist, and covering the period from 1569 to 1579, and index. [London], 1909. pp. 352.

LONDON. London County Council. Centenary of London's main drainage, 1855-1955. ([Publications]. No. 3900) London, 1955. pp. 30. 21cm. x 28cm.

- Social conditions

BOOTH (Right Hon. CHARLES) Charles Booth's London: a portrait of the poor at the turn of the century, drawn from his "Life and labour of the people in London;" selected and edited by Albert Fried and Richard M. Elman; [reprinted from the works originally published 1889-1903]. London, Hutchinson, 1969. pp. xxxix, 342. bibliog. 23cm.

LONDON. London County Council. Some interesting facts and figures about the Council's service, 1951. ([Publications]. No. 3726). London, 1951. pp. 48. 18½cm.

BOOTH (Right Hon. CHARLES) On the city: physical pattern and social structure: selected writings, edited and with an introduction by Harold W. Pfautz. Chicago, U. of Chicago P., 1967. pp. vi, 314. bibliog. 20½cm. (Heritage of Sociology)

HUBERT (JANE) and others. Methods of study of middle-class kinship in London: a working-paper on the history of an anthropological project, 1960-65. London, University, London School of Economics and Political Science, Department of Anthropology, 1968. pp. iv, 149. 30cm. (Occasional Papers)

PARKER (TONY) People of the streets. London, Cape, 1968. pp. 256. 19½cm.

FIRTH (RAYMOND WILLIAM) and others. Families and their relatives: kinship in a middle-class sector of London; an anthropological study by Raymond Firth [and others] with the team of the 'London Kinship Project'. London, [1970]. pp. 476.

LAND (HILARY) Large families in London: a study of 86 families. London, 1969. pp. 154. (Social Administration Research Trust. Occasional Papers on Social Administration. No.32)

WILLIAMS (TREVOR) Social gradients in the city: a trend surface analysis of enumeration district data for Inner London. London, 1969. fo. 8. (London. University. London School of Economics and Political Science. Graduate Geography Department. Discussion Papers. No.32)

YOUTH SERVICE INFORMATION CENTRE. Reports. 1. The Blenheim project, 1964-1969, etc. Leicester, 1970. pp. 17.

MARSHALL (HONOR) Twilight London: a study in degradation. London, [1971]. pp. 192.

HAY (HOPE) Friends and neighbours in Islington: ...the story of Friends Neighbourhood House. London, 1972. pp. 26.

- Social history

WOHL (ANTHONY STEPHEN) The housing of the artisans and laborers in nineteenth century London, 1815-1914:...thesis submitted in partial fulfillment of the requirements for the degree of Doctor of Philosophy in the Department of History at Brown University. 1966. fo. 511. bibliog. Xerographic copy.

BELL (QUENTIN) Bloomsbury. London, Weidenfeld & Nicolson, [1968]. pp. 126. bibliog. 21½cm. (Pageant of History)

MARSHALL (DOROTHY) Dr. Johnson's London. New York, Wiley, [1968] pp. xv, 293. 21cm. (New Dimensions in History. Historical Cities)

RUBINSTEIN (DAVID) School attendance in London, 1870-1904: a social history. Hull, 1969. pp. 137. bibliog. (Hull. University. Occasional Papers in Economic and Social History. No 1.)

CHESNEY (KELLOW) The Victorian underworld. London, [1970]. pp. 398. bibliog.

FORBES (THOMAS ROGERS) Chronicle from Aldgate: life and death in Shakespeare's London. New Haven, 1971. pp. 251. bibliog.

STEDMAN-JONES (GARETH) Outcast London: a study in the relationship between classes in Victorian society. Oxford, 1971. pp. 424. bibliog.

- Social life and customs

[TAYLOR (JOHN) the Water Poet] Saint Hillaries teares shed upon all professions from the iudge to the petty fogger, from the spruce dames of the exchange to the durty walking fishmongers, etc. London, N.V[avasour] and I.B., 1642. pp. 8. 18½cm. Wing T 507.

SAUNDERS (NICHOLAS) Alternative London. 2nd ed. London, 1971. pp. 282.

- Stock Exchange

BRISTON (R.J.) The Stock Exchange and investment analysis. London, 1970. pp. 493. bibliog.

- Stock Exchange - Anecdotes, facetiae, satire, etc.

ATKIN (GEORGE DUCKWORTH) compiler. House scraps; collected by G. Duckworth Atkin, with illustrations by Geo. Cruickshank, [and others]. London, 1887. pp. 183. Privately printed.

- Streets

LONDON. Metropolitan Board of Works. Streets Committee. Extract from report of the...Committee, submitting copy of letter to the Southwark and Vauxhall Water Company, urging the laying down of water mains in the subway under Southwark Street, instead of breaking up the thoroughfare for that purpose; together with the reply of the company thereto. [London], 1865. pp. 7.

LONDON - Streets (Cont'd.)

LONDON. Metropolitan Board of Works. Report...in answer to objections to their proposed scheme of metropolitan street improvements raised by Mr. Haywood in his report to the City Commissioners of Sewers upon the same subject; by J. W. Bazalgette. London, 1872. pp. 21.

LONDON. London County Council. List of streets and places within the administrative county of London, etc. (with Supplements 1929-1939). London, 1929-40. 7 pts. (in 1 vol.)

LONDON. London County Council. Names of streets and places in the administrative county of London; (with Supplement...for 1955-1966). 4th ed. London, 1955-67. 2 vols.

- Theatres

LONDON. London County Council. The site of the Globe Playhouse Southwark; with an appendix by the architect to the Council on the architecture of the building. London, 1921. pp. 43.

LONDON. London County Council. Committee of Inquiry on Sadler's Wells. Report of the independent Committee of Inquiry set up to advise the London County Council: [Sir Frederic Hooper, chairman]. [London, 1959]. pp. 26.

LONDON. Greater London Council. Survey of London. vol. 35. The Theatre Royal, Drury Lane, and the Royal Opera House, Covent Garden. London, 1970. pp. 132, 68.

- Tower of London

LONDON. Court of Common Council. A petition of the Major, aldermen, and Common-Councell of the citie of London, to His Majestie; together with His Majesties gracious answer thereunto. London, Barker and Bill, 1641. pp. 14. 18½cm. Wing P 1819.

A TRUE relation of the cruell and unparallel'd oppression which hath been illegally imposed upon the gentlemen, prisoners in the Tower of London; presented to the view of all Christians and all men of honour, etc. [London], 1647. pp. 20. 18½cm. Wing T 2938.

- Transit systems

LONDON. Metropolitan Board of Works. Report upon metropolitan railway schemes of session 1863; by J.W. Bazalgette, engineer. London, 1863. pp. 15.

LONDON. Metropolitan Board of Works. Report upon metropolitan railway and other schemes, session 1876; by Sir J. W. Bazalgette. London, 1876. pp. 29.

LONDON. London County Council. Highways Committee. Tramway legislation in London; and tramways belonging to local authorities; by A. Bassett Hopkins. rev. ed. London, 1891. pp. 90.

[SUTHERST (THOMAS)] Street traffic reform: municipal trams and 'buses: remedy for overwork. London, [imprint], [1891]. pp. 6.

LONDON. London County Council. Architect's Department. Report upon railway and other schemes affecting the administrative county of London. London, 1898. pp. 14.

LONDON. London County Council. Tramways. Rules and regulations for the staff in force and after 1st January, 1900. London, 1900. pp. 44.

LONDON. London County Council. Quarterly return of workmen's trains and other cheap morning trains between the London termini and each station in London and the neighbourhood, and of workmen's trams...; containing also information with regard to the...Council's dwellings for workmen and evening classes, etc. London, 1907. pp. 149.

LONDON. London County Council Highways Committee. London tramways guide. London, 1909. pp. 170.

LONDON. London County Council. Tramway map of London and suburbs including the county of London showing the L.C.C. tramways and their connections with other tramways and tube railways. London, 1910.

LONDON. London County Council Highways Committee London traffic: report, presented to the Council on 9th May, 1922, dealing with the passenger transport systems of Greater London, with special reference to the Council's tramways. London, 1922. pp. 28.

LONDON. London County Council. Tramways, trolley vehicles and motor omnibuses compared. [London, 1924]. pp. 8.

MAHON (JOHN A.) London.traffic: the menace of monopoly. London, Transport Workers' Minority Movement, 1928. pp. 16. 21½cm.

TRANSPORT AND GENERAL WORKERS' UNION. Bus Section. Committee of Rank and File Delegates. The London busmen's case. London, [c.1930]. pp. 16.

LABOUR RESEARCH DEPARTMENT. The London traffic combine: a study of the finances and ramifications of the London traffic combine. London, [1932?]. pp. 16.

LONDON. London Busmen's Rank-and-File Movement. The public, the busmen and the Transport Board. [London, 1935?]. pp. 15.

The FUTURE of passenger transport in London: statement adopted by the Conference of Communist Transport Workers at the Conway Hall, December 3rd, 1944. [London, 1944]. pp. 8.

COWDEROY (J.E.) Public co-operation in transport. 2. An address. [London, 1948]. pp. 25.

LONDON. University. London School of Economics and Political Science. Graduate Geography Department. Discussion Papers. No. 2. Regression analysis of the journey to work to central London, 1951; [by] R. Leigh. London, 1966. fo. 7. 30cm.

LONDON. University. London School of Economics and Political Science. Graduate Geography Department. Discussion Papers. No. 7. Journey to work definitions of the London region in 1921 and 1951; [by] Roger Leigh. London, 1967. fo. 8. 30cm.

MUNT (P.W.) and WOODHALL (R.) A study of travel times by private and public transport in Greater London. [London], 1967. unpaged. (London. Greater London Council. Department of Highways and Transportation. Research Memoranda. 44.)

MUNT (P.W.) and YATES (L.B.) A study of bus passenger movements in the Vauxhall-Wandsworth area. [London], 1967. pp. (14). (London. Greater London Council. Department of Highways and Transportation. Research Memoranda. 42)

BALINT (MAGDA) L[ondon-] M[idland] R[egion] Survey (Watford Line); information on tabulations. [London], 1968. pp. various. (London. Greater London Council. Department of Highways and Transportation. Research Memoranda. 127)

BALINT (MAGDA) L[ondon-] M[idland] R[egion] Survey (Watford Line); report of method. [London], 1968. pp. various. (London. Greater London Council. Department of Highways and Transportation. Research Memoranda. 119.)

COON (A.G.) and CHOWDHURI (R.H.) Unit travel costs for use in cost benefit studies. [London], 1968. pp. 12. (London. Greater London Council. Department of Highways and Transportation. Research Memoranda. 61.)

CRAWFORD (K.A.J.) Accuracy of the transportation model. [London], 1968. pp. 12. (London. Greater London Council. Department of Highways and Transportation. Research Memoranda. 76.)

CRAWFORD (K.A.J.) Future transportation survey programme: 1971 update. [London], 1968. pp. 3,2. (London, Greater London Council. Department of Highways and Transportation. Research Memoranda. 107)

CRAWFORD (K.A.J.) Future transportation survey programme: pilot study outline. [London], 1968. pp. 5. (London. Greater London Council. Department of Highways and Transportation. Research Memoranda. 108)

CRAWFORD (K.A.J.) Future transportation survey programme: preliminary timetable. [London], 1968. pp. 3. (London. Greater London Council. Department of Highways and Transportation. Research Memoranda. 63.)

CRAWFORD (K.A.J.) Future transportation survey programme: timetable. [London], 1968. pp. 2. (London. Greater London Council. Department of Highways and Transportation. Research Memoranda. 106)

CRAWFORD (K.A.J.) Outline proposals for updating the London Transportation Study. [London], 1968. pp. 4. (London. Greater London Council. Department of Highways and Transportation. Research Memoranda. 118)

LAMB (G.M.) Thamesmead: the journey to work. [London], 1968. pp. 16. bibliog. (London. Greater London Council. Department of Highways and Transportation. Research Memoranda. 62)

LEIGH (ROGER) The journey to work to Central London, 1921-1951: a geographical analysis; [Ph. D. (London) thesis]. 1968. fo. 408. bibliog. 25cm. Typescript; unpublished. This thesis is the property of London University and may not be removed from the Library.

LONDON. Greater London Council. Department of Highways and Transportation. Research Memoranda. 113. Off-peak journeys in Thamesmead. [London, 1968]. pp. 9. bibliog.

MUNT (P.W.) Strategic cordon and screen line studies: the Central Area cordon, 1968. [London], 1968. pp. various. bibliog. (London. Greater London Council. Department of Highways and Transportation. Research Memoranda. 126)

POWELL (A.E.) The design of a study to investigate the effects of the opening of the Victoria Line on the pattern of movement. [London], 1968. pp. various. (London. Greater London Council. Department of Highways and Transportation. Research Memoranda. 78)

SMITH (PAUL PRESTWOOD) and others. The building of a public transport policy level network. [London], 1968. pp. 7. (London. Greater London Council. Department of Highways and Transportation. Research Memoranda. 86)

STOPHER (P.R.) Preliminary note on the measurement of the value of comfort. [London], 1968. pp. 5,2. (London. Greater London Council. Department of Highways and Transportation. Research Memoranda. 88)

STOPHER (P.R.) Report on sampling for the household interview survey in the Victoria Line study. [London], 1968. pp. 4. (London. Greater London Council. Department of Highways and Transportation. Research Memoranda. 98.)

STOPHER (P.R.) Report on the journey to work survey; 1966. [London], 1968. pp. 8. bibliog. (London. Greater London Council. Department of Highways and Transportation. Research Memoranda. 48)

THRASHER (P.A.) and others. Motorway Box Area study. [London], 1968. 2 pts. (London. Greater London Council. Department of Highways and Transportation. Research Memoranda. 93-94.)

YATES (L.B.) Traffic flows during rail 'go slow', December 1967. [London], 1968. pp. 2. bibliog. (London. Greater London Council. Department of Highways and Transportation. Research Memoranda. 102.)

YATES (L.B.) Traffic surveys in London. [London], 1968. pp. 9. bibliog. (London. Greater London Council. Department of Highways and Transportation. Research Memoranda. 95.)

LONDON - Transit systems (Cont'd.)

WEBSTER (F.V.) A theoretical estimate of the effect of London car commuters transferring to bus travel. Crowthorne, Road Research Laboratory, 1968. pp. 40, (1). bibliog. 30cm. (U.K. Road Research Laboratory. Reports. LR 165.)

BALINT (MAGDA) Railheading study (phase 1). London, 1969. pp. 21. (London. Greater London Council. Department of Highways and Transportation. Research Memoranda. 162)

BAYLISS (DAVID) Notes on the interpretation of the L[ondon] T[ransportation] S[tudy] phase 3 tabulations. [London], 1969. pp. 24. (London. Greater London Council. Department of Planning and Transportation. Research Memoranda. 193.)

CRAWFORD (K.A.J.) L[ondon] T[ransportation] S[tudy] update: a discussion paper. [London], 1969. pp. 13. (London. Greater London Council. Department of Highways and Transportation. Research Memoranda. 177.)

HARRISON (W.J.) Central London traffic survey (R.R.L. method), April-May 1968. [London], 1969. pp. 10. bibliog. (London. Greater London Council. Department of Highways and Transportation. Research Memoranda. 124.)

HARRISON (W.J.) Journey times and traffic flows in Central London during the British Rail work-to-rule, June 1968. [London, 1969]. pp. 2. bibliog. (London. Greater London Council. Department of Highways and Transportation. Research Memoranda. 145.)

HEWING (R.B.) and HOFFMAN (M.L.H.) Public transport network sensitivity test (P.T.2). [London], 1969. pp. 2,4. (London. Greater London Council. Department of Highways and Transportation. Research Memoranda. 179)

HOLDER (D.R.) Model development note 4: the interaction of road and public transport systems: improved schemes for modal split. [London], 1969. pp. (4). (London. Greater London Council. Department of Highways and Transportation. Research Memoranda. 166.)

KOSTANOWICZ (H.) Movement in London: sources of data. [London], 1969. pp. 9. (London. Greater London Council. Department of Highways and Transportation. Research Memoranda. 203.)

LONDON. Greater London Council. Movement in London: transport research studies and their context. London, 1969. pp. 158. (Publications. No. 251.)

MAY (A.D.) and ALLEN (B.L.) A comparative study of traffic performance in the Blackwall tunnel under two-way and one-way operation. [London], 1969. pp. 6. (London. Greater London Council. Department of Highways and Transportation. Research Memoranda. 183.)

MUNT (P.W.) The effect of the opening of the duplicated Blackwall tunnels and the southern approach roads on traffic crossing the lower Thames, 1968-69. [London], 1969. pp. 4. (London. Greater London Council. Department of Planning and Transportation. Research Memoranda. 185.)

NESS (M.P.) Proposed preliminary tabulations and an outline of the ultimate analysis of the Victoria Line survey. [London], 1969. pp. 4, 2. (London. Greater London Council. Department of Highways and Transportation. Research Memoranda. 81.)

SMITH (J.E.R.) Automatic taxi studies. [London], 1969. pp. 5. (London. Greater London Council. Department of Highways and Transportation. Research Memoranda. 156.)

SMITH (J.E.R.) Central Area trip movements, London Traffic Survey data 1962. [London], 1969. fo. various. (London. Greater London Council. Department of Highways and Transportation. Research Memoranda. 133.)

SMITH (J.E.R.) A procedure for calculating unit travel costs for use in cost benefit studies. [London], 1969. pp. 13. (London. Greater London Council. Department of Highways and Transportation. Research Memoranda. 175.)

SMITH (J.E.R.) Six years on. [London], 1969. pp. 10. (London. Greater London Council. Department of Highways and Transportation. Research Memoranda. 164)

SMYTH (R.B.) Borough transportation studies: preliminary notes. [London], 1969. pp. 9, various. bibliog. (London. Greater London Council. Department of Highways and Transportation. Research Memoranda. 197.)

SPELLER (S.M.) Economic evaluation programs. [London], 1969. pp. 14. (London. Greater London Council. Department of Highways and Transportation. Research Memoranda. 171)

YATES (L.B.) and HOWARD (T.J.) Journey times by car in Central London. [London], 1969. pp. 3. bibliog. (London. Greater London Council. Department of Highways and Transportation. Research Memoranda. 150)

LONDON TRANSPORT EXECUTIVE. Annual report and accounts. a., 1970 [1st]- London.

BAYLISS (DAVID) A guide to strategic transport tests in London. [London], 1970. pp. 9. (London. Greater London Council. Department of Planning and Transportation. Research Memoranda 276.)

BAYLISS (DAVID) The scale of travel demand in London, 1962-1981-1991. [London], 1970. pp. 7. (London. Greater London Council. Department of Planning and Transportation. Research Memoranda. 247.)

BUCHANAN (COLIN) AND PARTNERS. North East London: some implications of the Greater London development plan; a report to the Greater London Council. [London], 1970. pp. 140.

CHAKRABORTI (S.) and others. Test 14 preliminary report. [London], 1970. pp. various. (London. Greater London Council. Department of Planning and Transportation. Research Memoranda. 254.)

CHAKRABORTI (S.) and others. Test 15 preliminary report. [London], 1970. pp. 8. (London. Greater London Council. Department of Planning and Transportation. Research Memoranda. 255.)

CHAKRABORTI (S.) and others. Test 17 preliminary report. [London], 1970. pp. (9). (London. Greater London Council. Department of Planning and Transportation. Research Memoranda. 256.)

CROCKFORD (R.J.) **The effect of students on a public transport trip matrix.** [London], 1970. pp. 5. (London. Greater London Council. Department of Planning and Transportation. Research Memoranda. 261.)

DALLIMORE (DAVID COLIN) Sources of data used in chapter 6 (transport) of the Report of Studies (G[reater] L[ondon] D[evelopment] P[lan]). [London], 1970. pp. various. (London. Greater London Council. Department of Planning and Transportation. Research Memoranda. 231.)

EYLES (DAVID R.) and DALLIMORE (DAVID COLIN) Effects on demand for road space. [London], 1970. pp. 9. (London. [Greater London Council. Department of Planning and Transportation.] Research Memoranda. 232.)

KOSTANOWICZ (H.) Movement in London, chapter 1: sources and comments. [London], 1970. pp. 6. (London. Greater London Council. Department of Planning and Transportation. Research Memoranda. 211.)

LONDON. Greater London Council. The future of London transport: a paper for discussion. [London, 1970.] pp. 52.

LONDON. Greater London Council. Transport in London: a balanced policy. [London, 1970.] pp. 19.

"MOVEMENT in London": proceedings of seminars; by D. Bayliss [and others]. London, 1970. pp. 57. (London. Greater London Council. Department of Planning and Transportation. Research Memoranda. 240)

NESS (M.P.) Victoria Line study: before and after household surveys, August 1968/August 1969: data collection manual. [London], 1970. pp. 42. (London. Greater London Council. Department of Planning and Transportation. Research Memoranda. 216.)

SPILLER (C.J.) The 1991 fixed matrix. [London], 1970. pp. 8. (London. Greater London Council. Department of Planning and Transportation. Research Memoranda. 259.)

SPILLER (C.J.) The production of trip ends for the 1981 and 1991 G[reater] L[ondon] D[evelopment] P[lan] tests. [London], 1970. pp. 25. (London. Greater London Council. Department of Planning and Transportation. Research Memoranda. 236)

- Transit systems - Rates

COMMUNIST PARTY OF GREAT BRITAIN. London District Committee. **More fares please.** [London, 1939?]. pp. 16.

U.K. Transport Tribunal. 1963-64. [Proceedings]... in the matter of the application (1963 No. 2) made by the British Railways Board for an order entitled The London Fares (British Railways) Order 1963 and in the matter of the application (1963 No. 3) made by the London Transport Board for an order entitled The London Fares (London Transport Order 1963; (and Reasons for decision). London, 1963-64. 11 pts.

U.K. Transport Tribunal. 1964. The London Fares (British Railways) Order 1963 (Variation) Order 1964, confirmed by order dated the 25th June 1964. London, [1964]. pp. 4.

U.K. Transport Tribunal. 1964. The London Fares (London Transport) Order 1964 (Variation) Order 1964, confirmed by order dated the 25th June 1964. London, [1964]. pp. 4.

U.K. Transport Tribunal. 1968. [Proceedings] in the matter of the application (1968 No.1) made by the London Transport Board for an order entitled the London Fares (London Transport) Order 1968; (with Reasons for decision and The London Fares (London Transport Order) 1968. London, 1968. 6 pts. (in 1 vol.) 33½cm.

U.K. Transport Tribunal. 1968. [Proceedings] in the matter of the application (1968 No.2) made by the British Railways Board for an order entitled the London Fares (British Railways) Order 1968; with Reasons for decision and The London Fares (British Railways) Order 1968. London, 1968. 7 pts. (in 1 vol.) 33½cm.

- Water-supply

LONDON. Metropolitan Board of Works. Streets Committee. Extract from report of the...Committee, submitting copy of letter to the Southwark and Vauxhall Water Company, urging the laying down of water mains in the subway under Southwark Street, instead of breaking up the thoroughfare for that purpose; together with the reply of the company thereto. [London], 1865. pp. 7.

KAY-SHUTTLEWORTH (UGHTRED JAMES) 1st Baron Shuttleworth. The water supply of London: a speech delivered in the House of Commons, May 23, 1871;...[and] A speech delivered in the same debate; by Lyon Playfair. London, Ridgway, 1871. pp. 33. 21½cm.

ST. MARYLEBONE. Vestry. The Metropolis Water Supply Bill: report of the proceedings at a meeting...held on Thursday, the 16th of March 1871. [London, 1871] pp. 8.

LONDON. London County Council. Special Committee on Water Supply and Markets. London Water Supply Enquiry. Engineer's reports dated 8th and 29th October, 1890. London, 1890. pp. 26.

LONDON. London County Council. Special Committee on Water Supply and Markets. London Water Supply Enquiry. Engineer's report on the London water supply from the Thames and Lea, dated 1st September, 1891. London, 1891. pp. 52.

LONDON - Water supply (Cont'd.)

LONDON. London County Council. Special Committee on Water Supply and Markets. London Water Supply Enquiry. London water supply: report by the Chief Engineer on the steps necessary for completing the inquiry on the water question, etc. London, 1891. pp. 8.

LONDON. London County Council. Special Committee on Water Supply and Markets. London Water Supply Enquiry. Preliminary report on the possibility of obtaining a supply of water for London within the Thames Basin; by W. Whitaker and A. H. Green. London, [1891]. pp. 20.

LONDON. London County Council. Summary of evidence presented to the Royal Commission on Metropolitan water supply; prepared by A. Bassett Hopkins, chairman of the Special Water Committee of the...Council. London, 1892-93. pp. 173.

LONDON. London County Council. The position of the London water companies considered from a parliamentary and legal point of view: a report...; by Henry Lawrence Cripps. London, [1892]. pp. 134,151.

LONDON. London Liberal and Radical Union. Four speeches on the present position of the London water supply delivered by W.H. Dickinson [and others] at a meeting held by the...Union...on April 23rd, 1896, etc. London, 1896. pp. 31.

DICKINSON (WILLOUGHBY HYETT) 1st Baron Dickinson. Water for London: speech... on moving the reception of the Committee's report recommending the promotion of bills in Parliament dealing with the purchase of Metropolitan Water Companies, etc. London, the Union, 1899. pp. 16. (London. London Reform Union. Pamphlets. No. 78)

LONDON. Metropolitan Water Board. The Metropolitan Water Board. London, [1903]. pp. 40,9.

LONDON. Metropolitan Water Board. Standing orders of the Board and references to committees; revised to 24th November, 1905. London, 1905. pp. 58.

LONDON, DECLARATION OF, 1909

BRISTOL. Incorporated Chamber of Commerce and Shipping. Special General Meeting. The Declaration of London: Bristol protests against ratification; great commercial gathering; Mr. T. Gibson Bowles' powerful indictment. Bristol, Times and Mirror, [1911]. pp. 30. 21½cm.

DEVLIN (PATRICK ARTHUR) Baron Devlin. The House of Lords and the Naval Prize Bill, 1911. Cambridge, C.U.P., 1968. pp. 30. 18½cm. (Cambridge. University. Rede Lectures. 1968)

LONDON AND NORTH WESTERN RAILWAY

NOCK (OSWALD STEVENS) North Western: saga of the premier line of Great Britain, 1846-1922. London, Allan, [1968]. pp. xii, 311. 21cm.

LONDON CORRESPONDING SOCIETY

LONDON. London Corresponding Society. A seasonable caution... to their fellow citizens, and the public in general. London, 1794. single sheet.

LONDON MIDLAND AND SCOTTISH RAILWAY

ELLIS (CUTHBERT HAMILTON) London Midland and Scottish: a railway in retrospect. London, 1970. pp. 224.

LONDON NAVAL TREATY, 1930

HARADA (KUMAO) Baron. Saionji-Harada memoirs: fragile victory; Prince Saionji and the 1930 London Treaty issue from the memoirs of Baron Harada Kumao; translated with an introduction and annotations by Thomas Francis Mayer-Oakes. Detroit, Wayne State U.P., 1968. pp. 330. 25½cm.

LONDON UNIVERSITY

LONDON. University. Library. Incunabula in the libraries of the University of London: a handlist. London, the University, 1963 [or rather 1964]. pp. iii, 40. 25cm.

STANDING CONFERENCE OF LIBRARIANS OF LIBRARIES OF THE UNIVERSITY OF LONDON. Guide to the admission of academic staff, students and other visitors to libraries within the University of London. [London], 1968. pp. 19. 21½cm.

BELLOT (HUGH HALE LEIGH) The University of London: a history. [London?], 1969. pp. 54.

HANSFORD-MILLER (F.H.) The visitorial jurisdiction of London University. London, [1970]. pp. 20.

- Birkbeck College

LONDON. University. Birkbeck College. Academic Advisory Committee. Report...on Birkbeck College; with an introduction by Eric H. Warmington. London, 1967. pp. xii, 87. bibliog.

HODGKIN (DOROTHY) Birkbeck, science and history. [London, 1969]. pp. 16. (London. University. Birkbeck College. Bernal Lectures. 1969)

LONDON. University. Birkbeck College. Statement of development policy, 1972-77. [London], 1970. pp. 33.

- London School of Economics and Political Science

LONDON. University of London. London School of Economics and Political Science. Department of Social Science and Administration. Link; [jubilee 1912-1962]. London, 1962. pp. 34.

LONDON. University. London School of Economics and Political Science. Carr-Saunders Hall. London, 1968. pp. 6.

KIDD (HARRY) The trouble at L.S.E., 1966-67. London, O.U.P., 1969. pp. (vii), 199. 21½cm.

WEST (JILL) "Thugs and wreckers": the case of the L.S.E. London, May Day Manifesto, [1969]. pp. 24. 30cm.

LONDON. University. London School of Economics and Political Science. Undergraduate geography at the London School of Economics, 1970-71. London, [1970]. pp. 26.

STUDENTS in conflict: L.S.E. in 1967; by Tessa Blackstone [and others]. London, [1970]. pp. 320. bibliog. (London. University. London School of Economics and Political Science. Research Monographs. 5)

- School of Oriental and African Studies

FEUCHTWANG (STEPHAN D.R.) and others. The struggle for democracy at SOAS. [London], 1969. pp. 11.

- University College

LONDON. University. University College. Memorandum by the chairman of the Committee of Management on the financial condition of the college. [London, 1897?]. pp. 19.

LONDON. University. University College. Report of the Committee of Management on the financial condition of the college. [London, 1898]. pp. 15.

- University College - Bartlett School of Architecture

ABERCROMBIE (MINNIE LOUIE JOHNSON) and others. Selection and academic performance of students in a university school of architecture. London, 1969. pp. 141. bibliog. (Society for Research into Higher Education. Research into Higher Education Monographs)

LONDONDERRY, Marquises of
See VANE-TEMPEST-STEWART FAMILY

LONDONDERRY

- Bridges

IRELAND, NORTHERN. H.C. 1962. Second report by the Joint Select Committee on Unopposed Bills: being a report upon the Londonderry Corporation Bill; together with the proceedings of the Committee and minutes of evidence. Belfast, 1969. pp. 114.

- Cemeteries

IRELAND, NORTHERN. H.C. 1962. Second report by the Joint Select Committee on Unopposed Bills: being a report upon the Londonderry Corporation Bill; together with the proceedings of the Committee and minutes of evidence. Belfast, 1969. pp. 114.

- Civic improvement

MUNCE (JAMES) PARTNERSHIP. Londonderry area plan. [Belfast, imprint, 1968]. pp. (x), 155. bibliog. 30cm.

- Industries

IRELAND, NORTHERN. 1966. Londonderry as a location for new industry. (Economic Council) Belfast, [1966]. pp. 20. 24½cm.

LONG (HUEY PIERCE)

WILLIAMS (THOMAS HARRY) Huey P. Long. Oxford, Clarendon Press, 1967. pp. 23. 21½cm. (Oxford. University. Inaugural Lectures. 1967)

GRAHAM (HUGH DAVIS) ed. Huey Long. Englewood Cliffs, N.J., [1970]. pp. 184. bibliog.

WILLIAMS (THOMAS HARRY) Huey Long. London, 1970. pp. 884. bibliog.

LONG ISLAND (NEW YORK)

- Social conditions

SOBIN (DENNIS P.) Dynamics of community change: the case of Long Island's declining "Gold Coast" Port Washington, Friedman, 1968. pp. xv, 205. bibliog. 23cm.

LONG MARCH, 1934-1935

SMEDLEY (AGNES) The great road: the life and times of Chu Teh. New York, Monthly Review P., 1956. pp. xviii, 461. 21cm.

SIKIRIANSKAIA (LIIA ABRAMOVNA) Великий поход китайской Красной армии, 1984-1936 гг. Москва, ИВЛ, 1962. pp. 92. 20cm.

WILSON (RICHARD GARRATT) The Long March, 1935: the epic of Chinese Communism's survival. London, 1971. pp. 331. bibliog.

LONGJUMEAU

NELIDOV (NIKOLAI VASIL'EVICH) and BARCHUGOV (PAVEL VASIL'EVICH) Leninskaia shkola v Lonzhiumo. Moskva, 1967. pp. 78.

LOOMS

INDIA. Powerloom Enquiry Committee. 1964. Report of the Powerloom Enquiry Committee. New Delhi, Ministry of Industry, 1964. pp. 208. 24cm.

LORRAINE

- Economic conditions

FRANCE. Direction de la Documentation. La Documentation Française. Notes et Études Documentaires. No. 2,955. L'économie de la Lorraine; [by] Pierre Prefol. Paris, 1963. pp. 51. bibliog. 30½cm. Map in end-pocket.

- Foreign population

NICOLAY (THÉODORE) Quelques aspects démographiques et sociologiques des immigrations d'étrangers dans le bassin houiller de Lorraine. Nancy, 1967. fo. 184.

- History - Sources

FRANCE. Direction des Archives de France. 1967. Lorraine, marche de France: deuxième centenaire du rattachement des duchés de Lorraine et de Bar à la France, 1766-1966. Paris, 1967. pp. 139.

LORRAINE (Cont'd.)

- Industries

BUZELAY (ALAIN) Crise de l'industrie textile vosgienne et politique économique. Nancy, Centre d'Études pour la Région Économique de Lorraine, 1967. pp. vi, 103. bibliog. (Études)

- Population

FABERT (YVON) Croissance démographique et développement de la région lorraine, (1861-1985); [prepared for the] Institut de Démographie de l'Université de Nancy [and the] Comité Régional du Bassin Lorrain. [Nancy], 1965. pp. 12, fo. (45). 27½cm.

LOS ANGELES

- Civic improvement

BARTLETT (DANA W.) The better city: a sociological study of a modern city. Los Angeles, Neuner, 1907. pp. 248. 19cm.

LOS ANGELES. Department of City Planning. Background information for the Los Angeles comprehensive plan 2. Analysis of the land use characteristics. Los Angeles, 1968. pp. 36. (Research Monographs)

- Economic conditions

LOREN (EUGENE L.) Economic background: the Los Angeles riot study. Los Angeles, 1967. pp. 48. (California University. Institute of Government and Public Affairs. [Publications]. MR-86)

- History

FOGELSON (ROBERT M.) The fragmented metropolis: Los Angeles, 1850-1930. Cambridge, Harvard U.P., 1967. pp. xviii, 362. bibliog. 24cm. (Massachusetts Institute of Technology, and Harvard University Joint Center for Urban Studies. Publications)

- Poor

MARSHALL (DALE ROGERS) The politics of participation in poverty: a case study of the board of the Economic and Youth Opportunities Agency of Greater Los Angeles. Berkeley, [Calif.], 1971. pp. 210. bibliog.

- Race question

BULLOCK (PAUL) ed. Watts: the aftermath; an inside view of the ghetto, by the people of Watts; edited, with an introduction, notes, and a concluding chapter. New York, [1969]. pp. 285.

- Riots

CALIFORNIA. Governor's Commission on the Los Angeles Riots. 1965. Transcripts, depositions consultants' reports, and selected documents. Los Angeles, 1965. 18 vols. Microfilm: 5 reels.

LOREN (EUGENE L.) Economic background: the Los Angeles riot study. Los Angeles, 1967. pp. 48. (California University. Institute of Government and Public Affairs. [Publications]. MR-86)

MORRIS (RICHARD THACKER) and JEFFRIES (VINCENT) The white reaction study. Los Angeles, 1967. pp. 71,43. (California University. Institute of Government and Public Affairs. [Publications]. MR-84)

- Transit systems

CALIFORNIA. Division of Highways. 1963. Los Angeles regional transportation study: vol. 1: base year report 1960. [Los Angeles], 1963. pp. xii, 61. 30cm.

CALIFORNIA. Division of Highways. 1967. Los Angeles regional transportation study: [vol. 2]: 1980 progress report. Los Angeles, [1967?] pp. (viii), 46. 21½cm. x 28cm.

LOT-ET-GARONNE (DEPARTMENT)

- Economic conditions

FRANCE. Institut National de la Statistique et des Études Économiques. Direction Régionale de Bordeaux. 1960. Quelques données caracteristiques sur l'économie du Lot-et-Garonne. Bordeaux. 1960. fo. 20. 27cm.

BALLAN (J.J.) and others. Les comptes économiques du département du Lot-et-Garonne. Paris, Gauthier-Villars, 1967. pp. 276. 27½cm. (Bordeaux. Université. Faculté de Droit. Institut d'Économie Régionale du Sud-Ouest. Techniques Économiques Modernes. No. 7)

LOTTERIES

- New Zealand

SALMOND (JAMES DAVID) The cult of the golden Kiwi: a plea for concern for our young New Zealanders, Pakehas and Maoris. Christchurch, [N.Z.], Presbyterian Bookroom, 1962. pp. 16. 21½cm.

NEW ZEALAND. Lottery Profits Board of Control. Report. a., 1966/7- Wellington.

LOUGHBOROUGH

- Civic improvement

CLARK (DAVID M.) ed. People and priorities in urban renewal: Wellington Street, Loughborough. Loughborough, 1970. pp. 56. (College of Education, Loughborough. Loughborough Occasional Papers in Social Studies. No. 2)

LOUGHBOROUGH UNIVERSITY OF TECHNOLOGY

LOUGHBOROUGH UNIVERSITY OF TECHNOLOGY. A report to industry. Loughborough, [1967]. pp. 63.

LOUIS IX, King of France, Saint

LABERGE (MARGARET WADE) Saint Louis: the life of Louis IX of France. London, Eyre & Spottiswoode, 1968. pp. 303. bibliog.

LOUIS XIV, King of France

GOUBERT (PIERRE) Louis XIV et vingt millions de Français. Paris, Fayard, [1966]. pp. 253. bibliog. 21½cm. (L'Histoire sans Frontières)

LOSSKY (A.) The nature of political power according to Louis XIV. in Krieger (Leonard) and Stern (Fritz Richard) eds. The responsibility of power. Garden City, 1967.

THOMSON (MARK ALMÉRAS) and others. William III and Louis XIV: essays, 1680-1720, by and for Mark A. Thomson; edited by Ragnhild Hatton and J.S. Bromley; with an introductory memoir by Sir George Clark. Liverpool, Liverpool U.P., 1968. pp. xi, 332. 23½cm.

WOLF (JOHN BAPTIST) Louis XIV. London, Gollancz, 1968. pp. xix, 678. 23cm.

LOUIS XIV and the craft of kingship: [based on a conference held at Ohio State University, 1964]; edited by John C. Rule. [Columbus, Ohio, 1969]. pp. 478. bibliog.

LOUIS XV, King of France

EGRET (JEAN) Louis XV et l'opposition parlementaire, 1715-1774. Paris, [1970]. pp. 246. bibliog.

LOUISIANA

- Economic conditions

BEARD (THOMAS R.) ed. The Louisiana economy. Baton Rouge, [1969]. pp. 232.

- History

HAIR (WILLIAM IVY) Bourbonism and agrarian protest: Louisiana politics, 1877-1900. Baton Rouge, [1969]. pp. 305. bibliog.

- Politics and government

HAIR (WILLIAM IVY) Bourbonism and agrarian protest: Louisiana politics, 1877-1900. Baton Rouge, [1969]. pp. 305. bibliog.

LOUISVILLE

- Commerce

CURRY (LEONARD P.) Rail routes south: Louisville's fight for the southern market, 1865-1872. Lexington, 1969. pp. 150. bibliog.

LOURDES

McCABE (JOSEPH) The Lourdes miracles: a candid inquiry. London, 1925. pp. 71.

LOURMARIN

- History

SHEPPARD (THOMAS F.) Lourmarin in the eighteenth century: a study of a French village. Baltimore, [1971]. pp. 248. bibliog. (Johns Hopkins University. Studies in Historical and Political Science. Series 88. [No.] 2)

LOUTH TOWNSHIP

- Description

FACTORS affecting land use in a selected area in Southern Ontario: a land use and geographic survey of Louth Township in Lincoln County; by the Ontario Department of Agriculture [and others]...; compiled by R.M. Irving. [Toronto] 1957. pp. x, 145. 27½cm.

LOUVAIN UNIVERSITY

ESSEN (LÉON VAN DER) L'Université de Louvain: son origine son histoire, son organisation: 1425-1953. Bruxelles, [imprint, 1953]. pp. 52. 22½cm.

LOUVAIN. Université. Association du Corps Académique et du Personnel Scientifique. L'opinion publique belge et l'Université de Louvain: enquête sociologique sur les problèmes de l'Université et divers problèmes connexes. [Louvain, Non Evertetur], 1967. pp. 81. 24cm.

- Students

LANOO (I. DE) De Leuvense studentenbevolking; evolutie en vooruitzichten 1947-1975. [Louvain], Université, Institut de Recherches Économiques, Sociales et Politiques, Centre de Recherches Sociologiques, 1964. pp. 102. bibliog. 24½cm. (Politica, Speciaal Nummer, 1964)

STUDENTEN over Leuven;(...samengesteld door de Universitaire Werkgemeenschap met medewerking van Robert Beutels [and others]. [Louvain, 1967]. pp. 174.

LANOO (IVAN DE) Stratifikatieproblemen en demokratisering van het universitair onderwijs: een onderzoek naar de demokratiseringstondensen bij de Leuvense studenten 1934/1966. Antwerpen, 1969. pp. 431. bibliog. With English summary.

LOVE

BEDBOROUGH (GEORGE) Love and happiness: letters to Tolstoy;...written in 1897 and now first published. Letchworth, 1917. pp. 35.

LOVE (THEOLOGY)

CHRISTS banner of love: set up to call all Christians to serve in love and unity under it, but especially directed to the saints of both kingdoms. London, Wright, 1648. pp. 6. 18½cm. Wing C 3966.

WOOD (WILLIAM) F.L.S., Dissenting Minister. The Christian duty of cultivating a spirit of universal benevolence amidst the present unhappy national hostilities; a sermon preached July 4, 1781, at Bradford in Yorkshire, before an assembly of dissenting ministers and published at their request. Leeds, Wright, 1781. pp. 32.

BEDBOROUGH (GEORGE) Love and happiness: letters to Tolstoy;...written in 1897 and now first published. Letchworth, 1917. pp. 35.

LOVE (THEOLOGY) (Cont'd.)

TOLSTOI (LEV NIKOLAEVICH) Count. The law of love and the law of violence; translated by Mary Koutouzow Tolstoy, with a forword by Baroness Budberg. London, [1970].

LOW (SETH)

NEW YORK (CITY). Citizens' Union. Seth Low for mayor: his life and public record. New York, [1897?]. pp. 16.

LOWER AUSTRIA

- Economic conditions

CREDITANSTALT-BANKVEREIN. Volkswirtschaftliche Abteilung. Sonderhefte. 1. Die österreichi schen Bundesländer: Niederösterreich, 1955-1964. [Vienna], the Bankverein, 1965. pp. 73. bibliog. 29½cm.

LOWER SAXONY

- Census

LOWER SAXONY. Amt für Landesplanung und Statistik. Veröffentlichungen. Reihe F. Band 1. Heft 2. Amtliches Gemeindeverzeichnis für Niedersachsen auf Grund der Volkszählung 1950: Gebietsstand: 1. Oktober 1951. Hannover, 1952. pp. 164.

- Economic conditions

SCHULENBURG (GUENZEL VON DER) Graf. Die Wirtschafts- und Sozialstruktur ländlicher Gemeinden in der Umgebung des Volkswagenwerkes. Bonn, Forschungsgesellschaft für Agrarpolitik und Agrarsoziologie, 1964. pp. vii, 194. bibliog. 29cm.

STAVENHAGEN (GERHARD) and SCHMIDT (KARL HEINZ) Der selbstständige gewerbliche Mittelstand in Niedersachsen. Göttingen, 1967. pp. 250. bibliog.

TREUE (WILHELM) and SCHRADER (KAETHE) Die Demontagepolitik der Westmächte nach dem zweiten Weltkrieg: unter besonderer Berücksichtigung ihrer Wirkung auf die Wirtschaft in Niedersachsen. Göttingen, Musterschmidt, 1967. pp. 110. bibliog. 21cm.

- Industries

SCHMIDT (KARL HEINZ) Das Handwerk im Zonenrandgebiet dargestellt am Beispiel Niedersachsens. Göttingen, Schwartz, 1966. pp. 116, iv, 23cm. (Göttingen. Universität. Seminar für Handwerkswesen. Göttinger Handwerkswirtschaftliche Studien. Band 10)

SANDER (ECKART) Verkehrsstruktur und Industriebesatz in den niedersächsischen Seehäfen. Göttingen, 1969. pp. 290. bibliog.

- Politics and government

LOTZ (ERICH WALTER) and GLATZEL (FRANK) Niedersächsische Landschaftsgliederung. 2nd ed. Braunschweig, Amt für Statistik und Wahlen, 1950. pp. 67. 24cm. (Kommunalpolitische Schriften der Stadt Braunschweig. Heft 8)

- Population

HOLSTEIN (WOLFGANG) Untersuchung über die Bevölkerungsstruktur und die Bevölkerungsentwicklung in Niedersachsen. Göttingen, 1961. pp. 136. bibliog.

LOWRY (IRA S.)

WILSON (ALAN GEOFFREY) Generalising the Lowry model. London, 1970. pp. 28. bibliog. (Centre for Environmental Studies. Working Papers. 56)

LOWTHER (JOHN) 1st Viscount Lonsdale

The LIFE and character of John Lord Viscount Lonsdal only two copies printed for the Rev. F. Wrangham. [Hunmanby?, c. 1820]. pp. 23. Privately printed

LOYALTY

HIRSCHMAN (ALBERT O.) Exit, voice and loyalty: responses to decline in firms, organizations and states. Cambridge, Mass., 1970. pp. 162.

LOYALTY OATHS

- Germany

BOETTCHER (REINHARD) Die politische Treupflicht der Beamten und Soldaten und die Grundrechte der Kommunikation. Berlin, [1967]. pp. 179. bibliog.

LOYALTY-SECURITY PROGRAM, 1947-

HARPER (ALAN D.) The politics of loyalty: the White House and the communist issue, 1946-1952. Westport, Conn., [1969]. pp. 318. bibliog.

STERN (PHILIP M.) The Oppenheimer case: security on trial;... with the collaboration of Harold P. Green. London, 1971. pp. 591. bibliog.

LOZIS

GLUCKMAN (HERMAN MAX) The judicial process among the Barotse of Northern Rhodesia. [Manchester], Manchester University Press, 1955. pp. xxiii, 386. bibliog. 21½cm.

PETERS (DAVID URLIN) Land usage in Barotseland ... edited by N.W. Smyth. Lusaka, the Institute, 1966. pp. xiv, 60, fo. (29). bibliog. 24½cm. (Rhodes-Livingstone Institute. Communications. No. 19)

CAPLAN (GERALD L.) The elites of Barotseland, 1878-1969: a political history of Zambia's Western Province. London, [1970]. pp. 270. bibliog.

LUANDA DE SAO PAULO

- History

A LITTLE true forraine newes better than a great deale of domestick spurious false newes, etc. London, Butter, 1641. pp. 1-8. 17½cm. Wing L 2553.

LUAPULA VALLEY

- Social conditions

CUNNISON (IAN GEORGE) Kinship and local organisation on the Luapula: a preliminary account of some aspects of Luapula social organization. Livingstone, Rhodes-Livingstone Institute, 1950, repr. 1965. fo. (iii), 32. 32½cm. (Communications. No. 5)

LUBAS

INSTITUTIONS traditionnelles et forces politiques au Congo: le cas de la société luba du Kasai. Bruxelles, 1970. fo. 37. (Centre de Recherche et d'Information Socio-Politiques. Etudes Africaines du C.R.I.S.P. [Series] 1)

LUBIENIECKI (STANISŁAW)

JORDT-JØRGENSEN (K. E.) Stanisław Lubieniecki: zum Weg des Unitarismus von Ost nach West im 17.Jahrhundert. Göttingen, [1968]. pp. 188. bibliog.

LUBIN (DAVID)

FOOD AND AGRICULTURE ORGANIZATION. 1969. David Lubin (1849-1919): an appreciation. [Rome, 1969.] pp. 15. bibliog.

LUBKE (HEINRICH)
See LUEBKE (HEINRICH)

LUBLIN

- History

MENCEL (TADEUSZ) ed. Powstanie styczniowe na Lubelszczyźnie: pamiętniki. Lublin, Wydawnictwo Lubelskie, 1966. pp. 243. 23cm.

LUBLIN (PROVINCE)

- Industries

WOŁCZEW (WSIEWOŁOD) Przemysł lubelszczyzny w okresie władzy Ludowej. Lublin, 1969. pp. 245. bibliog.

- Rural conditions

TUROWSKI (JAN) and BORNUS (ALEKSY) Drogi modernizacji wsi: przenikanie innowacji do rolnictwa i wsi województwa Lubelskiego. Warszawa, 1970. pp. 306. With Russian and English summaries.

LUBSKO

WĄSICKI (JAN) ed. Pierwsze lata Ziemi Lubuskiej w Polsce Ludowej: materiały sesji naukowej poświęconej XX-leciu wyzwolenia Ziemi Lubuskiej. Poznań, Wydawnictwo Poznańskie, 1967. pp. 209. 24cm.

LUCAS (CHARLES) M. P.

A CRITICAL review of the liberties of British subjects; with a comparative view of the proceedings of the H-e of C-s of I-d, against an unfortunate exile [Charles Lucas] of that country...; by a gentleman of the Middle-Temple. 2nd ed. London, printed for R. Watkins, 1750. pp. 119.

LUCAS (Sir CHARLES) Royalist

LUCAS (Sir CHARLES) Royalist. Sir Charles Lucas his last speech at the place of execution, where hee was shot to death. London, Smithurst, 1648. pp.6. 17½cm. Wing L 3390.

LUCCA (CITY)

- Social history

SARDI (CESARE) Vita lucchese nel Settecento; [originally published in 1905]. Lucca, [1968]. pp. 139.

LUCCA (PROVINCE)

- Politics and government

LUCCA (PROVINCE) La provincia di Lucca, 1956-1960. Lucca, [1960]. pp. 146. 29cm.

LUCE (HENRY ROBINSON)

KOBLER (JOHN) Luce: his time, life, and fortune. London, Macdonald, 1968. pp. vii, 296. bibliog. 21½cm.

LUCERNE (CITY)

- Economic conditions

KUEHN (ALFRED ROLF) Der Finanzhaushalt der Stadt Luzern von 1953-1965 unter besonderer Berücksichtigung der wirtschaftlichen und demographischen Entwicklung. Zürich, Kolb, 1967. pp. 195. bibliog. 24cm.

LUDDITES

UNITED KINGDOM. Assizes (Yorkshire, held at York). Proceedings under the Special Commission at York, before Baron Thompson and Mr. Justice Le Blanc, which commenced on Saturday the second of January, 1813, and closed on Tuesday the twelfth of the same month, for the trial of offences connected with the late disturbances in the West-Riding of this county. Leeds, Baines, 1813. pp. 71.

PEEL (FRANK) The risings of the Luddites, Chartists and Plug-drawers. 4th ed. London, Cass, 1968. pp. xv, 349. 21½cm.

LUDDITES (Cont'd.)

THOMIS (MALCOLM I.) The Luddites: machine-breaking in Regency England. Newton Abbott, 1970. pp. 196. bibliog.

LUDWIGSBURG

- Economic history

SCHIFFERER (OTTO) Die Wirtschafts- und Sozialstruktur der Stadt Ludwigsburg von der Weimarer Republik bis zur Bundesrepublik. [Tübingen?], 1968. pp. various. bibliog.

- Social history

SCHIFFERER (OTTO) Die Wirtschafts- und Sozialstruktur der Stadt Ludwigsburg von der Weimarer Republik bis zur Bundesrepublik. [Tübingen?], 1968. pp. various. bibliog.

LUDWIGSHAFEN

- Industries

KUBE (HELGA) Die Industrieansiedlung in Ludwigshafen am Rhein bis 1892; Chemie und Metallverarbeitung. [Stuttgart, imprint], 1962. pp. 247. bibliog.

LUEBECK

- Commerce - Sweden

WEIBULL (CURT) Lübeck och Skånemarknaden: studier i Lübecks pundtullsböcker och pundtullskvitton 1368-1369 och 1398-1400. Lund, 1922. pp.80. (Fahlbeckska Stiftelse. Skrifter. 2)

- Constitutional history

DAHL (HELMUT P.) Lübeck im Bundesrat 1871-1914: Möglichkeiten und Grenzen einzelstaatlicher Politik im Deutschen Reich. Lübeck, 1969. pp. 168. bibliog. (Lübeck. Archiv. Veröffentlichungen zur Geschichte der Hansestadt Lübeck. Band 23)

KRABBENHOEFT (GUENTER) Verfassungsgeschichte der Hansestadt Lübeck: eine Übersicht. Lübeck, [1969]. pp. 72. bibliog.

- Economic history

ROERIG (FRITZ) Wirtschaftskräfte im Mittelalter: Abhandlungen zur Stadt- und Hansegeschichte; herausgegeben von Paul Kaegbein. 2nd ed. Wien, 1971. pp. 748. bibliog.

- Economic history - Sources

WEIBULL (CURT) Lübeck och Skånemarknaden: studier i Lübecks pundtullsböcker och pundtullskvitton 1368-1369 och 1398-1400. Lund, 1922. pp.80. (Fahlbeckska Stiftelse. Skrifter. 2)

- History

WINTER (DAVID ALEXANDER) Geschichte der jüdischen Gemeinde in Moisling/Lübeck; mit einer Biographie des Verfassers von Hans Chanoch Meyer. Lübeck, 1968. pp. 224. (Lübeck. Archiv. Veröffentlichungen zur Geschichte der Hansestadt Lübeck. Band 20)

- Industries

KREUTZFELDT (BERND) Der Lübecker Industrie-Verein: eine Selbsthilfeeinrichtung lübeckischer Bürger 1889-1914. Lübeck, 1969. pp. 180. bibliog. (Lübeck. Archiv. Veröffentlichungen zur Geschichte der Hansestadt Lübeck. Band 22)

- Politics and government

DAHL (HELMUT P.) Lübeck im Bundesrat 1871-1914: Möglichkeiten und Grenzen einzelstaatlicher Politik im Deutschen Reich. Lübeck, 1969. pp. 168. bibliog. (Lübeck. Archiv. Veröffentlichungen zur Geschichte der Hansestadt Lübeck. Band 23)

LUEBKE (HEINRICH)

HEINRICH Lübke, president of the West German Federal Republic in the service of Bonn neo-colonialism: a documentation. Dresden, Zeit im Bild, [1966]. pp. 80. 21cm.
R(P)

HERMANNS (JOHANNES) Heinrich Lübke. Freudenstadt, Lutzeyer, [1966]. pp. 47. 20cm. (Persönlichkeiten der Gegenwart. Heft 1)

IS that true, Herr Lübke? documents accuse the West German federal president of crimes against humanity and international law. [Dresden, Verlag Zeit im Bild, 1966]. pp. 47. 20cm.

KOPPEL (WOLFGANG) ed. Heinrich Lübke Präsident der Deutschen?: Dokumentation; Textwiedergabe der Lübke-Dokumente. Karlsruhe, Antifaschistische Arbeitsgemeinschaft, [1967]. pp. 134. 29cm.

LUENEBURG

- Economic history

LUNTOWSKI (GUSTAV) Die Industrie- und Handelskammern und die Entwicklung von Industrie, Handel und Verkehr im Regierungsbezirk Lüneburg: Festschrift zum hundertjährigen Bestehen der Industrie- und Handelskammer, etc. Lüneburg, [1966?]. pp. 208. bibliog.

LUGANSK (OBLAST')

- Politics and government

EMCHENKO (GRIGORII IAKOVLEVICH) and others. Так начинались битвы: большевики Луганщины накануне и в период первой русской революции, 1900-1907. вып.1. Харьков, 1966. pp. 148. 21½см. (Луганский Машиностроительный Институт. Кафедка Истории КПСС и Основ Научного Коммунизма. Из Истории Луганской Областной Партийной Организации) R(Coll.)/Russ:J:1485:1/3428t

LUGBARAS

MIDDLETON (JOHN) The study of the Lugbara: expectation and paradox in anthropological research. New York, [1970]. pp. 78.

LUGO DI ROMAGNA

- History

MARTELLI (MINO) Storia del Monte di Pietà in Lugo di Romagna, 1546-1968: un aspetto di vita romagnola in oltre quattro secoli di vicende religiose, politiche, economiche e sociali. Firenze, Olschki, 1969. pp. 456. 24cm. (Archivio Storico Italiano. Biblioteca. 17)

LUISI (PAULINA)

SCARONE (ARTURO) Dra. Paulina Luisi: datos biograficos del libro Uruguayos contemporáneos. Montevideo, 1938. pp. 15.

LUKÁCS (GEORG)

FESTSCHRIFT zum achtzigsten Geburtstag von Georg Lukács; herausgegeben von Frank Benseler. Neuwied, [1965]. pp. 709. bibliog.

VACATELLO (MARZIO) Lukács da Storia e coscienza di classe al guidizio sulla cultura borghese. Firenze, La Nuova Italia, 1968. pp. viii, 157. 21cm. (Maestri e Compagni. Biblioteca di Studi Critici e Morali. 33)

BEYER (WILHELM RAIMUND) Vier Kritiken: Heidegger, Sartre, Adorno, Lukácz [sic]. Köln, [1970]. pp. 232.

PARKINSON (GEORGE HENRY RADCLIFFE) ed. Georg Lukacs: the man, his work and his ideas. London, [1970]. pp. 254. bibliog. (Reading. University. Graduate School of Contemporary European Studies. Studies on Contemporary Europe. 4.)

ŁUKASIEWICZ (JULIUSZ)

ŁUKASIEWICZ (JULIUSZ) Diplomat in Paris, 1936-1939: (papers and memoirs...); edited by Wacław Jedrzejewicz. New York, 1970. pp. 408. bibliog.

LUMBER TRADE

- Germany

TRAENKNER (HUBERT) Grundlagen und Dynamik des sächsischen Holzmarktes; [with] Einleitung: Die Ordnung des deutschen Holzmarktes; von Kurt Mantel). Neudamm, Neumann, 1939. pp. xxxix, 158. bibliog. 22cm. (Dresden. Technische Hochschule. Institut für Forstpolitik. Mitteilungen. Nr. 8)

- United States

HOWARD (JOHN C.) The negro in the lumber industry. Philadelphia, [1970]. pp. 97. (Pennsylvania University. Wharton School of Finance and Commerce. Industrial Research Unit. Racial Policies of American Industry. Reports. No. 19.)

LUMBERING

- Canada

HAZENBERG (G.) Wages in logging and forest operations in New Brunswick. Fredericton, Department of Labour, 1963. pp. iv, 108. 28cm.

CANADA. 1966. Manpower implications of prospective technological changes in the Eastern Canadian pulpwood logging industry; by Duncan R. Campbell and Edward B. Power. (Department of Manpower and Immigration Program Development Service Research Monographs. No. 1) Ottawa, 1966. pp. xii, 154. bibliog. 23cm.

- New Zealand

FORESTRY DEVELOPMENT CONFERENCE, WELLINGTON, 1969. Production Forestry Working Party. Logging and Transport Sub-Committee. Report on logging and transport for...[the] Working Party, etc. [Wellington, Government Printer, 1969.] pp. 21.

LUMBERMEN

- Canada - New Brunswick

NEW BRUNSWICK. Department of Labour. Studies. No.3. Some aspects of the manpower problem in New Brunswick woodlands. Fredericton, 1967. pp. ii, 53. bibliog. 28½cm.

- Russia

BRONINA (ALINA BORISOVNA) and CHUBAIS (BORIS MAREEVICH) Trudovye prava rabotnikov lesnoi promyshlennosti: spravochnoe posobie. Moskva, 1969. pp. 142.

- United States

UNITED STATES. 1965. Labor-management relations in the lumber industry in the West; [by] John L. Dana. (Bureau of Labor Statistics Regional Reports. No. 7) San Francisco, 1965. pp. 14. 27cm.

LUMPA CHURCH

ZAMBIA. 1965. Report of the commission of inquiry into the former Lumpa Church. Lusaka, 1965. pp. 36. 25½cm.

LUMUMBA (PATRICE)

OLISAH (OKENWA) The life story and death of Mr. Lumumba. Onitsha, [1961?]. pp. 56. 20½cm.

SKURNIK (W.A.E.) ed. African political thought: Lumumba, Nkrumah and Toure; [by] Réne Lemarchand [and others]. Denver, [1968]. pp. 147. (Denver. University. Social Science Foundation and Graduate School of International Studies. Monograph Series in World Affairs. vol. 5. nos. 3 and 4)

McKOWN (ROBIN) Lumumba: a biography. Garden City, N.Y., 1969. pp. 202. bibliog.

LUNACHARSKII (ANATOLII VASIL'EVICH)

ELKIN (ANATOLII SERGEEVICH) Lunacharskii. Moskva, 1967. pp. 303. bibliog.

LUNACHARSKII (ANATOLII VASIL'EVICH) Воспоминания и впечатления; (составление сборника, предисловие и примечания Н. А. Трифонова). Москва, 1968. pp. 376.

TRIFONOV (N.A.) А.В. Луначарский и М. Горький. in Muratova (К.D.) М. Горький и его современники. Ленинград, 1968.

FITZPATRICK (SHEILA) The commissariat of enlightenment: Soviet organization of education and the arts under Lunacharsky, October 1917-1921. Cambridge, 1970. pp. 380. bibliog. (National Association for Soviet and East European Studies. Soviet and East European Studies)

LUNACHARSKII (ANATOLII VASIL'EVICH) Neizdannye materialy. Moskva, 1970. pp. 671. (Akademiia Nauk SSSR. Institut Mirovoi Literatury. Literaturnoe Nasledstvo. t.82)

ZORINA (N.G.) V.I. Lenin i A.V. Lunacharskii. in V.I. Lenin i problemy pechati. Leningrad, 1970.

LUNDAS

CHIWALE (JACQUES CHILEYA) Royal praises and praise names of the Lunda Kazembe of Northern Rhodesia: their meaning and historical background. Lusaka, the Institute, 1962. pp. ii, 70. bibliog. 25cm. (Rhodes-Livingstone Institute. Communications. No.25)

LUNDBERG (ERIK)

ON incomes policy; papers and proceedings from a conference in honour of Erik Lundberg, [held by] the Industrial Council for Social and Economic Studies. [Stockholm, 1969]. pp. 275.

LUNGS

- Cancer

BUCK (S.F.) and BROWN (D.A.) Mortality from lung cancer and bronchitis in relation to smoke and sulphur dioxide concentration, population density, and social index. London, Tobacco Research Council, 1964. pp. 29. 33cm. (Research Papers. No. 7)

WICKEN (ALAN JOHN) and BUCK (S.F.) Report on a study of environmental factors associated with lung cancer and bronchitis mortality in areas of North East England. London, Tobacco Research Council, 1964. pp. 33. 33cm. (Research Papers. 8)

WICKEN (ALAN JOHN) Environmental and personal factors in lung cancer and bronchitis mortality in Northern Ireland, 1960-62. London, Tobacco Research Council, 1966. pp. 84. 24cm. (Research Papers. [No.] 9)

- Diseases

JOULES (HORACE) Stop that cough!: a study of preventable bronchitis. London, [1953?]. pp. 12.

- Dust diseases

U.K. 1967. Ministry of Social Security. Pneumoconiosis and allied occupational chest diseases: diagnosis and procedure for claiming industrial injuries benefits. London, 1967. pp. iv, 24. 21½cm.

LUNSFORD (Sir THOMAS)

LUNSFORD (Sir THOMAS) A speech made by Sr. Thomas Lunsford, Colonell, when he was apprehended; with a full relation, where, when, and how, he was taken, etc. London, 1642. pp. (6). 18½cm. Wing L 3488.

A MOST strange letter which was found in the Old-Change the 16 day of Jan. and directed with this mark, +, to the Right Reverend Father in God, Matthew, Lord Bishop of Ely...; also, the attachment of Colonel Lunsford at Windsor...the 19 day of Jan. 1642, etc. London, Greensmith, 1642. pp. (6). 17½cm. Wing M 2923A.

A TERRIBLE plot against London and Westminster discovered: shewing how Colonell Lunsford the Papist that should have bin Lieutenant in the Tower, should in a conspiracy among the Jesuites and other Papists have blowne up the city of London, etc. London, Greensmith, 1642. pp. (5). Wing T 774.

The TWELVE bishops called to the Parliament to answere the manifold articles whereof they were impeached, Ian. 17 [1642]; with the votes of both Houses...concerning the accused bishops; likewise an order from the Parliament in apprehension of Colonel Lunsford, and the Lord Digby, joyned his confederate, etc. London, Hammond, 1642. pp. (5). 17½cm. Wing T 3396.

LUOS (NILOTIC TRIBE)

OGOT (BETHWELL A.) Peoples of East Africa: history of the Southern Luo. vol. 1. Migration and settlement, 1500-1900. Nairobi, East African Publishing House, 1967. pp. 250. bibliog. 21½cm.

- Bibliography

DUPRÉ (CAROLE E.) The Luo of Kenya: an annotated bibliography. Washington, Institute for Cross-Cultural Research, [1968]. pp. ix, 164. 22½cm. (ICR Studies. 3)

LUSAKA

- Civic improvement

COLLINS (JOHN) Architect. Lusaka: the myth of the garden city. [Lusaka], 1969. pp. 32. (Zambia University. Institute for Social Research. Zambian Urban Studies. No. 2)

LUSATIA

- Economic history

SOŁTA (JAN) Die Beuern der Lausitz: eine Untersuchung des Differenzierungsprozesses der Bauernschaft im Kapitalismus. Bautzen, 1968. pp. 269. bibliog. (Deutsche Akademie der Wissenschaften zu Berlin. Institut für Sorbische Volksforschung in Bautzen. Schriftenreihe. 36)

LUSITANIA, THE

HISTORICUS, junior, pseud. The 'Lusitania' case: was Bryan's resignation justified?. New York, Masterson, 1915. pp. 71. 22½cm.

LUTHER (MARTIN)

WARING (LUTHER HESS) The political theories of Martin Luther. Port Washington, 1968. pp. 293. bibliog. First published 1910.

ATKINSON (JAMES) Martin Luther and the birth of protestantism. Harmondsworth, Penguin Books, 1968. pp. 352. bibliog. 18cm. (Pelican Books. A 865)

WIESENMUELLER (HERBERT) Die Wirtschaftsethik Thomas von Aquins, Luthers und Calvins und das deutsche Unternehmertum des Vor- und Frühkapitalismus. [Erlangen-Nürnberg, 1968?]. pp. 340. bibliog.

SCHEIBLE (HEINZ) ed. Das Widerstandsrecht als Problem der deutschen Protestanten, 1523-1546. Gütersloh, [1969]. pp. 100. bibliog.

WINCKLER (LUTZ) Martin Luther als Bürger und Patriot: das Reformationsjubiläum von 1817 und der politische Protestantismus des Wartburgfestes. Lübeck, 1969. pp. 88. bibliog.

LUTHERAN CHURCH

A REVELATION of Mr. Brigtmans [sic] revelation, wherein is shewed, how all that which Mr. Brightman on the revelation, hath fore-told concerning Germany, Scotland, and England, hath beene fulfilled,...in a dialogue betweene a Minister of the Gospell, and a citizen of London, whereby it is manifest, that Mr. Brightman was a true prophet. [London], 1641. pp. 37. 18½cm. Wing R 1190.

- Missions

BERNANDER (GUSTAV) Lutheran wartime assistance to Tanzanian churches, 1940-1945. Lund, Gleerup, [1968]. pp. 170. bibliog. 23½cm. (Studia Missionalia Upsaliensia. 9)

WRIGHT (MARCIA) German missions in Tanganyika, 1891-1941: Lutherans and Moravians in the Southern Highlands. Oxford, 1971. pp. 249. bibliog.

LUTHERAN CHURCH IN BRAZIL

HAMBURG. Archiv der Hansestadt. Bunte Reihe. Heft Verzeichnis der Gemeinden und Register der evangelischen Deutschen in Brasilien. Hamburg, Friederichsen, 1941. pp. 87. 21cm.

LUTHERAN CHURCH IN DANZIG

GUELZOW (GERHARD) Kirchenkampf in Danzig 1934-1945: persönliche Erinnerungen. Leer (Ostfriesl.), [1968]. pp. 46.

LUTHERAN CHURCH IN EASTERN GERMANY

BORGMANN (LUTZ) Zwischen gestern und morgen: evangelische Gemeinden in der Deutschen Demokratischen Republik. Berlin, [1970]. pp. 202.

LUTHERAN CHURCH IN GERMANY

WENTORF (RUDOLF) ed. Trotz der Höllen toben: Dokumente berichten aus dem Leben Paul Schneiders, der zum Prediger von Buchenwald wurde. Berlin, 1967. pp. 272. bibliog.

EVERTZ (ALEXANDER) Die evangelische Kirche und die Revolution von links. Velbert, [1968]. pp. 82.

KIRCHENARCHIVTAG, 1968. Kirche und Staat im 19. und 20. Jahrhundert: Vorträge, Aufsätze, Gutachten. Neustadt an der Aisch, 1968. pp. 284. bibliog. (Arbeitsgemeinschaft für das Archiv- und Bibliothekswesen in der evangelischen Kirche. Veröffentlichungen. 7)

MEIER (KURT) Kirche und Judentum: die Haltung der evangelischen Kirche zur Judenpolitik des Dritten Reiches. Göttingen, 1968. pp. 153. (Evangelische Kirche in Deutschland. Kommission für die Geschichte des Kirchenkampfes. Arbeiten zur Geschichte des Kirchenkampfes. Ergänzungsreihe. Band 7)

PERTIET (MARTIN) Das Ringen um Wesen und Auftrag der Kirche in der nationalsozialistischen Zeit. Göttingen, Vandenhoeck & Ruprecht, 1968. pp. 339. bibliog. 23cm. (Evangelische Kirche in Deutschland. Kommission für die Geschichte des Kirchenkampfes. Arbeiten zur Geschichte des Kirchenkampfes. Band 19)

SCHAEFER (GERHARD) and FISCHER (RICHARD) Pfarrer. eds. Landesbischof D. Wurm und der nationalsozialistische Staat 1940-1945: eine Dokumentation. Stuttgart, [1968]. pp. 507. bibliog. 23cm.

STROHM (THEODOR) Kirche und demokratischer Sozialismus: Studien zur Theorie und Praxis politischer Kommunikation. München, 1968. pp. 203. bibliog.

BAIER (HELMUT) and HENN (ERNST) compilers. Chronologie des bayerischen Kirchenkampfes 1933-1945. Nürnberg, 1969. pp. 284. bibliog. (Verein für Bayerische Kirchengeschichte. Einzelarbeiten aus der Kirchengeschichte Bayerns. Band 47)

BOYENS (ARMIN) Kirchenkampf und Ökumene 1933-1939: Darstellung und Dokumentation. München, [1969]. pp. 486. bibliog.

DEMOKRATISCHE Traditionen im Protestantismus; [by] Joachim Staedtke [and others]. München, [1969]. pp. 107. (Hanns-Seidel-Stiftung. Akademie für Politik und Zeitgeschehen. Schriftenreihe. Heft 2)

KANTZENBACH (FRIEDRICH WILHELM) Geschichte des Protestantismus von 1789-1848. Gütersloh, [1969]. pp. 176. bibliog.

KIRCHE und Nationalsozialismus: zur Geschichte des Kirchenkampfes; Beiträge von Helmut Baier [and others]. München, 1969. pp. 286. bibliog. (Tutzing. Evangelische Akademie. Tutzinger Texte. Sonderbände. 1)

LUTHER (CHRISTIAN) Das kirchliche Notrecht, seine Theorie und seine Anwendung im Kirchenkampf 1933-1937. Göttingen, 1969. pp. 204. bibliog. (Evangelische Kirche in Deutschland. Kommission für die Geschichte des Kirchenkampfes. Arbeiten zur Geschichte des Kirchenkampfes. Band 21)

LUTHERAN CHURCH IN GERMANY (Cont'd.)

MOTSCHMANN (CLAUS) Evangelische Kirche und preussischer Staat in den Anfängen der Weimarer Republik: Möglichkeiten und Grenzen ihrer Zusammenarbeit. Lübeck, 1969. pp. 147. bibliog.

NIEMOELLER (WILHELM) Wort und Tat im Kirchenkampf: Beiträge zur neuesten Kirchengeschichte. München, 1969. pp. 403.

RUEPPEL (ERICH GUENTER) Die Gemeinschaftsbewegung im Dritten Reich: ein Beitrag zur Geschichte des Kirchenkampfes. Göttingen, 1969. pp. 258. bibliog. (Evangelische Kirche in Deutschland. Kommission für die Geschichte des Kirchenkampfes. Arbeiten zur Geschichte des Kirchenkampfes. Band 22)

SPIEGEL-SCHMIDT (FRIEDRICH) Die Kirche und das deutsche Volk: Auseinandersetzung mit der protestantischen Rechten. Berlin, [1969]. pp. 79.

STUDNITZ (HANS GEORG VON) Ist Gott Mitläufer?: die Politisierung der evangelischen Kirche: Analyse und Dokumentation. Stuttgart-Degerloch, [1969]. pp. 307.

WINCKLER (LUTZ) Martin Luther als Bürger und Patriot: das Reformationsjubiläum von 1817 und der politische Protestantismus des Wartburgfestes. Lübeck, 1969. pp. 88. bibliog.

MOEGLICHKEIT und Grenze politischer Wirksamkeit der Kirche: wie konkret sollen kirchliche Denkschriften sein?; [lectures given at a meeting held under the auspices of the Evangelische Akademie Baden in conjunction with the Kanzlei der Evangelischen Kirche in Deutschland]; Herausgeber Wolfgang Bohme und Erwin Wilkens. Stuttgart, [1970]. pp. 89.

LUTHERANS IN THE UNITED STATES

KERSTEN (LAWRENCE K.) The Lutheran ethic: the impact of religion on laymen and clergy. Detroit, 1970. pp. 309.

LUXEMBOURG

- Bio-bibliography

VEKENE (EMIL VAN DER) Die luxemburger Drucker und ihre Drucke bis zum Ende des 18. Jahrhunderts: eine bio-Bibliographie. Wiesbaden, 1968. pp. 571.

- Census

LUXEMBOURG. Census, 1966. Recensement de la population au 31 décembre 1966. Luxembourg, 1968. pp. 189.

LUXEMBOURG. Census, 1971. Recensement de la population au 31 décembre 1970: premiers résultats. Luxembourg, 1971. pp. 16.

- Commercial treaties

SCHMIT (JOSEPH) Les conventions économiques avec l'étranger conclues par le Grand-Duché de Luxembourg. Luxembourg, 1968. pp. 44. (Luxembourg (City). Université Internationale de Sciences Comparées. Etudes Economiques Luxembourgeoises)

- Description and travel

SEVRIN (ROBERT) Géographie de la Belgique, des Pays-Bas et du Luxembourg. Paris, 1969. pp. 126. bibliog.

- Economic conditions

LAMALLE (DESIRE) Le Luxembourg en péril de mort. [Dinant, imprint], 1969. pp. 349.

SEVRIN (ROBERT) Géographie de la Belgique, des Pays-Bas et du Luxembourg. Paris, 1969. pp. 126. bibliog.

KIRSCH (RAYMOND) La croissance de l'économie luxembourgeoise. Luxembourg, 1971. pp. 250. bibliog. (Luxembourg. Service Central de la Statistique et des Etudes Economiques. Cahiers Economiques. No.48)

- Economic history

KIRSCH (RAYMOND) La croissance de l'économie luxembourgeoise. Luxembourg, 1971. pp. 250. bibliog. (Luxembourg. Service Central de la Statistique et des Etudes Economiques. Cahiers Economiques. No.48)

- Economic policy

ORGANISATION FOR ECONOMIC CO-OPERATION AND DEVELOPMENT. Manpower and Social Affairs Committee. 1970. Manpower policy in Luxembourg. Paris, 1970. pp. 149. (Reviews of Manpower and Social Policies. 8)

- Foreign economic relations

LUXEMBOURG. Ministère d'État. Service Information et Presse. 1952. Le Grand-Duché de Luxembourg et la Communauté Européenne du Charbon et de l'Acier: plan Schuman. [Luxembourg], 1952. pp. 130. bibliog.

LUXEMBOURG. Conseil National de l'Énergie Nucléaire. 1957. Le Grand-Duché de Luxembourg et la Communauté Européenne de l'Énergie Atomique. [Luxembourg], 1957. pp. 168. Extrait du Bulletin de Documentation du Service Information et Presse du Gouvernement, no. 11, novembre, 1957.

- History

HERCHEN (ARTHUR) History of the Grand Duchy of Luxembourg; [edited and translated by A.H. Cooper-Prichard]. Luxembourg, Linden, 1950. pp. xvii, 299. 23½cm.

- Industries

LAMALLE (DESIRE) Le Luxembourg en péril de mort. [Dinant, imprint], 1969. pp. 349.

- Politics and government

WEIL (GORDON LEE) The benelux nations: the politics of small-country democracies. New York, [1970]. pp. 260. bibliog.

- Statistics

GERMANY (BUNDESREPUBLIK). Statistisches Bundesamt. Länderkurzberichte: Luxemburg. irreg., 1967 [1st issue]- Wiesbaden.

LUXEMBOURG. 1967. Album de graphiques territoire, climat, population, etc. (Service Central de la Statistique et des Etudes Économiques) Luxembourg, [1967]. pp. v, 33. 30cm.

LUXEMBURG (ROSA)

ADLER (MAX) Helden der sozialen Revolution. Berlin, 1926. pp. 53.

CIOŁKOSZ (ADAM) Róża Luksemburg a rewolucja rosyjska. Paryż, 1961. pp. 259. (Biblioteka "Kultury". tom 62. Dokumenty. 9)

LUXEMBURG (ROSA) Pagine scelte: Sciopero generale, partito e sindacati; con la 3a edizione di "Centralismo o democrazia?: replica a Lenin; (a cura dei gruppi d'Azione Carlo Pisacane). Milano, Azione Comune, [1963]. pp. 103.

NOSKOV (M.A.) Sudebnye presledovaniia Rosy Liuksemburg nakanune pervoi mirovoi imperialisticheskoi voiny. in Mordovskii Gosudarstvennyi Universitet. Uchenye Zapiski. No. 51. Seriia Istoricheskikh Nauk. vyp. 1. Saransk, 1965.

BADIA (GILBERT) Le spartakisme: les dernières années de Rosa Luxemburg et de Karl Liebknecht, 1914-1919. Paris, L'Arche, [1967]. pp. 438. bibliog. 18cm.

HANNOVER-DRUECK (ELISABETH) and HANNOVER (HEINRICH) eds. Der Mord an Rosa Luxemburg und Karl Liebknecht: Dokumentation eines politischen Verbrechens. Frankfurt am Main, Suhrkamp, 1967. pp. 185. 18cm.

ALEKSEEV (G.A.) Русский 1905 год и революционная концепция Р. Люксембург. in Историческая наука и некоторые проблемы современности: статьи и обсуждения. Москва, 1969.

PARTISANS. No. 45. Rosa Luxemburg vivante. Paris, 1969. pp. 141.

NATAF (ANDRE) Le marxisme et son ombre: Rosa Luxembourg. Paris, [1970]. pp. 204.

WILDE (HARRY) Rosa Luxemburg: ich war, ich bin, ich werde sein; eine Biographie mit Auszügen aus Rosa Luxemburgs Reden und Schriften. Wien, [1970]. pp. 264. bibliog.

SCHIEL (ILSE) and MILZ (ERNA) eds. Karl und Rosa: Erinnerungen; zum 100. Geburtstag von Karl Liebknecht und Rosa Luxemburg. Berlin, 1971. pp. 300. bibliog.

TROTSKII (LEV DAVYDOVICH) Martyrs of the Third International; Karl Liebknecht, Rosa Luxemburg. London, [1971]. pp. 15.

LUXURY

PALMIERI (G.) Osservazioni sul lusso;... estratte dalla seconda edizione [1788] della di lui opera. in [Custodi (Pietro) Barone, ed.] Scrittori classici italiani di economia politica. vol. 49. Roma, 1967.

LAVELEYE (EMILE DE) Baron. Le luxe. Verviers, 1887. pp. 135. bibliog.

SOMBART (WERNER) Luxury and capitalism; introduction by Philip Siegelman. Ann Arbor, University of Michigan Press, [1967]. pp. xxxii, 200. bibliog. 21cm.

LUZZATTI (LUIGI)

LUZZATTI (LUIGI) Memorie...; a cura di Elena de Carli [and others]. Milano, 1966 in progress.

L'VOV

- Economic conditions

SOTSIAL'NYE... Социальные проблемы экономической реформы: материалы научной конференции, г.Львов, 21-22 февраля 1967 г. Львов, Каменяр, 1967. pp. 208. 20см.

- Industries

KIS' (IAROSLAV PAVLOVYCH) Промисловість Львова у період феодалізму, XIII-XIX ст. Львів, 1968. pp. 223.

- Social conditions

SOTSIAL'NYE... Социальные проблемы экономической реформы: материалы научной конференции, г.Львов, 21-22 февраля 1967 г. Львов, Каменяр, 1967. pp. 208. 20см.

L'VOV (OBLAST')

- Industries

CHERNYSH (MARIIA ANDRIIVNA) Oblasna partiina orhanizatsiia v borot'bi za industrializatsiiu m. L'vova, 1939-1955. L'vov, 1969. pp. 182.

- Intellectual life

SOTSIALISTYCHNA kul'tura L'vivshchyny: zbirnyk arkhivnykh dokumentiv i materialiv, 1939-1962. L'viv, 1964. pp. 199.

- Social history - Sources

SOTSIALISTYCHNA kul'tura L'vivshchyny: zbirnyk arkhivnykh dokumentiv i materialiv, 1939-1962. L'viv, 1964. pp. 199.

- Statistics

L'VOV (OBLAST') Statystychne Upravlinnia. Народне господарство Львівської області в 1965 році: статистичний збірник. Львів, 1966. pp. 281.

L'VOV UNIVERSITY

LAZARENKO (EVGENII KONSTANTINOVICH) 300 лет Львовского университета. Львов, 1961. unpaged.

LYAUTEY (LOUIS HUBERT GONZALVÉ)

SCHAM (ALAN) Lyautey in Morocco: protectorate administration, 1912-1925. Berkeley, 1970. pp. 272. bibliog.

LYME REGIS

- Siege, 1644

JESOP (WILLIAM) A more exact and full relation of many admirable passages which happened during the whole siege of Lime, etc. [London], Walbanke, 1644. pp. 5. 19cm. Wing J 685A.

LYNCHING

RAPER (ARTHUR FRANKLIN) The tragedy of lynching; [reprint of original edition of 1933]. New York, 1970. pp. 499.

LYNMOUTH

- Floods

DELDERFIELD (ERIC RAYMOND) The Lynmouth flood disaster. 5th ed. Exmouth, E.R.D. Publications, 1969. pp. 170. 18cm.

LYONNAIS

- Social life and customs

GONON (MARGUERITE) La vie quotidienne en Lyonnais d'après les testaments, XIVe-XVIe siècles. Paris, [1969]. pp. 579. (Institut de Linguistique Romane de Lyon. Publications. vol. 25)

LYONS

- History

GREENBERG (LOUIS M.) Sisters of liberty: Marseille, Lyon, Paris and the reaction to a centralized state, 1868-1871. Cambridge, Mass., 1971. pp. 391. bibliog. (Harvard University. Harvard Historical Monographs. 62)

- Orphans and orphan-asylums

FAYARD (ENNAMOND) Histoire administrative de l'oeuvre des enfants trouvés abandonnés et orphelins de Lyon: suivie des noms de recteurs et administrateurs des hospices et hôpitaux depuis la fondation de l'Hospice de la Charité jusqu'en 1859. Paris, 1859. pp. 432.

- Siege, 1793

BITTARD DES PORTES (RENÉ) Contre la terreur: l'insurrection de Lyon en 1793; le siège, l'expédition du Forez; d'après des documents inédits. 3rd ed. Paris, Émile-Paul, 1906. pp. xi, 586. 22½cm.

LYSENKO (TROFIM DENISOVICH)

MEDVEDEV (ZHORES ALEKSANDROVICH) The rise and fall of T.D. Lysenko;...translated by I. Michael Lerner, etc. New York, 1969. pp. 284.

JORAVSKY (DAVID) The Lysenko affair. Cambridge, Mass., 1970. pp. 459. bibliog. (Harvard University. Russian Research Center. Studies. No. 61)

LYTTELTON (OLIVER) 1st Viscount Chandos

LYTTELTON (OLIVER) 1st Viscount Chandos. From peace to war: a study in contrast, 1857-1918. London, Bodley Head, 1968. pp. 208. 21½cm.

M. N. R. A.
See MOVIMIENTO NACIONALISTA REVOLUCIONARIO

MAASTRICHT

- History

WOUTERS (H.H.E.) Grensland en bruggehoofd: historische studies met betrekking tot het Limburgse Maasdal en, meer in het bijzonder, de stad Maastricht. Assen, 1970. pp. 472. bibliog. (Limburg. Sociaal Historisch Centrum. Maaslandse Monografieën. 11) With French and German summaries.

MABINI (APOLINARIO)

REYNO (ADRIANO C.) The political, social, and moral philosophy of Apolinario Mabini. Manila, 1964. pp. 88. bibliogs. (University of San Carlos. San Carlos Publications. Series A. No. 2)

McADAM (JOHN LOUDON)

DEVEREUX (ROY) pseud. [i.e. Margaret Rose Roy PEMBER-DEVEREUX] John Loudon McAdam: chapters in the history of highways. London, O.U.P. 1936. pp. xi, 184. bibliog. 22cm.

MACARTHUR (DOUGLAS)

BROWDER (EARL RUSSELL) The meaning of MacArthur: a letter to a friend. n.p., [1951]. pp. 13.

UNITED STATES. Army Department. Reports of General MacArthur: the campaigns of MacArthur in the Pacific. Washington, 1966 in prog.

VORONTSOV (VLADILEN BORISOVICH) "Kumiry" bez prikras: D. Makartur i dal'nevostochnaia politika SShA. Moskva, 1968. pp. 214. bibliog.

MACAULAY (NEILL)

MACAULAY (NEILL) A rebel in Cuba: an American's memoir. Chicago, 1970. pp. 199.

McCABE (JOSEPH)

McCABE (JOSEPH) Twelve years in a monastery. 3rd ed. London, [1912] repr. 1931. pp. 259.

McCARTHY (EUGENE JOSEPH)

HERZOG (ARTHUR) McCarthy for president. New York, 1969. pp. 309.

McCARTHY (JOSEPH RAYMOND)

WATKINS (ARTHUR V.) Enough rope: the inside story of the censure of Senator Joe McCarthy by his colleagues, etc. Englewood Cliffs, [1969]. pp. 302.

MACCHIAVELLI (NICCOLÒ)

GILBERT (ALLAN H.) Machiavelli's "Prince" and its forerunners: "The Prince" as a typical book de regimine principum. New York, 1938, repr. 1968. pp. 266. bibliog.

MACCHIAVELLI (NICCOLO) (Opere complete; con introduzione di Giuliano Procacci e a cura di Sergio Bertelli). [Milan, 1960 in progress]. bibliogs.

CLOUGH (CECIL H.) Machiavelli researches. Napoli, 1967. pp. 109. (Naples. Istituto Universitario Orientale. Pubblicazioni della Sezione Romanza. Studi. vol. 3)

CRAWFORD (RAYMOND MAXWELL) "Per quale iddio" : Machiavelli's second thoughts. Sydney, 1967. pp. 23. (Australian Humanities Research Council. Annual Lectures. 1966)

GRAY (H. H.) Machiavelli: the art of politics and the paradox of power. in Krieger (Leonard) and Stern (Fritz Richard) eds. The responsibility of power. Garden City, 1967.

KLUXEN (KURT) Politik und menschliche Existenz bei Machiavelli: dargestellt am Begriff der Necessità. Stuttgart, Kohlhammer, [1967]. pp. 146. bibliog. 23cm.

PREZZOLINI (GIUSEPPE) Machiavelli; (translated by Gioconda Savini). London, Hale, 1968. pp. 346. bibliog. 21½cm.

ANGLO (SYDNEY) Machiavelli: a dissection. London, Gollancz, 1969. pp. 300. bibliog. 21½cm.

WHITFIELD (J.H.) Discourses on Machiavelli. Cambridge, 1969. pp. 243.

MACCHIAVELLIANISM (PSYCHOLOGY)

CHRISTIE (RICHARD) and GEIS (FLORENCE L.) Studies in machiavellianism. New York, 1970. pp. 415. bibliog.

GUTERMAN (STANLEY S.) The Machiavellians: a social psychological study of moral character and organizational milieu. Lincoln, Neb., [1970]. pp. 178. bibliog.

McCORMICK (CYRUS HALL)

HUTCHINSON (WILLIAM THOMAS) Cyrus Hall McCormick; [reprint of the edition published 1930-35 by Appleton-Century]. New York, 1968. 2 vols. bibliog.

McCREERY (MICHAEL)

EVANS (A.H.) Once again truth will out. [London David-Goliath Publications, 196-?]. pp. (79). 25cm.

McCULLOCH (JOHN RAMSAY)

O'BRIEN (DENIS PATRICK) J.R. McCulloch: a study in classical economics. London, 1970. pp. 452. bibliog.

MACDONALD (ALEXANDER)

CHALLINOR (RAYMOND) Alexander MacDonald and the miners. London, 1968. pp. 34. (Communist Party of Great Britain. Historians' Group. Our History. No. 48)

MACDONALD (JAMES RAMSAY)

CARLTON (DAVID) MacDonald versus Henderson: the foreign policy of the second Labour government. London, 1970. pp. 239. bibliog.

MACDONALD (MALCOLM JOHN)

MACDONALD (MALCOLM JOHN) People and places: random reminiscences. London, Collins, 1969. pp. 254. 21cm.

MACDONALD (MALCOLM) Thoughts on the human family. London, 1970. pp. 19. (Colchester. University of Essex. Noel Buxton Lectures. 1970)

MACEDONIA
For the federal republic within Yugoslavia see MACEDONIAN REPUBLIC

- Bibliography

ANDONOV-POLJANSKI (HRISTO) ed. Britanska bibliografija za Makedonija; British bibliography on Macedonia. Skopje, 1966. pp. 516. In Macedonian and English.

- History - Sources

ARHIV NA MAKEDONIJA. Dokumenti za Istorijata na Makedonskiot Narod. Turski dokumenti za istorijata na makedonskiot narod; Documents turcs sur l'histoire du peuple macédonien. serija 1. 1607-1699. Skopje, 1963 in progress.

ARHIV NA MAKEDONIJA. Dokumenti za Istorijata na Makedonskiot Narod. Britanski dokumenti za istorijata na makedonskiot narod; pod redakcija na Hristo Andonov-Poljanski; British documents on the history of the Macedonian people, etc. Skopje, 1968 in progress.

ARHIV NA MAKEDONIJA. Dokumenti za Istorijata na Makedonskiot Narod. Francuski dokumenti za istorijata na makedonskiot narod; pod redakcija na Andrija Lainović [and others]; Documents français sur l'histoire du peuple macédonien, etc. Skopje, 1969 in progress.

MACEDONIA (Cont'd.)

- Nationalism

RISTOVSKI (BLAŽE) "Лозарите" во развитокот на македонската национална мисла. Скопје, 1968. pp. 32.

- Politics and government

BALKAN COMMITTEE. Macedonia in the winter of 1907-8. [London, 1908]. pp. (4).

- Population

KONDOV (N. K.) Demographische Notizen über die Landbevölkerung aus dem Gebiet des unteren Strymon in der ersten Hälfte des XIV Jahrhunderts. in Études balkaniques. 2-3. Sofia, 1965.

- Relations (general) with Bulgaria

ČAŠULE (VANGA) БКП и македонското прашање, 1944-1968. Скопје, 1968. pp. 32.

RISTOVSKI (BLAŽE) "Лозарите" во развитокот на македонската национална мисла. Скопје, 1968. pp. 32.

RISTOVSKI (BLAŽE) Македонскиот народ и македонската национална свест. Скопје, 1968. pp. 63.

MACEDONIAN QUESTION

BALKAN COMMITTEE. The Macedonian crisis: the...Committee presents the following summar of the situation in the Near East. [London, 1903?]. pp. 8.

The POPULATION of Macedonia: evidence of the Christian schools: being the statistics of the schools, scholars, and teachers in the Vilayets of Salonika, and Monastir...added to which is a list of the Greeks killed at the instance of the Bulgarian Committees in Macedonia, from 1897 to November, 1904. London, 1905. pp. 46.

ANDONOVIĆ (M. J.) Македонски су Словени Срби: у одбрану оправданих српских права и интереса на Балкану. Београд, Наумовић и Стефановић, 1913. pp. 119. bibliog. 23cm.

STANEV (NIKOLA) Война за освобождението на Македония: исторически, икономически и критичен поглед. София, Стайков, 1914. pp. 176. 19cm.

DERZHAVIN (NIKOLAI SEVAST'IANOVICH) Българско-Сръбските взаимни отношения и Македонския Въпрос; преде...Ракаров. София, 1916. pp. 140.

MAKEDONIIA... Македония: минало и нови борби. София, Печатница Божинови, [1980?]. pp. 290. bibliog. 16½см.

DOOLAARD (A. DEN) pseud. [i.e. Cornelis Johannes George SPOELSTRA] Quatre mois chez les comitadjis: meurtriers patentés. Paris, Bossuet, [1932]. 19cm. pp. 143.

IAVOROV (P. K.) Съчинения...; под редакцията на Владимир Василев. т. 4. Статии върху македонския въпрос. София, 1935. pp. 183.

MARTULKOV (ALEKSO) Моето учество во револуционерните борби на Македонија. Скопје, 1954. pp. 388. (Институт за Националн*а* Историја. Материјали за Македонската Национал-Револуционерна Историја. кн.6)

HRISTOV (ALEKSANDAR T.) КПЈ во решавањето на македонското прашање, 1937-1944. Скопје, Култура, 1962. pp. 104. 19см. (Историско-Популарна Библиотека)

MIHAJLOV (IVAN) Spomeni. [v.]3. Osvoboditelna borba, 1924-1934 g. [Brussels, Macedonian Cultural Fellowship], 1967. pp. 1029.

ČAŠULE (VANGA) БКП и македонското прашање, 1944-1968. Скопје, 1968. pp. 32.

RISTOVSKI (BLAŽE) "Лозарите" во развитокот на македонската национална мисла. Скопје, 1968. pp. 32.

RISTOVSKI (BLAŽE) Македонскиот народ и македонската национална свест. Скопје, 1968. pp. 63.

NIAZI-BEY (AHMED) The Balkans:...an authoritative Turkish testimonial regarding the character of the Macedonian Slavs; (from the memoirs of Niazi-Bey, etc). Indianapolis, 1970. pp. 24. In English and Turkish.

MACEDONIAN REPUBLIC

- Constitution

MACEDONIAN Socialist Republic. Constitution. Устав, etc. in Yugoslavia. Constitution. 1963. Ustav Socijalističke Federativne Republike Jugoslavije sa Ustavima Socijalističkih Republika i Statutima Autonomnih Pokrajina. Beograd, 1963.

- History

HRISTOV (ALEKSANDAR T.) Sozdavanje na makedonskata država. Skopje, 1971. pp. 404.

- Sobranje - Biography

SAVEZNA i republičke skupštine. Beograd, Sedma Sila, 1964. pp. 314. 22cm. (Politička Dokumentacija. 5)

- Statistics

STATISTIČKI GODIŠNIK NA SR MAKEDONIJA; ([pd. by] Republički Zavod za Statistika [Macedonian Republic]). a., 1969- Skopje.

MACEDONIANS

HRON (KARL) Народноста на македонските Словени; редакција и коментари... Христо Андонов-Полјански; Das Volksthum der Slaven Makedoniens; Redaktion und Kommentare... Hristo Andonov-Poljanski. Скопје, 1966. pp. xviii, 66. 24cm. Facsimile of German original of 1890, with Macedonian translation and editorial matter.

RISTOVSKI (BLAŽE) Македонскиот народ и македонската национална свест. Скопје, 1968. pp. 63.

MACEO (ANTONIO)

HERNANDEZ (EUSEBIO) Maceo: dos conferencias historicas. La Habana, 1968. pp. 170.

MACEO GRAJALES (ANTONIO)
See MACEO (ANTONIO)

MACERATA (PROVINCE)

- Economic conditions

MACERATA (PROVINCE). Ufficio Provinciale di Statistica. Lineamenti economici e prospettive di sviluppo dell'economia maceratese. Macerata, Camera di Commercio, Industria, Artigianato e Agricoltura, 1967. pp. (iii), 71.

- Economic policy

MACERATA (PROVINCE). Ufficio Provinciale di Statistica. Lineamenti economici e prospettive di sviluppo dell'economia maceratese. Macerata, Camera di Commercio, Industria, Artigianato e Agricoltura, 1967. pp. (iii), 71.

McGEE (THOMAS D'ARCY)

SLATTERY (T. P.) The assassination of D'Arcy McGee. Toronto, Doubleday, 1968. pp. xix, 527. bibliog. 23cm.

McGRANE (REGINALD CHARLES)

BEAVER (DANIEL R.) ed. Some pathways in twentieth century history; essays in honor of Reginald Charles McGrane. Detroit, 1969. pp. 313. bibliog.

MACH (ERNST)

BRIDGMAN (P. W.) The Mach principle. in Bunge (Mario Augusto) ed. The critical approach to science and philosophy. New York, [1964].

ERNST Mach, physicist and philosopher; edited by Robert S. Cohen and Raymond J. Seeger; [a symposium held at the annual meeting of the American Association for the Advancement of Science in 1966]. Dordrecht, [1970]. pp. 295. bibliog. (Boston Colloquium for the Philosophy of Science. Boston Studies in the Philosophy of Science. vol. 6)

KORNEEVA (ANNA IVANOVNA) Leninskaia kritika makhizma i bor'ba protiv sovremennogo idealizma. Moskva, 1971. pp. 239.

MACHAJSKI (WACŁAW)

ZAREMBA (ZYGMUNT) Słowo o Wacławie Machajskim. Paryż, 1967. pp. 146.

MACHIAVELLIANISM (PSYCHOLOGY)
See MACCHIAVELLIANISM (PSYCHOLOGY)

MACHINE ACCOUNTING

ITALY. Ragioneria Generale dello Stato. 1959. La meccanizzazione della contabilità generale dello stato. Roma, 1959. 2 vols. 26½cm.

LI (DAVID H.) Accounting, computers, management information systems. New York, McGraw-Hill, [1968]. pp. xiv, 370. 22½cm. (Series in Accounting)

PROCESSING incomplete records with special reference to the use of a computer; [a] summer course [held at] Churchill College, Cambridge, 17-21 September, 1969; (by F. C. Rudd). [London, 1969]. pp. 38.

MACHINE-SHOPS

- Technological innovations

CANADA. Department of Labour. Economics and Research Branch. 1967. Technological changes in the railway industry: employment effects and adjustment process: C.P.R. Angus Workshop Montreal; (By C.Glyn Williams under the supervision of Phillip Cohen). Ottawa, 1967. pp. xi, 161. 24½cm.

MACHINE THEORY

GINSBURG (SEYMOUR) An introduction to mathematical machine theory. Reading, Mass., [1962]. pp. 148. bibliog.

MINSKY (MARVIN) Computation: finite and infinite machines. Englewood Cliffs, [1967]. pp. 317. bibliog.

MACHINE-TOOLS

- Numerical control

UNITED STATES. Labor Statistics Bureau. Bulletins. No. 1437. Outlook for numerical control of machine tools. Washington, 1965 pp. vii, 63. bibliog.

- Trade and manufacture

OTTWASKA (DIETER) Das Leistungspotential der Werkzeugmaschinenindustrie der Bundesrepublik Deutschland: eine Untersuchung über Struktur, Produktion und Weltmarktabsatz im internationalen Vergleich 1950-1960. [Mannheim?], 1964. pp. various. bibliog.

UNITED STATES. Business and Defense Services Administration. World trade in machine tools, 1961-1964. Washington. pp. iv, 32.

MACHINE TOOLS (Cont'd.)

- Trade and manufacture - Armenia

MEZHLUMIAN (S.G.) Некоторые проблемы комплексной механизации. in Эффективность комплексного развития техники в промышленности. Москва, 1966.

- Trade and manufacture - Italy

UNIONE COSTRUTTORI ITALIANI MACCHINE UTENSILI. L'Italia come fonte d'approvvigionamento di macchine utensili per mercati d'Europa, America, Africa, Asia: statistiche delle importazioni di macchine utensili di 53 paesi. Milano, 1967. pp. (vii), 185.

- Trade and manufacture - New Zealand

NEW ZEALAND. Department of Industries and Commerce. 1969. The New Zealand toolmaking industry. [Wellington], 1969. pp. 57.

- Trade and manufacture - Russia

MATEVOSOV (IURII DAVIDOVICH) Экономические проблемы развития станкостроительной промышленности в Закавказье. Ереван, АН Армянской ССР, 1968. pp. 160. 19½см.

- Trade and manufacture - United Kingdom

U.K. Board of Trade. Business monitor: Production series P 76. Numerically controlled metalworking machine tools. London, 1968 to date.

ECONOMIC DEVELOPMENT COMMITTEE FOR MACHINE TOOLS. Industrial report...on the economic assessment to 1972. London, National Economic Development Office, 1970. pp. 28.

P-E CONSULTING GROUP LIMITED. A handbook for marketing machinery, based on an international study of successful marketing practice in the British machine tool industry; prepared for the Machine Tools E[conomic] D[evelopment] C[ommittee]. London, H.M.S.O., 1970. pp. 100.

U.K. Machine Tool Expert Committee. 1970. The machine tool industry: report...; under the chairmanship of Sir Richard Way. London, 1970. pp. 131.

- Trade and manufacture - United States

WAGONER (HARLESS D.) The U.S. machine tool industry from 1900 to 1950. Cambridge, M.I.T. Press, [1968]. pp. xiv, 421. bibliog. 23cm.

MACHINE TRANSLATING

BOOTH (ANDREW DONALD) Machine translation. Amsterdam, North-Holland Publishing Company, 1967. pp. xi, 529. bibliog. 23cm.

DROSTE (F.G.) Vertalen met de computer : mogelijkheden en moeilijkheden. Groningen, 1969. pp. 169. bibliog.

MITCHELL (RUTH K.) Information science and computer basics: an introduction;...programmed by Richard W. Hostrop. London, [1971]. pp. 101. bibliog.

MACHINERY

- Trade and manufacture

WEBER (PETER) Dr. Die Organisationsstruktur des Absatzbereiches in Unternehmungen der Maschinenindustrie. Winterthur, Schellenberg, 1967. pp. (vi), 259. bibliog. 22½cm.

DEMICHEV (ALEKSANDR IVANOVICH) Spetsializatsiia promyshlennogo proizvodstva. Moskva, 1969. pp. 164.

- Trade and manufacture - Canada

CANADA. Department of Industry, Trade and Commerce. Machinery program analysis : imports. a., 1969 [1st issue]- Ottawa.

- Trade and manufacture - Communist countries

KORMNOV (IURII FILIPPOVICH) Международная специализация производства: экономические проблемы на примере сотрудничества стран СЭВ в области машиностроения. Москва, Экономика, 1968. pp. 802. 19½см.

- Trade and manufacture - Czechoslovakia

K dějinám Závodů V. I. Lenina. Plzeň. Plzeň Krajské Nakladatelství, 1964. pp. 279,17. 24cm.

- Trade and manufacture - Denmark

DENMARK. Statistiske Departement.1964. Industrieksporten fra Danmark og nogle andre lande siden 1953. 3. haefte. Ikke-elektriske maskiner; [by] Erik Holm. København, 1964. pp. 71. (Statistiske Undersøgelser. [Nr.13])

DENMARK. Statistiske Departement. 1965. Industrieksporten fra Danmark og nogle andre lande siden 1953. 4. haefte. Elektriske maskiner og instrumenter; [with] Supplement: Den konkurrencemaessige stilling for dansk maskineksport i 1961-63; [by] Erik Holm. København, 1965. pp. 46. (Statistiske Undersøgelser. [Nr. 16])

- Trade and manufacture - India

INDIA. Ministry of Commerce and Industry. Development Wing. 1962. Production and programmes of manufacture of machinery and equipment in 1961 and in the third five year plan of India. [Delhi], 1962. pp. 274.

INDIA. Planning Group for Machinery Industries. 1965. Fourth five year plan: report. Delhi, 1965. pp. 152.

- Trade and manufacture - Russia

EL'IASHEVICH (A.B.) and others. Ekonomika sotsialisticheskogo mashinostroeniia. Moskva, 1957. pp. 475.

"DINAMO", MOSKOVSKII ELEKTROMASHINOSTROITEL'NYI ZAVOD. История завода "Динамо". кн.1. "Динамо" на путях к Октябрю; [by] Л. А. Карлова. Москва, Профиздат, 1961. pp. 179. 20см.

MITEL'MAN (M.) and others. Istoriia Putilovskogo zavoda, 1801-1917. 3rd ed. Moskva, 1961. pp. 718. (Kommunisticheskaia Partiia Sovetskogo Soiuza. Leningradskii Oblastnoi Komitet. Istoriia Kirovskogo/byv. Putilovskogo/ Metallurgicheskogo i Mashinostroitel'nogo Zavoda v Leningrade. [vol.1])

UNITED STATES. Business and Defense Services Administration. The Soviet challenge to U.S. machine building. Washington. pp. vi, 73. bibliog.

BELOKHOLUNITSKOMY... Белохолуницкому машиностроительному заводу - 200 лет: 1764-1964 гг. Киров, 1965. pp. 168.

KOSTIUCHENKO (STANISLAV ALEKSEEVICH) and others. Istoriia Kirovskogo zavoda, 1917-1945. Moskva, 1966. pp. 702.

BITUNOV (V. V.) and BURYNDIN (R. M.) eds. Povyshenie effektivnosti tekhnicheskogo progressa na materialakh mashinostroeniia. Moskva, 1967. pp. 173.

SIRYI (P. O.) ed. Энергетическое машиностроение, 1917-1967. Ленинград, 1967. pp. 231. bibliog.

CHEREVKO (IVAN ALEKSANDROVICH) Нормирование сроков освоения проектных мощностей. Москва, 1968. pp. 151.

FIRSOV (VASILII GAVRILOVICH) Завод работает в новых условиях: из опыта Невского машиностроительного завода имени В. И. Ленина. Ленинград, 1968. pp. 119. (Школа Социалистического Хозяйства)

SHURGIN (MIKHAIL ALEKSEEVICH) Slovo o zavode: rasskaz o Nevskom mashinostroitel'nom zavode imeni Lenina. Leningrad, 1970. pp. 127.

DOKUKIN (VLADIMIR IGNAT'EVICH) ed. Rezervy rosta proizvoditel'nosti truda v mashinostroenii. Moskva, 1971. pp. 263. bibliog.

KUROCHKIN (BORIS ALEKSANDROVICH) and KHANEEV (OLEG PETROVICH) Zavod i liudi: ocherk istorii leningradskogo zavoda "Reduktor". Leningrad, 1971. pp. 199.

- Trade and manufacture - Spain

SPAIN. Comisaría del Plan de Desarrollo Económico y Social. 1964. Construcción de maquinaria y productos químicos, abonos y papel: [anexo al Plan de... 1964 a 1967]. [Madrid, 1964]. pp. 244. 30cm.

SPAIN. Comisaria del Plan de Desarrollo Economico y Social. 1967. (II Plan de desarrollo economico y social): maquinaria y bienes de equipo. [Madrid, 1967]. pp. 138.

- Trade and manufacture - Switzerland

HOFMANN (HANNES) Die Anfänge der Maschinenindustrie in der deutschen Schweiz 1800-1875. Zürich, 1962. pp. 220. bibliog.

- Trade and manufacture - Ukraine

ADAMENKO (ELLA MOISEEVNA) Резервы повышения экономической эффективности механизации производства. Харьков, Университет, 1968. pp. 184. 21см.

- Trade and manufacture - United Kingdom

GRINYER (PETER HUGH) A study of optimal purchasing rules for mechanical plant in the construction industry; [Ph.D. (London) thesis]. 1968. 2 vols. bibliog. 25½cm. Typescript: unpublished. This thesis is the property of London University and may not be removed from the Library.

[WELLWORTHY LIMITED] Wellworthy: the first fifty years. [Lymington, 1969]. pp. 191.

- Trade and manufacture - United States

ROSENBERG (NATHAN) ed. The American system of manufactures: the Report of the Committee on the Machinery of the United States 1855 and the special reports of George Wallis and Joseph Whitworth 1854. Edinburgh, Edinburgh U.P., 1969 repr. pp. (v), 440. 24½cm.

UNITED STATES. Business and Defense Services Administration. The Soviet challenge to U.S. machine building. Washington. pp. vi, 73. bibliog.

- Trade and manufacture - Uzbekistan

EKONOMIKA... Экономика машиностроения Узбекистана. Ташкент, АН УзССР, 1963. pp. 291. 21½см.

IAKUBOV (I.) and others. Problemy razvitiia i spetsializatsii mashinostroeniia Uzbekistana. Tashkent, 1971. pp. 270.

MACHINERY IN INDUSTRY

CENTRAL CO-OPERATIVE BOARD. Land, labour and machinery. Manchester, [1888]. pp. 22. 16cm.

HANSON (NILS H.) The onward sweep of the machine process; [with] Industrial efficiency and its antidote; by T. Glynn; [and] The diesel motor; by Barbara Lily Frankenthal. Chicago, [1932?], pp. 32.

BURKART (LUTZ) and WILLENER (ALFRED) Niveau de mécanisation et mode de rémunération:...rapport de synthèse d'une recherche effectuée dans la sidérurgie par des instituts des six pays de la Communauté. Luxembourg. European Coal and Steel Community. 1960. pp. 149.

PFEIFER (UTA) Mechanisierung der Produktion in Zahlen der deutschen Wirtschaft: ein Versuch. Mannheim, imprint], 1965. pp. 103. bibliog.

MACHINERY IN INDUSTRY (Cont'd.)

ADAMENKO (ELLA MOISEEVNA) Резервы повышения экономической эффективности механизации производства. Харьков, Университет, 1968. pp. 184. 21см.

MACIVER (ROBERT MORRISON)

MACIVER (ROBERT MORRISON) As a tale that is told: the autobiography. Chicago, U. of Chicago P., 1968. pp. ix, 269. 20½cm.

MACKENZIE DELTA

- Bibliography

JONES (MARY JANE) ed. Mackenzie Delta bibliography. Ottawa, 1969. pp. 119. (Canada. Northern Science Research Group. MDRP [Reports]. 6)

- Economic conditions

COOPER (P. F.) The Mackenzie delta: technology. Ottawa, 1967. pp. 69. bibliog. (Canada. Northern Co-ordination and Research Centre. MDRP [Reports]. 2)

WOLFORTH (JOHN R.) The Mackenzie Delta: its economic base and development: a preliminary study. Ottawa, [1967?]. pp. 85. bibliog. (Canada. Northern Co-ordination and Research Centre. MDRP [Reports]. 1)

McKINLEY (WILLIAM) President of the United States

COLETTA (PAOLO ENRICO) ed. Threshold to American internationalism: essays on the foreign policies of William McKinley. New York, [1970]. pp. 334.

MACLEAN CLAN

MACLEAN (JAMES NOEL MACKENZIE) The Macleans of Sweden. Edinburgh, 1971. pp. 61.

McLUHAN (MARSHALL)

FINKELSTEIN (SIDNEY) Sense and nonsense of McLuhan. New York, [1968]. pp. 122.

ROSENTHAL (RAYMOND) translator, ed. McLuhan: pro and con. New York, [1968]. pp. 308.

WEST (Dame REBECCA) pseud. [i.e. Cicily Isabel ANDREWS]. McLuhan and the future of literature. [London], 1969. pp. 19.

MILLER (JONATHAN WOLFE) McLuhan. London, 1971. pp. 139. bibliog.

MACMILLAN (HAROLD)

MACMILLAN (HAROLD) Tides of fortune, 1945-1955. London, Macmillan, 1969. pp. xx, 729. 21½cm.

MACMILLAN (HAROLD) Riding the storm, 1956-1959. London, 1971. pp. 786.

McNAMARA (ROBERT STRANGE)

ROHERTY (JAMES M.) Decisions of Robert S. McNamara: a study of the role of the Secretary of Defense. Coral Gables, Fla., [1970]. pp. 223.

McREYNOLDS (DAVID)

McREYNOLDS (DAVID) We have been invaded by the 21st century. New York, 1970. pp. 270.

MADAGASCAR

DESCHAMPS (HUBERT) Madagascar. Paris, P.U.F., 1968. pp. 128. bibliog. 17½cm. (Que Sais-Je? No. 529)

HESELTINE (NIGEL) Madagascar. London, 1971. pp. 334. bibliog.

- Commerce

MADAGASCAR. 1962. Statistiques du commerce extérieur de Madagascar: séries retrospectives, 1949-1961. (Service de Statistique et des Études Socio-Économiques) [Tananarive, 1962]. pp. 108. 27cm.

- Commerce - Europe

FRANCE. 1962. Commerce extérieur des états d'Afrique et de Madagascar de 1949 à 1960. [Fasc. 1] (Institut National de la Statistique et des Études Économiques). For Fasc. 2 see FRANCE.1963. Paris, [1962]. pp. 59. 27cm.

- Commercial policy

BOSCH (JUERGEN) Die Vanilleausfuhrpolitik der malagassischen Republik 1960-1969: ein Beitrag zur Aussenwirtschaftspolitik von Entwicklungsländern. Ludwigsburg, [1971]. pp. 311. bibliog.

- Constitution

CONGRÈS DES ASSEMBLÉES PROVINCIALES DE MADAGASCAR, TANANARIVE, 1958. Procès-verbaux du Congrès..., session d'octobre 1958. Tananarive, 1959. pp. 99.

MASSIOT (MICHEL) L'organisation politique administrative financière et judiciaire de la République Malgache. [Tananarive, 1970]. pp. 487. bibliog.

- Constitutional history

BARDONNET (DANIEL) La succession d'états à Madagascar: succession au droit conventionnel et aux droits patrimoniaux. Paris, 1970. pp. 877. bibliog.

MASSIOT (MICHEL) L'administration publique à Madagascar: évolution de l'organisation administrative territoriale de Madagascar de 1896 à la proclamation de la République Malgache. Paris, 1971. pp. 472. bibliog.

-Description and travel

GUILCHER (ANDRE) and BATTISTINI (RENE) Madagascar: géographie régionale. [2nd ed.] Paris, 1967. pp. 137. bibliog.

- Economic conditions

    GUILCHER (ANDRE) and BATTISTINI (RENE)
    Madagascar: géographie régionale. [2nd ed.]
    Paris, 1967. pp. 137. bibliog.

    FRANCE. Secrétariat d'Etat aux Affaires Etrangères.
    Direction des Relations et des Financements.
    1969. Economie et plan de développement:
    République malgache. [Paris, 1969]. pp.
    407.

- Economic conditions - Statistics

    MADAGASCAR. Institut National de la
    Statistique et de la Recherche Economique.
    1966. Inventaire socio-économique de
    Madagascar, 1960-1965. [Tananarive,
    1966?]. 2 pts. bibliogs.

- Economic policy

    MADAGASCAR. Statutes, etc. 1956-1957.
    La loi-cadre du 23 juin 1956 portant réforme
    des institutions politiques, économiques
    et sociales de Madagascar et les textes
    d'application, décrets, arretés et
    délibérations. 2nd ed. Tananarive, 1957.
    pp. 459.

    MADAGASCAR. Statutes, etc. 1960. Ordonnance no.
    60-125 portant adoption et promulgation du pro-
    gramme triennal 1959-1962 de développement écon-
    omique et social. (Journal officiel de la
    République Malgache. 76e année, nouvelle série,
    no. 128) Tananarive, 1960. pp. 2129-2178.
    33cm.

    MADAGASCAR. 1964. Plan quinquennal, 1964-1968.
    (Commissariat Général au Plan) Tananarive,
    [1964]. pp. 256. 31cm.

    VINAY (BERNARD) Fiscalité, épargne et
    développement. Paris, Colin, [1968].
    pp. 304. 16½cm.

    FRANCE. Secrétariat d'Etat aux Affaires Etrangères.
    Direction des Relations et des Financements.
    1969. Economie et plan de développement:
    République malgache. [Paris, 1969]. pp.
    407.

- Executive departments

    MADAGASCAR. Présidence de la République. Rapport
    sur l'activité du gouvernement. Tananarive,
    annual, 1964/5 (2nd ed.) to date.

    MASSIOT (MICHEL) L'organisation politique administ-
    trative financière et judiciaire de la République
    Malgache. [Tananarive, 1970]. pp. 487. bibliog.

- Government publications

    UNITED STATES. Library of Congress. Madagascar and
    adjacent islands: a guide to official publications.
    Washington, 1965. pp. xiii, 58.

- Industries - Statistics

    MADAGASCAR. 1963. Denombrement des établissements
    exerçant une activité économique à Madagascar.
    (Service de la Statistique et des Études Socio-
    Économiques) [Tananarive], 1963. pp. 3, 16. 26cm

- Maps

    ATLAS de Madagascar; préparé par l'Association
    des Géographes de Madagascar...sous la direc-
    tion de Françoise le Bourdiec [and others], etc.
    Tananarive, Bureau pour le Développement de la
    Production Agricole, Agence de Madagascar, 1969
    in progress. Loose-leaf binder.

- Nationalism

    BOITEAU (PIERRE) Mouvement national et problèmes
    de classes à Madagascar. Paris, the Centre,
    [1966]. fo. 29. 27cm. (Centre d'Études et de
    Recherches Marxistes. Cahiers. No. 44)

- Politics and government

    MADAGASCAR. Statutes, etc. 1956-1957.
    La loi-cadre du 23 juin 1956 portant réforme
    des institutions politiques, économiques
    et sociales de Madagascar et les textes
    d'application, décrets, arretés et
    délibérations. 2nd ed. Tananarive, 1957.
    pp. 459.

    LEJAMBLE (GEORGES) Le fokonolona et le
    pouvoir. Tananarive, Université de
    Madagascar, Centre de Droit Public et
    de Science Politique, 1963. fo. 81.
    bibliog. 27cm.

    MADAGASCAR. Présidence de la République. Rapport sur
    l'activité du gouvernement. Tananarive, annual,
    1964/5 (2nd ed.) to date. 23½cm.

    MASSIOT (MICHEL) L'administration publique à
    Madagascar: évolution de l'organisation admini-
    strative territoriale de Madagascar de 1896 à
    la proclamation de la République Malgache.
    Paris, 1971. pp. 472. bibliog.

- Population

    FRANCE. Institut National de la Statistique et
    des Études Économiques. Service de Coopération
    1967. Afrique Noire, Madagascar, Comores:
    démographie comparée. Paris, 1967. 2 vols
    (in one). bibliogs. 27cm.

- Rural conditions

    ALTHABE (GERARD) Oppression et libération dans
    l'imaginaire: les communautés villageoises
    de la côte orientale de Madagascar. Paris,
    1969. pp. 354.

- Social conditions

    LEJAMBLE (GEORGES) Le fokonolona et le
    pouvoir. Tananarive, Université de
    Madagascar, Centre de Droit Public et
    de Science Politique, 1963. fo. 81.
    bibliog. 27cm.

- Social conditions - Statistics

    MADAGASCAR. Institut National de la
    Statistique et de la Recherche Economique.
    1966. Inventaire socio-économique de
    Madagascar, 1960-1965. [Tananarive,
    1966?]. 2 pts. bibliogs.

- Social life and customs

    BLOCH (MAURICE E.F.) Placing the dead: tombs,
    ancestral villages and kinship organization
    in Madagascar. London, 1971. pp. 241. bibliog.

MADAGASCAR (Cont'd.)

- Social policy

MADAGASCAR. Statutes, etc. 1956-1957. La loi-cadre du 23 juin 1956 portant réforme des institutions politiques, économiques et sociales de Madagascar et les textes d'application, décrets, arretés et délibérations. 2nd ed. Tananarive, 1957. pp. 459.

MADAGASCAR. Statutes, etc. 1960. Ordonnance no. 60-125 portant adoption et promulgation du programme triennal 1959-1962 de développement économique et social. (Journal officiel de la République Malgache. 76e année, nouvelle série, no. 128) Tananarive, 1960. pp. 2129-2178. 33cm.

MADAGASCAR. 1964. Plan quinquennal, 1964-1968. (Commissariat Général au Plan) Tananarive, [1964]. pp. 256. 31cm.

FRANCE. Secrétariat d'Etat aux Affaires Etrangères. Direction des Relations et des Financements. 1969. Economie et plan de développement: République malgache. [Paris, 1969]. pp. 407.

- Statistics

EUROPEAN COMMUNITIES. Office Statistique. Associés: annuaire statistique des E.A.M.A. (Etats africains et malgache associés). a., 1969 [1st issue]- Luxembourg.

- Statistics, Vital

MADAGASCAR. Institut National de la Statistique et de la Recherche Economique. 1966. Etat civil, année 1965. [Tananarive, 1966?]. pp. 52.

MADARIAGA (SALVADOR DE)

BRUGMANS (HENDRYK) and MARTINEZ NADAL (RAFAEL) eds. Liber amicorum: Salvador de Madariaga; recueil d'études et de témoignages édité a l'occasion de son quatre-vingtieme anniversaire. Bruges, 1966. pp. 415. (College of Europe. Cahiers de Bruges. Numéro Hors Série) In various languages.

MADEJCZYK (JAN)

MADEJCZYK (JAN) Wspomnienia. Warszawa, Ludowa Spółdzielnia Wydawnicza, 1965. pp. 219. 20cm.

MADHYA BHARAT

- Economic policy

MADHYA BHARAT. General Administration (Planning) Department. 1954. The first five-year plan, 1951-56. [Indore?], 1954. pp. 184.

- Social policy

MADHYA BHARAT. General Administration (Planning) Department. 1954. The first five-year plan, 1951-56. [Indore?], 1954. pp. 184.

MADHYA PRADESH
See also CENTRAL PROVINCES AND BERAR

- Economic conditions

MADHYA PRADESH. 1955. Madhya Pradesh in Indian economy. (Directorate of Economics and Statistics) Nagpur, 1955. pp. (iii), 63. $24\frac{1}{2}$cm.

NAG (D.S.) ed. Development potential of Madhya Pradesh. Bhopal, Kailash, [1966]. pp. (vi), 186. $21\frac{1}{2}$cm.

- Economic conditions - Statistics

MADHYA PRADESH. 1960. Economic development of Madhya Pradesh: a statistical study. (Directorate of Economics and Statistics) [Bhopal, 1960]. pp. 49. $18\frac{1}{2}$cm.

- Economic policy

MADHYA PRADESH. 1960. Third five-year plan of Madhya Pradesh, 1961-62 to 1965-66. Pt. 1. A draft outline. Bhopal, 1960. pp. 362.

NAG (D.S.) ed. Development potential of Madhya Pradesh. Bhopal, Kailash, [1966]. pp. (vi), 186. $21\frac{1}{2}$cm.

- Industries

NATIONAL COUNCIL OF APPLIED ECONOMIC RESEARCH. Industrial programmes for the fourth five year plan for Madhya Pradesh. vol.1. Gwalior, Government Regional Press, 1966. pp. 178.

- Social policy

MADHYA PRADESH. 1960. Third five-year plan of Madhya Pradesh, 1961-62 to 1965-66. Pt. 1. A draft outline. Bhopal, 1960. pp. 362.

MADISON (JAMES) President of the United States

MADISON (JAMES) President of the United States. The papers...; edited by William J. Hutchinson and William M. E. Rachal. Chicago, University of Chicago Press, 1962 in progress. $23\frac{1}{2}$cm.

BRANT (IRVING) James Madison and American nationalism. Princeton, Van Nostrand, [1968]. pp. 223. bibliog. 19cm. (Anvil Books. 94)

BURNS (EDWARD McNALL) James Madison, philosopher of the Constitution. 2nd ed. New York, Octagon Books, 1968. pp. xi, 240. bibliog. 20cm. (Rutgers University. Studies in History. vol.1.)

BEAM (GEORGE D.) Usual politics: a critique and some suggestions for an alternative. New York, [1970]. pp. 196.

BRANT (IRVING) The fourth president: a life of James Madison. London, 1970. pp. 681.

MADJAPAHIT

- Politics and government

SLAMETMULJANA ( ) The structure of the national government of Madjapahit. Djakarta, 1966. pp. 31. 22cm.

MADRAS

- Description and travel

MADRAS. 1959. Madras in maps and pictures. (Director of Information and Publicity) 3rd ed. Madras, 1959 pp. (viii), 168. 22½cm.

- Economic conditions

MADRAS. 1959. Madras in maps and pictures. (Director of Information and Publicity) 3rd ed. Madras, 1959. pp. (viii), 168. 22½cm.

- Economic policy

MADRAS. 1961. Third five-year plan, Madras State. [Madras, 1961.] pp. 272.

BALIGA (B.S.) Studies in Madras administration. rev. ed. Madras, Government of Madras, 1960. 2 vols.

- History

BALIGA (B.S.) Studies in Madras administration. rev. ed. Madras, Government of Madras, 1960. 2 vols.

- Industries

MADRAS. Industrial Planning Committee. 1948. Final report. Madras, 1948. pp. 214.

- Officials and employees - Salaries, allowances, etc.

MADRAS. Pay Commission. 1960. Report...1959-60. Madras, 1960. pp. 508.

- Politics and government

MADRAS. 1947. Handbook of information on the administration of the Province of Madras. Madras, 1947. pp. 125.

MADRAS. Governor. 1950. Special address by His Excellency the Governor at the commencement of the first session of the Madras Legislature under the constitution of India, Saturday, the 11th February 1950. Madras, 1950. pp. 5.

MADRAS. Governor. 1959. Address by Shri Bisnuram Medhi, Governor of Madras at the joint session of the Madras Legislature, Saturday, 5th December 1959. Madras, [1959]. pp. 4.

BALIGA (B.S.) Studies in Madras administration. rev. ed. Madras, Government of Madras, 1960. 2 vols.

- Social conditions

MADRAS. 1959. Madras in maps and pictures. (Director of Information and Publicity) 3rd ed. Madras, 1959. pp. (viii), 168. 22½cm.

- Social policy

MADRAS. 1961. Third five-year plan, Madras State. [Madras, 1961.] pp. 272.

- Statistics

MADRAS. Annual statistical abstract. a., 1956/7, 1958/9. Madras.

MADRAS (CITY)

- Harbour

NATIONAL COUNCIL OF APPLIED ECONOMIC RESEARCH. Traffic survey of Madras port. New Delhi, [1968]. pp. ix, 99. 23cm.

MADRID

- Suburbs and environs

GRAN San Blas: analíses socio-urbanístico de un barrio nuevo español; investigación dirigida por Mario Gaviria. [Madrid, 1968]. pp. 160. (Separata de la revista Arquitectura, Nos. 113-114, May-June 1968)

MAFEKING

- Water supply

SOUTH AFRICA. 1967. Report of the select committee on the Mafeking Waterworks (Private) Amendment Bill; (with Proceedings and Minutes of evidence) (S.C.5-'67) in SOUTH AFRICA. House of Assembly Select Committee reports, which see.

MAFIA

OVAZZA (MARIO) Il caso Battaglia. Palermo, Libri Siciliani, 1967. pp. 139. 17cm. (Viaggi in Sicilia di Ieri e di Oggi. 2)

DOLCI (DANILO) The man who plays alone;...translated from the Italian by Antonia Cowan. London, MacGibbon & Kee, 1968. pp. xx, 367. 22cm.

The MAFIA and politics: a cause célèbre; Danilo Dolci on trial; the allegations, the trial, the appeal, to be heard autumn 1968. London, [1968]. pp. 15.

MAAS (PETER) The canary that sang: (the Valachi papers). London, 1969. pp. 269.

PANTALEONE (MICHELE) Antimafia: occasione mancata. Torino, Einaudi, [1969]. pp. 220. 21½cm. (Saggi. 440)

RUSAKOV (N. P.) Из истории сицилийской мафии. Москва, 1969. pp. 179.

HESS (HENNER) Mafia: zentrale Herrschaft und lokale Gegenmacht. Tübingen, 1970. pp. 230. bibliog.

MAFIA (Cont'd.)

PANTALEONE (MICHELE) Il sasso in bocca: Mafia e Cosa Nostra. Bologna, 1970 repr. 1971. pp. 145. bibliog.

MAGADAN (OBLAST')

- Economic conditions

SEVERO-VOSTOCHNYI... Северо-Восточный экономический район. Магадан, Книжное Издательство, 1965. pp. 320. 16см.

PROBLEMY razvitiia proizvoditel'nykh sil Magadanskoi oblasti: materialy Vtorogo nauchnogo soveshchaniia po problemam razvitiia i razmeshcheniia proizvoditel' nykh sil Magadanskoi oblasti, 3-5 iiunia 1968 g. t.1. Magadan, 1969. pp. 266. bibliog.

- History

GARUSOV (IVAN SERGEEVICH) Разгром белогвардейщины в Охотско-Камчатском крае. Магадан, Книжное Издательство, 1963. pp. 71. 16½см.

MAGEE UNIVERSITY COLLEGE

IRELAND, NORTHERN. H.C. 1891. Magee University College Londonderry Bill: special report from the Joint Select Committee on opposed bill, etc. 1968. pp. 17. Belfast.

MAGIC

- Nigeria

MACLEAN (UNA) Magical medicine: a Nigerian case-study. London, 1971. pp. 166. bibliog.

MAGIC, MALAY

ROBERT (KATHERINE) The role of Malay magicians and medicine men: a study of their practices, their clients, and their relation to their clients in Singapore; [research paper, Department of Social Studies, University of Singapore]. 1959. fo. (iii), 134. bibliog. Microfilm of typescript.

ENDICOTT (KIRK MICHAEL) An analysis of Malay magic. Oxford, 1970. pp. 188. bibliog.

MAGNA CARTA

BUTTERFIELD (Sir HERBERT) Magna Carta in the historiography of the sixteenth and seventeenth centuries. [Reading], 1969. pp. 25. (Reading. University. Stenton Lectures. 1968)

MAGNESIUM

UNITED STATES. Mines Bureau. Information Circulars. 8201. Magnesium and magnesium compounds. Washington, [1963]. pp. x, 128. bibliog.

GINSBERG (HANS) and WEFERS (KARL) Aluminium und Magnesium. 2nd ed. Stuttgart, 1971. pp. 218. bibliog. (Die metallischen Rohstoffe: ihre Lagerungsverhältnisse und ihre wirtschaftliche Bedeutung. 15. Band)

MAGNETIC RECORDERS AND RECORDING

U.K. Board of Trade. Business monitor: Production series P 80. Tape recorders. London, 1968 to date.

MAGNETISM, TERRESTRIAL

GILBERT (WILLIAM) M.D. De magnete;...translated by P. Fleury Mottelay; [re-issue of translation published in 1893]. New York, Dover Publications, 1958. pp. lv, 368. 20½cm. (Dover Books Explaining Science)

MAGNITOGORSK

- History

IZ... Из истории Магнитогорского металлургического комбината и города Магнитогорска, 1929-1941 гг.: сборник документов и материалов. Челябинск, 1965. pp. 276.

MAHAN (ALFRED THAYER)

MAHAN (ALFRED THAYER) From sail to steam: recollections of naval life; [reprint of the work originally published in New York, 1907]. New York, 1968. pp. 325.

BOURNE (KENNETH) and BOYD (CARL) Captain Mahan's "war" with Great Britain. [Annapolis, 1968]. pp. irreg. (Reprinted from United States Naval Institute Proceedings, July, 1968)

MAHARASHTRA

- Boundaries

INDIA. Commission on Maharashtra — Mysore — Kerala Boundary Disputes. 1967. Report: [Mehr Chand Mahajan, sole commissioner]. Delhi, 1967. 2 vols.

ANTULAY (A. RAHMAN) Mahajan report uncovered. Bombay, Allied Publishers, 1968. pp. (iv), 192 21½cm.

- Economic conditions

MAHARASHTRA. Fact-finding Committee for Survey of Scarcity Areas in Bombay State. 1960. Report...Vol.1. (General report). Vol. 2. (District reports). Pt. 1. Maharashtra. [N.S. Pardasani, chairman]. Bombay, 1960. 2 vols.

- Economic policy

MAHARASHTRA. 1960. Draft third five year plan of the Maharashtra State (1961-62 to 1965-66); submitted to Planning Commission. Bombay, 1960. pp. 609.

- Politics and government

> GAIKWAD (VIJAY SINGH RAMESHWAR RAO) Panchayati raj and bureaucracy: a study of the relationship patterns. Hyderabad, 1969. pp. 77.

- Social history

> KUMAR (RAVINDER) Western India in the nineteenth century: a study in the social history of Maharashtra. London, Routledge & Kegan Paul, 1968. pp. (viii), 347. 21½cm. (Studies in Social History)

- Social policy

> MAHARASHTRA. 1960. Draft third five year plan of the Maharashtra State (1961-62 to 1965-66); submitted to Planning Commission. Bombay, 1960. pp. 609.

MAHE DE LA BOURDONNAIS (BERTRAND FRANÇOIS)

> TOULOUP (FRANÇOIS) Bertrand-François Mahé de la Bourdonnais et la Compagnie des Indes. [Paris?, 1967] pp. 213. bibliog.

MAI (HSIEN-TEH)

> BATTLE hero: Mai Hsien-teh; by a Liberation Army Daily correspondent. Peking, 1967. pp. 26.

MAIAKOVSKII (VLADIMIR VLADIMIROVICH)

> KOLOSKOV (ALEKSANDR IVANOVICH) Маяковский в борьбе за коммунизм. 2nd ed. Москва, ИПЛ, 1969. pp. 487. 20см.

> KEMRAD (SEMEN SAMUILOVICH) Maiakovskii v Amerike: stranitsy biografii. Moskva, 1970. pp. 271.

MAIASHVILI (GEORGII FELIKSOVICH)

> KANDELAKI (M. I.) Г. Ф. Маиашвили (Зданович): гражданин, журналист, критик. Тбилиси, 1969. pp. 241.

MAIDSTONE

- Charities

> MAIDSTONE. Dissenting Charity School. The regulations and rules of the Charity School, established by the protestant dissenters at Maidstone, October 21, 1799, for the educating, clothing, and apprenticing of poor children. Maidstone, [imprint], 1800. pp. (ii), 11. 17cm.

- Schools

> MAIDSTONE. Dissenting Charity School. The regulations and rules of the Charity School, established by the protestant dissenters at Maidstone, October 21, 1799, for the educating, clothing, and apprenticing of poor children. Maidstone, [imprint], 1800. pp. (ii), 11. 17cm.

MAIL-ORDER BUSINESS

> GEPPERT (HUBERT) Der deutsche Universalversandhandel unter besonderer Berücksichtigung seiner Preis-, Sortiments- und Werbepolitik. [Erlangen, imprint, 1969?]. pp. 221. bibliog.

> ELI (MAX) and LAUMER (HELMUT) Der Versandhandel: Struktur und Wachstum im internationalen Vergleich. Berlin, 1970. pp. 114. bibliog. (IFO-Institut für Wirtschaftsforschung. Struktur und Wachstum. Reihe Absatzwirtschaft. Heft 1)

MAILBOXES

> FARRUGIA (JEAN YOUNG) The letter box: a history of post office pillar and wall boxes. Fontwell, 1969. pp. 282. bibliog.

MAILER (NORMAN)

> MAILER (NORMAN) The armies of the night: history as a novel, the novel as history. Harmondsworth, 1970. pp. 300.

MAINE (Sir HENRY JAMES SUMNER)

> FEAVER (GEORGE ARTHUR) From status to contract: a biography of Sir Henry Maine, 1822-1888. London, Longmans, 1969. pp. xx, 366. bibliog. 21½cm.

MAINZ

- History

> KEIM (ANTON M.) ed. Tagebuch einer jüdischen Gemeinde 1941/43; (herausgegeben und kommentiert von Anton Keim). Mainz, [1968]. pp. 112. bibliog.

- History - Sources

> FRANCE. Commission des Archives Diplomatiques. Recueil des Instructions données aux Ambassadeurs et Ministres de France depuis les Traités de Westphalie jusqu'à la Révolution Française. 28. Etats allemands. tome 1. L'électorat de Mayence; avec une introduction et des notes par Georges Livet. Paris, Centre National de la Recherche Scientifique, 1962. pp. lxix, 307. 24½cm.

- Intellectual life

> DREYFUS (FRANÇOIS GEORGES) Sociétés et mentalités à Mayence dans la seconde moitié du XVIIIe siècle. Paris, Colin, 1968. pp. 617. bibliog. 24cm.

- Social history

> DREYFUS (FRANÇOIS GEORGES) Sociétés et mentalités à Mayence dans la seconde moitié du XVIIIe siècle. Paris, Colin, 1968. pp. 617. bibliog. 24cm.

MAISKII (IVAN MIKHAILOVICH)

> MAISKII (IVAN MIKHAILOVICH) B. Shou i drugie: vospominaniia. Moskva, 1967. pp. 120. With an appendix of photographs.

MAISTRE (JOSEPH MARIE DE) Comte

NADA (N.) Tra Russia e Piemonte: lettere inedite di Giuseppe de Maistre a Carlo Emanuele Alfieri di Sostegno, 1816-1818. in Miscellanea Walter Maturi. Torino, 1966.

PESANTE (M. L.) Un inedito di Walter Mature; il pensiero di Giuseppe de Maistre. in Miscellanea Walter Maturi. Torino, 1966.

BRUNELLO (BRUNO) Joseph de Maistre: politico e filosofo. Bologna, Pàtron, [1967]. pp. viii, 330. bibliog. 22cm. (Scienze Filosofiche. 3)

TRIOMPHE (ROBERT) Joseph de Maistre: étude sur la vie et sur la doctrine d'un matérialiste mystique. Genève, Droz, 1968. pp. 637. bibliog. 24cm. (Travaux d'Histoire Éthico-Politique.14)

MAITLAND (FREDERIC WILLIAM)

FIFOOT (CECIL HERBERT STUART) Pollock and Maitland. Glasgow, 1971. pp. 26. (Glasgow. University. Lectures on the David Murray Foundation. No 31)

MAIZE

GURRÍA URGELL (JOSÉ MARÍA) La moneda-maíz. México, Paz-México, [1965]. pp. 126. 22½cm.

- Costa Rica

COSTA RICA. Dirección General de Estadística y Censos. 1965. Diseño de la encuesta agrícola por muestreo de arroz, maíz y frijol, 1965; por José G. Baptista and Mario Murillo M. [San José], 1965. pp. 55.

- Kenya

KENYA. Maize and Produce Board. Annual report. Nairobi, annual, 1966/7 (1st) to date. 34cm.

- Rhodesia

SOUTHERN RHODESIA. Maize Control Board. Annual report. Salisbury, annual, 1932/3, 1934/5, 1936/7, 1939/40. 33cm.

- Siam

SIAM. 1964. Maize from Thailand. (Ministry of Economic Affairs). [Bangkok, 1964]. pp. 20. 19cm.

- South Africa

SOUTH AFRICA. Report of the Controller and Auditor-General on the accounts of the Maize Board. 1969/70 to date included in SOUTH AFRICA. Parliament. House of Assembly. Votes and proceedings; (with Printed annexures).

- Tanzania

SCHLAGE (C.) Polished versus whole maize: some nutritional and economic implications of the traditional processing of maize in northeastern Tanzania. Dar Es Salaam, 1968. pp. 18. bibliog. (Dar es Salaam. University College. Bureau of Resource Assessment and Land Use Planning. Research Papers. No.2)

MAJANGIRS

STAUDER (JACK) The Majangir: ecology and society of a southwest Ethiopian people. Cambridge, 1971. pp. 200. bibliog.

MAJORITIES

HERMENS (FERDINAND ALOYS) Demokratie oder Anarchie?: Untersuchung über die Verhältniswahl. 2nd ed. Köln, Westdeutscher Verlag, 1968. pp. xxiv, 346. 21cm.

MAKARIOS III., Archbishop and Ethnarch of Cyprus

ENOSIS and only Enosis: a briefing paper on the politics of Archbishop Makarios. [Nicosia], 1957. fo.7. 33½cm.

MAKEEV (A.S.)

MAKEEV (A.S.) Bog voiny - baron Ungern: vospominaniia byvshego ad"iutanta Nachal'nika Aziatskoi Konnoi Divizii. Shankhai, 1934. pp. 144.

MAKERERE COLLEGE

GOLDTHORPE (JOHN ERNEST) An African elite: Makerere College students, 1922-1960. Nairobi, Oxford University Press, 1965. pp. ix, 109. bibliog. 24cm. (East African Institute of Social Research. East African Studies. No.17)

MAKHACHKALA

- Economic history

KAZHLAEV (ALI NAZHMUTDINOVICH) Возникновение и экономическое развитие Махачкалы. Махачкала, 1967. pp. 235.

MAKHNO (NESTOR)

KUBANIN (M.I.) Makhnovshchina: krest'-ianskoe dvizhenie v stepnoi Ukraine v gody grazhdanskoi voiny. Leningrad, [1926]. pp. 228.

MAKHNO (NESTOR) Makhnovshchina i ee vcherashnie soiuzniki - bol'sheviki: otvet na knigu M. Kubanina "Makhnovshchina". Parizh, 1928. pp. 62. Xerographic copy.

MAKONDES

LIEBENOW (J. GUS) Colonial rule and political development in Tanzania: the case of the Makonde. Evanston, Ill., 1971. pp. 360. bibliog.

MALARIAL FEVER

- Africa, Subsaharan

GELFAND (MICHAEL) Rivers of death in Africa: an inaugural lecture given in the University College of Rhodesia and Nyasaland on 10 October, 1963. London, O.U.P., 1964. pp. 100. 21½cm.

- Ceylon

CEYLON. Parliament. Sessional Papers, 1936. 5. Report on the relief of distress due to sickness and shortage of food: September, 1934, to December, 1935; by H.E. Newnham. Colombo, 1936. pp. 72.

MALAWI

MALAWI: land of progress; (produced for the Malawi Department of Information). irreg., 1969 (v.2)- [Zomba?]

- Bibliography

BROWN (EDWARD E.) and others, compilers. A bibliography of Malawi. Syracuse, 1965. pp. 161. (Syracuse University. Maxwell Graduate School of Citizenship and Public Affairs. Program of Eastern African Studies. Eastern African Bibliographical Series. No. 1)

SYRACUSE UNIVERSITY. Maxwell Graduate School of Citizenship and Public Affairs. Program of Eastern African Studies. Occasional Bibliographies. No.13. A supplement to A bibliography on Malawi; [compiled] by John B. Webster [and] Paulus Mohome. Syracuse, N.Y., [1968?]. fo. 54.

- Census

NYASALAND. Census, 1945. Report on the census of 1945. Zomba, 1946. pp. 52.

MALAWI. Census, 1966. Population census, 1966: provisional (and Final) report. Zomba, [1966-69]. 2 pts. (in 1 vol.) 33½cm.

- Economic conditions

FEDERATION OF RHODESIA AND NYASALAND. 1955. Opportunity in Rhodesia and Nyasaland. (Federal Information Department) Salisbury, [1955]. pp. 66.

SMIT (P.) Current trends of development in Malawi. Pretoria, [1968?]. fo. 13. (Africa Institute. Occasional Papers. No. 2)

- Economic conditions - Statistics

MALAWI. National Statistical Office. Annual survey of economic activities: larger establishments. Zomba, annual, 1967 [1st] to date.

- Economic history

PACHAI (B.) The story of Malawi capitals: old and new, 1891-1969. Blantyre, [1970]. pp. 22. (Reprinted from the Society of Malawi Journal, January 1970, vol.23, no.1)

BAKER (C. A.) Malawi's early road system. Blantyre, [1971]. pp. 15. (Reprinted from the Society of Malawi Journal, January 1971, vol.24, no.1)

- Economic policy

NYASALAND. 1945. Report of the post-war development committee: [Juxon Barton, subsequently D.W. Saunders-Jones, chairmen] Zomba, 1945. pp. 145. For revised report see NYASALAND. 1947.

- Foreign economic relations - South Africa

LEISTNER (G.M.E.) Malawi, South Africa, and the issue of closer economic co-operation. Pretoria, [1967?]. fo. 7. (Africa Institute. Occasional Papers. No. 13)

- Foreign relations - Treaties

MALAWI TREATY SERIES; (produced and ed. by Ministry for External Affairs). a., 1964/5 (ed. 1-2) [1st issue] - Zomba.

- Government publications

UNITED STATES. Library of Congress. The Rhodesias and Nyasaland: a guide to official publications. Washington, 1965. pp. xv, 285.

- History

GANN (LEWIS H.) Central Africa: the former British states. Englewood Cliffs, [1971]. pp. 180. bibliog.

- Industries

MALAWI. National Statistical Office. Annual survey of economic activities: larger establishments. Zomba, annual, 1967 [1st] to date.

- Race question

MWASE (GEORGE SIMEON) Strike a blow and die: a narrative of race relations in colonial Africa;...edited and introduced by Robert I. Rotberg. Cambridge, Mass., Harvard University Press, 1967. pp. xliii, 135. 21cm.

- Statistics

COMPENDIUM OF STATISTICS FOR MALAWI; [published by] National Statistical Office, Malawi. Zomba, annual, 1966 [2nd issue] to date. 33cm.

MALAWI. 1966. Compendium of statistics, 1965. (Ministry of Development and Planning) [Zomba], 1966. pp. iii, 62. 33cm.

MALAY ARCHIPELAGO AND PENINSULA

- Description and travel

MOOR (J.H.) Notices of the Indian archipelago and adjacent countries, etc.; [facsimile reprint of the edition of 1837]. London, Cass 1968. pp. (iv),vii,277,117. 25cm.

MALAY RACE

ROBERT (KATHERINE) The role of Malay magicians and medicine men: a study of their practices, their clients, and their relation to their clients in Singapore; [research paper, Department of Social Studies, University of Singapore]. 1959. fo. (iii), 134. bibliog. Microfilm of typescript.

MALAY RACE (Cont'd.)

BIN AHMAD (WAN ABDUL RAHMAN) The island Malays: a study of a group of Malays in an island off Singapore: their life, customs, beliefs, and the degree to which they communicate with other places to meet their various needs; [research paper, Department of Social Studies, University of Singapore]. 1960. fo. 191. bibliog. Microfilm of typescript.
R (Microfilm) Film 108 (2nd item) M 774

KRAUSE (DIETER) Die panindonesische Idee: Entstehung und Entwicklung in Malaya und Singapur bis 1963. Freiburg im Breisgau, Arnold-Bergstraesser-Institut für Kulturwissenschaftliche Forschung, 1967. pp. 226. bibliog. 21cm.

MAHATHIR BIN MOHAMAD. The Malay dilemma. Singapore, 1970. pp. 188.

MALAYA

- Economic conditions

MALAYAN INFORMATION AGENCY. 1912. British Malaya:... trade and commerce. London, 1912. pp. 64.

- Economic history

JACKSON (R.N.) Immigrant labour and the development of Malaya, 1786-1920. [Kuala Lumpur], Government Press, 1961. pp. 162. bibliog.

- Emigration and immigration

SANDHU (KERNIAL SINGH) Indians in Malaya: some aspects of their immigration and settlement, 1786-1957. Cambridge, 1969. pp. 345. bibliog.

- History

FOOK-SENG (PHILIP LOH) The Malay States, 1877-1895: political change and social policy. Singapore, 1969. pp. 233. bibliog.

KENNEDY (JOSEPH) M.A. A history of Malaya. 2nd ed. London, 1970. pp. 364. bibliog.

CLUTTERBUCK (RICHARD LEWIS) Riot and revolution in Singapore and Malaya, 1945-1963; (Ph.D. (London) thesis]. 1971. fo. 334. bibliog. Typescript: unpublished. This thesis is the property of London University and may not be removed from the Library. Not to be consulted without the author's permission until 1989.

- Officials and employees - Salaries, allowances, etc.

REPORT of the Commissions appointed by...the Governor of the Straits Settlements and the High Commissioner of the Federated Malay States to enquire into certain matters relating to the public service, to wit, the salaries, and the conditions of service, etc.; (with Text of oral evidence taken by the Commissions); [and letters of transmittal, etc.] [John A. Bucknill, president]. Singapore, Government Printing Office, 1919. 3 vols.

- Politics and government

FEDERATED MALAY STATES. Federal Council. Papers to be laid before the...Council by command of His Excellency the High Commissioner. Kuala Lumpur, irreg., 1941 (nos. 1, 2, 5, 7-11, 14, 15, 19). 33½cm.

MOVEMENT FOR COLONIAL FREEDOM. No to Malaysia! London, [1963?]. 1 pamphlet (unpaged).

MALAYAN peoples' experience refutes revisionist fallacies: sixteenth anniversary of the Malayan peoples' armed struggle. Peking, 1965. pp. 16. (Reprinted from Malayan Monitor, June 30, 1964)

KRAUSE (DIETER) Die panindonesische Idee: Entstehung und Entwicklung in Malaya und Singapur bis 1963. Freiburg im Breisgau, Arnold-Bergstraesser-Institut für Kulturwissenschaftliche Forschung, 1967. pp. 226. bibliog. 21cm.

HORLEMANN (JUERGEN) Modelle der kolonialen Konterrevolution: Beschreibung und Dokumente. Frankfurt a.M., [1968]. pp. 197.

STENSON (MICHAEL R.) Repression and revolt: the origins of the 1948 communist insurrection in Malaya and Singapore. Athens, Ohio, [1969]. pp. 31. (Ohio University. Center for International Studies. Papers in International Studies. Southeast Asia Series. No. 10)

- Sanitary affairs

MALAYA. Medical Departments. Annual report. Singapore, annual, 1939. 24cm.

MALAYSIA

GROSSMAN (BERNHARD) ed. Malaysia. Frankfurt, Metzner, [1966]. pp. xi, 222. bibliogs. 24cm. (Hamburg. Institut für Asienkunde. Studien zur Entwicklung in Süd- und Ostasien. Neue Folge. Teil 4)

UNITED STATES. Army Department. Pamphlets. No. 550-45. Area handbook for Malaysia and Singapore. Washington, [1966]. pp. xii, 745. bibliog.

GULLICK (JOHN MICHAEL) Malaysia. London, Benn, 1969. pp. 304. bibliog. 21½cm. (Nations of the Modern World)

- Commerce

POPENOE (OLIVER) Malay entrepreneurs: an analysis of the social backgrounds, careers and attitudes of the leading Malay businessmen in Western Malaysia; [Ph.D. (London) thesis]. 1970. fo. 539. bibliog. Typescript: unpublished. This thesis is the property of London University and may not be removed from the Library.

- Constitution

SHERIDAN (LIONEL ASTOR) and GROVES (HARRY E.) The constitution of Malaysia. rev. ed. Dobbs Ferry, Oceana, 1967. pp. xxxiv, 398. 22½cm.

- Economic conditions

   RUTHERFORD (JOHN) Geographer, and others. New viewpoints in economic geography: case studies from Australia, New Zealand, Malaysia, North America. London, Harrap, 1966, repr. 1967. pp. xiii, 466. bibliogs. 24cm.

   GOULD (JAMES W.) The United States and Malaysia. Cambridge, Mass., 1969. pp. 267. bibliog.

   KANAPATHY (V.) The Malaysian economy: problems and prospects. Singapore, 1970. pp. 240. bibliog.

- Economic conditions - Bibliography

   CHALLIS (JOYCE) compiler. Annotated bibliography of economic and social material in Singapore (and West Malaysia). vol. [1] is of the 2nd ed. Singapore, 1968-9. 3 vols. (Singapore. University. Economic Research Centre. Research Bibliography Series. Nos. 1-3)

- Economic policy

   FEDERATION OF MALAYSIA. 1965. First Malaysia plan, 1966-1970. Kuala Lumpur, 1965. pp. 190, map.

   FEDERATION OF MALAYSIA. 1965. Techniques used for developing Malaysia. (Ministry of National and Rural Development) Kuala Lumpur, 1965. pp. 19. 18½cm. x 26cm.

   FREEMAN (ROGER A.) Socialism and private enterprise in equatorial Asia: the case of Malaysia and Indonesia. Stanford, University, Hoover Institution on War, Revolution and Peace, 1968. pp. xiii, 130. bibliog. 20cm. (Hoover Institution Studies. 20)

   RAZAK BIN HUSSEIN (TUN ABDUL) Strategy for action: the selected speeches...; edited by J. Victor Morais. Kuala Lumpur, Malaysian Centre for Development Studies, 1969. pp. xxxix, 518. 22cm.

   KANAPATHY (V.) The Malaysian economy: problems and prospects. Singapore, 1970. pp. 240. bibliog.

   FEDERATION OF MALAYSIA. 1971. Second Malaysia plan, 1971-1975. Kuala Lumpur, 1971. pp. 267, 1 map.

- Foreign relations

   BOYCE (PETER) ed. Malaysia and Singapore in international diplomacy: documents and commentaries. Sydney, Sydney U.P., 1968. pp. xii, 268. 23½cm.

   RAZAK BIN HUSSEIN (TUN ABDUL) Strategy for action: the selected speeches...; edited by J. Victor Morais. Kuala Lumpur, Malaysian Centre for Development Studies, 1969. pp. xxxix, 518. 22cm.

- Foreign relations - Singapore

   CHAN (HENG CHEE) Singapore: the politics of survival, 1965-1967. Singapore, 1971. pp. 65. bibliog.

- Foreign relations - United States

   GOULD (JAMES W.) The United States and Malaysia. Cambridge, Mass., 1969. pp. 267. bibliog.

- Government publications

   NATIONAL ARCHIVES OF MALAYSIA. ...Accessions list 1957-1967. [Petaling Jaya, 1969]. pp. 185.

   Government
   Publications
   Department

- History

   RYAN (NEIL JOSEPH) The making of modern Malaysia: a history from earliest times to 1966. Kuala Lumpur, O.U.P., 1967. pp. xix, 259. bibliogs. 22cm.

   SMITH (THOMAS EDWARD) and BASTIN (JOHN) Malaysia. Oxford, O.U.P., 1967. pp. 128. bibliog. 18cm. (The Modern World. 12)

   ALLEN (Sir RICHARD HUGH SEDLEY) Malaysia: prospect and retrospect; the impact and aftermath of colonial rule. London, O.U.P., 1968. pp. xiv, 335. bibliog. 21½cm.

   GULLICK (JOHN MICHAEL) Malaysia. London, Benn, 1969. pp. 304. bibliog. 21½cm. (Nations of the Modern World)

- Occupations

   INTERNATIONAL LABOUR OFFICE. Development Programme: Technical Assistance Sector. [Malaysia]. R.23. Report to the government of Malaysia on the development of the national classification of occupations. (ILO/TAP/Malaysia/R.23). Geneva, 1968. pp. 30.

- Officials and employees

   SCOTT (JAMES C.) Political ideology in Malaysia: reality and the beliefs of an elite. New Haven, Yale U.P., 1968. pp. xiii, 302. 23½cm. (Yale University. Yale Southeast Asia Studies. 3)

- Parliament - Elections

   RATNAM (K.J.) and MILNE (ROBERT STEVEN) The Malayan Parliamentary election of 1964. Singapore, 1967 repr. 1969. pp. 467.

- Politics and government

   ALLEN (Sir RICHARD HUGH SEDLEY) Malaysia: prospect and retrospect; the impact and aftermath of colonial rule. London, O.U.P., 1968. pp. xiv, 335. bibliog. 21½cm.

   SCOTT (JAMES C.) Political ideology in Malaysia: reality and the beliefs of an elite. New Haven, Yale U.P., 1968. pp. xiii, 302. 23½cm. (Yale University. Yale Southeast Asia Studies. 3)

   FLETCHER (NANCY McHENRY) The separation of Singapore from Malaysia. Ithaca, 1969. pp. 98. bibliog. (Cornell University. Department of Asian Studies. Southeast Asia Program. Data Papers. No. 73)

   GOULD (JAMES W.) The United States and Malaysia. Cambridge, Mass., 1969. pp. 267. bibliog.

MALAYSIA - Politics and government
(Cont'd)

>The MAY tragedy in Malaysia: a collection of essays; [edited by Lee Kam Hing]. [Singapore], 1969. pp. 54.
>
>RAHMAN PUTRA (ABDUL), Tunku. May 13: before and after. Kuala Lumpur, 1969. pp. 207.
>
>RAZAK BIN HUSSEIN (TUN ABDUL) Strategy for action: the selected speeches...; edited by J. Victor Morais. Kuala Lumpur, Malaysian Centre for Development Studies, 1969. pp. xxxix, 518. 22cm.
>
>SLIMMING (JOHN) Malaysia: death of a democracy. London, [1969]. pp. 82.
>
>GAGLIANO (FELIX V.) Communal violence in Malaysia, 1969: the political aftermath. Athens, Ohio, 1970. fo. 39. (Ohio University. Center for International Studies. Papers in the International Studies. Southeast Asia Series. No.13)
>
>MEANS (GORDON P.) Malaysian politics. London, [1970]. pp. 447. bibliog.

- Race question

>MAHATHIR BIN MOHAMAD. The Malay dilemma. Singapore, 1970. pp. 188.

- Relations (general) with Ceylon

>PARANAVITANA (SENARAT) Ceylon and Malaysia. Colombo, Lake House Investments, 1966. pp. xiii, 234. 21cm.

- Rural conditions

>WILSON (PETER J.) A Malay village and Malaysia: social values and rural development. New Haven, Hraf P., [1967]. pp. ix, 171. bibliog. 21cm.

- Social conditions

>ALWEE (A. WAHAB) Rembau: a study in integration and conflict in a village in Negri Sembilan, Malaya. Nedlands, University of Western Australia, Centre for Asian Studies, 1967. pp. vii, 60. bibliog. 26cm. (Working Papers in Asian Studies. No.1.)
>
>GOULD (JAMES W.) The United States and Malaysia. Cambridge, Mass., 1969. pp. 267. bibliog.

- Social conditions - Bibliography

>CHALLIS (JOYCE) compiler. Annotated bibliography of economic and social material in Singapore (and West Malaysia). vol. [1] is of the 2nd ed. Singapore, 1968-9. 3 vols. (Singapore. University. Economic Research Centre. Research Bibliography Series. Nos. 1-3)

- Social policy

>FEDERATION OF MALAYSIA. 1965. First Malaysia plan, 1966-1970. Kuala Lumpur, 1965. pp. 190, map.
>
>RAZAK BIN HUSSEIN (TUN ABDUL) Strategy for action: the selected speeches...; edited by J. Victor Morais. Kuala Lumpur, Malaysian Centre for Development Studies, 1969. pp. xxxix, 518. 22cm.
>
>FEDERATION OF MALAYSIA. 1971. Second Malaysia plan, 1971-1975. Kuala Lumpur, 1971. pp. 267, 1 map.

- Statistics - Bibliography

>CHALLIS (JOYCE) compiler. Annotated bibliography of economic and social material in Singapore (and West Malaysia). vol. [1] is of the 2nd ed. Singapore, 1968-9. 3 vols. (Singapore. University. Economic Research Centre. Research Bibliography Series. Nos. 1-3)

MALCOLM X, pseud.

>CLEAGE (ALBERT) and BREITMAN (GEORGE) Myths about Malcolm X: two views. New York, 1968 repr. 1969. pp. 30.
>
>EPPS (ARCHIE) ed. The speeches of Malcolm X at Harvard. New York, Morrow, 1968. pp. 191. 20½cm.
>
>JAMAL (HAKIM ABDULLAH) From the dead level: Malcolm X and me. London, 1971. pp. 240.

MALCOLM (NORMAN)

>LEWIS (HYWEL DAVID) Dreaming and experience. London, Athlone P., 1968. pp. 29. 21½cm. (London. University. London School of Economics and Political Science. Hobhouse Memorial Trust Lectures. No. 37)

MALEBRANCHE (NICOLAS)

>LUCE (ARTHUR ASTON) Berkeley and Malebranche: a study in the origins of Berkeley's thought. Oxford, 1934 repr. 1967. pp. 214.
>
>DUCASSÉ (PIERRE) Malebranche. 3rd ed. Paris, P.U.F., 1968. pp. 134. bibliog. 17½cm. (Philosophes)

MALEEV (LUKA)

>MALEEV (LUKA) Принос към истината за катастрофата на България през септември 1918 година: документи, факти и спомени из дневника на адютанта на главнокомандующия Действующата Армия, etc. [кн. 1]. София, 1921. pp. 262.

MALI (REPUBLIC)

- Economic conditions

>MALI. 1962. Comptes économiques de la République du Mali, 1959. (Ministère du Plan et de la Coordination des Affaires Économiques et Financières) [Bamako? 1962]. pp. 167. 27cm.
>
>COMPTES ECONOMIQUES DU MALI; [published by] Service de la Statistique, Mali. [Koububa], annual, 1964/5 1964/7 to date.

GALLAIS (JEAN) Le delta intérieur du Niger: étude de géographie régionale. Dakar, 1967. pp. 621. bibliog. (Institut Fondamental d'Afrique Noire. Mémoires. No. 79)

- History

MONTIEL (CHARLES) Les empires du Mali: étude d'histoire et de sociologie soudanaises. Paris, Maisonneuve et Larose, [1968]. pp. viii, 159. bibliog. 22½cm. (Extrait du Bulletin du Comité d'Études Historiques et Scientifiques de l'Afrique Occidentale Française. tome 12, nos.3-4, 1929)

- Population

MALI. 1962. Étude démographique du delta vif du Niger; (conduite sous la direction de R. Clairin). 2ème fasc. Résultats détaillés. (Mission Socio-Économique du Soudan) [Paris, 1962?]. pp. 203. 27cm.

MALI. Service de la Statistique. 1968. Enquête démographique au Mali, 1960-1961. [Paris], I.N.S.E.E., [1968?]. pp. 349. 26½cm.

- Sanitary affairs

MALI. Ministère de la Santé Publique et des Affaires Sociales. 1966. Plan décennal (1^{er}juillet 1966 - 30 juin 1976) de développement des services de santé. Bamako, 1966. pp. 210.

MALI FEDERATION

- Politics and government

CAIOLI (ALDO) Esperienze politiche africane: la federazione del Mali. Milano, Giuffrè, 1966. pp. 163. bibliog. 22cm. (Florence. Università degli Studi di Filenze. Istituto di Diritto Pubblico comparato. La Persona e la Comunità nella Problematica del Potere Politico. 12)

MALIK (MICHAEL ABDUL)

MALIK (MICHAEL ABDUL) From Michael de Freitas to Michael X. London, Deutsch, 1968. pp. 207. 21½cm.

MALINGERING

EISSLER (K. R.) Malingering. in Wilbur (George B.) and Muensterberger (Warner) eds. Psychoanalysis and culture:...[reprint of work originally published in 1951]. New York, 1967.

MALINOV (ALEKSANDR P.)

MALINOV (ALEKSANDR P.) Странички от нашата нова политическа история: спомени. 1. София, 1938. pp. 182. 18½см.

MALINOWSKI (BRONISŁAW)

LANGENDOEN (D. TERENCE) The London school of linguistics: a study of the linguistic theories of B. Malinowski and J.R. Firth. Cambridge, M.I.T. Press, [1968]. pp. xiii, 123. bibliog.

PANOFF (MICHEL) Bronislaw Malinowski. Paris, [1972]. pp. 157. bibliog.

MALLET (MARIE CONSTANCE) Lady

[MALLET (MARIE CONSTANCE) Lady] Life with Queen Victoria: Marie Mallet's letters from Court 1887-1901; edited by Victor Mallet. London, Murray, 1968. pp. xxiv, 245. 21½cm.

MALNUTRITION

CITIZENS' BOARD OF INQUIRY INTO HUNGER AND MALNUTRITION IN THE UNITED STATES. Hunger, U.S.A.: a report. Boston, Beacon P., 1968. pp. 96. 25½cm.

MALNUTRITION, learning and behavior; edited by Nevin S. Scrimshaw and John E. Gordon; proceedings of an International Conference, co-sponsored by the Nutrition Foundation, Inc., and the Massachusetts Institute of Technology, held at Cambridge, Massachusetts, March 1 to 3,1967. Cambridge, M.I.T. Press, [1968]. pp. xiii, 566. 22½cm.

A SUMMARY report on estimates of deficiencies in protein, iron and vitamin A in the Indian Union, 1966-67 to 1970-71. [New Delhi?, 1968?] pp. 12.

COLES (ROBERT) Still hungry in America. New York, [1969]. pp. 115.

MALNUTRITION is a problem of ecology; [papers presented at a conference at Bellagio, 1968]; edited by Paul György and O.L. Kline. Basel, 1970. pp. 224.

MAY (JACQUES M.) and McLELLAN (DONNA L.) The ecology of malnutrition in Eastern Africa and four countries of Western Africa, etc. New York, 1970. pp. 675. bibliogs.

REID (J.V.O.) Malnutrition: a paper prepared for the National Union of South African Students. Johannesburg, [1970]. pp. 16. (South African Institute of Race Relations. Topical Talks. No. 22)

SHARMAN (ANNE CLARK) Social and economic aspects of nutrition in Padhola, Bukedi District, Uganda; [Ph.D. (London) thesis]. 1969 [or rather 1970]. fo. 367. bibliog. Two reprints and errata sheets in end pocket. Typescript: unpublished. This thesis is the property of London University and may not be removed from the Library.

MALRAUX (ANDRÉ)

GOLDMANN (LUCIEN) Pour une sociologie du roman. [Paris, 1965 repr. 1969]. pp. 372.

MALRAUX (ANDRÉ) Antimémoires. [Paris], Gallimard, [1967 in progress] 19½cm. (Collection Soleil)

MOSSUZ (JANINE) André Malraux et le gaullisme. Paris, 1970. pp. 312. bibliog. (Fondation Nationale des Sciences Politiques. Cahiers. 177)

MALTA

- Census

MALTA. Census, 1967. Malta census, 1967: report on economic activities. Valletta, [1971?] 2 vols. (in 1).

- Economic conditions

VLORA (K.ALESSANDRO) Geografia delle attività economiche regionali, con esemplificazioni sulle Isole Maltesi. [Florence, imprint, 1967] pp. (7). bibliog. 24cm. (Estratto da Cultura e scuola, n.23, 1967)

JOINT STEERING COMMITTEE FOR MALTA. Annual report. Valletta, annual, 1968 [1st] to date.

LA GRANDVILLE (OLIVIER DE) Malte: réalité géographique et perspectives économiques. Genève, Droz, 1968. pp. 268. bibliog. 23cm. (Travaux de Droit, d'Économie, de Sociologie, et de Sciences Politiques. Nc. 69)

- Economic history - Bibliography

XUEREB (PAUL) Economic and social history of Malta in the 19th century: a bibliography based on the holdings of the Royal University of Malta Library. Msida, 1970. fo. 20.

- Economic policy

MALTA. 1959. Development plan for the Maltese Islands, 1959-64. [Valletta], 1959. pp. 96.

JOINT STEERING COMMITTEE FOR MALTA. Annual report. Valletta, annual, 1968 [1st] to date.

LA GRANDVILLE (OLIVIER DE) Malte: réalité géographique et perspectives économiques. Genève, Droz, 1968. pp. 268. bibliog. 23cm. (Travaux de Droit, d'Économie, de Sociologie, et de Sciences Politiques. Nc. 69)

- Foreign relations - United Kingdom

AUSTIN (DENNIS) Malta and the end of empire. London, 1971. pp. 132. bibliog.

- History

GULIA (OLIVER J.) The 'Consiglio Popolare': some considerations on the origin, composition, functions and extent of powers of the Ancient Popular Council of the Maltese People and on the various theories thereon. n.p., 1956. pp. 19. Typescript.

- Officials and employees - Salaries, allowances, etc.

MALTA. 1959. Government proposals on pay and grading structure of non-industrial employees in the Malta government service. [Valletta], 1959. fo. 16.

- Politics and government

AUSTIN (DENNIS) Malta and the end of empire. London, 1971. pp. 132. bibliog.

- Rural conditions

BOISSEVAIN (JEREMY FERGUS) Hal-Farrug: a village in Malta. New York, [1969]. pp. 104. bibliog.

- Social conditions

BOISSEVAIN (JEREMY FERGUS) Saints and fireworks: religion and politics in rural Malta; [with a postscript, 1968]. 2nd ed. London, Athlone P., 1969. pp. xii, 162. bibliog. 21½cm. (London. University. London School of Economics and Political Science Monographs on Social Anthropology. No. 30)

- Social history - Bibliography

XUEREB (PAUL) Economic and social history of Malta in the 19th century: a bibliography based on the holdings of the Royal University of Malta Library. Msida, 1970. fo. 20.

- Social life and customs

BOISSEVAIN (JEREMY FERGUS) Hal-Farrug: a village in Malta. New York, [1969]. pp. 104. bibliog.

- Social policy

MALTA. 1959. Development plan for the Maltese Islands, 1959-64. [Valletta], 1959. pp. 96.

- Statistics

GERMANY (BUNDESREPUBLIK). Länderkurzberichte: Malta. Wiesbaden, irreg., 1969 [1st issue] to date.

- Statistics, Vital

MALTA. Central Office of Statistics. 1960. Maltese life table, no. 2, 1957. Valletta, [1960] pp. 13. Maltese life table, no. 1, is printed on pp.xiv-xvii of the Malta census, 1948.

MALTA. Central Office of Statistics. 1963. An enquiry into family size in Malta and Gozo. Valletta, 1963. pp. 305.

MALTHUS (THOMAS ROBERT)

VODOVOZOV (NIKOLAI VASIL'EVICH) Mal'tus. Berlin, 1922. pp. 168.

ZINKE (GEORGE W.) The problem of Malthus must progress end in overpopulation? Boulder, U. of Colorado P., 1967. pp. 88. bibliog. 25½cm. (Colorado University Studies. Series in Economics. No.5)

MALTHUSIANISM

AN APPEAL to the editors of the Times newspaper in behalf of the working classes: being a survey of the conduct of that journal during the last autumn on the most important subjects of the day; by two lay members of the Church. London, Hatchard, 1845. pp. 77. 22cm.

MALVERN

- Water-supply

JENKING (R.C.) Metering at Malvern: a research study of the Standing Water Committee of the Institute [of Municipal Treasurers and Accountants] [London], 1969. pp. 64.

MAMELI (GOFFREDO)

BERTOTTI. (E.) Goffredo Mameli e Repubblica romana nel 1849. Genova, Studio Editoriale Genovese, 1927. pp. 151. bibliog. 20½cm.

MAMMALS

YOUNG (JOHN ZACHARY) The life of mammals. Oxford, Clarendon P., 1957, repr. 1966. pp. xv, 820. bibliog. 23½cm.

MAN

WITCHELL (CHARLES A.) The cultivation of man according to the teachings of common-sense: being a treatise on the application to man of the laws that he applies to all other creatures. London, 1904. pp. 168.

PANTSKHAVA (IL'IA DIOMIDOVICH) Chelovek, ego zhizn' i bessmertie. Moskva, 1967. pp. 191.

DOURNES (JACQUES) L'homme et son mythe. Paris Aubier-Montaigne, [1968]. pp. 219. 20cm. (Collection Recherches Economiques et Sociales)

JOURNEES INTERNATIONALES D'ETUDES SUR LES METHODES DE CALCUL DANS LES SCIENCES DE L'HOMME, ROME, 1966. Calcul et formalisation dans les sciences de l'homme: conférences prononcées lors des journées...sous les auspices du Centre International de Calcul etc. Paris, 1968. pp. 324. bibliogs. In English or French.

TURNEY-HIGH (HARRY HOLBERT) Man and system: foundations for the study of human relations. New York, Appleton-Century-Crofts, [1968]. pp. viii, 635. 24cm.

GUSTAVUS ADOLPHUS COLLEGE. Nobel Conference, 4th, 1968. The uniqueness of man; a discussion at the Nobel Conference...edited by John D. Roslansky. Amsterdam, 1969. pp. 189.

PROBLEMA... Проблема человека в современной философии. Москва, 1969. pp. 430.

BRIERLEY (JOHN K.) A natural history of man: a biologist's view, etc. London, 1970. pp. 184. bibliog.

THORSON (THOMAS LANDON) Biopolitics. New York, [1970]. pp. 216.

- Age determination

BOURLIÈRE (FRANÇOIS MARIE GABRIEL) The assessment of biological age in man. Geneva, World Health Organization, 1970. pp. 67. bibliog. (Public Health Papers. No. 37)

- Animal nature

MORRIS (DESMOND) The human zoo. London, 1969. pp. 256. bibliog.

MORRIS (DESMOND) Intimate behaviour. London, 1971. pp. 253. bibliog.

- Influence of environment

SPITZ (R. A.) Environment versus race: environment as an etiological factor in psychiatric disturbances in infancy. in Wilbur (George B.) and Muensterberger (Warner) eds. Psychoanalysis and culture...[reprint of the volume originally published in 1951]. New York, 1967.

SYMPOSIUM ON HEALTH IN A CHANGING ENVIRONMENT, BIRMINGHAM 1965. Report, etc. [London], 1966. pp. 51. bibliog. (Journal of the Royal College of General Practitioners. vol. 12. Supplement no. 1)

DUBOS (RENÉ JULES) Man, medicine, and environment. London, Pall Mall P., [1968]. pp. v, 125. 23½cm.

GENETIC and environmental influences on behaviour: a symposium held by the Eugenics Society in September 1967; edited by J.M. Thoday [and] A.S. Parkes. Edinburgh, Oliver & Boyd, 1968. pp. x, 217. 21½cm.

LONDON. University. London School of Economics and Political Science. Graduate Geography Department. Discussion Papers. No. 20. A review of behavior and location: foundations for a geographic and dynamic location theory; [by] John Adams. London, 1968. fo. 6. 30cm.

ENVIRONMENT, heredity and intelligence: compiled from the Harvard Educational Review. Cambridge, Mass., [1969] repr. 1971. pp. 246. bibliogs. (Harvard Educational Review. Reprint Series. No. 2)

MORRIS (DESMOND) The human zoo. London, 1969. pp. 256. bibliog.

PROSHANSKY (HAROLD) and others, eds. Environmental psychology: man and his physical setting. New York, [1970]. pp. 690. bibliogs.

STERN (GEORGE G.) People in context: measuring person-environment congruence in education and industry. New York, [1970]. pp. 402. bibliog.

GOODEY (BRIAN) Perception of the environment: an introduction to the literature. Birmingham, 1971. pp. 90. bibliog. (Birmingham. University. Centre for Urban and Regional Studies. Occasional Papers. No. 17)

- Influence on nature

PRIRODA... Природа и общество. Москва, Наука, 1968. pp. 846. bibliog. 21½см.

WESTERN RESOURCES CONFERENCE, 1967. Man and the quality of his environment; edited by J. Ernest Flack and Margaret C. Shipley. Boulder, U. of Colorado P., [1968]. pp. x, 251. (Western Resources Papers)

ANDERSON (WALT) ed. Politics and environment: reader in ecological crisis. Pacific Palisades, [1970]. pp. 362.

MAN - Influence on nature (Cont'd.)

BLACK (JOHN NICHOLSON) The dominion of man: the search for ecological responsibility. Edinburgh, 1970. pp. 169. bibliog.

CHALLENGE for survival, (1968): land, air, and water for man in megalopolis; [symposium presented by the New York Botanical Garden]; edited by Pierre Dansereau. New York, 1970. pp. 235. bibliogs.

NATIONAL BOOK LEAGUE and U.K. Nature Conservancy. Man and environment: (an annotated list). London, 1970. pp. 23.

NICHOLSON (MAX) The environmental revolution: a guide for the new masters of the world. [London], 1970. pp. 366.

NUCLEAR power and the public: [based on a symposium held at the University of Minnesota, 1969, and sponsored by the Center for Population Studies and the Center for Urban and Regional Affairs]: (Harry Foreman, editor). Minneapolis, [1970]. pp. 273. bibliogs.

STUDY OF CRITICAL ENVIRONMENTAL PROBLEMS. Man's impact on the global environment: assessment and recommendations for action; report of the Study...sponsored by the Massachusetts Institute of Technology. Cambridge, Mass., [1970]. pp. 319. bibliogs.

TAYLOR (GORDON RATTRAY) The Doomsday book. London, [1970]. pp. 335.

MAN (THEOLOGY)

SPECK (JOSEF) Karl Rahners theologische Anthropologie: eine Einführung. München, [1967]. pp. 233.

CRAGG (KENNETH) The privilege of man: a theme in Judaism, Islam and Christianity. London, Athlone P., 1968. pp. xii, 208. 21½cm. (London. University. School of Oriental and African Studies. Jordan Lectures in Comparative Religion. 8)

O'CONNELL (ROBERT J.) St. Augustine's early theory of man, A.D. 386-391. Cambridge, Mass., 1968. pp. 301.

MAN, PRIMITIVE

TINLAND (FRANCK) L'homme sauvage: homo ferus et homo sylvestris; de l'animal à l'homme. Paris, Payot, 1968. pp. 287. bibliog. 22½cm. (Bibliothèque Scientifique)

MANAGEMENT

ORGANISATION FOR EUROPEAN ECONOMIC CO-OPERATION. European Productivity Agency. Turin Conference on Business Management Education, 1956. [Papers]. [Paris, 1956]. 9 pts.

PELLIZZI (CAMILLO) La tecnica come classe dirigente: le idee di James Burnham, "The managerial revolution", 1940; le tesi di Luigi Fontanelli, "Logica della corporazione", 1934. Roma, [196-?] pp. 105.

EUROPEAN PRODUCTIVITY AGENCY. 1961. A study of post-war growth in management organisations: comparison of chemical and engineering firms of eight Western European countries; report of the International Co-ordinator, T. E. Chester. (Project No. 347) Paris, 1961. pp. 94. 27cm.

The IMPACT of psychiatry on American management: a conference presented by the New York State School of Industrial and Labor Relations... March, 1962. Ithaca, New York State School of Industrial and Labor Relations, 1962. pp. 35. 28cm. (Reprint Series. No. 129) (Reprinted from Industrial Medicine and Surgery, November, 1962)

ORGANISATION FOR ECONOMIC CO-OPERATION AND DEVELOPMENT. 1962. Modern management: principles and practices; ([by] Dick Carlson). [Paris, 1962]. pp. 183.

AUSSCHUSS FÜR WIRTSCHAFTLICHE VERWALTUNG. Schriftenreihe. No. 114. Organisation in amerikanischen Unternehmen: Ergebnisse einer Studienreis in die Vereinigten Staaten von Amerika. Wiesbaden, Gabler, [1963]. pp. 120. 21cm.

CHARNES (ABRAHAM) and STEDRY (A.) Further explorations in the theory of multiple budgeted goals. Evanston, 1963. fo. 31. bibliog. (Northwestern University. Technological Institute. O.N.R. Research Memoranda. No. 72)

CRAWFORD (Sir JOHN GRENFELL) Responsibilities of management in a growing economy;(the second John Storey memorial lecture,...Science House, University of New South Wales, Kensington, Tuesday, 19th November, 1963). n.p. [1963?]. pp. 22. (Australian Institute of Management. John Storey Memorial Lectures. 1963)

WAERENSKJOLD (E.) Noen tanker om administrativ ledelse i dag og i morgen. Bergen, 1964. pp. 14. (Norges Handelshøyskole. Kristofer Lehmkuhl Forelesning. 1964)

McDONOUGH (ADRIAN M.) and GARRETT (LEONARD J.) Management systems: working concepts and practices. Homewood, Irwin, 1965. pp. xviii, 311. 23cm. (Irwin Series in Management)

REUSS (GERHART ERNST) Management im Zeitalter des Elektronenrechners. Basel, Kyklos-Verlag, 1965. pp. vii, 54. 21cm. (List Gesellschaft. Zur Politik der Gegenwart. Band 3)

CULLEN (DONALD EUGENE) and GREENBAUM (MARCIA L.) Management rights and collective bargaining: can both survive? Ithaca, the School, 1966. pp. vii, 63. 23cm. (Cornell University. New York State School of International and Labor Relations. Bulletins. 58)

GRUENFELD (LEOPOLD W.) Management development effect on changes in values. [Ithaca], Cornell University, New York State School of Industrial and Labor Relations, [1966]. pp. (8). 23cm. (Reprint Series. No. 196) (Reprinted from Training and Development Journal, June 1966)

ISTOMIN (LEV IVANOVICH) and IGNAT'EV (DANIIL IVANOVICH) Применение математических методов и ЭВМ в управлении. Москва, Экономика, 1966. pp. 72. 19½cm. (Библиотечка Хозяйственного Руководителя)

WEISSMAN (JACOB IRA) ed. The social responsibilities of corporate management. Hampstead, N.Y., Hofstra University, 1966. pp. 328. bibliog. 28cm. (Yearbook of Business. Series 3, vol.2)

BEER (STAFFORD) Management science: the business use of operations research. London, Aldus Books, [1967]. pp. 192. bibliog. 21½cm. (Aldus Science and Technology Series)

BEHAVIOURAL sciences in management: [papers during a seminar presented in August, 1965, at the Indian Institute of Management, Calcutta]; edited by Suresh Srivastva. London, Asia Publishing House, [1967]. pp. xii, 326. bibliogs. 21cm.

GOLEMBIEWSKI (ROBERT T.) and GIBSON (FRANK KENNETH) Managerial behavior and organization demands: management as a linking of levels of interaction. Chicago, Rand McNally, [1967]. pp. viii, 440. 23cm. (Rand McNally Series in the Organization Sciences)

HUMBLE (JOHN WILLIAM) Management by objectives. London, Industrial, Educational and Research Foundation, [1967]. pp. (23). 21cm. (Occasional Papers. No.2)

LIKERT (RENSIS) The human organization: its management and value. New York, McGraw-Hill, [1967]. pp. xi, 258. bibliog. 23cm.

ROBERTS (TOM JOHN) Developing effective managers. London, Institute of Personnel Management, 1967. pp. 63. bibliog. 21cm.

WARNER (KENNETH OREN) and HENNESSY (MARY L.) Public management at the bargaining table. Chicago, Public Personnel Association, [1967] pp. xiv, 490. bibliog. 22½cm.

1968

ARGENTI (JOHN) Corporate planning: a practical guide. London, Allen and Unwin, 1968. pp. 272. 21½cm. (Studies in Management. No. 2)

BARRETT (GERALD V.) The international research groups on management information system. Pittsburgh, U. of Pittsburgh, Graduate School of Business, Management Research Center, 1968. pp. 10. bibliog. 28cm. (Technical Reports. 18)

BASI (RAGHBIR S.) Action administration: planning and implementation. London, Asia Publishing House, [1968]. pp. xi, 234. 21½cm.

BATTY (JOSEPH) ed. Developments in management accountancy. London, Heinemann, 1968. pp. xv, 507. 21cm. (Heinemann Accountancy and Administration Series)

BECKER (HEINZ ALFRED) Management als beroep: kenmerken van de managersgroepering in sociologisch perspectief. 's-Gravenhage, Nijhoff, 1968. pp. xi, 271. bibliog. 24cm.

BERGER (KARL HEINZ) Unternehmensgrösse und Leitungsaufbau. Berlin, 1968. pp. 188. bibliog.

BERNSTEIN (LESLIE) ed. Management development. London, Business Books, 1968. pp. x, 188. 21½cm. (Management in Action Series)

BLAKE (ROBERT R.) and MOUTON (JANE S.) Corporate excellence through grid organization development. Houston, Gulf Publishing Co., [1968]. pp. xvii, 374. 23cm.

BRITISH STANDARDS INSTITUTION. Universal decimal classification; English full edition..., BS 1000... UDC 65/651+657/659; industrial and business management and organization; communication. London, 1968. pp. 38. (International Federation for Documentation. Publications. No.179)

CLARKSON (GEOFFREY P.E.) ed. Managerial economics; selected readings. Harmondsworth, Penguin Books, 1968. pp. 429. bibliog. 18cm. (Penguin Modern Economics X 57)

CLOOT (P.L.) Management information: a systematic approach. Henley-on-Thames, 1968. pp. 26. (Henley-on-Thames. Administrative Staff College. Occasional Papers. No. 7)

EMMERSON (BRIAN F.) Long range planning and its significance for the accountant. [London, 1968]. pp. 51. (Institute of Chartered Accountants in England and Wales. Summer Courses. 1968)

GELLERMAN (SAUL WILLIAM) Management by motivation. New York, American Management Association, [1968]. pp. 286. 23½cm.

GEORGE (CLAUDE SWANSON) The history of management thought. Englewood Cliffs, Prentice-Hall, [1968]. pp. xix, 210. bibliog. 22½cm.

GMAEHLE (PETER) Betriebswirtschaftslehre und Nationalsozialismus. [Bamberg, imprint, 1968?]. pp. 291. bibliog.

GROSS (BERTRAM MYRON) Organizations and their managing; a condensed one-volume edition of The managing of organizations. New York, Free P., [1968]. pp. xli, 708. bibliog. 23½cm.

HOFMANN (MICHAEL) Das unternehmerische Element in der Betriebswirtschaft. Berlin, Duncker und Humblot, [1968] pp. 318. bibliog. 23½cm. (Beiträge zur Ganzheitlichen Wirtschafts und Gesellschaftslehre. Band 5)

JEYNES (PAUL H.) Profitability and economic choice. Ames, Iowa State P., 1968. pp. xvii, 622. bibliog. 23cm.

KARSH (B.) Human relations versus management. in Becker (Howard Saul) and others, eds. Institutions and the person. Chicago, 1968.

KING (WILLIAM R.) Probability for management decisions. New York, Wiley, [1968]. pp. xxi, 372. bibliogs. 22½cm. (Wiley Series in Management and Administration)

MANAGEMENT (Cont'd.)

KOONTZ (HAROLD DAYTON) and O'DONNELL (CYRIL) Principles of management: an analysis of managerial functions. 4th ed. New York, McGraw-Hill, [1968] pp. x, 822. bibliogs. 23½cm. (McGraw-Hill Series in Management)

KUEHN (D. A.) Stock market valuation and acquisitions: an empirical test of one component of managerial utility. Coventry, University of Warwick, Department of Economics, 1968. fo. 28. bibliog. 30cm. (Warwick Economic Research Papers. No.1)

LAZARUS (HAROLD) and WARREN (E. KIRBY) eds. The progress of management: process, behavior, and operations research; a book of readings. Englewood Cliffs, Prentice-Hall, [1968]. pp. vi, 330. bibliogs. 23½cm.

LHERMITTE (PIERRE) Le pari informatique d'après une étude du Conseil Économique et Social sur les conséquences prévisibles du développement de l'automatisation de la gestion des entreprises. Paris, France-Empire, [1968]. pp. 348. 19cm.

LI (DAVID H.) Accounting, computers, management information systems. New York, McGraw-Hill, [1968]. pp. xiv, 370. 22½cm. (Series in Accounting)

MORRIS (WILLIAM THOMAS) Management science: a Bayesian introduction. Englewood Cliffs, Prentice-Hall, [1968]. pp. xiii, 226. 23cm. (International Series in Management)

PERETTI (ANDRÉ DE) L'administration: phénomène humain. Paris, Berger-Levrault, 1968. pp. 351. 21cm. (L'Administration Nouvelle)

PERRIGO (A.E.B.) Modern managerial techniques. London, Van Nostrand, [1968]. pp. xiii, 392. bibliog. 22½cm.

PORTER (LYMAN W.) and LAWLER (EDWARD E.) Managerial attitudes and performance. Homewood, Irwin, 1968. pp. viii, 209. bibliog. 22½cm. (Irwin-Dorsey Series in Behavioral Science)

PRASAD (S. BENJAMIN) and NEGANDHI (ANANT R.) Managerialism for economic development: essays on India. The Hague, Nijhoff, 1968. pp. (xi), 170. 24cm. (Studies in Social Life. 11)

REHDER (ROBERT R.) compiler. Latin American management: development and performance. Reading, Mass., Addison-Wesley, [1968]. pp. xi, 267. bibliog. 23½cm. (Stanford University. Graduate School of Business. Series in Business Management)

ROETHLISBERGER (FRITZ JULES) Man-in-organization: essays. Cambridge, Belknap P., 1968. pp. xiii, 322. 23½cm.

SKERTCHLY (ALLAN R.B.) Tomorrow's managers. London, Staples, 1968. pp. xii, 240. bibliog. 24½cm.

SLAVIN (ALBERT) and others. Basic accounting for managerial and financial control. New York, Holt, [1968]. pp. xiv, 848. 23cm.

SMITH (GEORGE ALBERT) and others. Policy formulation and administration: a casebook of top management problems in business. 5th ed. Homewood, Irwin, 1968. pp. xviii, 895. 23cm.

SPENCER (MILTON H.) Managerial economics: text, problems, and short cases. 3rd ed. Homewood, Irwin, 1968. pp. xii, 515. bibliogs. 23cm. (Irwin Series in Economics)

TOP management development and succession: an exploratory study; by Albert S. Glickman [and others]. New York, Macmillan, 1968. pp. xv, 92. 23cm. (Columbia University. Graduate School of Business. Studies of the Modern Corporation)

WADIA (MANECK S.) ed. Management and the behavioral sciences: text and readings. Boston, [1968]. pp. xiii, 543. bibliogs.

WINGO (WALTER) Pattern for success: presenting the Harvard Business School Advanced Management Program. Kingswood, World's Work, 1968. pp. xi, 235. 21½cm.

1969

ANSELL (D. J.) and GILES (A. K.) The farmer and his time: an agricultural exercise in 'activity sampling'. Reading, 1969. pp. 16, 17 tables. (Reading. University. Faculty of Agriculture and Horticulture. Agricultural Economics Department. Miscellaneous Studies. No.46)

BLUMENTHAL (SHERMAN C.) Management information systems: a framework for planning and development. Englewood Cliffs, [1969]. pp. 219. bibliog.

BODDEWYN (J.) ed. Comparative management and marketing text and readings. [Glenview, 1969]. pp. 302. bibliogs.

BROWN (MICHAEL BARRATT) Opening the books. [Nottingham, 1969?]. unpaged. (Institute for Workers' Control. Pamphlet Series. No. 4)

CARSBERG (BRYAN VICTOR) and EDEY (HAROLD CECIL) eds. Modern financial management: selected readings. Harmondsworth, [1969]. pp. 411. bibliogs.

CHILD (JOHN) British management thought: a critical analysis. London, Allen & Unwin, 1969. pp. 272. 21½cm. (Studies in Management. No.5)

EWING (DAVID WALKLEY) The human side of planning: tool or tyrant? London, [1969]. pp. 216.

FLINK (SALOMON J.) and GRUNEWALD (DONALD) Managerial finance. New York, Wiley, [1969]. pp. xv, 639. 22½cm.

GAUGLER (EDUARD) ed. Verantwortliche Betriebsführung;...Professor Dr. Guido Fischer zum 70. Geburtstag am 8. Juni 1969. Stuttgart, 1969. pp. 316. In German or English.

GEE (KENNETH P.) A positive approach to corporate objectives. London, [1969]. pp. 15. bibliog.

GILLIS (FLOYD E.) Managerial economics: decision making under certainty for business and engineering. Reading, Mass., [1969]. pp. 296.

HAEUSLER (JOACHIM) Planung als Zukunftsgestaltung: Voraussetzungen, Methodik und Formen der Planung in soziotechnischen Systemen. Wiesbaden, [1969]. pp. 104. bibliog. (Berliner Arbeitskreis für betriebliche Führungskräfte. Fortschrittliche Unternehmensführung. Band 1)

HAGUE (DOUGLAS CHALMERS) Managerial economics: analysis for business decisions. [London], Longmans, [1969]. pp. vii, 356. 23½cm.

HARVEY (JOHN L.) and NEWGARDEN (ALBERT) eds. Management guides to mergers and acquisitions. New York, [1969]. pp. 319.

HODGE (BARTOW) and HODGSON (ROBERT N.) Management and the computer in information and control systems. New York, McGraw-Hill, [1969]. pp. xiv, 297. bibliog. 22½cm.

HOLLOMON (JOHN HERBERT) and others. Innovation and profitability: three contributions to discussion; [by] J. Herbert Hollomon, Peter G. Peterson [and] Gordon Fryers. London, [1969?]. pp. 29.

HOPEMAN (RICHARD J.) Systems analysis and operations management. Columbus, Ohio, [1969]. pp. 346. bibliog.

KELLY (JOE) Organizational behaviour. Homewood, Ill., 1969. pp. 666. bibliog.

KELLY (WILLIAM F.) Management through systems and procedures: the total systems concept. New York, [1969]. pp. 556.

KOSIOL (ERICH) Die Unternehmung als wirtschaftliches Aktionszentrum: Einführung in die Betriebswirtschaftslehre. Reinbek bei Hamburg, 1969. pp. 265. bibliog.

KRIVTSOV (ALEKSANDR MIKHAILOVICH) and SHEKHOVTSOV (VLADIMIR VLADIMIROVICH) Setevoe planirovanie i upravlenie. Moskva, 1969. pp. 66.

MEYER (JEAN) Le contrôle de gestion. Paris, 1969. pp. 126. bibliog.

NICHOLS (THEO.) Ownership, control and ideology: an enquiry into certain aspects of modern business ideology. London, 1969. pp. 272. bibliog.

ODIORNE (GEORGE STANLEY) Management decisions by objectives. Englewood Cliffs, Prentice-Hall, [1969]. pp. xvi, 252. 22½cm.

STEINER (GEORGE ALBERT) Top management planning. New York, Macmillan, [1969]. pp. xxvii, 795. bibliog. 25¼cm. (Columbia University. Graduate School of Business. Studies of the Modern Corporation)

STEVENS (W.G.R.) Modular programming and management. London, 1969. pp. 72.

STURT (HUMPHREY) and YEARSLEY (RONALD) eds. Computers for management. London, 1969. pp. 199.

TATHAM (LAURA ESTHER) The use of computers for profit: a businessman's guide. London, [1969]. pp. 291.

WEBB (JAMES E.) Space age management: the large-scale approach. New York, McGraw-Hill, [1969]. pp. xv, 173. 20½cm. (Columbia University. Graduate School of Business. McKinsey Foundation Lecture Series. 1968)

WEBBER (ROSS A.) Culture and management: text and readings in comparative management. Homewood, Irwin, 1969. pp. xi, 598. bibliogs. 23cm. (Series in Management)

WITHINGTON (FREDERIC C.) The real computer: its influence, uses, and effects. Reading, Mass., 1969. pp. 350.

WOOT (PHILIPPE DE) La fonction d'entreprise: formes nouvelles et progrès économiques. 2nd ed. Louvain, Nauwelaerts, 1969. pp. 484. bibliog.

WORTMAN (MAX S.) and LUTHANS (FRED) eds. Emerging concepts in management: process, behavioral, quantitative, and systems. London, [1969]. pp. 462. bibliogs.

1970

ALLAKHVERDIAN (DERENIK AKOPOVICH) ed. Khozraschet i upravlenie: teoriia, opyt, perspektivy. Moskva, 1970. pp. 319.

CHEDZEY (CLIFFORD S.) ed. Science in management: some applications of operational research and computer science. London, 1970. pp. 357.

COMPANY organization: theory and practice; ...written by M.C. Barnes [and others]. London, 1970. pp. 235. bibliog.

DRUCKER (PETER FERDINAND) Technology, management and society: essays. London, 1970. pp. 182.

FARRAR (DONALD E.) and MEYER (JOHN ROBERT) Managerial economics. Englewood Cliffs, [1970]. pp. 115. bibliog.

GOLDSCHMIDT (YAAQOV) Information for management decisions: a system for economic analysis and accounting procedures. Ithaca, 1970. pp. 310. bibliog.

GVISHIANI (DZHERMEN MIKHAILOVICH) Organizatziia i upravlenie: sotziologicheskii anatiz burzhnaznykh teorii. Moskva, 1970. pp. 184. bibliog.

HUMBLE (JOHN WILLIAM) ed. Management by objectives in action. London, [1970]. pp. 293. bibliog.

KATZ (ROBERT L.) Management of the total enterprise. Englewood Cliffs, N.J., [1970]. pp. 657.

LARNER (ROBERT J.) Management control and the large corporation. New York, [1970]. pp. 148. bibliog.

MAXWELL (W. DAVID) Price theory and applications in business administration. Pacific Palisades, [1970]. pp. 270. bibliogs.

NEWBOULD (GERALD D.) Management and merger activity Liverpool, [1970]. pp. 233.

OGDEN (RONALD) Imaginative management control. London, 1970. pp. 234. bibliog.

MANAGEMENT (Cont'd.)

L'ORGANISATION vivante: comportements d'ajustement et d'évolution au sein des organisations; ([by] J.M. Faverge, [and others]). Bruxelles, [1970]. pp. 198. (Brussels. Université Libre. Institut de Sociologie. Etudes de Psychologie Sociale et Industrielle)

PARAMONOV (IVAN VASIL'EVICH) Uchit'-sia upravliat': mysli i opyt starogo khoziaistvennika. 2nd ed. Moskva, 1970. pp. 182.

POPOV (GAVRIIL KHARITONOVICH) Problemy teorii upravleniia. Moskva, 1970. pp. 207.

SCHROETER (LOUIS C.) Organizational élan. [New York], [1970]. pp. 181. bibliog.

SIMMONS (JOHN R. M.) Management of change: the role of information; based on a research project sponsored by the Institute of Office Management. London, 1970. pp. 172.

SMITH (THOMAS DANIEL) Management: Europe wakes up. London, [1970]. pp. 24. (Economist, The. Briefs. 21)

SOFER (CYRIL) Men in mid-career: a study of British managers and technical specialists. Cambridge, 1970. pp. 376.

TECHNOLOGICAL change and management; the John Diebold Lectures, 1968-1970; David W. Ewing, editor. Boston, Mass., 1970. pp. 148.

WAGNER (HARVEY M.) Principles of management science, with applications to executive decisions. Englewood Cliffs, n.j., 1970. pp. 562.

ZIEGLER (HELMUT) Strukturen und Prozesse der Autorität in der Unternehmung: ein organisationssoziologischer Beitrag zur Theorie der betrieblichen Organisation. Stuttgart, 1970. pp. 295. bibliog.

1971

BROSTER (ERIC JAMES) Planning profit strategies. London, 1971. pp. 285. bibliog.

HELLER (FRANK A.) Managerial decision-making: a study of leadership styles and power-sharing among senior managers. London, 1971. pp. 140. bibliog.

STARR (MARTIN KENNETH) Management: a modern approach. New York, [1971]. pp. 716. bibliog.

STEWART (JOHN DAVID) Management in local government: a viewpoint. London, 1971. pp. 197.

HARRIS (STANLEY) ed. Drucker talks to Britain's managers: [a report based on a series of meetings organised by the British Institute of Management and addressed by Peter Drucker]. London, 1972. pp. 36.

- Bibliography

UNITED STATES. United States Information Service, London. Library. Books on labor and business management. London, 1960. pp. 54.

SETHI (NARENDRA K.) compiler. A bibliography of Indian management: with reference to the economic, industrial, international, labor, marketing, organizational, productivity, and the public administration perspectives. Bombay, Popular Prakashan, 1967. pp. xvi, 116. 21½cm.

LINDFORS (GRACE V.) ed. Bibliography: cases and other materials for the teaching of business administration in developing countries: South and Southeast Asia. Boston, 1968. pp. viii, 408.

- Case studies

HUNT (PEARSON) and ANDREWS (VICTOR L.) eds. Financial management: cases and readings. Homewood, Irwin, 1968. pp. ix, 936. 23cm.

TAGIURI (RENATO) and others. Behavioral science concepts in case analysis: the relationship of ideas to management action. Boston, Harvard University, Graduate School of Business Administration, Division of Research, 1968. pp. x, 147. bibliog. 20½cm.

GRAVES (DESMOND JAMES TURNER) The comparison of management role behaviour in three factories of an international electronics company; [M.Phil. (London) thesis]. 1970. fo. 292. bibliog. Typescript: unpublished. This thesis is the property of London University and may not be removed from the Library.

- Congresses

LECTURE and conference on management, labour and the community; [held for the Stafford Cripps Memorial, Bristol, 22 November 1958]. n.p., [1958]. pp. 42.

- Dictionaries and encyclopaedias

JOHANNSEN (HANO) and ROBERTSON (ANDREW B.) Management glossary; edited by E.F.L. Brech. London, Longmans, 1968. pp. (v), 146. bibliog. 21½cm. (Management Studies Series)

- Mathematical models

BRABB (GEORGE JACOB) Introduction to quantitative management. New York, Holt, [1968]. pp. xv, 576. 23cm.

SCHELLENBERGER (ROBERT E.) Managerial analysis. Homewood, Ill., 1969. pp. 461. bibliogs.

- Societies

BRITISH INSTITUTE OF MANAGEMENT. Report reappraising the aims and organisation of the British Institute of Management by a committee under the chairmanship of Sir Cecil Mead. London, 1968. pp. 65.

- Study and teaching

ORGANISATION FOR EUROPEAN ECONOMIC CO-OPERATION. European Productivity Agency. Management Education Series. No. 2. The importance of scientific research for the teaching of business administration; text of a talk given by E. Dassel...in January 1956. [Paris, 1956]. pp. 13.

ALL INDIA MANAGEMENT ASSOCIATION. Handbook of training institutions abroad. New Delhi, [196-?] pp. 66. 32½cm.

ORGANISATION FOR ECONOMIC CO-OPERATION AND DEVELOPMENT. 1962. Development of a body of management teachers: final report. [Paris], 1962. pp. 45.

FÉDÉRATION DES INDUSTRIES BELGES. Formation et perfectionnement des cadres d'entreprise. Bruxelles, [1963]. pp. 52. bibliog. 24cm.

ORGANISATION FOR ECONOMIC CO-OPERATION AND DEVELOPMENT. 1963. Evaluation of supervisory and management training methods: co-ordination of research; general rapporteur R. Meigniez, etc. [Paris, 1963]. pp. 159. bibliog.

TOBIN (P.A.) The syndicate system in management training; (a study of the development, operation and effectiveness of the syndicate method of training as practiced in a variety of institutions for the training of managers and administrators in the United Kingdom and other countries). Lahore, Pakistan Administrative Staff College, 1964. pp. 62.

WUNDERER (ROLF) Systembildende Betrachtungsweisen der allgemeinen Betriebswirtschaftslehre und ihr Einfluss auf die Darstellung des Unternehmens. Berlin, Duncker und Humblot, [1967]. pp. 263. bibliog. 21½cm. (Betriebswirtschaftliche Schriften. Heft 23)

HACON (RICHARD J.) ed. Organisational necessities and individual needs. Oxford, Blackwell, 1968. pp. viii, 84. (Association of Teachers of Management. Occasional Papers. No. 5)

NEUMANN (RUEDIGER) Das Hochschulstudium der Betriebswirtschaft in den USA und in der Bundesrepublik Deutschland: ein kritischer Vergleich unter besonderer Berücksichtigung neuerer Reformvorschläge in beiden Ländern. Göttingen, 1968. pp. 470. bibliog.

TAYLOR (HENRY JAMES BOSANQUET) The administrative staff colleges at home and overseas: report prepared for the Leverhulme Trust. London, Lyon, Grant & Green, 1968. pp. xiii, 104. 21½cm.

THOMAS (RAYMOND E.) Responsibilities of management decisions. [London, 1968?]. fo. 11. (Industrial Educational and Research Foundation. Occasional Papers. No. 1)

MARKWELL (D.S.) and ROBERTS (TOM JOHN) Organisation of management development programmes. London, 1969. pp. 182.

CHERRINGTON (PAUL) Wider business objectives in management education. London, [1970]. pp. 17. (Industrial Educational and Research Foundation. Occasional Papers. No. 8)

RAPOPORT (ROBERT NORMAN) Mid-career development: research perspectives on a development community for senior administrators...; with contributions by M.B. Brodie and E.A. Life. London, 1970. pp. 290.

- Study and teaching - Belgium

PROGRAMMES de perfectionnement (organisés...par les centres universitaires de perfectionnement à la direction, associés à la Fondation Industrie-Université): Vollmakings-programma's 1965-1966. [Brussels, 1965?]. pp. 63. Text in French and Flemish.

- Study and teaching - Brazil

TAYLOR (DONALD ARTHUR) Institution building in business administration: the Brazilian experience. East Lansing, Michigan, 1968. pp. 205. (Michigan State University. Institute for International Business and Economic Development Studies. MSU International Business and Economic Studies)

- Study and teaching - Germany

ADLER (JOHN) and CHERRINGTON (PAUL) Management education in West Germany: a short study of post experience courses made in 1965/6. Henley-on-Thames, the College, 1966. pp. 48. 22½cm. (Henley-on-Thames. Administrative Staff College Occasional Papers. No. 5)

KRIEGER (ERHARD) Die Idee der Höheren Wirtschaftsfachschule unter Berücksichtigung ausländischer Erfahrungen bei der Ausbildung mittlerer Führungskräfte für die Wirtschaft. [Giessen, imprint, 1966?]. pp. 189. bibliog.

ARNDT (HANS JOACHIM) and others. Weiterbildung, wirtschaftlicher Führungskräfte an der Universität. Düsseldorf, Econ Verlag, 1968. pp. xvi, 325. bibliog.

- Study and teaching - Netherlands

EVANS-VAUGHAN (G.F.) Management education in the Netherlands: a short study carried out in February 1966. Henley-on-Thames, 1966. pp. 19. (Henley-on-Thames. Administrative Staff College. Occasional Papers. No. 4)

- Study and teaching - United Kingdom

UNITED KINGDOM ADVISORY COUNCIL ON EDUCATION FOR MANAGEMENT. Management studies in technical colleges: first report...1962. [J.W. Platt, chairman]. London, H.M.S.O., 1962. pp. viii, 19. 24½cm.

U.K. 1965. Department of Education and Science. A memorandum on the diploma in management studies; [by] the committee for the diploma in management studies: [chairman: F.W. Oakley] London, 1965. pp. iii, 20. 21cm.

UNITED KINGDOM ADVISORY COUNCIL ON EDUCATION FOR MANAGEMENT. Management studies in technical colleges: second report...1965. [J.W. Platt, chairman]. London, H.M.S.O., 1965. pp. x, 25. 24½cm.

PEARSON (Sir JAMES DENNING) Technological and management education: the future role of technical colleges. London, British Institute of Management, 1967. pp. 15. 23cm. (Urwick Lectures. 3)

U.K. Central Training Council. Management Training and Development Committee. 1967. An approach to the training and development of managers: a report. [Sir Joseph Hunt, chairman]. London. 1967, pp. vii, 16. 21½cm.

ENGINEERING INDUSTRY TRAINING BOARD. Booklets. No. 6. The training of managers. London, the Board, [1968]. pp. 24. bibliog.

U.K. Committee for the Diploma in Management Studies. 1968. The diploma in management studies, 1961-1968. [London], 1968. pp. 28.

U.K. Committee for the Diploma in Management Studies 1968. A memorandum on the diploma in management studies. 2nd ed. London, 1968. pp. 26.

MANAGEMENT - Study and teaching - United Kingdom (Cont'd.)

U.K. Central Training Council. Management Training and Development Committee. 1969. Training and development of managers: further proposals: [Sir Joseph Hunt, chairman]. London, 1969. pp.vii, 50. 21cm.

NATIONAL ECONOMIC DEVELOPMENT COUNCIL. Management Education, Training and Development Committee. First report on the supply of teachers for management education. London, National Economic Development Office, 1970. pp. 24.

ROSE (HAROLD BERTRAM) Management education in the 1970s: growth and issues; a report prepared...in conjunction with D.G. Clark and E. Newbigging, for the Management Education, Training and Development Committee [of the National Economic Development Council]. London, H.M.S.O., 1970. pp. 160.

JOINT COMPUTER TRAINING POLICY COMMITTEE OF INDUSTRIAL TRAINING BOARDS. Computer appreciation courses for managers: report prepared and presented to the Department of Employment, etc. London, H.M.S.O., 1971. pp. 28.

MANAGEMENT GAMES

TERHUNE (K. W.) and KENNEDY (JOHN L.) Exploratory analysis of a research and development game. [Princeton?], 1963. fo. (48). 28cm.

BOUDEVILLE (JACQUES R.) and others. L'entreprise privée et l'économie nationale. Paris, Presses Universitaires de France, 1967. pp. viii, 114. bibliogs. 24cm. (Paris. Université. Faculté de Droit et des Sciences Economiques. Travaux et Recherches. Série "Sciences Économiques" No.3) R

FRIEDRICH (GERD) and others. Entscheidungsübung durch Fallmethode und Planspiel. Berlin, Die Wirtschaft, 1967. pp. 178. bibliog. 21½cm.

McKENNEY (JAMES L.) Simulation gaming for management development. Boston, Harvard University, 1967. pp. xvii 189. bibliog. 20½cm.

LANGHOLM (ODD) Foretaksspill. Oslo, Norges Handelshøyskole, 1968. pp. 13. 29½cm. (Saertrykk-Serie. Nr. 67) (Saertrykk av Bedriftsøkonomen, Nr. 9-10/67)

DYCKMAN (THOMAS R.) and others. Management decision making under uncertainty: an introduction to probability and statistical decision theory. New York, Macmillan, 1969. pp. xxiii, 662. bibliog. 25½cm.

EDSTRÖM (ANDERS) Computerized system control: a management game for education and research in online, realtime control systems. Göteborg, [1969]. pp. 110. bibliog. (Gothenburg. Handelshögskolan. Skriftserie. 1969. 3)

GRAHAM (ROBERT G.) and GRAY (CLIFFORD F.) Business games handbook. [New York, 1969]. pp. 480. bibliog.

GREENE (RICHARD M.) The management game: how to win with people. Homewood, Ill., 1969. pp. 281.

MANAGEMENT RIGHTS

CONGRES DES RELATIONS INDUSTRIELLES DE L'UNIVERSITE LAVAL, 15E, 1960. Droits de gérance et changements technologiques. in Congrès des Relations Industrielles de l'Université Laval. (Etudes, etc.) Québec, 1960.

MANCHESTER

- Clubs

MILLS (WILLIAM HASLAM) ed. The Manchester Reform Club, 1817-1921: survey of fifty years' history. Manchester, [imprint], 1922. pp. (iii), 134. 21cm. Privately printed.

- Description

BUTTERWORTH (JAMES) of Oldham. The antiquities of the town, and a complete history of the trade of Manchester; with a description of Manchester and Salford; to which is added an account of the late improvements in the town, etc. Manchester, the Author, 1822. pp. (v), v, 302, xii. 18cm.

- Economic conditions

JENKINS (MICK) What next for Manchester...: great communist crusade. [Manchester, 1938]. pp. 15.

CHARDONNET (JEAN) Métropoles economiques: deuxième série, Manchester, Rotterdam, Hambourg, Cologne, Salzgitter, Dunkerque, Grenoble, Bilbao, Bâle, Zürich, Lodz, Zagreb. Paris, Colin, 1968. pp. 243. bibliog. 24cm. (Fondation Nationale des Sciences Politiques. Cahiers. 158)

- Economic history

VIGIER (FRANÇOIS) Change and apathy: Liverpool and Manchester during the industrial revolution. Cambridge, Mass, [1970]. pp. 236. bibliog.

- Growth

VIGIER (FRANÇOIS) Change and apathy: Liverpool and Manchester during the industrial revolution. Cambridge, Mass, [1970]. pp. 236. bibliog.

- History

BUTTERWORTH (JAMES) of Oldham. The antiquities of the town, and a complete history of the trade of Manchester; with a description of Manchester and Salford; to which is added an account of the late improvements in the town, etc. Manchester, the Author, 1822. pp. (v), v, 302, xii. 18cm.

- Industries

BUTTERWORTH (JAMES) of Oldham. The antiquities of the town, and a complete history of the trade of Manchester; with a description of Manchester and Salford; to which is added an account of the late improvements in the town, etc. Manchester, the Author, 1822. pp. (v), v, 302, xii. 18cm.

- Politics and government

PLAIN CITIZEN, A, pseud. Open letters to Manchester men and women;...reprinted from the Manchester City News. Manchester, Cornish, 1911. pp. vii, 262.

JENKINS (MICK) What next for Manchester...: great communist crusade. [Manchester, 1938]. pp. 15.

VIGIER (FRANÇOIS) Change and apathy: Liverpool and Manchester during the industrial revolution. Cambridge, Mass, [1970]. pp. 236. bibliog.

- Social conditions

LEWIS (JOHN PARRY) The statistical study of urban change;...read 8th November, 1967. [Manchester], Manchester Statistical Society, 1967. pp. 26. 21½cm.

- Transit systems

DE LEUW, CATHER AND PARTNERS and HENNESSY, CHADWICK, O hEOCHA AND PARTNERS. Manchester rapid transit study. Manchester, 1968. 2 vols. (in 1)

"MANCHESTER MASSACRE", 1819

COMMUNIST PARTY OF GREAT BRITAIN. Peterloo: the story of the terrible massacre of the Lancashire workers at St. Peter's Fields, Manchester, on August 16th, 1819, and the lessons of Peterloo. London, 1928. pp. 15.

MANCHESTER. Public Libraries. Peterloo, 1819: a portfolio of contemporary documents; (explanatory text by Harry Horton). [Manchester], 1969. pp. various.

MARLOW (JOYCE) The Peterloo massacre. London, 1969. pp. 238. bibliog.

WALMSLEY (ROBERT) Peterloo: the case reopened. Manchester, Manchester U.P., [1969]. pp. xx, 585. bibliog. 23½cm.

MANCHESTER UNIVERSITY

UNIVERSITY perspectives; (edited by John Knapp [and others]). Manchester, [1970]. pp. 297.

MANCHURIA

- Boundaries

LEE (ROBERT H.G.) The Manchurian frontier in Ch'ing history. Cambridge, Mass., 1970. pp. 229. bibliog. (Harvard University. East Asian Research Center. Harvard East Asian Studies. 43).

- History

LEE (ROBERT H.G.) The Manchurian frontier in Ch'ing history. Cambridge, Mass., 1970. pp. 229. bibliog. (Harvard University. East Asian Research Center. Harvard East Asian Studies. 43).

- Politics and government

NATHAN (CARL F.) Plague prevention and politics in Manchuria, 1910-1931. Cambridge, Harvard U.P., 1967. pp. vi, 104. bibliog. 25cm. (Harvard University. East Asian Research Center. Harvard East Asian Monographs. 23)

MANDATES

AUSTRALIAN LEAGUE OF NATIONS UNION. New South Wales Branch. The League and its critics: a report...by a Committee appointed to investigate recent criticism of the League of Nations. Sydney, [1922?]. pp. 20.

- South West Africa

VAN WYK (JACQUES THEODORE) The United Nations, South West Africa and the law. Cape Town, University of Cape Town, 1968. pp. 30. 21½cm.

MANDEL (GEORGES)

FAVREAU (B.) Georges Mandel: un clémenciste en Gironde. Paris, [1969]. pp. 295. bibliog. (Bordeaux. Université. Institut d'Etudes Politiques Centre d'Etude et de Recherche sur la Vie Locale. Série Vie Locale. 1)
R : WA 0821

SHERWOOD (JOHN M.) Georges Mandel and the Third Republic. Stanford, 1970. pp. 393. bibliog.

MANDOBOS

BOELAARS (J.) Mandobo's tussen de Digoel en de Kao: bijdragen tot een etnografie. Assen, 1970. pp. 259.

MANGANESE MINES AND MINING

- India

INDIA. 1967. Report on survey of labour conditions in manganese mining industry in India, 1962-63. (Labour Bureau). [Delhi, 1967]. pp. iv, 69. 24cm.

- Ukraine

SHOSTAK (AFANASII GRIGOR'EVICH) Горно-добывающая промышленность Украинской ССР: горнорудная промышленность Украинской ССР: железная и марганцевая руда. Москва, 1967. pp. 235. bibliog.

MANGANESE ORES

- United States

BROOKS (DAVID BARRY) Low-grade and non-conventional sources of manganese. Baltimore, Johns Hopkins Press, [1966] pp. xi, 123. 22½cm.

MANGLA DAM

BIRKHEAD (GUTHRIE S.) ed. Mangla project administration; from a field research report by Muhammad Ashfaque, [and others]. Lahore, Pakistan Administrative Staff College, 1964. pp. 38. bibliog.

MANIAGO

-Politics and government

MANIAGO. Relazione della amministrazione comunale 1946-1951. [Maniago, 1952?]. pp. 28. 24cm.

MANIAGO. Relazione della Amministrazione Comunale 1951-1956. [Maniago 1956]. pp. 38. 24cm.

MANICHAEISM

POPKIN (R. H.) Manicheanism in the Enlightenment. in Wolff (Kurt Heinrich) and Moore (Barrington) eds. The critical spirit. Boston, [1967].

MANILA

- Economic history

QUAISON (SERAFIN D.) English "country trade" with the Philippines, 1644-1765. Quezon City, U. of the Philippines P., 1966. pp. xv, 230. bibliog. 22½cm.

- History - Sources

CAMDEN SOCIETY. [Publications]. 4th Series. vol. 8. Documents illustrating the British conquest of Manila, 1762-1763; edited...by Nicholas P. Cushner. London, 1971. pp. 222.

MANILA SUMMIT CONFERENCE, 1966

VIET-NAM (REPUBLIC). 1966. Manila Summit Conference. [Saigon?, 1966]. pp. (13). 21cm. x 27cm.

MANIN (DANIELE)

MANIN (DANIELE) and PALLAVICINO TRIVULZIO (GIORGIO GUIDO) Marquis. Daniele Manin e Giorgio Pallavicino: epistolario politico, 1855-1857; con note e documenti per B.E.Maineri. Milano, Bortolotti, 1878. pp. xc, 648. 23cm.

MANIPAL

- History

MENEFEE (SELDEN C.) The Pais of Manipal. London, [1969]. pp. 249.

MANITOBA

MANITOBA. 1914. First province of Western Canada: own a farm of your own in Manitoba. (Department of Agriculture and Immigration) [Winnipeg, 1914]. pp. 79. 24cm.

- Bibliography

SCOTT (MICHAEL M.) compiler. A bibliography of Western Canadian studies relating to Manitoba. Winnipeg, Western Canada Research Council, 1967. fo. (ii), 79. 28cm.

- Boundaries

CANADA. Commission Appointed to Demarcate the Boundary between the Province of Manitoba and the Province of Saskatchewan. 1965. Report of the Commission [etc.]: part 1: 1961-1962: latitude 56°20'-60°00'. [With atlas]. Ottawa, 1965. pp. vi, 55. 25cm; atlas 53cm.

- Economic conditions

MANITOBA. 1960. Economic survey of Southwest Manitoba; prepared for the Department of Industry and Commerce... [by the] Economic Research Corporation. Montreal, Economic Research Corporation, [1960]. pp. (iii), 160. bibliog. 27½cm.

- Economic policy

CANADA. Department of Forestry and Rural Development. 1967. Agreement covering a comprehensive rural development plan for the interlake area of Manitoba. Ottawa, 1967. pp. 51. 21½cm.

- Politics and government

CLARK (LOVELL) ed. The Manitoba school question: majority rule or minority rights? Toronto, [1968]. pp. 230. bibliog.

- Population

SHARP (EMMIT F.) and KRISTJANSON (G. ALBERT) The people of Manitoba: 1951-1961. Ottawa, 1966. pp. vii, 60. 28cm. (Canada. Department of Forestry and Rural Development. ARDA Research Reports. No. RE-2)

- Sanitary affairs

MANITOBA. Department of Health and Social Development. Annual report. a., 1970- [Winnipeg]

MANITOBA. Department of Health and Social Development. Annual statistical bulletin. a., 1971- [Winnipeg]

- Social conditions - Statistics

MANITOBA. Department of Health and Social Development. Annual statistical bulletin. a., 1971- [Winnipeg]

- Social policy

MANITOBA. Department of Health and Social Development. Annual report. a., 1970- [Winnipeg]

- Statistics, Vital

MANITOBA. Department of Health and Social Development. Annual statistical bulletin. a., 1971- [Winnipeg]

MANLEY (NORMAN WASHINGTON)

NETTLEFORD (REX) Manley and the politics of Jamaica: towards an analysis of political change in Jamaica, 1938-1968. Mona, Jamaica, 1971. pp. 72. (Social and Economic Studies. Supplements)

MANN (HEINRICH)

MANN (THOMAS) and MANN (HEINRICH) Briefwechsel 1900-1949; (auf Grund der 1965... von Ulrich Dietzel redigierten Ausgabe... herausgegeben von Hans Wysling). [Frankfurt/Main], S.Fischer, 1968. pp. Lxii, 373. 18½cm.

MANN (THOMAS)

MANN (THOMAS) and MANN (HEINRICH) Briefwechsel 1900-1949; (auf Grund der 1965... von Ulrich Dietzel redigierten Ausgabe... herausgegeben von Hans Wysling). [Frankfurt/Main], S.Fischer, 1968. pp. Lxii, 373. 18½cm.

- Bibliography

WENZEL (GEORG) compiler. Thomas Manns Briefwerk: Bibliographie gedruckter Briefe aus den Jahren 1889-1955. Berlin, 1969. pp. 265. bibliog. (Deutsche Akademie der Wissenschaften zu Berlin. Institut für Deutsche Sprache und Literatur. Veröffentlichungen. Reihe E. Quellen und Hilfsmittel zur Literaturgeschichte. 41)

MANN (TOM)

TOM MANN RELEASE MOVEMENT. Who dares - free speech? London, [1932?]. pp. 2.

POLLITT (HARRY) Tom Mann: born April 15, 1856, died March 13, 1941; a tribute. London, [1941?]. pp. 8.

MANNERHEIM (GUSTAF)

RINTALA (MARVIN) Four Finns; political profiles. Berkeley, 1969. pp. 120.

MANNHEIM (KARL)

GRIGOR'IAN (R.G.) Критика "социологии знания" Карла Маннгейма. in Проблемы познания социальных явлений. Москва, 1968.

NEUSUESS (ARNHELM) Utopisches Bewusstsein und freischwebende Intelligenz: zur Wissenssoziologie Karl Mannheims. Meisenheim a, Glan, Hain, 1968. pp. 302. bibliog. 23cm. (Marburger Abhandlungen zur Politischen Wissenschaft. Band 10)

REMMLING (GUNTER WERNER) Wissenssoziologie und Gesellschaftsplanung: das Werk Karl Mannheims. Dortmund, 1968. pp. 315. bibliog.

BORIS (DIETER) Krise und Planung: die politische Soziologie im Spätwerk Karl Mannheims. Stuttgart 1971. pp. 344. bibliog.

MANNHEIM

- History

OPPENHEIMER (MAX) Der Fall Vorbote: Zeugnisse des Mannheimer Widerstandes. Frankfurt/Main. 1969. pp. 248. bibliog.

- Social policy

KOBEL (KLAUS) Soziale Hilfe und Sozialpolitik einer industriellen Stadtgemeinde in der BRD, dargestellt am Beispiel der Stadt Mannheim. Düsseldorf, 1966. pp. xii, 359. bibliog.

MANNHEIM UNIVERSITY

MOENCH (WALTER) ed. Wirtschaftshochschule Mannheim; herausgegeben im Auftrag des Senats der Wirtschaftshochschule Mannheim. Berlin, Länderdienst, [1961?] pp. 85. 29½cm. (Bücherreihe von Universitäts- und Hochschul-Publikationen)

SCHLENKE (MANFRED) Von der Residenz zur Universität: das kurpfälzische Schloss und die Mannheimer Hochschule in Vergangenheit und Gegenwart. Mannheim, [1971]. pp. 19. bibliog. (Sonderdruck aus Mitteilungen der Gesellschaft der Freunde der Universität Mannheim e.V., Heft 1/71, 20. Jahrgang)

MANNING (Dame ELIZABETH LEAH)

MANNING (Dame ELIZABETH LEAH) A life for education: an autobiography. London, 1970. pp. 263.

MANORS

- Europe

KAY (CRISTOBAL) Comparative development of the European manorial system and the Latin American hacienda system: an approach to a theory of agrarian change for Chile. 1971. fo. 253. bibliog.

- Poland

SERCZYK (WŁADYSŁAW A.) Gospodarstwo magnackie w województwie podolskim w drugiej połowie XVIII wieku. Wrocław, Ossolineum, 1965. pp. 186. 24cm. (Polska Akademia Nauk. Oddział w Krakowie. Komisja Nauk Historycznych. Prace. nr.13)

RYCHLIKOWA (IRENA) Produkcja zbożowa wielkiej własności w Małopolsce w latach 1764-1805. Warszawa, PWN, 1967. pp. 147. 24cm. (Polska Akademia Nauk. Instytut. Historii Kultury Materialnej. Studia i Materiały z Historii Kultury Materialnej. tom 31 [being also] Studia z Dziejów Gospodarstwa Wiejskiego. tom 9, zeszyt 1) With French summaries.

- Russia

ANFIMOV (ANDREI MATVEEVICH) Крупное помещичье хозяйство европейской России, конец XIX - начало XX века. Москва, 1969. pp. 392.

- United Kingdom

LONDON. London County Council. Court rolls of Tooting Beck Manor. vol. 1. comprising the rolls in the Council's possession, dating from 1394 to 1422, with introduction, notes, appendix containing earlier rolls of the manor in the possession of King's College, Cambridge and index. London, 1909. pp. 259.

ASTON (T. H.) The origins of the manor in Britain; [first published in 1958]. in vol.1 of Minchinton (Walter Edward) ed. Essays in agrarian history...; reprints, etc. Newton Abbot, [1968].

TITOW (J. Z.) Some differences between manors and their effects on the condition of the peasant in the thirteenth century, [first published in 1962] in vol.1 of Minchinton (Walter Edward) ed. Essays in agrarian history...; reprints, etc. Newton Abbot, [1968].

HATCHER (JOHN) Rural economy and society in the Duchy of Cornwall, 1300-1500. Cambridge, 1970. pp. 322. bibliog.

NEWTON (K.C.) The manor of Writtle: the development of a royal manor in Essex, c.1086 - c.1500. London, 1970. pp. 131. bibliog.

MANPOWER.

Here are entered general works on the strength of a country in terms of available personnel, including industrial and military requirements and reserves from the non-working population Works dealing with the labour market and labour reserves are entered under LABOUR SUPPLY. Works on manpower in particular fields will be found under such headings as AGRICULTURAL LABOURERS; ENGINEERS; SCIENTISTS; etc.

NATO CONFERENCE ON MANPOWER RESEARCH IN THE DEFENCE CONTEXT, LONDON, 1967. Manpower research: the proceedings of a conference held under the aegis of the NATO Scientific Affairs Committee in London from 14th-18th August, 1967; edited by N.A.B. Wilson. London, 1969. pp. 463. bibliogs. In English or French.

MANSEL (HENRY LONGUEVILLE)

FREEMAN (KENNETH D.) The role of reason in religion: a study of Henry Mansel. The Hague, 1969. pp. 117.

MANSHARDT (CLIFFORD)

MANSHARDT (CLIFFORD) Pioneering on social frontiers in India. Bombay, Lalvani, 1967. pp. vii, 118. 21½cm. (Tata Institute of Social Sciences. Tata Institute of Social Sciences Series. No.17)

MANSVETASHVILI (IAKOV)

MANSVETASHVILI (IAKOV A.) Vospominaniia; perevod s gruzinskogo. Tbilisi, 1967. pp. 115.

MANTUA (PROVINCE)

- History

GABRIELI (MANLIO) ed. La ricostituzione della provincia di Mantova, 1866-1868. [Mantua, 1968]. pp. 170. (Comitato per il Centenario dell'Unione di Mantova all'Italia. Collana "Mantova nel Risorgimento". 8)

- Politics and government

VAINI (MARIO) Le origini del fascismo a Mantova, 1914-1922; prefazione di Gastone Manacorda. [Rome], Editori Riuniti, [1961]. pp. 266. 22cm. (Biblioteca del Movimento Operaio)

VAINI (MARIO) I contadini mantovani nella rivoluzione nazionale, 1848-1860: contributo al dibattito storiografico sulle vicende del Mantovano negli ultimi cento anni. Milano, Edizioni del Gallo, 1966. pp. 196. 29cm. (Strumenti di Lavoro: Archivi del Movimento Operaio. N. 10)

MANUAL TRAINING

- Methods and manuals

REBORA (GIOVANNI) ed. Un manuale di tintoria del quattrocento. Milano, 1970. pp. 178. (Genoa. Università. Istituto di Storia Economica. [Publications]. 3)

MANUEL (JACQUES ANTOINE)

BONNAL (EDMOND) Manuel et son temps: étude sur l'opposition parlementaire sous la Restauration. Paris, Dentu, 1877. pp. vii, 512. 23cm.

MANUFACTURERS

- Australia

HALL (C.R.) The manufacturers: Australian manufacturing achievements to 1960. Sydney, 1971. pp. 892.

- France

VISINET ( ) Aperçus économiques à propos de l'exposition des produits de l'industrie en 1844 et des doctrines d'organisation du travail de M. Louis Blanc en 1847. Paris, Guillaumin, 1849. pp. 123. 22cm.

- United Kingdom - Directories

STUBBS' DIRECTORY: manufacturers, merchant shippers, and professional. London, annual, 1968/9. 26½cm.

- United States

BLANTON (ALEXANDER M.) and TRAUT (JOSEPH) Computers and small manufacturers. New York, Computer Research and Publications Associates, [1967] pp. x, 159. bibliogs. 28cm.

BOSTON MASSACHUSETTS. Economic Development and Industrial Commission. Boston's industry: a profile based on a survey of manufacturers conducted by the... Commission. [Boston, 1970]. pp. 22.

MANUFACTURES

MUELLER (UDO) Ökonomische Probleme und Wirkungen vergleichender Konsumgütertests. n.p., 1965. pp. x, 263. bibliog. 21cm.

JARRETT (HAROLD REGINALD) A geography of manufacturing. London, 1969. pp. 349. bibliogs.

- Classification

FRANCE. Institut National de la Statistique et des Études Économiques. 1959. Nomenclature des activités économiques: index alphabétique; (and index analytique). Paris, 1959. 2 vols. 27cm.

- Costs

DALY (D.J.) and others. Scale and specialization in Canadian manufacturing. Ottawa, 1968. pp. 97. (Canada. Economic Council. Staff Studies. No. 21)

MANUS

SCHWARTZ (THEODORE) The Paliau Movement in the Admiralty Islands, 1946-1954. New York, 1962. (American Museum of Natural History. Anthropological Papers. vol. 49. pt. 2)

MANUSCRIPTS

HEPWORTH (PHILIP) Archives and manuscripts in libraries. 2nd ed. London, Library Association, 1964. pp. 70. bibliog. 21½cm. (Pamphlets. No.18)

[LEHMANN-HAUPT (HELLMUT)] ed. Homage to a bookman: essays on manuscripts, books and printing written for Hans. P. Kraus on his 60th birthday, Oct. 12, 1967. Berlin, Mann, 1967. pp. 271. 27cm.

- Bibliography

SCHAB (WILLIAM H.) GALLERY. Catalogues. 31. (Early printed and illustrated books, illuminated manuscripts): a fine collection of illuminated manuscripts including the Musgrave hours, illustrated and literary incunabula containing some outstanding Italian woodcut books, etc. New York, [1962?]. pp. 154.

SCHAB (WILLIAM H.) GALLERY. Catalogues. 37. (Book illustration and literature in the XV th to XIXth centuries: Americana, architecture, science and medicine, botany and natural history, early music). New York. [1964?]. pp. 144.

OWEN (A.E.B.) compiler. Summary guide to accessions of Western manuscripts, other than medieval, since 1867, ([to the] University Library, Cambridge). Cambridge, 1966. pp. 48.

- Catalogues - Canada

UNION list of manuscripts in Canadian repositories: ...Robert S. Gordon, editor; (joint project of the Public Archives of Canada and the Humanities Research Council of Canada). Ottawa, Public Archives of Canada, 1968. pp. x, 734. 28cm.

- Catalogues - United Kingdom

BRITISH MUSEUM. Department of Manuscripts. Catalogue of additions to the manuscripts in the British Museum, etc. London, the Museum, 1843 in progress. 25½cm.

U.K. Historical Manuscripts Commission. List of accessions to repositories. a., 1956- London.

U.K. Parliament. House of Lords. Record Office. Memoranda. No. 24. The Braye manuscripts bought by the Record Office on 26th January, 1961. [London, 1961] fo. 9. 33cm.

SKEAT (THEODORE CRESSY) The catalogues of the manuscript collections in the British Museum. rev. ed. [London], Trustees of the British Museum, 1962. pp. 45. 25cm. (Offprinted from the Journal of Documentation. vol. 7, no. 1)

OXFORD. Oxford Historical Society. [Publications] New Series. vol. 17. Summary catalogue of manuscripts in the Bodleian Library relating to the City, County, and University of Oxford: accessions from 1916 to 1962; by P. S. Spokes. Oxford, Clarendon Press, 1964. pp. xiii, 207. 22cm.

U.K. India Office, Library. 1964. Index of post-1937 European manuscript accessions. Boston, Hall, 1964. pp. 156. 36cm.

WAINWRIGHT (MARY DOREEN) and MATTHEWS (NOEL) compilers. A guide to western manuscripts and documents in the British Isles relating to South and South East Asia;...under the general supervision of J. D. Pearson. London Oxford University Press, 1965. pp. xix, 532. 25cm.

SOTHEBY AND COMPANY. Bibliotheca Phillippica, medieval manuscripts, new series, part 3: catalogue of forty-two manuscripts of the 7th to the 17th century from the celebrated collection formed by Sir Thomas Phillipps, 1792-1872, the property of the trustees of the Robinson Trust. London, 1967. pp. 141. 28cm.

CHESTER BEATTY (Sir ALFRED) The Chester Beatty western manuscripts, part 1: catalogue of the thirty-seven illuminated manuscripts of the 9th to the 16th century;...which will be sold by auction by Messrs. Sotheby and Co., ...3, December, 1968. London, Sotheby, 1968. pp. 106. 28cm.

SOTHEBY AND COMPANY. Bibliotheca Phillippica: catalogue of the celebrated collection of manuscripts... new series, fourth part, comprising [Italian and Greek manuscripts of papal bulls, correspondence, early texts]. London, 1968. pp. 142. 24½cm.

CHESTER BEATTY (Sir ALFRED) The Chester Beatty western manuscripts, part 2: catalogue of thirty-eight illuminated manuscripts of the 8th to the 17th century;...which will be sold by auction by Messrs. Sotheby and Co. ...24 June 1969. London, 1969. pp. 109.

SOTHEBY AND COMPANY. Bibliotheca Phillippica, medieval manuscripts, new series, part 5: catalogue of manuscripts on papyrus, vellum and paper, of the 13th century B.C. to the 18th century A.D., from the celebrated collection formed by Sir Thomas Phillipps, 1792-1872; etc. London, [1969]. pp. 105.

- Catalogues - United Kingdom - Scotland

SCOTLAND. National Library of Scotland. Catalogue of manuscripts acquired since 1925. Edinburgh, 1938 in progress. 24½cm.

- Conservation and restoration

CUNHA (GEORGE DANIEL MARTIN) Conservation of library materials: a manual and bibliography on the care, repair and restoration of library materials. Metuchen, Scarecrow P., 1967. pp. x, 405. 21½cm.

AKADEMIIA NAUK SSSR. Laboratoriia konservatsii i Restavratsii Dokumentov. Preservation of documents and papers: Problema dolgovechnosti dokumentov i bumagi...; (D.M. Flyate, editor); translated from Russian. Jerusalem, Israel Program for Scientific Translations, 1968. pp. vi, 134. bibliogs. 24cm.

- Rhodesia

BAXTER (T.W.) and BURKE (E.E.) Guide to the historical manuscripts in the National Archives of Rhodesia. Salisbury, National Archives of Rhodesia, 1970. pp. 527.

- United Kingdom

LAUD (WILLIAM) Archbishop of Canterbury. A letter sent...with divers manuscripts to the Vniversity of Oxford...with the answer which the Vniversitie sent him, wherein is specified their integrity, as he is their Chancellor,...; [translated from the Latin]. [London], 1641. pp. 5. 17½cm. Wing L 590.

KER (NEIL RIPLEY) Medieval manuscripts in British libraries. Oxford, 1969 in progress.

MUNBY (ALAN NOEL LATIMER) and TOWNER (LAWRENCE W.) The flow of books and manuscripts. Los Angeles, California University, William Andrews Clark Memorial Library, 1969. pp. v. 55. 23cm.

WATSON (ANDREW G.) The manuscripts of Henry Savile of Banke. London, 1969. pp. 102.

EXPORT control of documents: review of the regulations governing the export from the United Kingdom of manuscripts, documents and archives. London, H.M.S.O., 1970. pp. 15.

FREWER (LOUIS BENSON) compiler. Manuscript collections, excluding Africana, in Rhodes House Library, Oxford. Oxford, 1970. pp. 62.

READING. University. Library. Accessions of general manuscripts up to June 1970. [Reading], 1970. fo. 27.

MANUSCRIPTS, ANGLO-SAXON

AETHELGIFU. The will of Aethelgifu: a tenth century Anglo-Saxon manuscript; translated and examined by Dorothy Whitelock, with a note on the document by Neil Ker and analyses...by Lord Rennell. Oxford, 1968. pp. 91. Letter from Lord Rennell about the production of the book attached to the fly-leaf.

MANUSCRIPTS, ARABIC

ATIYA (A. S.) Codex Arabicus, Sinai Arabic Ms. No.514. in [Lehmann-Haupt (Hellmut)] ed. Homage to a bookman. Berlin, 1967.

MANUSCRIPTS, GREEK

SOTHEBY AND COMPANY. Bibliotheca Phillippica: catalogue of the celebrated collection of manuscripts... new series, fourth part, comprising [Italian and Greek manuscripts of papal bulls, correspondence, early texts]. London, 1968. pp. 142. 24½cm.

MANUSCRIPTS, GREEK (PAPYRI)

SAMUEL (A. E.) An early papyrus text of Isocrates, P. Yale Inventory 2082. in [Lehmann-Haupt (Hellmut)] ed. Homage to a bookman. Berlin, 1967.

MANUSCRIPTS, ITALIAN

SOTHEBY AND COMPANY. Bibliotheca Phillippica: catalogue of the celebrated collection of manuscripts... new series, fourth part, comprising [Italian and Greek manuscripts of papal bulls, correspondence, early texts]. London, 1968. pp. 142. 24½cm.

MANUSCRIPTS, LATIN

MARINIS (T. DE) Di un codice di Petrarca da Ritrovare. in [Lehmann-Haupt (Hellmut)] ed. Homage to a bookman. Berlin, 1967.

MARSTON (T. E.) The earliest known laws of an Italian city state. in [Lehmann-Haupt (Hellmut)] ed. Homage to a bookman. Berlin, 1967.

MANZONI (ALESSANDRO) Conte

BELOTTI (GIUSEPPE) Il messaggio politico-sociale di Alessandro Manzoni; vicende critiche, punti focali, abbozzo di sintesi. Bologna, Zanichelli, [1966]. pp. viii, 535. 23½cm.

MAO (TSE-TUNG)

The WHOLE country should become a great school of Mao Tse-Tung's thought: in commemoration of the 39th anniversary of the founding of the Chinese People's Liberation Army. Peking, 1966. pp. 18.

BURLATSKII (FEDOR MIKHAILOVICH) Maoizm ili marksizm? Moskva, 1967. pp. 128.

FOLLOW chairman Mao and advance in the teeth of great storms and waves. Peking, 1967. pp. 15.

KAPCHENKO (NIKOLAI IVANOVICH) Пекин: политика, чуждая социализму. Москва, 1967. pp. 282.

LEIBZON (BORIS MOISEEVICH) Melkoburzhuaznyi revoliutsionarizm: ob anarkhizme, trotskizme i maoizme. Moskva, 1967. pp. 159.

SCHRAM (STUART R.) Mao Tse-tung. new ed. London, Penguin P., 1967. pp. 351. 20cm.

ZHUKOV (VLADIMIR GEORGIEVICH) Куда ведет политика Мао. Москва, 1967. pp. 55.

BAUM (RICHARD) and TEIWES (FREDERICK C.) Ssu-Ch'ing: the socialist education movement of 1962-1966. Berkeley, University of California, Center for Chinese Studies, [1968]. pp. 128. 23cm. (China Research Monographs. No. 2.)

BURLATSKII (FEDOR MIKHAILOVICH) Маоизм - угроза социализму в Китае. Москва, ИПЛ, 1968. pp. 192. 20см.

MAO Tse-Tung's thought is the invincible weapon. Peking, 1968. pp. 80.

MORAVIA (ALBERTO) pseud. [i.e. Alberto PINCHERLE] La révolution culturelle de Mao; traduit de l'italien par Jean-Louis Faivre D'Arcier. Paris, Flammarion, 1968. pp. 219. 20cm.

MORAVIA (ALBERTO) pseud. [i.e. Alberto PINCHERLE] The red book and the great wall; translated from the Italian by Ronald Strom. London, Secker & Warburg, 1968. pp. 158. 19cm.

ON the revolutionary "three-in-one" combination. Peking, Foreign Languages P., 1968. pp. (iii), 38. 20¼cm.

RAKHIMOV (TURSUN RAKHIMOVICH) Национализм и шовинизм - основа политики группы Мао Цзэ-дуна. Москва, Мысль, 1968. pp. 119. 20см.

SCALIGERO (MASSIMO) Hegel, Marcuse, Mao: marxismo o rivoluzione? Roma, 1968. pp. 89.

WEAKLAND (JOHN H.) "The thought of Mao Tse-tung": communications analysis of a propaganda movement. Palo Alto, Mental Research Institute, 1968. fo. 51. 28cm. (Technical Reports. 3)

ALTAISKII (MIKHAIL LEONT'EVICH) and GEORGIEV (VLADIMIR GEORGIEVICH) Антимарксистская сущность философских взглядов Мао Цзэ-дуна. Москва, 1969. pp. 141.

ANTIMARKSISTSKAIA... Антимарксистская сущность взглядов и политики Мао Цзэ-дуна; сборник статей; под редакцией... Сладковского М. И., etc. Москва, 1969. pp. 802.

BARKAT (ANWAR) Ideology in the modern world: a Christian questioning of marxism and maoism. Tokyo, [1969]. pp. 35. (World Student Christian Federation. Asia Study Fellowship Series. No. 6)

BOGUSH (EVGENII IUL'EVICH) Maoizm i politika raskola v natsional'-no-osvoboditel'nom dvizhenii. Moskva, 1969. pp. 119.

BOORMAN (SCOTT A.) The protracted game: a wei-ch'i interpretation of maoist revolutionary strategy. New York, 1969. pp. 242.

DEVILLERS (PHILIPPE) Mao;...translated [from the German] by Tony White. London, Macdonald, 1969. pp. 317. 21 cm. (What They Really Said Series)

KRIVTSOV (V. A.) ed. Маоизм глазами коммунистов: мировая коммунистическая и рабочая печать о политике группы Мао Цзэ-дуна. Москва, 1969. pp. 416. Material first published in the Communist press 1966-68.

LIFTON (ROBERT JAY) Revolutionary immortality: Mao Tse-tung and the Chinese cultural revolution. London, Weidenfeld & Nicolson, 1969. pp. xiv, 178. 21cm.

MAO (TSE-TUNG) On revolution and war; edited... by M. Rejai. Garden City, Doubleday, 1969. pp. xxi, 355. bibliog. 21cm.

NADEEV (IVAN MIKHAILOVICH) "Культурная революция" и судьба китайской литературы. Москва, 1969. pp. 147.

Il PARTITO rivoluzionario: un problema aperto; contributo del movimento trotskista; critica del maoismo e dello spontaneismo. Roma, [1969]. pp. 103.

RENMIN RIBAO and others. Put Mao Tse-Tung's thought in command of everything: new year editorial for 1969. Peking, 1969. pp. 20.

SIDIKHMENOV (V. IA.) Классы и классовая борьба в кривом зеркале. Москва, 1969. pp. 131.

VLADIMIROV (OLEG EVGEN'EVICH) and RIAZANTSEV (VLADIMIR IVANOVICH) Stranitsy politicheskoi biografii Mao Tsze-duna. Moskva, 1969. pp. 79.

WANG (MING) O sobytiiakh v Kitae. Moskva, 1969. pp. 62.

KRITIKA teoreticheskikh kontseptsii Mao Tsze-duna. Moskva, 1970. pp. 292.

MAO (TSE-TUNG) Mao papers: anthology and bibliography; edited by Jerome Ch'en. London, 1970. pp. 221. bibliog.

SCHILLING (WERNER) Einst Konfuzius, heute Mao Tse-Tung: die Mao-Faszination und ihre Hintergründe. Weilheim/Oberbayern, 1971. pp. 333. bibliog.

SLADKOVSKII (M.I.) and others, eds. Lenin i problemy sovremennogo Kitaia: sbornik statei. Moskva, 1971. pp. 286.

URBAN (GEORGE R.) ed. The miracles of Chairman Mao: a compendium of devotional literature, 1966-1970. London, 1971. pp. 182.

MAORIS

NEW ZEALAND. Department of Maori Affairs. 1961. Report on Department of Maori Affairs, with statistical supplement, 24 August, 1960; by J.K. Hunn. Wellington, 1961. pp. 176.

NEW ZEALAND. Department of Maori and Island Affairs. Report. Wellington, annual, 1967/8 [1st] to date. 24½cm.

NEW ZEALAND. Department of Industries and Commerce, 1967. The Maori in the New Zealand economy. [Wellington], 1967. pp. (ii), 128. 26cm.

PEARCE (G.L.) The story of the Maori people;...drawings by Harry Dansey. Auckland, Collins, 1968, repr. 1969. pp. 164. bibliog. 21cm.

PEOPLE'S VOICE. Government plans the last big grab of Maori land, and in the process exposes 'capital democracy'; [reprint of articles]. n.p., 1968. pp. 7.

SCHWIMMER (ERIK) ed. The Maori people in the nineteen-sixties: a symposium. London, Hurst, 1968. pp. 396. bibliog. 21½cm.

SUTCH (WILLIAM BALL) Poverty and progress in New Zealand: a re-assessment. [2nd ed.] Wellington, [N.Z.], 1969. pp. 389. bibliog.

WARDS (IAN) The shadow of the land: a study of British policy and racial conflict in New Zealand, 1832-1852. Wellington, Historical Publications Branch, Department of Internal Affairs, 1968. pp. xx, 422. bibliog. 25cm.

WILLIAMS (JOHN A.) Politics of the New Zealand Maori: protest and cooperation, 1891-1909. Seattle, [1969]. pp. 204. bibliog.

MAPS

McAREVEY (MARY) compiler. A guide to definitive maps of public paths: a guide to the preparation of draft, provisional and definitive maps of public paths, revised maps and details of public rights of representation and objection. London, 1970. pp. 30.

- Bibliography - Catalogues

NATIONAL MARITIME MUSEUM. Library. Catalogue of the Library. London, H.M.S.O., 1968 in progress.

- Symbols

COLEMAN (ALICE M.) Land use survey handbook: an explanation of the second land use survey of Britain on the scale of 1:25,000. 5th ed. London, 1968. pp. 32.

MARANOS

NETANYAHU (BENZION MILEIKOWSKY) The Marranos of Spain, from the late XIVth to the early XVIth century: according to contemporary Hebrew sources. New York, American Academy for Jewish Research, 1966. pp. ix, 254. 23cm.

MARAT (JEAN PAUL)

RASPAIL (F. V.) Etude impartiale sur Jean Paul Marat le savant et Jean Paul Marat le révolutionnaire. in Raspail (François Vincent) François-Vincent Raspail, etc. Paris, 1968.

MARBLE INDUSTRY AND TRADE

- France

GADILLE (ROLANDE) L'industrie française de la pierre marbrière. Paris, Les Belles Lettres, 1968. pp. 138. bibliog. 24cm. (Besançon. Université. Annales Littéraires. [2e Série]. vol. 97)

MARC PROJECT

LONDON. University. Institute of United States Studies. Computer Committee. Proposals for a machine-readable catalogue of American studies material. London, 1970. pp. 26.

MARCEL (GABRIEL)

SCHMID (C.) Gabriel Marcel. in Boersenverein des deutschen Buchhandels. Friedenspreis des deutschen Buchhandels. Frankfurt am Main, [1967].

TROISFONTAINES (ROGER) De l'existence à l'être: la philosophie de Gabriel Marcel. 2nd ed. Namur, 1968. 2 vols. (in 1). bibliog. (Namur. Facultés Universitaires Notre-Dame de la Paix. Faculté de Philosophie et Lettres. Bibliothèque. fasc. 16)

MARCHENKO (ANATOLII TIKHONOVICH)

MARCHENKO (ANATOLII TIKHONOVICH) My testimony. London, 1969. pp. 415.

MARCHENKO (ANATOLII TIKHONOVICH) Мои показания. Париж, 1969. pp. 369.

MARCHES

- Economic conditions

UNIONE ITALIANA DELLE CAMERE DI COMMERCIO, INDUSTRIA E AGRICOLTURA. Monografic Regionali per la Programmazione Economica. Marche; a cura dell'Unione Regionale delle Camere di Commercio delle Marche. [Milan], Giuffrè, [1967]. pp. xvi, 313. bibliog. 24cm.

- Politics and government

CORRADINI (GIOVANNI) Liberali e cattolici nelle Marche, 1900-1915. Urbino, [1970]. pp. 268. bibliog.

- Population

BONELLI (FRANCO) Evoluzione demografica ed ambiente economico nelle Marche e nell' Umbria dell'ottocento. Torino, 1967. pp. 377. bibliog. (Italy. Istituto per la Ricostruzione Industriale. Archivio Economico dell'Unificazione Italiana. Serie 2. Vol. 12)

MARCOULE

- Economic conditions

FRANCE. 1964. Étude économique du site de Marcoule; par Henri Duprat. (Études Économiques du Commissariat à l'Énergie Atomique. [No.3]) [in English and French]. Paris, 1964. pp. 45. 27cm.

MARCUSE (HERBERT)

LEISS (W.) and others. Marcuse as a teacher. in Wolff (Kurt Heinrich) and Moore (Barrington) eds. The critical spirit.

HABERMAS (JUERGEN) ed. Antworten auf Herbert Marcuse;... mit Beiträgen von Alfred Schmidt [and others]. Frankfurt a.M., 1968. pp. 161. bibliog.

HOLZ (HANS HEINZ) Utopie und Anarchismus: zur Kritik der kritischen Theorie Herbert Marcuses. Köln, Pahl-Rugenstein, [1968]. pp. 134. (Kleine Bibliothek: Politik, Wissenschaft, Zukunft)

SCALIGERO (MASSIMO) Hegel, Marcuse, Mao: marxismo o rivoluzione? Roma, 1968. pp. 89.

AMBACHER (MICHEL) Marcuse et la critique de la civilisation américaine. Paris, [1969]. pp. 134.

MASSET (PIERRE) La pensée Herbert Marcuse. [Toulouse, 1969]. pp. 190.

NEF, LA. Nouvelle Série. 26e Année. No. 36. Marcuse, cet inconnu. Paris, 1969. pp. 197.

PERROUX (FRANÇOIS) François Perroux interroge Herbert Marcuse, qui répond. Paris, [1969]. pp. 211.

ROBINSON (PAUL A.) The Freudian left: Wilhelm Reich, Geza Roheim [and] Herbert Marcuse. New York, [1969]. pp. 253.

STEIGERWALD (ROBERT REINHOLD) Herbert Marcuses dritter Weg. Köln, 1969. pp. 366. bibliog.

MACINTYRE (ALASDAIR CHALMERS) Marcuse. London, 1970. pp. 95. bibliog.

NICOLAS (ANDRÉ) Herbert Marcuse; ou la quête d'un univers trans-prométhéen. Paris, [1970]. pp. 187. bibliog.

ROHRMOSER (GUENTER) Das Elend der kritischen Theorie: Theodor W. Adorno, Herbert Marcuse, Jürgen Habermas. Freiburg, [1970]. pp. 107.

ZUIDEMA (S.U.) De revolutionaire maatschappijkritiek van Herbert Marcuse. Amsterdam, 1970. pp. 205.

SZEWCZYK (JAN) Eros i rewolucja: krytyka antropologii filozoficznej Herberta Marcuse. Warszawa, 1971. pp. 195.

MARCUSE (LUDWIG)

MARCUSE (LUDWIG) Mein zwanzigstes Jahrhundert: auf dem Weg zu einer Autobiographie. Frankfurt am Main, Fischer, 1968. pp. 326.

MAREMMA

RETZLAFF (CHRISTINE) Kulturgeographische Wandlungen in der Maremma unter besonderer Berücksichtigung der italienischen Bodenreform nach dem Zweiten Weltkrieg. Kiel, Universität, Geographisches Institut, 1967. pp. 204. bibliog. 24cm. (Schriften. Band 27. Heft 2)

MARESCHAL-VEZET (JOSEPH JEAN BAPTISTE LUC HIPPOLYTE DE) Comte

DUGON (HENRI) Marquis. Au service du roi en exil: épisodes de la contre-révolution d'après le journal et la correspondance du président de Vezet, 1791-1804. [Macon, imprint], 1968. pp. 373. 23cm.

MARGAI (ALBERT MICHAEL)

ALBERT Margai of Africa. London, [1965]. pp. 24.

MARGARINE

MARGARINE DEFENCE ASSOCIATION. The case for margarine. London, [1899?]. pp. 19.

MANITOBA. 1960. Report of the Margarine Enquiry Commission...appointed... October 14, 1959: [W.J.Waines, commissioner]. [Winnipeg, 1960]. pp. 16. 25cm.

SVENDSEN (KJELL) and SILVER (ÅKE) En analys av den svenska smör- och margarinmarknaden 1952-1962. Stockholm, 1964. pp. 117. bibliog. (Jordbrukets Utredningsinstitut. Meddelanden. 1964. Nr. 3) With English summary.

STUYVENBERG (J.H.VAN) ed. Margarine: an economic, social and scientific history, 1869-1969. Liverpool, 1969. pp. 342. bibliog.

MARGATE

- Harbour

SMITH (JOHN) of Sandwich, Draper. To the right honorable the Lords and Commons assembled in Parliament the humble petition of Iohn Smith... in the behalf of himself and the inhabitants of Margate. [London, 1647]. pp. 8. 17½cm. Wing S 4121.

MARGINAL UTILITY

BUKHARIN (NIKOLAI IVANOVICH) L'économie politique du rentier: la théorie de la valeur et du profit de l'école autrichienne; critique de l'économie marginaliste. Paris, E.D.I. [1967]. pp. 204. 21cm.

FELLNER (W. J.) Operational utility: the theoretical background and a measurement. in Fellner (William John) and others. Ten economic studies in the tradition of Irving Fisher. New York, [1967].

LEHMANN (HERMANN) Grenznutzentheorie: Geschichte und Analyse eines bürgerlichen ökonomischen Lehrsystems. Berlin, Dietz, 1968. pp. 428. 20cm.

PAGE (ALFRED N.) ed. Utility theory: a book of readings. New York, [1968. pp. ix, 454.

MARI REPUBLIC

SVET... Свет Великого Октября: Марийская АССР за 50 лет Советской власти. Йошкар-Ола, 1967. pp. 265.

- History

OCHERKI... Очерки истории Марийской АССР с древнейших времен до Великой Октябрьской социалистической революции. Йошкар-Ола, Марийское Книжное Издательство, 1965. pp. 363. bibliog. 20cm.

- History - Revolution, 1917-1921

PASHUKOV (VASILII FEDOROVICH) Марийский край в годы гражданской войны, 1918-1920 гг. Йошкар-Ола, 1965. pp. 178.

- Intellectual life

KALACHEV (NIKOLAI MATVEEVICH) Социалистическая культура марийского народа. Йошкар-Ола, Марийское Книжное Издательство, 1965. pp. 107. 20см.

VASIN (KIM KIRILLOVICH) and others. Из истории развития философской и общественно-политической мысли в Марийском крае: дооктябрьский период; под редакцией С. А. Васенева. Йошкар-Ола, Марийское Книжное Издательство, 1966. pp. 154. 20см.

- Rural conditions

ISANOV (VITALII VASIL'EVICH) Новое в партийной работе на селе. Йошкар-Ола, 1967. pp. 120.

- Statistics

MARI REPUBLIC Statisticheskoe Upravlenie. 1967. Марийская АССР в цифрах: статистический сборник. Йошкар-Ола, 1967. pp. 209. 14см.

MARIÁTEGUI (JOSÉ CARLOS)

POSADA (FRANCISCO) Los origenes del pensamiento marxista en Latinoamerica: politica y cultura en Jose Carlos Mariategui. Madrid, 1968. pp. 96.

MARIETTA AND CINCINNATI RAILROAD

PIXTON (JOHN) The Marietta and Cincinnati Railroad, 1845-1883: a case study in American railroad economics. Pennsylvania, 1966. pp. 94. bibliog. (Pennsylvania State University. Penn State Studies. No. 17)

MARIHUANA

SOLOMON (DAVID) 1925- , ed. The marihuana papers. Indianapolis, Bobbs-Merrill, [1966]. pp. xxvi, 448. bibliogs. 22½cm.

GOODE (ERICH) ed. Marijuana. New York, 1969. pp. 197. bibliog.

SMITH (DAVID E.) ed. The new social drug: cultural medical, and legal perspectives on marijuana. Englewood Cliffs, [1970]. pp. 186. bibliog.

MARINE ACCIDENTS

NORWAY. Statistiske Centralbyrå. Sjøulykkesstatistikk: Marine casualties. a., 1970 [1st]- Oslo.

BOEHME (ECKART) Tankerunfälle auf dem Hohe Meer: die Zulässigkeit staatlicher Massnahmen zur Gefahrenabwehr. Hamburg, 1970. pp. 92. bibliog. (Hamburg. Hansische Universität. Forschungsstelle für Völkerrecht und Ausländisches Öffentliches Recht. Werkhefte. 13)

MARINE MINERAL RESOURCES

CHRISTY (FRANCIS T.) Economic criteria for rules governing exploitation of deep sea minerals. Washington, D.C., Resources for the Future, Inc., 1968. pp. 224-242. 23cm. (Reprint Series. 72) (Reprinted from The International Lawyer, Jan. 1968)

MARINE POLLUTION

MARX (WESLEY) The frail ocean. New York, 1967 repr. 1970. pp. 274. bibliog.

SIBTHORP (M.M.) Oceanic pollution: a survey and some suggestions for control. London, [1969]. pp. 53.

SCHACHTER (OSCAR) and SERWER (DANIEL) Marine pollution problems and remedies. New York, United Nations Institute for Training and Research, 1970. pp. 41,ix. (Research Reports. No.4).

MARINE RESOURCES

MIKHAILOV (STEPAN VASIL'EVICH) Экономика мирового океана. Москва, Экономика, 1966. pp. 272. 20cm.

BARDACH (JOHN) Harvest of the sea. London, 1969. pp. 303. bibliog.

FRIEDHEIM (ROBERT L.) Understanding the debate on ocean resources. Denver, Colo., [1969] pp. 38. (Denver. University. Social Science Foundation and Graduate School of International Studies. Monograph Series in World Affairs. Vol. 6, no. 3)

LOFTAS (TONY) The last resource. London, 1969. pp. 256. bibliog.

MIKHAILOV (STEFAN VASIL'EVICH) Мировой океан и человечество. Москва, 1969. pp. 397.

REED (LAURANCE) Ocean-space, Europe's new frontier: towards a long-range, concerted programme for exploiting the resources of the sea. London, 1969. pp. 60. (Bow Group. Pamphlets)

- Law and legislation

The RESOURCES of the ocean bed: report of a conference at Ditchley Park, 26-29 September 1969; by K. R. Simmonds, conference rapporteur. Enstone, Oxfordshire, [1969]. pp. 53. (Ditchley Foundation. Ditchley Papers. No. 23)

ANDRASSY (JURAJ) International law and the resources of the sea. New York, 1970. pp. 191. bibliog. (Columbia University. School of Law. International Legal Research Program. Publications)

- United States

PADELFORD (NORMAN JUDSON) Public policy for the seas. [rev. ed.] Cambridge, Mass., [1970]. pp. 338.

SPANGLER (MILLER B.) New technology and marine resource development: a study in government-business cooperation. New York, 1970. pp. 607.

MARINE RESOURCES/CONSERVATION

- Law and legislation

WORLD PEACE THROUGH LAW CENTER. Pamphlets Series. No.10. Treaty governing the exploration and use of the ocean bed. Geneva, 1967. pp. 27.

TOWARDS a better use of the ocean: contemporary legal problems in ocean development, by W.T. Burke; [with] comments and recommendations by an international symposium. London, 1969. pp. 231. (Stockholm International Peace Research Institute. SIPRI Monographs)

MARINE SERVICE

- Canada

APPLETON (THOMAS E.) Usque ad mare: a history of the Canadian coast guard and marine services. Ottawa, Department of Transport, 1968 [or rather] 1969. pp. xiii, 318. 23½cm.

MARITIME LAW

UNITED NATIONS. International Law Commission. [Documents]. A/CN. 4/17,42,51,60,69,79. Report[s] on the regime of the high seas. [New York], 1950-54. 6 pts.

UNITED NATIONS. International Law Commission. [Documents]. A/CN. 4/32. Memorandum on the regime of the high seas. [New York], 1950. pp. vi, 112.

UNITED NATIONS. International Law Commission. [Documents]. A/CN. 4/97 and Addenda. Questions relating to the law of the sea: report [with] summary of replies from governments and conclusions, etc. [New York], 1956. 4 pts.

UNITED NATIONS. International Law Commission. [Documents]. A/CN. 4/99 and Addenda. Comments by governments on the provisional articles concerning the regime of the high seas and the draft articles on the regime of the territorial sea adopted by the... Commission at its seventh session. [New York], 1956. 10 pts.

SINGH (NAGENDRA) Essays in maritime international law and organisation. Waltair, 1966. pp. 174. (Andhra University. Sir Alladi Krishnaswami Endowment Lectures. 1965)

TEITELBOIM V. (SERGIO) Chile y la soberania en el mar. Santiago de Chile, Bello, 1966. pp. 219. bibliog. 19cm.

ALEXANDER (LEWIS M.) ed. The law of the sea: offshore boundaries and zones; [proceedings of the first conference of the Law of the Sea Institute, Kingston, Rhode Island, 1966] [Columbus] Ohio State U.P., [1967] pp. xix, 321. 23cm.

BOYER (ALBERT) Le droit maritime. Paris, Presses Universitaires de France, 1967. pp. 128. bibliog. 17½cm. (Que Sais-Je? No. 1252)

MANUAL of international maritime law; [by] P.D. Barabolia [and others]. Springfield, Va., 1968. 2 pts. (in 1 vol.)

THOMMEN (THAMARAPPALLIL KOCHU) International legislation on shipping. (TD/32/Rev.1) New York, United Nations, 1968. pp. 34.

DYMLING (PETER) Haagreglerna och kyltransporter. Göteborg, 1969. pp. 107. bibliog. (Gothenburg. Handelshögskolan. Skriftserie. 1969.4)

FRIEDHEIM (ROBERT L.) Understanding the debate on ocean resources. Denver, Colo., [1969] pp. 38. (Denver. University. Social Science Foundation and Graduate School of International Studies. Monograph Series in World Affairs. Vol. 6, no. 3)

SHARP (MITCHELL WILLIAM) Law and arms control
on the seabed: an address by the Honorable
Mitchell Sharp, Secretary of State for
External Affairs, to the International Law
Association, Toronto, November 5, 1969.
Ottawa, 1969. pp. 6. (Canada. Department
of External Affairs. Information Division.
Statements and Speeches. No. 69/19)

TOWARDS a better use of the ocean: contemporary
legal problems in ocean development, by W.T.
Burke; [with] comments and recommendations by
an international symposium. London, 1969.
pp. 231. (Stockholm International Peace
Research Institute. SIPRI Monographs)

PACEM in maribus: ocean enterprises: a summary
of the prospects, and hazards, of man's impending
commercial exploitation of the underseas: a
special report on a preliminary conference held
in preparation for the Pacem in Maribus convocation
at Valletta, Malta, June 28th - July 3rd 1970:
edited by Elaine H. Burnell and Piers von Simson.
Santa Barbara, 1970. pp. 116. bibliog. (Center
for the Study of Democratic Institutions. Occasional
Papers)

QUENEUDEC (JEAN PIERRE) Droit maritime international: recueil de textes. Paris, 1971.
pp. 383

- Bibliography

UNITED NATIONS. International Law Commission.
[Documents]. A/CN. 4/26. Bibliography on the
regime of the high seas. [New York], 1950. pp. 20

- Congresses

DEUTSCHER VEREIN FUER INTERNATIONALES
SEERECHT. Schriften. Reihe B: Dokumente und Materialien. Heft 3. Die
Stockholmer Konferenz des Comité Maritime International vom 9. bis 15.
Juni 1963: Berichte und Materialien.
Hamburg, 1964. pp. 40.

- Belgium

La BELGIQUE et le droit de la mer: actes du
Colloque conjoint des 21 et 22 avril 1967.
[Brussels, 1969]. pp. 180. (Brussels. Université Libre. Institut de Sociologie. Centre de
Droit International and Louvain. Université.
Centre de Droit International. [Publications]. 3)

- Bolivia

BURGOS ÓRTEGA (EDUARDO) Bolivia y su derecho al
mar. Potosí, 1966. pp. 140. bibliog. 21cm.

- Colombia

ESCOBAR TÉLLEZ (JORGE ENRIQUE) Colombia frente
a las principales normas marítimas de derecho
laboral internacional. Bogotá, 1967. pp. 127.
bibliog. 24cm.

- France

RODIÈRE (RENÉ) Traité général de droit
maritime: affrètements et transports.
Paris, Dalloz, 1967. 2 vols. 24cm.

KRIEGER (KARL FRIEDRICH) Ursprung und Wurzeln
der Rôles d'Oléron. Köln, 1970. pp. 167. bibliog.
(Hansischer Geschichtsverein. Quellen und Darstellungen zur Hansischen Geschichte. Neue Folge.
Band 15)

- Germany

SEGELKEN (HANS) Kapitänsrecht. Hamburg,
Weltarchiv, 1967. pp. (v), 548. bibliog.
24cm.

DEUTSCHER VEREIN FUR INTERNATIONALES SEERECHT.
Schriften. Reihe A: Berichte und Vorträge.
Heft 12. Bemerkungen zum Entwurf einer
Seerechtlichen Verteilungsordnung: Vortrag
von Walther Richter gehalten in der Jahresversammlung...am 10. März 1969. Hamburg, 1969.
pp. 19.

- Italy

MANCA (PLINIO) The Italian code of navigation:
translation and commentary. Milano, Giuffrè,
1958. pp. xv, 475. 24cm. (Fonti e Documenti
del Diritto della Navigazione. 2)

BERLINGUER (LUIGI) Domenico Alberto Azuni:
giurista e politico, 1749-1827; un contributo
bio-bibliografico. Milano, Giuffrè, 1966.
pp. xiv, 291. 24cm. (Quaderni di "Studi
Senesi". 17)

- Russia

UNITED NATIONS. International Law Commission.
[Documents]. A/CN. 4/38. Memorandum on the
Soviet doctrine and practice with respect to
the regime of the high seas. [New York], 1950.
pp. 17.

MATEESCO (MIRCEA) Le droit maritime et
le droit aérien de l'U.R.S.S. à l'heure
de la coexistence pacifique. Paris,
Pedone, 1967. pp. 383. bibliog. 25cm.

ANDERSEN (WOLFGANG) Das Seerecht der
Sowjetunion. Hamburg, Hansischer Gildenverlag,
[1968]. pp. vi, 245. bibliog. 24cm.
(Ostrechtliche Schriften. 3)

TSENTRAL'NYI NAUCHNO-ISSLEDOVATEL'SKII
INSTITUT MORSKOGO FLOTA. Trudy. vyp.
95. Morskoe pravo. Leningrad, 1968.
pp. 113.

TSENTRAL'NYI NAUCHNO-ISSLEDOVATEL'SKII
INSTITUT MORSKOGO FLOTA. Trudy. vyp.
108. Morskoe pravo. Leningrad, 1969.
pp. 135.

- Sweden

HILDING (MATS) Om bevisning vid lossning av
sjötransporterat gods. Göteborg, 1964.
pp. 28. (Gothenburg. Handelshögskolan.
Skrifterserie. 1964. 4) With English summary.

- United Kingdom

CHORLEY (ROBERT SAMUEL THEODORE) 1st Baron Chorley,
and GILES (OTTO CHARLES FELIX WILLIAM) Shipping
law. 6th ed. London, 1970. pp. 405.

IVAMY (EDWARD RICHARD HARDY) Casebook on
shipping law. London, 1970. pp. 20.

WISWALL (F.L.) The development of Admiralty jurisdiction and practice since 1800: and English
study with American comparisons. Cambridge,
1970. pp. 223. bibliog. (Cambridge. University.
Yorke Prize Essays. 1968)

WISWALL (F.L.) The development of Admiralty jurisdiction and practice since 1800: an English study
with American comparisons. Cambridge, 1970. pp.
223. bibliog. (Cambridge. University. Yorke Prize
Essays. 1968)

MARITIME LAW - United Kingdom (Cont'd.)

CARVER (THOMAS GILBERT) Carriage by sea: twelfth edition by Raoul Colinvaux. London, 1971. 2 vols.

- United States

REISENER (WOLFGANG) Staatliche Regulierung der Linienschiffahrt in den USA: vom Shipping Act, 1916 zum Bonner Act von 1961. Hamburg, 1969. pp. 122. bibliog. (Hamburg. Hamburgisches Welt-Wirtschafts-Archiv. Veröffentlichungen)

PADELFORD (NORMAN JUDSON) Public policy for the seas. [rev. ed.] Cambridge, Mass., [1970]. pp. 338.

WISWALL (F.L.) The development of Admiralty jurisdiction and practice since 1800: an English study with American comparisons. Cambridge, 1970. pp. 223. bibliog. (Cambridge. University. Yorke Prize Essays. 1968)

MARITIME TERRITORY

MOROZOV (P.) Приморье - край пограничный. Владивосток, Приморское Книжное Издательство, 1958. pp. 56. 19½cm.

- History

OCHERKI... Очерки истории советского Приморья: от эпохи первобытнообщинного строя до настоящего времени. Владивосток, Приморское Книжное Издательство, 1963. pp. 224. bibliog. 21cm.

- History - Sources

PRIMORSKAIA kraevaia partiinaia organizatsiia v period Velikoi Otechestvennoi voiny, 1941-1945 gg.: sbornik dokumentov i materialov. t.1. Deiatel'nost kraevoi partiinoi organizatsii po rukovodstvu promyshlennost'iu, transportom, sel'skim khoziaistvom i ukrepleniiu tyla. Vladivostok, 1965. pp. 304.

- History - 1917-1921, Revolution

ETIKH dnei ne smolknet slava...: stat'i, ocherki i materialy o bor'be ze vlast' Sovetov v Primor'e v 1917-1922 gg. Vladivostok, 1966. pp. 240.

MARKET DRAYTON

- Social history

ROWLEY (N.) and ROWLEY (S.V.) Market Drayton: a study in social history. Market Drayton, N. Rowley, 1966. pp. iv, 68. 24½cm.

MARKET SURVEYS

UNITED NATIONS. Commission on International Commodity Trade. [Limited Series]. E/CN. 13/L. 1. Survey of primary commodity markets. [New York], 1954. pp.120.

CONFERENCE ON THE ROLE OF TRADE ASSOCIATIONS IN THE STUDY OF MARKETS, VIENNA, 1961. Report. [Paris, 1961?] pp. 104.

STROSCHEIN (FRITZ REINHARD) Die Befragungstaktik in der demoskopischen Marktforschung. Berlin, 1962. pp. 263. bibliog. With tables and diagrams in English.

SPIELBERGER (KARLHEINZ) Über die Möglichkeiten und Grenzen des standardisierten Interviews in der Marktforschung. [Erlangen-Nürnberg, 1967?]. pp. 175. bibliog.

- Bibliography

GENERAL AGREEMENT ON TARIFFS AND TRADE. 1967. A bibliography of market surveys by products and countries. Genève, 1967. pp. 187. In various languages.

- Canada

CANADA. Dominion Bureau of Statistics. Merchandising and Services Division. 1969. Market research handbook; Manuel statistique pour études de marché, 1969. Ottawa, 1969. pp. 645. In English and French.

- Germany, Eastern

FISCHER (HERBERT) of the Institut für Marktforschung in Leipzig, and KOEPPERT (WILLI) Konsumentenbefragung in der sozialistischen Marktforschung. Berlin, Verlag Die Wirtschaft, 1967. pp. 200. bibliog. 21½cm.

- Uganda

MARKETING DEVELOPMENT COMPANY, LTD. Market Surveys Uganda, 1956: a report. [Entebbe, Government Printer, 1957]. pp. 39.

- United Kingdom

ALLEN (DAVID ELLISTON) British tastes: an enquiry into the likes and dislikes of the regional consumer. London, 1968. pp. (iii), 256.

ANGLIA TELEVISION. A marketing guide to the East of England. [London, 1968]. pp. 120. 36cm. Map in end pocket.

PEARL AND DEAN LTD. The young market, 1971: a definitive report and analysis of the teenagers in Great Britain. London, 1971. pp. 126.

- United Kingdom - Wales

CREDLAND (G.D.) and LUBY (B.E.) An appraisal of the TWW marketing region. [London], T.W.W. Ltd., [1964?]. pp. 23.

- United States

SPRENGER (WALTER) Der Bedarf in langlebigen Konsumgütern: eine Marktstudie unter besonderer Berücksichtigung amerikanischer Verhältnisse. [Erlangen-Nürnberg, 1963?]. pp. 202. bibliog.

JOHNSON (ARNO HALLOCK) and others. The American market of the future. New York, New York University, School of Commerce, 1966. pp. xi, 138. 20cm. (Charles C. Moskowitz Lectures. No. 6)

ERDOS (PAUL L.) Professional mail surveys;...with the assistance of Arthur J. Morgan. New York, [1970]. pp. 289. bibliog.

MARKETING

NIGERIA. Nigeria Constitutional Conference, 1958. Report by the ad hoc meeting... held in Lagos in February 1958. Lagos, 1958. pp. 63. The report of the Conference proper is filed with the British Parliamentary Papers (Cmnd. 569)

MUNTHE (PREBEN) Produsentens vertikale markedspolitikk som pristeoretisk problem. Bergen, Norges Handelshøyskole, 1960. pp. 62. bibliog. 24cm. (Skrifter. Økonomiske Avhandlinger. Nr.4)

FABRIZI (C.) I canali di distribuzione nella teoria e nella pratica del marketing. in vol.2 of Saggi di economia aziendale e sociale in memoria di Gino Zappa. Milano, 1961.

MEERTENS (L. L. G. D.) Over de invloed van de commerciële visie; openbare les gehouden... 29 November 1962. Leiden, Stenfert Kroese, [1962]. pp. 20. bibliog. 22cm.

DISCH (WOLFGANG K. A.) ed. Aktuelle Absatzwirtschaft. Hamburg, Weltarchiv, 1964. pp. 310. 24cm.

VIDAL (CAETANO L'EGLISE DA CRUZ) A distribuição e o seu custo. Lisboa, 1964. pp. xxiv, 162. bibliog. 25cm.

PHILPOTT (BRYAN PASSMORE) Strategic and tactical planning in international marketing policies. [Christchurch, N.Z.,] the Unit, 1965. pp. 33-50. 20½cm. (Christchurch, New Zealand. University of Canterbury. Lincoln College; Agricultural Economics Research Unit. Publications. No. 25.) (Reprinted from the Proceedings of a Conference on Marketing, July 1965)

CANADA. Dominion Bureau of Statistics. Direct selling in Canada. [in English and French] a., 1966 [1st issue]- Ottawa.

KYN (O.) The market mechanism in a socialist economy. in St.Antony's Papers. No.19. Soviet affairs; No.4. London, 1966.

REVZAN (DAVID ALLEN) The marketing significance of geographical variations in wholesale/retail sales ratios. Berkeley, California University, Institute of Business and Economic Research, 1966. fo. iii, 57. bibliog. 28cm.(IBER Special Publications)

SCHEUING (EBERHARD) Einflussfaktoren und Ausdrucksformen des Absatzmarktverhaltens industrieller Unternehmungen. [Munich?], 1966. pp. 174. bibliog.

ALBERT (HANS) Marktsoziologie und Entscheidungslogik: ökonomische Probleme in soziologischer Perspektive. Neuwied an Rhein, Luchterhand, [1967]. pp. 531. bibliog. 19cm. (Soziologische Texte. Band 36)

BAIKOV (GRIGORII DANILOVICH) Sovershenstvovanie sviazei torgovli s promyshlennost'iu. Moskva, 1967. pp. 78.

BIDLINGMAIER (JOHANNES) and others, eds. Absatzpolitik und Distribution...; Karl Christian Behrens zum 60. Geburtstag. Wiesbaden, [1967]. pp. 455. bibliogs. 24cm.

DICHTL (ERWIN) Über Wesen und Struktur absatzpolitischer Entscheidungen. Berlin, Duncker und Humblot, [1967]. pp. 180. bibliog. 23cm. (Betriebswirtschaftliche Schriften. Heft 21)

GOTTLIEB DUTTWEILER-INSTITUT. Internationale Studientagung, 15., 1966. Wissenschaft und Handel: der Brückenschlag zwischen Theorie und Praxis; mit Beiträgen von W. Applebaum [and others]. Bern, 1967. pp. 199.

HANSEN (HARRY L.) Marketing: text. technique and cases. 3rd ed. Homewood, Irwin, 1967. pp xiii, 1024. 22½cm.

KATCHOURINE (ALEC) La psychologie sociale, clé du marketing: (apport de la psychologie sociale aux communications commerciales). Paris, S.A.B.R.I., [1967] pp. 145. bibliog. 25cm.

MOLL (KARL) 1941- Cash and Carry als absatzwirtschaftliches System im Westdeutschen Lebensmittelgrosshandel. München, 1967. pp. 171. bibliog.

MOYER (M.S.) and SNYDER (G) Trends in Canadian marketing. Ottawa, D.B.S., 1967. pp. xxi, 321. 23cm. (Canada. Dominion Bureau of Statistics. Census Division. 1961 Census Monographs.)

ŠIK (OTA) Plan and market under socialism. White Plains, International Arts and Sciences P., [1967]. pp. 382. bibliog. 20½cm.

SMIRNOV (PETR VASIL'EVICH) and TARAS'IANTS (RUBEN BOGDANOVICH) Organizatsiia i planirovanie sbyta promyshlennoi produktsii v SSSR. 2nd ed. Moskva, 1967. pp. 311.

STANTON (WILLIAM J.) Fundamentals of marketing. 2nd ed. New York, McGraw-Hill, [1967]. pp. xix, 743. bibliog. 23cm.

TAFEL (JOERG) Der Entscheidungsprozess beim Kauf von Investitionsgütern. Möglichkeiten und Grenzen seiner Beeinflussung durch Absatzstrategien der Hersteller. [Erlangen, imprint, 1967?]. pp. 167. bibliog.

ALDERSON (WROE) and HALBERT (MICHAEL H.) Men, motives, and markets. Englewood Cliffs, Prentice-Hall, [1968]. pp.(iv), 118. bibliog. 22½cm. (Foundations of Marketing Series)

BAUER (PETER TAMAS) and YAMEY (BASIL SELIG) Markets, market control and marketing reform; selected papers. London, Weidenfeld and Nicolson, [1968]. pp. (iii), 421. 21½cm.

BEADLES (NICHOLAS ASTON) and DREWRY (L. AUBREY) eds. Money, the market, and the state: economic essays in honor of James Muir Waller. Athens, U. of Georgia P., [1968]. pp. xiii, 225. 23½cm.

MARKETING (Cont'd.)

BIRKIGT (KLAUS) Verkaufsförderung: Analyse eines absatzwirtschaftlichen Phänomens, dargestellt am Beispiel der Konsumgüterindustrie. [Bamberg, imprint], 1968. pp. 152. bibliog.

DISCH (WOLFGANG K. A.) ed. Netzplantechnik im Marketing. Hamburg, Weltarchiv, 1968. pp. 217. bibliog. 20½cm. (Hamburg. Hamburgisches Welt-Wirtschafts-Archiv. Veröffentlichungen)

KERNAN (JEROME B.) and SOMMERS (MONTROSE S.) eds. Perspectives in marketing theory. New York, Appleton-Century-Crofts, [1968]. pp. xv, 462. 23½cm.

MOYER (REED) and HOLLANDER (STANLEY C.) eds. Markets and marketing in developing economies. Homewood, Irwin, 1968. pp. xiii, 264. bibliog. 22½cm.

NIESCHLAG (ROBERT) and others. Einführung in die Lehre von der Absatzwirtschaft: ein entscheidungstheoretischer Ansatz. Berlin, [1968]. pp. 361. bibliogs.

O'DELL (WILLIAM F.) The marketing decision. [New York], American Management Association, [1968]. pp. 320. 23½cm.

RICHTER (BERND) Über Wesen, Begriff und Formen der Verkaufsförderung. [Erlangen, imprint, 1968?]. pp. 258. bibliog.

SHAPIRO (STANLEY J.) and DOODY (ALTON F.) eds. Readings in the history of American marketing: settlement to civil war. Homewood, Irwin, 1968. pp. viii, 484. bibliog. 23cm.

ŠIK (OTA) Plán a trh za socialismu. [3rd ed.]. Praha, Academia, 1968. pp. 366. bibliog. 20½cm. 1st (1964) and 2nd (1965) eds. entitled K problematice socialistických zbožních vztahů.

TILLMAN (ROLLIE) and KIRKPATRICK (CHARLES ATKINSON) Promotion: persuasive communication in marketing. Homewood, Irwin, 1968. pp. xii, 477. 23cm.

WASSON (CHESTER R.) and McCONAUGHY (DAVID H.) Buying behavior and marketing decisions. New York, Appleton, [1968]. pp. vii, 547. bibliog. 23½cm.

BLACKBURN (A.J.) On a class of market share functions. London, 1969. pp. 7. (Centre for Environmental Studies. Working Papers. 27)

CORAM (TERRY) Cases in marketing and marketing research. London, Crosby Lockwood. 1969. pp. ix, 165. 21cm.

COWLING (KEITH) and RAYNER (A.J.) Price, quality, and market share. Coventry, 1969. fo. 28. bibliog. (University of Warwick. Department of Economics. Warwick Economic Research Papers. No. 7)

ELLING (KARL A.) Introduction to modern marketing: an applied approach. New York, Macmillan, [1969]. pp. xiv, 431. 23cm.

HANSEN (HANS ROBERT) ed. Unternehmung und Markt: Festschrift für Carl W. Meyer. Berlin, [1969]. pp. 381. bibliog.

LEVITT (THEODORE) The marketing mode: pathways to corporate growth. New York, 1969. pp. 354.

MATTSSON (LARS-GUNNAR) Integration and efficiency in marketing systems. Stockholm, EFI, 1969. pp. xiii, 342. bibliog. 24cm.

MICONI (BRUNO) Indagini empiriche e problemi teorici delle forme concorrenziali moderne: due saggi su teoria dell'impresa e strutture di mercato. Milano, 1969. pp. 74. (Rome. Università. Istituto di Politica Economica e Finanziaria. Pubblicazioni. 7)

MISSELBROOK (B.D.) and WEYER (D.V.) Bank marketing: two lectures on marketing and its application to banking. London, [1969]. pp. 35. (Institute of Bankers. Ernest Sykes Memorial Lectures. 1969)

PALDA (KRISTIAN S.) Economic analysis for marketing decisions. Englewood Cliffs, Prentice-Hall, [1969]. pp. xii, 260. 22½cm.

WINKLER (JOHN) Marketing for the developing company. London, Hutchinson, 1969. pp. xiv, 258. 22½cm. (Hutchinson Marketing Library)

ANDERSON (DOLE A.) Marketing and development: the Thailand experience. East Lansing, Mich., 1970. pp. 214. (Michigan State University. Institute for International Business and Economic Development Studies. MSU International Business and Economic Studies.)

AYLOTT (D. JOHN.) and BRINDLE-WOOD-WILLIAMS (DIGBY) Physical distribution in industrial and consumer marketing. London, 1970. pp. 214. bibliog.

BARTELS (ROBERT) Marketing theory and metatheory. Homewood, Ill., 1970. pp. 299.

MORRIS (B.) Multi-dimensional aspects of market structure and market performance. Coventry, 1970. pp. 27. bibliog. (University of Warwick. Department of Economics. Warwick Economic Research Papers. No. 12)

SHEPHERD (WILLIAM G.) Market power and economic welfare: an introduction. New York, [1970]. pp. 302. bibliog.

BERG (THOMAS L.) Mismarketing: case histories of marketing misfires. London, 1971. pp. 244.

HENRY (HARRY) Perspectives in management, marketing and research. London, 1971. pp. 401.

NARVER (JOHN C.) and SAVITT (RONALD) The marketing economy: an analytical approach. New York, [1971]. pp. 432. bibliogs.

YOSHINO (M.Y.) The Japanese marketing system: adaptations and innovations. Cambridge, Mass., [1971]. pp. 319. bibliog.

- Bibliography

WILLS (GORDON) and others, compilers. Sources of U.K. marketing information. London, Nelson, 1969. pp. xiii, 304. 21½cm. (Marketing Library)

- Congresses

> CONFERENCE ON THE EXPLORATION OF NEW MARKETS BY SMALL AND MEDIUM-SIZED FIRMS, 1961. Exploration of new markets by small and medium sized firms: report. Paris, [1962]. pp. 86.

- Information services

> KELLEY (WILLIAM THOMAS) Marketing intelligence: the management of marketing information. London, Staples P., 1968. pp. xii, 248. bibliog. 24½cm.
>
> WILLS (GORDON) and others, compilers. Sources of U.K. marketing information. London, Nelson, 1969. pp. xiii, 304. 21½cm. (Marketing Library)

- Mathematical models

> VERBOOM (EEUWOUT) Absatzpolitik im Polypol auf unvollkommenem Markte unter Berücksichtigung der Independenzen zur Investitions- und Finanzierungspolitik. Hamburg, 1968. pp. iv, 371. bibliog.
>
> BRESSLER (RAYMOND GEORGE) and KING (RICHARD A.) Markets, prices and interregional trade. New York, [1970]. pp. 426. bibliogs.
>
> DONNELLY (JAMES H.) and IVANCEVICH (JOHN M.) Analysis for marketing decisions. Homewood, 1970. pp. 397. bibliogs.
>
> GRIGGS (JOHN E.) Evaluating marketing change: an application of systems theory. East Lansing, 1970. pp. 131. bibliog. (Michigan State University. Institute for International Business and Economic Development Studies. MSU International Business and Economic Studies)
>
> KOTLER (PHILIP) Marketing decision making: a model building approach. New York, [1971]. pp. 720.

- Study and teaching - United Kingdom

> CONFERENCE OF BRITISH TEACHERS OF MARKETING AT ADVANCED LEVEL, 3RD, HARROGATE, 1968. Conference proceedings. Lancaster, [1969]. fo. 51.

- Terminology

> EUROPEAN ECONOMIC COMMUNITY. 1961-62. Terminologie de la distribution. Première partie: notions 1 à 26; résultats de l'enquête effectuée en 1961 en Allemagne, Belgique, France, Italie et aux Pays-Bas. ([With] English supplement) (Bureau de Terminologie) [Brussels], 1961-62. 2 pts. (in 1 vol.). In Dutch, French, German and Italian. For parts 2 and 3 see EUROPEAN ECONOMIC COMMUNITY. 1962 and 1965.
>
> EUROPEAN ECONOMIC COMMUNITY. 1962. Terminologie de la distribution. Deuxième partie: notions 27 à 51; résultats de l'enquête effectuée en 1962 en Allemagne, Belgique, France, Italie et aux Pays-Bas. (Bureau de Terminologie) [Brussels], 1962. pp. xliv, 497. 20½cm. x 29½cm. In Dutch, English, French, German and Italian. For parts 1 and 3 see EUROPEAN ECONOMIC COMMUNITY. 1961-62 and 1965.
>
> EUROPEAN ECONOMIC COMMUNITY. 1965. Terminologie de la distribution. Troisième partie: notions 52 à 78; résultats d'une enquête effectuée en 1964 en Allemagne, Belgique, France, Italie, aux Pays-Bas et dans le Royaume Uni. (Bureau de Terminologie) [Brussels], 1965. pp. xlix, 588. In Dutch, English, French, German and Italian. For parts 1 and 2 see EUROPEAN ECONOMIC COMMUNITY. 1961-62 and 1962.

MARKETING MANAGEMENT

> LYNN (ROBERT A.) Price policies and marketing management. Homewood, Irwin, 1967. pp. xi, 331. bibliogs. 23cm.
>
> MORSE (STEPHEN P.) The practical approach to marketing management. London, McGraw-Hill, [1967]. pp. 255. bibliog. 20½cm.
>
> GRANT (ROY) ed. Distribution management. London, Business Books, 1968. pp. x, 184. 21½cm. (Management in Action Series)
>
> LITVAK (ISAIAH A.) and others. Marketing management for the middleman: cases and readings prepared and edited for the Department of Manpower and Immigration. Ottawa, Department of Manpower and Immigration, 1968. pp. ix, 252. bibliog. 23cm.
>
> BODDEWYN (J.) ed. Comparative management and marketing; text and readings. [Glenview, 1969]. pp. 302. bibliogs.
>
> **BROWN (REX V.) Research and the credibility of estimates: an appraisal tool for executives and researchers.** Boston, 1969. pp. 257.
>
> MONTGOMERY (DAVID B.) and URBAN (GLEN L.) Management science in marketing. Englewood Cliffs, Prentice-Hall, [1969]. pp. xix, 376. 23cm. (Prentice-Hall International Series in Management)
>
> RATHMELL (JOHN M.) Managing the marketing function: concepts, analysis, and application. New York, Wiley, [1969]. pp. xxi, 636. 22½cm. (Marketing Series)
>
> MIRACLE (GORDON E.) and ALBAUM (GERALD S.) International marketing management. Homewood, Illinois, 1970. pp. 604.
>
> **PEARCE (ESMOND) Marketing and higher management.** London, 1970. pp. 250.

- India

> NEELAMEGHAM (S) ed. Marketing management and the Indian economy. Delhi, [1970]. pp. 459.

MARKETING RESEARCH

> CRISP (RICHARD D.) Marketing research organization and operation. New York, [1958]. pp. 70. (American Management Association. Research Studies. No. 35)
>
> AUSTRALIA. Department of Trade. Industries Division. 1960. Economic research organizations in Australia. [Canberra, 1960]. fo. (53).
>
> EUROPEAN PRODUCTIVITY AGENCY. 1960. Documentation service on research into distribution. (Project 6/03-B) [Paris, 1960?]. pp. 173. 24cm.

MARKETING RESEARCH (Cont'd.)

RADEL (FRITZ EMIL) Market research practice in South Africa. Pretoria, University of South Africa, Bureau of Market Research, 1960. pp. 55. 24½cm. (Research Reports. No. 1)

BELSON (WILLIAM A.) Group testing in market research. London, London School of Economics and Political Science, Survey Research Centre, 1963. pp. 39-43. bibliog. 25½cm. (Reprint Series. 31) (Reprinted from the Journal of Advertising Research, vol. 3, no. 2, 1963)

HENN (R.) Das Testen von Hypothesen in der Marktforschung. in Zukunftsaufgaben in Wirtschaft und Gesellschaft. Zürich, 1963.

KILGUS (ERNST) Teilerhebungen im Dienste der betriebswirtschaftlichen Marktforschung. Zurich 1964. pp. 263. bibliog

BELSON (WILLIAM A.) The effects of reversing the presentation order of verbal rating scales. London, 1966. pp. 11. (London. University. London School of Economics and Political Science. Survey Research Centre. Reprint Series. 37). (Reprintd from the Journal of Advertising Research. vol. 6. No.4. 1966)

LANDWIRTSCHAFTLICHE Marktforschung in Deutschland; Arthur Hanau zum 65. Geburtstag;...Beiträgen von Hans Eberhard Buchholz [and others]; herausgegeben von Günther Schmitt. München, Bayerischer Landwirtschaftsverlag, [1967]. pp. 339. bibliogs. 24cm.

LEONHARD (DIETZ) The human equation in marketing research. New York, American Management Association, [1967]. pp. 176. 22½cm.

NIEDEN (WALTER ZUR) Möglichkeiten der Marktforschung im westdeutschen Warenhausunternehmen. [Erlangen, imprint, 1968?]. pp. various. bibliog.

PROESCHEL (KLAUS) Marktforschung in der Kraftverkehrsversicherung: statistische Probleme bei der Gewinnung und Darstellung von Marktforschungsergebnissen. Karlsruhe, 1968. pp. 142. bibliog.

WILSON (AUBREY) The assessment of industrial markets. London, Hutchinson, 1968. pp. xiii, 406. bibliog. 22½cm. (Hutchinson Marketing Library)

CORAM (TERRY) Cases in marketing and marketing research. London, Crosby Lockwood. 1969. pp. ix, 165. 21cm.

HARDER (THEODOR) Introduction to mathematical models in market and opinion research: with practical applications, computing procedures, and estimates of computing requirements; [translated from the German by Peter H. and Eva H. Friedlander). Dordrecht, [1969]. pp. 104. bibliog.

LONDON. University. London School of Economics and Political Science. Survey Research Centre. The semantic differential scaling system in market research. 3. Interviewer deviations from instructions; by William A. Belson and Susan B. Quinn. London, [1969]. pp. various.

QUINN (SUSAN B.) and BELSON (WILLIAM A.) The effects of reversing the order of presentation of verbal rating scales in survey interviews. London, [1969]. pp. 64. (London. University. London School of Economics and Political Science. Survey Research Centre)

RANGANADHA (SRIPATI) Industrial management and market research: a conceptual framework. Meerut, [1969]. pp. 205. bibliog.

RASMUSSEN (ARNE) ed. Markedsanalyse i Danmark. København, 1969. pp. 221. bibliogs. (Copenhagen. Handelshøjskolen. Skriftraekke F. 41)

Det SEGMENTEREDE salg; [by] Arne Rasmussen [and others]. København, 1970. pp. 81. (Copenhagen. Handelshøjskolen. Skriftraekke F. 42)

SEIBERT (JOSEPH) and WILLS (GORDON) eds. Marketing research: selected readings. Harmondsworth, 1970. pp. 391. bibliogs.

ECONOMIC DEVELOPMENT COMMITTEE FOR THE MECHANICAL ENGINEERING INDUSTRY. Market research in action: a guide for company management. London, H.M.S.O., 1971. pp. 36.

KRACMAR (JOHN Z.) Marketing research in the developing countries: a handbook. New York, 1971. pp. 322. bibliog.

- Bibliography

FANNING (DAVID CHRISTOPHER) compiler. Market research. London, Library Association, 1964. pp. 22. 21½cm. (Special Subject Lists. No. 44)

- Directories

ADLER (MAX KURT) Directory of British market research organisations and services. 2nd ed. London, Crosby Lockwood. 1967. pp. (iv), 84. 21cm.

- Information services

UHL (KENNETH P.) and SCHONER (BERTRAM) Marketing research: information systems and decision making. New York, Wiley, [1969]. pp. xv, 538. bibliogs. 22½cm. (Marketing Series)

MARKETS

CLAVAL (PAUL) Géographie générale des marchés. Paris, 1962. pp. 360. bibliog. (Besançon. Université. Cahiers de Géographie de Besançon. No. 10).

CALOIA (ANGELO) Forme di mercato e modelli di localizzazione. Milano, Giuffrè, 1967. pp. viii, 154. 23cm. (Saggi di Teoria e Politica Economica. 14)

ZIEGEL (ROLAND) Les marchés publics dans les pays en voie de développement. Paris, Colin, [1968]. pp. 325. 16½cm.

- Africa, West

HODDER (BRAMWELL WILLIAM) and UKWU (U.I.) Markets in West Africa: studies of markets and trade among the Yoruba and Ibo. [Ibadan], Ibadan U.P., 1969. pp. xii, 254. bibliog. 21½cm.

INTERNATIONAL AFRICAN SEMINAR. 10th Seminar. Fourah Bay College, 1969. The development of indigenous trade and markets in West Africa; studies...edited with an introduction by Claude Meillassoux. London, 1971. pp. 444. bibliog. In English or French with a summary in the other language.

- China

YOSHINORI (SHIBA) and YUKIO (YAMANE) Markets in China during the Sung, Ming, and Ch'ing periods; .... translated by Wake A. Fujioka and Mitsugu Matsuda. Honolulu, Hawaii University, East-West Centre, Institute of Advanced Projects, 1967. fo. (iii), 142. 27½cm. (Occasional Papers of Research Publications and Translations. Translation Series.No. 23) (Reprinted from Tōyō Gakuhō, 44, Nos.1-2 and Shiron, No.8)

- Europe

FRAIN (JOHN) Transportation and distribution for European markets. London, 1970. pp. 198.

- France

FRANCE. Statutes, etc. 1833-1962. Recueil des textes relatifs aux marchés passés au nom de l'État: lois, décrets, arrêtés et instructions; établi par le Ministère des Finances. Direction de la comptabilité publique; édition mise à jour au 1er mai 1962. (Journal Officiel de la République Française. [Brochures]. No. 1028). Paris, 1962. pp. xvi, 488. 21cm.

VILLIERS (MICHEL DE) Les marchés d'intérêt national. [Paris], [1967]. pp. 407. bibliog.

- India

SINHA (DHARNIDHAR PRASAD) Culture change in an intertribal market: the role of the Banari intertribal market among the hill peoples of Chotanagpur. London, Asia Publishing House, [1968]. pp. xvi, 117. bibliog. 21cm.

- Mexico

DURSTON (JOHN WAGNER) The social organization of peasant marketing in Michoacan, Mexico; [Ph.D.(London) thesis]. 1970. fo. 393. bibliog. Typescript: unpublished. This thesis is the property of London University and may not be removed from the Library.

- Nigeria

ADALEMO (ISAAC AYINDE) Distribution of market centers, market periodicities, and marketing in Northwestern Nigeria. Ann Arbor, 1970. pp. 38-57. bibliog. (Michigan University. Center for Research on Economic Development. Discussion Papers. No. 12)

- Russia

KERBLAY (BASILE) Les marchés paysans en U.R.S.S. Paris, 1968. pp. 517. bibliog. (Paris. Ecole Pratique des Hautes Etudes. Section des Sciences Economiques et Sociales. Etudes sur l'Histoire, l'Economie et la Sociologie des Pays Slaves. 10)

- Uganda

GOOD (CHARLES M.) Rural markets and trade in East Africa: a study of the functions and development of exchange institutions in Ankole, Uganda. Chicago, 1970. pp. 252. bibliog. (Chicago. University. Department of Geography. Research Papers. No. 128)

- United Kingdom - Scotland

HALDANE (ARCHIBALD RICHARD BURDON) Old Scottish fairs and markets. [Edinburgh], 1961. pp. 14. 21½cm. (Reprinted from the 'Transactions of the Royal Highland and Agricultural Society of Scotland,' 1961.)

MARKIEVICZ (CONSTANCE GEORGINA DE) Countess

O'FAOLÁIN (SEÁN) Constance Markievicz. [new ed.] London, Sphere, [1967]. pp. 220. 18cm.

MARKOV PROCESSES

FERGUSON (THOMAS S.) An infinitely divisible Markov process. Los Angeles, University of California, Western Management Science Institute, 1962. fo. 13. bibliog. 28cm. (Working Papers. No. 21)

CHOVER (JOSHUA) ed. Markov processes and potential theory: proceedings of a symposium conducted by the Mathematics Research Center and the United States Army at the University of Wisconsin, Madison, May 1-3, 1967. New York, Wiley, [1967]. pp. x, 235 23cm. (Wisconsin University. Mathematics Research Center [of the] United States Army. Publications. 19)

BLUMENTHAL (R.M.) and GETOOR (R.K.) Markov processes and potential theory. New York, Academic P., 1968. pp. x, 313. bibliog. 23cm. (Pure and Applied Mathematics. 29)

HOEM (JAN M.) Application of time-continuous Markov chains to life insurance. Oslo, University of Oslo, Institute of Economics, 1968. fo. 59. bibliog. 29½cm. (Memoranda)

COLMAN (DAVID) and LEECH (DENNIS) Structural change in the dairy industry in England and Wales: an application of Markov chain analysis. Manchester, 1969. pp. 55. (Manchester. University. Department of Agricultural Economics. Bulletins. No. 125)

DYNKIN (E. B.) and IUSHKEVICH (ALEKSANDR A.) Markov processes: theorems and problems...; translated from Russian by James S. Wood. New York, 1969. pp. 237. bibliog.

CHUNG (KAI LAI) Lectures on boundary theory for Markov chains. Princeton, N.J., 1970. pp. 94. bibliog.

MARKS OF ORIGIN

EIRE. Merchandise Marks Commission. Reports. No. 4. Report on ceramic ware. Dublin, [1969]. pp. 8.

EIRE. Merchandise Marks Commission. Reports. No. 5. Report on aluminium holloware and containers and electric kettles. Dublin, [1969]. pp. 7.

MARKS OF ORIGIN (Cont'd.)

EIRE. Merchandise Marks Commission. Reports. No. 6. Report on biscuits. Dublin, [1969]. pp. 6.

EIRE. Merchandise Marks Commission. Reports. No. 7. Report on vitreous enamelled ware. Dublin, [1969]. pp. 8.

EIRE. Merchandise Marks Commission. Reports. No. 8. Report on plumbers' brassfoundry and compression couplings. Dublin, [1969]. pp. 9.

EIRE. Merchandise Marks Commission. Reports. No. 9. Report on stockings, socks and the like. Dublin, [1969]. pp. 6.

EIRE. Merchandise Marks Commission. Reports. No. 10. Report on men's and boy's outer garments. Dublin, [1970]. pp. 8.

EIRE. Merchandise Marks Commission. Reports. No. 11. Report on proposal to amend the Merchandise Marks (Restriction on Importation of Ceramic Ware) Order, 1969. Dublin, [1970]. pp. 3.

EIRE. Merchandise Marks Commission. Reports. No. 12. Report on knitted and crocheted clothing. Dublin, [1970]. pp. 8.

MARKUP

INSTITUT FÜR MITTELSTANDSFORSCHUNG. Abhandlungen zur Mittelstandsforschung. Einzelhandelspreis- und Handelsspannenvergleich zwischen der Ländern Belgien, Deutschland, Frankreich, Italien, den Niederlanden und der Schweiz. Köln, Westdeutscher Verlag, 1965. pp. xi, 138. 24cm.

MARMIER (XAVIER)

MÉNARD (JEAN) Xavier Marmier et le Canada; avec des documents inédits; relations franco-canadiennes au xixe siècle. Québec, Les Presses de l'Université Laval, 1967. pp. xi, 211. bibliog. 22½cm. (Vie des Lettres Canadiennes. 4)

MARNE (DEPARTMENT)

- Population

FRANCE. Institut National de la Statistique et des Études Économiques. Direction Régionale de Reims and CENTRE D'ÉTUDE ET DE LIAISON POUR L'AMÉNAGEMENT DE LA MARNE. 1960. Évolution démographique et socio-démographique du département de la Marne. Reims, [1960?]. pp. 71. 27cm.

MAROŃ (JÓZEF)

MAROŃ (JÓZEF) Życie było walką: ze wspomnień działacza KPP; opracował Jan Kita. Katowice, Śląsk, 1966. pp. 78. 20½cm. (Śląski Instytut Naukowy. Biblioteczka Wiedzy o Śląsku. Seria Historyczna. nr.7) With Russian and English summaries.

MARONGIU (ANTONIO)

INTERNATIONAL COMMISSION FOR THE HISTORY OF REPRESENTATIVE AND PARLIAMENTARY INSTITUTIONS. Studies. 34. Mélanges Antonio Marongiu: studies presented to the...Commission, etc. Bruxelles, Librairie Encyclopédique, 1968. pp. 322. 25cm. In English, French and Italian.

MARONITES

HARIK (ILIYA F.) Politics and change in a traditional society: Lebanon, 1711-1845. Princeton, Princeton U.P., 1968. pp. xi, 324. bibliog. 21½cm.
R : W 99,667 : 332896

MAROONS

GROOT (SILVIA W. DE) Van isolatie naar integratie: de Surinaamse Marrons en hun afstammelingen; officiele documenten betreffende de Djoeka's 1845-1863. 's-Gravenhage, Nijhoff, 1963. pp. vii, 100. bibliog. 24cm. (Instituut voor Taal-, Land- en Volkenkunde. Verhandelingen. Deel 41) With English summary.

MARQUESAN LANGUAGE

LAVONDÈS (H.) Observations on methods used in assembling oral traditions in the Marquesas. in Highland (Genevieve A.) and others, eds. Polynesian culture history. Honolulu, [1967].

MARRAKECH

- History

DEVERDUN (GASTON) Marrakech, des origines à 1912. Rabat, Éditions Techniques Nord-Africaines, 1959-66. 2 vols. bibliog. 25cm.

MARRIAGE

GREAVES (JAMES PIERREPONT) Memoir of James Pierrepont Greaves, advocate for infant education, and late friend and associate of Pestalozzi. Ham Common, Surrey, At the Concordium, 1843. pp. 20, 16. Lacking final pages of second sequence after 16.

DU CANN (CHARLES GARFIELD LOTT) Marriage: sacerdotal or secular?: an enquiry into whether the marriage ceremony is the business of the church or the state. [London, c.1945]. pp. 35.

UNIVERSITY HUMANIST FEDERATION. Annual Conference, 5th, 1964. Marriage and the place of women in society; proceedings. London, 1964. pp. 16. (University Humanist Federation. Bulletins. No. 14)

BLANCK (RUBIN) and BLANCK (GERTRUDE) Marriage and personal development. New York, Columbia U.P., 1968. pp. xvi, 191. bibliog. 21½cm.

BOHANNAN (PAUL) and MIDDLETON (JOHN) eds. Marriage, family and residence. Garden City, Natural History P., 1968. pp. xi, 411. bibliog. 20½cm. (American Museum of Natural History. American Museum Sourcebooks in Anthropology)

DOMINIAN (JACK) Marital breakdown. Harmondsworth, Penguin Books, 1968. pp. 172. bibliog. 18cm. (Pelican Books. A999)

KAUPP (PETER) Das Heiratsinserat im sozialen Wandel: ein Beitrag zur Soziologie der Partnerwahl. Stuttgart, 1968. pp. 119. bibliog.

KENSIT (CONNAIRE) and BUCHANAN (RUTH) Marriage and the family: a discussion document...proposed as policy for the British Humanist Association. London, [1968]. pp. 16. bibliog.

ROSENBAUM (SALO) and ALGER (IAN) eds. The marriage relationship: psychoanalytic perspectives. New York, [1968]. pp. 366.

BECKEL (ALBRECHT) ed. Ehe im Umbruch. Münster, 1969. pp. 280.

BLOOD (ROBERT OSCAR) Marriage. 2nd ed. New York, [1969] pp. 535. bibliog.

LANTZ (HERMAN R.) and SNYDER (ELOISE C.) Marriage: an examination of the man-woman relationship. 2nd ed. New York, [1969]. pp. 512. bibliogs.

NEUBECK (GERHARD) ed. Extramarital relations. Englewood Cliffs, [1969]. pp. 205. bibliogs.

HALKETT (JOHN G.) Milton and the idea of matrimony: a study of the divorce tracts and Paradise lost. New Haven, 1970. pp. 162. bibliog.

MAIR (LUCY PHILIP) Marriage. Harmondsworth, 1971. pp. 221. bibliog.

RETHINKING kinship and marriage: ([derived mainly] from material presented at a conference on kinship and marriage, sponsored by the Association of Social Anthropologists of the Commonwealth, held at the University of Bristol...1970); edited by Rodney Needham. London, 1971. pp. cxvii, 276. bibliogs.

- Annulment - France

LA PRADELLE (GÉRAUD DE) Les conflits de lois en matière de nullités: du droit interne français au droit international privé. Paris, Dalloz, 1967. pp. viii, 270. bibliog. 24cm. (Bibliothèque de Droit International Privé. vol. 8)

- Annulment - United Kingdom

U.K. Law Commission. Published Working Papers. No. 20. First programme -- Item x. Family law: nullity of marriage. London, 1968. pp. 52. 33cm.

U.K. Law Commission. Published Working Papers. No. 38. (Second programme, item XIX.) Family law: jurisdiction in suits for nullity of marriage. London, 1971. pp. 16.

- Bibliography

ALDOUS (JOAN) and HILL (REUBEN LORENZO) International bibliography of research in marriage and the family, 1900-1964. [Minneapolis], U. of Minnesota P., [1967]. pp. (iii), 508. 31cm.

- Catholic church

The BOND of marriage : an ecumenical and interdisciplinary study; [papers delivered at an interdenominational symposium] sponsored by the Canon Law Society of America [and held at the University of Notre Dame, October 15-18, 1967]; edited with notes and an introduction by William W. Bassett. Notre Dame, 1968. pp. 265.

STEININGER (VIKTOR) Divorce: arguments for a change in the church's discipline; ...translated by Edward Quinn. London, 1969. pp. 174.

WEST (MORRIS LANGLO) and FRANCIS (ROBERT) Scandal in the assembly: a bill of complaints and a proposal for reform on the matrimonial laws and tribunals of the Roman Catholic Church. London, 1970. pp. 188.

- Church of England

CANTERBURY (PROVINCE). Convocation, Commission on the Christian Doctrine of Marriage. Marriage, divorce and the Church: the report of a Commission appointed by the Archbishop of Canterbury to prepare a statement on the Christian doctrine of marriage. London, 1971. pp. 166.

- Jews

ISRAEL. Central Bureau of Statistics. Special Series. No. 194. Marriages among Jews in Israel, 1947-1962. Jerusalem, 1965. pp. xvi, 126, (15). 27cm. In English and Hebrew.

BERMAN (LOUIS A.) Jews and intermarriage: a study in personality and culture. New York, Yoseloff, [1968]. pp. 707. bibliog. 20cm.

- Abkhazia

KUCHBERIIA (L.E.) K voprosu o razvitii brachnykh obychaev i svadebnoi obriadnosti abkhazov. in Sovremennoe abkhazskoe selo. Tbilisi, 1967.

- Africa, West

LARSON (MARA KATHRYN) Changing marriage patterns in West Africa with special reference to Nigeria; [M. Phil. (London) thesis]. [1969]. fo. iv, 274. bibliog. 25½cm. Typescript: unpublished. This thesis is the property of London University and may not be removed from the Library.

- Belgium

WATTELAR (CHRISTINE) et WUNSCH (GUILLAUME) Étude démographique de la nuptialité en Belgique. Louvain, Université, Institut de Recherches Économiques, Sociales et Politiques, Departement Démographie, 1967. pp. 132. bibliog. 24cm.

- Brazil

RIVIERE (PETER) Marriage among the Trio: a principle of social organisation. Oxford, 1969. pp. 353.

- Dutch Guiana

RIVIERE (PETER) Marriage among the Trio: a principle of social organisation. Oxford, 1969. pp. 353.

- France

BELS (PIERRE) Le mariage des protestants français, jusqu'en 1685: fondements doctrinaux et pratique juridique. Paris, Pichon et Durand-Auzias, 1968. pp. 264. bibliog. 25cm. (Bibliothèque d'Histoire du Droit et Droit Romain. tome 12)

MICHEL (JACQUES) Les nouveaux droits de la femme. [Paris, 1970]. pp. 154.

MARRIAGE (Cont'd.)

- Greece, Ancient

PHARMAS (PHEBUS) Sociologie du mariage chez les Hellènes. Alexandrie, Apollon, [1930?]. pp. 225.

- Hong Kong

HONG KONG. Colonial Secretariat. 1967. White paper on Chinese marriages in Hong Kong. Hong Kong, 1967. pp. 33.

HONG KONG. Department of the Attorney General. 1967. The McDouall-Heenan report, 1965. Hong Kong, 1967. pp. 96.

- India

BANERJEE (BHAVANI) Marriage and kinship of the Gangadikara Vokkaligas of Mysore. Poona, Deccan College, 1966. pp. xxiv, 212. bibliog. 24½cm. (Deccan College Dissertation Series. 27)

MOKASHI (P.R.) Some social aspects of marriages in Poona district, 1955-56. Poona, 1968. pp. 184. bibliog. (Deccan College. Deccan College Monogram Series. 33)

KHATRI (ABBDULLAH AHMED) Marriage and family relationships in Gujarati fiction; [with subsidiary contributions]; [Ph.D.(London) thesis]. 1970. 2 vols. bibliog. Typescript: unpublished. This thesis is the property of London University and may not be removed from the Library.

- Israel

ISRAEL. Central Bureau of Statistics. Special Series. No. 194. Marriages among Jews in Israel, 1947-1962. Jerusalem, 1965. pp. xvi, 126, (15). 27cm. In English and Hebrew.

- Italy

UNIONE GIURISTI CATTOLICI ITALIANI. Convegno Nazionale di Studio, 20°, 1969. Indissolubilità del matrimonio e referendum popolare: dichiarazione e relazioni, etc. Roma, 1969. pp. 75. (Quaderni di Iustitia. 21)

- Kazakstan

KISLIAKOV (NIKOLAI ANDREEVICH) Очерки по истории семьи и брака у народов Средней Азии и Казахстана. Ленинград, 1969. pp. 238.

- New Guinea

GLASSE (ROBERT M.) and MEGGITT (MERVYN JOHN) eds. Pigs, pearlshells, and women: marriage in the New Guinea highlands; a symposium. Englewood Cliffs, [1969]. pp. 246. bibliog.

- Pakistan

HUSAIN (IMTIAZUDDIN) and AFZAL (MOHAMMAD) Muslim first marriages in Karachi: a paper submitted to the third All-Pakistan sociological conference, held at Ayubia from July 7-9, 1966. Karachi, 1966. pp. 10.

- Philippine Islands

QUISUMBING (LOURDES R.) Marriage customs in rural Cebu. Cebu City, 1965. pp. 77. bibliog. (University of San Carlos. San Carlos Publications. Series A. No. 3)

- Poland

ŁOBODZIŃSKA (BARBARA) Małżeństwo w mieście. Warszawa, 1970. pp. 319.

- Puerto Rico

DOHEN (DOROTHY MARIE) Two studies of Puerto Rico: religion data; the background of consensual union. Cuernavaca, [1967]. pp. 155. bibliog. (Centro Intercultural de Documentacion. Sondeos. No. 3.)

- Russia

PROBLEMY byta, braka i sem'i. Vil'nius, 1970. pp. 246. With Lithuanian and English summaries.

- South Africa

SOUTH AFRICA. Bureau of Statistics. Report on marriages: South Africa. [in English and Afrikaans] 1958/1964 [1st issue]; a., 1965- Pretoria.

- South West Africa

SOUTH AFRICA. Bureau of Statistics. Reports. 07-02-01. Report on marriages: South Africa and South West Africa, 1958-1964. Pretoria, 1967. pp. v, 133. 30cm. In Afrikaans and English.

- Soviet Central Asia

KISLIAKOV (NIKOLAI ANDREEVICH) Очерки по истории семьи и брака у народов Средней Азии и Казахстана. Ленинград, 1969. pp. 238.

- United Kingdom

BEYFUS (DRUSILLA) The English marriage: what it is like to be married today. London, Weidenfeld and Nicolson, [1968]. pp. xiii, 162. 21½cm.

MACFARLANE (ALAN DONALD JAMES) The regulation of marital and sexual relationships in seventeenth century England, with special reference to the county of Essex; [M.Phil.(London) thesis]. 1968. fo. 191. bibliog. 25½cm. Typescript: unpublished. This thesis is the property of London University and may not be removed from the Library.

THOMAS (DAVID NICHOLAS) Marriage patterns in the British peerage in the eighteenth and nineteenth centuries; [M.Phil.(London) thesis]. 1969. fo. 285. bibliog. Typescript: unpublished. This thesis is the property of London University and may not be removed from the Library.

MATTINSON (JANET) Marriage and mental handicap. London, 1970. pp. 231.

- United States

PRATT (PARLEY PETER) Marriage and morals in Utah: an address;... read in joint session of the Legislature, in the Representative Hall, Fillmore City, Dec. 31, 1855, by Mr. Thomas Bullock. Liverpool, 1856. pp. 8.

CARTER (HUGH SEIVER) and GLICK (PAUL CHARLES) Marriage and divorce: a social and economic study. Cambridge, Mass., 1970. pp. 451. (American Public Health Association. Vital and Health Statistics Monographs)

VEROFF (JOSEPH) and FELD (SHEILA) Marriage and work in America: a study of motives and roles. New York, [1970]. pp. 404. bibliog.

MARRIAGE (HINDU LAW)

ROCHER (L.) The theory of matrimonial causes according to the Dharmaśāstra. in Anderson (James Norman Dalrymple) ed. Family law in Asia and Africa. London, 1968.

MARRIAGE (JEWISH LAW)

FELDMAN (DAVID M.) Birth control in Jewish law: marital relations, contraception, and abortion as set forth in the classic texts of Jewish law, etc. New York, 1968. pp. xiii, 322. bibliog. 23cm.

MARRIAGE, MIXED

WILLIAMS (JOHN GORDON) Mixed marriages between Anglicans and Roman Catholics. London, S.P.C.K. 1967. pp. 15. 18½cm.

BERMAN (LOUIS A.) Jews and intermarriage: a study in personality and culture. New York, Yoseloff, [1968]. pp. 707. bibliog. 20cm.

- Italy

MARCHESELLI (GIOVANNI) I matrimoni misti in Italia. Brescia, [1969]. pp. 120. bibliog.

MARRIAGE CUSTOMS AND RITES

- Buryat Republic

BALDAEV (SERGEI PETROVICH) Buriatskie svadebnye obriady. Ulan-Ude, 1959. pp. 180. bibliog.

- China

CHIV (VERMIER YANTAK) Marriage laws and customs of China. Hong Kong, [1966]. pp. 238.

- Dutch Guiana

SPECKMANN (J. D.) Marriage and kinship among the Indians in Surinam. Assen, Van Gorcum, 1965. pp. (viii), 302. bibliog. 23½cm. (Non-European Societies. 4)

- Ukraine

VESILLIA. Kyïv, 1970. 2 vols.

MARRIAGE GUIDANCE

BLANCK (RUBIN) and BLANCK (GERTRUDE) Marriage and personal development. New York, Columbia U.P., 1968. pp. xvi, 191. bibliog. 21½cm.

WALLIS (JACK HAROLD) Marriage guidance: a new introduction. London, Routledge & Kegan Paul, 1968. pp. xi, 256. 21½cm.

HERBERT (WILLIAM LESLIE) and JARVIS (F.V.) Marriage counselling in the community. Oxford, 1970 pp. 79. bibliogs.

MONGER (MARK) Husband, wife and caseworker. London, 1971. pp. 178. bibliogs.

MARRIAGE LAW

UNITED NATIONS. Commission on the Status of Women. [Documents]. E/CN. 6/356 and Addenda. Consent to marriage, age of marriage and registration of marriages. [New York], 1939-60. 3 pts.

UNITED NATIONS. Commission on the Status of Women. [Documents]. E/CN. 6/317. Consent to marriage and the age of marriage. [New York], 1958. pp. 19,8.

UNITED NATIONS. Commission on the Status of Women. [Documents]. E/CN. 6/376. Observations of governments on the draft convention and draft recommendation on the minimum age of marriage, consent to marriage and registration of marriages. [New York], 1961. pp. 26.

SCHEFTELOWITZ (ERWIN ELCHANAN) Das religiöse Eherecht im Staat. Köln, 1970. pp. 189.

- Africa

COTRAN (E.) The changing nature of African marriage. in Anderson (James Norman Dalrymple) ed. Family law in Asia and Africa. London, 1968.

- Africa, Subsaharan

PHILLIPS (ARTHUR) and MORRIS (HENRY FRANCIS) Marriage laws in Africa. London, 1971. pp. 229. bibliog.

- China

CHIV (VERMIER YANTAK) Marriage laws and customs of China. Hong Kong, [1966]. pp. 238.

McALEAVY (H.) Some aspects of marriage and divorce in communist China. in Anderson (James Norman Dalrymple) ed. Family law in Asia and Africa. London, 1968.

- Colombia

BUENO DELGADO (RODRIGO) La estafa sexologica y el matrimonio por interes: tesis para optar al titulo de Abogado. Bogotá, 1968. pp. 81. bibliog.

Europe

COUDERT (FREDERIC RENÉ) Marriage and divorce laws in Europe: a study in comparative legislation. New York, 1893. pp. 108.

- France

SAYN (JEAN YVES) and CHEVALLIER (JEAN YVES) Les règles générales des régimes matrimoniaux, loi du 13 juillet 1965. Paris, P.U.F., 1968. pp. viii, 121. 24cm. (Paris. Université. Faculté de Droit et des Sciences Économiques. Travaux et Recherches. Série "Droit Privé". No. 4)

- India

DESAI (KUMUD) Indian law of marriage and divorce. Bombay, Popular Prakashan, 1964. pp. xii, 376.

- Italy

RICCIO (STEFANO) Il matrimonio nella costituzione italiana. Padova, 1968. pp. 231.

SPADA (ILO) Il matrimonio concordatario nell'attuale esperienza giuridica. Bologna, [1969]. pp. 297.

LOMBARDI (GABRIO) Divorzio, referendum, concordato. Bologna, [1970]. pp. 182.

MARRIAGE LAW (Cont'd.)

- Kenya

COTRAN (EUGENE) The law of marriage and divorce. London, Sweet & Maxwell, 1968. pp. xxxiv, 213. bibliog. 24½cm. (London. University. School of Oriental and African Studies. Restatement of African Law. Kenya. vol. 1.)

KENYA. Commission on the Law of Marriage and Divorce. 1968. Report. Nairobi, 1968. pp. 209. 24½cm.

- Malawi

IBIK (J.O.) The law of marriage and divorce. London, 1970. pp. 214. bibliog. (London. University. School of Oriental and African Studies. Restatement of African Law. Malawi. vol. 1)

- Roumania

POPESCU (TUDOR R.) and PASCU (MIHAI) Căsătoria, familia si dreptul. București, Editura Ştiinţifică, 1963. pp. 255. 19½cm.

- Russia

FUNDAMENTALS of legislation of the USSR and the Union Republics on marriage and the family. Moscow, [1968?]. pp. 29.

ORLOVA (NINA VLADIMIROVNA) Pravovoe regulirovanie braka v SSSR. Moskva, 1971. pp. 127.

- South Africa

HAHLO (H. R.) The matrimonial regimes of South Africa. in Anderson (James Norman Dalrymple) ed. Family law in Asia and Africa. London, 1968.

- Sweden

FORSSIUS (GUSTAV) La legislation suedoise sur le mariage. 2nd ed. Paris, 1970. pp. 143. bibliog.

- Uganda

MORRIS (H. F.) Marriage law in Uganda: sixty years of attempted reform. in Anderson (James Norman Dalrymple) ed. Family law in Asia and Africa. London, 1968.

- United Kingdom

BROUGHTON (GLADYS MARY) A consideration of the problems of marriage and divorce and the Royal Commission. London, Moore & Tomlinson, 1951. pp. 28. 20cm.

JACKSON (JOSEPH) The formation and annulment of marriage. 2nd ed. London, 1969. pp. 468. bibliog.

U.K. Law Commission. Published Working Papers. No. 35. Solemnisation of marriage in England and Wales...: provisional proposals of the Joint Working Party of the Law Commission and the Registrar General. (Second programme, item XIX. Family law). London, 1971. pp. 120.

MARRIAGE WITH DECEASED WIFE'S SISTER

MARRIAGE with a deceased wife's sister. Hawick, 1869. pp. 9.

MARRIED WOMEN

- Australia

DAWSON (MADGE) Graduate and married: a report on a survey of one thousand and seventy married women graduates of the University of Sydney; ...edited and prepared for press by John Rorke. Sydney, University, 1965. pp. xvi, 233. bibliog. 23cm.

- Denmark

SOCIETY OF DANISH WOMEN and NATIONAL COUNCIL OF DANISH WOMEN. The legal status of married women in Denmark. [Copenhagen, 196-?]. pp. 17.

- France

AFTALION (ALBERT) Les lois relatives à l'epargne de la femme mariée: leur importance pratique pour la protection de l'épouse dans les classes laborieuses. Paris, 1898. pp. 211.

PAILLUSSEAU (JEAN) and others. Quelques aspects de la nouvelle situation de la femme mariée. Paris, P.U.F., 1968. pp. viii, 118. 24cm. (Paris. Université. Faculté de Droit et des Sciences Économiques. Travaux et Recherches. Série "Droit Privé." No. 5)

- Iran

CHASTELAND (JEAN CLAUDE) and others. Etude sur la fécondité et quelques caracteristiques démographiques des femmes mariées dans quatre zones rurales d'Iran. Teheran, 1968. pp. 316.

- Sweden

BERGLIND (HANS) Valet mellan hem och yrke: en sociologisk analys av en valsituation med tillämpning på gifta sjuksköterskor. Stockholm, Kommunalförvaltningen, 1968. pp. 357. bibliog. 24½cm. (Monografier. 30)

LAVAL (GUSTAF DE) Familjecykeln och den gifta kvinnans förvärvsarbete: en explorativ-deskriptiv studie utförd vid sociologiska institutionen, Göteborgs universitet, (med ett bidrag av Sören Olsson). Lund, 1970. pp. 341. bibliog. (Sweden. Statistiska Centralbyrån. Monografiserie i Anslutning till Folk- och Bostadsräkningen i Sverige 1960. 6) With English summaries.

- United Kingdom

WILLIAMS (GERTRUDE) Lady. The marriage rate and women's employment. London, the College, 1966. pp. 17. 24½cm. (London. University. Bedford College. Fawcett Lectures. 1966-67)

MARSEILLES

- Economic conditions

FRANCE. French Embassy, London. Service de Presse et d'Information. 1969. The Marseilles - Fos metropolitan area. London, [1969]. pp. 27. 25½cm.

- History

GREENBERG (LOUIS M.) Sisters of liberty: Marseille, Lyon, Paris and the reaction to a centralized state, 1868-1871. Cambridge, Mass., 1971. pp. 391. bibliog. (Harvard University. Harvard Historical Monographs. 62)

- Religion

GOODRIDGE (RICHARD MARTIN) Religion and the city with reference to Bristol and Marseilles, 1830-1880: a study in the comparative sociology of religion; [M.Phil. (London) thesis]. 1969. fo. 447. bibliog. Typescript: unpublished. This thesis is the property of London University and may not be removed from the Library.

- Sanitary affairs

CARRIÈRE (CHARLES) and others. Marseille, ville morte: la peste de 1720. Marseille, Garçon, [1968]. pp. 353. bibliog. 20½cm.

MARSHALL (ALFRED)

KERR (CLARK) Marshall, Marx and modern times: the multi-dimensional society. Cambridge, 1969. pp. 138. (Cambridge. University. Marshall Lectures. 1967-68.)

MARSHALL (JOHN)

THAYER (JAMES BRADLEY) John Marshall; [reprinted from the original edition of 1901 together with a speech of that year by Oliver Wendell Holmes and an essay by Felix Frankfurter first published in 1955]. Chicago, U. of Chicago P., 1967. pp. xiv, 174. 20½cm. (The Court and the Constitution)

FAULKNER (ROBERT KENNETH) The jurisprudence of John Marshall. Princeton, Princeton U.P., 1968. pp. xxi, 307. 21½cm.

MARSHALL (STEPHEN)

MARSHALL (STEPHEN) A copy of a letter...for the necessary vindication of himself and his Ministry, against that altogether groundlesse...aspersion cast upon him by certaine malignants in the city, and lately printed at Oxford, etc. London, Rothwell, 1643. pp. 30. 18½cm. Wing M 750.

MARSON (CHARLES LATIMER)

RECKITT (M. B.) Charles Marson, 1859-1914 and the real disorders of the church. in Reckitt (Maurice Benington) ed. For Christ and the people. London, 1968.

MARTERER (FERDINAND VON) Freiherr

LORENZ (R.) Aus dem Kriegstagebuch des Generaladjutanten Freiherrn von Marterer. in Institut für Österreichische Geschichtsforschung and Vienna. Katholische Akademie. Österreich und Europa. Graz, 1965.

MARTÍ (JOSÉ)

MARTÍ (JOSÉ) Obras completas. Havana, 1963-65. 27 vols. vol. 26 contains indices; vol. 27 a guide to the collected works and a chronological biography of the author.

ROIG DE LEUCHSENRING (EMILIO) Marti anti-imperialist. Havana, 1967. pp. 79.

SHISHKINA (VALENTINA IVANOVNA) Социально-политические взгляды Хосе Марти. Москва, 1969. pp. 114.

MARTIAL LAW

- Cape Colony

COLERIDGE (JOHN DUKE) Baron Coleridge. The illegality of martial law in Cape Colony; a speech delivered...in the House of Lords on March 17th, 1902. Manchester, [1902]. pp. 8. (National Reform Union. Pamphlets) (Reprinted from the Parliamentary Debates)

- Ceylon

MINATTUR (JOSEPH) Martial law in India, Pakistan and Ceylon. The Hague, Nijhoff, 1962. pp. 99. bibliog. 22cm.

- India

MINATTUR (JOSEPH) Martial law in India, Pakistan and Ceylon. The Hague, Nijhoff, 1962. pp. 99. bibliog. 22cm.

- Nicaragua

NICARAGUA. Constitution. 1950. Constitution politica, ley de amparo y ley marcial de Nicaragua. Managua, Talleres Nacional, 1951. pp. iv, 220. 13½cm.

- Pakistan

MINATTUR (JOSEPH) Martial law in India, Pakistan and Ceylon. The Hague, Nijhoff, 1962. pp. 99. bibliog. 22cm.

- United Kingdom

WHITTINGTON (JOHN) London apprentice. No martiall law, but advice for the grand inquests of London and Middlesex, and may serve generally for the whole kingdome; written by a London apprentice, on the behalfe of his fellow apprentices, 1648. [London], 1648. pp. 6. 18½cm. Wing W 2045A.

MARTIN (BASIL KINGSLEY)

JONES (MERVYN) ed. Kingsley Martin: portrait and self-portrait. London, [1969]. pp. 166.

MARTIN (JOSE DE SAN)
See SAN MARTIN (JOSE DE)

MARTÍNEZ Y MARTÍNEZ (EMILIO)

PETIT (ALFREDO M.) Centenario del nacimiento del Dr. Emilio Martínez y Martínez, 1864-1948. (Cuadernos de Historia de la Salud Pública. 30) La Habana, 1965. pp. 158.

MARTINIQUE

FRANCE. Direction de la Documentation. La Documentation Française. Notes et Études Documentaires. No. 2744. La Martinique: département français d'outre-mer. Paris, 1961. pp. 76. 31cm.

- Economic conditions

FRANCE. Institut National de la Statistique et des Études Économiques. 1968. Étude sur les comptes économiques de la Martinique, 1965-1966-1967. Paris, 1968. fo. (18).

FRANCE. Institut National de la Statistique et des Etudes Economiques. 1970. Comptes économiques de la Martinique, 1968. [Paris, 1970?] pp. 27.

MARTINIQUE (Cont'd.)

- History - Sources

FRANCE. Archives Nationales. 1967- . Inventaires de la série "Colonies". C8A. Martinique (correspondance à l'arrivée). Paris, 1967 in progress. (Inventaires et Documents).

- Population - Statistics

FRANCE. Institut National de la Statistique et des Études Économiques. 1957. Statistique du mouvement de la population dans les départements d'outre-mer: Martinique, Guadeloupe, Réunion, années 1951 à 1956. Paris, 1957. pp. 162. 26½cm.

FRANCE. Institut National de la Statistique et des Études Économiques. 1966. Statistique du mouvement de la population dans les départements d'outre-mer: Martinique, Guadeloupe, Guyane, Réunion, années 1957 à 1964. Paris, 1966. pp. 228. 26½cm.

- Race question

HAYOT (EMILE) Les gens de couleur libres au Fort-Royal, 1679-1823. Paris, 1971. pp. 165. (Société Française d'Histoire d'Outre-Mer. Bibliothèque d'Histoire d'Outre-Mer)

- Social history

HAYOT (EMILE) Les gens de couleur libres au Fort-Royal, 1679-1823. Paris, 1971. pp. 165. (Société Française d'Histoire d'Outre-Mer. Bibliothèque d'Histoire d'Outre-Mer)

- Statistics

ANNUAIRE STATISTIQUE DE LA MARTINIQUE; [published by] Institut National de la Statistique et des Etudes Economiques [France]. Paris, irreg., 1952/1956 to date.

- Statistics, Vital

LERIDON (HENRI) and others. Féoondité et famille en Martinique: faits, attitudes et opinions. Paris, 1970. pp. 186. bibliog. (France. Institut National d'Etudes Démographiques. Travaux et Documents. Cahiers. No. 56.)

MARTINS (EDUARDO AUGUSTO DE AZAMBUJA)
See AZAMBUJA MARTINS (EDUARDO AUGUSTO DE)

MARTOV (IULII OSIPOVICH)

GETSLER (I. M.) compiler. Stat'i, posviashchennye Iu.O. Martovu, sobrannye iz raznykh istochnikov. New York, 1961. pp. 59. (Inter-University Project on the History of the Menshevik Movement)

MARTULKOV (ALEKSO)

MARTULKOV (ALEKSO) Моето учество во револуционерните борби на Македонија. Скопје, 1954. pp. 388. (Институт за Национална Историја. Материјали за Македонската Национал-Револуционерна Историја. кн.6)

MARTYNOV (A.) pseud.

MARTYNOV (A.) pseud. [i.e. Aleksandr Samoilovich PIKKER] Vom Menschewismus zum Kommunismus; mit einem Vorwort von Karl Radek. Hamburg, 1923. pp. 59.

MARX (KARL)

AMBROSINI (GASPARE) Marx, Mazzini e l'internazionale socialista: (conferenza pronunziata al Circolo di Cultura di Palermo, etc.). Campobasso, Colitti, 1917. pp. 35. 24cm. (Collana Colitti di Conferenze e Discorsi. Num. 25)

COOK (A.E.) The socialism of Karl Marx: with a biographical sketch of the life of Karl Marx, the socialist. [Glasgow, 1918]. pp. 29.

MUELLER (HERMANN) Sekretär des Zentral-Arbeitersekretariats Berlin. Karl Marx und die Gewerkschaften. Berlin, 1918. pp. 106.

ALHAIZA (JEAN ADOLPHE) Vérité sociologique gouvernementale et religieuse: succint résumé du sociétarisme de Fourier comparé au socialisme de Marx et de la doctrine dualiste. Paris, Daragon, 1919. pp. 79. 20cm.

COLMAN (E.) Short communication on the unpublished writings of Karl Marx dealing with mathematics, the natural sciences, technology, and the history of these subjects. London, [1931]. pp. 3.

LENIN (VLADIMIR IL'ICH) The teachings of Karl Marx. London, 1931 repr. 1937. pp. 47.

POSTGATE (RAYMOND WILLIAM) Karl Marx. London, 1933. pp. 91. bibliog.

ZINT (FRANK) Karl Marx und die grossen europäischen Mächte: Beitrag zu einer politischen Biographie. Frankfurt a.M., [imprint, 1937]. pp. 155. bibliog. 21cm.

BRACHT (WILHELM) Trier und Karl Marx. [Trier], 1946. pp. 21.

GLASSER (M.) Über die Arbeitsmethoden der Klassiker des Marxismus-Leninismus. Berlin, [1948]. pp. 102.

KISCH (EGON ERWIN) Karl Marx in Karlsbad. Berlin, Aufbau-Verlag, 1953. pp. 46. 20½cm.

LEFEBVRE (HENRI) Pour connaître la pensée de Marx. 2nd ed. [Paris, 1955]. pp. 284. bibliog.

BROWDER (EARL RUSSELL) Karl Marx and America. Yonkers, N.Y., [1957]. fo. 38.

WUNSCH (KARL) Zum Wortfeld "Arbeiter" bei Marx und Engels. Halle, Niemeyer, 1962. pp. 458-468. bibliog. 24cm. (from Beiträge zur Geschichte der Deutschen Sprache und Literatur. Band 84)

VODOLAZSKII (ANATOLII FEODOSIEVICH) Iz istorii bor'by Marksa i Engel'sa za kollektivnost' partiinogo rukovodstva. Tashkent, 1963. pp. 87.

AGEEV (D.P.) К. Маркс и Ф. Энгельс о проблеме войны и мира. in Uchenye Zapiski Kafedr Obshchestvennykh Nauk Vuzov g. Leningrada. Filosofiia. vyp.5. Проблемы научного коммунизма. Ленинград, 1964.

HAUFSCHILD (ULRICH) Partei und Klasse bei Marx und Engels. [Reinheim/Odw., imprint], 1965. pp. 234. bibliog.

SHEKHOVTSOV (ALEKSEI VLADIMIROVICH) Теория товарного фетишизма Карла Маркса, etc. Воронеж, 1965. pp. 199. bibliog.

ANDRÉAS (BERT) A proposito di una biografia di Marx. n.p., the Rivista, 1966. pp. 115-136. 21cm. (Reprinted from Rivista Storica del Socialismo. N.28, 1966)

BLUMENBERG (WERNER) Karl Marx in Selbstzeugnissen und Bilddokumenten. Reinbek bei Hamburg, Rowohlt, 1966. pp. 179. bibliog. 19cm. (Rowohlts Monographien)

BRUHAT (J.) La Révolution française et la formation de la pensée de Marx. in Société des Études Robespierristes. La pensée socialiste devant la Révolution française. Paris, 1966.

DUPRÉ (LOUIS K.) The philosophical foundations of marxism. New York, Harcourt, [1966]. pp. xiv, 240. 21cm.

GRAESER (HARRY) Das Verhältnis von Arbeit und Eigentum in der Frühschriften von Karl Marx. Varel, 1966. pp. 87. bibliog. 21cm.

KUX (ERNST EDUARD WALTER) Karl Marx: die revolutionäre Konfession. [Zurich, imprint], 1966. pp. 139. bibliog.

MARX (KARL) and ENGELS (FRIEDRICH) Karl Marx, Friedrich Engels; Studienausgabe in 4 Bänden; herausgegeben von Iring Fetscher. Frankfurt am Main, Fischer, 1966. 4 vols. bibliogs. 18cm. (Bücher des Wissens)

MENEZES (DJACIR) Proudhon, Hegel e a dialética. Rio de Janeiro, 1966. pp. 158.

RICHTER (ROBERT) 1938- . Studien zur Londoner Emigration. Berlin, 1966. pp. 149. bibliog.

SEREBRIAKOVA (GALINA IOSIFOVNA) Маркс и Энгельс. Москва, Молодая Гвардия, 1966. pp. 880. bibliog. 20cm. (Жизнь Замечательных Людей. Серия Биографий. вып. 4)

SIGNORINI (ALBERTO) Il giovane Gentile e Marx. Milano, Giuffrè, 1966. pp. 140. 22½cm. (Florence. Università degli Studi di Firenze. Istituto di Storia delle Dottrine Politiche. Pubblicazioni. 5)

ZYRO (EMILIA) Pojęcie sprawiedliwości u Karola Marksa. Warszawa, Książka i Wiedza, 1966. pp. 186. bibliog. 19½cm. (Biblioteka Studiów nad Marksizmem) With Russian and English summaries and tables of contents

1967

ABALKIN (LEONID IVANOVICH) ed. "Капитал" К. Маркса и политическая экономия социализма. Москва, 1967. pp. 216.

"CAPITALUL" lui Marx și contemporaneitatea: 100 de ani de la apariția "Capitalului". București, 1967. pp. 288.

EKONOMICHESKAIA... Экономическая теория Маркса-Ленина и современный капитализм. Москва, 1967. pp. 407.

GARAUDY (ROGER) Karl Marx: the evolution of his thought. London, Lawrence & Wishart, [1967]. pp. 223. 20cm.

KARL Marx: Das Kapital, 1867-1967; Beiträge über "Das Kapital" und marxistische politische Ökonomie; veröffentlicht anlässlich des 100. Jahrestages des Erscheinens des Hauptwerkes von Karl Marx. Frankfurt am Main, 1967. pp.88. (Marxistische Blätter. Sonderhefte. 1967, 2)

LIVERGOOD (NORMAN D.) Activity in Marx's philosophy. The Hague, Nijhoff, 1967. pp. xii, 109. bibliog. 24cm.

MALYI (IL'IA GRIGOR'EVICH) Voprosy statistiki v "Kapitale" Karla Marksa. Moskva, 1967. pp. 216.

MANDEL (ERNEST) La formation de la pensée économique de Karl Marx, de 1843 jusqu'à la rédaction du "Capital": étude génétique. Paris, Maspero, 1967. pp. 215. bibliog. 21½cm. ("Les Textes à l'Appui")

MARX (KARL) and ENGELS (FRIEDRICH) Ex libris Karl Marx und Friedrich Engels: Schicksal und Verzeichnis einer Bibliothek. Berlin, Dietz, 1967. pp. 229. 21½cm.

PETROVIĆ (GAJO) Marx in the twentieth century: a Yugoslav philosopher considers Karl Marx's writings. Garden City, Doubleday, 1967. pp. 237. 18cm. (Anchor Books. A584)

POPITZ (HEINRICH) Der entfremdete Mensch: Zeitkritik und Geschichtsphilosophie des jungen Marx. Frankfurt am Main, Europäische Verlagsanstalt, [1967]. pp. 105. bibliog. 20½cm. (Kritische Studien zur Philosophie)

RASKIN (B.V.) К. Маркс и Ф. Энгельс об отношении пролетариата к демократии, о значении борьбы за демократию для установления союза с крестьянством. in Kofman (F Ia.) Социальные проблемы здравоохранения Москва, 1967. pp. 208.

RASKIN (B.V.) Маркс и Энгельс о гегемонии пролетариата в буржуазно-демократической революции, о положении и здоровье трудящихся при капитализме. in Kofman (F.Ia.) Социальные проблемы здравоохранения. Москва, 1967. pp. 208.

RIAZANOV (DAVID BORISOVICH) Marx et Engels: conférences faites aux cours de marxisme près l'Académie Socialiste en 1922. Paris, Editions Anthropos, [1967]. pp. 226. 22cm.

MARX (KARL) (Cont'd.)

SABETTI (ALFREDO) Studi sul giovane Marx: lezioni del corso ufficiale di "storia della filosofia", anno accademico 1966-67. Napoli, Liguori, 1967. pp. 216. 23cm.

SUDA (JYOTI PRASAD) Manu, Marx and Gandhi. Meerut, 1967. pp. 188.

1968

Die AKTUELLE philosophische Bedeutung des "Kapital" von Karl Marx: [papers presented at a conference in Jena, November 1967]; herausgegeben von Georg Mende und Erhard Lange. Berlin, Deutscher Verlag der Wissenschaften, 1968. pp. 218. 21½cm.

ALTHUSSER (LOUIS) and BALIBAR (ÉTIENNE) Lire Le capital. [new ed.] Paris, Maspero, 1968. 2 vols. 18cm. (Petite Collection Maspero. 30, 31)

AVINERI (SHLOMO) The social and political thought of Karl Marx. Cambridge, C.U.P., 1968. pp. viii, 269. bibliog. 21½cm. (Cambridge Studies in the History and Theory of Politics)

BEDESCHI (GIUSEPPE) Alienazione e feticismo nel pensiero di Marx. Bari, 1968. pp. 211.

BLOCH (ERNST) Über Karl Marx. Frankfurt a.M., Suhrkamp, 1968. pp. 178. bibliog. 17½cm.

CARMICHAEL (JOEL) Karl Marx: the passionate logician. London, Rapp & Whiting, 1968. pp. ix, 262. bibliog. 21cm.

CHKHIKVADZE (VIKTOR MIKHAILOVICH) Karl Marks o gosudarstve i prave. Moskva, 1968. pp. 207. bibliog.

COGNIOT (GEORGES) Karl Marx, notre contemporain. Paris, Éditions Sociales, [1968]. pp. 222. bibliog. 17cm. (Notre Temps)

D'IAKOV (VLADIMIR ANATOL'EVICH) Marks, Engel's i pol'skoe osvoboditel'noe dvizhenie. Moskva, 1968. pp. 192.

FISCHER (ERNST) Was Marx wirklich sagte;(... unter Mitarbeit von Franz Marek). 2nd ed. Wien, [1968]. pp. 188.

FREILIGRATH (FERDINAND) and others. Briefwechsel mit Marx und Engels;... bearbeitet von Manfred Häckel. Berlin, Akademie-Verlag, 1968. 2 vols. 23½cm.

GEMKOW (HEINRICH) and others. Karl Marx: a biography. Dresden, 1968. pp. 426.

HERMANN (URSULA) Der Kampf von Karl Marx um eine revolutionäre Gewerkschaftspolitik in der 1.Internationale 1864 bis 1868. Berlin, Tribüne, 1968. pp. 320. 20cm.

INTER NATIONES E.V. Karl Marx 1818/1968; [by Golo Mann and others]. Bad Godesberg, 1968. pp. 263. bibliog.

К... К. Маркс: математические рукописи. Москва, 1968. pp. 639. bibliog.

К... К Маркс и социалистическая экономика. Москва, Экономика, 1968. pp. 382. 20см.

"Das KAPITAL" von Karl Marx und seine internationale Wirkung; Beiträge ausländischer Teilnehmer an der wissenschaftlichen Session "100 Jahre Das Kapital", veranstaltet vom ZK der SED...1967 in Berlin. Berlin, Dietz, 1968. pp. 382. 20cm.

KARL... Карл Маркс: биография. Москва, 1968. pp. 746.

KARL Marx, 1818-1968: neue Studien zu Person und Lehre; [by Hans Lamm and others]. Mainz, [1968]. pp. 270. bibliog.

KARL Marx and modern philosophy; collection of articles [by F.V. Konstantinov and others]; [translated from the Russian]. Moscow, [1968]. pp. 239.

KASHKAREVA (LIUDMILA NIKOLAEVNA) Организация К. Марксом и Ф. Энгельсом рабочей статистики труда; под редакцией проф. Петрова А. И. Москва, 1968. pp. 75.

KETTLE (ARNOLD CHARLES) Karl Marx: founder of modern communism. 2nd ed. London, Weidenfeld & Nicolson, 1968. pp. 125. 20½cm. (Pathfinder Biographies)

KISCH (EGON ERWIN) Karl Marx in Karlsbad. [2nd ed.]. Berlin, Aufbau-Verlag, 1968. pp. 76. 19cm.

KUNINA (VALERIA EMMANUILOVNA) Карл Маркс и английское рабочее движение, 1845-1883. Москва, Мысль, 1968. pp. 422. 10½см.

KUZIN (ALEKSANDR AVRAMIEVICH) К. Маркс и проблемы техники. Москва, Наука, 1968. pp. 112. bibliog. 20cm.

LAPIN (NIKOLAI IVANOVICH) Молодой Маркс. Москва, 1968. pp. 376.

LEFEBVRE (HENRI). The sociology of Marx:...translated from the French by Norbert Guterman. New York, [1968]. pp. 214.

LEONT'EV (LEV ABRAMOVICH) "Капитал" К. Маркса и современная эпоха. Москва, 1968. pp. 398.

MAIHOFER (WERNER) Demokratie im Sozialismus: Recht und Staat im Denken des jungen Marx. Frankfurt am Main, [1968]. pp. 81.

MARKS... Маркс - историк. Москва, 1968. pp. 711.

MARX (KARL) Karl Marx on colonialism and modernization: his despatches and other writings on China, India, Mexico, the Middle East and North Africa; edited with an introduction by Shlomo Avineri. New York, Doubleday, 1968. pp. xv, 464. 20½cm.

MONDOLFO (RODOLFO) Umanismo di Marx: studi filosofici 1908-1966. Torino, Einaudi, [1968]. pp. xlviii, 419. 21cm. (Biblioteca di Cultura Filosofica. 30)

PARINETTO (LUCIANO) La nozione de alienazione in Hegel, Feuerbach e Marx; a cura di Marina Lavaggi e Marcello Pitta. Milano, La Goliardica, [1968]. pp. ii, 272. 24cm.

PAYNE (PIERRE STEPHEN ROBERT) Marx. New York, Simon & Schuster, [1968]. pp. 582. bibliog. 23½cm.

RAURICH (HÉCTOR) Notas para la actualidad de Hegel y Marx. Buenos Aires, Marymar, 1968. pp. ix, 148. 19cm.

TSAGOLOV (NIKOLAI ALEKSANDROVICH) ed. Метод "Капитала" и вопросы политической экономии социализма. Москва, 1968. pp. 268.

TSAGOLOV (NIKOLAI ALEKSANDROVICH) and KIROV (V. A.) eds. "Kapital" K. Marksa i problemy sovremennogo kapitalizma. Moskva, 1968. pp. 512.

TUCHSCHEERER (WALTER) Bevor "Das Kapital" entstand: die Herausbildung und Entwicklung der ökonomischen Theorie von Karl Marx in der Zeit von 1843 bis 1858. Berlin, Akademie-Verlag, 1968. pp. 493. bibliog. 21½cm.

TURNER (DENYS) On the philosophy of Karl Marx. Dublin, 1968. pp. 82. bibliog.

VAZIULIN (VIKTOR ALEKSEEVICH) Логика "Капитала" К. Маркса. Москва, Университет, 1968. pp. 295. 19½см.

VOLK (S.S.) Karl Marks i Fridrikh Engel's o pechatnom slove. in Piat'sot let posle Gutenberga, 1468-1968. Moskva, 1968.

ZELENÝ (JINDŘICH) Die Wissenschaftslogik bei Marx und Das Kapital; (nach der...tschechischen Originalausgabe übertragen). Frankfurt, [1968]. pp. 332. bibliog.

1969

ANSART (PIERRE) Marx et l'anarchisme: essai sur les sociologies de Saint-Simon, Proudhon et Marx. Paris, 1969. pp. 556. bibliog.

ASPELIN (GUNNAR) Karl Marx, samhällsforskare och samhällskritiker: en kommentar till Kapitalet 1. Lund, [1969]. pp. 215. bibliog.

CERRONI (U.) La crítica de Marx a la filosofía hegeliana del derecho público. in Marx, el derecho y el estado. Barcelona, 1969.

GROSSMANN (HENRYK) Marx, die klassische Nationalökonomie und das Problem der Dynamik; mit einem Nachwort von Paul Mattick. Frankfurt a.M., [1969]. pp. 133.

HAMMEN (OSCAR J.) The red '48ers: Karl Marx and Friedrich Engels. New York, [1969]. pp. 428. bibliog.

HYPPOLITE (JEAN) Studies on Marx and Hegel...; translated [from the French] with an introduction, notes, and bibliography by John O'Neill. London 1969. pp. 202.

INSTITUT MARKSIZMA-LENINIZMA. Русские современники о К. Марксе и Ф. Энгельсе. Москва, 1969. pp. 334. Continuation of its К. Маркс, Ф. Энгельс и революционная Россия.

INSTITUT VOENNOI ISTORII. Карл Маркс и военная история. Москва, 1969. pp. 240. 20см.

KERR (CLARK) Marshall, Marx and modern times: the multi-dimensional society. Cambridge, 1969. pp. 138. (Cambridge. University. Marshall Lectures. 1967-68.)

LAMM (HANS) Karl Marx und das Judentum. München, 1969. pp. 78.

LEFEBVRE (HENRI) Marx. 2nd ed. Paris, 1969. pp. 135. bibliog.

LITERATURNOE... Литературное наследство К. Маркса и Ф. Энгельса: история публикации и изучения в СССР. Москва, 1969. pp. 511.

PELLICANI (LUCIANO) Introduzione a Marx. [Bologna, 1969]. pp. 248.

PEVZNER (IAKOV ALEKSANDROVICH) Методология "Капитала" К. Маркса и современный капитализм. Москва, 1969. pp. 227.

RAKHMAN (DAVID ARONOVICH) Великий учитель рабочего класса: жизнь и учение К. Маркса. Москва, 1969. pp. 541. bibliog.

REIPRICH (KURT) Die philosophisch-naturwissenschaftlichen Arbeiten von Karl Marx und Friedrich Engels. Berlin, 1969. pp. 144.

SANDERSON (JOHN B.) An interpretation of the political ideas of Marx and Engels. London, 1969. pp. 118.

STEDMAN-JONES (GARETH) Althusserian Marxism. n.p., [c.1969]. pp. 9.

SYMPOSIUM ON THE ROLE OF KARL MARX IN THE DEVELOPMENT OF CONTEMPORARY SCIENTIFIC THOUGHT, PARIS, 1968. Marx and contemporary scientific thought; (papers from the symposium...organised...by the International Council for Philosophy and Humanistic Studies and the International Social Science Council). The Hague, [1969]. pp. 612. (International Social Science Council. Publications. No. 13) In French or English.

VAN CANGH (JEAN MARIE) Introduction à Karl Marx. Gembloux, [1969]. pp. 127. bibliog.

VOLK (STEPAN STEPANOVICH) Карл Маркс и русские общественные деятели. Ленинград, 1969. pp. 214.

WYSS (DIETER) Marx und Freud: ihr Verhältnis zur modernen Anthropologie. Göttingen, [1969]. pp. 114.

1970

AERZTE um Karl Marx; Arbeit eines Studentenkollektivs der Medizinischen Fakultät an der Humboldt-Universität zu Berlin, unter Leitung von Helmut Dressler. Berlin, 1970. pp. 148.

MARX (KARL) (Cont'd.)

ALTHUSSER (LOUIS) and BALIBAR (ETIENNE) Reading Capital; translated [from the French] by Ben Brewster. London, 1970. pp. 340.

BALINKY (ALEXANDER) Marx's economics: origin and development. Lexington, Mass., [1970]. pp. 178. bibliog.

CHAGIN (BORIS ALEKSANDROVICH) Соsдание и развитие К. Марксом и Ф. Энгельсом теории научного коммунизма. Ленинград, 1970. pp. 329.

COCCOPALMERIO (DOMENICO) La teoria politica di Marx: analisi critica dello stato "borghese" negli scritti giovanili. Milano, 1970. pp. 314. (Trieste. Università. Facoltà di Giurisprudenza. Pubblicazioni. 8)

FISCHER (ERNST) of the Austrian Communist Party. Marx in his own words;... in collaboration with Franz Marek; translated [from the German] by Anna Bostock. London, 1970. pp. 187.

GABAUDE (JEAN MARC) Le jeune Marx et le matérialisme antique. Toulouse, [1970]. pp. 277. bibliog.

HARTMANN (KLAUS) Die Marxsche Theorie: eine philosophische Untersuchung zu den Hauptschriften. Berlin, 1970. pp. 593.

LEVIOVA (SOF'IA ZELIKOVNA) Marks v germanskoi revoliutsii 1848-1849 godov. Moskva, 1970. pp. 375. bibliog.

LOEWENSTEIN (JULIUS I.) Vision und Wirklichkeit: Marx contra Marxismus. Basel, [1970]. pp. 170. (List Gesellschaft. Veröffentlichungen. Band 65)

LOWY (MICHAEL) La théorie de la révolution chez le jeune Marx. Paris, 1970. pp. 224.

McLELLAN (DAVID) Marx before Marxism. London, 1970. pp. 233. bibliog.

MARKS i nekotorye voprosy mezhdunarodnogo rabochego dvizheniia XIX veka: stat'i i dokumenty. Moskva, 1970. pp. 479.

MÉSZÁROS (ISTVÁN) Marx's theory of alienation. London, [1970]. pp. 352. bibliog.

MORF (OTTO) Geschichte und Dialektik in der politischen Ökonomie: zum Verhältnis von Wirtschaftstheorie und Wirtschaftsgeschichte bei Karl Marx. 2nd ed. Frankfurt am Main, [1970]. pp. 299. bibliog.

PRITYTSKAIA (TAT'IANA IVANOVNA) K. Marks i F. Engel's o vsemirno-istoricheskoi roli proletariata i ego partii. Minsk, 1970. pp. 131.

SCHEFOLD (CHRISTOPH) Die Rechtsphilosophie des jungen Marx von 1842, mit einer Interpretation der 'Pariser Schriften' von 1844. München, [1970]. pp. 301. bibliog. (Munich. Universität. Institut für Politische Wissenschaft. Münchener Studien zur Politik. 15. Band)

VYGODSKII (VITALII SOLOMONOVICH) K istorii sozdaniia "Kapitala". Moskva, 1970. pp. 294. Continuation of his Istoriia odnogo velikogo otkrytiia Karla Marksa, which see.

WILDERMUTH (ARMIN) Marx und die Verwirklichung der Philosophie. Den Haag, 1970. 2 vols.

1971

BLOCH (ERNST) On Karl Marx; (translated by John Maxwell). New York, 1971. pp. 173.

CERRONI (UMBERTO) Teoria della crisi sociale in Marx: una reinterpretazione. Bari, 1971. pp. 270.

COGNIOT (GEORGES) Karl Marx and the Paris Commune. [London, 1971]. pp. 11. (Marx Memorial Library. Marx Memorial Lectures. 1971.)

DAHRENDORF (RALF) Die Idee des Gerechten im Denken von Karl Marx. 2nd ed. Hannover, [1971]. pp. 186. bibliog. (Friedrich-Ebert-Stiftung. Forschungsinstitut. Schriftenreihe. Band 80)

GIDDENS (ANTHONY) Capitalism and modern social theory: an analysis of the writings of Marx, Durkheim and Max Weber. London, 1971. pp. 261. bibliog.

McLELLAN (DAVID) of the University of Kent. The thought of Karl Marx: an introduction. London, 1971. pp. 237. bibliog.

MARX (KARL) A contribution to the critique of political economy,...with an introduction by Maurice Dobb. London, 1971. pp. 264.

MARX (KARL) Early texts; translated and edited by David McLellan. Oxford, 1971. pp. 223. bibliog.

MARX (KARL) Karl Marx: economy, class and social revolution, edited and with an introductory essay by Z.A. Jordan. London, 1971. pp. 332. bibliog.

OLLMAN (BERTELL) Alienation: Marx's conception of man in capitalist society. Cambridge, 1971. pp. 325. bibliog.

WOLFSON (MURRAY) Karl Marx. New York, 1971. pp. 68.

- Bibliography

LEVIN (L.A.) Библиография произведений основоположников марксизма-ленинизма в СССР. in Voprosy bibliografii obshchestvenno-politicheskoi literatury. Moskva, 1967.

AGRANOVSKII (IL'IA ISAKOVICH) Прочитаны впервые. Москва, 1968. pp. 110.

VELIKOE... Великое наследие: о втором издании Сочинений К. Маркса и Ф. Энгельса. Москва, 1968. pp. 286.

PAEGLIS (J.) and DRUVA (M.) compilers. K. Markss, F. Engelss, V._I. Lenins latviešu valodā: bibliografija; K. Marks, F. Ehgel's, V. I. Lenin na latyshskom iazyke: bibliografiia. Riga, 1969. pp. 361.

MARX-KÁROLY KOZGAZDASÁGTUDOMÁNYI EGYETEM

[BIRO (KLARA) and KOLOS (NIKOLAUS)] Karl Marx Universität für Wirtschaftswissenschaften, Budapest. [Budapest?], 1968. pp. 144.

MARX (WILHELM)

MARX (WILHELM) Der Nachlass des Reichskanzlers Wilhelm Marx;...bearbeitet von Hugo Stehkämper. Köln, 1968 in progress. (Cologne. Stadtarchiv. Mitteilungen. Hefte 52-55)

MARXISM

ENGELS (FRIEDRICH) Historical materialism. Edinburgh, 1892 repr. 1902. pp. 22.

BIERMANN (WILHELM EDUARD) Die Weltanschauung des Marxismus: an der materialistischen Geschichtsauffassung und an der Mehrwertlehre erörtert. Leipzig, Roth und Schunke, 1908. pp. 83. 24cm.

CRAIK (WILLIAM WHITE) Student's outlines... philosophic logic; the theory of historical development; economics, Marxian. Halifax, Halifax Branch of the Central Labour College, [191-?] pp. (iv), 72. 21cm.

PETRY (FRANZ) Der soziale Gehalt der marxschen Werttheorie. Jena, Fischer, 1916. pp. viii, 70. 23cm.

COOK (A.E.) The socialism of Karl Marx: with a biographical sketch of the life of Karl Marx, the socialist. [Glasgow, 1918]. pp. 29.

[WORKERS' BOOKSHOP LTD]. A lesson in elementary economics. London, Collet's Bookshops, [c. 192-?] pp. 16.

BERDNIKOV (A. I.) and SVETLOV (F.) Курс политграмоты: пособие для совпартшкол, рабфаков и вузов; под общей редакцией Н. И. Бухарина. Москва, Государственное Издательство, 1924. pp. 656. 25см.

PLEKHANOV (GEORGII VALENTINOVICH) Fundamental problems of marxism; ...edited by D. Ryazanov; (translation...by Eden and Cedar Paul). London, 1929. pp. 145.

FERRERO REBAGLIATI (RAUL) Marxismo y nacionalismo: estado nacional corporativo. [Lima, 193-?] pp. 264.

MANUILSKII (DMITRII ZAKHAROVICH) Marxism: the doctrine of proletarian dictatorship: address delivered in Moscow on the fiftieth anniversary of the death of Karl Marx, March 14, 1933. London, [1933]. pp. 48.

LENIN (VLADIMIR IL'ICH) The proletarian revolution and renegade Kautsky; [with explanatory notes]. London, 1935. pp. 110.

MASARYK (THOMAS GARRIGUE) Otázka sociální: základy marxismu, filosofické a sociologické. Praha, 1936. 2 vols. (Spisy T. G. Masaryka. kn.6, 7)

[PANNEKOEK (ANTON)] Lenin als Philosoph: kritische Betrachtung der philosophischen Grundlagen des Leninismus; von J. Harper [pseud.]. [Amsterdam], [1938]. pp. 112. (Gruppe Internationaler Kommunisten in Holland. Bibliothek der "Räte-korrespondenz". No.1)

TAGORE (SAUMYENDRANATH) Bourgeois-democratic revolution and India. Calcutta, 1939 repr. 1946. pp. 53.

The CRISIS: Marx versus Keynes; a criticism of the theories of Lord Keynes and of the policies arising therefrom. n.p., [194-?]. fo. 21.

LYNN (GREY) The return of Karl Marx. [London], 1941. pp. 117.

AMORIM (DIOGO PACHECO DE) Princípios fundamentais do pensamento marxista: conferência proferida em 23 de Janeiro de 1941, etc. Lisboa, the União, 1942. pp. 28. 23½cm. (União Nacional. Conferências. 6)

THOMPSON (JOAN) Scientific socialism. rev. ed. London, Lawrence and Wishart, [1942?]. pp. 32. bibliogs. 18cm. (Marx Memorial Library and Workers' School. Marx House Syllabuses. 1)

TROTSKII (LEV DAVYDOVICH) Their morals and ours. New York, 1942. pp. 48.

VOLPE (GALVANO DELLA) La libertà comunista [originally published 1946] con l'aggiunta dello scritto del 1962 Sulla dialettica. Roma, 1969. pp. 175.

BROWDER (EARL RUSSELL) Language and war: letter to a friend concerning Stalin's article on linguistics. [Yonkers, N.Y., 1950]. pp. 13.

KOFLER (LEO) Marxismus und Sprache: zu Stalins Untersuchung über den Marxismus in der Sprachwissenschaft. Köln, 1952. pp. 53.

VYSHESLAVTSEV (BORIS PETROVICH) Кризис индустриальной культуры: марксизм, неосоциализм, неолиберализм. Нью-Йорк, Чехов, 1953. pp. 352. 21½см.

GINDEV (PANAIOT) За някои категории на диалектическия материализъм и тяхното приложение в наказателното право и наказателния процес. София, БАН, 1956. pp. 264. bibliog. 20cm.

[NOVACK (GEORGE)] The irregular movement of history: the marxist law of the combined and uneven development of society; [by William F.] Warde, [pseud.]. London, 1957. pp. 51. (Labour Review. Pamphlets) First published in Labour Review, 1957, with the titles: The law of uneven and combined development; and, The coming American revolution.

MENDE (GEORG) Freiheit und Verantwortung: kleine Essays. Berlin, Deutscher Verlag der Wissenschaften, 1958. pp. 212. 21½cm.

NU, U. Towards a socialist state;...translation of speech...on January 29, 1958, at the third All-Burma congress of the A[nti-]F[ascist] P[eople's] F[reedom] L[eague]. [Rangoon, 1958]. pp. 68.

SOCJALIZM, marksizm, komunizm;... (slowo wstępne; [by] Zygmunt Zaremba). Paryż, "Światło", 1958. pp. 241. 17½cm. (Biblioteka Społeczna. t.3)

EVANS (A.H.) Once again truth will out. [London David-Goliath Publications, 196-?]. pp. (79). 25cm.

MARXISM (Cont'd.)

WEE (HERMAN VAN DER) De groei van het kapitalisme en van het marxisme: bijdrage tot de algemene beschavingsgeschiedenis en tot de economische geschiedenis. [Louvain?, 196-]. fo. 291.

MAKAROV (A. D.) and others, eds. Диалектический материализм. Москва, ВПШ и АОН, 1960. pp. 471. 22см.

FROMM (ERICH) ed. Marx's concept of man; with a translation from Marx's economic and philosophical manuscripts by T. B. Bottomore. New York, 1962. pp. xii, 260.

PETROCHENKOV (V.N.) Влияние идей марксизма на социально-политические взгляды русских революционных демократов. in Uchenye Zapiski Kafedr Obshchestvennykh Nauk Vuzov g. Leningrada. Filosofiia. vyp.3. Leningrad, 1961.

SVIDERSKII (V.I.) Проблема многокачественности явления в материалистической диалектике. in Uchenye Zapiski Kafedr Obshchestvennykh Nauk Vuzov g. Leningrada. Filosofiia. vyp.3. Leningrad, 1961.

LUKÁCS (GEORG) Marxist. Werke. Neuwied, [1962 in progress]. bibliogs. Band 8 is of the third edition.

SAMEDOV (V. IU.) Распространение марксизма-ленинизма в Азербайджане. Баку, 1962-66. 2 vols. bibliog.

MARXISME et existentialisme: controverse sur la dialectique; par Jean-Paul Sartre [and others]. Paris, Plon, [1962]. pp. xi, 97. 20cm. (Tribune Libre. 62)

MOLSKA (ALINA) ed. Pierwsze pokolenie marksistów polskich: wybór pism i materiałów źródłowych z lat 1878-1886. Warszawa, Książka i Wiedza, 1962. 2 vols. 20cm. (Biblioteka Myśli Socjalistycznej)

NARSKII (IGOR' SERGEEVICH) and SUVOROV (LEV NIKOLAEVICH) Pozitivizm i mekhanisticheskaia reviziia marksizma. Moskva, 1962. pp. 84.

HEMBERGER (ADOLF) Das historisch-soziologische Verhältnis des westeuropäischen Anarcho-Syndikalismus zum Marxismus. Heidelberg, 1963. pp. 252. bibliog.

SCHRAM (STUART R.) ed. Documents sur la théorie de la révolution permanente en Chine: idéologie dialectique et dialectique du réel. Paris, Mouton, 1963. pp. xlix, 65. 27cm. (Maison des Sciences de l'Homme. Matériaux pour l'Étude de l'Extrême-Orient Moderne et Contemporaine. Textes. 4)

VIAKKEREV (FEDOR FEDOROVICH) Dialekticheskoe protivorechie i marksistskaia politicheskaia ekonomiia. Moskva, 1963. pp. 96.

BERLIN. Humboldt-Universität. Fragen der Marxistischen Soziologie. Berlin, 1964 (Teil 2) to date.

BLAKELEY (THOMAS J.) Soviet theory of knowledge. Dordrecht, Reidel, [1964]. pp. vii, 203. bibliog. 22cm. (Freiburg (Switzerland). Universität. Ost-Europa Institut. Sovietica)

CHUNAEVA (A.A.) О современных приемах идеалистической критики диалектического материализма. in Uchenye Zapiski Kafedr Obshchestvennykh Nauk Vuzov g. Leningrada. Filosofiia. vyp.5. Проблемы научного коммунизма. Ленинград, 1964.

Das DIALEKTISCHE Gesetz. Bratislava, 1964. pp. 492.

FROM party of working class to party of entire Soviet people. [Moscow, 1964]. pp. 20.

HIRSZOWICZ (MARIA) Konfrontacje socjologiczne: marksizm i socjologia współczesna. Warszawa, Książka i Wiedza, 1964. pp. 423. 19½cm.

LABOUR REVIEW. [Pamphlets]. What is revolutionary leadership?; (4 articles)... by Brian Pearce [and others]. New York, [1964]. pp. irreg.

NEKOTORYE voprosy marksistsko-leninskoi teorii na sovremennom etape: sbornik statei. Saratov, 1964. pp. 176.

RASPROSTRANENIE idei marksistskoi filosofii v Evrope, konets XIX - nachalo XX vekov. Leningrad, 1964. pp. 188.

RAZIN (VLADIMIR IVANOVICH) Марксизм-ленинизм о сломе эксплуататорской государственной машины. Москва, Университет, 1964. pp. 52. 21½см.

ROCHET (WALDECK) Qu'est-ce que la philosophie marxiste? Paris, Éditions Sociales, [1964]. pp. 80. 18½cm. (Notre Temps)

TAUT (HEINRICH) Zur Dialektik von Arbeit und Bedürfnissen im Sozialismus und Kommunismus. Berlin, [1964?]. pp. 427.

TITARENKO (ALEKSANDR IVANOVICH) Прагматистский лжемарксизм - философия антикоммунизма: критика современной прагматистской фальсификации философии марксизма. Москва, Университет, 1964. pp. 292. 20см.

VECCHIO (GIORGIO DEL) Critica del materialismo storico. rev. ed., Roma, Signorelli, [1964]. pp. 16. 24cm.

VOLPE (GALVANO DELLA) Chiave della dialettica storica. Roma, [1964 repr. 1968] pp. 38.

ZA... За чистоту марксизма-ленинизма: материалы научной сессии Академии общественных наук при ЦК КПСС, Института марксизма-ленинизма при ЦК КПСС, Высшей партийной школы при ЦК КПСС и гуманитарных институтов Академии наук СССР. Москва, Мысль, 1964. pp. 328. 21½см.

ACTION CENTRE FOR MARXIST-LENINIST UNITY. Manifesto. Manchester, 1965. pp. 25.

COGNIOT (GEORGES) Le socialisme scientifique: la pénétration du marxisme en France. Paris, the Centre, [1965?] fo. 28. 27cm. (Centre d'Études et de Recherches Marxistes. Cahiers. 3 ième Série. 2)

COMMUNIST PARTY OF AUSTRALIA. Central Committee. Philosophy: a guide to action for the working man. [Sydney], 1965. pp. 36. bibliog.

CRUSE (HAROLD) and others. Marxism and the negro struggle. New York, 1965 repr. 1969. pp. 46.

GERMANY (BUNDESREPUBLIK). 1965. Marxistische Wirtschaftstheorie und sowjetische Wirtschaftspolitik; ([by] Lutz Köllner). (Schriftenreihe der Bundeszentrale für Politische Bildung. Heft 68) Bonn, 1965. pp. 92. bibliog. 24cm.

GUILLÉN (ABRAHAM) Teoría de la violencia: guerra y lucha de clases. Buenos Aires, Jamcana, [1965]. pp. 233. 17½cm. (Colección Estrella Federal)

KOLMAN (ARNOST) Considerations about the certainty of knowledge; edited...by Robert S. Cohen and Dirk J. Struik. New York, [1965]. pp. 12. (American Institute for Marxist Studies. Occasional Papers. No.2)

MARXISM and democracy: a symposium; edited by Herbert Aptheker. New York, [1965]. pp. 113. bibliog. (American Institute for Marxist Studies. Monograph Series. No. 1)

MOLODTSOV (VASILII SERGEEVICH) Vozniknovenie dialekticheskogo i istoricheskogo materializma - revoliutsiia v filosofii. Moskva, 1965. pp. 78.

MOLSKA (ALINA) Model ustroju socjalistycznego w polskiej myśli marksistowskiej lat 1878-1886. Warszawa, Książka i Wiedza, 1965. pp. 291. bibliog 19½cm. (Biblioteka Studiów nad Marksizmem. 8) With Russian and English summaries.

OSBORN (R.) pseud. [i.e. Reuben OSBERT]. Marxism and psycho-analysis. London, 1965. pp. xix, 160.

UCHENYE ZAPISKI KAFEDR OBSHCHESTVENNYKH NAUK VUZOV G. LENINGRADA. Filosofiia. вып.6. Ленинград, Университет, 1965. pp. 232. 21cm.

UCHENYE ZAPISKI KAFEDR OBSHCHESTVENNYKH NAUK VUZOV G. LENINGRADA. Filosofiia. вып.7. Философские и социологические исследования. Ленинград, Университет, 1965. pp. 215. 21½cm.

VOLOVIK (L. A.) and DROZDOVA (E. M.) Истина марксистской и домарксовой философии. Москва, Мысль, 1965. pp. 224. 19½cm.

VOPROSY... Вопросы материалистической диалектики и критика буржуазной идеологии. Ташкент, 1965. pp. 148. (Ташкент. Университет. Научные Труды. вып. 279. [being also] Философские Науки. кн.8)

BENNER (DIETRICH) Theorie und Praxis: Systemtheoretische Betrachtungen zu Hegel und Marx. Wien, Oldenbourg, 1966. pp. 188. bibliog. 22 cm. (Überlieferung und Aufgabe. 4)

BLAKELEY (T.J.) The salient features of the Marxist-Leninist theory of knowledge. in Adelmann (Frederick J.) ed. The quest for the absolute. Chestnut Hill, [1966].

BLANCO AMOR (JOSÉ) [and FERNÁNDEZ SANTOS (F.)] España y el marxismo. Buenos Aires, Theoria, 1966. pp. 101. 20cm. (Biblioteca de Ensayistas Contemporaneos)

GERMANY (BUNDESREPUBLIK). 1966. Totalitärer, marxistischer oder demokratischer Sozialismus?; ([by] Günter Bartsch). (Schriftenreihe der Bundeszentrale für Politische Bildung. Heft 72) Bonn, 1966. pp. 128. 24cm.

GIRARDI (GIULIO) Marxismo e cristianesimo. 2nd ed. Assisi, Cittadella, [1966] pp. 238. 21cm. (Sulle Vie del Concilio)

HUBER (EDUARD) Um eine "dialektische Logik": Diskussionen in der neueren Sowjetphilosophie. München, Pustet, [1966]. pp. 259. bibliog. 20½cm.

KUMPMANN (WALTER) Franz Mehring als Vertreter des historischen Materialismus. Wiesbaden, 1966. pp. 192. bibliog. (Osteuropa-Institut, München. Veröffentlichungen. Band 29)

MARCHESE (ANGELO) Marxisti e cristiani. Torino, Borla, 1966. pp. 158. 21cm. (Le Idee e la Vita. (2). 2)

MARX (KARL) and ENGELS (FRIEDRICH) Karl Marx, Friedrich Engels; Studienausgabe in 4 Bänden; herausgegeben von Iring Fetscher. Frankfurt am Main, Fischer, 1966. 4 vols. bibliogs. 18cm. (Bücher des Wissens)

MENEZES (DJACIR) Proudhon, Hegel e a dialética. Rio de Janeiro, 1966. pp. 158.

NOVACK (GEORGE) An introduction to the logic of Marxism. 4th ed. New York, 1966. pp. 124.

NOVACK (GEORGE) Who will change the world? the new left and the views of C. Wright Mills. Toronto, YSF Publication, [1966]. pp. 36. 21cm.

PARETO (V.) Marxisme et économie pure. in vol. 9 of Pareto (Vilfredo) Oeuvres completes. Genève, Droz, 1966.

PARSONS (HOWARD L.) Humanistic philosophy in contemporary Poland and Yugoslavia. New York, [1966]. pp. 12. bibliog. (American Institute for Marxist Studies. Occasional Papers. No. 4)

PHILIPS (A.) and others. The split in the revolutionary tendency: documents and correspondence of the 1962 rupture; etc. New York, [1966?]. fo. 33. (Spartacist. Marxist Bulletins. No. 3)

REVUNENKOV (VLADIMIR GEORGIEVICH) Marksizm i problema iakobinskoi diktatury: istoriograficheskii ocherk. Leningrad, 1966. pp. 176.

ROCHET (WALDECK) Le marxisme et les chemins de l'avenir. Paris, Éditions Sociales, [1966]. pp. 95. 17½cm.

SCHELER (HERMANN) ed. Historischer Materialismus und Sozialforschung: ein Sammelband, etc. Berlin, Deutscher Verlag der Wissenschaften, 1966. pp. 216. 21½cm.

SOVESHCHANIE PO SOVREMENNYM PROBLEMAM MATERIALISTICHESKOI DIALEKTIKI, MOSKVA, 1965. Материалы Совещания... 7-9 апреля 1965 г. Москва, Наука, 1966. 4 vols. 20cm.

MARXISM (Cont'd.)

VODZINSKII (EVGENII IVANOVICH) Russkoe neokantianstvo kontsa XIX - nachala XX vekov: marksistsko-leninskaia kritika ontologii i gnoseologii. Leningrad, 1966. pp. 79.

VOPROSY teoreticheskogo nasledstva V. I. Lenina. Krasnoiarsk, 1966. pp. 162.

1967

50 Jahre Triumph des Marxismus-Leninismus: die Grosse Sozialistische Oktoberrevolution und die Entwicklung des Marxismus-Leninismus; (...unter Leitung von Gertraud Teschner herausgegeben). Berlin, Dietz, 1967. pp. 328. 20cm.

ANTONIAN (MARLEN OGANESOVICH) Соотношение объективных условий и субъективного фактора при социализме. Ереван, АН Армянской ССР, 1967. pp. 238. 19½см.

BAUDY (NICOLAS) Le marxisme: le centenaire du "Capital". [Paris], Éditions Planète, [1967]. pp. 255. bibliog. 17½cm. (Encyclopédie Planète. 29)

BERLIN. Humboldt-Universität. Symposion von Lehrkörper und Studenten, 1967. 100 Jahre Kapital; ausgewahlte Materialien. Berlin, [1967?]. pp. 113. 21cm. (Fichte-Schriften.1)

BURLATSKII (FEDOR MIKHAILOVICH) Maoizm ili marksizm? Moskva, 1967. pp. 128.

"CAPITALUL" lui Marx şi contemporaneitatea: 100 de ani de la apariţia "Capitalului". Bucureşti, 1967. pp. 288.

CHAGIN (BORIS ALEKSANDROVICH) Lenin o roli subektivnogo faktora v istorii. Leningrad, 1967. pp. 147.

CHAGIN (BORIS ALEKSANDROVICH) and others. Razvitie V. I. Leninym istoricheskogo materializma posle Velikoi Oktiabr'skoi sotsialisticheskoi revoliutsii. Leningrad, 1967. pp. 152.

CORNU (AUGUSTE) Die Herausbildung des historischen Materialismus: in Marx' "Thesen über Feuerbach", Engels' "Die Lage der arbeitenden Klasse in England" und in "Die Deutsche Ideologie" von Marx und Engels. Berlin, 1967. pp. 30. (Deutsche Akademie der Wissenschaften zu Berlin. Vorträge und Schriften. Heft 104)

DASGUPTA (A.K.) Marx and Keynes. in Singh (Baljit) and Singh (Vidya Bhusan) eds. Social and economic change. Bombay, 1967.

DEUTSCHE AKADEMIE DER WISSENSCHAFTEN ZU BERLIN. Oktoberrevolution und Wissenschaft; herausgegeben...aus Anlass des 50. Jahrestages der Grossen Sozialistischen Oktoberrevolution. Berlin, Akademie-Verlag, 1967. pp. xi, 452. 24cm.

DIALEKTICHESKII i istoricheskii materializm. Moskva, 1967. pp. 320.

FROMM (ERICH) ed. Marx's concept of man; with a translation from Marx's economic and philosophical manuscripts by T.B. Bottomore; with an afterword by Erich Fromm. New York, Ungar, 1967. pp. xii, 263. 19½cm. (Milestones of Thought)

GARRIDO (JOSE M.) El materialismo historico: en torno a dos textos de Marx-Engels. Madrid, 1967. pp. 80.

GLEZERMAN (GRIGORII EFIMOVICH) Исторический материализм и развитие социалистического общества. Москва, ИПЛ, 1967. pp. 304. 20см.

GRITSENKO (IVAN IVANOVICH) Логическое и историческое - категории материалистической диалектики. Москва, 1967. pp. 94.

GROSSER (GUENTHER) ed. Studien zur marxistisch-leninistischen Revolutionstheorie. Leipzig, Karl-Marx-Universität, 1967. pp. xi, 400. 22½cm.

GUILLÉN (ABRAHAM) Dialéctica de la politica: los años decisivos del siglo XX; crisis, guerras y revoluciones. Montevideo, Cooperativa Obrera Grafica, [1967]. pp. 319. 16½cm.

GULANIAN (KHACHIK GRIGOR'EVICH) Марксистская мысль в Армении; в конце XIX - начале XX века. Ереван, 1967. pp. 259.

HEROLD (MANFRED) ed. Der Marxismus-Leninismus: die Wahrheit unserer Zeit: zum 100. Jahrestag des Erscheinens des ersten Bandes des "Kapitals" von Karl Marx und zum 50. Jahrestag des Erscheinens der Arbeit von W.I. Lenin "Der Imperialismus als höchstes Stadium des Kapitalismus. Berlin, 1967. pp. 378.

HIEBSCH (HANS) and VORWERG (MANFRED) Einführung in die marxistische sozialpsychologie. Berlin, Deutscher Verlag der Wissenschaften, 1967. pp. 236. 21½cm. With German, English and Russian summaries.

KARL Marx: Das Kapital, 1867-1967; Beiträge über "Das Kapital" und marxistische politische Ökonomie; veröffentlicht anlässlich des 100. Jahrestages des Erscheinens des Hauptwerkes von Karl Marx. Frankfurt am Main, 1967. pp.88. (Marxistische Blätter. Sonderhefte. 1967, 2)

KOREN (HENRY J.) Marx and the authentic man: a first introduction to the philosophy of Karl Marx. Pittsburgh, Duquesne U.P., [1967]. pp. 150. 20½cm.

KOSING (ALFRED) Wissenschaftstheorie als Aufgabe der marxistischen Philosophie. Berlin, 1967. pp. 31. (Deutsche Akademie der Wissenschaften zu Berlin. Sitzungsberichte. 1967. Nr. 1)

KOVALEV (ALEKSANDR MITROFANOVICH) Марксистско-ленинская теория социалистической революции и современность. Москва, 1967. pp. 70.

KRASIN (IURII ANDREEVICH) Ленин, революция, современность: проблемы ленинской теории социалистической революции. Москва, Наука, 1967. pp. 568. 20см.

KURSANOV (G.A.) ed. Problèmes fondamentaux du matérialisme dialectique. Moscou, Éditions du Progrès, 1967. pp. 455.

LEKOVIĆ (DRAGUTIN) Marksizam i filozofija; prevela s francuskog Vida Gostuski. Beograd, 1967. pp. 479. bibliog. (Institut za Izučavanje Radničkog Pokreta. Razvoj Socijalističke Misli. Studije i Monografije) Originally presented as doctoral thesis at the Sorbonne, 1963.

MARKSISTSKO-leninskaia filosofiia. Moskva, 1967. 2 vols.

MOHL (ERNST THEODOR) and others. Folgen einer Theorie: Essays über "Das Kapital" von Karl Marx. Frankfurt am Main, Suhrkamp, 1967. pp. 205. bibliog. 17½cm.

OPITZ (HEINRICH) Philosophie und Praxis: eine Untersuchung zur Herausbildung des Marxschen Praxisbegriffs. Berlin, Dietz, 1967. pp. 184. 20cm.

PARNIUK (MIKHAIL ALEKSEEVICH) Determinizm dialekticheskogo materializma. Kiev, 1967. pp. 260.

PŁUŻAŃSKI (TADEUSZ) Marksizm a fenomen Teilharda. Warszawa, Książka i Wiedza, 1967. pp. 311. bibliog. 19½cm.

PROBLEMY formirovaniia nauchnogo mirovozzreniia: sbornik statei. Riga, 1967. pp. 318. Articles in Russian or Latvian.

PROTIV fal'sifikatorov marksistsko-leninskoi filosofii: sbornik statei. Moskva, 1967. pp. 160.

RAZVITIE revoliutsionnoi teorii Kommunisticheskoi partiei Sovetskogo Soiuza. Moskva, 1967. pp. 455.

REZNIKOV (ANDREI ILLARIONOVICH) Роль теоретического наследия В. И. Ленина в борьбе за марксистскую философию против идеализма. Харьков, 1967. pp. 240.

SBORNIK... Сборник материалов 2-й научной сессии вузов центрально-черноземной зоны: философские зоны. Воронеж, 1967. pp. 232.

VITA (ROBERTO) Uomini e macchine nel Capitale di Marx, 1867-1967. Torino, Contessa, [1967]. pp. 280. 21cm. (Collana Aletheia.)

1968

BUHR (MANFRED) and IRRLITZ (GERD) Der Anspruch der Vernunft: die klassische bürgerliche deutsche Philosophie als theoretische Quelle des Marxismus. Berlin, 1968 in progress. With summaries in French, English and Russian.

BRITISH AND IRISH COMMUNIST ORGANISATION. On Stalin's 'Economic problems'. [Belfast, 1968-69]. 2 pts. (in 1).

ADELMANN (FREDERICK J.) From dialogue to epilogue: Marxism and Catholicism tomorrow. The Hague, Nijhoff, 1968. pp. (x), 89. bibliog. 23½cm.

ANDREW (EDWARD) Marx and the social nature of man: the role of economic exchange in human relationships; [Ph. D. (London) thesis]. 1968. fo. (iv), 363. bibliog. 30cm. Typescript: unpublished. This thesis is the property of London University and may not be removed from the Library.

BEYER (WILHELM RAIMUND) Tendenzen bundesdeutscher Marx-Beschäftigung. Köln, [1968]. pp. 151.

BLOCH (ERNST) Über Karl Marx. Frankfurt a.M., Suhrkamp, 1968. pp. 178. bibliog. 17½cm.

BOAVENTURA (JORGE) Marxismo: alvorada ou crepúsculo? Rio de Janeiro, 1968. pp. 189.

BRAUNREUTHER (KURT) Soziologische Gesichtspunkte sozialstruktureller Studien: eine Erörterung... im entwickelten System der sozialistischen Gesellschaft. Berlin, 1968. pp. 38. (Deutsche Akademie der Wissenschaften zu Berlin. Sitzungsberichte. 1968. Nr.8)

BREUER (GEORG) Kann der Weltuntergang verhindert werden?: Marxismus im Atomzeitalter. Wien, [1968]. pp. 147.

CHAGIN (BORIS ALEKSANDROVICH) Субъективный фактор: структура и закономерности. Москва, Мысль, 1968. pp. 218. 19½см.

COFRANCESCO (DINO) Appunti sull'ideologia: marxismo e libertà. Milano, [1968]. pp. 255.

CONDE SALGADO (REMIGIO) Sociedad, estado y derecho en la filosofía marxista. Madrid, Cuadernos para el Diálogo, 1968. pp. 232. bibliog. 18½cm. (Divulgación Universitaria. No. 2)

CORNFORTH (MAURICE CAMPBELL) The open philosophy and the open society: a reply to Dr. Karl Popper's refutations of marxism. London, Lawrence and Wishart, 1968. pp. 396. 21½cm.

DE GEORGE (RICHARD T.) The new marxism: Soviet and East European marxism since 1956. New York, [1968]. pp. 170. bibliog.

EN partant du "Capital"; (préparé et présenté par Victor Fay). Paris, [1968]. pp. 333.

FILOSOFIIA i sovremennost'. Moskva, 1971. pp. 375. Soviet contributions to the 14th International Congress of Philosophy, 1968.

FRANKFURT AM MAIN. Universität. Institut für Politikwissenschaft and EUROPAEISCHE VERLAGSANSTALT. Frankfurter Colloquium, 1967. Kritik der politischen Ökonomie heute: 100 Jahre "Kapital"; Referate und Diskussionen...herausgegeben von Walter Euchner und Alfred Schmidt. Frankfurt a. M., Europäische Verlagsanstalt, [1968]. pp. 359. 20½cm. (Politische Ökonomie, Geschichte und Kritik)

FRITSCH (BRUNO) Die Geld- und Kredittheorie von Karl Marx: eine Darstellung und kritische Würdigung. 2nd ed. Frankfurt, Europäische Verlagsanstalt, [1968]. pp. 183. bibliog. 21cm. (Politische Ökonomie, Geschichte und Kritik)

GIRARDI (GIULIO) Marxism and Christianity...; translated by Kevin Traynor. Dublin, Gill, 1968. pp. xi, 267. 20cm. (Logos Books)

MARXISM (Cont'd.)

GIRARDI (GIULIO) Marxisme et Christianisme; ...traduit de l'Italien. Paris, Desclée, [1968]. pp. 316. 20½cm. (L'Athéisme Interrogé)

GUICHARD (JEAN) Le marxisme de Marx à Mao: théorie et pratique de la révolution. [Lyon], Chronique Sociale de France, [1968]. pp. 312. bibliog. 22cm.

GULIAN (C.I.) Le marxisme devant l'homme: essai d'anthropologie philosophique; traduit du roumain par Jean Herdan. Paris, Payot, 1968. pp. 222. 23cm. (Bibliothèque Scientifique)

HAHN (ERICH) Historischer Materialismus und marxistische Soziologie: Studien zu methodologischen und erkenntnistheoretischen Grundlagen der soziologischen Forschung. Berlin, 1968. pp. 273.

HISTORICAL materialism: basic problems; Russian text edited by G. Glezerman and G. Kursanov; [translated from the Russian, edited by David Fidlon, written by G. Glezerman and others]. Moscow, Progress, [1968]. pp. 333. 20cm.

HOERZ (HERBERT) Physik und Weltanschauung: Standpunkte der marxistischen Philosophie zur Entwicklung der Physik. Leipzig, 1968. pp. 132.

HOERZ (HERBERT) and GRIESE (ANNELIESE) Philosophie und Naturwissenschaft: neue Aspekte im Verhältnis von Naturwissenschaft und marxistisch-leninistischer Philosophie, erläutert am Raum-Zeit-Problem. Berlin, 1968. pp. 109.

IAKHOT (O.) Qu'est-ce que le matérialisme dialectique? Moscou, Éditions du Progrès, [1968?]. pp. 302. 17½cm. (Essais et Documents)

IDEMITSU (SAZO) If Karl Marx had been born in Japan. n.p., [1968?]. pp. (v), 140. 25½cm.

INTER NATIONES E.V. Karl Marx 1818/1968; [by Golo Mann and others]. Bad Godesberg, 1968. pp. 263. bibliog.

IVIN (DANIEL) Revolution und Evolution in Jugoslawien. Bern, [1968]. pp. 80. (Schweizerisches Ost-Institut. Tatsachen und Meinungen. TM 3)

IZ... Из истории марксистско-ленинской философии в Узбекистане. Ташкент, Фан, 1968. pp. 159. 21см.

JAHN (WOLFGANG) Director of the Institut für Marxismus-Leninismus of The University of Halle. Das Kapital und wir. Halle, 1968. pp. 211. (Halle. Universität. Wissenschaftliche Beiträge. 1968/2 (A6))

"KAPITAL"... "Капитал" Маркса, философия и современность. Москва, 1968. pp. 759.

"Das KAPITAL" von Karl Marx und seine internationale Wirkung; Beiträge ausländischer Teilnehmer an der wissenschaftlichen Session "100 Jahre Das Kapital", veranstaltet vom ZK der SED...1967 in Berlin. Berlin, Dietz, 1968. pp. 382. 20cm.

KLASSEN und Klassenkampf heute: Beiträge zu einer internationalen wissenschaftlichen Konferenz zum 150. Geburtstag von Karl Marx... 1968 in Frankfurt/Main. Frankfurt am Main, 1968. pp. 212. (Marxistische Blätter. Sonderhefte. 1968, 2)

KOŁAKOWSKI (LESZEK) Toward a Marxist humanism: essays on the left today; translated from the Polish by Jane Zielonko Peel. New York, [1968]. pp. 220.

KUMPF (FRITZ) Probleme der Dialektik in Lenins Imperialismus-Analyse: eine Studie zur dialektischen Logik. Berlin, 1968. pp. 212.

LEFEBVRE (HENRI) Dialectical materialism; ... translated from the French by John Sturrock. London, Cape, 1968. pp. 170. bibliog. 18cm. (Cape Editions. 27)

LEFEBVRE (HENRI) L'irruption de Nanterre au sommet. Paris, Anthropos, [1968]. pp. 177. 19cm. (Sociologie et Révolution)

LEFEBVRE (HENRI) Le marxisme. 12th ed. Paris, P.U.F., 1968. pp. 128. bibliog. 17½cm. (Que Sais-Je? No. 300)

LEONT'EV (LEV ABRAMOVICH) "Капитал" К. Маркса и современная эпоха. Москва, 1968. pp. 398.

LEONT'EV (LEV ABRAMOVICH) A short course of political economy; [translated from the Russian by Don Danemanis] Moscow, Progress Publishers, 1968. pp. 415. 20cm.

LIZZIO (MARIA) Marxismo e metafisica: riflessioni sul pensiero di Ugo Spirito. Catania, [1968]. pp. 365.

LOJACONO (GIORGIO) L'ideologia marxista. Roma, [1968]. 3 vols.

MANDEL (ERNEST) Entstehung und Entwicklung der ökonomischen Lehre von Karl Marx, 1843-1863. Frankfurt, [1968]. pp. 224. bibliog.

MANDEL (ERNEST) An introduction to marxist economic theory. New York, 1968. pp. 78.

MANDEL (ERNEST) Marxist economic theory. London, Merlin P., 1968. 2 vols. bibliog. 21½cm.

MARKS i sovremennost'. Moskva, 1968. pp. 591.

MARKSIZM-LENINIZM... Марксизм-ленинизм о войне и армии. 5th ed. Москва, Воениздат, 1968. pp. 391. 21см.

[MARX (KARL) and ENGELS (FRIEDRICH)] Marxist social thought; edited by Robert Freedman. New York, Harcourt, [1968]. pp. xxxiv, 347. bibliog. 20cm (Harvest Books. 137)

MARXISM and Christianity: a symposium; edited by Herbert Aptheker. New York, [1968]. pp. 240. bibliog. (American Institute for Marxist Studies. Monograph Series. No. 3)

MARXISMUS in unserer Zeit: Beiträge zum zeitgenössischen Marxismus, veröffentlicht zum 150. Geburtstag von Karl Marx am 5. Mai 1968. Frankfurt a.M., [1968]. pp. 232. (Marxistische Blätter. Sonderhefte. 1, 1968)

MARXISTES et chretiens: entretiens de Salzbourg; traduit de l'allemand par Michel Louis. Paris, Mame, [1968]. pp. 366. 21½cm.

MARXISTISCHE Beiträge zur Rechtsgeschichte. Berlin, 1968. pp. 236. (Berlin. Humboldt-Universität. Wissenschaftliche Schriftenreihe)

MESTRE (MICHELE) Pour une histoire antique de la philosophie marxiste. Paris, [1968]. pp. 68.

MOMDZHIAN (KH. N.) The dynamic twentieth century; [translated from the Russian by Vic Schneierson]. Moscow, [1968]. pp. 302.

NOVA (FRITZ) Friedrich Engels: his contribution to political theory. London, Vision, 1968. pp. xxiii, 115. bibliog. 21½cm.

OCHERKI... Очерки истории идейной борьбы вокруг "Капитала" К. Маркса, 1867-1967. Москва, 1968. pp. 294.

OCHERKI... Очерки истории марксистско-ленинской философии в Белоруссии, 1919-1968. Минск, Наука и Техника, 1968. pp. 278. 19½см.

RAGIONIERI (ERNESTO) Il marxismo e l'Internazionale: studi di storia del marxismo. Roma, Editori Riuniti, 1968. pp. xii, 310. 21½cm. (Biblioteca di Storia. 16)

RAPP (FRIEDRICH) Gesetz und Determination in der Sowjetphilosophie: zur Gesetzeskonzeption des dialektischen Materialismus unter besonderer Berücksichtigung der Diskussion über dynamische und statistische Gesetzmässigkeit in der zeitgenössischen Sowjetphilosophie. Dordrecht, Reidel, [1968]. pp. xi, 174. bibliog. 22½cm. (Freiburg (Switzerland). Universität. Ost-Europa Institut. Sovietica)

SAVAGE (KATHERINE) Marxism and communism. London, Bodley Head, 1968. pp. 165. bibliog. 19½cm.

SCALIGERO (MASSIMO) Hegel, Marcuse, Mao: marxismo o rivoluzione? Roma, 1968. pp. 89.

SCARPELLI (UBERTO) Esistenzialismo e marxismo: saggio sulla giustizia. 3rd ed. Torino, 1968. pp. 124.

SKRZYPCZAK (HENRYK) Marx: Engels: Revolution: Standortbestimmung des Marxismus der Gegenwart. Berlin, Colloquium Verlag, [1968]. pp. 122. 21cm.

STALIN (IOSIF VISSARIONOVICH) Concerning marxism in linguistics: facsimile of a work originally published in 1950 with a new preface]. [Belfast, 1968]. pp. 40.

STIEHLER (GOTTFRIED) Dialektik und Praxis: Untersuchungen zur "tätigen Seite" in der vormarxistischen und marxistischen Philosophie. Berlin, Academie-Verlag, 1968. pp. 332.

TUGARINOV (VASILII PETROVICH) Теория ценности в марксизме. Ленинград, 1968. pp. 124. bibliog.

ULBRICHT (WALTER) Die Bedeutung und die Lebenskraft der Lehren von Karl Marx für unsere Zeit. Berlin, 1968. pp. 74.

VACATELLO (MARZIO) Lukács da Storia e coscienza di classe al giudizio sulla cultura borghese. Firenze, La Nuova Italia, 1968. pp. viii, 157. 21cm. (Maestri e Compagni. Biblioteca di Studi Critici e Morali. 33)

VARGA (JENÖ) Politico-economic problems of capitalism; (translated from the Russian). Moscow, Progress Publishers, 1968. pp. 351. 20cm.

ZELENÝ (JINDRICH) Die Wissenschaftslogik bei Marx und Das Kapital; (nach der...tschechischen Originalausgabe übertragen). Frankfurt, [1968]. pp. 332. bibliog.

1969

KLEIN (MATTHAEUS) and others. Zur Geschichte der marxistisch-leninistischen Philosophie in Deutschland. Berlin, 1969 in progress.

ACTUEEL marxisme: (teksten en discussieverslagen, behorende bij de algemene ledenvergadering van het Thijmgenootschap...gehouden te Nijmegen op 10 mei 1969); [by] W. van Dooren [and others].

ADELMANN (FREDERICK J.) ed. Demythologizing marxism: a series of studies on marxism. Chestnut Hill, 1969. pp. 240. bibliog. (Boston College. Studies in Philosophy. vol. 2)

ALTHUSSER (LOUIS) For Marx; translated by Ben Brewster. London, 1969. pp. 272.

ARANGUREN (JOSÉ LUIS L.) Le marxisme comme morale; traduction par André Serres. Toulouse, [1969]. pp. 109.

ARON (RAYMOND) D'une Sainte Famille à l'autre: essais sur les marxismes imaginaires. [Paris] Gallimard, [1969]. pp. 309. 18½cm. (Les Essais. 146)

ARON (RAYMOND) Marxism and the existentialists. New York, [1969]. pp. 176.

BAGIROV (Z. N.) V. I. Lenin i dialekticheskoe ponimanie otritsaniia. Baku, 1969. pp. 221.

BARAN (PAUL A.) The longer view: essays toward a critique of political economy; edited...by John O'Neill. New York, [1969]. pp. 444.

BARKAT (ANWAR) Ideology in the modern world: a Christian questioning of marxism and maoism. Tokyo, [1969]. pp. 35. (World Student Christian Federation. Asia Study Fellowship Series. No. 6)

BERGER (PETER L.) ed. Marxism and sociology: views from Eastern Europe. New York, [1969]. pp. 246.

BERNSTEIN (EDUARD) Die Voraussetzungen des Sozialismus und die Aufgaben der Sozialdemokratie; herausgegeben von Günther Hillmann. 2nd ed. Reinbek, 1969. pp. 250. bibliog.

BROGNARD (ANTOINE) Lutte de classe et morale marxiste. Paris, [1969]. pp. 392.

CARRÈRE D'ENCAUSSE (HÉLÈNE) and SCHRAM (STUART R.) eds. Marxism and Asia: an introduction with readings; (translation [from the French] with additions). London, 1969. pp. 404. bibliog.

MARXISM (Cont'd.)

Le CENTENAIRE du "Capital": exposés et entretiens sur le marxisme; [centenary celebrations sponsored by the Centre Culturel and held in July 1967]. Paris, 1969. pp. 341. (Centre Culturel International de Cerisy-la-Salle. Décades. Nouvelle Série. 10)

COLLETTI (LUCIO) Ideologia e società. Bari, 1969. pp. 321.

COLLETTI (LUCIO) Il marxismo e Hegel. Bari, 1969. pp. 437.

DAHM (HELMUT) Meuterei auf den Knien: die Krise des marxistischen Welt- und Menschenbildes. Olten, 1969. pp. 208. bibliogs.

DEVILLERS (PHILIPPE) Mao;...translated [from the German] by Tony White. London, Macdonald, 1969. pp. 317. 21½cm. (What They Really Said Series)

DOMMANGET (MAURICE) L'introduction du marxisme en France. Lausanne, [1969]. pp. 232.

FEUER (LEWIS SAMUEL) Marx and the intellectuals: a set of post-ideological essays. Garden City, N.Y., 1969. pp. 301. Originally published in various periodicals between 1948 and 1968.

FLAM (LEOPOLD) Démocratie et marxisme. Bruxelles, [1969]. pp. 193.

FLEISCHER (HELMUT) Marxismus und Geschichte. Frankfurt a. M., 1969. pp. 168.

FRANTSUZOVA (NADEZHDA PAVLOVNA) Marksistsko-leninskaia filosofiia - metodologiia estestvennykh i obshchestvennykh nauk. Moskva, 1969. pp. 93.

FURMAN (ALEKSEI EVGEN'EVICH) Материалистическая диалектика: основные категории и законы. Москва, 1969. pp. 221.

GANDHI (MADAN G.) Gandhi and Marx: study in ideological polarities. Chandigarh, [1969]. pp. 132. bibliog.

GARAUDY (ROGER) Perspectives de l'homme: existentialisme, pensée catholique, structuralisme, marxisme. 4th ed. Paris, 1969. pp. 435.

GEFTER (M.IA.) Страница из истории марксизма начала XX века. in Историческая наука и некоторые проблемы современности. Москва, 1969.

GEORGIEV (F. I.) and PETROVICHEVA (L. F. Problema protivorechiia. Moskva, 1969. pp. 212.

GOERLICH (J. WOLFGANG) Semantik und dialektischer Materialismus: Darstellung und Analyse der modernen marxistisch-leninistischen Wissenschaftstheorie in der DDR. Berlin, 1969. pp. 174. (Berlin. Freie Universität. Osteuropa-Institut. Philosophische und Soziologische Veröffentlichungen. Band 10)

GRIESE (ANNELIESE) and LAITKO (HUBERT) eds. Weltanschauung und Methode: (philosophische Beiträge zur Einheit von Natur- und Gesellschaftswissenschaften). Berlin, 1969. pp. 249. bibliog.

GRITSENKO (IVAN IVANOVICH) Istoricheskoe i logicheskoe v marksistskoi filosofii. Rostov-na-Donu, 1969. pp. 153.

GRUJIĆ (PREDRAG M.) Hegel und die Sowjetphilosophie der Gegenwart: zur materialistischen Dialektik. Bern, [1969]. pp. 97. bibliog.

GUERIN (DANIEL) Pour un marxisme libertaire. [Paris, 1969]. pp. 295.

HELMS (HANS G.) Fetisch Revolution: Marxismus und Bundesrepublik. Neuwied, [1969]. pp. 205. bibliog.

IOVCHUK (MIKHAIL TRIFONOVICH) and others, eds. Краткий очерк истории философии. 2nd ed. Москва, 1969. pp. 789.

KAMENKA (EUGENE) Marxism and ethics. London, Macmillan, 1969. pp. viii, 72. bibliog. 21½cm. (New Studies in Ethics)

KHRESTOMATIIA... Хрестоматия по научному коммунизму. Москва, 1969. pp. 494.

KIM (GEORGII FEDOROVICH) and KAUFMAN (ARKADII SERGEEVICH) Ленинизм и национально-освободительное движение. Москва, 1969. pp. 286.

KIRSCHENMANN (PETER) Kybernetik, Information, Widerspiegelung: Darstellung einiger philosophischer Probleme im dialektischen Materialismus. München, [1969]. pp. 311. bibliog.

KLIUCHNYKOV (VALENTYN PAVLOVYCH) Metodolohichni osnovy krytyky V. I. Leninym idealizmu. Kyïv, 1969. pp. 202.

KOŁAKOWSKI (LESZEK) Marxism and beyond: on historical understanding and individual responsibility; translated by Jane Zielonko Peel. London, [1969]. pp. 240.

KOPNIN (PAVEL VASIL'EVICH) В. И. Ленин и материалистическая диалектика. Киев, 1969. pp. 194.

KUENZLI (ARNOLD) Über Marx hinaus: Beiträge zur Ideologiekritik. Freiburg, [1969]. pp. 206. bibliog.

KURYLEV (ANATOLII KONSTANTINOVICH) and others, eds. Osnovy nauchnogo kommunizma: metodicheskoe posobie dlia prepodavatelei vuzov. Moskva, 1969. pp. 460.

LEFEBVRE (HENRI) The explosion: marxism and the French revolution; (translated from the French by Alfred Ehrenfeld). New York, Monthly Review, [1969]. pp. 157. 20½cm.

LEFF (GORDON) The tyranny of concepts: a critique of marxism. 2nd ed. London, 1969. pp. 256.

LEONT'EV (LEV ABRAMOVICH) Ленинская теория империализма. Москва, 1969. pp. 549.

MACINTYRE (ALASDAIR CHALMERS) Marxism and Christianity [rev. ed.] London, Duckworth, 1969. pp. xi, 143. 20½cm.

McLELLAN (DAVID) of the University of Kent. The young Hegelians and Karl Marx. London, Macmillan, 1969. pp. ix, 170. bibliogs. 21½cm.

MAKHNOVETS (VLADIMIR PETROVICH) Vladimir Akimov on the dilemmas of Russian Marxism, 1895-1903: The second congress of the Russian Social Democratic Labour Party; A short history of the Social Democratic Movement in Russia; two texts in translation, translated, edited, and introduced by Jonathan Frankel. London, C.U.P., 1969. pp. x, 390. bibliog. 21½cm. (Cambridge Studies in the History and Theory of Politics)

MANDEL (ERNEST) The inconsistencies of "state-capitalism". London, 1969. pp.25.

MANDEL (ERNEST) The Marxist theory of the state. New York, [1969]. pp. 31.

MAREK (FRANZ) Philosophy of world revolution: a contribution to an anthology of theories of revolution. London, Lawrence & Wishart, 1969. pp. 138. 20cm.

MARXISME et petite bourgeoisie. Paris, 1969. pp. 60.

MATTICK (PAUL) Marx and Keynes: the limits of the mixed economy. Boston, Mass., [1969]. pp. 364. bibliog.

MOLNÁR (ERIK) Válogatott tanulmányok. Budapest, 1969. pp. 519. bibliog.

MONNEROT (JULES) Sociologie de la révolution: mythologies politiques du 20e siècle Marxistes-léninistes et fascistes; la nouvelle stratégie révolutionnaire. [Paris, 1969]. pp. 772.

NELL-BREUNING (OSWALD VON) Auseinandersetzung mit Karl Marx. München, 1969. pp. 90.

NOVACK (GEORGE) An introduction to the logic of Marxism. 5th ed. New York, [1969]. pp. 144.

PASSALACQUA (GIUSEPPE) Marx giovane a Praga: citati; Rosa Luxemburg [and others]. Roma, [1969?]. pp. 59.

PENTZLIN (KURT) Marxisten überwinden Marx. Wien, 1969. pp.138.

PLEKHANOV (GEORGII VALENTINOVICH) Fundamental problems of Marxism; with an appendix of his essays, The materialist conception of history, and The role of the individual in history. London, 1969. pp. 190.

POMEROY (WILLIAM J.) ed. Guerrilla warfare and marxism: a collection of writings from Karl Marx to the present on armed struggles for liberation and for socialism. London, Lawrence & Wishart, 1969. pp. 336. 20½cm.

POST (WERNER) Kritik der Religion bei Karl Marx. München, [1969]. pp. 327. bibliog.

RAZVITIE... Развитие В. И. Лениным экономической теории социализма и коммунизма. Москва, 1969. pp. 413.

REDLOW (GOETZ) Weltanschauung in den Kämpfen unserer Tage. Berlin, 1969. pp. 90.

REIPRICH (KURT) Die philosophisch-naturwissenschaftlichen Arbeiten von Karl Marx und Friedrich Engels. Berlin, 1969. pp. 144.

ROUX (JEAN) Précis historique et théorique de marxisme - léninisme. Paris, [1969]. pp. 398. bibliogs.

ROZENTAL' (M. M.) ed. Ленин как философ. Москва, 1969. pp. 447.

SCHACK (HERBERT) Marx, Mao, Neomarxismus: Wandlungen einer Ideologie. Frankfurt am Main, [1969]. pp. 231.

SCHMIDT (ALFRED) of Frankfurt University, ed. Beiträge zur marxistischen Erkenntnistheorie:...Aufsätze von György Márkus [and others]. Frankfurt a.M., [1969]. pp. 264.

SCIENCE COUNCIL OF JAPAN. Division of Economics, Commerce and Business Administration. Economic Series. No. 45. Development of marxism and the contemporary age; by Fumio Moriya; [and] A study on the Ono-gumi; by Mataji Miyamoto. Tokyo, 1969. pp. 53.

SEVE (LUCIEN) Marxisme et théorie de la personnalité. Paris, [1969]. pp. 509.

SIEBER (ROLF) and RICHTER (HORST) Die Herausbildung der marxistischen politischen Ökonomie. Berlin, 1969. pp. 387.

SOFRI (GIANNI) Il modo di produzione asiatico: storia di una controversia marxista. Torino, [1969]. pp. 193.

SPRINGER (EGON) Marxismus-Leninismus und Gewerkschaften. Berlin, 1969. pp. 80.

STEIGERWALD (ROBERT REINHOLD) Herbert Marcuses dritter Weg. Köln, 1969. pp. 366. bibliog.

TELFORD (SHIRLEY) Economic and political peace. Portland, [1969]. pp. 224. bibliog.

TERRAY (EMMANUEL) Le marxisme devant les sociétés "primitives": deux études. Paris, Maspero, 1969. pp. 177. 21½cm. (Théorie, 5)

TIBI (BASSAM) ed. Die arabische Linke. Frankfurt am Main, [1969]. pp. 180. bibliog.

TOMBERG (FRIEDRICH) Basis und Überbau: sozialphilosophische Studien. Neuwied, [1969]. pp. 181.

TUCKER (ROBERT CHARLES) The Marxian revolutionary idea. London, 1970. pp. 240. bibliog.

TUSHUNOV (ANATOLII VASIL'EVICH) "Теории прибавочной стоимости" (IV том "Капитала") и их место в экономическом учении К. Маркса. Москва, 1969. pp. 221.

V... В. І. Ленін і критика буржуазної ідеології. Київ, 1969. - pp. 244.

V... В. И. Ленин и проблемы научного коммунизма. Москва, 1969. pp. 498.

VACCA (GIUSEPPE) Marxismo e analisi sociale. Bari, 1969. pp. 315.

WELLMER (ALBRECHT) Kritische Gesellschaftstheorie und Positivismus. Frankfurt a.M., 1969. pp. 147.

WOLFE (BERTRAM DAVID) An ideology in power: reflections on the Russian revolution...; introduction by Leonard Schapiro. New York, [1969]. pp. 406.

MARXISM (Cont'd.)

1970

ADAMO (HANS) Antileninismus in der BRD;... Tendenzen, Inhalt und Methoden der Leninfälschung in der Bundesrepublik, etc. Frankfurt/Main, [1970]. pp. 85.

ALEKSANDROV (V. S.) and LASHIN (A. G.) eds. Razvitie V. I. Leninym teorii nauchnogo kommunizma. Moskva, 1970. pp. 427.

ARON (RAYMOND) Marxismes imaginaires: d'une sainte famille à l'autre. [Paris, 1970]. pp. 377.

ARVON (HENRI) L'esthétique marxiste. Paris, 1970. pp. 110. bibliog.

BABIN (A. I.) F. Engel's - vydaiushchiisia voennyi teoretik rabochego klassa. Moskva, 1970. pp. 319.

BALINKY (ALEXANDER) Marx's economics: origin and development. Lexington, Mass., [1970]. pp. 178. bibliog.

BALINKY (ALEXANDER) Marx's economics: origin and development. Lexington, Mass., [1970]. pp. 178. bibliog.

BANKS (JOSEPH AMBROSE) Marxist sociology in action: a sociological critique of the marxist approach to industrial relations. London, 1970. pp. 324.

BENOIST (JEAN MARIE) Marx est mort. Paris, [1970]. pp. 251.

BRÓDY (ANDRÁS) Proportions, prices and planning: a mathematical restatement of the labor theory of value. Budapest, 1970. pp. 194. bibliog.

BUDDHISM: the marxist approach; by Rahul Sankrityayan [and others]. Delhi, 1970. pp. 86.

CHAGIN (BORIS ALEKSANDROVICH) Сcздание и развитие К. Марксом и Ф. Энгельсом теории научного коммунизма. Ленинград, 1970. pp. 329.

CONQUEST (ROBERT) Where Marx went wrong. London, 1970. pp. 126. bibliog.

CONSTANTINESCU (MIRON) and LIVEANU (VASILE) Problems of history and of social theory. Bucharest, 1970. pp. 170. (Academia Republicii Socialiste România. Secţia di Stiinţe Istorice, Filozofice şi Economico-Juridice. Bibliotheca Historica Romaniae. Studies. 30)

ENGEL'S - teoretik. Moskva, 1970. pp. 455.

FAVRE (PIERRE) and FAVRE (MONIQUE) Les marxismes après Marx. Paris, 1970. pp. 128.

GARAUDY (ROGER) Marxism in the twentieth century; translated by René Hague. London, 1970. pp. 224.

GOLLWITZER (HELMUT) The Christian faith and the marxist criticism of religion;... translated [from the German] by David Cairns. Edinburgh, 1970. pp. 173.

GUIDUCCI (ROBERTO) Marx dopo Marx: dalla rivoluzione industriale alla rivoluzione del terziario avanzato. [Milan], 1970. pp. 275.

HELLER (ÁGNES) Alltag und Geschichte: zur sozialistischen Gesellschaftslehre. Neuwied, [1970]. pp. 119.

IOVCHUK (MIKHAIL TRIFONOVICH) Leninizm, filosofskie traditsii i sovremennost'. Moskva, 1970. pp. 334. bibliog.

IOVCHUK (MIKHAIL TRIFONOVICH) and MSHVENIERADZE (V. V.) eds. Leninizm i filosofskie problemy sovremennosti. Moskva, 1970. pp. 652.

KEDROV (BONIFATII MIKHAILOVICH) Engel's i dialektika estestvoznaniia. Moskva, 1970. pp. 470.

KIRSCHENMANN (PETER) Information and reflection: on some problems of cybernetics and how contemporary dialectical materialism copes with them; translated by T.J. Blakeley. Dordrecht, [1970]. pp. 225. bibliog.

KOFLER (LEO) Stalinismus und Bürokratie: zwei Aufsätze. Neuwied, 1970. pp. 182.

KOPNIN (PAVEL VASIL'EVICH) Dialektik, Logik, Erkenntnistheorie: Lenins philosophisches Denken; Erbe und Aktualität; [translated from the Russian]. Berlin, 1970. pp. 543. bibliog.

KORSCH (KARL) Marxism and philosophy: and other articles; translated from the German and edited by Fred Halliday. London, 1970. pp. 159.

LENIN und die Wissenschaft:...Beiträge zum 100. Geburtstag von W.I. Lenin. Berlin, 1970. 2 vols.

LENINIZM... Ленинизм и диалектика общественного развития. Москва, 1970. pp. 444.

LENINIZM i sovremennye problemy istoriko-filosofskoi nauki. Moskva, 1970. pp. 619.

LEONHARD (WOLFGANG) Die Dreispaltung des Marxismus: Ursprung und Entwicklung des Sowjetmarxismus, Maoismus und Reformkommunismus. Düsseldorf, 1970. pp. 575. bibliog.

LEONT'EV (LEV ABRAMOVICH) Engels und die ökonomische Lehre des Marxismus; [translation of the second Russian edition]; herausgegeben...von Fred Oelssner. Berlin, 1970. pp. 532.

LOEWENSTEIN (JULIUS I.) Vision und Wirklichkeit: Marx contra Marxismus. Basel, [1970]. pp. 170. (List Gesellschaft. Veröffentlichungen. Band 65)

LOOMIS (CHARLES PRICE) and RYTINA (JOAN HUBER) Marxist theory and Indian communism: a sociological interpretation. [East Lansing, 1970]. pp. 148.

MANDEL (ERNEST) Revolutionary strategy in the imperialist countries. New York, 1970. pp. 15.

MANDEL (ERNEST) and NOVACK (GEORGE) The Marxist theory of alienation. New York, [1970]. pp. 63.

MARK (A.A.) O probleme cheloveka v istorii filosofii: o sushchnosti revoliutsionnogo perevorota v filosofii. Khar'kov, 1970. pp. 188.

MARX (KARL) Economic and philosophic manuscripts of 1844;...edited with an introduction by Dirk J. Struik; translated by Martin Milligan. London, 1970. pp. 255.

MAUKE (MICHAEL) Die Klassentheorie von Marx und Engels;...herausgegeben von Kajo Heymann [and others]. Frankfurt am Main, [1970]. pp. 175.

MODRZHINSKAIA (ELENA DMITRIEVNA) Leninizm i sovremennaia ideologicheskaia bor'ba. Moskva, 1970. pp. 350.

MONNEROT (JULES) Démarxiser l'université. Paris, [1970]. pp. 179.

NATAF (ANDRE) Le marxisme et son ombre: Rosa Luxembourg. Paris, [1970]. pp. 204.

NIKISHOV (SERAFIM IVANOVICH) ed. V.I.Lenin i aktual'nye problemy istoricheskogo materializma. Moskva, 1970. pp. 317.

NIKOLAEV (PETR ALEKSEEVICH) Vozniknovenie marksistskogo literaturovedeniia v Rossii: metodologiia, problemy realizma. Moskva, 1970. pp. 310.

OKULOV (ALEKSANDR FEDOROVICH) Sovetskaia filosofskaia nauka i ee problemy: kratkii ocherk. Moskva, 1970. pp. 220. bibliog.

PARKINSON (GEORGE HENRY RADCLIFFE) ed. Georg Lukács: the man, his work and his ideas. London, [1970]. pp. 254. bibliog. (Reading. University. Graduate School of Contemporary European Studies. Studies on Contemporary Europe. 4.)

PASHUKANIS (EVGENII BRONISLAVOVICH) La théorie générale du droit et le marxisme. Paris, [1970]. pp. 173.

PIROSCHKOW (VERA) Freiheit und Notwendigkeit in der Geschichte: zur Kritik des historischen Materialismus. München, [1970]. pp. 316. bibliog.

POLEVOI (IU.Z.) F. Engel's i nachalo marksizma v Rossii. in Engel's i problemy istorii. Moskva, 1970.

RACHKOV (PETR ALEKSANDROVICH) and others, eds. O strukture marksistskoi sotsiologicheskoi teorii: materialy diskussii. Moskva, 1970. pp. 91.

RAZVITIE V.I. Leninym teorii nauchnogo kommunizma v period podgotovki i provedeniia Velikoi Oktiabr'skoi sotsialisticheskoi revoliutsii. Minsk, 1970. pp. 223.

RIECHERS (CHRISTIAN) Antonio Gramsci: Marxismus in Italien. Frankfurt am Main, [1970]. pp. 251. bibliog.

SANDKUEHLER (HANS JOERG) and VEGA (RAFAEL DE LA) eds. Austromarxismus: Texte zu Ideologie und Klassenkampf von Otto Bauer [and others]. Frankfurt am Main, [1970]. pp. 410. bibliog.

SCHAFF (ADAM) Marxism and the human individual;... based on a translation by Olgierd Wojtasiewicz. New York, [1970]. pp. 268.

SHEPTULIN (ALEKSANDR PETROVICH) Filosofiia marksizma-leninizma. Moskva, 1970. pp. 384.

SIJES (B.A.) Enkele marxistische opvattingen betreffende de verovering van de politieke macht in de laatste zeventig jaar. Assen, 1970. pp. 34.

SILBER (IRWIN) The cultural revolution: a Marxist analysis. New York, [1970]. pp. 62.

SOHN-RETHEL (ALFRED) Geistige und körperliche Arbeit: zur Theorie der gesellschaftlichen Synthesis. Frankfurt am Main, 1970. pp. 212.

SOUYRI (PIERRE) Le marxisme après Marx. [Paris, 1970]. pp. 122. bibliog

SOVREMENNYE problemy teorii poznaniia dialekticheskogo materializma. Moskva, 1970. 2 vols.

STRUCTURALISME et marxisme; [by] Jean-Marie Auzias [and others]. [Paris, 1970]. pp. 317.

TEORIIA, preobrazuiushchaia mir: v pomoshch' izuchaiushchim marksizm-leninizm. Minsk, 1970. pp. 331. bibliog.

TORDAI (ZÁDOR) Az elidegenedés mítosza és valósága. Budapest, 1970. pp. 305.

V. I. Lenin i problemy filosofskikh nauk i nauchnogo kommunizma. Leningrad, 1970. pp. 163.

V... В. И. Ленин - великий теоретик. 2nd ed. Москва, 1970. pp. 468.

VOPROSY filosofskogo naslediia V.I.Lenina. Moskva, 1970. pp. 212.

VOPROSY filosofskogo naslediia V.I. Lenina. Riga, 1970. pp. 219. bibliog. (Latviiskii Gosudarstvennyi Universitet. Uchenye Zapiski. t.131)

1971

ALTHUSSER (LOUIS) Lenin and philosophy, and other essays; translated from the French by Ben Brewster. London, 1971. pp. 229.

APPEL (GOTFRED) Class struggle and revolutionary situation. [Copenhagen?], 1971. pp. 36.

APPEL (GOTFRED) There will come a day: imperialism and the working class. [Copenhagen?], 1971. pp. 31.

ARON (ROBERT) Le socialisme français face au marxisme. Paris, [1971]. pp. 280. bibliog.

BLOCH (ERNST) On Karl Marx; (translated by John Maxwell). New York, 1971. pp. 173.

BOECKELMANN (FRANK) Die schlechte Aufhebung der autoritären Persönlichkeit. München, 1971. pp. 107.

CARDAN (PAUL) History and revolution: a revolutionary critique of historical materialism. Bromley, 1971. pp. 35. (Solidarity: [for workers' power]. Pamphlets. No. 38)

DAHRENDORF (RALF) Die Idee des Gerechten im Denken von Karl Marx. 2nd ed. Hannover, [1971]. pp. 186. bibliog. (Friedrich-Ebert-Stiftung. Forschungsinstitut. Schriftenreihe. Band 80)

MARXISM (Cont'd.)

FIKENTSCHER (WOLFGANG) Zur politischen Kritik an Marxismus und Neomarxismus als ideologische Grundlagen der Studentenunruhen 1965/69. Tübingen, 1971. pp. 62.

GRAMSCI (ANTONIO) Selections from the prison notebooks...; edited and translated by Quintin Hoare and Geoffrey Nowell Smith. London, 1971. pp. 483.

ISTORIIA marksistskoi dialektiki: ot vozniknoveniia marksizma do leninskogo etapa. Moskva, 1971. pp. 536.

KHYDYROV (TESHLI) Rasprostranenie idei marksizma-leninizma v dooktiabr'skom Turkmenistane, 1900-1917 gg.; pod redaktsiei... G.O. Muradovoi i I.L. Sosonkina. Ashkhabad, 1971. pp. 235.

KOMMUNISTICHESKAIA PARTIIA SOVETSKOGO SOIUZA. Tsentral'nyi Komitet. Vysshaia Partiinaia Shkola. Lektsii po nauchnomu kommunizmu: materialy kursov perepodgotovki rukovodiashchikh partiinykh i sovetskikh kadrov v vysshei partiinoi shkole pri TsK KPSS. Moskva, 1971. pp. 264.

KORNEEVA (ANNA IVANOVNA) Leninskaia kritika makhizma i bor'ba protiv sovremennogo idealizma. Moskva, 1971. pp. 239.

KORSCH (KARL) Die materialistische Geschichtsauffassung und andere Schriften: [selected reprints of writings originally published 1924-1932]; herausgegeben von Erich Gerlach. Frankfurt am Main, [1971]. pp. 181.

KORSCH (KARL) Three essays on marxism. London, 1971. pp. 71.

LICHTHEIM (GEORGE) From Marx to Hegel and other essays. London, 1971. pp. 248.

LUKÁCS (GEORG) Marxist. History and class consciousness: studies in Marxist dialectics; translated by Rodney Livingstone. London, [1971]. pp. 356.

LUXEMBURG (ROSA) Selected political writings of Rosa Luxemburg; edited and introduced by Dick Howard. New York, [1971]. pp. 441.

MACINTYRE (ALASDAIR CHALMERS) Against the self-images of the age: essays on ideology and philosophy. London, 1971. pp. 284.

PANTSKHAVA (IL'IA DIOMIDOVICH) and PAKHOMOV (BORIS IAKOVLEVICH) Dialekticheskii materializm v svete sovremennoi nauki. Moskva, 1971. pp. 262.

SCHMIDT (ALFRED) 1931- The concept of nature in Marx. London, 1971. pp. 251. bibliog.

STIEHLER (GOTTFRIED) System und Widerspruch: zur Dialektik in der sozialistischen Gesellschaft. Berlin, 1971. pp. 119.

THERBORN (GÖRAN) Klasser och ekonomiska system, etc. [Lund], 1971. pp. 328. bibliogs.

- Bibliography

KLYKOVA (S. M.) compiler. Критика буржуазной и реформистской философии и социологии эпохи империализма: советская литература на русском языке, опубликованная в 1956-1965 гг. Москва, Наука, 1967. pp. 156. 21½cm.

LACHS (JOHN) Marxist philosophy: a bibliographical guide. Chapel Hill, U. of North Carolina P., [1967]. pp. xiv, 166. 21½cm.

LEVIN (L.A.) Библиография произведений основоположников марксизма-ленинизма в СССР. in Вопросы библиографии общественно-политической литературы. Москва, 1967.

MUNBY (LIONEL M.) and WANGERMANN (ERNST) eds. Marxism and history: a bibliography of English language works. London, Lawrence and Wishart, 1967. pp. (v), 62. 24cm.

BAXANDALL (LEE) compiler. Marxism and aesthetics: a selective annotated bibliography; books and articles in the English language. New York, Humanities P., 1968. pp. xxii, 261. bibliog. 27½cm. (American Institute for Marxist Studies. Bibliographical Series. No. 4)

- Dictionaries and encyclopaedias

WOERTERBUCH der marxistisch-leninistischen Soziologie; herausgegeben von Wolfgang Eichhorn [and others]. Köln, 1969. pp. 535.

- Historiography

CARRERA DAMAS (GERMÁN) Historiografía marxista venezolana y otros temas. Caracas, Universidad Central de Venezuela, Dirección de Cultura, 1967. pp. 159. 23cm. (Colección Humanismo y Ciencia. 3)

- Study and teaching

KEDROV (BONIFATII MIKHAILOVICH) Как изучать книгу В. И. Ленина "Материализм и эмпириокритицизм". 2nd ed. Москва, Политиздат, 1965. pp. 200. 20cm.

- Terminology

GOULD (L. HARRY) Marxist glossary and philosophical dictionary. 4th ed. Sydney, Current Book Distributors, 1967. pp. 101. 21cm.

MARXIST-LENINIST ORGANISATION OF BRITAIN

MARXIST-LENINIST ORGANISATION OF BRITAIN. Programmatic manifesto of the Marxist-Leninist organisation of Britain. [London, 1968]. pp. 64.

MARY, Queen of Scots

FRASER (Lady ANTONIA) Mary Queen of Scots. London, Weidenfeld & Nicolson, [1969]. pp. xv, 613. bibliog. 24cm.

MARYLAND

- Politics and government

CALLCOTT (MARGARET LAW) The negro in Maryland politics, 1870-1912. Baltimore, [1969]. pp. xv, 199. bibliog. (Johns Hopkins University. Studies in Historical and Political Science. Series 87. [No.] 1)

MARYLAND (LIBERIA)

- History

EASTMEN (ERNEST) A history of the state of Maryland in Liberia. Monrovia, Bureau of Information, Department of State, [1956]. pp. 108. bibliog. 21½cm.

MASARYK (JAN)

MASARYK (JAN) Volá Londýn. Praha, 1946. pp. 316.

MASARYK (THOMAS GARRIGUE)

MASARYK (THOMAS GARRIGUE) Světová revoluce, za války a ve válce, 1914-1918: vzpomíná a uvažuje. Praha, Orbis, 1925. pp. 650. 20cm.

MASARYK (THOMAS GARRIGUE) Die Weltrevolution: Erinnerungen und Betrachtungen, 1914-1918. Berlin, Reiss, 1925. pp. xviii, 556. 22½cm.

RYCHNOVSKY (ERNST) Masaryk. Prag, Staatliche Verlagsanstalt, [1930]. pp. 338. bibliog.

SOUKUP (FRANTIŠEK) T. G. Masaryk jako politický průkopník, sociální reformátor a president státu. Praha, 1930. pp. 380.

NANI (UMBERTO) T.G. Masaryk e l'unità cecoslovacca. Milano, Treves, 1931. pp. xi,246. bibliog. 21cm. (Biblioteca di Cultura Politica. 12)

RYCHNOVSKY (ERNST) and others, eds. Masaryk a židovství, etc. Praha, 1931. pp. 333.

MASARYK (THOMAS GARRIGUE) Otázka sociální: základy marxismu, filosofické a sociologické. Praha, 1936. 2 vols. (Spisy T. G. Masaryka. kn.6, 7)

BIRLEY (Sir ROBERT) Thomas Masaryk:...a centenary address given at the School of Slavonic and East European Studies on 7 March, 1950. London, 1951. pp. 17.

MASCARENE ISLANDS

- Commerce

TOUSSAINT (AUGUSTE) La route des îles: contribution à l'histoire maritime des Mascareignes. Paris, S.E.V.P.E.N., 1967. pp. 540. bibliog. 25cm. (Paris. Ecole Pratique des Hautes Etudes. Section des Sciences Economiques et Sociales. Centre de Recherches Historiques. Ports, Routes et Trafics. 22) In French and English.

MASHONA

GELFAND (MICHAEL) African crucible: an ethico-religious study with special reference to the Shona-speaking people. Cape Town, Juta, 1968. pp. xiii, 163. bibliogs. 21½cm.

MURPHREE (MARSHALL WARNE) Christianity and the Shona. London, 1969. pp. 200. bibliog. (London. University. London School of Economics and Political Science. Monographs on Social Anthropology. No. 36)

- Religion and mythology

GELFAND (MICHAEL) Shona ritual: with special reference to the Chaminuka cult. Cape Town, Juta, 1959. pp. (vii), 217. 21½cm.

GELFAND (MICHAEL) Shona religion: with special reference to the Makorekore. Cape Town, Juta, 1962. pp. (ix), 184. 21½cm.

MASLOW (ABRAHAM HAROLD)

HUIZINGA (GERARD) Maslow's need hierarchy in the work situation. Groningen, 1970. pp. 207 and appendices. bibliog.

MASON (JOHN) Trade unionist

JOHN MASON DEFENCE COMMITTEE. A brief outline of the life of John Mason. Rotherham, [1940]. pp. 9.

MASS (PHYSICS)

JAMMER (MAX) Concepts of mass in classical and modern physics. New York, Harper & Row, 1964. pp. xi, 230. 20½cm. (Harper Torchbooks. TB 571)

MARKOV (V.A.) and DANENGIRSH (G.M.) Problema sokhraneniia i printsip inertsii: filosofskie aspekty. Riga, 1970. pp. 243. (Latviiskii Gosudarstvennyi Universitet. Uchenye Zapiski. t.128)

MASS MEDIA
See COMMUNICATION

MASS SOCIETY

VIDA y cultura en la sociedad de masas. Montevideo, Fundación de Cultura Universitária, [1968]. pp. 289. 19½cm. (Biblioteca de Cultura Universitária. 4)

MASSACHUSETTS

- Economic history

HANDLIN (OSCAR) and HANDLIN (MARY FLUG) Commonwealth: a study of the role of government in the American economy: Massachusetts, 1774-1861. rev. ed. Cambridge, Mass., 1969. pp. 314. bibliog.

- Government publications - Bibliography

MASSACHUSETTS EXECUTIVE DEPARTMENT PUBLICATIONS; [published by] the Commonwealth of Massachusetts State Library. Boston, 1962/1966 [1st cumulative issue]; annual, 1967 to date. 27½cm. Monthly issues, Commonwealth of Massachusetts publications received, etc., are also kept until superseded by the annual issue.

MASSACHUSETTS (Cont'd.)

- House of Representatives

GOLDMAN (SHELDON) Roll call behavior in the Massachusetts House of Representatives: a test of selected hypotheses. Amherst, 1968. pp. 83.

- Politics and government

ZIMMERMAN (JOSEPH FRANCIS) The Massachusetts town meeting: a tenacious institution. Albany, State University of New York, [1967]. pp. ix, 137. bibliog. 22½cm.

O'CONNOR (THOMAS H.) Lords of the loom: the cotton Whigs and the coming of the Civil War. New York, Scribner, [1968]. pp. ix, 214. bibliog. 23½cm.

HANDLIN (OSCAR) and HANDLIN (MARY FLUG) Commonwealth: a study of the role of government in the American economy: Massachusetts, 1774-1861. rev. ed. Cambridge, Mass., 1969. pp. 314. bibliog.

LEAGUE OF WOMEN VOTERS OF MASSACHUSETTS. Massachusetts state government. 2nd ed. Cambridge, Mass., 1970. pp. 378.

MASTER AND SERVANT

- Germany

SCHMIDT (KLAUS) 1941- . Der Einfluss des Betriebs- und Betriebsinhaberwechsels auf die Arbeitsverhältnisse führender Angestellter. [Würzburg, imprint], 1966. pp. 156. bibliog.

HOHLFELD (KNUT) Arbeitnehmerhaftung und Wirtschaftsordnung, etc. Berlin, 1968. pp. 126. bibliog. (Berlin. Freie Universität. Osteuropa Institut. Berichte: Rechtswissenschaftliche Folge. Nr.2)

- United Kingdom

CRONIN (J.B.) and GRIME (R.P.) Labour law. London, 1970. pp. 500.

HEPPLE (BOB ALEXANDER) and O'HIGGINS (PAUL) Individual employment law: an introduction. London, 1971. pp. 203.

- United Kingdom - Scotland

MILLER (ISAAC P.) Industrial law in Scotland. Edinburgh, 1970. pp. 461.

MATARAZZO (FRANCISCO) Conde

MARTINS (JOSÉ DE SOUZA) Empresário e emprêsa na biografia do Conde Matarazzo. Rio de Janeiro, Universidade Federal, Instituto de Ciências Sociais, 1967. pp. 110. bibliog. (Monografias. 2)

MATCH INDUSTRY

- United Kingdom

PRESS AND PUBLIC RELATIONS LTD. Bryant and May: making matches, 1861-1961. [London], Neame, [1961]. pp. 28. 24½cm.

MATERA (PROVINCE)

- Politics and government

MATERA (PROVINCE). Relazione sull'attività svolta dalla amministrazione provinciale nel quadriennio 1956-1960. Matera, 1960. pp. 52. 29cm.

MATERIALISM

NOVACK (GEORGE) The origins of materialism. New York, 1965. pp. 300. bibliog.

PELLETIER (ANTOINE) and GOBLOT (JEAN JACQUES) Matérialisme historique et histoire des civilisations. Paris, [1969]. pp. 200.

GABAUDE (JEAN MARC) Le jeune Marx et le matérialisme antique. Toulouse, [1970]. pp. 277. bibliog.

MARX (KARL) and ENGELS (FRIEDRICH) The German ideology, part one, with selections from parts two and three, together with Marx's Introduction to a critique of political economy; edited and with an introduction by C.J. Arthur. London, 1970. pp. 158.

WITTICH (DIETER) ed. Vogt, Moleschott, Büchner: Schriften zum kleinbürgerlichen Materialismus in Deutschland. Berlin, 1971. 2 vols.

MATERIALS

PAVLOV (GELY T.) Methods of the analysis for the consumption of material resources per manufacturing products. Cairo, 1966. pp. 35. 28cm. (U.A.R. Institute of National Planning. Memos. No. 737)

UNITED NATIONS. Economic Commission for Europe. 1966. Aspects of competition between steel and other materials. (ST/ECE/STEEL/17). New York, 1966. pp. 121.

- Accounting

PAVLOV (GELY T.) Accountancy and registration on the consumption of material resources. Cairo, 1966. pp. 33. 28cm. (U.A.R. Institute of National Planning. Memos. No. 707.)

MATERIALS MANAGEMENT

STRAUSS (CARL JUERGEN) Materialwirtschaft im neuen ökonomischen System. Berlin, Staatsverlag der Deutschen Demokratischen Republik, 1967. pp. 138. 21cm.

LARGE scale provisioning systems: the proceedings of a conference under the aegis of the NATO Scientific Affairs Committee [held at] Athens 4th-8th September 1967; edited by J. Ferrier. London, English Universities Press, 1968. pp. (vi), 530. bibliogs. 23cm.

MATERNAL AND INFANT WELFARE

SOCIETY FOR THE HEALTH OF WOMEN AND CHILDREN. Rules. Christchurch, N.Z., n.d. pp. 8.

SOCIETY FOR THE HEALTH OF WOMEN AND CHILDREN. General Conference, 4th, 1914. Report. Dunedin, [N.Z.], 1914. pp. 32.

UNITED STATES. Children's Bureau. Aspects of maternal and child health in developing regions. [Washington], 1964. pp. 22.

INTERNATIONAL PLANNED PARENTHOOD FEDERATION. Working Papers. No.5. The relationship between family size and maternal and child health. London, 1970. pp. 26. bibliog.

- Canada

CANADA. 1967. Maternity protection for women workers in Canada; by Sheila Woodsworth. (Department of Labour) Ottawa, 1967. pp. (vi), 63. 25cm.

- Denmark

SKALTS (VERA) and NØRGAARD (MAGDA) Mothers' aid in Denmark: the organization and activity of the Danish Maternity Aid Centres. Copenhagen, Det Danske Selskab, 1965. pp. 29. 20cm. R(P)

- Germany, Eastern

GERMANY (DEUTSCHE DEMOKRATISCHE REPUBLIK). Amt für Information. 1950. Gesunde Familie, glückliche Zukunft. Berlin, [1950]. pp. 55. 21cm.

- Ireland (Republic)

COYNE (EDWARD J.) Mother and child service; ...on the moral issue; with contributions from John F. Cunningham and Alexis Fitzgerald on medical and financial aspects of the question. Dublin, Educational Company of Ireland, [1951]. pp. 31. 24cm. (Questions of the Day. No. 1) (Reprinted from Studies, June 1951)

- Kazakstan

BISENOVA (AKLIMA BISENOVNA) Materinstvo i detstvo: ocherki razvitiia okhrany materinstva i detstva v Kazakhstane. Alma-Ata, 1965. pp. 207. bibliog.

- Lebanon

INTERNATIONAL LABOUR OFFICE. Development Programme: Technical Assistance Sector. [Lebanon]. R.12. Rapport au gouvernement de la République Libanaise sur l'organisation de la branche maladie-maternité. (OIT/TAP/Liban/R.12) Genève, 1968. pp. 57.

- United Kingdom

YORK. [Public Health Department]. Report on the Maternity and Child Welfare Act, 1918, and its possible local development: part 1; [by] Edmund M. Smith. [York, 1919?]. pp. 14.

McLACHLAN (GORDON) and SHEGOG (RICHARD) eds. In the beginning; (studies of maternity services) London, 1970. pp. 186.

MATERNAL DEPRIVATION

BOWLBY (JOHN) Maternal care and mental health...; [and] Deprivation of maternal care: a reassessment of its effects; [by] Mary D. Ainsworth [and others] New York, Schocken, 1966. pp. 357. bibliog. 20cm.

SCHMALOHR (EMIL) Frühe Mutterentbehrung bei Mensch und Tier: entwicklungspsychologische Studie zur Psychohygiene der frühen Kindheit. München, Reinhardt, 1968. pp. 156. bibliog. 23½cm. (Erziehung und Psychologie. Nr. 50)

MATERNAL MORTALITY
See MOTHERS - Mortality

MATERNITY HOMES

- United Kingdom

NICHOLSON (JILL) Mother and baby homes: a survey of homes for unmarried mothers. London, Allen & Unwin, 1968. pp. 156. bibliog. 21½cm. (National Institute for Social Work Training. National Institute for Social Work Training Series. No. 13.)

MATHEMATICAL ANALYSIS

HÖRMANDER (LARS) An introduction to complex analysis in several variables. Princeton, N.J., 1966 repr. 1967. pp. 208. bibliog.

DRAPER (JEAN E.) and KLINGMAN (JANE S.) Mathematical analysis: business and economic applications. New York, Harper, [1967], repr. 1968. pp. vii, 568. 22½cm. (Harper International Editions)

GRATTAN-GUINNESS (IVOR OWEN) The historical development of mathematical analysis from Euler to Riemann [Ph. D. (London) thesis]. 1969. fo. 233. bibliog. Typescript: unpublished. This thesis is the property of London University and may not be removed from the Library.

INTERNATIONAL SYMPOSIUM ON THE APPLICATIONS OF MODEL THEORY TO ALGEBRA, ANALYSIS AND PROBABILITY, PASADENA, CALIFORNIA, 1967. Applications of model theory to algebra, analysis and probability; edited by W.A.J. Luxemburg. New York, [1969]. pp. 307. bibliogs.

LECTURES in modern analysis and applications; ([by] M. F. Atiyah [and others]); edited by C.T. Taam. Berlin, 1969 in progress. bibliogs.

BURKILL (J.C.) and BURKILL (H.) A second course in mathematical analysis. Cambridge, 1970. pp. 526. bibliog.

FRIEDMAN (AVNER) Foundations of modern analysis. New York, [1970]. pp. 250. bibliog.

KAWADA (TAKAYUKI) Continuity and Lipschitz condition of random fields. Kobe, 1970. fo. 16. bibliog. (Kobe. University. Institute of Economic Research. Working Papers in Economics and Management Science. No. 2)

MATHEMATICAL LINGUISTICS

FODOR (ISTVÁN) The rate of linguistic change: limits of the application of mathematical methods in linguistics. London, 1965. pp. 85. bibliog.

HARRIS (ZELLIG SABBETTAI) Mathematical structures of language. New York, Interscience, [1968]. pp. ix, 230. 22½cm. (Interscience Tracts in Pure and Applied Mathematics. No. 21)

MULLER (CHARLES) Initiation à la statistique linguistique. Paris, Larousse, [1968]. pp. 248. bibliog. 21cm. (Langue et Langage)

MATHEMATICAL MACHINE THEORY
See MACHINE THEORY

MATHEMATICAL MODELS

SHTOFF (VIKTOR ALEKSANDROVICH) Моделирование и философия. Москва, Наука, 1966. pp. 301. bibliog. 21cm.

KREISEL (GEORG) and KRIVINE (J.L.) Elements of mathematical logic: model theory. Amsterdam, North-Holland, 1967. pp. xi, 222. 22½cm. (Studies in Logic and the Foundations of Mathematics)

HARROD (Sir H.R.F.) What is a model? in Wolfe (James Nathaniel) ed. Value, capital, and growth. Edinburgh, 1968.

ANISIMOV-SPIRIDONOV (DMITRII DMITRIE-VICH) Методы и модели больших систем оптимального планирования и управления. Москва, 1969. pp. 359. bibliog.

BLALOCK (HUBERT M.) Theory construction: from verbal to mathematical formulations. Englewood Cliffs, N.J., [1969]. pp. 180.

FEDORENKO (NIKOLAI PROKOF'EVICH) ed. Экономико-математические модели. Москва, 1969. pp. 511.

HARDER (THEODOR) Introduction to mathematical models in market and opinion research: with practical applications, computing procedures, and estimates of computing requirements; [translated from the German by Peter H. and Eva H. Friedlander). Dordrecht, [1969]. pp. 194. bibliog.

RIGBY (PAUL H.) Models in business analysis. Columbus, Merrill Publishing Company, [1969]. pp. ix, 102. 22½cm. (Merrill's Mathematics and Quantitative Methods Series)

BADIOU (ALAIN) Le concept de modèle: introduction à une épistémologie matérialiste des mathématiques. Paris, 1969. pp. 94. bibliog.

SONQUIST (JOHN A.) Multivariate model building: the validation of a search strategy. Ann Arbor, [1970]. pp. 244. bibliog.

MATHEMATICAL OPTIMIZATION

FRISCH (RAGNAR) Optimal investments under limited foreign resources: part I and part II. Oslo, Institute of Economics, University of Oslo, 1959. fo. iv, 190. 29½cm. (Memoranda)

LEIVO (VEIKKO) Optimization of location and size of automobile dealerships. Helsinki, Helsinki Research Institute for Business Economics, 1965. pp. 122. bibliog. 24½cm. (Helsinki. Liiketaloustieteellinen Tutkimuslaitos. Julkaisuja. 28)

FISCHER (HANNELORE) and KLUGE (MANFRED) Mathematische Methoden in der Planung, mit Beispielen aus der Giessereiindustrie. Leipzig, Deutscher Verlag für Grundstoffindustrie, 1966. pp. 153. bibliog. 21½cm.

SYMPOSIUM ON RECENT ADVANCES IN OPTIMIZATION TECHNIQUES, PITTSBURGH, 1965. Recent advances in optimization techniques; edited by Abrahim Lavi and Thomas P. Vogl; proceedings of the symposium ... sponsored by the Systems Science and Cybernetics Group of the I.E.E.E and the Optical Society of America, etc. New York, [1966] repr. 1967. pp. 656. bibliog.

BECKER (KARL OTWIN) Die Wirtschaftlichen Entscheidungen des Haushalts. Berlin, Duncker und Humblot, [1967]. pp. 200. bibliog. 23½cm. (Frankfurt am Main. Universität. Wirtschafts- und Sozialwissenschaftliche Fakultät. Frankfurter Wirtschafts- und Sozialwissenschaftliche Studien. Heft 18)

BRANDES (OVE) Optimeringsproblem inom tidningsdistributionen. Göteborg, Gumperts, [1967]. pp. 110. bibliog. 22½cm. (Gothenburg. Handelshögskolan. Skriftserie. 1967. 4)

EREMIN (I. I.) ed. Matematicheskie metody v nekotorykh zadachakh optimal'nogo planirovaniia: sbornik trudov. Sverdlovsk, 1967. pp. 82.

LEITMANN (GEORGE) ed. Topics in optimization. New York, Academic P., 1967. pp. xv, 469. bibliogs. 22½cm. (Mathematics in Science and Engineering. 31)

TEREKHOV (LEV LEONIDOVICH) Otsenki v optimal'nom plane. Moskva, 1967. pp. 132. bibliog.

ZAVEL'SKII (MIKHAIL GRIGOR'EVICH) Optimizatsiia otraslevogo planirovaniia. Moskva, 1967. pp. 359.

DOBELL (A. RONALD) Characteristic features of optimal control problems in economic theory. [Toronto], 1968. fo. 32. bibliog. (Toronto. University. Institute for the Quantitative Analysis of Social and Economic Policy. Working Paper Series. No. 6811)

DOBELL (A. RONALD) Optimization in models of economic growth. Toronto, 1968. pp. 47. bibliog. (Toronto. University. Institute for the Quantitative Analysis of Social and Economic Policy. Working Paper Series. No. 6816)

GUMOWSKI (IGOR) and MIRA (CHRISTIAN) Optimization in control theory and practice. Cambridge, C.U.P., 1968. pp. ix, 242. bibliog. 22½cm.

KUENZI (HANS PAUL) and others. Numerical methods of mathematical optimization: with ALGOL and FORTRAN programs;... translated by Werner C. Rheinboldt and Cornelie J. Rheinboldt. New York, Academic P., 1968. pp. x, 171. bibliog. 22½cm. (Computer Science and Applied Mathematics)

PROBLEMY... Проблемы статистической оптимизации. Рига, 1968. pp. 228.

RECHERCHES récentes sur la fonction de production. Namur, 1968. pp. 242. (Namur. Centre d'Etudes et de Recherches Universitaire. Centre de Recherches Economiques et Sociales. Département d'Econométrie Collection Economie Mathématique et Econométrie. No. 2) In English, French or German.

TAN (AUGUSTINE HUI HENG) Differential protection, economic indices and optimal trade policies; [an abstract]. [Stanford, 1968]. unpaged.

WEIN (HAROLD H.) and SREEDHARAN (V.P.) The optimal staging and phasing of multi-product capacity. East Lansing, 1968. pp. 131. (Michigan University. Graduate School of Business Administration. Institute for International Business and Economic Development Studies. MSU Studies in Comparative and Technological Planning)

WILSON (ALAN GEOFFREY) Inter-regional commodity flows: entropy maximising approaches. London, 1968. pp. 39. bibliog. (Centre for Environmental Studies. Working Papers. 19)

BRYSON (ARTHUR EARL) and HO (YU-CHI) Applied optimal control: optimization, estimation and control. Waltham, Mass., [1969]. pp. 481. bibliog.

CHAKRAVARTY (SUKHAMOY) Capital and development planning. Cambridge, Mass., [1969]. pp. 344. bibliog.

DEHEM (ROGER) L'utopie de l'économiste; ou La rationalité économique collective. Paris, 1969. pp. 78. bibliog.

INTERNATIONAL CONFERENCE ON COMPUTING METHODS IN OPTIMIZATION PROBLEMS, 2ND, SAN REMO, 1968. Computing methods in optimization problems; papers presented at the 2nd international conference...San Remo, Italy, September 9-13, 1968. Berlin, 1969. pp. 191.

KHAMEI (ANVAR) Contribution à l'étude de l'utilité espérée et sa maximisation. n.p., [1969?]. pp. 247. bibliog.

LUENBERGER (DAVID G.) Optimization by vector space methods. New York, Wiley, [1969]. pp. xvii, 326. bibliog. 23cm. (Series in Decision and Control)

OPTIMIZATION: symposium of the Institute of Mathematics and its Applications, University of Keele...1968; edited by R.Fletcher. London, 1969. pp. 354.

CANON (MICHAEL D.) and others. Theory of optimal control and mathematical programming. New York, [1970]. pp. 285.

DADAIAN (VLADISLAV SURENOVICH) Ekonomicheskie zakony sotsializma i optimal'nye resheniia. Moskva, 1970. pp. 325.

FØRSUND (FINN R.) A note on the technically optimal scale curve in inhomogeneous production functions. Oslo, 1970. fo. 24. bibliog. (Oslo. Universitet. Socialøkonomiske Institutt. Memoranda)

HOROVITZ (MARCU) Modelul economic optim. Bucureşti, 1970. pp. 317. (Academia de Ştiinţe Sociale şi Politice a Republicii Socialiste România. Institutul de Cercetări Economice. Bibliotheca Oeconomica. 16) With English, French and Russian tables of contents.

INAGAKI (M.) Optimal economic growth: shifting finite versus infinite time horizon. Amsterdam, 1970. pp. 196. bibliog.

MARTI (KURT) Entscheidungstheoretische Grundlagen der stochastischen Optimierung. Mannheim, 1970. pp. 36. bibliog.

MOORE (PETER GERALD) and HODGES (S.D.) eds. Programming for optimal decisions: selected readings in mathematical programming techniques for management problems. Harmondsworth, 1970. pp. 359. bibliogs.

INTRILIGATOR (MICHAEL D.) Mathematical optimization and economic theory. Englewood Cliffs, [1971]. pp. 508. bibliogs.

MOHRING (HERBERT DICK) Optimization and scale economies in urban bus transportation. Minneapolis, 1971. fo. 38. bibliog. (Minnesota University. Center for Economic Research. Discussion Papers. No. 5)

MOISEEV (NIKITA NIKOLAEVICH) Chislennye metody v teorii optimal'nykh sistem. Moskva, 1971. pp. 424.

MATHEMATICAL PHYSICS

ULLMO (J.) The agreement between mathematics and physical phenomena. in Bunge (Mario Augusto) ed. The critical approach to science and philosophy. New York, [1964].

MATHEMATICIANS

IUSHKEVICH (A. P.) Georg Cantor und Sof'ja Kovalevskaja. in Steinitz (Wolfgang) and others, eds. Ost und West in der Geschichte des Denkens und der kulturellen Beziehungen. Berlin, 1966.

EVES (HOWARD) An introduction to the history of mathematics. 3rd ed. New York, [1969]. pp. 464. bibliogs.

MATHEMATICIANS, ENGLISH

WALLIS (PETER JOHN) A check list of British mathematical writers up to 1850; ([with] A check list of British Euclids up to 1850). Newcastle upon Tyne, University Department of Education, 1967. fo. 51, pp. 17.

MATHEMATICIANS, RUSSIAN

DELONE (B. N.) Петербургская школа теории чисел. Москва, Академия Наук, 1947. pp. 422. 21½cm.

MATHEMATICS

Das KONTINUUM und andere Monographien; [by H. Weyl and others; reprints of 4 monographs originally published 1918-29]. New York, [1960]. pp. various. bibliogs.

BLAKEY (JOSEPH) University mathematics: a textbook for students of science and engineering. 2nd ed. London, Blackie, 1958, repr. 1966. pp. (iii), 581. 21½cm.

KEMENY (JOHN G.) and others. Finite mathematical structures. Englewood Cliffs, Prentice-Hall, [1958, repr. 1959]. pp. xiii, 487. 23cm.

CAHIERS mathématiques. Paris, Mouton, 1966 in progress. (Paris. Ecole Pratique des Hautes Etudes. Section des Sciences Economiques et Sociales. Mathématiques et Sciences de l'Homme)

BARBUT (MARC) Mathématiques des sciences humaines. Paris, P.U.F., 1967-8. 2 vols. bibliogs. 17½cm. (Le Psychologue. 30,33)

EASTER CONFERENCE IN MATHEMATICS, BEDFORD COLLEGE, 1965. Exploring university mathematics, 1: lectures given at Bedford College, London, by P. Chadwick [and others]; edited by N.J. Hardiman. Oxford, 1967. pp. 120. bibliogs.

LLOYD (E.H.) The relevance of mathematics. in Lancaster. University. Inaugural lectures, 1965-1967; Lancaster, 1967.

MATHEMATICS (Cont'd.)

DANTZIG (GEORGE B.) and VEINOTT (ARTHUR F.) eds. Mathematics of the decision sciences; [proceedings of the 5th Summer Seminar, Stanford, 1967]. Providence, American Mathematical Society, 1968. 2 vols. bibliogs. 23cm. (Lectures in Applied Mathematics. vols. 11,12)

EASTER CONFERENCE IN MATHEMATICS, BEDFORD COLLEGE, 1966. Exploring university mathematics, 2: lectures given at Bedford College, London, by D.M. Burley [and others]; edited by N.J. Hardiman. Oxford, 1968. pp. 115. bibliogs.

INTERACTIVE systems for experimental applied mathematics; proceedings of the Association for Computing Machinery Inc. Symposium held in Washington D.C., August 1967; edited by Melvin Klerer [and] Juris Reinfelds. New York, Academic P., 1968. pp. xiv, 472. bibliogs. 22½cm.

PERSON (RUSSELL V.) Essentials of mathematics. 2nd ed. New York, Wiley, [1968]. pp. xi, 721. 22½cm.

RASHEVSKY (NICOLAS) Looking at history through mathematics. Cambridge, M.I.T. Press, [1968]. pp. xvii, 199. bibliog. 20cm.

RICHARDSON (WILLIAM H.) Finite mathematics. New York, Harper & Row, [1968]. pp. (xi), 191. 23½cm.

SCIENTIFIC AMERICAN. Mathematics in the modern world: readings from Scientific American; with introductions by Morris Kline. San Francisco, Freeman, [1968]. pp. (v), 409. 28cm.

BASHAW (W.L.) Mathematics for statistics. New York, [1969]. pp. 326.

CRAIG (ROBERT T.) Modern principles of mathematics. Englewood Cliffs, [1969]. pp. 400. bibliog.

EASTER CONFERENCE IN MATHEMATICS, BEDFORD COLLEGE, 1967. Exploring university mathematics, 3: lectures given at Bedford College, London, by Mary Bradburn [and others]; edited by N.J. Hardiman. Oxford, 1969. pp. 119. bibliogs.

GELBAUM (BERNARD R.) and MARCH (JAMES GARDNER) Mathematics for the social and behavioral sciences probability, calculus and statistics. Philadelphia, Saunders, 1969. pp. xii, 337. bibliog. 23½cm.

GENTZEN (GERHARD) The collected papers...; edited by M. E. Szabo. Amsterdam, 1969. pp. 338.

HACKWORTH (ROBERT D.) Mathematical systems: finite and infinite. New York, [1969]. pp. 314.

LEWIS (JOHN PARRY) An introduction to mathematics for students of economics. 2nd ed. London, 1969. pp. 590. bibliog. 21½cm.

BISHIR (JOHN W.) and DREWES (DONALD W.) Mathematics in the behavioral and social sciences. New York. [1970]. pp. 714. bibliogs.

O'BRIEN (R.J.) and GARCIA (G.G.) Mathematics for economists and social scientists. London, 1971. pp. 616. bibliog. (Southampton. University. Economics Series)

- History

BALL (WALTER WILLIAM ROUSE) A short account of the history of mathematics; [an unabridged republication of the 4th edition of 1908]. 4th ed. New York, Dover Publications, 1960. pp. xxiv, 522. 20½cm. (Dover Histories and Classics of Science. Paperbounds. T 630)

SARTON (GEORGE ALFRED LÉON) The study of the history of mathematics; and, The study of the history of science; two volumes bound as one; [reprinted unaltered from the first editions of 1936]. New York, Dover Publications, 1957. pp. (iii), 113, 75. bibliog. 20½cm.

SMITH (DAVID EUGENE) History of mathematics. New York, Dover Publications, 1958, repr. [196-?]. 2 vols. bibliog. 21½cm. (Paperbounds. T 429,430)

EVES (HOWARD) An introduction to the history of mathematics. New York, 1961. pp. 422. bibliogs. (Rinehart Books in Mathematics)

MILLER (M.) Ungelöste Probleme im Euler-Goldbach-Briefwechsel. in Steinitz (Wolfgang) and others, eds. Ost und West in der Geschichte des Denkens und der kulturellen Beziehungen. Berlin, 1966.

BOYER (CARL B.) A history of mathematics. New York, Wiley, [1968]. pp. xvii, 717. bibliogs. 22½cm.

KLEIN (JACOB) Greek mathematical thought and the origin of algebra...; with an appendix containing Vieta's Introduction to the analytical art, etc. Cambridge, Mass., M.I.T. Press, [1968]. pp. xv, 360. 20cm.

WILDER (RAYMOND L.) Evolution of mathematical concepts: an elementary study. New York, Wiley, [1968]. pp. xix, 224. bibliog. 21½cm.

EVES (HOWARD) An introduction to the history of mathematics. 3rd ed. New York, [1969]. pp. 464. bibliogs.

WHITESIDE (DEREK T.) The mathematical principles underlying Newton's Principia mathematica. Glasgow, 1970. pp. 28. (Glasgow. University. George A. Gibson Foundation Lectures. 1969)

- History - Sources

STRUIK (DIRK JAN) ed. A source book in mathematics, 1200-1800. Cambridge, Mass., 1969. pp. 427.

- Periodicals - Union lists

LONDON. University. Library. Union list of periodicals on mathematics and allied subjects in London libraries. 2nd ed. London, 1968. pp. (vi), 139. 21cm.

- Philosophy

LAUTMAN (ALBERT) Nouvelles recherches sur la structure dialectique des mathématiques. Paris, Hermann, 1939. pp. 32. 25½cm. (Actualités Scientifiques et Industrielles. 804)

BETH (EVERT WILLEM) L'existence en mathématiques. Paris, 1956. pp. 60.

HEYTING (AREND) Intuitionism: an introduction. 2nd ed. Amsterdam, North-Holland, 1966. pp. ix, 136. bibliog. 22½cm. (Studies in Logic and the Foundations of Mathematics)

RENYI (ALFRED) Dialogues on mathematics. San Francisco, Holden-Day, [1967] pp. 100. bibliog. 23cm.

THIEL (RAINER) Quantität oder Begriff?: der heuristische Gebrauch mathematischer Begriffe in Analyse und Prognose gesellschaftlicher Prozesse. Berlin, 1967. pp. 611.

FREY (GERHARD) Einführung in die philosophischen Grundlagen der Mathematik. Hannover, [1968]. pp. 116. bibliog.

HEERDEN (PIETER J. VAN) The foundation of mathematics. Wassenaar, Wistik, [1968]. pp. x, 50. bibliog. 23½cm.

KAC (MARK) and ULAM (STANISLAW MARCIN) Mathematics and logic: retrospect and prospects. New York, Praeger, 1968. pp. ix, 170. 23½cm.

FOUNDATIONS of mathematics: symposium papers commemorating the sixtieth birthday of Kurt Gödel; edited by Jack J. Bulloff [and others]. Berlin, Springer, 1969. pp. xii, 195. bibliogs. 23cm.

HINTIKKA (KAARLO JAAKKO JUHANI) ed. The philosophy of mathematics. London, 1969. pp. 186. bibliog.

WITTGENSTEIN (LUDWIG) Philosophische Grammatik...; herausgegeben von Rush Rhees. Oxford, [1969]. pp. 490.

KIELKOPF (CHARLES F.) Strict finitism: an examination of Ludwig Wittgenstein's Remarks on the foundations of mathematics. The Hague, 1970. pp. 192. bibliog.

- Programmed instruction

BAGGALEY (ANDREW R.) Mathematics for introductory statistics: a programmed review. New York, [1969] pp. 171. 21cm.

- Study and teaching

ORGANISATION FOR EUROPEAN ECONOMIC CO-OPERATION. Office for Scientific and Technical Personnel. 1961. New thinking in school mathematics. [Paris], 1961. pp. 246. bibliog.

CONFERENCE ON APPLIED MATHEMATICS FOR ENGINEERS, ROME, 1963. Engineering education in the computer age: report of an OECD Conference, etc. [Paris, 1964] pp. 105. (Applied Mathematics for Engineers)

DAVIES (T. V.) Applied mathematics in a university: an inaugural lecture delivered in the University of Leicester, 30 January 1968. Leicester, Leicester U.P., 1968. pp. 15. 21cm.

[SYMPOSIUM ON UTILISATION OF COMPUTERS IN MATHEMATICAL RESEARCH, BLARICUM, 1966]. Computers in mathematical research; editors R.F. Churchhouse [and] J.-C. Herz. Amsterdam, North-Holland Publishing Co., 1968. pp. xi, 185. bibliog. 22¼cm. In English or French.

DIENES (ZOLTAN PAUL) and JEEVES (MALCOLM ALEXANDER) The effects of structural relations on transfer. London, 1970. pp. 147.

- Study and teaching - Germany

RICHTER (L.) Die Anwendung der pädagogischen Grundsätze E.W. v.Tschirnhaus' am Collegium mathematicum des Zittauer Gymnasiums durch Christian Pescheck. in Steinitz (Wolfgang) and others, eds. Ost und West in der Geschichte des Denkens und der kulturellen Beziehungen. Berlin, 1966.

- Study and teaching - United Kingdom

LONDON. London County Council. Education Officer's Department. Mathematics in secondary schools. London, 1960. pp. 36.

LONDON. Greater London Council. Inner London Education Authority. Junior school mathematics. London, 1966. pp. 43. bibliog.

U.K. 1967. Department of Education and Science. Mathematics for the majority: a programme in mathematics for the young school leaver. (Schools Council Working Papers. No. 14) London, 1967. pp. v, 45. 24½cm.

BIGGS (E. E.) Mathematics in primary schools. 3rd ed. London, 1969. pp. xi,165. bibliog. 24½cm. (U.K. Department of Education and Science. Schools Council. Curriculum Bulletins. No. 1)

HEADING (JOHN) The present position of applied mathematics in the United Kingdom; an inaugural lecture delivered at the University College of Wales, Aberystwyth, 26 February, 1969. Cardiff, 1969. pp. 41.

- Study and teaching - United Kingdom - British Empire

MATHEMATICS in Commonwealth schools: report of a specialist Conference held at the University of the West Indies, Trinidad, September 1968. London, Commonwealth Secretariat, 1969. pp. 199. bibliog.

- Tables, etc.

GREENWOOD (JOSEPH ARTHUR) and HARTLEY (HARMON OTTO) Guide to tables in mathematical statistics. Princeton, 1962. pp. 1014.

UNITED STATES. National Standards Bureau. Applied Mathematics Series. 55. Handbook of mathematical functions with formulas, graphs, and mathematical tables. Washington, 1964. pp. xiv, 1046.

BROWN (HORACE PLESSAY) Growth rate tables. Canberra, Australian National University, 1965. pp. 31. 19½cm.

THERY (G.) Tables économiques et financières: notions et usages. Paris, 1968. pp. 116.

MATHEMATICS, GREEK

ARCHIMEDES. The works...; edited in modern notation with introductory chapters by T. L. Heath; with a supplement, The method of Archimedes; (an unabridged reissue of the Heath edition of 1897 [with] the supplement of 1912). New York, Dover Publications, [196-?]. pp. clxxxvi, 326, 51. 20½cm. (Dover Histories and Classics of Science. Paperbounds. S 9)

MATHEMATICS, GREEK (Cont'd.)

SZABÓ (A.) Theaitetos und das Problem der Irrationalität in der griechischen Mathematikgeschichte. [Budapest], 1966. pp. 303-358. (Magyar Tudományos Akademia. Acta Antiqua. Tomus 14. Fasc. 3-4)

MATHEMATICS TEACHERS

UNITED STATES. National Science Foundation. Secondary school science and mathematics teachers. Washington, 1963. pp. vi, 45.

MATO GROSSO

- Economic conditions

MATO GROSSO. Governor, 1958 (João Ponce de Arruda) Mensagem apresentada pelo governador do estado, Dr. João Ponce de Arruda, por ocasião da abertura da sessão legislativa de 1958. Cuiaba, 1958. pp. 125.

- Politics and government

MATO GROSSO. Governor, 1958 (João Ponce de Arruda) Mensagem apresentada pelo governador do estado, Dr. João Ponce de Arruda, por ocasião da abertura da sessão legislativa de 1958. Cuiaba, 1958. pp. 125.

- Social conditions

MATO GROSSO. Governor, 1958 (João Ponce de Arruda) Mensagem apresentada pelo governador do estado, Dr. João Ponce de Arruda, por ocasião da abertura da sessão legislativa de 1958. Cuiaba, 1958. pp. 125.

MATRICES

WOLD (H.) On infinite, non-negative definite, Hermitian matrices, and corresponding linear equation systems. in Uppsala. Universitet. Institute of Statistics. Selected Publications. vol. 1. [Uppsala, 1943].

EL-KAFRAWY (MOHAMED) Matrix inversion: post-multiplication method. (Part 6.) Cairo, 1961. pp. 10. (U.A.R. Institute of National Planning. Memos. No. 11)

KOERVER-STUEMPER (HANS JÜRGEN) Die Matrizenrechnung im Dienste der Kostenrechnung. [Mannheim?], 1965. pp. 173. bibliog.

FINKBEINER (DANIEL TALBOT) Introduction to matrices and linear transformations. 2nd ed. San Francisco, Freeman, [1966]. pp. xi, 297. 23½cm.

ROGERS (ANDREI) Matrix analysis of interregional population growth and distribution. Berkeley, U. of California P., 1968. pp. xiv, 119. bibliogs. 21½cm.

GREGORY (ROBERT T.) and KARNEY (DAVID L.) A collection of matrices for testing computational algorithms. New York, [1969]. pp. 154.

LANCASTER (PETER) Theory of matrices. New York, Academic P., [1969]. pp. xii, 316. bibliogs. 22½cm.

PESTON (MAURICE H.) Elementary matrices for economics. London, Routledge & Kegan Paul, 1969. pp. viii, 111. bibliog. 18½cm. (Students Library of Economics)

BACHARACH (MICHAEL) Biproportional matrices and input- output change. Cambridge, 1970. pp. 170. bibliog. (Cambridge. University. Department of Applied Economics. Monographs. [No.] 16)

NERING (EVAR D.) Linear algebra and matrix theory. 2nd. ed. New York, [1970]. pp. 352.

MATRILINEAL KINSHIP

INTERNATIONAL AFRICAN INSTITUTE. Ethnographic Survey of Africa. East Central Africa. Part 16. The matrilineal peoples of eastern Tanzania: Zaramo, Luguru, Kaguru, Ngulu, etc.; by T.O. Beidelman. London, 1967. pp. 94. bibliog. 24cm.

NAKANE (CHIE) Garo and Khasi: a comparative study in matrilineal systems. Paris, Mouton, [1967]. pp. 187. bibliog. 24cm. (Paris. École Pratique des Hautes Études. Section de Sciences Économiques et Sociales. Cahiers de l'Homme. Nouvelle Série. 2)

DUBE (LEELA) Matriliny and Islam: religion and society in the Laccadives. Delhi, 1969. pp. 125. bibliog. (University of Saugar. Monographs in Anthropology and Sociology)

MATRIMONIAL ACTIONS

- United Kingdom

U.K. Law Commission. Published Working Papers. No. 22. Second programme, item XIX. Family law: restitution of conjugal rights. London, 1969. fo. 8. 30cm.

U.K. Law Commission. Published Working Papers. No. 28. Family law: jurisdiction in matrimonial causes (other than nullity). London, 1970. pp. 60.

PASSINGHAM (BERNARD) Law and practice in matrimonial causes. London, 1971. pp. 421.

U.K. Law Commission. Published Working Papers. No. 34. Second programme, item XIX. Family law: jactitation of marriage. London, 1971. pp. 8.

MATSHANGANA TERRITORY

- Politics and government

SOUTH AFRICA. Report of the Controller and Auditor-General on the accounts of the Matshangana Territorial Authority and of the accounts of lower authorities in its area. 1969/70 [1st] to date included in SOUTH AFRICA. Parliament. House of Assembly. Votes and proceedings; (with Printed annexures).

MATTEOTTI (GIACOMO)

MORANDI (RODOLFO) Giacomo Matteotti: il combattente socialista e l'antesignano della Resistenza: discorso pronunciato a Fratta Polesine nella celebrazione del 30° anniversario della morte. Roma, [imprint, 1954?] pp. 30. 18½cm. (Politica del Partito. 6)

MATTER

BROGLIE (LOUIS DE) Matter and light: the new physics;....translated by W.H. Johnston; [reprint of the edition originally published in 1939]. New York, Dover Publications, [196-?]. pp. 300. 20cm. (Dover Books Explaining Science. Paperbounds. T35)

WEYL (HERMANN) Space, time, matter;... translated from the German by Henry L. Brose. New York, Dover Publications, 1952, repr. [196-?]. pp. xvii, 330. bibliog. 20½cm. (Paperbounds. S 267)

GUERLAC (HENRY EDWARD) Newton et Épicure;... conférence donnée au Palais de la Découverte le 2 Mars 1963: Histoire des sciences. Paris, Université de Paris, [1963]. pp. 41. 18cm.

McMULLIN (ERNAN) ed. The concept of matter in Greek and medieval philosophy;... contributors Joseph Bobik [and others]. Notre Dame, U. of Notre Dame P., 1965. pp. viii, 325. 20½cm.

HEISENBERG (WERNER KARL) Natural law and the structure of matter; (address delivered on the hill of the Pnyx, Athens, the 3rd June, 1964); English version by the author. [London, 1970]. pp. 45.

MATTHESON (JOHANN)

FELDMANN (F.) Der Hamburger Johann Mattheson, 1681-1764 und die Musik Mittel- und Ostdeutschlands. in Hamburg. Arbeits- und Sozialbehörde. Hamburger Mittel- und Ostdeutsche Forschungen. Band 5. Kulturelle und wirtschaftliche Studien in Beziehung zum gesamtdeutschen Raum. Hamburg, [1966].

MATTING

INDIA. Labour Investigation Committee. 1945. Report on labour conditions in coir mats and matting industry; by Ahmad Mukhtar. [Delhi], 1945. pp. 61.

MATURATION (PSYCHOLOGY)

HEATH (DOUGLAS H.) Growing up in college: liberal education and maturity. San Francisco, 1968. pp. 326. bibliog.

KENISTON (KENNETH) Young radicals: notes on committed youth. New York, Harcourt, Brace & World, [1968]. pp. xi, 368. bibliog. 21cm.

SANDSTRÖM (C.I.) The psychology of childhood and adolescence; translated by Albert Read. Harmondsworth, Penguin Books, 1968. pp. 259. bibliog. 18cm. (Pelican Books. A911)

MAUGHAM (ROBERT CECIL ROMER) 2nd Viscount Maugham

MAUGHAM (ROBERT CECIL ROMER) 2nd Viscount Maugham. The 1946 MS. London, 1943. pp. 44.

MAUI

- Economic conditions

HAWAII UNIVERSITY. Economic Research Center. An economic study of the County of Maui. Honolulu, 1965-7. 4 vols. bibliog. 28cm.

MAURICE, Prince, Son of Frederick I., King of Bohemia

RUPERT, Prince, Son of Frederick I., King of Bohemia, and MAURICE, Prince, Son of Frederick I., King of Bohemia. A declaration...directed to both Houses of Parliament, with their intentions; as also their desires to the Parliament sent from Oatlands and delivered on Tuesday last, the 30. of June, 1646. London, Coe, 1646. pp. (6). 19cm. Wing R 2292.

MAURICE (JOHN FREDERICK DENISON)

DUNSTAN (G.R.) A digger still: an inaugural lecture delivered at King's College, London, on Tuesday, 14 November, 1967. London, Epworth Press, 1968. pp. 31. 18½cm.

COULSON (SIDNEY JOHN) Newman and the common tradition: a study in the language of church and society. Oxford, 1970. pp. 279. bibliog.

MAURITANIA

- Economic conditions

INTERNATIONAL LABOUR OFFICE. Development Programme: Technical Assistance Sector. [Mauritania]. R.7. Rapport au gouvernement de la République islamique de Mauritanie sur l'évaluation et la planification de la main-d'oeuvre. (OIT/TAP/Mauritanie/R.7) Genève, 1967. pp. ii, 79. 30cm.

MAURITANIA. Ministère des Affaires Étrangères et du Plan. 1967. Plan quadriennal, 1963-1966: bilan de 3 années d'exécution. [Nouakchott, 1967]. fo. 80. 26½cm.

- Social conditions

MAURITANIA. Ministère des Affaires Étrangères et du Plan. 1967. Plan quadriennal, 1963-1966: bilan de 3 années d'exécution. [Nouakchott, 1967]. fo. 80. 26½cm.

- Statistics

MAURITANIA. Direction de la Statistique et des Etudes Economiques. Annuaire statistique. a., 1969- Nouakchott.

GERMANY (BUNDESREPUBLIK). Statistisches Bundesamt. Länderkurzberichte: Mauretanien. irreg., 1971 [1st issue]- Wiesbaden.

MAURITIUS

U.K. Central Office of Information. Reference Division. Reference Pamphlets. 83. Mauritius. London, 1968. pp. 33. bibliog. 23½cm.

- Constitution

RAINAUD (JEAN MARIE) Le problème constitutionnel de l'Île Maurice. Paris, 1965. pp. 39. (Université d'Aix-Marseille. Faculté de Droit et des Sciences Economiques d'Aix. Travaux et Mémoires)

- Economic conditions

REPORT ON THE ECONOMY OF MAURITIUS; ([pd.by] Mauritius Economic Planning Unit). a., 1967 (1st issue)- Port Louis.

MAURITIUS - Economic conditions (Cont'd.)

    MILLIKEN (M.) Dairying in Mauritius: a socio-economic survey. [Port Louis], 1968. pp. 64.

    MILLIKEN (M.) and FAT (F.C.LIM) Population growth, income and the demand for food in Mauritius. [Port Louis], 1968. pp. 323-377. (Reprinted from Revue Agricole et Sucrière de l'Ile Maurice, vol. 47, no. 4)

    KING (JOHN A.) Mauritius, Malthus and Professor Meade. Brighton, 1970. pp. 14. (Brighton. University of Sussex. Institute of Development Studies. Communications. No. 49)

- Economic policy

    MAURITIUS. 1971. 4-year plan for social and economic development, 1971-75. [Port Louis, 1971]. 2 vols.(in 1).

- Emigration and immigration

    HAZAREESINGH (K.) A history of Indians in Mauritius. [Port Louis, Mauritius?], General Printing and Stationery Company, 1950. pp. x, 231, 20. $18\frac{1}{2}$cm.

- Government publications

    UNITED STATES. Library of Congress. Madagascar and adjacent islands: a guide to official publications Washington, 1965. pp. xiii, 58.

- Officials and employees - Salaries, allowances, etc.

    MAURITIUS. 1957. Report on the review of the salaries of senior officers of the Mauritius civil service; by R.J.C. Howes. Port Louis, 1957. pp. (v), 43. $32\frac{1}{2}$cm.

- Population

    MILLIKEN (M.) and FAT (F.C.LIM) Population growth, income and the demand for food in Mauritius. [Port Louis], 1968. pp. 323-377. (Reprinted from Revue Agricole et Sucrière de l'Ile Maurice, vol. 47, no. 4)

    KING (JOHN A.) Mauritius, Malthus and Professor Meade. Brighton, 1970. pp. 14. (Brighton. University of Sussex. Institute of Development Studies. Communications. No. 49)

- Social conditions

    GUY (FRANÇOIS) and GUY (MICHÈLE) Ile Maurice: régulation des naissances et action familiale;...deux années avec l'Action Familiale et les problèmes démographiques de l'Ile Maurice, Océan Indien, 1965-1966. Lyon, Mappus, [1968]. pp. 342. bibliog. 21cm.

- Social policy

    MAURITIUS. 1971. 4-year plan for social and economic development, 1971-75. [Port Louis, 1971]. 2 vols.(in 1).

- Statistics

    GERMANY (BUNDESREPUBLIK). Statistisches Bundesamt. Länderkurzberichte: Mauritius. irreg., 1971 [1st issue]- Wiesbaden.

MAURRAS (CHARLES MARIE PHOTIUS)

    GWYNN (DENIS ROLLESTON) The "Action Française" condemnation. London, Burns Oates & Washbourne, 1928. pp. viii, 272. $18\frac{1}{2}$cm.

MAUSS (MARCEL)

    CAZENEUVE (JEAN) Sociologie de Marcel Mauss. Paris, P.U.F., 1968. pp. 129. bibliog. 18cm. (Le Sociologue. 14)

    LÉVI-STRAUSS (C.) Introduction à l'oeuvre de Marcel Mauss. in Mauss (Marcel) Sociologie et anthropologie. 4th ed. Paris, 1968.

MAUTHE (FRIEDRICH)

    GEHRING (PAUL) Friedrich Mauthe: Kaufmann und Uhrenfabrikant in Schwenningen. Schwenningen, 1966. pp. 164-186. (Schwenningen. Schriftenreihe. Band 4) (Sonderdruck aus 200 Jahre Schwenninger Uhren 1765-1965)

MAVERICK (FONTAINE MAURY)

    HENDERSON (RICHARD B.) Maury Maverick: a political biography. Austin, Texas, [1970]. pp. 386. bibliog.

MAX-PLANCK-INSTITUT FUR AUSLÄNDISCHES UND INTERNATIONALES PRIVATRECHT, TUBINGEN

    RHEINSTEIN (M.) Vierzig Jahre Kaiser-Wilhelm und Max-Planck-Institut, etc. in Die Anwendung ausländischen Rechts im internationalen Privatrecht. Berlin, 1968.

MAXIMILIAN I, Emperor of Germany

    FICHTENAU (H.) Reich und Dynastie im politischen Denken Maximilians I. in Institut für Osterreichische Geschichtsforschung and Vienna. Katholische Akademie. Osterreich und Europa. Graz, 1965.

MAXIMILIAN ALEXANDER FREDERICK WILLIAM, Prince of Baden

    PETZOLD (J.) "Ethischer Imperialismus": eine Studie über die politische Konzeption des Kreises um den Prinzen Max von Baden am Vorabend der deutschen Frühjahrsoffensive von 1918. in Klein (Fritz) ed. Politik im Krieg, 1914-1918. Berlin, 1964.

    MAXIMILIAN ALEXANDER FREDERICK WILLIAM, Prince of Baden. Erinnerungen und Dokumente; neu herausgegeben von Golo Mann und Andreas Burckhardt; mit einer Einleitung von Golo Mann. Stuttgart, Klett, [1968]. pp. 692. bibliog. $22\frac{1}{2}$cm.

MAXIMILIANUS, Transilvanus

    PALL (F.) Maximilien Transylvanus, auteur du récit de l'expédition de Magellan. in Comité National des Historiens de la République Socialiste de Roumanie. Nouvelles études d'histoire. Bucarest, 1965.

MAXTON (JAMES)

    JAMES Maxton,...: an appreciation with a number of tributes [by various authors]. [London, 1947]. pp. 30.

ANAND (VIDYA SAGAR) and RIDLEY (FRANCIS A.)
James Maxton and British socialism. London,
1970. pp. 32.

MAY DAY

TRACHTENBERG (ALEXANDER) The history of
May day. New York, [1931?]. pp. 31.

MAYAKOVSKY (VLADIMIR)
See MAIAKOVSKII (VLADIMIR VLADIMIROVICH)

MAYAS

GUATEMALA. Seminario de Integración Social
Guatemalteca. Cuadernos. Primera Serie.
No. 5. Cultura folk y cultura compleja
en el area maya meridional; ([by] Stephan
F. de Borhegyi). Guatemala, 1959. pp. 31.
bibliog. 21cm. (Reprinted from Ciencias
Sociales de la Unión Panamericana, vol. 5,
no. 26, abril de 1954)

GUATEMALA. Seminario de Integración Social
Guatemalteca. Cuadernos. Primera Serie.
No. 6. Los Mayas del Altiplano; ([by] E.
Michael Mendelson; versión de Jorge Luis
Arriola). Guatemala, 1959. pp. 21. 21cm.

OAKES (MAUD) The two crosses of Todos Santos:
survivals of Mayan religious ritual. Princeton,
N.J., 1969. pp. 274. bibliog. (Bollingen Foundation. Bollingen Series. 27)

VOGT (EVON ZARTMAN) Zinacantan: a Maya community
in the highlands of Chiapas. Cambridge, Mass.,
1969. pp. 733. bibliog.

NASH (JUNE) In the eyes of the ancestors: belief
and behavior in a Maya community. New Haven,
1970. pp. 368. bibliog.

MAYENNE

- Church history

DENIS (MICHEL) L'église et la République en Mayenne,
1896-1906. [Paris, Klincksieck, 1967]. pp.
289. bibliog. 24cm.

MAYER (JACOB ANTON)

CROUS (HELMUT A.) and FALTER (HELMUT) Festschrift
zum einhundertfünfzigjährigen Bestehen der
J.A. Mayer'schen Buchhandlung, (1817-1967).
[Aachen], Mayer, [1967]. pp. x, 280.
bibliog. 23cm.

MAYO

KREYSLER (J.) Uhuru na maji: health, water
supply and self reliance in Mayo village.
Dar Es Salaam, [1968]. pp. 15. bibliog.
(Dar Es Salaam. University College.
Bureau of Resource Assessment and Land
Use Planning. Research Paper. No. 3)

MAYO INDIANS

CRUMRINE (LYNNE SCOGGINS) Ceremonial exchange
as a mechanism in tribal integration among the
Mayos of northwest Mexico. Tucson, 1969. pp.
52. bibliog. (Arizona University. Anthropological Papers. No. 14)

MAYORS

- Germany

BRUECKNER (HEINZ) Personen und Parteieneinfluss
in süddeutschen Oberbürgermeisterwahlen: eine
vergleichende Analyse am Beispiel Mannheims 1955,
Heidelbergs 1958, Regensburgs 1959/60 und Ludwigsburgs 1960. [Heidelberg, imprint], 1962. pp.
262. bibliog.

- United States

CUNNINGHAM (JAMES V.) Urban leadership in
the sixties. Waltham, Mass., [1970]. pp.
93. (Lemberg Center for the Study of Violence.
Approaches to the Study of Violence)

MAYRISCH (EMILE)

EMILE Mayrisch, précurseur de la construction de l'Europe. Lausanne, Centre de
Recherches Européennes, 1967. pp. 64.
24cm.

MAZARIN (JULES) Cardinal

GRAND-MESNIL (MARIE NOËLE) Mazarin, la
Fronde et la presse, 1647-1649. Paris
Colin, [1967] pp. 308. bibliog. 18cm.
(Kiosque. 31)

JANSEN (P.) Attachée de recherches au C.N.R.S.
Le Cardinal Mazarin et le mouvement janséniste
français, 1653-1659; d'après les documents inédits
conservés dans les archives du Ministère des
Affaires Étrangères. Paris, Vrin, 1967. pp.
274. bibliog. 22½cm. (Société d'Histoire
Ecclésiastique de la France. Bibliothèque)

MAZIERES EN GATINE

- Social history

THABAULT (ROGER) Education and change in a village
community: Mazières-en-Gâtine, 1848-1914; translated by Peter Tregear. London, 1971. pp.
270.

MAZZINI (ANDREA LUIGI)

SAITTA (ARMANDO) Sinistra hegeliana e
problema italiano negli scritti di A.L.
Mazzini: [with appendix of Mazzini's works
reprinted]. Roma, 1967-1968. 3 vols.
(Istituto Storico Italiano per l'Età Moderna
e Contemporanea. Italia e Europa. Collezione
per il Primo Centenario dell'Unità.)

MAZZINI (GIUSEPPE)

[BAKUNIN (MIKHAIL ALEKSANDROVICH)] La teologia
politica di Mazzini e l'Internazionale. n.p.,
[1871?] pp. 3-14. Title-page missing.

MAZZINI (GIUSEPPE) Lettere inedite di
Giuseppe Mazzini ed alcune de'suoi
compagni d'esiglio; pubblicate da L. Ordoño
De Rosales. Torino, Bocca, 1898.
pp. xx, 227. 21cm.

AMBROSINI (GASPARE) Marx, Mazzini e l'internazionale socialista: (conferenza pronunziata al Circolo di Cultura di Palermo, etc.). Campobasso, Colitti, 1917,
pp. 35. 24cm. (Collana Colitti di
Conferenze e Discorsi. Num. 25)

MAZZINI (GIUSEPPE) (Cont'd.)

GHISLERI (ARCANGELO) Giuseppe Mazzini e gli operai. Roma, 1946. pp. 111.

SANCTIS (FRANCESCO DE) Mazzini e la scuola democratica; a cura di Carlo Muscetta e Giorgio Candeloro. [Turin], Einaudi, 1951. pp. li, 238. 22cm. (Opere di Francesco de Sanctis. 12)

MAZZINI (GIUSEPPE) Scritti editi ed inediti di Giuseppe Mazzini: nuova serie. Imola, 1965 in progress.

LEVI (ALESSANDRO) La filosofia politica di Giuseppe Mazzini;... a cura di Salvo Mastellone. new ed. Napoli, Morano, [1967]. pp. 285. 23cm. (Nobiltà dello Spirito. 11)

FIUMARA (FRANCESCO) Mazzini e l'Internazionale: contatti, rapporti, polemiche. Pisa, Nistri-Lischi, 1968. pp. 109. 22cm. Domus Mazziniana. Collana Divulgativa. 5)

BIONDI (A.) Mazzini uomo. Milano, 1969. pp. 401. bibliog.

MAZZUCCHELLI (LUIGI)

LUCATI (VENOSTO) Il garibaldino Luigi Mazzucchelli nelle battaglie per l'unità d'Italia e per l'ideale democratico: Cantù 1835 - Como 1896. Como, Noseda, 1961. pp. 32. bibliog. 24cm.

MBALMAYO

- Census

CAMEROUN. Service de la Statistique Générale. 1958. Résultats du recensement de la subdivision de Mbalmayo, 1956. [Yaoundé?, 1958?]. pp. 129. 27cm.

MBOWAMBS

STRATHERN (A.) and STRATHERN (M.) Marsupials and magic: a study of spell symbolism among the Mbowamb in Cambridge. University. Department of Archaeology and Anthropology. Cambridge Papers in Social Anthropology. No. 5. Dialectic in practical religion. Cambridge, 1968.

MDEWAKANTON INDIANS

LANDES (RUTH) The Mystic Lake Sioux: sociology of the Mdewakantonwan Santee. Madison, 1968. pp. 224. bibliog.

MEAD (GEORGE H.)

WHITAKER (HOWARD E.) Humane enterprise: an account of the Mead Corporation, 1846-1963. New York, the Society, 1963. pp. 24. 23cm. (Newcomen Society in North America. Newcomen Addresses. 1963)

MEADE (JOHN)

COUNTY of Down election, 1805; the patriotic miscellany or mirror of wit, genius, and truth; being a correct collection of all the publications during the late contested election between...John Meade and...Viscount Castlereagh. London, [1805]. pp. 104. 23cm.

MEANING

GOMPERZ (HEINRICH) Philosophical studies; edited by Daniel S. Robinson. Boston, Mass., [1953]. pp. 287. bibliogs.

LOGIC and language: studies dedicated to Professor Rudolf Carnap on the occasion of his seventieth birthday. Dordrecht, [1962]. pp. 246.

HAYAKAWA (SAMUEL ICHIYÉ) and others. Language in thought and action. 2nd ed. New York, Harcourt, [1964]. pp. xvii, 350. bibliog. 21½cm.

BENDIX (EDWARD HERMAN) Componential analysis of general vocabulary: the semantic structure of a set of verbs in English, Hindi and Japanese. Bloomington, 1966. pp. 190. bibliog.

FITZGERALD (JOHN JAMES) Peirce's theory of signs as foundation for pragmatism. The Hague, Mouton, 1966. pp. 182. bibliog. 21cm. (Studies in Philosophy. 11)

GUIRAUD (PIERRE) La sémantique. 5th ed. Paris, P.U.F., 1966. pp.128. Bibliog. 17½cm. (Que Sais-Je? No.655)

BUCHDAHL (G.) Semantic sources of the concept of law. in Boston Colloquium for the Philosophy of Science. Proceedings, 1964-1966. Boston studies in the philosophy of science, vol. 3. Dordrecht, 1967.

HALLETT (GARTH) Wittgenstein's definition of meaning as use. New York, Fordham U. 1967. pp. xi, 210. 23cm. (Orestes Brownson Series on Contemporary Thought and Affairs. No. 6)

DAVIES (EIRIAN) Aspects of general linguistics. London, 1968. pp. 107. (London. University. University College. Communication Research Centre Programme in Linguistics and English Teaching. Papers. No. 8)

PARKINSON (GEORGE HENRY RADCLIFFE) ed. The theory of meaning. London, O.U.P., 1968. pp. 188. bibliog. 20½cm. (Oxford Readings in Philosophy)

REZNIKOV (LAZAR' OSIPOVICH) Erkenntnistheoretische Fragen der Semiotik; (aus dem Russischen übertragen). Berlin, 1968. pp. 299.

STEGMUELLER (WOLFGANG) Das Wahrheitsproblem und die Idee der Semantik: eine Einführung in die Theorien von A. Tarski und R. Carnap. 2nd ed. Wien, Springer, 1968. pp. x, 328. bibliog. 22½cm.

DAS (J.P.) Verbal conditioning and behaviour. Oxford, 1969. pp. 163. bibliog.

FOUCAULT (MICHEL) L'archéologie du savoir. [Paris, 1969]. pp. 279.

GOERLICH (J. WOLFGANG) Semantik und dialektischer Materialismus: Darstellung und Analyse der modernen marxistisch-leninistischen Wissenschaftstheorie in der DDR. Berlin, 1969. pp. 174. (Berlin. Freie Universität. Osteuropa-Institut. Philosophische und Soziologische Veröffentlichungen. Band 10)

KIEFER (F.) ed. Studies in syntax and semantics. Dordrecht, [1969]. pp. 242. bibliogs. In English and French.

KLAUS (GEORG) Semiotik und Erkenntnistheorie. 2nd ed. Berlin, 1969. pp. 182. bibliog.

PRZELECKI (MARIAN) The logic of empirical theories. London, Routledge, 1969. pp. v, 108. bibliog. 17½cm. (Monographs in Modern Logic Series)

QUINE (WILLARD VAN ORMAN) Ontological relativity and other essays. New York, 1969. pp. 165. (Columbia University. John Dewey Essays in Philosophy. No. 1)

SCHMIDT (SIEGFRIED J.) Bedeutung und Begriff: zur Fundierung einer sprachphilosophischen Semantik. Braunschweig, 1969. pp. 176. bibliog.

WITTGENSTEIN (LUDWIG) On certainty;...edited by G.E.M. Anscombe and G.H. von Wright [and] translated by Denis Paul and G.E.M. Anscombe. Oxford, 1969. pp. various. In German and English.

CHAFE (WALLACE L.) Meaning and the structure of language. Chicago, 1970 repr. 1971. pp. 360. bibliog.

GREIMAS (ALGIRDAS JULIEN) Du sens; essais sémiotiques. Paris, [1970]. pp. 313.

LEHRER (ADRIENNE) and LEHRER (KEITH) eds. Theory of meaning. Englewood Cliffs, [1970]. pp. 216. bibliog.

STRAWSON (PETER FREDERICK) Meaning and truth;... an inaugural lecture delivered before the University of Oxford on 5 November 1969. Oxford, 1970. pp. 25.

TAYLOR (DANIEL M.) Explanation and meaning: an introduction to philosophy. Cambridge, 1970. pp. 202. bibliog.

KLAUS (GEORG) Sprache der Politik. Berlin, 1971. pp. 294.

SEMANTICHESKAIA struktura slova: psikholingvisticheskie issledovaniia. Moskva, 1971. pp. 216.

STRAWSON (PETER FREDERICK) Logico-linguistic papers. London, 1971. pp. 251.

MEASLES

LONDON. London County Council. Hospitals and Medical Services Committee. Measles: report of the Medical Officer of Health and School Medical Officer on the measles epidemic, 1935-36. London, 1938. pp. 94.

MEAT

- Packaging

ORGANISATION FOR ECONOMIC CO-OPERATION AND DEVELOPMENT. Documentation in Food and Agriculture. 1964 Series. 68. The economic effects of fresh meat prepackaging in member countries of the O.E.C.D.; (by D.L. Anderson). Paris, [1964]. pp. 148. bibliog.

- Taxation - United Kingdom

UNITED KINGDOM. Parliament. 1644. An ordinance of the Lords and Commons...touching the excise of flesh-victualls, and salt; [dated 9 January, 1644]. London, Cotes and Raworth, 1643[O.S.]. pp. 6. 18½cm. Wing E 2100.

MEAT INDUSTRY AND TRADE

- Law and legislation - Uruguay

URUGUAY. Statutes, etc. 1911-1953. El comercio de carnes en el Uruguay: disposiciones que lo rigen y sus proyecciones económicas; por...Guillermo Bernhard. Montevideo, 1953. pp. 120. 23½cm.

- Argentine Republic

ARGENTINE REPUBLIC. Junta Nacional de Carnes. Reseña. Buenos Aires, annual, 1967 [1st issue] to date. 22 x 33½cm.

SMITH (PETER H.) Politics and beef in Argentina: patterns of conflict and change. New York, Columbia U.P., 1969. pp. xii, 292. bibliog. 22½cm.

- Australia

UNITED STATES. Foreign Agricultural Service. FAS-M-164. The livestock and meat industry of Australia. [Washington], 1965. pp. vi, 20. bibliog.

MUTTON AND LAMB SITUATION, THE; published by Bureau of Agricultural Economics,...Australia. Canberra, annual, June 1966 (no.1) to date. 23½cm-24½cm.

AUSTRALIA. Bureau of Agricultural Economics. 1967. Household meat consumption in Sydney. Canberra, 1967. pp. ii, 100. (Beef Research Reports. No. 3)

WOODWARD (K.R.) An empirical investigation of the N.S.W. meat market. [Armidale], 1968. pp. 218. bibliog.

- Azerbaijan

RAZVITIE miasnoi i molochnoi promyshlennosti Azerbaidzhana. Baku, 1966. pp. 52. (Azerbaidzhanskii Institut Nauchno-Tekhnicheskoi Informatsii. Obzornaia Informatsiia: Seriia "Pishchevaia Promyshlennost' ")

- Belgium

BODDEZ (G.R.) La production de viande porcine et bovine, 1970-1980. Bruxelles, 1969. fo.18. bibliog. (Belgium. Institut Economique Agricole. Notes. No.14.)

- Botswana

PURNELL (GLEN R.) and CLAYTON (W.S.) Report to the government of the Bechuanaland Protectorate on the beef, cattle and meat industry. Rome, [Food and Agriculture Organization], 1963. fo. 60. bibliog.

- Canada

HOLMES (R. A.) The estimation of demand elasticities for substitute food products. [Ottawa, 1966]. pp. 101. (Agricultural Economics Research Council of Canada. Publications. No.3)

UNITED STATES. Foreign Agricultural Service. FAS-M-176. Canada's meat and livestock industry. [Washington], 1966. pp. iv, 11.

- Colombia

ANDERSON (A.W.) and BEJARANO (JULIO) La industria de carne en Colombia; estudio realizado. Bogota, 1961. pp. 56.

MEAT INDUSTRY AND TRADE - Colombia (Cont'd.)

CURRIE (LAUCHLIN) Algunas consideraciones sobre la industria de carne en Colombia. Bogota, 1961. pp. 15.

FEDERACION COLOMBIANA DE GANADEROS. Aspectos tecnologicos, economicos, financieros e instituciones de la ganaderia colombiana: informacion basica para la II Asamblea de la Confederacion Interamericana de Ganaderos. Bogota, 1967. pp. 76, (13).

- Europe

ORGANISATION FOR EUROPEAN ECONOMIC CO-OPERATION. European Productivity Agency. Documentation in Food and Agriculture. 1961 Series. 42. Organisation of the wholesale meat markets in Europe; (including results of the International Seminar on Marketing of Meat, 1960; by J. O'Mahony). Paris, 1961. pp. 74.

- European Economic Community countries

UNITED STATES. Agriculture Department. Economic Research Service. ERS Foreign 139. Meat import prospects of the European Economic Community. Washington, 1966. pp. iv, 28.

UNITED STATES. Agriculture Department. Economic Research Service. Foreign Agricultural Economic Reports. No. 31. The grain-livestock economy of the European Economic Community: a historical review, 1951-63. Washington, 1966. pp. vi, 58.

SCHUMACHER (BRUNO) Dr. Die schweizerische Vieh- und Fleischwirtschaft im Rahmen der Europäischen Wirtschaftsgemeinschaft. Aarau, Keller, 1967. pp. xiv, 169. bibliog. 22½cm.

RICKARD (R.C.) Beef and veal in the Common Market: an examination of the E.E.C. market regulations for beef and veal effective from July 1968; prepared for the Meat and Livestock Commission; ([with] E.E.C. beef and veal circulars). Exeter, U. of Exeter, Department of Agricultural Economics, 1968 in progress. 33cm.

- France

La PRODUCTION de viande dans Midi-Pyrénées; par Jean Chataigner [and others]. [Toulouse], Laboratoire d'Economie Rurale, Institut National de la Recherche Agronomique, 1966-1968. 3 vols (in 1). bibliog.

- Germany

BOECKENHOFF (EWALD) Marktstruktur und Preisbildung bei Schlachtvieh und Fleisch in der Bundesrepublik Deutschland. Bonn, Forschungsgesellschaft für Agrarpolitik und Agrarsoziologie, 1966. pp. (ix), 125. bibliog. 29cm. ([Publications]. 166)

WILLERS (BENNO) Fleischabsatz im Umbruch: Analyse der Vermarktungsstruktur in dichtbesiedelten Regionen dargestellt für Nordrhein-Westfalen. Hannover, Strothe, 1966. pp. 295. bibliog. 20½cm. (Agrarwirtschaft. Sonderhefte. 21)

HOLST (PETER) and FENDT (FRANZ) Die Versorgung westdeutscher Ballungsgebiete mit tierischen Erzeugnissen. Hamburg, Parey, 1967. pp. 186. bibliog. 21cm.

MANEGOLD (DIRK) Die Handels- und Bearbeitungsspannen für Rind- und Schweinefleisch: Eine Überprüfung der Berechnungsgrundlagen im Hinblick auf die Aussagekraft der Ergebnisse. Bonn, 1968. pp. 79. bibliog. (Forschungsgesellschaft für Agrarpolitik und Agrarsoziologie. [Publications]. 204)

- Ireland (Republic)

EIRE. Advisory Committee on the Marketing of Agricultural Produce. 1959. Report on the export of livestock and meat. Dublin, [1959]. pp. 42. 33cm.

EIRE. Survey Team for the Beef, Mutton and Lamb Industry. 1963. Report. Dublin, [1963]. pp. 167.

- Kenya

KENYA. Sessional Papers. 1961. No. 7. Report of the Commission of Inquiry into the Administration and Staff Relations of the Kenya Meat Commission: [government views and proposed action]. [Nairobi], 1961. pp. 3.

- New Zealand

NEW ZEALAND. Commission of Inquiry into the Meat Industry. 1959. Report...presented to the House of Representatives, etc. [D.M. Greig, Chairman]. Wellington, 1959. pp. 32.

LOACH (CYRIL) A history of the New Zealand Refrigerating Company. Christchurch, 1969. pp. 200. bibliog.

- Nigeria

NIGERIA (WESTERN REGION). Ministry of Economic Planning. Studies in the Marketing of Agricultural Products. No. 1. Some economic and technical aspects of beef marketing in Western Nigeria, with special reference to the consumption of beef in Ibadan; by A.M.M. McFarquhar. [Ibadan, 1959] pp. 11.

- Russia

PSHIKOV (ALEKSEI VASIL'EVICH) and TSVETKOV (ALEKSANDR MIKHAILOVICH) Miasnaia promyshlennost' Stavropol'ia. Stavropol', 1964. pp. 44.

FALEEV (GEORGII ANATOL'EVICH) Основные вопросы развития и размещения мясной промышленности СССР. Москва, Пищевая Промышленность, 1968. pp. 104. bibliog. 21cm.

- South Africa

SOUTH AFRICA. 1962. The history and role of the Livestock and Meat Industries Control Board in the Republic of South Africa. (Livestock and Meat Industries Control Board) [Pretoria?, 1962]. pp. 16. (bis). 23cm. In English and Afrikaans.

- South West Africa

> SOUTH AFRICA. Report of the Controller and Auditor-General on the accounts of the Meat Trade Control Board of South-West Africa. Oct. 1968/Sept. 1969 to date included in SOUTH AFRICA. Parliament. House of Assembly. Votes and proceedings; (with Printed annexures).

- Switzerland

> SWITZERLAND. Commission Fédérale du Contrôle des Prix. 1959. Les prix et les marges dans le commerce du bétail de boucherie et de la viande; rapport au chef du Département fédéral de l'économie publique. Berne, 1959. pp. 67, (46).

> SCHUMACHER (BRUNO) Dr. Die schweizerische Vieh- und Fleischwirtschaft im Rahmen der Europäischen Wirtschaftsgemeinschaft. Aarau, Keller, 1967. pp. xiv, 169. bibliog. 22½cm.

- United Kingdom

> PHILPOTT (BRYAN PASSMORE) and MATHESON (MARY J.) An analysis of the retail demand for meat in the United Kingdom. [Christchurch, University of Canterbury], Lincoln College, Agricultural Economics Research Unit, 1965. fo. 39. 25½cm. (Publications. No. 23)

> U.K. Board of Trade. 1966. Cadco Developments Limited, Royal Victoria Sausages Limited, Victoria Wholesale Meats Limited: investigation under Section 165(b) of the Companies Act, 1948; report by Rondle Owen Charles Stable and Horace Owen Harrison Coulson. London, 1966. pp. vi, 150. 33cm.

> MATHESON (MARY J.) and PHILPOTT (BRYAN PASSMORE) The regional pattern of the demand for meat in the United Kingdom. [Christchurch, N.Z.], 1967. fo. 16. (Christchurch. New Zealand. University of Canterbury. Lincoln College. Agricultural Economics Research Unit. Publications. No. 31)

- United Kingdom - Ireland, Northern

> IRELAND, NORTHERN. 1967. The production and marketing of Northern Ireland meat. (Ministry of Agriculture) Belfast, 1967. pp. (iv), 62. 24½cm.

- United States

> SWIFT AND COMPANY and AMALGAMATED MEAT CUTTERS AND BUTCHER WORKMEN OF NORTH AMERICA. Master agreement..., covering period August 11, 1950 to August 11, 1952. [Chicago, 1950]. pp. 48.

> AMALGAMATED MEAT CUTTERS AND BUTCHER WORKMEN OF NORTH AMERICA and ARMOUR AND COMPANY. Master agreement..., November 19, 1952. [Chicago, 1952]. pp. 84.

> ARMOUR AND COMPANY and AMALGAMATED MEAT CUTTERS AND BUTCHER WORKMEN OF NORTH AMERICA. Agreement made...on November 19, 1952 concerning a pension plan. [Chicago?, 1952]. pp. 27.

> SWIFT AND COMPANY and AMALGAMATED MEAT CUTTERS AND BUTCHER WORKMEN OF NORTH AMERICA. Master agreement... covering period November 10, 1952 to August 11, 1954. [Chicago, 1953]. pp. 85.

> ORGANISATION FOR ECONOMIC CO-OPERATION AND DEVELOPMENT. Documentation in Food and Agriculture. 1961 Series. 40 Application of marketing and consumer research for livestock products in the United States. [Paris], 1961. pp. iv, 158. bibliog.

> FOGEL (WALTER A.) The negro in the meat industry. Philadelphia, [1970]. pp. 146. (Pennsylvania University. Wharton School of Finance and Commerce. Industrial Research Unit. Racial Policies of American Industry. Reports. No. 12)

MEAT INSPECTION

- United Kingdom

> LONDON. London Butchers' Trade Society. Inspection of meat and milk: to the members of the London County Council. [London?, 1899]. pp. 8.

MECHANICAL ENGINEERING

> COUNCIL OF EUROPE. 1966. International classification of patents for invention under the European Convention of 19th December 1954: elaboration of section F, mechanics, lighting and heating; prepared by the classification working party of the committee of experts on patents, etc. Strasbourg, 1966. pp. xv, 691. 26½cm.

- Italy

> ITALY. Comitato Nazionale per la Produttività. Gruppo di Lavoro per l'Industria Meccanica. 1953. L'esportazione di prodotti dell'industria meccanica: rapporto del Gruppo...sulle possibilità di sviluppo delle esportazioni meccaniche italiane. Roma, 1953. pp. 34. 26cm.

- United Kingdom

> ECONOMIC DEVELOPMENT COMMITTEE FOR THE MECHANICAL ENGINEERING INDUSTRY. Mechanical engineering: short term trends, August 1967: a report by the working party. London, 1967. pp. 8.

> ECONOMIC DEVELOPMENT COMMITTEE FOR THE MECHANICAL ENGINEERING INDUSTRY. Short term trends. London, quarterly, Feb.1968 to date.

> ECONOMIC DEVELOPMENT COMMITTEE FOR THE MECHANICAL ENGINEERING INDUSTRY. Market - the world: a study of success in exporting. London, [1968]. pp. (iii), 80. 24½cm.

> ECONOMIC DEVELOPMENT COMMITTEE FOR THE MECHANICAL ENGINEERING INDUSTRY. Better delivery: how to make delivery promises more reliable, reduce delivery times, and improve profitability: report of a working party. London, H.M.S.O., 1969. pp. 32. bibliog.

> ECONOMIC DEVELOPMENT COMMITTEE FOR THE MECHANICAL ENGINEERING INDUSTRY. Industrial report...on the economic assessment to 1972. London, [H.M.S.O.], 1970. pp. 39.

> ECONOMIC DEVELOPMENT COMMITTEE FOR THE MECHANICAL ENGINEERING INDUSTRY. Market research in action: a guide for company management. London, H.M.S.O., 1971. pp. 36.

MECHANICAL ENGINEERING - United Kingdom (Cont'd.)

ECONOMIC DEVELOPMENT COMMITTEE FOR THE MECHANICAL ENGINEERING INDUSTRY. The mechanical engineering industry: (digest of statistical information). London, National Economic Development Office, 1971. pp. 67.

MECHANICAL ENGINEERS, AMERICAN

CALVERT (MONTE A.) The mechanical engineer in America, 1830-1910: professional cultures in conflict. Baltimore, Johns Hopkins P., [1967]. pp. xviii, 296. bibliog. 22½cm.

MECHANICS

HERTZ (HEINRICH RUDOLPH) The principles of mechanics, presented in a new form; ... authorized English translation by D.E. Jones and J.T. Walley; [re-issue of the edition originally published in 1900]. New York, Dover Publications, 1956. pp. xliv, 274. bibliog. 20½cm. (Paperbounds. S 317)

- History

CLAVELIN (MAURICE) La philosophie naturelle de Galilée: essai sur les origines et la formation de la mécanique classique. Paris, Colin, 1968. pp. 504. bibliog. 24cm. (Philosophies pour l'Age de la Science)

DRAKE (STILLMAN) and DRABKIN (I.E.) eds. Mechanics in sixteenth-century Italy: selections from Tartaglia, Benedetti, Guido Ubaldo, and Galileo. Madison, Wis., 1969. pp. 428. bibliog. (Wisconsin University. Publications in Medieval Science. No. 13)

MECHANICS (PERSONS)

MAKURIN (NIKOLAI DMITRIEVICH) Оплата труда в ремонтных мастерских государственных предприятий сельского хозяйства: справочник для рабочих и инженерно-технических работников ремонтных мастерских государственных сельскохозяйственных предприятий. Москва, 1962. pp. 134.

MECHANICS' INSTITUTES

UNION OF LANCASHIRE AND CHESHIRE INSTITUTES. Outline of the operations of the Union, 1839-1897. [Manchester, 1897?] pp. 12.

LEA (JOHN THOMAS) The history and development of the mechanics' institutions. Werneth Oldham, Lancs., 1968. pp. 15. bibliog.

MECKLENBURG

- Foreign relations - Russia

MEDIGER (WALTHER) Mecklenburg, Russland und England-Hannover 1706-1721: ein Beitrag zur Geschichte des Nordischen Krieges. Hildesheim, Lax, 1967. 2 vols. bibliog. 23cm. (Historischer Verein für Niedersachsen. Quellen und Darstellungen zur Geschichte Niedersachsens. Band 70)

- History

MEIRITZ (HEINZ) Die Grosse Sozialistische Oktoberrevolution und ihr Einfluss auf die Entwicklung der revolutionären Arbeiterbewegung in Mecklenburg-Schwerin, 1917-1920: (Oktoberecho in Mecklenburg; zur Geschichte der Arbeiterbewegung in Mecklenburg). [Schwerin, 1967]. pp. 71.

MEDIATION
See CONCILIATION (CIVIL PROCEDURE)

MEDIATION, INTERNATIONAL

COT (JEAN PIERRE) La conciliation internationale. Paris, Pedone, 1968. pp. iv, 389. bibliog. 24½cm. (Revue Générale de Droit International Public. Publications. Nouvelle Série. No.11)

HAMZEH (FUAD S.) United Nations conciliation commission for Palestine, 1949-1967. Beirut, 1968. pp. 68. (Institute for Palestine Studies. Monographs Series. No. 17)

BURTON (JOHN W.) Conflict and communication: the use of controlled communication in international relations. London, Macmillan, 1969. pp. xvii, 246. bibliog. 20½cm.

PUSHMIN (EDUARD ANDRIANOVICH) Posrednichestvo v mezhdunarodnom prave. Moskva, 1970. pp. 165.

MEDICAL AUXILIARIES

- Russia

ARTEM'EV (FEDOR ANDREEVICH) Трудовые права медицинских работников. Москва, Юридическая Литература, 1965. pp. 144. 20cm.

MEDICAL CARE

ABEL-SMITH (BRIAN) The major pattern of financing and organisation of medical services that have emerged in other countries; (paper given before Committee on Social Policy for Health Care, New York, Academy of Medicine Committee on Special Studies, March 20, 1964) n.p., [1964?]. fo. irreg.

FRENCH (RUTH M.) The dynamics of health care. New York, McGraw-Hill, [1968]. pp. xi, 140. bibliogs. 20cm.

BRYANT (JOHN) Health and the developing world. Ithaca, N.Y., 1969. pp. 345.

ROEMER (MILTON IRWIN) The organisation of medical care under social security: a study based on the experience of eight countries. Geneva, International Labour Office, 1969. pp. 241. bibliog. (Studies and Reports. New Series. No. 73)

SOCIOLOGICAL REVIEW, THE [published by] University of Keele. Monographs. [No.] 14. Sociological studies in economics and administration; edited by Paul Halmos. Keele, 1969. pp. 163.

MAEGRAITH (BRIAN) Medical aid in the emergent world. [Glasgow], 1970. pp. 47. bibliog. (Glasgow. University. Maurice Bloch Lectures. 11) (Glasgow. University. Publications. New Series. No. 140)

SYMPOSIUM ON SYSTEMS AND MEDICAL CARE, HARVARD UNIVERSITY, 1968. Systems and medical care: [papers presented at the symposium]; edited by Alan Sheldon [and others]. Cambridge, Mass., [1970]. pp. 360. bibliogs.

MEDICAL history and medical care: a symposium of perspectives arranged by the Nuffield Provincial Hospitals Trust and the Josiah Macy Jr. Foundation;...edited by Gordon McLachlan and Thomas McKeown. London, 1971. pp. 244.

MURRAY (DAVID STARK) Medical care: who gets the best service. London, 1971. pp. 16. bibliog. (Fabian Society. Fabian Occasional Papers. 6)

OFFICE OF HEALTH ECONOMICS. Studies in Current Health Problems. No. 37. Prospects in health. London, [1971]. pp. 24. bibliog.

- Africa, East

BECK (ANN FRANK) A history of the British medical administration of East Africa, 1900-1950. Cambridge, Mass., 1970. pp. 271. bibliog.

- Australia

HUTCHINSON (M.) Group practice, ancillary help and government controls: a study of general practice in four countries. [London], 1967. pp. 67. bibliog. (Journal of the Royal College of General Practitioners. Vol. 14. Supplement no. 1)

- Canada

CANADIAN MEDICAL ASSOCIATION. Journal. Special Supplements. Statement on medical care with conclusions and recommendations; prepared by the Special Committee on Policy of the Canadian Medical Association. Toronto, 1964. pp. 55. 28½cm. (In English and French)

[NATIONAL CONFERENCE ON HEALTH SERVICES], OTTAWA, 1965. Health services in Canada: report of a working conference on the implications of a health charter for Canadians. Ottawa, imprint, [1965]. pp. 182. bibliog. 21¼cm.

CANADIAN WELFARE COUNCIL. Committee on Health Aspects of Welfare. The medical care act: comments and recommendations. Ottawa, 1967. pp. 16.

HUTCHINSON (M.) Group practice, ancillary help and government controls: a study of general practice in four countries. [London], 1967. pp. 67. bibliog. (Journal of the Royal College of General Practitioners. Vol. 14. Supplement no. 1)

BLISHEN (BERNARD R.) Doctors and doctrines: the ideology of medical care in Canada. [Toronto, 1969]. pp. 202. bibliog.

- Canada - Saskatchewan

SASKATCHEWAN. Advisory Planning Committee on Medical Care. 1961. Interim report...to the government of Saskatchewan, September 1961: [W.P. Thompson, chairman]. [Regina, 1961]. fo. 148.

SASKATCHEWAN. Advisory Planning Committee on Medical Care. 1962. Interim [and final] report...to the government of Saskatchewan: [W.P. Thompson, chairman]. Regina, 1962. 2 vols. (in 1).

- East (Near East)

SIMON (JAN) Men and medicine in the Middle East: a factual and pictorial assessment of what 20 countries are doing to raise their peoples' health standards and how the World Health Organization (WHO) is assisting them. [Alexandria], World Health Organization, [1967]. pp. 242.

- Europe

OFFICE OF HEALTH ECONOMICS. Health services in Western Europe. London, [1963]. pp. 16.

- Finland

HAAVIO-MANNILA (ELINA) Need of domiciliary care in Finnish rural districts. [Helsinki, 1964]. pp. 55-61. (Helsinki. Yliopisto. Sosiologian Laitos. Publications. No.21) (Reprinted from International Nursing Review, no.2, vol.11, 1964)

The UTILIZATION of the medical services and its relationship to morbidity, health resources and social factors: a survey of the population of Finland prior to the national sickness insurance scheme; [by] Tapani Purola [and others]. Helsinki, Research Institute for Social Security, 1968. pp. 243. bibliog. (Finland. Kansaneläkelaitos. Julkaisuja. Sarja A.3)

- France

SAVY (BERNARD CLAUDE) Nouvelle politique de santé. Paris, [1969]. pp. 117.

SÉVENO (MAURICE) Le scandale de la santé en France. Paris, [1970]. pp. 243. bibliog.

- Germany

GESELLSCHAFT FÜR SOZIALEN FORTSCHRITT. Schriften. Band 18. Patient-Arzt, Krankenhaus-Krankenkasse: Referate und Diskussion auf einer Tagung...in Bonn-Bad Godesberg am 28. November 1969. Berlin, [1970]. pp. 92.

KNOEFERL (GUENTER) Die Nachfrage nach freiberuflichen ärztlichen Leistungen: Versuch der Grundlegung für eine empirische Nachfrageprognose. [Erlangen, imprint, 1971?]. pp. 278, xxxiii. bibliog.

- Greece

RITSATAKIS (ANNE WOOD) An analysis of the health and welfare services in Greece. Athens, 1970. pp. 227. bibliog. (Center of Planning and Economic Research [Athens]. Special Studies. Series. B.1)

- India

NATIONAL SEMINAR ON THE ROLE OF VOLUNTARY AGENCIES IN THE IMPLEMENTATION OF PUBLIC HEALTH, MEDICAL CARE AND FAMILY PLANNING PROGRAMMES UNDER FIVE-YEAR PLANS, MADRAS, 1965. National health seminar;... sponsored by Andhra Mahila Sabha, etc. Madras, [1966]. pp. 205.

- Israel

HUTCHINSON (M.) Group practice, ancillary help and government controls: a study of general practice in four countries. [London], 1967. pp. 67. bibliog. (Journal of the Royal College of General Practitioners. Vol. 14. Supplement no. 1)

MEDICAL CARE (Cont'd.)

- Latvia

KANEP (V.) Health service in Soviet Latvia. Riga, 1969. pp. 37.

- Malaya - Johore

JOHORE. [Medical Department]. Report of the medical and health services of the State of Johore (formerly Medical report, previously Territorial medical report). Johore Bahru, annual, 1922-1934 1936; 1938 (pt.2 only); 1940. 20-32cm.

- New Guinea

AMELSVOORT (VINCENTIUS FRANCIS PETRUS MARIA VAN) Early introduction of integrated rural health into a primitive society: a New Guinea case study in medical anthropology. Assen, Van Gorcum, [1964]. pp. xiv, 245. bibliog. 24cm.

- New Zealand

HUTCHINSON (M.) Group practice, ancillary help and government controls: a study of general practice in four countries. [London], 1967. pp. 67. bibliog. (Journal of the Royal College of General Practitioners. Vol. 14. Supplement no. 1)

MEDICAL ASSOCIATION OF NEW ZEALAND. Review of medical services: preliminary report; by a sub-committee. Wellington, 1967. pp. 48. 21½cm.

NEW ZEALAND. Department of Health. Trends in health and health services. [Wellington], irreg., 1968 [1st issue] to date. 28cm.

HEALTH administration in New Zealand: [papers presented at a convention in Hamilton, New Zealand, May, 1968]; edited by R.J. Latimer. Wellington, 1969. pp. 127. (New Zealand Institute of Public Administration. Studies in Public Administration. No. 15)

- Nigeria

NIGERIA MEDICAL ASSOCIATION. A health programme for the nation. [Ibadan, 1966]. pp. 154. 25cm.

- Russia

FRY (JOHN) Medicine in three societies:...a comparison of medical care in the USSR, USA and UK. Aylesbury, [1969]. pp. 249.

- Sudan

PHILOSOPHICAL SOCIETY OF THE SUDAN. The health of the Sudan: a study in social development. in its Conference. Proceedings, 8th, 1960. Khartoum, 1963.

- Sweden

ANDERSEN (RONALD) and others. Medical care use in Sweden and the United States: a comparative analysis of systems and behavior. Chicago, 1970. pp. 174. bibliog. (Chicago. University. Center for Health Administration Studies. Research Series. No. 27)

- United Kingdom

RUMSEY (HENRY WYLDBORE) Essays on state medicine. London, 1856. pp. 424.

The CASE for health centres: what they would mean to the doctor, and to the patient; by a general practitioner; issued by the Socialist Medical Association. London, Today and Tomorrow Publications, [1964]. pp. 16. 21½cm.

LIBERAL HEALTH COMMITTEE. Health and welfare: interim report, London, [1964?]. pp. 18. (Current Topics. Supplements)

PETERS (ROBERT JAMES) and KINNAIRD (J.) Health services administration: a source book. Edinburgh, 1965. pp. 500. bibliogs.

SYMPOSIUM ON THE QUALITY OF MEDICAL CARE, LIVERPOOL UNIVERSITY, 1965. Report, etc. [London], 1966. pp. 36. (Journal of the Royal College of General Practitioners. vol. 11. Supplement no. 3)

WOOD (BRUCE) The personal health and welfare services. London, London University, London School of Economics and Political Science, Greater London Group, 1966. pp. 45. 30cm. (Town Government in South East England. Research Studies. No. 2)

OFFICE OF HEALTH ECONOMICS. Symposia. Alive to forty-five: proceedings of a symposium... 27 November, 1966. London, the Office, [1967] pp. 36. 30cm.

OFFICE OF HEALTH ECONOMICS. Symposia. The provision of general medical care in new towns: proceedings of a symposium...19th and 20th April 1966; edited by John Fry and John McKenzie. London, the Office, [1967]. pp. 31. 30cm.

BUTTERFIELD (W.J.H.) Priorities in medicine. [London], Nuffield Provincial Hospitals Trust, 1968. pp. xiv, 198. bibliog. 21½cm. (Rock Carling Fellowship. 1968)

[HINKS (M. DOROTHY)] Working together: a study of coordination and cooperation between general practitioners, public health and hospital services. London, King Edward's Hospital Fund for London, 1968. pp. 76. bibliog. 21cm.

HOCKEY (LISBETH) Care in the balance: a study of collaboration between hospital and community services. [London], Queen's Institute of District Nursing, [1968]. pp. xviii, 163. bibliog. 21½cm.

McLACHLAN (GORDON) ed. Problems and progress in medical care: (essays on current research, third series) London, O.U.P., 1968. pp. ix, 170. 21½cm.

MEDICAL DEFENCE UNION. Consent to treatment. rev. ed. London, 1968. pp. 21.

ROBINSON (KENNETH) Partnership in medical care. Glasgow, 1968. pp. 28. (Glasgow. University. Maurice Bloch Lectures. 9)

FRY (JOHN) Medicine in three societies:...a comparison of medical care in the USSR, USA and UK. Aylesbury, [1969]. pp. 249.

BRITISH MEDICAL ASSOCIATION. Working Party on Primary Medical Care. Report. London, 1970. pp. 80. (British Medical Association. Planning Unit. Reports. No. 4)

BUTLER (JOHN R.) and PEARSON (MARY) Who goes home?; a study of long-stay patients in acute hospital care. London, 1970. pp. 75. bibliog. (Social Administration Research Trust. Occasional Papers on Social Administration. No. 34)

McLACHLAN (GORDON) ed. Problems and progress in medical care: essays on current research, fourth series. London, [1970]. pp. 204.

RESOURCES in medicine: a collection of papers based on a three-day seminar... held at St. Thomas' Hospital in 1969...; edited by Jane Collins. London, [1970]. pp. 76. bibliog.

LANCE (HILARY) Report on transport services in general practice: an experiment in five general practices. [London], 1971. pp. 67. (Journal of the Royal College of General Practitioners. vol. 21. Supplement no.3)

RUBECK (M.F.) Social and emotional effects of chronic bronchitis. London, [1971]. pp.64. bibliog.

SURVEY of general practitioners' care of their patients in the hospital service; report by a team appointed by the Department of Health and Social Security. [London], 1971. pp. 14. bibliog. (Journal of the Royal College of General Practitioners. vol.21. Supplement no.1)

- United Kingdom - Scotland

ORGANISATION of medical work in the hospital service in Scotland: first report of the joint working party: [J.H.F. Brotherston, chairman]. Edinburgh, H.M.S.O., 1967. pp. 79. 24½cm.

SIMPSON (JOHN) of Dundee University, and others. Custom and practice in medical care: a comparative study of two hospitals in Arbroath, Scotland, U.K. and Waterville, Maine, U.S.A. London, O.U.P., 1968. pp. (iii), 119. 21½cm.

- United States

HOSPITALS, medical care and public responsibility; four papers presented at a conference commemorating the tenth anniversary of the Program in Medical and Hospital Administration, Graduate School of Public Health, University of Pittsburgh, June 9, 1961. [Pittsburgh, 1962]. pp. 34.

UNITED STATES. Department of Health Education and Welfare.
Human investment programs: delivery of health services for the poor. Washington, 1967. pp.ii, 135.

CUMMING (ELAINE) and others. Systems of social regulation. New York, Atherton P., 1968. pp. xi, 324. 21½cm.

DUFF (RAYMOND S.) and HOLLINGSHEAD (AUGUST DE BELMONT) Sickness and society. New York, Harper & Row, [1968]. pp. xiii, 390. 23½cm.

FUCHS (VICTOR ROBERT) The growing demand for medical care. New York, National Bureau of Economic Research, 1968. pp. 8. bibliog. 25½cm. (Reports. 3. Supplement)

PENCHANSKY (ROY) ed. Health services administration: policy cases and the case method. Cambridge, Harvard U. P., 1968. pp. xix, 460. 23½cm.

TAPPAN (FRANCES M.) Toward understanding administrators in the medical environment. New York, Macmillan, [1968]. pp. xvii, 270. bibliogs. 21cm.

UNITED STATES. Public Health Service. Publications. No. 1774.
Conference - workshop on regional medical programs: proceedings. Washington, 1968. 2 vols.

FRY (JOHN) Medicine in three societies:...a comparison of medical care in the USSR, USA and UK. Aylesbury, [1969]. pp. 249.

GINZBERG (ELI) Men, money, and medicine. New York, 1969. pp. 291.

MEDICINE in the ghetto: (conference sponsored jointly by Harvard Medical School, the Boston Globe, and the National Center for Health Services Research and Development); editor John C. Norman. New York, [1969]. pp. 333.

POVERTY and health; a sociological analysis; edited by John Kosa [and others]. Cambridge, Mass., 1969. pp. 449.

AMERICAN ASSEMBLY. [37th Assembly, April 1970]. The health of Americans; (edited by Boisfeuillet Jones). Englewood Cliffs, N.J., [1970]. pp. 209.

ANDERSEN (RONALD) and others. Medical care use in Sweden and the United States: a comparative analysis of systems and behavior. Chicago, 1970. pp. 174. bibliog. (Chicago. University. Center for Health Administration Studies. Research Series. No. 27)

BABBIE (EARL R.) Science and morality in medicine: a survey of medical educators. Berkeley, 1970. pp. 261. bibliog.

CONFERENCE ON THE ECONOMICS OF HEALTH [AND MEDICAL CARE], 2ND, BALTIMORE, 1968. Empirical studies in health economics: proceedings...; (Herbert E. Klarman, editor). Baltimore, [1970]. pp. 433.

EARICKSON (ROBERT) The spatial behavior of hospital patients: a behavioral approach to spatial interaction in metropolitan Chicago. Chicago, 1970. pp. 138. bibliog. (Chicago. University. Department of Geography. Research Papers. No. 124)

FREIDSON (ELIOT) Professional dominance: the social structure of medical care. New York, 1970. pp. 242.

- United States - California

CALIFORNIA. 1960. Health care for California: a report of the Governor's Committee on Medical Aid and Health: [Roger O. Egeberg, chairman] (Department of Public Health) Berkeley, 1960. pp. v, 104. 28cm.

- United States - Maine

SIMPSON (JOHN) of Dundee University, and others. Custom and practice in medical care: a comparative study of two hospitals in Arbroath, Scotland, U.K. and Waterville, Maine, U.S.A. London, O.U.P., 1968. pp. (iii), 119. 21½cm.

MEDICAL CARE (Cont'd.)

- United States - New York

GOODRICH (CHARLES H.) and others. Welfare medical care: an experiment. Cambridge, Mass., 1970. pp. 343.

GINZBERG (ELI) and others. Urban health services: the case of New York. New York, 1971. pp. 250. bibliog.

- Vietnam

EVANS (BARBARA) Caduceus in Saigon: a medical mission to South Viet-Nam. London, Hutchinson, 1968. pp. xii, 210. 21cm.

MEDICAL CARE, COST OF

The COST of health: proceedings of a seminar held at the University of Adelaide; [arranged by the Department of Adult Education in the University], September 18-20, 1970. Adelaide, 1971. pp. 61. (Adelaide. University. Department of Adult Education. Publications. No.25)

- Canada

CANADA. Committee on Costs of Health Services. 1970. Task force reports on the cost of health services in Canada. Ottawa, 1970. 3 vols (in 1). bibliogs.

- Colombia

CAJA NACIONAL DE PREVISION SOCIAL, [COLOMBIA]. Costos del seguro de enfermedad y maternidad: prestaciones médicas, farmacéuticas y hospitalarias y subsidios en dinero en los años de 1957, 1958 y 1959. Bogota, 1960. pp. 16.

- Germany

WOLFSLAST (JUERGEN) Cost-Benefit-Analyse im Gesundheitswesen. Hamburg, 1968. pp. 229. bibliog. (Hamburg. Hamburgisches Welt-Wirtschafts-Archiv. Veröffentlichungen)

- United Kingdom

OFFICE OF HEALTH ECONOMICS. The costs of medical care. London, [1964]. pp. 32. bibliog. 20½cm.

HEALTH services financing: a report commissioned in 1967 by the British Medical Association and carried out by an advisory panel under the chairmanship of Dr. Ivor M. Jones. [London, 1969?]. pp. 605.

SHARPHOUSE (R.C.) The finance of the health services. London, 1971. pp. 37.

- United States

DICKINSON (FRANK GREENE) Medical care expenditures, prices and quantity, 1930-1950. Chicago, 1951. pp. 15. (Bureau of Medical Economic Research. Bulletins. No.87)

DICKINSON (FRANK GREENE) and RAYMOND (JAMES) The economic position of medical care, 1929-1953;...the story in charts of the Economic position of medical care, 1929-1953. Chicago, [1955]. 2 pts. (American Medical Association. Bulletins. 99 and 99A)

SOMERS (HERMAN MILES) Financing of medical care in the United States. [Boston, 1966]. pp. irreg. (Reprinted from the New England Journal of Medicine, 275, September 29, 1966)

ANDERSEN (RONALD) and ANDERSON (ODIN W.) A decade of health services: social survey trends in use and expenditure. Chicago, U. of Chicago P., 1967. pp. xix, 244. 23cm. (Chicago. University. School of Business Studies in Business and Society)

COSTS of health care facilities: (report of a conference convened by the National Academy of Engineering, December 5 and 6, 1967). Washington, 1968. pp. 244. bibliogs. (National Academy of Sciences. Publications. 1592)

MUNTS (RAYMOND) Collective bargaining for health as a form of health planning. [Wisconsin Madison, 1968]. pp. 81-89. (Wisconsin University. Industrial Relations Research Institute. Reprint Series. No. 109) (Reprinted from Public Health Service-Labor Seminar on Consumer Health Services, Washington, January 22-23, 1968)

YOST (EDWARD) The U.S. health industry: the costs of acceptable medical care by 1975. New York, 1969. pp. 138.

EHRENREICH (BARBARA) and EHRENREICH (JOHN) The American health empire: power, profits and politics; a Health-Pac book [based on research and analysis at the Center]. New York, [1970]. pp. 279.

[NEW YORK (CITY)]. Mayor's Commission on Inflation and Economic Welfare. Inflation and medical costs: staff report. [New York, 1970?] fo. 20, 4.

PAULY (MARK V.) Medical care at public expense: a study in applied welfare economics. New York, 1971. pp. 160. bibliog.

MEDICAL CENTRES

- United Kingdom

The CASE for health centres: what they would mean to the doctor, and to the patient; by a general practitioner; issued by the Socialist Medical Association. London, [1964]. pp. 16.

MEDICAL PRACTITIONERS' UNION. Design for family doctoring; the revised version of the... Health centre report, 1960, up-dated and extended to include all aspects of present-day practice organisation;...prepared by Peggy Follis. London, Medical World, 1967. pp. 96. 22½cm.

U.K. Department of Health and Social Security, 1970. Health centres: a design guide. London, [1970]. pp. 48.

- United Kingdom - London

LONDON. London County Council. Woodberry Down Health Centre, Stoke Newington: descriptive brochure. London, 1954. pp. 13.

LONDON. London County Council. Woodberry Down Health Centre, Stoke Newington: descriptive brochure. [rev. ed.] London, 1959. pp. 16.

- United Kingdom - Scotland

>SCOTLAND. Scottish Health Services Council. Standing Dental Advisory Committee. 1969. Dental services in health centres: report of a sub-committee: [J. Blair Hardie, chairman]. Edinburgh, 1969. pp. 21.

MEDICAL COLLEGES

- Germany

>GERMANY (BUNDESREPUBLIK). Wissenschaftsrat. 1968. Empfehlungen des Wissenschaftsrates zur Struktur und zum Ausbau der medizinischen Forschungs- und Ausbildungsstätten; (with Kurzfassung wichtiger Empfehlungen). [Tübingen, Mohr], 1968. pp. 293.

MEDICAL COOPERATION

>CONFERENCE FOR STAFF IN THE MENTAL HEALTH SERVICES, LONDON, 1966. Inter-professional co-operation: facts and fantasies; report. London, National Association for Mental Health, [1966]. pp. 39. 22cm.

MEDICAL ECONOMICS

>ABEL-SMITH (BRIAN) An international study of health expenditure and its relevance for health planning. Geneva, World Health Organization, 1967. pp. 127. bibliog. (Public Health Papers. No. 32).

>BOUDREAU (THOMAS J.) ed. L'économique de la santé; textes de F. Beaudoin [and others]. Sherbrooke, Université de Sherbrooke, Faculté de Médecine, Division de Médecine Sociale, 1967. fo. iv, 219. 27½cm.

>CONFERENCE ON THE ECONOMICS OF HEALTH [AND MEDICAL CARE], 2ND, BALTIMORE, 1968. Empirical studies in health economics: proceedings...; (Herbert E. Klarman, editor). Baltimore, [1970]. pp. 433.

- France

>MATHÉ (CATHERINE) and MATHÉ (GEORGES) La santé est-elle au dessus de nos moyens? Paris, [1970]. pp. 322. bibliog.

- United Kingdom

>MENCHER (SAMUEL) Private practice in Britain: the relationship of private medical care to the National Health Service. London, 1967. pp. 95. (Social Administration Research Trust. Occasional Papers on Social Administration. No. 24)

>OFFICE OF HEALTH ECONOMICS. About OHE: a description of the organisation and work of the Office of Health Economics. London, [1968]. pp. 12.

>OFFICE OF HEALTH ECONOMICS. Building for health. London [1970]. pp. 29. bibliog.

- United States

>UNITED STATES. National Institutes of Health. Resources for medical research. Washington, 1962 in prog.

>RAYACK (ELTON) Professional power and American medicine: the economics of the American Medical Association. Cleveland, World Publishing Company, [1967]. pp. xix, 298. 21cm. (World Series in Economics)

>TAX FOUNDATION. Research Publications. New Series. No. 15. Medicaid: state programs after two years. New York, 1968. pp. 72. 25½cm.

>CAMPBELL (RITA RICARDO) Economics of health and public policy. Washington, 1971. pp. 108. bibliog. (American Enterprise Institute for Public Policy Research. Special Analyses. No.5)

MEDICAL ETHICS

>MAUROIS (ANDRÉ) pseud. [i.e. Émile HERZOG] De la morale médicale: discours aux médecins; avec une lettre liminaire du Professeur Robert Debré. Paris, Pavillon, [1967]. pp. 73. 18cm.

>GELFAND (MICHAEL) Philosophy and ethics of medicine. Edinburgh, Livingstone, 1968. pp. viii, 174. 21½cm.

>EBLING (F.J.) ed. Biology and ethics: proceedings of a symposium held at the Royal Geographical Society, London...September 1968. London, 1969. pp. 145. (Institute of Biology. Symposia. No. 18)

>BABBIE (EARL R.) Science and morality in medicine: a survey of medical educators. Berkeley, 1970. pp. 261. bibliog.

>BEECHER (HENRY KNOWLES) Research and the individual: human studies. Boston, [1970]. pp. 358. bibliog.

>MORALS and medicine: (discussions from the BBC Third programme). London, 1970. pp. 123.

>RAMSEY (PAUL) The patient as person: explorations in medical ethics. New Haven, 1970. pp. 283. (Yale University. Lyman Beecher Foundation Lectures 1969.)

>STRINGER (PAUL) Ethics and judgement in surgery and medicine. London, 1970. pp. 126. bibliog.

>SYMPOSIUM ON MAN, MILIEU AND MALADY, ROYAL COLLEGE OF OBSTETRICIANS AND GYNAECOLOGISTS, 1969. Report of a symposium... held... London 23 March 1969 [by the Royal College of General Practitioners] London, 1970. pp. 37. (Journal of the Royal College of General Practitioners. vol. 19. Supplement no. 4)

MEDICAL FEES

>GLASER (WILLIAM A.) Paying the doctor: systems of remuneration and their effects. Baltimore, [1970]. pp. 323.

- United Kingdom

>BRITISH MEDICAL ASSOCIATION. Fees for part-time medical services. London, 1970. pp. 60.

MEDICAL GEOGRAPHY

- Africa

>MAY (JACQUES M.) and McLELLAN (DONNA L.) The ecology of malnutrition in Eastern Africa and four countries of Western Africa, etc. New York, 1970. pp. 675. bibliogs.

MEDICAL GEOGRAPHY (Cont'd.)

- France

ST. ANDRÉ (J.A.D.) Topographie médicale du département de la Haute-Garonne, contenant la description générale de toutes ses communes, et la topographie plus particulière de celle de Toulouse, etc. Toulouse, Douladoure, 1814. pp. xxxii, 592. 21½cm.

- Kazakstan

PROBLEMY fizicheskoi, ekonomicheskoi i meditsinskoi geografii Kazakhstana: materialy nauchnykh konferentsii, posviashchennykh 50-letiiu Velikoi Oktiabr'skoi sotsialisticheskoi revoliutsii. Alma-Ata, 1967. pp. 159. bibliog.

- St. Helena

SHINE (IAN) Serendipity in St. Helena: a genetical and medical study of an isolated community;...with the assistance of Reynold Gold. Oxford, 1970. pp. 187. bibliog.

- United Kingdom

SYMPOSIUM ON HEALTH IN A CHANGING ENVIRONMENT, BIRMINGHAM, 1965. Report, etc. [London], 1966. pp. 51. bibliog. (Journal of the Royal College of General Practitioners. vol. 12. Supplement no. 1)

HOWE (GEORGE MELVYN) National atlas of disease mortality in the United Kingdom;... [prepared] on behalf of the Royal Geographical Society. rev ed. London, 1970. pp. 197. 3 transparencies in end pocket.

MEDICAL JURISPRUDENCE

TAYLOR (ALFRED SWAINE) Principles and practice of medical jurisprudence; twelfth edition edited by Keith Simpson; the law revised by W.H.D. Winder; Psychiatry and the law by David Stafford-Clark, the sections on Toxicology by L.C. Nickolls. London, 1965. 2 vols.

MACRAE (ALASTAIR KENNETH MACAULAY) Not only murder. [Edinburgh, 1969]. pp. 15. (Edinburgh. University. Inaugural Lectures. No. 42)

MEYERS (DAVID W.) The human body and the law: a medico-legal study. Edinburgh, 1970. pp. 203.

DAUBE (DAVID) Legal problems in medical advance. Jerusalem, 1971. pp. 21. (Hebrew University. Lionel Cohen Lectures. 16th Series)

- United States

CAWLEY (CLIFFORD C.) The right to live. New York, 1969. pp. 303.

MEDICAL LAWS AND LEGISLATION

- Belgium

SCREVENS (R.) L'internement prévu par la loi de défense sociale et l'interdiction d'exercer l'art de guérin. in Brussels. Université Libre. Faculté de Droit. Travaux et Conférences. 7. Bruxelles, 1959.

- France

JEAN (PIERRE) and TORDEUX (JACQUELINE) Le médecin à l'hôpital public: réformes intervenues depuis 1958: statut et rémunération. Paris, Berger-Levrault, 1967. pp. 321. 18cm.

JAMOUS (HAROUN) Sociologie de la décision: la reforme des études médicales et des structures hospitalières. Paris, 1969. pp. 257. (Centre National de la Recherche Scientifique. Centre d'Etudes Sociologiques. Travaux)

- Germany

BOCKELMANN (PAUL) Strafrecht des Arztes. Stuttgart, Thieme, 1968. pp. viii, 135. bibliog. 19cm.

KOHLHAAS (MAX) Medizin und Recht. München, 1969. pp. vii, 164. 18½cm.

- Poland

RADZICKI (JÓZEF) Ryzyko zabiegów lekarskich w prawie karnym. Warszawa, Państwowy Zakład Wydawnictwo Lekarskich, 1967. pp. 244. bibliog. 20cm.

SOŚNIAK (MIECZYSŁAW) Cywilna odpowiedzialność lekarza. Warszawa, WP, 1968. pp. 210. bibliog. 21cm. With English, French and Russian summaries.

- Russia

BERDICHEVSKII (FELIKS IUL'EVICH) Ugolovnaia otvetstvennost' meditsinskogo personala za narushenie professional'nykh obiazannostei. Moskva, 1970. pp. 126.

- United Kingdom

ROBB (Sir DOUGLAS) Medicine and the law. 3rd ed. London, Medical Defence Union, [1967]. pp. 34. 21½cm.

INSTITUTE OF HOSPITAL ADMINISTRATORS. Subject index to statutory instruments issued under the authority of the National Health Service Acts, 1946-67, and official memoranda and circulars issued to hospital authorities, England and Wales, 1946-67. London, the Institute, [1968]. pp. 46.

FARNDALE (WILLIAM ARTHUR JAMES) Medical negligence. Beckenham, 1969. pp. 36.

MEDICAL LITERATURE

HAHN (ANDRÉ) and DUMAITRE (PAULE) Histoire de la médecine et du livre médical à la lumière de collections de la Bibliothèque de la Faculté de Médecine de Paris. Paris, Perrin, [1962]. pp. 432. bibliog. 27cm.

MEDICAL PERSONNEL

BRYANT (JOHN) Health and the developing world. Ithaca, N.Y., 1969. pp. 345.

- India

RAY (K.) Scientific and technical personnel. New Delhi, [1966]. pp. ix, 88. bibliog. 27cm. (India. Census, 1961. Monograph Series. No. 1.)

- Nigeria

NIGERIA. National Manpower Board. Manpower Studies. No. 9. Health manpower survey, 1965: hospitals and clinics, dispensaries and maternity centres, health centres, health offices and specialist units. Lagos, 1969. pp. 84. Map in end pocket.

- Norway - Salaries, pensions, etc.

NORWAY. Statistiske Centralbyrå. Lønnsstatistikk for ansatte i helseveen.. og barneomsorg. [in Norwegian and English] a., 1969- Oslo.

- Peru

PERU. Oficina Sectorial de Planificacion de Salud. 1965. Censo de recursos humanos de salud: informe preliminar; Peru: 1964. [Lima?], 1965. pp. 61.

PERU. Oficina Sectorial de Planificacion de Salud.1967. Recursos humanos de salud; Peru: 1967; [by Thomas L. Hall]. [Lima?], 1967. pp. 369. bibliog.

HALL (THOMAS L.) Health manpower in Peru: a case study in planning. Baltimore, [1969]. pp. 281.

- Turkey

TAYLOR (CARL E.) and others. Health manpower planning in Turkey: an international research case study. Baltimore, Maryland, [1968]. pp. 300.

- United Kingdom

OFFICE OF HEALTH ECONOMICS. Studies in Current Health Problems. No. 20. Medical manpower. London, [1966]. pp. 32. bibliog.

U.K. National Health Service. 1967. Terms and conditions of service of hospital medical and dental staff (England and Wales) and headquarters medical staff of regional hospital boards (England and Wales). [London], 1967. pp. 39. 20½cm.

McLACHLAN (GORDON) ed. Problems and progress in medical care: (essays on current research, third series) London, O.U.P., 1968. pp. ix, 170. 21½cm.

MEDICAL DEFENCE UNION. Advice on the investigation of complaints to executive councils. London, [1968]. pp. 12.

U.K. Committee on Hospital Scientific and Technical Services. Report, 1967-68: [Sir Solly Zuckerman, chairman]. London, H.M.S.O., 1968. pp. vi, 69.

MARTIN (MARGARET) Colleagues or competitors?: a study of the role of five of the professions supplementary to medicine. London, 1969. pp. 103. (Social Administration Research Trust. Occasional Papers on Social Administration. No. 31)

- United Kingdom - Salaries, pensions, etc.

U.K. Department of Health and Social Security. 1970. National Health Service superannuation scheme: allocation of pension: explanatory memorandum, with tables prepared by the Government Actuary. London, 1970. pp. 27.

- United Kingdom - Scotland

SHIPP (P.J.) Manpower planning in the Scottish National Health Service. London, 1971. pp. 33. (Institute for Operational Research. Health Reports. No.5)

- United Kingdom - Scotland - Salaries, pensions, etc.

U.K. Government Actuary's Department. 1959. National Health Service Act, 1947: National Health Service Superannuation Scheme for Scotland, 1948-1955; report. Edinburgh, 1959. pp. 26. 25cm.

U.K. Government Actuary's Department. 1967. National Health Service (Scotland) Act, 1947: National Health Service Superannuation Scheme for Scotland, 1955-1962: report. Edinburgh, 1967. pp. 20. 24½cm.

- United States

UNITED STATES. Labor Department. Manpower Research Bulletins. No. 14. Technology and manpower in the health service industry, 1965-75. [Washington], 1967. pp. vii, 109, bibliog

GREENFIELD (HARRY I.) and BROWN (CAROL A.) Allied health manpower: trends and prospects. New York, Columbia U.P., 1969. pp. xix, 195. 22cm.

MEDICAL RECORD LIBRARIANS

CANADA. Dominion Bureau of Statistics. Health and Welfare Division. Institutions Section. 1970. Health manpower in hospitals: medical record librarians, 1961-68. Ottawa, 1970. pp. 18.

MEDICAL RECORDS

ACHESON (E. D.) ed. Record linkage in medicine: proceedings of the international symposium, Oxford, July,1967. Edinburgh, Livingstone, 1968. pp. xvi, 399. 21½cm.

SWEDEN. Kommunikationsdepartementet. Landstingens Arkivutredning. 1968. Arkiv inom hälso- och sjukvård. Stockholm, 1968. pp. 141. (Sweden. Statens Offentliga Utredningar. 1968. 53)

U.K. National Health Computing Services Group. 1968. The use of computers in general practice and community health care. [London], 1968. pp. 15. 30cm.

U.K. National Health Computing Services Group. 1969. An approach to the evaluation of computer hardware and software; [and] Computer compatibility. [London], 1969. pp. 9.

McLACHLAN (GORDON) ed. Problems and progress in medical care: essays on current research, fourth series. London, [1970]. pp. 204.

WORKING CONFERENCE ON INFORMATION PROCESSING OF MEDICAL RECORDS, LYON, 1970. Information processing of medical records: proceedings of the IFIP-TC4 Working Conference...; edited by J. Anderson [and] J.M. Forsythe. Amsterdam, 1970. pp. 419.

MEDICAL RESEARCH

UNITED STATES. Public Health Service. International biomedical research: first National Institutes of Health international symposium. Washington, 1964. pp. 247.

WORLD HEALTH ORGANIZATION. 1969. The medical research programme of the World Health Organization, 1964-1968: report by the Director-General. Geneva, 1969. pp. 350. bibliogs.

BEECHER (HENRY KNOWLES) Research and the individual: human studies. Boston, [1970]. pp. 358. bibliog.

DAUBE (DAVID) Legal problems in medical advance. Jerusalem, 1971. pp. 21. (Hebrew University. Lionel Cohen Lectures. 16th Series)

- Canada

CANADA. Medical Research Council. Report of the President. [in English and French] a., 1970/71- Ottawa.

- United Kingdom

BUTTERFIELD (W.J.H.) Priorities in medicine. [London], Nuffield Provincial Hospitals Trust, 1968. pp. xiv, 198. bibliog. 21½cm. (Rock Carling Fellowship. 1968)

McLACHLAN (GORDON) ed. Problems and progress in medical care: (essays on current research, third series) London, O.U.P., 1968. pp. ix, 170. 21½cm.

McLACHLAN (GORDON) ed. Problems and progress in medical care: essays on current research, fourth series. London, [1970]. pp. 204.

- United States

UNITED STATES. National Institutes of Health. Resources for medical research. Washington, 1962 in prog.

UNITED STATES. Labor Department. Manpower Research Bulletins. No. 14. Technology and manpower in the health service industry, 1965-75. [Washington], 1967. vii, 109. bibliog.

The COMMUNITY as an epidemiologic laboratory: a casebook of community studies; [presented at seminars, sponsored by the Department of Chronic Diseases, of the Johns Hopkins University School of Hygiene and Public Health, in 1968]; edited by Irving I. Kessler and Morton L. Levin. Baltimore, [1970]. pp. 325. bibliogs.

MEDICAL SCREENING

GIRT (J.L.) and others. The multiple health screening clinic, Rotherham 1966: a social and economic assessment; (a report prepared by the Social Science Research Unit) London, 1969. pp. 110. bibliog. (U.K. Department of Health and Social Security. Reports on Public Health and Medical Subjects. No. 121)

MEDICAL SOCIAL WORK

BROCK (MARGARET GAUGHAN) Social work in the hospital organization. [Toronto, 1969]. pp. 117. bibliog.

- Bahamas

COMMUNITY WELFARE [BAHAMAS]. The story of Community Welfare and its wonderful service in the Bahamas. Nassau, 1957. 1 pamphlet (unpaged).

- United Kingdom

BUTRYM (ZOFIA T.) Medical social work in action: a report of a study of medical social work at Hammersmith Hospital. London, Bell, 1968. pp. 128. 21½cm. (Social Administration Research Trust. Occasional Papers on Social Administration. No. 26)

FORMAN (JAMES ADAM SHOLTO) and FAIRBAIRN (E.M.) Social casework in general pratice: a report on an experiment carried out in a general practice. London, O.U.P., 1968. pp. viii, 119. bibliog. 21½cm.

HUMAN relations in general practice; proceedings of a symposium held at the Royal College of General Practitioners, London, 15th September, 1968; chairman, Dr. John Fry, edited by John McKenzie. London, [1969]. pp. 48.

GARRAD (JESSIE) and ROSENHEIM (Sir MAX LEONARD) Social aspects of clinical medicine. London, 1970. pp. 174. bibliog.

- United Kingdom - Ireland, Northern

NORTHERN IRELAND COUNCIL OF SOCIAL SERVICE. Central Committee for the Handicapped. The young chronic sick in Northern Ireland: a survey. Belfast, [1971]. pp. 56.

- United States

SILVER (GEORGE ALBERT) Family medical care: a report on the Family Health Maintenance Demonstration. Cambridge, Mass., Harvard University Press, 1963. pp. xvi, 359. bibliog. 23½cm.

AMERICAN HOSPITAL ASSOCIATION. The volunteer in long-term care. Chicago, [1968]. pp. v, 52. bibliog. 22 cm.

- Viêtnam

EVANS (BARBARA) Caduceus in Saigon: a medical mission to South Viet-Nam. London, Hutchinson, 1968. pp. xii, 210. 21cm.

MEDICAL STATISTICS

U.K. 1951. Social Survey. Some effects of using a two month memory period on the survey of sickness; by P. G. Gray and Ann Cartwright. (Papers. Methodological Series. No.M.41) [London, 1951] pp. 4. 33cm.

BENJAMIN (BERNARD) Health and vital statistics. London, Allen & Unwin, 1968. pp. 307. bibliogs. 23½cm.

BOURKE (GEOFFREY J.) and McGILVRAY (JAMES) Interpretation and uses of medical statistics. Oxford, Blackwell, [1969]. pp. viii, 162. 22cm.

HILL (Sir AUSTIN BRADFORD) Principles of medical statistics. 9th ed. London, 1971. pp. 390.

MEDICINE

TOLAND (J.) Physic without physicians. in vol.2 of Toland (John) A collection of several pieces... now first publish'd from his original manuscripts. London, 1726.

GALDSTONE (IAGO) ed. Man's image in medicine and anthropology. New York, International Universities P., [1963]. pp. xvii, 525. 21½cm. (New York (City). Academy of Medicine. Institute of Social and Historical Medicine. Monographs. 4)

FLOREY (HOWARD WALTER) Baron Florey. The responsibilities of medicine in the modern world. Edinburgh, 1967. pp. 25. bibliog. (Edinburgh. Royal College of Physicians. Publications. No. 32)

DUBOS (RENÉ JULES) Man, medicine, and environment. London, Pall Mall P., [1968]. pp. v, 125. 23½cm.

LE GALL (ANDRÉ) and BRUN (RENÉ) Docteur en pharmacie. Les malades et les médicaments. Paris, P.U.F., 1968. pp. 128. bibliog. 17½cm. (Que Sais-Je? No. 1299)

NORTON (ALAN RALPH) The new dimensions of medicine. London, 1969. pp. 288.

SOURNIA (JEAN CHARLES) Mythologies de la médecine moderne: essai sur le corps et la raison. Paris, 1969. pp. 220.

ANTHROPOLOGY and the behavioral and health sciences; Otto von Mering and Leonard Kasdan, editors; [papers originally presented as a symposium at the annual meeting of the American Anthropological Association, 1966]. Pittsburgh, [1970]. pp. 340. bibliogs.

LEACH (GERALD) The biocrats. London, 1970. pp. 317.

MEDICAL practice and the community: (proceedings of a conference convened by the Australian National University...August 1968); R.G. Brown and H.M. Whyte, editors. Canberra, 1970. pp. 244.

- History

STEVENSON (LLOYD G.) and MULTHAUF (ROBERT P.) Medicine, science and culture: historical essays in honor of Owsei Temkin. Baltimore, [1968]. pp. 312. bibliog.

KING (LESTER S.) The road to medical enlightenment, 1650-1695. London, 1970. pp. 209.

KING (LESTER S.) ed. A history of medicine: selected readings. Harmondsworth, 1971. pp. 316. bibliog.

- Information services

ALDERSON (MICHAEL ROWLAND) Was Disraeli right? [Southampton], 1971. pp. 23. bibliog.

- Philosophy

GELFAND (MICHAEL) Philosophy and ethics of medicine. Edinburgh, Livingstone, 1968. pp. viii, 174. 21½cm.

SIIRALA (MARTTI) Medicine in metamorphosis: speech, presence and integration; [translated from the Finnish]. London, 1969. pp. 164. bibliog.

LEDERMANN (ERICH KURT) Philosophy and medicine. London, 1970. pp. 180.

- Practice

U.K. Social Survey. [Reports. New Series].197. General practice under the National Health Service; by P.G. Gray and Ann Cartwright: an inquiry made for the Committee on General Practice in February and March, 1952. [London], Central Office of Information, 1961. pp. ii, (33). bibliog. 33cm.

HUTCHINSON (M.) Group practice, ancillary help and government controls: a study of general practice in four countries. [London], 1967. pp. 67. bibliog. (Journal of the Royal College of General Practitioners. Vol. 14. Supplement no. 1)

MEDICAL PRACTITIONERS' UNION. Design for family doctoring; the revised version of the...Health centre report, 1960, up-dated and extended to include all aspects of present-day practice organisation;...prepared by Peggy Follis. London, Medical World, 1967. pp. 96.

MENCHER (SAMUEL) Private practice in Britain: the relationship of private medical care to the National Health Service. London, 1967. pp. 95. (Social Administration Research Trust. Occasional Papers on Social Administration. No. 24)

OFFICE OF HEALTH ECONOMICS. General practice today. London, [1968]. pp. 30.

FREIDSON (ELIOT) Profession of medicine: a study of the sociology of applied knowledge. New York, 1970. pp. 409.

ROYAL COLLEGE OF GENERAL PRACTITIONERS. Council. Reports from General Practice. 13. Present state and future needs of general practice. 2nd ed. [London], 1970. pp. 47. bibliog.

SOHN-RETHEL (JOAN) and CARRIER (JOHN) Private practice within the National Health Service. Birmingham, [1970?] pp. 36.

SYMPOSIUM ON A FUTURE IN GENERAL PRACTICE, UNIVERSITY COLLEGE OF SWANSEA, 1969. Report [of proceedings], 6 September 1969. [London], 1970. pp. 39. (Journal of the Royal College of General Practitioners. vol. 20. Supplement. no. 1)

TREATMENT or diagnosis: a study of repeat prescriptions in general practice; [by] Michael Balint [and others]. London, 1970. pp. 182.

DOPSON (LAURENCE) The changing scene in general practice. London, 1971. pp. 248.

- Study and teaching - Australia

AUSTRALIA. Committee on the Teaching Costs of Medical Hospitals. 1961. Report...to the Australian Universities Commission, 6th October, 1961:[Sir Leslie H. Martin, Chairman]. Canberra, 1961. pp. 47.

- Study and teaching - Europe, Eastern

WEINERMAN (E. RICHARD) and WEINERMAN (SHIRLEY B.) Social medicine in eastern Europe: the organization of health services and the education of medical personnel in Czechoslovakia, Hungary and Poland. Cambridge, Mass., 1969. pp. 201.

MEDICINE (Cont'd.)

- Study and teaching - France

JAMOUS (HAROUN) Sociologie de la décision: la reforme des études médicales et des structures hospitalières. Paris, 1969. pp. 257. (Centre National de la Recherche Scientifique. Centre d'Etudes Sociologiques. Travaux)

- Study and teaching - Germany

GERMANY (BUNDESREPUBLIK). Wissenschaftsrat. 1968. Empfehlungen des Wissenschaftsrates sur Struktur und zum Ausbau der medizinischen Forschungs- und Ausbildungsstätten; (with Kurzfassung wichtiger Empfehlungen). [Tübingen, Mohr], 1968. pp. 293.

- Study and teaching - Russia

UNITED STATES. Public Health Department. Plan of scientific research in the field of medicine in the USSR for the years 1961-1962: a translation from the Russian. Washington, 1964. pp. vi, 214.

POSTGRADUATE education for medical personnel in the USSR: report prepared by the participants in a study tour organized by the World Health Organization. Geneva, World Health Organization, 1970. pp. 52. (Public Health Papers. No. 39)

- Study and teaching - United Kingdom

WOLFENDEN (Sir JOHN FREDERICK) The report of the Royal Commission on medical education and its implications..., Wednesday, 2 October, 1968. [London, 1968]. pp. 12. (Institute of Dental Surgery. Wilkinson Memorial Lectures. 1968)

ACHESON (E.D.) University, medical school and community: an inaugural lecture delivered...on the 12th May 1970. [Southampton], 1970. pp. 16.

ROYAL COLLEGE OF PHYSICIANS OF LONDON. Training for consultants. [London], 1971. pp. 69.

- Study and teaching - United States

BABBIE (EARL R.) Science and morality in medicine: a survey of medical educators. Berkeley, 1970. pp. 261. bibliog.

- Africa

AUJOULAT (LOUIS PAUL) Santé et développement en Afrique. Paris, [1969]. pp. 288.

- Africa, Subsaharan

RAY (MARY M.) Inoculations and medical supplies for research workers in sub-Saharan Africa. Evanston, 1967. pp. 11. bibliog.

SANKALÉ (MARC) Médecins et action sanitaire en Afrique noire. Paris, Présence Africaine, [1969]. pp. 436. bibliog. 21½cm.

- Australia

MEDICAL practice and the community: (proceedings of a conference convened by the Australian National University...August 1968); R.G. Brown and H.M. Whyte, editors. Canberra, 1970. pp. 244.

- China

HORN (JOSHUA S.) "Away with all pests...": an English surgeon in People's China. London, [1969]. pp. 192.

NEEDHAM (JOSEPH) Clerks and craftsmen in China and the West: lectures and addresses on the history of science and technology;...based largely on collaborative work with Wang Ling [and others]. Cambridge, 1970. pp. 470. bibliog.

- China - Manchuria

NATHAN (CARL F.) Plague prevention and politics in Manchuria, 1910-1931. Cambridge, Harvard U.P., 1967. pp. vi, 104. bibliog. 25cm. (Harvard University. East Asian Research Center. Harvard East Asian Monographs. 23)

- Finland

PUBLIC health, medical care and the medical profession in Finland; [by Tapani Kosonen and others]. Helsinki, 1964. pp. 40.

- France

CARO (GUY) La médicine en question. Paris, 1969. pp. 193. bibliog.

FRANCE. Direction de la Documentation. La Documentation Française. Notes et Études Documentaires. No. 3,584. La consommation médicale des Français; [by] Clément Michel. Paris, 1969. pp. 55. 27cm.

- Georgia

NIKOBADZE (I.I.) and KURCHISHVILI (I.B.) Osnovnye etapy razvitiia meditsiny v Gruzii. t.2. Tbilisi, 1969. pp. 350.

- Germany

DZIALLAS (P.) Johann Crato von Krafftheim und Johann von Jessen. in Schulz (Eberhard G.) ed. Leistung und Schicksal. Köln, 1967.

- Guatemala

ADAMS (RICHARD NEWBOLD) Un análisis de las creencias y prácticas médicas en un pueblo indígena de Guatemala, con sugerencias relacionadas con la práctica de medicina en el área maya. Guatemala, 1952. pp. 106. (Guatemala. Instituto Indigenista Nacional. Publicaciones Especiales. No.17)

- Israel

SHUVAL (JUDITH T.) and others. Social functions of medical practice: (doctor-patient relationships in Israel). San Francisco, 1970. pp. 223. bibliog.

- Malawi

GELFAND (MICHAEL) Lakeside pioneers: socio-medical study of Nyasaland, 1875-1920. Oxford, Blackwell, 1964. pp. x, 330. bibliog. 22cm.

- Nigeria

MACLEAN (UNA) Magical medicine: a Nigerian case-study. London, 1971. pp. 166. bibliog.

- United Kingdom

OFFICE OF HEALTH ECONOMICS. New frontiers in health: a review of the incidence, impact and implications of minor and unrecognised illness in the community. London, [1964]. pp. 32.

MEDICAL PRACTITIONERS' UNION. Design for family doctoring; the revised version of the... Health centre report, 1960, up-dated and extended to include all aspects of present-day practice organisation;...prepared by Peggy Follis. London, Medical World, 1967. pp. 96. 22½cm.

KAY (RICHARD) 1716-1751. The diary of Richard Kay, 1716-51, of Baldingstone, near Bury, a Lancashire doctor; extracts edited...by W. Brockbank and F. Kenworthy. Manchester, Chetham Society, 1968. pp. (iii), 179. 21cm. (Remains, Historical and Literary, connected with the Palatine Counties of Lancaster and Chester. 3rd Series. vol. 16)

OFFICE OF HEALTH ECONOMICS. General practice today. London, [1968]. pp. 30.

OFFICE OF HEALTH ECONOMICS. Medicine in the 1990's. a technological forecast. London, [1969]. pp. 23.

ROYAL COLLEGE OF GENERAL PRACTITIONERS. Council. Reports from General Practice. 13. Present state and future needs of general practice. 2nd ed. [London], 1970. pp. 47. bibliog.

SYMPOSIUM ON A FUTURE IN GENERAL PRACTICE, UNIVERSITY COLLEGE OF SWANSEA, 1969. Report [of proceedings], 6 September 1969. [London], 1970. pp. 39. (Journal of the Royal College of General Practitioners. vol. 20. Supplement, no. 1)

- United States

CUNNINGHAM (ROBERT M.) The third world of medicine. New York, [1968]. pp. 266. Mainly articles reprinted form Modern Hospital.

KETT (JOSEPH F.) The formation of the American medical profession: the role of institutions, 1780-1860. New Haven, Yale U. P., 1968. pp. xi, 217. bibliog. 23½cm.

MAINSTREAMS of medicine: essays on the social and intellectual context of medical practice: [a symposium sponsored by the University of Texas Medical School]; edited by Lester S. King. Austin, [1971]. pp. 186.

STEVENS (ROSEMARY) American medicine and the public interest. New Haven, Conn., 1971. pp. 572. bibliog.

MEDICINE, CHINESE

OH SIEW CHOO, The Chinese physician in Singapore: a study of his popularity among the Chinese and people of other races; [research paper for the Department of Social Studies, University of Singapore]. 1955. fo. ix, 115. bibliog. Microfilm of typescript.

MEDICINE, INDUSTRIAL

BAKER (FRANK) of Harvard Medical School, and others, eds. Industrial organizations and health. London, Tavistock Publications, 1969 in progress. bibliogs. 21½cm.

- Portugal

BRUGES E SAAVEDRA (ANTONIO DE) and others. Temas de medicina do trabalho; (tabalhos apresentados ao 2.º Congresso Nacional de Prevenção de Acidentes de Trabalho e Doenças Profissionais). Lisboa, 1968. pp. 84. (Fundo de Desenvolvimento da Mão-de-Obra. Cadernos. 24) With abstracts in English, French and German.

- United Kingdom

BRIDGER (HAROLD) and others. The doctor and sister in industry: a study of change: an examination of the work of Unilever medical services in the United Kingdom, etc. London, 1964. pp. 34. (Reprinted from Occupational Health, 1963)

DANGER and disease at work; based on addresses given at the S[ocialist] M[edical] A[ssociation] Week-end School, 1969; [by] J.A. Selby [and others]. Birmingham, [1969]. pp. 15.

MEDICINE, MAGIC, MYSTIC AND SPAGIRIC

MIDDLETON (JOHN) Magic, witchcraft, and curing. Garden City, Natural History P., [1967]. pp. xi, 346. bibliog. 21cm. (American Museum of Natural History. American Museum Sourcebooks in Anthropology)

RODINSON (MAXIME) Magie, médecine et possession à Gondar. Paris, Mouton, 1967. pp. 203. bibliog. 24cm. (Paris. École Pratique des Hautes Études. Section des Sciences Économiques et Sociales. Le Monde d'Outre-Mer Passé et Présent. 2ième Série. Documents. 5)

MEDICINE, MILITARY

- New Zealand

NEW ZEALAND. Army. Medical Section. 1958. The first fifty years: a commentary on the development of the Royal New Zealand Army Medical Corps from its inception in 1908. Wellington, 1958. pp. 24.

MEDICINE, POPULAR

BOUTEILLER (MARCELLE) Médecine populaire d'hier et d'aujourd'hui. Paris, Maisonneuve et Larose, [1966]. pp. 369. bibliog. 24cm.

OFFICE OF HEALTH ECONOMICS. Without prescription: a study of the role of self medication. London, [1968]. pp. 30. bibliog.

MEDICINE, PREVENTIVE

RUMSEY (HENRY WYLDBORE) Essays on state medicine. London, 1856. pp. 424.

WAKEFIELD (JOHN) Social factors in the detection and treatment of cancer; read [to the Manchester Statistical Society] 13th March, 1968. Manchester, [1968]. pp. 21. bibliog.

- Bibliography

NEDERLANDS INSTITUUT VOOR PRAEVENTIEVE GENEESKUNDE. List of publications, 1930-1955. Leyden, the Instituut, [1956?]. pp. 47.

MEDICINE, PRIMITIVE

ADAMS (RICHARD NEWBOLD) Un análisis de las creencias y prácticas médicas en un pueblo indígena de Guatemala, con sugerencias relacionadas con la práctica de medicina en el área maya. Guatemala, 1952. pp. 106. (Guatemala. Instituto Indigenista Nacional. Publicaciones Especiales. No.17)

LAMBO (THOMAS ADEOYE) African traditional beliefs,concepts of health and medical practice: a lecture given before the Philosophical Society, University College, Ibadan, on 24 October, 1962. Ibadan, Ibadan U.P., 1963. pp. 11. bibliog. 21½cm.

KIEV (ARI) Curanderismo: Mexican-American folk psychiatry. New York, Free P., [1968]. pp. xiii, 207. bibliog. 21cm.

AKISANYA (A.) Old wine in new bottles; inaugural lecture delivered... 4 December 1968. [Lagos], 1969. pp. 17. (Lagos. University. Inaugural Lecture Series. 2)

LYNCH (L. RIDDICK) ed. The cross-cultural approach to health behavior. Rutherford, [1969]. pp. 463. bibliog.

ALLAND (ALEXANDER) Adaptation in cultural evolution: an approach to medical anthropology. New York, 1970. pp. 203. bibliog.

MACLEAN (UNA) Magical medicine: a Nigerian case-study. London, 1971. pp. 166. bibliog.

MEDICINE, PSYCHOSOMATIC

FIELD (MINNA) Patients are people: a medical-social approach to prolonged illness. 3rd ed. New York, Columbia U.P., 1967. pp. xvii, 294. bibliog. 21½cm.

SIIRALA (MARTTI) Medicine in metamorphosis: speech, presence and integration; [translated from the Finnish]. London, 1969. pp. 164. bibliog.

DODGE (DAVID LOW) and MARTIN (WALTER TILFORD) Social stress and chronic illness: mortality patterns in industrial society. Notre Dame, [1970]. pp. 331.

PERSONALITY and science: an interdisciplinary discussion [arranged by the Board for Social Responsibility of the Church of England and the Ciba Foundation]; edited by I. T. Ramsey and Ruth Porter. Edinburgh, 1971. pp. 158. (Ciba Foundation. Blueprints)

- Cases, clinical reports, statistics

ALEXANDER (FRANZ) and others, eds. Psychosomatic specificity. Chicago, 1968 in progress. bibliog.

MEDICINE, STATE

SCHICKE (ROMUALD K.) Die Stellung des Arztes im System der gesellschaftlichen Sicherung in der Bundesrepublik Deutschland, in England und in den USA und ihre Bedeutung für die Versorgung mit Gesundheitsgütern. Hamburg, 1969. pp. 309. bibliog.

- Europe, Eastern

WEINERMAN (E. RICHARD) and WEINERMAN (SHIRLEY B.) Social medicine in eastern Europe: the organization of health services and the education of medical personnel in Czechoslovakia, Hungary and Poland. Cambridge, Mass., 1969. pp. 201.

- France

FRANCE. Commission de l'Équipement Sanitaire et Social. 1966. Ve Plan, 1966-1970: rapport général. [Paris, La Documentation française 1966]. pp. 108. 27cm.

POUR une politique de la santé: rapports présentés à Robert Boulin. Paris, Ministère de la Santé Publique et de la Sécurité Sociale, 1971. 3 vols. (in 1).

- Ireland (Republic)

EIRE. Department of Health. 1970. Health Act, 1970: explanatory memorandum for members of both Houses of the Oireachtas dealing with the changes in the administration of the health services provided for in the Health Act, 1970. [Dublin, 1970.] pp. 13.

- Italy

BRUZZESE (UMBERTO) La situazione sanitaria assistenziale e previdenziale in Italia. 2nd ed. Roma, Istituto Editoriale Scientifico, [1967]. pp. 494. 21cm. (Documenti del Nostro Tempo)

- Rhodesia

SOUTHERN RHODESIA. National Health Services Inquiry Commission. 1946. Report of the... Commission, 1945. Salisbury, Government Stationery Office, 1946. pp. 124.

- Roumania

IVAN (C. I.) Administraţia de stat în ocrotirea sănătăţii. Bucureşti, 1968. pp. 239.

- Russia

SHABAILOV (VIKTOR IVANOVICH) Управление здравоохранением в СССР. Москва, 1968. pp. 182.

- Russia - Accounting

CHAIKOVSKAIA (NADEZHDA VITAL'EVNA) and GRIKUROVA (RIPSIMIIA VAGANOVNA) Планирование расходов на здравоохранение. Москва, Финансы, 1967. pp. 151. 20cm.

- United Kingdom

RUMSEY (HENRY WYLDBORE) Essays on state medicine. London, 1856. pp. 424.

SOCIALIST MEDICAL ASSOCIATION. Medicine tomorrow: a scheme for an immediate socialised medical service. [Northwood, Middx., 1940]. pp. 12. 21cm. (Reprinted from Medicine today and Tomorrow, September, 1940).

FELLOWSHIP FOR FREEDOM IN MEDICINE. A critical examination of the Guillebaud report on the cost of the National Health Service. [London], 1957. pp. 15.

[U.K. 1957. Social Survey]. The use of survey techniques in connection with the operation of a National Health Service; by Louis Moss; at a meeting of the Section of Epidemiology and Preventive Medicine of the Royal Society of Medicine on Operational Research in the National Health Service, 18.10.57. ([Papers. General Series]. No. G. 53) [London, 1957] pp. 15. 33cm.

U.K. Social Survey. [Reports. New Series].197. General practice under the National Health Service; by P.G. Gray and Ann Cartwright: an inquiry made for the Committee on General Practice in February and March, 1952. [London], Central Office of Information, 1961. pp. ii, (33). bibliog. 33cm.

SOCIETY OF CHIROPODISTS. Memorandum on chiropody in the national health service. London, 1964. pp. 9. 24½cm.

PETERS (ROBERT JAMES) and KINNAIRD (J.) Health services administration: a source book. Edinburgh, 1965. pp. 500. bibliogs.

SOCIALIST MEDICAL ASSOCIATION. Socialist charter for health. London, [1965]. pp. 12.

SOCIALIST MEDICAL ASSOCIATION. A socialist plan for an occupational health service. London, [1965]. pp. 16.

WOMEN'S COMMITTEE IN DEFENCE OF THE NHS. [Charter]. [London, 1965]. fo. 4.

MENCHER (SAMUEL) Private practice in Britain: the relationship of private medical care to the National Health Service. London, 1967. pp. 95. (Social Administration Research Trust. Occasional Papers on Social Administration. No. 24)

SOUTHWICK (ARTHUR F.) The doctor, the hospital, and the patient in England: rights and responsibilities under National Health Service. Ann Arbor, Michigan University, Bureau of Business Research, [1967]. pp. vii, 376. bibliog 22½cm. (Michigan International Business Studies. No. 6)

McLACHLAN (GORDON) ed. Problems and progress in medical care: (essays on current research, third series) London, O.U.P., 1968. pp. ix, 170. 21½cm.

MANCHESTER.REGIONAL HOSPITAL BOARD. A Green Paper published by the Ministry of Health, entitled "National Health Service: the administrative structure of the medical and related services in England and Wales": views of the Manchester Regional Hospital Board [with] Memorandum prepared by the Secretary of the Board. Manchester, 1968. pp. iv, 15. 25½cm.

NATIONAL HEALTH SERVICE TWENTIETH ANNIVERSARY CONFERENCE, LONDON, 1968. Report. London, H.M.S.O., 1968. pp. 107. 24cm.

OWEN (DAVID) ed. A unified health service. Oxford, Pergamon P., 1968. pp. viii, 148. 19½cm. (Commonwealth and International Library)

SELDON (ARTHUR) After the N.H.S.: reflections on the development of private health insurance in Britain in the 1970s. London, 1968. pp. 44. (Institute of Economic Affairs, Occasional Papers. 21)

U.K. Ministry of Health. 1968. National Health Service: the administrative structure of the medical and related services in England and Wales. London, 1968. pp. 29. 24½cm.

U.K. National Health Service. Supplementary Ophthalmic Services. 1968. Statement specifying the fees and charges for the testing of sight and the supply or repair of glasses ...; revised as from 1st Oct., 1968. London, 1968. pp. 11.

HEALTH services financing: a report commissioned in 1967 by the British Medical Association and carried out by an advisory panel under the chairmanship of Dr. Ivor M. Jones. [London, 1969?]. pp. 605.

OXFORD. Oxford Regional Hospital Board. The general practitioner and the hospital service in the 1970s. Oxford, the Board, 1969. pp. 33,v.

REIN (MARTIN) Social class and the utilization of medical care services: a study of British experience under the National Health Service. [Chicago], 1969. pp. 43-54. Xerox copy of article in Hospitals, vol. 43.

RURAL DISTRICT COUNCILS ASSOCIATION. Rural districts and the green paper: comments on the effects on rural district councils of the Green Paper on the National Health Service issued by the Ministry of Health. [London], 1969. pp. 8.

U.K. National Health Service. General Ophthalmic Services. 1969. Statement specifying the fees and charges for the testing of sight and the supply or repair of glasses...; revised as from the 1st April, 1969. London, 1969. pp. 11.

DRAPER (PETER) and others. The N H S: three views. London, 1970. pp. 23. (Fabian Society. Research Series [No.] 287)

GOODMAN (NEVILLE MARRIOTT) Wilson Jameson: architect of national health. London, 1970. pp. 216. bibliogs.

SOHN-RETHEL (JOAN) and CARRIER (JOHN) Private practice within the National Health Service. Birmingham, [1970?]. pp. 36.

U.K. Department of Health and Social Security. 1970. National Health Service: the future structure of the National Health Service. London, 1970. pp. 32.

U.K. National Health Service. General Ophthalmic Services. 1970. Statement specifying the fees and charges for the testing of sight and the supply or repair of glasses...; revised as from the 26th May, 1970. London, 1970. pp. 11.

DOPSON (LAURENCE) The changing scene in general practice. London, 1971. pp. 248.

GATHERER (ALEXANDER) and WARREN (MICHAEL DONALD) eds. Management and the health services: [a selection of papers from an annual series of short courses on administration in the health services]. Oxford, 1971. pp. 175. bibliogs.

MEDICINE, STATE - United Kingdom (Cont'd.)

O'BRIEN (JOHN PHILIP) Reform of the health services structure; [essay for the Diploma in Public Administration, London University]. 1971. fo. 18. bibliog. Typescript: unpublished. This essay is the property of London University and may not be removed from the Library.

SCAMMELLS (BRIAN) The administration of health and welfare services: a study of the provision of care to elderly people. Manchester, [1971]. pp. 124.

U.K. Department of Health and Social Security. 1971. National Health Service reorganisation: consultative document. London, 1971. pp. 13.

- United Kingdom - Bibliography

U.K. Ministry of Health. Library. 1967-1970. Selected bibliography on the National Health Service; revised to December, 1967; (with first supplement, January 1968 to February 1970) [London, 1967-1970.] 2 pts.

- United Kingdom - Ireland, Northern

IRELAND, NORTHERN. 1969. The administrative structure of the health and personal social services in Northern Ireland. Belfast, 1969. pp. 35.

- United Kingdom - Scotland

SCOTLAND. Scottish Home and Health Department. 1968. Administrative reorganisation of the Scottish health services. Edinburgh, 1968. pp. 28.

DOCTORS in an integrated health service: report of a Joint Working Party appointed by the Secretary of State for Scotland; [J.H.F. Brotherston, chairman]. Edinburgh, H.M.S.O., 1971. pp. 61.

- United Kingdom - Wales

U.K. Welsh Office. 1970. National Health Service: the reorganisation of the health service in Wales. Cardiff, 1970. pp. 25.

- United States

TAX FOUNDATION. Research Publications. New Series. No. 15. Medicaid: state programs after two years. New York, 1968. pp. 72. 25½cm.

MARMOR (THEODORE R.) The politics of Medicare. London, 1970. pp. 145. bibliog.

SKIDMORE (MAX J.) Medicare and the American rhetoric of reconciliation. Alabama, [1970]. pp. 198.

PAULY (MARK V.) Medical care at public expense: a study in applied welfare economics. New York, 1971. pp. 160. bibliog.

- United States - California

GREENFIELD (MARGARET) Medi-Cal, the California medicaid program, title XIX, 1966-1967. Berkeley, 1970. pp. 71.

MEDICINE AND RELIGION

GLASER (WILLIAM A.) Social settings and medical organization: a cross-national study of the hospital. New York, 1970. pp. 210.

MEDICINE AS A PROFESSION

FREIDSON (ELIOT) Profession of medicine: a study of the sociology of applied knowledge. New York, 1970. pp. 409.

MEDICINE-MAN

ROBERT (KATHERINE) The role of Malay magicians and medicine men: a study of their practices, their clients, and their relation to their clients in Singapore; [research paper, Department of Social Studies, University of Singapore]. 1959. fo. (iii), 134. bibliog. Microfilm of typescript.

MEDICINES, PATENT, PROPRIETARY, ETC.

YOUNG (JAMES HARVEY) The medical messiahs: a social history of health quackery in twentieth-century America. Princeton, Princeton U.P., 1967. pp. xiv, 460. bibliog. 21½cm.

PROPRIETARY ASSOCIATION OF GREAT BRITAIN. 50 years of home medicines: the story of the PACB. [London, 1969]. pp. 25.

MEDITERRANEAN

- Bibliography

SWEET (LOUISE E.) and O'LEARY (TIMOTHY J.) eds. Circum-Mediterranean peasantry: introductory bibliographies. New Haven, 1969. pp. 106. (Human Relations Area Files. Behavior Science Bibliographies)

- Commerce

MAGLIETTA (CLEMENTE) La sfida economica dell'Europa passa per il Mediterraneo: Mezzogiorno, trasporti, porti. Napoli, 1969. pp. 224. (Unione Regionale delle Camere di Commercio, Industria ed Agricoltura della Campania. Centro Studi e Ricerche Economico-Sociali. Studi. 3)

- Commerce - Russia

Il CITTADINO politico, e imparziale d'Amsterdam; o, Lettera di un Olandese ad un suo corrispondente di Marsilia sopra l'arrivo della flotta russa nel Mediterraneo: traduzione dal Francese. Cosmopoli, 1771. pp. 40.

- Economic conditions

SILVESTRI (STEFANO) ed. Il Mediterraneo: economia, politica, strategia. Bologna, [1968]. pp. 310. (Istituto Affari Internazionali. Quaderni. 9)

- Economic history

GOITEIN (SOLOMON DOB FRITZ) A Mediterranean society: the Jewish communities of the Arab world as portrayed in the documents of the Cairo Geniza. Berkeley, 1967. in progress.

- Economic policy

ORGANISATION FOR EUROPEAN ECONOMIC CO-OPERATION. Directorate for Scientific Affairs. 1961. Mediterranean Regional Project: Greek National Project: the role of regional factors in the Mediterranean Regional Project; by C. Doussis. Paris, 1961. pp. 4.

- Foreign relations

    ALBI (FERNANDO) La política del Mediterráneo en la postguerra: 1918-1928. Valencia, 1931. pp. 224. bibliog.

    INTERNATIONAL INSTITUTE FOR STRATEGIC STUDIES. Adelphi Papers. No. 51. Conflict and tension in the Mediterranean; by Curt Gasteyger. London, 1968. pp. 18.

    SILVESTRI (STEFANO) ed. Il Mediterraneo: economia, politica, strategia. Bologna, [1968]. pp. 310. (Istituto Affari Internazionali. Quaderni. 9)

- Foreign relations - Russia

    Il CITTADINO politico, e imparziale d'Amsterdam; o, Lettera di un Olandese ad un suo corrispondente di Marsilia sopra l'arrivo della flotta russa nel Mediterraneo: traduzione dal Francese. Cosmopoli, 1771. pp. 40.

- Historical geography

    VITA-FINZI (CLAUDIO) The Mediterranean valleys: geological changes in historical times. Cambridge, C.U.P., 1969. pp. ix, 140. bibliog. 24½cm.

- History

    ANDRÈ (GIANLUCA) L'Italia e il Mediterraneo, alla vigilia della prima guerra mondiale: i tentativi di intesa mediterranea, 1911-1914. Milano, Giuffrè, 1967. pp. 318. (Rome. Università. Istituto di Studi Storici e Politici. [Publications]. 16)

    MALINVERNI (BRUNO) Il primo accordo per il Mediterraneo: febbraio-marzo 1887. Milano, Marzorati, [1967]. pp. 192. 21½cm. (Collana di Studi Storici)

    MAIER (FRANZ GEORG) Die Verwandlung der Mittelmeerwelt. Frankfurt a. M., [1968]. pp. 384. bibliog.

    EARLE (PETER) Corsairs of Malta and Barbary. London, 1970. pp. 307. bibliog.

    SOLE (CARLINO) Sardegna e Mediterraneo: saggi di storia moderna. Cagliari, 1970. pp. 208.

- History, Naval

    HALPERN (PAUL G.) The Mediterranean naval situation, 1908-1914. Cambridge, Mass., 1971. pp. 415. bibliog. (Harvard University. Harvard Historical Studies. vol. 86)

- Relations (general) with the United States

    FIELD (JAMES A.) America and the Mediterranean world, 1776-1882. Princeton, 1969. pp. 485. bibliog.

- Rural conditions

    MEDITERRANEAN SOCIOLOGICAL CONFERENCE, 1963. Contributions to Mediterranean sociology: Mediterranean rural communities and social change; acts... edited by J.G. Peristiany. Paris, 1968. pp. 349. (Athens. Social Sciences Center. Publications. 4)

MEETINGS

LEWIN (ARTHUR) The law, procedure and conduct of meetings in South Africa. 3rd ed. Cape Town, Juta, 1966. pp. xvii, 228. 24½cm.

MEHEDINȚI (SIMION)

BĂLDESCU (EMIL) Simion Mehedinți: ĝinditor social-politic și pedagog. București, 1969. pp. 132.

MÉHÉGAN (GUILLAUME ALEXANDRE DE)

SPINK (J. S.) Un abbé philosophe à la Bastille, 1751-1753: G.A. de Méhégan et son Zoroastre. in Barber (William H.) and others, eds. The age of the enlightenment. Edinburgh, 1967.

MEHRING (FRANZ)

KUMPMANN (WALTER) Franz Mehring als Vertreter des historischen Materialismus. Wiesbaden, 1966. pp. 192. bibliog. (Osteuropa-Institut, München. Veröffentlichungen. Band 29)

MEIGHEN (ARTHUR)

GRAHAM (WILLIAM ROGER) Arthur Meighen: a biography. Toronto, Clarke, 1960 in progress. 23cm.

MEINECKE (FRIEDRICH)

MEINECKE (FRIEDRICH) Werke; herausgegeben...von Hans Herzfeld [and others]. v.p., 1958-69. 8 vols. Band 1 is of the 3rd edition.

HERZFELD (H.) Historian. Friedrich Meinecke: der Geschichtsdenker. in Dietrich (Richard) ed. Historische Theorie und Geschichtsforschung der Gegenwart. Berlin, 1964.

GILBERT (F.) Political power and academic responsibility: reflections on Friedrich Meinecke's Drei Generationen deutscher Gelehrtenpolitik. in Krieger (Leonard) and Stern (Fritz Richard) eds. The responsibility of power. Garden City, 1967.

CHABOD (FEDERICO) De Machiavel à Benedetto Croce; études présentées par Henri Lapeyre. Genève, 1970. pp. 239.

MEINONG (ALEXIUS)

BERGMANN (GUSTAV) 1906- . Realism: a critique of Brentano and Meinong. Madison, U. of Wisconsin P., 1967. pp. x, 458. bibliog. 23cm.

MEISNER (DMITRII IVANOVICH)

MEISNER (DMITRII IVANOVICH) Mirazhi i deistvitel'nost': zapiski emigranta. Moskva, 1966. pp. 302.

MEISSEN

- History

    SCHMIDT (O. E.) Meissen als Mikrokosmos der sächsischen und der deutschen Geschichte. in Hamburg. Arbeits- und Sozialbehörde. Hamburger Mittel- und Ostdeutsche Forschungen. Band 5. Kulturelle und wirtschaftliche Studien in Beziehung zum gesamtdeutschen Raum. Hamburg, [1966].

MEJPRATS

ELMBERG (JOHN ERIK) Balance and circulation: aspects of tradition and change among the Mejprat of Irian Barat. Stockholm, Ethnographical Museum, 1968. pp. 333. 24cm. (Monograph Series. No. 12)

MEKONG RIVER

U.S. International Development Agency. Atlas of physical, economic and social resources of the lower Mekong basin. Washington, 1968. pp. x, fo. 257.

SANSOM (ROBERT L.) The economics of insurgency in the Mekong delta of Vietnam. Cambridge, Mass., [1970]. pp. 283. bibliog.

MELANCHTHON (PHILIPP)

KISCH (GUIDO) Melanchthons Rechts- und Soziallehre. Berlin, De Gruyter, 1967. pp. 307.

MELANESIA

- Economic conditions

BROOKFIELD (HAROLD CHILLINGWORTH) and HART (DOREEN) Melanesia: a geographical interpretation of an island world. London, 1971. pp. 464. bibliog.

- Politics and government

WAIGANI SEMINAR, 4TH, 1970. The politics of Melanesia: papers delivered at the fourth Waigani Seminar sponsored...by the University of Papua and New Guinea [and others]...; edited by Marion W. Ward. Port Moresby, 1970. pp. 734.

MELANESIA - Religion and mythology
See also CARGO MOVEMENT

- Social conditions

LITTLE (EARL TENNYSON) Millenial movements and social change in Melanesia; [M.Phil. (London) thesis]. 1970. fo. 177. bibliog. Typescript: unpublished. This thesis is the property of London University and may not be removed from the Library.

MELBOURNE

- Civic improvement

MELBOURNE. Melbourne and Metropolitan Board of Works. 1967. The future growth of Melbourne: a report to the Minister for Local Government on Melbourne's future growth and its planning administration, etc. [Melbourne, 1967]. pp. 29.

PRYOR (ROBIN J.) Accessibility in Melbourne's urban fringe. [Sydney], 1968. pp. 20. (Sydney. University. Department of Geography and Geographical Society of New South Wales. Research Papers in Geography. No. 14)

- Social conditions

PRYOR (ROBIN J.) Accessibility in Melbourne's urban fringe. [Sydney], 1968. pp. 20. (Sydney. University. Department of Geography and Geographical Society of New South Wales. Research Papers in Geography. No. 14)

JONES (FRANK LANCASTER) Dimensions of urban social structure: the social areas of Melbourne, Australia. [Toronto, 1969]. pp. 149. bibliog.

PARSLER (RONALD) Social values and social class in Melbourne; [Ph.D. (London) thesis]. [1971]. fo. 372. bibliog. Typescript: unpublished. This thesis is the property of London University and may not be removed from the Library.

- Transit systems

MELBOURNE transportation study; prepared for the Metropolitan Transportation Committee by Wilbur Smith and Associates and Len T. Frazer and Associates: [V.F. Wilcox, chairman of the Committee]. [Melbourne, Government Printer, 1969]. 3 vols.

MELBY (JOHN F.)

MELBY (JOHN F.) The mandate of heaven: record of a civil war, China 1945-49; (photographs by Henri Cartier-Bresson). London, Chatto & Windus, 1969. pp. xiii, 313. 23½cm.

MELFORT

- Civic improvement

SASKATCHEWAN. Department of Municipal Affairs. Community Planning Branch. 1956. Melfort looks ahead: a guide for community development. Regina, 1956. pp. 74.

MELLOWS (LIAM)

BRITISH AND IRISH COMMUNIST ORGANISATION. Pamphlets. No. 8. Liam Mellowes. [London], 1966 repr. 1969. pp. 17.

GREAVES (CHARLES DESMOND) Liam Mellows and the Irish revolution. London, 1971. pp. 416.

MELO (ANTÔNIO)

MELO (ANTÔNIO) The coming revolution in Brazil...[an interview]; translation and introduction by Robert Menzel. New York, [1970]. pp. 54.

MELONS

UNITED STATES. Foreign Agricultural Service. FAS-M-178. Survey of Mexican vegetable and melon production. Washington, 1966. pp. iv, 7.

MEMEL

- Economic history

WILLOWEIT (GERHARD) Die Wirtschaftsgeschichte des Memelgebiets. Marburg (Lahn), 1969. 2 vols. bibliog. (Johann Gottfried Herder-Institut. Wissenschaftliche Beiträge zur Geschichte und Landeskunde Ost-Mitteleuropas. Nr. 85)

MEMMINGEN

- History

LINN (DOROTHEE) Das Schicksal der jüdischen Bevölkerung in Memmingen von 1933 bis 1945: Jahresbericht einer Primanerin. Stuttgart, [1968]. pp. 90. bibliog.

MEMORIALS

LONDON. London County Council. Local Government, Records and Museums Committee. Return of outdoor memorials in London, other than statues on the exterior of buildings, memorials in the nature of tombstones, memorial buildings and memorial trees. London, 1910. pp. 58.

MEMORY

HUNTER (IAN MELVILLE LOGAN) Memory. rev. ed. Harmondsworth, Penguin Books, 1964, repr. 1968. pp. 329. bibliog. 18cm. (Pelican Books. A405)

ADAMS (JACK A.) Human memory. New York, [1967]. pp. 326. bibliog.

CONFERENCE OF LEARNING, REMEMBERING AND FORGETTING, 2nd, PRINCETON, 1964. The organization of recall;...edited by Daniel P. Kimble;...sponsored by the New York Academy of Sciences, etc. New York, New York Academy of Sciences, Interdisciplinary Communications Program, [1967]. pp. 389. 23cm.

JOHN (ERWIN ROY) Mechanisms of memory. New York, 1967. pp. 468. bibliog.

CHAUCHARD (PAUL) Connaissance et maîtrise de la mémoire. [Paris, Denoël, 1968]. pp. 253. bibliog. 22cm. (Comprendre, Savoir, Agir)

HALBWACHS (MAURICE) La mémoire collective. 2nd ed. Paris, P.U.F., 1968. pp. xxiii, 204. 21½cm. (Bibliothèque de Sociologie Contemporaine)

PIAGET (JEAN) On the development of memory and identity;... translated by Eleanor Duckworth. [Worcester], Clark U.P., 1968. pp. ix, 42. bibliog. 21cm. (Heinz Werner Institute of Developmental Psychology. Heinz Werner Lectures. 1967)

PIAGET (JEAN) and INHELDER (BARBEL) Mémoire et intelligence. Paris, P.U.F., 1968. pp. viii, 487. 21½cm. (Bibliothèque Scientifique Internationale)

TALLAND (GEORGE A.) Disorders of memory and learning. Harmondsworth, Penguin Books, 1968. pp. 176. bibliog. 18cm. (Penguin Science of Behaviour)

NORMAN (DONALD A.) Memory and attention: an introduction to human information processing. New York, Wiley, [1969]. pp. xi, 201. bibliog. 22½cm. (Series in Psychology)

POSTMAN (LEO JOSEPH) and KEPPEL (GEOFFREY) eds. Verbal learning and memory: selected readings. Harmondsworth, 1969. pp. 501. bibliogs.

TALLAND (GEORGE A.) and WAUGH (NANCY C.) eds. The pathology of memory. New York, 1969. pp. 292. bibliogs.

ASSOCIATION DE PSYCHOLOGIE SCIENTIFIQUE DE LANGUE FRANÇAISE. Symposium, Genève, 1968. La mémoire;... par D. Bovet [and others]. Paris, 1970. pp. 301. bibliogs.

BIOLOGY of memory: [papers of the XVIII International Congress of Psychology, 1966, and the Fiftieth Anniversary Convention of the American Psychological Association, 1967]; edited by Karl H. Pribram [and] Donald E. Broadbent. New York, 1970. pp. 323. bibliogs.

LEARNING and memory; by Jean-François Le Ny [and others]; translated by Louise Elkington. London, 1970. pp. 376. bibliog.

- Mathematical models

HUNT (EARL BUSBY) Simulation and analytic models of memory. Los Angeles, University of California, Western Management Science Institute, 1962. fo. 28. bibliog. 28cm. (Working Papers. No. 23)

NORMAN (DONALD A.) ed. Models of human memory. New York, [1970]. pp. 537. bibliogs.

MEMPHIS

- Water supply

SORRELS (WILLIAM WRIGHT) Memphis' greatest debate: a question of water. Memphis, [1970]. pp. 139. bibliog.

MEN

BEDNARIK (KARL) Die Krise des Mannes. Wien, Molden, [1968]. pp. 256. 21cm.

TIGER (LIONEL SAMUEL) Men in groups. London, Nelson, 1969. pp. xviii, 254. bibliog. 21½cm.

BEDNARIK (KARL) The male in crisis;... translated from the German by Helen Sebba. London, 1970. pp. 194.

SEXTON (PATRICIA CAYO) The feminized male: classrooms, white collars and the decline of manliness. London, 1970. pp. 240.

MILLETT (KATE) Sexual politics. London, 1971. pp. 393. bibliog.

MEN HO

MEN Ho: good cadre boundlessly loyal to chairman Mao's revolutionary line. Peking, 1969. pp. 68.

MENANDRINUS (MARSILIUS) Patavinus

PINCIN (CARLO) Marsilio. Torino, Giappichelli, 1967. pp. 307. bibliog. 23cm. (Turin. Università. Istituto di Scienze Politiche. Pubblicazioni. vol. 17)

LAGARDE (G. de) Le Defensor pacis. in Lagarde (Georges de) La naissance de l'esprit laïque au déclin du moyen âge; (nouvelle édition refondue et complétée). vol.3. Louvain, 1970.

MENDE (ERICH)

BOLESCH (HERMANN OTTO) Kennen Sie eigentlich den?: Erich Mende. Bonn, [1965]. pp. 95.

MENDES

- Religion

HARRIS (W.I.) Methodist Missionary, and SAWYERR (HARRY) The springs of Mende belief and conduct: a discussion of the influence of the belief in the supernatural among the Mende. Freetown, Sierra Leone U.P., 1968. pp. xvi, 152. 21½cm.

MENDÈS-FRANCE (PIERRE)

SALEM (DANIEL) Pierre Mendès France et le nouveau socialisme. Paris, 1969. pp. 158. bibliog. (Paris. Université. Faculté de Droit et des Sciences Economiques. Travaux et Recherches. Serie "Science Politique". No.14)

MENDOZA (CRISTOBAL)

El DOCTOR Cristobal Mendoza, primer presidente de Venezuela: recopilacion de opiniones y documentos sobre la recia personalidad del ilustre trujillano. Trujillo, 1964. pp. 77.

MENDOZA (PROVINCE)

- Politics and government

STROUT (RICHARD ROBERT) The recruitment of candidates in Mendoza Province, Argentina. Chapel Hill, 1968. pp. 159. bibliog. (North Carolina University. James Sprunt Studies in History and Political Science. vol. 50)

MENGER (CARL)

LEUSCHNER (HANS JOACHIM) Kritische Analyse des Methodenstreits in der Nationalökonomie und das Problem seiner Überwindung. [Cologne, imprint, 1964?]. pp. 171. bibliog.

MENJOT (ANTOINE)

SCHOLTENS (MARGUERITE) Antoine Menjot: docteur en médecine, ami de Pascal, réformé au temps des persécutions; études historiques et psychologiques. Assen, Van Gorcum, 1968. pp. (xii), 136. bibliog. 23½cm.

MENNONITES

HORST (SAMUEL) Mennonites in the Confederacy: a study in Civil War pacifism. Scottdale, Herald P., [1967]. pp. 148. bibliog. 19½cm.

TOEWS (JOHN B.) Lost fatherland: the story of the Mennonite emigration from Soviet Russia, 1921-1927. Scottdale, Herald P., [1967]. pp. 262. bibliog. 21½cm. (Mennonite Historical Society. Studies in Anabaptist and Mennonite History. No. 12)

HOSTETLER (JOHN ANDREW) Amish society. 2nd ed. Baltimore, Johns Hopkins P., 1968. pp. xviii, 369. bibliog. 21cm.

MENNONITES
See also OLD COLONY MENNONITES

MENON (KUMARA PADMANABHA SIVA-SANKARA)

MENON (KUMARA PADMANABHA SIVASANKARA) Russia revisited. Delhi, [1971]. pp. 109.

MENON (VENGALIL KRISHNAN KRISHNA)

BRECHER (MICHAEL) India and world politics: Krishna Menon's view of the world. London, O.U.P., 1968. pp. xii, 390. 21½cm.

MENTAL DEFICIENCY

INTERNATIONAL ASSOCIATION FOR THE SCIENTIFIC STUDY OF MENTAL DEFICIENCY. Congress, 1st. Proceedings...; edited by B.W. Richards. Reigate, Jackson, 1968. pp. xliv, 982. bibliogs. 23½cm. In English and French.

KIRMAN (BRIAN HERBERT) Mental retardation: some recent developments in the study of causes and social effects of this problem. London, Pergamon P., 1968. pp. x, 39. bibliog. 20cm. (Institute for Research into Mental Retardation. Occasional Papers. No. 1)

SARASON (SEYMOUR BERNARD) and DORIS (JOHN) Psychological problems in mental deficiency. 4th ed. New York, Harper & Row, [1968]. pp. ix, 483. bibliog. 23½cm.

[INTERNATIONAL SYMPOSIUM IN MENTAL SCIENCE, 1st, HOUSTON, 1967.] Congenital mental retardation; a symposium arranged by William M. McIsaac [and others];...proceedings edited by Gordon Farrell. Austin, [1969]. pp. 356. bibliogs.

- Bibliography

UNITED STATES. President's Panel on Mental Retardation. Bibliography of world literature on mental retardation, January 1940 - March 1963; ([and] Supplement: March, 1963 - December 31, 1964). Washington, [1963-65]. 2 vols.

MENTAL HEALTH LAWS

- Canada

STALWICK (HARVEY NOEL) A history of asylum administration and lunacy legislation in Canada before confederation; [Ph. D. (London) thesis]. 1969. fo. v, 325. bibliog. 25½cm. Typescript: unpublished. This thesis is the property of London University and may not be removed from the Library.

- Ireland (Republic)

EIRE. Statutes, etc. 1945-61. Mental treatment acts, 1945 to 1961: statutory provisions, regulations and explanatory notes regarding the reception, treatment, detention and discharge of mentally ill patients. Dublin, [1962]. pp. xix, 133.

- United Kingdom

SENEX, pseud., Author of An address on the laws of lunacy. Chancery lunatics: a reply to the address made to the House of Commons, June 23rd, 1858, by Sir Hugh Cairns...in defence of the two acts of Parliament, passed in 1853, relating to Chancery lunatics. London, 1861. pp. 12.

KENYON (F.E.) Psychiatric emergencies and the law: the impact of the Mental Health Act, 1959. Bristol, 1968. pp. 137. bibliog.

ROLLIN (HENRY R.) The mentally abnormal offenders and the law: an inquiry into the working of the relevant parts of the Mental Health Act, 1959. Oxford, Pergamon, 1969. pp. xvi, 139. bibliog. 19½cm. (Commonwealth and International Library. Mental Health and Social Medicine)

GREENLAND (CYRIL) Mental illness and civil liberty: a study of mental health review tribunals in England and Wales. London, 1970. pp. 126. bibliog. (Social Administration Research Trust. Occasional Papers on Social Administration. No.38)

- United Kingdom - Scotland

SCOTLAND. 1961. Mental Health (Scotland) Act, 1960: local authority services; notes on part II of the Act. (Department of Health) Edinburgh, 1961. pp. 17. 25cm.

- United States

ALLEN (RICHARD C.) and others. Mental impairment and legal incompetency...: report of the mental competency study, an empirical research project, etc. Englewood Cliffs, Prentice-Hall, 1968. pp. xxiv, 401. bibliog. 24½cm.

LEVITT (MORTON) and RUBENSTEIN (BEN) eds. Orthopsychiatry and the law: a symposium. Detroit, 1968. pp. 255. bibliogs.

ROCK (RONALD S.) and others. Hospitalization and discharge of the mentally ill. Chicago, 1968. pp. 268.

MECHANIC (DAVID) Mental health and social policy. Englewood Cliffs, [1969]. pp. 171. bibliog.

WEIHOFEN (HENRY) Legal services and community mental health centers. Washington, 1969. pp. 73. bibliog.

MENTAL HYGIENE

In earlier volumes of the bibliography similar works have been entered under MENTAL PHYSIOLOGY AND HYGIENE

MENTAL HYGIENE

CANADA. 1964. Prevention of mental illness and social maladjustment: [based on] Academic Assembly conducted by the McGill University Department of Psychiatry and the McGill School of Social Work in Montreal, Que., April 29-May 1, 1964; (prepared by Jean McCrimmon). (Canada's Mental Health. Supplements. 44) Ottawa, 1964. pp. 23.

CANADA. 1964. Promoting mental health in the school: [by] S.R.Laycock. (Canada's Mental Health. Supplements. 40) (Adapted from an article in Pulse, March, 1963) Ottawa, 1964. pp. 11. bibliog.

BOWLBY (JOHN) Maternal care and mental health...; [and] Deprivation of maternal care: a reassessment of its effects; [by] Mary D. Ainsworth [and others] New York, Schocken, 1966. pp. 357. bibliog. 20cm.

REIMANN (HELGA) Die Mental Health Bewegung: ein Beitrag zur Kasuistik und Theorie der sozialen Bewegung. Tübingen, Mohr, 1967. pp. viii, 119. bibliog. 23½cm. (Heidelberg. Universität. Institut für Soziologie und Ethnologie. Heidelberger Sociologica. 5)

The ROLE of religion in mental health: papers presented at a conference organised by the National Association for Mental Health in conjunction with the Institute of Religion and Medicine. London, National Association for Mental Health, [1967]. pp. 78. 21cm.

KLEIN (DONALD C.) Community dynamics and mental health. New York, Wiley, [1968]. pp. xvii, 224. bibliog. 22½cm.

WILLIAMS (RICHARD HAYS) and OZARIN (LUCY D.) eds. Community mental health: an international perspective; [based on the Research Seminar on the Evaluation of Community Mental Health Programs, 1966, sponsored by The National Institute of Mental Health]. San Francisco, Jossey-Bass, 1968. pp. xxvii, 529. bibliogs. 23cm. (Jossey-Bass Behavioral Science Series)

TOWARDS community mental health; edited by John D. Sutherland; [based on papers of the 1966-67 session of the Psychotherapy Section of the Royal Medico-Psychological Association]. London, 1971. pp. 130. bibliogs.

- Bibliography

CANADA. 1964. Mental health pocketbooks and paperbacks; prepared by Benjamin Schlesinger. (Canada's Mental Health. Supplements. 43) Ottawa, 1964. pp. 27.

- Canada - British Columbia

AMERICAN PSYCHIATRIC ASSOCIATION. Survey of mental health needs and resources of British Columbia; editor: Mathew Ross. [Victoria, B.C., 1961]. pp. xiv, 158.

- Europe

UNITED STATES. National Institutes of Health. Community mental health services in Northern Europe. Bethesda, Md., [1965]. pp. xiv, 215.

- Israel

CHILDREN and families in Israel: some mental health perspectives; [edited by] Arie Jarus [and others]. New York, [1970]. pp. 634. bibliogs.

- Russia

U.S. Public Health Service. Publications. No. 1893. Special report: the first U.S. mission on mental health to the U.S.S.R. Washington, 1969. pp. 181.

- Tasmania

TASMANIA. Mental Health Services Commission. Report for the year. 1968/9 [1st] to date included in TASMANIA. Parliament. Journals and printed papers.

- United Kingdom

NATIONAL ASSOCIATION FOR MENTAL HEALTH. Mental Subnormality Series. 1. Special care units; with a foreword by Gordon Rose. London, [1963]. pp. 20. bibliog.

GATHERER (ALEXANDER) and REID (J.J.A.) Public attitudes and mental health education: Northamptonshire Mental Health Project, 1963. Northampton, Northamptonshire County Council, [1964?]. pp. 56. bibliog.

CONFERENCE FOR STAFF IN THE MENTAL HEALTH SERVICES, LONDON, 1966. Inter-professional co-operation: facts and fantasies; report. London, National Association for Mental Health, [1966]. pp. 39. 22cm.

PSYCHIATRIC REHABILITATION ASSOCIATION. The mental health of East London; [by] Peter McCowan [and others]. [London], 1966. fo. 48.

FRENCH (CECIL W.) A history of the development of the mental health service in Bedfordshire, 1948-1970. [Bedford], 1971. pp. 42.

MENTAL HYGIENE - United Kingdom (Cont'd.)

SOCIALIST MEDICAL ASSOCIATION. The mental health services. Birmingham, 1971. pp. 8.

- United Kingdom - Scotland

SCOTLAND. 1961. Mental health services of local health authorities: report by the Standing Advisory Committee on Local Authority Services. (Department of Health) Edinburgh, 1961. pp. 34. 25cm.

- United States

UNITED STATES. National Institutes of Health. Research Utilization Series. Public opinions and attitudes about mental health. Washington, 1963. pp. vi, 22.

UNITED STATES. Public Health Service. Report of the Surgeon General's Ad Hoc Committee on Mental Health Activities: mental health activities and the development of comprehensive health programs in the community. Washington, [1963]. pp. ix, 41.

UNITED STATES. National Institutes of Health. Concepts of community psychiatry. Bethesda, Md., [1965]. pp. x. 211. bibliog.

COWEN (EMORY LELAND) and others. Emergent approaches to mental health problems. New York, Appleton-Century-Crofts, [1967]. pp. xiv, 474. 23½cm. (Century Psychology Series)

GREENBLATT (MILTON) and others, eds. Poverty and mental health;...scientific papers and discussions of a regional research conference held April 22 and 23, 1966, at Boston State Hospital, etc. Washington, American Psychiatric Association, 1967. pp. (ix), 175. 23cm. (Psychiatric Research Reports. No. 21)

MARTIN (PETER A.) ed. Leisure and mental health: a psychiatric viewpoint. Washington, American Psychiatric Association, Committee on Leisure Time and its Uses, 1967. pp. (vii), 126. 23cm.

UNITED STATES. Public Health Service. Publications. No. 1568. Mental health program reports; prepared by Office of Program Analysis [and] Office of the Director. Bethesda, 1967. pp. vi, 301. bibliogs.

CONNERY (ROBERT HOWE) and others. The politics of mental health: organizing community mental health in metropolitan areas. New York, Columbia U.P., 1968. pp. xi, 595. 23cm.

DUHL (LEONARD J.) and LEOPOLD (ROBERT L.) eds. Mental health and urban social policy: a casebook of community actions. San Francisco, 1968. pp. 326.

EVANS (FRANCES MONET CARTER) The role of the nurse in the community mental health. New York, Macmillan, [1968]. pp. xi, 227. bibliogs. 23½cm.

HILLSIDE HOSPITAL. 2nd Conference, New York, 1967. Mental health services for adolescents; proceedings...edited by Sol Nichtern. New York, Praeger, 1968. pp. xiii, 232. 23½cm. (Praeger Special Studies in U.S. Economic and Social Development)

SYMPOSIUM ON COMPREHENSIVE MENTAL HEALTH, MADISON, 1966. Comprehensive mental health: the challenge of evaluation; edited by Leigh M. Roberts [and others]. Madison, U. of Wisconsin P., 1968. pp. x, 339. bibliog. 23½cm.

UNITED STATES. Public Health Service. Publications. No. 1873. The definition and measurement of mental health. Washington, 1968. pp. 280. bibliog.

NONPROFESSIONALS in the human services: [a conference held by the National Association of Social Workers and American Psychological Association in Washington, in May, 1967]; Charles Grosser [and others], editors. San Francisco, 1969. pp. 263.

RYAN (WILLIAM) Ph. D., ed. Distress in the city: essays on the design and administration of urban mental health services. Cleveland, [Ohio], 1969. pp. 270.

SHORE (MILTON F.) and MANNINO (FORTUNE V.) Mental health and the community: problems, programs, and strategies. New York, [1969]. pp. 209.

U.S. Public Health Service. Publications. No. 1906. The mental health of urban America: the urban programs of the National Institute of Mental Health. Washington, 1969. pp. 139.

AMERICAN ASSEMBLY. [37th Assembly, April 1970]. The health of Americans; (edited by Boisfeuillet Jones). Englewood Cliffs, N.J., [1970]. pp. 209.

- United States - Bibliography

UNITED STATES. National Institutes of Health. Bibliography of informational publications issued by State mental health agencies. Washington, 1964. pp. 66.

MENTAL ILLNESS

SYMPOSIUM ON MENTAL HEALTH AND THE FAMILY DOCTOR, LONDON, 1960. [Papers]; [read on] 20th November, 1960..., the College of General Practitioners, London. Amsterdam, [1960]. pp. 47. (Excerpta Medica Foundation. International Congress Series. No. 53)

NATIONAL ASSOCIATION FOR MENTAL HEALTH. Questions on our minds. 3rd ed. London, 1966. pp. 22.

SCHEFF (THOMAS J.) Being mentally ill: a sociological theory. London, Weidenfeld and Nicolson, [1966]. pp. xi, 210

SILVERSTEIN (HARRY) ed. The social control of mental illness. New York, Crowell, [1968]. pp. vii, 327. bibliogs. 20cm. (Selected Studies in Social Problems)

DOHRENWEND (BRUCE P.) and DOHRENWEND (BARBARA SNELL) Social status and psychological disorder: a causal inquiry. New York, [1969]. pp. 207. bibliog.

PLOG (STANLEY C.) and EDGERTON (ROBERT BRECKENRIDGE) eds. Changing perspectives in mental illness. New York, [1969]. pp. 752. bibliogs.

- Classification

U.K. General Register Office. Studies on Medical and Population Subjects. No. 22. A glossary of mental disorders ...: prepared by the Sub-committee on Classification of Mental Disorders of the Registrar General's Advisory Committee on Medical Nomenclature and Statistics. London, 1968. pp. iv, 28. 24cm.

- Canada

MALZBERG (BENJAMIN) Mental disease among Jews in Canada: a study of first admissions to mental hospitals, 1950-1952. Albany, Research Foundation for Mental Hygiene, 1963. fo. 88. 28cm.

MALZBERG (BENJAMIN) Mental disease among native and foreign-born in Canada 1950-1952. Albany Research Foundation for Mental Hygiene, 1963. fo. 37. 28cm.

MALZBERG (BENJAMIN) Mental disease in Canada, 1950-1952, among Italian-born. Albany, Research Foundation for Mental Hygiene, 1963. fo. 41. 28cm.

MALZBERG (BENJAMIN) Mental disease in Canada, 1950-1952, among Scandinavian-born. Albany, Research Foundation for Mental Hygiene, 1963. fo. 40. 28cm.

MALZBERG (BENJAMIN) Mental disease in Canada, 1950-1952, among those born in the United Kingdom: a study of first admissions to hospitals for mental disease. Albany, Research Foundation for Mental Hygiene, 1963. fo. 43. 28cm.

MALZBERG (BENJAMIN) Mental disease in Canada, 1950-1952, among those born in the United States. Albany, Research Foundation for Mental Hygiene, 1963. fo. 49. 28cm.

MALZBERG (BENJAMIN) Internal migration and mental disease in Canada, 1950-1952. Albany, Research Foundation for Mental Hygiene, 1964. fo. (iv), 112. bibliog. 28cm.

MALZBERG (BENJAMIN) Mental disease in Canada, 1950-1952: a study of comparative incidence of mental disease among those of British and French origin Albany, Research Foundation for Mental Hygiene, 1964. fo. (iii), 71. 28cm.

CANADA. Dominion Bureau of Statistics. Health and Welfare Division. Mental Health Section. 1968. Mental health statistics...: the expectation of admission to a Canadian psychiatric institution (joint expectancy measure); (La statistique de l'hygiène mentale...: probabilité d'hospitalisation dans un établissement psychiatrique du Canada (mesure de probabilité composée). Ottawa, 1968. pp. 37. In English and French.

- Israel

ISRAEL. Ministry of Health. Unit for Medical Economics and Statistics. 1964. Preliminary [and Final] report[s] on the census of mental in-patients in Israel... 1964; by H.S. Halevi [and others]. Jerusalem, 1964. 2 pts. bibliog.

- Russia

[MEE (CORNELIA)] The internment of Soviet dissenters in mental hospitals. Cambridge [imprint], [1971]. pp. 21.

- United Kingdom

KENNING (PHILIP) and others. Mental illness in the city and suburb, 1968: a study of the geographical distribution of psychiatric patients discharged to Hackney, Tower Hamlets, Haringey, Enfield and Waltham Forest. London, 1970. pp. 46.

- United States - New York (State)

MALZBERG (BENJAMIN) New data on mental disease among negroes in New York State, 1960-1961. Albany, Research Foundation for Mental Hygiene, 1965. fo. 105. 28cm.

MENTAL PHYSIOLOGY AND HYGIENE
See MENTAL HYGIENE

MENTAL TESTS

LONDON. London County Council. Education Officer's Department. Mental and scholastic tests: report by the Education Officer submitting three memoranda by Cyril Burt, M.A., Psychologist, on mental and scholastic tests. London, 1921. pp. 432.

FAUSTO (GALANTINO) Analisi di alcuni aspetti statistici del campione. Bologna, Il Mulino, [1958]. pp. 109. 21½cm. (Palermo. Università. Scuola di Statistica. Centro di Psicostatistica. Indagine sul Livello Intellettuale degli Alunni delle Scuole Elementari di Palermo. vol. 1)

WOODBURY (MAX A.) The stochastic model of mental testing theory and an application. Princeton, N.J., 1962. fo.7.

SHUEY (AUDREY M.) The testing of negro intelligence. 2nd ed. New York, Social Science P., 1966. pp. xv, 578. 24cm.

CAMPBELL (JOEL T.) and others. Effects of repeating on test scores of the Graduate Record Examinations. Princeton, the Service, 1967. fo. 31. bibliog. 28cm. (Educational Testing Service. Graduate Record Examinations. Special Reports. No. 67-1)

McREYNOLDS (PAUL) ed. Advances in psychological assessment. Palo Alto, Science and Behavior Books, 1968 in progress. bibliog 23cm.

ALBOU (PAUL) Les questionnaires psychologiques. Paris, P.U.F., 1968. pp. 206. bibliog. 17½cm. (Le Psychologue. 36)

ALLISON (JOEL) and others. The interpretation of psychological tests. New York, Harper & Row, [1968]. pp. x, 342. 21cm.

ANASTASI (ANNE) Psychological testing. 3rd ed. New York, Macmillan, [1968]. pp xiii, 665. bibliog. 23½cm.

CATTELL (RAYMOND BERNARD) and BUTCHER (H.JOHN) The prediction of achievement and creativity. Indianapolis, [1968]. pp. 386. bibliog.

DEBOLD (RICHARD C.) Manual of contemporary experiments in psychology. Englewood Cliffs, N.J., [1968]. pp. 245.

MENTAL TESTS (Cont'd.)

LORD (FREDERIC M.) and NOVICK (MELVIN R.) Statistical theories of mental test scores. Reading, Mass., Addison-Wesley, [1968]. pp. xvii, 568. bibliogs. 23½cm. (Addison-Wesley Series in Behavioral Science: Quantitative Methods)

SIMON (BRIAN) Intelligence, psychology and education: a marxist critique. London, 1971. pp. 280.

MENTALLY HANDICAPPED

SCHIEFELBUSCH (RICHARD L.) and others, eds. Language and mental retardation: empirical and conceptual considerations; [based on a series of papers presented... at a conference held at Lawrence, Kansas, December 1963]. New York, Holt, [1967]. pp. xi,208. bibliogs. 22½cm.

FARBER (BERNARD) Mental retardation: its social context and social consequences. Boston, Houghton Mifflin, [1968]. pp. xiii, 287. 21cm.

KATZ (ELIAS) The retarded adult in the community. Springfield, Thomas, [1968]. pp. xxiii, 267. 23cm.

BECK (HELEN L.) Social services to the mentally retarded. Springfield, Illinois, [1969]. pp. 207. bibliog.

HURLEY (RODGER L.) Poverty and mental retardation: a causal relationship. New York, [1969]. pp. 301.

- Bibliography

UNITED STATES. President's Panel on Mental Retardation. Bibliography of world literature on mental retardation, January 1940-March 1963; (and Supplement: March, 1963-December 31, 1964) Washington, [1963-65]. 2 vols.

- Education - United Kingdom

TREDGOLD (ALFRED FRANK) Some account of the report and recommendations of the Royal Commission in the care and control of the feeble-minded, 1908. [London, 1908.] pp. 17.

- Rehabilitation - United States

UNITED STATES. Vocational Rehabilitation Administration. Proceedings of a conference on special problems in vocational rehabilitation of the mentally retarded, Madison, Wisconsin, November 3-7, 1963. Washington, 1964. pp. v, 72. bibliog.

- Denmark

CARLSEN (JOHAN NILS GOTTLOB) Statistiske Undersøgelser angaaende Aandssvage i Danmark 1888-1889: Uddrag af et paa Foranstaltning af Kommissionen af 15. September 1888 indsamlet Materiale. Kjøbenhavn, Gjellerup, 1891. pp. (iv), 81. 25½cm. [with English summaries to chapters].

The DANISH national service for the mentally retarded: ten years of planning and building, 1959-1969. København, 1969. pp. 127.

- Ireland, (Republic)

EIRE. Department of Health. 1960. The problem of mentally handicapped. Dublin, [1960]. pp. 11. 24½cm.

- Netherlands

UNITED STATES. President's Panel on Mental Retardation. Report of the Mission to the Netherlands. Washington, [1963]. pp. vi, 97.

- Russia

UNITED STATES. President's Panel on Mental Retardation. Report of the Mission to the U.S.S.R. Washington, [1964] pp. iii, 64.

- Scandinavia

UNITED STATES. President's Panel on Mental Retardation. Report of the Mission to Denmark and Sweden. Washington, [1963]. pp. vii, 48.

- South Africa

SOUTH AFRICA. Committee of Inquiry into the Care of Mentally Deficient Persons. 1968. Report...1967 (R.P. 66/1968). in South Africa. Parliament. House of Assembly. Votes and proceedings (with Printed annexures).

- United Kingdom

WESSEX REGIONAL HOSPITAL BOARD. Provision of further accommodation for the mentally sub-normal: report of the Working Party. Winchester, 1966. 2 pts.(in 1.)

CRAFT (MICHAEL JOHN) and MILES (LEWIS) Patterns of care for the subnormal. Oxford, Pergamon Press, 1967. pp. x, 141. 19½cm. (Commonwealth and International Library).

NATIONAL ASSOCIATION FOR MENTAL HEALTH. The mentally subnormal in England and Wales. London, 1969. unpaged. 21cm.

MATTINSON (JANET) Marriage and mental handicap. London, 1970. pp. 231.

RESIDENTIAL care for the mentally retarded: a symposium held...on 28th November 1968 under the auspices of the Institute for Research into Mental Retardation, London; edited by Elspeth Stephen. Oxford, 1970. pp. 45. bibliog. (Institute for Research into Mental Retardation. Symposia. No. 1)

- United Kingdom - Scotland

MENTAL WELFARE COMMISSION FOR SCOTLAND. 'No folks of their own': a report on one aspect of community care of the mentally handicapped. Edinburgh, H.M.S.O., 1970. pp. 26.

- United States

UNITED STATES. President's Panel on Mental Retardation. Chart book: mental retardation. Washington, 1963. pp. 69.

UNITED STATES. President's Panel on Mental Retardation. Report of the Task Force on Education and Rehabilitation. Washington, [1963], pp. iv, 78.

HURLEY (RODGER L.) Poverty and mental retardation: a causal relationship. New York, [1969]. pp. 301.

- United States - Massachusetts

LEAGUE FOR PREVENTIVE WORK. Feeble-minded adrift: reasons why Massachusetts needs a third school for the feeble-minded immediately. [Boston, Mass.], 1916. pp. (21).

MENTALLY HANDICAPPED CHILDREN

JACOBS (JERRY) The search for help: a study of the retarded child in the community. New York, [1969]. pp. 135.

ILLINGWORTH (RONALD STANLEY) The development of the infant and young child, normal and abnormal. 4th ed. Edinburgh, 1970. pp. 382. bibliogs.

ADAMS (MARGARET) Mental retardation and its social dimensions. New York, 1971. pp. 315. bibliog.

- Education

CANADA. 1965. Education and the maladjusted child; [by] Sol Gordon. (Canada's Mental Health. Supplements. 45) Ottawa, 1965. pp. 11. bibliog.

CANADA. 1965. School achievement, learning difficulties and mental health; [by] Charles G. Stogdill. (Canada's Mental Health. Supplements. No. 48) Ottawa, 1965. pp. 17.

GUNZBURG (HERBERT C.) Social competence and mental handicap: an introduction to social education. London, Baillière, Tindall & Cassell, 1968. pp. (vi), 225. 22cm.

- Education - South Africa

SOUTH AFRICA. Committee of Inquiry into the Education of Children with Minimal Brain Dysfunction. 1969. Report (R.P. 72/1969). in South Africa. Parliament. House of Assembly. Votes and proceedings; (with Printed annexures).

- Education - United Kingdom

ENFIELD ASSOCIATION FOR THE ADVANCEMENT OF STATE EDUCATION. Special children: the schooling for our children with mental handicaps; report of study group, 1966-69. [London, 1969]. pp. 28.

- Education - United States

LONDON. Greater London Council. Inner London Education Authority. The education of brain injured children in the United States of America. London, [1967]. pp. 30. bibliog.

- America, Latin

SEMINARIO REGIONAL INTERAMERICANO SOBRE EL NIÑO CON RETARDO MENTAL, 1ST, MONTEVIDEO, 1967. Como organizar servicios para la prevencion, diagnostico y tratamiento del retardo mental en los paises en desarrollo: [primer] seminario regional...Mayo 7-14 de 1967. Montevideo, Instituto Interamericano de Niño, 1970. pp. 367. bibliogs.

- United Kingdom

NATIONAL SOCIETY FOR MENTALLY HANDICAPPED CHILDREN. Stress in families with a mentally handicapped child. London, [1967]. pp. xi, 36. bibliog. 21½cm.

BARANYAY (EILEEN P.) The mentally handicapped adolescent: the Slough project of the National Society for Mentally Handicapped Children; an experimental step towards life in the community. Oxford, 1971. pp. 164.

KING (ROY DAVID) A comparative study of residential care for handicapped children; [Ph.D. (London) thesis]. [1971]. fo. 461. bibliog. With three reprinted articles. Typescript: unpublished. This thesis is the property of London University and may not be removed from the Library.

- United States

UNITED STATES. Children's Bureau. Child health projects for mentally retarded children: the role of the social worker. [Washington], 1963. pp. 50.

THOMAS (ALEXANDER) and others. Temperament and behavior disorders in children. New York, 1968. pp. 309.

DIMINISHED people: problems and care of the mentally retarded; by 15 authors; edited by Norman R. Bernstein. Boston, [1970]. pp. 340. bibliogs.

SEGAL (ROBERT M.) Mental retardation and social action: a study of the associations for retarded children as a force for social change. Springfield, [1970]. pp. 211. bibliog.

MENTALLY ILL

- Care and treatment

POLLOCK (HORATIO MILO) ed. Family care of mental patients: a review of systems of family care in America and Europe...; [by] Edgar A. Doll [and others]. Utica, 1936. pp. 247. bibliog.

The TREATMENT of mental disorders in the community: the proceedings of a symposium held in London on November 24th, 1967; sponsored and organized by E.R. Squibb and Sons Limited, and with the support of the National Association for Mental Health; edited by Gerald R. Daniel and Hugh L. Freeman. London, Baillière, 1968. pp. viii, 83. bibliogs. 21cm.

CAINE (T.M.) and SMAIL (D.J.) The treatment of mental illness: science, faith and the therapeutic personality. London, [1969]. pp. 192. bibliog.

COMMUNITY life for the mentally ill: an alternative to institutional care; [by] George W. Fairweather [and others]. Chicago, 1969. pp. 357. bibliog.

CAPLAN (GERALD) The theory and practice of mental health consultation. London, 1970. pp. 397. bibliog.

- Care and treatment - Bibliography

UNITED STATES. Veterans Administration. Family care treatment of the mentally ill: a selectively annotated bibliography. Omaha, Nebraska, 1966. pp. 31.

- Care and treatment - France

DOERNER (KLAUS) Bürger und Irre: zur Sozialgeschichte und Wissenschaftssoziologie der Psychiatrie. Frankfurt a.M., [1969]. pp. 410. bibliog.

PARTISANS. No. 46. Garde-fous, arrêtez de vous serrer les coudes. Paris, 1969. pp. 123.

MENTALLY ILL (Cont'd.)

- Care and treatment - Germany

DOERNER (KLAUS) Bürger und Irre: zur Sozialgeschichte und Wissenschaftssoziologieder Psychiatrie. Frankfurt a.M., [1969]. pp. 410. bibliog.

- Care and treatment - Ireland (Republic)

EIRE. 1967. Commission of inquiry on mental illness, 1966 : report;[Seamus Henchy, chairman]. (Pr.9181) Dublin, [1967] pp. xliii, 181. bibliog. 25cm.

- Care and treatment - Israel

ISRAEL. 1967. A survey of ambulatory facilities for mental cases in Israel, by H.S. Halevi and Z. Cochavy. (Ministry of Health) Jerusalem, 1967. pp. (iii), 26, (13). bibliog. 27½cm.

- Care and treatment - New Zealand

CHRISTIE (KERRIN M.) A first assessment of the costs and benefits associated with drug usage in New Zealand mental hospitals. [Wellington, 1968?]. pp. 51. (New Zealand. Institute of Economic Research. Contract Research Unit. Publications. No. 1)

- Care and treatment - United Kingdom

HAMILTON (MARIAN W.) and HOENIG (JULIUS) The elderly psychiatric patient and the medical and social services. 1966. pp. 193-196. 29½cm. (Reprinted from the Medical Officer, no. 3037, vol. 116 no. 15, 1966)

U.K. 1967. Ministry of Health. Residential hostels for the mentally disordered. (Local Authority Building Notes.6) London, 1967. pp. (ii), 9. 30cm.

APTE (ROBERT ZARA) Halfway houses: a new dilemma in institutional care. London, Bell, 1968. pp. 126. 21½cm. (Occasional Papers on Social Administration. No. 27)

REHIN (GEORGE FAENDERICH) and MARTIN (F.M.) Patterns of performance in community care: a report of a community mental health services study. London, O.U.P., 1968. pp. (iii), 235. 21½cm.

DOERNER (KLAUS) Bürger und Irre: zur Sozialgeschichte und Wissenschaftssoziologie der Psychiatrie. Frankfurt a.M., [1969]. pp. 410. bibliog.

GREENLAND (CYRIL) Mental illness and civil liberty: a study of mental health review tribunals in England and Wales. London, 1970. pp. 126. bibliog. (Social Administration Research Trust. Occasional Papers on Social Administration. No.38)

DURKIN (ELIZABETH) Hostels for the mentally disordered. London, 1971. pp. 12. (Young Fabian Group. Young Fabian Pamphlets. 24)

[PSYCHIATRIC REHABILITATION ASSOCIATION]. Nicholas House: an exercise in residential care of the mentally ill. [London], 1972. pp.19.

- Care and treatment - United States

UNITED STATES. President's Panel on Mental Retardation. Report of the Task Force on Prevention, Clinical Services and Residential Care. Washington, 1963. pp. (iii), 57.

ANGRIST (SHIRLEY S.) and others. Women after treatment: a study of former mental patients and their normal neighbors. New York, Appleton, [1968]. pp. xi, 333. 21cm. (Sociology Series)

EVANS (FRANCES MONET CARTER) The role of the nurse in the community mental health. New York, Macmillan, [1968]. pp. xi, 227. bibliogs. 23½cm.

HOSPITAL and community adjustment as perceived by psychiatric patients, their families, and staff; by Robert B. Ellsworth [and others]. [Lancaster, Ia., 1968]. pp. 41. bibliog. (Journal of Consulting and Clinical Psychology. Monographs. vol. 32. No.5)

ROCK (RONALD S.) and others. Hospitalization and discharge of the mentally ill. Chicago, 1968. pp. 268.

SILVERSTEIN (MAX) Psychiatric aftercare: planning for a community mental health service. Philadelphia, U. of Pennsylvania P., [1968]. pp. ix, 158. bibliog. 21 cm.

MECHANIC (DAVID) Mental health and social policy. Englewood Cliffs, [1969]. pp. 171. bibliog.

- Rehabilitation

QUERY (WILLIAM T.) Illness, work, and poverty: the hospital/factory in rehabilitation. San Francisco, 1968. pp. 266. bibliog.

RAUSH (HAROLD LESTER) and RAUSH (CHARLOTTE L.) The halfway house movement: a search for sanity. New York, Appleton, [1968]. pp. xiv, 247. bibliog. 20½cm. (Century Psychology Series)

- Rehabilitation - United Kingdom

PSYCHIATRIC REHABILITATION ASSOCIATION. Mental illness in four London boroughs: a study of psychiatric patients discharged to Hackney, Tower Hamlets, Greenwich and Bexley in 1967; [by] Jack Clark [and others]. London, [1969]. fo. 62.

- Rehabilitation - United States

CANADA. 1965. Democracy's scrap-heap: rehabilitating long-stay, mental hospital patients; [by] Pansy Schmidt. (Canada's Mental Health. Supplements. 46) Ottawa, 1965. pp. 12.

UNITED STATES. Vocational Rehabilitation Administration. Rehabilitating the mentally ill. Washington, 1965. pp. ix, 54.

SILVERSTEIN (MAX) Psychiatric aftercare: planning for a community mental health service. Philadelphia U. of Pennsylvania P., [1968]. pp. ix, 158. bibliog. 21cm.

The FIRST year out: mental patients after hospitalization. Baltimore, [1969]. pp. 299. bibliog.

- Italy

ITALY. Istituto Centrale di Statistica. Note e Relazioni. N.5. Ricoverati per tubercolosi, tumori maligni e malattie mentali; (relazione del prof. Stefano Somogyi). Roma, 1958. pp. 164. 26cm.

- New Zealand

FOSTER (F. H.) Mental hospitals admission and release data: cohort study of first admissions, 1962. Wellington, 1967. pp. 51. 28cm. (New Zealand. Department of Health Special Report Series. 27.)

NEW ZEALAND. Department of Health. Special Reports Series. 30. Census of mental hospital patients, 1966. Wellington, 1968. pp. (ii), 62. 28cm.

- Sweden

EKBLOM (BENGT) Acts of violence by patients in mental hospitals;...(translated by Helen Frey). [Stockholm, 1970]. pp. 130. bibliog.

- United Kingdom

HOENIG (JULIUS) and HAMILTON (MARIAN W.) The desegregation of the mentally ill. London, 1969. pp. 266. bibliog.

YOUTH DEVELOPMENT TRUST. Young and sick in mind. Manchester, 1970. pp. 22.

U.K. Department of Health and Social Security. 1971. The Nottingham psychiatric case register findings, 1962 to 1969. London, 1971. pp. 47. (Statistical Report Series. No. 13)

- United States

SPITZER (STEPHAN P.) and DENZIN (NORMAN KENT) eds. The mental patient: studies in the sociology of deviance. New York, McGraw-Hill, [1968]. pp. xv, 486. bibliogs. 22½cm.

MENTANA, BATTLE OF, 1867

TORRE (PAOLO DALLA) L'anno di Mentana: contributo ad una storia dello Stato Pontificio nel 1867. Milano, Martello, [1968]. pp. xxvii, 548. bibliog. 22½cm.

MENZIES (Sir ROBERT GORDON)

HUGHES (COLIN ANFIELD) and WESTERN (JOHN S.) The prime minister's policy speech: a case study in televised politics. Canberra, Australian National University Press, 1966. pp. xvi, 227. bibliog. 24½cm.

PERKINS (KEVIN) Menzies: last of the Queen's men. London, Angus & Robertson, 1968. pp. (vii), 264. 23cm.

HOLT (EDGAR) Journalist. Politics is people the men of the Menzies era. Sydney, 1969. pp. 144.

MENZIES (Sir ROBERT GORDON) The measure of the years. London, 1970. pp. 300.

MERAMEC BASIN

ULLMAN (EDWARD L.) and others. The Meramec basin: water and economic development: report of the Meramec Basin Research Project to the Meramec Basin Corporation. St. Louis, Washington University, Meramec Basin Research Project, 1961-62. 4 vols. 28cm. 13 appendices bound in a separate volume.

MERANO

- Economic conditions

BIERSACK (WERNER) Der Fremdenverkehr im Kurort Meran. [Bozen], 1967. pp. 179. bibliog. (Südtiroler Wirtschafts- und Sozialinstitut. Schriftenreihe. Band 12)

MERCANTILE BUILDINGS

OTT (LEO GERRIT LEOPOLDUS ANTONIUS) Van luchtkasteel tot koopmansburcht. Rotterdam, 1969. pp. 194. (Rotterdam. Historisch Genootschap Roterodamum. [Publications]. 9)

MERCANTILE SYSTEM

MENGOTTI (FRANCESCO) Conte. Il colbertismo: dissertazione coronata dalla Reale Società Economica Fiorentina..., li 13 giugno 1792: nuova edizione con l'aggiunta di alcuni l'Istoria dell'arte della seta in Toscana. Firenze, [imprint]. 1819. pp. (iii), 151. 21cm.

LINDOW (CONRAD) Die Bedeutung der gewerblichen Sozialpolitik in der brandenburg-preussischen Merkantilzeit, insbesondere auf dem Gebiete des Bergbaues und der Eisen-Industrie. Giessen, 1928. pp. 115. bibliog.

AKADEMIE FÜR RAUMFORSCHUNG UND LANDESPLANUNG. Ausschuss Historische Raumforschung. Historische Raumforschung. 4. Raumordnung in Renaissance und Merkantilismus. Hannover, Jänecke, 1963. pp. vii, 125. 25cm.

BOUVIER-AJAM (MAURICE) and TINGUY (GABRIEL DE) Mercantilisme et physiocratie. Paris, the Centre, [1963?]. fo. 33. 26½cm. (Centre d'Études et de Recherches Marxistes. Cahiers. 1e Série. 1)

JOHANNSSON (HARALDUR) Mercantilist and classical theories of foreign trade: an introduction. Kuala Lumpur, Rayirath Publications, 1968. pp. 160. bibliog. 19cm.

KISCH (HERBERT) Prussian mercantilism and the rise of the Krefeld silk industry: variations upon an eighteenth-century theme. Philadelphia, 1968. pp. 50. (American Philosophical Society. Transactions. New Series. vol. 58, part 7)

COLEMAN (DONALD CUTHBERT) ed. Revisions in mercantilism. London, 1969. pp. 213. bibliog. (Reprinted from various periodical articles)

GERSCHENKRON (ALEXANDER) Europe in the Russian mirror: four lectures in economic history. Cambridge, 1970. pp. 158. (Cambridge. University. Ellen McArthur Lectures. 1968)

KAMMEN (MICHAEL G.) Empire and interest: the American colonies and the politics of mercantilism. Philadelphia, [1970]. pp. 186. bibliog.

MERCATI (GIOVANNI)

TISSERANT (EUGÈNE) Cardinal. Giovanni Mercati 1866-1957: commemorazione, etc. Roma, Accademia Nazionale dei Lincei, 1963. 26½cm. (Problemi Attuali di Scienza e di Cultura. Quaderni. N.63)

MERCENARY TROOPS

CLARKE (S.J.G.) The Congo mercenary; a history and analysis. Johannesburg, 1968. pp. 104. bibliog.

SCHRAMME (JEAN) Le Bataillon Léopard: souvenirs d'un Africain blanc. Paris, [1969]. pp. 356.

MERCHANT ADVENTURERS COMPANY

JOHNSON (THOMAS) Merchant. A plea for free-mens liberties; or, The monopoly of the Eastland marchants anatomized by divers arguments, wch. will also serve to set forth the unjustnesse of the Marchant-Adventurers monopoly, etc. London, 1646. pp. (7). 18½cm. Wing J 850.

MERCHANT MARINE

UNITED STATES. Maritime Administration. Merchant fleets of the world: seagoing steam and motor ships of 1,000 gross tons and over as of December 31, 1962. Washington, pp. 17. 1963.

STUCHTEY (ROLF) Die Beurteilung des Aufbaus nationaler Handelsflotten in unterentwickelten Ländern. Hamburg, 1968. pp. 141. bibliog. (Deutsches Übersee-Institut. Probleme der Weltwirtschaft)

UNITED NATIONS. Conference on Trade and Development. 1968. Establishment or expansion of merchant marines in developing countries: report by the Secretariat of UNCTAD. (TD/26/Rev.1) New York, 1968. pp. 65.

BABIĆ (MATE) Pomorske politike u svijetu. Zagreb, 1970. pp. 131. bibliog. With English and Russian summaries.

- Belgium

INSTITUT BELGE D'INFORMATION ET DE DOCUMENTATION. Transportation in Belgium: the merchant marine. Brussels, Ministry of Foreign Affairs and External Trade, 1968. pp. 10. (Belgian News. No.5a)

- France

FRANCE. French Embassy, New York. Service de Presse et d'Information. 1962. France and the merchant marine. [New York, 1962]. pp. 48. 25½cm.

FRANCE. Commission des Transports. Section des Transports Maritimes. 1967. Ve Plan, 1966-1970: marine marchande (flotte de commerce et construction navale). [Paris, La Documentatio française, 1967]. pp. 240. 27cm.

- Germany

EVERSBUSCH (WOLFGANG A.) Die deutsche Mexiko-Schiffahrt. Berlin, 1941. pp. 141. bibliog.

- Italy

ITALY. Ministero della Marina Mercantile. Ufficio Studi Economici. Notiziario. [Roma], quarterly, 1966 to date. 24cm.

VECCHIO (EDOARDO DEL) Di Robilant e la crisi nei rapporti marittimi italo-francesi. Milano, 1970. pp. 194. (Rome. Università. Istituto di Studi Storici e Politici. [Publications]. 19)

- Latvia

NA morskoi vakhte: ocherki o revoliutsionnykh, boevykh i trudovykh traditsiiakh na morskom transporte Sovetskoi Latvii. Riga, 1968. pp. 216.

- Mauritius

MAURITIUS. Marine Services. Annual report. Port Louis, annual, 1966/7 to date. 25cm.

- Poland

CZAPLIŃSKI (WŁADYSŁAW) Polska a Bałtyk w latach 1632-1648: dzieje floty i polityki morskiej. Wrocław, Towarzystwo Naukowe, 1952. pp. 152. bibliog. 23½cm. (Breslau. Wrocławsie Towarzystwo Naukowe. Prace. Seria A. Nr.44)

MAJCZYNO (JANUSZ) Polityka rozwoju żeglugi morskiej. Gdańsk, 1970. pp. 262. bibliog.

- Russia

ANAN'INA (VERA ZAKHAROVNA) Vzaimodeistvie zheleznodorozhnogo i morskogo transporta pri peregruzke navalochnykh gruzov. Moskva, 1966. pp. 88. bibliog.

POD flagom Rodiny: ocherk istorii Chernomorskogo parokhodstva. Odessa, 1967. pp. 455.

KRAMAROV (EFRAIM MENAKHIMOVICH) Внешняя торговля продукцией морского транспорта: невидимый экспорт и импорт. Москва, Транспорт, 1968. pp. 303. 21см.

GEORGETOWN UNIVERSITY. Center for Strategic and International Studies. Special Report Series. No. 10. Soviet sea power. Washington, D.C., 1969. pp. 131.

SOVIET merchant ships, 1945-1968. Havant, Mason, 1969. pp. xvi, 280. 24½cm.

ANAN'IN (VLADIMIR IVANOVICH) Fond razvitiia proizvodstva i fondoobrazuiushchie pokazateli na morskom transporte. Moskva, 1971. pp. 102. bibliog.

DOIBAN (ALEKSANDR MOISEEVICH) Khoziaistvennyi raschet na sudakh morskogo flota. Moskva. 1971. pp. 125. bibliog.

FAIRHALL (DAVID) Russia looks to the sea: a study of the expansion of Soviet maritime power. London, 1971. pp. 287. bibliog.

- Singapore

TREGONNING (KENNEDY GORDON) Home port Singapore: a history of Straits Steamship Company Limited, 1890-1965. Singapore, O.U.P., 1967. pp. xii, 321. bibliog. 25cm.

- Sweden

GRUVBERGER (NILS) Sveriges utrikes-
sjöfart, 1865-1885: företagsformer
och ägandestruktur. Stockholm,
Svenska Bokförlaget, [1965]. pp. 128.
bibliog. 22½cm. (Uppsala. Universitet.
Ekonomisk-Historiska Institution.
Ekonomisk-Historiska Studier. 2)
(Reprinted from Forum Navale, Nr. 22)
With summary in English.

- United Kingdom

UNITED KINGDOM. Parliament. 1643. The humble
petition of the merchant-strangers, and others
in the city of London, concerned in the importation of plate and bullion into this kingdome
presented to both Houses of Parliament; with
an ordinance or declaration of the Lords and
Commons...concerning the said petition: [dated
26 August, 1643]. London, Wright, 1643. pp. 6.
18½cm. Wing H 3561.

REDDAWAY (T. F.) and RUDDOCK (A. A.) eds. The
accounts of John Balsall, purser of the Trinity
of Bristol. in Camden Society. [Publications].
4th Series. vol.7. Camden miscellany. vol.23.
London, [1969].

- United States

BARKER (JAMES R.) and BRANDWEIN (ROBERT) The
United States Merchant Marine in national perspective.
Lexington, [1970]. pp. 301. bibliog.

KUECHLE (DAVID) The story of the Savannah: an
episode in maritime labor-management relations.
Cambridge, Mass., 1971. pp. 313.

- Uruguay

CENTRO DE ESTADISTICAS NACIONALES Y COMERCIO INTER-
NACIONAL DEL URUGUAY. Marina mercante uruguaya,
etc. Montevideo, [1969]. pp. 268. bibliog.

MERCHANT SHIPS, BRITISH

GREENHILL (BASIL) The merchant schooners. rev.ed.
New York, 1968. 2 vols.

MERCHANTS, BRITISH

CLAYPOOLE (JAMES) James Claypoole's letter book:
London and Philadelphia, 1681-1684; edited by
Marion Balderston. San Marino, Huntington
Library, 1967. pp. vii, 256.

GREENHILL (BASIL) and GIFFARD (ANN) Westcountrymen
in Prince Edward's Isle: a fragment of the great
migration. Newton Abbot, David & Charles, [1967]
pp. 248. bibliog. 21½cm.

CUNYNGHAM-BROWN (JOHN SJOVALD HOSEASON) The traders:
a story of Britain's south-east Asian commercial adventure. London, 1971. pp. 352. bibliog.

MERCHANTS, FOREIGN

- Portugal

FREMDE Kaufleute auf der ibirischen Halbinsel;
herausgegeben von Hermann Kellenbenz. Köln, 1970.
pp. 403. (Cologne. Universität. Forschungsinstitut für Sozial- und Wirtschaftsgeschichte.
Kölner Kolloquien zur internationalen Sozial-
und Wirtschaftsgeschichte. Band 1) In various
languages.

- Spain

FREMDE Kaufleute auf der ibirischen Halbinsel;
herausgegeben von Hermann Kellenbenz. Köln, 1970.
pp. 403. (Cologne. Universität. Forschungsinstitut für Sozial- und Wirtschaftsgeschichte.
Kölner Kolloquien zur internationalen Sozial-
und Wirtschaftsgeschichte. Band 1) In various
languages.

MERCHANTS, INDIAN

HAZLEHURST (LEIGHTON W.) Entrepreneurship and
the merchant castes in a Punjabi city. [Durham
N.C.], the Center, [1966]. pp. ix, 151. bibliog.
23cm. (Duke University. Commonwealth-Studies
Center. Program in Comparative Studies on Southern
Asia. Monographs and Occasional Papers Series.
No. 1)

MERCHANTS, ITALIAN

PIKE (RUTH) Enterprise and adventure:
the Genoese in Seville and the opening
of the new world. Ithaca, Cornell University Press, 1966. pp. xiii, 243.
bibliog. 21½cm.

MERCHANTS, JAPANESE

SCIENCE COUNCIL OF JAPAN. Division of Economics,
Commerce and Business Administration. Economic
Series. No. 45. Development of marxism and the
contemporary age; by Fumio Moriya; [and] A study
on the Ono-gumi; by Mataji Miyamoto. Tokyo,
1969. pp. 53.

MERCHANTS, MEXICAN

BRADING (DAVID A.) Miners and merchants in Bourbon
Mexico, 1763-1810. Cambridge, 1971. pp. 382.
bibliog.

MERCHANTS, PORTUGUESE

BOXER (CHARLES RALPH) Francisco Vieira
de Figueiredo: a Portuguese merchant-
adventurer in South East Asia, 1624-1667.
's-Gravenhage, Nijhoff, 1967. pp.
(iv), 118. bibliog. 24cm. (Instituut
voor Taal-, Land-, en Volkenkunde
Verhandelingen. Deel 52)

MERCHANTS, RUSSIAN

KAUFMANN-ROCHARD (JACQUELINE) Origines
d'une bourgeoisie russe, 16e et 17e
siecles: marchands de Moscovie. Paris, [1969]. pp. 303. bibliog.

MERCHANTS, SPANISH

LOHMANN VILLENA (GUILLERMO) Les Espinosa: une
famille d'hommes d'affaires en Espagne et aux
Indes à l'époque de la colonisation. Paris,
S.E.V.P.E.N., 1968. pp. 259. 24cm. (Paris.
École Pratique des Hautes Études. Section des
Sciences Économiques et Sociales. Centre de
Recherches Historiques. Affaires et Gens
d'Affaires. 32)

MERCURY

ALESSANDRO (L. D') Il mercato del mercurio. in
vol.1 of Saggi di economia aziendale e sociale in
memoria di Gino Zappa. Milano, 1961.

MERETSKOV (KIRIL AFANAS'EVICH)

MERETSKOV (KIRILL AFANAS'EVICH) На
службе народу: страницы воспоминаний
Москва, ИПЛ, 1968. pp. 464. 20см.
(О Жизни и о Себе)

MERIDA

- Description and travel

VILA (MARCO-AURELIO) Aspectos geográficos del
Estado Mérida. Caracas, 1967. pp. 356. bibliog.
(Venezuela. Corporación Venezolana de Fomento.
Sub-Gerencia de Servicios Técnicos. Monografías
Económicas Estadales).

- Economic conditions

VILA (MARCO-AURELIO) Aspectos geográficos del
Estado Mérida. Caracas, 1967. pp. 356. bibliog.
(Venezuela. Corporación Venezolana de Fomento.
Sub-Gerencia de Servicios Técnicos. Monografías
Económicas Estadales).

MERINAS
See HOVAS

MERLEAU-PONTY (MAURICE)

MURPHY (R. T.) A metaphysical critique of method:
Husserl and Merleau-Ponty. in Adelmann (Frederick J.) ed. The quest for the absolute. Chestnut Hill, [1966].

BONOMI (ANDREA) Esistenza e struttura: saggio
su Merleau-Ponty. Milano, Il Saggiatore, 1967.
pp. 254. bibliog. 21cm. (La Cultura: Biblioteca
di Filosofia, Psicologia e Scienze Umane. 16)

RABIL (ALBERT) Merleau-Ponty: existentialist of the social world. New York, Columbia
University Press, 1967. pp. xviii, 331.
bibliog. 21½cm.

ARON (RAYMOND) Marxism and the existentialists.
New York, [1969]. pp. 176.

MERRIMAN (JOHN XAVIER)

GARSON (N.G.) Louis Botha or John X. Merriman:
the choice of South Africa's first prime minister.
London, 1969. pp. 47. (London. University. Institute
of Commonwealth Studies. Commonwealth Papers.
[No.] 12)

MERSEYSIDE

- Description and travel

GRESSWELL (RONALD KAY) and LAWTON (RICHARD) Merseyside:
a description of the O.S. one-inch sheet 100;
Liverpool. Sheffield, 1964. pp. 36. bibliog.
(Geographical Association. British Landscapes
Through Maps. 6)

- Economic conditions

GRESSWELL (RONALD KAY) and LAWTON (RICHARD) Merseyside:
a description of the O.S. one-inch sheet 100;
Liverpool. Sheffield, 1964. pp. 36. bibliog.
(Geographical Association. British Landscapes
Through Maps. 6)

MERSEYSIDE: social and economic studies; [the
findings of the Merseyside Social and Economic
Survey organised by the University of
Liverpool]; edited by Richard Lawton and
Catherine M. Cunningham. London, 1970. pp.
504. bibliogs.

- Economic history

HARRIS (JOHN RAYMOND) ed. Liverpool and
Merseyside: essays in the economic and
social history of the port and its hinterland.
London, Cass, 1969. pp. xiv, 287. 21½cm.

- Industries

ALLEN (ERIC GEORGE WALTER) Post-war industrial
development in Lancashire and Merseyside.
[Manchester], Manchester Statistical Society,
[1963]. pp. 29. 21½cm.

- Social conditions

MERSEYSIDE: social and economic studies; [the
findings of the Merseyside Social and Economic
Survey organised by the University of
Liverpool]; edited by Richard Lawton and
Catherine M. Cunningham. London, 1970. pp.
504. bibliogs.

- Social history

HARRIS (JOHN RAYMOND) ed. Liverpool and
Merseyside: essays in the economic and
social history of the port and its hinterland.
London, Cass, 1969. pp. xiv, 287. 21½cm.

- Transit systems

TRAFFIC RESEARCH CORPORATION. Merseyside area
land use/transportation study: technical reports,
nos. 1-24. Liverpool, 1969. 3 pts. (in 5 vols.).

MERU (AFRICAN TRIBE)

NELSON (ANTON) The freemen of Meru. Nairobi,
O.U.P., 1967. pp. xii, 227. bibliog. 21cm.

MESHCHERIAKOV (NIKOLAI LEONIDOVICH)

KLIORINA (IRAIDA SAMONOVNA) Н. Л.
Мещеряков в Якутии. Якутск, Книжное Издательство, 1965. pp. 86.
20см.

MESLIER (JEAN)

CENTRE AIXOIS D'ÉTUDES ET DE RECHERCHES
SUR LE XVIIE SIÈCLE. Colloque international,
d'Aix-en-Provence, 1964. Etudes sur le curé
Meslier: actes, etc. Paris, Societé des
Études Robespierristes, 1966. pp.125.
25cm.

MESMERISM

DARNTON (ROBERT) Mesmerism and the end of the
enlightenment in France. Cambridge, Mass., 1968.
pp. 218. bibliog.

MESSIANISM

- Dictionaries and encyclopaedias

DESROCHES (HENRI CHARLES) and others. Dieux d'hommes:
dictionnaire des messianismes et millénarismes
de l'ere chrétienne. Paris, 1969. pp. 281.
bibliogs.

MESSIANISM, POLITICAL

QUEIROZ (MAURÍCIO VINHAS DE) Messianismo e conflito social: a guerra sertaneja do Condestado,
1912-1916. Rio de Janeiro, Civilização Brasileira, 1966. pp. (vii), 353. 21cm. (Retratos
do Brasil. vol.45)

METAL FURNITURE

U.K. Department of Trade and Industry. Business monitor: Production series. P 84. Metal furniture. London, 1970 to date.

METAL TRADE

- Australia

MACARTY (BEN) Industrial relations in the metal trades in Australia, 1966. [London], Engineering Employers' Federation, 1966. pp. 16. 20½cm.

- Communist countries

ZUBKOV (ANATOLII IVANOVICH) Mеждународное разделение труда и развитие металлургии социалистических стран. Москва, Наука, 1968. pp. 197. 19½см.

- France

FRANCE. Comité Fonderie, Transformation et Travail des Métaux. 1971. Préparation du VIe Plan...: rapport. Paris, 1971. pp. 51.

- Germany

KUBE (HELGA) Die Industrieansiedlung in Ludwigshafen am Rhein bis 1892; Chemie und Metallverarbeitung. [Stuttgart, imprint], 1962. pp. 247. bibliog.

NOÉ (CLAUS) Gebändigter Klassenkampf: Tarifautonomie in der Bundesrepublik Deutschland; der Konflikt zwischen Gesamtmetall und IG Metall vom Frühjahr 1963. Berlin, [1970]. pp. 351. bibliog.

- Ireland (Republic)

EIRE. Committee on Industrial Progress. 1970. Report on metal trades industry. Dublin, [1970]. pp. 80.

- Italy

SCIARELLI (SERGIO) L'industria metallurgica e meccanica in Campania. Napoli, [1970]. pp. 319. (Centro di Studi Aziendali Giuseppe Cenzato. Collana di Studi e Ricerche. 2)

- Kazakstan

IGENBAEV (AKYZHAN ABDYKARIMOVICH) Карагандинский металлургический завод: исторический очерк. Алма-Ата, Наука, 1966. pp. 112. 19½см.

- Poland - Silesia

ZALESKI (WOJCIECH) Dzieje górnictwa i hutnictwa na Górnym Śląsku do roku 1806. Madryt, Nakładem Antoniny Zaleskiej, 1967. pp. 445. bibliog. 22½cm. (Towarzystwo Imienia Romana Dmowskiego. Wydawnictwa. nr.5)

- Russia

MITEL'MAN (M.) and others. Istoriia Putilovskogo zavoda, 1801-1917. 3rd ed. Moskva, 1961. pp. 718. (Kommunisticheskaia Partiia Sovetskogo Soiuza. Leningradskii Oblastnoi Komitet. Istoriia Kirovskogo/byv. Putilovskogo/ Metallurgicheskogo i Mashinostroitel'nogo Zavoda v Leningrade. [vol.1])

OSINTSEV (ARKADII STEPANOVICH) Tekhnicheskii progress v chernoi metallurgii. Moskva, 1963. pp. 52.

IZ... Из истории Магнитогорского металлургического комбината и города Магнитогорска, 1929-1941 гг.: сборник документов и материалов. Челябинск, 1965. pp. 276.

KOSTIUCHENKO (STANISLAV ALEKSEEVICH) and others. Istoriia Kirovskogo zavoda, 1917-1945. Moskva, 1966. pp. 702.

SLAVNAIA... Славная история, 1757-1967: очерки истории Выксунского ордена Ленина металлургического завода. Горький, 1967. pp. 423

POLISHCHUK (F.P.) Трудовой подвиг металлургов в годы Великой Отечественной войны. in Из истории рабочего класса СССР. Москва, 1968.

- South Africa

SOUTH AFRICA. Board of Trade and Industries. Industrial Development Series. [Reports]. No.6. Investigation into the iron and steel, metallurgical and engineering industries. Pretoria, [1968-69]. 5 pts.

- Ukraine

VOLODIN (GRIGORII GRIGOR'EVICH) Po sledam istorii: ocherki iz istorii Donetskogo ordena Lenina metallurgicheskogo zavoda imeni V. I. Lenina. Donetsk, 1967. pp. 352.

- Uzbekistan

BURIAKOVA (E.IU.) Uzbekskii metallurgicheskii zavod im. V.I. Lenina. in Materialy po istorii Uzbekistana. Tashkent, 1963.

METAL-WORK

- Germany

KAISER (KURT) Vor- und Zulieferungen des Metall verarbeitenden Handwerks an die Industrie im Regierungsbezirk Düsseldorf. Essen, Rheinisch-Westfälisches Institut für Wirtschaftsforschung, 1964. pp. 46. 24cm. (Schriftenreihe. Neue Folge. 22)

- Switzerland

WAEBER (PAUL) Die Gesellschaft zu Schmieden in Bern: ihr Leben und ihre Entwicklung in sechs Jahrhunderten. Bern, [imprint], 1938. pp. (vi), 456. 25½cm.

METAL-WORKERS

INTERNATIONAL LABOUR ORGANISATION. Metal Trades Committee. 8th Session. The role of employers' and workers' organisations in programming and planning in the metal trades: report submitted to and proceedings of the eighth session... [held in] Geneva, 6-17 December 1965. Geneva, 1967. pp. 127. (Labour-Management Relations Series. No. 27.)

METAL WORKERS (Cont'd.)

OPEL (FRITZ) 75 Jahre Eiserne Internationale 1893-1968: 75 ans de L'Internationale du Fer 1893-1968. Frankfurt am Main, [1968]. pp. 201. bibliog. In German and French.

- France

FÉDÉRATION DES TRAVAILLEURS DE LA MÉTALLURGIE (FRANCE ET OUTRE-MER). Les comités d'entreprises: principes d'orientation, d'organisation et de fonctionnement. [Paris, imprint, 1946]. pp. 212. 21cm.

- Germany

ALTMANN-GOTTHEINER (ELISABETH) Die Entwicklung der Frauenarbeit in der Metallindustrie: Vortrag, gehalten auf der dritten Konferenz zur Förderung der Arbeiterinnen-Interessen... 1914. Jena, 1916. pp. 23. (Ständiger Ausschuss zur Förderung der Arbeiterinnen-Interessen. Schriften. Heft 8)

BRANDENBURG (HANS H.) Der Einfluss von Einstellungen auf Lebensplanung und Lebensgestaltung junger Metallarbeiter. [Erlangen, imprint, 1967?] pp. 180. bibliog.

LUEDERS (KLAUS) Aktive Lohnpolitik: zum Lohnkampf der westdeutschen Metallarbeitergewerkschaft. Berlin Verlag Tribüne, 1967. pp. 149. 20cm.

SCHARMANN (THEODOR) ed. Lebensplanung und Lebensgestaltung junger Arbeiter aus der Metallindustrie der Bundesrepublik und der Schweiz, etc. Bern, Huber, [1967]. pp. 368. bibliogs. 23cm. (Munich. Deutscher Jugendinstitut and Erlangen. Universität. Institut für Wirtschafts- und Sozialpsychologie. Der Junge Arbeiter: Studien zu einer Genealogie des Industriebürgers. Band 1).

KOLB (JOHANNES) Metallgewerkschaften in der Nachkriegszeit: der Organisationsaufbau der Metallgewerkschaften in den drei westlichen Besatzungszonen Deutschlands. Frankfurt am Main, [1970]. pp. 180. bibliog.

- Hong Kong

HONG KONG. Machine Shop and Metal Working Industrial Committee. 1969. Report...on the manpower survey of the machine shop and metal working trades (2nd April - 11th April, 1968) Hong Kong, 1968 [or rather 1969]. pp. 151.

- India

INDIA. 1966. Report on survey of labour conditions in metal rolling factories in India. (Labour Bureau) Delhi, 1966. pp. iv, 54. 24½cm.

- Poland

NAJDUCHOWSKA (HALINA) Pozycja społeczna starych robotników przemysłu metalowego: fragmenty opracowanych badań. Wrocław, Zakład Narodowy im. Ossolińskich, 1965. pp. 140. 24cm. (Z Badań Klasy Robotniczej i Inteligencji)

- Russia

TUL'SKII soiuz metallistov: ocherki i vospominaniia. Tula, 1967. pp. 248.

- Switzerland

BRANDENBURG (HANS H.) Der Einfluss von Einstellungen auf Lebensplanung und Lebensgestaltung junger Metallarbeiter. [Erlangen, imprint, 1967?]. pp. 180. bibliog.

SCHARMANN (THEODOR) ed. Lebensplanung und Lebensgestaltung junger Arbeiter aus der Metallindustrie der Bundesrepublik und der Schweiz, etc. Bern, Huber, [1967]. pp. 368. bibliogs. 23cm. (Munich. Deutscher Jugendinstitut and Erlangen. Universität. Institut für Wirtschafts- und Sozialpsychologie. Der Junge Arbeiter: Studien zu einer Genealogie des Industriebürgers. Band 1).

- Ukraine

LAVROV (IURII PAVLOVYCH) Metalurhy Ukraïny v avanhardi revoliutsiĭnoï borot'by, 1895-1904. Kyïv, 1970. pp. 187. With Russian summary and table of contents.

- United Kingdom

OUR reply to Sir Allan Smith; [by] W. Hannington [and others]. London, 1928. pp. 13.

- United States

ASSOCIATED SPRING CORPORATION. Barnes Gibson Raymond Division. Plymouth Plant [Management], and INTERNATIONAL UNION, UNITED AUTOMOBILE, AEROSPACE AND AGRICULTURAL IMPLEMENT WORKERS OF AMERICA. Local 236. Agreement [made at Plymouth, Michigan, on 19th June, 1953]. [Plymouth, Mich., 1953]. pp. 37.

METALLURGY

WATSON (JOSEPH YELLOLY) A compendium of British mining, with statistical notices of the principal mines in Cornwall; to which is added the history and uses of metals, and a glossary, etc. London, 1843; [Truro, Barton, 1968?]. pp. iv,84 21cm. Original printed privately. Photographic reprint.

- Russia

ARZUMANIAN (ASHOT MARTIROSOVICH) Taina Bulata. Erevan, 1967. pp. 255.

METALS

- Yearbooks

METAL BULLETIN HANDBOOK. London, annual, 1968 (1st) to date. 22cm.

METAMATHEMATICS

LORENZEN (PAUL) Métamathématique; traduit de l'allemand par J.B.Grize. Paris, Mouton, 1967. pp. 166. 23cm. (Paris. École Pratique des Hautes Études. Section des Sciences Économiques et Sociales. Mathématiques et Sciences de l'Homme. 6)

RASIOWA (HELENA) and SIKORSKI (ROMAN)
The mathematics of metamathematics.
2nd ed. Warszawa, Państowe Wydawnictwo
Naukowe, 1968. pp. 519. bibliog. 23½cm.
(Polska Akademia Nauk. Monografie
Matematyczne. tom 41)

METAPHYSICS

DE MONTMORENCY (HERVEY GUY FRANCIS
EDWARD) From Kant to Einstein.
Cambridge, Heffer, 1926; .pp. 39
21½cm.

HEIDEGGER (MARTIN) What is philosophy?, translated-
... by William Kluback and Jean T. Wilde. London,
Vision, [1958]. pp. 97. bibliog. 20cm. Text
in German and English.

AGASSI (J.) The nature of scientific problems and
their roots in metaphysics. in Bunge (Mario
Augusto) ed. The critical approach to science
and philosophy. New York, [1964].

BRADLEY (RAYMOND D.) Logic, physics &
metaphysics. Auckland, N.Z., 1967.
pp. 27.

KURTZ (P.) Meta-metaphysics, the categories, and
naturalism. in Anton (John Peter) ed. Naturalism and historical understanding. Albany, 1967.

POLS (EDWARD) Whitehead's metaphysics: a critical examination of process and reality. Carbondale, Southern Illinois U.P., [1967]. pp. xi,
205. 20½cm.

WARTOFSKY (M. W.) Metaphysics as heuristic for
science. in Boston Colloquium for the Philosophy
of Science. Proceedings, 1964-1966. Boston
studies in the philosophy of science, vol.3.
Dordrecht, 1967.

GRAM (MOLTKE S.) Kant, ontology, and the a priori.
Evanston, 1968. pp. 194.

LEYDEN (WOLFGANG VON) Seventeenth-century metaphysics: an examination of some main concepts
and theories. London, Duckworth, 1968. pp.
xvi, 316. 21½cm.

LIZZIO (MARIA) Marxismo e metafisica: riflessioni
sul pensiero di Ugo Spirito. Catania, [1968].
pp. 365.

MARTIN (GOTTFRIED) General metaphysics: its problems
and its method. London, Allen & Unwin, 1968.
pp. 368 bibliog. 21½cm.

SELLARS (WILFRID STALKER) Science and
metaphysics: variations on Kantian themes.
London, Routledge & Kegan Paul, 1968. pp.
x, 246. 21½cm. (International Library of
Philosophy and Scientific Method)

TROTIGNON (PIERRE) L'idée de vie chez
Bergson, et la critique de la métaphysique.
Paris, 1968. pp. 635. bibliog.

YOLTON (JOHN W.) Metaphysical analysis.
London, Allen & Unwin, 1968. pp. xviii,
216. bibliog. 22½cm.

AYER (Sir ALFRED JULES) Metaphysics and common
sense. London, 1969. pp. 267.

BUCHDAHL (GERD) Metaphysics and the philosophy
of science: the classical origins, Descartes
to Kant. Oxford, 1969. pp. 714. bibliog.

HEIDEGGER (MARTIN) Identity and difference; translated and with an introduction by Joan Stambaugh.
New York, [1969]. pp. 146. In English with German
text in the appendix.

PENELHUM (TERENCE) and MACINTOSH (JOHN JAMES)
eds. The first critique: reflections on Kant's
Critique of pure reason. Belmont, Calif., [1969].
pp. 146.

ROUNER (LEROY S.) Within human experience: the
philosophy of William Ernest Hocking. Cambridge,
Mass., 1969. pp. 378. bibliog.

SIMON (JOSEF) Sprache und Raum: philosophische Untersuchungen zum Verhältnis
zwischen Wahrheit und Bestimmtheit von
Sätzen. Berlin, de Gruyter, 1969.
pp. xvi, 327. bibliog. 23cm.

SOLL (IVAN) An introduction to Hegel's metaphysics. Chicago, 1969. pp. 160. bibliog.

SONTAG (FREDERICK) The existentialist prolegomena:
to a future metaphysics. Chicago, 1969. pp.
223.

DREITZEL (HORST) Protestantischer Aristotelismus
und absoluter Staat: die Politica des Henning
Arnisaeus, ca. 1575-1636. Wiesbaden, 1970.
pp. 458. bibliog. (Institut für Europäische Geschichte. Veröffentlichungen. Band 55)

FINDLAY (JOHN NIEMEYER) Ascent to the absolute:
metaphysical papers and lectures. London, 1970.
pp. 271.

TOULMIN (STEPHEN EDELSTON) and others. Metaphysical
beliefs: three essays...with a preface by Alasdair
MacIntyre. London, 1970. pp. 206.

MÉTAYER SYSTEM

CHEUNG (STEVEN N.S.) The theory of share tenancy:
with special application to Asian agriculture
and the first phase of Taiwan land reform.
Chicago, 1969. pp. 188. bibliog.

- Brazil

JOHNSON (ALLEN W.) Sharecroppers of the sertão:
economics and dependence on a Brazilian plantation.
Stanford, 1971. pp. 153. bibliog.

- Italy

ASSOCIAZIONI CRISTIANE DEI LAVORATORI ITALIANI.
Presidenza Nazionale. Settore Terra. La
mezzadria oggi. [Rome, 1968]. pp. 174.
bibliog.

METEOROLOGICAL SATELLITES

- Law and legislation

PRAVOVYE aspekty ispol'zovaniia is-
kusstvennykh sputnikov dlia tselei
meteorologii i radiosviazi. Moskva,
1970. pp. 170.

METEOROLOGICAL STATIONS

- Atlantic Ocean

INTERNATIONAL CIVIL AVIATION ORGANIZATION, 1960.
Acts on the joint financing of the North Atlantic
Ocean stations, 1954 and 1960; (and Supplement
No. 1) (Doc, 8080) Montreal, 1960. pp. 45, 5.
24cm.

METEOROLOGY

UNITED STATES. Weather Bureau. World weather records, 1951-60. Washington, 1965 to date.

PENGUIN SCIENCE SURVEY: physical sciences. Harmondsworth, annual, 1968 to date. 18cm.

DESSENS (HENRI) La maitrise des climats. Paris, P.U.F., 1968. pp. 160. bibliog. 18cm. (La Science Vivante)

DURAND-DASTÈS (FRANÇOIS) Géographie des airs. Paris, P.U.F., 1969. pp 275. bibliog. 18cm. (Magellan: la Géographie et ses Problèmes. 4)

METEOROLOGY

- Charts, diagrams, etc.

UNITED STATES. Naval Air Systems Command. NAVAIR 50-1C-52. Selected level heights, temperatures and dew points for the northern hemisphere. Washington, 1970. pp. various. bibliog.

- Russia

NEZDIUROV (DMITRII FILIPPOVICH) Ochevki razvitiia meteorologicheskikh. nabliudenii v Rossii. Leningrad, 1969. pp. 223. bibliog.

METHANE

ITALY. Direzione Generale delle Imposte Dirette. 1959. Distribuzione del gas metano: studio approvato dagli Ispettori Compartimentali nella riunione di Firenze dal 12 al 15 novembre 1958. Rome, 1959. pp. 35. 20cm.

METHODISM

NEWTON (JOHN A.) Susanna Wesley and the puritan tradition in Methodism. London, Epworth P., 1968. pp. 216. bibliog. 21½cm.

METHODIST CHURCH IN THE UNITED KINGDOM

PACKER (JAMES INNELL) ed. The Church of England and the Methodist Church: a consideration of the report, Conversations between the Church of England and the Methodist Church; ten essays. Abingdon, Berkshire, [1963]. pp. 63.

PROBERT (JOHN CHARLES CRIPPS) An introduction to the sociology of Cornish Methodism: the formative years. [Redruth], 1964. pp. 48. (Cornish Methodist Historical Association. Occasional Publications. No. 8)

PROBERT (JOHN CHARLES CRIPPS) Fore Street Methodist Church, Redruth, 1865-1965: a social history. Redruth, [imprint 1965]. pp. (iii), 44. 21½cm.

CURRIE (ROBERT) Methodism divided: a study in the sociology of ecumenicalism. London, Faber, 1968. pp. 348.

ANDREWS (STUART) Methodism and society; [a study with supporting documents]. London, 1970. pp. 140. bibliog.

FARMER (LESLIE) The Putney story: a history of Putney Methodism. n.p. [1970]. pp. 20.

HALÉVY (ELIE) The birth of Methodism in England; translated and edited by Bernard Semmel. Chicago, 1971. pp. 81.

METHODISTS IN THE UNITED KINGDOM

WILSON (D. DUNN) Many waters cannot quench: a study of the sufferings of eighteenth-century Methodism and their significance for John Wesley and the first Methodists. London, 1969. pp. 213. bibliog.

METHODISTS IN THE UNITED STATES

PILKINGTON (JAMES PENN) The Methodist Publishing House: a history. Nashville, Abingdon P., 1968 in progress. 23cm.

METHODOLOGY

GIEDYMIN (J.) Strength, confirmation, compatibility. in Bunge (Mario Augusto) ed. The critical approach to science and philosophy. New York, [1964].

HEISKANEN (ILKKA) Theoretical approaches and scientific strategies in administrative and organizational research: a methodological study. Helsinki, Societas Scientiarum Fennica, 1967. pp. 199. bibliog. 25cm. (Commentationes Humanarum Litterarum. XXXIX. 2)

INTERNATIONAL COLLOQUIUM IN THE PHILOSOPHY OF SCIENCE, LONDON, 1965. Criticism and the growth of knowledge; proceedings ...vol. 4; edited by Imre Lakatos [and] Alan Musgrave. Cambridge, 1970. pp. 282. bibliogs.

METRIC SYSTEM

INDIA. Railway Board. Railway Metric Committee. 1957. Adoption of the metric system of weights and measures on Indian railways: report. [S.L. Kumar, chairman]. [New Delhi], 1957. pp. 148, xlv.

EIRE. Metric System and Decimal Coinage Committee. 1960. Report of the.... Committee, 1959.[A.W.Bayne,chairman]. Dublin,[1960]. pp. 100. bibliog. 24½cm.

UNITED STATES. Senate. Commerce Committee. Conversion to metric system: hearing. Washington, 1964. pp. ii, 68. bibliog.

U.K. 1967. Ministry of Public Building and Works. Going metric in the construction industry: why and when. (Going Metric Bulletins.1) London, 1967. pp. 15. 30cm.

AUSTRALIA. Parliament. Senate.Select Committee on the Metric System of Weights and Measures. 1968-71. Report; (with Minutes of evidence); [K.A. Laught, chairman]. in Australia. Parliament. Parliamentary papers, 1968, vol. 8, which see.

KELLAWAY (FRANCIS WILLIAM) ed. Metrication. Harmondsworth, Penguin Books, 1968. pp. 124. bibliog. 18cm.

METRIC units with reference to water, sewage and related subjects: report of working party, [W.H. Norris, chairman]. London, H.M.S.O., 1968. pp. 10. 24½cm.

U.K. Standing Joint Committee on Metrication. Change to the metric system in the United Kingdom. London, H.M.S.O., 1968. pp. iv, 10. 24½cm.

METRICATION BOARD [U.K.] **Annual report.** a., [May/Dec. 1969] (1st)- London.

EIRE. Department of Local Government. 1969. Metric programme for the building industry. Dublin, 1969. pp. 15.

The METRIC system: report of the Working Committee of Officials: [J.P. Lewin, chairman]. Wellington, [Government Printer], 1968 [or rather 1969]. pp. 51.

NATIONAL BUILDING AGENCY. Metric housing: what it means. London, 1969. pp. 23.

BUREAU INTERNATIONAL DES POIDS ET MESURES. S.I.: the international system of units; [translated from the French; prepared jointly by the National Physical Laboratory and the National Bureau of Standards, USA]. London, H.M.S.O., 1970. pp. 45.

CANADA. Department of Industry, Trade and Commerce. 1970. White Paper on metric conversion in Canada; Livre blanc sur la conversion au système métrique au Canada. Ottawa, 1970. pp. 22. In English and French.

DONOVAN (FRANK ROBERT) Prepare now for a metric future. New York, [1970]. pp. 212.

SINGAPORE. Ministry of Science and Technology. 1970. Report on a study of the proposed conversion to the metric system in Singapore. Singapore, 1970. pp. 26. bibliog. (Singapore. Parliament. Sessional Papers. 1970. Cmd.35.)

VERMAN (LAL C.) and KAUL (JAINATH) eds. Metric change in India. New Delhi, Indian Standards Institution, 1970. pp. 529.

CONSERVATIVE POLITICAL CENTRE. [Publications]. No. 484. Measure for measure: a viewpoint on metrication. London, 1971. pp. 22.

- Bibliography

ATKINS (JOHN LESLIE) ed. Metrication: a bibliography. Coventry, 1968 fo. 19.

- Conversion tables

U.K. Ministry of Housing and Local Government. 1968. Public Health Act 1961: the Building Regulations 1965: metric equivalents of dimension. London, 1968. pp. 45. 30cm.

ASSOCIATION OF TEACHERS IN TECHNICAL INSTITUTIONS. Metrication, decimalisation, and SI units. [London], 1969. pp. 16. bibliog.

U.K. Ministry of Housing and Local Government. 1969. Public Health Act, 1961: the building regulations, 1965: metric values: consultative proposals. London, 1969. pp. 101.

- Study and teaching

SCOTLAND. Consultative Committee on the Curriculum. 1968. Going metric: implications for the primary school. Edinburgh, 1968. pp. 7. 24½cm. (Curriculum Papers. 4.)

SCOTLAND. Consultative Committee on the Curriculum. 1968. Going metric: implications for secondary schools. Edinburgh, 1968. pp. 13. 24½cm. (Curriculum Papers. 5.)

U.K. Department of Education and Science. Schools Council. 1968. Change for a pound: a teaching guide for the introduction of decimal currency and the adoption of metric measures. London, 1968. pp. 48. bibliog.

U.K. Department of Education and Science. Schools Council. 1969. Change for a pound: a teaching guide for the introduction of decimal currency and the adoption of metric measures. 2nd ed. London, 1969. pp. 51. bibliog.

METROPOLITAN AREAS

LINGE (GODFREY JAMES RUTHERFORD) The delimitation of urban boundaries for statistical purposes, with special reference to Australia: a report to the Commonwealth Statistician. Canberra, Australian National University, 1965. pp. ix, 147. 32cm. (Australian National University. Research School of Pacific Studies. Department of Geography. Publications. G/2)

SAZANAMI (HIDEHIKO) Housing in metropolitan areas. Toronto, 1967. pp. 91. (Centennial Study and Training Programme on Metropolitan Problems. Papers. No. 10)

WILSON (ALAN GEOFFREY) Metropolitan growth models;...paper prepared for an International Colloquium on the Mastery of Urban Growth, organised by Mens en Ruimte, Brussels, December 1969. London, 1969. pp. 41. (Centre for Environmental Studies. Working Papers. 55)

METROPOLITAN problems: international perspectives: a search for comprehensive solutions; [based on the Centennial Study and Training Programme on Metropolitan Problems]: edited by Simon R. Miles. Toronto, [1970]. pp. 534. (International Association for Metropolitan Research and Development. Metropolitan Studies Series)

- Bibliography

HALÁSZ (D.) compiler. Metropolis: a select bibliography of administrative and other problems in metropolitan areas throughout the world. 2nd ed. The Hague, Nijhoff, 1967. pp. xiii, 265. 22½cm. (International Union of Local Authorities. [Publications]. 59)

- France

ORGANISATION D'ETUDES D'AMENAGEMENT DE L'AIRE METROPOLITAINE MARSEILLAISE. Schéma d'aménagement de l'aire métropolitaine marseillaise; métropoles d'équilibre et aires métropolitaines. [Paris, 1970]. pp. 224. bibliog. (France. Délégation à l'Aménagement du Territoire et à l'Action Régionale. Travaux et Recherches de Prospective. 5)

ORGANISATION D'ETUDES D'AMENAGEMENT DE L'AIRE METROPOLITAINE NANTES-SAINT-NAZAIRE. Schéma d'aménagement de l'aire métropolitaine Nantes-Saint-Nazaire; métropoles d'équilibre et aires métropolitaines. [Paris], 1970. pp. 80. (France. [Délégation à l'Aménagement du Territoire et à l'Action Régionale]. Travaux et Recherches de Prospective. 11)

METROPOLITAN AREAS - France (Cont'd.)

ORGANISATION D'ETUDE D'AMENAGEMENT DE L'AIRE METROPOLITAINE LYON-SAINT-ETIENNE-GRENOBLE. Schéma d'aménagement de la métropole Lyon-Saint-Etienne-Grenoble; métropoles d'équilibre et aires métropolitaines. [Paris], 1971. pp. 240. bibliog. (France. Délégation à l'Aménagement du Territoire et à l'Action Régionale. Travaux et Recherches de Prospective. 10) 3 maps in end pocket.

ORGANISATION REGIONALE D'ETUDES D'AMENAGEMENT NORD-PAS-DE-CALAIS. Aménagement d'une région urbaine: le Nord-Pas-de-Calais; métropoles d'équilibre et aires métropolitaines. [Paris, 1971], pp. 422. bibliog. (France. Délégation à l'Aménagement du Territoire et à l'Action Régionale. Travaux et Recherches de Prospective. 19)

- Italy

CAFIERO (SALVATORE) and BUSCA (A.) Lo sviluppo metropolitano in Italia. Roma, 1970. pp. 240. (Associazione per lo Sviluppo dell'Industria nel Mezzogiorno. Centro per gli Studi sullo Sviluppo Economico. Collana di Monografie).

- Poland

SŁUZEWSKI (JERZY) Działalność organów państwowych na obszarze aglomeracji miejskich. Warszawa, Wydawnictwo Prawnicze, 1965. pp. 214. 21cm. With Russian and English summaries.

- United Kingdom

MASSER (I.F.) A test of some models for predicting intermetropolitan movement of population in England and Wales. London, 1970. pp. 51. bibliog. (Centre for Environmental Studies. University Working Papers. 9)

ROSE (GORDON) Local councils in metropolitan areas. London, 1971. pp. 32. (Fabian Society. Research Series. [No.] 296)

- United States

CENTENNIAL STUDY AND TRAINING PROGRAMME ON METROPOLITAN PROBLEMS. San Francisco Bay Area Study Group. A critical commentary on "Metropolitan transportation problems". Berkeley, 1967. fo. 36.

TORRES (JUAN DE) Economic dimensions of major metropolitan areas: population, housing, employment and income. New York, [1968]. pp. 52. bibliog.

WILLIAMS (EDWARD A.) Open space: the choices before California: the urban metropolitan open space study. San Francisco, [1969]. pp. 187. bibliog.

BOLLENS (JOHN CONSTANTINUS) and SCHMANDT (HENRY J.) The metropolis: its people, politics, and economic life. 2nd. ed. New York, 1970. pp. 488. bibliog.

ELAZAR (DANIEL JUDAH) Cities of the prairie: the metropolitan frontier and American politics. New York, [1970]. pp. 514. bibliog. (Temple University. Center for the Study of Federalism. Studies in Federalism)

STANBACK (THOMAS M.) and KNIGHT (RICHARD V.) The metropolitan economy: the process of employment expansion. New York, 1970. pp. 279.

- United States - Statistics

UNITED STATES. Advisory Commission on Intergovernmental Relations. Directory of federal statistics for metropolitan areas. Washington, 1962. pp. viii, 118.

METROPOLITAN FINANCE

HICKS (URSULA KATHLEEN) Financing metropolitan government. Toronto, 1967. pp. 84. (Toronto. Bureau of Municipal Research. Centennial Study and Training Programme on Metropolitan Problems. Papers. No.3)

BAHL (ROY W.) Metropolitan city expenditures: a comparative analysis. Lexington, 1969. pp. 140.

METROPOLITAN GOVERNMENT

ROBSON (WILLIAM ALEXANDER) ed. Great cities of the world: their government, politics and planning. 2nd ed. London, Allen and Unwin, 1957. pp. 814. bibliog. 24½cm.

JANOWITZ (MORRIS) and others. Public administration and the public: perspectives toward government in a metropolitan community. Ann Arbor, the University, 1958. pp. vii, 140. 23cm. (Michigan. University. Michigan Governmental Studies. No. 36)

DAVIS (MORRIS) and WEINBAUM (MARVIN G.) Metropolitan decision processes: an analysis of case studies. Chicago, [1969]. pp.131.

- Canada

ONTARIO. 1961. A report on the Metropolitan Toronto system of government; prepared for the Special Committee of the Metropolitan Council on Metropolitan Affairs; by the Ontario Department of Economics. [Toronto] 1961. fo. (2),90. 35½cm.

- United States

GULICK (LUTHER HALSEY) third of the name. (Metro: growth and the problems of government in the metropolitan areas of the U.S.A.): changing problems and lines of attack. Washington, Governmental Affairs Institute, [1957]. pp. ii, 30. 23cm.

UNIVERSITY OF PENNSYLVANIA LAW REVIEW. vol. 105, no. 4. A symposium on metropolitan regionalism: developing governmental concepts. Philadelphia, University of Pennsylvania Law School, 1957. pp. 439-616. 26cm.

GOVERNMENT AFFAIRS FOUNDATION. Metropolitan surveys: a digest. Chicago, Public Administration Service, [1958]. pp. xvi, 256. 26½cm.

UNITED STATES. 1959. Metropolitan problems and urban development: hearings. (House of Representatives. Committee on Government Operations. Executive and Legislative Reorganization Subcommittee) Washington, 1959. pp. iv, 151. 23½cm.

CONNERY (ROBERT HOUGH) and LEACH (RICHARD H.) The Federal Government and metropolitan areas. Cambridge, Mass., Harvard University Press, 1960. pp. xi, 275. bibliog. 21cm.

SCOTT (ILEY STANLEY) and CULVER (WILLIS)
Metropolitan agencies and concurrent
office-holding: a survey of selected districts
and authorities. Berkeley, the Bureau, 1961.
pp. 31. 28cm. (California University. Bureau
of Public Administration. 1961 Legislative
Problems. No. 7)

SNOWISS (SYLVIA) Urban problems and governmental organization. Los Angeles, 1967.
fo. 21. bibliog. (California University.
Institute of Government and Public Affairs.
[Publications]. MR-88)

SNYDER (MARY E.) and ZIMMERMAN (JOSEPH
FRANCIS) The 1967 survey of metropolitan
planning: emerging trends. Albany, [1967?].
fo. 17.

CEASE (RONALD C.) and SAROFF (JEROME R.) eds.
The metropolitan experiment in Alaska: a study
of borough government. New York, Praeger, 1968.
pp. xxi, 449. bibliog. 23½cm. (Praeger Special
Studies in U.S. Economic and Social Development)

GOODHALL (LEONARD E.) The American metropolis.
Columbus, Merrill, [1968]. pp x, 246. bibliogs.
22½cm.

GREENE (LEE SEIFERT) and others. The states
and the metropolis. Alabama, U. of Alabama P.
[1968]. pp. 145. 21cm.

COMMITTEE FOR ECONOMIC DEVELOPMENT. Research and
Policy Committee. Statements on National Policy.
Reshaping government in metropolitan areas.
New York, 1970. pp. 83.

HAWLEY (AMOS HENRY) and ZIMMER (BASIL GEORGE)
The metropolitan community: its people and government.
Beverly Hills, [1970]. pp. 154.

- United States - Bibliography

GOVERNMENT AFFAIRS FOUNDATION. Metropolitan communities: a bibliography with special emphasis upon
government and politics. Chicago, [1957].
pp. xxiii, 392.

METTERNICH-WINNEBERG (CLEMENS WENZESLAUS NEPOMUK LOTHAR VON) Prince

KANN (R. A.) Metternich: a reappraisal of his
impact on international relations. in Black
(Eugene Charlton) ed. European political history,
1815-1870. New York, 1967.

BERTIER DE SAUVIGNY (GUILLAUME DE) Metternich
et la France après le Congrès de Vienne.
[Paris], Hachette, [1968 in progress]. 26cm.
(Bibliothèque des Recherches Historiques et
Littéraires)

WALKER (MACK) ed. Metternich's Europe.
London, Macmillan, 1968. pp. vi, 352.
bibliogs. 23cm. (The Documentary History of
Western Civilization)

METTERNICH-WINNEBURG (FRANZ GEORG KARL JOSEPH JOHANN NEPOMUCENUS) Graf.

MATHY (HELMUT) Franz Georg von Metternich, der
Vater des Staatskanzlers: Studien zur österreichischen
Westpolitik am Ende des 18. Jahrhunderts. Meisenheim
am Glan, 1969. pp. 249. bibliog.

MEULAN

- Population

LACHIVER (MARCEL) La population de Meulan du
XVIIe au XIXe siècle, vers 1600-1870: étude de
démographie historique. Paris, 1969. pp. 339.
bibliog. (Paris. Ecole Pratique des Hautes
Etudes. Section des Sciences Economiques et
Sociales. Centre de Recherches Historiques.
Démographie et Sociétés. 13)

MEUSEBACH (JOHN O.)

KING (IRENE MARSHALL) John O. Meusebach: German
colonizer in Texas. Austin, U. of Texas P.,
[1967]. pp. xiii, 192. bibliog. 23cm.

MEUSEBACH (OTFRIED HANS VON) Freiherr
See MEUSEBACH (JOHN O.)

MEVISSEN (GUSTAV VON)

KUSKE (BRUNO R.) Gustav Mevissens Stellung in der
Wirtschaftsentwicklung: ein Beitrag zur Geschichte
der deutschen und rheinischen Wirtschaftstendenzen;
Vortrag, gehalten am Stiftungstag der Universität.
30. Mai 1920. Köln, Müller, 1921. pp. 16. 23 cm.
(Kölner Universitätsreden. 2)

MEXICAN NEWSPAPERS

- Indexes

SIERRA BRABATA (CARLOS J.) La prensa liberal
frente a la intervención y el imperio.
Mexico, 1962. pp. 205.

MEXICANS

- Psychology

RODRIGUEZ SALA DE GÓMEZGIL (MARIA LUISA) El estereotipo
del Mexicano: estudio psicosocial. Mexico, the
Instituto, 1965. pp. 217. bibliog. 17½cm. (Mexico
City. Universidad Nacional Autónoma de México.
Instituto de Investigaciones Sociales. Cuadernos
de Sociología)

KIEV (ARI) Curanderismo: Mexican-American folk
psychiatry. New York, [1968]. pp. xiii, 207.
bibliog.

FROMM (ERICH) and MACCOBY (MICHAEL) Social
character in a Mexican village: a sociopsychoanalytic study. Englewood Cliffs,
[1970]. pp. 303. bibliog.

MEXICANS IN THE UNITED STATES

MINNESOTA. 1948. The Mexican in Minnesota:
a report...by the Governor's Interracial
Commission. [St.Paul], 1948. pp. 64.
20cm. For revised edition see MINNESOTA.
1953.

MINNESOTA. 1953. The Mexican in
Minnesota, revised: a report...by the
Governor's Interracial Commission.
[St.Paul], 1953. pp. 84. 20cm. For
first edition see MINNESOTA. 1948.

SINGLETON (ROBERT) and BULLOCK (PAUL) Some
problems in minority-group education in the
Los Angeles public schools. Los Angeles,
California University, Institute of Industrial
Relations, 1963. pp. 137-145. 24½cm.
(Reprints. No. 120.) (Reprinted from the
Journal of Negro Education, Spring, 1963)

MEXICANS IN THE UNITED STATES (Cont'd.)

FOGEL (WALTER A.) Mexican Americans in southwest labor markets. Los Angeles, 1967. pp. 222. (California University. Graduate School of Business Administration. Division of Research. Mexican-American Study Project. Advance Reports. 10)

KIEV (ARI) Curanderismo: Mexican-American folk psychiatry. New York, Free P., [1968]. pp. xiii, 207. bibliog. 21cm.

GAMIO (MANUEL) Mexican immigration to the United States: [reprint of the work first published in 1930]. New York, 1969. pp. 262. bibliog.

The MEXICAN American: a selected and annotated bibliography. [Stanford], 1969. pp. 139.

CLARK (MARGARET) Health in the Mexican-American culture: a community study. 2nd ed. Berkeley, 1970. pp. 253. bibliog.

GREBLER (LEO) and others. The Mexican-American people: the nation's second largest minority. New York, [1970]. pp. 777. bibliog.

MOORE (JOAN W.) and CUELLAR (ALFREDO) Mexican Americans. Englewood Cliffs, 1970. pp. 172. bibliog.

SERVIN (MANUEL PATRIC) ed. The Mexican-Americans: an awakening minority. Beverly Hills, 1970. pp. 235.

STEINER (STAN) La raza: the Mexican Americans. New York, [1970]. pp. 418. bibliog.

GALARZA (ERNESTO) Barrio boy. Notre Dame, [1971]. pp. 275.

MOQUIN (WAYNE) and VAN DOREN (CHARLES) eds. A documentary history of the Mexican Americans. New York, 1971. pp. 399. bibliog.

SAMORA (JULIAN) Los mojados: the wetback story. Notre Dame, [1971]. pp. 205. bibliog.

VIDAL (MIRTA) Chicano liberation and revolutionary youth. New York, 1971. pp. 15.

MEXICO

- Army

LIEUWEN (EDWIN) Mexican militarism: the political rise and fall of the revolutionary army, 1910-1940. Albuquerque, U. of New Mexico P., [1968]. pp. xvi, 194. bibliog. 23½cm.

- Biography

DICCIONARIO biografico de Mexico. Monterrey, 1968-1970. 2 vols.

ALISKY (MARVIN) ed. Who's who in Mexican government. Tempe, Arizona, 1969. pp. 64.

- Biography - Bibliography

IGUINIZ (JUAN B.) compiler. Bibliografia biografica mexicana. Mexico, 1969. pp. 433. (Mexico City. Universidad Nacional Autonoma de Mexico. Instituto de Investigaciones Historicas. Serie Bibliografica 5)

- Census

MEXICO. Census, 1970. 9° censo general de poblacion, 1970: 28 de enero de 1970. Datos preliminares sujetos a rectificacion. Mexico, 1970. pp. 55.

- Civilization

GARCÍA RIVAS (HERIBERTO) Aportaciones de México al mundo: lo que México ha dado al mundo en vegetales, minerales, animales, inventos, sistemas doctrinas y aportaciones a la cultura universal. México, Diana, 1964. 2 vols. (in 1). 18cm. (Colección Moderna. 11, 21)

- Commerce

BIANCONI (F.) Le Mexique à la portée des industriels, des capitalistes, des négociants importateurs et exportateurs et des travailleurs. Paris, [imprint], 1889. pp. 144. 18cm.

GARCIA REYNOSO (PLACIDO) Integracion economica latinoamericana: primera etapa 1960-1964. Mexico, 1965. pp. 282.

LERDO DE TEJADA (MIGUEL) Comercio exterior de México desde la conquista hasta hoy; (edición original...1853). México, Banco Nacional de Comercio Exterior, 1967. pp. xvii, 63, (246) bibliog. 25½cm. Facsimile reprint.

DURSTON (JOHN WAGNER) The social organization of peasant marketing in Michoacan, Mexico; [Ph.D.(London) thesis]. 1970. fo. 393. bibliog. Typescript: unpublished. This thesis is the property of London University and may not be removed from the Library.

HAMNETT (BRIAN R.) Politics and trade in southern Mexico, 1750-1821. Cambridge, 1971. pp. 214. bibliog.

- Commerce - Statistics

MEXICO. Direccion General de Estadistica. Censo Comercial, 1966. V censo comercial, 1966; datos de 1965: resumen general. Mexico, 1968. pp. 400.

- Commerce - Germany

EVERSBUSCH (WOLFGANG A.) Die deutsche Mexiko-Schiffahrt. Berlin, 1941. pp. 141. bibliog.

- Commerce - Latin American Free Trade Association Countries

MEXICO. Direccion General de Estadistica. Anuario estadistico del comercio de los Estados Unidos Mexicanos con los paises de la Asociacion Latinoamericana de Libre Comercio. a., 1964, 1969- Mexico.

- Commerce - United States

UNITED STATES. International Commerce Bureau. 1963 Trade Mission report on Mexico. Washington, [1963]. pp.19.

LITTLE (ARTHUR D.) INCORPORATED (MEXICO). Manufacturing in Mexico for the U.S. market: report to Centro Bancario de Tijuana, A.C. [Mexico?,] 1966. fo. 65.

– Commerce – Venezuela

ARCILA FARIAS (EDUARDO) Comercio entre Venezuela y México en los siglos XVI y XVII. México, Colegio de México, 1950 pp. 324. bibliog. 21cm.

MEXICO – Commercial policy
See also LATIN AMERICAN FREE TRADE ASSOCIATION – Mexico

– Constitution

MARTINEZ BAEZ (A.) Las ideas juridicas en el Congreso constituyente de 1856-1857. in Mexico City. Universidad Nacional Autonoma de Mexico. Escuela Nacional de Economia. [Cursos de Invierno. 1956]. El liberalismo y la reforma en Mexico. Mexico, 1957.

MEXICO. Constitution. 1917. Constitución política de los Estados Unidos Mexicanos: texto vigente. 23rd ed. México, Porrua, 1963. pp. 108. 16½cm. (Colección Porrua. Leyes y Códigos de México)

ORGANIZATION OF AMERICAN STATES. 1964. Constitution of the United Mexican States, 1917, as amended. (Department of Legal Affairs) Washington, 1964. pp. iii, 63. 27½cm.

ORGANIZATION OF AMERICAN STATES. Legal Division. 1968. Constitution of Mexico, 1917; (as amended) Washington, 1968. pp. 63.

– Constitutional history

BENSON (NETTIE LEE) ed. Mexico and the Spanish Cortes, 1810-1822: eight essays. Austin, University of Texas Press, [1966]. pp. 243. bibliog. 23cm. (Texas University. Institute of Latin American Studies. Latin American Monographs. No. 5)

HORN (HANS RUDOLF) México: Revolution und Verfassung; der mexikanische Weg zur politischen Stabilität. Hamburg, 1969. pp. 164. bibliog. (Institut für Iberoamerika-Kunde. Schriftenreihe. 10)

VELAZQUEZ (MANUEL) Revolucion en la constitucion: perspectiva de la constitucion, la ideologia y los grupos de presion en Mexico. Mexico, [1969]. pp. 311.

– Description and travel

RAMOS ARIZPE (MIGUEL) Report...to the august congress on the natural, political and civil condition of the provinces of Coahuila, Nuevo Leon, Nuevo Santander, and Texas of the four eastern interior provinces of the kingdom of Mexico; translation, annotations and introduction by Nettie Lee Benson; (originally published in 1950). New York, 1969. pp. 61. bibliog. (Texas University. Institute of Latin-American Studies. Latin-American Studies. 11)

BATAILLON (CLAUDE) Les régions géographiques au Mexique. Paris, 1967. pp. 212. bibliogs. (Paris. Université. Institut des Hautes Etudes de l'Amérique Latine. Travaux et Mémoires. 20)

– Economic conditions

BIANCONI (F.) Le Mexique à la portée des industriels, des capitalistes, des négociants importateurs et exportateurs et des travailleurs. Paris, [imprint], 1889. pp. 144. 18cm.

MOLINA ENRIQUEZ (ANDRES) Los grandes problemas nacionales. Mexico, Carranza, 1909. pp. 363. 28cm.

MAROF (TRISTAN) México de frente y de perfil. Buenos Aires, [1934]. pp. 156.

FERNANDEZ (ROBERTO D.) La miseria de México: sus causas y su único remedio. México, El Insurgente, 1939. pp. 16. 19½cm.

AMERICAN UNIVERSITIES FIELD STAFF. Reports. Mexico and Caribbean Area Series. New York, 1954 (vol. 1) to date.

AMERICAN MANAGEMENT ASSOCIATION. Management Bulletins. 57. Doing business in Mexico: prospects in a growing market. New York, [1964]. pp. 24. 28cm.

INTERNATIONAL GEOGRAPHICAL UNION. Conferencia Regional Latinoamericana, Mexico City, 1966. Guia de la excursión al centro de México. [México], Sociedad Mexicana de Geografía y Estadística, [1966]. pp. 127. 22½cm.

UNITED STATES. International Commerce Bureau. A market for U.S. products in Mexico. Washington, 1966. pp. vii, 66.

BATAILLON (CLAUDE) Les régions géographiques au Mexique. Paris, 1967. pp. 212. bibliogs. (Paris. Université. Institut des Hautes Etudes de l'Amérique Latine. Travaux et Mémoires. 20)

FERNÁNDEZ BRAVO (VICENTE) Temas socio-económicos: problemas nacionales, integración latinoamericana. México, Costa-Amic, 1967. pp. 151. bibliog. 21cm.

URQUIDI (VÍCTOR L.) and LAJOUS VARGAS (ADRIÁN) Educación superior, ciencia y tecnología en el desarrollo económico de México: un estudio preliminar. [Mexico City], Colegio de México, Centro de Estudios Económicos y Demográficos, [1967]. pp. viii, 86. bibliog. 22cm. (Publicaciones. 1)

BENNEWITZ (WOLFDIETRICH) Probleme des regionalen Ungleichgewichts in Entwicklungsländern, dargestellt am Beispiel von Mexico. [Munich, 1968?]. pp. 308. bibliog.

CAMPOS SALAS (OCTAVIANO) El sentido dinámico de el México económico de nuestros días, 1968. [México], Sela, [1968]. pp. 436. 23½cm. (Pensamiento Económico Mexicano)

El DESARROLLO económico de México: ciencia y tecnologia; cinco ensayos; [by] Rafael Pérez Rubio [and others]. México, Centro Nacional de Productividad, 1968. pp. ix, 184. 18½cm. (Colección Ciencia y Tecnologia. 3)

NAVARRETE R. (ALFREDO) Finanzas y desarrollo económico. México, SELA, 1968. pp. 183. 23cm. (Pensamiento Económico Mexicano)

OLÍZAR (MARYNKA) Guia a los mercados de México. 3rd ed. México, 1968. pp. 323. 30cm.

OPIE (REDVERS) Selected papers on the Mexican and international economies from 1966 to 1968;... edited by J.L. Hodgson, F.W. Schloesser [and] W. Z. Bairey. [Mexico City, 1968]. pp. 91. (University of the Americas. Department of Economics Tlatelolco Economic Monographs. Tianguisco Series. No. 1)

MEXICO - Economic conditions (Cont'd.)

SINGER (MORRIS) Growth, equality, and the Mexican experience. Austin, [1969]. pp. 341. bibliog. (Texas University. Institute of Latin American Studies. Latin American Monographs. No. 16)

HUMBOLDT (FRIEDRICH HEINRICH ALEXANDER VON) Baron. Tablas geograficas politicas del reino de Nueva España y Correspondencia mexicana. Mexico, Direccion General de Estadistica, 1970. pp. 161.

SOLIS M. (LEOPOLDO) La realidad económica mexicana: retrovision y perspectivas. Mexico, 1970. pp. 356.

- Economic history

PARRA (MANUEL GERMAN) La industrializacion de Mexico. Mexico, 1954. pp. 203.

AGUIRRE (MANUEL J.) Cananea: las garras del imperialismo en las entrañas de Mexico. Mexico, 1958. pp. 400.

LÓPEZ ROSADO (DIEGO) História económica de México. México, 1965 in progress. bibliog. (Colección Pormaca.)

LOPEZ CAMARA (FRANCISCO) La estructura economica y social de Mexico en la epoca de la reforma. Mexico, 1967. pp. 244. bibliog.

LÓPEZ GALLO (MANUEL) Economía y política en la história de México. 2nd ed. México, Grijalbo, 1967. pp. 608. 20cm. (Colección Norte)

AGUILAR MONTEVERDE (ALONSO) Dialectica de la economia mexicana: del colonialismo al imperialismo. Mexico, 1968. pp. 207.

MEYER (LORENZO) Mexico y Estados Unidos en el conflicto petrolero, 1917-1942. Mexico, 1968. pp. 273.

FLORESCANO (ENRIQUE) Precios del maiz y crisis agricolas en Mexico, 1708-1810: ensayo sobre el movimiento de los precios y sus consecuencias economicas y sociales. Mexico, 1969. pp. 254. bibliog. (Mexico City. Colegio de Mexico. Centro de Estudios Historicos. Nueva Serie. 4)

KING (TIMOTHY) Mexico: industrialization and trade policies since 1940; (edited by Ian Little [and others]). London, 1970. pp. 160. bibliog. (Organisation for Economic Co-operation and Development. Development Centre. Industry and Trade in Some Developing Countries)

LINK (MAX) Die Ursachen des industriellen Aufstiegs Mexikos. Zürich, [1970]. pp. 229. bibliog.

REYNOLDS (CLARK WINTON) The Mexican economy: twentieth-century structure and growth. New Haven, 1970. pp. 468. bibliog.

SOLIS M. (LEOPOLDO) La realidad económica mexicana: retrovision y perspectivas. Mexico, 1970. pp. 356.

BRADING (DAVID A.) Miners and merchants in Bourbon Mexico, 1763-1810. Cambridge, 1971. pp. 382. bibliog.

HANSEN (ROGER D.) The politics of Mexican development. Baltimore, [1971]. pp. 267. bibliog.

- Economic policy

BULNES (FRANCISCO) Los grandes problemas de México. México, El Universal, 1926. pp. xv, 350. 19½cm.

ENRIQUEZ FILHO (ANTONIO) Nueva economia social: plan sexenal mejicano, 1935-40. Mejico, 1935. pp. 160. 21cm.

SEMINARIO SOBRE PLANEACIÓN SOCIO-ECONÓMICA, DERECHO ADMINISTRATIVO Y ADMINISTRACIÓN PUBLICA, 1964. Memoria. Mexico, [1965]. pp. 222. 23cm.

SEMINARIO SOBRE PROBLEMAS ECONOMICOS DE MEXICO, 1°, Cuernavaca, 1965. Bases para la planeacion economico y social de Mexico. Mexico, 1966 repr. 1970. pp. 269.

AGUILAR MONTEVERDE (ALONSO) and CARMONA (FERNANDO) Mexico: riqueza y miseria; dos ensayos. [Mexico City], Nuestro Tiempo, [1967]. pp. 140. 21cm. (Colección Los Grandes Problemas Nacionales.)

CUMBERLAND (CHARLES CURTIS) ed. The meaning of the Mexican Revolution. Boston, Heath, [1967]. pp. xvi, 110. bibliog. 23½cm. (Problems in Latin American Civilization)

NAVARRETE (IFIGENIA MARTÍNEZ DE) Los incentivos fiscales y el desarrollo económico de México. México, Universidad Nacional Autónoma de México, Instituto de Investigaciones Economicas, 1967. pp. 171. bibliog. 21cm. (Textos Universitarios)

NAVARRETE (IFIGENIA MARTÍNEZ DE) Sobrepoblación y desarrollo económico. México, Universidad Nacional Autónoma de México. Dirección General de Publicaciones, 1967. pp. 34. 21cm.

AGUILAR MONTEVERDE (ALONSO) Dialectica de la economia mexicana: del colonialismo al imperialismo. Mexico, 1968. pp. 207.

BENNEWITZ (WOLFDIETRICH) Probleme des regionalen Ungleichgewichts in Entwicklungsländern, dargestellt am Beispiel von Mexico. [Munich, 1968?]. pp. 308. bibliog.

KOEHLER (JOHN E.) Economic policy-making with limited information: the process of macro-control in Mexico. Santa Monica, 1968. pp. 64. bibliog. (Rand Corporation. Research Memoranda. 5682)

NAVARRETE R. (ALFREDO) Finanzas y desarrollo económico. México, SELA, 1968. pp. 183. 23cm. (Pensamiento Económico Mexicano)

OPIE (REDVERS) Selected papers on the Mexican and international economies from 1966 to 1968;... edited by J.L. Hodgson, F.W. Schloesser [and] W. Z. Bairey. [Mexico City, 1968]. pp. 91. (University of the Americas. Department of Economics. Tlatelolco Economic Monographs. Tianguisco Series. No. 1)

BOHRISCH (ALEXANDER) Probleme privater Auslandsinvestitionen in México. Hamburg, 1969. pp. 130. bibliog. (Institut für Iberoamerika-Kunde. Schriftenreihe. 11)

LA CASCIA (JOSEPH S.) Capital formation
and economic development in Mexico. New
York, Praeger, 1969. pp. xix, 190. bibliog.
23½cm. (Special Studies in International
Economics and Development)

SINGER (MORRIS) Growth, equality, and the Mexican
experience. Austin, [1969]. pp. 341. bibliog.
(Texas University. Institute of Latin American
Studies. Latin American Monographs. No. 16)

BARKIN (DAVID) and KING (TIMOTHY). Regional economic
development: the river basin approach in Mexico.
Cambridge, 1970. pp. 262.

BENVENISTE (GUY) Bureaucracy and national planning: a sociological case study in Mexico.
New York, 1970. pp. 141. bibliog.

KING (TIMOTHY) Mexico: industrialization and trade
policies since 1940; (edited by Ian Little [and
others]). London, 1970. pp. 160. bibliog.
(Organisation for Economic Co-operation and Development. Development Centre. Industry and Trade
in Some Developing Countries)

REYNOLDS (CLARK WINTON) The Mexican economy:
twentieth-century structure and growth. New
Haven, 1970. pp. 468. bibliog.

HANSEN (ROGER D.) The politics of Mexican development. Baltimore, [1971]. pp. 267. bibliog.

ROSS (JOHN B.) The economic system of Mexico.
Stanford, Calif., [1971]. pp. 131. bibliog.

- Emigration and immigration

DURON GONZALEZ (GUSTAVO) Problemas migratorios
de México: apuntamientos para su resolución.
México, 1925. pp. 178, vi. bibliog. 20½cm.

GAMIO (MANUEL) El inmigrante mexicano: la historia
de su vida; notas preliminares de Gilberto Loyo
sobre la inmigracion de mexicanos a los Estados
Unidos de 1900 a 1967. Mexico, 1969. pp. 271.

GAMIO (MANUEL) El inmigrante mexicano: la historia
de su vida; notas preliminares de Gilberto Loyo
sobre la inmigracion de mexicanos a los Estados
Unidos de 1900 a 1967.

GAMIO (MANUEL) Mexican immigration to the United
States: [reprint of the work first published
in 1930]. New York, 1969. pp. 262. bibliog.

MEXICO - Foreign economic relations
See also LATIN AMERICAN FREE TRADE
ASSOCIATION - Mexico

- Foreign economic relations - United States

QUINTANA (MIGUEL A.) La nueva política comercial
americana con el exterior y sus efectos en la
economía de México. México, [Universidad
Nacional de México, 1930]. pp. 148. 14cm.

MEYER (LORENZO) Mexico y Estados Unidos en el
conflicto petrolero, 1917-1942. Mexico,
1968. pp. 273.

- Foreign relations

MEXICO. 1963-64. Pensamiento en acción; ([by]
Adolfo López Mateos). (Presidencia de la
República) Mexico, 1963-64. 2 vols. 23cm.

KATZ (F.) Die deutsche Verschwörung in Mexico
1914-1916. in Klein (Fritz) ed. Politik im
Krieg, 1914-1918. Berlin, 1964.

MEXICO. Ministerio de Relaciones Exteriores.
Dirección General de Prensa y Publicidad.
1966. México en la II Conferencia Interamericana Extraordinaria. México, 1966.
pp. 586, (v). 23cm.

MEXICO. Ministerio de Relaciones Exteriores.
Dirección General de Prensa y Publicidad.
1967. México en la Tercera Conferencia
Interamericana Extraordinaria, Buenos
Aires...1967. México, 1967. pp. 481.
23cm.

- Foreign relations - America, Latin

Las RELACIONES diplomaticas de Mexico con
Sud-America: coleccion de documentos pre-
cedidos de un prologo por Jesus Guzman y Raz
Guzman. Mexico, 1925. pp. 185. (Archivo
Historico Diplomatico Mexicano. Serie 1. Num. 17)

- Foreign relations - Guatemala

GUATEMALA. Ministerio de Relaciones Exteriores.
1959. Libro blanco de Guatemala sobre el
incidente del 31 de diciembre de 1958.
Guatemala, 1959. pp. 142. 26cm.

- Foreign relations - Spain

BENSON (NETTIE LEE) ed. Mexico and the
Spanish Cortes, 1810-1822: eight essays.
Austin, University of Texas Press,
[1966]. pp. 243. bibliog. 23cm.
(Texas University. Institute of Latin
American Studies. Latin American Mono-
graphs. No. 5)

- Foreign relations - United Kingdom

GRAJALES (GLORIA) compiler. Mexico y la
Gran Bretaña durante la intervencion,
1861-1862: [documentos]. Mexico, Secretaria
de Relaciones Exteriores, [1962] [or rather]
1963. pp. 255. bibliog. (Archivo Historico
Diplomatico Mexicano. Serie 2. No. 15.)

- Foreign relations - United States

MAYO (ROBERT) M.D. Political sketches of eight
years in Washington; in four parts with annotations to each, etc.[pt. 1]. Baltimore, 1839.
pp. viii, 216. This volume contains only the
introduction, the first part entitled Sketches
of the duplicity of the Jacksonian democracy,
with annotations and a postscript.

TRAVESI (GONZALO G.) La revolución de México y
el imperialismo yanqui. Barcelona, Maucci, 1914.
pp. 255. 19cm.

MANNING (WILLIAM RAY) Early diplomatic relations
between the United States and Mexico; [re-
print of the work originally published by the
Johns Hopkins Press in 1916]. New York,
Greenwood P., 1968. pp. xi, 406. 20½cm.
(Johns Hopkins University. Walter Hines Page
School of International Relations. Albert Shaw
Lectures on Diplomatic History. 1913)

GILL (MARIO) Nuestros buenos vecinos.
[Havana?], Editora Popular de Cuba y
del Caribe, 1960. pp. 300. 16½cm.
(Primer Festival del Pensamiento
Político. 8)

MEXICO - Foreign relations - United States (Cont'd.)

CARREÑO (ALBERTO MARIA) La diplomacia extraordinaria entre México y Estados Unidos, 1789-1947. 2nd ed. México, Jus, 1961. 2 vols. (in 1). (Figuras y Episodios de la Historia de México. Nos.96-97)

ZORRILLA (LUIS G.) Historia de las relaciones entre Mexico y los Estados Unidos de America, 1800-1958. Mexico, 1965-66. 2 vols.

CALLAHAN (JAMES MORTON) American foreign policy im Mexican relations. New York, Cooper Square, 1967. pp. xi, 644. 23cm. (Library of Latin American History and Culture)

PRICE (GLENN W.) Origins of the war with Mexico: the Polk-Stockton intrigue. Austin, U. of Texas P., [1967]. pp. xiii, 189. bibliog. 22½cm.

TEITELBAUM (LOUIS M.) Woodrow Wilson and the Mexican revolution, 1913-1916: a history of United States-Mexican relations from the murder of Madero until Villa's provocation across the border. New York, Exposition P., [1967]. pp. viii, 435. 20cm. (Exposition-University Books)

BARQUIN Y RUIZ (ANDRES) Agustin de Iturbide, campeon del hispanoamericanismo. Mexico, 1968. pp. 203.

GRIEB (KENNETH J.) The United States and Huerta. Lincoln, Nebraska, [1969]. pp. 233. bibliog.

HALEY (P. EDWARD) Revolution and intervention: the diplomacy of Taft and Wilson with Mexico, 1910-1917. Cambridge, Mass., [1970]. pp. 294. bibliog.

- History

BARBA GONZALEZ (SILVANO) La lucha por la tierra. Mexico, 1956-64. 4 vols.

SIERRA (JUSTO) Evolución política del pueblo mexicano. 2nd ed. México, Universidad Nacional Autónoma de México, 1957. pp. 426. 23½cm. (Obras Completas del Maestro Justo Sierra. tomo 12)

ELGUERO (JOSÉ) España en los destinos de México. 3rd ed. México, 1962. pp. 136.

LÓPEZ GALLO (MANUEL) Economía y política en la história de México. 2nd ed. México, Grijalbo, 1967. pp. 608. 20cm. (Colección Norte)

SIMPSON (LESLEY BYRD) Many Mexicos. 4th ed. Berkeley, U. of California P., 1967. pp. xv, 389. bibliog. 20cm.

CUMBERLAND (CHARLES CURTIS) Mexico: the struggle for modernity. New York, O.U.P., 1968. pp. xi, 394. bibliog. 21cm. (Latin American Histories)

SIERRA (JUSTO) The political evolution of the Mexican people; translated by Charles Ramsdell. Austin, [1969]. pp. 406.

- History - Bibliography

RAMOS (ROBERTO) Bibliografia de la revolución mexicana. México, 1931-35. 2 vols. 20cm. (Monografias Bibliográficas Mexicanas. No. 21, 30)

SIERRA BRABATA (CARLOS J.) La prensa liberal frente a la intervención y el imperio. Mexico, 1962. pp. 205.

- History - Historiography

SILVA HERZOG (JESÚS) El pensamiento económico, social y político de México, 1810-1964. México, Instituto Mexicano de Investigaciones Economicas, 1967. pp. 748. bibliog. 23cm.

- History - Sources

GONZÁLEZ RAMÍREZ (MANUEL) ed. Manifiestos políticos, 1892-1912. Mexico, Fondo de Cultura Económica, 1957. pp. lxi, 685. 24cm. (Fuentes para la Historia de la Revolución Mexicana. 4)

LEMOINE VILLICAÑA (ERNESTO) Morelos: su vida revolucionaria a traves de sus escritos y de otros testimonios de la epoca. Mexico, 1965. pp. 715.

REED (JOHN) Insurgent Mexico. [new ed]. New York, International Publishers, [1969]. pp. xxvi, 326. 20½cm. (New World Paperbacks)

WILKIE (JAMES W.) and MONZON DE WILKIE (EDNA) Mexico visto en el siglo XX: entrevistas de historia oral; Ramon Beteta, Marte R. Gomez, Manuel Gomez Morin, etc. Mexico, 1969. pp. 770. bibliog.

- History - Conquest, 1519-1540

VALERO SILVA (JOSÉ) El legalismo de Hernán Cortés como instrumento de su conquista. México, Universidad Nacional Autónoma de México, Instituto de Investigaciones Históricas, 1965. pp. 73. bibliog. 22cm. (Cuadernos. Serie Histórica. No. 13)

PADDEN (R.C.) The hummingbird and the hawk: conquest and sovereignty in the Valley of Mexico, 1503-1541. [Columbus, 1968]. pp. 319. bibliog.

- History - Spanish colony, 1540-1810

BRADING (DAVID A.) Miners and merchants in Bourbon Mexico, 1763-1810. Cambridge, 1971. pp. 382. bibliog.

- History - Wars of Independence, 1810-1821

ROBINSON (WILLIAM DAVIS) Memoirs of the Mexican revolution; including a narrative of the expedition of General Xavier Mina; to which are annexed some observations on the practicability of opening a commerce between the Pacific and Atlantic oceans, through the Mexican isthmus, etc. London, Lackington, 1821. 2 vols. 21½cm.

CHÁVEZ (EZEQUIEL A.) Morelos. 2nd ed. México, Jus, 1965. pp. 222. 23cm. (Colección México Heroico)

- History - 1821-1861

HALE (CHARLES A.) Mexican liberalism in the age of Mora, 1821-1853. New Haven, Yale U.P., 1968. pp. xi, 347. bibliog. 23½cm. (Caribbean Series. 11)

- History - European intervention, 1861-1867

MAXIMILIANO y la restitucion de la esclavitud en Mexico 1865-1866; investigacion y prologo de Luis Chavez Orozco. Mexico, 1961. pp. 168. (Archivo Historico Diplomatico Mexicano. Serie 2. Num. 13)

GRAJALES (GLORIA) compiler. Mexico y la Gran Bretaña durante la intervencion, 1861-1862: [documentos]. Mexico, Secretaria de Relaciones Exteriores, [1962] [or rather] 1963. pp. 255. bibliog. (Archivo Historico Diplomatico Mexicano. Serie 2. No. 15.)

- History - 1867-1910

DOMINGUEZ CASTILLA (JOSE M.) Ensayo criticohistorico sobre la revolucion de la Noria. Mexico, 1934. pp. 279.

VALADÉS (JOSÉ C.) El porfirismo: historia de un régimen. México, Editorial Patria, 1948. 2 vols. 23cm.

CARR (BARRY) The peculiarities of the Mexican North, 1880-1928: an essay in interpretation. [Glasgow], 1971. pp. 21. (Glasgow. University. Institute of Latin-American Studies. Occasional Papers. No. 4)

- History - 1910-1946

OTERO SILVA (MIGUEL) México y la revolución mexicana; [and] Un escritor venezolano en la Unión Soviética. Caracas, Universidad Central de Venezuela, Dirección de Cultura, 1966. pp. 55. 21cm. (Cuadernos de Nuestro Tiempo)

LIEUWEN (EDWIN) Mexican militarism: the political rise and fall of the revolutionary army, 1910-1940. Albuquerque, U. of New Mexico P., [1968]. pp. xvi, 194. bibliog. 23½cm.

- History - Revolution, 1910-1929

TRAVESI (GONZALO G.) La revolución de México y el imperialismo yanqui. Barcelona, Maucci, 1914. pp. 255. 19cm.

BULNES (FRANCISCO) Los grandes problemas de México. México, El Universal, 1926. pp. xv, 350. 19½cm.

RAMOS (ROBERTO) Bibliografia de la revolución mexicana. México, 1931-35. 2 vols. 20cm. (Monografias Bibliográficas Mexicanas. No. 21, 30)

FIGUEROA URIZA (ARTURO) Ciudadanos en armas: antecedencia y datos para la historia de la revolucion mexicana. Mexico, 1960. 2 vols.

MEXICO. 1961. La mujer en la revolución mexicana; ([by] Angeles Mendieta Alatorre). (Biblioteca del Instituto Nacional de Estudios Historicos de la Revolución Mexicana). Mexico, 1961. pp. 187.

ROMERO FLORES (JESUS) La revolución como nosotros la vimos. Mexico, 1963. pp. 179. (Mexico. Biblioteca del Instituto Nacional de Estudios Historicos de la Revolucion Mexicana. 27)

SILVA HERZOG (JESÚS) Trayectoria ideológica de la revolución mexicana, 1910-1917. México, Cuadernos Americanos, 1963. pp. 139. 21cm.

TARACENA (ALFONSO) Venustiano Carranza. México, Editorial Jus, 1963. pp. 319. 23 cm. (Colección "Mexico Heroico." 22)

AMAYA C. (LUIS FERNANDO) La Soberana Convencion Revolucionaria, 1914-1916. Mexico, 1966. pp. 468. bibliog.

O'HEA (PATRICK A.) Reminiscences of the Mexican revolution. Mexico, [1966]. pp. 212.

CUMBERLAND (CHARLES CURTIS) ed. The meaning of the Mexican Revolution. Boston, Heath, [1967]. pp. xvi, 110. bibliog. 23½cm. (Problems in Latin American Civilization)

TEITELBAUM (LOUIS M.) Woodrow Wilson and the Mexican revolution, 1913-1916: a history of United States-Mexican relations from the murder of Madero until Villa's provocation across the border. New York, [1967]. pp. viii, 435.

CALVERT (PETER) The Mexican revolution, 1910-1914: the diplomacy of Anglo-American conflict. Cambridge, U.P., 1968. pp. x, 331. bibliog. 21½cm. (Cambridge Latin American Studies. 3)

COCKCROFT (JAMES D.) Intellectual precursors of the Mexican revolution, 1900-1913. Austin, [1968]. pp. 329. bibliog. (Texas. University. Institute of Latin American Studies. Latin American Monographs. No. 14)

ATKIN (RONALD) Revolution!: Mexico 1910-1920. London, 1969. pp. 354. bibliog.

MILLON (ROBERT PAUL) Zapata: the ideology of a peasant revolutionary. New York, International Publishers, [1969]. pp. 159. bibliog. 20½cm. (New World Paperbacks. NW-104)

REED (JOHN) Insurgent Mexico. [new ed]. New York, International Publishers, [1969]. pp. xxvi, 326. 20½cm. (New World Paperbacks)

WOMACK (JOHN) Zapata and the Mexican revolution. London, 1969. pp. 435. bibliog.

HALEY (P. EDWARD) Revolution and intervention: the diplomacy of Taft and Wilson with Mexico, 1910-1917. Cambridge, Mass., [1970]. pp. 294. bibliog.

CARR (BARRY) The peculiarities of the Mexican North, 1880-1928: an essay in interpretation. [Glasgow], 1971. pp. 21. (Glasgow. University. Institute of Latin-American Studies. Occasional Papers. No. 4)

- Industries

BASIC industries in Texas and Northern Mexico: conference sponsored by the Institute of Latin-American Studies of the University of Texas, June 9-11, 1949; [reprint of work first published in 1950]. New York, 1969. pp. 193. (Texas University. Institute of Latin-American Studies. Latin-American Studies. 9)

AUBEY (ROBERT T.) Nacional financiera and Mexican industry; a study of the financial relationship between the government and the private sector of Mexico. Los Angeles, California University, Latin American Center, 1966. pp. 205. bibliog. 23cm. (Latin American Studies, vol. 3)

MEXICO - Industries (Cont'd.)

LITTLE (ARTHUR D.) INCORPORATED (MEXICO). Manufacturing in Mexico for the U.S. market: report to Centro Bancario de Tijuana, A.C. [Mexico?], 1966. fo. 65.

BANCO DE MÉXICO. Departamento de Investigaciones Industriales. La estructura industrial de México en 1960. [Mexico City], 1967. pp. 285. 27½cm.

MEXICO. Direccion General de Estadistica. Censo Industrial, 1966. VIII censo industrial, 1966; datos de 1965: resumen general. Mexico, 1967. pp. 871.

BULLARD (FREDDA JEAN) Mexico's natural gas: the beginning of an industry. Austin, 1968. pp. 336. bibliog. (Texas University. Bureau of Business Research. Studies in Latin-American Business. No. 5)

STRASSMANN (WOLFGANG PAUL) Technological change and economic development: the manufacturing experience of Mexico and Puerto Rico. Ithaca, Cornell U.P., 1968. pp. xix, 353. 23cm.

LINK (MAX) Die Ursachen des industriellen Aufstiegs Mexikos. Zürich, [1970]. pp. 229. bibliog.

LAVELL (ALLAN MICHAEL) Industrial development and the regional problem: a case study of Central Mexico; [Ph.D. (London) thesis]. [1971]. 2 vols. bibliogs. Typescript: unpublished. This thesis is the property of London University and may not be removed from the Library.

- Intellectual life

HADDOX (JOHN HERBERT) Vasconcelos of Mexico: philosopher and prophet. Austin, U. of Texas P., [1967]. pp. xi, 103. bibliog. 20cm. (Texas Pan American Series)

COCKCROFT (JAMES D.) Intellectual precursors of the Mexican revolution, 1900-1913. Austin, [1968]. pp. 329. bibliog. (Texas. University. Institute of Latin American Studies. Latin American Monographs. No. 14)

- Moral conditions

DEMARIS (OVID) Poso del mundo: inside the Mexican-American border, from Tijuana to Matamoros. Boston, [Mass.], [1970]. pp. 244.

- Nationalism

TURNER (FREDERICK C.) The dynamic of Mexican nationalism. Chapel Hill, U. of North Carolina P., 1968. pp. xii, 350. bibliog. 23cm.

- Native races

CARDENAS (LAZARO) El problem indigena de Mexico. [Mexico], Departamento de Asuntos Indigenas, 1940. pp. 11.

MEXICO. Direccion General de Asuntos Indigenas. 1953. Las comunidades de promocion indigena en Mexico. [Mexico, 1953?]. pp. 64.

- Officials and employees

MEXICO. Direccion de Pensiones Civiles de Retiro. Departamento de Estadistica. 1933. Segundo censo de empleados sujetos a la ley general de pensiones civiles de retiro, 1932. Mexico, 1933. pp. 61.

- Politics and government

MOLINA ENRIQUEZ (ANDRES) Los grandes problemas nacionales. Mexico, Carranza, 1909. pp. 363. 28cm.

BLASCO IBÁÑEZ (VICENTE) El militarismo mejicano: estudios publicados en los principales diarios de los Estados Unidos. Valencia, 1920. pp. 251.

MAROF (TRISTAN) México de frente y de perfil. Buenos Aires, [1934]. pp. 156.

CARDENAS (LAZARO) Discurso del Presidente de la Republica pronunciado...el 17 de marzo de 1940, con motivo del segundo aniversario de la expropiacion petrolera. Mexico, Direccion General de Informacion, [1940?]. pp. 11.

RAMOS ARIZPE (MIGUEL) Report...to the august congress on the natural, political and civil condition of the provinces of Coahuila, Nuevo Leon, Nuevo Santander, and Texas of the four eastern interior provinces of the kingdom of Mexico; translation, annotations and introduction by Nettie Lee Benson; (originally published in 1950). New York, 1969. pp. 61. bibliog. (Texas University. Institute of Latin-American Studies. Latin-American Studies. 11)

AMERICAN UNIVERSITIES FIELD STAFF. Reports. Mexico and Caribbean Area Series. New York, 1954 (vol. 1) to date.

LLANO (RODRIGO DE) México y las elecciones de 1958. México, 1957. pp. 67. 21cm.

ROMEROVARGAS YTURBIDE (IGNACIO) Organizacion politica de los pueblos de Anahuac. Mexico, 1957. pp. 435. bibliog.

BANEGAS GALVAN (FRANCISCO) El porqué del Partido Católico Nacional. México, 1960. pp. 87.

SILVA HERZOG (JESÚS) Trayectoria ideológica de la revolución mexicana, 1910-1917. México, Cuadernos Americanos, 1963. pp. 139. 21cm.

SCOTT (ROBERT EDWIN) Mexican government in transition. rev. ed. Urbana, 1964. pp. 345. bibliog.

SIERRA BRABATA (CARLOS J.) Presencia de Juárez en los gobiernos de la revolución 1911-1963. Mexico, Secretaria de Hacienda y Credito Publico, 1964. pp. 135.

SEMINÁRIO SOBRE PLANEACIÓN SOCIO-ECONÓMICA, DERECHO ADMINISTRATIVO Y ADMINISTRACIÓN PUBLICA, 1964. Memoria. Mexico, [1965]. pp. 222. 23cm.

SIERRA BRABATA (CARLOS J.) Juárez en la inmortalidad del 21 de Marzo. Mexico, Secretaria de Hacienda y Credito Publico, 1965. pp. 162.

DÍAZ ORDAZ (GUSTAVO) Ideas políticas del presidente Gustavo Diaz Ordaz; recopiladas por Roberto Amorós. México, Editorial Ruta, 1966. pp. xvii, 365. 20cm.

COS (JOSÉ MARÍA) Escritos políticos. México, Universidad Nacional Autónoma de México, 1967. pp. 189. 20cm. (Biblioteca del Estudiante Universitario. 86)

FERNÁNDEZ BRAVO (VICENTE) Temas socio-económicos: problemas nacionales, integración latinoamericana. México, Costa-Amic, 1967. pp. 151. bibliog. 21cm.

LOMBARDO TOLEDANO (VICENTE) A un joven socialista mexicano. México, Empresas Editoriales, 1967. pp. 57. bibliog. 18½cm. (Colección de los Mensajes)

LÓPEZ GALLO (MANUEL) Economía y política en la história de México. 2nd ed. México, Grijalbo, 1967. pp. 608. 20cm. (Colección Norte)

PARRA (PORFIRIO) Sociología de la reforma. 2nd ed. México, Empresas Editoriales, 1967. pp. 244. 17cm. (El Liberalismo Mexicano en Pensamiento y en Acción. 8)

CASTRO LEAL (ANTONIO) Adónde va México?: reflexiones sobre nuestra historia contemporánea. Mexico, 1968. pp. 213. bibliog.

GONZÁLEZ NAVARRO (MOISÉS) La confederación nacional campesina: un grupo de presión en la reforma agraria mexicana. México, 1968. pp. 335. bibliog.

NORTH AMERICAN CONGRESS ON LATIN AMERICA. Mexico 1968: a study of domination and repression. [New York, 1968]. pp. 51.

RODRIGUEZ LOZANO (RUBEN) El gran chantaje. Mexico, 1968. pp. 238.

ALISKY (MARVIN) ed. Who's who in Mexican government. Tempe, Arizona, 1969. pp. 64.

BALAM (GILBERTO) Tlatelolco: reflexiones de un testigo. 3rd ed. Mexico, 1969. pp. 110.

FURTAK (ROBERT K.) Revolutionspartei und politische Stabilität in Mexico. Hamburg, [1969]. pp. 133. bibliog. (Institut für Iberoamerika-Kunde. Schriftenreihe. Band 12)

HORN (HANS RUDOLF) México: Revolution und Verfassung; der mexikanische Weg zur politischen Stabilität. Hamburg, 1969. pp. 164. bibliog. (Institut für Iberoamerika-Kunde. Schriftenreihe. 10)

JARDON ARZATE (EDMUNDO) De la Ciudadela a Tlatelolco: Mexico, el islote intocado. Mexico, 1969. pp. 403.

KAHLE (GUENTER) Militär und Staatsbildung in den Anfängen der Unabhängigkeit Mexikos. Wien, 1969. pp. 267. bibliog. (Jahrbuch für Geschichte von Staat, Wirtschaft und Gesellschaft Lateinamerikas Beihefte. Lateinamerikanische Forschungen. Band 1)

SCHOLES (WALTER V.) Mexican politics during the Juárez regime, 1855-1872. Columbia, Missouri, 1969. pp. 190. (Missouri University. Studies. vol.30)

WILKIE (JAMES W.) and MONZON DE WILKIE (EDNA) Mexico visto en el siglo XX: entrevistas de historia oral; Ramon Beteta, Marte R. Gomez, Manuel Gomez Morin, etc. Mexico, 1969. pp. 770. bibliog.

ADLER (JUDITH) The politics of land reform in Mexico, with special reference to the Comarca Lagunera, 1935-1967; [M.Phil. (London) thesis]. 1970. fo. 246. bibliog. Typescript: unpublished. This thesis is the property of London University and may not be removed from the Library.

GONZALEZ CASANOVA (PABLO) Democracy in Mexico;...translated by Danielle Salti. New York, 1970. pp. 245.

HANSEN (ROGER D.) The politics of Mexican development. Baltimore, [1971]. pp. 267. bibliog.

JOHNSON (KENNETH F.) Mexican democracy: a critical view. Boston, [Mass., 1971]. pp. 190.

REYNA (JOSE LUIS) An empirical analysis of political mobilization: the case of Mexico. [Ithaca], 1971. pp. 213. bibliog. (Cornell University. Latin American Studies Program. Dissertation Series. No. 26)

- Population

GUTIÉRREZ DE MACGREGOR (MARÍA TERESA) Desarrollo y distribuición de la población urbana en México. México, 1965. pp. 59 and box of maps. bibliog.

NAVARRETE (IFIGENIA MARTÍNEZ DE) Sobrepoblación y desarrollo económico. México, Universidad Nacional Autónoma de México, Dirección General de Publicaciones, 1967. pp. 34. 21cm.

LEÑERO OTERO (LUIS) Investigacion de la familia en Mexico: presentacion y avance de resultados de una encuesta nacional. Mexico, 1968. pp. 359.

OLDEN (DANIEL) The spatial distribution of population in relation to wealth and welfare in Colombia, Mexico, and Peru; [M.Phil. (London) thesis]. [1971]. fo. 170. Typescript: unpublished. This thesis is the property of London University and may not be removed from Library.

- Public works

MEXICO. Secretaria de Obras Publicas. Memoria de labores. [calendar yr.] irreg., 1958/1959, 1962, 1963, 1964/1970- Mexico.

MEXICO. Secretaria de Obras Publicas. Informe de labores. [fiscal yr.] a., 1959/60-1961/62, 1966/7- Mexico.

- Race question

GONZALEZ NAVARRO (MOISES) Raza y tierra: la guerra de castas y el henequén. Mexico, 1970. pp. 392. bibliog. (Mexico City. Colegio de Mexico. Centro de Estudios Historicos. Nueva Serie. No. 10)

- Relations (general) with Spain

ELGUERO (JOSÉ) España en los destinos de México. 3rd ed. México, 1962. pp. 136.

MEXICO (Cont'd.)

- Relations (general) with the United States

MYERS (CHARLES NASH) U.S. university activity abroad: implications of the Mexican case. New York, [1968]. pp.35.

- Rural conditions

DOZIER (CRAIG L.) Land development and colonization in Latin America: case studies of Peru, Bolivia and Mexico. New York, 1969. pp. 229. bibliog.

DURSTON (JOHN WAGNER) The social organization of peasant marketing in Michoacan, Mexico; [Ph.D.(London) thesis]. 1970. fo. 393. bibliog. Typescript: unpublished. This thesis is the property of London University and may not be removed from the Library.

WILKIE (RAYMOND) San Miguel: a Mexican collective ejido. Stanford, Calif., 1971. pp. 190. bibliog.

- Sanitary affairs

MEXICO. Instituto Mexicano del Seguro Social. Departamento de Estudios y Promoción. 1955. Manual de geomedica mexicana...;[by] Miguel Huerta Maldonado. Mexico, 1955. pp. 285. bibliog.

SALUD PÚBLICA DE MÉXICO: organo oficial de la Secretaría de Salubridad y Asistencia, [México]. México, every months, nov./dic.1964 (núm.especial: epoca 5, vol.6, núm.6); nov./dic.1965 (vol.7, núm.6); sept./oct.1966 (vol.8, núm.5); 1968 (vol.10) to date. 28½cm.

SCHENDEL (GORDON) Medicine in Mexico: from Aztec herbs to betatrons;...written with the collaboration of José Alvarez Amézquitta [and] Miguel E. Bustamante. Austin, [1968]. pp. xviii, 329. bibliog.

- Social conditions

CASTILLO Y PIÑA (JOSÉ) La cuestion social en México. México, 1921. pp. 81.

MAROF (TRISTAN) México ue frente y de perfil. Buenos Aires, [1934]. pp. 156.

AMERICAN UNIVERSITIES FIELD STAFF. Reports. Mexico and Caribbean Area Series. New York, 1954 (vol. 1) to date.

LEWIS (OSCAR) The children of Sánchez: autobiography of a Mexican family. New York, 1961. pp. 499.

KAHL (JOSEPH A.) The measurement of modernism: a study of values in Brazil and Mexico. Austin, U. of Texas P., [1968]. pp. xvii, 210. bibliog. 22½cm. (Texas University. Institute of Latin American Studies. Latin American Monographs. No. 12)

GWALTNEY (JOHN L.) The thrice shy: cultural accommodation to blindness and other disasters in a Mexican community. New York, 1970. pp. 219. bibliog.

NELSON (CYNTHIA) The waiting village: social change in rural Mexico. Boston, [1971]. pp. 160. bibliog.

- Social history

TORRES QUINTERO (GREGORIO) México hacia el fin del Virreinato español: antecedentes sociológicos del pueblo mexicano. Paris, Bouret, 1921. pp. 157. 23½cm.

LOPEZ CAMARA (FRANCISCO) La estructura economica y social de Mexico en la epoca de la reforma. Mexico, 1967. pp. 244. bibliog.

VILLORO (LUIS) El proceso ideologico de la revolucion de independencia. 2nd ed. Mexico, 1967. pp. 250.

HORTON (INEZ) Copper's children: (the rise and fall of a Mexican copper mining camp). New York, Exposition P., 1968. pp. 202. 20½cm.

FRIEDRICH (PAUL WILLIAM) Agrarian revolt in a Mexican village. Englewood Cliffs, [1970]. pp. 158. bibliog.

- Social life and customs

GALARZA (ERNESTO) Barrio boy. Notre Dame, [1971]. pp. 275.

- Social policy

DÍAZ ORDAZ (GUSTAVO) Ideas políticas del presidente Gustavo Diaz Ordaz; recopiladas por Roberto Amorós. México, Editorial Ruta, 1966. pp. xvii, 365. 20cm.

SEMINARIO SOBRE PROBLEMAS ECONOMICOS DE MEXICO, 1°, Cuernavaca, 1965. Bases para la planeacion economico y social de Mexico. Mexico, 1966 repr. 1970. pp. 269.

- Statistics

MEXICO. Direccion General de Estadistica. 1960. Catalogo general de las estadísticas nacionales; (and Indice). Mexico, 1960. 2 pts. (in 1)

MEXICO CITY

- Riots

BALAM (GILBERTO) Tlatelolco: reflexiones de un testigo. 3rd ed. Mexico, 1969. pp. 110.

MEXICO UNIVERSITY

GONZALEZ COSIO (ARTURO) Historia estadistica de la Universidad [of Mexico], 1910-1967. Mexico, 1968. pp. 107, 28 graphs.

MEY (ABRAHAM)

ABRAM Mey tachtig jaar: liber amicorum. Bussum, 1970. pp. 198. bibliog. In various languages.

MEZHDUNARODNYI BANK EKONOMICHESKOGO SOTRUDNICHESTVA
See INTERNATIONAL BANK FOR ECONOMIC COOPERATION

MIASNIKOV (ALEKSANDR KONSTANTINOVICH)

MIASNIKOV (ALEKSANDR KONSTANTINOVICH) and others, defendants. Дело Мясниковых: стенографический отчет И.К. Маркузе. Санкт-Петербург, 1872. pp. viii, 406.

MIASNIKOV (IVAN KONSTANTINOVICH)

MIASNIKOV (ALEKSANDR KONSTANTINOVICH) and others, defendants. Дело Мясниковых: стенографический отчет И.К. Маркузе. Санкт-Петербург, 1872. pp. viii, 406.

MICA

- Canada - Ontario

HEWITT (D.F.) Phlogopite mica in Ontario. Toronto, 1968. pp. viii, 85. bibliog. 27½cm. (Ontario. Department of Mines. Mineral Resources Circulars. No. 8.)

- India

INDIA. Labour Bureau. 1967. Report on survey of labour conditions in mica mining industry in India, 1962-63. [Delhi, 1967]. pp. 60.

MICHEL (LOUISE)

THOMAS (EDITH) Louise Michel; ou, La Velléda de l'anarchie. [Paris, 1971]. pp. 477. bibliog.

MICHELS (ROBERT)

PFETSCH (FRANK) Die Entwicklung zum faschistischen Führerstaat in der politischen Philosophie von Robert Michels. [Heidelberg?], 1964. pp. 149. bibliog.

EBBIGHAUSEN (ROLF) Die Krise der Parteiendemokratie und die Parteiensoziologie: eine Studie über Moisei Ostrogorski, Robert Michels und die neuere Entwicklung der Parteienforschung. Berlin, [1969]. pp. 89. bibliog. (Berlin. Freie Universität. Wirtschafts- und Sozialwissenschaftliche Fakultät. Soziologische Abhandlungen. Heft 11)

MICHIGAN

- Economic conditions

MICHIGAN. State Resource Planning Division. Technical Reports. No. 10B. Michigan's future: its population and its economy; prepared by Leonard D. Bronder [and] John M. Koval. Lansing, 1967. pp. xiii, 92. 28cm.

- Economic history

MICHIGAN. State Resource Planning Division. Technical Reports. No. 10A. Michigan's economic past: basis for prosperity; prepared by Leonard D. Bronder [and] John M. Koval. Lansing, 1967. pp. xii, 109. 28cm.

- Industries

BACON (FRANK R.) and REMPP (KATHERINE A.) Electronics in Michigan: (a study of the electronic industry in Michigan in its national and international setting). Ann Arbor, Michigan University, Institute of Science and Technology, Industrial Development Division, 1967. pp. ix, 141. bibliog. 23cm.

- Politics and government

ANGEL (D. DUANE) Romney : a political biography. New York, Exposition P., [1967]. pp. xv, 266. 20cm. (Exposition-Banner Books)

- Population

MICHIGAN. Department of Public Health. 1965. Michigan population handbook; compiled and edited by R. Raja Indra. Michigan, 1965. pp. xxvii, 120. 28cm.

MICHIGAN. State Resource Planning Division. Technical Reports. No. 10B. Michigan's future: its population and its economy; prepared by Leonard D. Bronder [and] John M. Koval. Lansing, 1967. pp. xiii, 92. 28cm.

MICHON (JEAN HIPPOLYTE)

SAVART (CLAUDE) L'abbé Jean-Hippolyte Michon, 1806-1881: contribution à l'étude du libéralisme catholique au XIXe siècle. Paris, 1971. pp. 290. bibliog. (Lyons. Université. Faculté des Lettres et Sciences Humaines. Bibliothèque. Fasc. 27)

MICKIEWICZ (ADAM)

LUTZOWA (HANNA) ed. Listy Legionistów Adama Mickiewicza z lat 1848-1849;... wstęp Stefana Kieniewicza. Wrocław, Zakład Narodowy im. Ossolińskich, 1963. pp. 432. 24½cm. (Polska Akademia Nauk. Biblioteka Historyczna Roku Mickiewicza. Seria 1. Źródła do Dziejów Polskich Walk Narodowowyzwoleńczych)

MICRONESIA

DE SMITH (STANLEY ALEXANDER) Microstates and Micronesia: problems of America's Pacific islands and other minute territories. New York, 1970. pp. 193.

MICROSCOPE AND MICROSCOPY

HOOKE (ROBERT) Micrographia; or, Some physiological descriptions of minute bodies made by magnifying glasses, with observations and inquiries thereupon; (facsimile reproduction of the first edition published...in 1665, and the index from the 1745 and 1780 editions). New York, Dover, 1961. pp. x, (xxxvii), 274. 21½cm.

MICU (SAMUIL)

MICU (SAMUIL) Scrieri filozofice: studiu introductiv și ediție critică de Pompiliu Teodor și Dumitru Ghișe. București, 1966. pp. 284. bibliog.

MIDDLE AGE

OWEN (ROGER) ed. Middle age. London, British Broadcasting Corporation, 1967. pp. 152. 18cm. Talks from the series broadcast on BBC Television in October and November 1967.

MIDDLE AGES

ARCARI (PAOLA MARIA) Idee e sentimenti politici dell'alto medioevo. Milano, Giuffrè, 1968. pp. xi, 1023. 25cm. (Cagliari. Università. Facoltà di Giurisprudenza. Pubblicazioni. Serie 2. vol. 1)

GOSSMAN (LIONEL) Medievalism and the ideologies of the enlightenment: the world and work of La Curne de Sainte-Palaye. Baltimore, Johns Hopkins P., [1968]. pp. xvii, 377. 22½cm.

MORRALL (JOHN BRIMYARD) The medieval imprint: the founding of the western European tradition. Harmondsworth, 1970. pp. 173. bibliog.

MIDDLE AGES (Cont'd.)

SOUTHERN (RICHARD WILLIAM) Medieval humanism and other studies. Oxford, [1970]. pp. 261.

- History

LAGARDE (GEORGES DE) La naissance de l'esprit laïque au déclin du moyen âge; (nouvelle édition refondue et complétée). vol.1 is of the 3rd ed., vol.2 of the 2nd. Louvain, 1956-70. 5 vols.

AKADEMIE FÜR RAUMFORSCHUNG UND LANDESPLANUNG. Ausschuss Historische Raumforschung. Historische Raumforschung. 4. Raumordnung in Renaissance und Merkantilismus. Hannover, Jänecke, 1963. pp. vii, 125. 25cm.

QUELLER (DONALD E.) The office of ambassador in the middle ages. Princeton, U.P., 1967. pp. xiii, 251. bibliog. 23½cm.

BRUEHL (CARLRICHARD) Fodrum, gistum, servitium regis: Studien zu den wirtschaftlichen Grundlagen des Königtums im Frankenreich und in den fränkischen Nachfolgestaaten Deutschland, Frankreich und Italien vom 6. bis zur Mitte des 14. Jahrhunderts. Köln, 1968. 2 vols. bibliog. Pagination continuous. 7 maps and list in end pocket of vol. 2.

JACOB (ERNEST FRASER) Essays in later medieval history. Manchester, Manchester U.P., [1968]. pp. (iv), 223. 21½cm.

WERVEKE (HANS VAN) Miscellanea mediaevalia: verspreide opstellen over economische en sociale geschiedenis van de middeleeuwen. Gent, Story, 1968. pp. xliii, 402. bibliog. 23½cm. In Dutch, French, German or English.

MYERS (ALEC REGINALD) The study of medieval history; an inaugural lecture delivered 7 November 1968. Liverpool, 1969. pp. 35.

PACAUT (MARCEL) Les structures politiques de l'Occident médiéval. Paris, Colin, [1969]. pp. 410. bibliogs. 23cm. (Collection U: Série Histoire Médiévale)

EASTERN and Western Europe in the Middle Ages; [by] F. Graus [and others]; (edited with an introduction by Geoffrey Barraclough). London, [1970]. pp. 216. bibliog.

FOSSIER (ROBERT) Histoire sociale de l'Occident médiéval. Paris, [1970]. pp. 382. bibliogs.

HILL (BENNETT D.) ed. Church and state in the middle ages. New York, [1970]. pp. 210. bibliog.

LOPEZ (ROBERT SABATINO) The commercial revolution of the middle ages, 950-1350. Englewood Cliffs, [1971]. pp. 177. bibliog.

STRAYER (JOSEPH REESE) Medieval statecraft and the perspectives of history. Princeton, 1971. pp. 425. bibliog.

- History - Bibliography

DAVIS (RALPH HENRY CARLESS) compiler. Medieval European history, 395-1500: a select bibliography. 2nd ed. [London], Historical Association, 1968. pp. 48. 21cm. (Helps for Students of History. No. 67)

- History - Sources

BAUTIER (ROBERT HENRI) and SORNAY (JANINE) Les sources de l'histoire économique et sociale du moyen âge. Paris, Éditions du Centre National de la Recherche Scientifique, 1968 in progress. 26½cm.

HERLIHY (DAVID) ed. Medieval culture and society. London, Macmillan, 1968. pp. xv, 410. bibliogs. 23cm. (Documentary History of Western Civilization)

LA RONCIÈRE (CHARLES DE) and others, eds. L'Europe au moyen âge: documents expliqués. Paris, Colin, [1969 in progress]. 23cm. (Collection U: Série Histoire Médiévale)

- History - Study and teaching

PACAUT (MARCEL) Guide de l'étudiant en histoire médiévale. Paris, P.U.F., 1968. pp. 169. 18cm.

MIDDLE CLASSES

GATTI (VITTORIO) La borghesia e le riscosse attuali. Milano, Dumolard, 1886. pp. 37. 19cm.

LAMALLE (DESIRÉ) La bourgeoisie veut-elle mourir? [Anvers?], Les Éditions Jicistes, [1939?]. pp. 144. 20cm. (Collection Réaliser. No.15)

ROZITCHNER (LEÓN) Moral burguesa y revolución. 2nd ed. Buenos Aires, Ediciones Procyon, 1963. pp.219. 19½cm.

GAROSCI (A.) Sul concetto di "borghesia": verifica storica di un saggio Crociano. in Miscellanea Walter Maturi. Torino, 1966.

MISSIROLI (MARIO) Come si distrugge una borghesia: salviamo le classi medie. Roma, Frattina, [1967?]. pp. 79. 18cm.

VAZ (EDMUND W.) ed. Middle-class juvenile delinquency: [readings]. New York, [1967]. pp. 289.

PONTEIL (FÉLIX) Les classes bourgeoises et l'avènement de la démocratie, 1815-1914. Paris, Michel, [1968]. pp. 573. bibliog. 18cm (L'Evolution de l'Humanité. 4)

VACATELLO (MARZIO) Lukács da Storia e coscienza di classe al guidizio sulla cultura borghese. Firenze, La Nuova Italia, 1968. pp. viii, 157. 21cm. (Maestri e Compagni. Biblioteca di Studi Critici e Morali. 33)

MARXISME et petite bourgeoisie. Paris, 1969. pp. 60.

NITSCHE (ROLAND) Der hässliche Bürger: Leistungen, Versagen, Zukunft. Wien, [1969]. pp. 303.

WILMS (BERNARD) Revolution und Protest; oder, Glanz und Elend des bürgerlichen Subjekts. Stuttgart, [1969]. pp. 112.

BERL (EMMANUEL) Mort de la pensée bourgeoise. [rev. ed.] [Paris, 1970]. pp. 139.

MANDEL (ERNEST) The changing role of the bourgeois university. London, [1971]. pp. 13. (Spartacus League. Pamphlets)

- Africa, Subsaharan

TUMANOVA (LENA KAZIMIROVNA) Формирование африканской буржуазии. Москва, 1969. pp. 161. bibliog.

- America, Latin

FRANK (ANDRE GUNDER) Lumpenburguesia: lumpendesarrollo; dependencia, clase y politica en Latinoamerica. Montevideo, 1970. pp. 151. bibliog.

- Argentine Republic

JAURETCHE (ARTURO) El medio pelo en la sociedad argentina: apuntes para una sociología nacional. 7th ed. [Buenos Aires], Peña Lillo, 1967. pp. 372. 20cm. (Biblioteca de Estudios Americanos. 5)

- Belgium

LAMALLE (DESIRÉ) La bourgeoisie veut-elle mourir? [Anvers?], Les Éditions Jicistes, [1939?]. pp. 144. 20cm. (Collection Réaliser. No.15)

- China

BERGERE (MARIE CLAIRE) La bourgeoisie chinoise et la révolution de 1911. Paris, 1968. pp. 155. bibliog. (Maison des Sciences de l'Homme. Matériaux pour l'Etude de l'Extrême-Orient Moderne et Contemporain. Travaux. 3)

MAO (TSE-TUNG) On the question of the national bourgeoisie and the enlightened gentry, March 1, 1948. Peking, 1969. pp. 9.

- Ecuador

KOENIG (MECHTHILD) Die Rolle der Mittelschichten in der wirtschaftlichen Entwicklung Ecuadors: Besonderheiten und Ähnlichkeiten im Rahmen Lateinamerikas. Göttingen, [1969]. pp. 256. bibliog. (Göttingen. Universität. Ibero-Amerika-Institut für Wirtschaftsforschung. Arbeitsberichte. Heft 6)

- France

ELLUL (JACQUES) Métamorphose du bourgeois. Paris, Calmann-Lévy, [1967]. pp. 302. 21cm. (Liberté di l'Esprit)

GROETHUYSEN (BERNARD) The bourgeois: Catholicism vs. capitalism in eighteenth-century France;..translated from the French by Mary Ilford. London, Barrie & Rockliff, [1968]. pp. xvii, 268. 20½cm.

LE GALLO (YVES) Études sur la marine et l'officier de marine: Brest et sa bourgeoisie sous la monarchie de juillet; [with the text of the diary kept by Jean François Broumiche, February 1844 to March 1845]. Paris, P.U.F., 1968. 2 vols. bibliog. 24cm. (Rennes. Université. Faculté des Lettres et Sciences Humaines. Publications. Série 1. vol.12)

MANDRIN (JACQUES) L'Enarchie; ou, Les mandarins de la société bourgeoise. [Paris], La Table Ronde de Combat, [1968]. pp. 169. 20cm. (Les Brulots. 5)

DIERKES (MEINOLF) Der Beitrag des französischen Mittelstandes zum wirtschaftlichen Wachstum. Köln, 1969. pp. 365. bibliog. (Institut für Mittelstandsforschung. Abhandlungen zur Mittelstandsforschung. Nr. 39)

PERNOUD (REGINE) Les origines de la bourgeoisie. 4th ed. Paris, 1969. pp. 128. bibliog.

LARERE (PHILIPPE) Une nouvelle classe moyenne: l'avènement des techniciens. Paris, [1970]. pp. 127.

- Germany

BENDER (GERD M.). Der Mittelstand ist nicht vergessen; herausgegeben im Auftrag des Bundesministeriums für Wirtschaftlichen Besitz des Bundes. Bad Godesberg, Verlag für Publizistik, 1959. pp. 32. 23½cm.

INSTITUT FÜR MITTELSTANDSFORSCHUNG. Abhandlungen zur Mittelstandsforschung. Nr. 1, etc. Soziologische Probleme mittelständischer Berufe. Köln, 1962 in progress.

BICKEL (WOLFGANG) Das unbestrittene Feld kleiner und mittlerer Wirtschaftseinheiten in der gewerblichen Wirtschaft der Bundesrepublik Deutschland: ein Beitrag zur Frage der Existenzberechtigung des gewerblichen Mittelstandes. [Heidelberg, imprint], 1962. pp. 175. bibliog.

NORTH RHINE-WESTPHALIA. 1965. Der Mittelstand im hochindustrialisierten Wirtschaftsraum; ([by] Raymund Krisam). (Forschungsberichte des Landes Nordrhein-Westfalen. Nr. 1538) Köln, Westdeutscher Verlag, 1965. pp. 330. bibliog. 24cm.

NELLESSEN (WALTER) and NOLD (KLAUS) Möglichkeiten zur Ausgestaltung der deutschen amtlichen Statistik unter dem Aspekt einer quantitativen Abgrenzung der Mittelschichten. Köln, Westdeutscher Verlag, 1966. pp. 92. 24cm. (Institut für Mittelstandsforschung. Abhandlungen zur Mittelstandsforschung. Nr 20)

KOELVER (DIETER) Die Berücksichtigung der Problematik der mittelständischen Gewerbebetriebe in der deutschen Gesetzgebung. Köln, Westdeutscher Verlag, 1967. pp. 122. bibliog. 24cm. (Institut für Mittelstandsforschung. Abhandlungen zur Mittelstandsforschung. Nr. 22) R

LEVERKUS (J. CHRISTOPH) and WIEKEN (KLAUS) Eigentumsbildung und Altersvorsorge bei Angehörigen des selbständigen Mittelstandes. Köln, Westdeutscher Verlag, 1967. pp. 198. 24cm. (Institut für Mittelstandsforschung. Abhandlungen zur Mittelstandsforschung. Nr.30)

STAVENHAGEN (GERHARD) and SCHMIDT (KARL HEINZ) Der selbstständige gewerbliche Mittelstand in Niedersachsen. Göttingen, 1967. pp. 250. bibliog.

LENK (LEONHARD) Augsburger Bürgertum im Späthumanismus und Frühbarock, 1580-1700. Augsburg, Mühlberger, 1968. pp. 256. bibliog. 23cm.

GEWANDT (HEINRICH) ed. Die Zukunft des Mittelstandes: Strukturpolitik in einer dynamischen Wirtschaft. Düsseldorf, 1969. pp. 277.

LEBOVICS (HERMAN) Social conservatism and the middle classes in Germany, 1914-1933. Princeton, 1969. pp. 248. bibliog.

MIDDLE CLASSES - Germany (Cont'd.)

MOELLER (HELMUT) Die kleinbürgerliche Familie im 18. Jahrhundert: Verhalten und Gruppenkultur. Berlin, 1969. pp. 341. bibliog.

- Goa, Daman and Diu

ALMEIDA (JOSE C.) Engel's curves, income elasticities of demand and consumer price index number for the middle class employees families in the Panjim City. [Panjim, imprint, 1967]. pp. (v), 374. bibliog. 27cm. In English and Portuguese.

- India

TAGORE (SAUMYENDRANATH) Bourgeois-democratic revolution and India. Calcutta, 1939 repr. 1946. pp. 53.

CHHIBBAR (YASH PAL) From caste to class: a study of the Indian middle classes. New Delhi, Associated Publishing House, 1968. pp. viii, 142. 21½cm.

PRASAD (BHAGWAN) Socio-economic study of urban middle classes. Delhi, Sterling Publishers, 1968. pp. (v), 85. bibliog. 21½cm.

- Netherlands

NETHERLANDS. [Ministerie van Economische Zaken]. 1954. Middenstandsnota, 1954. 's-Gravenhage, 1954. pp. 95,77.

- Poland

IHNATOWICZ (IRENEUSZ) Obyczaj wielkiej burżuazji warszawskiej w XIX wieku. Warszawa, 1971. pp. 233. bibliog.

- Russia

DIAKIN (VALENTIN SEMENOVICH) Русская буржуазия и царизм в годы первой мировой войны, 1914-1917. Ленинград, 1967. pp. 373.

LAVERYCHEV (VLADIMIR IAKOVLEVICH) По ту сторону баррикад: из истории борьбы московской буржуазии с революцией. Москва, Мысль, 1967. pp. 288. 20см.

KAUFMANN-ROCHARD (JACQUELINE) Origines d'une bourgeoisie russe, 16e et 17e siecles: marchands de Moscovie. Paris, [1969]. pp. 303. bibliog.

LEBAKOVA (EL'ZA ROBERTOVNA) Opyt KPSS po priobshcheniiu melkoi burzhuazii goroda k stroitel'stvu sotsializma. Moskva, 1970. pp. 94.

- Spain

MADRAZO MADRAZO (SANTOS) Las dos Españas: burguesia y nobleza; los orígenes del precapitalismo español. Madrid, 1969. pp. 192.

- United Kingdom

McCREERY (MICHAEL) Notes on the lower middle class and the semi-proletariat in Britain. London, 1964. pp. 8.

BELL (COLIN) Middle class families: social and geographical mobility. London, 1968. pp. 191.

HUBERT (JANE) and others. Methods of study of middle-class kinship in London: a working-paper on the history of an anthropological project, 1960-65. London, University, London School of Economics and Political Science, Department of Anthropology, 1968. pp. iv, 149. 30cm. (Occasional Papers)

PARKIN (FRANK IORWETH) Middle class radicalism: the social bases of the British Campaign for Nuclear Disarmament. Manchester, U.P., 1968. pp. vii, 207. 21½cm.

FIRTH (RAYMOND WILLIAM) and others. Families and their relatives: kinship in a middle-class sector of London; an anthropological study by Raymond Firth [and others] with the team of the 'London Kinship Project'. London, [1970]. pp. 476.

RAYNOR (JOHN) The middle class. London, 1969. pp. 125.

PAHL (J.M.) and PAHL (RAYMOND EDWARD) Managers and their wives: a study of career and family relationships in the middle class. London, 1971. pp. 326. bibliog.

- United States

HOROWITZ (IRVING LOUIS) C. Wright Mills' White collar: a critical commentary. New York, American R.D.M. Corporation, 1967. pp. 49. bibliog. 21cm. (Study Master Publications. 701).

SENNETT (RICHARD). Families against the city: middle class homes of industrial Chicago, 1872-1890. Cambridge, Mass., 1970. pp. 258. (Massachusetts Institute of Technology and Harvard University. Joint Center for Urban Studies. Publications)

KRONUS (SIDNEY) **The black middle class.** Columbus, Ohio, [1971]. **pp. 182. bibliog.**

- Venezuela

GARCÍA PONCE (GUILLERMO) Política y clase media. Caracas, La Muralla, 1966. pp. 281. 18cm.

- Vietnam

CHESHKOV (MARAT ALEKSANDROVICH) Особенности формирования вьетнамской буржуазии. Москва, 1968. pp. 182. bibliog.

MIDDLESBROUGH

- History

LILLIE (WILLIAM) The history of Middlesbrough: an illustration of the evolution of English industry. Middlesbrough, Corporation, 1968. pp. xiv, 492. 21cm.

MIDDLESEX

- Economic history

MARTINDALE (LAWRENCE) Demography and land use in the late seventeenth and eighteenth centuries in Middlesex; [Ph.D.(London) thesis]. [1968]. fo. xi, 483. bibliog. 25½cm. Typescript: unpublished. This thesis is the property of London University and may not be removed from the Library.

- Population

> MARTINDALE (LAWRENCE) Demography and land use in the late seventeenth and eighteenth centuries.in Middlesex; [Ph.D.(London) thesis]. [1968]. fo. xi, 483. bibliog. 25 cm. Typescript: unpublished. This thesis is the property of London University and may not be removed from the Library.

MIDDLETON GRAMMAR SCHOOL

> PAUL (ROBERT SHIER) and SMITH (WILLIAM JOHN) A history of Middleton Grammar School, 1412-1964. Middleton, Queen Elizabeth's Grammar School, 1965. pp. vi, 41. bibliog. 21cm.

MIDGLEY FAMILY

> MIDGLEY (SARAH) and SKILBECK (RICHARD) The diaries of Sarah Midgley and Richard Skilbeck: a story of Australian settlers, 1851-1864. Melbourne, Cassell Australia, 1967. pp. viii, 208. 24cm.

MIDLAND AND GREAT NORTHERN JOINT RAILWAY

> WROTTESLEY (A.J.F.) The Midland and Great Northern Joint Railway. Newton Abbot, [1970]. pp. 221. bibliog.

MIDLAND RAILWAY

> BARNES (ERIC GEORGE) The Midland main line, 1875-1922. London, 1969. pp. 280.

MIDWIVES

- United Kingdom

> U.K. Central Health Services Council. Standing Maternity and Midwifery Advisory Committee. 1970. Domiciliary midwifery and maternity bed needs: report of the Sub-Committee: [Sir John Peel, chairman]. London, 1970. pp. 135. bibliog.

- United Kingdom - Ireland, Northern

> NORTHERN IRELAND COUNCIL FOR NURSES AND MIDWIVES. Statement of accounts... together with the Report of the Comptroller and Auditor-General. [Jan.]/March 1971 [1st] to date included in IRELAND, NORTHERN. Parliament. House of Commons. [Papers].

- United Kingdom - Scotland

> SCOTLAND. 1965. The staffing of the midwifery services in Scotland: report by a committee of the [Scottish Health Services[Council: [Mrs. J. Wolrige-Gordon, chairman]. Edinburgh, 1965. pp. 51. 24cm.

MIGRANT LABOUR

> ORGANISATION FOR ECONOMIC CO-OPERATION AND DEVELOPMENT. 1965. Adaptation of rural and foreign workers to industry: international joint seminar, Wiesbaden, 10th-13th December 1963; final report; (edited by Magda Talamo and Elie Dimitras; with supplement). (International Seminars. 1963. 4) Paris, 1965. 2 pts. 24cm - 29cm.

> ALFONSO (VICENZO ROBERTO) La sicurezza sociale del lavoratore italiano all'estero e dello straniero in Italia: tutela giuridica e previdenziale, convenzioni internazionali; manuale teorico-pratico etc. Milano, Pirola, 1967. pp. 447. bibliog. 24cm.

> NELSON (JOAN M.) Migrants, urban poverty, and instability in developing nations. Cambridge, Mass., 1969. pp. 81. (Harvard University. Center for International Affairs. Occasional Papers in International Affairs. No. 22).

- Belgium

> RONSE (EDMOND) L'émigration saisonnière belge. Gand, Het Volk, [1913]. pp. 257. bibliog. 20cm. (International Association on Unemployment. Section Belge. Brochures. No. 4)

- Bolivia

> ANTEZANA (FERNANDO) Los braceros bolivianos: drama humano y sangria nacional. La Paz, Icthus, [1966]. pp. 44. 21cm.

- Ceylon

> DUTTA (AMITA) Effect of international labour migration on trade and real income: a case study of Ceylon, 1920-38; [Ph. D. (London) thesis]. [1969]. fo. 233. bibliog. Typescript: unpublished. This thesis is the property of London University and may not be removed from the Library.

- Europe

> COUNCIL OF EUROPE. Co-ordinated Research Fellowships in the Social Field. 1968. Social services for migrant workers: report prepared by [Miss A. Gasc and others] Strasbourg, 1968. pp. 92. (Social Co-operation in Europe)

> FERRACUTI (F.) European migration and crime. in Wolfgang (Marvin Eugene) ed. Crime and culture. New York, [1968].

- European Economic Community countries

> EUROPEAN ECONOMIC COMMUNITY. Commission Administrative pour la Securité Sociale des Travailleurs Migrants. Guides. No. 1. Assurance maladie-maternité des travailleurs immigrant en Allemagne [and other European Economic Community countries] avec leur famille. [Brussels, 1961]. 6 pts. 15½cm.

> EUROPEAN ECONOMIC COMMUNITY. Commission Administrative pour la Securité Sociale des Travailleurs Migrants. Guides. No. 2. Assurance maladie-maternité-accidents du travail pendant un séjour temporaire dans un pays de la Communauté autre que le pays de résidence. [Brussels, 1961]. pp. 43. 14½cm.

> EUROPEAN ECONOMIC COMMUNITY. Commission Administrative pour la Securité Sociale des Travailleurs Migrants. Guides. No. 3. Assurance maladie-maternité-accidents du travail en cas de transfert de résidence d'un pays de la Communauté dans un autre pendant une maladie ou une maternité ou à la suite d'un accident du travail. [Brussels, 1961]. pp. 21. 15½cm.

MIGRANT LABOUR - European Economic Community countries (Cont'd.)

EUROPEAN ECONOMIC COMMUNITY. Commission Administrative pour la Securité Sociale des Travailleurs Migrants. Guides. No. 4. Assurance maladie-maternité-accidents du travail des travailleurs détachés temporairement d'un pays de la Communauté dans un autre. [Brussels, 1961]. pp. 44. 15½cm.

EUROPEAN ECONOMIC COMMUNITY. Commission Administrative pour la Securité Sociale des Travailleurs Migrants. Guides. No. 5. Assurance maladie-maternité des membres de la famille résidant en Allemagne [and other European Economic Community countries] alors que le travailleur est occupé dans un autre pays de la Communauté. [Brussels, 1961]. 6 pts. 15½cm.

EUROPEAN ECONOMIC COMMUNITY. Commission Administrative pour la Securité Sociale des Travailleurs Migrants. Guides. No. 6. Assurance maladie-maternité des titulaires de pensions ou de rentes résidant en Allemagne [and other European Economic Community countries. [Brussels, 1962]. 3 pts. 15½cm.

EUROPEAN ECONOMIC COMMUNITY. 1962. Dictionnaire comparatif des professions donnant lieu le plus souvent à migrations dans les pays de la C[ommunauté] E[conomique] E[uropéenne]. (Commission) [Brussels, 1962]. pp. iv(bis), v-xi, 146. 22½cm x 30cm. In Dutch, French, German and Italian; for second edition see EUROPEAN ECONOMIC COMMUNITY. 1965.

EUROPEAN ECONOMIC COMMUNITY. Commission Administrative pour la Securité Sociale des Travailleurs Migrants. Guides. No. 7. Allocations familiales [in European Economic Community countries] [Brussels, 1963]. 6 pts. 15½cm.

EUROPEAN ECONOMIC COMMUNITY. Commission Administrative pour la Securité Sociale des Travailleurs Migrants. Guides. No. 8. Indemnisation des travailleurs migrants en cas de chômage dans la république fédérale d'Allemagne [and in other European Economic Community countries] [Brussels, 1963]. 6 pts. 14½cm.

EUROPEAN ECONOMIC COMMUNITY. 1965. Dictionnaire comparatif des professions donnant lieu le plus souvent à migrations dans les pays de la C[ommunauté] E[conomique] E[uropéenne]. (Commission) 2nd ed. [Brussels, 1965]. pp. i-vi(bis), vii-xviii(249). 20½cm x 29cm. In Dutch, French, German and Italian; for first edition see EUROPEAN ECONOMIC COMMUNITY. 1962.

- **France**

INSTITUT D'ÉTUDES POLITIQUES, [LYON]. Les travailleurs étrangers dans la région Rhone-Alpes. Lyon, Chronique Sociale de France, [1966?]. pp. 76. bibliog. 26½cm.

- **Germany**

NANN (EBERHARD) Die Kriminalität der italienischen Gastarbeiter im Spiegel der Ausländerkriminalität. Hamburg, Kriminalistik Verlag, 1967. pp. 207. bibliog. 22½cm. (Deutsche Kriminologische Gesellschaft. Kriminologische Schriftenreihe Band 28)

BINGEMER (KARL) and others, eds. Leben als Gastarbeiter: geglückte und missglückte Integration. Köln, 1970. pp. 235. bibliog.

- **Italy**

RABETTI (EDOARDO) and VASA (GIUSEPPE) Lettere di emigrati ai compagni del Mezzogiorno d'Italia. Milano, 1969. pp. 39.

- **Poland - Silesia**

BROŻEK (ANDRZEJ) Robotnicy spoza zaboru pruskiego w przemyśle na Górnym Śląsku, 1870-1914. Wrocław, Zakład Narodowy im. Ossolińskich, 1966. pp. 220. bibliog. 24cm. (Monografie Śląskie Ossolineum) With English summary.

- **Siam**

TEXTOR (ROBERT B.) From peasant to pedicab driver: a social study of northeastern Thai farmers who periodically migrated to Bangkok and became pedicab drivers. New Haven, Yale University, [Council on] South East Asia Studies, 1961. pp. viii, 83. 28cm. (Cultural Report Series. No. 9)

- **South Africa**

RANDALL (PETER) Migratory labour in South Africa; a talk given to a Christian institute study group, Johannesburg, March 1967. [Johannesburg, 1967]. pp. 10. (South African Institute of Race Relations. Topical Talks. No.1)

- **Sweden**

LITTMARCK (ROBERT) Mälardalens nomader: en socialstatistisk studie över statarnas förhållanden...i södra och mellersta Uppland under åren 1925-1929. Stockholm, [1930]. pp. 84. bibliog.

- **United States**

KERR (CLARK) Migration to the Seattle labor market area, 1940-1942. Seattle, 1942. pp. 129-188. (Seattle. University of Washington. Publications in the Social Sciences. vol. 11, no. 3)

FOGEL (WALTER A.) Mexican Americans in southwest labor markets. Los Angeles, 1967. pp. 222. (California University. Graduate School of Business Administration. Division of Research. Mexican-American Study Project. Advance Reports. 10)

BEHAVIOR in new environments: adaptation of migrant populations; (prepared as resource material for a conference...supported by...the Center for Studies of Metropolitan and Regional Mental Health Problems of the National Institute of Mental Health) edited by Eugene B. Brody. Beverley Hills, Calif., [1970]. pp. 479. bibliogs.

NELKIN (DOROTHY) On the season: aspects of the migrant labour system. Ithaca, 1970. pp. 85. bibliog. (Cornell University. New York State School of Industrial and Labor Relations. ILR Paperbacks. No.8)

MIGRATIONS OF NATIONS

MARYAŃSKI (ANDRZEJ) Współczesne wędrówki ludów: zarys geografii migracji. Wrocław, Zakład Narodowy im. Ossolińskich, 1966. pp. 220. bibliog 24cm. With English summary.

MIHAILOVIĆ (DRAŽA)

AVAKUMOVIĆ (IVAN) Mihailović prema nemačkim dokumentima. London, 1969. pp. 181. bibliog. With English summary.

MIHAJLOV (IVAN)

MIHAJLOV (IVAN) Spomeni. [v.]3. Osvoboditelna borba, 1924-1934 g. [Brussels, Macedonian Cultural Fellowship], 1967. pp. 1029.

MIHAJLOV (MIHAJLO)

MIHAJLOV (MIHAJLO) Абрам Терц, или бегство из реторты; (несколько слов об авторе [Я. Трушновича]) [Frankfurt], Посев, 1969. pp. viii, 8-87. Cover bears subtitle: о творчестве Синявского.

MIKHAILOV (MIKHAIL ILLARIONOVICH)

SHELGUNOV (NIKOLAI VASIL'EVICH) and others. Vospominaniia... N. V. Shelgunova (L. P. Shelgunovoi i M. L. Mikhailova) Moskva, 1967. 2 vols.

FATEEV (PETR STEPANOVICH) Михаил Михайлов - революционер, писатель, публицист. Москва, Мысль, 1969. pp. 376. 20см.

MIKHAILOV (MIKHAIL LARIONOVICH)
See MIKHAILOV (MIKHAIL ILLARIONOVICH)

MIKHAILOVSKII (NIKOLAI KONSTANTINOVICH)

KAZAKOV (ANATOLII PAVLOVICH) Teoriia progressa v russkoi sotsiologii kontsa XIX veka: P.L. Lavrov, N.K. Mikhailovskii, M.M. Kovalevskii. Leningrad, 1969. pp. 129.

MIKIRS

SAIKIA (PADMA DHAR) Changes in Mikir society: a report on socio-economic resurvey of Kanther Terang Village in the United Mikir and North Cachar Hills district, Assam. Jorhat, Agro-Economic Research Centre for North East India, 1968. pp. ii,xiv, 82. 24½cm. (Studies in Rural Change. Assam Series)

MIKOIAN (ANASTAS IVANOVICH)

MIKOIAN (ANASTAS IVANOVICH) Mysli i vospominaniia o Lenine. Moskva, 1970. pp. 238.

MILAN (CITY)

- Borsa

PIVATO (GIORGIO) Il mercato mobiliare. Milano, Giuffrè. 1965. pp. xvi, 789. 25cm. (Milan. Università Commerciale Luigi Bocconi. Istituto di Economia Aziendale. Serie 2. N. 2)

- Buildings

MILAN. Servizi Statistici. Distribuzione territoriale e differenziazione strutturale dei vari sistemi sociali che compongono l'ambiente urbano. 2. Risultanze di una indagine sui fabbricati a Milano: distribuzione territoriale dei fabbricati a Milano. Milano, [1964?] pp. 175. 24½cm. (Milan. Documenti della Città di Milano. 27)

- History

CATTANEO (CARLO) L'insurrezione di Milano nel 1848 e la successiva guerra; a cura di Lilia Borri Motta. Torino, Loescher, 1968. pp. 315. 21½cm.

AMBROSOLI (LUIGI) ed. La insurrezione milanese del marzo 1848: memorie di Cesare Correnti [and others]. Milano, 1969. pp. 167.

CLINI (PIERO) Le speranze d'Italia nelle cinque giornate di Milano. Milano, 1970. pp. 279. bibliog.

- Industries

CAROZZI (LUIGI) L'industria dei guanti in Milano. Milano, 1908. pp. 47. bibliog. (Società Umanitaria. Ufficio del Lavoro. Pubblicazioni. No.16)

- Politics and government

ANIASI (ALDO) Sindaco a Milano. Milano. [1970]. pp. 119.

- Population

ALASIA (FRANCO) and MONTALDI (DANILO) Milano, Corea: inchiesta sugli immigrati. Milano, 1960. pp. 341.

- Social conditions

ALASIA (FRANCO) and MONTALDI (DANILO) Milano, Corea: inchiesta sugli immigrati. Milano, 1960. pp. 341.

MELOTTI (UMBERTO) Cultura e partecipazione sociale nella città in trasformazione; ricerca sociologica sui nuovi circoli culturali periferici e sulla situazione della cultura a Milano. Milano, La Culturale, [1967]. pp. 495. 21cm. (Biblioteca di Cultura Sociale)

- Suburbs and environs

BINI (VITTORIO) Studi e ricerche urbanistiche sulla periferia di Milano. Milano, Tamburini, 1967. pp (iii), 101. 30cm.

MILAN (PROVINCE)

- Economic conditions

ZIGNOLI (V.) Sulla struttura economico-produttiva delle provincie di Milano e Torino. in vol. 3 of Saggi di economia aziendale e sociale in memoria di Gino Zappa. Milano, 1961.

- Rural conditions

BARBERIS (CORRADO) Famiglie coltivatrici e attività non agricole: [province of Milan]; indagine dello Istituto Nazionale di Sociologia Rurale. Roma, [1969?]. pp. 94.

- Social conditions

MILAN (PROVINCE). Analfabetismo e istruzione in provincia di Milano. Milano, [1960]. pp. 70. 26½cm.

MILAN CATHOLIC UNIVERSITY

MILAN. Università Cattolica del Sacro Cuore. Storia di 3 occupazioni, repressioni e serrate. [Milan], Relazioni Sociali, 1968. pp. 135. 21cm. (Supplementi)

MILBANK MEMORIAL FUND

MILBANK MEMORIAL FUND. Organization policy and program. [New York, 1963]. pp. 13.

MILEJÓW

TUROWSKI (JAN) Przemiany wsi pod wpływem zakładu przemysłowego: studium rejonu Milejowa. Warszawa, PWN, 1964. pp. 231. 23½cm. (Polska Akademia Nauk. Komitet Przestrzennego Zagospodarowania Kraju. Studia t.8)

MILHAUD (EDGARD)

HOMMAGE à Edgard Milhaud, 1873-1964. Liège, CIRIEC, 1964. pp. 45. 21cm.

MILITARISM

GERASIMOV (VLADIMIR DANILOVICH) Вопросы воспроизводства общественного капитала в условиях милитаризации экономики. Москва, Высшая Школа, 1968. pp. 111. 19½см.

SCHNEIDER (FERNAND THIÉBAUT) L'armée face au pouvoir. Paris, France-Empire, [1968]. pp. 283. bibliog. 19cm.

DOORN (JAC A.A. VAN) ed. Military profession and military regimes: commitments and conflicts. The Hague, [1969]. pp. 304.

FARAMAZIAN (RACHIK ARTASHESOVICH) SShA: militarizm i ekonomika. Moskva, 1970. pp. 343.

- Brazil

HAHNER (JUNE E.) Civilian-military relations in Brazil, 1889-1898. Columbia. S. C., 1969. pp. 232. bibliog.

- China

KUHN (PHILIP A.) Rebellion and its enemies in late imperial China: militarization and social structure, 1796-1864. Cambridge, Mass., 1970. pp. 254. bibliog. (Harvard University. East Asian Research Center. Harvard East Asian Series. 49)

- Germany

BEBEL (AUGUST) and LIEBKNECHT (WILHELM PHILIPP MARTIN CHRISTIAN LUDWIG) Gegen den Militarismus und gegen die neuen Steuern: zwei Reichstags-Reden am 27. und 20. November 1893. Berlin, 1893. pp. 56.

PAULUS (G.) Der Bankrott der Militärdiktatur 1918. in Klein (Fritz) ed. Politik im Krieg, 1914-1918. Berlin, 1964.

ANSCHUETZ (OSKAR) Der Militarismus: seine Herkunft und sein Wesen, seine Entwicklung und seine Überwindung; ein Beitrag zu einer Philosophie des Unbewussten. Nürnberg, the Author, 1967. pp. 192. 19cm.

RITTER (GERHARD) The sword and the scepter: the problem of militarism in Germany;...translated from the German by Heinz Norden. Coral Gables, [1969 in progress].

GUS (MIKHAIL SEMENOVICH) Bezumie svastiki. Moskva, 1971. pp. 399.

PROEKTOR (DANIIL MIKHAILOVICH) Oruzhenostsy tret'ego reikha: germanskii militarizm, 1919-1939 gg. Moskva, 1971. pp. 197.

- Germany, Eastern

KABEL (RUDOLF) Die Militarisierung der Sowjetischen Besatzungszone Deutschlands: Bericht und Dokumentation. Bonn, 1966. pp. 316. 21cm. (Germany (Bundesrepublik). Bundesministerium für Gesamtdeutsche Fragen. Bonner Berichte aus Mittel - und Ostdeutschland)

- Indonesia

INDONESIA. Department of Information. 1967. The armed forces/army civic mission is not militarism. [Djakarta], 1967. pp. 92. 18cm.

INDONESIA. Department of Information. 1967. Participation in state affairs of the armed forces of the Republic of Indonesia is not militarism. [Djakarta], 1967. pp.20. 18cm.

- Israel

HELOU (ANGELINA) Interaction of political, military and economic factors in Israel. Beirut, 1969. pp. 175. bibliog. (Palestine Research Centre. Palestine Monographs. 16)

- Japan

LET us oppose the revival of Japanese militarism. Pyongyang, 1970. pp. 87.

DOWN with revived Japanese militarism. Peking, 1971. pp. 76.

- Mexico

BLASCO IBÁÑEZ (VICENTE) El militarismo mejicano: estudios publicados en los principales diarios de los Estados Unidos. Valencia, 1920. pp. 251.

KAHLE (GUENTER) Militär und Staatsbildung in den Anfängen der Unabhängigkeit Mexikos. Wien, 1969. pp. 267. bibliog. (Jahrbuch für Geschichte von Staat, Wirtschaft und Gesellschaft Lateinamerikas. Beihefte. Lateinamerikanische Forschungen. Band 1)

- United States

BOSCH (JUAN) Pentagonism: a substitute for imperialism; translated by Helen R. Lane. New York, [1968]. pp. 141.

BOSCH (JUAN) El pentagonismo: sustituto del imperialismo. Madrid, Guadiana de Publicaciones, [1968]. pp. 157. 21cm. (Colección Crónica de Un Siglo. 2)

The PENTAGON watchers: students report on the national security state; edited by Leonard S. Rodberg and Derek Shearer. New York, 1970. pp. 416. bibliog.

MILITARY ART AND SCIENCE

MARX (KARL) and ENGELS (FRIEDRICH) Articles in the New American Cyclopaedia; edited with a historical introduction by Hal Draper; [originally published in 1858-63]. Berkeley, [1969]. pp. 211. bibliog.

MAUDE (FREDERIC NATUSCH) Science of organisation and the art of war: a lecture. London, Association of Standardised Knowledge, [1912]. pp. 13. $24\frac{1}{2}$cm.

PISACANE (CARLO) Opere complete...a cura di Aldo Romano. Milano, 1957-64. 8 vols.

MACCHIAVELLI (NICCOLO) (Opere complete; con introduzione di Giuliano Procacci e a cura di Sergio Bertelli). [Milan, 1960 in progress]. bibliogs.

SUN TZU. The art of war; translated and with an introduction by Samuel B. Griffith; with a foreword by B.H. Liddell Hart. Oxford, Clarendon Press, 1963, repr. 1965. pp. xvii, 197. bibliog. $21\frac{1}{2}$cm. (United Nations Educational Scientific and Cultural Organization. Collection of Representative Works: Chinese Series)

RUSSIA (U.S.S.R.). Ministerstvo Oborony. 1965. Вопросы стратегии и оперативного искусства в советских военных трудах, 1917-1940 гг. Москва, 1965. pp. 768. 21см.

CROSS (J. E.) Security decisions and military technology. in Jordan (Amos Azariah) ed. Issues of national security in the 1970s. New York, 1967.

WALLACH (JEHUDA L.) Die Kriegslehre von Friedrich Engels. Frankfurt a.M., [1968]. pp. 78. bibliog

CELERIER (PIERRE) Géopolitique et géostratégie. Paris, 1969. pp. 127.

JACOBS (WALTER DARNELL) Frunze: the Soviet Clausewitz, 1885-1925. The Hague, 1969. pp. 231. bibliog.

KUROCHKIN (P. A.) ed. Osnovy metodiki voenno-nauchnogo issledovaniia. Moskva, 1969. pp. 247. bibliog.

TROTSKII (LEV DAVYDOVICH) Military writings. New York, [1969]. pp. 158.

The FOURTH dimension of warfare: [public lectures delivered in the autumn of 1967]; ...by S.G.F. Brandon [and others]; edited by Michael Elliott-Bateman. Manchester. [1970 in progress].

BABIN (A. I.) F. Engel's - vydaiushchiisia voennyi teoretik rabochego klassa. Moskva, 1970. pp. 319.

MRAZEK (JAMES) The art of winning wars. London, 1970. pp. 218. bibliog.

VO NGUYEN GIAP. The military art of people's war: selected writings...; edited and with an introduction by Russell Stetler. New York, [1970]. pp. 332.

- History

SMAIL (RAYMOND CHARLES) Crusading warfare, 1097-1193. Cambridge, C.U.P., 1956, repr. 1967. pp. xi, 272. bibliog. $21\frac{1}{2}$cm. (Cambridge Studies in Medieval Life and Thought. New Series. vol.3)

HOWARD (MICHAEL ELIOT) Studies in war and peace: [essays originally published between 1959 and 1969]. London, 1970. pp. 262.

HALE (J.R.) Armies, navies and the art of war. in vol. 3 of The New Cambridge modern history. Cambridge, 1968.

AZOVTSEV (NIKOLAI NIKOLAEVICH) V. I. Lenin i sovetskaia voennaia nauka. Moskva, 1971. pp. 359. bibliog.

MILITARY ASSISTANCE, FRENCH

- Laos

FRANCE. Mission Militaire Française près le Gouvernement Royal Lao. 1961. La mission militaire française près le gouvernement royal Lao. Vientiane, [1961]. pp. 36. $24\frac{1}{2}$cm.

MILITARY ASSISTANCE, GERMAN

HAFTENDORN (HELGA) Militärhilfe und Rüstungsexporte der BRD. Düsseldorf, [1971]. pp. 144. bibliog.

MILITARY ASSISTANCE, RUSSIAN

JOSHUA (WYNFRED) and GIBERT (STEPHEN P.) Arms for the third world: Soviet military aid diplomacy. Baltimore, [1969]. pp. 169. bibliog.

- Mongolia

SORKIN (NAUM SEMENOVICH) Vnachale puti: zapiski instruktora Mongol'skoi armii. Moskva, 1970. pp. 126.

MILITARY ATTACHÉS

VAGTS (ALFRED) The military attaché. Princeton, Princeton U.P., 1967. pp. xiv, 408. bibliog. $21\frac{1}{2}$cm.

MILITARY ATTACHÉS (Cont'd.)

- Austria-Hungary

ALLMAYER-BECK (J. C.) Die Archive der k.u.k. Militär-bevollmächtigten und Militär-Adjoints in Kriegs-archiv Wien; in Institut für Österreichische Geschichtsforschung and Vienna. Katholische Akademie. Österreich und Europa. Graz, 1965.

MILITARY ATTACHÉS, GERMAN

KEHRIG (MANFRED) Die Wiedereinrichtung des deutschen militärischen Attachédienstes nach dem Ersten Weltkrieg, 1919-1933. Boppard am Rhein, Boldt, [1966]. pp. ix, 254. bibliog. 24cm. (Militaergeschichtliches Forschungsamt. Wehrwissenschaftliche Forschungen. Militärgeschichtliche Studien. 2)

MILITARY BASES

- United States

The IMPACT of large installations on nearby areas: accelerated urban growth; [by] Gerald Breese and others. Beverly Hills, Sage, [1965]. pp. v, 632. bibliog. 27½cm.

LYNCH (JOHN E.) Local economic development after military base closures. New York, 1970. pp. 350. bibliog.

MILITARY BASES, AMERICAN

- Okinawa

ASSOCIATION FOR PROMOTION OF OKINAWA'S LIBERATION AND ITS RETURN TO THE FATHERLAND. Okinawa, island of tragedy. Tokyo, 1963. pp. (iii), 87. 25½cm.

- Philippine Islands

DODD (JOSEPH W.) Criminal jurisdiction under the United States - Philippine military bases agreement: a study in conjurisdictional law. The Hague, Nijhoff, 1968. pp. xiv, 143. bibliog. 24cm.

- United Kingdom - British Empire

TRINIDAD AND TOBAGO. 1958. Documents relating the bases leased to the United States of America, etc. [Port-of-Spain], 1958. pp. 46. Special Supplement to the Gazette Extraordinary, vol. 127, no. 83, dated 9th August, 1958.

MILITARY DISCHARGE

- United Kingdom

YOUNG (KEN) Civil liberties and service recruitment: the plight of reluctant servicemen. London, 1970. pp. 23.

MILITARY DISCIPLINE

- Switzerland

FLUETSCH (HANS-JUERG) Die rechtliche Natur des militärischen Befehls. Zürich, 1969. pp. 122. bibliog. (Zürich. Universität. Rechts- und Staatswissenschaftliche Fakultät. Zürcher Beiträge zur Rechtswissenschaft. Neue Folge. Heft 327)

MILITARY EDUCATION

- Canada

PRESTON (RICHARD ARTHUR) R.M.C. and Kingston: the effect of imperial and military influences on a Canadian community. [Durham, N.C., 1968]. pp. irreg. (Duke University. Commonwealth Studies Center. Reprint Series. No. 27) (Reprinted from Ontario History vol. 60. No. 3)

- Russia

KASHKENBAEV (Z. SH.) Voenno-organizatorskaia rabota kompartii respublik Srednei Azii i Kazakhstana v gody Velikoi Otechestvennoi voiny. Alma-Ata, 1970. pp. 297.

SHATUNOV (GEORGII PAVLOVICH) Leninskii vsevobuch. Moskva, 1970. pp. 102.

RUSSIA (U.S.S.R.). Ministerstvo Oborony. 1971. Soldat i voina: problemy moral'no-politicheskoi i psikhologicheskoi podgotovki sovetskikh voinov. Moskva, 1971. pp. 318.

- United States

HEISE (J. ARTHUR) The brass factories: a frank appraisal of West Point, Annapolis and the Air Force Academy. Washington, D.C., 1969. pp. 190.

MILITARY GEOGRAPHY

- United States - Illinois

ILLINOIS. Division of the State Geological Survey. Bulletins. No. 39. The environment of Camp Grant; by Rollin D. Salisbury and Harlan H. Barrows. Urbana, 1918. pp. 75. 25½cm.

MILITARY GOVERNMENT

UNITED STATES. Office of the Chief of Military History. United States Army in World War II. Special Studies. Civil affairs: soldiers become governors. Washington, 1964. pp. xxiii, 932.

The ROLE of federal military government of Nigeria to-day. n.p., 1966. pp. 32.

DOORN (JAC A.A. VAN) ed. Military profession and military regimes: commitments and conflicts. The Hague, [1969]. pp. 304.

CONFERENCE OF SCHOLARS ON THE ADMINISTRATION OF OCCUPIED AREAS, 1943-1955, INDEPENDENCE, 1970. Conference of Scholars on the Administration of Occupied Areas... at the Harry S. Truman Library;... transcript edited by Donald R. McCoy and Benedict K. Zobrist. Independence, [1970]. fo. 109.

MILITARY HISTORY

HOWARD (MICHAEL ELIOT) Studies in war and peace: [essays originally published between 1959 and 1969]. London, 1970. pp. 262.

HATTON (RAGNHILD) War and peace, 1680-1720;... an inaugural lecture delivered on 1 May 1969. London, [1969]. pp. 26.

INSTITUT VOENNOI ISTORII. Карл Маркс и военная история. Москва, 1969. pp. 240. 20см.

MILITARY LAW

- Germany

GRUETER (STEPHAN BERNWARD) Der minderjährige Soldat: ein Beitrag zum Recht des Minderjährigen. [Cologne, 1966?]. pp. 154. bibliog.

SACHAU (MANFRED) Wehrhoheit und auswärtige Gewalt: ein Beitrag zur Auslegung des Artikel 32 Absatz 1 des Grundgesetzes für die Bundesrepublik Deutschland. Berlin, Duncker & Humblot, [1967]. pp. 238. bibliog. 23½cm. (Schriften zum Öffentlichen Recht. Band 61)

DOEHRING (KARL) Befehlsdurchsetzung und Waffengebrauch: europäische Menschenrechtskonvention und deutsches Recht. Bad Homburg, 1968. pp. 77.

- Poland

MUSZYŃSKI (JERZY) Zasady ustrojowe sądownictwa wojskowego i prokuratury wojskowej w Polsce Ludowej. Warszawa, 1964. pp. 256. bibliog. 20½cm.

POLAND. Najwyższy Sąd Wojskowy. 1964. Orzecznictwo... za lata 1959-1962. Warszawa, 1964. pp. 388. 25cm.

POLAND. Ministerstwo Obrony Narodowej. 1967. Przestępstwo wojskowe a przewinienie dyscyplinarne w polskim prawie wojskowym; [by] Jerzy Muszyński. Warszawa, 1967 pp. 227. bibliog.

POLAND. Sąd Najwyższy. Izba Wojskowa. 1968. Orzecznictwo... za lata 1962-1967. Warszawa, 1968. pp. 360. 25cm

POLAND. Ministerstwo Obrony Narodowej. 1969. Podstawowe wiadomości o prawie wojskowym: według stanu prawnego na dzień 30 czerwca 1969 roku. Warszawa, 1969. pp. 261.

- Russia

RUSSIA (U.S.S.R.). Ministerstvo Oborony. 1965. Дисциплинарный Устав Вооруженных Сил Союза ССР. Москва, 1965. pp. 47.

RUSSIA (U.S.S.R.) Ministerstvo Oborony. 1967. Distsiplinarnyi ustav Vooruzhennykh Sil Soiuza SSR. Moskva, 1967. pp. 48.

- United Kingdom

U.K. 1956-65. Ministry of Defence. Manual of military law. pts. 1 and 3. (With Appendices and Amendments) 9th ed. London, 1956-65. 2 pts. 21½cm. For the 8th ed. see U.K. 1952-64. War Office; for the 10th ed. see U.K. 1961-63. War Office.

- United States

CONSCIENCE and command: justice and discipline in the military; edited by James Finn. New York, [1971]. pp. 300.

MILITARY MINIATURES

HAWLEY (E.J.) The toy soldier: a children's peace story. [Leicester, Leicester Peace Society], n.d. pp. 7. 16½cm.

MILITARY OCCUPATION

HOLZHAUER (GEORG) Barzahlung und Zahlungsmittelversorgung in militärisch besetzten Gebieten. Jena, Fischer, 1939. pp. x, 115. bibliog. 24cm.

OCCUPANTS-occupés, 1792-1815; (actes du) colloque de Bruxelles, 29 et 30 janvier 1968 [sponsored by the Institut de Sociologie]. Bruxelles, [1969]. pp. 406. (Brussels. Université Libre. Institut de Sociologie. Centre d'Histoire Economique et Sociale)

MILITARY POLICY

GERBER (JOHANNES) Betriebswirtschaftliche Grundlagen für die Führung von Streitkräften. [Mannheim?], 1962. pp. 194. bibliog.

JORDAN (AMOS AZARIAH) ed. Issues of national security in the 1970's: essays presented to Colonel George A. Lincoln on his sixtieth birthday. New York, Praeger, 1967. pp. viii, 336. 21cm.

SOKOLOV (P. V.) ed. Военно-экономические вопросы в курсе политэкономии. Москва, 1968. pp. 304.

INTERNATIONAL INSTITUTE FOR STRATEGIC STUDIES. Adelphi Papers. No. 62,68. Military logistic systems in Nato: the goal of integration; by Geoffrey Ashcroft. London, 1969-70. 2 pts.

BOBROW (DAVIS BERNARD) ed. Weapons system decisions: political and psychological perspectives on continental defense. New York, Praeger, 1969. pp. xiv, 285. 23½cm. (Special Studies in U.S. Economic and Social Development)

BURLAKOV (MIKHAIL IVANOVICH) Военное потребление и капиталистическое воспроизводство. Москва, 1969. pp. 279.

NATO CONFERENCE ON MANPOWER RESEARCH IN THE DEFENCE CONTEXT, LONDON, 1967. Manpower research: the proceedings of a conference held under the aegis of the NATO Scientific Affairs Committee in London from 14th-18th August, 1967; edited by N.A.B. Wilson. London, 1969. pp. 463. bibliogs. In English or French.

INTERNATIONAL INSTITUTE FOR STRATEGIC STUDIES. Adelphi Papers. No. 72. Military manpower and political purpose; by Erwin Häckel. London, 1970. pp. 31.

KAPLAN (MORTON A.) ed. Great issues of international politics: the international system and national policy. Chicago, 1970. pp. 432.

MILITARY RESEARCH

- United States

UNITED STATES. 12164/1182. Basic scientific and astronautic research in the Department of Defense: a report, etc. Washington, 1959. pp. ix, 33.

SNYDER (W. P.) Policy oriented research: contractors and advisers. in Jordan (Amos Azariah) ed. Issues of national security in the 1970's. New York, 1967.

BERKOWITZ (MARVIN) The conversion of military-oriented research and development to civilian uses. New York, 1970. pp. 649.

MILITARY RESEARCH (Cont'd.)

- United States - Directories

KLARE (MICHAEL) compiler. The university-military complex: a directory and related documents. New York, [1969?]. pp. 58.

MILITARY SERVICE, COMPULSORY

LUPTON (ARNOLD) Voluntary service versus compulsory service. London, 1915. pp. (3).

LUPTON (ARNOLD) Are you in favour of conscription? if not, vote against it. London, 1916. s.sh.

LUPTON (ARNOLD) Recruits for the army: inequality of sacrifice. London, 1915. pp. 4.

LIGT (BARTHÉLEMY DE) Beim Teufel zur Beichte: eine Antwort auf das internationale Manifest gegen die Wehrpflicht. Berlin, 1927. pp. 14.

PRASAD (DEVI) and SMYTHE (TONY) eds. Conscription: a world survey; compulsory military service and resistance to it. London, War Resisters' International, 1968. pp. xii, 166. 21½cm.

- Australia

CONSCRIPTION in Australia; edited by Roy Forward and Bob Reece. St. Lucia, Queensland, 1968. pp. 284.

ALBINSKI (HENRY STEPHEN) Politics and foreign policy in Australia: the impact of Vietnam and conscription. Durham, N.C., 1970. pp. 238.

- Canada

GRANATSTEIN (J.L.) Conscription in the Second World War, 1939-1945: a study in political management. Toronto, [1969]. pp. 85. bibliog.

- France

SIMON (JULES FRANÇOIS) Suppression des armées permanentes: organisation démocratique de l'armée; discours prononcés au Corps Législatif, etc. Paris, Degorce-Cadot, [1868]. pp. 23. 20cm.

DORLY (J.P.) Les réquisitions personnelles. Paris, 1965. pp. 362. bibliog.

- Netherlands

IEMHOFF (W.G.J.) Oorlog, dienstplicht, dienstweigering. Baarn, [1966]. pp. 132.

- United Kingdom

LANSBURY (GEORGE) A speech...on industrial conscription. [Southampton, 191-]. 1 pamphlet (unpaged)

[DEWAR (HUGO)] Resist the register. London, [1939]. 1 pamphlet (unpaged).

INDEPENDENT LABOUR PARTY. What's this "national service"? London, [1939]. pp. 8.

NATIONAL YOUTH CAMPAIGN. No conscripts: but free volunteers for a collective peace policy. [London, 1940?] pp. 14.

- United States

BLUM (ALBERT A.) Drafted or deferred: practices past and present. [Ann Arbor], University of Michigan, Graduate School of Business Administration, Bureau of Industrial Relations, [1967]. pp. (viii), 275. 23cm.

STUDENT UNION FOR PEACE ACTION. Toronto Anti Draft Programme. Escape from freedom: immigration to Canada as an alternative to the draft. Toronto, [1967?]. pp. 23.

UNITED STATES. Selective Service System. Special Monographs. No. 18. Evaluation of the selective service program: (with Appendices). Washington, 1967. 3 vols.

AMERICAN FRIENDS SERVICE COMMITTEE. Peace Education Division. The draft?: a report. New York, Hill & Wang, 1968. pp. xi, 112. bibliog. 20cm.

CHAPMAN (BRUCE K.) Our unfair and obsolete draft, and what we can do about it. new ed. New York, 1968. pp. 204. (Originally published under the title The wrong man in uniform)

MARMION (HARRY A.) Selective service: conflict and compromise. New York, Wiley, [1968]. pp. (254). 23cm.

NATIONAL SERVICE CONFERENCE, 2ND, WASHINGTON, 1967. National service: a report of a conference; edited by Donald J. Eberly. New York, 1968. pp. 598. bibliog.

BRADFORD (DAVID F.) Deferment policy in selective service. Princeton, N.J., 1969. pp. 64. (Princeton University. Department of Economics and Sociology. Industrial Relations Section. Research Report Series. No. 113)

LITTLE (ROGER W.) ed. Selective service and American society. New York, 1969. pp. 220. bibliog.

TATUM (ARLO) and TUCHINSKY (JOSEPH S.) Guide to the draft. Boston, Beacon P., [1969]. pp. xx, 281. 20cm.

BERRIGAN (DANIEL) The trial of the Catonsville nine. Boston, [1970]. pp. 122.

KENDALL (DAVID E.) and ROSS (LEONARD) The lottery and the draft: where do I stand? New York, 1970. pp. 159.

SHAPIRO (ANDREW O.) and STRIKER (JOHN M.) Mastering the draft: a comprehensive guide for solving draft problems. Boston, [Mass., 1970]. pp. 626.

SUTTLER (DAVID) IV-F: a guide to medical, psychiatric and moral unfitness standards for military induction. New York, [1970]. pp. 171.

GERHARDT (JAMES M.) The draft and public policy: issues in military manpower procurement, 1945-1970. Columbus, 1971. pp. 425.

MARMION (HARRY A.) The case against a volunteer army. Chicago, 1971. pp. 107.

POLITISK asyl åt Vietnamkrigsvägrare: artiklar och uttalanden av bl. a. Sara Lidman, amerikanska och svenska jurister ...; sammanställd och med inledning av Stockholms Forskningskollektiv. Stockholm, [1971?]. pp. 38.

WILLIAMS (ROGER NEVILLE) The new exiles: American war resisters in Canada. New York, [1971]. pp. 401.

MILITARY SERVICE AS A PROFESSION

RATTENBACH (BENJAMIN) El sector militar de la sociedad: principios de sociologia militar. Buenos Aires, Circulo Militar, 1965. pp. 95. (Biblioteca del Oficial. Colección Cultura General. vol. 555)

BUSQUETS BRAGULAT (JULIO) El militar de carrera en España: estudio de sociología militar. Barcelona, Ariel, 1967. pp. 224. 19cm. (Demos. Biblioteca de Sociología. 1)

UNIVERSITIES-SERVICES STUDY GROUP, SCOTLAND. The services and society in the 1970s and beyond: report and papers of the Group, Lent term, 1968. [Edinburgh], 1968. pp. irreg. bibliog.

JOHNSTON (JEROME) and BACHMAN (JERALD G.) Young men look at military service: a preliminary report; [with up-dating supplement]. Ann Arbor, 1970. pp. 115. bibliog. (Michigan University. Survey Research Center. Youth in Transition Documents. No. 193)

YOUNG (KEN) Civil liberties and service recruitment: the plight of reluctant servicemen. London, 1970. pp. 23.

ABRAHAMSSON (BENGT) Military professionalization and political power. [Stockholm, imprint, 1971] pp. 184. bibliog.

MILIUKOV (PAVEL NIKOLAEVICH)

SMIRNOV (S.A.) and others, eds. P.N. Miliukov: sbornik materialov po chestvovaniiu ego semidesiatiletiia, 1859-1929. Parizh, [1930]. pp. 355. bibliog.

MILIUKOV (PAVEL NIKOLAEVICH) Political memoirs, 1905-1917; ... edited by Arthur P. Mendel; translated by Carl Goldberg. Ann Arbor, U. of Michigan P., [1967]. pp. xviii, 508. 22½cm.

RIHA (THOMAS) A Russian European: Paul Miliukov in Russian politics. Notre Dame, [1969]. pp. 373. bibliog.

MILIUTIN (DMITRII ALEKSEEVICH)

MILLER (FORRESTT A.) Dmitrii Miliutin and the reform era in Russia. [Nashville], Vanderbilt U.P., 1968. pp. ix, 246. bibliog.

MILK

- Analysis and examination

TUBERCULOSIS (ANIMALS) COMMITTEE. Report of proceedings of the deputation to the Presidents of the Local Government Board and the Board of Agriculture and fisheries 12th March, 1908 on legislation and the milk supply. London, [1908]. pp. 23.

NATIONAL LEAGUE FOR PHYSICAL EDUCATION AND IMPROVEMENT. Leaflets. No.6. The case for clean milk. [London, the League, 1910?]. pp. (4).

- Prices

EIRE. Two-Tier Milk Price Study Group. 1967. Report: [M.J. Costello, chairman]. Dublin, [1967]. fo. 57.

DESAI (MEGHNAD J.) The computer simulation of the California dairy industry: a report prepared for the Giannini Foundation of Agricultural Economics. [Berkeley?], U. of California, Agricultural Experiment Station, Division of Agricultural Sciences, 1968. pp. viii, 190. 27cm.

MILK, DRIED

ROECKSEISEN (ARMIN) Der Markt für Milchpulver in der Bundesrepublik Deutschland. Bonn, Forschungsgesellschaft für Agrarpolitik und Agrarsoziologie, 1968. pp. xii, 217. bibliog. 29cm. ([Publications]. 193)

JEPHCOTT (Sir HARRY) The first fifty years: an account of the early life of Joseph Edward Nathan and the first fifty years of his merchandise business that eventually became the Glaxo Group. [London?, 1969]. pp. 118.

MILK CONSUMPTION

- Belgium

ACKERMAN (L.) and DUMEEZ (M.) La consommation de lait en Belgique; [prepared] sous la direction de A. Verkinderen. Bruxelles, 1968. 2 vols. 29cm. (Belgium. Cahiers de l'Institut Économique Agricole. Nos. 80-81.)

- Canada

JOHNSTONE (CHARLOTTE I.) Urban family expenditure for certain milk products, 1957. Ottawa, 1963. pp. 36.

- United Kingdom

UNITED KINGDOM. Social Survey. [Reports]. New Series. Regional. H. 11. Consumption of milk, February 1943. [mimeographed]. n.p. 1943. pp. 16. 33cm.

- United States

UNITED STATES. Department of Agriculture. Statistical Bulletins. No. 312. Fluid milk and cream consumption in selected marketing areas, 1950-59. Washington, 1962. pp. 43.

MILK SUPPLY

ORGANISATION FOR ECONOMIC CO-OPERATION AND DEVELOPMENT. 1965. Co-operative research to improve input/output data in cow milk production: report of the 1964 Seminar on co-operation between agricultural natural scientists and agricultural economists in research for selected input/output data. (Documentation in Food and Agriculture. 1965 Series. 71) [Paris, 1965]. pp. 264. 24cm.

COOK (R.S.) and UPTON (M.) The phasing of milk production for maximum profitability. [Reading], 1971. pp. 28. (Reading. University. Department of Agricultural Economics and Management. Miscellaneous Studies. No.48)

MILK SUPPLY (Cont'd.)

- Kenya

KENYA. Sessional Papers. 1960. No. 12. The Mariakani milk scheme. Nairobi, 1960. fo. (19).

- Mexico

DAVIES (J.L.) The milk industry in a developing country. Sutton Bonington, Nottingham, University School of Agriculture, Department of Agricultural Economics, 1967. pp.12. 23½cm. (Heath Memorial Lectures. No. 11)

- Russia

DOBRYNIN (VLADIMIR ALEKSANDROVICH) Экономика молочного скотоводства. Москва, 1969. pp. 254.

- United Kingdom

NORWICH. Health Committee. Report... to the Council on the milk supply of the city. Norwich, 1904. pp. 8.

CASON (R.G.) Supply response in milk production: a study in methodology for the prediction of milk supply based on a survey...in South West England, 1967. Exeter, 1969. pp. 47. bibliog. (Exeter. University. Department of Agricultural Economics Reports. No. 176)

LONDON. University. Wye College. School of Rural Economics and Related Studies. National investigation into the economies of milk production: results for the South East of England, April 1968 to March 1969. [Wye], 1969. pp. 14.

WALKER (ROSEMARY F.) Milk production economics, 1968-69: retrospect and prospect. [Manchester], 1970. pp. 67. (Manchester. University. Department of Agricultural Economics. Bulletins. No. 133)

U.K. Ministry of Agriculture, Fisheries and Food. 1971. Aspects of dairy economics, 1966-1969: a summary and critique of further research into the economics of milk production. London, 1971. pp. 79. bibliog.

- United Kingdom - Ireland

IRELAND. Commission of Inquiry into the Resources and Industries of Ireland. 1920. Ad interim report on milk production, March, 1920. Dublin, 1920. pp. 24.

MILK TRADE

- Argentine Republic

ARGENTINE REPUBLIC. Direccion de Economia Lechera. 1960. 10 anos de industria lechera en cifras 1950-1959. [Buenos Aires], 1960. fo. (33).

- Azerbaijan

RAZVITIE miasnoi i molochnoi promyshlennosti Azerbaidzhana. Baku, 1966. pp. 52. (Azerbaidzhanskii Institut Nauchno-Tekhnicheskoi Informatsii. Obzornaia Informatsiia: Seriia "Pishchevaia Promyshlennost' ")

- Belgium

ACKERMAN (L.) La commercialisation des dérivés liquides du lait; [prepared] sous la direction de A. Verkinderen. Bruxelles, 1970. fo. 54. (Belgium. Institut Economique Agricole. Cahiers. No.111)

- Canada - British Columbia

CANADA. Prices and Incomes Commission. 1970. Wholesale milk prices, [Vancouver area]. [Ottawa], 1970. fo. 10.

- Canada - Ontario

CANADA. Restrictive Trade Practices Commission. [Reports]. RTPC. No. 30. Report of an alleged combine in the matter of the sale and distribution of milk in the Ottawa, Ontario, area. Ottawa, 1964. pp. 25.

CANADA. Prices and Incomes Commission. 1970. Wholesale and retail milk prices, Ottawa area. [Ottawa], 1970. fo. 5.

- Europe

ORGANISATION FOR EUROPEAN ECONOMIC CO-OPERATION. European Productivity Agency. 1959. Development of farmers' marketing co-operatives for milk, milk products and eggs. [Paris], 1959. pp. 129.

ORGANISATION FOR EUROPEAN ECONOMIC CO-OPERATION. European Productivity Agency. Documentation in Food and Agriculture. 1959. Series. 13. Improved methods of distribution in the retail trade for milk and milk products. [Paris], 1959. pp. 20.

ORGANISATION FOR ECONOMIC CO-OPERATION AND DEVELOPMENT. Documentation in Food and Agriculture. 1962 Series. 55. Organisation and structure of the milk markets in O.E.C.D. member countries; (by E. Esche). [Paris, 1962]. pp. 546. bibliogs.

- European Economic Community countries

HAENSLI (JUERG) Der schweizerische Konsummilchmarkt und die europäische Wirtschaftsgemeinschaft. Aarau, Keller, 1966. pp. xix, 106. bibliog. 23cm.

- France

FRANCE. Ministère de l'Agriculture. Statistique agricole. Supplement. Série Etudes. No.60. Étude des structures de l'industrie laitière en 1966 au niveau des unités de production; [by M.F. Labouesse and others]. Paris, 1970. pp. 123.

- Germany

STAMER (HANS) Distributionswege von Milch und Milcherzeugnissen, ausgenommen Butter, in der Bundesrepublik Deutschland. Bonn, Forschungsgesellschaft für Agrarpolitik und Agrarsoziologie, 1966. pp. viii, 136. bibliog. 29cm. ([Publications]. 167)

SCHARRER (HANS WERNER) Die Ordnung des Marktes für Milch und Molkereiprodukte in der Bundesrepublik Deutschland. [Erlangen, imprint, 1968?]. pp. 323. bibliog.

SEIDLER (KARL) Der Vertrieb von Trinkmilch und Frischprodukten in Molkereien. Bonn, 1969. pp. 283. bibliog. (Forschungsgesellschaft für Agrarpolitik und Agrarsoziologie. [Publications]. 202)

- Pakistan, East

EAST PAKISTAN. Agricultural Marketing Directorate. 1962. Report on the marketing of milk in East Pakistan. Dacca, 1962. pp. 56.

- Switzerland

HAENSLI (JUERG) Der schweizerische Konsummilchmarkt und die europäische Wirtschaftsgemeinschaft. Aarau, Keller, 1966. pp. xix, 106. bibliog. 23cm.

- United Kingdom

REPORT on a complaint by Messrs. G. Padfield, G.L. Brock and H. Steven, milk producers in the South-Eastern Region, as to the operation of the Milk Marketing Scheme, 1933 (as amended); [prepared by the] Committee of Investigation for England and Wales: [David Karmel, chairman]. [London, H.M.S.O., 1969], pp. 121.

STINSON (DAVID J.) Agricultural Marketing Act, 1958: proposed amendment to the Milk Marketing Scheme 1933 (as amended): report...on the public inquiry held on 4th and 5th June, 1969. [London, H.M.S.O., 1969?] pp. 60.

JENKINS (ALAN) Drinka pinta: the story of milk and the industry that serves it; published on the occasion of the fiftieth anniversary of the National Milk Publicity Council;...with a foreword by the Rt. Hon. Cledwyn Hughes. London, 1970. pp. 242. bibliog.

WHETHAM (EDITH H.) The London milk trade, 1900-1930. [Reading], 1970. pp. 16. (Reading. University. Institute of Agricultural History. Research Papers. No. 3)

WHETSTONE (LINDA) The marketing of milk: an empirical study of the origins, performance and future of the Milk Marketing Board. London, 1970. pp. 60. (Institute of Economic Affairs. Research Monographs. 21)

- United States

UNITED STATES. Agriculture Department. Economic Research Service. Agricultural Economic Reports. No. 67. Nature of competition in fluid milk markets. Washington, 1965. pp. iv, 76. Bibliog.

MILL (JOHN STUART)

[VASEY (GEORGE)] Individual liberty, legal, moral, and licentious; in which the political fallacies of J.S. Mill's essay "On liberty" are pointed out; by Index [pseud.]. London, Vasey, 1867. pp. xii, 172.

THORNTON (NEIL SYLVESTER) Mill's individualism. [Brisbane, 1964?]. fo. 22.

ROBSON (JOHN MERCEL) The improvement of mankind: the social and political thought of John Stuart Mill. Toronto, U of Toronto P., [1968]. pp xiv, 292. bibliog. 23cm.

SCHNEEWIND (JEROME B.) ed. Mill: a collection of critical essays. Garden City, N.Y., 1968. pp. 455. bibliog.

SCHWARTZ (PEDRO) La nueva economía política de John Stuart Mill. Madrid, Tecnos, 1968. pp. 412. bibliog. 23cm. (Biblioteca Tecnos de Ciencias Económicas. No. 10.)

THORNTON (NEIL SYLVESTER) The problem of liberalism in the thought of John Stuart Mill; [Ph. D. (London) thesis]. [1969]. fo. 335. bibliog. 25½cm. Typescript: unpublished. This thesis is the property of London University and may not be removed from the Library.

RYAN (ALAN) John Stuart Mill. New York, [1970]. pp. 268. bibliog.

RYAN (ALAN) The philosophy of John Stuart Mill. London, 1970. pp. 268. bibliog.

MILLENIUM

MUEHLMANN (WILHELM EMIL) and others. Messianismes révolutionnaires du tiers monde;.. traduit de l'allemand, etc. [Paris], Gallimard, [1968]. pp. 389. bibliogs. 22cm. (Bibliothèque des Sciences Humaines)

TUVESON (ERNEST LEE) Redeemer nation: the idea of America's millennial role. Chicago, U. of Chicago P., 1968. pp. xiii, 238. bibliog. 21½cm.

BUCHHOLZ (ERICH) Alternative Gottesreich: unterwegs zur künftigen Gesellschaft. Bellnhausen über Gladenbach (Hessen), [1969]. pp. 299. bibliog.

BURRIDGE (KENELM O. L.) New heaven, new earth: a study of millenarian activities. Oxford, 1969. pp. 191. bibliog.

LITTLE (EARL TENNYSON) Millenial movements and social change in Melanesia; [M.Phil. (London) thesis]. 1970. fo. 177. bibliog. Typescript: unpublished. This thesis is the property of London University and may not be removed from the Library.

- Dictionaries and encyclopaedias

DESROCHES (HENRI CHARLES) and others. Dieux d'hommes: dictionnaire des messianismes et millénarismes de l'ère chrétienne. Paris, 1969. pp. 281. bibliogs.

- History of doctrines

LAMONT (WILLIAM MONTGOMERIE) Godly rule: politics and religion, 1603-60. London, 1969. pp. 200. bibliog.

COHN (NORMAN) The pursuit of the millennium: revolutionary millenarians and mystical anarchists of the middle ages. rev. ed. London, 1970. pp. 412. bibliog.

MILLINERY

- United Kingdom

U.K. Department of Trade and Industry. Business monitor: Production series. P110. Hats, caps and millinery. London, 1971 to date.

MILLIONAIRES

ENGELMANN (BERNT) Die Macht am Rhein: meine Freunde, die Geldgiganten. München, [1968 in progress].

JUNGBLUT (MICHAEL) Die Reichen und die Superreichen in Deutschland. Hamburg, 1971. pp. 383.

MILLS (CHARLES WRIGHT)

NOVACK (GEORGE) Who will change the world? the new left and the views of C. Wright Mills. Toronto, YSF Publication, [1966]. pp. 36. 21cm.

MILNER (ALFRED) 1st Viscount Milner

NIMOCKS (WALTER) Milner's young men: the "kindergarten" in Edwardian imperial affairs. Durham, Duke U.P., 1968. pp. xiii, 234. bibliog. 23½cm.

MILTON (JOHN)

HALKETT (JOHN G.) Milton and the idea of matrimony: a study of the divorce tracts and Paradise lost. New Haven, 1970. pp. 162. bibliog.

MILTON KEYNES

- Civic improvement

LLEWELYN-DAVIES WEEKS [AND PARTNERS]. Milton Keynes plan: interim report to the Milton Keynes Development Corporation. London, 1968. pp. (ix), 172. 29½cm.

MILTON KEYNES DEVELOPMENT CORPORATION. Milton Keynes: the existing towns. Wavendon, 1970. pp. 18.

MILTON KEYNES DEVELOPMENT CORPORATION. The plan for Milton Keynes: presented by the...Development Corporation to the Minister of Housing and Local Government; main consultants Llewelyn-Davies Weeks Forestier-Walker and Bor. Wavendon, 1970. 2 vols.

- Sanitary affairs

BUCKINGHAMSHIRE. Department of Health and Welfare. Medical Planning Group. Report: (A health service for Milton Keynes). Aylesbury, 1968. pp. 42. bibliog.

MILWAUKEE

- Economic history

KORMAN (GERD) Industrialization, immigrants and Americanizers: the view from Milwaukee, 1866-1921. Madison, State Historical Society of Wisconsin, [1967] pp. x, 225. bibliog. 21½cm.

MINAS GERAIS

- Rural conditions

ESTADO de Minas Gerais: orçamentos familiares rurais; [by Sylvio Wanick Ribeiro and others]. [Rio de Janeiro?], 1970. pp. 274.

- Statistics

ESTADO de Minas Gerais: orçamentos familiares rurais; [by Sylvio Wanick Ribeiro and others]. [Rio de Janeiro?], 1970. pp. 274.

MIND AND BODY

KNEALE (WILLIAM CALVERT) On having a mind. Cambridge, 1962. pp. 56. (Cambridge University. Arthur Stanley Eddington Memorial Lectures. 1962)

LANGER (SUSANNE KNAUTH) Mind: an essay on human feeling. Baltimore, Johns Hopkins P., [1967 in progress]. bibliog. 23cm.

FEIGL (HERBERT) The "mental" and the "physical": the essay and a postscript. Minneapolis, U. of Minnesota P., [1967]. pp. ix, 179. bibliogs. 20cm.

GIEGEL (HANS JOACHIM) Die Logik der seelischen Ereignisse: zu Theorien von L. Wittgenstein und W. Sellars. Frankfurt a. M., [1969]. pp. 163. bibliog.

LASZLO (ERVIN) System, structure, and experience: toward a scientific theory of mind. New York, [1969]. pp. 112.

LEWIS (HYWEL DAVID) The elusive mind; based on the first series of the Gifford Lectures, delivered in the University of Edinburgh, 1966-1968. London, 1969. pp. 347.

BORST (C.V.) ed. The mind-brain identity theory; ...contributors D.M. Armstrong [and others]. London, 1970. pp. 261. bibliog.

LEDERMANN (ERICH KURT) Philosophy and medicine. London, 1970. pp. 180.

MEILAND (JACK W.) The nature of intention. London, 1970. pp. 136. bibliog.

ROSENBLUETH (ARTURO) Mind and brain: a philosophy of science. Cambridge, Mass., [1970]. pp. 128. bibliog.

SPICKER (STUART F.) ed. The philosophy of the body: rejections of Cartesion dualism: [readings]. Chicago, [1970]. pp. 367. bibliog.

TRIMMER (ERIC JAMES) Understanding anxiety in everyday life. London, 1970. pp. 140.

MINE ACCIDENTS

LUCAS (REX A.) Men in crisis: a study of a mine disaster. New York, [1969]. pp. 335. bibliog.

MINE EXPLOSIONS

SYMPOSIUM ON COAL AND GAS OUTBURSTS, NÎMES, 1964. Symposium [held at] Nîmes, France 25-27 November 1964; [proceedings and reports]. (ST/ECE/COAL/17) New York, United Nations, 1967. pp. v, 289, 8. 27½cm.

MINE INSPECTION

TRADES UNION CONGRESS. Trades union deputation to the Rt. Hon. Sir Wm. Vernon Harcourt, M.P. in support of Mr. Burt's motion for an increase in the number of mine inspectors, July 2nd, 1884. Manchester, 1884. pp. 8.

MINE RAILWAYS

SELLICK (ROGER J.) The West Somerset Mineral Railway and the story of Brendon Hills iron mines;...with contributions by J.R. Hamilton and M.H. Jones. 2nd ed. Newton Abbot, 1970. pp. 128. bibliog.

MINERAL AGGREGATES
See AGGREGATES (BUILDING MATERIALS)

MINERAL INDUSTRIES

MINING: annual review. a., 1947/8- , with gap (1954/5). London. File includes w. Mining jl., 1921-1963 (v. 134-261), with gap (1958, no.6389).

HERFINDAHL (ORRIS CLEMENS) Three studies in minerals economics. Washington, D.C., [1961]. pp. 63.

CANADA. Mines Branch. Information Circulars. 149. Mines Branch contributions to the United Nations Conference on the Application of Science and Technology for the Benefit of the Less Developed Areas, Geneva, February 4-20, 1963. Ottawa, 1963. pp. 47. bibliogs. With French summaries.

MINERALS QUARTERLY; pd. by the Commonwealth Secretariat. q., Ap-Oc 1969 (v. 1, nos. 1-3); ceased pbln. London.

- History

FREIBERG. Bergakademie. Freiberger Forschungshefte. [Reihe] D.46. Montangeschichte; Beiträge zur Geschichte des Bergbaus, Hüttenwesens und der Montanwissenschaften, 16. bis 20. Jahrhundert. Band 1. Leipzig, Deutscher Verlag für Grundstoffindustrie, [1964]. pp. 127. bibliog. 24cm.

- Africa, Subsaharan

CANADA. Mineral Resources Division. Mineral Information Bulletins. 58. A survey of the mineral industry in Southern Africa; by R.B. Toombs; (prepared as a record of the seventh Commonwealth Mining and Metallurgical Congress, 1961). Ottawa, 1962. pp. 275. bibliog. Maps in end pocket.

- America, Latin

JARA (ALVARO) Tres ensayos sobre economía minera hispanoamericana. Santiago de Chile, Universidad de Chile, Centro de Investigaciones de Historia Americana, 1966. pp. 119. 22½cm. (Economía Minera Hispanoamericana. 1)

- Australia - Western Australia

WESTERN AUSTRALIA. Commonwealth Bureau of Census and Statistics. Western Australian Office. Statistics of Western Australia: Non-rural primary industries. a., 1968/9 [1st] to date. Perth.

- Canada

CANADA. Mineral Resources Division. Mineral Information Bulletins. 75. Canadian minerals in national and international perspective; [by] R.B. Toombs. Ottawa, 1964. pp. 63. With French summary.

- Canada - Taxation

CANADA. Mineral Resources Division. Mineral Information Bulletins. 73. Summary review of federal taxation and legislation affecting the Canadian mineral industry...; compiled by E.C. Hodgson and W.J. Beard. rev. ed. Ottawa, [1964]. pp. 27.

- Canada - British Columbia

HEDLEY (M.S.) The mineral industry of British Columbia. [Victoria], 1969. pp. 23.

- Canada - North-West Territories

CANADIAN BECHTEL LIMITED. Feasibility study: lead-zinc smelter, Pine Point, N.W.T.; prepared for government of Canada. Ottawa, Q.P., 1968. pp. (iii, 26). 28cm.

ARMSTRONG (GRAHAM T.) and FREYMAN (ANDREW J.) Cost-benefit analysis of a lead-zinc smelter in the Northwest Territories. Ottawa, Q.P., 1969. pp. vi,(75). 28cm.

- Canada - Nova Scotia

NOVA SCOTIA. 1966. Plan for the mining sector. (Voluntary Planning Board) [Halifax, N.S.], 1966. pp. (iii), 47. 24½cm.

- Ecuador

ECUADOR. División de Estadística y Censos. 1969- . Segundo censo de manufactura y minería, 1965. Quito, [1969 in progress]. 31cm.

ECUADOR. División de Estadística y Censos. 1969. Encuesta de manufactura y minería, 1966. Quito, [1969?]. pp. 194.

- Europe

ABRATE (MARIO) L'industria metallurgica in Europa nella prima metà del XIX secolo: una valutazione piemontese. Torino, Edizioni Minerva Tecnica, 1958. pp. 183. 21½cm.

- New Zealand

NATIONAL DEVELOPMENT CONFERENCE, WELLINGTON. 1969. Minerals Committee. Report. Wellington, Government Printer, 1969. pp. 67. ([Reports]. N.D.C. 8)

- Nigeria

NIGERIA. Ministry of Mines and Power. 1971. Policy paper on the development of solid minerals in Nigeria. Lagos, 1971. pp. 10.

- Peru

PERU. Direccion Nacional de Estadistica y Censos. 1967. Censo economico, 1963: resultados del censo de mineria y directorio. Lima, 1967. pp. 65.

- Peru - Safety measures

INTERNATIONAL LABOUR OFFICE. Regular Programme of Technical Assistance. [Peru]. R.12. Informe al gobierno de la Republica del Peru sobre la seguridad minera. (OIT/OTA/Peru/R.12) Ginebra, 1968. pp. 63.

MINERAL INDUSTRIES (Cont'd.)

- Rhodesia

RHODESIA. Report of the Secretary for Mines. Salisbury, annual, 1968 [1st] to date. 25½cm.

- South Africa

CARTWRIGHT (ALAN PATRICK) Golden age: the story of the industrialization of South Africa and the part played in it by the Corner House group of companies, 1910-1967. Cape Town, Purnell, [1968]. pp. xviii, 363. 23½cm.

- United Kingdom

REES (WILLIAM) Industry before the industrial revolution: incorporating a study of the Chartered companies of the Society of Mines Royal and of Mineral and Battery Works. Cardiff, U. of Wales P., 1968. 2 vols. bibliog. 24½cm.

- United Kingdom - Ireland, Northern

IRELAND, NORTHERN. Ministry of Commerce. Mineral Development Act (Northern Ireland) 1969: statement. 1970/71 [1st] included in IRELAND, NORTHERN. Parliament. House of Commons. [papers].

- Zambia

ZAMBIA. Ministry of Trade, Industry and Mines. Annual report. a., 1968- Lusaka.

MINERS

- Diseases and hygiene

INTERNATIONAL LABOUR OFFICE. Development Programme: Technical Assistance Sector. [India]. R.23. Report to the government of India on physiology in mines. (ILO/TAP/India/R.23). Geneva, 1967. pp. 26. 30cm.

- Australia

WILLIAMS (CECIL WALLACE EDGAR) Yellow, green and red. [Brisbane, 1967]. pp. 408.

- Bolivia

BEDREGAL (GUILLERMO) La nacionalización minera y la responsabilidad del sindicalismo: mensaje del Presidente de la Corporación Minera de Bolivia ...el 30 de noviembre de 1959. La Paz, 1959. pp. 58.

- Czechoslovakia - Pensions

HOUSER (JAROSLAV) Vývoj hornického pojištění: k bojům našich horníků za kapitalismu. Praha, Ceskoslovenská Akademie Věd, 1960. pp. 153. 20½cm. (Československá Akademie Věd. Sekce Ekonomie, Práva a Filosofie. Právněhistorická Knižnice. sv.5)

- Germany

KNAPPSCHAFTS-BERUFSGENOSSENSCHAFT. Drittes Statut der Knappschafts-Berufsgenossenschaft: gültig von 1. Januar 1902 ab. Berlin, 1901. pp. 127.

DOERNEMANN (MANFRED) Die Politik des Verbandes der Bergarbeiter Deutschlands von der Novemberrevolution 1918 bis zum Osterputsch 1921 unter besonderer Berucksichtigung der Verhältnisse im rheinisch-westfälischen Industriegebiet, etc. Bochum, [1965]. pp. 270, bibliog. 20½cm.

- India

INDIA. 1967. Report on survey of labour conditions in manganese mining industry in India, 1962-63. (Labour Bureau). [Delhi, 1967]. pp. iv, 69. 24cm.

INTERNATIONAL LABOUR OFFICE. Development Programme: Technical Assistance Sector. [India]. R.23. Report to the government of India on physiology in mines. (ILO/TAP/India/R.23). Geneva, 1967. pp. 26. 30cm.

INDIA. Central Wage Board for Iron Ore Mining Industry. 1968. Report... 1967. [Delhi, 1968.] pp. 116.

- Norway

NORWAY. Statistiske Centralbyrå. Lønnsstatistikk for arbeidere i bergverksdrift og industri: Wage statistics for workers in mining and manufacturing. Oslo, annual, 3. kvartal 1969 to date. 29cm.

- Peru

MAYER (DORA) The conduct of the Cerro de Pasco Mining Company. Lima, 1913. pp. 51.

- Poland

SOCJALDEMOKRATYCZNY ZWIĄZEK ZAWODOWY ROBOTNIKÓW PRZEMYSŁU GÓRNICZEGO I HUTNICZEGO. Ustawa, etc. Sosnowiec, 1912. pp. 14.

MROZEK (WANDA) Rodzina górnicza: przekształcenia społeczne w górnośląskim środowisku górniczym. Katowice, Śląsk, 1965. pp. 244. bibliog. 24cm. (Śląski Instytut Naukowy w Katowicach. Górnośląskie Studia Socjologiczne. tom 2) With English and Russian summaries.

PIETRASZEK (EDWARD) Wiejscy robotnicy kopalń i hut: dynamika przemian społeczno-kulturowych w sierszańskim ośrodku górniczym w XIX i XX wieku. Wrocław, Ossolineum, 1966. pp. 186. 24cm. (Polska Akademia Nauk. Oddział w Krakowie. Komisja Socjologiczna. Prace. Nr.5) With English and Russian summaries.

- Russia

KISELEV (A.) Die Gewerkschafts-Bewegung der Bergarbeiter in Sowjet-Russland. Leipzig, Frankes, 1920. pp. 20. 23cm.

PRUDINSKII (ARKADII MIKHAILOVICH) Трудовое законодательство о приеме на работу и переводе рабочих и служащих предприятий горной промышленности. Москва, 1964. pp. 102.

- South Africa

NAUDÉ (LOUIS) Dr. A. Hertzog, die Nasionale Party en die mynwerker. Pretoria, [1969]. pp. 284.

- United Kingdom

[INSTITUTE FOR WORKERS' CONTROL]. Archives in Trade Union History and Theory. Series 1. No. 2. The miners' next step; by Noah Ablett and others; [reprint of the work first published in 1912]. [Nottingham, 1965?] unpaged.

INSTITUTE FOR WORKERS' CONTROL. Archives in Trade Union History and Theory. Series 1. No. 6. Industrial democracy for miners; by William Ferris Hay and others; [reprinted from works published in 1919]. Nottingham, [1968?]. fo. 15.

PROUDFOOT (D.) and McARTHUR (J.) Barriers of the bureaucrats: Fife breaks through, call for new Scottish union;... foreword by W. Allan. [London, 192-?]. pp. 32.

(HORNER (ARTHUR LEWIS) and ALLAN (W.)] The miners' next task: an open letter to all miners on the next big step, one miners' union. London, National Minority Movement, [1926]. pp. 15. 21cm.

STEPHENSON (TOM) and BRANNAN (HUGH) The miner's case. London, Independent Labour Party, [1942]. pp. 19. 21½cm.

HARDIMENT (MELVILLE) The indestructibles: a portrait of a mining community. n.p. [1960?]. pp. 32. 21¼cm.

BARTON (DENYS BRADFORD) ed. Historic Cornish mining scenes underground. Truro, Truro Bookshop, 1967. pp. 56. 19½cm.

BEST (GEOFFREY FRANCIS ANDREW) Bishop Westcott and the miners; (Lecture given in Cambridge on 18 November, 1966). Cambridge, [1967]. pp. 39. (Cambridge. University. Bishop Westcott Memorial Lectures. 1966)

HOUSE (JOHN WILLIAM) and KNIGHT (E.M.) Pit closure and the community. [Newcastle-upon-Tyne], University, Department of Geography, 1967. pp. (iv), 144. 30cm. (Papers on Migration and Mobility in Northern England. No. 5)

CHALLINOR (RAYMOND) Alexander MacDonald and the miners. London, 1968. pp. 34. (Communist Party of Great Britain. Historians' Group. Our History. No. 48)

KNIGHT (E.M.) Men leaving mining: West Cumberland, 1966-67;...report to the Ministry of Labour. Newcastle-upon-Tyne, University of Newcastle-upon-Tyne, Department of Geography, 1968. pp. (iii), 40. (Papers on Migration and Mobility in Northern England. No. 6)

- United States

UNITED MINE WORKERS OF AMERICA. Constitution of the international union..., adopted at Cincinnati, Ohio on October 10, 1960. [Washington, D.C., 1960]. pp. 102.

- Zambia

ZAMBIA. 1966. Government paper on the report of the commission of inquiry into the mining industry, Brown report, 1966. (Government Papers. 1966. No.1 [bis]) Lusaka, 1966. pp. 4. 25½cm. For the report see ZAMBIA. 1966. Report, etc.

ZAMBIA. 1966. Report of the commission of inquiry into the mining industry, 1966; under the chairmanship of Roland Brown. Lusaka, 1966. pp. vii, 170. 25½cm. For the government paper on the report see ZAMBIA. 1966. Government paper, etc.

BATES (ROBERT H.) Unions, parties, and political development: a study of mineworkers in Zambia. New Haven, 1971. pp. 291. bibliog.

MINES AND MINERAL RESOURCES

MOREAU (GEORGES) L'industrie minière: ses principes fondamentaux, ses bases économiques. Paris, 1929. pp. 167.

PARK (CHARLES F.) and FREEMAN (MARGARET C.) Affluence in jeopardy: minerals and the political economy. San Francisco, [1968]. pp. 368. bibliog.

- Africa, East

MOELLER (TIES) Bergbau und regionale Entwicklung in Ostafrika. München, [1971]. pp. 202. bibliog. (Ifo-Institut für Wirtschaftsforschung. Afrika-Studien. 67) With English summary; 3 maps in end pocket.

- Africa, Subsaharan

FRANCE. [Bureau de Documentation Minière. 1961]. Eléments relatifs à l'industrie minière en Mauritanie, Sénégal, Mali, Côte d'Ivoire, Haute Volta, Niger... année 1960. [Paris, 1961?]. pp.(iv), 75. 27cm.

- Australia - Victoria

BLAINEY (GEOFFREY) The rise of Broken Hill. Melbourne, 1968. pp. 184.

- Bolivia - Government ownership

BOLIVIA. Subsecretaria de Prensa, Informaciones y Cultura. Departamento de Publicaciones. 1952. El libro blanco de la independencia economica de Bolivia. La Paz, 1952. pp. 188.

BEDREGAL (GUILLERMO) La nacionalización minera y la responsabilidad del sindicalismo: mensaje del Presidente de la Corporación Minera de Bolivia ...el 30 de noviembre de 1959. La Paz, 1959. pp. 58.

BEDREGAL (GUILLERMO) Recuperación de la mineria nacionalizada: un plan revolucionario, un drama de producción; (exposición del Presidente de la Corporación Minera de Bolivia...ante la Honorable Cámara de Diputados en fecha 17 de agosto de 1961). La Paz, Departamento de Relaciones Publicas de la Corporacion Minera de Bolivia, [1961]. pp. 39.

- Brazil

BRAZIL. Superintendencia do Plano de Valorização Economica da Amazonia. Comissão de Planejamento. Sub-Comissão de Recursos Naturais. 1959. Notas sobre os depositos de evaporitos da Bacia Amazon Amazonica, minerio de bauxita fosforosa do Maranhão e reconhecimentos geologicos em areas do estado do Amazonas e territorios de Rio Branco e Rondonia; etc. Belem, 1959. 2 vols. (Serie Recursos Naturais.5)

MINES AND MINERAL RESOURCES - Brazil (Cont'd.)

BRAZIL. Departamento Nacional da Produçao Mineral. 1967. Plano mestre decenal para avaliação de recursos minerais do Brasil, 1965-1974. 3rd ed. [Rio de] Janeiro, 1967. pp. 124. 32cm. (Publicaçãoes Especiales. No.3)

ANTONIL (ANDRÉ JOÃO) pseud. [i.e. João Antonio ANDREONI] Cultura e opulencia do Brasil por suas drogas e minas; texte de l'édition de 1711; traduction française et commentaire critique par Andrée Mansuy. Paris, [Université], Institut des Hautes Études de l'Amérique Latine, [1968]. pp. 627. bibliog. 24cm. (Travaux et Memoires. 21)

- Canada

ATLANTIC DEVELOPMENT BOARD. Background Studies. No. 4. Mineral resources in the Atlantic Provinces. Ottawa, Q.P., 1969. pp. xiv, 94. 27½cm.

CANADA. Mineral Resources Division. Mineral Information Bulletins. 100. Mineral resource development in the Atlantic Provinces. Ottawa, 1969. pp. 117.

STEWART (KEITH J.) The Atlantic Provinces: a chronicle of mineral development. Ottawa, 1969. pp. vii, 41. 24½cm. (Canada. Mineral Resources Division. Mineral Information Bulletins. 96.)

BUCK (W. KEITH) Factors influencing the mineral economy of Canada: past, present and future. Ottawa, 1970. pp. 21. (Canada. Mineral Resources Division. Mineral Information Bulletins. 106)

- Canada - Manitoba

MANITOBA. Department of Mines and Natural Resources. Mines Branch. 1962. Geology and mineral resources of Manitoba; by J.F. Davies [and others]. Winnipeg, 1962. pp. 190. bibliogs.

- Canada - New Brunswick

NEW BRUNSWICK. Commissioner of Mines. 1960. Final report of the Commissioner of Mines in New Brunswick. Fredericton, 1960. fo. 23.

- Canada - Northwest Territories

CANADA. Department of Indian Affairs and Northern Development. Northern Economic Development Branch. Mines and minerals north of 60: mining activity in the Yukon and the Northwest Territories. a., 1970 [1st?]- Ottawa.

- Canada - Ontario

HEWITT (D.F.) Pegmatite mineral resources of Ontario. Toronto, 1967. pp. vi, 83. bibliog. 28cm. (Ontario. Department of Mines. Industrial Mineral Reports. No. 21)

HEWITT (D.F.) Phosphate in Ontario. Toronto, 1967. pp. vi, 63. bibliog. 27½cm. (Ontario. Department of Mines. Mineral Resources Circulars. No. 6.)

HEWITT (D.F.) Pyrite deposits of Ontario. Toronto, 1967. pp. vii, 64. bibliog. 27½cm. (Ontario. Department of Mines. Mineral Resources Circulars. No. 5.)

HEWITT (D.F.) Uranium and thorium deposits of Southern Ontario. Toronto, 1967. pp. vii, 76. bibliog. 27½cm. (Ontario. Department of Mines. Mineral Resources Circulars. No. 4.)

ANNUAL STATISTICAL REPORT OF THE MINERAL PRODUCTION OF ONTARIO; [pd. by] Ontario Department of Mines. a., 1968 (v.1)- Toronto.

HEWITT (D.F.) Phlogopite mica in Ontario. Toronto, 1968. pp. viii, 85. bibliog. 27½cm. (Ontario. Department of Mines. Mineral Resources Circulars. No. 8.)

JOHNSTON (F. J.) Molybdenum deposits of Ontario. Toronto, 1968. pp. vii, 98. bibliog. 28cm. (Ontario. Department of Mines. Mineral Resources Circulars. No. 7.)

COPPER, nickel, lead and zinc deposits of Ontario; edited by Roman Shklanka. [rev. ed.] Toronto, 1969. pp. 394. (Ontario. Department of Mines. Mineral Resources Circulars. No. 12.)

- Canada - Ontario - Bibliography

ONTARIO. Department of Mines. Bulletins. No. 25. List of publications: vol. 1, 1891-1965. [With supplements, 1966 and 1967.] 11th ed. Toronto, 1966. pp. viii, 112. 26cm. 6 maps, 4 supplements in end pocket.

- Canada - Yukon Territory

CANADA. Department of the Interior. Mining Lands and Yukon Branch. 1916. The Yukon Territory: its history and resources; issued by direction of W.J. Roche, Minister of the Interior. Ottawa, 1916. pp. 233.

- Canada - Yukon

CANADA. Department of Indian Affairs and Northern Development. Northern Economic Developemant Branch. Mines and minerals north of 60: mining activity in the Yukon and the Northwest Territories. a., 1970 [1st?]- Ottawa.

- Communist countries

EROFEEV (BORIS NIKONOVICH) and GOLOV (ALEKSEI EGOROVICH) Geologicheskoe stroenie i poleznye iskopaemye stran-chlenov SEV: kratkii ocherk. Moskva, 1968. pp. 56. bibliog.

- Europe

JACKSON (R.T.) Mining settlements in western Europe: the landscape and the community. in Beckinsale (Robert P.) M.A. and Houston (James M.) eds. Urbanization and its problems. Oxford, 1968.

- France

GARIN (HENRI) Les mines. Paris, 1969. pp. 125. bibliog.

- Germany

HEMPEL (GUSTAV) Die deutsche Montanindustrie: ihre Entwicklung und Gestaltung. Essen, [1969]. pp. 231. bibliog.

- India

STATISTICS OF MINES IN INDIA (formerly Indian coal statistics); ([published by Department of Labour and Employment [India]). Calcutta, annual, 1907, 1909-1920, 1939, 1945-1948, 1951 to date. 20-33cm.

- Indo-China

> FRANCE. Commissariat Général du Plan de Modernisation et d'Equipement. Commission de Modernisation des Territoires d'Outre-Mer. Sous-Commission Indochine. 1948. Rapport général de la Section Mines. Saigon, 1948. pp. 29. (Indo-China. Affaires Statistiques. Bulletin économique de l'Indochine. Suppléments. No. 15)

- Iran

> IRAN. Bureau of Statistics. 1966. Time series of mining statistics in Iran. [Tehran], 1966. pp. 40. 27½cm.

- Israel

> SOME aspects of Israel; [reports of three lectures and two essays, 1960-61]; (by Solomon Gaon) [and others]. London, [1963]. pp. 54.

- Korea

> KOREA (REPUBLIC). Economic Planning Board. 1967. Report on mining and manufacturing census, [19]66. [Seoul, 1967]. 3 vols. 26cm. In English and Korean.

- Liberia

> LIBERIA. Information Service. 1958. Liberia's mineral resources. [London, 1958]. pp.(3)

- Madagascar

> UNITED STATES. Mines Bureau. Information Circulars. 8196. Mineral resources of the Malagasy Republic. Washington, 1963. pp. vi, 147. Bibliog.

- Mexico

> MEXICO. Consejo de Recursos Naturales no Renovables. Departamento de Estudios Economicos. 1969. Los recursos minerales de Mexico. Mexico, 1969. 2 vols. (in 1). bibliog.

- New Zealand

> COMMERCIAL BANK OF AUSTRALIA. New Zealand and its mineral resources. Melbourne, 1968. pp. (v), 68. 28cm.

- Rhodesia

> SOUTHERN RHODESIA. 1962. A handbook of useful information regarding base minerals; by R.B. Anderson. (Mines Department Bulletins. No. 6) 2nd ed. Salisbury, 1962. pp. xv, 197.

- Russia

> KUROCHKIN (GRIGORII DANILOVICH) Issledovaniia mineral'nykh resursov ekspeditsiiami Akademii nauk SSSR, 1919-1959 gg. Moskva, 1969. pp. 245.

> LOGINOV (VIKTOR PETROVICH) Ekonomicheskie problemy tekhnicheskogo progressa v dobyche mineral'nogo syr'ia. Moskva, 1971. pp. 223. bibliog.

- Russia - Siberia

> ZYKIN (B. N.) Районные различия в производительности труда: на примере отраслей добывающей промышленности Сибири. Москва, Наука, 1965. pp. 183. 19½см.

- Siam

> SIAM. 1964. Minerals of Thailand. (Ministry of Economic Affairs). [Bangkok, 1964]. pp. 16. 19cm.

- Somaliland

> PALLISTER (JOHN WEAVER) Mineral resources of Somaliland Protectorate. London, 1959. pp. 154-165. bibliog. (Somaliland Protectorate. Geological Survey. Mineral Resources Pamphlets. No.2) Reprinted from Overseas Geology and Mineral Resources, vol.7, no.2.

> DANIELS (J. L.) Minerals and rocks of Hargeisa and Borama districts. Hargeisa, 1960. pp. 25. (Somali Republic (Northern Region). Ministry of Natural Resources. Mineral Resources Pamphlets. No.3)

- South Africa

> SOUTH AFRICA. Department of Mines. Mining statistics. in SOUTH AFRICA. Parliament. House of Assembly. Votes and proceedings; (with Printed annexures).

- Tanzania - Bibliography

> UNITED REPUBLIC OF TANZANIA. Mineral Resources Division. Library. Bibliography of the geology and mineral resources of Tanzania, to December, 1967; (guide to basic data on resource assessment and land use planning. Dodoma, 1969. pp. 249. (Dar Es Salaam. University College. Bureau of Resource Assessment and Land Use Planning. Research Notes. No. 5c)

- Uganda

> UGANDA. Geological Survey and Mines Department. Annual report. a., 1969- [Entebbe]

- United Kingdom

> THOMAS (CHARLES) Mining Agent. Mining fields of the West: being a practical exposition of the principal mines and mining districts in Cornwall and Devon; [reprint of the edition first published in 1871]. Truro, Bradford Barton, [1967]. pp.100. 19½cm.

- United Kingdom - Government ownership

> INSTITUTE FOR WORKERS' CONTROL. Archives in Trade Union History and Theory. Series 1. No. 5. Nationalisation of the mines; by Frank Hodges [and others]; [works originally published in 1919 and 1920]. Nottingham, [1968?]. pp. various.

> SLESSER (Sir HENRY HERMAN) A bill to nationalise the mines and minerals of the United Kingdom and to provide for the national winning, distribution and sale of coal and other minerals. London, [1919]. pp. 10.

- United Kingdom - Cornwall

> WATSON (JOSEPH YELLOLY) A compendium of British mining, with statistical notices of the principal mines in Cornwall, to which is added, the history and uses of metals, and a glossary of the terms and usages of mining. London, 1843; [Truro, 1962]. pp. 84. Facsimile reprint.

> PAYNTER (WILLIAM HENRY) Our old Cornish mines: East Cornwall. Liskeard, [imprint], [1964]. 1 pamphlet (unpaged).

MINES AND MINERAL RESOURCES - United Kingdom - Cornwall (Cont'd.)

BARTON (DENYS BRADFORD) ed. Historic Cornish mining scenes underground. Truro, Truro Bookshop, 1967. pp. 56. 19½cm.

BURT (ROGER) ed. Cornish mining: essays on the organisation of Cornish mines and the Cornish mining economy. Newton Abbot, [1969]. pp. 210.

- United Kingdom - Scotland

U.K. Institute of Geological Sciences. 1969. A summary of the mineral resources of the "crofter counties" of Scotland, comprising Argyllshire, Caithness, Inverness-shire, Orkney and Shetland, Ross and Cromarty, and Sutherland; compiled by N.G. Berridge. London, 1969. pp. 36. bibliog. (Reports. No. 69/5)

- United States

SMITH (DUANE A.) Rocky Mountain mining camps: the urban frontier. Bloomington, Indiana U.P., [1967]. pp. xii, 304. bibliog. 21cm.

- United States - Kentucky

KENTUCKY. 1926. Resumé of Kentucky's mineral resources; by Willard Rouse Jillson. (Geological Survey. Geologic Reports. Series 6. No. 7) Frankfort, 1926. pp. 11. 22½cm.

- United States - Nevada

UNITED STATES. 12622/87. Mineral and water resources of Nevada. Washington, 1964. pp. xi, 314. bibliogs.

- Uzbekistan

MINERAL'NAIA... Минеральная сырьевая база строительных материалов УзССР. Ташкент, 1967. pp. 599.

- White Russia

RAZVITIE mineral'no-syr'evoi bazy Belorusskoi SSR. Minsk, 1971. pp. 88. bibliog.

- Zambia

CIKIN (M.) A preliminary report on the geology and ore reserves of the Hippo Mine, Kafue National Park. [Lusaka], 1968. pp. 34. bibliog. (Zambia. Geological Survey Department. Economic Reports. No. 19.) 3 maps in end pocket.

MINING CORPORATIONS

- Canada

HUNT (ELDON L.) Corporate disclosure requirements as they pertain to mining companies. Ottawa, 1970. pp. 113. (Canada. Mineral Resources Division. Mineral Information Bulletins. 110)

- Canada - Ontario

ONTARIO. Royal Commission to Investigate Trading in the Shares of Windfall Oils and Mines Ltd, 1964. Report of the Royal Commission to Investigate Trading in the Shares of Windfall Oils and Mines Ltd. [Toronto], 1965. pp. xviii, 177.

MINING ENGINEERING

ORDISH (HENRY GEOFFREY) Cornish engine-houses: a pictorial survey. Truro, Bradford Barton, 1967. pp. 71. 20cm.

ORDISH (HENRY GEOFFREY) Cornish engine-houses: a second pictorial survey. Truro, Bradford Barton, 1968. pp. 64. 20½cm.

GARIN (HENRI) Les mines. Paris, 1969. pp. 125. bibliog.

SPENCE (CLARK C.) Mining engineers and the American West: the lace-boot brigade, 1849-1933. New Haven, 1970. pp. 407. bibliog.

MINING INDUSTRY AND FINANCE

MINING: annual review. a., 1947/8- , with gap (1954/5). London. File includes w. Mining jl., 1921-1963 (v. 134-261), with gap (1958, no.6389).

NORÉN (NILS-ERIK) Long-range decision models in mining. Stockholm, EFI, 1969. pp. 351. bibliog. 24cm.

- America, Latin

MONCHABLON (ALBERTO) and others. Estudio comparativo de la acción estatal de fomento minero en Chile, Peru, Bolivia: sugerencias aplicables a la Republica Argentina. Buenos Aires, 1959. pp. 98.

MIKESELL (RAYMOND FRECH) and others. Foreign investment in the petroleum and mineral industries: case studies of investor-host country relations;... [sponsored by] Resources for the future, Inc. Baltimore, [1971]. pp. 459. bibliog.

- Bolivia

CANELAS O. (AMADO) Mito y realidad de la Corporación Minera de Bolivia, COMIBOL. La Paz, Los Amigos del Libro, 1966. pp. 299. 21cm. (Colección Mito y Realidad. Bolivia, Hoy y Mañana)

- Canada

MAIDORN (WERNER) Kleinstaktien als Finanzierungsinstrument kanadischer Bergbauerschliessungsgesellschaften. [Nuremberg?, 1965]. pp. 343. bibliog. 21cm.

LIVERMORE (ROBERT) Bostonians and bullion: the journal of Robert Livermore, 1892-1915; edited by Gene M. Gressley. Lincoln, U. of Nebraska P., [1968]. pp. xxix, 193. 23cm.

QUIRIN (G. DAVID) Economic consequences on the primary mineral industries of the adoption of the recommendations of the Royal Commission on Taxation. Toronto, 1968. pp. 19. (Toronto. University. Institute for the Quantitative Analysis of Social and Economic Policy. Working Paper Series. No. 6804)

DAWSON (JOHN) of the Economic Council of Canada. Productivity change in Canadian mining industries. Ottawa, 1971. pp. 53. (Canada. Economic Council. Staff Studies. No. 30)

- Canada - Ontario

ONTARIO. Royal Commission to Investigate Trading in the Shares of Windfall Oils and Mines Ltd, 1964. Report of the Royal Commission to Investigate Trading in the Shares of Windfall Oils and Mines Ltd. [Toronto], 1965. pp. xviii, 177.

- European Economic Community countries

EUROPEAN COAL AND STEEL COMMUNITY. Direction Générale Administration et Finances. Division Etudes et Analysis. 1967. Bilanzen der Bergbauunternehmen der Gemeinschaft: Balance sheets of the coalmining companies of the Community, 1960-1965. [Luxembourg, 1967] fo. 113. In various languages.

EUROPEAN COAL AND STEEL COMMUNITY. Direction Générale Administration et Finances. Division Etudes et Analysis. 1967. Bilanzen der Bergbauunternehmen der Gemeinsbhaft; Balance sheets of the coalmining companies of the Community, 1966. [Luxembourg, 1967]. fo. 34. In various languages.

- France

MESTRALLET (MICHELE) Les étrangers et les mines savoyards au 18e siècle: la Compagnie Anglaise, 1740-1771. Chambéry, Société Savoisienne d'Histoire et d'Archéologie, 1965. pp. 64. bibliog. 23cm. (Mémoires et Documents. Tome 80)

- Germany

MAEMPEL (ARTHUR) Bergbau in Dortmund: von Pingen und Stollen bis zu den Anfängen des Tiefbaus. Dortmund, [1963]. pp. 143.

MAEMPEL (ARTHUR) Bergbau in Dortmund: die sechziger und siebziger Jahre bis zum Ende ihrer Hochkonjunktur um 1876. Dortmund, [1965]. pp. 141.

GROSS (HANS JUERGEN) Die Clausthaler Bergbaukasse: Geschichte, Bedeutung und Rechtsnatur. Göttingen, 1967. pp. 150. bibliog.

- Germany - North Rhine - Westphalia

NORTH RHINE-WESTPHALIA. 1967. Die Kapitalverflechtung der Montanindustrie in Nordrhein-Westfalen mit dem Ausland. (Forschungsberichte des Landes Nordrhein-Westfalen. Nr. 1681) Köln, Westdeutscher Verlag, 1967. pp. 225. 24cm.

- Germany - Prussia

LINDOW (CONRAD) Die Bedeutung der gewerblichen Sozialpolitik in der brandenburg-preussischen Merkantilzeit, insbesondere auf dem Gebiete des Bergbaues und der Eisen-Industrie. Giessen, 1928. pp. 115. bibliog.

- Germany, Eastern

HERTIG (WOLFRAM) Entwicklung der Selbstkosten für die Gewinnung von Rohbraunkohle in den Tagebauen des Industriezweiges Braunkohlenbergbau der DDR von 1957 bis 1961, etc. Leipzig, VEB Deutscher Verlag für Grundstoffindustrie, 1966. pp. 104. bibliog. 24cm. (Freiberg. Bergakademie. Freiberger Forschungshefte. A 359)

- Iran

IRAN. 1965. Summary results of mining survey, 1962-1963. (General Department of Industrial and Mining Statistics) Tehran, [1965?]. pp. 20. 27½cm.

- Korea

KOREA DEVELOPMENT BANK. Research Department. Report on sample survey for mining and manufacturing establishments;..'64. Seoul, [1965]. pp. 147. 26cm. In English and Korean.

- Poland - Silesia

POPIOŁEK (KAZIMIERZ) Górnośląski przemysł górniczo-hutniczy w drugiej połowie XIX wieku. Kraków, PWN, 1965. pp. 245. bibliog. 23cm. With German, English and Russian summaries.

BIAŁY (FRANCISZEK) Górnośląski związek przemysłowców górniczo-hutniczych, 1914-1932. Wrocław, Ossolineum, 1967. pp. 225. bibliog. 24cm. With French summary.

ZALESKI (WOJCIECH) Dzieje górnictwa i hutnictwa na Górnym Śląsku do roku 1806. Madryt, Nakładem Antoniny Zaleskiej, 1967. pp. 445. bibliog. 22½cm. (Towarzystwo Imienia Romana Dmowskiego. Wydawnictwa. nr.5)

- Russia

BAKANOV (GRIGORII EVSTIGNEEVICH) Развитие горнорудной промышленности СССР. Томск, Университет, 1961. pp. 22. bibliog. 19½cm.

BARSUKOV (FEDOR ALEKSANDROVICH) and RACHKOVSKII (SOLOMON IAKOVLEVICH) Ekonomicheskaia effektivnost' kapital'nykh vlozhenii v zhelezorudnuiu promyshlennost'. Moskva, 1964. pp. 112. bibliog.

EGURNOV (GRIGORII PAVLOVICH) Ekonomika gornoi promyshlennosti. Moskva, 1966. pp. 223. bibliog.

SOBOLEVSKII (TRIFON FEDOROVICH) Sebestoimost' i pribyl' v gornorudnoi promyshlennosti. Moskva, 1967. pp. 149.

FEITEL'MAN (NINA GERMANOVNA) Экономическая эффективность затрат на подготовку минерально-сырьевой базы СССР. Москва. 1969. pp. 255. bibliog.

EKONOMICHESKAIA reforma i sistema finansovykh otnoshenii v ugol'noi promyshlennosti. Kiev, 1970. pp. 324. bibliog.

- South Africa

FRANKEL (SALLY HERBERT) Investment and the return to equity capital in the South African gold mining industry 1887-1965: an international comparison. Oxford, 1967. pp. x, 131.

- United Kingdom

BURT (ROGER) ed. Cornish mining: essays on the organisation of Cornish mines and the Cornish mining economy. Newton Abbot, [1969]. pp. 210.

MINING INDUSTRY AND FINANCE (Cont'd.)

- United States

LIVERMORE (ROBERT) Bostonians and bullion: the journal of Robert Livermore, 1892-1915; edited by Gene M. Gressley. Lincoln, U. of Nebraska P., [1968]. pp. xxix, 193. 23cm.

- Zambia

NORTHERN RHODESIA. Commission appointed to Inquire into the Mining Industry in Northern Rhodesia. 1962. Report: [Sir Ronald Morison, chairman]. Lusaka, 1962. pp. 60.

MINING LAW

KRAHMANN (MAX) Die Aufgaben der Bergwirtscaft im Rechts- und Kulturstaat;...1. Haupttex;... mit französischem und englischem Resümee und Epilog. Berlin, 1908. pp. 43.

- America, Latin

RAMOS PEREZ (DEMETRIO) Mineria y comercio interprovincial en Hispanoamerica: siglos XVI, XVII y XVIII. Valladolid, 1970. pp. 334. (Valladolid. Universidad. Facultad de Filosofia y Letras. Departamento de Historia Moderna. Estudios y Documentos. No. 31)

- Bolivia

HUET JORDAN (ROGER) and MIRANDA HELGUERO (HUGO) Legislacion minera de Bolivia: el codigo de mineria y las disposiciones legales vigentes, con una guia del derecho minero y un indice cronologico; con la colaboracion del abogado Pedro Valdivia Saa. [La Paz, 1969]. pp. 279.

- Brazil

BRAZIL. Statutes, etc, 1967. Código de mineração. Rio de Janeiro, 1966 [or rather 1967]. pp. 58. (Brazil. Divisão de Fomento da Produção Mineral. Avulsos. 93)

BRAZIL. Statutes, etc. 1967-1968. Código de mineração e legislação correlativa. Rio de Janeiro, 1968 in progress. 23cm. (Brazil. Departamento Nacional da Produção Mineral. Publicações Especiais. No. 6)

- Canada

CANADA. Mineral Resources Division. Mineral Information Bulletins. 73. Summary review of federal taxation and legislation affecting the Canadian mineral industry...; compiled by E.C. Hodgson and W.J. Beard. rev. ed. Ottawa, [1964]. pp. 27.

HODGSON (E.C.) compiler. Digest of mineral laws of Canada. [6th ed.] Ottawa, 1967. pp. 173. (Canada. Mineral Resources Division. Mineral Reports. 13)

- Germany

LEHMANN (WOLFGANG) 1932- . Die zwangsweise Nutzung und die Entziehung von Bergbauberechtigungen in ihrem Verhältnis zum Grundgesetz. Bonn, 1962. pp. 168. bibliog.

GROSS (HANS JUERGEN) Die Clausthaler Bergbaukasse: Geschichte, Bedeutung und Rechtsnatur. Göttingen, 1967. pp. 150. bibliog.

- Jamaica

JAMAICA. Industrial Development Corporation. Information Pamphlets. No.11. Legislation affecting the mining of minerals. Kingston, 1961. fo. 2. 28cm.

- Nigeria

NIGERIA (NORTHERN REGION). Ministry of Town and Country Planning. 1967. A handbook of the Ministry of Town and Country Planning on: A. Land. B. Mining titles. C. Administrative boundaries. Kaduna, [1967?]. pp. 205. Loose-leaf binder.

- Russia

LAPAI (ALEKSANDR PETROVICH) Trudovye prava shakhterov. Moskva, 1965. pp. 90.

SYRODOEV (NIKOLAI ALEKSEEVICH) Pravovoi rezhim nedr. Moskva, 1969. pp. 168.

- South Africa

SOUTH AFRICA. 1966. Report of the Commission of Enquiry regarding the Mining Rights Bill; [Petrus Cornelius Pelser, chairman] (R.P.37). in South Africa. Parliament. House of Assembly. Votes and proceedings; ([with] Printed annexures).

- South Africa - Transvaal

TRANSVAAL. Bewaarplaatsen Commissie. Report. Pretoria, 1910. pp. 19.

- United Kingdom

MINING ASSOCIATION OF GREAT BRITAIN. Compensation for Subsidence Bill: (notes on amendments). London, 1919. fo. 62.

MINING MACHINERY

CANADA. Tariff Board. 1963. Report...relative to the inquiry ordered by the Minister of Finance respecting machinery and equipment used in the mining industry and in the oil and gas industries. Ottawa, [1963]. 2 vols.

U.K. Department of Trade and Industry. Business monitor: Production series. P. 129. Mining machinery. q., 1971- London.

MINISTERIAL RESPONSIBILITY

- France

DESMOTTES (PIERRE) De la responsabilité pénale des ministres en régime parlementaire français. Paris, Pichon et Durand-Auzias, 1968. pp. 317. bibliog. 25cm. (Bibliothèque Constitutionnelle et de Science Politique. tome 23)

- United Kingdom

AKPAN (PIUS CUDJOE) Ministerial responsibility; [essay for the Diploma in Public Administration, London University]. 1971. fo. 26. Typescript: unpublished. This essay is the property of London University and may not be removed from the Library.

MINNEAPOLIS
See also TWIN CITIES METROPOLITAN AREA

MINNEAPOLIS

- Industries

ZWERMAN (WILLIAM L.) New perspectives on organization theory: an empirical reconsideration of the marxian and classical analyses. Westport, Conn., [1970]. pp. 219. bibliog.

MINNESOTA

- Emigration and immigration

LJUNGMARK (LARS) For sale, Minnesota: organized promotion of Scandinavian immigration, 1866-1873. [Gothenburg, 1971]. pp. 304. bibliog. (Göteborgs Universitet. Studia Historica Gothoburgensia. 13)

- History

HAGE (GEORGE S.) Newspapers on the Minnesota frontier, 1849-1860. [St. Paul], Minnesota Historical Society, 1967. pp. xiii, 176. 23cm.

- Politics and government

LEBEDOFF (DAVID) The 21st ballot: a political party struggle in Minnesota. Minneapolis, [1969]. pp. 218.

MITAU (G. THEODORE) Politics in Minnesota. 2nd ed. Minneapolis, [1970]. pp. 176. bibliog.

- Population

RIKKINEN (KALEVI) The net-migration of young people in Minnesota, 1950-1960. Helsinki, 1969. pp. 23. bibliog. (Academia Scientiarum Fennica. Annales. Ser. A. 3. Geologica-Geographica. 101)

- Race question

MINNESOTA. 1945. The Negro worker in Minnesota: a report...by the Governor's Interracial Commission. [St. Paul], 1945. pp. (ii), 57. 20cm.

MINNESOTA. 1948. The Mexican in Minnesota: a report...by the Governor's Interracial Commission. [St.Paul], 1948. pp. 64. 20cm. For revised edition see MINNESOTA. 1953.

MINNESOTA. 1949. The Oriental in Minnesota: a report...by the Governor's Interracial Commission. [St.Paul], 1949. pp. 63. 20cm.

MINNESOTA. 1952. The Indian in Minnesota, revised: a report...by the Governor's Interracial Commission. [St.Paul], 1952. pp. 79. 20cm.

MINNESOTA. 1953. The Mexican in Minnesota, revised: a report...by the Governor's Interracial Commission. [St.Paul], 1953. pp. 84. 20cm. For first edition see MINNESOTA. 1948.

MINNESOTA UNIVERSITY

NELSON (ROBERTA J.) ed. The ten-year story of IRC. Minneapolis, the Center, [1955]. pp. iii, 40. 23cm. (Minnesota University. Industrial Relations Center. Bulletins. 15)

MINORITIES

GUTTMANN (VIKTOR) Minderheitenpolitik und Minderheitenrecht: eine rechtssoziologische Untersuchung. Budapest, 1931. pp. 23. (Pécs. Tudományegyetem. Nemzetközi Jogi Intezet. Kiadványok. 16)

RABL (KURT O.) Das Selbstbestimmungsrecht der Völker: geschichtliche Grundlagen; Umriss der gegenwärtigen Bedeutung; ein Versuch, etc. München, [1963]. pp. 276. bibliog. With English summary.

PIZZORUSSO (ALESSANDRO) Le minoranze nel diritto pubblico interno, con un'appendice sulla condizione giuridica della minoranza tirolese nell'ordinamento italiano. Milano, Giuffrè, 1967. 2 vols. (in 1). bibliog. 25cm. (Pisa. Università. Facoltà di Giurisprudenza. Pubblicazioni. 19)

RIEDL (FRANZ HIERONYMUS) ed. Humanitas ethnica: Menschenwürde, Recht und Gemeinschaft: Festschrift für Theodor Veiter...dargeboten zum 60. Lebensjahr. Wien, [1967]. pp. 427. bibliog. (Forschungsstelle für Nationalitäten- und Sprachenfragen. Ethnos. Band 5)

GADGIL (DHANANJAYA RAMCHANDRA) Human rights in a multi-national society. Poona, Gokhale Institute of Politics and Economics, 1968. pp. viii, 28. 24½cm. (Gokhale Institute Studies. No. 53)

LEONHARDT (RUDOLF WALTER) Wer wirft den ersten Stein?: Minoritäten in einer züchtigen Gesellschaft. München, [1969]. pp. 435. bibliog.

TOBIAS (HENRY J.) and WOODHOUSE (CHARLES E.) eds. Minorities and politics. Albuquerque, [1969]. pp. 131.

YETMAN (NORMAN R.) and STEELE (C. HOY) eds. Majority and minority: the dynamics of racial and ethnic relations; [readings]. Boston, [1971]. pp. 621. bibliogs.

- Africa, Central

GHAI (YASH P.) and GHAI (DHARAM P.) The Asian minorities of East and central Africa. London, [1971]. pp. 39. (Minority Rights Group. Reports. No.4)

- Africa, East

GHAI (YASH P.) and GHAI (DHARAM P.) The Asian minorities of East and central Africa. London, [1971]. pp. 39. (Minority Rights Group. Reports. No.4)

- Algeria

ÉTIENNE (BRUNO) Les problèmes juridiques des minorités européennes au Maghreb. Paris, Centre National de la Recherche Scientifique, 1968. pp. 414. bibliog. 24cm. (Université d'Aix-Marseille. Faculté de Droit et des Sciences Économiques d'Aix. Centre de Recherches sur l'Afrique Méditerranéenne. Section Moderne et Contemporaine. Publications)

- Austria

VEITER (THEODOR) Das Recht der Volksgruppen und Sprachminderheiten in Österreich; mit einer ethnosoziologischen Grundlegung und einem Anhang (Materialien). Wien, 1970. pp. 890. bibliog.

MINORITIES (Cont'd.)

- Belgium

WILMARS (DIRK) Le problème belge: la minorité francophone en Flandre;... traduit du néerlandais et adapté par Edmond Knaeps. [Antwerp], Erasme, 1968. pp. 212. 18½cm.

- Bulgaria

RAZBOINIKOV (ANASTAS SP.) Народностният образ на Източния дел от Западна Тракия. София, 1944. pp. 128. Revised version of author's article in Известия на Българското Географско Дружество, 10, 1942.

- China

MOSELEY (GEORGE) A Sino-Soviet cultural frontier: the Ili Kazakh autonomous Chou. Cambridge, Harvard U.P., 1966. pp. viii, 163. 25½cm. (Harvard University. East Asian Research Center. Harvard East Monographs. 22)

- Europe

FRAGEN des mitteleuropäischen Minderheitenrechts; mit Beiträgen von Georg Geilke [and others] Herrenalb, 1967. pp. 340. bibliogs. (Munich. Institut für Ostrecht. Studien. Band 18)

ABO.Akademi. Acta Academiae Aboensis. Humaniora. 37. 1. The international protection of national minorities in Europe; by Tore Modeen. Abo, 1969. pp. 182.

- Germany

DOERDELMANN (BERNHARD) ed. Minderheiten in der Bundesrepublik. München, [1969]. pp. 254.

WEHLER (HANS-ULRICH) Sozialdemokratie und Nationalstaat : Nationalitätenfragen in Deutschland, 1840-1914. 2nd ed. Gottingen, [1971]. pp. 289. bibliog.

- Germany - Prussia

HUBATSCH (WALTHER) Masuren und Preussisch-Litthauen in der Nationalitätenpolitik Preussens, 1870-1920. Marburg, Elwert, 1966. pp. 91.

- Germany, Eastern

ZWAHR (HARTMUT) ed. Sorbische Volksbewegung: Dokumente zur antisorbischen Staatspolitik im preussisch-deutschen Reich...1872-1918: Quellenauswahl. Bautzen, [1968]. pp. 295. bibliog.

- Hungary

ORENDI-HOMMENAU (VIKTOR) Madjarisches, Allzumadjarisches: ein kleiner Beitrag zur Minderheitenfrage in Ungarn. Bukarest, 1940; München, 1968. pp. 18. Facsimile reprint.

SIMA (HORIA) Die rumänisch-ungarischen Beziehungen: Rede gehalten am 9 Oktober 1940, zu Brasov (Kronstadt). Bukarest, 1940; München, [1968?]. pp. 21. Facsimile reprint.

PACLIŞANU (ZENOVIE) Der Ausrottungskampf Ungarns gegen seine nationalen Minderheiten; nach magyarischen Geheimdokumenten. 2nd ed. Bukarest, 1941; [München, 1968]. pp. 200. Facsimile reprint.

PACLIŞANU (ZENOVIE) Was heisst ungarische Nationalität? Wie man Ungar werden konnte. Bukarest, 1941; München, 1968. pp. 13. Facsimile reprint.

- India

GHURYE (GOVIND SADASHIV) Social tensions in India. Bombay, 1968. pp. 552.

KABIR (HUMAYUN) Minorities in a democracy; [lectures delivered 1959-1968]. Calcutta, 1968. pp. 94.

- Iraq

MENTESHASHVILI (AL'BERT MIKHAILOVICH) Ирак в годы английского мандата. Москва, 1969. pp. 288. bibliog. With English summary.

- Italy

ITALY. Presidenza del Consiglio dei Ministri. 1960. The De Gasperi-Gruber Agreement on the Alto Adige, from the historical and political background to the implementation of the Agreement within the Italian constitutional system. Rome, 1960. 24½cm. pp. 211.

RUSINOW (DENNISON I.) Italy's Austrian heritage, 1919-1946. Oxford, 1969. pp. 423. bibliog.

ALCOCK (ANTONY EVELYN) The history of the South Tyrol question. London, 1970. pp. 535. bibliog.

WIDMOSER (EDUARD) Autonomie für Südtirol: der lange Weg. Innsbruck, [1970]. pp. 43.

- Nigeria

PROBLEMS of Nigerian minorities; being independent commentary on the proceedings of Sir Henry Willink Commission of Inquiry into the fears of Nigerian minorities and on the general set up of Nigerian politics. [Lagos, 196-?]. pp. 34.

BUHLER (JEAN) Tuez-les tous!: guerre de sécession au Biafra. Paris, Flammarion, [1968]. pp. 235. bibliog. 20cm.

- Poland

LOVELL (JERZY) Polska, jakiej nie znamy: zbiór reportaży o mniejszościach narodowych. Kraków, 1970. pp. 174.

- Roumania

FRUNZA (ION) Bessarabien: rumänische Rechte und Leistungen. Bukarest, 1941; München, 1968. pp. 88. Facsimile reprint.

MEHEDINŢI (S.) Was ist Siebenbürgen? Bukarest, 1941; München, 1968. pp. 104. Facsimile reprint.

- Russia

PRELOOKER (JAAKOFF) From holy orthodox Russia: a Stundist appeal to Christian Britain. Edinburgh, [189-?]. pp. 7.

SVERDLIN (MATVEI ABRAMOVICH) and ROGACHEV (PETR MIKHAILOVICH) Kommunizm i natsii. Elista, 1964. pp. 96. bibliog.

ANISIMOVA (TAT'IANA BORISOVNA) Gosudarstvenno-pravovye formy natsional'nykh otnoshenii v SSSR. Moskva, 1966. pp. 63.

GOLDHAGEN (ERICH) ed. Ethnic minorities in the Soviet Union. New York, Praeger, 1968. pp. xiv, 351. 21cm.

MAKAROVA (GALINA PETROVNA) Осуществление ленинской национальной политики в первые годы Советской власти, 1917-1920 гг. Москва, 1969. pp. 268.

BOURDEAUX (MICHAEL) and others. Religious minorities in the Soviet Union, 1960-70. London, 1970. pp. 38. bibliog. (Minority Rights Group. Reports. No. 1)

CONQUEST (ROBERT) The nation killers: the Soviet deportation of nationalities; (based in the main on the author's study, The Soviet deportation of nationalities). London, 1970. pp. 222.

TADEVOSIAN (EDUARD VRAMOVICH) V. I. Lenin o gosudarstvennykh formakh resheniia natsional'nogo voprosa v SSSR. Moskva, 1970. pp. 210.

ZAKHAROV (IVAN ZAKHAROVICH) Druzhba, zakalennaia v boiakh. Moskva, 1970. pp. 277.

- Siam

UNITED STATES. Army Department. Pamphlets. No. 550-107. Ethnographic Study Series. Minority groups in Thailand. Washington, 1970. pp. 1134. bibliogs.

- South Africa

RANDALL (PETER) ed. South Africa's minorities. Johannesburg, 1971. pp. 77. bibliog. (South African Council of Churches, and Christian Institute of Southern Africa. Study Project on Christianity in Apartheid Society. Occasional Publications. No. 2)

- Sweden

SCHWARZ (DAVID) ed. Svenska minoriteter: en handbok som kartlägger invandringspolitiken och befolknings-minoriteternas ställning inom det svenska samhället. Stockholm, Aldus, 1966. pp. 299. bibliog. 18 cm. (Aldusböckerna. A 172)

- Switzerland

BEGUELIN (ROLAND) Protection ethnique et revision de la constitution fédérale. [Delémont], 1966. pp. 23.

SCHAFFTER (ROGER) 1947-1967: vingt ans de lutte. [Delémont], 1967. pp. 30.

SCHAFFTER (ROGER) Despotisme démocratique ou négociation? [Delémont], 1967. pp. 15.

WILHELM (JEAN) La Romandie sous tutelle. [Delémont], 1967. pp. 10.

- Turkmenistan

GAFFERBERG (EDIT GUSTAVOVNA) Белуджи Туркменской ССР: очерки хозяйства, материальной культуры и быта. Ленинград, 1969. pp. 238.

- United Kingdom - Ireland

HART (JUDITH) Minorities in our society;...an address given at the annual general meeting of the National Council of Social Service. [London, 1968]. pp. 15.

BROWN (JOHN) Warden of the Cranfield Institute of Technology. The un-melting pot: an English town and its immigrants. London, 1970. pp. 240.

HIRO (DILIP) Black British, white British. London, 1971. pp. 384. bibliog.

KRAUSZ (ERNEST) Ethnic minorities in Britain. London, 1971. pp. 175. bibliog.

- United States

SINGLETON (ROBERT) and BULLOCK (PAUL) Some problems in minority-group education in the Los Angeles public schools. Los Angeles, California University, Institute of Industrial Relations, 1963. pp. 137-145. 24½cm. (Reprints. No. 120.) (Reprinted from the Journal of Negro Education, Spring, 1963)

BERGER (MORROE) Equality by statute: the revolution in civil rights. rev. ed. New York, Doubleday, [1967]. pp. ix, 253. bibliog. 21cm.

HUTHMACHER (J. JOSEPH) A nation of newcomers: ethnic minorities in American history. New York, 1967, repr. 1970. pp. 125. bibliog.

BRODY (EUGENE B.) and others. Minority group adolescents in the United States. Baltimore, Williams & Wilkins, 1968. pp. xi, 243. bibliogs. 22½cm.

MARDEN (CHARLES FREDERICK) and MEYER (GLADYS ELEANOR) Minorities in American society. 3rd ed. New York, American Book Co., [1968]. pp. xxi, 486. bibliog. 23½cm.

BAYLEY (DAVID HUME) and MENDELSOHN (HAROLD) Minorities and the police: confrontation in America. New York, Free Press, [1969]. pp. xiii, 209. 20½cm.

DINNERSTEIN (LEONARD) and JAHER (FREDERIC COPLE) eds. The aliens: a history of ethnic minorities in America. New York, [1970]. pp. 347.

HAWKINS (BRETT W.) and LORINSKAS (ROBERT A.) eds. The ethnic factor in American politics. Columbus, Ohio, [1970]. pp. 197.

KRAMER (JUDITH R.) The American minority community. New York, [1970]. pp. 293. bibliog.

ALLSWANG (JOHN M.) A house for all peoples: ethnic politics in Chicago, 1890-1936. Lexington, Ky., [1971]. pp. 253. bibliog.

GREELEY (ANDREW M.) Why can't they be like us?: America's white ethnic groups. New York, 1971. pp. 223. bibliog.

LEINWAND (GERALD) ed. Minorities all. New York, 1971. pp. 191. bibliog.

MINORITIES (Cont'd.)

- Yugoslavia

JANOSI (GABOR) Education and culture of nationalities in Yugoslavia. Beograd, Medunarodna Politika, 1965. pp. 47. 20cm. (Studies. No. 4)

MINORITY STOCKHOLDERS

DEUTSCH-ITALIENISCHE JURISTENKONGRESS, 1., ROME, 1966. Minderheitenschutz bei Kapitalgesellschaften; ([and] Pressefreiheit und Persönlichkeitsrecht in Deutschland und Italien): Verhandlungen des...Juristenkongresses, etc. Karlsruhe, 1967-68. 2 vols. (in 1). (Vereinigung für den Gedankenaustausch zwischen Deutschen und Italienischen Juristen. Heft 2-3)

- France

SCHMIDT (DOMINIQUE) Les droits de la minorité dans la société anonyme. Paris, 1970. pp. 264. bibliog.

MINSK

- Civic improvement

MINSK: poslevoennyi opyt rekonstruktsii i razvitiia. Moskva, 1966. pp. 179. 28cm.

- History

HISTORYIA Minska. Minsk, 1967. pp. 687.

MINTS

- Colombia

BARRIGA VILLALBA (A.M.) Historia de la Casa de la Moneda. Bogota, 1969. 3 vols. (Banco de la Republica, Colombia. Archivo de la Economia Nacional. 30)

- United Kingdom

U.K. Royal Mint. 1970. The Royal Mint: an outline history. 5th ed. London, 1970. pp. 35.

MINUSA

- Politics and government

BELIAEVSKII (STEPAN IVANOVICH) Большевики в Минусинской ссылке. Красноярск, Книжное Издательство, 1964. pp. 206. 20cm.

MIR

MALE (DONALD J.) Russian peasant organisation before collectivisation: a study of commune and gathering, 1925-1930. Cambridge, 1971. pp. 253. bibliog. (National Association for Soviet and East European Studies. Soviet and East European Studies)

MIRACLES

McCABE (JOSEPH) The Lourdes miracles: a candid inquiry. London, 1925. pp. 71.

MIRANDA (FRANCISCO DE)

[BIGGS (JAMES)] The history of Don Francisco de Miranda's attempt to effect a revolution in South America; in a series of letters by a gentleman who was an officer under that general, to his friend in the United States; to which are annexed sketches of the life of Miranda, etc. 2nd ed. Boston, Oliver, 1810. pp. xi, 312. 18cm.

- Description and travel

VILA (MARCO-AURELIO) Aspectos geográficos del Estado Miranda. Caracas, 1967. pp. 324. bibliog. (Venezuela. Corporación Venezolana de Fomento. Sub-Gerencia de Servicios Técnicos. Monografías Económicas Estadales)

- Economic conditions

VILA (MARCO-AURELIO) Aspectos geográficos del Estado Miranda. Caracas, 1967. pp. 324. bibliog. (Venezuela. Corporación Venezolana de Fomento. Sub-Gerencia de Servicios Técnicos. Monografías Económicas Estadales)

MISCEGENATION

FISCHER (EUGEN) Dr. med. Die Rehobother Bastards und das Bastardierungsproblem beim Menschen: anthropologische und ethnographische Studien am Rehobother Bastardvolk in Deutsch-Südwest-Afrika; [reprint of 1913 edition]. Graz, Akademische Druck- u. Verlagsanstalt, 1961. pp. xi, 323. bibliog. 24½cm.

LIPSCHUTZ (ALEJANDRO) El problema racial en la conquista de América, y el mestizaje. 2nd ed. Santiago de Chile, Bello, 1967. pp. 384. bibliog. 24cm.

MÖRNER (MAGNUS) Race mixture in the history of Latin America. Boston, Little, Brown, [1967]. pp. xiv, 178. bibliog. 21cm.

JOHNSTON (JAMES HUGO) Race relations in Virginia and miscegenation in the South, 1776-1860. Amherst, 1970. pp. 362. bibliog.

MISCONDUCT IN OFFICE

- Nigeria

NIGERIA. Commission of Inquiry into the Economics, Administration and Industrial Relations of the Nigerian Railway Corporation. 1960. Report of Elias Commission of Inquiry, etc. Lagos, 1960. pp. 93.

NIGERIA. Nigerian Railway Corporation Tribunal of Inquiry. 1966- Proceedings. Lagos, 1966 in progress. 24cm.

NIGERIA. Electricity Corporation of Nigeria Tribunal of Inquiry. 1967. Report. Lagos, 1967. pp. 217. 24cm.

NIGERIA. Nigerian Ports Authority Tribunal of Inquiry. 1967. Report...for the period October 1, 1960 to December 31, 1965. Lagos, 1967. pp. 287. 24cm.

NIGERIA. Nigerian Railway Corporation Tribunal of Inquiry. 1967. Lagos, 1967. pp. 431. 24cm.

NIGERIA. 1968. Comments of the Federal Military Government on the report of the Tribunal of Inquiry into the affairs of the Electricity Corporation of Nigeria for the period 1st January, 1961 to 31st December, 1965. Lagos, 1968. pp. 27. 24cm.

NIGERIA. 1968. Comments of the Federal Military Government on the report of the Tribunal of Inquiry into the affairs of the Nigerian Ports Authority. Lagos, 1968. pp. 48. 24cm.

NIGERIA. Lagos Executive Development Board Tribunal of Inquiry. 1968. Report...for the period 1st October, 1960 to 31st December, 1965. Lagos, 1968. pp. x, 292. 24½cm.

NIGERIA. Nigeria Airways Tribunal of Inquiry. 1968. Report of inquiry into the affairs of W.A.A.C. (Nigeria) Limited, otherwise known as Nigeria Airways, for the period 1st March, 1961 to 31st December, 1965. Lagos, 1968. pp. 418. 23½cm.

- Sierra Leone

REPORT of the Commission appointed to enquire into and report on the matters contained in the Director of Audit's Report on the Accounts of Sierra Leone for the Year 1960/61, and the government statement thereon. Freetown, Government Printer, [1963]. pp. 13, 194.

- South Africa

SOUTH AFRICA. Commission of Inquiry into certain matters relating to the Banana Control Board. Report (R.P. 47/1970). in South Africa. Parliament. House of Assembly. Votes and proceedings; (with Printed annexures).

- United Kingdom

CAMDEN SOCIETY. [Publications]. 4th Series. vol. 6. Records of the trial of Walter Langeton, Bishop of Coventry and Lichfield, 1307-1312; edited...by Alice Beardwood. London, Royal Historical Society, 1969. pp. v, 370. 21½cm.

MISSING PERSONS

WILLIAMS (RICHARD) of the Salvation Army. Missing!: a study of the world-wide missing persons enigma and the Salvation Army response. London, 1969. pp. 221.

MISSIONS

DAWES (WILLIAM) successively Bishop of Chester and Archbishop of York. A sermon preach'd before the Society for the Propagation of the Gospel in Foreign Parts on...February 18, 1708/9. London, Hills, 1709. pp. 16. 19cm.

BONNER (HYPATIA BRADLAUGH) Christianizing the heathen: first-hand evidence concerning overseas missions. London, 1922. pp. 170. bibliog.

CRAGG (KENNETH) Christianity in world perspective. London, 1968. pp. 227.

NEVE (HERBERT T.) Sources for change: searching for flexible church structures; a contribution to the ecumenical discussion on the structures of the missionary congregation, by the Commission on Stewardship and Evangelism of the Lutheran World Federation. Geneva, World Council of Churches, 1968. pp. 124. 21cm.

- Africa, East

MACLEAN (NORMAN) Africa in transformation. [2nd ed.] London, 1914. pp. 262.

- America, Latin

HOFMANN (HANS JOACHIM) Brot für die Welt in Südamerika: ein Bericht. [Stuttgart, 1964]. pp. 48.

MILITARISTS, merchants and missionaries: United States expansion in Middle America; essays written in honor of Alfred Barnaby Thomas; (edited by Eugene R. Huck and Edward H. Moseley). University, Alabama, [1970]. pp. 172. bibliogs.

- Angola

GILCRIST (SID) Angola awake. Toronto, Ryerson P., 1968. pp. xvii, 123. 20cm.

- Chile

KESSLER (J.B.A.) A study of the older Protestant missions and churches in Peru and Chile: with special reference to the problems of division, nationalism and native ministry. Goes, Oosterbaan & le Cointre, 1967. pp. xii, 369. bibliog. 24cm

- China

AH SIN, pseud. Letters of a Chinaman to English readers on English and Chinese superstitions and the mischief of missionaries; [introduction by] G.W. Foote. London, 1903. pp. 16. (Reprinted from The Freethinker)

LIN (SHAO-YANG) A Chinese appeal to Christendom concerning Christian missions. London, 1911. pp. 319.

MAXIM (Sir HIRAM STEVENS) compiler. Li Hung Chang's scrap-book. London, 1913. pp. 382.

WIRTH (BENEDICTA) Imperialistische Übersee- und Missionspolitik, dargestellt am Beispiel Chinas. Münster, Westfalen, [1968]. pp. 78. bibliog. (Münster in Westfalen. Westfälische Wilhelms-Universität. Institut für Missionswissenschaft. Veröffentlichungen. Heft 13) (Sonderdruck aus der Zeitschrift für Missionswissenschaft und Religionswissenschaft, 51. Jahrgang (1967))

- Congo (Kinshasa)

LIGUE POUR LA PROTECTION ET L'EVANGELISATION DES NOIRS. M. Vandervelde se refait une virginité: réponse..aux articles récents du Peuple contre les missionnaires. [Brussels], 1913. pp. 29. (Mouvement des Missions. Suppléments)

LAGERGREN (DAVID) Mission and state in the Congo: a study of the relations between Protestant missions & the Congo Independent State authorities with special reference to the Equator District, 1885-1903; [translated (from the Swedish) by Owen N. Lee]. [Lund], 1970. pp. 365. (Uppsala. Universitet. Studia Missionalia Upsaliensia. 13)

- Europe, Eastern

STASIEWSKI (B.) Zur Geschichte der Christianisierung Ostmitteleuropas. in Schulz (Eberhard G.) ed. Leistung und Schicksal. Köln, 1967.

MISSIONS (Cont'd.)

- Ghana

MOBLEY (HARRIS W.) The Ghanaian's image of the missionary: an analysis of the published critiques of Christian missionaries by Ghanaians 1897-1965. Leiden, 1970. pp. 180. bibliog. (Journal of Religion in Africa. Studies on Religion in Africa. 1)

- India

MADHYA PRADESH. 1957. Report of the Christian Missionary Activities Enquiry Committee, Madhya Pradesh, 1956. vol.1: [Dr. B.S. Niyogi, chairman] Indore, 1957. pp. ii, 187. bibliog. 24cm.

HESS (GARY R.) Sam Higginbottom of Allahabad: pioneer of point four to India. Charlottesville, U.P. of Virginia, 1967. pp. xv, 177. bibliog. 23½cm.

- Indonesia

MEERSMAN (ACHILLES) The Franciscans in the Indonesian archipelago, 1300-1775. Louvain, 1967. pp. 203. bibliog.

- New Guinea

BOCK (VALERIE) Ge hama. London, [1970]. pp. 67.

- Peru

KESSLER (J.B.A.) A study of the older Protestant missions and churches in Peru and Chile: with special reference to the problems of division, nationalism and native ministry Goes, Oosterbaan & le Cointre, 1967. pp. xi, 369. bibliog 24cm.

- Rhodesia

GELFAND (MICHAEL) ed. Gubulawayo and beyond: letters and journals of the early Jesuit missionaries to Zambesia, 1879-1887. London, Chapman, 1968. pp. 496. 21½cm.

- Singapore

LOH KENG AUN. Fifty years of the anglican church in Singapore Island, 1909-1959. Singapore, 1963. pp. 54. bibliog. (Singapore. University. Department of History. Singapore Studies on Malaysia. No. 4)

- South Africa

PHILIP (JOHN) D.D. Researches in South Africa; illustrating the civil, moral, and religious condition of the native tribes; including journals of the author's travels in the interior, etc. London, Duncan, 1828. 2 vols.

HOLDEN (WILLIAM CLIFFORD) British rule in South Africa: illustrated in the story of Kama and his tribe and of the war in Zululand. London, the author, [1879; Pretoria, State Library, 1969]. pp. viii, 218. 18cm. (Reprints. No.37) Facsimile reprint.

WILLIAMS (DONOVAN) When races meet: the life and times of William Ritchie Thomson, Glasgow society missionary, government agent and Dutch Reformed Church minister, 1794-1891. Johannesburg, A.P.B. Publishers, 1967. pp. ix, 246. bibliog. 21cm.

AYLIFF (JOHN) The journal of John Ayliff...; edited by Peter Hinchliff. Cape Town, 1971 in progress. (Rhodes University. Graham's Town Series. 1)

- Tanzania

BERNANDER (GUSTAV) Lutheran wartime assistance to Tanzanian churches, 1940-1945. Lund, Gleerup, [1968]. pp. 170. bibliog. 23½cm. (Studia Missionalia Upsaliensia. 9)

WRIGHT (MARCIA) German missions in Tanganyika, 1891-1941: Lutherans and Moravians in the Southern Highlands. Oxford, 1971. pp. 249. bibliog.

- United Kingdom

GARNETT (Mrs. CHARLES) The story of the Navvy Mission. London, 1898. pp. 24.

WRINTMORE (F.H.) God lifting men: stories of the London City Mission, its missioners and ministry. London, Oliphants, [1968]. pp. 126. 17½cm.

TUCK (J. ERSKINE) ed. 'Archbishop' of the gutter: the story of Ernest W. Walton-Lewsey and the London Embankment Mission;...foreword by Stephen F. Olford. London, [1969]. pp. 95.

- United States - Texas

WEDDLE (ROBERT SAMUEL) San Juan Bautista: gateway to Spanish Texas. Austin, Texas, 1968. pp. 469. bibliog.

- Zambia

GELFAND (MICHAEL) ed. Gubulawayo and beyond: letters and journals of the early Jesuit missionaries to Zambesia, 1879-1887. London, Chapman, 1968. pp. 496.

MISSIONS, AMERICAN

FIELD (JAMES A.) America and the Mediterranean world, 1776-1882. Princeton, 1969. pp. 485. bibliog.

MISSIONS, GERMAN

HOFMANN (HANS JOACHIM) Brot für die Welt in Südamerika: ein Bericht. [Stuttgart, 1964]. pp. 48.

WRIGHT (MARCIA) German missions in Tanganyika, 1891-1941: Lutherans and Moravians in the Southern Highlands. Oxford, 1971. pp. 249. bibliog.

MISSIONS, MEDICAL

- Kenya

KENYA. Sessional Papers. 1960/61. No. 8. Report of the Committee Appointed to Consider the Role of the Medical Services Rendered by the Missions in Relation to those Provided by Central and Local Government: [T.F. Anderson, chairman]. [Nairobi], 1960. pp. 37.

MISSIONS, PORTUGUESE

MEERSMAN (ACHILLES) The Franciscans in the Indonesian archipelago, 1300-1775. Louvain, 1967. pp. 203. bibliog.

MISSIONS, SPANISH

MEERSMAN (ACHILLES) The Franciscans in the Indonesian archipelago, 1300-1775. Louvain, 1967. pp. 203. bibliog.

WEDDLE (ROBERT SAMUEL) San Juan Bautista: gateway to Spanish Texas. Austin, Texas, 1968. pp. 469. bibliog.

HOEFFNER (JOSEPH) Kolonialismus und Evangelium: spanische Kolonialethik im Goldenen Zeitalter. 2nd ed. Trier, Paulinus, 1969. pp. vii, 455. bibliog. 21cm.

MISSISSIPPI

- History

HARRIS (WILLIAM C.) Presidential reconstruction in Mississippi. Baton Rouge, Louisiana State U.P., [1967]. pp. xiii, 279. bibliog. 22½cm.

MISSISSIPPI VALLEY

- Social history

CONFERENCE ON THE FRENCH IN THE MISSISSIPPI VALLEY, SOUTHERN ILLINOIS UNIVERSITY, 1967. Frenchmen and French ways in the Mississippi Valley; edited by John Francis McDermott. Urbana, 1969. pp. 304.

MISSOURI

- Industries

HARMSTON (FLOYD K.) and MONROE (CLAUDE E.) The inter-industry structure of Missouri, 1958. Columbia, University of Missouri, School of Business and Public Administration, Business and Public Administration Research Center, 1967. pp. (v), 153. bibliog. 25½cm. (Missouri Economy Studies. No. 10.)

-Politics and government

MERRING (JOHN VOLLMER) The Whig party in Missouri. Columbia, [1967]. pp. iii, 277. bibliog. (Missouri University. Studies. Vol. 41)

MITCHELL (FRANKLIN D.) Embattled democracy: Missouri Democratic politics, 1919-1932. Columbia, U. of Missouri P., [1968]. pp. (ix), 219. bibliog. 21½cm. (Missouri University. Studies. vol. 47)

MISTAKE (LAW)

- Poland

KOZACZKA (ADAM) Błąd jako wada oświadczenia woli: od błędu w pobudce do błędu usprawiedliwionego; De errore in verbis et voluntate, etc. Kraków, PWN, 1961. pp. 171. bibliog. 25cm. (Cracow. Uniwersytet Jagielloński. Rozprawy i Studia. tom 23) With Russian and German summaries.

- United Kingdom

STOLJAR (SAMUEL JACOB) Mistake and misrepresentation: a study in contractual principles. London, Sweet & Maxwell, 1968. pp. xvi, 160. 21½cm.

MISTRETTA

- Politics and government

MISTRETTA. Comune. Relazione sulla attività amministrativa: quadriennio, 1956-1960. Palermo, [imprint], 1960. pp. 24. 21½cm.

MISURATA

- Economic conditions

BLAKE (GERALD HENRY) Misurata: a market town in Tripolitania. Durham, 1968. pp. 34. bibliog. (Durham University. Department of Geography. Research Papers Series. No. 9)

MITKIEWICZ (LEON)

MITKIEWICZ (LEON) Z gen. Sikorskim na obczyźnie: fragmenty wspomnień. Paryż, Instytut Literacki, 1968. pp. 392. 21½cm. (Biblioteka "Kultury". tom 157. Seria Dokumenty. 21)

MITSKEVICH (SERGEI IVANOVICH)

MITSKEVICH (SERGEI IVANOVICH) Revoliutsionnaia Moskva, 1888-1905. Moskva, 1940. pp. 487. For 1st vol. of these memoirs see his Na grani dvukh epokh.

MITTERRAND (FRANÇOIS)

PARTI COMMUNISTE FRANÇAIS. Comité Central. Les raisons du soutien communiste à François Mitterrand: rapport de Waldeck Rochet, secrétaire général...;résolution. Drancy, Humanité Dimanche, 1965. pp. 29. 20cm.

NEF, LA. Nouvelle Série. 24e annee. No.30. Face à face: Edgar Faure, François Mitterrand. Paris, Tallandier, 1967. pp. 125. 20cm

MIXTEC INDIANS

MARROQUIN (ALEJANDRO) La ciudad mercado: Tlaxiaco. México, Imprenta Universitaria, 1957. pp. 275. 20cm. (Cultura Mexicana. 19)

MNEMONICS

GREY (RICHARD) D.D. Memoria technica; or, Method of artificial memory...; to which are subjoined Lowe's Mnemonics delineated, etc. new ed. Oxford, printed for J. Vincent, 1824. pp. xxiii, 216. 18 cm.

MOBS

RICHARDS (LEONARD L.) "Gentlemen of property and standing": anti-abolition mobs in Jacksonian America. New York, 1970. pp. 196. bibliog.

SINGER (BENJAMIN D.) and others. Black rioters: a study of social factors and communication in the Detroit riot. Lexington, Mass., [1970]. pp. 117. bibliog.

MOBUTU (JOSEPH)

KAMITATU (CLEOPHAS) La grande mystification du Congo-Kinshasa: les crimes de Mobutu. Paris, 1971. pp. 298.

MODALITY (LOGIC)

HUGHES (GEORGE EDWARD) and CRESSWELL (M.J.) An introduction to modal logic. London, Methuen, 1968. pp. xii, 388. bibliog. 21½cm.

HINTIKKA (KAARLO JAAKKO JUHANI) Models for modalities; selected essays. Dordrecht, [1969]. pp. 220.

MODEL ORDINANCES

- United Kingdom

U.K. Parliament. 1968. Model clauses: revised edition, 1968. London, 1968. pp. vi, 49. 24½cm.

MODEL THEORY

BELL (J.L.) and SLOMSON (A.B.) Models and ultra-products; an introduction. Amsterdam, 1969. pp. 322. bibliog.

FITTING (MELVIN CHRIS) Intuitionistic logic, model theory and forcing. Amsterdam, 1969. pp. 191. bibliog.

The PROCESS of model-building in the behavioral sciences; [a symposium held at Ohio State University in April, 1967; by] W. Ross Ashby [and others]; Ralph M. Stogdill, editor. Columbus, [1970]. pp. 181.

MODENA (DUCHY)

- Religion

MANNI (GRAZIANO) La polemica cattolica nel Ducato di Modena, 1815-1861. Modena, [1968]. pp. 326. bibliog.

MODENA (PROVINCE)

- History

ALBERGHI (PIETRO) Attila sull'Appennino: la strage di Monchio e le origini della lotta partigiana nella Valle del Secchia. Modena, 1969. pp. 253. bibliog. (Istituto Storico della Resistenza in Modena e Provincia. Quaderni. 7)

MODERNISM

- Catholic Church

GUASCO (MAURILIO) Romolo Murri e il modernismo. Roma, 1968. pp. 404. bibliog.

RANCHETTI (MICHELE) The Catholic modernists: a study of the religious reform movement, 1864-1907; translated by Isabel Quigly. London, 1969. pp. 230.

SCOPPOLA (PIETRO) Crisi modernista e rinnovamento cattolico in Italia. 2nd ed. Bologna, 1969. pp. 408. bibliog.

BEDESCHI (LORENZO) Buonaiuti, il concordato e la chiesa; con un'appendice di lettere inedite. Milano, 1970. pp. 469.

BEDESCHI (LORENZO) Lineamenti dell'antimodernismo: il caso Lanzoni. Parma, 1970. pp. 280.

MODERNISM (LITERATURE)

LEFEBVRE (HENRI) Introduction à la modernité: préludes. Paris, [1962]. pp. 375.

MODJOKUTO

- Social conditions

JAY (ROBERT RAVENELLE) Javanese villagers: social relations in rural Modjokuto. Cambridge, Mass., [1969]. pp. xiii, 468.

MODY (Sir HOMI)

MANNEKAR (D. R.) Homi Mody: a many splendoured life; a political biography. Bombay, 1968. pp. 255.

MOENCHENGLADBACH

- Industries

FRAENKEN (WILLY) Die Entwicklung des Gewerbes in den Städten Mönchengladbach und Rheydt im 19. Jahrhundert. Köln, 1969. pp. 245. bibliog. (Cologne. Archiv für Rheinisch-Westfälische Wirtschafts-geschichte. Schriften zur Rheinisch-Westfälischen Wirtschaftsgeschichte. Band 19)

MOESER (JUSTUS)

RUNGE (JOACHIM) Justus Mösers Gewerbetheorie und Gewerbepolitik im Fürstbistum Osnabrück in der zweiten Hälfte des 18. Jahrhunderts. Berlin, Duncker und Humblot, [1966]. pp. 162. bibliog. 23½cm. (Schriften zur Wirtschafts- und Sozialgeschichte. Band 2)

SHELDON (WILLIAM F.) The intellectual development of Justus Möser: the growth of a German patriot. Osnabrück, 1970. pp. 146. bibliog. (Verein für Geschichte und Landeskunde von Osnabrück. Osnabrücker Geschichtsquellen und Forschungen. 15) With German summary.

MOHAIR

UNITED STATES. Agriculture Dept. Statistical Bulls. No. 309. Wool and mohair...1909-59. Washington, 1962. pp. 35.

SOUTH AFRICA. Mohair Board. Report of the Controller and Auditor-General on the accounts of the...Board for the financial year. 1966/7 [1st] to date included in SOUTH AFRICA. Parliament. House of Assembly. Votes and proceedings; (with Printed annexures).

MOHAMMAD REZAPAULAVI, Shah of Iran

SANGHVI (RAMESH) Aryamehr: the Shah of Iran; a political biography. London, Macmillan, 1968. pp. xxvi, 390. bibliog. 21½cm.

MOHAMMEDAN COUNTRIES

ORGELS (BERNARD) La terre et les hommes dans le monde musulman. Bruxelles, Centre pour l'Étude des Problèmes du Monde Musulman Contemporain, [1965]. pp. 94. 24cm. (Correspondance d'Orient. No. 8)

- Commerce - Asia

ISLAM and the trade of Asia: a colloquium; edited by D.S. Richards;...under the auspices of the Near Eastern History Group, Oxford, etc. Oxford, [1970]. pp. 267, xvi. In English or French.

- History

HITTI (PHILIP KHURI) Makers of Arab history. London, Macmillan, 1968. pp. (vii), 268. 21½cm.

ISLAM and the trade of Asia: a colloquium; edited by D.S. Richards;...under the auspices of the Near Eastern History Group, Oxford, etc. Oxford, [1970]. pp. 267, xvi. In English or French.

- Politics and government

IRAQ. Embassy (U.K.) Office of the Press Attaché. 1965. Iraq: official statements of policy on internal, Arab and foreign affairs; (replacing the issue of the Bulletin of the Republic of Iraq for the months of November-December, 1965). London, 1965. pp. 63.

FLORY (MAURICE) and MANTRAN (ROBERT) Les régimes politiques des pays Arabes. Paris, P.U.F., 1968. pp. 469. bibliogs. 18cm. (Thémis)

MOHAMMEDAN EMPIRE

SPULER (BERTOLD) The Muslim world: a historical survey. Leiden, 1960 repr. 1968 in progress. bibliogs. Facsimile reprint.

MANTRAN (ROBERT) L'expansion musulmane, VIIe-XIe siècles. Paris, 1969. pp. 334 bibliog.

MOHAMMEDAN ETHICS

SHIRAVOV (KERIM ZAKAR'IAEVICH) Несовместимость нравственных поучений ислама с моральным кодексом строителя коммунизма. Махачкала, 1965. pp. 59.

MOHAMMEDAN SECTS

MITCHELL (RICHARD P.) The society of the Muslim brothers. London, 1969. pp. 349. bibliog.

MOHAMMEDANISM

SHIAH ISLAMIC SOCIETY. Thoughts on Islam and a brief account of the work of the Shiah Islamic Society, London. London, [1967]. pp. 58.

GEERTZ (CLIFFORD) Islam observed: religious development in Morocco and Indonesia. New Haven, Yale U.P., 1968. pp. xiii, 136. bibliog. 22cm. (Yale University. Terry Lectures. 1967)

JAMEELAH (MARYAM) Islam and modernism. 2nd ed. Lahore, 1968. pp. 251. bibliog.

LAMMENS (HENRI) Islam: beliefs and institutions;...translated by Sir E. Denison Ross; [reprint of the volume originally published in 1929]. London, Cass, 1968. pp. ix, 256. bibliog. 21cm. (Islam and the Muslim World)

PLANHOL (XAVIER DE) Les fondements géographiques de l'histoire de l'Islam. Paris, Flammarion, [1968]. pp. 442. bibliog. 21cm. (Nouvelle Bibliothèque Scientifique)

WATT (WILLIAM MONTGOMERY) What is Islam? London, Longmans, 1968. pp. x, 256. bibliog. 21½cm.

MAVLIUTOV (RASHID RAKHMATULLOVICH) Ислам. Москва, 1969. pp. 158.

HITTI (PHILIP KHURI) Islam: a way of life. London, 1970. pp. 198. bibliog.

KAMIL ('ABD-AL'-AZIZ' ABD-AL-QADIR) Islam and the race question. Paris, United Nations Educational, Scientific and Cultural Organization, 1970. pp. 65. (Race Question and Modern Thought)

SCHUON (FRITHJOF) Dimensions of Islam;... translated by P.N. Townsend. London, 1970. pp. 167.

MOHAMMEDANISM AND ECONOMICS

CHAPRA (M. 'UMAR) The economic system of Islam: a discussion of its goals and nature. London, 1970. pp. 54.

MOHAMMEDANISM AND POLITICS

HANIFI (MANZOOR AHMAD) A short history of Muslim rule in Indo-Pakistan. Dacca, 1964. pp. 317. bibliog.

SARKER (ABDUL BARI) The concept of Islamic socialism. Sylhet, 1964. pp. 139.

AHMAD (HAZRAT MIRZA NASIR) A message of peace and a word of warning. London, [1967?]. pp. 14.

ALL PAKISTAN POLITICAL SCIENCE CONFERENCE, 4TH, 1966. Proceedings...; edited by Muhammad Aziz Ahmad. [Karachi, 1968?]. pp. 284. bibliog. In English or Arabic.

HAQ (INAMUL) Islamic bloc: the way to honour, power and peace. Karachi, [1968?]. pp. 188.

KABIR (HUMAYUN) Muslim politics, 1906-47, and other essays. Calcutta, 1969. pp. 133.

BEHRMAN (LUCY CREEVEY) Muslim brotherhoods and politics in Senegal. Cambridge, Mass., 1970. pp. 224. bibliog.

KHADDURI (MAJID) Political trends in the Arab world: the role of ideas and ideals in politics. Baltimore, [1970]. pp. 298.

MOHAMMEDANISM AND STATE

MAKATOV (I. A.) Religioznye gruppy Amaia i Kunta-Khadzhi. Makhachkala, 1965. pp. 34.

SHIRAVOV (KERIM ZAKAR'IAEVICH) Несовместимость нравственных поучений ислама с моральным кодексом строителя коммунизма. Махачкала, 1965. pp. 59.

ALL PAKISTAN POLITICAL SCIENCE CONFERENCE, 4TH, 1966. Proceedings...; edited by Muhammad Aziz Ahmad. [Karachi, 1968?]. pp. 284. bibliog. In English or Arabic.

MOHAMMEDANISM AND STATE (Cont'd.)

[KHAN (MOHAMMAD AYUB)] Ideology and objectives. [Lahore?], 1968. pp. 173.

SAFDAR (MAHMOOD) and ZAFAR (JAVAID) Founders of Pakistan. Lahore, 1968. pp. 249.

WATT (WILLIAM MONTGOMERY) Islamic political thought: the basic concepts. Edinburgh, Edinburgh U.P., [1968]. pp. xi, 186. bibliog. 20cm. (Islamic Surveys. 6)

BRAEKER (HANS) Kommunismus und Weltreligionen Asiens: zur Religions- und Asienpolitik der Sowjetunion. Tübingen. 1969 in progress.

MOHAMMEDANS IN ABYSSINIA

ABIR (MORDECHAI) Ethiopia: the era of the princes; the challenge of Islam and the re-unification of the Christian Empire, 1769-1855. London, Longmans, 1968. pp. xxvi, 208. bibliog. 21½cm.

MOHAMMEDANS IN AFRICA

KRITZECK (JAMES) and LEWIS (WILLIAM H.) eds. Islam in Africa. New York, [1969]. pp. 339. bibliogs

FISHER (ALLAN GEORGE BARNARD) and FISHER (HUMPHREY J.) Slavery and Muslim society in Africa: the institution in Saharan and Sudanic Africa and the trans-Saharan trade. London, [1970]. pp. 182. bibliog.

MOHAMMEDANS IN ALBANIA

BARTL (PETER) Die albanischen Muslime zur Zeit der nationalen Unabhängigkeitsbewegung, 1878-1912. Wiesbaden, Harrassowitz, 1968. pp. 207. bibliog. 24cm. (Albanische Forschungen. Band 8)

MOHAMMEDANS IN ALGERIA

ALGERIA. Direction des Personnels et des Affaires Administratives. Sous-Direction L'Administration Générale. 1959. Stades d'évolution de la cellule familiale musulmane d'Algérie; synthèse réalisée par le Capitaine L.P. Fauque, etc. Alger, 1959. pp. 28. 24½cm.

MERAD (ALI) Le réformisme musulman en Algérie de 1925 à 1940: essai d'histoire religieuse et sociale. Paris, 1967. pp. 472. bibliog. (Maison des Sciences de l'Homme. Recherches Méditerranéennes. Études. 7)

AGERON (CHARLES ROBERT) Les Algériens musulmans et la France, 1871-1919. Paris, P.U.F., 1968. 2 vols. bibliog. 24cm. (Paris. Université. Faculté des Lettres et Sciences Humaines. Publications. Série Recherches. Tome 44-45)

MOHAMMEDANS IN BULGARIA

MIZOV (NIKOLAI) Isliamŭt v Bŭlgariia: sŭshtnost, modernizatsiia i preodoliavane. Sofiia, 1965. pp. 230.

MOHAMMEDANS IN CHINA

CHU (WEN-DJANG) The Moslem rebellion in Northwest China, 1862-1878: a study of government minority policy. The Hague, Mouton, 1966. pp. xiv, 232. bibliog. 24cm. (Central Asiatic Studies. 5)

CHAN (W. K. K.) The "Panthay Embassy" to Britain, 1872: an abortive diplomatic mission of the Moslem rebellion in Yunnan. in St.Antony's Papers. No.20. Far Eastern affairs; No.4. London, 1967.

MOHAMMEDANS IN DAGHESTAN

MAKATOV (I. A.) Religioznye gruppy Amaia i Kunta-Khadzhi. Makhachkala, 1965. pp. 34.

MOHAMMEDANS IN EGYPT

BERGER (MORROE) Islam in Egypt today: social and political aspects of popular religion. Cambridge, 1970. pp. 138. bibliog.

MOHAMMEDANS IN INDIA

THORPE (C.LLOYD) Education and the development of Muslim nationalism in pre-partition India. Karachi, Pakistan Historical Society, 1965. pp. iii, 89. bibliog. 23cm. (Publications. No. 44)

HAMID (ABDUL) Muslim separatism in India: a brief survey 1858-1947. [Lahore], 1967. pp. 263. bibliog.

DALWAI (HAMID) Muslim politics in India;... foreword by A.B. Shah. Bombay, 1968 repr. 1969. pp. 110.

HASSNAIN (S.E.) Indian Muslims: challenge and opportunity. Bombay, Lalvani, 1968. pp. 144. 22cm.

KARANDIKAR (MAHESHWAR ANANT) Islam in India's transition to modernity. Bombay, 1968 repr. 1969. pp. 414.

KABIR (HUMAYUN) Muslim politics, 1906-47, and other essays. Calcutta, 1969. pp. 133.

GREWAL (J.S.) Muslim rule in India: the assessments of British historians. Calcutta, 1970. pp. 218. bibliog.

ZAKARIA (RAFIQ) Rise of Muslims in Indian politics: an analysis of developments from 1885 to 1906. Bombay, [1970]. pp. 427. bibliog.

MOHAMMEDANS IN INDONESIA

GEERTZ (CLIFFORD) Islam observed: religious development in Morocco and Indonesia. New Haven, Yale U.P., 1968. pp. xiii, 136. bibliog. 22cm. (Yale University. Terry Lectures. 1967)

MUSKENS (MARTINUS PETRUS MARIA) Indonesië: een strijd om nationale identiteit; nationalisten, islamieten, katholieken. Bussum, 1969. pp. 597. bibliog. With English summary.

MOHAMMEDANS IN MOROCCO

GEERTZ (CLIFFORD) Islam observed: religious development in Morocco and Indonesia. New Haven, Yale U.P., 1968. pp. xiii, 136. bibliog. 22cm. (Yale University. Terry Lectures. 1967)

MOHAMMEDANS IN PAKISTAN

ABBOTT (FREELAND) Islam and Pakistan. Ithaca, Cornell U.P., 1968. pp. xvii, 242. 21cm.

MOHAMMEDANS IN RUSSIA

MUSBIURO... Мусбюро Р.К.П.(б) в Туркестане; с введением товарища Рыскулова. [Ташкент?], Туркестанское Государственное Издательство, [1920?]. pp. 94. 25½x36cm. Xerographic copy. Size of original 25½x18cm.

MAKATOV (I. A.) Religioznye gruppy Amaia i Kunta-Khadzhi. Makhachkala, 1965. pp. 34.

SHIRAVOV (KERIM ZAKAR'IAEVICH) Несовместимость нравственных поучений ислама с моральным кодексом строителя коммунизма. Махачкала, 1965. pp. 59.

VAGABOV (MUSTAFA VAGABOVICH) Ислам и женщина. Москва, 1968. pp. 230.

BRAEKER (HANS) Kommunismus und Weltreligionen Asiens: zur Religions- und Asienpolitik der Sowjetunion. Tübingen. 1969 in progress.

MAVLIUTOV (RASHID RAKHMATULLOVICH) Ислам. Москва, 1969. pp. 158.

MOHAMMEDANS IN SENEGAL

BEHRMAN (LUCY CREEVEY) The political influence of Muslim brotherhoods in Senegal. 1967. fo. 474. bibliog. Microfilm of typescript: 1 reel.

KLEIN (MARTIN A.) Islam and imperialism in Senegal: Sine-Saloum, 1847-1914. Stanford. Stanford U.P., 1968. pp. xviii, 285. bibliog. 23cm. (Stanford University. Hoover Institution on War Revolution and Peace. Hoover Institution Publications)

BEHRMAN (LUCY CREEVEY) Muslim brotherhoods and politics in Senegal. Cambridge, Mass., 1970. pp. 224. bibliog.

MOHAMMEDANS IN SENEGAL
See also MOURIDES

MOHAMMEDANS IN SUMATRA

SIEGEL (JAMES T.) The rope of God. Berkeley, 1969. pp. 308. bibliog.

MOHAMMEDANS IN THE CHECHEN-INGUSH REPUBLIC

MAKATOV (I. A.) Religioznye gruppy Amaia i Kunta-Khadzhi. Makhachkala, 1965. pp. 34.

MOHAMMEDANS IN THE LACCADIVE ISLANDS

DUBE (LEELA) Matriliny and Islam: religion and society in the Laccadives. Delhi, 1969. pp. 125. bibliog. (University of Saugar. Monographs in Anthropology and Sociology)

MOHAMMEDANS IN THE UNITED KINGDOM

BUTTERWORTH (ERIC) A Muslim community in Britain. London, Church Information Office, 1967. pp. 60. 21½cm.

MOHAMMEDANS IN TURKEY

HEYD (URIEL) Revival of Islam in modern Turkey; lecture delivered March 28, 1968, etc., Jerusalem, 1968. pp. 27.

MOHAMMEDANS IN WEST AFRICA

LEVTZION (NEHEMIA) Muslims and chiefs in West Africa: a study of Islam in the middle Volta Basin in the pre-colonial period. Oxford, Clarendon P., 1968. pp. xxvi, 228. bibliog. 21½cm. (Oxford Studies in African Affairs)

MOHAVE INDIANS

DEVEREUX (G.) The primal scene and juvenile heterosexuality in Mohave society. in Wilbur (George B.) and Muensterberger (Warner) eds. Psychoanalysis and culture: [reprint of work originally published in 1951]. New York, 1967.

MOINEAUX (JULES)

MOINEAUX (JULES) Lettres d'un forçat; précédées d'une préface et de la plaidoirie de Me Emile Royer prononcée devant la Cour d'assises de la province de Liége pour Jules Moineaux. Ixelles-Bruxelles, 1900. pp. 92.

MOIVRE (ABRAHAM DE)

WALKER (H. M.) Abraham de Moivre. in Moivre (Abraham de) The doctrine of chances;...[photographic reprint of the 3rd edition published in 1756, with a reprint of a bibliographical article on the author by Helen M. Walker]. New York, 1967.

MOKGATLE (MONYADIOE MORELEBA NABOTH)

MOKGATLE (MONYADIOE MORELEBA NABOTH) The autobiography of an unknown South African. London, [1971]. pp. 350.

MOLDAVIAN DIALECT

- Foreign elements

IL'IASHENKO (TAT'IANA PAVLOVNA) Iazykovye kontakty: na materiale slaviano-moldavskikh otnoshenii; kratkii ocherk. Moskva, 1970. pp. 205. bibliog.

MOLDAVIAN REPUBLIC
See also BESSARABIA

MOLDAVIAN REPUBLIC

- Commerce

FOKSHA (L. T.) Torgovlia Moldavskoi SSR v semiletke. Kishinev, 1959. pp. 100.

- Constitutional history

KARLOV (ALEKSANDR ALEKSANDROVICH) Молдавская ССР - суверенное советское государство в составе СССР. Киев, Наукова Думка, 1968. pp. 166. 20см.

MOLDAVIAN REPUBLIC (Cont'd.)

- Constitutional history - Historiography

SURILOV (A. V.) and STRATULAT (N. P.) O natsional'no-gosudarstvennom samoopredelenii Moldavskogo naroda: protiv fal'sifikatsii sovremennoi burzhuaznoi istoriografiei sovetskogo natsional'no-gosudarstvennogo stroitel'stva. Kishinev, 1967. pp. 147

- Constitutional history - Sources

NACHALO... Начало большого пути: сборник документов и материалов к 40-летию образования Молдавской ССР и создания Компартии Молдавии. Кишинев, Партийное Издательство, 1964. pp. 151. 20cm.

- Economic conditions

DIORDITSA (ALEKSANDR FILIPPOVICH) Молдавская ССР в новой пятилетке. Кишинев, Кфртя Молдовеняскэ, 1967. pp. 187. 16½см.

KOZUB (K.) and STUKALOV (G.) Расцвет экономики Молдавской ССР. Кишинев, 1969. pp. 148.

- Economic history

URSUI (D. T.) Razvitie obshchestvennykh otnoshenii v Sovetskoi Moldavii. Kishinev, 1967. pp. 375.

- Economic history - Sources

ISTORIIA Moldavii: dokumenty i materialy. t.5. Kishinev, 1961. pp. 599. Cover title: Krest'ianskoe dvizhenie v Moldavii epokhi imperializma.

ISTORIIA... История Молдавии: документы и материалы. т.4. Положение крестьян и общественно-политическое движение в Бессарабии, 1861-1895 годы, etc. Кишинев, Картя Молдовеняскэ, 1964. pp. 719. 22cm.

- Economic policy

DIORDITSA (ALEKSANDR FILIPPOVICH) Молдавская ССР в новой пятилетке. Кишинев Кфртя Молдовеняскэ, 1967. pp. 187. 16½см.

KOVIAZIN (F. IA.) Хозяйственный расчет и экономическая реформа в промышленности МССР. Кишинев, Картя Молдовеняскэ, 1968. pp. 128. 19½см.

GRADSHTEIN (IA.S.) and others, eds. Khoziaistvennaia reforma na predpriiatiiakh Moldavii: sbornik statei. Kishinev, 1969. pp. 100.

- History

ISTORIIA... История Молдавской ССР, etc. 2nd ed. Кишинев, Картя Молдовеняскэ, 1965-68. 2 vols. 24cm.

- History - Sources

LENIN nam put' ozaril: sbornik dokumentov i materialov. Kishinev, 1970. pp. 383.

- History - Revolution - 1917-1921

IVANOVA (ZOIA MIKHAILOVNA) Ревкомы в борьбе за упрочение Советской власти в левобережных районах Молдавии в 1919 - первой половине 1921 гг. Кишинев, Картя Молдовеняскэ, 1968. pp. 166. 22cm.

KORENEV (A. A.) and ROITMAN (I. D.) Uchastie trudiashchikhsia Moldavii v zashchite zavoevanii Oktiabria; под редактсией...S.IA. Afteniuka. Kishinev, 1968. pp. 86.

ITKIS (M. B.) Крестьянское движение в Молдавии в 1917 году и претворение в жизнь ленинского декрета о земле; под редакцией... И. И. Минца. Кишнев, 1970. pp. 299.

- History - (Revolution), 1917-1921 - Chronology

ZA... За власть Советсв! хроника революционных событий в Молдавии, март 1917 - январь 1918 гг. Кишинев, 1969. pp. 270.

- History - (Revolution), 1917-1921 - Sources

BEREZNIAKOV (NIKOLAI VASIL'EVICH) and others, compilers. Bor'ba trudiashchikhsia Moldavii protiv interventov i vnutrennei kontrrevoliutsii v 1917-1920 gg.: sbornik dokumentov i materialov. Kishinev, 1967. pp. 684.

BEREZNIAKOV (NIKOLAI VASIL'EVICH) and others, eds. Za vlast' Sovetskuiu: bor'ba trudiashchikhsia Moldavii protiv interventov i vnutrennei kontrrevoliutsii, 1917-1920 gg.: sbornik dokumentov i materialov. Kishinev, 1970. pp. 402.

- Industries

OB effektivnosti i stimulirovanii promyshlennogo proizvodstva v Moldavii. Kishinev, 1966. pp. 95.

GUDYM (A.) and TON (D.) Создание тяжелой промышленности в Молдавской ССР: основные проблемы и направления развития. Кишинев, 1967. pp. 145.

KOVIAZIN (F. IA.) Хозяйственный расчет и экономическая реформа в промышленности МССР. Кишинев, Картя Молдовеняскэ, 1968. pp. 128. 19½см.

PEISAKH (I. I.) and SILKIN (A. V.) Легкая индустрия Молдавии: ее вчера, сегодня и завтра, 1944-1970 годы. Кишинев, Картя Молдовеняскэ, 1968. pp. 152. bibliog. 19½см.

BAZIN (MIKHAIL IAKOVLEVICH) Союз земледелия и промышленности: о некоторых формах соединения сельскохозяйственного производства с промышленным в условиях Молдавии. Кишинев, 1969. pp. 201.

ROMANOVA (ZINAIDA GEORGIEVNA) Deiatel'nost Kommunisticheskoi partii Moldavii po razvitiiu promyshlennosti respubliki, 1924-1965gg.; pod redaktsiei...D.E. Shemiakova. Kishinev, 1970. pp. 234.

- Nationalism

 SURILOV (A. V.) and STRATULAT (N. P.)
 O natsional'no-gosudarstvennom samoopredelenii Moldavskogo naroda: protiv
 fal'sifikatsii sovremennoi burzhuaznoi
 istoriografiei sovetskogo natsional'no-
 gosudarstvennogo stroitel'stva. Kishinev, 1967. pp. 147.

- Politics and government

 IVANOV (IURII GRIGOR'EVICH) Uchastie moldavskogo naroda vo vse-
 rossiiskom revoliutsionnom dvizhenii. Kishinev, 1968. pp. 86.

- Rural conditions

 BODIUL (I. I.) Преодоление существен-
 ных различий между городом и деревней
 в условиях Молдавской ССР. Кишинев,
 Картя Молдовеняскэ, 1967. pp. 116.
 20см.

- Social history

 URSUI (D. T.) Razvitie obshchestvennykh otnoshenii v Sovetskoi Moldavii. Kishinev, 1967. pp. 375.

- Statistics

 MOLDAVIAN REPUBLIC. 1964. Советская
 Молдавия за 40 лет: статистический
 сборник. (Центральное Статистическое
 Управление) Кишинев, 1964. pp. 197.
 21½см.

 MOLDAVIAN REPUBLIC. Tsentral'noe Statisticheskoe Upravlenie. 1967. Советская Молдавия к 50-летию Великого Октября: статистический сборник.
 Кишинев, 1967. pp. 287.

MOLINA

- Rural conditions

 LANDSBERGER (HENRY A.) and CANITROT M. (FERNANDO)
 Iglesia, intelectuales y campesinos: la huelga
 campesina de Molina. Santiago de Chile,
 Pacífico, [1967]. pp. 358. 26cm.

MOLISE
 See ABRUZZI E MOLISE

MOLLY MAGUIRES

 COLEMAN (JAMES WALTER) The Molly Maguire riots:
 industrial conflict in the Pennsylvania coal
 region;... [reprint of original edition of 1936].
 New York, 1969. pp. 189. bibliog.

MOLNÁR (ERIK)

 MOLNÁR (ERIK) Válogatott tanulmányok.
 Budapest, 1969. pp. 519. bibliog.

MOLYBDENUM

 SCHNEIDER (V.B.) Molybdenum. Ottawa, 1963.
 pp. 176. bibliog. (Canada. Mineral Resources
 Division. Mineral Reports. 6)

 JOHNSTON (F. J.) Molybdenum deposits of
 Ontario. Toronto, 1968. pp. vii, 98.
 bibliog. 28cm. (Ontario. Department of
 Mines. Mineral Resources Circulars. No. 7.)

MOMBASA

- Politics and government

 [KENYA. 1956] The development of municipal government in Mombasa; by Fred
 Burke. [Mombasa, 1956]. fo. 31. 33cm.

 HORNE (ELEANOR ELIZABETH) A study of local
 government in Mombasa; [Ph. D. (London) thesis]
 1969. fo. 394. bibliog. 25½cm. Typescript:
 unpublished. This thesis is the property of
 London University and may not be removed
 from the Library.

MON LANGUAGE

- Phonology

 SHORTO (H. L.) Mon vowel systems: a problem in
 phonological statement. in Bazell (Charles
 Ernest) and others, eds. In memory of J.R. Firth
 London, 1966.

MONACO

- Economic conditions

 MONACO. Département des Finances et de l'Économie
 Nationale. 1958. Documents de la vie écono-
 mique; ([by] Victor Projetti); préface de
 Arthur Crovetto. Monaco, [1958]. pp. 78.

- History

 LABANDE (LÉON HONORÉ) Histoire de la
 Principauté de Monaco. 2nd ed. Monaco,
 [1934?]. pp. 534.

- Industries

 MONACO. Département des Finances et de l'Économie
 Nationale. 1957. Aspects industriels de la
 principauté, ([by] Victor Projetti). Monaco,
 [1957]. pp. 130.

MONARCHY

 The TRUE law of free monarchy; or, The recipro-
 call and mutuall duty betvvixt a free King and
 his naturall subjects; by a well affected subject of the kingdome of Scotland; [signed C.].
 London, T.F., 1642. pp. (14). 20cm.
 Wing C 2. Cropped.

 A SURVEY of monarchie; or, A discourse shewing
 the just bounds and limitts [sic] of
 monarchy,...; by a faithfull well-willer of
 the happy prosperity of Great-Britaine.
 London, 1644. pp. 13. 17½cm. Wing S 6197

 The KINGDOMES grand quere: what warrant there
 is for such proceedes about the King; resolved by a Presbyterian Minister; also a
 quere taken from the representation of the
 judgement of the ministers in the province of
 London, delivered to the Generall, Jan. 18.
 1648 [O.S.], etc. London, Cripps, 1648 [O.S.]
 pp. 9. 18½cm. Wing K 585.

 GENTILIS (ALBERICUS) Regales discursus tres: I.
 De potestate regis absoluta; II. De unione regno-
 rum Britanniae; III. De vi civium in regem semper
 injusta;...praefatione aucti. Helmestadii, sumptibus J. Heitmulleri, 1669. pp. (xiv), 104. 19cm.

MONARCHY (Cont'd.)

PATTON (ROBERT) The principles of Asiatic monarchies, politically and historically investigated, and contrasted with those of the monarchies of Europe: shewing the dangerous tendency of confounding them in the administration of the affairs of India; with an attempt to trace this difference to its source. London, Debrett, 1801. pp. xii, 374. 21cm.

[HEATHFIELD (RICHARD)] Argument for the general relief of the country from taxation and eventually from the corn laws, by an assessment on property. London, Limbird, 1839. pp. 16. 23cm.

[THOMSON (JAMES)] Author of "The City of Dreadful Night", etc. A commission of inquiry on royalty, etc.; by B.V. London, [1876]. pp. 16.

CANAVAL (GUSTAV A.) La monarquia, forma politica del mañana. Madrid, 1957. pp. 183.

PAGE (JAMES) Monarchy today. London, [1965]. fo. 8. (Monarchist Press Association. Occasional Papers)

MILLER (TOM) and others. An evolving monarchy. London, Bow Group, 1968. pp. 28. 21½cm.

SOCIETE JEAN BODIN. Recueils. 20-21. La monocratie. Bruxelles, 1969-70. 2 vols. bibliogs.

ALBANI (CLAUDIO) L'istituto monarchico nell'antica societa nordica. Firenze, 1969. pp. 198. (Milan. Università. Facoltà di Lettere e Filosofia. Pubblicazioni. 49)

BLACK (ANTONY J.) Monarchy and community: political ideas in the later conciliar controversy, 1430-1450. Cambridge, 1970. pp. 189. bibliog.

MONASTERIES

- France

LESTOCQUOY (JEAN) Etudes d'histoire urbaine: villes et abbayes, Arras au moyen-âge. Arras, 1966. pp. 179. (Pas-de-Calais. Commission Départementale des Monuments Historiques. Mémoires. Tome 12. Fascicule 2)

- Russia

BORISOV (A. M.) Хозяйство Соловецкого монастыря и борьба крестьян с северными монастырями в XVI-XVII веках. Петрозаводск, Карельское Книжное Издательство, 1966. pp. 282. 20cm.

- United Kingdom

WAITES (BRYAN) Moorland and vale-land farming in north-east Yorkshire: the monastic contribution in the thirteenth and fourteenth centuries. York, St. Anthony's P., 1967. pp. (ii), 35. 21½cm. (York. University. Borthwick Institute of Historical Research. Borthwick Papers. No. 32)

YOUINGS (J.A.) The terms of the disposal of the Devon monastic lands, 1536-58; ([with] Postscript). in vol. 1 of Minchinton (Walter Edward) ed. Essays in agrarian history...; reprints, etc. Newton Abbot, [1968].

PLATT (COLIN) The monastic grange in medieval England: a reassessment. London, Macmillan, 1969. pp. 272. bibliog. 21½cm.

- United Kingdom - Wales

WILLIAMS (DAVID H.) The Welsh Cistercians: aspects of their economic history. Pontypool, 1969. pp. 100. bibliog.

MONASTIC AND RELIGIOUS LIFE

McCABE (JOSEPH) Twelve years in a monastery. 3rd ed. London, [1912] repr. 1931. pp. 259.

MOORHOUSE (GEOFFREY) Against all reason. London, Weidenfeld and Nicolson, [1969]. pp. xiii, 436. bibliog. 21½cm.

MONASTICISM AND RELIGIOUS ORDERS

FISCHER (HUGO) Professor of Philosophy. Die Geburt der westlichen Zivilisation aus dem Geist des romanischen Mönchtums. München,]1969]. pp. 277.

KNOWLES (DAVID) Christian monasticism. London, Weidenfeld & Nicolson, [1969]. pp. 256. bibliog. 19cm. (World University Library)

MOORHOUSE (GEOFFREY) Against all reason. London, Weidenfeld & Nicolson, [1969]. pp. xiii, 436. bibliog. 21½cm.

- Missions

HAMANN (G.) Geistliche Forscher- und Gelehrtenarbeit im China des 17. und 18. Jahrhunderts. in Institut für Österreichische Geschichtsforschung and Vienna. Katholische Akademie. Österreich und Europa. Graz, 1965.

- Burma

SPIRO (MELFORD ELLIOT) Buddhism and society: a great tradition and its Burmese vicissitudes. London, 1971. pp. 510. bibliog.

- Italy

PENCO (GREGORIO) Storia del monachesimo in Italia. nell'epoca moderna. Roma, [1968]. pp. 429.

MONATTE (PIERRE)

MONATTE (PIERRE) Syndicalisme révolutionnaire et communisme: les archives de Pierre Monatte, 1914-1924; présentation de Colette Chambelland et Jean Maitron. Paris, Maspero, 1968. pp. 462. 21½cm. (Bibliothèque Socialiste. 12)

MONCKTON (WALTER TURNER) 1st Viscount Monckton

SMITH (FREDERICK WINSTON FURNEAUX) 2nd Earl of Birkenhead. Walter Monckton: the life of Viscount Monckton of Brenchley. London, Weidenfeld and Nicolson, 1969. pp. xii, 388. bibliog. 24cm.

MONEY

LLOYD (HENRY E.) An essay on the theory of money: [facsimile reprint of the work originally published by J. Almon in 1771]. [Rome], 1968. pp. 161.

GESELL (SILVIO) Internationale Valuta-Assoziation (Iva): Voraussetzung des Weltfreihandels, der einzigen für das zerrissene Deutschland in Frage kommenden Wirtschaftspolitik. Sontra in Hessen, 1920. pp. 43.

HUBER (JOHANNES) Neues kommunistisches Manifest. Basel, ["Basler Vorwärts"], 1922. pp. 67. 22½cm.

QUINTANA (MIGUEL A.) Los ensayos monetarios como consecuencia de la baja de plata: el problema de la plata y el de la moneda de plata en el mundo y en México. [Mexico, 1931] pp. 233.

HOLZHAUER (GEORG) Barzahlung und Zahlungsmittelversorgung in militärisch besetzten Gebieten. Jena, Fischer, 1939. pp. x, 115. bibliog. 24cm.

POUND (EZRA) What is money for?;... and, Introductory textbook. 2nd ed. London, Russell, 1951. pp. 15. 21½cm. (Money Pamphlets. No. 3)

EKONOMI, politik, samhälle: en bok tillägnad Bertil Ohlin på sextio-årsdagen; (redaktionskommitte: John Bergvall [and others]. [Stockholm, imprint, 1959]. pp. 305.

CARNEIRO (OTÁVIO AUGUSTO DIAS) Noções da teoria da renda. Recife, Comissão de Desenvolvimento Econômico, 1961. pp. 113. 23cm.

JOHNSON (HARRY GORDON) Recent developments in monetary theory; (text of a lecture delivered at the Instituto Torcuato Di Tella, Centro de Investigaciones Económicas, Argentina on the 30th July, 1963). [Delhi, 1963]. pp. 26 (Reprinted from Indian Economic Review. vol. 6, no. 4, August 1963)

KAMITZ (REINHARD) Monetary stability and free enterprise as prerequisites of successful economic integration. Zürich, [1963?]. pp. 29.

KILTHAU (MANFRED) Die Rechnung der Wirtschaftssubjekte in Geldeinheiten: Versuch eines theoretischen Beweises. Berlin, Duncker und Humblot, [1963]. pp. 74. bibliog. 23½cm. (Die Unternehmung im Markt. Band 8)

LIEBRUCKS (MANFRED) Zur Systematik der Geldillusion unter Berücksichtigung der Systemreaktionen. Berlin, 1963. pp. 75. bibliog.

MEINICH (PER) Patinkin without a price-index. Oslo, 1963. fo. 8. (Oslo. Universitet. Socialøkonomiske Institutt. Memoranda)

OESTERREICHISCHES FORSCHUNGSINSTITUT FÜR SPARKASSENWESEN. Schriftenreihe. 3. Jahrgang. Heft 2. Geld und Vermögen; aktuelle Betrachtungen. Wien, [1968]. pp. 55. 23cm.

GUTSCHER (JUERGEN) Gefüge und gegenseitige Abhängigkeit der Beteiligungsmärkte unter besonderer Berücksichtigung der Sparleistung. [Mannheim?], 1964. pp. 161. bibliog.

MARCHAL (JEAN) Monnaie et crédit: le système monétaire et bancaire français; suivi d'un aperçu sur les systèmes monétaires et bancaires en Grande-Bretagne et aux États-Unis; par Huguette Durand. Paris, Cujas, [1964]. pp. 476. bibliog. 18½cm.

MORGAN (EDWARD VICTOR) Monetary policy for stable growth. London, 1964. pp. 51. bibliog. (Institute of Economic Affairs. Hobart Papers. 27)

COLLIN (FERNAND) La deflation meconnue?; traduction de l'allocution...à l'Assemblée Générale des Actionnaires, Anvers, le 19 juin. [Brussels, Dredietbank, 1965]. pp. 15. 22½cm.

GURRÍA URGELL (JOSÉ MARÍA) La moneda-maíz. México, Paz-México, [1965]. pp. 126. 22½cm.

MONETAIRE theorie...; onder redactie van H.W.J. Bosman [and others]. Amsterdam, 1965. pp. 214.

MUNDELL (ROBERT ALEXANDER) The international monetary system: conflict and reform. [Montreal, 1965]. pp. 63.

WAGNER (ERNST) Dr. Untersuchungen über die Kostenabhängigkeit der Geldnachfrage: ein dynamisches Programmierungsmodell für die Kassenhaltung. Berlin, Duncker und Humblot, [1965]. pp. 79. bibliog. 23cm. (Frankfurt am Main. Universität. Wirtschafts- und Sozialwissenschaftliche Fakultät. Frankfurter Wirtschafts- und Sozialwissenschaftliche Studien. Heft 13)

ZOLOTAS (XENOPHON) Remodelling the international monetary system. Athens, the Bank, 1965. pp. 30. 23cm. (Bank of Greece. Papers and Lectures, 17)

DEBLETOGLOU (EUANGELOS A.) Devaluation and the stability of the trade balance. Athens, the Department, [1966]. pp. 80. bibliog. 23½cm. (Bank of Greece. Economic Research Department. Series of Special Economic Studies. 15)

GRAEBNER (WOLFGANG) Direkte Kontrollen als Mittel der Geldpolitik. Köln, 1966. pp. 86. bibliog. (North Rhine-Westphalia. Forschungsberichte des Landes Nordrhein-Westfalen. Nr. 1688.)

KIEL. Universität. Institut für Weltwirtschaft. Round-Table-Konferenz, 1966. Internationale Währungsprobleme: Vorträge... herausgegeben von Erich Schneider. Tübingen, Mohr, 1966. pp. 95. 23½cm.

KRITIKA sovremennykh burzhuaznykh teorii finansov, deneg i kredita. Moskva, 1966. pp. 264.

LAITY. No. 21. Towards a christian attitude to money. Geneva, World Council of Churches, Department on the Laity and the Department on the Cooperation of Men and Women in Church, Family and Society, 1966. pp. 96. 24cm.

WARBURTON (CLARK) Depression, inflation and monetary policy: selected papers, 1945-1953. Baltimore, [1966]. pp. 425.

1967

BOLOGNA CENTER CONFERENCE ON GOLD AND INTERNATIONAL MONETARY REFORM, 1967. Monetary reform and the price of gold: alternative approaches; edited by Randall Hinshaw. Baltimore, Johns Hopkins P., [1967]. pp. xi, 180. 22½cm.

MONEY

DELIBANES (DEMETRIOS) La contribution de la politique monétaire aux blocages de la croissance et du développement. Thessalonikē, Aristoteleion Panepistemion Thessalonikes, 1967. pp. 637-649. 24cm. (Reprinted from Epistēmonikē Epetēris Scholēs Nomikōn Kai Oikonomikōn Epistēmōn, tomos 12)

FRIEDRICH (HORST) Geldversorgung, Preisniveau und reales Wirtschaftswachstum bei alternativen Grundprinzipien der geldwirtschaftlichen Ordnung. Berlin, Duncker und Humblot, [1967]. pp. 205. bibliog. 23cm. (Bonn. Universität. Institut für das Spar-, Giro- und Kreditwesen. Band 33) With English and French summaries.

GRAMANN (ERNST AUGUST) Monetäre Voraussetzungen der gesamtwirtschaftlichen Nachfragesteuerung. Berlin, Duncker und Humblot, [1967]. pp. 124. bibliog. 23cm. (Volkswirtschaftliche Schriften. Heft 109)

GUENNICKER (FRANZ) Währungsmisere der freien Welt?: die Probleme der internationalen Währungsordnung. Stuttgart, Kohlhammer, [1967]. pp. 173. bibliog. 21cm.

HENRY (CLAUDE) L'affrontement des monnaies. Paris, Éditions Économie et Humanisme, [1967]. pp. 183. bibliog. 18cm. (Initiation Économique. 9)

HESTER (DONALD DENISON) and TOBIN (JAMES) eds. Financial markets and economic activity. New York, [1967]. pp. 256. (Yale University. Department of Economics. Cowles Foundation for Research in Economics. Monographs. 21)

KELLER (ALFRED) Die Idee des neutralen Geldes. Zürich, Keller, 1967. pp. xv, 118. bibliog.

MANFRA (MODESTINO REMIGIO) L'esercizio dei poteri monetari. Padova, Cedam, 1967. pp. 98. bibliog. 24½cm. (Ferrara. Università. Istituto di Economia e Finanza. Collana di Studi. 1)

MARCHAL (JEAN) Monnaie et crédit: le système monétaire et bancaire français; suivi d'un aperçu sur les systèmes monétaires et bancaires en Grande-Bretagne et aux États-Unis; par Huguette Durand. [3rd ed.] Paris, Cujas, [1967]. pp 535. bibliogs. 18cm.

PATINKIN (DON) On the nature of the monetary mechanism. Stockholm, Almqvist & Wiksell, 1967. pp. 37. 24cm. (Wicksell Lecture Society. Wicksell Lectures. 1967)

ROSSI (LIONELLO) Contraddizioni e paradossi della situazione monetaria mondiale: relazione svolta nella seduta ordinaria dell' 8 gennaio 1966. Roma, Accademia Nazionale dei Lincei, 1967. pp, 26 26½cm. (Problemi Attuali di Scienza e di Cultura. Quaderni. N. 82)

SYMPOSIUM ON MONEY, INTEREST RATES AND ECONOMIC ACTIVITY, WASHINGTON, D.C., 1967. Proceedings of a symposium...sponsored by the American Bankers Association; Thursday, April 6, 1967, etc. New York, American Bankers Association, [1967]. pp. vi, 161. 23cm.

U.K. Central Office of Information. Reference Division. 1967. International monetary reform. London, 1967. pp. 18. bibliog. 23½cm.

U.K. Treasury. 1967. International monetary co-operation. London, 1967. pp.8. 33cm.

VECCHIO (GUSTAVO DEL) Ricerche sopra la teoria generale della moneta. Padova, 1967. pp. xxix, 347. (Rome. Università. Istituto di Studi Economici, Finanziari e Statistici. Raccolta di Scritti. Serie 2. vol. 6)

1968

ANTINOLFI (RICCIOTTI) Considerazioni sul pensiero monetario contemporaneo;...lezioni tenute al centro per gli studi sullo sviluppo economico. Roma, 1968. pp. 67.

BEADLES (NICHOLAS ASTON) and DREWRY (L. AUBREY) eds. Money, the market, and the state: economic essays in honor of James Muir Waller. Athens, U. of Georgia P., [1968]. pp. xiii, 225. 23½cm.

BLANCO (FRANCISCO JAVIER) and others. Devaluación y crisis económica. Madrid, ZYX, [1968]. pp. 88. bibliog. 16½cm. (Colección Lee y Discute. Serie Roja. 30)

BUESCHGEN (HANS E.) ed. Geld, Kapital und Kredit: Festschrift zum siebzigsten Geburtstag von Heinrich Rittershausen. Stuttgart, Poeschel, 1968. pp. 480. 23cm.

CLAASSEN (EMIL M.) Monnaie, revenu national et prix. Paris, Dunod, 1968. pp. xx, 194. bibliog. 24cm. With English and German summaries.

DAY (ALAN CHARLES LYNN) The economics of money. 2nd ed. London, O.U.P., 1968. pp. vii, 151. bibliog. 20cm. (Oxford Paperbacks University Series. OPUS 31)

DE ZOETE AND GORTON. Monetary policy in the 'sixties, UK, USA and W. Germany; [by E. B. Chalmers]. London, [1968]. pp. xi, 176. 21½cm.

DIWOK (FRITZ) Gold, Dollar und unser Geld. Wien, Molden, [1968]. pp. 253. 21cm.

EINZIG (PAUL) Leads and lags: the main cause of devaluation. London, Macmillan, 1968. pp. xi, 169. bibliog. 21½cm.

ENTINE (ALAN D.) ed. Monetary economics: readings. Belmont, Wadsworth, [1968]. pp. xvii, 493. bibliogs. 23cm.

GELDTHEORIE und Geldpolitik: Günter Schmölders zum 65. Geburtstag; herausgegeben von C.A. Andreae [and others]; mit Beiträgen von Willi Albers [and others]. Berlin, Duncker & Humblot, [1968]. pp. xiii,355. bibliog. 23cm.

HABERLER (GOTTFRIED VON) and WILLETT (THOMAS D.) U.S. balance-of-payments policies and international monetary reform: a critical analysis. Washington, American Enterprise Institute for Public Policy Research, 1968. pp. (iv), 87. 21½cm.

HEILPERIN (MICHAEL ANGELO) Aspects of the pathology of money: monetary essays from four decades. London, Joseph, 1968. pp. 296. 23cm.

JACKENDOFF (NATHANIEL) Money, flow of funds, and economic policy. New York, Ronald P., 1968. pp. viii, 523. bibliogs. 22½cm.

JOHNSON (HARRY GORDON) Current issues in monetary policy. [New York], 1968. pp. 6. (Reprinted from Financial Analysts Journal, July-August 1968)

JOHNSON (HARRY L.) and WALKER (ERNEST W.) eds. Monetary issues of the 1960's. Austin, University of Texas, Bureau of Business Research, 1968. pp. x, 89. 23cm. (Studies in Banking and Finance. No. 8)

KEMENES (EGON) The reform of the international monetary system and the developing countries. Budapest, Hungarian Academy of Sciences, Center for Afro-Asian Research, 1968. pp. 21, 23½cm. (Studies on Developing Countries. No. 19)

MACHLUP (FRITZ) Remaking the international monetary system: the Rio Agreement and beyond. Baltimore, Johns Hopkins P., [1968]. pp. x, 161. 22½cm. (Committee for Economic Development. Supplementary Papers)

MAX (HERMANN) El porqué de las devaluaciones: política de cambios para paises en vías de desarrollo. Santiago de Chile, Editorial Universitaria, 1968. pp. 95. (Problemas de Nuestro Tiempo. No. 2)

MAYER (THOMAS) Elements of monetary policy. New York, Random House, [1968]. pp. xii, 143. bibliog. 18cm. (Random House Series in Money and Banking)

SEANZA CENTRAL BANKING COURSE. 7th, Colombo, 1968. SEANZA lectures; [by] W. Tennekoon [and others]. [Colombo, 1968]. pp. 729.

SHAPIRO (ELI) and others. Money and banking. 5th ed. New York, Holt, [1968]. pp. xvii, 715. bibliogs. 23½cm.

SMITH (HARLAN M.) The essentials of money and banking. New York, Random House, [1968]. pp. xv, 251. 20½cm. (Random House Series in Money and Banking)

STADNICHENKO (ALEKSEI IVANOVICH) Валютные потрясения на Западе. Москва, ИМО, 1968. pp. 111. 20см.

THOMSON (FRANCIS PAUL) Money in the computer age Oxford, Pergamon P., 1968. pp. xiv, 243. bibliog. 19½cm. (Commonwealth and International Library. Social Administration, Training, Economics and Production Division)

TRIFFIN (ROBERT) Our international monetary system; ...yesterday, today, and tomorrow. New York, Random House, [1968]. pp. xvii, 206. bibliog. 20cm. (Random House Studies in Economics. SE 14)

VEIT (OTTO) Währungspolitik als Kunst des Unmöglichen: zwölf Vorträge. Frankfurt am Main, Knapp, [1968]. pp. 237. 24cm.

WALTERS (A.A.) The demand for money expectations and short and long rates. in Wolfe (James Nathaniel) ed. Value, capital, and growth. Edinburgh, 1968.

WALTERS (ALAN A.) Money and exogeneity. [Birmingham], 1968. fo. 10. (Birmingham. University. Faculty of Commerce and Social Science. Discussion Papers. Series A. No.97)

WHITTLESEY (CHARLES RAYMOND) and WILSON (JOHN STUART GLADSTONE) eds. Essays in money and banking in honour of R.S.Sayers. Oxford, Clarendon P., 1968. pp. x, 327. bibliog. 21½cm.

YEAGER (LELAND BENNETT) The international monetary mechanism. New York, [1968]. pp. 154.

1969

JOHNSON (HARRY GORDON) [Lecture notes on macroeconomics: forty lectures for M.Sc: Economic Theory I, IV 1, final year]. 1969-1970. pp. various.
Book Counter :

ALTVATER (ELMAR) Die Weltwährungskrise. Frankfurt a.M., [1969]. pp. 149.

AMERICAN INTERNATIONAL INVESTMENT CORPORATION. World currency charts. 4th ed. Zurich, Hug, 1969. fo. (iv), 73. 35½cm.

AUBREY (HENRY G.) Behind the veil of international money. Princeton, 1969. pp. 32. (Princeton University. Department of Economics & Sociology. International Finance Section. Essays in International Finance. No. 71)

BARRAN (DAVID H.) and others. Rebuilding the liberal order. London, Institute of Economic Affairs, 1969. pp. 31. 21½cm. (Occasional Papers. 27)

BOS (P.C.) Money in development: the functions of money in equilibrium and disequilibrium, with special reference to developing countries;... with a preface by F. De Roos. [Rotterdam], 1969. pp. 183. bibliog.

CLOWER (ROBERT W.) ed. Monetary theory; selected readings. Harmondsworth, 1969. pp. 360. bibliog.

CONFERENCE ON INDICATORS AND TARGETS OF MONETARY POLICY, LOS ANGELES, 1966. Targets and indicators of monetary policy: [papers]; edited by Karl Brunner. San Francisco, [1969]. pp. 335.

DENIZET (JEAN) Monnaie et financement: essai de théorie dans un cadre de comptabilité économique;... préface de Valéry Giscard d'Estaing. 2nd ed. Paris, 1969. pp. 252. bibliog.

DUERR (ERNST WOLFRAM FRIEDRICH) ed. Geld- und Bankpolitik. Köln, Kiepenheuer & Witsch, [1969]. pp. 498. bibliog. 23cm. (Neue Wissenschaftliche Bibliothek. 28)

FRIEDMAN (MILTON) The optimum quantity of money; and other essays. London, 1969. pp. 296.

HABERLER (GOTTFRIED VON) Money in the international economy: a study in balance of payments adjustment, international liquidity and exchange rates...; with an introduction on "the international monetary system: some recent developments and discussions". 2nd ed London, 1969. pp. 66. (Institute of Economic Affairs. Hobart Papers. 31)

HAHN (LUCIEN ALBERT) Geld und Gold: Vorträge und Aufsätze 1962-1968; mit einem Geleitwort von Edgar Salin. Basel, 1969. pp. 285. bibliog. (List Gesellschaft. Veröffentlichungen. Band 64) In German or English.

HAJELA (PRAYAG DAS) Problems of monetary policy in underdeveloped countries with special reference to India. Bombay, 1969. pp. 298.

MONEY

HARROD (Sir HENRY ROY FORBES) Money. London, 1969. pp. 355.

HART (ALBERT GAILORD) and others. Money, debt and economic activity. 4th ed. Englewood Cliffs, [1969]. pp. 524. bibliogs.

HEINEMANN (KLAUS) Grundzüge einer Soziologie des Geldes. Stuttgart, 1969. pp. 160. bibliog.

HIRSCH (FRED) Money international. rev. ed. Harmondsworth, 1969. pp. 624. bibliog.

HORVITZ (PAUL M.) Monetary policy and the financial system. 2nd ed. Englewood Cliffs, Prentice-Hall, [1969]. pp. xvii, 525. bibliogs. 23cm.

HUDECZEK (KARL) Das internationale Währungssystem: Mängel und Reformen. Frankfurt am Main, [1969]. pp. 136. bibliog.

JOHNSON (HARRY GORDON) Essays in monetary economics. 2nd ed. London, Allen & Unwin, 1969. pp. xix, 15-332. 21½cm. (Unwin University Books. 52)

JOHNSON (HARRY GORDON) The international monetary crisis. n.p., [1969?]. pp. 105-120.

KAHN (JACQUES) Pour comprendre les crises monétaires. Paris, [1969]. pp. 159.

KLEINEWEFERS (HENNER) Theorie und Politik der Abwertung. Basel, Kyklos-Verlag, 1969. pp. ix, 137. bibliog. 23cm. (List Gesellschaft. Veröffentlichungen. Band 58)

LIPFERT (HELMUT) Einführung in die Währungspolitik. 4th ed. München, 1969. pp. 326. bibliog.

MAYNARD (GEOFFREY) The position of sterling and international monetary reform. [Reading], 1969. pp. 13. (Reading. University. Department of Economics Discussion Papers in Economics. No. 19)

MORFEY (K.M.V.) The effect of devaluation upon the trade balance in conditions of full employment. [Southampton], 1969. fo. 9. bibliog. (Southampton. University. Discussion Papers in Economics and Econometrics. No.6803)

MUNDELL (ROBERT ALEXANDER) and SWOBODA (ALEXANDER K.) eds. Monetary problems of the international economy. Chicago, 1969. pp. 405.

OFFICER (LAWRENCE H.) and WILLETT (THOMAS D.) eds. The international monetary system: problems and proposals. Englewood Cliffs, Prentice-Hall, [1969]. pp. xi, 238. bibliog. 20½cm. (Modern Economic Issues)

PRASAD (KAMTA) Role of money supply in a developing economy: a theoretical and empirical analysis. Bombay, Allied Publishers, 1969. pp. ix, 177. bibliog. 21½cm.

PRATHER (CHARLES LEE) Money and banking. 9th ed. Nobleton, 1969. pp. 738.

RANLETT (JOHN GRANT) Money and banking: an introduction to analysis and policy. 2nd ed. New York, [1969]. pp. 543. bibliogs.

SCITOVSKY (TIBOR) the Younger. Money and the balance of payments. London, Allen and Unwin, 1969. pp. ix, 188. bibliogs. 21½cm.

TEW (JOHN HEDLEY BRIAN) Monetary theory. London, 1969. pp. 61. bibliog.

1970

KOEHLER (CLAUS) Geldwirtschaft. Berlin, [1970 in progress]

AMERICAN INTERNATIONAL INVESTMENT CORPORATION. World currency charts. 5th ed. Zurich, 1970. fo.77.

BOCHUD (FRANÇOIS) Zahlungsbilanz und Währungsreserven: die Konzepte der Theorie und die Praxis. Basel, 1970. pp. 151. bibliog. (List Gesellschaft. Veröffentlichungen. Band 60)

CHUNG (PHAM) Money, banking, and income: theory and policy. Scranton, [1970]. pp. 655. bibliog.

CLAASSEN (EMIL M.) Analyse des liquidités et théorie du portefeuille. Paris, 1970. pp. 178. bibliogs.

CLAASSEN (EMIL M.) Probleme der Geldtheorie. Berlin, 1970. pp. 320. bibliog.

COHEN (STEPHEN D.) International monetary reform, 1964-69: the political dimension. New York, 1970. pp. 201. bibliog.

DUNKMAN (WILLIAM EDWARD) Money, credit, and banking. New York, [1970]. pp. 470. bibliogs.

FRIEDMAN (MILTON) The counter-revolution in monetary theory. London, 1970. pp. 28. (Institute of Economic Affairs. Occasional Papers. 33) (Wincott Foundation. Wincott Memorial Lectures. 1970)

HACCHE (JOHN) Economics of money and income. London, 1970. pp. 528. bibliog.

HAYASHI (TOSHIHIKO) The neutrality of money in a growing economy: the wealth theory approach. Kobe, 1970. fo. 27. bibliog. (Kobe. University. Institute of Economic Research. Working Papers in Economics and Management Science. No. 5.)

HENDRICKSON (ROBERT A.) The future of money. London, 1970. pp. 328.

JOHNSON (BRIAN) The politics of money. London, [1970]. pp. 339. bibliog.

JOHNSON (HARRY GORDON) Efficiency in domestic and international money supply...: a lecture delivered at the University of Surrey on 7 February, 1968. Guildford, 1970. pp. 16. (University of Surrey. International Economics. No. 3)

JOHNSON (HARRY GORDON) The Keynesian revolution and the monetarist counter-revolution. n.p., [1970]. fo. 17. bibliog. (American Economic Association. Richard T. Ely Lectures. 1970)

KLEIN (JOHN J.) Money and the economy. 2nd ed. New York, [1970]. pp. 488. bibliogs.

KONISHI (YASUO) The demand for monetary assets by firms: some empirical studies in Japan, 1950-67. Kobe, 1970. fo. 29. bibliog. (Kobe. University. Institute of Economic Research. Working Papers in Economics and Management Science. No. 4)

KRITIKA sovremennykh burzhuaznykh teorii finansov, deneg i kredita. Moskva, 1970. pp. 302. Continuation of book of same title published 1966.

MEINICH (PER) Effects of changes in risk on the demand for cash and bonds. Oslo, 1970. fo. 9. (Oslo.Universitet. Socialøkonomiske Instituttt. Memoranda)

MEISELMAN (DAVID) ed. Varieties of monetary experience. Chicago, 1970. pp. 391. (Chicago. University. Economics Research Center. Economics Research Studies)

MOSSÉ (ROBERT) Les problèmes monétaires internationaux au tournant des années 1970. 3rd ed. Paris, 1970. pp. 478. bibliog.

PAHLKE (JUERGEN) Steuerbedarf und Geldpolitik in der wachsenden Wirtschaft: Geldschöpfung als Mittel der Staatsfinanzierung. Berlin, 1970. pp. 118. bibliog.

REES (GRAHAM L.) International money; an inaugural lecture delivered at the University College of Wales, Aberystwyth, 3rd December, 1969. Cardiff, 1970. pp. 13.

RITTER (LAWRENCE S.) and SILBER (WILLIAM L.) Money. New York, [1970]. pp. 221. bibliog.

SCHUMPETER (JOSEPH ALOIS) Das Wesen des Geldes: aus dem Nachlass herausgegeben... von Fritz Karl Mann. Göttingen, 1970. pp. 341.

STADNICHENKO (ALEKSEI IVANOVICH) Valiutnyi krizis kapitalizma. Moskva, 1970. pp. 231.

WILLIAMSON (G.I.) International capital and money markets: their development and their application. Cairo, 1970. pp. 24. (National Bank of Egypt. Fiftieth Anniversary Commemoration Lectures)

1971

BRUNHOFF (SUZANNE DE) L'offre de monnaie: critique d'un concept. Paris, 1971. pp. 151.

COLLERY (ARNOLD) International adjustment, open economies, and the quantity theory of money. Princeton, N.J., 1971. pp. 33. (Princeton University. Department of Economics and Sociology. International Finance Section. Princeton Studies in International Finance. No. 28)

COOPER (RICHARD N.) Currency devaluation in developing countries. Princeton, N.J., 1971. pp. 31. (Princeton University. Department of Economics and Sociology. International Finance Section. Essays in International Finance. No. 86)

CRAMP (ALFRED BERNARD) Monetary management: principles and practice. London, 1971. pp. 142.

ECONOMIST INTELLIGENCE UNIT. Q[uarterly] E[conomic] R[eview] Specials. No. 9. Currencies in crisis: out of the Bretton Woods?; by Peter Jay. London, [1971]. pp. 28.

ERDÖS (PÉTER) Contributions to the theory of capitalist money, business fluctuations and crises. Budapest, 1971. pp. 466. bibliog.

FOLEY (DUNCAN K.) and SIDRAUSKI (MIGUEL) Monetary and fiscal policy in a growing economy. London, [1970]. pp. 304. bibliog.

INTERNATIONAL CURRENCY REVIEW. Currency portfolio. London, [1971?]. pp. 49.

McKINNON (RONALD I.) Monetary theory and controlled flexibility in the foreign exchanges. Princeton, N.J., 1971. pp. 32. (Princeton University. Department of Economics and Sociology. International Finance Section. Essays in International Finance. No. 84)

MUNDELL (ROBERT ALEXANDER) Monetary theory: inflation, interest, and growth in the world economy. Pacific Palisades, Calif., [1971]. pp. 189.

NATIONAL BUREAU OF ECONOMIC RESEARCH. Occasional Papers. 112. A theoretical framework for monetary analysis; [by] Milton Friedman. New York, 1971. pp. 69. bibliog.

NEWLYN (WALTER TESSIER) Theory of money. 2nd ed. Oxford, 1971. pp. 220.

OSSOLA (RINALDO) Towards new monetary relationships. Princeton, 1971. pp. 21. (Princeton University. Department of Economics and Sociology. International Finance Section. Essays in International Finance. No.87)

PICK (FRANZ) and SÉDILLOT (RENÉ) All the monies of the world: a chronicle of currency values. [2nd ed.] New York, [1971]. pp. 613. bibliog.

PRAGER (NONAS) ed. Monetary economics: controversies in theory and policy; [readings]. New York, [1971]. pp. 432. bibliog.

ROBBINS (LIONEL CHARLES) Baron Robbins. Money, trade and international relations: [essays]. London, 1971. pp. 282. Mainly reprints from his The economist in the twentieth century.

SHEFFIELD MONEY SEMINAR, 1970. Monetary theory and monetary policy in the 1970s: proceedings of the... seminar; edited by G. Clayton [and others]. Oxford, 1971. pp. 272.

SMITH (PAUL F.) Economics of financial institutions and markets. Homewood, Ill., 1971. pp. 287. bibliogs.

SOCHER (KARL) Koordination des Einsatzes geld- und finanzpolitischer Instrumente. Berlin, [1971]. pp. 140. bibliog.

TRIFFIN (ROBERT) How to arrest a threatening relapse into the 1930's. [Brussels, 1971]. pp. 33. (Translated from the Bulletin of the National Bank of Belgium, November, 1971)

WALLACE (NEIL) An approach to the study of money and nonmoney exchange structures. Minneapolis, 1971. fo. 15. (Minnesota University. Center for Economic Research. Discussion Papers. No. 6)

WILLMS (MANFRED) Zinstheoretische Grundlagen der Geldpolitik. Berlin, [1971]. pp. 112. bibliog. (Bonn. Universität. Institut für das Spar-, Giro- und Kreditwesen. Untersuchungen über das Spar-, Giro- und Kreditwesen. Band 53)

WRIGHTSMAN (DWAYNE) An introduction to monetary theory and policy. New York, [1971]. pp. 250. bibliogs.

CORDEN (WARNER MAX) Monetary integration. Princeton, N.J., 1972. pp. 41. bibliog. (Princeton University. Department of Economics and Sociology. International Finance Section. Essays in International Finance. No.93)

FLEMING (MILES) Monetary theory. London, 1972. pp. 63. bibliog.

MONEY

- Congresses - Bretton Woods International Monetary Conference, 1944

THELER (RENÉ) Die Institutionen von Bretton Woods in schweizerischer Sicht. Basel, [imprint], 1965. pp. 119. bibliog. 23cm.

- History

REISMAN (DAVID ALEXANDER) The monetary thought of Henry Thornton: the foundations of British monetary orthodoxy in the nineteenth century. 1966. fo. 47. 25½cm. (London. University. London School of Economics and Political Science. Gladstone Memorial Trust Prize Essays. 1966) Typescript.

HICKS (Sir JOHN RICHARD) Monetary theory and policy: a historical perspective. Nedlands, U. of Western Australia P., 1967. pp. 18. 23½cm. (Western Australia, University of. Edward Shann Memorial Lectures. 1967)

LECERF (JEAN) L'or et les monnaies: histoire d'une crise. [Paris, 1969]. pp. 185.

TEW (JOHN HEDLEY BRIAN) International monetary cooperation, 1945-70. 10th ed. London, 1970. pp. 278. bibliog.

WEIL (GORDON LEE) and DAVIDSON (IAN DOUGLAS) The gold war: the story of the world's monetary crisis. New York, [1970]. pp. 245.

PICK (FRANZ) and SÉDILLOT (RENÉ) All the monies of the world: a chronicle of currency values. [2nd ed.] New York, [1971]. pp. 613. bibliog.

- Law

ERNST (KLAUS ALFRED) Die Bedeutung des Gesetzeszweckes im internationalen Währungs- und Devisenrecht. Berlin, De Gruyter, 1963. pp. xix, 90. bibliog. 22cm. (Cologne. Universität. Rechtswissenschaftliche Fakultät. Neue Kölner Rechtswissenschaftliche Abhandlungen. Heft 26)

GOLD (JOSEPH) The International Monetary Fund and international law: an introduction. Washington, International Monetary Fund, 1965. pp. 26. (Pamphlet Series. [No.4])

TOMUSCHAT (CHRISTIAN) Die Aufwertung der Deutschen Mark: Staats- und völkerrechtliche Überlegungen zur Neufestsetzung der Währungsparität im Jahre 1969. Köln, 1970. pp. 48. (Max-Planck-Institut für Ausländisches Öffentliches Recht und Völkerrecht, Heidelberg. Beiträge zum Ausländischen Öffentlichen Recht und Völkerrecht. [Heft] 55)

HIRSCHBERG (ELIYAHU) The nominalistic principle: a legal approach to inflation, deflation, devaluation and revaluation. Ramat-Gan, [1971]. pp. 138. bibliog. (Bar-Ilan University. Bar-Ilan Research Monographs)

MANN (FRITZ A.) The legal aspect of money, with special reference to comparative private and public international law. 3rd ed. Oxford, 1971. pp. 615.

- Mathematical models

LLOYD (C.L.) Two classical monetary models. in Wolfe (James Nathaniel) ed. Value, capital, and growth. Edinburgh, 1968.

KUSKA (EDWARD ARTHUR) The theory of devaluation, uniform commercial policies and transfer payments; [Ph.D. (London) thesis.] 1969. fo. 160. Typescript: unpublished. This thesis is the property of London University and may not be removed from the Library.

SCADDING (JOHN L.) Some pitfalls in estimating the demand for money: an interpretation of Allais' procedure. Stanford, 1969. fo. 20. bibliog. (Stanford University. Institute for Mathematical Studies in the Social Sciences. Technical Reports. [New Series.] No.21)

SIMOND (ALAIN) Analyse critique des modèles théoriques de Gurley et Shaw. Paris, [1969]. pp. 237. bibliog. (Grenoble. Université. Centre de Recherche Economique et Sociale. Série Economie du Financement. Cahiers d'Etudes. No. 2)

STARRETT (DAVID) Money in the context of growth; a microeconomic approach. Stanford, 1970. fo. 26. bibliog. (Stanford University. Institute for Mathematical Studies in the Social Sciences. Technical Reports. [New Series.] No. 25)

ORR (DANIEL) Cash management and the demand for money. New York, 1971. pp. 212 bibliog.

- Programmed instruction

MASTEN (JOHN T.) and HAYNES (WILLIAM WARREN) Programmed text in money and banking. Englewood Cliffs, Prentice-Hall, [1969]. pp. 263. 28cm.

- Tables, etc.

OELSEN (E.S. VON) Zahlungsmittel, Masse, Gewichte der ganzen Welt. Berlin, Christian, 1930. pp. 120. bibliog. 21cm.

- Africa

VINAY (BERNARD) L'Afrique commerce avec l'Afrique: problèmes et impératifs africains de coopération économique et monétaire. Paris, P.U.F., 1968. pp. viii, 213. bibliog. 21cm. (Pays d'Outre-Mer. 1re Série: Études d'Outre-Mer. 8)

- Africa, East

NEWLYN (WALTER TESSIER) Money in an African context. Nairobi, O.U.P., 1967. pp. x, 156. bibliog. 21½cm. (Studies in African Economics. 1)

- Africa, Subsaharan

NEWLYN (W.T.) An African monetary perspective. in Whittlesey (Charles Raymond) and Wilson (John Stuart Gladstone) eds. Essays in money and banking in honour of R.S. Sayers. Oxford, 1968.

KLEIN (CHRISTIAN) Das zentralbankpolitische Instrumentarium der afrikanischen Entwicklungsländer im Commonwealth. [Erlangen, imprint, 1970?]. pp. 229. bibliog.

- America, Latin

> URI (PIERRE) and others. Una politica monetaria para America Latina. Mexico. 1966. pp. 172. (Centro de Estudios Monetarios Latinoamericanos. Estudios)

> URI (PIERRE) and others. A monetary policy for Latin America. New York, Praeger, 1968. pp. xviii, 147. 23cm. (Praeger Special Studies in International Economics and Development)

- Argentine Republic

> PREBISCH (RAUL) Moneda sana o inflación incontenible: plan de restablecimiento economico. [Buenos Aires], Secretaria de Prensa de la Presidencia de la Nacion, 1956. pp. 57.

> CUCCORESE (HORACIO JUAN) Historia económica financiera argentina, 1862-1930. Buenos Aires, El Ateneo, [1966]. pp. 126. bibliog. 26cm.

> DIFRIERI (JORGE ALBERTO) Moneda y bancos en la República Argentina. Buenos Aires, Abeledo-Perrot, [1967]. pp. 381. bibliog. 24cm.

> OLARRA JIMENEZ (RAFAEL) Evolucion monetaria argentina. Buenos Aires, [1968]. pp. 187. bibliog.

- Australia

> BUTLIN (SYDNEY JAMES) Foundations of the Australian monetary system, 1788-1851. Sydney, Sydney U. P., 1953, repr. 1968. pp. xvi, 727. bibliog.

> LONGMUIR (H. R.) The short term money market in Australia, December 1961. [Sydney], 1962. pp. 11. $24\frac{1}{2}$cm. (Reprinted from Jobson's Investment Digest Year Book, 1962)

> HENDERSON (RONALD FRANK) The role of monetary policy in promoting sound business growth. Melbourne, 1964. pp. 11. (Melbourne. University. Institute of Applied Economic Research. Reprint Series. No. 4)

> PHILLIPS (Sir JOHN GRANT) Recent developments in monetary policy in Australia. St. Lucia, U. of Queensland P., 1965. pp. 26. (Queensland University. English, Scottish and Australian Bank Limited Research Lectures. 1964)

> DEWALD (WILLIAM G.) The short term money market in Australia. St. Lucia, 1967. pp. 46. (English, Scottish and Australian Bank. Research Lectures. 1967)

> NORTON (W.E.) and others. A model of the monetary sector. Sydney, 1970. pp. 31. (Reserve Bank of Australia. Occasional Papers. No. 3D)

- Austria

> KUMMERER (WILLY) Struktur und Probleme des österreichischen Geldmarktes und die Stellung der Girozentrale der österreichischen Sparkassen Aktiengesellschaft am Geldmarkt. Wien, The Institut, [1963]. pp. 58. bibliog. 23cm. (Österreichisches Forschungsinstitut für Sparkassenwesen. Schriftenreihe. Jahrgang 3. Heft 1)

> SCHEITHAUER (MAX) Geldmarkt und Notenbank in Österreich. Wien, 1968. pp. 107. bibliog. (Österreichische Bankwissenschaftliche Gesellschaft. Schriftenreihe. Heft 30)

> OESTERREICHISCHER GEWERKSCHAFTSBUND. Volkswirtschaftliche Arbeitsgemeinschaft, and ARBEITSKREIS BENEDIKT KAUTSKY. Seminar, 1968-69. Geldwirtschaft in Österreich: Vorträge und Diskussionsbeiträge, etc. Wien, [1969]. pp. 118.

> GELDWERTSTABILITAET und Wirtschaftswachstum: Währungspolitik im Spannungsfeld des Konjunkturverlaufs; Festschrift für Andreas Korp; herausgegeben von Wolfgang Schmitz. Wien, [1971]. pp. 397.

- Bolivia

> BEDREGAL (GUILLERMO) Problemas de infraestructura, regimen monetario y desarrollo economico en Bolivia. La Paz, Departamento de Relaciones Publicas de la Corporacion Minera de Bolivia, 1962. pp. 40.

- Burgundy

> SPUFFORD (PETER) Monetary problems and policies in the Burgundian Netherlands, 1433-1496. Leiden, 1970. pp. 229. bibliog.

- Canada

> BINHAMMER (H.H.) Money, banking and the Canadian financial system. Toronto, [1968]. pp. 574. bibliogs.

> HAY (KEITH A. J.) Determinants of the Canadian money supply, 1875 - 1958. rev. ed. [Ottawa], 1968. fo. 30. (Carleton University. Carleton Economic Papers)

> RASMINSKY (LOUIS) Monetary policy and the defence of the Canadian dollar. [Victoria?, 1968]. fo. 18.

> MONEY and banking: analysis and policy in a Canadian context; [by] Gordon Boreham [and others]. [Toronto, 1969]. pp. 848.

> O'BRIEN (JOHN W.) and LERMER (G.) Canadian money and banking. 2nd ed. Toronto, [1969]. pp. 366. bibliog.

> LELART (MICHEL) La monnaie canadienne. Paris, [1970]. pp. 382. bibliog.

> PLUMPTRE (ARTHUR FITZWALTER WYNNE) Exchange-rate policy: experience with Canada's floating rate. Princeton, N.J., 1970. pp. 11. (Princeton.University Department of Economics and Sociology. International Finance Section. Essays in International Finance. No. 81)

> BEATTIE (J.R.) Remarks on "monetary policy". n.p., 1971. fo. 10.

- Ceylon

> GUNASEKERA (HILARION AUGUSTUS DE SILVA) From dependent currency to central banking in Ceylon: an analysis of monetary experience, 1825-1957. London, [1962]. pp. xi, 324. bibliog.

- Chile

> BANCO CENTRAL DE CHILE. Estudios monetarios. Santiago de Chile, 1968. pp. 181.

MONEY

- China

CHINA'S renminbi: one of the few most stable currencies in the world. Peking, 1969. pp. 32.

- Colombia

ABELLA (ARTURO) "Don Dinero" en la independencia. [Bogotá], Lerner, [1966]. pp. 213. 21½cm.

- Czechoslovakia

DOSTAL' (AELITA ARSEN'EVNA) Sotsialisticheskoe preobrazovanie i razvitie denezhno-kreditnoi sistemy Chekhoslovakii. Moskva, 1967. pp. 166.

- Egypt

MARZOUK (GIRGIS ABDO) Monetary and financial analyses in the Egyptian region. [Cairo], 1960. pp. 25, (12). bibliog. 23½cm. (United Arab Republic. Institute of National Planning. National Planning Series. 55) In English and Arabic.

- Europe

JAMES (E.) Unification monétaire en Europe. in Conférences économiques délivrées au séminaire du Professeur G.U. Papi. Milano, 1962.

SPUFFORD (P.) Coinage and currency. in The Cambridge economic history of Europe from the decline of the Roman Empire. vol. 3. Cambridge, 1963.

FEDERAL TRUST FOR EDUCATION AND RESEARCH. Federal Trust Reports. Special Series. No. 4. European monetary co-operation [edited report of a conference organised by the Federal Trust in London on 8-9th July, 1969]; [by] Harold Lever [and others]. London, 1969. pp. 94.

GARELLI (FRANÇOIS) Pour une monnaie européenne. Paris, [1969]. pp. 155.

COFFEY (PETER) Economist, and PRESLEY (JOHN R.) European monetary integration. London, 1971. pp. 131.

INTEGRATION durch Währungsunion?: Integration through monetary union?; Symposium Juni 1970 [held at the Institut für Weltwirtschaft an der Universität Kiel; with contributions by Otmar Emminger and others]; herausgegeben von Herbert Giersch. Tübingen, 1971. pp. 178. bibliog.

MAGNIFICO (GIOVANNI) European monetary unification for balanced growth: a new approach. Princeton, 1971. pp. 39. (Princeton University. Department of Economics and Sociology. International Finance Section. Essays in International Finance. No.88)

COOPER (RICHARD N.) Sterling, European monetary unification, and the international monetary system. [London], 1972. pp. 28.

- European Economic Community countries

CARDINALI (G.) La moneta scritturale nei Paesi del Mercato Comune Europeo. in Saggi di economia aziendale e sociale in memoria di Gino Zappa. vol. 1. Milano, 1961.

EUROPEAN ECONOMIC COMMUNITY. 1962. Les instruments de la politique monétaire dans les pays de la Communauté Économique Européenne. [Brussels], 1962. pp. 279. 25cm.

EUROPEAN ECONOMIC COMMUNITY. 1962. The instruments of monetary policy in countries of the European Economic Community. [Brussels], 1962. pp. 268. 25cm.

COLLIN (FERNAND) The priority of monetary integration in the European context. [Brussels, 1968?]. pp. 22.

KOHLER (BEATE) and SCHLAEGER (GERT) Ein Markt und eine Währung. Köln, [1968]. pp. 137. bibliog. (Bildungswerk Europäische Politik. Europäische Schriften. Band 17)

ROMETSCH (SIEGHARDT) Monetäre Integration: das Problem einer Währungsunion im Gemeinsamen Markt. Frankfurt am Main, [1968]. pp. 165. bibliog.

KATZ (SAMUEL I.) External surpluses, capital flows, and credit policy in the European Economic Community, 1958 to 1967. Princeton, University, Department of Economics and Sociology, International Finance Section, 1969. pp. 45. 22½cm. (Princeton Studies in International Finance. No. 22)

CARTOU (LOUIS) La politique monétaire de la C.E.E. Paris, [1970]. pp. 96. bibliog.

- Europe, Eastern

GROSSMAN (GREGORY) ed. Money and plan: financial aspects of East European economic reforms. Berkeley, 1968. pp. 188.

- Finland

SUOMEN PANKKI. Taloustieteellinen Tutkimuslaitos. Jalkaisuja. Sarja D.2. The index clause system in the Finnish money and capital markets. [Helsinki], 1969. fo. 18.

- France

NEURRISSE (ANDRÉ) Histoire du franc. 2nd ed. Paris, P.U.F., 1967. pp. 128. bibliog. 17½cm. (Que Sais-Je? No. 1082)

HERSCHTEL (MARIE LUISE) Die Bedeutung der Finanzgebarung der öffentlichen Hand für den Geldwert in Frankreich nach 1945. Berlin, Duncker & Humblot, [1968]. pp. 256. bibliog. 23½cm. (Bonn. Universität. Institut für das Spar-, Giro- und Kreditwesen. Untersuchungen über das Spar-, Giro- und Kreditwesen. Band 39)

GUILLAUMONT-JEANNENEY (SYLVIANE) Politique monétaire et croissance économique en France, 1950-1966. Paris, 1969. pp. 168. bibliog. (Fondation Nationale des Sciences Politiques. Service d'Etude de l'Activité Economique et de la Situation Sociale. Recherches sur l'Economie Française. 13)

MARJOLIN (ROBERT) and others. Rapport sur le marché monétaire et les conditions du crédit. [Paris], La Documentation Française, [1969]. pp. 57.

NETTER (MARCEL) Les institutions monétaires en France. 2nd ed. Paris, 1969. pp. 126.

VOLCOUVE (VICTOR) La crise du franc. Paris, [1969]. pp. 143.

MOURGUES (MICHELLE DE) Le marché monétaire dans le système financier français. Paris, 1971. pp. 303. bibliog.

- Germany

EROERTERUNG der Fragen: ob die Klagen über den zunehmenden Geldmangel in Deutschland gegründet seyn, woher derselbe entstehe und wie solchem zum Theil abgeholfem werden könne? 2nd ed. Frankfurt Lüdecke, 1771. pp. 110. 16½cm.

GERMANY (BUNDESREPUBLIK). Bundesministerium für Wirtschaft. Wissenschaftlicher Beirat. 1961. Aufwertung der Deutschen Mark. Bonn, 1961. pp. 3. 30cm.

ERNST (KLAUS ALFRED) Die Bedeutung des Gesetzeszweckes im internationalen Währungs- und Devisenrecht. Berlin, De Gruyter, 1963. pp. xix, 90. bibliog. 22cm. (Cologne. Universität. Rechtswissenschaftliche Fakultät. Neue Kölner Rechtswissenschaftliche Abhandlungen. Heft 26)

BLEILE (GEORG) Aktuelle Probleme der internationalen Währungsordnung unter besonderer Berücksichtigung der Aufwertung der deutschen Mark. Freiburg im Br., imprint, 1964 pp. v, 166, xix. bibliog. 20½cm.

KIRCH (ELEONORE) Die Neuordnung des Geldwesens, des Kreditmarktes und des Verkehrsmarktes der westdeutschen Wirtschaft nach der Währungsreform. Marburg, 1964. pp. 111. bibliog.

HAHN (LUCIEN ALBERT) Rückblick und Ausblick;... Vortrag, gehalten anlässlich seines 75.Geburtstags am 12. Oktober 1964, etc. Tübingen, Mohr, [1965]. pp. 32. 22½cm.

HUTTNER (FRANZ JOSEF) Auswirkungen der Aufwertung einer Währung auf die betriebliche Wirtschaftsrechnung. Marburg, 1965. pp. 246. bibliog.

LANG (PETER) War Aufwertung der D-Mark notwendig und erfolgreich? München, [imprint], 1966. pp. i-x. 187, xi-xvi. bibliog. 20½cm.

LANGER (WOLFRAM) Sicherung der Geldwertstabilität: eine Aufgabe der Konjunktur-, Struktur- und Wachstumspolitik. Kiel, Universität, Institut für Weltwirtschaft, 1966. pp. 20. 23½cm. (Kieler Vorträge. Neue Folge. 44)

GIERSCH (HERBERT) Lohnpolitik und Geldwertstabilität. Kiel, Universität, Institut für Weltwirtschaft, 1967. pp. 20. 24cm. (Kieler Vorträge. Neue Folge. 50)

IRMLER (HEINRICH) Geldwertstabilität und Wirtschaftswachstum. Kiel, Universität, Institut für Weltwirtschaft, 1967. pp. 21. 23½cm. (Kieler Vorträge. Neue Folge. 51)

ROEPER (HANS) Geschichte der D-Mark. Frankfurt a.M., Fischer, 1968. pp. 176. bibliog. 18cm. (Informationen zur Zeit. 890)

BUESCHGEN (HANS E.) Der deutsche Geldmarkt. Wien, 1969. pp. 69. bibliog. (Österreichische Bankwissenschaftliche Gesellschaft. Schriftenreihe. Heft 31)

FOEGEN (HERMANN) Geld- und Währungsrecht. München, 1969. pp. 175. bibliog.

GAUDE (BERNHARD) Die Mechanismen der Zentralbankgeldschöpfung und ihre Kontrollierbarkeit durch die Zentralbank. Berlin, [1969]. pp. 209. bibliog. (Bonn. Universität. Institut für das Spar-, Giro- und Kreditwesen. Untersuchungen über das Spar-, Giro- und Kreditwesen. Band 43) With English and French summaries.

STEUER (WERNER) Die Aufwertungsspekulation: Untersuchung...am Beispiel der Deutschen Mark. Berlin, [1969]. pp. 180. bibliog. (Bonn. Universität. Institut für das Spar-, Giro- und Kreditwesen. Untersuchungen über das Spar-, Giro- und Kreditwesen. Band 44) With English and French summaries.

FRITZSCHE (BRUNO) Deutschland wird zahlen: Geschichte und Probleme deutscher Währungspolitik. Köln, [1970]. pp. 248. bibliog.

HAESELBARTH (VOLKER) Der Geldmarkt der Bundesrepublik: eine experimentelle Untersuchung. Berlin, [1970]. pp. 181. bibliog. (Frankfurt am Main. Universität. Wirtschafts- und Sozialwissenschaftliche Fakultät. Frankfurter Wirtschafts- und Sozialwissenschaftliche Studien. Heft 22)

TOMUSCHAT (CHRISTIAN) Die Aufwertung der Deutschen Mark: Staats- und völkerrechtliche Überlegungen zur Neufestsetzung der Währungsparität im Jahre 1969. Köln, 1970. pp. 48. (Max-Planck-Institut für Ausländisches Öffentliches Recht und Völkerrecht, Heidelberg. Beiträge zum Ausländischen Öffentlichen Recht und Völkerrecht. [Heft] 55)

- Germany - Saarland

WEIDIG (CLAUS ELMAR) Das saarländische Geld- und Kreditwesen bei der Eingliederung des Saarlandes in die deutsche Bundesrepublik. Saarlouis, 1962. pp. xi, 127. bibliog. 20½cm.

- Greece

ZOLOTAS (XENOPHON) Current monetary and economic developments in Greece. Athens, 1966. pp. 25. (Bank of Greece. Papers and Lectures. 19)

ZOLOTAS (XENOPHON) Monetary planning. Athens, Bank of Greece, 1967. pp. 16. 23½cm. (Papers and Lectures. 22)

- Guatemala

GUATEMALA. Statutes, etc. 1945-46. Decreto 203: Ley Monetaria; Decreto 215: Ley Orgánica del Banco de Guatemala; Decreto 315: Ley de Bancos. 3rd ed. Guatemala, 1963. pp. (144). 20½cm.

- Hong Kong

LIN (TZONG-BIAU) Das monetäre System und das Verhalten des Angebotes an und Nachfrage nach Geld in Hong Kong. Freiburg im Breisgau, 1969. pp. 146. bibliog.

MONEY

- India

WACHA (Sir DINSHAW EDULJI) The Indian currency question: Mr. Wacha's speech, at the fourteenth Indian National Congress,... Madras...December 1898. [Bombay, imprint, 1898] pp. 27.

SHENOY (BELLIKOTH RAGHUNATH) The need for devaluation and consequences of devaluation. [Trivandrum, 1966]. pp. 52. (Kerala University. Ramaswamy Mudaliar Lectures. 1966)

SYMPOSIUM ON THE ECONOMIC CONSEQUENCES OF DEVALUATION, KANPUR, 1966. The economic consequences of devaluation; papers read in the symposium...held under the auspices of the Institute of Economic Research...; edited by S.N. Srivastava and J. Sahai. Kanpur, [1966]. pp. 152.

KAPURIA (R.S.) The Indian rupee: a study in retrospect and prospect. Bombay, Vora, 1967. pp. xi, 212. 21cm.

GANGULI (B.) Devaluation. in Appadorai (Angadipuram) ed. India. London, [1968].

SINGHVI (L.M.) ed. Devaluation of the rupee: its implications and consequences. 2nd ed. Delhi, Chand, 1968. pp. xii, 272. bibliog. 22cm.

TANEJA (S.K.) The Indian rupee in a maelstrom. Delhi, Sterling Publishers, 1968. pp. xv, 192. bibliog. 21½cm.

HAJELA (PRAYAG DAS) Problems of monetary policy in underdeveloped countries with special reference to India. Bombay, 1969. pp. 298.

PRASAD (KAMTA) Role of money supply in a developing economy: a theoretical and empirical analysis. Bombay, Allied Publishers, 1969. pp. ix, 177. bibliog. 21½cm.

GHATAK (SUBRATA) Rural money markets in India; [Ph. D. (London) thesis]. 1972. fo.290. bibliog. Typescript: unpublished. This thesis is the property of London University and may not be removed from the Library.

- Indonesia

ECK (DIRK VAN) Juridische aspecten van geld: valutaproblemen bij dekolonisatie. Deventer, 1970. pp. 358. bibliog. With English summary.

- Iraq

AL-ATRASH (MUHAMMAD HASSAN FAWZI) Monetary policy in an underdeveloped economy, with special reference to the experience of Egypt, Iraq and Syria, 1951-1958. 1962. fo. xiii, 254. bibliog. [typescript] Ph.D. (Econ.) (London) thesis: unpublished.

AL-KARAGHOLI (WAHBI ABDUL-RAZAK FATTAH) Le systeme monétaire en Irak. [Beyrouth, imprint, 1967]. pp. 188. bibliog. 23½cm.

- Israel

BEHAM (MIRIAM) Monetary aspects of the 1962 devaluation. Jerusalem, Maurice Falk Institute for Economic Research in Israel, 1968. pp. 106. 24cm.

- Italy

ITALY. Istituto Centrale di Statistica. 1954. Coefficienti per la trasformazione dei valori della lira dal 1871 al 1952. Roma, 1954. pp. vii, 25. 30cm.

ITALY. Istituto Centrale di Statistica. 1958. Coefficienti per la trasformazione dei valori della lira: estensione agli anni 1861-1870 e 1953-1957. Roma, 1958. pp. 19. 30cm.

CECCO (MARCELLO DE) Saggi di politica monetaria. Milano, Giuffrè, 1968. pp. (iii), 143. 25cm. (Rome. Università. Istituto di Politica Economica e Finanziaria. Pubblicazioni. 6)

FELLONI (GIUSEPPE) Il mercato monetario in Piemonte nel secolo XVIII. Milano, Banca Commerciale Italiana, 1968. pp. (iii), 369. bibliog. 24½cm. (Studi e Ricerche di Storia Economica Italiana nell' Età del Risorgimento)

- Japan

BANK OF JAPAN. Economic Research Department. Special Papers. No.12. Flow-of-funds during business adjustment period - monetary and economic developments during 1962 by flow-of-funds approach. Tokyo, 1963. pp. 7. (Reprinted from the July 1963 issue of the Monthly Economic Review, published by the... Bank of Japan)

BANK OF JAPAN. Economic Research Department. Special Papers. No. 30. Flow of funds of the Japanese economy in 1966. Tokyo, the Department, 1967. pp. 14. 27cm.

BANK OF JAPAN. Economic Research Department. The Japanese financial system: March 1969. [Tokyo], 1969. pp. 71.

BANK OF JAPAN. Economic Research Department. Special Papers. No. 37. Flow of funds of the Japanese economy in 1968. Tokyo, 1969. pp. 13.

BANK OF JAPAN. Economic Research Department. Special Papers. No. 41. Flow of funds of the Japanese economy in 1969. Tokyo, 1970. pp. 14.

FROST (PETER) The Bakumatsu currency crisis. Cambridge, Mass., 1970. pp. 79. bibliog. (Harvard University. East Asian Research Center. Harvard East Asian Monographs. 36)

YAO (JIRO) ed. Monetary factors in Japanese economic growth. Kobe, [1970]. pp. 241. (Kobe. University. Research Institute for Economics and Business Administration. Kobe Economic and Business Research Series. No. 3)

- Korea

BANK OF KOREA. Laws, decrees, ordinances. regulations and principles concerning emergency currency measures and emergency monetary measures. [Seoul], 1962. pp. 53. 25½cm.

- Liberia

MAYNARD (GEOFFREY) The economic irrelevance of monetary independence: the case of Liberia. [Reading], 1969. pp. 28. (Reading. University. Department of Economics. Discussion Papers in Economics. No. 20)

- Malta

BUSUTTIL (SALVINO) The decimalization of Maltese currency. [Valletta], 1968. pp. 31. 20½cm.

- Mexico

QUINTANA (MIGUEL A.) Los ensayos monetarios como consecuencia de la baja de la plata: el problema de la plata y el de la moneda de plata en el mundo y en Mexico. [Mexico, 1931]. pp. 233.

KOEHLER (JOHN E.) Economic policy-making with limited information: the process of macro-control in Mexico. Santa Monica, 1968. pp. 64. bibliog. (Rand Corporation. Research Memoranda. 5682)

- Netherlands

NETHERLANDS. Centraal Planbureau. Monografieën. No. 7. Monetary statement and monetary analysis; (by Th. A. Stevers). The Hague, 1959. pp. 24.

JONGMAN (C. D.) Handelsbanken en liquiditeitenmassa in Nederland; openbare les gehouden... 5 Februari 1963. Haarlem, Bohn, 1963. pp. 34. 24cm.

NATIONALE monetaire vraagstukken...; onder redactie van H.W.J. Bosman [and others]. Amsterdam, 1965. pp. 278.

GLASZ (CHRISTIAAN) and VLAK (G.J.M.) Geld en maatschappij: inleiding tot de financiële organisatie van de volkshuishouding. Leiden, 1968. pp. 214.

JONGMAN (C.D.) De monetaire politiek van de Nederlandsche Bank tijdens het presidentschap van M.W. Holtrop. Amsterdam, 1968. pp. 66. (Nederlands Instituut voor het Bank- en Effectenbedrijf. Publikaties. Nr. 1)

ECK (DIRK VAN) Juridische aspecten van geld: valutaproblemen bij dekolonisatie. Deventer, 1970. pp. 358. bibliog. With English summary.

- New Zealand

HOLMES (FRANK W.) Money, credit and credit policies in New Zealand. Wellington, N.Z., 1966. fo. 26.

DEANE (RODERICK S.) and LUMSDEN (M. A.) A model of the New Zealand monetary sector. Wellington, N.Z., 1971. pp. 44. bibliog. (Reserve Bank of New Zealand. Research Papers. No.2)

- Nigeria

NIGERIA. 1957. Report by J.B. Loynes on the establishment of a Nigerian central bank, the introduction of a Nigerian currency and other associated matters. Lagos, 1957. pp. 40.

- Norway

NAERINGSØKONOMISK FORSKNINGSINSTITUTT. Økonomi. Nr.47. En kritisk vurdering av innstillingen fra den penge- og kredittpolitiske komité; [by Rolf Pedersen]. Oslo, 1964. pp. 69. bibliog. 22cm.

SYRING (EDWARD M.) The demand for money in Norway: an econometric analysis. [Oslo, 1968]. pp. 234. bibliog.

- Pakistan

MEENAI (SAID AHMAD) Money and banking in Pakistan. Karachi, 1966. pp. 264. bibliog.

CHAUDHRI (FATEH M.) Money, prices and economic growth in the Pakistan economy; ...background paper presented to the seminar on economic problems of Pakistan, P.I.D.E., January 28-30, 1967. Karachi, 1967. pp. 6.

- Palestine

BEN-DAVID (ARYE) Jerusalem und Tyros: ein Beitrag zur palästinensischen Münz- und Wirtschaftsgeschichte, 126a.C-57p.C.; mit einem Nachwort: Jesus und die Wechsler, von Edgar Salin. Basel, 1969. pp. 55. (List Gesellschaft. Kleine Schriften zur Wirtschaftsgeschichte. Band 1)

- Peru

LIMA. Universidad Nacional Federico Villareal. Instituto de Investigaciones Económicas y Sociales. Evolución de la política monetaria y crediticia peruana. Lima, 1967. pp. 124. bibliog. 21½cm.

- Portugal

MARTIN VALLS (RICARDO) La circulación monetaria ibérica. [Valladolid], Universidad de Valladolid, 1967. pp. 183. 24cm.

- Portugal - Colonies

MAGALHÃES-GODINHO (VITORINO) L'économie de l'empire portugais aux XVe et XVIe siècles. Paris, 1969. pp. 857. bibliog. (Paris. Ecole Pratique des Hautes Etudes. Section des Sciences Economiques et Sociales. Centre de Recherches Historiques. Ports, Routes, Trafics. 26)

- Rome, Ancient

CALLU (JEAN PIERRE) La politique monétaire des empereurs romains de 238 à 311. Paris, 1969. pp. 562. bibliog. (Ecoles Françaises d'Athènes et de Rome. Bibliothèque. Fasc. 214).

- Roumania

KIRIȚESCU (COSTIN C.) Sistemul bănesc al leului și precursorii lui. București, Academia Republicii Socialiste România, 1964 in progress. 24cm.

CREAREA sistemului monetar național la 1867. București, 1968. pp. 125. bibliog. (Academia Republicii Socialiste România. Institutul de Cercetări Economice. Bibliotheca Oeconomica. 5)

- Russia

KATSENELENBAUM (Z. S.) Denezhnoe obrashchenie Rossii, 1914-1924. Moskva, 1924. pp. 192.

BAZILEVICH (KONSTANTIN VASIL'EVICH) Denezhnaia reforma Alekseia Mikhailovicha i vosstanie v Moskve v 1662 g. Moskva, 1936. pp. 115.

AIZENBERG (ISAAK PETROVICH) Osnovy ustoichivosti deneg pri sotsializme. Moskva, 1964. pp. 126.

MONEY - Russia (Cont'd.)

NEKOTORYE voprosy ispol'zovaniia tovarno-denezhnykh otnoshenii v razvitii sotsialisticheskoi ekonomiki. Kuibyshev, 1964. pp. 189. (Kuibyshevskii Planovyi Institut. Uchenye Zapiski. vyp.9)

BERKOV (NIKOLAI TIKHONOVICH) миграция денег и методы ее изучения. Москва, Финансы, 1966. pp. 120. 20cm.

KONNIK (IOSIF ISAAKOVICH) Den'gi v period stroitel'stva kommunisticheskogo obshchestva. Moskva, 1966. pp. 256.

SLAVNYI (ISAAK DAVIDOVICH) Denezhnoe obrashchenie i ekonomicheskaia reforma. Moskva, 1966. pp. 80.

KONNIK (IOSIF ISAAKOVICH) Закономерности взаимосвязи товарного и денежного обращения при социализме. Москва, 1968. pp. 207.

ATLAS (ZAKHARII VENIAMINOVICH) Социалистическая денежная система: проблемы социалистического преобразования и развития денежной системы СССР. Москва, 1969. pp.383.

KATSENELINBOIGEN (ARON IOSIFOVICH) and others. Optimal'nost' i tovarno-denezhnye otnosheniia. Moskva, 1969. pp. 122.

ROGOVA (OL'GA LEONIDOVNA) Методы планирования денежного обращения: вопросы моделирования наличноденежного обращения. Москва, 1969. pp. 122.

BARYREV (VLADIMIR MIKHAILOVICH) Tovarno-denezhnye otnosheniia; finansy i kredit v sotsialisticheskom khoziaistve: voprosy teorii; pod redaktsiei...IA. A. Kronroda. Moskva, 1970. pp. 215.

MEL'NIKOVA (A.S.) Tverdye den'gi. Moskva, 1971. pp. 79.

- Russia - Bibliography

DREMINA (Z. E.) and others, compilers. Finansy, den'gi i kredit SSSR: bibliograficheskii ukazatel', 1946-1966. Moskva, 1967. pp. 479.

- South Africa

KING (WILFRED THOMAS COUSINS) South Africa's growing money market. [Johannesburg, 1962]. pp. 161-170. (Extracted from Optima, September, 1962)

SOUTH AFRICA. Commission of Enquiry into Fiscal and Monetary Policy in South Africa. 1970. Fiscal and monetary policy in South Africa: third report: [Chairman, D.G. Franzsen] (R.P. 87/1970). in South Africa. Parliament. House of Assembly. Votes and proceedings; (with Printed annexures).

- Spain

MARTIN VALLS (RICARDO) La circulación monetaria ibérica. [Valladolid], Universidad de Valladolid, 1967. pp. 183. 24cm.

BLANCO (FRANCISCO JAVIER) and others. Devaluación y crisis económica. Madrid, ZYX, [1968]. pp. 88. bibliog. 16½cm. (Colección Lee y Discute. Serie Roja. 30)

- Sweden

SWEDEN. Finansdepartementet. 1957. Recept mot inflation: sex professorer har ordet. Stockholm, 1957. pp. 133. 19½cm.

- Switzerland

KUENZLE (ROBERT) Hochkonjunktur und Stabilisierung der Kaufkraft des Schweizerfrankens, 1954-1957. Winterthur, Keller, 1965. pp. viii, 151. bibliog. 22½cm.

FRANCE. Direction de la Documentation. La Documentation Française. Notes et Études Documentaires. No. 3,316. Le franc suisse et la politique monétaire et financière de la Suisse depuis 1960; [by] Rudolf Frei. Paris, 1966. pp. 37. bibliog. 30½cm.

BAUR (PETER) Wandlungen in der äusseren Währungspolitik der Schweiz seit dem Übergang zur Konvertibilität in Europa 1958-1964. Zürich, Juris, 1967. pp. vi, 251. bibliog. 22½cm.

HOCHULI (EMIL) the Younger. Die schweizerische Gold- und Dollarpolitik vom Beginn des Zweiten Weltkrieges im Herbst 1939 bis zur Pfundabwertung im Herbst 1949. Stuttgart, 1967. pp. v, 158. bibliog. 21cm.

SCHELBERT-SYFRIG (HEIDI) Empirische Untersuchungen über die Geldnachfrage in der Schweiz. Zürich, Polygraphischer Verlag, 1967. pp. xiii, 180. bibliog. 22½cm. (Zuerich. Universität. Rechts- und Staatswissenschaftliche Fakultät. Zürcher Volkswirtschaftliche Forschungen. Neue Folge. Band 12)

TOBLER (EWALD) Entwurf eines schweizerischen Mindestreservesystems auf der Grundlage ausländischer Methoden und Erfahrungen. Zürich, 1967. pp. 94. bibliog.

SIEBER (HUGO) and TUCHTFELDT (EGON) Probleme der schweizerischen Geldpolitik. Bern, [1969]. pp. 142.

- Tanzania

BINHAMMER (H.H.) Institutional arrangements for supplying credit and finance to the rural sector of the economy in Tanzania. Dar Es Salaam, [1968]. pp. 28. (Dar Es Salaam. University. Economic Research Bureau. ERB Papers. 68. 17)

LOXLEY (JOHN) The behaviour of the Tanzania money supply, 1966-1970, and the use of monetary indicators. [Dar Es Salaam, 1971]. pp. 46, 13. (Dar Es Salaam. University. Economic Research Bureau. ERB Papers. 71.3)

- Tunisia

BISTOLFI (ROBERT) Structure économique et indépendance monétaire: l'expérience monétaire de la Tunisie et ses enseignements. Paris, Cujas, [1967]. pp. 347. bibliog. 24cm. (Système et Structures Économiques. 3)

- Ukraine

TOVARNO-HROSHOVI... Товарно-грошові відносини та ексномічна реформа. Львів, Університет, 1967. pp. 282. 19½см.

- United Kingdom

CROSS (WILLIAM) A standard pound versus the pound sterling: a project for rendering the measure of value independent of the price of gold, and establishing the monetary system on a secure foundation. Edinburgh, 1856. pp. 32.

DOUGLAS (CLIFFORD HUGH) The breakdown of the employment system. Manchester, [1923]. pp. 11.

VICKERS (VINCENT CARTWRIGHT) Finance in the melting pot: reform or revolution?; the petition to His Majesty the King. London, 1936. pp. 31.

BEWLAY (SIMON) Devaluation: the crucial questions. [London, 1967]. pp. 13.

FRANCE. Direction de la Documentation. La Documentation Française. Notes et Études Documentaires. No. 3, 359. La livre sterling. Paris, 1967. pp. 47. bibliog. 30½cm.

[GOODHART (CHARLES C.A.E.)] British monetary policy, 1957-1967. [London, 1967]. fo. 80. bibliog.

LABOUR RESEARCH DEPARTMENT. Devaluation: questions and answers. London, 1967. pp. 19. 13½cm.

BURNS (EMILE) Money and inflation. London, Lawrence & Wishart, 1968. pp. 64. 18½cm.

CHALMERS (ERIC B.) U.K. monetary policy. London, Griffith, 1968. pp. 120. 18½cm.

DEANE (MARJORIE) Devaluation: why it must work. London, The Economist, 1968. pp. 24. 21½cm. (Briefs. 3)

MAASS (GUENTHER) Die Rolle des Pfund Sterlings in der Weltwirtschaft seit dem Zweiten Weltkrieg. Tübingen, 1968. pp. 185. bibliog. (Kiel. Universität. Institut für Weltwirtschaft. Kieler Studien. 90)

U.K. Central Office of Information. Reference Division. 1968. Devaluation and subsequent economic measures in Britain. London, 1968. pp. 5. 23½cm.

CHAPMAN (RICHARD A.) Decision making: a case study of the decision to raise the bank rate in September 1957. London, 1968, or rather 1969. pp. 118. bibliog.

CHOURAQUI (JEAN CLAUDE) Le marché monétaire de Londres depuis 1960. Paris, 1969. pp. 139. bibliog.

The LONDON discount market today;...by...Wilfred King [and others]. London, 1969. pp. 57. (Institute of Bankers. Ernest Sykes Memorial Lectures. 1962)

MORGAN (EDWARD VICTOR) Monetary policy for stable growth. 3rd ed. London, 1969. pp. 60. bibliog. (Institute of Economic Affairs. Hobart Papers. 27)

PARKIN (J.M.) and others. The portfolio behaviour of commercial banks. [Colchester], 1969. fo. 24. (Colchester. University of Essex. Department of Economics. Discussion Papers. No. 8)

ROWAN (D.C.) The monetary sector of the Southampton econometric model. [Southampton], 1969. fo. 22. bibliog. (Southampton. University. Department of Economics and Department of Econometrics. An Econometric Model of the U.K. Economy and its Trading Partners. Progress Papers. T. 5)

ROWAN (D.C.) and O'BRIEN (R.J.) Expectations, the interest rate structure and debt policy. [Southampton], 1969. fo. 53. bibliog. (Southampton. University. Department of Economics and Department of Econometrics. An Econometric Model of the U.K. Economy and its Trading Partners. Progress Papers. A. 5)

SHEPPARD (DAVID K.) Asset preferences and the money supply in the United Kingdom, 1880-1962. [Birmingham], 1969. pp. 24. (Birmingham. University. Faculty of Commerce and Social Science. Discussion Papers. Series A. No. 111)

WALTERS (ALAN A.) Money in boom and slump: an empirical inquiry into British experience since the 1880's. London, 1969. pp. 56. bibliog. (Institute of Economic Affairs. Hobart Papers. 44)

WALTERS (ALAN A.) The Radcliffe report: ten years after; a survey of empirical evidence ...; a paper to be presented at the "Radcliffe-ten years after" conference at Hove, Sussex, Oct. 24-26. [London, 1969?] fo.27.

WELHAM (P.J.) Monetary circulation in the United Kingdom: a statistical study. Oxford, 1969. pp. 118.

BAIN (ANDREW DAVID) The control of the money supply. Harmondsworth, 1970. pp. 175. bibliog.

GRIFFITHS (BRIAN) Monetary policy and resource allocation in the U.K. [London, 1970]. fo. 40.

HOCKLEY (G.C.) Monetary policy and public finance. London, 1970. pp. 301. bibliog.

HUTCHISON (TERENCE WILMOT) Economists and devaluation, (1963-1969). [Birmingham, 1970?] pp. 46. (Birmingham. University. Faculty of Commerce and Social Science. Discussion Papers. Series A. No. 119)

MONEY in Britain, 1959-1969: the papers of the Radcliffe report, ten years after; conference at Hove, Sussex, October, 1969; edited by David R. Croome and Harry G. Johnson. London, 1970. pp. 304. bibliog.

RANDS (R.S.J.) The problem of money: an appeal to students...: a brief explanation of the new economics: the way to combat inflation. London, 1970. pp. 55.

WALTERS (ALAN A.) Money in boom and slump: an empirical inquiry into British experience since the 1880's. 2nd ed. London, 1970. pp. 63. bibliog. (Institute of Economic Affairs. Hobart Papers. 44)

NEWLYN (WALTER TESSIER) Theory of money. 2nd ed. Oxford, 1971. pp. 220.

MONEY - United Kingdom (Cont'd.)

The POUND into Europe?: sterling, the City and EEC entry; [by] Raymond Barre [and others]. London, [1971]. pp. 52.

STRANGE (SUSAN) Sterling and British policy: a political study of an international currency in decline. London, 1971. pp. 363. bibliog.

- United Kingdom - Wales

JONES (IVOR WYNNE) Money for all: the story of the Welsh pound. 2nd ed. Llandudno, 1969. pp. 64.

- United States

WHICH do you want...free coinage or sound money? n.p., [1896]. pp. 16.

POUND (EZRA) America, Roosevelt and the causes of the present war; (translated by John Drummond). London, Russell, 1951. pp. 18. bibliog. 21½cm. (Money Pamphlets. No. 6)

HATANAKA (MICHIO) Quarterly estimation of the quantity of money, seasonally unadjusted, June 1923 -- December 1942. Princeton, Princeton University, Econometric Research Program, 1961. fo. (iii), 30. 28cm. (Research Papers. No. 6)

STERN (CLARENCE AMES) Golden Republicanism: the crusade for hard money. [Sioux City, the Author, 1964]. pp. ix, 118. bibliog. 21½cm.

UNITED STATES. House of Representatives. Committee on Banking and Currency. An alternative approach to the monetary mechanism. Washington, 1964. pp. xi, 131.

UNITED STATES. House of Representatives. Committee on Banking and Currency. A primer on money; (with Supplement: Money facts). Washington, 1964. 2 pts.

WARBURTON (CLARK) Depression, inflation and monetary policy: selected papers, 1945-1953. Baltimore, [1966]. pp. 425.

HUTCHINSON (HARRY DAVID) Money, banking, and the United States economy. New York, Appleton, [1967]. pp. xix, 456. 23½cm.

NUGENT (WALTER T.K.) The money question during reconstruction. New York, Norton, [1967]. pp. 127. bibliog. 20cm. (Norton Essays in American History)

SHERIDAN (JAMES R.) Employment of temporary funds for commercial banks. Boston, [1967]. pp. 132. bibliog.

SNIDER (DELBERT ARTHUR) Optimum adjustment processes and currency areas. Princeton, 1967. pp. 23. (Princeton University. Department of Economics and Sociology. International Finance Section. Essays in International Finance. No. 62.)

FRIEDMAN (MILTON) Dollars and deficits: living with America's economic problems. Englewood Cliffs, [1968]. pp. 279.

JACKENDOFF (NATHANIEL) Money, flow of funds, and economic policy. New York, Ronald P., 1968. pp. viii, 523. bibliogs. 22½cm.

JOHNSON (HARRY L.) and WALKER (ERNEST W.) eds. Monetary issues of the 1960's. Austin, University of Texas, Bureau of Business Research, 1968. pp. x, 89. 23cm. (Studies in Banking and Finance. No. 8)

PESEK (BORIS PETER) and SAVING (THOMAS R.) The foundations of money and banking. New York, Macmillan, [1968]. pp. xxvii, 525. 23½cm.

WHITTLESEY (CHARLES RAYMOND) and others. Money and banking: analysis and policy. 2nd ed. New York, [1968]. pp. 543.

BRENNAN (JOHN A.) Silver and the first New Deal. Reno, 1969. pp. 187. bibliog.

CHANDLER (LESTER VERNON) The economics of money and banking. 5th ed. New York, 1969. pp. 562. bibliogs.

COMMITTEE FOR ECONOMIC DEVELOPMENT. Research and Policy Committee. Program Committee. A stabilizing fiscal and monetary policy for 1970. New York, 1969. pp. 23.

FRIEDMAN (MILTON) and HELLER (WALTER W.) Monetary vs. fiscal policy. New York, [1969]. pp. 95. (New York (City). University. Graduate School of Business Administration. Arthur K. Solomon Lectures. 7th)

GOODHART (CHARLES A.E.) The New York money market and the finance of trade, 1900-1913. Cambridge, Harvard U.P., 1969. pp. vii, 235. bibliog. 21cm. (Harvard University. Harvard Economic Studies. vol. 132.)

HORVITZ (PAUL M.) Monetary policy and the financial system. 2nd ed. Englewood Cliffs, Prentice-Hall, [1969]. pp. xvii, 525. bibliogs. 23cm.

SUCHESTOW (MARCEL) The principle of the total picture: the first axiom in economic analysis. New York, 1969. pp. 163.

CHANDLER (LESTER VERNON) American monetary policy, 1928-1941. New York, [1971]. pp. 371. bibliog.

FRIEDMAN (MILTON) and SCHWARTZ (ANNA JACOBSON) Monetary statistics of the United States: estimates, sources, methods. New York, 1970. pp. 629. (National Bureau of Economic Research. Studies in Business Cycles. [No.] 20)

RICHARDSON (DENNIS W.) Electric money: evolution of an electronic funds-transfer system. Cambridge, Mass., [1970]. pp. 181. bibliog.

BACH (GEORGE LELAND) Making monetary and fiscal policy. Washington, [1971]. pp. 281. bibliog.

MUNDELL (ROBERT ALEXANDER) The dollar and the policy mix: 1971. Princeton, N.J., 1971. pp. 28. (Princeton University. Department of Economics and Sociology. International Finance Section. Essays in International Finance. No. 85)

- Uruguay

URUGUAY. Ministerio de Hacienda. 1962. La reforma cambiaria y monetaria del año 1959. [Montevideo], 1962. pp. 108. bibliog.

- Venezuela

CARRILLO BATALLA (TOMÁS ENRIQUE) Moneda, crédito y banca en Venezuela. Caracas, Banco Central de Venezuela, 1964. 2 vols. bibliog. 23cm.(Colección Cuatrocentenario de Caracas. 4)

DOWNTON (CHRISTINE VERONICA) A monetary study of Venezuela, 1950-1967; [Ph. D. (London) thesis]. [1970]. fo. 282. bibliog. Typescript: unpublished. This thesis is the property of London University and may not be removed from the Library.

- Yemen

SOUTHERN YEMEN. Currency Authority. Report. q., 1967/1968 (1st)- Crater.

MONEY, PRIMITIVE

LAUM (BERNHARD) Viehgeld und Viehkapital in den asiatisch-afrikanischen Hirtenkulturen. Tübingen, Mohr, 1965. pp. 60. 22½cm. (Recht und Staat. 308/309)

PANKHURST (RICHARD KEIR PETHICK) Primitive money: money and banking in Ethiopia. Addis Ababa, Commercial Bank of Ethiopia, 1967. pp. 54. 23½cm.

MONGOLIA

SANDERS (A. J. K.) The People's Republic of Mongolia: a general referance guide. London, O.U.P., 1968. pp. xi, 232. bibliog. 21½cm.

MONGOL'SKAIA Narodnaia Respublika. Moskva, 1971. pp. 438.

TITKOV (VASILII IVANOVICH) Mongol'skaia Narodnaia Respublika: obshchestvo, ekonomika, gosudarstvo, pravo. Moskva, 1971. pp. 104.

- Army - History

SORKIN (NAUM SEMENOVICH) Vnachale puti: zapiski instruktora Mongol'skoi armii. Moskva, 1970. pp. 126.

- Bibliography

TIULIAEVA (V.P.) compiler. Mongol'skaia Narodnaia Respublika: bibliografiia knizhnoi i zhurnal'noi literatury na russkom iazyke, 1935-1950 gg. Moskva, 1953. pp. 87. (Akademiia Nauk SSSR and Shinjleh Uhaany Akadyemi. Mongol'skaia Komissiia. Trudy. vyp.42)

- Constitutional history - Sources

PUNTSAGNOROV (TS.) ed. Революционные мероприятия народного правительства Монголии в 1921-1924 гг.: документы, etc. Москва, ИВЛ, 1960. pp. 211. 20cm.

- Description and travel

KATERINICH (ANATOLII NIKOLAEVICH) Десятилетия, равные векам. Москва, Политиздат, 1966. pp. 55. 20cm.

IVANENKO (VASILII IVANOVICH) Тропою памяти. Москва, 1968. pp. 120.

BURDUKOV (ALEKSEI VASIL'EVICH) В старой и новой Монголии: воспоминания, письма; (ответственный редактор И. Я. Златкин) Москва, Наука, 1969. pp. 419. bibliog. 20см.

- Economic conditions

FRANCE. Direction de la Documentation. La Documentation Française. Notes et Études Documentaires. No. 3,312. Le développement économique de la République populaire de Mongolie; [by] Léon Lavallée [and] Anne Bernolle. Paris, 1966. pp. 34. bibliog. 30½cm.

GUNGAADASH (B.) Mongoliia segodnia: priroda, liudi, khoziaistvo; perevod s mongol'skogo; predislovie i redaktsiia I. Kh. Ovdienko. Moskva, 1969. pp. 285. bibliog.

OCHERKI... Очерки экономики Монгольской Народной Республики. Москва, Наука, 1969. pp. 232. 20см.

- Economic history

NEKAPITALISTICHESKII put' razvitiia i opyt Mongol'skoi Narodnoi Respubliki. Moskva, 1971. pp. 303.

- Economic policy

PISAREV (VASILII IL'ICH) MNR na puti k zaversheniiu stroitel'stva sotsializma. Moskva, 1964. pp. 160.

- Foreign economic relations

GOMBOZHAV (DAMDINY) Rol' ekonomicheskogo sotrudnichestva v razvitii MNR. Moskva, 1969. pp. 110.

- Foreign economic relations - Russia

BERESINA (A.I.) Velikaia Oktiabr'skaia sotsialisticheskaia revoliutsiia i nachalo ekonomicheskogo sotrudnichestva Sovetskogo Soiuza i MNR. in Torzhestvo leninskoi natsional'noi politiki. Ulan-Ude, 1968.

ASONOV (BORIS ALEKSEEVICH) and PETROV (BORIS MIKHAILOVICH) Ekonomicheskoe sotrudnichestvo Sovetskogo Soiuza s MNR. Moskva, 1971. pp. 167.

- History

SHIRENDYB (B.) Монголия на рубеже XIX-XX веков: история социально-экономического развития. Улан-Батор, Комитет по Делам Печати, 1963. pp. 518. bibliog. 21½cm.

SANDAG (SH.) Борьба монгольского народа за государственную независимость и строительство новой жизни: научно-популярный очерк; под редакцией... В. Ширендыба. Улан-Батор, Госиздат, 1966. pp. 144. 20см.

ISTORIIA Mongol'skoi Narodnoi Respubliki. 2nd ed. Moskva, 1967. pp. 537.

BAWDEN (C.R.) The modern history of Mongolia. London, Weidenfeld and Nicolson, [1968]. pp. xvii, 460. bibliog. 21½cm. (Asia-Africa Series of Modern Histories)

MONGOLIA - History (Cont'd.)

50 let narodnoi revoliutsii v Mongolii: sbornik statei. Moskva, 1971. pp. 199.

SHIRENDYB (BAZARYN) Istoriia Mongol'skoi narodnoi revoliutsii 1921 goda; sokrashchennyi perevod s mongol'skogo. Moskva, 1971. pp. 399.

- Relations (general) with Russia

KISLOV (ALEKSEI NIKANOROVICH) Razgrom Ungerna: o boevom sodruzhestve sovetskogo i mongol'skogo narodov. Moskva, 1964. pp. 98.

SHIRENDYB (BAZARYN) Влияние Великой Октябрьской социалистической революции на Монголию; под общей редакцией Б. Болдо. Москва, 1967. pp. 99. (Великая Сила Идей Октября)

ISTORICHESKII opyt bratskogo sodruzhestva KPSS i MNRP v bor'be za sotsializm. Moskva, 1971. pp. 319.

SHIRENDYB (BAZARYN) Istoriia Mongol'skoi narodnoi revoliutsii 1921 goda; sokrashchennyi perevod s mongol'skogo. Moskva, 1971. pp. 399.

- Social conditions

FRANCE. Direction de la Documentation. La Documentation Francaise. Notes et Études Documentaires. No. 3,312. Le développement économique de la République populaire de Mongolie; [by] Léon Lavallée [and] Anne Bernolle. Paris, 1966. pp. 34. bibliog. 30½cm.

MONGOLIAN LANGUAGES

DARBEEVA (ANNA ANGADYKOVNA) Razvitie obshchestvennykh funktsii mongol'skikh iazykov v sovetskuiu epokhu. Moskva, 1969. pp. 151.

MONGOLISM

UNITED STATES. Children's Bureau. Publs. No. 401. Families of mongoloid children. Washington, 1963. pp (iii), 56. bibliog.

MONGOLS

VLADIMIRTSOV (BORIS IAKOVLEVICH) Общественный строй монголов: монгольский кочевой феодализм. Ленинград, 1934. pp. 223. bibliog.

STUDIA Mongolskie. Warszawa, 1969. pp. 132. (Polska Akademia Nauk. Instytut Historii Kultury Materialnej. Biblioteka Etnografii Polskiej. Nr.19) Illustrated. With Russian and English summaries.

TATARO-mongoly v Azii i Evrope: sbornik statei. Moskva, 1970. pp. 473.

- History

SPULER (BERTOLD) The Muslim world: a historical survey. Leiden, 1960 repr. 1968 in progress. bibliogs. Facsimile reprint.

GROUSSET (RENE) Conqueror of the world; translated [from the French] by Denis Sinor and Marian MacKellar, with preface notes and bibliography by Denis Sinor. Edinburgh, Oliver & Boyd, 1967. pp. xvii, 300.

MONGOLS IN RUSSIA

KARGALOV (VADIM VIKTOROVICH) Vneshnepoliticheskie faktory razvitiia feodal'noi Rusi: feodal'naia Rus' i kochevniki. Moskva, 1967. pp. 263.

MONIE (PETER WILLIAM)

CLAYTON (P.B.) and BARON (BARCLAY) Four men: (Herbert Plumer, Peter Monie, Ludovic Porter, Alec Paterson). London, 1948. pp. 40.

MONISM

GASMAN (DANIEL) The scientific origins of national socialism: social Darwinism in Ernst Haeckel. and the German Monist League. London, 1971. pp. 208. bibliog.

MONKEYS

HOOFF (J.A.R.A.M. VAN) The facial displays of the catarrhine monkeys and apes. in Morris (Desmond) ed. Primate ethology. London, [1967].

MONMOUTH'S REBELLION, 1685

CHENEVIX TRENCH (CHARLES POCKLINGTON) The western rising: an account of the rebellion of James Scott, Duke of Monmouth. London, 1969. pp. 293.

MONNET (JEAN)

FONTAINE (FRANÇOIS) Jean Monnet. Lausanne, Centre de Recherches Européennes, 1963. pp. 18. 24cm. (Reprinted from Réalités, December 1962)

BROMBERGER (MERRY) and BROMBERGER (SERGE) Jean Monnet and the United States of Europe. New York, [1969]. pp. 349.

RIEBEN (HENRI) and others. Jean Monnet. Lausanne 1971. pp. 121.

MONOPOLIES

REITZ (ERNST LUDWIG) Das bilaterale Monopol und die vollmonopolisierte Wirtschaft. Marburg, 1963. pp. 110. bibliog.

IUDANOV (IURII IGNAT'EVICH) Monopoliia-grabitel': kontsern "Iunilever". Moskva, 1967. pp. 64.

KINGSTON (WILLIAM HENRY GILES) Invention and monopoly. London, Woolwich Polytechnic, Department of Economics and Business Studies, [1967]. pp. 39. 21cm. (Woolwich Economic Papers. No.15).

BARNIKEL (HANS HEINRICH) ed. Wettbewerb und Monopol. Darmstadt, 1968. pp. 449.

GROENEWALD (HORST) Grundzüge regionaler Preisdifferenzierung: analytische Darstellung am Beispiel eines Monopolbetriebes. Meisenheim am Glan, 1968. pp. 67. bibliog.

TOWNSEND (HARRY) Scale, innovation, merger and monopoly: an introduction to industrial economics. Oxford, Pergamon P., 1968. pp. ix, 106. 19½cm. (Commonwealth and International Library)

HERMANIN (FEDERICO) and others, eds. Monopolkapital: Thesen zu dem Buch von Paul A. Baran und Paul M. Sweezy. Frankfurt a.M., [1969]. pp. 141.

HUNTER (ALEX) ed. Monopoly and competition; selected readings. Harmondsworth, 1969. pp. 429. bibliog.

KULIKOV (ALEKSANDR GEORGIEVICH) General'nye shtaby monopolii: soiuzy predprinimatelei v sisteme gosudarstvenno-monopolisticheskogo kapitalizma. Moskva, 1969. pp. 231.

MERHAV (MEIR) Technological dependence, monopoly, and growth. Oxford, Pergamon, 1969. pp. xi, 211. 21½cm.

RABOCHII... Рабочий класс и антимонополистическая борьба: материалы Международной научной конференции "50-летие Октября и международный рабочий класс". Москва, 1969. pp. 478.

SHILLING (NED) Excise taxation of monopoly. New York, 1969. pp. 254. bibliog.

DELILEZ (JEAN PIERRE) Les monopoles: essai sur le capital financier et l'accumulation monopoliste. Paris, [1970]. pp. 209.

GROSSER (DIETER) ed. Konzentration ohne Kontrolle. 2nd ed. Köln, 1970. pp. 314.

HEMPENIUS (ANTON LEENDERT) Monopoly with random demand. Rotterdam, 1970. pp. 87. bibliog.

JOLIET (RENE) Monopolization and abuse of dominant position: a comparative study of the American and European approaches to the control of economic power. Liège, 1970. pp. 329. bibliog. (Liège. Université. Faculté de Droit. Collection Scientifique. 31).

POLITICHESKAIA ekonomiia sovremennogo monopolisticheskogo kapitalizma. Moskva, 1970. 2 vols.

DRAGILEV (MIKHAIL SAMUILOVICH) and FAMINSKII (IGOR' PAVLOVICH) eds. Mezhdunarodnye formy gosudarstvenno-monopolisticheskogo kapitalizma. Moskva, 1971. pp. 318.

INTERNATIONAL CONFERENCE ON MONOPOLIES, MERGERS AND RESTRICTIVE PRACTICES, CAMBRIDGE, 1969. Papers and reports...; edited by J.B. Heath. London, H.M.S.O., 1971. pp. 285.

KHMEL'NITSKAIA (ELIZAVETA LEONIDOVNA) Ocherki sovremennoi monopolii. Moskva, 1971. pp. 207.

TEMPEL (GUDRUN) Als wär's der liebe Gott: die Weltmacht der Konzerne. Gütersloh, [1971]. pp. 237.

- Bibliography

U. K. Board of Trade. 1970. Competition, monopoly and restrictive practices: a select bibliography. London, 1970. pp. 127.

- Argentine Republic

BRAUN (OSCAR) Desarrollo del capital monopolista en Argentina. Buenos Aires, 1970. pp. 63.

- Canada

CANADA. Restrictive Trade Practices Commission. [Reports]. RTPC No. 27. Report on the production, distribution and supply of newspapers in the Sudbury-Copper Cliff area. Ottawa, 1963 [or rather 1964]. pp. 40.

CANADA. Restrictive Trade Practices Commission. 1965. Monopoly in distribution of propane, British Columbia: report in connection with the production, distribution and sale of propane in British Columbia. Ottawa, 1965. pp. 88.

CANADA. Restrictive Trade Practices Commission. [Reports]. RTPC. No. 33. Report relating to the acquisition in 1962 of the Times-Journal newspaper, published in Fort William, Ontario. Ottawa, 1965. pp. 25.

CANADA. 1966. Trade practices in the phosphorous products and sodium chlorate industries: a report concerning the production, distribution and sale of phosphates, other phosphorous chemicals and sodium chlorate. (Restrictive Trade Practices Commission [Reports]. RTPC. No. 41) Ottawa, 1966. pp. ix, 112. 25cm.

- European Economic Community countries

INTERNATIONAL LEAGUE AGAINST UNFAIR COMPETITION. Les monopoles dans le Marché Commun: l'article 37 du traité de Rome; travaux d'un groupe étude 1965-1967. Milano, Giuffrè, 1968. pp. 215. 25cm.

- France

BEAUMONT (RENE DE) L'aménagement des monopoles d'état français visés par l'article 37 du Traité de Rome. Paris, Pichon et Durand-Auzias, 1969. pp. (v), 361. bibliog. 25½cm. (Bibliothèque de Droit International. 51)

- Germany

REINHOLD (OTTO) Macht der Monopole, Macht des Staates: zur Entwicklung des staatsmonopolistischen Kapitalismus in Westdeutschland. Berlin, 1964. pp. 78. (Institut für Gesellschaftswissenschaften. ABC des Marxismus Leninismus)

DEUTSCHE HISTORIKERGESELLSCHAFT. Fachgruppe "Geschichte der Neuesten Zeit, 1917-1945". Tagung, 1965. Monopole und Staat in Deutschland 1917-1945. Berlin, Akademie-Verlag, 1966. pp. 202. 24cm.

MARTIN (PAUL CHRISTOPH) Die deutsche Wirtschaftsentwicklung vor der Weltwirtschaftskrise unter dem Einfluss der Monopolisierung und der amerikanischen Wirtschaftspolitik. [Bonn, 1966?], pp. 289. bibliog.

BOLLERT (GERHART) Patente, Konzentration und Konzentrationspolitik: eine Untersuchung volkswirtschaftlicher Probleme des Patentschutzes am Beispiel der Bundesrepublik Deutschland. Berlin, 1968. pp. 229. bibliog.

- India

MOHNOT (SOHAN RAJ) Monopoly, concentration and industrial licensing. Calcutta, 1968. pp. 171.

MONOPOLIES - India (Cont'd.)

SHANKAR (KRIPA) and PARAKAL (PAULY V.) Studies in Indian monopolies. New Delhi, 1970. pp. 80.

- Israel

SHEFER (MICHAEL) Monopoly and competition in small economies with special reference to Israel; [Ph. D. (London) thesis]. 1970. fo. 422. bibliog. Typescript: unpublished. This thesis is the property of London University and may not be removed from the Library.

- New Zealand

COLLINGE (JOHN) The law relating to the control of competition, restrictive trade practices and monopolies in New Zealand: an inquiry into the protection of public and private interests in the sphere of competitive trading. Wellington, 1969. pp. 444. bibliog.

- Russia

POGREBINSKII (A.P.) Некоторне итоги изучения монополистического капитализма в России в советской исторической литературе за последнее десятилетие. in Вопросы политической экономии: ученые записки. Москва, 1968.

- South Africa

SOUTH AFRICA. Commission of Inquiry into the Regulation of Monopolistic Conditions Amendment Bill. 1971. Report: [Chairman, W.C. Malan] (R.P. 40/1971). in South Africa. Parliament. House of Assembly. Votes and proceedings; (with Printed annexures).

- Spain

TAMAMES GÓMEZ (RAMÓN) Los monopolios en España. Madrid, Editorial ZYX, 1967. pp. 172. 20cm. (Biblioteca Promoción del Pueblo. 12)

- United Kingdom

MAHON (JOHN A.) London.traffic: the menace of monopoly. London, Transport Workers' Minority Movement, 1928. pp. 16. 21½cm.

LAMB (RICHARD) and SKEVINGTON (LEONARD) Expansion without inflation: a Liberal call to action against monopoly price rings and tariffs. [London, 1963]. pp. 19.

ALLEN (GEORGE CYRIL) Monopoly and restrictive practices. London, Allen & Unwin, 1968. pp. 183. bibliog. 21½cm.

SUTHERLAND (ALISTER) The Monopolies Commission in action. Cambridge, 1969. pp. 96. (Cambridge. University. Department of Applied Economics. Occasional Papers. 21)

HART (P.E.) Concentration in the United Kingdom. [Reading], 1970. pp. 30. (Reading. University. Department of Economics. Discussion Papers in Economics. No. 24)

JACQUES (MARTIN) The menace of the monopolies. [London, 1970] pp. 18. (Communist Party of Great Britain. Communist Party Pamphlets)

INDUSTRIAL POLICY GROUP. Studies. No. 8. The control of monopoly. London, 1971. pp. 35.

MOOS (S.) Aspects of monopoly and restrictive practices legislation in relation to small firms. London, 1971. pp. 32. (U.K. Committee of Inquiry on Small Firms. Research Reports. No. 13)

- United Kingdom - Bibliography

U. K. Board of Trade. 1970. Competition, monopoly and restrictive practices: a select bibliography. London, 1970. pp. 127.

- United States

CHAMBER OF COMMERCE OF THE UNITED STATES OF AMERICA. Economic Research Department. Measurement of Economic Concentration. No.2. The statistical bases of concentration ratios. Washington, 1957. pp. (iv), 26. 23cm.

COLLINS (NORMAN R.) and PRESTON (LEE E.) Concentration and price-cost margins in manufacturing industries. Berkeley, U. of California P., 1968. pp. xvi, 163. 21½c

GOULDEN (JOSEPH C.) Monopoly. New York, Putnam, [1968]. pp. 350. bibliog. 21cm.

RUCKER (BRYCE W.) The first freedom. Carbondale, Southern Illinois U.P., [1968]. pp. xvii, 322. 23½cm. (New Horizons in Journalism)

NUTTER (GILBERT WARREN) and EINHORN (HENRY ADLER) Enterprise monopoly in the United States, 1899-1958. New York, 1969. pp. 256. bibliog.

MONRAD (DITLEV GOTHARD) Bishop of Lolland and Falster

HEGERMANN LINDENCRONE (CAI DITLEV VON) Betragt ninger i Anledning af D.G. Monrads politiske Breve. Kjøbenhavn, 1875. pp. 189.

MONROE (JAMES) President of the United States

WILSON (CHARLES MORROW) The Monroe doctrine: an American frame of mind. Princeton, [1971]. pp. 155. bibliog.

MONROE DOCTRINE

PERKINS (DEXTER) A history of the Monroe doctrine; a new revision of the book originally published under the title Hands off: a history, etc. Boston, [Mass.], [1955 reprinted 1963]. pp. 462. bibliog.

RAMÍREZ NOVOA (EZEQUIEL) Monroismo y bolivarismo en América Latina. Buenos Aires, 195?. pp. 149.

KRAKAU (KNUD) Die kubanische Revolution und die Monroe-Doktrin: eine Herausforderung der Aussenpolitik der Vereinigten Staaten. Frankfurt am Main, 1968. pp. 220. bibliog.

WILSON (CHARLES MORROW) The Monroe doctrine: an American frame of mind. Princeton, [1971]. pp. 155. bibliog.

MONSOONS

SWAN (A.D.) The West African monsoon. Accra, 1958. pp. 11, fo. (7). (Ghana. Meteorological Department. Professional Notes. No. 8)

WALKER (H.O.) The monsoon in West Africa;... (write-up of a discourse given to a Symposium on the Monsoon of the World...February, 1958). Accra, 1958. pp. 6, fo. (4). (Ghana. Meteorological Department. Professional Notes. No. 9)

MONTAGNARDS

CHENU (JACQUES ETIENNE ADOLPHE) Les Montagnards de 1848; encore quatre nouveaux chapitres; précédés d'une réponse à Caussidière et autres democs-socs. Paris, Giraud et Dagneau, 1850. pp. 144. 17½cm.

MONTAGU (IVOR)

MONTAGU (IVOR) The youngest son: autobiographical sketches. London, 1970. pp. 384.

MONTAGUE (ANDREW JACKSON)

LARSEN (WILLIAM E.) Montague of Virginia: the making of a southern progressive. [Baton Rouge], Louisiana State U.P., [1965]. pp. xiii, 314. bibliog. 22½cm. (Southern Biography Series. vol. 20)

MONTAIGNE (MICHEL DE)

LA CHARITÉ (RAYMOND C.) The concept of judgment in Montaigne. The Hague, Nijhoff, 1968. pp. ix, 149. bibliog. 24cm.

POUILLOUX (JEAN YVES) Lire les "Essais" de Montaigne. Paris, 1969. pp. 118.

MONTALDEO

- Economic history

DORIA (GIORGIO) Uomini e terre di un borgo collinare dal XVI al XVIII secolo. Milano, Giuffrè, 1968. pp. xv, 435. 25cm. (Genoa. Università. Istituto di Storia Economica. [Publications]. 2)

MONTANA

- Government publications - Bibliography

SPEER (LUCILE) compiler. Montana state documents: a preliminary bibliography. Missoula, 1958. pp. 56. (Montana State University. Bureau of Government Research. Publications. No. 1)

- History

HOWARD (JOSEPH KINSEY) Montana: high, wide and handsome. new ed. New Haven, [1959] repr. 1968. pp. 347. bibliog.

CLINCH (THOMAS A.) Urban populism and free silver in Montana: a narrative of ideology in political action. [Missoula, 1970]. pp. 190. bibliog.

MONTE CARLO METHOD

MIKHAIL (WILLIAM MESSIHA) A study of the finite-sample properties of some econometric estimators; [Ph.D. (London) thesis]. 1969. fo. (iv), 254. bibliog. 25½cm. Typescript: unpublished. This thesis is the property of London University and may not be removed from the Library.

EVERETT (G.W.) Farm planning by the Monte Carlo method. London, Ministry of Technology, 1970. pp. 17.

MONTE CASSINO (BENEDICTINE MONASTERY)

- Siege, 1944

WAŃKOWICZ (MELCHIOR) Szkice spod Monte Cassino. Warszawa, 1969. pp. 175.

MONTEJO (ESTEBÁN)

MONTEJO (ESTEBÁN) The autobiography of a runaway slave; edited by Miguel Barnet; translated from the Spanish by Jocasta Innes. London, Bodley Head, 1968. pp. 223. 19½cm.

MONTENEGRO

- Economic policy

VUKČEVIĆ (RISTO) Проблеми привредног развоја Црне Горе. Цетиње, 1967. pp. 155. bibliog. With Russian summary.

MONTESINOS Y MOLINA (MANUEL)

DRAPKIN (I.) Manuel Montesinos y Molina: an almost forgotten precursor of penal reform in Spain. in Wolfgang (Marvin Eugene) ed. Crime and culture. New York, [1968].

MONTEVIDEO

- History

GRÜNWALDT RAMASSO (JORGE) Vida, industria y comercio en el antiguo Montevideo: 1830-1852. Montevideo, 1970. pp. 136.

- Statistics

URUGUAY. Direccion General de Estadistica y Censos. Departamento de Encuestas y Muestreo. Encuesta de hogares: ocupacion y desocupacion, Montevideo. s-a., Ja/Je 1969 (año 1, t.2)- Montevideo.

MONTGELAS DE GARNERIN (MAXIMILIAN JOSEPH) Graf.

WEIS (EBERHARD) Montgelas. München, [1971 in progress]. bibliog.

MONTINI (GIOVANNI BATTISTA) Pope Paul VI.
See PAUL VI., Pope (Giovanni Battista MONTINI)

MONTREAL

- Exhibitions

CANADIAN CORPORATION FOR THE 1967 WORLD EXHIBITION. General report on the 1967 world exhibition (EXPO '67). Ottawa, Queen's Printer, 1969. 5 vols.

MONTREAL (Cont'd.)

- Harbour

MONTREAL. Board of Trade. The port of Montreal and the St. Lawrence Seaway: a two-part discussion...April 25 and May 2, 1957 [led by Pierre Camu]; transcript of proceedings. [Montreal, 1957?]. pp. 65. 28cm.

- History

COOPER (JOHN IRWIN) Montreal: a brief history. Montreal, 1969. pp. 217. bibliog.

- Politics and government

QUEBEC (PROVINCE). Commission to Inquire into the Administrative System of Montreal. 1960-61. [Report]; [Paul E. Champagne, chairman]. [Quebec, 1960-1961]. 2 pts. bibliog.

- Population

ROSENBERG (LOUIS) Changes in the geographical distribution of the Jewish population of metropolitan Montreal in the decennial periods from 1901 to 1961 and the estimated possible changes during the period from 1961 to 1971: a preliminary study. Montreal, 1966. fo. 5. (Canadian Jewish Congress. Bureau of Social and Economic Research. Research Papers. Series A. No. 7)

MONTSERRAT

- Economic conditions

STARKEY (OTIS PAUL) Commercial geography of Montserrat. Bloomington, 1960. fo. 18. (Indiana University. Department of Geography. Technical Reports. No.6)

- Emigration and immigration

PHILPOTT (STUART BOWMAN) Mass migration in Montserrat; [Ph.D. (London) thesis]. 1971. fo. 349. bibliog. Typescript: unpublished. This thesis is the property of London University and may not be removed from the Library.

- Social conditions

PHILPOTT (STUART BOWMAN) Mass migration in Montserrat; [Ph.D. (London) thesis]. 1971. fo. 349. bibliog. Typescript: unpublished. This thesis is the property of London University and may not be removed from the Library.

MONUMENTS

- Belgium - Preservation

BELGIUM. Ministère des Affaires Etrangères et du Commerce Extérieur. 1968. The history and purpose of the "Institut Royal du Patrimoine Artistique". Brussels, 1968. pp. 10. (Memo from Belgium. No. 99.)

- Esthonia

WEISS (H.) Was geschieht für die Erhaltung historischer Baudenkmäler in Reval und Narva?: ein Beitrag zur Denkmalpflege im heutigen Estland. in Hamburg. Arbeits- und Sozialbehörde. Hamburger Mittel- und Ostdeutsche Forschungen. Band 5. Hamburg, [1966].

- Italy - Preservation

BONELLI (RENATO) Il problema piu urgente. Roma, [imprint], 1961. pp. 6. 26cm. (Estratto dalla Rivista l'Architetto Gennaio 1961, no. 1)

MOODY (DWIGHT L.)

FINDLAY (JAMES F.) Dwight L. Moody: American evangelist, 1837-1899. Chicago, 1969. pp. 440.

MOON

- Exploration

MAILER (NORMAN) A fire on the moon. London, [1970]. pp. 381.

MOONEY (FRED)

MOONEY (FRED) Struggle in the coal fields: the autobiography ...; edited by J.W.Hess. Morgantown, West Virginia University Library 1967. pp. xi, 194. bibliog. 21½cm.

MOONEY (THOMAS J.)

FROST (RICHARD H.) The Mooney case. Stanford, 1968. pp. 563.

MOORE (GEORGE EDWARD)

AMBROSE (ALICE) and LAZEROWITZ (MORRIS) eds. G. E. Moore: essays in retrospect. London, 1970. pp. 376.

KLEMKE (ELMER D.) The epistemology of G. E. Moore. Evanston, [Ill.], 1969. pp. 205. bibliog.

AYER (Sir ALFRED JULES) Russell and Moore: the analytical heritage. London, 1971. pp. 254. (Harvard University. William James Lectures on Philosophy and Psychology. 1970.)

MOORE (GILBERT)

MOORE (GILBERT) A special rage. New York, [1971]. pp. 276.

MOOS

- Social conditions

RUETTING (WERNER KARL) Die soziale Integrationsstruktur einer ländlichen Gemeinde: ein Beitrag zum soziologischen Problem der Integration, dargestellt an der Dorfgemeinde Moos im Landkreis Bühl. [Heidenberg, imprint], 1962. pp. 229. bibliog.

MORA (JOSÉ MARÍA LUIS)

HALE (CHARLES A.) Mexican liberalism in the age of Mora, 1821-1853. New Haven, Yale U.P., 1968. pp. xi, 347. bibliog. 23½cm. (Caribbean Series. 11)

MORAL CONDITIONS

GINSBERG (M.) Moral progress: a reappraisal. in Ayer (Sir Alfred Jules) ed. The humanist outlook. London, 1968.

MORAL EDUCATION

JOSEPHINE BUTLER SOCIETY. An equal moral standard: what does it mean? 2nd ed. London, 1925. unpaged.

KULIKOV (VLADIMIR NIKOLAEVICH) Воспитывать честность и правдивость у детей в семье. Иваново, 1961. pp. 64. bibliog.

WILSON (JOHN BOYD) and others. Introduction to moral education. Harmondsworth, Penguin, 1967. pp. 463. bibliog. 18cm.

HEMMING (J.) Moral education. in Ayer (Sir Alfred Jules) ed. The humanist outlook. London, 1968.

WISHY (BERNARD) The child and the republic: the dawn of modern American child nurture. Philadelphia, 1968. pp. 205. bibliog.

PAWLOWSKI (EMIL JOHN) Path to permanent peace. New York, Vantage P., [1969 in progress]. 20cm.

BULL (NORMAN JOHN) Moral education. London, 1969. pp. 183. bibliog.

MORALE

HIRSCHMAN (ALBERT O.) Exit, voice and loyalty: responses to decline in firms, organizations and states. Cambridge, Mass., 1970. pp. 162.

MORANDI (RODOLFO)

AGOSTI (ALDO) Rodolfo Morandi: il pensiero e l'azione politica. Bari, 1971. pp. 484.

MORAVIA

- Landtag - Elections

GISKRA (CARL) Wahlrede... für die Landtags-Candidatur des 2.Bezirks in Brünn im Augarten-Saale am 21.März 1861. Brünn, [imprint, 1861?]. pp. 29. 21cm.

MORAVIANS

- Missions

WRIGHT (MARCIA) German missions in Tanganyika, 1891-1941: Lutherans and Moravians in the Southern Highlands. Oxford, 1971. pp. 249. bibliog.

MORBIHAN

- History

DEBAUVE (HENRY JEAN LOUIS) La justice révolutionnaire dans le Morbihan: essai sur l'organisation judiciaire du Morbihan de 1790 à 1795. Paris, 1965. pp. 568. bibliog. 25cm.

MORDVINIAN REPUBLIC

POD... Под звездой Октября: Мордовская АССР за 50 лет Советской власти. Саранск, Мордовское Книжное Издательство, 1967. pp. 332. 21½см.

- Economic conditions

MATVEEV (GENNADII PETROVICH) and RODOSSKAIA (TAMARA LEONIDOVNA) Мордовская АССР: экономико-географический очерк. Саранск, Мордовское Книжное Издательство, 1967. pp. 215. bibliog. 20см.

- History

OCHERKI istorii Mordovskoi ASSR. t.2. 1917-1960 gg. Saransk, 1961. pp. 543.

- Politics and government

MORDOVSKII GOSUDARSTVENNYI UNIVERSITET Uchenye Zapiski. No.52. Seriia Obshchestvennykh Nauk. [Сборник статей] Саранск, 1966. pp 258.

OCHERKI istorii Mordovskoi organizatsii KPSS. Saransk, 1967. pp. 506

- Religious life and customs

MOKSHIN (N.F.) Proiskhozhdenie i sushchnost' mordovskikh dokhristianskikh religioznykh prazdnikov. in Mordovskii Gosudarstvennyi Universitet. Uchenye Zapiski. No.51. Seriia Istoricheskikh Nauk. vyp.1. Saransk, 1965.

- Statistics

MORDVINIAN REPUBLIC. Statisticheskoe Upravlenie. 1967. Мордовская АССР за годы Советской власти в цифрах: статистический сборник. Саранск, Мордовское Книжное Издательство, 1967. pp. 195. 16½см.

MORE (Sir THOMAS) Saint

PINEAS (RAINER) Thomas More and Tudor polemics. Bloomington, Indiana U.P., [1968]. pp. xi, 262. bibliog. 23cm.

WARTBURG (W. VON) Die Utopia des Thomas Morus: Versuch einer Deutung. in vol. 1 of Sieber (Marc) ed. Discordia concors. Basel, [1968].

JOHNSON (ROBBIN S.) More's Utopia: ideal and illusion. New Haven, 1969. pp. 166. bibliog.

PREVOST (ANDRE) Thomas More, 1477-1535, et la crise de la pensée européenne. [Tours, 1969]. pp. 409. bibliog.

MOREA

- Economic history - Sources

LONGNON (JEAN) and TOPPING (PETER W.) eds. Documents sur le régime des terres dans la principauté de Morée au 14e siècle. Paris, 1969. pp. 326. (Paris. Ecole Pratique des Hautes Etudes. Section des Sciences Economiques et Sociales. Documents et Recherches sur l'Economie des Pays Byzantins, Islamiques et Slaves et leurs Relations Commerciales au Moyen Age. 9)

MOREL (EDWARD DENE)

MOREL (EDMUND DENE) History of the Congo reform movement; [with supplementary chapters by] Wm. Roger Louis and Jean Stengers. Oxford, Clarendon, 1968. pp. xiv, 289. bibliog. 21½cm.

MORELLI (MICHELE)

MORELLI (ANTONIO) Michele Morelli e la rivoluzion napoletana del 1820-1821. 2nd ed. [Bologna], 1969. pp. 365. bibliog.

MORELOS Y PAVÓN (JOSÉ MARÍA)

CHÁVEZ (EZEQUIEL A.) Morelos. 2nd ed. México, Jus, 1965. pp. 222. 23cm. (Colección México Heroico)

LEMOINE VILLICAÑA (ERNESTO) Morelos: su vida revolucionaria a traves de sus escritos y de otros testimonios de la epoca. Mexico, 1965. pp. 715.

MORENO (MARIANO)

JUSTO LÓPEZ (MARIO) El mito de la constitución; y Tres ensayos sobre la democracia. Buenos Aires, Abeledo-Perrot, 1963. pp. 77. 23½cm.

MORGAN (CHARLES)

BAUGHMAN (JAMES P.) Charles Morgan and the development of Southern transportation. Nashville, Vanderbilt U. P., 1968. pp. xxxi, 302. bibliog. 23½cm.

MORGAN (LEWIS HENRY)

TERRAY (EMMANUEL) Le marxisme devant les sociétés "primitives": deux études. Paris, Maspero, 1969. pp. 177. 21½cm. (Théorie. 5)

FORTES (MEYER) Kinship and the social order: the legacy of Lewis Henry Morgan. London, 1970. pp. 347. bibliog. (Rochester, N.Y. University. Lewis Henry Morgan Lectures. 1963)

MORGENTHAU (HENRY) 1891-

BLUM (JOHN MORTON) From the Morgenthau diaries. Boston, [Mass.], 1959 in progress.

UNITED STATES. Senate. Judiciary Committee. Morgenthau diary, China. Washington, 1965. 2 vols.

MORIOLLES (ALEXANDRE NICOLAS LEONARD CHARLES MARIE DE) Comte

MORIOLLES (ALEXANDRE NICOLAS LÉONARD CHARLES MARIE DE) Comte. Mémoires...sur l'émigration, la Pologne et la cour du Grand-Duc Constantin, 1789-1833. Paris, Société d'Éditions Littéraires et Artistiques, 1902. pp. xx, 404. 23cm.

MORLEY (JOHN) Viscount Morley of Blackburn

HAMER (DAVID ALLAN) John Morley: liberal intellectual in politics. Oxford, Clarendon P., 1968. pp. xvi, 412. bibliog. 21½cm.

KOSS (STEPHEN E.) John Morley at the India Office, 1905-1910. New Haven, 1969. pp. 231. bibliog.

MORMONS AND MORMONISM

PRATT (PARLEY PETER) Marriage and morals in Utah: an address;... read in joint session of the Legislature, in the Representative Hall, Fillmore City, Dec. 31, 1855, by Mr. Thomas Bullock. Liverpool, 1856. pp. 8.

SMITH (JOSEPH) 1832-1914, and SMITH (HEMAN C.) History of the Church of Jesus Christ of Latter Day Saints. Lamoni, Iowa, 1897 in progress.

CHRISTIAN social order. n.p., [19--]. pp. 36.

KNISLEY (ALVIN) Dictionary of all proper names in the book of Mormon. Independence, Mo., [1909?]. pp. 118.

SMITH (WALTER W.) History of stewardships and consecration as practiced by the Latter Day Saints. Independence, Missouri, 1923. pp. 258-306. (Reprinted from Journal of History. vol 16, no. 3, July, 1923)

PHILLIPS (ARTHUR B.) The restoration movement and the Latter Day Saints: a book of ideals, pioneers, and martyrs. Independence, Missouri, 1928. pp. 335.

CARMICHAEL (ALBERT) Church finance: its relation to "the gathering". Independence, Missouri, 1929. pp. 29.

EDWARDS (F. HENRY) The background of church history: a topical study of the history of the Church of Jesus Christ of Latter Day Saints, from 1805 to 1920. Independence, 1929. pp. 38.

CARMICHAEL (ALBERT) The elements of stewardships and our social program. Independence, Missouri, [193-?]. pp. 104.

DAVIS (INEZ SMITH) A teachers' and students' guide to the story of the church: a one-volume history of the restoration;... prepared by F. Henry Edwards. Independence, Missouri, [193-?]. pp. 94.

VELT (HAROLD I.) The riddle of American origins. Independence, Missouri, [193-?]. pp. 96.

BLACKMORE (JOHN) Writer on religion. The church program for a new century. Independence, Missouri, 1930-31. 2 pts. (in 1). (Gospel Quarterly. vol.6, nos.1/2)

REORGANIZED CHURCH OF JESUS CHRIST OF LATTER DAY SAINTS. General Conference, 1932. Church objectives. [Independence, Missouri, 1932] pp. 32.

GOSPEL QUARTERLY. vol.9, no.2. Local and general church finance; [by A.B. Phillips and others]. Independence, Missouri, 1934. pp. 64.

DAVIS (INEZ SMITH) The story of the Church:... a history of the Church of Jesus Christ of Latter Day Saints, and of its legal successor, the Reorganized Church of Jesus Christ of Latter Day Saints. Independence, Missouri, 1938. pp. 480.

REORGANIZED CHURCH OF JESUS CHRIST OF LATTER DAY SAINTS. An open letter concerning the Reorganized Church of Jesus Christ of Latter Day Saints. Independence, Missouri, [194-?]. pp. 16.

CLINIC IN EVANGELISM, INDEPENDENCE, MISSOURI, 1941. The church and evangelism: the official report of the clinic...[organised by the] Reorganized Church of Jesus Christ of Latter Day Saints. Independence, Missouri, [1941]. pp. 406.

CHEVILLE (ROY A.) The Latter Day Saints and their changing relationship to the social order: a sociological approach to religious education. Independence, Mo., 1942. pp. 77. bibliog.

McDOWELL (FLOYD M.) That problem of leadership. Independence, 1943. pp. 100.

DELAPP (G. LESLIE) The problems of the gathering: (a study of Zionic procedure). rev. ed. Independence, Missouri, 1946. pp. 87.

DELAPP (G. LESLIE) Economic considerations: (a study of Zionic procedure). 2nd ed. Independence, Missouri, 1947. pp. 77

WIDTSOE (JOHN A.) and WIDTSOE (LEAH D.) The word of wisdom: a modern interpretation. rev. ed. [Salt Lake City], Deseret Book Company, 1950. pp. xii, 312. 19½cm.

[REORGANIZED CHURCH OF JESUS CHRIST OF LATTER DAY SAINTS]. Rules and resolutions. Independence, Missouri, 1952. pp. 215.

WHALEN (WILLIAM JOSEPH) The Latter-day Saints in the modern day world: an account of contemporary Mormonism. rev. ed. Notre Dame, University of Notre Dame Press, [1964]. repr. 1967. pp. 319. bibliog. 20cm.

REORGANIZED CHURCH OF JESUS CHRIST OF LATTER DAY SAINTS. An annual report to all members, 1965. Independence, Missouri, [1965]. pp. 28.

HIRSHSON (STANLEY P.) The lion of the lord: a biography of the Mormon leader, Brigham Young. London, 1971. pp. 397,xxvi. bibliog.

MOROCCO

UNITED STATES. Army Department. Pamphlets. No. 550-49. Area handbook for Morocco. Washington, [1966]. pp. x, 459.

- Boundaries

TROUT (FRANK E.) Morocco's Saharan frontiers. Geneva, 1969. pp. 561. bibliog.

- Commerce - United States

UNITED STATES. International Commerce Bureau. Market for U.S. products, Morocco. Washington, 1964. pp. viii, 56.

- Description and travel

JACKSON (JAMES GREY) An account of the empire of Morocco and the districts of Suse and Tafilelt ...; [facsimile reprint of the third edition of 1814]. London, Cass, 1968. pp. xvi, 328. 24½cm. (Cass Library of African Studies. Travels and Narratives. No. 42)

- Economic conditions

UNITED STATES. International Commerce Bureau. Market for U.S. products, Morocco. Washington, 1964. pp. viii, 56.

- Economic History - Sources

MIEGE (JEAN LOUIS) compiler. Documents d'histoire économique et sociale marocaine au XIXe siècle. Paris, 1969. pp. 359.

- Economic policy

MOROCCO. 1961. Plan quinquennal, 1960-1964: memento des objectifs de l'industrie. (Division de la Coordination Economique et du Plan) [Rabat], 1961. pp. 16. 23½cm.

MOROCCO. Division de la Coordination Economique et du Plan. 1968. Plan quinquennal, 1968-1972. [Rabat, 1968?] 4 vols.

- Foreign relations

MOREL (EDMUND DENE) Ten years of secret diplomacy: an unheeded warning; being a reprint of Morocco in diplomacy, etc. 5th ed. Manchester, 1918. pp. 198.

MOROCCO. 1958. Le Maroc à l'heure de l'indépendance; ([by] Sa Majesté Mohammed V. tome 1. 1955-1957; traduit de l'Arabe. (Ministère de l'Information et du Tourisme) Rabat, (1958?]. pp. 340. 21½cm.

TROUT (FRANK E.) Morocco's Saharan frontiers. Geneva, 1969. pp. 561. bibliog.

- Foreign relations - France

BERNARD (STEPHANE) Le conflit franco-marocain, 1943-1956. [Brussels, 1964]. 3 vols. (in 1). bibliog. (Carnegie Endowment for International Peace. Case Studies of International Conflict. 2)

CAILLÉ (JACQUES) Le consulat de Tanger: des origines à 1830. Paris, Pedone, 1967. pp. 132. bibliog. 25cm. (Petite Histoire des Consulats. 11)

BERNARD (STEPHANE) The Franco-Moroccan conflict, 1943-1956. New Haven, 1968. pp. 680. bibliog.

MIEGE (JEAN LOUIS) Une mission française à Marrakech en 1882; documents inédits avec introduction, commentaires et notes. Aix-en-Provence, 1968. pp. 451. bibliog. (Université d'Aix-Marseille. Faculté des Lettres. Travaux et Mémoires. No. 52)

- Foreign relations - Naples

IANNETTONE (GIOVANNI) Il Marocco negli atti consolari del Regno delle Due Sicilie, dal trattato del 1782 a quello del 1834. Napoli, [1967]. pp. 238.

- Foreign relations - United States

BLAIR (LEON BORDEN) Western window in the Arab world. Austin, [1970]. pp. 328. bibliog.

- History

HISTOIRE du MAROC, par J. Brignon [and others]. Paris, Hatier, [1967]. pp. 416. bibliogs. 23cm.

- History - Sources

MENDONÇA (JERONYMO DE) Jornada de Africa... copiado...da edição de...1607 por B.J. de Souza Farinha. Lisboa, Na Offic. de Joze da Silva Nazareth, 1785. pp. (xviii), 275. 17½cm.

- Industries

MOROCCO. 1961. Plan quinquennal, 1960-1964: memento des objectifs de l'industrie. (Division de la Coordination Economique et du Plan) [Rabat], 1961. pp. 16. 23½cm.

Writer on handicraft.
MUELLER (HERBERT) Das Handwerk in Marokko. Frankfurt a.M., Universität, Forschungsinstitut für Handwerkswirtschaft, 1968. pp. 62. bibliog. 21cm. (Studien und Berichte. Berichte.Nr. 40)

MOROCCO (Cont'd.)

- Intellectual life

LAROUI (ABDALLAH) L'idéologie arabe contemporaine: essai critique. Paris, Maspero, 1967. pp. xiii, 224. 21½cm. (Les Textes à l'Appui)

- Maps

ATLAS du bassin du Sebou; (with Livret explicatif). [Rabat?, Ministère de l'Agriculture et de la Réforme Agraire, 1970]. 2 vols.

- Nationalism

HALSTEAD (JOHN P.) Rebirth of a nation: the origins and rise of Moroccan nationalism, 1912-1944. Cambridge, Harvard U.P., 1967. pp. x, 323. bibliog. 21cm. (Harvard University. Center for Middle Eastern Studies. Harvard Middle Eastern Monographs. 18)

- Politics and government

MOROCCO. 1958. Le Maroc à l'heure de l'indépendance; ([by] Sa Majesté Mohammed V. tome 1. 1955-1957; traduit de l'Arabe. (Ministère de l'Information et du Tourisme) Rabat, (1958?]. pp. 340. 21½cm.

MOROCCO. 1958. The new government of Morocco. (Embassy of Morocco) Washington, 1958. pp. 27. 21½cm.

BEN BARKA (MEHDI) The political thought of Ben Barka. Havana, Tricontinental, 1968. pp. 189. 19cm.

SCHAM (ALAN) Lyautey in Morocco: protectorate administration, 1912-1925. Berkeley, 1970. pp. 272. bibliog.

WATERBURY (JOHN) The commander of the faithful: the Moroccan political élite...; a study in segmented politics. London, [1970]. pp. 367. bibliog.

- Population

NOIN (DANIEL) La population rurale du Maroc. Paris, [1970]. 2 vols. bibliog. (Rouen. Université. Publications. Série Littéraire, 8)

- Relations (general) with Europe

MIÈGE (JEAN LOUIS) Le Maroc et l'Europe, 1830-1894. Paris, Presses Universitaires de France, 1961 in progress. 24cm.

- Religion

GELLNER (ERNEST ANDRÉ) Saints of the Atlas. London, [1969]. pp. 317. bibliog.

- Rural conditions

COULEAU (JULIEN) La paysannerie marocaine. Paris, Centre National de la Recherche Scientifique, 1968. pp. 295. 24cm.

NOIN (DANIEL) La population rurale du Maroc. Paris, [1970]. 2 vols. bibliog. (Rouen. Université. Publications. Série Littéraire, 8)

- Social conditions

BENSIMON-DONATH (DORIS) Évolution du judaisme marocain sous le protectorat français, 1912-1956. Paris, 1968. pp. 149. bibliog. (Paris. École Pratique des Hautes Études. Section des Sciences Economiques et Sociales. Études Juives. 12)

- Social policy

MOROCCO. Division de la Coordination Economique et du Plan. 1968. Plan quinquennal, 1968-1972. [Rabat, 1968?] 4 vols.

MOROZOV (BORIS IVANOVICH)

PETRIKEEV (DMITRII IVANOVICH) Крупное крепостное хозяйство XVII в.: по материалам вотчины боярина Б. И. Морозова. Ленинград, 1967. pp. 229.

MORRIS (STUART)

MORRISON (SYBIL) The life and work of Stuart Morris. [London, 1969?]. pp. 27.

MORRIS (WILLIAM)

The BOOK of the opening of the William Morris Hall, Somers Road, Walthamstow, Saturday, Dec. 18, 1909. [Walthamstow, imprint], 1909. pp. 8.

THOMPSON (EDWARD PALMER) The communism of William Morris: a lecture...given on 4th May 1959 in the Hall of the Art Workers' Guild, London. London, William Morris Society, 1965. pp. 19. 22cm. (Transactions)

GOLDZAMT (EDMUND) William Morris a geneza społeczna architektury nowoczesnej. Warszawa, PWN, 1967. pp. 381. 19½cm. With English and Russian summaries.

SCHORSKE (C.E.) The quest for the Grail: Wagner and Morris. in Wolff (Kurt Heinrich) and Moore (Barrington) eds. The critical spirit. Boston, [1967].

DUFTY (ARTHUR RICHARD) Kelmscott; an illustrated guide. London, 1969. pp. 35.

HULSE (JAMES W.) Revolutionists in London: a study of five unorthodox socialists. Oxford, 1970. pp. 246. bibliog.

MORROW (JOHN HOWARD)

MORROW (JOHN HOWARD) First American ambassador to Guinea. New Brunswick, Rutgers U.P., [1968]. pp. xv, 291. 23½cm.

MORTALITY

BENOISTON DE CHATEAUNEUF (LOUIS FRANÇOIS) Mémoire sur la mortalité des femmes de l'âge de quarante à cinquante ans; lu à l'Academie de Sciences dans la séance du 13 mai 1818. Paris, Martinet, 1822. pp. iv, 32.

BENOISTON DE CHATEAUNEUF (LOUIS FRANÇOIS) Note lue à l'Academie Royale des Sciences, dans sa séance du 30 janvier 1826, sur les changemens qu'ont subis les lois de la mortalité en Europe, depuis un demi-siècle, 1775-1825. [Paris, imprint, 1826?]. pp. 10. (Extrait du Moniteur du 6 février 1826)

BENOISTON DE CHATEAUNEUF (LOUIS FRANÇOIS)
Mémoire sur la durée de la vie chez le riche
et chez le pauvre; communiqué à l'Académie
Royale des Sciences. [Paris, imprint, 1829?].
pp. 14. (Extrait du Moniteur du 11 mai 1829)

PICCINETTI (GIOVANNI) Quesiti di aritmetica politica relativi alla ricerca
della vita probabile, della vita media
ed ai vitalizj; proposti e risoluti.
Firenze, the Author, 1841. pp. 104.
21½cm.

DICKINSON (FRANK GREENE) and WELKER (EVERETT
LINUS) Mortality trends in the United States
1900-1949;...and an editorial and summary from
the Journal of the A.M.A. Chicago, 1952.
pp. 32. (American Medical Association. Bulletins. 92)

WASHINGTON (STATE). 1955. Mortality
trends in the State of Washington; by
Calvin F. Schmid [and others]. (Census
Board) Seattle, 1955. pp. iii, 73.
25cm.

OFFICE OF HEALTH ECONOMICS. Disorders which
shorten life: a review of mortality trends
for those between the ages of 15 and 44.
London, [1966]. pp. 33. bibliog. 20½cm.

HOEM (JAN M.) Some results on the estimation of
forces of decrement. Oslo, University of Oslo,
Institute of Economics, 1967. fo. 36. bibliog.
29½cm. (Memoranda)

MEEGAMA (SRINIWASA ANANDA) The decline in
mortality in Ceylon since the end of the
19th century, with particular reference
to economic and social development;
[Ph. D. (London) thesis]. 1968.
fo. vi, 345. bibliog. 25½cm. Typescript:
unpublished. This thesis is the property
of London University and may not be removed
from the Library

SHAPIRO (SAMUEL) and others. Infant, perinatal,
maternal, and childhood mortality in the United
States. Cambridge, Mass., 1968. pp. 388. bibliog.
(American Public Health Association. Vital and
Health Statistics Monographs)

ACSÁDI (GYORGY) and NEMESKÉRI (J.) History of
human life span and mortality; (translated by
K. Balás). Budapest, 1970. pp. 346. bibliog.

ARRIAGA (EDUARDO E.) Mortality decline and its
demographic effects in Latin America.
Berkeley, [1970]. pp. 232. bibliog.
(California University. Institute of International Studies. Population Monograph Series.
No. 6)

BENJAMIN (BERNARD) and HAYCOCKS (HERBERT WESTON)
The analysis of mortality and other actuarial
statistics. Cambridge, 1970. pp. 392.

DODGE (DAVID LOW) and MARTIN (WALTER TILFORD)
Social stress and chronic illness: mortality
patterns in industrial society. Notre Dame,
[1970]. pp. 331.

MARQUES (MANUEL PEDRO OLIVEIRA) Algumas
considerações sobre a mortalidade portuguesa.
Lisboa, Instituto Nacional de Estatistica,
1970. pp. 129.

PRESTON (SAMUEL H.) Older male mortality and
cigarette smoking: a demographic analysis.
Berkeley, [1970]. pp. 150. bibliog. (California
University. Institute of International Studies.
Population Monograph Series. No. 7)

- Tables

NETHERLANDS. Centraal Bureau voor de Statistiek.
1957. De sterfte in Nederland naar geslacht,
leeftijd en doodsoorzaken 1921-1955. Zeist,
1957. pp. 85.

BRUNO (VINCENZO) Evoluzione della mortalità per
cause di morte nella prima metà del secolo XX in
base alle tavole di mortalità del 1899-1902 e
1950-1953. Pisa, 1960. pp. 27. 24½cm.

GONIN (H.T.) Mortality trends in South Africa:
some comparisons with population and assured
lives' mortality in Great Britain and population
mortality in certain dominions. Pretoria,
University of South Africa, 1960. pp. 61.
21½cm. (Communications. Series B.14)

LEVIE (GUY) Tables de mortalité: l'utilisation
rationnelle des tables de mortalité pour la
capitalisation du manque à gagner d'une
victime d'accident ou de ses ayants droit.
2nd ed. Bruxelles, 1963. pp. 204. bibliog.

CANADA. Dominion Bureau of Statistics. Health
and Welfare Division. Vital Statistics Section.
1964. Provincial and regional life tables,
1960-1962. Ottawa, 1964. pp. 23. (Canada.
Dominion Bureau of Statistics. Reference Papers)
In English and French.

DENMARK. Statistiske Departement. 1965.
Nyere tendenser i dødeligheden; [by]
Jørgen Wedebye. København, 1965.
pp. 79. (Statistiske Undersøgelser.
[Nr. 15.])

URUGUAY. Direccion General de Estadistica y
Censos. 1965. Tablas de mortalidad, 1963,
1964. [Montevideo, 1965?]. pp. 51.

COPPLESTONE (J.F.) and ROSE (R.J.) Occupational
mortality among male population, other than
Maori, 20 to 64 years of age: based on deaths,
1959-63 and population census, 1961.
Wellington, 1967. pp. 74. 28cm. (New
Zealand. Department of Health. Special Report
Series. 28.)

SWITZERLAND. Bureau Fédéral de Statistique.
Statistiques de la Suisse. 399e fasc.
Schweizerische Volkssterbetafeln...1958/63:
Sterblichkeit nach Todesursachen...:
Ausscheide- und Überlebensordnungen nach
Zivilstand; (Tables de mortalité de la
population suisse 1958/63...: mortalité
par causes de décès...: ordres d'extinction
et de survie d'après l'état civil.) Bern,
1967. pp.38,47. bibliog. In German and
French.

HONG KONG. Census, 1966. Hong Kong life tables,
1963-1978; [by] K.M.A.Barnett. Hong Kong, 1968.
pp. v, 11. 35cm.

ROSE (RICHARD JOHN) Trends in health and health
services. [Wellington], Department of Health,
1968. pp. 134. 28cm.

DENMARK. Danmarks Statistik. 1969. Regionale
forskelle i dødeligheden; [by] Jørgen
Wedebye. København, 1969. pp. 23.
(Statistiske Undersøgelser. Nr. 23.)
In Danish and English.

MORTALITY - Tables (Cont'd.)

LEDERMANN (SULLY) Nouvelles tables-types de mortalité. [Paris], 1969. pp. 260. (France. Institut National d'Etudes Démographiques. Travaux et Documents. Cahiers. No. 53). 13 tables in end pocket.

NORWAY. Statistiske Centralbyrå. 1969. Dødelighetsforhold i fylkene, 1964-1967; Mortality rates in counties, 1964-1967. Oslo, 1969. pp. 47. (Norges Offisielle Statistikk. Rekke A. 298) In Norwegian and English.

MORTGAGE BANKS

- Germany

KNACKE (ERNEST) Die Hypothekenbanken. Frankfurt am Main, Knapp, [1964]. pp. 113. bibliog. 18cm. (Taschenbücher für Geld, Bank und Börse. Band 12)

SEIDEL (EBERHARD) Die Frage der Industriebeleihungen durch Pfandbriefinstitute. Berlin, 1966. pp. 190. bibliog.

BAEHRING (BERND) Hundert Jahre Centralboden: eine Hypothekenbank im Wandel der Zeiten 1870-1970; im Auftrage des Vorstandes der Deutschen Centralbodenkredit-Aktiengesellschaft Berlin-Köln. Frankfurt am Main, [1970]. pp. 146. bibliog.

MORTGAGE LOANS

- United Kingdom

BUILDING SOCIETIES INSTITUTE. Mortgage lending procedure: a model; report of a research group. 2nd ed. London, 1969. pp. 100.

MORTGAGES

- Canada

SMITH (LAWRENCE B.) Housing and mortgage markets in Canada. [Ottawa], 1970. pp. 110. bibliog. (Bank of Canada. Staff Research Studies. No. 6.)

- France

ALPHANDÉRY (CLAUDE) Les prêts hypothécaires et leur marché. Paris. P.U.F., 1968. pp. 128. bibliog. 17½cm. (Que Sais-Je? No.1326)

- Germany

LANDWEHR (GOETZ) Die Verpfändung der deutschen Reichsstädte im Mittelalter. Köln, Böhlau, 1967. pp. xxxi, 484. bibliog. 23cm. (Forschungen zur Deutschen Rechtsgeschichte. Band 5)

- Guatemala

GUATEMALA. Statutes, etc. 1929-1930. Leyes organica y reglamentaria de el Crédito Hipotecario Nacional de Guatemala. [Guatemala, 1930?]. pp. 57.

GUATEMALA. Ministerio de Gobernación. Comisión de Legislatión. 1932. Reforma hipotecaria: informe y proyecto de ley. 2nd ed. Guatemala, 1932. pp. 115. 26cm.

- Netherlands

ROES (J.B.M.) Hypotheek, een zakelijk recht. Arnhem, 1970. pp. 164. bibliog. With French summary.

- United Kingdom

FISHER (WILLIAM RICHARD) and LIGHTWOOD (JOHN MASON) Law of mortgage; eighth edition by E.L.G. Tyler. London, 1969. pp. 697.

- United States

UNITED STATES. Federal Housing Administration. FHA experience with mortgage foreclosures and property acquisitions. Washington, 1963. pp. vi, 81.

UNITED STATES. Housing and Home Finance Agency. Mortgage foreclosures in six metropolitan areas. [Washington], 1963. pp. vi, 192.

WEAVER (R.C.) FHA-FNMA policy and mortgage interest rate. in California University. Real Estate Research Program. Essays in urban land economics. Los Angeles, 1966.

GUTTENTAG (JACK M.) and BECK (MORRIS) New series on home mortgage yields since 1951. New York, 1970. pp. 357. (National Bureau of Economic Research. [Publications]. No. 92)

HERZOG (JOHN PHILLIP) and EARLEY (JAMES S.) Home mortgage delinquency and foreclosure. New York, 1970. pp. 170. (National Bureau of Economic Research. [Publications]. No. 91)

MORTIMER (WYDNHAM)

MORTIMER (WYNDHAM) Organize!: my life as a union man;...edited by Leo Fenster. Boston, [Mass.], [1971]. pp. 274.

MORUZI (ALEXANDRU D.)

SLĂVESCU (VICTOR J.) Viaţa şi opera economistului Alexandru D. Moruzi, 1815-1878. Bucureşti, 1941. pp. 366. Appendix of facsimiles.

MOSCOSO (TEODORO)

TEODORO Moscoso en Bolivia. [Usaid, imprint], 1962 pp. 10. 21½cm.

MOSCOW

- Description

FRANCE. Direction de la Documentation. La Documentation Française. Notes et Études Documentaires. No. 3,493. Les grandes villes du monde: Moscou; [by] B. Kerblay. Paris, 1968. pp. 79. bibliog. 30½cm.

- Economic history

POLETAEV (VLADIMIR EVGEN'EVICH) Рабочие Москвы на завершающем этапе строительства социализма, 1945-1958 Москва, 1967. pp. 276.

KONDRAT'EV (V. A.) and NEVZOROV (V. I.) eds. Из истории фабрик и заводов Москвы и Московской губернии, конец XVIII - начало XX в.: обзор документов. Москва, 1968. pp. 385. 21½см.

POLIAK (GEORGII BORISOVICH) Бюджет Москвы. Москва, Экономика, 1968. pp. 208. 20см.

- Economic history - Sources

DIAGILEV (D. V.) and others, eds. Iz istorii bor'by za razvitie kommunisticheskikh form truda: sbornik dokumentov i materialov. Moskva, 1967. pp. 502.

- Economic policy

SELIVANOV (TIMOFEI ALEKSEEVICH) and GEL'PERIN (MOISEI ABELEVICH) Planirovanie gorodskogo khoziaistva: na primere Moskvy. Moskva, 1970. pp. 229.

- Growth

PROMYSLOV (VLADIMIR FEDOROVICH) Развитие индустриального строительства в Москве. Москва, Стройиздат, 1967. pp. 544. 21½см.

- History

BAZILEVICH (KONSTANTIN VASIL'EVICH) Denezhnaia reforma Alekseia Mikhailovicha i vosstanie v Moskve v 1662 g. Moskva, 1936. pp. 115.

MITSKEVICH (SERGEI IVANOVICH) Revoliutsionnaia Moskva, 1888-1905. Moskva, 1940. pp. 487. For 1st vol. of these memoirs see his Na grani dvukh epokh.

ISTORIIA Moskvy v gody Velikoi Otechestvennoi voiny i v poslevoennyi period, 1941-1965. Moskva, 1967. pp. 566.

MOSKVA... Москва за 50 лет Советской власти, 1917-1967. Москва, 1968. pp. 487. bibliog. (Академия Наук СССР. Институт Истории. Труды по Истории Москвы)

- History - Revolution, 1917-1921

KOTELENETS (ANATOLII IVANOVICH) Во главе революционного крестьянства: борьба Московской большевистской организации за крестьянские массы в 1917 г. Москва, 1957. pp. 123.

KACHURINA (A. V.) Партия большевиков - вдохновитель и организатор Московского вооруженного восстания в октябре 1917 года: историографический очерк. Москва, 1967. pp. 48.

LUKASHEV (A. V.) and others. Oktiabr' v Moskve. Moskva, 1967. pp. 430.

- History - Revolution, 1917-1921 - Personal narratives

VOZNESENSKII (ARSENII NIKOLAEVICH) Moskva v 1917 godu. Moskva, 1928. pp. 196.

DVINOV (BORIS L.) Moskovskii Sovet Rabochikh Deputatov, 1917-1922: vospominaniia. New York, 1961. pp. 188. (Inter-University Project on the History of the Menshevik Movement. Paper no.1)

- History - Revolution, 1917-1921 - Sources

MOSKOVSKII... Московский военно-революционный комитет, октябрь-ноябрь 1917 года. Москва, 1968. pp. 304.

- Politics and government

MOROZOV (VIACHESLAV FEDOROVICH) Московские большевики в борьбе за создание вооруженных сил Советской республики в 1917-1918 гг. Москва, 1950. pp. 148.

OCHERKI... Очерки истории Московской организации КПСС, 1883-1965. Москва, 1966. pp. 767. bibliog.

KUZNETSOV (IVAN VASIL'EVICH) and SHUMAKOV (ANATOLII VASIL'EVICH) Большевистская печать Москвы. Москва, Московский Рабочий, 1968. pp. 456. bibliog. 19½см.

LENIN... Ленин и московские большевики. Москва, 1969. pp. 548.

MOSKOVSKIE... Московские большевики в борьбе с правым и "левым" оппортунизмом, 1921-1929 гг. Москва, 1969. pp. 320.

- Statistics

MOSCOW. Statisticheskoe Upravlenie. Москва в цифрах за годы Советской власти, 1917-1967 гг.: краткий статистический сборник. Москва, 1967. pp. 166.

MOSCOW. Statisticheskoe Upravlenie. Moskva v tsifrakh, 1966-1970 gg.: kratkii statisticheskii sbornik. Moskva, 1972. pp. 168.

- Transit systems

CHEREPANOV (VLADIMIR ALEKSANDROVICH) Транспорт в градостроительстве: на опыте Москвы. Москва, Стройиздат, 1964. pp. 392. 21см.

RUSOV (VLADIMIR ALEKSANDROVICH) 25 лет работы Филевского автобусно-троллейбусного парка. Москва, 1966. pp. 136.

MOSCOW (OBLAST')

- Economic conditions

MOSCOW (OBLAST') Planovaia Komissiia. Moskovskoe khoziaistvo v 1925 godu: opyt sostavleniia edinogo khoziaistvennogo plana na 1924/25 god; s prilozheniem administrativno-ekonomicheskoi karty Moskov. gub. Moskva, 1925. pp. 413.

- Economic history

KONDRAT'EV (V. A.) and NEVZOROV (V. I.) eds. Из истории фабрик и заводов Москвы и Московской губернии, конец XVIII - начало XX в.: обзор документов. Москва, 1968. pp. 385. 21½см.

- Industries

PODMOSKOVNYI... Подмосковный угольный бассейн. Москва, 1967. pp. 237.

MOSCOW (OBLAST) (Cont'd.)

- Politics and government

OCHERKI... Очерки истории Московской организации КПСС, 1883-1965. Москва, 1966. pp. 767. bibliog.

- Rural conditions

SPEKTOR (NAUM PAVLOVICH) and KULIKOV (VLADIMIR IVANOVICH) Одна цель двух классов. Москва, 1967. pp. 126.

- Statistics

MOSCOW (OBLAST'). Statisticheskoe Upravlenie. Московская область за 50 лет: статистический сборник. Москва, Статистика, 1967. pp. 256. 21½см.

MOSCOW, BATTLE OF, 1941-1942

GOLIKOV (FILIPP IVANOVICH) V Moskovskoi bitve: zapiski komandarma. Moskva, 1967. pp. 200.

MOSKOVSKOE... Московское ополчение: краткий исторический очерк. Москва, Воениздат, 1969. pp. 224. 20см.

MOSCOW TRIALS, 1930

LIEBERMANN (MATWEJ) Im Namen der Sowjets: aus Moskauer Gerichtsakten. Berlin, Malik-Verlag, [1980]. pp. 303. 18½cm.

MOSCOW TRIALS, 1931

KRYLENKO (NIKOLAI VASIL'EVICH) Acte d'accusation relatif au procès de l'organisation menchéviste contre-révolutionnaire de Gromann, Cher, Ikov, Soukhanov et autres. Paris, Bureau d'Éditions, 1931. pp. 98. 17½cm.

MOSCOW TRIALS, 1936-1937

HEISLER (FRANCIS) The first two Moscow trials: why?; preface by Roy E. Burt, etc. Chicago, 1937. pp. 190.

COMMISSION OF INQUIRY INTO THE CHARGES MADE AGAINST LEON TROTSKY IN THE MOSCOW TRIALS. Summary of the final report. [London, 1938?] pp. 24.

SERGE (VICTOR) pseud. [i.e. Viktor L'vovich KIBAL'CHICH] and others. L'assassinat politique et l'U.R.S.S.: crime à Lausanne en marge des procès de Moscou; la mort d'Ignace Reiss. Paris, [1938] pp. 95.

TROTSKII (LEV DAVYDOVICH) Stalin's frame-up system and the Moscow trials. New York, [1950]. pp. 144. bibliog.

KATKOV (GEORGE) The trial of Bukharin. London, 1969. pp. 255.

MOSCOW UNIVERSITY

TAUBMANN (WILLIAM) The view from Lenin Hills: Soviet youth in ferment. London, Hamilton, 1968. pp. vi, 249. 21½cm.

MOSELLE

- Navigation

KUTZ (MARLIES) and MILKEREIT (GERTRUD) Beiträge zur Geschichte der Moselkanalisierung. Köln, Rheinisch-Westfälisches Wirtschaftsarchiv, 1967. pp. 318. bibliogs. 24cm. (Schriften zur Rheinisch-Westfälischen Wirtschaftsgeschichte. Band 14)

COMMISSION DE LA MOSELLE. Rapport annuel. [in French and German]. a., 1968- Trier.

MOSER (JOHANN JAKOB)

MOSER (JOHANN JACOB) J.J. Moser: ein schwäbischer Patriot: Lebens-Geschichte Johann Jacob Mosers, von ihme selbst beschrieben; bearbeitet von Siegfried Röder. Heidenheim a.d. Brenz, [1971]. pp. 124.

MOSHESH

BECKER (PETER) of Johannesburg. Hill of destiny: the life and times of Moshesh, founder of the Basotho. London, 1969. pp. 294. bibliog.

MOSHESHOE
See MOSHESH

MOSLEY (Sir OSWALD ERNALD)

PRITT (DENIS NOWELL) The Mosley case. London, [1947]. pp. 32.

MOSLEY (Sir OSWALD ERNALD) My life. London, Nelson, 1968. pp. (vi), 521. 23cm.

MOSQUITIA

- History

FLOYD (TROY S.) The Anglo-Spanish struggle for Mosquitia. [Albuquerque], U. of New Mexico P., [1967]. pp. xii, 235. bibliog. 23½cm.

MOSS (ARTHUR B.)

HEAFORD (WILLIAM) Biographical sketch: Arthur B. Moss, London correspondent of the 'Truth Seeker'. Bradford, [1895?]. pp. 7. (Truth Seeker. Pamphlets. No.6) Reprinted from The Truth Seeker.

MOSSI (AFRICAN PEOPLE)

DENIEL (RAYMOND) De la savane à la ville: essai sur la migration des Mossi vers Abidjan et sa région. Paris, Aubier-Montaigne, [1968]. pp. 223. bibliog. 17½cm. (Tiers Monde et Développement)

MOSSI LANGUAGES

UNITED STATES. State Department. Moré: basic course. Washington, 1966. pp. xxxix, 340.

MOST (JOHANN)

VERITAS (ANONYMUS) pseud. Acht Jahre hinter Schloss und Riegel: Skizzen aus dem Leben Johann Most's. 2nd ed. New York, 1886. pp. 88.

MOST (LUDWIG OTTO)

MOST (LUDWIG OTTO) Drei Jahrzehnte an Niederrhein, Ruhr und Spree. Duisburg, 1969. pp. 110. (Duisburg. Stadtarchiv. Duisburger Forschungen. Beihefte. 11)

MOTHER AND CHILD

BOWLBY (JOHN) Attachment and loss. London, Hogarth P., 1969 in progress. bibliog. 21½cm. (Institute of Psycho-Analysis. International Psycho-Analytical Library. No. 79)

MOTHERS

BAYLY (MARY) Mrs., Author of "Ragged Homes", etc. Ragged homes, and how to mend them. London, 1860. pp. 264.

SWEDEN. Socialstyrelsen. 1957. Ensamstående mödrars sociala och ekonomiska förhållanden år 1955: (The social and economic conditions of single mothers 1955). Stockholm, 1957. pp. (iii), iii, 53. 24cm. (Statistiska Centralbyrån. Sveriges Officiella Statistik. Socialvård) With English summary.

RIEMER (DETLEF) Die soziale Situation der Mütter männlicher in öffentlicher Erziehung sich befindender Jugendlicher: eine soziologisch-empirische Analyse. Marburg/Lahn, 1968. pp. 354. bibliog.

MARSDEN (DENNIS) Mothers alone: poverty and the fatherless family. London, Penguin P., 1969. pp. xiv, 282. 22cm.

KRIESBERG (LOUIS) Mothers in poverty: a study of fatherless families. Chicago, 1970. pp. 356.

MOTHERS - Employment
See WOMAN - Employment

- Mortality

GREER (HENRY LITTLE HARDY). A report on maternal deaths in Northern Ireland, 1956 - 1959. Belfast, H.M.S.O., 1962. pp. 53. 24½cm.

U.K. Department of Health and Social Security. Reports on Public Health and Medical Subjects. No. 119. Report on confidential enquiries into maternal deaths in England and Wales, 1964-1966; by Humphrey Arthure [and others]. London, 1969. pp. v, 119. 24½cm.

MOTHERS' PENSIONS

- Canada

CANADA. Department of National Health and Welfare. Research and Statistics Directorate. General Series. Memoranda. No. 22. Changes in legislation in general assistance and mothers' allowances in Canada, 1966. [Ottawa, 1967]. pp. v, 38.

- Russia

MAKAROVA (V. S.) Государственные пособия многодетным и одиноким матерям: учебное пособие для студентов ВЮЗИ. Москва, 1968. pp. 51. bibliog.

MOTIER (MARIE JEAN PAUL ROCH YVES GILBERT) Marquis de la Fayette

SARRANS (BERNARD) Lafayette et la révolution de 1830: histoire des choses et des hommes de juillet. Paris, Desplaces, 1832. 2 vols. 21½cm.

GOTTSCHALK (LOUIS REICHENTHAL) and MADDOX (MARGARET) Lafayette in the French revolution: through the October Days. Chicago, Ill., 1969. pp. 414. bibliogs.

MOTIVATION (PSYCHOLOGY)

MADSEN (KAJ BERG) Theories of motivation: a comparative study of modern theories of motivation. 2nd ed. Cleveland, 1964. pp. 356. bibliog.

FELDMAN (SHEL) ed. Cognitive consistency motivational antecedents and behavioral consequents. New York, Academic P., 1966. pp. xiii, 312. bibliogs. 23cm.

PSYCHOLOGY OF LEARNING AND MOTIVATION, THE: advances research and theory. London, annual, 1967 (vol.1) to date. 23½cm.

BOLLES (ROBERT C.) Theory of motivation. New York, Harper & Row, [1967]. pp. (v), 546. 22½cm. (Harper International Edition)

DE CHARMS (RICHARD) Personal causation: the internal affective determinants of behavior. New York, Academic P., 1968. pp. xiii, 398. 22½cm.

GELLERMAN (SAUL WILLIAM) Management by motivation. New York, American Management Association, [1968]. pp. 286. 23½cm.

LARGUIER (J.) Une recherche sur les motivations para-criminologiques d'une activité ludique: l'abus de flippers: essai de pronostic d'un comportement antisocial. in L'Évolution du droit criminel contemporain. Paris, 1968.

LITWIN (GEORGE H.) and STRINGER (ROBERT A.) Motivation and organizational climate. Boston, Harvard University, Graduate School of Business Administration, Division of Research, 1968. pp. xiii, 214. bibliog. 20½cm.

LONDON. University. London School of Economics and Political Science. Graduate Geography Department. Discussion Papers. No. 14. On the concept of motivation in geography; [by] John D. Eyles. London, 1968. pp. 12. 30cm.

MADSEN (KAJ BERG) Theories of motivation: a comparative study of modern theories of motivation. 4th ed. Kent, Ohio, Kent State U.P., 1968. pp. 365. bibliog. 23½cm.

NEBRASKA SYMPOSIUM ON MOTIVATION, 16th, 1968. [Proceedings]; William J. Arnold, editor. Lincoln, 1968. pp. 337. (Current Theory and Research in Motivation. vol. 16)

BIRNEY (ROBERT CHARLES) and others. Fear of failure. New York, [1969]. pp. 280. bibliog.

GROSS (CHARLES G.) and ZEIGLER (HARRIS PHILIP) eds. Readings in physiological psychology: motivation. New York, [1969]. pp. 323. bibliogs.

HACKMAN (RAY C.) The motivated working adult. [New York], [1969]. pp. 206. bibliog.

MOTIVATION (PSYCHOLOGY) (Cont'd.)

McCLELLAND (DAVID CLARENCE) and WINTER (DAVID G.) Motivating economic development;...with Sara K. Winter [and others]. New York, Free P., [1969]. pp. xxii, 409. bibliog. 23cm.

NEBRASKA SYMPOSIUM ON MOTIVATION, 17TH, 1969. [Proceedings]; William J. Arnold and David Levine, editors. Lincoln, Nebraska, 1969. pp. 334. bibliogs.

SINHA (DURGANAND) Indian villages in transition: a motivational analysis. New Delhi, 1969. pp. 232. bibliog.

SINHA (DURGANAND) Motivation of rural population in a developing country. Bombay, 1969. pp. 51. (A.N. Sinha Institute of Social Studies. Monographs. 2)

VERNON (MAGDALEN DOROTHEA) Human motivation. Cambridge, 1969. pp. 189. bibliog.

ZIMBARDO (PHILIP G.) ed. The cognitive control of motivation: the consequences of choice and dissonance. Glenview, Illinois, [1969]. pp. 300. bibliog.

HUIZINGA (GERARD) Maslow's need hierarchy in the work situation. Groningen, 1970. pp. 207 and appendices. bibliog.

MASLOW (ABRAHAM HAROLD) Motivation and personality. 2nd ed. New York, [1970]. pp. 369. bibliog.

MOTIVATION RESEARCH (MARKETING)

RUPPEL (PETER) Die Bedeutung des Image für das Verbraucherverhalten. Göttingen, 1965. pp. 182. bibliog.

LISOWSKY (PETER UWE) Das Bedürfnis als absatzwirtschaftliches Problem. Zürich, 1968. pp. 109. bibliog.

MOTOR BUS LINES

- Cost of operation

MOHRING (HERBERT DICK) Optimization and scale economies in urban bus transportation. Minneapolis, 1971. fo. 38. bibliog. (Minnesota University. Center for Economic Research. Discussion Papers. No. 5)

- Germany

KLAAS (HERMANN) Konkurrenz im Personenlinienverkehr mit Omnibussen. Marburg, 1968. pp. 175. bibliog.

- Hong Kong

BUTLER (RICHARD) Ph.D. Bus operation in Hong Kong: a study of public and private enterprise; [Ph.D. (London) thesis]. [1971]. fo. 291. Typescript: unpublished. This thesis is the property of London University and may not be removed from the Library.

- India - Employees

INDIA. Labour Investigation Committee. 1946. Report on labour conditions in tram and bus services; by Ahmad Mukhtar. Delhi, 1946. pp. 124.

- Israel

HOVNE (AVNER) Bus services in Israel: co-operative form, monopolistic structure, public control. Jerusalem, 1966. pp. 161. bibliog. 27cm. [First published in Hebrew, 1951.]

- Russia

RUSOV (VLADIMIR ALEKSANDROVICH) 25 лет работы Филевского автобусно-троллейбусного парка. Москва, 1966. pp. 136.

- Tasmania

TASMANIA. Parliament. Legislative Council. Select Committee...appointed...to enquire into...the Road Transport Services of the Transport Commission, etc 1967. Transport Commission road services: report ...with minutes of proceedings. in Tasmania. Parliament. Journals and Printed Papers, 1967, no. 27.

- United Kingdom

MASON (ARNOLD JOSEPH) Transport in West Bromwich: a history of road passenger transport in West Bromwich from 1750 to 1963. London, [1963]. pp. 40.

ADAMS (BEN) The threat to the bus passenger. [London], Aims of Industry, 1967. pp. 17. 24cm. (Aims of Industry. Studies. No. 18)

HIBBS (JOHN ALFRED BLYTH) The history of British bus services. Newton Abbot, David and Charles, [1968]. pp. 280. bibliog. 21½cm.

WILLIAMS (WILLIAM IDRIS) The economic analysis of bus and coach licensing decisions under the Road Traffic Acts of 1930 and 1960; [Ph.D. (London, thesis]. [1968]. fo. 357. 25½cm. Typescript: unpublished. This thesis is the property of London University and may not be removed from the Library

HIBBS (JOHN ALFRED BLYTH) Transport for passengers: a study in enterprise without licence. 2nd ed. London, 1971. pp. 96. bibliog. (Institute of Economic Affairs. Hobart Papers. 23)

RUNCORN DEVELOPMENT CORPORATION. Runcorn busway. Runcorn, [1971?]. pp. 16.

OXFORD AND AREA RURAL BUS SERVICES. Steering Committee. Report on Oxford and area rural bus services [Oxford, 1972?]. pp. 108.

- United Kingdom - London

LONDON. London Busmen's Rank-and-File Movement. The public, the busmen and the Transport Board. [London, 1935?]. pp. 15.

MUNT (P.W.) and YATES (L.B.) A study of bus passenger movements in the Vauxhall-Wandsworth area. [London], 1967. pp. (14). (London. Greater London Council. Department of Highways and Transportation. Research Memoranda. 42)

WEBSTER (F.V.) A theoretical estimate of the effect of London car commuters transferring to bus travel. Crowthorne, Road Research Laboratory, 1968. pp. 40, (1). bibliog. 30cm. Road Research Laboratory. Reports. LR 165.)

- United Kingdom - London - Employees

PRACTICAL bus operation: [agreements between London Transport and the Transport and General Workers' Union]. London, [1970?]. 1 pamphlet (unpaged).

REDEPLOYMENT agreement between L[ondon] T[ransport] and T[ransport and] G[eneral] W[orkers'] U[nion]. London, [1970?]. pp. 7.

MOTOR BUSES

MOHRING (HERBERT DICK) Optimization and scale economies in urban bus transportation. Minneapolis, 1971. fo. 38. bibliog. (Minnesota University. Center for Economic Research. Discussion Papers. No. 5)

MOTOR FUELS

- Taxation - United Kingdom

BRITISH ROAD FEDERATION. Road user taxation and road investment: a pre-budget memorandum to the Chancellor of the Exchequer, etc. [London], 1970. pp. 9.

MOTOR SCOOTERS

NATIONAL COUNCIL OF APPLIED ECONOMIC RESEARCH. Demand for scooters. New Delhi, 1971. pp. 48. bibliog.

MOTOR-TRUCKS

CONNECTICUT. Tri-State Transportation Commission. Regional Profiles. Vol.1, No.6. Truck transportation. New York, the Commission, 1968. pp. 4. 28cm.

EVERALL (P. F.) Social benefits from minimum power-weight ratios for goods vehicles. Crowthorne, 1969. pp. 24. bibliog. (U.K. Road Research Laboratory. Reports. LR 291)

CANADA. Statistics Canada. For-hire trucking survey. [in English and French] a., 1970 (1st issue)- Ottawa.

MOTOR VEHICLES

EIRE. Fair Trade Commission. Fair Trading Rules. No. 20A. Entry into and trade in the sale and/or repair of motor vehicles. Dublin, [1962]. pp. 5. 24cm.

MOTT (LUCRETIA COFFIN)

HARE (LLOYD CUSTER MAYHEW) The greatest American woman: Lucretia Mott; [reprint of work first published in 1937]. New York, 1970. pp. 307.

MOTTOLA

- Economic history

CARAGNANO (STEFANO) Le condizioni economico-sociali di Mottola, 1900-1922. Mottola, Posa, 1966. pp.190. 24cm.

- Rural conditions

CARAGNANO (STEFANO) Le condizioni economico-sociali di Mottola, 1900-1922. Mottola, Posa, 1966. pp.190. 24cm.

MOULIN (JEAN)

MOULIN (LAURE) Jean Moulin. Paris, [1969]. pp. 482.

MOUNIER (EMMANUEL)

CAMPANINI (GIORGIO) La rivoluzione cristiana: il pensiero politico di Emmanuel Mounier. Brescia, Morcelliana, [1968]. pp. 341. bibliog. 21½cm.

MOUNTAINS

CANAC (ROGER) La montagne. Paris, Seuil, [1968]. pp. 187. 18cm. (Peuple et Culture. 20

- Czechoslovakia

ŠED'O (DANJEL) Problémy rozvoje JRD v horských a podhorských oblastiach. Bratislava, Vydavatel'stvo Politickej Literatúry, 1966. pp. 147. 20cm.

- Italy

ITALY. Cassa per Opere Straordinarie di Pubblico Interesse nell'Italia Meridionale. Convegno Tecnico, 2°, 1954. Atti...: i problemi della montagna nell' Italia Meridionale. Roma, 1955. pp. 288. 24½cm.

CONVEGNO SUI PROBLEMI DELLA MONTAGNA, 5°, 1968. Atti. Torino, [1968]. pp. 337.

- Sardinia

SARDINIA. Assessorato Agricoltura e Foreste. 1958. Direttive di politica montana; del Renato Saldarelli; a cura del Servizio Stampa e Propaganda dell'Ispettorato Regionale delle Foreste di Cagliari. Cagliari, 1958. pp. 64. ([Pubblicazioni]. 6)

MOUNTBATTEN (LOUIS FRANCIS ALBERT VICTOR NICHOLAS) 1st Earl Mountbatten of Burma

MOUNTBATTEN (LOUIS FRANCIS ALBERT VICTOR NICHOLAS) 1st Earl Mountbatten of Burma. Reflections on the transfer of power and Jawaharlal Nehru. Cambridge, 1968. pp. 36. (Cambridge. University. Jawaharlal Nehru Memorial Lectures. 1968)

TERRAINE (JOHN) The life and times of Lord Mountbatten: an illustrated biography based on the television history, etc. London, Hutchinson, 1968. pp. x, 197. 23cm.

MOURIDES

COUTY (PHILIPPE) and COPANS (JEAN) Entretiens avec des marabouts et des paysans du Baol. Dakar, ORSTOM, 1968. 2 vols. (in 1).

COUTY (PHILIPPE) and COPANS (JEAN) Travaux collectifs agricoles en milieu wolof mouride. Dakar, ORSTOM, 1968. fo. 55. bibliog.

COUTY (PHILIPPE) La doctrine du travail chez les Mourides. Dakar, ORSTOM, 1969. fo. 30. bibliog.

COUTY (PHILIPPE) Emploi du temps et organisation du travail dans un village wolof mouride (Darou Rahmane II). Dakar, ORSTOM, 1969. fo. 95. bibliog.

MOURIDES (Cont'd.)

OBRIEN (DONAL BRIAN CRUISE) The Mourides of Senegal: the socio-economic structure of an Islamic order; [Ph. D. (London) thesis]. 1969. fo. v, 526. bibliog. 25½cm. Typescript unpublished. This thesis is the property of London University and may not be removed from the Library.

O'BRIEN (DONAL BRIAN CRUISE) The Mourides of Senegal: the political and economic organization of an Islamic brotherhood. Oxford, 1971. pp. 321. bibliog.

MOURNING CUSTOMS

MORLEY (JOHN) Death, heaven and the Victorians. London, 1971. pp. 208. bibliog.

MOVEMENT, PSYCHOLOGY OF

VELDT (J. VAN DER) L'apprentissage du mouvement et l'automatisme: étude expérimentale. Louvain, 1928. pp. 350. bibliog.

HACKER (WINFRIED) Grundlagen der Regulation von Arbeitsbewegungen. Berlin, Deutscher Verlag der Wissenschaften, 1967. pp. 141. bibliog. 24cm. (Gesellschaft für Psychologie in der DDR. Probleme und Ergebnisse der Psychologie. Beihefte. 1) With English and Russian summaries.

BILODEAU (EDWARD ALFRED) and BILODEAU (INA McD.) eds. Principles of skill acquisition. New York, [1969]. pp. 368. bibliog.

PIAGET (JEAN) The child's conception of movement and speed...; translated from the French by G. E. T. Holloway and M. J. Mackenzie. London, 1970. pp. 306.

MOVIMIENTO NACIONALISTA REVOLUCIONARIO

FELLMANN VELARDE (JOSE) compiler. Album de la revolucion: (128 años de lucha por la independencia de Bolivia). [La Paz?], Subsecretaria de Prensa, Informaciones y Cultura, [1953?]. 1 vol. (unpaged).

GUEILER TEJADA (LYDIA) La mujer y la revolución: autobiografía política. La Paz, 1959. pp. 294. 18½cm.

MOVIMIENTO NACIONALISTA REVOLUCIONARIO. M.N.R.A.: exposición de motivos y declaración de principios. [La Paz], 1960. pp. 142. 19cm.

MOVIMIENTO NACIONALISTA REVOLUCIONARIO. Convención Nacional, 8°, La Paz, 1960. Convocatoria. [La Paz], 1959. pp. 13. 15½cm.

PATCH (RICHARD W.) The last of Bolivia's MNR?: tensions between personalism and party in politics. New York, American Universities Field Staff, 1964. pp. 25. 28cm. (American Universities Field Staff. Reports Service. West Coast South America Series. vol.11, no.5)

JUSTO (LIBORIO) Bolivia: la revolución derrotada, etc. Cochabamba, [Rojas Araujo], 1967. pp. (iv), 276. 24cm.

ZAVALETA MERCADO (RENÉ) Bolivia: el desarrollo de la conciencia nacional. [Montevideo, Diálogo], 1967. pp. 181. 17cm.

PANDO MONJE (MARIO) Los movimientistas en el poder: la revolucion boliviana; sus grandezas y frustraciones. La Paz, [1969?]. pp. 277. bibliog.

MALLOY (JAMES M.) Bolivia: the uncompleted revolution. Pittsburgh, 1970. pp. 396.

MOVIMIENTO NACIONALISTA REVOLUCIONARIO AUTENTICO
See MOVIMIENTO NACIONALISTA REVOLUCIONARIO

MOVING-PICTURE AUDIENCES

SOROKINA (V.N.) О некоторых результатах социологического исследования восприятия и оценки киноискусства зрителей. in Uchnye Zapiski Kafedr Obshchestvennykh Nauk Vuzov g. Leningrada. Filosofiia. vyp.6. Leningrad, 1965.

MOVING-PICTURE INDUSTRY

HUERFELD (WERNER) Die optimale Unternehmungsgrösse in der Filmproduktion. Düsseldorf, Droste, [1958] pp. 239. bibliog. 21cm. (Cologne. Universität. Industrieseminar. Filmwirtschaftliche Studien. 2)

BERGNER (HEINZ) Versuch einer Filmwirtschaftslehre. Berlin, Duncker und Humblot, [1962-66]. 4 vols. bibliogs. 23½cm. (Cologne. Universität. Industrieseminar. Filmwirtschaftliche Studien. Band 1)

VALTER (GERARD) Le régime de l'organisation professionnelle de la cinématographie, du corporatisme au régime administratif. Paris, 1969. pp. 285.

JARVIE (IAN CHARLES) Towards a sociology of the cinema: a comparative essay on the structure and functioning of a major entertainment industry. London, 1970. pp. 394. bibliog.

- Canada

CANADA. Dominion Bureau of Statistics. Motion picture theatres and film distributors. Ottawa, annual, 1958 to date. 28cm.

- Europe

GUBACK (THOMAS H.) The international film industry: Western Europe and America since 1945. Bloomington, [1969]. pp. 244. bibliog. (Indiana University. International Studies)

- France

FRANCE. French Embassy, London. Service de Presse et d'Information. 1967. The French cinema. London, [1967]. pp. 31.

LEGLISE (PAUL) Histoire de la politique du cinéma français: le cinéma et la IIIe République. Paris, 1970. pp. 325. bibliog.

- Germany - Finance

ADAM (WILFRIED) Das Risiko in der deutschen Filmwirtschaft. Wiesbaden-Dotzheim, [1959]. pp. 206. bibliog. (Cologne. Universität. Industrieseminar. Filmwirtschaftliche Studien. Band 3)

HERRIGER (HANS PETER) Die Subventionierung der deutschen Filmwirtschaft. Köln, Westdeutscher Verlag, 1966. pp. 56. bibliog. 24cm. (North Rhine-Westphalia. Forschungsberichte des Landes Nordrhein-Westfalen. Nr.1637)

- India

INDIA. Film Enquiry Committee. 1951. Report: (S.K. Patil, chairman]. New Delhi, 1951. pp. 339.

- Ireland (Republic)

EIRE. Film Industry Committee. 1968. Report. [John Huston, chairman]. Dublin, [1968]. pp. 61.

- United Kingdom

DAVIS (JOHN H.) F.C.I.S. The British film industry. [London, 1958]. pp. 15.

- United States

GUBACK (THOMAS H.) The international film industry: Western Europe and America since 1945. Bloomington, [1969]. pp. 244. bibliog. (Indiana University. International Studies)

MOVING-PICTURES

- Aesthetics

MITRY (JEAN) Esthétique et psychologie du cinéma. Paris, Éditions Universitaires, [1963-65]. 2 vols. 24cm. (Encyclopédie Universitaire)

- Censorship - United States

RANDALL (RICHARD S.) Censorship of the movies: the social and political control of a mass medium. Madison, U. of Wisconsin P., 1968. pp. xvi, 280. 23½cm.

- Psychological aspects

EMERY (FREDERICK E.) and MARTIN (DAVID) Psychological effects of the "western" film: a study in television viewing. [Melbourne], 1957. pp. 47. (Melbourne. University. Department of Audio-Visual Aids. Studies in Mass Communication. [No. 1])

MITRY (JEAN) Esthétique et psychologie du cinéma. Paris, Éditions Universitaires, [1963-65]. 2 vols. 24cm. (Encyclopédie Universitaire)

MUENSTERBERG (HUGO) The film: a psychological study: the silent photoplay in 1916. New York, 1970. pp. 100.

- Social aspects

GALLI (GIORGIO) and ROSITI (FRANCO) Cultura di massa e comportamento collettivo: società e cinema negli anni precedenti il new deal e il nazismo. Bologna, Il Mulino, [1967]. pp. 287. 23½cm. (Istituto "Agostino Gemelli". [Pubblicazioni]. 4)

[MICHARD (HENRI) and others.] The cinema and the protection of youth. Strasbourg, Council of Europe, 1968. pp. 167. bibliog.

CONVEGNO NAZIONALE DI ANTROPOLOGIA CRIMINALE, 3°, SIENA, 1968. Cinema e criminalità. Milano, 1970. pp. 142.

JARVIE (IAN CHARLES) Towards a sociology of the cinema: a comparative essay on the structure and functioning of a major entertainment industry. London, 1970. pp. 394. bibliog.

OSTERLAND (MARTIN) Gesellschaftsbilder in Filmen: eine soziologische Untersuchung des Filmangebots der Jahre 1949 bis 1964. Stuttgart, 1970. pp. 253. bibliog.

GLUCKSMANN (ANDRE) Violence on the screen...: a report on research into the effects on young people of scenes of violence in films and television; translated by Susan Bennett, with a foreword by Paddy Whannel and an afterword by Dennis Howitt. London, 1971. pp. 78.

GOLDMANN (ANNIE) Cinéma et société moderne: le cinéma de 1958 à 1968; Godard, Antonioni, Resnais, Robbe-Grillet. Paris, [1971]. pp. 252.

- Canada

CANADA. Parliament. House of Commons. Standing Committee on Broadcasting, Films and Assistance to the Arts. Minutes of proceedings and evidence. [from Nov. 19 1968 in English and French] Ottawa, irreg., March 24/April 21 1966 (27th Parl., 1st session, no.1) to date, with gap (27th Parl., 1st session, no.39). 25cm.

- Europe

QUINN (JAMES) The film and television as an aspect of European culture. Leyden, Sijthoff, 1968. pp. 168. 23cm. (Council of Europe. European Aspects Series A. Culture. No. 10)

- Germany

ALBRECHT (GERD) Nationalsozialistische Filmpolitik: eine soziologische Untersuchung über die Spielfilme des Dritten Reichs. Stuttgart, 1969. pp. 562. bibliog.

- United Kingdom

THURTLE (ERNEST) The case for Sunday cinemas. London, 1933. pp. 16.

- Uzbekistan

TESHABAEV (DZHURA) Киноискусство Советского Узбекистана. Москва, Союз Кинематографистов СССР, 1968. pp. 63. 20½см.

- Vietnam

IBRAGIMOV (AZHDAR) Киноискусство сражающегося Вьетнама. Москва, Бюро Пропаганды Советского Киноискусства, 1968. pp. 84. 20½см.

- White Russia

ISTORIIA Belorusskogo kino, 1945-1967. Minsk, 1970. pp. 255.

MOVING-PICTURES, DOCUMENTARY

MEYER (HAN) Joris Ivens, de weg naar Vietnam. Utrecht, 1970. pp. 260.

MOVING-PICTURES AND CHILDREN

LONDON. London County Council. London children and the cinema. ([Publications] No. 3742) London, 1951. pp. 18. bibliog., 18½cm.

[MICHARD (HENRI) and others.] The cinema and the protection of youth. Strasbourg, Council of Europe, 1968. pp. 167. bibliog.

MOVING-PICTURES IN ADVERTISING

SCREEN ADVERTISING ASSOCIATION. Media and the cinemagoer: a study of the 100% medium. London, [1964]. pp. 20. 19½cm.

MOVING-PICTURES IN EDUCATION

LONDON. London County Council. Education Officer's Department. Report on experiments in the use of films for educational purposes. London, 1937. pp. 63.

QUINN (JAMES) The film and television as an aspect of European culture. Leyden, Sijthoff, 1968. pp. 168. 23cm. (Council of Europe. European Aspects. Series A. Culture. No. 10)

MOVING-PICTURES IN PROPAGANDA

BALDELLI (PIO) and FILIPPI (ALBERTO) eds. Cinema e lotta di liberazione. Roma, 1970. pp. 74.

MOWRER (EDGAR ANSEL)

MOWRER (EDGAR ANSEL) Triumph and turmoil: a personal history of our time. London, 1970. pp. 454.

MOXOTÓ VALLEY

- Economic conditions

CAVALCANTI (CLÓVIS DE VASCONCELOS) and PESSOA (DIRCEU MURILO) Vale do Moxotó: análise sócio-econômica de uma bacia de açude público. Recife, Instituto Joaquim Nabuco de Pesquisas Sociais, 1970. pp. 272.

- Social conditions

CAVALCANTI (CLÓVIS DE VASCONCELOS) and PESSOA (DIRCEU MURILO) Vale do Moxotó: análise sócio-econômica de uma bacia de açude público. Recife, Instituto Joaquim Nabuco de Pesquisas Sociais, 1970. pp. 272.

MOYAMBA

- Social conditions

RANSON (BRIAN H. A.) A sociological study of Moyamba town, Sierra Leone. Zaria, Ahmadu Bello University, Institute of Administration, 1968. fo. v, 110. 25½cm. (Research Memoranda Series)

MOYOBAMBA

- Economic conditions

CENTRO DE INVESTIGACIONES SOCIALES POR MUESTREO. Aspectos sociales y economicos de la ciudad de Moyobamba; encuesta de hogares. Lima, 1968. pp. 41.

- Social conditions

CENTRO DE INVESTIGACIONES SOCIALES POR MUESTREO. Aspectos sociales y economicos de la ciudad de Moyobamba; encuesta de hogares. Lima, 1968. pp. 41.

MOZAMBIQUE

- Bibliography

COSTA (MÁRIO) compiler. Bibliografia geral de Moçambique; (contribuição para um estudo completo). Lisboa, Agência Geral das Colónias, 1946. pp. 359.

- Economic conditions

SALDANHA (EDUARDO D'ALMEIDA) Moçambique — União de África do Sul: as bases para a convenção. Lisboa, [imprint], 1928. pp. (256). 24cm.

- History - Sources

PORTUGAL. 1947. As campanhas de Moçambique em 1895 segundo os contemporaneos; prefacio e notas do Marcello Caetano. (Agencia Geral das Colonias). Lisboa, 1947. pp. 401.

- Industries

ASSOCIAÇÃO INDUSTRIAL DE MOÇAMBIQUE. Colectânea de estudos do Gabinete de Estudos Técnicos: Problemas de cabotagem em Moçambique, [and] Estrutura da indústria transformadora de Moçambique Lourenço Marques, 1968. pp. 104.

- Nationalism

MONDLANE (EDUARDO) The struggle for Mozambique. Harmondsworth, 1969. pp. 222. (Penguin African Library) Map in end pocket

- Politics and government

MONDLANE (EDUARDO) The struggle for Mozambique. Harmondsworth, 1969. pp. 222. (Penguin African Library) Map in end pocket.

MSIMANG (H. SELBY)

MSIMANG (H. SELBY) H. Selby Msimang looks back. Johannesburg, [1970?]. pp. 10. (South African Institute of Race Relations. Topical Talks. No. 25)

MUCH WENLOCK

- History

MUCH WENLOCK. Borough Council. Wenlock, 1468-1968; studies in the history of the town and borough, published in celebration of the quincentenary of the charter of Edward IV, 29 November, 1468; edited by L. C. Lloyd. Much Wenlock, 1968. pp. 53.

MUDIE (CHARLES EDWARD)

GRIEST (GUINEVERE L.) Mudie's circulating library and the Victorian novel. Bloomington, Ind., [1970]. pp. 272. bibliog.

MUELLER (HERMANN)

GERMANY. Reichskanzlei. 1928-1930. Das Kabinett Müller II, 28. Juni 1928 bis 27. März 1930; bearbeitet von Martin Vogt. Boppard am Rhein, 1970. 2 vols. bibliog. (Akten der Reichskanzlei, Weimarer Republik).

MUELLER (SIEGFRIED) German officer

ARNDT (MANFRED) ed. The laughing man: confessions of a murderer; program of a regime. [Dresden, 1966]. pp. 16.

MUENSTER VON DERNEBURG (GEORG HERBERT) Prince

NOSTITZ (HERBERT VON) Bismarcks unbotmässiger Botschafter: Fürst Münster von Derneburg 1820-1902. Göttingen, Vandenhoeck und Ruprecht, [1968]. pp. 326. bibliog. 21cm.

SUEHLO (WINFRIED) Georg Herbert Graf zu Münster, Erblandmarschall im Königreich Hannover: ein biographischer Beitrag zur Frage der politischen Bedeutung des deutschen Uradels für die Entwicklung vom Feudalismus zum industriellen Nationalstaat. Hildesheim, 1968. pp. 190. bibliog. (Historische Kommission für Niedersachsen. Veröffentlichungen. 32)

MULHOUSE

FRANCE. Direction de la Documentation. La Documentation Française. Notes et Etudes Documentaires. No.3,669. Les villes françaises: Mulhouse; [by] Paul Meyer [and others]. Paris, 1970. pp. 41. bibliog.

MULTILINGUALISM

VILDOMEC (VEROBOJ) Multilingualism. Leyden, Sythoff. 1963. pp. 262. bibliog. 24cm.

ANDERSON (NELS) ed. Studies in multilingualism. Leiden, 1969. pp. 153.

INTERNATIONAL AFRICAN SEMINAR. 9th Seminar, University College, Dar-es-Salaam, 1968. Language use and social change: problems of multilingualism with special reference to eastern Africa; studies...; edited with an introduction by W.H. Whiteley. London, 1971. pp. 406. bibliogs.

MULTIMACHINE ASSIGNMENTS

STORCH (JÜRGEN) and others. Mehrmaschinenbedienung: Normieurung der Arbeit, Entlohnung und Kostenermittlung. Berlin, 1966. pp. 180. bibliog. (Sozialistische Arbeitswissenschaft. [Publications]. 5.)

MULTIPLIER (ECONOMICS)

NEW SOUTH WALES. 1962. Multiplier effects of industry in country centres; (prepared by John Jackson and Associates); issued by J.B.Renshaw, Minister for Industrial Development and Decentralisation. [Sydney, 1962 reprinted] 1964. pp. 6. 21½cm.

ARCHER (BRIAN H.) and OWEN (CHRISTINE) Towards a tourist regional multiplier. Bangor, 1970. fo. 11. (Wales. University. University College of North Wales. Economic Research Papers. REG 1)

SADLER (P.G.) Regional multipliers and input-output analysis. Bangor, 1970. fo. 9. (Wales. University. University College of North Wales. Economic Research Papers. REG 2)

MULTIVARIATE ANALYSIS

CATTELL (RAYMOND BERNARD) ed. Handbook of multivariate experimental psychology. Chicago, [1966]. pp. 959. bibliog.

INTERNATIONAL SYMPOSIUM ON MULTIVARIATE ANALYSIS, DAYTON, 1965. Multivariate analysis; proceedings... edited by Paruchuri R. Krishnaiah. New York, Academic P., 1966. pp. xix, 592. bibliogs. 22½cm.

DEMPSTER (A. P.) Elements of continuous multivariate analysis. Reading, Mass., [1969]. pp. 388. bibliog.

INTERNATIONAL SYMPOSIUM ON MULTIVARIATE ANALYSIS, 2ND, DAYTON 1968. Multivariate analysis, II; proceedings...; edited by Paruchuri R. Krishnaiah. New York, 1969. pp. 696. bibliogs.

MATHER (PAUL M.) Principal components and factor analysis. [Nottingham], 1970. pp. 30. (Nottingham. University. Department of Geography. Computer Applications in the Natural and Social Sciences. No. 10)

THOMPSON (KENNETH H.) Cross-national voting behaviour research: an example of computer-assisted multivariate analysis of attribute data. Beverly Hills, [1970]. pp. 132-174. bibliog.

MUNICH

- History

HANKE (PETER) Zur Geschichte der Juden in München zwischen 1933 und 1945. München, Stadtarchiv, 1967. pp. 353. bibliog. (Munich. Stadtarchiv. Neue Schriftenreihe. Band 19)

BRETSCHNEIDER (HEIKE) Der Widerstand gegen den Nationalsozialismus in München von 1933 bis 1945. München, 1968. pp. 282. bibliog. (Munich Stadtarchiv. Neue Schriftenreihe. Band 20)

MORENZ (LUDWIG) Revolution und Räteherrschaft in München: aus der Stadtchronik 1918/1919. München, [1968]. pp. 135. (Munich. Stadtarchiv. Neue Schriftenreihe. Band 29)

SCHMOLZE (GERHARD) ed. Revolution und Räterepublik in München 1918/19 in Augenzeugenberichten. Düsseldorf, [1969]. pp. 426. bibliog.

- Politics and government

STEINBORN (PETER) Grundlagen und Grundzüge Münchener Kommunalpolitik in den Jahren der Weimarer Republik: zur Geschichte der bayerischen Landeshauptstadt im 20.Jahrhundert. München, 1968. pp. 604. bibliog. (Munich. Stadtarchiv. Neue Schriftenreihe. Band 21)

- Recreation areas

BRENDEL (RUEDIGER) Das Münchener Naherholungsgebiet im Bereich des Ammersees und des Starnberger Sees: eine sozialgeographische Studie. [Munich?], 1967. pp. 237. bibliog.

MUNICH FOUR-POWER AGREEMENT, 1938

LECTURES on the history of Munich: delivered at the international conference on the occasion of the 20th anniversary of Munich, Prague, 1958; edited by the Institute of International Politics and Economics, Prague. Prague, Orbis, 1959. pp. 103. 20cm.

KRÁL (VÁCLAV) ed. Politické strany a Mnichov: dokumenty. Praha, 1961. pp. 237.

SCOTT (W.E.) Neville Chamberlain and Munich: two aspects of power. in Krieger (Leonard) and Stern (Fritz Richard) eds. The responsibility of power. Garden City, 1967.

ROBBINS (KEITH GILBERT) Munich, 1938. London, Cassell, 1968. pp. (vi), 398. bibliog. 21cm.

SEELAND (ROLF) Appeasement: eine Methode zur Lösung internationaler Konflikte. Hamburg, 1968. pp. 156. bibliog.

DEML (FERDINAND) ed. München, 29. September 1938: vorher und nachher; eine Auswahl von Dokumenten. Bonn, [1969]. pp. 62.

LUNDGREEN (PETER) Die englische Appeasement-Politik bis zum Münchener Abkommen: Voraussetzungen, Konzeption, Durchführung. Berlin, [1969]. pp. 153. bibliog.

WERSTEIN (IRVING) Betrayal: the Munich Pact of 1938. Garden City, N.Y., [1969]. pp. 188.

MUNICH UNIVERSITY

PRANTL (KARL VON) Geschichte der Ludwig-Maximilians-Universität in Ingolstadt, Landshut, München, zur Festfeier ihres vierhundertjährigen Bestehens...; Neudruck der Ausgabe München 1872. Aalen, Scientia, 1968. 2 vols. 22cm.

SCHMIDBAUER (MICHAEL) Studienorientierung und Studienerfolg: Untersucht an Studenten der Volks- und Betriebswirtschaft der Universität München. München, [1968]. pp. 200. bibliog.

MUNICIPAL BONDS

- United States

SMITH (WILLIAM PAUL) Commercial bank entry into revenue bond underwriting: competitive impact and public benefits. Washington, Office of the Comptroller of the Currency, 1968. pp.x, 69. bibliog. 26½cm. (National Banking Studies)

- United Kingdom - Bedford

BEDFORDSHIRE. County Council. Proposed new county hall: (reports of George Brewis [and others]). [Bedford], 1963. pp. (iii), 36. 25cm.

MUNICIPAL CORPORATIONS

- Belgium

LIÈGE. Université. Faculté de Droit. Commission Droit et Vie des Affaires. L'entreprise dans la cité; séminaire organisé à Liège les 8, 9 et 10 décembre 1966. Liège, 1967. pp. 422. 24½cm. (Collection Scientifique. 27)

- Colombia

CORTÉS DÍAZ (BERNARDO) Estudio sobre el municipio y el alcalde en la legislación colombiana. Bogotá, 1963. pp. 55. bibliog. 24cm.

- Denmark

DAHL (FLEMMING) Københavns Kommunalforfatning af 1840: en Redegørelse for Anordning af 1. Januar 1840, etc. København, 1940. pp. 200.

- Germany

KUNTZMANN-AUERT (MARION) Rechtsstaat und kommunale Selbstverwaltung: die Vereinbarkeit rechtsstaatlicher Grundsätze mit einer von politischen Kräften getragenen Selbstverwaltung. Köln, Heymanns, 1967. pp. xxi, 145. bibliog. 20½cm.

- India - Maharashtra

MAHARASHTRA. Committee for Revision of the Acts relating to Municipal Corporations in Maharashtra State. 1965. Report. Bombay, 1965. pp. 40.

MAHARASHTRA. Committee for Unification of the Acts relating to Municipalities in Maharashtra State. 1965. Report. Bombay, [1965?]. pp. 67.

- Italy

MUSITELLI (LORENZO) Il Comune nell'ordinamento amministrativo: organi, funzioni, mezzi, servizi. Milano, 1969. pp. 261.

- Rome, Ancient

KUHN (EMIL) Die städtische und bürgerliche Verfassung des Römischen Reichs bis auf die Zeiten Justinians; Neudruck der Ausgabe Leipzig 1864-65. Aalen, Scientia Verlag, 1968. 2 vols. (in 1). 22cm. Facsimile reprint.

- United Kingdom

The LAW of corporations: containing the laws and customs of all the corporations and inferior courts of record in England, etc. London, Atkins, 1702. pp. (xxvii), 365. 19½cm.

- United States

URBAN LAND INSTITUTE. Technical Bulletins. No. 62. New zoning landmarks in planned unit developments; by Lenard L. Wolffe. Washington, [1968]. pp. 29.

MUNICIPAL COURTS

- United Kingdom

The LAW of corporations: containing the laws and customs of all the corporations and inferior courts of record in England, etc. London, Atkins, 1702. pp. (xxvii), 365. 19½cm.

MUNICIPAL ENGINEERING

ALESSI (NICOLO) Opere pubbliche comunali, ed esecuzione dei lavori pubblici nei grandi e piccoli comuni. Milano, 1969. pp. 425.

MUNICIPAL FINANCE
See LOCAL FINANCE

MUNICIPAL GOVERNMENT

GLADDEN (WASHINGTON) Civic religion. 5th ed. [Philadelphia], 1904. pp. 19. (National Municipal League. Leaflets. No.3)

BRITISH COMMITTEE FOR THE STUDY OF FOREIGN MUNICIPAL INSTITUTIONS. Municipal visit to Belgium and Germany. [London], 1905. pp. 35.

AYLES (WALTER H.) What a socialist town council would do. London, [192-?], pp. 15.

HANSON (ALBERT HENRY) The organisation and administration of municipal enterprises with emphasis on public transport, electricity, water: a comparative analysis. The Hague, Nijhoff, 1966. pp. 118. (International Union of Local Authorities. Management of Public Utilities by Local Authorities. 1)

PUBLIC ADMINISTRATION SERVICE and INTERNATIONAL CITY MANAGERS' ASSOCIATION. Automated data processing in municipal government: status, problems, and prospects. Chicago, [1966]. pp. 34.

WIDDEL (GUENTHER) Datenverarbeitung im kommunalen Einwohnerwesen: Integrationsmodelle für den Einsatz elektronischer Rechenanlagen. Göttingen, 1966. pp. 257. bibliog.

WALSH (ANN MARIE HAUCK) The urban challenge to government: an international comparison of thirteen cities. New York, Praeger, 1969. pp. xii, 294. bibliog. 23½cm.

McCANDLESS (CARL A.) Urban government and politics. New York, [1970]. pp. 517. bibliogs.

FUTURE directions in community power research: a colloquium [at the Institute of Governmental Studies, University of California]; Frederick M. Wirt, editor. Berkeley, 1971. pp. 228

MUNICIPAL GOVERNMENT
See also INTERNATIONAL UNION OF LOCAL AUTHORITY

- Africa, Subsaharan

CONFERENCE ON THE GOVERNMENT OF AFRICAN CITIES, LINCOLN UNIVERSITY, 1968. [Proceedings]. [Narberth?, 1968]. fo. 112.

- Algeria

DESCLOITRES (ROBERT) and CORNET (ROGER) Commune et société rurale en Algerie: administration locale et participation au développement dans l'Aurès. Aix-en-Provence, 1968. pp. 87. (Centre Africain des Sciences Humaines Appliquées. Collection des Travaux du CASHA. [No. 3])

- America, Latin - Bibliography

RABINOVITZ (FRANCINE F.) and others, compilers. Latin-American political systems in an urban setting: a preliminary bibliography. Gainesville, University of Florida, Center for Latin-American Studies, 1967. pp. 42. 23cm.

- Canada

CANADA. Department of Finance. 1865. [Miscellaneous statistics of Canada for the year 1864: part 2.] Municipal returns for upper and lower Canada. Quebec, 1865. pp. 27.

PLUNKETT (THOMAS J.) Urban Canada and its government: a study in municipal organization. Toronto, Macmillan, 1968. pp. (viii), 178. bibliog. 19½cm.

FELDMAN (LIONEL D.) and GOLDRICK (MICHAEL KEVIN D'ARCY) eds. Politics and government of urban Canada: selected readings. Toronto, [1969]. pp. 382. bibliogs.

CANADIAN FEDERATION OF MAYORS AND MUNICIPALITIES. Annual Conference, 32nd, 1969. Proceedings... Compte rendu, etc. [Ottawa, 1969]. pp. 114. In English or French.

CANADIAN FEDERATION OF MAYORS AND MUNICIPALITIES. Annual Conference, 33rd, 1970. Proceedings...: Compte rendu, etc. [Ottawa, 1971]. pp. 216. In English or French.

- Canada - British Columbia

BRITISH COLUMBIA. Department of Municipal Affairs. Report. Victoria, B.C., annual, 1939-1941, 1946-1949. 26½cm.

- Canada - Nova Scotia

OUTHIT (W.D.) Province of Nova Scotia: report on municipal boundaries and municipal representation and the effectiveness of existing law in relation to changes in boundaries and representation in the light of changing populations and the need for municipal services. Halifax, 1963. fo.103.

DALHOUSIE UNIVERSITY. Institute of Public Affairs. [Current Publications]. No. 58. Pictou county municipal coordination study: phase 1, report on possibilities for coordinating local services in Pictou county, Nova Scotia; Lawrence E. Sandford director of research; sponsored by towns of New Glasgow, etc. Halifax, 1967. pp. (x), xxxvii, 475. bibliog. 27½cm.

- Canada - Quebec

FRENETTE (JEAN-GUY) and others. Autorité municipale de la région pilote (BAEQ): étude des gouvernements municipaux et des commissions municipales; stratégie des officiers municipaux de la ville de Marchand: annexe technique au plan de développement pour la région pilote du Bas St-Laurent, de la Gaspésie et des Îles de la Madeleine. Ottawa, 1968. pp. i, 26. 28cm. (Canada. Department of Forestry and Rural Development. ARDA Rapports Abrégés. RA-No.16.)

FRENETTE (JEAN-GUY) and others. Municipal authorities in the pilot region (BAEQ): studies of municipal governments and municipal commissions, and the strategy used by municipal officers in the town of Marchand: a technical annex to the development plan, 1967-72, for the pilot region: Lower St.Lawrence, Gaspé and Iles-de-la-Madeleine. Ottawa, 1968. pp. (i), 25. 28cm. (Canada. Department of Forestry and Rural Development. ARDA Condensed Reports CR-No. 16.)

- Colombia

RIZO OTERO (HAROLD) Hacia una reforma integral de la administración local en Colombia y proyecto de reforma a la estructura administrativa del municipio de Cali. [Bogotá, 1968]. pp. 135. bibliog.

MUNICIPAL GOVERNMENT (Cont'd.)

- Egypt - Congresses

STUDIENKONFERENZ FÜR DIE V[EREINIGTE] A[RABISCHE] R[EPUBLIK], 2ND, 1962. Wesen, Aufbau und Funktion kommunaler und regionaler Verwaltungen. Berlin, Deutsche Stiftung für Entwicklungsländer, 1963. pp. 43. 29½cm.

- France

VERMEESCH (ALBERT) Essai sur les origines et la signification de la commune dans le nord de la France, XIe et XIIe siècles. Heule, U.G.A., 1966. pp. 197. bibliog. 25cm. (International Commission for the History of Representative and Parliamentary Institutions. Studies. 30)

PARTI RADICAL. Manifeste municipal, projet; [with] Annexe sur la réforme de la fiscalité locale. [Paris, 1970]. 2 pts. (in 1 vol.).

SAVIGNY (JEAN DE) L'état contre les communes? Paris, [1971]. pp. 222.

- Germany

BELOW (GEORG ANTON HUGO VON) Der Ursprung der deutschen Stadtverfassung; (Nachdruck der Originalausgabe 1892). Leipzig, 1968. pp. 147.

MUELHAUPT (LUDWIG) and OETTLE (KARL) eds. Gemeindewirtschaft und Unternehmerwirtschaft: Festgabe für Rudolf Johns zum 65. Geburtstag am 15. Juli 1965. Göttingen, Schwartz, 1965. pp. xi, 384. bibliog. 22½cm. (Frankfurt am Main. Forschungsgesellschaft für Staats- und Kommunalwirtschaft. Studien. Band 4)

WAGENER (F.) Unbeantwortete Fragen der Kommunalverwaltung an die Verwaltungswissenschaft. in Groeben (Klaus Von Der) and others. Über die Notwendigkeit einer neuen Verwaltungswissenschaft. Baden-Baden, [1966].

AMMON (ALF) Eliten und Entscheidungen in Stadtgemeinden: die amerikanische "Community Power"-Forschung und das Problem ihrer Rezeption in Deutschland. Berlin, Duncker und Humblot, [1967]. pp. 160. bibliog. 23½cm. (Berlin. Freie Universität. Wirtschafts- und Sozialwissenschaftliche Fakultät. Soziologische Abhandlungen. Heft 8)

SCHNELL (STEFAN) Der Deutsche Städtetag. Bonn, [1970]. pp. 112. bibliog.

- Germany - Saarland

MONZ (HEINZ) Die kommunale Neuordnung städtischer Ballungsräume: Lösungsmöglichkeiten dargestellt am Beispiel des Raumes Saarbrücken. Saarbrücken, 1962. pp. 148. bibliog.

- India

INDIA. Ministry of Health and Family Planning. Rural - Urban Relationship Committee. 1966. Report. New Delhi, 1966. 3 vols. (in 1). 24½cm.

ARGAL (R.) Municipal government in India. 3rd ed. Allahabad, 1967. pp. 245. bibliog.

ADMINSTRATION of the urban fringe;... proceedings of the seminar, Centre for Training and Research in Municipal Administration, (New Delhi, November 29-30, 1968). New Delhi, 1969. pp. 30.

BHATTACHARYA (MOHIT) State directorates of municipal administration. New Delhi, [1969]. pp. 113.

CABINET system in municipal government: proceedings of the seminar, September 15-16, 1969, New Delhi, [organised by the] Centre for Training and Research in Municipal Administration; [edited by Shri M. Bhattacharya]. New Delhi, [1970]. pp. 84.

- Italy

CONVEGNO NAZIONALE SUL DECENTRAMENTO DEMOCRATICO DEI COMUNI, 1969. Comuni e decentramento: atti. Roma, 1970. pp. 255.

- Italy - Lombardy

DILCHER (GERHARD) Die Entstehung der lombardischen Stadtkommune: eine rechts geschichtliche Untersuchung. Aalen, Scientia Verlag, 1967. pp. xix, 208. bibliog. 24½cm. (Untersuchungen zur Deutschen Staats- und Rechtsgeschichte. Neue Folge. Band 7)

- Mexico

MEXICO. Direccion General de Estadistica. 1960. División municipal de las entidades federativas, diciembre de 1959. Mexico, 1960. pp. 101.

GRAHAM (LAWRENCE S.) Politics in a Mexican community. Gainesville, 1968. pp. 73. bibliog. (Florida University. Monographs. Social Sciences. No. 35)

- Netherlands

VERENIGING VAN NEDERLANDSE GEMEENTEN. The position of the municipalities in the Netherlands within the general structure of the state. rev. ed. [The Hague?], 1967. pp. 12.

GEERAERT (A.) Jeugd en gemeentebeleid. Antwerpen. 1970. pp. 260.

GEMEENTELIJKE democratie; ([by] A.A.H. Stolk [and others; report of a committee appointed by Wiardi Beckman Stichting]. Deventer, 1970. pp. 98. (Wiardi Beckman Stichting. WBS Cahiers)

- New Zealand

STEWART (PETER J.) Port Chalmers Borough, 1866-1966: a short history on the occasion of the centennial of municipal government. Port Chalmers, [1966]. pp. 30.

- Pakistan, East

INTERNATIONAL CONFERENCE ON MUNICIPAL ADMINISTRATION, DACCA, 1967. Problems of municipal administration; collected papers...[of] the conference...under the joint sponsorship of the National Institute of Public Administration, Dacca, and Basic Democracies and Local Government Department,...Dacca, from May 29 - June 1, 1967; editor M.A. Husain Khan. Dacca, 1968. pp. 304. bibliog.

- Poland

SŁUŻEWSKI (JERZY) Działalność organów państwowych na obszarze aglomeracji miejskich. Warszawa, Wydawnictwo Prawnicze, 1965. pp. 214. 21cm. With Russian and English summaries.

NAROJEK (WINICJUSZ) System władzy w mieście; studium monograficzne. Wrocław, Ossolineum, 1967. pp. 274. 20½cm. With English and Russian summaries.

- Russia

SOROKIN (VALENTIN DMITRIEVICH) Administrativnye komissii pri ispolkomakh raionnykh gorodskikh Sovetov deputatov trudiashchikhsia. Moskva, 1964. pp. 76.

GABRICHIDZE (BORIS NIKOLAEVICH) Городские Советы депутатов трудящихся. Москва, Юридическая Литература, 1968. pp. 215. 20см.

- South Africa

JOHANNESBURG. Non-European Affairs Department. Activities of the Non-European Affairs Department. Johannesburg, 1964. pp. 29.

- South Africa - Natal

NATAL. Committee of Enquiry into the System of Management Committees for Local Authorities in Natal. 1968. Report: [Arthur Hopewell, chairman]. [Pietermaritzburg, 1968]. 2 vols. in 1.

- Switzerland

AARGAU (CANTON). Staatskanzlei. 1956. Gesetz über die Organisation der Gemeinden und Gemeinderäte vom 26. November 1841. Aarau, 1956. pp. 30. 21cm.

AARGAU (CANTON). Staatskanzlei. 1957. Organisation und Aufgaben der Gemeinden: Wegleitung für die Gemeinderäte. 2nd ed. Aarau, 1957. pp. 40. 21cm.

BUCHER (ERWIN) Der Gemeinderat der Stadt St. Gallen: Analyse eines schweizerischen Stadtparlamentes. Bern, [1970]. pp. 323. bibliog.

- Tasmania

TASMANIA. Commonwealth Bureau of Census and Statistics. Tasmanian Office. Compendium of municipal statistics. Hobart, irreg., 1957 [1st] to date. 30-33cm.

- Ukraine

ALEKSEENKO (ALEKSEI GRIGOR'EVICH) Городские Советы Украинской ССР, 1917-1920 гг. Киев, Университет, 1960. pp. 181. 22cm.

- United Kingdom

REPORT of an enquiry into the affairs of the Corporation of King's Lynn ... held before the Commissioners appointed for that purpose, in the Guildhall ... 1833; taken by John Thew. Stamford, Thew, 1833. pp.55. 23½cm.

SNELL (H.) 1st Baron Snell. The growth of municipal democracy. in London. University. London School of Economics and Political Science. Public lectures in celebration of the local government centenary, 1835-1935. [London, 1935].

ASSOCIATION OF MUNICIPAL CORPORATIONS. Annual report. London, annual, 1967/8 (88th rep.) to date.

MILLWARD (J.G.) Municipal work study. London, British Institute of Management, [1967]. pp. vii, 138. 25cm.

CLEMENTS (ROGER VICTOR) Local notables and the city council. London, 1969. pp. 207.

- United Kingdom - Bibliography

GROSS (CHARLES) A bibliography of British municipal history; including gilds and parliamentary representation. 2nd ed. Leicester, 1966. pp. 461. Originally published as vol. 5 of Harvard Historical Studies by Longmans Green, New York, in 1897.

- United States

CAPEN (SAMUEL BILLINGS) Opening address delivered... February 21, 1894. Boston, 1894. pp. 19. (Municipal League of Boston, [Massachusetts]. Tracts. No. 1)

CAPEN (SAMUEL BILLINGS) Our incompleted work: address delivered...at the meeting October 30, 1895, etc. Boston, 1895. pp. 36. (Municipal League of Boston, [Massachusetts]. Tracts. No. 3)

MUNICIPAL LEAGUE OF BOSTON, [MASSACHUSETTS]. Constitution and by-laws. Boston, 1896. pp. 8.

NEW YORK (CITY). Citizens' Union. Home rule in cities: the separation of elections, etc. 2nd ed. New York, [1897?]. pp. 32.

PHILADELPHIA. Municipal League. The declaration of principles and by-laws of the...League and the by-laws approved by the League for Ward and Division Associations. [Philadelphia], 1897. pp. 19.

NATIONAL MUNICIPAL LEAGUE. Leaflets. No. 2. The National Municipal League: what it is doing, what others have to say about it. [Philadelphia], 1899. pp. 20.

NATIONAL MUNICIPAL LEAGUE. Leaflets. No. 4. What others are sayong of the National Municipal League. [Philadelphia], 1900. pp. 27.

BONAPARTE (CHARLES JOSEPH) The essential element in good city government. 3rd ed. [Philadelphia, 1901] pp. 16. (National Municipal League. Leaflets. No. 5)

NATIONAL MUNICIPAL LEAGUE. The work of the League, 1894-1905. [Philadelphia], 1905. pp. 20.

AMMON (ALF) Eliten und Entscheidungen in Stadtgemeinden: die amerikanische "Community Power"-Forschung und das Problem ihrer Rezeption in Deutschland. Berlin, Duncker und Humblot, [1967]. pp. 160. bibliog. 23½cm. (Berlin. Freie Universität. Wirtschafts- und Sozialwissenschaftliche Fakultät. Soziologische Abhandlungen. Heft 8)

MUNICIPAL GOVERNMENT - United States (Cont'd.)

HOWE (FREDERIC CLEMSON) The city: the hope of democracy; [reprinted from the 1905 edition, with an introduction]. Seattle, U. of Washington P., [1967]. pp. xxix, 319. 21½cm. (Americana Library)

ADRIAN (CHARLES RAYMOND) and PRESS (CHARLES) Governing urban America. 3rd ed. New York, [1968]. pp. 530. bibliogs.

ELEY (LYNN W.) and CASSTEVENS (THOMAS W.) eds. The politics of fair-housing legislation: state and local case studies. San Francisco, [1968]. pp. 415. bibliog.

FARMER (DAVID J.) Civil disorder control: a planning program of municipal coordination and cooperation. Chicago, [1968]. pp. 60.

HAWLEY (WILLIS D.) and WIRT (FREDERICK M.) eds. The search for community power: [readings]. Englewood Cliffs, [1968]. pp. 379. bibliog.

WILSON (JAMES Q.) ed. City politics and public policy. New York, Wiley, [1968]. pp. ix, 300. 22½cm.

BANFIELD (EDWARD CHRISTIE) Urban government: a reader in administration and politics. rev. ed. New York, Free P., [1969]. pp. xvii, 718. bibliog. 23 cm.

CRAWFORD (CLAN) Strategy and tactics in municipal zoning. Englewood Cliffs, [1969]. pp. 205.

LOCKARD (DUANE) The politics of state and local government. 2nd ed. New York, [1969]. pp. 545. bibliog.

RABINOVITZ (FRANCINE F.) City politics and planning. New York, Atherton P., 1969. pp. xv, 192. 21¾cm.

WINTER (WILLIAM O.) The urban polity. New York, 1969. pp. 516.

EMERGING patterns in urban administration; edited by F. Gerald Brown [and] Thomas P. Murphy. Lexington, Mass., [1970]. pp. 288.

McCANDLESS (CARL A.) Urban government and politics. New York, [1970]. pp. 517. bibliogs.

MADGWICK (PETER JAMES) American city politics. London, 1970. pp. 117. bibliog.

WORKSHOP ON URBAN PROBLEMS, SANTA MONICA, 1967-68. Thinking about cities: new perspectives on urban problems; [papers from the Workshop ...organised by the Rand Corporation]; Anthony H. Pascal, editor. Belmont, Calif., [1970]. pp. 185.

EYESTONE (ROBERT) The threads of public policy: a study in policy leadership. Indianapolis, [1971]. pp. 197. bibliog.

FARKAS (SUZANNE) Urban lobbying: mayors in the federal arena. New York, 1971. pp. 335. bibliog.

- United States - Bibliography

GOVERNMENT AFFAIRS FOUNDATION. Metropolitan communities: a bibliography with special emphasis upon government and politics; [with] supplement, 1965-1967. Chicago, [1957-69]. 2 vols.

- United States - California

CALIFORNIA. 1959. Metropolitan government in California: a background study with recommendations; report to the Assembly Interim Committee on Conservation, Planning and Public Works by Pacific Planning and Research. (Assembly Interim Committee Reports, 1957-1959. vol.13, No.23) [Sacramento], 1959. pp. 51. bibliog. 23cm.

JAMIESON (JAMES B.) Park-bond voting in municipal elections. Los Angeles, 1965. fo. 31. (California University. Institute of Government and Public Affairs. [Publications]. MR-36)

- United States - New York

NEW YORK (CITY). City Vigilance League. Found: a municipal program; the greater and better New York; [program of a series of conferences of those interested in good municipal government...1894; with, Wanted: a municipal program; first series of 1894]. [New York, 1894]. pp. 31.

NEW YORK (CITY). City Club. Certain criticisms of the details of the proposed Greater New York charter, prepared for the use of the City Club's Committee on Greater New York Charter. New York, 1897. pp. 30.

NEW YORK (CITY). City Club. [Greater New York draft charter: suggestions made by the...Club] New York 1897. pp. 18.

WOMAN'S MUNICIPAL LEAGUE OF THE CITY OF NEW YORK By-laws of the...League, incorporated, April, 1904. [New York, 1904?] pp. 14.

- Venezuela

BREWER-CARIAS (ALLAN-RANDOLPH) El régimen de gobierno municipal en el distrito federal venezolano. Caracas, Gobernación del Distrito Federal, 1968. pp. xiii, 150. 19cm.

- Yugoslavia

PUSIC (EUGEN) and WALSH (ANN MARIE HAUCK) Urban government for Zagreb, Yugoslavia. New York, Praeger, 1968. pp. xiii, 150. 23½cm. (Praeger Special Studies in International Politics and Public Affairs)

MUNICIPAL INCORPORATION

- Germany

GAUPP (ERNST THEODOR) Über deutsche Städtegründung, Stadtverfassung und Weichbild im Mittelalter: besonders über die Verfassung von Freiburg im Breisgau, verglichen mit der Verfassung von Köln; Neudruck der Ausgabe Jena 1824. Aalen, Scientia, 1966. pp. xxiii, 406. 20½cm.

MUNICIPAL OWNERSHIP

- Germany

MUELHAUPT (LUDWIG) and OETTLE (KARL) eds. Gemeindewirtschaft und Unternehmerwirtschaft: Festgabe für Rudolf Johns zum 65. Geburtstag am 15. Juli 1965. Göttingen, Schwartz, 1965. pp. xi, 384. bibliog. 22½cm. (Frankfurt am Main. Forschungsgesellschaft für Staats- und Kommunalwirtschaft. Studien. Band 4)

- United Kingdom

SMART (WILLIAM) The limits of municipal enterprise. [Glasgow, 1899].
(Cutting from the Glasgow Herald, 5th June 1899)

LONDON. London Municipal Society. Municipal trading: report of a conference...on May 28th, 1902, to consider the question of municipal trading, etc. [London, 1902?] pp. 23.

LUBBOCK (JOHN) 1st Baron Avebury. Municipal trading; a speech delivered... at a dinner of the London Chamber of Commerce,...21st January, 1903. London, 1903. pp. 15.

INDUSTRIAL FREEDOM LEAGUE. Municipal trading: speeches delivered...at the annual meeting of the Industrial Freedom League, 30th June, 1905. London, 1905. pp. 36.

MORSE (SYDNEY) Municipal trading; an address delivered...before the Battersea Municipal Alliance, on 24th January, 1905. London, 1905. pp. 15.

HALL (FRED) L.C.C. tramways;...(lecture at Caxton Hall, Thursday, June 13th, 1912). London, 1912. pp. 16. (London. London Municipal Society. Municipal Reform Pamphlets. No. 51)

MUNICIPAL RESEARCH

COMPARATIVE urban research: the administration and politics of cities; [papers presented at a seminar held at the University of North Carolina, 1967]; edited by Robert T. Daland. Beverly Hills, Calif., [1969]. pp. 361. bibliog.

CENTRE FOR ENVIRONMENTAL STUDIES. Information Papers.22. Urban and regional research in the United Kingdom: a selective review; prepared...for the United Nations Economic Commission for Europe, Committee on Housing, Building and Planning, etc. London, 1970. pp. 62. bibliog.

- Directories

URBAN INSTITUTE. A directory of university urban research centers. Washington, D.C., [1969]. pp. 141.

- Canada - St. John

ST. JOHN, NEW BRUNSWICK. Town Planning Commission. Comprehensive community plan, St. John, New Brunswick: services; [survey by] Proctor, Redfern, Bousfield, and Bacon, [consulting engineers]. [Toronto], 1968-69. 2 vols.

MUNITION WORKERS

BRODRICK (WILLIAM ST. JOHN FREMANTLE) 1st Earl of Midleton. The Secretary of State for War's...reply to the Arsenal workers appeal for a living wage. [London, 1901?]. pp. 8.

MUNITIONS

PEETERS (EUGÈNE) Les forbans du patriotisme. Paris, Fédération Syndicale Internationale, 1937. pp. 331. bibliog. 25cm. (International Federation of Trade Unions. International Trade Union Library. 2nd Series. No. 3/4)

CALMANN (JOHN) European co-operation in defence technology: the political aspect. London, 1967. pp. iv, 23. (International Institute for Strategic Studies. Defence, Technology and the Western Alliance. No. 1)

HUNT (KENNETH) The requirements of military technology in the 1970s. London, 1967. pp. 36. (International Institute for Strategic Studies. Defence, Technology and the Western Alliance. No. 5)

JAMES (ROBERT RHODES) Standardization and common production of weapons in NATO. London, 1967. pp. 27. (International Institute for Strategic Studies. Defence, Technology and the Western Alliance. No. 3)

- Trade and manufacture

BULATSEL' (K.) Stop munitions! London, R.I.L.U., [1932]. pp. 24. 21cm.

WENISCH (GEORGES) and others. Organisation des programmes internationaux de production intégrée. 2. L'intégration administrative des pouvoirs publics. Liège, Institut de Sociologie, [1967]. pp. 127. 20½cm. (Sciences Sociales et Administration des Affaires. 10)

ENGELMANN (BERNT) The weapons merchants; translated from the German by Erica Detto. New York, Crown Publishers, [1968]. pp. 224. 20½cm.

FRANK (LEWIS A.) The arms trade in international relations. New York, Praeger, 1969. pp. xix, 266. bibliog. 23½cm. (Praeger Special Studies in International Politics and Public Affairs)

THAYER (GEORGE) The war business: the international trade in armaments. New York, [1969]. pp. 417. bibliog.

ALBRECHT (ULRICH) Der Handel mit Waffen. München 1971. pp. 216. bibliog.

- Trade and manufacture - Belgium

JAHN (GEORG MAX) Die Lüttischer Waffenindustrie. München, 1919. pp. 79. bibliog.

- Trade and manufacture - Canada

REFORD (ROBERT W.) Merchant of death? [Toronto] Canadian Institute of International Affairs, 1968. pp. 28. bibliog. 20cm. (Behind the Headlines. vol. 27, no. 4)

- Trade and manufacture - Germany

HAFTENDORN (HELGA) Militärhilfe und Rüstungsexporte der BRD. Düsseldorf, [1971]. pp. 144. bibliog.

- Trade and manufacture - Russia

KOVALENKO (DMITRII ALEKSANDROVICH) Oboronnaia promyshlennost' Sovetskoi Rossii v 1918-1920gg. Moskva, 1970. pp. 411.

MUNITIONS (Cont'd.)

- Trade and manufacture - Ukraine

"ARSENAL" imeni V. I. Lenina. Kyív, [1964]. pp. 319. bibliog. In Ukrainian.

- Trade and manufacture - United Kingdom

NATIONAL PEACE COUNCIL. The arms salesman. London, [1966?]. 1 pamphlet (unpaged).

CAMILLERI (JOSEPH) Britain and the death trade. London, [1971?]. pp. 16.

- Trade and manufacture - United States

BALDWIN (WILLIAM LEE) The structure of the defence market, 1955-1964. Durham, N.C., Duke U.P., 1967. pp. viii, 249. bibliog. 23½cm.

JAVITS (JACOB KOPPEL) and others. The defense sector and the American economy. New York, New York U.P., 1968. pp. xxi, 100. 20½cm. (New York (City). University. School of Commerce, Accounts and Finance. Charles C. Moskowitz Lectures. No. 8)

PIVETTI (MASSIMO) Armamenti ed economia: gli effetti della spesa militare e della produzione di armamenti nell'economia americana. Milano, 1969. pp. 142. bibliog.

- Canada

CANADA. Department of Defence Production. 1964. Canadian defence products. Ottawa, 1964. pp. 354.

- Germany

MANCHESTER (WILLIAM) The arms of Krupp, 1587-1968. London, Joseph, 1969. pp. 1053. bibliog. 21½cm.

- United States

SCHILLER (HERBERT I.) and PHILLIPS (JOSEPH D.) eds. Super-state: readings in the military-industrial complex. Urbana, Ill., [1970]. pp. 353. bibliog.

LENS (SIDNEY) The military-industrial complex. London, 1971. pp. 183.

MURAV'EV-APOSTOL (SERGEI IVANOVICH)

SLOBOZHAN (INNA IVANOVNA) S.I. Murav'ev-Apostol. Leningrad, 1967. pp. 42. bibliog.

MURDER

A TRUE and sad reration [sic] of the great and bloudy murder committed at Ratcliff in Stepney parish neer the city of London, etc. [London], B.A., 1647. pp. (6). 18½cm. Wing T 2581.

- Russia

POBEGAILO (EDUARD FILIPPOVICH) Умышленные убийства и борьба с ними: уголовно-правовое и криминологические исследование. Воронеж, Университет, 1965. pp. 205. 21cm.

BORODIN (STANISLAV VLADIMIROVICH) Квалификация убийства по действующему законодательству. Москва, Юридическая Литература, 1966. pp. 252. 20cm.

- United Kingdom

GIBSON (EVELYN) and KLEIN (S.) Murder, 1957 to 1968: a Home Office Statistical Division report on murder in England and Wales; (with Annex by the Scottish Home and Health Department on murder in Scotland). London, 1969. pp. 94. (U.K. Home Office. Home Office Research Studies. 3)

DEELEY (PETER) and WALKER (CHRISTOPHER) Murder in the Fourth Estate: an investigation into the roles of press and police in the McKay case. London, 1971. pp. 192.

MURDER, POLITICAL
See ASSASSINATION

MURIDS
See MOURIDES

MURMANSK (OBLAST')

- Population

DOBROV (VADIM VASIL'EVICH) Naselenie Kol'skogo Severa. Murmansk, 1967. pp. 71. bibliog.

- Statistics

MURMANSK (OBLAST'). Statisticheskoe Upravlenie. Narodnoe khoziaistvo Murmanskoi oblasti za 50 let Sovetskoi vlasti. Murmansk, 1967. pp. 95.

MURPHY (CHARLES FRANCIS)

WEISS (NANCY JOAN) Charles Francis Murphy, 1858-1924: respectability and responsibility in Tammany politics. Northampton, Mass., Smith College, 1968. pp. x, 139. bibliog. 23½cm. (Edwin H. Land Prize Essays)

MURPHY (EDGAR GARDNER)

BAILEY (HUGH C.) Edgar Gardner Murphy, gentle progressive. Coral Gables, [1968]. pp. 274. bibliog.

MURPHY (FRANK)

HOWARD (J. WOODFORD) Mr. Justice Murphy: a political biography. Princeton, Princeton U.P., 1968. pp. xi, 578. 23½cm.

MURRAY (ALFALFA BILL)
See MURRAY (WILLIAM HENRY DAVID)

MURRAY (JOHN HUBERT PLUNKETT)

WEST (FRANCIS JAMES) Hubert Murray: the Australian pro-consul. Melbourne, O.U.P., 1968. pp. vii, 296. bibliog. 21½cm.

MURRAY (TERENCE AUBREY)

WILSON (GWENDOLINE) Murray of Yarralumba. Melbourne, O.U.P., 1968. pp. xvii, 334. bibliog. 21½cm.

MURRAY (WILLIAM HENRY DAVID)

BRYANT (KEITH LYNN) Alfalfa Bill Murray. Norman, U. of Oklahoma P., [1968]. pp. xiii, 287. 22½cm.

MURRI (ROMOLO)

GUASCO (MAURILIO) Romolo Murri e il modernismo. Roma, 1968. pp. 404. bibliog.

ZOPPI (SERGIO) Romolo Murri e la prima democrazia cristiana. Firenze, Vallecchi, [1968]. pp. xiv, 229. bibliog. 21cm. (Problemi del Nostro Tempo)

BEDESCHI (LORENZO) Dal movimento di Murri all'appello di Sturzo, nel cinquantenario del Partito popolare italiano. Milano, [1969]. pp. 126.

MUSABEKOV (GAZANFAR MAKHMUDOVICH)

MUSABEKOV (GAZANFAR MAKHMUDOVICH) Избранные статьи и речи. Баку, 1960. 2 vols.

MUSCAT AND OMAN

- History

LANDEN (ROBERT GERAN) Oman since 1856: disruptive modernization in a traditional Arab society. Princeton, 1967. pp. xv, 488. bibliog.

- Politics and government

EDWARDS (ROBERT) The legal and historical aspects of the Oman question. London, [1963?]. pp. 14.

COMMITTEE FOR THE RIGHTS OF OMAN and MOVEMENT FOR COLONIAL FREEDOM. The Oman question and the United Nations. London, [1965?]. pp. 22.

MUSEUMS

- Directories

MUSEUMS ASSOCIATION. Museums calendar, 1970: including a directory of museums and art galleries of the British Isles together with a select list of institutions overseas. London, 1970. pp. 183.

- Pakistan

PAKISTAN. Central Bureau of Education. 1967. Second five-year plan development projects and their evaluation. [Karachi], 1967. pp. 56

- United Kingdom

WATSON (JOHN FORBES) The imperial museum for India and the colonies;... with a plan showing the proposed site on the Thames embankment. London, 1876. pp. 62.

U.K. Standing Commission on Museums and Galleries. 1968. Universities and museums: report on the universities in relation to their own and other museums; [The Earl of Rosse, chairman]. London, 1968. pp. vi, 48. 24½cm.

ADAMSON (DONALD) Dusty heritage: a national policy for museums and libraries. London, [1971]. pp. 41.

MUSEUMS IN EDUCATION

ZETTERBERG (HANS LENNART) Museums and adult education. London, 1968. pp. 89. bibliog.

MUSGRAVE (JOHN) Captain

MUSGRAVE (JOHN) Captain. A declaration...vindicating him against the misprisians [sic] and imputed reasons of his sad imprisonment for high treason against the state; with an order, or proclamation by the Committee of the City of London, with the Committee of Lords and Commons for safety, etc. London, Musgrave, 1647. pp. 6. 18½cm. Wing M 3147.

MUSIC

BAINTON (EDGAR L.) Music and socialism:... a lecture delivered to the Newcastle Socialist Society; with a preface by W.G. Whittaker. Manchester, [190-]. pp. 17.

- Bibliography

SMITH (WILLIAM CHARLES) and HUMPHRIES (CHARLES) A bibliography of the musical works published by the firm of John Walsh during the years 1721-1766. London, Bibliographical Society, 1968. pp. xx, 351. 21cm. (Publications. 1966)

- Germany

FELDMANN (F.) Der Hamburger Johann Mattheson, 1681-1764 und die Musik Mittel- und Ostdeutschlands. in Hamburg. Arbeits- und Sozialbehörde. Hamburger Mittel- und Ostdeutsche Forschungen. Band 5. Hamburg, [1966].

FELDMANN (F.) Der Anteil des deutschen Ostens an der Musikentwicklung in Deutschland. in Schulz (Eberhard G.) ed. Leistung und Schicksal. Köln, 1967.

SPEER (G.) Ostdeutsches Musikleben in Nordrhein-Westfalen. in Schulz (Eberhard G.) ed. Leistung und Schicksal. Köln, 1967.

- Russia

MUZYKA v sotsialisticheskom obshchestve: sbornik statei. Leningrad, 1969. pp. 220

- Russia - Instruction and study

UNITED STATES. Education Office. Fine arts education in the Soviet Union. Washington, 1963. pp. v, 74.

- United Kingdom

ARTS COUNCIL OF GREAT BRITAIN. A report on orchestral resources in Great Britain, 1970; [by a committee of enquiry, with Alan Peacock chairman]. London, [1970]. pp. 125.

MUSIC, POPULAR (SONGS, ETC.)

HIRSCH (PAUL) Sociologist. The structure of the popular music industry: the filtering process by which records are preselected for public consumption. Ann Arbor, Mich., [1967?]. pp. 72.

MUSIC AND SOCIETY

SILBERMANN (A.) Réflexions sur les conflits de groupes dans les milieux musicaux. in Atteslander (Peter M.) and Girod (Roger) eds. Soziologische Arbeiten. Bern, 1966.

MUSIC AND SOCIETY (Cont'd.)

HIRSCH (PAUL) Sociologist. The structure of the popular music industry: the filtering process by which records are preselected for public consumption. Ann Arbor, Mich., [1967?]. pp. 72.

ADORNO (THEODOR WIESENGRUND). Einleitung in die Musiksoziologie: zwölf theoretische Vorlesungen. [Reinbek bei Hamburg], 1968. pp. 252. bibliog.

LANG (P.H.) The composer. in Clifford (James Lowry) ed. Man versus society in eighteenth-century Britain. Cambridge, 1968.

SILBERMANN (ALPHONS) Les principes de la sociologie de la musique. Genève, Droz, 1968. pp. 191. 23cm. (Travaux de Droit, d'Économie, de Sociologie et de Sciences Politiques, No. 70)

MUSIC AND STATE

- Russia

BERGER (KARLHANNS) Die Funktionsbestimmung der Musik in der Sowjetideologie. Wiesbaden, Harrassowitz, 1963. pp. 128. bibliog. 25cm. (Berlin. Freie Universität. Osteuropa-Institut. Philosophische und Soziologische Veröffentlichungen. Band 4)

MUSIC AS A PROFESSION

CLERCQ (JACQUELINE DE) La profession de musicien: une enquête. Bruxelles, 1970. pp. 165. bibliog. (Brussels. Université Libre. Institut de Sociologie. Etudes de Sociologie de la Musique)

MUSIC TRADE

- Germany

HENLE (GUENTER) Weggenosse des Jahrhunderts: als Diplomat, Industrieller, Politiker und Freund der Musik. Stuttgart, Deutsche Verlags-Anstalt, 1968. pp. 367. 22½cm.

PASTICCIO auf das 250 jährige Bestehen des Verlages Breitkopf & Härtel: Beiträge zur Geschichte des Hauses. [Leipzig, 1968]. pp. 186.

- United Kingdom

U.K. Department of Trade and Industry. Business monitor: Production series. P 88. Musical instruments. q., 1970- . London.

MUSSOLINI (BENITO)

MONELLI (PAOLO) Mussolini piccolo borghese. 6th ed. Milano, Garzanti, 1965 repr. 1966. pp. 393. bibliog. 19cm. (Collezione I Rossi e i Blu)

ALESSI (RINO) Il giovane Mussolini rievocato da un suo compagno di scuola. Milano, [1969]. pp. 238.

SUSMEL (DUILIO) Nenni e Mussolini: mezzo secolo di fronte. Milano, 1969. pp. 356. bibliog.

VETTORI (VITTORIO) Mussolini antifascista. Roma, 1969. pp. 161.

WHITTLE (PETER) Journalist. One afternoon at Mezzegra. London, Allen, 1969. pp. 195. 21½cm.

CASSELS (ALAN) Mussolini's early diplomacy. Princeton, 1970. pp. 425. bibliog.

MUSTARD

INDIA. Ministry of Food and Agriculture. Directorate of Marketing and Inspection. Marketing Series. No.161. Report on the marketing of rapeseed and mustard in India. 2nd ed. Nagpur, [1967]. pp. viii, 234. 21cm.

MUTAGUCHI (RENYA)

SWINSON (ARTHUR) Four samurai: a quartet of Japanese army commanders in the Second World War. London, Hutchinson, 1968. pp. 266. bibliog. 22½cm.

MUTEZO (OBED)

SITHOLE (NDABANINGI) Obed Mutezo: the Mudzimu Christian nationalist. Nairobi, 1970. pp. 210.

MUTINY

- France

PEDRONCINI (GUY) Les mutineries de 1917. Paris, P.U.F., 1967. pp. 328. bibliog. 24cm. (Paris. Université. Faculté des Lettres et Sciences Humaines. Publications. Série "Recherches." tome 35)

PEDRONCINI (GUY) compiler. 1917: les mutineries de l'armée française. [Paris], Julliard, [1968]. pp. 289, 20cm. (Collection Archives. No. 35)

- Germany

STUMPF (RICHARD) War, mutiny and revolution in the German navy: the World War I diary of seaman Richard Stumpf; edited, translated...by Daniel Horn. New Brunswick, Rutgers U.P., [1967]. pp. iv, 442. 21cm.

MYRDAL (GUNNAR)

SINGER (HANS WOLFGANG) Keynesian models of economic development and their limitations: an analysis in the light of Gunnar Myrdal's "Asian Drama". Brighton, 1970. pp. 13. (Brighton. University of Sussex. Institute of Development Studies. Communications. No. 54)

MYSORE

- Boundaries

INDIA. Commission on Maharashtra — Mysore — Kerala Boundary Disputes. 1967. Report: [Mehr Chand Mahajan, sole commissioner]. Delhi, 1967. 2 vols.

ANTULAY (A. RAHMAN) Mahajan report uncovered. Bombay, Allied Publishers, 1968. pp. (iv), 192. 21½cm.

- Economic conditions

JORAPUR (P.B.) Economic overview of Dharwar block. Dharwar, [1964]. pp. various.

MYSORE. Department of Statistics. 1968. Mysore state in maps, 1966. Bangalore, 1968. fo.(iv),pp. 67. 35cm.

- Economic policy

> MYSORE. Planning, Housing and Social Welfare Department. 1961. Third five year plan. Vol. 1. Policy and programme. [Bangalore, 1961]. pp. 435.
>
> JORAPUR (P.B.) Economic overview of Dharwar block. Dharwar, [1964]. pp. various.

- Emigration and immigration

> KATTI (A. P.) Seasonal in-migrants in rural Shimoga, Mysore State. Dharwar, [1966]. pp. 101.

- Industries

> NATIONAL COUNCIL OF APPLIED ECONOMIC RESEARCH. Industrial programmes for the fourth plan: Mysore. New Delhi, [1969]. pp. 166.

- Maps

> MYSORE. Department of Statistics. 1968. Mysore state in maps, 1966. Bangalore, 1968. fo.(iv),pp. 67. 35cm.

- Population

> KATTI (A. P.) Seasonal in-migrants in rural Shimoga, Mysore State. Dharwar, [1966]. pp. 101.
>
> JORAPUR (P. B.) Demographic survey of Dharwar: a survey conducted in Dharwar town and 20 villages of Dharwar Taluka. Dharwar, 1968. pp. 145.
>
> KALE (B.D.) Population growth in Mysore State: regional variations. Dharwar, [1968?]. pp. 20.
>
> SEMINAR ON DEMOGRAPHIC ASPECTS OF MYSORE STATE, DHARWAR, 1967. Papers and proceedings, (19th, 20th March, 1967); edited by A. P. Katti. Dharwar, [1968]. pp. 155.

- Social policy

> MYSORE. Planning, Housing and Social Welfare Department. 1961. Third five year plan. Vol. 1. Policy and programme. [Bangalore, 1961]. pp. 435.

MYSTICISM

ZAEHNER (ROBERT CHARLES) Concordant discord: the interdependence of faiths. Oxford, 1970. pp. 464. (Gifford Lectures. 1967-1969)

MYTHOLOGY

CAMPBELL (J.) Bios and mythos: prolegomena to a science of mythology. in Wilbur (George B.) and Muensterberger (Warner) eds. Psychoanalysis and culture:...[reprint of the work first published in 1951]. New York, 1967.

ZOLOTAREV (ALEKSANDR MIKHAILOVICH) Родовой строй и первобытная мифология. Москва, Наука, 1964. pp. 328. bibliog. 21½см.

DOURNES (JACQUES) L'homme et son mythe. Paris, Aubier-Montaigne, [1968]. pp. 219. 20cm. (Collection Recherches Economiques et Sociales)

GEORGES (ROBERT A.) ed. Studies on mythology. Homewood, Dorsey P., 1968. pp. vii, 248. bibliog. 23cm. (Dorsey Series in Anthropology and Sociology)

LEACH (EDMUND RONALD) Genesis as myth, and other essays. London, 1969. pp. 124. bibliog.

MYTHS and symbols: studies in honor of Mircea Eliade; edited by Joseph M. Kitagawa [and others]. Chicago, 1969. pp. 438. bibliog.

LÉVI-STRAUSS (CLAUDE) The raw and the cooked: introduction to a science of mythology;... translated from the French by John and Doreen Weightman. London, 1970 in progress. bibliog.

KIRK (GEOFFREY STEPHEN) Myth: its meaning and functions in ancient and other cultures. Cambridge, 1970. pp. 299. (California University. Sather Classical Lectures. vol. 40)

SCHMIDBAUER (WOLFGANG) Mythos und Psychologie: methodische Probleme, aufgezeigt an der Ödipus-Sage. München, 1970. pp. 180. bibliog.

MYTHOLOGY, AFRICAN

GORDON (ROSEMARY) African mythology: the origin of death. [London], Guild of Pastoral Psychology, 1965. pp. 28. bibliog. 18½cm. (Guild Lectures. No. 129)

ZAHAN (DOMINIQUE) La viande et la graine: mythologie dogon. Paris, Présence Africaine, [1969]. pp. 179. 21½cm.

MYTHOLOGY, GREEK

GERNET (LOUIS) Anthropologie de la Grèce antique. Paris, Maspero, 1968. pp. 459. bibliog. 21cm. (Textes à l'Appui)

MYTHOLOGY, INDO-EUROPEAN

MYTH and law among the Indo-Europeans: studies in Indo-European comparative mythology; edited by Jaan Puhvel; [a symposium of the Center for the Study of Comparative Folklore and Mythology]. Berkeley, 1970. pp. 276. bibliog. (California University. Center for the Study of Comparative Folklore and Mythology. Publications. 1)

MYTHOLOGY, JEWISH

SNOWDEN (KEIGHLEY) Myth and legend in the Bible. London, 1915. pp. 200.

MYTHOLOGY, OCEANIC

POIGNANT (ROSLYN) Oceanic mythology: the myths of Polynesia, Micronesia, Melanesia, Australia. London, Hamlyn, [1967]. pp. 141. bibliog. 27½cm.

MYTHOLOGY, SLAVIC

RADOJIČIĆ (Đ. SP.) Der alte südslawische Text von den drei Kaiserreichen auf Erden. in Steinitz (Wolfgang) and others, eds. Ost und West in der Geschichte des Denkens und der kulturellen Beziehungen. Berlin, 1966.

MZABITES

FARRAG (AMINA A.M.) Mechanisms of social control amongst the Mzabite women of Beni-Isguen; [M.A. (London) thesis]. 1969. fo. 145. 25½cm. Typescript: unpublished. This thesis is the property of London University and may not be removed from the Library.

N. D. P. D.
See NATIONAL-DEMOKRATISCHE PARTEI DEUTSCHLANDS (D. D. R.)

N. P. D.
See NATIONALDEMOKRATISCHE PARTEI DEUTSCHLANDS (BUNDESREPUBLIK)

NABEUL

- Economic conditions

COQUE (ROGER) Nabeul et ses environs: étude d'une population tunisienne. [Paris], Presses Universitaires de France, [1964?]. pp. 169. bibliog. 27cm. (Tunis (City). Université. Centre d'Études de Sciences Humaines. Mémoires. vol. 9)

- Population

COQUE (ROGER) Nabeul et ses environs: étude d'une population tunisienne. [Paris], Presses Universitaires de France, [1964?]. pp. 169. bibliog. 27cm. (Tunis (City). Université. Centre d'Études de Sciences Humaines. Mémoires. vol. 9)

- Social conditions

COQUE (ROGER) Nabeul et ses environs: étude d'une population tunisienne. [Paris], Presses Universitaires de France, [1964?]. pp. 169. bibliog. 27cm. (Tunis (City). Université. Centre d'Études de Sciences Humaines. Mémoires. vol. 9)

NABUCO (JOAQUIM)

COSTA (JOÃO FRANK DA) Joaquim Nabuco e a política exterior do Brasil. Rio de Janeiro, Gráfica Récord, 1968. pp. 324. bibliog. 20½cm. (Coleção Diplomacia e Política. 3)

NACOZARI

HORTON (INEZ) Copper's children: (the rise and fall of a Mexican copper mining camp). New York, Exposition P., 1968. pp. 202. 20½cm.

NADARS

HARDGRAVE (ROBERT L.) The Nadars of Tamilnad: the political culture of a community in change. Berkeley, 1969. pp. 314. bibliog.

NAGALAND

ANAND (V.K.) Nagaland in transition. New Delhi, Associated Publishing House, 1967. pp. (iv), 144. 21½cm.

- Economic conditions

NATIONAL COUNCIL OF APPLIED ECONOMIC RESEARCH. Techno-economic survey of Nagaland. New Delhi, [1968]. pp. x, 136. 24cm.

NAGAS

ELWIN (VERRIER) ed. The Nagas in the nineteenth century: [an anthology]. London, 1969. pp. 650. bibliog.

FUERER-HAIMENDORF (CHRISTOPH VON) Freiherr. The Konyak Nagas: an Indian frontier tribe. New York, [1969]. pp. 111. bibliog.

HARTWIG (WERNER) Wirtschaft und Gesellschaftsstruktur der Naga in der zweiten Hälfte des 19. und zu Beginn des 20. Jahrhunderts. Berlin, 1970. pp. 274. bibliog. (Leipzig. Museum für Völkerkunde. Veröffentlichungen. Heft 20)

NAGASAKI

- History

CHINNOCK (FRANK W.) Nagasaki: the forgotten bomb. London, 1970. pp. 304. bibliog.

NAGORNYI KARABAKH

- Statistics

NAGORNYI KARABAKH. Statisticheskoe Upravlenie. Достижения осветского Нагорного Карабаха за 40 лет в цифрах: статистический сборник. Степанакерт, 1963. pp. 171. 21½cm.

NAGORNYI KARABAKH (AUTONOMOUS OBLAST')

- Statistics

NAGORNYI KARABAKH (AUTONOMOUS OBLAST'). Statisticheskoe Upravlenie. Nagornyi Karabakh za gody Sovetskoi vlasti: kratkii statisticheskii sbornik. Stepanakert, 1969. pp. 221.

NAGOYA

- Civic improvement

NAGOYA. City Council. Nagoya city: the dynamic metropolis of central Japan. [Nagoya, 1965]. pp. 68.

NAGOYA. Department of City Planning. The outline of city planning for Nagoya, 1966. [Nagoya, 1966]. pp. 52.

- Economic conditions

NAGOYA. City Council. Nagoya city: the dynamic metropolis of central Japan. [Nagoya, 1965]. pp. 68.

- Politics and government

NAGOYA. City Council. Nagoya city: the dynamic metropolis of central Japan. [Nagoya, 1965]. pp. 68.

NAILS AND SPIKES

CANADA. Tariff Board. 1961. Report...relative to the inquiry ordered by the Minister of Finance respecting nails of iron or steel. Ottawa, 1961. pp. 54.

NAIROBI

- Politics and government

KENYA. Commission of Inquiry into alleged Corruption or other Malpractices in relation to the Affairs of the Nairobi City Council, December, 1955-March, 1956. 1956. Report: [Sir Alan Rose, chairman]. Nairobi, 1956. pp. 60.

NALBANDIAN (MIKAEL LAZAR'EVICH)

DARONIAN (SERGEI KARPOVICH) Mikael Nalbandian i russkie revoliutsionnye demokraty. Moskva, 1967. pp. 255.

NAL'CHIK

KABANOV (ANDREI STEPANOVICH) Нальчик за десять лет, 1958-1963. Нальчик, Кабардино-Балкарское, 1964. pp. [80]. 21½см. With instructions.

NAMES

BAUDRILLARD (JEAN) Le système des objets. [Paris], Gallimard, [1968]. pp. 288. 18½cm. (Les Essais. 137)

- Dictionaries

LATHAM (EDWARD) A dictionary of names, nicknames and surnames of persons, places and things; [reprint of the work originally published in 1904]. Detroit, Gale, 1966. pp. vii, 334. 21½cm.

NAMES, GEOGRAPHICAL

- Dictionaries

WEBSTER'S geographical dictionary: a dictionary of names of places with geographical and historical information and pronunciations. rev. ed. Springfield Merriam, [1966]. pp. xxxi, 1293. 24½cm.

- Antarctic regions

UNITED STATES. Board on Geographic Names. Gazetteers. No. 14. Antarctica. 2nd ed. Washington, 1966. pp. v, 169.

- Burma

UNITED STATES. Board on Geographic Names. Gazetteers. No. 96. Burma. Washington, 1966. pp. v, 725.

- Burundi

UNITED STATES. Board on Geographic Names. Gazetteers. No. 84. Burundi. Washington, 1964. pp. ii, 44.

- Canada

CANADA. 1964. A list of named glaciological features in Canada; compiled by C.F. Stevenson. (Gazetteer of Canada. Special Supplements. No. 1) Ottawa, 1964. pp. 14.

- Canada - Bibliography

CANADA. Geographical Branch. Bibliographical Series. No. 30. Selected bibliography on Canadian toponymy. Ottawa, 1964. pp. 27.

- Dahomey

UNITED STATES. Board on Geographic Names. No. 91. Dahomey. Washington, 1965. pp. iv, 89.

- France

UNITED STATES. Board on Geographic Names. Gazetteers. No. 83. France. Washington, 1964. 2 vols.

- Germany - Schleswig - Holstein

SCHLESWIG-HOLSTEIN. Statistisches Landesamt. 1958. Wohnplatzverzeichnis Schleswig-Holstein: amtliches Verzeichnis der Ämter, Gemeinden und Wohnplätze; Gebietsstand; 30. September 1958, Bevölkerungsstand; 25. September 1956 und 31. Dezember 1957. Kiel, 1958. pp. 211. 29½cm.

- Guinea (Republic)

UNITED STATES. Board on Geographic Names. Gazetteers. No. 90. Guinea. Washington, 1965. pp. iv, 175.

- Ivory Coast

UNITED STATES. Board on Geographic Names. Gazetteers. No. 89. Ivory Coast. Washington, 1965. pp. iv, 250.

- Korea

UNITED STATES. Board on Geographic Names. Gazetteers. No. 95. South Korea. Washington, 1965. pp. iv, 370.

- Mali (Republic)

UNITED STATES. Board on Geographic Names. Gazetteers. No. 93. Mali. Washington, 1965. pp. v, 263.

- Niger

UNITED STATES. Board on Geographic Names. Gazetteers. No. 99. Niger. Washington, 1966. pp. iv, 207.

- Poland - Silesia

FIEDOR (KAROL) ed. Walka z nazewnictwem polskim na Śląku w okresie hitlerowskim, 1933-1939; Lutte contre la nomenclature polonaise en Silésie a l'époque de Hitler, 1933-1939. Wrocław, Zakład Narodowy im. Ossolińskich, 1966. pp. 158. bibliog. 20½cm.

- Ruanda

UNITED STATES. Board on Geographic Names. Gazetteers. No. 85. Rwanda. Washington, 1964. pp. iii, 44.

- Senegal

UNITED STATES. Board on Geographic Names. Gazetteers. No. 88. Senegal. Washington, 1965. pp. iv, 194.

- Siam

UNITED STATES. Board on Geographic Names. Gazetteers. No. 97. Thailand. Washington, 1966. pp. vi, 675.

- Sierra Leone

UNITED STATES. Board on Geographic Names. Gazetteers. No. 101. Sierra Leone. Washington, 1966. pp. ii, 125.

- Spain

MENENDEZ PIDAL (RAMON) Toponimia prerromanica hispana. Madrid, 1968. pp. 313.

- Tanzania

UNITED STATES. Board on Geographic Names. Gazetteers. No. 92. Tanzania. Washington, 1965. pp. vi, 236.

NAMES, GEOGRAPHICAL (Cont'd.)

- Togo

UNITED STATES. Board on Geographic Names. Gazetteers. No. 98. Togo. Washington, 1966. pp. iii, 100.

- United States

LYRA (E.) and LYRA (F.) Polish place-names in the U.S.A. in Polska Akademia Nauk. Instytut Geografii. Geografia Polonica. 11. Warszawa, 1967.

- Venezuela

VILA (MARCO AURELIO) Nomenclator geo-historico de Venezuela, 1498-1810. Caracas, Banco Central de Venezuela, 1964. pp. xxix, 502. bibliog. 23cm. (Colección Histórico-Económico Venezolana. vol. 10)

- Vietnam

UNITED STATES. Board on Geographic Names. Gazetteers. No. 79. Northern Vietnam. Washington, 1964. pp. v, 311.

- Zanzibar

PIGGOTT (P.H.) compiler. The gazetteer of Zanzibar Island. Zanzibar, 1962. pp. (11), 17.

UNITED STATES. Board on Geographic Names. Gazetteers. No. 76. Zanzibar. Washington, 1964. pp. iii, 36.

- France

LEBEL (PAUL) Les noms de personnes en France. 6th ed. Paris, P.U.F., 1968. pp. 128. 17½cm. (Que Sais-Je? No. 235)

NAMES, PERSONAL

- Greece

BIALOR (P.A.) What's in a name?: aspects of the social organization of a Greek farming community related to naming customs. in Lockwood (William G.) ed. Essays in Balkan ethnology. Berkeley, 1967.

- Hungary

PACLIȘANU (ZENOVIE) Was heisst ungarische Nationalität? Wie man Ungar werden konnte. Bukarest, 1941; München, 1968. pp. 13. Facsimile reprint.

- Russia - Dictionaries

SLOVAR'... Словарь собственных имен людей: украинско-русский и русско-украинский; Словник власних імен людей. 3rd ed. Київ, Наукова Думка, 1967. pp. 111. 17cm.

- Spain

ÁLVAREZ (GRACE DE JESÚS C.) Topónimos en apellidos hispanos. Garden City, Adelphi University, 1968. pp. 587. bibliog. 24cm. (Estudios de Hispanófila. 7)

MUGICA (JOSÉ A.) Apellidos vascos de Iberia: su origen y evolución. 3rd ed. Bilbao, Edili, [1968]. pp. 195. 21cm.

- Ukraine - Dictionaries

SLOVAR'... Словарь собственных имен людей: украинско-русский и русско-украинский; Словник власних імен людей. 3rd ed. Київ, Наукова Думка, 1967. pp. 111. 17cm.

- United Kingdom

U.K. 1957. Social Survey. Initial letters of surnames; [by] P. G. Gray. ([Papers. Methodological Series]. No.M.79) [London], 1957. single sheet. 33cm.

McKINLEY (R.A.) Norfolk surnames in the sixteenth century. Leicester, 1969. pp. 60. (Leicester. University. Department of English Local History. Occasional Papers. 2nd Series. No. 2)

NAMES, PERSONAL (CATALOGUING)

CHAPLIN (ARTHUR HUGH) and ANDERSON (DOROTHY) eds. Names of persons: national usages for entry in catalogues. Sevenoaks, IFLA, 1967. pp. ix, 57. 21cm. (International Manuals. No. 2)

NAMIER (Sir LEWIS BERNSTEIN)

NAMIER (JULIA) Lady. Lewis Namier: a biography. London, 1971. pp. 347. bibliog.

NANDIS

HOLLIS (Sir ALFRED CLAUD) The Nandi: their language and folk-lore;...edited with a new introduction by G.W.B. Huntingford. Oxford, 1909 repr. 1969. pp. 328. 21½cm.

NANTES

- Economic conditions

FRANCE. Direction de la Documentation. La Documentation Française. Notes et Études Documentaires. No. 3,362. Les grandes villes françaises: Nantes - Saint-Nazaire; par Claude Cabanne. Paris, 1967. pp. 45.

- History

LALLIÉ (A.) Les sociétés populaires à Nantes pendant la révolution. 2nd ed. Nantes, 1914. pp. 239.

NAOROJI (DADABHAI)

MASANI (Sir RUSTOM PESTONJI) Dadabhai Naoroji. Delhi, 1960. pp. 195. (Builders of Modern India)

NAPALM

TAKMAN (JOHN) ed. Napalm: Streitschrift und Dokumentation; (aus dem Schwedischen übersetzt, etc.) Berlin, [1968]. pp. 258.

NAPLES

- Commerce

GIURA (VINCENZO) Russia, Stati Uniti d'America e regno di Napoli nell'età del Risorgimento. Napoli, Edizioni Scientifiche Italiane, 1967. pp. xv, 362. bibliog. 25cm. (Naples. Istituto Universitario Navale. Facoltà di Economia Marittima. Istituto di Storia del Commercio. Fonti e Ricerche. 2)

- Economic conditions

ITALY. Ufficio Provinciale del Lavoro. Divisione Economico-Statistica. 1944. Studio comparativo tra il costo della vita e le retribuzioni di lavoro a Roma e a Napoli; [by] G. Galeotti [and] G. Togni. Roma, 1944. fo. 88, (3). 28cm.

RAO (ANTONIO) L'area d'influenza di Napoli. [Naples], Edizioni Scientifiche Italiane, [1967]. pp. 174. 24cm. (Geographica. 3) (Reprinted from Nord e Sud, 1965-66)

- Foreign relations - Morocco

IANNETTONE (GIOVANNI) Il Marocco negli atti consolari del Regno delle Due Sicilie, dal trattato del 1782 a quello del 1834. Napoli, [1967]. pp. 238.

- History

CESARE (RAFFAELE DE) La fine di un regno;...edizione definitiva con aggiunte, nuovi documenti e indice dei nomi [originally published 1908-09]. Milano, [1970]. pp. 1207.

CASSESE (LEOPOLDO) La spedizione di Sapri. Bari, 1969. pp. 248.

MASTELLONE (SALVO) Francesco D'Andrea, politico e giurista, 1648-1698: l'ascesa del ceto civile. Firenze, 1969. pp. 207.

MORELLI (ANTONIO) Michele Morelli e la rivoluzione napoletana del 1820-1821. 2nd ed. [Bologna], 1969. pp. 365. bibliog.

CINGARI (GAETANO) Mezzogiorno e Risorgimento: la Restaurazione a Napoli dal 1821 al 1830. Bari, 1970. pp. 263.

MARINI (LINO) Il Mezzogiorno d'Italia di fronte a Vienna e a Roma, e altri studi di storia meridionale. Bologna, [1970]. pp. 318.

- History - Sources

TANUCCI (BERNARDO) Lettere...a Carlo III di Borbone, 1759-1776; regesti a cura di Rosa Mincuzzi. Roma, 1969. pp. 1095. (Istituto per la Storia del Risorgimento Italiano. Pubblicazioni. 2a Serie: Fonti. vol. 59)

- Politics and government

ANTONELLIS (GIACOMO DE) La fine del fascismo a Napoli. Milano, Ares, 1967. pp. 223. bibliog. 18cm.

MACCIOCCHI (MARIA ANTONIETTA) Lettere dall'interno del P.C.I. a Louis Althusser: (il partito e: masse e. le forze rivoluzionarie nella densa corrispondenza fra una militante comunista e il filosofo francese). Milano, 1969. pp. 388.

NAPOLÉON I, Emperor of the French

DESCOTES (MAURICE) La légende de Napoléon et les écrivains français du XIXe siècle. Paris, 1967. pp. 277. bibliog.

HOLTMAN (ROBERT B.) The Napoleonic revolution. Philadelphia, Lippincott, [1967]. pp. 225. bibliog. 20cm. (Critical Periods of History)

LEFEBVRE (GEORGES) Napoleon;...translated from the French by Henry F. Stockhold [and] J.E. Anderson). London, Routledge & Kegan Paul, 1969. 2 vols. bibliogs. 21½cm.

RANKE-GESELLSCHAFT and MILITAERGESCHICHTLICHES FORSCHUNGSAMT. Tagung, Otzenhausen, 1968. Napoleon I. und die Staatenwelt seiner Zeit; ...herausgegeben von Wolfgang v. Groote. Freiburg i. Br., [1969]. pp. 213. bibliogs.

VILLEFOSSE (LOUIS DE) and BOUISSOUNOUSE (JANINE) L'opposition à Napoléon. [Paris], [1969]. pp. 419. bibliog.

LEAN (EDWARD TANGYE) The Napoleonists: a study in political disaffection, 1760-1960. London, 1970. pp. 402.

- Egyptian campaign, 1798-1799

SPILLMANN (GEORGES) Napoléon et l'Islam. Paris, [1969]. pp. 414. bibliog.

- Invasion of Russia, 1812

IZ... Из истории национально-освободительной борьбы в дореволюционной России. Волгоград, 1968. pp. 216. 20см.

- Campaigns of 1813-1814

IZ... Из истории национально-освободительной борьбы в дореволюционной России. Волгоград, 1968. pp. 216. 20см.

- Elba and the Hundred Days, 1814-1815

BRETT-JAMES (ANTONY) ed. The hundred days: Napoleon's last campaign from eye-witness accounts. London, Macmillan, 1964. pp. xi, 242. bibliog.

SAUNDERS (EDITH) The hundred days. London, Longmans 1964. pp. x, 323. bibliog.

- Captivity, 1815-1821

THORNTON (MICHAEL JOHN) Napoleon after Waterloo: England and the St. Helena decision. Stanford, Stanford U.P., 1968. pp. xiv, 241. 21½cm.

GORREQUER (GIDEON) St. Helena during Napoleon's exile: Gorrequer's diary; with introduction, biographies, notes and explanations, and index of pseudonyms by James Kemble. London, Heinemann, 1969. pp. ix, 298. 24cm.

- Relations with women

CHEVALLEY (E.) La théorie des différents ordres de lois, d'après Montesquieu, et son application à l'histoire: le divorce de Napoléon. Le Caire, [190-?]. pp. 163. 25cm.

- in fiction, drama, poetry, etc.

FREUND (MICHAEL) Historian. Napoleon und die Deutschen: Despot oder Held der Freiheit? München, [1969]. pp. 216.

NAPOLÉON III, Emperor of the French

BECKER (BERNHARD) Political Writer. Briefe deutscher Bettelpatrioten an Louis Bonaparte: eine gründliche Bearbeitung der sämmtlichen, im Buche: L'Allemagne aux Tuileries, französischer seits veröffentlichten Dokumente. Braunschweig, 1873. pp. 482.

SIMPSON (FREDERICK ARTHUR) The rise of Louis Napoleon. 3rd ed. London, 1950 repr. 1968. pp. 400.

ZELDIN (T.) The myth of Napoleon III. in Black (Eugene Charlton) ed. European political history, 1815-1870. New York, 1967.

GEUSS (HERBERT) Bismarck und Napoleon III.: ein Beitrag zur Geschichte der preussisch-französischen Beziehungen 1851-1871. Köln, Böhlau, 1959. pp. vi, 324. bibliog. 23cm. (Kölner Historische Abhandlungen. Band 1)

ROTHNEY (JOHN) Bonapartism after Sedan. Ithaca, Cornell U.P., 1969. pp. xv, 360. bibliog. 22½cm.

TACKE (KLAUS) Die sozialpolitischen Vorstellungen Napoleons III. [Cologne, imprint, 1969?]. pp. 325. bibliog.

NARANJA

- Social history

FRIEDRICH (PAUL WILLIAM) Agrarian revolt in a Mexican village. Englewood Cliffs, [1970]. pp. 158. bibliog.

NARAYAN (JAYAPRAKASH)

NARAYAN (JAYAPRAKASH) The evolution towards Sarvodaya: being a long letter...written to a friend in the Praja-Socialist Party in November 1957 explaining the reasons that led to his decision to withdraw from politics. Tanjore, 1957. pp. 53.

NARAYAN (SHRIMAN)

NARAYAN (SHRIMAN) India and Nepal: an exercise in open diplomacy. Bombay, 1970. pp. 172. bibliog.

NARCOTIC ADDICTS

- Rehabilitation

UNITED STATES. National Institutes of Health. Mental Health Monographs. 3. Rehabilitation in drug addiction: a report on a five-year community experiment of the New York Demonstration Center. Washington, 1963. pp. vii, 48.

UNITED STATES. Vocational Rehabilitation Administration. Rehabilitating the narcotic addict: report of Institute on New Developments in the Rehabilitation of the Narcotic Addict, etc. Washington, 1967. pp. ix, 392.

U.K. Advisory Committee on Drug Dependence. 1969. The rehabilitation of drug addicts: report [by the Rehabilitation Sub-Committee]: [Arthur Blenkinsop, chairman]. London, H.M.S.O., 1968[or rather 1969]. pp. vii, 28. 24½cm.

NARCOTIC HABIT

TOLSTOI (LEV NIKOLAEVICH) Count. Pourquoi les hommes usent-ils de stupéfiants? [Paris], Edition de la Revue l'Idée Libre, 1925. pp. 20. 22cm. (Les Meilleures Oeuvres des Auteurs Rationalistes des XVIIIe Siècles. Brochures. No. 5)

UNITED STATES. National Institutes of Health. Mental Health Monographs. No. 2. Narcotic drug addiction. Washington, 1963. pp. viii, 22.

COUNCIL OF EUROPE. Sub-Committee on Pharmaceutical Questions. 1964. Proprietary and other pharmaceuticals recognised as addiction-producing and on sale in 15 of the member states of the Council ...: document prepared by the Sub-Committee etc. 4th ed. Strasbourg, 1964. pp. 21. 21cm. In English and French.

McNICOL (JOHN) The chemical crutch: a handbook on drug addiction. [London, National Association of Drug Addiction, 1967]. pp. (8). 20½cm.

SILBERMAN (MARTIN) Aspects of drug addiction: a report on a survey, etc. London, Royal London Prisoners' Aid Society, 1967. pp. 112. 21½cm.

BECKER (H.S.) History, culture, and subjective experience: an exploration of the social bases of drug-induced experiences. in Becker (Howard Saul) and others, eds. Institutions and the person. Chicago, 1968.

WOOD (ANTONY J.) Drug dependence. 3rd ed. Bristol, 1968. pp. 32.

BRILL (LEON) and LIEBERMAN (LOUIS) Authority and addiction. Boston, [1969]. pp. 318.

EXPERIMENTAL approaches to the study of drug dependence; proceedings of an interdisciplinary research conference held at the University of Toronto, March 1965, under the sponsorship of the Alcoholism and Drug Addiction Research Foundation of Ontario; edited by Harold Kalant and Rosemary D. Hawkins. Toronto, [1969]. pp. 237. bibliog.

BEHIND the drug scene; by Michael Schofield [and others], London, [1970]. pp. 30.

DIJK (W. K. VAN) and HULSMAN (L. H. C.) eds. Drugs in Nederland. Bussum, 1970. pp. 254.

KRYSTAL (HENRY) and RASKIN (HERBERT A.) Drug dependence: aspects of ego function. Detroit, 1970. pp. 127. bibliog.

U.K. Department of Health and Social Security. 1970. Amphetamines, barbiturates, LSD and cannabis: their use and misuse; (by Sir Aubrey Lewis). London, 1970. pp. 75. bibliog. (Reports on Public Health and Medical Subjects. No. 124.)

[BARRITT (BRIAN)] Whisper: a timescript. London, 1971. pp. 128.

- Asia

BORG (GÉRARD) Le voyage à la drogue. Paris, [1970]. pp. 247. bibliog.

- Canada

   CANADA. Commission of Inquiry into the Non-Medical Use of Drugs. 1970. Interim report: [Gerald Le Dain, chairman]. Ottawa, 1970. pp. 557,(117). bibliogs.

- Hong Kong

   HONG KONG. Legislative Council. 1959. The problem of narcotic drugs in Hong Kong: a white paper laid before Legislative Council, 11th November, 1959. Hong Kong, 1959. pp. 20.

- India

   CARSTAIRS (G.M.) Bhang and alcohol: cultural factors in the choice of intoxicants. in Solomon (David) 1925- , ed. The marihuana papers. Indianapolis [1966].

- Ireland (Republic)

   EIRE. Working Party on Drug Abuse. 1971. Report: [K. Mullen, chairman]. Dublin, 1971. pp. 78. bibliog.

- Netherlands

   WIJBENGA (COR) ed. Soft drugs: sociale, medische en juridische aspecten; met bijdragen van J. van den Berg [and others]. Amsterdam, 1969. pp. 174.

- New Zealand

   NEW ZEALAND. Committee on Drug Dependency and Drug Abuse in New Zealand. 1970- . Drug dependency and drug abuse in New Zealand: [G. Blake-Palmer, chairman]. [Wellington], 1970 in progress. bibliog. (New Zealand. Board of Health Report Series No.14)

- South Africa

   SOUTH AFRICA. Committee of Inquiry into the Abuse of Drugs. 1970. Report: [Chairman, J.A. Grobler] (R.P. 97/1970). in South Africa. Parliament. House of Assembly. Votes and proceedings; (with Printed annexures).

   SOUTH AFRICA. Department of Social Welfare and Pensions. [Research Division]. 1970. Drug dependence and some of its concomitant aspects in the Republic of South Africa. [Pretoria], 1970. pp. 53. bibliog.(Research and Information. Publication 1970/No. 3.)

- United Kingdom

   NATIONAL COUNCIL FOR CIVIL LIBERTIES. Drugs and civil liberties. London, 1967. pp. 22 bibliog.

   OFFICE OF HEALTH ECONOMICS. Drug addiction. London, [1967]. pp. 32.

   DAWTRY (FRANK) ed. Social problems of drug abuse: a guide for social workers; edited on behalf of the National Association of Probation Officers. London, Butterworths, 1968. pp. 115. bibliog. 21½cm.

   TRENCH (SALLY) Bury me in my boots. London, 1968. pp. 191.

   U.K. Advisory Committee on Drug Dependence. 1968. Cannabis: report (of the Hallucinogens Sub-Committee): [Baroness Wootton of Abinger, chairman]. London, H.M.S.O., 1968. pp. vii, 79. bibliog. 24½cm.

   BINNIE (HUGH L.) The attitudes to drugs and drug takers of students at the university and colleges of higher education in an English Midland city. Leicester, 1969. pp. 29. (Leicester. University. Vaughan College. Papers. No.14)

   SOCIALIST MEDICAL ASSOCIATION. The problem of drugs. Birmingham, [1969?]. pp. 11.

   WIENER (RONALD STEVEN PAUL) Drugs and schoolchildren. London, 1970. pp. 238. bibliogs. Adaptation of a Ph. D. thesis, University of London, 1969.

   DEEDES (WILLIAM FRANCIS) The drugs epidemic. London, 1970. pp. 160.

   DRUG dependence: papers given in the 15th series of I[nstitute for the] S[tudy and] T[reatment of] D[elinquency] lectures,...October 1969-March 1970; [by] Sir Harry Greenfield [and others]. London, 1970. pp. 39.

   LEECH (KENNETH) Pastoral care and the drug scene. London, 1970. pp. 165. bibliog.

   PRESCRIPTION for drugs; [by] Anthony White [and others]. London, 1970. pp. 46. (Conservative Political Centre. [Publications]. No. 461)

   U.K. Advisory Committee on Drug Dependence. 1970. The amphetamines and lysergic acid diethylamide (LSD): report (by the Amphetamines Sub-Committee): [Baroness Wootton of Abinger, chairman]. London, 1970. pp. 51.

   BEAN (P. T.) Drug abuse in England and Wales since 1900; [M.Sc. (Econ.)(London) thesis]. [1971]. fo. 182. bibliog. Typescript: unpublished. This thesis is the property of London University and may not be removed from the Library.

   YOUNG (JOCK) The drug takers: the social meaning of drug use. London, 1971. pp. 240.

- United States

   UNITED STATES. Narcotics Bureau. Prevention and control of narcotic addiction. Washington, [1963]. pp. 32.

   SOLOMON (DAVID) 1925- , ed. The marihuana papers. Indianapolis, Bobbs-Merrill, [1966]. pp. xxvi, 448. bibliogs. 22½cm.

   UNITED STATES. President's Commission on Law Enforcement and Administration of Justice. Task Force Reports. Narcotics and drug abuse: annotations and consultants' papers. Washington, 1967. pp. vii, 158. bibliogs.

   CAREY (JAMES T.) The college drug scene. Englewood Cliffs, Prentice-Hall, [1968]. pp. ix, 210. 20cm. (Spectrum Books. S-186)

   GOODE (ERICH) ed. Marijuana. New York, 1969. pp. 197. bibliog.

   NEW YORK (CITY). Department of Health. The narcotics register: development of a case register. [New York?, 1969] fo. 7.

NARCOTIC HABIT (Cont'd.)

- United States - Kentucky

UNITED STATES. Public Health Service. Publications. No. 1881. Narcotic addicts in Kentucky. Washington, 1969. pp. 297.

- United States - Massachusetts

MARTIN (GORDON A.) and HALLGRING (ROBERT W.) Drug abuse in Boston: a report to Mayor Kelvin H. White and the mayor's Safe Streets Act Committee. [Boston], 1969. fo. 48. With separately indexed appendices.

- United States - New York

RAMIREZ (EFREM) The problem of narcotics addiction in New York city. [New York], 1966. fo. 14.

NARCOTIC LAWS

- Netherlands

DIJK (W. K. VAN) and HULSMAN (L. H. C.) eds. Drugs in Nederland. Bussum, 1970. pp. 254.

- United Kingdom

NATIONAL COUNCIL FOR CIVIL LIBERTIES. Drugs and civil liberties. London, 1967. pp. 22. bibliog.

JONES (TERENCE J.) Drugs and the police. London, Butterworths, 1968. pp. 80. 18½cm.

U.K. Advisory Committee on Drug Dependence. 1968. Cannabis: report (of the Hallucinogens Sub-Committee): [Baroness Wootton of Abinger, chairman]. London, H.M.S.O., 1968. pp. vii, 79. bibliog. 24½cm.

COON (CAROLINE) and HARRIS (RUFUS) The Release report on drug offenders and the law. London, Sphere Books, 1969. pp. 123. bibliog. 18cm.

U.K. Advisory Committee on Drug Dependence. 1970. Powers of arrest and search in relation to drug offences; report [by the Sub-Committee on Powers of Arrest and Search]: [William Deedes, chairman]. London, 1970. pp. 77.

- United States

DUSTER (TROY) The legislation of morality: law, drugs and moral judgment. New York, [1970]. pp. 274.

NARCOTICS

UNITED STATES. President's Advisory Commission on Narcotic and Drug Abuse. Final report. Washington, 1963. pp. iv, 123.

SOLOMON (DAVID) 1925-   , ed. The marihuana papers. Indianapolis, Bobbs-Merrill, [1966]. pp. xxvi, 448. bibliogs. 22½cm.

INTERNATIONAL NARCOTICS CONTROL BOARD. Comparative statement of estimates and statistics on narcotic drugs furnished by governments in accordance with international treaties. [in English and French] Geneva annual, 1967 [1st] to date. 28cm.

INTERNATIONAL NARCOTICS CONTROL BOARD. Statistics on narcotic drugs... and maximum levels of opium stocks. Geneva, annual, 1967 to date. 28cm.

WILLIAMS (JOHN B.) ed. Narcotics and hallucinogenics: a handbook. rev.ed. Beverly Hills, Glencoe P., [1967]. pp. viii, 277. bibliog.

WIJBENGA (COR) ed. Soft drugs: sociale, medische en juridische aspecten; met bijdragen van J. van den Berg [and others]. Amsterdam, 1969. pp. 174.

LAURIE (PETER) Drugs: medical, psychological and social facts. 2nd ed. Harmondsworth, 1971. pp. 191.

- Dictionaries and encyclopaedias

LINGEMAN (RICHARD R.) Drugs from A to Z: a dictionary. London, 1970. pp. 262.

NARCOTICS, CONTROL OF

INTERNATIONAL NARCOTICS CONTROL BOARD. Report. Geneva, annual, 1968 (1st) to date. 28cm.

- United States

UNITED STATES. President's Commission on Law Enforcement and Administration of Justice. Task Force Reports. Narcotics and drug abuse: annotations and consultants' papers. Washington, 1967. pp. vii. 158. bibliogs.

NARCOTICS AND YOUTH

DAVIES (EDWARD BERESFORD) Memorandum on the problem of illicit drug-taking and dependence, particularly among young people. [Cambridge], 1967. pp. 18.

BORG (GÉRARD) Le voyage à la drogue. Paris, [1970]. pp. 247. bibliog.

DRUG-taking in the younger generation: report of a conference at Ditchley Park, 7-10 November, 1969; by G.V. Stimson,... rapporteur. Ditchley Park, Enstone, [1970]. pp. 29. (Ditchley Foundation. Ditchley Papers. No. 24)

YOUNG (JOCK) The drug takers: the social meaning of drug use. London, 1971. pp. 240.

- United Kingdom

WIENER (RONALD STEVEN PAUL) A survey of drug taking among young people; [Ph. D. (London) thesis]. 1969. fo 458. bibliog. 25½cm. Typescript: unpublished. This thesis is the property of London University and may not be removed from the Library.

COCKETT (R.) Drug abuse and personality in young offenders. London, [1971]. pp. 166.

NARIMANOV (NARIMAN NADZHAFOVICH)

KAZIEV (MAMED IAKUBOVICH) Nariman Narimanov: zhizn' i deiatel'nost'. Baku, 1970. pp. 187.

NARVA

- History - Revolution of 1917-1921

KLEMENT (A.) Nekotorye voprosy bor'by trudiashchikhsia Narvy i Prinarcv'ia za pobedu sotsialisticheskoi revoliutsii. Narva, 1966. pp. 39.

NASJONAL SAMLING

LOOCK (HANS DIETRICH) Quisling, Rosenberg und Terboven: zur Vorgeschichte und Geschichte der nationalsozialistischen Revolution in Norwegen. Stuttgart, 1970. pp. 587. bibliog.

NASSAU, GERMANY

- Officials and employees - Salaries, allowances, etc.

LEWINSKI (MANFRED VON) Witwen- und Waisenkassen öffentlicher Bediensteter in Nassau und ihr Verhältnis zum Pensionsrecht. Göttingen, 1967. pp. 99. bibliog.

NASSER (GAMAL ABDEL)

GIBBONS (SCOTT) The conspirators. London, Baker, 1967. pp. (vi), 192. 19½cm.

COPELAND (MILES) The game of nations: the amorality of power politics. London, [1969]. pp. 272. bibliog.

LACOUTURE (JEAN) Quatre hommes et leurs peuples: sur-pouvoir et sous-développement. Paris, [1969]. pp. 282. bibliog.

MANSFIELD (PETER) Nasser. London, Methuen, 1969. pp. viii, 217. bibliog. 18cm. (Makers of the Modern World)

LACOUTURE (JEAN) The demigods: charismatic leadership in the Third World;...translated from the French by Patricia Wolf. London, 1971. pp. 300, vi. bibliog.

STEPHENS (ROBERT) Nasser: a political biography. London, 1971. pp. 635. bibliog.

NAST (THOMAS)

KELLER (MORTON) The art and politics of Thomas Nast. New York, O.U.P., 1968. pp. xi, 353. bibliog. 30cm.

NAT TURNER'S INSURRECTION
See SOUTHAMPTON INSURRECTION, 1831

NATAL

- Description and travel

MASON (GEORGE HOLDITCH) Life with the Zulus of Natal, South Africa; [facsimile reprint of the 1855 ed.]. London, Cass, 1968. pp. xii, 232. 21½cm. (Cass Library of African Studies. Travels and Narratives. No. 33)

PHIPSON (THOMAS) Letters and other writings of a Natal sheriff..., 1815-76; selected and introduced by R.N. Currey. Cape Town, O.U.P., 1968. pp. xxix, 248. 21cm.

- Economic conditions

NATAL UNIVERSITY. Natal Regional Survey. vol. 14. The Umgeni-Umbilo-Umlazi rivers catchment areas: the Durban-Pietermaritzburg region; general editor O.P.F. Horwood. [Pietermaritzburg]. 1967-69. 2 vols. bibliogs.

NATAL UNIVERSITY. Natal Regional Survey. Additional Reports. No. 5. A Natal Indian community: a socio-economic study in the Tongaat-Verulam area; by G.G. Maasdorp. [Durban], 1968. pp. 142. bibliog.

- Foreign population

NATAL UNIVERSITY. Natal Regional Survey. Additional Reports. No. 5. A Natal Indian community: a socio-economic study in the Tongaat-Verulam area; by G.G. Maasdorp. [Durban], 1968. pp. 142. bibliog.

- History

MARKS (SHULA) Reluctant rebellion: the 1906-8 disturbances in Natal. Oxford, 1970. pp. 404 bibliog.

- History - Sources

ROBINSON (Sir JOHN) A life time in South Africa: being the recollections of the first premier of Natal. London, Smith, 1900; [Pretoria, State Library, 1968]. pp. xxxix, 418. 17½cm. (Reprints. No.32) Facsimile reprint.

CHASE (JOHN CENTLIVRES) The Natal papers: a reprint of all notices and public documents connected with that territory including a description of the country and a history of events from 1498 to 1843; ... facsimile reprint [of the edition published in Graham's Town by Godlonton, 1843, with a new introduction, bibliography, and list of contents]. Cape Town, Struik, 1968. pp. xv, iv, 135, 320. bibliog. 21½cm. (Africana Collectanea. vol. 30)

PHIPSON (THOMAS) Letters and other writings of a Natal sheriff..., 1815-76; selected and introduced by R.N. Currey. Cape Town, O.U.P., 1968. pp. xxix, 248. 21cm.

- Social conditions

NATAL UNIVERSITY. Natal Regional Survey. Additional Reports. No. 5. A Natal Indian community: a socio-economic study in the Tongaat-Verulam area; by G.G. Maasdorp. [Durban], 68. pp. 142. bibliog.

- Social life and customs

MASON (GEORGE HOLDITCH) Life with the Zulus of Natal, South Africa; [facsimile reprint of the 1855 ed.]. London, Cass, 1968. pp. xii, 232. 21½cm. (Cass Library of African Studies. Travel and Narratives. No. 33)

NATAN (ZHAK)

BEILIS (ALEKSANDR SAMOILOVICH) Stanovlenie marksistskoi istoriografii v Bolgarii, s kontsa XIX v. do sotsialisticheskoi revoliutsii 1944 g.: problemy bolgarskogo Vozrozhdeniia. L'viv, 1970. pp. 239.

NATCHEZ

- History

JAMES (D. CLAYTON) Antebellum Natchez. Baton Rouge, Louisiana State U.P., [1968]. pp. xiv, 344. bibliog. 22½cm.

NATHAN (HARRY LOUIS) 1st Baron Nathan

HYDE (HARFORD MONTGOMERY) Strong for service: the life of Lord Nathan of Churt. London, Allen, 1968. pp. xii, 280. 21cm.

NATHAN (JOSEPH EDWARD)

JEPHCOTT (Sir HARRY) The first fifty years: an account of the early life of Joseph Edward Nathan and the first fifty years of his merchandise business that eventually became the Glaxo Group. [London?, 1969]. pp. 118.

NATIONAL-SOCIALISTISCHE BEWEGING IN NEDERLAND

JONGE (A.A. DE) Het nationaal-socialisme in Nederland: voorgeschiedenis, ontstaan en ontwikkeling. Den Haag, [1968]. pp. 199. bibliog.

NATIONAL ASSOCIATION FOR THE ADVANCEMENT OF COLOURED PEOPLE

MATTHEWS (JOSEPH BROWN) Communism and the N[ational] A[ssociation for the] A[dvancement of] C[oloured] P[eople]: [information presented... at a public hearing of the Florida Legislation Investigation Committee... February 10, 1958, etc.]. Atlanta, Georgia Commission on Education,[1958?]. 2 vols.

NATIONAL BANK OF PAKISTAN

The STORY of the National Bank of Pakistan...; issued for the Statistics Department of National Bank of Pakistan; [produced by the Public Relations Department, National Bank of Pakistan]. Karachi, United Advertisers, [1966]. pp. xii, 100. 18½cm.

NATIONAL CHARACTERISTICS

WERNER (HANS DETLEF) Klassenstruktur und Nationalcharakter: eine soziologische Kritik. Tübingen, Huth, [1967]. pp. (iv), 212. bibliog. 19½cm. (Das Wissenschaftliche Arbeitsbuch. VIII/4)

INTERNATIONAL SEMINAR FOR TEACHERS, ELSINORE, 1968. National stereotypes: an educational challenge...; report...edited by John Eppstein. London, Atlantic Information Centre for Teachers, [1968] pp. 37. 24½cm.

LYNN (RICHARD) Personality and national character. Oxford, 1971. pp. 200. bibliog.

NATIONAL CHARACTERISTICS, AMERICAN

RIESMAN (DAVID) and others. The lonely crowd: a study of the changing American character; [with an essay, Ten years later]. [new ed.] New Haven, Yale U.P., [1960?], repr. 1967. pp. xlviii, 386. 23½cm.

RISCHIN (MOSES) ed. The American gospel of success: individualism and beyond. Chicago, 1965. pp. 429. bibliog.

MÁRQUEZ (JAIRO) Anatomía del gringo: impresiones de un sudamericano; traducción de Mario Arrubla. Bogotá, Tercer Mundo, 1966. pp. 185. 20½cm. (Colección Problemas de América)

HARTSHORNE (THOMAS L.) The distorted image: changing conceptions of the American character since Turner. Cleveland, 1968. pp. 226. bibliog.

WOODWARD (COMER VANN) The burden of Southern history. rev. ed. Baton Rouge, Louisiana State U.P., [1968]. pp. xvii, 250. 21½cm.

HUDSON (WINTHROP S.) ed. Nationalism and religion in America: concepts of American identity and mission. New York, 1970. pp. 211.

SKIDMORE (MAX J.) Medicare and the American rhetoric of reconciliation. Alabama, [1970]. pp. 198.

NATIONAL CHARACTERISTICS, BRAZILIAN

RODRIQUES (JOSE HONORIO) The Brazilians: their character and aspirations; translated by Ralph Edward Dimmick. Austin, [1967]. pp. xxvii, 186. bibliog.

NATIONAL CHARACTERISTICS, BRITISH

GUARDIAN, THE. What's good about Britain: a Guardian inquiry. London, 1969. pp. 81.

GLYN (ANTHONY) The blood of a Britishman. London, 1970. pp. 328.

NATIONAL CHARACTERISTICS, CHILEAN

LEFEBVRE (ALFREDO) Artículos de malas costumbres. Santiago de Chile, Editorial Universitaria, 1961. pp. 105. 18cm.

NATIONAL CHARACTERISTICS, CUBAN

GARCIA (JOSÉ H.) Liborio speaks in English. New York, Vantage P., [1968]. pp. 95. 20cm.

NATIONAL CHARACTERISTICS, DUTCH

SCHMIDT (STEFFI) Die Niederlande und die Niederländer im Urteil deutscher Reisenden: eine Untersuchung deutscher Reisebeschreibungen von der Mitte des 17. bis zur Mitte des 19. Jahrhunderts. Siegburg, Schmitt, 1963. pp. 141. bibliog. 21cm. (Quellen und Studien zur Volkskunde. Band 5)

NATIONAL CHARACTERISTICS, FRENCH

AVENEL (GEORGES D') Vicomte. Les Français de mon temps. Paris, [1910]. pp. 350.

LEITES (NATHAN CONSTANTIN) The rules of the game in Paris;...translated by Derek Coltman. Chicago, 1969. pp. 355. bibliog.

NATIONAL CHARACTERISTICS, GERMAN

HERMANT (MAX) Idoles allemandes. Paris, [1935]. pp. 358.

VERRONA, pseud. The German mentality. rev. ed. London, 1946. pp. 344.

MONEY-KYRLE (R.) Some aspects of state and character in Germany. in Wilbur (George B.) and Muensterberger (Warner) eds. Psychoanalysis and culture: ...[reprint of the work first published in 1951]. New York, 1967.

INSTITUT FÜR STAATSBÜRGERLICHE BILDUNG RHEINLAND-PFALZ. Autoritarismus und Nationalismus - ein deutsches Problem?: Bericht über eine Tagung... in Ingelheim geleitet von Karl Holzamer. Frankfurt am Main, Europäische Verlagsanstalt, [1963]. pp. 96. 24cm. (Politische Psychologie. Band 2)

ENZENSBERGER (HANS MAGNUS) Deutschland, Deutschland unter anderm: Äusserungen zur Politik. Frankfurt am Main, Suhrkamp, [1967]. pp. 178. bibliog. 17½cm.

GROTE (BERND) Der deutsche Michel: ein Beitrag zur publizistischen Bedeutung der Nationalfiguren. Dortmund, Ruhfus, 1967. pp. 89. bibliog. 21cm. (Westfaelisch-Niederrheinisches Institut für Zeitungsforschung der Stadt Dortmund. Dortmunder Beiträge zur Zeitungsforschung. 11.Band)

NOELLE-NEUMANN (ELISABETH) and NEUMANN (ERICH PETER) eds. The Germans: public opinion polls 1947-1966; (translated from the German by Gerard Finan). Allensbach, Verlag für Demoskopie, 1967. pp. xvii, 630. 21cm. Selections from their Jahrbuch der öffentlichen Meinung, 1947-1955 and Jahrbuch... 1965-1967.

BACKHAUS (WILHELM) Sind die Deutschen verrückt?: ein Psychogramm der Nation und ihrer Katastrophen. Bergisch Gladbach, Lübbe, [1968]. pp. 323. bibliog. 20½cm.

MOELLER (JUERGEN) ed. Deutsche beschimpfen Deutsch: vierhundert Jahre Schelt- und Schmähreden. Hamburg, Claasen, 1968. pp. 390. 20½cm.

SUENDERMANN (HELMUT) ed. Die deutsche Frage: von den Anfängen bis 1933. Leoni, [1968]. pp. 220.

NEVEN-DU MONT (JUERGEN) After Hitler: report from a German city; translated by Ralph Mannheim. London, 1969. pp. 319.

PHILIPS (PETER) The tragedy of Nazi Germany. London, Routledge & Kegan Paul, 1969. pp. (viii), 241. bibliog. 21½cm.

ROHAN (KARL ANTON) Prinz. Die Deutschen und die Welt: wie sehen die anderen Völker die Deutschen? Wien, 1969. pp. 54.

NATIONAL CHARACTERISTICS, GUATEMALAN

CARDOZA Y ARAGÓN (LUIS) Guatemala: las lineas de su mano. México, 1955. pp. 304.

NATIONAL CHARACTERISTICS, NIGERIAN

ENAHORO (PETER) How to be a Nigerian. [Ibadan], Daily Times of Nigeria Limited, 1966, repr. 1967. pp. xii, 79. 18½cm.

NATIONAL CHARACTERISTICS, PERUVIAN

BELAUNDE (VÍCTOR ANDRÉS) Meditaciones peruanas. 2nd ed. Lima, [1963]. pp. 267. 20½cm.

NATIONAL CHARACTERISTICS, RUSSIAN

SOVETSKII... Советский характер. Москва, 1967. pp. 494.

NATIONAL CHILD LABOR COMMITTEE

TRATTNER (WALTER I.) Crusade for the children: a history of the National Child Labor Committee and child labor reform in America. Chicago, 1970. pp. 319. bibliog.

NATIONAL COUNCIL OF NIGERIA AND THE CAMEROONS

NIGERIA (EASTERN REGION). 1959. Government programme. Enugu, [1959]. pp. 19.

NATIONAL DEMOCRATIC PARTY (GERMANY)
See NATIONALDEMOKRATISCHE PARTEI DEUTSCHLANDS (BUNDESREPUBLIK); and NATIONAL-DEMOKRATISCHE PARTEI DEUTSCHLANDS (D. D. R.)

NATIONAL DEMOCRATIC PARTY (POLAND)

ORZECHOWSKI (MARIAN) Narodowa demokracja na Górnym Śląsku do 1918 roku. Wrocław, Zakład Narodowy im. Ossolińskich, 1965. pp. 302. bibliog. 25cm. (Monografie Śląskie. 9) With English summary.

NATIONAL INCOME

BOSSE (LOTHAR) Das Volkseinkommen. Wien, [1958]. pp. 30.

MARCHAL (J.) Contribution à la théorie de la répartition du revenu national: les catégories d'entrepreneurs. in Conférences économiques délivrées au séminaire du Professeur G.U. Papi, etc. Milano, 1962.

DE REVILLE (M. J. C.) Die verdeling van die volksinkome: teoretiese inleiding. Stellenbosch, Kosmo-Uitgewery, 1967. pp. 146. bibliog. 21cm.

PAVLOV (GELY T.) Problems of the analysis for inter-branch relationships in the planned inter-branch balance. Cairo, 1967. pp. 71. 28cm. (U.A.R. Institute of National Planning. Memos. No. 752.)

DAMALAS (BASILE V.) Revenu national et équilibre économique. Athènes, Papazissis, 1968. pp. xiv, 95. 21½cm.

INTERNATIONAL ECONOMIC ASSOCIATION. Conference, 1965. The distribution of national income: proceedings of a conference...; edited by Jean Marchal and Bernard Ducros. London, Macmillan, 1968. pp. xxx, 734. 21½cm.

AMES (EDWARD) Income and wealth. New York, [1969]. pp. 377. bibliog.

FEL'DMAN (GRIGORII ALEKSANDROVICH) Zur Wachstumstheorie des Nationaleinkommens; herausgegeben von O. Kratsch. Frankfurt, [1969]. pp. 126. Translation of 2 articles from Planovoe khoziaistvo nos.11 and 12, 1928, entitled "К теории темпов народного хозяйства".

BAILEY (MARTIN JEAN) National income and the price level: a study in macroeconomic theory. 2nd ed. New York, [1971]. pp. 278. bibliogs.

SCHULTZE (CHARLES L.) National income analysis. 3rd ed. Englewood Cliffs, [1971]. pp. 162. bibliog.

- Accounting

ÉTUDES ET CONJONCTURE: Économie mondiale. Numéros spéciaux hors série. Les comptabilités nationales dans le monde: comparaison des méthodes. Paris, 1952. pp. 256.

NATIONAL INCOME - Accounting (Cont'd.)

ORGANISATION FOR ECONOMIC CO-OPERATION AND DEVELOPMENT. National accounts statistics: expenditure, product and income. [in English and French] Paris, annual, 1955/1964 to date. 27-31cm. Each issue covers 10 years.

KUEHNAU (MARTIN) Der Formalaufbau der volkswirtschaftlichen Buchhaltung. Berlin, Duncker & Humblot, 1961. pp. 411. bibliog. 23½cm. (Berlin. Freie Universität. Wirtschafts- und Sozialwissenschaftliche Fakultät. Wirtschaftswissenschaftliche Abhandlungen. Heft 13)

ORGANISATION FOR EUROPEAN ECONOMIC CO-OPERATION. 1961. Input-output and national accounts; by Richard Stone. [Paris], 1961. pp. 202. bibliog.

ROSSI (N.) Le variazioni e la rimanenze di esercizio: alcune precisazioni terminologiche e concettuali. in vol. 3 of Saggi di economia aziendale e sociale in memoria di Gino Zappa. Milano, 1961.

STONE (JOHN RICHARD NICHOLAS) Mathematical models of the economy and other essays [originally published in various periodicals 1962-69]. London, 1970. pp. 335. bibliog.

HIRSCH (WERNER ZVI) and SONENBLUM (SIDNEY) Comments on Charles L. Leven's regional and interregional accounts in perspective; by Werner Z. Hirsch and Sidney Sonenblum. Los Angeles, 1963. fo. 6. bibliog. (California University. Institute of Government and Public Affairs. [Publications]. MR-1)

KURABAYASHI (YOSHIMASA) A note on basic concepts of national accounts. Tokyo, Institute of Economic Research, Hitotsubashi University, 1966. pp. 61-76. 25cm. (Reprint Series. No.48)

BECKERMAN (WILFRED) An introduction to national income analysis. London, Weidenfeld & Nicolson, [1968]. pp. x, 254. 21½cm.

FERRERI (CARLO) Criteri di analisi della dinamica degli aggregati del conto della produzione. Palermo, 1968. pp. 265. bibliog. (Palermo. Università. Facoltà di Economia e Commercio. Collana di Studi di Statistica Economica. 1)

HAIG (B.D.) and McBURNEY (S.S.) The interpretation of national income estimates. Canberra, 1968. pp. 120. bibliog.

KIRNER (WOLFGANG) Zeitreihen für das Anlagevermögen der Wirtschaftsbereiche in der Bundesrepublik Deutschland. Berlin, 1968. pp. 157. bibliog. (Deutsches Institut für Wirtschaftsforschung. DIW-Beiträge zur Strukturforschung. Heft 5)

QUARTERLY national accounts as data for economic policy: a report on progress in OECD countries prepared with the assistance of T.P. Hill. Paris, Organisation for Economic Co-operation and Development, 1968. pp. 90. bibliog. (Department of Economics and Statistics. Economic Studies)

ABRAHAM (WILLIAM I.) National income and economic accounting. Englewood Cliffs, Prentice-Hall, [1969]. pp. xv, 232. bibliog. 22½cm.

ORGANISATION FOR ECONOMIC CO-OPERATION AND DEVELOPMENT. Department of Economics and Statistics. 1970. National accounts statistics, 1950-1968. [Paris, 1970]. pp. 415. For annual of the same title see ORGANISATION FOR ECONOMIC COOPERATION AND DEVELOPMENT. National accounts statistics:... 1955/64 to date. In English and French.

O'LOUGHLIN (CARLEEN) National economic accounting. Oxford, 1971. pp. 192. bibliog.

- Mathematical models

SCOTT (ROBERT HANEY) Problems in national income analysis and forecasting. Glenview, Scott, [1966]. pp. (iii), 87. 28cm.

KATANO (HIKOJI) Factors to determine relative shares: the case of India. Tokyo, 1969. pp. 91. (Institute of Developing Economies. Occasional Papers Series. No. 5)

NEGREPONTI-DELIVANIS (MARIA) The distribution of national income during take off. Thessalonikē, 1969. pp. 260-284. (Reprinted from Epistēmonikē Epeteris Scholēs Nomikōn kai Oikonomikōn Epistēmōn, tom. 12, [pt.]5)

DUPREZ (COLETTE) and KIRSCHEN (ETIENNE SADI) eds. Megistos: a world income and trade model for 1975. Amsterdam, [1970]. pp. 668. bibliogs.

OLSEN (ERLING) International trade theory and regional income differences: United States, 1880-1950. Amsterdam, 1971. pp. 221.

- Statistics

USHER (DAN) The price mechanism and the meaning of national income statistics. Oxford, Clarendon, 1968. pp. xxiii. 180. 21½cm.

- Africa, Subsaharan - Accounting

ORGANISATION FOR EUROPEAN ECONOMIC CO-OPERATION. 1960. Systems of national accounts in Africa; by P.Ady and M. Courcier. [Paris], 1960. pp. 232.

- Argentine Republic

ARGENTINE REPUBLIC. Consejo Nacional de Desarrollo. 1965. Distribución del ingreso y cuentas nacionales en la Argentina; investigación conjunta CONADE-CEPAL. Buenos Aires, 1965. 5 vols. 26cm.

- Argentine Republic - Accounting

ARGENTINE REPUBLIC. Consejo Nacional de Desarrollo. 1964. Cuentas nacionales de la República Argentina: resumen de los resultados provisionales de la primera parte del programa de investigación CONADE CEPAL sobre "Distribución del ingreso en la República Argentina". Buenos Aires, 1964. pp. (xii), 213.

RGENTINE REPUBLIC. Consejo Nacional de Desarrollo. 1965. Distribución del ingreso y cuentas nacionales en la Argentina; investigación conjunta CONADE-CEPAL. Buenos Aires, 1965. 5 vols.

- Australia

DOWNING (RICHARD IVAN) National income and social accounts: an Australian study. 12th ed. Carlton, 1969. pp. 106.

- Botswana - Accounting

BOTSWANA. Central Statistics Office. National accounts. Gaberones, 1964/1966 [1st issue] to date. 33cm.

BOTSWANA. Report of the Director of Audit on the accounts of the Botswana Government. a., 1967/8- Gaborone.

- Canada - Accounting

DAS GUPTA (D. B.) An approach to a social accounting system for the Atlantic provinces. Fredericton, the Centre, 1966. fo. v,63,vi. bibliog. 28cm. (Atlantic Provinces Economic Council. Research Centre, Research Papers. No.4)

CANADA. Statistics Canada. System of national accounts: financial flow accounts. Ottawa, quarterly, 4th quarter 1968 (1st issue) to date.

CANADA. Dominion Bureau of Statistics. Financial Flows Section. 1969. System of national accounts: financial flow accounts, 1962-67: a preliminary report. Ottawa, 1969. pp. 270. 28cm.

NATIONAL ACCOUNTS OF CEYLON; [pd. by] Department of Census and Statistics [Ceylon]. a., 1963/1968 [1st Colombo.

- Colombia

ALFONSO (LUIS ALBERTO) Der Industrialisierungsprozess und seine Wirkungen auf die Entwicklung des Volkseinkommens in Kolumbien. Marburg, 1965. pp. 119. bibliog.

- Communist countries - Accounting

KUDROVA (EKATERINA STEPANOVNA) Статистика национального дохода европейских социалистических стран. Москва, Статистика, 1969. pp. 175. bibliog. 20cm.

- France - Accounting

FRANCE. Conseil National de la Comptabilité. Rapport d'activité. a.(approx.), [1962/3] (1er rapport)- Paris.

JEANNENEY (JEAN MARCEL) and QUIERS-VALETTE (SUZANNE) Essai d'une comptabilité interrégionale française pour 1954. Paris, 1968-71. 2 vols. (Fondation Nationale des Sciences Politiques. Service d'Étude de l'Activité Économique et de la Situation Sociale. Recherches sur L'Économie Française. 12, 17)

FRANCE. Institut National de la Statistique et des Etudes Economiques. Rapport sur les comptes de la nation. (Les Collections de l'I.N.S.E.E. Serie C) a., 1969- Paris.

- France - Colonies

FRANCE. Institut National de la Statistique et des Etudes Economiques. Comptes économiques des départements d'outre mer (sauf la Guyane). a., 1968- Paris.

- Germany

JECK (ALBERT) Wachstum und Verteilung des Volkseinkommens: Untersuchungen und Materialien zur Entwicklung der Einkommensverteilung in Deutschland, 1870-1913. Tübingen, 1970. pp. 310. bibliog. (Tübingen. Universität. Rechts- und Wirtschaftswissenschaftliche Fakultät. Wirtschaftswissenschaftliche Abteilung. Tübinger Wirtschaftswissenschaftliche Abhandlungen. Band 9)

- Germany, Eastern

STIEMERLING (KARL HEINZ) Wachstumsprobleme des Nationaleinkommens in der Deutschen Demokratischen Republik. Berlin, Dietz, 1968. pp. 187. 20cm.

- Guadeloupe

COMPTES ECONOMIQUES DE LA GUADELOUPE; [pd. by] Institut National de la Statistique et des Etudes Economiques [France]. a., 1969- [Paris]

- Hungary

HUNGARY. Központi Statisztikai Hivatal. Statisztikai Időszaki Közlemények. 28. kötet. A nemzeti jövedelem és a lakosság jövedelme 1958-ban. Budapest, 1959. pp. 68. with English summary.

HUNGARY. 1961. A nemzeti jövedelem és a lakosság életkörülményei a hároméves terv időszakában. (Statisztikai Időszaki Közlemények. 46. kötet) Budapest, 1961. pp. 101,(3). 28cm.

HUNGARY. Központi Statisztikai Hivatal. Közlemények. 56. kötet. A nemzeti jövedelem és a lakosság eletkörülményei, 1962. With English summary. Budapest, 1963. pp. 101.

HUNGARY. Központi Statisztikai Hivatal. Statisztikai Időszaki Közlemények. 65.kötet. A nemzeti jövedelem és a lakosság életkörülményei, 1963. Budapest, 1964. pp. 95. 29cm. With English summary.

HUNGARY. 1966. A nemzeti jövedelem és a lakosság életkörülményei a második ötéves terv időszakában. (Statisztikai Idő szaki Közlemények. 87. kötet) Budapest 1966. pp. 65,(2), 28cm. With English summary.

HUNGARY. Központi Statisztikai Hivatal. Statisztikai Időszaki Közlemények. 99. kötet. Jövedelemeloszlás magyarországon: a társadalmi rétegződés vizsgálatának adatai alapján. Budapest, 1967. pp. 387. 29cm.

HUNGARY. Központi Statisztikai Hivatal. Statisztikai Időszaki Közlemények. 103. kötet. A nemzeti jövedelem alakulása, 1966; A népgazdaság állóeszközei, 1960-1965. Budapest, 1967. pp. 53. 29cm.

HUNGARY. Központi Statisztikai Hivatal. Statisztikai Időszaki Közlemények. 130. kötet. A lakosság jövedelme és fogyasztása 1966-1967: az országos számítások és a háztartásstatisztikai megfigyelések eredményei. Budapest, 1968. pp. 183.

- India

INDIA. Central Statistical Organisation. 1963. National income statistics: a study of public sector undertakings in India. [New Delhi], 1963. pp. 57.

INDIA. Central Statistical Organisation. 1967. Brochure on revised series of national product for 1960-61 to 1964-65. [Delhi, 1967] pp. viii, 106.

NATIONAL INCOME - India (Cont'd.)

INDIA. Planning Commission. Perspective Planning Division. 1967. Draft fourth plan: material and financial balances 1964-65, 1970-71 and 1975-76: September 1966. [Delhi, 1967]. pp. 149. 27cm. Table in end pocket.

KATANO (HIKOJI) Factors to determine relative shares: the case of India. Tokyo, 1969. pp. 91. (Institute of Developing Economies. Occasional Papers Series. No. 5)

MUKHERJEE (M.) National income of India: trends and structure. Calcutta. 1969. pp. 521.

RAMANA (DUVVURI VENKATA) National accounts and input-output accounts of India. London, [1969]. pp. 100.

CHAVAN (B.W.) and CHAVAN (ANITA) National income in India: concepts and methods. Bombay, 1970. pp. 88. bibliog.

- India - Bengal, West

WEST BENGAL. State Statistical Bureau. 1956. State income of West Bengal, 1948-49 to 1951-52. [Calcutta, 1956]. pp. 172. 33½cm.

WEST BENGAL. State Statistical Bureau. 1965. Estimates of state income and its regional differentials, West Bengal. [Calcutta], 1965. pp. 44.

WEST BENGAL. State Statistical Bureau. 1966. Estimates of state income, West Bengal, 1964-65. [Calcutta], 1966. pp. 16.

- Iran

BANK MARKAZI IRAN. Economic Research Department. National income of Iran, 1962-67. [Tehran], 1969. pp. 195.

- Italy - Accounting

ERCOLANI (MARIO) and COTULA (FRANCO) I conti finanziari della Banca d'Italia. [Rome], Ente per gli Studi Monetari, Bancari e Finanziari Luigi Einaudi, [1969]. pp. 79. 24cm. (Quaderni di Ricerche. Num. 4)

- Jamaica

JAMAICA. Department of Statistics. 1966. The national income and product of Jamaica. 1964. Kingston, 1966. pp. iv, 91.

- Jamaica - Accounting

ROSE (DEXTER L.) A framework for revising the national accounts of Jamaica. [Kingston, 1964?] pp. vii, 254. bibliog. 28cm.

- Lebanon - Accounting

LEBANESE REPUBLIC. Direction Centrale de la Statistique. Comptes économiques. Beyrouth, annual, 1964 (vol. 1) to date, with gap (1964, vol. 2).

- Martinique

COMPTES ECONOMIQUES DE LA MARTINIQUE; [pd. by] Institut National de la Statistique et des Etudes Economiques. [France]. a., 1969- Paris.

- Netherlands

SCHILDERINCK (J.H.F.) and SINNER (H.J.N.) Production and income relations in the Netherlands: a semi-regional input-output analysis. Rotterdam, 1970. pp. 87. (Tilburg. Katholieke Hogeschool. Tilburg Institute of Economics. Tilburg Studies on Economics. 2.)

- Nicaragua

NICARAGUA. Consejo Nacional de Economía. Oficina de Planificación. Sector Público. 1965. Estudio del Sector Público de Nicaragua, 1950-1962. Managua, 1965. pp. xi, 314, 2. 27½cm.

- Nigeria

NIGERIA. Federal Ministry of Economic Development. 1962. Nigerian national accounts, 1950-57; [by] P.N.C. Okigbo. Enugu, [1962]. pp. 206.

- Norway - Accounting

NORWAY. Statistiske Centralbyrå. Nasjonalregnskap: National accounts. a., 1949/1965- Oslo. Each issue covers 5 yrs.

NORWAY. Statistiske Centralbyrå. 1970. Regionalt nasjonalregnskap, 1965; Regional national accounts, 1965. Oslo, 1970. pp. 111. (Norges Offisielle Statistikk. Rekke A. 376) In Norwegian and English.

- Pakistan - Accounting

PAKISTAN. Committee of Experts on the National Accounts of Pakistan. 1962. Report. [Henry J. Bruton, chairman]. Karachi, Institute of Development Economics. 1962. pp. (vi), 69. 24cm.

PAKISTAN. National Income Commission. 1966. Final report. [Karachi, 1966]. pp. 124.

- Poland

PRANDECKA (BARBARA KAROLINA) Analiza tworzenia i podziału dochodu narodowego Polski w układzie regionalnym. Warszawa, PWN, 1965. pp. 159. bibliog 24cm. (Polska Akademia Nauk. Komitet Przestrzennego Zagospodarowania Kraju) With Russian and French summaries.

- Réunion Island - Accounting

FRANCE. Institut National de la Statistique et des Etudes Economiques. Comptes économiques de la Réunion. 1965/1967 [1st issue]; a., 1968- Paris.

- Roumania

GRINDEA (DAN) Venitul national în Republica Socialistă România. București, 1967. pp. 552.

- Russia

PLYSHEVSKII (BORIS PAVLOVICH) Национальный доход СССР за 20 лет. Москва, Мысль, 1964. pp. 191. 20cm.

MAKOVETSKAIA (MARIIA IL'INICHNA) Экономия материальных затрат и рост национального дохода. Москва, Экономика, 1965. pp. 112. 20cm.

BECKER (ABRAHAM S.) Soviet national income, 1958-1964: national accounts of the USSR in the seven year plan period. Berkeley, 1969. pp. 606. bibliog.

FEL'DMAN (GRIGORII ALEKSANDROVICH) Zur Wachstumstheorie des Nationaleinkommens; herausgegeben von O. Kratsch. Frankfurt, [1969]. pp. 126. Translation of 2 articles from Planovoe khoziaistvo nos.11 and 12, 1928, entitled "К теории темпов народного хозяйства".

VAINSHTEIN (AL'BERT L'VOVICH) Narodnyi dokhod Rossii i SSSR: istoriia, metodologiia ischisleniia, dinamika. Moskva, 1969. pp. 167. bibliog.

ZVEREV (ARSENII GRIGOR'EVICH) Natsional'nyi dokhod i finansy SSSR. 2nd ed. Moskva, 1970. pp. 311.

- Siam

USHER (DAN) The price mechanism and the meaning of national income statistics. Oxford, Clarendon, 1968. pp. xxiii, 180. 21½cm.

- Sierra Leone - Accounting

SIERRA LEONE. Central Statistics Office. National accounts of Sierra Leone. a., 1963-4/1965-6 [2nd] 1963-4/1968-9 [4th]- Freetown.

- South Africa

SOUTH AFRICA. Bureau of Statistics. National Accounts and Finance Reports No. 11. Net national income, 1951-1952. Pretoria, 1953. pp. 12. 28cm. In English and Afrikaans.

- Sudan - Accounting

SUDAN. Department of Statistics. National accounts and supporting tables. a., 1966/7- [Khartoum]

- Switzerland - Accounting

BALTENSPERGER (MAX) Konzeption, Methoden und Quellen der nationalen Buchhaltung der Schweiz. Bern, 1967. pp. 151. bibliog.

- Tajikistan

AKHUNOV (I. I.) Proizvodstvo natsional'nogo dokhoda v Tadzhikskoi SSR. Dushanbe, 1967. pp. 115.

- Tunisia

TUNIS. 1954. Les comptes économiques de la Tunisie, [1953]. (Service des Statistiques) [Tunis, 1954?] fo. 24. 31cm.

- United Kingdom

LONDON. London Municipal Society. Department of Anti-Socialist Economics. Monographs for Parliamentary Candidates and their Workers. Statistical Series. No. 7. The income from abroad as related to the business done in the United Kingdom, unemployment in the United Kingdom, and the wages and salaries of the employees as compared with the profits of business taxed in the United Kingdom. London, [1909?]. pp. 8.

KUDROV (VALENTIN MIKHAILOVICH) Natsional'nyi dokhod Anglii v poslevoennyi period. Moskva, 1961. pp. 171.

U.K. Central Office of Information. Reference Division. 1968. Britain's national income statistics. London, 1968. pp. 5.

U.K. Central Statistical Office. 1968. National accounts statistics: sources and methods; edited by Rita Maurice. London, 1968. pp. vii, 502. 25cm.

- United States

UNITED STATES. 1960. Revisions of first estimates of quarter-to-quarter movement in selected national income series 1947-1958, seasonally adjusted data. (Bureau of the Budget Statistical Evaluation Reports. No. 2) Washington, 1960. pp. iii, 40. 26½cm.

SIRAGELDIN (ISMAIL ABDEL-HAMID) Non-market components of national income. Ann Arbor, [1969]. pp. 127. bibliog.

- United States - Accounting

DAVIE (BRUCE F.) and DUNCOMBE (BRUCE F.) Modern political arithmetic: the Federal budget and the public sector in national economic accounts. New York, [1970]. pp. 114.

RUGGLES (NANCY DUNLAP) and RUGGLES (RICHARD) The design of economic accounts. New York, 1970. pp. 184. bibliog. (National Bureau of Economic Research. [Publications]. No. 89)

- Yugoslavia

VINSKI (IVO) Nacionalno bogatstvo Jugoslavije. Zagreb, 1957. pp. 144. 24cm.

VINSKI (IVO) Procjena nacionalnog bogatstva po područjima Jugoslavije. Zagreb, 1959. pp. 282. With English summary.

POLAJNAR (A.) The enterprise and national income distribution; (translated by Danica Mijović). Beograd, 1963. pp. 53.

VINSKI (IVO) Uvod u analizu nacionalnog dohotka i bogatstva. Zagreb, 1967. pp. 402.

YUGOSLAVIA. Savezni Zavod za Statistiku. Studije, Analize i Prikazi. 45. Kretanj društvenog proizvoda i narodnog dohotka J goslavije 1952-1968. godine po oblastima privrede i socijalističkim republikama u cenema 1966: Social product and national income of Yugoslavia 1952-1968 by economic domains and socialist republics at 1966 prices. Beograd, 1969. pp. 139. With English summary.

VINSKI (IVO) Klasna podjela stanovništva i nacionalnog dohotka Jugoslavije u 1938. godini. Zagreb, 1970. pp. 190. bibliog. With English and Russian summaries.

NATIONAL INCOME - Yugoslavia (Cont'd.)

YUGOSLAVIA. Savezni Zavod za Statistiku. Studije, Analize i Prikazi. 51. Kretanje narodnog dohotka, zaposlenosti i produktivnosti rada u privredi Jugoslavije, 1947-1967: National income, employment and labour productivity in the economy of Yugoslavia, 1947-1967; [by] Branimir Marković. Beograd, 1970. With English summary.

- Yugoslavia - Accounting

YUGOSLAVIA. Savezni Zavod za Statistiku. Studije, Analize i Prikazi. 29. Privredni bilansi Jugoslavije, 1962-1965; Comptabilité nationale yougoslave, 1962-1965. Beograd, 1966. pp. 174. With French summary.

LYALL (KATHARINE) Yugoslav system of national accounts. Ljubljana, Urbanisticni Institut SRS, [1967]. fo. 14. bibliog. 29cm.

YUGOSLAVIA. Savezni Zavod za Statistiku. Studije, Analize i Prikazi. 39. Privredni bilansi Jugoslavije, 1965-1966; 1967, osnovni podaci; Comptabilité nationale yougoslave, 1965-1966; 1967, données fondamentales. Beograd, 1968. pp. 211. With French summary.

KITALJEVIĆ (BOŠKO) Sistem društvenih računa Jugoslavije i njegova evolucija. Zagreb, 1969. pp. 268. bibliog.

- Zambia - Accounting

FEDERATION OF RHODESIA AND NYASALAND. 1954. The national income and social accounts of Northern Rhodesia, 1945-1953. (Central African Statistical Office) Salisbury, 1954. pp. (iii), 70. 31½cm.

NATIONAL LIBERAL CLUB

NATIONAL LIBERAL CLUB. 80 years with the P and E, 1888-1968. London, 1968. pp. 26.

NATIONAL LIBERAL PARTY (GERMANY)

REISS (KLAUS PETER) ed. Von Bassermann zu Stresemann: die Sitzungen des nationalliberalen Zentralvorstandes, 1912-1917. Düsseldorf, Droste Verlag, [1967]. pp. 463. 24½cm. (Germany (Bundesrepublik). Quellen zur Geschichte des Parlamentarismus und der Politischen Parteien. 1. Reihe. Band 5)

NATIONAL MINORITY MOVEMENT

NATIONAL MINORITY MOVEMENT. National Minority Movement: constitution and structure. London, [192-?]. pp. 21.

NATIONAL MUNICIPAL LEAGUE

NATIONAL MUNICIPAL LEAGUE. Leaflets. No. 2. The National Municipal League: what it is doing, what others have to say about it. [Philadelphia] 1899. pp. 20.

NATIONAL MUNICIPAL LEAGUE. Leaflets. No. 4. What others are saying of the National Municipal League. [Philadelphia], 1900. pp. 27.

NATIONAL MUNICIPAL LEAGUE. The work of the League 1894-1905. [Philadelphia], 1905. pp. 20.

NATIONAL MUNICIPAL LEAGUE. Declaration of interdependence. New York, [1971]. 1 pamphlet (unpaged).

NATIONAL PARKS AND RESERVES

UNITED STATES. National Parks Service. First World Conference on national parks: proceedings, etc. Washington, [1964]. pp. xxiv, 471.

- Canada

LUCAS (PERCY HYLTON C.) Conserving New Zealand's heritage: report on a study tour of national park and allied areas in Canada and the United States. Wellington, Government Printer, 1970. pp. 94.

CANADIAN NATIONAL PARKS TODAY AND TOMORROW, CALGARY, 1968. Canadian parks in perspective; based on the conference...; [a selection from the papers prepared] edited by J.G. Nelson. Montreal, 1970. pp. 343.

- France

FRANCE. 1967. Nature conservation in France. (Ambassade de France, London). London, [1967]. pp. 15.

- Italy

SERRANI (DONATELLO) La disciplina normativa dei parchi nazionali. [Milan], 1971. pp. 306. bibliog. (Associazione per lo Sviluppo dell' Industria nel Mezzogiorno. Centro per gli Studi sullo Sviluppo Economico. Collana Francesco Giordani)

- New Zealand

NEW ZEALAND. Working Party on National Parks Administration in New Zealand. 1966. Report. [Wellington], 1966. pp. 71.

- Russia

EMEL'IANOVA (VALENTINA GEORGIEVNA) Zakonodatel'stvo o zapovednikakh, zakaznikakh, pamiatnikakh prirody. Moskva, 1971. pp. 62.

- South Africa

SOUTH AFRICA. Parliament. House of Assembly. Select Committee on the Paarl Mountain Disposal Bill. 1968. Report...(with Proceedings and Minutes of evidence). (S.C. 6-'68) in SOUTH AFRICA. Parliament. House of Assembly. Select Committee Reports.

- United Kingdom

PEAK PARK PLANNING BOARD. Peak District National Park Development Plan: first review; part 1: report and analysis of survey; part 2: written statement. [Bakewell], 1966. 2 pts. in 1.

NATIONAL TRUST FOR PLACES OF HISTORIC INTEREST OR NATURAL BEAUTY. Properties of the National Trust. London, 1969. pp. 247.

PEAK PARK PLANNING BOARD. The Peak: the story of a national park. [Bakewell], 1970. pp. 43.

JOHNSON (WARREN A.) Public parks on private land in England and Wales. Baltimore, [1971]. pp. 136. bibliog.

- United Kingdom - Ireland, Northern

IRELAND, NORTHERN. Nature Reserves Committee. Report for the year. Belfast, 1966/7 to date. in Ireland, Northern. Parliament. House of Commons. [Papers].

- United States

LUCAS (PERCY HYLTON C.) Conserving New Zealand's heritage: report on a study tour of national park and allied areas in Canada and the United States. Wellington, Government Printer, 1970. pp. 94.

NATIONAL PARTY (SOUTH AFRICA)

MALAN (MAARTEN PETRUS ALBERTUS) and VAN DER WALT (B. J.) Vrugte van die nasionale bewind 1948-1966. [Bloemfontein, Nasionale Party, 1966]. pp. 86.

NAUDÉ (LOUIS) Dr. A. Hertzog, die Nasionale Party en die mynwerker. Pretoria, [1969]. pp. 284.

NATIONAL SCHOOL OF LAW AND ADMINISTRATION (KINSHASA)

GOLAN (TAMAR) Educating the bureaucracy in a new polity: a case study of L'École Nationale de Droit et d'Administration, Kinshasa, Congo. New York, Teachers College P., [1968]. pp. xvi, 78. bibliog. 23cm.

NATIONAL SOCIALISM

BEYER (KARL) Die Ebenbürtigkeit der Frau in nationalsozialistischen Deutschland: ihre erzieherische Aufgabe; Vortrag, gehalten vor Hitlermädeln des Gaus Brandenburg am 7. Oktober 1932 in Potsdam. Leipzig, [1933]. pp. 21.

Die BRAUNHEMDEN im Reichstag: die nationalsozialistische Reichstagsfraktion 1932, VII. Wahlperiode; mit Abbildungen und Personalangaben der Mitglieder. München, 1933. pp. 154.

EWERS (HANNS HEINZ) Horst Wessel: ein deutsches Schicksal. Stuttgart, 1933. pp. 294.

HECKERT (FRITZ) Why Hitler in Germany?; the report of [the author], representative of the Communist Party of Germany, to the executive of the Communist International. London, [1933?]; Milano, 1967. pp. 48. Facsimile reprint.

PIATNITSKII (OSIP ARONOVICH) pseud. [i.e. Iosif Aronovich TARSHIS]. Die gegenwärtige Lage in Deutschland: ergänztes Stenogramm eines Referats in der "Internationalen Leninschule" vom...1933. 2nd ed. Hamburg, [1933]. pp. 104.

PIATNITSKII (OSIP ARONOVICH) pseud. [i.e. Iosif Aronovich TARSHIS] The present situation in Germany. London, 1933. pp. 44.

RELIEF COMMITTEE FOR VICTIMS OF FASCISM. The burning of the Reichstag; official findings of the legal commission of inquiry, London, Sept. 1933; chairman, D.N. Pritt. London, 1933. pp. 23.

ROSTEN (CURT) Das ABC des Nationalsozialismus. Berlin, 1933. pp. 226.

TROTSKII (LEV DAVYDOVICH) Qu'est-ce que le nazisme? Paris, [1933].

HITLER (ADOLF) Die Reden Hitlers als Kanzler: das junge Deutschland will Arbeit und Frieden. 3rd ed. München, Eher, 1934. pp. 64. 22cm.

KLINGER (MAX) Volk in Ketten: Deutschlands Weg ins Chaos. Karlsbad, Graphia, [1934]. pp. 104. 23cm.

[KRUEGER (OSKAR) ed.] 2. Mai 1933: die Befreiung des deutschen Arbeiters. München, 1934. pp. 216.

WENDT (HANS) Hitler regiert: Männer und Taten des ersten Jahres. 5th ed. Berlin, 1934. pp. 141.

FRIEDRICH (ERNST) Editor of Die Schwarze Fahne. Vom Friedensmuseum...zur Hitler-Kaserne: ein Tatsachenbericht über das Wirken von Ernst Friedrich und Adolf Hitler. Genf, 1935. pp. 187.

ROECKH (OTTO) Die Wahrheit über Danzig!: der Zusammenbruch des nationalsozialistischen Regimes. Wien, 1935. pp. 48.

LEY (ROBERT) Deutschland ist schöner geworden; herausgegeben von Hans Dauer und Walter Kiehl. Berlin, Mehden-Verlag, 1936. pp. xi, 275. 20cm.

DOERNER (CLAUS) ed. Freude, Zucht, Glaube: Handbuch für die kulturelle Arbeit im Lager; im Auftrage der Reichsjugendführung der NSDAP. Potsdam, [1937]. pp. 248. bibliog. 22cm.

HUDAL (ALOIS) Die Grundlagen des Nationalsozialismus: eine ideengeschichtliche Untersuchung. Leipzig, Günther, [1937]. pp. 294. bibliog. 21½cm.

VERMEIL (EDMOND JOACHIM) and GÉROME (PIERRE) L'Hitlérisme en Allemagne et devant l'Europe. Paris, Comité de Vigilance des Intellectuels Antifascistes, [1937.] pp. 95. 21½cm.

BOUHLER (PHILIPP) Kampf um Deutschland: ein Lesebuch für die deutsche Jugend. Berlin, 1938. pp. 107.

ENGLIŠ (KAREL) "Der deutsche Sozialismus" als Programm der Sudetendeutschen Partei: eine kritische Analyse;...Übersetzung aus dem Tschechischen. Prag, Orbis Verlag, 1938. pp. 102. 21cm.(Tschechoslowakische Quellen und Dokumente. Nr. 25)

FRANK (HANS) Nationalsozialistische Strafrechtspolitik. München, [1938]. pp. 50.

HITLER (ADOLF) Adolf Hitler, from speeches 1933-1938. Berlin, 1938. pp. 92. (Terramare Office. Publications. No. 8-10)

KOLLER (HELLMUT) Die nationalsozialistische Wirtschaftsidee im Völkischen Beobachter. München, [1989?]. pp. 175. bibliog.

NATIONALSOZIALISTISCHE DEUTSCHE ARBEITERPARTEI. Amt Schrifttumspflege. Ausstellung deutsche Grösse:...veranstaltet von der Dienststelle des Beauftragten des Führers für die Überwachung der gesamten geistigen und weltanschaulichen Schulung und Erziehung der NSDAP. München, 1940. pp. 395. bibliogs.

FOSTER (WILLIAM ZEBULON) and MINOR (ROBERT) The fight against Hitlerism. New York, 1941. pp. 32.

NATIONAL SOCIALISM (Cont'd.)

MASSON (P.R.) and JENSEN (BORGE) Hitler's policy is a Jewish policy: correspondence with a Jewish publicist. Liverpool, [1941]. pp. 23.

ECKART (DIETRICH) Dietrich Eckart: ein Vermächtnis; herausgegeben und eingeleitet von Alfred Rosenberg. 7th ed. München, Eher, 1942. pp. 252. 22cm.

BAEUMLER (ALFRED) Weltdemokratie und Nationalsozialismus: die neue Ordnung Europas als geschichtsphilosophisches Problem. Berlin, 1943. pp. 36. (Sonderdruck aus Internationale Zeitschrift für Erziehung, XI. Jahrgang, Heft 4/5, 1942)

INVESTIGATING COMMITTEE OF FREE JURISTS. Ex-Nazis in the service of the "German Democratic Republic". Berlin, [c.1945]. pp. 64.

HIPPEL (FRITZ VON) Die nationalsozialistische Herrschaftsordnung als Warnung und Lehre: eine juristische Betrachtung. Tübingen, Mohr, 1946. pp. 55. 23½cm. (Recht und Staat in Geschichte und Gegenwart. 129)

KERSTEN (FELIX) The Kersten memoirs, 1940-1945;...translated from the German by Constantine Fitzgibbon and James Oliver. London, 1956. pp. 314.

POLIAKOV (LÉON) and WULF (JOSEF) eds. Das Dritte Reich und seine Diener: Dokumente. Berlin-Grunewald, Arani, [1956]. pp. xv, 540. 23cm.

GOLLERT (FRIEDRICH) Dibelius vor Gericht. München, [1959]. pp. 193.

POLIAKOV (LÉON) and WULF (JOSEF) eds. Das Dritte Reich und seine Denker: Dokumente. Berlin-Grunewald, Arani, [1959]. pp. xi, 560. 23cm.

BEREND (IVÁN T.) and RÁNKI (GYÖRGY) Magyarország a fasiszta Németország "életterében", 1933-1939. Budapest, Közgazdasági és Jogi Könyvkiadó, 1960. pp. 221. 18½cm. With German summary.

GROSS (GUENTHER) Der gewerkschaftliche Widerstandskampf der deutschen Arbeiterklasse während der faschistischen Vertrauensräte-Wahlen 1934. Berlin, 1962. pp. 87. bibliog.

BENNECKE (HEINRICH) Die Reichswehr und der "Röhm-Putsch". München, Olzog, [1964]. pp. 93. bibliog. 23½cm. (Politische Studien. Beihefte. 2)

EVANGELISCHE Dokumente zur Ermordung der unheilbar Kranken unter der nationalsozialistischen Herrschaft in den Jahren 1939-1945. Stuttgart, [1964]. pp. 127. bibliog.

KAMIŃSKI (ANDRZEJ JÓZEF) Hitlerowskie obozy koncentracyjne i ośrodki masowej zagłady w polityce imperializmu niemieckiego. Poznań, Wydawnictwo Poznańskie, 1964. pp. 357. bibliog. 20½cm. With English summary.

FLITNER (ANDREAS) ed. Deutsches Geistesleben und Nationalsozialismus: eine Vortragsreihe der Universität Tübingen. Tübingen, [1965]. pp. 243.

BIBER (DUŠAN) Nacizem in nemci v Jugoslaviji, 1933-1941. Ljubljana, Cankarjeva Založba, 1966. pp. 480. 20cm.

Die DEUTSCHE Universität im Dritten Reich: acht Beiträge; [by] Helmut Kuhn [and others]. München, Piper, [1966]. pp. 282. 20½cm. (Piper Paperback)

FEYL (O.) Sozialdemokratischer Revisionismus und Reformismus und die Anfänge des "nationalen Sozialismus" in Böhmen. in Steinitz (Wolfgang) and others, eds. Ost und West in der Geschichte des Denkens und der kulturellen Beziehungen. Berlin, 1966.

JACOBSEN (HANS ADOLF) and JOCHMANN (WERNER) eds. Ausgewählte Dokumente zur Geschichte des Nationalsozialismus 1933-1945; [with] Kommentar). Bielefeld, [1966]. 3 vols. Vols. 1 and 2 are looseleaf.

OPPLER (FRIEDRICH) Das falsche Tabu: Betrachtungen über das deutsch-jüdische Problem. Stuttgart, Seewald, [1966]. pp. 331.

ROMANIK (FELIX) Österreichs wirtschaftliche Ausbeutung 1938-1945. Wien, Europa Verlag, [1966]. pp. 32. 19cm. (Dokumentationsarchiv des Österreichischen Widerstandes. Monographien zur Zeitgeschichte)

STEINMETZ (SELMA) Österreichs Zigeuner im NS-Staat. Wien, Europa Verlag, [1966]. pp. 64. bibliog. 19cm. (Dokumentationsarchiv des Österreichischen Widerstandes. Monographien zur Zeitgeschichte)

1967

AARSE (J.A.A.) and MARINUS (B.) "Houzee Kameraad!": een documentaire over de N[ationaal] S[ocialistische] B[eweging], etc. Amsterdam, 1967. pp. 299.

DEUTSCHE und Juden: Beiträge von Nahum Goldmann [and others]. Frankfurt a. M., [1967]. pp. 123.

FOERSTER (GERHARD) Totaler Krieg und Blitzkrieg: die Theorie des totalen Krieges und des Blitzkrieg in der Militärdoktrin des faschistischen Deutschlands am Vorabend des zweiten Weltkrieges. Berlin, 1967. pp. 256. bibliog. (Deutsche Akademie der Wissenschaften zu Berlin. Institut für Geschichte. Abteilung Militärgeschichte. Militärhistorische Studien. Neue Folge. 10)

GAIKIN (ALEKSANDR ABRAMOVICH) Germanskii fashizm. Moskva, 1967. pp. 399.

HAUG (WOLFGANG FRITZ) Der hilflose Antifaschismus: zur Kritik der Vorlesungsreihen über Wissenschaft und NS an deutschen Universitäten. Frankfurt a.M., Suhrkamp, 1967. pp. 159. bibliog. 17cm.

HEYEN (FRANZ JOSEF) compiler. Nationalsozialismus im Alltag: Quellen zur Geschichte des Nationalsozialismus vor-
nehmlich im Raum Mainz-Koblenz-Trier.
Boppard am Rhein, Boldt, [1967].
pp. xii, 372. 24cm.

KALOW (GERT) Hitler: das gesamtdeutsche
Trauma; zur Kritik des politischen
Bewusstseins. München, Piper, [1967].
pp. 135. 22cm.

KANTOROWICZ (ALFRED) Im 2. Drittel unseres Jahrhunderts: Illusionen, Irrtümer, Widersprüche,
Einsichten, Voraussichten. Köln, [1967]. pp.
216. 20½cm.

KESSEMEIER (CARIN) Der Leitartikler Goebbels in
den NS-Organen "Der Angriff" und "Das Reich".
Münster, Fahle, 1967. pp. 348. bibliog. 21cm.
(Münster in Westfalen. Westfälische Wilhelms-
Universität. Institut für Publizistik. Studien
zur Publizistik.Münstersche Reihe. Band 5)

NYOMARKAY (JOSEPH) Charisma and factionalism
in the Nazi Party. Minneapolis, University
of Minnesota Press, [1967]. pp. 161. bibliog.
23cm.

SCHMELZER (JANIS) Die braune Box: zu den
Anfängen der Zusammenarbeit; Monopole —
Nazismus — Neonazismus. Wolfen, 1967.
pp. 41.

SCHMELZER (JANIS) Europa-Patent: das IG-Farben
Projekt zur Neuordnung Europas. Wolfen, 1967.
pp. 51.

SODEIKAT (ERNST) Die Verfolgung und
der Widerstand der Katholischen
Kirche in der Freien Stadt Danzig
von 1933-1945. Hildesheim, 1967.
pp. 45. bibliog.

WERNER (KARL FERDINAND) Das NS-Geschichts-
bild und die deutsche Geschichtswissen-
schaft. Stuttgart, Kohlhammer, 1967.
pp. 123. 17½cm. (Lebendiges Wissen)

WISKEMANN (ELIZABETH) Undeclared war. 2nd ed.
London, Macmillan, 1967. pp. xiii, 332. 21½cm.

1968

CATHOLIC CHURCH IN GERMANY. Bishops.
Akten deutscher Bischöfe über die Lage
der Kirche, 1933-1945. Mainz, 1968
in progress. bibliog. (Katholische Akademie
in Bayern. Kommission für Zeitgeschichte.
Veröffentlichungen. Reihe A: Quellen. Band 5)

JUSTIZ und NS-Verbrechen: Sammlung deutscher
Strafurteile wegen nationalsozialistischer
Tötungsverbrechen 1945-1966; Redaktion: Fritz
Bauer [and others]. Amsterdam, University P.,
1968 in progress. 24cm.

ABEL (KARL DIETRICH) Presselenkung im
NS-Staat: eine Studie zur Geschichte der
Publizistik in der nationalsozialistischen
Zeit. Berlin, Colloquium, 1968. pp. xi,
172. bibliog. 23½cm. (Berlin. Freie
Universität. Friedrich Meinecke Institut.
Historische Kommission zu Berlin. Einzel-
veröffentlichungen. Band 2)

BLEUEL (HANS PETER) Deutschlands Bekenner:
Professoren zwischen Kaiserreich und
Diktatur. Bern, Scherz, [1968]. pp. 256.
bibliog. 20½cm.

BLUDAU (KUNO) Nationalsozialismus und Genossen-
schaften. Hannover, [1968]. pp. 240. bibliog.
(Friedrich-Ebert-Stiftung. Forschungsinstitut.
Schriftenreihe. B. Historisch-politische Schriften)
R : WA 8044

BRANDENBURG (HANS CHRISTIAN) Die Geschichte
der HJ: Wege und Irrwege einer Generation.
Köln, Wissenschaft und Politik, [1968].
pp. 348. bibliog. 20½cm.

BRECHT (BERTOLT) Schriften zur Politik
und Gesellschaft 1919-1956, etc.
Frankfurt am Main, Suhrkamp, 1968.
pp. 361,54. 19cm.

CONWAY (JOHN S.) The Nazi persecution of the
Churches, 1933-45. London, Weidenfeld &
Nicolson, [1968] pp. xxxi, 474. bibliog.
21½cm.

DUEWELL (KURT) Die Rheingebiete in der
Judenpolitik des Nationalsozialismus
vor 1942: Beitrag zu einer vergle-
chenden zeitgeschichtlichen Landeskunde. Bonn, Röhrscheid, 1968. pp.
328. bibliog. 23cm. (Bonn. Universität. Institut für Geschichtliche
Landeskunde der Rheinlande. Rheinisches
Archiv. 65)

EMMERICH (WOLFGANG) Germanistische Volkstumsideo-
logie: Genese und Kritik der Volksforschung
im Dritten Reich. Tübingen, 1968. pp. 368.
bibliog. (Tübingen. Universität. Ludwig Uhland
Institut für deutsche Altertumswissenschaft,
Volkskunde und Mundartenforschung. Volksleben.
20. Band)

GMAEHLE (PETER) Betriebswirtschaftslehre
und Nationalsozialismus. [Bamberg, imprint,
1968?]. pp. 291. bibliog.

GUELZOW (GERHARD) Kirchenkampf in Danzig 1934-1945:
persönliche Erinnerungen. Leer (Ostfriesl.),
[1968]. pp. 46.

HALBRITTER (KURT) Adolf Hitlers Mein Kampf: gezeichnete
Erinnerungen an eine grosse Zeit. [Frankfurt],
Bärmeier & Nikel, [1968]. pp. (238). 19cm.

HEINISCH (THEODOR) Österreichs Arbeiter für die
Unabhängigkeit, 1934 bis 1945. Wien, [1968].
pp. 39. (Dokumentationsarchiv des Österreichischen Widerstandes. Monographien zur Zeitgeschichte)

HEUSS (THEODOR) Hitlers Weg; eine Schrift
aus dem Jahre 1932...[reprinted] mit
einer Einleitung versehen von Eberhard
Jäckel. Tübingen, Wunderlich, [1968].
pp. i-liv, 168, lv-cxi. bibliog. 21cm.
Original subtitle: Eine historisch-
politische Studie über den Nationalsozialismus.

HOEPKE (KLAUS PETER) Die Deutsche Recht und der
italienische Faschismus: ein Beitrag zum Selbstverständnis und zur Politik von Gruppen und Ver-
bänden der deutschen Rechten. Düsseldorf, Droste,
[1968]. pp. 348. bibliog. 22cm. (Germany (Bundesr-
publik). Kommission für Geschichte des Parlamentarismus und der Politischen Parteien. Beiträge zur Geschichte des Parlamentarismus und
der Politischen Parteien. Band 38)

JASPER (GOTTHARD) ed. Von Weimar zu Hitler
1930-1933. Köln, Kiepenheuer & Witsch, 1968.
pp. 527. bibliog. 23cm. (Neue
Wissenschaftliche Bibliothek. 25)

NATIONAL SOCIALISM (Cont'd.)

KALOW (GERT) The shadow of Hitler: a critique of political consciousness;...translated from the German by Betty Ross. London, Rapp & Whiting 1968. pp. xii, 144. 21cm.

KEMPNER (ROBERT M. W.) Edith Stein und Anne Frank: zwei von Hunderttausend: die Enthüllungen über die NS-Verbrechen in Holland vor dem Schwurgericht in München: die Ermordung der "nichtarischen" Mönche und Nonnen. Freiburg im Br., 1968. pp. 189.

LANGE (KARL) Hitlers unbeachtete Maximen: "Mein Kampf" und die Öffentlichkeit. Stuttgart, [1968]. pp. 211.

MEIER (KURT) Kirche und Judentum: die Haltung der evangelischen Kirche zur Judenpolitik des Dritten Reiches. Göttingen, 1968. pp. 153. (Evangelische Kirche in Deutschland. Kommission für die Geschichte des Kirchenkampfes. Arbeiten zur Geschichte des Kirchenkampfes. Ergänzungsreihe. Band 7)

MORSEY (RUDOLF) ed. Das Ermächtigungsgesetz vom 24. März 1933. Göttingen, [1968]. pp. 84. bibliog.

PERTIET (MARTIN) Das Ringen um Wesen und Auftrag der Kirche in der nationalsozialistischen Zeit. Göttingen, Vandenhoeck & Ruprecht, 1968. pp. 339. bibliog. 23cm. (Evangelische Kirche in Deutschland. Kommission für die Geschichte des Kirchenkampfes. Arbeiten zur Geschichte des Kirchenkampfes. Band 19)

PETZINA (DIETER) Autarkiepolitik im Dritten Reich: der nationalsozialistische Vierjahresplan. Stuttga [1968]. pp. 204. bibliog. (Vierteljahrshefte zur Zeitgeschichte. Schriftenreihe. Nr. 16)

PFEIFER (EVA) Das Hitlerbild im Spiegel einiger rechtsgerichteter Tageszeitungen in den Jahren 1929-1933. 2nd ed. München, UNI-Druck, [1968]. pp. xi, 192. bibliog.

RUETHERS (BERND) Die unbegrenzte Auslegung: zum Wandel der Privatrechtsordnung im Nationalsozialismus. Tübingen, Mohr, 1968. pp. xx, 496. bibliog. 23cm.

SCHAEFER (GERHARD) and FISCHER (RICHARD)(Pfarrer,/eds. Landesbischof D. Wurm und der nationalsozialistische Staat 1940-1945: eine Dokumentation. Stuttgart, [1968]. pp. 507. bibliog. 23cm.

SIEWERT (CURT) Schuldig?: die Generale unter Hitler: Stellung und Einfluss der hohen militärischen Führer im nationalsozialistischen Staat, das Mass ihrer Verantwortung und Schuld. Bad Nauheim, Podzun, 1968. pp. 190. 20½cm.

VORLAENDER (HERWART) Kirchenkampf in Elberfeld, 1933-1945: ein kritischer Beitrag zur Erforschung des Kirchenkampfes in Deutschland. Göttingen, 1968. pp. 696. bibliog. (Evangelische Kirche in Deutschland. Kommission für die Geschichte des Kirchenkampfes. Arbeiten zur Geschichte des Kirchenkampfes. Ergänzungsreihe. Band 6)

WEINKAUFF (HERMANN KARL AUGUST) Die deutsche Justiz und der Nationalsozialismus: ein Überblick; [and] Die Umgestaltung der Gerichtsverfassung und des Verfahrens- und Richterrechts im nationalsozialistischen Staat; ([by] Albrecht Wagner). Stuttgart, Deutsche Verlags-Anstalt, 1968. pp. 383. 24cm. (Institut für Zeitgeschichte. Quellen und Darstellungen zur Zeitgeschichte. Band 16/1)

WILHELMI (HEINRICH) Die hamburger Kirche in der nationalsozialistischen Zeit, 1933-1945. Göttingen, 1968. pp. 326. (Evangelische Kirche in Deutschland. Kommission für die Geschichte des Kirchenkampfes. Arbeiten zur Geschichte des Kirchenkampfes. Ergänzungsreihe. Band 5)

WORMSER-MIGOT (OLGA) Le système concentrationnaire Nazi, 1933-1945. Paris, P.U.F., 1968. pp. vii, 660. bibliog. 24cm. (PARIS. Université. Faculté des Lettres et Sciences Humaines. Publications. Série Recherches. tome 39)

1969

ORLOW (DIETRICH) The history of the Nazi Party. Pittsburgh, [1969 in progress]. bibliog.

AIGNER (DIETRICH) Das Ringen um England: das deutsch-britische Verhältnis; die öffentliche Meinung 1933-1939; Tragödie zweier Völker. München, Bechtle, [1969]. 2 vols. bibliog. 22½cm.

ALBRECHT (GERD) Nationalsozialistische Filmpolitik: eine soziologische Untersuchung über die Spielfilme des Dritten Reichs. Stuttgart, 1969. pp. 562. bibliog.

ASSEL (HANS GUENTHER) Die Perversion der politischen Pädagogik im Nationalsozialismus. München, [1969]. pp. 156. bibliog.

BRACHER (KARL DIETRICH) Die deutsche Diktatur: Entstehung, Struktur, Folgen des Nationalsozialismus. Köln, Kiepenheuer & Witsch, [1969]. pp. vii, 580. bibliog. 23cm.

BREUNING (KLAUS) Die Vision des Reiches: deutscher Katholizismus zwischen Demokratie und Diktatur 1929-1934. München, 1969. pp. 403. bibliog.

BROCKDORFF (WERNER) Flucht vor Nürnberg: Pläne und Organisation der Fluchtwege der NS-Prominenz im "Römischen Weg". München, Welsermühl, [1969]. pp. 286. bibliog. 25½cm.

BROSZAT (MARTIN) Der Staat Hitlers: Grundlegung und Entwicklung seiner inneren Verfassung. München, 1969. pp. 472. bibliog.

CZARNIK (ANDRZEJ) Ruch hitlerowski na pomorzu zachodnim, 1933-1939. Poznań, 1969. pp. 172. (Polskie Towarzystwo Historyczne. Oddział w Słupsku. Biblioteka Słupska. t.22)

DEDEKE (DIETER) Das Dritte Reich und die Vereinigten Staaten von Amerika 1933-1937: ein Beitrag zur Geschichte der deutsch-amerikanischen Beziehungen. Bamberg, 1969. pp. 345. bibliog.

DIEHL-THIELE (PETER) Partei und Staat im Dritten Reich: Untersuchungen zum Verhältnis von N.S.D.A.P und allgemeiner innerer Staatsverwaltung 1933-1945. München, Beck, [1969]. pp. xv, 269. biblio 22cm. (Münch. Universität. Institut für Politische Wissenschaft. Münchener Studien zur Politik. 9. Band)

FABRY (PHILIPP WALTER) Mutmassungen über Hitler: Urteile von Zeitgenossen. Düsseldorf, 1969. pp. 265. bibliog.

FRIEDLANDER (SAUL) Counterfeit Nazi: the ambiguity of good;...translated from the French and German by Charles Fullman. London, Weidenfeld & Nicolson, 1969. pp. xvii, 228. 21½cm.

GERSTENBERGER (HEIDE) Der revolutionäre Konservatismus ein Beitrag zur Analyse des Liberalismus. Berlin, [1969]. pp. 171. bibliog. (Wilhelmshaven. Hochschule für Sozialwissenschaften. Sozialwissenschaftliche Abhandlungen. Heft 14)

GOERGEN (HANS PETER) Düsseldorf und der Nationalsozialismus: Studie zur Geschichte einer Grossstadt im Dritten Reich. Düsseldorf, [1969]. pp. 254. bibliog.

HAHN (HUGO) Bishop of Saxony. Kämpfer wider Willen: Erinnerungen des Landesbischofs von Sachsen D. Hugo Hahn aus dem Kirchenkampf 1933-1945; bearbeitet und herausgegeben von Georg Prater. Metzingen, [1969]. pp. 351.

HILDEBRAND (KLAUS) Vom Reich zum Weltreich: Hitler, NSDAP und koloniale Frage 1919-1945. München, 1969. pp. 955. bibliog. (Mannheim. Universität. Historisches Institut. Veröffentlichungen. Band 1)

JAECKEL (EBERHARD) Hitlers weltanschauung: Entwurf einer Herrschaft. Tübingen, Wunderlich, [1969]. pp. 160. 21cm.

JUNKER (DETLEF) Die Deutsche Zentrumspartei und Hitler 1932/33: ein Beitrag zur Problematik des politischen Katholizismus in Deutschland. Stuttgart, [1969]. pp. 247. bibliog.

KIMMEL (ADOLF) Der Aufstieg des Nationalsozialismus im Spiegel der französischen Presse 1930-1933. Bonn, 1969. pp. 218. bibliog.

KIRCHE und Nationalsozialismus: zur Geschichte des Kirchenkampfes; Beiträge von Helmut Baier [and others]. München, 1969. pp. 286. bibliog (Tutzing. Evangelische Akademie. Tutzinger Texte. Sonderbände. 1)

KRAUSE (WERNER) East German economist. Wirtschaftstheorie unter dem Hakenkreuz: die bürgerliche politische Ökonomie in Deutschland während der faschistischen Herrschaft. Berlin, 1969. pp. 247. (Deutsche Akademie der Wissenschaften zu Berlin Institut für Wirtschaftswissenschaften. Schriften. Nr. 31)

MESSERSCHMIDT (MANFRED) Die Wehrmacht im NS-Staat: Zeit der Indoktrination. Hamburg, [1969]. pp. 519. bibliog. 24cm.

MUELLER (KLAUS JUERGEN) Das Heer und Hitler: Armee und nationalsozialistisches Regime 1933-1940. Stuttgart, 1969. pp. 711. (Militärgeschichtliches Forschungsamt. Beiträge zur Militär- und Kriegsgeschichte. Band 10)

NEUMANN (GERD) Die Indoktrination des Nationalsozialismus in die Berufserziehung: Untersuchung zur Arbeits- und Erziehungsideologie während der Epoche zwischen 1933 und 1945. Hamburg, 1969. pp. 321. bibliog.

NIEMOELLER (WILHELM) Wort und Tat im Kirchenkampf: Beiträge zur neuesten Kirchengeschichte. München 1969. pp. 403.

PETERSON (EDWARD NORMAN) The limits of Hitler's power. Princeton, N.J., 1969. pp. 472. bibliog.

PHILLIPS (PETER) The tragedy of Nazi Germany. London, Routledge & Kegan Paul, 1969. pp. (viii), 241. bibliog. 21½cm.

REMAK (JOACHIM) ed. The Nazi years: a documentary history. Englewood Cliffs, [1969]. pp. 178.

RUEPPEL (ERICH GUENTER) Die Gemeinschaftsbewegung im Dritten Reich: ein Beitrag zur Geschichte des Kirchenkampfes. Göttingen, 1969. pp. 258. bibliog. (Evangelische Kirche in Deutschland. Kommission für die Geschichte des Kirchenkampfes. Arbeiten zur Geschichte des Kirchenkampfes. Band 22)

SAUER (PAUL) Die Schicksale der jüdischen Bürger Baden-Württembergs während der nationalsozialistischen Verfolgungszeit 1933-1945: statistische Ergebnisse. etc. Stuttgart, Kohlhammer, 1969. pp. xvi, 468. bibliog. 23½cm. (Baden-Württemberg. Staatlicher Archivverwaltung. Veröffentlichungen. Band 20)

SCHWARZ (WALTER) In den Wind gesprochen?: Glossen zur Wiedergutmachung des nationalsozialistischen Unrechts. München, 1969. pp. 95.

SPIEGEL (MARGA) Retter in der Nacht. Frankfurt/Main, [1969]. pp. 104.

STEINBERG (HANS JOSEF) Widerstand und Verfolgung in Essen 1933-1945. Hannover, [1969]. pp. 422. bibliog. (Friedrich-Ebert-Stiftung. Forschungsinstitut. Schriftenreihe. B. Historisch-politische Schriften)

TYRELL (ALBRECHT) ed. Führer befiehl...: Selbstzeugnisse aus der Kampfzeit der NSDAP; Dokumentation und Analyse. Düsseldorf, [1969]. pp. 403. bibliog.

UEBERHORST (HORST) ed. Elite für die Diktatur: die Nationalpolitischen Erziehungsanstalten 1933-1945: ein Dokumentarbericht. Düsseldorf, Droste, [1969]. pp. 441. 22cm.

WHEATON (ELIOT BARCULO) Prelude to calamity: the Nazi revolution, 1933-1935; with a background survey of the Weimar era. London, Gollancz, 1969. pp. xix, 523. bibliog. 21½cm.

1970

KERN (ERICH) pseud. [i.e. Erich Knud KERNMAYR] Adolf Hitler und seine Bewegung. Göttingen, [1970 in progress]. bibliog.

ANDRAE (FRIEDRICH) ed. Volksbücherei und Nationalsozialismus: Materialien zur Theorie und Politik des öffentlichen Büchereiwesens in Deutschland 1933-1945..Wiesbaden, 1970. pp. 200. (Deutscher Büchereiverband und Verein der Bibliothekare an Öffentlichen Büchereien. Beiträge zum Büchereiwesen. Reihe B. Quellen und Texte. Heft. 3)

DROEGE (FRANZ W.) Der zerredete Widerstand: zur Soziologie und Publizistik des Gerüchts im 2. Weltkrieg. Düsseldorf, [1970]. pp. 258. bibliog.

ECHTERHOELTER (RUDOLF) Das öffentliche Recht im nationalsozialistischen Staat. Stuttgart, 1970. pp. 343. (Institut für Zeitgeschichte. Quellen und Darstellungen zur Zeitgeschichte. Band 16/2)

FEST (JOACHIM C.) The face of the Third Reich;...translated from the German by Michael Bullock. London, 1970. pp. 402. bibliog.

HAGEMANN (JUERGEN) Die Presselenkung im Dritten Reich. Bonn, 1970. pp. 398. bibliog.

NATIONAL SOCIALISM (Cont'd.)

LINGELBACH (KARL CHRISTOPH) Erziehung und Erziehungstheorien im nationalsozialistischen Deutschland. etc. Weinheim, [1970]. pp. 341. bibliog.

MASER (WERNER VIKTOR) Hitler's Mein Kampf: an analysis...; translated by R.H. Barry. London, 1970. pp. 272. bibliog.

MATZERATH (HORST) Nationalsozialismus und kommunale Selbstverwaltung. Stuttgart, [1970]. pp. 503. bibliog. (Verein für Kommunalwissenschaften. Schriftenreihe. Band 29)

MOSSE (GEORGE L.) Germans and Jews: the Right, the Left and the search for a "third force" in pre-Nazi Germany. New York, 1970. pp. 260.

NOLTE (ERNST) Der Nationalsozialismus; [expanded version of a section of his Der Faschismus in seiner Epoche, published 1963]. Frankfurt/M, [1970]. pp. 250.

PLEWNIA (MARGARETE) Auf dem Weg zu Hitler: der völkische Publizist Dietrich Eckart. Bremen, [1970]. pp. 155. bibliog.

ROSENBERG (ALFRED) Grossdeutschland: Traum und Tragödie; Rosenbergs Kritik am Hitlerismus; [edited by Heinrich Härtle]. 2nd ed. München, [1970]. pp. 308.

SCHEEL (KLAUS) Krieg über Ätherwellen:...NS-Rundfunk und Monopole 1933-1945. Berlin, 1970. pp. 316. bibliog.

SCHLEUNES (KARL A.) The twisted road to Auschwitz: Nazi policy toward German Jews, 1933-1939. Urbana, [1970]. pp. 280. bibliog.

SCHOEPS (HANS JOACHIM) Bereit für Deutschland!: der Patriotismus deutscher Juden und der Nationalsozialismus; frühe Schriften 1930 bis 1939: eine historische Dokumentation. Berlin, [1970]. pp. 316.

SPEER (ALBERT) Erinnerungen. Berlin, 1969 repr. 1970. pp. 610.

SPEER (ALBERT) Inside the Third Reich: memoirs...; translated from the German by Richard and Clara Winston. London, 1970. pp. 596.

1971

AIGNER (DIETRICH) Die Indizierung "schädlichen und unerwünschten Schrifttums" im Dritten Reich. Frankfurt am Main, [1971]. cols. 933-1034. bibliog. (Sonderdruck aus dem Archiv für Geschichte des Buchwesens, Band XI, Lieferung 3-5, Frankfurt am Main 1971)

BRACHER (KARL DIETRICH) The German dictatorship: the origins, structure, and effects of National Socialism;...translated...by Jean Steinberg. London, 1971. pp. 553. bibliog.

BRANDT (WILLY) In exile: essays, reflections and letters, 1933-1947; translated from the German by R.W. Last; [with a] biographical introduction by Terence Prittie. London, [1971]. pp. 264.

CALIC (EDOUARD) Unmasked: two confidential interviews with Hitler in 1931. London, 1971. pp. 192. bibliog.

GANNON (FRANKLIN REID) The British press and Germany, 1936-1939. Oxford, 1971. pp. 314. bibliog.

GASMAN (DANIEL) The scientific origins of national socialism: social Darwinism in Ernst Haeckel and the German Monist League. London, 1971. pp. 208. bibliog.

GUS (MIKHAIL SEMENOVICH) Bezumie svastiki. Moskva, 1971. pp. 399.

KERN (ERICH) pseud. [i.e. Erich Knud KERNMAYR]. Meineid gegen Deutschland: eine Dokumentation über den politischen Betrug. Preussisch Oldendorf, [1971]. pp. 315.

PROEKTOR (DANIIL MIKHAILOVICH) Oruzhenostsy tret'ego reikha: germanskii militarizm, 1919-1939 gg. Moskva, 1971. pp. 197.

NATIONAL SOCIALISM
See also NATIONAAL-SOCIALISTISCHE BEWEGING IN NEDERLAND; also ANTI-NAZI MOVEMENT

- Congresses

HOFFMANN (HEINRICH) ed. Parteitag der Ehre: 73 Bilddokumente vom Reichsparteitag zu Nürnberg 1936. Berlin, [1936]. unpaged.

NATIONAL SOCIALISM IN LITERATURE

PFANNER (HELMUT F.) Hanns Johst: vom Expressionismus zum Nationalsozialismus. The Hague, 1970. pp. 326. bibliog.

RICHARD (LIONEL) Nazisme et littérature. Paris, 1971. pp. 202. bibliog.

NATIONAL SONGS

PRABHU (RAMCHANDRA KRISHNA) compiler. Songs of freedom: an anthology of national and international songs from various countries of the world. Bombay, Popular Prakashan, 1967. pp. xxxv, 513.

NATIONAL SONGS, ENGLISH

LONDON. London County Council Education Officer's Department. The national anthem: report by Education Officer submitting memoranda on the words and music of the national anthem by F. S. Boas and John E. Borland. London, 1916. pp. 21.

NATIONAL TRUST FOR PLACES OF HISTORIC INTEREST OR NATURAL BEAUTY

FEDDEN (HENRY ROMILLY) The continuing purpose: a history of the National Trust, its aims and work. London, Longmans, 1968. pp. xi, 226. 21½cm.

NATIONAL TRUST FOR PLACES OF HISTORIC INTEREST OR NATURAL BEAUTY. The National Trust: report by the Council's Advisory Committee on the Trust's constitution, organization and responsibilities, [chairman Sir Henry Benson]. [London], 1968. pp. 187. 24½cm.

NATIONAL TRUST FOR PLACES OF HISTORIC INTEREST OR NATURAL BEAUTY. Properties of the National Trust. London, 1969. pp. 247. 20cm.

NATIONALDEMOKRATISCHE PARTEI DEUTSCHLANDS (BUNDESREPUBLIK)

FREDERIK (HANS) ed. N[ationaldemokratische] P[artei] D[eutschlands]: Gefahr von Rechts? München, Verlag Politisches Archiv, [1966]. pp. 212. 20cm.

AUF dem Prüfstand der Demokratie: zur Analyse und geistigen Auseinandersetzung mit der NPD. Mainz, v. Hase und Koehler, [1967?]. pp. 64. 20½cm.

GOETZ (WOLFGANG) and BOSSLE (LOTHAR) Parolen und Realitäten: die NPD in Fragen und Antworten: Selbstzeugnisse Zitate, Urteile. Mainz, v. Hase und Koehler, [1967?]. pp. 96. 17cm.

KUEHNL (REINHARD) and others. Die N.P.D: Struktur. Programm und Ideologie einer neofaschistischen Partei. Berlin, Voltaire, [1967]. pp. vii, 260. 21cm.

RICHARDS (FRED H.) Die NPD: Alternative oder Wiederkehr?. München, Olzog, [1967]. pp. 160. 18cm. (Geschichte und Staat. Band 121)

DUVE (FREIMUT) ed. Die Restauration entlässt ihre Kinder; oder, Der Erfolg der Rechten in der Bundesrepublik. Reinbek bei Hamburg, Rowohlt, [1968]. pp. 184. 19cm.

LOMEIKO (VLADIMIR BORISOVICH) Есть ли шанс у нового Адольфа? Москва, 1968. pp. 208.

MAIER (HANS) and BOTT (HERMANN) Die NPD: Struktur und Ideologie einer nationalen Rechtspartei. 2nd ed. München, [1968]. pp. 99.

RUSSELL (EDWARD FREDERICK LANGLEY) 2nd Baron Russell of Liverpool. Return of the swastika? London, Hale, [1968]. pp. 197. 21½cm.

WINTER (FRANZ FLORIAN) Ich glaubte an die NPD. Mainz, Hase & Koehler, [1968]. pp. 136. 21cm.

BOCKEMUEHL (CHRISTIAN) Gegen die NPD: Argumente für die Demokratie. Bad Godesberg, [1969]. 1 vol. (unpaged). bibliog.

BROEDER (FRIEDRICH J.) Ein Sprachrohr des Rechtsradikalismus: die Deutschen Nachrichten; eine Studie zur Propagandatechnik und -methode. Mainz, [1969]. pp. 156. bibliog.

ESSAYS on modern politics and history, written in honor of Harold M. Vinacke; edited by Han-Kyo Kim. Athens, Ohio, [1969]. pp. 255.

KUEHNL (REINHARD) Deutschland zwischen Demokratie und Faschismus: zur Problematik der bürgerlichen Gesellschaft seit 1918. München, [1969]. pp. 186. bibliog.

KUEHNL (REINHARD) and others. Die NPD: Struktur, Ideologie und Funktion einer neofaschistischen Partei. Frankfurt am Main, 1969. pp. 397.

LIPPÓCZY (PIOTR) and SUŁEK (JERZY) Spadkobiercy swastyki. Warszawa, 1969. pp. 414. bibliog.

SCHMIDT (GISELHER) Hitlers und Maos Söhne: NPD und Neue Linke. Frankfurt am Main, [1969]. pp. 275. bibliog.

EFREMOV (ALEKSANDR EFREMOVICH) Korichnevaia ugroza. Moskva, 1970. pp. 152.

NAGLE (JOHN DAVID) The National Democratic Party: right radicalism in the Federal Republic of Germany. Berkeley, 1970. pp. 221. bibliog.

NATIONAL-DEMOKRATISCHE PARTEI DEUTSCHLANDS (D.D.R.)

STARITZ (DIETRICH) Die National-Demokratische Partei Deutschlands 1948-1953: ein Beitrag zur Untersuchung des Parteiensystems der DDR. Berlin, 1968. pp. 129. bibliog.

NATIONALISM

SCHNEE (HEINRICH) Nationalismus und Imperialismus. Berlin, [1928]. pp. 375.

ANDRÉ (PIERRE J.) Le réveil des nationalismes: la nouvelle évolution du monde. Paris, Berger-Levrault, 1958. pp. 464. 22½cm.

KOHN (HANS) Nationalism: its meaning and history. rev. ed. Princeton, [1965]. pp. 191. bibliog. 19cm.

SETON-WATSON (GEORGE HUGH NICHOLAS) Nationalism: old and new. Sydney, Sydney U.P., 1965. pp. 22. 21½cm. (Sydney. University. George Judah Cohen Memorial Lectures. 1964)

DEUTSCH (KARL WOLFGANG) and FOLTZ (WILLIAM J.) eds. Nation-building. New York, Atherton Press, 1966. pp. xix, 171. bibliog. 22cm. (Atheling Books)

IDEOLOGIIA... Идеология современного национально-освободительного движения. Москва, Наука, 1966. pp. 282. 20cm.

NATSIIA i natsional'nye otnosheniia. Frunze, 1966. pp. 143.

COUWENBERG (SERVATIUS WILLEM) Herlevend nationalisme: confrontatie met een oude uitdaging. Bilthoven, [1967]. pp. 79.

RIEDL (FRANZ HIERONYMUS) ed. Humanitas ethnica: Menschenwürde, Recht und Gemeinschaft: Festschrift für Theodor Veiter...dargebotenen zum 60. Lebensjahr. Wien, [1967]. pp. 427. bibliog. (Forschungsstelle für Nationalitäten- und Sprachenfragen. Ethnos. Band 5)

ROGACHEV (PETR MIKHAILOVICH) and SVERDLIN (MATVEI ABRAMOVICH) Нации, народ, человечество. Москва, 1967. pp. 189.

SINGH (HARMANDAR) ed. Nationalism after World War II. Jullundur City, Books International, India, 1967. pp. (iii), 106. 23½cm.

MOVEMENT FOR COLONIAL FREEDOM. Annual report. London annual, 1968 to date. 25½cm.

ASSOCIATION INTERNATIONALE DES SOCIOLOGUES DE LANGUE FRANÇAISE. 6e Colloque, Royaumont, 1965 Sociologie de la "construction nationale" dans les nouveaux états. Bruxelles, Université Libre, Institut de Sociologie, [1968]. pp. 376. 24cm. (Sociologie Générale et Philosophie Sociale)

NATIONALISM (Cont'd.)

BENAERTS (PIERRE) and others. Nationalité et nationalisme, 1860-1878. new ed. Paris, P.U.F., 1968. pp. 761. 21cm. (Peuples et Civilisations. Histoire Générale)

FOUGEYROLLAS (PIERRE) Pour une France féderale: vers l'unité européenne par la révolution régionale. [Paris], Denoël, [1968]. pp. 213. 21cm. (Collection Grand Format Médiations)

HENDERSON (JAMES LEWIS) and CALDWELL (MALCOLM) The chainless mind: a study of resistance and liberation. London, Hamilton, 1968. pp. 228. 21½cm. (Twentieth Century Themes)

IDEI... Идеи Октября и идеология национально-освободительного движения. Москва, 1968. pp. 183.

JOHNSON (HARRY GORDON) ed. Economic nationalism in old and new states. London, Allen & Unwin, 1968. pp. xiii, 145. 21½cm.

KOHN (HANS) Nationalism and realism, 1852-1879; volume II of a History of the European century, 1814-1917. Princeton, [1968]. pp. 191. bibliog.

LANGUAGE problems of developing nations: [papers prepared for a conference at Airlie House, Warrenton, Virginia, November 1-3, 1966, organized by the Committee on Sociolinguistics of the Social Science Research Council; edited by] Joshua A. Fishman [and others]. New York, Wiley, [1968]. pp. xvii, 521. bibliogs. 23cm.

LOTTE di liberazione e rivoluzioni in Africa nera, Egitto, Algeria, Cuba, Cina, Vietnam; ([by Gianni Sofri [and others]). Torino, Giappichelli, 1968. pp. xi, 359. 23cm. (Turin. Università. Facoltà di Magistero. Istituto di Storia. 4)

PONTEIL (FÉLIX) L'éveil des nationalités et le mouvement libéral, 1815-1848. new ed. Paris, P.U.F., 1968. pp. viii, 786. 21cm. (Peuples et Civilisations. 15)

SATYBALOV (ALLAUDIN ADZHAKOVICH) Metodologicheskie voprosy izucheniia istoricheskikh (etnicheskikh) tipov obshchnosti liudei. Leningrad, 1968. pp. 79.

SNYDER (LOUIS LEO) The new nationalism. Ithaca, N.Y., 1968. pp. 387.

KOTZÉ (DIRK JACOBUS) Nasionalisme, etc. Kaapstad. 1969-70. 3 vols. bibliog.

BOGUSH (EVGENII IUL'EVICH) Maoizm i politika raskola v natsional'no-osvoboditel'nom dvizhenii. Moskva, 1969. pp. 119.

DEUTSCH (KARL WOLFGANG) Nationalism and its alternatives New York, [1969]. pp. 200.

KALTAKHCHIAN (SUREN TIGRANOVICH) Ленинизм о сущности нации и пути образования интернациональной общности людей. Москва, 1969. pp. 461.

KIM (GEORGII FEDOROVICH) and KAUFMAN (ARKADII SERGEEVICH) Ленинизм и национально-освободительное движение. Москва, 1969. pp. 286.

LENGYEL (EMIL) Nationalism: the last stage of communism. New York, [1969]. pp. 369.

SULZBACH (WALTER) Die Zufälligkeit der Nationen und die Inhaltlosigkeit der internationalen Politik. Berlin, [1969]. pp. 170.

COHLER (ANNE M.) Rousseau and nationalism. New York, [1970]. pp. 212.

ISKENDEROV (AKHMED AKHMEDOVICH) Национально-освободительное движение: проблемы, закономерности, перспективы. Москва, 1970. pp. 391. bibliog.

LENIN... Ленин и национально-освободительное движение в странах Востока. Москва, 1970. pp. 504.

SMITH (ANTHONY DAVID STEPHEN) Nationalism and modernisation: a critical review of theories and typologies of nationalist movements; [Ph.D.(London) thesis]. 1970. fo. 588. Typescript: unpublished. This thesis is the property of London University and may not be removed from the Library.

BARCLAY (GLEN ST. JOHN) Twentieth century nationalism. London, [1971]. pp. 224. bibliog.

MILLER (NORMAN) Woodrow Wilson Fellow, Harvard University, and AYA (RODERICK) eds. National liberation: revolution in the third world. London, [1971]. pp. 307.

SMITH (ANTHONY DAVID STEPHEN) Theories of nationalism. London, 1971. pp. 344. bibliog.

LENINIZM i natsional'nyi vopros v sovremennykh usloviiakh. Moskva, 1972. pp. 567.

- Bibliography

DEUTSCH (KARL WOLFGANG) and MERRITT (RICHARD LAWRENCE) compilers. Nationalism and national development: an interdisciplinary bibliography. Cambridge, Mass., [1970]. pp. 517.

- Jews

HERMAN (SIMON N.) Israelis and Jews: the continuity of an identity. New York, [1970]. pp. 331. bibliog.

NATIONALISM AND EDUCATION

- Switzerland

CHEVALLAZ (GEORGES ANDRÉ) L'éducation du patriotisme: quelques réflexions. Lausanne, Payot, 1937. pp. 47. 23cm.

- Uganda

EVANS (DAVID R.) Teachers as agents of national development: a case study of Uganda. New York, 1971. pp. 245. bibliog.

NATIONALISM AND RELIGION

- Germany

WINCKLER (LUTZ) Martin Luther als Bürger und Patriot: das Reformationsjubiläum von 1817 und der politische Protestantismus des Wartburgfestes Lübeck, 1969. pp. 88. bibliog.

- Italy

GANAPINI (LUIGI) Il nazionalismo cattolico: i cattolici e la politica estera in Italia dal 1871 al 1914. Bari, 1970. pp. 224.

- Philippine Islands

DEATS (RICHARD L.) Nationalism and Christianity in the Philippines. Dallas, Southern Methodist U.P., [1967]. pp. xi, 207. bibliog. 23cm.

NATIONALISM AND SOCIALISM

NATIONAL-DEMOKRATISCHE PARTEI DEUTSCHLANDS. Nation und Nationalbewusstsein: einige Beiträge der National-Demokratischen Partei Deutschlands zur Entwicklung nationalen Denkens dabei Referat und Diskussionsbeiträge der Studientagung des Parteivorstandes... 1966, etc. Berlin, [1966]. pp. 154.

AGNELLI (ARDUINO) Questione nazionale e socialismo: contributo allo studio del pensiero di K. Renner e O. Bauer. Bologna, [1969]. pp. 249.

NATIONALLIBERALE PARTEI DEUTSCHLANDS
See LIBERAL PARTY - Germany

NATIVE RACES

BANNISTER (SAXE) Attorney General of New South Wales. Humane policy; or, Justice to the aborigines of new settlements essential to a due expenditure of British money, and to the best interests of the settlers, etc.; [reprint of the work first published in London in 1830]. London, Dawson, 1968. pp. vii, v-xii, 248, cclxxxii. 20cm. (Colonial History Series)

NATIVISM

LEONARD (IRA M.) and PARMET (ROBERT D.) American nativism, 1830-1860; [with documents]. New York, [1971]. pp. 185. bibliog.

NATIVISTIC MOVEMENTS.

MUEHLMANN (WILHELM EMIL) and others. Chiliasmus und Nativismus: Studien zur Psychologie, Soziologie und historischen Kasuistik der Umsturzbewegungen. Berlin, Reimer, [1961]. pp. 472. bibliog.

MUEHLMANN (WILHELM EMIL) and others. Messianismes révolutionnaires du tiers monde; traduit de l'allemand, etc. [Paris], Gallimard, [1968]. pp. 389. bibliogs. 22cm. (Bibliothèque des Sciences Humaines)

QUEIROZ (MARIA ISAURA PEREIRA DE) Réforme et révolution dans les sociétés traditionnelles: histoire et ethnologie des mouvements messianiques. Paris, Éditions Anthropos, [1968]. pp. xix, 394. bibliog. 19cm.

BURRIDGE (KENELM O. L.) New heaven, new earth: a study of millenarian activities. Oxford, 1969. pp. 191. bibliog.

- Africa, Subsaharan

BENZ (ERNST) ed. Messianische Kirchen, Sekten und Bewegungen im heutigen Afrika unter Mitarbeit von Ernst Dammann [and others]. Leiden, Brill, 1965. pp. x, 127. bibliog. 24½cm. (Zeitschrift für Religions- und Geistesgeschichte. Beihefte. 10)

NATURAL LAW

PILATI DI TASSULO (CARLO ANTONIO) L'esistenza della legge naturale impugnata sostenuta. Venezia, Zatta, 1764. pp. viii, 216.

CARRA (JEAN LOUIS) Système de la raison; ou, Le prophète philosophe. 3rd ed. Paris, Buisson, 1791; [Paris, Edhis, 1970]. pp. xvi, 84. Facsimile reprint.

DROSTE-HUELSHOFF (CLEMENS AUGUST MARIA ANTONIUS ALOYSIUS PAULUS VON) Baron zu Vischering. Lehrbuch des Naturrechts, oder der Rechtsphilosophie. Bonn, 1823; [Frankfurt am Main], 1970. pp. 280.

CHEVALLEY (E.) La théorie des différents ordres de lois, d'après Montesquieu, et son application à l'histoire: le divorce de Napoléon. Le Caire, [190-?]. pp. 163. 25cm.

GEIGER (OSCAR H.) Natural law in the economic world; address... at the Henry George Congress, ... New York, Sept. 13, 1927. New York, [1927?]. pp. 15.

GORDIS (ROBERT) The root and the branch: Judaism and the free society. Chicago, U. of Chicago P., 1962. pp. xv, 254. 21½cm.

KRUEGER (HERBERT) ed. Völkerrecht, Gewohnheitsrecht, Naturrecht: Referate zweier Seminare über die Problematik des Gewohnheitsrechts und seine Bedeutung als Völkerrechtsquelle. Hamburg, Metzner, 1967. pp. 295. 24cm. (Hamburg. Hansische Universität. Forschungsstelle für Völkerrecht und Ausländisches Öffentliches Recht. Hamburger öffentlich-rechtliche Nebenstunden. Band 1)

NEEDHAM (J.) Human law and the laws of nature. in Singh (Baljit) and Singh (Vidya Bhusan) eds. Social and economic change. Bombay, 1967.

ORDÓÑEZ NORIEGA (FRANCISCO) La fundamentación del derecho natural. Bogotá, Kelly, 1967. pp. 159. bibliog. 24cm.

BRENNER (GUENTER) Naturrecht und politische Ordnung. Mainz, v. Hase und Koehler, [1968]. pp. 99.

OSTROVSKII (IAKOV ARKAD'EVICH) ООН и права человека. Москва, 1968. pp. 191.

RUEPING (HINRICH) Die Naturrechtslehre des Christian Thomasius und ihre Fortbildung in der Thomasius-Schule. Bonn, 1968. pp. 191. (Bonn. Universität. Rechts- und Staatswissenschaftliche Fakultät. Bonner Rechtswissenschaftliche Abhandlungen. Band 81)

NATURAL LAW (Cont'd.)

SANDOVAL CAMPDERÁ (JUAN MARÍA) La solución del problema social institucional y privado; por la verdad, a la justicia social. Madrid, Aguado, [1968]. pp. 199. 21cm.

SCHELAUSKE (HANS DIETER) Naturrechtsdiskussion in Deutschland: ein Überblick über zwei Jahrzehnte 1945-1965. Köln, Bachem, 1968. pp. 384. bibliog. 22cm.

WATKINS (F.M.) Natural law and the problem of value-judgment. in Garceau (Oliver) ed. Political research and political theory. Cambridge, Mass., 1968.

HIPPEL (ERNST VON) Elemente des Naturrechts: eine Einführung. Berlin, 1969. pp. 147. bibliog

SAYAG (ALAIN) Essai sur le besoin créateur de droit. Paris, 1969. pp. 319. bibliog.

VECCHIO (GIORGIO DEL) Man and nature: selected essays...; Ralph A. Newman, editor; translated by A.H. Campbell. Notre Dame, [1969]. pp. 197.

CHIODI (GIULIO M.) Legge naturale e legge positiva nella filosofia politica di Tommaso Hobbes. Milano, 1970. pp. 197. (Milan. Università. Facoltà di Giurisprudenza Pubblicazioni. Serie 2a. Studi di Filosofia del Diritto.N.9)

LOSCHKE (JOHANNES) Das biologische Naturrecht: zugleich ein Beitrag zur Weltinnenpolitik und Friedensforschung. Varel, 1970. pp. 31.

PASSERIN D'ENTREVES (ALEXANDER) Natural law: an introduction to legal philosophy. 2nd ed. London, 1970. pp. 208.

NATURAL MONUMENTS

COWAN (I.M.) Conservation and man's environment. in Oehser (Paul Henry) ed. Knowledge among men. Washington, [1966].

- Law and legislation - Russia

EMEL'IANOVA (VALENTINA GEORGIEVNA) Zakonodatel'stvo o zapovednikakh, zakaznikakh, pamiatnikakh prirody. Moskva, 1971. pp. 62.

NATURAL OBLIGATIONS

WARNOTTE (DANIEL) Les origines sociologiques de l'obligation contractuelle. Bruxelles, Lamertin, 1927. pp. 119.

NATURAL RESOURCES

KNEESE (ALLEN V.) Economics and resource engineering. Washington, D.C., 1967. pp. irreg. (Reprints Series. No. 65) (Reprinted from Engineering Education, vol. 57, No. 10, June 1967)

DASMANN (RAYMOND FREDERICK) Environmental conservation. 2nd ed. New York, Wiley, [1968]. pp. xv, 375. 22½cm.

MACKAYE (BENTON) From geography to geotechnics;.. ited by Paul T. Bryant. Urbana, U. of Illinois P., 1968. pp. 194. 20½cm.

WATT (KENNETH E.F.) Ecology and resource management: a quantitative approach. New York, McGraw-Hill, [1968]. pp. xii, 450. bibliogs. (McGraw-Hill Publications in the Biological Sciences)

The ECOSYSTEM concept in natural resource management; edited by George M. Van Dyne; [papers of a symposium held at the annual meeting of the American Society of Range Management, 1968]. New York, 1969. pp. 383. bibliogs.

HERFINDAHL (ORRIS CLEMENS) Natural resource information for economic development...; a study sponored by the Latin American Institute for Economic and Social Planning, and Resources for the Future Inc. Baltimore, Johns Hopkins P., [1969]. pp. xv, 212. bibliog. 22½cm.

BARTELS (E.) Niet-zijn of welzijn: pleidooi voor een nieuw milieubeheer. Alphen aan den Rijn, 1970. pp. 210. bibliog.

CHICHVARIN (VLADIMIR AFANAS'EVICH) Okhrana prirody i mezhdunarodnye otnosheniia. Moskva, 1970. pp. 286. With brief English summary.

FAWCETT (JAMES EDMUND SANDFORD) International means of conservation of natural resources. London, [1970]. pp. 20.

- Bibliography

PAULSEN (DAVID F.) Natural resources in the governmental process: a bibliography, selected and annotated. Tucson, [1970]. pp. 99. (Arizona University. Institute of Government Research. American Government Studies. No.3)

FOOD AND AGRICULTURE ORGANIZATION. Documentation Center. 1971. Environment: (natural resources and the human environment: FAO publications and documents, 1967-1970); annotated bibliography; author and subject index. (DC/SP 21) [Rome], 1971. 1 vol. (unpaged)

- Research

INDIA. Committee on Natural Resources. 1962. [Report]. [New Delhi, 1962]. pp. 57.

INDIA. Committee on Natural Resources. 1965. [Report]. [New Delhi], 1965. pp. 30.

- America, Latin

ORGANIZATION OF AMERICAN STATES. Pan American Institute of Geography and History. Centro de Entrenamiento para la Evaluacion de Recursos Naturales. Programa de Cooperacion Technica de la Organizacion de los Estados Americanos. Proyecto 29. Los estudios sobre recursos naturales en las Americas. Mexico, 1953-54. 5 vols + 1 vol of maps.

ARGENTINE REPUBLIC. 1963. Comisión Económica para America Latina, C.E.P.A.L.: X periodo de sesiones Comite III, Industria y Recursos Naturales; conferencias de los delegados argentinos, representantes de las Secretarías de Estado de Industria y Minería y Energía y Combustibles. Buenos Aires, 1963. pp. 76. 17cm. For English summary see UNITED NATIONS Document No. E/CN.12/AC.55/SR.2,3.

GRUNWALD (JOSEPH) and MUSGROVE (PHILIP) Natural resources in Latin American development. Baltimore, [1970]. pp. 494.

- Argentine Republic

ARGENTINE REPUBLIC. Consejo Federal de Inversiones. 1961-1963. Evaluación de los recursos naturales de la Argentina (primera etapa). Vols 2-8. Buenos Aires, 1961-1963. 7 vols (in 9). bibliogs. 29½cm.

- Botswana

ROBERTS (SIMON) A restatement of the Kgatla law relating to land and natural resources. Gaborone, Government Printer, [1970]. pp. 33.

- Canada

CANADA. Department of Citizenship and Immigration. Canadian Citizenship Branch. Canadian Citizenship Series. [No. 4]. Our resources. Ottawa, 1963. pp. 132.

CANADA. Parliament. House of Commons. Standing Committee on National Resources and Public Works. Minutes of proceedings and evidence. Ottawa, irreg., Oct.29 1968 (28th Parl., 1st session no.2) to date, with gaps (28th Parl., 1st session, nos 5,7). 25cm.

CANADA. Department of the Secretary of State. Canadian Citizenship Branch. Canadian Citizenship Series. [No. 4]. Our resources. rev. ed. Ottawa, 1968. pp. 139.

LA FOREST (GERARD V.) Natural resources and public property under the Canadian constitution. [Toronto] [1969]. pp. 230.

ROBINSON (J. LEWIS) Resources of the Canadian Shield. Toronto, [1969]. pp. 136. bibliog.

RESOURCE management in the Great Lakes basin; edited by F.A. Butrico [and others]. Lexington, Mass., [1971]. pp. 190.

- Canada - Alberta

ALBERTA. Bureau of Statistics. 1968. Alberta industry and resources, 1968. Edmonton, 1968 pp. xii, 171. 28cm.

- Canada - Nova Scotia

RIMMINGTON (GERALD THORNEYCROFT) The resources of the Shubenacadie-Stewiacke area of Nova Scotia: a socio-economic study. Wolfville, Acadia University Institute, 1966. pp. vii, 96. bibliog. 28cm. ([Publications]. No. 23)

- Canada - Ontario

ONTARIO. Department of Commerce and Development. 1961. North Grey region conservation report, 1961: summary. Toronto, 1961. pp. 127. 24½cm.

ONTARIO. Department of Lands and Forests. Conservation Authorities Branch. 1962. Otter Creek conservation report, 1962. [Toronto], 1962. pp.x, 109. 25cm.

ONTARIO. Department of Lands and Forests. 1963. Ontario resources atlas. 4th ed. Toronto, 1963. fo. 33.

ONTARIO. Department of Lands and Forests. Conservation Authorities Branch. 1963. Big Creek region conservation report, 1963. [Toronto, 1963]. pp. x, 121. 25cm.

- Caribbean Area

CARLOZZI (CARL A.) and CARLOZZI (ALICE A.) Conservation and Caribbean regional progress. [Yellow Springs, Ohio., 1968]. pp. 151.

- Czechoslovakia

MĚKOTA (RUDOLF) Ochrana prírody v československom práve. Bratislava, SAV, 1968. pp. 199. bibliog. 20½cm. With Russian and German summaries.

- Egypt

AL SAYYAD (M.M.) Natural resources in the U.A.R. and their functional significance. in House (John William) ed. Northern geographical essays. Newcastle upon Tyne, 1966.

- India

INDIA. Committee on Natural Resources. 1962. [Report]. [New Delhi, 1962]. pp. 57.

INDIA. Committee on Natural Resources. 1965. [Report]. [New Delhi], 1965. pp. 30.

- Malawi

NYASALAND. Provincial Natural Resources Boards. Annual report. a., 1950 [1st], 1951. Zomba.

- Moldavian Republic

SHVARTS (KHANAN ISAAKOVICH) and TIUTEKIN (IURII IVANOVICH) Правовая охрана природы Молдавии: очерки советского природоохранительного права. Кишинев, 1964. pp. 296.

- New Zealand

NEW Zealand's wealth: studies in resource development and utilisation; edited by H.W.Bockemuehl. Palmerston North, N.Z., 1970. pp. 92.

- Nigeria

NIGERIA. (RIVERS STATE). Office of the Governor. Information Unit. 1968. Sources of wealth: the Rivers State. [Port Harcourt?, 1968]. pp. 42. 21cm.

- Roumania

PUIU (ALEXANDRU) Valorificarea superioară a resurselor naturale. București, 1969. pp. 299. bibliog. (Academia Republicii Socialiste România. Institutul de Cercetări Economice. Bibliotheca Oeconomica. 9) With English, French and Russian tables of contents.

- Russia

KOLOTINSKAIA (ELENA NIKOLAEVNA) Pravovaia okhrana prirody v SSSR: uchebnoe posobie dlia studentov-zaochnikov gosudarstvennykh universitetov; pod redaktsiei... N.D. Kazantseva. Moskva, 1962. pp. 194.

GEOGRAFICHESKIE problemy kompleksnogo razvitiia proizvoditel'nykh sil i osvoeniia estestvennykh resursov SSSR. Irkutsk, 1968. pp. 185. With English table of contents.

KURAZHSKOVSKII (IURII NIKOLAEVICH) Очерки природопользования. Москва, 1969. pp. 267. bibliog.

NATURAL RESOURCES - Russia (Cont'd.)

SHABAD (THEODORE) Basic industrial resources of the U.S.S.R. New York, 1969. pp. 393. bibliog

- Sierra Leone

SIERRA LEONE. 1961. White paper on natural resources policy. Freetown, [1961]. pp. 8.

- South Africa

SOUTH AFRICA. Natural Resources Development Council. 1964. Regional survey of the Western Cape Pretoria, 1964. fo. 113.

NATAL UNIVERSITY. Natal Regional Survey. vol. 14. The Umgeni-Umbilo-Umlazi rivers catchment areas: the Durban-Pietermaritzburg region; general editor O.P.F. Horwood. [Pietermaritzburg]. 1967-69. 2 vols. bibliogs.

- Switzerland

UNION DE BANQUES SUISSES. The natural resources and the industries of Switzerland. [Zurich, 1926]. pp. 35.

- United Kingdom

FAIRBROTHER (NAN) New lives, new landscapes. London, 1970. pp. 397. bibliog.

GOLDSMITH (EDWARD) ed. Can Britain survive? London, 1971. pp. 260. bibliogs.

- United States

PINCHOT (GIFFORD) The fight for conservation;...[reprint of the 1st ed. of 1910 with a new] introduction by Gerald D. Nash. Seattle, U. of Washington P., 1967. pp. xxvii, 152. 21½cm. (Americana Library)

UNITED STATES. White House Conference on Conservation 1962. Official proceedings. Washington, 1963. pp. iv, 103.

MURPHY (EARL FINBAR) Governing nature. Chicago, Quadrangle Books, [1967]. pp. xi, 333. bibliog. 21cm. (Problems of American Society)

FORD FOUNDATION. Ford Foundation grants in resources and environment. [New York, 1968]. pp. 22.

NASH (RODERICK) ed. The American environment: readings in the history of conservation. Reading, Mass. Addison-Wesley, [1968]. pp. xix, 236. bibliog. 21cm. (Themes and Forces in American History Series)

PATTON (DONALD J.) The United States and world resources. Princeton, Van Nostrand, [1968]. pp. 128. bibliog. 20cm. (Van Nostrand Searchlight Books. 39)

PENICK (JAMES) Progressive politics and conservation: the Ballinger-Pinchot affair. Chicago, U. of Chicago P., 1968. pp. xv, 207. bibliog. 20½cm.

HIGHSMITH (RICHARD MORGAN) and others. Conservation in the United States. 2nd ed. Chicago, [1969]. pp. 407.

OWEN (OLIVER S.) Natural resource conservation: an ecological approach. New York, [1971]. pp. 593.

RESOURCE management in the Great Lakes basin; edited by F.A. Butrico [and others]. Lexington, Mass., [1971]. pp. 190.

SMITH (GUY-HAROLD) ed. Conservation of natural resources;...contributors: Robert M. Basile [and others]. 4th ed. New York, [1971]. pp. 685. bibliogs.

- White Russia

ASTASHKIN (NIKOLAI DMITRIEVICH) Prirodnye resursy BSSR. Minsk, 1970. pp. 459. bibliog.

NATURAL SELECTION

LIMOGES (CAMILLE) La sélection naturelle: étude sur la première constitution d'un concept, 1837-1859. Paris, 1970. pp. 184. bibliog.

BAJEMA (CARL JAY) Natural selection in human populations: the measurement of ongoing genetic evolution in contemporary societies. New York, [1971] pp. 406. bibliogs.

NATURAL THEOLOGY

HUME (DAVID) the Historian. The natural history of religion;...with an introduction by John M. Robertson. London, 1889. pp. 75.

SEELEY (Sir JOHN ROBERT) Natural religion. 4th ed. London, 1895. pp. 305.

NATURALISM

FRIESS (H.L.) A naturalistic view of "functioning religiously". in Anton (John Peter) ed. Naturalism and historical understanding. Albany, [1967]

KURTZ (P.) Meta-metaphysics, the categories, and naturalism. in Anton (John Peter) ed. Naturalism and historical understanding. Albany, [1967].

STROMBERG (ROLAND N.) ed. Realism, naturalism, and symbolism: modes of thought and expression in Europe, 1848-1914. London, Macmillan, 1968. pp. xxxvi, 296. bibliog. 23cm. (Documentary History of Western Civilization)

WILLEMS (EDWIN P.) and RAUSH (HAROLD LESTER) eds. Naturalistic viewpoints in psychological research. New York, [1969]. pp. 294. bibliogs.

NATURALIZATION

- United Kingdom - Scotland

U.K. Parliament. The conference held the 25th day of February, anno 1606, betwene the Lords committees and the Commons, touching the naturalizinge of the Scots, etc. [first published in 1607]. in Somers (John) Baron Somers, and others, eds. A fourth collection of scarce and valuable tracts. vol. 1. London, 1752.

- United States

WIE man Bürger wird; Istruzioni per coloro che desiderano la naturalizzazione. In English, German and Italian. n.p., [c.1900]. pp. (7).

NATURE CONSERVATION

- United Kingdom

LUNN (A.G.) The distribution of countryside resources in northern England. in House (John William) ed. Northern geographical essays. Newcastle upon Tyne, 1966.

NAUCHNO-ISSLEDOVATEL'SKII FINANSOVYI INSTITUT

SITARIAN (STEPAN ARAMAISOVICH) ed. Эффективность общественного производства и финансы. вып. 2. Москва, Финансы, 1968. pp. 158. 20см.

NAUMANN (FRIEDRICH)

MEYER (H.C.) Naumann and Rathenau: Their paths to the Weimar Republic. in Krieger (Leonard) and Stern (Fritz Richard) eds. The responsibility of power. Garden City, 1967.

HAPP (WILHELM) Das Staatsdenken Friedrich Naumanns. Bonn, 1968. pp. 240. bibliog.

CHRIST (JUERGEN) Staat und Staatsraison bei Friedrich Naumann. Heidelberg, 1969. pp. 119. bibliog.

NAURU

- Politics and government

VIVIANI (NANCY) Nauru: phosphate and political progress. Canberra, 1970. pp. 215. bibliog.

NAUTICAL ALMANACS

SADLER (D.H.) Man is not lost: a record of two hundred years of astronomical navigation with 'The Nautical Almanac, 1767-1967. London, H.M.S.O., 1968. pp. 43. bibliog. 24½cm.

NAUTICAL TRAINING-SCHOOLS

[HANWAY (JONAS)] Proposal for county naval free-schools, to be built on waste lands, giving such effectual instructions to poor boys, as may nurse them for the sea service. [London, 1783]. pp. xxv, 141, 48. Lacking pp. v-viii. Bound with his Prudential, moral and religious advice, etc.

[HANWAY (JONAS)] Prudential, moral and religious advice, given to the respective scholars in the proposed naval free-schools, etc. [London, 1783]. pp. vii, 67. Bound with his Proposal for county naval free-schools, etc.

NAVAHO INDIANS

DYK (W.) Notes and illustrations of Navaho sex behavior. in Wilbur (George B.) and Muensterberger (Warner) eds. Psychoanalysis and culture: ...[reprint of the work first published in 1951]. New York, 1967.

KLUCKHORN (C.K.M.) and MORGAN (W.) Anthropologist. Some notes on Navaho dreams. in Wilbur (George B.) and Muensterberger (Warner) eds. Psychoanalysis and culture:...[reprint of the work first published in 1951]. New York, 1967.

UNITED STATES. 12705-2. An analysis of sources of information on the population of the Navaho. Washington, 1966. pp. v, 220. bibliog.

KLUCKHOHN (CLYDE KAY MABEN) Navaho witchcraft; [reprint of the 1944 edition with additions]. Boston, Beacon P., 1967. pp. xxii, 254. bibliog. 20½cm.

GILPIN (LAURA) The enduring Navaho. Austin, [1968]. pp. 263. bibliog.

- Government relations

KELLY (LAWRENCE C.) The Navajo Indians and federal Indian policy, 1900-1935. [Tucson], U. of Arizona P., [1968]. pp. x, 221. bibliog. 22½cm.

NAVAL ART AND SCIENCE

- Dictionaries

GRUSS (R.) Petit dictionnaire de la marine. 2nd ed. Paris, Challamel, 1945. pp. 211, 88 plates, viii. 18½cm.

NAVAL RESEARCH

- Belgium

CENTRE BELGE DE RECHERCHES NAVALES. La recherche en constructions navales en Belgique depuis 1949: vingt années d'activité du Ceberena, 1949-1968. Bruxelles, 1968. pp. 53.

NAVICERT SYSTEM

STOEDTER (ROLF) Handelskontrolle im Seekrieg: prisenrechtliche Betrachtungen zum Navicert-System. Hamburg, [1940]. pp. 83.

STEINICKE (DIETRICH) Kriegsbedingte Risiken der neutralen Seeschiffahrt: die Annahme eines Navicerts als feindselige Unterstützung; ein Beitrag zur Entwicklung des Instituts der feindseligen Unterstützung im modernen Seerecht. Hamburg, Hansische Universität, Forschungsstelle für Völkerrecht und Ausländisches Öffentliches Recht, 1968. pp. (iv), 51. bibliog. 23½cm. (Werkhefte. 5)

NAVIGATION

SADLER (D.H.) Man is not lost: a record of two hundred years of astronomical navigation with 'The Nautical Almanac, 1767-1967. London, H.M.S.O., 1968. pp. 43. bibliog. 24½cm.

NAVY-YARDS AND NAVAL STATIONS, AMERICAN

- Cuba

The U.S. naval base at Guantanamo: imperialist outpost in the heart of Cuba. Havana, [196-]. pp. 52.

NAYÓN

BEALS (RALPH LEON) Community in transition: Nayón-Ecuador. Los Angeles, University of California, Latin American Center, 1966. pp. 233. bibliog. 23cm. (Latin American Studies. vol. 2)

NDENDEULIS

GULLIVER (PHILIP HUGH) Neighbours and networks: the idiom of kinship in social action among the Ndendeuli of Tanzania. Berkeley, 1971. pp. 366. bibliog.

NDENI

- Social conditions

DAVENPORT (W.) Social structure of Santa Cruz island. in Goodenough (Ward Hunt) ed. Explorations in cultural anthropology. New York, [1964].

NE WIN

MAUNG, Maung. Burma and General Ne Win. London, [1969]. pp. 332. bibliog.

NEBRASKA

- Legislature

BRECKENRIDGE (ADAM CARLYLE) One house for two: Nebraska's unicameral legislature;... introduction by Frank Bane. Washington, Public Affairs Press, [1957]. pp. xi, 98. bibliog. 23cm.

- Politics and government

LUEBKE (FREDERICK C.) Immigrants and politics: the Germans of Nebraska, 1880-1900. Lincoln, Nebraska, [1969]. pp. 220. bibliog.

NECESSITY (LAW)

- Russia

PASHE-OZERSKII (NIKOLAI NIKOLAEVICH) Необходимая оборона и крайняя необходимость по советскому уголовному праву. Москва, Госюриздат, 1962. pp. 181. 20cm.

SHAVGULIDZE (TAMAZ GRIGOR'EVICH) Neobkhodimaia oborona. Tbilisi, 1966. pp. 158.

IAKUBOVICH (MARK IOSIFOVICH) Uchenie o neobkhodimoi oborone v sovetskom ugolovnom prave. Moskva, 1967. pp. 100.

TISHKEVICH (IVAN STANISLAVOVICH) Usloviia i predely neobkhodimoi oborony. Moskva, 1969. pp. 190.

NECKAR

- Navigation

MAUSHARDT (VOLKER) Die Neckarkanalisierung und ihre raumwirtschaftlichen Auswirkungen. Düsseldorf, Verlag Handelsblatt, 1966. pp. 120. bibliog. 24cm. (Cologne. Universität. Institut für Verkehrswissenschaft. Buchreihe. Nr.20)

NECKAR RIVER

- Regulation

SPAETH (RUDOLF) Die verkehrswirtschaftliche Bedeutung der Neckarkanalisierung im Raum Heilbronn-Plochingen. Karlsruhe, 1966. pp. 149. bibliog.

NEDERLANDS INSTITUUT VOOR PRAEVENTIEVE GENEESKUNDE
See NETHERLANDS INSTITUTE FOR PREVENTIVE MEDICINE

NEDERLANDSCH ZUID-AFRIKAANSCHE VEREENIGING

NEDERLAND-Zuid-Afrika: gedenkboek uitgegeven door de Nederlandsch Zuid-Afrikaansche Vereeniging bij gelegenheit van haar vijftig-jarig bestaan, 1881-1931. Amsterdam, 1931. pp. 279.

NEDERLANDSCHE BANK

JONGMAN (C.D.) De monetaire politiek van de Nederlandsche Bank tijdens het presidentschap van M.W. Holtrop. Amsterdam, 1968. pp. 66. (Nederlands Instituut voor het Bank- en Effectenbedrijf. Publikaties. Nr. 1)

NEGEV

EVENARI (MICHAEL) and others. The Negev: the challenge of a desert. Cambridge, Mass., 1971. pp. 345. bibliog.

- Population

MUHSAM (H.V.) Beduin of the Negev: eight demographic studies. Jerusalem, Jerusalem Academic P., 1966. pp. 123.

NEGLIGENCE

HOFFMANN (HANS JOACHIM) Die Abstufung der Fahrlässigkeit in der Rechtsgeschichte, unter besonderer Berücksichtigung der culpa levissima. Berlin, 1968. pp. 218. bibliog. (Cologne. Universität. Rechtswissenschaftliche Fakultät. Neue-Kölner Rechtswissenschaftliche Abhandlungen. Heft 54)

- Poland

BUCHAŁA (KAZIMIERZ) Bezprawność przestępstw nieumyślnych oraz wyłączające ją dozwolone ryzyko. Warszawa, 1971. pp. 271. With Russian and German summaries.

- United Kingdom

FARNDALE (WILLIAM ARTHUR JAMES) Medical negligence. Beckenham, 1969. pp. 36.

NEGOTIABLE INSTRUMENTS

BAXTER (NEVINS D.) The commercial paper market. Boston, Bankers Publishing Company, [1966]. pp. xv, 153. 22½cm.

NEGOTIATION

PRUITT (DEAN G.) and DREWS (JULIE LATANÉ) The effect of time pressure, time elapsed, and the opponent's concession rate on behavior in negotiation;...to the Office of Naval Research, Washington, D.C. Buffalo, State University of New York, Department of Psychology, 1967. fo. 40. 28cm. (Studies of the Dynamics of Cooperation and Conflict. Technical Reports. No. 3)

YOUNG (ORAN R.) The politics of force: bargaining during international crises. Princeton, Princeton U.P., 1968. pp. xii. 438. 21½cm.

CROSS (JOHN G.) The economics of bargaining. New York, [1969]. pp. 247.

KAPOOR (ASHOK) International business negotiations: a study in India. New York, 1970. pp. 361. bibliog.

NEGRI SEMBILAN

- Politics and government

NEGRI SEMBILAN. Administration report. Kuala Lumpur annual, 1920, 1923, 1924, 1929, 1930. 33cm.

NEGRO ATHLETES

EDWARDS (HARRY) The revolt of the black athlete. New York, [1969]. pp. 202.

NEGRO CHILDREN

BAUGHMAN (E. EARL) and DAHLSTROM (W. GRANT) Negro and white children: a psychological study in the rural South. New York, Academic P., 1968. pp. xxv, 572. 22½cm. (Social Psychology)

KOZOL (JONATHAN) Death at an early age: the destruction of the hearts and minds of Negro children in the Boston public schools. Harmondsworth, Penguin Books, 1968. pp. 223. 18cm. (Penguin Education Specials. X38)

TRUBOWITZ (JULIUS) Changing the racial attitudes of children: the effects of an activity group program in New York City schools. New York, [1969]. pp. 228. bibliog.

McDONALD (MARJORIE) Not by the color of their skin: the impact of racial differences on the child's development. New York, [1970]. pp. 242. bibliog.

NEGRO LITERATURE

FABRE (MICHEL) ed. Les noirs américains. Paris, Colin, [1967]. pp. 320. 16½cm. (Collection U/U2. Série "Études Anglo-américaines". 5)

NEGRO PRESS

DANN (MARTIN E.) ed. The black press, 1827-1890: the quest for national identity. New York, [1971]. pp. 384.

NEGRO RACE

HOLLY (JAMES THEODORE) and HARRIS (J. DENNIS) Black separatism and the Caribbean, 1860;...edited, with an introduction, by Howard H. Bell; [reprint of works first published in 1857 and 1860]. Ann Arbor, [1970]. pp. 184.

GARVEY (MARCUS) Minutes of proceedings of the meeting held at the Royal Albert Hall...June 6th, 1928, at 8 o'clock; speech presenting the case of the negro for international racial adjustment; [with new introduction by G.K. Osei]. London, 1928 [repr. 1968?]. pp. 30.

PAN-AFRICAN CONGRESS. 5th Congress, 1945. Colonial and coloured unity: a programme of action; history of the...Congress; edited by George Padmore. 2nd ed. London, Hammersmith Bookshop, 1963. pp. vi, 74. bibliog. 21½cm.

OSEI (GABRIEL K.) Fifty unknown facts about the African: with complete proof. London, African Publication Society, 1966. pp. 22. 21½cm.

LARSEN (MAY) and LARSEN (HENRY) Lointain tam-tam. Neuchâtel, La Baconnière, [1967]. pp. 199. bibliog. 21½cm.

TIMES NEWS TEAM. The black man in search of power: a survey of the black revolution across the world. London, Nelson, 1968. pp. (vi), 182. 21½cm.

DU BOIS (WILLIAM EDWARD BURGHARDT) The Negro; with a new introduction by George Shepperson. London, 1970. pp. 157. bibliog.

EGBUNA (OBI B.) Destroy this temple: the voice of black power in Britain. London, 1971. pp 157.

UYA (OKON EDET) ed. Black brotherhood: Afro-Americans and Africa. Lexington, [1971]. pp. 282. bibliogs.

- History

MALCOLM X, pseud. [i.e. Malcolm LITTLE]. Malcolm X on Afro-American history: expanded and illustrated edition. New York, 1970. pp. 74.

- Psychology - Bibliography

SOUTH AFRICA. 1966. Aptitudes and abilities of the black man in Sub-Saharan Africa, 1784-1963: an annotated bibliography; compiled by L.E.Ander; with an introduction by W.Hudson. (National Institute for Personnel Research) Johannesburg, 1966. pp. 174. bibliog.

NEGRO SONGS

CARAWAN (GUY) and CARAWAN (CANDIE) eds. Freedom is a constant struggle: songs of the freedom movement. New York, [1968]. pp. 224.

NEGRO STUDENTS

EDWARDS (HARRY) Black students. New York, [1970]. pp. 234. bibliog.

NEGRO TEACHERS

SCHULTZ (MICHAEL JOHN) The National Education Association and the black teacher. Coral Gables, Fla., [1970]. pp. 224.

NEGROES

FRAZIER (EDWARD FRANKLIN) Negro youth at the crossways: their personality development in the middle states;[reprint of the original edition of 1940] with an introduction by St. Clair Drake. New York, Schocken Books. 1967. pp xxxv, 299.. 20cm.

FRASER (R.S.) Marxist. For the materialist conception of the Negro question;...reprinted from S.W.P. Discussion Bulletin A-30, August, 1955. New York, Spartacist, [1964?]. fo. 26. 28cm. (Marxist Bulletins. No. 5)

BONTEMPS (ARNA) and CONROY (JACK) Anyplace but here; [originally published as 'They seek a city', 1945]. [rev. ed.] New York, Hill & Wang, 1966. pp. ix, 372. bibliog. 20cm. (American Century Series)

FABRE (MICHEL) ed. Les noirs américains. Paris, Colin, [1967]. pp. 320. 16½cm. (Collection U/U2. Série "Études Anglo-américaines". 5)

NEGROES (Cont'd.)

MORRIS (RICHARD THACKER) and JEFFRIES (VINCENT) The white reaction study. Los Angeles, 1967. pp. 71,43. (California University. Institute of Government and Public Affairs. [Publications]. MR-84)

MYRDAL (GUNNAR) The racial crisis in perspective: introductory lecture to symposium, University of California, Los Angeles, May 24, 1967. Stockholm, 1967. fo. 11.

SEABROOK (ISAAC DUBOSE) Before and after: or, The relations of the races at the South;...edited...by John Hammond Moore. Baton Rouge, Louisiana State U.P., [1967]. pp. vii, 157. 22½cm.

BILLINGSLEY (ANDREW) and BILLINGSLEY (AMY TATE) Black families in white America. Englewood Cliffs, Prentice-Hall, [1968]. pp. v, 218. 20cm. (Spectrum Books. S-189)

EPPS (ARCHIE) ed. The speeches of Malcolm X at Harvard. New York, Morrow, 1968. pp. 191, 20½cm.

FRAZIER (EDWARD FRANKLIN) E. Franklin Frazier on race relations: selected writings, edited and with an introduction by G. Franklin Edwards. Chicago, U. of Chicago P., 1968. pp. xx, 331. bibliog. 20cm. (The Heritage of Sociology)

GOLDSTON (ROBERT) The negro revolution. New York, Macmillan, [1968]. pp. (iii), 248. bibliog. 23cm.

KILLIAN (LEWIS MARTIN) The impossible revolution?: black power and the American dream. New York, Random House, [1968]. pp. xx, 198. bibliog. 20cm. (Studies in Sociology)

MUSE (BENJAMIN) The American negro revolution: from nonviolence to Black Power, 1963-1967. Bloomington, Indiana U.P., [1968]. pp. xiii, 345. 21cm.

SCHUCHTER (ARNOLD) White power - black freedom: planning the future of urban America. Boston, Beacon P., [1968]. pp. xvii, 650. bibliog. 20cm.

SLOAN (IRVING J.) The American negro: a chronology and fact book. 2nd ed. Dobbs Ferry, Oceana Publications, 1968. pp. xii, 112. bibliog. 23cm.

WRIGHT (NATHAN) Ready to riot. New York, Holt, [1968]. pp. (v), 148. 21cm.

BLACK anti-semitism and Jewish racism; [by] James Baldwin [and others]. New York, 1969. pp. 237.

BULLOCK (PAUL) ed. Watts: the aftermath; an inside view of the ghetto, by the people of Watts; edited, with an introduction, notes, and a concluding chapter. New York, [1969]. pp. 285.

CLEAVER (ELDRIDGE) Soul on ice. London, Cape, 1969. pp. xv, 210. 21½cm.

CRUDEN (ROBERT) The negro in reconstruction. Englewood Cliffs, N.J., [1969]. pp. 182. bibliog.

HILL (ADELAIDE CROMWELL) and KILSON (MARTIN) eds. Apropos of Africa: sentiments of negro American leaders on Africa from the 1800s to the 1950s. London, Cass, 1969. pp. xiv, 390. 21½cm. (Africana Modern Library. No. 7)

KATZ (IRWIN) and GURIN (PATRICIA) eds. Race and the social sciences. New York, [1969]. pp. 387.

LUZIK (KIRILL STEPANOVICH) Положение негров в США, 1950-1960 гг. Киев, 1969. pp. 218.

McKISSICK (FLOYD) Three-fifths of a man. London, [1969]. pp. 223. bibliog.

PELLEGRINI (EDGARDO) L'informazione negata: controgiornale afro-americano. Bari, 1969. pp. 277.

PICCIONI (LEONE) Troppa morte, troppa vita: viaggi e pensieri intorno agli USA. Firenze, 1969. pp. 199.

REDKEY (EDWIN S.) Black exodus: black nationalist and back-to-Africa movements, 1890-1910. New Haven, 1969. pp. 319. bibliog.

UNITED STATES. Census Bureau. Changing characteristics of the negro population: (a 1960 census monograph). Washington, 1969. pp. 259.

ALEXANDER (RAE PACE) and LESTER (JULIUS) eds. Young and black in America: [personal accounts by Frederick Douglass and others]; compiled by Rae Pace Alexander; introductory notes by Julius Lester. New York, [1970]. pp. 139. bibliog.

ALTSHULER (ALAN A.) Community control: the black demand for participation in large American cities. New York, [1970]. pp. 238.

BAKER (ROSS K.) ed. The Afro-American: readings. New York, [1970]. pp. 462.

The BLACK experience in America: selected essays; edited by James C. Curtis and Lewis L. Gould. Austin, [Texas]. [1970]. pp. 199.

CHACE (WILLIAM M.) and COLLIER (PETER) eds. Justice denied: the black man in white America; [an anthology]. New York, [1970]. pp. 548.

DUBOIS (WILLIAM EDWARD BURGHARDT) W.E.B. Du Bois speaks: speeches and addresses, 1890-(1963); edited by Dr. Philip S. Foner. New York, 1970. 2 vols. (in 1).

GLENN (NORVAL D.) and BONJEAN (CHARLES M.) eds. Blacks in the United States; ...expanded from The Social Science Quarterly, December, 1968. San Francisco, [1969]. pp. 621. bibliogs.

GREEN (ELY) Ely: too black, too white;... edited by Elizabeth N. and Arthur Ben Chitty. Amherst, 1970. pp. 637.

COLEMAN (JAMES SAMUEL) Resources for social change race in the United States. New York, [1971]. pp. 119. bibliog.

JACKSON (GEORGE LESTER) Soledad brother: the prison letters of George Jackson; introduction by Jean Genet. London, 1971. pp. 290.

UYA (OKON EDET) ed. Black brotherhood: Afro-Americans and Africa. Lexington, [1971]. pp. 282. bibliogs.

- Bibliography

WEST (EARLE H.) compiler. A bibliography of doctoral research on the Negro, 1933-1966. [Ann Arbor], 1969. pp. 134.

MILLER (ELIZABETH WILLIAMS) compiler. The negro in America: a bibliography;...second edition, revised and enlarged...by Mary L. Fisher. Cambridge Mass., 1970. pp. 351.

UNITED STATES. Library of Congress. The negro in the United States: a selected bibliography. Washington, 1970. pp. 313.

- Biography

METCALF (GEORGE R.) Black profiles. New York, McGraw-Hill, [1968]. pp. x, 341. bibliog. 21cm.

LOOK for me in the whirlwind: the collective autobiography of the New York 21; by Kuwasi Balagoon [and others]. New York, 1971. pp. 364.

- Civil rights

BAKER (RAY STANNARD) Following the color line; American Negro citizenship in the Progressive era; [reprint of work originally published in 1908, with corrections and a new introduction]. New York, 1964. pp. 311.

SAUNDERS (JOHN) of the Socialist Workers Party, and PARKER (ALBERT) The struggle for Negro equality. 3rd ed. New York, Pioneer Publishers, 1945. pp. 47. 20½cm.

SOCIALIST WORKERS PARTY (UNITED STATES). The class-struggle road to Negro equality. New York, Pioneer Publishers, 1957. pp. 23. 21½cm.

LYNN (CONRAD J.) Monroe, North Carolina: turning point in American history; two speeches. Detroit, Correspondence Publishing Co., [1962]. pp. 26. 19cm. (Correspondence Pamphlets. 5)

CRUSE (HAROLD) and others. Marxism and the negro struggle. New York, 1965 repr. 1969. pp. 46.

BUNDY (McGEORGE) Action for equal opportunity. New York, Ford Foundation, 1966. pp. 12. 23cm.

MALCOLM X, pseud. [i.e. Malcolm LITTLE]. Malcolm X speaks: selected speeches and statements. London, 1966. pp. 226.

ABBOTT (MARTIN) The Freedmen's Bureau in South Carolina, 1865-1872. Chapel Hill, U. of North Carolina P., [1967]. pp. ix, 162. bibliog. 21½cm.

CRUSE (HAROLD) The crisis of the negro intellectual. New York, Morrow, 1967. pp. 594. bibliog. 23½cm.

FRANKLIN (JOHN HOPE) and STARR (ISIDORE) eds. The negro in twentieth century America: a reader on the struggle for civil rights. New York, Vantage Books, [1967]. pp. xxii, 542. bibliog. 20cm. (Vantage Originals. V. 382)

LINCOLN (CHARLES ERIC) Sounds of the struggle: persons and perspectives in civil rights. New York, Morrow, 1967. pp. 252. 21cm.

TROTSKII (LEV DAVYDOVICH) On black nationalism and self-determination; [four discussions with Arne Swabeck and others]; (edited, with introductory notes, by George Breitman). New York, [1967]. pp. 66.

BELL (INGE POWELL) CORE and the strategy of non-violence. New York, [1968]. pp. 214.

BENNETT (LERONE) What manner of man: a biography of Martin Luther King, Jr. 3rd ed. Chicago, 1968. pp. (x), 251.

BLAUSTEIN (ALBERT P.) and ZANGRANDO (ROBERT L.) eds. Civil rights and the American negro: a documentary history. New York, Trident P., [1968]. pp. xv, 671. 21½cm.

DUBOIS (WILLIAM EDWARD BURGHARDT) The autobiography...: a soliloquy on viewing my life from the last decade of its first century. [New York], International Publishers, [1968]. pp. 448. bibliog. 21cm.

GOLDSTON (ROBERT) The negro revolution. New York, Macmillan, [1968]. pp. (iii), 248. bibliog. 23cm.

LIGHTFOOT (CLAUDE M.) Ghetto rebellion to black liberation. New York, International Publishers, [1968]. pp. 192. 20½cm.

LOCKARD (DUANE) Toward equal opportunity: a study of state and local antidiscrimination laws. New York, Macmillan, [1968]. pp. vii, 150. 21cm. (Government in the Modern World)

METCALF (GEORGE R.) Black profiles. New York, McGraw-Hill, [1968]. pp. x, 341. bibliog. 21cm.

NELSON (TRUMAN) The right of revolution. Boston, Beacon P., [1968]. pp. (v), 148. 20cm.

NEW JERSEY. Governor's Select Commission on Civil Disorder, State of New Jersey. 1968. Report for action: [Robert D. Lilley, chairman]. [Trenton?], 1968. pp. xii, 202. 28cm.

SMITH (JAMES WESLEY) The strange way of truth. New York, Vantage P., [1968]. pp. 145. bibliog. 20cm.

SOUTHERN (DAVID W.) The malignant heritage: Yankee progressives and the negro question, 1901-1914. Chicago, 1968. pp. 116. bibliog. (Loyola University. Department of History. William P. Lyons Master's Essay Award. 1967)

BLOCH (HERMAN D.) The circle of discrimination: an economic and social study of the black man in New York. New York, 1969. pp. 274.

COHEN (TOM) Three who dared. New York, Doubleday, [1969]. pp. 144. 20½cm. (Doubleday Signal Books)

LASCH (CHRISTOPHER) The agony of the American left. New York, 1969. pp. 212.

LECKY (ROBERT S.) and WRIGHT (H. ELLIOTT) eds. Black manifesto: religion, racism, and reparations. New York, [1969]. pp. 182. bibliog.

LESTER (JULIUS) Revolutionary notes. New York, 1969. pp. 209.

MASNATA-RUBATTEL (CLAIRE) L'Amérique blanche et les droits des noirs: la loi de 1964; contribution à l'étude du processus de décision aux États-Unis d'Amérique. Genève, Droz, 1969. pp. 295. bibliog. (Travaux de Droit, d'Économie, de Sociologie et de Sciences Politiques. No. 74)

NEGROES - Civil rights (Cont'd.)

SOCIOLOGICAL RESOURCES FOR THE SOCIAL STUDIES. Leadership in American society: a case study of black leadership. Boston, [Mass.], 1969. pp. 68. bibliog.

WAGSTAFF (THOMAS) Black power: the radical response to white America. London, 1969. pp. 150.

ALLEN (ROBERT L.) 1942- . A guide to black power in America: an historical analysis. London, 1970. pp. 251. bibliog.

BRANDES (VOLKHARD) and BURKE (JOYCE) USA: vom Rassenkampf zum Klassenkampf; die Organisierung des schwarzen Widerstandes. München, 1970. pp. 275. bibliog.

FACTOR (ROBERT L.) The black response to America: men, ideals and organization from Frederick Douglass to the NAACP. Reading, Mass., [1970]. pp. 385. bibliog.

GOLDSCHMID (MARCEL L.) ed. Black Americans and white racism: theory and research. New York, [1970]. pp. 434. bibliogs.

LESTER (JULIUS) Look out Whitey!: black power's gon' get your mama. London, 1970. pp. 150.

SMITH (WILLIAM GARDNER) Return to black America. Englewood Cliffs, [1970]. pp. 185.

WELLS (IDA BELL) Crusade for justice: the autobiography...; edited by Alfreda M. Duster. Chicago, 1970. pp. 434. bibliog.

PEEKS (EDWARD) The long struggle for black power. New York, [1971]. pp. 448.

WALTON (HANES) The political philosophy of Martin Luther King, Jr. Westport, Conn., [1971]. pp. 137. bibliog.

WILLIAMS (JOHN ALFRED) The King God didn't save: reflections on the life and death of Martin Luther King, Jr. London, 1971. pp. 222.

WOLK (ALLAN) The Presidency and black civil rights: Eisenhower to Nixon. Rutherford, [1971]. pp. 276. bibliog.

YETTE (SAMUEL F.) The choice: the issue of black survival in America. New York, [1971]. pp. 318.

- Economic conditions

UNITED STATES. Labor Dept. Bulls. S-3. The economic situation of negroes in the United States. rev. ed. Washington, 1962. pp. iii, 32.

MILLER (HERMAN P.) Poverty and the negro. Los Angeles, 1965. fo. 30. (California University. Institute of Government and Public Affairs. [Publications]. MR-37)

UNITED STATES. Public Health Service. Publications No. 1571. Graduates of predominantly negro colleges: class of 1964: by Joseph H. Fichter. Washington, 1967. pp. xix, 262.

FOLEY (EUGENE P.) The achieving ghetto. Washington, National P., [1968]. pp. 156. 21½cm.

AMERICAN ASSEMBLY. [35th Assembly, April, 1969]. Black economic development; [edited by William F. Haddad and G. Douglas Pugh]. Englewood Cliffs, N.J., [1969]. pp. 176.

CROSS (THEODORE L.) Black capitalism: strategy for business in the ghetto. New York, 1969. pp. 274. bibliog.

GIBSON (D. PARKE) The $30 billion negro. London, [1969]. pp. 311.

KAIN (JOHN F.) ed. Race and poverty: the economics of discrimination. Englewood Cliffs, [1969]. pp. 186. bibliog.

OVINGTON (MARY WHITE) Half a man: the status of the negro in New York; (with an introduction by Charles Flint Kellogg). New ed. New York, 1969. pp. 128.

TO the point of production: an interview with John Watson. Detroit, [1969]. pp. 9. (Reprinted from The Movement, July, 1969)

HENDERSON (WILLIAM L.) and LEDEBUR (LARRY C.) Economic disparity: problems and strategies for black America. New York, [1970]. pp. 360.

WOLTERS (RAYMOND) Negroes and the Great Depression: the problem of economic recovery. Westport, Conn., [1970]. pp. 398.

BECKER (GARY S.) The economics of discrimination. 2nd ed. Chicago, 1971. pp. 167. (Chicago. University. Economics Research Center. Economics Research Studies)

BLACK business enterprise: historical and contemporary perspectives; edited by Ronald W. Bailey. New York, [1971]. pp. 361. bibliog.

EPSTEIN (EDWIN M.) and HAMPTON (DAVID R.) Black Americans and white business. Encino, Calif., [1971]. pp. 447. bibliogs.

- Education

SINGLETON (ROBERT) and BULLOCK (PAUL) Some problems in minority-group education in the Los Angeles public schools. Los Angeles, California University, Institute of Industrial Relations, 1963. pp. 137-145. 24½cm. (Reprints. No. 120.) (Reprinted from the Journal of Negro Education, Spring, 1963)

BULLOCK (HENRY ALLEN) A history of negro education in the South from 1619 to the present. Cambridge, Mass., Harvard U.P., 1967. pp. xv, 339. 23½cm.

KVARACEUS (WILLIAM CLEMENT) and others. Poverty, education and race relations: studies and proposals. Boston, Allyn & Bacon, [1967]. pp. xi, 226. bibliog. 21cm.

UNITED STATES. Public Health Service. Publications No. 1571. Graduates of predominantly negro colleges: class of 1964: by Joseph H. Fichter. Washington, 1967. pp. xix, 262.

DAWSON (HELAINE S.) On the outskirts of hope: educating youth from poverty areas. New York, McGraw-Hill, [1968]. pp. xiv, 329. bibliog. 22½cm.

JAFFE (ABRAM J.) and others. Negro education in the 1960's. New York, Praeger, 1968. pp. xxvii, 290. bibliog. 23½cm. (Praeger Special Studies in U.S. Economic and Social Development)

KOZOL (JONATHAN) Death at an early age: the destruction of the hearts and minds of Negro children in the Boston public schools. Harmondsworth, Penguin Books, 1968. pp. 223. 18cm. (Penguin Education Specials. X38)

LEMELLE (TILDEN J.) and LEMELLE (WILBERT J.) The black college: a strategy for achieving relevancy New York, 1969. pp. 144.

AMERICAN COUNCIL ON EDUCATION. Annual Meeting. 1969. The campus and the racial crisis; edited by David C. Nichols and Olive Mills. Washington, [1970]. pp. 309

KING (KENNETH JAMES) Pan-Africanism and education: a study of race, philanthropy and education in the southern states of America and East Africa. Oxford, 1971. pp. 296. bibliog.

- Employment

MINNESOTA. 1945. The Negro worker in Minnesota: a report...by the Governor's Interracial Commission. [St. Paul], 1945. pp. (ii), 57. 20cm.

HANSLOWE (KURT L.) New York State Labor relations Law, 1964. [Ithaca], Cornell University, New York State School of Industrial and Labor Relations, [1964]. pp. 244-259. 23cm. (Reprint Series. No. 169) (Reprinted from Syracuse Law Review. vol. 16, no. 2, 1964)

MARSHALL (RAY) The negro worker. New York, Random House, [1967]. pp. viii, 180. bibliog. $18\frac{1}{2}$cm. (Studies in Labor)

BUSINESS leadership and the Negro crisis; [proceedings of a conference on urban minority problems, held by the Graduate School of Business of Columbia University, 1968]; edited by Eli Ginzberg. New York, McGraw-Hill, [1968]. pp. xi, 175. 20cm.

FERMAN (LOUIS A.) The negro and equal employment opportunities: a review of management experiences in twenty companies. New York, Praeger, [1968]. pp. xv, 195. $23\frac{1}{2}$cm. (Special Studies in U.S. Economic and Social Development).

FERMAN (LOUIS A.) and others, eds. Negroes and jobs: a book of readings. Ann Arbor, U. of Michigan P., [1968]. pp. xv, 591 bibliogs. 23cm.

JACOBSON (JULIUS) ed. The Negro and the American labor movement. Garden City, Doubleday, 1968. pp. vii, 430. 18cm. (Anchor Books. A 495)

KILLINGSWORTH (CHARLES C.) Jobs and income for negroes. Ann Arbor, 1968 repr. 1970. pp. 92. (Michigan University and Wayne State University. Institute of Labor and Industrial Relations. Policy Papers in Human Resources and Industrial Relations. No. 6)

KOZIARA (EDWARD CLIFFORD) and KOZIARA (KAREN S.) The negro in the hotel industry. Philadelphia, [1968]. pp. 74. bibliog. (Pennsylvania University. Wharton School of Finance and Commerce. Industrial Research Unit. Racial Policies of American Industry. Report No. 4)

MARSHALL (F. RAY) and BRIGGS (VERNON M.) Equal apprenticeship opportunities: the nature of the issue and the New York experience. Ann Arbor, 1968. pp. 57. (Michigan University and Wayne State University. Institute of Labor and Industrial Relations. Policy Papers in Human Resources and Industrial Relations. No. 10)

ROWAN (RICHARD L.) The negro in the steel industry. Philadelphia, [1968]. pp. 148. (Pennsylvania University. Wharton School of Finance and Commerce. Industrial Research Unit. Racial Policies of American Industry. Report No. 3)

BLOCH (HERMAN D.) The circle of discrimination: an economic and social study of the black man in New York. New York, 1969. pp. 274.

COUSENS (FRANCES REISSMAN) Public civil rights agencies and fair employment: promise vs. performance. New York, 1969. pp. 162.

KING (CARL B.) and RISHER (HOWARD W.) The negro in the petroleum industry. Philadelphia, [1969]. pp. 96. (Pennsylvania University. Wharton School of Finance and Commerce. Industrial Research Unit. Racial Policies of American Industry [Series] Reports. No. 5)

KOVARSKY (IRVING) The negro and fair employment. Iowa, 1969. pp. various. (Iowa University. College of Business Administration. Reprint Series. No.5)

NORTHRUP (HERBERT ROOF) The negro in the paper industry. Philadelphia, [1969]. pp. 233. (Pennsylvania University. Wharton School of Finance and Commerce. Industrial Research Unit. Racial Policies of American Industry. Report No.8)

NORTHRUP (HERBERT ROOF) and BATCHELDER (ALAN B.) The negro in the rubber tire industry. Philadelphia, P.A., [1969]. pp. 134. (Pennsylvania University. Wharton School of Finance and Commerce. Industrial Research Unit. Racial Policies of American Industry. Reports. No. 6)

QUAY (WILLIAM HOWARD) The negro in the chemical industry. Philadelphia, [1969]. pp. 110. (Pennsylvania University. Wharton School of Finance and Commerce. Industrial Research Unit. Racial Policies of American Industry. Report No. 7).

ANDERSON (BERNARD E.) Negro employment in public utilities: a study of racial policies in the electric power, gas, and telephone industries. (Studies of negro employment. vol. 3). [Philadelphia, 1970]. pp. 261. (Pennsylvania University. Wharton School of Finance and Commerce. Industrial Research Unit. Studies. No. 48)

CANTOR (MILTON) ed. Black labor in America; [collection of articles previously published in the Summer 1969 issue of Labor History]. Westport, Connecticut, [1970]. pp. 170.

FOGEL (WALTER A.) The negro in the meat industry. Philadelphia, [1970]. pp. 146. (Pennsylvania University. Wharton School of Finance and Commerce. Industrial Research Unit. Racial Policies of American Industry. Reports. No. 12)

HOWARD (JOHN C.) The negro in the lumber industry. Philadelphia, [1970]. pp. 97. (Pennsylvania University. Wharton School of Finance and Commerce. Industrial Research Unit. Racial Policies of American Industry. Reports. No. 19.)

NEGROES - Employment (Cont'd.)

> JEFFRESS (PHILIP W.) The negro in the urban transit industry. Philadelphia, [1970]. pp. 106. (Pennsylvania University. Wharton School of Finance and Commerce. Industrial Research Unit. Racial Policies of American Industry. Report No.18)
>
> LEONE (RICHARD D.) The negro in the trucking industry. Philadelphia, [1970]. pp. 149. (Pennsylvannia University. Wharton School of Finance and Commerce. Industrial Research Unit. Racial Policies of American Industry. Report No. 15)
>
> MORGAN (JOHN STEWART) and VAN DYKE (RICHARD L.) White-collar blacks: a breakthrough? [New York, 1970]. pp. 214.
>
> NORTHRUP (HERBERT ROOF) The negro in the tobacco industry;... with the assistance of Robert I. Ash. Philadelphia, [1970]. pp. 107. (Pennsylvania University. Wharton School of Finance and Commerce. Industrial Research Unit. Racial Policies of American Industry. Reports. No. 13.)
>
> NORTHRUP (HERBERT ROOF) and ROWAN (RICHARD L.) Negro employment in Southern industry: a study of racial policies in five industries. (Studies of negro employment. Vol.4). [Philadelphia, 1970]. 1 vol.(various pagings). (Pennsylvania University. Wharton School of Finance and Commerce. Industrial Research Unit. Studies. No. 49)
>
> OFARI (EARL) The myth of black capitalism. New York, [1970]. pp. 126. bibliog.
>
> ROWAN (RICHARD L.) The negro in the textile industry. Philadelphia, [1970]. pp. 172. (Pennsylvania University. Wharton School of Finance and Commerce. Industrial Research Unit. Racial Policies of American Industry. Report No. 20)
>
> RUBIN (LESTER) The negro in the shipbuilding industry. Philadelphia, [1970]. pp. 154. (Pennsylvania University. Wharton School of Finance and Commerce. Industrial Research Unit. Racial Policies of American Industry. Report No.17)
>
> SETHI (S. PRAKASH) Business corporations and the black man: an analysis of social conflict: the Kodak-FIGHT controversy. Scranton, [1970.]. pp. 184. bibliog.
>
> BLUMROSEN (ALFRED W.) Black employment and the law. New Brunswick, N.J., [1971]. pp. 416.
>
> RISHER (HOWARD W.) The negro in the railroad industry;...with the assistance of Marjorie C. Denison. Philadelphia, [1971]. pp. 202. (Pennsylvania University. Wharton School of Finance and Commerce. Industrial Research Unit. Racial Policies of American Industry. Report No.16)

- Health and hygiene

> MEDICINE in the ghetto: (conference sponsored jointly by Harvard Medical School, the Boston Globe, and the National Center for Health Services Research and Development); editor John C. Norman. New York, [1969]. pp. 333.

- History

> ALEXANDER (WILLIAM T.) History of the colored race in America; containing also their ancient and modern life in Africa, etc. [Kansas City?], 1887; New York, 1968. pp. 600. Facsimile reprint.
>
> FISHEL (LESLIE H.) and QUARLES (BENJAMIN) The negro American: a documentary history. New York, Morrow, [1967]. pp. (xi), 536. 23cm.
>
> KATZ (WILLIAN LOREN) Eyewitness: the negro in American history. New York, Pitman, [1967] repr. 1968. pp. xix, 554. 25½cm.
>
> OSOFSKY (GILBERT) ed. The burden of race: a documentary history of negro-white relations in America. New York, Harper & Row, [1967]. pp. xvii, 654. bibliog. 20½cm.
>
> APTHEKER (HERBERT) To be free: studies in American negro history. 2nd ed. New York, 1968. pp. 256.
>
> CONWAY (ALAN) The history of the Negro in the U.S.A. London, 1968. pp. 36. bibliog. (Historical Association. General Series. G. 67)
>
> DRIMMER (MELVIN) ed. Black history: a reappraisal. New York, Doubleday, [1968]. pp. xx, 553. bibliog. 20½cm.
>
> DROTNING (PHILLIP T.) A guide to negro history in America. New York, [1968]. pp. 247.
>
> HOOVER (DWIGHT W.) ed. Understanding negro history; edited with commentary, etc. Chicago, [1968]. pp. 432.
>
> VANDER (HARRY J.) The political and economic progress of the American negro, 1940-1963. Dubuque, Wm. C. Brown, [1968]. pp. ix, 111. bibliog. 23cm.
>
> BREWER (JAMES H.) The Confederate negro: Virginia's craftsmen and military laborers, 1861-1865. Durham, N.C., 1969. pp. 212. bibliog.
>
> GOODE (KENNETH G.) and JORDAN (WINTHROP D.) From Africa to the United States and then: a concise Afro-American history. [Glenview, 1969]. pp. 177. bibliog.
>
> STERNSHER (BERNARD) ed. The negro in depression and war,: prelude to revolution, 1930-1945. Chicago, [1969]. pp. 338. bibliog.
>
> DRAPER (THEODORE) The rediscovery of black nationalism. New York, 1970. pp. 211.
>
> MEIER (AUGUST) and RUDWICK (ELLIOTT M.) From plantation to ghetto. rev. ed. London, 1970. pp. 340. bibliog.
>
> ROUCEK (JOSEPH SLABEY) and KIERNAN (THOMAS) eds. The negro impact on western civilization. London, 1970. pp. 506. bibliogs.

- History - Historiography

> GENOVESE (EUGENE D.) In red and black: marxian explorations in southern and Afro-American history. London, 1971.. pp. 435.

- History - Sources

> FRAZIER (THOMAS R.) ed. Afro-American history: primary sources. New York, [1970]. pp. 514. bibliogs.

Ref
JAN 22 1974
Z
7161
L84
v.25
1969-72